The History of Printing from Its Beginnings to 1930

The History of Printing from Its Beginnings to 1930

THE SUBJECT CATALOGUE OF THE AMERICAN TYPE FOUNDERS COMPANY LIBRARY IN THE COLUMBIA UNIVERSITY LIBRARIES

WITH AN

INTRODUCTION BY

Kenneth A. Lohf

Volume Two

D - K

Kraus International Publications

Millwood, New York

A U.S. Division of Kraus-Thomson Organization Limited

©Copyright by the Trustees of Columbia University 1980

All rights reserved.
No part of this work covered by the copyright hereon may be reproduced or used in any form or by any means—graphic, electronic, or mechanical, including photocopying, recording or taping, information storage and retrieval systems—without written permission of the publisher.

First Printing

Printed in the United States of America

Library of Congress Cataloging in Publication Data

Columbia University. Libraries.
The history of printing from its beginnings to 1930.

1. Printing--Bibliography--Catalogs.
2. Printing--History--Sources--Bibliography--Catalogs. 3. Daystrom, inc. Typographic Library and Museum, Jersey City--Catalogs. 4. Columbia University. Libraries--Catalogs. I. Title.
Z117.C65 1980 016.6862 80-13377
ISBN 0-527-18763-1 (set)

TABLE OF VOLUMES

The History of Printing from Its Beginnings to 1930

D

D*** (Comte C.P. de Lasteyrie)

Cabinet MM | Shelf 2 | No. 43

Procédé actuel de la lithographie...Paris, 1818.

Has one folded plate.

Half morocco; 8½ x 5-3/8 x ¼ in.

DAFFIS, PAUL

Cabinet W | Shelf 3 | No. 114

Opinion de la presse sur les publications de la librairie Paul Daffis. Bibliothèque Elzévirienne...Paris, 1873. Brochure.

Item I in vol. with binder's title "Pamphlets Relating to Books - I. Bound 1932.

DAGUERRE, DOMINIQUE

Cabinet J | Shelf 3 | No. 15

Correspondence with Thomas Wedgwood.

See METEYARD, ELIZA. Group of Englishmen (1795 to 1818)...pp.43, 45, 46, 47, 50, 157.

DAGUERRE, LOUIS (1787-1851)

Cabinet Y | Shelf 2 | No. 23

Invention of daguerreotype, with an account of the inventor)

See LORCK, CARL B. Handbuch der geschichte...Leipzig, 1882-1883 (part 2, p.12)

DAHL, JOHANN CONRAD

Cabinet Y | Shelf 3 | No. 7

(Printing, historical) Buchdruckerkunst, ihre geschichte. von Poppe-Ebert-Dahl. [Excerpts from the] "Allgemeine Encyclopädie der Wissenschaften und Kunst", vol. 14. Leipzig, 1825.

Morocco; 11 x 9 in.

DAHL, SVEND

Cabinet Y | Shelf 3 | No. 117

Geschichte des buches. By Svend Dahl. [translated from the Danish by Lina Johnsson]. Leipzig, 1928. Illus.

Stamped cloth; 9¼ x 6¼ in.

DAILY ARGUS

See Newspapers

DAILY COLONIST (Victoria B.C.)

Cabinet | Shelf | No.

See Newspapers, Canada. Victoria.

DAILY FREEMAN, THE

Cabinet EE | Shelf 1 | No. 18

See SPECIMEN BOOKS, TYPES. Printers.

DAILY GRAPHIC, London.

Cabinet A | Shelf 3 | No. 1

No.1, January 4, 1890; the first issue.

Bound in with other newspapers; leaf 15.

DAILY GRAPHIC, an ILLUSTRATED NEWSPAPER.

Cabinet | Shelf | No.

see also

Newspapers, England.

(The) DAILY GRAPHIC

Cabinet C | Shelf 3 | No. 13 to 26

First illustrated evening newspaper

See JOURNALISM, ILLUSTRATED (The) Daily Graphic...1879

DAILY GRAPHIC (The), New York City.

Cabinet A — See Newspapers, special issues U.S. for a curious strike issue.

Shelf 3 — Bound in with other newspapers; leaf 15.

No. 11

DAILY OKLAHOMAN (The)

Cabinet — See Newspapers, special issues.

Shelf

No.

D'ALEMBERT

Cabinet — See Diderot et D'Alembert.

Shelf

No.

DAILY HERALD, THE

Cabinet NN — Bar Harbor, Maine, 1886, Vol. I. The Daily Herald. A summer journal of Mount Desert News. Joseph Wood, Editor - Publisher.

Shelf 7

No. 13

Cloth; 13 x 9 x ½ in.

DAILY TYPO ATHLETIC BULLETIN

Cabinet 47 — Chicago, Ill., 1909. Daily Typo Athletic Bulletin Published in the interests of the Typo Athletic Association.

Shelf 2

No. 13 — vol. 1, 1909

Cloth; 13-3/4 x 10¼ in.

DALEN, DANIEL VAN DEN.

Cabinet E — See Early Printing in Holland. Amsterdam, 1685. Hieronymus Sweerts.

Shelf 4

No. 81

DAILY MAIL, THE (Great Britain)

Cabinet 00 — "News of the future, Jan. 1, 2000" issue. London, 1928.

Shelf 6 — Extra illustrated, printed on colored paper.

No. 7

Buckram; 16½ x 12½ in.

DAILY UNION, SACRAMENTO — see

Cabinet A — Newspapers, California SACRAMENTO DAILY UNION

Shelf 3

No. 52

D'ALENCON, GODARD

Cabinet J — Memoire sur Godard d'Alencon. [Et] Le bois d'illustration au 19e siècles. Par Louis Dimier. Paris, 1925. Pamphlet, illus.

Shelf 3

No. 32 (env.)

Item in manila envelope.

DAILY (The) NATIONAL ERA (see)

Cabinet A — Newspapers, Washington, D.C. Daily (The) National Era...

Shelf 3

No. 5

DAKOTA LANGUAGE

Cabinet II — See LANGUAGE CHARACTERS. Examples of. Dakota Gospels...

Shelf 3

No. 50

DALLAS "NEWS"

Cabinet NN — Dealy, George B. owner of the news, his story of success.

Shelf 2 — See JOURNALISM (42) Pictures of Davy Crockett...

No. 2.02

DAILY NATIONAL INTELLIGENCER (Gales & Seaton).

Cabinet — See Newspapers, Washington, D.C.

Shelf

No.

DALAND, JUDSON

Cabinet FF — Evolution of modern printing, and the discovery of movable metal type by the Chinese and Koreans in the 14th century. Reprinted from the Journal of The Franklin Institute, vol. 212, No. 2, Aug. 1931. Brochure

Shelf 3

No. 9 Env. — Item in manila envelope.

D'ALLEGRE----?

Cabinet — See Specimens, Types. France. D'Allegre. (Successeurs de Cinier, A. C.?). Lyons, 1830.

Shelf

No.

"DAILY NEWS" THE LONDON

Cabinet 00 — Jubilee, The "Daily News".

Shelf 5 — see JOURNALISM, Great Britain. "Daily News" (The) Jubilee.

No. 9

DALBANNE, C. et E. DROZ

Cabinet V — L'Imprimerie a Vienne en Dauphiné au 15 siècle. Paris, 1930. Vol. II only. Illus. Bibliographical comparative study of three printers, 1478 to 1485.

Shelf 2

No. 69

Paper; 11¼ x 9 x 1-1/8 in.

d'ALLEMAGNE, HENRY-RENÉ

Cabinet L — (Les) Cartes a jouer du 14e au 20e siècle. Ouvrage contenant 3200 reproductions de carte dont 956 en couleur, 12 planches hors texte coloriées a l'aquarelle, 25 phototypies, 116 enveloppes illustrées pour jeux de cartes, et et 340 vignettes et vues diverses. Paris, 1906. (2 vols.)

Shelf 1

No. 50

Pictorial boards; 13 x 10-3/8 in.

DALLUT --

Cabinet Z Shelf 5 No. 32

Graveur et fondeur, Paris, n.d. [Specimens of types with prices of matrices and font]. Broadside.

Item in box labelled "French Type and Cut Specimens: Miscellaneous Collection."

DALMATINUS, (Gregorius)

Cabinet X Shelf 3 No. 14

Bibliographical note, with printer mark, Dalmatinus, Venice, 1482.

see

KRISTELLER, Dr. Paul. Italienischen buchdrucker ...p.86

DALMAZZO, GIANOLIO

Cabinet QQ Shelf 6 No. 22

Bodoni, Giambattista, ed il perche delle bellezze delle sue edizioni (Bodoni, and the reason for the beauty of his printed books)

Article in L'Arte Tipografica... Settembre, 1913, pp.17-35

DALMAZZO, GIANOLIO.

Cabinet AA Shelf 2 No. 33

(Il) Libro e l'art della stampa. Enciclopedia metodica per i cultori della tipografia e della arti affini, e per gli amatori del libro. Compilato ... per Gianolio Dalmazzo. Torino, 1926. Illus.

Full morocco; 9¾ x 7 x 3 in.

DALMAZZO, GIANOLIO

Cabinet MM Shelf 2 No. 16

(La) Tipografia: Storia, tecnica moderna, ed esercizio industriale dell'arte della stampa. ...per cura di Gianolio Dalmazzo, direttore della Regia Scuola Tipografica di Torino. Torino 1914. Illus.

Text book of printing. Historical, technical, biographical.

Cloth; 8½ x 6-1/8 x 1-5/8 in.

DALTON, MICHAEL (Type Founder)

Cabinet 61 Shelf 1 No. 5

Portrait, with brief biographical sketch of M. Dalton (1802-1879), of the Dickinson Type Foundry, Boston.

Article, with portrait in "The Paper World", vol.18, No.3, March, 1889, p.1

DALY, MARCUS

Cabinet Shelf No.

See Journalism, Montana. Anaconda Standard.

DALZIEL BROTHERS

Cabinet K Shelf 6 No. 12

Engravings for "The Cornhill Magazine", London, 1853.

see

CORNHILL GALLERY, THE. Wood engravings, one hundred...

DALZIEL BROTHERS, GEORGE AND EDWARD

Cabinet J Shelf 2 No. 17

Record of 50 years work in conjunction with many of the most distinguished artists of the period, 1840-1890. With selected pictures by, and autograph letters from Lord Leighton...and many others. London, 1901.

Cloth; 10¼ x 8 in.

DALZIEL BROTHERS

Cabinet K Shelf 6 No. 13

Wood engravings, one hundred pictures drawn by G. J. Pinwell, engraved by the Brothers Dalziel for "Dalziels' Illustrated Goldsmith". London, 1865.

Cloth, gilt; 11-3/4 x 7-5/8 x 1-1/8 in.

DAMASCENI, PETRUS

Cabinet D Shelf 1 No. 5

Liber de laudibus ac festis gloriosae virginis. Cologne (?). (1468?).

Begins: "Incipit liber de laudibus ac festis ... At end: Explicit Petrus Damaesceni de laudibus gloriose virginis Marie.

Mentioned in Hain, 5918.

Parchment, 10½ x 7¼ x ⅝ in.

DAMASCENUS, JOANNES.

Cabinet Shelf No.

See Joannes Damascenus.

DAMIAN, JEAN

Cabinet Shelf No.

See Early Printing in France. Literature. Troyes, 1568.

DAMON (Rev) SAMUEL C.

Cabinet G Shelf 2 No. 28

See Imprints, United States. Grabhorn, Edwin and Robert, San Francisco 1927.

DAMON & PEETS

Cabinet EE Shelf 4 No. 31

Favorite presses and cutters manufactured by Damon & Peets, 44 Beekman Street. New York.

Catalogue and price list.

Item in manila envelope.

DAMON-PEETS COMPANY

See Specimen Books - Types - U.S.

DAMRELL & MOORE

Cabinet K Shelf 6 No. 11

Imprint. Boston, 1853.

see

IMPRINTS, United States. Damrell & Moore...

DANA, CHARLES A.

Cabinet NN Shelf 2 No. 3

Blackmailing operations of Charles A. Dana's Sun. The biter bit; or the Robert Macaire of Journalism. Washington, D.C. 1870. Pamphlet.

Item 2 in vol. "Journalists and Journalism". Pamphlets.

DANA, CHARLES A.

Cabinet NN Shelf 2 No. 7

Journalism, Mr. Dana on. By H.T.P.
Excerpt from the Bookman, Nov., 1895.
With portrait.

Item 26 in bound collection "Journalism. Excerpts, etc."

DANA, CHARLES A.

Cabinet Shelf No.

see also

Journalism, New York City: Blackmailing operations of Charles A. Dana's "Sun."

DANA, JOHN COTTON

Cabinet PP Shelf 3 No. 30

Tribute to John Cotton Dana. 1856-1929. Newark, New Jersey, 1930. With portrait.
A selection from newspapers and magazines. 500 copies printed by D.B. Updike. The Merrymount Press, Boston. July 1930.

Boards, cloth back; 8½ x 6-1/8 x ½ in.

DANA, CHARLES ANDERSON

Cabinet NN Shelf 4 No. 22

Life of Charles A. Dana.

By James Harrison Wilson.
New York. 1907.
Frontispiece. Portrait.

Cloth: 8½ x 5½ in.

DANA, JOHN COTTON

Cabinet PP Shelf 3 No. 30.01

Address (an) by Frank Kingdon, President of Dana College. Given over Station W.O.R. on John Cotton Dana Day, October 6, 1935. Public Library, Newark, N. J. L935.

Pamphlet, in envelope.

DANA, JOHN COTTON

Cabinet QQ Shelf 1 No. 56

Who was cardelius? Edited by J.C. Dana. Issued by The Printing Art, The University Press, Cambridge, Mass. 1909.

A few letters, and a reply to the question; who was Cardelius?

Half morocco; 6 x 3-3/4 in. See also QQ/1/46.

DANA, CHARLES A.

Cabinet OO Shelf 3 No. 37

Master of facts - Charles A. Dana, one of the group of editors that flourished before and during the Civil War, was a master of facts. An intimate picture by Chester S. Lord. With portrait.
Excerpt from The Mentor, June 1, 1921, Vol. 9, No. 5, p. 29.

Cloth; 10¾ x 7 in.

DANA, JOHN COTTON

Cabinet QQ Shelf 2 No. 22

Business the civilizer. by Ernest Elmo Calkins. With an introduction by J.C. Dana. Boston, 1928. Illus.

Cloth; 9 x 6-3/8

DANA, JOHN COTTON.

Cabinet Shelf No.

See also

Imprints, United States. Elm Tree Press.
See also Libraries.

DANA, CHARLES A.

Cabinet 61 Shelf 1 No. 2

Modern American journalism, as illustrated by Charles A. Dana in the conduct of the New York Sun. With portrait.

Article in "The Paper World", vol. 4, No. 1, Jan., 1882

DANA, JOHN COTTON

Cabinet G Shelf 4 No. 15

Libraries, brief outline of the history of, by Justus Lipsius. Translated from the second edition...By John Cotton Dana. The Merrymount Press, Boston. 1907.

Boards; 6¾ x 4 in.

DANA, S.T.

Cabinet RR Shelf 4 No. 3

Paper birch in the Northeast. U.S. Department of Agriculture, Forest Service -- Circular 163. Washington, 1909. Pamphlet.

Item 14 in collection of pamphlets and excerpts with binder's title, "Paper-Making. Pamphlets".

DANA, CHARLES A.,

Cabinet NN Shelf 3 No. 17

Newspaper making, the art of.
Three lectures.
By Charles A. Dana.
New York. 1895.

Cloth: 7¼x4¾"

DANA JOHN COTTON.

Cabinet 67 Shelf 1 No. 13

See Libraries. Instructions concerning erecting of a library.

DANA'S "SUN", CHARLES A.

Cabinet NN Shelf 4 No. 8

(The) Biter bit - Being a narrative of some of the blackmailing operations of Charles A. Dana's "Sun".
By James B. Mix. Washington. 1870.

Bound in with two other campaign items.

Cloth: 9-7/8 x 7"

DANA, CHARLES ANDERSON

Cabinet Shelf No.

When Dana ruled the New York Sun. New biography of brilliant editor.
With representation of the bronze plaque by Saint-Gaudens.

Article in Editor & Publisher, vol. 64, p.13 May 23, 1931.

DANA, JOHN COTTON

Cabinet JJ Shelf 5 No. 7.02

"This our Noble Art of Printing is the Foster Mother of all Learning"...From the Latin of Cardelius, 1546.
("Who was Cardelius", answered by Mr. Dana) A Boston Society of Printers "Keepsake", 1909.

In envelope.

DANCE OF DEATH

Stack 15 Shelf 1 Number 64

Catalogues of books on death and dances of death.

See BOOK CATALOGUES, DEALERS.
[Dance of Death, etc.]

DANCE OF DEATH

Cabinet I Shelf 1 No. 35

Engravings on wood, with a dissertation on the several representations of the Dance of Death

See DOUCE, FRANCIS. Dance of Death... London, 1833.

"DANSE OF DEATH"

Cabinet K Shelf 5 No. 9

(Exhaustive account of a series of subjects which were frequently reproduced by the early wood engravers)

see PEIGNOT, GABRIEL. Recherches Historiques et litteraires sur les Danses des Morts...Dijon, 1826.

DANCE OF DEATH

Cabinet K Shelf 3 No. 4

(Die) Totentänze von Wolfgang Stammler. Leipzig, 1922. Band 47. Herausgegeben von Hans Tietz. (Representations of the "Dance of Death" from 1400 to 1872.

Marbled boards; 7 x 4¾ in.

DANCKERSZ, DANCKERT

Cabinet I Shelf 1 No. 11

Printer, Amsterdam, 1643-1664. His Imprint.

See BOSSE, ABRAHAM. Perspective op regel-lose...Anno 1664.

DANDO, J. CLIFF.

Cabinet LL Shelf 6 No. 20

Cost manufacturing, fundamental principles of ascertaining. Applied to manufacturing printing...Philadelphia, Dando Printing and Publishing Co. 1901. Brochure.

Item 18 in book with binder's title "Various items on printing shop practice". Bound 1919.

DANDO, J. CLIFF

Cabinet LL Shelf 6 No. 12

Fundamental principles of ascertaining cost of manufacturing. Applied to manufactured printing. Third edition. Philadelphia. Dando Printing & Publishing Co. 1901.

Roan; 12¼ x 9½ in.

DANDO COMPANY

Cabinet LL Shelf 4 No. 24

Little library of little brochures. Money making aids. Reprints from "Knowledge" A Journal of information, advice and suggestion for the Direct Advertiser. Published by the Dando Company, Philadelphia, Pa. 1915. Eleven brochures.

In board case; 6 x 3½ in.

DANEL, L.

Cabinet B Shelf 3 No. 6

Imprint of L. Danel, Lille, 1899. With printer device.

SEE IMPRINTS, France. Danel

DANEL LEONARD

Cabinet W Shelf 3 No. 71

Bi-centenaire de l'imprimerie L. Danel. Lille, 1698-1898. Souvenir de la Fete du 4 Septembre, 1898, au Kursaal de Dunkerque. Illus. Printer Mark.

Cloth, 11 x 7 in.

DANEL, LOUIS

Cabinet FF Shelf 5 No. 60

Presses mecaniques d'imprimerie Anglaises et Americaines (Extrait et traduit du Typographic Printing Machines et machine printing de Fred J. F. Wilson) Par Louis Danel. Lille, 1886. Illus.

With signature of L. Danel.

Half morocco; 10 x 6-5/8 x 5/8 in.

DANFORTH, HENRY RICHMOND.

Cabinet Shelf No.

See Memorials, Printers.

DANFRIE, PHILIPPE

Cabinet W Shelf 3 No. 27

Civilité, du caractère dit de, et des livres qui ont été imprimés avec ce caractère au XVIe siécle. Par Jerome Pichon. Paris [1850]. Pamphlet "Melanges", p.330.

Pichon denies credit to Danfrie for originating Civilite.

Item B (Mélanges) vol. with binders title "Eight French typographic items".

DANFRIE, PHILIPPE (Author)

Cabinet 69 Shelf 1 No. 57

Declaration de l'usage du graphometre... par Philippe Danfrie. Paris, Philippe Danfrie. 1597 Avec privilege du Roy.

Brunet declares: "that it is a curious work, printed in cursive letters [now called Civilitie] and embellished with 18 fine vignettes printed with the text."

Morocco; 7-3/4 x 5 x ½ in. Brunet 2, 485.

DANFRIE, PHILIPPE.

Cabinet 69 Shelf 1 No. 30

See Early Printing in France. Paris, 1558.

DANGERFIELD, THOS.

Cabinet X Shelf 4 No. 28

Answer to a certain scandalous lying pamphlet. Mr. France's answer to Mrs. Cellier's libel. Notes upon a late romance published by Elizabeth Cellier. 3 Pamphlets. London, 1680.

Paper board holder; 12-3/4 x 8½ in.

DANIEL, CHARLES HENRY OLIVE

Cabinet U Shelf 3 No. 89

Daniel Press, Oxford: Memorials of C. H. O. Daniel. [Provost and Printer], with a bibliography of the Press, 1845-1919. Oxford, 1921. Portrait frontispiece.

Boards; 9½ x 7¼ x 1-1/8 in.

DANIEL, C. H. O.

Cabinet S Shelf 4 No. 125

See Private Presses: Daniel Press, The.

DANIEL, ROGER

Cabinet E Shelf 3 No. 78

See Early Printing in England. Cambridge, 1644. Roger Daniel.

DANIEL, SAMUEL.

Cabinet 75 Shelf 1 No. 11

Emblem literature of Daniel.

See Redgrave, Gilbert R. Daniel and the emblem literature...

DANIEL, WILLIAM (or O'Donnell) see O'DONNELL, WILLIAM (Archbishop)

Cabinet Shelf No.

DANIEL PRESS, THE.

Cabinet 75 Shelf 2 No. 1

Frome and Oxford, At. Paper by Falconer Madan. With printer's mark.

In Transactions of the Bibliographical Society, "The Library," Vol. I, 1920-1921, pp. 65-68.

DANIEL PRESS

Cabinet T Shelf 4 No. 111

Types of Bishop Fell; Fell's "New-English" black letter-type, a few specimens of.

See STEELE, ROBERT T. (The) Revival of printing...London, 1912. pp.2, 7.

DANIEL PRESS, THE

Cabinet Shelf No.

See Private Presses: Daniel Press at Frome and Oxford.
" also Imprints, England. Daniel Press, The.
" also Prospectuses, Printers. Great Britain.

DANIELS, A. G.

Cabinet LL Shelf 4 No. 22

Potash and Perlmutter issue a catalog. By A.G. Daniels (After Montague Glass). Boston, Published by the author, 1914.

Copy signed by the author.

A story of a certain kind of instructive experience relating to advertising.

Limp leather 7-3/4 x 5¼ in.

DANIELS, A. G.

Cabinet QQ Shelf 3 No. 15

Potash and Perlmutter issue a catalog. By A.G. Daniels (After Montague Glass) Boston, 1923.

Dedicated to Henry Lewis Bullen "whose contributions to the literature of the craft have proved an inspiration to better printing.

Paper; 7¼ x 5 in.

DANIELS, MARK.

Cabinet 73 Shelf 2 No. 7

Green Symbols, The significance of form in growing things in the heritage of our common origin in the prime creation. With a note on trees by George Sterling. San Francisco, Printed by John Henry Nash, 1924.

Boards; 12½ x 9 in.

DANIELS, RALPH (Ink Manufacturer)

Cabinet Shelf No.

See Inks, Printing. [Specimen Books, U.S.]

DANISH

Cabinet II Shelf 3 No. 63 Box

Luke, Danish. New York, American Bible Society, 1914. Booklet.

Item in box labelled "MISCELLANEOUS LANGUAGE CHARACTERS: EXAMPLES".

DANNREUTHER --

Cabinet V Shelf 5 No. 2.01

Martin Mourot, imprimeur a Longeville, devant Bar-le-Duc (1501-15..). Sa marque typographique et son ensigne. Extrait du Bulletin historique et philologique, 1899.

Item 10 in vol. with binder's title "French printers and printing. Pamphlets". Bound, 1932.

DANSES DES MORTS

See Dance of Death.

DANTE

Cabinet AA Shelf 2 No. 44

Catalogo della mostra Dantesca...

See BIBLIOGRAPHY. Dantesca, catalogo della mostra alla Medicea Laurenziana...

DANTE

Cabinet E Shelf 2 No. 22

Con l'esposition di Christoforo Landino, et d'Allessandro Vellutello ... Con tavole, argumenti ... per Francesco Sansocino. Vinetia, Giovanbattista, Marchio Sessa, fratelli, 1578.

Tooled leather; 13 x 9 x 2¾ in. See Brown, "The Venetian Press."

DANTE

Cabinet 39 Shelf 2 No. 3

Il Dante. Con argomenti & dechiaratione de molti luoghi, novamente revisto & stampato. In Lione, per Giovan di Tournes. MDXXXXVI.

Morocco, gilt, 5¼ x 3¼ x 1¼ in.

DANTE ALIGIERI

Cabinet D Shelf 4 No. 30

De la volgare eloquenzia, tradotto in lingue Italiana. Stampata in Vicenza per Tolomeo Janiculo da Bressa. 1529.

Boards; 11 x 6¾ x ¾ in.

DANTE ALIGHIERI

Cabinet I Shelf 5 No. 26

Illustrations by Doré, 1861. His drawings reproduced in woodcuts by the then leading wood engravers. The binding designed probably by John Leighton ("Luke Limner") and executed by J. & J. Leighton then at 40 Brewer St., Golden Square, London, W.I. This Volume was exhibited in the International Exhibition 1862. Laid in are some of the original draughts of the pattern.

Parigi: Libreria di L. Hachette e Cie, 1861.

Morocco, gilt, tooled; 16-7/8 x 12 x 2

DANTE

Cabinet 71 Shelf 1 No. 57

See Imprints, United States. Nash, John Henry. San Francisco, 1922.

DANTE ALIGHERI

Cabinet See Imprints, United States. Nash, John Henry. San Francisco, 1929.

Shelf

No.

DANTE

Cabinet E Shelf 1 No. 11

Venice, 1544: Francesco Marcolini.

See Early Printing in Italy, Venice, 1544.

DARBY, JOHN

Cabinet X Shelf 4 No. 73

Habeas Corpus for John Darby, printer and Mrs.S.--1711.

see LIBERTY OF PRINTING. Great Britain. Copies taken from the records....London, 1763 p.17

DANTE

Cabinet 73 Shelf 2 No. 1

See Longfellow. Henry Wadsworth. Sonnets preceding the Inferno...Printed by John Henry Nash. San Francisco, 1925.

D'ANVERS, CALEB

See Craftsman's Doctrine, under "Liberty of Printing".

DARBY, J.

Cabinet X Shelf 4 No. 45

London, 1698 (Imprint), J. Darby.

see LIBERTY OF PRINTING. Great Britain. Letter to a member of parliament....

DANTE.

Cabinet 73 Shelf 2 No. 41

See Prospectuses, Printers. Nash, John Henry. San Francisco, 1929.

DANZIG see PRINTING, HISTORICAL. Germany

Cabinet

Shelf

No.

DARK, SIDNEY

Cabinet 00 Shelf 5 No. 20

Life of Sir Arthur Pearson...Newspaper proprietor and founder of St. Dunstan's Hostel... London, n. d. (1922). With portraits.

Cloth; $8\frac{3}{4}$ x 6 x $1\frac{3}{4}$ in.

DANTE, ALIGHIERI

Cabinet D Shelf 4 No. 31

Volgare eloquencia, de la. (Printed with the suggested letters of G. Trissino) Vicenza, 1529, Tolomeo Janiculo.

Bound in with Trissino's "Epistola", and "Dialogo", also the rare type specimen sheet of Arrighi italics.

Boards, leather back; $11\frac{1}{2}$ x 7-3/8 in.

DANZIGER ZEITUNG

Cabinet

Shelf

No.

See Newspapers, Germany. Anniversary Issue.

DaPONTE, (Gottardo)

Cabinet AA Shelf 2 No. 22

Biographical note, DaPonte, printer, Como, circa 1521.

see ARNEUDO, G.I. Dizionario...vol. 1, p.494

DANTE ALIGHERI

Cabinet 73 Shelf 1 No. 3

Purgatorio XXXIV. The Comedy of Dante Alighieri.

A trial sheet printed by John Henry Nash San Francisco, n.d.

Item 3 in John Henry Nash: His Work. San Francisco, v. d.

DaPONTE (Gottardo)

Cabinet X Shelf 3 No. 14

Bibliographical note, with printer mark, DaPonte, Milan, 1503-1535.

see KRISTELLER, Dr. Paul. Italienischen buchdrucker...p.30

DARLEY, FELIX O.C.

Cabinet K Shelf 5 No. 2

American illustrator, circa 1840.

see BIOGRAPHIES, ILLUSTRATORS. Darley...

DANTE.

Cabinet 73 Shelf 2 No. 1

Sonnets preceding the Inferno, Purgatorio, and Paradiso of the Comedy of Dante Alighieri of Florence. By Henry Wadsworth Longfellow. San Francisco: printed for Aurelia Henry Reinhardt by John Henry Nash. MDCCCCXXV.

Brochure No. 4, in John Henry Nash, Imprints San Francisco, 1910-1927.

DARBLAY, PERE et FILS

Cabinet RR Shelf 3 No. 31

Papeteries d'Essonne. Darblay Pere et Fils. (Extrait du Revue "Les grandes usines de Turgan", Sept., 1889.

Illustrated account of the Darblay paper mills at Essone, and of the machinery invented by the Darblays', father and son.

Paper; 11 x $7\frac{1}{2}$ in. In protective case.

DARLEY, FELIX O. C.

Cabinet K Shelf 5 No. 2

(Biographical sketch)

see ENGLISH, THOMAS DUNN. Darley...

DARLEY, FELIX OCTAVIUS CARR

Cabinet K Shelf 6 No. 39.01

Illustrator, 1822-1888.

see WEITENKAMPF, FELIX. "Illustrated by Darley"...

DATZ, P.

Cabinet LL Shelf 4 No. 1.01

Histoire de la publicite depuis les temps les plus recules jusqu'a nos jours. Tom premier, Orne de 16 illus. Paris, J. Rothschild, editeur. 1894.

History of advertising from the earliest times to the present.

Half morocco; 8-7/8 x 5½ x 3/4 in.

DAUPELEY-GOVERNEUR, G.

Cabinet LL Shelf 3 No. 44

(Le) Compositeur et le correcteur typographes. Paris, 1880.

Dedicated to Jules Claye "My former and esteemed master".

Half morocco; 7¾ x 5-1/8 x 1¼ in.

DARTNELL CORPORATION, THE

Cabinet LL Shelf 6 No. 70

Printed Salesmanship.

see PERIODICALS, PRINTING. United States. Printed Salesmanship...

DAUBY, J.

Cabinet KK Shelf 4 No. 6

Compositeur - typographe de Bruxelles (Brabant-Belgique)...By M. J. Dauby, compositeur - typographe. 1857.

Observations on the industrial organization of the family.

Paper; 9¾ x 6¼ in. In envelope.

DAVANNE, A.

Cabinet K Shelf 1 No. 21

(La) Photographie et les arts graphiques. Par A. Davanne.

Article included in "Coup d'oeil sur l'histoire de la gravure". Par Georges Duplessis. Paris, n. d. circa 1882.

Boards, morocco back; 12-7/8 x 9¾ x 7/8 in.

DARTNELL PUBLICATIONS

Cabinet 57 Shelf 2 No. 12 and fol.

Printing Art Quarterly; also Printed Salesmanship.

see PERIODICALS, PRINTING. United States.

DAUCHY & CAMPANY

Cabinet LL Shelf 4 No. 14

Circulars protesting against unfair competitive advertising practices of Geo. P. Rowell, Advertising Agent, New York, 1872.

Items inserted in back of Rowell, Geo.P. "Forty years an advertising agent", New York, 1906.

DAVANTES, PIERRE

Cabinet X Shelf 3 No. 15

Biographical note, with device of publisher, Davantes, Basel, 1572.

see HEITZ, PAUL. Basler büchermarken...pp.xxxviii, 107

DARU, Le COMTÉ

Cabinet X Shelf 5 No. 35

Notions statistiques sur la librairie pour servir a la discussion des lois sur la presse. Paris: Imprimerie de Firmin Didot. 1827.

Statistics of publishing in France from 1811 to 1825, to serve as a base for discussing the regulations of printing.

Half morocco; 12 x 9½ x 3/8 in.

DAUCHY & CO.

Cabinet Shelf No.

See also Specimen Books, Wood Types. United States. Page & Co., William Hamilton, Greeneville Conn. (Agency, Dauchy & Co. New York)

DAVENPORT (The Cartoonist)

Cabinet K Shelf 5 No. 2

Biographical sketch.

see BIOGRAPHIES, CARTOONISTS. Davenport...

DARWIN, BERNARD

Cabinet S Shelf 2 No. 165

(The) Dickens Advertiser: A collection of the advertisements in the original parts of novels by Charles Dickens. New York, 1930. The MacMillan Co. Illus.

Cloth; 9 x 5-3/4 x 5/8 in.

DAUGHADAY, J.W., & COMPANY

Cabinet EE Shelf 4 No. 114

Model Printing Press, Descriptive catalogue. n.d. circa 1860. Philadelphia Pa.

Item in manila envelope.

DAVENPORT, CYRIL

Cabinet PP Shelf 5 No. 15.01

Bagford's notes on bookbindings. A paper read before the Bibliographical Society. London, Nov. 16, 1903. Booklet.

In manila envelope.

DATES OF BOOKS see

Cabinet Shelf No.

BOOKS WITH DATES
CHRONOLOGY OF PRINTING

DAUNOU, PIERRE FRANCOIS

Cabinet V Shelf 3 No. 6

Analyse des opinions diverses sur l'origine de l'imprimerie. Par Daunou ... Paris, Frimaire An XI (1802).

Boards, leather back; 8-1/8 x 5-1/8 x 3/8 in.

DAVENPORT, CYRIL

Cabinet U Shelf 2 No. 4

Berthelet, Thomas, royal printer and bookbinder to Henry VIII, king of England: With special references to his book bindings. Published by the Caxton Club (Chicago). 1921. Illus.

Boards; 12-3/8 x 9-5/8 x 7/8 in.

DAVENPORT, CYRIL

Cabinet U Shelf 3 No. 103

Bindings of Samuel Mearne and his school, 1660. (Illustrated bio-bibliographical account).

See vol. 3, p.129 "Bibliographical"... London, 1895-1897.

DAVENPORT, CYRIL

Cabinet U Shelf 3 No. 103

Little Gidding bindings. (Bibliographical sketch)

See vol. 2, p.129 Bibliographica...London, 1895-1897.

DAVENPORT DEMOCRAT AND LEADER.

Cabinet Shelf No.

See Newspapers, Anniversary Issues. Davenport Democrat ... 1855-1930.

DAVENPORT, CYRIL

Cabinet U Shelf 5 No. 67

(The) Book, its history and developmetn. London, 1907. Illus.

Includes chapters on paper, illustration, bookbinding, etc.

Cloth; $8\frac{1}{4}$ x $5\frac{3}{4}$ x 1-1/8 in.

DAVENPORT, CYRIL

Cabinet U Shelf 3 No. 103

Payne, Roger, and his indebtedness to Mearne.

See vol. 3, p.371 Bibliographica...London, 1895-1897.

DAVEY COMPANY, THE

Cabinet Shelf No.

Bookbinder Boards, 1842-1932.

See Bookbinding. [Davey Co. (The)

DAVENPORT, CYRIL.

Cabinet 75 Shelf 1 No. 7

Bookbindings, Bagford's notes on. A paper read before the Bibliographical Society, Nov . 16, 1903.

In Trans. Biblio. Soc. Vol. VII, 1902-1904, pp. 123-159.

DAVENPORT, CYRIL

Cabinet PP Shelf 5 No. 16

Repairing and binding of books for Public Libraries. London: The Sound Leather Comm. of the Library Association, 1905.

One of four articles on bookbinding.

Cloth; $8\frac{3}{4}$ x $5\frac{1}{2}$ x $\frac{1}{2}$ in.

DAVID, CHARLES F. (Publisher)

Cabinet 61 Shelf 2 No.

Profitable Advertising, 1891-1893, founded and published by Charles F. David, Boston, Mass.

See PERIODICALS, ADVERTISING Profitable Advertising...

DAVENPORT, CYRIL

Cabinet U Shelf 5 No. 67.01

By ways among English books. With sixty-one drawings by the author and sixteen other illustrations. London, 1927.

Stamped cloth; 6-5/8 x 5 x 1 in.

DAVENPORT, HOMER

Cabinet K Shelf 5 No. 2

American cartoonist.

see BIOGRAPHIES, Cartoonists. Davenport, Homer...

DAVID, ROBERT

Cabinet U Shelf 5 No. 49

Memoir of The York Press, with notices of authors, printers, and stationers, in the 16th, 17th and 18th centuries. Westminster, 1868.

Bio-bibliographical account.

Tree calf binding by Zaehnsdorf; 8-3/4 x 5-3/4 x 1-1/8 in.

DAVENPORT, CYRIL.

Cabinet U Shelf 3 No. 103

Decoration of book-edges.

Historical biblio. sketch. Illus.

See vol. 2, p.385, Bibliographica...London, 1895-1897.

DAVENPORT, S.T.

Cabinet MM Shelf 7 No. 8

Engraving. [In "British Manufacturing Industries" edited by G. Phillips Bevan, pp.75-124]. London, 1876.

Cloth; 6-5/8 x $4\frac{3}{4}$ x $\frac{3}{4}$ in.

DAVIDS & CO. THADDEUS.

Cabinet 78 Shelf 1 No. 87

History of ink, including its etymology, chemistry and bibliography. New York, n.d. Printed by Francis Hart & Co. 63 Cortlandt Street.

Stamped cloth; $7\frac{3}{4}$ x $5\frac{1}{4}$ in.

DAVENPORT, CYRIL

Cabinet PP Shelf 4 No. 24

English embroidered bookbindings. The English Bookman's Library, edited by Alfred Pollard. London, 1899. Illus.

General introduction, historical, by A. Pollard.

Cloth; $8\frac{3}{4}$ x 7 x 1 in.

DAVENPORT, THOMAS.

Cabinet QQ Shelf 2 No. 27

Biography of Thomas Davenport, inventor of the electric motor. By Wlater Rice Davenport. With an introduction by The Hon. James Hartness...Montpelier, Vt., 1929. Illus.

Cloth; $9\frac{1}{4}$ x $6\frac{1}{4}$.

DAVIDSON, G.H.

Cabinet Shelf No.

See Imprints, England.

DAVIES, GERALD S.

Cabinet J Shelf 4 No. 15

Hans Holbein the younger. By Gerald S. Davies. London, 1903. Illus.

Biography with chronological list of works by Holbein.

Cloth; 15-1/8 x 10¼ x 2 in.

DAVIS, CHARLES, H. S.

Cabinet K Shelf 1 No. 26

Egyptian Book of the Dead: The most ancient and the most important of the extant religious texts of ancient Egypt. With 99 plates reproduced in facsimile. New York, 1894.

Cloth: 17½ x 12½ in.

DAVIS, RAY and Wm. H CUNNINGHAM

Cabinet LL Shelf 3 No. 42

English in school and out. Boston, 1929. Ginn and Company. Illus.

Cloth; 7½ x 5-1/8 in.

DAVIES, HUGH WM. (Compiler)

Cabinet I Shelf 5 No. 26

Bernard von Breydenbach and his journey to the Holy Land, 1483-4. A Bibliography. London, 1911. With 60 plates.

Only 200 copies printed.

Cloth, morocco back; 13½ x 10¼.

DAVIS, DANIEL

Cabinet FF Shelf 1 No. 6

Manual of magnetism. Including also electro-magnetism, magneto-electricity, and thermo-electricity. With a description of the electrotype process. For the use of students and literary institutions. With 100 original illustrations. Boston: Published by Daniel Davis Jr. 1842.

At end "The Medical application of electricity". Boston, 1846.

Cloth; 7½ x 5 in.

DAVIS, ROBERT H. (Inventor) see

Cabinet FF Shelf 6 No. 19

COMPOSING MACHINES. Davis, Robert H.

DAVIES, HUGH WILLIAM

Cabinet X Shelf 3 No. 51

Devices of the early printers, 1457-1560. Their history and development. With a chapter on portrait figures of printers. London: Grafton & Co. 1935.

Cloth; 8¾ x 5½ in.

DAVIS, ELMER

Cabinet NN Shelf 4 No. 25

History of The New York Times, 1851 1921.

By Elmer Davis, of The New York Editorial Staff. Illustrated. New York: The New York Times. 1921.

Copy signed by Adloph S. Ochs.

Cloth: 8¾x5¾x1½"

DAVIS, W.

Cabinet Shelf No.

See Specimen Books, Cuts

DAVIES, ROBERT

Cabinet U Shelf 5 No. 49

(A) Memoir of The York Press, with notices of authors, printers and stationers, in the 16th, 17th and 18th centuries. By Robert Davies, Westminster. Nichols and Sons, 1868.

Tree calf binding by Zaehnsdorf; 8¾ x 5¾ in

DAVIS, HENRY R.

Cabinet NN Shelf 6 No. 37

Providence Journal, half a century with. Being a record of the events and associates connected with the past fifty years of the life of Henry R. Davis, secretary of the Company. Compiled and issued by The Journal Company, 1904. For private distribution. Illus.

Cloth; 9¾ x 6¾ x 1-1/8 in.

DAVIS, WALTER B. (Linotyper)

Cabinet EE Shelf 1 No. 47

See LINOTYPE COMPOSITION...New York, 1909.

DA VINCI, LEONARDO

Cabinet Shelf No.

See LEONARDO DA VINCI.

DAVIS, JAMES (Printer)

Cabinet R Shelf 4 No. 155

Biography of Public Printer of North Carolina, 1749-82, J. Davis.

See Weeks, Stephen P. Pre-Revolutionary printers of North Carolina...(1915)

DAVIS, WALTER B.

See also

Specimen Books, Printers'.

DAVIS, ALBERT

Cabinet LL Shelf 3 No. 36

Style book and general information: An aid to standardization. Third edition. Issued by the United Typothetae and Franklin Clubs of America, 1916.

Half morocco; 7-7/8 x 5¼ x 3/8 in.

DAVIS, JOHN P.

Cabinet K Shelf 5 No. 3

Engraving, the new school of. With an engraving by the author. Excerpt from "The Century Magazine", Aug., 1889.

Item 6 in vol. labeled "Excerpts relating to engraving and engravers".

DAVIS TYPECASTER see

Cabinet FF Shelf 3 No. 36.01

TYPE CASTING MACHINES. Grant, Legros & Co. Ltd., London...

[DAVY, CHARLES]

Cabinet L Shelf 2 No. 3.01

Conjectural observations on origin and progress of alphabetic writing...[monogramm of author, C.D.] London.1762

With three plates of alphabets

Half morocco; 8½ x 5-3/8 in.

DAVY, CHAS. H.

Cabinet T Shelf 3 No. 13

Hansard, Thomas Curson. Typographia: an historical sketch of the origin and progress of the art of printing...By T.C. Hansard [London, 1867. Monthly sections from the Printers Journal]

A special copy gathered and bound by Chas. H. Davy, master-printer, London.

At end of this collection are many miscellaneous items relating to the history of printing.

Cloth; 10½ x 6-5/8 x 1½ in.

DAVY, CHAS. H.

Cabinet T Shelf 5 No. 54

(A) Typographical note. Dedicated to the memory of the three Williams, kings among printers, Caxton, Blades, Morris. London, 1907.

Bio-bibliographical account of the family of Davy. of The Dryden Press, established in London, 1784.

Calf, tooled; 4-5/8 x 2-3/4 x ½ in.

DAVY and SONS, J. (Dryden Press)

Cabinet Shelf No.

See Imprints, England, Dryden Press.

DAVY & SONS, JOHN (Dryden Press)

Cabinet Shelf No.

See SPECIMEN BOOKS, TYPES. Printers. Gr. Britain.

DAWE, EDWARD A.

Cabinet RR Shelf 2 No. 34

Paper and its uses. A treatise for printers, stationers and others. (2 vols.) By Edward A. Dawe. London, 1929. Illus.

Book 2 is composed of samples of papers and cards.

Cloth; 7¼ x 4-7/8 in.

DAWKS, ICHABOD

Cabinet T Shelf 2 No. 96

Morison, Stanley. Ichabod Dawks and his News-Letter: With an account of the Dawks family of booksellers and stationers, 1635-1731. Cambridge; at the University Press, 1931. With illus., facs. and specimens of type.

Cloth; 13 x 9 x ½ in.

DAWSON, ALFRED.

Cabinet U Shelf 1 No. 1b

What is the most beautiful book? A paper read by Mr. Dawson before the Nottingham Library Association, Sept., 1891.

In excerpts relating to printing from the Library, p.21 of pencilled folios.

DAWSON, THOMAS.

Cabinet 75 Shelf 2 No. 8

Printer, London, circa 1604.

See Early Printing in England. [Literature of]. Printers and publishers of "The Birth of Mankind," ...p. 36.

DAY, BENJAMIN H.

Cabinet Shelf No.

Portrait.

See NEWSPAPER CENTENNIALS. Three dailies, 4 weeklies round out 100 years...

DAY, BENJAMIN H.

Cabinet NN Shelf 7 No. 5

Printer and founder of The Sun, New York, [illegible].

see NEWSPAPERS, United States. Examples. Sun, The...

DAY, JOHN

Cabinet MM Shelf 3 No. 15

Account of J. Day, with portrait; books printed by him, 1546-1584; his device.

See JOHNSON, JOHN. Tyographia... London, 1824, vol.1, p.532

DAY, JOHN

Cabinet T Shelf 2 No. 6 [vol.4]

Books printed by John Day, London, 1546-1584. Bibliographical notes. With printer's device and portrait.

see DIBDIN'S "Typographical Antiquities" ...London, 1810-19, vol.iv, p.41

DAY, JOHN.

Cabinet 75 Shelf 2 No. 7

De Antiquitate Cantebrigiensis Academiae libri duo. His edition of 1574 [Printed in London by John Day]. A paper by Henry R. Plomer. [With facsimile title pages.]

In the Transactions of the Bibliographical Society, "The Library, " Vol. VII, 1926-27, pp. 253-268.

DAY, JOHN

Cabinet T Shelf 2 No. 2

Memoire, with portrait, of John Day, together with a list of books printed by him, 1546-1584.

see AMES, JOSEPH and WM. HERBERT. Typographical Antiquities...vol.1, pp.614-683

DAY, JOHN H. (Inventor) see

Cabinet FF Shelf 6 No. 19

TYPE WRITING MACHINES. Day, John H.

DAY, LEWIS F.

Cabinet L Shelf 2 No. 19

Alphabets old and new. For the use of craftsmen, with an introductory essay om "Art in the Alphabet". By Lewis F, Day. 2nd. ed. London, 1906.

Cloth; 7½ x 5 in.

DAY, MILLS

Cabinet S Shelf 3 No. 104

See Early Printing in Connecticut. New Haven. Mills Day's proposed Hebrew Bible.

DAY, RICHARD

Cabinet T Shelf 2 No. 6 [vol.4]

Books printed by Richard Day, London, 1578-1580. Bibliographical notes.

see DIBDIN'S "Typographical Antiquities" ...London, 1810-19, vol.iv, p.178

DAYE, STEPHEN

Cabinet R Shelf 3 No. 129

See Biographies, Printers. Daye, Stephen and his successors ... Cambridge, Mass., 1921.

DAYE, STEPHEN

Cabinet R Shelf 3 No. 122

See Roden, Robert F. The Cambridge Press ... the first printing press established in English America ... New York, 1905.

DAY & COLLINS, LTD.

Cabinet Shelf No.

See Specimen Books, Wood Types, Great Britain.

DAYE, STEPHEN

Cabinet S Shelf 5 No. 25.01

Earliest printer in this country. Ten copies reprinted from "Ten fac-simile reproductions relating to New England. By Samuel Abbot Green. Copyright 1902. Pamphlet.

Paper; 14½ x 10½ in. In box labelled "Colonial Printing and Printers. Miscellaneous Items".

DAYOT, ARMAND

Cabinet 68 Shelf No. 3

(La) Normandie monumentale et pittoresque. Heliogravures de Dujardin d'apres les photographies de E. Letellier...Avec une introduction par M. Armand Dayot. Havre, 1893

Half morocco; 19½ x 15½ in.

DAY and SON

Cabinet 68 Shelf No. 10

Imprint of Day and Son, London, 1856. Example of color printing.

See IMPRINTS, England. Day and Son...

DAYE, STEPHEN

Cabinet R Shelf 6 No. 5

Green, Samuel Abbott. Stephen Daye, the earliest printer in this country. [With] Ten fac-simile reproductions relating to New England Boston, 1902. Heliotype reproductions. Each reproduction is accompanied with several pages of text giving historical, biographical and historical facts.

Cloth; 15 x 10¾ in.

DAYTON JOURNAL (The)

Cabinet Shelf No.

See Newspapers, anniversary issues.

DAY BOOK (The)

Cabinet Shelf No.

See Newspapers, Virginia.

DAYE, STEPHEN

Cabinet R Shelf 4 No. 24.01

Historical sketch of the Stephen Daye Press, the first printing press in what was formerly British North America. Also a list of titles printed on this famous press from 1638 to 1658. With picture of the Press, now in the State Capitol at Montpelier, Vermont, and a picture of Daye's Book-Plate in 1642, supposed to be the earliest American book-plate.

This press was in operation for 150 years. Folder printed by and presented with the compliments of the University Press, of

cont'd

DAYTON RUBBER COMPANY see

Cabinet 78 Shelf 2 No. 90

ROLLERS, INKING, Rubber. Dayton Rubber Manufacturing Co...

DAYE, JOHN.

Cabinet E Shelf 2 No. 12

See Early Printing in Great Britain. London, 1573. John Daye.

DAYE, STEPHEN cont'd

Cabinet R Shelf 4 No. 24.01

Cambridge, Mass.

Folder, in manila envelope
Presented by University press, Cambridge.

DEABATE, GIUSEPPE

Cabinet AA Shelf 2 No. 12

Iacopo Suigo da San Germano celebre tipografo piemontese del secolo XV: per G. Deabate. Torino, 1889. Illus.

Limp vel., 9¼ x 6¼ in.

DAYE, JOHN

Cabinet S Shelf 5 No. 6

Birth and youth of English printing from Caxton to Daye. By H. M. D. An excerpt from Paper and Press. n. d. Illus.

Item 22 in collection "Various printers and their plants; excerpts from magazines," Vol. 2, 1918.

DAYE, STEPHEN

Cabinet R Shelf 4 No. 24

See Printing, Historical, Massachusetts. (Cambridge). The first folio of the Cambridge Press ... New York, 1889.

DEAN, AMOS

Cabinet NN Shelf 4 No. 39

Eulogy on the life and character of the late Judge Jesse Buel, pronounced before the New York State Agricultural Society, at their annual meeting, on the 5th February, 1840. Albany.

Printed by Charles Van Benthuysen.

Half morocco: 8½x5½"

DEAN, HENRY

Cabinet L — Shelf 3 — No. 12.01

Analytical guide to the art of penmanship...Also an historical account of the origin and progress of writing and printing. Second edition. New York (1808). Frontis.

Boards, leather back; 11-3/4 x 9 in.

DEARBORN, GEORGE

Cabinet 80 — Shelf 2 — No. 43

Publisher, New York, 1836

See Magazines, United States. American Monthly Magazine (The)...

DEARBORN, WALTER FENNO

Cabinet FF — Shelf 3 — No. 81

Psychology of reading. An experimental study of the reading pauses and movements of the eye ...Columbia University Contributions to Philosophy and Psychology, vol. XIV., No.1. New York, March, 1906. Illus.

Half morocco; 9½ x 6½ in.

DEARDEN, ROBERT R. Jr.

Cabinet S — Shelf 4 — No. 117

(The) Guiding light of the great highway. By Robert R. Dearden Jr. Philadelphia, 1929. Ills.

Historical and bibliographical account of Bibles in manuscript and Bibles printed before the year 1500 by famous printers.

Cloth; 9-1/8 x 6 in.

DEARING, O.A.

Cabinet MM — Shelf 7 — No. 10

Printing for profit, illustrating the "Dearing" specialties in printing office furniture. San Francisco, Palmer & Rey, publishers. 1885.

Buckram; 6¾ x 4½ x ¼ in.

De BEL, JOHANNES

Cabinet Y — Shelf 4 — No. 4

(Note on the DeBel press at Cologne, 1472-1482)

see VOULLIÉME, ERNST. (Die) Deutschen drucker des fünfzehnten Jahrhunderts...p.35

DE BERNY, ALEXANDRE

Cabinet FF — Shelf 3 — No. 23

Appreciation de son oeuvre. A la Memoire de Alexandre DeBerny. (Compiled by Ch. Tulen). Paris, 1882). With frontispiece portrait.

Morocco, gilt, 10½ x 8 in.

DEBERNY, ALEXANDER

Cabinet W — Shelf 3 — No. 70

Cinquantenaire des Institutions Patronales de Alexandre de Berny. Fete du 13 mars 1898. Assemblée Générale des Members de la Caisse de l'Atelier sous la Presidente de M. Charles Robert. Paris, Fonderie Typographique Deberny & Cie.

Full morocco; 10¼ x 8 in.

DEBERNY & COMPANY

Cabinet — Shelf — No.

See Specimen Books, Types. France. v.d.

" also Specimen Books, Types, France. Laurent et Deberny.

DE BERNY, FONDERIE.

See also Balzac, Honore de.

DEBERNEY ET PEIGNOT

Cabinet Z — Shelf 2 — No. 26

Portraits of members of this firm of type founders, 1799-1934, in Vol. I of their 1935 specimen book of types and materials.

Cloth; 10-3/8 x 7½ in.

DEBERNY et PEIGNOT.

Cabinet Z — Shelf 2 — No. 25

Specimens general. Fonderies Deberny et Peignot. [Paris], 1926. 2 vols.

Vol. I has a history of this type foundry.

Half cloth; 10¼ x 7-3/4 in.

DeBOM, EMMANUEL

Cabinet AA — Shelf 3 — No. 51

William Morris en zijn invloed op het boek. (William Morris and his influence on the book) Lezing gehouden door E. DeBom in het Museum Plantin-Moretus te Antwerpen den 25 Sept. 1904. Amsterdam, 1910. Frontispiece portrait, W. Morris.

Paper read by DeBom.

Boards; 9¼ x 6 in.

DeBOUBERS, JEAN LOUIS

Cabinet 83 — Shelf 2 — No. 25

Épreuves de caractères de la fonderie de J. L. Boubers. A Bruxelles. 1776.

In the preface the typefounder states that some of his types were designed by Gille and Rosart, and that the present specimens are comparable to the beautiful models of Baskerville.

Half morocco; 9¼ x 6¼ x 3/4 in.

DeBREBAN, CORRARD.

Cabinet — Shelf — No.

See BREBAN, CORRARD de

DeBURE, GUILLAUME-FRANCOIS

Cabinet V — Shelf 3 — No. 18

(Bio-bibliographical notes relating to DeBure family of printers-publishers, Paris, 1660-1788)

see WERDET, EDMOND. Histoire du livre en France...3me partie (2) p.314

De BURY, RICHARD.

Cabinet S — Shelf 5 — No. 51

Bishop of Durham, 1287-1345. First Year-Book of the De Burians of Bangor, Maine. By Samuel Lane Boardman. Bangor. Printed for private distribution, 1902. With plates.

Half niger morocco; 9½ x 6¼ x 3/8 in.

DeBUSSCHER, EDMOND

Cabinet J — Shelf 2 — No. 42

Biographie historique et artistique de J.-C. DeMeulemeester, de Bruges, graveur en taille-douce. Gand, n.d. circa 1837.

Portrait frontispiece.

Boards; 10-7/8 x 8½ in.

De BUSSCHER FRÈRES

Cabinet EE See SPECIMEN BOOKS, TYPES. Printers'. Belgium.
Shelf 3
No. 31

DECKER, GEORG

Cabinet 83 See Specimen Books, Types. Germany
Shelf 1
No. 47

DECORAH REPUBLICAN (The).

Cabinet See Newspapers, Iowa.
Shelf
No.

DECELLIER, CELIA

Cabinet 83 Épreuves de caractères de la fonderie de Decellier successeur de la fonderie de Jacques Francois Rosart. Troisieme édition augmentee. A Bruxelles. 1779.
Shelf 2
No. 27

Boards, linen back; 8-3/4 x 6¼ x 3/4 in.

DECKER, RUDOLPH

Cabinet See Specimen Books, Types. Germany.
Shelf
No.

DECORATION OF BOOKS

Cabinet See Typography, Decorative
Shelf " also Illustration, Book.
No.

DE CASTRO, IGNACIO Lima, Peru, 1784.

Cabinet F Del Ignacio de Castro, Rector del R. Colegio de S. Bernardo de la Ciudad del Cuzco, Examinador Sinodal del Obispado, Cura de San Geronimo: En Respuesta a lo que contra la primera, que publico sobre la concepcion de N. Senora, opone El P.M.F. Juan Prudencio De Osorio.
Shelf 1
No. 106

A dissertation between Ignacio de Castro and others on the conception of Maria Santisima. Lima, Peru, 1784.

DECKER, RUDOLPH LUDWIG.

Cabinet GG History of the Decker foundry at Berlin. Preface to the specimen book printed for the Exhibition of Works of Industry of all Nations, at London. By R. L. Decker, printer to His Majesty the King of Prussia. Berlin 1851.
Shelf 2
No. 1.01

Boards, leather back; 14 x 11 x 2½ in.

DECORATIVE ART

Cabinet U English revival in decorative art
Shelf 3
No. 54

See CRANE, WALTER. Morris, William to Whistler...London, 1911, p.47

DECIA, DECIO

Cabinet AA Battaglie di tipografi nel [1]500 (I Giunti e i Torrentino). Notize e documenti estratti dal lavoro di laurea "Annali delle edizioni dei giunti di Firenze". Florence, 1913.
Shelf 2 The battle of the Torrentino heirs over papal privileges accorded to the Giuntas.
No. 24

Half morocco; 9-3/4 x 6¼ in.

DECKER FAMILY, Printers, Typefounders.

Cabinet Y (Biographical historical notes and comments, brief.)
Shelf 2
No. 23

See LORCK, CARL B. Handbuch der geschichte...Leipzig, 1882-1883, (pp. 285, 358-62, 369, 402)

DECORATIVE DESIGN

Cabinet See Design
Shelf " also Typography, Decorative
No.

DeCHAMBRAY (R.F.S.D.C.)

Cabinet I Traité de la peinture de Leonardo da Vinci. Donne au publie et traduit d'Italien en Francois par R.F.S. [DeChambrey]. Paris, 1651.
Shelf 5
No. 21

Full morocco; 13½ x 11 x ¾ in.

DECKER FAMILY OF PRINTERS

Cabinet Y (History of the family Decker, printers 1596-1845: With genealogy showing the offices held by them as University Printers at Basle, State Printers at Colmar, and Court Printers at Berlin) Die abstammung der familie Decker. Festschrift bei hundertjahriger dauer des Koniglichen Privilegii der Geheim Ober-Hofbuchdruckerei. von Dr. August Potthaft. Berlin, 1863.
Shelf 5
No. 130

Half morocco; 13-1/8 x 10 x 3/8 in.

DECORATIVE TYPOGRAPHY

Cabinet See Typography, Decorative
Shelf
No.

DECKER, ALFONS de

Cabinet AA Antwerpsche drukkers in den vreemde: Bio-bibliographische schetsen. Door Alfons de Decker. Antwerpen, 1881. Facsimiles, printers marks. (Antwerp printers in foreign countries).
Shelf 3
No. 25

Half morocco; 9 x 6¼ in.

DECLARATION OF INDEPENDENCE (see)

Cabinet QQ AMERICANA
Shelf 5
No. 12.01

DE COSTA, WILLIAM HICKLING (Editor)

Cabinet NN In Memoriam. William Hickling DeCosta. b. 1825, d. 1878. With portrait.
Shelf 2
No. 8

De Costa edited and established the "Charlestown (Mass.) Advertiser".

Item 2 in Vol. "Various Editors: Excerpts and Pamphlets".

DE COSTA, WILLIAM HICKLING.

Cabinet See Journalism, Massachusetts: De Costa, In memoriam.

Shelf

No.

DEGAAST, GEORGES

Cabinet I Shelf 2 No. 58

"Photogravure et imprimerie. Par Georges Degaast. Preface de Victor Michel. Paris. 1925. Illus.

Paper; 9-3/8 x 6 in. Item in manila envelope

DEGEORGE, LEON

Cabinet W Shelf 4 No. 102

La Maison Plantin a Anvers ... aux XVIe et XVIIe siècles. Ouvrages orné d'un portrait de Plantin, d'un tableau généalogique de la famille, et de la marque du grand imprimeur. Deuxième édition augmentée d'un liste chronologique des ouvrages imprimes par Plantin, 1555 a 1589. Bruxelles, 1878.

Half morocco; 9¼ x 6 in.

DE FELICE

Cabinet V Shelf 5 No. 3

Encyclopedie ou dictionnaire des connoissances humaines. Mis en ordre par M. De Felice Tome XXIV. Jan - Inv. Yverdon, 1773.

See pp. 346-378 of this vol. for items relating to printing.

Illus. relating to pp.346-378, see V/5/3.01

Calf; 10 x 7-3/4 x 2¼ in.

DEGAAST, GEORGES

Cabinet W Shelf 1 No. 188

Typographie: Papyrus, numéro spécial...a été composé et fondu sur machine Monotype...Les vignettes, typographiques originales et hors commerce...décorant pages...de cet ouvrage ont été entièrement étudiees, dessinées, gravees et fondues par les Elèves de l'Ecole Estienne de Paris, 1922.

Half morocco; 11¼ x 9 in.

DEGERING, HERMANN

Cabinet Y Shelf 3 No. 76

(Tablet calendar for the year 1294. Its form and binding) Ein calendarium pugillare mit computus aus dem jahre 1294. (Mit 3 tafeln)

pp. 79-88 in Loubier, Hans (Tribute to) Buch und bucheinband...Leipzig, 1923.

DeFELICE----

Cabinet V Shelf 5 No. 3.01

Encyclopedie. Imprimerie-Marbreur. Yverdon, 1778

With many plates illustrating printing and printing appliances.

Tree calf; 10 x 7½ x 1 in.

DEGENER & WEILER

Cabinet Shelf No.

See Printing Presses. Degener & Weiler...

DE GONET

Cabinet X Shelf 5 No. 41

Code alphabetique. Dictionnaire des crimes, delits et contraventions commis par la voie de l'imprimerie, la librairie, la presse periodique, le colportage ... Montpellier, Imprimerie De Gras, 1859.

Laws relating to printing. Infractions and of fences, fines and punishments.

Half morocco; 8½ x 5-3/8 x ½ in.

DE FOE, DANIEL

Cabinet JJ Shelf 3 No. 38

Life and adventures of Robinson Crusoe...Edited by Peter Walker, a member of the Philadelphia Journeymen Printers Union, Philadelphia, 1850.

This was printed during a strike to provide employment to union printers.

Cloth; 9⅝ x 6¼ in.

DeGEORGE, L.

Cabinet V Shelf 5 No. 23

Historique de l'imprimerie E. Guyot. Notice détaillée sur l'ensemble des produits envoyés a l'Exposition Nationale de 1880. Bruxelles. Pamphlet, with one folded plate.

History of this house founded in 1856. Has detailed description of its technical equipment, various departments, workmen benefits, etc.

Item 6 in vol. with binder's title "Origin of Printing in France: Pamphlets".

De GROOT, E. J.

Cabinet LL Shelf 5 No. 52

Handleiding bij het prijsberekenen van drukwerk. Amsterdam. Naaml. Venn. Drukkerij "De Nieuwe Tijd". 1911.

Relates to Printing Accountancy.

Cloth; 7¼ x 5¼ x ¼ in.

DEFREES, JOHN D.

Cabinet 62 Shelf 2 No. 24

Open letter to Ebenezer B. Finley: a review of Mr. Finley's report on the Government Printing Office. J.D. Defrees, Public Printer, Washington, D. C., Feb.19, 1879.

Item inserted in book with title "HISTORY OF THE GOVERNMENT PRINTING OFFICE" ...by R. W. Kerr.

DEGEORGE, LEON

Cabinet V Shelf 3 No. 21

Imprimerie en Europe aux XVe et XVIe siecles: Les premières productions typographiques et les premiers imprimeurs Paris, 1892.

Chronological account of the first productions of the first printers in all parts of Europe.

Half morocco; 6-1/8 x 4 x ½ in.

De GROOT, J.

Cabinet 83 Shelf 2 No. 2

See Specimen Books, Types, Holland.

DEGAAST, GEORGES

Cabinet V Shelf 6 No. 37

(Les) Arts & Industries Graphiques au service de la Presse Technique. Rapport presente au 1er Congres International de la Presse Technique. Paris, 1925.

Summary: History of printing; Paper; Types; Illustration Printing; typography; Engraving; Lithography; etc.

Brochure, in manila envelope.

DE GEORGE, LEON

Cabinet W Shelf 4 No. 101.01

La Maison Plantin a Anvers. Relation détaillée: de visites faites a cette demeure celèbre lors de son acquisition par la ville d'Anvers, augmentée de documents historiques sur l'imprimerie. Ouvrage orné d'un portrait de Plantin, d'un tableau généalogique, d'un plan etc. 1555-1877. Bruxelles, 1877.

Original edition. Only 150 copies printed.

Original paper wrappers; 9 x 6-1/8.

DeHUS, PHILEMO

Cabinet X Shelf 3 No. 15

Biographical note, with device of DeHus, printer-publisher ? Basel, 1587

see

HEITZ, PAUL Basler büchermarken...pp.xxxvii, 105

DEJEAN, LUCIEN

Cabinet KK Shelf 4 No. 14

Étude et exposé des conditions du travail dans l'industrie du livre. Par Lucine Dejean... Préface de V. Breton. Paris, 1899.

Paper; 7¼ x 4⅝ x 3/8 in.

DELABORDE, HENRI

Cabinet K Shelf 6 No. 39.01

Notice sur deux estampes de 1406 et sur les commencements de la gravure en criblé. Extrait de la Gazette des Beaux-Arts, Mars, 1869, Paris.

Item 24 in bound collection with binder's title ENGRAVERS AND WOOD ENGRAVERS.

DELALAIN, JULES

Cabinet X Shelf 5 No. 124

Historique de la proprieté des brevets d'imprimeur. Paris, Oct., 1869.

Review of the influence upon the press of France of successive decrees for the regulating of printing.

Item in box labelled "Liberty of Printing. Various Items"

DeJERPHANION, G.

Cabinet K Shelf 2 No. 39

(La) Voix des monuments. Notes et études d'archélogie chretienne. Paris et Bruxelles. 1930.

Numerous illustrations.

Paper; 11¼ x 7-5/8 x 1-3/4 in.

De La CAILLE, Jean

Cabinet V Shelf 3 No. 18

(Bio-bibliographical notes relating to DelaCaille family of printers-publishers, Paris, 1612-1716)

see

WERDET, EDMOND. Histoire du livre en France...3me partie (2), p.227

DELALAIN, JULES

Cabinet W Shelf 2 No. 2

Typographie francaise et étrangère a l'Exposition Universelle de 1855. Compte rendu par Jules Delalain. Paris, 1856.

Report of the commission appointed by the Society of Printers, Paris, to examine the typographic exhibits of all countries represented.

Item (a) in book with binder's title "Pamphlets relating to French Typography. 1856-1923".

DE JETPHORT, CHOLET

Cabinet KK Shelf 4 No. 3

Projet d'organisation de l'imprimerie - librairie et des arts, etats et professions qui y sont attachés ou qui dépendent...Par M. Cholet DeJetphort. A Paris, 1807.

Plan to organize all arts and professions related to printing; bookbinders, publishers, paper makers, type founders, etc.

Half morocco; 10¾ x 8½ x ¾ in.

DELCAMBRE, ISIDORE.

Cabinet FF Shelf 2 No. 40

Inventor of Type Composing and Distributing Machine.
See Type Composing Machines. Delcambre.

Half morocco; 7-5/8 x 5 x 2 in.

DELALAIN, A. H. JULES .... TYPEFOUNDER.

Cabinet 83 Shelf 1 No. 7

See Specimen Books, Types. France.

DELABORDE (Le Vicomte) HENRI

Cabinet J Shelf 3 No. 18

Engraving: its origin, processes, and history. By Le Vicomte Henri Delaborde. Translated by R.A.M. Stevenson. With an additional chapter on English engraving by William Walker. London...1886.

Cloth; 7-5/8 x 5¼ x 1 in.

DELACOLONGE

Cabinet 83 Shelf 1 No. 6

See Specimen Books, Types. France.

DELALAIN, M.P.

Cabinet X Shelf 3 No. 12

Inventaire des marques d'imprimeurs et de libraires de la collection du Cercle de la Librairies. Deuxieme édition, revue et augmentée. Paris, 1892.

A brief biographical note accompanies the description of each mark which is arranged by countries. Preceded by an historical description of certain special signs in the marks.

Half morocco; 11¾ x 8½ x 1-3/8 in.

DELABORDE, HENRI

Cabinet K Shelf 3 No. 8

(La) Gravure. Précis élémentaire de ses origines, de ses procédes et de son histoire. Par le Vte. Henri Delaborde...Paris, n.d. (circa 1891) Illus.

Cloth; 8¾ x 5½ in.

DE LA FAYE

Cabinet W Shelf 5 No. 90

Catalogue complet "Des Republiques" imprimées en Holland in-24. Avec des rémarques sur les diverse éditions. Per De La Faye. Nouvelle edition revue, corrigee et augmentée per M. J. Chenu. Paris, 1854.

List of printed by the Elzeviers in Holland.

Item in manila envelope

DELALAIN, PAUL

Cabinet V Shelf 2 No. 24

L'Imprimerie et la Librairie à Paris de 1798 a 1813. Renseignements recueillis classés et accompagnés d'une introduction. Paris, 1899. Has three plans of Paris in 1810.

Classified list of the localities of the printers, publishers, engravers, type founders, etc., who exercised their professions in Paris, 1789 to 1813.

Half morocco; 10 x 6½ x 1½ in.

DELABORDE, HENRI

Cabinet L Shelf 1 No. 9

Lithographie en France: la lithographie dans ses rapports avec la peinture. Charlet, Verney...Gavarni (1816-1863) Excerpt from "Revue des deux mondes", Paris, 1863.

Item in manila envelope

DELALAIN, JULES

Cabinet W Shelf 2 No. 19

Didot, Ambroise Firmin, 1790-1876. [Biography. Excerpt from "Journal generale de l'Imprimerie et de la Librairie". Mars, 11, 1876.]

Item in manila envelope.

DELALAIN, PAUL

Cabinet V Shelf 5 No. 18

Libraires et Imprimeurs de l'Academie Francaise de 1634 a 1793. Notices biographiques Par Paul Delalain. Paris, 1907.

Half morocco; 10 x 6½ in.

DELALAIN, PAUL.

Cabinet V Shelf 5 No. 17

Notice suivie du catalogue des objets exposé a l'Exposition Universelle International de 1900, a Paris.
Reproductions of many printer marks.

Half morocco; 11½ x 7½ in.

DELALAIN FAMILY OF PRINTERS

Cabinet V Shelf 3 No. 18

(Bio bibliographical notes relating to this family of printers, Paris, 1764-1853.)

see WERDET, EDMOND. Histoire du livre en France...3me partie (2), p.333

De La LANDE

Cabinet Shelf No. with Illus. 491.04

Art de faire le papier (Art of making paper.) vol. 4 of "Description des arts et metiers. (Paris), 1762.
With 14 large engravings showing the complete process of making handmade paper, from cutting the rags to wrapping the finished paper.

Boards; 18½ x 12½ x 1-1/8 in.

De La LANDE

Cabinet RR Shelf 6 No. 3

Art de faire le papier (Art of making paper) Par M. De La Lande. (Paris), 1761.
With plates, 14, showing the complete process of making handmade paper. Same as RR/6/1.

Boards; 17½ x 12 x 1-1/8 in.

De La Lande

Cabinet RR Shelf 6 No. 2

Art du cartonier. (Art of making cardboard.) Par M. De La Lande, 1762. n.p.
With I engraved plate illustrating the apparatus used in making cardboard.

Board folder; 17 x 12 in.

De LAMA, GIUSEPPE

Cabinet AA Shelf 1 No. 23

Vita del Cavaliere Giambattista Bodoni, Tipografo Italiano, e Catalogo chronologico delle sue edizioni. [By G. de Lama]. Parma, 1816. 2 Vols. Vol. I. Portrait.
The first colume contains the life of Bodoni, the second a list of the works issued from his press.

Half morocco; 9-3/4 x 7½ in.

DE LA MORE PRESS

Cabinet M Shelf No.

See Imprints, England. De La More Press. Alexander Moring.

DELAMOTTE, PHILIP

Cabinet Shelf No.

See MOTTE, PHILIP H. De La.

DELANDINE, ANTOINE FRANCOIS

Cabinet V Shelf 3 No. 9

Histoire abrégée de l'imprimerie, ou precis sur son origine, son établissement en France, les divers caracteres qu'elle a employées, les premiers livres qu'elle a produit, les inventions successives qui la perfectionnèrent, ses ornemens, les noms de ceux qui l'introduisirent dans les principales villes de l 'Europe. Par Ant. Fr. Delandine... Paris [1814].

DELANDINE, ANTOINE FRANCOIS

Cabinet V Shelf 3 No. 9

Note following title page: This work forms the introduction to the catalogue of printed books in the Bibliothèque de Lyon.

Boards, cloth back; 8¾ x 5¾. Presentation copy to M. Peignot, with author's autograph

DeLaTour, LOUIS-DENYS

Cabinet V Shelf 3 No. 18

(Bio-bibliographical note relating to DeLaTour, printer, Paris, 1681-1736)

see WERDET , EDMOND. Histoire du livre en France...3me partie (2), p.310

DELBOS, GABRIEL and JEAN

Cabinet W Shelf 3 No. 55

See Printing, Historical, France (Tulle). Etienne Bleygeat, Francois Varolles, maitres-imprimeurs: Les frères Delbos...Limoges, 1895.

DELECLUZE, E.J.

Cabinet W Shelf 2 No. 1

Gutenberg, Jean. 1450: L'Imprimerie [The History, invention and progress of the art of printing]. Paris, n.d, Pamphlet.

Item 7 in volume "Gutenberg, l'inventeur de l'imprimerie - Melanges."

DELEEN, CARL ERIK.

Cabinet AA Shelf 5 No. 26

See Biographies, Printers. Deleen, Carl Erik. Stockholm, 1799-1846.

DELEN, A. J. J.

Cabinet I Shelf 4 No. 18

Histoire de la gravure dans les anciens Pays-Bas et dans les Provinces Belges, des origines jusqu'a la fin du 18e siecle. Premier Partie. Des origines a 1500. Paris et Bruxelles, 1924.
With 66 plates of reproductions.

Paper; 13 x 10 x 1½ in.

DELEN, J. J.

Cabinet 26 Shelf 1 No. 20

Bücherillustrationen von Peter Coeck von Alost. (Antwerp 1509-) Illus.
Bibliographical account.

Article in the "Gutenberg-Gesellschaft Jahrbuch" 1930, pp. 189-197.

DELESPINE, Charles-Jean Baptiste

Cabinet V Shelf 3 No. 18

(Bio-bibliographical notes relating to Delespine, printer-publisher, Paris, 1700-1787)

see WERDET, EDMOND. Histoire du livre en France...3me partie (2), p.302

DE LIGNAMINE, JOHN PHILIP

Cabinet S Shelf 1 No. 29

See De Vinne, Theodore Low. Notable printers of Italy ... New York, 1910. p.56

DELISLE, LEOPOLD.

Cabinet V Shelf 1 No. 48

Catalogue des livres imprimés ou publiés a Caen avant le milieu du XVI siècle: Suvie de recherches sur les imprimeurs et les libraires de la meme ville. Par Léopold Delisle. Caen, 1903. Facsimiles and printer marks. 2 vols.

Half morocco; 8¾ x 5½ x 1-3/8 in.

DELMAS, GABRIEL

Cabinet V Shelf 1 No. 24

Exposition Internationale Maritime de Bordeaux. Mai a Novembre, 1907. Section des Arts Graphiques. Rapport presenté par M. Gabriel Delmas, Président de la Section des Arts Graphiques. Président de l'Union des Maitres Imprimeurs de France. Illus.

Folder;

DELPORTE, ANTOINE

Cabinet W Shelf 1 No. 109

Rapport sur l'imprimerie. Présenté a l'administration communale de la ville de Bruxelles. Exposition Universelle d'Anvers. Par Antoine Creyson, Henri Steens, Antoine Delporte. Bruxelles, 1884.

Cloth; 9-7/8 x 6½ in. Bound in volume "Rapport sur l'imprimerie, Boston et Bruxelles, 1884-1885.

DeLISLE, LEOPOLD (Editor)

Cabinet B Shelf 3 No. 2

Gutenberg, Jean, a la memoire de: Hommage de l'Imprimerie Nationale et de la Bibliotheque Nationale. Paris, 1900.
With 17 plates

Morocco; 17 x 13 in.

DELMAS, GABRIEL (Compiler)

Cabinet QQ Shelf 6 No. 7

l'Imprimeurs chef d'industrie et commercant. Concours Delmas. Paris, 1909. Frontis.

On matters relating to labor conditions, printing shop equipment and management, legislation, and printing accountancy.

Cloth; 10¾ x 7¼ in.

DELPY, A

Cabinet L Shelf 3 No. 9.01

Essai d'une bibliographie spéciale des livres perdus, ignorés ou connus a l'état d'exemplair unique. (concerning lost books. unique copies, or books unknown)

Article (incomplete) in Bulletin...Le Vieux Papier. Paris, 1908, pp.224-250

DELISLE, LEORIER

Cabinet RR Shelf 2 No. 1

Oeuvres du Marquis de Villette. a Londres, 1786.

Dedication by Delisle in which he gives a brief clue as to his experimentations with papers, samples of which are at the end of this book.

Morocco, gilt; 4-3/4 x 3 x ½ in.

DELMAS, GABRIEL

Cabinet MM Shelf 2 No. 4

Petit questionnaire typographique a l'usage des apprentis compositeurs de 1re et 2e années. 2e édition. Bordeaux n.d. [1909].
Presentation copy, signed G. Delmas.

Cloth; 7¼ x 4 x ½ in.

DEMAREST, -

Cabinet RR Shelf 3 No. 22

Papier, art de fabriquer le. (Extrait du "Dictionnaire des arts et metiers mecaniques", Vol. 5, pp. 463-595, Paris, 1788. Copperplates at end.

Bound together with other items on paper making from the same volume.

Boards; 10-7/8 x 8⅛ in.

DELITSCH, HERMANN.

Cabinet 75 Shelf 2 No. 10

Geschichte der abendlandischen schreibschriftformen. Review of book with above title, by J. P. Gilson. London.
A History of western writing.

In Transactions of Bibliographical Society, "The Library," vol. 10, 1929. pp. 104-6.

DELON, CH.

Cabinet W Shelf 2 No. 140

Gutenberg, et l'invention de l'imprimerie. Par Ch. Delon. Deuxieme édition. Paris. Hachette et Cie. 1884. Bibliothèque des ècoles et des familles. Illus.

Half morocco; 5-7/8 x 3-3/4 in.

DEMAREST -

Cabinet RR Shelf 3 No. 19

Premier mémoire sur les principales manipulations qui font en usage dans les papeteries de Hollande, avec l'explication physique des résultats de ces manipulations. Par M. Desmarets.

(With other items on the same subject of paper making. Extracts from "Mémoires de l'Academie Royale des Sciences", 1771-4)

Half morocco; 11 x 8-5/8 in.

DELLA ROBBIA LIGHT

Cabinet 27 Shelf 2 No. 27

First showing of the type design Della Robbia Light, designed by Thomas Maitland Cleland, who also designed the heavier Della Robbia type design, his first type design.

see THE AMERICAN BULLETIN, June, 1918, pp. 11-14.

DELOYE, A.

Cabinet W Shelf 3 No. 114

(Des) Cornua des livres dans l'antiquite, à propos de deux petites cornes en bronze du Musée Calvert. Paris, 1872. (Extrait de la Revue des Sociétés Savantes, 5e série, tome III, 1872).

Item 9 in vol. with binder's title "Pamphlets Relating to Books - I. Bound, 1932".

DEMAREST -

Cabinet RR Shelf 3 No. 19

Second mémoire sur la papeterie. Dans lequel, en continuant d'exposer la méthode Hollandoise, l'on traite de la nature et des qualités des pâtes Hollandoises et Francoises...Lû December, 1774.

(With other items on the same subject of peper making. Extracts from "Mémoires de l'Academie Royale des Sciences", 1771-4).

Half morocco; 11 x 8-5/8 in.

DELLAGANA, JAMES.

Cabinet FF Shelf 2 No. 40

Early inventor of papier mache Stereotyping. Patent for typehigh plates issued to him in 1885. See Inventions, Patents for. Abridgments of specifications, No. 2104, p. 502, Vol. I...London, 1859.

Half morocco; 7-5/8 x 5 x 2 in.

DELPIT, JULES

Cabinet V Shelf 1 No. 82

Origines de l'imprimerie en Guyenne par Jules Delpit. Bordeaux, 1869.
Includes documentary evidence by Gaullieur that printing was introduced into Bordeaux by a German, Svelier, in 1486.

Paper; 9¼ x 6 x ½ in.

DeMARINIS, TAMMARO

Cabinet AA Shelf 2 No. 42

Catalogue d'une collection d'anciens livres à figures Italiens appartenant a Tommaro De Marinis. Préface de Seymour de Ricci. Milano, 1925. Illus.

Paper; 13 x 9½ x 1½ in.

De MARINIS, T. et C.

Cabinet J Shelf 5 No. 3

Woodcuts, types, and typographical devices reproduced from early printed books. Libreria Antiquaria T. Marinis e C. Via Vecchietti, 5. Firenze 1913.

Portfolio, boards, linen back; 18 x 13 in.

DE MONTFORT PRESS (Raithby, Lawrence & CO.)

Cabinet Shelf No.

See TYPOGRAPHY. Reithby, Lawrence & Co. (De Montfort Press)...

DENIDEL, ANTOINE.

Cabinet 75 Shelf 1 No. 13

Printers Erasmus' first volume, circa 1496.

See Allen, P. S. Erasmus' relations with his printers.

DeMEULEMEESTER, J.-C. (Engraver, 1771-1836)

Cabinet J Shelf 2 No. 42

Biographical sketch

see DeBusscher, Edmond. Biographie historique....circa 1837

"DEMOTIC ALPHABET"

Cabinet II Shelf 3 No. 63

See LANGUAGE CHARACTERS. Examples of. English demotic alphabet...

DENIS, FERDINAND

Cabinet N Shelf 1 No. 15

Histoire de l'ornementation des manuscrits. Par Ferdinand Denis. Paris. L. Curmer, editeur, 1857.

In Vol. 1 of the Imitation of Jesus-Christ, appendice a...Paris, 1858.

Morocco, tooled gilt; 11 x 7-1/8 in.

DEMOCRAT (The) Boston.

Cabinet Shelf No.

See Newspapers, Massachusetts.

DEMPSEY & CARROLL

Cabinet K Shelf 3 No. 36

[Society Stationers] "Love"... Edited by Mr. G.D. Carroll. Published by Dempsey & Carroll, the Art Stationers and Engravers to the Bon Ton. New York City, 1883.

Specimens of copperplate engraving, monograms, envitations, stationery, etc.

Cloth, oblong; $7\frac{1}{4}$ x 10-3/8 in.

DENIS, MICHAEL.

Cabinet Y Shelf 2 No. 93

Wiens buchdruckergeschicht bis 1560 (History of printing in Vienna to the year 1560). Wien, 1782.

Bio-bibliographical account.

Boards; $10\frac{1}{4}$ x 8-3/8 x $2\frac{1}{4}$ in.

DEMOCRATIC PRESS (The), Philadelphia.

Cabinet Shelf No.

See Newspapers, Pennsylvania.

De NECKER, JOST

Cabinet Shelf No.

See JOST de NECKER

DENMARK.

Cabinet 75 Shelf 2 No. 5

Bibliography of books printed before 1550.

See Nielsen, Lauritz (Bibliography)...

DEMOCRATIC REVIEW (see)

Cabinet Shelf No.

PERIODICALS, United States Democratic Review...

DENHAM, HENRY

Cabinet U Shelf 1 No. 1d

See Early Printing in England. London, 1560: Henry Denham.

DENMARK

Cabinet AA Shelf 5 No. 36

Boghistoriske studier til Dansk bibliografi, 1550-1000. Lauritz Nielsen. Copenhagen, 1923. Facsimiles.

Bio-biblio-historical account.

Half morocco; $11\frac{3}{4}$ x $8\frac{1}{2}$ in.

DEMOCRIET [Pseud.]

Cabinet QQ Shelf 1 No. 28

(XII) Volks-Liedekens op bekende wijzen, ter vervrolijking van Lourens Jansz Kosters vierde eeuw-feest. Te Haarlem, bii Vincent Loosjes. 1823.

Twelve songs in celebration of the alleged fourth centenary of Koster.

Morocco, limp; $6\frac{3}{4}$ x $4\frac{1}{4}$ in.

DENHAM, ROBERT S.

Cabinet LL Shelf 5 No. 70

Cost-finding, the science of. Applied to factories making products to special or shop orders. The Denham Costfinding Company, Cost Engineers, Cleveland, Ohio. n.d.

Has portrait of author.

Cloth; 6 x 4-1/8 x $\frac{1}{2}$ in.

DENMARK.

Cabinet 75 Shelf 2 No. 1

(Early typography of Denmark). Dansk Bibliografi 1482-1550. Af Lauritz Nielsen. Copenhagen, 1919. Review of book with above title, by Victor Scholderer.

In Transactions of the Bibliographical Society, "The Library," Vol. I, 1920-1921, pp. 179-182.

DENMARK

Cabinet NN Newspapers and journalism
see
Shelf 2 NEWSPAPERS, Denmark. Literature of
No. 13

DENNIE, JOSEPH (Oliver Oldschool)

Cabinet See Journalism, Massachusetts, Dennie, Joseph (Oliver Oldschool), Life of Joseph Dennie, Esq.
Shelf
No.

DENNISON, E. W.

Cabinet RR Memorial to E. W. Dennison. n. p. (1916). Portraits and illustrations. Printed at The Plimpton Press, Norwood, Mass., 1916.
Shelf 3
No. 11

Cloth; 9½ x 6¼ x 6/8 in.

DENMARK

Cabinet T (A) Short history of printing in Denmark
Shelf 5 See PEDDIE, R. A. Printing, a short history of the art...p.210
No. 135

DENNIE, JOSEPH ("OLIVER OLDSCHOOL") Philadelphia, 1816.

Cabinet 80
Shelf 2 See Periodicals, United States. Port Folio, The (No. iv, April 1816)
No. 34

DENNISON, E. W.

Cabinet 61 Story of the Dennison Manufacturing Co. An interesting instance of the saying "Some tall oaks from little acorns grow". Illus. With portrait.
Shelf 1
No. 2

Article in "The Paper World", vol. 4, No. 4, April, 1882.

DENMARK

Cabinet AA Skriftskoberier Danmarks. Af C. Nyrop. Kjobenhaven. Industriforeningens Maanedsskrift...10de Aargang-Januar. Thieles bogtrykkerei, 1875.
Shelf 5 Historical, bibliographical account of printing, in Denmark, with some references, to type founding, 1691-1846.
No. 34

Cloth; 8-3/8 x 5¼ x 3/8 in.

DENNIE, JOSEPH and ROYALL TYLER.

Cabinet NN Editor, 1796, "New Hampshire Journal and Farmers' Museum".
see
Shelf 2 JOURNALISM. United States (New England) Joseph Dennie...
No. 8

DENT, J.M.

Cabinet U Memorial Lectures at Stationers Hall, London, The first J.M. Dent. By Basil Blackwell. London, 1931. Pamphlet
Shelf 4 With portrait frontispiece.
No. 114

In envelope.

DENMARK

Cabinet U Spread of printing in Denmark
Shelf 5 (see) DUFF, E. GORDON. Early printed books...p.113
No. 28

DENNIG, FINCK & CO.

See Specimen Books, Types, Germany.

DENT, J. M. MEMORIAL LECTURES at the

Cabinet Q London School of Printing.
see
Shelf 1 LONDON SCHOOL OF PRINTING. Dent, J. M. Memorial Lectures...
No. 29.01

DENMARK

Cabinet See also
Early Printing in Denmark. Danske Palaeotyper trykte i Paris...
Shelf
No.

I - Early Printing in Denmark.
II - " " " " (Literature of)

DENNISON, CHARLES S.

Cabinet RR Round Robin Memorial, 1912. Biographical sketch, extracts from letters of condolence, etc. Portraits.
Shelf 3
No. 12

Limp board; 10 x 8 x ¼ in.

DENUCE, JAN

Cabinet AA Oud-Nederlandsche kaartmakers in betrekking met Plantin (Plantins relations with the early Netherland cartographers). Door Jan Denuce. Antwerp, 1912. Facsimiles, portraits, illus. 2 Vols.
Shelf 3
No. 37
2 Vols. Half morocco; 9¼ x 6¼ in.

DENNIE, JOSEPH (Editor)

Cabinet NN Life of Joseph Dennie. In the Port Folio, May, 1816. [Excerpt, with portrait.]
Shelf 2 X
No. 1

Item I in vol. with binder's title "Journalists. Various excerpts".

DENNISON, E. L.

Cabinet S Vancouver industries, place of printing in. (Newspaper excerpt, n.d. circa 1900)
Shelf 5
No. 50.01

In envelope.

DENVER POST (The), Denver, Colorado.

Cabinet See Newspapers, special issues.
Shelf
No.

DENVER TYPE FOUNDRY COMPANY

Cabinet QQ Shelf 5 No. 10

Specimen of their Tiffany upright series, 1911. The Denver Type Foundry Company, Denver, Colo. 1911.

Half morocco; 8½ x 14 x ½ in.

"DEPOSITO CORNUTI"

Cabinet LL Shelf 1 No. 2

Schmatz, Daniel Michael. Deposito cornuti typographici...Sultzbach, gedruckt by Johann Holsten, 1684.
Bound in with Schmatz's "Neu vorgestelltes auf der loblichen kunst buchdruckerey gebrauchliches format buch"...1684.

Leather; 6-7/8 x 4¼ x ½ in.

DEREUME, AUGUST

Cabinet Shelf No.

See Reume, August De.

DePASSE & MENNE

Cabinet Z Shelf 1 No. 2

See Specimen Books, Types, Holland. DePasse & Menne.

"DEPOSITO CORNUTI" (Bibliography)

Cabinet U Shelf 5 No. 9

An account of the German morality play entitled Depositio Cornuti Typographici, as performed in the 17th & 18th centuries...By William Blades...London, 1885.
With numerous facsimiles, and illus.

Half pigskin; 9 x 7¼ x ¾ in.

De RICCI, SEYMOUR

Cabinet Shelf No.

See Ricci, Seymour De.

DEPEW, CHAUNCEY M.

Cabinet X Shelf 5 No. 124

(The) Liberty of the Press. Address before the New York State Press Association at the Madison Square Theatre, New York, June. 19, 1888.

Brochure, in box labelled "Liberty of Printing: Various Items".

DERBY, GEORGE

Cabinet QQ Shelf 3 No. 24

Anniversary calendar, the Derby (Perpetual.) Being the records of 6000 noteworthy events, anniversaries, birthdays, etc., in American history. Compiled and edited by George Derby. New York, 1903.

Has dates of birth of editors, journalists, etc.

Cloth; 5-1/8 x 3¾ x 5/8 in.

De RIS, L. CLEMENT (Comte)

Cabinet V Shelf 2 No. 56

Typographie en Touraine, 1467-1830: Par Comte L. Clement de Ris. Paris, 1878.
Bibliographical account.

See Ris...

Half morocco; 9 x 5½ x 3/8 in.

DEPOSITIO CORNUTI

Cabinet LL Shelf 1 No. 21

(Apprentices and the "Cornuti" in early times) Rückblick auf der Cornutenstand und das Postulat in früherer zeit.
See pp.175-189 in Hilderbrand's Handbuch fur buchdrucker-lehrlinge...Eisenach, 1835.

DERBY, J. C.

Cabinet Q Shelf 2 No. 5

Fifty years among authors, books and publishers. New York, 1886. Many portraits.

Cloth; 9½ x 6¾ in.

DERMOTYPOTEMNIE

Cabinet L Shelf 4 No. 2

(Color printing method)

see AUMERLE, ERNEST. Dermotypotemnie ...Issoudan, 1867.

DEPOSITIO CORNUTI TYPOGRAPHICI

Cabinet LL Shelf 1 No. 8

(Leipzig, 1743). Depositio cornuti typographici; ...(Or apprentices initiation ceremony).
Follows p.464, Gessner's "Der in der Buchdruckerei wohl unterrichtete Lehr-Junge" ...Leipzig, 1743.

Vellum; 6-7/8 x 4¾ x 1-5/8 in.

DERBY, JAMES C.

Cabinet Q Shelf 2 No. 6

Fifty years among authors, books and publishers. By J. C. Derby. New York, 1886. Frontis.

Cloth; 7-3/8 x 5-1/8 x 1¾ in.

DeROOS, S. H.

Cabinet Y Shelf 3 No. 101

(Modern types and bookmaking in the Netherland) Ueber die neuzeitliche buchkunst und schrift gestaltung in den Niederland.

Essay, with illustrations in the Deutscher Verein für Buchwesen U. Schriftum...1933-34, p.3

"DEPOSITO CORNUTI TYPOGRAPHICI"

Cabinet Shelf No.

See Rist, Johann "Depositio Cornuti Typographici"

DE RENNE, WYMBERLEY JONES

Cabinet PP Shelf 6 No. 5

Books relating to the history of Georgia in the library of W. J. DeRenne, of Wormsloe, Isle of Hope, Chatham County, Georgia. Compiled and annotated by Oscar Wegelin, 1911. Facsimile.

Paper; 13¼ x 10½ x 1-3/8 in.

DE ROOS, S. H.

Cabinet 26 Shelf 2 No. 14

Ueber die neuzeitliche Buchkunst und Schriftgestaltungin den Niederlanden. (On modern typography in Holland and Belgium.)

Illus. article in Jahrbuch VII-VIII, 1933-34, p. 3, Deutscher Verein für Buchwesen und Schrifttum.

DeROSSI, GIOVANNI GHERARDO

Cabinet 50 Shelf 1 No. 48

Scherzi poetici e pittorici (At the end) Parma co' tipi Bodoniani, 1795.
The title and illustrations by Rosaspina are colored. Book dedicated to D. Allessandro de Sousa e Holstein.
Brooks, 599.

Half morocco; 12-3/8 x 9½ x 1-1/8 in.

DE ROSSI, Johannes Bernardus

Cabinet X Shelf 1 No. 79

Annales Hebraeo-typographici, sec. XV., descripsit fusoque commentario illustravit. Parmae, 1795.
Annales of Hebrew printing, with a brief account of the origin of Hebrew types.

Boards; 12¼ x 9-1/8 x 1 in.

DE ROSSI, JOHANNES BERNARDUS

Cabinet X Shelf 1 No. 80

Annales Hebraeo-Typographici ab an [.no] MDI ad MDXL. Digessit notisque hist.-criticis instruxit. Parmae, 1799.
Annales of Hebrew types, printing and printers, 1501 to 1540.

Half leather; 10-3/4 x 8 x ½ in.

Ex Regio Typographeo.

DE ROSSI, JOHANNIS BERNARDI

Cabinet 50 Shelf 1 No. 10

(De) Hebraicae typographiae origine ac primitiis, seu antiquis ac rarissimis. Hebraicorum librorum. Editionibus seculi XV. Disquitio historico-critica. Parmae. Ex regio typographeo. 1776.

Half morocco; 9-3/4 x 7½ in.

DE ROSSI, JOHANNES BERNARDUS

Cabinet X Shelf 1 No. 76

De Hebraicae typographiae ac primitiis; seu antiquis ac rarissimis Hebraicorum librorum editionibus seculi XV. Disquisitio historico-critica. Recudi curavit G. F. Hufnagel. Erlangae. 1778.
History of Hebrew printing.

Half morocco; 7-3/8 x 4-5/8 x ½ in.

DE ROSSI, JOHANNES BERNARDUS

Cabinet X Shelf 1 No. 77

(De) Typographia Hebraeo-Ferrariensi commentarius historicus, quo Ferrarienses Judaeorum editiones hebraicae, hispanicae, lusitanae recensentur et illustrantur. Parmae, 1780.
History of Hebrew printing in Ferrara.

Half morocco; 8-7/8 x 5-7/8 x ½ in.

Ex Regio Typographeo

DE ROSSI, JOHANNES BERNARDUS

Cabinet X Shelf 1 No. 78

Typographia Hebraeo-Ferrariensi commentarius historicus, quo Ferrarienses. Judaeorum editiones Hebraicae, Hispanicae, Lusitanae recensentur et illustratur. Editis altera. Accessit cel. auctoris Epistola qua nonnula Ferrariensis typographiae capita. Erlangae, 1781.
Origin and progress of Hebrew printing in Ferrara.

Half morocco; 6-3/4 x 4½ in.
Sumtibus Ioannis Jacobi Palm.

DERRIEY, CHARLES.

Cabinet Z Shelf 5 No. 32

Cadrats pour cintres inventes par Charles Derriey. Paris, n.d. Broadsides.

Item in box labelled "French Type and Cut Specimens: Miscellaneous Collection."

DERRIEY, CHARLES (PRESIDENT)

Cabinet FF Shelf 3 No. 21

International Association of Typographical Engravers & Founders to prevent remmolding and counterfeiting of their products by electrotyping or other process. Paris, 1859.

Half morocco; 9¼ x 6 in.

DERRIEY, CHARLES

Cabinet Shelf No.

See also index cards under the following sub-heads:

I Specimen Books, Types. France
II " " Vignettes. "

DERRIEY, JULES

Cabinet EE Shelf 5 No. 64

(Catalog, 1879) Jules Derriey's rotary perfecting printing machines. From the web or hand feeding. Paris, at Jules Derriey, 31, boulevard de Belleville. London at James Dellagana, 172 Saint-John Street. 1879.

Item in manila envelope.

DESARNOD, JOSEPH - FRANCOIS

Cabinet QQ Shelf 2 No. 6

Mémoire sur les foyers économiques et salubres... et auquel on a joint une notice fur les foyers de M. Franklin...Paris-Lyon, 1789. With 8 folded plates.
Bound in with L'Art d'économiser le bois...Par Jean Henri Sachtleben. Traduit de l'allemand par J. Goy. Paris, 1792.

Boards, tree-calf back; 8-1/8 x 5 x 1¼ in.

DESBARREAUX-BERNARD

Cabinet V Shelf 2 No. 51

Etablissement de l'imprimerie dans la province de Languedoc. Par Desbarreaux-Bernard. Toulouse, 1875. With some printers' marks, facsimiles, and paper marks.

Half morocco; 8 x 5½ x 1¼ in.

DESCHAMPS, (G)

Cabinet Shelf No.

See Specimen Books, Cuts, France.
" also Specimen Books, Vignettes, France.

DESERET NEWS (Utah).

Cabinet A Shelf 3 No. 52

See Newspapers, Utah.

DESFOSSÉ et KARTH

Cabinet RR Shelf 3 No. 23

Manufacture de papiers peints. De M. M. Desfossé et Karth. (Manufacture of wall-papers).
Illus. excerpt from "Grandes Usines", Clichy, n. d. circa 1860, pp. 113-128.

Bound with item "La papeterie d' Essonne".

Cloth; 10½ x 7-1/8 x 4/8 in.

DESIGN

Cabinet K Shelf 6 No. 1

Advertising Art...

see
TYPOGRAPHY, DECORATIVE. Advertising Art...

DESIGN

Cabinet 26 Shelf 1 No. 19

(Alphabets of the renaissance, the Italian studies of)

See BERTIERI, RAFFAELO. Gli studi italiani sull'alfabeto...

DESIGN

Cabinet K Shelf 2 No. 36

Ancient painting from the earliest times to the period of Christian art. By Mary Hamilton Swindler, New Haven, 1929.

With 640 illus. and 16 plates in black and white and colored.

Cloth; 11 x 8 in.

DESIGN

Cabinet K Shelf 2 No. 25

Arts au Moyen Age et a l'époque de la Renaissance ...Par Paul Lacroix. Paris, 1871.

Profusely illustrated

Morocco, gilt; 11-3/8 x 8-3/8 in.

DESIGN

Cabinet RR Shelf 6 No. 34

Cover designing, constructive. A book of 76 original designs...The Hampden Glazed Paper and Card Co., Holyoke, Mass., 1923. With an introduction by Frank Randolph Southard.

Half morocco; 13-3/4 x 10½ x 1-3/4 in.

DESIGN

Cabinet 68 Shelf No. 13

(Arabic-Norman design in the architecture of Sicily) L'Architettura Arabo-Normanna e el rinascimento in Sicilia. Giulio V. Arata. Prefazione di Corrado Ricci. Milano, 1925.

Designs by the author.

Portfolio; 19½ x 13¾ in.

DESIGN

Cabinet K Shelf 5 No. 7

Chinese book of designs, ideographs, symbolic figures, pictorial.

Paper: 12 x 7¼ x ⅝ in.

DESIGN

Cabinet K Shelf 3 No. 20

Decorative design: an elementary text book of principles and practice. By Frank G. Jackson. (7th ed.) LOndon, 1905. Illus.

Cloth; 8¾ x 5-5/8 in.

DESIGN

Cabinet J Shelf 4 No. 5

L'Art du dessin d'une manier claire et precise. Par Jean Cousin. Revue, corrigé et augmentée par P.T. Le Clere...A. Paris. Chez Jean, Rue Jean de Beauvais, No.32. n.d. circa 1550 [Title page and 24 plates, copperplate engravings].

Bound in with GUIFFREY'S "La famille de Jean Cousin...Paris, 1881.

Half morocco; 15¾ x 12 x ½ in.

DESIGN

Cabinet K Shelf 1 No. 22

Copperplate engravings, miscellaneous collection of initials, borders, ornaments and other decorative typographical material. Specimens mounted, 50 plates.

In box.

DESIGN

Cabinet K Shelf 1 No. 24

(Decorative design, examples) Modelli d'arte decorativa. Bestetti et Tumminelli, Milano-Roma. n. d. 19__. (Vols. 1, 2, 3, 4, 5, 6, 8.)

Portfolios, each with 60 plates.

Linen; 14 x 10 in.

DESIGN

Cabinet K Shelf 2 No. 9

L'Art Hollandais a l'Exposition Internationale des Arts Decoratifs et Industriels Modernes. Paris, 1925.

pp.28-43 show typographic designs.

This is the first book printed in the Lutetia types designed by van Krimpen, made by Enschede, Haarlem.

Cloth; 11-5/8 x 8¾ in.

DESIGN

Cabinet K Shelf 1 No. 4

Copperplates by Callot (?) circa 1630. Original.

Fastened tohether in the form of a book; paper, leather back; 8½ x 11 in.

DESIGN

Cabinet K Shelf 5 No. 37 5 vols.

(Decorative design of all peoples, and all times. Illustrated history of 1)

Geschichte des kunstgewerbes aller zeiten und völker. In verbindung fachgelehrten. Herausgegeben von Dr. H. Th. Bossert. Berlin, 1928-1932. (5 vols.) Illus.

Quarter morocco; 10½ x 7-5/8 in.

DESIGN

Cabinet K Shelf 4 No. 13.01

Art in industry. By Charles R. Richards. Being the report of an industrial art survey conducted under the auspices of The National Society for Vocational education...New York, 1922. Illus.

On printing, pp.227-250.

Cloth; 9½ x 6-1/8 x 1½ in. See also K/4/13.02. (1929 ed.)

DESIGN

Cabinet Q Shelf 1 No. 33.01

Copyright registration of design.

See COPYRIGHT, United States. Act amending the statutes of the United States...

DESIGN

Cabinet K Shelf 3 No. 21

Decorative designs for of all ages and for all purposes. With numerous engravings and diagrams. Edited by Paul N. Hasluck. London, 1903.

Cloth; 7 x 4-1/8 in.

DESIGN

Cabinet K Shelf 4 No. 11

Art of decorative design...By C. Dresser. London, 1862. Illus.

Cloth: 9¾ x 6½ in.

DESIGN

Cabinet RR Shelf 3 No. 48

Cover design. Princess cover papers. Manufactured at Windsor Locks, Conn., by C.H. Dexter & Sons.

Cloth; 11 x 9 in.

DESIGN

Cabinet K Shelf 1 No. 15

Deutsche bucherillustrationen der gothik und fruhrenaissance (1460-1530) von Richard Muther. Munchen, 1884. (2 vols. in one)

Boards, morocco back; 14½ x 10½ x 1-5/8 in.

DESIGN

Cabinet K Shelf 3 No. 13

Drawing for printers

see KNAUFFT, ERNEST. Drawing for printers...

DESIGN.

Cabinet K Shelf 4 No. 34

(German trade marks, ex libris).

See BRAUNGART, RICHARD. (Das) Moderne deutsche gebrauchs-exlibris ...

DESIGN

Cabinet P Shelf 2 No. 36.01

Historic design in printing. Reproductions of book covers, borders, initials, decorations, printers' marks and devices comprising reference material for the designer, printer advertiser, and publisher. With introduction and notations by Henry Lewis Johnson. Boston, 1923.

This is a duplicate of P/2/36 in another form.

Cloth; 12¼ x 9 1/8 x ⅝ in.

DESIGN

Cabinet PP Shelf 3 No. 43.01

Eskimos, the graphic art of the.

See HOFFMAN, WALTER JAMES. Graphic arts of the eskimos...

DESIGN

Cabinet J Shelf 5 No. 6

Grammar of ornament. By Owen Jones. Illustrated by examples from various styles of ornament. One hundred and twelve plates. London (1856).

Cloth, gilt; 13-3/8 x 9-3/8 x 1¾ in.

DESIGN

Cabinet K Shelf 4 No. 9

(History of decorative design and ornament) Ornamentstich. Geschichte der vorlagen des kunsthandwerks seit dem mittelalter. von Peter Jessen. Berlin, 1920. Illus.

Boards, linen back; 9½ x 6-3/8 x 7/8 in.

DESIGN

Cabinet K Shelf 6 No. 3

Examples of Mediaeval art applicable to modern purposes. (Illus. article by) Henry Shaw.

see "ART JOURNAL, THE". Wood engravings etchings, etc...1849, London. pp. 14, 57, 117, 217, 235, 341, 361.

DESIGN

Cabinet K Shelf 4 No. 17.01

Graphic Design...By Leon Friend and Joseph Hefter. New York, 1936. Illus.

A survey of the graphic arts in text and illustration. Includes lettering, reproduction, book design, etc.

Cloth; 11 x 8; pp. 407

DESIGN.

Cabinet I Shelf 3 No. 11

History of the rise and progress of the arts of design in the United States. By William Dunlap. A new edition, illustrated. Edited by Frank W. Bayley and Charles E. Goodspeed. In three volumes. Boston, 1918.

Cloth; 9¼ x 6-5/8 in.

DESIGN

Cabinet K Shelf 4 No. 12

Floral designs

See McFarland, J. Horace (Compiler) Floral designs...(Harrisburg, Pa.) 1888.

DESIGN

Cabinet K Shelf 3 No. 23

(Die) Grotesklinie und ihre spiegelvariation im modernen ornament und in der dekorationsmalerei. Herausgegeben von Julius Klinger und Hanns Anker. Berlin-Koln. n.d.

Consists of 64 plates of decorative motives, mostly printed in colors.

In portfolio, cloth; 6¾ x 8¼ in.

DESIGN

Cabinet J Shelf 4 No. 15

Holbein's designs for the handicrafts.

See DAVIES, GERALD S. Hans Holbein... London, 1903. Plate facing p.201.

DESIGN

Cabinet J Shelf 4 No. 8

(French 16th century) La gravure dans le livre et l'ornement. La gravure en France au 16e siècle. Par J. Lieure. Paris et Bruxelles, 1927. G. Vanoest, Editeur.

72 plates of illustration.

Paper; 13 x 9-7/8 x 1¼ in.

DESIGN

Cabinet P Shelf 2 No. 47.01

Gummed papers (110) suggestions.

see TYPOGRAPHY . Suggestions (110) for gummed paper labels...

DESIGN

Cabinet U Shelf 5 No. 87

Islamic Book, its art and history, 7th to 18th century.

See ARNOLD, THOMAS W. and Prof. A. GROHMANN. The Islamic Book...

DESIGN

Cabinet K Shelf 5 No. 27

(French 18th century head and tail pieces, borders, monograms, initials, etc.)

see AUDIN, MARIUS. Essai sur les graveurs sur bois en France...Paris, 1925.

DESIGN

Cabinet K Shelf 1 No. 25

(Hieroglyphics and emblems, their function and adaptation in decorative art). Bilder schriften der renaissance: hieroglyphic emblematik in ihren beziehungen und fortkungen. von Ludwig Volkmann. Leipzig, 1923. Illus.

Cloth; 13½ x 9¾ x 3/8 in.

DESIGN

Cabinet K Shelf 6 No. 3

Italian fictile wares of the renaissance.

see ART JOURNAL, THE. Wood engravings, etchings, etc...1849, London. pp. 80-3.

DESIGN

Cabinet K Shelf 4 No. 36

(ITalian laces, old and new.) Elisa Ricci. Ricami Italiani antichi e moderni. Firenze: Felice Le Monnier, Editore. n.d. Illus.

Embossed leather; 11 x 9 x 1-1/8 in.

DESIGN

Cabinet K Shelf 4 No. 8

Manual of historic ornament

See Glazier, Richard. Manual...London-New York, 1906.

DESIGN

Cabinet J Shelf 5 No. 9

Peasant art in Europe...Reproducing 2100 examples of peasant ornament. Selected and arranged by H. Th. Bossert. New York, 1927. Printed in Germany.

100 plates in full colours, 32 plates in black and white.

Cloth; 15-3/8 x 11¼ x 1¾ in.

DESIGN

Cabinet J Shelf 5 No. 15

Japanese design.

See GONSE, LOUIS. L'Art Japonais...Paris, 1883.

DESIGN

Cabinet K Shelf 1 No. 12

Meister des ornamentstichs: Gothik und Renaissance. 200 bildtafeln. Ausgewahlt von Peter Jessen. (Band I) Berlin, n. d. circa 1926.

200 plates of design.

Boards, cloth back; 13¼ x 9-7/8 x 1 in.

DESIGN

Cabinet J Shelf 5 No. 7

Polychromatic ornament. One hundred plates...comprising upwards of two thousand specimens of the various styles of ancient, oriental and mediaeval art...Selected and arranged by A. Racinet. With explanatory text and general introduction, translated from the French. London, 1873.

Morocco, gilt; 16¼ x 12 x 2 in. In slip case.

DESIGN

Cabinet K Shelf 5 No. 5

Japanese designs suggested or in use for purposes similar to our book marks. Text and designs lithographed in imitation of block book printing.

Limp cloth, oblong; 7-3/8 x 10¼ x 1¼ in.

DESIGN

Cabinet K Shelf 1 No. 27

Menus and programmes...du 17 siécle jusqu'a nos jours.

See MAILLARD, LÉON. Menus et programmes...Paris, 1898.

DESIGN

Cabinet K Shelf 3 No. 15

Practical handbook of drawing for modern methods of reproduction. By Charles G. Harper. Illus with drawings by several hands...(2nd. ed.) London, 1901.

Cloth; 8-7/8 x 5¾ in.

DESIGN

Cabinet Shelf No.

Lay-Out...

See TYPOGRAPHY

DESIGN

Cabinet K Shelf 6 No. 3

Original designs for manufactures. Illus. article.

see ART JOURNAL, THE. Wood engravings, etchings, etc...1849, London. pp. 26, 125, 152, 190, 273.

DESIGN

Cabinet K Shelf 4 No. 13

Principles of design. By Ernest A. Batchelder. .. Chicago: The Inland Printer Company. Publisher. 1906. Illus.

Cloth: 9-1/8 x 6 x ¾ in.

DESIGN

Cabinet I Shelf 1 No. 1

Letter design, the first treatise on.

See PACIOLO, LUCAS. Divina proportione... Venice, 1509.

DESIGN

Cabinet J Shelf 5 No. 8

Ornament in applied art...

See WEYHE, E. (Editor) Ornament in applied art...New York, 1924.

DESIGN

Cabinet K Shelf 3 No. 22

Projective ornament. By Claude Bragdon. Rochester N.Y., The Manas Press, 1915. Illus.

Cloth; 8½ x 5¾ in.

DESIGN

Cabinet K Shelf 4 No. 1 & 2

Lost language of symbolism. An inquiry into the origin of letters, words... By Harold Bayley. London, 1912. (2 vols. illus.)

Cloth: 9¾ x 6¼ in.

DESIGN

Cabinet J Shelf 5 No. 10

L'Ornament polychrome dans tous les styles historiques...Par Alexandre Speltz, Architecte ...Premier Partie. L'Antiquité. Librairie Baumgartner, Leipzig (1915).

Collection of 60 plates printed in three or four colours, with illustrated text.

Cloth portfolio; 15 x 11¼ in.

DESIGN

Cabinet Q Shelf 1 No. 33.09

Registrations of designs and certain enactments relating to trade marks, and an act to amend the Patents and Design Acts (Aug. 28, 1907 and Dec. 23, 1919. London, H.M. Stationery Office.

Pamphlet with other items in manila envelope

DESIGN

Cabinet P Shelf 2 No. 37.01

Resources for motifs in book and catalogue covers. Second part. By Henry Lewis Johnson. Excerpt from The New England Printer, August, 1924.

In envelope.

DESIGN.

Cabinet K Shelf 4 No. 32

(Symbolic bookplates).

See KISSEL, CLEMENS. Symbolic bookplates...London, 1894.

DESIGN

Cabinet Shelf No.

Type Design

see TYPE DESIGN

DESIGN

Cabinet K Shelf 1 No. 11

Rococco engravings, two hundred plates of the 18th century selected by Fr. Peter Jessen, and reproduction in collotype. London, 1922.

Cloth: 13½ x 10¼ x 7/8 in.

DESIGN

Cabinet K Shelf 4 No. 2

Symbolism for artists.

see BAILEY, HENRY TURNER and ETHEL POOL. Symbolism for artists...

DESIGN

Cabinet K Shelf 2 No. 6

Typographic ornaments

see GRASSET, EUGENE (Compiler) Ornaments typographiques...

DESIGN

Cabinet K Shelf 2 No. 20

(Russia, graphic arts in)

see MITROCHIN, D.I. Russische graphische kunst...

DESIGN

Cabinet K Shelf 2 No. 40

Technical arts and sciences of the ancients. By Albert Neuburger. Translated by Henry L. Brose. With 676 illustrations. New York, 1930.

Cloth; 9-3/8 x 6½ x 1-5/8 in.

DESIGN

Cabinet K Shelf 1 No. 8

Typographic ornaments, 460 copperplate engravings.

See GUERINET, ARMAND (Editor.) Recueil de 460 ornaments typographiques...

DESIGN

Cabinet K Shelf 6 No. 3

Ships, ancient ships. Illus.

see ART JOURNAL, THE. Wood engravings, etchings, etc...1849, London. pp. 7, 41, 62, 187, 346.

DESIGN

Cabinet K Shelf 3 No. 19

Theory and practice of design. An advanced text book on decorative art. By Frank G. Jackson. With 700 illustrations. 4th ed. London, 1903.

Cloth; 9 x 6 in.

DESIGN

Cabinet K Shelf 2 No. 39

(La) Voix des monuments. Notes et études d'archélogie chretienne. G. De Jerphanion, S.J. Paris et Bruxelles, 1930.

Numerous illustrations.

Paper; 11¼ x 7-5/8 x 1-3/4 in.

DESIGN

Cabinet K Shelf 3 No. 33

Sources of design...

see IVINS, WILLIAM M. Jr. Prints and books...pp.294-352.

DESIGN.

Cabinet K Shelf 4 No. 45

Towards a reform of the paper currency.

See DWIGGINS, W. A. Towards a reform etc. New York, 1932.

DESIGN

Cabinet K Shelf 4 No. 14

Zeichen-buchlein (von Gustav Wolf). Verlag Seldwyla.. Bern. n. d.

Illustrated description of the manner in which designs are built up from symbolic figures.

Boards, linen back; 10 x 7-1/8 in.

DESIGN

Cabinet K Shelf 2 No. 23

Suggestions in design...for the printer in colors, engraver, etc. By Luke Limner, pseud. [John Leighton] London, 1853.

Morocco, gilt; 11½ x 8¾ in.

DESIGN

Cabinet C Shelf 2 No. 10

(Turkish ceramics, design and color in.) Altturkische keramik in Kleinasien und Konstantinople. Mit ein einfuhrung von Karl Wulzinger Munchen, 1922.

Author's name Alexander Raymund

Boards; 19½ x 14½ in.

DESIGN

Cabinet Shelf No.

See also cards with following sub-head: DRAWING.

DESIGN REGISTRATION

Cabinet Q Shelf 1 No. 33.02

Proceedings of the Design Registration Convention of manufacturers, etc. Held at Hotel Astor, New York, Friday, Nov. 21, 1913, under the jount auspices of The National Registration League and the committee representing the Federation of Trade Press Associations in the U. S.

Brochure, in envelope.

DESIGNERS, PRINTING TYPE

Cabinet Shelf No.

See TYPE DESIGNERS

DESIGNING

Cabinet Shelf No.

Alphabets

See ALPHABETS...

DESIGNING

Cabinet MM Shelf 6 No. 73

Applied design: A handbook of the principles of arrangement, with brief comment on the periods of design which have most strongly influenced prin ing. By Harry Lawrence Gage. "Typographic Technical Series for Apprentices". Part VII, No.43. The United Typothetae of America, 1920. Illus.

Cloth; 8 x 5 in.

DESIGNING

Cabinet G Shelf 1 No. 23

Bradley, Will. Peter Poodle, toy-maker to the king. Illustrated. By Will Bradley. New York, 1906.

Printed in black and red.

Boards; $11\frac{1}{4}$ x 9 in.

DESIGNING

Cabinet G Shelf 3 No. 62

Initials and title page, based on flowers of. Palestine, and drawn by Miss E.H. McLauthlin for "The Sower and other Poems", by Rev. Wm. P. McKenzie. Cambridge, 1903.

Above book printed at the Sparrell Press, Boston.

Boards; $7\frac{1}{4}$ x $5\frac{1}{4}$ in.

DESIGNING.

Cabinet I Shelf 5 No. 22

Leonardo Da Vinci. Les manuscrits ... publies en fac-similes phototypiques. Avec transcriptions litterales, traductions françaises ... Par Charles Ravisson-Mollien, Paris, 1890.

Half morocco; $18\frac{3}{4}$ x $11\frac{1}{2}$ x $1\frac{1}{2}$ in.

DESIGNING.

Cabinet I Shelf 5 No. 21

Leonardo Da Vinci. Traite de la peinture ... Paris, 1511.

See LEONARDO DA VINCI. Traite de la peinture ...

DESIGNING

Cabinet 67 Shelf 2 No. 30

Letters: Of the Just Shaping of. By Albrecht Durer. Translated by R. T. Nichol from the latin text of the edition of 1535. Printed for The Grolier Club by Bruce Rogers, at The Mall Press, London, 1917.

Paper boards; $12\frac{1}{2}$ x $8\frac{1}{2}$ in.

DESIGNING

Cabinet M Shelf 1 No. 50

Morris, William. Some hints on pattern designing. Printed at the Chiswick Press with the Golden type designed by William Morris for the Kelmscott Press, and finished on the fourth day of October, 1899.

Boards; $8\frac{3}{4}$ x $5\frac{3}{4}$ x $\frac{1}{4}$ in.

DESIGNING.

Cabinet M Shelf 1 No. 50

Some hints on pattern designing. By William Morris. Printed at the Chiswick Press with the Golden type designed by William Morris for the Kelmscott Press, and finished on the fourth day of October, 1899.

Boards; $8\frac{3}{4}$ x $5\frac{3}{4}$ x $\frac{1}{4}$ in.

DESIGNING

Cabinet G Shelf 3 No. 61

Title page, initials and decorations based on the pansy. "Heartsease hymns", by Rev. Wm. P. McKenzie, Cambridge, 1901. Imprint: Printed by the Sparrell Press, Boston.

Boards; $8\frac{1}{2}$ x $6\frac{1}{2}$ in.

DES JARDINS, BENJAMIN M.

Cabinet FF Shelf 6 No. 54

Patent interference suits Nos. 21,694 and 23,998. Alexander Dow vs. Benjamin M. Des Jardins. Subject: Type justifying machines. Record for Des Jardins. Washington, 1905.

Half morocco; $9\frac{1}{4}$ x $6\frac{1}{4}$ in.

DESK BOOK

Cabinet Shelf No.

See Specimen Books, Types. United States. American Type Founders' Co. 1900.

DESLANDES, VENANCIO

Cabinet AA Shelf 5 No. 24

Documentos para a historia da typographia Portugueza nos seculos XVI e XVII. Publicados por Venancio Deslandes. Lisboa, Imprensa Nacional, 1888.

Chronological bio-bibliographical account gathered and arranged from documents.

Half morocco; $9\frac{1}{4}$ x 6-3/4 in.

DESORMES, E. and ARNOLD MULLER

Cabinet MM Shelf 7 No. 67

Dictionnaire de l'Imprimerie et des arts graphiques en général. Paris, 1912.

Half morocco; 7 x 4 x $\frac{3}{4}$ in.

DESPIERRES, GERASIME. MME.

Cabinet V Shelf 1 No. 6

Establissement d'imprimeries a Alencon de 1529-1575. Paris: Ernest Leroux, editeur, 1894.

Includes facsimile pages.

Half morocco; 9-7/8 x 6-5/8 x $\frac{1}{2}$ in.

DESPIERRES, GERASIME (MME.

Cabinet V Shelf 5 No. 1

L'Imprimerie a Alencon de 1529 a 1575. Communication de Mme. Gerasime Despierres. Bulletin Historique et Philologique...Paris, 1893. Pamphlet.

Bound in volume "French Typographical Pamphlets", item 10.

DESPREAUX, NICOLAS BOILEAU

Cabinet F Shelf 5 No. 1

Oeuvres de Nicolas Boileau Despreaux...Enrichie de figures gravées par Bernard Picart le Romain. Tome premier. A la Haye, chez Pierre de Hondt. 1729.

Leather; $14\frac{3}{4}$ x $9\frac{1}{2}$ x 2 in.

DESPREZ, Guillaume

Cabinet V Shelf 3 No. 18

(Bio-bibliographical notes relating to Desprez family of printers-publishers, Paris, 1651-1741)

see

WERDET, EDMOND. Histoire du livre en France...3me partie (2), p.208

DESROCHES, J.

Cabinet Y Shelf 2 No. 5

(Neue untersuchung uber den ursprung der buchdruckerkunst.) Translated from the French Nouvelles recherches sur l'imprimerie, par J. Desroches. In Breitkopf, Geschichte der erfindung der buchdruckerkunst...Leipzig, 1779.

Half calf; $8\frac{1}{2}$ x 7 in.

DESROCHES, J.

Cabinet V Shelf 4 No. 8

Nouvelles recherches sur l'origine de l'imprimerie, dans lesquelles on fait voir que la premier idée en est due aux Brabançons. Par M. Des Roches. Lues à la Séance du 8 Janvier 1777. Bruxelles, L'Academie de Bruxelles.

The first printer, according to this theory was a native of Brabant.

Half morocco; 10 x 8 in.

DETROIT FREE PRESS (The)

Cabinet A Shelf 1 No. 79

See Newspapers, anniversary issues. U.S.

DETROIT NEWS (George G. Booth, Pub.)

Cabinet OO Shelf 3 No. 40

Booth gives fortune to unique school. The Detroit publisher established Cranbrook Cultural Community as a youth to develop its talents. Illus. and portrait.

Newspaper clipping, "New York Times", Sunday, Jan. 1, 1928.

Item in envelope.

DETROIT NEWS (The)

Cabinet NN Shelf 6 No. 18

(A) Record of progress, 1873-1917.

see

WHITE, LEE A. Detroit News, The., 1873-1917...

DETROIT NEWS

See also

Newspapers.

DETROIT SUNDAY TIMES, THE

Cabinet A Shelf 1 No. 80

New home edition. Nov. 17, 1929. Illus.

Buckram; $21\frac{1}{4}$ x 16-7 /8 x $\frac{1}{4}$ in.

DETROIT TIMES, THE

Cabinet OO Shelf 3 No. 61

Specimens of headings and samples of type. n. d.

Paper; $8\frac{1}{4}$ x 5-3/8 in.

DETTERER, ERNST

Cabinet S Shelf 1 No. 112

See Types, Detterer, Ernst ... Nicolas Jenson, a new type designed by Ernst Detterer.

DETTERER, ERNST F.

Cabinet Shelf No.

See Imprints, United States.

DEUTSCH-AMERIKANISCHES BUCHDRUCKER-ZEITUNG

Cabinet 33 Shelf 2 No. 2

Officieles organ der Deutsch-Amerikanisches Typographie...

See PERIODICALS, PRINTING, United States Deutsche-Amerikanisches...

DEUTSCHE-AMERIKANISCHEN TYPOGRAPHIA

Cabinet JJ Shelf 5 No. 18

(Reports 1894 to 1925. Branch of the International Typographical Union. Report of 1898 contains a history of the German-American organization.) Deutsche-Amerikanischen Typographia. Jahres-Bericht. Zweig der I.T.U. von 1894 bis 1925.

18 items.

Boards; 11 x $7\frac{1}{2}$ in.

DEUTSCHE BUCHGEWERBEHAUS

Cabinet 13 Shelf No. 2

Plans of the proposed building to house this Society, Leipzig, 1899

See SOCIETIES, BOOKSELLERS. Des Deutsche Buchgewerbehaus...

DEUTSCHE BUCHMUSEUM, Leipzig.

Cabinet Y Shelf 3 No. 99

(Handbook for paper production, Japan, 1798. Facsimile, 1925) Kamisuki Choho-ki." Kumihigashi Iibei, Naniwa (Osaka) 1798.

Japanese text. Concluding remarks in German by Dr. Albert Schramm. Facsimile by the Deutsche Buchmuseum, Leipzig, 1925.

Paper; $8\frac{3}{4}$ x 6-1/8 in.

DEUTSCHE EIN-BLATT HOLZSCHNIT (16th cent.)

Cabinet 1 & 5 Shelf Portfolios 1 to 40

Facsimile reprints. About 1660 plates

See GEISBERG, MAX (German single-plate woodcuts...)

DEUTSCHE MUSEUM FÜR BUCH UND SCHRIFT

Cabinet Y Shelf 3 No. 100

(Account of the founding, purpose and contents of this museum, 1884-1934)

Das Deutsche Museum für Buch und Schrift. von Hans H. Bockwitz. Deutscher Verein für Buchwesen und Schrifttum, zu Leipzig, 1934.

In envelope. Paper; 12-1/8 x 9-1/8 in.

DEUTSCHE PORCUPEIN und LANCASTER ANZEIGS-

Cabinet A NACHRICHTEN.

See Newspapers. Pennsylvania; see also Newspapers, German-American.

Shelf 3

No. 9

DEUTSCHER VEREIN FÜR BUCHWESEN UND SCHRIFTTUM

Cabinet 26 Jahrbuch IV, 1930. Schriftprobleme. Schriftleitung Dr. Hans H. Bockwitz. Verlag des Deutschen Vereins für Buchwesen und Schrifttum zu Leipzig.

Shelf 2

Illus. essays on alphabets, Semetic, Indian, etc.

No. 12

Paper; 12½ x 9¼ in.

DEUTSCHER VEREIN FUR BUCHWESEN U. SCHRIFTTUM

Cabinet Y (Das) Deutsche Museum fur Buch und Schrift 1884-1934. von Dr. Hans H. Bockwitz. Leipzig.

Shelf 3

No. 100.01

Paper wrapper: 12½ x 9¼ in.

Deutsche und italienische inkunabeln.

Stack B see INCUNABULA. (Facsimile, German and Italian.) Monumenta Germaniae et Italiae typographica ...

Shelf 3

Number 14

DEUTSCHER VEREIN FUR BUCHWESEN UND SCHRIFTTUM

Cabinet 26 Jahrbuch V. Jahrgang 1931. Illus. Sur Geschichte des Kupferstich und der Lithographie. Schriftleitung: Dr. Hans Bockwitz. Verlag des Deutschen Vereins für Buchwesen und Schrifttum zu Leipzig.

Shelf 2

No. 13

Paper; 12½ x 9¼ in.

DEUTSCHER VEREIN FÜR BUCHWESEN UND SCHRIFTTUM

Cabinet 26 (Das) Deutsche Museum für Buch und Schrift. Sein Werden und seine Ziele. (Librarian) Dr. H. Bockwitz. Leipzig, 1930.

Shelf 2

Illus. account of this Museum, its collections, its aims.

No. 11

Paper; 12¼ x 3¼ in.

DEUTSCHEN BUCHGEWERBE VEREINS

Cabinet Y Amerikareise eines deutschen buchdruckers. Oktober, 1924. von Alexander Oldenbourg. (A printers tour of the United States as a delegate of the D. B. V.

Shelf 4

No. 78

Pamphlet, in envelope.

DEUTSCHER VEREIN FÜR BUCHWESEN U. SCHRIFTUM

Cabinet 26 Buchkunst: Beiträge zur entwicklung der graphischen künste und der kunst im buche. Herausgegeben von der Staatl. Akademie für Graphische Künste und Buchgewerbe zu Leipzig.

Buch und Schrift. Jahrbuch des Deutschen Vereins für Buchwesen und Schriftum. Buchkunst 1. Vll/Vlll (Doppel) Jahrgang 1933-34.

Shelf 2

No. 14

Paper; 12½ x 9 in.

DEUTSCHER VEREIN FÜR BUCHWESEN UND SCHRIFTTUM

Cabinet 26 Zeitschrift des Deutschen Vereins für Buchwesen und Schrifttum. VIII Jahrgang, Nummer 1-2, 3-4, 1925. Schriftleitung, Prof. Dr. Albert Schramm. Leipzig.

Shelf 2

Nos. 1 to 4 illus. description of this Museum and some of its contents.

No. 10

Two items in one envelope.

DEUTSCHEN BUCHGEWERBE VEREIN

Cabinet See also

Shelf SOCIETIES, PRINTERS'. Germany.

No.

DEUTSCHER VEREIN FÜR BUCHWESEN U. SCHRIFTTUM

Cabinet 26 Jahrbuch VII-VIII (Doppel) Jahrgang 1933-1934. Buchkunst I. Beiträge zur entwicklung der Graphischen Künste und der Kunst im Buche. Herausgegeben von der Staatl. Akademie für Graphische Künste und Buchgewerbe zu Leipzig.

Buchkunst II, IX Jahrgang, 1935.

Shelf 2

No. 14 & 15

Paper; 12½ x 9-1/8 in.

DEUTSCHES BUCHMUSEUM, Leipzig

Cabinet Y Inkunabeln. Kataloge des Deutschen Buchmuseum zu Leipzig. Die Inkunabeln. von Albert Schramm, Leipzig, 1925.

Shelf 3 ~~2~~

An illustrated bibliographical account of the incuabula in the Deutsches Buchmuseum. Has names of printers, places of printing, etc.

No. 100

Paper; 12¼ x 9-1/8 in.

DEUTSCHEN BUCHMUSEUMS

Cabinet PP (Brief descriptive guide through the rooms of the German book Museum.) Kurzer fuhrer durch die raume des deutschen Buchmuseums. von Albert Schramm, Leipzig, 1923. Illus. pamphlet.

Shelf 3

No. 51

Paper 8-3/4 x 5½ in.

DEUTSCHER VEREIN FÜR BUCHWESEN U. SCHRIFTTUM

Cabinet 26 Buchkunst. Beiträge zur entwicklung der graphischen kunste und der künste im buche. Band 11. Staatliche Akademie für Graphische Künste und Buchgewerbe zu Leipzig. 1X Jahrgang, 1935.

Shelf 2

No. 15

Paper; 12½ x 9 in.

DEUTSCHES BUCHMUSEUM (Leipzig, 1925)

Cabinet Y Kataloge des Deutschen Buchmuseums zu Leipzig. Die Inkunabeln. von Albert Schramm. Leipzig, 1925. Illus.

Shelf 3

No. 100

Paper; 12-1/8 x 9-1/8. In envelope.

DEUTSCHER BUCHDRUCKER-VEREIN

Cabinet KK Vereinigung der buchdruckereibesitzer deutschlands. Berlin. Marz 1928.

Shelf 2

Master Printers Associations of Germany. Book which contains rules, list of clubs, prices of printing, etc.

No. 60

Cloth; 6-3/8 x 4-5/8 x ¾ in.

DEUTSCHER VEREIN FÜR BUCHWESEN U. SCHRIFTTUM

Cabinet 26 Jahrgang IX, 1935. Buchkunst: Beiträge zur Entwicklung der Graphischen Künste und der Kunst im Buch. II Band. Staatliche Akademie für Graphische Kunst und Buchgewerbe zu Leipzig.

Shelf 2

Illus. articles on modern printing, illustrating, commercial art.

No. 15

Paper; 12½ x 8-7/8 in.

DEUTSCHES MUSEUM FÜR BUCH UND SCHRIFT

Cabinet B (Der) Bilderschmuck der frühdrucke. von Prof. Albert Shramm. Leipzig. [Herausgegeben von Deutsches Museum für Buch und Schrift]

Shelf 2

Published in parts, Nos 1 to ~~1~~3, for years 1922 to 193~~4~~5.

No.s 1 to ~~1~~3

On the illustrations [wood engravings] in books printed in the 15th century.

Half morocco, or board, morocco backs; 17½ x 13½ in

DEVAUX, A.

Cabinet L Shelf 3 No. 9.01

Papiers et parchmins timbres de France. Par A. Devaux.

Illus. article in Bulletin...le Vieux Papier, Paris, 1908, pp.232-243

DeVEZE, CAMILLE

Cabinet MM Shelf 6 No. 55

Job composition, first steps in. "Typographic Technical Series for Apprentices, Part II, No.18. Published by the United Typothetae of America, 1918.

Cloth; 8 x 5 in.

DE VEZE, CAMILLE

Cabinet S Shelf 4 No. 34

Report to the Washington Convention of the Clubs of Printing House Craftsmen, on the Fust and Schoeffer mark, with copies of letters from various authorities (Bullen, Winship, Pollard, Grannis, etc.). In galley form, folded, with signed letter from Mr. De Veze inserted. New York, 1920.

Half morocco; 7½ x 6-3/8 in.

DEVICES, PRINTERS.

Cabinet Shelf No.

See Printers' Marks.

DEVICES, PUBLISHERS

Cabinet 70 Shelf 1 No. 34

De Pre, Galliot. Paris, 1528.

See Early Printing in France. Paris, 1528.
Pierre Vidoue. Les XXI Epistres Davide....

DEVIEU, GUSTAVE.

Cabinet W Shelf 2 No. 51

Imprimeurs de Paris Piece en un acte, melee de couplets. Par M. G. Devieu, ancien eleve du College de Saint-Barbe. Paris, circa 1841.

Authors signature on original paper cover.

Cloth; 7-3/8 x 4½ x ¼ in.

DEVIEU, M.G.

Cabinet W Shelf 2 No. 51

Imprimeurs de Paris (Les). Piece en un acte, melée de couplets, par M.G.Devieu, Paris, 1840?

A play which takes place in the printing shop of one Bernard, Paris.

Linen; 7½ x 4-5/8 x 3/8 in.

DEVIL (The)

Cabinet 41 Shelf 2 No. 3

New York, 1887-8. The Devil. Published by the office of E.L. Megill.

Vol. 1(1887), Nos.1,2,3,4
" 2(1888), " 5

Unbound issues, in manila envelope

DEVIL

Cabinet 41 Shelf 2 No. 3

Published by E. L. Megill, New York

Vol.1, 1887, Nos.1,2,3,4
" 2, 1888, " 5

Items in manila envelope

DeVILLIERS, P.

Cabinet U Shelf 4 No. 87

(The) Signature of Gutenberg. London, 1878. With folding sheet, facsimile of the letters of Indulgence, 1455.

The author analyzes the various strokes in the supposed signatures.

Half morocco; 10¼ x 6½ x 3/8 in.

DeVILLIERS, P.

Cabinet W Shelf 2 No. 1

(The) Signature of Gutenberg: Found in the Letters of Indulgence, 1454 and 1455. Described by P. DeVilliers. London, 1878. Pamphlet.

Author's presentation copy, signed, "To A. Claudin, Author of the Monuments Typographiques."

Item 17 in volume "Gutenberg, l'inventeur de l'imprimerie - Melanges."

DeVINNE, DANIEL

Cabinet S Shelf 1 No. 12

Memorial of the Rev. Daniel DeVinne. Born Feb. 1, 1793. Died Feb. 10, 1883: And his autobiography as given on the occasion of the completion of his fiftieth year in the ministry. Printed for his family. New York, 1883.

Was father of Theodore L. DeVinne.

Half morocco; 9¼ x 6¼ in.

De VINNE, REV. DANIEL

Cabinet 27 Shelf 2 No. 26

Portrait of Rev. Daniel DeVinne, father of Theodore Low DeVinne, America's First Great Printer, in article on Theodore Low DeVinne, by Henry Lewis Bullen.

see
THE AMERICAN BULLETIN, April, 1914, p. 6.

DeVINNE, THEODORE LOW

Cabinet S Shelf 5 No. 12

About large types. By T. L. DeVinne, in The Literary Collector, Dec., 1901. Illus.

Bound in collection "Pamphlets and excerpts relating to typographical matters", item 14.

DE VINNE, Theodore Low.

Cabinet S Shelf 5 No. 6

An account of his death: A laudatory recognition of his many years active association with The Century Magazine, in The Century Magazine, May, 1914.

Bound with other items in Various Printers and their Plants, item 14, vol.2.

DeVINNE, THEODORE LOW

Cabinet S Shelf 1 No. 33

Adaptability of paper, The. By Theo. L. DeVinne. New York, n.d. An excerpt from "The Bookman."

Item 8 in volume "Writings of Theodore Low DeVinne."

Half morocco; 9¾ x 6-5/8 in.

DeVINNE, THEODORE LOW

Cabinet S Shelf 5 No. 19

American Printing [Brief historical survey] By Theodore Low DeVinne. Written for "ONe Hundred years of American Commerce," 1895.

In volume Excerpts on American Printing, etc."

DeVINNE, THEO. LOW.

Cabinet G Shelf 1 No. 58.05

An antidote against melancholy. Compounded of choice poems...At New York. Printed by T.L.D.V. for Pratt Manufacturing Company, No.46 Broadway, near Bowling Green. Christmas 1884.

Half morocco; 8-7/8 x 7-1/8 x 5/8 in.

DeVINNE, THEODORE LOW

Cabinet S Shelf 1 No. 33

Attractiveness in books. By Theodore Low DeVinne. An excerpt from "The Independent." n.d. Specimens of type.
Item 13 in volume "Writings of Theodore Low DeVinne."

Half morocco; 9¾ x 6-5/8 in.

DeVINNE, THEODORE LOW

Cabinet S Shelf 1 No. 50

Century Roman (Specimens of the the) Designed by Theodore Low DeVinne and cut by The American Type Founders Company for The Century Magazine. Pamphlet.
See DeVinne Scrap Book, p. 10.

Half morocco; 13½ x 10½ in.

DeVINNE, THEODORE LOW

Cabinet S Shelf 1 No. 33

Coöperation. By a New York Master Printer. A series of articles written about printers and printing ... Compiled and arranged by Alexander . Collins, Pittsburgh, Pa. 1912.
Item 4 in volume "Writings of Theodore Low DeVinne."

Half morocco; 9¾ x 6-5/8 in.

DeVINNE, THEODORE LOW

Cabinet S Shelf 1 No. 50

Autograph documents and letters relating to printing, all signed by Theodore Low DeVinne
In the "DeVinne Scrap Book, souvenirs of the Typothetae of New York."

DEVINNE, THEODORE L.

Cabinet BB Shelf 2 No. 19 also C-2-31

American Type Founders Co.
"Specimens of the Century romans". [c1899]

Pamphlet. 5 ll. 7¼ x 10-1/8

Includes essay: "The Century's new types", by Theodore L. DeVinne. His portrait in etching on cover.

DeVINNE, THEODORE LOW

Cabinet MM Shelf 5 No. 68

Correct composition. A treatise on spelling, abbreviations...with observations on punctuation and proof reading. Second edition. New York, 1904.

Cloth; 7½ x 5-3/8 x 1-1/8 in.

DeVINNE, THEODORE L.

Cabinet S Shelf 4 No. 99

(The) Building of a book: A series of practical articles ... With an introduction by Theodore L. De Vinne. Edited by Frederick H. Hitchcock. New York, 1906.

Cloth; 8½ x 5½ in.

DeVINNE, THEODORE LOW

Cabinet S Shelf 1 No. 33

(The) Century's Printer on The Century's Type: In the "Open Letters" section of The Century Magazine. An excerpt. Illus.
Mr. DeVinne discourses on the improvement of typographic taste, and the printers and type designers who were influential in developing that taste away from light face types to the stronger black Roman letters.
Item 7 in volume "Writings of Theodore Low DeVinne."

Half morocco; 9¾ x 6-5/8 in.

De VINNE, THEODORE LOW

Cabinet 27 Shelf 2 No. 26

DeVinne, Theodore Low, Printer. "His life began in 1828 and ended in 1914. He made good use of every year. His fame will endure forever.' Article by Henry Lewis Bullen with seven portraits of DeVinne, one of his father, Rev. Daniel DeVinne, one of Francis Hart, first partner of DeVinne and one of the main entrance of the DeVinne Press, 393-399 Lafayette St., New York. Erected by DeVinne, 1887.
see
THE AMERICAN BULLETIN, April, 1914, pp. 5, 6, 7 and 8.

DeVINNE, THEODORE LOW

Cabinet S Shelf 1 No. 38

Bullen, Henry Lewis. Theodore Low DeVinne, printer: Biographical Sketch. Privately printed, New York, 1915. Frontispiece portrait.
Includes: Memorials Addresses;, Resolutions of Corporations; Societies; and Clubs; Informal tributes; Bibliography of books written by Mr. DeVinne.

Boards; 10½ x 7 in.

DeVINNE, THEODORE LOW.

Cabinet S Shelf 1 No. 50

Chap-Book and its outgrowths, the (Excerpt) The Literary Collector, vol. 5, Nov. 1902. Illus.

Item 28 in DeVinne Scrap Book. Souvenirs of the Typothetae of New York.

DeVINNE, THEODORE LOW

Cabinet S Shelf 1 No. 50

(The) DeVinne Press. By Daniel B. Updike. An excerpt from The Literary Review, Jan. 20. 1923.
Biographical eulogy.
p. 24 in "DeVinne Scrap Book. Souvenirs of the Typothetae of New York.

Half morocco; 13¼ x 10¼ in.

DEVINNE, THEODORE LOW

Cabinet J Shelf 1 No. 6

Card of D. DeVinne, Pastor of M. E. Chrüch.

See Scrap Book. Trade cards mostly issued by New York business houses.

DeVINNE, THEO L.

Cabinet S Shelf 1 No. 18

Christopher Plantin and The Plantin-Moretus Museum at Antwerp. By Theo. L. DeVinne. With illustrations by Joseph Pennell, and others. Printed for The Grolier Club, New York, 1888.

Half morocco; 10-1/8x 7¼ in.

DE VINNE, THEODORE LOW

Cabinet S Shelf 1 No. 51

De Vinne Scrap Book No.2. Contains items personal to De Vinne and also relating to the organization (in 1865) of the Typothetae of New York City, of which he was the first secretary. With portraits of him at various ages; also of his father and elder brother Daniel.
This scrapbook was begun by De Vinne; several additions have been made since his death.

Half morocco; 15½ x 9 in.

DeVINNE, THEODORE LOW.

Cabinet S Shelf 1 No. 57

Catalogue of work of The DeVinne Press. Exhibited at The Grolier Club on the occasion of the one hundredth anniversary of the birth of Theodore Low DeVinne. December 25, 1828. The Grolier Club. New York, 1929.
One of three copies on special paper. Presented by Mr. James W. Bothwell.

Half morocco; 9-7/8 x 6-3/8 x 5/8 in.

DE VINNE, THEODORE LOW

Cabinet S Shelf 1 No. 50

Colophon of Theo. L. De Vinne, literal translation of. With brief biographical notes. The De Vinne - Hallenbeck Company, Inc. New York City, 1928.

Small broadside, with portrait. In De Vinne Scrap Book, fol. 31.

DeVINNE THEODORE LOW

Cabinet 25 Shelf 2 No. 5

Editor of The Printers Miscellany, 1859

See PERIODICALS, PRINTING. United States (The) Printers Miscellany

DeVINNE, THEODORE LOW

Cabinet S Shelf 1 No. 33

(The) First editor, Aldus Pius Manutius. By Theo. Low DeVinne. A series of articles written about printers and printing that have been extracted from various magazines ... Compiled by Alexander W. Collins. Pittsburgh, Pa. 1912. Illus. and portraits.

Half morocco; 9¾ x 6-5/8 in.

DeVINNE, THEODORE LOW

Cabinet S Shelf 1 No. 33

(The) Gutenberg Anniversary. By Theodore L. De Vinne, honorary Vice-President of the Gutenberg Festival. [Mainz, 1901?]. Excerpt from "The Outlook." n.d. Illus.

Item 11 in volume "Writings of Theodore Low DeVinne."

Half morocco; 9¾ x 6-5/8 in.

DeVINNE, THEODORE LOW

Cabinet S Shelf 5 No. 24

Invention of Printing by T. L. DeVinne. Book reviewed in Scribner's Monthly, Aug. 1878. An excerpt.

Pp. 146-147 in Collection "Printing Excerpts"

DeVINNE, THEODORE LOW

Cabinet S Shelf 5 No. 17

French method of making book margins. By T.L. DeVinne. Excerpt from The Engraver and Printer. Jan. 29, 1895.

Item 20 in collection "Miscellaneous items relating to printing; excerpts from magazines, 1918.

De VINNE, THEODORE LOW

Cabinet Y Shelf 4 No. 76

Gutenberg Museum, Mainz. Gifts to the municipal collection of the. Brief account. Together with the annual statement...Mainz, 1902-3. Brochure, German text.

Item in manila envelope

DeVINNE, THEODORE LOW

Cabinet S Shelf 1 No. 50

Inventory of the printing plant of Francis Hart 4 Thames Street, New York. [1847]. Now (1915) The DeVinne Press.

Entering as a journeyman Mr. DeVinne eventually became sole owner.

Leaflet, 4 pp. in DeVinne's Scrap Books, p. 11.

DeVINNE, THEODORE LOW

Cabinet S Shelf 1 No. 50

(A) Great printer. By Robert Underwood Johnson. An excerpt from The Literary Review. Jan. 20, 1923.

Biographical eulogy.

P. 25 in DeVinne Scrap book. Souvenirs of the Typothetae of New York.

Half morocco; 13½ x 10½ in.

DeVINNE, THEODORE LOW

Cabinet S Shelf 1 No. 16

Historic printing types. A lecture read before the Grolier Club of New York, January, 25, 1885, with additions and new illustrations. The Grolier Club, 1886. [Printed by T.L. DeVinne]

Presentation copy, with inscription and letter from Mr. DeVinne to Thomas MacKellar.

Boards; 10¼ x 8¼ in.

DeVINNE, THEODORE LOW

Cabinet L Shelf 4 No. 7

Italy, the glory of. An illustrated calendar for year 1909. Presented to T.L.DeVinne by the editor, Comm. Piero Barbèra, Florence.

In oblong box; 9-1/8 x 11 x 5/8 in.

DeVINNE, THEODORE LOW

Cabinet S Shelf 5 No. 14

(The) Growth of wood-cut printing: Early methods in the hand-press. 1450-1850. By T. L. De Vinne. Excerpts from Scribner's, April-May, 1880. Illus.

Bound with items in collection "Printing Processes", item 21.

DeVINNE, THEODORE LOW

Cabinet PP Shelf 2 No. 10

Historic printing types. An address. Printed in the Transactions of the Grolier Club, Part I, 1885, p.32.

Paper; 9½ x 7-1/8 in.

DeVINNE, THEODORE LOW

Cabinet S Shelf 5 No. 24

John Gutenberg. By T. L. DeVinne. An excerpt from Scribner's Monthly, May, 1876.

Bio-bibliographical account.

pp. 1-13 in collection "Printing Excerpts."

DeVINNE, THEODORE LOW

Cabinet S Shelf 1 No. 33

(The) Growth of Woodcut Printing. Part I: Early methods on the hand-press. 1450-1850. Part 2: The growth of woodcut printing. The modern method by machines. Illus.

Item 2 in volume "Writings of Theodore Low DeVinne."

Half morocco; 9¾ x 6-5/8 in.

DeVINNE, THEODORE LOW

Cabinet S Shelf 1 No. 9

(The) Invention of printing. A collection of facts and opinions description of early prints and playing cards, the block-books of the fifteenth century, the legends of Lourens Janszoon Custer, of Haarlem, and the work of John Gutenberg and his associates. Illustrated with facsimiles of types, and woodcuts By Theo. L. DeVinne ... New York, 1876.

Half morocco; 9½ x 6¾ in.

DeVINNE, THEODORE LOW

Cabinet S Shelf 1 No. 33

John Gutenberg, By Theo. Low DeVinne. An article extracted from a magazine ... Pittsburgh, Pa. 1912. Illus.

Item I in volume "Writings of Theodore Low DeVinne."

Half morocco; 9¾ x 6-5/8 in.

DE VINNE, THEODORE L.

Cabinet S Shelf 5 No. 4

(The) Gutenberg anniversary, 1400-1900, by T.L. De Vinne in the Outlook, May 5, 1900.

Bound with other items in "Various printers and their plants", item 15 and 16, vol.1.

DeVINNE, THEODORE LOW

Cabinet S Shelf 1 No. 10

Invention of Printing. A collection of facts descriptive of early prints and playing cards the block-books of the fifteenth century, the legends of Lourens Janszoon Coster of Haarlem and the work of John Gutenberg ... Illus. with facsimiles of early types and woodcuts. New York, George Bruce's Son & Co., typefounders, New York, 1878.

Composed in the form of specimens of type made by George Bruce's Son & Co.

Half morocco; 12¼ x 9¾ in.

Also in CC-2-13 and CC-2-15

DEVINNE, THEODORE L.

Cabinet S Shelf 5 No. 12

Kelmscott Press - Kelmscott Style by T. L. DeVinne. Illus. with specimen of the works from this Press. Jan . 1902.

Bound with "Pamphlets and excerpts relating to typographical matters, Item 23.

DeVINNE, THEODORE LOW

Cabinet S Shelf 5 No. 12

(The) Kelmscott style. By Theodore Low DeVinne. Excerpt from the Bibliographer, Jan. 1902. Specimens.

Item 23 in collection "Pamphlets and excerpts relating to various typographical matters".

DeVINNE, THEODORE LOW

Cabinet MM Shelf 6 No. 56

"Modern methods of book composition". Revised and arranged by J.W. Bothwell. [For] Typographic Technical Series for apprentices, Part II, No.20. Published by the United Typothetae of America, 1918.

Cloth; 8 x 5 in.

DEVINNE, THEODORE LOW

Cabinet LL Shelf 3 No. 2

Office manual, for the use of workman in the printing house of T. L. DeVinne & Co., 63 Murray St. N. Y. n.d.

Bound in with "Various items on proofreading." item 1.

DeVINNE, THEODORE LOW

Cabinet Y Shelf 3 No. 79

(Key to the discovery of the art of printing: An extract from "The invention of printing" Translated by Dr. Oscar Jolles). Der schlüssel zur erfindung der typographie. Ein abschnitt aus dem werke "The Invention of printing", by T. L. DeVinne, New York. 1876. Aus dem Englischen Übersetzt von Dr. Oscar Jolles. Berlin, 1921.

Boards; 11¼ x 8¼ x ¼ in.

DeVINNE, THEODORE LOW

Cabinet S Shelf 2 No. 169 2 Vols.

Moxon, Joseph: Mechanick Exercises, or the doctrine of handy-works applied to the art of printing. London, 1683. A facsimile reprint published by the Typothetae of New York, prefaced and printed by Theodore Low DeVinne, New York, 1896.

Half Levant; 10 x 7 in.

DeVINNE, Theodore Low

Cabinet S Shelf 1 No. 51

On the printing of "The Century". Excerpt from The Century, pp.808-9, n.d.

Item of folio 53 of "DeVinne Scrap Book, 2. Early Typothetae Items".

DeVINNE, THEODORE LOW.

Cabinet S Shelf 1 No. 58

Library of the late Theodore Low DeVinne. To be sold Jan. 12-16,1920 at The Anderson Galleries, 489 Park Avenue, New York.

Half morocco; 9-1/4 x 6-1/4 in.

DeVINNE, THEODOR LOW

Cabinet 61 Shelf 1 No. 2

(A) Notable New York Printing House.

See PRINTING HOUSES, United States. DeVinne...

DE VINNE, THEODORE LOW

Cabinet MM Shelf 5 No. 65

(The) Practice of typography. A treatise on the processes of type-making, the point system, the names, sizes, styles and prices of plain printing types. New York. The Century Co. 1900.

Cloth; 7½ x 5½ in.

DeVINNE, THEODORE LOW

Cabinet S Shelf 5 No. 24

Manutius, Aldus, The first editor. By Theodore Low DeVinne. Excerpt from Scribner's Monthly, Oct. 1881. Illus. Bio-bibliographical account.

pp. 23-32 in collection "Printing Excerpts."

DeVINNE, THEODORE LOW

Cabinet S Shelf 1 No. 29

Notable printers of Italy during the fifteenth century. Illustrated with facsimiles from early editions, and with remarks on early and recent printing. By Theodore Low De Vinne. New York, The DeVinne Press, 1910. Presentation copy, with signature.

Boards; 13 x 9¾ in.

DE VINNE, THEODORE LOW

Cabinet MM Shelf 5 No. 66

(The) Practice of typography. A treatise on the processes of type making, the point system, the names, sizes, styles, and prices of printing types. Second edition. New York, 1902.

Cloth; 7¾ x 5¼ in.

DeVINNE, THEODORE LOW

Cabinet MM Shelf 5 No. 69

Modern methods of book composition. A treatise on type-setting by hand and by machine, and on the proper arrangement and imposition of pages. New York, The Century Co. 1904.

Cloth; 7-5/8 x 5¼ x 1-1/8 in.

DeVINNE, THEODORE LOW

Cabinet LL Shelf 5 No. 36

Notice commending "How to succeed in the printing business."

Article pp.257-260 of Nathan's Printing business, how to make money in it...New York, 1900.

DeVINNE, THEODORE LOW

Cabinet MM Shelf 5 No. 67

(The) Practice of typography. A treatise on title-pages. With numerous illustrations in facsimile and some observations on the early and recent printing of books, New York, The Century Co. 1902.

Cloth; 7¾ x 5¼ in.

DeVINNE, THEODORE LOW.

Cabinet S Shelf 1 No. 50

Modern methods of book composition. A treatise on type-setting by hand and machine. (A review). The Literary Collector, March, 1905.

Item 27 in the DeVinne Scrap Book. Souvenirs of the Typothetae of New York.

DeVINNE, THEODORE LOW

Cabinet LL Shelf 3 No. 2

Office Manuel for the use of workmen in the printing house of Theo. L. DeVinne & Co., 63 Murray Street, New York. 1883. Pamphlet; 5-3/8 x 3-1/8 in.

Item I in book with binder's title "Various items on proofreading."

DeVINNE, THEODORE LOW

Cabinet S Shelf 5 No. 24

(A) Printer's Paradise. The Plantin-Moretus Museum at Antwerp. By Theo. Low DeVinne. An excerpt from The Century Magazine, June 1888. Illus.

pp. 54-74 in collection "Printing Excerpts."

DeVINNE, THEODORE LOW

Cabinet S Shelf 1 No. 34

(A) Printer's Paradise: The Plantin-Moretus Museum at Antwerp. By T. L. DeVinne. Illustrated extract from The Century Magazine [1912]. Vol. XXXVI, pp. 225-45.

Half morocco; 10 x 7 in.

DeVINNE, THEODORE LOW

Cabinet S Shelf 1 No. 33

(A) Printer's Paradise. The Plantin-Moretus Museum. Illus.
Item 5 in volume "Writings of Theodore Low DeVinne."

Half morocco; 9¾ x 6-5/8 in.

DeVINNE, THEODORE LOW

Cabinet LL Shelf 5 No. 24

Printers' price list: A manual for the use of clerks and bookkeepers in job printing offices. New York, 1869. Proof copy.
Besides prices, the book includes a vast amount of valuable practical information for printers.

Full morocco; 6-3/4 x 4-1/8 x 3/4 in.

DeVINNE, THEODORE LOW

Cabinet LL Shelf 5 No. 25

Printers' price list. A manual for the use of clerks and book-keepers in job printing offices. New York, Francis Hart and Company, 1871.
A valuable text book of printing. Interesting advertisements at end.

Leather; 7½ x 5-1/8 x 1 in.

DeVINNE, THEODORE LOW

Cabinet S Shelf 1 No. 43

Printing in the Nineteenth Century. By Theodore Low DeVinne. New York, 1901.
This item originally appeared in the New York Evening Post, Jan. 12, 1901. Reprinted as a private edition by the Lead Mould Electrotype Foundry, Inc., New York, Dec. 1924. and presented to members of the American Institute of Graphic Arts.

Cloth; 9½ x 6¼ in.

DeVINNE, THEODORE LOW

Cabinet S Shelf 5 No. 12

Printing of fine books. By Theodore Low De Vinne. An excerpt from The Outlook, Dec. 4, 1897. Illus.

Bound in collection "Pamphlets and excerpts relating to typographical matters", item 12.

DeVINNE, THEODORE LOW

Cabinet S Shelf 1 No. 33

Printing of fine books. By Theo. L. DeVinne n.d. An excerpt from "The Outlook," New York. With facsimiles and specimens.
Item 10 in volume "Writings of Theodore Low DeVinne."

Half morocco; 9¾ x 6-5/8 in.

DeVINNE, THEODORE LOW

Cabinet S Shelf 5 No. 24

Printing of "The Century." By Theo Low De Vinne. An Excerpt from The Century, Nov. 1890. Illus
Technical description of the various processes as practised at the "DeVinne Press'

pp. 132-144 in collection "Printing Excerpts'

DeVINNE, THEODORE LOW

Cabinet S Shelf 1 No. 20

(The) Printing of "The Century." An excerpt from The Century Magazine, Nov. 1890. Illus.
Mr. DeVinne discourses upon the practical processes of printing.

Half morocco; 10 x 7 in.

DeVINNE, THEODORE LOW

Cabinet S Shelf 1 No. 33

Printing of "The Century," Illustrated extract from The Century Magazine. Illus.
Item 6 in volume "Writings of Theodore Low DeVinne."

Half morocco; 9¾ x 6-5/8 in.

DE VINNE, Theodore Low.

Cabinet S Shelf 5 No. 6

Printing of "The Century," in The Century Magazine, Nov. 1890.

Illustrated with interior and outside views of the De Vinne printing establishment.

Bound with other items in "Various Printers and their Plants," items 6,14, vol.2.

DeVINNE, THEODORE LOW

Cabinet S Shelf 1 No. 33

(The) Printing of William Morris. By Theo. L. DeVinne. An excerpt from "The Book Buyer for Nov. 1895. Facsimiles.
Item 9 in volume "Writings of Theodore Low DeVinne."

Half morocco; 9¾ x 6-5/8 in.

DeVINNE, THEODORE L.

Cabinet S Shelf 1 No. 5

Profits of book composition. By Theo. L. De Vinne. New York, 1864. Pamphlet.
Bound in with "Scale of Prices" as adopted by the New England Franklin Club, July 1, 1864. Boston.

Cloth; 9¾ x 6 in.

DeVINNE, THEODORE LOW

Cabinet LL Shelf 5 No. 26

Record of production of 22 printing presses operated in the press room of Francis Hart & Co., N. Y. City, (circa 1871) at a time when DeVinne was superintendent. The count was taken by tokens of 250 impressions.
The book was opened by DeVinne himself, the writing in the heavier ink is his.
H.L. Bullen. Nov. 19, 1928.

Boards; 8½ x 5-5/8 x 5/8 in.

DE VINNE, THEODORE LOW.

Stack A Shelf 1&2 Number 64

Sale of the De Vinne library, by Henry Lewis Bullen, in The Inland Printer, vol. LXIV, p. 693.

DeVINNE, THEODORE LOW

Cabinet S Shelf 1 No. 50

Scrap Book kept by DeVinne containing early printed and manuscript documents relating to the Typothetae of New York, to which is added by H.L. Bullen, a collection of souvenirs, photographs etc, of De Vinne and his family.

Half morocco; 13½ x 10½ in.

DeVINNE, THEODORE LOW

Cabinet S Shelf 1 No. 23

Title-Pages as seen by a printer. With numerous illustrations in facsimile and some observations on the early and recent printing of books. By Theo. L. DeVinne. The Grolier Club, New York, 1901.

Half moroco; 10 x 7 in.

DE VINNE, THEODORE LOW

Cabinet 21 Shelf 2 No. 4

Trade Unions. Historical account of trade unions, their practices, usefulness, etc.

Articles in "The Printer", Vol. V, Nos., 10, 11, 12, Oct., Nov., Dec., 1864.

DeVinne, Theodore Low

Cabinet FF Shelf 3 No. 16

Type casting machines, about. A letter in the "American Newspaper Reporter" (circa 1884).

Pasted in back of Bruce's History (Ms.) of type founding in America...

DeVINNE, THEODORE LOW

Cabinet S Shelf 1 No. 50

Types, about large. (Illus. excerpt) The Literary Collector, Dec. 1901.

Item 29 in DeVinne Scrap Book. Souvenirs of the Typothetae of New York.

DeVINNE, THEODORE LOW

Cabinet S Shelf 1 No. 33

Typographical effects. By Theodore L. De Vinne. An excerpt from "The Independent" n.d.

Item 12 in volume "Writings of Theodore Low DeVinne."

Half morocco; 9¾ x 6-5/8 in.

DeVINNE, THEODORE LOW

Cabinet S Shelf 1 No. 33

(The) Writings of Theodore Low DeVinne, A.m. A series of articles written about printers and printing that have been extracted from various magazines printed during the past thirty-six years ... some with illustrations Compiled by Alexander W. Collins. Pittsburg Pa. 1912. Portrait.

Half morocco; 9¾ x 6-5/8 in.

De VINNE, THEODORE LOW

Cabinet R Shelf 5 No. 32

See Scientific American. Printing industry issue. November 14, 1903. p. 339.

DeVINNE, THEODORE LOW

Cabinet

See also cards with following sub-heads:

I - Biographies, Printers

Shelf II - Imprints, United States. DeVinne Press.

III - Plants, Printing. United States (New York City) DeVinne Press.

No. IV - Specimen Books. Printers'. Francis Hart & Co.

DE VINNE-HALLENBECK COMPANY, INCORPORATED

Cabinet S Shelf 1 No. 50

Centenary of the birth of Theo. Low De Vinne. Brief biographical memoir, with notice of consolidation of De Vinne Hallenbeck Co. in 1926. Also literal translation of De Vinne colophon.

Small broadside, with De Vinne portrait. De Vinne Scrap Book, fol. 31.

DE VINNE PRESS, THE

Cabinet S Shelf 1 No. 21

Grolier Club. A description of the early printed books owned by the Grolier Club, with a brief account of their printers and the history of typography in the 15th century. Printed by De Vinne, for the Grolier Club. New York, May 1895.

Half morocco; 12 x 8 in.

DeVINNE PRESS, THE

Cabinet LL Shelf 3 No. 2

List of variable spellings compiled from the American dictionaries...n.d. circa 1901. Pamphlet 7½ x 4¾ in.

Item 6 in book with binder's title "Various items on proofreading".

DeVINNE PRESS, THE

Cabinet LL Shelf 3 No. 5

Office manual for the use of workmen in the printing house of Theo. L. DeVinne & Co. 63 Murray Street, New York. n.d. Printed by Horace Hart, Oxford University Press.

[circa 1880]

Cloth; 5½ x 3 x ½ in.

DeVINNE PRESS, THE

Cabinet S Shelf 1 No. 20

Printing of "The Century", by Theodore Low De Vinne: An excerpt from The Century Magazine, November, 1890. Illus.

Mr. DeVinne Discourses upon the practical process of printing a periodical.

Half morocco; 10 x 7 in.

DeVINNE PRESS, THE

Cabinet S Shelf 5 No. 17

Profit sharing adopted by the DeVinne Press. The event is signalized by a banquet. Account written by "A. Guest," for The Inland Printer June, 1892.

Item 22 in collection "Miscellaneous items relating to printing; excerpts from magazines 1918.

DeVINNE PRESS, THE

Cabinet EE Shelf 1 No. 12

Roman and Italic printing types in the printing house of Theodore L. DeVinne & Co. 12 Lafayette Place. New York. The DeVinne Press, 1891.

Cloth; 9¾ x 6-5/8 x 3/8 in.

DeVINNE PRESS, THE

Cabinet EE Shelf 1 No. 11

Specimen book of types from the DeVinne Press. Theo. L. DeVinne & Co. 63 and 65 Murray Street. New York. 1883-1905.

Has signature of Theo. L. DeVinne & Co.

Cloth; 9½ x 6-3/8 x 1 in.

DeVINNE PRESS, THE

Cabinet EE Shelf 1 No. 13

Types of the DeVinne Press. Specimens for the use of compositors, proofreaders and publishers. New York, No.395 Lafayette Street, 1907.

Has frontispiece picture, exterior view of DeVinne Press.

Cloth; 9½ x 6-3/8 x 1-7/8 in.

DEVISES.

Cabinet Shelf No.

See Emblems.

DeVOTO, BERNARD

Cabinet S Shelf 4 No. 129

Mark Twain's America. Illustrated by M.J. Gallagher. Boston: Little, Brown, and Company. 1935.

Cloth; 8½ x 5-5/8 in.

De VRIES, JOHN

Cabinet S Shelf 2 No. 61

(In) Memoriam. John De Vries, died August 29, 1894. Published by the Typothetae of New York. Signed by the president, Theodore L. De Vinne.

Printed on Vellum.

Full limp morocco; 9 x 6½ in.

DeVRIES, R.W.P. Jr.

Cabinet 26 Shelf 1 No. 20

Niederlanden, der moderne holzschnitt in den (Modern wood engraving in the Netherlands) von R.W.P. DeVries Jr. Illus.

Article in the "Gutenberg-Gesellschaft Jahrbuch", 1930, pp.289-295.

DEWAR, DANIEL

Cabinet X Shelf 5 No. 57

Authorized Master Printer for Scotland, 1859

see LIBERTY OF PRINTING, Great Britain (Scotland 1859)

DeWEESE, TRUMAN A.

Cabinet LL Shelf 4 No. 13

Principles of practical publicity. Being a treatise on "The art of advertising". Buffalo, N.Y. 1906.
With specimens of advertising.

Cloth; 7-5/8 x 5¼ x 1-3/8 in.

DEWEY, F.E. & B.A.

Cabinet EE Shelf 4 No. 32

Detailed price list of the Springfield ruling machinery and attachments. Manufactured by F.E. & B.A. Dewey. Springfield, Mass. 1912.

Pamphlet in manila envelope.

DEXTER and SONS, C.H.

Cabinet RR Shelf 3 No. 48

Princess cover papers. (Samples) Manufactured at Windsor Locks, Conn., by C.H. Dexter & Sons. n.d.

Cloth; 11 x 9 in.

DEXTER, C. H. & SONS

Cabinet S Shelf 5 No. 3

See also Paper Mills, Connecticut.

DEXTER FOLDER COMPANY

Cabinet EE Shelf 4 No. 33

Catalogues and price lists of the Dexter folding and feeding machinery. Pearl River, and Fulton, New York. 1892, 1901. Pamphlets.

Has views of Dexter factories.

In manila envelope.

DE YOUNG, MICHAEL L. (Journalist) see

Cabinet NN Shelf 2 No. 8

JOURNALISM, United States. California journalism...

"DIADEM, THE"

Cabinet K Shelf 2 No. 29

Carey & Hart, Philadelphia, 1846.

see KEEPSAKES, or, GIFT BOOKS. Diadem, The...

DIAMANT, E. M.

Cabinet FF Shelf 2 No. 26.01

Rapid typo-calculator. Compiled by William P. Lillicrapp for E. M. Diamant Typographic Service. New York, 1928.

Item in manila envelope.

DIARY OF LADY WILLOUGHBY

Cabinet M Shelf 1 No. 42

First edition in original decorated paper binding, 8-5/8 x 7 x 1¼ in. Printed by C. Whittingham, Chiswick, 1844. See M/1/43 for fourth edition, 1846, in small format, also set in Caslon Oldstyle types.

The Caslon Oldstyle types, which had been out of use for half a century were revived to print this book, with such good effect that gradually this fine type series came into use again with ever increasing popularity.

(Cont'd)

DIARY OF LADY WILLOUGHBY (cont'd)

Cabinet Shelf No.

Decorated Paper over boards; 8-5/8 x 7 x 1¼ in.

DIARY OF LADY WILLOUGHBY

Cabinet M Shelf 1 No. 43

The fourth edition, Printed by C. Whittingham (nephew), Chiswick, 1846.

See M/1/113 for the first edition, 1844, in larger format.

In original decorated paper binding. 7 x 4-3/4 x 3/4 in.

DIAZ, Fernando

Cabinet X Shelf 3 No. 19

Brief bio-bibliographical note, with printer mark, Diaz (Granada), 1568-1588.

see HAEBLER, KONRAD. (Spanish and Portugese printer marks...p.xxxiii

DIBDIN, THOMAS FROGNALL

Cabinet T Shelf 3 No. 3

Bibliographical, antiquarian and picturesque tour in France and Germany. By the Rev. Thomas Frognall Dibdin. London. Printed for the author by W. Bulmer and N. Nichols, Shakspeare Press, 1821. (3 vols. illus.)

Morocco, gilt; 10¾ x 6¾ in.

DIBDIN, THOMAS FROGNALL

Cabinet T Shelf 3 No. 2 3 Vols.

Bibliographical Decameron; or, ten days pleasant discourse upon illuminated manuscripts, and subjects connected with early engraving, typography and bibliography. London: Printed for the author, by W. Bulmer & Co. 1817. Illus. 3 vols.
Inserted in Vol. I: A.L.S., the author.

Full morocco, back tooled, gilt; each vol. 11¾ x 7¾ in.

DIBDIN, THOMAS FROGNALL

Cabinet T Shelf 3 No. 1

Bibliomania; or book-madness, containing the account of the history, symptoms, and cure of the fatal disease. In an epistle address ed to Richard Heber. London, 1876. Reprinted from the first ed. published in 1809 Illus.

Cloth, leather back; 11½ x 7-5/8 x 2-3/8 in.

DIBDIN, THO. FROGNALL

Cabinet V Shelf 5 No. 6

See Books about Books. Crapelet, G.A. Lettre Trentième ... Paris, 1821.

DIBDIN, T.F.

Cabinet U Shelf 5 No. 52

Caxton imprints; Caxtons Chronicle; Statutes; Romance of Jason.
See pp.6-13 in Bibliographical Notes of The Gentleman's Magazine.

DIBDIN, THOMAS FROGNALL

Cabinet PP Shelf 2 No. 3

Descriptive catalogue of the books printed in the 15th century, lately forming part of the library of the Duke di Cassano Serra... London, 1823. Nicol

Boards, leather back; 10-7/8 x 7-1/8 x 1-1/8 in.

DIBDIN, Rev THOMAS FROGNALL

Cabinet T Shelf 2 No. 5

(An) Index to Dibdin's Edition of the Typographical Antiquities first compiled by Joseph Ames, with some references to the intermediate edition by William Herbert. Printed from a copy in the Library of Sion College. London: Printed for the Bibliographical Society, Dec., 1899.

Half morocco; 8-5/8 x 6-7/8 x ½ in.

DIBDIN, THOMAS F.

Cabinet PP Shelf 1 No. 5

Introduction to the knowledge of rare and valuable editions of the Greek and Roman Classics, being in part a tabulated arrangement from Dr. Harwood's "view" ... With notes from Maittaire, DeBure, Dictionnaire Bibliographique and references to ancient and modern catalogues ... Glocester, 1802. Printed by Ruff.
Presentation inscription on fly-leaf.

Half morocco (by Zaehnsdorf) 7-7/8 x 5 in.

DIBDIN, THOMAS FROGNALL

Cabinet T Shelf 2 No. 6

Typographical antiquities, or the history of printing in England, Scotland and Ireland... Begun by the late Joseph Ames. Considerably augmented by William Herbert...and now greatly enlarged with copious notes by the Rev. T.F. Dibdin. London, 1810-19. Four vols. Illus.

Quarter calf; each vol., 11¾ x 9 in.

(THE) DIBDIN CLUB

Cabinet Q Shelf 1 No. 8

Three centuries of English booktrade bibliography. By A. Growall. Also a list of the catalogues etc. published for the English booktrade from 1595-1902. By Wilberforce Eames. New York: Published for The Dibdin Club, 1903. Illus.

Half morocco; 9¾ x 6¼ in.

DICEY, A. V.

Cabinet NN Shelf 7 No. 16

(An) English scholar's appreciation of Godkin.

see
NATION, THE. Semi - centennial, 1865-1915, p. 51.

DICKINS, CHARLES

Cabinet NN Shelf 2 No. 2.02

Bright Chanticleer [Seven Dials literature]. Excerpt from Household Words, vol. VII, No.9, 1855.

Item 3 in vol. with binder's title "Journalists and Journalism -- III. Pamphlets".

DICKENS, CHARLES

Cabinet G Shelf 3 No. 51

Christmas Carol. Printed for the friends of William Edwin Rudge. Christmas 1930, at Mount Vernon, N.Y. Typography and binding by Frederic Warde. 2 vols.

Morocco; gilt tooling; 6-3/4 x 4¼ in. Two vols. in board protective case.

DICKENS, CHARLES

Cabinet S Shelf 6 No. 7

(The) Great Red Book [The London Post-Office Directory]
Excerpt from Household Words, Dec., 9, 1854.

More or less humorous account of the methods used in the compilation of "The Great Red Book".

Item (s) in book with binder's title: Early printed books: Various excerpts and pamphlets. 1854- 1931.

DICKENS, CHARLES

Cabinet NN Shelf 2 No. 14

Household Words: A Weekly Journal. Conducted by Charles Dickens.
(Article "The unknown public".
Excerpt from The Household Words, Aug.,21, 1858)

Item 6 in bound collection with binder's title "Periodicals, various exerpts".

DICKENS, CHARLES

Cabinet 71 Shelf 1 No. 21

What Christmas is as we grow older. By C. Dickens. Presentation copy from the publishers and printers, Taylor, Nash and Taylor. San Francisco, 1912. Illus.

Boards; 5-7/8 x 4¼ in. pp. 11.

DICKENS, CHARLES, author-editor.

Cabinet Shelf No.

See also
Periodicals, British: Unknown public, The.

DICKENS ADVERTISER, THE

Cabinet S Shelf 2 No. 165

Collection of the advertisements in the original parts of novels by Charles Dickens. Edited by Bernard Darwin, New York 1930. The MacMillan Co. Illus.

Cloth; 9¼ x 5-3/4 x 5/8 in.

DICKES, WILLIAM

Cabinet J Shelf 3 No. 14

Color printing of Wm. Dickes, with brief biographical sketch.

See LEWIS, COURTNEY. Story of picture printing in England during the 19th century ...pp.117-

DICKINSON, C. W.

Cabinet S Shelf 5 No. 14

Copper, steel, and bank-note engraving. By C. W. Dickinson. An excerpt from Popular Science Monthly, March, 1895. Illus.
Brief account of the origin and technique, with some notes concerning inventors and artists.

Bound with other items in collection "Printing Processes", item 9.

DICKINSON, JOHN AND COMPANY, LTD.

Cabinet RR Shelf 3 No. 13

Firm of John Dickinson and Company, Limited. With an appendix on ancient paper making. London, 1896. Portrait. Illus.

Cloth; 10½ x 8 x 5/8 in.

DICKINSON, CHARLES W. (Inventor) see

Cabinet FF Shelf 6 No. 19

COMPOSING MACHINES. Dickinson, Charles W...

DICKINSON, S. N.

Cabinet 80 Shelf No.

Boston Almanac, 1837 to 1850. S.N. Dickinson, Printer and Publisher.

See ALMANACS. Boston Almanac...

DICKINSON, S. N.

Cabinet 80 Shelf 1-a No. 4

Rotary Press, The. Specimens of card printing. Pasted in front and back of Boston Almanac for 1839.

See ALMANACS. Boston Almanac...1839.

DICKMAN, THOMAS (Printer)

Cabinet NN Shelf 7 No. 11

First publisher - printer, 1792, of the Greenfield Gazette, Greenfield, Mass. Biographical account of the.

see

NEWSPAPERS, ANNIVERSARY ISSUES. Greenfield Gazette. Centennial Edition, 1792 - 1892, p. 3.

DICKINSON, SAMUEL NELSON

Cabinet A Shelf 3 No. 7

Description of his printing house in Boston.

See p.4 of Boston Notion-Extra. Dec. 11, (ca. 1839)

On folio 55 in vol. labelled "Early printing in New England".

DICKINSON, SAMUEL N.

Cabinet Shelf No.

See also
Specimen Books, Types. U.S. [v.d.]

DICKMAN, THOMAS

Cabinet A Shelf 3 No. 5

Greenfield (Mass.), printer, 1792.

See "NEWSPAPERS, Massachusetts". Impartial Intelligencer...

DICKINSON, SAMUEL N.

Cabinet 81 Shelf 2 No. 34

Boston type and printing office. Sketch by Mr. Dickinson. Newspaper clipping.

See MUNSELL, JOEL. "Printers Scraps", vol. V., p.113.

DICKINSON & CO., JOHN

See Specimen Books, Types, Great Britain, Caslon (Chiswell Street.)

DICKSON, ROBERT

Cabinet U Shelf 1 No. 73

Introduction of the art of printing into Scotland. Aberdeen, 1885. Facsimiles, title-pages, illus. etc.
Historical, bibliographical account.

Stamped cloth; 9¼ x 5-7/8 x ½ in.

DICKINSON, SAMUEL N.

Cabinet LL Shelf 5 No. 16

(A) Help to printers and publishers: being a series of calculations, showing the quantity of paper required for a given number of signatures in book work...Also an extensive table for job work. Boston: Printed and published at 52 Washington Street. 1835.

Cloth; 8¼ x 5-1/8 x 7/8 in.

DICKINSON TYPE FOUNDRY

Cabinet 61 Shelf 1 No. 5

History of the house, its founders, its progress, and decline. Illus., portraits.

Article in "The Paper World", vol.18, No.3, March, 1889, p.1

DICKSON, ROBERT

Cabinet U Shelf 1 No. 72

Who was Scotland's first printer? Une compendious and breve tractate in commendation of Androw Myllar. Compylit be Robert Dickson, London. 1881.

Vellum; 7½ x 4-7/8 in.

DICKINSON, SAMUEL NELSON.

Cabinet G Shelf 1 No. 61

See Imprints, United States.

DICKINSON TYPE FOUNDRY

Cabinet 31 Shelf 2 No. 16

"Type" (January, 1889.Published by the Dickinson Type Foundry, Boston, Mass.

One issue only, item in manila envelope

DICKSON, ROBERT and J. P. EDMOND.

Cabinet U Shelf 1 No. 74

Annals of Scottish printing, from the introduction of the art in 1507 to the beginning of the 17th century. By Robert Dickson, and John Philip Edmond. Cambridge, 1890. Illus. facsimiles, printers marks, etc.
Bibliographical historical account.

Cloth; 11-7/8 x 9-1/8 x 2 in.

DICKINSON, S. N.

Cabinet 80 Shelf 1-a No. 6

Notice that in addition to his extensive facilities for Book and Job Printing, he has added the "very important item of Casting his own Type". Boston, 1843.

See ALMANACS. Boston Almanac for the year 1843...p.135.

DICKINSON TYPE FOUNDRY

Cabinet Shelf No.

See also
Specimen Books, Types. United States.
" also " " " " American Type Founders Co. Boston, 1902.
" also Specimen Books, Cuts. United States.

DICTIONARIES.

Cabinet F Shelf 5 No. 16

Diderot et D'Alembert: Encyclopedie, ou Dictionnaire Raisonne des Sciences des Arts et des Metieres....
Colophon: De l'Imprimerie de Le Breton, Imprimeur ordinaire du Roy. Paris, 1751.
See Page 650 for article on Types. (Caracteres) with specimens of 23 different types from the Fournier Foundry.

Tree calf; 15¾ x 10 x 2¼ in. Brunet 2, 701.

DICTIONARIES

Cabinet 70 — Shelf 2 — No. 15 (2 vols.)

Doleto, Stephano: Commentariorum linguae Latinae. [Two vols.] Apud Seb. Gryphium, Lugduni, 1536-1538. [Printer Mark]

Second vol. has same title and imprint, but is dated 1538. Both have woodcut title borders and printer marks.

DICTIONARIES

Cabinet V — Shelf 5 — No. 2

Encyclopédie ou dictionnaire des connoissances humaines. Mis en ordre Par M. De Felice. Tome XXIV. Jan - Inv. Yverdon, 1773.

See pp. 346-378 of this vol. for items relating to printing.

Calf; 10 x 7-3/4 x $2\frac{1}{4}$ in.

DICTIONARIES

Cabinet 40 — Shelf 1 — No. 22

(Hebrew). Thesaurus linguae sanctae. Ex R. David Kimchi...autnore. Ex officina Robertii Stephani typographi Regii. Ex privilegio Regis. 1548.

Tooled pigskin in buckram case; 9 x $6\frac{1}{4}$ x $3\frac{1}{2}$ ins.

DICTIONARIES

Cabinet QQ — Shelf 5 — No. 2

Pronouncing gazetteer and geographical dictionary of the Philippine Islands, United States of America, with maps, charts, and illustrations...with a complete indes. Prepared in the Bureau of Insular Affairs, War Department, 1902, Washington, Government Printint Office, 1902.

Cloth: $9\frac{1}{4}$ x 6 x $\frac{3}{4}$ in.

DICTIONARIES

Cabinet S — Shelf 5 — No. 25

Webster-Merriam Dictionary, century old. New dictionary is launched at celebration, June 25, 1934, Springfield, Mass. [Newspaper excerpt, illus. report of the event.]

Item in box labelled "History of Printing. U.S. Miscellaneous items."

DICTIONARIES

Cabinet 81 — Shelf 2 — No. 33

Webster's Dictionaries: The battle of the dictionaries. Articles and letters on the merit of Webster's Dictionary. Newspaper clippings, circa 1855.

Items in MUNSELL, JOEL. "Printers Scraps". Vol. IV, pp.1-4.

DICTIONARIES OF ART

Cabinet I — Shelf 1 — No. 31

Biographical dictionary, containing an historical account of all the engravers from the earliest period of the art of engraving to the present time...To which is prefixed an essay on the rise and progress of the art of engraving, with specimens. (2 vols.) By Joseph Strutt. London, 1785-6.

Calf; 12 x $9\frac{1}{4}$ in.

DICTIONARIES OF ART

Cabinet I — Shelf 1 — No. 30

Fontenai (l'Abbé de). Dictionnarie des artistes, ou notice historique et raisonnée des architectes, peintres, graveurs...imprimeurs. (2 vols.) A. Paris: 1776.

Calf; each vol., $6\frac{3}{4}$ x 4-3/8 in.

DICTIONARIES, COMMERCIAL

Cabinet QQ — Shelf 5 — No. 3

(Commercial dictionary, Spanish, Portugese, English) Nomenclature commercial commercial. Publicada por especial recomendacion de la conferencia internacional. Abril de 1897, Washington.

Cloth; 12 x $8\frac{3}{4}$ x 1-3/8 in.

DICTIONARIES, Greeks.

Cabinet 40 — Shelf 2 — No. 42

Thesaurus Graecae linguae. Ab. Henrico Stephano constructo....

Imprint: Henr. Stephani Oliva. Cum privilegio Caes. maiestatis, et christianiss Galliarum regis [Geneva 1572]

Morocco, 15[illegible] x $9\frac{3}{4}$ x $2\frac{3}{4}$ ins. Add to card.

DICTIONARIES, Illustrated.

Cabinet 69 — Shelf 1 — No. 40

La Prosopographie ou description des personnes insignes, enrichie de plusieurs effigies ....Par Antoine du Verdier...

Printed by Antoine Gryphe, Lyon, 1573. [Includes portraits of Gutenberg, Gryphe, etc., with an account of the invention of printing.]

Calf; $9\frac{1}{4}$ x 6-7/8 x 2 ins.

DICTIONARIES, MUSIC

Cabinet QQ — Shelf 2 — No. 8

Brossard, Sebastien de. Dictionaire de musique...Troisième édition. Amsterdam, n. d. circa, 1704.

Sheepskin; 7 x $4\frac{1}{2}$ in.

DICTIONARIES OF PAPER and PAPER MAKING TERMS

Cabinet RR — Shelf 4 — No. 20

Chemical terms, a dictionary of, together with a glossary of various papers, with brief notes as to origin of same, and use of papers.

See SINDALL, R. W. Paper technology... London, 1906, pp.216-236.

DICTIONARIES, PHOTO-MECHANICAL TERMS

Cabinet I — Shelf 2 — No. 53

Glossary of photo-mechanical terms.

See Appendix, p.403, AMSTUTZ, N.S. Amstutz' hand-book of photoengraving...

DICTIONARIES, PHOTO-MECHANICAL TERMS

Cabinet I — Shelf 2 — No. 49

Glossary of words and terms used in the photo-engraving business. [By Stephen H. Horgan.] Submitted to 31st Annual Convention of the American Photo-Engravers Association. Washington, D.C., July 14, 15, 16, 1927. Pamphlet.

Item in manila envelope.

DICTIONARIES, PHOTO-MECHANICAL TERMS

Cabinet I — Shelf 2 — No. 47

Photo-engraving: How to order and where to buy it. By Stephen H. Horgan...New York, 1914. Illus.

Has glossary of terms used in engraving.

Cloth; 7 x 4-3/8 in.

DICTIONARIES, Printers' Slang

Cabinet V — Shelf 2 — No. 16

Boutmy, Eugene. Les typographes Parisiens suivis d'un Petit Dictionnaire de la Langue Verte Typographique. Paris, 1874.

The human side of the French printer, with his slang words.

Half leather; 10 x 6-3/8 x $1\frac{1}{4}$ in.

DICTIONARY, PRINTERS' SLANG.

Cabinet QQ — Shelf 1 — No. 47

Boutmy, Eugene. Dictionnaire de la langue verte typographique...Paris, 1878.

Half morocco; 6-3/8 x $4\frac{1}{4}$ x $\frac{1}{2}$ in.

DICTIONARIES, PRINTERS' SLANG

Cabinet QQ Shelf 1 No. 37

Brimmer, George. The composing room. A serio-comico-satirico-poetico production--Oh!... London, 1835.
"This poem abounds in the slang of the printing office, and gives a very vivid picture of the manners and customs of the compositors of the period". B.& W.

Half morocco; $8\frac{1}{4}$ x $5\frac{1}{4}$ in.

DICTIONARIES OF PRINTING

Cabinet V Shelf 5 No. 3.01

DeFelice---Encyclopedie. Imprimeur-Marbreur. Yverdon, 1778.

With many plates illustrating printing and printing appliances.

Tree calf; 10 x $7\frac{3}{4}$ x 1 in.

DICTIONARIES OF PRINTING

Cabinet T Shelf 5 No. 109

Gesta Typographica, or a medley for printers and others. Collected by Chas. T. Jacobi, London, 1897.

Boards, linen back; 7 x $4\frac{1}{2}$ in.

DICTIONARIES, PRINTERS' SLANG. France

Cabinet LL Shelf 3 No. 46

L'Argot des typographes précédé d'une monographie du compositeur d'imprimerie. Par Eugene Boutmy. Paris, 1883.

Half morocco; 7-5/8 x 5-1/8 x 5/8 in.

DICTIONARIES OF PRINTING

Cabinet T Shelf 3 No. 27

Dictionary of typography and its accessory arts. Supplements to Printers Register. London, 1871.

Cloth; $10\frac{1}{4}$ x $8\frac{1}{4}$ x 3/8 in.

DICTIONARIES OF PRINTING

Cabinet MM Shelf 7 No. 70

Heir, Martin (Compiler). The twentieth century encyclopedia of printing. Chicago, 1930. Illus.

Has an introduction by Douglas C. McMurtrie.

Embossed leather; 9-3/8 x $6\frac{3}{4}$ x $1\frac{1}{2}$ in.

DICTIONARIES OF PRINTING

Cabinet S Shelf 2 No. 168

American dictionary of printing and bookmaking, containing a history of these arts in Europe and America, with definitions of technical terms and biographical sketches. [Pasko]. New York: Lockwood & Co., publishers. 1894.

Half morocco; 10-3/4 x $8\frac{1}{4}$ x 1-7/8 in.

DICTIONARIES OF PRINTING.

Cabinet MM Shelf 7 No. 67

Dictionnaire de l'imprimerie et des arts graphiques en général. Par E. Desormes et Arnold Muller. Paris, 1912.

Half morocco; 7 x 4 x $\frac{3}{4}$ in.

DICTIONARIES OF PRINTING

Cabinet I Shelf 1 No. 30

(Historical, biographical dictionary of artists, engravers, printers, etc. 2 vols.) By l'Abbé Fontenai. Paris, 1776.

Calf; each vol., $6\frac{3}{4}$ x 4-3/8 in.

DICTIONARIES OF PRINTING

Cabinet S Shelf 2 No. 167

American Encyclopedia of Printing. Edited by J. Luther Ringwalt. Philadelphia, 1871. Illus.
Bio-bibliographical, historical, and technical items.

Cloth; 11 x $7\frac{3}{4}$ in.

DICTIONARIES OF PRINTING

Cabinet LL Shelf 2 No. 44

Ferencz, Pustai. Nyomdászati encziklopédia az osszes grafikai tudományok ismettara... Budapest, 1902.

DICTIONARIES OF PRINTING

Cabinet 78 Shelf 1 No. 85

Kriegel, Harry G. Encyclopedia of printing inks. Secrets, formulae and helpful hints for craftsmen in the graphic arts. Published by Harry G. Kriegel, president of Superior Printing Ink Co., N.Y. City, 1932.

Cloth; $8\frac{1}{4}$ x 5-3/4 in.

DICTIONARIES OF PRINTING

Cabinet AA Shelf 2 No. 22 3 vols.

Arneudo, Giuseppe Isidoro. Dizionario esegetico, tecnico-storico per le arti grafiche, con speciale riguardo alla tipografia. Illustrqzione e tavole. (3 vols.) Torino, 1917.

Cloth; 8-3/8 x $5\frac{3}{4}$ in. each vol.

DICTIONARIES OF PRINTING.

Cabinet MM Shelf 1 No. 30

Frey, A. Manuel nouveau de typographie. Contenant les principes théoriques et pratiques de l'imprimeur-typographe...Orné de planches. Deux partie. Paris, 1835. (Forming part of the Encyclopedia Roret) 2 v.

Boards, leather back; 5-3/4 x $3\frac{1}{2}$ in.

DICTIONARIES OF PRINTING

Cabinet MM Shelf 7 No. 4

Morgan, H. A dictionary of terms used in printing. Madras, 1863.

Cloth; $8\frac{3}{4}$ x $5\frac{1}{4}$ in. Second copy MM/7/60.

DICTIONARIES OF PRINTING.

Cabinet AA Shelf 2 No. 33

Dalmazzo, Gianolio. Libro e l'art della stampa. Enciclopedia metodica per i cultori della tipografia e della affini, e per gli amatori del libro. Compilato ... per Gianolio Dalmazzo. Torino,,1926. Illus.

Full morocco; $9\frac{3}{4}$ x 7 x 3 in.

DICTIONARIES OF PRINTING.

Cabinet MM Shelf 1 No. 37 2 vols.

Frey-Bouchez. Nouveau manuel complet de typographie, contenant les principes théoriques et pratiques de cet art. Nouvelle édition, rrevue, corrigee et augmentée par M. E. Bouchez, Paris 1857. [2 vols]
These form part of the "Encyclopedie Roret".

Cloth; 6 x 3-5/8 in.

DICTIONARIES OF PRINTING

Cabinet MM Shelf 7 No. 4.01

Morgan, H. Dictionary of terms used in printing. Printed at the Military Male Orphan Asylum Press, by William Thomas, Madras, 1863.

"Mostly taken from Savage. The author describes himself as of the Government Printing Establishment".

Cloth; $8\frac{3}{4}$ x $5\frac{1}{2}$ x $\frac{1}{2}$ in.

DICTIONARIES OF PRINTING

Cabinet MM Shelf 3 No. 1

(Moxons, 1683) A dictionary alphabetically explaining the abstruse words and phrases that are used in typography...

Numb. XXIII, p.367 in Moxon's Mechanick Exercises...1677-1683.

DICTIONARIES OF PRINTING

Cabinet MM Shelf 3 No. 25

Timperley, C.H. A dictionary of printers and printing...London, 1839.

The first edition of this valuable work, with which is bound the "Printers' Manual" by the same author. London, 1838.

Half morocco; 10-1/8 x 6½ x 3-1/8 in.

DICTIONARIES OF PRINTING

Cabinet Y Shelf 4 No. 37

Waldow, Alexander. Illustrierte encyklopädie der graphischen künste und der verwandten zweige. (Buch-stein- und kufferdruk, lithographie, etc. etc.) Leipzig, 1884.

Half morocco; 10 x 6-5/8 x 2¼ in.

DICTIONARIES OF PRINTING.

Cabinet LL Shelf 1 No. 24

Neuburger, Hermann. Encyklopädie der buchdruckerkunst. Leipzig, 1844.

Boards; 8½ x 5¼ x ½ in.

DICTIONARIES OF PRINTING

Cabinet T Shelf 3 No. 24

Timperley, C.H. Encyclopaedia of literary and typographical anecdote; being a chronological digest of the history of printing from the earliest period to the present... Biographical sketches of booksellers, printers, and type founders, etc. London, 1842.

Important work.

Bound in with "The Printers' Manual.... by C. H. Timperley, London, 1838.

Cloth; 10½ x [illegible] 6-3/8 in.

DICTIONARIES OF PRINTING

Cabinet LL Shelf 2 No. 14

Hebel, Oskar. Hand-lexicon der deutschen presse und des graphischen gewerbes. Ein encyclopädie des wissens und der erfahrung in der praxis des verlegers und druckers...Leipzig, 1905. Illus.

Cloth; 9½ x 6-5/8 x 1¼ in.

DICTIONARIES OF PRINTING.

Cabinet Y Shelf 3 No. 33

(Pocket manual of printers and publishers from Gutenberg's time to the present day.) Taschen-Lexicon der buchdrucker u. buchhändler seit Gutenberg bis auf die gegenwart. von Paul Heicken. Leipzig, 1884. Illus.

Half morocco; 5-3/4 x 3-3/4 x 3/4 in.

DICTIONARIES OF PRINTING.

Cabinet MM Shelf 1 No. 8

Traité élémentaire de l'imprimerie, ou le manuel de l'imprimeur. Avec 36 planches en taille-douce. Par Ant. F. Momoro. Paris 1796.

A practical manual of printing treated in an encyclopaedic style.

See also MM/1/7.

Boards; 7-7/8 x 5¼ x 1¼ in.

DICTIONARIES OF PRINTING TERMS

Cabinet FF Shelf 3 No. 36

Common technical terms, glossary.

See Legros & Grant. Typographical printing surfaces... London, 1916/ pp. XXI-XIV

DICTIONARIES OF PRINTING

Cabinet T Shelf 3 No. 21

Savage, William: Dictionary of the art of printing. London, 1841. Illus.

A practical book of reference useful for the printer, author, and librarian.

Half morocco; 8¾ x 5¾ in.

DICTIONARIES OF PRINTING

Cabinet R Shelf 3 No. 193

Typographical Miscellany. By Joel Munsell. Albany, 1850.

Historical and practical work, encyclopedic in content, but not in arrangement.

Cloth; 9-1/8 x 5¾ in.

DICTIONARIES, PRINTING TERMS

Cabinet EE Shelf 2 No. 9

Dictionary of printing terms...presented through the courtesy of the Porte Printing Company... Salt Lake City, Utah.

p. 509 of FREDERIC NELSON PHILLIPS Inc. "Type faces" New York, 1929.

Latin, embossed; 9¼ x 6 x 2 in.

DICTIONARIES OF PRINTING

Cabinet MM Shelf 7 No. 61

Southward, John. Dictionary of typography and its accessory arts. Presented to the subscribers of the Printers' Register. London, 1870-1871. Illus.

Issued as supplements, 4 pp. each month to the "Printers' Register".

Boards, leather back; 9¾ x 8 in.

DICTIONARIES OF PRINTING

Cabinet QQ Shelf 6 No. 15

Van Huffel, N.G. Encyclopedisch handboek der graphische werkwijzen ten dienst van plaatdrukkers, uitgevers...Met 34 afbeeldingen tusschen den tekst. Door Dr. N.G. van Huffel Utrecht, 1926.

Boards; 9 x 7¼ in.

DICTIONARIES, PRINTING TERMS

Cabinet LL Shelf 3 No. 42.01

Dictionary of terms used in the printing and allied trades. Reprinted from The L. & M. News. Linotype & Machinery Ltd. London, England. (1935)

Pamphlet; 9-5/8 x 6; pp. 45.

DICTIONARIES OF PRINTING.

Cabinet MM Shelf 7 No. 62 Two copies

Southward, John. Dictionary of typography and its accessory arts. Second edition, London, 1875. At the end: The literary almanack, compiled by William Blades, 1875. London.

Frontispiece portrait of Gutenberg; at the end of book, printing trade advertisements.

Roan; 8½ x 5¼ in.

DICTIONARIES OF PRINTING.

Cabinet Y Shelf 4 No. 37

Waldow, Alexander. Illustrierte encyklopädie der graphischen kunst und der verwandten zweige: (buch,-stein-und kupferdruck, lithographie... Leipzig, 1884. Druck und Verlag von Alex. Waldow.

Half morocco; 10 x 6-5/8 x 2¼ in.

DICTIONARIES, PRINTING TERMS

Cabinet MM Shelf 3 No. 52

(English) Glossarial index of technical terms and phrases. Compiled from the author's (C.T. Jacobi) "Printers vocabulary of technical terms" etc. 1888.

pp.401-429 in Jacobi's "Printing: A practical treatise...London, 1919.

DICTIONARIES, PRINTING TERMS

Cabinet MM Shelf 7 No. 64

(English) Charles Thomas Jacobi. The printers' vocabulary: a collection of some 2500 technical terms, phrases, abbreviations and other expressions mostly relating to letterpress printing, many of which have been in use since the time of Caxton. London: The Chiswick Press, 1888.

Cloth; 7¾ x 5¼ x ½ in.

DICTIONARIES, PRINTING TERMS

Cabinet LL Shelf 1 No. 6

(German) Chr. Fr. Gessner. Versuch eines wohl eingerichteten worterbuchs...

pp.164-258, vol.I, of GESSNER'S Die so nithig als nutzlich buchdruckerkunst... Leipzig, 1740.

DICTIONARIES, PRINTING TERMS

Cabinet LL Shelf 1 No. 13

(German) Christian Gottlob Taeubel. Typographisches worterbuch...nach dem alphabet eingerichtet...Leipzig, 1791.

Second section of TAEUBEL'S "Praktisches Handbuch...Leipzig, 1791.

Boards; 7¾ x 4¾ x 1¼ in.

DICTIONARIES, PRINTING TERMS

Cabinet MM Shelf 7 No. 69

(English) Hugo Jahn, (Compiler). The dictionary of graphic arts terms. A book of technical words and phrases used in the printing and allied industries. Published by...United Typothetae of America, 1928.

Cloth; 8 x 5-1/8 x ⅞ in.

DICTIONARIES, PRINTING TERMS

Cabinet MM Shelf 7 No. 63

(German) Linus Irmisch. Wörterbuch der buchdrucker und schriftgiesser. Etwa 1700 fachgewerbliche und fachgesellschaftliche wörter... Braunschweig, 1901.

Buckram; 8 x 5¼ x ¾ in.

DICTIONARIES, PRINTING TERMS

Cabinet LL Shelf 1 No. 8

German. Fortgesetzter versuch eines wohl eingerichteten wörterbuchs, worinnen die meister kunstwörter welche bey buchdruckereyen gebrauchlich sind.

See Gessner, Chr. Friedrich. Der in den buchdruckerei wohl unterrichtete lehrjunge...Leipzig, 1843, pp.433-61, 187-224 following the "Deposito Cornuti"

DICTIONARIES, PRINTING TERMS

Cabinet MM Shelf 6 No. 35

(English) A.A. Stewart, (Compiler). The printer's dictionary of technical terms. A handbook of definitions and information about processes of printing. With a brief glossary of terms used in book binding. Boston, Mass. Published by the School of Printing, North End Union, 1912.

Cloth; 6-7/8 x 4 x 1¼ in.

DICTIONARIES, PRINTING TERMS

Cabinet LL Shelf 3 No. 53

(German) Die deutsche druckersprache. von Dr. Heinrich Klenz. Strassburg, 1900.

At end of book, pp.115-128, poetry of printing.

Half morocco; 8¼ x 5½ in.

DICTIONARIES, PRINTING TERMS

Cabinet LL Shelf 2 No. 18 & 19

(German) Wörterbuch der haufigsten buchgewerblichen fachausdrucke...

pp.6-20 in SAUBERLICH, OTTO, Buchgewerbliches hilfsbuch...Leipzig 1921, also 1923.

Boards; 8¾ x 6½ x 5/8 in.

DICTIONARIES, PRINTING TERMS.

Cabinet MM Shelf 7 No. 71

(English) Technical terms relating to printing machinery. Compiled by the editor of the "Printing Times & Lithographer". London, Wyman & Sons. n.d.

Cloth; 7½ x 5 in.

DICTIONARIES, PRINTING TERMS

Cabinet MM Shelf 7 No. 63

(German) Marahrens, Aug. Vollständiges Real-Lexicon der Buchdruckerkunst, und der ihr verwandten graphischen künste und gewerbe. Unter mitwirkung mehrerer fachgenossen... Erster Band A - L. Fulda, 1877.

Half morocco; 9½ x 6½ x 1 in.

DICTIONARIES, PRINTING TERMS

Cabinet EE Shelf 1 No. 52

Glossary of printing and publishing terms.

pp.407-433 LITTLE'S Type, specimen pages and book papers...New York, 1923.

DICTIONARIES, PRINTING TERMS

Cabinet MM Shelf 4 No. 19

(English) Technical terms relating to printing machinery, a list of. Compiled by the editor of the "Printing Times & Lithographer (C.W.H. Wyman). Wyman's Technical Series. London, Wyman & Sons, n.d. circa 1883.

On fly leaf, autograph of C.W.H. Wyman, distinguished printer, bibliographer, editor.

Cloth; 7-3/8 x 5 x 3/8 in.

DICTIONARIES, PRINTING TERMS

Cabinet LL Shelf 1 No. 14

(German) Christian Gottlob Taeubel. Allgemeines theoretisch-practisches wörterbuch der buchdruckerkunst und schriftgiesserey...Zwey bände. Wien, 1805. Illus.

Half leather; 8-7/8 x 7½ x 1¼ in.

DICTIONARIES, PRINTING TERMS

Cabinet LL Shelf 2 No. 44

(Hungarian) Pusztai Ferencz. Nyomdoszati enczi-klopedie az osszes grafikai tudomanyok ismerettara. Budapest, 1902.

Half niger; 9½ x 6-3/8 x 1½ in.

DICTIONARIES, PRINTING TERMS

Cabinet MM Shelf 7 No. 68

(German) Karl Albert. Lexikon der graphischen techniken...Verlag von W. Knapp, Halle (Saale) 1927.

Half morocco; 9¾ x 6-5/8 x ¾ in.

DICTIONARIES, PRINTING TERMS

Cabinet LL Shelf 1 No. 12

(German) C.G. Taeubel. Halle-Leipzig, 1785. Typographisches wörterbuch, welches diejenigen kunstwörter in alphabetischer ordnung ekläret, die dem corrector zu wissen nöthig sind...

See following p.344 in TAEUBEL'S "Orthotypographisches handbuch"...1785.

DICTIONARIES, Printing Terms

Cabinet I Shelf 2 No. 47

Photo-mechanical processes, terms of.

See HORGAN'S Photo-engraving. How to order...New York, 1914, p.33.

DICTIONARIES, PRINTING TERMS

Cabinet LL Shelf 1 No. 8

(Polyglot) Printing terms in German, French, and Italian, pp.433-461 in Gessner, der in der Buchdruckerei wohl unterrichtete Lehr-Junge ...Leipzig, 1743.

Vellum; 6-7/8 x 4¼ x 1-5/8 in.

DICTIONARIES, PRINTING TERMS

Cabinet LL Shelf 3 No. 35

(Polyglot) Technical vocabulary [English, French, German]. By L.A. Legros and O. Eckenstein. Excerpt from Typographical Printing-Surfaces, by L.A. Legros and John Cameron Grant. William Clowes and Sons, Ltd. London, 1915.

Cloth; 10 x 6¼ x 3/8 in.

DICTIONARIES, PRINTING TERMS

Cabinet Y Shelf 5 No. 26

(Polyglot) Typographical terms in English, German, French, Italian.

See AUSTRIA. Geschichte der K.K. Hof-Und Staatsdruckerei in Wien"...Wien 1851.

DICTIONARIES, PRINTING TERMS

Cabinet LL Shelf 1 No. 35 2 vols.

(Polyglot) Typographisch-technisches parallel-wörterbuch der deutschen, franzosischen und englischen sprache...

pp.376-487 (vol.2) MARAHRENS "Vollstandiges theoretisch-praktisches handbuch der Typographie". Leipzig, 1870.

DICTIONARIES, PRINTING TERMS

Cabinet LL Shelf 1 No. 18

(Polyglot) Typographisches wörterbuch: Teutsch, Fransösisch, Engländisch, Italienisch.

pp.777 to 817 in "Andreasch Handbuch"... Frankfurt a.M. 1827.

DICTIONARIES, PRINTING TERMS

Cabinet C Shelf 1 No. 9

Short dictionary of printing terms.

See MANCHESTER GUARDIAN. Craft of printing, the...May 23, 1922, p.X

DICTIONARIES OF PRINTING TERMS

Cabinet T Shelf 4 No. 80

Short glossary of bibliographical and typographical terms in more general use.

In Jacobi's "Books and printing... London, 1902, p. 75

DICTIONARIES, PRINTING TERMS

Cabinet MM Shelf 2 No. 22

(Spanish) Vocabulario del tecnicismo tipografico.

pp.256-279 in Giraldez, José, Tratado de la tipografia...Madrid, 1884.

DICTIONARIES, PRINTING TERMS

Cabinet MM Shelf 2 No. 21

(Spanish) Vocabulario tipografico.

Chap. 18, p.137 in Villamur's Manual de la tipografia Espanola. Barcelona, 1882.

DICTIONARIES OF PRINTING TERMS

Cabinet FF Shelf 3 No. 36

Technical vocabulary: English, French, German.

See Legros ... and Grant. Typographical printing surfaces... London, 1916, p. 669.

DICTIONARIES, Printing Terms.

Cabinet V Shelf 4 No. 7

Vocabulaire des terms usités dans l'imprimerie-librairie.

See Printing, Historical. Art de l'imprimerie - librairie...In Arts et Metiers n. n. n. d. [1773]. p. 591

DICTIONARIES, PROCESSWORKERS

Cabinet I Shelf 2 No. 46

Processworkers' glossary. An endeavour to standardize most of the terms commonly used in a new and constantly changing business. By S.H. Horgan.

See HORGAN'S Half-tone and photo mechanical processes...Chicago, 1913, p.201.

DICTIONARIES, Rhyming

Cabinet LL Shelf 3 No. 39

Brewer, R.F. Orthometry: The art of versification and the technicalities of poetry. With a new and complete rhyming dictionary. By R.F. Brewer. New and revised edition. Edinburgh, 1925.

Cloth; 8¼ x 5½ x 1½ in.

DICTIONARY OF AMERICAN...ENGRAVERS.

Cabinet I Shelf 3 No. 12

Fielding, Mantle. Dictionary of American painters, sculptors and engravers. Philadelphia, n.d. circa 1926. Illus.

Cloth; 10-5/8 x 7¾ x 2-5/8 in.

DICTIONARY OF PHOTOGRAPHY

Cabinet L Shelf 1 No. 40

Reference book

See WALL, E. J. Dictionary of photograph...London, n.d.

DIDEROT, DENIS

Cabinet X Shelf 5 No. 124

(Booksellers controversy regarding their method of disposal of Diderot's "Encyclopedia".

See LIBERTY OF PRINTING. France. Memoire a consulter...Paris, 1770.

DIDEROT et D'ALEMBERT

Cabinet F Shelf 5 No. 16

Encyclopedie, ou dictionnaire raissoné des sciences, des arts et des metiers...Paris, 1751. De l'Imprimerie de Le Breton. Tome second.

See p.650 for article on types. Includes specimens from the Fournier foundry.

Tree calf; 15⅝ x 10 x 2¼ in. Brunet 2, 701.

DIDOT, ALFRED FIRMIN

Cabinet RR Shelf 3 No. 33

Papier, III Groupe de l'Exposition Technologique de 1882. Partie moderne. Rapport...M. Alfred Firmin - Didot. Paris, 1883. (Union Centrale des Arts Decoratifs)

Report on typography, illustration, paper, photography. Has names of exhibitors, with brief biographical notes.

In folder

DIDOT, AMBROISE FIRMIN.

Cabinet W Shelf 2 No. 16

Alde Manuce et l'Hellénisme a Venise. Orné de quatre portraits et d'un facsimile. Paris 1875.
Biographical, bibliographical and technical account of the production of the Aldine press from 1495 to 1514.

Half morocco; 9 x 6 in.

DIDOT, AMBROISE FIRMIN

Cabinet V Shelf 4 No. 19

Essai sur la Typographie: Extrait du tome XXVI de l'Encyclopédie Moderne. Paris, 1855. Plates (4).

Boards; 9½ x 6 in. See also V/4/20

DIDOT, AMBROISE FIRMIN (Author)

Cabinet W Shelf 2 No. 147

Gutenberg (Jean ou Hans Gensfleisch). Par M. Ambroise Firmin Didot. Extrait de la Nouvelle Biographie Générale. Paris, 1858.
Bound in with "Notice sur la vie et les travaux de ... Didot." Par Wallon, Paris, 1886.

Half morocco; 11 x 9 in,

DIDOT, AMBROISE FIRMIN

Cabinet K Shelf 5 No. 16

Apocalypses figurées, manuscrites et xylographiques. Deuxième appendice au catalogue raisonné des livres de la bibliothèque de M. Ambroise Firmin Didot. Paris, 1870. Illus.

Half vellum; 9-1/8 x 6-3/8 x ¼ in.

DIDOT, AMBROISE FIRMIN

Cabinet W Shelf 2 No. 14

(Les) Estienne, Henri I: Francois I et II: Robert I, II et III., Henri II; Paul et Antoine. Extrait de la Nouvelle Biographie Générale, publiée par Mm. Firmin Didot frères Paris, [1856.]

Half morocco; 8½ x 5½ in.

DIDOT, AMBROISE FIRMIN

Cabinet W Shelf 2 No. 1

Gutenberg (Jean ou Hans Gensfleisch) par Ambroise Firmin Didot. Extrait de la Nouvelle Biographie Générale, publiée par MM. Firmin Didot, frères et fils.
Bio-bibliographical account.

Item 10 in volume "Gutenberg, l'inventeur de l'imprimerie - Melanges."

DIDOT, AMBROISE FIRMIN

Cabinet W Shelf 2 No. 123

Banquet offert le 20 Mars 1873 a M. Ambroise Firmin Didot a l'occasion de sa reception a l'Institut (Academie des Inscriptions de Belles-Lettres).
Includes Didot's speech of acceptance.

Half morocco; 9-3/4 x 6¼ in.

DIDOT, AMBROISE FIRMIN

Cabinet J Shelf 2 No. 14

Etude sur Jean Cousin, suivi de notices sur Jean Leclerc et Pierre Woeiriot. Par Ambroise Firmin Didot. Orne d'un portrait inedit de Jean Cousin, de la reproduction photographique des cinq portraits peints par lui ...Paris, 1872.
Includes a bio-bibliographical section relating to the early printed books illustrated by Cousin.

(cont'd)

DIDOT, AMBROISE-FIRMIN

Cabinet V Shelf 4 No. 20

Histoire de la typographie: Extrait de l'Encyclopédie modern. Paris, 1882.

Cloth, 9 x 5-3/4 in. See also V/4/19.

DIDOT, AMBROISE-FIRMIN.

Cabinet W Shelf 2 No. 19

Biographical sketch, by Alfred Franklin. Excerpt from Bulletin du Bouquiniste, No. 437, March 1, 1876. Paris, chez Aug. Aubrey.

In folder labelled "Miscellaneous items relating to the Didot Family of Printers."

DIDOT, AMBROISE FIRMIN (cont'd)

Cabinet Shelf No.

Half morocco; 9-7/8 x 6½ x 1 in.

DIDOT, AMBROISE FIRMIN

Cabinet O Shelf 1 No. 95

l'Imprimerie la Librairie et la Papeterie a l'Exposition Universelle de 1851. Rapport du 17e Jury. Presente par M. Ambroise Firmin Didot. 2e ed. avec quelques additions. Paris, 1884.
Bound in with two other exhibition items

Cloth; 9 x 5¾ in.

DIDOT, AMBROISE FIRMIN

Cabinet W Shelf 2 No. 19

[Biography] M. Ambroise Firmin Didot, 1790-1876. Par Jules Delalain.
Excerpt from "Journal generale de l'Imprimerie et de la Librairie", 11 Mars, 1876.

Item in manila envelope.

DIDOT, AMBROISE FIRMIN.

Cabinet I Shelf 3 No. 14 2 vols.

Graveurs de portraits en France. Catalogue raisonne de la collection des portraits de l'ecole Francaise appartenant a Ambroise Firmin Didot. Precede d'une introduction. Ouvrage posthume. (2 vols.) Paris, 1875-1877.
With very brief biographical notes.

DIDOT, AMBROISE -FIRMIN

Cabinet V Shelf 5 No. 7

Imprimeur recoit la visite de Benjamin Franklin. Donne les premiers notions de l'imprimerie a son petit-fils William Temple Franklin. (Franklin's visit to the printing office of Didot.)
see CRAPELET, CH. "Étude sur la typographie...Paris, 1837, p.216 (tome 1)

DIDOT, AMBROISE FIRMIN

Cabinet V Shelf 3 No. 12

Essai sur la typographie. Paris, 1851. With Plates.
Bound in with Histoire de la Gravure sur bois. Paris, 1863. Presentation copy, signed by the author.

Boards; leather back; 9½ x 6 in.

DIDOT, AMBROISE FIRMIN.

Cabinet W Shelf 2 No. 15

Gutenberg (Jean ou Hans Gensfleisch), par M. Ambroise Firmin Didot. Extrait de la Nouvelle Biographie Générale. Paris, 1858.
Historical, bibliographical and biographical account.

Morocco; 9¼ x 5½ in.

DIDOT, AMBROISE FIRMIN.

Cabinet W Shelf 2 No. 18

Inauguration de la statue de M. Ambroise Firmin Didot, élevée sur la Place Publique de Saint-Roch, commune de Sorel-Moussel (Eure-et-Loir) le 21 juin, 1891. Mesnil-sur l'Estrée (Eure).

Boards; 11¾ x 7½ in.

DIDOT, AMBROISE FIRMIN

Cabinet W, Shelf 2, No. 19

(Sale of Didot's library, the third session of.) La troisieme vente Ambroise Firmin Didot. n.d. Probably 1880.

Bibliographical.

Item in manila envelope.

DIDOT, FIRMIN.

Cabinet W, Shelf 2, No. 12

Bucoliques de Virgile, precédées de plusieurs Idylles de Théocrite ... Traduites en vers Francais par Firmin Didot. Gravé, fondu et imprimé par le traducteur. A Paris, a la librairie de Firmin Didot, 1806.

Boards; 8-3/8 x 5¼ in.

DIDOT, FIRMIN

Cabinet W, Shelf 2, No. 19

Typographe, litteratur, depute. [Excerpt from "Biographie des Hommes du Jour". Paris, circa 1840].

Biographical.

Item in manila envelope.

DIDOT, AMBROISE-FIRMIN

Cabinet RR, Shelf 4, No. 38

Sur le prix du papier dans l'antiquité. Lettre de M. Egger a M. Ambroise-Firmin Didot, et réponse de M.A. Firmin Didot...Paris, 1857.

Letters exchanged between Egger and Didot on the subject of the price of paper in ancient times.

Pamphlet; 9-3/4 x 6½ in. With other French pamphlets relating to paper. In board folder.

DIDOT, FIRMIN.

Cabinet Z, Shelf 2, No. 29

Caractères de la fonderie de Firmin Didot. Paris, n.d. [Broadsides].

Items in manila envelope.

DIDOT, FIRMIN.

Cabinet 20, Shelf 2, No. 7

Visit to the typefoundry and printing house of Firmin Didot, Paris, 1837.

Brief account in German.

Journal für Buchdruckerkunst, Feb.,1838, No.2, col.27.

DIDOT, AMBROISE FIRMIN

Cabinet W, Shelf 2, No. 147

Wallon, M. H.: Notice sur la vie et les travaux de M. Ambroise Firmin Didot. Par M. H. Wallon, Paris, 1886.

Half morocco; 11 x 9 in.

DIDOT, FIRMIN

Cabinet Z, Shelf 4, No. 6

Laboulaye et Cie. successeurs de Firmin Didot. Paris, n.d. [cir. 1860]. Fonderie Générale des caractères Francais et étrangers. Ch. Laboulaye et Cie.

A specimen book of types, cuts, vignettes, etc., from the several combined type foundries.

Cloth; 16¼ x 10¼ x 1-3/8 in.

DIDOT, FIRMIN (le jeune)

Cabinet X, Shelf 4, No. 32

Arrêt (du 2 Septembre, 1786) qui condamne les compagnons imprimeurs des imprimeries des sieurs Didot...Signé, Breteüil, Paris.

Printers in the shop of the Didots, ordered to apologise for acts of misbehavior.

Item 31 in volume with binder's title: French Legislation Affecting Printing, 1573-1810.

DIDOT, A.F. and Family

Cabinet, Shelf, No.

I Early Printing in France. Didot.
II Imprints. France. Paris [v.d.].
III Medals, Printers'.

DIDOT, FIRMIN (Freres)

Cabinet W, Shelf 1, No. 73

Memoire de MM. Firmin Didot Freres concernant la propriete litteraire dans les oeuvres collectives. Decembre, 1853.

Didot freres comment at length upon the copyright laws; also give the history of such laws in France.

Half morocco; 10¾ x 8½ in.

DIDOT, FIRMIN (2nd)

Cabinet F, Shelf 5, No. 24

Types engraved by Firmin Didot, son of Didot l'aine. Paris, 1788. Types used in a special edition of Fables de la Fontaine, printed at the printing office of Didot l'aine, Paris, 1788.

Morocco, gilt; 12½ x 9¼ in.

DIDOT, FIRMIN

Cabinet V, Shelf 5, No. 7

Alexandre Ire (l'empereur) de Russie, passe deux heures a examiner la typographie de M. Firmin Didot, en 1814.

see CRAPELET, Ch. "Études.. sur la typographie...Paris, 1837, p.215 (tome 1)

DIDOT, FIRMIN (Author).

Cabinet W, Shelf 2, No. 13

Poésies de Firmin Didot, député d'Eure-et-Loir: Suivies d'observations littéraires et typographiques sur Robert et Henri Estienne. Paris, Typographie de Firmin Didot Frères. 1834.

Half morocco; 8-7/8 x 5½ in.

DIDOT, FIRMIN AMBROISE

Cabinet 26, Shelf 2, No. 6

Review of the book L'origine et des debuts de l'imprimerie in Europe; par M. Aug.. Bernard.

In German.

Journal fur Buchdruckerkunst, 1853, No.19, cols. 222-233.

DIDOT, FIRMIN

Cabinet FF, Shelf 3, No. 65.01

Boileau...vs.Firmin Dodot, Paris, 1806.

Relating to a type designed, engraved and cast by Firmin Didot, claimed by Boileau as his own design.

In envelope.

DIDOT, FIRMIN

Cabinet V, Shelf 6, No. 22

Roman types engraved by Firmin Didot, 1811. See Imprimerie Royale. Notice sur les types etrangers...Paris, 1847.

DIDOT, FRANCOISE AMBROISE (II)

Cabinet F, Shelf 4, No. 91

See Early Printing in France. Paris, 1785. Francois-Ambroise (2) Didot.

DIDOT, FRANCOIS-AMBROISE, l'aine.

Cabinet F Shelf 5 No. 24

See Early Printing in France. Paris, 1788. Francois-Ambroise Didot l'aine.

DIDOT, FRANCOIS AMBROISE L'AINE

Cabinet W Shelf 2 No. 11

Essai de Fables Nouvelles dédieés au roi; suvies de poésies diverses, et d'une épitre sur les proges de l'imprimerie. Par Didot fils ainé. A Paris: imprimé par Franc. Ambr. Didot l'ainé, avec les caracteres de Firmin son 2d fils, 1786.

Half morocco; 6-7/8 x 4¼ in.

DIDOT, JULES.

Cabinet 83 Shelf 1 No. 8

(A) mon fils. C'est pour toi, Jules, mon Chere fils ... Par Pierre Didot, l'aine. Paris, 1819.
Dedicatory verse following title to Didot's "Specimen des nouveau caractères." Paris, 1819.

Boards; 10 x 6-7/8 x ½ in.

DIDOT, JULES

Cabinet W Shelf 2 No. 17

Particularité concernant un volume sorti des presses de Jules Didot. Et vers inédits de Pierre Didot. Par M. Alkan ainé. Neuilly (Seine), 1886. Extrait de la Bibliographie de la France, 19 December 1885. Pamphlet.
Has author's sign.

Folder; 10¼ x 6-3/4 in.

DIDOT, JULES

Cabinet W Shelf 3 No. 114

Particularité concernant un volume sorti des presses de Jules Didot et vers inédits de Pierre Didot. Par Alkan Ainé. Neuilly (Seine), 1886.

Has authors signature.

Item 12 in volume with binder's title "Pamphlets Relating to Books - I. Bound, 1932".

DIDOT, JULES

Cabinet W Shelf 2 No. 99

Verse in praise of Jules, by his father Pierre Didot.
Rough translation inserted in Werdet, La famille des Didot. Paris, 1864.

Half morocco; 9-1/8x 5-5/8 x 3/8 in.

DIDOT, PIERRE, l'aine (Author)

Cabinet 83 Shelf 1 No. 8

(A) Mon fils. C'est pour toi, Jules, mon chere fils...
Dedicatory verse following title to Didot's Specimen des nouveau caracteres. Paris, 1819.

Boards; 10 x 6-7/8 x ½ in.

DIDOT, PIERRE

Cabinet QQ Shelf 1 No. 9

Épitre sur les progrès de l'imprimerie. Par Didot, fils aine. A Paris. Imprimé chez Didot l'aine, avec les italiques de Firmin, son second fils. 1784.

Half morocco; 8-3/4 x 5-3/8 in.

DIDOT, PIERRE, the Elder

Cabinet 68 Shelf No. 12

Horatius, Flaccus (Quintus. Parisiis, 1799. Excudebam Petrus Didot, natu major.
Printed in the types cut by Firmin Didot. Vignettes designed by Charles Percier.

Morocco; 19 x 14½ in. In protective case

DIDOT, PIERRE

Cabinet W Shelf 2 No. 19

Né a Paris en 1762, fils ainé de F. Ambroise... (Bio-bibliographical sketch. Excerpt from unidentified French encyclopedia.)

Item in manila envelope.

DIDOT, PIERRE

Cabinet W Shelf 2 No. 19

Refutation pour M. Landon, peintre, auteur et editeur du journal "Annales du Musee, de le prétendue reponse de M.P. Didot, a son premier ecrit: Quelques Ides, etc. Paris, n.d.
Landon combats Didots accusations of plagiarism in regard to certain illustrations used in his magazine "Annales du Musee".

Item in manila envelope.

DIDOT, PIERRE.

Cabinet W Shelf 2 No. 17

Vers inédits de Pierre Didot et particularité concernant un volume sorti des presses de Jules Didot. Par M. Alkan aine. Neuilly (Seine), 1886.
Concerning some unpublished verse by Pierre Didot and a volume printed by Jules Didot.

Boards; 10¼ x 6⅝ in.

DIDOT FAMILY OF PRINTERS

Cabinet V Shelf 3 No. 18

(Bio-bibliographical notes relating to this notable family of printers, Paris, 1713-1852

see
WERDET, EDMOND. Histoire du livre en France...3me partie (2), p.205

DIDOT FAMILY OF PRINTERS

Cabinet Y Shelf 2 No. 23

(Bio-biblio. account of the Didot family, 1750-1881.)

See LORCK, CARL B. Handbuch der geschichte...Leipzig, 1882-1883 (part 2, pp. 178-183)

DIDOT FAMILY OF PRINTERS

Cabinet V Shelf 5 No. 7

Bio-bibliographical notes.
see
CRAPELET, CH. "Études pratiques...sur la typographie." Paris, 1837 (see index)

DIDOT FAMILY OF PRINTERS

Cabinet S Shelf 3 No. 91

Contributions to the art of printing; their handmade paper; their type; great type founders; their editions; their presswork.
See Index to Orcutt's "The kingdom of books." Boston, 1927.

DIDOT FAMILY OF PRINTERS

Cabinet V Shelf 3 No. ~~18~~ 13

Études bibliographiques; Les Didots, leurs devanciers et contemporains, 1500-1789.
See Werdet, Edmond. Histoire du Livre en France, Tome II, partie 3, Paris, 1864.

DIDOT FAMILY OF PRINTERS

Cabinet W Shelf 2 No. 99

Études bibliographiques sur la famille des Didot, imprimeurs, libraires, graveurs, fondeurs de caracteres, fabricants de papiers, etc., 1713-1864. Par Edmond Werdet. Paris, 1864.
This is an extract from "l'Histoire du livre en France" by the same writer.

Half morocco; 9¼ x 5¼ in.

DIDOT FAMILY.

Stack
See also
Biographies, printers. Didot dynasty of printers, The.

Shelf

Number

DIDOT FAMILY OF TYPEFOUNDERS

Cabinet Z
See Specimen Books, Types. France.

Shelf 1

No. 17

DIDOT, (H.), LEGRAND et Cie

Cabinet Z
Specimen des caracteres de la fonderie polyamatype de H. Didot, Legrand et Cie. Paris, 1828.
Price list of types inserted.
See also Z/2/28.

Shelf 2

No. 27

Half morocco; 9 x $5\frac{1}{2}$ x 1 in.

DIDOT (H.), LEGRAND & CO.

see also

Specimen Books, Types, France.

DIDOT SYSTEM

See Typefounding.

DIEDERICH, EUGEN.

Cabinet I
Deutsches leben der vergangenheit in bildern. Ein atlas mit 1760 nachbildung alter kupfer und holzschnitte aus dem 15[ten] - 18[ten] jahrhundert. Mit einfurnung von H. Kienzle. Kerausgegeben von Eugen Diederich (2 vols.) Jena, 1908.

Shelf 4

No. 21

2 vols.

Boards, vellum back; $15\frac{3}{4}$ x $11\frac{1}{2}$ x $1\frac{1}{4}$ in.

DIEDERICHS, EUGEN

Cabinet 26
Printer, brief biography of.

Shelf 1

No. 21

In Gutenberg-Gesellschaft Jahrbuch, 1931", pp.328-335.

DIEHL, ROBERT

Cabinet Y
Ratdolt, Erhard, ein meisterdrucker des 15 und 16 jahrhunderts. von Dr. Robert Diehl. Mit 56 abbildungen und eine beilage. Wien, 1933. Herbert Reichner Verlag.

Shelf 2

No. 40

Cloth; 9-3/4 x $6\frac{1}{2}$ in.

DIETERICHS, KARL

Cabinet Y
Buchdruckpresse, von Johannes Gutenberg bis Friedrich König. von Karl Dieterichs, oberingenieur der schnellpressen fabrik Frankenthal Albert & Cie. Aktien-Ges-Frankenthal (Pfalz). Verlag der Gutenberg-Gesellschaft, Mainz 1930. Illus.

Shelf 1

No. 99

Boards; $9\frac{1}{4}$ x 6 in.

DIETRICH, J. C. u. H.

Cabinet EE
See VOGTLANDISCHE MASCHINENFABRIK. A.G.

Shelf 5

No. 107

DIEZ, JULIUS

Cabinet
See Specimen Books, Vignettes. Germany, Bauer'sche Giesserei.

Shelf

No.

DIFFENDERFER, F.R.

Cabinet R
Early German printers of Lancaster and the issues of their press. By F.R. Diffenderfer A paper read before the Lancaster County Historical Society. January 1, 1904.
Bio-bibliographical account.
Bound in volume "Early printing in Lancaster County, Pa."

Shelf 5

No. 33

Half morocco; $9\frac{3}{4}$ x $6\frac{1}{4}$ in.

DIFFENDERFER, F.R.

Cabinet R
Early German printers of Lancaster Co., and the issues of their Press. Paper read before the Lancaster County Historical Society, Jan. 1, 1904. Vol. VIII, No. 3.
Bound in with other tracts.

Shelf 5

No. 33

Item in book with binder's title "Early printing in Lancaster County, Pa."

Half morocco; $9\frac{3}{4}$ x $6\frac{1}{4}$ in.

DIFFENDERFFER, F. R.

Cabinet R
(The) Newspapers of Lancaster County, Penn., 1752-1902. By F. R. Diffenderffer: A paper read before the Lancaster County Historical Society, May 2, 1902.
Bound in with another item, "Our early German printers: Who they were and what they did."

Shelf 5

No. 35

Cloth; 9-3/4 x 6 in.

DIFFENDERFFER, F.R.

Cabinet R
Newspapers of Lancaster County. A paper read before the Lancaster County Historical Society, May 2, 1902. Vol. VI No. 8.
Bound in with another item "Our early German printers"...
In vol. with binders title "Early German printing in America".

Shelf 5

No. 35

Cloth; $9\frac{3}{4}$ x 6 in. See also R/5/33.

DIFFENDERFER, F.R.

Cabinet R
Newspapers of Lancaster County. Paper read before the Lancaster County Historical Society. May 2 and June 6, 1902. Vol. VI, No.8.
Has facsimile of The Lancaster Gazette, the first newspaper in Lancaster Co.
Bound in with other tracts.

Shelf 5

No. 33

Item 2 in book with binders title "Early printing in Lancaster County, Pa."

Half morocco; $9\frac{3}{4}$ x $6\frac{1}{4}$ in.

DIFFENDERFER, F. R.

Cabinet R
(The) Oldest daily paper of Lancaster County. By F. R. Diffenderfer: A paper read before the Lancaster County Historical Society, Oct. 2, 1896.
Item I in volume "Early printing in Lancaster County." Item II, same publication: A bibliography of newspapers, 1752-1902.

Shelf 5

No. 33

Half morocco; $9\frac{3}{4}$ x $6\frac{1}{4}$ in.

DIFFENDERFER, F. R.

Cabinet R
(Our) Early German printers: who they were and what they did. Biographical sketches of some with an account of the issues of their presses ... A paper read before the Lancaster County Historical Society, Jan. 1, 1904 by F. R. Diffenderfer.
Newspaper clippings inserted in volume "Early German printing in America."

Shelf 5

No. 35

Cloth; 9-3/4 x 6 in.

DIGRAFS EI and IE

Cabinet LL Shelf 3 No. 22

On the use of the digrafs in English spelling. A paper read before the Chicago Society of Proofreaders, by Samuel Willard. Chicago, 1901.
Bound in with the "Stylebook of the Chicago Society of Proofreaders". Chicago, 1898.

Cloth; 7½ x 5¼ x 3/8 in.

DILNOT, GEORGE (Compiler)

Cabinet 00 Shelf 6 No. 1

Romance of the Amalgamated Press, the. Compiled by George Dilnot. London, 1925.
Has portraits, illustrations of printing works, paper making operations, printing presses, etc.

Half morocco; 13-1/8 x 10¾ x 1¼ in.

DINCKMUT, KONRAD

Cabinet Y Shelf 4 No. 4

(Note on Dinckmut and his printing at Ulm, 1476)
see
VOULLIÉME, ERNST. (Die) Deutscher drucker des fünfzehnten jahrhunderts...p.118

Di ISOARDI (Lazzaro) see

Cabinet Shelf No.

SOARDI, LAZZARO

DIME NOVELS

Cabinet R Shelf 5 No. 148

(The) Extinction of the Dime Novels. By Firmin Dredd. An excerpt from The Bookman, March, 1900.
An account of the origin development, evolution, and degeneration of the Dime Novel in America.

Excerpt 16 in volume "Chap Books, Almanacs, Annuals.

DINGELSTEDT, FRANZ

Cabinet W Shelf 2 No. 93

Jean Gutenberg, premier maitre imprimeur, ses faits et discours les plus dignes d'admiration, et sa mort...traduit de l'allemand en Francois par Gustave Revilliod. Geneve, 1858. Etchings by Gandon.

Boards; 12 x 8 in.

Historical novel.

DIJK, JACOB VAN (see)

Cabinet Shelf No.

VAN DIJK, JACOB

DIME NOVELS

Cabinet Shelf No.

see also
BEADLES DIME NOVELS.

DINGELSTEDT, FRANZ

Cabinet X Shelf 2 No. 22

Sechs jahrhundert aus Gutenberg's leben. Kleine gabe zum grossen feste. Cassel, 1840. Illus.
A poem in six cantos. The historical events of the century are sung under the dates of the centenaries of the invention of printing.

Half morocco; 14¼ x 10-3/8 x 3/8 in.

DIJON

Cabinet Shelf No.

See Printing, Historical, France (Dijon)

DINCKMUT, KONRAD

Cabinet B Shelf 2 No. 6

(Illustrated books printed by Dinckmut at Ulm, 1478-1497)
see
SCHRAMM, ALBERT. (Der) Bilderschmuck der frühdrucke...Leipzig, 1923.

DINGLEY, NELSON, JR. (Editor)

Cabinet NN Shelf 6 No. 11

Autobiography of Nelson Dingley, Jr. Lewiston (Maine): Published at the Journal Office, 1874.

Half morocco; 8-3/8 x 6 in.

DILL (Francis P.) and Garnett (Porter)

Cabinet S Shelf 4 No. 106

Ideal Book, The. Two essays jointly awarded the prize offered by the Limited Editions Club for the best essay upon the Subject, by Francis P. Dill and Porter Garnett. New York: The Limited Editions Club. 1932.

Boards; 8¼ x 5¼ in.

DIMIER, LOUIS

Cabinet J Shelf 3 No. 32 (env.)

(Le) Bois d'illustration au 19e siècle. Recherches sur ses origines. Memoire sur Godard d'Alencon. Paris, 1925. Pamphlet, illus.

Item in manila envelope.

DYONISIUS, ALEXANDRINUS (Periegetes)

Cabinet 29 Shelf 1 No. 3

De situ orbis. Eloquentissimi viri domini Antonii Becherie Veronensis proemium in Dyonisii traductionem ... Impressum est hoc opusculum Venetiis per Bernardum Pictor, Erhard Ratdolt and Petro Löslein. Venice, 1477.

Vellum; 8½ x 6¼ x ¼ in.

DILLON, PETER (Inventor) see

Cabinet FF Shelf 6 No. 19

COMPOSING MACHINES. Dillon, Peter
see also TYPE CASTING MACHINES. Dillon, Peter...

DIMIER, L.

Cabinet J Shelf 3 No. 32 (env.)

L'Estampe anglaise d'il y a cent ans. (18th century English engravings.)
Illus. excerpt from unidentified periodical. n.d.

Item in manila envelope.

DIONYSIUS [Periegetes]

Cabinet 29 Shelf 1 No. 3

De situ orbis. Venice: Ratdolt, Maler (Pictor) and Löslein, 1477.

See Incunabula. Dionysius [Periegetes]. De situ orbis.

DIPPY, ROBERT H.

Cabinet MM Shelf 6 No. 1

Embossing, how it is done. New York, Oswald Publishing Company, 1910. Brochure.

Item 4 in book with binder's title "Various items on printing". Bound 1919.

DIRECT MAIL ADVERTISING

Cabinet Shelf No.

See Advertising.

DIRECTORIES

Cabinet Q Shelf 7 No. 21

Australian Handbook (Incorporating New Zealand, Fiji, and New Guinea). Shippers, importers and professional directory and business guide. 1901 (32nd year of issue). Published by Gordon & Gotch...London.

Cloth printed cover; $9\frac{1}{4}$ x $6\frac{1}{4}$ in.

DIRECTORIES

Cabinet S Shelf 6 No. 8

First directory printed in New York City in 1786.

See HEBERMANN, C.G. New York's first directory...

DIRECTORIES

Cabinet QQ Shelf 5 No. 11

New York, the World's Metropolis, 1623-4--1923-4. A presentation of the greater city...The 300th anniversary of its founding... Commemorative edition. with complete index. New York City Directory. R.L.Polk & Co., Inc., Publishers. New York, 1924. Illus.
Includes articles relating to printing and allied crafts. With brief biographical notes of printers, press builders, editors, publishers, etc.
Cloth:13 x$9\frac{1}{2}$ x 2 in.

DIRECTORIES

Cabinet Q Shelf 7 No. 32

New Zealand Official Year Book, 1900. (9th year of issue). Prepared under the instructions from Rt. Hon. R.J. Seddon, P.C. Premier... Wellington, N.Z. 1900.

Cloth; $8\frac{1}{2}$ x $5\frac{1}{2}$ in.

DIRECTORIES

Cabinet Q Shelf 4 No. 25, 26

Paper Box Trade, and its allied branches (1919, 1922), directory of the. Edited by E. Geo. Ertman. Published by The Ravenswood Press Publishing Company, Chicago, Ill.

Cloth; 8 x 5 in.

DIRECTORIES, ADVERTISING

Cabinet Q Shelf 4 No. 19, 20

McKittricks Directory of Advertisers, their advertising managers and advertising agents. Advertisers Directory Association, Copyright by George McKittrick. New York.

LIBRARY HAS
vol.6, 1905
vol.xiv, 1913

Cloth; $9\frac{1}{4}$ x 6-7/8 in.

DIRECTORIES, BOOKBINDERS France

Cabinet PP Shelf 4 No. 7

(Paris, 1686-1749) Liste des maitres relieurs et doreurs de livres...
pp.195-204 in "Statuts et reglements pour la communaute des maistres relieurs... Paris, 1750.

Morocco; $6\frac{3}{4}$ x 3-5/8 in.

DIRECTORIES, BOOKBINDERS (Great Britain)

Cabinet PP Shelf 4 No. 6

London, 1812. A list of bookbinders, vellum binders, bookbinders' tool makers, book clasp makers, book and card edge gilders, and manufacturers or dealers in milled boards.
[In] A bookbinders manual. Containing a full description of leather...London, 5th ed., n.d. circa 1812. See pp.115-126

Morocco; gilt, 6 x $3\frac{3}{4}$ in.

DIRECTORIES, Booksellers

Cabinet Q Shelf 7 No. 46

Adressbuch der Antiquare. Deutschland und des gesamten ausländes...Verlag, Straubing & Muller. Weimar, 1926.

Cloth; $9\frac{1}{4}$ x 6-1/8 in.

DIRECTORIES, Booksellers

Cabinet Q Shelf 7 No. 47

Adressbuch des deutschen buchhandels (1927). Bearbeitet von der Adressbücher-Redaktion der Geschäftsstelle des Börsenverein der Deutschen Buchhändler zu Leipzig, 1927. Mit bildnis und biographie. von Carl Engelhorn. Leipzig.

Cloth; 9-3/4 x 6-3/4 in.

DIRECTORIES, BUSINESS

Cabinet Q Shelf 2 No. 17, 18

American Trade Index. Descriptive and classified membership directory of the National Association of Manufacturers of the U.S. Arranged for the convenience of foreign buyers...Philadelphia, 1899.
(Also 1905 for New York City)

Cloth; $8\frac{3}{4}$ x 6 in.

DIRECTORIES, BUSINESS

Cabinet Q Shelf 4 No. 3

Book and Stationery Trades of the United States, containing a full list of the publishers, booksellers, stationers and printers throughout the Union. New York, 1860.
With advertisements.

Cloth; 6 x 4 x $\frac{1}{2}$ in.

DIRECTORIES, BUSINESS

Cabinet Q Shelf 4 No. 2

New York Business Directory for 1841 and 1842. Alphabetical arrangement. Second edition of 1000 copies. Second year of the publication, with additions and improvements. New York; J. Doggett Jr., publisher and proprietor. Stereotyped edition, 1841.

Boards; $7\frac{1}{2}$ x $4\frac{3}{4}$ x $\frac{3}{4}$ in.

DIRECTORIES, CITY

Cabinet Q Shelf 4 No. 1

New York City, 1786. The first New York City Directory. One hundred years ago. (facsimile reprint, New York, 1886). Also Annals of New York City for the year 1786, compiled fr[om] newspapers of the day". Published by The Trow City Directory Company.
Original wrappers bound in. Partly interleaved with advertisements.

Half morocco; 8 x 6 in.

DIRECTORIES, CONGRESSIONAL

Cabinet QQ Shelf 5 No. 4,5,6

Official Congressional Directory...Second edition corrected to January 18, 1930. Washington, D. C., 1930.
also Directories for
1929
1933

Cloth; $9\frac{1}{4}$ x 6 x 1 in.

DIRECTORIES, NEWSPAPERS

Cabinet Q Shelf 4 No. 24

Advertisers' directory of leading publications. vol.25, 1914. Price $5.00. Published by Charles H. Fuller Company. Main Office, Chicago, Ill.

Cloth; $9\frac{1}{4}$ x 6-1/8 in.

DIRECTORIES, Newspapers

Cabinet Q Shelf 6 No. 1

American newspaper rate-book, containing advertising rates of leading newspapers, arranged with index. New York: Geo. P. Rowell & Co., 1870.

Bound in with "Men who Advertise"... 1870.

Cloth; 10¾ x 6¾ in.

DIRECTORIES, NEWSPAPERS

Cabinet NN Shelf 5 No. 25

(The) Golden Dozen: Some facts and figures compiled from the Edition of the American Newspaper Directory for December, 1901, concerning notable newspaper circulations...Copyright by the J. N. Matthews Company.

Frontispiece portrait of J. N. Matthews, editor Buffalo Commercial 1860 - 1877; editor Buffalo Express 1878 - 1888; founder of The Matthews - Northrup Works.

Morocco; 6-3/8 x 4-5/8 x 3/8 in.

DIRECTORIES, Newspapers

Cabinet Q Shelf 4 No. 21.01 22 & 23

Remington's, Edward P., newspaper directory for 1900, 1912, 1913. A list of all newspapers and other periodical publications of the United States and Canada. Pittsburg, Pa. [3 vols.]

Cloth; 9 x 6 in.

DIRECTORIES, NEWSPAPERS

Cabinet Q Shelf 4 No. 5

American newspapers, 1776-1876. A complete list of.

see ROWELL, GEO. P. and Company. Centennial Newspaper Exhibition, 1876 (Philadelphia)...

DIRECTORIES, Newspapers

Cabinet NN Shelf 5 No. 23

Leading newspapers. Considered from the advertisers standpoint. Seven separate selections compiled by the editor of "Printers' Ink"...Geo. P. Rowell & Co., Publishers, New York, 1902.

Frontispiece portrait of Geo. P. Rowell.

Cloth; 5 x 3 x 5/8 in.

DIRECTORIES, NEWSPAPERS

Cabinet Q Shelf 4 No. 15

REXFORD. R. W. (Fairleigh), Boston, 1894. Business Man's Hand-book. 2nd ed., 1894. Containing a selected list of representative newspapers published in the United States and Canada...And some interesting facts about advertising.

Cloth; 9 x 6 in.

DIRECTORIES, NEWSPAPERS

Cabinet Q Shelf 7 No. 33

Australia and New Zealand. The Advertisers' and Publishers Guide, 1932-1933. Compiled and published by Newspaper News, Sydney, N.S.W.

Cloth; 8¾ x 5¾ in.

DIRECTORIES, NEWSPAPERS

Cabinet Q Shelf 7 No. 28.01

New Jersey Rate Book (1929-1930). Dailies, semi-weeklies, weeklies. New Jersey Newspapers Inc., New York City.

Has "Revision Sheet 7", of Feb., 1932.

Paper; 12 x 9 in.

DIRECTORIES, Newspapers

Cabinet Q Shelf 6 No. 2 to 7

Rowell, Geo.P. & Co's. American newspaper directory. Containing accurate lists of all the periodicals in the United States and Territories, and the Dominion of Canada and British Colonies of North America. Illus. [For years], 1871, 1876,1894,1895,1896, 1899 (the 31st year)

Cloth; 10¼ x 7 in.

DIRECTORIES, Newspapers

Cabinet Q Shelf 6 No. 10 11

Ayer N.W. and Son. American newspaper annual, containing a catalogue of American newspaper ...lists of monthly and weekly publications of general circulation, religious and agricultural publications, etc. Philadelphia, 1905. With maps.

Also Newspaper Annual for 1929

Cloth; 9¾ x 6½ in.

DIRECTORIES, Newspapers

Cabinet Q Shelf 7 No. 26 28

Newspaper press directory and advertisers guide, containing full particulars relative to each journal published in the United Kingdom and the British Isles...26th Annual issue, 1871. C. Mitchell and Co., Contractors for Advertising. London.

Also for year 1901

Boards; 11 x 7½ in.

DIRECTORIES, NEWSPAPERS

Cabinet Q Shelf 4 No. 21

Rowell, George P. New York, 1906. Newspapers worth counting...All that print 1000 copies. According to the ratings assigned to the latest edition of Rowell's American Newspaper Directory. Edited by Geo. P. Rowell. Printer's Ink Publishing Co., New York, 1906.

Frontis. portrait of Rowell.

Paper; 8¾ x 5-3/8 in.

DIRECTORIES, Newspapers

Cabinet Q Shelf 6 No. 9

Chesman, Nelson & Company. Newspaper rate book, including a catalogue of newspapers and periodicals in the United States and Canada. Nelson Chesman & Co., St. Louis, 1905.

Cloth; 8½ x 6 in.

DIRECTORIES, NEWSPAPERS

Cabinet Q Shelf 4 No. 12, 13

Pacific States Newspaper Directory...Arranged alphabetically by towns. 6th ed. Copyrighted and published, 1894 by Palmer & Rey Type Foundry, proprietors of Pacific States Advertising Bureau. San Francisco.

<u>Library also has</u>

7th ed., 1895. American Type Founders Co., proprietors. Palmer & Rey Branch, San Francisco.

Cloth; 8¾ x 5¾ in.

DIRECTORIES, NEWSPAPERS

Cabinet Q Shelf 7 No. 52

(Spain, 1930). Catalogo de prensa España. Con apéndice para Portugal. Rudolf Mosse Ibérica, S.A. Barcelona, 1930.

Brochure; 10-3/4 x 8 in.

DIRECTORIES , Newspapers

Cabinet Q Shelf 7 No. 9

Editor and Publisher, 1933. Market guide for advertisers...

<u>see</u> ADVERTISING. Editor and Publisher. The Fourth Estate Market Guide...

DIRECTORIES, NEWSPAPERS.

Cabinet LL Shelf 5 No. 3

Pocket directory of the American Press for 1905 ...

See Lord & Thomas. Pocket directory...

DIRECTORIES, Newspapers

Cabinet Q Shelf 7 No. 2

Western Newspaper Lists. 5971 weekly newspapers. Kellog & Western Lists. Proprietors Geo. A. Joslyn... Chicago-New York, 1914.

Item in manila envelope

DIRECTORIES, NEWSPAPERS

Cabinet Q Shelf 7 No. 4

Western Newspaper Union. Country newspapers, 4278. Kellog & Western Lists. Chicago-New York. 1922

Boards; 11 x 8½ in.

DIRECTORIES, Printers

Cabinet AA Shelf 2 No. 33

Indice bio-geografico contente i nomi dei tipografi, artisti, incisori, inventori, etc. che nelle localita appresso indicate hanno visuta e lavorata ...

A biographical geographical list of names of the artists, etchers, inventors, printers, and of all those who have served the arts of the book.

See Gianolio, Dalmazzo: Il libro e l'art della stampa ... Torino, 1926. Sec. "Biografia della Stampa."

DIRECTORIES, PRINTERS France

Cabinet Q Shelf 5 No. 22

France, 1813. Annuaire de l'imprimerie et de la librairie de l'Empire Francais, pour l'annee 1813. Paris, chez Tillet.

Boards, leather back; 5-5/8 x 3-3/8 in.

DIRECTORIES, PAPER MANUFACTURERS

Cabinet Q Shelf 7 No. 8

Waldens Stationer. With which is incorporated Waldens Red Book. January, 1926. New York.

Paper; 11-3/8 x 8½ in.

DIRECTORIES, PRINTERS'

Cabinet FF Shelf 2 No. 25.01

Type Face Directory for 1935. Issued for readers of "Printing" by Walden, Sons & Mott, Inc. New York City.

Paper; 9 x 5-7/8; pp. 96.

DIRECTORIES, PRINTERS' France

Cabinet Q Shelf 5 No. 24

France, 1845. Annuaire de la typographie Parisienne et Départmentale. 2e année...Par E.M. Prétot, Typographe, Paris, 1845.

Half morocco; 6¼ x 4 in.

DIRECTORIES, Printers

Cabinet Q Shelf 7 No. 45

Addressbuch der buch und steindruckereien in Deutschland, Oesterreich und in der Schweiz. von Karl Klimsch, Frankfurt a.M., 1876.

Half morocco; 9¾ x 6¼ in.

DIRECTORIES, PRINTERS, Belgium

Cabinet AA Shelf 3 No. 28

(De) Boekdrukkers boekverkoopers en uitgevers in Antwerpen ... Door Frans Olthoff. Antwerpen 1891. [Alphabetic arrangement of Dutch printers who practised in Antwerp from the earliest period of printing to our own time. With portraits and printers marks.]

Half morocco; 10 x 8 in.

DIRECTORIES, Printers, France

Cabinet Q Shelf 5 No. 25 & 86

France, 1925. Annuaire de l'imprimerie. Par Arnold Muller. 35e année. Paris.

Also Annuaire for year 1926

Cloth; 7 x 4½ in.

DIRECTORIES, PRINTERS'

Cabinet Y Shelf 4 No. 56

Artists of the book; typographers, type designers, illustrators, etc.

See Schramm's "Taschenbuch zur buckerfreund"...Leipzig, 1925, pp.154

DIRECTORIES, Printers' (etc.) France

Cabinet Q Shelf 5 No. 21

Almanach de la Librairie. Contenant un tableau de tous libraries et imprimeurs de Paris et du Royaume. Les noms et les adresses des graveurs en lettres et en musique...A Paris, chez Moutard, 1781.

Cloth; 6½ x 4 in.

DIRECTORIES, PRINTERS' France

Cabinet Q Shelf 5 No. 23

France, 1829. Annuaire des imprimeurs et des libraires de France et de l'etranger. Par M.C. Bancelin-Duterte. Paris, 1829.

2nd year issue, with supplement

Half morocco; 6¼ x 4 in.

DIRECTORIES, PRINTERS'

Cabinet Q Shelf 7 No. 45

Austrian printers 1876 addressbook of.

see KLIMSCH, KARL. Addressbuch der buch und steindruckereien...Frankfurt a.M., 1876.

DIRECTORIES, Printers, France

Cabinet V Shelf 2 No. 70

Annuaire de l'imprimerie, de la presse, et de librairie Rédigé édité et exécuté par V. Eug. Gauthier, ouvrier, typographe. Paris, 1855-56.

Half morocco; 9¾ x 6½ x 5/8 in.

DIRECTORIES, PRINTERS, France.

Cabinet W Shelf 1 No. 63

Liste générale des imprimeurs de Paris, depuis 1469 jusqu'en 1789.

See Crapelet, G. A: De la profession d'imprimeur ... Paris, 1840 [P. 108]

DIRECTORIES, PRINTERS'

Cabinet KK Shelf 1 No. 33

English printers, type founders, etc.

see MASTER PRINTERS' ANNUAL. Typographical year book...London, 1920, 1924, 1927, 1928, 1929, 1930, 1931, 1932.

DIRECTORIES, Printers, France

Cabinet V Shelf 4 No. 25

Documents sur les imprimeurs ... ayant exercer a Paris de 1450 a 1600. Par Ph. Renouard. Paris, 1901.

Alphabetic arrangement of proper names. An appendix on the printers in the French provinces.

Half morocco; 9½ x 6¼ x 1½ in.

DIRECTORIES, Printers, France.

Cabinet V Shelf 2 No. 24

(Paris) L'Imprimerie et la Libraire à Paris de 1789 à 1813. Renseignments recueillis classés et accompagnés d'une introduction. Par Paul Delalain. Paris, 1899.

Half morocco; 10 x 6¼ x 1¼ in.

DIRECTORIES, PRINTERS, France

Cabinet V, Shelf 5, No. 12

(Paris). Liste des imprimeurs de Paris au XVI siècle.
See p. 245 in Maddan's Lettres d'un Bibliographe...Cinquième série. Paris, 1878.

DIRECTORIES, Printers, France.

Cabinet W, Shelf 2, No. 88

(Paris). Liste des imprimeurs du roi qui ont exerce a Paris depuis l'institution de cette charge.
See p. 230 of Bernard's "Geofroy Tory, peintre et graveur, premier imprimeur royal ...Paris, 1857.

DIRECTORIES, Printers. France

Cabinet Q, Shelf 5, No. 21

Paris, 1781, list of printers.

see DIRECTORIES, France. Almanach de la Librarie...1781

DIRECTORIES, Printers, France

Cabinet V, Shelf 3, No. 16

Paris, 1789. Les 36 imprimeurs de Paris au 14 Juillet, 1789.
See Werdet, Edmond. Histoire du Livre en France: Transformation du livre, 1470-1789. Partie II, p. 307. Paris, 1861

DIRECTORIES, PRINTERS', France

Cabinet Q, Shelf 7, No. 41

Paris, 1811-1870 Liste des imprimeurs typographes de Paris du ler Avril 1811 au 10 Sept. 1870. Extrait de la Bibliographie de la France (Sept.-Oct. 1899)

Half morocco; 11 x 7½ in.

DIRECTORIES, PRINTERS. France

Cabinet MM, Shelf 1, No. 40

Paris, 1869. Names and addresses of printers in Paris.
See pp.54-56 of Munier's Nouveau Guide Illustré de l'Imprimerie...Paris, 1869.

DIRECTORIES, PRINTERS, France

Cabinet MM, Shelf 1, No. 42

Paris, 1872. Noms et adresses des imprimeurs de Paris.
pp. 54-56 in Munier's "Almanach illustré de l'imprimerie"...Paris, 1872.

Boards, cloth back; 7-1/8 x 4½ x 3/8 in.

DIRECTORIES, PRINTERS, Germany & European Cities

Cabinet Q, Shelf 7, No. 44

Europe (Central), 1854. Adressbuch der buchdruckereien von Mitteleuropa. Herausgegeben von Dr. Heinrich Meyer, Braunscgweig, 1854.

Half morocco; 9¼ x 5-3/4 in.

DIRECTORIES, PRINTERS' Great Britain

Cabinet Q, Shelf 7, No. 29

Kelly's Directory of stationers, printers, booksellers, publishers, and paper makers of England, Scotland, and Wales, and most of the principal towns in Ireland. Fifth edition. London: Printed and published by Kelly & Co., Branch Offices...1889.

Cloth; 10-3/8 x 6¾ in.

DIRECTORIES, PRINTERS' Great Britain

Cabinet Q, Shelf 7, Nos. 34, 35, 36, 37, 39

London, Caxton Year Books for years: 1928, 1929, 1930, 1931, 1933,

Boards, cloth back; 10¾ x 8-3/8 in.

DIRECTORIES, Printers, Great Britain

Cabinet X, Shelf 5, No. 2

(London and vicinity). A complete and private list of all the Printing Houses in and about the Cities of London and Westminster, together with the printers names, what newspaper they print...(London, circa 1800). Broadside.

P. 6 in volume "Historical Documents relating to Printing."

DIRECTORIES, Printers, Great Britain

Cabinet X, Shelf 5, No. 2

(London and vicinty). A complete and private list of all the Printing Houses in and about the Cities of London and Westminster, together with the printers names, what newspaper they print ... [London, circa 1800]. Broadside.

P. 6 in volume "Historical Documents relating to Printing."

DIRECTORIES, PRINTERS. Great Britain

Cabinet MM, Shelf 3, No. 12

London and vicinity, 1823. List of master printers, lett r founders, printing ink makers...
pp.28-32 in Mason's Printer's Assistant ...London, 1823.

DIRECTORIES, PRINTERS. Great Britain

Cabinet MM, Shelf 3, No. 15

London and vicinity, 1824. Alphabetical list of printers, and the professions connected with the art, in the British metropolis and its environs.
vol. 2, pp.649-652 in Johnson's "Typographia, or the printer's instructor"... London, 1824.

DIRECTORIES, PRINTERS. Great Britain

Cabinet U, Shelf 3, No. 103

London printers in the year 1649, a list of. Compiled by Henry R. Plomer.

See vol. 2, p.225 Bibliographica...London, 1895-1897.

DIRECTORIES, PRINTERS (Gr. Britain)

Cabinet KK, Shelf 1, No. 34 to ~~43~~ 45

Master Printers Annuals, 1920-~~1934~~ 1936

See MASTER PRINTERS ANNUAL and Typographical Year Book...

DIRECTORIES, Printers. Great Britain

Cabinet 76, Shelf 1, No. 2-3

Plomer, H.R. Dictionary of booksellers and printers who were at work in England, Scotland and Ireland from 1641 to 1725. Edited by Arundell Esdaile. Printed for the Bibliographical Society, London, 1922. (2 vols.)

Boards, cloth backs; 8¾ x 7-1/8 in.

DIRECTORIES, PRINTERS, Holland

Cabinet AA, Shelf 4, No. 3

Alfabetische lijst der boekdrukkers, boekverkoopers en uitgevers in Noord-Nederland. sedert de uitvinding van de boekdrukkunst tot den aanvang der negentiende eeuw. Door A.M. Ledeboer. Utrecht, 1876.
Printer marks of Waesberghen and three other printers; at end of volume.

Half morocco; 11 x 9¼ in.

DIRECTORIES, Printers Holland

Cabinet AA Shelf 4 No. 4

Amsterdam, 16th century: Amsterdamsche boekdrukkers in de zestiende eeuw. Door E.W. Moes. Amsterdam, 1900, 1907, 1910, 1915 - 4 Vols.

Bio-bibliographical. Vol. 4 has name lise of Amsterdam printers.

Half morocco; 9½ x 7¼ in.

DIRECTORIES, PRINTERS, Italy

Cabinet AA Shelf 2 No. 2

Dizionario dei tipografi e dei principali correttori ed itagliatori che operarono negli stati Sardi di Terraferma e piu specialmente in Piemonte sino all'anno 1821. Barone Vernazza di Freney. Torino, 1859.

The work is incomplete owing to the death of the author.

Half calf; 10½ x 8¼ in.

DIRECTORIES, PRINTERS, United States.

Cabinet R Shelf 4 No. 87

Check list of printers in the United States; from Stephen Daye to the close of the War of Independence, with a list of places in which printing was done. Compiled by Chas. F. Heartman, New York, 1915.

Boards; 9½ x 6½ in.

DIRECTORIES, Printers Holland

Cabinet AA Shelf 3 No. 23

De boekdrukkers boekverkoopers en uitgevers in Noord-Nederland sedert de uitvinding van de boekdrukkunst tot den aanvang der negentiende eeuw. Door A.M. Ledeboer. Decenter, 1872.

Alphabetical register of Dutch printers.

Half morocco; 10½ x 9½ in.

DIRECTORIES, Printers' Italy

Cabinet Q Shelf 5 No. 27

Italy, 1924. Annuario Italiano delle arti grafiche. vol. 16, 1924. Editori Carpigiani & Zipoli. Firenze. Illus.

Cloth; 6¼ x 4 in.

DIRECTORIES, PRINTERS' United States

Cabinet Q Shelf 5 No. 9

Eastern Edition, 1933: Tenth annual printing trades blue book. Edited and published by A.F. Lewis & Co. of New York, Inc.

Cloth; 9 x 5½ in.

DIRECTORIES, Printers Holland

Cabinet AA Shelf 3 No. 24

Chronologische Register...Alfabetische lijst der boekdrukkers, boekverkoopers en uitgevers in Noord-Nederland sedert het jaar 1440 tot het begin dezen eeuw. (1440-1800). Door A.M. Ledboer. Utrecht, 1877.

This chronological register of Dutch printers is intended as an appendix to AA/3/23.

Half morocco; 10-7/8 x 9-1/8 in.

DIRECTORIES, PRINTERS, Italy.

Cabinet AA Shelf 2 No. 2

Vernazza, di Freney, (Barone G.) Dizionario dei tipografi e dei principali correctori ed intagliatori che operarono negli stati Sardi di Terraferma, e pie specialmente in Piedmonte sino all'anno 1821. Opera e stampa che remaste imperfetta per la morte dell'autore. Torino, 1859.

Bio-bibliographical account, alphabetic arrangement, printers and printing in Piedmont from it introduction to the year 1821. Half calf; 10½x 8½ in.

DIRECTORIES, PRINTERS' United States

Cabinet Q Shelf 4 No. 6,7,8,9

FARLEY'S Reference Directory of booksellers, stationers and printers in the United States and Canada, Publisher by A. C. Farley & Co., Philadelphia.

LIBRARY HAS for years:

1885, 1886-7, 1888-9, 1889-90.

Cloth; 9¼ x 6-1/8 in.

DIRECTORIES, PRINTERS, Holland.

Cabinet AA Shelf 3 No. 47

Nederlandsche bibliographie van 1500 tot 1540, door Wouter Nijhoff en M.E. Kronenberg. 'S-Gravenhage, 1923.-40

v. 1-2

Half morocco; 10-1/8 x 6½ x 3½ in.

DIRECTORIES, PRINTERS, Spain

Cabinet AA Shelf 5 No. 16

See Haebler, Conrado: Bibliografia Iberica del siglo XV ... Leipzig, 1903. pp. 364-85.

DIRECTORIES, PRINTERS' United States

Cabinet Q Shelf 4 No. 10

Fyfe & Boss. Directory of the printing trades in Chicago, 1889.

Paper; 7 x 4-1/8 in.

DIRECTORIES, PRINTERS, Holland.

Cabinet W Shelf 5 No. 57

Tableau chronologique des villes, bourgs etc., ou l'art typographique a été exercé dans les Pays-Bas au quinziéme siécle, avec les noms des imprimeurs.

See Holtrop, John William: Monuments, typographiques des Pays-bas ... La Haye, 1868.

DIRECTORIES, PRINTERS' United States

Cabinet Q Shelf 4 No. 11

(The) Ben Franklin Co. Chicago, Ill., 1890. Directory of the printing trades in Chicago.

see also Q/4/10

Paper; 7 x 4-1/8 in.

DIRECTORIES, PRINTERS, United States

Cabinet Q Shelf 4 No.

Graphic Arts Board of Trade

see GRAPHIC ARTS BOARD OF TRADE. Rating book....

DIRECTORIES, PRINTERS', India

Cabinet Q Shelf 7 No. 16

(The) Asian Printers' and Stationers' Annual Diary and Directory, 1923. Published by Game, Norton and Company. Bombey (India)

Boards; 9 x 6-1/8 in.

DIRECTORIES, PRINTERS United States

Cabinet 80 Shelf 1-a No. 5

Boston, 1842, printers, lithographers, engravers, addresses of.

See ALMANACS. Boston Almanac for the year 1842...

DIRECTORIES, PRINTERS' United States

Cabinet Q Shelf 4 No. 14

Industrial Information Co., of New Jersey (Formerly Farley's) Reference-Directory of booksellers, stationers and printers of the United States and Canada (Including all kindred trades), 1895.

Limp morocco; 9¼ x 6 in.

DIRECTORIES, Printers' United States

Cabinet Q Shelf 4 No. 16

Lockwood, Howard & Co. New York, 1893-4. Directory of the paper, stationery and allied trades...Price two dollars. New York.

Cloth; 9½ x 6¼ in.

DIRECTORIES, Printing. United States

Cabinet Q Shelf 5 No. 7

Printing Trades Blue Book (Illinois Edition, 16th Annual, 1925. A. F. Lewis & Company, Chicago Illinois.

Cloth; 7-7/8 x 5¼ in.

DIRECTORIES, PRINTERS' United States

Cabinet JJ Shelf 2 No. 63

United Typothetae of America, directory of International and Local Officers and Committees. (Revised January 1, 1931) Typothetae Bulletin. Monday, January 19, 1931, Vol. 32, No. 16.

Boards; 12 x 9¼ in.

DIRECTORIES, PRINTERS United States

Cabinet JJ Shelf 6 No. 39

New York City, 1894, 1896. Souvenir directory and specimen book of prominent establishments engaged in press work and kindred industries. Compiled by the Adams and Cylinder Press Printers' Association, No.51.

Two items bound together.

Half morocco; 11-7/8 x 9-3/8 in.

DIRECTORIES, PRINTERS. United States

Cabinet Q Shelf 5 No. 8

Printing Trades Blue Book (Mid-Western Edition, 1929). Edited and published by A. F. Lewis & Company, Chicago, Ill.

Cloth; 8 x 5½ in.

DIRECTORIES, PRINTERS' United States

Cabinet Q Shelf 7 No. 5,6,7

Walden's Red Book: An annual buyers guide covering the printing...and allied trades. Edited by Van Rensselaer Walden. Walden, Sons & Mott. New York.

For years; 1923, 1924, 1925.

Paper; 11-3/8 x 8½ in.

DIRECTORIES, PRINTERS. United States

Cabinet Q Shelf 5 No. 4

Printing Trades Blue Book (Eastern Edition, 2nd Annual, 1925). Edited and published by A.F. Lewis & Company, New York.

Cloth; 7¾ x 5½ in.

DIRECTORIES, PRINTERS. United States

Cabinet Q Shelf 5 No. 3

Printing Trades Blue Book (National Edition, 6th Annual, 1925). A business directory for busy people. Edited and published by A. F. Lewsi & Company, Chicago, Illinois.

Cloth; 7¾ x 5½ in.

DIRECTORIES, PRINTERS' United States

Cabinet Q Shelf 7 No. 8

Walden's Stationer. With which is incorporated Walden's Red Book. January, 1926. New York.

Paper; 11-3/8 x 8½ in.

DIRECTORIES, PRINTERS. United States

Cabinet Q Shelf 5 No. 1

Printing Trades Blue Book, 1918. Greater New York and surrounding towns edition. Edited and published by A. F. Lewis & Co., New York.

Cloth; 7¾ x 5½ in.

DIRECTORIES, PRINTERS. United States

Cabinet Q Shelf 5 No. 6

Printing Trades Blue Book (Western Edition, 3rd. Annual, 1925). Edited and published by A.F. Lewis & Company. San Francisco, California.

Cloth; 7¾ x 5-3/8 in.

DIRECTORIES, PUBLISHERS'

Cabinet Q Shelf 7 No. 10

Directory of booksellers, stationers, publishers and libraries in the United States and Canada. 2nd. ed. Minneapolis. The H. W. Wilson Co., Publishers. 1903.

Cloth; 10½ x 6-7/8 in.

DIRECTORIES, PRINTERS. United States

Cabinet Q Shelf 5 No. 5

Printing Trades Blue Book for Greater New York and the State of New Jersey. Tenth Annual Edition 1925. Edited and published by A. F. Lewis & Company, New Yorl.

Cloth; 7¾ x 5½ in.

DIRECTORIES, PRINTERS' UNITED STATES

Cabinet Q Shelf 7 No. 1

Reference book and directory of the book and job printers, newspaper, magazine and book publishers; also paper manufacturers and paper warehouses...Compiled and published by J. Arthurs Murphy & Co., New York, 1871-72.

Boards; 11 3/8 x 9 in.

DIRECTORIES, Publishing Houses.

Cabinet Q Shelf 5 No. 28

Germany, 1926. Deutschlands verlagsbuchhandel. von Albert Schramm. Leipzig, 1926.

Cloth; 6¼ x 4-5/8 in.

DIRECTORIES, PRINTERS, United States

Cabinet Q Shelf 5 No. 2

Printing Trades Blue Book (Illinois edition, 1918). A business directory for busy people. Edited and published by A. F. Lewis & Co. Chicago, Illinois.

Cloth; 7¾ x 5½ in.

DIRECTORIES, PRINTERS' United States

Cabinet Q Shelf 7 No. 3

(The) Typo Mercantile Agency. Credit book of the paper, book, stationery, printing, publishing, and kindred trades in the U.S. and Canada. Reference book and complete directory., July, 1917.

Cloth; 11¼ x 8¼ in.

DIRECTORIES, Trade

Cabinet Q Shelf 7 No. 51

Indice del comercio Americano. Directorio descriptivo y clasificado de los miembros de la Asociacion Nacional de Manufacturers de los Estados Unidos. Arreglado para conveniencia de los compradores extranjeros. National Association of Manufacturers. Philadelphia, Pa., 1899.

Cloth; 8¾ x 6 in.

DIRECTORIES, TRADE SCHOOLS

Cabinet Q Shelf 4 No. 4

Trade and Industrial Schools, directory of. Issued by the Federal Board for Vocational Education, Washington, D.C., 1930.

Paper; 5-3/4 x 3½ x 5/8 in.

DIRECTORIES, TYPE FOUNDRIES, France.

Cabinet 26 Shelf 2 No. 1

Paris, 1838. Alphabetic arrangement of addresses.

In Journal fur Buchdruckerkunst, Sept., 1838, No. 9, cols. 144-145.

DIRECTORIES, TYPE FOUNDRIES. Germany

Cabinet LL Shelf 1 No. 25

(Address of the more celebrated type foundries: With notes concerning some of their earliest type specimen books, 1834-1841)
See pp.280-285 in Henze's Handbuch der Schriftgiesserei...Weimar, 1841.

DIRECTORIES, TYPE FOUNDRIES, Germany.

Cabinet 20 Shelf 2 No. 7

German type foundries in 1838. Addresses of. Listed by towns.

In Journal fur Buchdruckerkunst, April, 1838, No. 4. cols. 63-64.

DIRECTORIES, Typefoundries. Great Britain

Cabinet MM Shelf 3 No. 9

London typefounders in 1808.

p.518 in Stower's Printers' Grammar... London, 1808.

DIRECTORY, LONDON POST-OFFICE

Cabinet S Shelf 6 No. 7

(The) Great Red Book. By Charles Dickens. Excerpt from Household Words, Dec. 9, 1854.
Bibliographical; more or less humorous account of the methods used in the compilation of "The Great Red Book".

Item (a) in book with binder's title: Early printed books: Various excerpts and pamphlets, 1854-1931.

DIRECTORY, PERIODICALS.

Cabinet Shelf No.

See PERIODICALS DIRECTORY.

DIRECTORY AND RECORD OF THE PRESS

Cabinet NN Shelf 3 No. 6

Accurate list of all the newspapers, magazines - in the United States and British Provinces of North America. Compiled by Daniel J. Kenny. New York. 1861.

Cloth: 7-5/8 x 5 in.

DIRKS, J.

Cabinet K Shelf 1 No. 19

Atlas van platen, behoorende bij het 2e deel (nieuwe reeks), van de verhandelingen intgeven door Teylers tweede genootschap. Haarlem, 1879.

143 plates of reproductions of Guild medals, tokens, trade marks, professional marks etc. of many cities in Holland.

Paper board, 11 x 7¼ x ¾ in.

DIRKS, JACOB

Cabinet QQ Shelf 4 No. 42

(De) Noord-Nederlandsche Gildepenningen wetenschappelijk en historische beschreven en afgebeeld. Uitgeven door Teylers Tweede Genootschap. Haarlem, 1878. (2 vols.)

Guilds of Holland

Paper; 9½ x 6-3/8 in.

DISASTERS

Cabinet QQ Shelf 2 No. 15

Flood souvenir. Views of Hamilton, Ohio, during and after the disastrous flood of March 1913. Published by The Republican Publishing Company. Hamilton, Ohio.

Paper; 6¼ x 9¼ in.

DISCURSIONS OF A RETIRED PRINTER

Stack A Shelf 1 & 2 Number 37-40

Bullen, Henry Lewis ("Quadrat") An historical account of American typemakers and typefounders from the 1870. Continued monthly in The Inland Printer. Illus.
Vols. XXXVII, 1906, pp. 513, 657, 817; Vol. XXXVIII, pp. 194, 353, 513, 673, 856; Vol. XXXIX, pp. 193, 353, 513, 675, 833; Vol. XL, pp. 38, 534.

DISEASES, PRINTERS

Cabinet Shelf No.

See PRINTERS' DISEASES.

DISLE, HENRY

Cabinet T Shelf 2 No. 6 [vol.4]

Books printed by Henry Disle (Dyszell, or Disley) London, 1576. Bibliographical note.

see
DIBDIN'S "Typographical Antiquities" ...London, 1810-19, vol. iv, p.186

DISPLAY COMPOSITION

Cabinet Shelf No.

See Composition. Display composition.

DISPLAYOTYPE (E.E. Wilson) see COMPOSING MACHINES.

Cabinet FF Shelf 6 No. 27

Displayotype...

DISPUTES, LABOR see

Cabinet Shelf No.

LABOR QUESTIONS

SEE ALSO-- LABOR CONDITIONS

DISREALI, ISAAC

Cabinet S Shelf 5 No. 12

Early printing: Excerpts from his Cusiosities of Literature. Prospectus of John Murray, London, 1823.
Briefly historical

Bound in collection "Pamphlets and excerpts relating to typographical matters", item 2.

DISTRIBUTING MACHINES

See Composing Machines.

DISTRIBUTIONS OF TYPES

Cabinet Shelf No.

See Non-distribution of types.

DITCHFIELD, P. H.

Cabinet X Shelf 5 No. 96

Books fatal to their authors. The Book-Lover's Library. Edited by Henry B. Wheatley. London, 1895.

Boards, linen back; 7-3/8 x 4-5/8 x 3/4 in.

DITCHFIELD, P. H.

Cabinet QQ Shelf 5 No. 13

City Companies of London, and their good works: a record of their history, charity and treasure. By P.H. Ditchfield. London, 1904. Illus.

Cloth; 11-5/8 x 9½ in.

DIX, E.R.

Cabinet 76 Shelf 1 No. 17

Dictionary of printers ... in Ireland from 1726 to 1775.

See BIBLIOGRAPHICAL SOCIETY, England. Dictionary of the printers ... Ireland. Printed for the Bibliographical Society, 1932 (for 1930).

DIX, E. R. Mc.

Cabinet U Shelf 1 No. 111

Dublin printing, the earliest, with list of books, proclamations, etc., printed in Dublin prior to 1601. Dublin, 1901.

Bio-bibliographical account.

Half morocco; 7¼ x 5 x 3/8 in.

DIX, E.R.

Cabinet U Shelf 1 No. 111

Dublin printing, the earliest, with list of books, proclamations, etc., printed in Dublin prior to 1601. Dublin: O'Donoghue and Co., 1901.

Half morocco; 7¼ x 5 in. Original covers bound in.

DIX, E. R. McCLINTOCK

Cabinet 75 Shelf 1 No.

(The) Earliest Dublin printer and the Stationers Company (II) The Dublin printers and the Guild of St. Luke the Evangelist. A paper read before the Bibliographical Society, March 16, 1903.

In Trans. Biblio. Soc. Vol. VII, 1902-1904. pp..76-85.

DIX, E. R. McC.

Cabinet 75 Shelf 2 No. 2

Initial letters and factotums used by John Franckton, printer in Dublin (1600-18).

In Transactions of the Bibliographical Society, "The Library," Vol. II, 1921-22, pp. 43-48.

DIX, E. R. McCLINTOCK

Cabinet 75 Shelf 1 No. 8

Ornaments used by John Franckton, printer at Dublin. A paper on. For the Bibliographical Society.

In Trans. Biblio. Soc., Vol. VIII, pp. 221-227. 1904-1906.

DIXON, J. M.,

Cabinet NN Shelf 2 No. 8

Valley and the shadow, comprising the experiences of a blind ex-editor, a literary biography, a chapter of Iowa journalism, etc. New York. 1868.

Cloth: 7¼x5"

DIXON, ROLAND B.

Cabinet II Shelf 4 No. 2

Maidu (or Pujunan) stock of American Indians. Illustrative sketch of their language and dialects.

See BOAS, FRANZ. American Indian languages, handbook of...Bulletin 40, Washington, 1911, pp.683-726.

DOBBS, JOHN FRANKLIN

Cabinet LL Shelf 3 No. 41 2 copies

Proof reading and style for composition in writing and printing. Second edition. New York: John F. Dobbs, Publisher. The Academy Press, 1928.

One copy a presentation copy signed; the second copy, on inside front cover, a statement written by hand as follows: "Written by John Franklin Dobbs to encourage grammatic uniformity in the use of capital letters and punctuation marks in printing".

Cloth; 7-7/8 x 5-1/8 x 1 in.

DOBELL, BERTRAM

Cabinet Q Shelf 2 No. 22.01

Bookseller and man of letters, Bertram Dobell. By S. Bradbury. London, 1909. With portrait. Brochure.

In envelope.

DOBELL, BERTRAM

Cabinet S Shelf 2 No. 95

Walt Whitman, the man and the poet. By James Thomson. With an introduction by Bertram Dobell. London, 1910.

Cloth; 8 x 5½ in.

DOBSON, AUSTIN (see)

Cabinet J Shelf 3 No. 23

ABBEY, EDWIN A. and ALFRED PARSONS. [Engravings of..] New York, 1890

DOBSON, AUSTIN

Cabinet K Shelf 6 No. 8

Bewick, Thomas, and his pupils. By Austin Dobson. With ninety-five illustrations. Boston, 1884. Frontispiece portrait.

No. 34 of 200 copies printed.

Boards; 11-3/4 x 9 x 1-3/8 in.

DOBSON, AUSTIN

Cabinet U Shelf 3 No. 103

Bibliotheca Meadiana. (Richard Mead, London, 1754)

Bio-bibliographical account.

See vol. I, p.404 Bibliographica... London, 1895-1897.

DOBSON, AUSTIN

Cabinet U Shelf 1 No. 1c

Books and their associations. Bibliographical historical account. "The Library," 1908.

In Excerpts relating to printing from "The Library," 1908, pp. 132-142.

DOBSON, AUSTIN

Cabinet U Shelf 1 No. 1h

Millar, Andrew (Publisher), and Fielding. [An account of the career of a notable eighteenth century bookseller]. Includes book prices.

In excerpts relating to printing from "The Library," 1915-17, pp. 109-122 of pencilled folios.

DOBSON, WILLIAM T.

Cabinet U Shelf 1 No. 30

History of the Bassandyne Bible: The first printed in Scotland. With notice of the early printers of Edinburgh. With facsimiles and other illustrations. Edinburgh, 1887.

Stamped cloth; 9¼ x 5-7/8 x 1 in.

DOCTRINA BREVE in Fac-Simile

Cabinet 79 Shelf 2 No. 16

Published in the City of Tenochtitlan, Mexico, June 1544, by Right Rev. Juan Zumarraga, First Bishop of Mexico. To which are added The earliest books in the New Worls. By Rev. Zephyrin Englehardt, and a technical appreciation of the first American printers, by Stephen H. Horgan. New York: The United States Catholic Historical Society. Monograph Series X. 1928.

Cloth; 9½ x 6-3/8 in.

DOCTRINA CHRISTIANA.

Cabinet E Shelf 2 No. 88

Bellarmini, D. Robert (Cardinal). Doctrina Christiana, nunc primum ex Italico idiomata in Arabicum transtata. Romae, ex typographia Savariana, excudebat Steph. Paulinus, 1613.

Vellum; 6-3/8 x 4¼ x ½ in.

DOCTRINA CHRISTIANA

Cabinet 26 Shelf 1 No. 21

First book printed in South America, 1544.

Bio-bibliographical essay.

In "Gutenberg-Gesellschaft Jahrbuch, 1931", pp.214-220.

DOCTRINA CRISTIANA

Cabinet AA Shelf 5 No. 13

Intento bibliografico de la Doctrina Cristiana del P. Jerónimo de Ripalda. Publicado en la "Revista Cultura Española". Madrid, 1908

Bibliographical study.

DOCTRINA CRISTIANA

Cabinet Shelf No.

See Marroquin, Francisco.

DOCUMENTS, Historical

Cabinet R Shelf 6 No. 36

See Broadsides, Early: Historical documents relating to printing.

DODD, GEORGE

Cabinet T Shelf 4 No. 57

Curiosities of Industry. Printing: its modern varieties. London, 1853. Pamphlet.
One of a series of pamphlets descriptive of the Great Exhibition of 1852.

Cloth; 8½ x 5½ x 3/8 in.

DODD, GEORGE

Cabinet MM Shelf 7 No. 3

Days at the factories; or, the manufacturing industry of Great Britain described, and illustrated by numerous engravings of machines and processes. Series I. London 1843.

On pp.326-362 is given an account with many illustrations of Clowes & Sons printing office in Stamford Street, Blackfriars.

Half leather; 7¾ x 5½ x 1¼ in.

DODGE, PHILIP T.

Cabinet QQ Shelf 2 No. 24

Mergenthaler Linotype Company. Brief note on P.T. Dodge.

see

ILES, GEORGE. Leading American Inventor ...New York, 1912, pp.425

DODGE, PHILIP T.

Cabinet FF Shelf 6 No. 13.01

Portrait of Philip T. Dodge, President of the Mergenthaler Linotype Company.
Excerpt from The Printing Machinery Record- March, 1913.

With other items in manila envelope

DODGSON, CAMPBELL

Cabinet J Shelf 4 No. 3

Colour-prints, old French. By Campbell Dodgson. Keeper of Prints and Drawings at the British Museum. London, 1924.

With 87 plates, some of which are printed in colors.

Cloth, parchment back; 12-5/8 x 10-1/8 x 1-3/8 in.

DODGSON, CAMPBELL

Cabinet K Shelf 6 No. 14

Woodcut, contemporary English. London, 1922. Printed by the Baynard Press.

No. 284 of 550 copies printed.

Boards, cloth back; 12¼ x 10-1/8 x 5/8 in.

DODSLEY, R.

Cabinet M Shelf 1 No. 9

Economy of human life. In two parts. Kelso: Printed by James Ballantyne. 1802.

Calf; 8¾ x 5-3/8 x ¾ in.

DODSLEY, R.

See also

Imprints.

DODSLEY, ROBERT

Cabinet NN Shelf 2 No. 2.01

Bookseller and poet. London, 1703-1764. Biographical sketch of Robert Dodsley. Excerpt from "Self-Made Men", By C.C.B. Seymour. N.Y. 1858.

Item 2 in vol. with binder's title "Journalists and Journalism -- II. Pamphlets".

DODSLEY, ROBERT

Cabinet Q Shelf 1 No. 1

Robert Dodsley, an 18th. century publisher. By Edward Fuller.
Excerpt from the Bookman, July, 1910.

Item 22 in volume with binder's title "Publishing. Various Excerpts".

DODSLEY, ROBERT.

Cabinet Shelf No.

See also

Publisher, Great Britain: Dodsley, Robert.

DODSON, WILLIAM C.

Cabinet Shelf No.

See Specimen Books, Types. United States. Dodson, William C.

DOESBORGH, JAN van

Cabinet 76 Shelf 2 No. 2

See Bibliographical Society, England. Jan van Doesborgh.

DOESBORGH, JAN van

Cabinet U Shelf 1 No. 1b

(A) Biographical, bibliographicalessay, By Robert G. C. Proctor.

In Excerpts relating to printing from "The Library," p. 78 of pencilled folios.

DOESBORG, JAN van

Cabinet U Shelf 5 No. 24

English books printed by J. van Boesborg, 1505-1530.

see

POLLARD, A. W. Fine Books... London, 1912, p.230

DOESBORCH, J. Van

Cabinet 75 Shelf 2 No. 9

Prints books for the English market, Antwerp, circa 1504.

See Kronenberg, M. E. English printing, early 16th century in the Low Countries, p. 141.

DOGGETT, J. Jr. Publisher

Cabinet Q Shelf 4 No. 2

Business Directory for 1841, New York.

SEE

DIRECTORIES, Business. New York Business Directory...

DOGWOOD PRESS, THE

Cabinet Shelf No.

See Imprints, United States. McCaffrey, Frank; Dogwood Press.

[DOISSIN, LUDOVICO]

Cabinet I Shelf 1 No. 20

(La) Gravure: Poeme. A Paris, chez P.G. Le Mercier, 1753. (French and Latin).

First edition published in 1752 was entirely in Latin.

Paper; 7 x 4-3/8 x $\frac{3}{4}$ in.

DOLCIBELLI del MANZO

Cabinet X Shelf 3 No. 14

Bibliographical note, with printer mark, Dolcibelli, Carpi, 1506.

see

KRISTELLER, Dr. PAUL Italienischen buchdrucker...p.10

DOLET, ÉTIENNE

Cabinet W Shelf 5 No. 45

[Biographical sketch of the martyr printer]. By Eugene Asse. [French text, 1863]. Portrait frontispiece.

Boards; $13\frac{1}{4}$ x 10-3/8 in.

DOLET, STEPHEN(Etienne or Estienne Dolet)

Cabinet 27 Shelf 2 No. 26

Biographies of Famous Printers: No. 1, Stephen Dolet. With portrait and other illustrations. By Henry Lewis Bullen.

see

THE AMERICAN BULLETIN, August, 1912, pp. 6-9; also small article on the finding of the ashes of Stephen Dolet in Paris, in the October, 1912 issue of THE AMERICAN BULLETIN, page 21.

DOLET, ETIENNE

Cabinet W Shelf 2 No. 87

Boulmier, Joseph. Études sur le seizième siècle Estienne Dolet, sa vie, ses oeuvres, son martyre. Par Joseph Boulmier. Paris, August Aubry, 1857. Frontispiece portrait, leaf at end with device of Dolet.

Half calf; 8-3/4 x 5 in.

DOLET, ESTIENNE (Author).

Cabinet 70 Shelf 2 No. 15

Commentariorum linguae Latinae. Tomus Primus. Stephano Doleto Gallo avrelio autore [Printer Mark. 2 vols. Lugduni apud Seb. Gryphium, 1536.
Second vol. has same title and imprints, but is dated 1538. Both have wood-cut title borders, and printer mark.

Calf; $13\frac{1}{2}$ x $9\frac{1}{2}$ x $2\frac{1}{2}$ in. Brunet 2, 794.

DOLET, ETIENNE (Stephan)

Cabinet 70 Shelf 2 No. 15 (2 vols.)

Commentariorum linguae latinae ... Lugduni Seb. Gryphium. 1536-8. (2 vols.)

Calf; $13\frac{1}{2}$ x 9 3/8 x $2\frac{1}{2}$ in.

DOLET, ETIENNE

Cabinet 70 Shelf 1 No. 49

Dialogus de Imitatione Ciceroniana, adversus Desiderium Erasmum Roterodamum, pro Christophoro Longolio. Lugduni, apud Seb. Gryphium. 1535.

Calf; 8-3/4 x 6 x $\frac{1}{2}$ in. Gresswell I, 296.

DOLET, ETIENNE, author.

Cabinet 70 Shelf 1 No. 49

Dialogus Stephani Doleti, de Imitatione Ciceroniana, adversus Desiderium Erasmum Roterdamum, pro Christophoro Longolio. Printer Mark. Lugduni apud Seb. Gryphium, M.D.XXXV.

Calf; 8-3/4 x 6 x $\frac{1}{2}$ in. Gresswells' Parisiam Greek Press I, 296.

DOLET, ESTIENNE.

Cabinet W Shelf 2 No. 110

Estienne Dolet et ses luttes avec la Sorbonne. Par Jacques Alary. Paris, 1898.

Half morocco; $9\frac{1}{2}$ x $5\frac{3}{4}$ in.

DOLET, ESTIENNE.

Cabinet W Shelf 5 No. 45

Etude historique. Par L. Duval-Arnould. Editions des "Questions Actuelles." Paris [1875?]. Pamphlet.
Bound in with "Asse-Estienne Dolet. [France 1863]."

Boards; $13\frac{1}{4}$ x $10\frac{1}{2}$ in.

DOLET, ETIENNE

Cabinet W Shelf 2 No. 111

Famille Dolet a Troyes. Par Louis Morin. Archiviste Municipal. Troyes, 1917. Extrait de l'Annuaire de l'Aube. Pamphlet.
Biographical, genealogical account.
Bound in with "Notes sur Étienne Dolet" Par René Sturel, 1913.

Half morocco; 9-3/4 x 6¼ in.

DOLET, ETIENNE. (Author-Printer)

Cabinet 69 Shelf 1 No. 7

Gestes (Les) de Francoys de Valois Roy de France...Premierement composé en Latin par Estienne Dolet: et apres pay luy memes translaté en langué Francoyse. [Printer Mark]

Imprint: A Lyon, chés Estienne Dolet. M.D.XL. Avec privileige pour dix ans.

Half morocco; 7¼ x 6 x 3/8 in.

DOLET, ESTIENNE

Cabinet D Shelf 4 No. 54

Imprint, 1540, Lyon.

See IMPRINTS, FRANCE. Dolet, Estienne, Lyon, 1540

DOLET, ÉTIENNE

Cabinet U Shelf 4 No. 63

(The) Martyr of the renaissance. A biography. By Richard Copley Christie. London, 1880.

Cloth; 9-1/8 x 5-7/8 x 1¼ in. See also U/4/65.

DOLET, ÉTIENNE

Cabinet U Shelf 4 No. 65

Martyr of the renaissance, 1508-1546. A biography By Richard Copley Christie. New edition, revised and corrected. London, 1899.

Cloth; 9-1/8 x 5-7/8 x 1¼ in. See also U/4/63

DOLET, ETIENNE

Cabinet W Shelf 2 No. 03

See Née de la Rochelle. Vie d'Etienne Dolet, imprimeur...Paris...1779.

DOLET, ÉTIENNE

Cabinet W Shelf 2 No. 111

Notes sur Étienne Dolet. D'apres des inédits. Par René Sturel. Extrait de la Revue du Siezième Siècle, tome I, 1913. Paris, 1913.
Bio-bibliographical account.
Bound in with "La famille Dolet a Troyes" par Louis Morin, Troyes, 1917.

Half morocco; $9\frac{3}{4}$ x $6\frac{1}{4}$ in.

DOLET, ETIENNE

Cabinet 70 Shelf 1 No. 50

See POETRY OF PRINTING. Epigrams in Latin verse in honor of printers.

DOLET, ETIENNE (Author)

Cabinet W Shelf 2 No. 109

Second enfer d'Etienne Dolet, suivi de sa traduction des deux dialogues platoniciens, l'Axiochus et l'Hipparchus. Notice bio-bibliographique par un bibliophile. Paris, 1868.

Half morocco; 7¼ x 5 in.

DOLET, ETIENNE

Cabinet W Shelf 2 No. 03

Vie d'Étienne Dolet, imprimeur a Lyon dans le seizieme siécle; avec une notice des libraires et imprimeurs auteurs que l'on a pu découvrir jusqu'a ce jour. Gogue & Nee de la Rochelle. Paris, 1779.

Boards; 8¼ x 5¼ in.

DOLET, ETIENNE

See also Imprints.

DOLHOPFF, GEORG ANDREAS

Cabinet X Shelf 3 No. 13

Brief bio-bibliographical note, with printer mark, Dolhopff, Strassburg, 1662-1711.

see

HEITZ, PAUL.
Elsässische büchermarken...p.xxvii, plate lii

DOLLAR SIGN

Stack Shelf Number

See Bullen, Henry Lewis: History of U.S. Dollar Sign.

DOLLAR SIGN

Cabinet PP Shelf 1 No. 37

Explanation of the possible origin of the American (U.S.) dollar sign. By Professor Florian Cajori.

Brief newspaper excerpt pasted in front of book with title "Morgan's Arithmetical Books"...London, 1847.

DOLLAR SIGN

Cabinet LL Shelf 3 No. 1.01

Origin of the $ mark, and when first used. [Excerpt from the "Historical Magazine", Apr., June, Aug. & Sept. 1857.

Item 12 in vol. with binder's title "Proofreading: Pamphlets". Bound, 1932.

DOLPHIN PRESS, THE

Cabinet M Shelf 2 No.

See Imprints, England. Jones, Geo. W. The Dolphin Press, London, v.d.

DOMEL, GEORG

Cabinet Y Shelf 1 No. 61

Gutenberg: die erfindung des typengusses, und seine frühdrucke. Mit 19 beilagen. Koln, 1919. Facsimiles (Gutenberg: the invention of typecasting and his earliest impressions) Author's signed copy.

Stamped cloth; 9-3/8 x 6¼ x 3/4 in.

DONALDSON FAMILY OF PRINTERS

Cabinet U Shelf 1 No. 90

(A) Notable family of Scots printers. By Robert T. Skinner. Edinburgh, 1928. Illus. and portraits.

Stamped limp leather; 10¼ x 7-3/4 x 3/4 in.

DONI, ANTOINE-FRANCOIS

Cabinet E Shelf 2 No. 31

La libraria ... Divisa in tre trattati. Vinegia. Giolito de Ferrari. 1558.

Boards; 6 x 4 x ½ in. Brunet 2, 814.

DOMINICA (British West Indies)

Cabinet Shelf No.

First printing in Dominica. Some historical information, the fruit of original research. By Douglas C. McMurtrie.

Article in British & Colonial Printer, vol. 110, No.186, May, 19, 1932, p.460.

DONAT FRAGMENTS

Cabinet 14 Shelf 2 No. 4

Reproductions of Gutenberg's

see FACSIMILES. Donat (Fragments)....

DONI, ANTOINE-FRANCOIS

Cabinet E Shelf 2 No. 30

La libraria Fiorentino; nella quale sono scritti tutti gli autori volgari, con centro discorsi sopra quelli ... Vinegia, 1580. Altobello Salicato.

Bound in with "La seconda libraria del Doni." Vinegia, 1551. Francesco Marcolini.

Half morocco; 5½ x 3 x 7/8 in. Brunet 2,814.

DON QUIXOTE

Cabinet M Shelf 5 No. 5 2 Vols.

Historie of Don Quixote of the Mancha: Translated out of the Spanish by Thomas Shelton. 2 Vols. 1927-28

Colophon:..First printed for E. Blount in 1620. Now newly reprinted by Charles H. St. John Hornby assisted by G. Faulkner...at his private press called The Ashendene Press, Shelley House in the County of London. The printing was begun in May...1927 and ended...in July 1928. Theborders and initials were de-

Cont'd.

DONDÉ, FR. ANTOINE

Cabinet E Shelf 4 No. 53

(Les) Figures et abregé de la vie, de la mort, et des miracles de Saint Francois de Paul...A Paris, chez Francois Muguet, 1671.

Has more than 40 beautifully executed engravings by Abraham Bosse and Francois de Poilly.

Morocco; 14½ x 10 x 1 in.

DONKIN, BRYAN.

Cabinet FF Shelf 2 No. 40

Early inventor of printing presses, etc. 1818. See Inventions, Patents for. Abridgments of specifications, Vol. I...London, 1859. pp. 128, 141 for Patents issued to him.

Half morocco; 7-5/8 x 5x2in.

Cabinet Shelf No.

signed by Louis Powell... Laus deo. Printer mark.

Full morocco; 17 x 12 in.

DONDEY-DUPREY fils

Cabinet QQ Shelf 1 No. 1

L'Imprimerie, ode Francaise et Latine, dediée au General Baron de Pommereul...Paris, 1812. Pamphlet.

Bound in with other items in binder labelled: Poetry of Printing. Various items.

DONLEVY, JOHN

Cabinet I Shelf 2 No. 71

Rise and progress of the graphic arts: including notices of illumination, chalcography, wood-engraving, typography, lithography...and elucidating the new art of chromo-glyphotype, invented by John Donlevy. New York, 1854.

Half morocco; 11-5/8 x 9-3/8 in.

DONALD, ROBERT

Cabinet OO Shelf 4 No. 51

Canada, the Imperial Press Conference in. Foreword by Viscount Burnham...London, New York, Toronto, n. d. (circa 1920). Illus. and portraits.

Cloth; 9½ x 6¼ x 1½ in.

DONELLUS, HUGO

Cabinet 2 Shelf 2 No. 13

Iurisconsulti commentarii. Ad titulos digestorum qui infra scripti sunt...Antverpiae, ex officina Christophori Plantini. 1582.

Vellum; 13¾ x 9 x 1½ in.

DONNAUD, E.

Cabinet LL Shelf 3 No. 45

Vade-Mecum typographique. Règles a suivre dans la composition. Paris, Imprimerie de E. Donnaud. 1866.

Half leather; 7-5/8 x 4-7/8 in.

DONALDSON, THOMAS

Cabinet S Shelf 2 No. 93

Walt Whitman, the man. New York, 1896. Portrait, illus., and facsimiles.

Cloth; 8 x 5¾ in.

DONHAM, WALLACE B.

Cabinet G Shelf 1 No. 11.01

Printing education, present status of

See PRINTING EDUCATION. Present status of...

DONNE, JOHN

Cabinet M Shelf 1 No. 34

Devotions upon emergent occasions. Edited by John Sparrow, with a bibliographical note by Geoffrey Keynes. Cambridge: At the University Press. 1923. With frontispiece portrait.

Boards, cloth back; 8¾ x 7 x 1 in.

DONNELLEY, RUEBEN R.

Cabinet S Shelf 2 No. 53

Memorial of R. R. Donnelley. By the Chicago Typothetae. Chicago, Ill. 1899, Portrait.

Boards; 9 x 6 in.

DONNELLEY, R. R. AND SONS CO. (Lakeside Press)

Cabinet S Shelf 6 No. 13

Exhibitions of printing.

see

EXHIBITIONS OF PRINTING. United States. Lakeside Press...

DONNELLEY, R. R. & SONS COMPANY

Cabinet PP Shelf 5 No. 24

Extra binding at The Lakeside Press. Chicago, Ill. 1925. Illus.

oards; 10½ x 7½ x ½ in.

DONNELLEY R. R. AND SONS CO.

Cabinet R Shelf 6 No. 13

Lakeside Press announces that William A. Kittredge is now in charge of its Design and Typography. R. R. Donnelley and Sons Co. Chicago, 1922.

Half morocco; 16-1/8 x 10½ in.

DONNELLEY and SONS, R.R.

Cabinet JJ Shelf 3 No. 26

Relations with the Chicago Typothetae.

See

BROWN, EMILY CLARK. Book and job printing in Chicago...Chicago, Ill., 1931. [see index].

DONNELLEY, R. R. & SONS COMPANY

Cabinet PP Shelf 5 No. 25

(A) Rod for the back of the binder. Some considerations of binding with reference to the ideals of The Lakeside Press. R. R. Donnelley & Sons Company. Chicago, Ill. 1928. Illus.

Cloth; 10½ x 7¾ x 3/8 in.

DONNELLEY & SONS CO., R. R.

See Imprints, Lakeside Press.

DORÉ, GUSTAVE

Cabinet 26 Shelf 1 No. 17

Buchillustrator. von Albert Kolb.
Article in the Gutenberg-Gesellschaft Jahrbuch 1928. pp.118-141.

DORÉ, GUSTAV

Cabinet I Shelf 5 No. 26

Dante illustrations by Doré in 1861.

see

DANTE, ALIGHIERI. Illustrations by Doré...

DORE, J. R.

Cabinet U Shelf 1 No. 33

Old Bibles: An account of the early versions of the English Bible.. Second edition. With the preface to the version of 1611 added at the request of the late Right Rev. Christopher Wordsworth, Lord Bishop of Lincoln. London, 1888.

Cloth; 8 x 5-5/8 x 1 in.

DORÉ et CO.

Cabinet Z Shelf 3 No. 43

See Ink Manufacturers, France.

DORLAN, A.

Cabinet V Shelf 5 No. 23

Quelques mots sur l'origine de l'imprimerie, ou résumé des opinions qui en attribuent l'invention a Jean Mentel, natif de Schlestadt. Schlestadt, 1840. Portrait and six plates of facsimiles.
An examination of the theory which ascribes the invention of printing to John Mentel.

Item 2 in vol. with binder's title "Origin of Printing in France: Pamphlets".

DORMAN, J. F. W., Co.

Cabinet EE Shelf 4 No. 34

Manufacturers the Baltomorean Printing Presses.

See PRINTING PRESSES, LETTER-PRESS. Catalogue.

DORNE, JOHN

Cabinet U Shelf 5 No. 40

Bookseller, J. Dorne, 1520, notes on books sold by him.

See Bradshaw, Henry. Collected papers...Cambridge, 1889, pp. 427-442

DORNEMANN & CO. Magdeburg.

Cabinet II Shelf 2 No. 32

See SPECIMEN BOOKS, IRON TYPE. Germany

[DORRINGTON, W.]

Cabinet LL Shelf 6 No. 49

Manual (a) for young printers. By An Old Printer. Published at the Press News Office. Printed by C. and H. Dorrington, London, 1878.
Pamphlet; 5 x 7½.

In box with various other items relating to apprentice ship

DORSTEN, Johann von (and son)

Cabinet X Shelf 3 No. 20

Cologne, 1488-1523

see

HEITZ, PAUL. Kölner büchermarken.... p.xxxiv

DOTTESIO, LUIGI

Cabinet AA Shelf 1 No. 49

Luigi Dottesio da Como, e la Tipografia Elvetica di Capolago, 1840-1851. Ricordi di Alessandro Repetti. Roma, 1887. Pamphlet.
Dottesio, native of Como, was the director of the Tipografia Elvetica di Capolago He was hung at Venice by the Austrians.

Item 4 in volume "Four Italian Typographic Items."

DOTTRINA CRISTIANA

Cabinet 83 Shelf 2 No. 40.01

Composta dall'Emo, e Rmo Cardinale Robert Bellarmino...In Roma 1786. Nella stamperia dell Sag. Congr. di Propaganda Fide.
Specimens of Arabic and Ethiopian types.

Boards; 10 x 7-3/8 x 3/8 in.

DOUBLEDAY, PAGE and COMPANY

Cabinet S Shelf 3 No. 34

See Country Life Press, The. Doubleday, Page & Company.

DOUGLAS, ROBERT K.

Cabinet U Shelf 3 No. 103

Chinese illustrated books.

Historical bibliographical paper.

See vol. 2, p.452, Bibliographica...London, 1895-1897.

DOUAI (or Douay) France

Cabinet OO Shelf 4 No. 5

Earliest newspaper printed in Douay in 1563.
Facsimile, with translation and notes.

see
JOURNALISM, France. Literature of. Douay, 1563. An early news-sheet...

DOUBLET, CH., Typefounder

See Specimen Books, Types, France.

DOUGLAS, R.K.

Cabinet U Shelf 3 No. 103

Japanese illustrated books (Historical bibliographical illustrated account).

See Bibliographica...London, 1895-1897. vol. 3, p.1.

DOUAI

Cabinet Shelf No.

See also
Printing, Historical, France (Douai)

DOUBLET, PRADELLES et CHAPELLE.

Cabinet Z Shelf 4 No. 5

See Specimen Books, Types. France.

DOUNOU, PIERRE CLAUDE FRANCOIS

Cabinet W Shelf 1 No. 59

Notice historique sur la vie et les ouvrages de M. Van Praet. Par M. Daunou. Paris, 1839. Printed throughout on vellum.
M. Van Praet was a celebrated bibliographer who contributed several important works. relating to the history of typography.

Morocco, Gilt; 10¼ x 8¼ in.

DOWAY BIBLE

Cabinet Shelf No.

See Early Printing in England. Doway, 1609-1610.

DOUCE, FRANCIS

Cabinet I Shelf 1 No. 35

Dance of Death: Exhibited in elegant engravings on wood with a dissertation of the several representations of that subject, but more particularly on those ascribed to Macaber and Hans Holbein...London, 1833. With 49 plates.

Half morocco; 9 x 5¾ in.

DOVER, SIMON

Cabinet X Shelf 4 No. 24

London, 1664

see
LIBERTY OF PRINTING. Great Britain
(An) Exact narrative of the tryal....

DOUAI BIBLE

Cabinet W Shelf 3 No. 114

Notice sur une traduction anglaise de l'ecriture sainte, publiée au 17e siecle et désignée ordinairement sous le titre de Bible de Douai...Douai, 1841: Imprimerie de V. Adam. Pamphlet.

Item 11 in vol. with binder's title "Pamphlets Relating to Books - I. Bound, 1932".

DOUGHERTY, ANDREW

Cabinet QQ Shelf 4 No. 4

Biographical sketch of an American playing card manufacturer in 1876.

see
INDUSTRIAL AMERICA. Manufacturers ...New York, 1876, p. 367.

DOVER TELEGRAPH

Cabinet OO Shelf 6 No. 39

Dover, New Hampshire, 1846-1847.

see
NEWSPAPERS, WEEKLY. United States.

DOUAY OLD TESTAMENT

Cabinet Shelf No.

See Bibles: English translation of the Bible, also English Bible, The.

DOUGLAS, LESTER

Cabinet P Shelf 4 No. 17

(The) Battle of the Fifty Books. Address by Lester Douglas at the opening of the Fifty Books of the Year. Feb. 9th, 1932. A. I. G. A. New York Public Library.
Printed for the members of the American Institute of Graphic Arts by the Condé Nast Press, Greenwich, Conn., March, 1935. Typography by L. D.

Brochure, in envelope.

DOVES PRESS

Cabinet 18 Shelf 1 No. 2

(Goethes Faust printed by Cobden Sunderson and Emery Walker) Goethes Faust gedruckt in der Doves Press von T.J.Cobden-Sanderson und Emery Walker. Beschrieben von Jean Loubier. Facsimiles.

In Zeitschrift für Bücherfreunde, 1907-8, part 1, p.243.

DOVES PRESS, THE

Cabinet U Shelf 3 No. 66

Sanderson-Cobden, T. J. Catalogue raisonne of books printed and published at the Doves Press, No. 1 The Terrace, Hammersmith. May 1908.

Boards; 9-3/8 x 6-5/8 in.

DOVES PRESS.

Cabinet 71 Shelf 2 No. 37

Sanderson-Cobden, T. J. Salve aeternum aeternumque vale. By Cobden Sanderson.

Brief account of the aims of the press in The Library of William Andrews Clark, Jr. The Kelmscott and Doves Presses, pp. 77.

Boards, linen backs; 10 x 7½ in.

DOVES PRESS

See also index cards under the following sub-heads:

I Bibliography of Printing. Doves Press.
II Private. Presses.
III Imprints, England. Doves Press. Cobden-Sanderson.

Cabinet Shelf No.

DOW, ALEXANDER

Cabinet FF Shelf 6 No. 18

Composing and justifying machine, New York, 1896. Illustrations on folio 38 of scrap book compiled by John S. Thompson.

Scrap Book

DOW, ALEXANDER vs. BENJAMIN M. DES JARDINS

Cabinet FF Shelf 6 No. 54

Patent interference suits Nos. 21,694 and 23,998. Subject: Type Justifying Machines. Record for Des Jardins. Washington, 1905.

Half morocco; 9¼ x 6¾ in.

DOW, LORENZO (Inventor) see

Cabinet FF Shelf 6 No. 19

COMPOSING MACHINES. Dow, Lorenzo...

DOW, LORENZO (Inventor) see

Cabinet FF Shelf 6 No. 18

COMPOSING MACHINES.- Single Types. Dow...

DOWNING, J.

Cabinet T Shelf 1 No. 22

London, 1720. J. Downing. [His Imprint].

See Early Printing in England. London, 1720. J. Downing ...

DOYEN, E.

Cabinet Shelf No.

See Specimen Books, Types, France.

DOYLE, JOHN

Cabinet NN Shelf 2 No. 2.01

Publisher, New York City, circa 1817. Biographical sketch of John Doyle. By Thomas F. Meehan. Excerpt from U.S. Cath. Hist. Soc. Hist. Records & Studies, vol. 10, Jan. 1917.

Item 7 in vol. with binder's title "Journalists and Journalism -- II. Pamphlets".

DRACH, PETER

Cabinet Y Shelf 4 No. 4

(Note on Drach and his printing at Speyer, 1476-1481)

see

VOULLIÉME, ERNST. (Die) Deutschen drucker des fünfzehnten jahrhunderts...p.101

DRACH & COMPANY, CHARLES

Cabinet Shelf No.

See Specimen Books, Cuts. United States

DRAEGER FRERES

Cabinet DD Shelf 2 No. 49

Composition on the Linotype, distinguished. Specimen pages of book and commercial printing produced in Paris by Draeger Freres...For the Mergenthaler Linotype Company, Brooklyn N.Y. June 1927.

In box marked Linotype. Miscellaneous specimen sheets, v.d.

Box

DRAKE, ALEXANDER WILSON.

Cabinet Shelf No.

See Biographies, illustrators. Drake, Alexander Wilson.

DRAKE, ALEXANDER WILSON

Cabinet K Shelf 5 No. 2

Illustrator, for forty three years art director of the "Century Magazine". By Clarence Clough Buell. Excerpt from the "Century Magazine", May, 1916. With portrait.

Item 25 in vol. with title "Wood engravers and illustrators"...

DRAPER, JOHN.

Cabinet Shelf No.

See Early Printing in New England. Boston, v.d. John Draper.

DRAPER, R. and S.

Cabinet 80 Shelf 1 No. 44

Boston printers, 1766 (Imprint).

See ALMANACS. Ames's Almanack (1766)...

DRAPER, RICHARD.

Cabinet Shelf No.

See Early Printing in New England. Boston, 1760. Richard Draper.

DRAWING

Cabinet I Shelf 1 No. 21

(Alphabets) Anleitung von form-und stahl-schneiden, wie buchstaben...Ganze alphabeter, character und zeichen, was bey buchdruckey und giesserei vorkommt...Erfurt, druckts und verlegts Elias Sauerlander, 1754. Illus.

Half morocco; 7 x 4¾ x ½ in.

DRAWING

Cabinet I Shelf 1 No. 7

(Perspective, letters in).

See LENCKER, HANS. Perspectiva literaria ...Nurmberg, 1596.

DRAWING

Cabinet I Shelf 1 No. 2

(Proportion, principles of correct. Albrecht Durer, Nuremberg, 1525)

See DURER, ALBRECHT. (Proportion...) in truck gebracht im jar, 1525, Nuremberg.

DRAWING

Cabinet K Shelf 3 No. 16

Applied mechanical drawing...By Frank Elliot Mathewson and Judson L. Stewart. The Haytol Series of text books for industrial education. Springfield, Mass. 1911.

Cloth; 9 x 5¾ in.

DRAWING

Cabinet I Shelf 1 No. 11

Perspective op regel-lose buyten - gedaanten, van de. A. Bosse...t'Amsterdam. By Dansker Danckersz, in de Kalverstraat, Anno 1664.

Engraved title, plates and diagrams.

Boards; 6-3/8 x 4 x 3/8 in.

DRAWING

Cabinet K Shelf 3 No. 19

Theory and practice of design. An advanced text book on decorative art. By Frank G. Jackson. With 700 illustrations. 4th ed. London, 1903.

Cloth; 9 x 6 in.

DRAWING

Cabinet K Shelf 3 No. 20

Decorative design: an elementary text book.

see JACKSON, FRANK G. Decorative design...

DRAWING

Cabinet I Shelf 1 No. 9

Perspectives, diverses methodes universelles... A Paris, Chez Melchior Tavernier et Francois L'Anglois, 1642.

Vellum; 9½ x 6-5/8 x 1-1/8 in.

DRAWING

Cabinet K Shelf 4 No. 22

Theory of pictorial art. A guide to the study of light, colour, line and composition. By H. W. Harrison. With a foreword by W. L. Wyllie. London, 1931. Illus.

Boards, cloth back; 9¼ x 6-5/8 x ½ in.

DRAWING

Cabinet J Shelf 2 No. 13.01

(Human figure, drawing the. Described and demonstrated by Jean Cousin) La vraye science de la pourtraicture descrite et demonstree. Par maistre Jean Cousin...A Lyon, chez Francois I Demasso, 1672.

Boards, oblong; 7 x 9½ in.

DRAWING

Cabinet I Shelf 1 No. 12

Polygraphice, or the arts of drawing, engraving, etching...By William Salmon. London: Printed by E.T. and R.H. for R. Jones, 1673.

With engraved plates.

Original sheep; 7 x 4¾ in.

DRAWING (see also)

Cabinet Shelf No.

DESIGN

DRAWING

Cabinet K Shelf 3 No. 27

Maps, elliptical functions applied to

See ADAMS. OSCAR S. Elliptical functions...Washington, 1925.

DRAWING

Cabinet I Shelf 1 No. 3

(Proportion and symetry of the human figure, principles of).

See DURER, ALBRECHT. Clarissimi pictoris et geometrae de symetria...Norimberger, 1532.

DRAWING FOR PRINTERS (see)

Cabinet K Shelf 3 No. 13

KNAUFFT, ERNEST. Drawing for printers...

DRAWING

Cabinet K Shelf 3 No. 17

(Perspective) Notice historique et bibliographique sur Jean Pèlerin, dit le Viateur, Chanoin de Toul, et sur son livre "De artificiale perspectiva". Par Anatole de Montaiglon. Paris, 1861.

Bio-biblio-historical account of Jean Pèlerin.

Cloth; 9 x 5½ in.

DRAWING

Cabinet I Shelf 1 No. 1

(Proportion, explanation of the principles of)

See PACIOLO, LUCAS. Divina Proportione... Venice, 1509.

DRAWING FOR REPRODUCTION

Cabinet K Shelf 3 No. 28

Modern methods of book illustration...

see WHEATLY, HENRY B. (Editor). Modern methods...London, 1887, p.234

DRAWINGS

Cabinet J; Shelf 2; No. 34

Lawrence, Sir Thomas. Exhibition of 60 drawings by. London, April 23, 1913. Descriptive illustrated catalogue. By Algernon Graves. Foreword by Reginald Grundy.

Cloth; 11-1/8 x $8\frac{1}{2}$ in.

DRESDNER-SCHNELLPRESSEN-FABRIK

Cabinet EE; Shelf 5; No. 65

(Catalog, printing presses) Planeta. Buchdruck-schnellpressen. Dresdner Schnellpressen-fabrik Akt.-Ges. Coswig in Sa. Illus. With prices.

Also catalogue: Victoria-Buchdruck-Schnell-pressen. Machinenfabrik Rockstroh & Schneider Nachf. A.G. Dresdner-Heidenau.

Both items in manila envelope.

DREW, THOMAS BRADFORD

Cabinet S; Shelf 6; No. 8

Celebrating the birth of William Bradford. Three hundredth anniversary. By Thomas Bradford Drew. Excerpt from Mag. of Amer. Hist. March, 1890.

Item 15 in vol. with binder's title "Early printing and printers. Pamphlets".

DREDD, FIRMIN

Cabinet R; Shelf 5; No. 148

Extinction of the Dime Novel. By Firmin Dredd. An excerpt from The Bookman, March, 1900.

An account of the origin, developement, evolution, and degeneration of the Dime Novel.

Excerpt 16 in volume "Chap Books, Almanacs, Annuals, etc.

DRESLER, FR., and ROST-FINGERLIN.

Cabinet; Shelf; No.

See Specimen Books, Types, Germany.

DRIOUX, L'ABBÉ

Cabinet K; Shelf 2; No. 6

Typographic ornaments designed by l'Abbe Drioux, 1880.

See GRASSET, EUGENE (Compiler) Ornaments typographiques...

DREI, GIOVANNI

Cabinet AA; Shelf 1; No. 53

(I) Viotti, stampatori e librai Parmigiani dei sec XVI - XVII Giovanni Drei. Portrait, facsimiles, genealogy.

Biographical, historical, and bibliographical account.

In volume "Parma Grafica." Parma, 1925. pp. 13 - 37.

Half morocco; $12\frac{1}{2}$ x $9\frac{1}{2}$ in.

DRESLER'SCHEN GIESSEREI (C. Meyer)

Cabinet; Shelf; No.

See Specimen Books. Types. Germany.

DROUET.

Cabinet F; Shelf 4; No. 88

See Books, Copperplate Pygmalion: Scene Lyrique de Mr. J.J. Rousseau.....1775.

DRESDEN

Cabinet X; Shelf 2; No. 2

(History of printing in Dresden. Historie derer Dresdnischen buchdrucker...Gehorsamst ersucht. Christian Schöttgen, Dresden, 1740.

Bound in with "Der löblichen buchdruckergesellschaft zu Dresden"...1740

Boards; 8-3/8 x 7 in.

DRESSER, C

Cabinet K; Shelf 4; No. 11

Art of decorative design. With an appendix, giving the hours of the day at which flowers open...By C. Dresser. London, 1862. Illus.

Cloth: $9\frac{1}{4}$ x $6\frac{1}{2}$ in.

DROUY, Guillermo

Cabinet X; Shelf 3; No. 19

Brief bio-bibliographical note, with publisher-printer ? mark, Drouy (Madrid), 1578-1599.

see

HAEBLER, KONRAD (Spanish and Portugese printer marks...p.xxxvii

---

DRESDEN PRESS, THE (Vermont)

Cabinet R; Shelf 5; No. 82

See Early Printing in Vermont.

DREUX, ANDRÉ

Cabinet II; Shelf 6; No. 16

(La) Bibliothèque des aveugles. Avec une preface de Pierre Loti. Association Valentin Haüy. Paris, 1917.

With 18 photogravures. Stereotyping machines, printing presses for braille.

Paper; $6\frac{1}{2}$ x 4-7/8 x $\frac{3}{4}$ in.

DROZ, E.

Cabinet W; Shelf 1; No. 90

L'Abuze en Court: Le doctrinale du temps present. [Lyon, typographe indetermine, vers 1484] Notice de E. Droz. Publiee par L'Association Guillaume du Roy. Lyon, n.d. Facsimile.

Bibliographical study.

Half morocco; 11-1/8 x 9-3/8 x $\frac{1}{2}$ in.

DRESDNER-HEIDENAU

Cabinet EE; Shelf 5; No. 65

Printing presses. Catalogue of.

See ROCKSTROH & SCHNEIDER.

DREW, BENJAMIN

Cabinet LL; Shelf 3; No. 16

Pens and types, or hints and helps for those who write, print, read, teach, or learn. A new and improved edition. Boston, 1891.

Cloth; $7\frac{1}{2}$ x $5\frac{1}{4}$ in.

DRUCKENORDEN (Der) see

Cabinet Y; Shelf 4; No. 74

BUSCH, JORG

DRUGULIN, W.

Cabinet See Specimen Books, Types, Germany.

Shelf

No.

DUBLIN

Cabinet 75 (The) Earliest Dublin printers and the Company of Stationers of London. (Part II) The Guild of St. Luke the Evangelist. A paper read by E. R. McC. Dix, 1903.

Shelf 1

No. 7

In Trans Biblio. Soc. Vol. VII, 1902-1904. pp. 75-85.

DUBUQUE VISITOR, THE

Cabinet R (The) First newspaper in Iowa, first issued May, 11, 1836: Reprint of the Articles of agreement between John King and Wm. Carey Jones.

See Franklin, Benjamin: Proceedings of the Commemoration of the 177th Anniversary 1885. Introduction to the above.

Shelf 2

No. 36

DRYDEN, JOHN

Cabinet 73 "All for Love: or The World well lost." A tragedy, as it is acted at the Theatre-Royal, and written in Shakespeare's Stile. By John Dryden ... In the Savoy: Printed by Tho. Newcomb, for Henry Herringman, 1678. Printed in facsimile for Wm. Andrews Clark, Jr., by John Henry Nash, San Francisco, 1929. Illus. and colored plates.

Shelf 2

No. 47

Boards; $8\frac{1}{2}$ x 6-1/8 x $\frac{1}{4}$ in. In protective case; 13[illegible] x 9-3/8 x 1-7/8 in.

DUBLIN

Cabinet U Printing in Dublin prior to 1601.

see

Mc.DIX, E.R. Dublin printing...

Shelf 1

No. 111

DUCAREL, ANDRÉ COLLÉE

Cabinet T Letters to Mr. Meerman, Ducarels.--Mr. Meerman"s answers to Dr. Ducarel: A supplement to the (Origin of Printing. London, 1781.

Shelf 1

No. 24

Brochure, in manila envelope

DRYDEN PRESS (JOHN DAVY & SONS)

Cabinet EE See SPECIMEN BOOKS, TYPES. Printers'. Gr. Britain.

Shelf 2

No. 52

DUBOIS, FREDERIC

Cabinet W Discours de M. Frédérie Dubois, administrateur de l'imprimerie Chaix, prononcés sur la tombe de M. Chaix. Le 29 aout, 1897. Portrait.

Shelf 3

No. 64

Half morocco; 9-3/4 x 6-3/8 in.

DUCHARTE, PIERRE -LOUISE

Cabinet K L'Imagerie Orleanaise: Ouvrage precede d'une etude sur le origines et les sources d'inspiration des imagiers. Par Pierre-Louise Ducharte. Notices biographiques per Dr. Maurice Garsonnin. Paris (1928).

Shelf 1

No. 9

Half morocco; $11\frac{1}{2}$ x 8-7/8 x 1 in.

DRYDEN PRESS (J. Davy & Sons)

Cabinet See also Imprints, England. Dryden Press.

Shelf

No.

DuBOIS, HENRI PENE

Cabinet PP Four private libraires of New-York. A contribution to the history of bibliophilism in America. First Series. Preface by Octave Uzanne. New York, 1892. Illus.

DeVinne Press.

Shelf 3

No. 6

Cloth; $9\frac{1}{4}$ x $6\frac{1}{4}$ in.

DUCHARTE, PIERRE-LOUIS and SAULNIER, R.

Cabinet K L'Imagerie populaire: les images de toutes les provinces Francaises du xv siecles au Second Empire. Les complaintes, contes, chansons, legendes qui ont inspire les imagiers. Paris, 1925. Illus.

Origin and evolution of illustratio[n] traced in every province and city of France.

Shelf 2

No. 1

Boards; $11\frac{1}{4}$ x 9 in.

DUANE, WILLIAM

Cabinet NN [Biographical, historical account] By Allen C. Clarke. Read before the Columbia Historical Society, Washington, D.C., Feb.13, 1905. Has frontispiece portrait.

Shelf 2

No. 19

Cloth; $9\frac{3}{4}$ x $6\frac{1}{2}$ in.

DUBOIS, JEAN

Cabinet X Biographical note, with publishers book mark, Dubois, Basel, 1583-1591.

see

HEITZ, PAUL. Basler büchermarken...pp.xxxviii, 107

Shelf 3

No. 15

DU CHEMIN, NICOLAS

Cabinet J Imprimeur - libraire, Paris, 1541-1576. Brief bio-bibliographical notes.

See Didot, Ambroise Firmin. Etude sur Jean Cousin ....Paris, 1872, p. 198.

Shelf 2

No. 14

DUANE, WILLIAM

Cabinet NN Senate documents, Feb. 26, 1800. Report, in part, of the Committee of Privileges on the form of proceedings in the case of William Duane (editor of General Advertiser, or Aurora, Philadelphia).

Shelf 2

No. 18

Half morocco; $9\frac{1}{4}$ x 5-3/4 in.

"DUBUQUE GRIT" see

Cabinet NN JOURNALISM, COMIC. Example of. "Dubuque Grit".

Shelf 7

No. 1

DuCLOSEL ET CO. F.

Cabinet Z See SPECIMEN BOOKS, TYPES. France.

Shelf 3

No. 10

DUCOURTIEUX, P.

Cabinet LL Shelf 6 No. 49

(Les) Apprentis dans l'imprimerie. Cinquième Congrès des Maitres Imprimeurs de France. Limoges, 1898. Pamphlet.

With other items in box labelled "Apprenticeship. Various items".

DUCOURTIEUX, PAUL and LOUIS BOURDERY.

Cabinet V Shelf 1 No. 95

Une imprimerie et une librairie a Limoges vers la fin du seizième siècle. Par Paul Ducourtieux et Louis Bourdery. Limoges, 1898.
Includes signature of Jacques Barbou, plan of his house, and initial letters used by the first Barbous.

Half morocco; 10 x 6-3/8 x 3/8 in.

DUDIN --

Cabinet IF Shelf 5 No. 5

Art du relieur. Doreur de livres. Par M. Dudin. [Neuchatel, 1722] With plates.

Half morocco; $9\frac{3}{4}$ x $7\frac{3}{4}$ x $\frac{1}{2}$ in.

DUDLEY, HOWARD

Cabinet QQ Shelf 3 No. 20

History and antiquities of Horsham. Illustrated wood engravings and lithograph views. London, 1836.
This entire book was set up and printed by the writer, who lithographed the plates and cut the wood blocks. He also bound all the copies, and performed this task at the age of fifteen.

Cloth; $7\frac{1}{2}$ x 5 x $\frac{1}{4}$ in.

DUFART, C.

Cabinet X Shelf 5 No. 124

Printer, Paris, n.d. circa 1820.

See LAW SUITS RELATING TO PRINTING. Dufart vs. Prudhomme...

DUFF E. GORDON.

Cabinet U Shelf 1 No. 1c

Assertio septem sacramentorum (Henry VIII contra Luther): Bibliographical description, by Gordon E. Duff.

In Excerpts relating to printing from The Library, pp.1-16.

DUFF, E. GORDON

Cabinet T Shelf 2 No. 81

Caxton, William. By E. Gordon Duff, M. A. Oxon. Chicago, The Caxton Club. 1905. Facsimiles.
Bio-bibliographical account.

Boards; 12-3/8 x $9\frac{1}{2}$ x $1\frac{1}{4}$ in.

DUFF, E. GORDON

Cabinet U Shelf 5 No. 30

(A) Century of the English book trade: Short notices of all printers, stationers, bookbinders, and others connected with it from the issue of the first dated book in 1457 to the incorporation of the Company of Stationers in 1557. London, 1905.

Cloth; 8-7/8 x 7 x $1\frac{1}{4}$ in.

DUFF, E. GORDON

Cabinet U Shelf 1 No. 86

Early career of Edward Raban, afterwards first printer in Aberdeen. By E. Gordon Duff. Read before the Bibliographical Society. London, 1922.

Half morocco; 8-7/8 x 7-1/8 x 3/8 in.

DUFF, E. GORDON.

Cabinet 75 Shelf 2 No. 2

Early career of Edward Raban, afterwards first printer at Aberdeen. A paper read before the Bibliographical Society, December 19, 1921.

In Trans. Biblio. Soc., "The Library," Vol. II, 1921-1922, pp. 239-256.

DUFF, E. GORDON

Cabinet R Shelf 6 No. 42

Early English printing. A series of facsimiles of all the types used in England during the 15th century, with some of those used in the printing of English books abroad. With an introduction by E. Gordon Duff. London, 1896. (40 facsimile plates, 4o pp. text).

Linen portfolio, tied; 16 x 12 in.

DUFF, E. GORDON.

Cabinet U Shelf 5 No. 28

Early printed books: A short account of the introduction of printing into the principal countries and towns of Europe. London, 1893. Illus.
Series "Books about books." edited by Alfred W. Pollard.

Cloth; 8-3/8 x 5-1/8 x $1\frac{1}{4}$ in.

DUFF, E. GORDON.

Cabinet U Shelf 1 No. 1a

Egmondt, Frederick, an English fifteenth century stationer, by E. Gordon Duff.
Includes an account of some of the earliest works printed in England.

In Excerpts relating to printing from "The Library," [n.d.] p. 172 of pencilled folios.

DUFF, E. GORDON.

Cabinet 75 Shelf 1 No. 8

English book trade before the incorporation of the Stationers Company: A paper read before the Bibliographical Society, London, Jan. 16, 1905.
Summary.

In Trans. Biblio. Soc. Vol. VIII, 1904-1906. pp. 10-14.

DUFF, E. GORDON.

Cabinet 76 Shelf 2 No. 18

English books, fifteenth century: A bibliography of books and documents printed in England, and of books for the English market printed abroad. Printed for the Bibliographical Society, at the Oxford University Press, 1917.
Illus. monograph XVIII.

Boards; $11\frac{1}{4}$ x 9 in.

DUFF, E. GORDON.

Cabinet 75 Shelf 1 No. 9

English 15th century broadsides. A paper read before the Bibliographical Society. London, December 16th, 1907.

In Trans. Biblio. Soc., Vol. IX, pp. 211-227. 1906-1908.

DUFF, E. GORDON.

Cabinet 76 Shelf 2 No. 40

English printing on vellum to the end of the year 1600. A paper read before the Bibliographical Society of Lancashire, Dec. 20, 1900. Printed by the Aberdeen University Press Limited, 1902.
Publication No. I.

Paper; $10\frac{1}{4}$ x 8 in.

DUFF, E. GORDON

Cabinet T Shelf 5 No. 125

English provincial printers, stationers and bookbinders to 1557. The Sanders Lectures, 1911. Cambridge, 1912. Illus.
Bio-bibliographical, historical account.

Cloth; $7\frac{1}{2}$ x 5 x 5/8 in

DUFF, EDWARD GORDON.

Cabinet 75 Shelf 2 No. 5

Memorial Notice, A. (1863-1924). By Falconer Madan.

In Transactions of the Bibliographical Society, "The Library," Vol. V, 1924-1925, pp. 264-266.

DUFF, GORDON E.

Cabinet 67 Shelf 2 No. 35

Spare your good. (London, T. Marshe? ab.1555) Reprinted from the only known copy with an introduction by E.G. Duff, Cambridge, 1919.

Full morocco, 9 x 6¾ ins., pp.22.

DU MARTEAU, PIERRE

See Marteau, Pierre du, under Biographies, Printers'.

DUFF, E. GORDON

Cabinet U Shelf 1 No. 1a

Notary, Julian: A new English 15th century printer earlier than 1498, in which year appeared his edition of the Sarum Missal.

In Excerpts relating to printing from "The Library," [n.d.] p. 32 of pencilled folios.

DUFF, E. GORDON

Cabinet U Shelf 3 No. 103

Stationers at the Sign of the Trinity, 1504-1538.

Bibliographical account.

See vol. I, pp.92-113, 175-192, 499 in Bibliographica...London, 1895-1897.

DU MAURIER, GEORGES

Cabinet K Shelf 5 No. 2

Bohemia with Du Maurier, in. Recollections of artist life in the fifties. By Felix Moschelles. With sketches by Du Maurier. Excerpt from "The Century Magazine", May, 1896.

Item 20 in vol. with binder's title "Wood engravers and illustrators".

DUFF, E. GORDON.

Cabinet U Shelf 1 No. 1c

Notes on stationers from the lay subsidy rolls of 1523-4, by E. Gordon Duff.

An investigation which resulted in shedding much light on the careers of early English printers.

In excerpts relating to printing from The Library, 1908, pp.257-266.

DUFF, E. GORDON

Cabinet U Shelf 4 No. 27

Sweynheym and Pannartz: Notes and collation. A paper read before the Edinburgh Bibliographical Society. Nov. 14, 1907. pp. 21-36 of Proceedings of the Edinburgh Bibliographical Society, 1906-1907, 1907-1908.

Half morocco; 9-58 x 8 x ½ in.

DU MAURIER, GEORGES

Cabinet K Shelf 5 No. 2

London society, and Du Maurier. By Henery James, Jr. Illus. excerpt from "the Century Magazine", May, 1883.

Item 19 in vol. with binder's title "Wood engravers and illustrators".

DUFF, E. GORDON

Cabinet T Shelf 5 No. 121

Printers, stationers and bookbinders of Westminster and London from 1476 to 1535. By E. Gordon Duff. Cambridge, 1906. Illus. Bio-bibliographical account.

Cloth; 7½ x 5-1/8 x 1-1/8 in.

DU-GARDIANIS

Cabinet E Shelf 4 No. 7

See Early Printing in England. London, 1651.

DUMEREY, CHARLES

Cabinet RR Shelf 4 No. 8

Bibliographie de la papeterie. Par Charles Dumerey. (Extrait de l'Industrie Moderne) Bruxelles, 1888.

Half morocco; 9½ x 6½ in. Orig. wrappers bound in.

DUFF, E. GORDON.

Cabinet 75 Shelf 1 No. 5

Printers, stationers and bookbinders of York up to 1600. A paper read before the Bibliographical Society. London, May 1899.

In Trans. Biblio. Soc., Vol. V, 1898-1900, pp. 87-107

DUHALT et RENAULT

Cabinet Z Shelf 3 No. 43

See Specimen Books, Brass Rule, France.

Du MONCEAU, DUHAMEL

Cabinet RR Shelf 6 No. 6

Art du cartier (Art of making cardboard.) Par M. Duhamel Du Monceau. (Paris), 1762.

With 5 engraved plates showing the process of making cardboard and playing cards.

Board folder; 15 x 12 in.

DUFF, E. GORDON

Cabinet 75 Shelf 1 No. 15

Scottish bookbinding, armorial and artistic. A paper read before the Bibliographical Society, Feb. 18, 1918.

In Trans. Biblio. Soc. Vol. XV, 1917-1919. pp. 95-113.

DULSSECKER, JOHANN REINHOLD

Cabinet X Shelf 3 No. 13

Brief bibliographical notes, with book marks, Dulssecker (father and son), publishers and printers, Strassburg, 1696-1737, 1735-1775.

see HEITZ, PAUL. Elsässische büchermarken...pp.xxix-xxx

DUMONT, JEAN

Cabinet FF Shelf 3 No. 26

Fonderie et gravure typographiques A. & F. Vanderborght. Notice historique, Bruxelles: Imprimerie speciale de l'etablissement, rue Verte, 138. Dedication dated January 1888.
Has portraits, exterior view of the Vanderborght establishment, price list of types and printing materials.
Cloth: 11½x8¾"

DUMONT, JEAN

Cabinet MM Shelf 2 No. 9

Vade-Mecum du typographe. Deuxième édition, revue, augmentée, et mise a la portée des commencants. Bruxelles, 1894. Illus.

Has one folding plate.

Half morocco; 9 x 5-7/8 x 1-1/8 in.

DUMOULIN, JOSEPH

Cabinet W Shelf 3 No. 61

Charlotte Guillard, imprimeur au XVI siècle. Par M. Joseph Dumoulin. Paris, 1896. Extrait du Bulletin du Bibliophile, 15 Nov., 1896.

Half morocco; 9½ x 6 in.

DUMOULIN, JOSEPH

Cabinet W Shelf 3 No. 85

Vie et oeuvres de Féderic Morel, imprimeur a Paris depuis 1557 jusqu'a 1583. Par Joseph Dumoulin. Paris, 1901. Facsimile, types used by Morel, his various printer marks.

Bibliographical, biographical and historical account.

Half morocco; 10¼ x 7 in.

DUNBAR, H.M (Compiler)

Cabinet K Shelf 2 No. 38.01

Catalogue of a loan exhibition "Twentieth Century Prints" from several important American Collections. Compiled by H.M. Dunbar, Albert Rouillier Art Galleries. [Exhibition at the] Lakeside Press Galleries, Chicago, Dec.1932, Jan.-Feb.,1933. Illus.

With article on how prints are made, by Atherton Curtis.

Paper; 10-3/8 x 8 in.

DUNBAR, JAMES

Cabinet RR Shelf 2 No. 13

Practical paper maker: a complete guide to the manufacture of paper. By James Dunbar. Leith, London, New York, 1880.

Cloth; 6-5/8 x 4-3/8 in.

DUNCAN, H. M.

Cabinet FF Shelf 6 No. 58.03

Lanston Monotype Composing Machine. Miscellaneous biographical material relating to Mr. Duncan's connection with the inventor and the invention of the Lanston Monotype.

Information in letters addressed to H.L.Bullen, dated March 20th,1924, signed, H.M.Duncan.

Items in manila envelope

DUNCAN, HAROLD M.

Cabinet FF Shelf 6 No. 58.03

Machine substitutes for the composition of types by hand.

Illus. article in The Journal of the Franklin Institute, Philadelphia., vol.144, 1897, pp.241-281

With other items in manila envelope

DUNCAN, HENRY

Cabinet X Shelf 5 No. 57

Authorized Master Printing for Scotland, 1859.

see LIBERTY OF PRINTING, Great Britain. (Scotland 1859)....

DUNCAN, RICHARD

Cabinet U Shelf 1 No. 60

Glasgow printers 1638 to 1800. [From Mason's "Public and Private Libraries of Glasgow", p. 148], and added as an appendix to Notices and Documents illustrative of the literary history of Glasgow. Presented to members of the Maitland Club, by Richard Duncan. Verbatim reprint, Glasgow: Thomas D. Morison, 1886.

Boards; 10-7/8 x 8-3/8 x 7/8 in.

See also U/1/59

DUNCAN, RICHARD

Cabinet U Shelf 1 No. 59

Notices and Documents illustrative of the literary history of Glasgow during the greater part of last (18th) century. Presented to members of the Maitland Club. Glasgow, 1831.

Contains notices regarding the history of printing in Glasgow; Catalogue of books printed by Robert and Andrew Foulis etc.

Half morocco; 10¼ x 8-3/8 x 7/8 in.

Verbatim reprint, with a chronological list of Glasgow printers, 1638 to 1800 in U/1/60.

DUNDEE COURIER see

Cabinet OO Shelf 4 No. 41

JOURNALISM, Great Britain (Scotland)

DUNDEE, COURIER

See Newspapers.

DUNLAP, WILLIAM

Cabinet I Shelf 3 No. 11

History of the rise and progress of the arts of design in the United States. A new edition illustrated. Edited with additions by Frank W. Bayley and Charles E. Goodspeed. In three volumes. Boston, 1918.

Cloth; 9¼ x 6-5/8 in.

DUNLOP, ANDREW

Cabinet OO Shelf 4 No. 10

Fifty years of Irish journalism. By Andrew Dunlop, Dublin, 1911.

Cloth; 7-7/8 x 5 x 1-3/8 in.

DUNLOP and CLAYPOOLE

Cabinet Shelf No.

See Newspapers, Pennsylvania: American Daily Advertiser.

DUNLOP AND CLAYPOOLE'S AMERICAN ADVERTISER

Cabinet Shelf No.

See Newspapers, Pennsylvania.

DUNN, F. T.

Cabinet S Shelf 6 No. 9.01

Report of the Assembly of the State of California, 29th session, relative to printing of State School Text Books. By F. T. Dunn, Expert. Sacramento: State Office, A. J. Johnson, Supt. State Printing, 1891.

Brochure, in manila envelope.

DUNN, HARVEY HOPKINS

Cabinet G Shelf 3 No. 20

Princeton University Press, Princeton, N.J. 1927. Twenty-fifth anniversary class of 1902. University of Pennsylvania. Philadelphia. [Booklet] Designed by H.H.Dunn, and printed at the University Press.

Boards; 6-3/8 x 4-3/8 x ½ in.

DUNSTERKOOP, J. J. (J. J. D.)

Cabinet FF Shelf 3 No. 1

Haerlemse zangen...en in nederduytse dichtmaat overgebragt door J. J. D. Te Haerlem. Gedrukt ter Musicq-Drukkery van Izaak en Johannes Enschede. 1761.

Half mor. oblong: 9½x11½ in.

DUNTON, CHARLES L. (Compiler)

Cabinet MM Shelf 6 No. 60

Pressroom hints and helps. Describing some practical methods of pressroom work, with directions and useful information relating to a variety of printing-press problems, "Typographic Technical Series for Apprentices", Part IV, No.28. United Typothetae of America.

Cloth; 8 x 5 in.

DUNTON, GEORGE E.

Cabinet FF Shelf 1 No. 1

(A) Black leading paradox. A philosophical treatise on black leading. By Geo. E. Dunton. New York and London, 1914. Printed by the Charles Francis Press, N.Y.

Item 5 in vol. with binder's title: ELECTROTYPING AND STEREOTYPING PAMPHLETS.

DUNTON, GEORGE E.

Cabinet FF Shelf 1 No. 1

Electrotyping brochure series. Book I. May 1910: Supplement to Book I. December 1910: Book 2, 1914 (Pamphlets)

Nos. 2, 3 and 5 in. vol. with binders' title; Electrotyping and Stereotyping Pamphlets.

DUNTON, GEORGE E.

ELECTROTYPING BROCHURE SERIES, Book II - See Dunton, George E.: A Black-Leading Paradox.

DUNTON, GEORGE E.

Cabinet FF Shelf 1 No. 1

Mechanical processes past and future. Address delivered before the International Association of Electrotypers of America, by George E. Dunton. At the Waldorf Astoria Hotel, New York. Oct. 7, 1914.

Item 7 in vol. with binders' title: Electrotyping and Stereotyping Pamphlets.

DUNTON, GEORGE E.

Cabinet FF Shelf 1 No. 20

Treatise on electrotyping; and illustrated catalogue of improved machinery for electrotyping, stereotyping and photo-engraving, manufactured by The Ostrander-Seymour Co., Chicago, 1900.

Bound in with Dunton's Electrotyping Brochure Series. Book I. May 1910 and Supplement to Book I. Dec. 1910.

Cloth; 10 x 7 in.

DUNTON, GEORGE E.

Cabinet FF Shelf 1 No. 21

Treatise on electrotyping; and illustrated catalogue of improved machinery for electrotyping, stereotyping and photo-engraving; manufactured by The Ostrander-Seymour Company. Chicago, U. S. A. 1900.

Treatise and catalogue are on alternate pages.

Paper; 10 x 6¾ in.

DUNTON, JOHN

Cabinet X Shelf 5 No. 3

Author and bookseller, London, 1659-1735. [Biographical sketch] Extract from "The Book of Days." n.d.

p. 35 in vol. with binder's title "Scrap-Book, 1705-1891, relating to printing."

DUNTON, JOHN

Cabinet 00 Shelf 4 No. 23

First English periodical (1693, John Dunton's Ladies Mercury) for women. By Bertha-Monica Stearns.

Excerpt from "Modern Philology", London, Aug. 1930, Vol. 28, No. 1, p. 45.

DUNTON, JOHN

Cabinet Q Shelf 1 No. 1

John Dunton was a citizen.

Excerpt from "Household Words", vol. 9, No.15, 1854

Item 7 in volume with binder's title "Publishing. Various Excerpts"

DUNTON, JOHN

Cabinet R Shelf 3 No. 107

Letters from New England; The publications of the Prince Society. Boston, 1867.

Historical, bibliographical, and biographical of printing and publishing in Boston.

Half morocco; 8½ x 7¼ in.

DUNTON, JOHN

Cabinet T Shelf 1 No. 26

Life and errors of John Dunton, late citizen of London; written by himself ... London, printed for S. Malthus, 1705.

John Dunton was an author-bookseller better known as a pamphleteer than a publisher. He was born 1659, died 1733.

Half morocco; 6¾ x 4-3/8 x 1½ in. See also T/1/27.

DUNTON, JOHN

Cabinet T Shelf 1 No. 26

Life and errors of John Dunton, late citizen of London; written by himself in solitude... London: Printed for S. Multhus, 1705.

Half morocco; 6-3/4 x 4¼ x 1¼ in.

DUNTON, JOHN

Cabinet T Shelf 1 No. 27

(The) Life and errors of John Dunton, citizen of London; with the lives and characters of more than a thousand contemporary Divines, and other persons of literary eminence...And a faithful portrait of the author. Printed by and for J. Nichols, Son, and Bentley. London, 1818. 2 vols.

Binding by Hayday: Calf, paneled, gilt edges; 8-3/4 x 5¼ in.

DUNTON, JOHN

Cabinet T Shelf 1 No. 27

Life and errors of John Dunton. London, 1818 (2 vols.).

Binding by Hayday: Calf, paneled, gilt edges; 8¾ x 5½ in.

DUODECIMOS, THE

Cabinet R Shelf 3 No. 38

Prospectus of "The Duodecimos" containing list of members of the Club. Bound in with Facsimile of Poor Richard's Almanack for 1733. New York (DeVinne Press), 1894.

Full morocco, gilt; 7¼ x 5¼ in.

DUODECIMOS

Cabinet Shelf No.

See also Societies, Booklovers.

DUPIN, Mr

Cabinet W · Shelf 1 · No. 41

Notices historiques, critiques et bibliographiques, sur plusieurs livres de jurisprudence Francaise ... Par Mr Dupin. Paris, 1820.

Half morocco; 8½ x 5½ in.

DUPLESSIS, GEORGES

Cabinet J · Shelf 4 · No. 6

Catalogue de l'Exposition de gravures anciennes et modernes. 4 Juillet, 1881. Paris. [Avec] Coup d'oeil sur l'histoire de la gravure. Par Georges Duplessis. Paris, 1881.

With many examples of engraving and color printing methods.

Boards, leatherette back; 13 x 9⅞ x 1½ in.

DUPLESSIS, GEORGES

Cabinet K · Shelf 1 · No. 21

Coup d'oeil sur l'histoire de la gravure. Par Georges Duplessis. Paris, n. d. circa 1882.

(Together with) Catalogue de l'Exposition de gravures anciennes et modernes. 4 Juillet, 1881. Paris. Illus.

Includes also an article "La photographie et les arts graphiques". Par A. Davanne.

Boards, morocco back; 12-7/8x9⅝x7/8 in.

DUPLESSIS, GEORGES

Cabinet K · Shelf 6 · No. 39.01

Essai bibliographiques sur les différentes éditions des Icones Veteris Testamenti d' Holbein. Lu dans la séance du 25 juillet, 1883.

Pamphlet

Item 8 in bound collection with binder's title ENGRAVERS AND WOOD ENGRAVERS

DUPLESSIS, GEORGES

Cabinet J · Shelf 3 · No. 28

Gravures sur bois dans les livres de Simon Vostre, libraire d'Heurs. Par Jules Renouvier. Avec un avant-propos par Georges Duplessis. Paris, 1862. Illus.

Half morocco; 8¾ x 5-5/8 x ¾ in.

DUPLESSIS, GEORGES

Cabinet K · Shelf 2 · No. 2

Histoire de la gravure en Italie, en Espagne, en Allemange, dans les Pays-Bas, en Angleterre, et en France...Par Georges Duplessis. Paris, 1880.

With 73 reproductions of ancient engravings.

Half morocco; 11 x 8 in.

DUPLESSIS, GEORGES

Cabinet K · Shelf 4 · No. 6

Livres a gravures du 16e siecle: Les emblems d'Alciat. Par Georges Duplessis. Paris, 1884. Illus.

Bibliographical study of "Emblems d'Alciat", with chronological table of editions, 1531 to 1781.

Cloth: 9-5/8x 6-3/8 x 3/8 in.

DUPLESSIS, GEORGES

Cabinet K · Shelf 3 · No. 9

(Les) Mervilles de la gravure. Par Georges Duplessis. 2m édition. Ouvrage illustre de 34 vignettes par P. Sellier. Paris, 1871.

On p. 306 picture of the interior of a copperplate printing shop. engraving by Abraham Bosse, circa 1640.

Cloth; 7¼ x 4½ in.

DUPLESSIS, GEORGES

Cabinet K · Shelf 6 · No. 39.01

(De) Quelques estampes en bois de l'ecole de Martin Schongeuer. Lu dans la seance du juillet 30, 1884.

Illus. pamphlet.

Item 1 in bound collection with binder's title ENGRAVERS AND WOOD ENGRAVERS

DUPLEX PRINTING PRESS COMPANY

Cabinet EE · Shelf 4 · No. 35

Catalogues and price lists of printing presses built by the Duplex Printing Press Company, Battle Creek, Mich. 1909-10.

Illus. pamphlet.

In manila envelope.

DUPONT, PAUL

Cabinet V · Shelf 6 · No. 5

Essais pratiques d'imprimerie precédés d'une notice historique. Typographie-Lithographie Paris, Imprimerie Paul Dupont, 1849.

Many specimens of types, bibliography, chronological table of acts relating to the Liberty of the Press 1488-1848, history of l'Imprimerie Nationale.

Boards, 14 x 10½ in.

DUPONT, PAUL

Cabinet W · Shelf 2 · No. 106

Exposition universelle de 1867. Notice sur les établissements de M. Paul Dupont, imprimeur a Paris. Described as follows: I. Imprimerie; II: Lithography; III: librairie administive; IV: librairie classique; V: établissement de Clichy; VI: inventions et procédés nouveaus VII: organisation ouvriére, VIII: organisation financière.

Half morocco; 10-3/4 x 7½ in.

DUPONT, PAUL.

Cabinet V · Shelf 3 · No. 14

Histoire de l'imprimerie. Paris, 1854 [2 vols].

Describes recording and communicating ideas before and since the invention of print ing; printing in France under the different regimes; lithography and the Imperial Printing Office. Has also a bibliography of printing; and a chronological table of the principal facts connected with the art from its origin.

Half morocco; 7½ x 5-1/8 in.

DUPONT, PAUL

Cabinet V · Shelf 4 · No. 15

Histoire de l'Imprimerie. Paris, 1854. 2 vols.

Vol. 1: Découverte de l'Imprimerie, pp. 23-64. L' Imprimerie en France, pp. 65-351. L'Imprimerie dans les diverses contrées de la terre, p. 401.

Vol. II: La profession d'imprimeur, pp, 1-106... Imprimerie Impériale, p. 461: Legislation: Tableau Chronologique.

Half morocco; 11 x 7½ in.

DUPONT, PAUL.

Cabinet V · Shelf 4 · No. 16

Histoire de l'Imprimerie. [Review of book by Alphonse Levray, Protê] Paris, 1856.

Pamphlet 221: Société Fraternelle des Protes des Imprimeries Typographiques de Paris.

Boards; 9 x 6-3/8 in.

DUPONT, PAUL

Cabinet W · Shelf 2 · No. 107

Imprimerie administrative de M. Paul Dupont. [France, 1860] Illus.

Cloth; 10½ x 7¼ in.

DUPONT, PAUL

Cabinet W · Shelf 2 · No. 105

Imprimerie (Une) en 1867. Par M. Paul Dupont Paris, 1867.

Full Illustrated and descriptive account of this printing house, its working methods quality and quantity of production.

Half morocco; 10-3/4 x 7½ in.

DUPONT, PAUL

Cabinet W · Shelf 2 · No. 104

Instruction générale a MM. les correspondents de l'imprimerie et de la libraire administratives. Première partie. Paris, 1862.

An account of the activities and methods of this printing house, which at this time was being conducted on the co-operative principle, its numerous services to employees, etc.

Buckram; 9¾ x 6 x 3/8 in.

DUPONT, PAUL

Cabinet KK Shelf 4 No. 7

Mémoire pour les ouvriers typographes. Par Armand Levy, leur defenseur. Paris, 1862.

Relates to prosecution of compositors employed by Paul Dupont.

Cloth; 11 x 9 in.

DUPONT, PAUL

Cabinet KK Shelf 4 No. 30

Notes sur les maisons ouvriers de l'imprimerie Paul Dupont: organisation financière basée sur un systeme nouveau. Loyers bon marché - reductions successives de ces loyers. Amortissement du capital engagé. Paris, 1867.

Notes on the various benefit societies of this printing firm.

Paper; $11\frac{1}{2}$ x $8\frac{1}{2}$ in.

DUPONT, PAUL

Cabinet V Shelf 4 No. 14

Notice historique sur l'imprimerie. Par Paul Dupont. Paris: Imprimerie Paul Dupont 1849.

Subjects include: workmen's associations in France, government printing office, liberty of the press, brief biographies, etc.

Half morocco; 11 x $7\frac{1}{4}$ in.

DUPONT, PAUL

Cabinet Z Shelf 3 No. 15

Specimen des caracteres de la Fonderie de Paul Dupont. Clichy, 12 rue du Bac-d'Asnieres. 1882.

See also Z/3/13

Boards; 12 x 8-7/8 x 3/4 in.

DUPORTAL, Melle J.

Cabinet I Shelf 4 No. 15

(La) Gravure en France au 18e siecle. La gravure de portraits et de paysages. Par Melle. J. Duportal. Avec 124 reproductions en heliotypie. Paris et Bruxelles, 1926.

Paper; 13 x 10 x $1\frac{1}{4}$ in.

DUPRAT, F. A.

Cabinet V Shelf 6 No. 23

Precis historique sur l'Imprimerie Nationale et ses types. Paris 1848.

The author was the "Chef-du-service" of the foundry department, and controller of the letter press-work of the National Printing Office at Paris.

Half morocco; 9-1/8 x 6 in.

DU PRE, GALLIOT.

Cabinet U Shelf 1 No. 1c

(A) Paris bookseller of the 16th century. Galliot Du Pre. (Bibliographical, historical account By Arthur Tilley.

In Excerpts relating to printing from "The Library," 1908. pp. 36-65, 143-172.

DUPUIS FAMILY OF PRINTERS

Cabinet V Shelf 3 No. 18

(Bio-bibliographical notes relating to the Dupuis family of printers and booksellers, Paris, 1539-1769)

see

WERDET, EDMOND. Histoire du livre en France...3me partie (2), p.68

Du PUYS, JACQUES.

Cabinet 69 Shelf 2 No. 19

See Early Printing in France. Paris, 1580.

DURAND, GEORGES.

Cabinet V Shelf 1 No. 60

Imprimeurs typographes de Chartres depuis 1482. Par Georges Durand. 1900.

[Extract of a work in preparation on the printers and booksellers of Chartres: A genealogy.]

Folded plate, paper board covers; 10-1/8 x $6\frac{1}{2}$ in.

DURAND, PIERRE

Cabinet V Shelf 3 No. 18

(Bio-bibliographical notes relating to Durand family of printers and booksellers, Paris, 1606-1772)

see

WERDET, EDMOND. Histoire du livre en France...3me partie (2), p.167

DURANDUS, GUILLELMUS

Cabinet 10 Shelf 2 No. 1

Rationale divinorum officiorum. n. p. d. [Basel. Berthold Ruppel v. Hanau, circa 1468-70].

Gesamt-Kat. ; Hain 6463.

Original pigskin, clasps; $16\frac{1}{4}$ x $11\frac{3}{4}$ x 3 in.

DURANDUS, GUILLELMUS

Cabinet D Shelf 1 No. 31

Speculum judiciale. Milan, 1478. Begninus et Johan Ant. de Honate.

Gesamt-Kat. ; Hain 6510.

Original covers with metal corners; 17 x $11\frac{1}{2}$ x $4\frac{1}{4}$ in.

DURANT, JEAN.

Cabinet 69 Shelf 2 No. 13

See Early Printing in France. Lyons, 1572.

DURANT, WILLIAM (Journalist)

Cabinet NN Shelf 6 No. 15

Boston Transcript (The), 1834-1884. A semi-centennial. Banquet and presentation to William Durant, treasurer and Manager. By the Boston Transcript Company. Hotel Vendom February 18, 1884. Privately printed.

Frontispiece portrait, Wm. Durant.

Cloth; 9 x $6\frac{3}{4}$ in.

DURANT, WILLIAM (Journalist)

Cabinet NN Shelf 6 No. 16

Sixty years service. Complimentary dinner to William Durant, by his fellow employees of The Boston Transcript Company. Given on Monday Evening, Feb.,19, 1894, at the Copley Square Hotel, Boston. Privately printed.

With portrait frontispiece.

Cloth; 9 x $6\frac{3}{4}$ in.

DURANTIS (Hieronymus de)

Cabinet X Shelf 3 No. 14

Bibliographical notes, books published by Durantis and printed by Ganibus, Pavia, 1483-1488. With publishers device.

see

KRISTELLER, Dr. Paul. Italienischen buchdrucker...p.44

DURELL, WILLIAM

Cabinet Shelf No.

See First Occurrences. First American edition of Josephus History of the Jews ... New York, 1792.

DÜRER, ALBRECHT.

Cabinet E Shelf 3 No. 5

See Adamo, Melchiore. Vitae Germanorum philosophorum. p.66.

DURER, ALBRECHT.

Cabinet I Shelf 3 No. 1

Biography.

See BIOGRAPHIES, ENGRAVER, Durer, Albrecht.

DURER, ALBRECHT

Cabinet G Shelf 3 No. 7

Great procession from the Church of Our Lady at Antwerp, as seen and described by Albrecht Durer, about 1620. Reprinted from a volume by Sir Martin Conway. The Museum Press (H.W. Kent), Metropolitan Museum of Art printing department, New York, 1919.

Half morocco; 8¼ x 5½ in. pp.6, (last blank)

DURER, ALBRECHT

Cabinet I Shelf 1 No. 4

Albertus Durerus Nurembergensis pictor huius aetatis celeberrimus, versus e Germanica lingua in Latinam...Aedo exacte quatuor his suarum Institutionum Geometricarum libris... Parisiis: Ex Officina Christiani Wecheli, sub scuto Basiliensi, 1535.

With woodcuts and diagrams. Part III gives rules for construction of letters.

Boards, leather back; 12¾ x 8½ x 5/8 in.

DURER, ALBRECHT.

Cabinet D Shelf 2 No. 43

Brant, Sebastien. Stultifera Navis. Basel, 1498. Printed by J. Bergmann,de Olpe.

This book contains 118 woodcuts from the original blocks, and by authorities now assigned to the hand of Durer.

Full morocco, 8½ x 6¼ ins.

DÜRER, ALBERT

Cabinet J Shelf 2 No. 21

Life and work of Albert Dürer. Being a lecture delivered to the Print Collectors Club on Nov. 15, 1922. By T.D. Barlow. With notes on watermarks, a chronological list of his woodcuts & engravings, & illustrations of his work. Printed in London by Sanders Phillips and Company Ltd. At the Baynard Press.

Boards; 9¼ x 7¼ x 3/8 in.

DURER, ALBRECHT.

Cabinet I Shelf 5 No. 23

Apocalipsis cum figuris [16 plates]. Impressa denuo Nurnberge p. Albertum Durer pictorem. Anno christiano millesimo quingentesimo undecimo (1511).

Following colophon a warning of punishment to imitators of these wood engraved plates.

Modern pigskin; 16½ x 12 in.

DURER, ALBRECHT

Cabinet I Shelf 1 No. 3

Clarissimi pictoris et geometrae de symetria partium in rectis formis humanorum corporum. Libri in latinum conversi...Norimbergaer excudebatur opus...1532, in aedib (us) biduae Durerianae. Numerous wood cuts.

On the symetry and proportion of the human figure.

Half morocco; 11-5/8 x 7¾ x 5/8 in.

DURER, ALBRECHT

Cabinet Y Shelf 2 No. 23

(Life and works of Durer. Brief comments)

See LORCK, CARL B. Handbuch der geschichte...Leipzig, 1882-1883. (part 1, pp.108-113)

DÜRER, ALBRECHT

Cabinet S Shelf 5 No. 17

[Biographical and technical essay]. By N. Peacock. An excerpt from The Connoisseur. Sept. 1902. Illus.

Item 16 in collection "Miscellaneous items relating to printing; excerpts from Magazines 1918.

DURER, ALBRECHT.

Cabinet 67 Shelf 2 No. 61

Construction (The) of Roman letters. Reprinted by Bruce Rogers, at the Printing House of William Edwin Rudge, New York, 1924.

Centaur types. Reproductions within red rules.

Boards, 7-7/8 x 4-3/4 ins., pp. 39.

DURER, ALBRECHT

Cabinet J Shelf 2 No. 19

Life of Albrecht Dürer of Nurnberg. With a translation of his letters...By Mrs. Charles Heaton, London, 1881.

Portrait and illustrations.

Cloth; 8½ x 6 x 1¼ in.

DURER, ALBRECHT

Cabinet I Shelf 3 No. 1

Biographical essay. Excerpt from The National Magazine. Nov. 1853. Illus.

Has picture of Durer's house in Nuremberg.

Item 2 in vol. with binder's title "Various Engravers and About Engravers."

DURER, ALBRECHT

Cabinet T Shelf 3 No. 12

Engraver of wood-cuts, Albrecht Durer, a brief sketch of his life

see HANSARD, THOMAS CURSON Typographia...London, 1825, pp.28-30

DURER, ALBRECHT

Cabinet J Shelf 2 No. 20

Literary remains of Albrecht Dürer. By William Martin Conway. With transcripts from the British Museum manuscripts and notes upon them by Lina Eckerstein. Cambridge (England), at the University Press, 1889. With plates.

Cloth; 10-7/8 x 7½ in.

DÜRER, ALBRECHT

Cabinet K Shelf 5 No. 2

Biographical sketch.

see LA FARGE, JOHN. Dürer...

DURER, ALBRECHT

Cabinet 5 Shelf Nos 22, 23

Facsimile reprints of some of the Durer woodcuts, 1471-1528

Facs. in Cabinet 5, portfolios, 22, 23, also portfolio 38-2

DURER, ALBRECHT

Cabinet J Shelf 2 No. 22

(The) Man in his own eyes and in the eyes of his neighbors. With a complete list of his prints from wood, copper, and iron. By Louis A. Holman. (Goodspeeds Monographs No.5) Boston, 1922.

Portrait frontispiece.

Half morocco; 7-7/8 x 5 in.

DURER, ALBRECHT.

Cabinet 10 Shelf 2 No. 14

Nuremberg Chronicle. Anthony Coburger, 1493. Has about 2000 wood engravings by Wolgemut and Plegdenwurff under whom Durer served his apprenticeship to wood engraving.

DURER, ALBRECHT

Cabinet 67 Shelf 2 No. 30

Of the just shaping of letters. Translated by R. T. Nichol from the Latin Text of the edition of 1535. New York, The Grolier Club, 1917.

Paper boards; 12½ x 8½ in. Warde 126.

DURER, ALBRECHT

Cabinet J Shelf 2 No. 18

Passion of our Lord Jesus Christ, pourtrayed by Albert Durer. Edited by Henry Cole, London, 1844.

Reprint of 37 engravings, a fourth impression from the original blocks of 1511

Leather, adaptation German binding of the period; 8 x 5½ in.

DURER, ALBRECHT

Cabinet I Shelf 1 No. 2

(Proportion, principles of correct) Underweisung der messung, mit dem zirckel und richtscheyt in linien eben und ganzen corporen, durch Albrecht Durer zusamen getzogē und zu nutz alle kunstlieb habenden mit gehorigen figuren in truck gebracht im jar, 1525. Nuremberg. Numerous geometric figures, alphabets...

Durer Imprint. First ed. rebound.

Half morocco; 10¾ x 8-5/8 x ¾ in.

DURER, ALBRECHT.

Cabinet G Shelf 4 No. 20

Records of a journey to Venice and the Low Countries, by A. Durer. Edited by Roger Fry. Printed by D.B. Updike at the Merrymount Press, Boston, 1913.

Boards, 9-3/4 x 6¼ ins., pp. 117.

DURER, ALBRECHT

Cabinet D Shelf 4 No. 38

Eyn Schön Nützlich Buchlin...der Kunst des Messens (perspectiva zu Latin genant.).

Colophon: Getruckt uund volnendet, zū Siemern uff dem huneszrucke; in verlegung Hieronimi Rodler...1531.

Boards, fol., 12-1/8 x 8 ins.; pp. not num., sig. A-h.

Brunet 2-913.

DURER, ALBRECHT.

Cabinet D Shelf 4 No. 38

See Early Printing in Germany. Siemeren. [Hundsrück] 1531. Hieronymi Rodler.

DURER, ALBRECHT.

Cabinet 20 Shelf 2 No. 10

See Wood Engraving, Early. Weiteres zu Hans Sachsischen Einzeldrucken mit Holzschnitten bestimmter Meister.

DURER, ALBRECHT

Cabinet Shelf No.

See also
ENGRAVING: Durer, Albrecht.
also BIOGRAPHIES, Engravers.
" Designs.
" EARLY PRINTING IN GERMANY
" WOOD ENGRAVING, Early.

DURER, ALBRECHT (Widow)

Cabinet I Shelf 1 No. 3

Nuremberg, 1532, Imprint.

See IMPRINTS, Germany. Durer, Albrecht (Widow)...

DURER, HANS

Cabinet 5 Shelf No. 23

Facsimile reprints of some of the Durer woodcuts, 1490-1538.

Facs. in Cabinet 5, portfolio 23

DUROUCHAIL, P.

Cabinet Z Shelf 3 No. 43

[Circular letter to printers informing them that Laurent et Deberny have acquired the ornaments and stereotypes engraved by P. Durouchail]. J'ai l'honneur de vous informer que je viens de céder a Messieurs Laurent et Deberny mon fonds d'ornamens typographiques.

p. 379 in Miscellaneous collection of French type and cut specimens ... 1829-1844.

DUROUCHAIL, P.

Cabinet Z Shelf 3 No. 43

See Specimen Books, Types. France.

DURRIEU (COMTE PAUL)

Cabinet I Shelf 5 No. 3

(La) Miniature flamande au temps de la cour de Bourgogne, 1415-1530...Accompagne de 153 reproductions de miniatures. Bruxelles et Paris, 1921.

Half morocco; 14 x 10½ x 1 3/4 in.

DURSTINE, ROY S.

Cabinet LL Shelf 4 No. 28

Making advertisements, and making them pay New York, 1920.

Boards, linen back; 8½ x 5½ x 1-1/8 in.

DURSTINE, ROY S.

Cabinet LL Shelf 4 No. 29

This advertising business. By Roy S. Durstine, New York, 1928.

Instructive and practical articles reprinted from "The Nations Business", "Printer's Ink",etc.

Boards; 8 x 5½ x 1 in.

DUSCHNES, PHILIP C.

Cabinet Shelf No.

Walpole Printing Office, New Rochelle. Imprint.

See IMPRINTS, United States. Walpole Printing Office (Philip C. Duschnes...

DUST JACKETS ON BOOKS see

Cabinet Shelf No.

BOOK JACKETS.

DUTCH

Cabinet II Shelf 3 No. 63 Box

New Testament.

See BRITISH AND FOREIGN BIBLE SOCIETY. Dutch New Testament...1914.

DUTTON AND WENTWORTH

Cabinet 80 Shelf 2 No. 38

Boston, 1828, imprint and advertisement of the "Printing Office" of Dutton & Wentworth.

See Magazines, United States. Bower of Taste, The...Printed and published by Dutton & Wentworth.

DUYCKINCK, EVERT A.

Cabinet J Shelf 2 No. 4

Early American wood engravings by Dr. Alexander Anderson and others. With an introductory preface by Evert A. Duyckinck. New York, 1877.

Impressions from a series of wood blocks engraved for tracts and juvenile books.

Half morocco; 8 x 5-3/8 x ½ in.

DUTHILLOEUL, H.R.

Cabinet V Shelf 1 No. 76

Bibliographie Douaisienne, ou catalogue historique et raisonné des livres imprimes a Douai, depuis l'année 1563 jusqu'a nos jours Par H.R. Duthilloeul. Douai: 1842.

Contains biographical notices of the printers who exercised their art in Douai since the discovery of printing.

Paper boards; 9¾ x 6½ x 1½ in.

DUTUIT, EUGÈNE

Cabinet B Shelf 3 No. 6

Collection Dutuit. Livres et manuscrits. Paris, 1899. [illus., facs.]
Imprime par L. Danel de Lille, 1899.

Boards; 18-3/8 x 12¼ x 1-7/8 in.

DWELLY, EDWARD

Cabinet U Shelf 1 No. 120

Souvenirs and history of E. Dwelly's (E. MacDonald & Co.'s) self-made Gaelic Dictionary. The Gaelic Press, Herne Bay, England. Collated and bound by the Typographic Library and Museum, Jersey City, June, 1911.

Mr. Dwelly spent about twenty years on an illustrated Gaelic Lexicon, for which he set the type, engraved the blocks, stereotyped the forms, and did the printing.

Cloth; 10-1/8 x 7-7/8 x 1 in.

DUTREIX et CIE.

Cabinet Shelf No.

See Specimen Books, Types, France.

DUVAL, LOUIS

Cabinet V Shelf 1 No. 7

L'Imprimerie et la librairie a Alencon et dans le diocese de Sées. Par Louis Duval, Alencon, 1900.

Bio-bibliographical historical account.

Half morocco; 11-5/8 x 8¼ x ½ in.

DWIGGINS, W. A.

Cabinet G Shelf 1 No. 3

Caslon Flowers: An appreciation. Paper read before The Society of Printers, Boston. The Advertisers Paper Mills, New York, 1913.

Boards; 10¼ x 7 in.

DUTTON, A.

Cabinet X Shelf 4 No. 69

Letter to such of the servants of Christ who may scruple about the lawfulness of printing anything written by a woman...By A.D. London: Printed by J. Hart, 1743.

Half morocco; 7¼ x 4¼ in.

DUVAL-ARNOULD, L.

Cabinet W Shelf 5 No. 45

Dolet, Estienne. Etude historique. Editions d des "Questions Actuelles." Paris [1875]. Pamphlet.

Bound in with Asse-Estienne Dolet. [France, 1863].

Boards; 13¼ x 10½ in.

DWIGGINS, W.A.

Cabinet G Shelf 4 No. 28

Complete Angler (The) by Isaak Walton. Decorations by W.A. Dwiggins. Printed by D.B. Updike. The Merrymount Press, Boston, in the month of April, 1928.

Decorated boards; 7 x 4¾ x 1¼ in.

DUTTON, E. P. & CO.

Cabinet Q Shelf 3 No. 7

Seventy-five years, or the joys and sorrows of publishing and selling books at Duttons from 1852 to 1927. Compiled from a variety of original sources, and lavishly illustrated... Printed in Brooklyn on Long Island for Duttons, and for sale in their store across the way from St. Thomas's in New York. (1927)

Half morocco; 7½ x 4½ x 3/8 in.

DuVERDIER, ANTOINE.

Cabinet 69 Shelf 1 No. 40

Prosopographie (La) ou description des personnes insignes, enrichie de plusieurs effigies. A Lyon, par Antoine Gryphe, 1573.

Portraits here include that of Gutenberg, Seb. Gryphius (the father of Antoine), Dolet, Durer etc., with accompanying descriptive text.

Calf; 9¼ x 6-7/8 x 2 in.

DWIGGINS, W. A.

Cabinet G Shelf 4 No. 28.01

Electra, a new type face designed by W.A.D., for the Mergenthaler Linotype Co., Brooklyn, N.Y. 1935.

Pamphlet. In envelope.

DUTTON, MEIRIC K.

Cabinet FP Shelf 4 No. 40

Historical sketch of bookbinding as an art. Norwood (Mass.) The Holliston Mills, Inc. 1926.

Cloth; 8¾ x 5-7/8 x ¾ in.

DUVERGER, E.

Cabinet V Shelf 6 No. 3

Histoire de l'invention de l'imprimerie par les monuments. Album typographique exécuté a l'occasion du Jubilé Européen de l'invention de l'imprimerie. Paris, 1840. Facsimiles, representations of early typefounding apparatus, portraits of Gutenberg, and engraving of a type-mould made by Garamond.

Boards; 13½ x 10½ in.

DWIGGINS, W.A.

Cabinet G Shelf 4 No. 28.01

Emblems, a bakers' dozen. Drawings by W.A. Dwiggins...and Electra: A new Linotype face from the hand of the said W.A.D. Mergenthaler Linotype Company, Brooklyn, N.Y., 1935.

Pamphlet. in envelope.

DWIGGINS, W. A.

Cabinet S Shelf 4 No. 28

Extracts from an investigation into the physical properties of books as they are at present published. Undertaken by the Society of Calligraphers. Published by W. A. Dwiggins. Boston, 1914.

Half morocco; 8¾ x 6 in.

DWIGGINS, W.A.

Cabinet Shelf No.

See also Title Pages.

DZIATZKO, KARL

Cabinet Y Shelf 1 No. 25

Gutenbergs fruheste druckpraxis. Auf grund einer mit holfer der herren Dr. Phil. W. Bahrdt,; Dr. Phil. Karl Meyer und Cand. Phil. J. Schnorrenberg ausgefuhrten vergleichung der 42 zeiligen und 36 zeiligen Bibel. Dargestell von Karl Dziatzko. Berlin, 1890.

Boards; morocco back, 9-3/4 x 6¼ in.

DWIGGINS, W.A.

Cabinet G Shelf 3 No. 52

Form letters: Illustrator to author...an assortment of opinions about the proper function of illustration, and the relation between pictures and text. New York, William Edwin Rudge, 1930.

Half cloth; 9-5/8 c 6½ x ½ in.

DWIGGINS, W.A. (Herman Püterschein)

Cabinet L Shelf 5 No. 34

Society of Calligraphers, 7th May, 1925, voted to admit Henry Lewis Bullen as an honorary member. Broadside. Signed Herman Püterschein, President; W.A. Dwiggins, Secretary.

Portfolio; 18-3/4 x 12¼ in.

DZIATZKO, Dr.

Cabinet U Shelf 5 No. 38

Treatise on the 42-line Bible [Bibliographical notes on the]

see

PROCTOR, ROBERT. Bibliographical essays...London, 1905, pp.45, 49, 42

DWIGGINS, WILL

Cabinet Shelf No.

See Imprints, United States, Goudy, Fred and Bertha...."Rabbi Ben Ezra," illustrations by Dwiggins.

DWIGGINS, W. A.

Cabinet K Shelf 4 No. 45

Towards a reform of the paper currency, particularly in point of true design. A text and specimens furnished by W. A. Dwiggins, published for 452 subscribers by The Limited Editions Club, New York, 1932.

Signed copy. No. 378 of an edition of 452 copies.

Boards; 10½ x 7½ x ½ in.

DZIATSKO, KARL

Cabinet S Shelf 4 No. 68.01

Johann Gutenberg and the invention of printing. Translated from the German by E.F. Kunz. July, 1903. Excerpt from the "Literary Collector".

Portrait of J.G. from a woodcut by an unknown master of the 16th cent.

In box marked "Pamphlets and excerpts relating to Gutenberg".

DWIGGINS, W.A.

Cabinet A Shelf 2 No. 91

New kind of printing calls for new design. Old standards of excellence suddenly superceded because of the complex of new processes in the industry -- Still the opportunity for blending common sense with artistic taste.

Article in the Graphic Arts Section of the Boston Evening Transcript, Aug. 29, 1922, part three, p.6.

DWIGHT, HENRY OTIS

Cabinet Q Shelf 3 No. 8

Centennial history of the American Bible Society. By Henry Otis Dwight. New York, 1916. Illus.

Cloth; 7¾ x 5⅛ in.

DWIGGINS, W. A.

Cabinet P Shelf 4 No. 16

Notes on the structure of a book. Foreword to "Fifty Books of the Year exhibited by the Institute" (A.I.G.A.), 1926. New York.

Boards, cloth back; 12½ x 9½ in.

DYING, CRAFT OF

Cabinet QQ Shelf 3 No. 46

Book of the craft of dying.

see

COMPER, FRANCES M. M. Book of the craft of dying...

DWIGGINS, W. A.

Cabinet G Shelf 1 No. 56.03

Printer marks (2) designed by Dwiggins for the Cygnet Press, Cambridge, Massachusetts. 1929.

Small prospectus in manila envelope.

DYOTYPE AUTOMATIC COMPOSER (see)

Cabinet FF Shelf 6 No. 18

COMPOSING MACHINES.- Single Types. Dyotype...

E

"EAGLE", Brooklyn

Cabinet
Shelf
No.

See BROOKLYN EAGLE

EAMES, WILBERFORCE

Cabinet S, Shelf 3, No. 104

(A) Bio-bibliographical narrative: Works and contributions. By Victor Hugo Paltsits, New York Public Library.
P. 23 in volume Wilberforce Eames ... Bibliographical essays: A tribute to ... Cambridge, 1924.

Cloth; 9½ x 6-3/8 in.

EAMES, WILBERFORCE

Cabinet R, Shelf 5, No. 132

Preface to facsimile reprint of the Bay Psalm Book, the first edition printed in English America, at Cambridge, Mass., by Stephen Daye, 1640.

Boards; 8 x 5½ in.

EAMES, WILBERFORCE

Cabinet S, Shelf 3, No. 104

Bibliographical essays: A tribute to Wilberforce Eames. Cambridge, 1924. Portraits and facsimiles.

Contains 31 essays of great interest. Includes: The first work with American types. (L.C. Wroth). -- Elizabethan Americana. (G.W. Cole). -- Mills Days proposed Hebrew Bible. (O. Wegelin). --16th Century Mexican imprints. (H.R. Wagner). -- Ann Franklin, Printer. (H.M. Chapin). -- Etc.

Cloth; 9½ x 6 3/8 in.

EAMES, WILBERFORCE

Cabinet R, Shelf 5, No. 121

Early New England Catechisms: A bibliographical account of some Catechisms published before the year 1800, for use in New England.
Read before The American Antiquarian Society Worcester, Oct. 21, 1897, by Wilberforce Eames.

Half morocco; 9-3/8 x 6¼ in.

EAMES, WILBERFORCE

Cabinet R, Shelf 3, No. 187

Press in Western New York, The history of the. By Frederick Follett. Reprint with preface by Wilberforce Eames. No. 34 of Heartman's Historical Series, New York, 1920. Facsimile.

Half morocco; 9¼ x 6¼ in.

EAMES, WILBERFORCE.

Cabinet 75, Shelf 2, No. 7

Bibliographical Essays: A tribute to Wilberforce Eames. Harvard University Press, 1924.
Book with same title reviewed by Alfred W. Pollard.

In Transactions of the Bibliographical Society, "The Library," Vol. VII, 1926-1927, pp. 103-11.

EAMES, WILBERFORCE

Cabinet R, Shelf 4, No. 91

(The) First year of printing in New York, May, 1693 to April, 1694. By Wilberforce Eames, LL. D. ... New York, 1928.
Autorgraphed by the author for "My friend Mr. Henry L. Bullen", March 4, 1928.

Half morocco; 10¼ x 7¼ in.

EAMES, WILBERFORCE

Cabinet K, Shelf 6, No. 34

Wood engraving (1505) illustrating the South American Indians, description of the. Excerpt from the Bulletin of the New York Public Library. Sept. 1923.

Bound in volume "Wood Engraving: Various excerpts," item 12.

EAMES, WILBERFORCE.

Cabinet S, Shelf 6, No. 3

Bio-bibliographical narrative. By Victor Hugo Paltsits. Reprinted from Bibliographical Essays. A tribute to Wilberforce Eames. Cambridge, 1925. Brochure.

In box labelled "Excerpts and brochures relating to printing and printers in America.

EAMES, WILBERFORCE

Cabinet Q, Shelf 1, No. 8

List of catalogues, etc., published for the English booktrade from 1595 to 1902.
With Growoll, A. Three centuries of English booktrade bibliography. New York, 1903. Illus.

Half morocco; 9¾ x 6¼ x 1 in.

EAMES, WILBERFORCE.

Cabinet S, Shelf 5, No. 12

See also
Printing Early: Bradford, William

EARHART, JOHN F.

Cabinet L Shelf 4 No. 39

Color Plan, The Earhart. Color plan with demonstration case. By J. F. Earhart. Fernbank, Cincinnati, O.

Set presented to Henry L. Bullen, April 16, 1925, with the authors compliments.

In folded paper case; 7-3/8 x $12\frac{1}{4}$ in.

EARHART, JOHN F.

Cabinet L Shelf 4 No. 37

Color printer, the. A treatise on the use of colors in typographical printing. By John F. Earhart. Cincinnati, Ohio. 1892.

Frontispiece portrait of the author. In envelope at back of book, pictorial section of Cincinnati Commercial Tribune, Sunday, Nov. 27, 1921, showing some of the paintings by J. F. Earheart, also his portrait.

Cloth; 11 x $8\frac{1}{4}$ x 1-3/8 in.

EARHART, JOHN F.

Cabinet L Shelf 4 No. 38

Harmonizer, The. By John F. Earhart, Cincinnati, Ohio. Earhart & Richardson, 1897.

Cloth: 7-3/8 x 4-7/8 x 7/8 in.

EARHART AND RICHARDSON

Cabinet 21 Shelf 2 No. 15 and following

(The) Superior Printer

See PERIODICALS, PRINTING. United States (The) Superior Printer.

EARLY PRINTERS IN ENGLAND

Cabinet T Shelf 2 No. 8

Catalogue of English Printers from the year 1471 to 1600, most of them at London. A revised and corrected list on four pages. Published by Joseph Ames in Wappin, England. n.d.

This appears to have been a List prepared by Joseph Ames prior to his publication of his Typographical Antiquities which was issued in 1749.

Item in ~~max~~ manila envelope.

EARLY PRINTING IN AFRICA (Example)

Cabinet A Shelf 3 No. 13

Liberia (Monrovia), 1820.

See Newspapers, Liberia (Africa). Liberia Herald.

EARLY PRINTING IN AUSTRIA

Cabinet D Shelf 3 No. 8

Ölmutz, 1502. Conrad Baumgarten.

Title: Sancte Romane ecclesie fidei defensionis clippeum adversus wasdensium weu pickardorum heresim. Heinricū Institoris. [Wood cuts]
Colophon: Opus perutile in defensio sancte Roma.. per magistrum Conradum Baumgarthē impressus finit....anno...MCCCCCII.XX.die Marcii [Printer Mark]

Modern binding: 12 x 8-3/4 x 3/4 in.

EARLY PRINTING IN AUSTRIA

Cabinet E Shelf 5 No.

Vienna, 1766-1790. Johann Thomas Trattner.
Title: Lambecius, Petrus: Commentariorum de augustissima bibliotheca caesarea vindobonensi...Edita altera, opera et studio Adami Francisci Kollarii (9 vols. illus.)
Imprints: Typis et sumpt. Joan. Thomae nob. de. Trattnern. Caes. Reg. Aul. Typogr. et bibliopol.

Calf; 15 x $9\frac{1}{2}$ x in. Each vol.

EARLY PRINTING IN BELGIUM.

Cabinet D Shelf 4 No. 27

Antwerp, 1525. Christopher Eynhoven. Provinciale Constitutiones. William Lynwood [Oxford, England]
Colophon: Explicit opus Wilhelmi Lin-/dewode super constitutiones pro-/vinciales Anglie... Chri/stophori Endovien. Antwerpie impressum.. Impensis vero Francisei Brickman/honesti mercatoris Anno salutis nostre millesimo quingentesimo vicesimo quinto dicesimo quinto XX die Decembris.

cont'd

EARLY PRINTING IN BELGIUM cont'd

Cabinet D Shelf 4 No. 27

Vellum covers; 11 x $8\frac{1}{4}$ x $1\frac{1}{2}$ in.

EARLY PRINTING IN BELGIUM.

Cabinet 2 Shelf 1 No. 1

Antwerp, 1555. Plantin-Moretus Press: Christopher Plantin.
Title: La institutione de una fanciulla nata nobilmente...Traduite de langue Tuscane en Francois. En Anvers. Chez Iehan Bellère a l'enseigne du Faucon.
Colophon: De l'Imprimerie de Chr. Plantain, 1555.

This is the first book printed by Christopher Plantin. Note how he spells his surname.
Vellum; $5\frac{1}{2}$ x 3 x $\frac{1}{2}$ in. Modern case, marbled boards

EARLY PRINTING IN BELGIUM

Cabinet 6 Shelf 2 No. 1 to 8

Antwerp, 1569-72. Christopher Plantin.

Title: Biblia Sacra. Hebraice, Chaldaice, Graece, & Latine; cura et studio Benedicti Ariae Montani. 8 vols. the last volume being the lexicon.
Imprint: Christoph Plantinus excud. Antverpiae.

Gilt morocco; 16-3/4 x $11\frac{1}{2}$ in. Brunet 1, 851.

EARLY PRINTING IN BELGIUM

Cabinet L Shelf 5 No. 1

Antwerp, 1569, Christopher Plantin.
Title: Esercitatio alphabetica nova et utitissima... edita, Clementi Perreti Bruxellani.
34 plates with examples of writing and ornaments engraved on copper by Corn. de Hooghe.
Imprint lacking but see Brunet 4-511; also Funck "Le livre Belge en graveur",p.378

Parchment; 10 x $12\frac{1}{4}$ in. In protective case.

EARLY PRINTING IN BELGIUM.

Cabinet 2 Shelf 2 No. 7

Antwerp, 1575. Plantin-Moretus Press: Christopher Plantin.
Title: P. Virgilius Maro, et in eum Commentationes & Paralopomena Germani Valentis Guellii, PP. Eiusdem Virgilii Appendix, cum Josephi Scaligeri commentariis & castigationibus, Printer Mark.
Imprint: Ex Officina Christophori Plantini, Architypographi Regii, M.D.LXXV.

Paper boards; leather back; $13\frac{1}{2}$ x $9\frac{1}{2}$ x 2 in.

EARLY PRINTING IN BELGIUM

Cabinet 2 Shelf 1 No. 5

Antwerp, 1581. Plantin-Moretus Press: Christopher Plantin.
Title: Omnia Andreae Alciati v.c. emblemata, cum commentariis....per Claudium Minoem. Editio tertio. Ex Officina Christophori Plantini... M.D.LXXXI.
Colophon: Antverpiae: excudebat Christophorus Plantinus, Architypographus regius, sub finem anni M.D.LXXXI.

Embossed vellum over board; 6-3/4 x $4\frac{1}{2}$ x 1-7/8 in.

EARLY PRINTING IN BELGIUM

Cabinet 2 Shelf 2 No. 13

Antwerp, 1582. Plantin-Moretus Press: Christopher Plantin.
Title: Hugonis Donelli, jurisconsulti commentarii ...
Imprint: Ex officina Christophori Plantini. M.D.LXXXII.

Vellum; $13\frac{3}{4}$ x 9 x $1\frac{1}{2}$ in.

EARLY PRINTING IN BELGIUM

Cabinet 2 Shelf 1 No. 11

Antwerp, 1585. Christopher Plantin
Title: I. Lipsi Saturnalium sermonum libri duo, qui de Gladiatoribus. Noviter correcti ...
Imprint: Antverpiae, apud Christophorum Plantinum. 1585.

Tree calf; $8\frac{1}{4}$ x $5\frac{3}{4}$ x $\frac{1}{2}$ in.

EARLY PRINTING IN BELGIUM

Cabinet 2 Shelf 1 No. 16

Antwerp, 1590. Plantin-Moretus Press: Widow Balthasar (I) Moretus, and John (III) Moretus.
Title: Vitae sanctorum ... per R.D. Franciscum Haraeum.
Imprint: Ex Officina Plantiniana apud viduam & Ioannem Moretum. M.D.XC.
Colophon: Antverpiae: in Officina Plantiniana, ultima Iulii, Anno M.D.XC.

Vellum; 7 x $4\frac{1}{2}$ x 2 in.

EARLY PRINTING IN BELGIUM.

Cabinet 2 — Antwerp, 1595. Plantin-Moretus Press: Widow Christopher Plantin & son-in-law John (I) Moretus.
Shelf 2 — Title: Descriptio publicae gratulationis spectaculorum et ludorum in adventu Sereniss. Principis Ernesti Archiducis Austriae.....
No. 22 — Omnia a Ioanne Bochio...conscripta. Antwerp. Ex officina Plantiniana M.D.XCV.

cont'd

EARLY PRINTING IN BELGIUM. cont'd

Cabinet 2 — Colophon: Ex officina Plantiniana apud viduam et Ioannem Moretum. M.D.XCV.
Shelf 2 — Leather; 15 x 9-3/4 x 7/8 in.
No. 22

EARLY PRINTING IN BELGIUM

Cabinet 2 — Antwerp, 1599. Plantin- Moretus Press: John (1) Moretus.
Title: Iusti Lipsi Poliorceton sive de machinis
Shelf 1 — Tormentis telis. Libri quinque.
Imprint: Antverpiae, ex officina Plantiniana, apud Ioannem Moretum. M. D. XCIX.
No. 22

Vellum over boards; 9¼ x 6 3/4 x 1 in.

EARLY PRINTING IN BELGIUM.

Cabinet 2 — Antwerp, 1599. Plantin-Moretus Press: John (I) Moretus.
Title: Iusti Lipsi Poliorceticon, sive, de ma-
Shelf 1 — chinis tormentis. Telis. Illus. Printer Mark.
Imprint: Ex Officina Plantiniana, apud Ioannem Moretum. M.D.XCIX.
No. 22

Vellum; 9¼ x 6½ x 1¼ in.

EARLY PRINTING IN BELGIUM

Cabinet 2 — Antwerp, 1602. Plantin-Moretus Press: John (I) Moretus.
Title: Iuste Lipsi: De bibliothecis, syntagma.
Shelf 1 — Printer Mark.
Imprint: Ex Officina Plantiniana, apud Ioannem Moretum. MDCII.
No. 25 — Paper boards; 10¼ x 7½ x ¼ in.

EARLY PRINTING IN BELGIUM.

Cabinet 2 — Antwerp, 1613. Plantin-Moretus Press: Widow and sons of John (III) Moretus.
Shelf 1 — Title: Notitia Episcopatuum orbis Christiani.... Libri V. Aubertus Miraeus, Bruxellensis. Printer Mark.
No. 28 — Imprint: Antverpiae, ex Officina Plantiniana, apud Viduam & Filios Io. Moreti. M.DC.XIII.

Calf; 6-3/4 x 4-1/8 x 1¼ in.

EARLY PRINTING IN BELGIUM.

Cabinet 2 — Antwerp, 1617. Plantin-Moretus Press: Balthasar (I) & John (II) Moretus.
Title: De prima scribendi origine et universa
Shelf 1 — rei literariae antiquitate....Hermannus Hugo.
Imprint: Antverpiae: Ex Officina Plantiniana,
No. 30 — apud Balthasarem & Ioannem Moretos. M.DC.XVII.

Tooled morocco; 7¼ x 4-3/4 x 1-1/8 in.

EARLY PRINTING IN BELGIUM.

Cabinet 2 — Antwerp, 1617. Plantin-Moretus Press: Balthasar and John Moretus.
Shelf 1 — Title: Thomae a Kempis....De imitatione Christi. Libri Quatuor....
Imprint; Antverpiae: Ex officina Plantiniana,
No. 31 — apud Balthasarem & Ioannem Moretos. M.DC.XVII.

Vellum; 5-7/8 x 3¼ x 1-3/4 in.

EARLY PRINTING IN BELGIUM.

Cabinet 2 — Antwerp, 1619. Plantin-Moretus Press: Balthasar Moretus, and widow of John Moretus and John Meurs.
Shelf 1 — Title: Heriberti Ros-Weydi e Societate Iesu. Anti-Capellus sive Explosio Naeniarum Iaacobi Capelli....
No. 34 — Imprint: Ex Officina Plantiniana apud Balthasarem Moretum & Viduam Ioannis Moreti & Io Meursium. M.DC.XIX.

Vellum; 7¼ x 4-3/4 x 1½ in.

EARLY PRINTING IN BELGIUM.

Cabinet 2 — Antwerp, 1627 and 1630. Plantin-Moretus Press: Balthasar (I) Moretus, widow John (III) Moretus, and John Meurs.
Shelf 1 — Title: Missale Romanum....Pii V. Pont. Max. issu editum, et Clementis VIII.....Ex Officina Plantiniana, apud Balthasarem et Io. Meursium,
No. 39 — M.DC.XXVII.
Colophon: Antverpiae, ex Officina Plantiniana: Balthasaris Moreti, M.DC.XXX.
Second title: "Graduale" is dated 1627.

Leather; 7½ x 5½ x 2-3/8 in.

EARLY PRINTING IN BELGIUM

Cabinet 2 — Antwerp, 1629. Plantin-Moretus Press: Balthasar (II) Moretus.
Shelf 1 — Title: Sacrae Litaniae, variae cum brevi piaque quotidiana exercitatione...
Imprint: Ex officina Plantiniana, apud Balthas-
No. 41 — arem Moretum. M.DC.XXIX.

Contemporary vellum with clasps; 5-3/4 x 3-3/8 x 1¼ in.

EARLY PRINTING IN BELGIUM.

Cabinet 2 — Antwerp, 1632. Plantin-Moretus Press: Balthasar (II) Moretus.
Shelf 2 — Title: L. Annaei Senecae: Opera a Iusto Lipsio emendata et Scholiis illustrata....
Imprint: Ex officina Plantiniana: Balthasaris
No. 26 — Moreti M.DC.XXXII.

Vellum; 15-3/4 x 10½ x 2-3/4 in. Brunet 5, 276.

EARLY PRINTING IN BELGIUM

Cabinet 2 — Antwerp, 1634. Plantin-Moretus Press Balthasar (I) Moretus.
Title: Sacrum sanctuarium crucis et patientae,
Shelf 1 — cruciferorum emblematicis imaginibus laborantium et aegrotantium ornatum. Auctore R.P. Petro Bivero.
No. 46 — Imprint: Antverpiae, ex officina Plantiniana: Balthasaris Moreti. M.DC.XXXIV.
Many full page copper plate engravings and vignettes printed with the text.

Calf; 8-3/4 x 6½ x 2½ in. Brunet 1,955

EARLY PRINTING IN BELGIUM.

Cabinet 2 — Antwerp, 1634. Plantin-Moretus Press: Balthasar (II), Moretus.
Title: De Symbolis heroicis. Libri IX. Auctore,
Shelf 1 — Silvestro Petrasancta, Romano E. Soc. Iesu. Illus.
Imprint: Antverpiae, ex Officina Plantiniana
No. 45 — Balthasaris Moreti. M.DC.XXXIV.
Title page engraved by Galle after a design by Rubens.

Morocco; 8¼ x 6-3/8 x 1-5/8 in.

EARLY PRINTING IN BELGIUM.

Cabinet 2 — Antwerp, 1642. Plantin-Moretus Press: Balthasar (II) Moretus.
Shelf 2 — Title: Concordantia Bibliorum sacrorum....Emendate Francisco Luca....
Imprint: Ex officina Plantiniana: Balthasaris
No. 31 — Moreti, M.DC.XLII.

Leather; 14-3/4 x 9-3/4 x 2-3/4 in.

EARLY PRINTING IN BELGIUM.

Cabinet 2 — Antwerp, 1645. Plantin-Moretus Press: Balthasar (II) Moretus.
Title: Les marques d'honneur de la maison de
Shelf 2 — Tassis. [Par J. Chiflet]
Imprint: A Anvers, en l'Imprimerie Plantinienne de Balthasar Moretus, M.DC.XLV.
No. 35 — Title page a wood engraving designed by Nic. vander Horst, Michael Nataha, engraver.

Vellum over boards; 15-1/8 x 9-3/4 x 1¼ in.

EARLY PRINTING IN BELGIUM

Cabinet 2 — Antwerp, 1650. Plantin-Moretus Press: Balthasar Moretus.
Shelf 2 — Title: Chifletius, Joannes Jacobus. Alsatia, ivre propietatis et protectionis Philippo IV.
Imprint: Ex officina Plantiniana: Balthasaris
No. 37 — Moreti M.DC.L.

Bound with other items.

Calf; 12¼ x 8¼ x 7/8 in.

EARLY PRINTING IN BELGIUM

Cabinet 2 — Antwerp, 1650. Plantin-Moretus Press: Balthasar Moretus.
Title: Chifletius, Joannes Jacobus: Opera Politi-
Shelf 2 — co-Historica.....
Imprint: Antverpiae, ex officina Plantiniana: Balthasaris Moreti, M.DC.L.
No. 36

Bound with other items.
Calf; 12¼ x 8¼ x 7/8 in. Brunet 1, 1843.

EARLY PRINTING IN BELGIUM.

Cabinet 2 — Shelf 2 — No. 40

Antwerp, 1652. Plantin-Moretus Press: Balthasar (II) Moretus.

Title: Lipsius, Justus. Opera L. Annae Seneca.
Imprint: Ex officina Plantiniana: Balthasaris Moreti. M.DC.LII.

Vellum over board; 15½ x 10 x 3-1/8 in.
Brunet 5,276.

EARLY PRINTING IN BELGIUM

Cabinet 2 — Shelf 1 — No. 50

Antwerp, 1677. Ex Officina Plantiniana: Apud Viduam & Heredes Balth. Moreti.
Title: Officium B. Mariae Virg. Illus.
Signatures a to y, untrimmed and unbound.

In morocco case; 4 3/4 x 3½ x in.

EARLY PRINTING IN BELGIUM.

Cabinet 6 — Shelf 2 — No. 18

Plantin-Moretus Press, Antwerp. Box containing 6 items incompleted after printing.
(A) Officium B. Mariae Virg. 1677: complete set of sheets, as they left the press, not folded not trimmed; 64 pp. to sheet; imposed to cut in sheets of 16 pp; illus. with copperplate engravings; size of type pages, red and black 2-3/8 x 1-5/16 in. (very sloppy craftsmanship
(B) Offices propres a l'usage....de l'ordre de S. Ursule, 1705: complete set of sigs. crudely sewn (as if by learner), but untrimmed

cont'd

EARLY PRINTING IN BELGIUM cont'd

Cabinet 6 — Shelf 2 — No. 18

size of type pages, black and red, 4-3/4 x 2-3/8 in; illus and a few initials on copper.
(C) Processionale juxta usum Fratrum B.V. Mariae, 1711: complete set of sheets after printing before binding; Fratrum B.V. Mariae, 1711: complete set of sheets after printing, before binding; 16 pp. on sheet; illus. and initials on copper; music notation and text in black and red; size of type page 6¼ x 3-5/8 in.

cont'd

EARLY PRINTING IN BELGIUM cont'd

Cabinet 6 — Shelf 2 — No. 18

(D) Officium Beatae Mariae Virginis, 1835; complete set folded sigs, not trimmed nor sewn; copper illus. black and red; size of pp.4 x 2 in.
(E) Horae Diurnae...S. Francisci, 1866; complete set folded sigs. not trimmed nor sewn; in black and red; size of pp. 7¼ x 4 in.
(F) Preces ante et post Missam, 1817; complete set folded sigs, not trimmed nor sewn; in black and red; size of pp. 5½ x 3 in.

EARLY PRINTING IN BELGIUM.

Cabinet 2 — Shelf 1 — No. 52

Antwerp, 1680. Plantin-Moretus Press: Widow Balthasar (III) Moretus and sons.
Title: Decreta et statuta tam in synodis provincialibus archiepiscopatus Mechliniensis, quam in synodis episcopatus Antverpiensis... Printer Mark.
Imprint: Ex officina Plantiniana, apud Viduam & Heredes Balthasaris Moreti M.DC.LXXX.

Leather; 6-3/4 x 4½ x 1-5/8 in.

EARLY PRINTING IN BELGIUM.

Cabinet 2 — Shelf 1 — No. 55

Antwerp, 1683. Plantin-Moretus Press: Balthasar (III) Moretus.
Title: Psalterium Davidis cum canticis sacris & selectis aliquot oriationibus...Printer Mark on last page.
Imprint: Ex Officina Plantiniana, Balthasaris Moreti. M.DC.LXXXIII.

Old morocco with clasps; 6¼ x 3-3/4 x 1½ in.

EARLY PRINTING IN BELGIUM.

Cabinet 2 — Shelf 1 — No. 60

Antwerp, 1712. Plantin-Moretus Press: Balthasar (III) Moretus.
Title: Officia propria sanctorom ecclesiae cathedrales et diocesios Antverpiensis, redacta ad formam Breviarii Romani Clementis VIII & Urbani VIII.
Imprint: Ex Typographia Plantiniana, M.DCC.XII.

Calf; 6½ x 4 x ¾ in.

EARLY PRINTING IN BELGIUM.

Cabinet 2 — Shelf 1 — No. 65

Antwerp, 1746. Plantin-Moretus Press:
Title: Martyrologium Romanum.....
Imprint: Ex Architypographia Plantiniana. MDCCXLVI.

Calf; 8-3/4 x 5-3/4 x 1½ in.

EARLY PRINTING IN BELGIUM

Cabinet 2 — Shelf 1 — No. 69

Antwerp, 1760. Plantin-Moretus Press. John Jacob Moretus Youngest brother of Balthasar (IV).
Title: Officium in festo et per octavam pentecostes.....
Imprint: Antverpiae, ex Architypographia Plantiniana. M.DCC.LX.

Leather; 6-3/8 x 3-3/4 x 3/4 in.

EARLY PRINTING IN BELGIUM

Cabinet 2 — Shelf 2 — No. 46

Antwerp, 1779. Plantin-Moretus Press. Widow Balthasar (VII) Moretus.
Title: Canones et decreta sacrosancti oecumenici et generalis concilii tridentini sub. Paulo III, Iulo III, Pio III, Pontificus Max.
Imprint: Antverpiae, ex architypographia Plantiniana. M.D.CC.LXXIX.

Calf; 11½ x 9-3/4 x 2 in.

EARLY PRINTING IN BELGIUM

Cabinet E — Shelf 1 — No. 67

Brussels, c. 1510. Thomas van der Noot.
Title: Het eerste Nederlandsche gedrukte kookboek (Brussel, Thomas van der Noot, c. 1510) Facsimile uitgave naar het eenig bekende exemplaar in de Bayerische Staatsbibliothek, München. 's-Gravenhage, Martinus Nijhoff, 1925.
[Facsimile. The first cook book printed in the Netherlands.]

Paper; 9 x 5¾ in.

EARLY PRINTING IN BELGIUM

Cabinet X — Shelf 4 — No. 6

Bruxelles, 1570: Michel de Hamont.
Title: Ordonnance, statut et edict...
Imprint: Imprimé en la ville de Bruxelles, par Michiel de Hamont, imprimeur juré...

Half morocco; 7-1/8 x 5 in.

EARLY PRINTING IN BOHEMIA

Cabinet E — Shelf 3 — No. 34

Prague, 1627. [Printer Unknown]

See Halevi, Isaac ben Samuel. Siah Yizhak, Prague.

EARLY PRINTING IN BOHEMIA

Cabinet D — Shelf 4 — No. 24

Vilemov, 1521, Monastery of the Bohemian Brotherhood.

See Chelcicky, Pierre. "Filet de la Foi"...

EARLY PRINTING IN ENGLAND. Example

Cabinet A — Shelf 3 — No. 1

Bath, 1756, Thomas Boddely, (his Imprint)

See Newspapers, England. Bath Journal (The)...1756.

EARLY PRINTING IN ENGLAND

Cabinet 30 — Shelf 1 — No. 1

Birmingham, 1758: John Baskerville.
Title: Paradise lost...Paradise regained. By John Milton. [2 vols.].
Imprint: Printed by John Baskerville for J. and R. Tonson in London. 1758.

Half calf; 9 x 6 in. each vol.

EARLY PRINTING IN ENGLAND

Cabinet 30 — Shelf 1 — No. 3

Birmingham, 1761: John Baskerville.
Title: D. Junii Juvenalis et auli Persii Flacci satyrae.
Imprint: Birminghamiae: Typis Johannis Baskerville.

Full morocco; gilt; 12 x 9-5/8 x 1 in.

EARLY PRINTING IN ENGLAND

Cabinet 30 Shelf 1 No. 4

Birmingham, 1766. John Baskerville.
Title: The works of Virgil Englished by Robert Andrews.
Imprint: Birmingham, printed by John Baskerville for the author.

Morocco; $9\frac{3}{4}$ x 6-1/8 x $1\frac{1}{2}$ in.

EARLY PRINTING IN ENGLAND cont'd

Cabinet F Shelf 4 No.

Half morocco; 8 x 4-7/8 in.

EARLY PRINTING IN ENGLAND. Example of

Cabinet FF Shelf 4 No. 6

Kentish Town, 1827, Julian Hibbert.
Title: The Book of Orphic Hymns...
Imprint: Printed in uncial letters as a typographical experiment...1827 (Next page): Printed and Published by Julian Hibbert, No. I, Fitzroy Place, Kentish Town.

Half calf; 8-3/8 x $5\frac{1}{4}$ x 3/8 in.

EARLY PRINTING IN ENGLAND

Cabinet F Shelf 4 No. 25

Birmingham, 1767. Robert Martin [Successor to Baskerville].
Title: The Chase, a Poem. By William Somerville.
Imprint: Birmingham: Printed by Robert Martin, and sold by A. Donaldson at his shop, near Norfolk Street in the Strand, London. 1767.

Paper boards; 9 x $6\frac{1}{4}$ x $\frac{3}{4}$ in.

EARLY PRINTING IN ENGLAND

Cabinet QQ Shelf 3 No. 20

Horsham, 1836, Howard Dudley.

see

DUDLEY, HOWARD. History and antiquities of Horsham...

EARLY PRINTING IN ENGLAND

Cabinet RR Shelf 2 No. 3

Lewes, 1809, J. Baxter (His imprint)

See PAPER. Sister arts...Lewes, 1809.

EARLY PRINTING IN ENGLAND

Cabinet 30 Shelf 1 No. 5

Birmingham, 1772: John Baskerville.
Title: Catulli, Tibulli, et propertii opera.
Imprint: Birminghamiae: Typis Johannis Baskerville.

Tree calf; 7 x 4 x $\frac{3}{4}$ in.

EARLY PRINTING IN ENGLAND

Cabinet M Shelf 3 No. 10

Kent, near Canterbury, 1813: Lee Priory Press, Sir Egerton Brydges, proprietor, Johnson and Warwick, printers.
Title: The poems of Sir Walter Raleigh.
Imprint: Printed by John Warwick at the Private Press of Lee Priory.

Boards, leather back and corners; 12 x 9-1/8 x 1-1/8 in.

EARLY PRINTING IN ENGLAND

Cabinet M Shelf 3 No. 16

Liverpool, 1805. James McCreery.
Title: The life and pontificate of Leo the Tenth. In 4 volumes. By William Roscoe.
Imprint: Liverpool: Printed by J. McCreery; for T. Cadell and W. Davis, Strand. London, 1805.

Calf, tooled; $10\frac{3}{4}$ x $8\frac{1}{2}$ in. each vol.

EARLY PRINTING IN ENGLAND

Cabinet E Shelf 3 No. 78

Cambridge, 1644. Roger Daniel.
Title: Apxaionomia, sive de precis Anglorum Legibus libri. [The laws of the Brigish kings, years 712 to 1135. Preceding p.l, a map of England, engraved by William Hole].
Imprint: Cantabrigiae: Ex officina Rogeri Daniel celeberrimae Academiae Typographi, 1644.

Calf; 14 x $9\frac{1}{4}$ in.

EARLY PRINTING IN ENGLAND

Cabinet M Shelf 3 No. 11

Kent, near Canterbury, 1817. Lee Priory Press. Sir Egerton Brydges, proprietor, John Warwick printer.
Title: List of pictures at the seat of T.B. Brydges Barrett, Esq., at Lee Priory.
Imprint: Printed at the Private Press at Lee Priory, by John Warwick.

Half morocco; 9 x 6 in.

EARLY PRINTING IN ENGLAND

Cabinet T Shelf 2 No. 40

London [1491]. Caxton, William.
Title: A reprint in facsimile of a treatise spekynge of the art and craft to know well to dye. Translated oute of French in englysshe by William Caxton. London. Sold by the Assigns of Edward Lumley, deceased, 1875.

Boards; 12-7/8 x $9\frac{3}{4}$ x 1/8 in.

EARLY PRINTING IN ENGLAND

Cabinet E Shelf 2 No. 83

Doway, 1609-1610. Lawrence Kellam
Title: The Holy Bible. Faithfully translated into English out of the authentic Latin...By the English College of Doway. 2 vols.
Imprint: Printed at Doway by Lawrence Kellam at the signe of the holie Lamb.

Vellum; 8-7/8 x 7 in. each vol.

EARLY PRINTING IN ENGLAND

Cabinet M Shelf 3 No. 12

Kent, near Canterbury, 1820: Lee Priory Press. Sir Egerton, proprietor, John Warwick
Title: The engravings on wood at Lee Priory.
Imprint: Kent. Printed at the Private Press of Lee Priory. By John Warwick.

Boards; $10\frac{1}{4}$ x 8 in.

EARLY PRINTING IN ENGLAND

Cabinet D Shelf 1 No. 57

London, 1493-1527: Wynkyn de Worde.

See Incunabula. Wynkyn de Worde.

EARLY PRINTING IN ENGLAND

Cabinet F Shelf 4 No. 27

Gloucester, 1775. Robert Raikes.
Title: An humble address and earnest appeal to those...fittest to decide, whether a connection with, or a separation from the continental Colonies of America, be most for the National advantage of these Kingdoms. By Josiah Tucker.
Imprint: Gloucester: Printed by R. Raikes; and sold by T. Cadell, London, 1776. Price one shilling and sixpence.

cont'd

EARLY PRINTING IN ENGLAND

Cabinet M Shelf 3 No. 13

Kent, near Canterbury, 1821: Lee Priory Press
Title: Letters from the Continent. By Sir Egerton Brydges, Bart. (2 vols)
Imprint: Kent. Printed at the private press of Lee Priory, by John Warwick.

Boards; $9\frac{1}{4}$ x 5-7/8 in.

EARLY PRINTING IN ENGLAND

Cabinet D Shelf 4 No. 63

London, 1510, Richard Pynson.

(6 fols. from Richard III. Gothic type).

In box labeled "Early 16th century Printing. Loose leaves".

EARLY PRINTING IN ENGLAND

Cabinet M | Shelf 4 | No. 27

London, 1532-33, Wynkyn de Worde.

See FACSIMILES (The) Maner of the tryumphe of Caleys...

EARLY PRINTING IN ENGLAND

Cabinet D | Shelf 4 | No. 63

London, 1556, Richard Tottle.

(5 fols. from a work relating to monasticism in the reign of Henry 7th. Gothic type).

In box labeled "Early 16th century Printing. Original Leaves".

EARLY PRINTING IN ENGLAND

Cabinet E | Shelf 2 | No. 12

London, 1573. John Daye.
Title: Johannis Parkhursti ludicra sive eipgrammata Iuvenilia...Londini Apud Iohannem Dayum Typographum. An. 1573. Cum gratia & privilegio Regiae Maiestatis.

Leather over boards; 7½ x 5¼ x ½ in.

EARLY PRINTING IN ENGLAND

Cabinet E | Shelf 2 | No. 26

London, 1579. Hugh Singleton.
Title: The Sheapeardes Calender conteyning twelve Aeglogues...to the noble and vertuous... Philip Sidney. [Edmund Spenser]. At London: Printed by Hugh Singleton, dwelling in Creede Lane neere unto Ludgate at the signe of the gylden tunne and are there to be sold. [Facsimile].
Colophon: Imprinted at London by Hugh Singleton, dwelling in Creede lane at the sign of the

cont'd

EARLY PRINTING IN ENGLAND cont'd

Cabinet E | Shelf 2 | No. 26

gylden tunn neere unto Ludgate. [Printer Mark.]

Boards; 10¼ x 8 x ½ in.

EARLY PRINTING IN ENGLAND

Cabinet E | Shelf 2 | No. 58

London, 1600. Thomas Fisher.
Title: A midsommer nights dreame. As it hath beene sundry times publickely acted... written by William Shakespeare. [Facsimile].
Imprint: Imprinted London, for Thomas Fisher, and are to be soulde at his shoppe, at the signe of the White Hart, in Fleetstreete. 1600. [Printer Mark].

cont'd

EARLY PRINTING IN ENGLAND cont'd

Cabinet E | Shelf 3 | No. 53

Boards; 8¼ x 1-1/8 x ½ in.

See a dictionary of Printers and booksellers in England etc. Bibl. Soc. 1910, p. 105.

EARLY PRINTING IN ENGLAND

Cabinet E | Shelf 2 | No. 66

London, 1602. Adam Islip.
Title: A discourse upon the meanes of wel governing...a kingdome...against Nicolas Machiavell the Florentine. Translated into English by Simon Patericke. [Printer Mark].
Imprint: London, Printed by Adam Islip. 1602.

Boards; 11 x 7¼ x 1¼ in.

EARLY PRINTING IN ENGLAND

Cabinet E | Shelf 2 | No. 73

London, 1607. John Norton.
Title: A world of wonders...or a preparation treatise to the Apologie for Herodotus... written in Latine by Henry Stephen... translated out of the best corrected French copie. Printer Mark.
Imprint: London, Imprinted for John Norton, 1607.

Calf tooled; 11⅜ x 7-7/8 in.

EARLY PRINTING IN ENGLAND

Cabinet E | Shelf 3 | No. 7

London, 1616. Richard Field.
Title: A commentarie of M. Doctor Martin Luther upon the epistle of S. Paul to the Galatians ...
Imprint: London: Imprinted by Richard Field dwelling in Great Woodstreete. 1616 [Printer Mark].

Calf; 8 x 5½ x 1½ in.

EARLY PRINTING IN ENGLAND

Cabinet E | Shelf 3 | No. 22

London, 1623. William Jaggard.
Title: The Theater of Honor and Knighthood... containing...the First Institution of Armes, Emblazons, King's Heralds and Pursuivants of Armes...The order of the Holy Ghost, Order of the Star...Andrew Favine.
Imprint: London: Printed by William Jaggard, dwelling in Barbican, and are to be sold there. 1623.

Polished Calf; gold tooled, 12⅜ x 8¼ x 2½ in.

EARLY PRINTING IN ENGLAND

Cabinet E | Shelf 3 | No. 47

London, 1632. John Haviland.
Title: The Essayes of counsels, civill and morall of Francis Lo. Verulam, Viscount St. Alban. Newly enlarged.
Imprint: Printed by John Haviland, in the little old Bayley. 1632.

Original calf; 7½ x 5½ x 1-1/8 in.

EARLY PRINTING IN ENGLAND

Cabinet E | Shelf 3 | No. 52

London, 1633. Bernard Alsop and Thomas Fawcet.
Title: Saturni Ephemerides sive tabula historico-chronologice containing...as also a succession of kings and rulers over most kingdomes. ..of the worls...By Henry Isaacson, Londoner.
Colophon: Printed by Bernard Alsop, and Thomas Fawcet, for Henry Seile, and Humphrey Robinson, and are to be sold at their shops in St. Paules Church-Yard. M.DC.XXXIII. FINIS.

cont'd

EARLY PRINTING IN ENGLAND cont'd

Cabinet E | Shelf 3 | No. 52

Calf; 17¼ x 11 x 2¼ in.

EARLY PRINTING IN ENGLAND.

Cabinet X | Shelf 4 | No. 16

London, 1641, Robert Cotton.
Title: Express Commands (London, 1641) from both the Honourable Houses of Parliaments ...
Imprint: London, printed by Robert Cotton. Brochure.

In folder labelled "Documents Relating to Liberty of Printing, 1641-1647."

EARLY PRINTING IN ENGLAND.

Cabinet X | Shelf 4 | No. 16

London, 1642. Printed for John Wright.
See Liberty of Printing, Great Britain. Declaration (London, 1642).

EARLY PRINTING IN ENGLAND

Cabinet E | Shelf 4 | No. 7

London, 1651. Du Gardianis.
Title: Joannis Miltoni, Angli. Pro populo Anglicano defensio. Contra Claudii Anonymi, alias Salmasii, defensionem Regiam. Editio emendatior.
Imprint: Londini, Typis Du-Gardianis. Anno Domini 1651.

Calf; 13 x 9 x 1 in. Brunet, 3, 1731.

EARLY PRINTING IN ENGLAND Example

Cabinet 00 | Shelf 4 | No. 1

London, 1656-1657. Thomas Newcomb.

see MERCURIUS, POLITICUS. Comprising the sum of foreine intelligence...

EARLY PRINTING IN ENGLAND Example of.

Cabinet II
Shelf 3
No. 24

London, 1657, Tho. Maxey.
Title: The Universal Character...By Cave Beck. With engraved title.
Imprint: London, Printed by Tho. Maxey, for William Weekley, and are to be sold at his shop in Ipswich, 1657.

Calf; 6-5/8 x 4-1/8 x 3/4 in.

EARLY PRINTING IN ENGLAND, cont'd

Cabinet E
Shelf 4
No. 56

See pp. 3 and 4 for Marvell's famous ironical apostrophe to the printing art.
This copy was the property of Isaac Disraeli.

Calf; $5\frac{1}{2}$ x $3\frac{1}{4}$ x $\frac{1}{2}$ in.

EARLY PRINTING IN ENGLAND

Cabinet E
Shelf 4
No. 74

London, 1681. Andrew Sowle.
Title: A brief examination and state of Liberty Spiritual...Written for the establishment of the faithful...by a Lover of True Liberty, William Penn.
Imprint: London, Printed by Andrew Sowle, and sold at his Shop in Devonshire Buildings, without Bishops-Gate, 1681.

Half morocco; $7\frac{1}{2}$ x $5\frac{3}{4}$ x $\frac{1}{4}$ in.

EARLY PRINTING IN ENGLAND

Cabinet 78
Shelf 1
No. 1

London, 1660. [John Martin].
Title: De atramentis cujuscunque generis... Auctore, Pedro Maria Caneparío.
Imprint: Londini, excudebat J.M. Impensis Jo. Martin. Ja. Alestry...ad insigne Campana, in Coemeterio Paulino, 1660.

Calf; 7-7/8 x 5-7/8 x 1-3/8 in. [Arber, T.C., 1., p.398.]

EARLY PRINTING IN ENGLAND Example

Cabinet I
Shelf 1
No. 12

London, 1673, E.T. and R.H. for R. Jones.

See SALMON, WILLIAM. Polygraphice...

EARLY PRINTING IN ENGLAND

Cabinet RR
Shelf 4
No. 1

London, 1694, Charles Bill (his imprint).

See PAPER. (Act of Parliament, 1694...)

EARLY PRINTING IN ENGLAND

Cabinet E
Shelf 4
No. 30

London, 1661. Henry Herringman.
Title: Humane industry, or a history of most manual arts....[Includes the invention of printing, p.62]
Imprint: Printed for Henry Herringham, and are to be sold at his shop, at the Blew-Anchor, in the lower walk of the New Exchange, 1661.

Half morocco; $6\frac{1}{2}$ x $4\frac{1}{4}$ x 5/8 in.

EARLY PRINTING IN ENGLAND

Cabinet E
Shelf 4
No. 60

London, 1674. Thomas Roycroft.
Title: A tutor to astronomy and geography...With an appendix showing the use of the Ptolomaick Sphere. Third Edition enlarged. By Joseph Moxon...
Imprint: London, printed by Thomas Roycroft, for Joseph Moxon: and sold at his shop on Ludgate-Hill at the sign of Atlas, M.DC.LXXIV.

Calf; 8 x 6 x 1-1/8 in.

EARLY PRINTING IN ENGLAND

Cabinet E
Shelf 4
No. 94

London, 1695. [Printer Unknown]
Title: Some discourses upon Dr. Burnet and Dr. Tillotson; occasioned by the late Funeral Sermon of the former upon the later.
Imprint: London. Printed in the year MDCXCV.

Half morocco; 8 x 6-3/8 x 3/8 in.

EARLY PRINTING IN ENGLAND

Cabinet E
Shelf 4
No. 38

London, 1664. [Printer Unknown]
Title: Vindicie Pietatis or, a vindication of godliness...By R.A. [llein M.A. of St. Alban's Hall, Oxford]. London, Printed in the year, 1664.

There are two armorial bookplates of Sir Richard Fust, who claimed descent from Fust, partner with Gutenberg, 1450-1455.

Morocco; 6-1/8 x 4 x 1-1/8 in.

EARLY PRINTING IN ENGLAND

Cabinet E
Shelf 4
No. 65

London, 1676. J.D. for M.K.
Title: Narration of the late wars risen in New England...with an account of the fight, the 19th December last, 1676. London, February 17th, 167-6/8. Licensed, Henry Oldenburg. A facimile.
Imprint: London, Printed by J.D. for M.D., and are to be sold by the Booksellers, 1676.

Boards; 8-3/8 x 6-1/8 in.

Printed for the Society of Colonial Wars in the State of Rhode Island. 1912

EARLY PRINTING IN ENGLAND (Example)

Cabinet F
Shelf 4
No. 2

London, 1700-1702: Henry Rhodes.
Title: Present state of Europe; or the historical and political Monthly Mercury...
Imprint: London, Printed for Henry Rhodes...and Eliz. Harris.

Old calf; $7\frac{1}{2}$ x $5\frac{1}{2}$ in.

EARLY PRINTING IN ENGLAND

Cabinet E
Shelf 4
No. 49

London, 1668. Thomas Roycroft.
Title: The fables of Aesop paraphras'd in verse... The second edition. By John Ogilby. [With many full page engravings].
Imprint: London. Printed by Thomas Roycroft, for the author, M.DC.LXVIII.

Boards; $15\frac{1}{2}$ x 10 x $1\frac{1}{4}$ in. Brunet 1, 102.

EARLY PRINTING IN ENGLAND. Example of

Cabinet E
Shelf 3
No. 88

London, 1676. Thomas Bassett and R. Chiswell.
Title: The theatre of Great Britain...Geography and atlas of the world. By John Speed.
Imprint: Printed for Thomas Bassett and Richard Chiswell. London, 1676.

Half morocco; $17\frac{1}{4}$ x $12\frac{1}{4}$ x $1\frac{1}{2}$ in.

EARLY PRINTING IN ENGLAND

Cabinet F
Shelf 4
No. 1

London, 1704. Henry Woodfall.
Title: Monsieur de Pourceaugnac...Done into English from a Comedy of Moliere's...for the diversion of the French King in the year 1679.
Imprint: Printed for William Davis, at the Black Bull against the Royal Exchange, and Bernard Lintott...in Fleet Street. 1704.

Cloth covered boards; $8\frac{1}{2}$ x $6\frac{1}{2}$ in.

EARLY PRINTING IN ENGLAND.

Cabinet E
Shelf 4
No. 56

London, 1672. A.B. [Printer unknown].
Title: The rehearsal transpros'd...shewing what grounds there are of fears and jealousies of Popery. The second edition, corrected.
Imprint: London, printed by A.B. for John Calvin and Theodore Beza at the sign of the King's indulgence, on the South side of the Lake Lemane, 1672.
This book, unlicensed and secretly printed has a spurious imprint.

(Cont'd).

EARLY PRINTING IN ENGLAND

Cabinet E
Shelf 4
No. 75

London, 1681-85. [Benjamin Tooke?]
Title: Leabhuir....The books of the Old Testament translated into Irish by....Doctor William Bedel. 1685. [With the New Testament in the Irish character, translated by William O'Donnell. London, 1681.
Imprint: Printed at London, Anno Dom. MDCLXXXV.

Calf; $9\frac{1}{2}$ x $7\frac{1}{4}$ x $3\frac{1}{4}$ in.

EARLY PRINTING IN ENGLAND

Cabinet X
Shelf 1
No. 23

London, 1709, Benj. Motte.
Title: Stephanorum historia...Michele Maittaire.
Imprint: Londini: Typis Benj. Motte, impensis Christophe Bateman.

Half morocco; 7-3/4 x 5 x 1-3/4 in.

EARLY PRINTING IN ENGLAND

Cabinet F
Shelf 4
No. 3

London, 1709. William Bowyer, Sr.
Title: An English-Saxon homily on the birthday of St. Gregory....By Elizabeth Elstob. Engraved frontispiece by S. Gribelin.
Imprint: London: Printed by W. Bowyer MDCCIX.

Full morocco, tooled; 9-1/8 x 5¾ x ¾ in.

EARLY PRINTING IN ENGLAND cont'd

Cabinet F
Shelf 4
No. 10

Leather; 6½ x 3-7/8 x ¾ in.

EARLY PRINTING IN ENGLAND

Cabinet F
Shelf 4
No. 14

London, 1726. Samuel Palmer.
Title: The religion of nature dilineated. By William Wollaston. Portrait, frontispiece.
Imprint: London. Printed by Samuel Palmer, in Bartholomew Close, 1726.
"On this book Franklin worked as a compositor at Palmer's in 1725."

Old red morocco, tooled gilt border; 11¾ x 9-1/8 x 1-3/8 in.

EARLY PRINTING IN ENGLAND

Cabinet RR
Shelf 4
No. 1

London, 1710-11, Thomas Newcomb and Henry Hills (Imprint)

See PAPER. (Act of Parliament, 1710...)

EARLY PRINTING IN ENGLAND

Cabinet F
Shelf 4
No. 11

London, 1717. Paul and Isaac Vaillant. (Imprint)

See RAMAZZINI, BERNARDINI. Opera omnia ...Londini, 1717.

EARLY PRINTING IN ENGLAND

Cabinet X
Shelf 4
No. 71

London, 1734, John Baskett, King's printer.
Title: An act for granting to Samuel Butler...
Imprint: London. Printed by John Baskett, printer to the King's most excellent majesty, 1734.
Bound in with another Act of 1754.

Boards; 12¼ x 7-7/8 in.

EARLY PRINTING IN ENGLAND

Cabinet 73
Shelf 2
No. 33

London, 1711. William Lewis, publisher.
Title: An essay on criticism by Alexander Pope. Printed for W. Lewis in Russel-Street, Covent Garden...MDCCXI. A facsimile.
Colophon: Printed...for William Andrews Clark, Jr. by John Henry Nash in the City of San Francisco, in nineteen hundred and twenty-eight.

Paper boards, in case; 13 x 9½ x 1-3/8 in.

EARLY PRINTING IN ENGLAND

Cabinet RR
Shelf 4
No. 1

London, 1718, John Baskett...(Imprint).

See PAPER. (Act of Parliament, 1713...) Printed 1718.

EARLY PRINTING IN ENGLAND

Cabinet L
Shelf 3
No. 4

London, 1737. William and Cluer Dicey (Imprint)

See IMPRINTS, England. Dicey, William...

EARLY PRINTING IN ENGLAND

Cabinet NN
Shelf 5
No. 2

London, 1712. The Examiner, for the year 1711. London, printed for John Morphew, 1712.
Reprint of political and literary tracts issued weekly during 1710-11.

Leather; 5¼ x 3¼ in.

EARLY PRINTING IN ENGLAND

Cabinet T
Shelf 1
No. 22

London, 1720. J. Downing.
Title: An extract of letters relating to... printing the New Testament and Psalter in the Arabick language...
Imprint: London: Printed by J. Downing, in Bartholomew-Close, near West-Smithfield, 1720.

Cloth; 7 x 4½ in.

EARLY PRINTING IN ENGLAND

Cabinet QQ
Shelf 3
No. 35

London, 1756, Luke Hinde. (Imprint)

see BOWNAS, SAMUEL. Account of the life...London, 1756.

EARLY PRINTING IN ENGLAND

Cabinet F
Shelf 4
No. 8

London, 1713. Jacob Tonson and John Watts.
Title: Vita Sallustii. By Michael Maittaire.
Imprint: Londini: Ex Officina Jacobi Tonson & Johannis Watts. M.DCC.XIII. Cum privilegio.
"The....Maittaire's Classicks would alone have immortalized his memory, (John Watts') both for correctness and neatness." Plomers Booksellers & Printers, 1668-1725.

Leather; 6-1/8 x 3¾ x ¾ in.

EARLY PRINTING IN ENGLAND

Cabinet F
Shelf 4
No. 13

London, 1725. Samuel Palmer.
Title: The religion of nature. By William Wollaston.
Imprint: London: Printed by S. Palmer, and sold by B. Lintott, W. and J. Innys, J. Osborn... 1725.
[Franklin, Autobiography, p.43: "At Palmer's I was employed in composing for the second edition of Wollaston's "Religion of nature"]

cont'd

EARLY PRINTING IN ENGLAND

Cabinet M
Shelf 4
No. 17

London, 1758. Strawberry Hill Press: Horace Walpole.
Title: A parallel; in the manner of Plutarch... By the Rev. Mr. Spence.
Imprint: Printed at the Strawberry Hill Press by William Robinson, and sold by Messieurs Dodsley, at Tully's Head. 1758.

½ Morocco; 7¼ x 4½ x 3/8 in.

EARLY PRINTING IN ENGLAND

Cabinet F
Shelf 4
No. 10

London, 1715. John Nicholson (Bookseller)
Title: The history of many memorable things lost ...Written originally in Latin by Guido Pancirollus....And now done into English. Vol. 2.
To this English Edition is added, first A supplement to the Chapter of printing, shewing the time of its beginning...
Imprint: London. Printed for John Nicholson in Little-Britain, and sold by John Morphew near Stationers-Hall. 1715.

cont'd

EARLY PRINTING IN ENGLAND cont'd

Cabinet F
Shelf 4
No. 13

Original sheep; 9¾ x 8 x 7/8 in.

EARLY PRINTING IN ENGLAND

Cabinet M
Shelf 4
No. 18

London, 1760. Strawberry Hill Press: Horace Walpole.
Title: M. Annaei Lucani. Pharsalia cum notis Hugonis Grotie et Richardi Bentleii...
Imprint: Strawberry Hill, 1760.

Calf; 11¾ x 9-1/8 x 1¾ in. Brunet 3, 1200.

EARLY PRINTING IN ENGLAND

Cabinet F · Shelf 4 · No. 5

London, 1772. William Bowyer and John Nichols.
Title: The poems of Mark Akenside, M.D.
Imprint: London, printed by W. Bowyer and J. Nichols; and sold by J. Dodsley, in Pall Mall, 1772.

Leather; $8\frac{3}{4}$ x 5-3/8 x $1\frac{1}{2}$ in.

EARLY PRINTING IN ENGLAND

Cabinet RR · Shelf 4 · No. 1

London, 1773, Charles Eyre and William Strahan. (Imprint)

See PAPER. (Act of Parliament, 1768-73...)

EARLY PRINTING IN ENGLAND

Cabinet M · Shelf 4 · No. 19

London, 1781. Strawberry Hill Press: Horace Walpole.
Title: The muse recalled, an ode...By William Jones, Esq.
Imprint: Strawberry Hill: Printed by Thomas Kirgate.

Half morocco; $9\frac{3}{4}$ x 8 in.

EARLY PRINTING IN ENGLAND

Cabinet L · Shelf 3 · No. 7

London, 1784, John Nichols
Title: Origin and progress of writing...By Thomas Astle. London, 1784.
Colophon: From the Press of J. Nichols.

Half morocco; 12 x 10 in.

EARLY PRINTING IN ENGLAND Example.

Cabinet QQ · Shelf 1 · No. 11

London, 1785. (Printed for J. Dodsley)
Title: The newspaper: a poem, by George Crabbe.
Imprint: London: Printed for J. Dodsley, in Pall-Mall. 1785.

Morocco; 11 x 9 in.

EARLY PRINTING IN ENGLAND

Cabinet RR · Shelf 4 · No. 1

London, 1792, Charles Eyre and Andrew Strahan (Imprint)

See PAPER (Act of Parliament, 1790-1792) ...

EARLY PRINTING IN ENGLAND.

Cabinet F · Shelf 4 · No. 16

London, 1794. Robert Bassam.
Title: A curious hieroglyphic bible.
Imprint: London: Printed and sold by Robert Bassam, No. 53, St. John's-Street.

Half morocco; 10 x $7\frac{1}{2}$ x $\frac{3}{4}$ in.

EARLY PRINTING IN ENGLAND

Cabinet M · Shelf 1 · No. 26

London, 1794. Thomas Bensley.
Title: Q. Horatii Flacci quae supersunt, recentsuit et notulis instruxit Gilbertus Wakefield ...Londini: Impensis Kearsley. M.DCC.XCIV. (2 vols.)
Colophon imprint: Typis T. Bensley.

Tree calf; $8\frac{3}{4}$ x 5-3/8 in.

EARLY PRINTING IN ENGLAND

Cabinet 30 · Shelf 2 · No. 1

London, 1795. W. Bulmer and Co. Shakspeare Printing Office.
Title: Milton: The poetical works of. [2 vols.]
Imprint: London: Printed by W. Bulmer and Co. Shakspeare Printing Office, for John and Josiah Boydell, and George Nicol; from the types of W. Martin. 1795.

Morocco; gilt; $7\frac{1}{2}$ x $13\frac{1}{4}$, each vol.

EARLY PRINTING IN ENGLAND

Cabinet 30 · Shelf 1 · No. 30

London, 1795. W. Bulmer: Shakspeare Printing Office.
Title: Poems by Goldsmith and Parnell. [Illus. with wood engravings by the Bewicks].
Imprint: London. Printed by W. Bulmer and Co. Shakspeare Printing Office. Cleveland-Row, 1795.

Calf, tooled; 12 x 9-3/8 x $1\frac{1}{2}$ in.

EARLY PRINTING IN ENGLAND

Cabinet 30 · Shelf 1 · No. 32

London, 1796. W. Bulmer and Co. Shakspeare Printing Office.
Title: The Chase. A poem by W. Somerville. wood engravings by Bewicks, Thomas and brother.
Imprint: London: Printed by W. Bulmer and Co. Shakspeare Printing Office, Cleveland-Row, 1796.

Tree calf; $11\frac{3}{4}$ x 9-3/8 x $1\frac{1}{4}$ in.

EARLY PRINTING IN ENGLAND

Cabinet 30 · Shelf 1 · No. 33

London, 1800. W. Bulmer and Co.
Title: The father's revenge...by Frederick Earl of Carlisle.
Imprint: London: Printed by W. Bulmer and Co. Shakspeare Printing Office, Russel-Court Cleveland-Row, St. James's.

Morocco, tooled; $11\frac{1}{2}$ x $9\frac{1}{4}$ x $1\frac{1}{4}$ in.

EARLY PRINTING IN ENGLAND

Cabinet 30 · Shelf 1 · No. 34

London, 1802. W. Bulmer and Co.
Title: Anacreontis Oderia...Accedunt variae lectiones cura Edvardi Forster. [Greek text].
Imprint: Londini, sumptibus editoris excudebant Gul. Bulmer et soc...1802.

Pigskin; 8-1/8 x $5\frac{1}{2}$ x 1 in.

EARLY PRINTING IN ENGLAND

Cabinet 30 · Shelf 1 · No. 35

London, 1804. W. Bulmer and Co.
Title: Outlines from the figures of Greek, Roman, and Etruscan vases of the late Sir William Hamilton; with engraved borders...by the late Mr. Kirk.
Imprint: London; published by William Miller; printed by W. Bulmer and Co.,

Morocco; tooled; $11\frac{3}{4}$ x $9\frac{1}{2}$ x $1\frac{1}{2}$ in.

EARLY PRINTING IN ENGLAND

Cabinet 30 · Shelf 1 · No. 35. 01.

London, 1804. Bulmer, W. and Co.
Title: Rasselas, by Dr. Johnson. Printed with patent types in a manner never before attempted. Rushe's Edition. Banbury...1804. London: Printed by W. Bulmer and Co. Cleveland-Row, St. James.

Half morocco; $8\frac{1}{2}$ x $5\frac{1}{4}$ x 5/8 in.

EARLY PRINTING IN ENGLAND

Cabinet 30 · Shelf 1 · No. 39 36

London, 1807. William Bulmer and Co.
Title: Richardi Bentleii, Epistotae.
Imprint: Londini, Typis Bulmerianis.

Half morocco; 13 x $10\frac{1}{2}$ x $1\frac{3}{4}$ in.

EARLY PRINTING IN ENGLAND

Cabinet 30 · Shelf 1 · No. 40 36.01 · 2 vols.

London, 1808: William Bulmer.
Title: Utopia. By Sir Thomas More...A new edition with copious notes and a biographical and literary introduction by T.F. Dibdin.
Imprint: London, 1808. Printed by William Bulmer ...For William Miller.

Boards; 8 x $5\frac{1}{4}$ x 7/8 in. each vol.

EARLY PRINTING IN ENGLAND

Cabinet M · Shelf 1 · No. 37

London, 1809. Thomas Bensley.
Title: Gertrude of Wyoming: A Pennsylvania tale ...By Thomas Campbell.
Imprint: London: Printed by T. Bensley, Bolt Court. 1809.

Half calf; marbled boards; $11\frac{3}{4}$ x $9\frac{1}{2}$ x $\frac{1}{2}$ in.

EARLY PRINTING IN ENGLAND.

Cabinet PP Shelf 1 No. 7

London, 1810. W. Bulmer & co.
Title: Bibliosophia, or book-wisdom ... By an Aspirant ...
Imprint: London: Printed for William Miller, Albemarle Street, by W. Bulmer and Co. Cleveland-Row, 1810.

Half morocco; 7 x 4½ in.

EARLY PRINTING IN ENGLAND Example

Cabinet A Shelf 3 No. 1

London, 1837, John Norris (Imprint of)

See Periodicals, England. Weekly Chronicle (The)...1837.

EARLY PRINTING IN ENGLAND. Example

Cabinet A Shelf 3 No. 1

London, 1840. John Hetherington (his Imprint)

See Periodicals, England. Odd Fellow (The) ...1840.

EARLY PRINTING IN ENGLAND

Cabinet 30 Shelf 1 No. 42

London, 1813. William Bulmer and Co.
Title: Hobbinol, field sports. By W. Somerville. [Engravings by Nesbit and Thurston].
Imprint: London: Printed by William Bulmer and Co. Shakspeare Printing Office, for R. Ackermann, In the Strand.1813.

Half morocco; 12 x 9-5/8 x 7/8 in.

EARLY PRINTING IN ENGLAND. Example

Cabinet A Shelf 3 No. 1

London, 1838, Murdo Young.

See Newspapers, Englan . Sun (The)...June 28, 1838.

EARLY PRINTING IN ENGLAND. Example

Cabinet A Shelf 3 No. 1

London, 1840. Penny Weekly Dispatch.

See periodicals, England. Penny...

EARLY PRINTING IN ENGLAND

Cabinet M Shelf 1 No. 28

London, 1817. Bensley and Son.
Title: The institutions of physiology. By J. Fred Blumenbach...Translated from the Latin.
Imprint: London: Printed by Bensley and Son, Bolt Court, Fleet Street, for S. Cox and Son, ...1817.
This is the first book printed on a cylinder press.

Half calf; 9 x 5¼ x 1-1/8 in.

EARLY PRINTING IN ENGLAND

Cabinet M Shelf 5 No. 8

London, 1838. Samuel Bentley.
Title: The ceremonies to be observed at the Royal Coronation.
Colophon: Printed by Samuel Bentley. Dorset Street, Fleet Street, London.

Half morocco; 13½ x 8½ in.

EARLY PRINTING IN ENGLAND

Cabinet M Shelf 1 No. 29

London, 1848: Bentley, Wilson and Fley.
Title: L'Allegro and il Penseroso. By John Milton. With thirty illustrations designed expressly for the Art-Union of London.
Imprint: S. & J. Bentley, Wilson and Fley.

Calf, tooled; 11¼ x 8¾ x ½ in.

EARLY PRINTING IN ENGLAND

Cabinet T Shelf 1 No. 27

London, 1818. Nichols, J., Son and Bentley.
Title: Life and errors of John Dunton.
Imprint: Printed by and for J. Nichols, Son and Bentley. London, 1818. (2 vols.)

Binding by Handay: Calf, paneled, gilt edges; 8¾ x 5½ in.

EARLY PRINTING IN ENGLAND

Cabinet L Shelf 4 No. 20

London, 1838. Willoughby and Company.(Imprint)

See Color Printing, Willoughby and Company, printers, 109 Goswell Street, London, 1838.

EARLY PRINTING IN ENGLAND

Cabinet M Shelf 2 No. 39

London, 1850. George Henry and Co.
Title: Haydock's Bible translated from the Latin Vulgate...
Imprint: London. George Henry and Co., 64 Bartholomew Close, [1850].

Tooled calf; 12½ x 9¾ x 4 in.

EARLY PRINTING IN ENGLAND

Cabinet II Shelf 4 No. 3

London, 1820. Richard Watts.
Title: Irish Testament. Translated into the Irish language by William O'Donnell.
Imprint: London: Printed by Richard Watts... 1820.

Calf; 7 x 4¼ x 1-3/8 in.

EARLY PRINTING IN ENGLAND

Cabinet L Shelf 4 No. 20

London, 1838, Willoughby and Company (Imprint)

see COLOR PRINTING. Willoughby and Company

EARLY PRINTING IN ENGLAND. Example

Cabinet X Shelf 5 No. 4

Newark-upon-Trent, 1794, Daniel Holt.

See Liberty of Printing. Great Britain. Holt, Daniel, printer of The Newark Herald.

EARLY PRINTING IN ENGLAND

Cabinet L Shelf 4 No. 18

London, 1822, William Savage

See Savage, William, Practical hints on decorative printing...London, 1822.

EARLY PRINTING IN ENGLAND Example

Cabinet A Shelf 3 No. 1

London, 1839. Leukin Jones. (his Imprint)

See Periodicals, England. Paul Pry: A Swindler's Register...1839-1840.

EARLY PRINTING IN ENGLAND

Cabinet F Shelf 4 No. 18

Newcastle, 1742. James White and William Ged.
Title: The life of God in the Soul of Man....By Henry Scougal...
Imprint: Newcastle: Printed by J. White, from plates made by W. Ged. Goldsmith, in Edinburgh, 1742.

Half calf; 4-7/8 x 3 in. Timperley, p.678.

EARLY PRINTING IN ENGLAND

Cabinet F
Shelf 4
No. 21

Oxford, 1771. Clarendon Press.
Title: Tracts relating to the antiquities and laws of England. By William Blackstone. Third edition.
Imprint: Oxford, printed at the Clarendon Press. M.DCC.LXXI.

Leather; 11 x $8\frac{1}{2}$ x $1\frac{1}{2}$ in.

EARLY PRINTING IN FRANCE cont'd

Cabinet 70
Shelf 1
No. 45

Bound in with the Historia Tripertita of Cassiodorus. Lyons. Jacques Giunta, 1534.

Calf; $7\frac{1}{4}$ x $4\frac{3}{4}$ x $1\frac{1}{2}$ in. Baudrier VI 150.

EARLY PRINTING IN FRANCE

Cabinet 70
Shelf 1
No. 50

Lyons, 1538. Sebastien Gryphium. Bound in with another book.
Title: Gilberti Ducherii (Ducher) Vultonis Aquapersani Epigrammaton, libri duo. Apud Seb. Gryphium Lugduni, 1538. pp.165.

This volume contains epigrams in verse in honor of printers: Dolet, Gryphius, Colines, Stephanus, Barbous and Romanus.

Leather; $6\frac{1}{2}$ x $4\frac{1}{2}$ x $1\frac{1}{2}$ in.

EARLY PRINTING IN ENGLAND

Cabinet F
Shelf 4
No. 23

York, 1735. Thomas Gent. (Printer and Author).
Title: Annales Regioduni Hullini: or, the History of the Royal and beautiful town of Kingston-upon-Hull...Faithfully collected by Thomas Gent....Woodcuts and plates.
Imprint: Sold at the printing office near the Star in Stone-Gate, York....MDCCXXXV.

Leather; $7\frac{3}{4}$ x 5 x 1 in.

EARLY PRINTING IN FRANCE

Cabinet 40
Shelf 1
No. 25

Lyons, 1535. Melchior and Gaspar Trechsel.
Title: Lexicon de partibus aedium Francisci Marii Grapaldi. [Printer Mark of Vicenti] Lugduni apud haeredes Simonis Vicentii M.D.XXXV.
Colophon: Excudebant Lugduni Melchior et Gaspar Trechsel fratres, 1535.

Bound with two items of Robert Stephanus (Estienne) Paris, 1548 and 1550.

Tooled leather; $6\frac{3}{4}$ x $4\frac{1}{2}$ x $1\frac{3}{4}$ ins.

EARLY PRINTING IN FRANCE

Cabinet D
Shelf 4
No. 54

Lyon, 1540, Estienne Dolet
Title: La chirugie de Paulus Aegineta
Imprint: Ches Estienne Dolet, a Lyon, 1540.

With printer mark on title page.

Vellum; $6\frac{1}{2}$ x $4\frac{3}{4}$ in.

EARLY PRINTING IN FRANCE.

Cabinet I
Shelf 4
No. 9

Lyons, 1483, Mathieu Husz et Pierre Hongre ...

See FACSIMILES. Jacques de Voragine, la legénde dorée en francais...

EARLY PRINTING IN FRANCE

Cabinet 70
Shelf 1
No. 49

Lyons, 1535. Sebastian Gryphe.

Title: Stephani Doleti dialogus, de Imitatione Ciceroniana...Printer Mark.
Imprint: Lugduni apud Seb. Gryphium, M.D.XXXV.

Calf; 8-3/4 x 6 x ½ in. Gresswell's Early Parisian Greek Press, I, 296.

EARLY PRINTING IN FRANCE

Cabinet 69
Shelf 1
No. 7

Lyons. 1540. Etienne Dolet.

Title: Les Gestes de Francoys de Valois Roy de France...Premierement composé en Latin par Estienne Dolet: et aprés par luy mesmes translaté en langue Francoyse. [Printer Mark].
Imprint: A Lyon, chés Estienne Dolet. M.D.XL. avec privileige pour dix ans.

Half morocco; $7\frac{1}{2}$ x 6 x 3/8 in.

EARLY PRINTING IN FRANCE

Cabinet 70
Shelf 2
No. 6

Lyons, 1528. Sebastien Gryphe.
Title: Adagiorum opus des Erasmi Roterdami... Printer Mark.
Imprint: Sebastianus Gryphus Germanus excudebat Lugduni. Anno M.D.XXVIII.

Calf; 12-3/4 x 9 x 1½ in.

EARLY PRINTING IN FRANCE

Cabinet 70
Shelf 2
No. 15
(2 vols.)

Lyons, 1536-1538. Sebastian Gryphe.
Title: Commentariorum linguae Latinae. Tomus Primus. Stephano Doleto Gallo autore.[Printer Mark]. 2 vols.
Imprint: Lugduni apud Seb. Gryphium, 1536.

Second vol. has same title and imprint but is dated 1538. Both have wood cut title borders and printer mark.
Calf; $13\frac{1}{2}$ x $9\frac{1}{2}$ x 2p in. Brunet 2, 794.

EARLY PRINTING IN FRANCE

Cabinet 39
Shelf 2
No. 3

Lyons, 1547. Jean (I) de Tournes.

Title: Il Dante. Con argomenti & dichiaratione de molti luoghi, novamente revisto & stampato.
Imprint: In Lione, per Giovan di Tournes. M.D.XXXXVII.

Morocco, gilt: 5¼ x 3¼ x 1¼ in. Vingtrinier. Histoire de L'Imprimerie à Lyon, 209.

EARLY PRINTING IN FRANCE.

Cabinet 70
Shelf 2
No. 8

Lyons, 1529. Jean Crespin.
Title: Opera Virgiliana cum decem commentis exposita...a Servio, Donato, Mancinello et Probo cum adnotionibus Beroaldinis. Augustino Datho, Calderino, Jodoco Badio Ascesio...M.D.XXIX. Illus. Wood engravings
Colophon: Lugduni in typographia officina Ioannis Crespini, anno virginei partus MDXXIX

Tooled leather over original wood cover; 13 x 8-3/4 x 3 in.

EARLY PRINTING IN FRANCE

Cabinet 70
Shelf 1
No. 50

Lyons, 1537. Joannes Barbous for Michael Parmenter. Bound in with another book.
Title: Joannis Vulteii (Vulteis, Voulte) Remensis Epigrammatum Libri I - IIII, eiusdem Xenia. [Printer Mark] Lugduni, suv scuto Basiliensi apud Michaelem Parmenterium, M.D.XXXVII. pp. 282 (iii)
Colophon: Lugduni, excudebat Ioannes Barbous, M.D.XXXVII.

cont'd

EARLY PRINTING IN FRANCE

Cabinet 69
Shelf 1
No. 12

Lyons, 1547. Jean Frellon.

Title: Icones historiarum veteris testamenti.... Lugduni, apud Ioannem Frellonium. 1547. [Woodcuts designed by Hans Holbein]
Colophon: Lugduni, Excudebat Ioannes Frellonius, 1547.

Calf; 7-3/8 x 5¼ x 3/8 in.

EARLY PRINTING IN FRANCE.

Cabinet 70
Shelf 1
No. 45

Lyons, 1533-4. Jacques and Franciscus Giunte
Title: Historia ecclesiastica Eusebii ... collecto & emendato...Habes...Gaufridus Boussardus sacrae Theologiae doctor huic operi praeponi curavit. 1533.
Colophon:...Impssa lugduni per Benedictum Bonnyn calcographum. Sumptibus vero ... Jacobi q. Francisci di Giuncta et socorum Florentini anno dni MCCCCCXXXIII mensis Septembris die VI. Printer mark.

Cont'd.

EARLY PRINTING IN FRANCE cont'd

Cabinet 70
Shelf 1
No. 50

This vol. contains epigrams in verse in honor of printers: Dolet, Gryphius, Colines Stephanus, Barbous and Rhomanus.

Leather; $6\frac{1}{2}$ x $4\frac{1}{2}$ x $1\frac{1}{2}$ in.

EARLY PRINTING IN FRANCE

Cabinet 69
Shelf 2
No. 1

Lyons, 1550. Guillaume Roville.
Title: Ioannis Corasii Tolosatis, iurisconsulti clarissimi, in....Pandectarum, de verbor. obligationibus, scholia....Senatum Tolosanum. [Printer Mark]
Imprint: Lugduni, Apud Gulielmum Rovillium, sub scuto Veneto, 1550. Cum privilegio regis.
[Bound with another item by Aemylio Ferreto. Printer, Matthieu Bonhomme, Lyons, 1552.]

cont'd

Vellum; 13 x 8½ x 2 in.

EARLY PRINTING IN FRANCE cont'd

Cabinet 6, Shelf 2 No.

Vellum; 13 x 8½ x 2 ins.

EARLY PRINTING IN FRANCE

Cabinet 39 Shelf 2 No. 9

Lyons, 1554. Jean (I) de Tournes.

Title: Figure del Vecchio Testamento con versi Toscani per Damian Maraffi nuovamente composti illustrate. [Printer Mark]
Imprint: In Lione per Giovanni de Tournes M.D.LIIII.
Bound with Tournes' Nuovo Testemento, 1577.

Morocco; 6¼ x 4½ x 7/8 in.

EARLY PRINTING IN FRANCE

Cabinet 39 Shelf 2 No. 14

Lyons, 1558. Jean (I) de Tournes.
Title: Illustratione degli epitaffi et medaglie antiche, di M. Gabriel Symeoni. [Illus.]
Imprint: In Lione, per Giovan di Tournes. M.D.LVIII.

Wood cuts and borders by Bernard Salomon.

Limp vellum; 8½ x 6¼ x ½ in. Brunet 5, 392.

EARLY PRINTING IN FRANCE

Cabinet 39 Shelf 2 No. 5

Lyons, 1550. Jean (I) de Tournes.
Title: Physionomie naturelle. Extraite de plusieurs Philosophes anciens...par M. Antoine du Moulin Masconnois. [Printer Mark].
Imprint: A Lyon, par Jean de Tournes. M.D.XXXXX. Avec privilege du Roy pour dix ans.
Following index: Ce present oeuvre fut acheve d'imprimer le premier jour de Mars. mille cinq cens cinquante.

Morocco; 6½ x 4¼ x ½ in.

EARLY PRINTING IN FRANCE

Cabinet 39 Shelf 2 No. 11

Lyons, 1555. Jean (I) de Tournes.
Title: Xenophon. La Cyropedie de Xenophon, de la vie...de Roy des Perses. Traduite de Grec par Iaques des Comtes de Vintemille Rhodien.
Imprint: A Lion, par Ian de Tournes, MD.LV....

Title in wood cut borders. Initials and ornaments.

Vellum; 9¼ x 6 x 1 in. Brunet 5, 1498.

EARLY PRINTING IN FRANCE

Cabinet 39 Shelf 2 No. 15

Lyons, 1558. Jean (I) de Tournes.

Title: D. Magni Ausonir. Burdigalensis Poëtae, augustorum praeceptoris, virique Consularis opera....
Imprint: Lugduni, apud Ioan Tornaesium M.D.LVIII.

Morocco, gilt; 6½ x 4 x 3/4 in. Brunet 1, 576.

EARLY PRINTING IN FRANCE.

Cabinet 69 Shelf 1 No. 18

Lyons, 1550. Mathias Bonhomme.
Title: Emblemata D.A. Alciati....autore recognita ac quae desiderabantur, imaginibus locupletata....Lugd. Apud Guliel. Rovilium. 1550. [Emblems and borders. Copper engravings]
Colophon: Lugduni, Excudebat Mathias Bonhomme.

Vellum; 7 x 4¾ x 3/4 in. Brunet 1, 148.

EARLY PRINTING IN FRANCE

Cabinet 69 Shelf 1 No. 26

Lyons, 1555. Sebastien Gryphe.

Title: Nicolai Leonici Thomaei. De varia historia libri tres. [Printer Mark].
Imprint: Apud Seb. Gryphium, Lugduni, 1555.
[Bound in with Libanius, sophista. Greek translation printed at Lyons by Jean Jullieron 1614]

Boards, leather back; 4¾ x 3-7/8 x 1 in.

EARLY PRINTING IN FRANCE.

Cabinet 39 Shelf 2 No. 19

Lyons, 1559. Jean (I) de Tournes.
Title: La Vita et metamorfoso d'Ovidio, figurato & abbreviato ... da Gabriello Symeoni. [Illus.]
Imprint: A Lione per Giovanni di Tornes nella via Resina. 1559.
Printed with italic types designed by Robert Granjon: engravings, borders, ornaments etc. by Bernard Salomon.

Tooled calf; 7 x 4- x 5/8 in. Brunet 4, 287. Updike I, 203-4.

EARLY PRINTING IN FRANCE

Cabinet 39 Shelf 2 No. 7

Lyons, 1552. Jean (I) de Tournes.
Title: Vitruvius, Pollionis. De Architecture libri decem....Accesserunt. Gulielmi Philandri.... [Printer Mark]
Imprint: Lugduni, apud Ioan. Tornaesium. M.D.LII. Cum privilegio ad sexennium.

Boards; 9-3/4 x 6-5/8 x 1 in. Brunet 5, 1327.

EARLY PRINTING IN FRANCE

Cabinet 69 Shelf 1 No. 28

Lyons, 1556. Guillaume Roville and Mathieu Bonhomme.
Title(1): Orlando furioso de M. Ludovico Ariosto. Traduzido en Romance Castel. por el S. don Hieronimo de Vrrea....[Printer Mark]. A Lyon en casa de Gulielmo Roville, 1556.
Title (2): Exposicion de todos los lugares difficultosos....con una breve demonstracion. [Printer Mark]. En Leon, en casa de Gulielmo Rovillio, en el anno del S.M.D.LVI.

cont'd

EARLY PRINTING IN FRANCE

Cabinet 69 Shelf 1 No. 33

Lyons, 1560 and 1562. Jean (II) Frellon.
Title: Scholia Pauli Manutii, quibus Ciceronis philosophia partim corrigitur, partim explanatur...[Printer Mark]
Imprint: Lugduni. Apud Ioannem Frellonium. 1560. [Bound in with two additional commentaries each with own title page, printer mark, and imprint, dated 1562. Colophon of last two sections: Lugduni, excudebat Symphorianus Barbierus.

Cont'd

EARLY PRINTING IN FRANCE.

Cabinet 69 Shelf 2 No. 1

Lyons, 1552. Matthieu Bonhomme.
Title: Aemylii Feretti iurisconsultorum huis aetatis facile principis in titul de.... Aemylius Ferrettus. [Printer Mark]
Imprint: Lugduni, Apud Mathiam Bonhomme, MDLII. Cum privilegio regis.
[Bound with another item by Joannis Corasii Tolosatis. Printed by G. Roville, Lyons, 1550].

Vellum; 13 x 8½ x 2 ins.

EARLY PRINTING IN FRANCE cont'd

Cabinet 69 Shelf 1 No. 28

Colophon, following second title. Fue impresso el present libro en la inclita cuidad de Leon, en casa de Mathias Bonhomme.

Morocco; 9¼ x 6½ x 1-5/8 in. Baudrier, IX, 250.

EARLY PRINTING IN FRANCE cont'd

Cabinet 69 Shelf 1 No. 33

Calf; 6-7/8 x 4-1/4 x 2½ ins. Baudrier V, 252.

EARLY PRINTING IN FRANCE

Cabinet 70 Shelf 1 No. 55

Lyons, 1552: Sebastien Gryphe.
Title: Aonii Palearii verulani di animorum imortalitate. Libri III.
Imprint: Apud Seb. Gryphium. Lugduni, 1552.

Translation of preface laudatory to Gryphius included. Translation by R. C. McMahon, a scholarly bookseller.

Paper cover; 6-5/8 x 4½ in.

EARLY PRINTING IN FRANCE

Cabinet 39 Shelf 2 No. 13

[Lyons, 1557?] Jean (I) de Tournes.
Title: Thesaurus amicorum. Variis iconibus iisq̄ perelegantibus illustratus. [Printer Mark]
Imprint: Apud Ioann. Torneasium.
Portrait medallions (184) with mottoes in various languages each with appropriate type. Wood cut borders.

Boards; 6-3/4 x 4½ x 1¼ in.

EARLY PRINTING IN FRANCE

Cabinet 69 Shelf 1 No. 35

Lyons, 1561. Guillaume Roville.

Title: Description de Limagne d'Auvergne en forme de dialogue...Traduit du livre Italien de Gabriel Symeon en langue Francoyse par Antoine Chappuys du Dauphine. [Printer Mark].
Imprint: A Lyon, par Guillaume Roville, 1561.
[Illus. with engravings of many medals]

Boards; 8½ x 6¼ x ½ in. Brunet 5, 391.

EARLY PRINTING IN FRANCE

Cabinet 39 Shelf 2 No. 21

Lyons, 1561. Jean (I) de Tournes.
Title: Alliances genealogiques des rois et princes de Gaule. Par Claude Paradin. [Printer Mark].
A Lion. Par Ian de Tournes M.D.LXI.
Colophon: A Lyon en rue Raizin, à l'enseigne des deux Viperès.
Illus. with wood cut heraldic devices.

Tooled morocco; 13½ x 8¼ x 2½ in. Brunet 4, 358.

EARLY PRINTING IN FRANCE.

Cabinet 69 Shelf 2 No. 8

Lyons, 1566. Guillaume Roville.

Title: Biblia Sacra...cum Hebraicorum,Caldeorum et Graecorum nominum interpretatione. [Wood cut title page. Many fine initials and decorative pieces.]
Imprint: Lugduni, Apud Guliel. Rovillium. M.D.L.XVI.

Vellum; 16¼ x 10½ x 3¾ ins.

EARLY PRINTING IN FRANCE

Cabinet 69 Shelf 2 No. 13

Lyons, 1572. Jean Durant.

Title: Oeuvre de la diversite des termes dont on use en Architecture....Par Hugues Sambin. A Lyon, par Jean Durant, M.D.LXXII. [Illus]

Colophon: Imprimé à Lyon par Iean Marcorelle. 1572.

Boards; 13-3/8 x 8¾ x 3/8 in. Brunet 5,104; Baudrier 1, p.139.

EARLY PRINTING IN FRANCE

Cabinet 69 Shelf 1 No. 40

Lyons, 1573. Antoine Gryphe.

Title: La Prosopographie ou description des Personnes insignes...Par Antoine du Verdier ...[Printer Mark]

Imprint: A Lyon par Antoine Gryphius. M.D.LXXIII. [An attempt at an illustrated dictionary of universal biography. Includes portraits of printers and items on the invention of

cont'd

EARLY PRINTING IN FRANCE cont'd

Cabinet 69 Shelf 1 No. 40

printing.]

Calf; 9¼ x 6-7/8 x 2 ins.

EARLY PRINTING IN FRANCE

Cabinet 39 Shelf 2 No. 9

Lyons, 1577. Jean (I) de Tournes.
Title: Figure del Nuovo Testamento. Illustrate da versi vulgari Italiani. [Wood Engravings]
Imprint: In Lione, per Gio. de Tornes MDLXXVII.

Bound with "Vecchio Testamento," 1554. Lyons, Jean de Tournes.

Morocco; 6¾ x 4½ x 7/8 in.

EARLY PRINTING IN FRANCE.

Cabinet 69 Shelf 1 No. 48

Lyons, 1581. Guillaume Roville.

Title: Promptuarii iconum insigniorum a seculo hominum...[Printer Mark.]

Imprint: Lugduni. Apud Gulielmum Rovillium.1581. [Portraits on medals representing important personages of antiquity.]

Vellum; 9½ x 7 x 2¼ ins. Brunet 4,900.

EARLY PRINTING IN FRANCE

Cabinet E Shelf 2 No. 85

Lyon, 1612-13. Horatio Cardon.
Title: Adagialium Sacrorum veteris et novi testamenti: collectore ac interprete, Martino del Rio Antverpiensi...[Printer Mark] 2 vols.
Imprint: Lugduni, sumptibus Horatii Cardon MDCXII Cum privilegio S. Caesar Maiest & Christianiss. Franc & Navarr. Regis.

Leather covered boards, each vol; 10 x 7¼ x 1¾ in.

EARLY PRINTING IN FRANCE.

Cabinet 69 Shelf 1 No. 26

Lyons, 1614. Jean Jullieron.
Title: Libanii sophistae characteres [hoc est] ... nunc primum cum Latina interpretatione edita ...
Imprint: Lugduni typis Iannis Iullieron. M.DCXIIII. [Bound in with De Varia historia Leonicus. Printed at Lyon by Sebastien Gryphe, 1555].

Boards, leather back; 4¾ x 3-7/8 x 1 in. See Brunet 3, 1049.

EARLY PRINTING IN FRANCE

Cabinet X Shelf 4 No. 44

Lyon, 1696: Declaration du roy portant règlement pour les libraires et imprimeurs de la ville de Lyon. Le 7 Fevrier, 1696. Imprimé à Paris par Christophe Ballard.
Regulations for Lyons printers, booksellers, typefounders, apprentices, widows of printers, etc.

Half morocco; 9-3/4 x 7E x 3/8 in.

EARLY PRINTING IN FRANCE

Cabinet D Shelf 2 No. 53

Paris, 1500. Philippe Pigouchet
Title: Altissiodorensis. Summa in IV libros sententiarum...Impressa est Parissiis maxima Philippi Pigoucheti cura...
Printer mark on title page.

Hain 8324

Tooled leather over boards; 11-3/8 x 8½ x 2½ in.

EARLY PRINTING IN FRANCE

Cabinet D Shelf 4 No. 61

Paris, circa 1501, Gaspard Philippe.

23 loose leaves from Bonaventura: Tractatus qui vocatur lignum Vitae. pp. 5-1/8 x 3½ in. Interesting chapter initials.

In box labeled "Early Printing: 1500-1616".

EARLY PRINTING IN FRANCE

Cabinet 29 Shelf 1 No. 41

Paris, 1503. Thielman Kerver.
Title: Hore intemerate Virginis marie secundū usum Romanum. [Printer Mark]....
Colophon: Ces presentes heures...furet acheves le V. iour de Ianier Lan mil cinq ces et troys. Par Thielman Kerver imprimeur et libraire...de Paris. Pour Gillet Remacle, aussi libraire iure: demourant sur le pont saint Michela a lenseigne de la Licorne. Printed on vellum. Illuminated.
Calf; 7-3/8 x 5 x 1¼ in. ex.cab.72

EARLY PRINTING IN FRANCE.

Cabinet 40 Shelf 1 No. 8

Paris, 1506. Robert I. Estienne.
Title: Dere horteli libellus ... [Various botanical-medical works bound together, of which Charles (Carolus), brother of Robert was author.]

Tooled leather; 7 x 4¾ in.

EARLY PRINTING IN FRANCE

Cabinet 29 Shelf 1 No. 44

Paris, 1506. Thielman Kerver.
Title: Decreti huius plenissimū argumentum.... [Printer Mark] Decretum aureum domini Gratiani....
Colophon: In nomine sancte et trinitatis Tripartitum Decreti aurei opus...finem accepit in alma Parisiensi achademia, expensis et opera Iohannis parui et Thielmani kerver bibliopolarum parisiensium in vico diva Iacobi...et Johānis cabillier mercatoris benemeriti Lug-

cont'd

EARLY PRINTING IN FRANCE cont'd

Cabinet 29 Shelf 1 No. 44

duni moram trahētis. Anno salutis millesimo quingentesimo sexto die XXI. Octobris.

Boards; 9-7/8 x 7¼ x 3¾ in.

EARLY PRINTING IN FRANCE

Cabinet 70 Shelf 1 No. 2

Paris, 1507. Josse Bade (Badius Ascensius)
Title: Prima pars operu Baptiste Mantuani.... [First Badius mark with the second earliest known picture of a printing office] Venundatur in vico sancti Iacobi in aedibus Ascensianis & sub Pelicano.
Colophon: Finis ex edibus Ascensianis nonis Septembris M.D.VII.

Vellum; 6¾ x 4½ x 1½ in.

EARLY PRINTING IN FRANCE

Cabinet 40 Shelf 1 No. 1

Paris, 1507. Stephanus (Henri Estienne I)

Title: Theologia Damasceni: Sancti patris Ioannis Damascini orthodoxe fidei...interprete Iacob Fabro Stapulensi.
Colophon: Sancti patris...cōsummatus est et absolutus:....Parisiis per Henricum Stephanum...Anno domini...millesimo quingentesimo septimo, decima quinta Aprilis.

Calf; 8¼ x 5¾ x 1 in.

EARLY PRINTING IN FRANCE

Cabinet 29 · Shelf 2 · No. 3

Paris, 1507. Thielman Kerver.
Title: Decretales dñi pape Gregorii nòni accurata diligētia emēdate...[Printer Mark]...
Colophon: Decretales Gregorii...Impresse Parisiis solerti cura Thielmani Kerver impressoris ac librarii...Parisienso. In magno vico divi Jacobi ad signu cratis ferri cōmorantis. Impensis Johanis petit et Johannis Cabiller. Anno dni M.CCCCC.VII. nònis Januarii.
Calf; $9\frac{1}{4}$ x $6\frac{3}{4}$ x $2\frac{1}{4}$ in.

EARLY PRINTING IN FRANCE.

Cabinet 70 · Shelf 1 · No. 5

Paris, 1508. Ulrich Gering and Bernard Renbolt.
Title: Beatissimi Gregorii pape totius ecclesie luminis. In septe psalmos penitētiales.... Device of Bernard Rembolt.
Colophon: In Sole aureo Parisius vicoqz Sorbonico Opera Udabrici gering e Mgr̄i Berchtoldi rēbolt sociox. Anno MCCCCCVIII die XX Marcii.

Mottled paper over card; 8-3/8 x 5-3/4 x 3/8 in.

EARLY PRINTING IN FRANCE

Cabinet 70 · Shelf 1 · No. 8

Paris, 1511. Guillaume Eustace.
Title: Missale ad consuetudinem ecclesie Romane ....In alma Parisioru academia. Anno domini virtutu...M.quingētesimo undecimo III kalendas Decembris. [Printer Mark]. Venundant in vico Judaico ad intersigniū duor Sagittariom; aut in Palacio regio tertio pilari.
Colophon: Missale...Etiā cum cantu et notulis noviter additis finit feliciter. Impensis honesti bibliopole Guillermi Eustace in alma

cont'd

EARLY PRINTING IN FRANCE cont'd

Cabinet 70 · Shelf 1 · No. 8

Parisiorum sub intersignio Saggitariorū vici Judaici comorantis Anno dñi M.CCCCXI. III kal decēbris.

Calf; gilt tooled edges: 7-1/8 x 5 x $1\frac{1}{2}$ in.

EARLY PRINTING IN FRANCE.

Cabinet 29 · Shelf 2 · No. 6

Paris, 1511. Thielman Kerver.
Title: Hore dive vgis Marie scdm verūsum Romanū. [Title page composed of the Kerver wood cut printers device. Printed on vellum. Illuminated initial letters].
Colophon: Finit offici bte marievirgis scdm usum Romanū...Impssum parisai Thielmanu Kerver. Anno dñi M.CCCCCXI die xxiiii Iulii.

Full morocco; 7 x 4-3/8 in. In protective case.

EARLY PRINTING IN FRANCE.

Cabinet 70 · Shelf 2 · No. 1

Paris, 1512. Berthold Rembolt.
Title: Trithemius. Liber scriptoribus Ecclesiasticis. [Printer mark of Jehan Petit].
Imprint: Venudatur Parrhisi a magistro Bertholdo Rembolt (ubi impressus ē.) Et a Joane Parvo: In vico sancti Jacobi sub sole et lilio aureis: quonum expe(n)sis i(m)pressē.

Calf; 8 x 5-3/8 x 1-1/8 in.

EARLY PRINTING IN FRANCE

Cabinet D · Shelf 4 · No. 61

Paris, 1512, Berthold Rembolt and Jean Waterloo.

(Original page).

In box labeled "Early Printing, 1500-1600."

EARLY PRINTING IN FRANCE

Cabinet 70 · Shelf 2 · No. 2

Paris, 1514. Berthold Rembolt.
Title: Cornucopie D. Nicolai Perotti....ad exēplar Aldinum recentius repositū: it diligētia excuttū a Bertholdo Rembolt Germano. Printed in red and black with Printer Mark.
Colophon:...impressum in Sole aureo vici divi Iacobi Per magistrum Bertholdum Rembolt. Anno gratiae Millesimo Quingentesimo decimoq̄rto Die vero. XII. Iulii.

Tooled Leather over boards; 4-3/4 x 10 x $2\frac{1}{2}$

EARLY PRINTING IN FRANCE

Cabinet 70 · Shelf 1 · No. 16

Paris, 1518. Michel Le Noir.
Title: Le rebours de Matheolus. Verso: Printer Mark.
Colophon: Cy finist le resolu en mariage nouvellement imprimé à Paris par Michel le noir Libraire demourāt en la rue sainct Jacques le onziesme iour de may. Lan mil cinq cens et dixhuit [Facsimile lithographed on veneered wood].

Morocco; $7\frac{1}{2}$ x $4\frac{1}{4}$ x 6/8 in.

EARLY PRINTING IN FRANCE

Cabinet 70 · Shelf 1 · No. 15

Paris, 1518. Nicolas de la Barre.
Title: La mer des croniques et mirover historical de Frãce iadis cōpose en latin par Robert Gaguin....[Printer Mark]. On les vent en la rue des carmes a lenseigne sainct iehan Baptiste.
Colophon: Cy finit la mer des Croniques...lequel traicte de touts les faicts advenuz depuis la destruction de Troye iusques en lan mil CCCCC et XVIII. Nouvellemet imprimez a Paris par maistre Nicolle de la barre.

Calf; $10\frac{1}{2}$ x $7\frac{1}{2}$ x $1\frac{1}{4}$ in.

EARLY PRINTING IN FRANCE cont'd

Cabinet 70 · Shelf 1 · No. 15

par maistre Nicolle de la barre.

Calf; $10\frac{1}{2}$ x $7\frac{1}{2}$ x $1\frac{1}{4}$ in.

EARLY PRINTING IN FRANCE.

Cabinet 70 · Shelf 1 · No. 19

Paris, 1520. Simon Vostre.
Title: Horae Beatae Virginis ad usum Romanum. Printed on vellum. illuminated. Printer Mark.
Imprint: Les presentes heures a lusaige de Rome.. ont est faictes a Paris pour Symo Vostre Libraire demourat...a leseigne s. ioha levagel.

Calf; $7\frac{1}{4}$ x $4\frac{3}{4}$ x $1\frac{1}{4}$ in.

In Ex.Cab.No.9

EARLY PRINTING IN FRANCE

Cabinet 29 · Shelf 2 · No. 9

Paris, 1523. Thielman Kerver [Widow]
Title: Hore deipare virginis marie secūdū usum Romanū, plerisqz biblie figuris atqz...effigiebs adornate...1523. [Printer Mark]
Colophon: Finiuntur hore...Parisiis, opera & impensis vidue defuncti...Thielmani kerver in vico sancti Iacobi ad signum Univornis, & ibide venales habent. Anno dni MDXXIII die XXX Martii....
[Wood cuts and borders. Printed in black and red]

cont'd

EARLY PRINTING IN FRANCE cont'd

Cabinet 29 · Shelf 2 · No. 9

Vellum; $6\frac{1}{2}$ x 4-1/8 x 1 in.

Ex. Cab. 72.

EARLY PRINTING IN FRANCE

Cabinet 70 · Shelf 2 · No. 3

Paris, 1524. Badius Ascensius (Josse Badé)

Title: De Asse et partibus eius Libri quinqz Gulielmi Budei Parisiensis Secretarii Regii. [Printer Mark]. Vaenundtur in aedibus Ascensianis.
Colophon: Finis libri Quinti & Ultimi de Asse & partibus eius...In chalcographia Ascensiana Pridie Nonas Ianua. Anno ad calculum Romanū MDXXIIII.

Vellum; 12 x $8\frac{1}{2}$ x $1\frac{1}{2}$ in.

EARLY PRINTING IN FRANCE

Cabinet 70 · Shelf 1 · No. 23

Paris, 1524. Philippe Lenoir.
Title: Les illustrations de Gaul et Singularitez de Troye. Fratris Petri...On les vend a Paris par Philippe le noir marchãt libraire et relieure de Paris....
Colophon: Imprime a Paris au moys de Juillet Lan Mil Cinq Cens et XXIIII par Philippe le Noir....de Paris demourāt en la grant Rue Sainct Jacques a lenseigne de la Rose blance couronne. Printed in four parts, each part with Lenoir imprint, colophon, and printer

cont'd

EARLY PRINTING IN FRANCE cont'd

Cabinet 70 · Shelf 1 · No. 23

mark.

Morocco over boards, clasps; $10\frac{3}{4}$ x $7\frac{3}{4}$ x $1\frac{3}{4}$in

EARLY PRINTING IN FRANCE.

Cabinet 70 · Shelf 1 · No. 26

Paris [1525]. Pierre Roffet.
Title: Horae [Engraved title page with border, and printer mark].
Imprint: Les presentes heures ... ont este faictes a Paris pour Pierre Roffet, libraire demourent en la rue neusue: a lesei. dū feulcheur. n.d.

Tooled leather; $8\frac{3}{4}$ x 6 x 1 in.

EARLY PRINTING IN FRANCE

Cabinet 70 · Shelf 1 · No. 27

Paris, 1525. Geofroy Tory.
Title: Heures a la louange de la vierge Marie, selon lusage de Rome...Printer Mark.
Colophon: Ces presentes heures achevees de imprimer le mardy dixsetiesme iour de Ianuier Mil cinq cens vingtcinq: pour maistre Geofroy Tory de Bourges...a Paris sus Petit pont ioignant lhostel. Dieu a lenseigne du Pot casse. Borders and illus.

Old calf, gold tooled; 8-3/4 x 5½ x 1 in.

EARLY PRINTING IN FRANCE cont'd

Cabinet 70 · Shelf 1 · No. 37

Casse...

Tooled Leather; 10 x 7 x 1 in.

EARLY PRINTING IN FRANCE

Cabinet 70 · Shelf 1 · No. 41

Paris, 1532. Claude Chevallon.

Title: Psalmorum omnium iuxta Hebraica veritate paraphrastica interpretatio, autore Ioanne Cāpensi...Printer Mark. Parisiis ex officina Claudii Chevallon, anno 1532.
Colophon: Parisiis, ex officina Claudii Chevallonii. Anno 1532.

Calf; 4-3/4 x 3 x 1-1/8 in.

EARLY PRINTING IN FRANCE.

Cabinet 70 · Shelf 1 · No. 30

Paris, 1526. Badius Ascensius (Josse Badé)
Title: Gulielmi Budaei Parisiensis, Contemptu rerum fortuitarum Libri Tres. At foot: Printer Mark. Venundantur in officina Ascensiana, cum Gratia & privilegio in Triennium.
Second title: Latinae linguae flosculi ad operis D. Gulielmi Budei...Below: Printer Mark. Venundantur ut opus ipsum, Badio.
Bound together; printer mark on each title.
Boards; 7½ x 5-5/8 x 3/4 in.

EARLY PRINTING IN FRANCE

Cabinet 40 · Shelf 2 · No. 1

Paris, 1530. Blaublom. Ludovici [or Louis Cyanus]
Title: Veterinariae medicinae libri II Iohanne Ruellio, Svessionensi interprete. Parisiis: apud Simonem Colinaeum. 1530. Cum privilegio regio ad quinquennium.
Colophon: Parisiis, ex chalcographia Ludovici Blaublomii Gandavi, impensis Simonis Colinaei. M.D.XXX.

cont'd

EARLY PRINTING IN FRANCE

Cabinet 40 · Shelf 1 · No. 77

Paris, 1531. Colines, Simon de.

Title: Silii Italici clarissimi poetae de bello punico libri septemdecim. Cum argumentis Hermanni Buschii. [Printer Mark]. Parisiis apud Simonem Colineum. 1531.
Colophon: Parisiis in aedibus Simonis Colinaei anno M.D.XXXI, mense Novembri.

Vellum; 6¾ x 4-3/8 x 1½ in. Brunet 5, 383.

EARLY PRINTING IN FRANCE

Cabinet 40 · Shelf 1 · No. 6

Paris, 1526. Robert Estienne (Stephanus)

Title: Prisciani libellus de accentibus. [Printer Mark]. Parisiis ex officina Roberti Stephani eregione scholae decretorum, M.D.XXVI.
Colophon: Excudebat Robertus Stephanus. Parisiis, anno M.D.XXVII.X calend. Iunii

Tooled morocco; 6¼ x 4¼ x 3/8 in.

EARLY PRINTING IN FRANCE cont'd

Cabinet · Shelf · No.

Boards; 13 x 9 x 1-1/8 in. See Renouard, Imprimeurs Parisiens, p.89.

EARLY PRINTING IN FRANCE

Cabinet 70 · Shelf 2 · No. 11

Paris, 1532. Gerard Morrhy and Jean Pierre.
Title: Orontii Finei. Protomathesis: Opus varium. Parisiis. Anno 1532. [Woodcut title border, many diagrams, cuts, head pieces and large initials.]
Colophon: Excusum est autem ipsum opus Parisiis in vico Sorbonico, impensis Gerardi Morrhii & Ioannis Petri. Anno M.D.XXXII. Vaenundatur autem in eodem vico Sorbonico & Iacobaeo apud eundem Ioannem Petrum sub insigni D. Barbarae.

Vellum; 14½ x 10½ x 2 in. Renouard, Imprimeurs Parisiens, 299.

EARLY PRINTING IN FRANCE.

Cabinet 40 · Shelf 2 · No. 19

Paris, 1526. Simon de Colines.
Title: Francisci Sarzosi Cellanti Aragonei, in Aequatorem planetarum ...
Imprint: Parisiis. Apud Simonem Colinaeu, 1526. [Two books in one. First book printed by Andreas Wechel. Paris, 1564].

Calf; 13 x 9 x 2¼ in.

EARLY PRINTING IN FRANCE

Cabinet 40 · Shelf 1 · No. 9

Paris, 1530. Simon de Colines.

Title: Aediloquium ceu Disticha, partibus Aedium urbanarum & rusticarum suis...Gotofredo Torino.
Imprint: Parisiis, apud Simonem Colineum, 1530.

Morocco, hand tooled (by Lortic); 6¼ x 4 x ¼ in. Brunet 5, 888-9.

EARLY PRINTING IN FRANCE

Cabinet 40 · Shelf 2 · No. 5

Paris, 1532. Robert (I) Estienne.
Title: P. Virgilii Maronis Opera. Mauri Servii Honorati Grammatici in eadem commentarii... Castigationes & Varietates Virgilianae lectionis, per Ioannem Pierium Valerianum. Parisiis: Ex officina Roberti Stephani. [Printer Mark]
Colophon: Excudebat Rob. Stephanus. Parisiis, anno M.D.XXXII. XVII. cal. Augusti. [Following colophon a full page engraving of the Estienne mark]

Morocco, gilt edges; 12-3/4 x 8¼ x 2-1/8 ins. Brunet 5, 1283.

EARLY PRINTING IN FRANCE.

Cabinet 70 · Shelf 1 · No. 34

Paris, 1528. Pierre Vidoue
Title: Les XXI. Epistres Davide translatees de latin en Frācoys Par...monseigñr Levesque Dangoulesme. [Publisher's device]....Ils se vendent...en la boutique de Galliot du pre marchāt. M.D.XXVIII.
Colophon: Cy finent les XXI. epistres Davide imprimees a Paris par maistre Pierre Vidoue Pour Galliot du pre...de Paris, Ayāt sa boutique au premier pillier de la grand salle du pallais.

Morocco; 5-3/8 x 3¼ x ½ in.

EARLY PRINTING IN FRANCE.

Cabinet 40 · Shelf 2 · No. 1

Paris, 1530. Simon de Colines. Ludovico Blaublom.
Title: Veterinariae medicinae libri II. Johanne Ruellio.
Imprint: Parisiis apud Simonem Colinaeum.
Colophon: Parisiis, ex chalcographia Ludovici Blaublomii Gandivi, impensis Simonis Colinaei 1530.

Boards; 13-1/8 x 8-7/8 x 1 in.

EARLY PRINTING IN FRANCE Example

Cabinet I · Shelf 1 · No. 4

Paris, 1535: Christian Wechel.

See DURER, ALBRECHT. Albertus Durerus Nurembergensis pictor...

EARLY PRINTING IN FRANCE

Cabinet 70 · Shelf 1 · No. 37

Paris, 1529. Geofroy Tory.
Title: Champ Fleury...& est a vendre a Paris sus Petit Pont a Lenseigne du Pot Casse par Maistre Geofroy Tory de Bourges, Libraire & Autheur du dict Livre...Below: Printer Mark.
Colophon: Cy finist ce present livre, avec Laddition de Treze diverses facōs de Lettres... Qui fut acheve dimprimer Le mercredy XXVIII. Iour du Mois Dapril Lan Mil Cincq Cens XXIX. Pour Maistre Geofroy Tory de Bourges, autheur dudict Livre demourāt a Paris, qui le vent sus Petit Pont a Lenseigne du Pot

cont'd

EARLY PRINTING IN FRANCE

Cabinet 40 · Shelf 1 · No. 78

Paris, 1530 and 1531. Colines, Simon de
Title (1): L. Fenestellae de magistratibus Romanorum libellus, iam primum nitori restitutus. ...Parisiis apud Simonem Colineum. 1530. [Printer Mark]
Title (2): Historia de Vita et moribus imperatorum Romanorum, excerpta ex libris Sexti Aurelii victoris...[Printer Mark]
Imprint: Parisiis apud Simonem Colinaeum M.D.XXXI

Wood cut title page in "maniere crible", by Geofroy Tory.

Boards; 7 x 4¼ x 1 in.

EARLY PRINTING IN FRANCE.

Cabinet 40 · Shelf 1 · No. 8

Paris, 1536. Robert Estienne I. [Various botanical-medical works, bound together, of which his brother Charles (Carolus) was author].
First Title: De re hortesi libellus, vulgaria herbarum, florum ... Parisiis: Ex officina Roberti Stephani, M.D.XXXVI. pp. 96 xv.
Second Title: Seminariu sive plantarium arborum ... [no imprint: colophon dated July 21, 1536] pp. 107, xvii.

(Cont'd)

EARLY PRINTING IN FRANCE. cont'd

Cabinet
Shelf
No.

Third Title: De vasculis libellus ... Parisiis: Ex officina Rob. Stephani M.D.XXXVI, pp. 56 vii.
Fourth Title: De re vestiaria libellus ... secunda editio. [Same imprint as on third title] pp. 68, viii. [Colophon dated May 3, 1536.]

Stamped leather; 7 x 4¾ in.

EARLY PRINTING IN FRANCE.

Cabinet 40
Shelf 2
No. 8

Paris, 1536. Simon de Colines.
Title: De natura stirpium libri tres, Ioanne Ruellio authore. [Title within a border in the manner of Geofroy Tory].
Imprint: Cum privilegio regis. Parisiis, ex officina Simonis Colinaei. 1536.

Morocco; 15 x 10 x 2½ in. Brunet 4,1451.

EARLY PRINTING IN FRANCE.

Cabinet 70
Shelf 2
No. 18

Paris, 1538. Michael Vascosan.
Title: Appiani Alexandrini, Sophistae de Civilibus Romanorũ historiarum libri quinque ...
Second Title: P.Velli paterculi historiae Romanae duo volumina [Each title with picture of Ascensian Press].
Imprint: Parisiis, ex officina Michaelis Vascosani. M.D.XXXVIII.

Calf; 13 x 8½ x 1¾ in.

EARLY PRINTING IN FRANCE

Cabinet 40
Shelf 2
No. 10

Paris, 1538. Robert (I) Estienne.
Title (I): Tullii Ciceronis epistolae. Parisiis. Ex officina Roberti Stephani. M.D.XXXVIII.
Title (2): M. Tullii Ciceronis philosophica.
Title (3): Petri Victorii Explicationes suarum in Ciceronem castigationum. [Each title page with imprint and large device of Robert Estienne.]

Old leather; 14¼ x 10-1/8 x 3¼ in.

EARLY PRINTING IN FRANCE

Cabinet 69
Shelf 1
No. 5

Paris, 1539. Conrad Neobar.
Title: Aristoteles: Rhetoric [In Greek. Printer Mark].
Imprint: Parisiis. Per Conradum Neobarium. Regium Typographum. 1539.
[Bound with another Greek item with the imprint of Turnèbe, and colophon of G. Morel, Paris, 1555.]
Contemporary calf; gilt edges, tooled with a floral design; 10½ x 8 x 1½ in.

EARLY PRINTING IN FRANCE

Cabinet 69
Shelf 1
No. 1

Paris, 1539. Denys Janot.
Title: Le théatre des bons engins, auquel sont contenuz cent Emblemes moraulx. Composé par Guillaume de la Perriere Tolosain:....De l'imprimerie de Denys Ianot, imprimeur & libraire.
Colophon: Imprime a Paris par Denys Ianot....demourant en la rue neufve nostre Dame, à l'enseigne sainct Iean Baptiste pres saincte Geneiefue des Ardents. [Printer Mark].
Morocco; 6½ x 4-1/4 x 1/2 in.

EARLY PRINTING IN FRANCE

Cabinet 40
Shelf 1
No. 10

Paris, 1539. Estienne. Francois (1) (Stephanus).
Title: Vita beatissimi patris, D. Petri Caelestini Quinti, Pontificis Maximi...[Printer Mark].
Imprint: Parisiis apud Franciscum Stephanum. 1539.

Vellum; 9¼ x 6½ x / in. See Renouard. Imprimeurs Parisiens.

EARLY PRINTING IN FRANCE.

Cabinet 40
Shelf 2
No. 13

Paris, 1539. Robert (I) Estienne.
Title: M.T. Ciceronis Opera. Ex Petri Victorii codicibus maxima ex parte descripta...eiusdem Victorii explicationes suarum in Ciceronem castigationum. Index rerum et verborum. [Printer Mark]. Parisiis: Ex officina Roberti Stephani. M.D.XXXIX.
Colophon: Excudebat Robertus Stephanus. Parisiis, Ann. M.XXXIX. Idib. Augusti.

Leather; 14-3/4 x 10-1/8 x 2½ ins.

EARLY PRINTING IN FRANCE

Cabinet 69
Shelf 1
No. 8

Paris, 1540. Claude Chevallon (Veuve). [Charlotte Guillard]
Title: Les apophthegmes...Translatez de latin en fracois, par lesleu Macault notaire, secretaire, & vallet de chambre du Roy.
Imprint: On les vend a Paris au soleil dor, en la rue saint Iacques. 1540. [Printer's name appears in the privilege which follows title]

Morocco; 4-7/8 x 3 x 1½ in.

EARLY PRINTING IN FRANCE.

Cabinet 60
Shelf 2
No. 18

Paris, 1540. Michel Vascosan.
Title: Jacobi Lodoici Strebaei in dialogis M.T. Ciceronis ...
Imprint: Parisiis. Ex officina Michaelis Vascosan, sub fonte, in via quae est at divum Jacobum. 1540.
Bound in with a 1554 Paul Manutius item.

Vellum; 13 x 9 x 1-3/8 in.

EARLY PRINTING IN FRANCE.

Cabinet 69
Shelf 1
No. 10

Paris, 1542. Christian Wechel.
Title: Clarissimi viri D. Andreae Alciati emblematum libellus....[Printer Mark]
IMPRINT; Parisiis. Apud Christianum Wechelum, sub scuto Basiliensi, in vico Iacobeo: & sub Pegaso in vico Bellouacensi M.D.XLII.

Half morocco; 6-1/8 x 4 x 1/2 in. Brunet, 1, 147.

EARLY PRINTING IN FRANCE

Cabinet 70
Shelf 2
No. 20

Paris, 1542. Michael Vascosan.
Title: M. Fabii Quintiliani. Institutionum oratoriarum libri XII; declamationum liber, additae sunt P. mosellani et Jo. Camerarii annotationes et Ant. Pini comment...
[Borders and initials; wood engraving]
Imprint: Parisiis, ex officina Michaelis Vascosani, in via...M.D.XLII. [Separate title page for second part, same date and imprint with Ascensian Press mark]

cont'd

EARLY PRINTING IN FRANCE cont'd

Cabinet
Shelf
No.

Calf; 13½ x 9 x 1¾ in. Brunet 4, 1025.

EARLY PRINTING IN FRANCE

Cabinet 40
Shelf 2
No. 23

Paris, 1544. Simon de Colines
Title: Orontii Finaei Delphinatis, Regii Mathematicarum Lutetiae professoris, in sex libros geometricorum...
Imprint: Lutetiae Parisiorum, apud Simonem Colineum 1544...[Woodcut title border, initials, head ornaments, and mathematical diagrams].

Boards covered with part of 15 cen. manuscripts; 12 x 8¼ x 7/8 in.

See also 40/2/22

EARLY PRINTING IN FRANCE

Cabinet 40
Shelf 1
No. 12

Paris, 1543. Robert (I) Estienne (Stephanus)
Title: C. Suetonii Tranquilli XII Caesares. [Printer Mark]. Parisiis. Ex officina Roberti Stephani typographi Regii M.D.XLIII.
Colophon: Excudebat Rob. Stephanus typographus Regius, Parisiis an. M.D.XLIII.XV cal. Decembr.

Calf; 6-3/4 x 4¼ x 7/8 in.

EARLY PRINTING IN FRANCE

Cabinet 40
Shelf 1
No. 11

Paris, 1543. Robert Estienne (Stephanus)
Title: Libri de re rustica, M.Catonis Lib.1. M. Terentii Varronis Lib. III. Per Petrum Victoriu....suae integritati restituti. [Printer Mark]. Parisiis. Ex officina Roberti Stephani typographi Regii M.DXLIII.
Colophon: Excudebat Rob. Stephanus, typographus regius, Parisiis. An. M.D.XLIII.XVI. cal. Augusti.

Morocco; 6¾ x 4-3/8 x 1 in.

EARLY PRINTING IN FRANCE

Cabinet 70
Shelf 2
No. 23

Paris, 1544. Charlotte Guillard.
Title: D. Hilarii Pictavorum episcopi lucubrationes olim per Des. Erasmum Rot. haud. mediocribus...emendate...[Printer Mark]
Imprint and Colophon: Parisiis. Ex officina Carolae Guillard, sub Sole aureo via ad divum Iacobum. 1544.

Boards; 13½ x 9-1/8 x 1½ in.

EARLY PRINTING IN FRANCE

Cabinet 40
Shelf 1
No. 15

Paris, 1544. Robert Estienne (Stephanus)
Title: Dion Cassius Nicaeus Aelius Spartianus Iulius capitolinus. Aelius Lampridius. Vulcatius Gallicanus. Iohannis Baptiste Egnatii ....annotationes. [Printer Mark]. Parisiis. Ex officina Roberti Stephani typographi Regii M.D.XLIIII.
Colophon: Excudebat Rob. Stephanus typographus Regius Parisiis, Ann. M.D.XLIIII. Idib Iun.

cont'd

EARLY PRINTING IN FRANCE, cont'd

Cabinet
Shelf
No.

Leather; 6½ x 4¾ x 7/8 in.

EARLY PRINTING IN FRANCE

Cabinet 40
Shelf 1
No. 16

Paris, 1544-45. Robert Estienne (Stephanus).

Title: Valerii Maximi dictorum factorumque memorabilium exempla....[Printer Mark]. Lutetiae. ex officina Roberti Stephani typographi Regii M.D.XLIIII.
Colophon: Excudebat Rob. Stephanus, typographus Regius Lutetiae. Ann. M.D.XLV. VII Id. Ian.

Calf; 6¾ x 4¼ x 7/8 in.

EARLY PRINTING IN FRANCE cont'd

Cabinet 40
Shelf 2
No. 28

M.D.XLVIII, Prid. cal. Febr.

Calf; 13¼ x 9 x 1½ in.

EARLY PRINTING IN FRANCE

Cabinet 40
Shelf 2
No. 20

Paris, 1544. Robert (I) Estienne.
Title: Ecclesiasticae Historiae. [Title in Greek and Latin] [Printer Mark] Lutetiae Parisiorum: ex officina Roberti Stephani typographi Regii, Regiis typis M.D.XLIIII. Cum privilegio regis.
Colophon: Excudebat Robertus Stephanus typographus regius Lutetiae Parisiorum. Anno MDXLIIII. Pridie cal. Iul. [Second variation of printer mark]

cont'd

EARLY PRINTING IN FRANCE

Cabinet 40
Shelf 1
No. 19

Paris, 1546. Robert Estienne (Stephanus)

Title: La coltivatione di Luigi Alamanni al Christianissimo re Francesco primo [Printer Mark]
Imprint: Stampato in Parigi da Roberto Stephano Regio Stampatore. M.D.XLVI.

Morocco, gilt ornamental tooling, 8-3/8 x 5-3/4 x 7/8 in.

EARLY PRINTING IN FRANCE

Cabinet 40
Shelf 1
No. 22

Paris, 1548. Robert (I) Estienne (Stephanus)

Title: Thesaurus linguae sanctae. Ex R. David Kimchi....authore..[Printer Mark]. Ex officina Robertii Stephani typographi Regii. Ex privilegio Regis.
Colophon: Excudebat Rob. Stephanus typographus Regius ann. M.D.XLVIII.XII. cal. Feb.

Tooled Pigskin in buckram case; 9 x 6¼ x 3½ in.

EARLY PRINTING IN FRANCE cont'd

Cabinet
Shelf
No.

Calf; 13¾ x 10 x 2¾ ins.

EARLY PRINTING IN FRANCE

Cabinet 69
Shelf 1
No. 13

Paris, 1547. Estienne (I) Groulleau.

Title: La Cyropedie de Xenophon....Traduite de Graec en langue Françoyse, par Iaques de Vintemille, Rhodien. [Printer Mark]. A Paris, de l'Imprimerie d'Estienne Groulleau. ...
Colophon: Fin du huytiesme & dernier livre de la Cyropedie de xenophon imprime a Paris par Estienne Groulleau: pour luy Ian Longis &

cont'd

EARLY PRINTING IN FRANCE.

Cabinet 40
Shelf 1
No. 25

Paris, 1548-50. Robert Estienne (Stephanus)
Title (1): Seminarium et plantarium...[Printer mark]. Parisiis, ex officina Rob. Stephani typographi Regii. M.D.XLVIII.
Title (2): Caroli Stephani, de nutrimentis ad Baillyum, libri tres. [Printer Mark]. Parisiis ex officina Rob. Steph. typographus regius Lutetia Ann. M.D.XLVIII.III.id decemb.

cont'd

EARLY PRINTING IN FRANCE

Cabinet 40
Shelf 1
No. 81

Paris, 1544. Simon de Colines.
Title: Martialis epigrammaton, libri 14, summa diligentia castigati ...
Imprint: Parisiis. Apud Simonem Colinaeum. 1544. With printer mark.

Calf; 4½ x 2¾ x 7/8 in.

EARLY PRINTING IN FRANCE cont'd

Cabinet
Shelf
No.

Vincent Sertenas, Libraires. 1547.

Morocco, gilt edges; 9¼ x 6½ x 7/8 in.

EARLY PRINTING IN FRANCE cont'd

Cabinet 40
Shelf 1
No. 25

Morocco, 6¾ x 4½ x 1¾ ins. These are bound together with a Trechsel item, Lyons, 1535.

EARLY PRINTING IN FRANCE.

Cabinet 40
Shelf 2
No. 22

Paris, 1544. Simon de Colines.
Title: Orontii Finaei Delphinatis. Regii mathematicarum Lutetiae professoris, in sex priories libros geometricorum elementorum Euclidis ... interpretatione latina Bartholamaei Zamberti Veneti. Omnia ad fidem ... per eundē Orontium recognita.
Imprint: Lutetiae Parisiorum, apud Simonem Colinaeum 1544. Cum privilegio regis. Virescit vulnere virtus.
Boards; 11¾ x 8-3/8 x 5/8 in.

EARLY PRINTING IN FRANCE

Cabinet 69
Shelf 1
No. 15

Paris, 1548. Conrad Badius.

Title: Theodori Bezae Vezlii. Poemata. [Ascensius woodcut printing press device]. Lutetiae. Ex officina Conradi Badii sub prelo Ascensiano ē regione gymnasii D. Barbarae. M.D.XLVIII...
Colophon: Lutetiae Robert Stephano regio typographo, et sibi Conradus Badius excudebat, idibus Iul.II. M.D.XLVIII.

Mottled calf; 6-3/4 x 4-1/8 x 3/8 in. Brunet 1,841.

EARLY PRINTING IN FRANCE

Cabinet 40
Shelf 1
No. 27

Paris, 1549. Robert (I) Estienne.
Title: Jovius Paulus. Vitae duodecim vicecomitum Mediolani principum... [Printer Mark]
Imprint: Lutetiae. Ex officina Rob. Stephani, typographi Regii. M.D.XLIX. Ex privilegio Regis.
Includes wood cut portraits, all with the Lorraine cross of Geofroy Tory. The ornamental initials are also the work of G.T.

Vellum; 10 x 6-7/8 x 7/8 in. Brunet 3, 584. Updike I, 235.

EARLY PRINTING IN FRANCE.

Cabinet 40
Shelf 2
No. 21

Paris, 1544. Simon Colines.
Title: Orontii Finaei Delphinatis, regii mathematicorum Lutetiae professoris. Quadratura circuli, tandem inventa et clarissime demonstrata ...
Imprint: Lutetiae Parisorum, apud Simonem Colinaeum, 1544.

Vellum manuscript, with straps; 12-7/8 x 8-5/8 x ½ in.

EARLY PRINTING IN FRANCE

Cabinet 40
Shelf 2
No. 28

Paris, 1548. Robert (I) Estienne

Title:....Dionis Romanarum historiarum libri XXIII, à XXXVI ad LVIII usque. Ex bibliotheca regia [In Greek; printer mark on title page]. Lutetiae: Ex officina Rob. Stephani, typographi regii, typis regiis. M.D.XLVIII. Ex privilegio regis.
Colophon: Excudebat Robertus Stephanus typographus regius. Lutetiae Parisiorum. Anno

cont'd

EARLY PRINTING IN FRANCE.

Cabinet 40
Shelf 2
No. 16

Paris, 1550. Robert (I) Estienne.
Title: Novum Iesu Christi D.N. Testamentum. Ex bibliotheca Regia. [Printer Mark] Lutetiae. Ex officina Roberti Stephani typographi Regiis typis. M.D.L.[Greek]
Colophon: Excudebat Robertus Stephanus typographus regius Lutetiae Parisiorum, anno M.D.L. XVII. cal Iul.

Calf; 13¼ x 9 x 1-3/4 in.

EARLY PRINTING IN FRANCE

Cabinet 40 Shelf 2 No. 34

Paris, 1551. Charles Estienne.
Title: Appiani alexandrini romanarum historiarum [in Greek]. Ex bibliotheca regia. [Printer Mark].
Imprint: Lutetiae: typis regiis, cura ac diligentia Caroli Stephani, M.D.LI. Cum privilegio regio.

Vellum; 13¼ x 9 x 1½ in. Brunet 1, 356.

EARLY PRINTING IN FRANCE

Cabinet 69 Shelf 1 No. 23

Paris, 1553. Gaultherot, Vivant.
Title: Cosmographia Petri Apiani, per Gemmam Frisium vindicata....[Woodcut of sphere on title page]. Parisiis, Vaeneunt apud Vivantium Gaultherot, via Iacobea: sub intersignio D. Martini. 1553.
Colophon: Parisiis impressum expensis Vivantii Gaultherot Anno domini. 1551.

Half vellum; 9 x 6¾ x 3/4 in.

EARLY PRINTING IN FRANCE.

Cabinet 69 Shelf 2 No. 3

Paris, 1560. Richard Roux [For Jean I, Ruelle].
Title: Annales et croniques de France ... Nicole Gilles ... Corrigées et annotes par le Seigneur Denis Sauvage. [Printer Mark]. A Paris, Par Iean Ruelle ... al'Enseigne Sainct Nicolas, 1566. [Illus].
Colophon: Fin du second et dernier volume ... continues iusques en l'an mil cinq cens soixante. Imprimees a Paris, par Richard Roux

Cont'd.

EARLY PRINTING IN FRANCE.

Cabinet 40 Shelf 1 No. 29

Paris, 1551. Robert (I) Estienne.
Title: Dionis Nicae rerum Romanarum ... [Greek and Latin text]
Imprint: Lutetiae, ex officina Roberti Stephani Typographi Regii, Regiis typis. 1551.

Vellum; 9¾ x 6¾ x 2 in.

Brunet 5, 1504

EARLY PRINTING IN FRANCE

Cabinet 40 Shelf 1 No. 15

Paris, 1554. Charles Estienne (Stephanus)
Title: De Latinis et Graecis nominibus arborum... ex Aristotele, Theophrasto...Quarto aeditio. [Printer Mark]
Imprint: Lutetiae. Apud Carolum Stephanum, Typographum Regium M.D.LIII.

Morocco; 6¾ x 4½ x 1¾ ins. Bound together with a Trechsel item, Lyons, 1535 and Robert

cont'd

EARLY PRINTING IN FRANCE cont'd

Cabinet Shelf No.

imprimeur ... Sainct Victor, a l'Enseigne Sainct Catherine.

Calf; 13¼ x 8½ x 1½ in. Brunet 2, 1596.

EARLY PRINTING IN FRANCE

Cabinet 40 Shelf 1 No. 30

Paris, 1551-1552. Charles Estienne (Stephanus).
Title (1): Apologia cuiusdam regiae famae studiosi ....
Title (2): Altera apologia pro rege christianissimo contra Caesarianos: [Both titles with printer marks].
Colophon; 1 and 2: Lutetiae, apud Carolum Stephanum typographum regium, e regione scholae Decretorum. M.D.LI-M.D.LII. Cum privi-

cont'd

EARLY PRINTING IN FRANCE cont'd

Cabinet 40 Shelf 1 No. 25

Estienne items of 1535, 1548 and 1550. See Renouard Imprimeurs Parisiens.

EARLY PRINTING IN FRANCE

Cabinet 29 Shelf 2 No. 14

Paris, 1561. Jacques Kerver
Title: Hypnerotomachie ... de Poliphile ... Nouvellement traduit de langage Italian en Francois.
Imprint: A Paris. Pour Jacques Kerver a la Licorne, rue S. Jacques, 1561.

Tree calf; 13¼ x 9 x 1½ in.

EARLY PRINTING IN FRANCE cont'd

Cabinet 40 Shelf 1 No. 30

legio. [Both items bound together].

Vellum; 8¾ x 6-3/8 x 3/8 in.

EARLY PRINTING IN FRANCE.

Cabinet 40 Shelf 1 No. 36

Paris, 1554. Henri Estienne (Stephanus).
Title: Anacreontis teii odae [Greek] ab Henrico Stephano luce & Latinitate nunc primum donatae.
Imprint: Lutetiae. Apud Henricum Stephanum. M.D.LIIII. Ex privilegio regis.

Morocco; 8 x 5-3/4 x 5/8 in. Brunet 1, 250.

EARLY PRINTING IN FRANCE

Cabinet 29 Shelf 2 No. 13

Paris, 1561. Jacques Kerver.
Title: Polygraphie et Universelle escriture cabalistique de M. I. Tritheme Abbé...
Imprint: Pour Iaques Kerver demeurant en la rue sainct Iaques a l'enseigne de la Licorne, 1561.

Calf; 10 x 8 x 2-1/8 in.

EARLY PRINTING IN FRANCE.

Cabinet 69 Shelf 1 No. 21

Paris, 1552. Adrien Turnèbe.
Title: Aeschyli Tragoediae sex. [Greek; Printer Mark]
Imprint: Parisiis. Ex officina Adriani Turnebi. Typographia Regii, M.D.LII. Typis Regis.

Contemporary binding; pigskin, gilt; 6-3/4 x 4¼ x ½ in. Brunet I, 77.

EARLY PRINTING IN FRANCE

Cabinet 69 Shelf 1 No. 5

Paris, 1555. Adrien Turnèbe and Guillaume Morel.
Title: Aristoteles. De Moribus ad Nicomachum lib. X. [In Greek and Latin]
Imprint: Parisiis M.D.LV. apud Adrianum Turnebum ....
Colophon: Excudebat...Guil. Morelius. M.D.LV [Bound in with Aristoteles Rhetoric: Printed in Greek, Conrad Neobar, Paris, 1539.]

Contemporary calf, gilt edges tooled with a floral design; 10½ x 8 x 1½ in.

EARLY PRINTING IN FRANCE

Cabinet 40 Shelf 2 No. 19

Paris, 1564. Andreas Wechel.
Title: Gorraeus (J) Definitionum medicarum ...
Imprint: Lutetiae Parisiorum. Apud Andream Wechelum, sub Pegaso, in vico Bellovaco. 1564.
[Two books in one. Second book printed by Simon de Colines. Paris, 1526].

Calf; 13 x 9 x 2-3/4 in.

EARLY PRINTING IN FRANCE.

Cabinet 40 Shelf 1 No. 32

Paris, 1552. Robert Estienne.
Title: ad censuras theologorum, quibus Biblia a Robert Stephano typographo Regio excusa calumniose notarunt ...
Imprint: [Paris]. Oliva Roberti Stephani. 1552.

Morocco; 7-1/8 x 4-5/8 x 3/4 in.

EARLY PRINTING IN FRANCE.

Cabinet 69 Shelf 1 No. 30

Paris, 1558. Philippe Danfrie and Richard Breton.
Title: Le discours de la court. Avec le plaisant recit. [Printed in a peculiar "Civilite Type'
Imprints: A Paris, De l'imprimerie de Philippe Danfrie, et Richard Breton, rue sainct Jacques, a lescrevisse. M.D.LVIII. Avec privilege du roy.

Calf; 6½ x 4 x 3/8 in.

EARLY PRINTING IN FRANCE

Cabinet 40 Shelf 1 No. 51

Paris, 1568. Robert (II) Estienne.
Title: Edict du Roy par lequel il erige et institue en tiltre d'office...[Printer Mark]
Imprint: A Paris par Rob. Estienne Imprimeur du Roy. M.D.LXVIII.

Half morocco; 6 3/4 x 4-3/8 x 3/8 in.

EARLY PRINTING IN FRANCE.

Cabinet 40 Shelf 1 No. 54

Paris, 1569. Robert (II) Estienne.
Title: [Bible: Greek]. Novum Testamentum ex bibliotheca Regia. Lutetiae (Paris) ex officina Roberti Stephani typographi Regii, Typis Regiis. M.D.LXVIII.
Colophon: Excudebat Rob. Stephanus typographus Regius Parisiis Idib. Ianvar. Anno M.D.LXIX [Printer Mark].

Morocco; 5 x 3-1/4 x 1-5/8 in.

EARLY PRINTING IN FRANCE

Cabinet 69 Shelf 2 No. 11

Paris, 1571. Jean (I) Charron.
Title: Theatrum vitae humanae....Primum à Conrado Lycosthene...Theodori Zvinggeri. [Printer Mark]. Apud Nicolaum Chesneau, via Iacobea, sub scuto Frobeniano & Quercu viridi M.D.LXXI. Cum privilegio regis.
Colophon: Cudebat typis 'que mandabat Ioannes Charron typographus, impensis Nicolai Chesnau et Sonnii Bibliopolarum. Anno Domini, milesimo quingnetesimo septuagesimo primo, septimo Idus Augusti, 1571.

Calf; 14-3/8 x $9\frac{1}{4}$ x $4\frac{1}{4}$ ins.

EARLY PRINTING IN FRANCE

Cabinet 69 Shelf 2 No. 14

Paris, 1572. Michel de Vascosan.
Title: Les oeuvres morales et meslées de Plutarque. Translatées du Grec en François par Missire Iacques Amyot. [Woodcut initials; ruled in red throughout. 2 vols.]
Imprint: A Paris, de l'Imprimerie de Michel de Vascosan. M.D.LXXII. Avec privilege du Roy.

Vellum; $15\frac{1}{2}$ x 10 x 2 ins. Brunet 4, 737.

EARLY PRINTING IN FRANCE.

Cabinet 69 Shelf 1 No. 43

Paris, 1575. Frederic (I) Morel.
Title: Octo cantica sacra e sacris bibliis...A Io Matthaeo Toscano: praefixis argumentis Io. Aurati...
Imprint: Parisiis. Ex officina Federici Moreli Typographi Regii. 1575.

Calf; 6-7/8 x 4-3/8 x $\frac{1}{2}$ in.

EARLY PRINTING IN FRANCE

Cabinet 69 Shelf 2 No. 19

Paris, 1580. Jacques du Puys.
Title: Recueil des roys de France, leurs couronne et maison...par Iean du Tillet. [Printer Mark.]
Imprint: A Paris chez Iaques du Puys, Libraire iure in l'Université de Paris, rue sainct Iean de Latran à la Samaritaine. M.D.LXXX. Avec prévilege du Roy.

Mottled calf; $12\frac{1}{2}$ x $8\frac{1}{2}$ x 1-3/4 in.

EARLY PRINTING IN FRANCE

Cabinet 69 Shelf 1 No. 51

Paris, 1584. Pierre l'Huillier.
Title: De la Vicissitude ou variete des choses en l'univers...Par Loys le Roy dict Regius. [Printer Mark].
Imprint: A Paris, A l'Olivier de Pierre l'Huillier, M.D.LXXXIIII. Avec privilege du Roy.

Vellum; 6-5/8 x $4\frac{1}{4}$ x $1\frac{1}{2}$ in. Brunet 3,1000-1.

EARLY PRINTING IN FRANCE.

Cabinet 40 Shelf 1 No. 64

Paris, 1587. Mamert Patisson & Robert Estienne.
Title: Premieres ouvres de Philippes des Portes
Imprint: A Paris, par Mamert Patisson. Imprimeur de Roy, chez Robert Estienne.

Vellum; $5\frac{3}{4}$ x 3-3/8 x $1\frac{1}{4}$ in.

EARLY PRINTING IN FRANCE

Cabinet 40 Shelf 1 No. 88

Paris, 1587. Mamert Patisson.
Title: Les premieres oeuvres de Philippes des Portes....Reveues, corrigees & augmentees outre les precedentes impressions. [Printer Mark].
Imprints: A Paris par Mamert Patisson Imprimeur du Roy, chez Robert Estienne. M.D.LXXXVII.

Vellum; 5/ x $3\frac{1}{4}$ x 1-3/8 in. See Renourd Imprimeurs Parisiene.

EARLY PRINTING IN FRANCE

Cabinet X Shelf 4 No. 8

Orleans, 1594, Fabian Hotot (Imprint)

see
PRINTING, HISTORICAL, France
(Edict of the King of France, 1594)...

EARLY PRINTING IN FRANCE

Cabinet 69 Shelf 1 No. 57

Paris, 1597. Philippe Danfrie.
Title: Declaration de l'usage du graphometre, par la...mesurer toutes distances des choses de remarque qui se pourront voir...du lieu où il sera posé...par Philippe Danfrie. [Illus.
Imprint: A Paris, chez ledict Danfrie, rue des Carmes. Avec privilege du Roy.
[Curious work in cursive characters created by Robert Granjon, and now known as Civilitie.]

cont'd

EARLY PRINTING IN FRANCE, cont'd

Cabinet Shelf No.

Morocco; $7\frac{3}{4}$ x 5 x $\frac{1}{2}$ in. Brunet 2, 485.

EARLY PRINTING IN FRANCE

Cabinet 2 Shelf 1 No. 20

Paris, 1598. Plantin-Moretus Press: Hadrian Perier, son-in-law of C. Plantin, who established a printing office for him in Paris.
Title: Caii Solii Apollinaris Sidonii, Arvernorum episcopi opera. Io. Savaronis studio & diligentia castigatius recognita. Printer Mark
Imprint: Officina Plantiniana, apud Hadrianum Perier, via Iacobaea. M.D.XCVIII.
Vellum; $7\frac{1}{4}$ x 4-3/8 x 1-3/8 in. Brunet 5, 373-4.

EARLY PRINTING IN FRANCE.

Cabinet 69 Shelf 1 No. 60

Paris, 1600. Matthieu (1) Guillemot.
Title: Le tableau des riches inventions: couvertes du voile des feintes amoureuses, qui sont representées dans le Songe de Poliphile.... exposees par Beroald [de Verville].
Imprint: A Paris, chez Matthieu Guillemot, au Palais, en la gallerie des prisonniers. Avec privilege du Roy. 1600.

Half morocco; $10\frac{1}{2}$ x $7\frac{1}{2}$ x 3/4 in. Brunet 4,779.

EARLY PRINTING IN FRANCE

Cabinet E Shelf 2 No. 80

Paris, 1609. Le Bé (Guillaume III).
Title: Linguae hebraicae institutiones absolutissimae, Johanne Quinquarboreo...authore. Cum annotationibus Petri Vignalii...Et alphabetum Rabbinicum ad calcem Grammatices. Omnia per...diligenter recognita.
Imprint: Lutetiae: Ex officina & Typis Gulielmi Lebé, in angulo viarum S. Iohannis Bellovacensis & Lateranensis. M.DC.IX.
Vellum; $8\frac{3}{4}$ x $6\frac{1}{2}$ x $\frac{3}{4}$ in.
See Renouard, Imprimeurs Parisiens.

EARLY PRINTING IN FRANCE

Cabinet E Shelf 3 No. 60

Paris, 1638. Gilles Morel.
Title: Isidori Pelusiota [S]. De interpretatione divinae Scripturae epistolarum libri V. [Greek and Latin] quorum tres priores ex interpretatione Jac. Billii, Conrado Rittershusio, et Andrea Schotto...nunc primum in Gallia prodeunt. [Printer Mark].
Imprint: Parisiis, sumptibus Aegidii Morelli, via Iacobea, ad insigne fontis. M.DC.XXX.VIII. Cum privilegio regis.

cont'd

EARLY PRINTING IN FRANCE cont'd

Cabinet E Shelf 3 No. 60

Leather; $15\frac{1}{2}$ x 10 x 2-3/4 ins. Brunet 3,463.

EARLY PRINTING IN FRANCE

Cabinet E Shelf 3 No. 64

Paris, 1640. Imprimerie Royale.
Title: De imitatione Christi Libri IV.
Imprint: Parisiis. Anno MDCXL E Typogra'phia Regia.

Morocco; 15_{4} x $10\frac{1}{2}$ x 2 in. Bigmore and Wyman vol.1, p.357.

EARLY PRINTING IN FRANCE

Cabinet E Shelf 3 No. 72

Paris, 1642. L'Imprimerie Royale.
Title: Les principaux poincts de la foy catholique defendus contre l'escrit addresse au roy par l'eminentissime Cardinal duc de Richelieu.
Imprint: A Paris de l'imprimerie Royale du Louvre MDCXLII [Below imprint the name Mettan, the designer and engraver of title page.]

Original leather; 15 x $10\frac{1}{2}$ x $1\frac{1}{2}$ in. Bigmore and Wyman, vol. 1, p.357.

EARLY PRINTING IN FRANCE

Cabinet I · Shelf 1 · No. 9

Paris, 1642, Melchior Tavernier. [Imprint]

See TAVERNIER, MELCHIOR. Perspective pratique. A Paris, chez Melchior Tavernier ...

EARLY PRINTING IN FRANCE

Cabinet E · Shelf 3 · No. 85

[Paris, 1649. Mascurat or Jean Camusat?]
Title: Jugement de tout ce qui a esté imprimé contre le Cardinal Mazarin, depuis le sixieme janvier jusques à la declaration du premier avril mil six cens quarante neuf. n.p.
Following Title: l'imprimeur au favorable lecture. ..que tu seras satisfait de Mascurat & de mon impression.

12 x 8½ x 1⅛ in.

EARLY PRINTING IN FRANCE

Cabinet E · Shelf 4 · No. 34

Paris, 1662. Antoine Vitre.

Title: Biblia Sacra. Vulgate editionis...Parisiis, excudebat Antonius Vitre, Regis & Cleri Gallicani typographus. M.DC.LXII. Cum privilegio Regis...
Imprint: Execudebat Antonius vitre, Regis & Cleri Gallicani Typographus.

Calf; 16 x 10¾ x 2½ ins. Brunet 1, 879.

EARLY PRINTING IN FRANCE

Cabinet E · Shelf 3 · No. 76

Paris, 1644. Pierre Moreau.

Title: Metamorphoses os les changemens miraculeux de quelques grands Saints....Par I. Baudoin.
Imprint: A Paris, en l'imprimerie des nouveaux caracthères de P. Moreau....Imprimeur ordre du Roy, Et se vend en boutique au Palais.... a l'Enseigne de la Verité 1644.

Leather; 8¼ x 6¼ x 1-1/8 in. Werdet. Histoire

cont'd

EARLY PRINTING IN FRANCE

Cabinet X · Shelf 1 · No. 6

Paris, 1650, Robert Ballard
Title: Mentelin, Jacques. De vera typographiae...
Imprint: Parisiis, ex officina Roberti Ballard, Architypographi rei Musices Regis, ad signum Parnassi Montis, in vico Sancti Joannis. Bellovacensis. 1650.

Calf; 8-3/4 x 6½ x ½ in.

EARLY PRINTING IN FRANCE

Cabinet E · Shelf 4 · No. 48

Paris, 1668. (Veuve) Nic. de la Coste.
Title: nouvelle methode pour se disposer aisement. ..a Confessione...Par R.P.Christophle Liutbrevver.
Imprint: A Paris, chez la Veuve Nic. de la Coste, a l'Escu de Bretagne, a la petite Porte du Palais, qui regarde le Quay des Augustins M.DC.LXVIII....

Calf; 5¾ x 3¼ x 3¼ ins.

EARLY PRINTING IN FRANCE cont'd

Cabinet E · Shelf 3 · No. 76

du livre en France; IIIme partie (II), p.190.

EARLY PRINTING IN FRANCE

Cabinet I · Shelf 5 · No. 21

Paris, 1651. Jacques Langlois.

Title: Traitté de la peinture de Leonard De Vinci Donné au public et traduit d'Italien en Francois par R.F.S. De Chambray.
Imprints: A Paris, de l'Imprimerie de Jacques Langlois, Imprimeur ordinaire du Roy, au mont Saincte Genevievfe, vis à vis la Fonteine à la Reyne de Paix. M.DC.LI...

Morocco; 15-3/4 x 11-3/4 x 1 in.

EARLY PRINTING IN FRANCE

Cabinet E · Shelf 4 · No. 53

Paris, 1671, Francois Muguet.
Title: Les figures et l'abregé de la vie, de la mort, et des miracles de Saint Francois de Paule...
Imprint: A Paris, chez Francois Muguet...1671.

Has more than 40 beautifully executed engravings by Abraham Bosse and Francois de Poilly.

Morocco; 14½ x 10 x 1 in.

EARLY PRINTING IN FRANCE.

Cabinet E · Shelf 3 · No. 77

Paris, 1644. Typographia Regia.

Title: D. Iunii Iuvenalis satyrae. [Royal escutcheon]
Imprint: Parisiis, E. Typographia Regia. M.DC.XLIV.

Morocco, gold coat-of-arms; 14½ x 10½ x 1¼ in.

EARLY PRINTING IN FRANCE.

Cabinet E · Shelf 4 · No. 12 · 2 Vols.

Paris, 1653. Sebastian Cramoisy.
Title: (1): Biblia sacra. Parisiis, MDCLIII. E Typographia regia. Illus.
Title: (2): Biblio sacra. Vulgate editionis ... Parisiis ...
Colophon: Parisiis, e Typographia Regia, curante Sebastiano Cramoisy, Regis, & Reginae architypographo MDCLIII. Illus.

Morocco; 9½ x 7 x 1¼ in.

EARLY PRINTING IN FRANCE

Cabinet V · Shelf 4 · No. 16

Paris, 1689. Jean de la Caille.

See CAILLE (JEAN DE LA) Histoire de l'imprimerie...

EARLY PRINTING IN FRANCE

Cabinet J · Shelf 2 · No. 13

Paris, 1647, Guillaume Le Be.
Title: La vraye science de la pourtraicture,..
Imprint: A Paris, chez Guillaume Le Be, rue sainct Jean de Beauvais, pres le puits certain. 1647.

With 39 plates of wood engravings.

Boards, leather back, oblong; 8 x 10½ in.

EARLY PRINTING IN FRANCE.

Cabinet E · Shelf 4 · No. 21

Paris, 1658. Adrien Moreau.
Title I: L'eneide de Virgile fidelement traduit en vers. A Paris chez Estienne Loyson. MDCLVIII.
Title II: L'eneide traduite in vers francois ... Seconde partie. A Paris. Chez Iean Pasle ... MDCLVIII. [Illus].
Second part, p.464: Privilege to Adrien Moreau].

Calf; 10½ x 8 x 2¼ in.

EARLY PRINTING IN FRANCE

Cabinet V · Shelf 3 · No. ~~4~~ 1

Paris, 1728. Claude-Louis Thiboust.
Title: Connubia florum latino carmine demonstrata. Anctore D. Mac-Eneroe, M. D. Cum interpretatione Gallica. Parisiis
Imprint: Ex Typographia Theobustea, è Regione Collegii Regii. M. DCC.XXVIII.
Bound in with "L'Excellence de l'imprimerie", by C. L. Thiboust, 1754.

Calf; 7¾ x 4¾ x ¾ in.

EARLY PRINTING IN FRANCE.

Cabinet E · Shelf 3 · No. 82

Paris, 1648. Sebastian Cramoisy (Imprimerie Royale).
Title: Georgius Codinus cura plata, de officiis magnae ecclesiae ... cura et opera P. Jacobi Goar.
Colophon: Parisiis in Typographia Regia, curante Sebastiano Cramoisy.

Tooled calf; 16½ x 11 x 2½ in.

EARLY PRINTING IN FRANCE

Cabinet E · Shelf 4 · No. 27

Paris, 1660. Frederic Léonard.
Title: Idea principis christiano politici. Symbolis CI expressa a Didaco Saavedra Faxardo.... [Illus.]
Imprint: Parisiis. Apud Fridericum Leonardum, 1660.

Following dedication: Picture of a printing press, and an account of the invention of printing, addressed to the reader.

Vellum; 5¼ x 3 x 1 in.

EARLY PRINTING IN FRANCE.

Cabinet F · Shelf 4 · No. 79 · 3 vols.

Paris, 1745: Antoine Urban (II) Coustelier.

Title: Vergilii Opera, curis et studio Stephani Andreae Philippe. [Printer mark]. Copperplate engravings by Cochin. 3 vols.
Imprint: Lutetiae Parisiorum. Sumptibus Ant. Urb. Coustelier. 1745.

Morocco, gilt; 6 x 3½ x 7/8 in. Brunet 5, 1291.

EARLY PRINTING IN FRANCE.

Cabinet F · Shelf 4 · No. 82

Paris, 1750: l'Imprimerie Royale.
Title: Oeuvres de M. de Crebillon de l'Academie Francoise. 2 vols. with engravings designed by F. Boucher, Peintre du Roy.
Imprint: A Paris, de l'Imprimerie Royale, 1750.

Leather; $10\frac{1}{4}$ x $8\frac{3}{4}$ x $1\frac{1}{4}$ in. Brunet 2, 412.

EARLY PRINTING IN FRANCE

Cabinet PP · Shelf 4 · No. 7

Paris, 1750, P.G. Le Mercier
Title: Statuts et reglements des maitres relieurs ....
Imprint: A Paris, de l'Imprimerie de P.G. Le Mercier, rue S. Jacques, au Livre d'Or.

Morocco; $6\frac{1}{4}$ x 3-5/8 in.

EARLY PRINTING IN FRANCE.

Cabinet F · Shelf 5 · No. 16

Paris, 1751. Le Breton.
Title: Encyclopedie, ou Dictionnaire Raisonne des Sciences, des Arts et des Metieres.... Mis en ordre & public par M. Diderot...par M. D'Alembert. Tome second.
Colophon: De l'Imprimerie de Le Breton, Imprimeur ordinaire du Roy.

Article under caracteres gives the history of type casting and type founding, with "Examples de tous les caracteres ro-
cont'd

EARLY PRINTING IN FRANCE cont'd.

Cabinet F · Shelf 5 · No. 16

mains et italiques" from the Foundry of S.P.Fournier, and in theprinting establishment of Le Breton.

Treated calf; $15\frac{3}{4}$ x 10 x $2\frac{1}{4}$ in. Brunet, 2, 701.

EARLY PRINTING IN FRANCE.

Cabinet F · Shelf 5 · No. 18

Paris, 1755. Charles-Antoine Jombert.
Title: Fables choisies mises en vers par J. de la Fontaine. 2 vols. Full page etchings and decorative pieces designed by J.B. Oudrÿ, engraved by C.N. Cochin le fils.
Imprint: A Paris, M.DCC.LV. De l'Imprimerie de Charles-Antoine Jombert.

Leather; $16\frac{1}{2}$ x $11\frac{1}{4}$ x $2\frac{1}{2}$ in.

EARLY PRINTING IN FRANCE.

Cabinet F · Shelf 5 · No. 20

Paris, 1766. Simon, Pierre-Guillaume.
Title: Bibliotheque des artistes...L'Abbe Petity. 3 vols.
Imprint: Paris, chez P-G. Simon, imprimeur du Parlement.

Tree calf, each vol., $10\frac{1}{4}$ x $8\frac{1}{2}$ in.

EARLY PRINTING IN FRANCE.

Cabinet 40 · Shelf 1 · No. 72

Paris, 1768. Jacques Estienne.
Title: Le spectacle de la nature, tome huitieme.. ...second partie.
Imprint: A Paris, chez les Freres Estienne, rue S. Jacques à la Vertu. M.DCC.LXVIII. Avec Approbation & Privilege du Roi.

Leather; $6\frac{3}{4}$ x 4 x 1-1/8 in.

EARLY PRINTING IN FRANCE.

Cabinet F · Shelf 4 · No. 85

Paris, 1773. Grangé.
Title: Chefs-D'Oeuvre dramatiques...Par M. Marmontel.
Imprint: A Paris, de l'Imprimerie de Grangé, rue de la Parcheminerie, 1773. Avec approbation et privilege du roi.

Paper boards; $11\frac{3}{4}$ x $9\frac{1}{4}$ x 1 in.

EARLY PRINTING IN FRANCE.

Cabinet F · Shelf 4 · No. 91

Paris, 1785. Francoise-Ambroise (II) Didb t.
Title: Idee's d'un militaire pour la dispositions de troupes.....Par M. Fosse. Several folded plates, colored engravings by Bonnet who claimed to have been the inventor of this crayon stipple method.
Imprint: De l'Imprimerie de Franc. Amb. Didot l'aine. A Paris. Chez Alexandre Jombert, Jeune. 1785.
Cloth; $11\frac{3}{4}$ x 9 x 1 ih.

EARLY PRINTING IN FRANCE

Cabinet F · Shelf 4 · No. 92

Paris, 1785. L'Imprimerie de Monsieur.
Title: Précis historique de la vie de M. de Bonnard. Par M. Garat.
Imprint: A Paris, de l'Imprimerie de Monsieur.

Quarter morocco; $5\frac{5}{8}$ x 3-3/8 x 3/8 in.

EARLY PRINTING IN FRANCE.

Cabinet F · Shelf 5 · No. 24

Paris, 1788. Francois-Ambroise Didot, l'ainé
Title: Fables de la Fontaine. Imprimé par ordre du roi pour l'education de Monseigneur le Dauphin. De l'Imprimerie de Didot l'ainé 1788.
Colophon: Cette édition a été imprimée....avec les nouveaux caracteres de la fonderie de Didot l'aine, gravés par Firmin son 2nd fils ....

Morocco gilt; $12\frac{1}{2}$ x $9\frac{1}{4}$ x 2-1/8 in. Brunet 3, 751.

EARLY PRINTING IN FRANCE

Cabinet F · Shelf 5 · No. 28

Paris, 1789. Société Litteraire-Typographique
Title: La Henriade. Poeme suivi de quelques autres poemes de Voltaire. [Full page engravings by Moreau].
Imprint: De l'Imprimerie de la Société Litteraire-Typographique. 1789.

Leather; $12\frac{1}{2}$ x 10 x $2\frac{1}{4}$ in.

EARLY PRINTING IN FRANCE.

Cabinet F · Shelf 5 · No. 31

Paris, 1793. Defer de Maisonneuve.
Title: Galatee, roman pastoral; imite de Cervantes, par M. de Florian...Edition ornee de Figures en couleur, d'apres les dessins de Monsiau.
Imprint: A Paris, chez Defer de Maisonneuve, rue du Foin S. Jacques.

Leather, gilt; $13\frac{1}{4}$ x $10\frac{1}{4}$ x 1 in. Brunet 2, 1307.

EARLY PRINTING IN FRANCE.

Cabinet F · Shelf 5 · No. 34

Paris, 1795. Pierre Didot l'aine.
Title: M. Annaei Lucani. Pharsalia. Ex optimis exemplaribus emendata.
Imprint: Parisiis: Studio et impensis Ant. Aug. Renouard. Typis P. Didot natu majores. An Reipubl. III. 1795.

Tooled leather; gilt fore-edge decoration; $14\frac{3}{4}$ x 10 x $1\frac{3}{4}$ in.

EARLY PRINTING IN FRANCE.

Cabinet F · Shelf 5 · No. 36

Paris, 1796. Pierre Didot l'ainé.
Title: La Jérusalem Delivrée, en vers Francois par L.P.M.F. Baor-Lormian. 2 vols. Many full page engravings by C.N.Cochin.
Imprint: A Paris, de l'Imprimerie de P.Didot l'ainé. L'an IV de la République. 1796.

Half cloth; 13 x 10 x $1\frac{1}{2}$ in. Brunet 5, 667.

EARLY PRINTING IN FRANCE.

Cabinet F · Shelf 4 · No. 95

Paris, 1800. Pierre Didot [Son of Francoise-Ambroise II].
Title: Quintus Horatius Flaccus. Editio Stereotypa. Monogram.
Imprint: Parisiis, ex Officina Stereotypa. Petri Didot natu maj. et Firmin Didot. Anno VIII (1800)

Vellum; $6\frac{1}{4}$ x 3-7/8 x $1\frac{1}{4}$ in. Brunet 3, 323.

EARLY PRINTING IN FRANCE

Cabinet X · Shelf 5 · No. 9

Paris, 1804. Delance et Lesueur. Plaidoyers pour le sieur Baudelocque contre...le sieur Lefebvre, imprimeur; prononcés par M. Delamalle. Paris, 1804.

The case of libel agianst the printer Lefebvre, and a plea for the reformation of previous acts regulating printing.

EARLY PRINTING IN FRANCE. Exemple

Cabinet II · Shelf 4 · No. 39

Paris, 1821, Georg Crapelet.
Title: Specimen novae typographiae indicae... curavit Aug. Guil. Schlegel...
Imprint: Lutetiae Parisiorum. Ex Officina Georgii Crapelet. 1821.

Half morocco: 8-3/8 x 5-5/8 in.

EARLY PRINTING IN FRANCE

Cabinet E, Shelf 3, No. 28

Rouen, 1626. Jean Osmont
Title: Essay des merveilles de nature et des plus nobles artifices....Par René François, Predicateur du Roy...
Imprint: A Rouen: Chez Iean Osmont, dans la Cour du Palais. M.DC.XXVI. Avec privilege du Roy. Illus.

See P.302 for [Facts about Printing]. Du fait de l'imprimerie.
Morocco: $9\frac{1}{4}$ x $6\frac{3}{4}$ x $1\frac{1}{4}$ in.

EARLY PRINTING IN GERMANY

Cabinet D, Shelf 1, No. 29

Augsburg, 1476. Anton Sorg.
Title: Bonaventura, St. Speculum beatae Mariae Virginis.
Colophon: Devotissimi...Non quidem cyrographatus sed p. fide dignum viru Anthonium Sorg conduem Autustensem qz diligenter impressus.

Gesamt-Kat. ; Hain 3566.

Boards; 12 x $8\frac{1}{4}$ x $\frac{1}{4}$ in. In protective case.

EARLY PRINTING IN GERMANY.

Cabinet D, Shelf 4, No. 39

Augsburg, 1531. Heinrich Steiner (Siliceus or Stayner). Cicero. Officia M.T.C. Woodcuts by Burgkmair and borders by Weiditz.
Colophon: Gedruckt in der keyserlichen statt Augspurg/durch Heynrichen Stayner. vollendet/ am. VII. Tag Decembris. Im/ M.D.XXXI. Jar.

Boards; $11\frac{1}{2}$ x 8 x $\frac{1}{2}$ ins. 2 copies.

EARLY PRINTING IN FRANCE.

Cabinet E, Shelf 3, No. 51

Sedan, 1633. Jean Jannon.
Title: La Bible, qui est toute la saincte escriture du vieil et nouveau testament...
Imprint: A Sedan, par Jean Jannon, imprimeur de l'Academie M.DC.XXXIII.

Morocco; 5-3/4 x $3\frac{1}{4}$ x 1-3/4 ins. See Arneudo Dizionario Esegetico, p.1206.

EARLY PRINTING IN GERMANY.

Cabinet 10, Shelf 2, No. 10

Augsburg, 1478. Monastery of SS. Ulrich and Afra.

See Incunabula. Salomon. Epistola (etc)

EARLY PRINTING IN GERMANY

Cabinet D, Shelf 4, No. 40

Augsburg, 1533. Heinrich Steiner (or Steyner)
Title: Cicero. Officia M.T.C... Wolchs auf begere Herren Johansen von Schwartzenbergs etc. verteutschet.
Imprint: Gedruckt inn der Keyserlichen Stadt Augspurg durch Heinrichen Steyner vollendet.

Boards; $11\frac{1}{2}$ x 8 x $\frac{1}{2}$ in.

EARLY PRINTING IN FRANCE (Alsace-Lorrain)

Cabinet X, Shelf 2, No. 38

Strassburg, 1840. Imprint of the widow Levrault

See CELEBRATIONS, Printers. 1840, Strassburg,

EARLY PRINTING IN GERMANY

Cabinet 29, Shelf 1, No. 34

Augsburg, 1503: Erhard Ratdolt.
Title: Missale Pataviense: [With wood cuts].
Colophon: With printer mark facing p.305: Erhardi Ratdolt felicia conspice signa/ testata artificem qua valet ipse manum.
Printed in red and black; 33 leaves with music.

Original tooled pigskin with clasps; 9-3/4 x $7\frac{1}{4}$ x 2-3/4 ins.

EARLY PRINTING IN GERMANY

Cabinet J, Shelf 5, No. 19

Bamberg, 1461, Albert Phister.

See FACSIMILES (Der) Edelstein von Ulrich Boner...

EARLY PRINTING IN FRANCE

Cabinet 70, Shelf 1, No. 43

Troyes [1533 or 1544?]. Jean II Lecoq.
Title: La vie de ma dame Saincte Marguerite vierge et martyre. Facsimile.
Imprint: Imprime a Troyes chez Jean Lecoq, n.d. Printer mark.
The design of the printer mark is said to indicate that this small booklet must have been printed by the Widow Lecoq, Thibaut Trumen, or Jean II Lecoq.

Marbled paper; $7\frac{1}{4}$ x 4-7/8 in. pp. 16.

EARLY PRINTING IN GERMANY

Cabinet 29, Shelf 1, No. 35 and 36

Augsburg, 1515. George Ratdolt. Breviarium Ratisbonense. [Printed in red and black]
Title: Pars hyemal Breviarii Ratispoñ. [Woodcut].
Imprint: De iussa ac consensu Reve/rendissimi... Co/mit Palatini Rheni: ac ducis Bavarie... hic liber...Sed expēsis et sumptibris Georgi ratdolt/civis Augusteñ. Anno domi/ni 1515 vicesima die mensis/ Novembris.

Original tooled pigskin; $7\frac{1}{2}$ x 3 x $2\frac{1}{4}$ in.
[second copy marked No.36 same shelf)

EARLY PRINTING IN GERMANY.

Cabinet F, Shelf 4, No. 52

Breslau, 1711. Christian Bauch.
Title: Vitae...illustrum virorum ut et Helenae Cornarae et Cassandrae fidelis...ac in unum volumen redactae. [Various authors]
Imprint: Vratislaviae, sumptibus Christiani Bauchii, 1711.
Includes the life of J. Cporirus, printer, Basle. 1507-1568.

Vellum; $6\frac{3}{4}$ x 4-1/8 x $1\frac{1}{2}$ in.

EARLY PRINTING IN GERMANY

Cabinet E, Shelf 2, No. 67

Amberg, [Bavaria] 1602. Forster. [Georg?]
Title: Nova reperta, sive rerum memorabilium recens inventarum....Guidonis Pancirol.... Liber secundus. Iam primum ex Italico Latine redditus & commentariis illustratus ab Henrico Salmuth.
Imprint: Amberg'ae. Typis Forsterianis M.D.CII.

Vellum; $6\frac{1}{2}$ x 4-1/8 x 2 in. See Brunet IV, 339.

EARLY PRINTING IN GERMANY.

Cabinet D, Shelf 3, No. 61

Augsburg, 1519. Schoensperger, Hans. Tewrdannckh [Facsimile]. Holbein Society, London, 1884.
Colophon: Gedruckt in der Kayserlichen/Stat Augspurg durch/ den eltern Hansen/Schonsperger/im jar Tausent funff hun/dert und im/ neuntze/henden.

Cloth; $14\frac{1}{2}$ x $10\frac{1}{4}$ x $2\frac{3}{4}$ ins.

EARLY PRINTING IN GERMANY.

Cabinet I, Shelf 3, No. 30

Cologne, 1438? (Photographic facsimile).
Title: Ars Moriendi.

See WEIGEL, T. O. (PUBLISHER). Ars Moriendi ... Leipzig, 1869.

EARLY PRINTING IN GERMANY

Cabinet D, Shelf 1, No. 18

Augsburg [Augustae Vindelicorum], 1472. Günther Zainer. Etymologiarum, lib.XX, Isidorus.
Colophon: Isidori iunioris hispalensis episcopi Ethimlogiarum libri/numero vigincifiniunt soelicter per Gintherum Zainer ex/Reutlingen progenitum literis impressi ahenis Anno/ ab incarnatione domini. Millesimo quadringentesimo/Septuagesimo secundo Decimanona die Mensis nouebris.

Gesamt-Kat. ; Hain 9273, Brunet 3,463; folio.
Old morocco; 12 x $8\frac{1}{4}$ x 2-3/4 ins.

EARLY PRINTING IN GERMANY.

Cabinet D, Shelf 3, No. 65

Augsburg, 1520: Sigmund Grimm & Marr Wirsung.

Title: Hans Burgkmair's leben and leiden Christi Illus. Facsimile reprinted by Knorr & Hirth, Munich, 1823.

Paper boards; 8-1/8 x 6 x 3/8 in.

EARLY PRINTING IN GERMANY.

Cabinet D, Shelf 1, No. 5

Cologne (?), 1468 (?), Peter Damasceni. Liber de Laudibus ac Festis Gloriosae Virginis. Explicit.....Petrus Damasceni.

Mentioned in Hain, 5918. Parchment; $10\frac{1}{2}$ x $7\frac{3}{4}$ x $\frac{3}{4}$ in.

EARLY PRINTING IN GERMANY

Cabinet D Shelf 2 No. 16

Cologne [1491, Heinrich Quentell?].
Title: Gouda. Tractatus de expositione missae.
Colophon: Tractatus fr tris Guilhelmi Gouda ordinis minorum de observantia de expone... finit feliciter. Impressus Colonie circa summum cuilibet sacer doti summa necessarius.

Gesamt-Kat. ; Hain 7828.

Paper board; 8-1/8 x 5-3/8 in.

EARLY PRINTING IN GERMANY

Cabinet D Shelf 2 No. 47

Cologne, 1499. Johann Koelhoff [The younger].
Title: Chronica van der hilliger Stat van Coellen.
Colophon:...Ind hait gedruckt mit groissem ernst ind vliss Iohan Koelhoff, burger in Coellen ...

Gesamt-Kat. ; Hain 4989.

Tooled leather over boards; 12$\frac{3}{8}$ x 8$\frac{3}{4}$ in.

EARLY PRINTING IN GERMANY

Cabinet D Shelf 2 No. 17

Cologne, 1499. Heinrich Quentell
Title: Sabunde: Viola anime per modum dyalogi.
Colophon: Finit...in septe distinctus dyalogus Colonie impensis honesti viri Henrici Quentell faustissime iam p̄mo impressus.

Gesamt-Kat. ; Hain 14070.

Mottled calf; 8 x 5$\frac{1}{2}$ x $\frac{3}{4}$ in.

EARLY PRINTING IN GERMANY

Cabinet D Shelf 4 No. 61

Cologne, 1501, Hermann Bungart.

(3 leaves from a liturgical work, printed by Bungart, probably circa 1501.)

In box labeled "Early Printing, 1500-1600."

EARLY PRINTING IN GERMANY.

Cabinet D Shelf 2 No. 18

Cologne, 1538: Peter Quentell.
Title: Des Ertzstiffts Coeln Reformation.
Colophon: Gedruckt durch den Ersamen Peter Quentell, Burger der Stat Coeln.
Title within wood engraved border.

Paper boards; 12-1/8 x 8$\frac{1}{4}$ x $\frac{3}{4}$ in.

EARLY PRINTING IN GERMANY

Cabinet X Shelf 1 No. 5

Cologne, 1639, Johann Kinchius
Title: Mallingkrot, Bernard von. De ortu ac progressu artis typographicae dissertatio historica.
Imprint: Coloniae Agrippinensium, apud Joannem Kinchium, sub Monocerose veteri. Anno M.D.C. XXIX.

Vellum 8 x 6$\frac{1}{4}$ x 3/4 in.

EARLY PRINTING IN GERMANY Example

Cabinet X Shelf 1 No. 76

Erlangen, 1778, Fridr. Andr. Schleich
Title: De Hebraicae typographiae origines...
Imprint: Erlangae: Apud Fridr. Andr. Schleich.

Half morocco; 7-3/8 x 4-5/8 in.

EARLY PRINTING IN GERMANY.

Cabinet E Shelf 1 No. 40

Frankfort A.M., 1564. Christian Egenolff. (Successors).
Title: Des heiligen Romischen Reichs Hoffgericht zu Rotweil ordnung und process.
Colophon: [Effigies Christiani Egenolphi Typographi]. Gedruckt zu Franckfurt am Meyn bei Christian Egenolff, erben. Im jar M.D.LXIV.
With two large woodcuts (by Jost Amman?) and portrait of the printer Chris Egenolff at the end.
Boards; 12$\frac{1}{4}$ x 8 x $\frac{3}{4}$ in.

EARLY PRINTING IN GERMANY.

Cabinet E Shelf 1 No. 39

Frankfort a.M., 1564. Christian Egenolff (Successors).
Title: Des heiligen Romischen Reichs Hoffgericht zu Rotweil ordnung und process.
Colophon: [Effigies Christiani Egenolphi Typographi]. Gedruckt zu Franckfurt am Mein bei Christian Egenolff, Erben. Im jar M.D.LXIV.
With 2 large woodcuts by (Jost Amman?) and portrait of printer, Christ. Egenolff at the end.
Paper; 11$\frac{1}{2}$ x 7$\frac{1}{2}$ in. Duplicate, E/1/40.

EARLY PRINTING IN GERMANY.

Cabinet E Shelf 1 No. 46

Frankfort a M., 1566. Sigmund Feyerabend, Simon Hüter, and George Rabner.
Title: Thurnier-Buch, von anfang, ursachen, Ursprung und herkommen der Thurnier...[by Georg Ruxner.]
Colophon: Gedruckt zu Franckfurt am Main bey Georg Raben in verlegung Sigmund Feyrabends und Simon Hüters. [Printers Mark]: als man zalt nach Christi geburt tausent funffhundert sechss und sechtsig jar.
cont'd

EARLY PRINTING IN GERMANY cont'd

Cabinet E Shelf 1 No. 46

Many of the wood engravings in this book are attributed to Jost Amman.

Vellum over boards, gilt edges; 12 x 8 1$\frac{3}{4}$ in.
Brunet IV, 1471.

EARLY PRINTING IN GERMANY

Cabinet I Shelf 1 No. 5

Frankfort a.M. 1568. Karl Feyerabend.
Title: Panoplia omnium illiberalium mechanicarum aut sedentiarum artium genere continens... per Hartman Schopperum.
Colophon: Impressum Francfurti ad Moenum, apud Georgium Coruinum, impensis Sigismundi Feyerabent.
A book of engravings of trades and professions by Jost Amman, whose initials (I.A.) are on many of the designs.

(cont'd)

EARLY PRINTING IN GERMANY (cont'd)

Cabinet Shelf No.

Morocco; 5$\frac{3}{4}$ x 3$\frac{1}{2}$ x $\frac{3}{4}$ in.

EARLY PRINTING IN GERMANY

Cabinet I Shelf 1 No. 6

Frankfort A.M., 1574. Sigismund Karl Feyerabent.
Title: De omnibus illiberalibus sive mechanicis artibus...Auctore Hartmanno Schoppero. [Illus. by Jost Amman.] Francofurti ad Moenum, cum...privilegio. M.D.LXXIIII.
Colophon: Impressum Francofurti ad Moenum, apud Georgium Coruinum, impensis Sigismundi Caroli Feyerabent. [Printer Mark]. M.D.LXXIIII.

(cont'd)

EARLY PRINTING IN GERMANY (Cont'd)

Cabinet Shelf No.

Tooled leather, with clasps; 6$\frac{1}{2}$ x 3$\frac{3}{4}$ x 1-1/8 in. See Becker "Jost Amman," pp.64-5.

EARLY PRINTING IN GERMANY

Cabinet E Shelf 2 No. 35

Frankfort a.M., 1584. Andrea Wechel.
Title: P. Rami, regii eloquentiae et philosophiae professoris, liber de moribus veterum Gallorum, ad Carolum Lotharingum...[Printer Mark].
Imprint: Francofurti apud haeredes Andreae Wecheli M.D.LXXXIIII.

Morocco; 7 x 4$\frac{1}{4}$ x $\frac{1}{2}$ in.

EARLY PRINTING IN GERMANY

Cabinet E Shelf 3 No. 31

Frankfort a.M., 1626. Lucas Jennis.
Title: Piazza Universale...aller professionen, kunsten, geschäfften, handeln und handwerken ....durch Thomam Garzonum. [Title enclosed within a border, woodcut, illustrating the arts and trade; printing press included].
Imprint: Frankfurt am Mayn. In verlegung Lucae Jennisii. M.DC.XXVI.

Half morocco; 12 x 7$\frac{3}{4}$ x 2$\frac{3}{4}$ in. Brunet 2, 1497.

EARLY PRINTING IN GERMANY

Cabinet E Shelf 3 No. 43

Frankfort a.M. 1631. Caspar Rotel.

Title (1): Guidonis Pancirolli. Rerum memorabilium....Pars Prior. Commentariis....Henrico Salmuth. Ambergensium Sijndico Emerito Francofurti sumptibus Godefridi Tampachii.
Title (2): Guidonis Pancirolli clarissimi nova reperta....recens inventarum....Pars posterior....Henrico Salmuth....

Cont'd

EARLY PRINTING IN GERMANY cont'd

Cabinet E
Shelf 3
No. 43

Imprint: Francofurti, sumptibus Godefridi Tampachii, Typis Casparis Rotelli. M.DC.XXXI
[Two parts in one volume. Printer Mark]

EARLY PRINTING IN GERMANY

Cabinet Y
Shelf 3
No. 102

Lübeck, 1714: Samuel Struck.
Title: Depositio cornuti typographici.
Imprint: Gedruckt in Luneberg, by Samuel Struck, 1714.
A facsimile reprinted by Genzsch & Heyse. Hamburg, 1925.

Boards; $9\frac{1}{4}$ x $6\frac{1}{4}$ x $\frac{1}{4}$ in.

EARLY PRINTING IN GERMANY cont'd

Cabinet 14
Shelf 1
No. 15

geburt/unsers lieben herrn Jesu/Christi/ M.D.XLI, 2 Printers marks.

Original vellum covered boards; 12 x 8 x 3 ins.

EARLY PRINTING IN GERMANY Example

Cabinet 80
Shelf 2
No. 1 - 2, 3 - 4

Frankfurt am Main, 1831-4. Sigismund Latomi.

See PERIODICALS, Germany. Mercurii Gallobelgici succneturiati...

EARLY PRINTING IN GERMANY.

Cabinet 14
Shelf 1
No. 5

Mainz, 1515. Johann Schoeffer I. Compendium sive Brevarium primi voluminis Analium (etc). ... Trithemius.
Colophon: Impressum et completum est presens Chronicarum opus anno domini MDXV in vigilia Margaretae virginis in nobile famosaque urbe Moguntina hujus artis impressorie inventrice prima per Joa. Schoeffer, nepotem quondam honesti viri Joa. Fusth civis Moguntina (etc) With printer mark.

Vellum; $12\frac{1}{4}$ x $8\frac{1}{4}$ x $\frac{1}{2}$ ins.

EARLY PRINTING IN GERMANY.

Cabinet 22
Shelf 1
No. 17

(Mecklenburg, 1475-1707. See Early Printing in Germany, Rostock.

EARLY PRINTING IN GERMANY.

Cabinet 14
Shelf 1
No. 11

Hagenau, 1529. Johann Secerius. Compen/diariae titulo/rum Codicis Iustini/ani Exegeses./ Authore Christophoro Hegendorphino. With printer's mark.
Colophon: Haganoe in aedibus Iohannis Secerii/ anno M.D.XXIX. Mense Augusto.
Bound in with "Placentini", printed by Johann Schoeffer I, Mainz, 1531.

Original covers; $6\frac{1}{4}$ x 4 x $1\frac{1}{4}$ ins.

EARLY PRINTING IN GERMANY.

Cabinet 14
Shelf 1
No. 7

Mainz, 1518. Johann Schoeffer I. Livius, Historia, Duobus voluminibus recens. ex vetusto codice Moguntin Bibliothecae auctus, cum Flori Epitome.
Colophon: Moguntiae in ae/ditus Joannis/ Schaeffer, men/se Novembri/ an MDXVIII.
This contains the preface in which the invention of printing is attributed to the father of the printer.

Original boards; 13 x $8\frac{1}{2}$ x $2\frac{3}{4}$ ins.

EARLY PRINTING IN GERMANY

Cabinet E
Shelf 1
No. 23

Munich, 1553. Thain Ambtman.
Title: Bayerische Landts ordnung: In diesem buch Bayrischer...wie dieselben reformirt, gebössert und in fünfszehenhundert dreyundfunfftzigisten jar seind publiciert worden.
Colophon: Und nachdem dieser Erklarung...und durch Thainen Ambtman in seinem abzug weggefurt werden soll...das solche nachdruch kainen glauben habñ in unser furstenthums gebracht..

cont'd

EARLY PRINTING IN GERMANY

Cabinet 18
Shelf 1
No. 15

Hamburg, 1683. [Various Printers]

See Journalism, Germany. History of Hamburg newspapers.

EARLY PRINTING IN GERMANY.

Cabinet 14
Shelf 1
No. 9

Mainz, 1530. Johann Schoeffer I. Julius Caesar An Julii Cesaris des gross-mechtigen ersten Romischen Keysers historien vom Gallier (etc). Printers Mark.
Colophon: Gedruckt zu Meyntz durch Johan-/ nem Schoffer im jar nach der geburt Christi/ unsers Herrn Tausent Funffhun-/dert und dreissigsten/ im Septemb.

Original boards; 13 x 8 x $1\frac{1}{2}$ ins.

EARLY PRINTING IN GERMANY cont'd

Cabinet E
Shelf 1
No. 23

oder verkauft werden soll...GEDRUCK ZU MUNCHEN.

Vellum; $12\frac{1}{2}$ x 8-3/8 x 2 ins.

EARLY PRINTING IN GERMANY.

Cabinet E
Shelf 3
No. 5

Heidelberg, 1615. Johann Lacellori.
Title: Vitae Germanorum philosophorum qui seculo superiori....collectae Melchiore Adamo. (woodcut)
Imprint: Haidelbergae. Impensis Jonae Rosae Librarij Francos. Typis Johannis Lacellori, Acad Typograph. Anno MDCXV.

Calf; $7\frac{1}{4}$ x $4\frac{1}{2}$ x $1\frac{1}{2}$ in.

EARLY PRINTING IN GERMANY.

Cabinet 14
Shelf 1
No. 11

Mainz, 1531. Johann Schoeffer I. Placen-/tini. Rogerio. Cum praefatione Nicolai Rho-/dii, qui hos autores e tenebris eru-/tos in lucem aeditit. Printer Mark.
Colophon: Compendii sive summae Rogerii de/ diversis praescriptiōibus...finis mo/gūtia ex aedibus Joan-/nis Scheffer mense Februarios/ANNO. M.D./XXXI. Bound in with "Compendiariae" etc., printed in Hagenau by Johannes Secerius, 1529.
Original covers: $6\frac{1}{4}$ x 4 x $1\frac{1}{2}$ ins.

EARLY PRINTING IN GERMANY

Cabinet 10
Shelf 2
No. 6

Nuremberg, 1473. Anton Koberger.
Title: De consolatione philosophiae, Boethius, cum commentario S. Thomae de Aquino.
Colophon: Hic liber...finit feliciter anno domini M.CCCC.LXXIII mensis July...Antonius Coburger.

Boards; $16\frac{1}{2}$ x $11\frac{1}{4}$ x $2\frac{3}{4}$ in.

EARLY PRINTING IN GERMANY

Cabinet 20
Shelf 2
No. 19

Lübeck, 1495: Stephan Arndes.

See Bibles. Narrenbible. Das Rätsel das Narrenbible.

EARLY PRINTING IN GERMANY

Cabinet 14
Shelf 1
No. 15

Mainz, 1541. Ives Schoeffer. [Grandson of Peter Schoeffer I]. Titi Livii des aller redsprechsten und hochberümpsten geschichte....Römische Historien (etc) Gedruckt iñ der Churfürstlichen Statt Meyntz durch Ivonem Scheffer, im jare M.D.XLI.
Colophon: Gedruckt iñ der loblichen uñ Chur-/ fürstlichen Statt Meyntz, durch Ivonem Schöf-/fer. Vollendet am dritten tag des herbstmo-/nates als man zallt nach der

cont'd

EARLY PRINTING IN GERMANY

Cabinet 10
Shelf 2
No. 8

Nuremberg, 1480. Anthony Koberger.

Title: Biblia Latina.
Colophon:...In oppido Nurnbergu per Antonius Coburger...fabresactum.

Stamped leather (clasps missing); 16 3/4 x $11\frac{1}{4}$ x 4 3/4 in.

EARLY PRINTING IN GERMANY

Cabinet I — Shelf 5 — No. 23

Nürnberg, 1511, Albrecht Dürer.
Title: Apocalipsis cum figuris (16 wood engraved plates)
Colophon: Impressa denuo Nurnberge p. Albertum Durer pictorem anno christiano, 1511.

Modern binding; pigskin, 16-1/8 x 12 in.

EARLY PRINTING IN GERMANY.

Cabinet D — Shelf 4 — No. 38

Siemeren [Hundsrück]. 1531. Hieronymi Rodler. Eyn Schön nützlich buchlein...der kunst des Messens [Based on Durer's book dealing with the problems of perspective].

Imprint: Getruckt unnd volnendet, zu Siemern uff dem huneszrucke, in verlegug Hieronimi Rodler...1531.

Boards; 12 x 8 x ½ in. Brunet 2, p.914.

EARLY PRINTING IN GERMANY

Cabinet D — Shelf 4 — No. 61

Strassburg, 1513, Renatus Beck.
(2 leaves, one with colophon of Beck, ane leaf from Life of Alexander the Great).

In box labeled " Early Printing, 1500-1600"

EARLY PRINTING IN GERMANY

Cabinet D — Shelf 3 — No. 60

[Nürnberg, 1517], Hans Shönsperger.
Title: Die geuerlicheiten...geschichten des Ritters Tewrdannncks.
Colophon: Gedruckte in der Kayserlichen Stat Nürnberg durch den eltern Hannsen Schönsperger, burger zu Augsburg.

Plush over boards; 14 x 10½ x 2½ in.

EARLY PRINTING IN GERMANY.

Cabinet D — Shelf 4 — No. 37

Strassburg, Peter Schoeffer II, second son of Peter Schoeffer of Fust and Schoeffer, Mainz.
See Imprints, Germany. Schoeffer, Peter II.

EARLY PRINTING IN GERMANY

Cabinet E — Shelf 1 — No. 38

Strassburg, 1530, Christian Egenolph.
Title: De mirandis Germaniae antiquitatibus, sermones.
Imprint XXXXXXXX: Argentorati apud Christianum Egenolphum.

Printer mark on title page.

Boards; 8 x 5¾ in.

EARLY PRINTING IN GERMANY

Cabinet I — Shelf 1 — No. 7

Nurenberg, 1596, Paul Kauffmann.

See LENCKER, HANS. Perspectiva literaria ...Gedruckt zu Nurmberg, durch Paulum Kauffmann, 1596.

EARLY PRINTING IN GERMANY

Cabinet 10 — Shelf 2 — No. 4

Strassburg [1472 Johann Mentelin]

Title: Summa de casibus conscientia.

Hain 1889. Pr. 211. B.M.C. 1, 56.

Stamped pigskin with brass bosses; 17 x 12 x 4¾ in.

EARLY PRINTING IN GERMANY

Cabinet E — Shelf 2 — No. 47

Strassburg, 1590. Bernard Jobinus
Title: Icones sive imagines virorum literis illustrium....Ex secunda recognitione Nicolai Reusneri.[Illus]
Imprint: Curante Bernhardo Iobino. Privigelio Caesareo. Argentorati: 1590. [Printer Mark]

Morocco; 6½ x 4½ x 1¾ in. Brunet IV, 1255.

EARLY PRINTING IN GERMANY

Cabinet X — Shelf 1 — No. 44

Nuremberg, 1748, Joh. Jos. Fleischmann
Title: Librorum ab anno 1 usque ad annum L. sec. XVI (1501-1550)...Editus C.C. Hirschio.
Imprint: Noribergae Prostat apud Felseckeros. Prelo Joannis Josephi Fleischmanni.

Boards, vellum back; 8-5/8 x 7 in.

EARLY PRINTING IN GERMANY.

Cabinet D — Shelf 1 — No. 51

Strassburg, 1487. Printer unknown.
Title: Sermonew Dormi secure vel Dormi fina cura....
Colophon: Ad laudem et honorem omnipotentis dei v̄ginisqz matris eius gloriose necnō vtilitate totis̄ ecelesie finiunt....Impressi Argentini. Anno dn̄i M.CCCCLXXXVII. Finita circa festum sancte Iohannis baptiste.

Gesamt-Kat. ; Hain 15959. Paper boards; 11½ x 8½ 3/4 in.

EARLY PRINTING IN GERMANY.

Cabinet X — Shelf 2 — No. 37

Strassburg, 1641. Eberhard Zetzner.
Title: Gott zu lob. Drey christliche danck predigten: Wegen ders im jahr 1440, und also vor zweyhundert Jahren, durch Gottliche Eingebung, in Strassburg erfundenen hochwerthen Buchdrucker-Kunst.
Imprint: Strassburg. In verlegund Eberhard Zetzners buchhandlers. Anno M.DC.XLI.

Boards; 8 x 6½ x ½ in. Bigmore and Wyman 11, 315.

EARLY PRINTING IN GERMANY.

Cabinet F — Shelf 4 — No. 55

Nurnberg, 1762. Johann Andreas Endter.

Title: Herrn Johann Arndts...Sechs Bucher vom Wahren Christenthum...Nebst dasselben Paradiessgartlein....
Imprint: Nurnberg, zu finden in der Johann Andrea Endterischen Buchhandlung, 1762.

Leather; 9 x 7¼ x 3½ in.

EARLY PRINTING IN GERMANY

Cabinet D — Shelf 3 — No. 13

Strassburg, 1505, Johann Prüss.
Title: Epithoma rerum Germanicarum usque ad nostra tempora. Jacob Wimpheling.
Colophon: Ioannes Prüss in aedibus Thiergarten Argentinae imprimabat ... Anno M.D.V. quinto Idus Martij. [Edited by Tho. Wolphius, jun., whose full page wood cut coat-of-arms appears on verso of last leaf].

Cont'd.

EARLY PRINTING IN GERMANY

Cabinet LL — Shelf 1 — No. 2

Sulzbach, 1684, Johann Holst. [Imprint].

See SCHMATZ, DANIEL MICHAEL. Neuvorgestelltes auf der loblichen kunst...

EARLY PRINTING IN GERMANY

Cabinet D — Shelf 3 — No. 11

Pforzheim, 1503. Thomas Anshelm.
Title: De laudibus sancte crucis. Rabanus.
Colophon:...in aedibus Thome Anshelmi...
From the De Vinne collection.
In regard to contents of this curious work see note inserted at end of book.

Brunet 4,1035; Pr.11747

Parchment over boards; 12¼ x 8½ ½ in.

Cabinet D — Shelf 3 — No. 13

Chap. LXV has an account of the invention of printing.
Chap. LXVIII gives an account of current pictorial art with the first mention of Martin Schongaur and Albrecht Durer.

Vellum, edges gilt; 8¼ x 6 x ½ in.

EARLY PRINTING IN GERMANY.

Cabinet 14 — Shelf 1 — No. 12

Worms, 1527. Peter Schoeffer II. (Grandson of Peter I of Mainz). Alle propheten nach hebraischer sprach verteutscht [Printer mark.]
Colophon: Getruckt zu Worms bei Peter Schöffern/und volendet am dreizehenden tag des/ Aprillen im jar nach der geburt/ Christi unsers selig-/machers./M.D.XXVII.

Boards, 12½ x 8¼ x 1 ins.

EARLY PRINTING IN GERMANY.

Cabinet E, Shelf 1, No. 19

Worms, 1551. Gregorium Hofman.
Title: Ein kurtzweilige lobrede ... Beschreiben durch Casparum Scheidt von Wormbs.
Colophon: Gedruckt zu Wormbs durch Gregorium Hofman.

Boards; 7-7/8 x 6 in.

EARLY PRINTING IN HOLLAND.

Cabinet 39, Shelf 1, No. 10

Amsterdam, 1664. Ex officina Elzeviriana. [Ludwig and Daniel Elzevier.]
Title: Geographia generalis, in qua affectiones generales Telluris explicantur. Autore, Bernh. Varenio. Engraved title page.
Imprint: Amstelodami. Ex officina Elzeviriana, 1664.

Half morocco; 5½ x 3 x 1¾ in. Ledeboer 31.

EARLY PRINTING IN HOLLAND.

Cabinet 39, Shelf 2, No. 48

Amsterdam, 1678: [Daniel Elzevier]

Title: Lettres choisies du Sr. de Balzac.
Imprint: A Amsterdam. Chez les Elzeviers.1678.

Vellum; 5-3/8 x 3 x 1-1/4 in.

EARLY PRINTING IN HOLLAND

Cabinet 00, Shelf 6, No. 2

Amsterdam, 1620-1621. George Veseler.

see **FACSIMILES, NEWSPAPERS, the first of England printed in Holland, 1620-1621.**

EARLY PRINTING IN HOLLAND

Cabinet 39, Shelf 1, No. 12

Amsterdam, 1665. Daniel Elzevier.
Title: Arnoldi Vinnii, J.C. In quatuor libros Institutionum Imperialium Commentarius. Editio Quarto. Printer Mark.
Imprint: Amstelodami, Apud Danielem Elzevirium, 1665.

Rebound, half morocco; 9½ x 7-3/4 x 2-3/8 in. Pieters, Annales Elsevirienne, p.229, 8.

EARLY PRINTING IN HOLLAND.

Cabinet E, Shelf 4, No. 81

Amsterdam, 1685. Hieronymus Sweerts.
Title: Martelaers Spiegel der doopsgesinde of weereloose Christenen....Door T.J.V. Braght. Den Tweeden Druk (The second edition) Illus.
Imprint: Tamsterdam, by Hieronymus Sweerts, Jan ten Hoorn, Jan Bouman, en Daniel van den Dalen. In Compagnie, 1685.

Leather; 16¼ x 11 x 5 ins. The original from which the Ephrata Book of Martyrs was translated and printed in Ephrata, Pa. 1748.

EARLY PRINTING IN HOLLAND

Cabinet 39, Shelf 2, No. 50

Amsterdam and Leyden, 1648. Ludwig Elzevire and Frans Hack
Title: Historia naturalia Brasiliae...Guilielmo Pisonis.
Imprint: Lugdun. Batavorum, apud Franciscum Hackium et Amsteldomi, apud Lud. Elzevirium.

Paper, vellum back, 15-3/4 x 10 in.

EARLY PRINTING IN HOLLAND

Cabinet E, Shelf 4, No. 44

Amsterdam, 1667. Joseph Athias.
Title: Biblia Hebraica. Accuratissima, notis Hebraicis...A Johanne Leusden, philosophiae doctore & lingua sancte...professore.Amstelodami typis et sumptibus Josephi Athias. Anno M.DC.LXVII.
Colophon: Amstelodami Typis Joseph Athias, in vico S. Antonii volgo S. Antonis Breestraet. 1667.

Vellum; 8¼ x 5 x 3¼ ins.

EARLY PRINTING IN HOLLAND — Example

Cabinet I, Shelf 1, No. 14

Amsterdam, circa 1753, Reinier en Josua Ottens. (Imprint)

See LUIKEN, JOHANNES. Afbeelding der menschelyke bezigheden...

EARLY PRINTING IN HOLLAND

Cabinet E, Shelf 4, No. 18

Amsterdam, 1657. Blaeu, Johan.
Title: Hugonis Grotii. Annales et historiae de rebus Belgicis.
Imprint: Amsteledami, ex Typographeio Joannis Blaeu. M.DC.LVII. Cum privilegiis S.C. Majestatis; et ordd. Belgicae Federatae, nec non Holl. West-Frisieque, per annos quindecim.

Calf; 14 x 9½ x 2½ ins. Brunet 2, 1767.

EARLY PRINTING IN HOLLAND.

Cabinet 39, Shelf 1, No. 15

Amsterdam, 1671. Daniel Elzevier.
Title: Polydori Vergilii Urbinatis de Inventoribus libri VIII. et de Prodigiis, Libri III Cum indicibus locupletissimis. Engraved title page.
Imprint: Amstelodami, Apud Danielem Elzevirium 1671.

Calf; 5-3/8 x 3 x 1½ in. Pieters, 255, 18.

EARLY PRINTING IN HOLLAND.

Cabinet F, Shelf 4, No. 63

Amsterdam, 1769. Unidentified printer.

Title: Les Saisons, poeme...[James Thompson]. Engraved frontispiece, head and tail-pieces by P.P. Chauffard and others.
Imprint: A Amsterdam, 1769.

Leather; 7-1/8 x 5 x 1-7/8 in.

EARLY PRINTING IN HOLLAND.

Cabinet 39, Shelf 1, No. 7

Amsterdam, 1659. Ludwig and Daniel Elzevier
Title: Posthumus Pacianus; sev Definitiones ... Cl. Iulii Pacii a Beriga IC., posthumus ... Editio altera. Recognita & amplissima dote locupletata ab Arnoldo Corvino, a Belderen. Printer Mark.
Imprint: Amsteleedami, Apud Ludovicum & Danielem Elzevirios. 1659.

Vellum; 5½ x 3 x 1¼ in. Pieters 216, 3.

EARLY PRINTING IN HOLLAND.

Cabinet 39, Shelf 1, No. 16

Amsterdam, 1671. Daniel Elzevier.
Title: Reflexions, Sentences, ou Maximes royales et politiques. Traduites de l'Espagnol par le Reverend Pere D'Obeilh. Printer Mark.
Imprint: A Amsterdam, chez Daniel Elzevier. M.DC.LXXI.

Vellum; 5¼ x 3-1/8 x 1 in.

EARLY PRINTING IN HOLLAND

Cabinet F, Shelf 4, No. 65

Amsterdam and Paris, 1771-1772. Printer unknown.
Title (1): Le Jugement de Paris. Par Imbert. Amsterdam, 1772. Engravings by Moreau, Eisen, Choffard, etc.
Title (2): Idilles de St. Cyre. [Attributed to J. Dorat]. Amsterdam. 1771. Engravings by. Marillier.
Title (3): Phrosine et Melidore. A Messine, et se trouve a Paris...1772.

cont'd

EARLY PRINTING IN HOLLAND.

Cabinet 39, Shelf 1, No. 24

Amsterdam, 1663. Ludwig and Daniel Elzevier
Title: Corpus Juris Civilis ... Addito textu Graeco ... cum notis, Dionysii Gothofredi ... Printer Mark. Amstelodami, apud Joannem Blaeu, Ludovicum & Danielem Elzevirios. Lugd Batavorum Apud Franciscum Hackium M.DC.LXIII.
Colophon, end of first part, p. 796: Amsterdami Typis Ludovici & Danielis Elzeviriorum MDCLXIII. 2 vols. in one.
Calf; 16 x 10 x 4½ in. Pieters 221; Brunet 3, 608.

EARLY PRINTING IN HOLLAND

Cabinet 39, Shelf 1, No. 20

Amsterdam, 1674. Daniel Elzevier.
Title: Catalogus librorum qui in bibliopolio Danielis Elsevirii venales extant. Printer Mark.
Imprint: Amstelodami, ex Officina Elseviriana M.DC.LXXIV.

Vellum; 5½ x 3¼ x 1½ in. See Pieters, Annales Elsevirienne, p.LV.

EARLY PRINTING IN HOLLAND — cont'd

Cabinet F, Shelf 4, No. 65

Morocco, gilt; 8-5/8 x 5⅝ x 1-1/8 in.

EARLY PRINTING IN HOLLAND.

Cabinet 14 Shelf 1 No. 20

Bois-le-Duc, 1585. Johann Schoeffer III. Die Gulden Letanien. Woodcut.
Imprint: Gheprent Tshertogenbossche by Jan/ Scheffer.

Boards; 5½ x 3¾ x 1/8 ins.

EARLY PRINTING IN HOLLAND.

Cabinet D Shelf 3 No. 37

Daventry, 1515. Theodorici (Dirk) de Borne. Fratris rvtgerisicam/bri canonici regula/ris prognostica/ Vera (etc). Picture of a printing press with printer mark D.B.
Colophon: Excussum Daventriae in officina/ literaria Theodorici de Borne/ anno domini, M.D/XV.

Morocco; 7¼ x 4½ x ¼ ins.

EARLY PRINTING IN HOLLAND.

Cabinet F Shelf 4 No. 60

's Gravenhagen, 1717. Gysbregt Gazinet.
Title: De schoonste, of het ontzet van Scheveningen; Bly-spel. [Diderik Buisero]. Printer Mark.
Imprint: In 's Cravenhage. By Gysbregt Gazinet. Boekverkooper in t'Kort-Agterom, MDCCXVII.

Half morocco; 6¼ x 4 in.

EARLY PRINTING IN HOLLAND.

Cabinet E Shelf 1 No. 35

Haarlem. 1561. Jan van Zuren.
Title: Officia Ciceronis. Leerende wat yeghelijck in allen staten behoort de doen... vertaelt in nederlandtscher spraken door Dierick Coornhert. [Printer Mark]
Imprint: Tot Haerlem, by Ian van Zuren, 1561...
In this book Coster was first named as first inventor of printing.

Vellum; 5½ x 3½ x 7/8 in. See Ledebor, Boekdrukkers Nord-Nederland, p.205.

EARLY PRINTING IN HOLLAND

Cabinet E Shelf 3 No. 12

Haarlem, 1620. Vincent Casteleyn.
Title: Tractatus Brevis. De variis ac diversis maleficiis....apprime utilis, ac necessarius. Autore Ioanne Gael, Harlemensi Batavo ...Advocato Hollandiae.
Imprint: Harlemi; Apud Vincentium Casteleyn, sub signo Typographiae. Anno M.DC.XX. [Printers Mark.]
Boards; 6 x 3¾ x 1/2 in. See Ledeboer, Boekdrukkers Noord-Nederland, p.196.

EARLY PRINTING IN HOLLAND

Cabinet 00 Shelf 6 No. 2

Hague (The), 1620, Adrian Clarke.

see FACSIMILES, NEWSPAPERS, the first of England printed in Holland, 1620-1621.

EARLY PRINTING IN HOLLAND

Cabinet F Shelf 5 No. 1

Haye (La) 1729. Pierre de Hondt.
Title: Oeuvres de Nicolas Boileau Despreaux... nouvelle Edition revue...Enrichie de figures gravees par Bernard Picart le Romain. Tome Premier.
Imprint: A la Haye, chez Pierre de Hondt. MDCCXXIX.

Leather; 14¾ x 9½ x 2 in.

EARLY PRINTING IN HOLLAND.

Cabinet 2 Shelf 2 No. 17

Leyden, 1584. Plantin-Moretus Press: Christopher Plantin.
Title: Hadriani Barlandi: Hollandae comitum historia et icones; Caroli Burgundiae ducis vita; ejusdem argumenti libellus, auctore Gerardo Noviomago. Printer Mark.
Imprint: Lugduni Batavorum, ex officina Christophori Plantin, M.D.LXXXIV.

Paper boards; 12½ x 8¼ x ½ in.

EARLY PRINTING IN HOLLAND.

Cabinet 2 Shelf 1 No. 8

Leyden, 1585. Plantin-Moretus Press: Christopher Plantin.
Title I: Tive-spraack vander Nederduitsch letterkunst....uytghegheven. Tot Leyden by Christoffel Plantyn.
Title II: Kort begrip des redenkavelings....Tot Keyden by Christoffel Plantyn. M.D.LXXXV.

Bound in with a third item printed in same office 1587 by Francois Raphelengen.

EARLY PRINTING IN HOLLAND.

Cabinet 2 Shelf 1 No. 8

Leyden, 1587. Plantin-Moretus Press: Francois Raphelengen.
Title: Rederijck-kunst (Rhetoric)....
Imprint: Tot Leyden, by Franchoys Raphelinghen M.D.LXXXVII.

Bound in with two items printed in 1585 by Christopher Plantin.

Vellum; 6½ x 4½ x 1¼ in.

EARLY PRINTING IN HOLLAND.

Cabinet 2 Shelf 1 No. 13

Leyden, 1588. Plantin-Moretus Press: Francois Raphelengen.
Title: Hadriani Iunii Hornani, medici, Batavia. In qua praeter gentis & insulae antiquitatem, originem, decora, mores...Printer Mark.
Imprint: Ex Officina Plantiniana; Apud Franciscum Raphelengium. Leyden, 1588.
In this book, The History of Holland, by Adrian Junius, the claim was first advanced (p.253-55) that the honor of the in-

cont'd

EARLY PRINTING IN HOLLAND cont'd

Cabinet 2 Shelf 1 No. 13

vention of printing belonged to Holland and not to Germany, thus starting the Coster-Gutenberg controversy.

¾ morocco; 8½ x 6-1/8 x 1¾ in.

EARLY PRINTING IN HOLLAND.

Cabinet 2 Shelf 1 No. 15

Leyden, 1590. Plantin-Moretus Press: Francois Raphelengen.
Title: I. Lipsi: Saturnalium Sermonum. Libri duo, qui de Gladiatoribus. Editio ultima, auctior & ornatior....Illus. Printer Mark.
Imprint: Lugduni Batavorum, ex Officina Plantiniana, apud Franciscum Raphelengium. M.D.XC.

Morocco; 7-3/4 x 6 x 5/8 in.

EARLY PRINTING IN HOLLAND.

Cabinet E Shelf 2 No. 66

Leyden, 1602. [Jan van Hout].
Title: Dienst-Bovc der Stadt Leyden ... door Ian van Hovt.
Imprint: Gedruct opt Raedthuys der voorschreven stede, inden Iare zestien-hondert ende tvvee.

Vellum; 12 x 8 x ½ in.

EARLY PRINTING IN HOLLAND.

Cabinet E Shelf 3 No. 17

Leyden, 1615-1618. Erpenius (or Van Erp) Thomas.
Title: Historia Josephi Patriarchae, ex Alcorano, Arabice Cum triplici versione Latina, a scholijs Thomae Erpenii.
Imprint: Leidae, Ex typographia Erpeniana linguarum Orientalium, 1617.
Has two printer marks.

Bellum; 7-3/8 x 5-4/8 x 1 in.

EARLY PRINTING IN HOLLANL

Cabinet E Shelf 3 No. 18

Leyden, 1622. Erpenius [Thomas]
Title:...Pentateuchus mosis. Arabicè.
Imprint: Lugduni Batavorum: Ex typographia Erpeniana linguarum Orientalium. Prostant apud Iohannem Maire. 1622.
Boards; 7¾ x 6¼ x 1½ in. See Ledeboer, Boek drukkers Noord-Nederland. p.251.

EARLY PRINTING IN HOLLAND

Cabinet 39 Shelf 1 No. 3

Leyden, 1622. Isaac Elzevier
Title: Tabacologia: hoc est Tabaci seu Nicotianae descriptio...per Iohannem Neanorum, Bremanum. Printer Mark.
Imprint: Lugduni, Batavorum, Ex officina Isaaci Elzeviri Iurati Academia Typographi. 1622.

Calf; 8-3/4 x 6¼ x 1¼ in. Pieters 56, 9.

EARLY PRINTING IN HOLLAND.

Cabinet 39 Shelf 1 No. 4

Leyden, 1626. Ex officina Elzeviriana. [Bonaventura and Abraham].
Title: Emblemata Florentii Schoonhovii I. C. Goudani ...
Imprint: Lugduni Batavorum, Ex Officina Elzeviriana. Anno M.DC.XXVI.

Vellum; 8¼ x 6¾ x 1-3/8 in. Pieters, 74, 13.

EARLY PRINTING IN HOLLAND.

Cabinet 39 Shelf 1 No. 25

Leyden, 1663. Johann Elzevier [Widow].
Title: Biblia, ;.. vervattende alle de canonijcke Boecken des ouden en des nieuwen testament. [Printers mark].
Imprint: Tot Leyden. By de Weduwe ende Ersgenamen van Johan Elzevier, 1663.

Calf; tooled, with iron corners and clasps; 19 x 12 x 6 in. Pieters, 153.

EARLY PRINTING IN HOLLAND

Cabinet E Shelf 4 No. 68

Leyden, 1678. Gaesbeeck. Daniel.
Title: D. Justiniani...Institutionum libri quator. Additi sunt tituli digestor de verborum significatione et regulis juris.
Imprint: Lugd. Batav. Apud Danielum à Gaesbeeck, M.DC.LXXVIII.

Morocco, gilt edges; 5¼ x 3¼ x ½ in. Brunet, 3,612.

EARLY PRINTING IN HOLLAND

Cabinet 39 Shelf 1 No. 23

Leyden, 1683-1712. Abraham Elzevier.

A collection of title and other pages printed by him.

In folder, 9½ x 7 in.

EARLY PRINTING IN HOLLAND.

Cabinet E Shelf 4 No. 52

Nimwegen, 1671. Reynier Smetius (or Smeding)
Title: Polydori vergilii urbinatis de rerum inventoribus libri octo in quibus omnium scientiarum ... brevissime continetur. [Contains an account of the invention of printing].
Imprint: Noviomagi Batavorum. Ex Typographia Reineri Smetii, 1671.

Vellum; 5 x 3 x 1½ in.

EARLY PRINTING IN HOLLAND.

Cabinet D Shelf 1 No. 34

[Utrecht] 1479 [Joh. Veldener]. Omelien. Gregorius Magnus Papa. (Without indication of typographer or place.)
On f.1. Dit is die prologues of die voerspreke in sin/ to Gregorius omelie in duutschen/ f.212; Hier eynden ende gaen wt allen/ etc. f. 310: Dit boec is gheprint int iaer doe men screef M.CCCC.LXXIX/ op den tweentwintichste dach/ in april. deo gracias.

cont'd

EARLY PRINTING IN HOLLAND. cont'd

Cabinet D Shelf 1 No. 34

Gesamt-Kat. ; Proctor 8856; Campbell 854. p.236.

Boards, leather back; 9 x 6 x 1½ in.

EARLY PRINTING IN HOLLAND

Cabinet 39 Shelf 2 No. 47

Utrecht, 1670. Peter Elzevier.
Title: Prima Scaligerana, nusquam antehac edita, cum praefatione T. Fabri.
Imprint: Ultrajecti, apud Petrum Elzevirium, M.DC.LXX.
It is doubtful whether Peter Elzevier printed the above work, as he was only a publisher of books. This is probably a false Elzevier.
See Willems, re "False Elzevier."

Calf; 6¼ x 4 x 5/8 in.

EARLY PRINTING IN HUNGARY.

Cabinet D Shelf 1 No. 21

Buda, 1473. Andrea Hess. Chronica Hungarorum. [Facsimile]. With an explanatory essay by Wilhelm Fraknoi.
Title: Chronica/Hungarorum/ Impressa Budae 1473.
Colophon: Finita Bude Anno dni M.CCCC.LXXIII. in vigilia penthecostes: per Andrea Hess.

Half morocco: 12 x 9½ x ½ in.

EARLY PRINTING IN INDIA

Cabinet II Shelf 3 No. 26

Colombo, 1742. Imprimerie de la compagnie des Indes Orientales.

See CEYLON. Singaleesch belydenis bocke, na kerken -ordre...April, 1742.

EARLY PRINTING IN INDIA

Cabinet II Shelf 4 No. 47

Columbo (Capital of Ceylon), 1754. Johann Bernhardt Arnhardt. [Imprint].

See LANGUAGE CHARACTERS. Examples of. Tamul...1754.

EARLY PRINTING IN IRELAND

Cabinet C Shelf 2 No. 8

Cork, 1778, T.M. Vize (Imprint)

See BROADSIDES. Lerkin, George Sr. Essay on the origin...of printing

EARLY PRINTING IN IRELAND

Cabinet L Shelf 2 No. 5

Dublin, 1815, Graisberg and Campbell (Imprin
Title: Essay on the invention of alphabet writing. By Andrew Carmichael.

Half morocco; 10¼ x 8½ in.

EARLY PRINTING IN ITALY.

Cabinet F Shelf 4 No. 70

Bassno, 1744. Ciovanni Battista Remondini.
Title: Verita eterna esposte in lezioni....Raccolte dal P. Carlo Gregorio Rosignoli. Della Compangnia di Gesu.
Imprint: In Bassano. Nella Stamperia Remondini. Con licenza de' Superiori.
The printing house of Remondini continued until 1860.

Vellum; 6-1/8 x 3¼ x 1 in. See Arneudo,

cont'd

EARLY PRINTING IN ITALY cont'd

Cabinet F Shelf 4 No. 70

Dizionario Grafiche, p.1812.

EARLY PRINTING IN ITALY.

Cabinet E Shelf 1 No. 54

Brescia, 1568. Vincenzo de Sabbio [or Vicenzo Niccolini]
Title: Rime de gli Academici Occulti con le loro impresse et discorsi.
Colophon: In Brescia, appresso Vincenzo de Sabbio MDLXVIII.

Parchment; 9-3/4 x 7¼ x 1¼ in. See Arneudo Dizionario Esegetico. p.1557; Niccolini (Fratelli) detti da Sabbio.

EARLY PRINTING IN ITALY

Cabinet E Shelf 1 No. 65

Cremona, 1585. Ippolito Tromba and Ercoliano Bartoli.
Title: Cremona fedelissima citta et nobilissima Colonia de Romani rappresentata in disegno... da Antonio Campo....In Cremona in casa.... auttore. [Wood cut borders, initials, ornaments, head and tail pieces]
Colophon: In Cremona in casa dell'auttore. Per Hippolito Tromba & Hercoliano Bartoli M.D.LXXXV...Printer Mark.

cont'd

EARLY PRINTING IN ITALY cont'd

Cabinet E Shelf 1 No. 65

Morocco; 15¾ x 10¼ x 1-1/8 ins. Brunet I, 1526

EARLY PRINTING IN ITALY

Cabinet D Shelf 3 No. 15 and 16

Fano, 1507. Hieronymus Soncinus.
Title: Marci Vigerii Saonensis San. Mariae transtibe. Praesbi. Car. Senogallien Decachordum Christianum Iulio II. Pont. Max. dictum. Illus. Many beautiful woodcuts and borders.
Colophon:...Quod Hieronymus Soncinus de Urbe Fani his caracteribus impressit die X Augusti. M.D.VII...
Morocco, blind tooled; 12½ x 8¼ x 2 ins. Brunet 5, 1216.

EARLY PRINTING IN ITALY.

Cabinet D · Shelf 2 · No. 35

Ferrara, 1497. Lorenzo Rozzi (de Valenza)
Title: De claris mulieribus. Jacobus Philippus (Foresti) Bergomensis.
Colophon:....Gerrarie ip̄ressus. Opera et īpensa Magistri Laurentii de rubeis de Valentia. tertio kal.' maias. anno salutis nr̄e. M.ccccLxxxvij.....

Morocco; 12 x $8\frac{1}{4}$ x $1\frac{1}{4}$ in. Hain #2813.

EARLY PRINTING IN ITALY.

Cabinet D · Shelf 2 · No. 38

Ferrara, 1497. Lorenzo Rossi (de Valenza).
Title: Epistolae. S. Hieronymus.
Colophon: Impressa e la presente opera....ne la inclita & florentis/ sima cita de Ferrara: per maestro Lorenzo/ di Rossi da Valenza: ne gli anni MCCCCXCVII. a. di: XX/ de Octobre...

Gesamt-Kat. Brunet 998; folio, vol.2.

EARLY PRINTING IN ITALY.

Cabinet E · Shelf 1 · No. 21 (2 vols)

Florence, 1553. Laurentius Torrentinus.
Title: Digestorum seu Pandectarum libri quinquaginta. ex florentinis pandectis repraesentati. [2 vols.]
Imprint: Florentiae. In officina Laurentii Torrentini Ducelis Typographi. MDLIII ...

Calf; $16\frac{1}{4}$ x $10\frac{1}{4}$ x 3 and 4 ins. Bruent 3, 615.

EARLY PRINTING IN ITALY

Cabinet E · Shelf 1 · No. 56

Florence, 1568. Giunta.
Title: Le vite de piu excellenti pittori, scultori, ed architetti. Scritte da Georgio Vasari... In Fiorenza, Appresso i Giunta 1568. [With portraits] . 2 vols.
Colophon: In Fiorenza, appresso i Giunta, 1568.

Boards, vellum backs; $9\frac{1}{2}$ x 6 3/4 x $2\frac{1}{2}$ ins. Brunet, V. 1096.

EARLY PRINTING IN ITALY

Cabinet AA · Shelf 2 · No. 28

Florence, 1587 or 1588. Georgi Marescotti
Title: Oratio de Francisci Medices Etruriae ducis laudabus habita ab Aldo Manutius ... [Aldus Manutius, author].
Imprint: Florentiae, ex typographia Georgii Marescotti. With printer mark.

Full morocco, gilt; 7-5/8 x $5\frac{1}{2}$ x $\frac{1}{4}$ in.

EARLY PRINTING IN ITALY.

Cabinet E · Shelf 2 · No. 70

Florence, 1604. [Giunta].
Title: Catalogus librorum qui in Iunctarum bibliotheca Philippi Haeredum Florentiae prostant. [Printer Mark] Florentiae MDCIV
Dedication at end of vol: Per illustri ac Rev.mo D.D. Alexandro Burghio...Iunctae fratres Philippi FF.S.DD.

Vellum $5\frac{3}{4}$ x 3 x $1\frac{1}{4}$ ins.

EARLY PRINTING IN ITALY

Cabinet F · Shelf 5 · No. 49

Florence, 1791, Gaetano Cambiagi. (Imprint)

See IMPRINTS, Italy. Cambiagi, Gaetano ...

EARLY PRINTING IN ITALY

Cabinet F · Shelf 4 · No. 76

Florence, 1827, Giuse pi Molini.

See IMPRINTS, Italy. Molini, Giuseppi e Co.

EARLY PRINTING IN ITALY

Cabinet 75 · Shelf 1&2 · No.

Foligno, 1474.

See Scholderer, Victor. Fologno edition of 1474.

EARLY PRINTING IN ITALY.

Cabinet D · Shelf 3 · No. 27

Fossombrone, 1513. Ottaviano Petrucci. Paulina de recta Paschae celebratione: et de Passionis Domini nostri Iesu Christi. Paulus Germanus de Middelburgo. 2 vols.
Colophon: Impressum Forosempronii....virū Octavianū petru/tiā cive Forosemproniesem ipressoriae artis peritissimū Anno Domini M.D.XIII, die octava Iulii, cu privilego, etc. Printer Mark.

Vellum; 11-3/4 x 7-3/4 x 1-3/4 in.

EARLY PRINTING IN ITALY

Cabinet D · Shelf 3 · No. 28

Fossombrone, 1513. Ottaviano Petrucci.
Title: Paulina de recta Paschae celebratione: et die Passionis domini nostri Iesu Christi. 2 parts in one volume.
Colophon: Impressum Forosempronii per spectabilē virū Octavianū petrutiū civē Forosemproniēsem īpressoriae artis peritissimū Anno Domini M.D.XIII. die octava Iulii....Printer Mark.

Original tooled calf with clasps; $12\frac{1}{2}$ x $8\frac{1}{2}$ x $3\frac{1}{4}$ in.

EARLY PRINTING IN ITALY

Cabinet D · Shelf 3 · No. 44

Genoa, 1516. Petrus-Paulus Porrus
Title: Psalterium [Polyglot. Printed in types proper to each language].
Colophon: Impressit miro ingenio. Petrus Paulus Porrus, genuae in aedibus Nicolai Justiniani Pauli...

Boards; 13 x $9\frac{1}{4}$ x1 in. Brunet 4, 919

EARLY PRINTING IN ITALY.

Cabinet D · Shelf 3 · No. 45 · 2nd and better copy.

Genoa, 1516. Petrus-Paulus Porrus.
Title: Psalterium hebraeum, graecum, arabicum et chaldaeum, cum tribus latinis interpretat, et glossis studio Aug. Justiniani.
Colophon: Impressit miro ingenio, Petrus Paulus Porrus, Genuae in aedibus Nicolai Justiniani 1516. Printer Mark.
Said to be the first Polyglot edition printed in the types proper to each language.
Paper boards; 13 x $9\frac{1}{2}$ x $1\frac{1}{4}$ in. Brunet 4, 919.

D/3/44 Copy 1.

EARLY PRINTING IN ITALY

Cabinet D · Shelf 1 · No. 26

Mantua, 1475. Johannes Schall.
Title: Scrutinium Scripturarum. Paulus de S. Maria.
Colophon: Nota cp iste libellus videtur fuisse... et cum diligenti emeda per me Johannem/ Schallus artiū doctorē Mantue impressus sub annis pre/fati domī nostri Jhesu xp̄i M.CCCC.LXXV.

Gesamt.-Kat. Half morocco; 12 x $8\frac{1}{4}$ x $2\frac{1}{2}$ in.

EARLY PRINTING IN ITALY

Cabinet D · Shelf 1 · No. 31

Milan, 1478. Benignus et Johan Ant. de Honate.

See Incunabula. Durandus. Speculum Judiciale.

EARLY PRINTING IN ITALY

Cabinet F · Shelf 4 · No. 78

Milan, 1816. Regiis Typis.

See IMPRINTS. Italy. Regiis Typis. Milano. 1816...

EARLY PRINTING IN ITALY.

Cabinet E · Shelf 2 · No. 9

Naples, 1573. Horatio Salviani.
Title: Rerum a societate Iesu in oriente gestarum volumen. In q.o haec ferme continentur... Commentarius Emmanuelis Acostae...Neapoli, apud Horatium Saluianum.

Has on pp.246-228 the first European explanation of Japanese written characters.

Vellum covered boards; $8\frac{1}{2}$ x $6\frac{1}{4}$ x $1\frac{1}{4}$ in.

EARLY PRINTING IN ITALY

Cabinet D · Shelf 3 · No. 56

Ortona, 1518. Girolamo Soncino. Opus toti christiane Reipublice maxime utile, des arcanis/ catholice veritatis contra obstinatissimam Iudeorū/. Petrus Galatinus.
Colophon: Impressum vero Orthonae maris, summa cum diligentia per Hieronymum Suncinum: Anno christiane navitatis M.D.XVIII quintodecimo kalendas martias, etc.

Vellum, $12\frac{1}{2}$ x $9\frac{1}{4}$ x $2\frac{1}{4}$ ins. First book printed in this town (Olschki).

EARLY PRINTING IN ITALY (EXAMPLE)

Cabinet FF
Shelf 5
No. 1

Padua, 1656, Francesco Bertelli.
Title : Novo teatro di machine et edificii... di Vittorio Zonca.
Imprint: In Padova; appresso Francesco Bertelli.

Engraved title page and 42 full page copperplate illustrations.

Boards; 11¾ x 8½ in.

EARLY PRINTING IN ITALY.

Cabinet 50
Shelf 1
No. 1

Parma, 1769. Giambattista Bodoni.
Title: Le festa d'Apollo ...
Imprint: Parma nella Stamperia Reale.

Leather; 9½ x 7 x 7/8 in. Brooks, 8.

EARLY PRINTING IN ITALY

Cabinet 50
Shelf 1
No. 17

Parma, 1783. Giambattista Bodoni.
Title: Gestorum ab Episcopis Salvtiensibus.... Iosephus Ioachimus Lovera. Patricius Savillianensis. [Ornaments, borders, etc.]
Colophon: Parmae. Ec regio typographeo M.DCC.LXXXIII.

Calf; 9½ x 6¼ x 1 in. Brooks No.228.

EARLY PRINTING IN ITALY

Cabinet RR
Shelf 3
No. 6

Parma, 1762, Fratelli Borsi.
Title: Osservazioni intorno all'arte di fabbricare la carta...
Imprint: Fratelli Borsi, Stampatori, e Librai.

Tree calf; 10½ x 8 x ½ in.

EARLY PRINTING IN ITALY

Cabinet 50
Shelf 1
No. 7

Parma, 1774. Giambattista Bodoni.

Title: Pel solenne battesimo di S.A.R. Ludovico, Principe de Parma...
Colophon: Impresso nella R. Stamperia di Parma. L'anno M.DCC.LXXIV. Il giorno 18 de Aprile. [Preface by Bodoni, followed by twenty inscriptions in as many exotic types and languages.]

Half morocco; 11¼ x 8½ x 3/8 in. Brooks No.50

EARLY PRINTING IN ITALY

Cabinet 50
Shelf 1
No. 19

Parma, 1784. Giambattista Bodoni.

Title: Il calendario di corte per l'anno bissestile MDCCLXXXIV.

Imprint: Parma;Nella Stamperia Reale.

Morocco; 4¾ x 2¾ x 5/8 in. Brooks No.1386.

EARLY PRINTING IN ITALY.

Cabinet 50
Shelf 1
No. 2

Parma, 1771. Giambattista Bodoni.
Title: Fregi e majuscule incise e fuse da Giambattista Bodoni ...
Imprint: A Parma nella stamperia stessa.

Original paper cover, 7-7/8 x 4-3/4 x 3/8 in.
In cloth protective case.

EARLY PRINTING IN ITALY

Cabinet 50
Shelf 2
No. 3

Parma, 1775. Giambattista Bodoni.

Title: Epithalamia exoticis linguis reddita.
Imprint: Parmae ex Regio Typographeo. [With many beautiful copperplate engravings, head and tail pieces.]

Morocco; 17½ x 13 x 1½ in. Brooks No.70.

EARLY PRINTING IN ITALY

Cabinet 50
Shelf 1
No. 21

Parma, 1785. Giambattista Bodoni.
Title: Anacreontis...[Alternating Greek and Latin text in Majuscule types].
Imprint: Parmae. Ex Regio typographeio.

Half morocco; 12 x 9-1/8 x 1 in. Brooks, 287.

EARLY PRINTING IN ITALY.

Cabinet 50
Shelf 1
No. 4

Parma, 1773. Giambattista Bodoni.
Title: Giornata Villereccia. Poemata in tre canti ...
Imprint: Parma. Dalla Stamperia Reale. 1773.

Paper; 8¾ x 5¾ x 3/8 in. Brooks, 38.

EARLY PRINTING IN ITALY.

Cabinet 50
Shelf 1
No. 10

Parma, 1776. Giambattista Bodoni.
Title: Origine ac primitiis de hebraicae typographia ... Johannis Bernardi de-Rossi.
Imprint: Parmae. Ex regio typographeo. 1776.

Half morocco; 9-3/4 x 7½ in.

EARLY PRINTING IN ITALY.

Cabinet 50
Shelf 1
No. 22

Parma, 1785. Giambattista Bodoni.

Title: Lettre de J.B. Bodoni, Typographe du Roi d'Espagne et Directeur de l'Imprimerie de S.A.R. l'Infant Duc de Parme à Monsieur de Marquis de Cubieres.

Half morocco; 11¾ x 8 x ¼ in. Brooks No. 292.

EARLY PRINTING IN ITALY.

Cabinet 50
Shelf 1
No. 3

Parma, 1773. Giambattista Bodoni.
Title: La marcia. Commedia del signor abate Francesco Maruchi di Milano.
Imprint: Parma. Dalla Stamperia Reale.

Half morocco; 11¼ x 8 x ¾ in.

EARLY PRINTING IN ITALY

Cabinet 50
Shelf 1
No. 13

Parma, 1778. Giambattista Bodoni.

Title: Elogio Funebre. Recitato dal signor Conti Antonio Cerati....

Colophon: Parma. Dalla Reale Stamperia. (1778) Con approvazione.

Calf; 11 x 8 x ½ in.

EARLY PRINTING IN ITALY.

Cabinet 50
Shelf 1
No. 24

Parma, 1786. Giambattista Bodoni.
Title: Gli amori pastorali di Dafni e di Cloe ... Tradotti dalla lingua Greca.
Imprint: Crispoli. Impresso co'caratteri Bodoniani.

Morocco, tooled; 12 x 8¾ x 1½1/8 in. Brooks, 309.

EARLY PRINTING IN ITALY.

Cabinet 50
Shelf 1
No. 5

Parma, 1773. Giambattista Bodoni.
Title: Saggio di poesie. Italiane dell'Abate ... Alberti.
Imprint: Parma dalla Stamperia Reale.

Original boards; 10 x 8¼ x 3/8 in. Brooks, 34.

EARLY PRINTING IN ITALY.

Cabinet 50
Shelf 1
No. 15

Parma, 1779. Giambattista Bodoni.

Title: Atti della solenne coronazione...Dna Maria Maddalena Morelli Fernandez...
Colophon: Impresso nella Stamperia Reale di Parma il di XXX Giugno dell'anno di nostra riparata saluta M.DCC.LXXIX.

Flowered Japanese paper; 8½ x 5-7/8 x 7/8 in Brooks No.135.

EARLY PRINTING IN ITALY

Cabinet 50
Shelf 1
No. 25

Parma, 1786. Giambattista Bodoni.

Title: Characterum ethicorum Theophrasti Eresii ....quae ex cod. ms. Vaticano saeculi XI graece edidit latine vertit praefatione... Christophorus Amadutius.
Imprint: Parmae. Ex Regio Typographeo.

Boards; 11 x 8 x 3/8 in. Brooks No.315.

EARLY PRINTING IN ITALY

Cabinet 50
Shelf 1
No. 28

Parma, 1788. Giambattista Bodoni.

Title: Osservazioni di Ennio Quirino Visconti...

Imprint: In Parma. Dalla Reale Tipografia, MDCCLXXXVIII.

Mottled calf; $8\frac{1}{2}$ x $5\frac{3}{4}$ x $\frac{1}{2}$ in. Brooks No.359

EARLY PRINTING IN ITALY

Cabinet 50
Shelf 1
No. 29

Parma, 1788. Giambattista, Bodoni.

Title: Serie de Caratteri Greci di Giambatista, Bodoni.

Boards; $9_{\frac{1}{4}}$ x 6 x 3/8 in. Brooks No.355.

EARLY PRINTING IN ITALY.

Cabinet 50
Shelf 2
No. 5

Parma, 1788. Giambattista Bodoni.

Title: Serie di Majuscole e caratteri cancellereschi. [Without imprint. "I have had the great pleasure of receiving... It is one of the most beautiful that Art has hitherto produced, B. Franklin".]

Half morocco, 20 x $13\frac{1}{2}$ x 1 in. Brooks No.357 Updike II, p.166.

EARLY PRINTING IN ITALY.

Cabinet 50
Shelf 1
No. 34

Parma, 1789. Giambattista Bodoni.

Title: .minta, favola boschereccia di Torquato Tasso ...

Imprint: Crispoli. Impresso co'caratteri Bodoniani. 1789.

Half morocco; $11\frac{1}{2}$ x $9\frac{1}{4}$ in. Brooks, 379.

EARLY PRINTING IN ITALY

Cabinet 50
Shelf 1
No. 36

Parma, 1791. Giambattista Bodoni.

Title: Anakreontis...Odea.

Imprint: Parma, In aedibus Palatiuis, 1791.

Full morocco, gilt edges; 6 x 4-3/8 x 1 in. Brooks 422; Brunet 1, 252.

EARLY PRINTING IN ITALY.

Cabinet 50
Shelf 1
No. 37

Parma, 1791: Giambattista Bodoni.

Title: Saggio di memoria de la Tipografia Parmense del secolo XV del Padre Ireneo Affo...

Imprint: Parma dalla stamperia Reale. M.DCC.XCI.

Half morocco; 10 x $8\frac{1}{4}$ x $\frac{1}{2}$ in.

EARLY PRINTING IN ITALY

Cabinet 50
Shelf 2
No. 8

Parma, 1792. Giambattista Bodoni.

Title: Britannia, Lathmon, Villa Bromhamensis. [On frontispiece, portrait of the author, John Trevor].

Imprint: Parmae. Aedibus Palatinis. Typis Bodonianis. MDCCXCII.

Full morocco, $17\frac{3}{4}$ x $11\frac{3}{4}$ x $1\frac{1}{4}$ in. Brooks, p.89

EARLY PRINTING IN ITALY.

Cabinet 50
Shelf 2
No. 7

Parma, 1792. Giambattista Bodoni.

Title: Callimaco. Greco-Italiano...[Dedication]. Per le nozze della R. Principessa di Parma Carolina Teresa di Borbone...[Printed in Greek and Italian].

Imprint: Parma, nel Regal Palazzo, MDCCXCII. Co' tipi Bodoniani.

Boards; 18 x 12 x 1 in.

EARLY PRINTING IN ITALY.

Cabinet 50
Shelf 1
No. 40

Parma, 1792. Giambattista Bodoni.

Title: Le Stanze di Messer Angelo Poliziano di nuovo pubblicate.

Imprint: Parma nel Regal Palazzo MDCCXCII. Co' tipi Bodoniani.

Orig.mottled calf; $13\frac{3}{4}$ x $8\frac{1}{2}$ x $\frac{3}{4}$ in. Brooks No.451.

EARLY PRINTING IN ITALY

Cabinet 50
Shelf 1
No. 42

Parma, 1793. Giambattista Bodoni.

Title: La tavola di Cebete Tebano. [This is the second title; the first part of the book being a Greek Version of the same subject].

Imprint: Parma nel Regal Palazzo MDCCXCIII. co' tipi Bodoniani.

Calf; $7\frac{1}{2}$ x 5 x $\frac{1}{2}$ in. Brooks No.510.

EARLY PRINTING IN ITALY.

Cabinet 50
Shelf 1
No. 44

Parma, 1794. Giambattista Bodoni.

Title: Pel Virgilio.

Imprint: Stampato in Parma in due volumi. 1791. [Sonnets in praise of printing in which the names of Aldo, Gryphe and Giolito are mentioned; also "Alcippo," the Arcadian name for Bodoni.

Brochure, paper covers. Brooks, 543.

EARLY PRINTING IN ITALY

Cabinet 49
Shelf 1
No. 4

Parma, 1794. Giambattista Bodoni.

Title: La Gerusalemme liberate di Torquato Tasso.

Imprint: Parma, nel regal Palazzo, MDCCXCIV. Co'tipi Bodoniani.

Copy presented to H.L. Bullen, by A. Lobetti Bodoni, grandson of Bodoni's sister.

Paper covers; 15 x 10 x 1 in. Brooks No.563.

EARLY PRINTING IN ITALY

Cabinet 50
Shelf 1
No. 45

Parma, 1794. Giambattista Bodoni.

Title: The Seasons. By James Thomson.

Imprint: Parma. Printed by Bodoni. MDCCXCIV.

Half calf, gilt: $11\frac{1}{2}$ x 9 x 1 in. Brooks No.531.

EARLY PRINTING IN ITALY.

Cabinet 50
Shelf 1
No. 48

Parma, 1795. Giambattista Bodoni.

Title: Scherzi poetici e pittorici. (At end). Parma, co' tipi Bodoniani. Title and illustrations by Rosaspina are colored. Book dedicated to D. Allessandro de Sousa e Holstein. Brooks, ,599.

Holf morocco; 12-3/8 x $9\frac{1}{2}$ x 1-1/8 in.

EARLY PRINTING IN ITALY

Cabinet 50
Shelf 1
No. 52

Parma, 1796. Giambattista Bodoni.

Title: Poesie de Maria Luisa Cicci...

Imprint: Parma. Co'tipi Bodoniani, 1796. [This is one of only two copies printed on vellum.]

Boards; 6-3/4 x $4\frac{1}{2}$ x 3/4 in. cased. Brooks No. 627.

EARLY PRINTING IN ITALY.

Cabinet 50
Shelf 1
No. 55

Parma, 1799. Giambattista Bodoni.

Title: Odi dell'Abate Giuseppe Parini già divolgate.

Imprint: Parma. Co'tipi Bodoniani. 1799.

Boards; $6\frac{1}{2}$ x $4\frac{1}{2}$ x 5/8 in. Brooks No.760.

EARLY PRINTING IN ITALY.

Cabinet 50
Shelf 2
No. 9

Parma, 1800. Giambattista Bodoni.

Title: Aesop Phrygii fabulae. Graecae Latine conversae.

Imprint: Parmae. Ex regio typographeo. 1800.

Calf; 16 x $11\frac{1}{2}$ in. Brunet I, 87; Brooks 796.

EARLY PRINTING IN ITALY

Cabinet 50
Shelf 1
No. 59

Parma, 1800. Giambattista Bodoni.

Title: Per le nozze del nobil uomo Signor Conte Alessandro Bonacossi....

Imprint: Parma. Co'tipi Bodoniani, MDCCC

Boards; $6\frac{3}{4}$ x $4\frac{1}{2}$ x $\frac{1}{2}$ in. Brooks No.764.

EARLY PRINTING IN ITALY

Cabinet 50 Shelf 1 No. 58

Parma, 1800. Giambattista Bodoni.
Title: Pitture di Antonio Allegri detto Il Correggio.
Imprint: Parma nel Regal Palazzo. MDCCC.Co'tipi Bodoniani.

Boards; $10\frac{3}{4}$ x $7\frac{3}{4}$ x $\frac{3}{4}$ in. Brooks 777.

EARLY PRINTING IN ITALY

Cabinet 50 Shelf 2 No. 13

Parma, 1806-1807. Giambattista Bodoni.
Title: Bodoniana 2: Bodoni in honor of Napoleon.
Imprints [Various].

Scrap book. Half morocco; $18\frac{1}{2}$ x 13 in.

EARLY PRINTING IN ITALY

Cabinet 50 Shelf 2 No. 11

Parma, 1806. Giambattista Bodoni.
Title: Oratio Dominica in CLV linguas versa et exoticis characteribus plerumque expressa.
Colophon: Parmae typis Bodonianis MDCCCVI.
[The Lord's Prayer in 155 languages set in types of each language made by G. Bodoni.]

Boards; 17 x 11 x 2 in. Brooks No.1003; Updike II p.168-169.

EARLY PRINTING IN ITALY.

Cabinet 49 Shelf 1 No. 6

Parma, 1809. Giambattista Bodoni.

Title: Le piu insigni pitture Parmensi indicate agli amatori delle Belle Arti.
Imprint: Parma dalla Tipografia Bodoniana. MDCCCIX.

Half morocco; $12\frac{1}{4}$ x 9 x $1\frac{1}{2}$ in. Brooks No.1059.

EARLY PRINTING IN ITALY.

Cabinet 49 Shelf 1 No. 10

Parma, 1818. Giambattista Bodoni.

Title: Di Q. Orazio Flacco satira V. Traduzione italiana con rami allusivi.
Imprint: Parma. Co'tipi Bodoniani MDCCCXVIII.

Half morocco; 12 x 9 x $\frac{1}{2}$ in. Brooks, No.1212.

EARLY PRINTING IN ITALY.

Cabinet 49 Shelf 1 No. 9

Parma, 1818. Giambattista Bodoni.
Title: Manuale tipografico del cavaliere G. Bodoni.
Imprint: Parma, presso la Vedova, MDCCCXVIII. [2 vols.]
Include specimens of more than 250 different type designs: Latin, Greek, Russian, etc.

Original boards; 13 x $9\frac{1}{2}$ x 2 in. Brooks 1216; Brunet, 1, 1027-8.

EARLY PRINTING IN ITALY.

Cabinet 50 Shelf 1 No. 63

Parma, 1821. Giambattista Bodoni.
Title: Regolamento per la Ducale Tipografia. Firenze 28. Settembre 1821.
Includes prices for printing, wages, discipline, etc., in the printing house established by Bodoni.

Boards; 8-7/8 x 5-5/8 in.

EARLY PRINTING IN ITALY

Cabinet F Shelf 5 No. 50

Pisa, 1811. Tipografia Società Letteraria. Imprint.

See IMPRINTS. Italy. Tipografia Società Letteraria...

EARLY PRINTING IN ITALY.

Cabinet D Shelf 1 No. 33

Rome, 1479. Francisci di Cinquinis.
Title: Apologia Heremitarum. Ulmeus [Paulus] Bergomensis....
Colophon: Impressum Rome in domo nobilis Francisci de Cinquinis apud sanctam Maria de pplo Anno dni 1479 die 18, mensis Iulii.

Gesamt-Kat. ; Hain 6086. 10238. Paper boards; 9 x $6\frac{1}{4}$ x $\frac{1}{2}$ in.

EARLY PRINTING IN ITALY

Cabinet D Shelf 1 No. 55

Rome, 1490. Peter de Turre. Ptolemaei Cosmographia: Registrum alphabeticum/super octo libros Ptolo-/mei incepit feliciter.
Colophon: Hoc opus....impressum fuit et completum Rome anno....MCCCCLXXXX....arte ac impensio Petri di Turre; folio.

Gesamt-Kat. Brunet 4, 954. Hain 13541. Calf; 16-3/8 x 11 x $1\frac{1}{2}$ in.

in vestibule cabinet

EARLY PRINTING IN ITALY

Cabinet D Shelf 4 No. 19

Rome, 1522. [Calliergi or Kaliergi, Zaccaria, from the island of Crete]
Title: Chrysoloras, Manuel [Greek Grammar].... Erotemata chrysolorae/ de formatione tem-/porum ex libro chalcondylae.
Colophon: Impressum Romae. M.D.XXII. Mense Iunis [Without printers name]

Boards; $6\frac{1}{4}$ x 4 x $\frac{3}{4}$ in. See Arneudo, Dizionario esegetico....p.252.

EARLY PRINTING IN ITALY.

Cabinet D Shelf 4 No. 53

Rome, 1534. Antonio Blado. Oratione de la pace di M. Claudio Tolomei. Con gratia, & prohibitione del sommo pontefice, che nessuno possa stampare....sotto la penna (etc).
Colophon: Composto da l'authore nel MDXXIX/ d'Aprile & stampata poi in Roma da Antonio Blado Asolano nel M.D./XXXIIII. di Marzo. [with printer's mark]

Boards; $8\frac{1}{4}$ x $5\frac{1}{2}$ x 3/8 ins.

EARLY PRINTING IN ITALY

Cabinet L Shelf 3 No. 4.02

Rome, 1540, Baldassarre di Francesco Cartloari. (His colophon)

See IMPRINTS, Italy. Cartolari...
Roma, 1540

EARLY PRINTING IN ITALY

Cabinet 60 Shelf 2 No. 21

Rome, 1562-3. Paulus Manutius, Aldi F.

Title (I): Theodoretus. In visiones Danielis prophetae Commentarius, Ioanne Baptista Gabio Veronensi interprete. [Printer Mark] Romae, M.D.LXII.
Title (II & III): Beati Theodoriti episcopi Cyrensis...[Printer Mark] Romae M.D.LXIII. Apud Paulum Manutium, Aldi F. Cum privilegio Pii IIII. Pont. Max.

"In canticum cantorum: and
"In Ezechielem prophetem." cont'd

EARLY PRINTING IN ITALY cont'd

Cabinet 60 Shelf 2 No. 21

Full morocco; $13\frac{1}{2}$ x $9\frac{1}{4}$ x 1-3/4 in. Renouard II, 18 & 28.

EARLY PRINTING IN ITALY.

Cabinet 60 Shelf 2 No. 23

Rome, 1563. Paulus Manutius, Aldi F.
Title: Divi Caecilii Cypriani Episcopi Carthaginiensis, et gloriosissimi martyris, Opera .....Alia eidem Cypriano adscripta.... [Printer Mark]
Imprint: Romae, M.D.LXIII. Apud Paulum Manutium, Aldi F. Cum privilegio Pii IIII Pont.Max.

Calf; $12\frac{1}{2}$ x $8\frac{3}{4}$ x $1\frac{3}{4}$ in. Renouard II, 29; Brunet 2, 459.

EARLY PRINTING IN ITALY

Cabinet 60 Shelf 1 No. 39

Rome, 1563. Paulus Manutius.
Title: Francisci Vargas....De episcoporum jurisdictione et pontificis max. auctoritate responsum. [Printer Mark].
Imprint: Romae, M.D.LXIII. Apud Paulum Manutium Aldi F. In aedibus populi Romani.

Parchment; $7\frac{3}{4}$ x $5\frac{1}{2}$ x 5/8 in. Brunet 5, 1088. Goldsmid. Aldine Press, No.564.

EARLY PRINTING IN ITALY

Cabinet E Shelf 2 No. 38

Rome, 1585. Vincento Accolti.
Title: Historia de las cosas mas notables, ritos y costombres del gran Reyno dela China... Maestro Fr. Ioan Gonzalez de Mendoça... 1580...Con un Itinerario del nuevo Mundo.
Imprint: En Roma, a costa de Bartholome Grassi, en la stampa de Vincentio Accolti, 1585.

Morocco; $6\frac{1}{2}$ x $4\frac{1}{4}$ x 1 in.

EARLY PRINTING IN ITALY.

Cabinet E
Shelf 2
No. 49

Rome, 1590, Typographia Medicea-Orientale.
Title: Evangelium Sanctum Domini nostri Jesu Christi. [In Arabic].
Colophon: Romae in Typographia Medicea, 1590.

This printing office was under the direction of the learned orientalist, Giovanni Battista Raimondi, elected by Cardinal Ferdinando de Medici.

Half leather; 13-3/8 x $9\frac{1}{4}$ x 1-3/8 in.

EARLY PRINTING IN ITALY.

Cabinet E
Shelf 2
No. 75

Rome, 1608. Giacomo Ruffinello.
Title: Vago e dilettevole giardino di varie lettioni di mutio Panza...et infinite altre cose curiose....In Roma, appresso Giacomo Mascardi. MDCVIII. ad instanza di Giovanni Martinelli. Illus.
Colophon: In Roma, appresso Giacomo Ruffinello Ad istanza di Gio. Martinelli M.D.XC. [Printer Mark of G. Martinelli]

Vellum; 9 x $6\frac{1}{2}$ x 1 in.

EARLY PRINTING IN ITALY.

Cabinet E
Shelf 2
No. 88

Rome, 1613. Savary de Breves [et] Steph. Paulinus.
Title: Dotrina Christiana D. Robert Card. Bellarmini. [Text in Arabian and Latin].
Imprint: Romae. ex typographia Savariana. Excudebat Stephanus Paulinus. 1613.

Vellum; 6-3/8 x $4\frac{1}{4}$ x $\frac{1}{2}$ in.

EARLY PRINTING IN ITALY

Cabinet E
Shelf 3
No. 37

Rome, 1628. Vicentius Gherardus.
Title: Odegia [In Greek]
Imprint: In Roma, nella stampa della S. Congr. de propag. Fide. MDCXXVIII.
Imprimatur: Fr. Vincentius Gherardus Socius. Reverendissimi P.F.Nicolai Rodulfii, Sacri & Apost. Pal. Mag. Ord. Praed.

$5\frac{3}{4}$ x 3 x 1-1/8 in.

EARLY PRINTING IN ITALY

Cabinet X
Shelf 4
No. 78-01

Rome, 1670. Camera Apostolica Tipographia.
Title: Index librorum prohibitorum Clementis X...
Imprint: Romae, ex Typographia Rev-Cam(era)-Apost(olica). 1670.

Vellum; $6\frac{1}{4}$ x 3-7/8 x 7/8 in.

EARLY PRINTING IN ITALY.

Cabinet F
Shelf 5
No. 6

Rome, 1736. Giovanni Maria Salvioni: Vatican Printer.
Title: Parentalia Mariae Clementinae, Magn. Britan. Franc et Hibern. Regin. Iussu clements XII. Pont Max. Engraved title page and two folded plates by Pannini.
Colophon: In Roma. Appresso Giovanni Maria Salvioni. Stampator Vaticano.

Paper boards, leather back: $16\frac{3}{4}$ x $11\frac{3}{4}$ in.

EARLY PRINTING IN ITALY.

Cabinet F
Shelf 5
No. 12

Rome, 1758. Niccolo et Marco Pagliarini.
Title: Componimenti poetici per le felicissime nozze di sua eccellenza il Signor Giovanni Correr con sua eccellenza la Signora Andriana Pesaro...Da Marco Antonio Fadalti. Many engraved vignettes, and initials by Gio Barbault.
Imprint: Dalla Stamperia di Pallade. Appresso Niccolo e Marco Pagliarini....

Paper boards; $14\frac{1}{2}$ x 10 x $\frac{1}{2}$ in.

EARLY PRINTING IN ITALY.

Cabinet F
Shelf 5
No. 9

Rome, 1763-65. Joannes Zempel.
Title: P. Virgilii Maronis. Bucolica, Georgica, et Aeneis. Ex cod. Mediceo-Laurentiano descripta ab Antonio Ambrogi Florentino S.J. Italico versus reddita...Aere incisis et Cl. Virorum illustrata. 3 vols.
Imprint: Excudebat Joannes Zempel prope montem Jordanum Venantii monaldini Bibliopolae sumptibus.

Paper boards; 17 x 12 in. Brunet 5, 1306.

EARLY PRINTING IN ITALY

Cabinet PI
Shelf 3
No. 3

Rome, 1803. Gio. Batista Cannetti. (Imprint)

See LAWS RELATING TO PUBLISHING. Rome, 1803.

EARLY PRINTING IN ITALY

Cabinet LL
Shelf 3
No. 57

Siena, 1585. Luca Bonetti
Title: L'Arte del puntar...da Orazio Lombardelli.
Imprint: In Siena, appresso Luca Bonetti. 1585. Con licenza dé Superiori.
Has printer mark on title page. Bound in with another item by same author, with imprint of M. Florimi, Siena, 1608.

Boards, leather back; $6\frac{1}{4}$ x $4\frac{1}{4}$ x 1 in.

EARLY PRINTING IN ITALY

Cabinet LL
Shelf 3
No. 57

Siena, 1608. Matteo Florimi.
Title: I riscontri gramaticali d'Orazio Lombardelli. La terza volta stampati.
Imprint: In Siena, appresso Matteo Florimi. 1608. Con licenza de Superiori.
Has printer mark. Bound in with another item by same author, with imprint of Luca Bonetti, Siena, 1585.

Boards, leather back; $6\frac{1}{4}$ x $4\frac{1}{4}$ x 1 in.

EARLY PRINTING IN ITALY

Cabinet F
Shelf 4
No. 77

Torino, 1842. Stamperia Reale (Imprint)

See IMPRINTS. Italy. Stamperia Reale. Torino, 1842...

EARLY PRINTING IN ITALY

Cabinet 6
Shelf 1
No. 2

Venice, 1470. Nicolas Jenson.
Title: Eusebius Pamphilius: De evangelica praeparatione....
Colophon: Hoc Ienson veneta Nicolaus in urbe volumen Prompsit: cui foelix gallica terra parens. Scrire placet tempus: Mauro christophorus vrbi Dux erat aequa animo musa retecta suo est. Quid magis artificem peteret Dux christus: et auctor: Tres facit aeternos ingeniosa manus. MCCCCLXX.
This is the first book printed by Jenson. Stitched only; in morocco slip case; 14 x $10\frac{1}{4}$ x 2 in. Hain 2, 6696

EARLY PRINTING IN ITALY.

Cabinet 6
Shelf 1
No. 4

Venice, 1472: Nicolas Jenson.
Title following preface: Caii Plynii secundi Naturalis Historiae.
Colophon: Caii Plynii secundi Naturalis Historiae libri tricesimiseptimi et ultimi finis impressi Venetiis per Nicolaum Jenson Gallicum. M.CCCC.LXXII. Nicolao Trono inclyto Venetiarum Duce.

In eighteenth century morocco; 16 x 11 x 4 in. Hain 4, 13089.

EARLY PRINTING IN ITALY.

Cabinet D
Shelf 1
No. 37

Venice, [1474] . Johanes de Colonia.

See Incunabula. Antoninus. Summa confessionum.

EARLY PRINTING IN ITALY.

Cabinet 6
Shelf 1
No. 6

Venice, 1475. Nicolas Jenson.

See Incunabula. Augustinus, Aurelius: De civitate dei......

EARLY PRINTING IN ITALY

Cabinet D
Shelf 1
No. 28

Venice, 1476. Jacobus Rubeis. Also known as Rosso or Rossi.
Title: Bonifacius VIII. Decretales.
Colophon: Finitur hic prima pars....sexto libro decretalium: Impssa Venetiis...Jacobum de Rubeis gallicum...Anno M.ccc.Lxxvi quarto Idus septembris.

Gesamt-Kat. Original boards; 17 x $11\frac{1}{4}$ x $3\frac{1}{2}$ in.

EARLY PRINTING IN ITALY

Cabinet 29
Shelf 1
No. 4

Venice, 1477: Ratdolt, Maler (Pictor) and Löslein.
Title: Appianus, Historia Romano. (In two parts)
Colophon: Impressum est hoc opus Venetiis per Bernardu pictorem & Erhardum ratdolt de Augusta una cum Petro Löslein de Langencen correctore ac socio. 1477.

Calf; $11\frac{1}{2}$ x $8\frac{1}{8}$ in.

EARLY PRINTING IN ITALY.

Cabinet 6, Shelf 1, No. 10

Venice, 1480. Nicolas Jenson.
Title: Johannes, Carthusiensis (Giov. de Dio)
Nosce te ipsum.
Imprint: Actum hoc opus ... a officina Nicolai Jenson Gallici, 4 kal. Jul. 1480.

Boards; $8\frac{1}{4}$ x $5\frac{1}{2}$ x 7/8 in.

EARLY PRINTING IN ITALY

Cabinet D, Shelf 1, No. 39

Venice, 1481. Johann Herbort.
Title: Baysio, Guido de. Rosarium decretorum
Colophon: Exactum insigne hoc opus ductū auspitiis optimōz, Iohannis de Colonia Nicolai Jenson sociorum...

Gesamt-Kat. ; Hain 2717.

Original binding, tooled velum; 18 x $11\frac{1}{2}$ in.

EARLY PRINTING IN ITALY.

Cabinet D, Shelf 1, No. 44

Venice, 1482. Franciscus Renner de Heilbronn

See Incunabula. Ausimo, Nicolaus de Liber qui dicitur supplementum.

EARLY PRINTING IN ITALY.

Cabinet 6, Shelf 1, No. 8

Venice, 1483. Andreas Torresanus and Bartholomaeus de Blavis.
Title: Bonifacius VIII. Sextus Decretalium.
With the incorrect Colophon: Sexti libri decretalium...Nicolai Jenson Gallici Venetiis impressus feliciter explicit Olympiadib' domini nostri iesu christi M.CCC.LXXIX. nona calendarum decembris.

Bound in with another volume in same format and types, printed by Jenson's successors in 1483. Jenson died in 1480.

Gilt russia; 17 x $11\frac{1}{2}$ x 1-3/4 in. Hain 1,3598

EARLY PRINTING IN ITALY

Cabinet 6, Shelf 1, No. 8

Venice, 1483. Andrea d'Asola.
Title: Clement V. Constitutiones una cum apparatu Joannis Andreae.
Colophon: Clementarium opus perutile enucleatius castigatum elimatuqz; Impensa atqz diligentia singulari Bartholomei de alexandria Andreeqz de Asula sociox Venetijs impressum feliciter explicit. Anno salutis christiane M.CCCC.LXXXIIj. tertio calendas novembris.
Bound in with another volume in same
cont'd

EARLY PRINTING IN ITALY cont'd

Cabinet, Shelf, No.

format and types

Gilt Russia; 17 x $11\frac{1}{2}$ x $1\frac{3}{4}$ in.
Hain 2, 5431.

EARLY PRINTING IN ITALY.

Cabinet D, Shelf 1, No. 47

Venice, 1483. Ottaviano Scottus.

See Incunabula. Hieronymus. Vitas Patrum.

EARLY PRINTING IN ITALY

Cabinet D, Shelf 1, No. 49

Venice, 1486. Nicolaus Battibovis.

See Incunabula. Lucanus, Marcus Annaes. Pharsalia.

EARLY PRINTING IN ITALY.

Cabinet 6, Shelf 1, No. 16

Venice, 1487: Andrea de Torresanus de Asula
Title: Sabellicus. Rerum venetiarum ab urbe condita lib. XXXIII.
Colophon: Hoc opus Impressum Venetiis Arte & industria optimi viri Andreae de Toresanis de Asula Anno M.CCCLXXXVII. Die XXI. Madii Augustino Barbadico Inclyto principe.

Printed in Jenson's Roman and Gothic types.

Morocco; 16-3/4 x $11\frac{1}{2}$ x $2\frac{1}{4}$ in. Brunet 5, 6. Hain 4, 14053.

EARLY PRINTING IN ITALY.

Cabinet D, Shelf 2, No. 19

Venice, 1492. Bernardino Rizzo. Supplementum chronicarum. [Printer mark]
Colophon: Ac sic demu....fuit idi/bus octobris anno a natali xpiano, 1486 in civitate nostra Bergomi..../Impressum autem Venetiis per Magistrum Bernardinuz ricium de novaria: Anno a nativita te dñi M.CCCC.LXXXXii die decimo quinto Februarii: regnante inclyto duce Augustino barbadico. [Illus]

Gesamt-Kat. ; Hain 2809.

EARLY PRINTING IN ITALY

Cabinet D, Shelf 2, No. 20

Venice, 1492. Hieronymus de Pagininis
Title: Biblia Latina
Colophon:..Impressa vero in felici Venetorum civitate sumptibus arte Hieronymi de Paganinis Brixiensis...

Gesamt-Kat. ; Hain 3112, 3114.

Calf; 6-7/8 x $4\frac{1}{4}$ x $2\frac{1}{4}$ in.

EARLY PRINTING IN ITALY

Cabinet D, Shelf 2, No. 31

Venice 1496. Bartholomaeus de Zanis.
Title: Plutarchus: Vitae illustrium virorum.
Colophon:...Venetiis impressae Bartolumeu de Zanis de Portefio...

Gesamt-Kat. Hain 13130.

Vellum over board; $12\frac{1}{4}$ x 8-1/8 x $2\frac{1}{2}$ in.

EARLY PRINTING IN ITALY

Cabinet D, Shelf 2, No. 42

Venice, 1498. Joannes and Gregorius de Gregoriis.
Title: Hieronymus. Commentaria in Biblia.
Colophon:..Ioanis & Graegorii de Gregoriis fretus officio ea noviter impressa commentaria...

Gesamt-Kat. ; Hain 8581

Calf; $12\frac{3}{4}$ x $9\frac{1}{2}$ in.

EARLY PRINTING IN ITALY

Cabinet 13, Shelf 4, No.

Venice, 1499. Lucantonio Giunta.Graduale Romanum [Edited by Franciscus de Brugio], Venice. Johannes Emericus de Spira, 1499-1500. Sept. 28 to March 1.
Title: Graduale am morem sancte Romane ecclesia...
Colophon:.. Impressum Venetiis cura nobil viri Luce Antonii de Giunta, florentini... Anno incarnationis dnice 1499. Kl. Octobris.

Boards covered with red vellum; brass bosses. 23 x $15\frac{5}{8}$ x 5 in.

EARLY PRINTING IN ITALY

Cabinet D, Shelf 2, No. 48

Venice, 1499. Zacharias Callierges.
Title: Etmologikum magnum graece.
Colophon:...sumptibus Domini Nicolai Blasti... Labore et dexteritate Zachariae Calliergi Cretensis...[With printer mark].

Gesamt-Kat. ; Hain 6691.

Vellum $15\frac{1}{2}$ x 10 x 2 in.

EARLY PRINTING ITALY.

Cabinet 60, Shelf 2, No. 1

Venice, 1500. Aldus Manutius.
Title: Epistole devotissime de Sancta Catharina da Siena. [Illus. and Woodcuts]
Colophon: Stampata in la Inclita Cita de Venetia in Casa de Aldo Manutio Romano adi XV Septembrio M.CCCCC.

Mottled paper over boards; calf back 12-3/4 x 9 x 3 ins. Renouard. Annales....des Aldes, I, p.55.

Ex.Cab.9

EARLY PRINTING IN ITALY

Cabinet 10, Shelf 2, No. 12

Venice, 1504. Baptista de Tortis. Gratianus. Decretales.
Title: De Tortis. Decretum Gratiani cādidissime lector habe bis cū multis notabilibus i margine in locis congruis positis: necnō cū multis cōcordātiis sacrarum scripturarū novi e veteris testamēti que in aliis nūquam fuerūt impresse.
Colophon: Cum privilegio ne quis audeat hoc opus imprimere citra decem annos sub pena in
cont'd

EARLY PRINTING IN ITALY, cont'd

Cabinet 10, Shelf 2, No. 12

eo contenta. Venetiis per Baptistam de Tortis. M.CCCCC.IIII. die XII. februarii. Printers mark.

Original stamped leather with clasps, $18\frac{1}{2}$ x 13 x $3\frac{1}{2}$ ins.

EARLY PRINTING IN ITALY.

Cabinet 60 · Shelf 1 · No. 1

Venice, 1507-8. Aldus Manutius.
Title: Institutionum grammaticarum libri quatuor ... Venice, Julio 1508. (One signature only). A prospectus with 1507 preface.
See Renouard "Annales des Aldes." Vol. I, pp. 123-232.
See also Brunet 3, 1382.

In paper envelope.

EARLY PRINTING IN ITALY.

Cabinet 60 · Shelf 1 · No. 9

Venice, 1515. Aldus Manutius.
Title: Lucanus. Civilis belli.
Imprint: Venetiis aedibus Aldi, et Andreae soceri, Mense Iulio M.D.XV. [Printer Mark]

Vellum; 6¼ x 3½ x 1-1/8 in. Brunet 3, 1199. Renouard. Annales....des Aldes I, p.171.

EARLY PRINTING IN ITALY.

Cabinet D · Shelf 4 · No. 20

Venice, 1522: Alex. Paganinus.
Title: Cornucopiae, sive linguae latinae commentarii. [Per Nic. Perothum].
Colophon: Thusculani, apud Benacum in aedibus Alexandri Paganini. Mense April, M.CCCCC.XII

Printed in curious seemingly upright italic types "minute cursive condensed" the invention of which is attributed to Paganini.

Calf; 9-1/8 x 5-7/8 x 1-7/8 in.

EARLY PRINTING IN ITALY

Cabinet 60 · Shelf 1 · No. 5

Venice, 1509. Aldus Manutius.
Title: C. Crispii Salustii. De conivratione Catilinae eiusdem de bello Jugurthino, oratio contra M.T. Ciceronem. M.T. Ciceronis oratio contra C. Crispii Sallustium ...
Colophon: Venetiis in Aedibus Aldi, et Andrea Asulani soceri Mense Aprili, MDIX. [Printer Marks.]

Tooled calf; 6½ x 4 x 7/8 in. Renouard Annales ... des Aldes. I, p. 133.

EARLY PRINTING IN ITALY.

Cabinet D · Shelf 3 · No. 36

Venice, 1515. Pietro Liechtenstein. Missale Saltzeburgeñ/ nouiter impressum....ex of/ficina litteraria Petri Liech-/tenstein Coloniensis/ anno. 1515.
Colophon: Missale....[as above]....anno saluti-/gero. 1515. Die. 15. Octob̄/Dino ac semp̄ augusto Maximiliano p̄mo Imperiale (etc)
Last leaf; printers mark:

Orig. boards covered with calf; 13x8½x2¼ ins

EARLY PRINTING IN ITALY.

Cabinet D · Shelf 4 · No. 22

Venice, 1523. Luca Antonio Giunta. Missale Romanum.
Colophon: Clauditur missale...in quo celebraturus sacerdos nullo labore querendi fatigbitur quoniã singula suis sunt in locis collocata. Venetiis impressum in edibus domini Luce antonii giunta...M.D.XXIII.Die X Januarii Laus deo. Registrum...

Morocco; tooled; 14_4 x 10 x 2¼ ins.

EARLY PRINTING IN ITALY.

Cabinet D · Shelf 3 · No. 18

Venice, 1509. Paganinis (de) Paganinus. Euclidis megarensis philo/sophi....interprete fidissimo tralata....Lucas pacio....emendavit. A. Paganius Paganinus characteribus elegantissimis accuratissime imprimebat.
Colophon: Euclidis....finit/....Venetiis impressum per probum Virum Paganinum de Paganinis de Brixia....Anno redemptionis nostre M.D.VIIII. Klen XI Junii.

Boards; 12 x 8 x 1 ins.

EARLY PRINTING IN ITALY.

Cabinet 60 · Shelf 2 · No. 8

Venice, 1516. Aldi et Andrea [d'Asola] Soceri.
Title: Rhodiginus, Ludovicus Coelius: Lectionum antiquarum libri XVI.....
Colophon: Venetiis in aedibus Aldi, et Andreae Soceri. Mense Februario M.D.XVI [Printer Marks]

Vellum gilt edges: 12½ x 8-3/4 x 2-3/4 in. Renouard. Annales...de Aldes, I. p.178.

From the library of Wm. Morris, with his label

EARLY PRINTING IN ITALY.

Cabinet 60 · Shelf 2 · No. 12

Venice, 1528. Aldi & Andreae Asulani.
Title: Paulus Aegineta. Opera medica optimi libri septem...Venetiis...[Greek Printing]
Colophon: Venetiis in aedibus Aldi, et Andreae Asulani soceri, mense Augusto M.D.XXVIII.

Bound in with Aetius Amidensu Librorum medicinalum tomus primus. Venetiis, 1534.

Vellum over boards; 12½ x 8½ x 2-3/4 in. Brunet I, 59. Renouard I, 251.

EARLY PRINTING IN ITALY

Cabinet D · Shelf 3 · No. 21

Venice 1511, Lazzaro de Soardi
Title: Plauti, M. Commoediae xx, ex emendationibus, adque commentariis...
Colophon: Impressum Venetiis per Lazarum Soardum. Die XIIII, Augusti M.D. XI.

Calf 12¼ x 8½ x 1¾ in.

EARLY PRINTING IN ITALY.

Cabinet 60 · Shelf 1 · No. 12

Venice, 1518. Aldi et Andrea di Asola Soceri.
Title: Sacrae scripturae veteris, noveaque omnia. Old and New Testament in Greek
Colophon: Venetiis in aedib Aldi et Andrea Soceri. M.D.CVIII. Mense Februario: Printer Mark

Blind stamped vellum over boards; 12 x 8¼ x 2 3/4 in. Renouard. Annales...des Aldes I, p. 192.

EARLY PRINTING IN ITALY

Cabinet D · Shelf 4 · No. 35

Venice, 1530? Andrea Vavassore.

Title: Opera nova contemplativa......
Colophon: Opera di Giovaniandrea Vavassore ditto Vadagni no: Stampata novame [n] te nella inclita citta di Vinegia. Laus Deo.

Last of the block books, but printed on a press.

Limp vellum; 6 x 4 in.

EARLY PRINTING IN ITALY.

Cabinet 60 · Shelf 2 · No. 5

Venice, 1514. Aldus Manutius.
Title: Suida [Greek]
Colophon: Venetiis in aedibus Aldi et Andreae [d'Asola]. Soceri, Mense Feb. M.V.XIIII.

Vellum, stamped 13½ x 8½ x 2-3/8 in. Brunet 5, 587 Renouard. Annales....des Aldes I., p.153.

EARLY PRINTING IN ITALY.

Cabinet 60 · Shelf 1 · No. 15

Venice, 1520. Aldine Press. Aldi and Andrea d'Asola.
Title: Polybii Historiarum libri quinque in Latiam conversi linguam, Nicolao Perotto interprete.
Colophon: Venetiis in aedibus Aldi et Andreae soceri, mense Decembri, M.D.XX [Printer Mark]

Calf; 12 x 8¼ x 3/4 in.

EARLY PRINTING IN ITALY.

Cabinet 60 · Shelf 2 · No. 12

Venice, 1534. Aldi Manutii & Andreae Asulani.
Title: Aetius Amidenus. Librorum medicinalum tomus primus...[Greek] Venetiis MD.XXXIIII.
Colophon: Venetiis, in aedibus haeredum Aldi Manutii & Andreae Asulani, mense Sept. MDXXXIIII.
Bound in with Pauli Aeginatae libri septem, graece, 1528.
Vellum over boards; 12½ x 8½ x 2-3/4 in. Brunet I, 103. Renouard I, 267.

EARLY PRINTING IN ITALY

Cabinet D · Shelf 3 · No. 30

Venice, 1514. Luca Antonio Giunta.
Title: Decretales pape Gregorii noni...
Colophon:...Impressas Venetiis suma cum diligentia i edibo Luce Antonii Giõta florentini. Anno. M.CCCCC.XIIII.

Tooled leather over boards, with clasps; 8½ x 6¼ x 2¾ in.

EARLY PRINTING IN ITALY

Cabinet D · Shelf 4 · No. 16

Venice, 1520. Luca Antonio Giunta.
Title: Pontificale ritus Romane ecclesia cum multis additionibus...
Colophon: Ad honore et gloria dei...In floretissima Venetiarum urbe per spectabilez virum dnm Lucam antonium de Giuta...impressus.

Morocco, gilt: 13¾ x 9-5/8 x 2-1/8 in.

EARLY PRINTING IN ITALY.

Cabinet E · Shelf 1 · No. 3

Venice, 1535: Bernardino Bindoni.
Title: Bergomensis. Supplementum supplementi delle croniche.
Imprint: Finisse ... Impresso Veneti per Bernardino Bindoni.
Curious make-up: Reference to printing under date 1458; to America under 1493. See translation re printing at end of book.

Vellum leaves over boards; 11¾ x 8½ x 2⅛ in.

EARLY PRINTING IN ITALY

Cabinet E · Shelf 1 · No. 4

Venice, 1540: Gabriel Giolito de Ferrari (Comin da Trino).
Title: I sei primi libri del Eneide di Vergilio tradotti...Tolomei de Borghesi... Title with in border .
Colophon:..Stampato on Vinetia per Comin de Trino ...nel anno MDXL. Adi. XII del Mese de Otto bre..

Half morocco; 6 x 4 in.

EARLY PRINTING IN ITALY

Cabinet E · Shelf 1 · No. 6

Venice, 1542. Giunta (Heirs of Luc Antonio).
Title: P. Virgilii/maronis opera/ cum servii donati,...Venetiis apud Iuntas./M.D.XLII. Illus. [Printer Mark]
Colophon: Venetiis apud Haeredes Luceantonii Iuntae Florentini Anno a partu Virginis M.D.XLII, mense Ianvario.

Leather covered boards; 12 x 8¾ x 3 in.

EARLY PRINTING IN ITALY.

Cabinet 14 · Shelf 1 · No. 17

Venice, 1542. Peter Schoeffer II. Opera toscane di Luigi Alamanni. Venetiis apud haeredes Lucae Antonii Iuntae Anno. M.D.XLII. Printer Mark, L.A.
Colophon: Stampato in Vinigia per Pietro Sceffer Germano/Maguntino, ad instantia delli heredi di M. Lucantonio giunta il primo di Luglio/ L'anno/ M.D.XLII.

Vellum covered boards; 6¼ x 4 x 1 ins.

EARLY PRINTING IN ITALY

Cabinet E · Shelf 1 · No. 10

Venice, 1544. Francesco Marcolini.
Title (full page woodcut): Il terzo libro di Sabastiano Serlio Bolognese...con nove additioni...Illus.
Colophon: Impresso per Francesco Marcolini in Venetia. Al Segno de la Verita. M.D.XLIIII. Con Privilegii. [Printer mark].

Boards; 14¼ x 9¾ x 1 in. See Essling, vol. III, 670.

EARLY PRINTING IN ITALY

Cabinet E · Shelf 1 · No. 11

Venice, 1544: Francesco Marcolini.
Title: La comedia di Dante Aligieri con la nova espositione di Alessandro Vellutello. Con gratia... che nessuno la possa imprimere... sotto le pene che in quella si contengono. [Illus., with curiously painted woodcuts]
Colophon: Impressa in Vinegia per Francesco Marcolini...del mese di Gugno lanno MDXLIIII.

Calf; 9½ x 6¼ x 2½ in.

EARLY PRINTING IN ITALY

Cabinet 60 · Shelf 1 · No. 19

Venice, 1546. Paul Manutius [Aldi Filio]
Title: De Oratore, Ciceronis and Q. Fratrem. Libri III [Printer Mark].
Imprint: Corrigente Paulo Manutio, Aldi filio. Venetiis, M.D.XLVI.
[Three vols. in one; each part with separate title, colophon, and mark]

Calf; 8-3/8 x 5½ x 2 ins.

EARLY PRINTING IN ITALY.

Cabinet E · Shelf 1 · No. 14

Venice, 1547: Francesco Bindoni and Mapheo Pasini.
Title: Benedictu., S. Regula del S. Benedetto tradutta. [With wood cut on title-page and printer's device on the last leaf].
Colophon: Stampata in Vinegia per Francesco di Alessandro Bindoni, & Mapheo Pasini, compagni. 1547.

Morocco; 5-7/8 x 3¾ x ½ in.

EARLY PRINTING IN ITALY

Cabinet E · Shelf 1 · No. 15

Venice, 1547. Gabriel Giolito.
Title: Il Petrarca corretto da M. Lodovico Dolce et alla sua integrita ridotto. [Printer Mark].
Imprint: In Vinegia appresso Gabriel Giolito de Ferrari, MDXLVII. [This is followed by a preface by G.G. to the readers in which he explains the advantages of this special small format.]

Calf; 5-1/8 x 3-1/8 x 3/4 in. Brunet, vol.4, 551.

EARLY PRINTING IN ITALY

Cabinet 60 · Shelf 1 · No. 22

Venice, 1548. Aldi Filii.
Title: Le Epistole famigliari de Cicerone. tradotte....della lingua volgare. Ristampate di nuovo. [Printer Mark]. Con privilegio... M.D.XLVIII.
Colophon: In Vinegio, nell'anno M.D.XLVIII. In casa de figliuoli di Aldo.

Half morocco, modern; 6¼ x 4-1/8 x 1¼ in. Brunet 2, 46.

EARLY PRINTING IN ITALY

Cabinet E · Shelf 1 · No. 17

Venice, 1549. Gabriel Giolito.
Title: La nobilta della donne di M. Lodovico Domenichi. [Printer Mark]. In Vinetia appresso Gabriel Giolito di Ferrarii. MDXLIX.
Colophon: In Vinegia apresso Gabriel Giolito de Ferrari. MDXLIX

Vellum; 6½ x 4¼ x 1½ ins.

EARLY PRINTING IN ITALY.

Cabinet E · Shelf 2 · No. 30

Venice, 1551. Francesco Marcolini
Title: La seconda libraria del doni. Al S. Ferrante Carassa. [Wood cut]: In Vinegia MDLI con privilegii.
Colophon: In Venetia per Francesco Marcolini MDLI nel mese di Lugno. [Printer Mark] [Bound in with LA LIBRARIA DEL DONI FIORENTINO, printed by Atobello Salicato, Venice, 1580].

Half morocco; 5½ x 3 x/4 in. Brunet 2,814.

EARLY PRINTING IN ITALY

Cabinet 60 · Shelf 2 · No. 15

Venice, 1551. Paulus Manutius. [Aldi filii]
Title: Petri Bembi Cardinalis Historiae Venetae. [Printer Mark] Cum privileigiis. Venetiis M.D.LI.
Colophon: Venetiis, apud Aldi filios. M.D.LI.

Vellum over boards; 12¼ x 8½ x 1-5/8 in. Brunet I, 767: Renouard I, 364.

EARLY PRINTING IN ITALY.

Cabinet 60 · Shelf 2 · No. 18

Venice, 1554. Paulus Manutius.
Title: Iovatae Rapocoo Brixiani di numero oratorio libri quinque ... [Printer Mark]. Cum privilegio Iulii III ... Venetiis M.D.LIIII.
Colophon: Venetiis, in aedibus Pauli Manutii, Alde filii, M.D.LIIII.
Bound with a 1540 Vascosen item.

Vellum; 13 x 9 x 1-3/8 in. Renouard I, 383.

EARLY PRINTING IN ITALY

Cabinet 60 · Shelf 1 · No. 28

Venice, 1556. Paulus Manutius.
Title: Athenagora...Tradotto in lingua Italiana da Girolamo Faleti. [Printer Mark].
Imprint: Aldus in Venetia, M.D.LVI.

Parchment, 8 x 5-3/4 x ½ in. Goldsmid, The Aldine Press, No.455.

EARLY PRINTING IN ITALY.

Cabinet E · Shelf 2 · No. 31

Venice, 1558. Gabriel Giolito.
Title: La libreria del doni Florentino [Anton Francesco.] Printer Mark.
Imprint: In Vinegia appresso Gabriel Giolito de Ferrari. MDLVIII.

Boards; 6 x 4 x ¾ in.

EARLY PRINTING IN ITALY

Cabinet 60 · Shelf 1 · No. 31

Venice, 1558. Academia Veneta [Paulus Manutius, printer]
Title: De dei locutione Marci Antonii Nattae. Astensis Oratio.
Imprint: In Academia Veneta, M.D.LVIII.

Vellum; 8¼ x 6 x ¼ in. Renouard. Annales ....des Alde II, p.221.

EARLY PRINTING IN ITALY

Cabinet 60 · Shelf 1 · No. 30

Venice, 1558. Paul Manutius.
Title: Archimedis opera non nulla a Federico Commandino Urbinate nuper in Latinam conversa....illustrata. [Printer Mark]
Imprint: Cum privilegio in annos x. Venetiis, apud Paulum Manutium, Aldi F. M.DLVIII.

Three-quarters morocco; 11-3/4 x 7-7/8 x 1 in. Brunet 1, 384. Renouard. Annales..... des Aldes II, p. 417. Goldsmid. The Aldine Press, 485.

EARLY PRINTING IN ITALY

Cabinet 60 · Shelf 1 · No. 35

Venice, 1559. Academia Veneta. [Paulus Manutius, printer].
Title: Summa Librorum, quos in omnibus scientiis ac nobilioribus artibus variis linguis conscriptos,...in lucem emittet Academia Veneta.
Imprint: In Academia Veneta, M.D.LIX.

Morocco; 8 x 5½ x ¼ in. Brunet 5, 592. See Goldsmid. The Aldine Press, vol.II, p.57.

EARLY PRINTING IN ITALY.

Cabinet E, Shelf 1, No. 43

Venice, 1564. Giorgio Cavalli.
First Title: Delle Istorie di Mona. Giovio ... Printer Mark. In Venetia appresso Ciorgio de Cavalli, 1564.
Second Title: La Selva divaria Istorie di Carlo Passi. In Venetia appresso Giorgio de Cavalli. 1564.
Allusions to history of printing on p. 381, translation of which is inserted at end of book.
Parchment; $8\frac{1}{4}$ x 6 in.

EARLY PRINTING IN ITALY.

Cabinet E, Shelf 2, No. 30

Venice, 1580. Atobello Salicato.
Title: La libraria del doni Fiorentino...[Printer Mark].
Imprint: In Vinegia, presso Altobello Salicato. M.D.LXXX.
[Bound together with LA SECONDA LIBRARIA DEL DONI, printed by Francesco Marcolini, Venice, 1551].
Half morocco; $5\frac{1}{2}$ x 3 x $\frac{3}{4}$ in. Brunet 2,814.

EARLY PRINTING IN ITALY.

Cabinet F, Shelf 4, No. 75

Venice, 1784. Carlo Palese.
Title: Orazione per solenne ingresso di sua eccellenza il Signor...e Signore di Ascalona. Frontispiece, engraved by Daniotto.
Imprint: In Venezia nella stamperia di Carlo Palese. 1784.
Paper; $11\frac{3}{4}$ x $8\frac{3}{4}$ in.

EARLY PRINTING IN ITALY.

Cabinet 60, Shelf 2, No. 48

Venice, 1566. Paulus Manutius, Aldi F.
Title: I. Livii Patavini, Historiarum ab urbe condita....Adiunctis Scholiis Caroli Signoii ....secunda editis [Printer Mark]
Imprint: Cum privilegio Pontificis Maximi....ad annos XX. Venetiis, apud Paulum Manutium, Aldo F. M.D.LXVI.
Calf; $12\frac{1}{2}$ x $8\frac{1}{2}$ x 2-3/4 in. Renouard II, 62.

EARLY PRINTING IN ITALY

Cabinet 60, Shelf 1, No. 47

Venice, 1585. Aldus Manutius.
Title: La vicissitudine ō mutabile varietà della cose, nell'universo, di Luigi Regio Francese: Tradotta dal Sig. Cavalier Hercole Cato. Engraved title page; also printer mark.
Imprint: In Vinetia, 1585. Presso Aldo.
Boards; 8 x 6 x 1 in.

EARLY PRINTING IN ITALY.

Cabinet D, Shelf 4, No. 30

Vicenza,1529. Tolomeo Janiculo. Dante/ de la volgare/ eloquenzia. (Printer mark T.IA)./ Giovanni de Boccaccio da Certaldo, ne la vita di Dante'/ (etc)
Imprint: Stampata in Vicenza, per Tolomeo Janiculo da Bressa,/ nel anno MDXXIX./ Del mese di Genaro./ Con la grazia, e prohibizione come ne l'altre.
11 x $6\frac{3}{4}$ x $\frac{1}{4}$ in.

EARLY PRINTING IN ITALY.

Cabinet 60, Shelf 1, No. 42

Venice, 1571. Aldus [Manutius] Junior.
Title: Epistolarum Pauli Manutii. Libri X.... [Printer Marks, also portraits (2) of Aldus Senior]
Imprint: Venetiis. MDLXXI. In aedib Manutianis.
Vellum; $6\frac{1}{4}$ x $4\frac{1}{4}$ x 1-3/4 in. Goldsmid. Aldine Press. No.674.

EARLY PRINTING IN ITALY.

Cabinet E, Shelf 3, No. 26

Venice, 1625. Antonio Pinelli.
Title: Illustrium anchoretarum elogio ... Jacob Cavicio.
Imprint: Venetiis in typographia Pinelliana. [Has full page wood engravings by Fr. Valesio
Vellum; $10\frac{1}{2}$ x 8-1/8 x 1-1/8 in.

EARLY PRINTING IN ITALY

Cabinet D, Shelf 4, No. 31

Vicenza, 1529, Tolomeo Janiculo.
Title: Epistolo del Trissino. (Bound in with Trissino's "Dialogo", and "Dante")
Colophon: Stampata in Vicenza, per Tolomeo Janiculo da Brescia, nel anno 1529, del mese di Febraio. Printer mark on title page.
This is the first book printed by Janiculo with the Arrighi italics.
Boards, leather back; $11\frac{1}{2}$ x 7-3/8 in.

EARLY PRINTING IN ITALY

Cabinet E, Shelf 2, No. 16

Venice, 1574. Domenico and Giambattista Guerra.
Title: Le due deche dell' historia di Sicilia, del R.P.M. Tomaso Fazello...[Printer Mark]: In Venetia, appresso Domenico & Gio. Battista Guerra, Fratelli.M.D.LXXIIII.
Vellum, 9 x $6\frac{3}{4}$ x $2\frac{3}{4}$ in.

EARLY PRINTING IN ITALY — Example

Cabinet E, Shelf 4, No. 57

Venice, 1672: Combi (Sebastien de), & LaNou
Title: Histoire cronologiche della vera origine de tutti gl'ordini equestri...Da Bernardo Giustiniano.
Imprint: Venetia: Presso Combi, e LaNou, 1672.
Has extensive list of errata on page following dedication.
With numerous wood engravings, and copper engravings.
Vellum; $10\frac{1}{2}$ x $7\frac{1}{2}$ x $1\frac{1}{2}$ in.

EARLY PRINTING IN JAPAN — Example

Cabinet II, Shelf 4, No. 9

Said to be the first Japanese book printed from individual engraved characters, circa 18th century.
Paper; 10-7/8 x 8 x 3/8 in.

EARLY PRINTING IN ITALY

Cabinet E, Shelf 2, No. 22

Venice, 1578. Giambattista and Marchio Sessa
Title: Dante con l'espositioni di Christoforo Landino et d'Allesandro Vellutello... In Venetia, appresso Giovambattista, Marchio Sessa & Fratelli, 1578. Illus.
Colophon: In Venetia, Appresso gli heredi di Francesco Rampazetto. Ad instantia di Giovambattista, Marchio Sessa, et Fratelli M.DLXXVIII. (Printer Mark)
cont'd

EARLY PRINTING IN ITALY.

Cabinet F, Shelf 4, No. 72

Venice, 1753. Giambatista Albrizzi.
Title: Dissertazioni Vossiane di Apostolo Zeno. ...Tomo secondo. Vignette and head and tail pieces.
Imprint: In Venezia, MDCCLIII. Per Giambattista Albrizzi Q. Gir. Con Licenza de'Superiori
Biographical sketches of latin scholars from the 15th to the 17th cen., their works, and where and by whom their works were printed.
Boards; 10-5/8 x 8 x $1\frac{1}{4}$ in.

EARLY PRINTING IN MEXICO.

Cabinet E, Shelf 2, No. 77

Mexico, 1609. Jeronimo Balli.
Title: Ortografia castellane ... Mateo Aleman.
Imprint: Con previlejio por diez anos. En Mexico. En la emprenta de Jeronimo Balli. Ano, 1609.
Medina, La imprenta en Mexico II, 244.
Calf; 8 x $5\frac{1}{2}$ in.

EARLY PRINTING IN ITALY cont'd

Cabinet E, Shelf 2, No. 22

Tooled Leather; 13 x 9 x $2\frac{3}{4}$ in. See Brown, The Venetian Press.

EARLY PRINTING IN ITALY

Cabinet F, Shelf 5, No. 14

Venice, 1764. Albrizzi Press.
Title: Componimenti poetici per l'ingresso solenne...il Signor Lodovico Manin. Engraved frontispiece, borders, head and tail pieces n.a.n.
Colophon: nella stamperia Albrizzi. Con privilegio del Ecc. mo Senato per tutti li rami che adornano le di lui stampe.
Paper; $14\frac{1}{2}$ x $10\frac{1}{2}$ x $\frac{1}{2}$ in.

EARLY PRINTING IN MEXICO

Cabinet E, Shelf 3, No. 61

Mexico, 1638. Bernardo Calderon.
Title: Tratado del estado de las Philipinas. Por el Don Geronimo de Banuelos y Carrillo.
Imprint: En Mexico, con licencia de su Excelencia, en la imprenda Bernardo Calderon, impressor, y mercardor de libros.
Medina, La imprenta en Mexico II, 498.
Old leather with ribbon ties, $7\frac{1}{2}$ x $5\frac{3}{4}$ in. In protective case.

EARLY PRINTING IN MEXICO.

Cabinet F Shelf 1 No. 101

Mexico City, 1735: Imprenta Real.
Title: Vida del venerable padre Don Pedro de Arellano y Sossa...Por el Dr. D. Juan Joseph de Eguiara y Eguren...
Imprint: En Mexico: En la Imprenta Real del Superior Gobierno y del nuevo Rezado de Dona Maria de Rivera en el Empedradillo. Ano de 1735.

Hand tooled calf; 8½ x 6¼ in. Medina IV, 3364; p.400.

EARLY PRINTING IN MEXICO

Cabinet F Shelf 1 No. 105

Mexico, 1770, Joseph Jauregui.
Title: Descripcion del barreno ingles, instrumento muy util...para los mineros. Por D. Joseph Antonio de Alzate y Remirez.
Imprint: Impresso en Mexico en la Imprenta del Lic. D. Joseph de Jaurequi. Los caracteres de esta impression han sido fabricados en esta cividad por D. Francisco Favier de Ocampo....

cont'd

EARLY PRINTING IN MEXICO cont'd

Cabinet F Shelf 1 No. 105

Half morocco; 7-7/8 x 5-7/8 in. Medina VI, 5322; p.47.

EARLY PRINTING IN MEXICO.

Cabinet F Shelf 1 No. 104

Puebla de Los Angeles, 1770, Palafox Seminary: Cardinal Ximenez.
Title: Missa gothica seu mozarabica et officium ....ad usum per celebris mozarabum sacelli Toleti a munificentissimo Cardinali Ximenio ....
Imprint: Angelopoli: Typis Seminarii Palafoxiani. Anno Domini. M.DCC.LXX.

Contemporary calf, border around sides, enclosed in morocco case. Medina "La imprenta ... Los An- geles, p.434.

EARLY PRINTING IN MEXICO

Cabinet 79 Shelf 2 No. 16

Tenochtitlan, 1544. Johann Cromberger.
See Doctrina Breve in fac-simile.

EARLY PRINTING IN HAWAII

Cabinet 00 Shelf 6 No. 24

Honolulu, 1835-1871. A collection of newspapers. Bound as one vol.

Cloth; 17¾ x 12-1/8 in.

Example of.

EARLY PRINTING IN PACIFIC ISLANDS.

Cabinet II Shelf 3 No. 54

Honolulu, 1847, Mea Pai Palapala Na Na Misionari ...

See PACIFIC ISLANDS. Imprint of 1847. He helu kamalii ...

EARLY PRINTING IN PORTUGAL

Cabinet L Shelf 3 No. 3

Lisboa, 1718 or 1722 ? Bernardo da Costa de Carcatho (imprint)

See IMPRINTS, Portugal. DeCarvalho, Bernardo da Costa. Lisboa Occidental...

EARLY PRINTING IN ROUMANIA. Example.

Cabinet II Shelf 4 No. 37

Psalter, printed in 1847, Town where printed? Printer's name?

Calf tooled, with clasps, 8¾ x 7 x 1-1/8 in.

EARLY PRINTING IN RUSSIA Example of

Cabinet E Shelf 4 No. 98

[Moscow, circa 1799. Without name of printer]. Russian Bible.

"This work is not printed in the ordinary Russian, but in the Russian which in Church Russian is called Sloviansky".

Leather; 12¾ x 7-7/8 x 2¼ in.

EARLY PRINTING IN SCOTLAND

Cabinet E Shelf 3 No. 55

Aberdeen, Edward Raban, 1635.
Title: Funerals of a Right Reverend Father in God, Patrick Forbes, of Corse, Bishop of Aberdeen....
Imprint: Aberdeen, imprinted by Edward Raban, 1635.
The two last pages contain a poem entitled "Raban's Regrate...and signed, Edward Raban, Master Printer, the first in Aberdeen."

Calf; 8¼ x 5½ x 1½ in.

EARLY PRINTING IN SCOTLAND.

Cabinet F Shelf 4 No. 36

Edinburgh, 1706-1711. James Watson.

Title: A choice collection of comic and serious Scots Poems, both ancient and modern. By several hands. In 3 parts.
Imprint: Printed by James Watson, and sold at his shop next door to the Red-Lyon, opposite to the Lucken-booths.
There are three title pages. The first one is a substitution of more than a century later date.

Russia; 7¼ x 4¾ x 1 in.

EARLY PRINTING IN SCOTLAND.

Cabinet F Shelf 4 No. 40

Edinburgh, 1757. G. Hamilton and John Balfour.

Title: Phaedri. Augusti Liberti. Fabularum Aesopiarum. Libri quinque. Alexandri Cuningamii.
Imprint: Edinburgi. Apud G. Hamilton & J. Balfour, Academiae Typographos. 1757.

Morocco; 7½ x 4-3/4 x ½ in. Brunet 4, 589.

EARLY PRINTING IN SCOTLAND.

Cabinet F Shelf 4 No. 43

Glasgow, 1751. Robert and Andrew Foulis.

Title: Boetius. Consolationis philosophiae. Libri quinque.
Imprint: Glasguae: In aedibus Academicis. Excudebant Robertus et Andreas Foulis. Academiae Typographi. M.DCC.LI.

Leather; 7-3/4 x 6 x ½ in. Brunet, 1, 1035.

EARLY PRINTING IN SCOTLAND.

Cabinet F Shelf 4 No. 45

Glasgow, 1756. Robert and Andrew Foulis.

Title: Euclidis elementorum libri priores sex ex versione latina Federici Commandini; curante a Roberto Simson, M.D.
Imprint: Glasguae, in aedibus Academicis excudebant Robertus et Andreas Foulis. Academiae Typographi. 1756.

Leather; 11¾ x 9¼ x 1¾ in. Brunet 2, 1082.

EARLY PRINTING IN SCOTLAND

Cabinet F Shelf 4 No. 47

Glasgow, 1758. Robert and Andrew Foulis.

Title: Publii Virgilii maronis. Bucolica, Georgica, et Aeneis. ex editione Petri Burmanni.
Imprint: Glasguae: in Aedibus Academicis. Excudebant Robertus et Andreas Foulis. Academiae Typographi. 1758.

Half morocco; gilt; 6-3/8 x 4 x 1¼ in. Brunet 5, 1293.

EARLY PRINTING IN SCOTLAND.

Cabinet F Shelf 4 No. 49

Glasgow, 1763. Robert and Andrew Foulis.

Title: Dionysii Longini de Sublimate ex edition tertia. Zachariae Pearce. In Greek and Latin
Imprint: Glasguae: In Aedibus Academicis excudebant Robertus et Andreas Foulis. Academiae Typographi. 1763.

Morocco, gilt; 8¼ x 6-3/8 x 1-1/8 in. Brunet 3, 1152.

EARLY PRINTING IN SCOTLAND

Cabinet M Shelf 1 No. 9

Kelso, 1802: James Ballantyne.
Title: The economy of human life. In two parts. By R. Dodsley.
Imprint: Kelso. Printed by James Ballantyne for... and A. Constable, Edinburgh.

Calf; 8¾ x 5-3/8 x ¾ in.

EARLY PRINTING IN SPAIN

Cabinet D Shelf 4 No. 5 1-6

Alcala, 1514-17. Arnald Guillen de Brocar.
Title: Complutensian Polyglot Bible. 6 Vols.
Colophon: [Vol. 6]: Explicit grāmatica hebraiça noviter impssa in hac p̄clarissima cōplutensi universtate. De mādato...F.Francisci Ximenez de Cineros...Industria & solertia honorabilis viri Arnaldi Guilielmi de Brocario artis impressorie magistri. Anno dñi M.D.XV

Cont'd.

EARLY PRINTING IN SPAIN cont'd

Cabinet Shelf No.

mensis Maii die ultima.
See Printing types, Updike, Vol. 2, pp. 63-67.

Calf; 15 x 10½ x 2 in.

EARLY PRINTING IN SPAIN.

Cabinet F Shelf 5 No. 44

Madrid, 1772. Joachin Ibarra.
Title: La conjuración de Catilina y la guerra de Jugurta por Cayo Salustio Crispo.
Colophon: En Madrid: Por Joachin Ibarra, Impresor de Camara del Rei Nuestro Senor, 1772.
"This book with reason is regarded as a typographic masterpiece," Brunet 5, 91. also Updike 2, 55.

Leather; gilt; 14 x 10½ x 1-3/4 in.
Duplicate in same cabinet. 7/5/44.

EARLY PRINTING IN SPAIN

Cabinet AA Shelf 5 No. 5

(Madrid, 1799). Imprenta Real.
Title: Reglamento para la dirección y gobierno de la Imprenta Real.
Imprint: Madrid. En la misma Imprenta Real, año de 1799.

Marbled boards; 8 x 5½ in.

EARLY PRINTING IN SPAIN.

Cabinet E Shelf 4 No. 97

Valencia, 1695. Vincente Cabrera.
Title: Idea de un principe politico y christiano, representada en cien empressas. Por D. Diego Saavedra Faxardo ...
Imprint: En Valencia, por Vincente Cabrera.

Boards; 8¼ x 5½ x 1½ in.

EARLY PRINTING IN SPANISH AMERICA (Peru).

Cabinet F Shelf 1 No. 106

Lima, 1784, Baquijano y Carrillo.
Title: Segunda disertacion del D.D.Ignacio de Castro ...
Imprint: Lima, 1784. Con las licensias necesarias.

Vellum; 6 x 4-7/8 in.

EARLY PRINTING IN SWITZERLAND

Cabinet 10 Shelf 2 No. 1

Basle [1468-70] Rudolph Ruppel.
Title: Rationale divinorum officiorum. Guil. Durandus. N. p. d.
Colophon ends:..Misericordissimu indice p. peccatis meis devotas oraciones essundant. Deo gracias.

Original pigskin with two clasps; 16¼ x 11¾ x 3 in.

EARLY PRINTING IN SWITZERLAND.

Cabinet D Shelf 1 No. 43

Basel, 1482. Bernhard Richel.

See Incunabula. Rolewinck, Werner. Fasciculus temporum.

EARLY PRINTING IN SWITZERLAND.

Cabinet D Shelf 2 No. 25

Basel, 1494. Johann Froben.

See Incunabula. Gregorious IX. Decretales.

EARLY PRINTING IN SWITZERLAND

Cabinet D Shelf 2 No. 43

Basel, 1498. J. Bergmann de Olpe.

See Incunabula. Brant Sebastien. Stultifera navis....

EARLY PRINTING IN SWITZERLAND. Example

Cabinet D Shelf 3 No. 38

Basle, 1515, Johann Froben.

See Facsimile. Erasmi Roterodami. Encomium moriae. With marginal drawings of Hans Holbein, the younger.

EARLY PRINTING IN SWITZERLAND.

Cabinet D Shelf 3 No. 47

Basel, 1516. Johannes Froben, Aeneae Platonici, Camaldulensis interpr.; Athenagoras Athen, Marsilio Ficino interpr.; xysti Pythagorici Sententiae interpr. Frontispiece by Hans Holbein [signed].
Colophon: Basileae apud Joannem/Frobenium mense/viii bri. an./M.D.XVI.

See Heckethorn, The Printers of Basle, p.98.
Boards, 8½ x 6½ ins., ½ in. thick.

EARLY PRINTING IN SWITZERLAND.

Cabinet D Shelf 3 No. 55

Basle; 1518. John Froben.
Title: De optimo reip. statu deque nova insula Utopia...Thomae Mori in clytae civitatis Londinensis...Epigramata. Des Erasmi Roterodami.
Colophon: Basileae apud Io. Frobenium mense Martio, an. MD.XVIII. [With Printer Mark]

Leather; 8½ x 6¼ x 1¼ in.

EARLY PRINTING IN SWITZERLAND.

Cabinet D Shelf 4 No. 23

Basel, 1523. Valentinus Curio [or Schaffner]. Strabonis geographicorum. [Many woodcut borders. tail pieces, large initials, and printer device].

Imprint: Basileae in aedibus valen/tini curionis M.D./XXIII. Mense Martio.

See Heckethorn, p.168. Vellum; 12½ x 8¼ x 2 in.

EARLY PRINTING IN SWITZERLAND.

Cabinet E Shelf 1 No. 2

Basel, 1535. Jerome Froben and Nicolaus Episcopius.
Title: Paraphraseon des Erasmi Roterodami, in Novum Testamentum. [Two vols. in one, and divided into six parts, each part with separate title, printer mark, and imprint; the last imprint dated 1532.]
Colophon: Basileae in officina Frobeniana, per Hieronymum Frobenium & Nicolaum Episcopium.

cont'd

EARLY PRINTING IN SWITZERLAND.

Cabinet Shelf No. 2

M.D.XXXII.

Embossed leather over boards, with clasps; 13 x 9 x 3¼ ins.

See Heckethorn: The printers of Basle, p.203.

EARLY PRINTING IN SWITZERLAND

Cabinet D Shelf 4 No. 55

Basle, 1540, Michele Isingrin (Imprint)

See VERGILIUS, POLYDORUS. (De) Rerum inventoribus...1540.

EARLY PRINTING IN SWITZERLAND

Cabinet E Shelf 1 No. 22

Basle, 1554, Jacob Parcum.
Title: Virgil. De Rerum inventoribus libro octo ...
Imprint: Basileae, anno, M.D. LIIII
Colophon: Basileae per Jacobū Parcum, expensis Michaelis Isingrinei anno 1553, mense Augusto.

Stamped pigskin, with leather clasps; 6¾ x 4¾ x 2 in.

EARLY PRINTING IN SWITZERLAND

Cabinet E Shelf 1 No. 28

Basel, 1555. Nicolaus Episcopius, the younger.
Title: Io. Lodovici. Vivis Valentini opera in duos. distincta tomos...[Printer Mark]... Basileae Anno MDLV.
Colophon: Basilae, per Nic. Episcopium Iuniorem, anno M.D.LV.

Original vellum; 13 x 8¾ x 2½ ins.

EARLY PRINTING IN SWITZERLAND

Cabinet E Shelf 1 No. 50

Basel, 1569. Eusebius Episcopius
Title: P. Rami Scholarum mathematicarum libri unus et triginta.[Printers device].
Imprint: Basileae, per Eusebium Episcopium, Nicolai Fratris haeredes. Anno M.D.LXIX.

Vellum; 9½ x 7¼ x 1½ in. Brunet IV, 1098-9

EARLY PRINTING IN SWITZERLAND

Cabinet E Shelf 2 No. 5

Basel, 1572. Sebastien Henricpetri.
Title: Pauli Aemilii und Arnoldi Ferronii der kön. May in Frankreich...Dergleichen in Teutscher sprache...durch Christian Wurstisen...Getruckt zu Basel.
Colophon: Getrucket zu Basel durch Sebastian Henricpetri. Im Jar MDLXXII (Printer Mark).

Boards covered with tooled leather; 13½ x 8½ x 2¾ in.
Heckethorn, The printers of Basel, pp.143-61.

EARLY PRINTING IN SWITZERLAND.

Cabinet 22 Shelf 1 No. 7

(Basle, 1578. Ambrosius Froben, printer of the Talmud.) Ambrosius Froben von Basle als Drucker des Talmud, von Heinrich Pallman.

Description of a bad piece of printing which resulted in a law suit and non acceptance of completed work.

In Archiv für Deutschen Buchhandels, 1882, vol.VII, p.44.

EARLY PRINTING IN SWITZERLAND

Cabinet E Shelf 2 No. 47

Basel, 1589. Conrad Valdkirch.
Title: Icones sive imagines viuae literis Cl. virorum. Italiae, Graeciae, Germaniae, Galliae, Angliae, Ungariae. Ex typis Valdkirchianis in lucem productae: cum elogiis variis: per Nicolaum Revsnerivm I.C.& P.C.

Bound in with an Icones by same author, printed by Bernard Jobinus, Strassburg, 1590.

EARLY PRINTING IN SWITZERLAND

Cabinet F Shelf 3 No. 70

Basel, 1789, Wilhelm Hass dem Sohne.
Title: Poetische Versuch. von Gottlieb Conrad Pfeffel...(3 vols.)
Imprint: Basel: Bey Wilhelm Hass dem Sohne, 1789.

Boards; 6½ x 4 in.

EARLY PRINTING IN SWITZERLAND.

Cabinet 40 Shelf 1 No. 32

[Geneva] 1552. Robert (I) Estienne (Stephanus).
Title: Ad censuras theologorum Parisiensium quibus Biblia à Roberto Stephano typographo Regis excusa calumniose notarunt, eiusdem Roberti Stephani responsio. [Printer Mark].
Imprint [n.p.] Oliva Roberti Stephani M.D.LII.

Morocco; 7-1/8 x 4-5/8 x 3/4 in. See Renouard Imprimeurs Parisiens. p.124.

EARLY PRINTING IN SWITZERLAND

Cabinet E Shelf 1 No. 42

Geneva, 1564. Jean Crespin.
Title: Actes des Martyrs deduit en sept livres, depuis...Wiclef & de Hus, jusques à present.. [Printer Mark]. A Geneve. Par I.Crespin, M.D.LXIIII.I. Steiger.
Colophon: Larger copy of the printer device.

Vellum with original gilt edges; 12½ x 8 x 2½ ins.

EARLY PRINTING IN SWITZERLAND.

Cabinet 40 Shelf 1 No. 44

[Geneva] 1566. Henri (II) Estienne. [n.n.n. p.]
Title: L'introduction au traite de la conformité des merveilles anciennes avec les modernes. Ou Traite préparatif à l'apologie pour Herodote....[Estienne printer mark. Printer's name not given]
Imprint: L'an M.D.LXVI. au mois de Novembre.

Calf; 6¼ x 4-3/8 x 1½ in. See Renouard. Imprimeurs Parisiens, p.126.

EARLY PRINTING IN SWITZERLAND.

Cabinet 40 Shelf 1 No. 48

Geneva, 1567. Estienne, Henri (II). (Stephanus).
Title: Polemonis, Himerii, et aliorum quorundam declamationes nunc primum editae. [First Greek edition. Printer Mark]
Imprint: Excudebat Henr. Stephanus, illustris viri Huldrichi Fuggeri typographus, M.D.LXVII

Old vellum 9½ x 6-3/8 x ½ in. Brunet 4, 775. See also Schottenloher. Das alte buch, p.195.

EARLY PRINTING IN SWITZERLAND.

Cabinet 40 Shelf 1 No. 56

Geneva, 1569, Henri Estienne.
Title: Artis typographicae Querimonia, de illiteratis quisdam typographis, propter quos in contemtum venit. Autore Henrico Stephano Epitaphia Graeca & Latina...
Imprint: Anno M D LXIX. Excudebat Henricus Stephano.

Half morocco; 8½ x 6 in.

EARLY PRINTING IN SWITZERLAND.

Cabinet 40 Shelf 1 No. 65

[Geneva] 1569. Henri Estienne.

Title: Henrici Stephani epistola, qua ad multorum amicorum respondet, de suae typographiae statu, nominatimque de suo thesauro linguae Graecae....Index librorum qui ex officina eiusdem Henrici Stephani hactenus prodierunt [Printer Mark]
Imprint: Anno M.D.LXIX. Excudebat Henricus Stephanus.

Morocco; 7 x 4¼ x ¼ in.

EARLY PRINTING IN SWITZERLAND

Cabinet 40 Shelf 2 No. 38

[Geneva] 1570. Henri (II) Estienne (Stephanus).
Title: Conciones, sive orationes, ex graecis Latinisque historicis excerptae...[Greek and Latin. Printer Mark]
Imprint: Anno M.D.LXX, Excudebat Henricus Stephanus.

Vellum; 12½ x 8 x 1-3/4 in. Brunet 2, 212.

EARLY PRINTING IN SWITZERLAND

Cabinet 40 Shelf 2 No. 42

[Geneva 1572?] Henri (II) Estienne.

Title: Thesaurus graecae linguae ab Henrico Stephano constructus...[Printer Mark]
Imprint: Henr. Stephani Oliva. Cum privilegio Caes. Maiestatis, et Christianiss. Galliarum regis.

Morocco; 15¼ x 9-3/4 x 2-3/4 ins.

EARLY PRINTING IN SWITZERLAND.

Cabinet 40 Shelf 1 No. 75

Geneva. 1574. Henri (II) Estienne.
Title: Francofordiense emporium, sive francofordienses nundinae. Quam varia mercium genera in hoc emporio prostent pagina septima indicabit. Henr. Stephanus....[Printer Mark]. Anno M.D.LXXIIII. Excudebat Henricus Stephanus.

Parchment cover; 6-7/8 x 4-1/4 x 1/2 in. Brunet 2, 1082.

EARLY PRINTING IN SWITZERLAND.

Cabinet 40 Shelf 1 No. 60

[Geneva]. 1576, Henri Estienne.
Title: De latinitate falso suspecto. Expostulatio Henrici Stephani.
Imprint: Anno M.D.LXXVI. Excudebat Henricus Stephanus.

Leather; 6 x 3¾ x 1 in.

EARLY PRINTING IN SWITZERLAND.

Cabinet E Shelf 2 No. 32

Geneva, 1580. Jean de Laon.
Title: Icones id est verae imagines virorum doctrina simul et pietate illustrium ... Theodore Beza auctore. [Printer mark].
Imprint: Geneva, apud Ioannem Laonium, M.D.LXXX.

Boards; 8¾ x 6¼ x ¾ in. Brunet 1, 842.

EARLY PRINTING IN SWITZERLAND

Cabinet E Shelf 2 No. 33

[Geneva] 1581. Jean de Laon.
Title: Les vrais pourtraits des hommes illustres en piete et doctrine...plus quarante quatre emblemes chrestiens. Traduicts du latin de Theodore d Beze. [Printer Mark]. Illus.
Imprint: Par Jean de Laon. [Geneva]. M.D.LXXXI.

Calf; 8 x 6 x 1 in. Brunet I, 843.

EARLY PRINTING IN SWITZERLAND.

Cabinet E
Shelf 2
No. 48

Geneva, 1590. Jean le Preux.
Title: Tractatus pius et moderatus de vera excommunicatione, & christiano Presbyterio ... Theodoro Beza, vezelio auctore. [Printer Mark: A printing office, men working at press and setting types.]
Imprint: Genevae: Apud Ioannem le Preux. M.D.XC

Boards; 9 x 6¼ x ½ in. Brunet 1, 841.

EARLY PRINTING IN SWITZERLAND.

Cabinet 40
Shelf 1
No. 93

[Geneva]. 1599. Paul Estienne.
Title: Publii Virgilii Maronis Poemata. Henrici Stephani scholiijs ... excerpta dedit.
Imprint: Excudebat Paulus Stephanus. Anno M.D.XCIX.

Tertia editio.

Vellum; 6-3/4 x 4-3/4 x 1½ in.

EARLY PRINTING IN SWITZERLAND.

Cabinet 39
Shelf 2
No. 26

Geneva, 1612. Jean [Antoine] de Tournes.
Title: Xenophontis philosophi et ... historiarum de Cyri ... Libri octo.
Imprint: Apud Ioann. Tornaesium. 1612. Geneuae.

Vellum; 4-7/8 x 3-1/8 x 1½ in.

EARLY PRINTING IN SWITZERLAND.

Cabinet 39
Shelf 2
No. 35

Geneva, 1672. Tournes, Jean Antoine and Samuel de. Geneva. 1672.
Title: Rodolphi Hospiniani de Templis hoc est, de origine, progressu usu et abusu templorum & rerum ad templa pertinentium. Libri quinqui ... [Printer Mark].
Imprint: Genevae, Sumptibus Ioannis Antonii & Samuelis De Tournes, M.DC.LXXII.

Calf; 14 x 9½ x 1¼ in.

EARLY PRINTING IN SWITZERLAND

Cabinet E
Shelf 4
No. 61

Geneva, 1674. Widerholt, Johann Hermann.

Title: Petri della valle. Eines...reise beschreibung in unterschiedliche theile der welt. ..Erster theil. Illus. [Title repeated for second part, including printer mark.]
Imprint: Getruckt zu Genff. In verlegung Johann-Herman Widerholde M.DC.LXXIV.

Vellum; 13 x 8½ x 2-3/4 ins.

EARLY PRINTING IN SWITZERLAND

Cabinet 39
Shelf 2
No. 40

Geneva, 1684. Samuel de Tournes.
Title; Lucii Annaei Flori rerum Romanarum. Libri quatuor....Cum notis....Davidis Constantii [Printer Mark]
Imprint: Geneva, apud Samuelem de Tournes. M.DC.LXXXIV.
[Engraved title precedes printed title page.]

Old leather, 5-3/4 x 3½ x 1¼ in.

EARLY PRINTING IN SWITZERLAND

Cabinet E
Shelf 2
No. 42

Zurich, 1586. Christopher Froschauer.
Title: Gemeiner löblicher Eydgnoschafft Stetten Handen und Volckeren Chronick thaaten beschreybung...Hierinn wirt auch die gelegenheit der gantzen Europe...[Printer Mark]. Illus.
Imprint: Getruckt zu Zürych in der Froschow. M.D.LXXXVI.

Calf; 13½ x 9 x 5 ins.

EARLY PRINTING IN TURKEY Example of

Cabinet II
Shelf 4
No. 49

Constantinople, 1730 [Ibraham Basmadzi]
Title: Grammaire Turque...
Imprint: A Constantinople, M,D.CCC,XXX.

This is the first European book printed in Constantinople.

Contemporary native binding: Half calf; 8-3/8 x 6 x 7/8 in.

EARLY PRINTING IN UNITED STATES

EARLY PRINTING IN CALIFORNIA

Cabinet F
Shelf 3
No. 57

San Francisco, 1859, Towne & Bacon

Decade sermons. Two historical sermons ...Samuel H. Willey. San Francisco. Printed and Published by Towne & Bacon, No.125 Clay Street, corner Sansome. 1859.

Brochure, in manila envelope.

EARLY PRINTING IN CONNECTICUT.

Cabinet F
Shelf 3
No. 35

Hartford, 1789: Nathaniel Patten.

Title: a view of the internal evidence of the Christian religion...By Soame Jenyns. The sixth edition.
Imprint: Hartford: Printed by Nathaniel Patten. 1789.

Leather; 6½ x 4 x 1 in. Evans 7, 21904, p.327

EARLY PRINTING IN CONNECTICUT

Cabinet 80
Shelf 1
No. 40

Hartford, 1807, Hudson & Goodwin [Imprint]

See ALMANACS. Beers's Almanac for... 1807.

EARLY PRINTING IN CONNECTICUT

Cabinet 80
Shelf 1
No. 64

Hartford, 1823-1830: Roberts & Burr and H. Burr Jun.

See ALMANACS. Newtonian Reflector...By Anson Allen...

EARLY PRINTING IN CONNECTICUT.

Cabinet F
Shelf 3
No. 33

New Haven, 1757: James Parker and Company.

Title: Some remarks on Mr. President Clap's history and vindication of the doctrines...of the New England churches... [Thomas Darling].
Imprint: New Haven: Printed by J. Parker and Company, 1757.

Half morocco; 8 x 5½ in. Evans 3, 7881, p.163

EARLY PRINTING IN GEORGIA Example of.

Cabinet II
Shelf 3
No. 28

New Echota, 1883, John F. Wheeler and John Candy.
Title: Acts of the Apostles translated into Cherokee...
Imprint: New Echota Georgia : John F. Wheeler and John Candy, Printers. 1833.

Paper; 4 3/4 x 2 3/4 in. Item in manila envelope.

EARLY PRINTING IN GEORGIA

Cabinet II
Shelf 3
No. 30

Park Hill, Cherokee (Mission Press). John Candy, Printer, 1844.
Title: The Gospel according to Matthew. Translated into the Cherokee language. 4th ed.
Imprint: Park Hill. Mission Press, John Candy, Printer. 1844.

Leatherette; 5 x 3 x 1-1/8 in.

EARLY PRINTING IN ILLINOIS

See Newspapers: Missouri and Illinois, for list of early newspapers.

EARLY PRINTING IN IOWA

Cabinet
Shelf
No.

Pioneer printing in Iowa. Illus. By D.C. McMurtrie.

Article in National Printer Journalist, vol. 50, No.12, Dec., 1932, pp.22-23, 80, 81.

EARLY PRINTING IN LOUISIANA

Cabinet F · Shelf 4 · No. 80

New Orleans, 1764, Denis Braud ?

See BRAUD, DENIS. New Orleans, 1764 (Imprint)...

EARLY PRINTING IN MARYLAND

Cabinet 00 · Shelf 6 · No. 51

Baltimore, 1773, William Goddard.

see FACSIMILES. NEWSPAPERS. Maryland Journal...Aug. 20, 1773.

EARLY PRINTING IN MARYLAND

Cabinet X · Shelf 5 · No. 12

Baltimore, 1808. The case of Baptis Irvine in a matter of contempt of court. With an appendix by a Gentleman of the Bar....Printed by S. Magill, Baltimore, 1808.

Irvine as editor of "The Whig" was arrested with several others as being promoters of a riot; the complainants being two discharged printers.

Half morocco; 9¼ x 5-3/4 x 3/8 in.

EARLY PRINTING IN MARYLAND

Cabinet F · Shelf 2 · No. 95

Baltimore, 1819, Benjamin Edes (Imprint)

A sermon delivered at the ordination of Rev. Jared Sparks...By Wm. Ellery Channing. Baltimore: Printed by Benjamin Edes.

Brochure, in manila envelope

EARLY PRINTING IN NEW ENGLAND.

Cabinet F · Shelf 1 · No. 1

Boston, 1677. John Foster. Four pages of Hubbards: A narrative of the trouble with the Indians in New England. pp.4 only. (sig.H2, H3) pp.51-54.

See Evans, No.231, vol.1 p.43.

EARLY PRINTING IN NEW ENGLAND.

Cabinet F · Shelf 1 · No. 4

Boston, 1685: Richard Pierce.
Title: A practical discourse concerning the choice benefit of communion with God in His house...By Joshua Moody.
Imprint: Boston in New England: Printed by Richard Pierce for Joseph Brunning, and are to be sold at his shop at the corner of Prison-Lane next the Exchange, 1685.

Old calf; 5⅝ x 3¼ in. Evans I, 396, p.67.

EARLY PRINTING IN NEW ENGLAND

Cabinet F · Shelf 1 · No. 13

Boston, 1706: Bartholomew Green.
Title: Considerations to prevent murmurings and promote patience in Christians under afflictive providence. In a lecture sermon preached September 19,1706, in Boston by Benj. Wadsworth.....
Imprint: Boston: N.E.Printed by B.Green. Sold by Nicholas Boone at his Shop,1706.

Cloth case; 6 x 4¼ in. Evans I, 1282, p.186.

EARLY PRINTING IN NEW ENGLAND

Cabinet F · Shelf 1 · No. 14

Boston, 1708. Bartholomew Green.
Title: Sacramental meditations upon divers select passages of Scripture. Sixth edition enlarged. By John Flavel.
Imprint: Boston in N.E., 1708. Printed by B. Green for Benj. Eliot; Sold at his shop, 1708.
At end: List of books sold by Benj.Eliot

Leather, 5½ x 3½ in. Evans I, 1351, p.195.

EARLY PRINTING IN NEW ENGLAND

Cabinet F · Shelf 1 · No. 7

Boston, 1717: T. Crump.
Title: The nature and manner of man's blessing God; with obligations thereto. A sermon preached....by John Barnard...in Marblehead.
Imprint:Boston: Printed by T. Crump for Samuel Gerrish. 1717.

In morocco case, 6½ x 4 in. Evans I, 1865; p.253.

EARLY PRINTING IN NEW ENGLAND

Cabinet F · Shelf 1 · No. 65

Boston, 1718: James Franklin.
Title: A sermon delivered by Thomas Prince, M.A. at his ordination...Together with The charge by the Reverend Increase Mather, D.D.....
Imprint: Boston: Printed by J. Franklin for S. Gerrish, and sold at his shop near the Old Meeting House, 1718.

Paper boards; leather back; 7-3/8 x 5-1/8 in. Evans I, 1996, p.269.

EARLY PRINTING IN NEW ENGLAND.

Cabinet F · Shelf 1 · No. 68

Boston, 1721: James Franklin.
Title: English liberties, or the free-born subjects inheritance...Compiled first by Henry Care, and continued with additions by W.N. of the Middle-Temple, Esq. The fifth edition.
Imprint: Boston: Printed by J. Franklin, for N. Buttolph and D. Henchman and sold at their shops, 1721.

Calf; 6½ x 4-1/8 in. Evans I, 2208, p.292.

EARLY PRINTING IN NEW ENGLAND

Cabinet F · Shelf 1 · No. 15

Boston, 1725: Bartholomew Green, Jr.
Title: The reasonableness of personal reformation, and the necessity of conversion.... By John Flavell.
Imprint: Boston, N.E. Reprinted by B. Green, Jun for D. Henchman at his Shop in Corn-Hill, 1725.

Leather; 5½ x 3¼ in. Evans I, 2634, p.342.

EARLY PRINTING IN NEW ENGLAND

Cabinet F · Shelf 1 · No. 17

Boston, 1726: Bartholomew Green and Samuel Kneeland.
Title: A compleat body of divinity in two hundred and fifty lectures....By Samuel Willard,M.A. ...
Imprint: Boston in New England: Printed by B. Green and S. Kneeland for B. Eliot and D. Henchman, and sold at their shops. MDCCXVI.
The first book printed in black and red in the British-American colonies.
Leather: 13½ x 8½ x 3 in. Evans I, 2828, p.365.

EARLY PRINTING IN NEW ENGLAND.

Cabinet F · Shelf 1 · No. 18

Boston, 1727: Bartholomew Green.
Title: The duty of a people to pray to, and bless God for their Rulers. A sermon preached before the....of the Massachusetts-Bay, in New England, May 31st, 1727.
Imprint: Boston in N.E. Printed by B. Green. Sold by Samuel Gerrish, at the lower end of Corn-hill, 1727.

Half morocco; 7 x 4¼ in. Evans I, 2841, p.366.

EARLY PRINTING IN NEW ENGLAND

Cabinet F · Shelf 1 · No. 25

Boston, 1737: For Daniel Henchman.
Title: A faithful servant of Christ described and rewarded....Tuesday lecture, in Harvard College. By Edward Wigglesworth, D.D.....
Imprint: Boston: Printed for D. Henchman. 1737.

Half morocco; 7½ x 4½ in. Evans 2, 4209, p.121.

EARLY PRINTING IN NEW ENGLAND.

Cabinet F · Shelf 1 · No. 48

Boston, 1739: John Draper.
Title: A sermon preached at Andover South Parish. Occasioned by the death of Mr.Abiel Abbot....By John Barnard...Prefaced by Samuel Phillips.
Imprint: Boston. Printed by J. Draper, for D. Henchman in Cornhill. 1739.

Half morocco; 6-1/8 x 4 in. Not in Evans.

EARLY PRINTING IN NEW ENGLAND

Cabinet F · Shelf 1 · No. 50

Boston, 1740: John Draper.
Title: The doctrine of predestination unto life ....by William Cooper.
Imprint: Boston: Printed by J. Draper, for J. Edwards and H. Foster, in Cornhil. MDCCXL.

Leather; 6½ x 4 in. Evans 2, 4497. p.155.

EARLY PRINTING IN NEW ENGLAND.

Cabinet F · Shelf 1 · No. 20

Boston, 1741: Samuel Kneeland and Timothy (2) Green.
Title: An answer to the Rev. Mr. Garden's three first letters to the Rev. Mr. Whitefield... Andrew Crosswell.
Imprint: Boston: Printed and sold by S. Kneeland and T. Green, over against the prison in Queenstreet, 1741.

Half morocco; 7¼ x 4½ in. Evans 2, 4705, p.179.

EARLY PRINTING IN NEW ENGLAND.

Cabinet F Shelf 2 No. 53

Boston, 1743: Gamaliel Rogers and Daniel Fowle.
Title: The fulfilling of the Scripture.... By the Reverend Mr. Robert Fleming.... With a preface by Mr. Foxcroft.
Imprint: Boston, New England: Printed by Rogers and Fowle for Walter McAlpine near the Mill Bridge. 1743.

Leather; $6\frac{3}{4}$ x 4 x 2 in. Evans, 2, 5185, p.237.

EARLY PRINTING IN NEW ENGLAND

Cabinet F Shelf 1 No. 23

Boston, 1743: Green, Bushell, and Allen.
Title: Marrow of modern divinity....By E. Fisher. The tenth edition. With the commendatory epistles of divers Divines in the City of London.
Imprint: Boston: Printed by Green, Bushell, and Allen, for D. Henchman in Cornhill. 1743.

Leather; $5\frac{3}{4}$ x $3\frac{1}{2}$ in. Evans 2, 5182, p.236.

EARLY PRINTING IN NEW ENGLAND.

Cabinet F Shelf 1 No. 22

Boston, 1743: Green, Bushell and Allen.
Title: Some brief sacramental meditations preparatory for Communion at the Great Ordinance of the Supper. By Samuel Willard, M.A. Second edition.
Imprint: Boston: Printed by Green, Bushell, and Allen, for D. Henchman in Cornhill. 1743.

Leather; 5-7/8 x 4-7/8 x 7/8 in. Evans 2, 5315, p.253.

EARLY PRINTING IN NEW ENGLAND

Cabinet F Shelf 2 No. 55

Boston, 1744. Gamaliel Rogers and Daniel Fowle.
Title: Nicodemus: or a treatise against the fear of man. Translated by August Herman Franck ....Third edition.
Imprint: Boston: Printed by Rogers and Fowle, for N. Proctor at the Bible and Dove in Ann Street. 1744.

Leather; $5\frac{1}{2}$ x 3 x $\frac{1}{2}$ in. Evans 2, 5394, p.262.

EARLY PRINTING IN NEW ENGLAND

Cabinet 80 Shelf 2 No. 5

Boston, 1745: Gamaliel Rogers and Daniel Fowle. [Imprint of].

See PERIODICALS, United States. American Magazine, Boston, 1745.

EARLY PRINTING IN NEW ENGLAND

Cabinet F Shelf 1 No. 25.02

Boston, 1746, D. Henchman...and S. Kneeland and T. Green.

See PRINCE, THOMAS. Sermon delivered in Boston, August 14, 1746.

EARLY PRINTING IN NEW ENGLAND.

Cabinet F Shelf 2 No. 57

Boston, 1747. Gamaliel Rogers and Daniel Fowle.
Title: The imperfection of the creature, and the excellence of the Divine Commandment. By John Barnard.
Imprint: Boston, New England: Printed and sold by Rogers and Fowle in Queen Street and sold by D. Gookin in Marlborough Street, MDCCXLVII

Leather; 8 x 5 x 1-1/8 in. Evans 2, 5905; p.325.

EARLY PRINTING IN NEW ENGLAND

Cabinet F Shelf 2 No. 59

Boston, 1748. Gamaliel Rogers and Daniel Fowle.
Title: A strong rod broken and withered....By Jonathan Edwards, A.M., Pastor of the First Church in Northampton.
Imprint: Boston: Printed by Rogers and Fowle for J. Edwards in Cornhill, 1748.

Half calf; $7\frac{1}{4}$ x 4-3/8 in. Evans 2, 6130: p.355.

EARLY PRINTING IN NEW ENGLAND

Cabinet F Shelf 1 No. 53

Boston, 1750: John Draper.
Title: A sermon preached at Boston....of the Province of Massachusetts-Bay in New-England, on May 30th, 1750. Being the anniversary for the election of His Majesty's Council for the said Province. By Samuel Phillips.
Imprint: Boston, New-England: Printed by John Draper, Printer to His Honor the Lieutenant Governor and Council. 1750.
Half morocco; 8-5/3 x $5\frac{1}{2}$ in. Not in Evans.

EARLY PRINTING IN NEW ENGLAND.

Cabinet F Shelf 1 No. 28

Boston, 1752. Samuel Kneeland.
Title: A defence of the Divine Right of infant baptism....By Peter Clark, A.M., Pastor of a church in Salem.
Imprint: Boston, New England: Printed and sold by S. Kneeland, in Queen Street, 1752.

Leather; $7\frac{3}{4}$ x 4-7/8 x 1-3/8 in. Evans?

EARLY PRINTING IN NEW ENGLAND.

Cabinet F Shelf 2 No. 73

Boston, 1751. Thomas Fleet.
Title: Some distinguishing characters of the extraordinary and ordinary Ministers of the Church of Christ.....
By Edward Wigglesworth, D.D.
Imprint: Boston: Printed and sold by Thomas Fleet, at the Heart and Crown in Cornhill, 1754.

Half morocco; 7 x $4\frac{1}{4}$ in. Evans 3, 7338, p.94.

EARLY PRINTING IN NEW ENGLAND.

Cabinet F Shelf 2 No. 63

Boston, 1755: Daniel and Zechariah Fowle.
Title: The duty of God's People when engaged in war: A sermon.....By Samuel Checkley.
Imprint: Printed and sold by D. Fowle in Ann Street, and Z. Fowle in Middle Street, below the Mill Bridge, 1755.

Half calf; $7\frac{1}{2}$ x 5-7/8 in. Evans 3, 7364; p.100.

EARLY PRINTING IN NEW ENGLAND.

Cabinet F Shelf 1 No. 55

Boston, 1755. John Draper.
Title: A day of darkness: A sermon preached before his Excellency William Shirley, Esq.... By Samuel Checkley.
Imprint: Boston, N.E. Printed by John Draper, printer to his Excellency the Governor and the Honorable his Majesty's Council. MDCCLV.

Half morocco; $7\frac{1}{4}$ x $4\frac{3}{4}$ in. Evans 3, 7383; p.100.

EARLY PRINTING IN NEW ENGLAND.

Cabinet F Shelf 1 No. 31

Boston, 1758: John Green and Joseph Russell.
Title: A rejoinder to the Reverend Mr. Robert Abercrombie...by B.J.Parsons and D. McGregore.
Imprint: Boston: Printed and sold by Green and Russell at their Printing-Office in Queen Street, M.DCC.LVIII.

Half morocco; $7\frac{1}{2}$ x 5 in. Evans 3, 8224; p.207.

EARLY PRINTING IN NEW ENGLAND.

Cabinet F Shelf 1 No. 60

Boston, 1760: Benjamin Mecom. [Nephew of B. Franklin]
Title: The interest of Great Britain considered with regard to her Colonies....[By Benjamin Franklin]...
Imprint: London, printed. MDCCLX. Boston, reprinted; by B. Mecom, and sold at the New Printing Office near the Town-House. 1760.

Half morocco; $7\frac{1}{4}$ x $4\frac{1}{2}$ x $\frac{1}{2}$ in. Evans, 3,8601, p.254.

EARLY PRINTING IN NEW ENGLAND.

Cabinet F Shelf 1 No. 34

Boston, 1760: Daniel and John Kneeland.
Title: A sermon...in Rowley, after the death of Mr. John Noyes...By Jedidiah Jewett.
Imprint: Boston. Printed by D. and J. Kneeland, in Queen Street. 1760.

Half leather; 7 x 4-5/8 in. Not in Evans.

EARLY PRINTING IN NEW ENGLAND

Cabinet F Shelf 1 No. 58

Boston, 1760: Richard Draper.
Title: A discourse occasioned by the death of the honorable Stephen Sewall, Esq.....By Jonathan Mayhew.
Imprint: Boston. Printed by Richard Draper, in Newbury-Street, Edes & Gill in Queens-Street; and T & J. Fleet, in Cornhill. MDCCLX.

Half morocco; $7\frac{1}{8}$ x $4\frac{3}{4}$ in. Evans, 3, 8666; p.262.

EARLY PRINTING IN NEW ENGLAND

Cabinet F Shelf 1 No. 37

Boston, 1761: John Green and Joseph Russell.
Title: Pietas et Gratulatio Collegii Cantabrigiensis apud Novanglos.
Imprint: Bostoni-Massachusettensium. Typis J. Green & J. Russell. M.DCC.LXI.
This is the first printing with Greek types executed in the North American Colonies.

Full morocco; 10-1/8 x 8 in. Evans 3, 8877, p.286.

EARLY PRINTING IN NEW ENGLAND.

Cabinet F Shelf 1 No. 35

Boston, 1763: Daniel and John Kneeland.

Title: A new version of the Psalms of David....
Imprint: Boston: Printed by D. and J. Kneeland, for J. Edwards, in Corn-Hill. MDCCLXIII.

Leather; 6 x 3-5/8 x 1-1/8 in. Evans 3, 9344; p.345.

EARLY PRINTING IN NEW ENGLAND.

Cabinet F Shelf 2 No. 77

Boston, 1774: John Boyle.

Title: Seven Sermons.....By Robert Russell. At Wardhurst in Sussex. Fifty-First edition.
Imprint: London, printed: Boston, reprinted, and sold by J. Boyle in Marlborough Street, 1774.

Half board and leather; 5-7/8 x 3½ in. Evans 5, 13593, p.69.

EARLY PRINTING IN NEW ENGLAND.

Cabinet F Shelf 3 No. 8

Boston, 1791: Isaiah Thomas and Ebenezer T. Andrews.

Title: An eulogy on the honorable James Bowdoin, Esq. Late President of the American Academy of Arts and Sciences...By John Lowell.
Imprint: Printed at Boston, by Isaiah Thomas and Ebenezer T. Andrews, at Faust's Statue, No.45 Newbury Street, 1791.

Half morocco; 11½ x 9 in. Evans 8, 23513, p.172.

EARLY PRINTING IN NEW ENGLAND.

Cabinet F Shelf 1 No. 39

Boston, 1763. Samuel Kneeland.

Title: Animadversions on the Reverend Mr. Croswell's late letter....By A. Cumming, A.M.
Imprint: Boston: Printed and sold by S. Kneeland, in Queen Street, M,DCC,LXIII.

Half leather; 7¼ x 5 in. Evans?

EARLY PRINTING IN NEW ENGLAND.

Cabinet F Shelf 2 No. 80

Boston, 1775: Thomas Leverett (Bookseller)

Title: A discourse preached December 15, 1774... By William Gordon.
Imprint: Boston: Printed for, and sold by Thomas Leverett, in Corn-Hill. 1775.

Half morocco; 7 x 4¾ in. Evans 5, 14073, p.136.

EARLY PRINTING IN NEW ENGLAND.

Cabinet F Shelf 2 No. 92

Boston, 1791. Samuel Hall.

Title: New version of the Psalms of David.... By N. Brady and N. Tate.
Imprint: Boston. Printed and sold by Samuel Hall, No.53 Cornhill. 1791.

Paper boards; 6½ x 3½ in. Not in Evans.

EARLY PRINTING IN NEW ENGLAND

Cabinet F Shelf 2 No. 78

Boston, 1764, Edes and Gill (Imprint)
The right of the British Colonies asserted and proved. By James Otis. Boston: Printed and sold by Edes and Gill.

Brochure, in manila envelope

EARLY PRINTING IN NEW ENGLAND.

Cabinet F Shelf 2 No. 75

Boston, 1776. Thomas and John Fleet.

Title: Observations on the nature of civil liberty, the principles of government, and the justice and policy of the war with America....By Richard Price.
Imprint: London, printed 1776: Boston re-printed and sold by T. and J. Fleet.

Half morocco; 7-3/8 x 4-5/8 in. Evans, 5, 15032, p.272.

EARLY PRINTING IN NEW ENGLAND

Cabinet F Shelf 2 No. 90

Boston, 1793, Alexander Young (Imprint)
Dr. Thatcher's sermon on the death of Governor Hancock. Printed at Boston, by Alexander Young, State Street, 1793.

Brochure, in manila envelope

EARLY PRINTING IN NEW ENGLAND.

Cabinet F Shelf 1 No. 43

Boston, 1769. John Kneeland and Seth Adams.

Title: A discourse occasioned by the death of the Reverend Dr. Joseph Sewall....By Charles Chauncy, Pastor of the First Church in Boston.
Imprint: Boston, N.E. Printed and sold by Kneeland and Adams, in Milk-Street. MDCCLXIX.

Half leather: 7¼ x 4½ in. Evans 3, 11206; p.170.

EARLY PRINTING IN NEW ENGLAND.

Cabinet F Shelf 2 No. 89

Boston, 1784: Edward E. Powars & Nathaniel Willis.

Title: The benevolence of the Diety...By Charles Chauncy, D.D. Senior Pastor of the first Church of Christ in Boston.
Imprint: America: Massachusetts; Boston. Printed by Powars & Willis, MDCCLXXXIV.

Half russia; 8 x 5 in. Evans 6, 18397; p.276.

EARLY PRINTING IN NEW ENGLAND

Cabinet F Shelf 2 No. 94

Boston, 1793: Manning & Loring.

Title: New version of the Psalms of David. By N. Brady and N. Tate.
Imprint: Printed at Boston, by Manning & Loring, for J. Thomas and E. T. Andrews, Faust's Statue, No.45, Newbury Street, 1793.

Leather; 7-1/8 x 4¼ x 1¼ in. Not in Evans.

EARLY PRINTING IN NEW ENGLAND.

Cabinet F Shelf 2 No. 79

Boston, 1774: Benjamin Edes and John Gill.

Title: The misery and duty of an oppress'd and enslav'd people, represented in a sermon.... By Samuel Webster, Pastor of a Church in Salisbury.
Imprint: Boston: Printed by Edes and Gill, in Queen Street, 1774.

Half leather; 8 x 5 in. Evans 5, 13758, p.94.

EARLY PRINTING IN NEW ENGLAND.

Cabinet F Shelf 2 No. 83

Boston, 1786. Benjamin Edes and Son.

Title: The shortness and afflictions of human life. By John Steele.
Imprint: Edinhurgh printed: Boston reprinted and sold by B. Edes & Son, No.42, Cornhill, 1786.

Half morocco; 8¼ x 5¼ in. Evans 7, 20008, p.71.

EARLY PRINTING IN NEW ENGLAND

Cabinet F Shelf 3 No. 12

Boston, 1799, John Russell (Imprint)
An oration...By Thomas Paine. Boston, Printed by John Russell.

Brochure, in manila envelope

EARLY PRINTING IN NEW ENGLAND

Cabinet F Shelf 2 No. 80

Boston, 1774, Edes and Gill (Imprint)
Observation on the Act of Parliament... By Josiah Quincy, jun'r. Boston: N.E. Printed and sold by Edes and Gill, in Queen Street, 1774.

Brochure, in manila envelope

EARLY PRINTING NEW ENGLAND

Cabinet 80 Shelf 2 No. 14

Boston, 1789, Nathaniel Coverly, his imprint.

See PERIODICALS, UNITED STATES. Gentlemen and Ladies Town and Country Magazine...

EARLY PRINTING IN NEW ENGLAND

Cabinet F Shelf 2 No. 91

Boston, 1800, Young & Minns (Imprint)
Dr. Thatcher's Century Sermon. Boston. Printed by Young & Minns, State Street.

Brochure, in manila envelope

EARLY PRINTING IN NEW ENGLAND

Cabinet X
Shelf 5
No. 6

Boston, 1801, David Carlisle [his imprint].

See "IMPARTIAL CITIZEN". Dissertation upon the constitutional freedom of the Press ...1801.

EARLY PRINTING IN NEW ENGLAND

Cabinet F
Shelf 2
No. 100.01

Boston, 1834, Garrison & Knapp (Imprint)

Debate...Speech...Letter against the American Colonization Society. Boston, Publisher by Garrison & Knapp.

Brochure, in manila enveolpe

EARLY PRINTING IN NEW ENGLAND

Cabinet F
Shelf 2
No. 96

Dedham, 1804. H. Mann (Imprint)

A tribute of respect to the memory of Samuel Adams...By Thomas Thatcher, Dedham: Printed and sold by H. Mann, January, 1804.

Brochure, in manila envelope

EARLY PRINTING IN NEW ENGLAND

Cabinet 80
Shelf 2
No. 26

Boston, 1808 Ephraim C. Beal, (his imprint).

See New England Association of Inventors... (The Useful Cabinet.)

EARLY PRINTING IN NEW ENGLAND

Cabinet II
Shelf 3
No. 63
Box

Boston, 1835. Crocker & Brewster.

See FLEMING, REV. JOHN. Short Sermon... Boston, 1835 [Imprint].

EARLY PRINTING IN NEW ENGLAND

Cabinet F
Shelf 2
No. 93

Newburyport(Mass.), 1795, Blunt and March (Imprint).

Family Exercises..By the Rev. T. Priestley.

Brochure, in manila envelope.

EARLY PRINTING IN NEW ENGLAND

Cabinet 80
Shelf 1
No. 51

Boston, 1812-1816, E.G. House [his imprint]

See ALMANACS. Clergyman's Almanack for 1812...

EARLY PRINTING IN NEW ENGLAND.

Cabinet A
Shelf 3
No. 7

Boston, 1845. Smith, Bryam & Co.

See Newspapers, Massachusetts. Sun (The), Boston (weekly)...

EARLY PRINTING IN NEW ENGLAND

Cabinet F
Shelf 3
No. 13

Newburyport, 1799, Angier March (Imprint)

Discourse at the ordination of Rev. Leonard Woods in Newbury, Dec., 5, 1798, by David Osgood. Printed by Angier March, Newburyport, 1799.

Brochure, in manila envelope

EARLY PRINTING IN NEW ENGLAND.

Cabinet R
Shelf 5
No. 144

Boston, James Loring, 1815-1830.

Title: The New England Primer ... Adorned with cuts.

Imprint: Boston: Printed by James Loring. Sold at wholesale and retail at his bookstore No. 2, Cornhill.

Unbound copy attached to back of Heartman's Bibliography of New England Primers.

EARLY PRINTING IN NEW ENGLAND

Cabinet F
Shelf 1
No. 9

Cambridge, 1663. Samuel Green and Marmaduke Johnson.

Title: The first American Bible. A leaf [original] from a copy translated into the Indian Language by John Eliot. With an account of the two printers. By George Parker Winship.

Imprint: Boston. Printed by D. B. Updike...1929.

Stamped cloth; 7-7/8 x 6 x ¼ in.

EARLY PRINTING IN NEW ENGLAND

Cabinet F
Shelf 3
No. 14

Portland (Maine), 1809, J. M'Kown (Imprint)

A sermon...By Thomas Barnard. Printed by J. M'Kown, Portland, 1809.

Brochure, in manila envelope

EARLY PRINTING IN NEW ENGLAND

Cabinet F
Shelf 2
No. 97

Boston, 1821, Sewell Phelps (Imprint)

Two discourses...By Henry Ware. Boston: Published by James W. Burditt, Sewell Phelps. Printer, 1821.

Brochure, in manila envelope

EARLY PRINTING IN NEW ENGLAND

Cabinet F
Shelf 1
No. 10

Cambridge, 1682: Samuel Green.

Title: A seasonable discourse wherein sincerity and delight in the service of God...By the Reverend and learned Urian Oakes. Harvard College.....

Imprint: Cambridge: Printed by Samuel Green, 1862.

Half morocco; 7¼ x 5⅝ x 3/8 in. Evans 325, vol.1, p.54.

EARLY PRINTING IN NEW ENGLAND

Cabinet F
Shelf 2
No. 98

Portland (Me.), 1814. Arthur Shirley (Imprint)

A Discourse...by Edward Payson. Portland. Printed by Arthur Shirley, 1814.

Brochure, in manila envelope

EARLY PRINTING IN NEW ENGLAND

Cabinet A
Shelf 3
No. 7

Boston, 1831, Stephen Foster. Printer of Garrison's The Liberator.

See Newspapers, Massachusetts. Liberator (The): Journal of the Times...

EARLY PRINTING IN NEW ENGLAND

Cabinet 80
Shelf 2
No. 23

Cambridge, 1804: William Hilliard, his imprint.

See PERIODICALS, United States. Literary Miscellany (The)...Cambridge (Mass.) 1804.

EARLY PRINTING IN NEW ENGLAND

Cabinet F
Shelf 2
No. 88

Salem, 1783, Samuel Hall (Imprint)

A sermon preached at the ordination of William Bently...By John Lathrop. Salem: Printed by Samuel Hall, near the Court-House, 1783.

Brochure, in manila envelope

EARLY PRINTING IN NEW ENGLAND

Cabinet F, Shelf 2, No. 99

Salem, 1819, John D. Cushing (Imprint)
Discourse...by John Bartlett. Salem, Printed by John D. Cushing, 1819.

Brochure, in manila envelope

EARLY PRINTING IN NEW ENGLAND.

Cabinet F, Shelf 3, No. 9

Worcester, 1791: Isaiah Thomas.
Title: Holy Bible, containing the Old and New Testaments: Together with the Apocrypha... with engraved frontispiece.
Imprint: Printed at the Press in Worcester, Massachusetts, by Isaiah Thomas. Sold by him in Worcester; and by him and Company, at Faust's Statue, No.45, Newbury Street, Boston.

Leather; $11\frac{3}{4}$ x $9\frac{1}{4}$ x $3\frac{1}{2}$ in. Evans 8, 23185, p.125.

EARLY PRINTING IN NEW HAMPSHIRE

Cabinet F, Shelf 2, No. 67

Portsmouth, 1760. Daniel Fowle.
Title: Preaching Christ the great business of the Gospel-Ministry.....By Samuel Haven.
Imprint: Portsmouth: Printed and sold by Daniel Fowle, 1760.

Half leather; $7\frac{3}{4}$ x 4-7/8 in. Evans 3, 8616; p.256.

EARLY PRINTING IN NEW ENGLAND.

Cabinet G, Shelf 1, No. 97 56

Salem, 1822. John D. and Thomas C. Cushing.
Title: The ruins of Paestum and other compositions in verse.
Imprint: Salem: Massachusetts. Printed by John D. and Thomas C. Cushing.

Half morocco; 9-7/8 x $7\frac{1}{4}$ x $\frac{1}{2}$ in.

EARLY PRINTING IN NEW ENGLAND.

Cabinet F, Shelf 3, No. 11

Worcester, 1795: Isaiah Thomas.
Title: Elegiac sonnets. By Charlotte Smith. The first Worcester edition from the sixth London edition.
Imprint: Printed at Worcester, by Isaiah Thomas, sold by him in Worcester, and by said Thomas and Andrews in Boston. 1795.
Colophon: From the Old Press of Isaiah Thomas at Worcester.
Advertisement by the editor "Printed on

cont'd

EARLY PRINTING IN NEW HAMPSHIRE.

Cabinet F, Shelf 2, No. 70

Portsmouth, 1765. Daniel and Robert Fowle.
Title: An impartial examination of Mr. Robert Sandeman's letters on Theron and Aspasio.... By Samuel Langdon.
Imprint: Portsmouth, in New Hampshire, N.E. Printed by Daniel & Robert Fowle, MDCCLXV.

Cloth; 9 x $5\frac{1}{2}$ ins. Evans 4, 10035; p.19.

EARLY PRINTING IN NEW ENGLAND

Cabinet F, Shelf 2, No. 81

Watertown, 1775: Benjamin Edes.
Title: A sermon preached before the Honorable House of Representatives [19 July, 1775]. By William Gordon.
Imprint: Watertown: Printed and sold by Benjamin Edes. 1775.

Half morocco; $7\frac{3}{4}$ x 5 in. Evans 5, 14073; p.136.

EARLY PRINTING IN NEW ENGLAND cont'd.

Cabinet F, Shelf 3, No. 11

paper the first manufactured by the Editor, Isaiah Thomas." The plates are engraved by Joseph Seymour" -- an artist who obtained his knowledge in this country."

Leather; 5-7/8 x $4\frac{3}{4}$ x 5/8 in. Evans 10, 29523, p.200.

EARLY PRINTING IN NEW HAMPSHIRE

Cabinet F, Shelf 2, No. 71

Portsmouth, 1799, William Treadwell (Imprint)
Mr. Sewell's eulogy on the late General Washington. Portsmouth, N.H. Printed by William Treadwell.

Brochure, in manila envelope

EARLY PRINTING IN NEW ENGLAND

Cabinet 80, Shelf 1, No. 63

Wendell, Mass., 1823, 1824, 1828, J. Metcalf, Printer: (His imprint).

See ALMANACS. Farmer's, Mechanic's and Gentleman's Almanack...By Nathan Wild.

EARLY PRINTING IN NEW HAMPSHIRE

Cabinet A, Shelf 3, No. 7

Dover, N.H. July 27, 1833. New Hampshire Globe. Edwin R. Locke & Co., publishers.

On folio 51 in vol. labelled "Early printing in New England".

EARLY PRINTING IN NEW HAMPSHIRE

Cabinet A, Shelf 3, No. 7

Portsmouth, 1830. Miller & Brewster.

See Newspapers, New Hampshire. Portsmouth Journal (daily)

EARLY PRINTING IN NEW ENGLAND

Cabinet F, Shelf 3, No. 5

Worcester, Mass., 1787. Isaiah Thomas.
Title: The history of little goody twoshoes... The first Worcester Edition. Illus.
Imprint: Printed at Worcester, Massachusetts by Isaiah Thomas, and sold wholesale and retail at his book store.

Half morocco; $4\frac{1}{2}$ x 3 x $\frac{1}{2}$ in.

EARLY PRINTING IN NEW HAMPSHIRE

Cabinet 80, Shelf 1, No. 48

Keene, N.H. 1806, 1810. John Prentiss. [Imprint]

See ALMANACS. Houghton's Genuine Alamanac (1806)... John Prentiss.

EARLY PRINTING IN NEW JERSEY

Cabinet 80, Shelf 1, No. 50

Burlington, 1775-1778, Isaac Collins.

See TRUEMAN, TIMOTHY, pseud. [Burlington Almanack for...1775..]

EARLY PRINTING IN NEW ENGLAND.

Cabinet F, Shelf 3, No. 6

Worcester, 1789. Isaiah Thomas.
Title: Elements of general history. Translated from the French of Abbe Millot. First American edition. vol.5.
Imprint: Printed at Worcester, Massachusetts, by Isaiah Thomas. Sold at his book store in Worcester, and by him and Company, in Boston 1789.

Leather: $8\frac{1}{4}$ x $5\frac{1}{4}$ x $1\frac{3}{4}$ in. Evans 7, 21965-6, p.336.

EARLY PRINTING IN NEW HAMPSHIRE

Cabinet F, Shelf 2, No. 65

Portsmouth, 1756. Daniel Fowle.
Title: Good news from a Far Country. In seven discourses. Delivered at the Presbyterian Church in Newbury.
Imprint: Portsmouth, in New Hampshire: Printed and sold by Daniel Fowle, 1756.
First book printed in New Hampshire.

Leather; 7 x $4\frac{1}{2}$ in. Evans 3, 7746; p.146.

EARLY PRINTING IN NEW JERSEY.

Cabinet F, Shelf 3, No. 46

Trenton, 1791: Isaac Collins.
Title: The Holy Bible containing the Old and New Testament....
Imprint: Trenton: Printed and sold by Isaac Collins. 1791.

Leather; 11 x 9 x 3 ins. Evans 8, 23184, p.124.

EARLY PRINTING IN NEW JERSEY

Cabinet 80 Shelf 2 No. 7

Woodbridge, 1759: James Parker his imprint.

See PERIODICALS, United States. (The) New American Magazine: No. XIV...

EARLY PRINTING IN NEW YORK CITY.

Cabinet F Shelf 3 No. 24

Childs, Francis, and John Swaine. The first government Printers in America, 1789-91.

Title: Acts of the First Congress of the United States of America in New York, 1789. [Contains the first official printing of the Constitution of the United States, and the Treaty of Peace with Great Britain.]

Imprint: New York: Printed by Francis Childs and John Swaine, printers to the United States.

" (2): Printers to the Congress of the United States.

cont'd

EARLY PRINTING IN NEW YORK CITY.

Cabinet F Shelf 3 No. 22

Gaine, Hugh. Hanover Square, 1785.

Title: Poems upon several occasions. By the Rev. Mr. John Pomfret....

Imprint: London, printed: New York, reprinted by Hugh Gaine, at the Bible, in Hanover Square. 1785.

Paper boards; 6½ x 4 in. Evans 6, 19195, p.375.

EARLY PRINTING IN NEW YORK.

Cabinet G Shelf 4 No. 36

Albany, 1802: Charles R. and George Webster

Title: A farewell sermon delivered September 26th, 1802 in the North Dutch Church, Albany. By John B. Johnson....

Imprint: Albany: Printed by Charles R. and George Webster. 1802.

Half morocco; 9-5/8 x 5-3/4 in.

EARLY PRINTING IN NEW YORK CITY cont'd

Cabinet F Shelf 3 No. ~~61~~ 24

Paper boards; 12¾ x 8½ in. Evans 8, 23902, p.224.

EARLY PRINTING IN NEW YORK CITY.

Cabinet S Shelf 2 No. 3

Inslee, Samuel and Ant. Car. On Moor's Wharf 1772.

Title: The American Village, a poem by Philip Freneau. Reprint in facsimile.

Imprint: Printed by S. Inslee and A. Car, on Moor's Wharf. 1772.

This is the third publication of the club of Colonial reprints of Providence, Rhode Island. 1906.

Half vellum; 9 x 6 3/4 in.

EARLY PRINTING IN NEW YORK

Cabinet 80 Shelf 1 No. 66

Albany, 1837: Packard and Van Benthuysen. Imprint.

See ALMANACS. Temperance Almanac...1837.

EARLY PRINTING IN NEW YORK CITY

Cabinet 80 Shelf 2 No. 36

Clark & Reser, Printers, New York, 1821.

SEE Periodicals, UNITED STATES. Saturday Magazine, vol.1, No.23, Dec.8, 1821.

EARLY PRINTING IN NEW YORK CITY. Example

Cabinet X Shelf 5 No. 7

Johnson & Stryker. 1801.

See Liberty of Printing. United States. Enquiry concerning the liberty...

EARLY PRINTING IN NEW YORK

Cabinet F Shelf 1 No. 111

Lansingburgh, Rensselaer County, 1797: William W. Wands.

Title: The American Accomptant; being a plain practical and systematic compendium of Federal Arithmetic...By Chauncy Lee.

Imprint: Lansingburgh: Printed by William W. Wands. 1797.

Leather; 6-7/8 x 4¼ x 1¼ in.

EARLY PRINTING IN NEW YORK CITY Example of

Cabinet NN Shelf 7 No. 5

New York City, 1833, Benjamin H. Day

see NEWSPAPERS, United States. Example of. Sun, The. New York, Sept. 3, 1833, No. I...

EARLY PRINTING IN NEW YORK CITY

Cabinet JJ Shelf 3 No. 1

New York City, 1802, Southwick and Crooker.

Title: An address delivered before the Franklin Typographical Association of New York, on July 5th. By Thomas Ringwood.

Imprint: Printed by Southwick and Crooker, No. 354, Water Street, 1802.

Half morocco; 8¼ x 5¼ x ¼ in.

EARLY PRINTING IN NEW YORK

Cabinet F Shelf 3 No. 40

Schenectady, 1797: Cornelius P. Wyckoff.

Title: Letters on Missions... By Melville Horne ...

Imprint: Schenectady: Printed by C.P. Wyckoff, in State Street.

Following page 124, printers advertisement: "Cornelius P. Wyckoff, at his Book-Store... has for sale the following"...

Leather; 6 3/4 x 4½ x ½ in.

EARLY PRINTING IN NEW YORK CITY Example

Cabinet X Shelf 5 No. 5

Forman, George, 1800.

Title: A treatise concerning political enquiry and the liberty of the press. By Tunis Wortman.

Imprint: Printed by George Forman, No.64 Water-Street, for the author. 1800.

Boards; 9¼ x 6 in.

EARLY PRINTING IN NEW YORK CITY.

Cabinet F Shelf 3 No. 28

Swords, T. & J. Pearl Street, 1798.

Title: The Botanic Garden. A Poem in two parts... [By Erasmus Darwin]. The first American Edition [Engravings by Benjamin Tanner 1775-1848.]

Imprint: New York: Printed by T. & J. Swords, Printers ot the Faculty of Physic of Columbia College, No.99 Pearl Street.

Calf; 8½ x 5½ x 1½ in.

EARLY PRINTING IN NEW YORK CITY.

Cabinet F Shelf 3 No. 16

Brown, Samuel. 1766.

Title: Theological Theses...by Isaac Sigfrid and Daniel Wyttenbach...Translated from the Latin.

Imprint: New York: Printed and sold by Samuel Brown at the foot of Pat-Baker's-Hill, between the New Dutch Church and Fly-Market, 1766.

Half russia; 6½ x 4¾ in. Evans 4, 10493, p.78.

EARLY PRINTING IN NEW YORK CITY.

Cabinet F Shelf 3 No. 20

Gaine, Hugh: Hanover Square, 1768.

Title: Every man his own lawyer...[By Jacob Giles]

Imprint: New York: Printed by Hugh Gaine, printer, bookseller and stationer, at the Bible and the Crown, in Hanover-Square, 1768.

Leather; 7¾ x 5 in. Evans 4, 10935, p.136.

EARLY PRINTING IN NEW YORK STATE

Cabinet JJ Shelf 3 No. 3

New York City, 1811, C. S. Van Winkle.

Title: An oration delivered before the New York Typographical Society on the 4th of July, 1811. By George Ashbridge.

Imprint: New York: Printed by C. S. Van Winkle, No. 56 Pine Street, 1811.

Half morocco; 8-5/8 x 5¼ x 3/8 in.

EARLY PRINTING IN NEW YORK CITY

Cabinet G — Shelf 4 — No. 35

Watts, John & Co., New York, 1813.
Title: The larger catechism...with proofs from the scripture, revised by Alexander M'Leod, D.D. The first book ever stereotyped in America.
Imprint: New York: Stereotyped and printed by J. Watts & Co. for Whiting & Watson, Theological and classical Booksellers. June, 1813.

Calf; 7-1/8 x 4¼ in.

EARLY PRINTING IN NEW YORK.

New York City. See also Zenger, John Peter.

EARLY PRINTING IN PENNSYLVANIA.

Cabinet F — Shelf 5 — No. 48

Ephrata, 1748. Ephrata Press.
Title: Der blutige Schau-Platz oder Martyrer... von T.J.V. Braght Nun aber sorgfaltigst ins hochteutsche ubersetzt... Printer Mark.
Imprint: Ephrata in Pensylvanien. Drucks und verlags der Bruderschaft. Anno MDCCXLVIII.
Printed in two parts, each part with title page. The largest book printed in the U.S. prior to the Revolution.

Leather, metal corners; 15 x 9¾ x 4¾ in. Evans 2, 6256 p.371.

EARLY PRINTING IN PENNSYLVANIA

Cabinet F — Shelf 2 — No. 15

Ephrata, 1770: The Ephrata Press [Peter Miller].
Title; Christliches Gemuths-Gesprach von dem Geistlichen und seligmachenden Glauben und Erkantnuss der Warheit...[von Gerhard Roosen].
Imprint: Ephrata: Typis Societatis. Anno MDCCLXX.

Leather, clasp; 6½ x 4 in. Thomas History of Printing, 2; p.87.

EARLY PRINTING IN PENNSYLVANIA.

Cabinet F — Shelf 2 — No. 17

Ephrata: The Ephrata Press, 1786.
Title: Chronicum Ephratense...Zusamen getragen von Br. Lamech u. Agrippa. Steel engraving.
Imprint: Ephrata: Gedruckt Anno MDCCLXXXVI.

Half morocco; 9½ x 8 x 1 in. Sachse German Sectarians.

EARLY PRINTING IN PENNSYLVANIA

Cabinet F — Shelf 2 — No. 21

Germantown, 1739: Christopher (I) Sauer.
Title: Zionitischer Weyrauchs-Hugel oder: Myrrhen Berg, Worinnen Allerley liebliches und wohlriechendes nach apotheker-Kunst zubereitetes Ruach-Werck zu finden....
Imprint: Germantown: Gedruckt bey Christoph Saur, 1739.
This is the first book printed with German types in the United States.
Leather; 6½ x 4½ x 2-7/8 in., Evans, 2, 4466, p.151.

EARLY PRINTING IN PENNSYLVANIA

Cabinet F — Shelf 2 — No. 24

Germantown, 1751: Christopher (II) Sauer.
Title: Ausbund, das ist: etliche schone Christliche Lieder....
Imprint: Germantown: Gedruckt bey Christoph Sauer. 1751.

A second title page at end of book with imprint "Gedruckt im Jahr 1752."

Leather with clasps; 6½ x 4 x 2-3/8 in. Evans 3, 6632, p.2.

EARLY PRINTING IN PENNSYLVANIA

Cabinet F — Shelf 2 — No. 27

Germantown, 1757: Christopher (II)Sauer.
Title: Some gospel treasures, or the holiest of all unvailing.....In several sermons. By John Everard.
Imprint: London printed in 1653. And now reprinted in Germantown by Christopher Sower, 1757.

Original leather; 8¼ x 6¾ x 2¼ in. Evans, 3, 7889, p.164.

EARLY PRINTING IN PENNSYLVANIA.

Cabinet F — Shelf 2 — No. 30

Germantown, 1759: Christopher(II) Sauer.
Title: A discourse on mistakes concerning religion, enthusiasm, experiences, etc. By Thomas Hartley.
Imprint: London printed. Germantown reprinted by Christopher Sower, 1752.

Quarter morocco; 7-1/8 x 4¾ x ¾ in. Not in Evans.

EARLY PRINTING IN PENNSYLVANIA.

Cabinet F — Shelf 2 — No. 29

Germantown, 1759: Christopher (II)Sauer.
Title: The way to the Sabbath of rest. Or the soul's progress in the work of the new birth...Thomas Bromley.
Imprint: Germantown: Reprinted and sold by Christopher Sower; also sold by Solomon Fussell and Jonathan Zane in Philadelphia, 1759.

Leather; 7¾ x 5 x 1½ in. Evans 3, 8309, p.219.

EARLY PRINTING IN PENNSYLVANIA

Cabinet F — Shelf 2 — No. 33

Germantown, 1762: Christopher (II)Sauer.
Title: Gesang-Buch in sich haltend eine Sammlung...welche von langer zeit her bey den Bekennern...gewesen....
Imprint: Germantown, gedruckt bey Christoph Sauer, auf Kosten vereinigter Freunden, 1762.

Leather; with clasps; 7½ x 5¼ x 2 in. Not in Evans.

EARLY PRINTING IN PENNSYLVANIA

Cabinet F — Shelf 2 — No. 36

Germantown, 1770: Christopher (II) Sauer.
Title: Ein geistliches magazine....Zweiter Theil.
Imprint: Germantown. Gedruckt bey Christoph Saur,1770.

Number 12, p.136, of this publication has note in German as follows: Printed with the first types that were cast in America.

cont'd

EARLY PRINTING IN PENNSYLVANIA cont'd

Cabinet F — Shelf 2 — No. 26

Half morocco; 8¾ x 5¾ in. See Thomas, History of Printing 2, p.83.

EARLY PRINTING IN PENNSYLVANIA.

Cabinet F — Shelf 2 — No. 38

Germantown, 1774: Christopher (II) Sauer.
Title: The Ready Reckoner; or trader's useful assistant...The seventh edition...By Daniel Fenning.
Imprint: London, printed, Germantown reprinted by Christopher Sower, 1774.

Leather; 6½ x 4 x 1-1/8 in.

EARLY PRINTING IN PENNSYLVANIA

Cabinet F — Shelf 2 — No. 40

Germantown, 1776: Christopher (II) Sauer.
Title: Biblia, das ist die ganze Heilige Schrift alten und neuen Testaments, nach der Deutschen uebersetzung Martin Luthers....
Imprint: Germantown: Gedruckt und zu finden bey Christoph Sauer, 1776.

Original leather over boards; 10½ x 8 x 3-7/8 in.

EARLY PRINTING IN PENNSYLVANIA

Cabinet F — Shelf 2 — No. 12

Germantown, 1798: Michael Billmeyer.
Title: Kirchen-formularien der evangelische-reformirten gemeinen.
Imprint: Germantown: Gedruckt bey Michael Billmeyer, 1798.

Paper covers; 7¼ x 4¼ x ¼ in.

EARLY PRINTING IN PENNSYLVANIA

Cabinet F — Shelf 2 — No. 46

Germantown, 1809: Michael Billmeyer.
Title: Der psalter des kōnigs und propheten David, verdeutschet von D. Martin Luther... Die siebente auflage.
Imprint: Germantown: Gedruckt bey Michael Billmeyer, 1809.

Calf; 5½ x 3-1/8 x 1-1/8 in.

EARLY PRINTING IN PENNSYLVANIA

Cabinet F — Shelf 1 — No. 71

Philadelphia, 1720-1721. Samuel Keimer.
Title: The Independent Whig. [No.1. January 20, 1720. No.53. January 4, 1721]
Imprint: Printed and sold by S. Keimer in Philadelphia.
Reprinted from the London edition [Thomas Gordon], in weekly numbers for the first twenty numbers, which were used with the remainder to make up the complete work.

Marbled boards; 8 x 6 x 7/8 in. Evans 1, 2536, p.331.

EARLY PRINTING IN PENNSYLVANIA

Cabinet F | Shelf 1 | No. 72

Philadelphia, 1728: Samuel Keimer.
Title: The history of the rise, increase, and progress of the Christian people called Quakers....By William Sewell. The third edition, corrected.
Imprint: Printed and sold by Samuel Keimer in Second Street, MDCCXXVIII.
This book was completed by Benjamin Franklin and his partner Hugh Merideth: They printed all following page 533.
Leather; 12 x 7-3/4 in. Evans I, 3104,p.397.

EARLY PRINTING IN PENNSYLVANIA

Cabinet F | Shelf 1 | No. 75

Philadelphia, 1730: Benjamin Franklin.
Title: Mystische und sehr geheyme sprueche....
Imprint: Zu Philadelphia: Gedruckt bey B. Franklin in jahr 1730.

This book is a facsimile of the first book printed in the German language in America.

Half morocco; $7\frac{1}{2}$ x $5\frac{1}{4}$ in.

EARLY PRINTING IN PENNSYLVANIA

Cabinet F | Shelf 1 | No. 79

Philadelphia, 1742. Benjamin, Franklin.

Title: The Charters of the Province of Pensilvania and City of Philadelphia. [Edited by John Kinsey.]
Imprint: Printed and sold by B. Franklin, MDCCXLII. [Two other title pages follow, each with the Franklin imprint.]

Calf; $11\frac{1}{2}$ x $7\frac{1}{4}$ x 1-7/8 in. Evans, 2, 5033; p.217.

EARLY PRINTING IN PENNSYLVANIA

Cabinet F | Shelf 1 | No. 81

Philadelphia, 1744: Benjamin Franklin.
Title:M.T. Cicero's Cato Major, or his discourse of old-age. [Translated].With explanatory notes [by James Logan]
Imprint: Philadelphia; Printed and sold by B. Franklin, MDCCXLIV.
This is generally considered to be the best specimen of printing produced by Franklin's Press.
Gilt morocco; 8-1/8 x $5\frac{1}{2}$ x 3/8 in. Evans 2, 5361, p.258.

EARLY PRINTING IN PENNSYLVANIA.

Cabinet F | Shelf 2 | No. 3

Philadelphia, 1747: William Bradford (II).
Title: An exhortation of the inhabitants of the province of South Carolina...By Sophia Hume...
Imprint: Philadelphia: Printed by William Bradford [1747].

Leather; $7\frac{1}{2}$ x $4\frac{3}{4}$ in. Evans, 2, 5974; p.335.

EARLY PRINTING IN PENNSYLVANIA.

Cabinet F | Shelf 2 | No. 5

Philadelphia, 1754: William Bradford (II)
Title: The Life and Death of Riches and Poverty: or the ready way to true content...[n.a.n: Preface signed: Thy friend, N.D.]
Imprint: Philadelphia: Printed and sold by W. Bradford, at the Sign of the Bible, in Second Street, M.DCC.LIV.

Half morocco; $6\frac{1}{4}$ x $3\frac{3}{4}$ in.

EARLY PRINTING IN PENNSYLVANIA.

Cabinet F | Shelf 2 | No. 7

Philadelphia, [1758] William Bradford.

Title: The grants, concessions, and original constitutions of the province of New Jersey between 1664, and 1682...By Aaron Leaming and Jacob Spicer.
Imprint: Philadelphia. Printed by W. Bradford printer to the King's Most Excellent majesty for the Province of New Jersey.

Original calf; $11\frac{3}{4}$ x $7\frac{1}{2}$ in. Evans 3, 8205; p.204.

EARLY PRINTING IN PENNSYLVANIA.

Cabinet F | Shelf 2 | No. 48

Philadelphia, 1770: Robert Bell.

Title: The history of the reign of Charles the Fifth..... In three volumes. By William Robertson.... Volume the third.
Imprint: America: Printed for the subscribers.
The history is preceded by an address to the subscribers concerning copyright signed by Robert Bell.

Leather; $8\frac{1}{4}$ x 5-1/4 x $1\frac{3}{4}$ in. Evans 4, 11837; p.250.

EARLY PRINTING IN PENNSYLVANIA

Cabinet NN | Shelf 3 | No. 1

Philadelphia, 1770, William Goddard. The partnership: or the history of the rise and progress of the Pennsylvania Chronicle. Philadelphia. Printed and sold by William Goddard in Arch Street, between Front and Second Streets. 1770.

Half morocco; $7\frac{1}{2}$ x 4-3/4 in.

EARLY PRINTING IN PENNSYLVANIA

Cabinet 80 | Shelf 2 | No. 11

Philadelphia, 1787, 1792, Mathew Carey.

See PERIODICALS, UNITED STATES. American Museum, or repository of ancient and modern ...

EARLY PRINTING IN PENNSYLVANIA Example

Cabinet A | Shelf 3 | No. 9

Philadelphia, 1789, Eleazer Oswald.

See Newspapers, Pennsylvania. Independent Gazetteer...May 15, 1789.

EARLY PRINTING IN PENNSYLVANIA.

Cabinet F | Shelf 2 | No. 44

Philadelphia, 1791: Samuel Sauer.

Title: Der neue hoch Deutsche Americanische Calender, auf das Jahr Christi 1792....
Imprint: Chestnut Hill, Gedruckt und zu finden bey Samuel Saur....
Full page wood engraving showing a printing office with furniture, precedes title page.

Half morocco; 7-7/8 x $6\frac{1}{2}$ x $\frac{1}{4}$ in. Seidensticker, p.128.

EARLY PRINTNG IN PENNSYLVANIA.

Cabinet F | Shelf 1 | No. 88

Philadelphia, 1792: Mathew Carey.

Title: Epicteti Enchiridion. Ex editione Joannis Upton. Accurate expressum.
Imprint: Philadelphiae: Impensis Mathaei Carey. 1792.

First book printed with Greek types in America.

Calf; $5\frac{3}{4}$ x $3\frac{1}{2}$ in. Not in Evans.

EARLY PRINTING IN PENNSYLVANIA. Example

Cabinet A | Shelf 3 | No. 9

Philadelphia, 1796-1799, Benjamin Franklin Bache.

See Newspapers, Pennsylvania. General Advertiser, daily [also known as Aurora]

EARLY PRINTING IN PENNSYLVANIA.

Cabinet F | Shelf 1 | No. 93

Philadelphia, 1796. Robert Campbell. [Bookseller.]
Title: British honor, or American patience, as exemplified in the modest publications... of William Cobbett...By a friend to regular government.
Imprint: Philadelphia: Printed for and sold by Robert Campbell No.40, South Second Street, 1796.

Half morocco; $9\frac{1}{4}$ x $5\frac{1}{2}$ in. Not in Evans.

EARLY PRINTING IN PENNSYLVANIA.

Cabinet F | Shelf 2 | No. 10

Philadelphia, 1796: Thomas Bradford.
Title: A New Year's Gift to Democrats...or, a vindication of Mr. Randolph's resignation. By Peter Porcupine [William Cobbett].
Imprint: Philadelphia: Published by Thomas Bradford, printer, bookseller & stationer, No.8, South Front Street, 1796.

Boards, cloth back; $8\frac{3}{4}$ x $5\frac{1}{2}$ in.

EARLY PRINTING IN PENNSYLVANIA.

Cabinet G | Shelf 5 | No. 17 | 2 vols.

Philadelphia, 1798. John Thompson and Abraham Small. [The Hot Press of John Thompson].
Title: The Holy Bible, containing the Old and New Testament: Together with the Apocrypha. 2 vols.
Imprint: Philadelphia. Printed for John Thompson & Abraham Small. [From the Hot-Press of John Thompson]. 1798.

Calf; each vol; $16\frac{3}{4}$ x $10\frac{1}{4}$ in.

EARLY PRINTING IN PENNSYLVANIA.

Cabinet G | Shelf 4 | No. 34

Philadelphia, 1806. John Watts.
Title: Xenophontis de Cyri institutis.
Imprint: Excudebat Johannis Watts, impensis Wm. Payntell et Soc.
This is the first Greek book printed from the first Greek type cast in the United States of America.

Calf; 9 x $5\frac{1}{2}$ in.

EARLY PRINTING IN PENNSYLVANIA

Cabinet II | Shelf 3 | No. 32

Philadelphia, 1831, John Grigg.
Title: The case of the Cherokee Nation against the State of Georgia...
Imprint: Philadelphia: John Grigg, 9 North Fourth Street. 1831.

Cloth; 10 x $6\frac{1}{4}$ in.

EARLY PRINTING IN RHODE ISLAND

Cabinet R | Shelf 3 | No. 155

Newport, 1728. James Franklin.
Title: The Rhode Island Almanack for the year 1728. Being the first ever printed in that Colony. Carefully reproduced in exact facsimile ... Together with a brief account of James Franklin, the printer ... [Ed. by George Parker Winship. Providence, 1911.

Half morocco; $6\frac{1}{2}$ x 5 in.

EARLY PRINTING IN RHODE ISLAND.

Cabinet F | Shelf 1 | No. 69

Newport, 1752: James Franklin.
Title: Catechism and confession of faith.... by R.B. a servant of the Church of Christ.
Imprint: Newport: Printed by James Franklin at the Town-School House, 1752.

Original leather; 6-1/8 x $4\frac{1}{4}$ x $\frac{1}{2}$ in.
Not in Evans.

EARLY PRINTING IN RHODE ISLAND.

Cabinet F | Shelf 3 | No. 2

Providence, 1774: John Carter.
Title: English liberties or the free-born subjects inheritance...Compiled first by Henry Care, and continued...by William Nelson.
Imprint: Providence, Rhode Island: Printed and sold by John Carter at Shakespear's Head, in Meeting Street, near the Court House. 1774.

Leather; $6\frac{3}{4}$ x $4\frac{3}{8}$ x $1\frac{1}{2}$ in. Evans 5, 13185, p.14.

EARLY PRINTING IN RHODE ISLAND

Cabinet 00 | Shelf 6 | No. 52

Providence, 1786 - 1797. Printers: John Carter, Bennett Wheeler, and Nathaniel Phillips.
Imprints of the three printers as above, on three "Acts". Single sheets bound in one Vol.

Cloth; $15\frac{3}{8}$ x $10\frac{1}{4}$ in.
Carter, 1786, Providence
Wheeler, 1786, Providence

Phillips, 1797, Warren, R.I.

EARLY PRINTING IN RHODE ISLAND

Cabinet 00 | Shelf 6 | No. 52

Warren (R.I.), 1797, Nathaniel Phillips.
Title: State of Rhode Island, etc. in General Assembly. October Session, A.D., 1797.
Imprint: Warren (Rhode Island). Printed by Nathaniel Phillips, printer to the State.

Bound in with other items.

Cloth; $15\frac{3}{8}$ x $10\frac{1}{4}$ in.

EARLY PRINTING IN RHODE ISLAND.

Cabinet | Shelf | No.

See Printing press of the French fleet, Providence, R.I. 1781.

Bound with other items in "Various printers and their plants", item 6, vol.1.

EARLY PRINTING IN SOUTH CAROLINA

Cabinet F | Shelf 3 | No. 51

Charles-Town, 1737: Timothy Lewis.
Title: Collection of Psalms and Hymns. Charles-Town. Printed by Lewis Timothy.
Imprint: Facsimile Reprint. Printed by A. Pearson ... London, 1742.

Cloth; 7 x 4-3/4 x 3/8 in.

EARLY PRINTING IN SOUTH CAROLINA.

Cabinet F | Shelf 3 | No. 54

Charles-Town, 1770: Charles Crouch.
Title: A discourse on the death of Rev. George Whitefield...By Josiah Smith.
Imprint: Charles-Town: Printed by Charles Crouch 1770.

Half morocco; $7\frac{3}{4}$ x $4\frac{3}{4}$ in. Evans 4, 11862, p.254.

EARLY PRINTING IN VIRGINIA.

Cabinet S | Shelf 5 | No. 65

Williamsburg, 1730: William Parks.
Title: Typographia, an ode on printing ...
Imprint: Williamsburg: Printed by William Parks, 1730.
Photographic reprint by the Stone Printing Co. Roanoke, Virginia. For the American Institute of Graphic Arts, New York, 1926.

Folder; $11\frac{1}{4}$ x $8\frac{1}{2}$ in.

EARLY PRINTING IN VIRGINIA

Cabinet A | Shelf 3 | No. 5

Williamsburg, 1776. The Virginia Gazette.

See Newspapers, Virginia. Virginia Gazette. Williamsburg, No.78, July 26, 1776.

EARLY PRINTING IN CANADA.

Cabinet F | Shelf 1 | No. 121

Montreal, 1776. Fleury Mesplet & Charles Berger.
Title: Réglement de la confrerie de l'adoration perpétuelle du S. Sacrement.....
Imprint: A Montreal; Chez F. Mesplet & C.Berger, Imprimeurs & Libraires; près le Marché, 1776.
First book printed in Canada.

Limp morocco; $4\frac{1}{2}$ x $3\frac{1}{4}$ x 1/8 in. Thomas 2, p.181.

EARLY PRINTING [Literature of]

Cabinet S | Shelf 3 | No. 104

Americana, Elizabethan. By George Watson Cole, Librarian of the Henry E. Huntington Library San Gabriel, California.
P. 159 in volume Wilberfore Eames ... A tribute to. Cambridge, 1924.

EARLY PRINTING LITERATURE OF

Cabinet J | Shelf 2 | No. 1

Amman, Jost, zeichner und formschneider.... von C. Becker, Leipzig, 1854. Illus.

A bibliographical account of early printed books with illustrations by Amman. 1564 to 1586.

Half morocco; $8\frac{1}{4}$ x 6-1/8 x $\frac{3}{4}$ in.

EARLY PRINTING Literature of

Cabinet Y | Shelf 3 | No. 50

(Art of book printing, 16th, 17th and 18th centuries. With numerous full page reproductions, ornaments, and vignettes). Buchkunst. Mit zahlreichen vollbildern, zum teil in tondruck und vielen vignetten und zierleisten. von Felix Poppenberg. Berlin, 1908.

Boards; 6-3/8 x 4-3/4 x $\frac{1}{2}$ in.

EARLY PRINTING [Literature of]

Cabinet U | Shelf 1 | No. 1c

Assertio septem sacramentorum (Henry VIII contra Luther). Bibliographical description by Gordon E. Duff.

In Excerpts relating to printing from "The Library," 1908. pp. 1-36

EARLY PRINTING [Literature of]

Cabinet S | Shelf 4 | No. 116

(The) Bible from the beginning. By Rev. P. Marion Simms. New York, 1929.
Historical, bibliographical account.

Cloth; 8-1/8 x 5-1/8 x 1-1/8 in.

EARLY PRINTING [Literature of]

Cabinet S | Shelf 4 | No. 113

Bibles, Fifteenth Century: A study in Bibliography. By Wendell Prime, New York, 1888.

Boards; $9\frac{1}{2}$ x $6\frac{1}{4}$ in.

EARLY PRINTING [Literature of]

Cabinet S, Shelf 4, No. 117

(Bibles). The guiding light of the great highway. By Robert R. Dearden, Jr. Philadelphia, 1929. Illus.

Historical and bibliographical account of Bibles in manuscript and Bibles printed before the year 1500 by famous printers.

Cloth; 9-1/8 x 6 in.

EARLY PRINTING

Cabinet U, Shelf 5, No. 40

Bibliographical account of the printer of "Historia S. Albani", 1467-77? (with one plate)

In Bradshaw's "Collected Papers"... Cambridge, 1889, p.149.

EARLY PRINTING Literature of

Cabinet 18, Shelf 1, No. 15

(Bibliographical history of the 16th and 17th century books relating to Ahasverus.) Zur geschichte und Bibliographie des Volksbuchs von Ahasverus, von Leonhard Neubaur, Elbing.

In ZEITSCHRIFT FUR BUCHERFREUNDE, 1913-14, part 2, p.211.

EARLY PRINTING Literature of

Cabinet Y, Shelf 3, No. 45

(Book printing of the early masters, 15 to the 18th centuries: A guide to the collection of Han Grisebach) Fuhrer durch die sonderausstellung die buchkunst der alten meister. Gestande der vormaligen sammlung Hans Griesbach. Berlin, 1906.

Half morocco; 7 x 5 x ¼ in.

EARLY PRINTING [Literature of]

Cabinet T, Shelf 1, No. 57

Bowyer, William: Miscellaneous tracts by the late William Bowyer, printer, and several of his learned friends; including letters on literary subjects by Mr. Markland, Mr. Clark, etc. Collected and illustrated with occasional notes by John Nichols, printer...London, 1785.

Half calf; 10½ x 8½ x 1-7/8 in.

EARLY PRINTING [Literature of]

Cabinet S, Shelf 1, No. 189

Catalogue of books [compiled by A. W. Pollard], mostly from the presses of the first printers showing the progress of printing with movable metal types through the second half of the 15th. century. Collected by Rush C. Hawkins ...and deposited in the Annmary Brown Memorial at Providence, Rhode Island. Printed at the cost of General Rush C. Hawkins at the University Press, Oxford, 1910.

Cloth; 11½ x 9 x 1⅔ in.

EARLY PRINTING. Literature of

Cabinet W, Shelf 1, No. 15

Catalogus librorum qui extant apud Joanneum Anisson, typographes Regis Praefectum. Paris, 1702.

Bound in with "Supplementum Bibliographiae Anissonianae" published by Claude Rigaud, Anisson's successor, in 1709.

Half morocco; 6¼ x 3-3/4 in.

EARLY PRINTING

Cabinet S, Shelf 6, No. 9

Children's books, the history of. By C.M. Hewins. Excerptfrom the "Atlantic", Jan., 1888.

Item 13 in vol. with binder's title "Early printing and printed books. Pamphlets". Bound, 1932.

EARLY PRINTING Literature of

Cabinet S, Shelf 5, No. 12

Concerning authors, by Charles Nordhoff: An excerpt from The Ladies' Repository, Sept. 1856

Briefly traces the history of printing, book printing, journalism, with brief mention of some celebrated early writers.

Bound with "Pamphlets and excerpts relating to typographical matters," item 16.

EARLY PRINTING

Cabinet S, Shelf 6, No. 9

Debt of medical science to the early printers, the. By Dr. Jas. J. Walsh. Excerpt from "Scientific Monthly", Feb., 1924.

Item 11 in vol. with binder's title "Early printing and printed books. Pamphlets". Bound, 1932.

EARLY PRINTING Literature of

Cabinet S, Shelf 1, No. 16

DeVinne, Theodore Low: Historic printing types A lecture read before the Grolier Club of New York, January 25, 1885, with additions and new illustrations. New York: The Grolier Club, 1886.

Boards; 10¼ x 8¼ in.

EARLY PRINTING. Literature of

Cabinet S, Shelf 5, No. 12

Disraeli, Isaac. Early printing: Excerpts from Curiosities of Literature. A prospectus from John Murray, London, 1823.

Brief historical outline.

Bound in collection "Pamphlets and excerpts relating to typographical matters", item 4. 2

EARLY PRINTING. Literature of

Cabinet 18, Shelf 1, No. 13

[Earliest editions of the "Prognostications" of Nostradamus: A Nostradamus bibliography] Die altesten ausgaben der "Prophetics" des Nostradamus. von Carl Klinckowstroem. Munich, 1913. [With facsimiles]

In Zeitschrift fur Bucherfreunde, 1913, part 2, p.361.

EARLY PRINTING [Literature of]

Cabinet 75, Shelf 1, No. 5

Earliest printers of Greek and their types, The: A paper read before the Bibliographical Society, by Mr. Robert Proctor, Jan. 1909.

In Trans. Biblio. Soc., Vol. V. 1898-1900, pp. 174-177.

EARLY PRINTING [Literature of]

Cabinet 75, Shelf 1, No. 3

English books printed abroad. A paper read by Alfred W. Pollard. The Bibliographical Society, April. 20. 1896.

In Trans. Biblio. Soc. Vol. 3, 1895-1896. pp. 195-209.

EARLY PRINTING Literature

Cabinet LL, Shelf 3, No. 1.01

(An) Essay on the introduction of the consonants J and V in printing. Translated from Desmolet's Continuation of Sallengre's Memoires de Litterature; Paris, 1749. [Excerpt from the Literary Collector, Sept., 1903].

Item 7 in vol. with binder's title "Proofreading: Pamphlets". Bound, 1932.

EARLY PRINTING. [Literature of]

Cabinet 75, Shelf 2, No. 5

Euclid's Elements, 1482-1600. Early editions of. A paper read before the Bibliographical Society by C. Thomas-Stanford, November 19, 1923.

In Trans. Biblio. Soc., "The Library," Vol. 5, 1924-1925, pp. 39-42.

EARLY PRINTING. Literature of

Cabinet 18, Shelf 1, No. 14

(Forgeries in printed works and early manuscripts.) Fälschungen in alten Handschriften und Druckwerken, von Johannes Schinnerer, Leipzig. Illus.

In Zeitschrift für Bücherfreunde, 1913-14, part 1, p.97.

EARLY PRINTING. Literature of

Cabinet S Shelf 6 No. 7

Greek New Testament, the four-hundredth anniversary of the publication of the first. By Bernhard Peck.
Bibliographical examination. Excerpt from The Open Court, March, 1916.

Item (g) in book with binder's title "Early printed books, various excerpts and pamphlets". 1854-1931.

EARLY PRINTING. Literature of

Cabinet 20 Shelf 1 No. 16

(History of early Herbals). Alten Kraüterbücher: Ein beitrag zur geschichte des nachdrucks, von W.L. Schreiber, Potsdam.

Brief description of the earliest herbals with reference to the early printers of them.

In Zietschrift für Bücherfreünde, 1904-5, p.393.

EARLY PRINTING Literature of

Cabinet Y Shelf 1 No. 97

(Manuscripts and printed books in the 15th and 16th centuries, an investigation concerning) Handschriftenforschung und buchdruck im XV und XVI jahrhundert. von Karl Schottenloher.

Essay in the "Gutenberg-Gesellschaft Jahrbuch, 1931", pp.73-106.

EARLY PRINTING Literature of

Cabinet S Shelf 5 No. 14

(The) Growth of wood-cut printing: Early methods in the hand press, 1450-1850. By Theodore Low De Vinne. Excerpts from Scribners, April-May, 1880. Illus.

Bound with items in collection "Printing Processes", item 21.

EARLY PRINTING. Literature of

Cabinet S Shelf 5 No. 12

History of printing and some printed books briefly told by Isaac Disraeli: An excerpt from Curiosities of Literature, London, 1823.

Bound in with "Pamphlets and excerpts relating to various typographical matters," item 2.

EARLY PRINTING. [Literature of]

Cabinet T Shelf 6 No. 11

Masterpieces of early printers and engravers. A series of facsimiles from rare and curious books remarkable for illustrative devices, beautiful borders, decorative initials, printers marks, elaborate title pages, etc. By Jenry Noel Humphreys. London, 1870.

Stamped cloth; 14½ x 10¼ x 1¼ in.

EARLY PRINTING [Literature of]

Cabinet S Shelf 5 No. 18

Hawkins, Rush C. A letter "To the editor of The Bookmart, Oct. 1886.
Concerns the invention controversey.

Bound in collection "Dawn of Printing", item 13.

EARLY PRINTING Literature of

Cabinet T Shelf 4 No. 9 & 10

History of the Horn Book. By Andrew W. Tuer. London, 1896, 2 vols. Illus. with enclosures of original Horn Books. 1897 2nd ed. in one vol. Illus.

1st. ed. Vellum; 10 x 8-5/8 x 2 in.
2nd. ed. Cloth; 10 x 8-5/8 x 2 in.

EARLY PRINTING Literature of

Cabinet W Shelf 5 No. 35

Mémoire sur les différentes branches d'industrie et de commerce suiventes en 1776. (1): caractères à imprimeur; (2):cartes a jouer; (3): livres, cartes geographiques, estampes et tableau. Par Alexandre Pinchart. (Extrait du tome VIII de Bulletin Bibliophile belge).

Morocco; 9½ x 6 in.

EARLY PRINTING. Literature of

Cabinet 20 Shelf 1 No. 16

(Herbals: A supplementary study ot the history of early Herbals) Alten Kräuterbucher. Ein Beitag zue geschichte des nachdrucks, von prof. W.L. Schreiber, Potsdam.

In Zeitschrift für Bücherfreünde, 1904-5, part 2, p.297.

EARLY PRINTING [Literature of]

Cabinet V Shelf 3 No. ~~180~~ 21

Imprimerie en Europe aux XVe et XVIe siecles: Les premières productions typographiques et les premiers imprimeurs. Par Leon De George. Paris, 1892.
Chronological account of the first productions of the first printers in all parts of Europe.

Half morocco; 6-1/8 x 4 x ½ in.

EARLY PRINTING Literature of

Cabinet W Shelf 1 No. 147

Misset, E. Le premier livre connu: Un Missel spécial de Constance, oeuvre de Gutenberg avant 1450. Étude liturgique et critique. Par E. Misset. Paris, 1899.

Half morocco; 9-3/4 x 6½ in.

EARLY PRINTING [Literature of]

Cabinet 75 Shelf 1 No. 6

"Herbarius" and "Hortus Sanitatis" on the. A paper read before the Bibliographical Society, Jan. 21, 1901, by Joseph Frank Payne. Illus.

In Trans. Biblio. Soc. Vol. 6, 1900-1902. pp. 63-126.

EARLY PRINTING [Literature of]

Cabinet 20 Shelf 2 No. 18

Kalender und Almanache. von Dr. Vita von Lieres in Frankfurt a.M. Illus.
Brief historical account of Almanac production from the 15th to the 20th century.

In Zeitschrift für Bücherfreunde, 1926, pp. 101-114.

EARLY PRINTING Lit. of

Cabinet AA Shelf 2 No. 13

Monumenta Typographica. Catalogue LIII. Primordii artis typographicae completens editiones qua apud equitem Leonem S. Olschki, bibliopolam. Illus. Florence, 1903.

Half morocco; 11¾ x 8 in.

EARLY PRINTING [Literature of]

Cabinet Y Shelf 3 No. 93

Hiersemann, Karl W. Werden und wirken. Ein festgruss. Zugesand am 3 Sept. 1924 sum siebzigsten geburtstag und vierzigjahrigen bestehen seiner firma (A series of essays on printers, printing, bibliography, bookbinding, etc.) Leipzig, 1924. Illus.

Boards; 11 x 7-7/8 x 2 in.

EARLY PRINTING [Literature of]

Cabinet 18 Shelf 1 No. 14

(Leaves of otherwise unknown books found in bindings)

(Waste Paper: A glance in a bookbinding shop of the 16th century.) Einband-Makulatur, von G. Kohfeldt Rosteck.

In Zeitschrift für Bücherfreunde, 1913-14, part 1, p.11.

EARLY PRINTING. Literature of.

Cabinet V Shelf 5 No. 22

Morison, Stanley. L'Art de l'Imprimerie: Deux cent cinquante reproductions des plus beaux specimens de la typographie depuis 1500 jusqu'a 1900. Paris, [1925].

Cloth; 11 x 8¾ x ½ in.

EARLY PRINTING. Literature of

Cabinet 75 | Shelf 2 | No. 7

Notes on old books. The order of printing the forms, by W. W. Greg.

In Transections of the Bibliographical Society, "The Library," Vol. VII, 1926-1927, pp. 216-220.

EARLY PRINTING. Literature of

Cabinet R | Shelf 1 | No. 90

Printing and printers of Franklin's time, by Chas. T. Jacobi, in The American Printer: Franklin number, Jan.20, 1923. p.60. Portraits.

Half morocco; 12 x 8-7/8 ins.

EARLY PRINTING [Literature of]

Cabinet Y | Shelf 3 | No. 61

Schwenke, Paul Beiträge zum bibliotheks und buchwesen. Berlin, 1913. Facsimiles. A collection of essays on libraries, books, printing and publishing by bibliophiles. Dedicated to Paul Schwenke.

Half morocco; 11¼ x 8-5/8 x 1-3/8 in.

EARLY PRINTING Literature of

Cabinet 18 | Shelf 1 | No. 5

(On the study of types used in the XV century) zur typenkunde des XV Jahrhunderts, by Konrad Haebler, Berlin, 1909.

In Zeitschrift für Bücherfreunde, 1909, part 1, p.136.

EARLY PRINTING. Literature of

Cabinet S | Shelf 5 | No. 6

Printing in the XV and XIX centuries: review of article in "Penny Magazine."

Bound in with other items in "Various Printers and their Plants," item I, vol.2.

EARLY PRINTING [Literature of]

Cabinet S | Shelf 4 | No. 13

(Some) Early printers and their colophons. By Joseph Spencer Kennard, Philadelphia, 1902.

Illuminated vellum; 9 x 5¾ in.

EARLY PRINTING. Literature of

Cabinet K | Shelf 4 | No. 5

(Ornamental initial lett rs, 15th to 18th century...History of)

See Boffito, Giuseppe. Iniziali istoriate... Firenze, 1925.

EARLY PRINTING. Literature of

Cabinet X | Shelf 5 | No. 3

Printing in the fifteenth and in the nineteenth centuries. n.a.n. Excerpt from The Penny Magazine of the Society for the Diffusion of Useful Knowledge. Nov.30 to Dec.31, 1837. Illus

Describes the Mayence festival on the occasion of the erection of the Statue to John Gutenberg, and enumerates the various benefits to mankind through the invention of printing.

p. 25 in vol. with binder's title "Scrap-Book, 1705-1891, relating to printing."

EARLY PRINTING [Literature of]

Cabinet S | Shelf 5 | No. 24

Some late statements about early printing. By Rush C. Hawkins. An excerpt from The Bibliographer, Feb. 1902.

pp. 15-22 in collection "Printing Excerpts".

EARLY PRINTING Literature of

Cabinet 18 | Shelf 1 | No. 10

(Pamphlets of Gusmao, 1709, relating to air-ships.) Die Gusmao-Flugblatter von 1709, von Carl von Klinckowstroem, Munich. Facsimile title pages, etc.

In Zeitschrift für Bücherfreunde, 1911, part 1, p.36.

EARLY PRINTING

Cabinet S | Shelf 6 | No. 9

"Rarities" in old world libraries. By D. Haveloc Fisher. Excerpt from the "Editorial Review", Aug., 1912.

Item 9 in vol. with binder's title "Early printing and printed books. Pamphlets". Bound, 1932.

EARLY PRINTING

Cabinet J | Shelf 1 | No. 20

Specimen collection of woodcuts: Initials, head and tail pieces, borders, coats-of-arms, etc. Early 17th century. Scrap book.

Boards: 9-5/8 x 7-3/8 "

EARLY PRINTING. Literature of

Cabinet 76 | Shelf 1 | No. 1-3

Plomer, H.R. Dictionary of printers and booksellers in England, Scotland and Ireland, and of Foreign printers of English books from 1557 to 1725, by H.R. Plomer. Printed for the Bibliographical Society, London, 3 vols. 1907, 1910, 1922.

Boards, canvas backs, 8-3/4 x 7 ins.

EARLY PRINTING Literature

Cabinet LL | Shelf 3 | No. 1.01

Recherches historiques sur la coquilles des imprimeurs. Par Arnould Locard. Lyon, 1892. Pamphlet.

Item 13 in vol. with binder's title "Proof-reading: Pamphlets". Bound, 1932.

EARLY PRINTING Literature

Cabinet J | Shelf 1 | No. 19

Specimens of early woodcuts, printing and printers marks (period of Caxton). No title page, n.p. n.d.

Boards: 10x7¼"

EARLY PRINTING. Literature of

Cabinet 18 | Shelf 1 | No. 5

(Pope Nicolas V. (1447-1455) as a friend of the book) Papst Nikolaus V. als Bucherfreunde, by Klemens Loffler, Breslau.

An account of his collection of incunabula and manuscripts which formed the foundation for the Vatican Library.

In Zeitschrift fur Bucherfreunde, 1909, part 1, p.174.

EARLY PRINTING. [Literature of]

Cabinet 22 | Shelf 1 | No. 5

(Schmalkalden, 1591. A printer's warning to printers and publishers against piracy.) Ein mahnruf an lied nachdrucker 1591. Communicated by A. Kirchhoff.

The warning appears in a book printed by Michael Schmuck.

In Archiv für Deutschen Buchhandels, vol.V, p.310.

EARLY PRINTING

Cabinet S | Shelf 6 | No. 9

Temperance novels, 1848 to 1870. [Bibliographical Account] By Edmund Lester Pearson. With illustrations. Excerpt from "Scribners", Nov., 1924.

Item 18 in vol. with binder's title "Early printing and printed books. Pamphlets". Bound, 1932.

EARLY PRINTING [Literature of]

Cabinet V Shelf 3 No. 30

Thibaudeau, F. La lettre d'imprimerie: Origine, developpement ... et 12 notices illustrées sur les Arts du livre ... Paris, 1921. 2 Vols.
Many facsimiles, reproductions of types, etc.

Cloth; 8-7/8 x 6-3/8 in.

EARLY PRINTING IN AUSTRIA [Literature of]

Cabinet X Shelf 1 No. 82

Braun, Placidus: Notitia historico-litteraria de libris ab artis typographicae inventione usque ad annum 1500 impressis: in bibliotheca monasterii ad SS. Uldaricum et Afram Augustae extantibus. Augustae Vindelicorum, 1788.
Notice of 15th century printed books in the library of the monastery Sts. Uldaric and Afra at Vienna, with plates delineating the alphabets of the several printers.

Paper boards; 10 x 8½ x 3/4 in.

EARLY PRINTING IN AUSTRIA Literature

Cabinet Y Shelf 2 No. 93

(Vienna, 1482-1560) Wiens buchdruckergeschichte bis 1560. von Michael Denis. Wien, 1782. [printed by] Christian Fried. Wappler.

Bio-bibliographical history

Boards; 10¼ x 8-3/8 in.

EARLY PRINTING [Literature of]

Cabinet S Shelf 4 No. 12

Triumphs of early printing: A paper read at the Annual Meeting of the Club of Odd Volumes, at the University Club, Dec. 26, 1901, by the President, James Frothingham Hunnewell. Boston, Club of odd Volumes, 1902.

Half boards; 8-7/8 x 7 in.

EARLY PRINTING IN AUSTRIA. [Literature of]

Cabinet 22 Shelf 1 No. 7

(Carniola, 1561. Primus Truber, Hasn Freiherr, and partners.)

A biographical account in German of the men who were most instrumental in introducing printing in the German language into Austrian-Hungarian towns.

In Archiv für Deutschen Buchhandels, vol. VII, p.62.

EARLY PRINTING IN AUSTRIA Literature

Cabinet 26 Shelf 1 No. 20

(Vienna, 1500) Wappenholzschnitte aus Wiener fruhdrucken. von Hedwig Gollob. Illus. Bibliographical.

Article in the "Gutenberg-Gesellschaft Jahrbuch" 1930, pp.166-174.

EARLY PRINTING

Cabinet J Shelf 4 No. 17

Type Facsimile Society. Publication of the Society for the years 1900-1909. Printed by Horace Hart. At the Oxford University Press, Oxford.
Plates with type specimens 15th century printers. For any particular printer, see Index.

(2 boxes; 13½ x 10½ x 4 in.)

EARLY PRINTING IN AUSTRIA. [Literature of]

Cabinet 22 Shelf 1 No. 4

Gratz, 1564. Printing and book trade in the 16th century.) Grazer buchdruck und buchhandel im sechzehnten jahrhundert, von Anton Schlossar.

In Archiv für Deutschen Buchdrucker, vol.IV p.54

EARLY PRINTING IN AUSTRIA. [Literature of]

Cabinet 20 Shelf 2 No. 19

Vienna, (1545?), Therese Andreter.

See Bibles. Narrenbible. Das Rätsel das Narrenbible.

EARLY PRINTING,

Cabinet 75 Shelf 2 No. 2

Use of the galley in Elizabethan Printing, by R.B. McKerrow.

In Transactions of the Bibliographical Society, "The Library," Vol. II, 1921-1922, pp. 97-108.

EARLY PRINTING IN AUSTRIA [Literature of]

Cabinet 22 Shelf 1 No. 19

(Laibach, 1575-1580. Johann Manuel, Laibach's first printer.) Johann Manuel, Laibach's erster buchdrucker, von Friedrich Ahn.

In Archiv für Deutschen Buchhandels, vol. XIX, p.45.

EARLY PRINTING IN BELGIUM Literature of

Cabinet U Shelf 1 No. 49

Antwerp, 1525-1614.

See POLLARD, ALFRED W. Records of the English Bible...London, 1911.

EARLY PRINTING [Literature of]

Cabinet AA Shelf 5 No. 15

Vindel, Pedro. Bibliografia grafica: Reproduccion en facsimil de partatas, retratos, colofones, y otras curiosidades utiles a los bibliofilos. Reunida y publicada por Pedro Vindel. Madrid, 1910. 2 Vols.

Half morocco; 9½ x 7 in.

EARLY PRINTING IN AUSTRIA. [Literature of]

Cabinet 22 Shelf 1 No. 4

(Leopold, Alexander, The first printer in Graz, 1559: Printing and bookselling in Graz in the 16th century.) Grazer Buchdruck und Buchhandel im sechzehnten Jahrhundert. von Anton Schloffar.

Survey of the business methods, with prices of labour and materials.

In Archiv für Deutschen Buchhandels, vol.IV, 1879, p.54.

EARLY PRINTING IN BELGIUM Literature

Cabinet W Shelf 2 No. 2.01

(Antwerp, 1540 to 1625, family of Martin Nuyts (Nutius)

see NUTIUS (Nuyts), C.J. Essai sur l'imprimerie de...

EARLY PRINTING, Literature of (see also

Cabinet Shelf No.

BIBLE LITERATURE
BIBLES
BIBLIOGRAPHY
BOOKS ABOUT BOOKS
BOOK CATALOGUES
INCUNABULA
INCUNABULA, Literature of

EARLY PRINTING IN AUSTRIA. [Literature of]

Cabinet 22 Shelf 1 No. 15

See Publishing, Austria. Siebenburgen (Transylvania.) 1500 to 1890.

EARLY PRINTING IN BELGIUM (Literature of)

Cabinet 76 Shelf 1 No. 7

Bruges, Early printing at: A paper read before the Bibliographical Society, by W.H. James Weale, London, May 16, 1898.

Half; morocco; 8 3/4 x 7 in. pp.14

EARLY PRINTING IN BELGIUM. (Literature of)

Cabinet V Shelf 1 No. 42

Bruges: Recherches sur les imprimeurs brugeois Par Albert Visart de Bocarmé. A Bruges, 1928
Biographies printers, printer mark, facsimile, etc.
Printed by Desclée de Brouwer et Cie, on the occasion of the fiftieth anniversary of their establishment at Bruges.

Half morocco; 11½ x 8 3/4 in.

EARLY PRINTING IN BELGIUM. Literature of.

Cabinet I Shelf 3 No. 28

[Illustrated books before the 18th century. Engravings, Belgium].

See FUNCK M. Livre Belge a gravures ... Paris et Bruxelles. 1925.

EARLY PRINTING IN BELGIUM Literature

Cabinet B Shelf 2 No. 21

Netherlands, 1500-1540

see

NIJHOFF, WOUTER. l'Art typographique dans les Pays-Bas...

EARLY PRINTING IN BELGIUM (Literature of)

Cabinet W Shelf 4 No. 30

Bruges, 1476. L'Imprimeur Colard Mansion et le Boccace de la bibliotheque d'Amiens. Par Henry Michel. Ouvrage accompagné de XI planches en phototypie. Pour le Société Française de Bibliographie. Paris, 1925.
Bio-bibliographical account.

Half morocco; 13-1/8 x 10-1/8 in.

EARLY PRINTING IN BELGIUM. [Literature]

Cabinet 75 Shelf 2 No. 9

Importation of Low Country and French books into England, 1480 and 1502-3.

See Plomer, H. R. Importations...

EARLY PRINTING IN BELGIUM (Lit. of)

Cabinet U Shelf 1 No. 1a

Plantin, Christopher, by Reginald S. Faber.

In excerpts relating to printing from "The Library," pp. 108-123, 129-147 of pencilled folios.

EARLY PRINTING IN BELGIUM (Literature of)

Cabinet 76 Shlef 2 No. 2

Doesburg, Jan van, printer at Antwerp. By Robert Proctor. Printed for the Bibliographical Society, London, Dec., 1894. With plates (12).
Biographical.

Half morocco; 11 x 9 in.

EARLY PRINTING IN BELGIUM. [Literature of]

Cabinet 18 Shelf 2 No. 1

See Journalism, Belgium. Newspapers in Belgium. The history of.

EARLY PRINTING IN BELGIUM. Literature of

Cabinet S Shelf 5 No. 3

Plantin, Christopher: A review of four books dealing with the subject of Plantin, his life, works, correspondence, house, etc. Paris, 1866. Excerpt from unidentified publication.

Bound in collection "Printers and their Plants," item 17.

EARLY PRINTING IN BELGIUM. [Literature of]

Cabinet 75 Shelf 1 No. 4

Early printing at Bruges: A paper read before the Bibliographical Society, by W. H. James Weale, May 16, 1898.

In Trans. Biblio. Soc., Vol. IV, pp. 202-212.

EARLY PRINTING IN BELGIUM. [Literature of]

Cabinet V Shelf 3 No. 5

See Lambinet, Pierre. Origine de l'imprimerie d'apres les titres authentiques.. , des établissemens de cet art dans la Belgique... Paris, 1810.

EARLY PRINTING IN BELGIUM. Literature of

Cabinet 6 Shelf 2 No. 14

Plantin-Moretus, le Museum. Contenant la vie et l'oeuvre de Chriostphe Plantin et de ses successeurs, les Moretus, ainsi que la déscription de Musée et des collections qu'il renferme. Par Max Rooses, conservateur. Anvers, 1914-16.

Full morocco; 17-7/8 x 13-3/8 x 2-3/4 in.

EARLY PRINTING IN BELGIUM (Lit. of)

Cabinet 18 Shelf 2 No. 1

See First Occurrences. Belgian newspapers The first Belgian Newspapers.

EARLY PRINTING IN BELGIUM. [Literature]

Cabinet 75 Shelf 2 No. 1

Mansion Colard, by Seymour de Ricci. Abstract of a paper read before the Bibliographical Society, March 22, 1926.

In Trans. Biblio. Soc. "The Library," Vol. I, 1920-1921, pp. 95-6.

EARLY PRINTING IN BELGIUM [Literature of]

Cabinet V Shelf 3 No. 4

See Printing, Historical, Lambinet, Pierre: Recherches historical...sur l'origine de l'imprimerie; particulièrement...dans la Belgium...Bruxelles [1799]

EARLY PRINTING IN BELGIUM. Literature

Cabinet FF Shelf 3 No. 50

[Flemish printers of the 16th century, and the Civilite-types of Robert Granjon] Die civilité-schriften des Robert Granjon in Lyon und de flämischen drucker des 16 Jahrhunderts. von Maurits Sabbe und Marius Audin. Wien, 1929. Facs.

Boards; 11¼ x 7½ in.

EARLY PRINTING IN BELGIUM. Literature of

Cabinet W Shelf 5 No. 31

See MOTTELEY, CHARLES. Aperçu sur les errors de la Bibliographie spéciale des Elzevirs... Paris, 1848.

EARLY PRINTING IN BELGIUM. Literature of

Cabinet W Shelf 4 No. 38

Recherches historiques et critiques sur la vie et les éditions de Thierry Martens (Martinus Mertens). Par feu M.J. de Gand, d'Alost. Alost, 1845.

Cloth; 8½ x 5½ in.

EARLY PRINTING IN THE BERMUDA ISLANDS. (Lit.)

Cabinet S Shelf 5 No. 25-03

Project for printing in Bermuda, 1772. By Douglas C. McMurtrie. Chicago. Privately printed, 1928. Pamphlet.

In folder labelled McMurtrie. Pamphlets relating to the history of printing.

EARLY PRINTING IN BOHEMIA. Literature of

Cabinet 26 Shelf 1 No. 16

Prague, 1487-1620. By Paul Krasnopolski. [Biobiblio. essay].

See "Gutenberg-Gesellschaft Jahrbuch, 1927," pp.72-84.

EARLY PRINTING IN BOHEMIA. Literature

Cabinet D Shelf 1 No. 59

Prague, 1495, Jan Kamp. The Utraquist Passional of 1495. (Bibliographical account of) By Zdenek Tobolka, Prague, 1926.

Paper; $12\frac{1}{4}$ x 8 in. Item in case.

EARLY PRINTING IN BOHEMIA (Lit. of)

Cabinet 75 Shelf 2 No. 2

(Prague, 1562). A little-known Bohemian Herbal. A paper by S. Savage, and read before the Bibliographical Society, London. Sept, 1921. Illus.

In Trans. Biblio. Soc. "The Library," vol. II, 1921-1922. pp. 117-131.

EARLY PRINTING IN CANADA. (Lit. of)

Stack A Shelf 1&2 Number 53

Bullen, Henry Lewis. Histories of printing in the Dominion of Canada. In The Inland Printer, vol. 53, p.555. Illus.

EARLY PRINTING IN CANADA. Literature

Cabinet Shelf No.

[Manitoba] The first printing in Manitoba. Illus. by Douglas C. McMurtrie.

Article in Printing Review of Canada, Vol. 6, No. 5, Oct. 1930. pp. 22-27.

EARLY PRINTING IN CANADA. Literature

Cabinet Shelf No.

Printing in Canada from 1752 to 1931.

Article in British & Colonial Printer, vol. 109, No.166, Dec. 31, 1931, p.634.

EARLY PRINTING IN CANADA Literature

Cabinet S Shelf 5 No. 50.01

Vancouver industries, the place of printing in. By L.E. Dennison. (Newspaper excerpt, n.d. circa 1900.)

In envelope.

EARLY PRINTING IN BR. COLUMBIA Literature

Cabinet R Shelf 4 No. 173

Victoria; a print shop tells the history of a province. By Stephen Wentworth. Excerpt from "Man-to-Man" Aug. 1910, pp.535-39

Has portrait of Wolfenden, King's printer, and picture of the first Victoria Provincial Printing Plant.

Item in manila envelope

EARLY PRINTING IN NOVA SCOTIA

Cabinet 00 Shelf 4 No. 48

Halifax, 1751. Early journalism in Nova Scotia. A paper read by J. J. Stewart, Dec. 8, 1887.

On p. 91 of the Collections of the Nova Scotia Historical Society for the year 1887-88, Vol. VI, Halifax, N. S.

Boards; $8\frac{3}{4}$ x 5-7/8 in.

EARLY PRINTING IN CHINA Literature of

Cabinet V Shelf 5 No. 19

[Bibliography of books printed and published in China by Europeans, in the 17th and 18th centuries).

See CORDIER, HENRI. L'Imprimerie Sino-Europeenne en Chine...Paris, 1901.

EARLY PRINTING IN CHINA (Literature of)

Stack A Shelf 1&2 No. 53

Bullen, Henry Lewis. Histories of printing and paper: China and Japan, in The Inland Printer, vol.LIII, p.860

EARLY PRINTING IN CHINA. [Literature of]

Cabinet T Shelf 4 No. 17

Certain old Chinese notes or Chinese paper money. A communication presented to the American Academy of Arts and Sciences, by Andrew McFarland Davis. Boston, 1915. Illus.

Cloth; 9-5/8 x $6\frac{1}{2}$ x $\frac{1}{2}$ in.

EARLY PRINTING IN CHINA (Literature)

Cabinet 20 Shelf 2 No. 19

Chinesische Buchdruck. Von...Dr. Adolf Schmidt of Darmstadt.

In Zeitschrift für Bücherfreunde, 1927, pp. 11-20

EARLY PRINTING IN CHINA Literature

Cabinet Y Shelf 1 No. 95.01

I - Chinesischen buchdruckerkunst, von der alten. II Der unbewegliche holzschnittdruck: Die enstehung. III - Buchdruck mit beweglichen lettern. von Ting Wen-Yuan.

Article in the "Gutenberg-Gesellschaft Jahrbuch" 1929, pp.9-17.

EARLY PRINTING IN CHINA [Literature of]

Cabinet 79 Shelf 1 No. 7

(Macao, 1590) Nota bibliografica sobre un libro impreso en Macao en 1590. Por José Toribio Medina. Sevilla, 1894.

Cloth; $9\frac{1}{2}$ x $6\frac{3}{4}$ in.

EARLY PRINTING IN DENMARK (Lit. of)

Cabinet AA Shelf 5 No. 36

Boghistoriske studier: Til Dansk bibliografi, 1550-1660. Lauritz Nielsen, Copenhavn, 1923. Facsimiles, reproductions of types, initials, borders, ornaments, etc.

Bio-bibliographical account, with consideration of the type material used by the printers of Denmark.

Half morocco; $11\frac{3}{4}$ x $8\frac{1}{2}$ in.

EARLY PRINTING IN DENMARK (Lit of)

Cabinet 18 Shelf 1 No. 2

(Concerning the history of printing in Northern Germany and Denmark] Zur danischen und norddeutschen Druckergeschichte.

An account and summary of booklet published to celebrate the tricentenary in 1906 of the founding of the Royal Library in Copenhagen.

In Zeitschrift für Bücherfreunde, 1907-8, part 1, p.177.

EARLY PRINTING IN DENMARK (Literature of)

Cabinet AA, Shelf 5, No. 32

Copenhagen, 1574-1583. Andreas Gutterwitz. Et Okant Kopenhammstrych av ar 1582. Ragner Dalhberg, Helsingfors, 1925.
Bibliographical essay in Collijn's "Bok-ock biblioteks historika studier ... Uppsala 1925. pp. 295-301.

Boards; 11 x 8½ x 2 in.

EARLY PRINTING IN DENMARK. (Lit. of)

Cabinet AA, Shelf 5, No. 32 (33)

Dansk Bibliografi, 1482-1550: Med saerligt hensyn til Dansk bogtrykkerkunst historie. Af Lauritz Nielsen, Kobenhavn og Kristiania. 1919. Facsimiles, reproduction letters, borders, vignettes, etc.
Bio-bibliographical historical account.

Half morocco; 11¾ x 9¼ in.

EARLY PRINTING IN DENMARK. (Lit. of)

Cabinet AA, Shelf 5, No. 32

Danske Palaeotyper tryke i Paris [Christiern Pedersen, 1507]. Sofus Larson, Kópenhamn, 1925. Reproductions.
Bio-bibliographical essay in Collijn's "Bok-ock biblioteks historika studier ... Uppsala, 1925. pp. 183-197.

Boards; 11 x 8¼ x 2 in.

EARLY PRINTING IN DENMARK. [Literature]

Cabinet 75, Shelf 2, No. 1

Denmark, Early typography of. A review by Victor Scholderer of the book "Dansk Bibliografi, 1482-1550," by Af Lauritz Nielsen, Copenhagen, 1919.

In Transactions of the Bibliographical Society, "The Library," Vol. I, 1920-1921, pp. 179-182.

EARLY PRINTING IN DENMARK (Lit. of)

Cabinet S, Shelf 5, No. 12

(Horn books and primers in Denmark). Bidrag til ABC-litteraturens historie I Danmark. Af Julius Clausen. Excerpt from Tidsskriftet, Copenhagen, 1896. Illus.

Bound in collection " Pamphlets and excerpts relating to typographical matters," item 25.

EARLY PRINTING IN DENMARK [Literature of]

Cabinet AA, Shelf 5, No. 35

Lorentz Benedicht, bogtrykker og xylograf i Kobenhavn i sidst halvdel af det XVI aarhundrede. Bibliografi med indledning af R. Paulli, Kobenhavn, 1920. Facsimiles.
Bio-bibliographical account.

Half morocco; 10¼ x 7½ in.

EARLY PRINTING IN EAST INDIES. (Lit. of)

Cabinet S, Shelf 5, No. 1

(First printers in Batavia, East Indies.) De eerste compagnies drukkers te Batavia, by J. W. Enschede, Amsterdam, 1911.

Bound in collection "Various Printing Plants Brochures," item 8.

EARLY PRINTING IN ENGLAND. (Lit. of)

Cabinet U, Shelf 1, No. 1f

Abree, James, printer and bookseller of Canterbury, by Henry R. Plomer.

In excerpts relating to printing from The Library, 1912-13, p.82 of pencilled folios.

EARLY PRINTING IN ENGLAND. (Literature of)

Cabinet 76, Shelf 1, No. 5

Abstracts from the wills of English printers and stationers from 1492 to 1630, by Henry R. Plomer. Printed for the Bibliographical Society, London, Feb. 1903.

Half morocco, 8-3/4 x 7 ins. pp. 54.

EARLY PRINTING IN ENGLAND. [Literature of]

Cabinet 76, Shelf 2, No. 17

Almanacks and prognostications, English printed: A bibliographical history to the year 1600, by Eustace Bosanquet. Printed for the Bibliographical Society at the Chiswick Pres. London, 1917.
Illus. Monograph XVII.

Boards; 11 x 9 in.

EARLY PRINTING IN ENGLAND. Literature of

Cabinet 75, Shelf 1, No. 5

Bath books early (16th century). A paper read before the Bibliographical Society, London, Dec. 1898.
(Brief Summary).

In Trans. Biblio. Soc., Vol. V, 1898-1900, pp. 6-7.

EARLY PRINTING IN ENGLAND Literature

Cabinet T, Shelf 2, No. 95

Bell, John, 1745-1831, bookseller, printer, publisher, typefounder, journalist, etc...
By Stanley Morison. Printed for the author at the University Press. Cambridge, 1930. Illus.

Cloth; 10 x 6½ x 1½ in.

EARLY PRINTING IN ENGLAND. [Literature of]

Cabinet 75, Shelf 1, No. 8

Berthelet, Thomas, notes on the types, borders, etc., used by. A paper by W. W. Greg, for the Bibliographical Society.

In Trans. Biblio. Soc., Vol. VIII, 1904-1906, pp. 187-220.

EARLY PRINTING IN ENGLAND. Literature of

Cabinet U, Shelf 1, No. 12

Bibles printed in England and Scotland, 1541 to 1811, chronological list of.

See BIBLE SOCIETIES IN SCOTLAND. Memorial ...Edinburgh, 1824.

EARLY PRINTING IN ENGLAND. [Literature of]

Cabinet U, Shelf 1, No. 1c

See Biographies, printers. Bynneman, Henry, printer, 1566-83.

EARLY PRINTING IN ENGLAND. [Literature

Cabinet 75, Shelf 2, No. 7

Birchley Hall Secret Press, The. A paper read before the Bibliographical Society, by Arthur J. Hawkes, with a criticism of the paper by C. A. Newdigate. Feb. 15, 1926. Facsimile of title page.

In Transactions of the Bibliographical Society, "The Library," Vol. VII, 1926-1927, pp. 303-320.

EARLY PRINTING IN ENGLAND Literature

Cabinet JJ, Shelf 2, No. 13

Birth and youth of English printing. By H. M. Duncan.

Illus. article in United Typothetae of America Official Souvenir. Eighth Annual Convention, Philadelphia, Sept.,1894, p.33

Stiff paper; 10½ x 7-3/8. In envelope.

EARLY PRINTING IN ENGLAND. Literature

Cabinet T, Shelf 5, No. 29

Bolton bibliography and jottings of book-lore; with notes on local authors and printers. By Jas. C. Scholes, Manchester, 1886.

Cloth; 7-5/8 x 5-1/8 in.

EARLY PRINTING IN ENGLAND Literature

Cabinet Q Shelf 1 No. 12

Book-trade, 1557-1625. By H.G. Aldis. Reprinted from The Cambridge History of English Literature, Vol. IV, 1909. Pamphlet.

Item in envelope.

EARLY PRINTING IN ENGLAND. (Lit. of)

Cabinet U Shelf 1 No. 1f

Cambridge fragments; with more important additions than that in previous article in The Library for 1911. By Charles Sayle.

In Excerpts relating to printing from The Library, 1912-13, p.42 of pencilled folios.

EARLY PRINTING IN ENGLAND Literature

Cabinet T Shelf 2 No. 71

Caxton, William, and the development of the art of printing in England and Scotland.

See Bullen, George. Caxton Celebration 1877...pp. 1-49, and sections 1-V11.

EARLY PRINTING IN ENGLAND. [Literature of]

Cabinet 75 Shelf 2 No. 8

Books and readers, 1591-4: Variations in methods of entry in the Stationers' Register. By G. B. Harrison. Read before the Bibliographical Society, 17 Oct., 1927.

In Trans. Biblio. Soc., Vol. VIII, 1927-1928, pp. 273-302.

EARLY PRINTING IN ENGLAND. Literature

Cabinet 75 Shelf 2 No. 2

Cambridge University Press: A review of S. C. Robert's History, by A. W. Pollard.

In Transactions of the Bibliographical Society, "The Library," Vol. II, 1921-1922, pp. 205-9.

EARLY PRINTING IN ENGLAND. (Lit. of)

Cabinet S Shelf 4 No. 120

Caxton (The) Celebration of 1877; Lessons of. By J. G. Shea. An excerpt from the Catholic World, June, 1877.
Item 3 in volume "About the Bible; Excerpts from Magazines".

Half morocco; 10¼ x 6-7/8 in.

EARLY PRINTING IN ENGLAND. Literature

Cabinet 75 Shelf 2 No. 5

Border-pieces used by English printers before 1641: Paper read before the Bibliographical Society, by Ronald B. McKerrow, Jan. 21, 1924.

In Trans. Biblio. Soc., "The Library," Vol. V, 1924-25, pp. 1-37.

EARLY PRINTING IN ENGLAND Literature

Cabinet U N Shelf 2 No. 142

Cambridge University Press, and John Siebercht the first printer of.

See BOWES, ROBERT and G.J.GRAY Siberch, John...

EARLY PRINTING IN ENGLAND. (Lit. of)

Cabinet U Shelf 1 No. 1g

Cirencester, 1753. Samuel Rudder: An account by Roland Austin.

In excerpts relating to printing from The Library, 1914-15, p.136 of pencilled folios.

EARLY PRINTING IN ENGLAND (Lit. of)

Stack A Shelf 1&2 Number 54-57

Bullen, Henry Lewis: Great Britain: The literature of typography. In the Inland Printer, vol. 54, p. 797;,vol. 55, pp. 60, 493, 635, 779; vol. 56, pp. 60, 345; Vol. 57, pp. 635, 781. Illus.

EARLY PRINTING IN ENGLAND. (Lit. Of)

Cabinet U Shelf 1 No. 1f

Canterbury, 1717, Thomas Reeve: "The Kentish Post" and "Canterbury News Letter." Bibliographical note by William F. Cock.

In Excerpts relating to printing from "The Library," 1912-13, p. 137 of pencilled folio

---

EARLY PRINTING IN ENGLAND. [Literature]

Cabinet 75 Shelf 1 No. 14

City printers, The. by Charles Welch. A brief account of the printers who were chosen to fill this official position. With some bibliographical extracts from the Corporation Records at Guildhall.

In Trans. Biblio. Soc., Vol. XIV, 1915-1917, pp. 175-241.

EARLY PRINTING IN ENGLAND. Literature of.

Cabinet 76 Shelf 1 No. 15

Cambridge, 1504 to 1699. Abstracts from the wills of printers, binders and stationers of Cambridge, from 1504 to 1699. By George J. Gray and William Mortlock Palmer. London: Printed for the Bibliographical Society, 1915.

Half morocco; 8-5/8 x 6-7/8 x ¾ in.

EARLY PRINTING IN ENGLAND (Literature of)

Stack A Shelf 1&2 Number 67

Caslon, William and his types, by Henry Lewis Bullen, in The Inland Printer, vol.LXVII, p.51. Illus.

EARLY PRINTING IN ENGLAND Literature of

Cabinet U Shelf 4 No. 108

Commemoration of the first folio tercentenary. With a catalogue of Shakespeariana exhibited in the Hall of The Worshipful Company of Stationers, illustrative facsimiles, and introduction by Sir Israel Gollancz. London. 1923. Pamphlet.
Bound in with three other items relating to The Stationers Company.

Half morocco; 11¼ x 8-3/4 x 1 in.

EARLY PRINTING IN ENGLAND. (Lit. of)

Cabinet U Shelf 1 No. 1e

Cambridge fragments, by Charles Sayle. Includes one folded sheet and one plate.
Miscellaneous specimen of early printing and engraving found during the process of architectural reconstruction of the University.

In excerpts relating to printing from "The Library," 1911-12, p. 238 of pencilled folio

---

EARLY PRINTING IN ENGLAND. [Lit. of].

Cabinet U Shelf 4 No. 102

Catalogue of an exhibition of books, etc. illustrative of the history and progress of printing and bookselling in England 1477-1800. Held at Stationers' Hall, 25-29 June 1912.

Cloth; 8½ x 6½ x ¾ in.

EARLY PRINTING IN ENGLAND [Literature of]

Cabinet BB Shelf 2 No. 19
also BB-2-33
C-2-31,p.10

American Type Founders Co.
"A compend of the origin and growth of the Roman Letter in Reed's Old English Letter-Founders." [c1905]

Pamphlet. 24 pp. 9" x 11-1/2"

BB-2-33 copy differs slightly. Also lacks insert.

EARLY PRINTING IN ENGLAND. (Literature of)

Cabinet U — Shelf 1 — No. 1f

Copland, Robert, and Pierre Gringoire, by William E.A. Axon.

In excerpts relating to printing from The Library, 1912-13, p.77 of pencilled folios.

EARLY PRINTING IN ENGLAND. Literature of.

Cabinet 75 — Shelf 1 — No. 6

Curriculum and text books of English schools in the first half of the seventeenth century: A paper read before the Bibliographical Society by Professor Foster Watson, Feb. 1, 1902.

In Trans. Biblio. Soc. Vol. VI, 1900-1902, pp. 159-267.

EARLY PRINTING IN ENGLAND. Literature

Cabinet T — Shelf 2 — No. 96

Dawks, Ichabod, 1635-1731, and his News-Letter. With an account of the Dawks family of booksellers and stationers. By Stanley Morison. Cambridge: at the University Press, 1931. With illus., facs and specimens of type.

Cloth; 13 x 9 x $\frac{1}{2}$ in.

EARLY PRINTING IN ENGLAND. Literature.

Cabinet 75 — Shelf 2 — No. 3

Day, John. Note by W. W. Greg on two issues of the Isle of Gulls.

In Transactions of the Bibliographical Society, "The Library," Vol. III, 1922-23, pp. 307-9.

EARLY PRINTING IN ENGLAND [Literature of]

Cabinet X — Shelf 4 — No. 16

Declaration of the Lords and Commons assembled in Parliament...concerning irregular printing and for the suppressing of all false and scandalous pamphlets. Die Sabbathi, Aug. 27, 1642. Ordered by the Lords and Commons... London. Small brochure.

Bound in with 5 other items on the same subject, for the years 1641, 1642, and 1647.

Boards; 7-5/8 x 6 in.

EARLY PRINTING IN ENGLAND. Literature of.

Cabinet 76 — Shelf 1 — No. 17

Dictionary of the printers and booksellers who were at work in England, Scotland and Ireland from 1726 to 1775. By H. R. Plomer ... Printed for the Bibliographical Society, at the Oxford Press, 1932 (for 1930).

Boards, linen back; $8\frac{3}{4}$ x 7 x 1-5/8 in.

EARLY PRINTING IN ENGLAND. (Literature of)

Stack A — Shelf 1&2 — Number 62

(Dr.) Fell and the University Press at Oxford, by Henry Lewis Bullen, in (Collectanea Typographica) The Inland Printer, vol.LXII, p. 527.

EARLY PRINTING IN ENGLAND. (Lit. of)

Cabinet U — Shelf 1 — No. 1a

Duff, E. Gordon: Frederick Egmondt, an English XV Century stationer.

Bibliographical account of the earliest printing in England.

In Excerpts relating to printing from "The Library" [n.d.] p. 172 of pencilled folios.

EARLY PRINTING IN ENGLAND. (Lit. of)

Cabinet T — Shelf 1 — No. 26

Dunton, John, 1659-1733. London, Life and letters of. Written by himself Printed by S. Malthus, 1705. London.

Dunton was an eccentric publisher author. His book gives some interesting accounts of his relations with British and New England printers.

Half morocco; $6\frac{3}{4}$ x 4-3/8 x $1\frac{1}{2}$ in. See also T/1/27.

EARLY PRINTING IN ENGLAND. [Literature of]

Cabinet 75 — Shelf 1 — No. 5

Earliest Latin grammars in English. A paper read before the Bibliographical Society by Rev. A. E. Shaw, Feb. 20, 1899. Illus. Wood Cuts.

In Trans. Biblio. Soc., Vol. V, 1898-1900, pp. 39-65.

EARLY PRINTING IN ENGLAND. (Literature of)

Cabinet 75 — Shelf 2 — No. 8

Earliest tables of the highways of England and Wales, 1541-61. By Sir Herbert George Fordham. London, Dec., 1927. Facsimile.

In Transactions of the Bibliographical Society, 1927-1928. Vol. VIII, pp. 349-54. "The Library."

EARLY PRINTING IN ENGLAND. Literature

Cabinet 75 — Shelf 2 — No. 3

Early printed books at Corpus Christi College, Cambridge, with hand-list. Compiled by Stephen Gaselee. A review of book with above title.

In Transactions of the Bibliographical Society, "The Library," Vol. III, 1922-23, pp. 61-2.

EARLY PRINTING IN ENGLAND. Literature.

Cabinet 75 — Shelf 2 — No. 3

Eliot's Court Press. Decorative blocks and initials by Henry R. Plomer.

Includes facsimiles of decorative blocks and initial letters.

In Transactions of the Bibliographical Society, "The Library," Vol. III, 1922-23, pp. 194-209.

EARLY PRINTING IN ENGLAND. Literature.

Cabinet 75 — Shelf 2 — No. 2

Eliot's court printing house, The. 1584-1674: a paper by H. R. Plomer.

In Transactions of the Bibliographical Society, "The Library," Vol. II, 1921-22, pp. 175-184.

EARLY PRINTING IN ENGLAND. [Literature]

Cabinet 75 — Shelf 2 — No. 4

Elizabethan printer and his copy, An. A paper by W. W. Greg.

In Transactions of the Bibliographical Society, The Library, "Vol. IV, 1923-24, pp. 102-118.

EARLY PRINTING IN ENGLAND. [Literature of]

Cabinet 75 — Shelf 2 — No. 5

Elizabethan printers and the composition of reprints. By Ronald B. McKerrow.

In Transactions of the Bibliographical Society, "The Library," Vol. V. 1924-1925, pp. 357-364.

EARLY PRINTING IN ENGLAND. [Literature of]

Cabinet 76 — Shelf 2 — No. 30

English and Scottish printing types, 1501-35, 1508-41. Collected and annotated by Frank Isaac. Printed for the Bibliographical Society, at the Oxford University Press, 1930. Facsimiles and Illustrations No. II.

Boards; $11\frac{1}{4}$ x 9 in.

EARLY PRINTING IN ENGLAND Literature

Cabinet U — Shelf 1 — No. 49

English Bible printing, 1525-1611.

See POLLARD, ALFRED W. Records of the English Bible...London, 1911.

EARLY PRINTING IN ENGLAND. [Literature of]

Cabinet 75 Shelf 1 No. 8

English book trade before the incorporation of the Stationers' Company: A paper read before the Bibliographical Society, by Mr. E. Gordon Duff, Jan. 16, 1905.
Summary.

In Trans. Biblio. Soc., Vol. VIII, 1904-1906, pp. 10-14.

EARLY PRINTING IN ENGLAND. Literature of

Cabinet T Shelf 1 No. 7 to 9

English literature 1668 to 1709 A.D. The term catalogue.

See ARBER, EDWARD. Term catalogues, 1668-1709...London, 1903 to 1906.

EARLY PRINTING IN ENGLAND. (Literature of)

Cabinet U Shelf 1 No. 1J

Extra gill and the full quart pot: A bibliographical study. By George Watson Cole, London, 1919. Facsimile pages.

A critical examination of methods practised by the early printers to secure uniformity of close spacing.

In Excerpts relating to printing from The Library, 1915-17, pp.249-67 of pencilled folios.

EARLY PRINTING IN ENGLAND. [Literature]

Cabinet 75 Shelf 1 No. 13

English current writing and early printing. By Hilary Jenkinson. A paper read before the Bibliographical Society, Feb. 15, 1915.

In Trans. Biblio. Soc., Vol. XIII, 1913-15, pp. 273-295.

EARLY PRINTING IN ENGLAND. [Literature]

Cabinet 75 Shelf 2 No. 8

English printed almanacks and prognostications. A bibliogrpahical history to the year 1600 By E. F. Bosanquet.

In Transactions of the Bibliographical Society, "The Library," Vol. VIII, 1927-28, pp. 456-477.

EARLY PRINTING IN ENGLAND (Literature of)

Cabinet U Shelf 1 No. 1d

False dates in Shakespearian quartos, by William Jaggard.

In excerpts relating to printing from The Library, 1909, p.71 of pencilled folios.

EARLY PRINTING IN ENGLAND. [Lit. of]

Cabinet 76 Shelf 1 No. 12

English editions ... of Greek and Latin Classics printed before 1641. By Henrietta R. Palmer With an introduction by Victor Scholderer. London: Printed for the Bibliographical Society, Dec. 1911.

Boards, linen back; 8-7/8 x 7 x 5/8 in.

EARLY PRINTING IN ENGLAND. (Lit. of)

Cabinet 75 Shelf 1 No. 4

English printers and booksellers of the 16th century, new documents on. By H. R. Plomer. Paper read Nov. 15th, 1897 before the Bibliographical Society.

In Trans. Biblio Soc. Vol. 4, 1896-1898. pp. 153-183.

EARLY PRINTING IN ENGLAND. (Literature of)

Cabinet U Shelf 1 No. 1e

False dates in Shakespeare quartos, by A.W. Pollard.

In excerpts relating to printing from The Library, 1911-12, p.49 of pencilled folios.

EARLY PRINTING IN ENGLAND. Literature.

Cabinet 75 Shelf 1 No. 9

English fifteenth century broadsides. A paper read before the Bibliopgraphical Society by E. Gordon Duff. December 16th, 1907

In Trans. Biblio. Soc., Vol. IX, 1906-1908, pp. 211-227.

EARLY PRINTING IN ENGLAND. Literature

Cabinet T Shelf 6 No. 61

English printing, 1700-1925. A note by Strickland Gibson M.A.
Booklet presented "With the compliments of Dulau & Company " London, 1925.

In box labelled "English printing and printers. Shakespeariana. Misc. v.d."

EARLY PRINTING IN ENGLAND. [Literature]

Cabinet 75 Shelf 2 No. 7

Fell, John. Specimens of books at Oxford with the types given to the University by. Book with same title reviewed by R. B. McKerrow.

In Transactions of the Bibliographical Society, "The Library," Vol. VII, 1926-27, pp. 225-7.

EARLY PRINTING IN ENGLAND. Literature

Cabinet R Shelf 6 No. 42

English 15th century printing. A series of facsimiles of all the types used in England during the 15th century...With an introduction by E. Gordon Duff. London, 1896.

Linen portfolio, tied; 16 x 12 in.

EARLY PRINTING IN ENGLAND. (Literature)

Cabinet U Shelf 4 No. 111 2 vols.

English tracts, pamphlets and printed sheets: A Bibliography. By J. Harvey Bloom. Vol. I (Early period) 1473-1650. (Suffolk). Vol. II (Early Period) Leicestershire, Staffordshire, Warwickshire and Worcestershire. London, 1922
Bibliography is arranged alphabetically under authors, noteworthy people and places.

Cloth; 9 x 5-7/8 in.

EARLY PRINTING IN ENGLAND Literature of

Cabinet U Shelf 5 No. 3

Field, Richard, London, circa 1588, his relation with Vautrollier, printer of Shakespeare editions.

See BLADES, WILLIAM. Shakespeare and typography...London, 1772, pp.26-32

EARLY PRINTING IN ENGLAND. Literature

Cabinet 75 Shelf 1 No. 9

English Herbals: A summary of books under this denomination which were printed in England. A paper read before the Bibliographical Society by Dr. J. F. Payne, Feb. 17, 1908.

In Trans. Biblio. Soc., Vol. IX, 1906-1908, pp. 120-123.

EARLY PRINTING IN ENGLAND Literature

Cabinet T Shelf 1 No. 42

Enquiry into the origin of printing in Europe... By a Lover of Art (John Baptist Jackson), London, 1752. Printed for N. Gibson.

Half morocco; $7\frac{3}{4}$ x 5 in.

EARLY PRINTING IN ENGLAND. [Literature of]

Cabinet 76 Shelf 2 No. 18

Fifteenth century English books. A bibliography of books and documents printed in England, and of books for the English market printed abroad, by E. Gordon Duff. Printed for the Bibliographical Society at the Oxford University Press, 1917.
Illus. monograph XVIII.

Boards; $11\frac{1}{4}$ x 9 in.

EARLY PRINTING IN ENGLAND. [Literature]

Cabinet 75 Shelf 2 No. 4

Fifth edition of Robert Burton's Anatomy of Melancholy: A paper read before the Bibliographical Society, by E. Gordon Duff, March, 19, 1923.

In Trans. Biblio. Soc., "The Library," Vol. IV, 1923-1924, pp. 81-101.

EARLY PRINTING IN ENGLAND (Literature of)

Cabinet 76 Shelf 1 No. 8

Hand-lists of English printers, 1501-1556, by E.G. Duff, H.R. Plomer, A.W. Pollard. Printed for the Bibliographical Society, London, 1913.

2 vols. parts I to IV. Illus.

Half morocco, each 8-3/4 x 7 in.

EARLY PRINTING IN ENGLAND (Lit. of)

Cabinet U Shelf 1 No. 1c

Jaggard, William: On certain false dates in Shakespearian quartos. By W.W. Greg.

In Excerpts relating to printing from "The Library," 1908-pp. 113-131.

EARLY PRINTING IN ENGLAND. Literature.

Cabinet 75 Shelf 2 No. 3

First English printers and their patrons, The. A paper read before the Bibliographical Society on behalf of Prof. H. B. Lathrop. February 20, 1922.

Includes classified list of works printed by William Caxton.

In Trans. Biblio. Soc., "The Library," Vol. III, 1922-23, pp. 69-96.

EARLY PRINTING IN ENGLAND. (Lit. of)

Cabinet X Shelf 5 No. 3

Hazlitt, W. Carew. Notes on early British printers: Bibliographical notes, printers and printing from 1477 to 1565. Excerpt n.n.n.d. [circa 1888].

p. 61 in vol. with binder's title "Scrap-Book, 1705-1891, relating to printing."

EARLY PRINTING IN ENGLAND. (Lit. of)

Cabinet U Shelf 1 No. 1g

Law suit [1677?] as to an early edition of Pilgrim's Progress. Account by R. Plomer.

In Excerpts relating to printing from "The Library," 1914-15, p. 30 of pencilled folios

---

EARLY PRINTING IN ENGLAND Literature

Cabinet 00 Shelf 5 No. 1 (2 vols.)

(The) Fourth Estate: Contributions towards a history of newspapers, and of the liberty of the press. By F. Knight Hunt. In two vols...London, 1850.

Cloth; 8 x 5-1/8 in.

EARLY PRINTING IN ENGLAND Literature

Cabinet 00 Shelf 5 No. 2 (2 vols.)

History of British Journalism, from the foundation of the newspaper press in England to the repeal of the stamp act in 1855. By Alexander Andrews. In 2 vols., with index. London, 1859.

Cloth; 8 x 5 x 1 in.

EARLY PRINTING IN ENGLAND Literature

Cabinet X Shelf 5 No. 115

L'Estrange, Sir Roger: a contribution to the history of the press in the 17th century. By George Kitchen, London, 1913. Illus.

Cloth; 8-3/4 x 5-3/4 in.

EARLY PRINTING IN ENGLAND. [Literature of]

Cabinet 75 Shelf 2 No. 8

Future work on the short-title catalogue of English books, 1475-1640. By Alfred W. Pollard. A paper read before the Bibliographical Society, 21 November, 1927.

In Trans. Biblio. Soc., "The Library," Vol. VIII, 1927-1928, pp. 377-394.

EARLY PRINTING IN ENGLAND. [Literature of]

Cabinet 75 Shelf 1 No. 7

Initial letters in early English printed books: A paper read before the Bibliographical Society by Charles Sayle, Nov. 17, 1902.

In Trans. Biblio. Soc., Vol. VII, 1902-1904, pp. 15-47.

EARLY PRINTING IN ENGLAND. [Literature of]

Cabinet 75 Shelf 2 No. 5

Ling, Nicholas and England's Helicon. Paper by J. William Hebel.

In Transactions of the Bibliographical Society, "The Library," Vol. V, 1924-1925, pp. 153-160.

EARLY PRINTING IN ENGLAND. (Lit. of)

Cabinet U Shelf 1 No. 1g

Gloucester, 1721. Robert Raikes, the elder, and the Glouscester Journal, by Roland Austin.

In excerpts relating to printing from The Library, 1914-15, p.99 of pencilled folios.

EARLY PRINTING IN ENGLAND. (Lit. of)

Cabinet U Shelf 1 No. 1d

Ipswich, 1548. John Oswen. A new Ipswich book of 1548. Communicated by F. G. Beck. Bibliographical description.

In Excerpts relating to printing from "The Library," p. 9 of pencilled folios.

EARLY PRINTING IN ENGLAND Literature

Cabinet T Shelf 2 No. 32

London, 1476, William Caxton.

See CAXTON, WILLIAM. Relic of the past...

EARLY PRINTING IN ENGLAND Literature

Cabinet 00 Shelf 4 No. 17

Handlist, 1620-1920, of English and Welsh newspapers. [With a history of the origin of newspapers, and early press laws]. London: The Times, 1920.

Cloth; $9\frac{3}{4}$ x $6\frac{1}{4}$ x 1 in.

EARLY PRINTING IN ENGLAND. [Literature]

Cabinet 75 Shelf 2 No. 5

Italian books printed in England before 1640. A paper read before the Bibliographical Society, by Harry Sellers. February 18, 1924. Illus.

In Transactions of the Bibliographical Society, "The Library," Vol. V, 1924-1925, pp. 105-128.

EARLY PRINTING IN ENGLAND. [LITERATURE OF]

Cabinet 75 Shelf 1 No. 3

London [ca. 1530--], Robert Wyer.

See Plomer, H. R. Wyer, Robert.

EARLY PRINTING IN ENGLAND. [Literature of]

Cabinet T Shelf 4 No. 62

London, 1536. Thomas Petyt. The A.B.C. both in Latyn and Englysch: Being a facsimile reprint of the earliest extant English reading book. With and introduction by E. S. Schuckburgh. London, 1889.

Leather; 9 x 6 x ¼ in.

EARLY PRINTING IN ENGLAND. [Literature of]

Cabinet 75 Shelf 2 No. 10

(London, 1617). Edward Allde, a typical trade printer. A paper read before the Bibliographical Society by R. B. McKerrow. London, 18 Feb. 1929. Illus. with types, devices, initials, and ornaments.

In Trans. Biblio. Soc. "The Library," vol. 10, 192-30. pp. 121-62.

EARLY PRINTING IN ENGLAND. (Literature of)

Cabinet 18 Shelf 1 No. 14

(Luther's writing in England) Luther's Schriften in England. Review of an article on same subject.

Includes a bibliographical account of the works, also the printers.

In Zeitschrift fur Bucherfreunde, 1913-14, part 1, p. 213, of Supplement ("Beiblatt")

EARLY PRINTING IN ENGLAND. Literature.

Cabinet 75 Shelf 1 No. 17

London, 1556-1571.

See Pickering, William. Earliest bookerseller on London Bridge...

EARLY PRINTING IN ENGLAND. (Lit. of)

Cabinet 75 Shelf 2 No. 8

(London, 1640). Relations between London and Edinburgh printers and stationers. A paper by F. S. Ferguson. The Bibliographical Society, 21 Feb. 1927.

In Trans. Biblio. Soc. "The Library," Vol. VIII, 1927-1928. pp. 145-198.

EARLY PRINTING IN ENGLAND. (Lit. of)

Cabinet U Shelf 1 No. 1d

Marprelate Press (1588). A new tract from the. Communicated by John Dover Wilson to "The Library," London, 1909.

In Excerpts relating to printing from "The Library," p. 78 of pencilled folios.

EARLY PRINTING IN ENGLAND. (Lit. of)

Cabinet U Shelf 1 No. 1d

London, 1560: Henry Denham, printer. Account by Henry R. Plomer, London, 1909. Bio-bibliographical historical account.

In Excerpts relating to printing from "The Library," p. 94 of pencilled folios.

EARLY PRINTING IN ENGLAND [Literature of]

Cabinet T Shelf 1 No. 17

(London, 1678) Orders, Rules and Ordinances ordained, devised and made by the Master and Keepers or Wardens and comminalty of the mystery or art of Stationers of the City of London, for the well governing of that Society. London, printed for the Company of Stationers, 1678.

Half calf; 7½ x 5½ x ¼ in. See also T/1/18

EARLY PRINTING IN ENGLAND. Literature

Cabinet T Shelf 4 No. 1

Marprelate tracts, the printers of.

See PIERCE, WILLIAM. Historical introduction fo the Marprelate Tracts...London, 1908 (see index)

EARLY PRINTING IN ENGLAND (Lit. of)

Cabinet U Shelf 1 No. 1c

London, 1566-83. Henry Bynneman, printer. By Henry R. Plomer.

In Excerpts relating to printing from "The Library," 1908, pp. 225-244.

EARLY PRINTING IN ENGLAND [Literature]

Cabinet X Shelf 4 No. 41

(London, 1693) Appeal of murther from certain unjust judges...containing a relation of the tryal, behavior and death of W. Anderton, executed June 16, 1693, at Tyburn for pretended high treason.

Andertons crime consisted in printing a pamphlet in which he was supposed to have referred to the Prince of Orange as "Hooknose".

Half morocco; 7½ x 5-7/8 x ¼ in.

EARLY PRINTING IN ENGLAND. [Literature of]

Cabinet 75 Shelf 2 No. 5

Medieval England.

See Chambers, R. W. Lost literature of.

EARLY PRINTING IN ENGLAND. (Lit. of)

Cabinet 75 Shelf 2 No. 7

London, 1574: John Day. The 1574 edition of Dr. John Caius's De Antiquitate Canterbrigiensis Academiae libri duo. By Henry R. Plomer. Illus.

In Transactions of Bibliographical Society, "The Library," Vol. VII, 1926-1927. pp. 253-268.

EARLY PRINTING IN ENGLAND. Literature.

Cabinet 75 Shelf 2 No. 6

London, 1726. Benjamin Motte. The early editions of Gulliver's Travels. By Harold William. Read before the Bibliographical Society, 16, Nov., 1925. Facsimile.

In Transactions of the Bibliographical Society, "The Library," Vol. Vi, 1925-1926. pp. 229-262.

EARLY PRINTING IN ENGLAND. [Literature]

Cabinet 75 Shelf 2 No. 4

Milton, Salmasius, and Dugard, by F. F. Madan. Facsimile title pages.

An account of the first edition of Milton Pro Populo Anglicano Defensio, and the printer of them, William Dugard.

In Transactions of the Bibliographical Society, "The Library," Vol. IV, 1923-1924, pp. 119-145.

EARLY PRINTING IN ENGLAND. Literature

Cabinet U Shelf 3 No. 103

London, 1600. John Allde, the printer at the Long Shop.

See vol. 2, p.168 Bibliographica...London, 1895-1897.

EARLY PRINTING IN ENGLAND (Literature of)

Cabinet L Shelf 4 No. 18

London, 1822, William Savage.

see SAVAGE, WILLIAM. Practical hints on decorative printing....

EARLY PRINTING IN ENGLAND. (Lit. of)

Cabinet U Shelf 1 No. 1e

"The mirror for magistrates." By Henrietta C. Bartlett.

The book with above title is an early compilation of the tragedies of English history prior to the reign of Elizabeth.

In excerpts relating to printing from The Library, 1911-12, p.262. of pencilled folios.

EARLY PRINTING IN ENGLAND Literature

Cabinet 00 Shelf 4 No. 19

Muddiman, J. G. King's journalist, 1659-1689. Studies in the reign of Charles II. With 14 illustrations. London, (1923).

Cloth; $8\frac{3}{4}$ x 6 x $1\frac{1}{2}$ in.

EARLY PRINTING IN ENGLAND. (Lit. of)

Cabinet U Shelf 1 No. 1a

Notary, Julian: A new English 15th century printer earlier than 1498, in which year appeared his edition of the Sarum Missal. An account by E. Gordon Duff.

In Excerpts relating to printing from "The Library," [n.d.]. p. 32 of pencilled folios.

EARLY PRINTING IN ENGLAND Literature

Cabinet U Shelf 3 No. 103

Notices of printers and printing in the State papers. By Henry R. Plomer.

Bibliographical sketch, with a list of printers in London and other parts of England in the year 1649.

See vol. 2, p.204, Bibliographica...London, 1895-1897.

EARLY PRINTING IN ENGLAND. (Literature of)

Cabinet Shelf No.

Munday, Anthony: His romances of chivalry. A paper by Gerald R. Hayes.

In Transactions of the Bibliographical Society,"The Library," vol. VI, pp. 57-81

EARLY PRINTING IN ENGLAND. [Literature of]

Cabinet 75 Shelf 1 No. 11

Notes on English books printed abroad, 1525-48. by Robert Steele, a paper read before the Bibliographical Society, London, Jan 16, 1911.

In Trans. Biblio. Soc., Vol. XI, 1909-1911, pp. 189-236.

EARLY PRINTING IN ENGLAND LITERATURE OF

Cabinet U Shelf 5 No. 57

Nottinghamshire printed Chap-Books, with notices of their printers and vendors. By Percy J. Cropper. Nottingham, 1892. Illus. and facsimiles.

Half morocco; 10 x $7\frac{1}{2}$ x 3/8 in.

EARLY PRINTING IN ENGLAND. [Literature of]

Cabinet 76 Shelf 2 No. 11

Music printing, the earliest English: A description and bibliography of English printed music to the close of the 16th century. By Robert Steele. London: Printed for the Bibliographical Society at the Chiswick Press December 1903.

Illus. Monograph XI.

Half morocco; 11 x 9 in.

EARLY PRINTING IN ENGLAND. Literature.

Cabinet 75 Shelf 2 No. 3

Notes on old books: A study of worm-holes, by W. W. Greg.

In Transactions of the Bibliographical Society, "The Library," Vol. III, 1922-23 pp. 53-57.

EARLY PRINTING IN ENGLAND. (Lit. of)

Cabinet 75 Shelf 2 No. 6

Ogilby, John, 1600-1676: His Britannia and the British Itineries of the eighteenth century. By Sir Herbert George Fordham. Facsimile, and portrait of John Ogilby.

In Transactions of the Bibliographical Society, vol. VI, 1925-1926. pp. 157-178. "The Library"

EARLY PRINTING IN ENGLAND. (Literature of)

Cabinet U Shelf 1 No. 1b

New Copy of the Speculum Vite Christi 1494, by Wynkyn de Worde. By Wm. May. Facsimile of one page.

In excerpts relating to printing from The Library, p.232 of pencilled folios.

EARLY PRINTING IN ENGLAND. Literature.

Cabinet 75 Shelf 2 No. 3

Notes on Shakespeare's printers and publishers. A paper read before the Bibliographical Society, by Harry Farr, November 20, 1922. Facsimiles of title pages, and imprints.

In Trans. Biblio. Soc., "The Library," Vol. III, 1922-23, pp. 225-260.

EARLY PRINTING IN ENGLAND (Lit. of)

Cabinet V Shelf 4 No. 23

Origines de l'imprimerie et son introduction en Angleterre. D'Apres de recentes publications Anglaises. Par A. Quantin. Paris, 1877.

Half morocco; $11\frac{3}{4}$ x $8\frac{1}{4}$ in.

EARLY PRINTING IN ENGLAND Literatur

Cabinet T Shelf 2 No. 33

New discovery: An Indulgence of 1476. Earliest printing in England. By Alfred W. Pollard. [Excerpt from The London Times, Feb.7, 1928]

Pasted in vol.1 of Blades "Life and typography of William Caxton"...London, 1861.

EARLY PRINTING IN ENGLAND. (Lit. of)

Cabinet U Shelf 1 No. 1j

Notes on the seventeenth century printing press of the English college of Saint Omers. By C. A. Newdigate, S. J. London, 1919.

Includes reproductions of intials, borders, tail pieces, and device. Also a list of books printed at St. Omers College Press.

In Excerpts relating to printing from "The Library," 1918-19, pp. 208-27, 277-88 of pencilled folios.

EARLY PRINTING IN ENGLAND. (Lit. of)

Cabinet U Shelf 1 No. 1d

Oxford (1517). A new Oxford book of 1517, by A.W. Pollard.

Mr. Pollard collates this unique book which might be considered as the earliest known production of the second Oxford Press.

In excerpts relating to printing from The Library, 1909, p.75 of pencilled folios.

EARLY PRINTING IN ENGLAND (Literature of)

Cabinet Shelf No.

New documents on English printers and booksellers of the sixteenth century: A paper read before the Bibliographical Society, by H.R. Plomer, Nov. 15, 1897.

In Transactions of the Bibliographical Society, vol. IV, pp. 153 - 183.

EARLY PRINTING IN ENGLAND. Literature of

Cabinet 75 Shelf 1 No. 6

Notices of English stationers in the archives of the City of London. By H. R. Plomer. A Paper read Oct. 15, 1900, before the Bibliographical Society.

In Trans. Biblio. Soc., Vol. VI, 1900-1902, pp. 13-27.

EARLY PRINTING IN ENGLAND [Literature of]

Cabinet U Shelf 2 No. 135

Oxford and Cambridge, 1634-1684: Early printing in the Universities of.

Manuscript typewritten copy, extracted from book "Collectanea Curiosa". Oxford, 1781.

Cloth; 8-5/8 x 11 x $\frac{1}{4}$ in.

EARLY PRINTING IN ENGLAND. (lit. of)

Cabinet 75 Shelf 2 No. 6

Oxford Press, The. 1650-75: The struggle for a place in the sun. A paper read before the Bibliographical Society, by Falconer Madan. March 16, 1925.

In Transactions of the Bibliographical Society, vol. VI, 1925-1926. pp. 113-147.

EARLY PRINTING IN ENGLAND. Literature.

Cabinet 75 Shelf 2 No. 3

Oxford University Press, 1468-1921. Some account of the Oxford University Press. A brief review of a book with same title. In "The Library," 1922.

In Transactions of the Bibliographical Society, "The Library," Vol. III, 1922-23, pp. 66-7.

EARLY PRINTING IN ENGLAND Literature of

Cabinet OO Shelf 4 No. 6

Pictorial Press, The. Its origin and progress. By Mason Jackson. With 150 illustrations. London, 1885.

Cloth; 9 x 5-5/8 x $1\frac{1}{4}$ in.

EARLY PRINTING IN ENGLAND. (lit. of)

Cabinet U Shelf 1 No. 1a

Oxford Press, Curiosities of. By Falconer Madan. London, n. d.

In Excerpts relating to printing from "The Library," [n.d.], p. 154 of pencilled folios

---

EARLY PRINTING IN ENGLAND. (Lit. of)

Cabinet U Shelf 1 No. 1e

Oxford University Press and the Stationer's Company, by R.L. Steele.

In excerpts relating to printing from The Library, 1911-12, p.273 of pencilled folios.

EARLY PRINTING IN ENGLAND. (Lit. of)

Cabinet U Shelf 1 No. 1h

Plomer, Henry R. Some Elizabethan book sales.

In Excerpts relating to printing from "The Library," 1915-17. pp. 158-169 of pencilled folios.

EARLY PRINTING IN ENGLAND. [Literature of]

Cabinet 75 Shelf 1 No. 9

Oxford Press during the Civil War, The: A paper read before the Bibliographical Society, by Mr. Falconer Madan, Oct. 21, 1907

In Trans. Biblio. Soc., Vol. IX, 1906-1908, pp. 107-110.

EARLY PRINTING IN ENGLAND [Literature of]

Cabinet T Shelf 1 No. 31 & 32

Palmer, Samuel, London, 1732-33: A general history of printing; from the first invention of it in the City of Mentz, to its propagation and progress...Particularly the introduction and success of it here in England...By S. Palmer, printer, London, 1732. Second ed. 1733.

Calf; 9-3/4 x $8\frac{1}{4}$ x $1\frac{1}{2}$ in.

EARLY PRINTING IN ENGLAND (Lit. of)

Cabinet U Shelf 1 No. 1h

Pollard, Alfred W. Authors, players and pirates in Shakespeare's day: A lectur delivered at Cambridge, Nov., 1915.

In Excerpts relating to printing from "The Library," 1915-17, 79-107 of pencilled folio

---

EARLY PRINTING IN ENGLAND. [Lit. of]

Cabinet 76 Shelf 2 No. 12

Oxford printing 1468-1900, with notes and illustrations, by Falconer Madan. Printed for the Bibliographical Society at the Oxford University Press, Feb., 1904.
Illus. Monograph XII.

Half morocco; 11 x 9 in.

EARLY PRINTING IN ENGLAND. [Literature of]

Cabinet 75 Shelf 2 No. 5

'Paterson's Roads," 1738-1825, his mark and itineraries. By Sir Herbert George Fordham. Facsimiles.

In Transactions of the Bibliographical Society, "The Library," Vol. V, 1924-1925, pp. 333-356.

EARLY PRINTING IN ENGLAND. (Lit. of)

Cabinet U Shelf 1 No. 1c

Pollard, Alfred W. Recent English purchases at the British Museum.
Brief bio-bibliographic account of English printers and printing.

In Excerpt relating to printing from "The Library," 1908, pp. 323-332.

EARLY PRINTING IN ENGLAND. Literature

Cabinet U Shelf 2 No. 119

Oxford, printing in, and Oxford Bibles. By H. Latham. Oxford, 1870.

Morocco; $5\frac{3}{4}$ x 3-3/8 x $\frac{1}{2}$ in.

EARLY PRINTING IN ENGLAND. (Lit. of)

Cabinet U Shelf 1 No. 1h

Petition of Eleanor Playford (1686) that she may continue to keep up her printing house.

In Excerpts relating to printing from "The Library," 1915-17, pp. 172-178.

EARLY PRINTING IN ENGLAND. (Lit. of)

Cabinet 75 Shelf 1 No. 6

Pollard, Alfred W. Some notes on English illustrated books. A paper read before the Bibliographical Society, Nov. 19th, 1900. Illus.

In Trans. Biblio. Soc. Vol. 6, 1900-1902. pp. 29-61.

EARLY PRINTING IN ENGLAND Literature

Cabinet U Shelf 2 No. 127

Oxford University Press, a brief account of the. With illustrations. Together with a chart of Oxford printing. By Falconer Madan, Oxford, 1908.

Half morocco; 9 x 6-7/8 in.

EARLY PRINTING IN ENGLAND. (Lit. of)

Cabinet U Shelf 1 No. 1j

Petitions for appointment as master printers called forth by the Star Chamber Decree of 1637. By Henry R. Plomer. London.

In Excerpts relating to printing from "The Library," 1918-19, pp. 138-53 of pencilled folios.

EARLY PRINTING IN ENGLAND. [Literature]

Cabinet 75 Shelf 2 No. 9

(A) Pore helpre and its printers (16th century). By M. Channing Lenthicum. [Bibliographical]

In Transactions of the Bibliographical Society, "The Library," Vol. IX, 1928-29, pp. 164-8.

EARLY PRINTING IN ENGLAND. Literature.

Cabinet 75 Shelf 2 No. 7

Portuguese books before 1640. English translation of. Paper by Henry Thomas. London, 1926.

In Transactions of the Bibliographical Society, "The Library," Vol. VII, 1926-27, pp. 1-30.

EARLY PRINTING IN ENGLAND Literature of

Cabinet U Shelf 4 No. 110

Proof-reading in the sixteenth, seventeenth and eighteenth centuries. By Percy Simpson. London: Oxford University Press, 1935.
Contents: Author's Proof-Reading.
Early Proofs and Copy.
Correctors of the Press.
The Oxford Press and its Correctors.
etc.
Boards, cloth back; 11-1/8 x 7-5/8 in.

EARLY PRINTING IN ENGLAND Literature of

Cabinet K Shelf 6 No. 21

Printers' ornaments, English. By Henry R. Plomer. London, 1924. Illus.

Historical.

Boards; 11-5/8 x 9½ x 1¼ in.

EARLY PRINTING IN ENGLAND. Lit. of

Cabinet KK Shelf 1 No. 25

Preston (Leeds). The romance of a Preston printer, Edward Baines.

see "LEEDS MERCURY, THE". Two centuries of journalistic work...

EARLY PRINTING IN ENGLAND. Literature

Cabinet U Shelf 3 No. 103

Provincial presses, English, 1478-1556. Papers on. By W.H. Allnutt.

See vol. II, pp.23-46, 150-180, 276-308, Bibliographica...London, 1895-1897.

EARLY PRINTING IN ENGLAND. [Literature of]

Cabinet A Shelf 3 No. 93

Raikes, Robert, and W. Dicey. Gloucester, 1722. An account of the first book printed in Gloucester, by them.

In the Gloucester Journal: Bi-centenary Historical Supplement, 1722-1922.

Buckram 22 x 19 x ½ in.

EARLY PRINTING IN ENGLAND. (Lit. of)

Cabinet U Shelf 1 No. 1d

Printers and books in Chancery. Communication by Robert Lewis Steele. n.d.
Bio-bibliographical.

In Excerpts relating to printing from "The Library," p. 24 of pencilled folios.

EARLY PRINTING IN ENGLAND. Literature

Cabinet U Shelf 3 No. 103

Rastell, John, and his contemporaries. By Henry R. Plomer.

Bibliographical.

See vol. 2, p.437 Bibliographica...London, 1895-1897.

EARLY PRINTING IN ENGLAND. [Literature of]

Cabinet A Shelf 3 No. 93

Raikes, Robert, and W. Dicey. Gloucester, 1923. An account of the first book in Gloucester by them.

In the Gloucester Journal, 1722-1922: Bi-centenary Historical Supplement, April 8, 1922.

EARLY PRINTING IN ENGLAND. [Literature of]

Cabinet 75 Shelf 2 No. 8

Printers and publishes of "The Birth of Mankind:" Thomas Raynold, 1540: Richard Jugge, 1560: John Cawood, 1561: Richard Watkins, 1598: Thomas Adams, 1604: Thomas Dawson, 1613: James Boler, 1620: Brief biographical account of these printers.

In Transactions of the Bibliographical Society, vol. VIII, 1927-1928. pp. 34-37. "The Library."

EARLY PRINTING IN ENGLAND. [Literature of]

Cabinet U Shelf 1 No. 1h

Regulation of the book trade in the sixteenth century: A lecture delivered by Alfred Pollard at Cambridge, Nov., 1915.

In Excerpts relating to printing from "The Library", 1915-17. pp. 38-63 of pencilled folios.

EARLY PRINTING IN ENGLAND. [Literature of]

Cabinet 75 Shelf 1 No. 11

Schilders, Richard and the English Puritans. A paper read before the Bibliographical Society by J. Dover Wilson, October 17th, 1910. This item includes many facsimile reproductions of title pages, initials and ornaments.

In Trans. Biblio. Soc., Vol. XI, 1909-1911, pp. 65-134.

EARLY PRINTING IN ENGLAND. Literature.

Cabinet 75 Shelf 2 No. 2

Printing of the Beaumont and Fletcher folio of 1647, The: A brief account by W. W. Greg, The Library, Sept. 1921.

In Transactions of the Bibliographical Society, "The Library," Vol. II, 1921-22, pp. 109-115.

EARLY PRINTING IN ENGLAND. [Literature of]

Cabinet S Shelf 3 No. ~~172~~

Robinson Crusoe and its printing 1719-1731. A bibliographical study. By Henry C. Hutchins With a foreward by A. Edward Newton. New York, 1925. Illus.

Cloth; 10 x 7½ in.

EARLY PRINTING IN ENGLAND. [Literature of]

Cabinet R Shelf 6 No. 42

(A) Series of facsimiles of all types used in England during the 15th century, with some of those used in the printing of English books abroad. With an introduction by E. Gordon Duff. London, 1896. (40 facsimiles plates, 40 pp. text).

Linen portfolio, tied; 16 x 12 in.

EARLY PRINTING IN ENGLAND Literature

Cabinet QQ Shelf 1 No. 2

Private printer and his ballad book...no author name, no place [London? circa 1875]. Illus. and facs.

Has brief notes concerning the printers of these early ballads.

Boards; 8-3/4 x 6-3/4 x ½ in.

EARLY PRINTING IN ENGLAND Literature

Cabinet Q Shelf 1 No. 26

(The) Romance of bookselling: A history from the earliest times to the twentieth century. By Frank A. Mumby. With a bibliography by W. H. Peet. London, 1910. Illus.

Cloth; 9 x 6 x 2¼ in.

EARLY PRINTING IN ENGLAND Literature

Cabinet X Shelf 5 No. 120

Shakespear's fight with the pirates, and the problems of the transmission of his text. By Alfred W. Pollard, London, 1917.

Boards; 10¼ x 6-5/8 in.

EARLY PRINTING IN ENGLAND. [Literature of]

Cabinet 75 Shelf 1 No. 9

Signs of booksellers in St. Paul's Churchyard: A paper read before the Bibliographical Society by Henry B. Wheatley, March 18, 1907.

In Trans. Biblio. Soc., Vol. IX, 1906-1908, pp. 67-106.

EARLY PRINTING IN ENGLAND. [Literature of]

Cabinet U Shelf 1 No. 1c

Stationers from the lay subsidy rolls of 1523-4, notes on. By E. Gordon Duff.
Historical investigation which resulted in gathering information concerning the lives and activities of early English printers.

In Excerpts relating to printing from "The Library," 1908, pp. 257-266.

EARLY PRINTING IN ENGLAND. [Literature of]

Cabinet U Shelf 1 No. 1J

Two lost causes: The Oxford "Jerome" printed in 1468, and a supposed Shakespeare autograph in the Bodleian Library. By F. Madan. London, April, 1918.

In Excerpts relating to printing from The Library, 1915-17, pp.158-74 of pencilled folios.

EARLY PRINTING IN ENGLAND. [Literature of]

Cabinet 75 Shelf 1 No. 7

Some devotional books printed by the earliest English printers: A paper read by the Right Rev. F. A. Gasquet before the Biographical Society, on Jan. 18, 1904.

In Trans. Biblio. Soc., Vol. VII, 1902-1904, pp. 163-189.

EARLY PRINTING IN ENGLAND. [Literature of]

Cabinet 75 Shelf 2 No. 1

Strahan, Wm. printer of Fieldings' works, 1715-85, by J. Paul De Castro.

In Transactions of the Bibliographical Society, "The Library," Vol. I, 1920-1921. pp. 257-70.

EARLY PRINTING IN ENGLAND [Literature of]

Cabinet T Shelf 2 No. 1

Typographical Antiquities; being an historical account of printing in England, with some memoirs of our ancient printers, and a register of the books printed by them from 1471 to 1600; with an appendix concerning printing in Scotland and Ireland to the same time. By Joseph Ames, London, 1749.

Half morocco; 10-3/4 x 8¼ x 2 in.

EARLY PRINTING IN ENGLAND. [Literature of]

Cabinet 75 Shelf 1 No. 7

Some notes on the Oxford Press, with special reference to the fluctuations in its issues: A paper read before the Bibliographical Society by Mr. Falconer Madan, Oct. 20, 1902.

In Trans. Biblio. Soc., Vol. VII, 1902-1904, pp. 1-3.

EARLY PRINTING IN ENGLAND. [Literature of]

Cabinet 75 Shelf 2 No. 4

Surreptitious edition of Michael Drayton's "Peirs Gaueston." A paper by J. William Hebel.

In Transactions of the Bibliographcial Society, "The Library," Vol. IV, 1923-24, pp.151-55.

EARLY PRINTING IN ENGLAND Literature

Cabinet U Shelf 5 No. 3

Vautrollier, Thomas, London, circa 1564, and his Shakespeare editions.

BLADES, WILLIAM. Shakespeare and typography...London, 1772, pp.26-32

EARLY PRINTING IN ENGLAND. [Literature

Cabinet 75 Shelf 2 No. 6

Spanish Tragedy, The. A Leading Case? A paper by W. W. Greg.

In Transactions of the Bibliographical Society, "The Library," Vol. VI, 1925-26, pp. 47-56.

EARLY PRINTING IN ENGLAND. [Literature of]

Cabinet U Shelf 1 No. 1g

Sussex. Notes on the introduction of printing into Sussex up to the year 1850; with a chronology of Sussex printers to that date, by A. Cecil Piper.

In Excerpts relating to printing from "The Library, 1914-15. p. 67 of pencilled folios

---

EARLY PRINTING IN ENGLAND. (Lit. of)

Cabinet 75 Shelf 2 No. 8

Whitchurch, Edward. London, 1548. The Whitchurch compartment in London and Mexico. By Lucy Eugenia Osborne. London, Dec. 1927. Facsimile.
The author attempts to establishe some connection between the original user of the decorative wood-cut and the imitator in Mexico.

In Transactions of the Bibliographical Society, vol. VIII, 1927-1928. pp. 303-311. "The Library."

EARLY PRINTING IN ENGLAND. [Literature of]

Cabinet U Shelf 1 No. 1b

Spenser Society and its work, The: A paper read before the Library Associaton at Belfast, By William E. A. Axon, Sept. 1894.
Includes a list of early books reprinted by the Society.

In Excerpts relating to printing from "The Library," p. 193 of pencilled folios.

EARLY PRINTING IN ENGLAND. (Literature

Cabinet U Shelf 3 No. 103

Tottel, Richard, printer and publisher of "Tottel's Miscellany" London (circa 1557). By H.R. Plomer.

Bibliographical account.

See vol. 3, p.378 Bibliographica...London, 1895-1897.

EARLY PRINTING IN ENGLAND [Literature of]

Cabinet U Shelf 1 No. 1h

Winchester, 1549-1789. The book trade in Winchester, 1549-1789. Extracts from the local records of the city. Gathered and arranged by A. Cecil Piper, Librarian.

In excerpts relating to printing from The Library, 1915-17, pp.123-129 of pencilled folios.

EARLY PRINTING IN ENGLAND Literature

Cabinet U Shelf 3 No. 103

Stationers at the Sign of the Trinity, 1504-1538. By Duff E. Gordon.

Bibliographical account.

See vol. I, pp.92-113, 175-192, 499 in Bibliographica...London, 1895-1897.

EARLY PRINTING IN ENGLAND.

Cabinet U Shelf 4 No. 4

(Tracts and broadsides, 1819-1870). Curiosities of English literature. A collection of "Cocks," or "Catchpennies," Street drolleries, squibs, histories, etc. London: Reeves & Turner, 1871.

Cloth;leather back; 10-5/8 x 9 x 1-1/8 in.

EARLY PRINTING IN ENGLAND. [Literature]

Cabinet 75 Shelf 2 No. 1

Winchester 1691 - The early printers and booksellers of Winchester. By A. Cecil Piper. A paper for the Bibliographical Society.

In Trans. Biblio. Soc., "The Library," Vol. I, 1920-1921, pp. 103-110.

EARLY PRINTING IN ENGLAND. [Literature of]

Cabinet 76 Shelf 1 No. 6

Wyer, Robert, printer and bookseller, 1530-1536. A paper read before the Bibliographical Society, by Henry R. Plomer, Jan. 21st, 1925.

Half morocco; 8-3/4 x 7 ins. pp.59 (6)

EARLY PRINTING IN FRANCE [Literature of]

Cabinet U Shelf 1 No. 1a

(Avignon, 1444-1446?) Procope Valdfoghel, goldsmith and printer. By S. J. Aldrich.

In Excerpts relating to printing from "The Library," [n.d.] p. 179 of pencilled folios

---

EARLY PRINTING IN FRANCE. [Literature of]

Cabinet V Shelf 5 No. 1

Bordeaux, 1572-1623: Simon Mellanges, imprimeur a Bordeaux. Communication de M. Dast de Boisville. Bulletin Historique et Philologique...Paris, 1898. Pamphlet.

Bound in volume "French Typographical Pamphlets", item 12.

EARLY PRINTING IN ENGLAND. [Literature of]

Cabinet U Shelf 1 No. 1g

Wyer, Robert. some rogueries of. By H. B. Lathrop.

In Excerpts relating to printing from "The Library," 1914-15. p. 83 of pencilled folios.

EARLY PRINTING IN FRANCE Literature

Cabinet V Shelf 5 No. 2.01

Avignon, 1558, Pierre Roux.

See ROUX, PIERRE. Imprimeur a Avignon...

EARLY PRINTING IN FRANCE [Literature of]

Stack A Shelf 1&2 Number 54

Bullen, Henry Lewis. Literature of Typography: France. In The Inland Printer, vol.LIV, pp.537, 676.

EARLY PRINTING IN ENGLAND. [Literature of]

Cabinet U Shelf 1 No. 1g

Wynkyn de Worde, 1553. An inventory of Wynkyn de Worde's house "The Sun in Fleet Street" in 1553, by Henry R. Plomer.

In excerpts relating to printing from The Library, 1914-15, p.129 of pencilled folios.

EARLY PRINTING IN FRANCE [Literature of]

Cabinet 18 Shelf 1 No. 14

[Barbou Family of Printers, 1524-1820] Franzosische Buchdrucker und Buchhandler-familie der Barbou (1524-1820) von Bernhard Kabuse in Paris.

In Zeitschrift fur Bucherfreunde, 1913-14, part I, p.18.

EARLY PRINTING IN FRANCE [Literature of]

Cabinet V Shelf 4 No. 28

Christian, Arthur. Débuts de l'imprimerie en France: L'Imprimerie Nationale: L'Hotel de Rohan. Paris, 1905. Préface de M. Jules Claretie. Illus. Many type specimens, facsimile, and printer marks.

Half morocco; $11\frac{1}{4}$ x 8 x$1\frac{1}{4}$ in.

EARLY PRINTING IN ENGLAND. Literature of

Cabinet 75 Shelf 1 No. 5

York, 1493-1600. The printers, stationers and bookbinders of York up to 1600. By E. Gordon Duff. A paper read before the Bibliographical Society, May, 1899.

In Trans. Biblio. Soc., Vol. V, 1898-1900, pp. 87-107.

EARLY PRINTING IN FRANCE [Literature of]

Cabinet W Shelf 1 No. 123

Bibliographie des principales éditiones original et d'écrivains Francaise du XVe au XVIIIe siècle. Par Jules Le Petit. Ouvrage contenant environ 300 fac-similes de titres des livres décrito. Paris, 1888.

A bibliographical account. The notes, and illustrations form a comprehensive history of printing in France.

Half morocco; $10\frac{3}{4}$ x $7\frac{1}{2}$ in.

EARLY PRINTING IN FRANCE. [Literature of]

Cabinet U Shelf 1 No. 1b

Claudin, A. (Review) Seven books dealing with printing in France. Paris, 1894.

In Excerpts relating to printing from "The Library," p. 188 of pencilled folios.

EARLY PRINTING IN ENGLAND (see also)

Cabinet Shelf No.

LIBERTY OF PRINTING, Great Britain

EARLY PRINTING IN FRANCE. Literature.

Cabinet 75 Shelf 2 No. 3

Books printed at Lyons in the sixteenth century. A paper read before the Bibliographical Society by Alfred Forbes Johnson, October 15, 1922.

In Trans, Biblio. Soc., "The Library," vol. 3 1922-23, pp. 145-174.

EARLY PRINTING IN FRANCE. [Literature of]

Cabinet V Shelf 5 No. 7

Crapelet, G.-A. Études pratiques et littéraires sur la typographie. Tome premier. Paris 1837

Half morocco; 9-5/8 x $6\frac{1}{2}$ in.

EARLY PRINTING IN FRANCE Literature

Cabinet K Shelf 2 No. 3

Almanachs Francaise. Bibliographie-iconographie ...(1600-1895). Par John Grand-Carteret, Paris, 1896.

Bibliography of almanachs and other annual publications edited at Paris, 1600-1895.

Half morocco; $10\frac{1}{2}$ x 7 in.

EARLY PRINTING IN FRANCE. (Lit. of)

Cabinet 18 Shelf 1 No. 3

(Booksellers and printers of the French Academy from 1634 to 1793) Les Libraires et imprimeurs de l'Academie francaise de 1634-1793: Review of book with same title, by Jos. Thron.

In Zeitschrift für Bücherfreunde, 1907-8, part 2, p. 343.

EARLY PRINTING IN FRANCE. [Literature of]

Cabinet V Shelf 4 No. 12

(Crapelet, G. A.). Progrès de l'Imprimerie en France et en Italie au XVI siècle, et de son influence sur la littérature; avec les Lettres-Patentes en date du 17 Janvier, 1538, qui instituent le premier Imprimeur Royal pour le Grec. Par G. A. Crapelet, Imprimeur. Paris, 1836.

Half morocco; $9\frac{1}{2}$ x $6\frac{1}{4}$ in.

EARLY PRINTING IN FRANCE. [Literature]

Cabinet 75 Shelf 2 No. 7

Diane de Poitiers and her books. A paper by George H. Bushnell.
Includes a sketch of her life, library, devices and bindings.

In Transactions of the Bibliographical Society, "The Library," Vol. VII, 1926-1927, pp. 283-302.

EARLY PRINTING IN FRANCE Literature

Cabinet KK Shelf 4 No. 12

Essai sur la police des compagnons imprimeurs sous l'ancine regime. Par Louis Morin, Typographe. Lyon, 1898.

An organization of French printers, 17th and 18th centuries.

Half morocco; 10 x 6½ x ¼ in.

EARLY PRINTING IN FRANCE Literature of

Cabinet S Shelf 6 No. 7

(Hawkers literature of France since the 15th century) Histoire des livres populaires, ou de la littérature du colportage, depuis le XVem siècle jusqu'a l'etablissement de la Commission de l'Examen des Livres du Colportage 2 vols. Par Charles Nisard, Paris, 1852.
Review of book with above title. Excerpt from Edinburgh Review, Jan. 1858.

(cont'd)

EARLY PRINTING IN FRANCE. [Literature of]

Cabinet V Shelf 3 No. 14

Dupont, Paul. Histoire de l'Imprimerie en France Paris, 1854. 2 Vols.
See Vol. I, pp. 65-351 of above.

Half morocco; 11 x 7½ in.

EARLY PRINTING IN FRANCE. [Literature of]

Stack A Shelf 1&2 Number 67

Estienne, Robert and Henry, and the Estienne dynasty of printers, by Henry Lewis Bullen, in The Inland Printer, vol. LXVII, p.198. Illus.

EARLY PRINTING IN FRANCE Lit. of (cont'd)

Cabinet Shelf No.

Item (b) in book with binder's title: Early printed books: Various excerpts and pamphlets, 1854-1931.

EARLY PRINTING IN FRANCE. (Lit. of)

Cabinet U Shelf 1 No. 1c

Du Pre, Gallot, 1512-1560: A Paris bookseller of the sixteenth century - Gallot du Pre, by Arthur Tilley.

In excerpts relating to printing from The Library, 1908, pp. 36-65, 143-172.

EARLY PRINTING IN FRANCE. (Lit. of)

Cabinet V Shelf 5 No. 1

Etude sur l'origine et la propagation de l'imprimerie a Toulouse au XVe siecle: Communication de M.Macoris a la Bulletin Historique et Philologique, Paris, 1897.

Bound in volume "French Typographical Pamphlets," item 12.

EARLY PRINTING IN FRANCE. (Lit. of)

Cabinet V Shelf 5 No. 1

Histoire de l'imprimerie a Castelsarrasin, par M. Em. Forestie, neveu, Montauban (France), 1900. An excerpt from Recueil de l'Academie des Science ... et Arts, de Tarn-et-Garonne.

Bound in volume "French Typographical Pamphlets," item 8.

EARLY PRINTING IN FRANCE. [Literature of]

Cabinet 18 Shelf 1 No. 13

(Earliest editions of the "Prophets" of Nostradamus.) Die Altesten Ausgaben der "Prophe-ties" des Nostradamus, ein Beitrag zur Nostradamus-Bibliographie, von Carl v. Klinckowstroem, Munich. Many facsimiles of title pages.

In Zeitschrift für Bücherfreunde, 1913, part 2, p.361.

EARLY PRINTING IN FRANCE Literature of

Cabinet V Shelf 3 No. 22 2 vols.

Evolution de la lettre d'imprimerie: A l'oeuvre francaise de l'èpoque gothique au XIX siècle. With many facsimiles, printer marks, specimen of types, etc.

See Tome I, pp.112-409, La lettre d'imprimerie. Par F. Thibaudeau. Paris, 1921.

Cloth; 8-7/8 x 6-3/4 in.

EARLY PRINTING IN FRANCE Literature

Cabinet KK Shelf 4 No. 1

Histoire de toutes les noblesses, sous la direction litteraire de M. C. Fournier. 1 livraison. Second Serie - No. I. Corporation des Imprimeurs. Paris, n. d. Illus.

On early printing, early printers in France and their privileges.

Half morocco; 11 x 7 in.

EARLY PRINTING IN FRANCE. [Literature of]

Cabinet 75 Shelf 2 No. 1

Earliest French itineries, The. 1552 and 1591. A paper read before the Bibliographical Society by Sir. H. George Fordham, November 15, 1920.
Facsimile reproductions of title pages, printers marks, etc.

In Transactions of the Bibliographical Society, "The Library," Vol. I, 1920-1921, pp. 193-224.

EARLY PRINTING IN FRANCE (Lit. of)

Cabinet 75 Shelf 2 No. 1

French atlases, 1594-1637, note on a series of. By Sir H. George Fordham. The Bibliographical Society.

In Trans. Biblio. Soc. Vol. I, 1920-1921. "The Library," pp. 145-152.

EARLY PRINTING IN FRANCE. Literature of.

Cabinet I Shelf 3 No. 18 to 21

Histoire illustree de la gravure en France. Des origines a 1660-19^e siecle. Par Francois Courboin. Paris, 1923-1929. [4 parts].
Many allusions to printers, historical and biographical, bibliographical See index of each part.

Paper; 12¾ x 8-7/8 in.

EARLY PRINTING IN FRANCE. [Literature of]

Cabinet 75 Shelf 2 No. 5

Early French Books at the British Museum. A review of Short-title Catalogue of Books, printing in France and of French books printed in other countries from 1470 to 1600 now in the British Museum. London, 1924, By Arthur Tilley.

In Transactions of the Bibliographical Society, "The Library," Vol. V, 1924-25, pp. 161-168.

EARLY PRINTING IN FRANCE Literature of

Cabinet U Shelf 4 No. 34

French 16th century printing. By A.F. Johnson. With fifty illustrations. London: Ernest Benn,Ltd., 1928.

Boards; 9¾ x 7-3/8 in.

EARLY PRINTING IN FRANCE. Literature.

Cabinet J Shelf 5 No. 29 3 Vols.

Histoire illustrée de la gravure en France. Par Francois Courboin. Paris, 1923.

3 portfolios with 1392 plates, reproductions from the earliest printed books. With bio-bibliographical descriptions.

Portfolio, 17¾ x 12-5/8 x 4 in.

EARLY PRINTING IN FRANCE. (Lit. of)

Cabinet U Shelf 1 No. 1b

History of printing in France: A review of eight monographs contributed by A. Claudin.

In excerpts relating to printing from The Library, p. 188 of pencilled folios.

EARLY PRINTING IN FRANCE Literature

Cabinet X Shelf 4 No. 32

Legislation affecting French printing. A collection of broadsides, leaflets, etc., from 1573 to 1810)

37 Items bound in one volume, with binder's title: "French Legislation Affecting Printing". 1573-1810.

EARLY PRINTING IN FRANCE. [Literature of]

Cabinet 18 Shelf 1 No. 14

(Lyon, 1524-1820. The Barbou family of printers and publishers.) Die Französische Buchdrucker und Buchhandlerfamilie der Barbou, von Bernhard Kabuse, Paris.

In Zeitschrift für Bucherfreunde, 1913-14, part 1, p.18.

EARLY PRINTING IN FRANCE Literature

Cabinet V Shelf 6 No. 16.02

(Illustrated articles concerning books and early printing in France).

See BULLETIN OFFICIEL DES MAITRES IMPRIMEURS (1930)

EARLY PRINTING IN FRANCE. Literature.

Cabinet 75 Shelf 2 No. 3

Listes generales des postes de France, 1708-79, and the Jaillot's, Geographes ordinaires du roi, by Sir H. George Fordham, Facsimile title pages.

In Transactions of the Bibliographical Society, "The Library," Vol. III, 1922-23, pp. 115-136.

EARLY PRINTING IN FRANCE [Literature of]

Cabinet U Shelf 1 No. 1j

Lyons, 1555. Jean de Tournes. Notes critical and bibliographical, on Louis Labe. By E. M. Cox. London, 1915.

In Excerpts relating to printing from "The Library," 1918-19, pp. 45-59 of pencilled folios.

EARLY PRINTING IN FRANCE [Literature of]

Cabinet V Shelf 5 No. 1

L'Imprimerie a Alencon de 1529 a 1575. Communication a Bulletin Historique et Philologique de Mme. Gerasime Despierres, Paris, 1893.

Bound in volume "French Typographical Pamphlets," item 10.

EARLY PRINTING IN FRANCE Literature

Cabinet V Shelf 5 No. 2.01

Longeville (Bar-le-Duc), 1501-15..), Martin Mourot.

See DANNREUTHER -- Martin Mourot, imprimeur a Longeville...

EARLY PRINTING IN FRANCE Literature

Cabinet V Shelf 5 No. 23

Lyon, 1581-1583, Francois Conrado.

See BAUDRIER, J. Acquisition en 1582 d'un materiel d'imprimerie...

EARLY PRINTING IN FRANCE. (Lit. of)

Cabinet U Shelf 1 No. 1a

L'Imprimerie a Avignon en 1444. Par L'Abbe Requin, Paris, 1890: Brief review of book with same title by S.J. Aldrich.

In excerpts relating to printing from "The Library," p. 170 of pencilled folios.

EARLY PRINTING IN FRANCE [Literature of]

Cabinet V Shelf 1 No. 109 (6 vols.) Series 1 to 6. SHELF 2 NO. 1 (6 vols.) Series 7 to 12.

(Lyon) Bibliographie Lyonnaise: Recherches sur les imprimeurs, libraires, relieurs et fondeurs de lettres de Lyon au XVI siecle. Par le President Baudrier. Publiees et continuees par J. Baudrier. Lyon: Series 1 to 12, 1895 to 1921.

Innumerable reproductions in facsimile, and of printer marks.

EARLY PRINTING IN FRANCE. [LITERATURE OF]

Cabinet 75 Shelf 1 No. 14

Lyons as a literary centre in the fifteenth and sixteenth centuries. A paper read before the Bibliographical Society by Dr. E. Marion Cox. November 15, 1915.

In Trans. Biblio. Soc., Vol. XIV, 1915-17, pp. 23-37.

EARLY PRINTING IN FRANCE. Literature of

Cabinet J Shelf 4 No. 7

L'Imprimerie et la gravure en Gevaudan. Imagerie Lozérienne avec des bois anciennes. Par Robert Barroux...à Mende (Lozere.) 1924. Illus.

Paper; $3\frac{1}{4}$ x $9\frac{3}{4}$ in.

EARLY PRINTING IN FRANCE Literature

Cabinet Y Shelf 3 No. 61

Lyons, 1482, die drucker von Buyers ausgabe der werke des Bartolus.

Bibliographical account in "Beitrage zum bibliothek und buchwesen", Paul Schwenke, Leipzig, 1913.

Half morocco; $11\frac{1}{4}$ x 8-5/8 in.

EARLY PRINTING IN FRANCE. (Lit. of)

Cabinet V Shelf 5 No. 1

Mourot, Martin. Imprimeur a Longeville devant Barle-Duc (1501-15). Sa marque typographique et son ensign. Communication de M. Dannseuther: An excerpt from "Bulletin historique du Comite des travaux Historiques, 1898.

Bound in volume "French Typographical Pamphlets," item 7.

EARLY PRINTING IN FRANCE. [Literature]

Cabinet 75 Shelf 1 No. 14

Laws regulating printing and publishing in France. A paper read before the Bibliographical Society by G. F. Barwick, February 21, 1916.

In Trans. Biblio. Soc., Vol. XIV, 1915-1917, pp. 69-107.

EARLY PRINTING IN FRANCE [Literature of]

Cabinet W Shelf 1 No. 90

Lyon, circa 1484. [Printer not known]. L'abuze en Court. Le doctrinale du temps present. Notice de E. Droz. Publiee par l'Association Guillaume du Roy. Lyon, n.d. Facsimile. Bibliographical study.

11 -1/8 x 9-3/8 x $\frac{1}{2}$ in.

EARLY PRINTING IN FRANCE. Literature

Cabinet 26 Shelf 1 No. 20

(Nancy, Alsace-Lorrain 1572-1600) Die anfänge der drukkunst in Nancy. von Albert Kolb. Illus.

Bio-bibliographical account.

Article in the "Gutenberg-Gesellschaft Jahrbuch" 1930, pp.209-225.

EARLY PRINTING IN FRANCE Literature

Cabinet V Shelf 5 No. 23

(Nantes, 15th to 18th century) Notes sur les anciens imprimeurs Nantais (XVe a XVIIIe siècle). Par Mis. de Granges de Surgères. Paris, 1898.

Bio-bibliographical notes.

Item 5 in vol. with binder's title "Origin of Printing in France. Pamphlets".

EARLY PRINTING IN FRANCE. [Literature of]

Cabinet 76 Shelf 2 No. 6

(Paris, 1470-1472). The first Paris Press. An account of the books printed for G. Fichet and J. Heynlein in the Sorbonne. By A. Claudin. Printed at the Chiswick Press for the Bibliographical Society, London, 1898. Facsimiles of colophons, alphabets, and pages.
Illus. monograph VI.

Half morocco; 11 x 9 in.

EARLY PRINTING IN FRANCE Literature

Cabinet X Shelf 4 No. 32

(Paris, 1706). Names of 36 printers elected for the city of Paris.

Item 3 in volume with binder's title : French Legislation Affecting Printing, 1573-1810.

EARLY PRINTING IN FRANCE. [Literature of]

Cabinet U Shelf 1 No. 1b

Notes on the history of book production in France, with special reference to the French books exhibited at the Bibliotheque Nationale Communicated to the Library Association by Alfred W. Pollard, Paris, Sept. 1892.

In excerpts relating to printing from "The Library, p. 98 of pencilled folios.

EARLY PRINTING IN FRANCE Literature of

Cabinet J Shelf 3 No. 27

Paris, 1488, Anthoine Verard.

See RENOUVIER, J. Gravures en bois dans les livres d'Anthoine Verard...

EARLY PRINTING IN FRANCE [Literature of]

Cabinet X Shelf 5 No. 2

Paris, 1706. Par le Roy. Extrait du Conseil d'Etat prive du Roy. Requeste presentee par les Syndic ... des libraries et imprimeurs de Paris (Complaint against excessive and unjust charges by Municipal Officials). Paris 1706. De L'Imprimerie Denys Thierry. Broadside.

Item 31 in volume "Historical documents relating to printing."

EARLY PRINTING IN FRANCE [Literature of]

Cabinet W Shelf 1 No. 41

Notices historiques, critiques et bibliographiques sur plusieurs livres de jurisprudence Francaise ... Par M^{r}. Dupin. Paris, 1820.

Half morocco; 8½ x 5½ in.

EARLY PRINTING IN FRANCE [Literature of]

Cabinet U Shelf 1 No. 1j

Paris, 1504: Jehan Trepperel. Notes on a fragment of a lost edition of Theseus de Cologne. By F. W. Bourdillon.

In Excerpts relating to printing from "The Library," 1918-19, pp. 29-39 of pencilled folios.

EARLY PRINTING IN FRANCE Literature

Cabinet X Shelf 4 No. 38

(Paris, 1723, laws regulating printing in). Reglement pour la librairie et imprimerie de Paris, arreste au Conseil d'Etat du Roy le 28 Fevrier, 1723. A Paris. De l'Imprimerie de P.A. Le Mercier, Pere, 1731.

Vellum; 5½ x 3¾ x ½ in.

EARLY PRINTING IN FRANCE. [Literature of]

Cabinet U Shelf 4 No. 73

Paris: Annals of Parisian typography. Containing an account of the earliest typographical establishments of Paris...By the Rev. William Parr Greswell. London, 1818. Portrait of Gering.

Half morocco; 9 x 5-3/4 x 1 in. See also U/4/74

EARLY PRINTING IN FRANCE. [Literature of]

Cabinet U Shelf 1 No. 1c

Paris, 1512-1560: A Paris bookseller of the sixteenth century--Galliot Du Pre. Bibliographical account by Arthur Tilley.

In Excerpts relating to printing from "The Library," 1908, pp. 36-75, 143-172.

EARLY PRINTING IN FRANCE [Literature of]

Cabinet X Shelf 5 No. 2

Paris, 1728: Declaration du roy concernant les imprimeurs. Donne a Versailles le 10 May, 1728. Registree en Parlement le 29 May, 1728. [Printed by] la veuve Jacob & Charles Jacob, a Orleans. Broadside.

Item 32 in volume "Historical documents relating to printing."

EARLY PRINTING IN FRANCE. [Literature]

Cabinet 75 Shelf 2 No. 8

(Paris). Basle ornaments on Paris books, 1519-36. By A. F. Johnson. London, Dec. 1927. Illus.

In Transactions of the Bibliographical Society, "The Library," Vol. VIII, 1927-28, pp. 355-360.

EARLY PRINTING IN FRANCE Literature of

Cabinet W Shelf 3 No. 115

(Paris, 17th century) Les libraires et imprimeurs a Paris, au 17e siècle. [Illus. excerpt from "Magasine Pittoresque". Paris, circa 1848].

Item 4 in vol. with binder's title "Pamphlets Relating to Books - II. Bound, 1932".

EARLY PRINTING IN FRANCE. [Literature of]

Cabinet X Shelf 4 No. 98

Paris 1793. Gueffier V. Mehee. Memoir et denonciation pour le Sr. Gueffier, imprimeur.
Before presenting his case, Gueffier gives a brief biographical sketch of his family, booksellers and printers in Paris since 1582.

Paper; 7-3/8 x 4⅝ x ¼ in.

EARLY PRINTING IN FRANCE. [Literature of]

Cabinet 20 Shelf 1 No. 17

(Paris. The family of Estienne (Stephanus). Die Druckfamilie der Estienne, von Wilhelm Kothe, Gottingen, Aug., 1905.

In Zeitschrift für Bücherfreünde, 1905-6, part 1, p.179.

EARLY PRINTING IN FRANCE [Literature]

Cabinet X Shelf 4 No. 35

Paris, 1686. Edit du roy pour le reglement des imprimeurs et les libraires de Paris. Registré en Parlement le 21 Aout, 1686. A Paris, de l'Imprimerie de Le Mercier, 1731.
See also X-4-95 and X-4-97.

Boards; 5½ x 3¾ x ½ in.

EARLY PRINTING IN FRANCE Literature

Cabinet V Shelf 2 No. 23

Parisian Greek Press.

see

GRESWELL (Rev.) W. P. (A) View of the early Parisian Greek Press...

EARLY PRINTING IN FRANCE. [Literature of]

Cabinet V Shelf 2 No. 32

(Poitiers,) 1479-1515. Monuments de l'Imprimerie a Poitiers. Recueil de fac-similes des premiers livres imprimés dans cette ville. Specimens de caractères, lettres ornées, filigranes de paperiers, etc. Par A. Claudin, Paris, 1897. Facsimiles.

Half morocco; 10 x 6¾ x 1¾ in.

EARLY PRINTING IN FRANCE. [Literature of]

Cabinet U Shelf 1 No. 1b

Pollard, Alfred W. Notes on the history of book-production in France...Communicated to the fifteenth Annual Meeting of the Library Association, Paris, Sept. 1892.

In Excerpts relating to printing from "The Library," p. 98 of pencilled folios.

EARLY PRINTING IN FRANCE LITERATURE OF

Cabinet J Shelf 2 No. 14

Printers and publishers of books illustrated by Jean Cousin, circa 1560-89.

See Didot, Ambroise Firmin. Etude sur Jean Cousin...Paris, 1872.

EARLY PRINTING IN FRANCE Literature

Cabinet U Shelf 3 No. 103

Private presses in France during the 15th century. By A. Claudin.

See vol. 3, p.344 "Bibliographica"... London, 1895-1897.

EARLY PRINTING IN FRANCE . Literature of

Cabinet 26 Shelf 1 No. 21

(Provence, 15th century printing)

See Liturgical Literature. (Les) Premiers livres liturgiques...

EARLY PRINTING IN FRANCE. [Literature of]

Cabinet 75 Shelf 1 No. 5

Reinhard, Marcus & Johann Grüninger: A paper read before the Bibliographical Society by Robert Proctor, 1899.

In Trans. of Biblio. Soc., Vol. V, 1898-1900, pp. 143-160.

EARLY PRINTING IN FRANCE Literature of

Stack-15 ~~Cabinet~~ Shelf 4 No. 31.01

Renaissance in France. Catalogue of books printed For sale by E.P. Goldschmidt & Co., London. Illus.

EARLY PRINTING IN FRANCE. [Literature]

Cabinet V Shelf 2 No. 39

Rouen, 1525. Un typographe Rouennais oublie. Maitre J.G., imprimeur d'une edition de Commines en 1525. Par A. Claudin. Paris, 1896.

Boards; 9½ x 5¼ in.

EARLY PRINTING IN FRANCE Literature of

Cabinet K Shelf 6 No. 19

(Series of wood engravings of the 15th century, with some valuable typographical information elucidations of old printers' marks, etc.)

see
LABITTE, A. Gravure sur bois ...Paris, 1868.

EARLY PRINTING IN FRANCE Literature of

Cabinet X Shelf 2 No. 53

Strassburg, 1685, Friedrich Wilhelm Schmuck, founder of the house of Berger-Levrault. Historical accont. German text. By Louis F. Mohr.

Half morocco; 9-7/8 x 6¾ x ¼ in.

EARLY PRINTING IN FRANCE Literature of

Cabinet KK Shelf 4 No. 9

(Tours, 16th century. With brief biographies of printer) Une association d'imprimeurs et de libraires de Paris refugies a Tours au 16 siecle...[Par Dr. E. Giraudet] Tours, 1877.

Half morocco; 11 x 7¾ in.

EARLY PRINTING IN FRANCE Literature of

Cabinet K Shelf 6 No. 25

Troyes, 15th, 16th, 17th and 18th centuries.

see
VARUSOLTIS. Xylographie de l'imprimerie Troyenne...Troyes...Paris, 1859.

EARLY PRINTING IN FRANCE. (Literature)

Cabinet V Shelf 2 No. 61

Troyes, 1568. Un imprimeur Troyen apocryphe (Jean Damian, 1568). Questions bibliographiques.

Excerpt, unknown source, circa 1908. In envelope pasted in back of Morin's L'Imprimerie a Troyes, Paris, 1912.

Paper; 9 x 5-5/8 x 3/8 in.

EARLY PRINTING IN FRANCE Literature of

Cabinet V Shelf 5 No. 23

Troyes, 1598-1607, Estienne de la Hupreye, le Jeune.

See SOCARD, ALEXIS. Sur un imprimeur de Troyes...

EARLY PRINTING IN FRANCE. (Lit.)

Cabinet 76 Shelf 2 No. 7

Verard, Antoine, 1485, an account by John MacFarlane. Printed for the Bibliographical Society, London, 1900. Illustrated monograph No. VII.

Includes facsimiles of types, devices, initials, etc.

Half morocco; 11 x 9 in. (XXIX), pp. 1-139.

EARLY PRINTING IN FRANCE Literature

Cabinet V Shelf 5 No. 2.01

Vitre, Antoine, et ses caractères orientaux...

See BERNARD, AUGSUTE-ANTOINE. Antoine Vitré...

EARLY PRINTING IN FRANCE. Literature.

Cabinet 75 Shelf 2 No. 4

Wechel, Christian, 1534. The first Paris edition of the emblems of Alciat. A paper by Eustace F. Bosauquet.

In Transactions of the Bibliographical Society, "The Library," Vol.IV, 1923-1924, pp. 326-331.

EARLY PRINTING IN GERMANY (Lit. of)

Cabinet 18 Shelf 1 No. 2

See Advertising, early (Counterfeit money notices in the early period of printing.)

EARLY PRINTING IN GERMANY. (Lit. of)

Cabinet 22 Shelf 1 No. 17

(Apiarius family of printers in Strassburg. Bern and Basle, 1533-1592) Die buchdruckenfamilie Apiarius ... von J. W. Roth.
Bio-bibliographical historical account.

In Archiv fur Deutschen Buchhandels, vol. 17. p. 26.

EARLY PRINTING IN GERMANY [Literature of]

Cabinet V Shelf 6 No. 1

Bamberg, 1462. Albert Pfister. Notice d'un livre imprimé à Bamberg in 1462, par Albert Pfister, et contenu dans un volume nouvellement arrivé à la Bibliothèque nationale. Par Armand Gaston Camus. Paris, An VII (1799).

Calf; 14 x 10¼ in.

EARLY PRINTING IN GERMANY. (Lit. of)

Cabinet 22 Shelf 1 No. 10

See Bookbinding, early. Bookbinder and publisher in Germany in the 16th and 17th century.

EARLY PRINTING IN GERMANY [Literature of]

Cabinet 18 Shelf 1 No. 6

(Astronomical broadsides of the XVI and XVII centuries) Die Kometen-Flugschriften des XVI und XVII Jahrhunderts von H. Ludendorf, Potsdam.

In Zeitschrift für Bücherfreunde, 1908-9, part 2, p.501.

EARLY PRINTING IN GERMANY [Literature of]

Cabinet U Shelf 1 No. 1e

Bamberger Pfisterdruck und die 36 zeiliege Bibel, von Prof. Dr. Gottfreid Zedler: A review of book with same title, by Victor Scholderer.

In excerpts relating to printing from "The Library," 1911-12, p. 284 of pencilled folios.

EARLY PRINTING IN GERMANY. [Literature of]

Cabinet 22 Shelf 1 No. 13

(Breitkopf, Johann, Leipzig, 1765; complaints about abuses in the printing trades.) Johann Gottlob Immanuel Breitkoph im kampfe gegen missbrauche in den druckereien.

In Archiv für Deutschen Buchhandels, 1890, vol.XIII, p.204.

EARLY PRINTING IN GERMANY Literature of

Cabinet 75 Shelf 1 No. 2

Augsburg, 1471-1500. The Augsburg Printers of the Fifteenth Century: A paper read before the Bibliographical Society by Stephen J. Aldrich, April 16, 1894.

In Transactions of the Bibliographical Society, vol. II, pp. 25-48. 1893-1894.

EARLY PRINTING IN GERMANY. [Literature of]

Cabinet 22 Shelf 1 No. 6

(Baumann Georg, Breslau, 1590) The Breslauer bookseller and printer. Documents.) Die Breslauer Buchhandler und der Buchdrucker Georg Baumann. Documents. Communicated by A. Kirchhoff.

In Archiv für Deutschen Buchhandels, 1881, Vol.VI, p.94.

EARLY PRINTING IN GERMANY. [Literature of]

Cabinet 22 Shelf 1 No. 4

(Breslau, 1590. Peddler, Printer, Bookbinder, and Bookseller in the 16th century) Hausirer und buchbinder in Breslau im 16 jahrhundert.

An account gleaned from the original manuscript.

In Archiv für Deutschen Buchhandels, vol.IV, p.35.

EARLY PRINTING IN GERMANY Literature

Cabinet Z Shelf 5 No. 37

Augsburg, 1485-1522. Erhard Ratdolt.

See Schottenloher's Liturgischen druckwerke Erhard Ratdolts...Verlag Gutenberg-Gesellschaft, 1922.

EARLY PRINTING IN GERMANY [Literature of]

Cabinet 18 Shelf 1 No. 10

(Berger, Thiebold, Strassburg, 1551-1584. Unknown books printed by Thiebold Berger) Unbekannte Ausgaben zeistlicher und weltlicher gedruckt von Thiebold Berger, von Paul Heitz.

In Zeitschrift für Bücherfreunde, 1911, part 1, p.21.

EARLY PRINTING IN GERMANY. [Literature of]

Cabinet 18 Shelf 1 No. 16

(Broadsides of the 15th century.) A bibliographical inventory published by the Commission for the complete catalogue of Incunabula.

Brief summary of the history of German broadsides.

In Zeitschrift für Bücherfreunde, 1914, part 1, p.132.

EARLY PRINTING IN GERMANY (Lit. of)

Cabinet 20 Shelf 1 No. 16

(Ballhorn impressions from the Kiel University Library, 1536) Ballhorn-Drucke (1536) der Kieler Universitats - Bibliothek, von Dr. W. Ludtke, Kiel, Illus. Initials, title pages, and wood engravings.

In Zeitschrift fur Bucherfreunde, 1904-5, part 2, p. 281.

EARLY PRINTING IN GERMANY. [Literature of]

Cabinet 22 Shelf 1 No. 7

(Berlin, 1540-1700, Printing and bookselling in Brandenburg-Prussia in 1540-1740) Buchdruck und Buchhandel in Brandenburg-Preussen, namentlich in Berlin, in den Jahren 1540-1740, von F. Kapp.

In Archiv für Deutschen Buchhandels, 1887, vol.VII, p.6-43.

EARLY PRINTING IN GERMANY (Lit. of)

Stack A Shelf 2 Number 54

Bullen, Henry Lewis. The literature of typography in Germany, the Netherlands, and Switzerland. The Inland Printer, vol. 54. p. 61.

EARLY PRINTING IN GERMANY Literature

Cabinet 26 Shelf 1 No. 20

Bamberg, 1452-1491. Quellen zur geschichte des Bamberger buchdrucks im fünfzehnten jahrhundert. von Gottfried Zedler.

Article in the "Gutenberg-Gesellschaft Jahrbuch" 1930, pp.149-157.

EARLY PRINTING IN GERMANY Literature

Cabinet 26 Shelf 1 No. 20

(Berlin 1574-1596. Voltz, Hilden, Mellemann. A contribution to Berlin printing in the 16th century) Zur geschichte des Berliner buchdrucks im 16. jahrhundert. von Ernst Crous. Illus.
Bio-bibliographical account.

Article in the "Gutenberg-Gesellschaft Jahrbuch" 1930, pp.226-235.

EARLY PRINTING IN GERMANY [Literature of]

Cabinet 18 Shelf 1 No. 15

[Catalogue of the books of the first half of the eighteenth century of the publishing house of M. Georg Weidman in Leipzig.] Katalog der Weidmannsehen Buchhandlung aus der ersten Halfte des XVIII. Jahrhunderts. von Karl Baerent.

In Zeitschrift fur Bucherfreunde, 1913-14, part 2, p.236.

EARLY PRINTING IN GERMANY (Lit. of)

Cabinet 18 Shelf 1 No. 12

(Catalogue of the Church Library in Sommerfeld, 1515) Ein verzeichnis der Kirchenbibliothek zu Sommerfeld aus dem Jahr 1515, von Fritz Schillman. Berlin.

In Zeitschrift für Bücherfreunde, 1912, part 2, p. 326.

EARLY PRINTING IN GERMANY Literature of

Cabinet U Shelf 1 No. 1f

Cologne, 1474, Arnold Therhoernen. The edition of the "Fasciculus Temporum" printed by Arnold Ther Hoernen. An account by A.G.W. Murray.

In Excerpts relating to printing from "the Library," 1912-13, p. 93 of pencilled folios.

EARLY PRINTING IN GERMANY. (Lit. of

Cabinet 20 Shelf 1 No. 19

Cologne, 1479. Die Kolner bilderbibel und die beziehungen des druckers Nicholaus Goetz zur Helman und Quentel von Otto Zaretsky, Koln, June, 1906. Facsimiles.

The Cologne Bible and the relationship of the printer, Nikolaus Goetz with Helman and Quentel.

In Zeitschrift für Bücherfreunde, 1906-7, part 1, p. 101.

EARLY PRINTING IN GERMANY Literature of

Cabinet U Shelf 1 No. 19

Cologne, 1525, Peter Quentel.

See ARBER, EDWARD. Facsimile Texts. The first English New Testament...p.65.

EARLY PRINTING IN GERMANY [Literature of]

Cabinet U Shelf 1 No. 1f

Cologne, Basle and Cologne printing in 1484-1485. A note by V. Scholderer.

In excerpts relating to printing from "The Library," 1912-13, p. 205 of pencilled folios.

EARLY PRINTING IN GERMANY [Literature of]

Cabinet 18 Shelf 1 No. 9

(Concerning some publishers and illustrators of Hans Sach's works) Uber einige verleger und Illustratoren des Hans Sachs, von Reinhard Buchwald, Leipzig, illus.

In Zeitschrift fur Bucherfreunde, 1910-11, part 1, p. 233.

EARLY PRINTING IN GERMANY Literature

Cabinet Y Shelf 3 No. 76

Crous, Ernst. Die anfänge des antiquadrucks in Deutschland und seinen nachbarländern... (With 6 facs.)

pp. 33-42 in Loubier, Hans (Tribute to) Buch und bucheinband...Leipzig, 1923.

EARLY PRINTING IN GERMANY. [Literature of]

Cabinet 22 Shelf 1 No. 7

(Dorpat, 1630. The development of the book industry.) Die entwickelung des Buch-Gewertes in Dorpat, von Wilhelm Stieda.

Includes prices of types.

In Archiv fur Deutschen Buchhandels, 1882, vol.VII, p.163.

EARLY PRINTING IN GERMANY [Literature of]

Cabinet 18 Shelf 2 No. 2

[Dresden, The earliest printing in]. Der alteste Dresdner Buchdruck. von Dr. Otto Gunther. Leipzig, 1916. With facsimiles and reproductions of initials.

In Zeitschrift fur Bucherfreunde, 1916-17, part 2, p.174.

EARLY PRINTING IN GERMANY (Lit. of)

Cabinet 18 Shelf 1 No. 4

(Early school books) Alte Fibeln. von Paul Hennig. Charlottenberg. Illus.

In Zeitschrift für Bückerfreunde, 1908-9, part 1, p. 1.

EARLY PRINTING IN GERMANY [Literature of]

Cabinet 22 Shelf 1 No. 10

See Engraving, early. Did the early printers use engravings or metal, etc.

EARLY PRINTING IN GERMANY [Literature of]

Cabinet 20 Shelf 2 No. 18

Entstehung (Die) der modelbücher, 1525-1600. (Origin of handwork pattern books). von Arthur Lotz in Berlin. Facsimile.

In Zeitschrift für Bücherfreunde, 1926, pp. 45-56.

EARLY PRINTING IN GERMANY Literature

Cabinet Y Shelf 3 No. 61

Erfurt, 1474. Geschichte einiger Erfurter typem des 15 jahrhunderts. von Ernst Voullieme.

Essay (p. 261) in Beitrage zum bibliothek und buchwesen", Paul Schwenke, Leipzig, 1913.

Half Morocco; 11¼" x 8-5/8"

EARLY PRINTING IN GERMANY [Literature of]

Cabinet 22 Shelf 1 No. 10

(Erfurt, 1479-1700, History of printing and publishing in Erfurt from the 15th century to the 17th century.) Geschichte der buchdruckerkunst und Buchhandler Erfurts im 15 bis 17. Jahrhundert von J. Braun.

Includes chronological list with brief biographies of printers and booksellers with reference to their works.

In Archiv für Deutschen Buchhandels, vol. X, p.59.

EARLY PRINTING IN GERMANY [Literature of]

Cabinet 20 Shelf 2 No. 19

Felssecker und Fillion [1683]: Zur Verlegerfrage bei Grimmelshausen. Von Richard Alewyn of Heidelberg. [Felssech, publisher: Fillion, printer: An Inquiry concerning the publisher and place of publication of Grimmelshausen "Simplissimus"].

In Zeitschrift für Bücherfreunde, 1927. pp. 38-40: See also 20/2/18. pp. 11.-20.

EARLY PRINTING IN GERMANY. [Literature of]

Cabinet 22 Shelf 1 No. 13

Feyerabend, Sigmund, and his itinerant stock in Leipzig in 1570) Sigmund Feyerabend's Wanderlager in Leipzig von A. Kirchhoff.

In Archiv für Deutschen Buchhandels, 1890, vol.XIII, p.103.

EARLY PRINTING IN GERMANY (Lit. of)

Cabinet 22 Shelf 1 No. 9

(Feyerabend's Sigmund, book record for 1565). Ein mesregister Sigmund Feyerabend's aus dem jahre 1565. Von Heinrich Pallmann.

Includes an alphabetical list of Feyerabend's clients.

In Archiv fur deutschen buchhandels, vol. 9, p. 5.

EARLY PRINTING IN GERMANY Literature

Cabinet Y Shelf 3 No. 111

(Frankfurt a.M. 1473 - 1516, Franz Renner von Heilbronn and Nicolaus von Frankfurt). Bibliographical - historical study.

See Sondheim, Mortiz, Gesammelte schriften...Frankfurt, 1927, p. 244 and fol.

EARLY PRINTING IN GERMANY Literature

Cabinet Y, Shelf 3, No. 111

Frankfort a. M. 1511-12. Bibliographical literary study of printing in.

See Sondheim, Moritz, Gesammelte schriften...Frankfurt, 1927, p. 36

EARLY PRINTING IN GERMANY. [Literature of]

Cabinet 22, Shelf 1, No. 18

(Haselberg, Johann, Reichenau, 1515-1538. The printer and publisher.) Johann Haselberg, von Archivar, W.C. Roth.

Documentary contributions relating to the man, his works, and governmental contacts.

In Archiv für Deutschen Buchhandels, vol. XVIII, p.16.

EARLY PRINTING IN GERMANY Literature

Cabinet Y, Shelf 1, No. 95.01

Leipzig. Kachelofen, Konrad und Johannes. von Victor von Klemperer. Illus. facsimiles and printers' marks.

Bio-bibliographical account of two celebrated 15th century printers.

Article in the "Gutenberg-Gesellschaft Jahrbuch" 1929, pp.134-151.

EARLY PRINTING IN GERMANY Literature.

Cabinet 75, Shelf 2, No. 2

Frankfort and the history of early printing, by V. Scholderer. A review of the book Frankfurter Urkendenbuch zur Fruhgeschicte des Buchdrucks, by W. K. Zulch und Gustav Mori.

In Transactions of the Bibliographical Society, "The Library," Vol. II, 1921-22, pp. 59-63.

EARLY PRINTING IN GERMANY [Literature of]

Cabinet AA, Shelf 5, No. 32

Heidelberg, 1478-1484. Heinrich Knoblochtzer. Zur bibliographie Heinrich Knoblocktzers in Heidelberg. Ernst Voulliéme, Berlin, 1925. Facsimile, repro. types.

Bibliographical essay in Collijns "Bokock biblioteks-historika studier ... Uppsala 1925. pp. 137-151.

Boards; 11 x 8½ x 2 in.

EARLY PRINTING IN GERMANY Literature

Cabinet 26, Shelf 1, No. 17

Leipzig, 1497. Konrad Kachelofens. Ein druck: Historia Sancti Albini. von Adolf Schmidt.

Bio-bibliographical account. German text.

Article in the Gutenberg-Gesellschaft Jahrbuch 1928, pp. 79-86.

EARLY PRINTING IN GERMANY. [Literature of]

Cabinet 22, Shelf 1, No. 20

(Frankfort, 1664-1678. From the correspondence of the Frankfort printer, Johann Arnold Cholinus.) Aus dem briefwechsel des Frankfurter buchdruckers Johann Arnold Cholinus, von F. Buchwald.

In Archiv für Deutschen Buchhandels, vol. XX, p.86.

EARLY PRINTING IN GERMANY [Literature of]

Cabinet 22, Shelf 1, No. 11

(The history of printing to 1500 gleaned from the administrative records in the archives of Basle.) Registen zur geschichte des Buchdruchs bis zum jahre 1500. Aus dem Buchern des Basler gerichtsarchivs von Karl Stehlen

Includes name index of printers and publishers.

In Archiv für Deutschen Buchhandels, 1888, vol.XI, p.5, vol.XII, p.6.

EARLY PRINTING IN GERMANY. [Literature of]

Cabinet 18, Shelf 2, No. 3

(Leipzig, 1511-28. The printer of Luther's indulgence thesis of 1517). Die drucker von Luther's Ablassthesen 1517, von Otto Gunther Leipzig. Facsimiles.

Brief controversial item which by type comparison establishes Jacob Tanner as the first Leipzig printer, and not Lotter.

In Zeitschrift für Bücherfreunde, 1917-18, part 2, p.259.

EARLY PRINTING IN GERMANY (Lit.)

Cabinet 22, Shelf 1, No. 8

(Fruitful gleanings from 17th century Acts of the Saxony Book Commissioners in Leipzig.) Lesefruchte aus den Acten der Kurf. sachsischen Bucher-Commission zu Leipzig von Albrecht Kirchhoff.

Account of strike regulations: Book tax of 1666: censorship: Printers.

In Archiv für Deutschen Buchhandels, 1883, vol.VIII, p.62, vol.IX, pp;47, 255, vol.X, p.117.

EARLY PRINTING IN GERMANY (Lit. of)

Cabinet U, Shelf 1, No. 1f

Hoernen, Arnold Ther, 1474. The edition of the "Fasciculus Temporum" printed by Arnold Ther Hoernen in 1474: An account by A.G.W. Murray.

Probably the first or second illustrated book printed in Cologne.

In excerpts relating to printing from "The Library," 1912-13, p. 93 of pencilled folios.

EARLY PRINTING IN GERMANY. [Literature of]

Cabinet 22, Shelf 1, No. 12

(Leipzig, 1517. Pantsschman's publishing house: An additional history of the Leipzig book fairs.) Pantschman's Buchhandel. Ein weiterer beitrag zur geschichte der Leipziger Buchermesse, von A. Kirchoff.

In Archiv für Deutschen Buchhandels, 1889, vol. XII, pp.71, 178.

EARLY PRINTING IN GERMANY (Lit. of)

Cabinet 20, Shelf 1, No. 16

Goslar, 1614). Johann Vaigt establishes the first printing and publishing house in). Zur verlagsgeschichte.

German text, Brief historical account.

In Zeitschrift für bücherfreunde, 1904-5, part 2, p. 333.

EARLY PRINTING IN GERMANY. [Literature of]

Cabinet 22, Shelf 1, No. 10

(Koburger, Anthony, Nurnberg, 1500. Municipal assistance to the earliest booksellers.) Förderung des altesten buchhandels, durch die Stadthorden, von O. Hase.

Item includes book prices, and excerpts from governmental letters concerning business relations between A, Koburger and others.

In Archiv für Deutschen Buchhandels, 1886, vol.X, p.27.

EARLY PRINTING IN GERMANY (Lit. of)

Cabinet 18, Shelf 1, No. 14

Leipzig, 1518. Michael Roswick, or Koswick.

See Printing, Historical, Koswick, Michael known as Roswick.

EARLY PRINTING IN GERMANY LITERATURE OF

Cabinet K, Shelf 1, No. 17

Hagenau, 1516 - 1523, Thomas Anshelm.

See Heitz, Paul (Die) Zierinitialen in dem drucken der Thomas Anshelm...

EARLY PRINTING IN GERMANY. [Literature of]

Cabinet 18, Shelf 1, No. 14

(Koswick, Michael, named Roswick, 1516: An investigation into the confusing biographical information relating to this printer, publisher or monk) Michael Koswick, Roswick genannt, von Paul Emil Richter, Dresden.

In Zeitschrift für Bücherfreunde, 1913-14, part 1, p.14.

EARLY PRINTING IN GERMANY. [Literature of]

Cabinet 22, Shelf 1, No. 15

(Leipzig, 1534-1578. Christopher Birck, bookbinder and bookseller.) Christopher Birck. Buchbinder und Buchführer in Leipzig. von A. Korchhoff.

Brief sketch of this bookbinder's relation with his contemporary printers.

In Archiv für Deutschen Buchhandels, vol. XV, p.11.

EARLY PRINTING IN GERMANY. [Literature of]

Cabinet 22 Shelf 1 No. 11

(Leipzig, 1550-1650. The Book Fair in Leipzig, 1550-1650) Die Leipziger Büchermesse von 1550-1650. Communicated by A. Kirchhoff.

In Archiv für Deutschen Buchhandels, 1888, vol.XI, p.163.

EARLY PRINTING IN GERMANY [Literature of]

Cabinet 22 Shelf 1 No. 13

(Leipzig, 1559-78. Ernst Vogelin's and his types.

Brief account in German in which the writer remarks upon the absence of recent French innovations.

In Archiv fur Deutschen Buchhandels, vol. XIII, p.251.

EARLY PRINTING IN GERMANY. [Literature of]

Cabinet 22 Shelf 1 No. 10

(Leipzig, 1606. The first suggestion of privileges came from the Leipzig council.) Die anfange der insimation von privilegien durch der Rath zu Leipzig. von A. Kirchhoff.

In Archiv für Deutschen Buchhandels, 1886, vol.X, p.257.

EARLY PRINTING IN GERMANY. [Literature of]

Cabinet 22 Shelf 1 No. 12

(Leipzig, 1608. Gleanings from the acts in the Leipzig State archives: Contribution to the understanding of the book trade during the 17th century.) Lesefrüchte aus den Acten des staatischen archivs zu Leipzig von Albrecht Kirchhoff.

In Archiv für Deutschen Buchhandels, vol.XII, p.120, vol.XIII, p.177, vol.XIV, p.196.

EARLY PRINTING IN GERMANY. [Literature of]

Cabinet 22 Shelf 1 No. 17

(Leipzig, 1652. Privileges for the production of elementary school books. Prejudices after the Thirty Years War.) Die privilegien uber die elementar-schulbucher kriege, von A. Kirchhoff.

In Archiv für Deutschen Buchhandels, vol.XV, p.79.

EARLY PRINTING IN GERMANY [Literature of]

Cabinet X Shelf 2 No. 6

Leipzig, 1740. Gepriesens andenken von erfindung der buchdruckerey, wie solches beym schluss des dritten jahrhunderts...gefeyert worden. (In praise of printing: Historical-bibliographical miscellany relating to the origin, development and diffusion of printing. The tri-centenary celebration of the invention of printing.

Cloth; 8-3/4 x 7-1/8 x 7/8 in.

EARLY PRINTING IN GERMANY. [Literature of]

Cabinet 22 Shelf 1 No. 6

(Leipzig, 1767. Statistics concerning the Leipzig printer and copperplate engraver in 1676) Zur statistik der Leipziger buchdrucker und kupferstecher im Jahre 1767.

Includes cost of publishing privileges, prices of printing, etc.

In Archiv für Deutschen Buchhandels, vol. VI, p.273.

EARLY PRINTING IN GERMANY [Literature of]

Cabinet 18 Shelf 1 No. 10

(Letter of indulgence for Neuhausen, Worms, 1461 and 1462) Die Ablassbrief fur Neuhausen bei Worms, von Adolf Schmidt, Darmstadt. Facsimiles including seal.

In Zeitschrift für Bücherfreunde, 1911, part 1, p.65.

EARLY PRINTING IN GERMANY Literature

Cabinet Y Shelf 3 No. 93

Lübeck, 1499-1518, Georg Richolff

See COLLIJN, ISAK. (Der) Buchdrucker Georg Richolff...

EARLY PRINTING IN GERMANY [Literature of]

Cabinet 20 Shelf 2 No. 2

Lubeck [1530-1603] Johann Ballhorn. Ballhorn ABC von Arthur Kopp, Marburg, 1916.

Brief account of the production of Ballhorn A.B.C. Books.

In Zeitschrift fur Bucherfreunde, 1915-16, part 2, p.191.

EARLY PRINTING IN GERMANY [Literature of]

Cabinet Y Shelf 2 No. 74

(Magdeburg, 1483-1504). Altere geschichte der buchdruckerkunst in Magdeburg. (I). Abtheilung: Die drucker des 15 jahrhunderts. von Dr. Ludwig Goetze. Magdeburg, 1872. Illus.

"Only 120 copies were printed of this first part,-all that was published". B & W.

Half morocco; 9¼ x 6 x 5/8 in.

EARLY PRINTING IN GERMANY (Lit. of)

Cabinet 22 Shelf 1 No. 13

Magdeburg, 1591.

See Bookselling early. Francke, Johann, Magdeburg.

EARLY PRINTING IN GERMANY. Literature of

Cabinet W Shelf 2 No. 1

Excerpt re printing in Mainz in 1463.

Bound in volume "Gutenberg inventeur de l' imprimerie. Melanges."

EARLY PRINTING IN GERMANY Literature

Cabinet Y Shelf 3 No. 19

Mainz, 1480, Johann Numeister

see

KELCHNER, Dr. ERNST. (Mainz Ecclesiastical Acts of 1480...

EARLY PRINTING IN GERMANY [Literature of]

Cabinet X Shelf 1 No. 84

(Mainz, 15th century). Wurdtwein, Etienne Alexander: Bibliotheca Moguntina libris saeculo primo typographico Moguntiae impressis instructa hinc inde addita inventae typographiae historia. Augustae Vindel (Augsburg), 1789.

Bibliographical history of books printed in Mainz during the first century of the invention

Half morocco; 9 x 7-3/8 x 1-1/8 in.

EARLY PRINTING IN GERMANY Literature

Cabinet Y Shelf 2 No. 25

Mainz, 1540, Franz Behem. Ein beitrag zur geschichte des buchhandels des 16 jahrhunderts....von Simon Widmann, Paderborn, 1889.

Bio-bibliographical of a 16th cent. printer and bookseller.

Half morocco; 8¾ x 5½ x 3/8 in.

EARLY PRINTING IN GERMANY [Literature of]

Cabinet Y Shelf 5 No. 134

(Marienthal, 1463- Brothers of the Common Life. A bibliographical study of the Marienthal impressions now in the Municipal Library in Frankfurt a.M. With facsimiles). Die Marienthaler drucke der Stadt-Bibliothek... Bibliographisch beschreiben. von Dr. Ernst Kelchner. Frankfurt a.M. 1883.

Half morocco; 14-7/8 x 11 x ½ in.

EARLY PRINTING IN GERMANY [Literature of]

Cabinet Y Shelf 2 No. 77

(Munich, 1482-1500). Die wiegendruck Münchens: Ein bibliographische verzeichnis mit neun typentafeln. Zusammengestellt von Ernst Weil Munchen, 1923.

The incunabula of Munich: A bibliographical account, with specimens of types designed by Schaur for Schobser, the first printer in Munich.

Boards; 9½ x 6¼ x 3/8 in.

EARLY PRINTING IN GERMANY Literature

Cabinet Y Shelf 3 No. 93

Münster, 1499-1518, Georg Richolff

See COLLIJN, ISAK (Der) Buchdrucker Georg Richolff...

EARLY PRINTING IN GERMANY. [Literature of]

Cabinet 18 Shelf 1 No. 9

(Nuremberg, 1570) See Publishing, early. Illustrators and publishers of the works of Hans Sachs.

EARLY PRINTING IN GERMANY [Literature of]

Cabinet 18 Shelf 1 No. 10

(Printed medical books 1546-1700: Tarquinius Schnellenberg and his work "Practica deutsch) An account in German by Franz Tetzner, Leipzig

In Zeitschrift für Bücherfreunde, 1911, part 1, p.169.

EARLY PRINTING IN GERMANY [Literature of]

Cabinet 22 Shelf 1 No. 10

(Nuremberg, 1470. Earliest example of business partnership in the printing trade.) Zum gesellschaftsbetrieb im druckgewerbe: Fruhestes Nurnberger beispiel. Communicated by Oskar Hase.

In Archiv fur Deutschen Buchhandels, vol. X, p.5.

EARLY PRINTING IN GERMANY Lit of

Cabinet Y Shelf 5 No. 20

(Nurnberg, 1658-1908) Zum 250 jahr geschaftsjubilaum der Konigl. Bayer Hofdruckerei und verlagshandlung von U.E. Sebald. Nurnberg, 1908. With portraits and other illustrations.

Half morocco; 12¼ x 9¼ x 3/8 in.

EARLY PRINTING IN GERMANY. [Literature of]

Cabinet 22 Shelf 1 No. 18 & 19

(Prussia. History of printing and bookselling in the dukedom of Prussia) Geschichte des buchdrucks und des buchhandels im herzogthum Preussen, von Karl Lohmeyer.

Includes brief biographies of the early printers.

In Archiv fur Deutschen Buchhandels, vol. XVIII, p.38, vol. XIX, p.179.

EARLY PRINTING IN GERMANY (Lit. of)

Cabinet Y Shelf 2 No. 26

Nuremberg, 1472-1540. Die Koberger, seine darstellung des buchhändlerischen geschäftsbetriebes in der zeit des uberganges vom miltelatter zur neuzeit. von Oscar Hase. [Second ed.] Leipzig, 1885. Facsimiles.

Boards; 9½ x 6 x 1½ in.

EARLY PRINTING IN GERMANY Literature of

Cabinet K Shelf 1 No. 1

Nuremberg and Altdorf, 1726-42. Joh. Dan. Tauber, haeredes (Successors of Johann Daniel Tauber). Imprint.

See Roth-Scholtzius (Fredericus). Icones bibliopolarum et typographorum... Norimbergae et Altdorfi, 1726- 42.

EARLY PRINTING IN GERMANY. [Literature of]

Cabinet 18 Shelf 1 No. 5

Reinhard, Marcus, Kirchheim, 1491 (An unknown German Horae B.M.V. of the 15th century) Ein unbekannte deutsche Ausgabe des Horae B.M.V aus dem XV Jahrhundert von Otto Zaretski, Cologne. Facsimile.

In Zeitschrift für Bücherfreunde, 1909, part 1, p.22.

EARLY PRINTING IN GERMANY Literature

Cabinet Y Shelf 2 No. 97

Nürnberg, 1473. Ein merkwürdiger stützsatz in einem drucke Friedrich Creussners von Nürnberg. von Adolf Schmidt.

Bibliographical.

Article in Gutenberg-Gesellschaft Jahrbuch, 1932, p.114.

EARLY PRINTING IN GERMANY (Lit. of)

Cabinet 75 Shelf 1 No. 3

Oppenheim Press [Jacob Köbel, 1494], some early book illustrations of the. A paper read by Gilbert R. Redgrave.

In Transactions of the Bibliographical Society, vol. 3, 1895 - 1896, pp. 71-80.

EARLY PRINTING IN GERMANY [Literature of]

Cabinet 18 Shelf 1 No. 13

[Remarkable changes in the printing of Luther portraits.] Denkwurdige Reformationsdruck mit dem Bilde Luthers. Dr. Karl Schottenloher. Munich, 1913.
Illus. with portraits and facsimile title pages of early Luther editions.

In Zeitschrift fur Bucherfreunde, 1913, part 2, p. 221.

EARLY PRINTING IN GERMANY [Literature of]

Cabinet Y Shelf 2 No. 72

Nuremberg, 1525, Johannes Petreius. Eine schriftprobe vom jahre 1525. von K. Burger, Leipzig, 1895. Facsimile, and printer mark.
Brief biography, with bibliographical account of a presumably first dated type specimen sheet. Includes a list of books published or printed by Petreius.

Half morocco; 13 x 9½ x ¾ in.

EARLY PRINTING IN GERMANY (Lit. of)

Cabinet 18 Shelf No.1 3

(Pamphlets during the early years of the Reformation) Flugschriften aus den ersten jahren der Reformation, von Karl Schottenloher, Bamberg.

In Zeitschrift fur Bucherfreunde, 1907-8, part 2, p. 464.

EARLY PRINTING IN GERMANY [Literature of]

Cabinet 18 Shelf 1 No. 13

(Remarkable impression of the Reformation period with portraits of Luther) Denkwurdige Reformationsdrucke mit dem Bilde Luthers, von Karl Schottenloher. Munchen. Illus.

In Zeitschrift für Bücherfreunde, 1913, part 2, p.221.

EARLY PRINTING IN GERMANY [Literature of]

Cabinet 22 Shelf 1 No.

(Nuremberg, 1527) See Bookselling, Germany. Nuremberg, Johann Herrgott.

EARLY PRINTING IN GERMANY [Literature of]

Cabinet 18 Shelf 1 No. 15

(Playing Cards. The earliest German Playing Cards: Reminiscences of an Antiquarian.) Die Altest deutsche Spielkarte. Aus den erinnerungen eines antiquars, von Erwin Volckmann. Illus.

In Zeitschrift für Bücherfreunde 1913-14, part 2, p.323.

EARLY PRINTING IN GERMANY [Literature of]

Cabinet U Shelf 5 No. 52

Reutlingen, Ulm, 1473: John Czeiner.
See pp.20-22 in Bibliographical Notes: Gentleman's Magazine.

EARLY PRINTING IN GERMANY [Literature of]

Cabinet 22 Shelf 1 No. 17

(Rostock, 1475-1707. Studies related to the history of printing and publishing in Mecklenburg.) Studien zur geschichte des buchdrucks und buchhandels in Mecklenburg. von Wilh. Stieda.

In Archiv für Deutschen Buchhandels, vol. XVII, p.119-325.

EARLY PRINTING IN GERMANY Literature

Cabinet Y Shelf 3 No. 72

(Strassburg, 1490, Peter Attendorn) Peter Attendorn, ein buchhandler in drucker in Strassburg um 1490.)

See BOOKS ABOUT BOOKS. Aufsaetse... Leipzig, 1921, pp.344-353

EARLY PRINTING IN GERMANY Literature

Cabinet 22 Shelf 1 No. 2

Tubingen, 1522-1700. Zur geschichte des buchhandels in Tubingen. von Th. Schott in Stuttgart.

In "Archiv für Deutschen Buchhandles, 1879. p.241, vol. 2, 1879.

EARLY PRINTING IN GERMANY. Literature of

Cabinet 26 Shelf 1 No. 16

Salzburg, 1550-1557, Hans Baumann.

See "Gutenberg-Gesellschaft Jahrbuch, 1927", pp.68-71

EARLY PRINTING IN GERMANY. [Literature of

Cabinet 75 Shelf 1 No. 11

Strassburg, 1492 et sub. The Schotts of Strassburg and their Press, by S. H. Scott. A paper read before the Bibliographical Society, London, December 19, 1910.

In Trans. Biblio. Soc., Vol. XI, 1909-1911, pp. 165-188.

EARLY PRINTING IN GERMANY [Literature of]

Cabinet 20 Shelf 2 No. 10

Weiters zu Hans Sachsischen Einzeldrucken mit Holzschnitten bestimmter meister. Von Prof. Dr. Georg Stuhlfauth of Berlin.

In Zeitschrift für Bücherfreunde, 1921, pp. 117-19.

EARLY PRINTING IN GERMANY [Literature of]

Cabinet 22 Shelf 1 No. 14

(Selling methods of the first booksellers.) vertriebsmittel der altesten buchhandler, von F. Herm. Meyer.

Excerpts from prospectuses advertising books of the earliest printers, Peter Schoeffer and others.

In Archiv für Deutschen Buchhandels, vol. XIV, p.1.

EARLY PRINTING IN GERMANY. [Literature of]

Cabinet 22 Shelf 1 No. 5

(Strassburg, 1500-1590) Introduction of printing and bookselling into Strassburg.) Die anfange der Buchdruckerkunst in Strassburg, n.n. Leipzig, 1880.

Includes chronological list of the printers with brief biographies of each, also bibliography of their productions.

In Archiv fur Deutschen Buchhandels, 1880, vol.V, pp.1 - 145.

EARLY PRINTING IN GERMANY (Lit. of)

Cabinet 75 Shelf 1 No. 3

Wittenberg, the Lutheran Press at. A paper by G. F. Barwick, and read before the Bibliographical Society, Feb. 18th, 1895. Facsimiles.

In Trans. Biblio. Soc. Vol. 3, 1895-1896. pp. 9-25.

EARLY PRINTING IN GERMANY. [Literature of]

Cabinet 18 Shelf 2 No. 2

(Stockel, Wolfgang, Dresden, 1524. The earliest printing in Dresden) Der alteste Dresdner Buchdruck, von Otto Gunther, Leipzig. Facsimile.

In Zeitschrift für Bücherfreunde, 1916-17, part 2, p.174.

EARLY PRINTING IN GERMANY [Literature of]

Cabinet 20 Shelf 2 No. 16

Strassburg, 1532-1546. Jakob Cammerlander. Unbekannte Drucke von Jakob Cammerlander. Von Dr. Otto Clemen of Zwickau.

In Zeitschrift für Bücherfreunde, 1925, pp. 12-15.

EARLY PRINTING IN GERMANY. [Literature of]

Cabinet 22 Shelf 1 No. 19

(Wittenberg, 1537. George Rhau the Wittenberg printer and author of theological works.) Der Wittenberger buchdrucker Georg Rhau als "theologischer Schriftsteller," von Georg Buchwald.

Description of his books.

In Archiv für Deutschen Buchhandels, vol. XIX, p.38.

EARLY PRINTING IN GERMANY (Lit. Of)

Cabinet AA Shelf 5 No. 32

Strasburg, 1464-1489. Adolf Rusch. Notes pour la collation des deux tirages de l'edition du Speculum doctrinale, s. inc. typ. (Unidentified types). [Strasbourg, Adolphe Rusch. Par M.-Louis Polain, Bruxelles, Paris 1925.

Bibliographical essay based on type comparison. In Collijn's "Bok-ock biblioteks-historika studier ... Uppsala, 1925. pp. 111-120.

Boards; 11 x 8 1/2 x 2 in.

EARLY PRINTING IN GERMANY (Bavaria) Lit. of

Cabinet Y Shelf 2 No. 97

Tegensee, 1568, die anfänge des buchdrucks in der Abtei. Mit zwei abbildungen. von Alois Mitterwieser.

Article in Gutenberg-Gesellschaft Jahrbuch, 1932, p.178.

EARLY PRINTING IN GERMANY Literature

Cabinet 1 & 5 Shelf No. 1 - 41

(Wood engraving in first half of the 16th century) Der Deutsche einblatt-holzschnitt in der ersten halfte des 16 jahrhunderts. Max Geisberg, editor. Munich: Hugo Schmidt Verlag, 1928.

In 40 portfolio volumes, 22 x 16 in. and 32 x 22 in. with Index No. 41 in separate octavo vol.

EARLY PRINTING IN GERMANY. Literature of

Cabinet Y Shelf 5 No. 89

Strassburg, 1466, bibliographical description of the first Bible printed in.

See STEIGENBERGER, GERHOLD. Literarische-kritische abhandlung uber die zwo alleräl-teste gedruckte deutsche Bibeln...Munchen, 1787.

EARLY PRINTING IN GERMANY [Literature of]

Cabinet 20 Shelf 2 No. 10

(Title compartments of the Reformation period). Bermerkungen zu einigen Titeleinfassungen der Reformationszeit. von Dr. Otto Clemen in Zwickau. Illus.

In Zeitschrift für Bucherfreunde, 1921, pp. 65-68.

EARLY PRINTING IN GERMANY. Literature of

Cabinet Y Shelf 1 No. 94

Worms, 1521, Johann von Erfurt.

See "SCHOTTENLOHER, KARL". Hans Werlich, genannt Hans von Erfurt...

EARLY PRINTING IN GERMANY. [Literature of]

Cabinet 22 · Shelf 1 · No. 20

(Wurzburg, 1479-1618. History of printing and publishing in Wurzburg.) Geschichte der verlagsgeschafte und buchdruckereien zu Wurzburg, von J.W. Roth.

Includes biographies of the earliest printers and publishers.

In Archiv für Deutschen Buchhandel, vol. XX, p.67.

EARLY PRINTING IN HOLLAND. Literature of

Cabinet W · Shelf 5 · No. 31

Apercu sur les errors de la Bibliographie speciale des Elzevirs et de leurs annexes, avec quelques découvertes curieuse sur la typographie Hollandaise et Belge du 17e siecle. Motteley, Charles, Paris, 1848.

An attempt to distinguish the false from the true Elzeviers by their typography.

Half morocco; 7 x 4¼ in.

EARLY PRINTING IN HOLLAND [Literature of]

Cabinet S · Shelf 5 · No. 1

Enschede, John W. Een Nederlansache handleiding voor boekdrukwerk uit 1761. (Netherland printing materials in 1761). Illus. excerpt n.d.

Bound in collection "Various printing plants excerpts." item 9.

EARLY PRINTING IN GERMANY. [Literature of]

Cabinet 22 · Shelf 1 · No. 15

(WURZBURG, 1481-1548. Exemption for printers, 1481-1548.) Wurzburger befreiungen fur buchdrucker, 1481-1548, von F. Herm. Meyer.

In Archiv für Deutschen Buchhandels, vol. XV, p.4.

EARLY PRINTING IN HOLLAND (Lit. of)

Stack A · Shelf 1 & 2 · Number 54

Bullen, Henry Lewis: Germany, the Netherlands and Switzerland: The literature of typography, in The Inland Printer. vol. LIV p. 61.

EARLY PRINTING IN HOLLAND. [Literature of]

Cabinet AA · Shelf 3 · No. 46

Erasmus en zijn drukkers-uitgevers. Een fragment uit hun briefwisseling, bewerkt door B. Kruitwagen, O.F.M. Amsterdam, 1923.

Produced by the typefounders, Voorheen N. Tetterode, to introduce their new type Erasmus-Mediaeval, designed by S.-H. de Roos.

Half morocco; 9½ x 6-3/8 in.

EARLY PRINTING IN GERMANY. Literature.

Cabinet 75 · Shelf 2 · No. 7

Zell, Ulrich, his early quartos. A paper read at Cambridge as a Sandars lecture, by Francis Jenkinson, Dec. 4, 1908.

In Transactions of the Bibliographical Society, "The Library," Vol. VII, 1926-27, pp. 46-66.

EARLY PRINTING IN HOLLAND. [Literature of]

Cabinet W · Shelf 4 · No. 92

Campbell, M. F. A. G. Annales de la typographie Neerlandaise au XVe siècle. [Bibliography]

Supplements: 1, 2, 3, and 4: 1878 to 1890 bound in one volume.

See also W/4/91.

Half morocco; 9-3/4 x 6¼ in.

EARLY PRINTING IN HOLLAND. [Literature of]

Cabinet U · Shelf 1 · No. 1b

French clandestine press in Holland: Communicated to the sixteenth annual meeting of the Library Association, by Robert Harrison, Aberdeen, Sept. 1893.

In Excerpts relating to printing from "The Library," p. 121 of pencilled folios.

EARLY PRINTING IN GERMANY [Literature of]

Cabinet 22 · Shelf 1 · No. 16

(Zwickau, 1512, M. Stephen Roth: His importance to the booksellers and the literature of the Reformation period.) Stadtschreiber M. Stephen Roth in seiner literarisch-buchhandlerischen bedeutung fur die Reformationszeit.

A contribution towards the history of printing and bookselling.

In Archiv für Deutschen Buchhandels, vol. XVI, pp.6-354.

EARLY PRINTING IN HOLLAND [Literature of]

Cabinet AA · Shelf 3 · No. 37 · 2 Vols.

Denuce, Jan: Oud-Nederlandsche kaartmakers in betrekking met Plantijn. Door Jan Denuce. Antwerp, 1912. (2 Vols.) Facsimile, portraits, illus.

Early Netherland cartographers, and Plantin's relations with them. Bibliographical historical study.

Half morocco; 9¼ x 6¼ in.

EARLY PRINTING IN HOLLAND. (Lit. of)

Cabinet 18 · Shelf 1 · No. 17

Historical review of a Catalogue of Bibles printed in Holland from 1479. German text.

In Zeitschrift für Bücherfreunde, 1914-15, part 2, p. 293 of Supplement ("Beiblatt")

EARLY PRINTING IN HOLLAND. [Literature of]

Cabinet AA · Shelf 4 · No. 4 · 4 Vols.

Amsterdamsche boekdrukkers en uitgevers in de zestiende eeuw (16th. cent.(Door E.W. Moes, Amsterdam, 1900, 1907, 1910, 1915. (4 Vols). Facsimiles.

Bio-bibliographical. Vol. 4 has a name list of the Amsterdam printers.

Half morocco; 9 x 7¼ in.

EARLY PRINTING IN HOLLAND. (Lit. of)

Cabinet U · Shelf 1 · No. 1b

Doesborgh, Jan van, by Robert G.C. Proctor.

Mr. Proctor's attempt to throw some light on the history of printing in the Netherlands Includes notes of types, and devices.

In excerpts relating to printing from "The Library," p. 78 of pencilled folios.

EARLY PRINTING IN HOLLAND Literature

Cabinet 26 · Shelf 1 · No. 20

Holländische frühdruck und die ersten versuche Gutenbergs in Strassburg. von Gottfried Zedler.

Bibliographical account: The first printing in Holland and Gutenberg's first experiments in Strassburg.

Article in the "Gutenberg-Gesellschaft Jahrbuch" 1930, pp.53-72.

EARLY PRINTING IN HOLLAND. [Literature of]

Cabinet AA · Shelf 3 · No. 36

(Antwerp, 1572-1652). Abraham Verhoeven, zijn leven: Ontstaan van het nieuwsblad te Antwerpen. Door F. Jos. Van den Branden, Antwerp, 1902.

The life of Abraham Verhoeven, printer-publisher, and the origin of the first newspaper in Antwerp.

Half morocco; 7¾ x 5-1/8 in.

EARLY PRINTING IN HOLLAND [Literature of]

Cabinet S · Shelf 5 · No. 4

Elseviers, Famous Dutch Printers, by Baroness Althea Salvador, in New Science Review, Jan. 1895.

A brief historical account with genealogy of the Elzeviers.

Item 21 in collection "Various printers and their plants; Excerpt from magazines, I."

EARLY PRINTING IN HOLLAND. [Literature of]

Cabinet AA · Shelf 4 · No. 5 · 2 Vols.

Kleerkooper, M.M.: Te Boekhandel te Amsterdam in de 17e eeuw ... 'S - Gravenhage, 1914-16 2 Vols.

See "Zaak-en Plaatsnaamregister," p. 1718 of the above work.

Half morocco; 9½ x 6½ in.

EARLY PRINTING IN HOLLAND [Literature of]

Cabinet AA Shelf 3 No. 39

Knuttel, W.P.C.: Verboden boeken in de Republiek der Vereenigde Nederlanden. Beredeneerde catalogus. Door Dr. W.P.C. 'S-Gravenhage, 1914. (Prohibited books in the Republic of the United Netherlands).
Bibliographical account.

Half morocco; 9½ x 6 in.

EARLY PRINTING IN HOLLAND. Literature of

Cabinet J Shelf 5 No. 57

Monuments typographiques des Pays-Bas au Quinsième Siècle. Collection de facsimile d'apres les originaux conserves a la Bibliotheque royale de la Haye et ailleurs. Par John William Holtrop. La Haye, 1868. Facsimile.
At the end a map of Holland in the 15th century, also a chronological table of the towns where printing was exercised in the 15th century in Holland, with the names of the printers.

(cont'd)

EARLY PRINTING IN HOLLAND Literature of

Cabinet W Shelf 5 No. 106

Nouvelles études sur la bibliographie Elzevirienne. Supplement a l'ouvrage sur les Elzevier de M. Alphonse Willems. Par G. Berghman. Stockholm, 1897.
Bibliographical account.

Half morocco; 10 x 6¼ in.

EARLY PRINTING IN HOLLAND. [Literature of]

Cabinet AA Shelf 3 No. 24

Ledeboer, A.M.: Chronologische Register ... Alfabetische lijst der boekdrukkers, boekverkoopers en uitgevers in Noord-Nederland sedert het jaar 1440 tot het begin dezen eeuw. (1440-1800). Door A.M. Ledeboer. Utrecht, 1877.
This chronological register of Dutch printers is intended as an appendix to AA/3/23..

Half morocco; 10-7/8 x 9-1/8 in.

EARLY PRINTING IN HOLLAND. Lit. of. (cont'd)

Cabinet Shelf No.

Boards; 14¾ x 11 in.

EARLY PRINTING IN HOLLAND [Literature of]

Cabinet AA Shelf 3 No. 45

Ontwikkeling der boekdrukkunst in Nederland: Catalogus der Tentoonstelling, in het Paviljoen te Haarlem. 1923. (The development of printing in Holland: Catalog of an exhibition). Facsimile.
Includes many historical accounts relating to printing and its history in all its branches, by several authors.

Half morocco; 9½ x 6¼ in.

EARLY PRINTING IN HOLLAND. [Literature of]

Cabinet AA Shelf 3 No. 19

Ledeboer, A.M: Het geslacht van Waesberghe: eene bijdrage tot de geschiedenis der boekdrukkunst en van den boekhandel in Nederland. Door A.M. Ledeboer. 's Gravenhagen, 1869. With printer marks and facsimile.

Half leather; 10½ x 6½ in.

EARLY PRINTING IN HOLLAND. [Literature of]

Cabinet AA Shelf 3 No. 47

Nederlandsche bibliographie van 1500 tot 1540, door Wouter Nijhoff en M.E. Kronenberg. 'S-Gravenhage, 1923.—40
A bibliography with alphabetical lists of places and names of printers.

Half morocco; 10-1/8 x 6½ x 3½ in.

EARLY PRINTING IN HOLLAND [Literature of]

Cabinet 18 Shelf 1 No. 16

[Typography in the Low Countries, 1500-1540. By Wouter Nijhoff] L'Art typographique dans les Pays-Bas, 1500-1540. Wouter Nijhoff. [Review of book with same title, by M.D. Henkel.]

In Zeitschrift fur Bucherfreunde, 1914-15, part I, p.7 of "Beiblatt."

EARLY PRINTING IN HOLLAND. (Lit. of)

Cabinet 20 Shelf 1 No. 17

Leeu, Geraert, Antwerp, 1491. Eine Buchanzeige des Antwerpener Druckers Geraert Leeu in neederlandischer Sprache. von Karl Schorbach Strassburg, July, 1905. Illus.
Brief account of the advertising notices used by early printers and publishers.

In Zeitschrift für Bücherfreunde, 1905-6, part 1, p. 139.

EARLY PRINTING IN HOLLAND Literature

Cabinet AA Shelf 3 No. 48

Nederlandsche bibliographie van 1500 tot 1540. Door Wouter Nijhoff en M.E. Kronenberg. 'S-Gravenhage. 1925-34.
Supplements to the bibliography of Netherland printing. See also AA/3/47.
Afl. 1-4

Boards; 10¼ x 6¼ in.

EARLY PRINTING IN HOLLAND. [Literature of]

Cabinet 18 Shelf 1 No. 14

(Typography in the Netherlands, 1500-1540) L'art typographique dans les Pays-Bas: Brief review of book with same title, by M.D. Henkel, Amsterdam.

References to the earliest unrecorded printers.

In Zeitschrift für Bücherfreunde, 1913-14, part 1, pp.153-4 of Supplement ("Beiblatt")

EARLY PRINTING IN HOLLAND. [Literature of]

Cabinet U Shelf 2 No. 7

Leyden, The Pilgrim Press. The story of the Pilgrim Fathers', 1606-1623 A.D., as told by themselves, their friends, and their enemies. Edited from the original texts, by Edward Arber. London, 1897.

Stamped cloth; 7-7/8 x 5¼ x 1-7/8 in.

EARLY PRINTING IN HOLLAND Literature

Cabinet B Shelf 2 No. 21

Netherlands, 1500-1540
see
NIJHOFF, WOUTER. l'Art typographique dans les Pays-Bas...

EARLY PRINTING IN HUNGARY [Literature of]

Cabinet AA Shelf 5 No. 37

History of Printing and of Book Trade in Hungary in the 18th century. By Albert Gardonyi. Budapest, 1917. Hungarian text. With facsimile.

Half morocco; 9½ x 6-3/8 in.

EARLY PRINTING IN HOLLAND [Literature of]

Cabinet U Shelf 4 No. 40

List of the founts of type and woodcut devices used by printers in Holland in the 15th century. By Henry Bradshaw. London, 1871.

Cloth; 8-3/4 x 5-5/8 x ¼ in.

EARLY PRINTING IN HOLLAND [Literature of]

Cabinet 75 Shelf 2 No. 9

Notes on English printing in the Low Countries (Early sixteenth century). A paper read before the Bibliographical Society, 19 March 1928, by M.E. Kronenberg.
Bibliographical account of the productions of the presses of Jan van Doesborch, C. van Ruremund etc.

In Trans. Bibl. Soc. "The Library" vol. IX pp. 139-163. 1928-1929.

EARLY PRINTING IN HUNGARY. [Literature of]

Cabinet 22 Shelf 1 No. 19

(Laibach, 1575-1580. Johann Manuel, Laibach's first printer.) Johann Manuel, Laibach's erster buchdrucker, von Friedrich Ahn.

In Archiv für Deutschen Buchhandels, vol. XIX, p.45.

EARLY PRINTING IN HUNGARY. Literature of

Cabinet 26 Shelf 1 No. 16

Leutschau, 1625-1705, the Brewer family of printers.

See "Gutenberg-Gesellschaft Jahrbuch, 1927", pp.91-95.

EARLY PRINTING IN IRELAND. (Lit. of)

Cabinet U Shelf 1 No. 1b

Account of some notable books printed in Belfast: A paper read before the Library Association by Robert M. Young, Belfast, Sept., 1894.

In excerpts relating to printing from "The Library," p. 173 of pencilled folios.

EARLY PRINTING IN IRELAND (Lit. of)

Cabinet 75 Shelf 2 No. 4

Irish characters in print, 1571-1923. By E. W. Lynam. A paper for the Bibliographical Society, London. March, 1924-. Facsimiles.

In Trans. Biblio. Soc. Vo. IV, 1923-1924. pp. 286-325. "The Library."

EARLY PRINTING IN HUNGARY. Literature of

Cabinet 26 Shelf 1 No. 16

[Pressburg, 1715-1848. The Royer family of printers in Hungary. A bio-biblio. essay]. Die buchdrucker familie Royer in Ungarn. von Josef Fitz, Budapest.

See "Gutenberg-Gesselschaft Jahrbuch, 1927", pp.85-90.

EARLY PRINTING IN IRELAND. Literature

Cabinet 75 Shelf 2 No. 2

Bibliographical sketch of Ireland, The. by T. Percy C. Kirkpatrick.

In Transactions of the Bibliographical Society, "The Library," Vol. II, 1921-1922, pp. 201-204.

EARLY PRINTING IN IRELAND. [Literature]

Cabinet 75 Shelf 2 No. 7

King's printers, The: A brief comment b. Robert Steele.

In Transactions of the Bibliographical Society, "The Library," Vol. VII, 1926-27, pp. 321-22.

EARLY PRINTING IN HUNGARY (Literature of)

Cabinet 26 Shelf 1 No. 21

(Reprints of German devotional writings in Hungarian printing offices of the 17th century.) Nachdrucke deutscher erbauungsschiften aus Ungarländischen offizinen des 17 jahrhunderts. Von Bela von Pukanszky. With facsimiles.

Essay in "Gutenberg-Gesellschaft Jahrbuch, 1931", pp.244-249.

EARLY PRINTING IN IRELAND. [Literature of]

Cabinet 75 Shelf 1 No. 7

Earliest Dublin printers and the Company of Stationers of London: A paper read before the Bibliographical Society by E. R. McC. Dix, Mary 16th, 1903.

In Trans. Biblio. Soc., Vol. VII, 1902-1904, pp. 75-85.

EARLY PRINTING IN IRELAND. [Literature]

Cabinet 75 Shelf 1 No. 8

Ornaments used by John Franckton, printer at Dublin, 1529-1618: A paper prepared for the Bibliographical Society by E. R. McC. Dix, Facsimile.

In Trans. Biblio. Soc., Vol. VIII, 1904-1906, pp. 221-227.

EARLY PRINTING IN HUNGARY Literature

Cabinet 26 Shelf 1 No. 17

(Die) Vergangenheit der buchdruckerkunst im Burgenland. von Andre Csatkai.
Article, German text, in the Gutenberg-Gesellschaft Jahrbuch 1928. pp.172-174.

EARLY PRINTING IN IRELAND Literature

Cabinet 00 Shelf 5 No. 3 (2 vols.)

History of Irish periodical literature... [Many references to early printers and printing].

see Index to MADDEN'S History of Irish periodical literature...London, 1867.

EARLY PRINTING IN IRELAND Literature of

Cabinet S Shelf 2 No. 151

Sixteenth century printing in Ireland. By P.P. Lennox.
Article, excerpt from the Catholic University Bulletin, March, 1909.

EARLY PRINTING IN HUNGARY Literature

Cabinet 26 Shelf 1 No. 20

(The Vienna printer Rafael Hoffhalter and his son in Hungary in 1563) Der Wiener buchdrucker Rafael Hoffhalter und sein sohn in Ungarn. von Paul Gulyas.

Article in the "Gutenberg-Gesellschaft Jahrbuch" 1930, pp.198-108.

EARLY PRINTING IN IRELAND. Literature.

Cabinet 75 Shelf 2 No. 2

Initial letters and factotums used by John Franckton, printer in Dublin, 1600-18. A brief note by E. R. McC. Dix. Facsimiles.

In Transactions of the Bibliographical Society, "The Library," Vol. II, 1921-22, pp. 43-48.

EARLY PRINTING IN IRELAND [Literature of]

Cabinet T Shelf 2 No. 1

Typographical Antiquities; being an historical account of printing in Ireland from 1471 to 1600. By Joseph Ames. London, 1749.

Half morocco; 10-3/4 x 8¼ x 2 in.

EARLY PRINTING IN ICELAND. [Literature of]

Cabinet AA Shelf 5 No. 41

Borgfirdingur, Jon. Jonsson: Soguagrip um prentsmidjur og prentara a Islandi. Reykjavik, 1867. Hofundur og utgefari: Jon Jonsson Borgfiringur.
Bio-historical account of printers and printing in Iceland, 1524 to 1854.

Boards; 7¼ x 5½ in.

EARLY PRINTING IN IRELAND. (Lit. of)

Cabinet 20 Shelf 2 No. 1

(Ireland's contribution to the art of the book). Die verdienste Ireland um schrift und buchwesen, von Ernst Schultze, Hamburg, 1915.

In Zeitschrift für Bücherfreunde, 1915-16, part 1, p. 82.

EARLY PRINTING IN ITALY (Lit. of)

Cabinet 75 Shelf 2 No. 6

Aldine Pliny of 1508. By George Parker Winship, for The Bibliographical Society, March, 1926

In Trans. Biblio. Soc. "The Library," vol. VI, 1925-1926. pp. 358-369.

EARLY PRINTING IN ITALY Literature

Cabinet 26 Shelf 1 No. 19

Bologna 1467 to 1495. Enrico di Colonia ed altri tipografi Tedeschi a Bologna nel sec. XV. Albano Sorbelli.
Article in the "Gutenberg-Gesellschaft Jahrbuch" 1929, pp.109-126.

EARLY PRINTING IN ITALY [Literature of]

Cabinet AA Shelf 1 No. 20

Florence, 1503?-1563: Lorenzo Torrentino. Annali della Tipografia Fiorentina di Lorenzo Torrentino [By Domenico Moreni]. Firenze, 1811.
Historical and biographical account.

Half calf; 8-3/4 x 6 in.

EARLY PRINTING IN ITALY Literature of

Cabinet K Shelf 4 No. 17

Italian book illustrations, chiefly of the 15th century. By Alfred W. Pollard. London, 1894. Illus.

Imitation leather; 10½ x 7-1/8 x ½ in.

EARLY PRINTING IN ITALY [Literature of]

Cabinet S Shelf 1 No. 115

(The) Book in Italy during the 15th and 16th centuries shown in facsimile reproductions from the most famous printed volumes ... together with an introduction by Guido Biagi, Florence. Explanatory text and comment by William Dana Orcutt. New York, 1928.

Boards; 12½ x 9-5/8 in

EARLY PRINTING IN ITALY. Literature of

Cabinet K Shelf 6 No. 18

Florentine (15th and 16th centuries) printers and publishers, index of.

see
KRISTELLER, PAUL. Early Florentine woodcuts...London, 1897.

EARLY PRINTING IN ITALY. [Literature of]

Cabinet 75 Shelf 1 No. 8

Italian section of Mr. Proctor's index of early printed books, 1501-1520: A paper read for Mr. Alfred W. Pollard beforethe Bibliographical Society, October 16, 1905.

In Trans. Biblio. Soc., Vol. VIII, 1904-1906, pp. 63-66.

EARLY PRINTING IN ITALY [Literature of]

Stack A Shelf 1&2 Number 54

Bullen, Henry Lewis. Literature of Typography Italy. In The Inland Printer, vol.LIV. p.219.

EARLY PRINTING IN ITALY (Lit. of)

Cabinet 75 Shelf 2 No. 5

(Foligno, 1474). A supposed Foligno edition of 1474. By Victor Scholderer. A paper read before the Bibliographical Society.

In Trans. Biblio. Soc. "The Library," Vol. V. 1924-1925. pp. 169-70.

EARLY PRINTING IN ITALY [Literature of]

Cabinet U Shelf 4 No. 31

Italian 16th century, The. By A. F. Johnson. With fifty illustrations. In series of handbooks "Periods of Typography", edited by Stanley Morison, London, 1926.

Boards; 9-7/8 x 7¼ x 3/8 in.

EARLY PRINTING IN ITALY Literature

Cabinet AA Shelf 2 No. 38

Editori et stampatori del quattrocento. Note bio-bibliographiche. Introduzione di Raffaello Bertieri. Libreria Antiquaria V. Hoepli, Milano, 1929. Has 108 plates, reproductions, facsimiles, and printer marks.
Bio-bibliographical notes of 15th century Italian publishers, printers, etc. A sale catalogue.

Paper; 12¼ x 9¼ x 1¼ in.

EARLY PRINTING IN ITALY Literature

Cabinet 26 Shelf 1 No. 20

(Genoa and Naples, 1474, 1475-1491. Matthias Moravus) Nota per Mattia Moravo. Di Tamaro di Marinis. Illus.
Bio-biblio account.

Article in the "Gutenberg-Gesellschaft Jahrbuch" 1930, pp.104-114.

EARLY PRINTING IN ITALY. [Literature of]

Cabinet 75 Shelf 2 No. 7

Italian XVI Century typography. By A. F. Johnson. London, 1926. Reviewed by A. W. Pollard.

In Transactions of the Bibliographical Society, "The Library," Vol. VII, 1926-27, p. 111.

EARLY PRINTING IN ITALY. [Literature of]

Cabinet 18 Shelf 1 No. 14

(Editors of the Renaissance) Gli Editori del Risorgimento: Brief review in German of book with same title.

Lists the first printers and printers work in Italy.

In Zeitschrift für Bücherfreunde, 1913-14, part 1, p.145-7, of Supplement ("Beiblatt")

EARLY PRINTING IN ITALY. Literature of.

Cabinet Y Shelf 2 No. 97

Iesi, 1471. Federico de'Conti and the first book printed at Iesi. By Victor Scholderer. With 2 figures.

Article in Gutenberg-Gesellschaft Jahrbuch, 1932. p. 110.

EARLY PRINTING IN ITALY. Literature

Cabinet 75 Shelf 1 No. 14

Laws regulating printing and publishing in Italy, by G. F. Barwick.

In Trans. Biblio. Soc., Vol. XIV, 1915-1917, pp. 311-323.

EARLY PRINTING IN ITALY Literature

Cabinet X Shelf 1 No. 77

(Ferrara) De Typographia Hebraeo-Ferrariensi, [1470-1577] commentarius hidtoricus...de Joh. Bernardi De Rossi. Parma. Ex Regio Typographeo, 1780.

Half morocco; 8-7/8 x 5-7/8 in.

EARLY PRINTING IN ITALY (Lit. of)

Cabinet V Shelf 2 No. 251 -10

(Les) Imprimeurs Rouennais en Italy au XVe siecle ... Par Emile Picot. Rouen, 1911.

¾ Morocco; 9¾ x 6½ x ½ in.

EARLY PRINTING IN ITALY Literature

Cabinet Y Shelf 4 No. 73

("Leiden Christi"), the earliest printed work in Italy. A bibliographical study.)

See HAEBLER, KONRAD. (Die) Italianische fragmente vom Leiden Christi...

EARLY PRINTING IN ITALY. Literature of

Cabinet 26 (Messina, 1473-1478. Enrico Alding)

Shelf 1 See Boselli, Antonio. (Alding, Enrico in Messina...)

No. 21

EARLY PRINTING IN ITALY. Literature.

Cabinet AA (Piedmont printers and printing in the 15th century. Typographic observations). Ozzervazioni tipografiche sobra libri impressi in Piedmonte nel secolo 15. Del Barone Vernazza. Bassano, Tipografia Remondiniana, 1807.

Shelf 2

No. 1

Boards; 8½ x 5½ x 3/8 in.

EARLY PRINTING IN ITALY [Literature of]

Cabinet X Rome, 1572. Gregorii papae XIII. Privilegium D. Paulae Bladae, et eius filiis concessum, imprimendi ... cum inhibitione contra alios impresores (Exclusive privilege in favor of Paul Blado and son).

Shelf 5

No. 2

Item 39 in volume "Historical documents relating to printing."

EARLY PRINTING IN ITALY Literature

Cabinet 26 Modena, 1489-1495. Tipografia Modenese del quattrocento e specialmente sulle edizione silografiche.Di Dominico Fava.

Shelf 1 Article in the "Gutenberg-Gesellschaft Jahrbuch", 1929, pp.164-185.

No 19

EARLY PRINTING IN ITALY [Literature of]

Cabinet AA (Piemonte). Cenni storici intorno all'origine dell'arte tipografica e suoi progressi in Piemonte, dall' invenzione della stampa sino al 1835 ... Angelo Brofferio. Guisia le memorie ed i documenti somministratigli dal tipografo, Giuseppe Pomba. Milano, 1876.

Shelf 1

No. 46

Half morocco; 9¼ x 6½ in.

EARLY PRINTING IN ITALY (Lit. of)

Cabinet U Rome, 1648 . Sixtus Riessinger's first Press at Rome, by V. Scholderer.

Shelf 1

No. 1g

In excerpts relating to printing from "The Library," 1914-15, p. 78 of pencilled folios.

EARLY PRINTING IN ITALY [Literature of]

Cabinet AA Olschki, Leo S.: Le Livre en Italie a travers les siècles. Role joué par l'Italie dans le developpement de l'art de l'imprimerie et de l'illustration du Livre, du XV au XIX siècle. Florence, 1914. Facsimiles, illus. and tables of names and places.

Shelf 2

No. 25

Half morocco; 9-3/4 x 7 in.

EARLY PRINTING IN ITALY Literature of

Cabinet QQ Presses of Italy, 16th century. Brief notes concerning the Aldine and other presses.

Shelf 3 see BUTLER, CHARLES. Erasmus, the life of...London, 1825, p. 85.

No. 29

EARLY PRINTING IN ITALY [Literature of]

Cabinet AA Sardini, Giacomo: Esame sui principi della Francese ed Italiana tipografia, ovvero storia critica di Nicolas Jenson ... da Giacomo Sardini. Lucca. 1796, 1797, 1798. [Bound in one volume]. Plates showing facsimile of types used by Jenson.

Shelf 1

No. 17

oards, vellum back; 15 x 10½ in.

EARLY PRINTING IN ITALY literature of

Cabinet K Pagine de antichi maestri della typografia Italiana. Conferenza da Raffaello Bertieri.. . Milano, 1921.

Shelf 2 35 facsimiles of title pages tipped in.

No. 7

Half morocco; 10 x 7-3/8 in.

EARLY PRINTING IN ITALY [Literature of]

Cabinet S (The) Prince printers of Italy. By Catherine Mary Phillimore. An excerpt from the Eclectic, May 1874.

Shelf 5 Biographical, biblio-historical account.

No. 4

Item 18 in collection "Various printers and their plants; excerpts from magazines, I".

EARLY PRINTING IN ITALY. Literature of

Cabinet 75 (Sicily). Printing in Sicily, 1478-1554: A paper read before the Bibliographical Society by Reginald Stanley Faber, on Feb. 19, 1900. Includes a bibliography of printing in Sicily.

Shelf 1

No. 5

In Trans. Biblio. Soc. Vol. V,1898-1900, pp. 183-211.

EARLY PRINTING IN ITALY [Literature of]

Cabinet AA Parma, 1768. Un esempio [Bodoni], un augurio, un monito immortale. Da Umberto Bernassi.

Bibliographical historical account of Parma Printing, printers, and Bodoni's immortal achievements.

Shelf 1 In volume "Parma Grafica." Parma, 1925. pp. 55-62.

No. 53

Half morocco; 12½ x 9½ in.

EARLY PRINTING IN ITALY [Literature of]

Cabinet U (Rome) Sweynheym and Pannartz: Notes and collation. A paper read before the Edinburgh Bibliographical Society, by E. Gordon Duff. Nov. 14, 1907.

Shelf 4 pp.21-36 of Proceedings of the Edinburgh Bibliographical Society, 1906-1907, 1907-1908

No. 27

Half morocco; 9-5/8 x 8 x ½ in.

EARLY PRINTING IN ITALY [Literature of]

Cabinet U Sweynheym and Pannartz. Petition to Pope Sixtus IV. March 13, 1472. By Victor Scholderer.

Shelf 1

No. 1g

In Excerpts relating to printing from "The Library," 1914-15. p. 123 of pencilled folios.

EARLY PRINTING IN ITALY. Literature

Cabinet U Pavia, 15th century. Books with woodcuts printed at Pavia. By Paul Kristeller.

Shelf 3 Illus. bibliographical account.

No. 103

See vol. I, p.347 in Bibliographica... London, 1895-1897.

EARLY PRINTING IN ITALY (Lit. of)

Cabinet U Rome, 1472. The petition of Sweynheym and Panmartz of Sixtus IV., by V. Scholderer.

Shelf 1

No. 1g

In excerpts relating to printing from The Library, 1914-15, p. 123 of pencilled folios

---

EARLY PRINTING IN ITALY [Literature of]

Cabinet AA Torino, Gli incunaboli ed i tipografi Piedmontesi del secolo XV. Indice bibliografici. Francesco Consentini. Torino, 1914.

Shelf 2

No. 26

Half morocco; 8-3/4 x 6½ in.

EARLY PRINTING IN ITALY. Literature of

Cabinet AA Shelf 1 No. 49

(Trieste). Antonio Turini, primo stampatore in Trieste nel 1625, e di Giovan Maria Petreuli, scrittore delle prime storie di Trieste date alle Stampe. Lettera di P. Kandler al Nicola Bottacin. Con documenti. Trieste, 1860. Pamphlet.

Item 3 in volume "Four Italian Typographic items."

Half morocco; 9-3/4 x 6½ in.

EARLY PRINTING IN ITALY. (Literature)

Cabinet U Shelf 3 No. 103

Venice, 1497, Filippo Finzi, printer of the Celsus' "De Medicina", a book once the property of Jean Grolier. By W.Y. Fletcher.

Bibliographical account.

See vol. I, p.1 in Bibliographica...London, 1895-1897.

EARLY PRINTING IN JAPAN [Literature of]

Stack Shelf Number

Bullen, Henry Lewis. Histories of printing and paper; China and Japan, by Henry Lewis Bullen, in The Inland Printer, vol.LIII, p. 860. Illus.

EARLY PRINTING IN ITALY. [Literature of

Cabinet 75 Shelf 1 No. 10

Venice, the Cioliti and their press at. A paper read before the Bibliographical Society by A.J. Butler, January 18, 1909. Illus.

In Trans. Biblio. Soc., Vol. X, 1908-1909, pp. 83-107.

EARLY PRINTING IN ITALY [Literature of]

Cabinet S Shelf 5 No. 4

Venice, 1512-1578. Gabriele Giolito, printer-publisher. By Horatio F. Brown. Excerpt from the Atlantic Monthly, Feb. 1892.

Bound with other items in "Various printers and their plants", item 8, vol.I.

EARLY PRINTING IN MEXICO [Literature of]

Cabinet 79 Shelf 2 No. 14

Bibliografia Mexicana del siglo XVI. Primera parte. Catalogo razonado de libros impresos en Mexico de 1539 a 1600. Con biografias de autores y otras ilustraciones. Precedido de una noticia acerca de la introduccion de la imprenta en Mexico. Por Joaquin Garcia Icazbalceta, Mexico, 1886.

Half morocco; 12 x 8¾ in.

EARLY PRINTING IN ITALY. Literature.

Cabinet I Shelf 5 No. 16 to 20 5 vols.

(Venice, 1450 to 1525). Les livres a figures Venetiens ... Par Prince d'Essling, Florence Paris, 1907-1914.

Bibliographical. With over 2,000 reproductions ofwoodcuts.

Half morocco; 17½ x 12 in.

EARLY PRINTING IN ITALY. [Literature of]

Cabinet 18 Shelf 1 No. 9

(Vercellensi, Bernhard, Venice, 1501: A remarkable broadside.) Ein merkwurdiger einblatt-druck, von Loescher, Rome. Facsimiles.

In Zeitschrift für Bucherfreunde, 1910-11, part 1, p.227.

EARLY PRINTING IN MEXICO. [Literature of]

Cabinet S Shelf 3 No. 74

[Harrisse, Henry]. A brief disquisition concerning the early history of printing in America. New York, privately printed, 1866. Extracted from the Bibliotheca Americana Vetustissima, pp. 365-377. Includes a list of works printed in America between the years 1540 and 1600.

Half morocco; 10½ x 7½ in.

EARLY PRINTING IN ITALY (Lit. of)

Cabinet 75 Shelf 2 No. 5

(Venice 1469-1481) Printing at Venice to the end of 1481. By Victor Scholderer. Read before the Bibliographical Society, 17 March 1924. Illus.

In Trans. Biblio. Soc. Vol. V, 1924-1925. pp. 129-152. "The Library."

EARLY PRINTING IN ITALY. [Literature of]

Cabinet AA Shelf 1 No. 43

Verona, 1742 to 1826. Della tipografia Veronese; saggio storico-letterario. Per Giamb. Carlo Co. Giuliari. Verona, 1871.

Half morocco; 10-1/8 x 7½ x 7/8 in.

EARLY PRINTING IN MEXICO. [Literature of]

Cabinet 79 Shelf 1 No. 23

(Querétaro, 1821) Notas bibliograficas referentes les primas producciones de la imprenta en algunas cindades de la America-Española. Por José Toribio Medina. Santiago de Chile, 1904.

Cloth; 9½ x 6¼ in. Chiappa 146

EARLY PRINTING IN ITALY [Literature of]

Cabinet Y Shelf 2 No. 41

(Venice, 1476-1485, by Erhard Ratdolt, books printed in) Buchdruckergeschichte Augsburgs ...Diejeniger bücher welcher Erhard Ratdolt in Venedig vom jahr 1476 bis 1485 gedruckt hat...von Georg Wilhelm Zapf. Augsburg, 1786. With facsimiles.

Boards; 9½ x 7½ x 5/8 in.

EARLY PRINTING IN ITALY. [Literature of]

Cabinet 18 Shelf 1 No. 14

(Zanetti, Camillo Bartolomeo, Rome, 1516. An identified scribe and printer) Ein identifizierte Handschriftenschreiber und Buchdrucker.

Brief account of the identification of scribe and printer with description of his works.

In Zeitschrift für Bücherfreunde, 1913-14, part 1, p.218 of Supplement ("Beiblatt.")

EARLY PRINTING IN HAWAII. Literature

Cabinet 81 Shelf 2 No. 36

Afraquits, first printing done at. Excerpt newspaper clipping.

Item in MUNSELL, JOEL. "Printers Scraps", vol.VII, p.78

EARLY PRINTING IN ITALY Literature

Cabinet Y Shelf 4 No. 75

Venice, 1486. Konrad Zeninger. Ein neu-aufgefundener einblatt-Kalender. von Hanns Bohatta. Separatdruck aus Katalog 168, Gilhofer & Ranschburg. Wien. Pamphlet. Reproduction of broadside calendar. Bibliographical account by Bohatta.

In box marked "Miscellany relating to German Printers and Printing. v.d."

EARLY PRINTING IN ITALY [Literature of]

Cabinet AA Shelf 1 No. 7

Zatta, Antonio: Venice, 1762. Stampa. (Documents regulating Italian printers. Italian text. Compilation).

Half morocco; 11½ x 8-1/8 in.

EARLY PRINTING IN HAWAII. Literature

Cabinet Shelf No.

Bullen, Henry Lewis. The literature of typography: Hawaii.

Article in the Inland Printer, vol 53, p.396

EARLY PRINTING IN HAWAII Literature

Cabinet R Shelf 5 No. 113

First Hawaiian printing. By Rev. W.B. Westervelt. n.d. Facsimiles.
Excerpt from periodical "Paradise of the Pacific".
Bound in with "History of the Hawaiian Mission Press."

Half morocco, 12¼ x 9½ in.

EARLY PRINTING IN PORTUGAL [Literature of]

Cabinet AA Shelf 5 No. 25

(A) Imprensa em Portugal nos seculos XV e XVI. As ordenacões d'el - rei D. Manuel. Por Brito Aranha. Lisboa, 1898. Imprensa Nacional. 1898. Reproductions.
Ordinances printed for King Manuel with bibliographical - historical account.

Half morocco; 10 x 6½ in.

EARLY PRINTING IN RUSSIA. [Literature of]

Cabinet 18 Shelf 1 No. 16

(Fedorow, Iwan, Moscow, 1564) Moskauer Brief, von Arthur Luther, May, 1914.

Briefly recounts the historical typographic possessions of Russia, and with particular notice of Iwan Fedorow, who printed the first book in Russia.

In Zeitschrift für Bücherfreunde, 1914, part 1, pp.118-21.

EARLY PRINTING IN HAWAII Literature

Cabinet S Shelf 5 No. 25

History of the Hawaiian Mission Press, with a bibliography of the earlier publications. By Howard M. Ballau and George R. Carter. Presented to the Society, August 27, 1908. Papers of the Hawaiian Historical Society, No.14.

Item in box labelled "History of Printing, United States. Miscellaneous items".

EARLY PRINTING IN PORTUGAL [Literature of]

Cabinet V Shelf 3 No. ~~12~~ 10

(Née de la Rochelle, J.-Fr.). Recherches historiques et critiques sur l'établissement de l'Art Typographiques en Espagne et en Portugal, pendant le quinzieme siécle: Extraites des récréations historiques et bibliographiques. Paris, 1830.

Half morocco; 8½ x 5 in.

EARLY PRINTING IN RUSSIA [Literature of]

Cabinet 18 Shelf 1 No. 7

(Introduction of the art of printing into Russia) Die Einfuhrung der Buchdruckerkunst in Russland, von K. Baerent, St. Petersburg.

Brief account of the first printer in Russia (Georg Czernowic, 1493) and the works printed by him and some of his immediate followers.

In Zeitschrift für Bucherfreunde, 1910, part 1, p.29.

EARLY PRINTING IN HAWAII Literature

Cabinet R Shelf 5 No. 114

Story of three old buildings in Honolulu. By Mrs. R.W. Andrews, secretary emeritus, Honolulu, 1926. Illus. pamphlet.

Has picture and account of the first pri printing house in Hawaii, completed Aug. 30, 1823.

Item in manila envelope

EARLY PRINTING IN PORTUGAL [Literature of]

Cabinet AA Shelf 5 No. 23

Noronho, Tito de: Imprensa Portugueza durante o seculo XVI. Por Tito de Noronho. Porto, 1874.
Chronological bibliographical account.

Cloth; 9½ x 6-3/4 in.

EARLY PRINTING IN RUSSIA [Literature of]

Cabinet AA Shelf 5 No. 43

Olgin, P. T.: Johann Guttenburg, book printer. [Russian text]. St. Petersburg, 1900. Facsimiles, reproduction of bust erected to Ivan Fedoroff, printer of the first book in Russia.

Cloth; 9¾ x 7 in.

EARLY PRINTING IN POLAND [Literature of]

Cabinet 18 Shelf 1 No. 1

(Art of printing in Poland to the middle part of the 17th century) Buchdruckerkunst in Polen bis zur mitte des XVII jahrhunderts von K. von Kozycki, Munich.

In Zeitschrift fur Bucherfreunde, 1906-7, part 2, p.487.

EARLY PRINTING IN PORTUGAL [Lit. of]

Cabinet 76 Shelf 2 No. 4

Printers of Spain and Portugal, early. By Konrad Haebler. Printed for the Bibliographical Society, March, 1897.
Illus. Monograph IV.

Half morocco; 11 x 9 in.

EARLY PRINTING IN RUSSIA [Literature of]

Cabinet 22 Shelf 1 No. 6

(Riga 1620. History of bookselling in Riga.) Zur geschichte des buchhandels in Riga, von Wilhelm Stieda.

Includes notices of governmental privileges for prints, bookbinders, and booksellers: Items taken from original documents.

In Archiv für Deutschen Buchhandels, vol. VI, p.114.

EARLY PRINTING IN POLAND. [Literature of]

Cabinet AA Shelf 5 No. 42

Stanislas, Lam: Le livre Polonaise au XV et XVI siecle ... Edite et imprime par l'Imprimerie de Wl. Lazarski, a Varsovie [1923]. Facsimiles and reproductions.

Paper wrapper in board case; 9-1/8 x 7¼ in.

EARLY PRINTING IN PORTUGAL Literature of

Cabinet 18 Shelf 1 No. 4

(Talmud issued in Portugal before 1500, A) Eine portugiesische Talmud, ausgabe vor 1500, von E. Slijper, Leiden. Facsimile.

In Zeitschrift für Bücherfreunde, 1908-9, part 1, p. 207.

EARLY PRINTING IN SCOTLAND. Literature.

Cabinet 75 Shelf 1 No. 17

Aberdeen, 1620, Edward Raban.

See Duff, E. Gordon. Early career of Edward Raban...

EARLY PRINTING IN PORTUGAL [Literature of]

Cabinet AA Shelf 5 No. 24

Documents para a historia da typographia Portugueza nos seculos XVI e XVII. Publicados por Venancio Deslandes. Lisboa: Imprensa Nacional, 1888.
Chronological bio-bibliographical account gathered and arranged from documents.

Half morocco; 9½ x 6-3/4 in.

EARLY PRINTING IN PRUSSIA. [Literature of]

Cabinet 22 Shelf 1 No. 18 & 19.

(History of printing and bookselling in the dukedom of Prussia.) Geschichte des buchdrucks und des buchhandels im herzogthum Preussen. von Karl Lohmeyer.

Includes brief biographies of the early printers.

In Archiv für Deutschen Buchhandels, vol. XVIII, p.33, vol.XIX, p.179.

EARLY PRINTING IN SCOTLAND. [Literature of]

Cabinet U Shelf 1 No. 1a

Annals of Scottish printing. By Dickson and Edmond: A review of book with title as above.

In Excerpts relating to printing from "The Library," [n.d.], p. 191 of pencilled folios

EARLY PRINTING IN SCOTLAND. Literature of

Cabinet U — Shelf 2 — No. 62

Ballantyne Press and its founders, 1796-1908.

See BALLANTYNE PRESS, The. (The) Ballantyne Press and its founders...

See also U/2/62 and U/2/61.

EARLY PRINTING IN SCOTLAND. (Lit. of)

Cabinet 75 — Shelf 2 — No. 8

(Edinburgh - 1640). Relations between London and Edinburgh printers and stationers. By F.S. Ferguson. A paper read before the Bibliographical Society, 21 Feb. 1927.

In Trans. Biblio. Soc. "The Library," Vol. VIII, 1927-1928. pp. 145-198.

EARLY PRINTING IN SCOTLAND Literature of

Cabinet U — Shelf 1 — No. 88

Edinburgh printing 1775-1925. Commemorating the 150th anniversary of the foundation of the firm of H. & J. Pillans and W.S. Wilson. Illus.

Boards; 7-5/8 x 5-3/8 x 5/8 in.

EARLY PRINTING IN SCOTLAND. Literature of

Cabinet U — Shelf 1 — No. 12

Bibles printed in England and Scotland, 1541 to 1811, chronological list of.

See BIBLE SOCIETIES IN SCOTLAND. Memorial ...Edinburgh, 1824.

EARLY PRINTING IN SCOTLAND Literature

Cabinet 00 — Shelf 4 — No. 42 (2 vols.)

Edinburgh, 1642-1800. Bibliographical account of the newspapers, journals, and magazines ...By W. J. Couper. Stirling, 1908. 2 vols. illus.
Has index of names of persons.

Cloth; 9¼ x 6 x 1½ in.

EARLY PRINTING IN SCOTLAND. Literature

Cabinet U — Shelf 1 — No. 30

Edinburgh, the early printers of, [and] history of the Bassandyne Bible, the first printed in Scotland. By William T. Dobson. With facsimiles and other illustrations. Edinburgh, 1887.

Stamped cloth; 9¼ x 5-7/8 in.

EARLY PRINTING IN SCOTLAND. [Literature of]

Cabinet 75 — Shelf 2 — No. 10

Bibliography of Sir David Lindsay, 1490-1555. A paper read before the Bibliographical Society 21 Jan. 1929. by Douglas Hamer.
A history of the successive editions of Lindsay's works; being an addition to the history of Scottish printing before 1550.

In Trans. Biblio. Soc. "The Library", vol. 10, 1929-30. pp. 1 to 42.

EARLY PRINTING IN SCOTLAND [Literature of]

Cabinet X — Shelf 4 — No. 67

Edinburgh, 1740. Mr. Robert Freebairn, His Majesty's printer for Scotland, and Mr. John Baskett, His Majesty's printer for England, his partner, against the representatives of James Watson, printer in Edinburgh, deceast.

Half morocco; 7¼ x 6-1/8 x 3/8 in.

EARLY PRINTING IN SCOTLAND. Literature

Cabinet English and Scottish printing types, 1501-1558.

Cabinet 76 — Shelf 2 — No. 30

See ISAAC, FRANK. Types, English and Scottish printing, 1501-

---

EARLY PRINTING IN SCOTLAND. [Literature of]

Cabinet T — Shelf 1 — No. 68

Bruce, John, 1745-1826, Edinburgh: The letter book of John Bruce, January 3, 1817 to December 20, 1820. Manuscript.
These letters relate to matters of family and business affairs. John Bruce, historian joint king's printer for Scotland, and publisher.

Boards; 12¼ x 7¼ x 1¼ in.

EARLY PRINTING IN SCOTLAND Literature

Cabinet X — Shelf 4 — No. 67

Edinburgh, 1740, Robert Freebairn.

see LIBERTY OF PRINTING, Great Britain. Information (June 16th, 1740) for Mr. Robert Freebairn...

EARLY PRINTING IN SCOTLAND. Literature of

Cabinet U — Shelf 1 — No. 1g

Foulis, Andrew and Robert: The Foulis Exhibition Nov., 23, 1912.
An exhibition illustrative of the life and work of the brothers.

In Excerpts relating to printing from "The Library," 1912-13, p. 158 of pencilled folios.

EARLY PRINTING IN SCOTLAND Literature

Cabinet OO — Shelf 4 — No. 34

Documents (circa 1686-1705) relative to the printers of some early Scottish newspapers ...
("Collected and carefully transcribed ...from the Registers and original Warrants of the Privy Council of Scotland, by the care of...Mr. Macdonald") An excerpt, n. p. n. d.

Half morocco; 10½ x 8-1/8 ½ in.

EARLY PRINTING IN SCOTLAND. Literature.

Cabinet U — Shelf 1 — No. 54

Edinburgh, 1780-1781, John and Thomas Robertson ...

See ROBERTSON, JOHN and THOMAS, vs. SOC. OF SOLICITORS. Petition ...

EARLY PRINTING IN SCOTLAND. Literature of

Cabinet U — Shelf 1 — No. 1a

Foulis brothers and early Glasgow printing, by John Ferguson, Sept. 15, 1888.
Includes a list giving the date of the earliest work of each printer from 1638-1798.

In excerpts relating to printing from "The Library," pp. 11-26 of pencilled folios.

EARLY PRINTING IN SCOTLAND Literature of

Cabinet U — Shelf 1 — No. 84

Documents relative to the printers of some early Scottish newspapers, etc., 1686-1705.

Half morocco; 10¾ x 8¾ in.

EARLY PRINTING IN SCOTLAND [Literature of]

Cabinet U — Shelf 1 — No. 12

Edinburgh, Aberdeen, Glasgow. 1541 to 1811.
Memorial for the Bible Societies in Scotland: containing remarks on the complaint of His Majesties printers against the Marquis of Huntly and others. Edinburgh, 1824.
Concerns the liberty of Bible printing. Includes a chronological list of Bibles printed in England and Scotland, 1541 to 1811.

See also U/1/13.

Paper boards; 9-3/8 x 5-3/4 x 1¼ in.

EARLY PRINTING IN SCOTLAND. Literature of

Cabinet U — Shelf 1 — No. 83

Glasgow, 1638-1931. The Glasgow University Press. With some notes on Scottish printing in the last three hundred years. By James Maclehose. At the University Press, 1931. With portraits, illus., facs.

Boards, linen back; 9 x 5¾ x 1¼ in.

EARLY PRINTING IN SCOTLAND [Literature of]

Cabinet U Shelf 1 No. 1f

Glasgow, 1638-1781. The Foulis Exhibition: Organized by the Glasgow Bibliographical Society, February, 1912, to illustrate the life and work of the brothers Foulis.

In Excerpts relating to printing from "The Library," 1912-13, p. 158 of pencilled folios.

EARLY PRINTING IN SCOTLAND [Literature of]

Cabinet T Shelf 2 No. 1

Typographical Antiquities; being an historical account of printing...in Scotland, 1471 to 1600...By Joseph Ames. London, 1749.

Half morocco; 10-3/4 x 8¼ x 2 in.

EARLY PRINTING IN SPAIN [Literature of]

Cabinet 18 Shelf 2 No. 1

(Introduction of printing into Spain). Zur einführung des Buchdrucks in Spanien, von Konrad Haebler, Berlin.

In Zeitschrift für Bücherfreunde, 1915-16, part 2, p.177.

EARLY PRINTING IN SCOTLAND. [Literature of]

Cabinet 76 Shelf 2 No. 41

List of books printed in Scotland before 1700, including those printed abroad for Scottish booksellers. With brief notes on the printers and stationers, by Harry G. Aldis. Printed for the Edinburgh Bibliographical Society, 1904.

Boards; 11 x 9 in.

EARLY PRINTING IN SOUTH AFRICA (Lit. of)

Cabinet U Shelf 1 No. 1g

Birth of printing in South Africa, 1784: An account of A.C. Lloyd.
Includes a list which gives the earliest product from each press from 1784 to 1856.

In Excerpts relating to printing from "The Library," 1914-14, p. 1 of pencilled folios.

EARLY PRINTING IN SPAIN. [Literature of]

Cabinet 75 Shelf 1 No. 4

Laws regulating printing and publishing in Spain. (1502-1628): A paper read before the Bibliographical Society by G. R. Barwick, Jan. 18, 1897.

In Trans. Biblio. Soc., Vol. IV, 1896-1898, pp. 47-55.

EARLY PRINTING IN SCOTLAND. Literature

Cabinet S Shelf 5 No. 25.02

Notes on early printing in Scotland, 1507-1600. By J.T. Clark. Transactions 3rd annual meeting of the Library Assn. of the United Kingdom, 1881.

Pamphlet in box labelled "Pamphlets and excerpts relating to printers, their plants, and other typographical matters". Box No.2.

EARLY PRINTING IN SPAIN [Literature of]

Cabinet AA Shelf 5 No. 18

Bibliofilia: Recull d'estudis, observacions, comentaris. y noticies sobre llibres en general y sobre questions de llengua y literatura catalanes en particular. R. Miguel y Planas. Barcelona, 1911-1914. Illus. facsimiles.
Bibliographical historical notes on early and modern printing.

Half morocco; 11 x 8-3/8 x 1-3/4 in.

EARLY PRINTING IN SPAIN. Literature

Cabinet PP Shelf 2 No. 11

Martens, Thierry, and the Early Spanish Press. The earliest royal decree on printing, or Thierry Martens. An address by Prof. Wm. I. Knapp, delivered before the Grolier Club, March 12, 1886. Transactions of the Grolier Club, Part II, 1894, p.127.

Paper; 9-3/4 x 7-1/8 x 7/8 in.

EARLY PRINTING IN SCOTLAND Literature of

Cabinet U Shelf 1 No. 53

[Printers and printing in Scotland] History of the art of printing...and a preface by the publisher to The Printers in Scotland. Edinburgh: James Watson, 1713.

Calf; 6¾ x 4 in.

EARLY PRINTING IN SPAIN LITERATURE OF

Cabinet K Shelf 1 No. 18

Early book illustration in Spain. By James P. R. Lyell. With an introduction by Dr. Konrad Haebler. Illustrated with numerous reproductions. London, 1926.

Cloth; 11½ x 9 x 1¾ in.

EARLY PRINTING IN SPAIN [Literature of]

Cabinet AA Shelf 5 No. 3

Mendez, Fray Francisco: Tipographia Española, o historia de la introduccion, propagacion y progresos de arte de la imprenta en España ... Tomo I. Madrid, 1796.
The second volume of this history was never published, because of loss of the manuscript.

Tree calf; 8 x 6¼ in.

EARLY PRINTING IN SCOTLAND. [Literature of]

Cabinet 76 Shelf 2 No. 30

Printing types, English and Scottish, 1501-35, 1508-41. Collected and annotated by Frank Isaac. Printed for the Bibliographical Society, at the Oxford University Press, 1930. Facsimiles & Illustrations No. II.

Boards; 11¼ x 9 in.

EARLY PRINTING IN SPAIN [Literature of]

Cabinet AA Shelf 5 No. 8

Guasp, Gabriel, dinastia de impresores mas antiqua de Europe [1579 a 1897, Palma]. Noticias y documentos recogidos por Don Gabriel Llabrés y Quintana ... Mahon, 1897. (Extrait de la "Revista de Memoria")
Biographic genealogical account of a long practising family of printers.

Half morocco; 8-7/8 x 6-7/8 in.

EARLY PRINTING IN SPAIN [Literature of]

Cabinet AA Shelf 5 No. 20

Montserrat, Monastery of, 15th - 16th centuries. La impremta de Montserrat (segles XVe-XVIe). Per Dom M.a Albareda. Monestir de Montserrat 1919. Facsimile.
Historical-bibliographical account.

Half morocco; 11¼ x 9¼ in.

EARLY PRINTING IN SCOTLAND. Literature.

Cabinet 75 Shelf 2 No. 2

Raban, Edward, the first printer at Aberdeen A paper read before the Bibliographical Society by E. Gordon Duff, Dec. 19, 1921.

In Trans. Biblio. Soc., "The Library," Vol. II, 1921-1922, pp. 239-256.

EARLY PRINTING IN SPAIN. Literature.

Cabinet 75 Shelf 2 No. 6

Haebler, Konrad. Geschichte des spanischen Fruhdruckes in Stammbaumen. Book with title as above reviewed by V. Scholderer.

In Transactions of the Bibliographical Society, "The Library," Vol. VI, 1925-26 pp. 99-104.

EARLY PRINTING IN SPAIN. [Literature of]

Cabinet 75 Shelf 1 No. 3

Native printers in Spain in the fifteenth century: A paper by Dr. Konrad Haebler, and ready before the Bibliographical Society by Mr. Faber, June, 17, 1895.

In Trans. Biblio. Soc., Vol. III, 1895-1896, pp. 4-7.

EARLY PRINTING IN SPAIN [Literature of]

Cabinet V Shelf 3 No. 10

(Née de la Rochelle, J.-Fr.). Recherches historiques et critiques sur l'établissement de l'Art Typographiques en Espagne... pendant le quinzieme siècle. Paris, 1830

Half morocco; 8½ x 5 in.

EARLY PRINTING IN SPAIN. Literature of

Cabinet V Shelf 3 No. 10

Recherches historiques et critiques sur l'establissement de l'art typographique en Espagne et en Portugal, pendant le 15em siécle. De J.-Fr. Nee de la Rochelle. Paris, 1830.

Half morocco; 8¼ x 5-3/4 x 3/8 in.

EARLY PRINTING IN SWEDEN [Literature of]

Cabinet AA Shelf 5 No. 29

Lagerström, Hugo. Svensk bokkunst: Studier och anteckningar över särdragen i Svensk bokstavsform och Svenskt typtryck ... Av Hugo Lagerström. Stockholm, 1920. Facsimile and specimens.

History of the development of printing in Sweden, from 1483 to 1918. Swedish text.

Half morocco; 12 x 9 in.

EARLY PRINTING IN SPAIN. Literature.

Cabinet 75 Shelf 1 No. 15

Output of books in Spain in the sixteenth century, by Mr. Henry Thomas. A summary of a paper read before the Bibliographical Society, February 17, 1918.

In Trans. Biblio. Soc., Vol. XV, 1917-1919, pp. 111-155.

EARLY PRINTING IN SPAIN. Literature.

Cabinet 75 Shelf 2 No. 2

Spanish books: A review of H. Thomas' catalogue of, by S. Gaselee

In Transactions of the Bibliographical Society, "The Library," Vol. II, 1921-22, pp. 135-6.

EARLY PRINTING IN SWEDEN Literature

Cabinet Y Shelf 3 No. 61

Schwedische Donate. von Isak Collijn.

Essay in "Beitrage zum biblictheks-- und buchwesen". Paul Schwenke, Berlin, 1913, p. 47

Half morocco; 11¼ x 8 5/8 in.

EARLY PRINTING IN SPAIN. [Literature of]

Cabinet 75 Shelf 2 No. 1

Out-put of Spanish books in the sixteenth century. A paper read before the Bibliographical Society by Henry Thomas, Feb. 16, 1920.

In Trans. Biblio. Soc., "The Library," Vol. I, 1920-1921, pp. 69-94.

EARLY PRINTING IN SPAIN (Lit. of)

Cabinet 75 Shelf 2 No. 5.01

Spanish books in the library of Samuel Pepys. By Stephen Gaselee, for The Bibliographical Society, London, 1921.

Illustrative of the history of 16th cent. printing.

Trans. Biblio. Soc. Supplements 1-5, 1921-1926.

EARLY PRINTING IN SWEDEN [Literature of]

Cabinet AA Shelf 5 No. 32

Stockholm, 1618-1648: Peter van Selow. Peter van Selow stiljutare och boktryckare i Stockholm 1618-1648. Gustaf Rudbeck, Stockholm, 1925. Facsimile, head and tail pieces borders.

Bio-bibliographical essay in Collijn's "Bok ock biblioteks historika studier ... Uppsala, 1925. pp. 295-301.

Boards; 11 x 8½ x 2 in.

EARLY PRINTING IN SPAIN [Literature of]

Cabinet AA Shelf 5 No. 7

Pastor, Cristobal Pérez: La imprenta en Medina del Campa. Por Cristobal Pérez Pastor. Madrid, 1895.

Chronological bibliographical history. Following p. 478; biographies of some printers and editors, 1511 to 1621.

Half morocco; 10-3/4 x 8 in.

EARLY PRINTING IN SPAIN [Literature of]

Cabinet U Shelf 4 No. 32

Spanish 16th century printing. By Henry Thomas. With fifty illustrations. In series of handbooks "Periods of Typography", edited by Stanley Morison. London, 1926.

Boards; 9-7/8 x 7¼ x 3/8 in.

EARLY PRINTING IN SWEDEN [Literature]

Cabinet 75 Shelf 2 No. 5

Svend Dahls Bibliotekshandbok oversatt, bearbetad och med bidrag av svenska fackman, by Samuel Bing. A review of book with title as above.

In Transactions of the Bibliographical Society, "The Library," Vol. V. 1924-1925, pp. 379-381.

EARLY PRINTING IN SPAIN. Literature.

Cabinet 75 Shelf 2 No. 2

Pepy's, Samuel. Spanish Books. A paper read before the Bibliographical Society, by Stephen Gaselee, 17 January, 1921.

In Trans. Biblio. Soc., "The Library, " Vol. II, 1921-22, pp. 1-11.

EARLY PRINTING IN SPAIN. [Literature of]

Cabinet 75 Shelf 2 No. 7

Typography of the Spanish 16th century. By Henry Thomas. London, 1926. Reviewed by A. W. Pollard.

In Transactions of the Bibliographical Society, "The Library," Vol. VII, 1926-1927, p. 111.

EARLY PRINTING IN SWITZERLAND. Literature of

Cabinet U Shelf 4 No. 35

Basle in the 15th and 16th centuries, the printers of. By Charles William Heckethorn. London, 1897. Illus.

Cloth; 12 x 8 x 1¼ in.

EARLY PRINTING IN SPAIN. [Literature of]

Cabinet 76 Shelf 2 No. 4

Printers of Spain and Portugal, early. By Konrad Haebler. Printed for the Bibliographical Society. March, 1897.

Illus. Monograph IV.

Half morocco; 11 x 9 in.

EARLY PRINTING IN SPAIN (see also)

Cabinet Shelf No.

EARLY PRINTING IN SPAIN. Examples of

EARLY PRINTING IN SPAIN. Literature

PRINTING, HISTORICAL, Spain

EARLY PRINTING IN SWITZERLAND Literature

Cabinet U Shelf 5 No. 38

Basel, influence on printing in France; Basel printers in foreign countries.

see

PROCTOR, ROBERT. Bibliographical essays...London, 1905, pp.68, 156

EARLY PRINTING IN SWITZERLAND [Literature of]

Cabinet U, Shelf 4, No. 33

Basle. The first century of printing at. By A. F. Johnson. With fifty illustrations. In series of handbooks "Periods of Typography", edited by Stanley Morison, London, 1926.

Linen over boards; 9-7/8 x 7½ x 3/8 in.

EARLY PRINTING IN SWITZERLAND. [Lit. of]

Cabinet U, Shelf 1, No. 1d

Basel, 1477: Ludwig Hohenwang's second press at Basel. Communication by Victor Scholderer. n.d.

In Excerpts relating to printing from "The Library," p. 21 of pencilled folios.

EARLY PRINTING IN SWITZERLAND. [Lit. of]

Cabinet U, Shelf 1, No. 1f

Basle and Cologne printing in 1484-1485; A note by V. Scholderer.

In Excerpts relating to printing from The Library, 1912-13, p.205 of pencilled folios.

EARLY PRINTING IN SWITZERLAND. [Lit. of]

Cabinet V, Shelf 1, No. 19

(Basle). Les premiers incunables Bâlois et leurs dérivés: Toulouse, Lyon, Vienne-en-Dauphine, Spire, Eltvil, etc. 1471-1484: Essai de synthèse typographique. Par Henry Harrisse ... Seconde édition, revue et augmentée. Paris, 1902.
Historical bibliographical account.

Half morocco; 9-7/8 x 6-5/8 in.

EARLY PRINTING IN SWITZERLAND. [Lit. of]

Cabinet U, Shelf 1, No. 1d

Basel, 1477. Ludwig Hohenwang's second press at Basel, by Victor Scholderer.

In excerpts relating to printing from The Library, 1909, pp.21-23 of pencilled folios.

EARLY PRINTING IN SWITZERLAND. [Lit. of]

Cabinet 18, Shelf 1, No. 6

(Basle Book Marks to the year 1500) Basler Buchermarken bis zum Jahr 1550 von Hans, Koegler, Basel. Illus.

In Zeitschrift für Bücherfreunde, 1908-9, part 2, pp.283,328, 364, 440, 499,

---

EARLY PRINTING IN SWITZERLAND. (Lit. of)

Cabinet 22, Shelf 1, No. 5, 11 & 14.

Basle, 1462-1521: See Printing, Historical Records relating to the history, etc.

EARLY PRINTING IN SWITZERLAND [Lit. of]

Cabinet U, Shelf 1, No. 1g

Basle, 1490. Adam von Speir and the Chur Breviary. By Victor Scholderer.
Bio-bibliographical account.

In Excerpts relating to printing from "The Library," 1914-15, p. 14 of pencilled folios.

EARLY PRINTING IN SWITZERLAND. [Lit. of]

Cabinet 18, Shelf 1, No. 4

(Basle printers and their marks until the year (1550) Basle Büchermarken bis zum Jahre 1550, von Hans Koegler, Basle. Illus.

In Zeitschrift für Bücherfreunde, 1908-9, part 1, p.253.

EARLY PRINTING IN SWITZERLAND (Lit. of)

Cabinet 75, Shelf 2, No. 7

Basle, first century of printing at. By F. A. Johnson. London, 1926. Book with title as above reviewed by A. W. Pollard.

In Transactions of Bibliographical Society "The Library," vol. VII, p. 111, 1926-1927.

EARLY PRINTING IN SWITZERLAND. [Lit. of]

Cabinet 75, Shelf 2, No. 10

(Basle, 1504-8, Johann Schott). Bibliography of the editions of the "Margarita Philosophica" of Joh. Reisch, and printed by J. Schott. A paper by John Ferguson, for the Bibliographical Society, London, 1929.
With facs. of titles.

In Trans. Biblio. Soc. "The Library," vol. 10, 1929-30. pp. 194-216.

EARLY PRINTING IN SWITZERLAND. [Lit. of]

Cabinet 18, Shelf 1, No. 3

(Basle) Two re-discovered pamphlets from the press of Pamphilus Gengenbach in Basle) Zwei wiederfundene Flugblatter aus der press des Pamphilus Gengenbach in Basle, von Hans Koegler, Basle. Illus.

In Zeitschrift für Bücherfreunde, 1907-8, part 2, p.411.

EARLY PRINTING IN SWITZERLAND [Lit. of]

Cabinet 22, Shelf 1, No. 11, 12, 14.

(Basle, 1470-1521. Records relating to the history of printing, gathered from the archives in Basle.) Regesten zur geschichte des buchdrucks, 1501-1520. Aus den Basler Regesten von Karl Stehlin.

Brief biographical sketches.

In Archiv für Deutschen Buchhandels, vol.XI, p.5, vol.XII, p.6, vol.XIV, p.10.

EARLY PRINTING IN SWITZERLAND [Lit. of]

Cabinet AA, Shelf 1, No. 6

Basle, 1520-82: Pietro Perna.
See Manni, Domenico Maria. Vita di Pietro Perna ... Luca, 1763.

EARLY PRINTING IN SWITZERLAND. [Lit of.]

Cabinet 22, Shelf 1, No. 2

(Bern, 1537. Brief account of the introduction of printing into Bern.) Uber die einfuhrung der buchdruckerkunst in Bern, von G. Rettig.

Includes an account of the Liberty of Printing in Bern.

In Archiv für Deutschen Buchhandels, vol.2 pp.238-240; vol.IV, p.28.

EARLY PRINTING IN SWITZERLAND [Lit. of]

Cabinet U, Shelf 1, No. 1f

Basle, 1472, Michael Wenssler and his press. By Victor Scholderer.
Bio-bibliographical account.

In Excerpts relating to printing from "The Library," 1912-13, p. 1 of pencilled folios.

EARLY PRINTING IN SWITZERLAND. [Lit. of]

Cabinet 75, Shelf 2, No. 8

Basle, 1519-36. Basle ornaments on Paris books. By A. F. Johnson. London, Dec., 1927. Illus.

In Transactions of the Bibliographical Society, vol. VIII, 1927-1928. pp. 355-360. "The Library."

EARLY PRINTING IN SWITZERLAND. [Lit. of]

Cabinet 22, Shelf 1, No. 19

(Bern, Basel, Zurich and Geneva, 1480-1536.) Bern's relation to the printing houses in other towns.) Die Beziehungen Berns zu den Buchdruckern in Basel, Zurich und Genf. von Adolf Fluri.

In Archiv für Deutschen Buchhandels, vol. XIX, p.8.

EARLY PRINTING IN SWITZERLAND. [Lit. of]

Cabinet 22 Shelf 1 No. 4

See Biographies, printers. Apiarius, Mathias.

EARLY PRINTING IN SWITZERLAND. [Lit. of]

Cabinet 22 Shelf 1 No. 6

(Lucerne, 1541-1550. Two Lucerne printers and booksellers: Johann Spiegel, and Johann Hederlin.) Zwei Luzerner buchdrucker und buchhandler, von Franz Joseph Schiffman.

Includes a list of books printed by Hederlin.

In Archiv für Deutschen Buchhandels, vol. VI, p.255.

EARLY PRINTING IN SPANISH AMERICA. Literature

Cabinet 26 Shelf 1 No. 20

(Argentine) Ursprung der presse am Rio de la Plata, und das buch "de la diferencia entre lo temporal y eterno" des P. Juan Eusebio Nieremberg. von Carlo von Muller.
Biblio-historical account.

Article in the "Gutenberg-Gesellschaft Jahrbuch" 1930, pp.238-245.

EARLY PRINTING IN SWITZERLAND. [Lit. of]

Cabinet U Shelf 1 No. 1f

See Biographies, printers. Wenssler, Michael, and his press at Basel.

EARLY PRINTING IN SWITZERLAND. [Lit. of]

Cabinet 22 Shelf 1 No. 8

(Solothurns, 1565. Samuel Apiarius the first printer in Solothurns.) Samuel Apiarius, der älteste buchdrucker in Solothurns, von Franz Jos. Schiffmann.

Includes bibliography.

In Archiv für Deutschen Buchhandels, 1883, vol.VIII, p.5.

EARLY PRINTING IN SPANISH AMERICA [Lit. of]

Cabinet Shelf No.

Brazil (Rio de Janeiro, 1747) First book printed in. German text: Das erste in Brasilien buch.

Article on p.29 of the "Philobiblon", 5 Jahrgang, heft I, 1932.

EARLY PRINTING IN SWITZERLAND [Lit. of]

Stack A Shelf 1 & 2 Number 54

Bullen, Henry Lewis. Germany, the Netherlands and Switzerland: The Literature of Typography in The Inland Printer. Vol.LIV, p.61.

EARLY PRINTING IN TAHITI

Cabinet 81 Shelf 2 No. 36

First printing in Tahiti. Under the direction of Mr. Ellis, chief Pomare composed the first alphabet that ever was put in type in Polynesia. Brief note, Newspaper clipping.

Item in MUNSELL, JOEL. "Printers' Scraps", vol.VII., p.2.

EARLY PRINTING IN SP. AMERICA. [Lit. of]

Cabinet Shelf No.

(Brazil) First book was printed there in (Rio Janiero), early in 1747.

See short note in British and Colonial Printer and Stationer, vol. 109, No. 146, Aug., 13, 1931, p.168.

EARLY PRINTING IN SWITZERLAND [Lit. of]

Cabinet U Shelf 1 No. 1g

Chur Breviary of 1490 and its printer, Adam von Speier: An account of V. Scholderer.

Brief biographical sketch of the printer, and description of the Breviary.

In excerpts relating to printing from The Library, 1914-15, p.14 of pencilled folios.

EARLY PRINTING IN SPANISH-AMERICA Lit. of

Cabinet W Shelf 3 No. 115

Historical, bibliographic article. By R. Garnett. Excerpt from the "Book-Lover", Nov.-Dec., 1901.

Item 14 in vol. with binder's title "Pamphlets Relating to Books - II. Bound, 1932".

EARLY PRINTING IN SPANISH-AMERICA [Lit. of]

Cabinet 79 Shelf 1 No. 23

(Columbia: Popayan, 1816-1819) Notas bibliograficas referentes les primas producciones de la imprenta en algunas ciudades de la America-Españole. Por José Toribio Medina. Santiago de Chile, 1904.

Cloth; 9½ x 6¼ in. Chiappa 146

EARLY PRINTING IN SWITZERLAND. [Lit. of]

Cabinet 22 Shelf 1 No. 14

(Contribution to the history of printing 1501-1520. Taken from the Archives in Basle.) Regesten zur geschichte des buchdrucks 1501-1520. von Dr. Karl Stehlen.

Chronological and biographical account.

In Archiv für Deutschen Buchhandels, vol. XIV, p.10.

Literature
EARLY PRINTING IN AMERICA (Spanish-America)

Cabinet 79 Shelf 2 No. 26

Laws relative to the printing-press in Colonial America. By Virgilio Rodriquez Beteta.
Excerpt from "Inter-America. April, 1926. English: vol. IX, No. 4.

In envelope.

EARLY PRINTING IN SPANISH-AMERICA [Lit. of]

Cabinet 79 Shelf 1 No. 23

(Columbia: Santa Marta, 1816) Notas bibliograficas ...Por José Toribio Medina. Santiago de Chile, 1904.

Cloth; 9½ x 6¼ in. Chiappa 146

EARLY PRINTING IN SWITZERLAND. [Lit. of]

Cabinet 26 Shelf 2 No. 2

(Corrections concerning the facts related to the history of printing in Switzerland.) Einege bemerkungen uber der Rubrik "Schweiz" in der geschichte der Buchdruckerkunst, von Dr. Karl Falkenstein.

Journal fur Buchdruckerkunst, Jan., 1841, cols.5-8.

EARLY PRINTING IN SPANISH-AMERICA [Lit. of]

Cabinet 79 Shelf 1 No. 38

Medina, Jose Toribio. La primitiva inquisicion Americana (1493-1569) Estudio historico. Documentos. Santiago de Chile, 1914. Two vols. in one.
pp.51 to 66 refer to printing and censorship of books.

Half morocco; 10 x 7 x 1-5/8 in. Chiappa 226

EARLY PRINTING IN SPANISH-AMERICA [Lit. of]

Cabinet 79 Shelf 1 No. 23

(Columbia: Tunja, 1814) Notas bibliograficas referentes les primas producciones de la imprenta...Por José Toribio Medina. Santiago de Chile, 1904.

Cloth; 9½ x 6¼ in. Chiappa 146.

EARLY PRINTING IN SPANISH-AMERICA [Lit. of]

Cabinet 79 Shelf 1 No. 23

(Cuba: Santiago, 1796-1810) Notas bibliograficas referentes les primas produccions de la imprenta...Por José Toribio Medina. Santiago de Chile, 1904.

Cloth; 9½ x 6¼ in. Chiappa 146

EARLY PRINTING IN SPANISH-AMERICA [Lit. of]

Stack A Shelf 1 & 2 Number 53

(New Mexico) Bullen, Henry Lewis. Histories of printing in Spanish-speaking America. In The Inland Printer, vol. LIII, p. 697.

With bibliography of history relating to the same subject.

EARLY PRINTING IN SP. AMERICA. [Lit. of]

Cabinet S Shelf 3 No. 75.01

[Peru, 1584 et sub]. The printing press in South America. By George Parker Winship. Providence, 1912.

Bio-bibliographical.

Half morocco; 6¼ x 4¾ in.

EARLY PRINTING IN SPANISH-AMERICA. Lit. of.

Cabinet Shelf No.

(Dominica, British West Indies) First printing in Dominica. Some historical information. By Douglas C. McMurtrie.

Article in British & Colonial Printer, vol. 110, No. 186, May 19, 1932. p.460.

EARLY PRINTING IN SPANISH-AMERICA [Lit. of]

Stack A Shelf 1 & 2 Number 53

(New Mexico). Bullen, Henry Lewis. Literature of Typography, The. In The Inland Printer vol. LIII. p. 396.

EARLY PRINTING IN SP. AMERICA [Lit. of]

Cabinet S Shelf 3 No. 79

(Peru. Lima 1585-1800), books printed in, and books printed in Lima and elsewhere in South America after 1800. A list of books in The John Carter Brown Library. Providence, Rhode Island. The Merrymount Press, Boston, 1908.

Boards; 10¼ x 7 in.

EARLY PRINTING IN SPANISH-AMERICA. [Lit. of]

Cabinet 79 Shelf 1 No. 23

(Ecuador: Ambato, 1754-1758) Notas bibliograficas referentes a las primeras producciones de la imprenta en algunas ciudades de la America-Española...Por J.T. Medina, Santiago de Chile, 1904.

Cloth; 9½ x 6¼ in. Chiappa 146.

EARLY PRINTING IN SPANISH-AMERICA [Lit. of]

Cabinet 79 Shelf 2 No. 19

New Mexico. (La) Primera imprenta (1835) en Nuevo Mexico; su objecto y producto "El Crepusculo", primer periodico que se vio al Oeste del Rio Misuri,...Hasta la anexion de Nuevo Mexico a los Estados Unidos.

See p.29 in Memorias sobre la vida del Don Ant. Jose Martinez. Por Pedro Sanchez. Santa Fe. N.M. 1903.

Stamped cloth; 7½ x 5¼ in.

EARLY PRINTING IN SPANISH AMERICA Lit.

Cabinet C Shelf 2 No. 19

Historia y bibliografia de la imprenta en el antiguo vireinato del Rio de la Plata. Por José Toribio Medina. La Plata, Buenos-Aires, 1892. Illus.

Half morocco; 18¼ x 12½ in.

EARLY PRINTING IN SPANISH-AMERICA [Lit. of]

Cabinet 79 Shelf 1 No. 23

(Ecuador: Guayaquil, 1810 1822) Notas bibliograficas...Por J.T. Medina, Santiago de Chile, 1904.

Cloth; 9½ x 6¼ in. Chiappa 146

EARLY PRINTING IN SPANISH-AMERICA. [Lit. of]

Cabinet 79 Shelf 1 No. 23

(Panama, 1822-3) Notas bibliograficas referentes les primas producciones de la imprenta en algunas ciudades de la America-Española. Por José Toribio Medina. Santiago de Chile, 1904.

Cloth; 9½ x 6 in. Chiappa 146.

EARLY PRINTING IN SPANISH-AMERICA [Lit. of]

Cabinet 79 Shelf 1 No. 23

(Venezuela: Maracaibo, 1822) Notas bibliograficas referentes a las primas producciones de la imprenta en algunas ciudades de la America-Española. Por José Toribio Medina, Santiago de Chile, 1904.

Cloth; 9½ x 6¼ in. Chiappa 146

EARLY PRINTING IN SPANISH-AMERICA [Lit. of]

Cabinet 79 Shelf 2 No. 4

(Guatemala 1724) Doctrina Cristiana en lengua Guatemaltcca de Don Francisco Marroquin. Reimprose á plana y renglon del unico ejemplar conocido, y precedida de una biografia de su autor. José Toribio Medina. Santiago de Chile. Imprenta Elzeviriana. 1905.

Half morocco; 7-5/8 x 4⅛ in. Chiappa 163

EARLY PRINTING IN SPANISH AMERICA (Lit.)

Cabinet U Shelf 3 No. 103

Paraguayan and Argentine bibliography. By R. Garnett.

See vol. I, pp.262-73 in Bibliographica... London, 1895-1897.

EARLY PRINTING IN SPANISH-AMERICA. [Lit. of]

Cabinet 79 Shelf 1 No. 23

(Venezuela: Nueva Valencia, 1764-1813) Notas bibliograficas referentes les primas producciones de la imprenta en algunas ciudades de la America-Española. Por José Toribio Medina. Santiago de Chile, 1904.

Cloth; 9½ x 6¼ in. Chiappa 146

EARLY PRINTING IN SPANISH-AMERICA. Lit.

Cabinet S Shelf 6 No. 3

(Mexico, 1532). Early Spanish-American printing By R. Garnett. (Excerpt) Book-lover, Nov.-Dec, 1901.

Biblio-historical account.

Item in box labelled "Excerpts and brochures relating to printing and printers in America.

EARLY PRINTING IN SPANISH AMERICA. Lit. of

Cabinet 26 Shelf 1 No. 21

(Peru: Lima, 1544, Antonio Ricardo) Doctrina Christiana: das erste in Südamerika gedruckte buch. von Carla von Muller.

Essay in "Gutenberg-Gesellschaft Jahrbuch, 1931", pp.214-220.

EARLY PRINTING IN SP. AMERICA. [Lit. of]

Cabinet 79 Shelf 2 No. 25

(Venezuela. Tachira, 1845-1883) La imprenta en el Tachira. Por Luis F. Briceno, redactor de "El Porvenir" Caracas, 1883.

Cloth; 12⅛ x 8½ in.

EARLY PRINTING IN SPANISH-AMERICA [Lit. of]

Cabinet 79 Shelf 1 No. 23

(West Indies, British: Puerto Espana, 1876) Notas bibliograficas referentes les primas producciones de la imprenta en algunas ciudades de la America-Espanola. Por Jose Toribio Medina. Santiago de Chile, 1904.

Cloth; 9½ x 6¼ in. Chiappa 146

EARLY PRINTING IN WALES. [Literature of]

Cabinet U Shelf 1 No. 1d

Secret printing of a "popish book" in Wales, the earliest notice of. A new tract from the Marprelate Press. Communicated by J. D. Wilson to "The Library," London, 1909.

In Excerpts relating to printing from "The Library," p. 86 of pencilled folios.

EARLY PRINTING IN AMERICA, U.S. [Lit. of]

Cabinet S Shelf 4 No. 110

Bibles of America, Early; being a descriptive account of bibles published in the United States, Mexico and Canada. By Rev. John Wright, D.D. New York, 1894. Third edition illus.

Bio-bibliographical, historical account.

Half morocco; 9¾ x 6½ in.

EARLY PRINTING IN SPANISH AMERICA [Lit. of]

Cabinet 79 Shelf 1 No. 23

(West Indies, Dutch Curacao, 1819.) Notas bibliograficas referentes a las primeras producciones de la imprenta en algunas ciudades de la America-Espanola. Por J.T. Medina, Santiago de Chile, 1904.

Cloth; 9½ x 6¼ in. Chiappa 146

EARLY PRINTING IN AMERICA.(U.S.)Literature of

Cabinet II Shelf 3 No. 2

Algonquin language, bibliography of. [1660 to 1886]. By James Constantine Pilling. Washington, D.C. 1891. Facs.

Lists and describes 2,245 items, 1,926 of which relate to printed books and articles.

Cloth; 9¾ x 6-3/8 x 1½ in.

EARLY PRINTING IN AMERICA (U.S.) Literature

Cabinet W Shelf 3 No. 115

Bookselling and printing in Washington's days. [Historical biographical article: excerpt from the "Book-Lover", Jan.-Feb., 1902.

Item 16 in vol. with binder's title "Pamphlets Relating to Books - II. Bound, 1932".

EARLY PRINTING IN SPANISH-AMERICA [Lit. of]

Cabinet 79 Shelf 1 No. 23

(West Indies: Puerto Rico, 1808-1817) Notas bibliograficas referentes les primas producciones de la imprenta en algunas ciudades de la America-Española. Por José Toribio Medina. Santiago de Chile, 1904.

Cloth; 9½ x 6¼ in. Chiappa 146

EARLY PRINTING IN AMERICA.(U.S.) Literature

Cabinet TT Shelf 4 No. 15-26

American bibliography: a chronological dictionary of all books, pamphlets and periodical publications printed in the United States from 1639 to 1820. By Charles Evans. Printed for the author. Chicago, 1903-1934. (12vols.)

Vol. I, 1639-1729.	Vol. VI, 1779-1785.
" II, 1730-1750.	" VII, 1786-1789.
" III, 1751-1764.	" VIII, 1790-1792.
" IV, 1765-1773.	" IX, 1793-1794.
" V, 1774-1778.	" X, 1795-1796.
	" XI, 1796-1797.
	" XII, 1798-1799.

EARLY PRINTING IN AMERICA, U.S. [Lit. of]

Cabinet R Shelf 3 No. 71

Bradford, Andrew, founder of the Newspaper Press in the Middle States of America: An address delivered at the Annual Meeting of the Historical Society of Pennsylvania. By Horatio Gates Jones. Feb. 9, 1869.

Bound in with publications of the Historical Society of Pennsylvania. No. 11.

Half morocco; 9½ x 6 in.

EARLY PRINTING IN SPANISH-AMERICA [Lit. of]

Cabinet 79 Shelf 1 No. 23

(West Indies: Santo Domingo, 1821) Notas bibliograficas referentes les primas producciones de la imprenta...Por José Toribio Medina. Santiago de Chile, 1904.

Cloth; 9½ x 6¼ in. Chiappa 146

EARLY PRINTING IN AMERICA (U.S.) Literature

Cabinet U Shelf 5 No. 24

American colonies, early printing in.

see

POLLARD, A. W. Fine Books... London, 1912, pp.243-9

EARLY PRINTING IN AMERICA (U.S.) [Lit. of]

Cabinet R Shelf 3 No. 71

Bradford, William: Celebration of the two-hundredth birth-day of William Bradford, who introduced the art of printing into the Middle Colonies of British America. Reported by Horatio Gates Jones, New York, May 20, 1863.

Bound in with publications of the Historical Society of Pennsylvania. No. 5.

Half morocco; 9½ x 6 in.

EARLY PRINTING IN UKRANIA [Literature of]

Cabinet 26 Shelf 1 No. 15

(Ukranian printing of the 16th to the 18th centuries). Ukrainische druckkunst des 16. bis 18. jahrhunderts. von S. J. Masslow, Kiew. 1926. Illus.

p. 65 Gutenberg-Gesellschaft Jahrbuch, 1926.

EARLY PRINTING IN AMERICA, (U.S.) [Lit. of]

Cabinet S Shelf 3 No. 75

American imprints, the earliest. By George Parker Winship. Milwaukee, 1899. Reprinted from "American Book-Lore" for July, 1899.

Bio-bibliographical. Very brief account.

Half morocco; 6-3/4 x 4-3/8 x ¼ in.

EARLY PRINTING IN AMERICA, U.S. [Lit. of]

Cabinet Shelf No.

See Bradford Bi-Centennial celebration, New York, 1893.

Bound with other items in "Various printers and their plants", item 5, vol.1.

EARLY PRINTING IN WALES (Lit. of)

Cabinet U Shelf 1 No. 1d

See Early Printing in England (Literature of) Marprelate Press, (1588).

EARLY PRINTING IN AMERICA (U.S.)

Cabinet Shelf No.

Bibles (Title Pages of), printed in America 1768 to 1861. (Collection).

File drawer "A-Z" Envelope marked "Title Pages, No. 10."

EARLY PRINTING IN AMERICA (U.S.) Literature

Cabinet S Shelf 5 No. 12

Bradford, William: First American edition of Wither's Poems and Bacon's Essay, by Wilberforce Emes, in The Bibliographer, Jan., 1902.

Reproduced facsimile pages, also list of books printed and sold by W. Bradford in Philadelphia.

Bound with "Pamphlets and excerpts relating to typographical matters." Item 23.

EARLY PRINTING IN AMERICA (U.S.) Lit.

Cabinet S Shelf 5 No. 25.01

Bradford, William (and his successors). By Henry Simpson. Excerpt from "Lives of Eminent Philadelphians" Phila. 1859.
Has portrait.

Item in box labelled "Colonial printing and printers. Miscellaneous items."

EARLY PRINTING IN AMERICA (U.S.) Literature

Cabinet R Shelf 4 No. 87

Check list of printers in the United States; from Stephen Daye to the close of the War of Independence, with a list of places in which printing was done. Compiled by Chas. F. Heartman, New York, 1915.

Boards; 9½ x 6½ in.

EARLY PRINTING IN AMERICA (U.S.) Literature of

Cabinet QQ Shelf 3 No. 5

Curious Boston lectures: Revolutionary proclamations. (Brief historical notes of early printed proclamations and broadsides).

Paper; 7¾ x 5 in.

EARLY PRINTING IN AMERICA (U.S.) Literature

Cabinet MM Shelf 6 No. 81

Brief history of printing in America: containing a brief sketch of the development of the newspaper and some notes on publishers who have especially contributed to printing. By Frederick W. Hamilton. "Typographic Technical Series for Apprentices", Part VIII, No.54. The United Typothetae of America, 1918.

Cloth; 8 x 5 in.

EARLY PRINTING IN AMERICA, U.S. [Lit. of]

Cabinet R Shelf 5 No. 148

Children's Books, Early History of, in New England By Charles Welsh. Excerpt from New England Magazine, April, 1899.

Excerpt 20 in volume "Chap Books, Almanacs, Annuals, etc."

EARLY PRINTING IN AMERICA (U.S.) Literature

Cabinet R Shelf 5 No. 148

Dudley Leavitt's New Hampshire Almanac [1797]. With some observations on New England Almanacs. By John Albee. Excerpt from the New England Magazine, Jan. 1898. Illus.
Bio-bibliographical account.

Excerpt 15 in volume "Chap Books, Almanacs, Annuals, etc.

EARLY PRINTING IN AMERICA.LITERATURE.

Cabinet NN Shelf 3 No. 5

Buckingham's Reminiscences. Anecdotes, personal memoirs, and biographies of literary men, connected with newspaper literature, from 1690 to 1800. By Joseph T.Buckingham. With steel portraits of Isaiah Thomas and Benjamin Russell. (2 vols.) Boston. 1852. Illus.

Paper: 7½x4-5/8"

EARLY PRINTING IN AMERICA, U.S. [Lit. of]

Cabinet 75 Shelf 2 No. 7

Chronological survey of American printing. Contained in review of Book "Bibliographical Essays: A tribute to Wilberforce Eames. Harvard University Press. 1924.

In Transactions of Bibliographical Society, "The Library," Vol. VII, 1926-1927. pp. 103-111.

EARLY PRINTING IN AMERICA, U.S. [Lit. of]

Cabinet S Shelf 3 No. 104

Eames, Wilberforce. Bibliographical Essays: A tribute to. Cambridge, 1924.
Bio-bibliographical and historical essays.

Cloth; 9½ x 6-3/8 in.

EARLY PRINTING IN AMERICA. U.S. [Lit. of]

Stack A Shelf 1&2 Number 52

Bullen, Henry Lewis. Literature of typography: Histories of Printing in America, in The Inland Printer, vol.LII, pp.233-35, 396-99, 355-57, and continuing volumes.

EARLY PRINTING IN AMERICA. U.S. [Lit. of]

Cabinet R Shelf 5 No. 50

Colonial printer, the. By Lawrence C. Wroth. New York, The Grolier Club, 1931. Illus.
Chapters include the following: First presses of the Colonies -- The Colonial Printing House -- The Colonial Printing Press -- Printing Ink -- The Journeyman and Apprentice -- The product of the Colonial Press, etc.

Boards, linen back; 10-3/8 x 6-3/4 x 1 in.

EARLY PRINTING IN AMERICA Literature

Cabinet S Shelf 6 No. 9

Early American poetry. A compilation of titles of volumes of verse and broadsides issued during the 17th and 18th centuries. By Oscar Wegelin. [A review of above book. Excerpt from the "Literary Collector", Oct., 1903].

Item 14 in vol. with binder's title "Early printing and printed books. Pamphlets". Bound, 1932.

EARLY PRINTING IN AMERICA, U.S. [Lit. of]

Cabinet R Shelf 3 No. 122

Cambridge Press, 1638-1692: A history of the first printing press established in English America, together with a bibliographical list of the issues of the press. By Robert F. Roden, New York, 1905.

Boards; 7¾ x 5¾ in.

EARLY PRINTING IN AMERICA (U.S.) Literature

Cabinet JJ Shelf 3 No. 32

Colonial times to 1928, history of wages in the United States from the United States Bureau of Labor Statistics, Bulletin No. 499, Washington, D.C.

Chapters on the printing trades, with statistics.

Paper; 9 x 5¾ x ¾ in.

EARLY PRINTING IN AMERICA, U.S. [Lit. of]

Cabinet S Shelf 4 No. 111

(Early) Prayer Books of America; being a descriptive account of prayer books published in the United States, Mexico and Canada. By Rev. John Wright, D.D. St. Paul, Minn. 1896. Illus.
Bio-bibliographical.

Half morocco; 8¾ x 6¼ in.

EARLY PRINTING IN AMERICA (U.S.) Literature

Cabinet R Shelf 4 No. 5 2 vols.

Catalogue of publications in what is now the United States, prior to the Revolution of 1775-6.

See THOMAS, ISAIAH: History of printing in America...Worcester, Mass., 1810, also second edition, Albany, 1874.

EARLY PRINTING IN AMERICA. U.S. Literature

Cabinet PP Shelf 2 No. 23

(The) Cradle of the United States, 1765-1789. A collection of contemporary broadsides and pamphlets...Bibliographically, historically and sometimes sentimentally described by Charles F. Heartman, Metuchen, New Jersey, 1922-23. (2 vols.)

Boards; 11 x 7-5/8 in.

EARLY PRINTING IN AMERICA Literature

Cabinet S Shelf 5 No. 25

Early printing in the West. By Robert Clark, Cincinnati, Ohio.
Excerpt from Historical Magazine, May, 1873.

In box labeled "History of Printing. United States. Miscellaneous items".

EARLY PRINTING IN AMERICA (U.S) Literature

Cabinet 22 Shelf 4 No. 20

Establishment of the printing press in the Colonies.

see

BISHOP, J. LEANDER. History of American manufacturers...Philadelphia, 1868, pp. 152-194.

EARLY PRINTING IN AMERICA, U.S. [Lit. of]

Cabinet R Shelf 5 No. 127

Ford, Paul Leicester: The New-England Primer, a reprint of the earliest known edition, with many facsimiles and reproductions and a historical introduction. Edited by Paul Leicester Ford, New York, 1899.

Boards; $7\frac{1}{4}$ x $5\frac{1}{2}$ in.

EARLY PRINTING IN AMERICA,(U.S) [Lit. of]

Cabinet S Shelf 3 No. 74

[Harrisse Henry]. Brief disquisition concerning the early history of printing in America. New York, Privately printed, 1866.

Extracted from the Bibliotheca Americana Vetustissima, pp. 365-377.

Includes a list of works printed in America between the years 1540-1600.

Half morocco; 10 x 7 in.

EARLY PRINTING AND PRINTERS IN AMERICA, U.S.

Cabinet R Shelf 5 No. 15

Excerpts from Pennsylvania Magazine. Contents: Bradford Andrew; Anthony Armbruster; Friends Press, 1696-1712; Sauer's Almanac; Brandmiller, the Moravian Printer, 1761-1777; First Newspaper published in Harrisburg Pa; Quarrel between Christopher Sauer and Conrad Beissel, etc.

Half morocco; $9\frac{3}{4}$ x $6\frac{3}{4}$ in.

EARLY PRINTING IN AMERICA, (U.S.) [Lit. of]

Cabinet S Shelf 3 No. 106

Forgotten books of the American nursery. A history of the development of the American Story-book. By Rosalie V. Halsey. Boston, 1911. Illus.

Paper boards; 10-1/8 x $6\frac{3}{4}$ x 7/8 in.

EARLY PRINTING IN AMERICA, U.S. [Lit. of]

Stack A Shelf 1&2 Number 52

Histories of printing in America, by Henry Lewis Bullen, in The Inland Printer, vol.LII, pp.233-5, 396, 555, 709, 873. Illus.

With bibliography of histories relating to the same subject.

EARLY PRINTING IN AMERICA Literature

Cabinet S Shelf 5 No. 25

First book printed between Seneca - Lake and the Pacific Ocean. - In the Historical Magazine Bibliographical notes. By J.G. Shea.

Excerpt from Historical Magazine, Feb. 1872.

In box labeled "History of Printing, United States, Miscellaneous items".

EARLY PRINTING IN AMERICA, U.S. [Lit. of]

Cabinet S Shelf 2 No. 2

Freneau, Philip A. Bibliography of the separate and collected works of Philip Freneau, together with an account of his newspapers. By Victor Hugo Paltsits. New York, 1903.

Half morocco; $9\frac{3}{4}$ x $6\frac{1}{2}$ in.

EARLY PRINTING IN AMERICA Literature

Cabinet NN Shelf 2 No. 36

History of journalism in the United States. By George Henry Payne. New York, 1920.

Cloth; 8 x 5-3/8 in.

EARLY PRINTING IN AMERICA (U.S.) Lit. of

Cabinet 79 Shelf 2 No. 17

First book printed in North America. By S. H. Horgan. Excerpt from U. S. Cath. Hist. Society Hist. Researches & Studies, Vol.5, Part 2, April, 1909.

Bibliographical account of the "Doctrina Christiana", printed by Juan Cromberger, in the city of Tenochtitlan of Mexico, in 1544.

In envelope.

EARLY PRINTING IN AMERICA, U.S. [Lit. of]

Cabinet 22 Shelf 1 No. 1

German-American printing and bookselling business in the early part of the 18th century). Der Deutschamerikanische Buchdruck und Buchhandel im vorigen Jahrhundert, von Freidrich Kapp.

In Archiv für Deutschen Buchhandles, 1878, vol. 1, p. 56.

EARLY PRINTING IN AMERICA, U.S. [Lit. of]

Cabinet 26 Shelf 2 No. 2

(History of the introduction and development of printing in America) Uber die Einfuhrung und erste buchdruckerkunst in Amerika. Fabricus.

Journal fur Buchdruckerkunst, Oct., 1843, No. 10, cols. 129-35. Nov., No. 11, cols. 145-154.

EARLY PRINTING IN AMERICA (U.S.) [Lit. of]

Cabinet 26 Shelf 1 No. 15

(First printed work in English speaking North America) Die ersten drucke im English-sprachigen Nord-America. Von Douglas McMurtrie, New York. Facsimiles

pp. 136-143 Gutenberg-Gesellschaft Jahrbuch, 1926.

EARLY PRINTING IN AMERICA Literature

Cabinet R Shelf 5 No. 30

German printing in America, first century of, 1728-1830, preceded by a notice of the literary work of F.D. Pastorius, by Oswald Seidensticker. Published by the German Pionier-Verein of Philadelphia. Philadelphia, 1893.

Half morocco; 9x 6 in.

EARLY PRINTING IN AMERICA Literature

Cabinet R Shelf 3 No. 161

Houghton, Henry Oscar. An address delivered before the Vermont Historical Society at Montpelier, Oct. 25, 1894.

Half morocco; $8\frac{3}{4}$ x 5-7/8 in.

EARLY PRINTING IN AMERICA Literature

Cabinet S Shelf 5 No. 50

First (The) printers on the Continent of North America. With facs.

Chapter I in Fauteux, Aegidius "The introduction of printing into Canada...Montreal, 1930.

EARLY PRINTING IN AMERICA (U. S.) Lit. of

Cabinet 81 Shelf 2 No. 30

[Green, Samuel, the sixth generation of the Green family of printers, beginning in Cambridge Mass., in 1648]. Letter of S. Green, dated Hartford, Jan., 9, 1847, containing data relating to his ancestors.

In MUNSELL, JOESL. Printers' Scraps... vol. I, pp.87-88

EARLY PRINTING IN AMERICA (U.S.) [Lit. of]

Cabinet s Shelf 2 No. 87

See Huidekoper, Harm Jan...Cambridge, 1904.

EARLY PRINTING IN AMERICA, U.S. Lit. of.

Cabinet K Shelf 4 No. 43

(A) Hundred years of bank note engraving in the United States. By Robert Noxon Toppan. Read before the Trustees of the American Bank Note Company. New York, 1896.

Half morocco; 9¼ x 6 x 3/8 in.

EARLY PRINTING IN AMERICA(U.S.) Lit. of

Cabinet KK Shelf 6 No. 9

New Hampshire, 1868 -

see

NEW HAMPSHIRE PUBLISHERS ASSOCIATION. Annual reports...

EARLY PRINTING IN AMERICA Literature

Cabinet S Shelf 6 No. 9

Old time book shelf, an. By Blanche McManus. Excerpt from "Peterson's Magazine". Aug., 1897. Illus.

Item 6 in vol. with binder's title "Early printing and printed books. Pamphlets". Bound, 1932.

EARLY PRINTING IN AMERICA Literature

Cabinet S Shelf 6 No. 9

Lilies and languors. By Edmund Lester Pearson. With illustrations from old books. Excerpt from "Scribner's", Jan. 1924.

Item 10 in vol. with binder's title "Early printing and printed books. Pamphlets". Bound, 1932.

EARLY PRINTING IN AMERICA, U.S. Lit. of

Cabinet S Shelf 5 No. 25.01

New York printers and the celebration of the French Revolution of 1830. By Ruth Shepard Grannis, librarian of The Grolier Club, New York. 1926.

Item in box labelled "Colonial printing and printers. Miscellaneous items".

EARLY PRINTING IN AMERICA(U.S.) Literature

Cabinet R Shelf 5 No. 106

Oregon country, early printing in the. Written by Alfred Powers and published as a keepsake by the Portland (Oregon) Club of Printing House Craftsmen. n.d. (1933)

Boards; 11 x 8⅜ in.

EARLY PRINTING IN AMERICA. U.S. [Lit. of]

Cabinet R Shelf 4 No. 37

List of early American imprints belonging to the library of the Massachusetts Historical Society. With an introduction and notes by Samuel Abbott Green. Cambridge, Mass. 1895. With two supplements, 1899, 1903.

Half morocco; 9 x 6¼ in.

EARLY PRINTING IN AMERICA, U.S. [Lit. of]

Cabinet S Shelf 3 No. 104

New York Printers, and the celebration of the French revolution of 1830. By Ruth Shepard Granniss, Librarian of The Grolier Club. Biblio-historical account.

P. 193 in volume, Wilberforce Eames ... A tribute to. Cambridge, 1924.

EARLY PRINTING IN AMERICA, U.S. [Lit. of]

Stack A Shelf 1&2 Number 65

Pilgrim printers, The, by Henry Lewis Bullen, in The Inland Printer, vol. LXV, p. 55.

Inclunes a facsimile of a title page of a folio book printed by one of the Pilgrim Printers.

EARLY PRINTING IN AMERICA (U.S.) Lit. of

STACK 15 Shelf 1 No. 17.05

Louisiana. Broadside, 1769. Don Alexandre O'Reilly. Commandeurs de Benjayan dans l'Ordre de Alcantara...Donne en Notre Hotel, a la Nouvelle Orleans le Decembre 1769. Facs

Catalogue item No.87, the Library of Mr. Simon J. Schwartz. To be sold Nov., 8,9, 10, 1926, at The Anderson Galleries, New York.

EARLY PRINTING IN AMERICA Literature

Cabinet OO Shelf 3 No. 34

Newspapers, notes toward a history of American. Vol. I...By William Nelson. With reproductions. Published by Charles F. Heartman, New York, 1918.

No. 4 of 45 copies printed on special paper.

Half morocco; 11½ x 9¼ x 2½ in.

EARLY PRINTING IN AMERICA. U.S. [Lit. of]

Stack A Shelf 1&2 Number 66

Pilgrim printers of Plymouth in New England, The, by Henry Lewis Bullen, in The Inland Printer, vol.LXVI, p.334.

EARLY PRINTING IN AMERICA, U.S. Lit. of

Cabinet S Shelf 5 No. 25.01

Middle colonies, early printing in the. Addres delivered before The Historical Society of Pennsylvania, December 11, 1885, to commemorate the two hundredth anniversary of the introduction of printing into the middle colonies of North America.

Pamphlet in box labelled "Colonial printing and printers. Miscellaneous items."

EARLY PRINTING IN AMERICA, U.S. Lit. of

Cabinet S Shelf 5 No. 21

Notable editors between 1776 and 1800: The influence of the early American Press. By S.G.W. Benjamin. In Magazine of American History, Feb. 1887. Illus.

Bound with other items in " Excerpts relating to printing in America", pp.29-59.

EARLY PRINTING IN AMERICA, U.S. [Lit. of]

Cabinet S Shelf 5 No. 6

Pioneer printers of America. By S. R. Davis. Excerpt from Paper and Press, n. d.

Includes a brief chronology of the introduction of the printing-press in different parts of America.

Item 22 in collection "Various printers and their plants; excerpts from magazines," Vol. 2, 1918.

EARLY PRINTING IN AMERICA, U.S. [Lit. of]

Cabinet S Shelf 5 No. 12

(The) New England Primer printed in America prior to 1830. A bibliographical check list. Compiled by Charles F. Heartman, New York, 1917. Heartman's Historical Series, No. 15.

Item 10 in collection "Pamphlets and excerpts relating to various typographical matters".

EARLY PRINTING IN AMERICA Literature

Cabinet NN Shelf 2 No. 35

Notes toward the history of the American newspaper. By William Nelson, New York, 1918.

On the introduction of printing into every State of the Union. vol.1 comprises States under the alphabets A to N.

Cloth; 9½ x 6¼ in.

EARLY PRINTING IN AMERICA, U.S. Literature

Cabinet S Shelf 6 No. 3

Poetry, early American. A compilation of titles of verse and broadsides ... issued during the 17th and 18th centuries. By Oscar Wegelin. N.Y. published by the compiler, 1903. (An illus. review). Excerpt from the Literary Collector, Oct. 1903.

Item in box labelled "Excerpts and brochures relating to printing and printers in America."

EARLY PRINTING IN AMERICA, U.S. [Lit. of]

Cabinet 22 Shelf 1 No. 1&11

(Sauer, Christopher, and the introduction of German bookselling in America.) Der aufang des deutschen Buchhandels im Amerika, von F. Herm. Meyer.

This item is based on a letter written by Sauer himself.

In Archiv für Deutschen Buchhandels, 1888, vol.XI, p.359.

EARLY PRINTING IN AMERICA, U.S. [Lit. of]

Cabinet X Shelf 4 No. 57

Zenger, John Peter: The tryal of John P. Zenger, of New York, printer, who was lately try'd and acquitted for printing and publishing a libel against the Government...Second edition. London: Printed for J. Wilford, 1738.

Half morocco; 9-1/8 x 7-1/8 x 3/8 in.

EARLY PRINTING IN AMERICA, U.S. Lit. (New England)

Cabinet NN Shelf 7 No. 11

Greenfield, Mass., Thomas Dickman, 1792, first publisher of the Greenfield Gazette.

see

NEWSPAPERS ANNIVERSARY ISSUES. Greenfield Gazette. Centennial Edition, 1792 - 1892...

EARLY PRINTING IN AMERICA, U.S. [Lit. of]

Cabinet R Shelf 5 No. 135

School Books of New England, Early. By George E. Littlefield, Boston, Mass., The Club of Odd Volumes, 1904. Facsimiles.

Historical, bibliographical account.

Boards; 9¾ x 6¾ in.

EARLY PRINTING IN AMERICA, U.S. (Literature of)

Cabinet QQ Shelf 4 No. 8

New England, a narrative of the newspapers printed in. A letter to the President of the Historical Society.

In Massachusetts Historical Society. Collections...Boston, 1835, p. 208.)

Boards; 10¼ x 6¼ x ¾ in.

EARLY PRINTING IN AMERICA, U.S. [Lit. of]

Stack A Shelf 1 & 2 Number 67

(New England). Thomas, Isaiah. Biography of I. Thomas, America's most successful printer, by Henry Lewis Bullen, in The Inland Printer, vol. LXVII, p. 483. Illus.

Biographical sketch.

EARLY PRINTING IN AMERICA, U.S. [Lit. of]

Cabinet S Shelf 4 No. 3 2 Vols.

Specimens of newspaper literature: With personal memoirs, anecdotes, and reminiscences. By Joseph T. Buckingham. Boston, 1850. Second eidtion, 1852. (2 Vols.) Illus., portrait of I. Thomas; specimens, etc.

Historical, literary, and biographical of the earliest American printers.

Cloth; 8-1/8 x 5 in. See also S/4/4.

EARLY PRINTING IN AMERICA, U.S. [Lit. of]

Cabinet S Shelf 5 No. 12

(New England). Bay Psalm Book, The. By Edmund F. Carpenter, in The New England Magazine, Jan., 1897. Facsimile reproductions, reduced sizes of some pages of earliest editions.

Brief account of this Psalm Book's contents; its various editions, and final disposition.

Bound with "Pamphlets and excerpts relating to typographical matters," item 18.

Lit. of EARLY PRINTING IN AMERICA (Southern States)

Stack A Shelf 1&2 Number 53

BULLEN, Henry Lewis. Literature of Typography, The, in The Inland Printer, vol.LII, pp. 709, 873.

This section includes, Maryland, North and South Carolina, Virginia, and Kentucky.

EARLY PRINTING IN AMERICA Literature

Cabinet W Shelf 3 No. 115

Stationery trade, the. By John G. Bainbridge. Excerpt from "One hundred years of American commerce". New York, 1895. With portrait, J.G. Bainbridge.

Has brief outline of printing and bookselling in America.

Item 5 in vol. with binder's title "Pamphlets relating to books - II. Bound, 1932".

EARLY PRINTING IN AMERICA, U.S. [Lit. of]

Cabinet T Shelf 1 No. 26

(New England). Dunton, John, 1659-1733, life and letters of. Written by himself. Printed for S. Malthus, London, 1705.

Dunton was an excentric publisher author. His book gives some interesting accounts of his relations with British and New England printers.

Half morocco; 6¾ x 4-3/8 x 1½ in. See also T/1/27.

EARLY PRINTING IN AMERICA (Western States)

Stack A Shelf 1&2 Number 53

BULLEN, Henry Lewis. Literature of Typography, The, in The Inland Printer, vol. LIII, pp. 73, 236. 396.

This section includes, Ohio, Indiana, Missouri, Michigan, Illinois, and Wisconsin.

EARLY PRINTING IN AMERICA, U.S. Literature

Cabinet 26 Shelf 1 No. 20

Westward migration of the printing press in the United States, 1786-1836. By Douglas C. McMurtrie.

Illustrated article.

In the Gutenberg-Gesellschaft Jahrbuch, 1930, pp. 269-288

EARLY PRINTING IN AMERICA (U.S.) Literature

Cabinet R Shelf 5 No. 121

(New England). Early New England Catechisms, A bibliographical account of some Catechisms published before the year 1800, for use in New England. Paper read before The American Antiquarian Society at Worcester, Oct. 21, 1897, by Wilberforce Eames.

Half morocco; 9-3/8 x 6¼ in.

EARLY PRINTING IN AMERICA, U.S. (Lit. of)

Stack A Shelf 1&2 Number 53

(California) Bullen, Henry Lewis. Literature of typography, The. In The Inland Printer, vol. LIII, p. 396. Illus.

This section includes Iowa, New Mexico, Hawaii, Oregon.

EARLY PRINTING IN AMERICA, U.S. Literature.

Cabinet 75 Shelf 2 No. 3

Winship, George Parker. Literature of the history of printing in the United States. A survey.

In Transactions of the Bibliographical Society, "The Library," Vol. III, 1922-23, pp. 288-303.

EARLY PRINTING IN AMERICA, U.S. [Lit. of]

Cabinet S Shelf 5 No. 12

(New England). Eliot, John. The apostle of the Indians: by James De Normandie, in The New England Magazine, Nov., 1896. Facsimile reproductions, reduced sizes of pages of some books used for teaching the English language to the Indians.

Bound with "Pamphlets and excerpts relating to typography," item 19.

EARLY PRINTING IN AMERICA, U.S. [Lit. of]

Cabinet S Shelf 2 No. 73

(California). Cubery, William: Fifty years a printer. San Francisco [1857-1907]. n.d. Portrait.

Half morocco; 9-1/2 x 6-1/4 in.

EARLY PRINTING IN AMERICA, U.S. Lit. of

Cabinet S Shelf 5 No. 41

(California) History of California newspapers [By E.C. Kemble. See note "Explanatory" opposite title page]. Being a contemporary chronicle of early printing and publishing on the Pacific Coast. Reprinted for the first time from the Sacramento Daily Union of Dec. 25, 1858...Plendome Press, Imprinted at New York, N.Y. 1927.

Boards; 7½ x 5 x 1 in.

EARLY PRINTING IN AMERICA, U. S. [Lit. of]

Cabinet S Shelf 3 No. 104

(Connecticut: Hartford, 1764-1768). The work of Thomas Green, Hartford's first printer, By Albert Carlos Bates.
p. 345 in volume, Wilberforce Eames ... A tribute to. Cambridge, 1924.

EARLY PRINTING IN AMERICA, U.S. [Lit. of]

Cabinet S Shelf 3 No. 44

(Illinois, Chicago). Story of Chicago in connection with the printing business. Chicago: Regan Printing House, 1912. Illus.
Includes lists and short sketches of the old time job printers. Chicago's daily news papers, and periodicals.

Cloth; 8 x 5¼ in.

EARLY PRINTING IN AMERICA, U.S. [Lit. of]

Cabinet A Shelf 3 No. 52

(California). History of California newspapers: Included as a Christmas offering to the readers of the Sacramento Daily Union. Sacramento: Vol. XVI, No. 2417. Dec. 25, 1858.

Buckram; 24 x 18¾ x ½ in.

EARLY PRINTING IN AMERICA. [Literature of]

Cabinet 75 Shelf 2 No. 10

(Georgia, 1762). James Johnston, the first printer in Georgia. A paper by Douglas C. McMurtrie, for the Bibliographical Society, London, Jan. 1929.

In Trans. Biblio. Soc. "The Library," vol. 10, 1929-30. pp. 73-80.

EARLY PRINTING IN AMERICA. Lit. of

Cabinet NN Shelf 7 No. 14

Illinois, 1814 - 1868.

see BOSS, HENRY R. Illinois, early newspaper in...Chicago, 1870.

EARLY PRINTING IN AMERICA, (U.S.) [Lit. of]

Cabinet S Shelf 3 No. 77

(California) Spanish press in California, 1833-1844. By Robert E. Cowan. [Los Angeles, 1909]. Reprinted from the California Historic-Genealogical Society Publication III.
Copy signed by R.E.C.

Half morocco; 9-5/8 x 6-1/8 x ¼ in.

EARLY PRINTING IN AMERICA, U.S. [Lit. of]

Cabinet Y Shelf 2 No. 97

Idaho, the beginnings of printing in. By Douglas C. McMurtrie. With facs.

Article in Gutenberg-Gesellschaft Jahrbuch, 1932, p.234.

EARLY PRINTING IN AMERICA, U.S. [Lit. of]

Cabinet S Shelf 2 No. 104

(Iowa). Aldrich, Charles. In Memoriam. [Printer, editor]. Des Moines, 1909. Annals of Iowa. Vol. VIII No. 8. January, 1908. Third Series. Portrait.
Biographical, historical, by various members of the Historical Department of Iowa of which Aldrich was founder and curator.

Half morocco; 10 x 6½ in.

EARLY PRINTING IN AMERICA (U.S.) Literature

Cabinet QQ Shelf 3 No. 9

California. Three years in California. By Rev. Walter Colton. Illustrated. New York, 1850.

Account of first newspaper in California in English, issued by Colton, August 22, 1846, at Monterey. See p. 38 and after.

Cloth; 7¾ x 5¼ in.

EARLY PRINTING IN AMERICA (U.S.) Literature

Cabinet Shelf No.

(Illinois). Pioneer printing in Illinois. By Douglas C. McMurtrie.
Article in National Printer Journalist, Dec. 1931, Vol. 49, No. 12, pp. 20, 21, 78, 79.

EARLY PRINTING IN AMERICA Literatur

Stack Shelf Number

(Kansas) Story of Kansas journalism.
Radio talks by Prof. E.C. Rogers, Kansas State College, reported in The Publishers Auxiliary, 68th year, No.38, 1933, pp.1 and 6.

EARLY PRINTING IN AMERICA U.S. Literatur

Cabinet Shelf No.

California
see also
JOURNALISM, United States (California)...

EARLY PRINTING IN AMERICA (U.S.) Literature

Cabinet S Shelf 6 No. 8

(Illinois) An Irishman took the first printing press into the State of Illinois. By Mrs. Annie M. Stringfield. [Excerpt from the "Journal of American Irish Historical Society", vol. 22, N.Y. 1923] Pamphlet.

Item 3 in vol. with binder's title "Early printing and printers. Pamphlets".

EARLY PRINTING IN AMERICA (U.S.) Lit.

Cabinet Shelf No.

Kansas, pioneer printing in. By D.C. McMurtrie.

Illus. article in National Printer Journalist, vol. 51, No. 3, March 1933, pp.26-29

EARLY PRINTING IN AMERICA, U.S. [Lit. of]

Cabinet R Shelf 5 No. 73

(Connecticut, 1709-1800). List of books printed in Connecticut, By James Hammond Trumbull, Hartford, 1904.
Bibliography.

Half morocco; 11 x 8¾ in.

EARLY PRINTING IN AMERICA, U.S. [Lit. of]

Cabinet R Shelf 5 No. 108

(Illinois, Chicago). The first printers of Chicago; with a bibliography of the issues of the Chicago Press, 1836-1850. By Douglas C. McMurtrie, Chicago,,1927. Facsimiles.

Boards; 11¼ x 8 in.

EARLY PRINTING IN AMERICA, U.S. [Lit. of]

Cabinet S Shelf 5 No. 21

(Kentucky). The first newspaper west of the Alleghanies: The Kentucky Gazette, founded by John Bradford in 1787. By William H. Perrin, in Magazine of American History, 1887.

Bound with other items in volume "Excerpts relating to printing in America," pp. 89-95.

EARLY PRINTING IN AMERICA (U.S.) Literature

Cabinet Kentucky, the history of journalism in. By Victor B. Portmann.

Shelf

Article in The Publishers' Auxialiary, Oct.27, 1934, p.7

No.

EARLY PRINTING IN AMERICA (U.S.) Literature

Cabinet NN Maine, 1785 - 1872. History of the press of. Edited by Joseph Griffin. Second issue of the Press of Maine, 1872, with a supplement, 1874. Brunswick: From the press established A. D. 1819. Illus.

Shelf 6

No. 10

Cloth; 9-3/8 x 6 x 1-1/8 in.

EARLY PRINTING IN AMERICA(U.S.) Literature

Cabinet S (Massachusetts) William H. Whitmore and the early printed laws of Massachusetts. By Max Farrand.

Shelf 5

No. 54

See PUTNAM, HERBERT. Essays offered to... New Haven, 1929, P.146

EARLY PRINTING IN AMERICA, U.S. [Lit. of]

Cabinet R (Kentucky.) Pioneer Press of Kentucky, from the printing of the first paper West of the Alleghanies, Aug. 11, 1787, to the establishment of the daily press in 1830. By William Henry Perrin ... and read before the Filson Club, August, 1887. Louisville, Ky.

Shelf 5

No. 93

Cloth; $11\frac{1}{4}$ x 9 in.

EARLY PRINTING IN AMERICA. U.S. [Lit. of]

Cabinet 75 (Maryland). History of printing in Colonial Maryland, 1686-1716. By Lawrence C. Wroth: Brief reviews of this book and other books relating to the history of printing in America.

Shelf 2

No. 3

In transactions of the Bibliographical Society, "The Library," vol. III, pp. 224, 288, 298. 1922-23.

EARLY PRINTING IN AMERICA, U.S. Literature

Cabinet R **Massachusetts, 1638-1711. The early Massachusetts Press. By George E. Littlefield. Boston: The Club of Odd Volumes. 1907. Facsimiles.**

Shelf 4

No. 31

2 vols.

Half levant and boards; $9\frac{1}{2}$ x $6\frac{1}{2}$ in.

EARLY PRINTING IN AMERICA, U.S. Literature

Cabinet NN Kentucky , 1787, John Bradford

Shelf 2

No. 15

see NEWSPAPERS, United States. Literatur First newspaper west of the Allegenies...

EARLY PRINTING IN AMERICA (U.S.) Literature

Cabinet S (Maryland) The Maryland colonization tracts. By Lawrence C. Wroth.

Shelf 5

No. 54

See PUTNAM, HERBERT. Essays offered to... New Haven, 1929, p. 539

EARLY PRINTING IN AMERICA, U.S. [Lit. of]

Cabinet R (Massachusetts. 1681). An early Boston Imprint: "The Pilgrim's Progress" printed by Samuel Green, Boston, 1681. [With] Ten facsimile reproductions relating to various subjects. By Samuel A. Green, Boston, 1903.

Shelf 6

No. 6

Each reproduction is accompanied by several pages of text giving bio-bibliographical and historical facts relating to early Boston printers and printing.

Cloth; 15 x 10-3/4 in.

EARLY PRINTING IN AMERICA, U.S. [Lit. of]

Cabinet 79 (Louisiana, 1769-1810) Notas bibliographicas referentes a las primas producciones de la imprenta en algunas cindades de la America-Española. For José Toribio Medina, Santiago de Chile, 1904.

Shelf 1

No. 23

Cloth; $9\frac{3}{4}$ x $6\frac{1}{4}$ in. Chiappa 146

EARLY PRINTING IN AMERICA. U.S. [Lit. of]

Cabinet S (Maryland). A Maryland tract of 1646. By Lathrop C. Harper of New York City. An important historical document lacking names of author, publisher and printer.

Shelf 3

No. 104

p. 143 in volume, Wilberforce Eames ... A tribute to. Cambridge, 1924.

EARLY PRINTING IN AMERICA, U.S. Literatur

Cabinet NN **Massachusetts, 1689-1783. Historical digest of the provincial press...**

Shelf 2

No. 26

see WEEKS, HORACE L., and EDWIN M. BACON. Historical digest...

EARLY PRINTING IN AMERICA (U.S.) Lit. of

Stack 15 Louisiana, 1778. Black Code...a la Nlle. Orleans de l'Imprimerie d'Antoine Boudousquie, Imprmieur du Roi et du Cabildo. (Facs.)

Shelf 1

Number 17,05

Catalogue , item No.60, the library of Mr. Simon J. Schwartz. To be sold, Nov. 8, 9,10, 1926, at the Anderson Gelleries, New York

---

EARLY PRINTING IN AMERICA. U.S. [Lit. of]

Cabinet **(Maryland) Pioneer printing in Maryland. By Douglas C. McMurtrie.**

Shelf

No.

Article in NATIONAL PRINTER JOURNALIST, Vol. 50, No. 8, August, 1932, pp. 24, 25, 72, 73.

EARLY PRINTING IN AMERICA Literature

Cabinet NN **Massachusetts, 1704-1707.**

Shelf 2

No. 27 also NN-2-26

see WEEKS, HORACE L., and EDWIN M. BACON. Historical digest of the provincial press...

EARLY PRINTING IN AMERICA. U.S. [Lit. of]

Cabinet R (Louisiana: New Orleans). Early printing in New Orleans, 1764-1810: With a bibliography of the issues of the Louisiana Press. By Douglas C. McMurtrie, New Orleans, 1929. Facsimile, title pages, broadsides, etc.

Shelf 5

No. 105

Boards; $10\frac{1}{2}$ x $8\frac{1}{4}$ in.

EARLY PRINTING IN AMERICA. Literature

Cabinet X Massachusetts, the press in. 1639-1775.

Shelf 5

No. 105

See p.7 in Schuyler's Liberty of the press in the American Colonies...New York, 1905.

EARLY PRINTING IN AMERICA, U.S. [Lit. of]

Cabinet R (Massachusetts. 1726-1775). The Almanacks of Nathanial Ames, father and son of Dedham Mass., 1726-1775. With notes and comments by Sam Briggs. Cleveland, Ohio, 1891. Facsimiles.

Shelf 5

No. 119

Imprints on these almanacks form a comprehensive record of early printers and printing in Boston.

Cloth; 10 x 7 in.

EARLY PRINTING IN AMERICA. U.S. [Lit. of]

Cabinet R Shelf 5 No. 60

(Massachusetts, Boston). John Foster, the earliest American engraver, and the first Boston printer. By Samuel Abbott Green. Boston, 1909. Facsimiles, also bibliography of titles printed by Foster.
Bio-historical.

Cloth; $10\frac{1}{2}$ x $7\frac{3}{4}$ in.

EARLY PRINTING IN AMERICA. U.S. Literature

Cabinet Shelf No.

Minnesota, pioneer printing in (1849). Illus. By Douglas C. McMurtrie.

Article in National Printer-Journalist, vol. 50, No.2, Feb. 1932, pp.22, 23, 92.

EARLY PRINTING IN AMERICA Literature of

Cabinet NN Shelf 4 No. 33

New York, 18th century printing and printers.

See MARTIN, CHARLOTTE and BENJAMIN ELLIS. (The) New York press...

EARLY PRINTING IN AMERICA. U.S. [Lit. of]

Cabinet S Shelf 5 No. 21

(Massachusetts, Boston, 1778). Newspaper of the Revolution. The Independent Chronicle and the Universal Advertiser, printed by Powars and Willis. An account in Magazine of American History. By Horatio King. 1887.

Bound with other items in volume "Excerpts relating to printing in America." pp. 103-107.

EARLY PRINTING IN AMERICA (U.S.) Lit. of

Cabinet R Shelf 5 No. 150

(New Hampshire, Portsmouth). The celebration of the centennial anniversary of the introduction of the art of printing into New Hampshire, in the City of Portsmouth, October 6, 1856. A sketch of the proceedings, the oration, decorations, speeches etc. Portsmouth, Edward N. Fuller, Publisher, 1857.

Cloth; $8\frac{1}{2}$ x $5\frac{1}{2}$ in.

EARLY PRINTING IN AMERICA Literature

Cabinet X Shelf 5 No. 105

New York. the press in. 1686 to 1772.

See pp.34-67 in Schuyler's Liberty of the press in the American Colonies...New York, 1905.

EARLY PRINTING IN AMERICA. U.S. [Lit. of]

Cabinet S Shelf 5 No. 21

(Massachusetts, Essex, 1808). A literary curiosity: The Herald of Gospel Liberty.. By D. H. Lamson. In Magazine of American History. Facsimile.
An account of the earliest religious paper published in U.S.

Bound with other items in "Excerpts relating to printing in America." p. 109.

EARLY PRINTING IN AMERICA (U.S.) Lit. of

Cabinet NN Shelf 2 No. 2.02

New Hampshire, 1756 to 1840.

See NEWSPAPERS. UNITED STATES. Literature of. New Hampshire...

EARLY PRINTING IN AMERICA. U.S. [Lit. of]

Cabinet S Shelf 2 No. 23

(New York,Utica, Oneida County). An Oneida County Printer, William Williams, printer publisher, editor. With a bibliography of the press at Utica Oneida County, New York, from 1803 to 1838. By John C. Williams. New York, 1906. Portraits, facsimiles, head and tail pieces, alphabets.

Half vellum; $9\frac{1}{4}$ x $5\frac{3}{4}$ in.

EARLY PRINTING IN AMERICA. U.S. Literature of (Massachusetts)

Cabinet QQ Shelf 4 No. 21 (2 Vols)

Newburyport, 1764-1905. History of Newburyport, Mass., 1764-1905, with maps and illustrations. By John J. Currier. 2 Vols. Newburyport, Mass., 1906, 1909.
History of books, newspapers, printers, in Vol, I, p. 471.

Cloth; $9\frac{1}{4}$ x$6\frac{1}{4}$ in.

EARLY PRINTING IN AMERICA, U.S. [Lit. of]

Cabinet A Shelf 1&2 No. 70

(New Jersey). Bullen, Henry Lewis. Literature of typography, The. In The Inland Printers, vol. LII, p. 709, vol. LXX, p. 833.

EARLY PRINTING IN AMERICA. U.S. [Lit. of]

Cabinet R Shelf 3 No. 188

(New York State) Washington, Saratoga and Warren Counties State of New York, A brief history of the printing press in. Together with a check list of their publications prior to 1825...By William H. Hill. Privately Printed: Fort Edward, New York. Printed by the Tory Press, Rutland, Vermont.
No. 27 of an edition of 54 copies.

Cloth; $9\frac{1}{4}$ x 6-3/8 x 3/4 in.

EARLY PRINTING IN AMERICA. U.S.[Lit. of]

Cabinet R Shelf 5 No. 65

(Massachusetts). Salem Imprint, 1768-1825: A history of the first fifty years of printing in Salem, Massachusetts ... By Harriet Silvester Tapeley. Salem, Mass., 1927. Illus., Facsimiles, portraits, etc.

Cloth; $9\frac{1}{2}$ x $6\frac{1}{2}$ in.

EARLY PRINTING IN AMERICA. U.S. [Lit. of]

Cabinet R Shelf 4 No. 111

(New Jersey, Burlington, 1770, Isaac Collins). Reminiscences of Isaac and Rachel (Budd) Collins...together with a genealogy of the Collins family...Philadelphia, 1893. Illus.

Half morocco; $10\frac{1}{4}$ x 6-5/8 in.

EARLY PRINTING IN AMERICA. U.S. [Lit. of]

Cabinet R Shelf 4 No. 96

New York. (Buffalo, 1812-1850). Pamphlets and books printed in Buffalo prior to 1850, being an appendix to Vol. VI, Buffalo Historical Society Publication. Buffalo, 1903. Facsimiles.

Cloth; $9\frac{1}{2}$ x $6\frac{1}{2}$ in.

EARLY PRINTING IN AMERICA (U.S.) Literature

Cabinet Shelf No.

(Michigan) Pioneer printing in Michigan. Illus. By Douglas C. McMurtrie.

Article in National Printer Journalist, vol. 50, No.10, Oct., 1932, pp.20, 21, 92, 93.

EARLY PRINTING IN AMERICA. U.S. [Lit. of]

Cabinet R Shelf 4 No. 115

New Jersey. (Newark, 1776-1900). Books, pamphlets and newspapers printed at Newark, New Jersey, 1776-1900. A list compiled by Frank Pierce Hill...and V.L. Collins. Privately printed, 1902.

Cloth; 9 x $6\frac{1}{4}$ in.

EALRY PRINTING IN AMERICA (U.S.A.) Lit. of

Cabinet Shelf No.

North Carolina, pioneer printing in. By Douglas C. McMurtrie. With reproductions.

Article in National Printer Journalist, Vol. 50, No. 11, Dec. 1932. pp. 26, 27, 84,85.

EARLY PRINTING IN AMERICA. Literature

Cabinet R Shelf 4 No. 155

North Carolina, pre-Revolutionary printers of: Davis, Steuart, Boyd. By Stephen B. Weeks. (Lacks title page, n.d. (1915).

See also R/4/154.

Half morocco; 9-1/8 x 6 x 3/8 in.

EARLY PRINTING IN AMERICA U.S. Litera.

Cabinet Shelf No.

Oregon, the Lapwai Mission Press, first press in the Pacific Northwesr, 1839. By Prof. Elmer F. Beth, University of Idaho, Moscow.

Illus. article in National Printer Journalist, vol.51, NO.4, April, 1933, pp. 28-32.

EARLY PRINTING IN AMERICA (U.S.) Literature

Cabinet R Shelf 5 No. 13

(Pennsylvania). Notes on the provincial literature of Pennsylvania. By T. I. Wharton. Phila., 1864.

From Memoirs of the Historical Society of Pennsylvania, Vol. 1, Phila., 1826; reprinted, 1864.

Cloth; 9-3/4 x 6¼ in.

EARLY PRINTING IN AMERIC (U.S.) Literature

Cabinet Shelf No.

(North Dakota) The first printing in North Dakota. By Douglas C. McMurtrie.

Illus. article in the National Printer Journalist, vol.51, No.9, Sept.1933, pp. 18, 20

EARLY PRINTING IN AMERICA. U.S. [Lit. of]

Stack A Shelf 1&2 Number 53

(Oregon). Bullen, Henry Lewis. Literature of Typography, The. In The Inland Printer, vol. LIII, p. 396.

EARLY PRINTING IN AMERICA, U.S. Literature of

Cabinet R Shelf 2 No. 100

(Pennsylvania, 1759-1766.) A work-book of the printing house of Benjamin Franklin & David Hall. Described by George Simpson Eddy. New York Public Library, 1930. Brochure, Illus.

Item in manila envelope.

EARLY PRINTING IN AMERICA (U.S.) Literature

Cabinet NN Shelf 6 No. 34

Ohio, early newspapers of. (By C. B. Galbreath). Adopted from paper read at meeting of National Association of State Librarians, Waukesha, Wis., July 5, 1901.

Together with "Newspapers and Periodicals in Ohio State Library"...Compiled by C. B. Galbreath. Has facsimile of first newspaper northwest of the Ohio River, the "Centinel of the North-Western Territory, Nov. 9, 1793, publisher, William Maxwell.

Half morocco; 9⅝ x 6½ x 5/8 in.

EARLY PRINTING IN AMERICA. U.S. [Lit. of]

Cabinet S Shelf 4 No. 120

(Pennsylvania). Early German-American Bibles, by Daniel Miller, in The Pennsylvania-German, May, 1910.

In bound collection "About the Bible," item 8.

EARLY PRINTING IN AMERICA. U.S. [Lit. of]

Cabinet R Shelf 5 No. 29

(Pennsylvania. Germantown) Sower, Christopher I and II: Presentation of Tablet in memory of Christopher Sower, father and son, to the Church of the Brethren in Germantown [Pa.], January 1, 1899. By Charles G. Sower.

Biographical eulogistic memoire: Includes "Life and work of Bishop Christopher Sower." by M.G. Brumbaugh.

Half morocco: 8 x 5½ in.

EARLY PRINTING IN AMERICA U.S. Literature

Cabinet R Shelf 4 No. 158

(Ohio, Dayton). Early printing in Dayton, Ohio. By Douglas C. McMurtrie. Dayton, Ohio. Printing House Craftsmen's Club of Dayton and Vicinity. 1935

Brochure, in envelope.

EARLY PRINTING IN AMERICA, U.S. [Lit. of]

Cabinet R Shelf 5 No. 25

Pennsylvania (Ephrata Press). Chronicon Ephratense: a history of the community of Seventh Day Baptists at Ephrata, Lancaster County, Penna., by "Lamech and Agrippa." Translated from the original German by J. Max Hark. Lancaster, Pa., 1889.

Cloth; 9½ x 6½ in.

EARLY PRINTING IN AMERICA (U.S.) Literature

Cabinet FF Shelf 3 No. 49

(Pennsylvania) Germantown, 1743, Christopher Sauer.

See facsimile of title page, Bible, in MORI'S Die anfange des schriftgiesergewerbes in Frankfurt am Main...1928.

EARLY PRINTING IN AMERICA (U.S.) Literature

Cabinet JJ Shelf 5 No. 14

Ohio, 1811-1898. Columbus (Ohio) newspapers- past and present.

Article in Fiftieth Anniversary banquet celebration of Columbus Typographical Union No. 5 October 31, 1909.

Cloth; 12¼ x 9 3/8 in.

EARLY PRINTING IN AMERICA. U.S. [Lit. of]

Cabinet S Shelf 5 No. 21

(Pennsylvania). History of a newspaper: The Pennsylvania Gazette. By Paul L. Ford, in the Magazine of American History, April 1887.

Bound with other items in "Excerpts relating to printing in America. pp. 84-88.

EARLY PRINTING IN AMERICA, U.S. [Lit. of]

Cabinet R Shelf 5 No. 15

Pennsylvania. (Harrisburg). The first newspaper published in Harrisburg, Pennsylvania, n. n.

An editorial dispute anent the date of first newspaper in Harrisburg.

In volume "Early printing and printers in America. Excerpts from Pennsylvania Magazines". p.233.

Half morocco; 9-7/8 x 6-5/8 in.

EARLY PRINTING IN AMERICA. Literature of

Cabinet Shelf No.

Oklahoma, pioneer printing in. By Douglas C. McMurtrie.

Illus. article in National Printer Journalist, vol. 50, No.5, May 1932, pp.26-7, 100.

EARLY PRINTING IN AMERICA. U.S. [Lit. of]

Cabinet S Shelf 2 No. 99

(Pennsylvania). Mathew Carey, editor, author and publisher: A study in American literary development. By Earl L. Bradsher. New York, 1912.

Cloth; 9¼ x 6¼ in.

EARLY PRINTING IN AMERICA (U.S.) Literature

Cabinet R Shelf 5 No. 33

Pennsylvania. Lancaster County, early German printers in, and the issues of their press. Papers read before the Lancaster County Historical Society, Jan. 1, 1904. Vol. VIII, No.3.

Bio-bibliographical account.

Bound in with other tracts.

Item in book with binder's title "EARLY PRINTING IN LANCASTER COUNTY, PA."

EARLY PRINTING IN AMERICA (U.S.) [Lit. of]

Cabinet R Shelf 5 No. 33

Pennsylvania. Lancaster County. Newspapers of. (1752-1902) By F.R. Diffenderfer. Papers read before the Lancaster County Historical Society, May 2, 1902. Vol. VI, No. 8.

Has facsimile of The Lancaster Gazette, first paper in Lancaster Co.

Bound in with other tracts on early printing in Lancaster.

Half morocco; 9¾ x 6¼ in.

EARLY PRINTING IN AMERICA, U.S. [Lit. of]

Cabinet S Shelf 2 No. 13

(Pennsylvania: Pittsburgh, 1797-1900). A printer's reminiscences, 1842-1902. By John Francis Marthens: Read at a banquet given by Pittsburgh Typothetae, Jan. 17, 1902. Portrait of Marthens. At end names of Pittsburgh printers, 1797 to 1900.

Half morocco; 9½ x 6 in.

EARLY PRINTING IN AMERICA. Literature

Cabinet NN Shelf 6 No. 39

Texas, growth and development of printing in.

see

BAILLIO, F. B. History of the Texas Press Association, 1880 to 1915...p. 47-53.

EARLY PRINTING IN AMERICA, U.S. [Lit. of]

Cabinet S Shelf 5 No. 25.01

(Pennsylvania. Philadelphia, 1685). The first book printed in Philadelphia [by William Bradford]. Account by John William Wallace. Excerpted from the Historical Magazine, Aug. 1864.

In box labelled "Colonial printing and printers. Miscellaneous items".

EARLY PRINTING IN AMERICA Literature

Cabinet X Shelf 5 No. 105

Pennsylvania, the press in. 1685 to 1776.

See pp.23-33 in Schuyler's Liberty of the press in the American Colonies...New York, 1905.

EARLY PRINTING IN AMERICA U.S. Literature

Cabinet Shelf No.

Utah, pioneer printing in. Illus. By Douglas C. McMurtrie.

Article in the National Printer Journalist, vol. 51, No. 6, June, 1933, pp.18-20

EARLY PRINTING IN AMERICA (U.S.) Lit. of

Cabinet Y Shelf 3 No. 25

(Pennsylvania) Philadelphia, 1706-1777

See FABRICIUS, J.F. Notizen uber die einfuhrung...der buchdruckerkunst in America. Hamburg, 1841, pp.17-83

EARLY PRINTING IN AMERICA, U. S. [Lit. of]

Cabinet S Shelf 5 No. 4

(Rhode Island: Providence, 1781). Calendrier Francais pour l'annee 1781, and the printing press of the French fleet in American waters ... By H. M. Chapin. Reprinted from the Providence Magazine, 1914.

Item 6 in collection "Various printers and their plants; excerpts from magazines,"I.

EARLY PRINTING IN AMERICA (U.S.) Literature

Cabinet R Shelf 4 No. 170

(Utah) The story of printing and publishing in Utah. By John Elbridge Jones, Salt Lake City, 1933.

Reprint from "Utah resources and activities".

Metaloid cover. Brochure in envelope

EARLY PRINTING IN AMERICA Literature

Cabinet S Shelf 5 No. 25-03

(Pennsylvania) Philadelphia, 1754, the price of printing in. By Douglas C. McMurtrie. Chicago, privately printed. 1928. Pamphlet.

In folder labelled McMurtrie. Pamphlets relating to the history of printing.

EARLY PRINTING IN AMERICA, U.S. Literature

Cabinet Shelf No.

(Rhode Island) Pioneer printing in Rhode Island. By D.C. McMurtrie.

Article in NATIONAL PRINTER JOURNALIST. vol. 50, No.9, Sept. 1932, pp.18, 19, 72, 73.

EARLY PRINTING IN AMERICA, U.S. [Lit. of]

Cabinet S Shelf 3 No. 104

(Vermont 1779-1791). Note on the laws of the Republic of Vermont. By James Benjamin Wilbur of Manchester, Vermont.

Biblio-historical.

p. 277 in volume, Wilberforce Eames ... A tribute to. Cambridge, 1924.

EARLY PRINTING IN AMERICA, U.S. [Lit. of]

Cabinet S Shelf 3 No. 104

(Pennsylvania: Philadelphia). Chez Moreau de Saint-Méry, Philadelphie (1795-97). By Henry W. Kent of the Grolier Club, New York. With a list of Imprints enlarged by George Parker Winship.

p. 67 in volume Wilberforce Eames ... A tribute to. Cambridge, 1924.

EARLY PRINTING IN AMERICA Literature

Cabinet NN Shelf 6 No. 38

South Carolina, Charleston, the newspaper press of. A chronological biographical history embracing a period of 140 years. By William L. King. Charleston, S. C. 1882.

Cloth; 7-5/8 x 4¾ x 5/8 in.

EARLY PRINTING IN AMERICA. U.S. Literature

Cabinet R Shelf 4 No. 131

Vermont, 1814-1879. Simeon Ide.

See Flanders, Louis W. Ide, Simeon, yeoman, freeman, pioneer printer...Rutland, Vermont, 1931.

EARLY PRINTING IN AMERICA. U.S. [Lit. of]

Cabinet X Shelf 4 No. 100

(Pennsylvania: Philadelphia, 1798) Truth will out! The foul charges of the Tories against the editor of the Aurora: Repelled by positive proof and plain truth, and his base calumniators put to shame.

Attributed to B.F. Bache, the grandson of B. Franklin.

Half morocco; 8¼ x 5 x ¼ in.

EARLY PRINTING IN AMERICA. U.S. Literature

Cabinet Shelf No.

Tennessee, pioneer printers in. By Douglas C. McMurtrie. Illus.

Article in Printer Journalist, vol. 49, No.11, Nov. 1931, pp. 20, 21.

EARLY PRINTING IN AMERICA, U.S. [Lit. of]

Cabinet R Shelf 5 No. 82

(Vermont). Dresden Press, The. By Harold Goddard Rugg. Dartmouth, 1918. Facsimiles, and list of Dresden Imprints.

"This is an abstract of a paper read before the Ticknor Club of Dartmouth College, May 1, 1918." Bibliographical, biographical, historical.

Half morocco; 9¾ x 7 in.

EARLY PRINTING IN AMERICA, U.S. [Lit. of]

Cabinet S Shelf 5 No. 62

(Vermont). Invitations, some early Vermont, from the collection of Bella C. Landauer, New York, 1930.

Boards; $9\frac{3}{4}$ x $6\frac{1}{4}$ in.

EARLY PRINTING IN MASSACHUSETTS. Literature

Cabinet Q Shelf 1 No. 6

Boston, 1642-1711, early Boston booksellers. By George Emery Littlefield. Boston: The Club of Odd Volumes, 1910. Illus.
No. 10 of edition of 150 copies.
Printed at the University Press, Cambridge, Mass.

Boards, leather back; $9\frac{3}{4}$ x $6\frac{1}{2}$ in.

EARLY PRINTING IN AMERICA, U.S. [Lit. of]

Cabinet S Shelf 5 No. 12

(Cambridge, 1669). The first Indian Primer and Bible. John Eliot the Apostle of the Indian. By James De Normandie, in the New England Magazine, Nov. 1896. Facsimiles.

Bound in collection "Pamphlets and excerpts realting to typographical matters", item 19.

EARLY PRINTING IN AMERICA, U.S. Literature

Cabinet R Shelf 6 No. 109

Wisconsin, early printing in. With a bibliography of the issues of the press, 1833-1850. By Douglas C. McMurtrie. Printed and published by Frank McCaffrey at Seattle, Washington, 1931. Illus. facs.

Cloth; 12 x $8\frac{1}{2}$ in.

EARLY PRINTING IN MASSACHUSETTS. Literature

Cabinet Q Shelf 1 No. 5

Boston, 1679-1700.

see FORD, WORTHINGTON CHAUNCEY. (The) Boston book market...

EARLY PRINTING IN AMERICA(U.S.)Literature of

Cabinet QQ Shelf 4 No. 26

Cambridge, 1669.

see TOOKER, WILLIAM WALLACE. Eliot's John, first Indian teacher...

EARLY PRINTING IN AMERICA (U.S.) Literature

Cabinet JJ Shelf 5 No. 2

Albany, 1771 - - Historical souvenir and first year-book of Albany Typographical Union No.4. Half-century number. January, 1905. Illus., portraits, facs.

Cloth; $11\frac{1}{4}$ x $7\frac{1}{2}$ in.

EARLY PRINTING IN AMERICA, U.S. (Lit. of)

Cabinet X Shelf 4 No. 72

Boston 1754. A total eclipse of liberty: Being a true and faithful account of the arraignment and examination of Daniel Fowle...Octob. 24th 1754, barely on suspicion of his being concern'd in printing and publishing a pamphlet intitled "Monster of Monsters"...Written by himself. Boston 1755.

Cloth case; $7\frac{1}{4}$ x 5 in.

EARLY PRINTING IN AMERICA (U.S.) Literature

Cabinet S Shelf 6 No. 9

Cambridge, 1673, Samuel Green. The Connecticut law book of 1673. By Albert C. Bates. With facsimile. Excerpt from the "Literary Collector", Feb., 1903.

Item 16 in vol. with binder's title "Early printing and printed books. Pamphlets". Bound, 1932.

EARLY PRINTING IN AMERICA, U.S. [Lit. of]

Cabinet R Shelf 3 No. 107

(Boston). John Dunton's letters from New England Publications of the Prince Society. Boston, 1867.
Historical, bibliographical, and biographical of printing and publishing in Boston.

Half morocco; $8\frac{1}{2}$ x $7\frac{1}{4}$ in.

EARLY PRINTING IN AMERICA, U.S. Lit. of.

Cabinet S Shelf 6 No. 4

Boston, 1822-1829...Written contracts for executing the State Printing for the last ten years Taken from the Records of the Committee on Accounts...(Brochure).
Agreements included here are signed by the printers, Russell & Gardner; True & Greene; Dutton & Wentworth.

Item in box labelled "Brochures and excerpts relating to Government Printing and Printers, in U.S. A.

EARLY PRINTING IN AMERICA, U.S. Literature.

Cabinet S Shelf 6 No. 9 No. 16

Cambridge, Mass., 1673. Samuel Green. The Connecticut law book of 1673. By Albert C. Bates. (Excerpt). The Literary Collector, Feb. 1903.

EARLY PRINTING IN AMERICA Literature

Cabinet NN Shelf 2 No. 28

Boston newspapers, 1704-1780, a check list of. By Mary Farwell Ayer. With bibliographical notes by Albert Matthews. Publications of the Colonial Society of Massachusetts, vol. IX. Boston, 1907.

Cloth; 9-5/8 x $6\frac{3}{4}$ in.

EARLY PRINTING IN AMERICA, U.S. [Lit. of]

Cabinet R Shelf 3 No. 129

(Cambridge, 1639-1921). Stephen Daye and his successors: The establishment of a Printing Plant in...British North America and the development of the Art of Printing at The University Press of Cambridge, Mass. 1921. Illus.

Boards; 8 x $5\frac{1}{4}$ in.

EARLY PRINTING IN AMERICA, U.S. Lit. of

Cabinet S Shelf 5 No. 25.01

New York City. Bi-centennial celebration of the two hundredth anniversary of the introduction of printing in New York by William Bradford. Commemoration by the New York Historical Society on April 8, 1893.

Pamphlet in box labelled "Colonial printing and printers. Miscellaneous items".

EARLY PRINTING IN AMERICA, U.S. [Lit. of]

Cabinet R Shelf 3 No. 117

(Boston, 1638). Early printing in Boston and the manuscript sources of Massachusetts history. By Worthington Ford. Facsimiles.
Essay in Handbook for the twenty-fourth annual conference of the American Library Association. Boston, 1902. p.72.

Cloth; $7\frac{1}{2}$ x $5\frac{1}{2}$ in.

EARLY PRINTING IN AMERICA, U.S. [Lit. of]

Cabinet R Shelf 5 No. 132

(Cambridge, 1640, Stephen Daye). The Bay Psalm Book. Being a facsimile reprint of the first edition, printed by Stephen Daye at Cambridge, in New England in 1640.
A facsimile reprint with preface by Wilberforce Eames. New York, 1903.

Boards; 8 x $5\frac{1}{2}$ in.

EARLY PRINTING IN AMERICA, U.S. [Lit. of]

Cabinet R Shelf 3 No. 181

(New York City). Bradford, William, 1696. Reprint of the first book printed in New York. "A Letter of Advise to a young gentleman"... with introduction and notes by Frank C. Erb, New York, 1907. With facsimiles.

Cloth; 6 x $4\frac{3}{4}$ in.

EARLY PRINTING IN AMERICA, U.S. [Lit. of]

Cabinet S Shelf 5 No. 4

(New York). Reminiscences of printers, authors, and booksellers in New York. By John W. Francis, M.D. New York, Jan. 16, 1852. Reprinted in the International Magazine, Feb. 1852.

Item 11½ in collection "Various printers and their plants; Excerpts from magazines, I."

EARLY PRINTING IN AMERICA (U.S.) Literature

Cabinet S Shelf 6 No. 8

(New York City, 1786) Shepard Kollock, printer of New York's first directory. Bibliographical account by C.C. Herbermann. Excerpt from the "U.S. Cath. Hist. Soc. Hist. Records & Studies, vol. 5, No.I, Nov., 1907. Pamphlet

Item 4 in vol. with binder's title "Early printing and printers. Pamphlets".

EASTERN ARGUS, Portland, Maine.

Cabinet Shelf No.

See cards with following sub-heads.

I - NEWSPAPERS, Anniversary Issues.
II - " , Maine.

EARLY PRINTING IN AMERICA (U.S.) Lit. of.

Cabinet JJ Shelf 4 No. 13

New York City, 1693-1926.

See MORGAN, CHARLOTTE E. Origin and history of the New York Employing Printers' Association...

EARLY PRINTING IN AMERICA, U.S. [Lit. of]

Cabinet R Shelf 5 No. 148

(New York City, 1792). A Book of the past: First American edition of Josephus' History of the Jews. With many copper engravings. An account of the above book, by W. L. Andrews; excerpt from The Bookman, Feb. 1900.

Excerpt 11 in volume "Chap Books, Almanacs, Annuals, etc.

EASTERN BRASS TYPE FOUNDRY

Cabinet II Shelf 2 No.

Specimen books of type.

See SPECIMEN BOOKS, BRASS TYPE. United States.

EARLY PRINTING IN AMERICA. U.S. Lit. of

Cabinet S Shelf 5 No. 25.01

New York, 1693. Historical notes on the introduction of printing into New York. By George H. Moore, LL.D. Superintendent of the Lenox Library. New York. Printed for the author. 1888.

Pamphlet in box labelled "Colonial printing and printers. Miscellaneous items ".

EARLY PRINTING IN AMERICA. Literature

Cabinet NN Shelf 7 No. 9

New York City, 1826 - Methodist Book Concern...The first printers story - mechanical progress.- The first "Head Printers"- etc. Illus., facs., portraits.

see pp. 20 - 28, CHRISTIAN ADVOCATE, THE. Centennial number, 1826 - 1926.

Cloth; 13 x 9 x ½ in.

EASTERN MANUFACTURING COMPANY (Paper Mills)

Cabinet RR Shelf 3 No. 17

Modern manufacture of writing paper. A story concerning the modern processes of manufacturing an ancient product, with some side lights on its history. Compliments of the Eastern Manufacturing Company, New York. Mills at Bangor and Lincoln, Maine. n. d. Illus.

Half cloth; 10-7/8 x 8⅜ in.

EARLY PRINTING IN AMERICA, U.S. Literature.

Cabinet S Shelf 6 No. 3

(New York City, 1696, William Bradford). New York in 1696; A note to accompany the proclamation of Sept. 12, 1696. (Excerpt from) The Literary Collector, Sept. 1903. With reproduction of the proclamation with Bradford imprint.

Item in box labelled "Excerpts and brochures relating to printing and printers in America

---

EARLY PRINTING IN AMERICA (U.S.) Literature

Cabinet S Shelf 6 No. 9

Philadelphia, 1794. A curious antique treasure of 1794. Prospectus of the first American edition of Shakespeare. Excerpt from Mag. of Am. History, Aug., 1890.

Item 22 in vol. with binder's title "Early printing and printed books. Pamphlets". Bound, 1932.

EASY NAT: or Boston Bars and Boston Boys.

Cabinet Q Shelf 5 No. 45

(A) Tale of home trials. By one who knows them. Boston. Redding and Company, Boston, 1844.

Brochure. Item in envelope.

EARLY PRINTING IN AMERICA (U.S.) Literature

Cabinet S Shelf 6 No. 9

New York, 1730, Goelet, Jacob.

See BIBLIOGRAPHY. Dutch text book of 1730...

EARLY PRINTING IN AMERICA (U.S.) Lit. of

Cabinet 81 Shelf 2 No. 30

Philadelphia, early printing and publishing in. Festival (banquet) in honor of A. Hart (Cary & Hart) on his retirement from business. Full report. Addresses of great historical value, by Hart, Carey, McMitchel etc. n.d. circa 1840. Full newspaper report.

Item in MUNSELL, JOEL. Printers' Scraps... vol.I, pp.106-119.

EATON, RACHEL CAROLINE

Cabinet II Shelf 3 No. 37

Ross, John and the Cherokee Nation. By Rachel Caroline Eaton. Menasha, Wisconsin, 1914.

Cloth; 9¼ x 6 x 7/8 in.

EARLY PRINTING IN AMERICA (U.S.) Literature

Cabinet S Shelf 6 No. 8

(New York City, 1786) Shepard Kollock, printer of the first New York directory. By William Hall. Excerpt from Mag. of Am. History, Oct., 1886.

Item 13 in vol. with binder's title "Early printing and printers. Pamphlets".

EARLY PRINTING IN AMERICA, U.S. Literatur

Cabinet NN Shelf 2 No. 24

Salem (Massachusetts), 1768 to 1856).

see STREETER, GILBERT L. Account of the newspapers...Salem, 1856.

EATON, WALTER PRICHARD

Cabinet S Shelf 6 No. 8

Three great American printers [Bruce Rogers, Frederic W. Goudy, D.B. Updike]. Excerpt from the "Bookman", Aug. 1924.

Item 11 in vol. with binder's title "Early printing and printers. Pamphlets".

EBERT, F. A.

Cabinet Y Shelf 3 No. 7

(Printing, Historical) Buchdruckerkunst, ihre geschichte. von Poppe-Ebert-Dahl. [Excerpts from the] "Allgemeine Encyclopädie der Wissenschaften und Kunst", vol. 14. Leipzig, 1825.

Morocco; 11 x 9 in.

"ECCLESIASTES".

Cabinet Shelf No.

See Imprints. United States. Nash, John Henry. San Francisco, 1920.

ECKENSTEIN, O. (Co-author with L.A. Legros)

Cabinet LL Shelf 3 No. 35

See Legros, L.A. and O. Eckenstein.

"ECLECTIC MAGAZINE"

Cabinet NN Shelf 2 No. 1

See PERIODICALS. UNITED STATES. Eclectic Magazine.

L'ECOLE ESTIENNE

Cabinet C Shelf 1 No. 25

Work of the students of l'Ecole Estienne, Paris, circa 1924.

Scrap book collection of specimens of printing.

Cloth; 16½ x 14 in.

L'ECOLE ESTIENNE

Cabinet Shelf No.

See also SCHOOLS OF PRINTING, France L'École Estienne...

ECONOMICS OF THE PRINTING SHOP

Cabinet Shelf No.

See Prices of Printing.
" also, Printing Accountancy.
" " Wages, Printers.

ECUADOR

Cabinet 79 Shelf 2 No. 27

Printers of Quito, 1819-1934, brief biographies of.

see

SANCHEZ, CARLOS ENRIQUE. (La) Imprenta en el Ecuador...Quito, 1935, p. 137 and fol.

ECUADOR

Cabinet 79 Shelf 1 No. 29

Quito, 1760-1818, la imprenta en. Notas bibliográficas. Por José Toribio Medina, Santiago de Chile, 1904.

Cloth; 9½ x 6¼ in. Chiappa 152

ECUADOR see also

Cabinet Shelf No.

Early Printing in Spanish-America (Lit. of) PRINTING, HISTORICAL (Sp. America) Ecuador.

EDDY, GEROGE SIMPSON

Cabinet R Shelf 1 No. 20

Franklin, Benjamin, account books kept by. Ledger 1728-1739: Journal 1730-1737. Notes by G. S. Eddy. New York, 1928.

Boards; 10-3/8 x 7-1/8 in.

EDDY, GEORGE SIMPSON

Cabinet R Shelf 1 No. 21

Franklin, Benjamin, account books kept by. Ledger "D" 1739-1747. Vol. 2. Notes by G. S. Eddy. New York, 1929.

Boards; 10-3/8 x 7-1/8 in.

EDDY, GEORGE SIMPSON

Cabinet R Shelf 2 No. 100

(A) Work-book of the printing house of Benjamin Franklin & David Hall. 1759-1766. Described by G.S. Eddy. New York Public Library, 1931. Brochure, Illus.

Item in manila envelope.

EDDY, ISAAC

Cabinet S Shelf 3 No. 104

Isaac Eddy, printer-engraver. By Harold Goddard Rugg, Assistant Librarian, Dartmouth College Library.
Bibliographical account of early printing in Vermont.
p. 313 in volume, Wilberforce Eames ... A tribute to. Cambridge, 1924.

EDES, BENJAMIN

Cabinet Shelf No.

See Early printing in New England. Boston [v.d.]. Benjamin Edes.
" also Early Printing in New England, Watertown, 1775.

EDES, BENJAMIN

Cabinet F Shelf 2 No. 95

Baltimore, 1819, B. Edes (Imprint)

See EARLY PRINTING IN MARYLAND. Baltimore, 1819,...

EDES, BENJAMIN C.

Cabinet R Shelf 4 No. 34

Letter from Peter Edes, Printer, to his grandson Benjmain C. Edes, Feb. 16, 1836: With biography and notes by Harry H. Edes.
Excerpt from Proceedings of the Massachusetts Historical Society, 1871-1872.

Cloth; 9¾ x 6¼ in.

EDES, BENJAMIN AND SON.

Cabinet Shelf No.

See Early printing in New England. Boston, 1786: Benjamin Edes and Son.

EDES, PETER

Cabinet R Shelf 4 No. 45

Diary of Peter Edes, the oldest printer in the United States, written during his confinement in Boston, by the British, 107 days, in the year 1775, immediately after the Battle of Bunker Hill. Written by himself. Bangor [Maine]. Samuel Smith, printer, 1837

Half morocco; 8 x 5½ in.

EDINBURGH

Cabinet OO Shelf 4 No. 42 (2 vols.)

Periodical press of Edinburgh (1642-1800) Bibliographical account...By W. J. Couper. Stirling, 1908. (2 vols.) Illus.

Cloth; 9¼ x 6 x 1½ in.

EDINBURGH GAZETTE

Cabinet U Shelf 5 No. 52

First Scottish Newspaper, the Edinburgh Gazette, 1699.

See p.141 in Bibliographical Notes: The Gentleman's Magazine.

EDES, PETER

Cabinet R Shelf 4 No. 34

Letter from Peter Edes, printer, to his grandson Benjamin C. Edes, Feb. 16, 1836: With biography and notes by Harry H. Edes.

Excerpt from Proceedings of the Massachusetts Historical Society, 1871-1872.

Cloth; 9¾ x 6¼ in.

EDINBURGH

Cabinet KK Shelf 2 No. 30

Scales of prices agreed to by the employers and journeymen printers of Edinburgh. Adopted Jan. 1867, and amended Jan., 1872, Nov., 1872, and Dec., 1877. Edinburgh, 1878. Edinburgh, 22nd July 1881.

Morocco; 6-7/8 x 4-7/8 x ¼ in.

EDINBURGH TYPOGRAPHICAL SOCIETY see

Cabinet KK Shelf 2 No. 29

SOCIETIES, PRINTERS'. Great Britain. Edinburgh Typographical Society...

EDES, PETER.

Cabinet A Shelf 3 No. 7

See Newspapers, Maine: Herald of Liberty, Augusta, published by him.

EDINBURGH

Cabinet Shelf No.

See also Printing, Historical, Scotland (Edinburgh)

EDISON, THOMAS ALVA

Biographical article: "Edison as a printer". With facsimile of Edison's "Grand Trunk Herald", the first and only newspaper ever published on a train.

Article in THE AMERICAN ART PRINTER, Vol. IV, No. 3, Oct., 1890.

EDES, PETER

Cabinet R Shelf 4 No. 50

Pioneer printer in Maine, his diary while a prisoner by the British at Boston in 1775 ... Edited by Samuel Lane Boardman, Bangor: printed for the De Burians, 1901. Facsimiles

Half cloth; 8½ x 6½ in.

EDINBURGH BIBLIOGRAPHICAL SOCIETY

Cabinet U Shelf 4 No. 27

Abstract and proceedings, and list of members. Sessions 1906-1907, 1907-1908.

Includes articles as follows: Cataloguing 15th century books; Sweynheym and Pannartz, the first Roman printers. By J.P. Edmond; Sweynheym and Pannartz: notes and collation. By E. Gordon Duff.

Half morocco; 9-5/8 x 8 in.

EDISON, THOMAS ALVA

Cabinet QQ Shelf 4 No. 17

Dinner in honor of Thomas Alva Edison upon the occasion of the 50th anniversary of his invention of the elctric light, and of the dedication of the Edison Institute of Technology. Independence Hall, Greenfield, Michigan, Oct., 21, 1929.

Menu and program.

Paper; 10½ x 7-3/8 in.

EDINBURGH

Cabinet U Shelf 1 No. 30

Bassandyne Bible, the first printed in Scotland, history of. With notices of the early printers of Edinburgh. By William T. Dobson. With facsimiles and other illustrations. Edinburgh, 1887.

Stamped cloth; 9¼ x 5-7/8 in.

EDINBURGH BIBLIOGRAPHICAL SOCIETY.

Cabinet 76 Shelf 2 No. 41

List of books printed in Scotland before 1700, including those printed furth of the Realm for Scottish booksellers. With brief notes on the printers and stationers. By Harry G. Aldis. Printed for the Edin. Biblio. Soc. 1904.

Boards; 11 x 9 in.

EDISON, THOMAS ALVA.

Cabinet 66 Shelf 1 No. 3

Papers announcing death of T. A. Edison, with biographical and appreciative articles. Issued Oct., 19-22, 1932. Illus.

Times and Herald Tribune (New York).
San Francisco Chronicle.
Globe-Democrat and Post-Dispatch (St. Louis)
Etc.

Cloth, 21 x 17¾ in.

EDINBURGH

Cabinet Q Shelf 2 No. 11

Booksellers and bookselling in Edinburgh in the time of William IV, reminiscences of. An address delivered to a meeting of booksellers assistants, Edinburgh, Oct., 1904. Printed for private circulation of Oliver and Boyd, 1905. Frontis.

Boards; 8-3/8 x 6¾ in.

EDINBURGH (The) GAZETEER (see)

Cabinet A Shelf 3 No. 1

Newspapers, Scotland, Edinburgh...

EDISON INSTITUTE, THE

Cabinet PP Shelf 3 No. 51

Illustrated descriptive booklet of an educational project: The Edison Institute, founded by Henry Ford, Dearborn, Michigan.

Item in envelope.

EDITOR AND PUBLISHER

Cabinet Q Shelf 7 No. 9

Market guide for advertisers, 1933.

see

ADVERTISING. Editor and Publisher The Fourth Estate...

EDITOR AND PUBLISHER MARKET GUIDE (See)

Cabinet LL Shelf 6 No.

ADVERTISING. Editor and Publisher Market Guide...

EDITOR-JOURNALISTS see JOURNALISTS

Cabinet Shelf No.

EDITORS see

Cabinet Shelf No.

BIOGRAPHIES, EDITORS

ASSOCIATIONS, JOURNALISTS.

EDITORS, TRIBULATIONS OF

Cabinet see TRIBULATIONS OF EDITORS.

Shelf No.

EDMOND, J. P.

Cabinet U Shelf 1 No. 70 (4 vols.)

Aberdeen printers. Edward Raban to James Nicol. 1620-1736. Aberdeen. Edmond & Spark, 1884-86. In 4 parts.

Part 1, 1620-1638; part 2, 1638-1682; part 3, 1682-1736; part 4, 1620-1736: Historical notices, etc.

Bio-bibliographical historical account.

Boards; each vol. 11-5/8 x 7-3/4 in.

EDMOND, JOHN PHILIP

Cabinet U Shelf 4 No. 27

Sweynheym, Conrad and Arnold Pannartz, the first Roman printers. A paper read before the Edinburgh Bibliographical Society, Dec.8, 1904.

pp.13-20 of Proceedings, 1906-1907, 1907-1908.

Half morocco; 9-5/8 x 8 in.

EDMONTON DAILY BULLETIN (Canada)

Cabinet Shelf No.

See Newspapers, Canada.

EDMONTON-JOURNAL

Cabinet Shelf No.

See Newspapers, Canada.

EDUCATION, PRINTING see

Cabinet Shelf No.

I - PRINTING EDUCATION

II - SCHOOLS OF PRINTING.

EDWARDS, DAVID

Cabinet X Shelf 4 No. 73

Hebene Gompue fon Dowid Edwards, London, Oct. 14, 1694.

see

LIBERTY OF PRINTING, Great Britain Copies from the records...London, 1763, p.11

EDWARDS, ERNEST

Cabinet I Shelf 2 No. 25

Heliotype process, the. By Ernest Edwards. With twenty-eight illustrations. Boston: James R. Osgood and Company. 1876.

Boards; 12 x 10 x 5/8 in.

EDWARDS, GEORGE WHARTON

Cabinet S Shelf 5 No. 12

(The) Illustration of books. By G. W. Edwards in the Outlook. Dec. 4, 1897.

Bound in collection "Pamphlets and excerpts relating to typographical matters," item 12

EDWARDS, GEORGE WHARTON

Cabinet S Shelf 1 No. 33

Illustration of books, The. By George W. Edwards. An excerpt from "The Outlook," n.d.

Item 10 in volume "Writings of Theodore Low DeVinne."

Half morocco; 9½ x 6-5/8 in.

EDWARDS & FRANKLIN COMPANY

Cabinet S Shelf 6 No. 6

See Plants, Printing. United States.

EELLS, REV. M. (Compiler)

Cabinet II Shelf 3 No. 63 Box

Hymns in the Chinook jargon language. Compiled by Rev. M. Eells, Missionary of the American Missionary Association. 2nd revised ed. Portland, Oregon, 1889. Booklet.

Item in box labelled "MISCELLANEOUS LANGUAGE CHARACTERS: EXAMPLES".

EGENOLF, CHRISTIAN

Cabinet X Shelf 3 No. 13

Brief bio-bibliographical note, Strassburg, 1529-30.

see

HEITZ, PAUL. Elsässische büchermarken...p.xx

EGENOLFF, CHRISTIAN

Cabinet E Shelf 1 No. 40

See Early Printing in Germany. Frankfort a M. 1564.

Contains his portrait.

EGENOLFF, CHRISTIAN

Cabinet Y Shelf 2 No. 20

Ersten buchdrucker zu Frankfort a. M. und seine vorlaufer. von Dr. H. Grotefend Gedenkenblatt an die 350 jabrige jubelfeier der einfuhrung in Frankfort. Frankfort a. M. 1881. Illus.

Bio-historical sketch of Frankfort's first printer. Souvenir brochure of the 350th year celebration of the introduction of printing.

Half morocco; 11-5/8 x 9 in.

EGGER, E.

Cabinet RR Shelf 4 No. 38 2 cops

Sur le prix du papier dans l'antiquité. Lettre de M. Egger, a M. Ambroise-Firmin Didot, et réponse de M.A. Firmin Didot a M. Egger. (Extrait de la Revue Contemporaint du 15 Septembre, 1856.) Paris, 1857. Imprimerie de Dubuisson et Cie.

(On the price of paper in ancient times).

Pamphlet; 9-3/4 x 6¼ in. With other French pamphlets relating to paper. In board folder.

EGYPT

Cabinet U Shelf 1 No. 1d

Early Codices from Egypt. (Bibliographical communication). By H. I. Bell, London, 1909.

In Excerpts relating to printing from "The Library," 1909. p. 142 of pencilled folios.

EGENOLFF, CHRISTIAN

Cabinet Y Shelf 1 No. 41

Frankfurt a.M., Chr. Egenolff in. (Biographical account, with portrait)

See BÖRCKEL, ALFRED. "Gutenberg und seine berühmsten nachfolger"...Frankfurt a.M., 1900, pp.123-130

EGGESTEIN, HEINRICH

Cabinet Y Shelf 4 No. 4

(Note on Eggestein and his printing at Strasbourg, 1463)

see

VOULLIÉME, ERNST. (Die) Deutschen drucker des fünfzehnten jahrhunderts...p.105

EGYPT

Cabinet NN Shelf 7 No. 42

Editors of 1422 B. C.

see JOURNALISM. Editors of 1422 B. C. etc.

EGENOLFF-LUTHERSCHE SCHRIFTGIESSEREI

Cabinet FF Shelf 5 No. 6

Frankfurt am Main, 1735.

See MORI, GUSTAV. (Die) Egenolff-Luthersche Schriftgiesserei...Frankfurt am Main, 1926.

EGGESTEIN, HEINRICH

Cabinet D Shelf 1 No. 63

Strassburg, circa 1472.

see INCUNABULA (loose leaves) Eggestein...

EGYPT.

Cabinet K Shelf 1 No. 26

Egyptian book of the dead reproduced in facsimile. 99 plates.

See Davis, Charles, H. S. Egyptian book of the dead... New York, 1894.

EGGE, OTTO F.

Cabinet L Shelf 2 No. 28

Alphabet, the story of. Its evolution and development. By Otto F. Ege. Baltimore, Md. Compliments of Norman T. Munder & Co., 1921.

Illus. with double plate.

Boards; 9¾ x 3-7/8 in.

EGLINGTON, WILLIAM

Cabinet Shelf No.

See index cards with headings as follows:
Specimen Books, Cuts. Great Britain
" also: " " Wood Types. Great Britain.

EGYPT

Cabinet Shelf No.

Hieroglyphic writing

see HIEROGLYPHICS

EGGELING, ARTHUR

Cabinet PP Shelf 4 No. 39

Bookbinding by hand. Arthur Eggeling and his associates. New York, Eggeling Bookbindery. 1925. Illus.

Cloth; 9 x 6¼ in.

EGMONDT, FREDERICK

Cabinet U Shelf 1 No. 1a

(A) Fifteenth century English Stationer. By E. Gordon Duff.

Bio-bibliographical account.

In Excerpts relating to printing from "The Library," [n.d.], p. 172 of printed folios.

EGYPT

Cabinet 26 Shelf 1 No. 21

L'Imprimerie Nationale Egyptienne. History of.

See "GOVERNMENT PRINTING OFFICES, Egypt" Apercu historique...

EGGER, E.

Cabinet RR Shelf 2 No. 9

Papier dans l'antiquite et dans les temps modernes. Apercu historique. Par E. Egger. Paris, 1866.

Brief historical account.

Cloth; 6-1/8 x 3-3/4 x ¼ in.

EGYPT

Cabinet L Shelf 2 No. 17

Alphabet, a new Egyptian

See SPITTA, WILHELM. Egyptian alphabet ...The Landi Press, Florence, 1897

EGYPT

Cabinet PP Shelf 3 No. 9

Librarians, some old Egyptian. By Ernest Cushing Richardson. New York, 1911.

Boards; 7¼ x 4½ in.

EGYPT

Cabinet NN Shelf 2 No. 13

Newspapers in Egypt

see NEWSPAPERS, Egypt. Literature

EGYPT, GRECO-ROMAN

Cabinet L Shelf 3 No. 26

Greek literary texts from Greco-Roman Egypt. A study in the history of civilization. By Charles Henry Oldfather. University of Wisconsin Studies, No.9. Madison, Wis., 1923.

(A study of the types of literature and what authors were used in the schools.)

Brochure, in manila envelope.

EGYPTIAN CODICES.

Cabinet U Shelf 1 No. 1d

See Bookmaking, early. Early codices from Egypt.

In excerpts relating to printing from The Library, 1909, p.142.

EGYPTIAN PUBLICATIONS, PRESS OF THE (See)

Cabinet G Shelf 3 No. 82.01

IMPRINTS, United States. Press of the Egyptian Publications

EGYPTIAN TYPES, PRINTING

Cabinet FF Shelf 3 No. 20

Brusch, Henri. Memoir sur la reproduction imprimee des caracteres de l'ancienne ecriture demotique des egyptiens, au moyen de types mobiles et de l'imprimerie, Berlin, 1855.

Half morocco; 10 x 7 in.

EGYTERTES (Hungary)

Cabinet Shelf No.

See Newspepers, Hungary.

EHLERT & Co., HEINRICH

Cabinet Shelf No.

See Specimen Books, Types. Germany.

EHMCKE, F. H.

Cabinet Y Shelf 3 No. 87

(Development of book printing in Germany during three decades, 1890-1920) Drei jahrzehnte deutscher buchkunst. Eine bücherschau in dreiszig vitrinen nicht strong chronologisch, doch möglichst vorteilhaft angeordnet durch F. H. Emcke. Berlin, 1922.

Boards; 9 x 5-3/4 x ¼ in.

EHMCKE, F.H.

Cabinet 18 Shelf 1 No. 8

(My "Faust") Main "Faust" von F.H.Ehmcke,Dusseldorf. Facsimiles of pages and plates.

An item in German in which Mr. Ehmcke explains his reason for selection of certain method of composition, for an edition of "Faust."

In Zeitschrift für Bücherfreunde, 1910, part 2, p.263.

EHMCKE, F. W.

Cabinet Y Shelf 3 No. 89

(Historical development of occidental letter forms) Die historische entwicklung der abendlaendischen schriftformen. Ravensburg, 1927. Numerous specimens.

Includes a bibliography.

Boards; 10-5/8 x 7½ x 3/8 in.

EHRENHARD & GRAMM, Act-Ges.

Cabinet EE Shelf 5 No. 66

(Catalogue, 1900, and price list of printing machinery) Haupt-Katalog uber buchdruck schnellpressen. Ausgabe: Januar 1900. Worms a. Rh.

Cloth; 9-3/8 x 12½ in.

EHRENHARD & GRAMM, AKT.-GES.

Cabinet EE Shelf 5 No. 67

(Catalogue 1901, and price list of Wormser original treadle machines) Speziale-preis-liste uber Wormser Original-Tret-Maschinen. Schuellpressenfabrik Worms. Ehrenhard & Gramm, Akt.-Ges. Worms am Rheine. Gegrunded 1869.

Another catalogue in same envelope, printed in Dutch for J.E. Stolberg, Amsterdam, Agent for the Netherlands.

Pamphlet in manila envelope.

EICHENBERG, EDUARD

Cabinet 71 Shelf 1 No. 41

What the bird did at Hazel's Orchard. By E. Eichenberg.

Imprint: San Francisco: Printed for John F. Newbegin by John Henry Nash, 1916.

Paper boards; 7-3/4 x 5-3/4 in.

EICHLER, FERDINAND

Cabinet Y Shelf 3 No. 76

Lederschnitt und hornverzierung beim bucheinband.

pp.88-94 in Loubier, Hans (Tribute to) Buch und bucheinband...Leipzig, 1923.

EILERT, ERNEST FREDERICK, 1881-1931.

Cabinet G Shelf 1 No. 7

Testimonial dinner to E.F. Eilert, Sponsored by Printers' Supply Salesmen's Guild. New York Wednesday Evening. February 25, 1931. Hotel Astor. (Programm).

Printed for Printers' Supply Salesmen's Guild of New York with compliments of the American Type Founders Company.

Boards; 7-3/8 x 5-1/8 in.

EISEN, CHARLES

Cabinet Shelf No.

See Engravings. Copperplate. Jugement de Paris. Par J. Imbert...1772.

EISENBERG, BERNARD B.

Cabinet LL Shelf 6 No. 20

Estimating presswork. Read before the estimatimg class of the Ben Franklin Club of Cleveland. March 4, 1913. Brochure.

Item 3 in book with binder's title "Various items on printing shop practice." Bound 1919

EL CUZCO

Cabinet Shelf No.

See Printing, Historical, Peru.

ELDER, PAUL, Publisher.

Cabinet NN Shelf 3 No. 23

Extra!! Fairy tales up to now. The victims: Babes in the Wood. Cinderella. Jack the Giant-killer. Sleeping Beauty. Little Red Riding-hood. Paul Elder, the San Francisco publisher, brings to light the details of the tragedy. San Francisco, The Tomoyé Press.1904

Boards: 8x4-5/8". In slip case

ELECTRO MATRICES

Cabinet 21 Shelf 2 No. 1

Invented by James Conner. James Conner, a biography.

In "The Printer", Vol. 2, May, 1859, No. I, p. 3, 8th column.

ELECTROTYPE PLANTS

Cabinet Shelf No.

See Plants, Electrotype.

ELDER, WILLIAM

Cabinet Q Shelf 2 No. 19

Memoir of Henry C. Carey. Read before the Historical Society of Pennsylvania, Philadelphia, January 5, 1880. Philadelphia 1880. With portrait.

Cloth; 9¼ x 5-7/8 in.

ELECTROTINT

Cabinet FF Shelf 1 No. 5

Art of making painting ... See Electrotyping. Electrotint, or the art of making paintings... by T. Sampson, London, 1842.

ELECTROTYPERS, SOCIETIES OF

Cabinet Shelf No.

See SOCIETIES, ELECTROTYPERS'

ELDRIDGE- PARTON -- see "FERN FANNY"

Cabinet Shelf No.

ELECTROTYPE

Cabinet FF Shelf 1 No. 15

Being a description of the art of working in metal by voltaic electricity. With illustrations. To which is added a brief description of the calotype, daguerreotype, or photographic processes. By Vaughan Palmer...Eighth edition. London (1845)

Half morocco; 6¼x3-7/8 in.

ELECTROTYPES

Cabinet DD Shelf 5 No. 73

Mergenthaler Linotype Co. New York, 1895. Linotype faces. The specimens of Linotype print shown herein are printed from electrotypes made direct from Linotype slugs. Tribune Building. New York, October 1895.

Cloth; 18 x 11¾ x 3/8 in.

ELECTRIC MOTOR

Cabinet QQ Shelf 2 No. 27

Invention see DAVENPORT, THOMAS... Biography...

ELECTROTYPE and STEREOTYPE MACHINERY (Catalogue)

Cabinet FF Shelf 6 No. 19

Cottrell & Sons, C.B. Electrotype and Stereotype Machinery. Factory Westerly, Rhode Island. n.d. circa 1885.

Bound in at the end of volume lettered "Type Machines"

ELECTROTYPING

Cabinet S Shelf 5 No. 14

An American Art: The electrotype - It's application to printing purposes. An excerpt from the Inland Monthly, June, 1872.

Briefly outlines the history of invention, inventors, experiments, and improvements.

Bound with other items in collection "Printing Processes," item 7.

ELECTRICAL TESTING LABORATORIES

Cabinet RR Shelf 2 No. 15

Paper, testing of. For those who make, use, by or sell paper in any form. E.T.L. New York City. Illus. booklet.

Item in manila envelope.

ELECTROTYPE CUTS

Cabinet Shelf No.

See Specimen Books, Cuts.

ELECTROTYPING

Cabinet FF Shelf 1 No. 3

Application of plumbago to non-conducting substances for the production of voltatypes. London, 1841. (A discovery vital to the industry afterwards called electrotyping.) In transactions of the Society of Arts, Manufactures, and Commerce. Vol. 53.-Pt.2 For the session 1840-41, pp. 10-18

Half morocco: 8-5/8x5¾ in.

ELECTRO-DYNAMO

Cabinet FF Shelf 2 No. 51

Faraday machine.

See Faraday machine. Memorial meeting, Sept. 21, 1931 in Budapest, Hungary.

ELECTROTYPE JOURNAL (The) see

Cabinet 31 Shelf 2 No.

Periodicals, Printing, United States. Electrotype Journal...

ELECTROTYPING

Cabinet FF Shelf 1 No. 1

BARCLAY, G. The first steps in electrotype. "Facts not words". London: Published by G. Barclay, 22 Gerrard Street, Soho. 1841 Second edition. With folding plate.

Paper 4-½x2¾". Item I in vol. with binder's title: Electrotyping and Stereotyping Pamphlets.

ELECTROTYPING

Cabinet FF Shelf 1 No. 38

Blaney, Charles W., Boston's oldest electrotyper. With his portrait and description of his specialties. He did not work from type forms. He was an apprentice of John W. Wilcox, the originator of electrotyping of type forms in America by the method still used.

Newspaper excerpt in manila envelope.

ELECTROTYPING.

Cabinet 26 Shelf 2 No. 4

(Concerning the progress of Dr. Kobell's galvanography.) Uber die fortschritte der galvanographie: vom Professor Dr. Von Kobell.

Journal fur Buchdruckerkunst, 1845, No.5, cols. 66-70.

ELECTROTYPING

Cabinet FF Shelf 1 No. 8

Earliest history of the invention of electrotyping.

See pp XVII - XXX in Smee's Elements of electro-metallurgy ...London, 1843.

ELECTROTYPING

Cabinet FF Shelf 1 No. 54

Broadside: A brief graphic outline of the history of stereotyping and electrotyping, 1041 to 1933, n. p., n. d.

In envelope

ELECTROTYPING

Cabinet FF Shelf 1 No. 37

Copper electrotyping. Circular of the Bureau of Standards, No. 387. Issued Aug. 30, 1930. Washington, D. C., 1930.

Paper pamphlet in manila envelope.

ELECTROTYPING

Cabinet S Shelf 5 No. 14

Electrography or the electrotype. Instructions for the multiplication of works of Art in metal by Voltaic electricity; by Thomas Spencer: A review of book with same name, by B. Silliman, Jr., who also includes result of his experiments after having read the book. An excerpt from American Journal of Science, Jan. 1841. Illus.

Bound with other items in collection "Printing Processes," item 12.

ELECTROTYPING

Cabinet FF Shelf 1 No. 40

Cerotype process.

see

McLEES, FRANK & BROS. Cerotype advertisements...

ELECTROTYPING

Cabinet FF Shelf 1 No. 1

Dunton, George E. A black leading paradox. A philosophical treatise on black leading. New York and London, 1914. Printed by the Charles Francis Press, New York. Electrotyper's Brochure Series.

Item 5 in vol. with binders' title; Electrotyping and Stereotyping Pamphlets.

ELECTROTYPING

Cabinet 21 Shelf 2 No. 1

Electro - Metallurgy. Copyrighted by William Filmer, electrotyper and manufacturer of electrotyping appliances. Dutch and Fulton Streets, New York.

Claimed to be the "Oldest practical electrotyper in America." Picture of plant on p. 14.

Articles in "The Printer", Vol. I, begin No. 1, May 1858; continued on pp. 22, 46, 72, 93, 115, 189, 213, 236, 259 and conclude on p. 282.

ELECTROTYPING

Cabinet FF Shelf 1 No. 1

Collection of pamphlets relating to electrotyping and stereotyping. Bound 1919. Seven items, with index.

I - First steps in electrotyping
II & III Electrotyping. Dunton Process.
IV - Hints to stereotypers and electrotypers, etc. etc.

Half morocco, 10 x 7 in.

ELECTROTYPING

Cabinet FF Shelf 1 No. 1

DUNTON, George E. Mechanical processes past and future. Address delivered before the International Association of Electrotypers of America. Waldorf Astoria Hotel. New York, Wednesday, Oct. 7, 1914.

Item 7 in vol. with binders' title; Electrotyping and Stereotyping Pamphlets.

ELECTROTYPING

Cabinet FF Shelf 1 No. 5

Electrotint, or the art of making paintings in such a manner that copper plates and "blocks" can be taken from them by means of voltaic electricity. By Thomas Sampson. Published by Edward Palmer, Philosophical Instrument Maker. London, 1842. At end of book the patent, dated 1841, and plates.

Cloth; 10 x 6-½ in.

ELECTROTYPING

Cabinet 26 Shelf 2 No. 2

(Concerning galvanoplastic reproduction of pierced copperplates) Uber galvano-plastische nachbildung gestochener kupferplatten.

Journal fur Buchdruckerkunst, June, 1842, cols. 83-89.

ELECTROTYPING

Cabinet FF Shelf 1 No. 1

Dunton Brochure Series: Book I. May, 1910. Depositing metal by the agency of electricity. By George E. Dunton, New York City, Pamphlet.

Paper 8 x 5 in. Item 2 in vol. with binders' title: Electrotyping and Stereotyping Pamphlets.

ELECTROTYPING

Cabinet FF Shelf 1 No. 7

Electrotype, The; Pamphlet, 7 pp. extract from the "Classic". By J. n.p. n.d. circa 1843, American.

Insert in front of "Traite de Galvanoplastie". Paris, 1843.

Buckram; 10 x 6½ in.

ELECTROTYPING.

Cabinet 26 Shelf 2 No. 4

Concerning Glyphography: Methods and rules.

Journal fur Buchdruckerkunst, 1845, No.11, cols. 137-43: No.12, cols.145-149: No.13, cols. 163.

ELECTROTYPING

Cabinet FF Shelf 1 No. 1

Dunton Brochure Series. Supplement to Book I. December 1910. The electrotype de luxe: (Trade Mark) The Dunton Process. New York City.

Paper 8x5 in. Item 3 in vol. with binders' title: Electrotyping and Stereotyping Pamphlets.

ELECTROTYPING

Cabinet FF Shelf 1 No. 11

Electrotype manipulation. Containing theory, and plain instructions... By Charles V. Walker. Illustrated from wood cuts. From the 6th London edition. Carey and Hart. Philadelphia, 1844.

Two parts in one. Title page missing from part one.

Cloth; 6-1/8 x 4 in.

ELECTROTYPING

Cabinet FF Shelf 1 No. 13

Electrotype manipulation. Being the theory and plain instructions in the art of working in metals...by galvanic or voltaic electricity. Illustrated by wood cuts...by Charles V. Walker. 14th ed. London, 1844.
Two parts in one.
Part II : (Title same as above)...and plain instructions in the arts of electro-plating, electro-gilding and electro-etching....
Seventh ed. London, 1844
Cloth; 6½x4 in.

ELECTROTYPING

Cabinet FF Shelf 1 No. 8

First electrotype used in actual printing, April, 1840.

For account see P. XXll Smee's Elements of electro-metallurgy ...London, 1843.

ELECTROTYPING

Cabinet 26 Shelf 2 No. 2

Galvanography in Denmark: Some notes concerning the methods, by F. von Kobell, May, 1843.

In German language.

Journal fur Buchdruckerkunst, May, 1843, cols. 60-62.

ELECTROTYPING

Cabinet FF Shelf 1 No. 14

Electrotype manipulation: Being the theory and plain instructions in the art of working in metals... By Charles V. Walker. Illustrated by wood cuts. Second American, from the twenty-fifth English edition. Philadelphia, 1852.
Two parts in one volume.
Cloth; 7 x 4½ x ½ in.

ELECTROTYPING

Cabinet Shelf No.

First occurrences in the history and methods of electrotyping.

See First Occurrences.

ELECTROTYPING

Cabinet 26 Shelf 2 No. 2

Galvanoplastik, Die. Descriptive historical account of the invention, in German.

Journal fur Buckdruckerkunst, April, 1841, cols.49-60, May, cols.69-76, June, cols. 81-87, July, cols.97-100.

ELECTROTYPING

Cabinet 25 Shelf 2 No. 17

(_The) Electrotyper. Publisht quarterly by Schniedewend & Lee, Electrotypers, Chicago, Ill.
Vol.Vll, No.4(Dec.,1879); vol.Vlll, Nos. 1,2,3,4(1880)

Portfolio; 12½ x 9½ in.

ELECTROTYPING

Cabinet FF Shelf 1 No. 28.01

From xylographs to lead molds. A.D. 1440-A.D. 1921. Copyright 1921, The Rapid Electrotype Company. Cincinnati, Ohio.

Boards; 8 x 5 in.

ELECTROTYPING

Cabinet FF Shelf 1 No. 16

Galvanoplastik. Grundliche anleitung für buchdrucker, schriftgiesser, kupferstecher und hogzschneider, auf die einfachste und billigste art typen und kupferplätten darzustellen. von W. Hasper. Carlsruhe, 1855.

The author W. Hasper, was a Court Printer. He died at Carlsruhe in 1875, aged 75.

Half morocco; 7 x ¼ in.

ELECTROTYPING

Cabinet FF Shelf 1 No. 17

Electrotypers' Manual, The. By William Stuart Speirs. Buffalo, N. Y. 1869.

Paper; 8¾ x 6¼ in. In manila envelope

ELECTROTYPING

Cabinet FF Shelf 1 No. 33

From xylographs to lead molds. A. D. 1440-A. D. 1921. (Compiled by) H. C. Forster. The Royal Electrotype Company, Cincinnati, Ohio.

Boards; 8 x 5 in.

ELECTROTYPING

Cabinet FF Shelf 1 No. 18

(Die) Galvanoplastik und ihre anwendung in der buchdruckerkunst. Bearbeited von A. Hering. Leipzig, 1870. Illus.

Half morocco; 7 x 5 in.

ELECTROTYPING

Cabinet FF Shelf 1 No. 9

Elements of electro-metallurgy. By Alfred Smee, F.R.S....First American, from the third London edition. Illustrated with electrotypes and numerous woodcuts. New York, 1852.

Cloth; 8 x 5½ in.

ELECTROTYPING

Cabinet FF Shelf 1 No. 4

(Die) Galvanographie, eine methode, gemalde tuschbilder durch galvanische kupferplatten in drucke zu vervielfaltigen. von Franz von Kobell. Munchen, 1842.
illus. 7 plates.

Half levant, 12 x 9 in.

ELECTROTYPING.

Cabinet V Shelf 5 No. 14

See Gobin, Henry. L'Art de Peindre la Parole. Paris, 1874. Chap. IV.

ELECTROTYPING

Cabinet K Shelf 6 No. 3

Etching or engraving by electricity. Article by Robert Hunt.
see
ART JOURNAL, THE. Wood engravings, etchings, etc...1849, London, p. 9.

ELECTROTYPING.

Cabinet 26 Shelf 2 No. 2

Galvanography: Briefly descriptive of method and result. An excerpt in German taken from the Allgemeine Zeitung. 1842.

Journal fur Buchdruckerkunst, July, 1842, cols. 101-2, Oct., cols. 148-53.

ELECTROTYPING

Cabinet FF Shelf 1 No. 106

Guide for the production of plates by the papier mache and plaster processes. Stereotyping and electrotyping ....Fourth edition, By Frederick J. F. Wilson. London, n. d. E. Menken, "Wymans Technical series.

Cloth; 7-3/8 x 5¼ in.

ELECTROTYPING.

Cabinet 26 Shelf 2 No. 6

(Gutenberg's Monument and galvanoplastic) Die Galvanoplastic und das Gutenbergsdenkmal. Illus.

A German account of the above process used in casting the monument modeled by Launitz, and which was erected in Frankfort to celebrate the 4th centennial of the invention of printing.

Journal fur Buchdruckerkunst,1853,No.7,cols. 73-80.

ELECTROTYPING

Cabinet FF Shelf 1 No. 28

How to know values in electrotypes. n. p. (1915) Illus.

Published by the Royal Electrotype Company of Philadelphia.

Cloth; 7-1/8 x 4½"

ELECTROTYPING

Cabinet 25 Shelf 2 No. 5

Picture of the first electrotyping shop in the world, 152 Washington St. Boston, one door from corner of Milk Street, now the site of building occupied by Boston Transcript. It was established by John W Wilson in Dec., 1846. The floor below was occupied by J. G. Chandler, wood engraver, who assisted Wilson in perfecting his electrotyping plant.(H.L.B)

Item in vol. of misc. printing trade periodicals, circulars, etc

ELECTROTYPING

Cabinet MM Shelf 6 No. 54

Hatch, Harris B. Electrotyping and Stereotyping: A primer of information about the processes of electrotyping and stereotyping. Electrotyping, Part I, Stereotyping, Part II, By A.A. Stewart. "Typographic Technical Series for Apprentices", Part I, No.15. Published by the United Typothetae of America, 1918.

Cloth; 8 x 5 in.

ELECTROTYPING

Cabinet EE Shelf 5 No. 24

(lead moulding) Electrotypes exactly as good as the original. By means of the Dr. Albert Patent Lead Moulding process. F. Wesel Manufacturing Co., owners of the American patents. Brooklyn, N.Y. 1907.

Paper; 12 x 9 in. Item in manila envelope.

ELECTROTYPING

Cabinet FF Shelf 2 No. 15.01

[Plate making] Formschneidekunst, oder die herstellung von druckformen oder druckmodeln ...von Chr. Heinr. Schmidt, Weimar, 1852.

With folded plates.

Half morocco; 7-7/8 x 4-7/8 x ½ in.

ELECTROTYPING

Cabinet FF Shelf 1 No. 87

Hints on electrotyping and stereotypint . R. Hoe & Co. New York, 1875. Illus.

Cloth; 9-1/8 x 6¼ x 3/8 in.

ELECTROTYPING

Cabinet 26 Shelf 2 No. 4

(Making galvano relief plates to reproduce wood engravings.) Uber die galvanische anfertigung erhabener platten, welche gleich den holzschnitten gedruckt werden konnen, bei Dr. Kobell.

Journal fur Buchdruckerkunst, 1845, No.4 cols. 49-50.

ELECTROTYPING

Cabinet FF Shelf 1 No. 101

Practical notes on stereotyping and electrotyping From "The British Printer". Compiled by the editor. London. Raithby, Lawrence & Company, Limited, 1901. Illus.

Cloth; 8-5/8 x 5¾ in.

ELECTROTYPING

Cabinet FF Shelf 1 No. 19

Hints on electrotyping and stereotyping... R. Hoe & Co. New York. 1875. Illus.

Has autograph of Peter J. Hoe on title page.

Cloth; 8½ x 5¾ in.

ELECTROTYPING

Cabinet FF Shelf 1 No. 1

Multiplication of works of art in metal by voltaic electricity. Excerpt from the Living Age. Jan. 25, 1945.

Item 6 in vol. with binders' title: Electrotyping and Stereotyping Pamphlets.

ELECTROTYPING

Cabinet FF Shelf 1 No. 23

(A) Practical treatise on the art of electrotyping by the latest known methods. Containing historical review of the subject... By C. S. Partridge. Second edition. Chicago: The Inland Printer Company, 1908.

Cloth; 8 x 5½ in.

ELECTROTYPING

Cabinet FF Shelf 1 No. 41

History of electrotyping. The art that was born in a quart jar little more than a half a century ago..

Article in P.M., vol.2, No.1, Sept., 1935, p.4.

ELECTROTYPING.

Cabinet 26 Shelf 2 No. 3

Palmer, Edward. Glyphography, or galvanoplastic plates for printing on the type press after the manner of wood cuts, Patented, London, 1843.

Brief description, in German, of the inventor's method.

Journal fur Buchdruckerkunst, 1844, No.9, cols. 139-40.

ELECTROTYPING

Cabinet Y Shelf 2 No. 96

Pretsch, Paul den erfinder derphoto-galvanographie, festschrift zur enthüllungsfeier der gedenktafel fur. Herausgeben der Wiener Buchdruckerei und Schriftgiesserei Factore. Zusammengestellt von G. Fritz. Wien 1888.

In folder; 11 x 8 in.

ELECTROTYPING

Cabinet FF Shelf 1 No. 1

Hoe & Co., R.; Hints to stereotypers and electrotypers. R. Hoe & Co. (New York City). 1891.

Paper; 9½x6 in. Item 4 in vol. with binders' title: Electrotyping and Stereotyping Pamphlets.

ELECTROTYPING

Cabinet FF Shelf 1 No. 6.01

Parkes, Mrs. Mary: The electrotype as misapplied to engraving in the National Art-Union. A letter to Mr. Moon, of Threadneedle Street, by Mrs. Mary Parkes. 3rd. ed. with additions London, 1842.

Paper wrappers; 8 x 5 in. Item in manila envelope

ELECTROTYPING

Cabinet 33 Shelf 2 No. 9

Printers' Album and the Electrotyper.

See PERIODICALS, PRINTING, United States Printers' Album...

ELECTROTYPING

Cabinet EE Shelf 4 No. 66

Processes of electrotyping, a brief account.

See p.52 HOE'S (Catalogue and price list, 1871).

ELECTROTYPING

Cabinet FF Shelf 1 No. 2

Spencer, Thomas. Instructions for the multiplication of works of art in metal, by voltaic electricity. With an introductory chapter on electro-chemical decompositions by feeble currents. Glasgow, 1840

Cloth, leather back; 8-5/8 x 5-½ in.

ELECTROTYPING

Cabinet FF Shelf 1 No. 20

Treaties on electrotyping by George E. Dunton; and illustrated catalogue of improved machinery for electrotyping, stereotyping and photoengraving manufactured by The Ostrander Seymour Co., Chicago, 1900.

Bound in with Dunton's Electrotyping Brochure Series. Book I, May 1910, and Supplement to Book I, Dec. 1910.

Cloth; 10 x 7 in.

ELECTROTYPING

Cabinet FF Shelf 1 No. 41

Processing the electrotype. From the mould to finished plate. By Alfred R. Flower.

Illus. article in P.M., vol.2, No.1, Sept., 1935, p.6

ELECTROTYPING

Cabinet RR Shelf 1 No. 5

Standard electrotype scale. In effect May 1, 1925.

Together with "Information for the printer". Gilbert Paper Company, Menasha, Wisconsin.

Boards; 12¼ x 9 in.

ELECTROTYPING

Cabinet FF Shelf 1 No. 21

Treatise on electrotyping. By George E. Dunton, and illustrated catalogue of improved machinery for electrotyping, stereotyping and photo-engraving, manufactured by The Ostrander-Seymour Company, Chicago, U. S. A. Price $1.00.

Treatise and catalogue are on alternate pages.

Paper: 10 x 6¾ in.

ELECTROTYPING.

Cabinet FF Shelf 1 No. 35

Raisbeck Electrotype Company, New York, 1929. Process of electrotyping. Printing throughout (with exception of illustration on p.16) from Electrotypes. Copyright, 1929.

Boards; 12½ x 9-5/8 in.

ELECTROTYPING

Cabinet FF Shelf 1 No. 42

Standard Electrotype Scale of Net Prices. Based on cost production. New York, April 15, 1930. Lead Mould Electrotype Company. 216 West 18th Street, New York City.

Broadside, in envelope.

ELECTROTYPING

Cabinet 26 Shelf 2 No. 2

Uber die Galvanographie von Jacobi: An excerpt from the publication of the Academy of Sciences in St. Petersburg.

Journal fur Buchdruckerkunst, Feb., 1843, cols. 19-23.

ELECTROTYPING

Cabinet FF Shelf 1 No. 99

Reference book of electrotyping and stereotyping Giving information and instruction regarding processes, materials and machinery. By Charles S. Partridge. Chicago; The Inland Printer. 1905.

Cloth; 7 x 4¾ in.

ELECTROTYPING

Cabinet FF Shelf 1 No. 27

Ten two-minute talks. By Harris B. Hatch. Royal Electrotype Co. Philadelphia, Pa. 1910.

Boards; 8½ x 6 in.

ELECTROTYPING

Cabinet FF Shelf 1 No. 39

Unmounted electrotype shell: Declaration of Independence of the United States of America, Jul7 4, 1776.

Item in envelope

ELECTROTYPING

Cabinet JJ Shelf 6 No. 39

Scales for electrotyping. Adopted Oct., 17, 1906. In effect November I, 1906. Booklet.

With other items in manila envelope.

ELECTROTYPING

Cabinet FF Shelf 1 No. 37

Throwing power in chronium plates. By H.L.Farber and W. Blum. Research Paper, No.131, U.S. Department of Commerce. Washington, 1930. Pamphlet.

Item in manila envelope.

ELECTROTYPING

Cabinet S Shelf 5 No. 14

Wilcox, John A. An American art: the electrotype, its application to printing purposes. An xxx excerpt in which is related the early experiences of John W. Wilcox, the originator of the wax process of moulding type forms in electrotyping. This article is based on an interview with Wilcox in 1872. He died in 1875.

[Item 7 in collection of excerpts]

The wax process of moulding type forms for electrotyping was first used in Boston in 1847.

con't

ELECTROTYPING

Cabinet FF Shelf 1 No. 8

Smee battery for deposition of copper.

See pp. 10, 12, 23-30, 192 in Smee's Elements of electro metallurgy ...London, 1843.

ELECTROTYPING

Cabinet FF Shelf 1 No. 7

I Traite' de galvanoplastie' Par J. L. Paris, 1843.

II The electrotype. (Signed "J") Reprint from "The Classic", 1843. American.

Both articles bound together.

Buckram; 10 x 6-½ in.

ELECTROTYPING cont'd

Cabinet S Shelf 5 No. 14

See 25-2-5 in a Ruggles advertisement for a picture of the building in which Wilcox latterly conducted his business of electrotyping. It is located immediately above the premises used by Ruggles and had the sign "Electrotyping". It was on the site occupied by the Boston Evening Transcript. It is on penciled page 36. Wilcox began the used of his process of electrotyping from wax moulds at No.8 North Anderson Street, Boston.

ELECTROTYPING

Cabinet
Shelf
No.

See also cards with following sub-head:

CHEMITYPIE
PATENTS, ELECTROTYPING

ELECTROTYPING (Wilcox's)

Cabinet 81
Shelf 2
No. 35

Picture of First Electrotyping Plant in the world. Exterior view. In the S.P. Ruggles Press and Paper Cutter Manufactory, cor. Washington Street, Boston, circa 1845. Newspaper excerpt.

Item in MUNSELL, JOEL. "Printers Scraps", Vol.VI, p.66.

ELECTROTYPING MACHINERY

Cabinet FF
Shelf 5
No. 67

Claybourn Process Precision Machinery for modern plate making... Claybourn Process Company, Milwaukee, Wis., 1926. Illus. Brochure.

Item in manila envelope

ELECTROTYPING MACHINERY

Cabinet EE
Shelf 4
No. 69

Hoe, R. & Co. Catalogue of stereotyping and electrotyping machinery. New York, 1881.

Boards; 10-3/4 x $7\frac{1}{2}$ in.

ELECTROTYPING MACHINERY

Cabinet EE
Shelf 4
No. 71

Hoe, R., & Co. Catalogue, 1898, of machinery and materials for electrotyping...New York, 1898.

Pamphlet in manila envelope.

ELECTROTYPE MACHINERY

Cabinet EE
Shelf 4
No. 72

Hoe & Co., R. New York, 1910. Some of the rotary electrotype web perfecting presses for periodicals, magazine... printing. (Catalogues and price lists, 2)

Items in manila envelope

ELECTROTYPING MACHINERY

Cabinet EE
Shelf 5
No. 70 & 71

Hogenforst Maschinenfabrik. Leipzig, circa 1900.

See PRINTING EQUIPMENTS. Catalogue. Hogenforst Maschinenfabrik...

ELECTROTYPING MACHINERY, Catalogue

Cabinet EE
Shelf 5
No. 63

Boildieu et Fils, Paris, 1878.

See BOILDIEU & FILS. (Catalogue 1878...)

ELECTROTYPING MACHINERY. Catalogue

Cabinet EE
Shelf 4
No. 24

Cottrell, C.B., & Sons. New York, Chicago, 1890. Special catalogue of electrotype and stereotype machinery, tools and supplies.

Has frontispiece view of the Cottrell works at Westerly, R.I.

Pamphlet in manila envelope.

ELECTROTYPING MACHINERY. Catalogue

Cabinet EE
Shelf 4
No. 67

Hoe, Robert, & Co. (Catalogue and price list, 1873).

Cloth; 13 3/4 x 11 x 3/8

ELECTROTYPING MACHINERY. Catalogue

Cabinet EE
Shelf 4
No. 120

Ostrander, J.W. Chicago, Ill. 1889. Illus. catalogue of electrotyping and stereotype machinery

Item in manila envelope

ELECTROTYPING MACHINERY CATALOGUE

Cabinet FF
Shelf 1
No. 20

Ostrander-Seymour Company, Chicago, Ill. 1900. Illustrated catalogue of improved machinery for electrotyping, stereotyping and photo-engraving. (Together with) Treatise on electrotyping By George E. Dunton. Chicago, U. S. A. Price $1.00. Treatise and catalogue are on alternate pages

Cloth; 10 x 7 in. See also FF/1/ 21/

ELECTROTYPING MACHINERY. Catalogue

Cabinet EE
Shelf 4
No. 121

Ostrander-Seymour Co., Chicago, Ill. 1912. Catalogue No.18 of improved machinery for electrotyping and stereotyping.

Paper board; $10\frac{1}{2}$ x 8 x $\frac{3}{4}$ in.

ELECTROTYPING MACHINERY. Catalogues

Cabinet EE
Shelf 4
No. 123

Ostrander-Seymour Co. Chicago, Ill. 1916. Catalogue No.20. A complete catalogue of improved machinery for electrotyping and stereotyping. Tools, accessories and supplies. Manufactured by The Ostrander-Seymour Co.

Cloth; $10\frac{3}{4}$ x 8 x 7/8 in.

ELECTROTYPING MACHINERY. Catalogue

Cabinet EE
Shelf 4
No. 73

Wax machinery, moulding presses, melting furnaces and backing-up machines, plate planing and shaving machines, routing machinery and bits, punches, chisels, brushes, etc. R. Hoe & Company. New York - London. n.d.

Separate numbered bulletins bound together

Half morocco loose leaf binder; $8\frac{1}{2}$ x $12\frac{1}{4}$ in.

ELECTROTYPING MACHINERY. Catalogue

Cabinet EE
Shelf 5
No. 15

Wesel Manuf'g. Co. Brooklyn, N.Y. Catalogue of electrotyping, stereotyping, and photo-engraving machinery and materials.

Paper; $9\frac{3}{4}$ x 7 in.

ELECTROTYPING MACHINERY. Catalogue

Cabinet EE
Shelf 5
No. 14

Wesel Manufacturing Company. 72-80 Cranberry Street. Brooklyn, and N.Y. City. n.d. Electrotyping machinery. Moulding presses, case-making machinery, shavers, planers, bevelers, saws, trimmers, routers, and everything for the foundry.

Paper; $8\frac{1}{2}$ x 12 in.

ELECTROTYPING MACHINERY. Catalogue

Cabinet EE
Shelf 5
No. 17

Wesel Manufacturing Co., F. Catalogue of electrotyping, stereotyping and photo-engraving machinery and materials. Brooklyn, n.d. (1897).

Same as EE/5/16, with additional pages showing machines with electric motors attached to platemaking machinery.

This was the desk book of H.L. Bullen when manager of the F. Wesel Mfg. Co.

(cont'd)

ELECTROTYPING MACHINERY. Catalogue (con'd)

Cabinet | Boards; 10 x 7 in. Hand lettering on cover; "Henry L. Bullen".
Shelf
No.

ELECTROTYPING MACHINERY. Catalogue

Cabinet EE | Wesel Manufacturing Co. F. Catalogue of electrotyping, stereotyping...machinery and materials. New York, n.d. (1897).
Shelf 5
No. 17

Same as EE/5/16 which has additional pages showing machines with electric motors attached to platemaking machinery.

Cloth; 10 x 6 3/4 x ½ in.

ELECTROTYPING MACHINERY. Catalogue

Cabinet EE | Wesel Mfg. Co., 1902. Catalogue of electrotyping ...machinery and materials. Brooklyn.
Shelf 5
No. 19

Cloth; 10 x 7 x 1¼ in.

ELECTROTYPING MACHINERY. Catalogue

Cabinet EE | Wesel Manufacturing Co., F. Catalogue of machinery and appliances used in electrotyping, photo-engraving, stereotyping.[Compiled by Henry L. Bullen]. Brooklyn 1904.
Shelf 5
No. 22

Note: "Prepared entirely by H.L. Bullen, manager of the company. Frist complete platemaking machinery catalogue ever issued".

Cloth; 10½ x 7½ in.

ELECTROTYPING MACHINERY. Catalogue

Cabinet EE | Wesel Mfg. Co. Catalogue of electrotyping machinery and appliances... Brooklyn, N.Y. October I, 1906.
Shelf 5
No. 23

Paper; 10¼ x 7 in.

ELECTROTYPING MACHINERY Catalogue

Cabinet EE | Wesel Manfacturing Company. Complete price list of electrotyping machinery, tools, and appliance. July I, 1907, also 1909.
Shelf 5
No. 24

Items in manila envelope.

ELECTROTYPING MACHINERY. Catalogue

Cabinet EE | Wesel Manufacturing co. Frist supplement to the catalogue of electrotyping machinery, tools and appliances. Brooklyn, N.Y. March, 1911.
Shelf 5
No. 28

Has complete price list of first supplement inserted.

Paper; 10 x 7¼ in.

ELECTROTYPING MACHINERY. Catalogue

Cabinet EE | Western Engravers Supply Co. (Successors to Carl Schraubstadter, Jr.) Illustrated catalogue and price list of machinery and supplies for...electrotypers...manufactured by The Western Engravers Supply Company. St. Louis, Mo. 1894.
Shelf 5
No. 29

Two copies, one copy interleaved.

Both items in manila envelope.

ELECTROTYPOGRAPH

See Composing Machines: Turpain.

ELECTROTYPOGRAPH SETTING AND CASTING MACHINES

Cabinet FF | See COMPOSING MACHINES.-Single Types...
Shelf 6
No. 18

ELIOT, JOHN

Cabinet S | (The) Apostle of the Indians. By James De Normandie, in The New England Magazine, Nov., 1896. Facsimiles, reduced sizes of pages of some books used for teaching the English language to the Indians.
Shelf 5
No. 12

Bound in with "Pamphlets and excerpts relating to typography", item 19.

ELIOT, JOHN

Cabinet F | Bible of 1663. A leaf from a copy of the Bible the first American, translated into the Indian language by John Eliot, and printed at Cambridge. With an account of the translator and the two printers who reproduced the book, by George Parker Winship, Boston, 1929.
Shelf 1
No. 9

Stamped cloth; 7-7/8 x 6 x¼ in.

ELIOT, JOHN

Cabinet | (Die) Indianer-Bibel des John Eliot. [Bibliographical account with facsimile].
Shelf
No.

Article on p.26 of the "Philobiblon", 5 Jahrgang, heft I, 1932.

ELIOT, JOHN Jr.

Cabinet | See Imprints, United States.
Shelf
No.

ELIOT'S COURT PRESS.

Cabinet 75 | Decorative blocks and initials.
Shelf 2
No. 3

See Plomer, Henry R. Eliot's Court Press.

ELIOTS COURT PRESS

Cabinet 75 | See Early Printing in England. [Literature of] Eliots etc.
Shelf 2
No. 2

ELIZABETH DAILY JOURNAL

Cabinet A | One hundred and fiftieth anniversary issue, 1779-1929.
Shelf 2
No. 67

Includes facsimile of the first issue.

Buckram; 22½ x 17-5/8 x ½ in.

ELLENBOG, ULRICH von

Cabinet U | Bibographical sketch of von Ellenbog; paper on the press of St. Ulrich at Augsburg.
Shelf 5
No. 38

see PROCTOR, ROBERT. Bibliographicl essays...London, 1905, pp.73-88

ELLERMAN, HARMS & COMPANY

Cabinet AA Shelf 3 No. 35

See Plants, Printing. Holland.

ELLIOTT, CHARLES WYLLYS

Cabinet R Shelf 5 No. 148

(Some) Old Almanacs. By C. W. Elliot: An excerpt from The Galaxy, Jan. 1877.
Comments on the recorded contents of early Almanacs; with some historical references.

Excerpt 6 in volume "Chap Books, Almanacs, Annuals, etc.

ELLIOT, HENRY RUTHERFORD

Cabinet S Shelf 4 No. 120

Most popular book in the world: Curious facts about the printing, sale and distribution of the Bible. By Henry Rutherford Elliot. An excerpt from The Century Magazine, July, 1905.
Item 5 in volume "About the Bible: Excerpts from Magazines."

Half morocco; 10¼ x 6-7/8 in.

ELLIS, ALEXANDER JOHN

Cabinet L Shelf 2 No. 42

Paleotype, or the systematic notation of all spoken sounds by means of the ordinary printing types. London, 1868.

Advance pamphlet. Includes author's A.L.S.

Boards; 8¾ x 5¾ in.

ELLIS, ALEXANDER J.

Cabinet L Shelf 2 No. 44

Specimen of phonetic types from the foundry of Vincent anf James Figgins, in use at Mr. Alex J. Ellis's Phonetic Printing Office. London, 1849. Brochure.

Item C in book with binder's title "Various attempts at alphabets".

ELLIS, F. H. S.

Cabinet T Shelf 5 No. 112

(A) Royal Craft: Being notes on the history and progress of printing. London, n.d. Illus.

Cloth; 6⅝ x 4½ x 3/8 in.

ELLIS, GEORGE H.

Cabinet 61 Shelf 1 No. 6

House of George H. Ellis, Boston. A modern and model printing house. Its modest birth, vigorous growth and success.

Illus. article in "The Paper World", vol.23, No.4, Oct., 1891, p.1

ELLIS, GEORGE H.

Cabinet S Shelf 6 No. 6

See Plants, Printing. United States.

ELLIS, GEORGE H. and COMPANY

Cabinet EE Shelf 1 No. 43

See SPECIMEN BOOKS, TYPES. Printers.

ELLIS, JOHN ALEXANDER

Cabinet II Shelf 4 No. 30

Fonetic printing illustrated; or specimens of fonotips, lists of fonts, type-founders bil, plans of cases, etc., being the third appendix to A.J. Elisez "Esensalz ov Fonetics".

Bound in with two other items relating to phonetics.

Cloth; 9 x 6¼ x 3/8 in.

ELLIS, RICHARD W.

Cabinet Shelf No.

Georgian Press

see IMPRINTS, United States. Georgian Press...

ELM TREE PRESS.

Cabinet Shelf No.

See Imprints, United States.

ELPHINSTON, JAMES

Cabinet II Shelf 3 No. 64

Propriety ascertained in her picture; or, Inglish speech and spelling rendered mutual guides... London: Printed by Jon Walter. 1786. (2 vols. in one)

John Walter printer publisher was founder of the London Times.

Half morocco; 11-3/8 x 9 x 2¼ in.

ELROD RULE AND SLUG CASTER (see)

Cabinet FF Shelf 3 No. 55

TYPE FOUNDING MACHINERY. Elrod...

ELSON, A.W.

Cabinet MM Shelf 6 No. 61

Reproductive processes of the graphic arts. A brief description of relief, intaglio, and planographic printing processes..."Typographic Technical Series" Part IV, No.29. United Typothetae of America, 1920.

Cloth; 8 x 5 in.

ELSTOB, ELIZABETH.

Cabinet F Shelf 4 No. 3

English-Saxon homily on the birth-day of St. Gregory....By Elizabeth Elslob. Engraved frontispiece by S. Gribelin.

Imprint: London. Printed by W. Bowyer, 1709.

Leather; 8¾ x 5½ x ⅝ in.

ELSTON PRESS, THE.

Cabinet Shelf No.

See Imprints, United States. Elston Press.

ELTON, CHARLES I.

Cabinet U Shelf 3 No. 103

Christina of Sweden and her books.

Bibliographical account.

See vol. I, p.5 in Bibliographica...London, 1895-1897.

ELTON, C. and M.

Cabinet U Shelf 3 No. 103

Little books [Illus. biblio-historical account of miniature books].

See vol. 3, p.197 "Bibliographica"... London, 1895-1897.

ELTON'S FUNNY ALMANAC

Cabinet 80 Shelf 1 No. 69

New York, 1846. Elton's Funny Almanack. Elton, Publisher and Engraver, 18 Division St.

Item in manila envelope.

ELTVILLE

Cabinet W Shelf 2 No. 1

See Printing, Historical, Germany

ELY, MARGARET (Compiler)

Cabinet NN Shelf 3 No. 34

Newspaper editors, some great America. White Plains, N.Y. and New York City. 1916.

"The bibliographies of this series were prepared as graduation requirements at The Library School at the University of Wisconsin".

Bound with other items.

Half morocco; $7\frac{1}{8}$ x $5\frac{1}{4}$ in.

ELY, RICHARD T.

Cabinet NN Shelf 5 No. 19

(The) Printers and Mr. Childs (title missing). George W. Childs in his relations to his employees. By Richard T. Ely. [Also]: Celebration of the birthday of George W. Childs, May 12, 1888. Account taken from the "Printers' Circular". Philadelphia.

Half morocco; 6 x $4\frac{3}{4}$ in.

ELYAN, KASPAR

Cabinet Y Shelf 4 No. 4

(Note on the Elyan press at Breslau, 1475-1482)

see

VOULLIÉME, ERNST. (Die) Deutschen drucker des fünfzehnten jahrhunderts...p.27

ELZEVIER, ABRAHAM.

Cabinet 39 Shelf No.

See Early Printing in Holland. Leyden, 1683-1712.

ELZEVIER, DANIEL

Cabinet W Shelf 5 No. 93

Brieven van Daniel Elsevier aan Nicolaas Heinsius 9 Mai 1675-1 July 1679. Voorwoord bei W.R. Veder, Amsterdam, Dec., 1889.

Reprinted from the Journal of the Netherland Society of Publishers.

The original Elzevier letters are in the University Library at Utrecht.

Half morocco; $9\frac{1}{2}$ x 6 in.

ELZEVIER, DANIEL, EX OFFICINA ELSEVIRIANA

Cabinet 39 Shelf 1 No. 20

Catalogus librorum qui in bibliopolio Danielis Elsevirii venales extant. Printer mark. Amstelodami, Ex Officina Elseviriana. 1674.

Lists of works of theology, law and medicine. Lists of Italian, Spanish, and German works.

Vellum; $5\frac{1}{2}$ x $3\frac{1}{4}$ x $1\frac{1}{2}$ in. See Pieters, Annales Elzevirienne, p.LV.

ELZEVIER, DANIEL

Cabinet AA Shelf 4 No. 6.01

(Sojourn and business relations in England of D. Elzevier. Notations from official records.)

Daniel Elzeviers betrekkingen met Engeland.

Excerpt from some book or publication unidentified. circa 1910. Dutch text.

In envelope.

ELZEVIER, DANIEL

Cabinet 39 Shelf No.

See also
Early Printing in Holland. Leyden [v.d.]
" also " " " Amsterdam [v.d.]
Ex Officina Elzeviriana.

ELZEVIER, ISAAC

Cabinet 39 Shelf 1 No. 3

See Early Printing in Holland. Leyden, 1622. Isaac Elzevier.

ELZEVIER, JEAN

Cabinet W Shelf 3 No. 27

(Une) Lettre [1660 or 1661] du pere Pierre LeMayne a Jean Elzevier. Avec facsimile in phototypie. Publiée et annotée par H. Chérot. Extrait du Bulletin de la Societé historique de Langes, 1891.

Item G in vol. with binder's title "Eight French typographic items."

ELZEVIER, JOHANN

Cabinet AA Shelf 3 No. 29

De drukkerij van Johannes Elzevier in 1658. Door Mr. Ch. Enschedé [Haarlem, 1896].

A bibliographical critical account of the Johann Elzevier Press.

Linen; 8 x $5\frac{1}{2}$ in.

ELZEVIER, JOHANNES

Cabinet W Shelf 5 No. 72

De drukkerij van Johannes Elzevier in 1685. Door Ch. Enschede.

Concluding chapter in "Klaasesz Aankondiger", Hengelo, Holland. n.d. probably 1899.

Item in manila envelope.

ELZEVIER, JOHAN [Widow of]

Cabinet 39 Shelf 1 No. 25

See Early Printing in Holland. Amsterdam, 1663. Johann Elzevir.

ELZEVIER, LUDWIG

Cabinet 39. Shelf No.

See Early Printing in Holland. Amsterdam [v.d.] Ludwig and Daniel.

ELZEVIER, LUDWIG AND DANIEL.

Cabinet 39 Shelf 1 No.

See Early Printing in Holland. Amsterdam, [v.d.] Ludwig and Daniel Elzevier.

ELZEVIER, PETER

Cabinet 39 Shelf 2 No. 47

Scaligerana, Prima, nusquam antehac edita, cum praefatione T. Fabri. Ultrajecti, apud Petrum Elzevirium, 1670.
Peter Elzevier was not a printer, he was a publisher and could not have printed the above book. Probably a false Elzevier.
See Willems, re "False Elzevier."

Calf; 6½ x 4 x 5/8 in.

ELZEVIER FAMILY OF PRINTERS

Cabinet W Shelf 5 No. 73

Histoire et annales typographiques. Par Alphonse Willems. Bruxelles, 1880. 2 vols.

Half morocco; 10½ x 7-3/4 in.

ELZEVIER BIBLIOGRAPHY

Cabinet W Shelf 5 No. 103

See Bibliography. Elzevier.

ELZEVIER DYNASTY OF PRINTERS.

Stack Shelf Number

See Bullen, Henry Lewis. Elzevier dynasty of printers, The.

ELZEVIER FAMILY OF PRINTERS

Cabinet Y Shelf 2 No. 23

(Life and works of the Elzevier family, 1540-1669 Brief account)

See LORCK, CARL B. Handbuch der geschichte...Leipzig, 1882-1883 (part 1, 228-249)

ELZEVIER EDITIONS

Cabinet W Shelf 5 No. 106

See Early printing in Holland, Lit. of Nouvelles etudes ... Par F. Berghman. Stockholm, 1897.

ELZEVIER FAMILY OF PRINTERS

Cabinet W Shelf 5 No. 37

Annales de l'imprimerie des Elsévier, ou histoire de leur famille et de leurs éditions. Par Charles Pieters. A. Gand, 1851.

Half morocco; 9¼ x 6¼ in.

ELZEVIER FAMILY OF PRINTERS

Cabinet AA Shelf 5 No. 26

See Lundahl, Carl. Pro Novitate... Stockholm, 1898. Swedish text.

ELZEVIER EDITIONS, False.

Cabinet W Shelf 5 No. 31

Motteley, Charles. Apercu sur les erreurs de la bibliographie spéciale des Elzéviers ... avec quelques découvertes curieuse sur la typographie Hollandaise et Belge du 17e siecle. Paris, 1847.
An attempt to distinguish the false from the true Elzeviers by their typography.

3/4 Morocco; 7 x 4½ in.

ELZEVIER FAMILY

Cabinet U Shelf 4 No. 45

Bibliography Elzevieriana: A paper read before the Library Association at Glasgow, Sept. 1888. By Richard Copley Christie. London, 1888.

Cloth; 8-3/4 x 7 in.

ELZEVIER FAMILY OF PRINTERS

Cabinet W Shelf 5 No. 32

Recherches historiques, généalogiques et bibliographiques sur les Elsevier. Par A. De Reume. Bruxelles, 1847. Lithograph portrait of Mathieu Elsevier.

Half morocco; 10 x 6¼ in.

ELZEVIER PRESS, THE

Cabinet W Shelf 5 No. 90

Catalogue complete "Des Republiques" imprimées en Holland in-24. Avec des remarques sur les diverse éditions. Par De La Faye. Nouvelle édition revue, corrigee et augmentee. Par J.Chenu. Paris, 1854.

Item in manila envelope

ELZEVIER FAMILY OF PRINTERS

Cabinet S Shelf 5 No. 50.01

(The) Elseviers, famous Dutch printers. By Baroness Althea Salvador.
Biography, with genealogy. Excerpt from New Science Review, Jan., 1895.

In envelope.

ELZEVIER FAMILY OF PRINTERS

Cabinet W Shelf 5 No. 73

Willems, Alphonse: Histoire et annales typographiques. Par Alphonse Willems. Bruxelles, 1880. 2 vols.
"This is without doubt one of the best guides for those making collections of Elzevier editions."

Half morocco; 10½ x 7¾ in.

ELZEVIER PRESS, THE

Cabinet W Shelf 5 No. 103

Catalogue d'une collection unique de volumes imprimés par les Elzevier et divers typographes Hollandais du XVIIe siècle. Rédigé par Eduard Rahir. Précédé d'un avant-propos par M. Ferd. Brunetière, et d'une lettre de M. Alphonse Willems. Paris, 1896.
Has facsimiles of ornaments, devices, etc.

Half morocco; 9¾ x 6½ x 1½ in.

ELZEVIER FAMILY OF PRINTERS

Cabinet S Shelf 5 No. 4

Famous Dutch printers. By Baroness Althea Salvador. An excerpt from New Science Review. Jan. 1895.
Biographical account.

Item 21 in collection "Various printers and their plants; Excerpts from magazines, I."

ELZEVIR FAMILY

See also

Imprints.

ELZEVIER PRESS, THE

Cabinet U Shelf 4 No. 44

Complete catalogue of all the publications of the Elzevier Presses at Leyden, Amsterdam, the Hague, and Utrecht, with introduction, notes, and an appendix containing a list of...forgeries or anonymous publications generally attributed to these presses. By Edmund Goldsmid. 3 vols. [Bound together in 1 vol.]. Edinburgh 1888.

Half morocco; 8½ x 5-7/8 x 2-1/8 in.

ELZEVIR PRESS

Cabinet DD Shelf 2 No. 47

(The) Elzevirs and their work. With portrait of Daniel Elzevir. Short history of the Elzevirs. Mergenthaler Linotype Company. 29 Ryerson Street, Brooklyn, New York 1920.
The above brief history in specimen book of the Linotype showing the Elzevir No.3 Series.

Cloth; $12\frac{1}{2}$ x $9\frac{1}{2}$ x $\frac{1}{2}$ in.

ELZEVIER PRESS, The

Cabinet U Shelf 4 No. 50

Handlist of the productions of the Elzevier Presses at Leyden, Amsterdam, the Hague and Utrecht, with references to Willems, Berghman, Rahir and other bibliographers. By H. B. Copinger. London, 1927.

Cloth; 10 x 6-1/8 x 3/4 in.

ELZEVIER PRESS, THE

Cabinet W Shelf 5 No. 104

(List of books printed by the elzrviers. Reproduction of catalogue printed at Leyden in 1628. With introduction by Ernest Kelchner. Paris, 1880)
Catalogus librorum officinae Elzevirianae...Lugduni, Batavorum, ex officina Elzeviriana, 1628.

Parchment; $7\frac{1}{2}$ x 5 in. Item in manila envelope

ELZEVIER PRESS

Cabinet W Shelf 5 No. 38 Folder

Notice sur une collection unique de volumes imprimes par les Elzevier et divers typographes Hollandais du 17e siecle en vente chez D. Morgand, Paris, 1896. Pamphlet.

In folder labelled The Elzevier family of printers. Various pamphlets and excerpts.

ELZEVIER PRESS

Cabinet W Shelf 3 No. 114

Notice sur une collection unique de volumes imprimes par Les Elzevier et divers typographes hollandais du 17e siècle. En vente chez D. Morgand. Paris, 1896. Pamphlet.

Item 7 in vol. with binder's title "Pamphlets Relating to Books - I. Bound, 1932."

ELZEVIER PRESS

Cabinet W Shelf 5 No. 38 Folder

Premiér edition des maximes de la Rochefocauld imprimée par les Elzevier in 1664. Notice bibliographic. Par Alphonse Willens. Bruxelles, 1879. Pamphlet.

In folder labelled The Elzevier family of printers. Pamphlets and excerpts.

ELZEVIER TYPES

Cabinet EE Shelf 2 No. 73

(Elzevier types said to have been cast from original matrices).
See SPECIMEN BOOKS, TYPES. Printers'. France. Claye, Jules. Paris, 1875.

ELZEVIERS

Cabinet W Shelf 5 No. 49

See Walther, Ch. Fr. (Les) Elzevier de la Bibliotheque Imperiale Publique de St. Petersbourg ...St. Petersbourg, 1864.

ELZEVIRS

See also Imprints.

EMBLEMS

Cabinet 69 Shelf 1 No. 10

Alciati, Andrea. Clarissimi viri D. Emblematum libellus ... [Printer mark].
Imprint: Parisiis. Apud Christianum Wechelum sub scuto Basilieni in vico iacobeo: & sub Pegaso in vico Bellouacensi. M.D.XLII.

Half morocco; 6-1/8 x 4 x ½ in. Brunet 1, 147

EMBLEMS

Cabinet 69 Shelf 1 No. 18

Alciati, D. A. Emblemata. Lugd. Apud Guliel. Rovilium. 1550. Excudebat Mathias Bonhomme.

Vellum; 7 x 4-3/4 x 3/4 in.

EMBLEMS

Cabinet 2 Shelf 1 No. 5

Alciatus, Andreae : Omnia emblemata: cum commentariis...per Claudium Minoem. Editio tertia. Antverpiae, ex officina Christophori Plantini. 1581.

Embossed vellum over boards; 6-3/4 x 4½ x 1-7/8 in.

EMBLEMS.

Cabinet T Shelf 4 No. 19

Andrea Alciati and his book of emblems: a biographical and bibliographical study. By Henry Green. London, 1872. Illus.

Stamped cloth; $8\frac{3}{4}$ x $5\frac{3}{4}$ x 1 in.

EMBLEMS

Cabinet 2 Shelf 1 No. 46

Bivero, Petri. Sacrum sanctuarium crucis et patientiae cruciferorum emblematicis.... Antverpiae ex officina Plantiniana: Balthasarus Moreti. M.DC.XXXIV. Illus with copperplate engravings.

Calf; $8\frac{1}{4}$ x $6\frac{1}{2}$ x $2\frac{1}{2}$ in. Brunet 1, 955.

EMBLEMS

Cabinet K Shelf 2 No. 24

Cats, Jacob and Robert Farlie.
See
LEIGHTON, JOHN. Moral emblems of all ages and nations...London, 1860

EMBLEMS

Cabinet G Shelf 4 No. 28.01

Dwiggins, W. A., 1935
see
DWIGGINS, W. A. Emblems. a bakers' dozen...

EMBLEMS

Cabinet T Shelf 3 No. 46

Facsimile reprint of Whitney's choice of emblems. Edited by Henry Green, London, 1866.

Cloth; 10 x 7-3/4 in.

EMBLEMS.

Cabinet E Shelf 4 No. 27

Faxardo, Didaco Saavedra. Idea principis, Christiano, politici symbolis 101 expressa. Paris, Fr. Leonardum 1660.
Following deication: Picture of a printing press, and an account of the invention of printing addressed to the reader.

Vellum; $5\frac{1}{4}$ x 3 x 1 in.

EMBLEMS.

Cabinet E Shelf 4 No. 97

Faxarda, Diego Saavedra. Idea de un principe politico y christiano ... En Valencia, por Vicente Cabrera. 1695.

Boards; 8¼ x 5½ x 1½ in.

EMBLEMS Literature of

Cabinet K Shelf 4 No. 6

(Alciati, Andrea. Bibliographical study of the Alciati emblems, 1531 to 1781).

See Duplessis, Georges. Livres a gravures du 16^{e} siecle...Paris, 1884

EMBLEMS Literature of

Cabinet T Shelf 3 No. 2

Paradin, Claude, account of his work of emblems, and engravings from.

In DIBDIN'S Bibliographical Decameron...London, 1817, vol.1, pp.264-70

EMBLEMS.

Cabinet E Shelf 2 No. 32

Icones, id est verae imagines virorum doctrina simul et pietate illustrium ... additis eorundem vitae et operae descriptionibus ... Theodore Beze auctore. Geneva. Joannem Laonium. 1580.

Boards; 8¾ x 6¼ x ¾ in. Brunet 1,842.

EMBLEMS Literature of

Cabinet K Shelf 1 No. 25

Bilder schriften der renaissance: Hieroglyphie und emblematik in ihren beziehungen und fortwirkungen. von Ludwig Volkmann. Leipzig, 1923. Illus.

The relative function and adaptation of hieroglyphics and emblems in decoration.

Cloth; 12½ x 9¾ x 3/8 in.

EMBLEMS Literature of

Cabinet U Shelf 5 No. 24

Plantin's four emblem-books of 1562, 1564, 1565, and 1566.

see POLLARD, A.W. Fine Books... London, 1912, pp.275, 280

EMBLEMS

Cabinet K Shelf 2 No. 24

Moral emblems of all ages and nations, from Jacob Cats and Robert Farlie. With illustrations freely rendered from designs found in their works. By John Leighton. The whole translated and edited by Richard Pigot, London, 1860.

Engravings by Leighton, Dalziel, Jackson, etc.

Cloth, embossed; 10-7/8 x 8 in.

EMBLEMS. Literature of

Cabinet 75 Shelf 1 No. 11

Daniel and the emblem literature. Emblem books of the 16th and 17th centuries. A paper read by Gilbert R. Redgrave, before the Bibliographical Society, February 21,1910.

In Trans. Biblio. Soc., Vol. XI, 1909-1911. pp. 39-58.

EMBLEMS OF PRINTING

Cabinet Shelf No.

See ALLEGORIES OF PRINTING.

" PICTURES, ALLEGORIES OF PRINTING.

EMBLEMS.

Cabinet 69 Shelf 1 No. 1

Perriere, Guillaume. Paris, 1539. Le theatre des bons engins, auquel sont contenuz cent emblems moraulx. De l'imprimerie de Denys Ianot, imprimeur & libraire. Paris, 1539.

Morocco; 6½ x 4¼ x ½ in.

EMBLEMS. Literature of

Cabinet 75 Shelf 2 No. 4

First Paris edition of the Emblems of Alciat, 1534. By Eustace F. Bosanquet, for the Bibliographical Society, London, March, 1924. Illus.

In Trans. Biblio. Soc. Vol. IV, 1923-1924. pp. 326-331. "The Library."

EMBOSSED BOOKS

Cabinet II Shelf 6 No. 12

Revised braille-- grade one and a half. Books embossed, or selected for embossing in. Commission on Uniform Type for the Blind, Baltimore, MD. 1919

Item in manila envelope.

EMBLEMS

Cabinet 39 Shelf 1 No. 4

Schoonhovius, Emblemata ... Partim Moralia, partim etiam Civilia. Cum latiori eorunden, ejusdem Auctoris interpretatione ... Lugduni Batavorum, Ex Officina Elzeviriana. [Bonaventura and Abraham]. Anno 1626. Copperplate engravings.

Vellum, 8¼ x 6¼ x 1-3/8 in. Pieters, 74, 13

EMBLEMS, LITERATURE OF

Cabinet K Shelf 4 No. 1 & 2

Lost language of symbolism...

See Bayley, Harold, Lost language of symbolism...London, 1912 (2 vols.)

EMBOSSED TYPES

Cabinet II Shelf 6 No. 4

Specimen of printing with embossed types. Paris, 1819.

See PRINTING FOR THE BLIND. Guillé -- Notice historique...

EMBLEMS

Cabinet 2 Shelf 1 No. 45

Symbolis heroicis. Libri IX. Auctore Silvestro Petrasancta, Romano, E. Soc. Ieusu.
Imprint: Antverpiae, ex Officina Plantiniana: Balthasaris Moreti. M.DC.XXXIV.

Title page engraved by Galle after design by Rubens.

Morocco; 8¼ x 6-3/8 x 1-5/8 in.

EMBLEMS Literature of

Cabinet RR Shelf 3 No. 41

New light on the renaisance, displayed in contemporary emblems. By Harold Bayley. Illustrated with reproductions of numerous emblems. London, 1909.

Cloth; 10¼ x 7¼ in.

EMBOSSING

Cabinet LL Shelf 4 No. 3

Embossing in celluloid (in colors). Beautiful example of.

See Thompson Co. J. Walter. Advertising Media...1897.

EMBOSSING

Cabinet II Shelf 6 No. 19

Experimental sheets embossed by H.L. Bullen... demonstrating the practicability of embossing sheets on both sides simultaneously. Work done on a Colts Armory, with electric heated plate holder, from flat plate, in the printing department of the American Type Founders Co., Jersey City, N.J. in 1917. At request of United States War Dept.

Items in manila envelope.

EMBOSSING

Cabinet Shelf No.

See also cards with following sub-head:

PRINTING FOR THE BLIND.

EMERSON, EDWIN

Cabinet S Shelf 4 No. 68

(The) Gutenberg Bible on vellum in the Vollbehr Collection: An authentic story of the choicest book of Christendom, told anew by Edwin Emerson. New York, 1928. Illus. portrait. Bibliographical essay.

Half morocco; 9 x 6 in.

EMBOSSING

Cabinet RR Shelf 6 No. 5

Goffering (or) gaufering

See BOOKBINDING. Goffering...

EMBOSSING MACHINES. Catalogue

Cabinet EE Shelf 4 No. 37

Fuchs & Lang Mfg. Co.,...n.d. Catalogue and price list of litho supplies.

Cloth, stamped; 12¾ x 9¾ x 3/8 in.

EMERSON, EDWIN

Cabinet QQ Shelf 5 No. 12

Hoover and his times. Looking back through the years...Illustrated by contemporary cartoons. New York, 1932.

Presentation copy.

Cloth; 8½ x 5-5/8 x 1½ in.

EMBOSSING

Cabinet MM Shelf 6 No. 1

How it is done. By Robert H. Dippy. New York, Oswald Publishing Company, 1910.

Item 4 in book with binder's title "Various items on printing". Bound 1919.

EMBOSSING MACHINES. Catalogue

Cabinet EE Shelf 4 No. 41

Golding & Co. Boston, Mass. 1897. Catalogue and price list of machinery and tools for printing and embossing...

Booklet; 3½ x 6 in. Item in manila envelope.

EMERSON, WILLIAM A.

Cabinet K Shelf 5 No. 19

Practical instruction in the art of wood engraving...Also, a history of the art, from its origin to the present time. Illus. East Douglas (Mass.) 1876.

Cloth; 6-5/8 x 4-3/8 x ¼ in.

EMBOSSING

Cabinet MM Shelf 5 No. 73

Inland Printer Company, The. A practical guide to embossing. By an expert. Chicago, 1902. Bound in with "Easy embossing on any job press". The Orro Manufacturing Company, New York City, 1910.

Cloth; 7-5/8 x 5¼ x 3/8 in.

EMBOSSING PRESSES.

Cabinet Z Shelf 3 No. 43

Presse Gauffrer, advertised and illus., with price, by Ch. Giroudot Fils, Paris. [circa, 1840].

p. 401 in "Miscellaneous Collection of French Type Specimens," ... 1829-1844.

EMERY, P.

Cabinet X Shelf 4 No. 34

Printer of French Governmental Decrees, 1704-

See items 5, 6, in book with binder's title "French legislation relating to printing. Various items. vol. II, 1640-1793".

EMBOSSING

Cabinet II Shelf 6 No. 15

Interlinear embossing presses, pictures of.

See NEW YORK INSTITUTE FOR THE EDUCATION OF THE BLIND. Seventy-eighth annual report ...New York, 1914.

EMERALD, THE

Cabinet 80 Shelf 2 No. 25

Boston, 1806

See Periodicals, United States. Emerald (To be continued weekly)...Boston

EMIN, AHMED

Cabinet OO Shelf 5 No. 32

Development of modern Turkey as measured by its press. By Ahmed Emin. New York, 1914. Columbia University "Studies in History, Economics and Public Law", Vol. 59, No. I, Whole No. 142.

Half morocco; 9¾ x 6½ x ½ in.

EMBOSSING

Cabinet II Shelf 6 No. 13

Origin and development of embossed literature... With special reference to the educational interests of the blind in the United States. By William B. Wait. New York, 1890.

Half morocco; 9 x 5¾ in.

EMERICUS DE SPIRA, JOHANNES.

Cabinet 10 Shelf 1 No. 1

See Incunabula Graduate Romanum. Venice, 1499-1500.

EMMEL, SAMUEL

Cabinet X Shelf 3 No. 13

Brief bibliographical note, with printer mark, Emmel, Strassburg, 1554-1571.

see HEITZ, PAUL. Elsässische büchermarken...p.xxiv, plate xxxv

EMMETT, BURTON

Cabinet K Shelf 6 No. 39.01

Oldest woodcut, the. By Burton Emmett. Illus. excerpt from The Century Magazine, Dec.,1923.

item 8 in bound collection with binder's title ENGRAVERS AND WOOD ENGRAVERS.

EMMEUS, JOHANN FABER

Cabinet X Shelf 3 No. 15

Biographical note, with printer mark, Emmeus, Basel, 1526-1529.

see HEITZ, PAUL. Basler büchermarken... pp.xxix, 77

EMMONS, EARL H.

Cabinet QQ Shelf 1 No. 62

Mavericks. Illustrated by the author. New York, Oswald Publishing Company, 1924.

Boards; 7-5/8 x 5 x 3/4 in.

EMPEROR, MARTIN

Cabinet U Shelf 1 No. 49

Printer at Antwerp, Martin Emperour (otherwise Martin Caesar of Keyserer)

See POLLARD, ALFRED W. Records of the English Bible...London, 1911. pp.8, 10.

EMPIRE PRESS, THE (House of Jarrolds).

Cabinet U Shelf 3 No. 73

Brief history of one hundred years. The House of Jarrolds, 1823-1923. [Established 1770]. Printed at their works, The Empire Press, St. James, Norwich,.. Illus.

Has portraits of the founder of the house and his successors.

Half morocco; 9-5/8 x 6¾ x 5/8 in.

EMPIRE STATE TYPE FOUNDRY

Cabinet Shelf No.

See Specimen Books, Types. United States. Empire State Type Foundry.

EMPIRE TYPE FOUNDRY

Cabinet Shelf No.

See Specimen Books, Types. United States.

EMPIRE TYPESETTER AND AUTOMATIC JUSTIFIER.

Cabinet FF Shelf 6 No. 72

See COMPOSING MACHINES (Single Types) Empire Typesetter...

EMPIRE TYPE SETTING MACHINE

Cabinet FF Shelf 6 No. 40

Descriptive pamphlet.

See COMPOSING MACHINES, TYPE. Empire Typesetting Machine...

EMPLOYING ELECTROTYPERS & STEREOTYPERS ASSO. of NEW YORK.

Cabinet Shelf No.

See SOCIETIES, ELECTROTYPERS.

EMPLOYING PRINTER

Cabinet 27 Shelf 2 No. 9

St. Paul, Minnisota

See PERIODICALS, PRINTING, United States. Employing Printer...

EMPLOYING PRINTERS and JOURNEYMEN OF N.Y. CITY

Cabinet JJ Shelf 4 No. 4

Scale of prices for book and job work, April 27th 1869. New York. (Booklet, paper; 5 x 3 in.)

Printed by Francis Hart & Co.

Item in manila envelope

EMPLOYING PRINTERS ASSOCIATION see

Cabinet Shelf No.

SOCIETIES, PRINTERS. United States

EMPLOYING PRINTERS CONGRESS (Pacific Coast)

Cabinet JJ Shelf 2 No. 44

see SOCIETIES, PRINTERS'. United States

EMPLOYING PRINTERS' OF KANSAS CITY

Cabinet JJ Shelf 4 No. 11

Banquet, Oct., 28, 1910.

See SOCIETIES, PRINTERS'. Employing Printers of Kansas City...

EMPLOYING PRINTERS OF THE CITY OF NEW YORK

Cabinet JJ Shelf 4 No. 17

Prices for printing recommended, in Convention, February 2, 1864 [Proof copy to be used for revision only.]

3 items in manila envelope.

ENCYCLOPAEDIA LONDINENSIS

Cabinet T Shelf 3 No. 17

Printing: Illustrated article on the art or process of impressing letters, typography; also includes brief outline of the origin of printing. Excerpt from "Encyclopaedia." London, 1825.

Half morocco; 11 x 8-3/4 x 3/8 in.

ENCYCLOPAEDIA OF LITERARY & TYPOGRAPHICAL ANECDOTES. C. H. Timperley

Cabinet T Shelf 3 No. 24

See DICTIONARIES OF PRINTING Timperley, C.H...London, 1842

ENCYCLOPEDIA

Cabinet X Shelf 5 No. 124

Diderot, Denis, Paris, 1750-

See LIBERTY OF PRINTING, France. Memoire a consulter...Paris, 1770.

ENCYCLOPEDIE...UNIVERSEL RAISONNE

Cabinet FF Shelf 3 No. 5

Articles, illustrated with many copper-plates, relating to printing and type founding. From the Encylopedie, on Dictionnaire Universel Raisonne des Connoissances Humaines. Mis en ordre par M. De Felice. Yverdon. 1778.

Boards, leather back; $10\frac{3}{4}$ x $8\frac{3}{4}$ x 5/8 in.

ENDTER FAMILY OF PRINTER-PUBLISHERS

Cabinet Y Shelf 5 No. 19

Nurnberg, 1590-1740: Endter, eine Nürnberger buchhändlerfamilie. Monographische Studie. von Friedrich Oldenbourg. München und Berlin, 1911. Portraits.

Stamped cloth; 9-5/8 x 6-3/4 x 5/8 in.

ENCYCLOPEDIA.

Cabinet I Shelf 3 No. 2

Iconographic encyclopedia of arts and sciences ... Philadelphia, 1885.

Vol. 3 only, treats of "Sculpture and Painting." Beautiful illustrations.

Stamped cloth; $10\frac{3}{4}$ x $7\frac{1}{2}$ x $1\frac{3}{4}$ in.

END PAPERS

Cabinet S Shelf 5 No. 17

Bradley, William A. End papers. [An historical and illustrated account]. Excerpt from unidentified periodical, n.d.

Item 21 in collection "Miscellaneous items relating to printing; excerpts from magazines 1918.

ENDTERS, JOHANN ANDREA

Cabinet LL Shelf 1 No. 3 & 4

See First Occurrences. Earliest extended German text book.

The book was printed by the son and successor of J.A. Endters.

ENCYCLOPEDIA BRITANNICA

Cabinet U Shelf 2 No. 81

See Smellie, William. Memoirs of the life... Edinburgh, 1811.

ENDERS, JOHANN NEPOMUK (Johann von Hradisch)

Cabinet Y Shelf 2 No. 17

(Die) Buchdruckerkunst in ihrer welthistorischen bedeutung von der erfindung bis zur gegenwart. In kurzen umrissen geschildert. Neutitschein, 1866.

Half morocco; $6\frac{1}{2}$ x 4 x 3/8 in.

ENEMIES OF BOOKS

Cabinet U Shelf 5 No. 17

Blades, William. The enemies of books. With a preface by R. Garnett. Illustrated by Louis Gunnis and H.E. Butler. London, 1896.

Stamped cloth; $11\frac{1}{2}$ x 9 x 7/8 in.

ENCYCLOPEDIAS Literature

Cabinet S Shelf 6 No. 7

(History of cyclopaedias) English cyclopaedia; a new dictionary of universal knowledge. Conducted by Charles Knight. 22 vols. London, 1861.

Review of book with above title. Excerpt from London Quarterly Review. April 1863.

Item (d) in book with binder's title "Early printed books, various excerpts and pamphlets. 1854-1931.

ENDRES, HEINRICH

Cabinet Y Shelf 3 No. 76

Frenckel, Ulrich from Hirschau. A contribution to the history of Erfurt bookbindings of the 15th century). Meister Ulrich Frenckel aus Hirschau. Ein versuche zur geschichte des Erfurter bucheinbandes in 15 jahrhundert.

pp.176-182 in Loubier, Hans (Tribute to) Buch und bucheinband...Leipzig, 1923.

ENEMIES OF BOOKS

Cabinet 18 Shelf 1 No. 8

(Worms and method for their destruction) Insekten als Bucherfeinde und ein vorschlag zu ihre bekampfung, von Paul Hennig, Charlottenburg.

In Zeitschrift für Bücherfreunde, 1910, part 2, p.331.

ENCYCLOPEDIAS OF PRINTING (see)

Cabinet Shelf No.

Dictionaries of Printing

ENDTER, GEORG.

Cabinet Shelf No.

See Biographies, bookbinders, Endter, Georg, Nurnberg, 1550.

ENESS, A.

Cabinet S Shelf 5 No. 17

Analysis of Overlays. Excerpt from "An old pressman's souvenir," 1906.

Brief account of the involved technicalities, with notices of the patents and patentees.

Item 5 in collection "Miscellanesous items relating to printing; excerpts from magazines," 1918.

ENCYCLOPEDIE FELICE'S [Excerpts from

Cabinet FF Shelf 6 No. 2

Fonderie en caracteres d'imprimerie...[Yverdun, 1775].

Has plates with views of type foundries, printing offices, copper-plate engraving, and machinery, specimens of exotic types, etc.

Half morocco; 17 x 11 in.

ENDTER, JOHANN ANDREAS.

Cabinet F Shelf 4 No. 55

See Early Printing in Germany. Nurnberg, 1762. Johann Andreas Endter.

ENGEL-HARDT, RUDOLF

Cabinet P Shelf 4 No. 33

(Der) Goldene-Schnitt in buchgewerbe. Ein regelwerk fur buchdrucker und buchgewerben... Leipzig-Reudnitz (1919) Illus.

On proportion and the use of the sector by printers

Cloth; 9 x $5\frac{3}{4}$ x 5/8 in.

ENGELMANN, GODEFROY.

Cabinet 26 Shelf 2 No. 1

See Lithography. Engelmann, Godefroy.

ENGINEERING, PRINTING

Cabinet BB Shelf 3 No. 31.02

American Cut-Cost, a catalogue and description of the Cut-Cost Printing Plant Equipment. [Catalogue] Written and printed by Henry L. Bullen, the designer of the equipments shown, and manager of the Engineering Dept., of the American Type Founders Co., Jersey City, April, 1921.

Cloth; 7¾ x 5-3/8 in.

ENGINEERING, PRINTING

Cabinet BB Shelf 3 No. 30.01

American Cut-Cost Printing Plant Equipments. Catalogues, various, illus. v.d.

In box labelled "Engineering Department, A.T.F. Co. Catalogues".

ENGINEERING, PRINTING

Cabinet LL Shelf 6 No. 20

Laying out a factory floor plan. How a printing concern planned a factory arrangement that eliminated non-productive labor - the course that work now follows through the plant. By J.W. Stannard. Excerpt from "System", Aug. 1909.

Item 10 in book with binder's title "Various items on printing shop practice". Bound 1919.

ENGINEERING, PRINTING

Cabinet MM Shelf 7 No. 19

Modern composing room equipment. Some plans and pictures. The American Type Founders Co. Cleveland, Ohio. 1910.

Buckram; 9½ x 12½ in.

ENGINEERING, PRINTING

Cabinet MM Shelf 7 No. 15

Starting a printing office: being a handbook for those about to establish themselves...By Robert C. Mallette & William H. Jackson, New York. (1902). Illus.

Cloth; 9 x 6-1/8 x ½ in.

EMGINEERING, PRINTING.

Cabinet LL Shelf 6 No. 20

Stote Franklin A. Organization of a composing room. How a system in a large printing office shows the compositors how everything is located... [Excerpt]. System, Jan. 1907.

Item 13 in book with binder's title "Various items on printing shop practice". Bound 1919.

ENGINEERING, PRINTING. (Catalogue)

Cabinet BB Shelf 3 No. 30.01

American Cut-Cost Printing Plant Equipments.... With a statement of the services rendered to printers by our Efficiency Department. American Type Founders. 1923.

These Cut-Cost Printing Plant Equipments were designed personally by Henry L. Bullen. The catalogue is also his personal work in every detail.

Paper; 10-1/8 x 6-7/8 in. Item in manila envelope.

ENGINEERING IN PRINTING PLANTS

Cabinet 27 Shelf 2 No. 26

Engineering Department begun in 1911 at suggestion of Henry Lewis Bullen, who was its manager until Dec. 1923.

see articles "COURAGEOUS EFFICIENCY" and "EFFICIENCY ENGINEERING IN PRINTING PLANTS", both by Henry Lewis Bullen) in the AMERICAN BULLETIN, April-May, 1912, p. 3.

ENGLAND

Cabinet K Shelf 4 No. 21

(Illustrated book in England, 1790-1860)

See Rumann, Arthur (Das) Illustrierte buch des 19 jahrhunderts...Leipzig, 1930. pp. 13-113.

ENGLAND

Cabinet Shelf No.

See also Early printing in England.
" also " " " [Literature of]
" " Imprints, England
" " Newspapers, England.

ENGLISH, THOMAS DUNN

Cabinet K Shelf 5 No. 2

Darley, Felix O. C. [American illustrator]. Biographical sketch. With portrait. Excerpt from Sartain's, Nov., 1850.

Item 4 in vol. with binder's title "Wood engravers and illustrators".

ENGLISH DEMOTIC ALPHABET

Cabinet II Shelf 3 No. 63

Plea for the English demotic...

See KNUDSEN, C.W. English demotic...

ENGLISH SEA PRESSES (see)

Cabinet SEA PRESSES

Shelf

No.

ENGLISHMAN, THE

Cabinet A Shelf 2 No. 16

Centenary Edition, 1821-1921, of The Englishman, Calcutta, India. Illus.

Cloth; 23 x 19

ENGRAVED BOOKS

Cabinet I Shelf 1 No. 16

Cyphers, a new book of...By S. Sympson, London (1729)

The entire book is engraved. Has list of engravers, including Wm. Caslon.

Half morocco; 7 x 4½ in.

ENGRAVED STATIONERY

Cabinet MM Shelf 7 No. 23

See American Embossing Company, The.

ENGRAVERS.

Cabinet I Shelf 3 No. 10 2 vols.

American engravers upon copper and steel. Illustrated biographical sketches of.

See STAUFFER, DAVID McNEELY. American engravers ... Part I. The Grolier Club, 1907.

ENGRAVERS

Cabinet J Shelf 3 No. 8

Antwerp engravers who were members of the Guild of St. Luke. Brief biographies, with lists of work.

See Ter Bruggen, Edouard. Histoire metallique et histoire de gravure....Anvers, 1875, pp. 113-302.

ENGRAVERS

Cabinet K Shelf 5 No. 27

(French 18th century book illustrators, wood engravers)

see

AUDIN, MARIUS. Essai sur les graveurs sur bois en France....

ENGRAVERS

Cabinet V Shelf 4 No. 25

See Renouard, Ph. Documents sur les imprimeurs, libraires, cartiers, graveurs...ayant exercè à Paris de 1450-1600.

ENGRAVERS

Cabinet J Shelf 2 No. 43

Beeler, C.H., artist and wood engraver, 1826-1899. Examples of his work as designer and engraver, with a brief manuscript biography by his grandson.

These items in one manila envelope.

This eminent engraver was employed regularly and exclusively by MacKellar, Smiths & Jordan, type founders, for 50 years. All the cuts advertised by McK. Smiths & J. in their type specimen books were designed and engraved by Beeler. The series of

ENGRAVERS

Cabinet K Shelf 5 No. 28

(Japanese wood engravers) Les estampeurs Japonais, et les graveurs de Yédo.

see

BUSSET, MAURICE. (La) Technique moderne du bois gravé...Paris (1925), p. 51.

ENGRAVERS.

Cabinet I Shelf 3 No. 1

Sertain, John. his portrait, with brief biographical note.

Item 5 in vol. with binder's title: "Various Engravers and About Engravers."

ENGRAVERS (cont'd)

Cabinet J Shelf 2 No. 43

seals of the U.S. and foreign countries and the flags to be printed in the various proper colors were done by Beeler.

The engraved wood cuts of Beeler are preserved in this Library.

ENGRAVERS

Cabinet K Shelf 1 No. 2

Liste alphabetic d'une petite collection de portraits... Par J. T. Bodel Nyenhuis, Leyden, 1836-68.

List of portraits of printers, engravers, etc., with date of birth and date of the subject, and the painter and engraver of the portraits.

Boards, cloth back; 10-5/8x9¼ x ½ in.

ENGRAVERS

Cabinet 26 Shelf 2 No. 15

Schwinds Freischütz-Radierungen. von Otto Erich Deutsch. (The engravings for the "Freischutz" by Moritz von Schwind, 1824)

Illus. article in Jahrbuch IX, 1935, p. 81, Deutscher Verein für Buchwesen und Schrifttum.

ENGRAVERS

Cabinet U Shelf 3 No. 96

Cary, John, engraver, map, chart and print-seller and globe maker, 1754 to 1835...By Sir Herbert George Fordham. Cambridge, 1925.

Cloth; 9 x 6-7/8 in.

ENGRAVERS.

Cabinet I Shelf 3 No. 4

Masters of engraving: All schools, 14th to 19th centuries.

See WILLSHIRE, WILLIAM HUGHES. Ancient prints ... London, 1877.

ENGRAVERS

Cabinet K Shelf 6 No. 39.01

Shaw, Henry, London, 1834.

see

MANUSCRIPTS Literature of. Catalogue of the Arundal Manuscripts...

ENGRAVERS

Cabinet J Shelf 2 No. 42

DeMeulemeester, J.-C. Bruges, 1771-1836

see

BIOGRAPHIES, ENGRAVERS. DeMeulemeester...

ENGRAVERS

Cabinet J Shelf 3 No. 17

Names of great masters of engraving: With account of their lives and works.

See CHAPIN, WILLIS O. Masters and Masterpieces of engraving...[Index].

ENGRAVERS, BIOGRAPHIES OF

Cabinet Shelf No.

See Biographies, Engravers.

ENGRAVERS

Cabinet J Shelf 3 No. 22

Dictionary of engravers and their works, being an alphabetical list of the principal engravers and etchers.

See SLATER, J. HERBERT. Engravings and their value...New York, 1929. pp.85-704.

ENGRAVERS

Cabinet V Shelf 6 No. 36

Ostade, Adrian van, 1610-1685. Les eaux-fortes de. An essay by P.M., n.d. no place. Translates by G.R. Bullen.

Items in one manila envelope.

ENGRAVERS AND PRINTERS MACHINERY CO.

Cabinet EE Shelf 4 No. 36

Sag Harbor, New York.

see

PRINTING EQUIPMENTS. Catalogue.

ENGRAVERS' MONOGRAMS

Cabinet I Shelf 1 No. 23

Collection and explanation of the several marks of engravers, etc.

See pp.73-162 SCULPTURA-HISTORICO-TECHNICA (or) History and art of engraving ...London, 1747.

ENGRAVING

Cabinet K Shelf 2 No. 15

(Die) Altdeutsch malerei. von Curt Glaser. Munchen, 1924.

Profusely illustrated history of engraving and painting in Germany, 14th to 16th century.

Boards; 10¾ x 8¼ in.

ENGRAVING

Cabinet J Shelf 3 No. 12

Aquatint: Article by Malcolm C. Salaman.

p. 83 "Studio" Ltd. London,1917. The Graphic Arts of Great Britain...

Half morocco; 11½ x 8¼ in.

ENGRAVERS' MONOGRAMS

Cabinet I Shelf 1 No. 18

Dictionnaire des monogrammes...Paris, 1750.

See CHRIST, J. FRED. Dictionnaire des monogrammes, chiffres...Traduit de l'allemand [par Sellius]. Paris, 1750.

ENGRAVING.

Cabinet I Shelf 3 No. 1

American engravers, some pre-revolutionary. by Charles Allen Munn. [Excerpt from Art and Progress. Oct, 1914]. Illus.

Item 22 in vol. with binder's title:"Various Engravers and About Engravers."

ENGRAVING.

Cabinet I Shelf 3 No. 1

Art of engraving, on the. Excerpt from the "Eclectic," June, 1861.

Item 6 in vol. with binder's title: "Various Engravers and About Engravers."

ENGRAVERS' RULING MACHINES. Catalogue

Cabinet EE Shelf 5 No. 76

"Universal" Engraving machine, with specimens of the work executed on it. Klimsch & Co. Frankfort a.M.

Catalogue and price list.

Item in manila envelope.

ENGRAVING.

Cabinet I Shelf 3 No. 10

2 vols.

American engravers upon copper and steel. By David McNeely Stauffer. [2 vols.]

Part I - Biographical sketches, illustrated.
" II - Check list of the works of the earlier engravers.

The Grolier Club of the City of New York, 1907.

Cloth, linen back; 9-7/8 x 6½ in.

ENGRAVING.

Cabinet I Shelf 3 No. 1

Arts in black and white, by William Aspenwall Bradley. An excerpt from The Independant. Jan. 16, 1913. Illus.

Item 11 in vol. with binder's title:"Various Engravers and About Engravers."

ENGRAVERS' TOOLS

Cabinet J Shelf 5 No. 12

Pictures of engravers tools and equipment. Paris, 1740. (Nine plates).

Half morocco; 16¾ x 11 in.

ENGRAVING,

Cabinet S Shelf 5 No. 17

Anderson, Alexander, Dr., The American pioneer wood engraver: An excerpt from The American Historical Record, May, 1873.

Bound in collection "MISCELLANEOUS ITEMS RELATING TO PRINTING", item 3.

ENGRAVING.

Cabinet I Shelf 3 No. 26

[Authenticity of the date of 1418 on a wood cut. An important discovery]. Quelques mots sur la gravure sur bois au millesime de 1418. Par C. D. B. (Charles de Brou. Bruxelles, 1846. With 7 plates.

Half morocco; 11-3/8 x 8-5/8 x 3/8 in.

ENGRAVERS TOOLS AND WOODS. Catalogue.

Cabinet EE Shelf 4 No. 132

Sandberg & Co. Chicago, Ill. n.d. Illustated catalogue and price list of engravers' woods, tools and materials. Manufacturers, Sandberg & Co. 86 and 88 Dearborn Street. Chicago, Ill.

Item in manila envelope.

ENGRAVING

Cabinet J Shelf 2 No. 6

Andrews, Joseph (engraver). Report of the proceedings at the memorial meeting of the late Joseph Andrews, held at the Boston Art Club, May 17, 1873. Boston: published by the Boston Art Club.

Cloth; 9¾ x 6½ in.

ENGRAVING

Cabinet I Shelf 3 No. 1

Bank note engraving, wood and steel engraving. An excerpt from "Great Industries of the U.S." Hartford, 1872.

Item 1 in vol. with binder's title "Various Engravers and About Engravers."

ENGRAVING

Cabinet I Shelf 1 No. 19

Abregè historique de l'origine et des progrez de la gravure et des estampes en bois, et en taille douce. Par Mr. le Major H. [Humbert - de]. A Berlin, chez Haude & Spener, 1752.

Half morocco; 6½ x 3¾ in.

ENGRAVING

Cabinet I Shelf 1 No. 21

Anleitung von form und stahl-schneiden, wie buchstaben, zierrathen und alle vorkommende figuren in holz zu schneiden...nebst einer kurzen anweisung zu neuinventirten druckformen. Erfurt: Druckts und verlegts Elias Sauerlander, 1754. Illus.

Half morocco; 7 x 4¼ x ½ in.

ENGRAVING

Cabinet L Shelf 4 No. 26

Baxter's knowledge of engraving; his plates, etc.

See Lewis, C. T. Courtney. George Baxter, the picture printer...London n.d. (circa 1925) (See index).

ENGRAVING

Cabinet I
Shelf 4
No. 19

(Beginnings of illustration and printing. Many facsimiles). Die anfänge der buchdruckerkunst in bild und shrift ... Erlautert von T. O. Weigel und Dr. Ad. Zestermann. Leipzig, 1866 (2 vols.)

Embossed cloth; 15½ x 12 in.

2 vols.

ENGRAVING.

Cabinet I
Shelf 2
No. 28

British school of etching. Being a lecture delivered...by Martin Hardie, on July 8th, 1921. With a foreword by Sir Frank Short. Published by The Print Collectors Club. London, 1921. Illus.

Cloth; 9¾ x 7-3/8 in.

ENGRAVING.

Cabinet K
Shelf 4
No. 10

(Copper engravings, catalogue of, with brief biographical notes of engravers, 16th and 17th centuries). Katalog 26: Ornamentstiche. H. Gilhofer & H. Ranschburg, Luzerne. n. d. Catalogue, pp. 18, with 27 plates.

Another item, catallgue XV of "Precious ornament prints of the 16th to 18th century"

Items in manila envelope

ENGRAVING..

Cabinet I
Shelf 3
No. 28

[Belgian before the 18th century, illustrated books. Bio-biblio.-historical account].

See FUNCK, M. Livre Belge a gravures ... Paris et Bruxelles, 1925.

ENGRAVING.

Cabinet S
Shelf 5
No. 14

Bureau of Engraving and Printing. Washington, D. C. Printing our money and stamps. By Walden Fawcett. Excerpt from Van Norden Magazine, June, 1907. Illus.

Bound with other items in collection "Printing Processes: Excerpts from magazines", item 15.

ENGRAVING

Cabinet T
Shelf 2
No. 6
[vol.1]

Copperplate engraving, account of the origin of.

see

DIBDIN'S "Typographical Antiquities"... London, 1810-19, vol.i, pp.iv, xxiv

---

ENGRAVING

Cabinet I
Shelf 1
No. 31

Biographical dictionary...To which is prefixed an essay on the rise and progress of the art of engraving, both on copper and on wood. With several curious specimens. By Joseph Strutt. (2 vols.) London, 1785-6.

Calf; 12 x 9¼ in.

ENGRAVING

Cabinet 64
Shelf 3
No. 18

Bureau of Engraving and Printing. Washington, D.C. Report No.3220. To provide for printing government securities in the highest style of the art. Submitted by Mr. Wheeler to the House of Representatives. Aug.8, 1888.

Cloth; 9¼ x 6 in.

ENGRAVING

Cabinet 26
Shelf 2
No. 13

(Copperplate engraving, history of 18th century) Meister des Kupferstichs im 18 Jahrhundert und ihre techniken. von Hans H. Bockwitz.

Illus. account in Jahrbuch des Deutschen Vereins für Buchwesen und Schrifttum. V Jahrgang, 1931, p. 31.

ENGRAVING

Cabinet I
Shelf 1
No. 10

Bosse, Abraham. Traicte des maniere de graver en taille douce sur l'airain, par le moyen des eaux fortes, et des vernix durs et mols. Ensemble de la facon d'en emprimer les planches...A Paris. (De l'Imprimerie de Pierre Des-Hayes). 1645.

Engraved titles, (2) plates and diagrams.

Tree calf; 7 x 4½ in.

ENGRAVING.

Cabinet J
Shelf 3
No. 32
Env.

Calcographie des Piranesi, ou traité des arts d'architecture, peinture et sculpture, développés par la vue des principaux monumens antiques et modernes. A Paris: Les Piranesi, Freres. Au XII. - 1804.

Prospectus.

With other French items in manila envelope.

ENGRAVING

Cabinet 26
Shelf 1
No. 19

(Copperplate engraving) Kufferstichillustration des 15 Jahrhunderts. von Erich von Rath.

Article in the Gutenberg-Gesellschaft Jahrbuch, 1929, pp.186-192.

ENGRAVING

Cabinet I
Shelf 1
No. 32

Boydell, John and Josiah: An alphabetical catalogue of plates engraved by the most esteemed artists...Which compose the stock of...London, 1803. Printed by W. Bulmer and Co., 1803.

Quarter sheep; 10 x 7¼ in.

ENGRAVING

Cabinet U
Shelf 5
No. 40

Copper engraving first used for diagrams in a German book, 1476.

See Bradshaw, Henry. Collected papers...Cambridge, 1889, p. 238 and fol.

ENGRAVING

Cabinet J
Shelf 5
No. 12

(Copperplate engraving, practice of. 9 plates illustrated, showing tools and methods of application) Gravure en taille-douce en maniere noire, maniere de crayon, etc. Contenant neuf planches. [Excerpts, Paris, 1740].

Half morocco; 16¾ x 11 in.

ENGRAVING

Cabinet QQ
Shelf 2
No. 23

(Brief descriptive account. With 1 plate.)

See FOKKE, AREND. Museum der voornaamste uitvindingen...Amsteldam, n.d. circa 1795, pp.108-111.

ENGRAVING

Cabinet T
Shelf 1
No. 65

Copper engraving, the history of the art of

See Lemoine, Henry (Typographical Antiquities)...London, 1797, p. 106

ENGRAVING

Cabinet K
Shelf 1
No. 31

(Copperplate music title pages from the 12th to 16th century)

See VON ZUR WESTEN, WALTER Musik titel aus vier jahrhunderten... Leipzig, 1921.

ENGRAVING

Cabinet 18 Shelf 1 No. 11

(Copperplate Press of 1617). Eine Kupferdruckpress von 1617, von Franz M. Feldhaus, Fridnau. Illus.

A description and picture of this press was taken from the book "MACHINE NOVAE" by Fausto Veranzio, Venice, 1617.

In Zeitschrift für Bücherfreunde, 1912, part 1, p. 56.

ENGRAVING

Cabinet T Shelf 5 No. 111

Description of the different modes of engraving: brief account

See SOCIETY FOR PROMOTING CHRISTIAN KNOWLEDGE. History of printing... London, n.d. p.183

ENGRAVING

Cabinet I Shelf 1 No. 35

Douce, Francis. The Dance of Death exhibited in elegant engravings on wood: With a dissertation on the several representations of that subject, but more particularly on those ascribed to Macaber and Hans Holbein. London, 1833. With 49 plates.

Half morocco; 9 x 5¾ in.

ENGRAVING

Cabinet T Shelf 3 No. 12

Copperplate printing; engraving on metal which led to the art of.

see HANSARD, THOMAS CURSON Typographia...London, 1825, pp.22-28

ENGRAVING

Cabinet I Shelf 3 No. 5

Descriptive bibliography of the most important books in the English language relating to the art and history of engraving and the collecting of prints. By Howard C. Levis. London, 1912. Illus.

Half morocco; 11-3/4 x 9-3/4 in.

ENGRAVING.

Cabinet S Shelf 5 No. 17

Durer, Albrecht, by N. Peacock, in The Connoisseur, Sept. 1902. Illus.

Brief sketch of the artist, his life and works.

Bound in collection "Miscellaneous items relating to printing," item 16.

ENGRAVING.

Cabinet K Shelf 1 No. 21

Coup d'oeil sur l'histoire de la gravure. Par Georges Duplessis. Paris, n. d. circa 1882. (Together with) Catalogue de l'Exposition de graveurs anciennes et modernes. 4 Juillet, 1881. Illus.

Includes an article "La photographie et les arts graphiques. Par M. A. Davanne.

Boards, morocco back; 12-7/8x9¾ x 7/8 in.

ENGRAVING

Cabinet I Shelf 1 No. 30

Dictionnaire des artistes...graveurs etc. Par l'Abbé de Fontenai. Paris, 1776. (2 vols.)

Historical dictionary of the arts, and artists.

Calf; each vol., 6¾ x 4-3/8 in.

ENGRAVING

Cabinet J Shelf 2 No. 22

Durer, Albert: the man in his own eyes and in the eyes of his neighbors. With a complete list of his prints from wood, copper, and iron. By Louis A. Holman (Goodspeeds Monographs No.5) Boston, 1922.

Portrait frontispiece.

Half morocco; 7-7/8 x 5 in.

ENGRAVING

Cabinet 75 Shelf 2 No. 4

Crispijn Vande Pas, the younger (1614) and his "Hortus Floridus", by S. Savage, for the Bibliographical Society, London. Dec. 1923.

In Trans. Biblio. Soc. Vol. IV, 1923-1924. pp. 181-216. "The Library".

ENGRAVING.

Cabinet 22 Shelf 1 No. 10

(Did the early printers use engravings or metal at times as a substitute for wood?) Title in German: Die verwendung von metallschnitten in der typographischen ausstallung, von A Kirchhoff.

In Archiv für Deutschen Buchhandels, 1886, vol.10, p.225, vol.XI, p.358.

ENGRAVING.

Cabinet J Shelf 3 No. 22

Early history of engraving: Wood-engraving, line-engraving, etching, mezzotint, engraving in stipple...

See SLATER, J. HERBERT. Engravings and their value...New York, 1929, pp.1-42.

ENGRAVING

Cabinet J Shelf 2 No. 17

Dalziel Brothers, The: a record of 50 years work in conjunction with many of the most distringuished artists of the period, 1840-1890. With selected pictures and autographs. London, 1901.

Cloth; 10¼ x 8 in.

ENGRAVING

Cabinet C Shelf 2 No. 14

Documents iconographiques et typographiques de la Bibliotheque Royale de la Belgique. Fac-simile photo-lithographiques, avec texte historique et explicatif...Bruxelles, 1877.

On the origin and development of engraving on wood and metal.

Half cloth; 21½ x 14 in.

ENGRAVING

Cabinet J Shelf 3 No. 11

England, the old engravers of, in their relation to contemporary life and art. 1540-1800. By Malcolm C. Salaman. With 48 illustrations. London....Philadelphia, 1907.

Cloth; 8½ x 6 x 1½ in.

ENGRAVING

Cabinet MM Shelf 7 No. 8

Davenport, S.T. [Essay in "British Manufacturing Industries" edited by G. Phillips Bevan, pp. 75-124]. London. 1876.

Cloth; 6-5/8 x 4¾ x ¾ in.

ENGRAVING

Cabinet I Shelf 1 No. 20

[Doissin, Ludovico] La gravure: Poeme. A Paris, chez P.G. Le Mercier, 1753. (Latin with French translation)

First edition published in 1752 was entirely in Latin.

Paper; 7 x 4-3/8 x ½ in.

ENGRAVING.

Cabinet I Shelf 3 No. 25

[English, 18th century]. La gravure en Angleterre au 18e siecle. Par Andre Blum. Avec une preface by M. Campbell Dodgson. Paris, 1930. Illus.

Has lists of engravers of different processes.

Half morocco; 13-1/8 x 10 x 1½ in.

ENGRAVING.

Cabinet J Shelf 3 No. 18

English engraving, a chapter on.

See DELABORDE (Le Vicomte) HENRI. Engraving: its origin...London, 1886.

ENGRAVING

Cabinet Shelf No.

Etching.

See ETCHING.

ENGRAVING

Cabinet B Shelf 3 No. 4

France 15th and 16th centuries.

see RICCI, Seymour De. Documents sur la typographie et la gravure...

ENGRAVING.

Cabinet J Shelf 3 No. 13

English illustration 'The Sixties': 1855-70. By Gleeson White. With numerous illustrations by...London, 1906.

Stamped cloth; 10¼ x 7 x 2 in.

ENGRAVING.

Cabinet I Shelf 3 No. 1

[Etching, Japanese]. Art of Kuniyoshi, The, by Hamilton Easter Field. An excerpt from Arts and Decoration, March, 1917. Illus.

Item 34 with binder's title:"Various Engravers and About Engravers.

ENGRAVING.

Cabinet K Shelf 2 No. 1

(France, origin and evolution of popular illustration in.)

see DUCHARTE, LOUIS and SAULNIER, RÉNE L'Imagerie populaire...Paris, 1925

ENGRAVING

Cabinet QQ Shelf 4 No. 19

Engraving for printing purposes, brief article on.

see FREEDLEY, EDWIN. Leading pursuits and leading men...Philadelphia, 1854, p.165.

ENGRAVING.

Cabinet 18 Shelf 1 No. 1

(Figure designs in the Apostolic Confessionals of the Middle Ages) Mittelalterliche form schnittdarstellungen des Apostolischen Glaubensbekenntnisses, von Dr. W. Molsdorf, Breslau. Illus.

In Zeitschrift für Bücherfreunde, 1906-7, part 2, p.452.

ENGRAVING.

Cabinet I Shelf 3 No. 23

France, origines de le gravure en: les estampes sur bois et sur metal; les incunables xylographiques. Par Andre Blum. Paris et Bruxelles, 1927. Illus.

English translation of the above mentioned work, I/3/24.

Paper; 12-7/8 x 10 x 1¼ in.

ENGRAVING.

Cabinet I Shelf 3 No. 4

Engraving in general from the beginning of the 13th to the15th century.

See Chap. II, Vol. I, WILLSHIRE, WILLIAM HUGHES. Ancient prints ... London, 1877.

ENGRAVING

Cabinet K Shelf 2 No. 37

Five centuries of print making. From the collection of Lessing Rosenwald. The Print Club of Philadelphia, 1932.

Illus. descriptive catalogue.

Paper; 11 x 8½ in.

ENGRAVING

Cabinet J Shelf 4 No. 2

French colour prints of the 18th century, French. An introductory essay by Malcolm C. Salaman. Illustrated by 50 representative examples in colours. London, 1913.

Cloth, stamped; 13-5/8 x 10-1/8 x 1½ in.

ENGRAVING

Cabinet J Shelf 3 No. 32 (env.)

(Engravings in the Musee du Louvre). Chalcographie du Musee du Louvre. Par Henry de Chennevieres.

Illus. excerpt from unidentified French periodical. n.d.

Item in manila envelope.

ENGRAVING.

Cabinet R Shelf 5 No. 60

Foster, John, The earliest American engraver, and the first Boston printer. By Samuel Abbott Green. Boston, 1909. Facsimiles.

Bio-bibliographical historical.

Cloth; 10½ x 7¾ in.

ENGRAVING

Cabinet I Shelf 3 No. 1

French 18th century, some engravings of. Introduction by Fitz Roy Carrington. [Excerpt from Burr McIntosh Monthly, May, 1910]. Illus.

Item 27 in vol. with binder's title: "Various Engravers and About Engravers."

ENGRAVING.

Cabinet I Shelf 3 No. 16

l'Estampe francaise: Essai par Francois Courboin. Graveurs et marchands ... Brusselles et Paris G. Van Oest et Cie. 1914. Illus.

French engravers and engraving: bio-biblio historical, technical.

Half morocco; 10¼ x 7-1/8 x 1¼ in.

ENGRAVING.

Cabinet R Shelf 5 No. 59

Foster, John, the earliest engraver in New England. By Samuel A. Green. Cambridge, 1905.

Bio-historical account of the engraver-printer, who in 1675 set up the first press in Boston. See also R/5/60.

Half morocco; 9½ x 6½ in.

ENGRAVING.

Cabinet J Shelf 5 No. 29 3 Vols.

(French engraving from its origin to the 19th century, illustrated history of).

See COURBOIN, FRANCOIS. Histoire illustrèe ... A Paris, 1923.

ENGRAVING.

Cabinet I Shelf 3 No. 15

[French engravings and engravers]. L'Ancienne France. Peintres et graveurs. Ouvrage illustre de 200 gravures et d'une chromo-lithographie. Paris, 1888.

Bio-historical. Not well indexed.

Cloth; $10\frac{3}{4}$ x 7-1/8 x 1-3/8 in.

ENGRAVING

Cabinet K Shelf 3 No. 8

Gravure. Précis élémentaire de ses origines de ses procédés et de son histoire. Par le vte. Henri Delaborde... Paris, n.d. (circa 1891) Maison Quantin. Illus.

Cloth, $8\frac{1}{2}$ x $5\frac{1}{2}$ in.

ENGRAVING

Cabinet FF Shelf 4 No. 8

Henze, Adolph. Handbuch der schriftgiesserei und der verwandten nebenzweige... fur schriftgiesser, buchdrucker, stempelschneider, xylographen, graveure und andere kunstgenossen. Weinmar, 1844. With plates

Boards; 7-3/8 x 4-3/8 x 1 in.

ENGRAVING.

Cabinet J Shelf 3 No. 24

French portrait engraving of the 17th and 18th centuries. London, 1910. Illus.

Cloth; 9-5/8 x 7 x 1-5/8 in.

ENGRAVING.

Cabinet I Shelf 3 No. 27

(La) Gravure en Belgique ou notices biographiques sur les graveurs Anversois, Bruxellois et autres, depuis les origines de la gravure jusqu'a la fin du 18e siècle. Par Benjamin Linnig. Anvers, 1911. Illus.

Paper; 7-7/8 x $5\frac{3}{4}$ x 1 in.

ENGRAVING

Cabinet V Shelf 4 No. 18

Histoire de l'Imprimerie et des arts et professions qui se rattachent a la typographie... (Gravure sur bois et sur metal).

See BOOK MAKING. Le livre d'or des metiers...Paris, 1852.

ENGRAVING

Cabinet T Shelf 3 No. 3

French school of engraving, account of; with notices of a few of the more celebrated engravers.

see DIBDIN'S Bibliographical tour...London, 1821, vol.ii, pp.504-511

ENGRAVING

Cabinet J Shelf 4 No. 9

(La) Gravure en France au 18e siècle. La gravure d'illustration. Par Louis Reau. Paris, n.d. Illus.

Publisher's prospectus, with 3 plates.

Paper; 13 x 10 in.

ENGRAVING

Cabinet J Shelf 4 No. 6

L'Histoire de la gravure, cour d'oeil sur. Par Georges Duplessis. Paris, 1881. Illus.

Article above precedes Catalogue de l'Exposition de gravures anciennes et modernes. 4 Juillet.

Boards; $12\frac{3}{4}$ x $9\frac{3}{4}$ x $1\frac{1}{2}$ in.

ENGRAVING

Cabinet I Shelf 3 No. 1

Gillray's caricatures: historical and descriptive account of. [A review of two books dealing with above subject. Excerpt from the "Eclectic," Sept., 1853].

Item 4 in vol. with binder's title: "Various Engravers and About Engravers."

ENGRAVING.

Cabinet I Shelf 3 No. 17

(La) Gravure en France des origines a 1900. Par Francois Courboin. 204 reproductions, 8 planches hors texte en couleurs. Paris, Librairie Delagrave, 1923.

Bio-biblio. historical.

Paper; $11\frac{1}{4}$ x $1\frac{1}{4}$ in.

ENGRAVING

Cabinet I Shelf 4 No. 18

Histoire de la gravure dans les anciens Pays-Bas et dans les Provinces Belges, des origines jusqu'à la fin du 18e siècle. Par A.J.J. Delen. Premier partie, des origines a 1500. Paris et Bruxelles, 1924.

With 66 plates of reproductions.

Paper; 13 x 10 x $1\frac{1}{2}$ in.

ENGRAVING.

Cabinet J Shelf 3 No. 21

Golden age of engraving: An introductory essay on the old engravers. Reprinted by permission from Harpers Magazine. Frederick Keppel, New York, 1878. Pamphlet.

Paper; 11 x $7\frac{3}{4}$ in. In manila envelope.

ENGRAVING.

Cabinet I Shelf 3 No. 3

Guide de l'amateur de livres à vignettes de 18e siècles. Second édition ... Par Henry Cohen. Frontispiece a l'eau-forte par J. Chauvet.

Bibliography of 18th century illustrated books.

Half morocco; $9\frac{1}{4}$ x 5-7/8 x 1-1/8 in.

ENGRAVING

Cabinet K Shelf 2 No. 3

Histoire de la gravure en Italie, en Espagne, en Allemagne, dans les Pays-Bas, en Angleterre, et en France. Par Georges Duplessis. Contenant 73 reproductions de gravures anciennes. Paris, 1880.

Half morocco; 11 x 8 in.

ENGRAVING.

Cabinet J Shelf 3 No. 20

Golden age of engraving, the. A specialists story about fine prints. By Frederick Keppel. With 262 illustrations showing the progress of the art from the year 1465 to the year 1910. Third edition. New York, 1910.

Bibliography at end.

Cloth; $9\frac{1}{2}$ x $6\frac{3}{4}$ in.

ENGRAVING

Cabinet MM Shelf 7 No. 28

Hackleman, Charles W. Commercial engraving and printing. A manual of practical instruction and reference covering commercial illustrating and printing by all processes. Published by Commercial Engraving Publishing Company. Indianapolis, Indiana U.S.A. (1921)

With more than 2000 illus.

Cloth; $9\frac{1}{2}$ x $6\frac{1}{2}$ x 2-1/8 in.

ENGRAVING

Cabinet K Shelf 2 No. 4

Histoire de la gravure typographique. Conférence, 29 Janvier, 1875. Par Gaston Tissandier. [Paris]

Extrait de la Journal General de la Librairie et l'Imprimerie...du Fevrier, 1875. Illus.

Half morocco; $10\frac{1}{4}$ x $7\frac{1}{4}$ in.

ENGRAVING.

Cabinet I Shelf 3 No. 18 to 21

Histoire illustree de la gravure en France. Des origines a 19e siecles. [In 4 parts]. Par Francois Courboin. Paris, 1923 to 1929.

Part I - Des origines a 1660
" II - 1660 a 1800
" III - 19e siecle
" IV - Table generale.

Paper; 12¾ x 8-7/8 in.

ENGRAVING

Cabinet I Shelf 1 No. 33

Jansen, Hendrik: Essai sur l'origine de la gravure en bois et en taille-douce...Tome premiere, avec 20 planches. Paris, 1808.

Complete edition of this work, 2 vols. Paris, 1808, see I-1-33.01

Half morocco; 8-7/8 x 5 x 1¾ in.

ENGRAVING

Cabinet C Shelf 2 No. 17

Memorie spettanti alla storia della calcografia. Del Command. Conte Leopoldo Gigognara. Prato, 1830.

Illustrated record concerning the history of engraving.

Boards; 18½ x 12½ in.

ENGRAVING

Cabinet J Shelf 3 No. 8

Histoire métallique et histoire de la gravure d'Anvers... (Also pp.113-302) Gravures de Maîtres Anverois et des peintres graveurs qui ont été membres de la Gilde St.-Luc. Par Ed. Ter Bruggen. Antwerp, 1875.

Boards, morocco back; 9-5/8 x 6¼ x 7/8 in.

ENGRAVING

Cabinet J Shelf 3 No. 29

Japanese wood engraving.

See ANDERSON, WILLIAM. Japanese wood engravings.

ENGRAVING

Cabinet K Shelf 1 No. 27

Menus et programmes illustrés...du 17 siécle jusqu'a nos jours. Ouvrage orné de 460 reproductions. Par Léon Maillard. Paris, 1898.

Half morocco; 12¾ x 9½ in.

ENGRAVING.

Cabinet K Shelf 4 No. 9

(History of decorative design and ornamental engraving).

See Jessen, Peter. Ornamentstich... Berlin, 1920.

ENGRAVING

Cabinet I Shelf 2 No. 80

Leetle lessons in engraving. Illustrated by Alfred Leete. With the compliments of The Practical Etching Service Lts., London, n.d.

Brochure; 11 x 8 in.

ENGRAVING

Cabinet K Shelf 3 No. 9

(Les) Mervilles de la gravure. Par Georges Duplessis. 2m édition. Ouvrage illustré de 34 vignettes par P. Sellier, Paris, 1871.

Cloth; 7¼ x 4½ x ¾ in.

ENGRAVING.

Cabinet V Shelf 6 No. 12.01

(History of engraving). Histoire de la gravure La gravure sur bois; la gravure en taille-douce; la gravure des poincons typographiques.

See BULLETIN OFFICIEL DES MAITRES IMPRIMEURS (1925). L'Imprimeur et le bibliophile ... pp. 45-69.

ENGRAVING

Cabinet J Shelf 3 No. 12

Line-engraving: article by Malcolm C. Salaman.

p. 43 "STUDIO" LTD. London, 1917. The Graphic Arts of Great Britain....

Half Morocco; 11½ x 8¼ in.

ENGRAVING

Cabinet K Shelf 2 No. 40

Metal-working, coining, chasing and engraving... casting in metal, etc.

see

NEUBURGER, ALBERT. Technical arts and sciences of the ancients...pp.29-64

ENGRAVING.

Cabinet I Shelf 4 No. 20 2 Vols.

(History of German illustration). Geschichte der deutschen illustration vom ersten auftreten des formschnittes bis auf die gegenwart. von Th. Kutschmann. Goslar und Berlin. (1899). 2 vols.

Cloth; 12½ x 9½ in.

ENGRAVING

Cabinet I Shelf 5 No. 7 to 15 9 vols.

Manuel de l'amateur de la gravure sur bois et sur metal au XVe siecle. Par W. L. Schreiber Leipzig and Berlin, 1891-1910.
[9 vols. of text, 3 of facsimiles].

For subject of each volume, see SCHREIBER, W. L. Manuel ...

ENGRAVING

Cabinet 31 Shelf 2 No. 17

(The) Modern Engraver, Blomgren Bros. & Co., Chicago, Ill.

Vol.1, Nos., 1,2,3, 1890

Unbound issues, tied in bundle

ENGRAVING

Cabinet K Shelf 3 No. 5

(History of popular picture making) Histoire de l'imagerie populaire. Par Champfleurt. Paris, 1869. Illus.

Paper; 7-3/8 x 4-5/8 in.

ENGRAVING.

Cabinet J Shelf 3 No. 17

Masters and masterpieces of engraving. By Willis O. Chapin. Illustrated with 60 engravings and heliogravures. New York, 1894.

Half morocco; 10½ x 8 x 1½ in.

ENGRAVING

Cabinet K Shelf 6 No. 15

Modern woodcut, the. A study of the evolution of the craft. By Herbert Furst...London (1924) Illus.

Cloth; 11½ x 9 x 1½ in.

ENGRAVING

Cabinet K Shelf 6 No. 39.01

Notice sur deux estampes de 1406 et sur les commencements de la gravure en criblé. Par M. Henri Delaborde. Extrait de la Gazette des Beaux-Arts, Mars, 1869. Paris. Illus.

Item 24 in bound collection with binder's title ENGRAVERS AND WOOD ENGRAVERS.

ENGRAVING

Cabinet I Shelf 1 No. 34

Ottley, William Young: An inquiry into the origin and early history of engraving, upon copper and in wood...(2 vols.) London, 1816. Illus.

Half morocco; 11½ x 9 in.

ENGRAVING

Cabinet 75 Shelf 1 No. 4

Portraits in Books: A paper read before the Bibliographical Society by Henry B. Wheatley June 28, 1897.

In Trans. Biblio. Soc., Vol. IV, 1896-1898. pp. 129-136.

ENGRAVING

Cabinet J Shelf 4 No. 3

Old French colour prints. By Campbell Dodgson... London, 1924.

With 87 plates, some of which are printed in colors. Includes an outline of the history and development of color printing.

Cloth, parchment back; 12-5/8 x 10-1/8 x 1-3/8 in.

ENGRAVING

Cabinet Shelf No.

Photo-mechanical processes.

See PHOTO-ENGRAVING
" also PHOTO-ENGRAVING PROCESSES.

ENGRAVING,

Cabinet J Shelf 3 No. 15

Pottery, engraving on, supersedes painted ware.

See METEYARD, ELIZA. Group of Englishmen (1795 to 1818)...p.173.

ENGRAVING

Cabinet I Shelf 1 No. 28

(Origin of engraving, with a dissertation on the earliest illustrated books.) Idée générale d'une collection complette d'estampes. Avec und dissertation sur l'origine de la gravure et sur les premiers livres d'images. [Par le Baron Heinecken] A Leipsic et Vienne. Chez Jean Paul Kraus, 1771.

Half calf; 7¾ x 5 in.

ENGRAVING

Cabinet V Shelf 4 No. 3

Pictures of methods, tools, etc. Copperplate engravings by Abraham Bosse, Paris, 1643.

3 Folded plates at end of l'Histoire de l'Imprimerie", par Jean de la Caille, Paris, 1689.

ENGRAVING,

Cabinet G Shelf 4 No. 32

Revere's, Paul, own story...together with a brief sketch of his versatile career. Compiled by Harriet E. O'Brien. Privately printed. Perry Walton (Boston, Mass. 1929) Illus.

Boards, cloth back; 11¼ x 8-3/8 x 5/8 in. In protective case.

ENGRAVING

Cabinet K Shelf 2 No. 26

Origin of wood engraving...The masters of engraving.

see LACROIX, PAUL. Arts of the Middle Ages...London, 1875, p.315

ENGRAVING

Cabinet J Shelf 3 No. 7

Ploos van Amstel, Cornelis, en zijne mederwerkes en tijgenooten. Historische schets van de techniek der Hollandsche prentteekeningen zemaakt in de tweede helft de 18 eeuw. Door Dr. N.G. van Huffel. Utrecht, 1921.

With 28 cards of illustrations in portofolio attached to book.
Cloth; 10-3/4 x 8¼ in.

ENGRAVING

Cabinet J Shelf 2 No. 35

Rollinson, William, a monograph on. Prepared by Robert W. Reid and Charles Rollinson. New York. Privately printed, October, 1931.

With portraits and reproductions of the engravings of Rollinson.

Paper boards: 9 5/8 x 6½ in.

ENGRAVING.

Cabinet J Shelf 3 No. 18

Origin, processes and history. By Henri Delaborde. Translated by R.A.M. Stevenson. With an additional chapter on English engraving by William Walker. London...1886.

Cloth; 7-5/8 x 5¼ x 1 in.

ENGRAVING

Cabinet I Shelf 1 No. 12

Polygraphice; or the arts of drawing, engraving, etching...By William Salmon. London: Printed by E.T. and R.H. for R. Jones. 1673.

With engraved plates.

Original sheep; 7 x 4⅝ in.

ENGRAVING

Cabinet J Shelf 2 No. 37

(Rops, Félicien, French engraver, circa 1860. Biographical and critical sketches, with illustrated account of his works. In special number of "La Plume", No.172, June 15, 1896. Paris.)

Half morocco; 10¼ x 7¼ x 3/8 in.

ENGRAVING,

Cabinet 75 Shelf 2 No. 9

Origines de la gravure en France. Les estampes sur bois et sur metal. Les incunables xylographiques. Par Andre Blum. Paris et Bruxelles, 1927. Book reviewed by A.W. Pollard.

In Trans. Bibl. Soc. "The Library," Vol. IX pp.215-18. 1928-29.

ENGRAVING

Cabinet K Shelf 6 No. 39.01

Portrait engravers in France. Catalogue and bibliographical notes).

see ALKAN aîné. Graveure de portraits en France...Paris, 1879

ENGRAVING

Cabinet J Shelf 2 No. 38

Sartain, John, reminiscences of a very old man, 1808-1897, New York, 1900. Illus.

Cloth; 9 x 6¼ in.

ENGRAVING

Cabinet I Shelf 1 No. 25

Sculptura; or, the history and art of chalcography, and engraving in copper. To which is annexed a new manner of engraving, or mezzotint, communicated by His Highness Prince Rupert to the author of this treatise, John Evelyn. The second edition. With memoirs of the authors life. London: 1769.

Frontispiece portrait and I folded plate.

Calf; $7\frac{1}{4}$ x $4\frac{3}{8}$ in.

ENGRAVING.

Cabinet J Shelf 3 No. 22

Technical terms.

See SLATER, J. HERBERT. Engravings and their value...New York, 1929. p.69.

ENGRAVING

Cabinet Shelf No.

See also

ETCHING

ENGRAVING

Cabinet I Shelf 1 No. 23

Sculptura-Historica-Technica: or the history and art of engraving...London, 1747: Printed for S. Harding. With plates and engravers marks.

A revised and enlarged edition of John Evelyn's "Sculptura, or The History of Chalcography", London, 1662.

Half morocco; $6\frac{1}{4}$ x 3-7/8 in.

ENGRAVING

Cabinet J Shelf 3 No. 6.01

Walker Engraving Company. New York, 1926. Book of notable American illustrators. Illus.

Boards; $12\frac{1}{2}$ x $9\frac{1}{2}$ in.

ENGRAVING, BANK NOTE.

Cabinet I Shelf 3 No. 1

Evolution of bank notes. By Warren Luqueer Green, President of the American Bank Note Company. [Excerpt from the Editorial Review, August, 1910]. Illus.

Item 9 in vol. with binder's title: "Various Engravers and About Engravers.

ENGRAVING

Cabinet I Shelf 1 No. 24

Sculptura-Historico-Technica: or, the history and art of engraving...With copper plates. The third edition. London: Printed for J. Marks. 1766.

With plates, facsimiles of engravers marks, etc.

Calf; 7 x $4\frac{1}{4}$ in.

ENGRAVING

Cabinet J Shelf 2 No. 32

Wolf, Henry, life and work of. By Ralph Clifton Smith....Champlain, N.Y. 1927. Portrait frontis., illus.

Boards, cloth back; 10-3/4 x 7-5/8 in.

ENGRAVING, BANK NOTES.

Cabinet K Shelf 4 No. 41

How to detect forged bank notes. Illustrated. By Effingham Wilson. By permission of the Bank of England. London, 1856. Pamphlet.

Bound in with Report .. of the Society of Arts. London, 1819.

Half morocco; 10 x $6\frac{1}{2}$ in.

ENGRAVING

Cabinet I Shelf 1 No. 26

Sculptura-Historica-Technica (or), history and art of engraving...[By John Evelyn] The fourth edition. London. Printed for J. Marks, 1770.

With plates and facsimiles of marks and cyphers of engravers etc.

Calf; 6-7/8 x 4-1/8 x 7/8 in.

ENGRAVING

Cabinet K Shelf 1 No. 31

(Wood engraving, music title pages, 12th to 16th century)

See VON ZUR WESTEN, WALTER. Musik titel aus vier jahrhunderten...Leipzig, 1921.

ENGRAVING, Bank Note

Cabinet K Shelf 4 No. 43

(A) Hundred years of bank note engraving in the United States, 1795-1895. By Robert Noxon Toppan. Read before the Trustees of the American Bank Note Company. New York,1896.

Half morocco; $9\frac{1}{4}$ x 6 in.

ENGRAVING

Cabinet J Shelf 3 No. 19

Short history of engraving and etching. For the use of collectors and students. With a full bibliography, classified list and index of engravers. By A.M. Hind. With frontispiece in photogravure, and 110 illustrations in the text. Boston, 1908.

Cloth; $9\frac{1}{2}$ x $6\frac{1}{2}$ x $1\frac{3}{4}$ in.

ENGRAVING

Cabinet W Shelf 3 No. 115

Wood engraving, 17th century British.

See BROADSIDES. Old English broadsides ...of the 17th century.

ENGRAVING, Bank Note.

Cabinet I Shelf 3 No. 1

Processes of bank note engraving. Brief account An excerpt from "Great Industries of the U.S" Hartford, 1872.

Item 1 in vol. with binder's title "Various Engravers, and About Engravers"

ENGRAVING

Cabinet I Shelf 3 No. 1

Steel and copperplate printing. [Excerpt from] "Great Industires of U.S." Hartford, 1872.

Item 1 in vol. with binder's title "Various Engravers and About Engravers."

ENGRAVING

Cabinet Shelf No.

(Wood engraving)

See cards with following sub-heads:

I - WOOD ENGRAVING. Literature of
II - WOOD ENGRAVINGS

ENGRAVING, BANK NOTE.

Cabinet K Shelf 4 No. 40

Report ... on the mode of preventing the forgery of bank notes. Printed by order of the Society of Arts. London, 1819.

With 5 plates.

Boards, 10 x 6 $\frac{1}{2}$ in.

ENGRAVING, BANK NOTES.

Cabinet K Shelf 4 No. 41

Report ... on the mode of preventing the forgery of bank notes. Printed by order of the Society of Arts. London, 1819. With 5 plates.

Bound in with leaflet: The Bank Restriction Barometer booklet: How to detect forged bank notes. Wilson, 1856.

Half morocco, 10 x 6½ in.

ENGRAVING, BANK NOTE.

Cabinet K Shelf 4 No. 42

Security and manufacture of bank notes ...

See BRADBURY, HENRY. Security, etc. London, 1856.

ENGRAVING, BANK NOTE.

Cabinet K Shelf 4 No. 44

Specimens bank notes. Printed by John Leighton. London, 1856.

Items in manila envelope.

ENGRAVING, BANK NOTE.

Cabinet K Shelf 4 No. 44

Specimens of bank note printing. Bradbury & Evans, Bank Note Engravers & Printers, Whitefriars, London, circa 1856.

Items in Manila envelope.

ENGRAVING, BANK NOTE.

Cabinet K Shelf 4 No. 43

United States, a hundred years of bank note engraving in.

See Toppan, Robert Noxon. Bank note engraving in the United States ...

ENGRAVING, COPPERPLATE

Cabinet PP Shelf 1 No. 29

Finiguerra, Thomaso, (Florence, 1460) the first discoverer of engraving on copper.

See pp. 273, 274, vol. I, Horne's Introduction to the study of bibliography ... London, 1814.

ENGRAVING, COPPERPLATE

Cabinet FF Shelf 5 No. 1

[Printing Press, copper plate, of 1656. Full page copperplate engraving.)

The book with this engraving, has 42 other full page engravings showing various machines.

See Zonca's Novo teatro de machine... Padova, 1656.

ENGRAVING, COPPERPLATE

Cabinet 80 Shelf 2 No. 8

Revere's Paul, political cartoon "The Mitred Minuet", in the Royal American Magazine, Oct., 1774. Boston, Printed and sold at Greenleaf's [Joseph; Printing Office.

Item in manila envelope.

ENGRAVING, LAWS RELATING TO

Cabinet I Shelf 2-a No. 5

Fuld, Ludwig. Gesets, betreffend das urheberrecht an werken der bildenden künste und der photographie. Zweite auflage. Berlin, Leipzig, 1925.

Guttentasche Sammlung, No.81.

Cloth; 6-1/8 x 4¼ x 3/8 in.

ENGRAVING Literature of

Cabinet K Shelf 5 No. 11

Antiquity of engraivng.

see JACKSON, JOHN. Treatise on wood engraving...London, 1839, pp. 1-51.

ENGRAVING Literature of

Cabinet K Shelf 5 No. 11

Copperplate engraving, its invention.

see JACKSON, JOHN. Treatise on wood engraving...London, 1839. p. 25. (See index)

ENGRAVING, Literature of

Cabinet K Shelf 5 No. 1

Golden age of engraving. By F. Keppel. Illus. excerpt from Harper's New Monthly Magazine. Aug., 1878.

Item 4 in vol. with binder's title "Wood Engraving, Etc".

ENGRAVING Literature of

Cabinet K Shelf 6 No. 34

History of engraving from the earliest times to the present day. Excerpt from the United States Magazine. July, 1856. Illus.

Item 3 in vol. with binder's title "Wood engraving. Various excerpts."

ENGRAVING, Literature of

Cabinet K Shelf 5 No. 1

Magic line: a study in the technic of engraving. By Timothy Cole. Illus. excerpt from "The Century Magazine", Feb., 1917.

Item 16 in vol. with binder's title " Wood Engraving, Etc."

ENGRAVING, Literature of

Cabinet K Shelf 5 No. 2

Wolf, Henry, 1852-1916, American engraving.

see BIOGRAPHIES, ENGRAVINGS. Wolf, Henry, 1852-1916...

ENGRAVING, Literature of

Cabinet K Shelf 5 No. 1

Wood engraving and wood cut printing in New York, desultory thoughts on. [Unsigned article. Excerpt from "Knickerbocker Magazine", Jan., 1853].

Item I in vol. with binder's title "Wood Engraving, Etc"

ENGRAVING, Literature of

Cabinet K Shelf 6 No. 5 to 10

Wood engravings of Thomas and John Bewick.

see WOOD ENGRAVING. Literature of. Bewick, Thomas...

ENGRAVING Literature of

Cabinet K Shelf 6 No. 30

Woodcut, An Annual. Edited by Herbert Furst. Published by The Fleuron Limited. London, 1930. (With 20 contemporary woodcuts).

Includes article by Furst: The significance of Bewick.

Includes article by Johnson: Woodcut writing books.

Boards; 11 x 7½ x 3/8 in.

ENGRAVING Literature of

Cabinet K Shelf 6 No. 29

Woodcut Annual for 1925. Edited by Alfred Fowler. Kansas City, Mo. Illus.

Includes articles by Ruzicka, Guthrie, Teall, also a short bibliography, and list of contemporary woodcuts for 1924.

Boards; 12½ x 9½ x ¼ in.

ENGRAVING MACHINERY

Cabinet FF Shelf 5 No. 8

Benton's matrix engraving machine. Illus. description.

See Kaup, W. J. Modern automatic type making methods.

ENGRAVING MACHINERY

Cabinet FF Shelf 3 No. 54

Weibking Engraving Machine, facts concerning the. Has a list of some of the type families engraved in matrix form by Robert Weibking senior...Ms. signed Chas. Murray, President and General Manager Barnhart Brothers & Spindler. Chicago, Ill. Oct. 13. 1931.

Item in manila envelope.

ENGRAVING Literature of

Cabinet K Shelf 6 No. 25

Xylographie de l'imprimerie Troyenne pendant le 15e, le 16e, le 17e et le 18e siècle. Précéder d'une lettre du Bibliophile Jacob, sur l'histoire de la gravure en bois. Publiée par Varusoltis, de Troyes...Paris, 1859.

571 original woodcuts on 72 leaves of hand made paper.

Half morocco; 12½ x 9-3/4 x 7/8 in.

ENGRAVING MACHINERY

Cabinet FF Shelf 5 No. 9

Benton's Matrix Engraving Machine, No. 59. Instructions for setting up. Jersey City, 1917-22.

"The foregoing instructions were written by me and sent...to the Imperial Printing Bureau of Japan, at Tokio, on the occasion of shipping the first Benton Matrix Engraving Machine to that country" (signed) L. B. Benton.

Typescript.

Half morocco; 13¼ x 8½ in.

ENGRAVING MACHINERY. Catalogue

Cabinet EE Shelf 4 No. 36

Model C engraving machine. Engravers and Machinery Co. Sag Harbor, New York. n.d. Pamphlet.

In manila envelope.

ENGRAVING, Mezzotint.

Cabinet I Shelf 3 No. 1

Art of engraving, The: A brief sketch of the origin of mezzotint, with some account of other processes. An excerpt from the Eclectic, June, 1861.

Item 6 in vol. with binder's title: "Various Engravers and about Engravers."

ENGRAVING MACHINERY

Cabinet 26 Shelf 2 No. 1

(Line machines for copper engraving and lithography.) Linür Maschine fur Kupferstecher und Steindrucker.

Description of the machine (in German) by the inventor.

Journal fur Buchdruckerkunst, Mar.,1838, No.3, col.45.

ENGRAVING MACHINERY. CATALOGUE

Cabinet I Shelf 2-a No. 3

Royle, John & Sons. Efficient machinery for photo-engravers and others. (Catalogue No. 300) John Royle & Sons, Paterson, N.J., 1918. Illus.

Has views of the Royal works in 1860, and of present buildings.

Half morocco; 6¾ x 4-1/8 x 1 in.

ENGRAVING, Mezzotint.

Cabinet I Shelf 3 No. 1

[Mezzotint]. Sartain, John and his portrait: An excerpt from the Eclectic, May 1861.

Brief biography of the artist who first introduced mezzotint engraving into America.

Item 5 in vol. with binder's title "Various Engravers and About Engravers."

ENGRAVING MACHINERY

Cabinet 26 Shelf 2 No. 2

Relief Engraving Machines, first invented by Christ, Gobrecht, Philadelphia, 1817: An account in German by L. Karrig.

This invention which was improved by Wagner in Germany, Collas, in France and others; was said to have brought about a new era for line engraving.

Journal fur Buchdruckerkunst,Nov., 1841, cols.161-64.

ENGRAVING PLANTS

Cabinet S Shelf 3 No. 20

(United States) Suffolk Engraving & Electrotyping Co. Cambridge Mass. Pictures tell the story: A pictorial presentation of the plant. n.d. (cir. 1924).

Board paper; 6 x 9 in.

ENGRAVING, MEZZOTINT Literature of

Cabinet K Shelf 5 No. 1

Famous mezzotints. A beautiful form of engraving that reached its highest point in reproducing the work of Reynolds...By Royal Cortissoz. Illus. excerpt from "Munsey's", Feb., 1906.

Item 9 in vol. with binder's title "Wood Engraving, Etc".

ENGRAVING MACHINERY

Cabinet I Shelf 2-a No. 4

Routing machine...a sketch of the development of. By Vernon Royle. John Royle & Sons. Paterson, N.J. 1918. (Circular No.293, Illus.)

Morocco; 6¾ x 4¼ in.

ENGRAVING PROCESSES

Cabinet 27 Shelf 1 No. 8

Acid engraving on zinc. By J. Luther Ringwalt.

Illus article in the Printer's Circular, Vol.8 No.8, Oct., 1873, p.273

ENGRAVING, MEZZOTINTS. Literature of

Cabinet K Shelf 5 No. 1

On the revival of mezzotint as a painter's art By Seymour Haden. [Also] The isle of Purbeck. By Miss J. E. Panton. Illus. excerpt from Harper's New Monthly Magazine. Jan., 1885.

Item 5 in vol. with binder's title "Wood Engraving, Etc".

ENGRAVING MACHINERY

Cabinet FF Shelf 4 No. 4

Type engraving machine: Description d'une machine a graver...

See Rochon, M. l'Abbe'. Recueil de Memoires... Paris, 1783.

ENGRAVING PROCESSES

Cabinet V Shelf 6 No. 14

(French methods, various specimens of)

See ICONOGRAPHIE de l'IMPRIMERIE Bulletin Officiel...Paris, 1927

ENGRAVING PROCESSES

Cabinet 46 Shelf 2 Number 4

Gillot, Firmin, promotor of chemical engraving in France. Biographical note, with portrait.

Article in BULLETIN de l'IMPRIMERIE Mai, 1877, p. 101.

ENGRAVING PROCESSES, EXAMPLES OF

Cabinet J Shelf 1 No. 16

Chemilyiphic process, specimens of fruit and vegetable labels by the New Rose & Co. Designers, engravers, printers. Baltimore, Md. n.d. circa 1860.

Cloth; 6 x 8-5/8 in.

ENGRAVING PROCESSES, LITERATURE OF

Cabinet I Shelf 2 No. 16

Aquatint engraving: A chapter in the history of book illustration. By S.T. Prideaux. Illustrated by an original aquatint, two collotype plates and numerous half-tone plates. London (1909).

Cloth; 9-5/8 x 6¼ x 2 in.

ENGRAVING PROCESSES

Cabinet J Shelf 4 No. 11

(Half-tone copper engraving, line engraving, four color printing, facsimile printing. Examples of). 12 plates.

K.u.K. Hof. Photogr. Kunst-Anstalt. E. Angerer und Goschl. Wien, c.1905.

Cloth portfolio: 15-5/8 x 11¾ in.

ENGRAVING PROCESSES, EXAMPLES OF

Cabinet J Shelf 1 No. 14

Edinburgh, 1849. W.H. Lizars.

See LIZARS, W.H. Specimens of engraving ...

ENGRAVING PROCESSES, LITERATURE OF

Cabinet J Shelf 2 No. 40

Aquatint engraving, pioneer and populariser of, Rudolph Ackermann, 1764-1834.

See Ackermann, Rudolph. Populariser of aquatint engraving....

ENGRAVING PROCESSES.

Cabinet I Shelf 5 No. 2

Heliotype process, examples of.

See MANUSCRIPTS, ILLUMINATED. [Facsimiles]. Les tres belles miniatures ... Bruxelles et Paris, 1913.

ENGRAVING PROCESSES. Examples of

Cabinet 68 Shelf No. 3

Heliography. Plates by Letellier and Dujardin. Printed by Lemale et Cie, Havre, 1893.

La Normandie monumentale et pittoresque...Avec une introduction par M. Armand Dayot.

Half morocco; 19½ x 15½ in.

ENGRAVING PROCESSES. Literature of.

Cabinet V Shelf 6 No. 12.01

Arts de reproduction: Lithographie, photogravure, heliogravure etc. Bulletin Officiel des Maitres Imprimeurs. Paris, 1925.

Illustrated history and description of mechanical reproductive methods.

Paper; 12½ x 9½ x 1 in.

ENGRAVING PROCESSES.

Cabinet I Shelf 4 No. 15

[Heliotypie. Examples of].

See DUPORTAL, M$^{elle.}$ J. (La) Gravure en France en 18e siècle ... Paris et Bruxelles, 1926.

ENGRAVING PROCESSES, EXAMPLES OF

Cabinet 68 Shelf No. 5

(Lithography) Fac-similes of the miniatures and ornaments of Anglo-Saxon and Irish manuscripts. Executed by J.O. Westwood. Drawn on stone by W.R.Tymms. Chromo-lithographed by Day and Son, Ltd., London, 1868.

Half morocco; 22 x 14¾ in.

ENGRAVING PROCESSES Literature of

Cabinet K Shelf 6 No. 4

Arts du livre à l'Exposition Internationale des Arts Décoratifs et Industriels Modernes. Paris, 1925. (Illus. and descriptive catalogue)

Supplément au "Bulletin Officiel".

Item in envelope.

ENGRAVING PROCESSES

Cabinet K Shelf 3 No. 15

Photo engraving, a practical handbook of drawing for modern methods of reproduction. By Charles C. Harper. London, 1901. Illus.

Cloth; 8-7/8 x 5¾ in.

ENGRAVING PROCESSES Examples of

Cabinet J Shelf 1 No. 30

Moss' Process. Specimen sheets of portraits and figures, buildings, landscapes, machinery and apparatus. The Photo Engraving Co.(L.S Hobart, John C. Moss), New York, n.d. circa 1860.

On back of each issue, exterior view of the Photo Engraving Co. building.

Portfolio; 13½ x 10 in.

ENGRAVING PROCESSES. Literature of

Cabinet I Shelf 2 No. 11

Auer, Alois. l'Appareil polygraphique de l'Imprimerie Imperiale Royale de Vienne. Par Aloyse Auer. Vienne. Imprimerie Royal, 1855. Pamphlet.

French translation of I/2/1. Without the illustrations.

Item in manila envelope.

ENGRAVING PROCESSES

Cabinet LL Shelf 5 No. 15

Steps in making a line etching, a half tone, a woodcut. Illus.

See GREER, CARL RICHARD. Buckeye book of direct advertising...pp.161-174.

ENGRAVING PROCESSES, LITERATURE OF.

Cabinet I Shelf 3 No. 1

[Anastatic printing]. New arts of printing and drawing. Excerpt from the "Living Age," March 15, 1845.

Item 7 in vol. with binder's title: "Various Engraving and About Engravers."

ENGRAVING PROCESSES Literature of

Cabinet I Shelf 2 No. 10

Auer, Alois. Polygraphische apparat...der K.K. hof - und Staatsdruckerei zu Wien. I und II, vortrag. Wien, 1853. Illus.

Description of the different processes in use at the Imperial Royal Printing-office at Vienna.

Paper; 9½ x 6-1/8 x ½ in.

ENGRAVING PROCESSES, LITERATURE OF

Cabinet K Shelf 4 No. 15

Cantor lectures on book illustration old and new. By J. Comyns Carr. London, 1882.

Half morocco; $10\frac{3}{4}$ x $6\frac{3}{4}$ x 3/8 in.

ENGRAVING PROCESSES Literature of

Cabinet J Shelf 4 No. 6

Catalogue de l'Exposition de gravures anciennes et modernes. (Redigé par Georges Duplessis). Paris, 4 Juillet, 1881.

Has numerous engravings, and specimens of advertising typography.

Includes also a brief history of engraving and engraving processes.

Boards; $12\frac{3}{4}$ x $9\frac{3}{4}$ x $1\frac{1}{2}$ in.

ENGRAVING PROCESSES, LITERATURE OF.

Cabinet I Shelf 3 No. 1

Color prints of Mr. Edwards. By Russell Sturges. Excerpt from Scribners, January, 1906.

Item 24 in vol. with binder's title:"Various Engravers and about Engravers."

ENGRAVING PROCESSES Literature of

Cabinet L Shelf 4 No. 45

Colour printing and printers. By R.M.Burch. With a chapter on modern processes by W. Gamble. New York, 1910. Illus.

With 8 half tones and 22 colour prints

Cloth; $9\frac{3}{4}$ x $6\frac{3}{4}$ x 1-5/8 in.

ENGRAVING PROCESSES, Literature of

Cabinet R Shelf 5 No. 148

[Copperplate] Examples of early American copper engraving in the first American edition of Josephus' History of the Jews, printed by William Durell, New York, 1792: An Account of the above by W.L. Andrews; excerpt from the Bookman, Feb. 1900.

Excerpt 12 in volume "CHAP BOOKS, ALMANACS, ANNUALS, etc."

ENGRAVING PROCESSES, LITERATURE OF

Cabinet 20 Shelf 2 No. 10

[Copperplate] First book decorated with copper engravings said to have been the "Monte Santo di Dio, by Bishop A. Bettino, Florence, 1477.

Brief account of the above.

In ZEITSCHRIFT FUR BUCHERFREUNDE, 1921, pp.78-80.

ENGRAVING PROCESSES Literature of

Cabinet K Shelf 3 No. 6

[Copperplate] Geschichte der kupferstechkunst und der damit verwandten künste, holzschneide-und steindruck kunst. Dargestellt von Wilhelm von Lüdemann. Dresden, 1828.

Paper; $6\frac{1}{4}$ x 3-7/8 in.

ENGRAVING PROCESSES, LITERATURE OF

Cabinet M Shelf 3 No. 16

[Copperplate] Origin and progress of copper engraving.

See LEO, POPE THE TENTH. Life and pontificate of...vol. IV. p.260.

ENGRAVING PROCESSES Literature of

Cabinet K Shelf 3 No. 7

[Copperplate] Practical engraving on metal, including hints on saw-piercing, carving, iXX inlaying, etc. By G.A. Banner. Second edition. London, n.d. Illus.

Cloth; 6-7/8 x $4\frac{3}{4}$ in.

ENGRAVING PROCESSES, LITERATURE OF

Cabinet J Shelf 4 No. 6

Coup d'oeil sur l'histoire de la gravure. Par Georges Duplessis. [Avec] Catalogue de l'Exposition de gravures anciennes et modernes. 4 Juillet, 1881. Paris. Illus.

History of engraving.

Boards, leatherette back; 13 x $9\frac{3}{4}$ x $1\frac{1}{4}$ in.

ENGRAVING PROCESSES, Literature of

Cabinet QQ Shelf 6 No. 15

(Definition of engraving terms, with brief descriptions of processes)

See VAN HUFFEL, N. G. Encyclopedisch handboek...Utrecht, 1926.

ENGRAVING PROCESSES, LITERATURE OF

Cabinet FF Shelf 2 No. 40

Different styles of engraving...

See index to book with title: Patents for Inventions: Abridgments of specifications relating to printing...London, 1859.

Half morocco; $7\frac{3}{4}$ x 5-1/8 x 1-7/8 in.

ENGRAVING PROCESSES, LITERATURE OF.

Cabinet I Shelf 3 No. 25

[English 18th century: masters of mezzotint, stipple, wood and copper engraving].

See BLUM, ANDRE. (Le) Gravure en Angleterre au 18e siecle ... Paris, 1930.

ENGRAVING PROCESSES Literature of

Cabinet 43 Shelf 1 No.

(The) Engraver and Printer, 1893--

See PERIODICALS,PRINTING, United States (The) Engraver and Printer...

ENGRAVING PROCESSES, LITERATURE OF

Cabinet J Shelf 3 No. 22

Engravings and their value: wood engraving, line-engraving, etching, mezzotint, stipple, colour prints, etc.

See SLATER, J. HERBERT. Engravings and their value, a complete guide...New York, 1929.

ENGRAVING PROCESSES. Literature of

Cabinet I Shelf 2 No. 13

Essai historique, la gravure a l'eau-forte. Par Raoul de Saint-Arroman. [also] Comment je devins graveur a l'eau-forte. Par le Comte Lepic. Paris, 1876. Frontispiece.

Paper; $8\frac{3}{4}$ x $5\frac{1}{2}$ x 3/8 in.

ENGRAVING PROCESSES, LITERATURE OF.

Cabinet I Shelf 3 No. 1

[Etching]. Book illustration, old and new. Cantor Lectures on. By J. Comyns Carr. Delivered before the Society of Arts, May, 1882.

Item 10 in vol. with binder's title:"Various Engravers and About Engravers."

ENGRAVING PROCESSES, LITERATURE OF

Cabinet I Shelf 2 No. 78

Etching, engraving and the other methods of picture printing. By Hans W. Singer and William Strang. With ten original plates by, and four il ustrations after William Strang. London, 1897.

At end a list of books that treat of artistic and mechanical processes.

Cloth; $8\frac{3}{4}$ x 6-7/8 x 1-1/8 in.

ENGRAVING PROCESSES, LITERATURE OF.

Cabinet I, Shelf 4, No. 15

[Etching, French 18th century].

See DUPORTAL, M[elle.] J. (La) Gravure en France au 18e siècle ...

ENGRAVING PROCESSES, LITERATURE OF

Cabinet V, Shelf 3, No. 22

Gravure sur bois, zincogravure, photogravure, chromotypogravure, lithographie, etc.

See vol.11, p.475, THIBAUDEAU'S "La lettre d'imprimerie"...Paris, 1921.

ENGRAVING PROCESSES, LITERATURE OF.

Cabinet, Shelf, No.

Line engraving.

See PHOTO-ENGRAVING PROCESSES. [Line engraving].

ENGRAVING PROCESSES. LITERATURE OF

Cabinet I, Shelf 2, No. 79

Étude descriptive, historique et critique sur la gravure au 19e siécle. D'apres les éditions de M.L.H. Lefevre de Londres. Par Le Roy de Saint-Croix [Editeur]. Paris, 1882.

Paper; 7-1/8 x 4¾ x 3/8 in.

ENGRAVING PROCESSES Literature of

Cabinet J, Shelf 2, No. 29

Heliogravure und des rakeltiefdruckes, Karl Klietsch der erfinder der. von Karl Albert. Mit 25 tafeln in den von Klietsch erfundenen techniken hergestellt. Wien, 1927.

Boards; 9-7/8 x 8 x ½ in.

ENGRAVING PROCESSES Literature of

Cabinet I, Shelf 2, No. 15

Lostalot, Alfred de. Procédés de la gravure. Bibliotheque de l'enseignement des beaux-arts. Paris, 1886. Illus.

Paper; 8½ x 5½ in.

ENGRAVING PROCESSES, LITERATURE OF

Cabinet V, Shelf 5, No. 14

Etude sur la gravure. Par Henry Cobin. Paris, 1874.

Summary of articles on engraving contained in the book with title "L'Art de peindre la parole. Par MM. Gobin, Jeunesse, Kaeppelin...Paris, 1874, pp.103-139.

Paper; 9-7/8 x 6¼ in.

ENGRAVING PROCESSES, LITERATURE OF.

Cabinet I, Shelf 3, No. 27

[Historical, brief account of the beginnings of various engraving processes].

See LINNIG, BENJAMIN. (La) Gravure en Belgique ... Anvers, 1911. p. 9-39.

ENGRAVING PROCESSES, LITERATURE OF

Cabinet I, Shelf 2, No. 17

Machines versus engraving. An answer to an article by the editor of the Engravers Bulletin issue of April 1914: A discourse on the degeneracy of the engraving business by present day methods. Hass Bank Note Engraving Co., New York (1914). Pamphlet.

Item in manila envelope.

ENGRAVING PROCESSES, LITERATURE OF.

Cabinet I, Shelf 3, No. 16

[French engraving and engravers.]

See COURBOIN, FRANCOIS. l'Estampe francaise ... Paris, 1914. pp.

ENGRAVING PROCESSES Literature of

Cabinet K, Shelf 6, No. 34

History of engraving and engraving methods. Review of four books on the subject of engraving. Excerpt from the "North British Review," Nov. 1846.

Item 2 in vol. with binder's title "Wood engraving. Various excerpts."

ENGRAVING PROCESSES, LITERATURE OF.

Cabinet I, Shelf 4, No. 20, 2 vols.

Mechanical methods, several processes: Autotypie, heliogravure, lichtdruck, dreifarbendruck, etc. (Historical descriptive).

See KUTSCHMANN, TH. "Geschichte der deutschen illustration ... Goslar und Berlin (1899(Vol. II, pp. 367-383.

ENGRAVING PROCESSES, LITERATURE OF

Cabinet I, Shelf 2, No. 76

Geschichte der reproductionstechnik: funfzig jahre C. Angerer & Goschl. Wien, 1871-1921. With portraits.

Paper; 10 x 8 in. In manila envelope.

ENGRAVING PROCESSES Literature of

Cabinet K, Shelf 2, No. 38.01

How prints are made, brief description of various processes. By Atherton Curtis.

Article in catalogue of a loan exhibition "Twentieth Century Prints" from several important American Collectors...The Lakeside Press Galleries, Chicago, Dec.1932, Jan-Feb. 1933.

Paper; 10-3/8 x 8 in.

ENGRAVING PROCESSES, Literature of.

Cabinet S, Shelf 5, No. 17

Mezzotint, Invention of. By Ernest Radford in The Connoisseur, April, 1902. Illus.

Bound in collection "MISCELLANEOUS ITEMS RELATING TO PRINTING", item 17.

ENGRAVING PROCESSES. Literature of

Cabinet B, Shelf 3, No. 5

Graphic processes; intaglio, relief, planographic. A series of actual prints. Selected and arranged with notes, by Louis A. Holman. Boston, 1926.

Portfolio; 19 x 13¼ in.

ENGRAVING PROCESSES, LITERATURE OF

Cabinet J, Shelf 3, No. 30

Japanese wood engravings, their history, technique and characteristics. By William Anderson. New edition. London, 1908. Illus.

Cloth; 6 x 4½ x 5/8 in.

ENGRAVING PROCESSES, Literature of

Cabinet 35, Shelf 2, No. 1-12

Paper and Press: The arts pictorial illustrated.

See PERIODICALS, PRINTING. United States Paper and Press [beginning with vol.19,1894]

ENGRAVING PROCESSES, LITERATURE OF

Cabinet J
Shelf 3
No. 1

Pennell, Joseph. Illustration of books. A manual for the use of students, notes for a course of lectures at the Slade School, University College. New York - London (1895)

Cloth; 7½ x 4-7/8 x 5/8 in.

ENGRAVING PROCESSES, Literature of.

Cabinet
Shelf
No.

[Photogravure]. Cost of engraving and producing photogravure cylinders and plate.. By L. F. Holt.

Article in British and Colonial Printer and Stationer, Vol. 11, No. 196, July 28, 1932, pp. 88, 90.

ENGRAVING PROCESSES. LITERATURE OF

Cabinet I
Shelf 2
No. 12

[Photo-lithography; Essai sur les gravure chimiques en relief. Par C. Motteroz. Paris, 1871. With 2 vols.

Deals with the different processes of mechanical engraving, historical and biographical.

Half morocco; 8½ x 5-5/8 in.

ENGRAVING PROCESSES, LITERATURE OF

Cabinet MM
Shelf 4
No. 21

Printing Arts; an epitome of the theory, practice, processes of engraving, lithography and printing in black and in colors. By John W. Harland. London, 1892. Illus.

Cloth; 7½ x 5-1/8 x ¾ in.

ENGRAVING PROCESSES, LITERATURE OF

Cabinet S
Shelf 5
No. 12

Processes of engraving and printing for pictorial purposes from the sixteenth century to our own time, (exclusive of modern photo-mechanical processes,)in catalogue prepared by S.R. Koehler for the Graphic Arts section at Centennial Exposition, Cincinnati, 1888.

Bound with "Pamphlets and excerpts relating to various typographical matters," item 5.

ENGRAVING PROCESSES, LITERATURE OF

Cabinet A
Shelf 2
No. 91

Progress of engraving and process work -- Boston the home of the first American engravers -- Pioneer of the first illustrated weekly paper...By Stephen H. Horgan.

Illus. article in the Graphic Arts Section of the Boston Evening Transcript, Aug. 29, 1929, part four, p.5.

ENGRAVING PROCESSES, LITERATURE OF

Cabinet A
Shelf 2
No. 91

Steel and copper-plate engraving. Period of greatest mechanical development in this industry, which is nearly 500 years old. By Harry J. Fredd.

Article in the Graphic Arts Section, Boston Evening Transcript, Tues. Aug., 29, 1922, part four, p.14.

ENGRAVING PROCESSES. Literature of.

Cabinet I
Shelf 3
No. 1

[Steel Engraving]. An American invention, due to Jacob Perkins, of Newburypost, Mass. [circa 1800].

Biographical-historical account; excerpt from "Great Industries of the U.S." Hartford 1872.

Item 1 in vol. with binder's title "Various Engravers, and About Engravers"

ENGRAVING PROCESSES, LITERATURE OF

Stack A
Shelf 1 & 2
Number 63

[Steel engraving] Jacob Perkins, the inventor of steel-engraving, was an American. By Henry Lewis Bullen.

Article in The Inland Printer, vol.LXIII, p.403.

ENGRAVING PROCESSES, LITERATURE OF.

Cabinet I
Shelf 3
No. 4

Various processes or kinds of engraving, on the.

See Chap. III, Vol. I, WILLSHIRE, WILLIAM HUGHES. Ancient prints ... London, 1877.

ENGRAVING PROCESSES, LITERATURE OF.

Cabinet I
Shelf 3
No. 6

[Various processes; wood engraving; line engraving; lithography, etc.]

See HUBBARD, HESKETH. How to distinguish prints ... Wiltshire, England, 1926.

ENGRAVING PROCESSES, Literature of.

Cabinet Y
Shelf 2
No. 38.

[Wood and copper engravings. Historical account. illustrated].

See BOGENG, G.A.E. Geschichte der buchdruckerkunst ... pp. 65-208.

ENGRAVING PROCESSES, Literature of

Cabinet
Shelf
No.

Wood-block printing

see WOOD-BLOCK PRINTING

ENGRAVING PROCESSES, LITERATURE OF.

Cabinet I
Shelf 3
No. 1

Wood Blocks, by Henriette Boekman: An excerpt from the Internation Studio, October, 1916. Illus.

Brief historical, technical account.

Item 32 in vol. with binder's title:"Various Engravers and About Engravers."

ENGRAVING PROCESSES, LITERATURE OF.

Cabinet I
Shelf 4
No. 5

Wood engraving. Mode of transferring impressions; repairing wood blocks.

See SOTHEBY, SAMUEL LEIGH. Principia Typographica...London, 1858, Vol.I, pp.49-157, 158, 165.

ENGRAVING PROCESSES, LITERATURE OF.

Cabinet I
Shelf 3
No. 1

[Wood Engraving]. New art development in England: Color Printing from wood blocks done by a society of artists. Excerpt from the Craftsman, July, 1912. Illus.

Item 30 in vol. with binder's title:"Various Engravers and About Engravers."

ENGRAVING PROCESSES, LITERATURE OF

Cabinet I
Shelf 3
No. 1

[Wood engraving]. The German peoples artist, Ludwig Richter. By W. Henry Winslow, in The New England Magazine, Dec., 1897. Illus.

A summary of the life and work of the artist who is said to have had the greatest influence upon modern wood engraving.

Item 26 in vol. with binder's title: "Various Engravers and About Engravers."

ENGRAVING PROCESSES, LITERATURE of.

Cabinet I
Shelf 3
No. 1

[Wood Engraving, etc.] Book illustration, old and new, by J. Comyns Carr: A series of lectures delivered before the Societyof Arts, London, May, 1882.

Traces the progress of wood engraving through all its developments, with a consideration of the newer mechanical processes.

Item 10 in vol. with binder's title:"Various Engravers and About Engravers."

ENGRAVING PROCESSES, LITERATURE OF.

Cabinet I Shelf 3 No. 1

[Wood Engraving, etc.] Book illustrations, a chapter on. By B. B. Chamberlain. [Excerpt from Ladies Repository, Oct., 1869].

Illustrations: Wood engravers' tools, portraits of Durer, Bewick.

Item 14 in vol. with binder's title:"Various Engravers and About Engravers."

ENGRAVING PROCESSES, LITERATURE OF.

Cabinet I Shelf 3 No. 1

[Wood engraving, etc.] Illustration, some modern methods of. By Jas. B. Carrington. [Excerpt from the Bookman, August 1905]. Illus.

Item 21 in vol. with binder's title:"Various Engravers and About Engravers."

ENGRAVING PROCESSES, LITERATURE OF.

Cabinet I Shelf 3 No. 1

[Wood engraving, etc., Italian]. Modern Italian graphic art. Illustrated description of the work shown at an exhibition in London.

Item 33 in vol. with binder's title:"Various Engravers and About Engravers."

ENGRAVING PROCESSES, LITERATURE OF.

Cabinet I Shelf 4 No. 3

Wood Engraving in Europe, some account of the early useof, and the invention of chalcography by Maso Finiguerra (circa 1440).

See Introduction to Ottley's "Collection of 125 fac-similes of scarce and curious prints." ... London, 1828.

ENGRAVING PROCESSES, LITERATURE OF

Cabinet I Shelf 3 No. 1

[Wood Engraving of Felix Vollotton, Biographical technical account]. By Christian Brinton. Excerpt from the Critic, April, 1903.

With portraits of Vellotton, also specimens of his wood engravings.

Item 23 in vol. with binder's title:"Various Engravers and About Engravers."

ENGRAVING PROCESSES, LITERATURE OF.

Cabinet I Shelf 3 No. 1

Wood engraving, the return of. By Gardner Teall [Excerpt from the Bookman, May, 1909].

Illustrated article.

Item 16 in vol. with binder's title"Various Engravers and About Engravers."

ENGRAVING PROCESSES, METHODS OF.

Cabinet I Shelf 2 No. 57

[Air brush] A treatise on the air brush. With progressive lessons. By Samuel W. Frazier and George F. Stine. Boston, Mass., 1930. Illus.

Cloth; 10-1/8 x 6-7/8 x 5/8 in.

ENGRAVING PROCESSES, METHODS OF

Cabinet I Shelf 2 No. 4 Ref. B. & W. p.146

Anastatic printing, a brief description of the art, and of the uses to which it may be applied; with full directions for making drawings for transfers. S.W. Cowell, Ipswich, Suffolk, n.d.

Morocco; 9⅞ x 6¼ in.

ENGRAVING PROCESSES, METHODS OF.

Cabinet I Shelf 2 No. 2

Anastatic printing, a treatise on, or the art of reprinting from prints on paper, detailing a simple process invented by the author. With various applications and modifications...By C.J. Jordan. London, 1853.

Cloth; 8-1/8 x 5¾ in.

ENGRAVING PROCESSES, METHODS OF.

Cabinet I Shelf 2 No. 1

Anastatic printing and papyrography, on the various applications of. With illustrative examples. By Philip de la Motte. London, 1849.

Boards, illuminated; 8⅝ x 5⅝ x ¼ in.

ENGRAVING PROCESSES, METHODS OF.

Cabinet I Shelf 2 No. 3 Ref. B. & W. p.146

Anastatic printing, brief description of the art, and of the uses to which it may be applied, as practised by S.H. Cowell, Ipswich, Suffolk. n.d. (1868?).

Paper; 9¾ x 6-1/8 in. In manila envelope.

ENGRAVING PROCESSES, METHODS OF

Cabinet Shelf No.

Aquatone Printing Process and some of its predecessors.

Article in Inland Printer, vol. 86. Nov. 1930. pp. 55-57.

ENGRAVING PROCESSES, METHODS OF.

Cabinet I Shelf 4 No. 2

Aquatone Reproductions. Versatility. As produced by Edward Stern & Company, Inc. Philadelphia, n.d. circa, 1928.

Bound in with another process engraving item: "Aquatone Corporation," N. Y. n.d., circa, 1925.

Half morocco; 14-1/8 x 11¼ in.

ENGRAVING PROCESSES, METHODS OF

Cabinet I Shelf 2 No. 37

[Autotype] The autotype process: being a practical manual of instruction in the art of printing in carbon, or other permanent pigment. Third edition, revised and enlarged. Spencer, Sawyer, Bird & Co. London, 1873. Frontis.

Cloth; 8-3/8 x 6½ in.

ENGRAVING PROCESSES, METHODS OF

Cabinet I Shelf 2 No. 38

[Autotype] The autotype process: being a manual of instruction in the art of printing in permanent pigments; with a notice of the autotype mechanical process. 6th revised ed. By J.R. Sawyer. London, 1877. Frontis.

Cloth; 8 x 6¾ in.

ENGRAVING PROCESSES, METHODS OF

Cabinet I Shelf 2 No. ~~35~~ 36

[Autotypie] De natuur zich zelve afbeeldende. Handleiding tot het maken van zelfdrukken. Benevens eene reeks van autotypen. Door J.S. Wilson. Meppel, 1857.

Half morocco, oblong; 6¾ x 8½ in.

ENGRAVING PROCESSES, METHODS OF

Cabinet FF Shelf 2 No. 40

Chemitypy See Chemitypy, 1850

ENGRAVING PROCESSES, METHODS OF

Cabinet S Shelf 5 No. 56

(Collotype). History of the Society of Iconophiles of the City of New York 1895-1930 ... Compiled by Richard Hoe Lawrence, New York, 1930.

See the several prints in this book.

Quarter morocco; 11 x 8½ x 1¾ in.

ENGRAVING PROCESSES, METHODS OF

Cabinet I, Shelf 2-b, No. 1

[Copper engraving].

See BERTHIAUD -- Nouveau manuel complet ...Paris, 1837. Manuel Roret.

ENGRAVING PROCESSES, METHODS OF

Cabinet S, Shelf 5, No. 14

[Copperplate] Etching ground for engravers: Methods and ingredients, by Mr. Edmund Turrell, of Somerstown, Eng., 1825: An excerpt from the reports of the British Society of Arts.

Bound with other items in collection "PRINTING PROCESSES", item 6.

ENGRAVING PROCESSES, METHODS OF

Cabinet J, Shelf 3, No. 32

(Copperplate engraving and printing) Gravure et imprimerie en taille-douce. Par Ch. Jacques. [Illus. excerpt from "Magazine Pittoresque"]. n.p. n.d. circa 1860.

With illus. of interior of engraver's studio, printing press with men at work, engraving tools, etc.

Item in manila envelope.

ENGRAVING PROCESSES, METHODS OF

Cabinet V, Shelf 4, No. 16

Copperplate engraving, Paris, 1642, Abraham Bosse. Engraved broadsides illustrating and explaining process of copper engraving.

See CAILLE (JEAN DE LA). Histoire de l'imprimerie...1689.

ENGRAVING PROCESSES, METHODS OF

Cabinet L, Shelf 4, No. 2

Dermotypotemnie...

See Aumerle, Ernest. Dermotypotemnie... Issondun, 1867.

ENGRAVING PROCESSES, METHODS OF

Cabinet I, Shelf 2, No. 14

[Etching] Traite élémentaire de gravure a l'eau-forte, sur bois de buis, et sur bois de fil. d'apres Albert Durer, Callot, etc. Par V.M. Bouton. Paris, n.d. circa 1880. Illus.

Paper; 7¼ x 4⅝ in. With other items in manila envel.

ENGRAVING PROCESSES, METHODS OF.

Cabinet I, Shelf 2, No. 73.01

Exhibition illustrating the technical methods of the reproductive arts from the 15th century to the present time, with special reference to the photo-mechanical processes. January 8 to March 6, 1892. Boston Museum of Fine Arts, Print Department.

Cloth; 7-5/8 x 4⅝ x ⅛ in.

ENGRAVING PROCESSES, METHODS OF

Cabinet I, Shelf 2, No. 21

Glyphographie, die buchzeichnung oder. Enthaltend eine beschreibung dieser neuer erfindung nebst anleitung für künstler. Mit zahlreichen buchdruckzeichnungen. Leipzig, 1846.

Paper; 10½ x 6⅝ in.

ENGRAVING PROCESSES, METHODS OF

Cabinet I, Shelf 2, No. 22

Glypographie uit het etablissement van H.B. Bingen...Te Amsterdam. n.d. circa 1850.

With specimens.

Half morocco; 12-1/8 x 9¼ in.

ENGRAVING PROCESSES, METHODS OF

Cabinet I, Shelf 2, No. 20

Glyphography, instructions on. (Abdiel Hawkins) Glyphographic Office, 79 Shoe Lane, London, n.d. Pamphlet.

Has specimens.

Circular in manila envelope.

ENGRAVING PROCESSES, METHODS OF

Cabinet I, Shelf 2, No. 18

Glyphography, Palmer's Patent.

See PALMER, EDWARD. Glyphography...London, 1843.

ENGRAVING PROCESSES, METHODS OF

Cabinet K, Shelf 3, No. 10

(Die) Graphischen kunst. von C. Kampmann. Mit zahlreichen abbildungen und beilagen. Dritte, vermehrte und verbesserte auflage. Leipzig, 1909.

Cloth; 6-1/8 x 4-1/8 in.

ENGRAVING PROCESSES, METHODS OF

Cabinet I, Shelf 2, No. 26

[Graphotype] Prospectus of the Intagtiotype & Graphotype Engraving Company, New York, 1864. Pamphlet, illus.

Bound in with three pamphlets issued by the Moss Engraving Co. of N.Y. 1880-1884.

Cloth; 12⅝ x 907/8 x 3/8 in.

ENGRAVING PROCESSES, METHODS OF.

Cabinet I, Shelf 2, No. 39

[Heliochromy] A new principle in. By Frederic E. Ives. Philadelphia, 1889. Illus. Frontispiece portrait.

Cloth; 9-1/8 x 7 x ¼ in.

ENGRAVING PROCESSES, METHODS OF

Cabinet I, Shelf 2, No. 23

[Heliography] Gravure heliographique galvanoplastie. Traite pratique. Par Geymet & Alker. Paris...Bruxelles, 1870.

Paper; 7¼ x 4½ in.

ENGRAVING PROCESSES, METHODS OF

Cabinet I, Shelf 2, No. 24

[Heliotype] Description of heliotype process. With 12 specimens. The Heliotype Company Limited, London, 1872.

Cloth; 9¼ x 6⅝ x 3/8 in.

ENGRAVING PROCESSES, METHODS OF

Cabinet I, Shelf 2, No. 25

[Heliotype] The heliotype process. By Ernest Edwards. With 28 illustrations. Boston: James R. Osgood and Company, 1876.

Boards; 12 x 10 x 5/8 in.

ENGRAVING PROCESSES, METHODS OF

Cabinet 26, Shelf 2, No. 3

[Hyalography, or the art of printing from engraved glass plates] Uber die kunst glass zu atzen und zu drucken.

Specimens follow No.5 of publication below.

Journal fur Buchdruckerkunst, 1844, No.4, cols. 59-60, No.5, following cols. 79-80.

ENGRAVING PROCESSES, METHODS OF

Cabinet I Shelf 2 No. 26

[Intagliotype]

See INTAGLIOTYPE AND GRAPHOTYPE ENGRAVING CO. Prospectus...

ENGRAVING PROCESSES, METHODS OF

Cabinet Shelf No.

Multicel (The) composition without type. By Parker Hart. (A proposal seemingly of little value).

Article in The Platemakers Criterion, pp.97-99, July issue, 1931, vol.33, No.7.

ENGRAVING PROCESSES, METHODS OF

Cabinet I Shelf 2 No. 61

Photogravure: a text book on the machine and hand printed processes. By H. Mills Cartwright. Boston, 1930. Illus.

Cloth; 9-1/8 x 6-1/8 x ¾ in.

ENGRAVING PROCESSES. METHODS OF

Cabinet Shelf No.

Linoleum block printing.

see BLOCK PRINTING. Linoleum block printing...

ENGRAVING PROCESSES, METHODS OF.

Cabinet I Shelf 2 No. 30

[Olgemalde-Druck] erfunden und beschrieben. von J. Liepmann. Berlin, 1842. With diagrams, folded plates.

On chromo-lithographic printing.

Half morocco; 10-3/8 x 8½ x 3/8 in.

ENGRAVING PROCESSES, METHODS OF

Cabinet I Shelf 2 No. 60

Photogravure, elements of. Photo printing from copper plates. Screen photogravure simply explained with full working instructions, and an explanatory chapter on modern rotary gravure printing...By Colin N. Bennett. Boston-London, 1927. Illus.

Cloth; 7½ x 4-7/8 x ½ in.

ENGRAVING PROCESSES, METHODS OF

Cabinet V Shelf 5 No. 40 14

[Lithography]. Chromo-lithographie autographe, gravure sur pierre, machines a imprimer, Par D. Kaeppelin. Paris, 1874. Illus.

Description pp.77-101 in L'Art de peindre la parole...Par MM. Gobin, Jeunesse, Kaeppelin...

Paper; 9-7/8 x 6¼ in.

ENGRAVING PROCESSES, METHODS OF

Cabinet I Shelf 2 No. 26

[Photo-engraving line cuts]. Specimens of etched line engravings (3 pamphlets bound together (1 loose), issued by the Moss Engraving Co. of New York, circa 1880-1884; with picture of premises occupied by that company "Largest establishment of the kind in the world".

Cloth; 12¾ x 9¾ in.

ENGRAVING PROCESSES, METHODS OF

Cabinet I Shelf 2 No. 58

[Photogravure] "Photogravure et imprimerie". Par Georges Degaast. Preface de Victor Michel. Paris, 1925. Illus.

Paper; 9-3/8 x 6 in. Item in manila envelope

ENGRAVING PROCESSES, METHODS OF

Cabinet I Shelf 2 No. 27

[Map printing, colored]

See RITSCHEL Von HARTENBACH (J.) Neues system geographische charten...Leipzig, 1840.

ENGRAVING PROCESSES, METHODS OF

Cabinet I Shelf 2 No. 56

Photo engraving of today. Address by A.J. Powers ...Dec. 9, 1926. New York. Privately Printed Booklet.

Item in manila envelope.

ENGRAVING PROCESSES, METHODS OF.

Cabinet I Shelf 2 No. 59

Photogravure rotative, la. Historique, procedes, formules. Par F. Lamey. Mulhouse, 1924. Illus

Paper; 11-5/8 x 9-1/8 x ½ in.

ENGRAVING PROCESSES, METHODS OF

Cabinet I Shelf 2 No. 29

[Mezzotint] British mezzotints. Being a lecture delivered to the Print Collectors Club, Nov. 7, 1924. By Sir Frank Short...London, 1924. Illus.

Boards; 10 x 7½ x 3/8 in.

ENGRAVING PROCESSES, METHODS OF

Cabinet I Shelf 2 No. 55

Photo engraving, process and practice of. By Harry A. Groesbeck Jr. New York, 1924, (1st ed.) Illus.

Cloth; 11¼ x 8½ x 7/8 in.

ENGRAVING PROCESSES, METHODS OF

Cabinet I Shelf 2 No. 52

Photo-trichromatic printing in theory and practice. By C.G. Zander. Published by Raithby, Lawrence & Co., Ltd., Leicester, 1896. Illus.

Deals with three color printing.

Cloth; 8-3/8 x 6-1/8 x ½ in.

ENGRAVING PROCESSES, METHODS OF

Cabinet S Shelf 5 No. 17

[Mezzotint] Invention of mezzotint. By Ernest Radford. An excerpt from The Connoisseur, April, 1902. Illus.

Item 17 in collection "Miscellaneous items relating to printing; excerpts from magazines", 1918.

ENGRAVING PROCESSES, METHODS OF

Cabinet I Shelf 2 No. 77

[Photo-engraving processes, various]. Achievement in photo-engraving and letter-press printing, 1927. Compiled and edited by Louis Flader. Published by the American Photo-Engravers Association.

Has a number of technical articles by authorities; and with numerous illustrations.

Embossed leather; 12-3/4 x 9-3/8 x 2-3/4 in.

ENGRAVING PROCESSES, METHODS OF.

Cabinet I Shelf 2 No. 31

Plate printing and die stamping. How to operate a department for copperplate and steel die engraving and printing. By Robert F. Salade. New York, 1917.

Cloth; 7 x 5¼ in.

ENGRAVING PROCESSES, METHODS OF

Cabinet I, Shelf 2-b, No. 1 to 7

[Process engraving]

See GAMBLE, WILLIAM (Compiler) Penrose Process Pocket Book and Diary...

ENGRAVING PROCESSES, METHODS OF

Cabinet I, Shelf 2-b, No. 2

[Process engraving] By Carl Hentschel. The "What to be" books. Penny guides to trades and handicrafts for youths and girls. London, n.d. Booklet.

Paper; 5-3/8 x 3-3/8 in.

ENGRAVING PROCESSES, METHODS OF.

Cabinet I, Shelf 4, No. 1

[Process engraving] Discovery of the natural printing process ... Vienna, 1854.

See AUER, ALOIS. Discovery of the natural printing process ... Vienna, 1854.

ENGRAVING PROCESSES, METHODS OF

Cabinet I, Shelf 2, No. 63

[Process engraving]. Formulas, equipment, and methods of working. By Edward S. Pilsworth. New York, 1922. Illus.

Cloth; 7½ x 5 x ⅜ in.

ENGRAVING PROCESSES, METHODS OF.

Cabinet I, Shelf 2, No. 62

[Process engraving] I - Photographische schwierigkeiten. II - Augenblickliche lichtbilder...von Cadby Ponting...Mit einem alphabetisch geordneten sachregister und einem anhang uber Photo - Zinkographie in's deutsche ubertragen von Paul Grimm. Weimar, 1863.

Boards; 8¼ x 5½ in.

ENGRAVING PROCESSES, METHODS OF

Cabinet I, Shelf 2, No. 64

[Process engraving] Typon, a photographic material for...process engraving. For camera and contact. This booklet has been entirely reproduced by Typon and printed in Switzerland. n.p. n.d. circa 1928. Illus.

Item in manila envelope.

ENGRAVING PROCESSES, METHODS OF

Cabinet I, Shelf 2, No. 70

[Process engraving. Various methods] The art of engraving, with the various modes of operation under the following different divisions: etching, line engraving, mezzotint, lithography, photography..By T.H. Fielding. London, 1844. Illus.

Cloth; 9-3/4 x 6¼ in.

ENGRAVING PROCESSES, METHODS OF

Cabinet I, Shelf 2, No. 72

[Process engraving, various methods.] Des arts graphiques destinés à multiplier par l'impression, considérés sous le double point de vue historique et pratique. Par J.-M.-Herman Hammann. Genève - Paris, 1857

Half morocco; 7 x 4-1/8 x 1 in.

ENGRAVING PROCESSES, METHODS OF

Cabinet I, Shelf 2, No. 75

[Process engraving, various methods] Die herstellung von büchern, illustrationen, u.s.w. von Arthur W. Unger. Mit 178 figuren, 12 beilagen und 74 tafeln. Halle, A.S. 1910.

Cloth; 8½ x 5-5/8 x 2¼ in.

ENGRAVING PROCESSES, METHODS OF

Cabinet I, Shelf 2, No. 74

[Process-engraving, Various methods] Methods and processes adopted for production of the maps of the "Ordinance Survey" of the United Kingdom; drawn up by the officers of Royal Engineers. (Second edition). London. Printed for His Majesty's Stationery Office, by Darling & Son, Ltd. 1902. With diagrams, plates, etc.

Cloth; 12½ x 10-1/8 x 3/4 in.

ENGRAVING PROCESSES, METHODS OF.

Cabinet I, Shelf 2, No. 73

[Process engraving, various methods]. Procédés de reproductions graphiques appliquées à l'imprimerie. Par H.-L. Monet. Avec 103 figures intercalées dans le text et 13 planches hors text dont plusieurs en couleurs. Paris, 1888.

Half morocco; 10¼ x 6-7/8 x 1 in.

ENGRAVING PROCESSES, METHODS OF

Cabinet I, Shelf 2, No. 71

[Process engraving, Various methods.] Rise and progress of the graphic arts: including notices od illumination, chalcography...and elucidating the new art of chromo-glyphotype, invented by John Donlevy. New York, 1854.

Half morocco; 11-5/8 x 9-3/8 in.

ENGRAVING PROCESSES, METHODS OF.

Cabinet A, Shelf 3, No. 89

[Relief and wood engraving]

Article in the Special Graphic Arts number of The Times, London, Sept., 1912, p.33.

ENGRAVING PROCESSES, METHODS OF

Cabinet 26, Shelf 2, No. 6

(Relief engraved printing surfaces; A new method of) Neue Manier des hochdrucks.

Journal fur Bucheruckerkunst, 1853, No.6, cols. 63-67.

ENGRAVING PROCESSES, METHODS OF

Cabinet I, Shelf 2, No. 32

[Retouching].

See JOHNSON, ROBERT. Retouching photographic negatives...Boston, Mass., 1930.

ENGRAVING PROCESSES, METHODS OF

Cabinet V, Shelf 5, No. ~~40~~ 1-1

[Stereotypie]. Par Aug. Jeunesse. Paris, 1874.

Illustrated description, pp.63-76, in "L'Art de peindre la parole" ...Par MM. Gobin, Jeunesse, Kaeppelin, et Pierragi. Paris, 1874.

Paper; 9-7/8 x 6¼ in.

ENGRAVING PROCESSES, METHODS OF.

Cabinet I, Shelf 2-a, No. 1

[Various methods]. Nouveau manuel complet du graveur...Par A.M. Perrot, Paris, 1865. Manuels-Roret. With folding plates.

Paper; 6-1/8 x 3-7/8 x 1-1/8 in.

ENGRAVING PROCESSES, METHODS OF

Cabinet I, Shelf 2-a, No. 2

[Various processes] Manuel complete du graveur en creux et en relief. Contenant procédés anciens et modernes...Suivi de la fabrication du papier-monnaie, des timbres-postes, et des cartes à jouer. (2 vols.) Par A.M. Villon. Ouvrage orné de nombreuse figures intercalées dans le texte. Paris, 1914.

Paper; 6-1/8 x 3-3/4 in.

ENGRAVING PROCESSES, METHODS OF

Cabinet I Shelf 2 No. 34

[Wax engraving] Comparison in time, appearance and cost between hand-set tabular work and wax engraving. By Royal Electrotype Co. Philadelphia, circa 1926. Illus. pamphlet.

Item in manila envelope.

ENGRAVING PROCESSES, METHODS OF

Cabinet I Shelf 2 No. 33

[Wax engraving] The L.L. Poates Engraving Company. New York, 1913.

Specimen illustrations.

Paper; 10¼ x 7-5/8 in.

ENGRAVING PROCESSES, METHODS OF

Cabinet I Shelf 2 No. 35

[Wax process] Illustrated description of the.

See CLEMENTS, J.W. Co. - THE MATTHEWS NORTHRUP WORKS. Making of fine maps...

ENGRAVING PROCESSES, METHODS OF

Cabinet J Shelf 5 No. 12

(Wood and copperplate engraving. Nine plates with illustrated description of methods.) Gravure en taille-douce, en maniere noire, maniere de crayon, etc. Contenant neuf planches. (Excerpts, Paris, 1740].

Half morocco; 16¾ x 11 in.

ENGRAVING PROCESSES, METHODS OF

Cabinet I Shelf 2 No. 65

[Zincography] A practical guide to the art. By Josef Böck...Revised and enlarged edition. Translated by E. Menken. London, n.d.

Wyman's Technical Series.

Cloth; 7-3/8 x 5 in.

ENGRAVING PROCESSES, METHODS OF

Cabinet I Shelf 2 No. 66

[Zincography]. Proeven van reproductien en zink voor de boekdruppers. Roeloffzen & Hubner. Amsterdam, 1888.

Decorated cloth; 9-3/8 x 7 in.

ENGRAVINGS

Cabinet J Shelf 3 No. 23

Abbey, Edwin and Alfred Parsons. [Engravings in book entitled] "The quiet life". Certain verses by various hands. With a prologue and an epilogue by Austin Dobson. New York. Harper & Brothers, Printers and Publishers. 1890.

Morocco, gilt; 12 x 9¼ in.

ENGRAVINGS

Cabinet Z Shelf 5 No. 15

Bara et Gerard, Paris, circa 1837. Wood engravings. Specimen of printers cuts and ornaments.

Bound in with "Epreuves de la fonderie de J. A. Pasteur"...1823.

Half morocco; 16 x 10¼ x ½ in.

ENGRAVINGS

Cabinet Z Shelf 4 No. 7.01

Bara et Gerard, Paris, n.d. circa 1837, wood engravings of.

See SPECIMEN BOOKS, CUTS. France. Laurent et Deberny, Paris, circa 1837.

ENGRAVINGS

Cabinet F Shelf 5 No. 12

Barbault, Gio., Rome, 1758. Initials and vignettes, copperplate.

See EARLY PRINTING IN ITALY. Rome, 1758. Niccolo et Marco Pagliarini...

ENGRAVINGS

Cabinet M Shelf 2 No. 42

Bewick, Thomas, 1795. Steel engravings, facsimiles of.

See GOLDSMITH, OLIVER. Deserted Village ...Linotype and Machinery Limited. London. 1921.

ENGRAVINGS

Cabinet K Shelf 6 No. 10

Bewick, Thomas & John, wood engravings of. Portfolio of 13 plates, pictures mounted.

Boards; 11-3/8 x 9 x ½ in.

ENGRAVINGS

Cabinet K Shelf 3 No. 11

Bird's-eye view engravings, examples of. By Edward W. Spofford, illustrator. New York, 1910.

Cloth, oblong; 7-1/8 x 9-7/8 in.

ENGRAVINGS.

Cabinet F Shelf 4 No. 91

[Bonnet, (Louis Marin) engraver. France 1785].

See EARLY PRINTING IN FRANCE. Paris, 1785. Francoise-Ambroise (II) Didot.

ENGRAVINGS

Cabinet V Shelf 4 No. 16

Bosse, Abraham, Paris, 1642. Copper engravings showing processes of making copperplate engravings.

See CAILLE (JEAN DE LA). Histoire de l'imprimerie...1689.

ENGRAVINGS

Cabinet E Shelf 4 No. 53

Bosse, Abraham and Francois de Poilly, Paris, 1671, copperplate engravings of.

See EARLY PRINTING IN FRANCE. Paris, 1671, Francois Muguet...

ENGRAVINGS

Cabinet C Shelf 1 No. 11

Century Gallery (The). Selected proofs from The Century Magazine and St. Nicholas. New York, The Century Company, 1898.

Half morocco; 17½ x 13¼ x ½ in.

ENGRAVINGS

Cabinet F Shelf 5 No. 18

(Cochin, Charles-Nicolas le jeune. Paris, 1755.) Etchings.

See LA FONTAINE, JEAN DE. Fables Choisies mises en vers. Par J. de la Fontaine. Paris, 1755. 2 vols.

ENGRAVINGS

Cabinet K Shelf 6 No. 31

Contemporary Italian original woodcuts, 1924-5.

see WOODCUT MONTHLY (Italian) 1924-5. Xilografia...

ENGRAVINGS

Cabinet C Shelf 2 No. 13

(Copperplate, 18th century. Engravings provided for the Imprimerie Royale) Printed at l'Imprimerie Nationale, Paris, 1889.

Half calf; 20 x 13-7/8 in.

ENGRAVINGS.

Cabinet I Shelf 5 No. 23

Durer, Albrecht, 1511. Apocalipsis cum figuris. [16 plates of wood engravings]. Impressa denuo Nurnberge p. Albertum Durer pictorem. Anno christiano millesimo quingentesimo undecimo.

Following colophon, a warning of punishment to imitators of these engravings.

Modern pigskin; 16¼ x 12 in.

ENGRAVINGS

Cabinet 9 Shelf 2 No. 1 to 9

(Copper engravings depicting the antiquities of Herculaneum, 1757-92)

See BAJARDE, OTTAVIANO-ANTONIO. Antichita (le) di Ercolano...

ENGRAVINGS

Cabinet J Shelf 2 No. 12

(Copperplate engravings of Alfred Cossmann) Ein meister des kupferstiches. n.p. n.d. circa 1919.

8 plates of illustrations, includes a self portrait of the artist.

Boards; 9-5/8 x 6⅝ in.

ENGRAVINGS

Cabinet J Shelf 3 No. 32 (env.)

(English engraving, 18th century.) L'Estampe anglaise d'il y a cent ans. Par L. Dimier.

Illus. excerpt from unidentified periodical. n.d.

Item in manila envelope.

ENGRAVINGS

Cabinet 68 Shelf No. 1

Copper-engravings designed by Charles Percier, Paris, 1809.

See PERCIER, CHARLES and P.F.L. FONTAINE. Choix des plus célèbres maisons...

ENGRAVINGS

Cabinet K Shelf 1 No. 1

Copperplate engravings, portraits of printers, bibliophiles etc... Nuremberg and Altdorf, 1726 - 42.

See Roth-Scholtzius (Fredericus). Icones bibliopolarum et typographorum... Norimbergae et Altdorfee, 1726- 42.

ENGRAVINGS

Cabinet J Shelf 3 No. 22

Engravings and their value, a complete guide...

See SLATER, J. HERBERT. Engravings and their value...New York, 1929.

ENGRAVINGS

Cabinet E Shelf 4 No. 57

(Copper engravings (Venice 1672) of Mother Isabella Picini at the Monastery of the Holy Cross) "La Madre Suor Isabella Picini Monaco in S. Croce de Venetia incisi i Rami"...

See GIUSTINIANO, BERNARDO. Histoire cronologiche...Venetia: Presso Combie, e La Nou, 1672.

ENGRAVINGS.

Cabinet I Shelf 5 No. 21

[Copperplate in] Traité de la peinture de Leonardo da Vinci ... Traduit d'Italien en Francois, par R.F.S.D.C. A Paris, 1651. De l'Imprimerie de Jacques Langlois.

Full morocco; 18½ x 11 x ¾ in.

ENGRAVINGS

Cabinet M Shelf 3 No. 12

Engravings on wood at Lee Priory, printed on Chinese paper. Kent: Printed at the private Press of Lee Priory; by John Warwick, 1820.

Boards; 10¼ x 8 in.

ENGRAVINGS

Cabinet 17 Shelf 2 No. 1

Copperplate engraving. View of an ancient printing office. By Galle, after Jo. Stradanus.

Item on fol.1 of HENRY STEVEN'S "Typographical Miscellanies", vol.1-A

ENGRAVINGS

Cabinet K Shelf 2 No. 24

Copperplates from the designs of Adrien Van de Venne of Holland, 16th century

see ILLUSTRATION Engravings after the designs of Adrien Van de Venne...

ENGRAVINGS

Cabinet J Shelf 5 No. 25

L'Estampe moderne...Publication Mensuelle contenant quatre estampes originales inédites en couleurs et en noir. Editées par L'Imprimerie Champenois. Premiere volume, 1897-1898. Préface par Léonce Bénédite. Paris.

50 plates.

Stamped cloth; 16¼ x 12⅝ x ⅝ in.

ENGRAVINGS

Cabinet 5 Shelf 1 No.

Copperplate, 15th century. The Nova Reperta of Stradanus. n.p.n.d.

Collection of plates depicting the arts (trades) and professions. Includes 3 plates of maps of North and South America.

Boards, leather back; 19¼ x 29½ in.

ENGRAVINGS

Cabinet K Shelf 3 No. 4

[Dance of Death, as represented by artists, 1400 to 1872]

See STAMMLER, WOLFGANG (Die) Totentänze...

ENGRAVINGS

Cabinet Shelf No.

Etchings

See ETCHINGS

ENGRAVINGS.

Cabinet I, Shelf 3, No. 13

Exhibition of 100 notable American engravers, 1683-1850. Annotated list of prints. On exhibition at The New York Public Library, 1928. Illus. catalogue.

With brief biographical notes.

Item in manila envelope.

ENGRAVING

Cabinet 1 & 5, Shelf, No. 1-41

(German wood engraving in first half of 16th century) Der Deutsche einblatt-holzschnitt in der ersten hälfte des 16 jahrhunderts. Max Geisberg, editor. Munich: Hugo Schmidt Verlag. 1928.

In 40 portfolios, 22 x 16 in. and 32 x 22 in. with Index No. 41, in separate octavo vol.

ENGRAVINGS

Cabinet 17, Shelf 2, No. 1

Line engraving representing a monk writing a Ms. attended by cupidons holding books, and working a printing press.

Item on fol.4 of HENRY STEVEN'S "Typographical Miscellanies", vol.1-A

ENGRAVINGS

Cabinet 1 & 5, Shelf, No.

Facsimile reprints of woodcuts executed by unidentified Nuremberg and Augsburg, 16th century.

Facs. in Cabinet 1, portfolios 6,9,10.
also " " 5, " 23, 24

ENGRAVINGS

Cabinet 1 & 5, Shelf, No.

German woodcut engravings of the early 16th century, facsimile reprints of.

See MEISTER DER CELTIS ILLUSTRATIONEN

ENGRAVINGS

Cabinet E, Shelf 4, No. 81

Luken, Jan. Amsterdam, 1685. Etchings of.

See EARLY PRINTING IN HOLLAND. Amsterdam, 1685, Hieronymus Sweerts...

ENGRAVINGS,

Cabinet G, Shelf 5, No. 20

First book printing with wood cuts made ready by overlays, method originated by J.A. Adams.
The illuminated Bible, embellished with 1600 historical engravings by J.A. Adams... New York, Harper Brothers, publishers, 1846.

Embossed morocco; 13½ x 10 in.

ENGRAVINGS.

Cabinet U, Shelf 5, No. 55

[Great Britain] Banbury Chap Books of the 18th and early 19th centuries. With impressions from several hundred original wood-cut blocks, by T. & J. Bewick, Blake, Cruikshank, and others...With much that is valuable appertaining to the early typography of children's books. By Edwin Pearson. London, 1890.

Boards; 10-3/8 x 7-7/8 x ½ in.

ENGRAVINGS

Cabinet F, Shelf 5, No. 9

Mario, Carlona. Rome, 1763. Full page copper engravings.

See VIRGIL. P. Vergilii Maronis. Bucolica, Georgica et Aeneis...Romae, 1763. Excudebat Joannes Zempel...

ENGRAVINGS

Cabinet K, Shelf 4, No. 12

Floral designs by A. Blanc, engraver for florists. Philadelphia, Pa. 1888.

See McFarland, J. Horace (Compiler) Floral designs...Published by A. Blanc and J. Horace McFarland...

ENGRAVING.

Cabinet E, Shelf 4, No. 49

[Hollar, Wenzel. Great Britain, 1668].

See AESOP. Fables of Aesop paraphrased in verse...London, 1668.

ENGRAVINGS

Cabinet F, Shelf 4, No. 65

Moreau (Jean Michel), Amsterdam, 1772. Copper engravings.

See IMBERT, JEAN. Jugement de Paris... Amsterdam, 1772.

ENGRAVINGS

Cabinet V, Shelf 2, No. 17

Forestie, Eduard. Vignettes typographiques d'une Imprimerie Montalbanaise. Tri-centenaire. Montauban, 1900. Many folded plates.

Cloth; 10 x 6½ x 3/8 in.

ENGRAVINGS.

Cabinet I, Shelf 3, No. 2

Iconographic encyclopedia ... Illustrated with nearly 600 steel, wood, and lithographic prints from the original plates ... Iconographic Publishing Co., Philadelphia, 1885.

Stamped cloth; 10-¾ x 7½ x 1⅞ in.

ENGRAVINGS

Cabinet K, Shelf 5, No. 31

Nückel, Otto. New York, 1930. Destiny. A novel in pictures.

About 300 wood engravings.

Cloth; 8 x 6-3/4 x 1-1/8 in.

ENGRAVINGS.

Cabinet I, Shelf 4, No. 21, 2 vols.

German, 15th to 18th century copper and wood engravings, facsimiles of.

See DIEDERICH, EUGEN. Deutsches leben der vergangenheit ...

ENGRAVINGS

Cabinet K, Shelf 2, No. 5

Initial letters, a collection of decorated. Wood and copper engravings. Scrap book collection.

Calf; 10 x 7¾ in.

ENGRAVINGS

Cabinet K, Shelf 3, No. 25

Ornamental initial letters, circa 1766.

see VOLPI (Gio Ant. and Gaetano) Lettere iniziale...circa 1766

ENGRAVINGS

Cabinet C Shelf 3 No. 3

Pennell, Joseph. Stationers Hall, London. Original drawings (6 plates)

Portfolio; 21½ x 15¾ in.

ENGRAVINGS.

Cabinet G Shelf 1 No. 34

[Ruzicka, Rudolf. United States, 1915] Carteret Press, Newark, New Jersey, 1915. Rubaiyat of Omar Kkayyam. Wood engravings in color.

Orig. bds. linen back; 8½ x 5½ in.

ENGRAVINGS.

Cabinet 40 Shelf 1 No. 27

[Tory, Geoffroy. France, 1549]. French painter and engraver, the first Royal Printer.

See his initials, portraits, printers device (R. Estienne), and decorative designs in Jovius Paulus "Vitae Duodecim vicecomitum" ...Lutetia, Ex officina Rob. Stephani, 1549.

Vellum; 10 x 6-7/8 x 7/8 in. Brunet 3, 594.

ENGRAVINGS

Cabinet F Shelf 5 No. 1

Picart, Bernard, La Haye, 1729. Copperplate engravings of.

See DESPREAUX, NICOLAS BOILEAU. Oeuvres de...Tome Premier. A la Haye, chez Pierre de Hondt, 1729.

ENGRAVINGS

Cabinet K Shelf 2 No. 29

Sartain, John, his engravings in "The Diadem" for 1846. Philadelphia: Carey & Hart, 1846. (plate X) portrait of M. Carey.

Cloth, embossed; 11 x 9 in.

ENGRAVINGS.

Cabinet 70 Shelf 1 No. 27

[Tory, Geofroy. Paris, 1525]. Heures a la louange de la vierge Marie selon lusage de Rome... En sont vendre, per Maistre Geofroy Tory de Bourges, a Paris sus Petit pot a lenseigne du Pot casse.

Old calf; gold tooled; 8⅝ x 5½ x 1 in.

ENGRAVINGS

Cabinet 10 Shelf 2 No. 14

Pleydenwurff...Nuremberg, 1493. Wood engravings.

See NURNBERG CHRONICLE. Coberger, Anthony, 1493.

ENGRAVINGS

Cabinet 39 Shelf 1 No. 4

Schoonhovii, I.C. Leyden, 1626. Copperplate. Emblemata Florentii Schoonhovi, I.C. Goudani ...Lugduni, Batavorum, ex officina Elzeviriana. Anno, M.D.XXVI.

Vellum; 8¼ x 6¼ x 1-3/8 in.

ENGRAVINGS

Cabinet C Shelf 2 No. 5

Typographic decorative material: borders, head and tail pieces, initial letters, etc. Original woodcut and copperplate engravings taken from early printed books. Scrap book collection.

Boards; 22 x 13¾ in.

ENGRAVINGS

Cabinet M Shelf 1 No. 3

Polychrome borders and ornaments taken from illuminated Mss.

See IMPRINTS, England. Austin, Stephen. Hertford, 1855.

ENGRAVINGS

Cabinet F Shelf 3 No. 11

Seymour, Joseph H., Worcester (Mass.) 1795. Steel engraving, frontispiece to Eligiac Sonnets. By Charlotte Smith. First Worcester edition. Printed by Isaiah Thomas, 1795.

Leather; 5-7/8 x 4-3/8 x 5/8 in.

ENGRAVINGS

Cabinet 68 Shelf No. 11

Van Audernaerdt, Robert, Flemish artist-engraver, 1732.
Specimens of his work, copper-engravings.

See NUMISMATA.Berbadica gente...1732

ENGRAVINGS

Cabinet J Shelf 4 No. 12

Portfolio of proof impressions selected from Scribner's Monthly and St. Nicholas. Scribner and Company. New York, 1880.

Half morocco; 14 x 12 x 1 in.

ENGRAVINGS.

Cabinet I Shelf 3 No. 1

Shannon, Charles. Idylls of rural life: A series of woodcuts by Charles Shannon, A.R.A. and briefly described by Frank Gibson. Excerpt from the International Studio, October, 1916. Illus.

Item 35 in vol. with binder's title:"Various Engravers and About Engravers."

ENGRAVINGS

Cabinet R Shelf 6 No. 1

Wikström, B.A. The true story about Gutenberg's invention of printing. Complete in seven sheets. Drawn by B.A. Wikström, New York, 1882.

Half morocco; 16 x 12 in.

ENGRAVINGS

Cabinet U Shelf 3 No. 103

Printing presses, early representations of. (Reproductions).

See BOOKS ABOUT BOOKS. Bibliographica: papers on books...vol.I, pp.223, 499.

ENGRAVINGS

Cabinet J Shelf 4 No. 13

Steinlen...Catalogue descriptive et analytique suivi d'un essai de bibliographie et d'iconographie de son oeuvre illustré. Par E. de Crauzat. Preface de Roger Marx. Paris, 1913. Illus.

Paper; 13-7/8 x 10 x 1 in.

ENGRAVINGS

Cabinet 10 Shelf 2 No. 14

Wohlgemuth, Michael, Nuremberg. 1493. Wood engravings.

See NURNBERG CHRONICLE. Coburger, Anthony, 1493...

ENGRAVINGS

Cabinet K, Shelf 1, No. 28

Wood and copperplate engravings: facsimiles of music printing and manuscripts, 12th to 16th century. (28 plates). With brief notes.

Boards; $12\frac{1}{4}$ x 9 in.

ENGRAVINGS

Cabinet J, Shelf 1, No. 20

Woodcuts, and copper engravings, printers ornaments, etc. Early 17th century. Scrap book collection.

Boards; 9-5/8 x 7-3/8"

ENGRAVINGS

Cabinet 1 & 5, Shelf Portfolios 1 to 40

Woodcuts, German 16th century, facsimile reprints of.

See GEISBERG, MAX (German single-plate woodcuts...)

ENGRAVINGS

Cabinet J, Shelf 1, No. 18

Wood engravings. Collection of printers cuts and ornaments (1850-1860). Presented by Willis McDonald Mfg. Co. n.p. n.d.

Half morocco: $16x10\frac{1}{4}$"

ENGRAVINGS,

Cabinet J, Shelf 1, No. 17

(Wood Engravings). A brochure of American art. The Aldine Almanac, 1874, with illustrations by the best American artists. Printed and published by James Sutton & Company, New York.

Illuminated cover: $11\frac{1}{4}$x8".
In protective folder.

ENGRAVINGS
(Wood engraving)

Cabinet K, Shelf 6, No. 14

English woodcuts, contemporary. By Campbell Dodgson. London, 1922.

No. 284 of 550 copies printed.

Boards, cloth back; $12\frac{1}{4}$ x 10-1/8 x 5/8 in.

ENGRAVINGS

Cabinet J, Shelf 1, No. 19

Wood engravings. Reproduction of woodcuts, (period of Caxton) printers marks, early types, printers portraits. No title page, n. p. n. d.

Portraits include Caxton and John Daye.

Boards: $10x7\frac{1}{4}x\frac{1}{2}$"

ENGRAVINGS

Cabinet, Shelf, No.

See also cards with following sub-head:

"BLOCK BOOKS"
BOOK CATALOGUES, Dealers [Engravings]
ILLUSTRATED BOOKS

ENGRAVINGS, CATALOGUES OF.

Cabinet I, Shelf 3, No. 13

American engravers, 1683-1850, one hundred notable. Annotated list of prints. On exhibition at The New York Public Library. 1928, Illus. pamphlet.

With very brief biographical notes.

Item in manila envelope.

ENGRAVINGS (Catalogue)

Cabinet J, Shelf 4, No. 10

(Le) Cabinet d'estampes d'un amateur. Comprenant ...des maitres Italiens des XVe et XVIe siècles, estampes originales de Durer, Rembrandt, Schongauer...Vent les 16 et 17 Novembre, 1926. H. Gilhofer & Ranschburg Ltd. Lucerne. Illus.

Paper; $11\frac{3}{4}$ x 8-7/8 in.

ENGRAVINGS, (Catalogues of)

Cabinet K, Shelf 4, No. 10

(Copper engraving and engravers, 16th and 17th century). Catalogue 26, Gilhofer & Ranschburg. Luzerne, n. d. pp. 18, with 27 plates.

Another catalogue: Precious ornament-prints of the 16th to 18th century. Catalogue XV.

Items in manila envelope

ENGRAVINGS (Catalogue)

Cabinet K, Shelf 2, No. 19

(Copperplate and wood engravings of the old masters, 15th to 17th century. L. Gilhofer & Ranschburg, Luzerne, 1927.)

Eine kostbare privat-sammlung von kupferstichen und holzschnitten alter meister.

Paper; $11\frac{3}{4}$ x 8-5/8 in.

ENGRAVINGS (Catalogue)

Cabinet K, Shelf 2, No. 18

(English 18th century prints.) Doubletten der kupferstich sammlung Albertina in Wien. Englishe schabkunstblatter des 18 jahrhunderts. Gilhofer & Ranschburg, 1923.
56 Auktion.

Paper; 11-7/8 x 9 in.

ENGRAVINGS (Catalogue)

Cabinet K, Shelf 2, No. 27

English portraits, collection of 41 male. By early engravers in mezzotint, line, and stipple, after the paintings of Sir Henry Raeburn (1756-1823). For sale by Frederick B. Danielle & Son. London, n.d. circa 1900

Cloth; $10\frac{3}{4}$ x $8\frac{1}{4}$ in.

ENGRAVINGS, CATALOGUE OF.

Cabinet I, Shelf 3, No. 14

[French portrait engravings and engravers].

See DIDOT, AMBROISE FIRMIN. Graveurs de portraits en France ... (2 vols) Paris, 1875-1877.

ENGRAVINGS, Catalogue of

Cabinet K, Shelf 2, No. 38

Rosenwald, Lessing, J. Collection of prints. Catalogue of a loan exhibition of. Compiled by H.M. Dunbar, Chicago, Jan. Feb., March, 1932.

Paper; 10-3/8 x 8-1/8 in.

ENGRAVINGS, COPPERPLATE

Cabinet K, Shelf 4, No. 4

A' Dilettanti delle belle arti. B. Betti, inc. Fir. Appo il Pagni da Orsan Michele. n.p. n. d. Probably about 1785.

Book of copperplate prints; allegorical figures with letters of the alphabet, A to Z.

Oblong; half vellum; 10 x 11 in.

ENGRAVINGS, COPPERPLATE

Cabinet J, Shelf 4, No. 5

L'Art du dessin...Par Jean Cousin. Paris, n.d. circa 1550.

Title page and 24 plates.

Half morocco; $15\frac{1}{4}$ x 12 x $\frac{1}{2}$ in.

ENGRAVINGS, COPPERPLATE

Cabinet L Shelf 3 No. 4

Bickham, John and Geo. Jr., London, 1737. One-hundred curiously engraved copperplates ...Printed and sold by William and Cluer Dicey.

Calf, stamped; $8\frac{1}{2}$ x $5\frac{3}{4}$ in.

ENGRAVINGS, COPPERPLATE

Cabinet C Shelf 2 No. 13

(French, 18th century. Frontispieces, fleurons, head and tail pieces, etc., provided for the former l'Imprimerie Royale. Printed at l'Imprimerie Nationale, Paris, 1889)

Half calf; 20 x 13-7/8 in.

ENGRAVINGS, COPPERPLATE

Cabinet K Shelf 1 No. 22

Miscellaneous collection of initials, borders, ornaments and other decorative typographical material. Specimens mounted, 50 plates.

In box

ENGRAVINGS, COPPERPLATE

Cabinet K Shelf 1 No. 8

(Collection of 460 typographic ornaments, copper engravings, of the 1st Empire and Renaissance) Recueil de 460 ornaments typographiques et gravures sur cuivre des époques 1er Empire, Louis XVI, Louis XV, Louis XIV, et Renaissance Publié par Armand Guerient, Paris.

48 plates, in folder, 12" x 8-3/8 in.

ENGRAVINGS, COPPERPLATE

Cabinet J Shelf 5 No. 16

Gravure Francaise au XVIIIe siecle. Avec une suite de 44 estampes. Par Pierre Gusman. Paris, n.d. circa 1916.

With 44 plate engravings.

Portfolio; 18 x 13 in.

ENGRAVINGS, COPPERPLATE

Cabinet E Shelf 4 No. 61

[T.H.]. Geneva, 1674. Copper engravings, head pieces, initials, and many full page engravings bearing a monogram "T.H."

See VALLE, PIETRO Della. Reise beschreibung in unterschiecliche theile der welt...

ENGRAVINGS, COPPERPLATE

Cabinet L Shelf 5 No. 1

De Hoogh, Cornelis. Antwerp, 1569. Plates (34), examples of writing and border work.

See Perret, Clement. Exercitatio alphabetica nova et utilissima...(Antwerp) : 1569.

ENGRAVINGS, COPPERPLATE

Cabinet FF Shelf 6 No. 2

Imprimerie en taille-douce. Contenant deux planches. [Illus. plates with view of interior of printing office, and tools, for copper plate engraving].

See FELICE'S Encyclopedie...Excerpts from] Fonderie en caracteres...Yverdun, 1775.

Half morocco; 17 x 11 in.

ENGRAVINGS, COPPERPLATE

Cabinet I Shelf 1 No. 9

Tavernier, Melchior, Paris, 1641-1644. Copperplate engravings of.

See TAVERNIER, MELCHIOR. Perspective pratique...

ENGRAVINGS, COPPERPLATE

Cabinet J Shelf 3 No. 11

England, 1500-1840.

See SALAMAN, MALCOLM C. Old engravers of England....

ENGRAVINGS, COPPERPLATE

Cabinet J Shelf 5 No. 13

Initial letters, and printers decorative material, originals, on wood and copper. Scrap book.

Cloth; 18 x $13\frac{1}{4}$ in.

ENGRAVINGS, COPPERPLATE

Cabinet K Shelf 3 No. 2

(Trades and professions, 40 plates, late 18th or early 19th century)

see GALLERIE...KUNSTE UND HANDWERKE Lehrreiches und unterhaltendes bilderbuch...

ENGRAVINGS, COPPERPLATE

Cabinet I Shelf 1 No. 15

Etwas für alle, das ist: Eine kurtze beschreibung ...Wurtzburg, 1711.

See ABRAHAM à S. CLARA. Etwas für alle ...

ENGRAVINGS, COPPERPLATE

Cabinet K Shelf 4 No. 3

Initial letters, borders, head and tail pieces, illustrations, etc. Scrap book collection of typographic decorative material. Probably 17th and 18th century.

Half morocco; $9\frac{1}{2}$ x 7-1/8 x $\frac{3}{4}$ in.

ENGRAVINGS, COPPERPLATE

Cabinet K Shelf 3 No. 1

Vignettes (125), the work of several Italian engravers. Printed by Gio. M. Salvioni, [illegible] printer for the Vatican, Rome, circa 1730.

Parchment, oblong; $5\frac{3}{4}$ x $8\frac{1}{4}$ in.

ENGRAVINGS, COPPERPLATE.

Cabinet K Shelf 4 No. 33

Ex-Libris, twenty one copperplate prints of.

See ALLEN, CHARLES DEXTER. Ex-Libris. Essays of a collector ...

ENGRAVINGS, COPPERPLATE

Cabinet I Shelf 1 No. 13 & 14

Luiken, Johannes and Gaspaares. Amsterdam, 1694.

See LUIKEN, JOHANNES and GASPAARES. Het menselyk bedrye...t'Amsterdam, 1694.

ENGRAVINGS, COPPERPLATE

Cabinet Shelf No.

Zundt, Matthias. Nuremberg, 1596.

See LENCKER, HANS. Perspectivea literaria ...Gedruckt zu Nurnberg, durch Paulum Kauffmann, 1596.

ENGRAVINGS, Japanese.

Cabinet K, Shelf 5, No. 4

Woodcuts of Japanese warriors, scholars, etc. (some in two colors), including the text. Ei ō SanjurokKassen. Sadahida, Koka, 1848.

This is a block book printed and found prior to the introduction of typography in Japan.

Paper; 7-1/8 x 4-3/4 x ½ in.

ENGRAVINGS (Prints)

Stack, Shelf, Number

Catalogues of prints issued by dealers and auctioneers. Illustrated catalogues.

See BOOK CATALOGUES, DEALERS. [Engravings]

ENGRAVINGS, STEEL PLATE. (Examples of)

Cabinet J, Shelf 1, No. 3

Lowell, J. A. and Company. (Boston). Album of steel plate cards for menus, programs, pamphlets, calendars and general business purposes. n.d. circa 1880. (with prices in English Sterling).

These cards were very popular in the eighties.

Half levant: 15x10x2" See also J/1/2

ENGRAVINGS, WOOD

Cabinet, Shelf, No.

See cards with following sub-heads:

I - WOOD ENGRAVING. Literature of
II - WOOD ENGRAVINGS.

ENO, JOEL

Cabinet S, Shelf 4, No. 68.01

Gutenberg, the earlier work of. A review of Otto Hupp's argument. March, 1903. Excerpt from The Literary Collector, vol.5.

With facsimiles.

In box marked "Pamphlets and excerpts relating to Gutenberg"

ENSCHEDÉ, CHARLES

Cabinet AA, Shelf 3, No. 29

De drukkerij van Johannes Elzevier in 1658. Door Mr. Ch. Enschedé. [Haarlem, 1896].

A bibliographical account of the Elzevier Press, with notes concerning the origin of types used by them.

Linen; 8 x 5½ in.

ENSCHEDE, CH.

Cabinet W, Shelf 5, No. 72

De drukkerij van Johannes Elsevier in 1658.

Bio-bibliographical account. Concluding chapter p.73 in "Klaasesz Aankondiger". Hengelo, Holland. n.d. but probably 1899.

Item in manila envelope.

ENSCHEDÉ, CHARLES

Cabinet AA, Shelf 3, No. 30

Elzevier-van Dyck. Door Mr. Ch. Enschede, Haarlem, 1899 [Reprint from the "Klaasez Aankondiger"].

Comparative study of types cut by van Dyck, the type founder, for the Elzeviers.

Linen, 8½ x 5½ in.

ENSCHEDÉ, CHARLES

Cabinet W, Shelf 5, No. 125

Fonderies de caractères et leur matérial dans les Pays-Bas du XV au XIX siècle. Notice historique principalement d'après les données de la collection typographique de Joh. Enschedé en Zonen à Harlem. Par Ch. Enschedé. Haarlem, 1908.

Vellum gilt; 15 x 11¼ in.

ENSCHEDE, CHARLES

Cabinet AA, Shelf 3, No. 43

Laurens Jansz. Coster. De uitvinder van de boekdrukkunst. Door Mr. Ch. Enschede. Haarlem, 1904. Pamphlet.

Technical, historical investigation concerning the invention of printing.

Bound in volume "De Coster Legende." 1856, 1904, 1922.

Half morocco; 11 x 7¼ in.

ENSCHEDE, CH.

Cabinet AA, Shelf 3, No. 45

See Gutenberg-Coster Controversey. Uit de strijdschriften over de Hollandsche uitvinding.

ENSCHEDE, ISAAC and JEAN

Cabinet 83, Shelf 2, No. 4

See Specimen Books, Types, Holland. [v.d.]

ENSCHEDE, J. W.

Cabinet FF, Shelf 4, No. 17

(De) Boekletter in Nederland. Door J. W. Enschede. Amsterdam, 1902. In Specimen book of types used by Ipenbuur & van Seldam, printers.

Cloth; 8¾ x 5-7/8 in.

ENSCHEDE EN ZONEN, Joh.

Cabinet AA, Shelf 3, No. 15

Catalogus van der typographische verzameling van Joh. Enschede en Zonen. Haarlem 1916.

Catalogue of a collection of books relating to typography, engraving, invention of printing, types.

Paper cover; 9-1/8 x 6 in.

ENSCHEDÉ, JOHN W.

Cabinet S, Shelf 5, No. 1

(First printers in Batavia, East Indies). De Eerste Compagnies Drukkers to Batavia. Excerpt, n.d.

Historical, bibliographical account.

Bound in collection "Various printing plants brochures", item 8.

ENSCHEDE, JOHN W.

Cabinet S, Shelf 5, No. 1

(Netherland printing materials in 1761). Een Nederlandsche handleiding voor boekdrukwerk uit 1761. Illus. excerpt n.d.

Historical bibliographical account.

Bound in collection "Various printing plants-excerpts", item 9.

ENSCHEDE, J.W.

Cabinet AA, Shelf 3, No. 42

Spin, C.A. & Zoon: Amsterdam, 1818-1919. Gedenkenboek bij haar honderdjarig bestan. Door J.W. Enschede. Amsterdam, 10 Dec., 1919. Illustrated with portraits, views, printing presses, facsimile etc.

Historical bibliographical account.

Boards; 9½ x 6¾ in.

ENSCHEDÉ, JOH. EN ZONEN

Cabinet W, Shelf 5, No. 129

Exposition Nationale du Livre à Amsterdam...1910. Catalogue de l'Exposition de Joh. Enschedé en Zonen: Donnant un aperçu de l'art typographique dans les Pays-Bas depuis le XVe siècle jusque dans nos jours.

Half morocco; 9-1/8 x 5-7/8 in.

ENSCHEDE, JOHN & SONS

Cabinet FF Shelf 5 No. 4

Lettergieterii van Joh. Enschede en Zonen. Gedenkschrift ter gelegenheid van haas honderdvijftig - jarig bestaan. Op 9 Maart 1893. Haarlem. Illus. portraits.
The letter foundry of Joh. Enschede & Sons. Celebration 150 Years of its existence.

Stamped cloth; 12 x 9 in.

ENSCHEDE, JOH. en ZONEN

Cabinet J Shelf 5 No. 23

Proeven van reproductie in boekdruk. Haarlem, 1907.

Reproductive printing processes, proofs of.

Pictorial paper cover; 17-7/8 x 11-3/8 in.

ENSCHEDE JOH. en ZONEN

Cabinet 83 Shelf 2 No.

See Specimen Books, Types. Holland. [v.d.]

ENSCHEDE, JOH. AND SONS

Cabinet 18 Shelf 1 No. 12

See Type Foundries, Enschede, Joh. en Zonen.

ENSCHEDE (Joh.) en ZONEN

Cabinet AA Shelf 3 No. 15

Typographische versameling (Catalogus) van Joh. Enschede en Zonen. Haarlem, 1916.
Catalogue of books, 15th to 19th centuries, in the library of Enschede and sons. Brief bibliographical notes.

Paper; 9-5/8 x 7-3/8 x ½ in.

ENSCHEDÉ, JOH EN ZONEN

Cabinet AA Shelf 3 No. 14

Uitvinding der Boekdrukkunst. Haarlem, Joh. Enschedé en Zonen, 1854. Portrait of Coster Illus.
The writer credits Coster with the invention of printing, Gutenberg with its improvement, and Schoeffer with its perfecting: "Therefore I have joined their three portraits together."

Leather; 7-1/8 x 5-3/8 in.

ENSCHEDE & ZONEN, Johannes.
see also

Cabinet Shelf No.

Newspapers, Holland: Haarlemsche Courant.

ENSCHEDE FAMILY OF TYPEFOUNDERS

Cabinet Z Shelf 1 No. 18

See Specimen Books, Types. Holland.

ENSCHEDE FAMILY OF TYPEFOUNDERS

Cabinet Z Shelf 1 No. 17

Specimen des caractères de la fondérie normale à Bruxelles de Jules Didot et son père Pierre Didot. A Haarlem, chez Joh. Enschedé en Zonen. 1914.
The Didot type foundry was acquired by Johann Enschede in 1850. In 1914 the Enschedes issued this specimen of the Didot Types on their possession in that year.
All these types are of French origin.

Paper; 9-5/8 x 6-3/4 in.

ENSCHEDE FOUNDRY.

Cabinet T Shelf 3 No. 45

Sources of the material of the Enschede Foundry. Compiled from Ch. Enschede Fonderies de Caracteres etc. and from information supplied by Messrs. Joh. Enschede en Zonen themselves.
Chart in Birrell & Garnett's Catalogue of Type Founders Specimens ... London, 1928.

Half morocco; 11¼ x 8¾ x 5/8 in.

ENSCHEDE TYPE SPECIMENS

Cabinet F Shelf No.

(Description and historical account of the Enschede type specimens).

See Breitkopf's Nachricht von der stempelschneiderei...Leipzig, 1777.

ENVELOPE MAKING

Cabinet 81 Shelf 2 No. 40

Brief history of envelopes followed by description of the processes involved in making envelopes. Excerpt, newspaper clipping. circa 1860.

See MUNSELL, JOEL. "Printers Scraps", Vol.XI, pp.123-4.

ENVELOPES.

Cabinet FF Shelf 2 No. 40

[Earliest mention of manufacture of, 1849].
In Inventions, Patents for. Abridgments of specifications, Vol. I...London, 1859. pp. 296,297, No. 12,653, section 4, 1849. "Apparatus for pressing into required forms covers for notes on letters."

Half morocco; 7-5/8 x 5 x 2 in.

ENVELOPES

Cabinet RR Shelf 2 No. 32

Story of the envelope.

See LOGAN, JAMES. Envelope, story of the...

ENVELOPES

Cabinet R Shelf 5 No. 148

War-time envelopes. By Pleasant E. Todd. Excerpt from the Monthly Illustrator, 1895.

Excerpts 17 in volume "Chap Books, Almanacs, Annuals, etc.

EPEÖGRAPHY (or)

Cabinet II Shelf 4 No. 30

Notations of orthoëpy...

See MANNING, JOSEPH B. Epeography... Boston, 1829.

EPHRATA

Cabinet R Shelf 5 No. 26

Historic Ephrata, Lancaster County. Pennsylvania. Bi-Centennial celebration at Ephrata Cloister of Seven Day Baptist Society. Saturday, September 29, 1928. Souvenir. Illus.

Pamphlet, in envelope.

EPHRATA PRESS

Cabinet R Shelf 5 No. 25

Chronicon Ephratense; a history of the community of Seventh Day Baptists at Ephrata Lancasta County, Penna. By "Lamech and Agrippa." Translated from the original German by J. Max Hark. Lancaster, Pa., 1889.

Cloth; 9½ x 6½ in.

EPHRATA PRESS, The

Cabinet R Shelf 5 No. 32 — 2 vols.

(The) German Sectarians of Pennsylvania, 1708-1742: A critical and legendary history of the Ephrata Cloister and the Dunkers. By J. F. Sachse. Philadelphia, 1899 and 1900. 2 vols. Illus., facsimiles, and reproductionsof head and tail pieces, initial letters, vignettes, etc.

Cloth; 10 x 7 in.

EPHRATA PRESS

Cabinet Y Shelf 3 No. 111

(Historical account of the founding of the Ephrate Brotherhood Press in 1734 by Johann Conrad Beissel).

See Sondheim, Moritz. Gesammelte schriften...Frankfurt, 1927, p. 285

EPHRATA PRESS, THE

Cabinet 27 Shelf 1 No. 7

Second German printing press in Pennsylvania. Address by the Hon. Joseph R. Chandler.

Article in the Printers' Circular, vol. 7, No.10, Dec.,1872, p.362

EPHRATA PRESS, THE

Cabinet R Shelf 5 No. 15.

See Sower, Christopher. Quarrel between Christopher Sower, the Germantown printer, and Conrad Beissel.

EPHRATA PRESS.

Cabinet F Shelf 2 No. 15,17

See Early Printing in Pennsylvania. Ephrata [v.d.]: The Ephrata Press.

EPHRUSSI, CHARLES

Cabinet W Shelf 3 No. 40

Étude sur la Chronique de Nuremberg de Hartmann Schedel, avec les bois de Wolgemut & W. Pleydenwurff. Paris, 1894
Bibliographical account.

Half morocco; 10-1/8 x 6-5/8 x ½ in.

EPHRUSSI, CHARLES

Cabinet W Shelf 3 No. 114

Etude sur le Songe de Poliphile. (Venise 1499 et 1545 - Paris, 1546, 1883) Avec gravures sur bois. Par Charles Ephrussi, Paris, 1888.

Item 10 in vol. with binder's title "Pamphlets Releting to Books - I. Bound, 1932".

EPINAL

Cabinet K Shelf 1 No. 10

(Les) Images d'Epinal...

See Perout, Rene. (Les) Images d'Epinal...Nancy, 1912.

"EPINAL PICTURES."

Cabinet I Shelf 3 No. 1

Pellerin, Jean Charles. His pictures of Epinal.

See COLOR PRINTING. Pictures of Epinal ...

EPISCOPIUS, EUSEBIUS

Cabinet Shelf No.

See Early Printing in Switzerland . Basle, 1569.

EPISCOPIUS, NICOLAUS

Cabinet X Shelf 3 No. 15

Biographical sketch, with printers device, Episcopius, Basel, 1501-1564.

see HEITZ, PAUL.
Basler büchermarken... pp.xxii, 41, 43.

EPISCOPIUS, NICOLAUS

Cabinet E Shelf 1 No. 2

See Early Printing in Switzerland. Basel, 1535. Jerome Froben and Nicolaus Episcopius.

EPISCOPIUS, NICOLAUS, the younger.

Cabinet E Shelf 1 No. 28

See Early printing in Switzerland. Basel, 1555. Nicolaus Episcopius.

EPITAPHS, PRINTERS'

Cabinet QQ Shelf 1 No. 35

Caxton, William, John Day, Dr. Franklin, Christopher Barker, etc. Each with brief biographical note.

See pp.78-86 in TIMPERLEY'S Songs of the press...London, 1833.

EPITAPHS, PRINTERS'

Cabinet QQ Shelf 1 No. 42

Here lies a type of being who was wont... [By E.A. McLoughlin, proof-reader].

See p.298, Brentons Voices of the Press... New York, 1850.

EPITAPHS, PRINTERS'

Cabinet Shelf No.

(The) Printer says "Finis". By Charles H. Lea.

Article in Caxton Magazine, vol. 33, No.12, Dec. 1931, p.638.

EQUIPMENTS, LIBRARY AND MUSEUM (see)

Cabinet Shelf No.

LIBRARY EQUIPMENTS

EQUIPMENT-- PRINTING

Cabinet Shelf No.

See PRINTING EQUIPMENTS.

ERAGNY PRESS

Cabinet T Shelf 4 No. 111

"Brook" type, a specimen of.

See STEELE, ROBERT T. (The) Revival of printing...London, 1912. p.36.

ERASMUS, DESIDERIUS (ROTTERDAMUS)

Cabinet AA Shelf 3 No. 46

Erasmus en zijn drukkers - uitgevers. Een fragment uit hun briefwisseling, bewerkt door B. Kruitwagen. Amsterdam, 1923.

Produced by the Amsterdam type foundry, formerly Tetterode, to introduce their new type Erasmus-Mediaeval designed by S.H. de Roos.

Half morocco; 9½ x 6-3/8 in.

ERB, FRANK C.

Cabinet R Shelf 3 No. 181

Bradford, William, 1696. Reprint of the first book printed in New York " A letter of advise to young gentlemen"...with introduction and notes. New York, 1917. Facsimiles.

Cloth; 6 x 4-3/4 in.

ERAGNY PRESS, THE

Cabinet M Shelf No.

See Imprints, England. Eragny Press. Lucien and Esther Pissarro.

ERASMUS, DESIDERIUS (Rotterdamus).

Cabinet 75 Shelf 1 No. 13

Erasmus' relations with his printers, by P. S. Allen. A paper read before the Bibliographical Society March 15th, 1915.

In Trans. Biblio. Soc., Vol. XIII, 1913-15, pp. 297-321.

ERCOLANO (le) ANTICHITA di (see)

Cabinet 9 Shelf 2 No. 1 to 9

Bajardi, Ottaviano- Antonio. Antichite (le) di Ercolano...

ERASMUS, DESIDERIUS (ROTTERDAMUS)

Cabinet 70 Shelf 2 No. 6

Adagiorum: Opus Des. Erasmi Roterodami.... [Printer Mark] Sebastianus Gryphius Germanus, excudebat Lugduni. Anno M.D.XXVIII.

Calf; 13 x 9¼ x 1¼ in.

ERASMUS von Rotterdamus

Cabinet Q Shelf 2 No. 37

(Das) Leben Erasmus. von ihm selbst erzahlt. Ubersetzung und nachwort von Ernst Schulz. (Alternating Latin and German text) Dieser druck wurde als Neujahrsgabe 1935 Braus-Riggenbach vorm. Henning Oppermann, Basel... (No.244 of an edition of 900)

At back picture of Froben's house in which Erasmus lived as his guest from Aug., 1535 until July 1536.

Brochure in manila envelope

"ERFURT", HANS von (Hans Werlich)

Cabinet 26 Shelf 1 No. 16

Drucker des Wormser edikts (1518-1532), Hans Werlich genannt Hans von Erfurt. von Karl Schottenloher.

Illus. article in GUTENBERG-GESELLSCHAFT JAHRBUCH, 1927, p.53

ERASMUS, DESIDERIUS (ROTTERDAMUS)

Cabinet D Shelf 3 No. 38

Encomium, Moriae. With the marginal drawings of Hans Holbein. Published at Basle in 1515.

Facsimile published by Oppermann, Basle, ~~1918~~ 1931. With bibliographical introduction.

Boards; 9¼ x 6-5/8 in. In slip case.

ERASMUS

Cabinet QQ Shelf 3 No. 29

Life of Erasmus, the: with historical remarks on the state of literature between the 10th and 16th centuries. By Charles Butler. London, 1825.

Brief notes concerning early presses

Boards; 9 x 5⅝ x ¾ in.

ERFURT

Cabinet Y Shelf 4 No. 4

(Notes relating to 15th century printers and printing at Erfuts.)

see

VOULLIÉME, ERNST. (Die) Deutschen drucker des fünfzehnten jahrhunderts...p.42

ERASMUS, DESIDERIUS (ROTTERDAMUS)

Cabinet D Shelf 3 No. 55

Epigrammata clarissimi disertissimi qui viri Thomae mori Britanni. Basle, 1518. John Froben [This is bound in with the seconnd edition of Thomas More's Utopia in which there are two separate title pages by Hans Holbein, and two printers marks, differing in design]

Calf; 8½ x 6¼ x 1¼ in.

ERASMUS, DESIDERIUS (ROTTERDAMUS)

Cabinet E Shelf 2 No. 32

Portrait of. Wood cut. In Icones id est Verae imagines. Geneva, 1580. Sig. ciii.

ERFURT

see also

Gedenkbuch, Thuringsch-Erfurter.

ERASMUS, DESIDERIUS (ROTTERDAMUS)

Cabinet E Shelf 1 No. 2

Parphraseon in Novum Testamentum. Basel, 1535: Jerome Froben and Nicolaus Episcopius.[Two vols. in one, and divided into six parts, each part with separate title, printer mark and imprint; the last imprint dated 1532.

Embossed leather over boards, with clasps; 13 x 9 x 3½ in.

ERASMUS-DRUCK. Berlin

Cabinet EE Shelf 3 No. 15

See SPECIMEN BOOKS, TYPES. Printers'. Germany.

ERHARDT

Cabinet Shelf No.

See Specimen Books, Types. Germany.

ERHARDTISCHE GIESSEREI

Cabinet — Shelf — No. —

See Specimen Books, Types. Germany.

ERIE CANAL

Cabinet QQ — Shelf 1 — No. 30.01

Ode for the Canal written by Samuel Woodworth, printer, 1825.

see
WOODWORTH, SAMUEL. Ode...

ERLINGER, GEORG

Cabinet 5 — Shelf — No. 25

Facsimile reprints of the woodcut engravings of G. Erlinger, 1490-1541.

Facs. in Cabinet 5, portfolio 25

ERNESTI, JOH. HEINRICH GOTTFRIED

Cabinet LL — Shelf 1 — No. 3

(Die) Wol-eingerichtete buchdruckerey, mit hundert und ein und zwanzig Teutsch, Lateinisch, Griechisch und Hebraischen Schriften, vieler fremden sprachen alphabeten...Mit accurater abbildung der erfindung der löblichen kunst, nebst einer summarischen nachricht von den buchdruckern in Nürnberg ausgezieret. Am ende ist das gebrauchliche "Depositions" buchlein aufgefuget. Nurnberg, gedruckt und zu finden

(cont'd)

ERNESTI, JOH. HEINRICH GOTTFRIED (cont'd)

Cabinet — LL — Shelf 1 — No. 3

bey Johann Andrea Endters seel. Sohn und erben. 1721.
Engraved frontispiece representing the interior of a printing office.

Half vellum; 8 x 10 x 1-1/8 in.

ERPENIUS, THOMAS

Cabinet E — Shelf 3 — No. 18

See Early Printing in Holland. Leyden, 1622.

ERPENIUS, (or Van Erp), Thomas.

Cabinet E — Shelf 3 — No. 17

Historia Josephi Patriarchae, ex Alcoran, Arabice cum triplici versione Latine, et Scholiis Thomas Erpenii. Leidae, ex Typographia Erpeniana Linguarum Orientatium, 1617.
Included in the same binding: Pauli Apostoli ad Romanos Epistola, 1615. [in Arabic], and Canones de literarum apud Arabes, 1618. With notes Arabic and Latin notes by the author-printer, Erpenius.

Vellum, 7-3/8 x 5-3/8 x 1 in.

ERRATA (see)

Cabinet — Shelf — No. —

PROOFREADING

ERRONEOUS DATES ON IMPRINTS (see)

Cabinet — Shelf — No. —

FALSE DATES ON IMPRINTS

ERSKINE, THOMAS

Cabinet X — Shelf 4 — No. 97

Whole proceedings at the meeting of the friends of the Liberty of the Press....With the much admired speech of Mr. Erskine. Dec.22, 1792. [London]: Printed for T. Browne.

Half morocco: 7½ x 4-7/8 in.

ERTMAN, E. Geo. (Editor)

Cabinet Q — Shelf 4 — No. 25, 26

National Directory of the Paper Box Trade and its Allied Branches (1919, 1922). Published by the Ravenswood Press Publishing Co., Chicago, Ill.

Cloth; 8 x 5 in.

ESCODECA DE BOISSE (D')

Cabinet V — Shelf 6 — No. 26

Exposition Universelle de 1855. Quelques détails sur les produits de l'Imprimerie Impériale de France. Par M. D'Escodeca de Boisse. Paris, 1855.
The contents include detail of the specimens from the Imperial Printing Office.

Boards; 9¼ x 5-7/8 in.

ESCRIBANO, Alonso

Cabinet X — Shelf 3 — No. 19

Brief bio-bibliographical note, with printer mark Escribano (Sevilla) 1567-1577.

see
HAEBLER, KONRAD. (Spanish and Portugese printer marks...p.xxxiii

---

ESDAILE, ARUNDELL.

Cabinet 75 — Shelf 2 — No. 2

Author and Publisher in 1727: "The English Hermit," by Arundell Esdaile.

In Transactions of the Bibliographical Society, "The Library," Vol. II, 1921-22, pp. 185-192.

ESENWEIN, J. BERG

Cabinet K — Shelf 5 — No. 1

Japanese caricature: an imported national humor. By J. Berg Esenwein. Illus. excerpt from the "Bookman", May, 1904.

Item 7 in vol. with binder's title "Wood Engraving, Etc."

ESKIMO (Arctic Coast)

Cabinet II — Shelf 4 — No. 2

Languages of Alaska and Greenland. Illustrative sketch of. By William Thalbitzer.

See BOAS, FRANZ. American Indian languages, handbook of...Bulletin 40, Washington, 1911, pp.971-1066.

ESKIMOS

Cabinet PP — Shelf 3 — No. 43.01

Graphic art of the Eskimos

See HOFFMAN, WALTER JAMES. Graphic art ...

ESKRICH, PIERRE

Cabinet J — Shelf 2 — No. 23

Peintre et tailleur d'histoires a Lyon au XVI[e] siecle. Etude posthume de M. Natalis Rondot. Lyon, 1901.

Parchment; 11¼ x 7½ in.

ESPARTO PAPERS

Cabinet RR Shelf 4 No. 41

(History and use of Esparto papers) Presented with the compliments of the Association of Makers of Esparto Papers. (Edinburgh),1933

Paper; 9¾ x 7-3/8 in

ESPARTO PAPERS

Cabinet Shelf No.

History of Esparto

See PAPER. History of Esparto and Esparto papers...

ESPARTO PAPERS

Cabinet 61 Shelf 1 No. 5

Rise and progress of the Esparto trade.

Article in " The Paper World", vol.16, No.3, March, 1888, p.8

ESPERANTO

Cabinet II Shelf 3 No. 50.01

(The) American Esperanto Journal

See PERIODICALS, LANGUAGE Esperanto Journal...

ESPINOSA DE LOS MONTEROS, ANTONIO

Cabinet AA Shelf 5 No. 2

Provision Real de los Señores del Consejo para que se establezcan en la Ciudad de Segovia ... una imprenta: Escula de ... dibujo y el arte de hacer punzones e matrices de letras de imprenta, con el arte de fundirlas. Segovia, 1778.

Decree authorizing the establishment of a state printing and typefounding establishment also a school for teaching all branches of the graphic arts, including type design and type casting: Both under the direction of Antonio Espinosa de los Monteros.

Calf; 8 x 5-7/8 in.

ESPINOSA, ANTONIO

Cabinet 83 Shelf 2 No. 52

See Specimen Books, Types. Spain.

ESSEQUEBO and DEMERARY GAZETTE

Cabinet Shelf No.

See Newspapers, British Guiana.

ESSEX ALMANACK (see)

Cabinet 80 Shelf 1 No. 44.01

Almanacs. Essex Almanack....

ESSEX HOUSE PRESS, THE

Cabinet M Shelf 2 No.

See Imprints, England. Essex House Press. C.R. Ashbee.

ESSEX HOUSE PRESS

Cabinet M Shelf 2 No. 31

Private Press, The: A study in idealism. To which is added a bibliography of the Essex House Press. C.R. Ashbee author and printer, at the Essex House Press, Campden, Gloucestershire, 1909.

Boards; 10½ x 8 in.

ESSEX HOUSE PRESS

Cabinet T Shelf 4 No. 111

Specimens of the "Prayer Book" and the "Endeavour" types.

See STEELE, ROBERT T. (The) Revival of printing...London, 1912. p.51.

ESSEX REGISTER.

Cabinet Shelf No.

See Newspaper, Massachusetts.

ESSLING, (PRINCE D')

Cabinet I Shelf 5 No. 16 to 20 5 vols.

Etudes sur l'art de la gravure sur bois a Venise. Les livres a figures Vénetiens de la fin du XVe siècle et du commencement du XVIe. [5 vols.] Florence-Paris, 1907, 1908, 1909-1914. With photogravure plates and woodcut reproductions.

Tome I - Ouvrages imprimés de 1450 jusqu'a 1490.
" II - " " " 1491 " 1500

(Cont'd).

Essling (Prince d')

Cabinet I Shelf 5 No. 16-20

Tome III, (Part I). Ouvrages imprimes de 1501 jusqu'a 1517.
" " Part II. Ouvrages imprimés de 1518 jusqu'a 1525.
" IV Essais, appendice et tables.

Half morocco; 17½ x 12 in.

ESSLING, PRINCE d'

Cabinet U Shelf 1 No. 1c

Etudes sur l'art de la gravure sur bois a Venise. Les livres a figures venetians de la fin du XVe siecle et du commencement du XVIe. Florence, L. S. Olschki, n. d. [1907] Book with above title reviewed by A. W. Pollard.

In Excerpts relating to printing from "The Library," 1908. pp. 104-110.

ESSONNE (France)

Cabinet RR Shelf 3 No. 23

Paper mill of Essonne, description of.

see PAPER MILLS, France. Papeterie d'Essonne...

ESSONE

Cabinet RR Shelf 3 No. 31

Paper mills of Exxone.

see PAPER MILLS, France. Essone...

ESTIENNE, CHARLES (Author).

Cabinet 40 Shelf 1 No. 8

I: Dere horteli libellus, vulgaria herbarum ... Paris. Ex officina Roberti Stephani, 1536.
II: Seminariu[m] sive plantarium earum arborum, quae post hortos conseri solent ... Excudebat Rob. Stephanus. Parisiis.

Various botanical-medical works bound together, all of which were printed by Robert Estienne, brother of Charles.

Tooled leather; 7 x 4¾ in.

ESTIENNE, CHARLES (Author).

Cabinet 40 Shelf 1 No. 25

Seminarium et plantarium fructiferaerum praefertim arborum quae post hortos conseri solene ...(Carolus Stephanus). Parisiis, ex officina Rob. Stephani. 1548.
Bound in with "De Nutrimentis," Caroli Stephani, Parisiis, 1550; also another item, not by same author, printed by Melchior and Gaspar Trechsel, Lyons, 1535.

Tooled leather; 6-3/4 x 4½ x 1-3/4 in.

ESTIENNE, CHARLES

Cabinet 75 Shelf 2 No. 1

Earliest French itineraries, 1552 and 1591. Charles Estienne and Theodore de Mayerne-Turquet. By Sir H. George Fordham. Read before the Bibliographical Society, 15. Nov. 1920.

In Trans. Biblio. Soc. Vol. I, 1920-1921. pp. 193-224. "The Library."

ESTIENNE, CHARLES.

Cabinet 40 Shelf No.

See Early Printing in France. Paris. [v.d.]

ESTIENNE, CHARLES.

Cabinet 75 Shelf 2 No. 8

Published first regular road-book and itinery. Paris, 1552. Brief note.

In Transactions of the Bibliographical Society, "The Library," Vol. VIII, 1927-28, p. 352.

ESTIENNE, HENRI (Author).

Cabinet 40 Shelf 1 No. 36

Anacreon: [Translated into Latin from the Greek, by Henri Estienne]. Lutetiae. Apud Henricum Stephanum. 1554.

Morocco; 8 x 5¾ x 5/8 in. Brunet I,250.

ESTIENNE, HENRI (Author)

Cabinet 40 Shelf 1 No. 56

Artis typographicae Querimonia de illiteratis quibusdam typographis, propter quos in contemptum venit. Autore Henrico Stephano. Epitaphia Graeca & Latina doctorum quorundum typographorum, ab eodem scripta. Anno M D LXIX. Excudebat Henricus Stephanus. Printer Mark.
Poem on typography with epitaphs in honor of celebrated printers; Aldus Manutius; Johann Oporinus, etc.

Half morocco 8½ x 6 in.

ESTIENNE, HENRI (Author)

Cabinet W Shelf 2 No. 143 2 Vols.

Deux dialogues du nouveau langage français italianizé, et autrement desguizé, principalement entre les courtisans de ce temps. Par Henri Estienne avec introduction et notes par P. Ristelhuber. Paris, 1885. Two Vols.
The first edition of the "Deux dialogues" appeared in 1578.

Half morocco; 8¼ x 5¼ in.

ESTIENNE, HENRI (Author)

Cabinet 40 Shelf 1 No. 55

(1) Epistola, qua ad multorum amicorum respondet, de suae typographiae statu....de suo Thesauro linguae Graecae...(2). Index librorum qui ex officina Henrici Stephani hactenus prodierunt. [Two items in one binding] [Geneva] 1569.

Morocco; 7 x 4¼ x ¾ in.

ESTIENNE, HENRI, Author-Printer

Cabinet W Shelf 2 No. 83

(La) Foire de Francfort. Par Henri Estienne; traduit en Francais pour le premiere fois sur l'edition originale de 1574. Par Isidore Lizeux. Avec le text Latin en regard. Paris, 1875.

Half morocco; 6-1/8 x 3-3/4 x ½ in.

ESTIENNE, HENRI

Cabinet S Shelf 1 No. 107

Frankfort Book Fair: The Francofordiense Emporium of Henry Estienne [1574]. Edited with historical introduction, original Latin text with English translation on opposite pages and notes, by James W. Thompson. Chicago: The Caxton Club, 1911. Facsimiles, Illus., portraits.

Half vellum; 11½ x 7¾ in.

ESTIENNE, HENRI

Cabinet QQ Shelf 1 No. 10

Plainte de la typographie contre certains imprimeurs ignorans...Poëm latin, traduit en français par un imprimeur de Paris, du XVIIIe; On y a joint le tableau généalogique des Estienne. Paris, Chez Jean-Roch Lottin. 1785.

Morocco; 9¼ x 7½ in.

ESTIENNE, HENRI, author.

Cabinet E Shelf 2 No. 73

World of wonders...or a preparation treatise to the Apologie for Herodotus...written in Latin by Henry Stephen......translated out of the best corrected French copie. Printer Mark.
Imprint: London, Imprinted for John Norton, 1607.

Calf tooled; 11-3/4 x 7-7/8 in.

ESTIENNE, HENRI (Commentator)

Cabinet 40 Shelf 1 No. 68

Publii Virgilii Maronis. Poemata. Henrici Stephani Scholiis illustrata ... Tertia Editio ... [Printer mark: Excudebat Paulus Stephanus. Anno M.D.XCIV. (1599).

Vellum; 6½ x 4¼ x 1½ in.

ESTIENNE, HENRI

Cabinet W Shelf 2 No. 77

Essai sur la vie et les ouvrages de Henri Estienne. Suivi d'une étude sur Scévole de Sainte-Marthe. Par Léon Feugère. Paris, Imprimerie de Jules Delalain. 1853.

Half morocco; 7½ x 4½ in.

ESTIENNE, HENRI.

Cabinet Shelf No.

see also
Early Printing in France. Paris [v.d.]
Early Printing in Switzerland, Geneva.

ESTIENNE, HENRI, AND ROBERT

Cabinet W Shelf 2 No. 13

Didot, Firmin: Poésies de Firmin Didot, député d'Eure-et-Loir. Suivies d'observations littéraires et typographiques sur Robert et Henri Estienne. Paris, Typographie de Firmin Didot Frères. 1834.

Half morocco; 8-7/8 x 5½ in.

ESTIENNE, HENRI and ROBERT.

Cabinet T Shelf 6 No. 59

(A) Distinguished family of French printers of the 16th century, Henri and Robert Estienne. n.a.n. London: Linotype and Machinery Ltd. 1929. Printed by George W. Jones at The Sign of the Dolphin.

Boards; 13-3/8 x 8½ in.

ESTIENNE, HENRI and ROBERT

Cabinet M Shelf 2 No. 61

(A) Distinguished family of printers of the 16th century: Henri and Robert Estienne and their successors. (n.a.n.) The Mergenthaler Linotype Company. Brooklyn, New York. 1929. Printed in London by George W. Jones in Gough Square.

Boards, vellum back; 13-3/8 x 8-5/8 in. In protective case.

ESTIENNE (HENRI II)

Cabinet X Shelf 1 No. 36

Artis typographicae Iurimonia de illiteratis quibusdam Typographis propter quos in contemptum venit. Paris, 1569. (Poem, with epitaphs of celebrated printers; Aldus, Badius, etc.)

[In Wolf, "Monumenta Typographica", vol. I, p. 57]

ESTIENNE, HENRI (II) (author)

Cabinet 40 Shelf 1 No. 60

De latinitate falso suspecta. Expostulatis Henrici Stephani....eiusdam de Plauti latinitate dissertatio & ad lectionem illius progymnasa, [Printer Mark]. Anno M.D.LXXVI Excudebat Henricus Stephanus.

Leather; 6 x 3-3/4 x 1 in.

ESTIENNE, HENRI (II)

Cabinet 40 Shelf No.

See Early Printing in Switzerland, Geneva, (v.d.)

ESTIENNE, HENRI (II) (Author)

Cabinet 40 Shelf 1 No. 58

Francofordiense emporium, sive francofordiense nundinae. Quam varia mercium genera in hoc emporio prostent, pagina septima indicabit. Henr. Stephanus....Anno M.D.LXXIIII. Excudebat Henricus Stephanus.

Parchment cover; 6-7/8 x 4¼ x ½ in. Brunet 2, 1082.

ESTIENNE, HENRI (II) (author)

Cabinet 40 Shelf 1 No. 44

L'introduction au traité de la confromité des merveilles anciennes avec les modernes. [Geneva] 1556. [The Estienne device without the name of printer]

The first edition of a remarkable book by the most scholarly of the members of the Estienne family.

Calf; 6¼ x 4-3/8 x 1½ in. See Renouard, Imprimeurs Parisiens.

ESTIENNE, HENRI (II) (Author)

Cabinet 40 Shelf 2 No. 42

Thesaurus graecae linguae. ab Henrico Stephano constructus....[Printer Mark]

Imprint: Henr. Stephani Oliva. Cum privilegio Caes. maiestatis, et Christianiss Galliarum regis. [Geneva: 1572?]

Morocco; 15¼ x 9-3/4 x 2-3/4 ins.

ESTIENNE, JACQUES

Cabinet 40 Shelf 1 No. 72

See Early Printing in France. Paris, 1768.

ESTIENNE, PAUL.

Cabinet 40 Shelf 1 No. 68

See Early Printing in Switzerland. [Geneva] 1599.

For a detailed account of Paul Estienne, the grandson of Robert (I). See Didot. Les Estiennes, 1856. p.553.

ESTIENNE, ROBERT, The first of that name.

Cabinet S Shelf 5 No. 6

An account in French of the great scholar-printer who flourished in France and Geneva during the early part of the 16th century, by G. A. Crapelet.

Bound with other items in "Various printers and their plants." item 21, vol. 2.

ESTIENNE, ROBERT (Stephanus). (Author)

Cabinet 40 Shelf 1 No. 32

Ad censures theologorum Parisiensium, quibus Biblia à Roberto Stephano typographo Regia excusa calumnise notarunt, eiusdem Roberti Stephani responsio (Robert Estienne's reply to the theologians' false accusations. (Geneva) 1552.

Imprint: Oliva Roberti Stephani M.D.LII. French translation, facsimile 40/1/33.

Morocco; 7-1/8 x 4-5/8 x 3/4 in.

ESTIENNE, ROBERT I. (Author).

Cabinet 40 Shelf 1 No. 33

(Les) Censures des theologiens de Paris, par lesquelles ils avoyent faulsement condamne les Bibles imprimées par Robert Estienne imprimeur du Roy: Avec la response d'iceluy Robert Estienne. Traduictes de Latin en Francais. L'Olivier de Robert Estienne. 1552. Réimprimé par Jules-Guillaume Fick. Geneva, 1866.

Vellum; 9½ x 6¼ x 1½ in.
SEE also 40/1/32

ESTIENNE, ROBERT (1)

Cabinet 70 Shelf 1 No. 50

Epigrams.

see

POETRY OF PRINTING. Epigrams in honor of printers...Lyons, 1538

ESTIENNE, ROBERT

Cabinet Y Shelf 1 No. 41

Paris, Robert Etienne in. (Biographical account, with portrait, device, and specimen of printing).

See BÖRCKEL, ALFRED. Gutenberg und seine berühmsten nachfolger...pp.172-183

ESTIENNE, ROBERT I

Cabinet V Shelf 6 No. 9

See Portraits, Printers. Estienne (Stephanus) Robert.

ESTIENNE, ROBERT

Cabinet C Shelf 1 No. 12

Vita, Roberti Stephani. Basle, 1740. [Photostatic copy]

Life of Robert Estienne, with a list of books printed by him.

Half morocco; 17½ x 11½ in.

ESTIENNE, ROBERT I.

Cabinet 69 Shelf 1 No. 15

See Early Printing in France. Paris, 1548. Conrad Badius. Theodori Beza.

Estienne (Stephanus) Collaborated with Badius in printing this book.

ESTIENNE, ROBERT (Stephanus).

Cabinet Shelf No.

See Early Printing in France, Paris. [v.d.].

ESTIENNE, ROBERT.

Cabinet 40 Shelf 1 No. 64

See Early Printing in France. Paris, 1587. Mamert Patisson & Robert Estienne.

ESTIENNE, ROBERT (II)

Cabinet 40 Shelf 1 No.

See Early Printing in France, Paris, (v.d.)

ESTIENNE FAMILY

Stack A Shelf 1 & 2 Number 82

Last of a Great Family of printers, 1502-1928, by Henry Lewis Bullen. In Collectanea Typographica. The Inland Printer. Vol. 82, 1928-29. p.82. Illus. Portrait, and printer mark.

ESTIENNE FAMILY OF PRINTERS

Cabinet W Shelf 2 No. 14

Didot, Ambroise Firmin. Les Estienne. Henri I; Francois I et II, Robert I, II, et III; Henri II; Paul et Antoine. Extrait de la Nouvelle Biographie Générale, publiée par M.M. Firmin Didot frères. Paris, [1856].

Half morocco; 8½ x 5½ in.

ESTIENNE DYNASTY OF PRINTERS.

Stack A Shelf 1&2 Number 67

Estienne, Robert and Henry, and the Estienne dynasty of printers, by Henry Lewis Bullen, in The Inland Printer, vol. 67, p. 198. Illus.

ESTIENNE FAMILY

See Mattaire, Michael.

ESTIENNE FAMILY OF PRINTERS

Cabinet V Shelf 3 No. 17

(Dynasty of celebrated printers, Paris, 1502-1661. Bio-bibliographical account)

Henri-1502-20	Francois-1562-1582
Robert-1526-1559	Paul-1599-1627
Charles-1551-1564	Robert-1618-1644
Henri (2)-1556-1598	Antoine-1572-1644
Robert (2)-1556-1571	Henri-1646-1661

see WERDET, EDMOND. Histoire du livre en France...3me partie (1), pp.306-364

ESTIENNE (STEPHANUS), The family of.

Cabinet 20 Shelf 1 No. 17

Druckerfamilie der Estienne (Stephanus). von Wilhelm Kothe, Gottingen, Aug., 1905.

In Zeitschrift fur Bucherfreunde, 1905-6, part 1, p.179.

ESTIENNE FAMILY

Cabinet S Shelf 5 No. 6

(A) Notable family of printers. (Biographical) Excerpt from "Sunday at Home," reprinted in the National Repository, May, 1879.

Item 3 in collection "Various printers and their plants; excerpts from magazines," vol. 2, 1918.

ESTIENNE FAMILY OF PRINTERS

Cabinet Shelf No.

Francois Estienne restores the Greek upper case letters;- Paul Estienne;- Robert Estienne; R. Estienne as a printer of Greek, etc.

see PROCTOR, ROBERT. Bibliographical essays...London, 1912, pp.94-119.

ESTIENNE FAMILY

Cabinet W Shelf 2 No. 82

(Les) Estienne et les types Grecs de Francois 1er. Complément des annales Stéphaniennes. Renfermant l'histoire complete des types royaux ... Par Aug. Bernard, Paris. 1856. Specimens, and Genealogical chart. Bio-historical.

Boards; 9 x 5-3/4 in.

ESTIENNE, Family

see also Janssonius, Theodorus (De Vitis Stephanorum)

ESTIENNE FAMILY OF PRINTERS

Cabinet V

See Genealogies, Printers. Maddan. J. P. A. De quelques alliances favorables...du XVIe siècle.

ESTIENNE FAMILY

Cabinet W Shelf 1 No. 78

Etablissement des Estienne a Geneve. See Gaullieur, E. H. Études sur la Typographie. Genevoise ... Geneva, 1855. p.180.

ESTIENNE FAMILY OF PRINTERS

Cabinet V Shelf 5 No. 7

(Bio-bibliographical citations, notes, etc.)

see CRAPELET, CH. "Études pratiques...sur la typographie". Paris, 1837 (see index)

ESTIENNE FAMILY OF PRINTERS

Cabinet Y Shelf 2 No. 23

(Life and works of Robert Stephanus and his successors. Brief notes)

See LORCKE, CARL B. Handbuch... Leipzig, 1882-83, part 1, pp.202-208

ESTIENNE FAMILY.

Cabinet V Shelf 3 No. 17

Études bibliographiques: sur les imprimieurs et libraires de Paris les plus celèbre. See Werdet, Edmond. Histoire du Livre en France. Études Bibliographiques: Les Estienne. Tome I, partie 3, Paris. 1864, pp.69-353.

ESTIENNE FAMILY OF PRINTERS

Cabinet X Shelf 1 No. 15

(De) Vitis Stephanorum, celebrium typographorum. Dissertatio epistolica...Theodor Janson Almeloveen. Amsteldami, 1683. With frontis. portrait, R. Estienne. Bio-bibliogr. essay on the lives and works of the Estienne family.

Calf; 5-5/8 x 4-1/8 in.

ESTIENNE FAMILY OF PRINTERS

Cabinet U Shelf 4 No. 74

Parisian Greek Press, Early; including the lives of the Stephani; notices of other contemporary Greek printers of Paris, and various particluars of the literary and ecclesiastical history of their times. Edited by E. Greswell. Oxford 1833. Two vols.

2 vols. Half morocco; 9 x 5-3/4 x 1-1/8 in. See also U/4/73

ESTIENNE FAMILY OF PRINTERS

Cabinet W — Shelf 2 — No. 48

Renouard, Antoine-Augustin: Annales de l'imprimerie des Estienne, ou histoire de la famille des Estienne et de ses éditions, par Ant. Aug. Renouard. Second partie. Paris, 1838.

At the end, a tract dated 1838 "Note sur Laurent Coster, à l'occasion d'un ancien livre imprimé dans les Pays-Bas."

Calf; 8½ x 5½ in.

ESTIENNE FAMILY OF PRINTERS

Cabinet W — Shelf 2 — No. 144

Rossignol. Les Estienne, 1503-1620 [Par Rossignol, Paris, 1885?]. Portrait

Half morocco; 7½ x 4-3/4 in.

ESTIENNE FAMILY OF PRINTERS

Cabinet S — Shelf 5 — No. 25.02

Scholar - printers, 1502-1674. [Biographical account] by Louis K. Comstock. Montclair Dec. 25, 1928.

Pamphlet in box labelled "Pamphlets and excerpts relating to printers, their plants, and other typographical matters". Box No.2.

ESTIENNE FAMILY OF PRINTERS

Cabinet Q — Shelf 2 — No. 30

Scholar-printers-publishers. Biographical notes.

See PUBLISHING. Aldus, Froben, Jenson, Plantin, Estiennes...

ESTIENNE FAMILY OF PRINTERS

Cabinet X — Shelf 1 — No. 23

Stephanorum historia, vitas ipsorum ac libros complectens. (Michele Maittaire). Londini, Typis Benj. Motte.

Includes lists of the books printed by the Estiennes, 1556-1660

Half morroco; 7¾ x 5 x 1¾ in.

ESTIENNES, The or (Stephenses)

Cabinet S — Shelf 5 — No. 6

See "A notable family" in the "National Repository," London, May, 1879.

Bound with other items in "Various Printers and their Plants," item 3, vol.2.

ESTIENNE De La HUPROYE le JEUNE

Cabinet — Shelf — No.

See HUPROYE (Estienne de la) le Jeune.

ESTIENNE, L'ECOLE (see)

Cabinet — Shelf — No.

SCHOOLS OF PRINTING, France L'Ecole Estienne...

ESTIMATING COSTS

Cabinet — Shelf — No.

See Printing Accountancy.

ESTIMATING PRESSWORK

Cabinet — Shelf — No.

See Printing Accountancy.

ESTRADA, ANGEL

Cabinet — Shelf — No.

See Specimen Books, Types. South America.

ETCHERS

Cabinet J — Shelf 3 — No. 32

Struck, Hermann

see STRUCK, HERMANN.

ETCHING

Cabinet I — Shelf 1 — No. 10

Bosse, Abraham. Triacte des manieres de graver en taille douce...A Paris, 1645.

Has engraved titles (2), plates and diagrams.

Tree calf; 7 x 4½ in.

ETCHING.

Cabinet I — Shelf 2 — No. 28

British School of Etching, The. Being a lecture delivered to The Print Collectors Club by Martin Hardie, R.E., on July 8th, 1921, with a foreword by Sir Frank Short, R.A. Published by The Print Collectors Club, 5a, Pall Mall East, S.W. 1, Printers, Sanders Phillips & Co. The Baynard Press, London, 1921.

Linen over boards; 10 x 7½ x 3/8 in.

ETCHING

Cabinet J — Shelf 3 — No. 25

French etchers of the Second Empire. By William Aspinwall Bradley. With illustrations. Boston...1916.

Stamped cloth; 8¼ x 5½ in.

ETCHING

Cabinet J — Shelf 3 — No. 26

French etching, a history of, from the 16th century to the present day. By F.L. Leipnik. Illustrated with frontispiece and 106 reproductions in photogravures. London...New York, 1924.

Boards, cloth back; 11½ x 9 x 1-7/8 in.

ETCHING

Cabinet J — Shelf 3 — No. 19

History of engraving and etching, a short.

See HIND, A.M. Engraving & etching, a short history of...

ETCHING

Cabinet I — Shelf 1 — No. 34

Invention of chalcography, of the.

Chap. IV, p.259 of OTTLEY'S Inquiry into the origin and early history of engraving upon copper and in wood. (2 vols.) London, 1816. Illus.

Half morocco; 11⅛ x 9 in.

ETCHING.

Cabinet Process or examples of etching.

See ENGRAVING PROCESSES. Methods of [Etching].

Shelf

" also ENGRAVING PROCESSES, Literature of [Etching].

No.

ETCHING

Cabinet See also cards with following sub-heads:

I - ENGRAVING PROCESSES, LITERATURE OF. Etching.
Shelf II - " " METHODS OF. "

No.

ETCHINGS

Cabinet 68 Shelf No. 4

Croatto, Bruno, ten original etchings of.

See CROATTO, BRUNO. (Sicily, ten original etchings...)

ETCHINGS

Cabinet C Shelf 1 No. 7

Marussig, Guido....Ferrara. XXIV visioni del pittore. (24 visions of Guido Marussig, 3 of Carlo Parmeggia, and 4 of Ferrucio de Lupis)

Editori, Alfieri-Lacroix, Milano...n.d.

Pictorial boards; 16 x 13¼ in.

ETHERINGTON, CHRISTOPHER

Cabinet U Shelf 5 No. 49

York, 1770-1776, Chris. Etherington, printer. Biblio-biographical notes.

see DAVIS, ROBERT (A) Memoir of The York Press...1868, pp.331-38

ETTINGER, P.

Cabinet 26 Shelf 1 No. 17

Bibliophilie und buchkunst in Sowiet-Russland (Printing and book collecting in Soviet Russia).

Article in the Gutenberg-Gesellschaft Jahrbuch 1928. pp.129-171.

ETYMOLOGIKUM MAGNUM GRAECAE

Cabinet D Shelf 2 No. 48

Venice, 1499

see INCUNABULA. Etymologikum etc.

EUCLID

Cabinet F Shelf 4 No. ~~138~~

Euclidis Elementorum libri priores sex, libri priores sex. Ex versione latina Federici Commandini...Curante a Roberto Simson.

Imprint: Glasguae, in aedibus academicis excudebant Robertus et Andreas Foulis. Academiae Typographi. 1756.

Leather; 11¾ x 9¼ x 1¾ in. Brunet 2, 1082.

EUCLID

Cabinet D Shelf 3 No. 18

Euclidis megarensis philosophi acutissimi mathematicorum...A. Paganius Paganinus characteribus elegantissimis accuratissime imprimebat. [Venice, 1509.]

Paper boards; 12 x 8 x 1 in.

EUCLID

Cabinet 40 Shelf 2 No. 22

Orontii, Finaei Delphinatis. Regii mathematicarum. Lutetiae professoris in sex priores libros géometricorum...cum ipsius Euclidis textu graeca & interpretatione latina Bartholamaei Zamberti Veneti.

Imprint: Lutetiae Parisiorum, apud Simoneum Colinaeum. 1544. Cum priveligio regis.

Boards; 11-3/4 x 8-3/8 x 5/8 in.

EUCLID Bibliography

Cabinet 76 Shelf 2 No. 20

Early editions of Euclids Elements. By Charles Thomas-Stanford. London. Printed for the Bibliographical Society, 1926. Illus. monograph No.20.

Boards, cloth back; 11-1/8 x 8-7/8 x ½ in.

EUCLID. Bibliography

Cabinet 75 Shelf 2 No. 5

Early editions of Euclid's Elements. 1482-1600: A paper read before the Bibliographical Society by C. Thomas-Stanford, November, 19, 1923.

In Trans. Biblio. Soc., "The Library," Vol. 5, 1924-1925, pp. 39-42.

EULENBERG, HERBERT

Cabinet Y Shelf 1 No. 92.02

Huldigung an Gutenberg: Eine festdichtung zu seinem angedenken. Kleine druck der Gutenberg-Gesellschaft Nr. 6. n.d.

Play, theatrical, about the invention of printing in which the characters include Gutenberg, Ennel, his wife, Fust, Schoeffer, and Ortlieb, a boy.

With other items in manila envelope.

EUREKA STEREOTYPING MACHINE see STEREOTYPING.

Cabinet FF Shelf 1 No. 108

Eureka...

EUSEBIUS.

Cabinet 29 Shelf 1 No. 20 & 21

Chronicon, id est temporum breviarium incipit foeliciter ... Venice, Erhard Ratdolt impressit. 1483.

Calf; 9¼ x 6½ in. [Second copy] Morocco.

EUSEBIUS, PAMPHILIUS

Cabinet 6 Shelf 1 No. 2

De Evangelica praeparatione latinum ex graeco... Venice, Nicolas Jenson, 1470.

This is the first book printed by Jenson.

Stitched only; in morocco slip case; 14 x 10¼ x 2 in. Hain 2, 6696.

EUSEBIUS.

Cabinet 70 Shelf 1 No. 45

Historis ecclesiastica Eusebii. Impressa Ludguni per Benedictum Bonnym Calcographum. Sumptibus Jacobi et Francisci de Giunta, sociorum Florentini. 1533.

Bound in with another Giunta item, 1534.

Calf; 7¼ x 4¾ x 1½ in. Blaudelaire 6, 150.

EUSTACE, GUILLAUME

Cabinet 70 Shelf 1 No. 8

See Early Printing in France. Paris, 1511. Guillaume Eustace.

EVANS, A. B.

Cabinet L Shelf 1 No. 22

Short history of offset printing. By A.B. Evans. [Excerpt from The Modern Lithographer & Offset Printer, Feb., 1925]

Item in manila envelope

EVANS, CHARLES

Cabinet TT Shelf 4 No. 15-26

American bibliography: a chronological dictionary of all books, pamphlets and periodical publications printed in the United States of America from 1639 to 1820, with biographical notes. Privately printed for the author. Chicago, 1903, 4, 5, 7, 9, 10, 22, 24, 25, 29 and 1931, 1934

(cont'd)

EVANS, CHARLES (cont'd)

Cabinet TT Shelf 4 No. 15-26

Vol. I, 1639-1729. Vol. VI, 1779-1785.
" II, 1730-1750. " VII, 1786-1789.
" III, 1751-1764. " VIII, 1790-1792.
" IV, 1765-1773. " IX, 1793-1794.
" V, 1774-1778. " X, 1795-1796.
" XI, 1796-1797.
" XII, 1798-1799

Each vol. cloth; $11\frac{1}{2}$ x 9 in.

EVANS EDMUND

Cabinet L Shelf 4 No. 22

Gems from painters and poets. Embellished with eight facsimiles of water-colour drawings, and other illustrations...Engraved and printed by Edmund Evans. London (1869)

Embossed cloth, gilt; $9\frac{1}{2}$ x 7 in.

EVANS, HENRY R.

Cabinet R Shelf 5 No. 149

Benjamin Franklin and religion. Illus. Excerpt from The Master Mason. New Jersey Edition, August, 1925, No.2.

Item (j) in book with binder's title "Benjamin Franklin: various pamphlets". 1853-1926.

EVANS-WINTER-HEBB.

Cabinet Shelf No.

See Imprints, United States. Cleland, Thomas Maitland, Detroit, 1927. The new Cadillac

EVELYN, JOHN

Cabinet I Shelf 1 No. 23

History and art of engraving...Printed for S. Harding. London, 1747. With plates and engravers marks.

A revised and enlarged edition of the "Sculptura; or the history of chalcography" ...1662.

Half morocco; $6\frac{1}{2}$ x 3-7/8 in.

EVELYN, JOHN

Cabinet I Shelf 1 No. 25

Sculptura, or the history and art of chalcography and engraving in copper. To which is annexed a new manner of engraving, or mezzotinto, communicated by His Highness Prince Rupert to the author of this treatise, John Evelyn. The second edition...With memoirs of the author's life. London, 1769.

Portrait frontispiece, and 1 folded plate.

Calf; $7\frac{1}{4}$ x $4\frac{3}{4}$ in.

EVELYN, JOHN

Cabinet I Shelf 1 No. 26

Sculptura, or the history and art of chalcography and engraving...To which is now added a chronological and historical series of the painters from the 11th century. With copperplates. The fourth edition. London: Printed for J. Marks, 1770.

With reproductions of marks and cyphers of engravers.

Calf; 6-7/8 x 4-1/8 x 7/8 in.

"EVENING BULLETIN, THE" (Philadelphia)

Cabinet NN Shelf 3 No. 46

"One Day". This volume is designed to show how one copy of the Evening Bulletin appears when published in book form. The Evening Bulletin, Philadelphia, 1929.

Cloth; $7\frac{3}{4}$ x $5\frac{1}{8}$ x 1-1/8 in.

EVENING BULLETIN, The, San Francisco.

Cabinet Shelf No.

See Journalism California: Full and authentic account of the murder of James King.

EVENING EAGLE (Pittsfield and Dalton, Mass.)

Cabinet NN Shelf 7 No. 10

Industrial Edition of The Evening Eagle, illustrating Pittsfield and Dalton, Mass., in the year 1897. Facts relative to...their manufactures, trade, citizens, etc. Compiled and illustrated by John E. Thornton. Pittsfield, Mass., 1897.
History of the Evening Eagle on p. 2. -Paper industry, pp. 33 - 39.

Cloth; 13-7/8 x $10\frac{1}{4}$ in.

EVENING POST, Baltimore.

Cabinet Shelf No.

See Newspapers, Maryland.

EVENING POST, THE.

Cabinet 81 Shelf 2 No. 39

New York Weekly Evening Post.

See NEWSPAPERS. UNITED STATES. Lit. of. Evening Post, the first half century.

EVENING POST, (THE).

Cabinet Shelf No.

See Journalism, New York City.

Bound with other items in "Various newspapers and periodicals", item 6.

EVENING POST (The), New York City.

Cabinet A Shelf 1 No. 89

See Newspapers, anniversary issues. U.S.

EVENING POST see

Cabinet Shelf No.

NEW YORK EVENING POST

EVENING POST, THE NEW YORK see

Cabinet Shelf No.

NEW YORK EVENING POST

EVENING SUN (The)

Cabinet See Newspapers, New York City.

Shelf

No.

EVOLUTION OF TYPE FACES

Cabinet S Bullen, Henry Lewis: Notes toward the study of types. Taken from The Graphic Arts. Boston, 1911-12. Illus.

Shelf 1 Part 1, The power of the serif ...
" 2, Classification of type designs ...
" 3, Of color, contrast and clarity ...

No. 102 " 4, The type models ...
" 5, The Roman type model ...

Full morocco; 12½ x 9¼ in.

EXCERPTS RELATING TO ENGRAVING

Cabinet I Binder's title: Various engravers and about engravers.

Shelf 3

No. 1 Cards for items 1 to 38.

EVENING TELEGRAPH (The), Philadelphia.

Cabinet See Newspapers, Pennsylvania.

Shelf

No.

EWER (CHARLES) of Bedlington & Ewer

Cabinet

Shelf See: Specimen Books, Types, U.S.

No.

EXCERPTS RELATING TO HISTORY OF TYPOGRAPHY

Cabinet T From English periodicals of circa 1830.

Shelf 2

No. 7 In envelope, loosely mounted.

EVENING TIMES (The), Glasgow.

Cabinet See Newspapers, Scotland.

Shelf

No.

"EXAMINER, THE"

Cabinet NN Examiner for the year 1711.

see

Shelf 5 JOURNALISM, Great Britain. Examiners (the)...

No. 2

EXCERPTS RELATING TO LIBERTY OF PRINTING

Cabinet X Binders title: French legislation relating to printing. Various items. vol. I, 1500-1872.

Shelf 4

No. 33.01 Half morocco; 11 x 8½ in.

EVER READY LABEL CORPORATION

Cabinet EE Brief history of labels. Illus. pamphlet issued by the Ever Ready Label Corporation, 141-155 East 25th Street, New York, 1934.

Shelf 4

No. 87 Item in manila envelope.

EXAMINER, THE (Catskill, N.Y.)

Cabinet See Newspapers, Anniversary Issues. Examiner, The. Centennial Edition, 1830-1930.

Shelf

No.

EXCERPTS RELATING TO PRINTING (Collection)

Cabinet R Binder's title: Benjamin Franklin: Various pamphlets, 1853-1926.

Shelf 5

No. 149

Half morocco; 11¼ x 8 in.

"EVERYBODY'S see

Cabinet NN PERIODICALS, United States. Everybody's...

Shelf 2

No. 14

EXCELSIOR TYPE FOUNDRY (see)

Cabinet FF PRICES, TYPES. Excelsior...

Shelf 3

No. 59

EXCERPTS RELATING TO PRINTING

Cabinet S Binders title: "Dawn of Printing - Excerpts from Magazines" ... Bound, 1918.

Shelf 5

No. 18

Half morocco; 10-5/8 x 7-1/8 x 5-5/8 in.

EVOLA, FILIPPO

Cabinet AA Storia tipografico-letteraria del secolo XVI in Sicilia, con un catalogo ragionato delle edizioni in essa citate. Pel Rett. Filippo Evola. Palermo, 1878. Nine plates at end with printer marks, initials, borders, and wood engravings.

Shelf 2

No. 4

Half morocco; 9 x 6¼ in.

EXCERPTS, Printing Processes

Cabinet S Binders Title:"Printing Processes: Excerpts from Magazines, etc. Bound, 1918.

Shelf 5

No. 14

Half morocco; 10 x 6-7/8 x 1 in.

EXCERPTS RELATING TO PRINTING (Collection)

Cabinet S Binder's title: Early printed books. Various excerpts and pamphlets, 1854-1931.

Partial contents: Hawker's literature of France;

Shelf 6 Early editions of King James' Bible,
History of Cyclopedies

No. 7 First Greek New Testament
Romance of rare books
Monuments of printing, 1455-1500.

Half morocco; 10¾ x 7 x ⅜ in.

EXCERPTS RELATING TO PRINTING

Cabinet S Shelf 5 No. 19

Binders title; "Excerpts on American Printing, etc. N. Y., 1895".

Cloth; 11½ x 8¼ x 3/8 in.

EXCERPTS RELATING TO PRINTING

Cabinet S Shelf 5 No. 3

Binder's Title: Printers and their Plants: Collection of Pamphlets." Bound, 1918.

Half morocco; 8¾ x 5-5/8 x 1½ in.

EXEMPTION, PRINTERS'

Cabinet Shelf No.

See **Printers' Exemption.**

EXCERPTS RELATING TO PRINTING

Cabinet S Shelf 5 No. 21

Binders title: "Excerpts relating to printing in America."

Half morocco; 9-5/8 x 7-5/8 x ½ in.

EXCERPTS RELATING TO PRINTING.

Cabinet S Shelf 5 No. 24

Binder's title: Printing excerpts.

Cards for items pp. 1-13, 15-22, 23-32, 33, 40, 54-74, 76-86, 88-111, 112-131, 132-144, 146-147

EXHIBITIONS

Cabinet FF Shelf 3 No. 17.01

French Universal Exhibition, Paris, 1867

See FRENCH UNIVERSAL EXHIBITION, Paris, 1867 ...

EXCERPTS RELATING TO PRINTING.

Cabinet S Shelf 5 No. 17

Binders title: "Miscellaneous items relating to printing; excerpts from magazines. Bound, 1918.

Half morocco; 12½ x 9½ in.

EXCERPTS RELATING TO PRINTING.

Cabinet S Shelf 5 No. 23

Binders title: "Various items relating to printing." Bound, 1919.

Half morocco;; 11¼ x 8¾ in.

EXHIBITIONS, PRINTERS, England.

Cabinet X Shelf 5 No. 3

Islington, England. March 20, 1891. Sketches at the Printers' Exhibition. Illustrations of typecasting, the Linotype, type setting, with brief description. Excerpt from the Daily Graphic.

pp. 47, 49, 51 in vol. with binder's title Scrap-Book, 1705-1891, relating to printing.

EXCERPTS RELATING TO PRINTING

Cabinet S Shelf 5 No. 12

Binders title: "Pamphlets and excerpts relating to various typographical matters." Bound, 1910.

Half morocco; 12 x 8¾ x 2¼ in.

EXCERPTS RELATING TO PRINTING.

Cabinet S Shelf 5 No. 4

Binders title; "Various printers and their plants; Excerpts from magazines, 1." bound 1918.

Half morocco; 10-3/8 x 6-7/8 in.

EXHIBITIONS, Printers, United States.

Cabinet X Shelf 5 No. 3

Philadelphia, 1876. Printing wall-paper, in the Machinery Hall, the Ingram patent rotary printing machine, etc. Philadelphia Exhibition. Illus. Newspaper excerpt, n.n.

pp. 53, 55 in vol. with binder's title "Scrap Book, 1705-1891,,relating to printing."

EXCERPTS RELATING TO PRINTING. (Collection)

Cabinet W Shelf 2 No. 2

Binder's title: Pamphlets relating to French typography. 1856-1923.

Items lettered a to h.

Half morocco; 10¾ x 8¾ x 1-1/8 in.

EXCERPTS RELATING TO PRINTING

Cabinet S Shelf 5 No. 6

Binder's title: "Various printers and their plants, excerpts from magazines," [Vol. 2]. 1918.

Half morocco; 10-3/8 x 7½ in.

EXHIBITIONS, PRINTING Austria

Cabinet Y Shelf 5 No. 28

(Imperial and Government Printing House at the Universal Exhibition of Industry and Art, Paris, 1855). Die K.K.Hof-und Staatsdruckerei bei der allgemeinen industry und kunstausstellung in Paris.

Descriptive catalogue; text in four languages

Half morocco; 7-3/4 x 5-3/8 x 3/8 in.

EXCERPTS RELATING TO PRINTING.

Cabinet S Shelf 5 No. 2

Binder's title: "Printers and their plants; collection of pamphlets. Bound, 1918.

Half morocco; 12½ x 10 in.

EXCERPTS RELATING TO PRINTING

Cabinet S Shelf 5 No. 9

Binders title: "Various printers-Excerpts and Brochures." Bound 1919.

Half morocco; 11 x 8-1/8 in.

EXHIBITIONS, PRINTING, Austria

Cabinet Y Shelf 5 No. 24

(Imperial and Government Printing House, Vienna, exhibit at London, 1851. Description of the). Uebersicht d von der Wiener K.K. Hof-und Staatsdruckerei in London: ausgestellten gegenstaende aller graphischen kunstweize. Wien, 1851.

Cloth; 9-1/8 x 5-3/4 x 3/8 in.

EXHIBITIONS, Printing, Austria

Cabinet AA Shelf 5 No. 22

Vienna, 1873; Notice abrégée de l'Imprimerie Nationale de Lisbonne, suivie du catalogue des produits présesntés dans l'Exposition Universelle de Vienne en 1873. Lisbonne: Imprimerie Nationale, 1873. In French and German.

Catalogue is preceded by a brief history of printing in Portugal.

EXHIBITIONS, PRINTING. England

Cabinet 0 Shelf 1 No. 92

London, 1862. An address delivered before the Society of Antiquaries of London, at an exhibition of early printed books. By William Tite.

Half morocco; 7¾ x 5½ in.

EXHIBITIONS, PRINTING, France.

Cabinet 26 Shelf 2 No. 1

(Industrial exhibition in Paris, 1839. A review; in German, of the work exhibited, with historical and brief biographical sketches of exhibitors, typefoundries, engravers, printers, etc.

Journal fur Buchdruckerkunst, Sept. 1839, No.9, cols. 117-121: Oct., No.10.

EXHIBITIONS, PRINTING. Belgium.

Cabinet 0 Shelf 1 No. 93

Brussels, 1839. Rapport de l'Exposition de l'industrie Francaise, Typographie, lithographie, et reliure . Par J.B.A.M. Jobard. Bruxelles, 1842.

Half morocco; 8¾ x 6 x ½ in.

EXHIBITIONS, PRINTING, England

Cabinet U Shelf 1 No. 23

London, 1877, Caxton Ehibition. The Bibles in the Caxton Ehibition...1450 to 1877. Bibliographical description of nearly 1000 Bibles in various languages chronologically arranged...By Henry Stevens, London, 1878.

Cloth; 9½ x 6¼ in.

EXHIBITIONS, PRINTING. France

Cabinet W Shelf 2 No. 2

Paris, 1855. Exposition Universelle.

See Delalain, Jules. Typographie francaise et étrangère...

EXHIBITIONS, PRINTING. Belgium

Cabinet 0 Shelf 1 No. 94

Brussels, 1897. Exposition Internationale. Catalogue du Groupe de l'Imprimerie et des Industries du Livre.

Illustrated wit portraits of printers, interior views of early printing offices, etc. Includes history of printing in Belgium, with brief biographical notes.

Half morocco: 8-5/8 x 6-3/8 in.

EXHIBITIONS, PRINTING. England

Cabinet 0) Shelf 1 No. 85

London, 1910. Souvenir of an exhibition with a record. The 4th. International Printing, Stationary and Allied Trades' Exhibition at the Royal Agricultural Hall, London, 1910 Illus.

Cloth; 11¼ x 8-7/8 x ¼ in.

EXHIBITIONS, PRINTING, FRANCE

Cabinet FF Shelf 5 No. 46

Paris, 1855. New appliances and processes shown at the Paris Exhibition...A glance of the industrial position of England. (Excerpt from The Leisure Hour). July 15, 1858.

Item in manila envelope

EXHIBITIONS, PRINTING. Belgium

Cabinet 0 Shelf 1 No. 91

Gand (Ghent), 1904. Catalogue de l'Exposition du livre...Dans les annexes de la Bibliothéque de la Ville et de l'Université, à Gand, du 2 au 31 Juillet 1904.

Has alternating Flemish text. List of Gand printers with brief biographical sketches, reproductions of printer marks, etc.

Half morocco; 9½ x 6-3/8 in.

EXHIBITIONS, PRINTING. France

Cabinet V Shelf 1 No. 24

Bordeaux (France), Mai-Novembre, 1907.

See DELMAS, GABRIEL. Exposition Internationale Maritime de Bordeaux...

EXHIBITIONS, PRINTING. France

Cabinet 0 Shelf 1 No. 95

Paris, 1867. Exposition Universelle. Rapports du Jury International. Produits de l'Imprimerie et de la librairie Par Paul Boiteau. Paris, 1867.

Bound in with two other exhibition items, London 1851, and amsterdam 1884.

Cloth; 9 x 5¾ in.

EXHIBITIONS, PRINTING. China

Cabinet PP Shelf 2 No. 42

Peiping, 1935. Exhibition of modern American printing. A catalogue. Under the auspices of the National Library of Peiping. May, 1935.

Brochures (2) in envelope.

EXHIBITIONS, PRINTING, France

Cabinet V Shelf 2 No. 14

Orleans, 1884: Catalogue de l'Exposition Universitaire et Typographique. Exposition organisée (Mai-Juin 1884). Orléans, 1885.

Wood engravings, printer marks, typographic ornaments, and portraits of bibliophiles.

Half morocco; 10¼ x 6¼ x 3/4 in.

EXHIBITIONS, PRINTING. France

Cabinet KK Shelf 4 No. 39

Paris, 1878, Exposition Universelle Internationale Rapport sur l'imprimerie et la librairie. Par M. Emile Martinet. Paris, 1880.

Report on the section of printing, and bookmaking.

Paper; 9½ x 6-3/8 x ½ in.

EXHIBITIONS, PRINTING. England.

Cabinet 0 Shelf 1 No. 95

London, 1851. l'Imprimerie la librairie et la papeterie a l'Exposition Universelle de 1851. Rapport presente par M. Firmin Didot. 2e ed. avec quelques additions. Paris 1854

Bound in with two other exhibition items Paris 1867, and Amsterdam 1884.

Cloth; 9 x 5¾ in.

EXHIBITION, Printing **France**

Cabinet FF Shelf 3 No. 10

Paris, 1819 and 1823. Typographie: Notice pour le Concours des progres de l'Industrie Francaise. Par Joseph Gille, Paris, 1823.

Historical summary of type founding, printing, stereotype, machinery, type design, etc.

Half morocco; 11x8¼x½ in. See also FF/3/11

EXHIBITIONS, PRINTING. France

Cabinet W Shelf 2 No. 2

Paris, 1889. La typographie a l'Exposition Universelle de 1889. Rapport des délégués de la Chambre Syndicale. Société Typographique Parisienne.

Report on machinery, printing, types, printing schools, etc.

Item (c) in book with binder's title "Pamphlets relating to French typography. 1856-1923".

EXHIBITIONS, PRINTING. France

Cabinet V Shelf 6 No. 25

Paris, 1900. Exposition Universelle et Internationale. Vitrines de L'Imprimerie Nationale. Paris.
Catalogue of items exhibited, with brief historical account, and chronological table of the managers of the Imprimerie National from 1640 to 1895.

In folder marked "L'Imprimerie Nationale. Various Pamphlets." Paris, 1874.

EXHIBITIONS, Printing, France.

Cabinet V Shelf 5 No 17

Paris, 1900. Imprimerie. Classe 11. Exposition rétrospective. Notice suivie de Catalogue des objets exposés. Par Paul Delalain. Many printer marks.

Hal fmorocco; 11½ x 7½ in.

EXHIBITIONS, PRINTING. France

Cabinet 0 Shelf 1 No. 84

(Paris, 1911) 2e Exposition de l'Imprimerie. Organisee par la Ghambre Syndicale des Constructeurs. 2 au 25 Juillet, 1911. Illus.

Paper; 12½ x 9½ x ½ in.

EXHIBITIONS, Printing, France.

Cabinet W Shelf 1 No. 195

Paris, 1923: Pavillon de Marsan. Le livre Français, des origines à la fin du second empire. [A series of articles by various authors, articles based on the books shown in the exhibition]. Illus., facsimile etc.

3/4 Morocco; 11-3/4 x 9¼ in.

EXHIBITIONS OF PRINTING. France

Cabinet V Shelf 5 No. 38

Paris, 1925. Exposition des Arts du Livre Francais. Musee Galliera.
This was a brilliant, colorful exhibition It was this that inspired H.L. Bullen to form his Exhibition of European Printing. The annotations in this item were made by Bullen for catalogue, of which see S-4-27.01.

Item in manila envelope.

EXHIBITIONS OF PRINTING, France

Cabinet V Shelf 6 No. 36

Schmied, Francois Louis, catalogue of and exhibition of his work, in Paris, December, 1924. (see pp. 17-23 of catalogue)
On a visit to this exhibition H.L. Bullen was so impressed with the excellence of the work, that he bought duplicates of all for the Typographic Library. These were included by Bullen in an Exhibit of European Printing that was taken to New York, Boston, Detroit, Cleveland, Chicago, Los Angeles, San Francisco, Portland and

(cont'd)

EXHIBITIONS OF PRINTING, France (cont'd)

Cabinet V Shelf 6 No. 36

Seattle. Mr. Schmied's work recommended much attention, and created such a demand from collectors that he found it profitable to send a special exhibition of his own to New York.
See S-4-27.01 for Catalogue of the Bullen Exhibition of European Printing.

The Paris catalogue of 1924 is in a manila envelope with other Schmied items.

EXHIBITIONS, Printing, Germany

Cabinet 26 Shelf 2 No. 4

Berlin, 1845. Impressions gathered during an exhibition in Berlin of the type founding and printing industry.

Historical notes, in German language.

Journal fur Buchdruckerkunst, 1845, No.19, cols.233-38: No.20, cols. 249-54: No.21, cols. 261-71: No.24, cols. 301-2.

EXHIBITIONS, PRINTING, Germany

Cabinet Y Shelf 5 No. 99

Berlin, 1904-5: Guide to the exhibition of present day printing shown at the Art and Crafts Museum). Fuhrer fur die sonderausstellung die kunst im neueren buchdruck. Dezember 1904- Januer 1905. Kunstgewerbe Museum. Berlin, 1904.

Half morocco; 7-1/8 x 5¼ x ¼ in.

EXHIBITIONS, Printing, Germany

Cabinet Y Shelf 3 No. 45

(Berlin, 1906. Book printing of the early masters, 15th to 18th centuries: A guide to the collection of Hans Grisebach) Führer durch die sonderausstellung die buchkunst der alten meister. Gestände der vormaligen sammlung Hans Grisebach. Berlin, 1906.

Half morocco; 7 x 5 x ¼ in.

EXHIBITION, PRINTING, Germany.

Cabinet Y Shelf 4 No. 75

Berlin, 1929. Ausstellung Berliner buchdruck, einst und jetzt. Aus anlass des 50-jahrigen bestehens der Berliner Typographischen Gesellschaft. (Pamphlet catalogue).
Fifty years printing activities in Berlin. Includes brief bio-bibliographical notes.

In box marked "Miscellany relating to German printers and printing. v.d."

EXHIBITIONS, PRINTING. Germany.

Cabinet Y Shelf 3 No. 116

Cologne, 1928. International press exhibition, Cologne, 1928. First prospectus which gives a review, in outline, of the programme of the exhibition.

Prochure, in envelope.

EXHIBITIONS, Printing, Germany

Cabinet Y Shelf 3 No. 115

Cologne, 1928. Pressa: Kulturschau am Rhein. Internationalen Presse-Austellung. Koln, 1928. Illus.
Essays on the growth, development and cultural influence of the Press.

Stamped cloth; 11 x 9¼ x 1¼ in.

EXHIBITIONS, PRINTING. Germany

Cabinet Y Shelf 4 No. 77

Frankfurt, 1924. Drucke beruhmter offizinen von Aldus Manutius bis Bodoni. Zweite Ausstellung der Frankfurter Bibliophilen-Gesellschaft von 24 Februar bis 30 Marz. In den Raumen der Linel-Sammlung Frankfurter Kunstgewerbe-Museum. (von Moriz Sondheim)

Descriptive historical catalogue.

Item in manila envelope.

EXHIBITIONS, Printing, Germany

Cabinet 20 Shelf 2 No. 19

Internationale Buchkunstausstellung in Leipzig, 1927. von Dr. Julius Zeitler in Leipzig, Illus. Facsimile.

In Zeitschrift für Bücherfreunde, 1927, pp. 101-120.

EXHIBITIONS, PRINTING, Germany

Cabinet Y Shelf 4 No. 46

Leipzig, 1914. (Illustrated souvenir of the International Exhibition of Graphic Arts). Erinnerung an die weltausstellung für buchgewerbe. und graphik. Leipzig, 1914.

Half morocco; 9-5/8 x 6½ x 3/8 in.

EXHIBITIONS, PRINTING, Germany

Cabinet Y Shelf 4 No. 42

Leipzig, 1914. Internat. ausstellung fur buchgewerbe und Graphik: Halle der Kultur. I, Vorstufen der schrift und Graphik; 2, Die schrift entwicklung...und Ostasiatischen kulturen; Europa...Illus.
The different parts of the exhibition described, with historical notes on the history of writing, printing from the earliest times to the present, development and dispersal of printing in Europe, Asia, and Africa.

Half morocco; 8¼ x 5 3/4 x 7/8 in.

cont'd

EXHIBITIONS, PRINTING, Germany

Cabinet Y Shelf 4 No. 47

Leipzig, 1914. Internationale ausstellung fur buchgewerbe und Graphik. Amtlicher Katalog. (Official catalogue of the entire exhibition, historical and descriptive notes on printing, paper and ink making, publishing, machinery, etc.

Half morocco; 9¼ x 6¼ x 1-7/8 in.

EXHIBITIONS, PRINTING, Germany

Cabinet Y Shelf 4 No. 45

Leipzig, 1914. International Graphic Arts Exhibition. Variosa. (volume contains I; Map and Plan of Leipzig, 2; French description of the Exhibition, 3; Catalogues of Swiss, Holland, and Denmark divisions. 6 pamphlets bound in one volume).

Half morocco; 8-7/8 x 6¼ x 7/8 in.

EXHIBITIONS, Printing, Holland

Cabinet W Shelf 5 No. 129

(Amsterdam). Exposition Nationale du Livre à Amsterdam, 1910., Catalogue de l'exposition de Joh. Enschede en Zonen: Donnant un apercu de l'art typographique dans les Pays-Bas depuis le XVe siècle jusque dans nos jous. Haarlem 1910. Joh. Enschedé en Zonen.

Half morocco; 9-1/8 x 5-7/8 in.

EXHIBITIONS, PRINTING, Holland.

Cabinet AA Shelf 3 No. 45

Haarlem, 1923: Catalogus der Tentoonstelling van de ontwikkeling der boekdrukkunst in Nederland. November 1923, in het Paviljoen te Haarlem. Facsimile.

The development of printing in the Netherlands, several essays by several authors.

Half morocco; 9½ x 6¼ in.

EXHIBITIONS, PRINTING, Germany

Cabinet Y Shelf 4 No. 44

Leipzig, 1914. (Austrian Section). Internationale ausstellung für buchgewerbe und graphik. Leipzig, 1914. Österreichisches Haus. Illus.

Includes historical notes on the history and development of printing, papermaking, ink, schoolbooks, publishing, modern reproduction processes, bookbinding, etc. in Austria.

Half morocco; 9¼ x 6½ x 1¼ in.

EXHIBITIONS, PRINTING, Holland.

Cabinet O Shelf 1 No. 95

Amsterdam, 1884. Rapport sur l'Exposition Universelle d'Amsterdam presenté a la Typographie Parisienne par Jacques Alary. Paris 1884.

Bound in with two other exhibition items.

Half morocco; 9 x 5¾ in.

EXHIBITIONS OF PRINTING, Italy

Cabinet AA Shelf 2 No. 36

Firenza, 1928. L'Arte tipografica in Italia nella terza Fiera Internazionale del libro. Augusto Cabali. a cura de "gli amatori del libro." Stampato da Raffaello Bertieri.

Half morocco; 9-1/8 x 6½ in.

EXHIBITIONS, PRINTING, Germany

Cabinet Y Shelf 4 No. 43

Leipzig, 1914. (Swiss Section) Catalogue. Includes notes on statistics of printing and publishing in Switzerland, Benefit Societies, Unions, the paper industry, bookbinding, women in the printing trades, etc. Illus. (Internationale Austellung fur buchgewerbe und graphik. Leipzig, 1914. Schweiz, Katalog. Illus.

Half morocco; 8½ x 5¾ x 1 in.

EXHIBITIONS, PRINTING, Holland

Cabinet AA Shelf 3 No. 38

Amsterdam, 1913: International Graphic Arts Exhibition. Published by the G. J. Thieme Drukkerii, Arnhem in Nijmegen in honor of the occasion.

Illustrated descriptive account of the Thieme printing house.

Half morocco; 10¼ x 7-3/4 in.

EXHIBITIONS, PRINTING, Scotland.

Cabinet U Shelf 1 No. 1f

Glasgow, February 1912. The Foulis Exhibition organized by the Glasgow Bibliographical Society, to illustrate the life and work of the brothers Foulis.

In Excerpts relating to printing from "The Library" 1912-13, p. 158 of pencilled" folios.

EXHIBITIONS, PRINTING, Germany

Cabinet Y Shelf 4 No. 40

Leipzig, 1914. Souvenirs of the International Graphic Arts Exhibition: Programs, pamphlets with items relating to the history of printing, etc. Illus.

Half morocco; 12 x 8-3/8 x 1 in.

EXHIBITIONS, PRINTING, Holland.

Cabinet W Shelf 1 No. 109

Antwerp, 1884. Rapport sur l'imprimerie presenté à l'Administration Communale de la ville de Bruxelles. Par Antoine Greyson... Henri Steens ... Antoine Delporte. Pictures, printing press of M. Jullien.

Cloth; 9-7/8 x 6½ in. Bound in volume "Rapport sur l'Imprimerie, Boston et Bruxelles, 1884-1885."

EXHIBITIONS, PRINTING United States

Cabinet RR Shelf 4 No. 14

American Institute of Graphic Arts. New York, 1920. List of contemporary printing, books etc., which were printed on Japan Paper Company's paper.

See JAPAN PAPER COMPANY. Achievement... ...New York, 1920.

EXHIBITIONS, PRINTING, Germany

Cabinet Y Shelf 4 No. 41

Leipzig, 1914. (Women in the printing trades: A special group at the International Exhibition of Graphic Arts) Die frau im buchgewerbe und in der graphik. Sondergruppe fur buchgewerbe und graphik, Leipzig, 1914. 2. Auflage.

Half morocco; 7-7/8 x 5-1/8 x 7/8 in.

EXHIBITIONS, PRINTING, Holland

Cabinet AA Shelf 3 No. 50

Antwerp, 1925: Museum Plantin-Moretus. Catalogus der Tentoonstelhing van moderne Nederlandsche boekkunst in het Museum Plantin-Moretus te Antwerpen, van 18 Juli tot 15 Augustus, 1925.

Half morocco; 8¼ x 5 in.

EXHIBITIONS, PRINTING, United States

Cabinet P Shelf 4 No. 16

American Institute of Graphic Arts, N.Y. 1926.

See AMERICAN INSTITUTE OF GRAPHIC ARTS. Fifty books exhibited...

EXHIBITIONS, PRINTING. Great Britain

Cabinet KK Shelf 4 No. 31

(London) Delegations ouvrières a l'Exposition Universelle de Londres en 1862. Rapport des délégués de la typographie. Suivi de nouveau tarif. Publié par la Commission Ouvriere. Paris, 1862.

With alphabetic list of exhibitors and product exhibited. At end of book the new prices for composition.

Half morocco; 7½ x 4¾ in.

EXHIBITIONS, Printing, Holland

Cabinet N Shelf 2 No. 18.01

'S-Gravenhage, 1925. (Catalogue of books from Dutch printing houses.)

Brochure, in manila envelope with other items

EXHIBITIONS OF PRINTING, United States.

Cabinet S Shelf 3 No. 98

American Institute of Graphic Arts, New York, May 5 to June 1: Catalogue of an Exhibition held at the National Arts Club. With an introduction by Frederic W. Goudy.

Early books shown in eight cases by the American Type Founders Company [Typographic Library]. prepared by Henry Lewis Bullen.

Cloth; 9-1/8 x 5-5/8 in.

EXHIBITIONS, PRINTING, United States

Cabinet W Shelf 1 No. 109

Boston, 1885. Rapport du délégué de l'Imprimerie à l'Exposition de Boston. Paris, Imprimerie Nouvelle (Association ouvriere) 1884.

Cloth; 9-7/8 x 6½ in. Bound in volume "Rapport sur l'Imprimerie, Boston et Bruxelles, 1884-1885."

EXHIBITIONS, PRINTING, United States

Cabinet W Shelf 1 No. 132

Chicago, 1893. Exposition Internationale de Chicago en 1893. Imprimerie et Librairie: Rapports publies sous la direction de M. Camille Krantz ... Paris, Imprimerie Nationale, 1894.

Complete report on the exhibits of printing, and printing processes from Europe, and the United States.

Half morocco; 11-5/8 x 7-7/8 in.

EXHIBITIONS, PRINTING United States

Cabinet JJ Shelf 5 No. 11

New York City, 1900. Printing Exposition Embracing all the trades connected with The Art Preservative. Held by the New York Typographical Union No.6, on the occasion of its semi-centennial. May 2 to June 2, 1900. New York City.

Paper; 10 x 7 x ½ in.

EXHIBITIONS, PRINTING. United States

Cabinet R Shelf 5 No. 2

Bradford, William, his Philadelphia imprints 1685-1692; New York imprints, 1694-1714. Shown at N. Y. Public Library, December, 1935.

Bibliographical and historical account, excerpt from N. Y. Times Book Review, Sunday, Dec. 22, 1935.

Excerpt pasted on back cover of book R/5/2.

EXHIBITIONS, Printing, United States.

Cabinet S Shelf 5 No. 12

Cincinnati, 1888. Catalogue of the contributions of the section of Graphic Arts to the Ohio Valley Centennial Exposition, Cincinnati, 1888. Catalogue prepared by S. R. Koehler.

Bound in collection "Pamphlets and excerpts relating to various typographical matters, item5.

EXHIBITIONS, PRINTING. UNITED STATES

Cabinet JJ Shelf 3 No. 28

New York City, 1900. Printing Exposition embracing all the trades connected with The Art Preservative. Held by Typographical Union No. 6 on the occasion of its semi-centennial, from May 2nd until June 2nd, Grand Central Palace, New York City, 1900. Illus. official catalogue.

Portrait of Horace Greeley on front cover.

Paper; embossed, 10 x 7 in.

EXHIBITIONS, Printing. United States

Cabinet S Shelf 4 No. 27

Bullen, Henry Lewis. Catalogue: An exhibition of the evolution of the art of the book, and in praise of printing. Held at the Free Public Library, Newark, New Jersey, from Monday April 12, to Saturday, May 1, 1920.

The catalogue and the entire exhibition supplied and arranged by Mr. Bullen.

Half morocco; 8¼ x 4-3/4 in.

EXHIBITIONS OF PRINTING. United States

Cabinet S Shelf 4 No. 28

Circulars advertising an exhibit of European Find Book and Commercial Printing in Los Angeles Public Library, May 15 to 31, 1927, under the auspices of the Los Angeles Club of Printing House Craftsmen.

For description of above item see S-4-27.01.

Circulars in manila envelope.

EXHIBITIONS, PRINTING United States

Cabinet JJ Shelf 4 No. 15

New York City, 1915. Exhibit on the occasion of the Golden Anniversary of the Typothetae of the City of New York, as arranged and catalogued by Mr. Henry Lewis Bullen.

Half morocco; 9½ x 6½ in.

EXHIBITIONS OF PRINTING. United States

Cabinet S Shelf 4 No. 27.01

Catalogue of an Exhibition of recent European Fine Book and Commercial Printing. Loaned by the Typographic Library and Museum of the American Type Founders Co., Jersey City, N.J. With introduction by Henry Lewis Bullen. (Half morocco; 8½ x 6 in., pp.38.)

These exhibits were shown in Jersey City (at the Library), New York City (twice) Boston, Chicago, Detroit, Cleveland, Los Angeles, San Francisco, Portland and Seattle in 56 cases of the sort shown at an angle

(cont'd)

EXHIBITIONS, PRINTING, United States.

Cabinet P Shelf 4 No. 17

Fifty books of the year. An exhibition of American bookmaking. Selected and shown by the American Institute of Graphic Arts. New York, 1931.

Boards; 8½ x 5½ in.

EXHIBITIONS, PRINTING, United States.

Cabinet 28 Shelf 1&2 No.

New York Industrial Exhibition, July 15, 1853, reviewed and commented upon in German. Illus.

Journal fur Buchdruckerkunst, 1853, No. 18, cols. 203-212; No. 19, cols. 219-22; No. 22, cols. 269-73; No. 23, cols. 275-73.

(cont'd)

EXHIBITIONS OF PRINTING. United States

Cabinet S Shelf 4 No. 27.01

in the centre of the frontispiece. Stands were also forwarded by the library to hold the show cases. The exhibits, cases and stands, and the wall panels were returned to Jersey City in 1927, and in (1935) are still available for exhibition purposes.

This exhibit was the most extensive and representative that has been shown in the U.S. until the present time (1935)

EXHIBITIONS, PRINTING. United States.

Cabinet O Shelf 1 No. 96.

Franklin, Benjamin. Catalogue of an exhibition commemorating the 200th anniversary of the birth of. At the Grolier Club of the Cityy of New York, January 1906.

Half morocco; 7 x 4-3/8 in. Orig. covers bound in.

EXHIBITIONS, PRINTING, United States.

Cabinet S Shelf 5 No. 3

Newark, N. J., Jan. 25, 1904: The Art of Printing. A printing exhibition of tools, materials and products of the art of printing, held at the Free Public Library. Circular.

Item 10 in collection "Printers and their Plants: Collection of Pamphlets," 1918.

EXHIBITIONS, PRINTING, United States

Cabinet Q Shelf 1 No. 30

Chicago, 1893. Exposition de la Librairie Francaise...M. Emil Terquem, representant. Chicago, 1893.

Official catalogue, with brief biographical sketches of exhibiting French publishers and printers.

Half morocco; 10 x 7¾ in. Orig. covers bound in.

EXHIBITIONS OF PRINTING United States

Cabinet S Shelf 6 No. 13

Lakeside Press (R.R. Donnelley & Sons Co.) Chicago, Ill., June 1st to Nov. 1st, 1934.

I-An invitation to visit an International Exhibition of Contemporary Fine Printing:

II-To visit the exhibition of the work of The Lakeside Press. Illus. folder.

In envelope.

EXHIBITIONS, PRINTING, United States.

Stack A Shelf 1 & 2 Number 65

Newark, N. J. [circa 1916]. Carteret Book Club. Exhibition in praise of printing, illustrating the evolution of the art of the book Account by Henry Lewis Bullen, in The Inland Printer, vol. 65, p. 459.

EXHIBITIONS, PRINTING, United States.

Cabinet 67 Shelf 1 No. .02

Newark, N. J. 1916: An Exhibition of the work of Mr. Bruce Rogers, printer...under the auspices of The Carteret Book Club. Newark, N. J. Includes an essay by A. W. Pollard, with a list of books printed by Mr. Rogers.

Boards; 9-3/8 x 6 in.

EXHIBITIONS, PRINTING. United States.

Cabinet 0 Shelf 1 No. 90

Philadelphia, 1876. Exposition Universelle de Philadelphia. Catalogue du Cercle de la Librairie de L'Imprimerie, et des Industries qui s'y rattachent. A Paris, 1876.

Half morocco; $9\frac{3}{4}$ x $6\frac{1}{2}$ x $1\frac{1}{2}$ in.

EXHIBITIONS, Printing. United States

Cabinet AA Shelf 1 No. 45

Philadelphia, 1876. Luigi Moriendo: La Stampa in America. Note techniche raccolte all' Esposizione di Filadelfia e in un visita alla tipografia Munsell, Haerper etc. Torino, 1876.
An official report of the Typography at the Philadelphia Exhibition.

Half morocco; $9\frac{1}{2}$ x $6\frac{1}{4}$ in.

EXHIBITIONS, PRINTING, United States.

Cabinet S Shelf 3 No. 55

Philadelphia centennial exhibition of 1876. The National Printing Office at Lisbon: An historical and statistical notice, with the catalogue of the products exhibited. Lisbon National Printing Office, 1876.

Cloth; $8\frac{3}{4}$ x $5\frac{1}{2}$ in.

EXHIBITIONS, PRINTING. United States

Cabinet 0 Shelf 1 No. 89

Saint Louis, 1904. Exposition de la Librairie Francaise a.

Has history of "Cercle de la Librairie, 1847-1904, and views of its building in Paris.

Cloth; 9 x $7\frac{1}{4}$ in.

EXHIBITIONS, PRINTING, United States

Cabinet S Shelf 1 No. 105

St. Louis, Mo., Ben Franklin Club of St. Louis. Catalogue of Exhibit of Printing Art: a Section of the St. Louis Exposition of Industrial Arts and Crafts, Oct.15 to Nov. 11, 1919.
Case A-I contain an exhibit illustrating the History of Printing, described on 12 pages, from B.C.4200 to Bruce Rogers, in 1915. This exhibit prepared by Henry Lewis Bullen, founder of the Typographic Library and Museum, Jersey City, N.J.

With other items in manila envelope

EXHIBIITONS, PRINTING. United States.

Cabinet 0 Shelf 1 No. 86

San Francisco, 1915. Exposition Universelle et Internationale de San-Francisco, 1915; Librairie-Imprimerie-typographie. Fernand Nathan, rapporteur. Paris, 1916.

Paper; $11\frac{1}{2}$ x 7-5/8 in.

EXHIBITIONS. PRINTING EQUIPMENT

Cabinet EE Shelf 4 No. 86

London, England. April 11th to 15th. 1929. Eighth International Printing and Allied Trades [Equipment] Exhibition. Official catalogue. Illus.

Has alphabetical list of exhibitors.

Cloth; 11 x $8\frac{1}{2}$ x 7/8 in.

EXHIBITIONS. Printing Equipment

Cabinet EE Shelf 2 No. 77

Paris, 1911. Officiel catalogue de la 2me Exposition par la Chambre Syndicale des Constructeurs de Machines d'Imprimerie.

Many colored plates, and other illustrations showing machinery and tools for printers.

Cloth; 9-3/4 x 6-3/4 in.

EXHIBIITONS, PUBLISHERS. Belgium

Cabinet 0 Shelf 1 No. 88

Liege, 1905

See PUBLISHING. Belgium. Liege, 1905 ...

EXHIBIITONS, PUBLISHERS. France.

Cabinet 0 Shelf 1 No. 87

Paris, 1880. Cercle de la Librairie. Premiere Exposition. Paris, Juin, 1880. Catalogue.

Includes history of printing in France. Brief notes arranged alphabetically by towns or cities.

Cloth; $9\frac{1}{2}$ x 6-3/8 x $\frac{1}{2}$ in.

EXHIBITIONS OF TYPEMAKING

Cabinet S Shelf 5 No. 69

Travelling exhibition of type making appliances, improvements in type casting and American imprints of great historical significance to type-making and early 3-color process printing and electrotyping. Prepared in 1933 by Henry Lewis Bullen, in Four Cases, each 30 x 35 x 6 ins., of which this envelope there are four photographs reduced in size to $6\frac{3}{4}$ x $8\frac{1}{2}$ in.

EXHIBITIONS, Type Making Machines

Cabinet FF Shelf 3 No. 56.03

Awards given to American Type Founders Company, 1894.

see
AMERICAN TYPE FOUNDERS COMPANY. Awards given to Exhibit...

EX LIBRIS.

Cabinet Shelf No.

See Book Marks.

EXPORTS

Cabinet S Shelf 3 No. 30

(Manufactures for Printers) National Paper and Type Company: A sketch of its formation, aims, ideals and progress, 1900-~~1902~~ 1920. Printed in the General Offices, New York City, 1920.

Paper; 9 x 6-1/8 in.

EXPORTS see also

Cabinet RR Shelf 3 No. 50

UNITED STATES BULLETINS.

EXPOSITION (The)

Cabinet Shelf No.

See Newspapers, New York State.

EXPOSITION INTERNATIONALE, Bruxelles 1897.

See Belgium.

(The) EXTRA LOG CABIN

Cabinet C
Shelf 2
No. 12

Greeley, H. & Co. The Extra Log Cabin, July,4, 1840, vol.1, No.1. (one issue only)

Bound in with New York Tribune, vols.1 and 2, Jan.1, 1842 to Dec.24, 1842.

Half calf; 20-3/8 x 15-3/8 in.

EYNHOVEN, CHRISTOPHER

Cabinet D
Shelf 4
No. 27

See Early Printing in Belgium. Antwerp, 1525. Christopher Eynhoven.

EYRE, CHARLES and STRAHAN, WILLIAM

Cabinet RR
Shelf 4
No. 1

Imprint, London, 1773, Charles Eyre and William Strahan.

See PAPER (Act of Parliament, 1768-73...)

F

F****J.F.

Cabinet LL Shelf 1 No. 17

Handbuch der buchdruckerkunst fur angehende und praktische buchdrucker. Als anhang: Anweisung, papier auf alle art zu farben. Mit einem...formatbuche, der vorstellung einer correctur und vier kastenabbildungen in steindruck. Berlin, bei Theod. Christ. Fried. Enslin, 1820.

Boards; 6¾ x 4-1/8 x 5/8 in.

FABER, LOUIS and SCHLEICHER, ADOLF

Cabinet Y Shelf 3 No. 82

(Printing press builders. Offenbach a.M., 1871-1921).
Faber & Schleicher Aktien Gesellschaft. 20 November, 1871-1921. Illus.

Description of the development of the lithographic printing press, 1797 to 1921, with an account of the house of Faber & Schleicher.

Paper; 11¼ x 8¾ in.

FABER, REGINALD STANLEY

Cabinet 75 Shelf 1 No. 5

Printing in Sicily (1478-1554). A paper read before the Bibliographical Society, London, Feb. 19, 1900. Facsimiles.

In Trans. Biblio. Soc. Vol. V. 1898-1900. pp. 183-211.

FABER & SCHLEICHER, AKT.-GES.

Cabinet EE Shelf 5 No. 68

(Catalogue and price list No.104) Hochmoderne buchdruck-maschinen. Allerneueste Buchdruck-Schnellpressen "Gretel", "Merkur", "Tell". Faber & Schleicher, Offenbach a.M. Pamphlet.

Item in manila envelope.

FABES, GILBERT

Cabinet U Shelf 5 No. 81

Autobiography of a book. London, 1926.

Fictional description of the book; its birth, development, etc., with remarks about authors, booksellers, printers, etc.

Cloth; 9-1/8 x 6+1-3/8 in.

FABLES OF PRINTING

Cabinet QQ Shelf 1 No. 56

Who was Cardelius? Edited by John Cotton Dana. The University Press, Cambridge, Mass. 1909.

Includes 15th century verses in praise of printing.

Half morocco; 6 x 3¾ in.

FABRE, ADOLPH

Cabinet W Shelf 1 No. 89

Notice historique sur A. de Terrebasse, sa nie et ses oeuvres. Par Adolphe Fabre.. Vienne [France], 1873. Portrait frontispiece.

Half morocco; 9½ x 6¼ in.

FABRIANO

Cabinet RR Shelf 3 No. 28.02

(Industries of Fabriano, and the Fonari family. With brief notes on paper making in Fabriano

La famiglia Fornari di Fabriano. Da Giuseppi Consentino, Bologn, 1902

Paper; 8¼ x 5½ in.

FABRIANO

Cabinet RR Shelf 4 No. 39

Miliani, Pietro (paper maker at Fabriano.)

See MILIANI, PIETRO. Letter to Pietro Miliani from Giambattista Bodoni...

FABRIANO "Cartiere Pietro Miliani"

Cabinet AA Shelf 2 No. 22

Picture of this celebrated paper mill, with brief description. (Italian text)

See p.693, vol. A-F of Arneudo's Dizionario esegetico...Torino, 1917.

FABRIANO

Cabinet RR Shelf 6 No. 15

Samples of paper from the oldest paper mill in Italy. Fabriano, Cartiere Pietro Miliani. 1919.

Half morocco; 15¼ x 11½ x 3/8 in.

FABRICIUS, J. F.

Cabinet Y Shelf 3 No. 25

Notizen über die einführung und erste ausbreitung der buchdruckerkunst in America. Hamburg, 1841. (Notes on the introduction and development of printing in America).
Fabricius was a master-printer in Hamburg 1834-1875.

Half morocco; 6-7/8 x 4-3/8 x ¼ in.

FABRICIUS, BLASIUS

Cabinet X Shelf 3 No. 13

Brief bibliographical note, Fabricius, printer, Strassburg, 1549-1556.

see HEITZ, PAUL. Elsässische büchermarken ...p.xxiv

FACSIMILES

Cabinet W Shelf 1 No. 90

(L') Abuze en Court: Le doctrinale du temps present. [Lyon, typographe indetermine, vers 1484]. Notice de E. Droz. Publie par L'Association Guillaume du Roy. Lyon, n.d. Bibliographical study.

Half morocco; 11-1/8 x 9-3/8 x ½ in.

FACSIMILES

Cabinet A Shelf 2 No. 11

Arkansas Gazette. By Wm. E. Woodruff. Arkansas (Arkansas Ter.), Saturday, November 20, 1819, vol.1, No.1.

See NEWSPAPERS, ANNIVERSARY ISSUES. (U.S. Arkansas Gazette, 100 years, 1819-1919... p.38

FACSIMILE

Cabinet K Shelf 6 No. 4

Albertina - Facsimile.

see ALBERT, DR. E. Facsimile-Albertina...

FACSIMILES

Cabinet C Shelf 1 No. 3

Advertisements, 15th century broadsides of booksellers.

see BROADSIDES, Printers. (Fifteenth century printers and publishers...

FACSIMILES.

Cabinet I Shelf 3 No. 30

Ars Moriendi (Photographic facsimile).

See Weigel, T. C. (Publisher). Ars Moriendi ... Leipzig, 1869.

FABRITIUS, GUALTHERUS

Cabinet X Shelf 3 No. 20

Brief bio-bibliographical note, Fabritius, Cologne, 1553-1595.

see HEITZ, PAUL. Kölner büchermarken...p.xxv

FACSIMILES

Cabinet 60 Shelf 1 No. 2

Alphabetum Hebraicum. Aldus Manutius, Venedig, 1501.

Verlag der Munchner Drucke, Munchen, 1927.

Facsimile from one of only two known perfect copies.

Boards; 7½ x 5¼ in.

FACSIMILES.

Cabinet I Shelf 3 No. 31

Ars Moriendi (Editio princeps, circa 1450). A reproduction of the copy in the British Museum. With an introduction by George Bullen. Printed for the Holbein Society, London, 1881.

Cloth; 11¼ x 9½ x 3/8 in.

FABRITIUS, W.C. & SONS

Cabinet AA Shelf 5 No. 38

Mindeskrift l anledning Fabritius Boktrykkeris 75-Aars Jubilaeum. 1844. I Januar, 1919. Kristiania. Frontispiece portraits, wood engravings.

Bound in with "Femti aar i boktrykkerkunstens tjeneste av H. Scheibler" 1919. With Portrait. Both items are biographical and were published to commemorate long service in the printing trade.

Half morocco; 12¼ x 9-1/8 in.

FACSIMILES

Cabinet S Shelf 2 No. 3

(The) American Village. A poem by Philip Freneau Printed by S. Inslee and A. Car, New York, 1772. Reprinted with an introduction by Harry Lyman Koopman, and bibliographical data by Victor H. Paltsits. Providence, Rhode Island, 1906.

Half vellum; 9 x 6¾ in.

FACSIMILES

Cabinet U Shelf 2 No. 15

Baskerville types, facsimiles of.

Plates VII-XIII at end of STRAUS and DENT'S "Baskerville, John: A memoire..."

FACIOT, JEAN.

Cabinet Shelf No.

See Vulteii, Joan.

FACSIMILES

Cabinet 68 Shelf No. 5

Anglo-Saxon and Irish manuscripts, miniatures and ornaments of.

See WESTWOOD, J.O. Fac-similes... London, 1868.

FACSIMILES

Cabinet L Shelf 5 No. 10

(Basle manuscripts of the 15th and 16th centuries).

See Roth, Carl and Schmidt, Ph. Handschriftproben zur Basler geistesgeschichte...

FACKLER, S. A.

Cabinet NN Shelf 6 No. 50

Ups and downs of a country editor. Mostly downs. By S. A. Fackler. n. p. n. d. Illus.

Paper; 9 x 5¾ x 3/8 in.

FACSIMILES.

Cabinet I Shelf 4 No. 11

Apocelypse, (block-book) premier édition d'apres baron de Heinecken et cinquième d'après Sotheby. Reproduite en facsimile par Adam Pilinski. Précédeé une notice par Gustave Pawlowski ... Paris, 1882. (45 plates).

Half morocco; 13¾ x 10½ in.

FACSIMILES.

Cabinet R Shelf 5 No. 132

Bay Psalm Book, 1640. Cambrdige, Mass., printed by Stephen Daye.

A facsimile reprint prepared for the New England Society in New York, 1903. Prefaced by Wilberforce Eames.

Boards; 8 x 5½ in.

FACSIMILES

Cabinet 14 — Shelf 2 — No. 2

Bible of 42 lines. [Johann Gutenberg, Mainz, 1450-1544]. Leipzig.

Insel-Verlag, 1913.

2 vols.

FACSIMILES.

Cabinet I — Shelf 4 — No. 10

Biblia Pauperum. Reproduced in facsimile, from one of the copies in the British Museum, with an historical and bibliographical introduction, by J. Ph. Berjeau. London, 1859.

Quarter morocco; 15¼ x 11½ in.

FACSIMILES

Cabinet T — Shelf 5 — No. 85

Biblia Pauperum (1 plate)

See HANSARD, THOMAS CURSON Treatises on printing...(following p.234)

FACSIMILES

Cabinet 82 — Shelf 1 — No. 1.02

Binny & Ronaldson, 1809. A specimen of Metal Ornaments cast at the Letter Foundry of. Philadelphia, 1809. Printed by Fry & Kammerer

Reproduced in collotype by Meriden Gravure Co., Meriden, Connecticut, 1935.

Boards; 10 x 6½

FACSIMILE.

Cabinet I — Shelf 3 — No. 29

[Block Book, 15th Century]. Confessionale ou Beichtspiegel nach den zehn geboten ... Reproduit en fac-simile par E. Spanier. Avec une introdution par J. W. Holtrop. La Haye, 1861.

Facsimile with an account of a unique 15th century Block Book.

Boards; 10½ x 7 in.

FACSIMILES

Cabinet S — Shelf 5 — No. 25.01

Bradford, William, New York, 1693. Facsimile of t the first known prints of Wm. Bradford in New York; also facsimile of an early number of Bradford's "The New York Gazette", April, 4, 1726.

With menu of Dinner, April 12, 1893, celebrating the Introduction of Printing in New York by Wm. Bradford. The 200th Anniversary celebration.

Paper; 9-1/8 x 6¼. In box.

FACSIMILES

Cabinet R — Shelf 5 — No. 2.01

Bradford, William, facsimiles of imprints, 1693 to 1726. Included in programme of Dinner of the Printing and Allied Trades in celebration of the 200th anniversary of the introduction of printing in New York. April, 1893.

With misc. collection of items in envelope.

FACSIMILE

Cabinet FF — Shelf 3 — No. 4

Breitkopf, I. G. J. Leipzig, 1777. Nachricht von der stempelschneiderey und schriftgiesserey. Zur erlauterung der Enschedischen schriftprobe. Mit erganzungen aufs neue herausgegeben von Dr. Wilhelm Thitzig und Heinrich Schwartz. Mit Breitkopfs bildnes. Berlin 1925. H. Berthold A. G. Ableilung Privatdrucke.

Boards: 10¼x8¼ in.

FACSIMILES

Cabinet 71 — Shelf 1 — No. 80

Browning, Elizabeth Barret. Sonnets from The Portuguese (1847). Printed in facsimile for William Andrews Clark, Jr., by John Henry Nash of San Francisco, in the year 1927.

Paper, 6 x 4 in. Cased together with "Observation and bibliography" by W.A. Clark, Jr.

FACSIMILES

Cabinet D — Shelf 3 — No. 65

Burgkmair, Hans: Leben und leiden Christi. Nach der bei Grimm & Wyssung 1520 in Augsburg erschienen Ausgabe. Von G. Hirth's Verlag, 1923 new aufgelegt.

Imprint: Gedruckt von Knorr & Hirth, Munchen.

Paper boards; 8-1/8 x 6 x 3/8 in.

FACSIMILES

Cabinet I — Shelf 5 — No. 25

Buxheim St. Christopher of 1423.

See AMERICAN INSTITUTE OF GRAPHIC ARTS Busheim St. Christopher...

FACSIMILES

Cabinet T — Shelf 2 — No. 40

Caxton, William: A reprint in facsimile of a treatise spekynge of the art and craft to knowe well to dye. Translated oute of frenche in englysshe by William Caxton. London [1491]. Sold by the Assigns of Edward Lumley, deceased. 1875.

Boards; 12-7/8 x 9-3/4 x 1/8 in.

FACSIMILES

Cabinet T — Shelf 2 — No. 43

Caxton, William: Fac-similes illustrating the labours of William Caxton at Westminster, and an introduction of printing in England. With a memoir of our first printer, and bibliographical particulars of the illustrations. By Francis Compton Price. London, privately printed, 1877 The four hundredth anniversary .

Half morocco; 11-3/8 x 8-7/8 x ½ in.

FACSIMILES

Cabinet T — Shelf 2 — No. 33

Caxton, William; facsimiles of printing types and pages from the works printed by.

See BLADES, WILLIAM. Life and typography of William Caxton...London, 1861, 1863 (2 vols.)

FACSIMILES

Cabinet D — Shelf 1 — No. 23

Caxton, William. Game and playe of chesse. Cologne? Bruges? 1474. Reprinted by Vincent and James Figgins, London 1855.

"The types were especially cut and cast for this tribute in memory of Wm. Caxton, in facsimile of Caxton's first types."

Stamped calf; 11-3/8 x 8½ x ¾ in.

FACSIMILE

Cabinet T — Shelf 2 — No. 32

Caxton, William, 1476. Reproduction of a document which is an indulgence printed for the Abbot of Abingdon.

Item in manila envelope

FACSIMILES

Cabinet D — Shelf 1 — No. 22

Caxton, 1477. The story of Queen Anelida and the false Arcite: by Geoffrey Chaucer. Printed at Westminster about the year 1477.

[Reprinted] Cambridge, at the University Press, 1905.

Boards; 10½ x 7 in.

FACSIMILES

Cabinet T — Shelf 2 — No. 64

Caxton, William, 1483; his "Sex quam elegantissime epistolae" reproduced in facsimile by James Hyatt with an introduction by George Bullen. London, 1892.

Cloth; 8½ x 6½ x ½ in.

FACSIMILES

Cabinet M Shelf 1 No. 25

Chrestoleros: Seven books of epigrames written by T. B. Imprinted at London by Richard Bradcocke. 1598. Reprinted at the Beldornie Press, in the year 1842.

Boards; 5-7/8 x $4\frac{1}{2}$ x $\frac{3}{4}$ in.

FACSIMILES

Cabinet U Shelf 1 No. 38

Cromwell's Soldiers Pocket Bible: being a reprint in facsimile of "The Souldier's Pocket Bible", compiled by Edmund Calamy, and issued for the use of the commonwealth army in 1643. With a bibliographical introduction, and a preface, by Field Marshal...Viscount Wolseley. London, 1895.

Limp leather; $7\frac{3}{4}$ x $5\frac{1}{4}$ in.

FACSIMILES

Cabinet T Shelf 6 No. 9

Early books; manuscripts to books printed in the early part of the 16th century. (100 illus.)

see HUMPHREYS, NOEL. History of printing...London, 1867

FACSIMILES

Cabinet D Shelf 1 No. 21

Chronica Hungarorum. Buda, 1473. Andrea Hess. [This is an exact facsimile with explanatory notes of the first book printed in Hungary]

Imprint: Finita Bude anno dni M.CCCC.LXXIII in viglia penthecostes: per Andrea Hess.

Half morocco; 12 x $9\frac{3}{4}$ x $\frac{1}{2}$ in.

FACSIMILES

Cabinet Y Shelf 3 No. 102

Depositio cronuti typographici, das ist: Lust- oder freuder spiel...von Johann Rist. Lübeck, gedruckt bey Samuel Struck. 1714. [Facsimile by Genzsch & Heyse. Hamburg, 1925].

Boards; $9\frac{1}{4}$ x $6\frac{1}{4}$ x $\frac{1}{4}$ in.

FACSIMILES

Cabinet R Shelf 6 No. 42

Early English printing, 15th century. A series of facsimiles of all the types used in England during the xvth century, with some of those used in the printing of English books abroad. With an introduction by E. Gordon Duff. London, 1896. (40 pp. text and 40 plates facsimiles.)

Linen portfolio, tied; 16 x 12 in.

FACSIMILES.

Cabinet I Shelf 4 No. 3

Collection of 125 fac-similes of scarce and curious prints by early masters of the Italian, German and Flemish Schools ... By William Young Ottley. London, 1828.

Half morocco; 15 x $11\frac{1}{2}$ x 2 in.

FACSIMILES

Cabinet Q Shelf 4 No. 1

Directory, 1786, New York City. (Facsimile reprint. Published by The Trow Directory Company, New York, 1886)
Partly interleaved with advertisements

Half morocco; 8 x 6 in.

FACSIMILES

Cabinet J Shelf 5 No. 18

Early printed books in the British Museum. Selected pages from representative specimens of early printed books of Germany, Italy, France, Holland, and England, exhibited in the King's Library. London...1897.

32 plates with descriptive text.

Portfolio; $15\frac{1}{2}$ x $11\frac{1}{4}$ in.

FACSIMILES

Cabinet Y Shelf 3 No. 43

(Colophons (79) of German printers of the Reformation period)

In "Die hochdeutschen drucker"...von Alfred Götze, Strassburg, 1905.

Half morocco; $8\frac{3}{4}$ x $5\frac{1}{2}$ x 1-3/8 in.

FACSIMILES

Cabinet 79 Shelf 2 No. 16

Doctrina Breve by Right Rev. Juan Zumarraga, Mexico, 1544. [Printed by Johann Cromberger] Monograph Series X. The United States Catholic Historical Society. New York, 1928.

Cloth; $9\frac{1}{2}$ x 6-3/8 in.

FACSIMILES

Cabinet J Shelf 5 No. 19

(Der) Edelstein von Ulrich Boner. [Bamberg, 1461] Lichtdrucknachbildung der undatierten ausgabe im besitze der Kgl. Bibliotheque zu Berlin. Nebst sech tafeln nach der ausgabe der Herzogl. Bibliothek zu Wolfenbüttel. In Berlin bei Bruno Cassirer. Berlin, 1908.
A supposed first book printed in Germany with date and wood engravings.

Boards, linen back; 15-3/8 x 11 in.

FACSIMILES

Cabinet G Shelf 5 No. 23

Constitution of the United States of America -- The Declaration of Independence. The first reduced facsimile in legible form. Made and published by Norman T. A. Munder, Baltimore, 1935.

Brochure, in envelope.

FACSIMILES

Cabinet 14 Shelf 2 No. 4

Donat (Fragments) of Gutenberg. Reproduced at the Art Shop of Max Breslauer, Leipzig, 1926.

The original Donat are in the Library of the Deutschen Vereins fur Buchwesen und Schriftum, Leipzig.

Reproduced fragments in manila envelope.

FACSIMILE

Cabinet K Shelf 1 No. 26

Egyptian book of the dead...Reproduced from the Turin papyrus and the Louvre papyrus.

See Davis, Charles H. S. Egyptian book of the dead...New York, 1894.

FACSIMILES.

Cabinet E Shelf 1 No. 67

(Cook book, the first printed in the Netherlands (Brussel, Thomas van der Noot, c. 1510). Het eerste Nederlandsch gedrukt kookboek. 's-Gravenhage, Martinus Nijhoff, 1925.

Paper; 9 x $5\frac{3}{4}$ in.

FACSIMILES.

Cabinet 73 Shelf 2 No. 47

Dryden, John. All for love; or the world well lost. A tragedy ... Printed by Tho. Newcomb, for Herringman, 1678. Printed in facsimile for Wm. Andrews Clark, Jr., by John Henry Nash, San Francisco, 1929. Illus. and colored plates.

Boards; $8\frac{1}{2}$ x 6-1/8 x $\frac{1}{4}$ in. In protective case; $13\frac{1}{4}$ x 9-3/8 x 1-7/8 in.

FACSIMILES

Cabinet 73 Shelf 2 No. 13

Elegy wrote in a country church yard [By Thomas Gray]. London: Printed for R. Dodsley in Pall-Mall; 1751. Price Six-Pence.
Colophon: Printed in facsimile for William Andrews Clark, Jr., by John Henry Nash in the City of San Francisco, 1925.

Paper boards; 9-3/4 x 7-3/4 in. In slip case.

FACSIMILES

Cabinet T Shelf 3 No. 46

Emblems, Whitney's choice of

See WHITNEY, Geffrey. Emblems... London, 1866.

FACSIMILES

Cabinet FF Shelf 1 No. 105

First stereotyped books in 1701, facsimiles of pages of the.

see KUBLER, GEORGE A. Historical treatises...on stereotyping. New York, 1936, pp. 94, 96.

FACSIMILES

Cabinet 71 Shelf 1 No. 79

Goldsmith. Oliver. The Deserted Village. By Dr. Goldsmith. London: Printed for W. Griffin, at Garrick's Head, in Catherine-Street, Strand, 1770.
Printed in facsimile for William Andrews Clark, Jr., by John Henry Nash, San Francisco. 1926.

Boards; 9 x 7½ in. pp. 23: In case together with "An Introduction: Oliver Goldsmith..."

FACSIMILES

Cabinet 76 Shelf 2 No. 42

Engraved and etched title-pages, 1545-1691

see JOHNSON, ALFRED FORBES Catalogue of engraved and etched title-pages...

FACSIMILES.

Cabinet I Shelf 5 No. 3

(Flemish 15th century illuminated manuscripts, reproductions of).

See DURRIEU (Comte Paul) (La) miniature flamande...

FACSIMILES

Cabinet 14 Shelf 2 No. 10

Gutenberg, and Schoeffer imprints: Psalterium 1457: (one page) Bible of 42 and 36 lines (one leaf of each): Canon Missal 1458 (one page): Durandus 1459 (one page): Durandus 1459: (one leaf: Biblia Latina 1462: (one page): Missale Speciale 1470 (one page).

See Incunabula, [Literature of]: Gutenberg. Johann. Die buchkunst Gutenbergs und Schoffers, etc.

FACSIMILE

Cabinet D Shelf 3 No. 38

Erasmi Roterodami: Encomium moriae. With the marginal drawings of Hans Holbein the younger. Published at Basle in 1515. Facsimile of the Praise of Folly with bibliographical introduction. Oppermann, Basle, 1931.

Boards; 9¼ x 6-5/8 in. In slip case.

FACSIMILE

Cabinet R Shelf 1 No. 68

Franklin, B., Philadelphia, 1742. Title page of Laws of the Province of Pennsylvania, printed by B. Franklin.

see CLARY, WILLIAM W. Franklin, B., printer and publisher...p. 36.

FACSIMILES.

Cabinet 73 Shelf 1 No. 1

Gutenberg 42 line Bible. (1 page). Printed by John Henry Nash, San Francisco, n.d. [1901-1925].

Item 5 in John Henry Nash: His work, 1901-1925.

FACSIMILES

Cabinet 73 Shelf 2 No. 33

Essay on criticism by Alexander Pope. London. Printed for W. Lewis in Russel-Street, Covent Garden...MDCCXI (1711).

Colophon: Printed in facsimile for William Andrews Clark, Jr., by John Henry Nash in the City of San Francisco in Nineteen Hundred and Twenty-Eight.

Paper boards, in case; 13 x 9¼ x 1-3/8 in.

FACSIMILE

Cabinet R Shelf 1 No. 68

Franklin to Strahan, letter, July 5, 1775.

see CLARY, WILLIAM W. Franklin, B., printer and publisher...p. 80.

FACSIMILE

Cabinet Y Shelf 1 No. 54

Gutenberg's Turkenkalender für 1455. Facsimile with biographical study by Gustav Mori.
Kleiner Druck (1Xa and 1Xb) der Gutenberg Gesellshaft. Mainz, 1928

Item in manila envelope

FACSIMILES

Cabinet D Shelf 4 No. 24

Filet de la foi de Pierre Chelcicky. (Vilenov Monastery of bohemian Brotherhood, 1521) Facsimile, Prague, 1926.

Red morocco, tooled; 8 x 6 x 1¾ in.

FACSIMILE

Cabinet NN Shelf 7 No. 26

Gazette Francoise, 1780: With a bibliographical preface by Howard M. Chapin.

see GROLIER CLUB, THE. Gazette Francoise. A facsimile reprint...1926.

FACSIMILES

Cabinet L Shelf 3 No. 32

Hebrew incunabula typography

See FRIEMANN, A. (Editor) Thesaurus typographiae hebraicae...

FACSIMILES

Cabinet U Shelf 1 No. 19

First English New Testament translated by William Tyndale.

See TYNDALE, WILLIAM. English New Testament translated by William Tyndale...

FACSIMILES

Cabinet 1 & 5 Shelf No. Portfolios 1 to 40

German single-plate woodcuts of the first half of the 16th century. Edited by Max Geisberg, published by Hugo Schmidt, Munich, 1923-30)

About 1600 plates in 40 large portfolios. Plates arranged alphabetically, by artists.

Portfolios, 22 x 16¼ in.

FACSIMILE

Cabinet NN Shelf 7 No. 12

Herald of Gospel Liberty. By Elias Smith. Facsimile of first issue, Thursday evening, Sept. 1, 1808. Portsmouth, N. H.
Bound in with No. 100, 1908, Dayton, Ohio.

Cloth; 12¾ x 8-7/8 in.

FACSIMILES

Cabinet S Shelf 6 No. 9

Historica documents [Americana] in America archives. [Excerpt from Jour. of Amer. History, Jan., 1910].

Item 26 in vol. with binder's title "Early printing and printed books. Pamphlets". Bound 1932.

FACSIMILES

Cabinet B Shelf 3 No. 14

(Incunabula, German and Italian)

see BURGER, K. Monumenta Germanise et Italise....

FACSIMILES.

Cabinet I Shelf 5 No. 22

Leonardo Da Vinci, manuscrits de ... Avec transcriptions litterales, traductions francaises, avant-propos et tables methodiques. Par Charles Ravisson-Mollien. Paris, 1890.

Half morocco; $18\frac{3}{4}$ x $11\frac{1}{2}$ x $1\frac{1}{2}$ in.

FACSIMILES

Cabinet T Shelf 6 No. 10

History of the art of printing from its invention to its wide-spread development in the middle of the 16th century...By H. Noel Humphreys... Illustrated by 100 facsimiles in photo-lithography. Second iuuse. London, 1868.

Stamped cloth; 14 x 9-3/4 x 2 in.

FACSIMILES

Cabinet Y Shelf 1 No. 87

(Indulgences. Letters of, Mainz 1454 and 1455). Die Mainzer Ablassbriefe der jahre 1454 und 1455. von Dr. Gottfried Zedler. Verlag der Gutenberg-Gesellschaft, Mainz. 1913. Plates only (17).

For accompanying text, See Y/1/86.

FACSIMILES

Cabinet Y Shelf 3 No. 19

Mainz Ecclesiastical Acts of 1480

see KELCHNER, Dr. ERNST. (Mainz Ecclestiastical Acts, 1480...

FACSIMILES.

Cabinet I Shelf 5 No. 2

Illuminated manuscripts

See MANUSCRIPTS, ILLUMINATED. [Facsimiles].

FACSIMILES

Cabinet U Shelf 1 No. 111

Irish alphabet and catechism, facsimile of (1721) title page.

see Mc.Dix, E.R. Dublin printing...(frontispiece)

FACSIMILES

Cabinet M Shelf 5 No. 17

Mainz Psalter, 1457, Fust and Schoeffer. First page of the. Reproduced by wood cutting from the original copy on vellum in the King's Library of the British Museum. Printed by George W. Jones at the Sign of the Dolphin. London, England. 1927.

In folder marked "Broadsides, Printers (Various)." England 1927--

---

FACSIMILES.

Cabinet D Shelf 1 No. 21

See Incunabula. Chronica Hungorarum. Impressa Budae. Andrea Hess, 1473.

Facsimile [with history] of the first book printed in Hungary.

FACSIMILES.

Cabinet I Shelf 4 No. 9

Jacques de Voragine, la Légende dorée en francais. Imprime a Lion par les maistres Mattieu et Pierre Hongre, 1483. [Reproduit]. Par l'Association Guillaume le Roy. Lyon, n.d., circa, 1900.

French wood engravings of the 15th century.

In folder, 12 x 10 in.

FACSIMILES

Cabinet M Shelf 4 No. 27

(The) Maner of the tryumphe of Caleys and Bulleyn...Printed by Wynkyn de Worde, 1532-33.

[Facsimile] Edited by Edmund Goldsmid. Privately printed, Edinburgh, 1884.

Cloth; 7 x $4\frac{1}{2}$ in.

FACSIMILES

Cabinet C Shelf 1 No. 2

(Incunabula) Facsimiles of the earliest printed books. (13 plates)

Half morocco; $12\frac{3}{4}$ x $14\frac{3}{4}$ in.

FACSIMILE

Cabinet R Shelf 5 No. 2.01

Kalendarium Pennsilvaniense 1686...By Samuel Atkins. Printed and sold by William Bradford. Facsimile of The Historical Society of Pennsylvania, Dec., 1885.

Item in envelope.

FACSIMILES.

Cabinet I Shelf 5 No. 4

[Manuscripts, French 13th to 15th century, illuminated].

See MANUSCRIPTS, ILLUMINATED. Miniature francaise du 13e au 15e siecle.

FACSIMILE

Cabinet B Shelf 3 No. 11

Incunabula (German) in the British Museum. 152 facsimile plates.

see MORISON, STANLEY. German incunabula in the British Museum...

FACSIMILES

Cabinet U Shelf 2 No. 63

"Kelso Mail", first page of first issue, No.I. April 13, 1797.

Reduced facsimile of newspaper edited by James Ballantyne.

See "BALLANTYNE PRESS, THE". (The) Ballantyne Press and its founders. 1796-1908...p.4.

FACSIMILES

Cabinet L Shelf 5 No. 10

(Manuscripts of the 15th and 16th century, Basle.)

see ROTH, CARL and SCHMIDT, Ph. Handschriften proben zur Basle geistergeschichte...

FACSIMILES

Cabinet 70 Shelf 1 No. 16

Matheolus, Le Rebours de. Paris, 1518. Michel Le Noir.

A curious book, lithographed on veneered wood.

Morocco; 7½ x 4¼ x 6/8 in.

FACSIMILES

Cabinet K Shelf 1 No. 28

Music printing and manuscript, 12th to 16th century. Wood and copperplate engravings. With brief notes. (28 plates)

Each plate has imprint.

Boards; 12¼ x 9 in.

FACSIMILES

Cabinet OO Shelf 6 No. 2

Newspapers, the first of England printed in Holland, 1620-1621. A faithful reproduction made from the originals...The Hague, 1914.

Painted by George Veseler, Amsterdam, and Broer Johnson. Adrian Clarke, The Hague.

In cloth folder; 16¾ x 11-3/8 in.

FACSIMILES

Cabinet T Shelf 5 No. 85

Mentz Psalter and Colophon (1 plate)

See HANSARD, THOMAS CURSON Treatises on printing...(following p. 234)

FACSIMILE

Cabinet F Shelf 1 No. 75

Mystische und sehr geheyme sprueche welche in der Himlischen schule des heiligen geistes erlernet...Zu Philadelphia: Gedruckt bey B. Grnaklin in jahr 1730.

This is a reprint of the first book printed in the German language in America, and the earliest book with the imprint of "B. Franklin".

Half morocco; 7½ x 5¼ in.

FACSIMILES

Cabinet AA Shelf 3 No. 41

Niewsblad voor den Boekhandel. Woensdag, den I October, 1834. [Amsterdam]. No. 1 pp. 4, 8 x 6½ in.

This is the official organ of book receiving house (wholesale publishing house) in Amsterdam. Folded in "Het boek aan het bestelhuis en het niewsblad," door D. Smit.

Boards; 6½ x 4½ in.

FACSIMILES

Cabinet V Shelf 2 No. 30

Monuments de l'imprimerie à Poitiers. Recueil de fac-similes des premiers livres imprimés dans cette ville. Specimens de caractères, lettres ornées, filigranes de papiers, etc. Par A. Claudin. Paris, 1879

Half morocco; 10 x 6¾ x 1¾ in.

FACSIMILES

Cabinet E Shelf 4 No. 65

Narration of the late wars risen in New England ... With an account of the fight, the 19th December last, 1676. London, printed by J.D. for M.K. and to be sold by the Booksellers, 1676. Printed for the Society of Colonial wars in the State of Rhode Island, 1912.

Boards; 8¾ x 6-1/8 in.

FACSIMILES

Cabinet NN Shelf 7 No. 8

Old Flag (The). Lithographic reproduction of the three original issues, New York, 1867.

The Old Flag, first published by Union Prisoners at Camp Ford, Texas, 1864.

Cloth; 11½ x 9½ in.

FACSIMILES

Cabinet L Shelf 5 No. 7

Monumenta palaeographica Vindbonensia... [manuscripts]

see RITTER von KARABACEK, JOSEF Monumenta palaeographica Vindobonensia... Leipzig, 1910.

FACSIMILES

Cabinet B Shelf 2 No. 21

Netherlands, 1500-1540. Ornaments, initial letters etc. used by the printers in the.

see NIJOFF, WOUTER. l'Art typographique dans les Pays-Bas...

FACSIMILES

Cabinet X Shelf 4 No. 39

Orders, Rules and Ordinances - Stationers Company: London 1692.

Modern reprint (n.n.n.p.) from the original as above.

Half morocco; 8-1/8 x 6½ in.

FACSIMILES

Cabinet A Shelf 1 No. 22

Morning Post and Daily Advertiser. London, August 17, 1776. Printed by R. Haswell, in Blake Court. Reprinted by William E. Rudge. New York. July 1929.

Bound in volume "British Daily Newspapers".

Buckram, 19 x 14 x 1 3/4 in.

FACSIMILES

Cabinet QQ Shelf 5 No. 11

New York City and Brooklyn directory, 1786, 1796

See Bonner, William Thompson, New York, the World's Metropolis...pp.132-141.

FACSIMILES.

Cabinet V Shelf 6 No. 12

Origines et les débuts de l'imprimerie d'apres les recherches les plus récentes. Par Charles Mortet. Ouvrage accompagné de XXI planches en phototypie. Paris, 1922.

Explanatory text for these facsimiles in V/6/11.

Cloth; 13 x 10-3/8 x 5/8 in.

FACSIMILES

Cabinet S Shelf 2 No. 169 2 Vols.

Moxon, Joseph: Mechanick Exercises, or the doctrine of handy-words applied to the art of printing. London, 1683. 2 Vols.

A reprint with preface and notes by Theo. L. DeVinne. New York, 1896.

Half levant; 10 x 7 in.

FACSIMILE

Cabinet OO Shelf 6 No. 28

Newspaper, manuscript. Brazil, 1515.

see BRAZIL, "NEUEN ZEITUNG". Brazil.

FACSIMILES.

Cabinet M Shelf 1 No. 55

Oxford University, 1641: The life of Sr. Thomas Bodley, the honourable founder of the public library in the University of Oxford. Written by himself. Oxford, printed by Henry Hall, Printer to the University, 1647.

Reprinted by T. and A. Constable. Edinburgh, 1894.

Paper; 5¾ x 4½ in.

FACSIMILES

Cabinet Z Shelf 1 No. 69

Plantinini, Christophori, index characterum, 1567. Facsimile reprint with an introduction by Douglas C. McMurtrie. New York, 1924.

Boards; 11-1/8 x 7¾ x 3/8 in. In protective case.

FACSIMILES

Cabinet C Shelf 1 No. 3

Prospectuses, 15th century publishers.

See BURGER, KONRAD. Buchhändleranzeigen des 15 jahrhunderts...

FACSIMILES

Cabinet V Shelf 6 No. 38

Roman Calender printed by Jean de Tournes at Lyon in 1577. Facsimile with bibliographical notes by Marius Audin, Lyon, 1921.

In envelope.

FACSIMILES

Cabinet D Shelf 1 No. 60

Poliphi hypnerotomachia, ubi humana omnia non nisi somnium esse ostendit...
Facsimile reprint from the 1499 edition. Methuen & Co., London, 1904

Boards, cloth back; 13½ x 8¾ in.

FACSIMILES

Cabinet F Shelf 3 No. 51

Psalms and Hymns, collection of. Printed by Lewis Timothy. Charlestown (S. Carolina), 1737. (Reprinted) by A. Pearson ... London 1742.
Two pages in exact facsimile, other pages reset.

Cloth; 7 x 4¾ x 3/8 in.

FACSIMILES

Cabinet 00 Shelf 4 No. 5

Russian invasion of Poland in 1563, The. An exact facsimile of a contemporary account in Latin, published at Douay. Together with an introduction and historical notes, and a full translation into English. London: Chatto and Windus, Publishers, 1874.
Only 250 copies printed.

Boards; 8¼ x 5½ in.

FACSIMILES

Cabinet R Shelf 3 No. 38

Poor Richard, 1733. An almanack for the Year of Christ, 1733 ... By Richard Saunders, Philom. Philadelphia: Printed and sold by B. Franklin, at the new Printing Office near the Market. The Third Impression.
Facsimile done for "The Duodecimos" by the DeVinne Press, New York, 1894.

Full morocco, gilt; 7¼ x 5¼ in.

FACSIMILES

Cabinet T Shelf 2 No. 94.01

"Pylgremage of the Sowle". John Lydgate's. Printed by Wm. Caxton at Westminster, June 6, 1843. A hitherto unknown copy. Bibliographical description and facsimile pages. Wm. H. Robinson Ltd. London (1932)

Brochure; 12 x 10; pp. 11

FACSIMILE

Cabinet L Shelf 3 No. 2.02

Schreibbuch des Urban Wyss. Libellus valde doctus Zurich, 1549.
Facsimile-Ausgabe...November 1927, in Art Institute Orell Fuselli, Zurich.

No. 238 of 600 printed copies.

Boards, oblong; 7¼ x 9¾ in .

FACSIMILES

Cabinet 80 Shelf 1 No. 5

Poor Richard's Almanack for 1749

See ALMAANCS. Poor Richard's...

FACSIMILES

Cabinet D Shelf 1 No. 24

Regiomontanus: Deutsche Kalender, Blockbuch 1474. Text und bilder in Holz geschnitten von Hans Spoerer in Nurnberg.
Faksimile-Ausgabe, Munchen, J. Halle. 1927.

Paper; 8½ x 6 in.

FACSIMILES

Cabinet E Shelf 2 No. 58

Shakespeare's Midsummer Night's Dream. The first quarto. Imprinted at London for Thomas Fisher, 1600.
Facsimile in photo-lithography by William Griggs. London. 1880.

Boards; 8¾ x 6-1/8 x ½ in.

FACSIMILES

Cabinet B Shelf 3 No. 8

(Printing types of the 15th to the 18th century) Druckschriften des xv bis xviii jahrhunderts in getreuen nachbildungen. Herausgegeben von der Direction der Reichsdruckerei. Berlin, 1884-1887.
(100 plates of facsimiles)

Half morocco; 18¾ x 12½ x 1-3/8 in.

FACSIMILES

Stack 15 Shelf 2 Number 2

Reproductions (362) from early printed books. Catalogue (Parts 1-2). J.&J. Leighton, London. n.d.

Paper; 8¾ x 5-3/8 in.

FACSIMILES

Cabinet B Shelf 3 No. 10

Six hundred examples of the work of presses established during the years 1500 to 1914.

see MORISON, STANLEY. Four centuries of fine printing...

FACSIMILE

Cabinet S Shelf 6 No. 9

Proclamation issued by Gov. Fletcher, and printed by William Bradford, New York City, 1696.

Item 15 in vol. with binder's title "Early printing and printed books. Pamphlets". Bound, 1932.

FACSIMILES

Cabinet 86 Shelf 1 No. 3.01

Rhode Island Almanac of 1728. Being the first ever printed in that Colony...Printed and the Almanack reprinted, under the oversight of Will. Chatterton, Providence, 1911

Half morocco; 6¼ x 5 in.

FACSIMILES

Cabinet E Shelf 2 No. 26

[Spenser, Edmund] Shepheardes (The) Calender conteyning twelve Aeglogues...to the noble and Vertuous...Philip Sidney. At London: Printed by Hugh Singleton, 1579. [Facsimile of first edition, with commentaries and bibliographical notes by H. Oskar Sommer. London, 1890.

Boards; 10¾ x 8 x ½ in.

FACSIMILES.

Cabinet 71 Shelf 2 No. 38

Stevenson, Robert Louis: Father Damien: An open letter to the Reverend Dr. Hyde of Honolulu. Sydney, 1890. Printed in facsimile for William Andrews Clark, Jr., by John Henry Nash in San Francisco, California, in the year 1930.

Reprint, large edition, in same case.

This is copy No. 92 of an edition of 250 copies.

Boards; 8-3/8 x 5½ x ¼ in. In case; 13 x 9¼ x 1½ in.

FACSIMILES

Cabinet 84 Shelf 1 No. 3

Type Specimen Book, first English. Specimen of the several sorts of letter given to the University by Dr. John Fell, Oxford, 1693.

The first English type specimen book, reproduced in collotype facsimile from the most perfect copy known. London: James Tregaskis & Son, 1928.

Paper boards; 9½ x 6 in.

FACSIMILES

Cabinet D Shelf 1 No. 58

Utraquist Passional of 1495, Prague, Jan Kamp ?

See D/1/59 for bibliographical information relating to the "Passional"

Tooled leather; 12½ x 8¼ x 2¼ in.

FACSIMILES

Cabinet D Shelf 3 No. 61

Tewrdannchk. Augsburg, 1519. Hans Shoensperger. A reproduction of the edition printed for the Holbein Society, London, 1884.

Cloth; 14½ x 10¼ x 2-3/4 in.

FACSIMILES

Cabinet 84 Shelf 1 No. 3

Types, Dr. John Fell, Oxford. A specimen of the several sorts of letter given to the University by Dr. John Fell.

The first English Type Specimen Book, reproduced in collotype facsimile from the most perfect copy known. London: James Tregaskis & Son. 1928.

Paper boards; 9 x 5-7/8 x 3/8 in.

FACSIMILES

Cabinet 70 Shelf 1 No. 43

Vie de me Saincte Marguerite, vièrge et martyre. n.d. [1533 or 1544?]

Imprint: Imprimé à Troyes chez Jean Lecoq. Printer mark.

The design of this printer mark is said to indicate that this small booklet must have been printed by the Widow Lecoq, Thibaut Trumen, or Jean II Lecoq. See Breban: L'Imprimerie a Troyes.

Marbled paper; 7½ x 4-7/8 in. pp. 16.

FACSIMILES.

Cabinet 66 Shelf 1 No. 10

Times, New York Daily Times. Vol. I, No. I, New York, Thursday, Sept. 18, 1851.

See NEWSPAPERS, ANNIVERSARY ISSUES Times, New York, 1851-1931 ...

FACSIMILES

Cabinet 76 Shelf 2 No. 30

Types, English and Scottish printing, 1501-35. 1508-41, 1535-58, 1552-58. Collected and annotated by Frank Isaac. Printed for the Bibliographical Society at the Oxford University Bibliographical Society at the Oxford University Press, 1930 and 1932 (2 vols.)

Facsimiles & Illustrations No.II.
" " " III.

Boards; 11¼ x 9 in.

FACSIMILES.

Cabinet I Shelf 4 No. 14

Wood engravings. French 15th century.

See WOOD ENGRAVING. [French 15th century] ...

FACSIMILES

Cabinet AA Shelf 5 No. 15

[Title pages, colophons, borders, printer marks, specimens of early printing in all countries, exlibris, etc]. Bibliografia Grafica: Reproduccion en facsimil de portatos, retratos, colofones, y otras curiosidades utiles a los bibliofilos. Reunida y publicada por Pedro Vindel. Madrid, 1910. 2 Vols.

Half morocco; 9½ x 7 in.

FACSIMILES.

Cabinet I Shelf 4 No. 13

Types, woodcuts and capital letters used by early printers, a collection of facsimiles of 42 plates. London, 1840.

Boards; 14-3/8 x 9-7/8 in.

FACSIMILES, NEWSPAPERS

Cabinet 00 Shelf 6 No. 55

Arkansas Gazette, The. (Wm. E. Woodruff, founder), Arkansas, Nov. 20, 1819, Vol. I, No. I.

see NEWSPAPERS, ANNIVERSARY ISSUES. Arkansas Gazette, 1819-1919...(facing p. 38).

FACSIMILES

Cabinet K Shelf 2 No. 7

(Title pages, Italian 15th century. Facsimiles)

See BERTIERI, RAFFAELLO Pagini di antiche maestri della tipografia... Milano, 1920.

FACSIMILES

Cabinet S Shelf 1 No. 130

"Typographia, an ode on Printing, one of the earliest books printed in Williamsburg, Virginia, and is dated 1730. Printed by William Parks, the first to establish a printing office in Virginia. Photographic reprint by the Stone Printing Co. Roanoke Virginia. For the American Institute of Graphic Arts, New York, 1926.

Boards; 10½ x 7-1/8 in. In protective case.

FACSIMILES, Newspapers

Cabinet NN Shelf 7 No. 35

"Aurora de Chile", 1812 - 1813. Reimpresion paleografica a plana y renglón. Con una introducción por Julio Vicuña Cifuentes. Santiago de Chile, 1903.

Cloth; 13-5/8 x 10¼ x 1 in.

FACSIMILES

Cabinet J Shelf 4 No. 17

Type Facsimile Society. Publications of the Society for the years 1900-1909. Printed by Horace Hart. At the Oxford University Press. Oxford.

For any particular printer, see Index in box.

(2 boxes; 13¼ x 10½ x 4 in.)

FACSIMILES

Cabinet T Shelf 6 No. 5

Typography of the 15th century; a collection of facsimiles.

See Sotheby, Samuel. Typography of the 15th century...

FACSIMILES, Newspapers.

Cabinet R Shelf 3 No. 187

Bath Gazette, and Genesee Advertiser...Published by William Kersey and James Edie. 1797. Facsimile of the earliest newspaper of Western New York extant.

In Follett's "History of the press in Western New York"...New York, 1920. Heartmans Historical Series, No. 34.

Half morocco; 9¼ x 6½ in.

FACSIMILES, NEWSPAPERS

Cabinet NN Shelf 6 No. 14

Boston Transcript, July 24, 1831, vol.1, No.1

see
NEWSPAPERS, Massachusetts. Literature
Boston Transcripts fiftieth birthday...1880.

FACSIMILES, NEWSPAPERS

Cabinet OO Shelf 6 No. 38

Ulster County Gazette of January 4, 1800. With photostatic reproduction showing the heading of the original copy that is in the Library of Congress. Also circular relating to the Ulster County Gazette.

Items in envelope.

FAGE, RENÉ

Cabinet W Shelf 3 No. 55

Etienne Bleygeat, Francois Varolles, maîtres imprimeurs: Les frères Delbos, fondeurs en caractères. Par René Fage. Limoges, 1895.

Half morocco; $8\frac{3}{4}$ x $5\frac{1}{2}$ in.

FACSIMILES, NEWSPAPER

Cabinet OO Shelf 6 No. 51

Maryland Journal and Baltimore Advertiser. Vol. I, No. 1, Aug. 20, 1773. Printed by William Goddard.
Bound in with Baltimore American Anniversary Jubilee Edition, 1773-1905. Illus.

Cloth; 14 x $10\frac{3}{4}$ in.

FACSIMILES, SPECIMENS, Vignettes.

Cabinet 83 Shelf 2 No. 50.01

Trattner, Johann Thomas. Wien, 1760. Röslein und zierrathen, welche sich in der K.K. Hoffschriftgiesserey ... befinden, in jahr 1760. [Reprinted by] Bibliotheca Typographica, Wien, 1927.

Boards; $10\frac{1}{4}$ x $7\frac{1}{4}$ x $\frac{1}{2}$ in.

FAGE, RENÉ

Cabinet V Shelf 5 No. 23

Note pour servir a l'histoire de l'imprimerie en Tulle. Tulle, 1879.

Item 11 in vol. with binder's title "Origin of Printing in France: Pamphlets".

FACSIMILE, Newspaper

Cabinet OO Shelf 3 No. 26

Missouri Gazette, Vol. I, No. 8, July 26, 1808.

see
NEWSPAPERS, MISSOURI. Missouri Gazette, St. Louis, Mo.

FACSIMILES, TITLE PAGES

Cabinet FF Shelf 1 No. 105

Camus, A. G. Histoire et procedes du polytypage et du stereotypage. A Paris, X - 1802.

Facsimile of the Original Title Page.

see
KUBLER, GEORGE A. Historical treatises...on stereotyping. New York, 1936, p. 8.

FAHLGREN, CARL I.

Cabinet LL Shelf 2 No. 42

Handbok i boktryckerikonsten för Unga Sättare. Stockholm, Tryckt uti Joh. Beckmans Officin, 1853.
Has wood engraving of printing office on title page.

Morocco; 8-7/8 x 5-3/4 x 3/8 in.

FACSIMILES, Newspapers.

Cabinet A Shelf 2 No. 67

New Jersey Journal, Tuesday, Feb. 16, 1779. Vol. I. No. I. Supplement to the Elizabeth Daily Journal: Sesqui-centennial anniversary edition, 1779-1929.

Buckram; $22\frac{1}{4}$ x 17-5/8 x $\frac{1}{2}$ in.

FACSIMILES, TITLE PAGES

Cabinet FF Shelf 1 No. 105

Paroy (Marquis de). Precis sur stereotypie... Paris, 1882. Facsimile of the title page. Also: Sample of Pankotyping by the Paroy method.

see
KUBLER, GEORGE A. Historical treatises...on stereotyping. New York, 1936, p. 120 and following.

FAIRBAIRNS, W.H.

Cabinet MM Shelf 6 No. 102

Printer. (What to be series no. 1) London, n.d. Booklet.

With other items in manila envelope.

FACSIMILES, Newspapers

Cabinet NN Shelf 1 No. 9

New York Times, Sept.18,1851, Vol. I, No.I.

See Raymond, Henry J. New York Press for thirty years...Hartford, Conn. 1870, p.88.

FACSIMILE, TITLE PAGES

Cabinet FF Shelf 1 No. 105

Sallust, page 44, by William Ged, Edinburgh, 1739.

see
KUBLER, GEORGE A. Historical treatises...on stereotyping, New York, 1936, p. 18.

FAIRBANKS COMPANY, THOMAS N.

Cabinet RR Shelf 6 No. 35

Hand-made papers, samples, sample books, etc. This is portfolio No.50.

Boards; $15\frac{1}{4}$ x 11-3/4 x 2-3/4 in.

FACSIMILES, Newspapers

Cabinet NN Shelf 1 No. 9

New York Tribune, April 10,1841, Vol.I, No.I.

See Raymond, Henry J. New York Press for thirty years...Hartford, Conn. 1870. p. 38.

FAELLI (Johannes Baptiste)

Cabinet X Shelf 3 No. 14

Bibliographical note, with printer mark, Faelli, Bologna, 1526-34.

see
KRISTELLER, Dr. Paul. Italienischen buchdrucker...p.6

FAIRBANKS COMPANY, THOMAS N.

Cabinet RR Shelf 4 No. 39

Letter to Pietro Milini (paper maker at Fabriano) from Giambattista Bodoni, October 10, 1797. Reprinted by permission. Thomas N. Fairbanks Company, Import Division United States Envelope Company, New York, 1931. Leaflet.

Item with other excerpts and pamphlets relating to paper. Folder; $10\frac{1}{2}$ x $7\frac{1}{2}$ x 1 in.

FAIRBANKS COMPANY, THOMAS N.
See also
Imprints, Anonymous. (United States).
New York, 1930. Thomas N. Fairbanks Company.

Cabinet
Shelf
No.

FAIRCHILD, HELEN LINCKLAEN

Cabinet S · Shelf 2 · No. 86

Francis Adrian Van der Kemp, 1752-1829: An autobiography together with extracts from his correspondence. Edited with an historical sketch by Helen Lincklaen Fairchild. New York, 1903.

Cloth; $8\frac{1}{2}$ x 6 in.

FAIRLEY, JOHN A.

Cabinet U · Shelf 1 · No. 89

Agnes Campbell, Lady Roseburn, relict of Andrew Anderson the King's Printer. A contribution to the history of printing in Scotland. Aberdeen, 1925.

Cloth; 9-1/8 x 6 x 3/8 in.

FAIRLEY, JOHN A.

Cabinet U · Shelf 2 · No. 103

Buchan, Peter, printer and ballad collector. With a bibliography. Reprinted from the Transaction of the Buchan Field Club. Peterhead: P. Scrogie "Buchan Observer" Printing Works. 1903.

Half morocco; $8\frac{1}{4}$ x 6-3/4 in.

FAITHORN, WILLIAM. Engraver.

Cabinet E · Shelf 4 · No. 49

See Engravings, Hollar, Wenzel. Gt. Brit., 1668.

FALCKENBURG, HEINRICH

Cabinet X · Shelf 3 · No. 20

Cologne, 1590-1599

see
HEITZ, PAUL. Kölner büchermarken...p.xxxiii

FALCKNER, DANIEL

Cabinet R · Shelf 5 · No. 39

Falckner's Curieuse Nachricht von Pensylvania. The book that stimulated German emigration to Pennsylvania. A reprint of the Edition of 1702, amplified with the text of the Original manuscript in the Halle Archives. Together with an introduction and English translation. By Julius Freidrich Sachse. Philadelphia, 1905. Illus.

Cloth; 10 x $6\frac{3}{4}$ in.

FALK, FRANZ

Cabinet Y · Shelf 1 · No. 72

Canon Missal vom jahr 1458 in liturgischen beziehung. Verlag der Gutenberg-Gesellschaft. Mainz. 1904.
Bound in with another item by Heinrich Wallau.

Boards; $11\frac{1}{2}$ x $8\frac{3}{4}$ x $\frac{1}{2}$ in.

FALK, [Dr. F.]

Cabinet W · Shelf 2 · No. 1

Wittig, Jvo. von Hammelburg in Mainz. n.d. [1873]. Excerpt from Centralblatt fur bibliothekswesen. Leipzig.
Adverse to Hessel who in his new book "Haarlem the birth place of printing" declares Wittig to have been related to Gutenberg.

Item 18 in volume "Gutenberg l'inventeur de l'imprimerie - Melanges."

FALK, HERMANN

Cabinet Y · Shelf 1 · No. 92.05

Bodonis, Giambattista, typenkunst. Beilage zum 13 Jahresbericht der Gutenberg-Gesellschaft. Mainz, 1915. With type specimens.

Pamphlet in manila envelope.

FALKENSTEIN, Dr. KARL

Cabinet Y · Shelf 2 · No. 13

Geschichte der buchdruckerkunst in ihrer enstehung und ausbildung. Ein denkmal zur vierten säcular-feier der erfindung der typographie. Leipzig, 1840. Numerous facsimiles, and specimens of oriental types.
"This History of the Art of Printing is the most important of the works published in Germany, on the occasion of the 4th centenary of its invention. Still it is not always correct in its historical data." B & W.

cont'd

FALKENSTEIN, Dr. KARL **cont'd**

Cabinet
Shelf
No.

Boards; $11\frac{3}{4}$ x $9\frac{1}{4}$ x $1\frac{3}{4}$ in.

FALSE DATES ON IMPRINTS

Cabinet Y · Shelf 1 · No. 23

Chronological table of imprints with false dates, 1471-1499.

See LINDE, ANTONIOUS van der. Geschichte der erfindung...Berlin, 1886, vol.1, 5-9.

FALSE IMPRINTS

Cabinet U · Shelf 4 · No. 20

Aldine forgeries and doubtful editions.

See GOLDSMID, EDMUND. Bibliographical sketch of the Aldine Press...Edinburgh, 1887.

FALSE IMPRINTS.

Cabinet 60 · Shelf 1 · No. 6

C. Crispi Sallustii, de Conivratione Catilinae. Anonymous printer. np. nd.
A reprint of the same work issued by Aldus in 1509 (see 60/1/5). The date on this book is "Venetiis mense Aprili, 1510." A fleur-de-lis is substituted for the Dolphin and Anchor. Forty-five forgeries of Aldin books are known.

Vellum; $6\frac{1}{2}$ x 4 x $\frac{3}{4}$ in. See Renouard. Annales des Aldes, 11, p. 302. No. 23.

FALSE IMPRINTS.

Cabinet W · Shelf 1 · No. 51

Imprimeurs imaginaires et Libraires supposés. Etude bibliographique, suivi de recherches sur quelques ouvrages imprimés avec des indications fictives de lieux, ou avec des dates singulières. Par Gustave Brunet. Paris, 1866.
Deals with fictitious imprints or falsified localities.

Cloth; $8\frac{1}{2}$ x $5\frac{1}{2}$ x $1\frac{1}{4}$ in.

FALSE IMPRINTS

Cabinet 26 · Shelf 1 · No. 19

(Moretus imprints, false) Falsche Moretusdrucke von Maurits Sabbe.
Article in the "Gutenberg-Gesellschaft Jahrbuch" 1929, pp.193-214.

FALSE TITLES OF BOOKS

Cabinet
Shelf
No.

See Liberty of Printing. Books under false titles.

FAMOUS ENGLISH PRINTERS

Cabinet S Shelf 2 No. 151

Brief bio - bibliographical article. Excerpt from Living Age, Aug. 11, 1877.

In envelope.

FAQUES, WILLIAM

Cabinet T Shelf 2 No. 6 [vol.3]

Books printed by Faques, London, 1499-1508. Bibliographical notes. With printer's device.

see

DIBDIN'S "Typographical Antiquities" ...London, 1810-19, vol.111, pp.1-12

FARLEY, A. C. & Co.

Cabinet Q Shelf 4 No. 6,7,8,9

Philadelphia, 1885-1890

see

DIRECTORIES, PRINTERS'. Farley's Reference Directory....

FANFOLD FORMS (see)

Cabinet RR Shelf 1 No. 26

PAPER. Fanfold Forms

FAQUES, WILLIAM

Cabinet MM Shelf 3 No. 15

Notice of W. Faques; list of books printed by him; biographical account; his device, etc.

See JOHNSON, JOHN. Typographia... London, 1824, pp.476-480

FARLIE, ROBERT

Cabinet K Shelf 2 No. 24

Moral emblems of Jacob Cats and Robert Farlie.

see

LEIGHTON, JOHN. Moral emblems of all ages...London, 1860

FANFOLD SYSTEMS

Cabinet EE Shelf 2 No. 3

See GILMAN PRINTING COMPANY, A.S. Individuality in printing...

FARADAY, MICHAEL

Cabinet U Shelf 3 No. 94

Life of Michael Faraday, 1791-1867. By Wilfrid L. Randal. London, 1924. Portrait.

Faraday, the inventor, started his career as a bookbinder's apprentice, Oct. 7, 1805.

Cloth; 7½ x 5 x 7/8 in.

"FARM JOURNAL

Cabinet NN Shelf 4 No. 47

Wilmer Atkinson. An autobiography. Founder of the Farm Journal. Philadelphia. 1920. Illus. and frontispiece portrait.

Cloth: 8x5¼x1½"

FANN STREET LETTER FOUNDRY

Cabinet Shelf No.

See Specimen Books, Types. England. Reed and Fox, late Robert Besly Co.

" also under same classification: Specimen Books, Types: Reed & Sons, Sir Charles.

FARADAY MACHINE

Cabinet FF Shelf 2 No. 51

Memorial meeting, Sept. 21, 1931, in Budapest, by Academy of Science and Universities of Hungary. Illus.

Report in English, in Elektrotechnika (Faraday Number), vol. 24, Oct. 15, 1931. Budapest.

Faraday was a bookbinder by trade. Inventor of the electro-dynamo.

Item in manila envelope.

FARMER & SON TYPE FOUNDING CO., A.D.

Cabinet II Shelf 2 No.

Specimen books, brass type.

See SPECIMEN BOOKS, BRASS TYPE. United States.

FANN STREET LETTER FOUNDRY

Cabinet Shelf No.

See Specimen Books, Types. England. Thorowgood & Co. W. Fann Street Foundry.

" also Specimen Books, Types. England. R. Besley & Co. Fann Street Foundry.

" also Specimen Books Types, England. Reed & Fox (Late R. Besley & Co.) Fann Street Letter Foundry.

FARFENGO (Battista)

Cabinet X Shelf 3 No. 14

Bibliographical note, with printer device, Farfengo, Brescia, 1489-99.

see

KRISTELLER, Dr. Paul Italienischen buchdrucker...p.8

FARMER, A.D. & SON.

Cabinet A Shelf 1 No. 2

See Type Foundries. New York Type Foundry, 1810-1908.

FANTOZZI, FEDERIGO

Cabinet AA Shelf 1 No. 31

Notizie biografiche originali di Bernardo Cennini ... primo promotore della tipografia in Firenze ... Opuscolo dell'in geg.re Federigo Fantozzi. Firenze, 1839. dalla tipografia Galileiana. With genealogical chart.

Half morocco; 9½ x 6 in. See also AA/1/82.

FARKALL, AMAND

Cabinet X Shelf 3 No. 13

Bibliographical note, with printer mark, Farkall, Colmar (Alsace-Lorraine), 1522-1530.

see

HEITZ, PAUL. Elsässische büchermarken...p.xxxiii, plate, lxxiii

---

FARMER, AARON DWIGHT see

Cabinet Shelf No.

PORTRAITS, Type Founders

TYPE FOUNDERS, United States

FARMER, LITTLE & Co.

Cabinet — Shelf — No.

See Specimen Books, Types. United States. Farmer, Little & Co.

FARMERS ALMANACS

Cabinet — Shelf — No.

See ALMANACS. Farmers Almanacs...

FARMER'S CABINET (The)

Cabinet — Shelf — No.

See Newspapers, New Hampshire.

FARMERS' LIBRARY, The

Cabinet NN — Shelf 2 — No. 6

Lyon, Matthew, editor of The Framers' Library, etc

see JOURNALISM, United States. Lyon, Matthew (Col.)...

FARMERS REGISTER and MECHANICS and MANUFACTURERS JOURNAL.

Cabinet — Shelf — No.

See Newspapers, New York State.

FARNHAM, A.B.

Cabinet LL — Shelf 6 — No. 20

Cost (A) record for the publisher. A system by which a printing concern may ascertain and keep on file the exact cost of every piece of work done in the shop...[Excerpt] System, Aug. 1907.

Item 11 in book with binder's title "Various items on printing shop practice". Bound 1919.

FARR, HARRY.

Cabinet 75 — Shelf 2 — No. 3

Notes on Shakespeare's printers and publishers. A paper read before the Bibliographical Society, November 20, 1922.

In Trans. Biblio. Soc., "The Library," Vol. III, 1922-23, pp. 225-260.

FARRAND, MAX

Cabinet S — Shelf 5 — No. 54

Whitmore, William H. and the early printed laws of Massachusetts.
(Account of the Massachusetts Laws of 1648).

Article on p. 146 of "Herbert Putnam: Essays in honor of his thirtieth anniversary"... 1929.

FARRAR, GILBERT P.

Cabinet BB — Shelf 3 — No. 38

Facts about type. Farrar's Fact-A-Week about Type. For the Sales representatives of the American Type Founders Company, Elizabeth, New Jersey, 1935.

Talks on type, with specimens

In envelope.

FARRAR, GILBERT P.

Cabinet LL — Shelf 4 — No. 26

Typography of advertisements that pay: How to choose and combine type faces, engravings and all the other mechanical elements of modern advertisement construction. New York, 1917.

Cloth; 7-3/4 x 5-3/8 x 1¼ in.

FARRAR, JAMES ANSON

Cabinet X — Shelf 5 — No. 95

Books condemned to be burnt. The Book-Lover's Library. Edited by Henry B. Wheatley. London, 1892.

Boards, linen back; 7-3/8 x 4-5/8 x 3/4 in.

FARWELL, JOHN

Cabinet X — Shelf 4 — No. 31

Tryal of J. Farwell, London, 1682.

see LIBERTY OF PRINTING, Great Britain. (The) Tryal (1682) of Nathaniel Thompson, William Pain, and John Farwell....

"FASCICULUS TEMPORUM"

Cabinet U — Shelf 1 — No. 1f

Edition printed by Arnold Ther Hoernen in 1474, at Cologne. [Bibliographical account]. By A.G.W. Murray.

In Excerpts relating to printing from "The Library," 1912-13, p. 93 of pencilled folios

FASCICULUS TEMPORUM

Cabinet S — Shelf 3 — No. 104

(A) Genealogical survey of editions before 1480. By Margaret Bingham Stillwell.
P. 409 in volume, Wilberforce Eames ... A tribute to. Cambridge, 1924.

FASCICULUS TEMPORUM

Cabinet D — Shelf 1 — No. 43

Rolewinck, Werner. Fasciculus temporum. Basel, 1482. Bernhard Richel.
Colophon: Chronica q̄ dicit...edita in alma universitate colonie agrippine sup rhenum./... Sepius quidem iā impr̄ssa sed negligētia corrector/ in diversis locus a vero originiali minus iuste emēdata...per Bernardū Richel civem Basilien̄. Sub anno dn̄i M.CCCC.LXXXII. X. Kl. mēs marcii...

Gesamt-Kat. Hain 6932; boards; 11¾ x 8 x 1 in.

FASCICULUS TEMPORUM

Cabinet 29 — Shelf 1 — No. 23

[Rolewinck, Werner]. Fasciculus temporum. Venice: Erhard Ratdolt. 1485.
Dedication: Nicolao mocenico magnifici. D. Francisci/Patricio Veneto: Erhardus Ratdolt salutē.
Text: Fasciculus temporū omnes antiquoz chroni/cas strictim complectens felici numine incipit./Prologus:
Colophon: Erhardus Ratdolt Augustensi impressioni paravit:/ Anno salutis M.CCCC.LXXXV.VI. idus. Septembris/Venetiis inclyto principe mocenico
Gesamt-Kat. . Zapf, p. 168. Essling 280. Hain 6937. Redgrave 52. Boards; 10 x 8 x ½ in.

FAUCOU, LUCIEN

Cabinet X — Shelf 5 — No. 81

Mémoire sur les vexations qu'exercent les libraires et imprimeurs de Paris, publié d'apres l'imprimerie de 1725, et le manuscrit de la Bibliotheque de la Ville de Paris. Paris, 1879. [A reprint from the original of Pierre-Jacques Blondel, 1725].
Adverse to the publishers of Paris.

Quarter morocco; 10-3/8 x 8-3/8 x ½ in.

FAULKNER, GEORGE

Cabinet QQ — Shelf 1 — No. 5

Letter from Martin Gulliver to George Faulkner, printer. Printed in the year, 1730. n.p.

Poem advising Faulkner how to treat with his libellous enemies.

Half morocco; 6¼ x 4 x ¼ in.

FAULMANN, CARL

Cabinet L · Shelf 2 · No. 13

Buch der schrift, enthaltend die schriften und alphebete aller zeiten und aller volker des gesammtem erdkreises...und erlauteret von Carl Faulmann, Wien, 1878.
(Alphabets and writing of all peoples and countries. Each alphabet preceded by xx historical and philological notes.)

Cloth and boards; $11\frac{1}{4}$ x $8\frac{1}{4}$ in.

FAULMANN, KARL

Cabinet Y · Shelf 1 · No. 29

Erfindung der buchdruckerkunst nach den neuesten forschungen. Dem deutschen volke. Dargestellt von Prof. Karl Faulmann. Wein, 1891. Facsimiles.
Biographical historical account; includes genealogy of the Gensfleisch family.

Cloth; $9\frac{1}{4}$ x 6-5/8 x $\frac{1}{2}$ in.

FAULMANN, KARL

Cabinet LL · Shelf 2 · No. 12

Handbuch der buchdruckerkunst für schriftsetzer und korrektoren. Wien, 1884. Illus.

Cloth; $7\frac{3}{4}$ x $5\frac{1}{4}$ x $\frac{3}{4}$ in.

FAULMANN, KARL

Cabinet LL · Shelf 2 · No. 11

Illustrirte geschichte der buchdruckerkunst mit besonderer berücksichtigung ihrer technischen entwicklung bis zur gegenwart. Leipzig, 1882. Colored plates, supplements, and 380 illus. in the text.
"One of the best general histories of printing".

Cloth; $9\frac{1}{2}$ x $6\frac{1}{2}$ x 2-5/8 in.

FAULMANN, KARL

Cabinet L · Shelf 3 · No. 15

Illustrirte geschichte der schrift: popular-wissenschaftliche darstellung der schrift der sprache der zahlen sowie der schrift-systeme aller völker der erde. Wien, 1880.
(Writing systems of all peoples and nations)
With 15 plates

Cloth; $9\frac{1}{2}$ x $6\frac{3}{4}$ in.

FAUSTUS: (Johann Fust)

Cabinet QQ · Shelf 3 · No. 40

Life, death, and doom, Faustus. A romance in prose. Translated from the German. London, 1864.

Cloth; $7\frac{3}{4}$ x 5 x 1 in.

FAUSTUS ASSOCIATION

Cabinet JJ · Shelf 3 · No. 2

Boston, Mass., 1808

see
SOCIETIES, PRINTERS. United States Faustus Association...

FAUTES D'UN IMPRIMEUR see

Cabinet W · Shelf 1 · No. 107

LECSNE, HENRI...

FAUTEUX, AEGIDIUS

Cabinet R · Shelf 4 · No. 172

Introduction of printing into Canada. A brief history. Published by the Rolland Paper Company, Montreal, 1930. Illus. facs.

Cloth; $9\frac{1}{2}$ x $6\frac{1}{4}$ x 7/8 in. In protective case.

FAVA, DOMENICO

Cabinet 26 · Shelf 1 · No. 20

(La) Fortuna del pronostico di Giovanni Lichtenberger in Italia nel quattrocento e nel cinquecento. Illus.
Bibliographical account of 15th and 16th century astrological works.

Article in the "Gutenberg-Gesellschaft Jahrbuch" 1930, pp.126-148.

FAVA, DOMENICO

Cabinet 26 · Shelf 1 · No. 19

Tipografia Modenese del quattrocento e specialmente sulle edizioni silografichi.
Bibliographical account of 15th century printing in Modena, with special notice of books illustrated with wood engravings.
Article in the "Gutenberg-Gesellschaft Jahrbuch", 1929, pp.164-185.

FAVINE, ANDREW.

Cabinet E · Shelf 3 · No. 22

The Theater of Honor and Knighthood...containing...the first institution of Armes, Emblazons, King's Heralds and Pursuivants of Armes...The order of the Holy Ghost, Order of the Star....London: printed by William Jaggard, dwelling in Barbican, 1623.

Polished calf; gold tooled. $12\frac{3}{4}$ x $8\frac{1}{4}$ x $2\frac{1}{2}$ ins.

FAWCET, THOMAS

Cabinet E · Shelf 3 · No. 52

See Early Printing in Great Britain. London, 1633. Bernard Alsop and Thomas Fawcet.

FAWCETT, BENJAMIN

Cabinet L · Shelf 4 · No. 32

Colour printer and engraver, Benjamin Fawcett. By the Rev. M. C. F. Morris...Oxford University Press. 1925.

With protraits, and list of the Fawcett color prints.

Cloth: $7\frac{1}{2}$ x 5 x $\frac{3}{4}$ in.

FAWCETT, WALDON

Cabinet S · Shelf 5 · No. 14

Printing our money and stamps. By Waldon Fawcett, in Van Norden Magazine, June, 1907. Illus. excerpt.
Technical description of processes as employed at Washington, D. C.

Bound with other items in collection "Printing Processes: Excerpts from Magazines." Item 15.

FAWKES, RICHARD

Cabinet T · Shelf 2 · No. 6 [vol.3]

Books printed by Richard Fawkes, 1509-1530. Bibliographical notes. With printer's device.

see
DIBDIN'S "Typographical Antiquities" ...London, 1810-19, vol.iii, p.355

FAXARDO, DIDACUS SAAVEDRA

Cabinet E · Shelf 4 · No. 27

Idea principis Christiano politici symbolis Cl expresa...Parisiis, apud Fridericum Leonardum. 1660.

Dedication page to the reader has a picture of a printing press, then follows a brief history of the invention of printing.

Vellum; 5 x $3\frac{1}{4}$ in.

FAXON, FREDERICK WINTHROP.

Cabinet PP · Shelf 1 · No. 16

Literary annuals and gift books. A bibliography with a descriptive introduction. Boston, Mass. 1912.

Boards, cloth back; $8\frac{3}{4}$ x 5-7/8 x $\frac{3}{4}$ in.

FAZELLO, TOMASO

Cabinet E
Shelf 2
No. 16

Due deche dell'historia di Sicilia ... Divise in venti libri. Tradotte dal Latino in lingua Toscano ... Venetia, 1574. Domenico, & Gio. Battista Guerra, fratelli.

Vellum; 8-7/8 x $6\frac{3}{4}$ x $1\frac{1}{2}$ in.

FEATHER, WILLIAM

Cabinet QQ
Shelf 2
No. 20

Ideals and follies of business. Cleveland: The William Feather Company, Publishers. 1927.

Cloth; 7-7/8 x 5-1/8

FEDERAL ORRERY, published by Thomas Paine.

Cabinet
Shelf
No.

See Newspapers, Massachusetts.

FEDERATED MASTER PRINTERS OF SOUTH AFRICA

Cabinet KK
Shelf 2
No. 36

Printing and newspaper industry of South Africa. First National Conference. Johannesburg, Nov. 10 - 15th, 1919. Also March 29 - 31st, 1920. Reports of the proceedings. (2 pamphlets)
Conference between representatives of the Federated Master Printers of South Africa, and the newspaper press on one side, and representatives of the South African Typographical Union on the other.

Half morocco; $9\frac{3}{4}$ x 7-3/8 x $\frac{1}{2}$ in.

FEDERATION FRANCAISE DES TRAVAILLEURS DU LIVRE

Cabinet KK
Shelf 4
No. 43

see SOCIETIES, PRINTERS'. France. Federation Francaise...

FEDERATION OF MASTER PRINTERS

Cabinet LL
Shelf 4
No. 37

Advertising to increase your sales. British Federation of Master Printers, London, 1933.

Pamphlet,

FEDERATION OF MASTER PRINTERS, Great Britain

Cabinet LL
Shelf 5
No. 50

Cost-finding and accountancy systems. Explanation and specimen forms. London, 1919.

Cloth folder; 8-5/8 x 5-5/8 x $\frac{1}{2}$ in.

FEDERATION OF MASTER PRINTERS. Gr. Britain

Cabinet LL
Shelf 6
No. 20.01

Estimating: How to avoid a misfit. The Costing Committee. Federation of Master Printers, London, n.d. circa 1925.

Item 3 in vol. with binder's title "Printing Accountancy: Excerpts and Pamphlets". Bound, 1932.

FEDERATION OF MASTER PRINTERS, Great Britain

Cabinet LL
Shelf 5
No. 48

(London, England) Estimating for printers. Issued by the Costing Committee. London, 1916.

Cloth; $8\frac{3}{4}$ x $5\frac{1}{4}$ x 5/8 in.

FEDERATION OF MASTER PRINTERS. Great Britain

Cabinet LL
Shelf 5
No. 49

Estimating for printers. Issued by the Costing Committee, Federation of Master Printers. London, 1919.

Cloth; $8\frac{3}{4}$ x $5\frac{1}{4}$ x 5/8 in.

FEDERATION OF MASTER PRINTERS. Great Britain

Cabinet LL
Shelf 5
No. 47

(London, England) Profit for printers or what is "Cost"? Third impression, London, 1909.

Cloth; $8\frac{3}{4}$ x $5\frac{1}{4}$ x 3/8 in.

FEDERATION OF MASTER PRINTERS, Gt. Britain

Cabinet RR
Shelf 2
No. 14

Tables and data for printers. Paper standardization. Published by the Cost Committee. London (1926).

Booklet in manila envelope.

FEDERATION OF MASTER PRINTERS see

Cabinet
Shelf
No.

SOCIETIES, PRINTERS'. Great Britain.

FEDERATION TYPOGRAPHIQUE BELGE

Cabinet KK
Shelf 4
No. 40

Congrès International...Bruxelles, 1880.

see SOCIETIES, PRINTERS'. Belgium. Federation Typographique Belge...

FEDERICI (Dom. Maria)

Cabinet AA
Shelf 1
No. 24

Volpi-Cominiana, annali della tipografia. Colle notizio intorno la vita e gli studi de Fratelli Volpi. Padova, 1809.
History and bibliography of the famous printing house of Padua from 1717 to 1756.

Half morocco: 9 x $6\frac{1}{4}$ in.

FEDOROFF, IVAN

Cabinet AA
Shelf 5
No. 44

Diaconus Iohannes Fedorov, Moscoviae impressor primus, 1563-4.
See Printing, Historical, Russia: Origines Artis Typographicae Ucrainorum ... Leopoldi, 1924. p. 22.

FEDEROW, IVAN

Cabinet 26
Shelf 1
No. 15

(First printer in Moscow, bio-bibliographical account)

see MASSLOW, S.J. Ukrainische druckkunst...

FEDOROFF, IVAN

Cabinet AA
Shelf 5
No. 43

(First printer in Russia).
See Early Printing in Russia. Olgin, P.T. ... St. Petersburg, 1900.

FEENY, R.

Cabinet LL Shelf 6 No. 1

Master Printers' Price Manual, to which is added specimens of type in general use...Also a list of wholesale stationers, card makers, printers' brokers, wood engravers, etc. And numerous useful practical hints. Second edition. London, n.d. (After 1845, date of first edition).

Paper; 6½ x 4 in. In box labelled "Printing Accountancy, Misc."

FEKNO (P.P.)

Cabinet X Shelf 1 No. 36

Programma de duplici Germaniae invento, typographia et pulvere pyrio. Torgae, 1713.

[Reprinted in Wolf, "Monumenta Typographica", vol. 2, p. 867]

FELICE de -----

Cabinet FF Shelf 3 No. 5

Yverdon (France) 1778.

See Encyclopedie... Universal Raisonne. Articles, illustrated with many copperplates...Yverdon, 1778.

FELICE'S ENCYCLOPEDIE...[Excerpts from].

Cabinet FF Shelf 6 No. 2

I FONDERIE EN CARACTERES D'IMPRIMERIE... [Yverdun, 1775] [8 plates with drawings of tools used in type founding. Interior views of type foundries]

II IMPRIMERIE EN CARACTERES [19 plates: illus. explanatory text on composition, imposition, printing. With views of printing offices and printing tools.

III IMPRIMERIE EN TAILLE-DOUCE [Copper plate printing. Illus. and text. 2 plates]

(cont'd)

FELICE'S ENCYCLOPEDIE...[Excerpts from] (cont'd)

Cabinet FF Shelf 6 No. 2

IV CARACTERES ET ALPHABETS [Specimens of exotic types. With explanatory notes].

Half morocco; 17 x 11 in.

FELIX, J.

Cabinet X Shelf 5 No. 87

Anciens imprimeurs. Certificat l'examen universitaire d'un imprimeur Rouennais. Rouen, 1883.

Regulations governing examinations for apprentices and master printers at Rouen.

Half morocco; 8-3/4 x 5-3/4 x ¼ in.

FELL, DR. JOHN

Stack A Shelf 2 Number 62

Bullen, Henry Lewis. Dr. Fell and the University Press at Oxford. (Collectanea Typographica) In The Inland Priner, vol. LXII, p. 527. Illus.

FELL, JOHN.

Cabinet 75 Shelf 2 No. 6

His work for Oxford printing.

See Transactions of the Bibliographical Society, "The Library," Vol. VI, 1925-26, pp. 123-7.

FELL, Dr.

Cabinet U Shelf 2 No. 125

Letters by Robert Scott to Dr. Fell (1668-1670); as to types and other printing material for the University of Oxford. (Bodleian Mss.)

Appendix 3, part 1 of "Notes on a century of typography at the University Press, Oxford, 1693-1794"...By Horace Hart, Oxford, 1900.

Full morocco; 13¾ x 10¼ in.

FELL (Bishop)

Cabinet U Shelf 5 No. 24

Oxford, buys Dutch types for

see

POLLARD, A. W. Fine Books... London, 1912, p.298

FELL, JOHN.

Cabinet 75 Shelf 2 No. 7

Specimens of books printed at Oxford with the types given to the University by John Fell. Oxford. At the Clarendon Press, 1925. Reviewed by R. B. McKerrow.

In Transactions of the Bibliographical Society, "The Library," Vol. VII, 1926-27, pp. 225-7.

FELL TYPES

Cabinet P Shelf 3 No. 33

Specimens of the books printed (1674-1925) at Oxford with the types given to the University by John Fell...Oxford, at the Clarendon Press, in the year of the Centenary, 1925.

Cloth; 18 x 11½ in.

FELL TYPES

Cabinet 84 Shelf No.

See Specimen Books. Types. England. Oxford University Press Foundry, 1693.

" also Oxford University Foundry, England. Specimen...

FELLENFURST, AEGIDIUS

Cabinet Y Shelf 2 No. 55

(Books printed by Fellenfurst, Coburg, 1522--. Bibliographical notes).

see

HÖFER, CONRAD. Beitrag... Coburg, 1906, p.27

FELSECKER-SEBALD

Cabinet Y Shelf 5 No. 20

(Imperial and Government Printing House for Bayern, 1658-1908. Celebration of the 250th year Jubilee of the firm). Zum 250 jähr, geschäftsjubiläum der Königl. Bayer. Hofdruckerei und verlagshandlung von U. E. Sebald. Nürnberg, 9 May 1908. Portraits and other illus.

Half morocco; 12¼ x 9¼ x 3/8 in.

FELT, CHARLES W.

Cabinet FF Shelf 6 No. 23

Inventor, 1854, of a typesetting machine. Biographical and descriptive account of the inventor and the invention.

Article in The Atlantic Monthly, May, 1864, p.615.

Magazine with article in manila envelope.

FELT, CHARLES W.

Cabinet FF Shelf 6 No. 23

Lecture on Type-Setting Machines before the Boston Printers' Union.

Excerpt report from the Boston Post, Oct.12, 1863.

Item in manila envelope with other items.

FEMALE JOURNALISTS see

Cabinet Shelf No.

WOMEN JOURNALISTS

FENOT, CHARLES

Cabinet Z, Shelf 2, No. 36

See Specimen Books, Types. France.

FENTON, FRANCES

Cabinet OO, Shelf 3, No. 27

Influence of newspaper presentations upon the growth of crime and other anti-social activity: A dissertation...for the decree of Doctor of Philosophy. The University of Chicago. Chicago, Ill. 1911.

Half morocco; 9½ x 6¾ x ½ in.

FENTON, SAGIE VELLE

Cabinet NN, Shelf 3, No. 38

Some verses, travel letters and addresses.

By Sagie Velle Fenton.

Published by her mother, Mrs. C.O. Fenton. Indianapolis. 1917.

With portraits.
Limp leather: 7¼x4-7/8x¾"

FERCHL, FRANZ MARIA

Cabinet MM, Shelf 2, No. 52.01

Geschichte der errichtung der ersten lithographischen kunstanstalt bei der Feiertags-Schule fur Künstler und Techniker. Aus auftrag...bei gelegenheit des neunzigsten (90) geburtstages des erfinders der lithographie, Johann Aloys Senefelder. Geschichte diese ruhmvollen Münchener erfindung, nebst...vollständigen incunabeln-sammlung der lithographie. Munchen, 1862. Illus.

Boards; 9 x 5-3/4 x ½ in.
Lithographed signature of Senefelder on bill of Oct. 30, 1811 inserted at the end.

FERENCZ, PUSZTAI.

Cabinet LL, Shelf 2, No. 44

Nyomdoszati enciklopedia az osszes grafikai tudomanyok ismerettara. Budapest, 1902. Encyclopedia of graphic arts.

Half niger; 9½ x 6-3/8 x 1¼ in.

FERGUSON, F. S.

Cabinet 75, Shelf 2, No. 8

Relations between London and Edinburgh printers and stationers (-1640). By F. S. Ferguson. Read before the Bibliographical Society, 21 Feb. 1927.

In Trans. Biblio. Soc., "The Library," Vol. VIII, 1927-1928, pp. 145-198.

FERGUSON BROTHERS

Cabinet, Shelf, No.

See Specimen Books, Types. Scotland.

"FERN FANNY" (Eldridge-Parton)

Cabinet NN, Shelf 6, No. 26

Biographical sketch of a woman journalist of 1851.

see
BROWNE, JUNIUS HENRI (The) Great Metropolis; a mirror of New York...1870, p.633

FERNANDEZ ,Juan

Cabinet X, Shelf 3, No. 19

Brief bio-bibliographical note, with printer-publisher mark, Fernandez (Salamanca), 1586-1596.

see
HAEBLER, KONRAD. (Spanish and Portugese printer marks...p.xxxviii

---

FERNANDEZ, Valentin de Moravie

Cabinet X, Shelf 3, No. 19

Bio-bibliographical sketch, with printer mark, Fernandez (Lisbon), 1495-1514

see
HAEBLER, KONRAD. (Spanish and Portugese printer marks...p.xxiii

---

FERNANDEZ de CORDOBA (Diego and Francisco)

Cabinet X, Shelf 3, No. 19

Bio-bibliographical sketch, with printer mark, Fernandez (Medina del Campo), 1538-1589.

see
HAEBLER, KONRAD. (Spanish and Portugese printer marks...p.xx)

FERRAR, NICHOLAS

Cabinet U, Shelf 3, No. 103

Little Gidding bookbindings. By Cyril Davenport. Bibliographical sketch.

See vol. 2, p.129 Bibliographica...London, 1895-1897.

FERRARA

Cabinet U, Shelf 5, No. 24

Early printing at Ferrara

see
POLLARD, A.W. Fine Books... London, 1912, pp.68, 70, 140

FERRARA

Cabinet X, Shelf 1, No. 77

(Hebrew printing in Ferrara, 1470-1577)

See De ROSSI, JOHANNES BERNARDUS (De) Typographia hebrew-Ferrariensi...

FERRARA

Cabinet, Shelf, No.

See also
Printing, Historical, Italy. (Ferrara)

FERRARI de GIOLITIS (or GIOLITO de FERRARI)

Cabinet S, Shelf 5, No. 4

See Giolito, Gabriele, Printer-Publisher, Venice, 1512-1578.

FERRARIIS (de Nicolaus de Pralormio)

Cabinet X, Shelf 3, No. 14

Bibliographical note, with printer mark, Ferrarii, Venice, 1491.

see
KRISTELLER, Dr. PAUL. Italienischen buchdrucker...p.78

FERRER, Juan and Miguel

Cabinet X, Shelf 3, No. 19

Brief bio-bibliographical note, with printer mark, Ferrer (Toledo), 1547-1572)

see
HAEBLER, KONRAD. (Spanish and Portugese printer marks...p.xxvi

FERRIGNI, MARIO

Cabinet AA Shelf 2 No. 29

Aldo Manuzio: Invenione della stampa. Da Mario Ferrigini. Milano, 1925.
Biographical, with notes about books printed by Aldus, and his last will.

Half morocco; 7¾ x 5-3/8 x 3/4 in.

FERTEL, MARTIN DOMINIQUE.

Cabinet MM Shelf 1 No. 1

Science pratique de l'imprimerie. [Mss. copy Paris 1723]. Pen drawings.
Probably preceded the first printed editions, as the no. of pages is left blank in the description on page I.
Printed copy MM/1/2.

Boards; 8 x 6½ x 1 in.

FERTEL, MARTIN DOMINIQUE

Cabinet MM Shelf 1 No. 2

Science pratique de l'imprimerie... St. Omer 1723
Illus. in copper plates incorporated on same page with type display.
This is the first text book of printing issued in France. The first English book was issued in 1677 by Moxon. On page 2 of preface, French edition, reference is made to "De Germaniae miraculo optimo maximo, typis literarum", etc., issued in Leipzig without name of author or date of issue. The date is 1710, the author Paulus Pater, RR. Both books

(cont'd)

FERTEL, MARTIN DOMINIQUE (cont'd)

Cabinet MM Shelf 1 No. 2

are in this collection.

Calf; 9-5/8 x 7-3/8 x 1-1/8 in.

FERTEL, MARTIN DOMINIQUE

Cabinet MM Shelf 1 No. 3

(La) Science pratique de l'imprimerie. Contenenant des instructions tres faciles pour se confectionner dans cet art...Le tous représenté avec des figures en bois et en taille douce. A St. Omer, 1741.
Another edition of the earliest French text book of printing (1723). Printed by the author himself at St. Omers.
See earlier edition, MM/1/2.

Calf; 9-5/8 x 7-3/8 x 1-1/8 in.

FERTIAULT, F.

Cabinet W Shelf 1 No. 95

Amoureux du livre: Sonnets d'un bibliophile ... notes et anecdotes. Par F. Fertiault; preface du bibliophile Jacob (Paul Lacroix) Seize eaux-fortes de Jules Chevrier. Paris, 1877.

Half morocco; 9½ x 6¾ in.

FESSENDEN, THOMAS GREEN(pseud. Chris. Caustic)

Cabinet Q Shelf 3 No. 5

Terrible tractoration and other poems. By Christopher Caustic. Fourth American Edition. To which is prefixed Caustic's wooden booksellers and miseries of authorship. Boston, 1837. Frontispiece.

Cloth; 6-5/8 x 4¼ x ¾ in.

FESSIN

Cabinet Z Shelf 2 No. 33

Specimen de filets mixtes de la fonderie de Fessin, Rue des Boucheries St-Germain 19. Paris, 1841.
Brass rules.

Pamphlet; 10-1/8 x 7 in.

FESSIN, P. J.

Cabinet FF Shelf 2 No. 12

(Type founder, poet. Biographical sketch)
Notice sur P.J. Fessin, fondeur en caractères, poète et homme de lettres. Accompagnée d'un fac simile d'une lettre autographe inédite de Beranger. Par M. Alkan Aine. Paris, 1853. Brochure.

In Manila envelope.

FESTIVALS, PRINTERS

Cabinet Shelf No.

See Celebrations, Printers.

FETIS ___

Cabinet EE Shelf 3 No. 72

Specimen des caractères de musique...Précédé d'une notice sur la typographe musicale. Paris. Imprimerie de E. Duverger...1834.

Boards; 13-7/8 x 10-3/4 in.

FEUGÈRE, LÉON JACQUES

Cabinet W Shelf 2 No. 77

Essai sur la vie et les ouvrages de Henri Estienne. Suivi d'une étude sur Scévole de Sainte-Marthe. Par. Léon Feugère. Paris, Jules Delalain, 1853.

Half morocco; 7½ x 4½ in.

FEYERABEND, KARL.

Cabinet I Shelf 1 No. 6

See Early Printing in Germany. Frankfort a M., 1574.

FEYERABEND, SIGMUND

Cabinet Y Shelf 5 No. 63

(Biography of the man and an account of his works and business relationg) Sigmund Feyerabend sein leben und seine geschäftlichen verbindungen. Nach archivalischen quellen. Bearbeitet von Heinr. Pallman. Frankfurt a.M., 1881. Portrait frontispiece.
Has genealogy of Feyerabend family.

Half morocco; 11½ x 7¼ x ½ in.

FEYERABENDS, SIGMUND

Cabinet Y Shelf 3 No. 111

(Book catalogue of Sigmund Feyerabend, Frankfurt a.m. 1584, an unknown) Bibliographical study, illus.
See Bondheim, Moritz. Gesammelte schriften...Frankfurt, 1927, p. 274

FEYERABEND, SIGMUND.

Cabinet 22 Shelf 1 No. 2

Concerning a legal process against Feyerabend in Frankfort a.M, because of piracy and offence against the press laws of 1568-1570.

In Archiv für Deutschen Buchhandles, 1879, vol.2, p.47.

FEYERABEND, SIGMUND.

Cabinet 22 Shelf 1 No. 14

(Feyerabend, Sigmund, Frankfort, a.M. 1559. The publishing house of Sigmund Feyerabend.) Der Verlag Sigmund Feyerabend, von F. Herm. Meyer.

Chronological and descriptive list of books with prices.

In Archiv für Deutschen Buchhandels, vol. XIV, p.114.

FEYERABEND, SIGMUND (see also)

Cabinet Shelf No.

Biographies, Printers
Early Printing in Germany. Lit. of.
Early Printing in Germany. Frankfort a.M., 1566
Illustrated Books, Early. [Panoplia]
Imprints, Germany
Prices of Books. Feyerabend, Sigmund. 1565

FEYERABEND FAMILY OF PRINTERS.

Cabinet 22 Shelf 1 No. 1

Familie Feyerabend: Brief biographical account which includes genealogical table, compiled by A. Kirchhoff.

In Archiv für Deutschen Buchhandles, 1878. vol. 1, p. 187.

FICHET, GUILLAUME

Cabinet V Shelf 5 No. 2.01

Fichet, Guillaume, et sa famille, documents inédits sur. Par C. Couderc. Paris, 1900. "Extrait du Bulletin du Bibliophile". Pamphlet.

Fichet is credited with having introduced printing into France, through Ulric Gering.

Item 6 in vol. with binder's title "French printers and printing. Pamphlets". Bound, 1932.

FICHET, GUILLAUME

See also

Printers' Biographies.

FEYLE BROTHERS

Cabinet C Shelf 1 No. 13

Werden und wachsen eines deutschen druckhauses. Gedenkschrift zum 25 jährigen jubiläum der firma Geber. Feyl, Berlin, n.d. circa 1925. Illus.

Pictorial boards; 17 x 17-3/4 in.

FICHET, WILLIAM

Cabinet S Shelf 1 No. 135

(The) Fichet letter [Jan. 1, 1471], the earliest document ascribing to Gutenberg the invention of printing. By Douglas C. McMurtrie With reproduction of the letter in collotype and a translation of the text by W.A. Montgomery. New York, 1927.

Boards; $11\frac{1}{2}$ x 8-1/8 in.

FICK, JULES GUILLAUME

Cabinet J Shelf 5 No. 5

Anciens bois de l'Imprimerie Fick a Genève. A Genève. Par Jules Guillaume Fick, Imprimeur. 1863.

Book of initials and typographic ornaments from the original wood blocks engraved by Salomon Bernard for Tournes.

Half morocco; $17\frac{1}{4}$ x 11-5/8 in.

FIALA, ANTHONY

Cabinet NN Shelf 7 No. 8.01

Photo-engraver and leader of the Ziegler Polar Expedition, 1903.

see

PORTRAITS, PHOTO-ENGRAVERS. Fiala, Anthony...

FICHET, GUILLAUME

Cabinet U Shelf 5 No. 24

Invention of printing, letter on

see

POLLARD, A.W. Fine Books... London, 1912, pp.33, 44, 70

FICK, JULES-GUILLAUME, Printer

Cabinet 40 Shelf No.

See Imprints, Switzerland. Fick, Jules-Guillaume, Geneva, 1866.

FICHET, GUILLAUME

See

CHAMPION, PIERRE, Ed.: Les plus anciens monuments de la Typographie Parisienne. Paris, 1904

FICHET, GUILLERMO

Cabinet W Shelf 2 No. 1

(Letter to Robert Gaguinum (1 January 1472) in which Fichet mentions Gutenberg as the inventor of printing). Guillermi Fichet quam ad Robertum Gaguinum de Johanne Gutenberg et de artis impressoriae in Gallia primordiis nec de orthographiae utilitate conscripsit. Epistola ... Edidit Ludovicus Sieber. Basileae, 1887.

Item 16 in volume "Gutenberg, l'inventeur de l'imprimerie - Melanges."

FICTION, PRINTING

Cabinet QQ Shelf 3 No. 51

Easy Nat: or Boston bars and Boston boys. A tale of home trials. By one who knows them. Boston, Redding and Company, 1844.

Brochure. Item in envelope.

FICHET, GUILLAUME

Cabinet W Shelf 3 No. 80

Documents inédits sur Guillaume Fichet et sa famille. Par C. Couderc, Sous-bibliothécaire à la Bibliothèque Nationale. Paris, 1900.

Half morocco; 9 x 5-3/4 in.

FICHET, GUILLAUME

Cabinet W Shelf 3 No. 37

Proposal to erect a statue to the "Franklin" of French typography, in his home town of Petit - Bornand.

Excerpt from Courier des États-Unis, Dec. 4, 1935.

Pasted in back of book "Épitre addressée à Robert Gaguin", 1471. Paris, 1889.

Boards; 9-3/4 x 6-3/4 in.

FICTION, PRINTING

Cabinet QQ Shelf 3 No. 40

Faustus: life, death, and doom. A romance in prose. Translated from the German. London, 1864.

Cloth; $7\frac{3}{4}$ x 5 x 1 in.

FICHET, GUILLAUME

Cabinet W Shelf 3 No. 37

Épitre adressée a Robert Gaguin le 1, Janvier, 1472, par Guillaum Fichet, sur l'introduction de l'imprimerie a Paris.. Reproduction heliographique de l'exemplaire unique possedé par l'Université de Bâle. Paris, 1889.

Boards; 10 x $6\frac{3}{4}$ in.

FICHET, GUILLAUME

Cabinet W Shelf 3 No. 43

See Printing, Historical, France (Paris). Guillaume Fichet, sa vie, ses oeuvres.

FICTION, Printing

Cabinet R Shelf 3 No. 61

Franklin (A play in four acts). By Constance D. Mackay. New York, 1922. Frontispiece: Reproduction of McKenzie statue "The Youthful Franklin."

Cloth; $7\frac{1}{2}$ x $5\frac{1}{4}$ in.

FICTION, Printing

Cabinet S Shelf 3 No. 100

Goudy, Frederic W.: The City of Crafts, a phantasy: Being some account of a journey to the Court of the Printer's Guild. Told by [F.W. Goudy] a member of the American Institute of Graphic Arts. New York. Feb. 15, 1922.

Half morocco; 9¾ x 6¼ in.

FICTION, Printing

Cabinet S Shelf 5 No. 67

Sub-Rosa, or the rape of the printerie. Privately printed: San Francisco, California, 1930

Anonymous imprint

Paper; 9¼ x 6¾ in.

FIELD, JOHN

Cabinet X Shelf 4 No. 17

London, 1649

see LIBERTY OF PRINTING, Great Britain. Act (1649)...

FICTION, PRINTING

Cabinet X Shelf 2 No. 60

Gutenberg: historisches drama in vier akten. Nach der ersten fassen neu bearbeitet. von Alfred Börchel, Mainz, 1900.

Historical drama in four acts

Play in book with title "Gutenberg-Feier Mainz, 1900...von K. G. Bockenheimer.

FICTION, HUMOROUS OF PRINTING

Cabinet NN Shelf 5 No. 14

Our Joshua as a reporter. By Brother Jonathan... Fredericton, N. B. 1884.

Cloth; 7¼ x 5 in.

FIELD, RICHARD

Cabinet E Shelf 3 No. 7

See Early Printing in England. London, 1616. Richard Field.

FICTION, PRINTING

Cabinet Y Shelf 1 No. 92

(Gutenberg's dream of the invention.) Gutenbergs schöpfertraum. Erzählung von Hans Bleyer-Hörtl. Mainz, 1930. Verlag der Gutenberg-Gesellschaft. Pamphlet.

With other items in manila envelope.

FICTIONAL HISTORIES OF PRINTING

Cabinet Shelf No.

See Schmidt-Weissenfels.

FIELD, RICHARD

Cabinet U Shelf 5 No. 3

Shakespeare editions printed by Richard Field, London.

See BLADES, WILLIAM. Shakespeare and typography...London, 1872, pp. 26-32

FICTION, PRINTING

Cabinet S Shelf 6 No. 6

Pete's printing press. (A boy's business story) By Kate Gannett Wells.

Excerpt from Wide Awake, October, 1885.

Item (f) in book with binder's title "Printing and printing offices".

FICTITIOUS IMPRINTS

Cabinet Shelf No.

See FALSE IMPRINTS

FIELD & TUER (Leadenhall Press)

Cabinet NN Shelf 5 No. 9

Imprint of Field & Tuer, London, circa 1881.

see WILLIAM'S...Journalistic jumbles, or trippings in type...

FICTION, PRINTING

Cabinet LL Shelf 5 No. 66

Porte, Roy Trewin. Printers of Chiapolis. Reprinted by permission. Porte Publishing Company, Salt Lake City. 1922.

Each story attempts to point a moral as to right business methods in the printing business.

Leather; 7½ x 5¼ x ⅜ in.

FIELD, EUGENE

Cabinet 73 Shelf 2 No. 43

Immortal little Willie. By Eugene Field. Illus. by Dan Sweeney. Printed by John Henry Nash of San Francisco for "understanding mothers and fathers...February, 1929.

Marble paper boards; 17¼ x 12¼ in.

FIELD & TUER

Cabinet T Shelf 6 No. 62

Imprint of 1883.

see CRAWHALL, JOSEPH. Old ffrends wyth newe faces...

FICTION, Printing

Cabinet W Shelf 2 No. 93

Premier maître imprimeur: Ses faits et discours le plus dignes d'admiration, et sa mort. Ce récit fidèle, écrit par F. Dingelstedt est traduit de l'Allemand en Français par Gustave Revilliod. Geneva, 1858.

Boards; 12 x 8 in.

FIELD, EUGENE

Cabinet Q Shelf 5 No. 51

Story of two friars, the. Being a somewhat curious tale by Eugene Field. The same privately printed for Miles C. Holden at the shop of Frank and Emily Mathewson, Springfield, Mass., 1904.

Paper; 8⅜ x 6¼ in., pp. 10.

In envelope.

FIELD & TUER (THE LEADENHALL PRESS)

Cabinet J Shelf 1 No. 29

One thousand (1,000) quaint cuts from books of other days, including amusing illustrations from childrens story books...One-and-fourpence. A limited number printed on one side of the paper only at two-and-eightpence. London, E. C. no date.

Half morocco; 9-3/8 x 7-3/8 x 1-1/8 in.

FIELD and TUER
See also
IMPRINTS, England.

Cabinet
Shelf
No.

FIGARO, LE

Cabinet J Shelf 5 No. 22

Figaro photographe. Edition unique. Supplement du Figaro. A l'occasion de la première Exposition Internationale de Photographie, Paris, 1887. Illus.

History of photography and photographic processes.

Cloth; 16¾ x 12¾ in.

FIGUEIREDO, MANOEL

Cabinet L Shelf 3 No. 3

Nova escola para aprender a ler, escrever, e contar...Por Manoel de Andrede de Figueiredo Mestre desta arte nas citades de Lisboa. Occidental, e Oriental. Lisboa Occidental. Na Officina de Bernardo da Costa de Carvalho, impressor...[1718 or 1722].

Engraved title page, portrait opposite p.1, etc.

Tree calf; 12 x 8¼ in.

FIELDING, MANTLE.

Cabinet I Shelf 3 No. 12

Dictionary of American painters, sculptors and engravers. By Mantle Fielding. Printed for the subscribers. Philadelphia, n.d. circa 1926.

Cloth; 10-5/8 x 7¼ x 2-5/8 in.

FIGARO, LE

Cabinet J Shelf 5 No. 21 also 22

(Illustrations in le Figaro. Paris, 1887).

See ILLUSTRATION. Figaro-Salon, 1887.

FIGUIER, Mme. LOUIS

Cabinet QQ Shelf 1 No. 45

Gutenberg, drame historique. En cinq actes et en prose. Paris, 1869.

Half morocco; 7½ x 5-1/8 in.

FIELDING, T.H.

Cabinet I Shelf 2 No. 70

Engraving, the art of, with the various modes of operation, under the following different divisions: etching, aquatint, mezzotint, lithography...London, 1844. Illus.

Cloth; 9¾ x 6½ in.

FIGGINS, JAMES

Cabinet 27 Shelf 2 No. 16

Biographical sketch.

see
BIOGRAPHIES, Type Founders.

FIKENTSCHER, H. (Bookbinder) see

BOOKBINDING FIRMS, Germany.

Cabinet
Shelf
No.

FIELDS, REBECCA

Cabinet NN Shelf 2 No. 29

Publisher of Montgomery County Sentinel since 1871, oldest woman newspaper operator in the world. Announcement of the death of Mrs. Fields, a centarian.

Newspaper clipping, n.n.np.nd.

With other items in manila envelope

FIGGINS, JAMES

Cabinet T Shelf 4 No. 77

Type founding and printing during the nineteenth century: A short review. By James Figgins. London, 1900.

Paper; 9¾ x 7¼ in.

FILET DE LA FOI

Cabinet D Shelf 4 No. 25

Bibliographical accouht of the "Filet de la foi de Pierre Chelcicky. Vilenov, 1521.

Mss. translation of article by Zdenek V. Tobolka. Prague, 1926

Item in manila envelope

FIFTH ESTATE, THE

Cabinet R Shelf 1 No. 3

Delivered in connection with Centenary Celebrated of the founding of the Franklin Institute... Reprint.

Pamphlet No. 3 in vol. "Franklin Pamphlets", Bound 1928.

FIGGINS, VINCENT

Cabinet D Shelf 1 No. 23

See Caxton, William. Game and Playe of the Chesse.
" also Specimen Books, Types. England.

FILIGRANES

Cabinet 20 Shelf 2 No. 19

Ein entlegenes. Feld Bibliophiler betatigung. (Watermarks, a subject for the bibliophiles' inquiry). Von Armin Renker of Zerkall. Illus.

In Zeitschrift für Bücherfreunde, 1927. pp. 61-3

FIFTY BOOKS OF THE YEAR (See)

Cabinet P Shelf 4 No. 17

AMERICAN INSTITUTE OF GRAPHIC ARTS.
Fifty books of the year...

FIGGINS, VINCENT and JAMES

Cabinet
Shelf
No.

See Imprints, England. Figgins.

FILLION, JOHANN

Cabinet
Shelf
No.

See Early Printing in Germany. Felssecker und Fillion [1683].

FILLON, BENJAMIN

Cabinet W
Shelf 1
No. 97

Quelques mots sur le Songe de Poliphile. Par Benjamin Fillon. Extrait de la Gazette des Beaux-Arts, Juin et Juillet, 1879. Paris Illus.
Bibliographical account.

Half morocco; 11½ x 8-3/8 in.

FINE ARTS PRESS, Oregon.

Cabinet
Shelf
No.

See Nash, John Henry. Education and the State.
" also, Imprints, United States. Fine Arts Press.

FINE PRINTING

Cabinet S
Shelf 5
No. 37.01

Revival of printing: an illuminating article from "The Eighteen Nineties", by Holbrook Jackson.

Illus. article in ARS TYPOGRAPHICA, vol.1, No.1, 1918.

FINCH, I.

Cabinet QQ
Shelf 2
No. 31

Travels in the United States of America and Canada, containing some account of their scientific institutions...London, 1833.

Briefly mentions B. Franklin and Archibald Binny.

Half binding only, board; 8¾ x 5-5/8

FINE PRINTING.

Cabinet S
Shelf 3
No. 67

Biblio-Typographica: A Survey of contemporary fine printing style. By Paul Johnston. New York, 1930.
With many examples.

Cloth; 10½ x 7-1/8 x 1-1/8 in.

FINE PRINTING see also

Cabinet
Shelf
No.

MODERN PRINTING.

FINE ORONCE

Cabinet 40
Shelf 2
No. 23

Orontii Finaei Delphinatis, Regii mathematicarum Lutetiae professoris, in sex libros geometricorum...Lutetiae Parisiorum, apud Simonem Colineum, 1544...

Boards covered with part of 15th cent. manuscript: 12 x 8¼ x 7/8 in.

FINE PRINTING.

Cabinet Y
Shelf 2
No. 2

(Collection of beautifully printed books). Sammlung der kunstlerischen druck von Julius Rodenberg. Leipzig, n.d. Pamphlet.

Item in box labelled "German Pamphlets - History of Printing - Bibliography, etc."

FINESCHI, VINCENZIO

Cabinet AA
Shelf 1
No. 9

Notizie storiche sopra la stamperia di Ripoli le quali possono servire all' illustrazione della storia tipografica Fiorentina Raccolte, e pubblicate dal P. Vincenzio Fineschi. Firenze, 1781.
"Printing was introduced into the convent of St. Jacopo of Ripoli by the Dominican brothers, Domenica da Pistoja and Pietro da Pisa, who also introduced the casting of types."

Quarter morocco; 8¾ x 5¾ in.

FINE, ORONCE

Cabinet 70
Shelf 2
No. 11

Protomathesis: opus varium. Paris, 1532. Gerard Morrhy and Jean Pierre.

[Woodcut title-border, designs, cuts of mathematical instruments, ornaments, head pieces, and large initials, were designed by the author.]

Vellum; 14½ x 10½ x 2 in.

FINE PRINTING

Cabinet B
Shelf 3
No. 10

Four centuries of fine printing, 1500-1914

see MORISON, STANLEY. Four centuries of fine printing...

FINIGUERRA, MOZO (Tommaso)

Cabinet I
Shelf 4
No. 3

Chalcography, the invention of by Mozo Finiguerra (ca. 1440), account of.

See Introduction to Ottley's "Collection of 125 fac-similes of scarce and curious prints" ... London, 1828.

FINE, ORONCE

Cabinet 26
Shelf 1
No. 17

Illustrator of books, Oronce Fine. By A.F. Johnson.
Bibliographical account.
Article in the Gutenberg-Gesellschaft Jahrbuch 1928. pp.107-9.

FINE PRINTING

Cabinet S
Shelf 4
No. 105

Influence of fine printing. A lecture by W. Arthur Cole. Delivered at the Carnegie Institute of Technology, Feb. 9, 1928. Pittsburg. Department of Printing Carnegie Institute of Technology, 1929.

Boards; 8-3/4 x 5-5/8 x ¼ in.

FINIGUERRA, THOMASO

Cabinet T
Shelf 2
No. 6
[vol.i]

Copperplate engravings, account of the first specimens of: facsimile of the same.

see

DIBDIN'S "Typographic Antiquities"... London, 1810-19, vol.i, pp.iv, 363.

FINE ARTS PRESS, JOHN HENRY NASH

Cabinet G
Shelf 4
No. 6.03

Imprint of 1933. University of Oregon. John Henry Nash, Fine Arts Press.

See IMPRINTS, United States. University of Oregon...

FINE PRINTING

Cabinet B
Shelf 3
No. 12

Modern fine printing...

see MORISON, STANLEY. Modern fine printing...London, 1925

FINIGUERRA, THOMASO

Cabinet PP
Shelf 1
No. 29

Engraving on copper, the first discoverer of. Florence, 1460.

See pp. 273, 274, Vol. I, Horne's Introduction to the histroy of bibliography... London, 1814.

FINLAND

Cabinet NN Shelf 2 No. 13

Newspapers and journalism

see NEWSPAPERS, Finland. Literature

FINLAND

Cabinet T Shelf 5 No. 135

(A) Short history of printing in Finland

See PEDDIE, R.A. Printing, a short history of the art...p.235

FINLEY, EBENEZER B.

Cabinet 62 Shelf 2 No. 24

Defrees, J.D., Public Printer, to Ebenezer B. Finley. A review of Mr.Finley's report on the Government Printing Office. Washington D.C., Feb.19, 1879.

Item inserted in book with title "HISTORY OF THE GOVERNMENT PRINTING OFFICE".. by R. W. Kerr.

FINNISH LANGUAGE CHARACTERS

Cabinet Shelf No.

See LANGUAGE CHARACTERS. Finnish...

FIOL, SWEIPOLD

Cabinet AA Shelf 5 No. 44

Slavorum primi libri impressi (Notae librorum a Fiole, Cravoviae, 1491. cyrillicis characteribus impressorum ...

See Printing, Historical, Russia: Origines artis typographicae Ucrainorum ... Leopoldi, 1924.

FIRESTONE, HARVEY S. JR.

Cabinet QQ Shelf 2 No. 33

Romance and drama of the rubber industry. Radio talks delivered by Harvey S. Firestone Jr., Sept., 1931 to Sept., 1932. Portraits.

Paper; 8-5/8 x 5¾ in.

FIRST EDITION CLUB. England

Cabinet T Shelf 3 No. 5

Book Clubs and Printing Societies of Great Britain and Ireland. By Harold Williams. Printed at the Curwen Press, and published at the First Edition Club, London 1929.

Linen covered boards; 9¼ x 6-3/4 x 3/4 in.

FIRST EDITION CLUB. England

Cabinet U Shelf 3 No. 113

Book of signs which contains all manner of symbols used from the earliest times to the middle ages by primitive peoples and Early Christians. Collected, drawn and explained by Rudolf Koch. Translated by Vyvyan Holland. London 1930.

Cloth; 9½ x 7 x 3/8 in.

FIRST EDITION CLUB (London)

Cabinet M Shelf 4 No. 2.01

History of First Edition Club (from 1922), with rules and list of exhibitors and books published. n.d. circa 1928

Small brochures, in manila envelope

FIRST EDITION CLUB

Cabinet PP Shelf 2 No. 37

List of books published by the First Edition Club, London (1929). Includes list of members, benefactors, and of exhibitions.

Brochure, in manila envelope

FIRST OCCURRENCES

Cabinet 27 Shelf 1 No. 2

Advertisment, the first known, the paper called the "Impartial Intelligencer", published in the year 1648, in Candish, Suffolk, England.

Brief item in the Printers' Circular, vol.2, No.11, Jan., 1868, p.369

FIRST OCCURRENCES

Cabinet LL Shelf 4 No. 2

Advertisement newspaper (the first) appeared in the "Impartial Intelligencer", an English paper, in the year 1648.

Notice in article "Advertisements" By Kate A. Sanborn. Excerpt from The Galaxy, Aug., 1912.

Item 5 in book with binder's title "Various items on advertising".

FIRST OCCURRENCES.

Cabinet V Shelf 6 No. 13

Almanacks, the first in France. Historical account with brief notices alphabetically arranged. With facsimiles.

Article in the Bulletin Official de l'Union Syndicale des Maitres Imprimeurs. Paris, December, 1925.

Paper; 12½ x 9¼ x 1 in.

FIRST OCCURRENCES

Cabinet QQ Shelf 3 No. 5

America, first newspaper in.

see WHEILDON, WILLIAM. First newspaper in America...

FIRST OCCURRENCES

Cabinet LL Shelf 4 No. 2

American advertisement, the first appeared in the "News Letter" published in Boston in 1704.

Notice of the above in article "Advertisements" By Kate A. Sanborn. Excerpt from The Galaxy, Aug., 1912.

Item 5 in book with binder's title "Various items on advertising."

FIRST OCCURRENCES

Cabinet R Shelf 5 No. 148

(First) American edition of Josephus' History of The Jews. Printed by William Durell, New York. 1792. With many copper engravings: Account of the book by W. L. Andrews; an excerpt from The Bookman, Feb. 1900.

Excerpt 11 in volume "Chap Books, Almanacs, Annuals, etc.

FIRST OCCURRENCES

Cabinet S Shelf 6 No. 9

American edition of Shakespeare: prospectus of the first...

See SHAKESPEARIANA. Curious antique of 1794...

FIRST OCCURRENCES

Cabinet CC Shelf 2 No. 35

American system of interchangeable type bodies. Specimen book of the first point system t types. Marder, Luse & Co. Chicago Type Foundry. Chicago and St. Louis, 1881.

Cloth; 11¾ x 9½ x ⅝ in.

FIRST OCCURRENCES

Cabinet BB Shelf 1 No. 2

American Type Founders Co. First specimen book issued bearing the name of. The Blue Book containing specimens of type, printing machinery, printing material. American Type Founders Company. Central Type Foundry Branch, Fourth and Elm Streets, St. Louis Mo. 1895.
Has prices.

Leather; $7\frac{1}{4}$ x 5 x $1\frac{3}{4}$ in.

FIRST OCCURRENCES

Cabinet R Shelf 4 No. 143

Baltimore-Town, The first book printed in, Nicholas Hasselbach, printer. The book reprinted with a sketch of Hasselbach's life and work. By George W. McCreary. Baltimore, 1903. Facsimile.

Boards; $8\frac{3}{4}$ x $6\frac{1}{4}$ in.

FIRST OCCURRENCES

Cabinet FF Shelf 1 No. 69

Bible, first to be printed from stereotypes in America. By D. & G. Bruce, New York, 1815.

Copy present to Typographic Library by Wallace Bruce. Pasted in front A. L. S. Wallace Bruce.

Morocco; $6\frac{3}{4}$ x 4 x 1-5/8 in.

FIRST OCCURRENCES

Cabinet BB Shelf 1 No. 13

American Type Founders Co. First specimen book issued by them for Mexico, Central and South America. Libro de Muestras de tipos. American Type Founders Co., New York, Corner Rose and Duane Streets, Philadelphia Nos. 606 to 614 Sansom Street.
Preface is dated Dec. 1896.

Cloth; $9\frac{1}{2}$ x $6\frac{1}{2}$ x $1\frac{1}{8}$ in.

FIRST OCCURRENCES

Cabinet 18 Shelf 1 No. 14

Bank note, first in 1718.

Note in "Zeitschrift für Bücherfreunde"...1913-14 (part 1), p.62

FIRST OCCURRENCES

Cabinet II Shelf 6 No. 5

Bible for the blind, the first: The Gospel of St. John printed with angular types, the invention of James Gall. Edinburgh, 1832.

See GALL, JAMES. Historical sketch of the origin of literature for the blind... Edinburgh, 1834, pp.134-35.

FIRST OCCURRENCES

Cabinet R Shelf 5 No. 49

American Types, The first work with. By Lawrence C. Wroth ... Cambridge, 1925.
Biblio-historical account of the Pennsylvania Mercury, 1775, "The first work with American Types".

Half morocco; $9\frac{3}{4}$ x 6-3/8 in.

FIRST OCCURRENCES

Cabinet CC Shelf 1 No. 6

Barnhart Bros. & Spindler (Great Western Type Foundry) Chicago, 1873. First Specimen Book of this foundry.
Has price list.

Cloth; $9\frac{1}{4}$ x $6\frac{1}{4}$ x $\frac{3}{4}$ in.

FIRST OCCURRENCES

Cabinet S Shelf 4 No. 110

Bibles, the first published in America.

see
Myer, John Nicholas. "Colonists' Bible a "Bootleg' Book"....

FIRST OCCURRENCES.

Cabinet S Shelf 5 No. 17

Americas first lithography, by H. Merian Allen, in The International Studio, Jan., 1917. Illus.

Bound in collection "Miscellaneous items relating to Printing," item 12.

FIRST OCCURRENCES

Cabinet R Shelf 5 No. 132

Bay Psalm Book: First book printed in English North America. Printed by Stephen Daye, at Cambridge, 1640.
A facsimile reprint with preface by Wilberforce Eames, New York, 1903.

Boards; 8 x $5\frac{1}{8}$ in.

FIRST OCCURRENCES

Cabinet U Shelf 5 No. 68

Birmingham Journal (Warren's), 1733. Facsimile and description of Birmingham's first newspaper.

See
HILL, JOSEPH. Book makers of old Birmingham...1907.

FIRST OCCURRENCES

Cabinet AA Shelf 3 No. 36

Antwerp, the first newspaper in. Nieuwe Tydinghe, 1610-1629: Abraham Verhoeven, printer publisher. By Jos. Van der Branden. Antwerp, 1902.
Dutch text.

Half morocco; $7\frac{3}{4}$ x 5-1/8 in.

FIRST OCCURRENCES.

Cabinet 18 Shelf 2 No. 1

(Belgian Newspapers) The first Belgian newspapers were called "Nieuwe Tijdinghen" afterwards "Post-Tijdinghan," and were published in Antwerp by Abraham Verhoeven, 1604.

In Zeitschrift für Bücherfreunde, 1915-16, p.144.

FIRST OCCURRENCES

Cabinet II Shelf 6 No. 1

Blind printing for, the first, Paris, 1786. Essai sur l'education des aveugles. Par [Valentin] Hauy. Paris, 1876.

Calf; 10 x 8 in.

FIRST OCCURRENCES

Cabinet PP Shelf 1 No. 21

Australian book, first printed in Hobart Town in 1817.

see
GARNETT, RICHARD. Essays in librarianship...p. 125.

FIRST OCCURRENCES

Cabinet QQ Shelf 4 No. 20

Bible, first printed in America. (Brief notes on.)

see
BISHOP, J. LEANDER. History of American manufacturers...Philadelphia, 1868, pp. 157, 158, 159, 181, 183.

FIRST OCCURRENCES

Cabinet R Shelf 5 No. 2.02

"Book of Common Prayer", the first edition ever printed on the American Continent. Printed by William Bradford, 1710. Article by Horatio Gates Jones, 1870.

Brochure, in envelope.

FIRST OCCURRENCES

Cabinet S
Shelf 5
No. 25

Book printed between Seneca - Lake and the Pacific Ocean, the first. By J.G. Shea. Bibliographical notes.
Excerpt from Historical Magazine, Feb., 1872.

In box labeled "History of Printing, United States. Miscellaneous items".

FIRST OCCURRENCES.

Cabinet F
Shelf 1
No. 17

Book printed in black and red in the British American Colonies, The first. Boston, 1726: Bartholomew and Samuel Kneel...

Leather; 13$\frac{1}{2}$ x 8$\frac{1}{2}$ x 3 in. Evans I, 2828, p.365.

FIRST OCCURRENCES

Cabinet I
Shelf 1
No. 5

Bookbinder, the first engraving of a.

See AMMAN (JOST). Panoplia omnium illiberalium mechanicarum...1568, Frankfurt, p.21.

FIRST OCCURRENCES

Cabinet S
Shelf 5
No. 25

"Books printed in 1446 with a date". By S.H.P. Middleton, Conn., 1858.
Relates to first books, European and American, 1450 to 1795.

Excerpt from Historical Magazine, June, 1858.

In box labeled History of Printing, United States. Miscellaneous items.

FIRST OCCURRENCES

Cabinet CC
Shelf 2
No. 3

Boston Type Foundry, established in 1820. First type foundry in New England. Event mentioned in the Specimen Book of 1885.
Includes a history of the firm, and has a woodcut showing the Boston Type Foundry in Salem Street at it appeared from 1823 to 1830.

Cloth; 10$\frac{3}{4}$ x 9$\frac{1}{4}$ x $\frac{3}{4}$ in.

FIRST OCCURRENCES

Cabinet R
Shelf 3
No. 71

Bradford Prayer Book, printed under the auspices of Trinity Church, New York, 1710: The first edition of that book ever printed on the American Continent. [Pamphlet]. Privately printed for H. G. Jones, 1870.
Historical account. Bound in with publications of the Historical Society of Pennsylvania. No. 13.

Half morocco; 9$\frac{1}{4}$ x 6 in.

FIRST OCCURRENCES

Cabinet II
Shelf 6
No. 24

Braille, revised, a copy of the first book embossed in. "The Deserter". By Richard Harding Davis. The Perkins Institution for the Blind, Watertown, Mass. 1917.

Paper; 10$\frac{1}{4}$ x 13$\frac{1}{2}$ x $\frac{3}{4}$ in.

FIRST OCCURRENCES

Cabinet
Shelf
No.

Brazil, first book printed in.

See Brazil. First book printed in.

FIRST OCCURRENCE

Cabinet D
Shelf 1
No. 21

Buda, Hungary, 1473. The first book printed in.

See Incunabula. Chronica Hungarorum.

FIRST OCCURRENCES.

Stack A
Shelf 1&2
Number 62

Caille, Jean de la: The first historian of printing. See Bullen, Henry Lewis, Caille, Jean de la.

FIRST OCCURRENCES

Cabinet S
Shelf 5
No. 41

California, the first newspaper in, the "Californian", published by Colton & Semple, Monterey, 1846.

see PRINTING, HISTORICAL. United States. (California....New York, 1927, p.12

FIRST OCCURRENCES

Cabinet S
Shelf 5
No. 41

California, the first printing in Monterey, 1825 A.V. Zamorano, printer.

See PRINTING, HISTORICAL. United States. (California)....Plandone Press, N.Y. 1927, p.3

FIRST OCCURRENCES

Cabinet NN
Shelf 2
No. 13

California journalism; an account of "The Transcript", the first daily newspaper established in California in 1850. Article by J.M. Scanland.

Item 24 in volume with binder's title "Various newspapers and periodicals".

FIRST OCCURRENCES

Cabinet QQ
Shelf 3
No. 9

Californian newspaper, the first issued at Monterey, August 22, 1846, by Rev. Walter Colton.
Account in Colton's "Three years in California". Illus. New York, 1850. See p. 38 and after.

Cloth; 7$\frac{3}{4}$ x 5$\frac{1}{4}$ in.

FIRST OCCURRENCES

Cabinet 18
Shelf 1
No. 14

Cartography, 560 B.C.

Note in Zeitschrift für Bücherfreunde" ...1913-14 (part 1) p.62

FIRST OCCURRENCES

Cabinet EE
Shelf 5
No. 4

Catalogue, first, (1888) John Thomson (Colt's Armory Press).

See THOMSON, JOHN (Colt's Armory Press) Inclusive illus. catalogue...

FIRST OCCURRENCES

Cabinet EE
Shelf 5
No. 17

Catalogue (first) showing electric motors attached to platemaking machines. F. Wesel Mfg. Co's catalogue of electrotyping, stereotyping and photo-engraving machinery. Brooklyn, n.d. (1897)
"The first platemaking plant to be operated by connected individual electric motors was that of N.Y. Life Insurance Co. The first platemaking plant sold with connected electric motors was a Wesel plant made for the Galvanoplastik Co. of Berlin, Germany."

Boards; 10 x 7 in. H.L. Bullen

FIRST OCCURRENCES

Cabinet NN
Shelf 2
No. 12

Catholic newspaper, the first established in New York City, April 2, 1825.

Brief account

Item 19 in volume with binder's title "Various newspapers and periodicals"-2.

FIRST OCCURRENCES

Cabinet T Shelf 2 No. 45

Caxton's hand-bill advertisement, ante 1480. The first broadside printed in England. From the copy in Bodley's Library of Oxford. [A fragment in] Facsimiles illustrating the labours of William Caxton...By Frances Compton Price, London, 1877.

Half morocco; 11-3/8 x 8-7/8 in.

FIRST OCCURRENCES

Cabinet RR Shelf 6 No. 13

Cornstalk, the world's first newspaper printed on paper made from. The Sunday Commercial News, Danville, Ill., Dec., 16, 1928.

Item in manila envelope.

FIRST OCCURRENCES

Cabinet R Shelf 3 No. 203

Daily newspapers in the United States, the first.

see MOORE, JOHN W. Historical, Biographical, and Miscellaneous Gatherings...p.213

FIRST OCCURRENCES

Cabinet PP Shelf 1 No. 21

China, first book printed by Europeans in 1589.

see GARNETT, RICHARD. Essays in librarianship...p. 120.

FIRST OCCURRENCES

Cabinet A Shelf 2 No. 43

Cornstalks, First newspaper printed on paper made from: The Sunday Commercial-News. Danville, Ill., Dec., 16, 1928.

Cloth; 22 x 17½ in (2 copies in Library)

FIRST OCCURRENCES

Cabinet Q Shelf 4 No. 1

Directory, 1786, the first New York City.

see DIRECTORIES, CITY. New York City, 1786...

FIRST OCCURRENCES

Cabinet R Shelf 3 No. 203

Connecticut, first press in.

see MOORE, JOHN W. Historical, Biographical, and Miscellaneous Gatherings...p.19

FIRST OCCURRENCES.

Cabinet M Shelf 1 No. 28

Cylinder Press, First book printed on a. Bensley and Son. London, 1817.

See Imprints, England. Bensley and Son. London, 1817. The Institutiones of Psysiology ...

FIRST OCCURRENCES

Cabinet S Shelf 6 No. 8

Directory, the first printed in New York, 1786, by Sheprard Kollock.

See EARLY PRINTING IN AMERICA (U.S.) Literature (New York City, 1786) Shepard Kollock, printer...

FIRST OCCURRENCES

Cabinet II Shelf 4 No. 49

Constantinople, 1730, first European book printed in. "Grammaire Turque...(Printer) Ibraham Mutafarrika.

Contemporary native binding; half calf, 8-3/8 x 6 x 7/8 in.

FIRST OCCURRENCES

Cabinet S Shelf 3 No. 91

Cylinder press, the first in America.

See p. 169 of Orcutt's "The Kingdom of Books." Boston, 1927.

FIRST OCCURRENCES

Cabinet 26 Shelf 1 No. 21

"Doctrina Christiana", 1544, the first book printed in South America.

Bio-bibliographical essay.

In "Gutenberg-Gesellschaft Jahrbuch, 1931", pp. 214-220.

FIRST OCCURRENCES

Cabinet J Shelf 3 No. 11

Copper plate engraving in England, circa 1550, the first example of. by Thomas Gemini (or Geminus)

See SALAMAN, MALCOLM C. Old engravers of England.... p.2.

FIRST OCCURRENCES

Cabinet OO Shelf 3 No. 36

Daily newspaper, the first in the United States, "Philadelphia North American", 1784.

see BULLEN, HENRY LEWIS. Century old newspapers...1920.

FIRST OCCURRENCES

Cabinet J Shelf 3 No. 17

Earliest dated wood-cut. "St. Christopher", (1423) Reproduction.

See CHAPIN, WILLIS O. Masters and masterpieces of engraving...p.8.

FIRST OCCURRENCES

Cabinet 18 Shelf 1 No. 14

Copperplate printing, the first in 1420.

Note in "Zeitschrift für Bücherfreunde" ... (part 1) p.62

FIRST OCCURRENCES

Cabinet KK Shelf 6 No. 2

Daily newspapers,first established by women.

see WOMEN EDITORS. Women in journalism. First daily newspapers...

FIRST OCCURRENCES

Cabinet LL Shelf 1 No. 3

(Earliest extended German text book of printing.) Die wol-eingerichtete Buchdruckerey... Nurnberg: Johann Andrea Endters seel. Sohn and Erben, 1721).

Library has also the 1733 issue of above, LL/1/4.

The typography in two colors very characteristic of the period in Germany.

FIRST OCCURRENCES

Cabinet 83 Shelf 1 No. 38.01

Earliest known Specimen of Types used for advertising purposes, n.d., circa 1467-1469.
A broadside advertisement of the books printed by or for sale by Peter Schoeffer, with specimen of types as follows "hec est littera psalterii".

Photostat copy in envelope.

FIRST OCCURRENCES

Cabinet U Shelf 1 No. 19

English Bible, the first printed.

See ARBER, EDWARD. Facsimile Texts. The first English New Testament...London, 1871.

FIRST OCCURRENCES

Stack A Shelf 1&2 Number 82

First American Type Specimen Books. The earliest American. Printed and issued by Isaiah Thomas. Worcester, Mass. 1785. By Henry Lewis Bullen. In Collectanea Typographica, The Inland Printer. Vol. 82. March 1929. p. 90. Facsimile title page.

FIRST OCCURRENCES.

Cabinet Shelf No.

The earliest paper in France: The Journal des Petites Affiches, founded in 1612.

See Journalism, France: Newspaper and Periodical Press of France.

FIRST OCCURRENCES

Cabinet I Shelf 1 No. 5

Engraving of type foundry, the first.

See AMMAN (JOST). Panoplia omnium illiberalium mechanicarum...1568, Frankfurt, p.16.

FIRST OCCURRENCES

Cabinet D Shelf 3 No. 55

First attempt at a Phonetic Alphabet.

See Alphabets, Utopiensium.

FIRST OCCURRENCES

Cabinet U Shelf 5 No. 52

Edinburgh Gazette, 1699 first Scottish newspaper
See p.141 Bibliographical Notes: The Gentleman's Magazine.

FIRST OCCURRENCES.

Cabinet 40 Shelf 1 No. 36

Estienne, Henri. The first book printed by him. Paris, 1554.

Title: Anacreontis. Teij odae. Ab Henrico Stephano luce & Latinitate nunc primum Stephanus, M.D.LIIII. Ex privilegio regis.

Full morocco, gilt; 8 x $5\frac{3}{4}$ x 5/8 in. Brunet 1, 250.

FIRST OCCURRENCES

Cabinet RR Shelf 4 No. 3

First Bible printed in America. The Indian Bible printed in 1661 by John Eliot with the assistance of James Printer, an Indian: See The Nipmucks and their country, a pamphlet.

Bound with other items in "Paper-making Pamphlets, historical and technical," item 9.

FIRST OCCURRENCES

Cabinet FF Shelf 1 No. 6

Electrotype from copperplate engraving; the first in America. Boston, 1842.
Method of making described on p. 204 of Davis's Manual of Magnetism ... Boston, 1842.

Cloth; 7-$\frac{1}{4}$ x 5 in.

FIRST OCCURRENCES.

Cabinet S Shelf 5 No. 21

First aboriginal newspaper on the American Continent, The Phoenix, edited by Elias Bondinot, organ of the Cherokee Nation.

See Journalism, United States: Journalism among the Cherokee Indians.

FIRST OCCURRENCES.

Cabinet F Shelf 3 No. 46

First Bible printed in New Jersey: The Holy Bible, containing the Old and New Testament...

Imprint: Trenton: Printed and sold by Isaac Collins, 1791.

Leather; 11 x 9 x 3 in. Evans 8, 23184, p.124.

FIRST OCCURRENCES

Cabinet FF Shelf 1 No. 6

Electrotype from wood cut, the first made in America, Boston, 1842.
Method of making described on p.92 Fig.63, of Davis's Manual of Magnetism...Boston, 1842.

Cloth; $7\frac{1}{4}$ x 5 in.

FIRST OCCURRENCES

Cabinet F Shelf 1 No. 9

First American Bible. A leaf from a copy translated into Indian language by John Eliot, and printed at Cambridge in New England in the year 1663. With an account of the translator and of the two printers who produced the book, by George Parker Winship.

Stamped cloth; 7-7/8 x 6 x $\frac{1}{4}$ in.

FIRST OCCURRENCES.

Cabinet 20 Shelf 2 No. 10

First book decorated with copperplate engravings: Monte Santo di Dio, by Bishop A. Bettino. 1477.
For brief account see Printing, Historical, Italy. Florence. Nikolaus Laurentii und seine Danteausgabe vom jahr 1481.

In Zeitschrift fur Bucherfreunde, 1921, pp. 78-80.

FIRST OCCURRENCES

Cabinet FF Shelf 1 No. 8

Electrotyping. First electrotype actually used in printing appeared in the London Journal for April, 1840.

For account, see Smee's Elements of electro-metallurgy ...London, 1843. P.XXII

FIRST OCCURRENCES.

Cabinet S Shelf 5 No. 14

First American paper money: Facsimile reproduction in Harper's New Monthly magazine, Feb., 1862.

Bound with other itmes in collection "Printing Processes," item 11.

FIRST OCCURRENCES

Cabinet F Shelf 1 No. 121

First book printed in Canada, 1776.

Réglement de la confrerie de l'adoration perpétuelle du S. Sacrement.....

Imprint: A Montreal: Chez F. Mesplet & C. Berger, Imprimeurs & Libraires: près le Marché, 1776.

Limp morocco; $4\frac{1}{2}$ x $3\frac{1}{4}$ x 1/8 in. Thomas 2, p.181.

FIRST OCCURRENCES.

Cabinet S Shelf 5 No. 21

(First book printed in English-speaking North America.) The Massachusetts Bay Psalm Book, 1640: Its origin and history by Clement Ferguson, in Magazine of American History.

Bound with other items in "Excerpts relating to Printing in America." pp.112-113.

FIRST OCCURRENCES

Cabinet FF Shelf 1 No. 63

First book stereotyped by the new (Stanhope) process.

See Freylinghausen, John A. Abstract---of the Christian Religion...1804

FIRST OCCURRENCES

Cabinet A Shelf 1 No. 28

First newspaper established in Ontario, Canada, Jan. 16th, 1821: Centennial issues of the Brockville Recorder 1821-1921

FIRST OCCURRENCES

Cabinet F Shelf 2 No. 65

First book printed in New Hampshire: Good News from a Far Country.....By Jonathan Parsons. Portsmouth, 1756.

Imprint: Portsmouth, in New Hampshire: Printed and sold by Daniel Fowle, 1756.

Leather; 7 x $4\frac{1}{2}$ in. Evans 3, 7746; p.146.

FIRST OCCURRENCES

Cabinet I Shelf 2 No. 46

First dated and published halftone was in New York Daily Graphic, March 4, 1880. Method invented and halftone made by Stephen H. Horgan who also invented the apparatus which made possible the lithographic method used in the N. Y. Daily Graphic at that time.

see HORGAN, STEPHEN H. Horgan's Halftone...Chicago, 1913, p. 12.

FIRST OCCURRENCES

Cabinet R Shelf 5 No. 105

(First) Newspaper to be published in the Gulf States: "Moniteur de la Louisiane," New Orleans, La. 1794.

See p. 53 McMurtrie's "Early printing in New Orleans".

FIRST OCCURRENCES

Cabinet R Shelf 3 No. 181

[First Book printed in New York]. Reprint of the first book printed in New York, 1696, by William Bradford: A letter of advice to a young gentleman ... By R. L. With an introduction and notes by Frank C. Erb, New York, 1907. Facsimile.

Cloth; 6 x $4\frac{3}{4}$ in.

FIRST OCCURRENCES

Cabinet RR Shelf 6 No. 12

(First) Farm paper printed on paper made from cornstalk: The Prairie Farmer. Chicago, Ill. Dec., 1928. (2 copies in Library).

Buckram; $12\frac{1}{4}$ x $10\frac{1}{4}$ in.

FIRST OCCURRENCES.

Stack A Shelf 1&2 Number 61

First Newspapers: A list of newspapers and dates to serve as a starting point for further research into the history of newspapers. compiled by Henry Lewis Bullen, for (Collectanea Typographica) in The Inland Printer, vol.LXI, p. 720.

FIRST OCCURRENCES

Stack A Shelf 1&2 Number 82

First book printed on a cylinder press. London 1817.

See Bullen, Henry Lewis. Inventor's (The) account of the invention of the Cylinder Press.

FIRST OCCURRENCES.

Cabinet 75 Shelf 1&2 No. 1

First Greek book printed in England by Reynold Wolfe, 1543.

A brief account of this book and other matters pertinent to Wolfe's activities.

In Transactions of the Bibliographical Society, vol. XIII, pp. 171 - 192.

FIRST OCCURRENCES.

Cabinet Shelf No.

First newspapers in England and France.

See Journalism France: Progress of the Newspaper Press in France.

FIRST OCCURRENCES

Cabinet R Shelf 5 No. 15

(First) Book printed South of Massachusetts. Not Leed's Templeof Wisdom, but William Penn's Excellent Privilege of Liberty and Property: A lost work by the founder of Pennsylvania By C. R. Hildeburn.

In volume "Early Printing and printers in America. Excerpts from Pennsylvania Magazine." p. 61.

Half morocco; 9-7/8 x 6-5/8 in.

FIRST OCCURRENCES.

Stack A Shelf 1&2 Number 66

First Magazine and its originator, by Henry Lewis Bullen, in The Inland Printer, vol. LXVI, p.341.

FIRST OCCURRENCES

Cabinet R Shelf 6 No. 6

(First) Paper established in this country: The Boston News-Letter, April 24, 1704. Account in Samuel Abbott Green's "Facsimile reproductions relating to various subjects." Boston, 1903.

Cloth; 15 x $10\frac{3}{4}$ in.

FIRST OCCURRENCES

Cabinet F Shelf 1 No. 88

The first book printed with Greek types in America. Epicteti Enchiridion. ex editione Joannis Upton, accurate expressum.

Imprint: Philadelphia: Impensis Mathaei Carey, 1792.

Calf; $5\frac{3}{4}$ x $3\frac{1}{2}$ in. Not in Evans.

FIRST OCCURRENCES

Cabinet S Shelf 5 No. 21

First Newspaper at Lexington, Ky: The Kentucke Gazette, Aug. 11, 1787. Facsimile.

See Journalism, American, early: First newspaper West of the Alleghanies.

FIRST OCCURRENCEC

Cabinet NN Shelf 2 No. 13

First printing press brought to the American Colonies in 1693.: First product of printing press was "The Freeman's Oath"; second an almanac; third the Celebrated Day Psalm Book in metre...

Item 26 in volume with binder's title "Various newspapers and periodicals"-1

FIRST OCCURRENCES.

Cabinet S — Shelf 5 — No. 21

First religious newspaper published in the world.

See Periodicals, religious: A Literary Curiosity.

FIRST OCCURRENCES

Cabinet V — Shelf 4 — No. 28

(French Newspapers). The first French newspaper the "Gazette" established in 1630 by Théophraste Renaudot.

See pp. 61-68: Débuts de l'Imprimerie en France. Par Arthur Christian. Paris, 1905.

Half morocco; 11½ x 8 x 1¼ in.

FIRST OCCURRENCES.

Cabinet 75 — Shelf 1 — No. 13

Greek printer in England, Reynold Wolfe, the first.

See Sayle, C. Wolfe, Reynold [King's printer in Latin, Greek and Hebrew...]

FIRST OCCURRENCES

Cabinet FF — Shelf 5 — No. 50

First sheet printed on a power printing press by Frederick Koenig: Sig. H., part 2, commencing p. 113, of the "Annual Register of 1810.

With portraits and clippings.

Tree calf; 8¾ x 5¼ x 1½ in.

FIRST OCCURRENCES

Cabinet R — Shelf 5 — No. 32 — 2 vols.

(Geistlichs Magazine), first paper printed with American type.

See pp. 45-46 in Sachse's German Sectarians of Pennsylvania, 1708-1742. Vol. I.

FIRST OCCURRENCES

Cabinet F — Shelf 1 — No. 37

Greek printing executed in the North American Colonies, by John Green and Joseph Russell, Boston. 1761. Pietas et gratulatio Collegii Cantabrigiensis apud Novanglos.

Full morocco; 10¼ x 8 x 3/8 in.

FIRST OCCURRENCES.

Stack A — Shelf 1&2 — Number 67

First typefoundry in Chicago. See Bullen, Henry Lewis, Collectanea Typographia, Inland Printer, vol. 67, p. 223.

FIRST OCCURRENCES

Cabinet J — Shelf 5 — No. 19

German book, the first printed with date and wood engravings [Bamberg, 1461].

See FACSIMILES (Der) Edelstein von Ulrich Boner [Bamberg 1461].

FIRST OCCURRENCES.

Cabinet G — Shelf 4 — No. 34

Greek type first cast, and the first book printed with Greek types in the United States of America. Xenophontis de Cyri Institutione. Libri octo. Excudebat Johannis Watts, Philadelphia, 1806.

Calf; 9 x 5½ in.

FIRST OCCURRENCES

Cabinet U — Shelf 5 — No. 24

Foliation, or leef-numbers first used.

see POLLARD, A.W. Fine Books... London, 1912, p.62

FIRST OCCURRENCES

Cabinet F — Shelf 1 — No. 75

German printing in America: B. Franklin, Philadelphia, 1730: The first book printed in German in America. Facsimile.

Title: Mystische und sehr geheyme spruecht....

Imprint: Zu Philadelphia: gedruckt bey B. Franklin in jahr 1730.

Half morocco; 7¼ x 5¼ in.

FIRST OCCURRENCES

Cabinet MM — Shelf 5 — No. 6

Hand Press with double levers, similar to those used in present Washington Hand Press, invented in 1816 by John I. Wells, Hartford, Conn.

See description and account pp.335-337, Adams' Typographia...Philadelphia, 1837.

FIRST OCCURRENCES

Cabinet F — Shelf 1 — No. 72

Franklin, B: The first book printed by him as a master printer. Philadelphia, 1728.

See Imprints, United States. Franklin, B., and Hugh Meredith, Philadelphia, 1728.

FIRST OCCURRENCES

Cabinet F — Shelf 2 — No. 21

German Types: The first book printed in German Types in America. Germantown, Pa., 1739: Christopher Sauer, printer.

See Early Printing in Pennsylvania. Germantown, 1739: Christopher Sauer.

FIRST OCCURRENCES

Cabinet 21 — Shelf 2 — No. 2.01

House Organ, the first type founders ever issued. The Western Advertiser, Cincinnati, Ohio, Jan., 1839, vol.1, No.1. Issued by J.A. James, Type and Stereotype Foundry, Cincinnati, O.

Item in manila envelope

FIRST OCCURRENCES

Cabinet PP — Shelf 1 — No. 20

Free Library in the United States observes its 100th birthday. Illus.

Excerpt from N. Y. Times, April 2, 1933, and pasted on back cover of OGLE'S: Free Library, its history...London, 1897.

FIRST OCCURRENCES

Cabinet R — Shelf 4 — No. 34

Germantown, Pa. Important dates in Germantown history. A circular, 8pp. The first paper mill (1690); the first type was cast (1772); and the first Bible in a European language (1743) in America, etc.

Item in manila envelope.

FIRST OCCURRENCES

Cabinet 18 — Shelf 1 — No. 14

Hydraulic printing press, the first.

Note in Zeitschrift für bücherfreunde... 1913-1914 (part 1) p.62

FIRST OCCURRENCES

Cabinet C Shelf 3 No. 13 to 26

Illustrated evening newspaper; The Daily Graphic, the first.

See JOURNALISM, ILLUSTRATED (The) Daily Graphic...

FIRST OCCURRENCES

Cabinet PP Shelf 1 No. 21

Japan, on printing in.

see

GARNETT. RICHARD. Essays in librarianship...pp. 121, 122.

FIRST OCCURRENCES

Cabinet 6 Shelf 1 No. 2

Jenson, Nicolas: The first book printed by him at Venice, 1470.

See Incunabula. Eusebius Pamphilius: De evangelica praeparatione.....

FIRST OCCURRENCES.

Cabinet I Shelf 3 No. 1

Illustrated natural history, the first. "Ortus Sanitatis" by Von Cube, 1480.

See BIBLIOGRAPHY. Natural History, the first illustrated ...

Item 13.

FIRST OCCURRENCES

Cabinet NN Shelf 6 No. 2.01

Japan, the first newspaper said to have been printed with moveable wooden types.

"Shimbun Zassiji", January 30th 1876.

In envelope.

FIRST OCCURRENCES

Cabinet R Shelf 4 No. 144

Kansas, the first printing press operated in the State of.

see

KANSAS. Mystery of the Meeker Press...

FIRST OCCURRENCES

Cabinet OO Shelf 3 No. 39

Illustrated paper, the first. Account of.

see

Chap. XX, p. 217, WARRENS'S "JOURNALISM"...London, 1922.

FIRST OCCURRENCES

Cabinet II Shelf 4 No. 9

Japanese book (said to be the first) printed from individual engraved characters, circa 18th century. An experiment which proved less satisfactory than printing from pages wholly engraved.

Paper; 10-7/8 x 8 x 3/8 in.

FIRST OCCURRENCES

Cabinet R Shelf 5 No. 33

Lancaster Gazette. The first daily newspaper in Lancaster County. The oldest newspaper in Lancaster Co. A paper read by F.R. Diffenderfer before the Lancaster County Historical Society, Oct. 2, 1896.

Has facsimile of the Lancaster Gazette. Bound in with other pamphlets.

Half morocco; $9\frac{3}{4}$ x $6\frac{1}{4}$ in.

FIRST OCCURRENCES

Cabinet S Shelf 5 No. 12

Indian Primer and Bible (Cambridge, Mass. 1669) John Eliot the Apostle of the Indians. By James De Normandie, in the New England Magazine, Nov. 1896. Facsimiles, Illus.

Bound in collection "Pamphlets and excerpts relating to typographical matters", item 19.

FIRST OCCURRENCES

Cabinet NN Shelf 6 No. 2.02

Japanese newspaper, (Domestic and Foreign News) (Naigai Shimpo), No. 1-25 (omit No. 7) 4th Month 1865.

This is said to be the very first newspaper printed from wood blocks.

Item in exhibition cabinet, stack end of room.

FIRST OCCURRENCES

Cabinet LL Shelf 2 No. 5

Lining system of type bodies first proposed.

See pp.52-56 Smalian's "Practisches Handbuch"...Danzig, 1874.

Boards; $7\frac{1}{2}$ x 5 in.

FIRST OCCURRENCES

Cabinet R Shelf 2 No. 36

Iowa, The first newspaper in: The Dubuque Visitor first issued May 11, 1836: Reprint of the Articles of agreement between John King, and Wm. Carey Jones.

See Franklin, Benjamin: Proceedings of the Commemoration of the 177th Anniversary ... 1885. Introduction to the above.

FIRST OCCURRENCES

Cabinet II Shelf 1 No. 90

Japanese type specimen book published by Motogi & Hirano, Tokio. n.d. 18-- (Probable first) The Printers' handy book etc..

Levant, $9\frac{1}{4}$ x 7 in.

FIRST OCCURRENCES

Cabinet K Shelf 3 No. 32

List of important dates in the art of the book.

see IVINS, W.M. Jr. Arts of the book ..New York, 1924.

FIRST OCCURRENCES

Cabinet E Shelf 4 No. 75

Irish Bible. The first bible printed in the Irish language. 1681-85.

See Early Printing in England. London, 1681-85 [Benjamin Tooke?]

FIRST OCCURRENCES

Cabinet E Shelf 2 No. 9

Japanese written characters. First printing in Europe, 1573.

See Early Printing in Italy. Naples, 1573. Horatio Salviani.

FIRST OCCURRENCES

Cabinet U Shelf 5 No. 38

Lyon, first book printed at

see

PROCTOR, ROBERT. Bibliographical essays...London, 1905, p.44

FIRST OCCURRENCES

Cabinet QQ
Shelf 4
No. 20

Magazines, the first in England and America. (Brief notes on)

see

BISHOP, J. LEANDER. History of American manufacturers...Philadelphia, 1868, p. 186.

FIRST OCCURRENCES

Cabinet NN
Shelf 7
No. 44

Monthly magazine, the first in America.

see

YALE (The) LITERARY MAGAZINE. Oldest...

FIRST OCCURRENCES

Cabinet R
Shelf 5
No. 2.02

New York Newspaper, the first, Nov. 8, 1725. Article "The City Press attains its 200th birthday". By Allanson Shaw. Excerpt from N. Y. Times Magazine, Nov. 8, 1925.

With other items, in envelope.

FIRST OCCURRENCES.

Cabinet G
Shelf 5
No. 20

Make ready. First application of modern (present methods of make ready by overlays and cut outs applied by J. A. Adams on 1600 woodcuts engraved by him for Harper Bros. Bible of 1846.

See Imprints, United States. Harper & Bros. New York, 1846.

FIRST OCCURRENCES.

Cabinet
Shelf
No.

Neuen Zeitungen, 1518. Leipzig: The first newspaper printed in Leipzig.

See newspapers, Germany. Leipzig "Neuen Zeitungen", 1518.

FIRST OCCURRENCES

Cabinet OO
Shelf 3
No. 39

Newspaper, first printed in England, 1638. Facsimile of front page.

see

WARREN'S "JOURNALISM"...London, 1922, p. 19.

FIRST OCCURRENCES

Cabinet R
Shelf 5
No. 132

Massachusetts Laws of 1648. Most valuable American-printed book. Bibliographical account and story by Luther S. Livingston. Article, excerpt, from The Nation, July 5, 1906.

Article pasted on back cover of facsimile of "The Bay Psalm Book", 1640, printed by Stephen Daye, Cambridge.

FIRST OCCURRENCES

Cabinet NN
Shelf 2
No. 13

New England Magazine, the first, and its founder.

see

PERIODICALS, United States. "New England Magazine"...

FIRST OCCURRENCES

Cabinet Y
Shelf 3
No. 25

Newspaper, first German in Philadelphia, published by Joseph Grellius, 1743.

See (GRELLIUS, JOSEPH. Philadelphia printer-publisher, 1743...)

FIRST OCCURRENCES

Cabinet HH
Shelf 5
No. 29

Miller and Richards, Edinburg (circa 1896) issue their first point specimen book.

FIRST OCCURRENCES

Cabinet
Shelf
No.

New Hampshire, the first book printed in.

see

Article in THE LIBRARY (England) vol.XV, No.3, Dec.,1934, p.340-363

FIRST OCCURRENCES

Cabinet NN
Shelf 2
No. 2.02

Newspaper printed in America, the first, Boston, Sept, 25, 1690. Printed by P. Pierce.

See NEWSPAPERS, UNITED STATES. Literature of. First newspaper...

FIRST OCCURRENCES

Cabinet W
Shelf 1
No. 147

Missel Special de Constance: Premier livre imprimé connu, oeuvre de Gutenberg avant 1450. Étude liturgique et critique. Par E. Misset, Paris, 1899.

Half morocco; 9-3/4 x 6½ in.

FIRST OCCURRENCES

Cabinet R
Shelf 4
No. 121

(First) New Jersey imprint, printed by William Bradford in Perth Amboy, 1723.

See Nelson's New Jersey printers and printing in the 18th century ... April, 1911. p. 4.

FIRST OCCURRENCES

Newspaper, the first and only ever published on a train.

Article "Edison as a Printer" in THE AMERICAN ART PRINTER, Vol. IV, No. 3, Oct., 1890.

FIRST OCCURRENCES

Cabinet Y
Shelf 3
No. 20

(Mission Presses in all countries, from 16th to 18th century).

see

HUONDER, ANTON. (Die) Verdienst der katholischen Heidenmission...

FIRST OCCURRENCES

Cabinet NN
Shelf 4
No. 1

New Jersey, the first newspaper printed was the New Jersey Gazette, 1777, at Burlington N.J., printed by Isaac Collins.

Excerpt account from The Plainfield N.J Courier-News, June 2, 1933.

Item in envelope inserted in book "New Jersey Archives", First Series, vol.xi.

FIRST OCCURRENCES

Cabinet NN
Shelf 2
No. 34.01

Newspapers, the first (in United States and Europe).

Article in "Kablegram" for July, 1933, pp. 22, 23.

In envelope.

FIRST OCCURRENCES

Cabinet NN Shelf 2 No. 9

Newspaper, the first published in Canada

see JOURNALISM, Canada. Halifax Gazette...

FIRST OCCURRENCES

Cabinet NN Shelf 3 No. 4

Newspapers, the first in the world.

see HUDSON'S "Journalism in the United States"...pp.xxviii-XLl.

FIRST OCCURRENCES

Cabinet RR Shelf 1 No. 13

Paper made from wood, first. Account of.

See KOOPS, MATTHIAS. Historical account ...of paper. London, 1800, pp.85-91.

FIRST OCCURRENCES

Cabinet QQ Shelf 1 No. 35

Newspapers, first. Early newspapers, 1588-1724.

Brief historical note.

See p.95, TIMPERLEY'S Songs of the Press ...London, 1833.

FIRST OCCURRENCES

Cabinet NN Shelf 2 No. 9

Newspapers in the United States, list of the first issues. Excerpt in "The Republic", June, 1873.

Item 2 in volume with binder's title "Newspapers, various excerpts".

FIRST OCCURRENCES

Cabinet I Shelf 1 No. 5

Papermaker, first engraving of a.

See AMMAN (JOST). Panoplia omnium illiberalium mechanicarum...1568, Frankfurt, p.20.

FIRST OCCURRENCES

Cabinet NN Shelf 2 No. 8

Newspapers, first British. In the year 1611 Nathaniel Butter issued his "News - Letter from Spain". Brief account of

see BRIDGMAN'S "Famous Editors"... Munsey's Magazine, March, 1904.

FIRST OCCURRENCES

Cabinet 18 Shelf 2 No. 1

Nieuwe Tijdinghen, afterwards, Post-Tijdighen. The first newspaper in Belgium published in 1580 by Abraham Verhoeven, a copper engraver.

See Journalism, Belgium. Newspapers in Belgium, The history of.

FIRST OCCURRENCES

Cabinet R Shelf 3 No. 83

Paper making in America, The first: William Rittenhouse, Germantown, 1690.

See Jenkins, "Guide book to Historic Germantown," 1904. p. 130.

FIRST OCCURRENCES

Cabinet NN Shelf 2 No. 7

Newspapers, first printed journal in England.- first daily in London.- First newspapers in the Colonies.- First Daily in New York ...

Excerpt from "Great American Industries of the United States". Hartford, 1872.

Item 4 in bound collection "Journalism. Excerpts, etc."

FIRST OCCURRENCES

Cabinet 79 Shelf 2 No. 17

North America, first book printed in.

see HORGAN, STEPHEN H. (The) First book, etc.

FIRST OCCURRENCES

Cabinet QQ Shelf 1 No. 36

Paper Mill, the first erected in America, Boston, 1730.

See Appendix, p.299 Brenton's Voices of the Press...New York, 1850.

FIRST OCCURRENCES

Cabinet OO Shelf 3 No. 37

Newspapers in America, the first. Brief account of. Illus.

Excerpt from The Mentor, June 1, 1921, Vol. 9, No. 5, p. 29.

Cloth; 10¼ x 7 in.

FIRST OCCURRENCES

Cabinet V Shelf 5 No. 5

Pagination first used in the work of J. Bocace "de claris mulieribus", printed at Ulm by Jean Zeiner, 1473.

See Printing, Historical. Serne, Carlos de la. Mémoire sur l'origine...Bruxelles 1795. p. 26.

FIRST OCCURRENCES

Cabinet 18 Shelf 1 No. 14

Parchment, first use of in 263 B.C.

Note in Zeitschrift für Bücherfreunde"... 1913-14 (part 1) p.62

FIRST OCCURRENCES.

Cabinet V Shelf 6 No. 15

Newspapers in France, the first. Brief notices alphabetically arranged of the first newspapers in Paris and Provinces of France. With facsimiles.

Account in the Bulletin Officiel de l'Union Syndicale des Maitres Imprimeurs. Paris. December, 1925.

Paper; 12½ x 9½ x 1 in.

FIRST OCCURRENCES

Cabinet RR Shelf 1 No. 13

Paper made from straw, first. Account of.

See KOOPS, MATTHIAS. Historical account ...of.paper. London, 1800, pp. 1-82.

FIRST OCCURRENCES Ref.

Cabinet Shelf No.

Pennsylvania Gazette, 1754, published the drawing of a snake cut in eight parts. It symbolized the divided colonies, and under it he wrote "Join or Die". This woodcut illus. the earliest specimen of newspaper pictorial features.

In REED, PERLEY ISAAC. Writing Journalistic Features. New York, 1935, p. 5.

Book not in Library.

FIRST OCCURRENCES

Cabinet S Shelf 5 No. 25.01

Philadelphia, 1685, the first book printed in. [Account by] John William Wallace. Excerpted from the Historical Magazine; Aug. 1864.

In box labelled "Colonial printing and printers. Miscellaneous items."

FIRST OCCURRENCES

Cabinet FF Shelf 5 No. 50

Power platen press first use of, by the inventor Frederick Koenig in "Principal Occurrences in the year 1810", London 1811. (See sig. H. part D, commencing p.113.

With portrait and clippings inserted.

Tree calf; 8¾ x 5¼ x 1½ in.

FIRST OCCURRENCES

Cabinet QQ Shelf 1 No. 42

Printing in America: The first paper-mill was erected in Boston, in 1730. The first type-foundry, at Germantown, Penna, etc.

See Appendix, p.299, Brentons Voices of the Press...New York, 1850.

FIRST OCCURRENCES

Cabinet NN Shelf 2 No. 25

"Philadelphische Zeitung", the first German newspaper printed and published in America, by Benjamin Franklin, 1732.
Account by Julius F. Sachse, Philadelphia, 1900.

Half morocco; 9-3/8 x 6¼ in.

FIRST OCCURRENCES

Cabinet R Shelf 3 No. 203

Power Printing-Press, the first invented by Isaac Adams. Brief account of.

see
MOORE, JOHN W. Historical, Biographical, and Miscellaneous Gatherings... p.39

FIRST OCCURRENCES.

Cabinet V Shelf 6 No. 13

Printing in France, the first. Brief notices chronologically arranged, 1470 to 1790, of the introduction of printing in Paris and Provinces of France. With facsimile of the first book printed in Paris.
Account in the Bulletin Officiel de l'Union Syndicale des Maitres Imprimeurs. Paris, December, 1925.

Paper; 12½ x 9½ x 1 in.

FIRST OCCURRENCES

Cabinet PP Shelf 1 No. 21

Philippines, Juan de Vera first printer in the.

see
GARNETT, RICHARD. Essays in librarianship...p. 122.

FIRST OCCURRENCES

Cabinet OO Shelf 4 No. 5

Printed newspaper, the earliest...Douay, 1563.

see
FACSIMILES. Russian invasion of Poland in 1563...London, 1874.

FIRST OCCURRENCES

Cabinet NN Shelf 2 No. 3

Printing office and newspaper in Fitchburg, Mass., established in Oct., 1830, by J.E. Whitcomb & Co.

Account in a "Sketch of Journalism" in Fitchburg, Mass. By James F.A. Garfield. 1888. Pamphlet.

Item 4 in vol. "Journalists and Journalism". Pamphlets.

FIRST OCCURRENCES

Cabinet J Shelf 3 No. 16

Photography, the first inventor of, Tom Wedgwood.

See LITCHFIELD, R.B. Wedgwood, Tom, the first photographer...

FIRST OCCURRENCES

Cabinet X Shelf 1 No. 59

Printers, the first in various cities and countri[es] Brief notices of.

See QUIRINI, ANGELO MARIA (Cardinal) Liber singularis...Lindaugiae, 1761,

FIRST OCCURRENCES

Cabinet V Shelf 4 No. 27

Quebec. The first book printed in. The Catéchisme de Sens, 1765.
See Introduction of Printing, Canada. (Quebec). Débuts de l'imprimerie. Par Raoul Renault, 1905.

FIRST OCCURRENCES

Cabinet J Shelf 3 No. 15

Photography, the invention of Thomas Wedgwood, 1791.

See METEYARD, ELIZA. Group of Englishmen (1795 to 1815), being the record of the younger Wedgwoods...

FIRST OCCURRENCES

Cabinet 81 Shelf 2 No. 30

Printers' Festival, the first ever held in Western New York, Rochester, 1846. Report of the occasion. Newspaper excerpt.

Item in MUNSELL, JOEL. Printers' Scraps", Vol.I, pp.32-f - 32-p.

FIRST OCCURRENCES.

Cabinet II Shelf 3 No. 12.01

Reading book in Asamese, the first. Jaipur, 1842 American Baptist Mission Press.

Pictorial boards; 6-5/8 x 4-3/8 x ¼ in.

FIRST OCCURRENCES.

Cabinet 2 Shelf 1 No. 1

Plantin, Christopher. The first production of. "La Institutione de una fanciulla nata nobilment. Antwerp, 1555.

In the dedication of this volume it is styled "the first blossom from the garden of his (Plantin's) printing press."

vellum; 5½ x 3 x ½ in.

FIRST OCCURRENCES

Cabinet X Shelf 5 No. 3

Printing by steam: The Times, London, Nov. 29, 1814, the first newspaper printed by steam. Excerpt from unidentified publication, n.d.

p. 27 in vol. with binder's title "Scrap Book, 1705-1891, relating to printing."

FIRST OCCURRENCES

Cabinet 86 Shelf 1 No. 3.01

Rhode Island Almanack for year 1728, the first ever printed in that Colony. Carefully reproduced with a brief account of the printer, James Franklin, by G. P. Winship. Printed and the Almanack reprinted under the oversight of Will. Chatterton, Providence, 1911.

Half morocco; 6¼ x 5 in.

FIRST OCCURRENCES

Cabinet NN Shelf 2 No. 10

Rochester Advertiser, the first daily newspaper in the West, and the first telegraph line between the Atlantic and the Mississippi VAL Valley. Excerpt from the "Historical Magazine", Jan.,1907.

Item 11 in bound collection with binder's title "Description of various newspapers".

FIRST OCCURRENCES

Cabinet Shelf No.

Running Head (running title) first used by Gering in partnership with Rembolt, Paris, 1494.

Ref. Hain 8219.

Book not in this Library.

FIRST OCCURRENCES, Russia.

Cabinet 18 Shelf 1 No. 16

Federow, Iwan, printed the first book in Russia, in 1564.

Brief historical account of this printer and some of his successors.

In Zeitschrift für Bucherfreunue, 1914, part 1, pp.118-21.

FIRST OCCURRENCES.

Cabinet 75 Shelf 2 No. 5

Shakespeare. The first illustration to. By E. K. Chambers. [With facsimile].

In Transactions of the Bibliographical Society. "The Library," Vol. 5, 1924-1925, pp..326-330.

FIRST OCCURRENCES

Cabinet Y Shelf 2 No. 72

Specimen broadside of Johannes Petreius, 1525, the first dated.

see

BURGER, K. (Eine) Schriftprobe vom jahre 1525...

FIRST OCCURRENCES

Cabinet R Shelf 3 No. 203

Stamps, first American postage. Brief historical note on.

see

MOORE, JOHN W. Historical, Biographical and Miscellaneous Gatherings...p.482

FIRST OCCURRENCES

Cabinet DD Shelf 1 No. 4

Standard line type book, the first in the world. Inland Type Foundry, Saint Louis. 1895.

Half morocco; $7\frac{3}{4}$ x $5\frac{1}{4}$ in.

FIRST OCCURRENCES

Cabinet FF Shelf 1 No. 105

Stereotyped book, 1701, facsimile of a page of the first.

see

KUBLER, GEORGE A. Historical treatises...on stereotyping. New York, 1936, p. 94.

FIRST OCCURRENCES

Cabinet FF Shelf 1 No. 56

Stereotyped book, the first by the clay or plaster process: Ged's invention.

See Stereotyping (Ged's invention... 1739.

FIRST OCCURRENCES

Cabinet FF Shelf 1 No. 68

Stereotyped in America, the first book: The larger Catechism... Revised by Alex. McLeod. New York: Stereotyped and printed by J. Watts & Co. June, 1813.

Half morocco; $6\frac{3}{4}$ x 4 x 5/8 in.

FIRST OCCURRENCES

Cabinet G Shelf 4 No. 35

Stereotyping: The first book ever stereotyped in America. John Watts & Co., New York City, 1813.

Half morocco; $6\frac{3}{4}$ x 4 x 5/8 in.

FIRST OCCURRENCES

Cabinet M Shelf 5 No. 60

Strawberry Hill Press, first production of "Six Poems of M.T. Gray" with designs by R. Bentley. Printed for R. Dodsley in Pall Mall, 1753.

Half morocco; $15\frac{1}{2}$ x $11\frac{1}{2}$ in.

FIRST OCCURRENCES

Cabinet NN Shelf 7 No. 5

Sun, The New York: First issue, Sept. 3, 1833 to No. 166, March 15, 1884. Bound volume in this library.

Newspaper founded by Benj. H. Day, Printer.

Half calf; $11\frac{3}{4}$ x 8-7/8 x $1\frac{1}{2}$ in.

FIRST OCCURRENCES

Cabinet Shelf No.

Sunday newspapers in United States, New York Observer, came out 125 years ago.

Article in The Publishers Auxiliary, 69th year-No.6, Feb.,10, 1934, pp.1,6

FIRST OCCURRENCES

Cabinet MM Shelf 3 No. 1

Text book of printing, the first: The Mechanick exercises...By Joseph Moxon. London, 1677-1683.

Two vols. bound in one, of which vol. 2, (1683) is entirely devoted to the crafts related to type founding, printing, etc.

Leather; $7\frac{3}{4}$ x $6\frac{1}{4}$ x 2 in.

FIRST OCCURRENCES

Cabinet MM Shelf 1 No. 2

Text book of printing, the first in France. Martin Dominique Fertel. St. Omer, 1723.

See Text Books, Printing. France. Fertel, Martin Dominique.

FIRST OCCURRENCES

Cabinet I Shelf 2 No. 50.01

Three-Color Picture, the first published in America by the process, March, 1893. It was published in the Engraver and Printer, Boston (Henry Lewis Johnson, publisher and editor). The process was patented by W. Kurtz, Madison Square, New York, who made the color separation photographs. The plates were made under the supervision of F.A. Ringler by the Electro-Light Engraving Co., New York.

Specimens of work, and correspondence relating to this process are all in one manila envelope

---

FIRST OCCURRENCES

Cabinet CC Shelf 2 No. 3

Type-casting machine invented by Edwin Starr, introduced in the United States in 1826 by The Boston Type Foundry. In 1843 the same foundry developed and perfected the type-casting machine invented by David Bruce.

Above events briefly noted in the preface of the Boston Type Foundry book of specimens for 1885.

See Specimen Books, Types. United States. Boston Type Foundry (John K. Rogers, agent) 1885.

FIRST OCCURRENCES

Cabinet 81 Shelf 2 No. 40

Type cutter, Richard Starr, the first to cut a complete font of type punches in the United States. Brier note. Excerpt, newspaper clipping.

See MUNSELL, JOEL. "Printers Scraps", Vol.XI, p.35.

FIRST OCCURRENCES

Cabinet R Shelf 3 No. 83

Type first made in America, 1772 or 1773, by Chris. Sower at Germantown, Pa.
See Jenkins "Guide book to historic Germantown," pp. 44-45.

FIRST OCCURRENCES

Cabinet [illegible] Shelf 1 No. 42

Type foundry in America, the first, at Germantown, Penn.

See Appendix, p.299, Brenton's Voices of the Press...New York, 1850.

FIRST OCCURERENCES

Cabinet I Shelf 1 No. 5

Type making; first picture of.

See Illustrated Books, 16th Cent. In Library. [Panoplia] omnium illiberalium mechanicarm.... Frankfort a.m. 1568.

FIRST OCCURRENCES

Cabinet I Shelf 1 No. 5

Type punch cutter, the first engraving of a.

See AMMAN (JOST). Panoplia omnium illiberalium mechanicarum...1568, Frankfurt, p.18.

FIRST OCCURRENCES

Cabinet F Shelf 2 No. 36

Types: The first cast in America, and used to print "Ein Gestliches Magazine...Christopher (II) Sauer, Germantown, 1770, No.12, p.136.

Half morocco; $8\frac{3}{4}$ x $5\frac{3}{4}$ in. In ex. cab. 40.

FIRST OCCURRENCES

Cabinet S Shelf 3 No. 104

Types, The first work with American. By Lawrence C. Wroth, Librarian of the John Carter Brown Library.
P. 129 in volume, Wilberforce Eames ... A tribute to. Cambridge, 1924.

FIRST OCCURRENCES

Cabinet S Shelf 1 No. 130

"Typographia, an ode to printing": The First book printed in the American Colonies relating to the art of printing. Printed by William Parks, Williamsburg, Va., 1730. Photograph reissue for The American Institute of Graphic Arts, New York, 1926.

Boards; 10½ x 7-1/8 in. In protective case.

FIRST OCCURRENCES

Cabinet R Shelf 4 No. 171

Virginia, first printing in. By Douglas C. McMurtrie. Lexington, Va., 1935. Facs.

Pamphlet; 9-1/8 x 6. In envelope.

FIRST OCCURRENCES

Cabinet 00 Shelf 4 No. 23

Womens periodical, the first English, John Dunton's, 1693. Bibliographical account of Bertha-Monica Stearns.

Excerpt from "Modern Philology", London, Aug. 1930, Vol. 28, No. 1, p. 45.

FIRST OCCURRENCES

Cabinet DD Shelf 5 No. 53

Wood type, the first specimen book of. D. Wells, letter cutter, 161 Broadway (Rear of George Long's Book Store). New York, 1828.
Bound in with a brief biography of Darius Wells, the inventor of the routing machine [By Henry Lewis Bullen]

Half morocco; 13 x 8 x 3/8 in.

FIRST OCCURRENCES

Cabinet 18 Shelf 1 No. 14

Woodcut engraving, the first dated 1350.

Note in "Zeitschrift für Bücherfreunde" ... (part 1) p.62

FIRST OCCURRENCES

Cabinet G Shelf 5 No. 20

Woodcuts made ready by overlays, first book of. This method was originated by J.A. Adams, who not only engraved these 1600 woodcuts, but made them ready himself.
See The illuminated Bible, embellished with 1600 historical engravings...Harper & Brothers, publishers. New York, 1846.

Embossed morocco; $13\frac{1}{2}$ x 10 in.

FIRST OCCURRENCES

Cabinet 18 Shelf 1 No. 14

Zylographic impression, the first in 1439

Note in "Zeitschrift für Bücherfreunde" ...1913-14 (part 1) p.62

FIRST OCCURRENCES see also

Cabinet Shelf No.

INTRODUCTION OF PRINTING.

FISCHER, GOTTHELF

Cabinet Y Shelf 3 No. 4

(Typographical rarities, together with information on the invention of printing). Typographischen seltenheiten nebst beyträgen zur erfindungsgeschichte der buchdruckerkunst. Nurnberg and Mainz. 1801-1804. In 6 parts with numerous plates.

Half morocco; 8-7/8 x 5-7/8 x 3 in.

FISHER, GOTTHELF

Cabinet Y Shelf 1 No. 5

Essai sur les monumens typographiques de Jean Gutenberg, Mayencais, inventeur de l'imprimerie. Mayence l'an 10 [1802]. Portrait of Gutenberg, engraved title, engraved dedication plate, facsimiles.
Bibliographical historical account. p.90: Chronological list of the works from the press of Fust and Schoeffer, 1454-1478.

Boards; $9\frac{3}{4}$ x 7-7/8 x $\frac{1}{2}$ in.

FISCHER & WITTIG

Cabinet L Shelf 4 No. 14

Color printing, details of the process contained in a letter from the firm of Fischer & Wittig, Leipzig. 1929

Letter attached to copy of the "Monatshefte" for May, 1927, a publication with many colored prints, printed by the above house.

Paper; 10-3/8 x 7 x 3/8 in.

FISH, WILLISTON

Cabinet 73 Shelf 1 No. 9

(The) Last Will and Testament. Written by Williston Fish for Harper's Weekly, 1898. [Reprinte San Francisco: John Henry Nash, 1935.

Boards; 22½ x 11¾ in.

FISHER, T.

Cabinet MM Shelf 7 No. 5

Elements (The) of letterpress printing, composing and proof-reading. A practical manual for Indian artisans. Second edition. Enlarged and revised. Madras: Published by Higginbotham & Co. 1906. Illus.

Has advertisements at end of book, as examples of jobwork display.

Cloth; 9-7/8 x 6-7/8 x 1¼ in.

FITZ, JOSEF

Cabinet 26 Shelf 1 No. 16

Royer in Ungarn, die buchfamilie , 1715

Article in GUTENBERG-GESELLSCHAFT JAHRBUCH, 1927, pp.85-90

FISHER, D. HAVELOCK

Cabinet S Shelf 6 No. 9

Some "rarities" in old world libraries. Excerpt from the "Editorial Review", Aug., 1912.

Item 9 in vol. with binder's title "Early printing and printed books. Pamphlets". Bound, 1932.

FISHER, THOMAS

Cabinet E Shelf 2 No. 58

See Early Printing in England. London, 1600. Thomas Fisher.

FITZGERALD, DAVID

Cabinet X Shelf 4 No. 73

Habeas Corpus for David Fitzgerald, printer, 1701.

see

LIBERTY OF PRINTING, Great Britain. Copies from the records...London, 1763, xxii p.13

Fisher, Paul
An Uncommon Gentry Linotype School, Sch. of Journalism. University of Missouri, Columbia 1952.

Classify in Typographic Library

6/5/52

FISKE, BRADLEY A.

Cabinet QQ Shelf 2 No. 26

Invention the master-key to progress. By Rear-Admiral Bradley A. Fiske. New York, 1921. Illus.

On p.101 and continuing, a brief outline of the invention of printing.

Cloth; 8¼ x 5-5/8

FITZGERALD, JOSEPH

Cabinet NN Shelf 3 No. 10

Caseine: being rural meditations (pp. 182-24) "About Newspapers." By Joseph Fitzgerald, Cincinnati:

Published for the author by John P. Walsh, 190 Sycamore Street, 1869.

Stereotyped at the Franklin Type Foundry, Cincinnati, O.

Cloth: 7-3/8x4¾x7/8"

FISHER, S.

Cabinet T Shelf 1 No. 65

London, 1797, Imprint S. Fisher.

See Imprints, England, Fisher, S...

FITCH, CHARLES E.

Cabinet R Shelf 3 No. 175

(The) Press of Onondago: A lecture delivered before the Onodago Historical Association by Charles E. Fitch. Syracuse, 1868.
Has list of newspapers, with dates of publications, of all the newspapers in Onondago County. pp. 11-12.

Half morocco; 9 x 6 in.

FLACH, MARTIN, Jr.

Cabinet X Shelf 3 No. 13

Brief bio-bibliographical note, with printer mark, Flach, Strassburg, 1501-1539.

see

HEITZ, PAUL. Elsässische büchermarken...p.xvii, plate vi.

FISHER, SYDNEY GEORGE

Cabinet R Shelf 3 No. 42

(The) True Benjamin Franklin: An analysis of the life and character of B. Franklin. By George S. Fisher. Philadelphia, 1899. Illus. portraits and facsimile.

Cloth; 8½ x 5½ in.

FITCH, GEORGE HAMLIN.

Cabinet 71 Shelf 1 No. 20

Comfort found in good old books. Published by Paul Elder & Company. Printed at their Tomoye Press under the direction of John Henry Nash. San Francisco, 1911.

Stamped cloth; 7 x 4¼ x 5/8 in.

FLACH, MARTIN

Cabinet Y Shelf 4 No. 4

(Note on Flache and his printing at Strasbourg, 1487)

see

VOULLIÉME, ERNST. (Die) Deutschen drucker des fünfzehnten jahrhunderts...p.112

FISHER, SYDNEY GEORGE

Cabinet R Shelf 3 No. 43

(The) True Benjamin Franklin. Third edition; with an appendix. Philadelphia, 1900.

This edition contains further evidence of Franklin's having an illigitimate daughter.

Cloth; 8-1/8 x 5-1/8 x 1¼ in.

FITZ, JOSEPH

Cabinet 26 Shelf 1 No. 21

(Hungarian printers, 15th century, in Europe) Ungarische buchdrucker des XV jahrhunderts im Auslande.

Essay in the "Gutenberg-Gesellschaft Jahrbuch, 1931", pp.109-121.

FLADER, LOUIS (Compiler)

Cabinet I Shelf 2 No. 77

Achievement in photo-engraving and letter-press printing. 1927. Compiled and edited by Louis Flader. Published by the American Photo-Engravers Associations. Chicago, Ill.

Includes a number of technical articles by authorities; and with numerous illustrations.
Presentation copy to Henry L. Bullen.

Embossed leather; 12¾ x 9-3/8 x 2⅝ in.

FLAGS

Cabinet MM | Shelf 2 | No. 64

[Offset printing, early example of].

See Offset Printing (From Raised Surfaces)

FLAGS, UNITED STATES

Cabinet BB | Shelf 3 | No. 35

"Old Glory", United States Flags. Pamphlet issued by American Type Founders Co., from its Specimen Printing Dept., Jersey City, N.J. 1918.

16 pp. in red and blue, with note on "To prevent misuse of the flag". Shows extensive variety of the nation's flag.

Item in manila envelope.

FLAGS OF ALL NATIONS

Cabinet S | Shelf 4 | No. 73

National Geographic Magazine, The. vol. 32, No.4, October, 1917. Our Flag Number. The story of the American Flag.

also S/4/74

Half morocco; 10½ x 7 x ½ in.

FLANDER, MATHAEUS (Mathaeus Flander)

Cabinet W | Shelf 4 | No. 65

Imprimeur à Saragosse, de 1475-78.

See Meersch P.C. Van der: Recherches sur la vie et les travaux de quelques imprimeurs Belges établis a l'étranger. ... Gand, 1844-46. pp. 193-206.

FLANDERS, LOUIS W.

Cabinet R | Shelf 4 | No. 131

Ide, Simeon, yeoman, freeman, pioneer printer. With a genealogy of the Ide family compiled by Edith Flanders Dunbar. Bibliography of the imprints of Simeon Ide. By R.W.G. Vail. Rutland, Vermont, 1931. Has frontispiece portrait.

Cloth; 9-3/8 x 6-1/8 x 1¼ in.

FLANDERS

Cabinet X | Shelf 4 | No. 6

See Liberty of Printing. Belgium. Ordonnance, 1570.

FLANDRE

Cabinet | Shelf | No.

See Printing, Historical, France. (Flandre-Artois Picardie).

FLATHE, LUDWIG.

Cabinet X | Shelf 2 | No. 28

Vierte säcular-feier der erfindung Gutenbergs in Dresden und Leipzig. Ein gedenkenbuch für gegenwart und zukunft. Leipzig, 1840. Facsimiles.

Frontispiece representing Gutenbergs monument at Mayence.

Paper boards; 8 x 5-1/8 x 3/8 in.

FLAXON, WILLIAM, Publisher, Conn. 1822-1883.

Cabinet S | Shelf 5 | No. 6

An account of his career until he became a member of the Cabinet under Lincoln.

See A Typographical Galaxy, by Marcus A. Casey, in the Connecticut Quarterly, No.1, 1896.

Bound with other items in "Various Printers and their Plants," item 19, vol.2.

FLAXON, WILLIAM

Cabinet S | Shelf 5 | No. 6

See Biographies, Printers (Connecticut printers, 1709-1893.

FLEET, THOMAS

Cabinet | Shelf | No.

See Early printing in New England. Boston, [v.d.] Thomas Fleet.

FLEETWOOD BODY CORPORATION

Cabinet G | Shelf 5 | No. 3

Fleetwood coach work [Advertising brochure] Printed in U. S. A. By Bartlett Orr Press, from designs by Lucian Bernhard. 1929.

Boards; 13¼ x 12¼ in.

FLEISCHMAN, JOHANN JOSEPH (see)

Cabinet X | Shelf 1 | No. 44

EARLY PRINTING IN GERMANY. Nuremberg, 1746

FLEISCHMAN, Jo. Michael (Punch-cutter)

Cabinet Y | Shelf 1 | No. 23

Notes and comments on a celebrated punch cutter, F.M. Fleischman; with biographical notes concerning his relation with the Enschede type foundry in Haarlem. Fleischman died in 1768. With portrait.

See LINDE, ANTONIOUS van der Geschichte der erfindung...Berlin, 1886. vol.1, p.266 (see also index, vol.3 of the above work.)

FLEISCHMAN, JOAN MICHAEL

Cabinet 83 | Shelf 2 | No. 4

See Specimen Books, Types, Holland. Enschede, Joh. en Zoonen. Haarlem, 1806.

FLEMING, REV. JOHN

Cabinet II | Shelf 3 | No. 63 Box

Short sermon: Also hymns, in the Muskokee or Creek language. Boston, 1835. Booklet.

Item in box labelled "MISCELLANEOUS LANGUAGE CHARACTERS: EXAMPLES".

FLEMING & Co., Ltd.

Cabinet C | Shelf 1 | No. 14

Caroline Park House and Roystoun Castle. Printed for private circulation at the Cranford Press, Chiswick, W. 1896.

Caroline Park House, became and is the head office of A.B. Fleming & Co., Ltd., inkmakers of Edinburgh.

This book also includes "Specimens of fine illustration inks".

Cloth; 17 x 11¾ in.

FLEMISH

Cabinet II | Shelf 3 | No. 63 Box

Gospel of St. John...1913.

See BRITISH AND FOREIGN BIBLE SOCIETY. Flemish (Belgium) Het Heilig Evangelie...

FLEMISH PRINTERS

Cabinet — Shelf — No.

See EARLY PRINTING IN BELGIUM.

FLETTNER, PETER

Cabinet 5, Shelf, Nos 25, 26

Facsimile reprints of the woodcut engravings of P. Flettnet, German engraver, circa 1500-1546.

Facs. in Cabinet 5, portfolios 25,26 also, portfolio 38-2

FLINSCH, FERDINAND

Cabinet — Shelf — No.

See Specimens, Types. Germany. Dressler'sche Giesserei (F. Flinsch).
" also Specimen Books, Types. Germany. Flinsch.

FLETCHER, F. Morley

Cabinet K, Shelf 3, No. 12

Wood-block printing: a description of the craft of woodcutting and coloring based on the Japanese practice. With drawings and illustrations by the author and A. W. Seaby... London, 1916.
The Artistic Craft Series of Technical Handbooks. Edited by W.R.Lethaby.

Boards, linen back; 7½ x 4-7/8 in.

FLEURON, THE.

Cabinet 75, Shelf 2, No. 4

Reviewed by A. W. Pollard.

In Transactions of the Bibliographical Society, "The Library," Vol. IV, 1923-24, pp. 76-8, 342-3.

FLINSCH SCHRIFTGIESSEREI

Cabinet — Shelf — No.

See Specimen Books, Types. Germany

FLETCHER, W. Y.

Cabinet 75, Shelf 1, No. 4

Bagford, John, and his collection: A paper read before the Bibliographical Society by W. Y. Fletcher, Jan. 17, 1898.
This mass of material which consists of title pages, printers' devices, and other fragments pertaining to the history of printing, is now in the British Museum print room.

In. Trans. Biblio. Soc., Vol. IV, 1896-1898, pp. 185-201.

FLEURON BOOKS

Cabinet M, Shelf 2, No. 33

List of Fleuron Books to be published in the Autumn 1927. London. The Fleuron Limited, 101 Great Russell Street, W.C.

Brochure; 7¼ x 4⅝ in.

FLINT, J. N.

Cabinet NN, Shelf 2, No. 33

Advertising clinic: Diagnosis and treatment for lame, blind, anaemic, dyspeptic, lying, crazy and dead ads. A paper read before the Kansas Editorial Association at Wichita May 10, 1918.

Bound in with other items on journalism.

Half morocco; 10 x 7 in.

FLETCHER, W.Y.

Cabinet U, Shelf 3, No. 103

Copy (A) of Celsus, printed in Venice, 1497, by Filippo Pinzi, from the library of Grolier.

Bibliographical account.

See vol. I, p.1 in Bibliographica...London, 1895-1897.

FLEURON EN TYPOGRAPHIE see

Cabinet V, Shelf 6, No. 38

MEYNELL, F. and S. MORISON.
Fleuron...

FLINT, L.N.

Cabinet NN, Shelf 2, No. 33

Newspaper writing in High Schools: containing an outline for the use of teachers. Department of Journalism in the University of Kansas. [Lectures 1914 to 1918]

Lectures, several items bound into one volume.

Half morocco; 10 x 7 in.

FLETCHER, W.Y.

Cabinet U, Shelf 3, No. 103

English armorial book-stamps and their owners. (Bio-biblio. illus. account).

See vol. 3, p.309 "Bibliographica"... London, 1895-1897.

FLEURON PRESS, THE (U.S.)

Cabinet G, Shelf 2, No. 4

See Imprints, United States.

FLINT, TIMOTHY.

Cabinet NN, Shelf 1, No. 20

Pioneer, missionary, author, editor, 1780-1840. The story of his life. By John Ervin Kirkpatrick. Cleveland, Ohio, 1911. Illus.

Cloth; 9½ x 6-3/8 x 1½ in.

FLETCHER, WILLIAM YOUNGER

Cabinet PP, Shelf 6, No. 3

Foreign bookbindings in the British Museum ...Sixty - three examples...printed in facsimile by W. Griggs. London, 1896. Kegan Paul...& Company, Ltd.

Cloth; 13 x 11¼ x 1⅜ in.

"FLIEGENDE BLATTER"

Cabinet NN, Shelf 2, No. 13

German comic paper, a. "Fliegender Blatter, founded in 1844 by Caspar Braun and Freidrich Schneider. Illus. account of the career of this paper.
Excerpt from the Century, July, 1894

Item 10 in bound collection with binder's title "Various newspapers and periodicals"

FLORENCE

Cabinet X, Shelf 3, No. 14

Printing in Florence, 15th and early 16th centuries. Bibliographical notes.

see
KRISTELLER, Dr. Paul.
Italienischen buchdrucker...p.18

FLORENCE PRESS, THE. (Chatto & Windus)

Cabinet M Shelf 2 No.

See Imprints, England. Florence Press, The. Chatto & Windus.

FLORIDA TIMES-UNION.

Cabinet A Shelf 1 No. 59

See Newspapers, special issues. U.S.

FOGAZZARO, ANTONIO.

Cabinet G Shelf 2 No. 31

Eden Anto. Translated by Theo. Wesley Koch. Printed by Edwin and Robert Grabhorn for The Roxburgh Club. San Francisco, 1930.

Paper boards with ribbon ties: 11¼ x 7¾ x ¼ in.

FLORENCE PRESS, THE

Cabinet T Shelf 4 No. 111

Type, the "Florence Press" a specimen of.

See STEELE, ROBERT T. (The) Revival of printing...London, 1912. p.80.

FLORINI, MATTEO

Cabinet Shelf No.

See Early Printing in Italy. Siena, 1608.

FOIK, PAUL J. (C.S.C.)

Cabinet NN Shelf 2 No. 7

Pioneer efforts in Catholic journalism in the United States (1809-1840). Excerpt from the Catholic Historical Review, Oct., 1915.

Item 20 in bound collection "Journalism. Excerpts, etc."

FLORENTINE BOOK FAIR.

Cabinet G Shelf 2 No. 63

Book section of the Exposition of Decorative Arts The German book exhibit at Columbia University. Notes gathered by Theodore W. Koch. Printed for subscribers. The Lakeside Press, Chicago, 1926. Illus.

Cover paper 6½ x 5½ ins., pp.121.

FLORUS, LUCIUS ANNAEIUS

Cabinet 39 Shelf 2 No. 40

Lucii Anaei Flori rerum Romanarum. Libri quatuor....Cum notis....Davidis Constantii [Printer Mark] Geneva, apud Samuelem de Tournes, M.DC.LXXXIV.

Old leather; 5-3/4 x 3½ x 1¼ in.

FOILLET, JACQUES

Cabinet W Shelf 3 No. 97

Imprimeur, libraire and papetier. (1554-1616). See Biographies, Printers. Foillet, Jacques.

FLORIAN, FRÉDÉRIC

Cabinet J Shelf 2 No. 24

Biographies d'artistes contemporains - No.I. Frédéric Florian, dessinateur et graveur sur bois. Par Clément - Janin. Paris, 1911. Illus.

In folder; 12½ x 9¼ in.

FOBES, FRANCIS H.

Cabinet BB Shelf 3 No. 30.02

Sneill's Pace Press, Amherst, Mass., 1932.

See "SPECIMEN BOOKS, TYPES. United States Fobes...

FOIX, J.

Cabinet LL Shelf 5 No. 16.01

Méthode simplifiée de la tenue des livres a l'usage des maisons d'imprimerie. Deuxième édition. Auch ... Paris, 1858.

Bookkeeping methods for printing offices.

Cloth; 9 x 6¼ x ¾ in.

FLORIAN (J.P.Claris de)

Cabinet F Shelf 5 No. 31

Galatée, roman pastoral; imité de Cervantes, par M. de Florian...Edition ornee de figures en couleur, d'apres les dessins de Monsiau.

Imprint: A Paris, chez Defer de Maisonneuve, rue du Foin S. Jacques.

Leather, gilt; 13¼ x 10¼ x 1 in. Brunet 2, 1307.

FOCK, GUSTAV

Cabinet AA Shelf 1 No. 13

Aldine bibliotheca: A collection of 800 impressions of Aldus Manutius and his successors. With a bibliographical introduction. Offered for Sale. Buchhandlung G. Fock. Leipzig. [1930].

Paper; 8½ x 6½ x ½ in.

FOKKE, AREND

Cabinet QQ Shelf 2 No. 23

Museum der voornaamste uitvindingen en nuttige ontdekkingen in de Wetenschappen en handwerken. Te Amsteldam, n.d. circa 1795. (2 vols.) Plates.

On arts and crafts; p.50, bookbinding. pp.54-65, printing. pp.108-111, engraving.

Pictorial boards; 5½ x 4 in.

FLORIDA PRESS ASSOCIATION

Cabinet KK Shelf 5 No. 87

Proceedings of the 16th annual session held in Key West, Fla., and Havana, Cuba, April 9th to 12th 1894. Pamphlet.

Item in envelope.

FOELHOFF, JOHAN

See Imprints.

FOLDING MACHINES

Cabinet EE Shelf 4 No. 12

Brown Folding Machine Co. Erie, Pa. 1890-1891. Catalogue and price list.

In manila envelope.

FOLDING MACHINES. Catalogue

Cabinet EE Shelf 4 No. 19

Chambers Brothers Co. Philadelphia, Pa. 1891.
Folding machines and binders machinery.

Cloth, stamped; 8$\frac{3}{4}$ x 6-7/8 x $\frac{1}{4}$ in.

FOLDING MACHINES. Catalogue

Cabinet EE Shelf 4 No. 14

Circular and price list. With specimens of imposition. The Campbell Printing Press and Manufacturing Co. 160 William Street, New York. Works: Taunton, Mass.

Has pictures of the Taunton works.

Circular in manila envelope.

FOLDING MACHINES. Catalogue

Cabinet EE Shelf 4 No. 33

Dexter folding and feeding machines. Illus. catalogues and price lists. Factories, Pearl River, and Fulton, New York. 1892, 1901. Pamphlets.

Has views of Dexter factories.

In manila envelope.

FOLIGNO.

Cabinet 75 Shelf [illegible] No. 5

Edition of 1474.

See Scholderer, Victor. Foligno edition of 1474.

FOLLETT, FREDERICK

Cabinet R Shelf 3 No. 170

History of the press of Western New York; together with the proceedings of the printer's festival held on the 141st Anniversary of the birth-day of Franklin, in the City of Rochester, on Monday, Jan. 18, 1847.

Cloth; 9$\frac{1}{4}$ x 6 in.

FOLLETT, FREDERICK

Cabinet R Shelf 3 No. 187

History of the press in Western New York. From the beginning to the middle of the nineteenth century. By F. Follett. With a preface by Wilberforce Eames. New York, 1920. Facsimile of the earliest newspaper of Western New York extant.

Reprinted from the original pamphlet of 1847. This is No..34 of Heartman's Historical Series.

Half morocco; 9$\frac{1}{4}$ x 6$\frac{1}{2}$ in.

FOLLINGHAM, WILLIAM

Cabinet T Shelf 2 No. 6 [vol.iv]

Bio-bibliographical note relating to Wm. Follingham, printer, London, 1544.

see

DIBDIN'S "Typographical Antiquities" ...London, 1810-19, vol.iv, p.38

FOLZ, HANS

Cabinet Y Shelf 4 No. 4

(Note on Folz and his printing at Nuremberg, 1479)

see

VOULLIÉME, ERNST (Die) Deutschen drucker des fünfzehnten jahrhunderts...p.89

FONDERIA TIPOGRAFICA COOPERATIVA

Cabinet Z Shelf 4 No. 28

Milan, n.d. [cir. 1885]. Compionario della Fonderia...di Milano.

Specimens of types from the coöperative printing and type foundry in Milan.

Stamped cloth; 11-5/8 x 7$\frac{1}{4}$ x 5/8 in.

FONDERIE GENERALE

Cabinet Z Shelf 2 No. 15

Biesta, Laboulaye et Cie. Paris, 1843. Epreuves de caracteres. Biesta Laboulaye et Cie. successeurs de Firmin Didot, Mole, Lion, Tarbe, [illegible], [illegible], Laboulaye frères.

Has price list, also brief account of the merging of the foundries which finally became "La Fonderie Generale". Another copy of this book with somewhat different contents, Z/2/14, also Z/2/16.

Cloth; 10 x 6$\frac{3}{4}$ x 2$\frac{1}{4}$ in.

FONDERIE GÉNÉRALE (Adolphe René et Cie.)

Cabinet Shelf No.

See Specimen Books Types. France. Fonderie etc.

FONDERIE GÉNÉRALE (Adolphe René et Cie)

Cabinet Shelf No.

See Specimen Books, Types. France. René et Cie, Adolphe.

FONDERIE GÉNÉRALE, (Beaudoire et Cie)

Cabinet Z Shelf 2 No. 3

Beaudoire et Cie: Fonderie Générale. Paris, n.d. [1870].

Caractères Français et Étrangères. Beaudoire et Cie. Rue Duguay-Trouin, 13. Paris.

With prices.

Morocco; 6-3/8 x 9-3/8 x 3/8 in.

FONDERIE GÉNÉRALE (Laboulaye et Cie)

Cabinet Shelf No.

See Specimen Books, Types. France. Laboulaye et Cie. successeurs de Firmin Didot. . .

FONDERIE GÉNÉRALE (E. TARBE et CIE)

Cabinet Shelf No.

See Specimen Books, Types, France. Tarbé et Cie.

FONDERIE MODERNE (Laval et Cie).

Cabinet Z Shelf 2 No. 35

See Specimen Books, Types. France.

FONDERIE MAYEUR

Cabinet Shelf No.

See Specimen Books, Types. France.

FONDERIE TYPOGRAPHIE DE BATTENBERG

Cabinet Shelf No.

See Specimen Books, Types. France. Mayer, Gustave (Succ...) Paris 1877.

FONDERIE TYPOGRAPHIQUE

Cabinet 46 Shelf 2 No.

Organe de la Chambre Syndicale des Maitres Fondeurs Francais.

See PERIODICALS, PRINTING, France Fonderie Typographique...

FONDERIE TYPOGRAPHIQUE FRANCAISE

Cabinet Z Shelf 3 No. 18

Album d'alphabets pour la pratique du croquis-calque. Edite specialement pour le Manuel francais de Typographie Moderne de F. Thibaudeau. Paris, n.d. circa 1922.

Paper; 10½ x 8¾ x 3/8 in.

FONDERIES DEBERNY & PEIGNOT

Cabinet Shelf No.

See Specimen Books, Types. France. Deberny & Peignot.

FONTENAI (l'Abbe de)

Cabinet I Shelf 1 No. 30

Dictionnaire des artistes, ou notice historique et raisonnée des architectes, peintres, graveurs, sculpteurs, musiciens, imprimeurs ...(2 vols.) A Paris: 1776.

Calf; each vol., 6¾ x 4-3/8 in.

FONTENELLE, JULIA de et P. POISSON

Cabinet RR Shelf 2 No. 7

Nouveau manuel complet du marchand papetier et du regleur...Par MM. Julia de Fontenelle et P. Poisson. Nouvelle édition, entièrement refondue et ornée de figures. Paris, 1854. (Manuels-Roret).

4 folded plates at end of book.

Half calf; 6¼ x 3-5/8 x 1 in.

FOOTE & DAVIS COMPANY

Cabinet Shelf No.

See Plants, Printing. United States.

FOQUEL, Guillermo

Cabinet X Shelf 3 No. 19

Brief bio-bibliographical note, with printer mark, Foquel (Salamanca), 1587-1593.

see

HAEBLER, KONRAD. (Spanish and Portuguese printer marks...p.xxxix

---

FORBES, PATRICK.

Cabinet E Shelf 3 No. 55

Funerals of the Right Reverend Father in God, Patrick Forbes, of Corse, Bishop of Aberdeen.

Imprinted by Edward Raban, 1635.

First edition, woodcut ornaments and initial letters. Portrait inserted.

Calf; 8¼ x 5½ x 1½ in.

FORBES LITHO CO. (W. H. Forbes)

Cabinet S Shelf 5 No. 3

Boston, 1862. Brief illustrated description of the plant, with a portrait of the founder of the house, W. H. Forbes. Booklet.

Item 19 in collection "Printers and their Plant; Collection of Pamphlets," 1918.

FORBIDDEN BOOKS see

Cabinet Shelf No.

CENSORSHIP OF BOOKS

FORCE, PETER

Cabinet 81 Shelf 2 No. 30

Report of brief address at banquet of Columbia Typographic Society, Washington, D.C., Jan. 2, 1847.

In MUNSELL, JOEL. Printers' Scraps... vol.I, p.8.

FORD, HENRY

Cabinet PP Shelf 3 No. 51

Edison Institute, founded by Henry Ford, Dearborn Michigan. Illus. descriptive booklet.

Item in protective envelope

FORD, PAUL LEICESTER

Cabinet R Shelf 1 No. 1

Franklin as printer and publisher: The many sided Franklin. By Paul Leicester Ford in The Century Magazine, April 1899. Portraits.

Bound in volume "Franklin, excerpts from magazines," item 14.

FORD, PAUL LEICESTER.

Cabinet R Shelf 2 No. 44

Franklin Bibliography. A list of books written by, or relating to Benjamin Franklin, Brooklyn, 1889.

Half morocco, 9½ x 6¼ ins: pp.LXXI, (1), 467, half of which are blank.

FORD, PAUL LEICESTER

Cabinet R Shelf 2 No. 44

Franklin bibliography. A list of books written by, or relating to Benjamin Franklin. By P.L. Ford. Brooklyn, n.Y. 1889.

Half morocco; 9½ x 6¼ in.

FORD, PAUL LEICESTER.

Cabinet R Shelf 2 No. 55

Franklin, The many sided, by P.L. Ford, New York: The Century Company, 1899. Illus. Portraits and facsimiles.

Orig. cloth, 8½ s 6 ins., pp (XX), 516.

FORD, PAUL LEICESTER

Cabinet S Shelf 5 No. 21

History of a newspaper: The Pennsylvania Gazette. By Paul L. Ford in the Magazine of American History, April, 1887.

Bound with other items in"Excerpts relating to printing in America". pp. 84-88.

FORD, PAUL LEICESTER

Cabinet R Shelf 4 No. 80 2 Vols.

(The) Journals of Hugh Gaine, printer. Edited by Paul Leicester Ford. New York, 1902. 2 vols. illus., portrait, facsimiles.

Vol. I: Biography and Bibliography.

Vol. II: Journals and Letters.

Buckram, 10½ x 7 in.

FORD, PAUL LEICESTER

Cabinet R Shelf 5 No. 127

(The) New England Primer: A reprint of the earliest known edition, with many facsimiles and reproductions, and a historical introduction. Edited by Paul Leicester Ford. New York, 1899.

Boards; 7¼ x 5½ in.

FORD, PAUL LEICESTER

Cabinet S Shelf 5 No. 21

(The) Pennsylvania Gazette: History of a newspaper. By P. L. Ford in the Magazine of American History, n. d.

Bound in with other items in volume "Excerpts relating to printing in America," pp. 84-88.

FORD, PAUL LEICESTER

Cabinet R Shelf 3 No. 33

Poor Richard, The sayings of: The prefaces, proverbs, and poems of Benjamin Franklin, originally printed in ... 1733-1758. Collected and edited by Paul Leicester Ford. New York, 1890. Portrait frontispiece, 2 facsimiles.

Cloth; 5½ x 4 in.

[FORD, THOMAS]

Cabinet MM Shelf 3 No. 30

Compositor's (The) handbook: designed as a guide in the composing room. With the practice as to book, job, newspaper, law, and parliamentary work; the London scale of prices; appendix of terms, etc...London, 1854.

Cloth; 6¾ x 4½ x 5/8 in.

FORD, WORTHINGTON CHAUNCEY

Cabinet Q Shelf 1 No. 5

(The) Boston book market, 1679-1700. By Worthington Chauncey Ford. Boston: The Club of Odd Volumes, 1917. With facs. of early printed books.
Limited ed., 150 copies printed by D. B. Updike, The Merrymount Press.

Boards; 9¾ x 6-5/8 in.

FORD, WORTHINGTON C.

Cabinet R Shelf 3 No. 117

Early printing in Boston (1638), and the manuscript sources of Massachusetts History. By C. W. Ford. Boston, 1902. Facsimiles.
Essay in Handbook for the twenty-fourth annual conference of the American Library Association. Boston, 1902.

Cloth; 7½ x 5½ in.

FORD, WORTHING CHAUNCEY.

Cabinet R Shelf 1 No. 87

Franklin's account against Massachusetts: Includes Joseph Massie's letter, No.VIII, and letters of Barceu-Dubourg to Franklin; also Franklin to Hodgson, 1781-82.

In proceedings of the Massachusetts Historical Society, 1922, pp.94-161.

Half morocco, 9½ x 6¼ ins.

FORD, WORTHINGTON CHAUNCEY (compiler)

Cabinet R Shelf 1 No. 57

List of the Benjamin Franklin papers in the Library of Congress, Washington: Government Printing office, 1905.

Cloth, 11 x 7½ ins., pp.322.

FORD, WORTHINGTON CHAUNCEY

Cabinet S Shelf 3 No. 104

(The) New England Primer. By Worthington Chauncey Ford, Massachusetts Historical Society.
Bibliographical account.
p. 61 in volume, Wilberforce Eames ...
A tribute. Cambridge, 1924.

FORDHAM (Sir) HERBERT GEORGE

Cabinet U Shelf 3 No. 96

Cary, John, engraver, map, chart and printseller and globe maker, 1754 to 1835. A bibliography, with biographical notes. Cambridge, 1925.
facsimiles.

Cloth; 9 x 6-7/8 in.

FORDHAM, SIR HERBERT GEORGE.

Cabinet 75 Shelf 1 No. 11

Descriptive catalogues of maps. Hertfordshire Maps, 1579-1900. A paper read before the Bibliographical Society, November 21st, 1910.

In Trans. Biblio. Soc., Vol. XI, 1909-1911, pp. 135-164.

FORDHAM, SIR HERBERT GEORGE.

Cabinet 75 Shelf 2 No. 8

Earliest tables of the highways of England and Wales, 1541-61. By Sir Herbert George Fordham. London, Dec., 1927. Facsimile.

In Transactions of the Bibliographical Society, vol. VIII, 1927-1928. pp. 349-54. "The Library."

FORDHAM, HERBERT GEORGE.

Cabinet T Shelf 6 No. 61

Itineraries and road books, notes on British and Irish, 1577-1798. A paper read in the Geographical Section at the meeting of the British Association for the Advancement of Science, held at Dundee. Sept. 1912. Illus.

Booklet in box labelled "English printing and printers. Shakespeariana. Misc. v.d."

FORDHAM, SIR. H. GEORGE.

Cabinet 75 Shelf 2 No. 1

Note on a series of early French atlases, 1594-1637. Presented to the British Museum, 1920.

In Transactions of the Bibliographical Society, "The Library," Vol. I, 1920-1921, pp. 145-152.

FORDHAM (Sir) HERBERT GEORGE.

Cabinet 75 Shelf 2 No. 6

Ogilby, John, 1600-1676. His Britannia and the British itineraries of the 18th century.

In Transactions of the Bibliographical Society, "The Library," Vol. VI, 1925-1926, pp. 157-178.

FORDHAM (Sir) HERBERT GEORGE.

Cabinet 75 Shelf 2 No. 5

'Paterson's Roads," Daniel Paterson, his maps, and itineraries, 1738-1825.

In Transactions of the Bibliographical Society, "The Library," Vol. V, 1924-1925, pp. 333-356.

FORDHAM, SIR HERBERT GEORGE.

Cabinet 75 Shelf 1 No. 13

Road-Books and Itineries, biographically considered. A paper read before the Bibliographical Society, November 17, 1913.

In Trans. Biblio. Soc., Vol. XIII, 1913-1915, pp. 29-68.

FOREIGN LANGUAGE NEWSPAPERS see NEWSPAPERS, Foreign Language

Cabinet Shelf No.

FOREIGN LANGUAFES FOR THE USE OF Printers and translators

see PROOFREADING. Foreign languages

Cabinet LL Shelf 3 No. 30.02

FORGERIES, PRINTING

Counterfeit printing in Jacobean times. By Wm. A. Jackson.

Article in THE LIBRARY (England), vol.xv, No.3, Dec.1934, pp.364-376

Cabinet Shelf No.

FORMAN, H. BUXTON

Books of William Morris described. With some account of his doings in literature and in the allied crafts...Chicago, 1897. Illus.

With a biographical introduction.

Cloth; 9 x 5-7/8 x 1 in.

Cabinet U Shelf 3 No. 38

Foreman, Mrs. Carolyn Thomas

Oklahoma imprints 1835-1907 ... Norman, University of Oklahoma press, 1936.

Cabinet R Shelf 5 No. 107

FORGERIES, Printing.

Fälschungen in alten Handschriften und Druckwerken. vom Johannes Schinnerer, Museumdirektor in Leipzig. [Facsimiles].

In Zeitschrift fur Bucherfreunde, 1913-14, part I, p.97.

Cabinet 18 Shelf 1 No. 14

FORMAN, MAURICE BUXTON

Merdithiana, being a supplement to the bibliography of Meredith. Printed for the Bibliographical Society at The Dunedin Press, Edinburgh. 1924.

Boards; 8-7/8 x $7\frac{1}{4}$ in.

Cabinet 76 Shelf 1 No. 14

FORÉSTIE, ÉDUARD.

Vignettes typographiques d'une Imprimerie Montalbanaise. Tri-centenaire. Par Éduard Foréstie. Montauban, 1900. Many folded plates.

Cloth; 10 x $6\frac{1}{2}$ x 3/8 in.

Cabinet V Shelf 2 No. 10

FORGERIES, Printing

False imprints, etc.

See FALSE IMPRINTS.

Cabinet Shelf No.

FORMAT OF BOOKS

Format des livres, le. Notions pratiques suivies de recherches historiques. Avec quatre planches hors texte. Ch. Mortet, Paris, 1925.

Half morocco; 10 x 6-5/8 x 3/8 in.

Cabinet W Shelf 1 No. 196

FORGERIES

[Typographic forgeries]. Fälschungen aus dem Gebiete der Graphki. Dr. Emil Waldmann. Bremen, 1915. [Illus]

In Zeitschrift fur Bucherfreunde, 1915-16. part I, p.1.

Cabinet 18 Shelf 2 No. 1

FORGERY OF CHECKS, PREVENTION OF.

[Papers, Inks, Methods, etc.] Patents issued for in Great Britain up to 1857. See Index (p. 626) of Inventions, Patents for. Abridgments of specifications, Vol. I... London, 1859.

Half morocco; 7-5/8 x 5 x 2 in.

Cabinet FF Shelf 2 No. 40

FORMAT OF BOOKS

See also Text-books, Printing.

FORGERIES, BANK NOTES.

See BANK NOTE PRINTING.
" also ENGRAVING, BANK NOTE.

Cabinet Shelf No.

FORKERT, OTTO MAURICE

From Gutenberg to the Cuneo Press: An historical sketch of the printing press. Chicago, Ill. The Cuneo Press, 1933. Illus.

Brochure in box labelled "Pamphlets and excerpts relating to Gutenberg".

Cabinet S Shelf 4 No. 68.01

FORSTER, Rev., C.

Harmony of primeval alphabets,

Folded broadside chart of early alphabets showing their relation to each other and the Latin character.

In slip case; $9\frac{3}{4}$ x $5\frac{1}{2}$ in.

Cabinet L Shelf 2 No. 10

FORGERIES, Manuscripts.

See Forgeries, Printing. Falschungen in allen Handschriften....

Cabinet 18 Shelf 1 No. 14

FORMAN, ALLAN (Editor)

(The) Journalist, New York.

See PERIODICALS, JOURNALISM. (The) Journalist...

Cabinet 43 Shelf 2 No.

FORSTER [Georg?]

See Early Printing in Germany. Amberg [Bavaria] 1602.

Cabinet E Shelf 2 No. 67

FORSTER, H. C. (Compiler)

Cabinet FF Shelf 1 No. 33

From xylographs to lead molds. A. D. 1440 - A. D. 1921. Copyright, 1921 The Rapid Electrotype Company, Cincinnati, Ohio.

Historical, technical account.

Boards; 8 x 5 in.

FORT PITT TYPE FOUNDRY

Cabinet Shelf No.

See Specimen Books, Types. United States.

FORTIER, G.

Cabinet MM Shelf 2 No. 54

Photolithographie (La), son origine, ses procédés, ses applications. Paris, 1876.

Historical account followed by technical description and formulas.

Half morocco; $8\frac{1}{2}$ x $5\frac{3}{4}$ x $\frac{1}{2}$ in.

FORTNIGHTLY BOOK LIST

Cabinet 41 Shelf 1 No. 14

Philadelphia, 1859

See PERIODICALS, BOOKSELLING (The) Fortnightly...

FORTSAS, COUNT J. N. A. de

Cabinet PP Shelf 2 No. 41

Catalogue of the Library of M. le comte de Fortsas, Paris, 1840. Reprinted in The Miscellany, Oct., 1915, Kansas City, Mo.

Brochure in envelope.

FOSSILS, THE (see)

Cabinet NN Shelf 6 No. 55

AMATEUR JOURNALISM. Names of a few of the boys...

FOSTER, AGNESS GREENE

Cabinet 71 Shelf 1 No. 2.05

By the way, Travel letters written during several journeys abroad. Published by Paul Elder & Company. Printed by John Henry Nash The Tomoye Press. San Francisco, 1910.

Cloth; 7 x $4\frac{1}{4}$ x $\frac{3}{4}$ in.

FOSTER, AGNESS GREENE

Cabinet 71 Shelf 1 No. 17

To Friendship. By the author of "You & Some Others." Paul Elder & Co. Publishers. San Francisco. Printed by The Tomoye Press, under the direction of J.H. Nash, San Francisco, March, 1910.

Paper; $8\frac{1}{4}$ x 4-7/8 in.

FOSTER, GEO. E.

Cabinet II Shelf 3 No. 33

Se-Qua-Yeh, the American Cadmus and modern Moses. A complete biography of the greatest of Redmen...By Geo. S. Foster. Illustrated by C.S. Robbins. Philadelphia, 1885.

Cloth; 7 x 4-7/8 x 1 in.

FOSTER, JOHN

Cabinet Shelf No.

See Early Printing in New England. Boston, 1677.

FOSTER, JOHN

Cabinet R Shelf 5 No. 60

(The) Earliest American engraver, and the first Boston printer. By Samuel Abbott Green. Boston, 1909. Facsimiles.

Bio-bibliographical, historical.

Cloth; $10\frac{1}{2}$ x $7\frac{3}{4}$ in.

FOSTER, JOHN

Cabinet R Shelf 5 No. 59

Remarks on John Foster, the earliest engraver in New England. By Samuel A. Green. Cambridge, 1925.

Bio-historical account. See also R/5/60.

Half morocco; $9\frac{1}{2}$ x $6\frac{1}{4}$ in.

FOSTER, STEPHEN

Cabinet A Shelf 3 No. 7

Printer of Garrison's newspaper, The Liberator... 1831.

See Newspapers, Massachusetts. Liberator (The)...

FOSTER AND WINSTONE.

Cabinet Shelf No.

See Inks, Printing. [Specimen Books, England].
" also Prices, Printing Inks. England.

FOSTER PRINTING COMPANY

Cabinet S Shelf 5 No. 2

Memphis, Tenn. 1916. We know how to print: A booklet printed for the information of those who are unacquainted with their work and facilities for doing it. Illus.

Item 11 in volume with binders title "Printers and their plants." Bound, 1918.

FOSTER, ROE and CRONE

Cabinet G Shelf 1 No. 78

"Art Fakes". Foster, Roe and Crone, Art Printers, 140-142 Munroe St., Chicago, Ill. n.d. circa 1880.

Specimens of typography

Brochure, in protective envelope

FOUCHER, A.

Cabinet FF Shelf 3 No. 56

Automatic Casting machine, Foucher. Paris, France. Correspondence (original) between A. Foucher of Paris, and President Nelson of the American Type Founders Co., in 1910, re purchase of machine, with invoice for a trial machine with its accessories.

Includes blue prints, illustrated circulars, etc.

Items in manila envelope.

FOUCHER, A.

Cabinet FF Shelf 3 No. 57

Typefounding machinery. Broadside

See Typefounding Machinery. Foucher A. (Maison Foucher Freres).....circa 1880

FOUCHER, L. & A.

Cabinet FF Shelf 8 No. 39

Patent for type casting machine.

see PATENTS, TYPE CASTING MACHINES, AUTOMATIC. Foucher...

FOUCHER, LOUIS LEON

Cabinet AA Shelf 2 No. 22

French mechanic, 1817-1864, founder of a large establishment in Paris manufacturing tools and machinery for printers. Invented and constructed the type casting machine "Rapide-Universelle."

Illus. and brief historical description of type casting machines, pp.765-67, vol. A-F of Arneudo's Dizionario esegetico...Torino, 1917.

FOUCHER, LOUIS LEON

Cabinet FF Shelf 2 No. 40

See Type Casting Machines, Foucher.

FOUCHER et FILS (veuve)

Cabinet Shelf No.

Catalogue of printing materials, Paris, 1872.

See PRINTING MATERIALS. Catalogue. Foucher et Fils (veuve)

FOUCQUET, JEHAN

Cabinet J Shelf 2 No. 25

Vie et les oeuvres de Jehan Foucquet, 1450. Paris, 1866-7. L. Curmer, printer and publisher.

Luxurious work with Foucquet reproductions by means of chromolithographic process.

Morocco, gilt; $11\frac{1}{4}$ x 8 in.

FOUDRINIER PAPER-MAKING MACHINE

Cabinet RR Shelf 4 No. 2

Complete diagram and illustration of a Foudrinier paper making room and machine.

See BOWKER. RR. Paper, a sheet of..

FOULIS, ANDREW the younger

Cabinet U Shelf 1 No. 83

Glasgow printer.

See pp.195-203 Maclehose's Glasgow University Press, The, 16 9-1931.

FOULIS, ROBERT and ANDREW

Cabinet U Shelf 1 No. 1f

Foulis exhibition of 1912: Organized by the Glasgow Bibliographical Society to illustrate the life and work of the Foulis brothers.

In Excerpts relating to printing from "The Library," 1912-13, p. 158 of pencilled folios

---

FOULIS, ROBERT and ANDREW

Cabinet U Shelf 2 No. 47

(The) Glasgow Press, and Robert and Andrew Foulis. With some account of The Glasgow Academy of the Fine Arts. By David Murray. Glasgow, 1913. Frontispiece portrait medallion of Robert Foulis. Facsimiles.

Boards; $10\frac{1}{4}$ x 8 x 7/8 in.

FOULIS, ROBERT and ANDREW

Cabinet U Shelf 1 No. 83

Glasgow University Printers.

See pp.149-194 Maclehose's Glasgow University Press, The, 1638-1931.

FOULIS, ROBERT and ANDREW.

Cabinet F Shelf No.

See Early Printing in Scotland. Glasgow, v.d.

FOURDRINIER, HENRY

Cabinet X Shelf 5 No. 3

(Late (The) Mr. Henry Fourdrinier, patentee of the paper machine. With portrait. Excerpts from newspapers, 1778-1817.

Biographical with an account of his invention.

p. 69 in vol. with binder's title "Scrap-Book, 1705-1891, relating to printing."

FOURMAND, BERTRAND

Cabinet Z Shelf 3 No. 43

Presses Nantaises. Paris, 1828. Illustrated circular letter in which the inventor of the "Presses Nantaises" explains its superiority over that of the "Columbienne".

Pp. 383-384 in "Miscellaneous collection of French type specimens"..1829-1844

FOURNIER, EDOUARD

Cabinet FF Shelf 4 No. 19

L'Art de la reliure en France aux derniers siècles. Paris. J. Gay, Éditeur. 1864.

No. 250 of 300 examples on handmade paper.

Half morocco; $7\frac{1}{2}$ x $4\frac{1}{2}$ x $\frac{3}{4}$ in.

FOURNIER, EDOUARD

Cabinet FF Shelf 4 No. 20

L'Art de la reliure en France aux derniers siècles. (2 me ed.) Par Edouard Fournier. Paris, 1888. E. Dentu, Éditeur.

Half morocco; $6\frac{3}{4}$ x $4\frac{1}{2}$ in.

FOURNIER, EDOUARD

Cabinet V Shelf 4 No. 18

Collaborator with Paul Lacroix and Ferdinand Sere on "Histoire de l'imprimerie", Paris, 1852.

See LACROIX, PAUL.

FOURNIER, HENRY

Cabinet W Shelf 3 No. 25

See Biographies, Printers. Quatre leçons de la typographie parisienne. Par Alkan, Angers, 1889.

FOURNIER, HENRI.

Cabinet MM Shelf 1 No. 26

Traité de la typographie. Paris, 1825, Imprimerie de H. Fournier.

Text book of printing dedicated to Firmin Didot.

Boards, morocco back; 8-3/8 x 5-1/8 x 7/8 in.

FOURNIER, HENRI

Cabinet MM | Shelf 1 | No. 27

Traite de la typographie. Deuxième édition. Tours, 1854.

Boards; 6¼ x 4¼ x 7/8 in.

FOURNIER, HENRI.

Cabinet MM | Shelf 1 | No. 75

Traite de la typographie. Rapport de J. Cusset. Societe fraternelle des protes de Paris. Paris, 1873. Pamphlet.

In box labelled "Brochures relating to French typographical matters."

FOURNIER, HENRI

Cabinet MM | Shelf 1 | No. 28

Traité de la typographie. Quatrième édition entierement revuè et augmentée par Arthur Viot. Paris 1904.

Cloth; 7¼ x 4½ x 1¼ in.

FOURNIER, HENRI et ARTHUR VIOT

Cabinet MM | Shelf 1 | No. 29

Traité de la typographie. Par Henri Fournier, imprimeur. Nouvelle édition entierement revue et augmentée. Par Arthur Viot. Paris, 1919. Illus.

Half morocco; 7½ x 4¾ x 1¼ in.

FOURNIER, L.

Cabinet X | Shelf 4 | No. 32

Imprint, Fournier, Auxerre, 1793.

See LIBERTY OF PRINTING, France. Décret (du 28 Fevrier, 1793)...

FOURNIER, O.

Cabinet KK | Shelf 4 | No. 1

Histoire de toutes les noblesses, sous la direction littéraire de M. O. Fournier. 1 livraison. Second Serie - No. I. Corporation des Imprimeurs. Paris, n. d. Illus.

Brief history of printing, the first printers of France and their privileges.

Half morocco; 11 x 7 in.

FOURNIER, PIERRE SIMON

Cabinet U | Shelf 5 | No. 77

[Beaujon, Mr. Paul] Pierre Simon Fournier, Sept. 15, 1712 - Oct.8, 1768, and 18th century typography. Together with a specimen of Monotype Fournier Face. Lnaston Monotype Corporation, Ltd. London, 1926. The Monotype Recorder, Nos.212-13

Cloth; 12 x 9-1/8 in.

FOURNIER, PIERRE SIMON

Cabinet T | Shelf 3 | No. 1

Bibliographical notes concerning books by Fournier.

In DIBDIN'S "Bibliomania"... London, 1809, p.57 and fol.

FOURNIER, P.S. LE JEUNE

Cabinet 26 | Shelf 1 | No. 17

Breitkopf, J.G.I. und P.S. Fournier le jeune, Ein beitrag zur geschichte des notendrucks und der schrift-giesserei im 18 jahrhunderts. von Ludwig Volkmann. (Contribution to the history of music printing and of 18th century type foundries).

Article in Gutenberg-Gesellschaft Jahrbuch 1928, pp.118-141, also Gutenberg-Gesellschaft Jahrbuch 1929, p.312.

FOURNIER, PIERRE SIMON, le JEUNE

Cabinet FF | Shelf 4 | No. 3

Carter, Harry. Fournier on type founding: The text of the Manuel Typographique (1764-1766) translated into English and edited with notes by Harry Carter. Published by the Soncino Press. London, 1930. Illus.

Biographical note on pp. XII - XXXIII.

Cloth; 7-3/8 x 5¼ x 1¾ in.

FOURNIER, PIERRE SIMON (Fournier le jeune).

Cabinet V | Shelf 3 | No. 2

Dissertation sur l'Origine et les Progrès de l'Art de graver en bois, pour éclaircir quelques traits de l'histoire de l'Imprimerie et prouver que Guttemberg n'en est pas l'Inventeur. Par Fournier le jeune, Graveur and Fondeur de Caracteres d 'Imprimerie. A Paris de l'Imprimerie de J Barbou. 1758.

Bound in with Observations...Vindicae Typographicae 1760, and Lettre sur l'origine de l'Imprimerie, Strasbourg,1761.

Leather; 7½ x 4¾ x 1¾ in. See also V/3/3

FOURNIER, S.P. le jeune.

Cabinet 83 | Shelf 1 | No. 10

See genealogical manuscript notes of Fournier family from 1712 to 1768 in S.P. Fournier type specimen book of 1742.

FOURNIER, PIERRE SIMON

Cabinet V | Shelf 3 | No. 2

Lettre sur l'origine de l'imprimerie, servant de réponse aux Observations publiees par M. Fournier, sur l'ouvrage de M. Schoepflin, intitulé Vindiciae Typographicae. Strasbourg, 1761.

Bound in with Observations...Paris, 1760, and Dissertation sur l'origine de graver en bois. Paris, 1758.

Leather; 7½ x 4¾ x 1¾ in. See also V/3/3 .

FOURNIER (P. S.) LE JEUNE

Cabinet FF | Shelf 4 | No. 1

Manuel typographique, utile aux gens lettres et a ceux exercent les differentes parties de l'art de l'imprimerie. A Paris, Imprime par l'auteur...1764. (vol. I only) Frontispiece portrait.

Has signatures of James Ronaldson, Binny and Ronaldson, and L. Johnson & Co., 1847.

Half morocco; 6-7/8 x 4¾ x 1-1/8 in.

FOURNIER (PIERRE SIMON) LE JEUNE

Cabinet FF | Shelf 4 | No. 2 (2 vols.)

Manuel typographique, utile aux gens de lettres, et a ceux qui exercent les differentes parties de l'art de l'imprimerie. Par Fournior, le jeune. Tome I. A Paris, Imprime par l'auteur, rue des Postes, 1764. Plates & engr. frontispieces. (Tome II, 1766: specimens of type)

Full morocco; 6¾ x 4¼ in.

FOURNIER, Pierre Simon

Cabinet V | Shelf 3 | No. 2

Observations sur un ouvrage intitule: Vindiciae Typographicae, pour servie de suite ou traité de l'origine de l'imprimerie primitive en taille de bois. Paris, de l'Imprimerie de J Barbou. 1760.

Bound in with Dissertation sur l'origine et les Progrés de l'Art de graver en bois. Paris 1758, and Lettres sur l'origine [by E. Baer]. Strasbourg, 1761.

Leather; 7½ x 4¾ x 1¾ in. See also V/3/3

FOURNIER, PIERRE SIMON

Cabinet V | Shelf 3 | No. 3

Origine et des productions de l'imprimerie primitive en taille de bois...Par Fournier le jeune. Paris: De l'Imprimerie de J. Barbou, 1759.

[Bound in with other Fournier items.

Half morocco; 7½ x 4¾ x 1¾ ins. See also V/3/2 .

FOURNIER, PIERRE SIMON, le JEUNE

Cabinet FF | Shelf 4 | No. 2

Reponse a un Memoire en 1766 par MM. Gando au sujet des caracteres de fonte pour la musique.

Fournier here accuses the Gandos of plagiarism.

See pp. 289-306,Tome II, Fournier's Manuel Typographique...Paris, 1764-1766.

FOURNIER, SIMON-PIERRE, le jeune

Cabinet 83 See Specimen Books, Types, France

Shelf 1

No.

FOURNIER, P.S.

Cabinet

Shelf

No.

See also Specimen Books, Types, France.

FOWLE, Sachariah, Printer, Boston, 1747.

Cabinet S See Isaiah Thomas, The Patriot Printer; in the New England Magazine, Nov. 1901.

Shelf 5 Bound with other items in "Various printers and their plants", item 12, vol.2.

No. 6

FOURNIER, S.O. le jeune

Cabinet R Specimen of a font of script types designed by Benjamin Franklin, and cut and cast by S.P. Fournier le jeune, Paris, 1780.

Shelf 1

No. 3

In Frankliniana, p.33.

FOWLE, DANIEL

Cabinet R See Printing, Historical, New Hampshire, Celebration of the Centennial Anniversary ... Portsmouth, Oct. 1856. p. 24-5.

Shelf 3

No. 150

FOWLE, WILLIAM

Cabinet II He Helu Kamalii. (Arithmetic book (7th ed.) in Hawaiian tongue, by William Fowle). Honolulu: mea pai palapala na na Misionari, 1847. Paper booklet.

Shelf 3

No. 54

Item in manila envelope.

FOURNIER LE JEUNE

Cabinet FF Specimen of 1757. Facs.

Shelf 2

No. 7

See McMurtrie, Douglas C. Fournier le jeune's 1757 specimen ...

FOWLE, DANIEL

Cabinet X (A) Total eclipse of liberty: being a true account of the arraignment and examination of Daniel Fowle...Octob. 24th 1754, barely on suspicion of his being concerned in printing and publishing a pamphlet, intitled, "The Monster of Monsters"...Written by himself. Boston 1755.

Shelf 4

No. 72

Cloth case; $7\frac{1}{2}$ x 5 in.

FOWLE, ZECHARIAH

Cabinet See Early Printing in New England. Boston, 1755. Daniel and Zechariah Fowle.

Shelf

No.

FOURNIER, S.P, Paris, 1751.

Specimens of Types: See pp 663-665 of Encyclopedie ou Dictionnaire des Sciences, des Arts, et des Metiers, par un Société de gens de Lettres., Tome ii, Paris 1775.

See also: Specimen Books-Types-France

FOWLE, DANIEL

Cabinet See also Early Printing in New England. Boston, [v.d.] Gamaliel Rogers and Daniel Fowle. also Early Printing in New Hampshire, Portsmouth.

Shelf

No.

FOWLER, ALFRED (Editor)

Cabinet K Woodcut Annual (American). 1925.

Shelf 6 see WOODCUT ANNUAL (American)

No. 29

FOURNIER, SIMON-PIERRE, le jeune

Cabinet V Tableau des vingt corps de caractères, d'usage ordinaire dans l'Imprimerie: Qui nous ont été fournis par M. Fournier le jeune, graveur-fondeur de caractères.

Shelf 5 See Petity, Jean Ramond de. Encyclopédie élémentaire...Paris, 1767. pp. 307-316.

No. 4

FOWLE, DANIEL AND ZECHARIAH.

Cabinet F See Early Printing in New England. Boston, 1755: Daniel and Zecharia Fowle.

Shelf 2

No. 33

FOWLER, JOSEPH C. (Inventor)

Cabinet FF Fowler type casting and setting machine...The story of the most wonderful invention since the discovery of movable types. Introduction by J. Renwick Preston. National Mortgage & Bond Company, Chicago, Ill., 1907. Illus. pamphlet.

Shelf 6

No. 39

Item in manila envelope.

FOURNIER LE JEUNE (PIERRE-SIMON)

Cabinet FF Traite historique et critique sur l'origine et les progres des caracteres de fonte pour l'impression de la musique, avec des epreuves...Par M. Fournier le Jeune. A Berne, et a Paris. 1765.

Shelf 3

No. 2

Half mor.; $10\frac{1}{4}$ x $7\frac{3}{4}$ in.

FOWLE, ROBERT

Cabinet See Early Printing in New Hampshire. Portsmouth, 1765. Daniel and Robert Fowle.

Shelf

No.

FOWLER, JOSEPH C. (Inventor) see also

Cabinet FF COMPOSING MACHINES.-Slugs. Fowler...

Shelf 6

No. 18

FOWLER, NATHANIEL C., Jr.

Cabinet LL Shelf 4 No. 8

Advertising and printing. A concise, practical, and original manual on the art of local advertising. Boston: A.M. Thayer & Co., Pub. 1890.

Cloth; 8-7/8 x 6¾ x 7/8 in.

FOWLER, NATHANIEL C. Jr.

Cabinet LL Shelf 4 No. 9

Publicity, Fowler's. An encyclopedia of advertising and printing, and all that pertains to the public seeing side of business. New York, 1897.

With many specimens of advertisements.

Cloth; 11-3/8 x 9¼ x 2-5/8 in.

FOX, CHARLES-JAMES

Cabinet X Shelf 4 No. 95

Considerations of the respective rights of judge and jury: particularly upon trials for libel occasioned by motion of the Hon. Charles-James Fox. By John Bowles, London, 1791.

Paper boards; 8½ x 5-3/8 in.

FOX, GEORGE TOWNSHEND

Cabinet K Shelf 5 No. 10

Synopsis of the Newcastle Museum, late The Allan, formerly The Tunstall or Wycliffe Museum: To which is prefixed memoirs of Mr. Tunstall, the founder, and of Mr. Allan, the late proprietor of the collection... Newcastle, 1827.

With plates and wood cuts.

Half morocco; 8-5/8 x 5¼ x 3/4 in.

FOX, JOHN

Cabinet X Shelf 4 No. 48

(The) Benefit and invention of printing, by John Fox, that famous martyrologist...anno 1684: where he shews, when and by whom printing was invented, the excellency and usefulness of the art, the disadvantage that accru'd to popery, and the great advantage that the Protestant Religion hath reaped thereby... London, printed and sold by T. Sowle. 1704.

Paper boards; 8-3/8 x 6¼ in.

FOXIUS, (Annibel Parmensis)

Cabinet X Shelf 3 No. 14

Bibliographical note, with printer mark, Foxius, Venice, 1485-1487.

see KRISTELLER, Dr. PAUL. Italienischen buchdrucker...p.80

FOYOT, PHILIP

Cabinet X Shelf 3 No. 14

Bibliographical note, with printer mark, Foyot, Milan, 1521.

See KRISTELLER, Dr. Paul. Italienischen buchdrucker...p.22

FRACASSINI (Maffeo)

Cabinet X Shelf 3 No. 14

Bibliographical note, Fracassini, printer, Collio 1503-1515.

see KRISTELLER, Dr. Paul. Italienischen buchdrucker...p.10

FRAKTUR and ROMAN ANTICUA

Cabinet Shelf No.

See Types, Printing. Literature of.

FRAKTUR und ANTIQUA

Cabinet 18 Shelf 1 No. 12

Historische betrechtung zur schriftfrage. von Johannes Schinmerer. Leipzig. 1912.

Article in the Zeitschrift für Bücherfreunde, 1912, part 2, p.201.

FRAKTUR TYPE

Cabinet FF Shelf 4 No. 26

Origin and formation of fraktur types.

See Keutzsch, Rudolf. (Die) Entstehung der frakturschrift...

FRANCE

Cabinet QQ Shelf 2 No. 7

Agriculture in France in 1819.

see CHAPTAL, le COMTE. De l'industrie Francoise...Paris, 1819.

FRANCE

Cabinet QQ Shelf 2 No. 7

Apprenticeship in France in 1819.

see CHAPTAL, le COMTE. De l'industrie Francoise...Paris, Vol. 2, p. 299.

FRANCE

Cabinet Shelf No.

Bibliotheque Nationale, Paris.

see BIBLIOTHEQUE NATIONALE

FRANCE

Cabinet QQ Shelf 2 No. 7

(Commerce with foreign countries in 1819, with statistics for the years 1787 - 1789) L'industrie Francoise, par M. le Comte Chaptal...Paris, 1819. (2 vols.)

pp. 143, 197, 299, 310, 316, 328, relate to working conditions of papermakers, apprentices, journeymen, publishing, etc.

Quarter pigskin; 8¼ x 4-7/8 in.

FRANCE

Cabinet QQ Shelf 2 No. 7

Corporations in industry in France in 1819.

see CHAPTAL, le COMTE. De l'industrie Francoise...Paris, Vol. 2, p. 328.

FRANCE

Cabinet QQ Shelf 2 No. 7

Employers in France in 1819.

see CHAPTAL, le COMTE. De l'industrie Francoise...Paris, Vol. 2, p. 316.

FRANCE.

Cabinet J Shelf 5 No. 29 3 Vols.

(Engraving in France from its origin to 19th century).

See COURBOIN, FRANCOIS. Histoire illustrée de la gravure en France ... Paris, 1923.

FRANCE

Cabinet K Shelf 4 No. 21

(Illustrated book in France, 1790-1860)

See Rumann, Arthur. (Das) Illustrierte buch des 19 jahrhunderts...Leipzig, 1930, pp. 117-204.

FRANCE

Cabinet Y Shelf 1 No. 41

Paris, printing in, 1470-1572

See BORCKEL, ALFRED. Gutenberg und seine berühmsten nachfolger... pp.166-183

FRANCESCO DA BOLOGNA

Cabinet AA Shelf 1 No. 33

Chi era?

See Panizzi, Sir Anthony. Francesco da Bologna, Chi era? ... Londra, 1050.

FRANCE

Cabinet K Shelf 4 No. 20

(Illustrated book of the 15th century)

See Olschki, Leo A. Le livre illustre au XV siecle...Florence, 1926, pp.XXV-XXIX ...

FRANCE

Cabinet QQ Shelf 2 No. 7

Publishing in France in 1819.

see CHAPTAL, le COMTE. De l'industrie Francoise...Paris, Vol. 2, p. 197.

FRANCIS, CHARLES

Cabinet S Shelf 2 No. 115

The above booklet represents the specimens of a type-setting contest among the printing houses in connection with the program used for this occasion, the "Social Evening."

Limp morocco; 8¼ x 5¼ in.

FRANCE

Cabinet Shelf No.

Journalism in France.

see JOURNALISM, France

FRANCE

Cabinet U Shelf 5 No. 28

Spread of printing in France (see)

DUFF, E. GORDON. Early printed books...p.78

FRANCIS, CHARLES

Cabinet S Shelf 3 No. 121

Good Thoughts and Helpful Maxims. Selected and original. Compiled by Chas. Francis, New York. Charles Francis Press, Christmas, 1929. Frontispiece portrait.

Limp leather; 5¾ x 3½ x 3/8 in.

FRANCE

Cabinet QQ Shelf 2 No. 7

Journeymanship in France in 1819.

see CHAPTAL, le COMTE. De l'industrie Francoise...Paris, Vol. 2, p. 310.

FRANCE

Cabinet V Shelf 5 No. 26

Statistics of printing, 1874.

See STATISTICS OF PRINTING.

FRANCIS, CHARLES

Cabinet S Shelf 3 No. 120

How to buy printing: Charles Francis Press, New York, 1922. Illus.

Description of various technical points in book making, from preparation of copy to delivery. Last chapter devoted to "Practical informaion."

Imitation leather; 10¼ x 7¼ in.

FRANCE

Cabinet L Shelf 1 No. 9

Lithographie en France, 1816-1863

See DELABORDE, HENRI. Lithographie en France...

FRANCE (see also)

Cabinet Shelf No.

Early Orinting in France
Imprints "
Ink-Makers "
Journalism "
Liberty of Printing "
Newspapers "
Paper Making "
Periodicals "
Printing, Historical "
Schools of Printing "

FRANCIS, CHARLES

Cabinet S Shelf 2 No. 117

Memories of a great printer. Biographical sketches of the career of Charles Francis. By Charles H. Cochrane. The Charles Francis Press, New York, n.d. [1926]. Portrait.

Cloth; 8-7/8 x 5-5/8 in.

FRANCE

Cabinet QQ Shelf 2 No. 7

Paper, manufacturers of, in 1819.

see CHAPTAL, le COMTE. De l'industrie Francoise...Paris, 1819, Vol. 2, p. 143.

FRANCE (see also)

Cabinet Shelf No.

DIRECTORIES, France

FRANCIS, CHARLES

Cabinet S Shelf 5 No. 27

Printer at eighty. Souvenir, New York, 1928.

A scrap book containing menu cards of testimonial dinners: Sayings of Charles Francis: "Kind words uttered in connection with Testimonial Dinners, etc.

Half morocco; 11½ x 8¾ in.

FRANCIS, CHARLES

Cabinet LL Shelf 5 No. 56

Printing for profit. Written after completing fifty years of printing experience on three continents. New York, 1917. Illus.
Frontispiece portrait.

Cloth; 9 x 6 x 1¼ in.

FRANCIS, CHARLES

Cabinet NN Shelf 7 No. 33

Specimen of his early printing. "Otago Punch" (New Zealand) Sept. 1, 1866 to Jan. 19, 1867. Printed and published by Charles Francis.
Read printed notice on p. I following cover.

Half calf; 11 x 8½ x 5/8 in.

FRANCIS, CHARLES

Cabinet S Shelf 2 No. 115

Welcome to Charles Francis, Esq., of the Charles Francis Press Co., New York, after an absence of fifty-two years from Dunedin, N.Z. Social evening tendered by the Master Printer's Association...Saturday, April 16, 1921

Limp morocco; 8¼ x 5¼ in.

See also

Printing Plants: Charles Francis Press

FRANCIS, DARTOIS, et GABRIEL

Cabinet QQ Shelf 1 No. 29

L'Imprimeur sans caractère...Comédie-vaudeville en un acte. Representée, pour la premiére fois a Paris, sur le Théatre des Variétes, le 18 Aout 1824.

Half morocco; 8½ x 5¼ x ½ in.

FRANCIS, JABEZ

Cabinet MM Shelf 4 No. 8

Printing at home, with full instructions for amateurs...Second edition. Rochford, Essex: Printed and published by J. Francis & Son. n.d. (circa 1874). Illus.
Bound in with two other items on amateur printing by Joseph Watson, Boston, 1873 and 1875.

Cloth; 7¾ x 4⅝ x ½ in.

FRANCIS, JOHN M.

Cabinet NN Shelf 7 No. 21

Printer and founder of The Troy Daily Times, 1851. Biography, with portraits.

see
NEWSPAPERS, ANNIVERSARY ISSUES.
Troy Daily Times, The. 1851 - 1901.

FRANCIS, JOHN W. M.D.

Cabinet 21 Shelf 2 No. 3

Address by John Francis on the occasion of 50th anniversary of the New York Typographical Society, July 4, 1859. Reminiscences.
In "The Printer", Vol. 2, No. 3, July, 1859, p. 49.

FRANCIS, JOHN W. Dr.

Cabinet R Shelf 4 No. 63

New York during the last half century: A discourse in commemoration of the Fifty-Third Anniversary of the New York Historical Society ... By John W. Francis, M.D. New York, 1857.
Dr. Francis was first a printer, and later received his medical degree.
See pp. 206-221 for data on newspapers, journalism, publishing and authorship.

Half morocco; 9¼ x 6-1/8 in.

FRANCIS, JOHN W.

Cabinet R Shelf 4 No. 68

Old New York: Or reminiscences of the past sixty years. By John W. Francis, M.D. L.L.D. New York, 1866.
See pp. 332-336 for data on printing, journalism and publishing.
Dr. John W. Francis L.L.D., was in early life a printer, and his writings cotain facts about printing not elsewhere recorded.

Cloth; 8½ x 6 in.

FRANCIS, Dr. JOHN W., Printer

Cabinet A Shelf 3 No. 11

Portrait, full page woodcut, p.252, Frank Leslie's Illus. Newspaper, March 9, 1861.

On folio 56 of vol. labelled "Early printing in New York State".

FRANCIS, JOHN W.

Cabinet S Shelf 5 No. 4

Reminiscences of printers, authors and booksellers in New York. By John W. Francis, M. D. An address delivered at the Printers' Banquet in New York. Jan. 16, 1852. Reprinted in the International Magazine, Feb. 1852.

Item 11½ in collection "Various printers and their plants; Excerpts from Magazines, I."

FRANCIS, JOHN W.

Cabinet R Shelf 4 No. 57

Reminiscences of printers, authors and booksellers in New York. By John W. Francis,
Excerpt from The International Magazine, March, 1852; pp. 253-266.

Bound half morocco; 9½ x 6¼ in.

FRANCKTON, JOHN.

Cabinet 75 Shelf 1 No. 8

Ornaments used by John Frankton, printer at Dublin. By E. R. McC. Dix for the Bibliographical Society. Illus.
Bio-bibliographical account.

In Trans. Biblio. Soc., Vol. VIII, 1904-1906 pp. 221-227.

FRANCKTON, JOHN.

Cabinet 75 Shelf 2 No. 2

Printer in Dublin, 1600-18.

See Early Printing in Ireland. Literature of. Initials letters and factotums used by John Franckton...

FRANCO (et figli), SEBASTIANO

Cabinet Z Shelf 4 No. 32

See Specimen Books, Types. Italy.

FRANCOIS, RENÉ

Cabinet E Shelf 3 No. 28

Essay des merveilles de nature, et des plus nobles artifices ... A Rouen, Jean Osmont, 1626.
See p. 302 for (Facts about printing) "Du fait de l'imprimerie.

Morocco; 9¼ x 6¾ x 1¼ in.

FRANÇOIS, RENÉ

Cabinet E Shelf 3 No. 28

Essay des merveilles de nature, et des plus nobles artifices. A Rouen: Chez Jean Osmont. 1626.

Contains chapters on the histories of paper, and printing.

Morocco; 9¼ x 6-3/4 x 1¼ in.

FRANCOIS et ARNAL

Cabinet Shelf No.

See Ink Manufacturers, France.

FRANDOR COMPANY, THE

Cabinet RR Shelf 2 No. 22

Printer's Green Book for 1910. Containing a classified list of water-marked Bonds, Linens, Writings, and Ledgers...Published by the Frandor Company, Cleveland, Ohio.

Contains the names of all water-marked papers carried by jobbers throughout the country, average list price on same, and the names of jobbers who carry them.

Morocco; 6½ x 4¼ x ¼ in.

FRANK, JULIUS.

Cabinet 78 Shelf 1 No. 92

Pressman's ink manual, containing basic facts on colors and color mixtures. New York, 1928. Pamphlet.

Item in box labelled "Pamphlets and excerpts relating to ink and ink making."

FRANK LESLIE'S

Cabinet 00 Shelf C No. 57

Illustrated Newspaper. Vol. I, No. I, Dec. 15, 1855. New York.

Cloth; 16 x 11 in.

FRANK WIGGINS TRADE SCHOOL (see)

Cabinet Shelf No.

SCHOOLS OF PRINTING, United States. Frank Wiggins Trade School...

FRANKE, CARL AUGUST

Cabinet LL Shelf 1 No. 29

Handbuch der buchdruckerkunst. Nach eignen erfahrungen und denen anderer namhafter buchdrucker bearbeitet. Dritter vermehrte auflage. Weimar, 1863.

Boards; 6¾ x 4½ x 7/8 in.

FRANKE, CARL AUGUST

Cabinet LL Shelf 1 No. 30

Handbuch der buchdruckerkunst. Nach eignen erfahrungen und denen anderer namhafter buchdrucker bearbeitet. (3rd edition) Weimar, 1867.

Half morocco; 7¾ x 4-7/8 x 7/8 in.

FRANKE, CARL AUGUST (R. Wagner, Editor)

Cabinet LL Shelf 1 No. 33

Handbuch der buchdruckerkunst. Nach eignen erfahrungen und nach denen andrer namhafter buchdrucker. Bearbeitet von Carl August Franke. (Fifth edition, complete new revision) Herausgegeben von R. Wagner. Weimar, 1886.

Half morocco; 9-1/8 x 5-7/8 x ⅞ in.

FRANKE, CARL AUGUST

Cabinet LL Shelf 1 No. 27

Katechismus der buchdruckerkunst und der verwandten geschäftszweige. Mit 39 in den text gedruckten abbildungen. Leipzig, 1856.

"Gives a brief history of printing, also explains the practice of the art of printing in a catechetical form.

Half morocco; 7 x 4½ x ½ in.

FRANKE, CARL AUGUST

Cabinet LL Shelf 1 No. 28

Katechismus der buchdruckerkunst, und der verwandten geschaftszweige. Leipzig, 1856.

Also the second and improved edition, 1862. Two volumes bound as one. Illus.

Cloth; 7 x 4½ x 1 in.

FRANKE, CARL AUGUST (Alex. Waldow, Ed.)

Cabinet LL Shelf 1 No. 31

Katechismus der buchdruckerkunst. Fourth revised edition by Alexander Waldow. With 42 illus. Leipzig, 1879.

Cloth; 6¾ x 4½ in.

FRANKE, CARL AUGUST (Alex. Waldow, Ed.)

Cabinet LL Shelf 1 No. 32

Katechismus der buchdruckerkunst. von Carl August Franke. (Fifth enlarged, and improved edition, Alex. Waldow. With 43 illus. and plates) Leipzig, 1886.

Cloth; 6¾ x 4½ in.

FRANKE, JOHN

Cabinet U Shelf 1 No. 111

Biographical note relating to Franke (Frankton or Francton), printer, Dublin, circa 1602.

see
McDIX, E. R. Dublin printing....p.25

FRANKFORT.

Cabinet 75 Shelf 2 No. 2

(History of early printing in Frankfort). Frankfurter Urkundenbuch zur Fruhgeschichte des Buchdrucks. von Walter Carl Zulch und Gustav Mori. Frankfort, A. M. 1920.

In Transactions of the Bibliographical Society, "The Library," Vol. II, 1921-1922, pp. 59-63.

FRANKFORT

Cabinet X Shelf 3 No. 17

(Printer and publisher marks from the 15th to the 17th centuries) Frankfurter...drucker-und verlegerzeichen bis in das 17 jahrhundert. Paul Heitz. Strassburg, 1896. Illus.

Half cloth; 14½ x 11½ x ⅜ in.

FRANKFORT am MAIN

Cabinet FF Shelf 5 No. 49

Anfänge des schriftgiessergewerbes in Frankfurt am Main. von Gustav Mori....Dezember 1928.

Brochure, illus., in manila envelope.

FRANKFORT ON THE MAIN

Cabinet X Shelf 4 No. 9

Eines erbarn Raths ernewerte ordnung und artickel wie es forthin allen Truckereyen in dieser Statt Frankfurt soll gehalten werden. Gedruckt...durch Johann Saurn. 1598.

Rules and regulations for printing offices as ordered by the State as to rates of pay; relations of masters and men, etc.

Boards; 8 x 6-3/8 x 3/8 in.

FRANKFORT AM MAIN

Cabinet FF Shelf 5 No. 6

(History of the Egenolff - Luther type foundry, and its connection with the United States.)

See Mori, Gustav. (Die) Egenolff-Luthersche Schriftgiesserei...Frankfurt, a. M. 1926.

FRANKFORT BOOK FAIR.

Cabinet 40 Shelf 1 No. 58

Estienne, Henri (II) 1574. Francfordiense emporium sive Francofordienses nundinae ... Henr. Stephanus. Anno 1574. Excudebat Henricus Stephanus.

Parchment, 6-7/8 x 4¼ x ⅛ in. Brunet 2, 1082.

FRANKFORT BOOK FAIR.

Cabinet S Shelf 1 No. 107

Francofordiense emporium of Henri Estienne [1574]. Edited with historical introduction original Latin text with English translation on opposite pages and notes. By James Westfall Thompson. The Caxton Club. Chicago, 1911. Illus.

Half vellum; 11½ x 7¾ in.

FRANKFORT BOOK FAIR

Cabinet W Shelf 2 No. 83

See Estienne, Henri. Author-Printer. Foire de Francfort ... Paris, 1875.

FRANKFORT, Commonwealth (The)

Cabinet Shelf No.

See Newspapers, Kentucky.

FRANKLIN, ALFRED.

Cabinet W Shelf 2 No. 19

Didot, Ambroise-Firmin. Biographical sketch. Excerpt from Bulletin du Bouquiniste, No. 437, March I, 1876. Paris, chez Aug. Aubrey.

Item in folder labelled "Miscellaneous items relating to the Didot Family of Printers."

FRANKLIN, ALFRED

Cabinet V Shelf 2 No. 18

(La) Sorbonne, ses origines, sa bibliotheque, les debuts de l'imprimerie a Paris...Deuxième edition. Paris, 1875.

Half morocco; 8-1/8 x 5¼ x 1-1/8 in.

FRANKLIN, ANN

Cabinet S Shelf 3 No. 104

Ann Franklin of Newport, printer, 1736-1763. By Howard Millar Chapin, Librarian of the Rhode Island Historical Society.

Biographical. Sister-in-law of B. Franklin.

p. 337 in volume, Wilberforce Eames ... A tribute to. Cambridge, 1924.

FRANKLIN, BENJAMIN

Cabinet R Shelf 1 No. 20

Account books kept by Benjamin Franklin: Ledger 1728-1739: Journal 1730-1737. Notes by George Simpson Eddy. New York, 1928.

Boards; 10-3/8 x 7-1/8 in.

FRANKLIN, BENJAMIN

Cabinet R Shelf 1 No. 21

Account books kept by Benjamin Franklin. Ledger "D" 1739-1747. Vol. 2. Notes by George Simpson Eddy. New York, 1929.

Boards; 10-3/8 x 7-1/8 in.

FRANKLIN, BENJAMIN

Cabinet R Shelf 3 No. 31

Account of the discovery of the original manuscript of Dr. Benjamin Franklin's autobiography.

See Bigelow's "Recollections of the late Edouard Laboulaye" ... New York, 1888. p. 24.

FRANKLIN, BENJAMIN

Cabinet A Shelf 3 No. 9

Advertisement of the American Philosophical Society, in Independent Gazetteer, No.1067, May 15, 1789; "A stated meeting of the Am. Philosophical Society, will be held at the house of the President, Dr. Franklin, this evening, at six o'clock. May 15. R. Patterson, secretary

Folio 2 in vol. labelled "Early printing in Pennsylvania".

FRANKLIN, BENJAMIN

Cabinet A Shelf 3 No. 9

Advertisement offering for sale the type foundry Franklin bequeathed to his grandson in 1790, in the General Advertiser (Aurore) Dec. 31, 1798. Sold because of death of B.F. Bache

See top of third col. p. 1.

"Type Foundery to be sold: The whole of the extensive and valuable apparatus for casting and completing metal printing types...

Item on folio 3 in vol. labelled "Early printing in Pennsylvania".

FRANKLIN, BENJAMIN

Cabinet R Shelf 5 No. 32 2 Vols.

Agent for Sauer Bible; loans types to Sauer; gets German types from Sauer ...

See pp. 14, 45, 47, 48, 235 in Sachse's German Sectarians of Pennsylvania, 1708-1742. Vol I, also Vol. II.

FRANKLIN, BENJAMIN

Cabinet R Shelf 1 No. 1

Allegory, Franklin in. By C. H. Hart, in The Century Magazine, Dec., 1890.

Bound in volume "Franklin, excerpts from Magazine", item 6.

FRANKLIN, BENJAMIN

Cabinet LL Shelf 1 No. 21

(Also a printer) Auch ein buchdrucker.

Brief biography in Hilderbrand's Handbuch für buchdrucker-lehrlinge...Eisenach, 1835.

FRANKLIN, BENJAMIN

Cabinet R Shelf 2 No. 98

(The) Amazing Benjamin Franklin. [A collection of essays relating to his activities]. Compiled and edited by J. Henry Smythe, Jr. New York, 1929. Illus.

Cloth; 8-3/8 x 5-5/8 in.

FRANKLIN, BENJAMIN.

Cabinet R Shelf 1 No. 41

Ancestry and descendants of Franklin in the Colonel Louis Bache (1779) line to 1889, interspersed with historico-genealogical events, by William Bache, 1889.

Half morocco, 9¼ x 6 ins; pp.8

FRANKLIN, BENJAMIN

Cabinet R Shelf 1 No. 3

Anniversary of the birth of Franklin. Semi-centennial of the Franklin Typographical Society. A verbatim report in the Boston Transcript. Boston, Jan. 20, 1874.

In volume "Frankliniana", p. 58 to 64.

FRANKLIN, BENJAMIN

Cabinet R Shelf 5 No. 149

An apprentice comes to Philadelphia. By René Bache. Illus. biography.

Excerpt from The Outlook, Jan. 17, 1923.

Item (h) in book with binder's title "Benjamin Franklin: various pamphlets", 1853-1926.

FRANKLIN, BENJAMIN

Cabinet R Shelf 5 No. 149

Archimedes and Franklin. A lecture, November 29, 1853. By Robert C. Winthrop. Boston, Nov. 29, 1853. (Pamphlet)

Item (a) in book with binder's title "Benjamin Franklin: various pamphlets", 1853-1926.

FRANKLIN, BENJAMIN

Cabinet R Shelf 1 No. 3

Banquet to honor the memory of B. F., Hotel Astor New York, Jan., 18, 1924: Programme and menu, with list of guests.

In Frankliniana, p.55.

FRANKLIN, BENJAMIN

Cabinet R Shelf 2 No. 40

Benjamin Franklin as a man of letters. By John Bach McMaster. Boston, 1887. Frontispiece portrait, B.F., Aet-84, from the original painting in the possession of the Historical Society of Penn.

Cloth; 8-1/8 x 4¾ in.

FRANKLIN, BENJAMIN.

Cabinet R Shelf 1 No. 3

Association of Franklin Medal Scholars, formed Sept. 17, 1855: Certificate of membership, dated July 27, 1857, signed by Edward Everett, president.

In Frankliniana, p.25.

FRANKLIN, BENJAMIN

Cabinet R Shelf 1 No. 1

Ben Franklin and Tom Paine. By John McGovern, in The National Magazine, Jan., 1906.
Comment upon two heros of the Revolutionary period in America.

Bound in volume "Franklin, excerpts from magazines. Item 5.

FRANKLIN, BENJAMIN

Cabinet S Shelf 6 No. 8

Benjamin Franklin, bookman. By Asa Don Dickinson [A bibliographical account, with facsimiles]. Excerpt from the "Bookman", May, 1921. Pamphlet.

Item 5 in vol. with binder's title "Early printing and printers. Pamphlets".

FRANKLIN, BENJAMIN

Cabinet R Shelf 2 No. 26

Autobiography of Benjamin Franklin. Edited from his manuscript, with notes and an introduction by John Bigelow. Philadelphia, 1868.

Cloth; 8 x 5¼ in.

FRANKLIN, BENJAMIN

Cabinet JJ Shelf 3 No. 18

Benjamin Franklin, 1706 - 1908.

see POETRY OF PRINTING. Benjamin Franklin

FRANKLIN, BENJAMIN.

Cabinet R Shelf 1 No. 79

Benjamin Franklin, Founder: The remarkable record of a Philadelphia Institution from 1728 to 1915, Philadelphia, 1915.

Boards 9¾ x 6-3/8 ins., pp.53.

FRANKLIN, BENJAMIN.

Cabinet R Shelf 1 No. 64

Autobiography of Benjamin Franklin, The. Boston, 1906. Illus.

Orig. bds., 11¼ x 7-3/4 ins., pp.XX, 183. Portrait and 27 plates.

FRANKLIN, BENJAMIN

Cabinet R Shelf 1 No. 80

Benjamin Franklin and Germany: Thesis presented to the Faculty of the Graduate School of the University of Pennsylvania. By Beatrice M. Victory, 1915.
Includes a list of Franklin's works in German, also a chronological bibliography.

Cloth; 10¼ x 6¼ in.

FRANKLIN, BENJAMIN.

Cabinet R Shelf 1 No. 97

Benjamin Franklin in oil and bronze, by John Clycle Oswald. New York, 1926.

Printed linen, 12½ x 9-5/8 ins. pp.58.

FRANKLIN, BENJAMIN

Cabinet R Shelf 5 No. 149

Bagatelles, Franklin's. By J.G. Rosengarten. Reprinted from Proceedings of the American Philosophical Society, vol. XL. July 30, 1901. Pamphlet.
Bibliographical.

Item (e) in book with binder's title "Benjamin Franklin: various pamphlets", 1853-1926.

FRANKLIN, BENJAMIN

Cabinet R Shelf 2 No. 47

Benjamin Franklin and the University of Pennsylvania. Edited by Francis Newton Thorpe. Washington: Government Printing Office,1893. Circulation of Information No. 2. 1892.Illus
Biographical and historical account of the origin and development of Penn. University.

Half morocco; 9-1/8 x 6 in.

FRANKLIN, BENJAMIN

Cabinet R Shelf 3 No. 55

Benjamin Franklin, Printer. By John Clyde Oswald. New York: Associated Advertising Clubs of the World, 1917. Illus. Facsimile.

Half russia, 8 x 5½ in.

FRANKLIN, BENJAMIN.

Cabinet R Shelf 1 No. 3

Banquet in honor of the birthday of the immortal Franklin, Delmonico's, (New York), Jan., 17, 1872: Menu.

In Frankliniana, p.52.

FRANKLIN, BENJAMIN.

Cabinet R Shelf 1 No. 62

Benjamin Franklin as a Free Mason, by Julius Friedrich Sachse, Litt. D. librarian of the Grand Lodge of Pennsylvania, Philadelphia, 1906. Illus.

Cloth, 10 x 6¾ ins., pp. (VIII), 150.

FRANKLIN, BENJAMIN

Cabinet R Shelf 5 No. 5

Benjamin Franklin to William Bradford: Long credits in Old Philadelphia.
See Bradford, William: An Old Philadelphian: Colonel William Bradford ... 1776. By John W. Wallace, 1884. p. 447.

FRANKLIN, BENJAMIN.

Cabinet R Shelf 1 No. 33

Benjamin Franklin's life and writings: A bibliographical essay on the Stevens collection of books and manuscripts relating to Doctor Franklin. By Henry Stevens, London, 1881. Illus.

Cloth, 11¼ x 7-3/4 ins., pp. (VIII), 40.

FRANKLIN, BENJAMIN

Cabinet R Shelf 5 No. 149

[Biographical account, with portrait.]

Excerpt from "Electic", July, 1864.

Item (c) in book with binder's title "Benjamin Franklin: various pamphlets". 1853-1926.

FRANKLIN, BENJAMIN

Cabinet R Shelf 1 No. 2

Books printed by Benjamin Franklin...For sale by Dodd, Mead & Company. N.Y. City. April 1906.

Pamphlet I, in volume "Franklin Pamphlets" Bound 1928.

FRANKLIN, BENJAMIN

Cabinet R Shelf 1 No. 61.01

Bi-Centenary of the birth of Benjamin Franklin, Ceremony held in Paris to commemorate the. April 27, 1906. Compiled by the chairman of the Press Committee. Paris, 1906. Frontispiece; The Franklin Statue in Paris. Halftone.

Paper; 7-1/8 x 5-1/8 x ¼ in.

FRANKLIN, BENJAMIN

Cabinet JJ Shelf 3 No. 7

Birthday celebration, January 17, 1850.

see CELEBRATIONS, PRINTER'S. 1850, New York City, New York Typographical Society...

FRANKLIN, BENJAMIN

Cabinet A Shelf 2 No. 91

Boston's world printer-messenger. Manifold ways in which the great diplomat made himself conspicuous in his vocation -- A legacy of pride for all craftsmen of today -- Letter founding, engraving, ink making...By Carl C. Fowler.

Illus. article in the Graphic Arts Section of the Boston Evening Transcript, Tues. Aug., 29, 1922, part four, p.1.

FRANKLIN, BENJAMIN

Cabinet R Shelf 1 No. 61

Bi-Centenary of the birth of Right Worshipful Past Grand Master, Brother Benjamin Franklin Held in the Masonic Temple, in Philadelphia, March, A.D. 1906- A.L. 5906. Together with an account of the Memorial Service at his tomb. Grand Lodge of Pennsylvania. Philadelphia 1906. Frontispiece portrait; facsimiles and other illus.

Cloth; 9¾ x 6¾ x 1-3/8 in.

FRANKLIN, BENJAMIN

Cabinet JJ Shelf 4 No. 16

Birthdays of Benjamin Franklin and the celebrations by the Typothetae of New York, January 17, 1884 to January 17, 1893.

Annual dinners of the N.Y. Typothetae, reports of speeches, menus, etc.

Cloth; 8-7/8 x 6 x 5/8 in.

FRANKLIN, BENJAMIN

Cabinet R Shelf 2 No. 101

Brad Stephens proposes a Course in Franklin to Yale, on its acquisition of the Wm. S. Mason Collection of Frankliniana.

Excerpt from The Providence Journal, April 28, 1936.

In envelope.

FRANKLIN, BENJAMIN

Cabinet R Shelf 1 No. 66

Bi-centennial celebration under the auspices of the American Philosophical Society, Philadelphia, 1906. Vol. I; Vols. 2 to 6, Celendar of the papers of Benjamin Franklin in the Library of the American Philosophical Society. Edited by I. Minis Hays. Philadelphia, 1908.

Includes Chronology of Benjamin Franklin, in Vol. 2, pages immediately following preface.

Cloth; 10 x 7 in.

FRANKLIN, BENJAMIN

Cabinet R Shelf 3 No. 46

Book of remembrance. By Mrs. E.D. Gillespie. Philadelphia - London, 1901. Illus.

The author, Mrs. Gillespie, was a member of the Bache family (Franklin's descendants), and in this book of remembrance there are many references to B. Franklin.

Cloth; 7½ x 5¼ in.

FRANKLIN, BENJAMIN

Cabinet QQ Shelf 2 No. 31

Briefly mentioned in book of "Travels in the United States of America and Canada"....By I. Finch. London, 1833.

Boards; 8¾ x 5-5/8.

FRANKLIN, BENJAMIN

Cabinet R Shelf 5 No. 149

Bigelow, John: Autobiography of Benjamin Franklin, Edited from his manuscript, with notes and introduction. Philadelphia, 1868 (A review)

Excerpt from Historical Magazine, May, 1868.

Item (d) in book with binder's title "Benjamin Franklin: various pamphlets", 1853-1926.

FRANKLIN, BENJAMIN

Cabinet F Shelf 4 No. 13

Book upon which B. Franklin worked as a compositor while in London: "Wollaston's Religion of Nature", Printed by S. Palmer, London, 1725.

Calf; 9½ x 7-7/8 in.

FRANKLIN, BENJAMIN

Cabinet R Shelf 2 No. 3

Bronze bust of B. Franklin, by John J. Boyle, letter concerning the. By Henry Lewis Bullen. Illus.

Item in "The American Collector", Oct., 1926, vol.3, No.1, p.48

FRANKLIN, BENJAMIN.

Cabinet R Shelf 1 No. 3

[Biographical account. French text. Excerpt from "Hist. D'Amerique." n.d.n.p. Frontispiece portrait, engraved by C. N. Cochin.]

Item on p. 65 "Frankliniana."

FRANKLIN, BENJAMIN.

Cabinet R Shelf 1 No. 58

Books printed by B.F.: Books from the library of B.F.: Letters of B.F. and his son William Franklin, etc: A catalogue of sale (with prices realized) of library of Hon.Samuel W. Pennypacker, Philadelphia, Dec., 14, 1905. Facsimile.

Includes a facsimiles of two rare portraits of B.F.

Half morocco, 10 x 7 ins., pp (V), 90, 5.

FRANKLIN, BENJAMIN

Stack A Shelf 1&2 Number 68

Bullen, Henry Lewis. Benjamin Franklin and what printing did for him. By H. L. Bullen.

In The Inland Printer, vol. LXVIII, p. 201

FRANKLIN, BENJAMIN

Stack A · Shelf 1&2 · Number 70

Bullen, Henry Lewis: Benjamin Franklin's family and his descendants.

In The Inland Printer, Vol. LXX. p. 531.

FRANKLIN, BENJAMIN.

Stack · Shelf · Number

See Bullen, Henry Lewis: Benjamin Franklin's permanent bequests, etc.

FRANKLIN, BENJAMIN

Cabinet R · Shelf 1 · No. 91

Bullen, Henry Lewis: The greatness of Benjamin Franklin: An article in volume "The Pictorial Life of Benjamin Franklin," Philadelphia (Dill & Collins), 1923.

Imitation leather, label; 11¼ x 8-3/4 in.

FRANKLIN, BENJAMIN

Cabinet R · Shelf 1 · No. 91

Bullen, Henry Lewis: The Vitality of Benjamin Franklin's enterprise: An essay taken from the "Statlers Roundabout," Feb. 1927, and inserted in Volume "The Pictorial life of Benjamin Franklin," Philadelphia (Dill & Collins), 1923.

Imitation leather, label; 11¼ x 8-3/4 in.

FRANKLIN, BENJAMIN

Cabinet R · Shelf 1 · No. 66 · 6 Vols.

Calendar of the papers of Benjamin Franklin in the library of the American Philosophical Society, 5 Vols. (Vols. 11-VI, of Record of Celebration of two hundredth anniversary of birth of Franklin). Philadelphia, 1906 to 1908. 6 Vols.

Cloth, 10¼ x 7½ ins., pp. (XX), 573: (IX) 526: (IX) 560: (IX), 510: (IX), 325.

FRANKLIN, BENJAMIN

Cabinet R · Shelf 1 · No. 70

Calendar of the papers of Benjamin Franklin in Library of the University of Pennsylvania. Being an appendix of the "Calendar of the papers of the Benjamin Franklin in the Library of the American Philosophical Society," edited by I. Minis Hays. Philadelphia, 1908.

Cloth, 10 x 7 ins., pp. from 399 to 546.

FRANKLIN, BENJAMIN

Cabinet R · Shelf 2 · No. 48

Career of Benjamin Franklin. A paper read before the American Philosophical Society, Philadelphia, May 25, 1893, at the celebration of the 150th anniversary of its formation in that City. By Samuel Abbott Green, Groton, Mass. June, 1893.

Bound in with a reprint of the above, Philadelphia, 1893.

Half morocco; 9¾ x 6¼ in.

FRANKLIN, BENJAMIN

Cabinet O · Shelf 1 · No. 96

Catalogue of an exhibition commemorating the 200th anniversary of the birth of Benjamin Franklin. At the Grolier Club of the City of New York, January 1906.

Half morocco; 7 x 4-3/8 x ½ in.

FRANKLIN, BENJAMIN

Cabinet R · Shelf 1 · No. 44

Catalogue of works relating to Benjamin Franklin in the Boston Public Library, including the collection given by Doctor Samuel Abbott Green, with the titles of similar works not in the library. Boston, 1883.

(Also) Franklin portraits in the Boston Public Library (excerpt from "Bulletin", vol. XI, No. 2, 1892).

Bound in one volume: Half morocco; 11¼ x 7½ in pp. 139-150.

FRANKLIN, BENJAMIN

Cabinet R · Shelf 1 · No. 36

Catalogue of works relating to Benjamin Franklin in the Boston Public Library, including the collection given by Doctor Samuel Abbot Greer Published by order of the Trustees. Boston, 1883.

Half morocco; 11-1/8 x 7¼ in. Ford 969.

FRANKLIN, BENJAMIN

Cabinet R · Shelf 2 · No. 55

Ceremonies attending the unveiling of the Statue of Benjamin Franklin, June 14, 1899. Sculptor John J. Boyle. Presented to the City of Philadelphia by Mr. Justus C. Strawbridge. Philadelphia, 1899.

Cloth; 9½ x 6 in.

FRANKLIN, BENJAMIN

Cabinet R · Shelf 2 · No. 82

Ceremony held in Paris to commemorate the Bi-Centenary of the birth of Benjamin Franklin. Compiled by the Chairman of the Press Committee. Paris, April 27, 1906.

Portraits of the donor, John H. Harjes, and picture of the Franklin statue at Paris.

Cloth; 7½ x 5¼ in.

FRANKLIN, BENJAMIN

Cabinet X · Shelf 5 · No. 3

Character of Benjamin Franklin. Excerpt The Book of Days [London, n.d.], Portrait, and illus. of printing press worked at by Franklin in London.

p. 27 in vol. with binder's title "Scrap-Book, 1705-1891, relating toprinting."

FRANKLIN, BENJAMIN.

Cabinet R · Shelf 1 · No. 1

Character of Franklin, The. An excerpt from the North American Review, Oct., 1856.

Bound in volume "Franklin, excerpts from magazines," item 1.

FRANKLIN, BENJAMIN

Cabinet R · Shelf 1 · No. 66

Chronology of Benjamin Franklin: Bi-centennial celebration under the auspices of the American Philosophical Society, Philadelphia, 1906. (6 vols.)

Chronology in vol. 2, pages immediately following preface.

Cloth; 10 x 7 in.

FRANKLIN, BENJAMIN.

Stack A · Shelf 1&2 · Number 62

Circular printed by Franklin, which in 1918, sold for $1,300.00: An account given by Henry Lewis Bullen, in (Collectanea Typographica) The Inland Printer, vol.LXII, p.648.

FRANKLIN, BENJAMIN

Cabinet R · Shelf 1 · No. 83

Collection of Franklin Imprints in the Museum of the Curtis Publishing Company. With a short title check list of all the books, pamphlets broadsides, etc., known to have been printed by Benjamin Franklin. Compiled by William Campbell. Philadelphia, 1918. Facsimiles.

Note: This collection now in possession of University of Pennsylvania.

Cloth, 11-3/4 x 9 ins. pp. 333.

FRANKLIN, BENJAMIN

Cabinet R · Shelf 3 · No. 50

Commemoration of the two hundred and sixth anniversary of the birth of Benjamin Franklin: Annual Dinner of the Typothetae of the City of New York, 1912. Five folders designed by T.M. Cleland.

Each folder with same title, supplementary legend at bottom: B.Franklin from an etching T.L.DeVinne from bronze bust, Guests, Menu, Toasts.

In board case; 7½ x 5¼ in.

FRANKLIN, BENJAMIN.

Cabinet R Shelf 1 No. 1

Cradle of the Franklin's, The, by Arthur Branscombe, in Munsey's Magazine, July,1907.Illus.

Bound in volume "Franklin, excerpts from Magazines," item 12.

FRANKLIN, BENJAMIN.

Cabinet 26 Shelf 2 No. 2

See Early Printing, Historical. History of the introduction and development, etc.

FRANKLIN, BENJAMIN

Cabinet R Shelf 5 No. 149

Extracts from the autobiography and other writings of Benjamin Franklin. Suggested for use in the Public Schools of the City of Boston ...In connection with the observance of the 200th anniversary of Franklin's birth. Boston, 1906. (Pamphlet)

Item (f) in book with binder's title "Benjamin Franklin: various pamphlets". 1853-1926.

FRANKLIN, BENJAMIN.

Cabinet R Shelf 1 No. 3

Description of the process to be observed in making large sheets of paper in the Chinese manner, with a smooth surface. Communicated by Dr. B. Franklin to the American Philosophical Society, Philadelphia, n.d.

In Frankliniana p. 39.

FRANKLIN, BENJAMIN

Cabinet R Shelf 1 No. 7

Electricitat: A pamphlet written in German, printed in Germany after 1770, which describes Dr. Franklin's discoveries in electricity. No title, n.d.n.p.

Not in Ford. Possibly the earliest German work on B.F.'S invention: Alludes to publications issued in 1770; earliest German edition mentioned by Ford is in 3 vols. Dresden 1780.

Boards; $6\frac{3}{4}$ x $3\frac{3}{4}$ in. pp. 24.

FRANKLIN, BENJAMIN.

Cabinet R Shelf 1 No. 3

Faith of Franklin,The, poem by Harry Webb Farrington, with line portrait.

In Frankliniana, p.47

FRANKLIN, BENJAMIN.

Cabinet G Shelf 3 No. 31

Dialogue with the gout. With an account of the first editions by Luther S. Livingston. printed by Carl Purington Rollins at the Dyke Mill, Montague, Mass., 1917.

Full morocco, tooled, 8 x 5¼ ins., pp.16 (6)

FRANKLIN, BENJAMIN.

Cabinet R Shelf 1 No. 90

Eulogies of Benjamin Franklin, by presidents of the U.T.A: American Institute of Graphic Arts: National Editorial Association: Press Congress of the World, etc., p.67 in The American Printer: Franklin number, Jan. 20, 1923.

Half morocco, 12 x 8-7/8 ins.

FRANKLIN, BENJAMIN.

Cabinet R Shelf 1 No. 17

Features of Inauguration of the Franklin Statue in Boston, Sept., 17, 1856, by W.J.Knowles (A poem) Boston, 1856.

Stitched, $7\frac{1}{2}$ x $4\frac{3}{4}$ ins., pp.12. Inserted in back part Memorial of the Inauguration.

FRANKLIN, BENJAMIN.

Cabinet R Shelf 1 No. 3

(Dissertation on liberty and necessity, pleasure and pain: A pamphlet.) Excerpt from the London Telegraph, 6/6/13, relating how Stevens, bookseller, bought this pamphlet (written and published by B.F. in 1724) for 2/6 in 1850, and how Stevens son bought it back at auction in 1913 for £1005. (In 1881 the Library of Congress bought a copy for $500.00.)

In Franliniana, p.27

FRANKLIN, BENJAMIN

Cabinet R Shelf 2 No. 1

Eulogium on Benjamin Franklin, L. L. D. ... delivered March 1, 1791, in the German Lutheran Church ... By William Smith, D. D. ... Printed by Benjamin Franklin Bache, Philadelphia, 1792. Many portraits.

Half morocco; 9 x 6 in.

FRANKLIN, BENJAMIN

Cabinet R Shelf 1 No. 2

(The) Fifth Estate: Delivered in connection with the Centenary Celebration of the founding of the Franklin Institute...and published in the Journal of the Franklin Institute, vol. 198, No.5. By D. Little. Reprinted from The Chemical Foundation, Inc. through the courtesy of the Atlantic Monthly.

Pamphlet #3 in "Franklin Pamphlets". Bound 1928.

FRANKLIN, BENJAMIN

Cabinet R Shelf 5 No. 149

Dr. Ben Franklin. By Philip Guedalla. Forum Americana Series---I. Drawings by E.H. Suydam.

Excerpt from Forum, January, 1926.

Item (k) in book with binder's title "Benjamin Franklin: various pamphlets". 1853-1926.

FRANKLIN, BENJAMIN

Cabinet R Shelf 5 No. 149

Evans, Henry R. Benj. Franklin and religion. Illus.

Excerpt from The Master Mason. New Jersey Edition. August, 1925, No.2.

Item (j) in book with binder's title "Benjamin Franklin: various pamphlets". 1853-1926.

FRANKLIN, BENJAMIN

Cabinet QQ Shelf 2 No. 6

Fireplace, Franklin's Pennsylvania, descriptive analytic notice.

see

DESARNOD, JOSEPH-FRANCOIS. Mémoire sur les foyers économiques...Paris-Lyon, 1789.

FRANKLIN, BENJAMIN.

Cabinet R Shelf 1 No. 1

Early and private life of Benjamin Franklin, by Jacob Abbott, in Harpers' New Monthly Magazine, Jan.,1852. Illus., etchings.

Bound in volume "Franklin, excerpt from magazines," item 3.

FRANKLIN, BENJAMIN (Author)

Cabinet R Shelf 1 No. 5

Experiments and observations on electricity made at Philadelphia in America by Benjamin Franklin, L.L.D. and F.R.S. To which are added, letters and papers on philosophical subjects...and illustrated with copper plates London, 1769.

Boards; calf back; $9\frac{1}{4}$ x 7-1/8 in. Ford 303.

FRANKLIN, BENJAMIN

Cabinet NN Shelf 2 No. 8

First famous American journalist, who became editor of the Pennsylvania Gazette in 1729. Brief account, with portrait. In Famous Editors. By William S. Bridgman. Excerpt from Munsey's March, 1904.

Item 22 in Vol. "Various Editors. Excerpts and Pamphlets".

FRANKLIN, BENJAMIN.

Cabinet R Shelf 1 No. 3

First prospectus of constitution, by-laws, and form of application for membership in the International Benjamin Franklin Society, New York, 1893.

In Frankliniana, p.46.

FRANKLIN, BENJAMIN

Cabinet R Shelf 2 No. 79

Franklin as a man of Science and an inventor. Benjamin Franklin Trust Funds to Boston and Philadelphia. By Dr. Edwin James Houston. Philadelphia, 1906. In Journal of Franklin Institute, April and May, 1906. Illus.

Half morocco; 9¼ x 6¼ in.

FRANKLIN, BENJAMIN

Cabinet R Shelf 2 No. 23

Franklin Fund: A sketch of the origin, object and character of the Franklin Fund, for the benefit of young married mechanics of Boston, [By S. F. McCleary]. City Document--No.89. Boston, 1866.

Half morocco; 9¼ x 5¾ in.

FRANKLIN, BENJAMIN

Cabinet R Shelf 3 No. 170

Follett, Frederick. History of the press of western New York; together with the proceedings of the printers' festival held on the 141st Anniversary of the birthday of Franklin, in the City of Rochester, on Monday, Jan. 18, 1847.

Cloth; 9½ x 6 in.

FRANKLIN, BENJAMIN

Cabinet R Shelf 1 No. 3

Franklin as printer and publisher; The many sided Franklin, by Paul Leicester Ford, in The Century Magazine, April, 1899. Portraits.

Bound in volume "Franklin, excerpts from magazines," item 14

FRANKLIN, BENJAMIN.

Cabinet R Shelf 1 No. 1

Franklin in allegory, by C.H. Hart, in The Century Magazine, Dec., 1890.

Bound in volume "Franklin, excerpts from magazines," item 6.

FRANKLIN, BENJAMIN

Cabinet QQ Shelf 3 No. 36

Footprints of famous Americans in Paris. By John Joseph Conway. London-New York, 1912. Illus.

Chap. I on Benj. Franklin.

Cloth; 8-7/8 x 5-5/8 x 2 in.

FRANKLIN, BENJAMIN.

Cabinet R Shelf 1 No. 3

Franklin at Passy, 1777-1785, by Henri Bouchot Excerpt, pp.22, beautifully printed, Illus. with copperplates, first item in Frankliniana, a scrap book.

FRANKLIN, BENJAMIN

Cabinet R Shelf 1 No. 1

Franklin in France, by John Hay, in The Century Magazine, Jan., 1906. Portrait.

Bound in volume "Franklin, excerpts from magazines," item 8.

FRANKLIN, BENJAMIN

Cabinet R Shelf 2 No. 44

Ford, Paul Leicester. Franklin bibliography; a list of books written by or relating to Benjamin Franklin. Brooklyn, 1889.

Half morocco; 9¼ x 6¼ in.

FRANKLIN, BENJAMIN.

Cabinet R Shelf 2 No. 17

Franklin before the Privy Council, White Hall Chapel, London, 1774, on behalf of the Province of Massachusetts, to advocate the removal of Hutchinson and Oliver, Philadelphia 1860.

Engraving of this celebrated event at front with key to names of persons.

Orig. cloth, 9¼ x 6 ins., pp (V), 134.

FRANKLIN, BENJAMIN.

Cabinet R Shelf 2 No. 39

Franklin in France. From original documents, most of which are now published for the first time. By Edward E. Hale and Edward E. Hale, Jr. Boston, Robert Brothers, 1887. Illus.

Orig. cloth bds., 9¾ x 7 ins., pp. (XVI) 3 leaves, 478.

FRANKLIN, BENJAMIN

Cabinet R Shelf 1 No. 1

Franklin, the citizen, by Geo. W. Alger. in The American Magazine, Jan., 1906. Portraits.

Bound in volume "Franklin, excerpts from magazines," item 13.

FRANKLIN, BENJAMIN.

Cabinet R Shelf 1 No. 3

(Franklin Dinner.) Third annual dinner of the Franklin Literary Society of the City of Brooklyn in celebration of the birth of B.F. Jan., 18, 1886.

In Frankliniana p.57.

FRANKLIN, BENJAMIN.

Cabinet R Shelf 1 No. 1

Franklin in Germany, by J.G.Rosengarten, in Lippincott's, Jan., 1903.

Bound in volume "Franklin, excerpts from magazines," item 4.

FRANKLIN, BENJAMIN

Cabinet R Shelf 1 No. 22

Franklin and his Press at Passy: An account of the books, pamphlets and leaflets printed there, including the long-lost "Bagatelles." By Luther S. Livingston, New York: The Grolier Club, 1914.

Presentation copy from author to H.L. Bullen, A.L.S. of the author inserted.

Boards; 9¾ x 6½ in.

FRANKLIN, BENJAMIN

Cabinet R Shelf 1 No. 2

(The) Franklin Fund: Proceedings of the Massachusetts Historical Society. October Meeting, 1897.

Pamphlet #4 in volume "Franklin Pamphlets". Bound 1928.

FRANKLIN, BENJAMIN.

Cabinet R Shelf 1 No. 3

Franklin Institute of Boston, built with funds bequeathed by B.F. in his will, 1790; a halftone of the building.

In Frankliniana, p.41.

FRANKLIN, BENJAMIN

Cabinet 73 Shelf 1 No. 3

Franklin keepsake...Given by the Zellerbach Paper Company to Members of the American Institute of Graphic Arts. The portrait of Franklin was specially painted by Henry Raschen. Text by John Eugene Hasty. Printed by John Henry Nash in San Francisco, Sept. 1925. Broadside.

Item on p.30 of scrap book, "JOHN HENRY NASH: HIS WORK."

FRANKLIN, BENJAMIN

Cabinet R Shelf 1 No. 1

Franklin's home and host in France, by John Bigelow, in The Century Magazine, Mar., 1888. Illus.

Bound in volume "Franklin, excerpts from magazines," item 11.

FRANKLIN, BENJAMIN

Cabinet QQ Shelf 1 No. 42

His genius, life, and character. By John L. Jewett. An oration delivered before the New York Typographical Society, Jan. 17, 1849.

See p.185, Brenton's Voices of the Press ...New York, 1850.

FRANKLIN, BENJAMIN

Cabinet R Shelf 1 No. 1

Franklin manuscripts, The, by J. S. Loring in Historical magazine, Jan., 1859.

Bound in volume "Franklin, excerpts from magazines," item 15.

FRANKLIN, BENJAMIN

Cabinet R Shelf 1 No. 1

Franklin's place in the science of the last century, by Dr. J.W. Draper, in Harper's, July, 1880.

Bound in volume "Franklin, excerpts from magazines," item 7.

FRANKLIN, BENJAMIN

Cabinet S Shelf 5 No. 21

History of a newspaper: The Pennsylvania Gazette By Paul L. Ford, in the Magazine of American History, April, 1887.

Bound with other items in volume "Excerpts relating to printing in America", pp. 84-88.

FRANKLIN, BENJAMIN.

Cabinet R Shelf 1 No. 3

Frankliniana, a scrap book. Contains miscellanea relating to B.F.

Half mor., 13 x 10 in; 3 in. thick.

FRANKLIN, BENJAMIN

Cabinet R Shelf 1 No. 3

Franklin's printing press, The narrative of; brought from London to Boston in 1717, taken to Newport R. I. in 1732, returned to Boston in 1864 ... A typewritten broadside issued by the Massachusetts Charitable Mechanical Assoication.

In volume "Frankliniana," p. 29.

FRANKLIN, BANJAMIN

Cabinet R Shelf 3 No. 23

History of Franklin Lodge, Instituted June 24th, A.D. 1812 - A.L. 5812. Reorganized October 15th, A.D. 1846 - A.L. 5846. Philadelphia, 1868.

"The name "Franklin Lodge" adopted as a compliment to the grandson of B.F., Brother Richard Bache, its first Worshipful Master."

Cloth; $8\frac{3}{4}$ x 5-5/8 in.

FRANKLIN, BENJAMIN.

Cabinet R Shelf 1 No. 63

Frankliniana, from Bulletin of the New York Public Library, Jan., 1906.

Half morocco, $10\frac{1}{4}$ x $7\frac{1}{2}$ ins., pp.63

FRANKLIN, BENJAMIN

Cabinet NN Shelf 2 No. 25

German newspaper, 1732, printed and published by B. Franklin.

see

SACHSE, JULIUS F. First German newspaper published in America...

FRANKLIN, BENJAMIN

Cabinet R Shelf 2 No. 62

History of the Franklin Fund; being the agreed facts in Collins vs James H. Doyle et als., and the Attorney General. Boston, Municipal Printing Office, 1902.

Includes "Will and Codicil" of Benjamin Franklin. See also R/2/63.

Half morocco; $9\frac{1}{2}$ x 8 in.

FRANKLIN, BENJAMIN.

Cabinet R Shelf 1 No. 87

Franklin's account against Massachusetts: Includes Joseph Massie's letter, No.VIII, and letters of Barbeu-Dubourg to Franklin; also Franklin to Hudgson, 1781-82.

Proceedings of the Massachusetts Historical Society, 1922, pp.94-161.

Half Morocco, $9\frac{1}{2}$ x $6\frac{1}{4}$ ins.

FRANKLIN, BENJAMIN

Cabinet Y Shelf 1 No. 9

Gutenberg and Franklin. Eine festgabe zum vierten jubiläum der erfindung der buchdruckerkunst ...von Karl Preusker, Leipzig, 1840. With a lithographed title showing the portraits of Gutenberg and Franklin, and the statue of the former at Mainz.

Half morocco; 8-5/8 x $5\frac{1}{4}$ x $\frac{1}{4}$ in.

FRANKLIN, BENJAMIN

Cabinet R Shelf 3 No. 45

Home of the Franklins (in England): The cradle of the Washingtons and the home of the Franklins. By Arthur Branscombe. Profusely illustrated by the author.

Boards; $7\frac{1}{4}$ x 10 in.

FRANKLIN, BENJAMIN.

Cabinet R Shelf 1 No. 52

Franklin's account with the "Lodge of Masons," 1731-1737, as found upon the pages of his Daily Journal. Read before the Right Worshipful Grand Lodge F. and A.M. of Pennsylvania, Dec., 27, 1898 by Brother Julius Friedrich Sachse, Columbia Lodge, No.91. Philadelphia, 1899. Portrait and facsimile.

Half morocco, 12 x 9 ins., pp.21 with 4 plates.

FRANKLIN, BENJAMIN

Cabinet JJ Shelf 3 No. 6

His genius, life and character. An oration delivered before the New York Typographical Society on the occasion of the birthday of Franklin, at the Printers' Festival, held January 17, 1849. By John L. Jewett. Published by order of the Society. New York, 1849.

Cloth; 9-1/8 x $5\frac{3}{4}$ x $\frac{1}{4}$ in.

FRANKLIN, BENJAMIN.

Cabinet R Shelf 1 No. 90

How Benjamin Franklin became a publisher. A story of two hundred years ago. An article in The American Printer. Franklin number, Jan., 20, 1923, p.57. Facsimiles of some early newspapers.

Half morocco, 12 x 8-7/8 ins.

FRANKLIN, BENJAMIN

Cabinet R Shelf 1 No. 3

Important Franklin discovery, An, by Mary C. Crawford, in The Outlook, Jan., 20,1906. Facsimile reproductions of ode printed on the press set up at Passy by Franklin for his grandson.

Bound in volume "Franklin, excerpts from magazines," item 10.

FRANKLIN, BENJAMIN

Cabinet F Shelf 1 No. 75

Imprint, 1730, Philadelphia. The earliest book with imprint "B. Franklin".

See IMPRINTS, United States. Franklin, Benjamin, Philadelphia, 1730.

FRANKLIN, BENJAMIN

Cabinet 27 Shelf 2 No. 26

In article by Henry Lewis Bullen there is shown pictures of medals struck in honor of Benjamin Franklin and Giambattista Bodoni, with accounts of their printing art careers.

see THE AMERICAN BULLETIN, April-May, 1912, pp. 1-2.

FRANKLIN, BENJAMIN

Cabinet R Shelf 2 No. 65

Inaugural Address of Joseph H. Choate, American Ambassador, Oct. 23, 1903, as president of the Birmingham and Midland Institute.

Half morocco; 9 x 6 in.

FRANKLIN, BENJAMIN (Author)

Cabinet F Shelf 1 No. 60

Interest of Great Britain considered with regard to her Colonies and the acquisition of Canada and Guadaloupe....Boston: Reprinted by B. Mecom, and sold at the New Printing Office, near the Town-House, 1760.

Half morocco; $7\frac{1}{4}$ x $4\frac{1}{2}$ x $\frac{1}{2}$ in. Evans 3, 8601. p.254.

FRANKLIN, BENJAMIN

Cabinet R Shelf 2 No. 4

L'Inventeur du Paratonnerre, et auteur d'ouvrages utiles a tontes les classes de citoyens. Par Th. G. Clemson de Philadelphia. [1833]. With portrait.

In Vol. Montyon et Franklin, Societe , 1833-1834." pp. n.n.

Tooled calf; $8\frac{1}{4}$ x 5-3/8 x 1-1/8 in.

FRANKLIN, BENJAMIN

Cabinet 27 Shelf 2 No. 26

Last years of Benjamin Franklin. With full-page illustration of Benjamin Franklin at his home in Philadelphia(1787). Reproduced from an oil painting by Henry Bacon (1876) Article by Henry Lewis Bullen.

see THE AMERICAN BULLETIN, January, 1914, page 2 and frontispiece.

FRANKLIN, BENJAMIN.

Cabinet R Shelf 1 No. 3

Letter by John Bigelow on Franklin statuette supposed to be the work of Nini.

In Frankliniana, pp. 9-12.

FRANKLIN, BENJAMIN.

Letter to Lieut. Gov. Golden. See Stereotyping, Golden.

FRANKLIN, BENJAMIN

Cabinet R Shelf 2 No. 85

Letters from Benjamin Franklin to William Franklin, William Strahan, Marquis de Condorcet, and letters from William Franklin to William Strahan, 1748-1781. Philadelphia, 1909.

Half morocco; $9\frac{1}{2}$ x 7 in.

FRANKLIN, BENJAMIN.

Cabinet R Shelf 1 No. 1

Letters from Franklin: Excerpts from the Port Folio, May, 1812.

Two humorous and self-revealing letters.

Bound in volume "Franklin, excerpts from magazines," item 2.

FRANKLIN, BENJAMIN

Cabinet R Shelf 2 No. 61

Letters from James Parker to Benjamin Franklin relating to their partnership in a Printing Business in New York City and in New Jersey 1741 to 1770; with Letters from children of James Parker to B. Franklin, 1770-1773.

Excerpts from Proceedings of Massachusetts Historical Society, 1902.

Cloth; $9\frac{1}{2}$ x 6 in.

FRANKLIN, BENJAMIN.

Cabinet R Shelf 1 No. 63

Letters of Franklin printed from the originals in the New York Public Library.

In Frankliniana, pp.13-22.

FRANKLIN, BENJAMIN.

Cabinet R Shelf 1 No. 19

Letters to Benjamin Franklin, from his family and friends, 1751-1790. New York, 1859.

Includes portraits of Franklin's family.

Half morocco, 10 x $7\frac{1}{4}$ ins., pp.195.

FRANKLIN, BENJAMIN

Cabinet R Shelf 1 No. 25 2 vols.

Life and times of Benjamin Franklin, by James Parton, 2 vols. New York, 1865. Portraits of Franklin, his son and daughter. Cloth, large paper edition, 11 x 8 ins., vol. 1, pp. 627: vol. 2, pp. 707. Ford p. 371.

FRANKLIN, BENJAMIN

Cabinet R Shelf 1 No. 2

Life of Benjamin Franklin. n.a.n. In Illustrated Magazine of Art. July 1853. Illus.

Pamphlet #10 in volume "Franklin Pamphlets". Bound, 1928.

FRANKLIN, BENJAMIN

Cabinet R Shelf 3 No. 28

(The) Life of Benjamin Franklin. By O. L. Holley Philadelphia: John E. Potter & Co. [1885?]. Illus.

The wood engravings depicting scenes in the life of Franklin are from the originals by Alex. Anderson, son of a N.Y. master printer and a contemporary of B.F.

Cloth; $7\frac{1}{2}$ x $4\frac{3}{4}$ in.

FRANKLIN, BENJAMIN

Cabinet R Shelf 2 No. 7

Life of Dr. Franklin: A lecture by the Rev. Hugh M'Neile, A. M. as delivered at the Liverpool Royal Amphitheatre. In aid of The London Printers' Pension Society...Note to the reader, by John B. Murray of New York. London, 1841. Lithograph of A.L.S. by B. Franklin to G. Whitefield, dated New York, 1756.

Half morocco; $8\frac{3}{4}$ x $5\frac{1}{2}$ in.

FRANKLIN, BENJAMIN.

Cabinet R Shelf 1 No. 25 2 vols.

Life and times of Benjamin Franklin, by James Parton, 2 vols. New York, 1865. Portraits of Franklin, his son and daughter.

Cloth, large paper edition, 11 x 8 ins., vol.1, pp.627: vol2, pp.707. Ford p. 371.

FRANKLIN, BENJAMIN

Cabinet R Shelf 3 No. 4 2 Vols.

Memoirs of the life and writings of Benjamin Franklin, LL.D. ... Written by himself to a late period, and continued to the time of his death, by his grandson W. Temple Franklin London, 1818. Third Edition. 2 Vols. Portrait.

Bound as Vols. III and IV of complete works.

Cloth; 8½ x 5½ in. Ford 561-2.

FRANKLIN, BENJAMIN

Cabinet R Shelf 3 No. 58

(My) Printing experience. By Benjamin Franklin. Also a short biography of Franklin by Geo. E. Wray. Salt Lake City, 1921. Illus.

Imitation leather; 7½ x 5¼ in.

FRANKLIN, BENJAMIN.

Cabinet R Shelf 1 No. 63

List of works in the New York Public Library, by or relating to Benjamin Franklin, in 1906.

In Frankliniana, pp.29-57.

FRANKLIN, BENJAMIN.

Cabinet R Shelf 1 No. 17

Memorial of the Inauguration of the Statue of Franklin, Boston: Prepared and printed by authority of the City Council, 1857. Presentation copy to Hon. Robt. C. Winthrop, orator of the occasion, with his autograph.

Full morocco, tooled, gold fore-edge decoration. 11½ x 9½ ins., pp.412.

FRANKLIN, BENJAMIN

Cabinet R Shelf 5 No. 149

New view of Benjamin Franklin, a. By R. Tait McKenzie. Excerpt from the "Century" Magazine, July, 1914.

Has reproduction, color-tone, from the sculpture by McKenzie.

Item (g) in book with binder's title "Benjamin Franklin: various pamphlets", 1853-1926.

FRANKLIN, BENJAMIN.

Cabinet R Shelf 1 No. 57

List of the Benjamin Franklin papers in the Library of Congress, compiled under the direction of Worthington Chauncey Ford, Washington, Government Printing Office, 1905.

Cloth, 11 x 7½ ins., pp. 322.

FRANKLIN, BENJAMIN

Cabinet R Shelf 1 No. 16

Memorial of the Inauguration of the Statue of Franklin. Boston: Prepared and printed by authority of the City Council, 1857.

Cloth, 10 x 6½ in. pp. 42. See also R/1/17.

FRANKLIN, BENJAMIN.

Cabinet Shelf No.

See Newton, A. Edward. Strahan's (Mr.) dinner party.

FRANKLIN, BENJAMIN.

Cabinet R Shelf 2 No. 55

Many sided Franklin, The, by Paul Leicester Ford, New York: The Century Company, 1899. Illus. portraits and facsimiles.

Orign. Cloth, 8½ x 6 ins., pp. (XX), 516.

FRANKLIN, BENJAMIN

Cabinet R Shelf 1 No. 2

(The) Memory of Benjamin Franklin. An address delivered by Hon. James M. Beck...at a dinner of the International Benjamin Franklin Society on Jan. 18, 1924. New York City. Portrait.

Also includes chronological account of the principal events in the life of Franklin.

Pamphlet #9 in volume "Franklin Pamphlets". Bound 1928.

FRANKLIN, BENJAMIN

Cabinet NN Shelf 2 No. 37

Notes relating to B.F. as newspaper publisher, printer; his letters to newspapers, etc.

see BLEYER'S "Main currents in the history of American journalism... (index)

FRANKLIN, BENJAMIN

Cabinet S Shelf 5 No. 9

Master builder, A. By Helen Campbell: Excerpt from "Our Continent," Dec., 6, 1882.

Bound in collection "Various Printers--Excerpts and Brochures", item 16.

FRANKLIN, BENJAMIN

Cabinet R Shelf 1 No. 3

Monument to Franklin in Granary Burial Ground, Boston. Erected in 1827, with inscrition: "Within this graveyard lie buried the parents of Benjamin Franklin, who placed a marble slab over the spot with an inscription which has been transferred to the monument erected in 1827.

In Frankliniana, p.30.

FRANKLIN, BENJAMIN (Author)

Cabinet R Shelf 1 No. 9

Oeuvres de M. Franklin, Docteur des Lois, Membre de l'Academie Royale des Sciences... Traduites de l'Anglois sur la quatrieme édition par M. Barbeu Dubourg. Paris, 1773. Portrait, plates; 2 vols.

This is the first book by Franklin printed in the French language.

Boards; calf back; 11 x 8½ in. Ford 315.

FRANKLIN, BENJAMIN

Cabinet R Shelf 1 No. 12

Mémoire de la vie privée de Benjamin Franklin, écrits par lui-meme, et adressés a son fils ... A Paris, 1791.

The first edition of Franklin's autobiography, translation of which is attributed to Dr. Jacques Gibelin.

Boards; 8½ x 5½ in. See Ford 383.

FRANKLIN, BENJAMIN

Cabinet G Shelf 3 No. 80

Morals of chess, B. Franklin's. Book designed by F.W. Shaefer at Tri-Arts Press. n.p.n.d. (1932). Reprinted from an 1802 edition.

No.31 of 150 copies printed.

Boards; 5-1/8 x 5-3/8 x ¼ in. In case.

FRANKLIN, BENJAMIN

Cabinet FF Shelf 1 No. 65

On a new method of printing discovered by the late Lieut. Gov. Golden (in 1842) together with an original letter from the late Dr. Franklin... By the Editors of the Register.

From "The American Medical and Historical Register". 1810. Pages 439 to 450. Bound seperately.

Half morocco; 8½ x 5½ in.

FRANKLIN, BENJAMIN

Cabinet R Shelf 2 No. 13

Oration at the inauguration of the statue of Benjamin Franklin, in his native city, Sept. 17, 1856. By Hon. Robert C. Winthrop. Boston, 1856.

Half morocco; 9½ x 6 in.

FRANKLIN, BENJAMIN

Cabinet OO Shelf 6 No. 50

Pennsylvania Gazette [founded by B. Franklin], No. 2445, Nov. 1, 1775, pp. 2 only.

Item in envelope.

FRANKLIN, BENJAMIN

Cabinet R Shelf 3 No. 33

Poor Richard, The sayings of: The prefaces, proverbs, and poems of Benjamin Franklin, originally printed in ... 1733-1758. Collected and edited by Paul Leicester Ford. New York 1890. Portrait frontispiece, 2 facsimiles.

Cloth; 5½ x 4 in.

FRANKLIN, BENJAMIN

Cabinet R Shelf 1 No. 3

Oration by His Excellency Jean J. Jusserand, L.I.D. the French Ambassador at the 158th commencement of the University of Pennsylvania, June 17, 1914: A message from France.

Excerpt from Old Penn Weekly Review, in Frankliniana, p. 35.

FRANKLIN, BENJAMIN

Cabinet KK Shelf 3 No. 2

Pension Fund, the Franklin, account of.

see HODSON, JAMES SHIRLEY. History of printing trades charities...London, 1883, p. 57.

FRANKLIN, BENJAMIN

Cabinet R Shelf 1 No. 2

Poor Richard Club; Victory dinner of. Bellevue-Stratford Hotel. Jan. 17th, Philadelphia, 1919. Program.

Pamphlet #2 in volume "Franklin Pamphlets". Bound 1928.

FRANKLIN, BENJAMIN

Cabinet R Shelf 2 No. 81

Our debt to Franklin: Oration delivered on the two-hundredth anniversary ... at Boston, Jan. 17, 1906.

See pp. 49-77, Two hundredth anniversary of the birth of Franklin ... Boston, 1906.

Cloth; 9½ x 6½ in. See also R/2/80.

FRANKLIN, BENJAMIN.

Cabinet R Shelf 1 No. 91

Pictorial life of Benjamin Franklin, printer, typefounder, ink maker, bookbinder, copper-plate engraver and printer, stationer, merchant, bookseller, author, editor, publisher, etc. Published in commemoration of the 200th anniversary of the arrival of Franklin in Philadelphia, Dill & Collins & Co., Philadelphia, 1923. Portraits and views, some colored

Imitation leather, label, 11¼ x 8¾ ins., 3/8 in. thick, n.p.

FRANKLIN, BENJAMIN

Cabinet R Shelf 3 No. 38

Poor Richard's Almanack for 1733. With an introduction by John Bigelow, and notes on the portraits. New York: The Duodecimos (De Vinne Press), 1894.

Prospectus of "The Duodecimos" bound in.

Full morocco, gilt; 7¼ x 5¼ in.

FRANKLIN, BENJAMIN

Cabinet R Shelf 3 No. 53

Parable against persecution: With an account of early editions. By Luther S. Livingston. Cambridge, 1916. Facsimile.

Half morocco; 6½ x 5¼ in.

FRANKLIN, BENJAMIN

Cabinet R Shelf 3 No. 65

(The) Pith of Franklin's Letters. Edited by William S. Pfaff. New Orleans, 1927. Frontispiece: Reproduction of Shaffordshire Statuette of Franklin.

Boards; 9-1/8 x 6 in.

FRANKLIN, BENJAMIN

Cabinet R Shelf 5 No. 15

Portraits of Benjamin Franklin: A list of portraits of Franklin, with the names of their owners as far as is known.

In volume "Early printing and printers in America. Excerpt from Pennsylvania Magazine p. 173.

Half morocco; 9-7/8 x 6-5/8 in.

FRANKLIN, BENJAMIN

Cabinet G Shelf 4 No. 52

Parable against persecution. A proposed new chapter of the Bible. By Benjamin Franklin. From a unique copy of the edition of 1757 ? Boston: Brad Stephens. Composition by Carl Ourrington Rollins, Yale University Press, 1927.

Brochure.

FRANKLIN, BENJAMIN

Cabinet R Shelf 1 No. 14

Poem delivered before the Franklin Debating Society at their anniversary, January 17, 1831. Being the birth-day of Franklin. By Charles C. Beaman. Boston, 1831.

Half morocco; 9¼ x 5¾ in.

FRANKLIN, BENJAMIN

Cabinet R Shelf 1 No. 68

Printer and publisher, B. Franklin. By William W. Clary. The Los Angeles Club of Printing House Craftsmen. 1935. Dedicated to the memory of Arthur M. Ellis. Illus.

250 copies printed.

Boards, leather back; 9¾ x 6-1/8 in.

FRANKLIN, BENJAMIN.

Cabinet R Shelf 1 No. 94

Passports printed by Benjamin Franklin on his Passy Press. Printed by Bruce Rogers for The William L. Clements Library, Ann Harbor, Nov., 1925. Three broadsides in facsimile.

Boards 12½ x 9¼ ins., pp.10.

FRANKLIN, BENJAMIN

Cabinet QQ Shelf 1 No. 42

Poem "Franklin", By J. Bayard Taylor.

See p.119, Brenton's Voices of the Press ...New York, 1850.

FRANKLIN, BENJAMIN.

Cabinet R Shelf 1 No. 3

Printers Festival, Boston, Jan. 20,1874. Community anniversary of birth of Franklin, under the auspices of Franklin Typographical Society: Verbatim report in Boston Transcript.

In Frankliniana, pp.58-64.

FRANKLIN, BENJAMIN

Cabinet S Shelf 5 No. 1

See Printing Plants, Great Britain. Wyman & Sons: The history of Great Queen Street.

FRANKLIN, BENJAMIN.

Cabinet R Shelf 1 No. 3

Proof of types cast from matrices once owned by Benjamin Franklin, now in the possession of The Massachusetts Historical Society.

In Frankliniana, p.37.

FRANKLIN, BENJAMIN.

Cabinet R Shelf 1 No. 3

Resolution of the Senate and House of Representatives in acknowledgment of the tribute paid to the memory of B.F. by the National Assembly of France (June 11, 1790): Broadside, Washington, Mar., 2, 1791.

In Frankliniana, p.43.

FRANKLIN, BENJAMIN

Cabinet KK Shelf 3 No. 2

Printing - press at which Franklin worked when in England, 1725 - 26. Brief account of.

see

HODSON, JAMES SHIRLEY. History of printing trades charities...London, 1883, p. 57.

FRANKLIN, BENJAMIN.

Cabinet R Shelf 1 No. 3

(Prospectus of American Philosophical Society). A proposal for promoting useful knowledge among the British plantations in America: Broadside (facsimile) pp.2, written, printed and issued by B.F. Philadelphia, May 14,1743.

In Frankliniana p.49.

FRANKLIN, BENJAMIN

Cabinet R Shelf 1 No. 3

Sale of A.L.S. of B. F. and his wife Deborah, etc. Article excerpted from unidentified newspaper.

Item in vol. "Frankliniana", on p.67

FRANKLIN, BENJAMIN

Cabinet R Shelf 3 No. 3 2 Vols.

Private correspondence of Benjamin Franklin, LL.D., ... comprising a series of letters on miscellaneous, literary, and political subjects: written between the years 1753 and 1790. ... Published from the originals by his grandson William Temple Franklin. 2 Vols. Third Edition. London, 1818. Facsimile. B.F. Handwriting.

Cloth; 8½ x 5½ in. Ford 560.

FRANKLIN, BENJAMIN.

Cabinet R Shelf 1 No 1

Public Life of Benjamin Franklin, by Jacob Abbott, in Harpers' New Monthly Magazine, Feb., 1852.

Bound in volume "Franklin, excerpts from magazines," item 3.

FRANKLIN, BENJAMIN.

Cabinet R Shelf 1 No. 90

Scenes reminiscent of Franklin: An American printer's dash through Europe, by E.E.Gress. In The American Printer: Franklin number, Jan. 20, 1923. p.64. Illus.

Half morocco, 12 x 8-7/8 ins.

FRANKLIN, BENJAMIN

Cabinet R Shelf 1 No. 2

Proceedings in The House of Representatives of the United States, on the presentation of the Sword of Washington and the Staff of Franklin, February 7, 1843. Washington.

Pamphlet #6 in volume "Franklin Pamphlets". Bound, 1928.

FRANKLIN, BENJAMIN

Cabinet R Shelf 1 No. 66 6 Vols.

Record of the celebration of the two hundredth anniversary of the birth of Benjamin Franklin, under the auspices of the American Philosophical Society for promoting useful knowledge, April 17 to 20, 1906. Philadelphia, 1906 to 1908. 6 Vols.

Cloth, 10¼ x 7¼ ins., pp. XIX, 321.

FRANKLIN, BENJAMIN

Cabinet JJ Shelf 4 No. 19

Scheme for printing office to be established in New Haven, Conn., as drawn up by Benjamin Franklin to William Straham. [From the original in Yale University Library.]

Article in the Franklin Anniversary Number of the Typothetae News, vol.5, No.5, January 19, 1926, Pittsburgh, Pa.

Item in manila envelope.

FRANKLIN, BENJAMIN

Cabinet R Shelf 2 No. 36

Proceedings of the Commemoration of the 177th Anniversary of the birth of Benjamin Franklin By the Editors, Publishers, Reporters and Printers of Dubuque, Iowa. January 17th, 1885.

Half morocco; 9 x 6 in.

FRANKLIN, BENJAMIN

Cabinet R Shelf 2 No. 31

Record of the proceedings and ceremonies pertaining to the erection of the Franklin Statue in Printing-House Square. Presented by Albet de Groot to the Press and Printers of the City of New York. 1872. With photograph of the Statue.

Has autograph of T. L. De Vinne.

Half morocco; 9 x 6½ in. Also Typothetae Duplicate: R/2/32.

FRANKLIN, BENJAMIN

Cabinet C Shelf 3 No. 2

(La) Science du bonhomme Richard. Par Benjamin Franklin. Paris, imprimé par C.L.F. Panckoucke.

Half morocco; 20 x 15½ in.

FRANKLIN, BENJAMIN.

Cabinet 67 Shelf 2 No. 45

Project for Universal Peace. By Pierre-Andre Gargoz. Originally printed by B.F. at Passy in the year 1782. Here reprinted (wtih an English Version) by Bruce Rogers. At the Printing House of W. E. Rudge, New York, 1922.

Boards, buckram back; 7¼ x 4¼ in.

FRANKLIN, BENJAMIN

Cabinet S Shelf 2 No. 86

References to him in Fairchild's Francis Adrian Van der Kemp, 1752-1829. (See Index).

Cloth; 8½ x 6 in.

FRANKLIN, BENJAMIN

Cabinet R Shelf 5 No. 149

Seymour, C.C.B. Benjamin Franklin. (Biographical account) With portrait.

Excerpt from "Self Made Men", N.Y. 1858.

Item (b) in book with binder's title "Benjamin Franklin; various pamphlets". 1853-1926.

FRANKLIN, BENJAMIN

Cabinet R Shelf 1 No. 3

Sketches of American characters: Franklin. From the monthly Repository, Oct., 1831, with wood cut portrait.

In Frankliniana, p.31.

FRANKLIN, BENJAMIN

Cabinet R Shelf 1 No. 2

Smoky torches in Franklin's honor. By R.M. Bache, in The Critic, June, 1906.

Pamphlet #8 in volume "Franklin Pamphlets." Bound, 1928.

FRANKLIN, BENJAMIN

Cabinet R Shelf 3 No. 67

Some sayings of Benjamin Franklin. Privately printed by Typographic Craftsmen, New York, August, 1928.

Boards; 6-3/8 x 4-7/8 in.

FRANKLIN, BENJAMIN

Cabinet R Shelf 2 No. 99

Souvenir of the annual birthday celebration of The New York Employing Printers' Association By Lindsay Swift. Hotel Astor, New York, Friday, Jan. 17, 1930. Portrait frontispiece Biographical chronological account.

Cloth; 6 x 3-7/8 x 5/8 in.

FRANKLIN, BENJAMIN.

Cabinet R Shelf 1 No. 3

Specimen of a font of script types, designed by Benjamin Franklin, and cut and cast by S. P. Fournier le jeune, Paris, 1780.

In Frankliniana, p.33.

FRANKLIN, BENJAMIN.

Cabinet 22 Shelf 1 No. 1

(Statesman, and printer in Philadelphia, 1706-1790). Franklin, Benjamin, Staatsmann, Schriftsteller und Buchdrucker in Philadelphia.

German article entitled: Der deutschamerikanische buchdruck und buchhandel in vorigen jahrhundert.

In Archiv fur Deutschen Buchhandels, vol.1, pp.61, 62, 69, 73, 74.

FRANKLIN, BENJAMIN

Cabinet R Shelf 1 No. 2

Story of a famous book. [Autobiography of B.F.] By Samuel A. Greene. In The Atlantic, Feb., 1871.

Pamphlet #5 in volume "Franklin Pamphlets" Bound 1928.

FRANKLIN, BENJAMIN

Cabinet R Shelf 3 No. 62

(The) Story of the Whistle, by Benjamin Franklin With an introductory note by Luther S. Livingston and a bibliography to 1820. Cambridge, 1922. The Livingston Reprints. Frontispiece in facsimile.

Full morocco; 8 x 5-1/8 in.

FRANKLIN, BENJAMIN.

Cabinet 75 Shelf 2 No. 3

Strahan, William and his ledgers. A paper read before the Bibliographical Society, by Austen Leigh. December, 18th, 1922.

In Trans. Biblio. Soc., "The Library," Vol. III, 1922-23, pp. 261-287.

FRANKLIN, BENJAMIN

Cabinet R Shelf 4 No. 47

Suggestions relating to a Museum and Library of the Graphic Arts in the Franklin Memorial, Philadelphia. (In 2 parts): I, Historic background of the Franklin Memorial and the Franklin Institute, and their activities in fulfillment of Franklin's educational ideas; II, Frankliniana worthy of a place in the Franklin Memorial. By Henry Lewis Bullen. Jersey City, N. J. Oct. 24, 1932.

Typescript copies (2), in envelope.

FRANKLIN, BENJAMIN

Cabinet S(R?) Shelf 3 No. 43

(The) True Benjamin Franklin. By Sydney George Fisher. Third Edition; with an appendix. Philadelphia, 1900.

This edition contains furhter evidence of Franklin having an illigitimate daughter.

Cloth; 8-1/8 x 5-1/8 x $1\frac{1}{4}$ in.

FRANKLIN, BENJAMIN

Cabinet R Shelf 3 No. 42

(The) True Benjamin Franklin: An analysis of the life and character of B. Franklin. By George S. Fisher. Philadelphia, 1899. Illus portraits, and facsimile.

Cloth; $8\frac{1}{4}$ x $5\frac{1}{4}$ in.

FRANKLIN, BENJAMIN

Cabinet R Shelf 2 No. 80

Two hundredth anniversary of the birth of Benjamin Franklin, 1706-1906. Franklin, Massachusetts. Under the auspices Franklin Business Association: Franklin, Massachusetts, 1906. Illus.

Half morocco; $7\frac{3}{4}$ x $4\frac{3}{4}$ in. See also R/2/81.

FRANKLIN, BENJAMIN

Cabinet R Shelf 2 No. 81

Two-hundredth anniversary of the birth of Benjamin Franklin. Celebration by the Commonwealth of Massachusetts and the City of Boston, in Symphony Hall, Boston. January 17, 1906.

Cloth; $9\frac{1}{2}$ x $6\frac{1}{2}$ in. See also R/2/80.

FRANKLIN, BENJAMIN

Cabinet R Shelf 5 No. 149

Type founder.

See Bache, Benjamin Franklin. Benjamin Franklin, typefounder.

FRANKLIN, BENJAMIN

Cabinet R Shelf 2 No. 100 Env.

Typefounder, Benjamin Franklin. A note to accompany a facsimile reproduction of the type specimen of Benjamin Franklin Bache. The equipment for which was assembled by Benjamin Franklin. By Douglas C. McMurtrie. Privately printed, 1925. Brochure.

With other items in manila envelope.

FRANKLIN, BENJAMIN

Cabinet R Shelf 1 No. 3

Types cast from matrices once owned by Benjamin Franklin, now in possession of The Massachusetts Historical Society. (Proof of types)

In Frankliniana, p. 37.

FRANKLIN, BENJAMIN

Cabinet R Shelf 2 No. 52

(A) Typical American, Benjamin Franklin. An address delivered before the Old-Time Printers' Association of Chicago, Jan. 17th 1896, by Joseph Medill. Chicago, 1896. Portraits.

Inserted excerpt: Times-Herald, June 7, 1896, in which there is a line etching of Statue of Franklin erected at Lincoln Park, Chicago.

Half morocco; $8\frac{3}{4}$ x 6in.

FRANKLIN, BENJAMIN

Cabinet R Shelf 1 No. 1

Unpublished letters of Benjamin Franklin, by John Bigelow, in The Century Magazine, June, 1886.

Bound in volume "Franklin, excerpts from magazines," item 9.

FRANKLIN, BENJAMIN

Cabinet R Shelf 1 No. 74

Who was the mother of Franklin's son: An inquiry demonstrating that she was Deborah Read, wife of Benjamin Franklin. By Charles Henry Hart. Philadelphia, 1911.

Half morocco; 10 x 7 in.

FRANKLIN, BENJAMIN

Cabinet R Shelf 2 No. 92

(The) Youthful Franklin: An address at the unveiling of a statue to B. Franklin at the University of Pennsylvania, June, 16, 1914. By James M. Beck, LL.D. Philadelphia.

Half morocco; 8-3/4 x 5½ in.

FRANKLIN, BENJAMIN.

Cabinet R Shelf 1 No. 3

Very brief and very comprehensive life (of) Ben Franklin, printer, done into quaint verse by one of the types (B.F.Shillaber), Boston, Sept. 17, 1856: Broadside.

In Frankliniana, p.45.

FRANKLIN, BENJAMIN

Cabinet R Shelf 2 No. 63

Will of Benjamin Franklin and proceedings of managers and courts relating thereto. Boston, Municipal Printing Office, 1904.

Inserted are reports on Franklin Trust Funds for 1908.

Cloth; 9½ x 6 in.

FRANKLIN, BENJAMIN

Cabinet Shelf No.

See also
Early Printing in Pennsylvania. Philadelphia, [v.d.]
also Early Printing in Great Britain, London 1725. Samuel Palmer.
also Imprints, United States.

FRANKLIN, BENJAMIN.

Cabinet R Shelf 2 No. 9

Vie de Franklin, a l'usage de tout le monde. Par [F.M.A.] Mignet, Paris, 1848.

Half morocco; 6½ x 4½ x ¾ in.

FRANKLIN, BENJAMIN.

Cabinet F Shelf 4 No. 13

Wollaston's Religion of Nature: London, 1725.

Imprint: London: Printed by S. Palmer, and sold by B. Lintott, W. and J. Innys, J. Osborn... 1725.

[Much of the composition work on this book was done by Franklin. It was his first employment on reaching London. See Autobiography p.43.]

Original sheep; 9-3/4 x 8 x 7/8 in.

FRANKLIN, BENJAMIN

Cabinet Shelf No.

See also
Imprints, United States. Franklin, B., and Hugh Meredith, Philadelphia, 1728.

FRANKLIN, BENJAMIN

Cabinet V Shelf 5 No. 7

Visite l'imprimerie d'Ambroise Didot. Ce qu'il dit aux ouvriers imprimerus.

see CRAPELET, CH. "Études pratiques...sur la typographie", Paris, 1837 (tome 1)

FRANKLIN, BENJAMIN

Cabinet R Shelf 3 No. 13

(The) Works of Dr. Benjamin Franklin; consisting of Essays, humorous, moral and literary, with his life, written by himself. Boston, 1825. Portrait.

Cloth, calf back; 6 x 3¾ in.

FRANKLIN, BENJAMIN

Cabinet Shelf No.

See also
stereotyping, Colden, C.D.

FRANKLIN, BENJAMIN

Cabinet R Shelf 3 No. 60

When Franklin advertised: Being excerpts from Franklin's Autobiography, together with notes collected and arranged by the Franklin Press and The Franklin Offset Co. Detroit, 1922. Portrait and facsimile.

Paper, 7 x 5 in.

FRANKLIN, BENJAMIN

Cabinet R Shelf 2 No. 73 10 Vols.

(The) Writings of Benjamin Franklin. Collected and edited with a life and introduction by Albert Henry Smyth. New York, 1905-1907. 10 Vols. Portraits.

Cloth; 9¼ x 6¼ in. each vol.

FRANKLIN, BENJAMIN, IN PICTURES

Cabinet R Shelf 1 No. 3

Monument erected by B.F. in honor of his father and mother in Tremont Street burial ground Boston: A woodcut.

In Frankliniana, p.30.

FRANKLIN, BENJAMIN.

Cabinet G Shelf 3 No. 54

Whistle, The: Extract from a letter written by Franklin to Mme. Brillon, Nov., 1779. Published by Brad Stephens & Company, Boston, Mass., 1921. Booklet. Colored. Illus.

Boards, 6 x 4 ins., pp.8, not numbered.

FRANKLIN, BENJAMIN

Cabinet R Shelf 1 No. 2

Wyman & Sons, Ltd. The story of. By Arthur Lawrence. Reprinted from the "Daily Mail", 21st February, 1907. Illus.

B. Franklin was employed as a journeyman printer at their former premises at 75 Great Queen Street, London.

Pamphlet #7 in volume "Franklin Pamphlets". Bound 1928.

FRANKLIN, BENJAMIN, IN PICTURES.

Cabinet R Shelf 1 No. 3

View of Passy from east bank of Seine; portrait in copper of B.F. with fur cap (bust), line sketch of Franklin presenting his grandson to Voltaire for his benediction; allegory in copper of B.F. defying the lightning and dethroning kings; portrait in copper of B.F. seated at window overlooking shipping; contemporary view from B.F.'s residence at Passy, showing ascension of first balloon.

These in excerpt Franklin at Passy in "Frankliniana, " a scrap book (first item, pp.22)

FRANKLIN, BENJAMIN, Monuments

Cabinet R Shelf 1 No. 3

Unveiling of statue of "Franklin in 1723", gift of the University of Pennsylvania by the class of 1904, with an address by Hon. James M. Beck.

Excerpt from Old Penn Weekly Review in Frankliniana, p.35.

FRANKLIN, JAMES Sr.

Cabinet R Shelf 2 No. 3

Printer of Boston and Newport, James Franklin, Senior. By Hope Frances Kane. Article with facs.

Item in "The American Collector", Oct., 1926, vol.3, No.1, p.17

FRANKLIN, WILLIAM TEMPLE

Cabinet R Shelf 3 No. 4 2 Vols.

Memoirs of the life and writings of Benjamin Franklin, LL.D. ... Written by himself to a late period, and continued to the time of his death. By his grandson William Temple Franklin. London, 1818. Third edition. 2 Vols. Portrait.

Bound as vols. III and IV of complete works.

Cloth; $8\frac{1}{2}$ x $5\frac{1}{2}$ in. Ford 561-2.

FRANKLIN, BENJAMIN, Portraits.

Cabinet Shelf No.

See Portraits, Printers.

FRANKLIN, JAMES

Cabinet 86 Shelf 1 No. 3.01

Rhode Island Almack of 1728.

see ALMANACS. Rhode Island...

FRANKLIN, WILLIAM TEMPLE

Cabinet R Shelf 3 No. 3 2 Vols.

Private correspondence of Benjamin Franklin LL.D. ... A series of letters on miscellaneous, Literary, and political subjects ... published from the originals by his grandson William Temple Franklin. 2 Vols. Third Edition. London, 1818. Facsimile of B.F. handwriting.

Cloth; 8- x $5\frac{1}{2}$ in. Ford 560.

FRANKLIN, Printing

Cabinet R Shelf 3 No. 61

Franklin (A play in four acts). By Constance D. Mackay. New York, 1922.

Frontispiece: Reproduction of the McKenzie statue, "The Youthful Franklin."

Cloth; $7\frac{1}{2}$ x $5\frac{1}{2}$ in.

FRANKLIN, JAMES.

Cabinet Shelf No.

See also

See Early Printing in Rhode Island. Newport, 1752: James Franklin.

" also Newspapers, Rhode Island: The Newport Mercury.

" also Imprints, United States.

also Early Printing in New England. Boston, [v. d.] James Franklin

FRANKLIN ALMANAC

Cabinet 80 Shelf 1 No. 6

Poor Richard's Franklin Almanac, 1807...Boston: Printed and published by A. Newall.

Item in manila envelope.

FRANKLIN, BENJAMIN & David Hall

Cabinet R Shelf 2 No. 100

Work-book of the printing house of Benjamin Franklin & David Hall, 1759-1766. Described by George Simpson Eddy. New York Public Library. 1930. Brochure, Illus.

Item in manila envelope.

FRANKLIN, RICHARD

Cabinet X Shelf 4 No. 52

Trial of R. Franklin, 1731

see LIBERTY OF PRINTING, Great Britain. Trial (1731) of Richard Franklin.....

FRANKLIN BEFORE THE PRIVY COUNCIL.

Cabinet R Shelf 2 No. 17

See Franklin, Benjamin: Franklin before the Privy Council.

See also Pictures in Frames.

FRANKLIN, JAMES.

Cabinet A Shelf 3 No. 7

Brother of Benjamin Franklin, and founder of the Newport Mercury.

See Newspapers. Rhode Island. Newport Mercury (The)

FRANKLIN, R.

Cabinet X Shelf 4 No. 73

Warrant for the arrest of R. Franklin, printer, 1729.

see LIBERTY OF PRINTING. Great Britain Copies taken from the records....London, 1763, p.30

FRANKLIN CLUB BULLETIN,(The)

Cabinet 33 Shelf 1 No. 12-13

Milwaukee, Wisconsin, 1907-1912

See PERIODICALS, PRINTING, United States (The) Franklin Club Bulletin...

FRANKLIN, JAMES.

Cabinet R Shelf 1 No. 3

Narrative of his printing press, brought from London to Boston in 1717, taken to Newport, R.I. in 1732, returned to Boston in 1864 as a gift to the Mass. Charitable Mechanic Association: A typewritten broadside issued by the M.C.M.A.

In Frankliniana, p.29.

FRANKLIN, WILLIAM TEMPLE

Cabinet V Shelf 5 No. 7

(Learns the printing trade in the shop of Ambroise Didot, Paris)

see CRAPELET, CH. "Études pratiques...sur la typographie". Paris, 1837, p. 216 (tome 1)

FRANKLIN, BEN, CLUB OF AMERICA see

Cabinet 27 Shelf 2 No. 26

BEN FRANKLIN CLUB OF AMERICA.

FRANKLIN CLUB OF NEW ENGLAND.

Cabinet S, Shelf 1, No. 5

See Associations Printers, United States.

FRANKLIN CLUBS OF AMERICA see

Cabinet, Shelf, No.

UNITED TYPOTHETAE & FRANKLIN CLUBS OF AMERICA.

FRANKLIN ENGRAVING AND ELECTROTYPING CO.

Cabinet 31, Shelf 2, No.

Electrotype Journal (The)

See PERIODICALS, PRINTING, United States Electrotype Journal...

FRANKLIN FOUNDRY, CINCINNATI, OHIO

Cabinet, Shelf, No.

Branch of MacKellar, Smiths & Jordan, Philadelphia.
See Specimen Books, Types, United States. MacKellar, Smiths, & Jordan. Philadelphia, 1868. The Johnson Type Foundry. Established 1796.
See also Specimen Books, Types. Franklin Type Foundry.

FRANKLIN FOUNDRY. Cincinnati

Cabinet, Shelf, No.

See Specimen Books, Types. United States. Johnson & Co. Lawrence. Philadelphia, 1865.

FRANKLIN FUND

Cabinet R, Shelf 2, No. 62

History of the Franklin Fund; being the agreed facts in Collins vs James H. Doyle et als., and the Attorney General. Boston, Municipal Printing Office, 1902.
Includes "Will and Codicil" of Benjamin Franklin. See also R/2/63.

Half morocco; 9½ x 8 in.

FRANKLIN FUND

Cabinet R, Shelf 2, No. 81

History of the Franklin Fund, by Dr. Henry S. Pritchett.
See pp. 41-45, Two-hundredth anniversary of the birth of Benjamin Franklin ... Boston, 1906.

Cloth; 9½ x 6½ in. See also R/2/80.

FRANKLIN FUNDS

Cabinet R, Shelf 2, No. 23

Franklin Fund: A sketch of the origin, object and character of the Franklin Fund, for the benefit of young married mechanics of Boston [By S. F. McCleary] City Document -- No. 89. Boston, 1886.

Half morocco; 9¼ x 5⅞ in.

FRANKLIN FUNDS

Cabinet R, Shelf 2, No. 79

Franklin Trust Funds to Boston and Philadelphia. by Dr. Edwin James Houston. In Journal of Franklin Institute. April and May, 1906. Illus.

Half morocco; 9¼ x 6¼ in.

FRANKLIN IMPRINTS

Cabinet R, Shelf 1, No. 83

Franklin Imprints in the Museum of The Curtis Publishing Company. Compiled by William J. Campbell. Philadelphia: The Curtis Publishing Company, 1918. Facsimiles.
Note: This collection now owned by the University of Pennsylvania.

Cloth; 11¾ x 9 in.

FRANKLIN INSTITUTE

Cabinet R, Shelf 5, No. 11

See Bowen, Daniel. A history of Philadelphia ...1839. p. 176

FRANKLIN INSTITUTE

Cabinet R, Shelf 2, No. 79

Houston, Edwin James: Franklin as a man of Science and an Inventor. An address by Dr. Edwin J. Houston, Before the Franklin Institute, Philadelphia, Feb. 21, 1906. Illus. In Journal of Franklin Institute, April and May, 1906.

Half morocco; 9¼ x 6¼ in.

FRANKLIN INSTITUTE, JOURNAL OF THE

Cabinet FF, Shelf 3, No. 9

Evolution of modern printing and the discovery of movable metal type by the Chinese and Koreans in the 14th century. By Judson Daland. Reprinted from the Journal of the Franklin Institute, vol. 212, No. 2, Aug. 1931. Illus. Brochure.

Item in manila envelope.

FRANKLIN INSTITUTE (Memorial)

Cabinet, Shelf, No.

View of exterior of Franklin Memorial (house of th the Franklin Institute), Parkway at 20th Street, Philadelphia. A postal card view.
The Memorial was formally opened in 1934.
Item on folio 69 of Scrap Book, "Frankliniana".

FRANKLIN LETTER FOUNDRY. Albany N.Y.

Cabinet, Shelf, No.

See Specimen Books, Types. United States. Franklin Letter Foundry (A.W. Kinsley & Co.) Albany N.Y.

FRANKLIN MEDAL SCHOLARS

Cabinet, Shelf, No.

See Franklin Benjamin: Association of Franklin Medal Scholars

---

FRANKLIN (Benjamin) MEMORIAL

Cabinet PP, Shelf 6, No. 9

Book of designations (architects drawings). The Benjamin Franklin Memorial and the Franklin Institute Museum. Philadelphia (1932)

Portfolio, boards; 12¾ x 10 in.

FRANKLIN OFFSET CO., THE

Cabinet R, Shelf 3, No. 60

See Advertising. Franklin, Benjamin. When Franklin advertised ... Detroit, 1922.

(The) FRANKLIN PRINTER

Cabinet 21 Shelf 2 No. 16 and 17

Western Master Printers Association Official Publication, "The Franklin Printer"

See PERIODICALS, PRINTING. United States (The) Franklin Printer, etc.

FRANKLIN PRINTING CATALOGUE DIGEST

Cabinet LL. Shelf 5 No. 68

Porte Publishing Co., Utah.
Franklin Printing Catalogue Digest.
April, 1934.
Partial contents:
Figuring Printing Costs
Country newspapers comments
Answers to questions
Comments by readers
etc.

Brochure.

FRANKLIN PRINTING COMPANY

Cabinet R Shelf 2 No. 92

See Imprints, United States

FRANKLIN PRINTING HOUSE.

Cabinet R Shelf 1 No. 79

Benjamin Franklin, Founder: The remarkable record of a Philadelphia Institution from 1728 to 1915. Philadelphia, 1915. Portrait.

Boards 9¾ x 6-3/8 ins., pp.53.

FRANKLIN REPOSITORY.

Cabinet See Newspapers, anniversary issues.

Shelf

No.

FRANKLIN REPOSITORY (The)

Cabinet See Newspapers, Pennsylvania

Shelf

No.

FRANKLIN SOCIETY, THE

Cabinet 21 Shelf 2 No. 10

Printing Press The

See PERIODICALS, PRINTING. United States. (The) Printing Press, etc

FRANKLIN SOCIETY (Chicago, Ill.)

Cabinet NN Shelf 7 No. 14

Early newspapers in Illinois: A paper read before the Franklin Society by Henry R. Boss, Jan. 20, 1870. (Franklin Society Publications II)

Half morocco; 12½ x 9½ in.

FRANKLIN SOCIETY OF CHICAGO

Cabinet 21 Shelf 2 No. 7

(The) Printer: Read before the Society by James W. Sheehan, Oct.,27, 1869.
Franklin Society Publication No.1

Item in manila envelope

FRANKLIN SOCIETY OF CHICAGO

Cabinet S Shelf 1 No. 145

See Societies, Printers.

FRANKLIN TYPE FOUNDRY

Cabinet 21 Shelf 2 No. 17.01

Allison, Smith & Johnson, proprietors of the Franklin Type Foundry pictured in an advertisement of 1875. Exterior view.

See PERIODICALS, PRINTING, United States (The) Composing Stick...

FRANKLIN TYPE FOUNDRY

Cabinet FF Shelf 3 No. 20.01

Documents relating to the partnership of Allison (Robert), Smith (Charles H.) and Johnson,(Howard L.)

See TYPE FOUNDING, United States Franklin Type Foundry...

FRANKLIN TYPOGRAPHICAL ASSOCIATION

Cabinet R Shelf 6 No. 15

Price list submitted to Master Printers of City of New York, circa 1850?

Broadside (double), in envelope.

FRANKLIN TYPOGRAPHICAL SOCIETY. Boston

Cabinet JJ Shelf 3 No. 18.01

Anniversary Entertainment. Celebrating the 202nd anniversary of the birth of Benjamin Franklin. Boston, Jan.16th, 1908.

Item in envelope.

FRANKLIN TYPOGRAPHICAL SOCIETY. Boston

Cabinet JJ Shelf 3 No. 45.01

Constitution and Catalogue of Library of the F.T.S., instituted 1824, incorporated 1825. [Ideal fraternal union our security]. Boston, 1850.

Brochure, in envelope.

FRANKLIN TYPOGRAPHICAL SOCIETY. Boston

Cabinet JJ Shelf 3 No. 18

Few facts relating to the F.T.S. its aims and purposes, together with some things it has done in the past seventy-five years . Boston, 1900.
Has list of members.

Brochure, in envelope.

FRANKLIN TYPOGRAPHICAL SOCIETY

Cabinet S Shelf 2 No. 110

(Boston). Henry Clay Whitcomb: In memoriam. Read before the Franklin Typographical Society, Sept. 3, 1914. by Willard H. Fobes Boston, printed for the Society, 1914. Portrait.

Cloth; 9 x 6 in.

FRANKLIN TYPOGRAPHICAL SOCIETY. Boston

Cabinet JJ Shelf 3 No. 18.02

Miscellaneous printed forms used in the transactions of the Franklin Typographical Society. v.d. Most of them carry the seal of the Society.

In envelope.

FRANKLIN TYPOGRAPHICAL SOCIETY. Boston

Cabinet JJ Shelf 3 No. 18.01

Noted Hub Organization rounds out One Hundred Years.
Excellent newspaper report of Centennial Anniversary Dinner and of the history of the F.T.S. With list of donors to the general charitable fund.

In envelope.

FRANKLINIANA

Cabinet C Shelf 3 No. 1

(The) North American Franklin bi-centennial issue, April 17, 1906.

See NEWSPAPERS, Anniversary Issues (U.S.) North American Franklin...

FRANKLINIANA: PRINTS

Cabinet Shelf No.

Portrait of B.F., bust, cap on head and spectacles, in circle, somewhat like Ninis medallion. 7¼ x 5¼ in.

Value $3.00

In frame 4 of pedestal frames.

FRANKLIN TYPOGRAPHICAL SOCIETY

Cabinet R Shelf 1 No. 3

Semi-centennial of the F.F.S. Boston, Jan. 20, 1874: Verbatim report in Boston Transcript.

In Frankliniana, pp.58-64.

FRANKLINIANA: PRINTS

Cabinet Shelf No.

Franklin Court, Philadelphia, an alley adjacent to B. F.'s last residence, in which he died in 1790. 10 x 7¼ in.

Value $3.00

In Frame 4 of Pedestal Frames.

FRATELLI BOYER E C., Typefounders

See Specimen Books, Types, Italy: Boyer.

FRANKLIN TYPOGRAPHICAL SOCIETY, Boston

Cabinet JJ Shelf 3 No. 18.02

(Various items). (1), Constitution and By-Laws, with list of members 1825: (2), Constitution and By-Laws, with list of members, 1902: (3), Broadside relating to the activities of the Society: (4), Ballot ticket for use in 102nd annual election, Jan.7, 1926.

In envelope.

FRANKLINIANA: PRINTS

Cabinet Shelf No.

Portrait (wood engraving) bust of B.F. by P. Grassby. Issued by Franklin Printing Co., Philadelphia. 11¼ x 13 in.

Value $3.50

In frame 4 of pedestal frames.

FRATERNITIES, PRINTERS (see)

Cabinet Shelf No.

SOCIETIES, PRINTERS

FRANKLIN TYPOTHETAE OF CINCINNATI

Cabinet JJ Shelf 4 No. 6

Activities and aims of the Franklin Typothetae of Cincinnati. Copyright 1929. Illus. pamphlet.

Paper; 9¼ x 6 in.

FRANKLIN'S PRINTING OFFICE (A reproduction made in 1926)

Cabinet R Shelf 6 No. 33

Attempt to revive a part of Franklin's printing office, at the Sesquicentennial Exposition, Philadelphia, 1926.
Exhibit prepared by Henry Lewis Bullen for Curtis Publishing Co. Photographed before shipping to Philadelphia, where it presented a more realistic appearance. Franklin operated three printing presses; he of course worked at night by candlelight.

Items in manila envelope.

FRAZIER, JULIUS LEROY

Cabinet S Shelf 4 No. 102

Biographical sketch, with portrait of J.L. Frazier, printer, artist, and editor. Sent to you by Advertisers Paper Mills, Holyoke, Mass.

Brochure, in envelope

FRANKLIN UNION (City of New York)

Cabinet Shelf No.

See SOCIETIES, PRINTERS'. Franklin Union...

FRASER, C. LOVAT

Cabinet Shelf No.

See Imprints, England. Hazel, Watson & Viney, Ld., London and Aylesburg, 1922.

FRAZIER, SAMUEL W. and GEO. F. STINE

Cabinet I Shelf 2 No. 57

Air brush, a treatise on the. With progressive lessons. By Samuel W. Frazier and George F. Stine. Boston, Mass. 1930. Illus.

Cloth; 10-1/8 x 6-7/8 x 5/8 in.

FRANKLINIANA

Cabinet 80 Shelf 1 No. 5

Facsimile reproduction of "Poor Richard's Almanac for 1733.

Franklin keepsake, the Times-Mirror Printing and Binding Company, Los Angeles, California, January, 1933

With other items in manila envelope

FRASER COMPOSING and DISTRIBUTING MACHINE

Cabinet FF Shelf 6 No. 77

Prospectus, illus. issued by Alexander Fraser, patentee, Edinburgh, circa 1886.

Item in manila envelope

FREDERICK. C. STANLEY

Cabinet L Shelf 5 No. 22

Color chart of C. Stanley Frederick. Origination, construction, drawings and presswork by C. Stanley Frederick. Copyright applied for by C. Stanley Frederick. n.p.n.d.

Item in manila envelope

FREDONIA (N.Y.) HISTORICAL SOCIETY

Cabinet NN Shelf 6 No. 46

(The) Pioneer press of Chautauqua County. [Read before the Fredonia Historical Society, March 14, 1879, by W. McKinstry, Pres. Also "Letters published in the Fredonia Censor at various times between 1842 and 1894.

Cloth; 9-1/8 x 6-1/8 x 1 in.

FREEMAN, E.L. & Sons

See also

Printing Plants

FREITAG, (Andrea)

Cabinet X Shelf 3 No. 14

Bibliographical note, with printer mark, Freitag, Rome, 1492-96.

see KRISTELLER, Dr. Paul. Italienischen buchdrucker...p.54

FREE PRESS (The), Detroit, Michigan.

Cabinet See Newspapers, special issues.

Shelf

No.

FREEMAN'S FRIEND.

Cabinet See Newspapers, Maine.

Shelf

No.

FRELLON, JEAN.

Cabinet 69 Shelf 1 No. 12

See Early Printing in France. Lyons, 1547.

FREE SPEECH LEAGUE

Cabinet X Shelf 5 No. 111

Free press anthology. Compiled by Theodore Schroeder. Published by The Free Press League...New York City. 1909.

Cloth; $9\frac{1}{2}$ x $6\frac{3}{4}$ x $\frac{3}{4}$ in.

FREEBAIRN, ROBERT

Cabinet X Shelf 4 No. 67

King's printer for Scotland, 1740. Information ...

see LIBERTY OF PRINTING, Great Britain. Information (June 16th, 1740) for Mr. Robert Freebairn...

FRELLON, JEAN (II)

Cabinet 69 Shelf 1 No. 33

See Early Printing in France. Lyons, 1560 and 1562.

FREEBAIRN, ROBERT

Cabinet X Shelf 4 No. 68

Additional petition of Mr. Robert Freebairn, his Majesty's printer, pursuer; against Mr. Thomas Heriot, defender. [Edinburgh]. 1742.

Boards; 9 x 7-1/8 in.

FREEDLEY, EDWIN

Cabinet QQ Shelf 4 No. 19

Leading pursuits and leading men. A treatise on the principal trades and manufactures of the United States...Illustrated by sketches of distinguished mercantile and manufacturing firms. Philadelphia, 1854.

see articles on the Book Trade, p. 42, Engraving, on p. 165.

Cloth; 9-3/8 x 6 x 5/8 in.

FRENCH, FRANK.

Cabinet K Shelf 6 No. 33

See Biographies, engravers'. French, Frank.

FREEMAN, EDMUND

Cabinet 80 Shelf 2 No. 10

Imprint and magazine: The Boston Magazine for April, 1786. Printed, published, and sold by Edmund Freeman.

Item in manila envelope.

FREEZ, FREDERICK and GERARD

Cabinet U Shelf 5 No. 49

Bio-bibliographical notes relating to F. and G. Freez, printers, bookbinders, stationers, York, 1497-1515.

see DAVIES, ROBERT (A) Memoir of The York Press...1868, pp. 7-14

FRENCH, FRANK

Cabinet K Shelf 5 No. 3

Wood engravers in camp. With engravings by the author. Illus. excerpt from "The Century", Aug. 1889.

Item 6 in vol. labeled "Excerpts relating to engraving and engravers".

FREEMAN, E. L. & SONS

Cabinet S Shelf 3 No. 22

Providence, Pawtucket, Central Falls, 1896. Pictorial description of their plant bound in with other typographical items.

Half morocco; 6 x $8\frac{3}{4}$ in.

FREIMANN, A. (Editor)

Cabinet L Shelf 3 No. 32

Thesaurus typographiae hebraicae saeculi 15. (Typography of Hebrew incunabula). Frankfort a.M.

Parts 1 to 4, 1924. About 200 single plates.
" 5 " 7, 1925. 150 single plates
" 8 1931. 50 " "

Reproductions of full size specimen pages, with titles, illus., ornaments, colophons, et etc.

Portfolios; Paper wrappers.

FRENCH, GEORGE

Cabinet LL Shelf 5 No. 12

Advertising, 20th, century. New York, 1926.

Cloth, $9\frac{1}{4}$ x 6-1/8 x 1-7/8 in.

FRENCH, GEORGE

Cabinet P Shelf 4 No. 26

Brief biographical sketch, with portrait of George Brench, printer, editor, advertising man.

Article excerpted from The American Printer, Dec.20, 1923.

In envelope.

FRENCH, GEORGE

Cabinet S Shelf 4 No. 96

Bookmaking: An address before the Rowfant Club in Cleveland by George French. Cleveland, Ohio, 1904.

Cloth; 6¾ x 4-1/8 in.

FRENCH, GEORGE

Cabinet S Shelf 3 No. 32

(The) Imperial Press, Cleveland, Ohio: A Critique. By George French. Cleveland, Ohio. 1902. Illus.

Cloth; 7¼ x 4¾ in.

FRENCH, GEORGE

Cabinet S Shelf 4 No. 97

Books in the making. By George French, Buffalo: The Matthews-Northrup Works, 1904. Advertising booklet for the Matthew-Northrup Company.

Buckram; 4½ x 2¾ in.

FRENCH, GEORGE

Cabinet S Shelf 6 No. 9

Books as books in England and America. Excerpt from "The Literary Collector" May, 1905.

Item 1 in vol. with binder's title "Early printing and early printed books. Pamphlets". Bound, 1932.

FRENCH, GEORGE.

Cabinet S Shelf 4 No. 94

Printing in relation to graphic art. Cleveland, The Imperial Press, 1903.

Boards; 8¼ x 5¼ x 5/8 in.

FRENCH FLEET IN AMERICA (see)

Cabinet SEA PRESSES

Shelf

No.

FRENCH JOURNALISM AND JOURNALISTS

Cabinet See Journalism, France: French Journalists and Journalism.

Shelf

No.

FRENCH REVOLUTION OF 1830

Cabinet QQ Shelf 1 No. 30.01

Ode by Samuel Woorworth, Printer.

see WOODWORTH, SAMUEL. Ode...

FRENCH UNIVERSAL EXHIBITION, Paris, 1867

Cabinet FF Shelf 3 No. 17.01

United States documents concerning the event, and correspondence of Geo. Bruce, Typefounder, N.Y. City -- muchado about one specimen book of the Bruce Typr Foundry.

Item in manila envelope

FRENCKEL, HEINRICH (Bookbinder, 15th cent.)

Cabinet See Endres, Heinrich. (Frenckel, Ulrich...

Shelf

No.

FRENEAU, PETER

Cabinet NN

Biographical account, the man and his works.

Shelf 1

See Thomas, E.S. Reminiscences... Hartford, 1840, Vol. II, pp. 74-83.

No. 1

2 Vols.

FRENEAU, PHILIP

Cabinet S Shelf 2 No. 2

Bibliography of the separate and collected works of Philip Freneau. Together with an account of his newspapers. By Victor Hugo Paltsits, New York, 1903.

Half morocco; 9¾ x 6½ in.

FRENEAU, PHILIP

Cabinet S Shelf 2 No. 3

(The) American Village. A poem by Philip Freneau. Reprinted in facsimile from the original 1772 New York edition, with an introduction by Harry Lyman Koopman, and bibliographical data by Victor H. Paltsits. Providence, Rhode Island, 1906.

Half vellum; 9 x 6¾ in.

FRENEAU, PHILIP

Cabinet R Shelf 4 No. 121

(The) Poet of the Revolution, and founder of the Jersey Chronicle, 1792.

See Nelson, William: New Jersey printers in the 18th century... April, 1911. p.29

FRENEAU, PHILIP

Cabinet S Shelf 2 No. 1

Poet of the Revolution, Philip Freneau. A history of his life and times. By Mary S. Austin. Edited by Helen Kearny Vreeland, great granddaughter of the poet. New York, 1901. Portraits and facsimiles.

Cloth; 9¼ x 6½ in.

FRENEAU, PHILIP

See also Portraits.

FRÉNY et CIE, A.

Cabinet Z Shelf 3 No. 43

See Ink Manufacturers. France.

"FREORIF" or Complete Language

Cabinet II — Shelf 4 — No. 60

Universal alphabet, prospectus of an

See ALPHABETS. Universal Alphabet...

FRÈRE, ED

Cabinet V — Shelf 4 — No. 17

Considérations sur les origines typographiques. Par Ed. Frère...Rouen, 1850.

Half morocco; 9½ x 6¾ in.

FRÈRE, EDUARD.

Cabinet V — Shelf 2 — No. 36

De l'Imprimerie et de la Librairie à Rouen, dans les XVe et XVIe siècles et de Martin Morin, célèbre imprimeur rouennais. Par Ed. Frère. Rouen, 1843.

Devise of Martin Morin adorns the title page; there is also a list of Norman printers and publishers from 1480 to 1550; and a catalogue of the productions of M. Morin.

Half morocco; 8 x 6¼ x ¼ in.

FRETZ GEBR., A.G.

Cabinet EE — Shelf 3 — No. 27

See SPECIMEN BOOKS, TYPES. Printers'. Switzerland.

FREY, A.

Cabinet LM — Shelf 1 — No. 30 — 2 vols.

Manuel nouveau de typographie. Contenant les principes théoriques et pratiques de l'imprimeur-typographe...Orné de planches. Deux partie. Paris, 1835. (Forming part of the Encyclopedia Roret.)

Boards, leather back; 5? x 3? in.

FREY, A.

Cabinet MM — Shelf 1 — No. 37 — 2 vols.

Nouveau manuel complet de typographie, contenant les principes théoriques et pratiques de cet art. Nouvelle édition, revue corrigée et augmentée par M.E. Bouchez. Paris 1857.

These two vols. form part of the "Encyclopedie Roret".

Cloth; 6 x 3-5/8 in.

FREYLINGHAUSEN, JOHN A.

Cabinet FF — Shelf 1 — No. 63

Abstract (An) of the whole doctrint of the Christian Religion...The first book stereotyped by the new (Stanhope) process. London: Stereotyped and printed by A. Wilson ...1804.

Facing title: Standing Rules of the Stereotype Office.

Boards; 10¾ x 7¼ in.

FREZISE, F.J.

Cabinet — Shelf — No.

See Imprints, United States.

FRIEDBERG, PETER

Cabinet Y — Shelf 4 — No. 4

(Notes on the Friedberg 15th century press at Mainz)

see

VOULLIÉME, ERNST. (Die) Deutschen drucker des fünfzehnten jahrhunderts...p.80

FRIEND, LEON and HEFTER, JOSEPH

Cabinet K — Shelf 4 — No. 17.01

Graphic Design: a library of old and new masters in the graphic arts. By Leon Friend and Joseph Hefter. Whittlesey House. McGraw Hill Book Co., New York, 1936. Illus.

A survey of the graphic arts in text and illustration. Includes lettering, printing, reproduction, photography, book design, advertising, poster, etc.

Cloth; 11 x 8; pp. 407

FRIENDS PRESS, THE

Cabinet R — Shelf 5 — No. 15

Interregnum of the Bradfords (1696-1712). By John William Wallace.

In volume "Early printing and printers in America. Excerpts from Pennsylvania Magazine pp. 32-44.

Half morocco; 9-7/8 x 6-5/8 in.

FRIES, AUGUSTIN

Cabinet X — Shelf 3 — No. 16

Brief bibliographical note, Fries, printer, Zurich, 1540-1546.

see

HEITZ, PAUL. Zürcher buchermarken... p.6

FRIES, AUGUSTIN

Cabinet X — Shelf 3 — No. 13

Brief bibliographical note, with printer mark, Fries, Strassburg, 1551-1554.

see

HEITZ, PAUL. Elsässische büchermarken...p.xxiv, plate xxxvi

FRIES, WALTER

Cabinet Y — Shelf 3 — No. 98

Guldemund, Hans, der Nürnberger briefmaler. (Bibliographical account of illustrated books, colored, or printed by Guldemund. 1521-1555)

Article in Zeitschrift für Buchkunde, vol. 1, 1924, p.36.

FRIJLINK, J.

Cabinet Z — Shelf 1 — No. 23

See Specimen Books, Types. Holland.

FRISBEE, HENRY C.

Cabinet NN — Shelf 6 — No. 46

Founder of the "Fredonia Censor", 1821.

see

FREDONIA (N.Y.) Historical Society. (The) Pioneer press of Chautauqua County... By W. McKinstry...1879. pp. 46 - 89.

FRISCH, ERNST von

Cabinet 26 — Shelf 1 — No. 16

Baumann, Hans, der erster buchdrucker in Salzburg, 1550, 1557. von Ernst von Frisch.

Illus. article in GUTENBERG-GESELLSCHAFT JAHRBUCH, 1927, p.68

FRITSCH (AHASUERUS)

Cabinet X — Shelf 1 — No. 36

Dissertatio de Typographis. De artis typographicae origine remissive..

[Reprinted in Wolr, "Monumenta Typogrhica", vol. 2, pp. 503-550.

FRITSCH (AHASUERUS)

Cabinet X Shelf 1 No. 36

Dissertationes duae historico-political, altera de Abusibus Typographiae tollendis, altera de Zigenorum Origine, Vita, ac Moribus Jenae, 1664.

[In Wolf"Monumenta Typographicae", vol. 2, p. 428.]

FRITZ, G.

Cabinet Y Shelf 2 No. 96

Paul Pretsch den erfinder der photo-galvanographie, festschrift zur enthullungsfeier der gedenktafel fur. Herausgegeven der Wiener Buchdruckerei und Schriftgiesserei-Factore. Wien 1888. With portrait, heliogravure.

In folder; 11 x 8 in.

FROBEN JEROME

Cabinet Shelf No.

See Early Printing in Switzerland. Basel, 1535.

FRITSCH, AHASUERUS

Cabinet X Shelf 1 No. 12

Dissertationes duae historico-politicae, altera de abusibus typographiae tollendis, altera de Zygenorum origine, vita ac moribus. Jenae, 1664. Second ed.

Two historical-political dissertations on the freedom of printing, together with the origin, life and habits of Gypsies. Reprinted in Wolf "Monumenta Typographica", vol II, pp. 428-455.

Typis ac sumptibus Georgi Sengenwaldi.

Half morocco; 7-3/8 x 6¼ x 3/8 in.

FRITZ, G.

Cabinet Y Shelf 5 No. 33

(Die) K.K. Hof-und Staatsdruckerei und deren technische einrichtungen. Mit text illustrationen, anrichten und plänen. Wien, 1894. (The Imperial and Government Printing Office in Vienna, and its technical equipment).

Stamped cloth; 9½ x 6¾ x ¾ in.

FROBEN, JOHN

Cabinet T Shelf 3 No. 2

Account of the life of John Froben, printer, Basel, and of the books printed by him, his portrait, his devices, etc.

In DIBDIN'S Bibliographical Decameron...London, 1817, vol.2, pp.171-76

FRITSCH, AHASUERUS

Cabinet X Shelf 1 No. 12

Dissertationes duae...1664

See LIBERTY OF PRINTING, Germany. Fritsch, Ahasuerus...

FRITZ, GEORG

Cabinet MM Shelf 2 No. 55

Photo-lithography. Translated by E.J. Wall, London, 1895.

Historical technical account.

Cloth; 8-3/4 x 5-5/8 x ½ in.

FROBEN, JOHANN.

Cabinet E Shelf 3 No. 5

See Adamo, Melchiore. Vitae Germanorum philosophorum, p.63.

FRITSCHE, RUDOLF

Cabinet MM Shelf 2 No. 65

Photo-lithography. Explanation and practical instructions of modern methods for photo-lithographic plates, including, preparation and treatment of reverse and deep etch plates. Vol. I. Rydolf Fritsche. New York, N.Y. Pamphlet, n.d. Illus.

Item in manila envelope.

FRITZ, JOHANN FRIEDRICH

Cabinet L Shelf 2 No. 1

Alphabete derer Europaisch-asiatisch-Africanisch und Americanischen volker...Johann Friedrich Fritz, Leipzig, 1748. With folded plates.

Illus description of the alphabets and languages of Europeans, Asiatics, Africans, etc. (part 2): The Lord's Prayer in more than 200 languages.

Half morocco; 7 x 4¼ in.

FROBEN, JOHANN

Cabinet Y Shelf 1 No. 41

Basel, Johann Froben in. (Biographical account, with portrait and device)

See BÖRCKEL, ALFRED. "Gutenberg und seine berühmsten nachfolger...pp.150-159

FRITSCHEN, GASPAR

Cabinet Shelf No.

Imprint, Leipzig, 1741.

See Koehler's Hochverdiente...chrenrettung Johann Gutenbergs...Leipzig 1741.

FROBEN, AMBROSIUS (and Aurelius)

Cabinet X Shelf 3 No. 15

Biographical sketch, with printer marks, Froben, Basel, 1564-1590.

see HEITZ, PAUL.

Basler büchermarken... pp.xxi, 41, 43

FROBEN, JOHANNES.

Cabinet D Shelf 3 No. 47

See Early Printing in Switzerland. Basle, 1516.

FRITZ, GEORG

Cabinet FF Shelf 3 No. 46

Geschichte der Wiener schriftgiesserien, 1482-1923, seit einfuhrung der buchdruckerkunst im jahr 1482 bis zur gegenwart. Wien, 1924. Gedruckt auf veranlassung der H. Berthold Ges. M.B.H. Wien, 1924. Portraits, facs., etc. Illus.

Boards, cloth; 11¼ x 8-1/8 x 5/8 in.

FROBEN, AMBROSIUS.

Cabinet 22 Shelf 1 No. 7

See Early Printing in Switzerland, Basle 1578, Ambrosius Froben, printer, etc.

FROBEN, JOHN.

Cabinet D Shelf 3 No. 55

See Early Printing in Switzerland. Basel, 1518. John Froben.

FROBEN, JOHANN

Cabinet D Shelf 2 No. 25

See Incunabula. Gregorious IX. Decretales. Basel, Switzerland, 1494.

FROBEN, JOHANN

Cabinet S Shelf 5 No. 25.02

Scholar - printer, 1460-1528. [Biographical account] by Louis K. Comstock, Montclair, Dec., 25, 1928.

Pamphlet in box labelled "Pamphlets and excerpts relating to printers, their plants, and other typographical matters". Box No.2.

FROBEN, JOHN

Cabinet Q Shelf 2 No. 30

Scholar-printer-publisher. Biographical sketch

See PUBLISHING. Aldus, Froben,... Montclair, 1928.

FROBEN, JOHN

See also

Imprints.

FROBEN, (Johann and Hieronymus)

Cabinet X Shelf 3 No. 15

Brief biographical sketch, with printer mark, Froben, Basel, 1490-1527, 1501-1563.

see

HEITZ, PAUL. Balser büchermarken...pp.xx, xxi, 23-37-41.

FROELICH, JACOB (Jucundus)

Cabinet X Shelf 3 No. 13

Brief bio-bibliographical note, with printer mark, Froelich, Strassburg, 1531-1557.

see

HEITZ, PAUL. Elsässische büchermarken...p.xxi

FROME MINIATURE GAZETTE.

Cabinet 75 Shelf 2 No. 1

Printed by the Daniel Press, 1850.

See p. 67, In Transactions of the Bibliographical Society, "The Library," Vol. I, 1920-1921.

FROMMOLD, EBERHARD

Cabinet T Shelf 2 No. 17

Basel printer, circa 1480. Bibliographical notes.

See PRINTING, HISTORICAL. Switzerland. Basel, a note on Eberhard Frommolt...

FROMMOLT, EBERHARD

Cabinet Y Shelf 4 No. 4

(Note on the Frommolt press at Basel, 1461)

see

VOULLIÉME, ERNST. (Die) Deutschen drucker des fünfzehnten jahrhunderts...p.25

FROSCHAUER, CHRISTOPHER

Cabinet T Shelf 3 No. 2

Account of books printed by Froschauer at Zurich

In DIBDIN'S Bibliographical Decameron...London, 1817, vol.2, pp.196-201

FROSCHAUER, JOHANN

Cabinet U Shelf 5 No. 38

Books printed by Froschauer containing the "Accipies" cut.

see

PROCTOR, ROBERT. Bibliographical essays...London, 1905, p.5

FROSCHAUER, CHRISTOPH

Cabinet 20 Shelf 2 No. 2

See Wood Engraving, Early. Baldung, Hans. His work.

Hans Baldung was the designer and engraver of some of the Froschauer printer devices.

FROSCHAUER, CHRISTOPH

Cabinet Y Shelf 1 No. 41

Zürich, Chr. Froschauer in. (Biographical account with portrait and device)

See BÖRCKEL, ALFRED. Gutenberg und seine berühmsten nachfolger...pp.160-165

FROSCHAUER, CHRISTOPHER

Cabinet Shelf No.

See also

Early Printing in Switzerland. Zurich, 1586.

" also Biographies, Printers (Collective), Zürich Printers.

FROSCHAUER FAMILY OF PRINTERS

Cabinet V Shelf 5 No. 11

Printing establisment of the Froschauers at Zurich.

See Madden, J.P.A. Lettres d'un Bibliographe. Tome IV, 1875. pp. 250-254.

FROSCHAUER FAMILY OF PRINTERS

Cabinet X Shelf 3 No. 16

Zurich, 1519-1591. Bibliographical notes.

see

HEITZ, PAUL. Zürcher büchermarken...pp.5-6

FROST, THOMAS

Cabinet 00 Shelf 5 No. 5

Reminiscences of a country journalist. London, 1886.

Cloth; 9 x 5-7/8 x $1\frac{1}{4}$ in.

FROST, THOMAS

Cabinet 00 Shelf 5 No. 6

Reminiscences of a country journalist. New edition. London, 1888.

Cloth; $8\frac{1}{4}$ x $5\frac{3}{4}$ x 1-1/8 in.

FROTHINGHAM, OCTAVIUS BROOKS

Cabinet NN Shelf 5 No. 11

Ripley, George. By O. B. Frothingham. Fourth edition. [For series] American men of letters. Edited by Charles Dudley Warner. Boston, 1884. Frontispiece.

Cloth; 7-1/8 x 4-5/8 x 1-1/8 in.

FRY, FRANCIS

Cabinet U Shelf 2 No. 51

Brief memoir of Francis Fry, F. S. A., of Bristol. By his son Theodore Fry. Not published. 1887. Portraits and a facsimile of a page of Tyndale's New Testament, 1525.
Biographical account.

Cloth; 10½ x 6-7/8 x ½ in.

FRY & STEELE

Cabinet Shelf No.

See Specimens, Types. England

FRY, EDMUND

Cabinet P Shelf 1 No. 10

Pantographia: containing accurate copies of all the known alphabets in the world, with an English explanation of the peculiar force or power of each letter; to which are added specimens of all well-authenticated oral languages; forming a comprehensive digest of Phonology. London, 1799.
One of two copies printed on vellum

Pigskin; 10½ x 6¾ x 2½ in.

FRY, JOSEPH

Cabinet Shelf No.

See Specimen Books, Types, Gt. Britain.

FUCHS, LEONARD, PHYSICIAN-BOTANIST, 1501-1566

Cabinet S Shelf 6 No. 7

See Bibliography (Botanical and medical works.)

FRY, EDMUND

Cabinet P Shelf 1 No. 10.01

Pantographia; containing accurate copies of all the known alphabets in the world; together with an explanation of the peculiar force or power of each letter; to which are added specimens of all well-authenticated oral languages; forming a comprehensive digest of phonology. By Edmund Fry, Letter-Founder Type Street. London. Printed by Cooper and Wilson, 1799.

Half morocco; 9¾ x 6½; pp. XXXVI, 320.

FRY & KAMMERER

Cabinet Shelf No.

See Imprints, United States.

FUCHS, LOUIS F. (Editor-Publisher)

Cabinet 27 Shelf 2 No. 10

(The) Stick, vol.1, 1904-5 (all issued). Published monthly, at 207 North 11th Street, St. Louis Mo.

Cloth; 9¾ x 6 in.

FRY, EDMUND & Co.

Cabinet Shelf No.

See Specimen Books, Types, Gt. Britain.

FRY & SON, EDMUND

Cabinet Shelf No.

See Specimen Books, Types, Gt. Britain.

FUCHS & LANG MANUFACTURING COMPANY

Cabinet EE Shelf 4 No. 37

Catalogue and price list of litho supplies, machinery, printing inks, bronze powders, photo engravers supplies. Fuchs & Lang Mfg. Co. New York, Chicago, etc. n.d.

Cloth, stamped; 12¼ x 9¼ x 3/8 in.

FRY, EDMUND and Co.

Cabinet Shelf No.

See Specimen Books, Types. England.

FRY AND SONS, JOSEPH

Cabinet Shelf No.

See Broadsides, Specimens of Type. England.
" also Specimen Books, Types. England.

FUGGER, ULRICH

Cabinet 40 Shelf 1 No. 48

See Early Printing in Switzerland. Geneva. 1567. Estienne, Henri (II) (Stephanus).

For further information concerning Fugger's relations with the Estiennes; See Schottenloher. Das alte buch. p.195.

FRY, EDMUND and ISAAC STEELE

Cabinet Shelf No.

See Specimen Books, Types. England.

FRY, JOSEPH, and SONS.

Cabinet Shelf No.

(A) Specimen of printing types, by Joseph Fry and Sons, Letter Founders, Worship Street, Moorfields, London, 1785.
Printed on both sides.

Value $22.50

In Frame 5 of Pedestal Frames.

FUGGER, ULRICH.

Cabinet 40 Shelf 1 No.

See Imprint, Switzerland. Estienne, Henri (II) and Ulrich Fugger.

FUHRMANN, OTTO W.

Cabinet (The) Five hundredth anniversary of printing. Illus. with arms of the Gensfleisch family; a modern portrait of Gutenberg, seal of Johann Gutenberg, Strassburg, 1442.
Shelf

Article in P.M., Vol. 2, No. 8, April, 1936, p. I
No.

FUHRMANN, OTTO W.

Cabinet 26 More about the printing house craftsmen. By Otto W. Fuhrmann
Shelf 1

Article in GUTENBERG-GESELLSCHAFT JAHRBUCH, 1926, p.111
No. 15

FULD, LUDWIG

Cabinet I Gesets, betreffend das urheberrecht an werken der bildenden künste und der photographie. Zweite auflage. Berlin, Leipzig, 1925.
Shelf 2-a

Guttentasche Sammlung, No.81.
No. 5

Deals with legal matters, copyright etc., pertaining to the reproductive arts.

Cloth; 6-1/8 x 4¼ x 3/8 in.

FULDA MONASTERY

Cabinet AA See Libraries, Monastic. Fulda.
Shelf 5
No. 32

FULIN R.

Cabinet AA Documenti per servire alla storia della tipografia Veneziana. (Estratto dall' Archivio Veneto, Tome XXlll, Parte 1). Venezia, 1882.
Shelf 1
No. 15.01

Boards; 9-1/8 x 6-1/8. Original wrappers bound in.

FULLER, CHARLES H. Company

Cabinet Q Advertisers' Directory
Shelf 4
No. 24

see DIRECTORIES, NEWSPAPERS. Advertisers' directory of leading publications....

FULTON, ROBERT

Cabinet L Illustrated book of pigeons. With standards for judging. By Robert Fulton. Edited by Lewis Wright. Illustrated with fifty life-like coloured plates, from paintings by J. W. Ludlow, Cassell & Company, Limited. London...(n.d.) circa. 1880.
Shelf 4
No. 23

Stamped cloth; 10-7/8 x 8-5/8 x 2 in.

FUMAGALLI, GIUSEPPE

Cabinet AA Bodoni, Giambattista, notizia biografica.
Shelf 1

See BERTIERI, RAFFAELLO. L'Arte di Giambattista Bodoni...Milano, n.d. circa 1913.
No. 51.01

FUMAGALLI, G.

Cabinet T Italy, a short history of the art of printing in.
Shelf 5

p.38 in "Printing; a short history". Edited by R. A. Peddie, London, 1927.
No. 135

Cloth; 7¾ x 5-1/8 in.

FUNCK, M.

Cabinet I Livre Belge a gravures. Guide de l'amateur de livres illustrees imprimes en Belgique avant le 18e siecle. Par le Dr. M. Funck. Paris et Bruxelles. G. Van Oest, editeur, 1925. Illus.
Shelf 3
No. 28

Bio-bibliographical historical account of Belgian illustrated books before the 18th century.

Paper; 10 x 6¾ x 1½ in.

FUNDICION BAUER

Cabinet See Specimen Books, Types. Spain. Fundicion Bauer. Suc. de J. de Neufville.
Shelf
No.

FUNDICION MEXICANO DE TIPOS.

Cabinet See Specimen Books, Types. Mexico: American Type Founders Co.
Shelf
No.

FURNO, Antonio de

Cabinet X Brief bio-bibliographical note, with publisher book device, Furno (Saragossa ?), 1567
Shelf 3

see HAEBLER, KONRAD. (Spanish and Portugese printer marks...p.xxxii
No. 19

FURST, HERBERT

Cabinet K Bewick and his school of engraving, the significance of. Illus. article.
Shelf 6

see WOODCUT ANNUAL (British) 1930. pp. 1-16.
No. 30

FURST HERBERT

Cabinet K Woodcut, the modern. A study of the evolution of the craft. By Herbert Furst ('Tis') with a chapter on the practice of xylography W. Thomas Smith, with over 200 illustrations in black and white and 16 plates in color. London. (1924)
Shelf 6
No. 15

Printed cloth: 11½ x 9 x 1½ in.

FURTER, MICHAEL

Cabinet X Bio-bibliographical sketch, with printer mark. Furter, Basel, 1483 --
Shelf 3

see HEITZ, PAUL. Basler büchermarken...pp.xvii, 15, 17
No. 15

FURTER, MICHAEL

Cabinet Y (Note on the Fuerter press at Basel, 1483)
Shelf 4

see VOULLIÉME, ERNST. (Die) Deutschen drucker des fünfzehnten jahrhunderts...p.23
No. 4

FUST, SR. FRANCIS.

Cabinet E Rare armorial bookplates (2) of Sir Richard Fust. Sir Francis Fust claimed descent from Fust the famous 15th century printer and partner of Schoeffer.
Shelf 4

See Alleine, Richard. Vindiciae Pietatis ... London, 1664.
No. 38

FUST, JOHANN

Cabinet T Shelf 3 No. 2

Account of Fust's connections with Gutenberg, Schoeffer, his printing office, his types, account of works printed by Fust, etc.

In DIBDIN'S Bibliographical Decameron... London, 1817, vol.1, pp.309-41

FUST, JOHANN

Cabinet W Shelf 2 No. 1

(Law suit of Fust against Gutenberg). Der prozess Fust's gegen Gutenberg im jahre 1455. von Ludw. Wilhelm Mayr. Munchen, 1858.

Item 2 in volume "Gutenberg inventeur de l'imprimerie - Melanges."

FUST AND SCHOEFFER

Cabinet U Shelf 5 No. 42

Works of Faust and Schoeffer--legend of the printer's devil--etc.

In Skeen's "Early Typography". Ceylon, 1872, p. 349

FUST, JOHANN

Cabinet Y Shelf 4 No. 4

(Bio-bibliographical notes relating to Fust)

see

VOULLIÉME, ERNST (Die) Deutschen drucker des fünfzehnten jahrhunderts...p.75

FUST, JOHANN.

Cabinet 75 Shelf 2 No. 2

Printer mark, note by Dr. Johnson on his printer's mark.

See Transactions of the Bibliographical Society, "The Library," Vol. II, 1921-1922, p. 270.

FUST, SIR RICHARD

Cabinet E Shelf 4 No. 38

See armorial bookplate in Early Printing in Great Britain. London 1664 [Printer Unknown].

Sir Richard Fust claimed to be a descendant of Johann Fust, partner with Gutenberg 1450-1455.

FUST, JOHANN

Cabinet X Shelf 2 No. 25

Druckhause des Johann Fust und Peter Schoeffer. (The printing house of Johann Fust and Peter Schoeffer, with biographical sketch of these printers.)

In Gedenk-buch der vierten jubelfeier in Mainz". Mainz, 1840.

Boards; $9\frac{3}{4}$ x $6\frac{1}{2}$ in.

FUST JOHANN.

Cabinet 22 Shelf 1 No. 10

See Printing, Historical. Mysterious fragments from a document dated 1505.

FYFE & BOSS

Cabinet Q Shelf 4 No. 10

Directory of the printing trades in Chicago. Chicago: Fyfe & Boss, publishers., 1889.

Paper; 7 x 4 1-8 in.

FUST, JOHANN

Cabinet Y Shelf 1 No. 2

Faust von Mainz. Ein gemahlde aus der mitte der funfzehnten jahrhunderts. In vier aufzuegen. von J. M. Komareck. Leipzig, 1794.

A drama in four acts.

Half morocco; 6-3/4 x $4\frac{1}{4}$ x 3/8 in.

FUST (Johann) and GUTENBERG (Johann)

Cabinet T Shelf 3 No. 3

Original depositions relating to the lawsuit between Fust and Gutenberg, at Strasburg.

see DIBDIN'S Bibliographical tour...London, 1821, vol.iii, p.53

FYNER, KONRAD

Cabinet Y Shelf 4 No. 4

(Notes relating to the Fyner 15th century pares at Esslingen.)

see

VOULLIÉME, ERNST. (Die) Deutschen drucker des fünfzehnten jahrhunderts...p.46

FUST, JOHANN

Cabinet Y Shelf 1 No. 23

Genealogical account of J. Fust

See LINDE, ANTONIOUS van der. Geschichte der erfindung...Berlin, 1886. vol.1, pp.10-41

FUST and MENTELIN

Cabinet V Shelf 5 No. 10

Did Fust or Mentelin first print "De Arte et modo praedicandi" of St. Augustin?

See Madden, J. P. A. Lettres d'un Bibliographe. Deuxième Série. 1873 [Letters 8 to 10].

FUST (or FAUST), JOHANN

Cabinet T Shelf 1 No. 73

Invention of printing attributed to Fust: Causes of Law-Suit with Gutenberg...

See HODGKIN, JOHN ELIOT. "Rariora"... (1858-1900) London, vol.2, pp.2, 3-4, 17-20.

FUST and SCHOEFFER

Cabinet B Shelf 2 No. 14

(Illustrated printed books of Fust & Schoeffer, Mainz,)

see

SCHRAMM, ALBERT (Der) Bilderschmuck der frühdrucke...

G

GABI, SIMONE (see)

Cabinet / Shelf / No.

BEVILAQUE, Simone

GAELIC DICTIONARY

Cabinet U / Shelf 1 / No. 120

Dwelly, E. (E. MacDonald & Co.), Herne Bay, England. Souvenirs and history of a self-made Gaelic Dictionary. Collated and bound by the Typographic Library and Museum, Jersey City, June, 1911.

Includes title pages of vols. I and II; Specimens of Dictionary (five signatures); part of original manuscript, etc.

Cloth; 10-1/8 x 7-7/8 x 1 in.

GAESBEECK, DANIEL.

Cabinet E / Shelf 4 / No. 68

See Early Printing in Holland. Leyden, 1678.

GAGE, FRED W.

Cabinet MM / Shelf 6 / No. 27

Modern Presswork. Chicago, The Inland Printer Co. 1909.

Cloth; $7\frac{3}{4}$ x $5\frac{1}{4}$ in.

GAGE, HARRY LAWRENCE

Cabinet MM / Shelf 6 / No. 73

Applied design: A handbook of the principles of arrangement, with brief comment on the periods of design which have most strongly influenced printing. "Typographic Technical Series for Apprentices" Part VII, No.43. The United Typothetae of America, 1920. Illus.

Cloth; 8 x 5 in.

GAGE, W.J. & COMPANY, Limited

Cabinet S / Shelf 5 / No. 2

Story of 65 successful years, 1844-1909. Toronto, Canada.

With portraits.

Item 8 in vol. Printers and their Plants. Collection of pamphlets.

GAGE & SONS, WM. C.

Cabinet S / Shelf 3 / No. 24

Briefly historical and descriptive of the printing plant of Wm. C. Gege & Sons, Fine Job Printers, Battle Creek, Mich. 1883-1900.

Cloth; 5-5/8 x $7\frac{3}{4}$ in.

GAGNIARD, E.

Cabinet V / Shelf 2 / No. 38

Progrès de l'imprimerie a Rouen, au XIX siècle et des arts qui s'y rattachent. Rouen, 1881. With printer marks.

Half morocco; 10 x $7\frac{1}{2}$ in.

GAGUIN, ROBERT

Cabinet W / Shelf 3 / No. 37

Épitre adressée a Robert Gaguin le Ie janvier 1472 par Guillaum Fichet, sur l'introduction de l'imprimerie a Paris. Reproduction heliographique de l'exemplaire unique possedé par l'Universite de Bâle. Paris, 1889.

With historical and explanatory preface signed L.D.

Boards; 10 x $6\frac{3}{8}$ in.

GAGUIN, ROBERT.

Cabinet 70 / Shelf 1 / No. 15

(La) Mer des croniques et mirouer historial de France iadis compose en latin par Robert Gaguin ... Nouvellement translate de latin en francoys, additionne de plusieurs additions ... avec les genealogies de France. On les vent en la rue des carmes a lenseigne Saint Jehan Baptiste. Nicolas de la Barre. Paris. 1518.

Calf; $10\frac{1}{2}$ x $7\frac{1}{2}$ x $1\frac{1}{4}$ in.

GAINE, HUGH

Stack A / Shelf 1 & 2 / Number 70

Bullen, Henry Lewis: Hugh Gaine, printer. [Biographical account]. In The Inland Printer, Vol. LXX, 1922, p. 377. Portrait. Illus.

GAINE, HUGH.

Cabinet F / Shelf 3 / No. 20

See Early Printing in New York City. Gaine, Hugh: Hanover Square, 1768.

GAINE, HUGH.

Cabinet F · Shelf 3 · No. 22

See Early Printing in New York City.
Gaine, Hugh. Hanover Square, 1785.

GAINE, HUGH

Cabinet R · Shelf 3 · No. 178

Irish printer, and his Journalistic Straddle.
See pp. 72-88 in Hildeburn, Sketches of printers and printing in Colonial New York.

GAINE, HUGH

Cabinet R · Shelf 4 · No. 80 · 2 Vols.

(The) Journals of Hugh Gaine, printer! Edited by Paul Leicester Ford, New York, 1902. 2 vols. illus., portrait, facsimiles.
Vol. I : Biography and Bibliography
Vol. II: Journals and Letters.

Buckram, 10¼ x 7 in.

GAINES, Hugh.

Cabinet A · Shelf 3 · No. 11

See Newspapers, New York City: The New York Gazette and the Weekly Mercury, of which he was publisher.

Bound in with other newspapers; leaves 2, 2a, 2b.

GALATINUS, PETRUS (The Franciscan)

Cabinet D · Shelf 3 · No. 56

Opus toti christiane republice maxime utile de arcarnis catholice, contra obstinatissimam Judeorum nostre tempestatis...Ortona Hieronymus Soncino. 1518.
"First book printed in this town", Olschki.

Vellum; 12½ x 9½ x 2¼ in.

GAINE, HUGH, Printer-Bookseller

Cabinet · Shelf · No.

See also
Early printing in New York City.

GALBREATH, C. B.

Cabinet NN · Shelf 6 · No. 34

Early newspapers of Ohio. Adopted from paper read at meeting of National Association of State Librarians, Waukeska, Wis., July 5, 1901.
Has facsimila of first newspaper northwest of the Ohio River, the "Centinel of the North-Western Territory, Nov. 9, 1793, publisher, William Maxwell,

Half morocco; 9¾ x 6½ x 5/8 in.

GALBREATH, C. B. (Compiler)

Cabinet NN · Shelf 6 · No. 34

Newspapers and periodicals in Ohio State Library, other Libraries of the State, and lists of Ohio newspapers in the Library of Congress and Historical Society of Wisconsin. Columbus, Ohio, 1902.
Preceded by "Early newspapers of Ohio". Historical account.

Half morocco; 9¾ x 6½ x 5/8 in.

GALENA WEEKLY GAZETTE (The).

Cabinet · Shelf · No.

See Newspapers, anniversary issues.

GALES, JOSEPH

Cabinet NN · Shelf 2 · No. 13

Biographical account of the founder of the National Intelligencer, 1809.
Excerpt from The Atlantic, Oct.,1860.

Item 7 in bound collection with binder's title "Various newspapers and periodicals"

GALES, JOSEPH, Jr.

Cabinet · Shelf · No.

See Newspapers, Washington, D.C.: National Intelligencer, April 2 and 4, 1811.

GALES and SEATON

Cabinet II · Shelf 3 · No. 35.01

Imprint of 1832. Washington.

See CHEROKEE NATION. Opinion of the Supreme Court of the United States... Washington, 1832.

GALES & SEATON.

Cabinet · Shelf · No.

See also
See Newspapers, Washington, D.C.
Daily National Intelligencer.
National Intelligencer.
Weekly National Intelligencer.

GALHARTE, Germão

Cabinet X · Shelf 3 · No. 19

Bio-bibliographical sketch, Galharte (Lisboa), 1519-1560.

see
HAEBLER, KONRAD. (Spanish and Portugese printer marks...p.xvii

---

GALIGNANI (Jean-Antoine et William)

Cabinet Q · Shelf 1 · No. 31

Biographical sketch of the Galignani brothers, publishers and editors, Paris.
Excerpt from unidentified publication

With other French items, in envelope

GALL, JAMES

Cabinet II · Shelf 6 · No. 5

Historical sketch of the origin and the progress of literature for the blind: and practical hints and recommendations as to their education. With an appendix, containing directions for teaching reading and writing to the blind. By James Gall. Edinburgh, 1834.
Preceding title, a page of angular types printed in relief, the invention of James Gall, printer-author.

Cloth; 9½ x 5-7/8 x 1 in.

GALLATIN, A. E.

Cabinet S · Shelf 3 · No. 148

Modern fine printing in America. An essay by A. E. Gallatin. New York. Privately printed, 1921. Bruce Rogers Item. Warde 152

Boards; 9-5/8 x 6-7/8 in

GALLATIN, A.E.

Cabinet S · Shelf 6 · No. 8

Modern fine printing in America. Illus. article. Excerpt from American Magazine of Art. Nov., 1920.

Item 8 in vol. with binder's title "Early printing and printers. Pamphlets".

GALLAY ET GRIGNON

Cabinet Z · Shelf 3 · No. 23

See Specimen Books, Types. France.

GALLAY, fils

Cabinet · Shelf · No.

See Specimen Books, Types, France.

GALLE, PHILIPPE

Cabinet 2 · Shelf 1 · No. 45

Engraver and publisher. Antwerp, circa 1540.

See Emblems. Symbolis heroicis. Libri IX. Auctore Silvestro.....

GALLERIE...KUNSTE UND HANDWERKE

Cabinet K · Shelf 3 · No. 2

Lehrreiches und unterhaltendes bilderbuch fur die jugned. Neue verbesserte auglage mit 40 schwarzen kupfern. In der Trachs'lerschen Buchhandlung, Zurich. n.d. circa 1830.

5 Plates showing printing offices, bookbindery, copperplate making, paper making, etc.

Boards, oblong; $4\frac{1}{2}$ x 6 x $\frac{3}{4}$ in.

GALLEY, PRINTERS'.

Cabinet 75 · Shelf 2 · No. 2

Use of the galley in Elizabethan printing, by R. B. McKerrow.

In Transactions of the Bibliographical Society, "The Library," Bol. II, 1921-22, pp. 97-108.

GALLY UNIVERSAL PRESSES

Cabinet EE · Shelf 4 · No. 38

Descriptive catalogue [Written and planned by Henry Lewis Bullen.] Published by the American Type Founders Company. Jersey City. n.d. after 1900. Booklets (2).

Has portrait of M. Gally.

In manila envelope.

GALVANOGRAPHY

Cabinet · Shelf · No.

See Electrotyping.

GALVANOPLASTIK (Electrotyping)

Cabinet · Shelf · No.

See Electrotyping.

GAMA, J. P.

Cabinet W · Shelf 2 · No. 1

Esquisse historique de Gutenberg. Paris, 1857. Pamphlet.

A short sketch of the life of the inventor of printing. At the end, is an account of the discovery of an old oil painting representing Gutenberg.

Item 8 in volume "Gutenberg, l'inventeur de l'imprimerie - Melanges."

GAMBLE, W.

Cabinet L · Shelf 4 · No. 45

Colour printing and colour printers. By R.M. Burch. With a chapter on modern processes by W. Gamble. New York, 1910. Illus.

Cloth; $9\frac{3}{4}$ x $6\frac{3}{4}$ x 1-5/8 in.

GAMBLE, WILLIAM

Cabinet · Shelf · No.

(Distinguished authority on process engraving) Biographical appreciation, the man and his work. By T,C. Kamer. With portrait.

Article in the British and Colonial Printer and Stationer, vol.111, No.247, July, 1933, pp.57 and 77

GAMBLE, WILLIAM.

Cabinet · Shelf · No.

Halftone, novel screen effects in. By W. Gamble. Article in British and Colonial Printer and Stationer, Vol. 109, No. 145, Aug. 6, 1931. p. 141.

GAMBLE, WILLIAM (Translator)

Cabinet I · Shelf 2 · No. 42

Half-tone on the American basis. By Wilhelm Cronenberg. Translated by William Gamble (Editor of "Process Work" and "Process Year Book".) London 1896. Illus.

Cloth; $7\frac{1}{4}$ x 4-7/8 x 5/8 in.

GAMBLE, William

Cabinet L · Shelf 4 · No. 45

Modern processes of colour printing. By W. Gamble [a chapter in] "Colour printing and colour printers", by R. M. Burch. New York, 1910.

Cloth; $9\frac{1}{2}$ x $6\frac{3}{4}$ in.

GAMBLE, WILLIAM

Cabinet MM · Shelf 3 · No. 58

Music engraving and printing. Historical and technical treatise. London, 1923. Illus. Pub. Sir Isaac Pitman & Sons, Ltd.

Cloth; 8-3/8 x $6\frac{3}{4}$ x 1 in.

GAMBLE, WILLIAM (Compiler)

Cabinet I · Shelf 2b · No. 8

Penrose process engraving pocket book and diary for 1922. Published by A.W. Penrose & Co. Ltd. London.

Cloth; 6 x 3 x 3/8 in.

GAMBLE, WILLIAM (Compiler)

Cabinet I · Shelf 2-b · No. 3 to 7

Penrose Process Pocket Book and Diary. Published by A.W. Penrose & Co., Ltd. London.

For the years, 1908, 1912, 1913, 1914, 1915.

Morocco, or cloth; 5-7/8 x 3 in.

GAND, MICHEL JOSEPH DE

Cabinet W · Shelf 4 · No. 38

Recherches historiques et critiques sur la vie et les éditions de Thierry Martens (Martinus Marten). Par feu M.J. de Gand, d'Alost Alost, 1845.

Martens was the first Belgian printer.

Cloth; $8\frac{1}{2}$ x $5\frac{1}{2}$ in.

GAND

Cabinet W Shelf 5 No. 114

See Printing, Historical, Belgium.

GANDO, NICOLAS

Cabinet FF Shelf 4 No. 2

Reponse (Par Fournier, le jeune), a un Memoire en 1766 par MM. Gando au sujet des caracteres de fonte pour la musique.

Fournier here accuses the Gandos of plagiarism.

See pp. 289-306, Tome II, Fournier's Manuel Typographique...Paris, 1764-1766.

GANDO, NICOLAS

Cabinet 83 Shelf 1 No. 16

See Specimen Books, Types. France.

GANDO FAMILY OF TYPEFOUNDERS

Cabinet Z Shelf 1 No. 18

See Specimen Books, Types. France: Gando, Nicholas Pierre and Theodore Simon (father and son.)

GANS, RICHARD, TYPE FOUNDER

Cabinet FF Shelf 5 No. 16

Recuerdo del trigesimo aniversario de la fundacion del establecimiento e' inauguracion de los nuevos y reformados talleres, 1881 - 1911. Fundicion Richard Gans, Madrid. With portrait, interior and exterior views, etc.

Boards; 13 x 10 in.

GANTZ, W.H.

Cabinet NN Shelf 3 No. 30

Postal riders and raiders. Are we fools? If we are not fools, why continue to act foolishly ...By "The man on the ladder". Issued By The Independent Postal League. Chicago, 1912.

Frontispiece, showing tree bark for paper mills.

Cloth; 8-1/8 x 5-5/8 x 1-1/8 in.

GARALDI, (Bernardino)

Cabinet X Shelf 3 No. 14

Bibliographical notes, with printer marks, Garaldi, Pavia, 1498-1521.

see KRISTELLER, Dr. Paul. Italienischen buchdrucker...p.46

GARAMOND, CLAUDE

Cabinet 73 Shelf 1 No. 3

[Biographical historical account of the French type founder who died in 1561. With portrait].

See AMERICAN INSTITUTE OF GRAPHIC ARTS. Garamond keepsake...1927.

GARAMOND, CLAUDE.

Cabinet 73 Shelf 1 No. 1

See Biographies, Printers. Garamond, Claude and his place in the Renaissance, By Edward F. O'Day.

GARAMOND, CLAUDE

Cabinet EE Shelf 1 No. 51

Bullen, Henry Lewis. Garamond and his famous types. A history...

[Together with] An exhibit of Garamond type...of Redfield-Kendrick-Odell Co. Printers and Map Makers. Tenth Avenue at Thirty-Sixth Street, New York, 1927.

Boards; 10¼ x 7¼ x ¼ in.

GARAMOND, CLAUDE

Cabinet S Shelf 1 No. 29

See De Vinne, Theodore Low. Notable printers of Italy ... New York, 1910. p. 134.

GARAMOND, CLAUDE

Cabinet BB Shelf 3 No. 36

First type founder and his types, Claude Garamond. By Henry Lewis Bullen, 1918. The American Type Founders Company, Jersey City. Illus. brochure.

The Garamond types were revived at the suggestion of Mr. Bullen after being in disuse for about 138 years.

Item in manila envelope, with other items.

GARAMOND, CLAUDE

Cabinet V Shelf 5 No. 23

Grecs du Roi en 1556, Inventaire des.

See GRECS DU ROI. Inventaire...

GARAMOND, CLAUDE.

Cabinet V Shelf 4 No. 22

See Le Be, Guillaume. Specimens de caracteres hebreux graves a Venise, etc.

GARAMOND, CLAUDE

Cabinet 67 Shelf 2 No. 86

(A) Note on Claude Garamond. By Wm. Ivins, Jr. on pp.20-23 of "Monotype", vol.9, No.6, 1923.

GARAMOND, CLAUDE

Cabinet V Shelf 6 No. 22

Roman types attributed to Garamond. 1640

See Imprimerie Royale. Notice sur les types étrangers...Paris, 1847. p. 46.

GARAMOND, CLAUDE.

Stack A Shelf 1&2 Number 68

Tory, Geofroy, A great typographer, and his apprentice Claude Garamond, by Henry Lewis Bullen, in The Inland Printer, vol.LXVIII, p.635, Facsimiles.

GARAMOND, CLAUDE

Cabinet V Shelf 6 No. 3

Type mould made by him.

See TYPEFOUNDING, (Duverger, E.) Histoire de l'invention de l'imprimerie par les monuments. Paris, 1840.

GARAMOND, CLAUDE

Cabinet U
Shelf 5
No. 38

Typefounder, Claude Garamond, makes the Royal Greek Types.

see PROCTOR, ROBERT. Bibliographical essays...London, 1905, p.95

GARAMOND, CLAUDE

Cabinet
Shelf
No.

See Types. Garamond, Claude, Paris, 1540.

GARAMOND TYPE

Cabinet FF
Shelf 3
No. 48

Exhibit of Garamond Type with appropriate ornaments. Redfield-Kendrick-Odell Co. New York 1927.

Together with "History of Garamond and his Famous Types". By Mr. Henry Lewis Bullen

Boards; 10¾ x 7½ x 3/8 in.

GARAT, M.

Cabinet F
Shelf 4
No. 92

Précis historique de la vie de M. de Bonnard. A Paris, de l'imprimerie de Monsieur. 1785.

Quarter morocco; 5⅝ x 3-3/8 x 3/8 in.

GARCIA, J. A. HIJOS de

Cabinet
Shelf
No.

See Specimen Books, Types. Spain.

GARDEN BOOKS

Cabinet S
Shelf 6
No. 9

Paradisi in sole Paradisus Terrestris (1629) By John Parkinson.

See BIBLIOGRAPHY. Paradisi in sole Paradisus...

GARDEN CITY TYPE FOUNDRY

Cabinet EE
Shelf 4
No. 39

Price list printers' cabinets, furniture, etc. Also type, printers' machinery and supplies. Chicago, Ill. 1884. Pamphlet.

In manila envelope.

GARDENERS CALENDAR

Cabinet
Shelf
No.

See Almanacks, Gardeners.

GARDINER, ROBT. S.

Cabinet S
Shelf 2
No. 150

History of the rail-road ticket. By Robert S. Gardiner. President Rand Avery Supply co. Boston. 1836-1898. Printed for private circulation. Illus.

Limp morocco; 7-7/8 x 6-1/8 in.

GARDONYI, ALBERT

Cabinet AA
Shelf 5
No. 37

History of Printing and of Book Trade in Hungary in the 18th century. [Hungarian text]. By Albert Gardonyi. Budapest, 1917. With facsimile.

Half morocco; 9½ x 6-3/8 in.

GARDTHAUSEN, V.

Cabinet Y
Shelf 3
No. 55

(Das) Buchwesen im altertum und in byzantinischen mittelalter. Zweite auflage. Mit 38 figuren. (Book making in ancient times and in the Byzantine Middle Ages). Leipzig, 1911.

Half morocco; 9½ x 6-3/4 x 3/4 in.

GARDTHAUSEN, V.

Cabinet L
Shelf 2
No. 25

Protokoll, text und schrift. (The Egyptian text and writing in the "Protokoll", circa 527-565).

Srticle in Zeitschrift des Deutschen Vereins für Buchwesen u. Schriftum. Sept-Okt., 1910. pp.97-107

GARFIELD, JAMES F.D.

Cabinet NN
Shelf 2
No. 3

Sketch of journalism in Fitchburg, Mass. Reprinted...Fitchburg; Press of Blanchard & Brown, 1888. Pamphlet. Illus.

Item 4 in vol. "Journalists and Journalism". Pamphlets.

GARNETT, PORTER (Compiler)

Cabinet G
Shelf 4
No. 53

(A) Conspectus of type design from 1454 to the present day. Advance sheets (without illustrations). Printed at The Laboratory Press, Pittsburg, Pennsylvania. Pamphlet.

In envelope.

GARNETT, PORTER

Cabinet S
Shelf 3
No. 3

(A) Documentary account of the beginnings of The Laboratory Press, Carnegie Institute of Technology. By Porter Garnett. Pittsburgh, The Laboratory Press, 1927. Facsimiles.

Includes innumerable specimens of typography of America's leading printers, with critical reviews of their works.

Boards; 10 x 7½ in.

GARNETT, PORTER

Cabinet G
Shelf 2
No. 55.01

(The) Fine book: a symposium. Being divers essays and articles by T.J. Cobden-Sanderson, Henri Focillon, etc. Edited with an introduction by Porter Garnett. Pittsburg, The Laboratory Press, 1934.

Morocco; 8¼ x 5¼ in.

GARNETT, PORTER

Cabinet FF
Shelf 5
No. 55

(The) Hand Press. Reprinted from "The Dolphin", vol.1, No.1, 1933

Item in manila envelope

GARNETT, PORTER

Cabinet S
Shelf 4
No. 106

Ideal Book, The. Two Essays.

See Dill (Francis P.) and Garnett (Porter)

GARNETT, PORTER see also

Cabinet IMPRINTS, United States. Laboratory Press, Pittsburgh, Pa.

Shelf

No.

GARNETT, R.

Cabinet U Preface to William Blades "Enemies of books". London, 1896.

Shelf 5

No. 17

Stamped cloth; $11\frac{1}{2}$ x 9 x 7/8 in.

GARRISON, WILLIAM LLOYD

Cabinet A Liberator (The): Journal of the Times. Boston, vol.I, No.I, Jan.1, 1931. Published by W.L. Garrison and Isaac Knapp.

Shelf 3 Printer, Stephen Foster.

No. 7

Item on folio $43\frac{1}{2}$ of vol. labelled "Early printing in New England".

GARNETT, RICHARD

Cabinet U Colophons of some of the early printers: A paper read before the Library Association, London, Oct. 1889.

Shelf 1

No. 1a

In Excerpts relating to printing from "The Library," [n.d.], p. 139 of pencilled folios.

GARNETT, R.

Cabinet W Spanish-American printing, early. (Bibliographical account of early Mexican printing). Excerpt from the Book-lover, Nov.-Dec. 1901.

Shelf 3

No. 115

No. 14

Item in box labelled "Excerpts and brochures relating to printing and printers in America.

GARRISON, WILLIAM LLOYD

Cabinet S Story of his life, 1805-1879. Told by his children. 4 Vols. Illus. London, 1885-1889.

Shelf 2

No. 7

4 Vols.

Cloth; $9\frac{1}{2}$ x $6\frac{1}{4}$ in.

GARNETT, R.

Cabinet W Early Spanish-American printing [Bibliographical excerpt from the "Book-Lover", Nov.-Dec., 1901].

Shelf 3

No. 115

Item 14 in vol. with binder's title "Pamphlets Relating to Books - II. Bound 1932".

GARRISON, WENDELL P.

Cabinet K Holbein and John Bewick: A chapter in the history of wood engraving.

Shelf 5 Illus. excerpt from "The Bibliographer", Feb., 1902.

No. 3 Item I in vol. labeled "Excerpts relating to wood engraving and engravers".

GARRISON and KNAPP

Cabinet F Boston, 1834. Garrison & Knapp (Imprint)

Shelf 2 See EARLY PRINTING IN NEW ENGLAND. Boston, 1834...

No. 100.01

GARNETT, RICHARD

Cabinet PP Essays in librarianship and bibliography. New York - London. 1899.

Shelf 1

No. 21

Cloth; 7-5/8 x 4-7/8 in.

GARRISON, WENDELL PHILLIPS

Cabinet LL Punctuation, a dissolving view on. Excerpt from the "Atlantic", Aug. 1906.

Shelf 3

No. 2

Item 9 in book with binder's title "Various items on proof reading".

GARZANI, TOMASO

Cabinet E Piazza Universale...aller professionem... Thomam Garzonum. Frankfort a.M. In Verlegung Lucae Jennisii, M.DC.XXVI (Universal mart of all professions...arts, trade...)

Shelf 3

No. 31

Half morocco; 12 x $7\frac{3}{4}$ x $2\frac{3}{4}$ in. Brunet 2, 1497.

GARNETT, RICHARD

Cabinet U Notable books, 30. added to the Library of the British Museum under the keepership of Richard Garnett, 1890-1899. Printed by T. and A. Constable, Edinburgh. March, 1899.

Shelf 3 Has portrait of Dr. Garnett and numerous facsimiles.

No. 14

Half morocco; $11\frac{3}{4}$ x 8 in.

GARRISON, WENDEL P.

Cabinet NN Two editors. E. L. Godkin and W. P. Garrison. By Viscount Bryce.

Shelf 7 see NATION, THE. Semi - centennial number, 1863 - 1915, p. 41.

No. 16

GASELEE, STEPHEN (Compiler)

Cabinet 75 Corpus Christi College, Cambridge, early printed books at. Review of book with above title.

Shelf 2

No. 3

In Transactions of the Bibliographical Society, "The Library," Vol. III, 1922-23, pp. 61-2.

GARNETT, R.

Cabinet U Paraguayan and Argentine bibliography.

Shelf 3

No. 103 See vol. I, pp.262-73 in Bibliographica... London, 1895-1897.

GARRISON, WILLIAM LLOYD.

Cabinet R Letter read at banquet commemorating the semi-centennial of the Franklin Typographical Society, Boston, Jan. 20, 1874: A verbatim report in Boston Transcript.

Shelf 1 In Frankliniana, pp.58-64.

No. 3

GASELEE, STEPHEN

Cabinet 26 Incunabula and their future, small private collections of.

Shelf 1

No. 19

Article in the "Gutenberg-Gesellschaft Jahrbuch" 1929, pp.303-311.

GASELEE, STEPHEN

Cabinet 76 Shelf 1 No. 13.01

Spanish books in the library of Samuel Pepys. Printed at the Oxford University Press for The Bibliographical Society, 1921.

Brochure; $8\frac{3}{4}$ x 7 in.

GASELEE, STEPHEN

Cabinet 75 Shelf 2 No. 5.01

Spanish books in the library of Samuel Pepys. by Stephen Gaselee for the Bibliographical Society, London. 1921.

Bibliographical, illustrative of the history of early printing in Spain.

Trans. Biblio. Soc., Supplements 1-5, 1921-1926.

GASELEE, STEPHEN.

Cabinet 75 Shelf 2 No. 2

Spanish books in the library of Samuel Pepys. A paper read before the Bibliographical Society, January 17, 1921.

In Trans. Biblio. Soc., "The Library," Vol. II, 1921-22, pp. 1-11.

GASELEE, STEPHEN.

Cabinet 75 Shelf 2 No. 3

An unrecorded Spanish incunable by Stephen Gaselee.

In Transactions of the Bibliographical Society, "The Library," Vol. III, 1922-23, pp. 304-6.

GASKILL, JACKSON

Cabinet MM Shelf 3 No. 38

Printing-machine (The) manager's complete practical handbook; or the art of machine managing fully explained. For the use of master printers, as well as for the practical instruction and special guidance of machine managers. London, 1877. Illus.

Cloth; $6\frac{1}{2}$ x 4-1/8 x $\frac{1}{2}$ in.

GASQUET, REV. F. A.

Cabinet 75 Shelf 1 No. 7

Bibliography of some of the earliest devotional books printed by the earliest English printers. A paper read before the Bibliographical Society, January 18, 1904.

In Trans. Biblio. Soc., Vol. VII, 1902-1904, pp. 163-189.

GASQUET, REV. ABBOT.

Cabinet 75 Shelf 1 No. 9

Books and bookmaking in early chronicles and accounts: A paper read before the Bibliographical Society by the Rev. Abbott Gasquet, November 19, 1906.

In Trans. Biblio. Soc., Vol. IX, 1906-1908, pp. 15-30.

GASQUET, REV. F. A.

Cabinet 75 Shelf 1 No.

Devotional books printed by the earliest English printers. Read before the Bibliographical Society on Jan. 18, 1904.

In Trans. Biblio. Soc. Vol. VII, 1902-1904. pp. 163-189.

GAST, MATIAS (and successors)

Cabinet X Shelf 3 No. 19

Brief bio-bibliographical note, with printer mark, Gast (Salamanca), 1562-1592.

see

HAEBLER, KONRAD. (Spanish and Portugese printer marks...p.xxx

---

GATTEAUX, NICOLAS MARIE

Cabinet FF Shelf 1 No. 105

Portrait, with brief biography.

see

KUBLER, GEORGE A. Historical treatises...on stereotyping. New York, 1936, p. 52.

GAUDENZI, PIETRO

Cabinet C Shelf 1 No. 8

L'Anima et l'arte di Pietro Gaudenzi. Per Ettore Cozzani, l'Eroica, Milano. n.d.

The works of Gaudenzi.

Cloth; $16\frac{1}{2}$ x $13\frac{1}{4}$ in.

GAULLIEUR, E. H.

Cabinet W Shelf 1 No. 78

Études sur la Typographie Genevoise du XV au XIX siècle ét sur l'Origine de l'Imprimerie én Suisse. Geneva, 1855. Facsimile.

"Ce memoire est extrait et broché à part du tome II du Bulletin de l'Institue, 1855, ce qui explique la pagination defecteuse."

Half morocco; 8-3/4 x 5-3/4 in.

GAULLIEUR, ERNEST

Cabinet V Shelf 1 No. 82

Documents qu'il a découverte. Interprétation par Ernst Gaullieur.

[Documentary evidence that printing was introduced into Bordeaux by a German, Svelier, in 1846].

See Delpit's "Origines de l'imprimerie en Guyenne", Bordeaux, 1869.

Paper; $9\frac{1}{4}$ x 6 x $\frac{1}{2}$ in.

GAULLIEUR, ERNEST.

Cabinet V Shelf 1 No. 21

L'Imprimerie à Bordeaux en 1486. Par Ernest Gaullieur. Bordeaux, 1869.

Documentary evidence to establish the date of the arrival of Michel Svierler and Jehan Waltear in Bordeaux.

Cloth; 10 x $6\frac{1}{2}$ x $\frac{1}{4}$ in.

GAULLIEUR, ERNEST

Cabinet V Shelf 5 No. 23

L'Imprimerie a Bordeaux en 1486. Bordeaux, 1869. (Pamphlet). Typ. E. Farastie et Fils.

With authors signature.

Item 7 in vol. with binder's title "Origin of Printing in France: Pamphlets".

GAULTHEROT, VIVANT

Cabinet 69 Shelf 1 No. 23

See Early Printing in France. Paris, 1553.

GAUTHIER, EUGENE V.

Cabinet V Shelf 2 No. 70

Annuaire de l'Imprimerie, de la presse et de la librairie pour 1855-56. Troisieme année. Juillet, 1855. Rédigé, édité et exécuté par V. Eugène Gauthier, ouvrier typographe. Paris

Includes list of 192 new publications, 480 newspapers appearing regularly in Paris, addresses of printing material supply shops, addresses of printers and their usual type of work, statistic, reports, etc.

Half morocco; $9\frac{3}{4}$ x $6\frac{1}{2}$ x 5/8 in.

GAUTHIER, (V. EUGÈNE)

Cabinet FF Shelf 3 No. 21.04

Concordance du point typographique avec le système métrique, ou méthode pour compter au centimètre ou au mètre des quantités de lignes...Par V.-Eugène Gauthier...Nice, 1871. Pamphlet.

Item in manila envelope.

GAUTHIER, JULES

Cabinet RR Shelf 3 No. 8

L'Industrie du papier dans les hautes vallées franc-comtoises du 15e et 18e siècle. (The paper industry in the high valleys of France in the 15th to the 18th centuries.) Extrait des mémoires de la Societe d'Émulation de Montbéliard. 1897.
With 9 plates, facsimiles, watermarks.

Paper; 9¾ x 6½ in. In folder.

GAUTIER D. AGOTY, JACQUES

Cabinet L Shelf 4 No. 1

Observations sur l'histoire naturelle sur la physique et sur la peinture. Avec des planctes imprimers en couleur. Cet ouvrage renferme les secrets des arts, les nouvelles deconvertes, et les disputes des philosophes et des artistes modernes. Paris 1752. (3 parts in one vol.)
With 46 plates printed in colors by Gautier.

Boards: 10¼ x 7¾ in.

GAZINET, GYSBREGT

Cabinet Shelf No.

See Early printing in Holland. S'Gravenhagen, 1717. Gysbregt Gazinet.

GAUTHIER, FRÈRES et Cie

Cabinet Shelf No.

See Printing Presses, France. Columbian Press; Stanhope Press.

GAVARNI

Cabinet K Shelf 5 No. 2

Parisian prince of the pencil. By A. Rhodes. Excerpt from Scribner's. May, 1873. Illus.

Item 5 in vol. with binder's title "Wood engravers and illustrators".

GAZLAY, THEODORE

Cabinet MM Shelf 5 No. 18

Practical printer's assistant; containing numerous schemes of imposition, definite directions for making composition rollers, and many useful tables. Cincinnati: Stereotyped and published by J.A. James & Co. 1836.

At end of book, an advertisement of J.A. James & Co. Type and Stereotype Founders, Cinn., Ohio.

Cloth; 7¾ x 4-5/8 x 3/8 in.

GAUTHIER-VILLARS

Cabinet EE Shelf 2 No. 71

Imprimerie de Gauthier-Villars, (successeur de Mellet-Bachelier) Rue de Seine, Saint Germaine, 10. Paris, 1867.

This printing house, established exclusively for the production of scientific and technical works published by the same firm, was founded in 1791 by J.M. Courcier.

Boards; 10¾ x 8½ x 5/8 in.

GAY, JEAN

Cabinet X Shelf 4 No. 43

Saisie de livres prohibés faite aux couvents des Jacobins et des cordeliers a Lyon, en 1694... Augmentee d'un repetoire bibliographique; par Jean Gay. Turin, 1876.
Bibliographical account of condemned books seized in the Dominican and Franciscan convents in Lyons in 1694.

Half morocco; 7¾ x 5¼ x 3/8 in.

GED, WILLIAM

Cabinet FF Shelf 1 No. 58

Biographical memoires of William Ged, including particular account of his progress in the art of block printing, Newcastle: Printed by S. Hodgson, 1819.

Half morocco; 7¾ x 5¼ in.

GAUTIER, ÉMILE

Cabinet W Shelf 3 No. 8

Guéraud, Armand-Laurent, imprimeur-libraire. 1824-1860. Nantes, 1862.
Bio-bibliographical account.

Boards; 12 x 9½ in.

GAZANIIS, Lazaro de

Cabinet X Shelf 3 No. 19

Bio-bibliographical note, with printer mark, de Gazaniis (Toledo), 1498-1503.

see

HAEBLER, KONRAD. (Spanish and Portugese printer marks...p.ix

GED, WILLIAM

Cabinet FF Shelf 1 No. 105

Biographical memoire of William Ged; including a particular account of his progress in the art of Block Printing. Newcastle, 1819.
With facsimile of the original title page of memoirs as above.

In KUBLER, GEORGE A. Historical treatises ...on stereotyping. New York, 1936, p. 130 and fol.

GAUTIER, ÉMILE

Cabinet V Shelf 5 No. 2.01

Notice sur Armand-Laurent Géraud, imprimeur-libraire...Nantes, 1862. Pamphlet.

Item I in vol. with binder's title "French printers and printing. Pamphlets". Bound, 1932.

GAZETTE (The), York, Pa.

Cabinet A Shelf 1 No. 116

See Newspapers, anniversary issues.

GED, WILLIAM

Cabinet F Shelf 4 No. 18

See Early Printing in Great Britain. Newcastle, 1742. James White and William Ged.

Ged was inventor of the clay or plaster of paris method of stereotyping.

GAUTIER, (Jacq. D'Agoty)

Cabinet L Shelf 4 No. 1.01

Lettres a l'auteur du MERCURE sur l'invention et l'utilité de l'art d'imprimer les tableaux. Par Mxx M. Gautier, pensionnaire du Roi. (Paris, 1756).
Excerpt pp.306-324 of Gautier's "Observations sur la phisique, l'histoire naturelle et la peinture", 1752-55.

In envelope/

GAZETTE FRANCOISE

Cabinet NN Shelf 7 No. 26

Facsimile reprint, with bibliography of a newspaper printed at Newport in 1780, by the French fleet in American waters.

see

GROLIER CLUB. Gazette Francoise. A facsimile reprint.

GED, WILLIAM

Cabinet FF Shelf 1 No. 56

First book printed from plates made by clay or plaster process. The invention of Wm. Ged.

C. Crispi Sallusti, Edinburgi. Gulielmus Ged, non typis mobilibus sed tabellis seu laminis fusis, excudebat 1739.

Calf; 5-3/8 x 3-½ in.

GED, WILLIAM, Endinburg, 1725.

Cabinet S Shelf 5 No. 23

Stereotyping and Electrotyping: Item in pamphlet "Great American Industries of U.S." Hartford, 1875. p.175.

Item 2, in bound volume of "Various items relating to printing."

GEER, ELIHU

Cabinet S Shelf 5 No. 6

See Biographies, Printers (Connecticut printers 1709- 1893)

GEER, ELIHU

Cabinet Shelf No.

See Imprints, United States. Geer, Elihu, Hartford, Conn. 1845.

GEER, ELIHU, Printer-Publisher, Conn. circa.

Cabinet S Shelf 5 No. 6

1817-1875.

See A Typographical Galaxy, by Marcus A. Casey in the Connecticut Quarterly, No.1, 1896.

Bound with other items in "Various Printers and their Plants," item 19, vol.2.

GEIGER, WILLI

Cabinet 26 Shelf 2 No. 14

(Appreciation of the work of Willi Geiger, German artist, printer, lithographer, etc.

Illus. article in Jahrbuch VII-VIII, 1933-34, p. III, Deutscher Verein für Buchwesen und Schrifttum.

GEIGER, WILLI

Cabinet Y Shelf 3 No. 101

(Artist illustrator, Willi Geiger, account of. Illus. article.)

Article in
DEUTSCHER VEREIN FUR BUCHWESEN U. SCHRIFTTUM...Jahrbuch 1933-34

GEISBERG, MAX.

Cabinet I Shelf 3 No. 32

Bilder-katalog zu Max Geisberg "Der Deutsche Einblatt-Holzschnitt in der ersten Halfte des 16 jahrhunderts." 1600 verkleinerte wiedergaben. Harausgegeben von Hugo Schmidt, Verlag, Munchen, n.d. circa 1929. Frontispiece.

Catalogue of all the illustrations (reduced size) conatained in Geisberg's monumental work on German wood engravings of the early 16th century, the original of which is in this Library.

Cloth; 10-3/8 x 8-3/4 x 3/4 in.

GEISBERG, MAX

Cabinet J Shelf 4 No. 23

Deutsche buchillustration in der ersten hälfte des 16e jahrhunderts. Herausgegeben von Professor Dr. Max Geisberg. Munchen. Hugo Schmidt Verlag. [Parts 1 to 9, 1929 to 1932].

Issued in parts, 5 issues per year for the space of ten years. Each issue with 50 plates. Still continuing.

Paper; 15¾ x 10¾ in.

GEISBERG, MAX

Cabinet 1 & 5 Shelf Portfolios 1 to 40

(German single-plate woodcuts in the first half of the 16th century. Facsimile reprints. Edited by Max Geisberg. Hugo Schmidt, publisher, Munich, 1923-1930)

About 1600 plates in 40 portfolios numbered 1 to 40. Plates arranged alphabetically, by artists.

38-40 (6v.) in closet Room 653
Portfolios; 22 x 16¼ in.

GEISBERG, MAX

Cabinet 1 Shelf 1 No.

(Index, complete, to Geisberg's "Deutsche einblatt holzschnitt"...)

Der Deutsche einblatt-holzschnitte in der ersten halfte des 16 jahrhunderts. Die gesamtverzeichnis. Hugo Schmidt Verlag, Munchen, 1931.

Index with important alterations in margins, with pen.

Cloth; 21½ x [illegible] in.

GEMINIE, THOMAS

Cabinet T Shelf 2 No. 6 [vol.4]

Books printed by Thomas Geminie, London, 1556-59. Bibliographical notes.

see
DIBDIN'S "Typographical Antiquities" ...London, 1810-19, vol IV, p.537

GEMINI (or Geminus), Thomas

Cabinet J Shelf 3 No. 11

English printer, circa 1556, said to have been the first person to engrave on copper in England.

See SALAMAN, MALCOLM C. Old engravers of England....p.2.

GEMINIANO (Dominicus de Sancto)

Cabinet D Shelf 1 No. 28

Prima pars lecturae super VI decretalium... Impressa Venetiis per magistrum Jacobum de Rubeis: Anno 1470, 4 id. Sept.

Hain-7539, Gesamt-Kat.

Original boards; 17 x 11¼ x 3½ in.

GENEALOGIES

Cabinet Shelf No.

Plantin-Moretus Family. 1514-1880.

See Insert following p. 82: Antwerpsche Boekdrukkers by Frans Olthoff.

GENEALOGIES, PRINTERS

Cabinet U Shelf 2 No. 16

Baskerville, John (1706-1775), the printer, his ancestry...By Thomas Cave. Kidderminster, 1923.

Half morocco; 10-3/8 x 8-1/8 in.

GENEALOGIES, Printers

Cabinet AA Shelf 4 No. 2

Blaeu, Willem Janszoon.
See Baudet, P.J.H.: Leven en werken van Willem Jansz. Blaeu ... Utrecht, 1871. p.160.

GENEALOGIES, Printers

Cabinet S Shelf 2 No. 55

Boss, Henry Rush: An inquiry concerning the Boss Family and the name of Boss: Correspondence between William Graham Boss of Edinburgh, Scotland, and Henry Rush Boss, Chicago, 1902. Portrait.

Half morocco; 9 x 6½ in.

GENEALOGIES, Printers

Cabinet R Shelf 5 No. 9

Bradford, William, 1660-1752: Arrived in Ship "Welcome", 1682 with William Penn. Compiled by Henry Darrach, Philadelphia, July 1906.

Half morocco; 10 x 8 in.

GENEALOGIES, Printers

Cabinet R Shelf 5 No. 173

Bradford, William and family: Genealogical Memorials of William Bradford, the printer. By Samuel S. Purple. New York: privately printed, 1873. Frontispiece: woodcut reproduction of tombstone of William Bradford the first.

Cloth; $10\frac{3}{4}$ x $8\frac{1}{8}$ in.

GENEALOGIES, Printers

Cabinet AA Shelf 3 No. 43

Coster, Laurens Janszoon and family. 1355-1589. See Vos. K. De Coster Legende outward? ... Haarlem, 1922.

GENEALOGIES, Printers.

Cabinet W Shelf 5 No. 32

Elzevier family. See Reume, Aug. de: Recherches historiques, genealogiques ... Elzevier. Bruxelles, 1847. facing p. 86 and following.

GENEALOGIES, Printers

Cabinet AA Shelf 1 No. 31

Cennini, Bernardo. Florence, 1415-98. See Fantozzi, Federigo. Notizie biografiche originali di Bernardo Cennini ... Firenze, 1839.

GENEALOGIES, Printers

Cabinet AA Shelf 5 No. 21

Cromberger, Johann and family, 1508. Spain. See Printing, Historical, Spain. Seville Noticias inéditos de impresores Sevillanos... J. Gestosos y Pérez ... Seville, 1925. Following p. 26.

GENEALOGIES, Printers

Cabinet W Shelf 5 No. 73

Elzevier family, The: See tome I, following p. CXXV of Willems, "Les Elzevier: Histoire ...Bruxelles ... 1880", 2 Vols.

GENEALOGIES, Printers

Cabinet V Shelf 2 No. 67

(Chaillau, Vincent et Francois) Les imprimeurs et les libraires du départment de la Vienne (hors Poitiers) Par M.A. de la. Boubalière Poitiers, 1896. Facing p.280.

Half morocco; 10 x $6\frac{1}{2}$ x $\frac{1}{2}$ in.

GENEALOGIES, PRINTERS'

Cabinet T Shelf 2 No. 96

Dawks family of [printers], booksellers and stationers, 1635-1731.

See Appendix I to Morison's, Ichabod Dawks and his News-Letter...University Press, 1931.

GENEALOGIES, Printers

Cabinet S Shelf 5 No. 4

Elzevier family of Dutch printers. By Baroness Althea Salvador. An excerpt from New Science Review. Jan., 1895.

Item 21, 346 in collection "Various printers and their plants, Excerpts from magazines, I"

GENEALOGIES, PRINTERS

Cabinet V Shelf 5 No. 18

Coignard family of printers, 1677-1787.

See folded plate at end of Delalain's Libraires et Imprimeurs de l'Academie Francaise...Paris, 1907.

GENEALOGIES, Printers

Cabinet T Shelf 3 No. 29

Didot family, 1689-1826. See Bigmore & Wyman: Bibliography of printing.

GENEALOGIES, Printers.

Cabinet W Shelf 5 No. 37

(Elzeviers who were publishers or printers during 129 years, 1583 to 1712). Tableau généalogique des quatorze Elzevier qui ont été libraires ou imprimeurs pendant 129 ans, depuis 1583 jusqu'en 1712. See p. LIII, in Pieters, Charles, "Annales de l'Imprimerie Elzevirienne."

GENEALOGIES, Printers.

Cabinet R Shelf 4 No. 111

Collins, Isaac. 1770: Burlington, New Jersey. Reminiscences of Isaac and Rachel (Budd) Collins ... together with a genealogy... Philadelphia, 1893. Illus.

Half morocco; $10\frac{1}{4}$ x 6-5/8 in.

GENEALOGIES, Printers

Cabinet W Shelf 2 No. 111

Dolet. La Famille a Troyes. Par Louis Morin, Archiviste Municipal. Troyes, 1917. Extrait de l'Annuaire de l'Aube. Pamphlet. Bound in with "Notes sur Étienne Dolet. Par René Sturel, Paris, 1913.

Half morocco; $9\frac{3}{4}$ x $6\frac{1}{2}$ in.

GENEALOGIES PRINTERS

Cabinet W Shelf 2 No. 82

Estienne family. Tableau généalogique et héraldique de la famille Estienne, originaire de Provence, depuis l'an 1270 jusqu'en 1826 ...

See Folded broadside preceding title of Aug. Bernard's "Les Estienne." Paris, 1856.

GENEALOGIES, PRINTERS

Cabinet Y Shelf 1 No. 23

Coster, Laurens Janszoon

See LINDE, ANTONIOUS van der. Geschichte der erfindung ... Berlin, 1886, vol.1, p.274

GENEALOGY, Printers

Cabinet S Shelf 5 No. 50.01

Elseviers, the famous Dutch printers. By Baroness Althea Salvador. Biography, with genealogy. Excerpt from the New Science Review, Jan., 1895.

In envelope.

GENEALOGIES, PRINTERS

Cabinet QQ Shelf 1 No. 10

Estienne family of printers and booksellers, since the year 1500.

See p.27 of ESTIENNE'S Plainte de la typographie...Paris, 1785.

GENEALOGIES, Printers

Cabinet Y Shelf 5 No. 63

Feyerabend, Sigmund sein leben...Bearbeitet von Heinr. Pallman. Frankfurt a.M., 1881. Portrait frontispiece.

Half morocco; 11¼ x 7¾ x ½ in.

GENEALOGIES, PRINTERS

Cabinet U Shelf 4 No. 35

Froben, John, and his family, 1491-1600.

See HECKETHORN, CHARLES WILLIAM. The printers of Basle in the 15th and 16th centuries...p.86.

GENEALOGIES, PRINTERS'

Cabinet AA Shelf 5 No. 8.01

Guasp Family of Printers. Palma de Mallorca. 1579 - 1931.

p. 65 in La Antiguedad de la Imprenta de Guasp. Por Felipe Guasp y Pou. Imprenta de Guasp. 1931. Illus.

Paper; 8½ x 5¾ x 3/8 in.

GENEALOGIES, Printers.

Cabinet 22 Shelf 1 No. 1

(Feyerabend, the family of) Die familie Feyerabend. von A. Kirchoff.

In "Archiv für geschichte des Deutschen buchhandels," vol. 1, 1878. pp. 187-89.

GENEALOGIES, Printers

Cabinet S Shelf 2 No. 7 4 Vols.

Garrison, William Lloyd. Ancestry of (1764-1805) See pp. 1 - 20. Garrison, William Lloyd. Story of his life.

GENEALOGIES, Printer's

Cabinet Y Shelf 1 No. 3

Gutenberg, Johann. Erste stammtafel des ädelichen geschlechts der von Sorgenloch genannt Gänsfleisch...

Folding plates pp.77 and 83 in Kochler's Hochverdiente...ehren-rettung Johann Guttenbergs. Leipzig, 1741.

GENEALOGIES, Printers

Cabinet W Shelf 2 No. 48

Estienne family of printers.

See Renouard's "Annales de l'imprimerie des Estienne," Paris, 1838: [Following p.202.]

GENEALOGIES, PRINTERS

Cabinet X Shelf 2 No. 59

Gensfleisch family, the genealogy of

see HARTWIG, OTTO (Compiler) Festschrift...Mainz, 1900, pp.80, 118

GENEALOGIES, Printers

Cabinet W Shelf 2 No. 73

Gutenberg, Johann: Ne en 1412 a Kuttenberg en Boheme.

See Winaricky, Charles: Jean Gutenberg ...

GENEALOGIES, Printers

Cabinet R Shelf 1 No. 41

Franklin family: Ancestry and descendants in the Colonel Louis Bache (1779) line to 1889, interspersed with historico genealogical events and appendix added. By William Bache, 1889.

Half morocco; 9¼ x 6-1/8 in.

GENEALOGIES, PRINTERS

Cabinet LL Shelf 2 No. 11

Gensfleisch, stammtafel der familie.

Facing p.96 in Faulmann's "Illusthirte geschichte der buchdruckerkunst"...Vienna, 1882.

GENEALOGIES, Printers

Cabinet R Shelf 4 No. 131

Ide, Simeon, and the Ide family.

See Vermont. Simeon Ide, yeoman, freeman, pioneer printer...

GENEALOGIES, PRINTERS

Cabinet V Shelf 5 No. 12

(French families of printers and their favorable alliances with German printers in the early part of the 16th century.)

Guillard; Rembolt; Chevallon; Badius, etc.

See MADDEN, J.P.A. Lettres d'un bibliographie...Paris, 1878, p.261

GENEALOGIES, Printers

Stack A Shelf 1 & 2 Number 70

Franklin, Benjamin: His family and descendants. By H. L. Bullen.

In The Inland Printer, Vol. LXX, p. 531.

GENEALOGIES, Printers

Cabinet R Shelf 4 No. 133

Kollock family of Sussex County, Delaware, 1657-1897. By Edwin Jaquett Sellers. Philadelphia, 1897.

Shephard Kollock, printer and founder of "The New Jersey Journal," 1779, and "The New York Gazeteer and Country Journal." New York City, 1783.

See Nelson's "New Jersey Printers and Printings." ... April, 1911. pp. 18-21.

Cloth; 9¾ x 6⅛ in.

GENEALOGIES, Printers

Cabinet S Shelf 2 No. 1

Freneau, Philip Morin, 1752. New York and New Jersey. See pp. 49-68. Freneau, Philip, poet of the Revolution. By Mary S. Austin. New York, 1901.

Cloth; 9¼ x 6½ in.

GENEALOGIES, Printers

Cabinet X Shelf 1 No. 86

(Giunta family of printers. Annals of the press of the Giuntas at Florence, Venice, and Lyons) De Florentina Juntarum typographia. Angelo Maria Bandini. Lucae, 1791.

Half morocco; 9 x 6 x 1¼ in.

GENEALOGIES, Printers

Cabinet AA Shelf 5 No. 8

Guasp, Gabriel, and heirs, 1579 to 1897. Palma, Spain.

See Guasp family of printers. Dinastie de impresores mas antiqua de Europa..... Mahon, 1897.

GENEALOGIES, Printers.

Cabinet W Shelf 3 No. 85

Morel, Federic, 1523-1583.
See Dumoulin, Joseph. Vie et oeuvres de Féderic Morel ... Paris, 1901. p. 97.

GENEALOGIES, Printers

Cabinet U Shelf 2 No. 38

Raikes, pedigree of the family of. Formerly of Kingston-upon-Hull...Compiled from the Wills, Parish Registers, and other documents collected by Lieut.-Colonel G. A. Raikes.

Cloth; 10 x 6-3/4 x 3/8 in. See also U/2/37

GENEALOGIES, Printers

Cabinet AA Shelf 3 No. 19

Waesberghe, Van family: Amsterdam, Antwerp, Utrecht Rottedam etc; 1561-1829.
See Ledeboer, A.M. Het geslacht van Waesberghe ... 's Gravenhagen, 1869.

GENEALOGIES, Printers

Cabinet S Shelf 2 No. 19

Munsell, Joel, and family, 1681-1876. Biographical sketch of Joel Munsell. By George R. Howell. To which is appended a genealogy of the Munsell family, by Frank Munsell. Boston, 1880. Portrait.

Half morocco; 9-7/8 x 6¼ in.

GENEALOGIES, PRINTERS

Cabinet AA Shelf 3 No. 14.01

Schoeffer, het geslacht, later Scheffer en Scherffers te 's-Hertogenbosch, van 1541-1706, in betrekking tot de boekdrukkunst. Door Ch. C. V. Verreyt. 's-Gravenhage, 1888.

Half morocco, 8-3/8x5½x½ in.

GENEALOGIES, Typefounders

Cabinet S Shelf 2 No. 109

Pelouze, Louis. Autobiography of Edmond Pelouze (1765-1845), with a brief biography of his wife. Introductory remarks by Wm. Nelson Pelouze. Published privately in the year A.D. 1923.
Edmond Pelouze was the brother of a printer, and father of Louis Pelouze, typefounder, Philadelphia, 1849.

Boards; 7½ x 5-1/8 in.

GENEALOGIES, Printers

Cabinet AA Shelf 3 No. 28

Plantin, Christophe--Joanna Rivière.
See Olthoff, Frans. De Boekdrukkers boekverkoopers ... in Antwerpen...Antwerp, 1891. Following p. 82.

GENEALOGIES, PRINTERS

Cabinet W Shelf 4 No. 42

Schoeffer, Pierre: Les descendants Pierre Schoeffer, qui exercèrent l'imprimerie à Bois-le-Duc de père en fils, depuis l'années 1541 jusqu'en 1796. Gand, 1846.
Reprinted from the "Messager des Sciences", Gand, 1846, pp. 435-445.

Half morocco; 8-7/8 x 5¾ in.

GENERAL ADVERTISER, or, AURORA

Cabinet NN Shelf 2 No. 18

Philadelphia, 1800, Willaim Duane, editor.

see LIBERTY OF PRINTING, United States. Duane, William, Senate report...

GENEALOGIES, Printers.

Cabinet W Shelf 4 No. 102

Plantin-Moretus. France and Antwerp, 1514 to 1804.
See Degeorge, Leon (La) maison Plantin a Anvers ... Bruxelles, 1878. p. 10.

GENEALOGIES, Printers

Cabinet R Shelf 5 No. 23

Sower, Christopher: Genealogical chart of the descendants of Christopher Sower, printer of Germantown, Philadelphia, Pa. Compiled by Charles G. Sower. Philadelphia, 1887.
Bio-bibliographical. With picture of the house of Sowers' I and II.

Folding Chart, 125 x 42 in. In box, 11 x 9 in., which also contains a notice (reprint) of David Sower.

GENESEE MESSENGER.

Cabinet Shelf No.

See Newspapers, New York State.

GENEALOGIES, Printers

Cabinet AA Shelf 3 No. 17

Plantin-Moretus family: Geslagt-lyste der merkomelingen van den vermaerden ... waeby gevoeged is eenen geslagt-lyste der familie Mourentorff, alias Moretus. door J. B. Van der Straelen. Antwerpen, 1853.
Biographical genealogy.

Half cloth 14 x 9-3/4 in.

GENEALOGIES, PRINTERS'

Cabinet B Shelf 2 No. 23

(Spanish 15th and 16th century printers. Biographies of, with genealogies.)

In Haebler's "Geschichte des spanischen frühdruckers...Leipzig, 1923.

Cloth over boards; 16¾ x 13 x 1½ in.

GENGENBACH, PAMPHILUS

Cabinet X Shelf 3 No. 15

Bio-bibliographical sketch, with printer mark, Gegenbach, Basel, 1480-1524.

see HEITZ, PAUL.
Basler büchermarken... pp.xix, 21, 23

GENEALOGIES, Printers.

Cabinet W Shelf 3 No. 3

Monnoyer family of printers, established in France 1618, still in existence in 1883. Imprimerie Monnoyer. Paris, 1878-83.

Cloth; 9-3/4 x 6¼ in.

GENEALOGIES, Printers

Cabinet AA Shelf 1 No. 53

Viotti famiglia, 1507-1702. Parma, Italy.
Viotti, stampatori e librai Parmigiani. Giovanni Drei. Parma, 1925.
In volume "Parma Grafica." Parma, 1925. pp. 37 - 38.

Half morocco; 12½ x 9½ in.

GENNEP, JASPAR von

Cabinet X Shelf 3 No. 20

Brief bio-bibliographical note, von Gennep, Cologne, 1536-1564.

see HEITZ, PAUL.
Kölner büchermarken...p.xxviii

GENOA

Cabinet RR Shelf 3 No. 10

(Paper and paper marks of Genoa, 1154 to 1700)

see

BRIQUET, C. M. Papiers et filigranes des archives de Gênes...Genève, 1888.

GENOA

Cabinet Shelf No.

See also
Early Printing in Italy. Literature. Genoa and Naples, 1474, 1475-1491. Matthias Moravus.

GENSFLEISCH FAMILY

Cabinet X Shelf 2 No. 60

[Guild disputes and the Genschfleisch family] Die Zunftkämfe in Mainz und der anteil der familie Gensfleisch. von J.B. Seidenberger, Mainz, 1900.

Essay in book with title "Gutenberg-Feier, Mainz, 1900"...von K.G. Bockenheimer.

GENT, THOMAS. (Author-Printer)

Cabinet F Shelf 4 No. 23

Annales Regioduni Hullini: or, the History of the Royal and beautiful town of Kingston upon-Hull...Faithfully collected by Thomas Gent. York, 1735. Frontispiece portrait, woodcuts, and plates.

Imprint: Sold at the Printing-Office, near the Star in Stone-Gate, York.....MDCCXXXV.

Leather; 7-3/4 x 5 x 1 in.

GENT, THOMAS

Cabinet U Shelf 5 No. 49

Bio-bibliographical notes concerning Th. Gent, printer-publisher, York, 1724-1778.

see

DAVIES, ROBERT
(A) Memoir of The York Press...1868, p.144

GENT, THOMAS

Cabinet U Shelf 2 No. 22

Life of Mr. Thomas Gent, printer, of York [1691-1778]; Written by himself. London, 1832.

Half morocco; 8-7/8 x 5$\frac{3}{4}$ x $\frac{3}{4}$ in.

GENT, THOMAS

Cabinet S Shelf 5 No. 17

Quaint romance of Thomas Gent, printer of York. Excerpt from The Caxton Magazine, 1890. Portrait and illus.

Item 14 in collection "Miscellaneous items relating to printing; excerpts from magazines 1918.

(The) Gentleman's Diary (see)

Cabinet 80 Shelf 1 No. 88

Almanacs. (The) Gentleman's Diary

GENTLEMAN'S EVENING JOURNAL (The)

Cabinet Shelf No.

See Newspapers, Massachusetts.

GENTLEMAN'S MAGAZINE, The

Cabinet U Shelf 5 No. 52

Bibliographical notes: A classified collection of the chief contents of "The Gentleman's Magazine" from 1731-1868. London, 1889.

Includes notes on special books; notes on printers and early printing; early English newspapers, almanacks, origin of cards, etc.

Boards; 9$\frac{1}{4}$ x 6 x 1$\frac{1}{4}$ in.

GENTLEMAN'S MAGAZINE see

Cabinet NN Shelf 2 No. 14

PERIODICALS, Great Britain. (A) very old gentleman...

GENTLEMEN'S AMERICAN MONTHLY REVIEW see

Cabinet 80 Shelf 2 No. 47

PERIODICALS, United States. Burton's Magazine (The Gentlemens American Monthly Review...

GENZSCH, EMIL JULIUS

Cabinet FF Shelf 6 No. 14

(Celebration publication in honor of his fifty years active service with the firm of Genzsch & Heyse). Fünfzig jahre schriftgiesser. Emil Genzsch, ihrem seniorchef zum goldenen berufsjubiläum gewidmet von den firmen Genzsch & Heyse, Hamburg und E.J. Genzsch, Munchen. Ostern A.D. 1906.
Has portrait, also specimens of type.

Half morocco; 14$\frac{3}{4}$ x 10 in.

GENZSCH, EMIL JULIUS (Typefounder).

Cabinet Y Shelf 5 No. 114

Funfzig jahre schriftgiesser: Ihrem seniorchef zum goldenen berufsjubiläum gewidmet von den firmen Genzsch, Munchen. Ostern A.D. 1906. With portrait.
Includes many type specimens from the house of Genzsch & Heyse.

3/4 Morocco; 14-3/8 x 10-1/8 x 1 in.

GENZSCH, EMIL JULIUS

Cabinet Shelf No.

See Specimen Books, Types. Germany. Genzsch, Emil Julius. München, 1902.

GENZSCH & HEYSE.

Cabinet Y Shelf 5 No. 115

Chronik der schriftgiesserei von Genzsch & Heyse in Hamburg. Zum jubilaum des 75- jahrigen bestehens der firma. 1833-1908. With portraits of the founder and his successors.

Parchment; 7 x 5 x $\frac{1}{2}$ in.

GENZSCH & HEYSE

Cabinet FF Shelf 4 No. 20

Chronik der schriftgiesserei von Genzsch & Heyse in Hamburg, 1833-1908.

History of the firm.

Vellum; 6$\frac{3}{4}$ x 5 x 3/8 in.

GENZSCH & HEYSE

Cabinet FF Shelf 3 No. 35

Erinnerungen an das Jubiliaum des 75 jahrigen bestehens der schriftgiesserei von Genzsch & Heyse in Hamburg. 28 Februar, 1833-1908. (With many Illus.)

Half morocco; 10-3/4 x 7-3/4 "

GENZSCH & HEYSE

Cabinet CG Shelf 2 No. 34

(Der) Schonsten schriften aus 100 jahren schaffen, 1833-1933. Genzsch & Heyse, Hamburg.

Specimens of the 50 most beautiful type produced during 100 years by the firm of Genzsch & Heyse. The real value of this item is the history on pp. 5-19

Cloth over boards; 12 x 9 in.

GENZSCH & HEYSE

Cabinet Y Shelf 5 No. 113

Schriftgiesserei Genzsch & Heyse in Hamburg, 70 jahre, 1833-1903. Pamphlet.

Each page of this commemorative pamphlet, is composed in a different series of types, with a brief description of each.

Paper; 9¾ x 7½ in.

GENZSCH & HEYSE

Cabinet FF Shelf 3 No. 33

Universal Schriftlinie System. Genzsch & Heyse. Munchen-Hamburg. Illus. Brochures (2)

Point system, adopted in Germany in 1904, confroming with the American.

Items in manila envelope.

GENZSCH & HEYSE

Cabinet Shelf No.

See also index cards with following sub-heads:

I Specimen Books, Types. Germany
II Type Foundries, Germany.

GEOGRAPHICAL SIGNS

Cabinet MM Shelf 4 No. 15

See p.120 Crisp's Printers' Universal book of reference...London, 1875.

GEOMETRICAL SIGNS

Cabinet MM Shelf 4 No. 15

See p.120 of Crisp's Printers' Universal book of reference...London, 1875.

GEORGE, HENRY

Cabinet S Shelf 2 No. 132

Achievements of Henry George, printer's apprentice, foreman in printshop, politician, and idealist. 1839-1897.

See Weinstein, Gregory. Reminiscences of an interesting decade ... Chap. XIV.

GEORGIA

Cabinet FF Shelf 6 No. 5

Books relating to the history of Georgia in the library of W. J. DeRenne, of Wormsloe County, Georgia. Compiled and annotated by Oscar Wegelin, 1911.

Paper; 13¼ x 10½ x 1-3/8 in.

GEORGIA

Cabinet S Shelf 3 No. 104

Promotion literature of Georgia. By Verner W. Crane, Assistant professor of American History, Brown University.

Bibliographical.

P. 281 in volume, Wilberforce Eames ... A tribute to. Cambridge, 1924.

GEORGIA

Cabinet Shelf No.

See also "EARLY PRINTING IN GEORGIA".

EARLY PRINTING IN AMERICA. [LITERATURE OF] PRINTING, HISTORICAL, Georgia.

GEORGIA WEEKLY PRESS ASSOCIATION

Cabinet KK Shelf 5 No. 88

Minutes, eighth annual meeting, held at Milledgeville and Atlanta Ga., Aug, 7th, 8th, 9th, 1894.

Item in envelope.

GEORGIAN PRESS

Cabinet Shelf No.

See Imprints, United States

GEPRIESENES ANDENKEN

zu Erfindung der Buchdruckerey..

See Andenken, Gepriesenes.

GÉRARD de FLANDRE

Cabinet W Shelf 4 No. 65

Imprimeur à Trévise, Vicence, Venise, Friuli et Udine, de 1471-1499.

See Meersch, P. C. Van der: Recherches sur la vie et les travaux de quelques imprimeurs Belges ... Gand, 1844 - 1846. pp. 1 - 70.

GÉRAUD, H.

Cabinet W Shelf 1 No. 64

Essai sur les livres dans l'antiquité, particulièrement chez les Romans. Par H. Géraud. Paris, 1840.

Boards; 8½ x 5¼ in.

GERDIL, GIACINTO

Cabinet PP Shelf 3 No. 3

Statuti della venerabile compagnia, ed universita dé librari di Roma. Sotto l'invocazione de S. Thomaso d'Aquino...In Roma, 1803. Nella Stamperia de Gio. Batista Cannetti.

Statutes relating to booksellers.

Vellum; 9½ x 7 in.

GERING, CONRAD and FRIBURGER

Cabinet T Shelf 3 No. 2

First printers at Paris, account of the

In DIBDIN'S Bibliographical Decameron...London, 1817, vol.2, pp.20-4

GERING, ULRICH

Cabinet S Shelf 1 No. 29

See De Vinne, Theodore Low. Notable printers of Italy ... New York, 1910. p. 131.

GERING, ULRICH.

Cabinet 70 Shelf 1 No. 5

See Early Printing in France. Paris, 1508. Ulrich Gering.

GERING, ULRIC

Cabinet V Shelf 6 No. 9

See also
Monuments, Printers.
Portraits, Printers.
Partnership of Printers. Early. Gering, Ulric

GERMAN MASTER PRINTERS' UNION

Cabinet KK Shelf 2 No. 60.01

Deutschen Buchgewerbe Verein.

see SOCIETIES, PRINTERS'. Germany Deutschen Buchgewerbe Verein.

GERING, ULRICH

Cabinet V Shelf 5 No. 2.01

Mémoire sur le projet d'elever une statue a Ulrich Gering.

See ALKAN Ainé. Memoire sur le projet... Paris, 1879.

GERLACH, A.

Cabinet Shelf No.

See Specimen Books, Types. Germany.

GERMAN MASTER PRINTERS VISIT AMERICA, U.S.A.

Cabinet Y Shelf 4 No. 55

Account of German printers activities and entertainments while on a visit to America, Oct.15-18, 1924.
Die America fahrt deutscher buchdrucker. Zur 28 versammlung der U.T.A. Eine sammlung von Berichten...Berlin, 1925. Illus.

Half morocco; $8\frac{1}{4}$ x $5\frac{3}{4}$.

GERING, ULRIC

Cabinet W Shelf 2 No. 1

Nouveau document sur Gutenberg. Témoinage d'Ulric Gering, le premier imprimeur parisien, et de ses compagnous en faveur de l'invention de l'imprimerie. Par A. Claudin Extrait du Livre. 4e Année. pp. 369-72. Paris, 1883.

Item 14 in volume "Gutenberg, l'inventeur de l'imprimerie - Melanges."

GERLACH, MARTIN (EDITOR)

Cabinet K Shelf 1 No. 16

(Das Alte buch und seine ausstattung, von 15 bis 19 jahrhundert, buchdruck, buchschmerck, einband. Mit einem vorwort von Dr. Heinrich Rottinger. 1376 abbildungen auf 74 doppelseitigen buch und lichtdrucktafeln. Herausgegeben von Martin Gerlach. Wien - Leipzig (1912 ?)
"Die Quelle mappe XIII".

Portfolio, boards; 12 x 10 in.

GERMAN PRINTING IN AMERICA (Early)

Cabinet 22 Shelf 1 No.

Deutschamerikanische buchdruch und buchhandels im vorigen jahrhundert (German-American printing and publishing, 1683-1872). von Friedrich Kapp.

In "Archiv für geschichte Deutschen buchhandels." vol. 1, 1878. pp. 56-77.

GERING, ULRICH

Cabinet Y Shelf 1 No. 41

Paris, Ulrich Gering in (Biographical account, with portrait)

See BÖRCHEL, ALFRED. Gutenberg und seine berühmsten nachfolger...pp.166-171

GERLI, (Leonardo)

Cabinet X Shelf 3 No. 14

Bibliographical note, with printer mark, Gerlie, Pavia, 1485-98.

see KRISTELLER, Dr. Paul. Itelienischen buchdrucker...p.46

GERMAN PRINTING IN AMERICA (Early)

Cabinet S Shelf 4 No. 120

Early German-American Bibles. By Daniel Miller. An excerpt from The Pennsylvania-German, May 1910.
Item 8 in volume "About the Bible," Excerpts from Magazines.

Half morocco; $10\frac{1}{4}$ x 6-7/8 in.

GERING, ULRIC

Cabinet V Shelf 4 No. 4

Premier imprimeur de Paris, Ulric Gering, histoire de.

See CHEVILLIER, ANDRÉ. l'Origine de l'Imprimerie de Paris...Paris, 1694.

GERMAIN, A.

Cabinet X Shelf 5 No. 64

Martyrolage de la presse, 1789-1861. Paris, 1861.

Half morocco; $7\frac{1}{2}$ x 4-7/8 x 1 in.

GERMAN PRINTING IN AMERICA, Early.

Cabinet R Shelf 5 No. 30

(The) First century of German printing in America, 1728-1830: Preceded by a notice of the literary work of F. D. Pastorius. By Oswald Seidensticker. Philadelphia, 1893.
Bibliographical account; has aldo a list of places of German printing arranged in the order of first issues.

Half morocco; 9 x 6 in.

GERING, ULRICH

Cabinet V Shelf 4 No. 2

See Printing, Historical, France. Chevillier, Andre. L'origine de l'imprimerie de Paris. [Parts I and II of this work]. Paris,1689.

GERMAN AND GERMANY (GUIDE CARDS)

Cabinet Shelf No.

See cards immediately following this.

See also cards with following sub-heads.
I - NEWSPAPERS, Germany
II - JOURNALISM, Germany
III - PERIODICALS, Germany
IV - EARLY PRINTING IN GERMANY
V - " " " " [Lit. of]
VI - IMPRINTS
VII - INCUNABULA
VIII - PRINTING, HISTORICAL
IX - SPECIMEN BOOKS, TYPES.

GERMAN PRINTING IN AMERICA, Early

Cabinet R Shelf 5 No. 35

Our Early German Printers: Who they were and what they did. Biographical sketches of some, with an account of the issues of their presses. By F. R. Diffenderffer. A paper read before the Lancaster County Historical Society, Jan. 1, 1904. (Newspaper report of the address).

Cloth; $9\frac{3}{4}$ x 6 in.

GERMAN PRINTING IN AMERICA, Early

Cabinet R · Shelf 5 · No. 33

(Pennsylvania). Early German printers of Lancaster and the issues of their press. By F. R. Diffenderfer: A paper read before the Lancaster County Historical Society. January, 1, 1904.
Bound in volume "Early printing in Lancaster County, Pa."

Half morocco; 9¾ x 6¼ in.

GERMAN PRINTING IN AMERICA, Early

Cabinet R · Shelf 5 · No. 35

(Pennsylvania). Newspapers of Lancaster Co., Penn., 1752-1902. By F. R. Diffenderffer: A paper read before the Lancaster County Historical Society, May 2, 1902.
Bound in with another item "Our Early German Printers: who they were and what they did." By the same author.

Cloth; 9¾ x 6 in.

GERMAN PRINTING IN AMERICA, Early

Cabinet 27 · Shelf 1 · No. 7

(Pennsylvania) The old Ephrata press, the second German-press in Pennsylvania. Address by the Hon. Joseph R. Chandler.

Article in the Printers' Circular, vol.7, No.10, Dec., 1872, p.362

GERMAN PRINTING IN AMERICA, Early

Cabinet R · Shelf 5 · No. 37

Researches in the first century of German printing in America, 1728-1830. By Rev. A. Stapleton. Two essays in the Pennsylvania-German, Vol. V. Nos. 2 and 4. pp. 81-89; 183.

Buckram; 9¼ x 6 in.

GERMAN SINGLE-PLATE WOODCUTS (16th cnetury)

Cabinet 1 & 5 · Shelf · Portfolios · No. 1 to 40

Facsimile reprints, about 1600 plates

See GEISBERG, MAX

(German single-plate woodcuts of the first half of the 16th century...)

GERMAN TYPES

Cabinet 26 · Shelf 1 · No. 17

United States as a market for German types. By Melbert B. Cary, Jr.

Article in the Gutenberg-Gesellschaft Jahrbuch 1928. pp.175-179.

GERMANTOWN, Pa.

Cabinet R · Shelf 4 · No. 34

Important dates in Germantown History: a circular, 8pp. n.d.
The first paper mill (1690); The first Type was cast (1772); and the first Bible in a European language (1743 in America and several other important First Occurrences.

Item in manila envelope.

GERMANY

Cabinet X · Shelf 2 · No. 26

Erfurt, 1802-1840 list of printers, and booksellers exercising in. (German text)

See Celebrations, Printers 1840, Erfurt: Gutenberg 400th anniversary... p. 197

GERMANY

Cabinet A · Shelf 3 · No. 89

Fine Printing in Germany, p.16 special graphic arts number of The Times, Sept. 10, 1912.

GERMANY

Cabinet K · Shelf 4 · No. 20

(Illustrated book of the 15th century)

See Olschki, Leo S. Le livre illustre' au XV[e] siecle...Florence, 1926. pp.111-X19...

GERMANY

Cabinet K · Shelf 4 · No. 21

(Illustrated book in Germany, 1790-1860)

See Rumann, Arthur (Das) Illustrierte buch des 19 jahrhunderts...Leipzig, 1930. pp. 221-352.

GERMANY

Cabinet Q · Shelf 1 · No. 17

(Leipzig, the old and new home of the booksellers society. Celebration)

see
PUBLISHING, Germany. (Das) Alte und neue buchhändlerheim...

GERMANY

Cabinet FF · Shelf 3 · No. 33

(Point system adopted in Germany in 1904)

See Genzsch & Heyse. Universal Schriftline system.

GERMANY

Cabinet U · Shelf 5 · No. 28

Spread of printing in Germany (see)

DUFF. E. GORDON. Early printed books.. p.39

GÉRONVAL, AUDOIN de

Cabinet MM · Shelf 1 · No. 24

Manuel de l'imprimeur, ou traité simplifié de la typographie. Paris 1826. Illus.

Half morocco, gilt; 5-7/8 x 3-5/8 x 1-1/8 in.

GERRING, CHARLES

Cabinet K · Shelf 3 · No. 29

Notes on book illustration. Oposculum x. The Nottingham Sette of Odde Volumes. Privately printed. Nottingham, January, 1898. Illus.

Half morocco; 5¾ x 4-5/8 in.

GERRING, CHARLES

Cabinet PP · Shelf 4 · No. 26

Notes on bookbinding. Vol. III, the Nottingham Sette of Odde Volumes, opusculum XII. Nottingham. Privately printed, 1899. Illus.

Half morocco; 8 x 5¾ x 3/8 in.

GERRING, CHARLES

Cabinet U · Shelf 5 · No. 64

Printers and booksellers, Notes on. With a chapter on Chap Books. Dedicated to the late Mr. Bernard Quaritch. London, 1900. Facsimiles and other illus.
Bio-bibliographical historical account.

Half morocco; 9¼ x 6 x 7/8 in.

GERSTINGER, HANS

Cabinet 68 Shelf No. 7 (2 parts)

(Die) Griechische buchmalerei. Mit 22 abbildungen im textband und 28 tafeln nach originalen der Nationalbibliothek in Wien. Wien, 1926. (In 2 parts)

Part 1, Text
" 2, Plates

Boards; 20 x 15 in.

GERWER, K.

Cabinet Y Shelf 4 No. 24

Basel "Typographia" und ihre 50 jahriger wirksamkeit, 1857-1907 (The Basel society "Typographia", and its 50 years activity). Basel, 1917.
A History of the Basel printer's society "Typographia", preceded by a brief historical account of printing in Basel.

Half morocco; 9-1/8 x 6¼ x 3/8 in.

GESAMTKATALOG DER WIEGENDRUCK

Cabinet Shelf No.

See Pollard, Alfred W. Gesamtkatalog etc: A review.

GESCHICHTE DER K. K. HOF-

... und Staats-Druckerei in Wien.

See Auer, Alois.

GESELLSCHAFT FÜR TYPENKUNDE

Cabinet B Shelf 2 No. 22

Veröffentlichungen der Gesellschaft fur typenkunde des 15 jahrhunderts. Halle, 1907-1930. Nos.1-1888.

Issued in portfolios. Reproductions of 15th century type specimens.
Inserted in vol.1, various interesting documents relating to the Society for the Stu of Types.

As issued, 29 parts, 17 x 12 in. Index to reproductions in manila envelope: B/2/22. 01

GESNER, ANDREAS

Cabinet X Shelf 3 No. 16

Bibliographical note, gesner, printer, Zurich, 1535-1560.

see
HEITZ, PAUL.
Zurcher büchermarken...p.7

GESNER, ANDREAS.

Cabinet Shelf No.

See Biographies, Printers (Collective)
Zurich printers, 1504-1560.

GESSLER, JÖRG

Cabinet Y Shelf 4 No. 4

(Note on Gessler and his printing at Zweibrücker, 1492)

see
VOULLIÉME, ERNST (Die)
Deutschen drucker des fünfzehnten jahrhundert...p.123

GESSNER, CHR. FR.

Cabinet LL Shelf 1 No. 6 (4 vols)

(Die) So nothig als nutzliche buchdruckerkunst und schriftgiesserei, mit ihren schriften, formaten, und allen dazu gehorigen instrumenten abgebildet... Mit einer vorrede Herrn Johann Erhard Kappen. Leipzig, 1740-45.
4 vols. with numerous plates.
Bound in back of vol.4 of above, "Der in der buchdruckerei wohl unterrichtete lehr-junge", Leipzig, 1743. This includes type specimens from the foundries of

cont.

GESSNER, CHR.FR. cont'd

Cabinet LL Shelf 1 No. 6

Erhardt and Zincken, also the "Deposito Cornuti".

vols. 1,2,3, Calf; 7 x 4¾ in., vol. IV, Half vellum, 7 x 4¾ in.

GESSNER, CHRISTIAN FRIEDRICH

Cabinet LL Shelf 1 No. 6

Der in der buchdruckerei wohl unterrichtete lehr-junge, Oder: bey der loblichen buchdruckerkunst nothig und nutzliche anfangsgrunde...Leipzig, 1743. Many engraved plates.
Includes specimens of type from the foundries of Erhardt and Zincken, and the "Depositio Cornuti Typographici".
Bound in the back of vol. IV, of Gessner's

(cont'd)

GESSNER, CHRISTIAN FRIEDRICH (cont'd)

Cabinet Shelf No.

Die so nothig als nutzlich buchdruckerkunst ...Leipzig, 1740-1745.

Half vellum; 6¾ x 4½ in.

GESTA TYPOGRAPHICA

Cabinet T Shelf 5 No. 109

Medley for printers and others. By Chas. T. Jacobi, London, 1897.

Historical notes on printers and printing.

Boards, linen back; 7 x 4½ in.

GESTOSO Y PEREZ, JOSÉ

Cabinet 79 Shelf 2 No. 11

Introduccion de la imprenta en America, Carta que al Sr. D. José Gestoso y Perez dirige J.T. Medina. Santiago de Chile, 1910.
Letter by Medina in answer to a previous letter of Gestoso y Perez.

Cloth; 10¼ x 7 in. Chiappa 190

GETHER & DREBERT COMPANY

Cabinet Shelf No.

See Specimen Books, Types. United States. Gether and Drebert.

GÉVAUDAN (France)

Cabinet J Shelf 4 No. 7

See PRINTING, HISTORICAL. France. (Gévaudan)

GEYMET and ALKER

Cabinet I Shelf 2 No. 23

Gravure heliographique, galvanoplastie. Traite pratique. Par Geymet & Alker. Paris... Bruxelles, 1870.

Paper; 7¼ x 4½ in.

GHEMART, ADRIAN

Cabinet X Shelf 3 No. 19

Brief bio-bibliographical note, with printer mark, Ghemart (Valladolid) 1551-1572.

see
HAEBLER, KONRAD. (Spanish and Portuguese printer marks...p.xxvii

GHENT

Cabinet U Shelf 5 No. 38

Types and devices used at Ghent by the early printers

see PROCTOR, ROBERT. Bibliographical essays...London, 1905, p.146

GHERARDO, Querino

Cabinet X Shelf 3 No. 19

Brief bio-bibliographical note, with printer mark, Gherardo (Alcalá) 1580-1583.

see HAEBLER, KONRAD. (Spanish and Portugese printer marks...p.xxxvii

GHERARDUS, VINCENTIUS.

Cabinet E Shelf 3 No. 37

See Early Printing in Italy. Rome, 1628.

GHOTAN, BARTHOLOMAEUS

Cabinet Y Shelf 4 No. 4

(Notes on Ghotan's 15th century press at Magdeburg)

see VOULLIÉME, ERNST. (Die) Deutschen drucker des fünfzehnten jahrhunderts...p.67

GIANOLIO

Cabinet Shelf No.

See "DALMAZZO, GIANOLIO".

GIBBINGS, ROBERT

Cabinet M Shelf No.

See Imprints, England. Golden Cockerel Press, The. Robert Gibbing.

GIBSON, CHARLES R.

Cabinet L Shelf 1 No. 38

Romance of modern photography. Its discovery and its achievements. By Charles R. Gibson. With 63 illustrations. London, 1910.

Cloth; 8 x 5¼ in.

GIBSON, DAVIS.

Cabinet G Shelf 1 No. 34.01

A Buyer of Printing. Some confessions, By Davis Gibson. The Caxton Company, Cleveland. April 1915.

Boards; 8-1/8 x 5½ in.

GIBSON, STRICKLAND

Cabinet 76 Shelf 1 No. 11

Abstracts from the wills and testamentary documents of binders, printers, and stationers of Oxford from 1493 to 1638. London: Printed for the Bibliographical Society, by Blades, East & Blades. Feb., 1907.

Half morocco; 8¾ x 7½ in.

GIBSON, STRICKLAND.

Cabinet 75 Shelf 1 No. 8

Book bindings, the localization of books by their. A paper read before the Bibliographical Society, February 20, 1905.

In Trans. Biblio. Soc., Vol. VIII, 1904-1906, pp. 25-38.

GIBSON, STRICKLAND.

Cabinet T Shelf 6 No. 61

English printing, 1700-1925. A note on. Booklet presented "With the compliments of Dulau & Company," London, 1925.

In box labelled "English Printing and Printers. Shakespeariana. Misc. v.d."

GIBSON, STRICKLAND

Cabinet PP Shelf 3 No. 13

Oxford libraries, some. By Strickland Gibson. Oxford University Press. Oxford, 1914. Illus.

Cloth; 6⅞ x 4¾ in.

GIBSON, STRICKLAND.

Cabinet 75 Shelf 2 No. 3

Recent books on bookbinding. A review.

In Transactions of the Bibliography Society, "The Library," Vol. III, 1922-23, pp. 137-140.

GIBSON, THOMAS

Cabinet T Shelf 2 No. 6 [vol.3]

Books printed by Thomas Gibson, London, 1535-1539. Bibliographical notes.

see DIBDIN'S "Typographical Antiquities" ...London, 1810-19, vol.iii, p.400

GIEBEN, K.J.

Cabinet Shelf No.

See SPECIMEN BOOKS, TYPES. Printers'. Holland.

GIESSER, HANS

Cabinet X Shelf 3 No. 19

Bio-bibliographical note, with printer mark, Giesser, printer (Salamanca), 1501-1520.

see HAEBLER, KONRAD. (Spanish and Portugese printer marks...p.xiv

GIFFING

Cabinet Shelf No.

See: Cortelyou & Giffing. Specimen Books, Types, U.S.

GIFT BOOKS.

Cabinet Shelf No.

See ANNUALS AND GIFT BOOKS.

CICOGNARA, LEOPOLDO

Cabinet C Shelf 2 No. 17

Memorie spettanti all storia della calcografia. Del Commend. Conte Leopoldo Giogonare. Prato, 1830.

Illustrations which bear upon the history of engraving.

Boards; 18½ x 12¼ in.

GILDEA & COMPANY Inc., DAVID

Cabinet EE Shelf 1 No. 53

See SPECIMEN BOOKS, TYPES. Printers.

GILKS, THOMAS

Cabinet K Shelf 5 No. 17

Wood engraving, the art of. A practical handbook. By Thomas Gilks. With numerous illustrations by the author. 3rd edition. London, 1871.

Explains the different processes involved in wood engraving, describes the tools and materials used, etc.

Paper; 7 x 4-3/4 x 3/8 in.

GIL, GERONIMO

Cabinet Shelf No.

See Specimen Books, Types. Spain. [Gil. etc.] 1787.

GILDER, JEANNETTE L.

Cabinet Q Shelf 1 No. 4

(Goschen) A famous German publisher. Biographical comments. Excerpt from The Critic, July, 1903.

Item 9 in vol. with binder's title "Various items on Publishing."

GILKS, THOMAS

Cabinet K Shelf 5 No. 18

Wood engraving, the art of. A practical handbook. By Thomas Gilks. With numerous illustrations by the author. Sixth edition. London, n.d.

Half morocco; 7-3/8 x 5 x 3/8 in.

GILBERT and RIVINGTON

Cabinet Shelf No.

See Specimen Books, Types England

GILDER, RICHARD WATSON

Cabinet NN Shelf 2 No. 16

(The) Newspaper, the magazine and the public. An interview with Richard Watson Gilder, by Clifton Johnson.

Excerpt from the Outlook, Feb.4, 1899. with portrait.

Item 7 in vol. with binder's title; "Journalism: Pamphlets. Bound, 1932".

GILL, ERIC

Cabinet Y Shelf 2 No. 97

Essay on typography - The two worlds. [Brief review of above]. by Noel Carrington.

Article in Gutenberg-Gesellschaft Jahrbuch, 1932, p.292.

GILBERT ISLANDS (South Pacific)

Cabinet II Shelf 3 No. 51

Gospel of Saint John. (American Bible Society, N.Y., 1866. Booklet.

Cloth; 6 x 4 in.

GILDER, RICHARD WATSON

Cabinet Shelf No.

see also BIOGRAPHIES, Editors.

GILL, ERIC

Cabinet K Shelf 5 No. 26

Introduction to R. John Beedham's "Wood Engraving". Printed and published at S. Dominic's Press, Ditchling, Sussex. 1920. Illus.

Boards; 7-3/4 x 5-1/8 x ¼ in.

GILBERT PAPER COMPANY

Cabinet RR Shelf 1 No. 5

Information book for the printer. Compliments of Gilbert Paper Company, Menasha, Wisconsin. n.d. After 1925.

Includes standard scales for color process plates, photo-engraving, and electrotype.

Boards; 12¼ x 9 in.

GILDERSLEEVE, BASIL L.

Cabinet NN Shelf 7 No. 16

Reviewing, the hazards of. The founder of the "American Journal of Philology" relates the inner history of reviewing for the "Nation".

see NATION, THE. Semi - centennial, 1863-1915, p. 49.

GILL, JOHN

Cabinet F Shelf 2 No. 79

See Early Printing in New England. Boston, 1774: Benjamin Edes and John Gill.

GILCHRIST, A.S. and COMPANY

Cabinet Shelf No.

See Specimen Books, United States. Knickerbocker Type Foundry, A.S. Gilchrist & Co.

GILES, HERBERT A.

Cabinet J Shelf 3 No. 10

Introduction to the history of Chinese pictorial art. With illustrations. (Second edition, revised and enlarged) London, 1918. Bernard Quaritch.

Half morocco; 9-7/8 x 6-5/8 in.

GILLE, J.

Cabinet FF Shelf 3 No. 10

Notice sur l'Exposition de 1819. Typographic Notice pour la Concours des progres de l'Industrie Francaise en 1823.

Two broadsides bound in at end.

Historical summary of type founding, and printing in France.

Half morocco; 11x8½x4½ in.

GILLÉ, J. (Author-Printer)

Cabinet FF | Shelf 3 | No. 11

Typographie. L'Exposition de l'industrie en 1823. Paris. Illus. of medals presented to Gillé.

The author briefly outlines the account of the discovery of printing, and its progress, particularly in France.

Half morocco; 10¼ x 8-1/8 x 3/8 in.

GILLÉ, J.G.

Cabinet MM | Shelf 1 | No. 18

Manuel de l'imprimerie, contenant: [long list of contents follows]. Seconde édition, corrigée et augmentée. Paris, 1817. Plates, illus.

Text book of printing.

Boards; 7-7/8 x 5 x 3/8 in.

GILLÉ, J.G.

Cabinet MM | Shelf 1 | No. 19

Manuel de l'imprimerie, contenant [long list of contents follows]. Seconde édition, corrigée et augmentée. Paris, 1817. With plates.

Typothetae copy.

Boards; 7-7/8 x 5 x 3/8 in.

GILLÉ, fils, J. G.

Cabinet Z | Shelf 5 | No. 47

Caractères de la fonderie et l'Imprimerie de Gillé fils, rue Jean de Beauvais, à Paris. (Broadside, no. 11, 22; fols. 23 to 25)

Also specimens of vignettes, fols. 12 to 17. With prices.

Fols. 12 to 17 in vol. labelled "Broadsides, Specimens of types, Spain, 1832-1840".

GILLÉ, fils, J. G.

Cabinet | Shelf | No.

See also Specimens, Vignettes. France.

GILLÉ, JOSEPH

Cabinet | Shelf | No.

See Specimen Books, Types. France.

GILLES, NICOLE.

Cabinet 69 | Shelf 2 | No. 3

Annales et croniques de France...Nicole Gilles....Corrigées et annotées par le Seigneur Denis Sauvage. [Printer Mark]. À Paris. Par Jean Ruelle, libraire, demourant en la rue sainct Jaques, à l'Enseigne sainct Nicolas. 1566.

Colophon: Fin du second et dernier volume.... continuées jusques en l'an mil cinq cens soixante. Imprimées....par Richard Roux, imprimeur (etc)

Calf; 13¼ x 8½ x 1½ in. Brunet 2, 1596.

GILLES, NICOLE cont;d

Cabinet | Shelf | No.

Calf; 13¼ x 8½ x 1½ in. Brunet 2, 1596.

GILLES de GOURMONT see

Cabinet | Shelf | No.

COURMONT, Gilles de

GILLESPIE, MRS. E.D.

Cabinet R | Shelf 3 | No. 46

Book of remembrance. By Mrs. E.D. Gillespie. Illustrated. Philadelphia - London, 1901.

Contains material on the Bache family (Franklin descendants).

Cloth; 7½ x 5¼ in.

GILLIODTS-van SEVEREN, LOUIS

Cabinet | Shelf | No.

See Severen, Louis Gilliodts, van.

GILLIS, STEPHEN EDWARD

Cabinet S | Shelf 2 | No. 30

Steve Gillis, printer. Memories of Mark Twain and Steve Gillis. By Wm. R. Gillis. Sonora, Calif, 1924. Portraits, illus.

Biographical.

Cloth; 9-3/8 x 6½ in.

GILLIS, WM. R.

Cabinet S | Shelf 2 | No. 30

Memories of Mark Twain and Steve Gillis. By Wm. R. Gillis. Sonora, California, 1924. Portraits, illus.

Biographical of Gillis and Twain.

Cloth; 9-3/8 x 6½ in.

GILLISS, WALTER

Cabinet S | Shelf 5 | No. 37

Printing career of Walter Gilliss, 1869-1925.

Article in ARS TYPOGRAPHICA, vol.2, No.2, Oct.,1925, p.175

GILLISS, WALTER

Cabinet S | Shelf 2 | No. 43

Recollections of The Gilliss Press and its work during fifty years, 1869-1919. By Walter Gilliss. New York, The Grolier Club, 1926. Portrait of Walter Gilliss.

Boards; 9¼ x 5-7/8 in.

GILLISS, WALTER

Cabinet S | Shelf 2 | No. 38

Story of a motto and a mark: being a brief sketch of a few printers' marks and containing the facts concerning the mark of The Gilliss Press. New York: The Gilliss Press, 1902. Illus.

Paper; 7 x 4¾ in.

GILLISS, WALTER

Cabinet S | Shelf 2 | No. 40

Tributes to my Beloved have been collected and are sent to his friends and mine as a remembrance at Christmas time 1925. Frank Le G. Gilliss. New York, 1925.

Boards; 7 x 4¼ in.

GILLIS, WALTER.

Cabinet | Shelf | No.

See also Imprints, United States, Gillis Press, The.

GILLISS PRESS, THE

Cabinet S Shelf 2 No. 43

Imprints, The Gilliss Press: Short-title list of the imprints of Gilliss Brothers, Gilliss Brothers and Turnure ... Recollections of the Gilliss Press, 1869-1919. The Grolier Club, New York, 1926.

Boards; 9¼ x 6 x 5/8 in.

GILLISS PRESS, THE

Cabinet S Shelf 2 No. 37

See also Imprints, United States

GILLOT, FIRMIN

Cabinet 46 Shelf 2 Number 4

Promoteur de la gravure chimique, Firmin Gillot, 1820 - 1877.

Brief biographical article, with portrait, in BULLETIN de l'IMPRIMERIE, Mai, 1877, p. 101.

GILLRAY, JAMES.

Cabinet I Shelf 3 No. 1

[Biographical sketch, by Ralph Nevill]. Illustrated excerpt from the Connoisseur. May, 1902. Illus.

Item 38 in vol. with binder's title; "Various Engravers and About Engravers."

GILLRAY, JAMES.

Cabinet I Shelf 3 No. 1

Caricatures of James Gillray.

See ENGRAVING, LITERATURE OF. Gillray's caricatures ...

GILMAN (Mrs) CAROLINE

Cabinet NN Shelf 6 No. 38

Editor of "The Southern Rose-bud, Charleston, S.C. 1831. Brief biographical account.

see

KING, WILLIAM L. (The) Newspaper press of Charleston, S. C...1882, p. 85.

GILMAN, M. D.

Cabinet R Shelf 5 No. 79

(The) Bibliography of Vermont, or a list of books and pamphlets relating in any way to the State. With biographical and other notes Prepared by M. D. Gilman, Montpelier, Vt., 1897.

Cloth; 10¾ x 7½ in.

GILMAN, WINTHROP S.,

Cabinet NN Shelf 3 No. 2

"Alton Trials" of Winthrop S. Gilman, who was indicted with .. for the crime of riot, committed on the night of the 7th of November, 1837, while engaged in defending a printing press, from an attack made on it by an armed mob. New York, 1838.

Frontispiece showing the mob attacking the warehouse of Godfrey Gilman & Company.

GILMAN, WINTHROP S. (cont'd)

Cabinet NN Shelf 3 No. 2

Embossed cloth; 7-1/8 x 4½ x ½ in.

GILMAN PRINTING COMPANY, A.S.

Cabinet EE Shelf 2 No. 3

Individuality in printing. Gilman Fanfold Systems. The A.S. Gilman Printing Co. Cleveland, Ohio. n.d. circa, 1923.

Has pictures of printing plants, exterior and interior.

Boards; 12¼ x 8-7/8 in.

GILMORE, JAMES R. ("Edmund Kirke")

Cabinet NN Shelf 4 No. 18

(The) New York "Tribune" in the draft riot. The story of a member of the staff...By James R. Gilmore. Preiodical excerpt, n.n.n.d.

With other items, in manila envelope

GILSON, F. H.

Cabinet QQ Shelf 4 No. 3

History of shaped or character notes. With specimens. Boston, F. H. Gilson, 1889. Pamphlet.

Item in envelope.

GILSON COMPANY, F.H.

Cabinet MM Shelf 6 No. 4

Music book printing. With specimens. Boston, 1897.

Text book.

Cloth; 8½ x 6½ in.

GILSON COMPANY, F.H. (Stanhope Press)

Cabinet EE Shelf 1 No. 32

See SPECIMEN BOOKS, TYPES. Printers'

GIMSON, ERNEST

Cabinet Shelf No.

See Griggs, F.L. Gimson, Ernest: His Life & Work.

GINN, EDWIN

Cabinet Q Shelf 1 No. 4

(The) School book, the publisher and the public. By Edwin Ginn. Excerpt from Independent, Aug. 4, 1910. Has portrait of E. Ginn.

Item 5 in vol. with binder's title "Various items on publishing".

GINN, EDWIN.

Cabinet P Shelf 4 No. 3

See Publishing: School book (The), the publisher and the public.

GINN AND COMPANY (Athenaeum Press, The)

Cabinet Shelf No.

Athenaeum Press (Ginn & Co.) Imprints of.

See IMPRINTS, United States. Athenaeum Press ...

GINN & COMPANY

Cabinet S Shelf 5 No. 1

Boston, Mass., 1915. Quality and cost in the making of text books. Ginn and Company's part in the making of American text books. Brochure. Illus.

Item 2 in volume with binders' title "Various printing Plants. Brochures."

GINN & CO., Publishing & Printing House,

Cabinet S Shelf 5 No. 4

Cambridge, Mass.

A pamphlet, illus., describing the Atheneum Press of this firm, n.d.

Bound with other items in "Various printers and their plants", item 12, vol.1.

GINN and COMPANY

Cabinet S Shelf 5 No. 3

Quality and cost in making of text books. Ginn and Company: The Athenaeum Press. Boston, n. d.

Item 16 in collection "Printers and their Plants; Collection of Pamphlets", 1918.

GINN & COMPANY
See also

Cabinet G Shelf 2 No. 10

Plants, Printing, United States.
also Imprints, United States.

GINOUX, P.-F.

Cabinet LL Shelf 6 No. 33

Comptes-faites typographiques a l'usage des imprimeurs, libraires, auteurs et editeurs, ou tarif général pour labeurs. Par P.-F. Ginoux, Imprimeur-Typographe. (Paris, circa 1858).

Printing accountancy. With detailed tables showing price of composition, etc.

Boards; 11¼ x 9 in.

GINOUX, P.F.

Cabinet LL Shelf 5 No. 20

Vade Mecum de l'imprimeur...et un extrait du tarif général pour labeurs. Deuxieme edition, revue et perfectionnée. Laigle (Orne) - 1860.

Has folding plates with costs, and prices for labor.

Cloth; 8¾ x 5-5/8 x 3/8 in.

GINSBURG, CHRISTIAN DAVID

Cabinet S Shelf 5 No. 26.01

Massoretic Bible.

See Bible Literature. Massoretic Bible. Ginsburg's...

GIOLITO (Bernardino Ferrari) Stagnino

Cabinet X Shelf 3 No. 14

Bibliographical notes, with printer marks, Giolito (cognomen, Stagnino), Venice, 1478-1537 ?

see
KRISTELLER Dr. Paul.
Italienischen buchdrucker...pp.120,122

GIOLIOT, GABRIEL dé Ferrari

Cabinet AA Shelf 2 No. 10 2 Vols.

Annali di Gabriel Giolito dé Ferrari da Trino de Monferrato, stampatore [1536-1599] in Venezia. Descritti ed illustrati da Salvatore Bongi. Roma, 1890-1897. 2 Vols.

Biographical, bibliographical, and historical account.

Half morocco; 9 x 6½ in.

GIOLITO, GABRIELE, Printer-Publisher,

Cabinet S Shelf 5 No. 4

Venice, 1512-1578.

Venetian printer-publisher in the sixteenth century (A), by Horatio F. Brown, in the Atlantic Monthly, Feb. 1892.

Bound with other items in "Various printers and their plants", item 8, vol.1.

GIOLITO, GABRIEL.

Cabinet 75 Shelf 1 No. 10

Venice, the Gioliti and their Press at. A paper read before the Bibliographical Society, by A. J. Butler, Jan. 18, 1909. Illus.

In Trans. Biblio. Soc., Vol. X, 1908-1909, pp. 83-107.

GIOLITO, GABRIEL DE FARRARI (Comin de Trino)

Cabinet Shelf No.

See also
Early Printing in Italy. Venice, 1540: Gabriel Giolito de Ferrari.
Early Printing, dates of 1547, 1549, 1558.

GIOVANNETTO de CASTIGLIONE

Cabinet X Shelf 3 No. 14

Bibliographical note, with printer mark, Giovannetto, Milan, 1506-1521.

see
KRISTELLER, Dr. Paul
Italienischen buchdrucker...p.36

GIOVANNI DA SPIRA

Cabinet AA Shelf 1 No. 16

See Pellegrini (Domenico Maria). Della prima origine della stampa in Venezia ... Venezia, 1794.

GIOVANNINI, GAETANO

Cabinet RR Shelf 1 No. 4

Industria della carta. Bologna, Trieste. Bologna, Aprile, 1921.

New Year's presentation to the clinets of the paper house of G. Giovannini. Contains a list of the various kinds of papers manufactured by this house, also exterior and interior views of the establishment.

Paper boards; 12½ x 9-5/8 in.

GIRÁLDEZ, JOSÉ

Cabinet MM Shelf 2 No. 22

Tratado de la tipografia ó arte de la imprenta. Madrid 1884.

Practical treatise on the art of printing. A text book.

Morocco; 8-7/8 x 5-7/8 x 5/8 in.

GIRARD, PIERRE

Cabinet J Shelf 4 No. 7

Imprimeurs de Mende, 1682-1711.

See PRINTING, HISTORICAL. France (Gévaudan)...A Mende (Lozère), 1924.

GIRARD & CIE (Successeurs de Deberny & Tuleu)

Cabinet Z Shelf 4 No. 7.01

Paris, 1923.

see
SPECIMEN BOOKS, TYPES. France. Girard & Cie...

GIRARDENGO, (Francesco)

Cabinet X — Bibliographical note, with printer mark, Girardengo, 1480-1484, Pavia.

Shelf 3 — see KRISTELLER, Dr. Paul. Italienischen buchdrucker...p.48

No. 14

GIRAUDET, E.

Cabinet KK — Association d'imprimeurs et de libraires de Paris réfugiés a Tours au 16 siecle... Tours: Imprimerie Rouille - Ladeveze, 1877.

Shelf 4 — No. 97 of 175 copies printed.

No. 9

Half morocco; 11 x 7¾

GIRAUDET, E.

Cabinet V — Association d'imprimeurs et de libraires de Paris, refugiés a Tours au XVI siècle [E. Giraudet] Tours: Imprimerie Rouille-Ladeveze, 1877.

Shelf 2 — Biographies of eight printers who formed the association, together with the signed document of agreement; signatures in facsimile.

No. 52

Paper; 11 x 7½ in.

GIRAUDET, E.

Cabinet V — Origines de l'imprimerie à Tours, 1467-1550. Contenant la nomenclature des imprimeurs depuis la fin du XV siècle jusqu'en 1850. Par le docteur E. Giraudet. Tours, 1881.

Shelf 2 — Among the biographies of printers, are those of Rouille, Jenson, Plantin.

No. 54

Half morocco; 11 x 7½ x ½ in.

GIROUDOT

Cabinet FF — Notice sur les presses mecaniques et celles a la Stanhope. De Giroudot, Inginieur-mecanicien... a Paris (1835).

Shelf 5 — With I folding plate

No. 44

Cloth; 8 x 5¼ in.

GIROUDOT Fils, Ch.

Cabinet Z — Gutenbergeoise and Stanhope Presses sold by Ch. Giroudet fils, engineers, rue du Val-de Grace 6, Paris. Illus. Prices.

Shelf 3 — All-iron lever press, probably of German and English manufacture.

No. 43

pp. 399, 400, 401 in "Miscellaneous collection of French type specimens"...1829-1844.

GIROUDOT fils. CH

Cabinet — See also Prices, Printing Materials, France also Prices, Printing Presses "

Shelf

No.

GIST, GEORGE

Cabinet S — See Sequoyah

Shelf 5

No. 6

GIULIARI, G. CARLO

Cabinet AA — (Della) Tipografia Veronese; saggio storico-letterario. Verona, 1871.

Shelf 1 — Bio-bibliographical historical account of printing in Verona, 1472 to 1826.

No. 43

Half morocco; 10-1/8 x 7½ x 7/8 in.

GIULIARI FAMILY OF PRINTERS

Cabinet U — Veronese typography, 15th-19th century; with some account of the private press of the Giuliari family. By C. H. E. Carmichael. In Transactions of the Royal Society of Literature, second series, vol. XI. part I. London, 1874.

Shelf 4

No. 37

Half morocco; 8¾ x 5½ in.

GIUNTA, FILIPPO and JACOPO

Cabinet AA — Heirs of Bernardo Giunta, 1550. (Battle of the typographers in the 15th century: The Giunti and the Torrentino). Battaglie di tipografi nel 1500 (I Giunti e i Torrentino) notize e documenti estratti dal lavoro di laurea "Annali della edizioni dei Giunti di Firenze." By Decio Decia. Florence, 1913.

Shelf 2

No. 24

Half morocco; 9-3/4 x 6¼ in.

GIUNTA, LUCA ANTONIO.

Cabinet D — See Early Printing in Italy. Venice, 1514.

Shelf 3

No. 30

GIUNTA, FRANCISCO

Cabinet — See Early Printing in France. Lyons, 1533-4. Jacques and Franciscus Giunta.

Shelf

No.

GIUNTA, JACQUES.

Cabinet 70 — See Early Printing in France. Lyons, [v.d.]

Shelf 1

No. 45

GIUNTA, LUCA ANTONIO

Cabinet D — See Early Printing in Italy. Venice, 1520.

Shelf 4

No. 16

GIUNTA, LUCA ANTONIO.

Cabinet D — See Early Printing in Italy. Venice, 1523.

Shelf 4

No. 22

GIUNTA, LUC ANTONIO.

Cabinet 14 — See Early Printing in Italy. Venice, 1542. Peter Schoeffer II.

Shelf 1

No. 17

GIUNTA [Heirs of Luc Antonio]

Cabinet E — See Early Printing in Italy. Venice, 1542.

Shelf 1

No. 6

GIUNTA, PHILIP

Cabinet X Shelf 3 No. 14

Bibliographical notes, with printer marks (5), Philippus Giunta, Florence, 1497-1518.

see KRISTELLER, Dr. Paul. Italienischen buchdrucker...p.14

GIUNTA, PHILIP.

Cabinet E Shelf 2 No. 70

Catalogues librorum qui in Junctarum Bibliotheca Phillipi haeredum Florentiae prostant. [Giunta]. Florence, 1602.

Vellum; $5\frac{3}{4}$ x 3 x $1\frac{1}{4}$ in.

GIUNTA FAMILY OF PRINTERS

Cabinet X Shelf 1 No. 86

Bandini, Angelo Maria: De Florentina Juntarum typographia, eiusque censoribus ex qua graeci, latini, turci scriptores...Lucae, 1791.
Annals of the press of the Giuntas of Florence, Venice and Lyons. With biography and genealogy of the Giunta family.

Half morocco; 9 x 6 x $1\frac{1}{4}$ in.

GIUNTA FAMILY OF PRINTERS

Cabinet Y Shelf 2 No. 23

(Life of Luc-Antonius Giunta, and his successors Brief bio-bibliographical account)

See LORCK, CARL B. Handbuch der geschichte...Leipzig, 1882-1883 (part 1, p.184)

GIUSTINIANI, LORENZO

Cabinet AA Shelf 1 No. 14

Saggio storico-critico sulla tipografia del regno di Napoli di Lorenzo Giustiniani. Napoli, 1793. Has index of printers names.

Boards; $10\frac{1}{2}$ x $8\frac{1}{4}$ in.

GIVEN, JOHN L.

Cabinet NN Shelf 3 No. 27

Making a newspaper. by John L. Given, late of the New York "Evening Sun". New York. 1907.

Cloth: $7\frac{1}{2}$x$5\frac{1}{4}$"

GLASER, CURT

Cabinet K Shelf 2 No. 15

(Die) Altdeutsch malerei. von Curt Glaser. Munchen, 1924.

Profusely illustrated history of engraving and painting in Germany, 14th to 15th century.

Boards; $10\frac{3}{4}$ x $8\frac{1}{4}$ in.

GLASER, WILHELM CHRISTIAN

Cabinet X Shelf 3 No. 13

Brief bibliographical note, Glaser, printer, Strassburg, 1624-1636.

see HEITZ, PAUL. Elsässische büchermarken...p.xxiii

GLASGOW

Cabinet KK Shelf 3 No. 1

Royal Technical College, The.

see SCHOOLS OF PRINTING. Great Britain. Glasgow...1915.

GLASGOW

Cabinet QQ Shelf 5 No. 14

Trades House of Glasgow, records of 1605-1678. Glasgow: Printed for the Trades House of Glasgow, 1910. With facs.

Cloth; 10 x 7 x 2 in.

GLASGOW ADVERTISER

Cabinet Shelf No.

See Newspapers, Scotland.

GLASGOW BIBLIOGRAPHICAL SOCIETY

Cabinet U Shelf 1 No. 82

(A) Century of books printed in Glasgow 1638-1686. Shown in the Kelvingrove Galleries, by the courtesy of the Corporation of Glasgow. Printed for the Society. Glasgow, 1918. Illus.

Half morocco; $9\frac{3}{4}$ x 7-1/8 x 3/8 in.

"GLASGOW HERALD"

Cabinet 00 Shelf 4 No. 37

Newspaper life, 1845-1895.

see SINCLAIR, ALEXANDER (of the "Glasgow Herald")

"GLASGOW HERALD", THE

Cabinet 00 Shelf 4 No. 35

see also cards with following sub-heads:

I-JOURNALISM, Great Britain. "Glasgow Herald".

II-NEWSPAPERS, Scotland (Literature of) "Glasgow Herald".

GLASGOW HERALD (The)

Cabinet Shelf No.

See also
Newspapers, anniversary issue.

Newspapers. Scotland

GLASGOW LETTER FOUNDRY

Cabinet Shelf No.

See Specimen Books, Types. Scotland. Wilson & Sons, Alex.
" also Specimen Books, Types. England. Wilson, Alex & Sons. London, 1834.
" also Specimen Books, Types. Scotland. Macbrayne & Stirling.

GLASGOW PRINTING AND PRINTERS

Cabinet U Shelf 1 No. 59

Notices and documents illustrative of the literary history of Glasgow...Presented to the members of the Maitland Club. By Richard Duncan, Glasgow, 1831.
Bio-bibliographical account. Reprint edition of 1886 in U/1/60, has a chronological list of Glasgow printers, 1638 to 1800.

Half morocco; $10\frac{1}{4}$ x 8-3/8 x 7/8 in.

GLASGOW UNIVERSITY PRESS

Cabinet U Shelf 1 No. 83

Maclehose, James. The Glasgow University Press, 1639-1931. With some notes on Scottish printing in the last three hundred years. Glasgow: At the University Press. 1931. Illus. portraits, facs.

Boards, linen back; 9 x $5\frac{3}{4}$ x $1\frac{1}{4}$ in.

GLASGOW WEEKLY HERALD.

Cabinet See Newspapers, special issues.

Shelf

No.

GLASS, ENGRAVING ON

See Engraving, Hyalographie. (449/I/5)

GLAZIER, RICHARD

Cabinet K Manual of historic ornament. Treating upon the evolution, tradition, and development of architecture and the applied arts. Prepared for the use of students and craftsmen. By Richard Glazier. Second edition. With 600 illustrations by the author. London.,. New York, 1906.

Shelf 4

No. 8

Cloth: 9¾ x 6¼ x 5/8 in.

GLEASON'S PICTORIAL DRAWING-ROOM COMPANION

Cabinet 00 Boston, 1851. A weekly.

see PERIODICALS, ILLUSTRATED. United States. Gleason's...

Shelf 6

No. 40

GLEASON'S PICTORIAL DRAWINGROOM COMPANION

See also Periodicals

GLEDITSCH & SOHNE, JO. FRIDER

Cabinet X Leipzig, 1710. Imprint.

See Imprint on Pater's De Germania miraculo...Leipsiae, 1710.

Shelf 1

No. 19

GLIDDON, THOMAS

Cabinet S Memorial address of William Randle Wells: Read before the Rochester Typographical Union, on Saturday evening, June 7, 1862. Published by the Union, Rochester, 1862. Portrait.

Shelf 2

No. 64

Cloth; 7 x 4½ in.

GLIMM, GIOVANNI (Gleim)

Cabinet German printer at Savigliano in 1470, together with Cristoforo Beggiamo.

For account see Berlan's "Introduzione della stampa in Savigliano ... Torino, 1887.

Shelf

No.

GLOBUS PRINTING ART INSTITUTE

Cabinet EE Budapest, Hungary.

Shelf 3 See SPECIMEN BOOKS, TYPES. Printers'. Hungary.

No. 87

GLOSSARIES, BOOKBINDING

Cabinet PP Bib-li-op-e-gis-tic (pertaining to the art of binding books.-Dibdin), to which is appended a glossary of some terms used in the craft. With illustrations of fine bindings. The Trow Press, Printers and Binders, New York. n.d. ~~Pamphlet~~

Shelf 4

No. 2

Half morocco; 8¾ x 5-7/8 in.

GLOSSARIES OF BOOKBINDING

Cabinet EE Glossary of printing and publishing terms...

pp.407-433 LITTLE'S Type, specimen pages and book papers...New York, 1923.

Shelf 1

No. 52

GLOSSARIES, BOOKBINDING. French

Cabinet PP Vocabulaire des termes techniques employés par les relieurs et en usage dans les principales industries, qui se rattachent a la relieure.

Shelf 5

See pp. 310 - 318, BOSQUET'S Traité théorique et pratique de l'art du relieur ...Paris, 1890.

No. 8

GLOSSARY OF PRINTING TERMS

Cabinet See Dictionaries, Printing Terms.

Shelf

No.

GLOUCESTER JOURNAL, THE

Cabinet U Robert Raikes, the elder, and the Gloucester Journal, 1721. By Roland Austin.

Shelf 1

No. 1g

In Excerpts relating to printing from "The Library," 1914-15. p. 99 of pencilled folios

---

GLOUCESTER JOURNAL (England)

Cabinet See Newspapers, England.

Shelf

No.

GLOUCESTER JOURNAL

Cabinet A See Newspapers, England. Gloucester Journal: Bi-centenary Historical Supplement, April 8, 1922.

Shelf 3

No. 93

GLOUZOT, HENRI

Cabinet V Notes pour servir à l'histoire de l'imprimerie à Niort et dans les Deux-Sèvres. Niort, 1891.

Shelf 2

No. 12

Half morocco; 9½ x 6½ x ½ in.

GLYPHOGRAPHY

Cabinet I Binger, M.H. Amsterdam (1850).

See BINGER, M.H. Glypographie uit het etablissement...

Shelf 2

No. 22

GLYPHOGRAPHY

Cabinet I Shelf 2 No. 21

Buchdruckzeichnung oder glyphographie. Enthaltend eine beschreibung dieser neuer erfindung nebst anleitung fur künstler. Mit zahlreichen buchdruckzeichungen. Leipzig, 1846.
Glyphographisches Institut.

Paper; $10\frac{1}{2}$ x $6\frac{3}{4}$ in.

GOBIN, HENRY

Cabinet V Shelf 5 No. 14

L'Art de Peindre la Parole. Paris, 1874. Illus.
Chap. I: L'Imprimerie et les livres. Historiques.
" II: La librairie à l'Exposition de 1867.
" III: La matérial: Machines à composer etc.
" IV: La fonderie en caractères. Clichage etc. Par Aug. Jeunesse.
" V: Lithographie...gravure sur pierres, machines à imprimer. Par D. Kaeppelin.
" VI: Étude sur la Gravure. Par Henry Gobin.

(cont'd)

GODDARD, WILLIAM

Cabinet NN Shelf 3 No. 1

Partnership (The): or the history of the Pennsylvania Chronicle. By William Goddard. Philadelphia. 1770.

Printed by William Goddard, in Arch Street, between Front and Second Streets, Philadelphia.

Half Morocco: $7\frac{1}{2}$x$4\frac{1}{4}$"

GLYPHOGRAPHY

Cabinet I Shelf 2 No. 20

Instructions on glyphography for the amateur. (Abdiel Hawkins) Glyphographic Office, 79 Shoe Lane, London, n.d.).

Has specimens; glyphograph map, ornaments, landscapes, etc.

Circular in manila envelope.

GOBIN, HENRY (cont'd)

Cabinet V Shelf 5 No. 14

Chap. VII: Les cartes et les globes. Par Endymion Pierragi.

Bibliothèque Scientifique-Industrielle et Agricole...Paris, 1874. Illus.

Paris; 9-7/8 x 6-5/8 in.

GODDARD, WILLIAM.

See also Early Printing in Pennsylvania, Philadelphia, 1770, William Goddard.

GLYPHOGRAPHY

Cabinet FF Shelf 1 No. 8

Invention of E. Palmer described.

See pp. 279 - 283 Smee's Elements of Electro-Metallurgy. London, 1843.

GOBIN, HENRY

Cabinet V Shelf 5 No. 14

Étude sur la gravure.

See ENGRAVING PROCESSES, LITERATURE OF.

Étude...Paris, 1874.

GODEY, LOUIS A.

Cabinet 80 Shelf 2 No. 44

Ladies Book and Ladies American Magazine, 1838.

See Periodicals, United States. Lady's Book and Ladies American Magazine...

GLYPHOGRAPHY

Cabinet I Shelf 2 No. 18

Palmer's Patent: Glyphography; or engraved drawing, for printing at the ty e press after the manner of woodcuts. With full directions and specimen illustrations. Second edition.
Edward Palmer's Patent. London, n.d. (1843)

Bound in with two items on architecture.

Half calf; $8\frac{1}{4}$ x $5\frac{1}{2}$ in.

GODDARD, DELANO A.

Cabinet NN Shelf 4 No. 31

Newspapers and newspaper writers in New England. 1787-1815. Read before the New England Historic, Genealogical Society, Feb. 4, 1880. Boston.

Cloth: 9-1/8x6"

GODEY, LOUIS A. see also

Cabinet Shelf No.

PERIODICALS, United States. Godey's..

PORTRAITS, Editors. Godey...

GLYPHOGRAPHY

Cabinet I Shelf 2 No. 19

Palmer's Patent Glyphography.

See PALMER, EDWARD. Glyphography... London, n.d.

GODDARD, PLINY EARLE

Cabinet II Shelf 4 No. 2

Athapascan (Hupa) language. Illustrative sketch of.

See BOAS, FRANZ. American Indian languages, handbook of...Bulletin 40. Washington, 1911, pp.91-158.

GODEY'S LADY'S BOOK.

Cabinet S Shelf 5 No. 4

Collins, Tillinghast K. and Philip G. Collins. A day's ramble through the mechanical department of the "Lady's Book". Philadelphia, Oct. 1852. Illus. Description.

Item 4 in collection "Various printers and their plants; Excerpts from Magazines, I".

GLYPHOGRAPHY

Cabinet 26 Shelf 2 No. 4

See Process Engraving.

GODDARD, WILLIAM

Cabinet 00 Shelf 6 No. 51

Baltimore printer, 1773, his imprint.

see FACSIMILES, NEWSPAPERS. Maryland Journal...Aug. 20, 1773.

GODEY'S LADY'S BOOK

Cabinet Shelf No.

See also

PERIODICALS, United States. Literature. Godey's...

PERIODICALS, American (U.s.): Godey's past and present.

GODEY'S MAGAZINE AND LADY'S BOOK

Cabinet 80 Shelf 2 No. 51

Philadelphia, 1845

see

PERIODICALS, United States

Godey's Lady's Book...

GODFRAY, THOMAS

Cabinet T Shelf 2 No. 6 [vol.3]

Books printed by T. Godfrey, London, 1522-1532. Bibliographical notes.

see

DIBDIN'S "Typographical Antiquities" ...London, 1810-19, vol.iii, pp.62-72

GODKIN, EDWIN LAWRENCE (Journalist)

Cabinet NN Shelf 2 No. 1

Biographical sketch of E.L. Godkin of the "Nation". By Eugene Benson. Excerpt from The Galaxy, June, 1869.

Item 8 in vol. with binder's title "Journalists, various excerpts".

GODKIN, EDWIN L.

Cabinet NN Shelf 7 No. 16

English scholar's appreciation of Godkin. By A. V. Dicey.

see

NATION, THE. Semi - centennial, 1863-1915, p. 51.

GODKIN, EDWIN L.

Cabinet NN Shelf 7 No. 16

"Nation", former editors of the. By Edwin Lawrence Godkin, founder and first editor of the "Nation".

see

NATION, THE. Semi - centennial, 1863 - 1915, p. 68.

GODKIN, E. L.

Cabinet NN Shelf 2 No. 7

Newspapers and abroad. Excerpted article from North American Review, Feb., 1890.

Item 11 in bound collection "Journalism. Excerpts, etc."

GODKIN, EDWIN LAWRENCE,

Cabinet NN Shelf 2 No. 8

"Reflections and Comments". By Edwin Lawrence Godkin. [Review of book with title as above]. By H. T. Peck. Excerpt from the Bookman, Feb., 1896. Has portrait.

Item 15 in vol. "Various Editors. Excerpts and Pamphlets".

GODKIN, EDWIN L.

Cabinet NN Shelf 7 No. 16

Two editors. Recollections of E. L. Godkin and W. P. Garrison. By Viscount Bryce.

see

NATION, THE. Semi - centennial number, 1863 - 1915, p. 41.

GODWIN, PARKE (Journalist)

Cabinet NN Shelf 2 No. 1

New York Journalists: Parke Godwin. By Eugene Benson. Excerpt from The Galaxy, Feb. 1869.

Item 9 in vol. with binder's title "Journalists, various excerpts".

GOEBEL, THEODOR

Cabinet Y Shelf 5 No. 85

(Friedrich Koenig: A memoir of the inventor of the cylinder printing machine, compiled from original sources). Friedrich Koenig und die erfindung der schnellpresse. Ein biographisches denkmal. Stuttgart, 1883. Illus.

Stamped cloth; 13 x 9¾ x 7/8 in.

GOEBEL, THEODORE

Cabinet FF Shelf 5 No. 49

Friedrich König und der erfindung der schnellpresse. Ein gedankblatt zum 17 April 1875. Braunschweig, 1875.

Reprinted from the Journal fur Buchdruckerkunst.

Quarter morocco; 8 x 5-1/8 x ¼ in

GOEBEL, THEODOR

Cabinet J Shelf 4 No. 20

(Die) Graphischen kunst der gegenwart. Neue folge. Herausgegeben von Felix Krais. Stuttgart, 1902. Illus.

Handsome exhibit of letter press and lithograph printing, embossing, designing, and illustrating in Germany.

Cloth; 14¼ x 10½ x 2¾ in.

GOEBEL, THEODOR.

Cabinet 78 Shelf 1 No. 48

Graphischer Abreiss-Kalender (1896) von Gebr. Jänecke & Fr. Schneemann, buch und steindruckfarben-fabriken. Hannover.

Calender pertaining to printing and printers for the year 1896. A compilation.

Stamped cloth; 7¾ x 5 x ⅝ in.

GOEBEL, THEODOR

Cabinet Y Shelf 5 No. 111

Karl Krause und sein werk. Die machinenfabrik in Leipzig. Zur feier des jubiläums des fünfzigjährigen bestehens der fabrik. Leipzig, 1905. Illus. and portraits.

Issued on the 50th anniversary of the firm of machine builders.

Stamped cloth; 12½ x 15¾ in.

GOEBEL, THEODOR

Cabinet FF Shelf 5 No. 64

Koenig, Friedrich, und die erfindung der schnellpresse. Ein biographisches denkmal. Zweite auflage. Stuttgart, 1906. Illus.

Cloth; 8½ x 6 in.

GOEBEL, THEODOR

Cabinet EE Shelf 5 No. 84.01

Krause, Karl und sein werk, (1855-1905). Zür feier des Jubiläums des fünfzigjährigen bestehens der fabrik. Leipzig, Verlag der Maschinenfabrik Karl Krause. 1905.

Portraits, illus., views exterior and interior.

Printed silk over board; oblong; 12¼ x 15¾

GOEBEL, THEODOR

Cabinet EE Shelf 5 No. 96

(Die) Maschinenfabrik Johannisberg, Klein, Forst & Bohn nachfolger zu Geisenheim a Rh. Beschrieben von Theodor Goebel. 1897.

Illustrated descriptive account of the above firm, together with a history of the development of printing presses from the earliest times.

Cloth; 12¼ x 15½ in.

GOEBEL, THEODOR

Cabinet 78 Shelf 1 No. 47

Unserer farbe: historisch und technisch betrachtet. St. Gallen, 1886.

Historical technical account of printing inks. With three folded plates, illustrations showing interior and exterior views of the ink manufacturing house of Jänacke & Shneemann in Hannover.

Stamped cloth; 6-1/8 x 4-3/8 x ¼ in.

GOELET, JACOB

Cabinet S Shelf 6 No. 9

Printer, New York, 1730.

See BIBLIOGRAPHY. Dutch text book of 1730...

GOEWEY COLLECTION

Cabinet 71 Shelf 1 No. 43

Descriptive catalogue of the Goewey Collection of Browning pictures, 1908-1918. Together with an introductory paper. Printed by John Henry Nash. San Francisco, 1917.

Boards; 11-3/4 x 8½ in. pp. 40.

GOLDEN COCKEREL PRESS.

Cabinet M Shelf 2 No. 37

Prospectuses, 1931, of the following publications Shakespeare's "Twelfth Night"; Fielding's "Jonathan Wild," F. T. Powys' "When thou wast naked;" Eric Gill's "An Essay on the Nude."

In box marked "Golden Cockerel Press: Miscellany, 1931--

GOETHE, WOLFGANG

Cabinet RR Shelf 5 No. 21

(Don) Stefano Merola's paper mill [at Trajetto, Italy]. From the biographical sketch of Philip Hackert by Johann Wolfgang Goethe. New York: Japan Paper Company, 1931.

Boards; 8½ x 6¼ in.

GOEZ, HUGO

Cabinet U Shelf 5 No. 49

Bio-bibliographical notes relating to Hugo Goez, printer, York, 1509)

see DAVIES, ROBERT (A) Memoir of The York Press...1868, p.15

GOLDEN COCKEREL PRESS, THE

Cabinet M Shelf 2 No. 35

Taylor, G. S. The Golden Cockerel Press, Waltham Saint Lawrence, Berkshire. 1923. The XI Books of the Golden Asse of Lucius Apuleius ... Translated out of Latine in English. Printed at the Golden Cockerel Press, and finished on the 13th of August, 1923.

Boards; 10½ x 7-7/8 x 1¼ in.

GOETZ, NIKOLAUS, von Schlettstadt

Cabinet X Shelf 3 No. 20

Brief bio-bibliographical note, with printer mark, Goetz, Cologne, 1473-1478.

see HEITZ, PAUL. Kölner büchermarken...p.xvi

GOFFERING (or) GAUFERING

Cabinet Shelf No.

See EMBOSSING.

GOLDEN COCKEREL PRESS, THE

Cabinet M Shelf No.

See also Imprints, England. Golden Cockerel Press, The. Robert Gibbings.

GOETZ, NIKOLAUS

Cabinet B Shelf 2 No. 8

(Illustrated books printed by Goetz, Cologne, 1474-1478)

see SCHRAMM, ALBERT (Der) Bilderschmuck der frühdrucke...Leipzig, 1924.

GOGGLES, PHIL

Cabinet QQ Shelf 1 No. 3

Bro-de-hed-da: A song of slaughter. Originally written and published in the Sunday Transcript. Philadelphia. n.d.

Poetry about the steam printing press.

Buckram; 7¾ x 5 in.

GOLDEN CROSS PRESS (Edmund Thompson)

Cabinet G Shelf 4 No. 57

Announcement of two books from the Golden Cross Press, with miniatures by Valenti Angelo. New York, 1936.

Small folder, in envelope.

GOETZ, NOCOLAUS

Cabinet Y Shelf 4 No. 4

(Note on the Goetz press at Cologne, 1474-)

see VOULLIÉME, ERNST. (Die) Deutschen drucker des fünfzehnten jahrhunderts...p.32

GOLD LEAF.

Cabinet Shelf No.

See BOOKBINDING, [Gold Leaf] ...

GOLDEN EAGLE PRESS (THE) see IMPRINTS, United States.

Cabinet G Shelf 4 No. 54

GOETZE, LUDWIG

Cabinet Y Shelf 2 No. 74

Aeltere geschichte der buchdruckerkunst in Magdeburg. I Abtheilung: Die drucker des 15. jahrhunderts. (History of printing in Madgeburg). Magdeburg. 1872. With illus.

"Only 120 copies were printed of this first part,-all that was published". B & W.

Half morocco; 9¼ x 6 x 5/8 in.

GOLDBERG, E.

Cabinet L Shelf 1 No. 37

Farbenphotographie und farbendruck. Mit 8 abbildungen in text und 12 tafeln mit monochromen sowie 16 mehrfarbigen abbildungen. Leipzig, 1908.

Band 2, Monographien des Buchgewerbes.

Half morocco; 6-5/8 x 4¾ in.

GOLDING & COMPANY, Boston

Cabinet FF Shelf 5 No. 47

Bullen, Henry Lewis: Recent improvements in platen presses: a description of the Golding Jobber, illus. This press is not now made in the U. S., but is made in England.

In envelope.

GOLDING and COMPANY.

Cabinet / Shelf / No.

Catalogues and price lists, 1887 to 1914.

See Cards immediately following this.
See also cards with following sub-heads:

I PRINTING EQUIPMENTS. Catalogue.
II SPECIMEN BOOKS, TYPES, United States.
III PRINTING PRESSES, Catalogue.

GOLDING and COMPANY

Cabinet EE · Shelf 4 · No. 41

Catalogue and price list of machinery, tools, material for printing, embossing, cutting and binding. Furniture and material... Golding & Co., Boston. Mass. 1897.

Booklet; 3½ x 6 in. Item im manila envelope.

GOLDING and COMPANY

Cabinet EE · Shelf 4 · No. 41

Catalogue, 1889, of printing presses and printers tools made by Golding & Co. Boston, Mass.

Limp leather; 8-7/8 x 5-3/4 in. In manila envelope.

GOLDING and COMPANY

Cabinet EE · Shelf 4 · No. 41

Catalogue, 1908, of printing machinery. Printing presses, paper cutters and printers' tools. Golding Mfg. Co. Franklin, Mass.

Frontispiece exterior view of Golding factories and general office.

Item in manila envelope.

GOLDING and COMPANY

Cabinet EE · Shelf 4 · No. 41

Price list (circa 1885) of printing presses and accessories made by Golding & Co. Boston, Mass.

Item in manila envelope.

GOLDING & COMPANY

Cabinet 27 · Shelf 2 · No. 14.01

(The) Printers' Review

see

PERIODICALS, PRINTERS'. United States. (The) Printers' Review...

GOLDING AND COMPANY.

Cabinet 25 · Shelf 2 · No. 17

(The) printers' Review, Boston, 1880

See PERIODICALS, PRINTING. United States

(The) Printers' Review...

GOLDING AND COMPANY

Cabinet · Shelf · No.

See Specimen Books, Types. United States. Golding & Company. Boston, Mass. 1891.

GOLDSCHMIDT, E. PH.

Cabinet PP · Shelf 5 · No. 39 (2 vols.)

Gothic and Renaissance bookbindings. Exemplified and illustrated from the author's collection. (2 vols.) London...New York ...1928.

Vol. I - text
Vol. II - plates

Tooled cloth: 11½ x 8-7/8 in.

GOLDSCHMIT, E. P.

Cabinet 75 · Shelf 2 · No. 10

Theodore Gottlieb: a reformer of the history of bookbinding. [Paper] By E. P. Goldschmidt.

In Transactions of the Bibliographical Society, "The Library," Vol. X, 1929-1930, pp. 274-9.

GOLDSMID, EDMUND

Cabinet U · Shelf 4 · No. 20

Bibliographical sketch of the Aldine Press at Venice, forming a catalogue of all the works issued by Aldus and his successors, from 1494 to 1597, and a list of all known forgeries or imitations. Translated and abridged from Ant. Aug. Renouard's "Annales des Aldes". Revised and corrected by E. Goldsmid. Edinburgh, 1887. 3 vols. in I.

Half morocco; 6-7/8 x 4½ x 7/8 in.

GOLDSMID, EDMUND

Cabinet U · Shelf 4 · No. 44

Elzevier Presses, The: A complete catalogue of all the publications of the Elzevier Presses at Leyden, Amsterdam, the Hague, and Utrecht ...and an appendix containing a list of all works whether forgeries or anonymous, and publications generally attributed to these presses. 3 vols. [Bound together in 1 vol.]. Edinburgh, 1888.

Half morocco; 8½ x 5-7/8 x 2-1/8 in.

GOLDSMITH, OLIVER

Cabinet 71 · Shelf 1 · No. 79

See Clarke, William Andrews Jr. Facsimile 1770 edition of The Deserted Village... San Francisco, 1926.

GOLDSMITH, OLIVER

Cabinet K · Shelf 6 · No. 13

Dalziels' Illustrated Goldsmith...

see

WOOD ENGRAVINGS. Dalziels' Illustrated Goldsmith...London, 1865.

GOLDSMITH, OLIVER.

Cabinet M · Shelf 2 · No. 21

Deserted Village, The. Published by Linotype and Machinery Limited. London, 1921.
Colophon:...woodcuts which are facsimiles of those engraved by the Bewicks for Bulmer's 1795 edition, has been superintended by Geo. W. Jones, who has linotyped the work and printed it on a Miehle Press at his office at The Sign of The Dolphin, Gough Square, Fleet Street, London.
Paper; 12 x 9 in.

GOLLANCZ, Sir ISRAEL

Cabinet U · Shelf 4 · No. 107

In Commemoration of the first folio tercentenary. A resetting of the preliminary matter of the first folio, with a catalogue of Shakespeariana. Exhibited in the Hall of the Worshipful Company of Stationers. With facsimiles. London. George W. Jones, printer. 1923.

Half morocco; 10-1/8 x 6½ x ½ in.

GOLLOB, HEDWIG

Cabinet 26 · Shelf 1 · No. 20

Wappenholzschnitte aus Wiener frühdrucken. Illus. Bibliographical.

Article in the Gutenberg-Gesellschaft Jahrbuch" 1930, pp.166-174.

GOLLOB, HEDWIG.

Cabinet I · Shelf 3 · No. 33

(Der) Wiener holzschnitt in den jahren von 1490 bis 1550, seine bedeutung fur die nordische kunst, seine entwicklung, seine blute und seine meister. Zusammengestellt und beschreiben von Hedwig Collob. Mit 91 abbildungen. Wien, 1926.

Boards; 11x 8-5/8 x 3/8 in.

COMEZ, ALONSO

Cabinet X Shelf 3 No. 19

Brief bio-bibliographical note, with publisher book mark, Comez (Medina del Campo), 1564-1584.

see HAEBLER, KONRAD. (Spanish and Portugese printer marks...p.xxxi

GOODSON GRAPHOTYPE COMPOSING and CASTING MACHINE, invented by George A. Goodson

Cabinet FF Shelf 6 No. 18

See COMPOSING MACHINES.- Single Types. Goodson...

GOPS, GOSWIN von EUSKIRCHEN

Cabinet Y Shelf 4 No. 4

(Note on the Gops press at Cologne, 1475)

see VOULLIÉME, ERNST. (Die) Deutschen drucker des fünfzehnten jahrhunderts...p.31

GOMME, GEORGE LAURENCE (Editor)

Cabinet U Shelf 5 No. 52

Bibliographical Notes. A classified collection of the chief contents of "The Gentleman's Magazine" from 1731 to 1868. London, 1889.

Boards; 9½ x 6 x 1½ in.

GOODSPEED, CHARLES E.

Cabinet Q Shelf 2 No. 29.01

How Goodspeed Began. (Biographical sketch) By Charles E. Goodspeed. Foreword XVIII pp. to Catalogue 250. Goodspeed's Book Shop, Incorporated, 7 Ashburton Place, Boston, Mass. October 30, 1935.

Paper; 9 x 5-7/8 in.

GORDON, COSMO.

Cabinet 75 Shelf 1 No. 13

Books on accountancy, 1490-1600. A paper read before the Bibliographical Society, March 16, 1914.

In Trans. Biblio. Soc., Vol. XIII, 1913-1915, pp. 145-170.

GONCALVEZ, Antonio

Cabinet X Shelf 3 No. 19

Brief bio-bibliographical note, Concalvez (Lissabon), 1568-1576.

see HAEBLER, KONRAD. (Spanish and Portugese printer marks...p.xxxiii

GOODWIN, GEORGE

Cabinet 61 Shelf 1 No. 1

Publisher od the Connecticut Courant for 58 years. Bio-historical account. With portrait

Article in "The Paper World", vol.2, No.4, April, 1881, p.1

GORDON, GEORGE P.

Cabinet QQ Shelf 4 No. 4

Biographical sketch of the inventor of many styles of printing presses.

see INDUSTRIAL AMERICA. Manufacturers ...New York, 1876, p. 387.

GONSE, LOUIS

Cabinet J Shelf 5 No. 15

L'Art Japonais. Par Louis Gonse. Paris, 1883.

Illustrated descriptive prospectus of forthcoming book with title as above.

Paper; 14-3/8 x 10¾ in. In folder.

GOOLD, WILLIAM

Cabinet RR Shelf 4 No. 3

Paper mills of New England, early. By Hon. William Goold. Paper read before the Maine Historical Society, Bath, Feb. 19, 1874.

Pamphlet presented by Nathan Goold.

Item I in bound collection of pamphlets and excerpts with binder's title "Paper-Making. Pamphlets".

GORDON, GEORGE PHINEAS.

Stack A Shelf 1&2 Number 70

Famous inventor, A, by Henry Lewis Bullen, in The Inland Printer, vol.LXX, p.91.

Brief sketch of the man, his invention of the "Gordon" press and its subsequent development.

GOODHUE, BERTRAM GROSVENOR

Cabinet G Shelf 4 No. 3

See Imprints, United States. University Press, The. John Wilson and Son, 1897. Shakespear's Sonnets.

GOOVAERTS, ALPHONSE

Cabinet FF Shelf 4 No. 11

Histoire et bibliographie de la typographie musicale dans les pay-bas...Avec neuf phototypies par M. Jos. Maes...Anvers,1880.

Bibliography and history of printing in the Netherlands.

Half morocco; 8-3/8 x 6 in. Dupl. original paper covers, in vestibule.

GORDON, GEORGE P.

Cabinet 25 Shelf 2 No. 5

(Platen Printing Presses), Geo. P. Gordon's earliest. Pictures of

Item in vol. of miscellaneous trade periodicals, printing trade circulars, etc.

GOODMAN, JOSEPH

Cabinet MM Shelf 2 No. 59

Metalithography, practical modern. Being a complete, practical, and technical handbook... Garden City Press, Ltd. Letchworth, Herts, 1914. Illus.

Half morocco; 8¾ x 6 x 1 in.

GOPFERDTSCHEN OFFICINI.

Cabinet Shelf No.

See Specimen Books, Types, Germany.

GORDON, GEORGE P.

Cabinet Shelf No.

See also Printing Presses. Degener & Weiler, George P. Gordon, R. Hoe & Co.

Press: Gordon Press.

GORDON, JOHN

Cabinet S Shelf 3 No. 167

(A) Memorial to the "Tramp Printer" ... Also a collection of old-time literature of great interest to anyone in the printing trade ... Compiled and printed by John Gordon at The Gordon Press, South Brewer, Maine, 1927. Illus.

Boards; 7 x 4¼ in.

GORDON, Robert

Cabinet X Shelf 5 No. 57

Authorized Master Printer for Scotland, 1859

see LIBERTY OF PRINTING, Great Britain. (Scotland 1859)....

GORDON, SAUL

Cabinet QQ Shelf 5 No. 3.01

Standard annotated forms of agreement. By Saul Gordon. New York: Prentice - Hall, Inc., 1935.

Cloth; 9½ x 6-7/8 in.

GORDON-CUMMING, CONSTANCE F.

Cabinet FF Shelf 2 No. 18

Inventor (Rev. W.H. Murray) of the numeral-type for China. By the use of which illiterate Chinese, both blind and sighted can very quickly be taught to read and write fluently. A new edition. London, 1889.

With frontispiece portrait.

Cloth; 7½ x 5 in.

GORDON PRESS WORKS

Cabinet EE Shelf 4 No. 44

Franklin Printing Press, Gordon's. Depot: Bennett Building, 97 Nassau St., New York. Works, Rahway, N.J. November 1, 1880.

Illus. catalogue and price list.

Item in manila envelope.

GOSCHEN, GEORG JOACHIM

Cabinet Q Shelf 1 No. 4

(A) Famous German publisher (Goschen) By Jeannette L. Gilder. Ecerpt from The Critic, July, 1903.

Item 9 in vol. with binder's title "Various items on Publishing".

GOSCHEN, GEORG JOACHIM

Cabinet U Shelf 3 No. 99 2 vols.

Life and times of Georg Joachim Goschen, publisher and printer of Leipzig, 1752-1828. By his grandson, Viscount Goschen. 2 vols. Illus. London, 1903.

Stamped cloth; 9 x 5-3/4 x 2 in.

GOSCHEN, GEORG JOACHIM, Printer-Publisher.

Cabinet P Shelf 4 No. 3

See Publishing, Germany. Famous German publisher A (Goschen)

GOSLAR, Germany

Cabinet 20 Shelf 1 No. 16

Voigt, Johann establishes the first printing and publishing house in Goslar, 1614. Brief account. German text.

In Zeitschrift für bücherfreunde, 1904-5 part 2, p. 333.

GOSPELS

Cabinet Shelf No.

See BIBLES or BIBLE LITERATURE.

GOSS PRINTING PRESS CO. Ltd.

Cabinet EE Shelf 4 No. 45

Descriptive catalogue of Goss Patented Printing Presses. Main office and works. Hayes, Middlesex, England. 1911.

Has views of the works, also a reprint from the British and Colonial Printer, No. 1695, vol.68, No.12. March 23, 1911, in which are illustrations of the new works, printing presses, etc.

In manila envelope.

GOSSE, EDMUND

Cabinet S Shelf 3 No. 140

Elizabethan dedications of books. By Edmund Gosse. Illus. excerpt from Harper's Monthly Magazine, June, 1902.

See Books about Books. Short articles about books ... Collected by the Typographic Library, Jersey City, 1912. p. 49.

GOTARD, Hubert

Cabinet X Shelf 3 No. 19

Brief bio-bibliographical note, with publisher book mark, Gotard (Barcelona), 1581-1591)

see HAEBLER, KONRAD. (Spanish and Portugese printer marks...p.xxxvii

GOTHA, ALMANAC de

Cabinet 80 Shelf 1 No. 91

(Brief history of the Almanac de Gotha) Excerpt from Chamber's Journal, June 5, 1850.

Item in manila envelope.

GOTHIC vs. LATIN (see)

Cabinet L Shelf 2 No. 24

REINECKE, ADOLF. Deutsche buchstabenschrift... Leipzig-Borsdorf, 1910.

GOTTLIEB, THEODORE.

Cabinet 75 Shelf 2 No. 10

Reformer of the history of bookbinding. By E. P. Goldschmidt. A paper for the Bibliographical Society, London, 1929.

In Trans. Biblio. Soc. "The Library," vol. 10, 1929-30. pp. 274-9.

GOTTSCHALK, PAUL.

Cabinet 14 Shelf 2 No. 10

Buchkunst (Die) Gutenbergs und Schöffers, mit einem einleitenden versuch uber die entwicklung der buchkunst von ihren frühesten anfangen....Berlin, 1918. With facsimiles.

Buckram, 18 x 13 x ½ in.

GOTTWALD, EDUARD

Cabinet X Shelf 2 No. 24

Erinnerungsblätter an die vierte säcularfeir der erfindung der buchdruckerkunst. (Souvenir pages of the 400th anniversary of printing, together with a brief history of printing in Dresden from 1524 to 1840. With biographical sketches). Dresden, 1840. Portraits.

Full morocco; 8½ x 5 x 3/8 in.

GÖTZE, ALFRED

Cabinet Y Shelf 3 No. 43

(German printers of the Reformation period) Die hochdeutschen drucker der reformationszeit. Strassburg, 1905. Facsimiles.
Bio-bibliographical account.

Half morocco; 8¼ x 5½ x 1-3/8 in.

GOUDY, FREDERIC W.

Cabinet S Shelf 3 No. 100

(The) City of Crafts, a phantasy: Being some account of a journey to the Court of the Printer's Guild. Told by [Frederic W. Goudy] a member of the American Institute of Graphic Arts ... Wednesday, February 15, 1922. New York.

Half morocco; 9⅝ x 6¼ in.

GOUDY, FREDERIC

Cabinet CC Shelf 5 No. 22

Goudy Type Family: A composity showing of Goudy types. A pamphlet supplementing the specimen book of 1923. The American Type Founders Company. 1927.

Paper; 12½ x 9½ x 3/8 in. In box marked: Goudy, Frederic. Type Specimens, Various. 1926-1931.

GOUDY, BERTHA M.

Cabinet S Shelf 5 No. 37.01

Portrait of Bertha M. Goudy, with article on "Type Design", by Frederic W. Goudy.

Article in ARS TYPOGRAPHICA, vol.1, No.4, Autumn, 1934

GOUDY, FREDERIC WILLIAM

Cabinet S Shelf 6 No. 6

[Eulogistic biography]. By Robert O. Ballou.
Excerpt from American Mercury, February, 1926.

Item (j) in book with binder's title "Printing and printing offices".

GOUDY, FREDERIC W.

Cabinet S Shelf 5 No. 37.01

Hand press printing: a plea for a lost craft.

Article in "ARS TYPOGRAPHICA", vol.1, No.3, 1918, p.33

GOUDY, FREDERIC W.

Cabinet S Shelf 6 No. 8

Appreciative account of the man and his work.

See EATON, WALTER PRICHARD. Three great American printers...

GOUDY, FREDERIC W.

Cabinet A Shelf 2 No. 91

Evolution of printing types...A brief review of the steps leading to the present forms.

Illus. article in the Graphic Arts Section of the Boston Evening Transcript, Aug. 29, 1922, part three, p.14.

GOUDY, FREDERIC W.

Cabinet DD Shelf 2 No. 33

Kennerly Type. [Designed by Goudy] The circumstances which brought about its conception. Article written by Mitchel Kennerly for the Special Kennerly Issue "Monotype" May 1924 Number 70. Lanston Monotype Machine Company. Philadelphia.

Pamphlet in box marked 2, "Monotype Recorder" (House Organ) Philadelphia Pa. and London, England.

GOUDY, FREDERIC W.

Cabinet S Shelf 5 No. 37 and 37.01

ARS TYPOGRAPHICA, vols.1 (1918-1934), Nos.1-4; vol.2, 1925, Nos.1-4; vol.3, 1926, No.1

Half morocco; 12¼ x 8 in.

GOUDY, FREDERIC W.

Cabinet S Shelf 3 No. 42.01

(The) Friendly Goudys: The story of a visit to Deepdene. By Sidney S. Wheeler. Boston, The Typographical Laboratory, 1932. Illus.

Boards, linen back; 11-5/8 x 7-5/8 in.

GOUDY, FREDERIC W.

Cabinet DD Shelf 2 No. 33

Monotype faces, two new. Goudy Text and Lombardic Capitals. Designed by Frederic W. Goudy. Lanston Monotype Machine Company. Philadelphia Pa. n.d.
Advance specimen sheet.

In box marked 2, "Monotype Recorder" (House Organ) Philadelphia Pa. and London, England.

GOUDY, FREDERIC W.

Cabinet S Shelf 5 No. 9

See Biographies, printers: Goudy, Frederic W.

GOUDY, FREDERICK.

Cabinet G Shelf 3 No. 42

Goudy: An address by Temple Scott at a meeting of the American Institute of Graphic Arts, May22nd, 1923. Printed from Monotype (Goudy) Garamond. Booklet.

Boards; 7-3/4 x 4 ins.,pp.13.

GOUDY, FREDERIC W.

Cabinet S Shelf 5 No. 37

Roman alphabets, its origin and esthetic development.

Illus. article in ARS TYPOGRAPHICA, vol.2, No.3, Jan.,1926, p.185

GOUDY, FREDERIC W.

Cabinet S Shelf 5 No. 37.01

Bulmer, William and the Shakspear Press.

Illus. article in ARS TYPOGRAPHICA, vol.1, No.2, 1918, p.17

GOUDY, FREDERIC W. see

Cabinet 27 Shelf 2 No. 27

GOUDY OLDSTYLE. First showing of this popular type design.

GOUDY, FREDERICK W.

Cabinet S Shelf 3 No. 42

Speaking of type faces: A little story about the genius of the Village Letter Foundry. Told for you by Advertisers Paper Mills, Holyoke, Massachusetts. N. d. [1929].

Paper; 6¾ x 3-3/8 in.

GOUDY, FREDERIC W.

Cabinet S Shelf 3 No. 43

(The) Story of the Village Type. By its designer Frederic W. Goudy. New York: The Press of the Woolly Whale, 1933.

With a chronological list of types designed by Frederic W. Goudy, 1896-1932.

Boards, cloth back; $9\frac{1}{4}$ x $6\frac{1}{4}$ in.

GOUDY, Frederic W.

Cabinet S Shelf 5 No. 37.01

Type designs old and new. By F.W.G.

Article in ARS TYPOGRAPHICA, vol.1, No.1, 1918, p.38

GOUDY, FREDERIC W.

Cabinet S Shelf 3 No. 41

(The) Village Press and Letter Foundry. A novel type foundry. Specimens of the types, borders and page ornaments designed and sold by Frederic W. Goudy. New York, 1914.

Half morocco; $8\frac{1}{2}$ x 5-1/8 in.

GOUDY, FREDERIC W.

Cabinet S Shelf 5 No. 37.01

What printing is.

Article in ARS TYPOGRAPHICA, No.2, vol.1, 1918, p.37

GOUDY. FRED W. AND BERTHA

Cabinet Shelf No.

See Imprints, United States

GOUDY OLDSTYLE

Cabinet 27 Shelf 2 No. 27

First showing of this popular type design of Fred.W. Goudy.

see THE AMERICAN BULLETIN, June, 1916, pp. 9-18.

GOUGH, (or Gowghe), JOHN

Cabinet T Shelf 2 No. 6 [vol.3]

Books printed by John Gough, London, 1536-1543. Bibliographical notes. With printer's device.

see DIBDIN'S "Typographical Antiquities" ...London, 1810-19, vol.iii, p.402

GOUGH, JOHN

Cabinet T Shelf 2 No. 2

Memoire of J. Gough, together with a list of books printed by him or for him, 1536-1543

see AMES, JOSEPH and WM. HERBERT Typographical Antiquities...vol.1, pp. 491-499

GOUGH, RICHARD

Cabinet T Shelf 2 No. 6 [vol.1]

Memoirs of Joseph Ames. By the late Richard Gough. (With portrait of Ames)

see DIBDIN'S "Typographical Antiquities" ...London, 1810-19, vol.i, pp.19-51

GOULD, FRANCES CARRUTHERS

Cabinet K Shelf 5 No. 2

British cartoonist.

see BIOGRAPHIES. CARTOONISTS. Gould...

GOULD, JOSEPH

Cabinet MM Shelf 3 No. 37.01

Compositors guide and pocket book; being the whole routine of work as practised in various offices...Also complete diagrams of imposition. By Joseph Gould. London, 1878.

Cloth; 4-1/8 x 2-5/8 x $\frac{1}{4}$ in.

GOULD, JOSEPH

Cabinet MM Shelf 3 No. 37

Letter-press printer, the; A complete guide to the art of printing, containing practical instructions for learners at case, press, and machine. Embracing the whole practice of book work...(Third thousand) London, 1876.

Cloth; $6\frac{1}{2}$ x $4\frac{1}{4}$ x $\frac{1}{2}$ in.

GOUNILHOU, GUSTAVE.

Cabinet V Shelf 1 No. 23

Histoire d'une imprimerie Bordelaise 1600-1900. Les imprimeries de G. Gounouilhou; La Gironde; La Petite Gironde. Bordeaux, 1901. Illus. facsimiles.

Part 1 - L'Imprimerie a Bordeaux de 1486-1850.
" 2 - L'Imprimerie G. Gounilhou, 1851-1900.

Half morocco; 13 x 10 x $2\frac{1}{2}$ in.

GOUNOUILHON, G.

Stack A Shelf 1&2 Number 66

See Bullen, Henry Lewis.

GOURMONT, GILLES

Cabinet Shelf No.

See Greek Printing, France. Paris, 1507:Gilles Gourmont.

GOURMONT, JÉROME et BENOIT

Cabinet V Shelf 5 No. 23

Paris, 1535 l'Imprimerie de Saint-Denis.

See PRINTING, HISTORICAL, FRANCE. (Paris, 1535) L'Imprimerie de Saint-Denis...

GOVERNMENT PRINTERS

Cabinet V Shelf 6 No. 38

Lyon, 1545-1793. Chronological list, with notes by Marius Audin, Lyon, 1925.

Pamphlet.

In envelope.

GOVERNMENT PRINTERS. France

Cabinet V Shelf 6 No. 24

Imprimerie Nationale, 1809-1847.

See Imprimerie Nationale. Bernard, August. Notice historique...Paris, 1848.

GOVERNMENT PRINTERS, France

Cabinet V (Lyons, 1558-1793)
Shelf 6
No. 36

See Printing, Historical. France. Lyon, 1925.

GOVERNMENT PRINTERS, France

Cabinet V
Shelf 6
No. 36

(Lyons, 1545-1793) L'Imprimeur de la ville. a Lyon. Marius Audin. 1925.

With other items in manila envelope.

GOVERNMENT PRINTERS'. France

Cabinet X
Shelf 4
No. 32

[Pierres Philippe-Denys, 1785, is made printer to the King] Lettres-Patentes du Roi qui créent en faveur du Sieur Pierres, la charge de l'Imprimerie Ordinaire de Sa Majesté...De 9 Juillet...A Versailles, de l'Imprimerie de Ph.-D. Pierres.

Item 33 in vol. with title "French legislation affecting printing, 1573-1810."

GOVERNMENT PRINTERS, Great Britain

Cabinet 75
Shelf 1
No. 13

Reynold, Wolfe, 1547, King's printer in Latin, Greek and Hebrew, the first in England.

See Sayle, C. Wolfe Reynold [King's printer in Latin, Greek and Hebrew].

GOVERNMENT PRINTERS, Holland

Cabinet F
Shelf 4
No. 66

Aelbert Hendricxz, 1578.

Types used by him in a reprint by Johannes Enschedé en Zonen, Haarlem, 1778.

See IMPRINTS, HOLLAND. Enschede, Johannes in Zonen, Haarlem, 1778.

GOVERNMENT PRINTERS, Holland

Cabinet AA
Shelf 4
No. 5
2 Vols.

Kleerkooper, M.M.: De boekhandel te Amsterdam in de 17e eeuw ... 'S - Gravenhage, 1914-16. 2 Vols.

See "Stadsdrukkers," p. 1737 of "Zaak-en Plaatsnaamregister" of the above work.

Half morocco; $9\frac{1}{2}$ x $6\frac{1}{2}$ in.

GOVERNMENT PRINTERS, United States.

Cabinet F
Shelf 3
No. 24

Childs, Francis and John Swaine. New York, 1789.

The first printers to the United States of America. They printed the Acts of the First Congress which contains the first official printing of the Constitution of the United States, and the Treaty of Peace with Great Britain.

See Early Printing in New York City.
cont'd

GOVERNMENT PRINTERS, United States, cont'd.

Cabinet F
Shelf 3
No. 51

Childs, Francis and John Swaine....1791.

GOVERNMENT PRINTERS.

Cabinet NN
Shelf 3
No. 4

Public printers and printing, United States, 1692-1846.

see

HUDSON'S "Journalism in the United States... (index)

GOVERNMENT PRINTERS (U.S.)

Cabinet 27
Shelf 2
No. 16

Rounds, Sterling P.

see

BIOGRAPHIES, Printers. Rounds, Hon. Sterling P...

GOVERNMENT PRINTERS'

Cabinet NN
Shelf 2
No. 8

Steedman, James Blair. Public Printer, Washington, D. C., circ 1853. Oration at the unveiling of the monument of Maj. Gen. James B. Steedman. By Gen. John C. Smith. At Toledo, Ohio, May 26, 1887. Frontspiece reproduction of monument. Pamphlet.

Item 7 in vol. "Various Editors. Excerpts and Pamphlets"

GOVERNMENT PRINTERS, United States.

Cabinet NN
Shelf 2
No. 8

Steedman, James B. U. S. Public Printer, 1858. Ovation at the unveiling of monument erected to the memory of Maj. Gen. James B. Steedman ... at Toledo, Ohio. May 26, 1887.

Bound with other items in "Various editors," item 7.

GOVERNMENT PRINTERS, United States

Cabinet QQ
Shelf 4
No. 20

Wendell, Cornelius, Washington, D. C., 1868. Biographical sketch.

see

BISHOP, J. LEANDER. History of the American manufacturers...Philadelphia, 1868, p. 672.

GOVERNMENT PRINTING

Cabinet
Shelf
No.

Statistics of printing

see

STASTICS OF PRINTING

GOVERNMENT PRINTING United States.

Cabinet 81
Shelf 2
No. 31

Congressional printing. State and Congress printing. vol.2 of "Printers' Scraps" collected by Joel Munsell of Albany, prior to 1860. With index.

See pp.1-32.

Half morocco; 8-7/8 x 7-1/8 in.

GOVERNMENT PRINTING, United States

Cabinet 62
Shelf 2
No. 21.01

Madisonian, J. B. Jones, proprietor, Washington, D. C. An appeal to the public for support January 1, 1844. A one leaf broadside.

Jones complains that though he has loyally supported the policies of the President, the Senate bestows its printing on The Intelligencer, and the House, on The Globe. Both houses have passed a joint resolution taking from the President the power to select a printer. Jones promises to support the President provided the public supports Jones.

In envelope. (over)

GOVERNMENT PRINTING, United States

Cabinet 62
Shelf 2
No. 21.01

Madisonian, J. B. Jones, proprietor, Washington, D. C. An appeal to the public for support January 1, 1884. A one leaf broadside.

Jones complains that though he has loyally supported the policies of the President, the Senate bestows its printing on The Intelligencer, and the House, on The Globe. Both houses have passed a joint resolution taking from the President the power to select a printer. Jones promises to support the President provided the public supports Jones.

(cont'd)

GOVERNMENT PRINTING, United States (cont'd)

Cabinet 62
Shelf 2
No. 21.01

Daily paper $10; Tri-Weekly $5 - in advance. In 1844 there was no Government Printing Office.

In envelope.

GOVERNMENT PRINTING, United States

Cabinet S
Shelf 5
No. 4

Problem of Federal Printing (The), by William S. Rossiter, in the Atlantic Monthly, Sept., 1905.

Bound with other items in "Various printers and their plants" item 10, vol. 1.

GOVERNMENT PRINTING BUREAU. Japan

Cabinet 44
Shelf 2
No. 18

Statistics of type characters.

see NAKAMURA, NOBUO. (A) statistical survey...

GOVERNMENT PRINTING United States

Cabinet 81
Shelf 2
No. 31

Ohio State printing. State and Congress printing. vol.2 of "Printers Scraps" collected by Joel Munsell of Albany, prior to 1860.

See p.2.

Half morocco; 8-7/8 x 7-1/8 in.

GOVERNMENT PRINTING United States

Cabinet 81
Shelf 2
No. 31

(Pennsylvania State Printing) State and Congress printing. vol.2 of "Printers' Scraps" collected by Joel Munsell of Albany, prior to 1860. With index.

See pp.18-19.

Half morocco; 8-7/8 x 7-1/8 in.

GOVERNMENT PRINTING HOUSES, Bavaria

Cabinet Y
Shelf 5
No. 20

(Nurnberg, 1658-1908. Anniversary 250th year of Felsecker-Sebald, Imperial and Government printers and publishers for Bavaria, Historical account). Zum 250 jähr geschäftsjubilaum der Konigl. Bayer Hofdruckerei und verlagshandlung von U.E. Sebald. Nurnberg von U.E. Sebald. Nurnberg, 9 May, 1908. Portraits and other illus.

Half morocco; 12¼ x 9¼ x 3/8 in.

GOVERNMENT PRINTING HOUSES. Germany

Cabinet X
Shelf 2
No. 43

Weimar 1592- Sur geschichte der entstehung der Hofbuchdruckerei in Weimar. von Dr. Panze. Weimar 1840.

History of the State Printing House of Weimar, together with a collection of essays contributed by various writers, in celebration of the fourth centenary of printing.

GOVERNMENT PRINTING HOUSES, Russia.

Cabinet RR
Shelf 4
No. 3

(St. Petersburgh). Catalogue of exhibits of the Imperial Russian State Paper Manufactory, at World's Columbian Fair, Chicago, 1893. This establishment was actually the government printing house in which printing, engraving, platemaking, type founding and paper-making were carried on: the exhibits represent these various departments (See also Paper-making, Russia.)

cont'd

-2-

Cabinet RR
Shelf 4
No. 3

Bound with other items in "Paper-making Pamphlets, historical and technical," item 12.

GOVERNMENT PRINTING OFFICES, Austria

Cabinet Y
Shelf 5
No. 34

(Imperial Printing Office, Vienna, 1804-1904: Centennial celebration) Did K.K. Hof-und Staats Druckerei von der grundung bis zur gegenwart. Vienna, 1904. Illus.

Half morocco; $16\frac{1}{4}$ x 12-1/8 x 1 in.

GOVERNMENT PRINTING OFFICES, Austria

Cabinet Y
Shelf 5
No. 26

Vienna, 1851. (A history of the Imperial and Government printing establishment at Vienna. By one of its members. (I) History. (II) Description) Geschichte der K.K. Hof-und Staatsdruckerei in Wien...1851. Numerous illus. of technical equipment. Views, interior and exterior. Text in four languages.

Includes a dictionary of typographical terms in four languages.

Half morocco; 9-3/8 x 6 x $2\frac{1}{4}$ in.

GOVERNMENT PRINTING OFFICES, Austria

Cabinet Y
Shelf 5
No. 33

Vienna, 1894 (The technical equipment of the Imperial and Government printing office) Die K.K. Hof-und Staatsdruckerei und deren technische einrichtungen. Mit text, illustrationen, ansichten und planen. von G. Fritz. Wien. 1894.

Stamped cloth; $9\frac{1}{2}$ x $6\frac{1}{4}$ x $\frac{1}{4}$ in.

GOVERNMENT PRINTING OFFICES - Austria

Cabinet 20
Shelf 1
No. 17

Vienna, (K.K. Hof-und Staatsdruckerei.

See Loubier, Dr. Jean. Celebration of the hundredth anniversary.

GOVERNMENT PRINTING OFFICES. Austria

Cabinet
Shelf
No.

Vienna: K. und K. Hof-und Staatsdruckerei.

See Specimen Books, Types. Austria. K.K. Hof-und Staatsdruckerei in Wien.

GOVERNMENT PRINTING OFFICES. Austria

Cabinet Y
Shelf 5
No. 25

Vienna, 1850. (A History of the Imperial and Government printing establishment at Vienna. By one of its members) Geschichte der K.K. Hof-und Staats-Druckerei in Wien. von einem typographen dieser anstalt. Wien, 1850. Frontispiece, allegorical subject. German text only; for translation see Y/5/26.

Half morocco; 9-3/8 x 5-3/4 x 3/8 in.

GOVERNMENT PRINTING OFFICES, Austria

Cabinet Y
Shelf 5
No. 24

Vienna, 1851. (Imperial and Government Printing House exhibit at London, 1851. Description of the) Uebersicht de von der Wiener K.K. Hof-und Staatsdruckerei in London: ausgestellten gegenstaende aller graphischen kunstweize. Wien, 1851.

Cloth; 9-1/8 x $8\frac{3}{4}$ x 3/8 in.

GOVERNMENT PRINTING OFFICES, Austria

Cabinet Y
Shelf 5
No. 28

Vienna, 1855. (Imperial and Government Printing House at the Universal Exhibition of Industry and Art, Paris, 1855). Die K.K. Hof-und Staatsdruckerei bei der allgemeinen industry und kunstausstellung in Paris.

Descriptive catalogue; text in four languages.

Half morocco; $7\frac{3}{4}$ x 5-3/8 x 3/8 in.

GOVERNMENT PRINTING OFFICES (Dutch East Ind.

Cabinet 62
Shelf 2
No. 9.01

Batavia. Annual Reports, 1911 to 1927. Illus.

15 items, paper and cloth covers, tied in one bundle.

GOVERNMENT PRINTING OFFICES (Dutch East Ind.,

Cabinet 62
Shelf 2
No. 9.02

Batavia. Jaarverslag (Report) van de Landsdrukkerij 1931... Batavia. Department van Governmentsbedrijven in Nederl-Indie, 1933.

Brochure, in manila envelope.

GOVERNMENT PRINTING OFFICES (Dutch East Ind.)

Cabinet 62 Shelf 2 No. 9

Batavia Landsdrukkery. (View book, photographs, etc.)

Cloth; $10\frac{1}{2}$ x $13\frac{1}{2}$ in.

GOVERNMENT PRINTING OFFICES (Ecuador)

Cabinet 79 Shelf 2 No. 27

(Quito). Brief account of the establishment of a Government Printing Office at Quito. Illus.

see

SANCHEZ, CARLOS ENRIQUE. (La) Imprenta en el Ecuador...Quito, 1935, p. 55 and fol.

GOVERNMENT PRINTING OFFICES, Egypt

Cabinet 26 Shelf 1 No. 21

Aperçu historique sur l'Imprimerie Nationale Egyptienne. Par Mohamed Amine Bahgat Bey. (Brief historical account, with facsimile of the first number of the "Journal Officiel".)

Essay in the "Gutenberg-Gesellschaft Jahrbuch, 1931", pp.275-77.

GOVERNMENT PRINTING OFFICES (France)

Cabinet V Shelf 5 No. 1

Exhibits of the French Government (Imprimerie Nationale.) Universal and International Exhibition, Saint-Louis, U.S.A. 1904.
Another copy entirely in French.

Bound in volume "French Typographical Pamphlets." items 13 and 14.

GOVERNMENT PRINTING OFFICES, France

Cabinet V Shelf 6 No. 25

L'Imprimerie Nationale depuis sa fondation jusqu'a ce jour, tabliea des directeurs de. 1640-1895. Pamphlet.
Brief historical account in catalogue of Exposition Universelle et Internationale de 1900. Vitrines de L'Imprimerie Nationale.

In folder marked "L'Imprimerie Nationale. Various Pamphlets." Paris 1874.

GOVERNMENT PRINTING OFFICES, France

Cabinet B Shelf 3 No. 2

L'Imprimerie Nationale, et la Bibliothèque Nationalè. Hommage a la mémoire de Jean Gutenberg. Paris: Imprimérie Nationale, Juin 1900. [With 17 plates]

Morocco; 17 x 13 in.

GOVERNMENT PRINTING OFFICES, France

Cabinet V Shelf 6 No. 23

L'Imprimerie Nationale et ses Types, precis historique sur. Par F.A. Duprat, chef du service de la Fonderie, etc. Paris, 1848.
Has specimens of types.

Half morocco; 9-1/8 x 6 in.

GOVERNMENT PRINTING OFFICES. FRANCE

Cabinet FF Shelf 5 No. 35

L'Imprimerie Royale, 1783. Description d'une nouvelle presse executee pour le service du Roi. A Paris, de l'Imprimerie Royale, 1783. With colored plates.
Inserted, an autograph letter from M. Anisson le fils, the inventor.

Full morocco; gilt; $10\frac{1}{2}$ x 8 in.

GOVERNMENT PRINTING OFFICES, France.

Cabinet V Shelf 6 No. 19

Rapport fait par Brival, au nom d'une commission spéciale, composée des citoyens Vieguy, Rabaud-Rommier et Brival; sur une résolution du 11 pluviose, relative a l'imprimerie de la République. Séance du 16 Floréal, an V. Paris (1795?).

Half morocco; $8\frac{1}{2}$ x 5-3/4 in.

GOVERNMENT PRINTING OFFICES, Germany

Cabinet Y Shelf 5 No. 46

(Berlin, 1885. The Imperial Printing Office in). Die Reichsdruckerei in Berlin. 1885. Illus. Technical, statistical and historical account.

Portfolio, stamped cloth; 11-3/4 x 9 in. See also Y/5/47.

GOVERNMENT PRINTING OFFICES, France
SEE ALSO

Cabinet Shelf No.

See Imprimerie Imperial
" Nationale
" de la République
" Royale du Louvre

Early Printing in France.
Paris, 1642, 1644, 1648.

GOVERNMENT PRINTING OFFICES. Germany

Cabinet Y Shelf 5 No. 45

Berlin, Reichsdruckerei, 1879-1929. Funfzig Jahre: mit einem rückblick auf den Berliner Buchdruck für hof und staat bis zur begrundung der Reichsdruckerei. Verfasst und herausgegeben von der direktion der Reichsdruckerei unter mitwirkung Dr. Ernst Crous. Mit zahlreichen abbildungen. Berlin, 1929. Gedruckt und verlegt von der Reichdruckerei.

Morocco; 12 x $8\frac{1}{2}$ x $1\frac{3}{4}$ in. In protective case.

GOVERNMENT PRINTING OFFICES, Germany

Cabinet Y Shelf 5 No. 47

(Berlin, 1895. The Imperial Printing Office in.) Die Reichsdruckerei in Berlin. 1895.
Statistical, technical and historical account.

Portfolio, leather; 12-3/8 x $9\frac{1}{2}$ x $\frac{1}{2}$ in. See also Y/5/46.

GOVERNMENT PRINTING OFFICES. Germany

Cabinet L Shelf 2 No. 29

Berlin, 1924. Alphabeten und schriftzeichen des morgen und des abendlandes...Herausgegeben, gedruckt und verlegt von der Reichsdruckerei Berlin.
Specimens of oriental and occidental alphabets. With historical and philological notes.

Cloth; 10-7/8 x 8-18 in.

GOVERNMENT PRINTING OFFICES. Germany

Cabinet Y Shelf 2 No. 52

Breslau Statbuchdruckerey, 1504-1804. Geschichte der seit dreihundert jahren in Breslau befindlichen Statbuchdruckerey...[von J. E. Scheibel. Breslay, 1804. Portraits.
Historical account. Genealogical table of the Bauman family of printers.

Half morocco; 9-3/4 x 8-3/4 x 7/8 in.

GOVERNMENT PRINTING OFFICES. Germany

Cabinet B Shelf 3 No. 8

Reichsdruckerei. Druckschriften des xv bis xviii jahrhunderts in getreuen nachbildungen. Herausgegeben von der Direction der Reichsdruckerei. Berlin, 1884-7.

100 plates of facsimiles of types of the 15th and 16th centuries.

Half morocco; $18\frac{3}{4}$ x $12\frac{1}{2}$ x 1-3/8 in.

GOVERNMENT PRINTING OFFICES, Germany.

Cabinet X Shelf 2 No. 11

(Weimar, 1740, Brief history of the Hoch-Furstlich Sachsen-Weimarischen Hof-Buchdruckerey).
See Schroen, Wolffgang, A. (History of the Imperial Printing Office at Weimar).

GOVERNMENT PRINTING OFFICES. Great Britain

Cabinet Shelf No.

His majesty's printers (H.M. Stationery Office)

Article in London Typographical Journal, Dec. 1930, No.300, vol.25, p.4.

GOVERNMENT PRINTING OFFICES. Great Britain

Cabinet MM Shelf 4 No. 6

H.M. Stationery Office. Questions and answers in typography. A guide to the City and Guilds Institute of London, and H.M. Stationery Office examinations. Leicester, Raithby, Lawrence & Co. Ltd. n.d.

Paper; 7¼ x 4-7/8 in.

GOVERNMENT PRINTING OFFICES. Great Britain

Cabinet X Shelf 5 No. 53

House of Commons, 1832-37: Report from Select Committee on King's Printers' Patents: With the Minutes of Evidence, and Appendix. Ordered, by the House of Commons, to be printed, 8 August 1832. (At end:) Report from the Select Committee on King's Printers' Patent (Scotland). 1837.

Boards; 14 x 8½ in.

GOVERNMENT PRINTING OFFICES (Great Britain)

Cabinet X Shelf 5 No. 53

King's Printers' Patents. Report of the Select Committee

See King's Printers' Patents

GOVERNMENT PRINTING OFFICES, Great Britain

Cabinet 62 Shelf 2 No. 1

Report of the select committee on printing (House of Parliament, etc.) Together with the proceedings of the committee, minutes of evidence, appendix and index. Ordered by The House of Commons to be printed, 1st August, 1855.

Half morocco; 13-1/8 x 8½ in.

GOVERNMENT PRINTING OFFICES. Holland

Cabinet 62 Shelf 2 No. 10

Annual reports, 1913 to 1916. (4 items)

In manila envelope

GOVERNMENT PRINTING OFFICES, Holland

Cabinet 62 Shelf 2 No. 11

Verslag aan zijne excellente den van...de Algemeene Landsdrukkerij. Uitgebracht door de commissie, bij beschikking van Januari 1910, No.718, Afdeeling A/Z.C., Ingesteld. Gedruckt in de Electrische Drukkerij "T. Kasteel van Amstel", Amsterdam, 1912.

Cloth; 14½ x 9½ in.

GOVERNMENT PRINTING OFFICES. India

Cabinet EE Shelf 3 No. 77

Imprense Nacional, Nova Goa, 1887. Specimen de typos.

Nova Goa, a Portuguese possession on the Malabar coast.

Boards, leather back; 11-5/8 x 7-3/4 x 3/4 in. See also EE/3/78.

GOVERNMENT PRINTING OFFICES, India, British

Cabinet 62 Shelf 2 No. 4

Calcutta. Note on the subject of State owned printing establishments and their competition with private trade, 28th August, 1922. Lal Chand & Sons, Government of India and General Printers.

Circular in manila envelope.

GOVERNMENT PRINTING OFFICES, India, British

Cabinet 62 Shelf 2 No. 5

Calcutta. State-owned printing presses and their competition with private trade. Extract from the Proceedings of the Associated Chambers of Commerce of India and Ceylon. Calcutta, 9th January, 1923. Illus.

Half morocco; 13¼ x 8½ in.

GOVERNMENT PRINTING OFFICES, India, British

Cabinet 62 Shelf 2 No. 3

Ceylon. Administration reports, 1883-1907 (Part IV.- Miscellaneous). Government Printing Office.

Presented by H.C. Cottle, Esq., Government Printer. Includes his A.L.S.

Cloth; 13 x 9 in.

GOVERNMENT PRINTING OFFICES, India, British

Cabinet 62 Shelf 2 No. 2

Madras. Annual reports of the Government Presses, 1913 to 1916. (3 items)

Paper; 13¼ x 8½ in.

GOVERNMENT PRINTING OFFICES. India

Cabinet MM Shelf 7 No. 5

(Madras) The elements of letterpress printing, composing and proofreading: A practical manual for Indian artisans. By T. Fisher, Superintendent Government Press. Second edition. Illus. Madras, 1906.

Cloth; 9-7/8 x 6-7/8 x 1¼ in.

GOVERNMENT PRINTING OFFICES. India (British)

Cabinet MM Shelf 7 No. 4

(Madras, 1863) A dictionary of terms used in printing. By H. Morgan, Government Printing Establishment. Madras, printed at the Military Male Orphan Asylum Press, by William Thomas, 1863.

The contents of this book "was mostly taken from Savage". B.&W.

Cloth; 8¾ x 5¼ in. Second copy MM/7/60.

GOVERNMENT PRINTING OFFICES. India

Cabinet LL Shelf 5 No. 60

Madras Government Press. 1917.

See STYLE BOOKS, PRINTERS. Madras (India) Government Press...

GOVERNMENT PRINTING OFFICES, Italy

Cabinet AA Shelf 1 No. 25

Rome, 1820. Stato generale dell'prodotte e delle passivitá dell'appatto della Stamperia Camerale dell'Anno 1821.

Generale statement of accounts for tools, machinery, cost of production, hygiene in the printing office, etc. with prices charged for the printing.

Half morocco; 12½ x 9¼ x ½ in.

GOVERNMENT PRINTING OFFICES. Italy

Cabinet F Shelf 4 No. 77

Torino, 1740-1872. Stamperia Reale. (Imprint of 1842)

See IMPRINTS, Italy. Stamperia Reale, Torino, 1842.

GOVERNMENT PRINTING OFFICE, Japan

Cabinet Q Shelf 7 No. 16

Account of the founding and the directors of the Japan Government Printing Office. In The Asian Printers' and Stationers' Annual and Directory, 1923. Bombey (India) p.13.

Boards; 9 x 6-1/8 in.

GOVERNMENT PRINTING OFFICES. Japan

Cabinet 62 Shelf 2 No. 14

Brief history of fifty years of the operation of the Imperial Government Printing Bureau, Tokyo, Japan, 1923. Illus.

Half morocco; 9 x 6 in.

GOVERNMENT PRINTING OFFICES, Japan

Cabinet 62 Shelf 2 No. 14

Imperial Government Printing Bureau, Tokyo. "Brief history of fifty years", Tokyo, Japan. Together with "Choyo Kai (Morning Sun Association)". History of the establishment and aims of this Japanese Society.

Half morocco; 9 x 6 in.

GOVERNMENT PRINTING OFFICE, Japan

Cabinet J Shelf 5 No. 26

(The) Insatsu Kyoku. The Imperial Government Printing Bureau, Tokyo, 1935.
"The Kokka Yoho". (Catalogue of the treasures in the Emperor's Royal Art Gallery. Published by this office in the early part of the Meiji Era (1880). Now out of print. In three parts. Presented by S. Sugi on behalf of Dr. Yano, head of the Government Printing Bureau, Tokyo, 1935. Figured silk over boards; 13 x 9¾ in. In protective case.

GOVERNMENT PRINTING OFFICES. Japan

Cabinet II Shelf 1 No. 91

Tokyo: Imperial Printing Office (Seibundō)? n.d. Specimens of Japanese and Chinese characters at the Seibundo, Tokyo. 188-
This copy was presented by Imperial Printing Office, Tokyo.

Japanese paper binding; 8¾ x 6¼ x ⅜ in.

GOVERNMENT PRINTING OFFICES. Mexico

Cabinet F Shelf 1 No. 101

Imprenta Real. Mexico City, 1735.
See Early printing in Mexico. Mexico City, 1735. Imprenta Real.

GOVERNMENT PRINTING OFFICES, Pacific Islands

Cabinet 62 Shelf 2 No. 16

Manila. Annual reports of the Director of Bureau of Printing, 1912, 1913.
Picture of printing plant, 1916.
Comments on system of vocational training by John S. Leech, Director.

Items in manila envelope.

GOVERNMENT PRINTING OFFICES. Philippine Islands

Cabinet LL Shelf 6 No. 64

Manila, P.I., 1913. Annual report of the director of printing for the fiscal year ended June 30, 1913. To the Hon. The Secretary of Public Instruction. Bureau of Printing, 1913.

In envelope.

GOVERNMENT PRINTING OFFICES. Philippine Isls.

Cabinet LL Shelf 3 No. 31

Manila, 1910. Bureau of Printing (John A. Leech, Director for Printing) Desk Book; A revised manual of style, useful informations, and specimens of type used by the Bureau of Printing, Government of the Philippine Islands.
Book presented by Hon. John S. Leech.

Full morocco; 10 3/4 x 7 x 1 in.

GOVERNMENT PRINTING OFFICES, Portugal

Cabinet AA Shelf 5 No. 22

Imprensa Nacional (Impressão Regio), Lisbonne. Founded in 1769 under the technical direction of Miguel Manescal da Costa.
For history of above Government Printing Office, see Exhibitions of Printing. Vienna 1873: Notice abrégée de l'Imprimerie Nationale de Lisbonne ... 1873.

GOVERNMENT PRINTING OFFICES, Portugal.

Cabinet S Shelf 3 No. 55

(Lisbon). National Printing Office at Lisbon: An historical and statistical notices, with the catalogue of the products exhibited. (Philadelphia Exhibition of 1876). Lisbon, National Printing Office, 1876.

Cloth; 8¾ x 5½ in.

GOVERNMENT PRINTING OFFICES, Portugal

Cabinet S Shelf 3 No. 55

Lisbon, 1876: National Printing Office at Lisbon: an history and statistical notice, with the catalogue of products exhibited at the Centennial Exhibition (Philadelphia) of 1876. Lisbon: National Printing Office, 1876.

Cloth; 8¾ x 5½ in.

GOVERNMENT PRINTING OFFICES. Russia

Cabinet II Shelf 2 No. 7

Imperial Academy of Sciences, St. Petersburg.

See SPECIMEN BOOKS, TYPES. Russia. Imperial...

GOVERNMENT PRINTING OFFICES. Russia

Cabinet RR Shelf 4 No. 3

Russian Imperial State Paper Manufactory. (History in English, distributed at Columbian Exposition, Chicago, 1893. Printed at the I.S.P.M. St. Petersburg, 1893. Pamphlet.

Second title: Catalogue of exhibits of the Imperial Russian State Paper Manufactory, Columbian Exposition, Chicago, 1893. Pamphlet.

(cont'd)

GOVERNMENT PRINTING OFFICES. Russia. (cont'd)

Cabinet RR Shelf 4 No. 3

(This is also a printing, engraving, typefounding and electrotyping establishment)

Items 12, 13, in collection of pamphlets and excerpts with binder's title "Paper-Making. Pamphlets".

GOVERNMENT PRINTING OFFICES. South America

Cabinet EE Shelf 3 No. 74

Imprensa Nacional. Rio de Janeiro, 1889. Specimen de typos e ornatos.

Boards; 11-3/8 x 8¼ x 3/4 in.

GOVERNMENT PRINTING OFFICES. Spain

Cabinet 83 Shelf 2 No. 60

Imprenta Real, Madrid. 1799. Muestras de los punzones y matrices de la letra que se funde en el obrador de la Imprenta Real. Año de 1799.
Specimen of punches and matrices of the types that are cast in the workroom of the Imprenta Real.

Paper boards; 8½ x 6-3/4 x 3/4 in.

GOVERNMENT PRINTING OFFICES, Spain

Cabinet AA Shelf 5 No. 5

Imprenta Real: Reglamento para la dirección y gobierno de la Imprenta Real y demas ramos. Madrid: En la misma Imprenta Real, año de 1799.
Regulations for the management and government of the Imprenta Real and its branches

Marbled boards; 8 x 5½ in.

GOVERNMENT PRINTING OFFICES, Spain

Cabinet AA Shelf 5 No. 2

(Segovia, 1778). Privision Reale ... para que se establezcan en la Ciudad de Segovia ... una imprento ... Baxo la dirección de Don Antonio Espinosa de los Monteros, gravador principal de la Casa de Moneda de dicha Ciudad. Segovia, 1778.

Calf; 8 x 5-7/8 in.

GOVERNMENT PRINTING OFFICES (Sp. America)

Cabinet Shelf No.

(Guatemala, National Printing Office). La Tipografia Nacional de Guatemala, y su director el senor Nicolas Reyes O.

Has picture of building, and portrait of Reyes.

Article in El Arte tipografico, Ano 28, No.4, Oct-Nov-Dec., 1931, p.139.

GOVERNMENT PRINTING OFFICE — United States

Cabinet LL Shelf 3 No. 30.01

Abridged style manual. April, 1933. U.S. Government Printing Office, Washington, D.C.

Paper; 9 x 5-7/8 in.

GOVERNMENT PRINTING OFFICE — United States

Cabinet S Shelf 6 No. 4

Amazing story of the Government Printing Office. By Henry Litchfield West. [Excerpt from the "Bookman", Dec.,1918, Jan., 1919]

Item in box labelled "Brochures and Excerpts relating to Government Printing and Printers in U.S.A.

GOVERNMENT PRINTING OFFICE — United States

Cabinet 64 Shelf 2 No. 3

Annual Reports of the Congressional and Public Printers, for years, 1870, 1878,1880,1881, 1883,1884,1885.

7 items (brochures) tied in one bundle.

GOVERNMENT PRINTING OFFICE — United States

Cabinet 64 Shelf 2 No. 4

Annual Report of the Public Printer (Th. E. Benedict)...for the fiscal year ending June 30, 1886. Washington, Government Printing Office, 1887.

Cloth; 9 x $5\frac{3}{4}$ in.

GOVERNMENT PRINTING OFFICE — United States

Cabinet 64 Shelf 2 No. 5

Annual Report of Public Printing (F.W. Palmer, Public Printer), 1891-1894. Washington, D.C.

Cloth, 9 x $5\frac{3}{4}$ in.

GOVERNMENT PRINTING OFFICE, — United States

Cabinet QQ Shelf 4 No. 46

Annual report of the Government Printer for the year ended June 30, 1895. U.S. Government Printing Office, Washington, D. C.

Calf; 9 x $5\frac{3}{4}$ in

GOVERNMENT PRINTING OFFICE — United States

Cabinet 64 Shelf 2 No. 6

Annual Report of the Public Printer (Th. E. Benedict), 1895-1896. Washington, D.C.

Cloth; 9 x 6 in.

GOVERNMENT PRINTING OFFICE — United States

Cabinet 64 Shelf 2 No. 7

Annual Report of the Public Printer (F.W. Palmer), 1897-1898. Washington, D.C.

Cloth; 9 x 6 in.

GOVERNMENT PRINTING OFFICE — United States

Cabinet 64 Shelf 2 No. 8

Annual Report of the Public Printer (F.W. Palmer), 1899. Washington, D.C.

Cloth; $9\frac{1}{4}$ x 6 in.

GOVERNMENT PRINTING OFFICE — United States

Cabinet 64 Shelf 2 No. 9

Annual Report of the Public Printer (F.W. Palmer), 1900-1901. Washington, D.C.

Cloth; $9\frac{1}{4}$ x 6 in.

GOVERNMENT PRINTING OFFICE — United States

Cabinet 64 Shelf 2 No. 10

Annual Report of the Public Printer (F.W.Palmer), 1902-1903. Washington, D.C.

Cloth; $9\frac{1}{4}$ x 6 in.

GOVERNMENT PRINTING OFFICE — United States

Cabinet 64 Shelf 2 No. 11

Annual Report of the Public Printer (F. W. Palmer) 1904-1905. Washington, D. C.

Cloth; $9\frac{1}{4}$ x 6 in.

GOVERNMENT PRINTING OFFICE — United States

Cabinet 64 Shelf 2 No. 12

Annual Report of the Public Printer (Chas.A. Stillings), 1906-7. Washington, D.C.

Cloth; $9\frac{1}{4}$ x 6 in.

GOVERNMENT PRINTING OFFICE — United States

Cabinet 64 Shelf 2 No. 13

Annual Report of the Public Printer (Sam'l. B. Donnelly), 1908. Washington, D.C.

Cloth; $9\frac{1}{4}$ x 6 in.

GOVERNMENT PRINTING OFFICE — United States

Cabinet 64 Shelf 2 No. 14

Annual Report of the Public Printer (Sam'l B. Donnelly), 1910-part 1. Washington, D.C.

Cloth; $9\frac{1}{4}$ x $5\frac{3}{4}$ in.

GOVERNMENT PRINTING OFFICE — United States

Cabinet 64 Shelf 2 No. 15

Annual Report of the Public Printer (Sam'l B. Donnelly), 1911. Washington, D.C.

Cloth; $9\frac{1}{4}$ x $5\frac{3}{4}$ in.

GOVERNMENT PRINTING OFFICE — United States

Cabinet 64 Shelf 2 No. 16

Annual Report of the Government Printer (Sam'l B. Donnelly), 1912. Washington, D. C.

Cloth; $9\frac{1}{4}$ x $5\frac{3}{4}$ in.

GOVERNMENT PRINTING OFFICE — United States

Cabinet 64 Shelf 2 No. 17

Annual Report of the Public Printer (Cornelius Ford), 1913. Washington, D.C.

Cloth; $9\frac{1}{4}$ x $5\frac{3}{4}$ in.

GOVERNMENT PRINTING OFFICE United States

Cabinet 64 Shelf 2 No. 18

Annual Report of the Government Printer (Cornelius Ford), 1914. Washington, D. C.

Cloth; 9¾ x 5¾ in.

GOVERNMENT PRINTING OFFICE United States

Cabinet 64 Shelf 2 No. 19

Annual Report of the Government Printer (Cornelius Ford), 1915. Washington, D. C.

Cloth; 9¾ x 5¾ in.

GOVERNMENT PRINTING OFFICE United States

Cabinet 64 Shelf 2 No. 20

Annual Report of the Public Printer (Cornelius Ford), 1916. Washington, D. C.

Cloth; 9¾ x 5¾ in.

GOVERNMENT PRINTING OFFICE United States

Cabinet 64 Shelf 2 No. 21

Annual Report of the Public Printer (Cornelius Ford), 1917. Washington, D.C.

Cloth; 9¾ x 5¾ in.

GOVERNMENT PRINTING OFFICE United States

Cabinet 64 Shelf 3 No. 1

Annual Report of the Public Printer (Cornelius Ford), 1918. Washington, D.C.

Cloth; 9¾ x 6 in.

GOVERNMENT PRINTING OFFICE United States

Cabinet 64 Shelf 3 No. 2

Annual Report of the Public Printer (Cornelius Ford), 1919. Washington, D. C.

Paper; 9¾ x 6 in.

GOVERNMENT PRINTING OFFICE United States

Cabinet 64 Shelf 3 No. 3

Annual Report of the Public Printer (Cornelius Ford), 1920. Washington, D.C.

Cloth; 9¾ x 6 in.

GOVERNMENT PRINTING OFFICE United States

Cabinet 64 Shelf 3 No. 4

Annual Report of the Public Printer (George H. Carter), 1921-1928. Washington, D.C.

Cloth; 9¾ x 6 in.

GOVERNMENT PRINTING OFFICE United States

Cabinet 64 Shelf 3 No. 5

Annual Report of the Public Printer (George H. Carter), 1929. Washington, D.C.

Cloth; 9¾ x 6 in.

GOVERNMENT PRINTING OFFICE United States

Cabinet 64 Shelf 3 No. 6

Annual Report of the Public Printer (George H. Carter), 1930. Washington, D.C.

Cloth; 9¾ x 6 in.

GOVERNMENT PRINTING OFFICE United States

Cabinet 64 Shelf 3 No. 7

Annual Report of the Public Printer (George H. Carter), 1931. Washington, D.C.

Cloth; 9¾ x 6 in.

GOVERNMENT PRINTING OFFICE United States

Cabinet 64 Shelf 3 No. 8

Annual Report of the Public Printer (George H. Carter), 1932. Washington, D. C.

Cloth; xxxx 9¾ x 6 in.

GOVERNMENT PRINTING OFFICE United States

Cabinet 64 Shelf 3 No. 9

Annual Report of the Public Printer (George H. Carter), 1933. Washington, D.C.

Cloth; 9¾ c 6 in.

GOVERNMENT PRINTING OFFICE United States

Cabinet 64 Shelf 3 No. 10

Annual Report of the Public Printer (A.E. Giegengack), 1934. Washington, D.C.

Cloth; 9¾ x 6 in.

GOVERNMENT PRINTING OFFICE, United States

Cabinet 62 Shelf 2 No. 8

Base printing plant of the A.E.F., at Langres, France. View Book, 1918.

Half morocco; 7½ x 9½ in.

GOVERNMENT PRINTING OFFICE, United States

Cabinet 62 Shelf 2 No. 25

Bond, Speech on resolution to separate Government from the Press (p.7, Reform in Public Printing), Washington, D.C. April, 1838. Brochure.

With other items in manila envelope

GOVERNMENT PRINTING OFFICE, United States.

Cabinet S Shelf 6 No. 4

(Boston, Mass. 1822-29). H.R.-No. 7 Commonwealth of Massachusetts. In House of Representatives June 9, 1829. The Clerk of the House, who was directed by order of the 8th inst. to procure copies of the written contracts for executing the State Printing ... (Brochure).

Item in box labelled "Brochures and excerpts relating to Government printing and printers in U.S.A.

GOVERNMENT PRINTING OFFICE, United States

Cabinet 62 Shelf 2 No. 18

Boston, 1846-89. City documents relating to printing in Boston: Reports, Acts and Ordinances, Contracts for Printing, etc.

Half morocco; 9 x 5-7/8 in.

GOVERNMENT PRINTING OFFICE, United States.

Cabinet 8 Shelf 6 No. 4

Boston, 1889. Publication of the Province Laws A stenographic report of the hearing before the joint standing committee on printing of the legislature of 1889...To investigate the work of the Commission on the Province Laws. Brochure.

In box labelled "Brochures and excerpts relating to Government Printing and Printers in U.S.A.

GOVERNMENT PRINTING OFFICE, United States

Cabinet 62 Shelf 2 No. 20

Boston, 1897. Reports, majority and minority of the joint standing committee on printing, on thr purchase of a municipal printing plant. Boston, 1897.

Morocco; 9 x 5-3/4 x 1-3/8 in.

GOVERNMENT PRINTING OFFICE, United States

Cabinet 62 Shelf 2 No. 19

Boston, 1897-98. Annual report of the printing department of the City of Boston. Boston: Municipal Printing Office, 1908. Illus.

Limp morocco, 9¼ x 6 in.

GOVERNMENT PRINTING OFFICES, United States

Cabinet 62 Shelf 2 No. 20.01

Boston, 1902-1903. Annual report of the printing department of the City of Boston.

Cloth 9¼ x 5-3/4 in.

GOVERNMENT PRINTING OFFICE, United States

Cabinet 62 Shelf 2 No. 20.02

Boston, 1909-12, 1913-17, 1922-28. Annual reports of the printing department of the City of Boston.

Also list of obsolete documents and where located. Communication from City Clerk to Board of Alsermen, Boston, May 8, 1899.

17 Pamphlets in one bundle

GOVERNMENT PRINTING OFFICE, United States

Cabinet LL Shelf 6 No. 11

Boston Municipal Printing Office. 1910. Price list of printing for the municipal printing department. Revised to Sept. 1, 1900.

Folded in: a letter to Theo. L. DeVinne commenting the excessive cost of printing in the Boston municipal plant. Letter dated Nov. 12, 1900. Signed by Cushing of the Norwood Press.

Cloth, stamped; 8 x 5¼ in.

GOVERNMENT PRINTING OFFICES, United States

Cabinet 8 Shelf 6 No. 9.01

(California) Laws in force governing the State Printing of California. Sacramento: State Office, J. D. Young, Supt. State Printing, 1887.

Brochure, in manila envelope.

GOVERNMENT PRINTING OFFICES, United States

Cabinet S Shelf 6 No. 9.01

(California) Report of the Assembly of the State of California...By F. T. Dunn, Expert. Sacramento: State Office, A. J. Johnson, Supt. State Printing, 1911.

Brochure, in manila envelope.

GOVERNMENT PRINTING OFFICE, United States

Cabinet 62 Shelf 2 No. 25

Complaint of John C. Rives, Public Printer, complaint of loss of money under the term of his contract. August 13, 1850, Washington, D.C. Circular

With other items in manila envelope

GOVERNMENT PRINTING OFFICE United States

Cabinet S Shelf 6 No. 4

(The) Congressional Record. By Hilton Butler. (Excerpt from the "American Mercury", Dec., 1925)

Account of the function of the Congressional Record, with statistics of printing same.

Item in box labelled "Brochures and Excerpt Relating to Government Printing and Printer in U.S.A.

GOVERNMENT PRINTING OFFICE United States

Cabinet 64 Shelf 2 No. 2

Congressional Reports on Proceedings on public printing, binding, etc.,April 21, 1858. Superintendent of Printing, Geo.W. Bowman.

Item in Congressional Proceedings, 1851-59. (Pencilled pages, 71-459)

Half calf; 9½ x 5¾ in.

GOVERNMENT PRINTING OFFICE United States

Cabinet LL Shelf 3 No. 30

Correct orthography of geographic names, revised to January 1911. U.S. Government Printing Office, Washington, D.C.

Cloth; 9¼ x 6 in.

GOVERNMENT PRINTING OFFICE United States

Cabinet 64 Shelf 3 No. 19

Covode Investigation, naval contracts, Public Printing, etc., 1860. Washington, D.C.

Cloth; 9 x 5¾ in.

GOVERNMENT PRINTING OFFICE United States

Cabinet LL Shelf 6 No. 49

Dedication of Harding Hall in the United States Government Printing Office, Friday, May 23, 1930. Washington, D.C. Illus. brochure.

Item in box labelled "Apprenticeship: Various Items".

GOVERNMENT PRINTING OFFICE United States

Cabinet 62 Shelf 2 No. 24

Defrees, John D., Public Printer, to Ebenezer B. Finley. An open letter: a review of Mr. Finley's report on the Government Printing Office. Washington D. C., Feb.19, 1879.

Item inserted in book with title "HISTORY OF THE GOVERNMENT PRINTING OFFICE" ...by R. W. Kerr

---

GOVERNMENT PRINTING OFFICE, United States

Cabinet 21 Shelf 2 No. 3

Description of the Public Printing Office in Washington, D.C., 1859.

Illus. exterior and interior views.

Article in THE PRINTER, vol.2, July, 1859, p.60

GOVERNMENT PRINTING OFFICE, United States.

Cabinet LL Shelf 6 No. 49 Box

Exercises on the occasion of the graduation of apprentices. United States Government Printing Office, Class of 1930, June 4. Illus. Pamphlet.

On p.3 "A printer's prayer" by Henry Lewis Bullen.

In box labelled "Apprenticeship: Various items".

GOVERNMENT PRINTING OFFICE United States

Cabinet S Shelf 6 No. 4

Harding Hall Dedicated. (Reprinted article from "Printing", New York City, May 31, 1930).

Brochure. Includes program, list of attendants, ets.

Item in box labelled "Brochures and Excerpts relating to Government Printing and Printers in U.S.A.

GOVERNMENT PRINTING OFFICE United States

Cabinet 62 Shelf 2 No. 21

Historical sketch of the Government Printing Office in Washington, D.C. 1861-1916. Illus.

Half morocco; 10¼ x 6-3/4 in.

GOVERNMENT PRINTING OFFICE United States

Cabinet S Shelf 2 No. 159

Making Uncle Sam's Money. By Joseph E. Ralph. Extra illustrated. With portrait of J.E. Ralph, director of Bureau of Engraving and Printing. Washington, D.C., 1909.

Half morocco; 9½ x 6¾ in.

GOVERNMENT PRINTING OFFICE United States

Cabinet EE Shelf 1 No. 38

Our type faces. Job division. A complete showing of the printing types, borders, ornaments, brass rules, cuts, etc. U.S. Government Printing Office. Washington, D.C, 1900

Cloth; 11 x 8¾ in.

GOVERNMENT PRINTING OFFICE, United States

Cabinet 62 Shelf 2 No. 24

History of the Government Printing Office at Washington, D.C. With a brief record of the public printing for a century, 1789-1881. By R. W. Kerr, of the Government Printing Office. Lancaster, Pa., 1881. Illus.

Cloth; 9½ x 6 in.

GOVERNMENT PRINTING OFFICE United States

Cabinet LL Shelf 3 No. 27

Manual of style for use of copy editors, proof readers, operators, and compositors ~~xxxxxx~~ engaged in the production of executive, congressional, and departmental publications (1st ed.), Sept., 1908. Government Printing Office. Washington, D.C.

Cloth; 9½ x 5¾ in.

GOVERNMENT PRINTING OFFICE United States

Cabinet S Shelf 5 No. 30

Printing and Publishing. Census of manufactures for 1905. Bulletin 79. Department of Commerce and Labor. Washington, D.C., 1907.

Half morocco; 11¾ x 9¼ in.

GOVERNMENT PRINTING OFFICE United States

Cabinet 61 Shelf 1 No. 2

History of the Government Printing Office; its magnitude and its work. The newly appointed Public Printer, Sterling P. Pounds.

Article in "The Paper World", vol.4, No.5, May 1882, p.5.

GOVERNMENT PRINTING OFFICE United States

Cabinet LL Shelf 3 No. 28

Manual of style for use of copy editors, proof-readers, operators, and compositors engaged in the executive, congressional and departmental publications. Second edition, Nov., 1909. U.S. Government Printing Office. Washington, D.C.

Cloth; 9½ x 6 in.

GOVERNMENT PRINTING OFFICE, United States.

Cabinet S Shelf 5 No. 14

Printing our money and stamps, by Waldon Fawcett, in Van Norden Magazine, June, 1907: An illustrated article describing the processes as practiced in Washington, D. C.

Bound with other items in collection "Printing Processes," item 15.

GOVERNMENT PRINTING OFFICE, United States

Cabinet 62 Shelf 2 No. 25

Investigation of Public Printing, May 31, June, 12, 1860. Majority and minority views and reports. In the Senate, 36th Congress, 1st Session, Wehington, D.C.

Brochure, with other items in manila envelope

GOVERNMENT PRINTING OFFICE, United States.

Cabinet S Shelf 5 No. 1

Nation's print shop and its methods, The. by J. D. Whelpley, in The American Review of Reviews Nov., 1903; A brief account which includes description of plant, reasons for the government doing its own printing, how the system grew up, wages, etc. Illus.

Bound in collection "Various Printing Plants-Brochures, item 13.

GOVERNMENT PRINTING OFFICE United States

Cabinet 64 Shelf 3 No. 18

Report, 1888. To provide for printing government securities in the highest style of the art. Submitted by Mr. Wheeler.

An examination into the work and management of the Bureau of Engraving and Printing.

Cloth; 9¼ x 6 in.

GOVERNMENT PRINTING OFFICE United States

Cabinet MM Shelf 6 No. 25

(The) Making of a book. Operations that lead to its proper construction, together with useful tables and information. Prepared for use in the several divisions of the Government Printing Office, Washington, D.C. 1909

Cloth; 9½ x 6 in.

GOVERNMENT PRINTING OFFICE United States

Cabinet 62 Shelf 2 No. 26

Official manual and constitution book of the Government Printing Office Mutual Relief Association, Washington, D.C. Organized April, 1883. Incorporated April 5, 1889. Illus.

Cloth; 7¾ x 6 in.

GOVERNMENT PRINTING OFFICE United States

Cabinet 64 Shelf 3 No. 21

Report on Government Printing. No.2494 of Senate reports, 2nd Session, 51st Congress, 1890-91. Washington, D.C.

Calf; 9 x 6 in.

GOVERNMENT PRINTING OFFICE United States

Cabinet MM Shelf 6 No. 25.01

Making of a book (The). Information for the instruction of apprentices in the U.S. Government Printing Office...Prepared under the direction of John Green, Deputy Public Printer, Washington, 1933.

Cloth; 9⅛ x 6 in.

GOVERNMENT PRINTING OFFICE United States

Cabinet 62 Shelf 2 No. 27

Official Manual and Constitution of the Government Printing Office Mutual Relief Association. Organized April, 1883, Incorporated April 15, 1889. Washington, D.C. Illus. [n.d. After 1902]

Paper wrapper; 7 x 8½ in.

GOVERNMENT PRINTING OFFICE United States

Cabinet 64 Shelf 3 No. 20

Report on Public Printing Office. Senate executive documents, 2nd Session, 51st Congress, 1890-1891, vol.1, Nos.1 to 75 inclusive.

See index p.viii as marked

For Cherokee Nation (see index p.4)

Calf; 9¼ x 6 in.

GOVERNMENT PRINTING OFFICE United States

Cabinet 64 Shelf 3 No. 24

Report on the administration of the Government Printing Office under Mr. Defrees, 1879.
Reports Nos. 119, 169-291 in Reports of Committees, 1878-79. Washington, D.C.

Calf; 9 x 6 in.

GOVERNMENT PRINTING OFFICE, United States

Cabinet 62 Shelf 2 No. 25

Speech of the Hon. James L. Orr, of S. Carolina, delivered in the House of Representatives, Feb. 12, 1851, on the bill to indemnify the Public Printer. Washington: Printed at the Congressional Globe Office, 1851. Circular

With other items in manila envelope

GOVERNMENT PRINTING OFFICE United States

Cabinet 62 Shelf 2 No. 22

Suppressed documents. Treasuary inventigation. Report on theprinting of the public money. Washington, D. C., 1864.

Cloth; 9¼ x 6 in.

GOVERNMENT PRINTING OFFICE United States

Cabinet 64 Shelf 3 No. 23

Report on the administration of the Government Printing Office under Public Printer, Mr. Benedict. Washington, D.C.
Report in House Reports, 1887-1888.

Cloth; 9 x 6 in.

GOVERNMENT PRINTING OFFICE, United States

Cabinet 62 Shelf 2 No. 25

Speech of the Hon. John A. Curley, of Ohio, on the subject of Public Printing. Delivered in the House of Representatives, May, 30th, 1860, Washington, D.C.

Brochure, with other items in manila envelop

GOVERNMENT PRINTING OFFICE, United States

Cabinet A Shelf 2 No. 91

Uncle Sam as world's greatest printer. Story of the Government Printing Office in Washington ...Great reforms in operation and morale under the new Public Printer, George H. Carter.
Article with portrait of G.H.C. in the Graphic Arts Section of the Boston Evening Transcript, Aug., 29, 1923, part four, p.7.

GOVERNMENT PRINTING OFFICE United States

Cabinet 64 Shelf 3 No. 22

Report on the enlargement of the Public Printing Office.
Report No.30 of House Reports, 3rd Session 46th Congress, 1880-81. vol.1.

Calf; 9 x 6 in.

GOVERNMENT PRINTING OFFICE United States

Cabinet S Shelf 6 No. 4

Speech of Hon. Truman Smith of Conn., on printing the returns of the Seventh Census, and on congressional and departmental printing generally.: Delivered in the Senate of the U.S., Jan.12, 1852. Printed by John T. Towers.

Item in box labelled "Brochures and Excerpt Relating to Government Printing and Printers in U.S./ A.

GOVERNMENT PRINTING OFFICE United States

Cabinet 61 Shelf 1 No. 6

Uncle Sam' paper and printing bills. Article with exterior views of the U.S. Government Printing Office and the Bureau of Engraving and Printing. Washington, D.C.

Illus.article in "The Paper World", vol.20, No.5, May 1890, p.1

GOVERNMENT PRINTING OFFICE United States

Cabinet S Shelf 5 No. 31

Report to the President [of the U.S.A.] by Wm.S. Rossiter upon conditions prevailing in the Government Printing Office. Reply thereto by Chas. A. Stillings, Public Printer. Washington, D.C., 1908.

Cloth; 9¼ x 6 in.

GOVERNMENT PRINTING OFFICE, United States

Cabinet 62 Shelf 2 No. 25

Speech of the Hon. Truman Smith of Conn., on printing the return of the seventh census, and on Congressional and Departmental printing generally: Delivered in the Senate of the U.S. January 12, 1852. Washington: Printed by John T. Towers. Circular.

With other items in manila envelope

GOVERNMENT PRINTING OFFICE United States

Cabinet EE Shelf 4 No. 72

What may be seen in the Government Printing Office in Washington D.C. Booklet which shows some of the machines supplied to the various printing departments of the U.S. Goverment Printing Office.
R. Hoe & Co., New York-London. Illus. Brochure.
Has views of R.Hoe & Co's works in London.

Item in manila envelope.

GOVERNMENT PRINTING OFFICE United States

Cabinet LL Shelf 3 No. 1

Simplified spelling. For the use of Government Departments. By Chas. A. Stillings, Public Printer. Washington, D.C. 1906.
Brochure, 1st ed.

Item in box labelled "Proof Reading: Various Items".

GOVERNMENT PRINTING OFFICE, United States

Cabinet 81 Shelf 2 No. 31

State and Congress printing. vol.2 of "Printers' Scraps" collected by Joel Munsell of Albany, prior to 1860.

Half morocco; 8-7/8 x 7-1/8 in.

GOW, LEONARD.

Cabinet M Shelf 2 No. 55

Collection of Chinese porcelain. A set of plates printed by Geo. W. Jones. Gough Square, London, England, 1931.

In Folder; 13 x 10½ in.

GOVERNMENT PRINTING OFFICE United States

Cabinet 62 Shelf 2 No. 23

Souvenir of a complimentary dinner given to Almon M. Klapp, by gentlemen connected with the Government Printing Office, at the Arlington Hotel, Sept.,2, 1876. Washington City. Printed by Richard A. Mecomb, 1876. With portrait Mr. Klapp.

Signed presentation copy.

Half morocco; 9¼ x 6¾ in.

GOVERNMENT PRINTING OFFICE United States

Cabinet LL Shelf 3 No. 29

Style Book: A compilation of rules governing executive, congressional and departmental printing...Including the Congressional Record. Government Printing Office. Washington, D.C., 1911.

Cloth; 9¼ x 6 in.

GRABERG, FREDERIC

Cabinet Z Shelf 4 No. 16

(Specimens of vignettes etc., nine leaves) Graves et fondus par Frederic Graberg a Z Zurich. n.d. circa 1860.

Item in manila envelope.

GRABHORN, EDWIN & ROBERT.

Cabinet See Imprints, United States.

Shelf

No.

GRAFTON, RICHARD

Cabinet T Books printed by Richard Grafton, London, 1537-1553. Bibliographical notes. With printer's device and portrait.

Shelf 2 see

No. 6 DIBDIN'S "Typographical Antiquities" ...London, 1810-19, vol.iii, p.421

[vol.3]

GRAHAM, JOHN

Cabinet LL Compositor's text-book: or instructions in the elements of the art of printing; consisting of an essay on punctuation, directions on the use of the capitals; rules for distributing and composing; with various schemes of imposition...Glasgow, 1848.

Shelf 3

No. 11

Cloth; 7-5/8 x 4½ in.

GRABHORN, FLORENCE AND EDWIN

Cabinet S Typography of Shakspere's Midsommer Nightes Dreame. By Mark Harvey Liddel. Printed in the City of Indianapolis, U.S.A. by Florence and Edwin Grabhorn at their shop, The Studio 10th Oct. 1918.

Shelf 4

No. 26

Half morocco; 7-7/8 x 5¾ x ¼ in.

GRAFTON, RICHARD

Cabinet T Memoire of R. Grafton, together with a list of books printed by him, 1537-1571.

Shelf 2 see

No. 2 AMES, JOSEPH and WM. HERBERT Typographical Antiquities...vol.1, pp. 501-538

GRAHAM, MICHAEL

Cabinet 00 Glasgow Press, The early: a paper read to the members of The Old Glasgow Club, on March 19, 1906. Glasgow.

Shelf 4

No. 38

Half morocco; 8½ x 6¾ x ½ in.

GRACIAN, Juan

Cabinet X Brief bio-bibliographical note, with printer mark, Gracian (Alcalá) 1572-1578

Shelf 3 see

HAEBLER, KONRAD. (Spanish and Portuguese printer marks...p.xxxv)

No. 19

GRAFTON PRESS, THE

Cabinet G Nonnes preestes tale of the cok and hen. Published 1902 by The Grafton Press, New York City. Printed by Theodore L. DeVinne & Co.

Shelf 1

No. 60

Boards; 9 x 6¾ in.

GRAHAM'S Magazine

Cabinet 31 Philadelphia, Pa., Graham's Magazine, vols.1 & 2, 1853-4

Shelf 1

No. 10 & 11

Half morocco; 9¾ x 6½ in.

GRADUALE ROMANUM

Cabinet 13 See Incunabula. Graduale Romanum [Edited by Franciscus de Brugis] Venice, Johannes Emericus de Spira, 1499-1500.

Shelf 1

No. 4

GRÄGER, U. (Translator)

Cabinet RR (Die) Entfarbung und das bleichen der hadern. von E. Bourdilliat...Ins Deutsche ubertragen von E. Grager. Mit 5 lithographerten figuren. Weimar, 1867.

Shelf 2

On bleaching and dying rags for paper making.

No. 12

Paper bds; 7 x 4-5/8 x ½ in.

GRAMINAUS, THEODOR

Cabinet X Cologne, 1569-1594

Shelf see

HEITZ, PAUL.

No. 3 Kölner büchermarken...p.xxxi

20

GRADUALE ROMANUM

Cabinet 13 Venice, 1499-1500, Luca Antonio Giunta

Shelf 2 vols.

No. 4 See INCUNABULA. Graduale Romanum...

GRAHAM, GEORGE R.

Cabinet 80 Graham's Lady's & Gentleman's Magazine.

Shelf 2 see

PERIODICALS, United States Graham's Lady's & Gentleman's Magazine...

No. 54

GRAMMAR

Cabinet Principles of grammar.

Shelf See PROOF READING.

No.

GRAFTON, RICHARD

Cabinet MM Account of R. Grafton, with portrait; list of book printed by him; his device.

Shelf 3

No. 15 See JOHNSON, JOHN. Typographia... London, 1824, vol.1, p.513

GRAHAM, J. B.

Cabinet S Handset reminiscences. Recollections of an old-time printer and journalist. By J.B. Graham, Salt Lake City, Utah, 1915. Portrait.

Shelf 4

No. 103

Cloth; 8½ x 5½ in.

GRAN, HEINRICH

Cabinet X Brief bibliographical note, with printer marks, Gran, Hagenau (Alsace-Lorraine), 1489-1523.

Shelf 3 see

HEITZ, PAUL.

No. 13 Elsässasiche büchermarken...p.xxii, plate lxiii

GRAN, HEINRICH

Cabinet Y Shelf 4 No. 4

(Notes relating to the Gran 15th century press at Hagenau)

see VOULLIÉME, ERNST. (Die) Deutschen drucker des fünfzehnten jahrhunderts...p.50

GRAND-CARTERET, JOHN

Cabinet K Shelf 2 No. 3

Almanachs Francais, bibliographie-iconographie des almanachs...et autres publications annuelles éditées a Paris (1600-1895). Ouvrage illustré de 5 planches coloriées et de 36 vignettes. Paris, 1896.

Bibliography of almanachs and other annual publications edited ** Paris, 1600-1895.

Half morocco; 10½ x 7 in.

GRAND-CARTERET, JOHN

Cabinet RR Shelf 1 No. 16

Papeterie et papetiers de l'ancien temps. A l'Expostition Universelle Internationale de 1900, a Paris. Rapport du Comite d'Instalation. Illus. Paris, 1900.

Historical account of paper selling and sellers. Includes alphabetic list of paper makers in France, 1691 to about 1856.

Half morocco; 11¼ x 8 x 1-3/8 in.

GRANDJEAN, PHILIPPE

Cabinet V Shelf 6 No. 22

Roman types engraved by Grandjean et Alexandre, 1693 for the Imprimerie Royale. Specimen See Imprimerie Royale. Notice sur les types étrangers...Paris, 1847. p. 46.

GRANGÉ

Cabinet F Shelf 4 No. 85

See Early Printing in France. Paris, 1773. Grangé.

GRANGIER, PIERRE

Cabinet V Shelf 5 No. 2.01

Printer, Dijon (France), circa 1530.

See URSEL, C. Notes sur le libraire et imprimeur Dijonnais Pierre I. Grangier...

GRANJON, ROBERT.

Cabinet Shelf No.

Biographical and bibliographical relating to Robert Granjon.

In the L&M. NEWS, vol.6, No.5, Feb., 1933, p.118

GRANJON, ROBERT.

Cabinet W Shelf 2 No. 155

Caractères de civilité de Robert Granjon, et les imprimeurs Flamands. Maurits Sabbe et Marius Audin. Lyon, 1921.

Brief bibliographical comparison of Granjon's Civilite types, and those of Flemish design in the possession of Plantin.

Has signature of Stanley Morison on cover.

Boards; 11½ x 7¾ in.

GRANJON, ROBERT

Cabinet W Shelf 3 No. 27

Civilité, du caractère dit de, et des livres qui ont été imprimés avec ce caractère au XVIe siécle. Par Jerome Pichon. Paris [1850].

Item B (Mélanges) in vol. with binder's title "Eight French typographic items".

GRANJON, ROBERT

Cabinet FF Shelf 3 No. 50

Civilité-schriften (die) des Robert Granjon in Lyon und die Flamischen drucker des 16th Jahrhunderts. von Maurits Sabbe et Marius Audin. Wien, 1925. Facs.

Boards; 11¼ x 7½ in.

GRANJON, ROBERT.

Cabinet 69 Shelf 1 No. 57

Civilite types created by Robert Granjon. Used by Philippe Danfrie in his printed work "Declaraction de l'Usage du graphometre." Paris, 1597.

Morocco; 7¾ x 5 x ½ in. Brunet 2, 485.

GRANJON, ROBERT

Cabinet Z Shelf 1 No. 21.01

Civilité types, designed by Robert Granjon of Lyon, France in 1557. Reproduced by Enschedé in Zonen. Haarlem, 1926.

Specimen book which includes a brief account of the engraving and engravers of the types known as "Civilité". See pp.38-39.

Boards; 9-3/4 x 7-3/4 x ½ in.

GRANJON, ROBERT

Cabinet U Shelf 5 No. 38

Greek types for Plantin cut by Granjon of Lyon. Account of

see PROCTOR, ROBERT. Bibliographical essays...London, 1905, p.108

GRANJON, ROBERT

Cabinet M Shelf 2 No. 56

Typecutter and printer of the 16th century. [Printed by Geo. W. Jones, London, 1931, for the] Mergenthaler Linotype Co., Brooklyn, New York, 1931.

Shows specimens of types. Has Granjon device.

Boards, vellum back; 13½ x 8½ in. In slip case.

GRANNIS, RUTH S.

Cabinet S Shelf 1 No. 38

List of the writings of Theodore Low DeVinne Compiled by Miss Ruth S. Grannis for the year book of The Grolier Club for 1914.

In Volume "Theodore Low DeVinne, printer" p. 97.

Boards; 10¼ x 7 in.

GRANNIS, RUTH SHEPARD

Cabinet S Shelf 5 No. 25.01

New York printers and the celebration of the French Revolution of 1830.

Excerpt from "Bibliographical Essays: A tribute to Wilberforce Eames". Reprinted in the "Belles-Lettres Repository", vol.II, Saturday May 29, 1926.

Item in box labelled "Colonial printing and printers. Miscellaneous items".

GRANNISS, RUTH SHEPARD

Cabinet S Shelf 3 No. 104

(The) New York printers and the celebration of the French Revolution of 1830. By Ruth Shepard Granniss, Librarian of The Grolier Club.

Biblio-historical account.

P. 193 in volume, Wilberforce Eames ... A tribute to. Cambridge, 1924.

GRANT, JAMES

Cabinet OO Shelf 4 No. 4

Newspaper Press, The. Its origin, progress and present position. By James Grant. In 3 vols. London, 1871-2.

Cloth; 9 x 5-5/8 in.

GRANT, JOHN CAMERON

Cabinet S Shelf 5 No. 14

Typographical printing surfaces. The Technology and mechanism employed in their production ...By Lucien A. Legros ... and John Cameron Grant. London, 1914. Prospectus.

Bound with other items in collection"Printing Processes", item 10.

GRAPHIC ART ASSOCIATION

Cabinet JJ Shelf 3 No. 39

Proceedings...June 27th, and 28th, 1926.

See

SOCIETIES, PRINTERS. Graphic Arts Association...

GRAPHIC ARTS BOARD OF TRADE

Cabinet Q Shelf 4 No. 27

Rating book for the guidance of members who sell printing, publishing...paper box and paper trades. 4th ed. January, 1919.

Limp cloth; 6-5/8 x 4¾ in.

GRANT, JOHN CAMERON & L.A. LEGROS.

Cabinet FF Shelf 3 No. 36

Typographical printing surfaces. Technology and mechasim of their production. By Lucien Alphonse Legros and John Cameron Grant, London. 1916. Illus.

Cloth: 10x6¾x2-1/8"

GRAPHIC ARTS

Cabinet V Shelf 6 No. 37

(Les) Arts & Industries Graphiques...

see

DEGAAST, GEORGES. (Les) Arts... Paris, 1925.

GRAPHIC ARTS BOARD OF TRADE

Cabinet Q Shelf 4 No. 28

Rating Book...14th ed., January, 1923. Containint the entire United States.

Limp cloth; 6½ x 4½ in.

GRANT, LEGROS & Co.

Cabinet FF Shelf 3 No. 36.01

Davis Typecasting machine. Miscellaneous advertisements, articles, etc. relating to the Davis Typecaster, which appears to have been acquired by G.L.& Co.

Items in manila envelope.

(The) GRAPHIC ARTS

Cabinet 43 Shelf 1 No.

Johnson, Henry Lewis, editor, The Graphic Arts.

See PERIODICALS, PRINTING, United States (The) Graphic Arts...

GRAPHIC ARTS BOARD OF TRADE

Cabinet Q Shelf 4 No. 29

Rating book...18th ed. Oct.31, 1924. Revised to December 31st 1934. Containing the entire United States.

Limp cloth; 6½ x 4½ in.

GRANTOFF, OTTO

Cabinet K Shelf 2 No. 12

Entwicklung der modernen buchkunst in Deutschland. von Otto Grantoff. Zweites tausend. Leipzig (1910).

The development of modern decorative typography in Germany. Illus. in text, with 8 plates, some printed in colors.

Cloth; 10-3/8 x 7¾ in.

GRAPHIC ARTS, THE

Cabinet NN Shelf 7 No. 25

Prospectus of a new monthly magazine dedicated to the printers of America...Edited by Henry Lewis Johnson. Published by National Arts Publishing Company, 200 Summer Street, Boston, 1910. With portraits.

Half morocco; 12¾ x 9½ in.

GRAPHIC ARTS ENGINEERING AND RESEARCH

Cabinet B Shelf 3 No. 15

Project for a department of Graphic Arts Engineering at the Massachusetts Institute of Technology, Cambridge, Mass. n.d. (1929)

Morocco; 11-3/4 x 15-3/4 in.

GRAPHEUS, NIKOLAUS

Cabinet X Shelf 3 No. 20

Cologne, 1562-1582.

see

HEITZ, PAUL. Kölner büchermarken...p.xxxi

GRAPHIC ARTS see also

Cabinet Shelf No.

ART OF THE BOOK

ADVERTISING ART

BOOKMAKING

COMMERCIAL ART

TYPOGRAPHY, DECORATIVE

GRAPHIC ILLUSTRATED NEWSPAPER

Cabinet OO Shelf 6 No. 3

London, Dec. 1869 to June 1870, Vol. I.

Cloth; 16¼ x 12¼ x 2 in.

GRAPHIC, The Daily.

Cabinet Shelf No.

See Daily Graphic.

GRAPHIC ARTS AND CRAFTS YEAR BOOK, (The)

Cabinet 43 Shelf 2 No.

Edited by Joseph Meadon, Hamilton, Ohio, 1907-

See PERIODICALS, PRINTING. United States. (The) Graphic Arts and Crafts Year Book...

GRAPHISCHEN CLUB IN WIEN

Cabinet Shelf No.

See LIBRARIES, Graphic arts.

GRAPHOTYPE CASTER

Cabinet FF Shelf 6 No. 40

Descriptive pamphlet.

See TYPE CASTING MACHINES. Graphotype Caster...New York, n.d. circa 1902.

GRAPULDUS, FRANCISCUS MARIUS

Cabinet 40 Shelf 1 No. 15

Lexicon de partibus aedium...Lyons, 1535.

See Early Printing in France. Lyons, 1535. Melchior and Gaspar Trechsel.

GRASSAL vs. HERHAN

Cabinet FF Shelf 1 No. 64

Stereotyping invention, controversy.

See STEREOTYPING. French invention, controversy over...Paris (1805).

GRASSBY, PERCY

Cabinet Shelf No.

See Imprints, United States.

GRASSET, EUGENE (Compiler)

Cabinet K Shelf 2 No. 6

Ornaments typographiques: lettres ornées tetes de pages et fins de chapitres. Dessinés et publiés en 1880 Par. M. l'Abbé Drioux. Paris, n.d. circa 1888.

Cloth; 11 x $7\frac{1}{2}$ in.

GRASSIS (Gabriel de Papia)

Cabinet X Shelf 3 No. 14

Bibliographical notes, with printer marks, Grassis, Venice, 1485.

see KRISTELLER, Dr. PAUL, Italienischen notes...p.84

GRATAZL, EMIL

Cabinet T Shelf 3 No. 76

(Islam manuscript bindings) Islamische handschriften bande der Bayerischen Staatsbibliothek. (Mit I tafel)

pp. 118-147 in Loubier, Hans (Tribute to) Buch und bucheinband...Leipzig, 1923.

GRATIANUS

Cabinet 10 Shelf 2 No. 12

Decretales. Venice, 1504.

See Early Printing in Italy. Venice, 1504. Baptista de Tortis.

GRAPULDUS, FRANCISCUS MARIUS

Cabinet 40 Shelf 1 NO. 15

Lexicon de partibus aedium...Lyons, 1535.

See Early Printing in France. Lyon, 1535. Melchior and Gaspar Trechsel.

GRATIANUS.

Cabinet 14 Shelf 2 No. 15

Decretum [With commentaries]. Aug. 13, 1472, Mainz. Peter Schoeffer.
Rubricated and illuminated copy.
14/2/16, a second copy entirely without illumination and rubrication.

Gesamt-Kat.

Morocco; 19 x $14\frac{1}{4}$ x 3 in.

GRATIANUS.

Cabinet 14 Shelf 2 No. 16

Decretum. Mainz, 1472. Peter Schoeffer [Second copy entirely without illumination and rubrication]
See 14/2/15

Gesamt-Kat.

Morocco; 19 x 13-3/4 x $4\frac{1}{4}$ in.

GRATIANUS

Cabinet 29 Shelf 1 No. 44

Decreti huius plenissimum argumentum...[Printer's device] Decretum aureum domini Gratiani... Paris, Thielman Kerver, 1506.

Boards; 9-7/8 x $7\frac{1}{4}$ x 3-3/4 in.

GRATTAN, EDWARD

Cabinet MM Shelf 5 No. 20

(The) Printer's companion: being practical directions for filling the various situations in a printing office: embodying a system of punctuation, and copious original directions for composing Greek and Hebrew. Philadelphia, 1846.

Cloth; $5\frac{1}{2}$ x $3\frac{1}{4}$ x 3/8 in.

GRAVELOT

Cabinet 26 Shelf 1 No. 16

Buchillustrator, Gravelot's werk als. von Richard Oehler, Breslau.

Illus. article, with list of books illustrated by Gravelot. In GUTENBERG-GESELLSCHAFT JAHRBUCH, 1927, p.105

GRAVES, HENRY S.

Cabinet RR Shelf 4 No. 39

Paper and pulp industry, the conservation problem of the. By Prof. Henry S. Graves. Yale Forest School. Excerpt from The Scientific Monthly, March, 1925.

Item with other excerpts and pamphlets relating to paper. Folder; $10\frac{1}{2}$ x $7\frac{1}{2}$ x 1 in.

GRAY, GEORGE J.

Cabinet 76 Shelf 2 No. 13

Cambridge stationers and bookbinders, The earlier and the first Cambridge printer. Printed for the Bibliographical Society, at the Oxford University Press, October 1904.
Illus. monograph XIII.

Half morocco; 11 x 9 in.

GRAY, GEORGE J.

Cabinet 75 Shelf 2 No. 8

(The) Cambridge University Press and John Siberch. Bio-bibliographical essay.

In Transactions of the Bibliographical Society, "The Library," Vol. VIII, 1927-28, pp. 260-3.

GRAY, G. J.

Cabinet 75 Shelf 1 No. 17

Pickering, William: The earliest bookseller on London Bridge, 1556-1571. A paper read before the Bibliographical Society, March 15, 1897. Pamphlet, illus.

With other items in manila envelope.

GRAY, G. J.

Cabinet 75 Shelf 1 No. 4

Pickering, William, the earliest bookseller on London Bridge, 1556-1570. A paper read before the Bibliographical Society, March 15, 1897. Facsimiles.
Bio-bibliographical. Has list of works published by Pickering.

In Trans. Biblio. Soc. Vol. 4, 1896-1898. pp. 57-102.

GRAY, G. J.

Cabinet U Shelf 2 No. 142

Sieberch, John, the first Cambridge (England) printer. Bibliographical notes by Robert Bowes and G.J. Gray...London, 1906. Facs.

Boards; 8-1/8 x 6 in.

GRAY, GEORGE J. and W. M. PALMER.

Cabinet 76 Shelf 1 No. 15

Abstracts from the wills and testamentary documents of printers, binders and stationers of Cambridge, from 1504 to 1699. London: Printed for the Bibliographical Society, 1915

Half morocco; 8-5/8 x 6-7/8 x $\frac{3}{4}$ in.

GRAY, NEIL, Jr.

Cabinet EE Shelf 4 No. 127

History of the Oswego Machine Works, and Brown & Carver Paper Cutters. (Manuscript), Oswego, 1910.

Together with a collection of circulars and catalogues of Oswego Machine Works.

Cloth; $12\frac{1}{4}$ x 9 x 1-1/8 in.

GRAY, NIEL JR.

Cabinet MM Shelf 6 No. 50

Paper-Cutting Machines: A primer of information about paper and card trimmers, hand-lever cutters, power cutters and other automatic machines for paper cutting. "Typographic Technical Series for Apprentices", Part 1, No.10. Published by the United Typothetae of America, 1918.

Cloth; 8 x 5 in.

GRAY, THOMAS

Cabinet 73 Shelf 2 No. 13

Elegy written in a country church yard. [Facsimile, 1751 ed. and reprint, 1925]. With a foreword by William Andrews Clark, Jr., and frontispiece by William Wilke.
Imprint: Printed for William Andrews Clark, Jr. by John Henry Nash in San Francisco, 1925.

Paper boards; facsimile, 9-3/4 x 7-3/4 in.; 12 x $9\frac{1}{4}$ in. Both in one slip case.

GRAY PRINTING COMPANY (Printing Plant)

Cabinet S Shelf 5 No. 1

Our new home. Fosteria, Ohio, 1918. Brochure. Descriptive.

Bound in collection "Various Printing Plants-Brochures", item 6.

GRAYDON, SAMUEL.

Cabinet Shelf No.

See Imprints, United States. Wynkoop Hallenbeck Crawford Co.

GRAYSON, ROBERT

Cabinet P Shelf 2 No. 4

Designs and suggestions for job work. Reprinted from vol.VII of "The British Printer". Leicester, 1894.

Paper; $9\frac{3}{4}$ x $7\frac{1}{4}$ in.

GREAT BRITAIN

Cabinet J Shelf 3 No. 12

Graphic arts of Great Britain: Drawing, line-engraving, etching, mezzotint, aquatint, lithography, wood-engraving, color-printing. Edited by Charles Holme. Text by Malcolm C. Salaman. "Studio" Ltd. London, 1917.

Half morocco; $11\frac{1}{2}$ x $8\frac{1}{4}$ in.

GREAT BRITAIN

Cabinet U Shelf 5 No. 28

Spread of printing in Great Britain

See DUFF, E. GORDON. Early printed books...p.174

GREAT WAR (Base Printing Plant)

Cabinet Shelf No.

See Plants, Printing. Base printing plant of the 29th Engineers A.E.F.

GREAT WAR NEWSPAPER

Cabinet A Shelf 3 No. 1

British News (The) No.129, May 30, 1918. Printed and published in Amsterdam, Holland, by interned British and American Army men.

Item on folio 29 of vol. labelled "Early printing in Great Britain and Europe".

GREAT WESTERN TYPE FOUNDRY. Chicago

Cabinet Shelf No.

(Barnhart Bros. & Spindler). See its history in a letter secured in CC-1-6 and in the preface to CC-1-25

GREAT WESTERN TYPE FOUNDRY

Cabinet 27 Shelf 2 No. 14

Periodical "The Type Founder" issued by Barnhart Bros. & Spindler, proprietors of G. W. T. F., Chicago, Ill.

see PERIODICALS, TYPE FOUNDERS. United States. (The) Type Founder...

GREAT WESTERN TYPE FOUNDRY

Cabinet Shelf No.

See also Specimen Books, Types. United States. Great Western Type Foundry.

also Specimen Books, Types. United States. Barnhart Bros. & Spindler.

GREBO (Western Africa)

Cabinet II Shelf 3 No. 52

See LANGUAGE CHARACTERS. Examples of. Grebo ...

GRECS DU ROI

Cabinet V Shelf 6 No. 18

See Imprimerie Royale. Essai historique. Sur l'origine des caracteres Orientaux...et sur les caracteres Grecs du Francois 1er... Par M. de Guignes. n.d. [circa 1780]

GRECS DU ROI

Cabinet V Shelf 5 No. 23

Inventaire des Grecs du Roi en 1556. Par H.O. (Extrait du Bulletin de la Société de Histoire de Paris, Juillet-Aout, 1881).

Item 12 in vol. with binder's title "Origin of Printing in France: Pamphlets".

GREEK PRINTING. England Example

Cabinet FF Shelf 2 No. 10

Hibbert, Julian. Kentish-Town, 1828.
Title: Plutarchus and Theophrastus on superstition; with various appendices and a life of Plutarch.
Imprint: Printed A.D. 1828. Price, One Guilea. Printed by Julian Hibbert.

Has preface by the printer, with prices of printing.

Half calf; 8-3/8 x 5-3/8 x ⅝ in.

GREEK PRINTING IN FRANCE. [Example of]

Cabinet 40 Shelf 1 No. 29

Paris, 1551. Robert Estienne.
Title: Dionis Nicae rerum Romanarum ... [Greek and Latin text].
Imprint: Lutetiae, ex officina Roberti Stephani, typographi Regii, Regiis typis.

Vellum; 9¾ x 6⅝ x 2 in.

GREECE

Cabinet T Shelf 5 No. 135

(A) Short history of printing in Greece

See PEDDIE, R.A. Printing, a short history of the art... p.301

GREEK PRINTING IN FRANCE [Example of]

Cabinet 69 Shelf 1 No. 5

Paris, 1539. Conrad Neobar.
Title: Aristotles: Rhetoric. [Printer Mark]. Parisiis per Conradum Neobarium. Regium Typographum. 1539.
[Bound with another Greek item with the imprint of A. Turnèbe, and colophon of G. Morel, Paris, 1555].

Calf; gilt edges tooled with a floral design. 10½ x 8 x 1½ in.

GREEK PRINTING IN FRANCE [Example of]

Cabinet 69 Shelf 1 No. 21

Paris, 1552: Adrien Turnebe. (De Tournebus).
Title: Aeschyli tragoediae.

Contemporary binding; 6-3/4 x 4-1/8 x 5/8 in. Brunet 1, 77

GREECE

Cabinet Shelf No.

Manuscript books of Greece, masterpieces of

See also MANUSCRIPT BOOKS, Greece

GREEK PRINTING IN FRANCE [Example of]

Cabinet 40 Shelf 2 No. 20

Paris, 1544. Robert (I) Estienne.
Title: Ecclesiasticae Historiae. [Title in Greek and Latin. Printer Mark]
Imprint: Lutetiae Parisiorum: Ex officina Roberti Stephani typographi Regii, Regiis typis M.D.XLIIII. Cum privilegio regis.

Calf; 13-3/4 x 10 x 2-3/4 ins.

GREEK PRINTING IN FRANCE [Example of]

Cabinet 40 Shelf 1 No. 36

Paris, 1554; Henri Estienne (Stephanus)
Title: Anacreontis teii odae., ab Henrico Stephano luce & Latinitate nunc primum donatae.
Imprint: Lutetiae. Apud Henricum Stephanum. M.D.LIIII. Ex privilegio regis.

Morocco; 8 x 5¾ x 5/8 in. Brunet 1, 250.

GREEK

Cabinet L Shelf 3 No. 26

Literary (The) texts from Greco-Roman Egypt. A study in the history of civilization. By C.H. Oldfather. University of Wisconsin Studies., No.9. Madison, Wis., 1923.
(A study of the types of literature and what authors were used in the schools.)

Brochure, in manila envelope.

GREEK PRINTING IN FRANCE [Example of]

Cabinet 40 Shelf 2 No. 28

Paris, 1548. Robert Estienne.
Title: Dionis Romanarum historiarum libri 23, à 36 ad 58 usque.
Imprint: Lutetiae, Ex officina Rob. Stephani, typographi Regii, typis Regiis. 1548.

Calf; 13¼ x 9 x 1½ in.

GREEK PRINTING IN FRANCE [Example of]

Cabinet 69 Shelf 1 No. 21

Paris, 1552: Adrien Turnèbe. (De Tournebus).
Title: Aeschlyi tragoediae.

Contemporary binding; 6-3/4 x 4-1/8 x 5/8 in. Brunet 1, 77

GREEK PRINTING, England Example

Cabinet 30 Shelf 1 No. 34

Bulmer, William and Co. London, 1802. Anacreontis Odaria...Accedunt variae lectiones cura Edvari Forster.

Pigskin; 8-1/8 x 5½ x 1 in.

GREEK PRINTING IN FRANCE. [Example of]

Cabinet 40 Shelf 2 No. 16

Paris, 1550. Robert (I) Estienne.
Title: Novum Testamentum. Ex Bibliotheca Regia...
Imprint: Lutetiae, ex officina Roberti Stephani typographi Regii, Regiis typis.

Calf; 13¼ x 9 x 1¾ in.

GREEK PRINTING, France. [Example of]

Cabinet 40 Shelf 1 No. 54

Paris, 1569. Robert (II) Estienne.
Title: Novum Testamentum ex bibliotheca regia Lutetiae. Ex officina Roberti Stephani typographi Regiis, M.D.LXVIII.

Morocco; 5 x 3¾ x 1-5/8 in.

GREEK PRINTING, England Example

Cabinet FF Shelf 4 No. 6

Hibbert, Julian, Kentish Town, 1827. The Book of Orphic Hymns. Printed in uncial letters as a typographical experiment.
Copy signed by the printer-publisher.

Half calf; 8-3/8 x 5¼ x 3/8 in.

GREEK PRINTING IN FRANCE. [Example of]

Cabinet 40 Shelf 2 No. 34

Paris, 1551. Charles Estienne.
Title: Appiani Alexandrini romanarum historiarum. Ex bibliotheca regia.
Imprint: Lutetiae : Typis regiis, cura ac diligentia Caroli Stephani. 1551.

Vellum; 13¼ x 9 x 1½ in. Brunet 1,356.

GREEK PRINTING IN FRANCE. [Example of]

Cabinet E Shelf 3 No. 60

Paris, 1638. Gilles Morel.
Title: Isiodorus ... Interpretatione div. Scripturae epistolarum ...
Imprint: Paris, Aegid Morellius.

Calf; 13¼ x 9½ x 2¼ in. Brunet 3, 464.

GREEK PRINTING IN FRANCE [Example of]

Cabinet 69 | Shelf 1 | No. 5

Paris, 1555. Adrien Turnèbe.
Title: Aristoteles. De Moribus ad Nicomachum lib X Parisiis M.D.LV. Apud Adrianum Turnebum ...
Colophon: Excudebat, et cum Graecis Latina coniungebat Guil. Morelius. M.D.LV. XII Cal. Martias

Contemporary calf; gilt edges tooled with a floral design; 10½ x 8 x 1½ in.

GREEK PRINTING IN FRANCE [Example of]

Cabinet E | Shelf 3 | No. 82

Paris, 1648. Sebastien (II) Cramoisy. [Imprimerie Royale]
Title: Gerogius Codinus...De officiis magnae ecclesiae...In hae editioné praeter comparatum cum Regiis MM.SS. Graecum textum ...
Imprint: Parisiis. E typographia Regia.

Tooled calf; 16-3/4 x 11-1/8 x 2¼ in.

GREEK PRINTING IN FRANCE [Example of]

Cabinet 6 | Shelf 2 | No. 1 to 8

See Bibles. Polyglottes. Christopher Plantin, 1569-72.

GREEK PRINTING IN ITALY Example of

Cabinet F | Shelf 4 | No. 78

Milan, 1816. Dionysii Halicarnassei Romanarum Antiquitatem, codicum Ambrosianorum ab Angelo Maio...Milan, 1816.
Engraved portrait frontispiece.

Calf gilt; 12 x 9 x 7/8 in.

GREEK PRINTING IN ITALY. [Example of]

Cabinet 50 | Shelf 1 | No. 21

Parma, 1785. Giambattista Bodoni.
Title: Anakreontoz ...
Imprint: Parmae. Ex regio typographeio.

Half morocco; 12 x 9-1/8 x 1 in. Brooks,287.

GREEK PRINTING IN ITALY. [Example of]

Cabinet 50 | Shelf 2 | No. 7

Parma, 1792. Giambattista Bodoni.
Title: Callimaco. Greco-Italiano ... Per le nozze dell R. Principessa di Parma ...
Imprint: Parma, nel Regal Palazzo. Co'tipi Bodoniani.

Boards; 18 x 12 x 1 in.

GREEK PRINTING IN ITALY. [Example of]

Cabinet 50 | Shelf 2 | No. 9

Parma, 1800. Giambattista Bodoni.
Title: Aesop Phrygii fabulae. Graecae Latine conversae.
Imprint: Parmae. Ex regio typographeo.

Calf; 16 x 11½ in. Brunet I, 87; Brooks, 796.

GREEK PRINTING IN ITALY [Example of]

Cabinet D | Shelf 4 | No. 19

Rome, 1522. Calliergi or Kaliergi, Zaccaria, from the island of Crete.
Title: Chrysoloras, Manuel [Greek Grammar].
Colophon: Impressum Romae. 1522. Mense Iunis. [Without name of printer].

Boards; 6¼ x 4 x 3/4 in.

GREEK PRINTING IN ITALY [Example of]

Cabinet E | Shelf 3 | No. 37

Rome, 1628. Congr. de Propag. fide. Vincent Ghrardus, Printer.
Title: Odegia.
Imprint: In Roma, nella stampa della S. Congr. de Propag. fide. Fr. Vincentius Gherardus, socius ...

Half vellum; 5¾ x 3 x 1-1/8 in.

GREEK PRINTING IN ITALY [Example of]

Cabinet D | Shelf 2 | No. 48

Venice, 1499. Zacharias Kallierges.
Title: Etmologikum magnum graece.
Colophon: Sumptibus Domini Nicolai Calliergi Cretensis...[With printer mark].
Gesamt-Kat. Hain 6691.

Vellum; 15¼ x 10 x 2 ins.

GREEK PRINTING IN ITALY. [Example of]

Cabinet 60 | Shelf 2 | No. 5

Venice, 1514. Aldus Manutius and Andreae d'Asola.
Title: Suida.
Colophon: Venetiis in aedibus Aldi et Andreae [d'Asola]. soceri. Mense Feb. 1514.

Vellum, stamped; 13½ x 8½ x 2-3/8 in. Brunet 5, 587; Renouard I, p. 153.

GREEK PRINTING IN ITALY. [Example of]

Cabinet 60 | Shelf 1 | No. 12

Venice, 1518. Aldi et Andrea [di Asola] Soceri. Sacrae scripturae veteris, novaeque omnia. [Old and New Testament].
Colophon: Venetiis in aedib. Aldi et Andrea Soceri. MDXVIII. Mense Febrario.

Blind stamped vellum over boards; 12 x 8¼ x 2-3/4 in. Renouard. Annales....des Aldes I, p.192.

GREEK PRINTING IN ITALY. [Example of]

Cabinet 60 | Shelf 2 | No. 12

Venice, 1528. Aldus Manutius & Andreae d'Asolani.
Title: Paulus Aegineti. Opera medica.
Colophon: Venetiis in aedibus Aldi et Andreae Asolani soceri. Mense Augusto 1528.
Bound in with Aetius Amidenus "Librorum medicinalum". Venetiis, 1534.

Vellum over boards; 12½ x 8½ x 2[illegible] in. Brunet I, 59; Renouard I, p. 251.

GREEK PRINTING IN ITALY. [Example of]

Cabinet 60 | Shelf 2 | No. 18

Venice, 1534. Aldus Manutius and Andreae Asulani.
Title: Aetius Amidenus. Librorum medicinalum ...
Colophon: Venetiis, in aedibus haeredum Aldi Manutii & Andreae Asulani. Mense Sept. 1534.
Bound in with Pauli Aeginetae "Opera medica." Venetiis, 1528.

Vellum over boards; 12½ x 8½ x 2¼ in. Brunet 1, 103. Renouard 1, 267.

GREEK PRINTING IN SCOTLAND Example

Cabinet F | Shelf 4 | No. 49

Glasgow, 1763. Robert and Andrew Foulis.
Title: Dionysii Longini de Sublimate. Ex edition tertia. [Greek and Latin text].
Imprint: Glasguae: In Aedibus Academicis excudebant Robertus et Andreas Foulis. Academiae Typographi. 1763.

Morocco; 8¾ x 6-3/8 x 1-1/8 in. Brunet 3, 1152.

GREEK PRINTING IN SWITZERLAND. [Example of]

Cabinet 40 | Shelf 1 | No. 48

Geneva, 1567. Estienne, Henri (II), and Ulrich Fugger.
Title: Polemonis, Himerii, et aliorum quorundam declamationes, nunc primum edite. [Alternating title in Greek.]
Imprint: Excudebat Henr. Stephanus, illustris viri Huldrichi Fuggeri typographus, 1567.

Old vollume; 9½ x 6-3/8 x ½ in.

GREEK PRINTING IN SWITZERLAND [Example of]

Cabinet 40 | Shelf 2 | No. 38

[Geneva]. 1570. Henri (II) Estienne (Stephanus).

Title: Conciones, sive orationes, ex graecis Latinisque historicis excerptae...[Printer Mark]. Anno M.D.LXX, Excudebat Henricus Stephanus.

Vellum; 12½ x 8 x 1-3/4 in. Brunet 2, 212.

GREEK PRINTING IN SWITZERLAND [Example of]

Cabinet 40 | Shelf 2 | No. 42

[Geneva, 1572?]. Henri (II) Estienne.

Title: Thesaurus graecae linguae. ab Henrico Stephano...cum privilegio caes. Maiestatis et christianiss Galliarum regis.

Morocco; 15¼ x 9-3/4 x 2-3/4 ins.

GREEK PRINTING IN UNITED STATES. [Example of]

Cabinet F Shelf 1 No. 37

Boston, 1761: John Green and Joseph Russel.
Title: Pietas et Gratulatio Collegii Cantabrigiensis apud Novanglos.
Imprint: Boston-Massachusettensium. Typis J. Green & J. Russell, M.DCC.LXI.

This is the first printing with Greek types executed in the North American Colonies.

Full morocco; 10-1/8 x 8 in. Evans 3, 8877, p.286.

GREEK PRINTING

Cabinet V Shelf 2 No. 23

Parisian Greek Press, the early.

see

GRESWELL (Rev.) W. P. (A) View of the early Parisian Greek Press...

GREEK PRINTING IN FRANCE Literature of

Cabinet V Shelf 5 No. 23

Incunable Grec de l'imprimerie Parisienne au XVI siècle (Extrait du Bulletin de la Société de l'Histoire de Paris...Juillet-Aout, 1886.

Item 13 in vol. with binder's title "Origin of Printing in France: Pamphlets".

GREEK PRINTING IN UNITED STATES [Example of]

Cabinet F Shelf 1 No. 88

Philadelphia, 1792. Mathew Carey.
Title: Epicteti Enchiridion. Ex editione Joannis Upton.
Imprint: Philadelphiae: Impensis Mathaei Carey. 1792.
This is the first book printed with Greek types in America.

Calf; 5¾ x 3½ in. Not in Evans.

GREEK PRINTING. [Literature of]

Cabinet 76 Shelf 2 No. 8

Printing of Greek in the fifteenth century, by Robert Proctor. Printed for the Bibliographical Society at the Oxford University Press, December 1900.
Illus. Monograph VIII.

Half morocco; 11 x 9 in.

GREEK PRINTING, France [Literature of]

Cabinet V Shelf 4 No. 12

Paris, 1507:Gilles Gourmont. Progrès de l'Imprimerie en France...auXVI siècle...avec les Lettres-Patentes en date du Janvier, 1538, qui instituent le premier Imprimeur Royal pour le Grec. Par G. A. Crapelet, Paris, 1836.

Half morocco; 9½ x 6¼ in.

GREEK PRINTING IN UNITED STATES. [Example of]

Cabinet G Shelf 4 No. 34

PHIladelphia, 1806. John Watts. Xenophontis de Cyri institutis. Execudebat Johannis Watts, impensis Wm. Payntell et Soc.
This is the first Greek book printed from the first Greek type cast in the U. S.of America.

Calf; 9 x 5½ in.

GREEK PRINTING. [Literature of]

Cabinet T Shelf 6 No. 53

Types. Greek printing, 1465-1927. Facsimiles from an exhibition of books illustrating the development of Greek printing shown in the British Museum, 1927. With an historical introduction by V. Scholderer. London, 1927.

Boards, linen back; 15-1/8 x 10-3/8 x 3/4 in.

GREEK PRINTING IN FRANCE [Literature of]

Cabinet U Shelf 4 No. 74 2 vols.

View of the early Parisian Greek Press; including the lives of the Stephani; notices of other contemporary Greek printers of Paris, and various particulars of the literary and ecclesiastical history of their times. Edited by E. Greswell. Oxford 1833. 2 vols.

Half morocco; 9 x 5-3/4 x 1-1/8 in. See also U/4/73

GREEK PRINTING Literature

Cabinet U Shelf 5 No. 38

French Royal Greek Types, paper on; Notes on Greek printing in England in the 16th century.

see

PROCTOR, ROBERT. Bibliographical essays...London, 1905, pp.89-119

GREEK PRINTING IN FRANCE [Literature of]

Cabinet V Shelf 4 No. 4

...Découvre l'origine de l'impression Grecque et Hebraique...Par André Chevillier. Paris, 1694.

See Chevillier, André. L'Origine de l'imprimeri de Paris... Part IV of this work.

GREEK PRINTING IN ITALY. [Literature of]

Cabinet M Shelf 3 No. 16

Leo the Tenth establishes a Greek Press at Rome.

See Leo, Pope the Tenth. Life and pontificate of...vol.2. p.253.

GREEK PRINTING. Literature.

Cabinet LM Shelf 6 No. 1

Greek in type: An essay for printers. By Herbert W. Williams. Gisborne. N.Z. No date. Brochure.

Historical technical account.

Item 1 in book with binder's title "Various items on printing". Bound 1919.

GREEK PRINTING IN FRANCE [Literature of]

Cabinet U Shelf 2 No. 32

Estienne (Les) et les types grecs de Francois I, complément des annales Stephaniennes renferment l'histoire complète des types royaux, enrichie d'une notice historique sur les premières impressions grecques. Par Aug. Bernard. Paris, 1856.

Boards; 9 x 5¾ in.

GREEK TYPES.

Cabinet S Shelf 3 No. 91

Aldus cuts first complete font ...
See Index to Orcutt's "The kingdom of books," Boston, 1927.

GREEK PRINTING Literature of

Cabinet U Shelf 5 No. 38

Oxford, Joseph Barnes prints Greek books at.

see

PROCTOR, ROBERT. Bibliographical essays...London, 1905, p.110

GREEK PRINTING IN FRANCE. [Literature of]

Cabinet 75 Shelf 1 No. 7

French Royal Greek Types and the Eton Chrysostom. By Robert Proctor. Read before the Bibliographical Society, Feb. 16, 1903. Facsimiles,

In Trans. Biblio. Soc. vol. VII, 1902-1904. pp. 49-74.

GREEK TYPES

Cabinet BB Shelf 3 No. 30.02

Benner Greek, designed by Francis H. Fobes. Amherst, Mass., 1932. At the Snail's Pace Press.

Specimen, three sizes.

With other items in manila envelope.

GREEK TYPES.

Cabinet 75 Shelf 1 No. 4

Brescia, incunabulum of.

See Christie, R. C. Incunabulum of Brescia.

GREEK TYPES.

Cabinet 75 Shelf 1 No. 5

Earliest printers of Greek and their types. A paper read before the Bibliographical Society by Mr. Robert Proctor. Jan. 1909.

In Trans. Biblio. Soc., Vol. V, 1898-1900, pp. 174-177.

GREEK TYPES

Cabinet V Shelf 6 No. 18

See Imprimerie Royale. Essai historique. Sur l'origine des caractères Orientaux...et sur les caractères Grecs du Francois 1er... Par M. de. Guignes. n.d. [circa 1780].

GREEK, TYPES.

Cabinet 30 Shelf 1 No. 34

See Imprints, Great Britain. Bulmer W. & Co., London, 1802. Anacreontis.

GREEK TYPES

Cabinet Z Shelf 1 No. 18

Lamesle, Claude. Paris, 1737.
Grecs originaires de la fonderie de.
See Specimen Books, Types. France. Gando, Nicolas Pierre and Theodore Simon (father and son)...(2, p.55)

GREEK TYPES

Cabinet AA Shelf 2 No. 21

Manutius, Aldus and his Greek types.
See Lambiasi, Enrico. Aldo Pio Manutius, tipografo e letterato: Milano, 1911. p.19.

GREEK TYPES.

Cabinet 75 Shelf 2 No. 7

Pollard, Alfred W. Greek types, old and new [With specimen pages.]

In Transactions of the Bibliographical Society, "The Library," Vol. VII, 1926-27, pp. 414-18.

GREEK TYPES.

Cabinet 75 Shelf 2 No. 7

Scholderer, Victor designs a fount of Greek types for the Lanston Monotype Corporation. Two specimen pages in facsimile.

In Transactions of the Bibliographical Society, "The Library," Vol. VII, 1926-27, p. 418.

GREEK TYPES

Cabinet V Shelf 6 No. 28

(Les) Types Grecs de Francois I.
See Bernard, Auguste. Histoire de l'Imprimerie Royale de Louvre. Paris, 1867. pp. 1-39.

GREELEY, HORACE

Cabinet JJ Shelf 5 No. 16

Address at a meeting of printers in 1850...
Biographical sketch of Horace Greeley...His interest in the general labor movement.

See STEVENS, GEORGE A. New York Typographical Union No.6. Study of... Albany, 1912. [see index].

GREELEY, HORACE

Cabinet JJ Shelf 3 No. 7

Address at the printer's banquet held by the New York Typographical Society, on the occasion of Franklin's birthday, Jan. 17, 1850, at Niblo's, Broadway, New York.
Together with the proceedings at the banquet, menu, toasts, etc.

Half morocco; 9¼ x 5-7/8 x 3/8 in.

GREELEY, HORACE

Cabinet NN Shelf 2 No. 2.01

[Biographical sketch] By Gamaliel Bradford. Excerpt from The American Mercury, April, 1924.

Item 21 in vol. with binder's title "Journalists and Journalism -- II. Pamphlets".

GREELEY, HORACE

Cabinet 81 Shelf 2 No. 38

Biographical sketch, Horace Greeley, of New York, printer. With portrait. Excerpt, newspaper clipping.

See MUNSELL, JOEL. "Printers Scraps". Vol.IX, pp. 15-18.

GREELEY, HORACE

Cabinet [illegible] Shelf 1 No. 46

Biographical sketch of a distinguished American journalist, and founder of The New York Tribune.

Includes pictures of Greeley's birthplace, and his first school house.

See pp.17-24, Harpel's Poets and poetry of printerdom...Cincinnati, 1875.

GREELEY, HORACE

Cabinet NN Shelf 2 No. 6

Biography gone mad (Bennett and Greeley). Excerpt from Blackwood's, March, 1856.

The author of this article severely criticises the American method of distorting facts.

Item 1 in bound collection "Biographies of Journalists".

GREELEY, HORACE

Cabinet NN Shelf 2 No. 2.01

[Biography of Horace Greeley] By W.H. Bidwell, editor of the Eclectic.] Excerpt from the Eclectic, April, 1870.

Item 10 in vol. with binder's title "Journalists and Journalism -- II. Pamphlets".

GREELEY, HORACE

Cabinet NN Shelf 6 No. 26

Brief biographical sketch of H.G., editor-in-chief of the New York Tribune.

see

BROWNE, JUNIUS HENRI (The) Great Metropolis...1870, p.214

GREELEY, HORACE

Cabinet NN Shelf 5 No. 43

Centenary 1811 - 1911, of founder of the Tribune. Exercises at Chappaqua, Amherst, etc. Newspaper clippings with full account of the life and activities of Greeley. With portraits and illus.

Item in folder 17 x 12½ in. Lying flat on shelf.

GREELEY, HORACE

Cabinet NN (The) Comic life of Horace Greeley. By a professional biographer.

Shelf 4 Published at "Wild Oats" Office, 113 Fulton St., New York. 1872.

No. 8 Bound in with two other campaign items.

Cloth; 9-7/8 x 7 "

GREELEY, HORACE

Cabinet 81 Gentleman, Mr. Greeley as a. Letter concerning Mr. Greeley. Excerpt from the "Round Table". Newspaper clipping.

Shelf 2

No. 37 Item in MUNSELL, JOEL. "Printers Scraps". Vol.VIII, p.72.

GREELEY, HORACE

Cabinet NN Shelf 7 No. 27

One hundreth anniversary of the birth of Horace Greeley, first President of Typographical Union No. 6. New York Theatre, Feb. 5, 1911 Under the auspices of "Big" 6. With portrait.

Cloth; 10¾ x 7 in. With other items in box labeled "Horace Greeley. Various items".

GREELEY, HORACE

Cabinet NN Shelf 4 No. 15

Comic life pf Horace Greeley...Together with what he knows about farming. By a Professional Biographer. Published at "Wild Oats" Office New York [1879] Illus.

Half morocco; 10 x 6½ in.

GREELEY, HORACE

Cabinet NN Shelf 2 No. 7

Humor and tragedy of the Greeley campaign. By Henry Watterson.
Excerpt from The Century, Nov., 1912.
With portraits.

Item 28 in bound collection "Journalism. Excerpts, etc."

GREELEY, HORACE

Cabinet NN Shelf 7 No. 27

Oration at the grave of Horace Greeley. By L. M. Lawson. Horace Greeley Post, 557. May 30, 1889.
Frontispiece portrait of Horace Greeley done entirely in brass rules, by F. B. Crewe, New York, 1889.

Item in box labeled "Horace Greeley. Various Items".

GREELEY, HORACE

Cabinet NN Shelf 2 No. 2

Editorial Chair of The Tribune. (Biographical account of Horace Greeley, his career as an editor, his political relations, etc.

Item 4 in vol. "Journalists and Journalism", Bound 1918.

GREELEY, HORACE

Cabinet NN Life of Horace Greeley, editor of "The New York Tribune".
From his birth to the present time.

Shelf 4 By James Parton. Boston. 1872. Illus.

No. 10 Cloth; 7-3/4 x 5¼ x 1¼ in.

GREELEY, HORACE

Cabinet NN Shelf 4 No. 14

Proceedings at the unveiling of a memorial to Horace Greeley at Chappagua, N.T., Feb. 3, 1914.

With reports on other Greeley celebrations related to the centennial of his birth, Feb. 3, 1911.

Published under the auspices of the State Historian. Albany. 1915. Illus.
Cloth:9x6"

GREELEY, HORACE

Cabinet NN Shelf 2 No. 1

Editors that I have known. By Alexander Wilder. (Excerpt from Belford's, August 1890).

Item 2 in vol. with binder's title "Journalists. Various excerpts".

GREELEY, HORACE

Cabinet NN Shelf 4 No. 11

Life of Horace Greeley: Founder of the New York Tribune, with extended notices of many of his contemporary statesmen and journalists.
By L. D. Ingersoll. Chicago, Ill. 1873. Illus.

Leather: 9¼x6½"

GREELEY, HORACE

Cabinet NN Shelf 4 No. 7

Recollections of a busy life: including reminiscences of American politics, - to which are added Miscellanies: "Literature as a vocation" by Horace Greeley. New York. 1869. Illus.

Cloth: 9x6¼"

GREELEY, HORACE

Cabinet NN Fiftieth anniversary of the founding of "The Tribune," celebrated April 10, 1891 at the Metropolitan Opera House. New York.

Shelf 4 Description of the event, addresses of tribute by eminent people; a brief history of "The Tribune", and biographical sketches of its founder.

No. 16

Cloth; 10 x 6-3/4 in.

GREELEY, HORACE

Cabinet NN Shelf 4 No. 12

Memorial of Horace Greeley.

Published by The Tribune Association New York. 1873.

With portraits.

Cloth: 8¾x5¾"

GREELEY, HORACE

Cabinet NN Shelf 6 No. 25

Scrap Book of newspaper clippings (1867-1868), relating to journalists, journalism, Horace Greeley, etc. Has historical data relative to history of New York newspapers.

Clippings pasted over a school report.

Boards; 9 x 6 in.

GREELEY, HORACE

Cabinet NN Shelf 4 No. 13

Founder and editor of The New York Tribune, Horace Greeley.

By William Alexander Linn. New York. 1903. Illus.

Cloth: 7¾x5¼"

GREELEY, HORACE

Cabinet NN Shelf 7 No. 27

Monument, The Greeley, unveiled at Greenwood, December 4, 1876. New York: Francis Hart & Company, 1877. Illus. pamphlet.

Account of the event. With brief biographical notes.

In box labeled "Horace Greeley. Various Items".

GREELEY, HORACE

Cabinet QQ Shelf 1 No. 42

Sonnet. - Portrait of a lady...

See p.56, Brenton's Voices of the Press ...New York, 1850.

GREELEY, HORACE

Cabinet NN Shelf 4 No. 12.02

Tribune Association, The. Organization and by-laws. New York, 1872.
With 2 portraits of Horace Greeley

Brochure, in manila envelope

GREELEY, HORACE

Cabinet NN Shelf 4 No. 12.01

Tribute to Horace Greeley: The Greeley Monument. Unveiled at Greenwood, Dec.,4, 1876. New York: Francis Hart & Co., 1877.

Brochure; 9 x 5¾ in.

GREELEY, HORACE

Cabinet NN Shelf 4 No. 9

What I know about farming:
Founded on the experience of Horace Greeley.
By Joseph Hull, of Oswego, N.Y. 1871
Illus.
II The Greeley record. 1872
III Greeley illustrated. (illus. by Th. Nast. 1872)
Three campaign items in one folder.

Boards: 10x7"

GREEN, BARTHOLOMEW.

Cabinet F Shelf No.

See Early Printing in New England. Boston, [various dates].

GREEN, BARTHOLOMEW, JR.

Cabinet F Shelf 1 No. 15

See Early Printing in New England. Boston, 1725; Bartholomew Green, Jr.

GREEN, BUFORD L.

Cabinet Shelf No.

[Invention of a method of operating type composing machine telegraphically.]

Illus. descriptive article in "Printing", vol. 55, No.9, pp.28, 29, April 2, 1932.

GREEN, BUFORD (Inventor)

Cabinet Shelf No.

"Semagraph". Electric eye which sets type automatically. Illus. description, with portrait of the inventor.

Article in Editor and Publisher, vol. 64, April 2, 1932, pp.7, 40.

GREEN (H.H.), New Orleans Type Foundry

Cabinet C Shelf 2 No. 6

Announcement (A), dated 1858, of his acquisition of Sole Agency of George Bruce's New York Type Foundry, etc. (B), advertisement of Greens removal at same time, and (C) Reading Notice from the New Orleans True Delta.

p.55 in Scrap book "Souvenirs of Bruce Family".

GREEN, H.H.

Cabinet Shelf No.

See also
Specimen Books, Types. United States. Green, H.H. New York.

GREEN, HENRY

Cabinet T Shelf 4 No. 19

Alciati, Andrea, and his book of emblems: a biographical and bibliographical study. London, 1872. Illus.

Stamped cloth; 8¾ x 5¾ x 1 in.

GREEN, JOHN

Cabinet MM Shelf 6 No. 25.01

Making of a book (The). Information for the instruction of apprentices in the U.S. Government Printing Office. Together with standard imposition layouts for flat-bed and web presses. Washington, 1933.

Cloth; 9½ x 6 in.

GREEN, JOHN. Printer.

Cabinet F Shelf 1 No. 22&31

See Early Printing in New England. Boston, 1743 and 1758. Green, Bushell, and Allen.

GREEN, JOHN AND JOSEPH RUSSEL

Cabinet Shelf No.

See Early Printing in New England. Boston. [v.d.]
John Green and Joseph Russell

GREEN, SAMUEL

Cabinet F Shelf 1 No.

See Early Printing in New England. Cambridge, [v.d.]

GREEN, SAMUEL

Cabinet S Shelf 6 No. 9

Imprint of 1673, Cambridge. [Facsimile]

See EARLY PRINTING IN AMERICA (U.S.) Literature. Cambridge, 1673, Samuel Green...

GREEN, SAMUEL ABBOTT

Cabinet R Shelf 2 No. 48

Career of Benjamin Franklin. A paper read before the American Philosophical Society, Philadelphia, May 25, 1893, at the celebration of the 150th anniversary of its formation in that City. Groton, Mass. June, 1893
Bound in with a reprint of the above, Philadelphia, 1893.

Half morocco; 9¾ x 6¼ in.

GREEN, SAMUEL ABBOTT

Cabinet R Shelf 6 No. 5

Daye, Stephen, the earliest printer in this country. [With] ten fac-simile reproductions relating to New England. By S. A. Green, Boston, 1902.
Each reproduction is accompanied with several pages of text giving biographical, bibliographical, and historical facts relating to New England printers and printing.

Cloth; 15 x 10¾ in.

GREEN, SAMUEL ABBOTT

Cabinet S Shelf 5 No. 25.01

Daye, Stephen, the earliest printer in this country. Reprinted from "Ten fac-simile reproductions relating to New England". Copyright 1902. Pamphlet.

Paper; 14½ x 10½ in. In box labelled "Colonial Printing and Printers. Miscellaneous Items".

GREEN, SAMUEL ABBOTT

Cabinet R Shelf 6 No. 5

Facsimile reproduction (10) relating to New England. By Samuel A. Green, Boston, 1902. Heliotype reproductions.
Each reproduction is accompanied with several pages of text giving biographical, bibliographical facts relating to early Boston printers and printing.

Cloth; 15 x 10⅝ in.

GREEN, THOMAS

Cabinet S Shelf 5 No. 6

See Biographies, Printers (Connecticut printers, 1709 - 1893.)

GREEN BOOK

See PAPER: Printers' Green Book for 1910.

GREEN, SAMUEL ABBOTT

Cabinet R Shelf 6 No. 6

Fac-simile reproductions (10) relating to various subjects. By Samuell Abbott Green. Boston, 1903. Heliotype reproductions.
Contents: Some engraved portraits of the Mather family: An early Boston imprint, 1681: The Boston News-letter, 1704,; Reprints of early Boston Newspapers, etc.

Cloth; 15 x 10⅝ in.

GREEN, THOMAS

Cabinet S Shelf 3 No. 104

(The) Work of Hartford's first printer. (Thomas Green, 1764-1768). By Albert Carlos Bates. Bio-bibliographical.
p. 345 in volume, Wilberforce Eames ... A tribute to. Cambridge, 1924.

GREEN, BUSHELL and ALLEN.

Cabinet F Shelf 1 No. 23

See Early Printing in New England. Boston, 1743.

GREEN, SAMUEL ABBOTT

Cabinet R Shelf 5 No. 60

Foster, John, the earliest American engraver and the first Boston printer. By Samuel Abbott Green. Boston, 1909. Facsimiles, and bibliographical list of titles printed by Foster.
Bio-historical.

Cloth; 10½ x 7¾ in.

GREEN, TIMOTHY (2)

Cabinet F Shelf 1 No. 20

See Early Printing in New England. Boston, 1741: Samuel Kneeland and Timothy (2) Green.

GREEN, LOW & DOLGE, INC.

Cabinet RR Shelf 6 No. 37

Oxford papers, how and where they are made. Green Low & Dolge, Inc., Paper Distributers, New York. Mills: Rumford, Maine.

Boards; 19 x 12½ in.

GREEN, SAMUEL A.

Cabinet R Shelf 5 No. 59

Foster, John. The earliest engraver in New England. By Samuel A. Green. Cambridge 1905.
John Foster set up the first printing press in Boston in 1675. See also R/5/60.

Half morocco; 9½ x 6¼ in.

GREEN, WARREN L.

Cabinet I Shelf 3 No. 1

Evolution of bank notes. [Excerpt from the Editorial Review, August 1910]. Illus.

Item 9 in vol. with binder's title: "Various Engravers and About Engravers."

GREENE, CHARLES GORDON

Cabinet 61 Shelf 1 No. 2

Boston Post (The), C.G. Greene, editor and founder of the. Biographical account, with portrait.

Article in "The Paper World," vol.5, Aug., 1882, p.1.

GREEN, SAMUEL A.

Cabinet R Shelf 4 No. 37

List of Early American Imprints belonging to the Library of the Massachusetts Historical Society. With an introduction and notes by Samuel A. Green. Cambridge, Univerity Press, 1895.

Half morocco; 9 x 6¼ in.

GREEN, WILLIAM (see)

Cabinet JJ Shelf 2 No. 1.01

TYPOTHETAE OF THE CITY OF NEW YORK. Testimonial meeting, February, 11, 1907...

GREENE, SAMUEL A.

Cabinet R Shelf 1 No. 2

Story of a famous book (Autobiography of Benjamin Franklin. By Samuel A. Greene. In The Atlantic, Feb., 1871.

Pamphlet #5 in volume "Franklin Pamphlets" Bound 1928.

GREEN, SAMUEL ABBOTT

Cabinet R Shelf 6 No. 5

(The) Stamp Act, 1765. [With] Ten fac-simile reproductions relating to New England. By Samuel Abbott Green, Boston, 1902.

Cloth; 15 x 10⅝ in.

GREEN, FAMILY OF PRINTERS

Cabinet 81 Shelf 2 No. 30

Data contained in a letter of Samuel Green, dated Hartford, Jan. 9, 1847, concerning his ancestors, the Green family of printers, beginning in Cambridge, Mass., in 1648. Newspaper clipping.

In MUNSELL, JOEL. Printers' Scraps... vol.I, pp.87-88.

GREENFIELD (Mass.) GAZETTE ("The Impartial Intelligencer")

Cabinet NN Shelf 7 No. 11

Centennial Edition, 1792 - 1892. Greenfield, Mass., February 1, 1892. The history of one hundred years. Illus., facs. portraits.
Includes biographical sketches of the Gazette's principal publishers, etc.

Cloth; 13-3/8 x 11 x ½ in.

GREENLAND

Cabinet T Shelf 5 No. 135

(A) Short history of printing in Greenland

See PEDDIE, R. A. Printing, a short history of the art...p.243

GREENLEAF, JOSEPH

Cabinet 80 Shelf 2 No. 8

Boston, 1774, Imprint of Joseph Greenleaf.

See PERIODICALS, United States. Royal (The) Magazine, or Universal Repository...Oct., 1774.

GREENWOOD, GRACE (Editor)

Cabinet 00 Shelf 4 No. 43.01

Little Pilgrim, The. Philadelphia, 1857. Edited by Grace Greenwood.

Item in manila envelope

GREENWOOD, J. M.

Cabinet R Shelf 4 No. 153

Life of Col. Robert T. Van Horn, printer, editor, and publisher. By J. M. Greenwood: An address delivered before the Greenwood Club of Kansas City, Missouri, March 10, 1905. An excerpt from Missouri Historical Review.

Cloth; 9½ x 6½ in.

GRAY, THOMAS

Cabinet 73 Shelf 2 No. 13

Elegy written in a country church yard. (Facsimile, 1751 ed. and reprint, 1925). With a foreword by William Andrews Clark, Jr., and frontispiece by William Wilke.
Imprint: Printed for William Andrews Clark, Jr. by John Henry Nash in San Francisco, 1925.

Paper boards; facsimile, 9-3/4 x 7-3/4 in.; reprint 12 x 9¼ in. Both in one slip case.

GREER, CARL RICHARD

Cabinet LL Shelf 5 No. 15

Buckeye book of direct advertising. By Carl Richard Greer, the Buckeye Cover Man. The Beckett Paper Company, Hamilton, Ohio. (1925)

Boards, cloth back; 9¼ x 6-1/8 x 1-1/8 in.

GREER, CARL RICHARD (The Buckeye Cover Man)

Cabinet LL Shelf 4 No. 34

Across with the Ad-Men. International Advertising Convention, London, 1924. By The Buckeye Cover Man (Carl Richard Greer) at The Beckett Paper Co. Hamilton, Ohio, 1924.

Boards; 8-3/8 x 5 3/4 x 1 in.

GREER, CARL RICHARD

Cabinet RR Shelf 2 No. 33

What a Buckeye Cover Man saw in Europe and at home. By Carl Richard Greer in collaboration with Thomas Beckett. The 75th anniversary of The Beckett Paper Company, Hamilton, Ohio. U.S.A., 192[illegible]. Illus.
Contains a history of the Beckett Paper Company.

Boards; 8[illegible] x 5-5/8 x 1 in.

GREETINGS, Printers

Cabinet S Shelf 1 No. 151

Caxton Company, Cleveland, Ohio. 1920: Christmas in Caxton's time ... as prevailed through the festive season during the life time of this illustrious printer. Made up and presented as the season's greetings by the Caxton Company at Cleveland, Ohio. Xmas,1920

Half morocco; 11-1/8 x 7¾ in.

GREETINGS, PRINTERS'

Cabinet J Shelf 1 No. 42

Collection of Christmas greetings received from printers, artists, bookmen,and others. Between years 1925 and 1936.

In envelope.

GREFFIER, DESIRE

Cabinet LL Shelf 3 No. 1.01

Manuel des signes de la correction typographique a l'usage des auteurs, correcteurs et compositeurs...Paris, n.d. Pamphlet.

Item I in vol. with binder's title "Proofreading: Pamphlets". Bound, 1932.

GREG, W. W.

Cabinet 75 Shelf 1 No. 12

Bibliography, what is? A paper read before the Bibliographical Society, February 19, 1912.

In Trans. Biblio. Soc., Vol. XII, 1911-1913, pp. 39-53.

GREG, W. W.

Cabinet 75 Shelf 2 No. 3

Day, John, and two issues of the "Isle of Gulls," 1606.

In Transactions of Bibliographical Society, "The Library," 1922-1923, vol. 3, p. 307-9

GREG, W. W.

Cabinet 75 Shelf 2 No. 4

Elizabethan printer and his copy, An. A paper read before the Bibliographical Society.

In Trans. Biblio. Soc., "The Library," vol. IV, pp. 102-118. 1923-1924.

GREG, W. W.

Cabinet 75 Shelf 2 No. 4

Greek numerals of John of Basing. A paper read before the Bibliographical Society.

In Trans. Biblio. Soc. "The Library," vol. IV, pp. 53-58. 1923-24.

GREG, W. W.

Cabinet 75 Shelf 2 No. 5

More Massinger corrections. With a note on simultaneous printing.

In Transactions of the Bibliographical Society, "The Library," Vol. V, 1924-25, pp. 59-91.

GREG, W. W.

Cabinet 75 Shelf 2 No. 3

Notes on old books. A study of worm-holes.

In Transactions of the Bibliographical Society, "The Library," Vol. III, 1922-1923, pp. 53-57.

GREG, W. W.

Cabinet 75 Shelf 2 No. 7

Notes on old books. The order of printing the forms.

In Transactions of Bibliographical Society, "The Library," Vol. VII, 1926-1927, 216-220.

GREG, W. W.

Cabinet 75 Shelf 1 No. 8

Notes on the types, borders, etc., used by Thomas Berthelet, 1528. A paper read to the Bibliographical Society.

In Trans. Biblio. Soc., Vol. VIII, 1904-1906, pp. 187-220.

GREG, W. W.

Cabinet 75 Shelf 2 No. 8

Stationers Company, decrees and ordinances of, 1576 - 1602. Read before the Bibliographical Society, Dec. 19, 1927.

In Trans. Biblio. Soc., vol. VIII, 1927-1928, pp. 395-425. "The Library."

GREG, W. W.

Cabinet 75 Shelf 2 No. 7

Stationers' Company, some notes on its Register, by W. W. Greg.

In Transactions of the Bibliographical Society, "The Library," Vol. VII, 1926-1927, pp. 376-386.

GREG, W. W.

Cabinet 75 Shelf 2 No. 6

Type-facsimiles and others. A paper read before the Bibliographical Society, Dec. 21, 1925.

In Transactions of the Bibliographical Society, "The Library," Vol. VI, 1925-1926, pp. 321-28.

GRÉGOIRE ---

Cabinet W Shelf 3 No. 115.01

Convention Nationale. Rapport sur la bibliographie ...Paris, circa 1793.

Item 4 in vol. with binder's title "French bibliographical items, 1731-1873". Bound, 1932.

GREGORI (Giovanni e Gregorio de)

Cabinet X Shelf 3 No. 14

Bibliographical notes, with printer marks, Gregorio, Venice, 1480-1516.

see KRISTELLER, Dr. PAUL. Italienischen buchdrucker...p.84

GREGORIIS, JOANNES and GREGORIUS DE.

Cabinet D Shelf 2 No. 42

See Incunabula. Hieronymus Commentaria in Biblia. Venice, 1498.

GREER, CARL RICHARD (The Buckeye Cover Man)

Cabinet LL Shelf 4 No. 34

Across with the Ad-Men. International Advertising Convention, London, 1924. By The Buckeye Cover Man (Carl Richard Greer) at The Beckett Paper Co. Hamilton, Ohio, 1924.

Boards; 8-3/8 x 5-3/4 x 1 in.

GREGORIUS IX

Cabinet 29 Shelf 2 No. 3

Decretales dn̄i pape Gregorii noni accurata dilige̅tia eme̅data. [Printer Mark: Thielmān Kerver. 1507]

Colophon:....Impresse Pariis solerti cura Thielmani Kerver impressoris ac librarii iurati alme universitatis Parisiensis. In magno vico diui Jacobi ad signu cratis ferri comorantis...Anno dni M.CCCCC.vij nonis Januarii.

Calf; 9_{4} x $6\frac{3}{4}$ x $2\frac{1}{4}$ in.

GREGORIUS IX.

Cabinet D Shelf 3 No. 30

Decretales dn̄i pape Gregorii noni acurata diligentia novissime...pluribus cum exemplaribus emendate...Venice Luca Antonio Giunta. 1514.

Tooled leather over boards, with clasps; $8\frac{3}{4}$ x $6\frac{1}{4}$ x $2\frac{1}{4}$ in.

GREGORIUS MAGNUS

Cabinet D Shelf 1 No. 34

Homelien. Utrecht, 1479. Jan Veldener.

Gesamt-Kat. ; Proctor 8856; Campbell 854.

Boards, leather back; 9 x 6 x $1\frac{1}{2}$ in.

GRENOBLE

Cabinet U Shelf 5 No. 38

First book printed at Grenoble

see PROCTOR, ROBERT. Bibliographical essays...London, 1905, pp.39-44

GREER, CARL RICHARD

Cabinet LL Shelf 5 No. 15

Buckeye book of direct advertising. By Carl Richard Greer (The Buckeye cover man) The Beckett Paper Company, Hamilton, Ohio, 1925. Illus.

Boards, cloth back; $9\frac{1}{4}$ x $6\frac{1}{4}$ x $1\frac{1}{4}$ in.

GREGORIOUS IX

Cabinet D Shelf 2 No. 25

Decretales. Basle, 1494. Johann Froben.

Gesamt-Kat. ; Original covers with clasps; 9 x $6\frac{1}{4}$ x 3-1/8 in.

GRESHAM PRESS, THE (Unwins Bros. Ltd.)

Cabinet U Shelf 3 No. 75

Century of progress, 1826-1926. Being a record of the rise and present position of the Gresham Press. London and Woking. Illus.

Half morocco; $9\frac{1}{4}$ x $6\frac{1}{2}$ x $\frac{1}{2}$ in.

GRESS, EDMUND G.

Cabinet MM Shelf 6 No. 17 2 copies.

American (The) handbook of printing, containing in brief and simple style something about every department of the art and business of printing. New York, Oswald Publishing Co. 1907. Illus.

One copy with marginalia by H.L. Bullen.

Cloth; 7-5/8 x $5\frac{1}{4}$ x 1 in.

GRESS, EDMUND G.

Cabinet MM Shelf 6 No. 18

American Handbook of Printing, containing in brief and simple style something about every department of the art and business of printing. (Second edition) New York. Oswald Publishing Company, 1909. Illus.

Cloth; 7-5/8 x $5\frac{1}{2}$ x 1 in.

GRESS, EDMUND G.

Cabinet MM Shelf 6 No. 20

American (The) handbook of printing, containing in brief and simple style something about every department of the art and business of printing. (Third edition) New York. Oswald Publishing Company, 1913. Illus.

Cloth; $7\frac{1}{2}$ x $5\frac{1}{4}$ x 1 in.

GRESS, EDMUND G.

Cabinet QQ Shelf 3 No. 26

Dash through Europe, with snapshots by the way. Including how I planned the trip, and what I found out of value to others. New York, 1923. Illus.
Tells of visits to ancient printing offices, to living printers, of a visit to Passy where Franklin lived in France, brief notes on early printing, etc.

Cloth back; 7-5/8 x 5 x ¾ in.

GREYFF, MICHEL

Cabinet Y Shelf 4 No. 4

(Note on Greyff and his printing at Reutlingen, 1486)

see VOULLIÈME, ERNST. (Die) Deutschen drucker des fünfzehnten jahrhunderts...p.97

GRIFFIN, JOSEPH

Cabinet NN Shelf 6 No. 10

Maine, history of the press of. Edited by Joseph Griffin, 1872. Second issue of the Press of Maine, with a supplement, 1874. Brunswick: From the press established A. D. 1819. Illus.
Collection by several authors, according to counties. Includes a brief history of printing.

Cloth; 9-3/8 x 6 x 1-1/8 in.

GRESWELL, E.

Cabinet U Shelf 4 No. 74 2 vols.

View of the early Parisian Greek Press; including the lives of the Stephani; notices of other contemporary Greek printers of Paris, and various particulars of the literary and ecclesiastical history of their times. Edited by E. Greswell. Oxford 1883. 2 vols.

Half morocco; 9 x 5¾ x 1-1/8 in. See also U/4/73

GREYFF, MICHAEL

Cabinet D Shelf 4 No. 62

Reutlingen, circa 1486.

see INCUNABULA (loose leaves) Greyff, Michael...

GRIFFIS, WILLIAM ELLIOT

Cabinet Q Shelf 1 No. 4

(The) New world of books in Japan. Illustrated. Excerpt from The Critic, Aug., 1905.

Item 7 in vol. with binder's title "Various items on Publishing".

GRESHAM PRESS, THE (Unwin Brothers)

Cabinet EE Shelf 2 No. 41

See SPECIMEN BOOKS, TYPES. Printers'. Great Britain. Unwin Brothers (The Gresham Press).

GRIERSON FAMILY OF PRINTERS. see POETRY OF PRINTING. Grierson, Mrs. Constantia...

Cabinet QQ Shelf 1 No. 55

GRIFFITH, ARTHUR

Cabinet U Shelf 2 No. 110

Journalist and statesman. (first president Irish Free State). Stephens. Written in the morning of his triumph. Dublin, n.d. [1922]. Photo.
Biographical.

Half morocco; 8 x 5-3/8 x 3/8 in.

GRESWELL (Rev.) WILLIAM PARR

Cabinet U Shelf 4 No. 73 also U/4/74

Annals of Parisian typography. Containing an account of the earliest typographical establishments of Paris; and notices and illustrations of the most remarkable productions of the Parisian gothic press...By the Rev. William Parr Creswell. London, 1818. Illus.
Printed by R. & W. Dean of Manchester.

Half morocco; 9 x 5¾ in.

GRIFFIN, A.P.C

Cabinet PP Shelf 3 No. 15.01

Bibliography of American Historical Societies. 2nd.ed. Annual report of the American Historical Association for the year 1905. Washington Government Printing Office, 1907.

Cloth; 9¼ x 5¾ x 2-5/8 in.

GRIFFITH, ROY

Cabinet 78 Shelf 2 No. 51

Twelve homilies on printers' rollers. With illustrations by the author. Wild & Stevens, Inc. Roller Manufacturers since 1864. Boston, Mass., 1930.

Boards; 6 x 4½ x ⅜ in.

GREVENBRUCH, Gerhard

Cabinet X Shelf 3 No. 20

Cologne, 1583-1642

see HEITZ, PAUL. Kölner büchermarken...p.xxxii

GRIFFIN, A.P.C.

Cabinet 79 Shelf 1 No. 19

Library of Congress: A list of books (with reference to periodicals) on the Philippine Islands, in the. With a chronological list of maps in the Library of Congress. By P. Lee Phillips. Washington, 1903. Senate Documents vol. 8.

Calf; 9¼ x 6 x 2 in.

GRIFFITH-STILLINGS PRESS.

Cabinet S Shelf 5 No. 2

See Plants, Printing. United States. (Boston, Mass.)

GREY, DOUGLAS

Cabinet FF Shelf 5 No. 61

Co-author with Fred J. F. Wilson

See Wilson, Fred. J. F. and Douglas Grey.

GRIFFIN, G. W.,

Cabinet NN Shelf 3 No. 11

Studies in literature: George D. Prentice, poet-journalist. Philadelphia. 1871.
SECOND EDITION

Paper: 7½x4¾"

GRIFFITH-STILLINGS PRESS

Cabinet S Shelf 5 No. 3

Something in both of us. [Description of their methods and aims.] The Griffith-Stillings Press, Boston, 1907. Booklet.

Item 4 in collection "Printers and their Plants; Collection of Pamphlets", 1918.

GRIGG, JOHN

Cabinet TT Shelf 3 No. 32

Printer, 1831, Philadelphia (Imprint)

See EARLY PRINTING IN PENNSYLVANIA. Philadelphia, 1831, John Grigg...

GRIGGS, F.L.

Cabinet M Shelf 4 No. 15

Gimson, Ernest: His life & work. Preface and line drawings by F.L. Griggs. Shakespeare Head Press, Stratford-upon-Avon, 1924.

Paper boards; 12 c 8¾ x 1-1/8 in.

GRIMALDI'S BREVIARY

Cabinet S Shelf 5 No. 18

See Breviaries [Grimaldis]

GRIMM, PAUL (Translator)

Cabinet I Shelf 2 No. 62

Photographische schwierigkeiten...von Cadby Ponting...Mit einem alphabetisch geordneten sachregister und einem anhange uber photo-zinkographie. In's deutsch ubertragen von Paul Grimm, Weimar, 1863.

Boards; 8¾ x 5½ in.

GRESS, E.E.

Cabinet R Shelf 1 No. 90

Scenes reminiscent of Franklin: An American printer's dash through Europe. By E. E. Gress. In The American Printer: Franklin number, Jan. 20, 1923. p. 64. Illus.

Half morocco; 12 x 8-7/8 in.

GRIMSDITCH, HERBERT B. (TRANSLATOR).

Cabinet K Shelf 1 No. 20

Book illustration in France, by Leon Pichon.

See Pichon, Leon. Book illustration in France, the new...London, 1924.

GRISWOLD, KATE E. (Editor)

Cabinet 61 Shelf 2 No.

Profitable Advertising bought by Kate E. Griswold from Chas. F. David. The new owner assumes management of the publication with the Nov., 1895 issue.

See PERIODICALS, ADVERTISING. Profitable Advertising...

GROESBECK, HARRY A. Jr.

Cabinet I Shelf 2 No. 55

Process and practice of photo engraving. [1st ed.] Garden City, N.Y. 1924.

Cloth; 11¼ x 8½ x 7/8 in.

GROHMANN, ADOLF (collaborator with)

Cabinet U Shelf 5 No. 87

Arnold, Thomas W.

see ARNOLD, THOMAS W. and Prof. A. GROHMANN

GRESWELL, (Rev.) W. P.

Cabinet V Shelf 2 No. 23

(A) View of the early Parisian Greek Press; including the lives of Stephani; notices of other contemporary Greek Printers of Paris; and various particulars of the literary and ecclesiastical history of their times. 2 vols. Oxford, 1833.

Review of book with title as above. Excerpt from Select Journal of Foreign Periodical Literature, July, 1834.

In envelope.

GROLIER, JEAN.

Cabinet S Shelf 5 No. 12

See Book Collectors: Grolier, Jean.

GROLIER, JEAN

Cabinet W Shelf 2 No. 115

Catalogue alphabétique des ouvrages manuscrits ou imprimes qui proviennet de la biblio-theque de J. Grolier. Par M. le Roux de Lincy. Paris, 1866.

Half morocco; 10¾ x 7¼ in.

GROLIER, JEAN

Cabinet S Shelf 5 No. 12

France's first bibliophile. By John C. Covert, in The Critic, March, 1905. Illus.

Contains a brief account of Grolier's influence in book appreciation, suitable coverings, and his association with the printers of the 15th. century.

Bound in collection "Pamphlets and excerpts relating to typographical matters", item 20.

GROLIER, JEAN.

Cabinet 18 Shelf 1 No. 13

(Historical contribution towards the history of Grolier bindings.) Zur entstehungsgeschichte der Grolier-Einbande, von J. Rudbeck in Stockholm. Illus.

In Zeitschrift für Bücherfreunde, 1912, part 2, p.319.

GROLIER, JEAN

Cabinet T Shelf 5 No. 1

Library and acquaintance with bookbinding; specimen of his book embellishment.

See p.141 of Arnett's Inquiry into the nature and form of books...London, 1837.

GROLIER, JEAN

Cabinet S Shelf 3 No. 91

Patronage of the Aldine Press ... His relations with Tory ...

See Index to Orcutt's "The kingdom of books." Boston, 1927.

GRIMM, SIGMUND.

Cabinet D Shelf 3 No. 65

See Early Printing in Germany. Augsburg, 1520. Sigmund Grimm.

GROLIER, JEAN

Cabinet AA Shelf 5 No. 32

Versuch einer klassifizierung der Einbande fur Jean Grolier. Bei Hans Loubier, Berlin, 1925.

Bibliographical essay in Collijn's "Bok-ock biblioteks historika studier ... Uppsala 1925.

GROLIER, JEAN (Bibliophile)

Cabinet PP Shelf 2 No. 10

Biography. A sketch of the life and services of Grolier.

See p.9, GROLIER CLUB. Transactions... 1885.

GROLIER CLUB (THE) cont'd

Cabinet S Shelf 1 No. 57

One of three co ies on special paper. Presented by Mr. James W. Bothwell.

Half morocco; 9-7/8 x 6-3/8 x 5/8 in.

GROLIER CLUB, THE

Cabinet QQ Shelf 1 No. 58

Depositio cornuti typographici...Originally printed at Lüneburg [1621]: Reprinted as acted at the Grolier Club, 1911. Printed by D.B. Updike, The Merrymount Press, Boston.

Boards; cloth back; 9½ x 6-1/8 in. In protective case.

GROLIER, BOOKBINDINGS

Cabinet Y Shelf 3 No. 76

(Origin of the Grolier bindings) Über die herkunft der Grolier-einbände...von Johannes Rudbeck. Mit 3 tafeln.

pp. 183-190 in Loubier, Hans (Tribute to) Buch und bucheinband...Leipzig, 1923.

GROLIER CLUB, THE

Cabinet 67 Shelf 1 No. 29

Champ Fleury. By Geofroy Tory. Translated into English and annotated by George B. Ives. At the Printing House of William Edwin Rudge [under the direction of Bruce Rogers]. Mount Vernon, New York, 1927.

One of an edition of 390 copies.

Boards; 12½ x 8¾ x 1¼ in.

GROLIER CLUB, THE

Cabinet PP Shelf 2 No. 34

Description of the early printed books owned by The Grolier Club, with a brief account of their printers and the history of typography in the 15th century. Printed for The Grolier Club, New York, May, 1895. Illus.

One of an edition of 400 copies printed by Theo. L. DeVinne.

Cloth, pigskin back; 12 x 8 in.

GROLIER CLUB, THE.

Cabinet I Shelf 3 No. 10

2 vols.

American engravers upon copper and steel. By David McNeely Stauffer. [In two parts.]
Part I - Biographical sketches, Illustrated.
" II - Check list of the works of the earlier engravers.
The Grolier Club of the City of New York, 1907.

Cloth, linen back; 9-7/8 x 6½ in.

GROLIER, JEAN

Cabinet W Shelf 2 No. 115

Recherches sur Jean Grolier, sur sa vie et sa bibliothèque, suivies d'un catalogue des livres qui lui ont appartenu. Par Le Roux de Lincy. Paris, 1866. Facsimile (Lithograph plates)

Half morocco; 10-3/4 x 8 in.

GROLIER CLUB, THE

Cabinet S Shelf 1 No. 21

Description of the early printed books owned by The Grolier Club; with a brief account of their printers and the history of typography in the 15th century. Printed for The Grolier Club, New York. The DeVinne Press, 1895. Illus. & Facsimiles.

Quarter calf; 12 x 8 x ½ in.

GROLIER CLUB, THE.

Cabinet G Shelf 3 No. 49

Boswell, James: Catalogue of an exhibition of the private papers from Malahide Castle. Held at the Grolier Club, New York, Dec., 18 1930 to Feb. 7th, 1931. Printed by Wm. E. Rudge, Inc. New York, 1930.

Paper; 9-3/8 x 6¼ x 5/8 in.

GROLIER CLUB, THE

Cabinet G Shelf 1 No. 48

Compromise of the king of the Golden Isles by Lord Dunsany. Designed and printed by T.M. Cleland, for The Grolier Club, 1924.

Boards, cloth back; 11¾ x 8¼ x ½ in. pp.25.

GROLIER CLUB, THE

Cabinet S Shelf 1 No. 16

DeVinne, Theodore Low: Historic printing types. A lecture read before the grolier Club of New York, Jan. 25, 1885, with additions and illustrations. The Grolier Club, 1886. [Printed by T.L. DeVinne.]

Presentation copy, with inscription and letter from Mr. DeVinne to Thomas MacKellar.

Boards; 10¼ x 8¼ in.

GROLIER CLUB

Cabinet O Shelf 1 No. 96

Catalogue of an exhibition commemorating the 200th. anniversary of the birth of Benjamin Franklin. At the Grolier Club of the City of New York, January 1906

Half morocco; 7 x 4-3/8 x ½ in. Orig. covers bound in

GROLIER, JEAN

Cabinet Shelf No.

See also Bookbinding, Early. Origin of the Grolier bindings.

GROLIER CLUB, THE

Cabinet S Shelf 1 No. 29

DeVinne, Theodore Low. Notable printers of Italy during the fifteenth century. Illustrated with facsimiles from early editions, and with remarks on early and recent printing. By Theo. L. DeVinne. The DeVinne Press, New York, 1910.

Boards; 13 x 9½ in.

GROLIER CLUB, (The).

Cabinet S Shelf 1 No. 57

(A) Catalogue of the work of The DeVinne Press. Exhibited at The Grolier Club on the occasion of the one hundredth anniversary of the birth of Theodore Low DeVinne. December 25, 1828. The Grolier Club, New York, 1929.

Half morocco; 9-7/8 x 6-3/8 x 5/8 in.

GROLIER CLUB, THE

Cabinet R Shelf 5 No. 50

(The) Colonial printer. By Lawrence C. Wroth. New York, The Grolier Club, 1931. Illus.

Boards, linen back; 10-3/8 x 6-3/4 x 1 in.

GROLIER CLUB, THE.

Cabinet 67 Shelf 2 No. 30

Durer, Albrecht, of the just shaping of letters. Translated by R. T. Nichol from the Latin Text of the edition of 1535. New York. The Grolier Club, 1917. (Printed at The Mall Press, Bruce Rogers, Emery Walker et al). Hammersmith, 1917.

Paper boards; 12½ x 8½ in. Warde 126.

GROLIER CLUB

Cabinet R Shelf 1 No. 22

Franklin and his Pressat Passy: An account of the books, pamphlets and leaflets printed there, including the long-lost "Bagatelles." By Luther S. Livingston, New York: The Grolier Club, 1914.

Presentation copy from author to H. L. Bullen, A.L.S. of the author inserted.

Boards; 9$\frac{3}{4}$ x 6$\frac{1}{8}$ in.

GROLIER CLUB, THE

Cabinet S Shelf 3 No. 82

Mores, Edward Rowe: A dissertation upon English typographical founders and foundries. With appendix by John Nichols. [A reprint of the 1779 edition]. Edited and printed by D. B. Updike: The Merrymount Press, Boston, for The Grolier Club, New York, 1924. Illus.

Linen boards; 9$\frac{3}{4}$ x 6 in.

GROLIER CLUB, THE

Cabinet S Shelf 1 No. 23

Title-Pages as seen by a printer. With numerous illustrations in facsimile and some observations on the early and recent printing of books. By Theo. L. DeVinne. The Grolier Club, New York, 1901.

Half morocco; 10 x 7 in.

GROLIER CLUB, THE

Cabinet NN Shelf 7 No. 26

Gazette Francoise. A facsimile reprint of a newspaper printed at Newport on the printing press of the French fleet in American waters during the Revolutionary War. With an introduction by Howard M. Chapin. New York. The Grolier Club, 1926.

Boards; 12$\frac{3}{4}$ x 8$\frac{3}{4}$ x 3/8 in.

GROLIER CLUB, New York

Cabinet S Shelf 4 No. 64

Portraits of Johannes Gutenberg, to be found in the Library [of the Grolier Club, New York] n.d.

Half morocco; 6-7/8 x 4$\frac{1}{4}$ in.

GROLIER CLUB, THE

Cabinet S Shelf 2 No. 43

Recollections of the Gilliss Press and its work during fifty years, 1869-1919. By Walter Gilliss. New York, The Grolier Club, 1926.

Boards; 9$\frac{1}{4}$ x 5-7/8 in.

GROLIER CLUB, THE

Cabinet S Shelf 2 No. 43

Gilliss Press Imprints: Short-title list of the imprints of Gilliss Brothers, Gilliss Brothers and Turnure, and the Gilliss Press. Including other volumes, periodicals, etc., with the printing of which Walter Gilliss was connected: Recollections of the Gilliss Press, 1869-191. The Grolier Club, New York, 1926.

Boards; 9$\frac{1}{4}$ x 6 x 5/8 in.

GROLIER CLUB (The)

Cabinet PP Shelf 2 No. 10

Price list of publications and exhibition catalogues, February 1, 1932. The Grolier Club, New York.

Attached to front cover of "Transaction of the Grolier Club...New York, 1885.

GROLIER CLUB

Cabinet PP Shelf 2 No. 10

Transactions of the Grolier Club from its foundation January 1884 to July 1885. Part I. New York, The Grolier Club, 64 Madison Avenue, 1885.

Has list of members, also articles by Robert Hoe, "The artistic history of bookbinding", and "Historic printing types" by Theo. DeVinne.

Paper; 9$\frac{1}{2}$ x 7-1/8 in.

GROLIER CLUB

Cabinet PP Shelf 2 No. 34.01

Microscopic books, a short list of in the Library of the Grolier Club. Mostly presented by Samuel P. Avery. New York, 1911.

Brochure, in manila envelope

GROLIER CLUB

Cabinet 67 Shelf 2 No. 51

Rogers, Bruce. New York, 1923. Pierrot of the Minute, by Ernest Dowson. Printed for the Grolier Club. Deberny types and vignettes.

Boards; 7$\frac{1}{4}$ x 4$\frac{1}{2}$ in. pp. 48.

GROLIER CLUB

Cabinet PP Shelf 2 No. 11

Transactions of the Grolier Club of the City of New York, from July 1885 to February 1894. Part II. New York, Twenty-nine East Thirty-Second Street. 1894.

Has exterior and interior views of the Club building.

Paper; 9-3/4 x 7-1/8 x 7/8 in.

GROLIER CLUB, THE.

Cabinet G Shelf 2 No. 9

Culprit fay and other poems, by J. Rodman Drake. Printed for The Grolier Club, by Walter Gillis, The Gillis Press, New York, MCMXXIII. Illus.

Boards; 9 x 6 ins., $\frac{1}{4}$ in. thick, pp.XV, (1) 49.

GROLIER CLUB, THE

Cabinet G Shelf 3 No. 32

Stevenson, R.L. A lodging for the night... Printed by Carl Purrington Rollins, New Haven, at the invitation of The Grolier Club, New York, 1923.

Boards; 8$\frac{1}{4}$ x 5-3/8 in.

GROLIER CLUB

Cabinet U Shelf 2 No. 69

Whittinghams (Charles), the printers. By Arthur Warren, New York: The Grolier Club, 1896. Illus.

Half morocco; 9$\frac{3}{4}$ x 7 in.

GROLIER CLUB, THE

Cabinet PP Shelf 5 No. 7

Modern bookbinding practically considered. A lecture read before the Grolier Club of New York, March 25, 1885...By William Matthews. New York, The Grolier Club, 1889.

Cloth; 10$\frac{1}{2}$ x 8$\frac{1}{4}$ x 3/8 in.

GROLIER CLUB, THE.

Cabinet G Shelf 2 No. 19

Three essays: Book-buying: Bookbinding: The Office of literature, by Augistine Birrel. Composed by Mrs. Goudy with types designed by Mr. Goudy. Printed for The Grolier Club, M.CM.XXIV.

Boards; 11-3/4 x 8$\frac{1}{2}$ ins., pp.XVI.

GROLIER CLUB, THE.

Cabinet Shelf No.

See also

Imprints, United States. Cleland, Thomas Maitland.

GROLIER CLUB, THE

Cabinet X Shelf 5 No. 24.01

Milton, John. Areopagita. A speech of Mr. John Milton for the liberty of unlicensed printing, to the Parliament of England. With an introduction by James Russell Lowell. New York, The Grolier Club, 1890.

Boards; 6-3/4 x 4-3/8 x 7/8 in.

GROPALL, JOHN (Lumbard)

Cabinet U Shelf 1 No. 1h

(An) Exeter bookseller, his friends and contemporaries [1553]. By Henry R. Plomer.

In Excerpts relating to printing from "The Library," 1916-17, pp. 180-187 of pencilled folios.

GROVER, EDWIN OSGOOD

Cabinet S Shelf 4 No. 125

Angel Alley Press, Winter Park. Florida. 1926-1928. Check list of books printed.
See Ransome, Will: Private presses and their books. p. 199.

GROLIER CLUB, THE.

Cabinet 71 Shelf 1 No. 54

Quattrocentisteria: How Sandro Botticelli saw Simonetta in the Spring. By Maurice Hewlett. Printed by John Henry Nash of San Francisco for The Grolier Club of New York, in the month of October, MCMXXI.

Boards, linen back; 12 x 8½ x ins., pp.19.

GROSS, CHARLES

Cabinet QQ Shelf 5 No. 22

Gild merchant: a contribution to British municipal history. By Charles Gross, Oxford, 1890. (2 vols.)

Cloth; 9 x 6 in.

GROVER, ISAAC

Cabinet U Shelf 1 No. 1●

See Wills, Printers.

GROLIER CLUB

Cabinet X Shelf 4 No. 11

Decree of Star Chamber concerning printing, made July 11, 1637. Reprinted by the Grolier Club from the first edition by Robert Barker, 1637. New York, 1884. Press of Theo. L. De Vinne & Co.

Stamped vellum; 9¼ x 6 x ½ in. In protective case.

GROSVENOR, CHATER and COMPANY LTD.

Cabinet RR Shelf 3 No. 46

Sample book. Grosvenor Chater & Co., Limited, paper makers, wholesale and export stationers. London, 1890. Frontispiece.

Price list pasted on back cover.

Cloth; gilt; 10¼ x 8-1/8 x 1¼ in.

GROWOLL, A.

Cabinet Q Shelf 1 No. 1

Literary production of the world. With statistical tables.
Excerpt from the "Independent", Nov. 19, 1903.

Item 26 in volume with binder's title "Publishing. Various Excerpts"

GRONAU, WILHELM

Cabinet Shelf No.

See Specimen Books, Types. Germany

GROTEFEND, DR. H.

Cabinet Y Shelf 2 No. 20

Christian Egenolff der erster buchdrucker zu Frankfort, a. M. und seine vorlaufer. Gedenkenblatt an die 350 jabrige jubelfeier der einfuhrung der buchdruckrunst in Frankfort. Frankfort a. M. 1881. Illus.
Biographical sketch of Egenolff, the first printer in Frankfort. Souvenir brochure of the 350th year celebration of the introduction of printing in Frankfort.

Half morocco; 11-5/8 x 9 in.

GROWOLL, A.

Cabinet Q Shelf 1 No. 8

Three centuries of English booktrade bibliography: an essay on the beginnings of booktrade bibliography since the introduction of printing, and in England since 1595. New York, 1903. Illus. Published for The Dibdin Club.

Half morocco; 9¾ x 6¾ x 1 in.

GRONINGEN

Cabinet AA Shelf 3 No. 18

See Printing, Historical, Holland.

GROTIUS, HUGONIS

Cabinet E Shelf 4 No. 18

Annales et historiae de rebus belgicis. Amsteledami, 1657. Johan Blaeu.

Calf; 14 x 9½ x 2½ ins. Brunet 2, 1767.

GROWOLL, ADOLF

Cabinet S Shelf 5 No. 10

See Biographies, Editors.

GROOT, J. de

Cabinet Shelf No.

See Specimen Books, Types, Holland.

GROULLEAU, ESTIENNE (I)

Cabinet 69 Shelf 1 No. 13

See Early Printing in France. Paris, 1547.

GRUBER, CARL ANTON

Cabinet X Shelf 1 No. 92

Elogia et epigraphia. Quibus accedit diagnosis librorum ab arte typographica inventae, usque ad annum 1560 typis editorum. Posonii (Presburgh, Germany) 1805.
Brief account of printing and books from the invention of moveable types to the year 1560. First title "Elogia et epigraphia" has nothing to do with printing.

Half leather; 8-3/4 x 7-1/8 x 3/8 in.

GRUEL, LEON

Cabinet Manuel historique et bibliographique de l'amateur de reliures. Par Léon Gruel, relieur. Paris, 1887. Gruel et Engelmann, Editeurs. Illus.
II Shelf 5 No. 37

Author's ex - libris pasted in.

Half morocco; 12½ x 10 x 1-3/8 in.

GRÜNINGER, JOHANN

Cabinet U Shelf 5 No. 38

Types, identy of Johann Grüninger's; true name of Grüninger.

see
PROCTOR, ROBERT. Bibliographical essays...London, 1905, pp.7, 20, 21

GUADALAJARA

Cabinet Mexico. Shelf No.

See "MEXICO", Guadalajara...

GRUEL, LÉON

Cabinet X Shelf 3 No. 44

Recherches sur les origines des marques anciennes qui se recontrent dans l'art et dans l'industrie du XV au XIXe siècle. Par rapport au chiffre quatre. Paris et Bruxelles, 1926. Illus.

History of the origin of devices in its relation to the figure 4, as used in art and industry of the 15th century.

Half morocco; 11½ x 7-5/8 in.

GRÜNINGER [Reinhard], JOHANN

Cabinet Shelf No.

See also
Incunabula. [Verdena, Johannes de]. Sermones ...Strassburg, 1487.

GUADALAJARA DE MÉXICO

Cabinet Shelf No.

See Printing, Historical. Mexico.

GRÜNINGER, JOHANNES

Cabinet X Shelf 3 No. 13

Bio-bibliographical notes, Grüninger, printer, Strassburg, 1483-1531. With printer marks.

see
HEITZ, PAUL. Elsässische büchermarken...p.xvi, plate 1.

GRUWELL, J. P.

Cabinet L Shelf 2 No. 44

English language, a reformed alphabet of the. By J.P. Gruwell...Aliance, Ohio. n.d. circa 1891. Brochure

Item B in book with binder's title "Various attempts at alphabets".

GUALTIERE, THOMAS

Cabinet T Shelf 2 No. 6 [vol.4]

Books printed by Thomas Gaultiere. London, 1550 1553. Bibliographical notes.

see
DIBDIN'S "Typographical Antiquities" ...London, 1810-1819, vol.IV, p.332

GRÜNINGER, JOHANN.

Cabinet 75 Shelf 1 No. 5

Biography.

See Biographies, Printers. Grüninger, Johann ...

GRUYER, GUSTAVE

Cabinet K Shelf 6 No. 16

Illustrations des écrits de Jérome Savonarole publiés en Itali au 15e et au 16e siècle, et les paroles de Savonarole sur l'art. Par Gustave Gruyer. Ouvrage accompagné de 33 gravures executées d'après les bois originaux. Paris, 1879.

Paper; 11 x 8-7/8 x ½ in.

GUARDIAN PRESS (Taylor, Garnett Evans & Co. Ltd.)

Cabinet Shelf No.

See SPECIMEN BOOKS, TYPES. Printers'. Gr. Britain

GRUNINGER (John Reinhardt)

Cabinet U Shelf 5 No. 52

Excerpt relating to Gruninger editions, 1496, 1498, 1501, 1502, reprinted in Bibliographical Notes of The Gentleman's Magazine, pp.14-16. Article signed, Observator.

GRYPHIUS, SEBASTIEN.

Cabinet 70 Shelf 1 No. 50

See Poetry of Printing. Epigrams in honor of printers in Vulteis. "Epigrammatum", Lyons, 1538.

GUARIN, THOMAS

Cabinet X Shelf 3 No. 15

Biographical sketch, with printer mark, Guarin, Basel, 1529-1592.

see
HEITZ, PAUL
Basler büchermarken... pp.xxxvi, 103, 105

GRÜNINGER, JOHANN

Cabinet Y Shelf 4 No. 4

(Note on Grüninger and his printing at Strasbourg, 1480)

see
VOULLIÉME, ERNST. (Die)
Deutschen drucker des fünfzehnten jahrhunderts...p.110

GRYPHIUS (Gryphe), SEBASTIENE

Cabinet Shelf No.

See also
Early Printing in France. Lyons, [various dates].
also Imprints, France. Gryphe.

GUARINO DEI GUARINI (Paolo)

Cabinet X Shelf 3 No. 14

Bibliographical note, with printer mark, Guarino, Forli, 1495.

see
KRISTELLER, Dr. Paul
Italienischen buchdrucker...p.20

GUASP, FELIPE

Cabinet AA Shelf 5 No. 8.01

(La) Antiguedad de la Imprenta de Guasp. Fundada en 1579) Datos historicos, bibliografia y resena del acto celebrado el día 19 de Marzo de este año 1931. Por Felipe Guasp y Pou. Palme de Mallorca.

With genealogy of Guasp family of printers, facsimiles, portrait, picture of old printing press. This house was founded in 1579.

Paper; 8½ x 5-3/4 x 3/8 in.

GUASP FAMILY OR PRINTERS

Cabinet AA Shelf 5 No. 8

Dinastie de impresores mas antiqua de Europa (1579 a 1897, Palma). Noticias y documentos recogidos por Don Gabriel Llabrés y Quintana ... Mahon, 1897. (Extrait de la "Revista de Menorca")

Biographic genealogical account of a long practising family of Spanish printers.

Half morocco; 8-7/8 x 6-7/8 in.

GUATEMALA

Cabinet 79 Shelf 2 No. 4

Doctrina Cristiana (1724) en lengua Guatemalteca ...Reimpresa del unico ejemplar conocido y precedida de una biografia de su autor. Por Jose Toribio Medina. Santiago, 1905.

Half morocco; 7-5/8 x 4½ in. Chiappa 163

GUATEMALA

Cabinet 79 Shelf 1 No. 5

(La) Imprenta en Guatemala (1660-1821.) Por José Toribio Medina. Santiago de Chile, 1910. Facs.

Bio-bibliographical account.

Cloth; 12 x 8½ x 1¾ in. Chiappa 199

GUATEMALA (Central America)

Cabinet 79 Shelf 2 No. 27

Introduction of printing, 1660 by Pineda Ibarra, and spread of printing in Guatemala.

see

SANCHEZ, CARLOS ENRIQUE. (La) Imprenta en el Ecuador...Quito, 1935, p. 29.

GUATEMALA

Cabinet Shelf No.

See also cards with following sub-heads:

I Printing, Historical (Sp. America) Guatemala
II Early Printing in Spanish America "
III Government Printing Offices (Sp. America). Guatemala.

GUAZZO, BROTHER FRANCESCO MARIA

Cabinet M Shelf 1 No. 54

Compendium maleficarum, collected in 3 books from many sources...Edited with notes by The Rev. Montague Summers. Translated by E.A. Ashwin. Printed in Great Britain by Richard Clay & Sons, Limited, Bungay Suffolk. 1929.

The original "Compendium Maleficarum" was issued in Milan in 1608.

Cloth; 10½ x 7¾ x 1 in.

GUEDALLA, PHILIP

Cabinet R Shelf 5 No. 149

Dr. Ben Franklin. Forum Americana Series---I. Drawings by E.H. Suydam.

Excerpt from Forum, January, 1926.

Item (k) in book with binder's title "Benjamin Franklin: various pamphlets". 1853-1926.

GUEDON, REMIGIUS

Cabinet X Shelf 3 No. 13

Bibliographical note, Guedon, printer, Strassburg, 1549.

see

HEITZ, PAUL. Elsässische büchermarken...

GUEFFIER V. MEHÉE

Cabinet X Shelf 4 No. 98

Memoire et dénonciation pour le Sr. Gueffier, imprimeur, Paris 1793.

Before presenting his case, Gueffier gives a brief biographical sketch of his family, booksellers and printers, in Paris since 1582.

Paper; 7-3/8 x 4-3/4 x ¼ in.

GUEINTZIUS (C.)

Cabinet X Shelf 1 No. 36

Encomium nobilis atque utilis artis typographicae

[Printed in Wolf, "Monumenta Typographica) vol. I, p. 1040

GÜEMES, FR. CECILIO

Cabinet Shelf No.

See Pérez (FR. Angel) y FR. Cecilio Güemes.

GUÉRAUD, ARMAND-LAURENT

Cabinet W Shelf 3 No. 8

Notice sur Armand-Laurent Guéraud, imprimeur-libraire. Par Émile Gautier. Nantes, 1862.

Boards; 12 x 9½ in.

GUÉRAUD, ARMAND-LAURENT

Cabinet V Shelf 5 No. 2.01

(Printer-publisher, Nantes, 1824-1859.)

See Gautier, Émile. Notice sur Armand-Laurent Géraud...

GUÉRIN, Hippolyte-Louis

Cabinet V Shelf 3 No. 18

(Bio-bibliographical notes relating to the Guerin family of printers-publishers, Paris, 1606-1789)

see

WERDET, EDMOND. Histoire du livre en France...3me partie (2), p.298

GUERINET, ARMAND (EDITOR)

Cabinet K Shelf 1 No. 22 3

Recueil de 460 ornaments typographiques et gravures sur cuire, des epoques 1er Empire, Louis XVI, Louis XV, Louis XIV et Renaissance, Publie par Armand Guerinet, Editeur. Paris, n. d.

48 plates, in folder; 12 x 8-3/8 in.

GUERNIER, LOUIS

Cabinet MM Shelf 1 No. 60

Conseils pratiques sur la composition typographique. Conférences faites aux cours du soir de l'École Estienne. Paris, 1903.

Cloth; 8¼ x 5-5/8 x 3/8 in.

GUERNSEY, A.H.

Cabinet S Shelf 5 No. 14

Making Money: The American Bank Note Company. An excerpt from "Harper's New Monthly Magazine." Feb. 1862.

Item 11 in volume "Printing Processes: Excerpts from Magazines, etc."

GUERRA, DOMENICO and GIAMBATTISTA

Cabinet E Shelf 2 No. 16

See Early Printing in Italy. Venice, 1574. Domenico and Giambattista Guerra.

GUIFFREY, JULES

Cabinet W Shelf 3 No. 10

Famille de Jean Cousin, peintre et verrier du seizième siècle. Par Jules Guiffrey. Paris, 1881. Extrait des Mémoires de la Société nationales des Antiquaires de France, tome XLI.

Half morocco; 9 x 5¾ in.

GUILD OF WOMEN-BINDERS

Cabinet Shelf No.

See WOMEN-BINDERS GUILD

GUIANA

Cabinet Shelf No.

See British Guiana
" also Dutch "
" " French "

GUIFFREY, JULES

Cabinet J Shelf 4 No. 5

(La) Famille de Jean Cousin, peintre et verrier du 16e siècle. Par Jules Guiffrey. Lu dans les séances des 18 Mai et 15 Juin, 1881. (Paris). Excerpt.

Bound in with "L'Art du dessin...Par Jean Cousin. Paris, n.d. circa 1550.

Half morocco; 15¼ x 12 x ½ in.

GUILDHALL (THE) OF THE CITY OF LONDON

Cabinet QQ Shelf 3 No. 28

Short account of its historic associations... Compiled by Sir John James Baddeley, J.P. Fifth revised edition. London, 1921. Illus.

Concerning the library and its contents, see p. 99.

Paper; 8½ x 5½ x ½ in.

GUIDE BOOKS.

Cabinet 18 Shelf 1 No. 17

(Bibliography of Italian guide books, and Italy's early explorers.) Romischer Brief.

In Zeitschrift fur Bucherfreunde, 1914-15, part 2, p.453 of Supplement ("Beiblatt")

GUIFFREY, J.

Cabinet FF Shelf 3 No. 9 Env.

(Le) Polytipe de Mm. Hoffmann, graveurs, 1783-1787. Documents communiques et annotes par M. J. Guiffrey.

Excerpt in manila envelope.

GUILDS

Cabinet T Shelf 2 No. 33

Account of Trade Guilds

See BLADES, WILLIAM. Life and typography of William Caxton...London, 1861 (vol.1, index)

GUIDE BOOKS.

Cabinet 18 Shelf 1 No. 15

Guide books as seen from a bibliphiles point of view: History and desirability as collectors items.

In Zeitschrift für Bücherfreunde, 1913-14, part 2, p.475 of Supplement ("Beiblatt")

GUIGNES, JOSEPH de.

Cabinet V Shelf 6 No. 18

Essai historique. Sur l'origine des caractères Orientaux de l'imprimerie royale, sur les ouvrages qui ont été imprimés en Paris, en Arabe...et sur les caractères Grecs de François 1er appelés communément Grecs du Roi. Par M. de Guignes. [ca. 1780]

Half morocco; 10-7/8 x 8½ in.

GUILDS

Cabinet QQ Shelf 5 No. 23

Authentic records of the Guild merchant of Preston in the year 1822. Carefully compiled by I. Wilcockson. Preston, 1822.

Has portrait of Grimshaw, Guild Mayor in 1802-1822; also a print of the procession of trades.
Bound in with " Charters granted by different sovereigns", Preston, 1821

Half calf; 8 x 5 in.

GUIDE BOOKS.

Cabinet S Shelf 6 No. 7

Red Book, The Great.

See Directories, London Post-Office. The Great Red Book.

GUIGNES, JOSEPH de

Cabinet T Shelf 4 No. 50

Historical essay on the origin of Oriental characters in the Royal Printing-House, on the works which have been printed at Paris, in Arabic, Syriac, Armenian, etc., and on the Greek characters of Francis I. commonly called the King's Greek. Translated from the French. London, 1789. 2 Vol. bound in 1.
Extracts of manuscripts in the library of the King of France.

Half calf; 8-3/8 x 5¼ x 2-3/8 in.

GUILDS.

Cabinet T Shelf 6 No. 12

Banquet at Guild Hall, London, Nov. 10, 1884. The Invitation; the Souvenir, and Musical Programme; the Menu, a note relating to the printing for the occasion.

Portfolio, boards; 12¼ x 10½ in.

GUIDE BOOKS (see) also

Cabinet Shelf No.

MAPS

TIMETABLES

GUILD OF HANDICRAFT (England)

Cabinet M Shelf 2 No. 26

(An) Endeavour towards the teaching of John Ruskin and William Morris...Being an account of the aims of the Guild of Handicraft. By C.R. Ashbee, London, 1901.
This is the first book printed at the Essex House Press in the new type designed by C.R. Ashbee.

Vellum; 8½ x 6 in.

GUILDS

Cabinet QQ Shelf 5 No. 13

City Companies of London and their good works: A record of their history, charity and treasure By P.H. Ditchfield. London, 1904. Illus.

Cloth; 11-5/8 x 9½ in.

GUILDS

Cabinet U Shelf 3 No. 63

Cobden-Sanderson, T.J. Ecce mundus: Industrial ideals and the book beautiful. Hammersmith (London). Printed at the Chiswick Press: Charles Whittingham & Co., 1902.

Boards; 8½ x 6-1/8 in.

GUILDS

Cabinet V Shelf 5 No. 25

(Historical study) Étude historique sur les corporations professionnelles chez les Romains, depuis les origines jusqu'a la chute de l'Empire d'Occident. Par J.-P. Waltzing. Louvain. 1925, 1926. (2 vols.)

Paper; 8-5/8 x 5-5/8 in.

GUILDS

Cabinet QQ Shelf 5 No. 21

Worshipful Company of Grocers: an historical retrospect, 1345-1923. By J. Aubrey Rees, London, 1923. Illus.

Cloth; 8¾ x 5½ in.

GUILDS

Cabinet QQ Shelf 5 No. 18

(Flemish guilds and their emblems) Description de mereau et autres objets amiens des gildes et corps de metiers, eglises etc. Par L. Minard-Van HOOrebeke. Gand. 1877,1878. (2 vols. illus).

Boards, cloth back; 13½ x 10¼ in.

GUILDS

Cabinet K Shelf 1 No. 19

Medals, tokens, trade and professional marks of many cities in Holland. Reproductions of.

See Dirks, J. Atlas van platen... Haarlem, 1879.

GUILDS (see also)

Cabinet Shelf No.

Labor Questions
Societies, Printers

GUILDS

Cabinet QQ Shelf 5 No. 22

Gild merchants: a contribution to British municipal history. By Charles Gross. Oxford, 1890. (2 vols.)

Cloth; 9 x 6 in.

GUILDS

Cabinet QQ Shelf 5 No. 20

Merchant and craft guilds: a history of the Aberdeen incorporated trades. By Ebenezer Bain, Aberdeen, 1887. Illus.

Cloth; 9¼ x 5¾ in.

Guilds, Bookbinders.

Cabinet 22 Shelf 1 No. 19

(Rules for German bookbinders.) Deutsche buchbinder-Ordnungen, von Karl Bucher.

Includes history of bookbinding, with excerpts from documents dated 1550 relating to handwork, hours of work, etc.

In Archiv für Deutschen Buchhandels, vol. XIX, p.305-376.

GUILDS

Cabinet QQ Shelf 5 No. 19

Glasgow, sketch of the rise and progress of the Trades' House of, its constitution, funds, and bye-laws. By George Crawford. Glasgow 1858.

Cloth: 9¼ x 5¾ x 1 in.

GUILDS

Cabinet QQ Shelf 4 No. 42

(de) Noord-Nederlandsche Gildepenningen wetenschlappelijk en historisch beschreven en afgebeeld. Door Mr. Jacob Dirks. Uitgeven door Teyler's Tweede Genootschap. Haarlem, 1878. (2 vols.)

Paper; 9½ x 6-3/8 in.

GUILDS, Printers

Cabinet AA Shelf 4 No. 5 2 Vols.

Kleerkooper, M.M.: De boekhandel te Amsterdam voornamelijk in de 17e eeuw ... 'S - Gravenhage, 1914-16. 2 Vols.

See "Zaak-en Plaatsnamregister," p. 1727 of the above work.

Half morocco; 9½ x 6⅞ in.

GUILDS

Cabinet QQ Shelf 5 No. 14

Glasgow, 1605-1678, records of the Trades House of. Glasgow: Printed for the Trades House of Glasgow, 1910. With facs.

Cloth; 10 x 7 x 2 in.

GUILDS

Cabinet X Shelf 4 No. 77

(Printers and bookbinders guilds , Holland, 1769, regulations of)
Ordonnantie voor het boek-en-konst verkoopers, nevens boek-kaart-pleat drukkers... Amsterdam, by Pieter Mortier, 1769.

Boards; 8-1/8 x 6½ in.

GUILDS, Printers

Cabinet 75 Shelf 1 No. 7

St. Luke the Evangelist and the Dublin printers. A paper read before the Bibliographical Society by E. R. McC. Dix.

In Trans. Biblio. Soc. Vol. VII, 1902-1904. pp. 75-85.

GUILDS

Cabinet QQ Shelf 2 No. 17

Historical account of guilds. Chap. 8, p. 139 in "Romance of Commerce. By H. Gordon Selfridge. London, 1923. Illus.

Cloth; 8-7/8 x 5-7/8 x 2-1/8 in.

GUILDS

Cabinet S Shelf 4 No. 128

Production marks in the regulation of trade by the Guilds and Companies.

See Schecter, Frank I. The historical foundations of the law relating to trademarks ... pp. 38-77.

GUILFORD and JONES

Cabinet Shelf No.

See Specimen Books, Types. United States. Ohio Type Foundry.

GUILLARD, CHARLOTTE

Cabinet V Shelf 5 No. 12

Genealogical biographical notes and comments concerning a celebrated early 16th century women printer.

See MADDEN, J.P.A. Lettres d'un bibliographie...Paris, 1878, p.261

GUILLARD, CHARLOTTE

Cabinet W Shelf 3 No. 61

Imprimeur au XV siècle. Par M. Joseph Dumoulin. Paris, 1896.

Half morocco; 9½ x 6 in.

GUILLARD, CHARLOTTE

Cabinet TT Shelf 5 No. 91

Notice of C. Guillard, 1490-1540, the widow of Berthold Rembolt.

See Stark, Adam. Printing: Its antecendents...London, 1855

GUILLARD, CHARLOTTE

Cabinet T Shelf 5 No. 91

Notice of Charlotte Guillard, printer, widow of Claude Chevallon, and Berthold Rembolt. Paris, 1490-1540.

see STARK, ADAM. Printing: Its antecedents...London, 1855.

GUILLARD, CHARLOTTE

Cabinet V Shelf 5 No. 7

(Widow of Rembolt, c. Guillard manages the printing office during fifty years.)

see CRAPELET, CH. "Études pratiques...sur la typographie".Paris,1837. P.18 (tome 1)

GUILLARD, CHARLOTTE (see also)

Cabinet Shelf No.

EARLY PRINTING IN FRANCE. Paris 1540
1544
EARLY PRINTING IN FRANCE. Paris, 1540 Claude Chevallon (Veuve)...
BIOGRAPHIES, Printers
WOMEN PRINTERS.

GUILLAUME le BÉ

Cabinet Shelf No.

See Le Bé, Guillaume.

GUILLÉ (Doctor)

Cabinet W Shelf 1 No. 37

Essai sur l'instruction des aveugles, ou exposé analytique des procédés employés pour les instruire; par le Docteur Guillé. Paris, imprimé par les aveugles. 1817. Illus.

Boards; 8-3/4 x 5¼ in.

GUILLIÉ (Docteur)

Cabinet II Shelf 6 No. 3

Essai sur l'instruction des aveugles, ou exposé analytique des procédes employés pour les instruire...A Paris, imprimé par les aveugles, 1817. With engravings.

Bound in with English translation of above essay: London, 1819.

Half calf; 8½ x 5-1/8 x 1-1/8 in.

GUILLÉ --

Cabinet II Shelf 6 No. 4

Notice historique sur l'instruction des jenues aveugles...Paris, Imprimé par les jeunes aveugles, 1819.

Printed throughout in embossed types.

Boards; 11½ x 8½ x 1-3/8 in.

GUILLEMOT, MATTHIEU.

Cabinet 69 Shelf 1 No. 60

See Early Printing in France. Paris, 1600.

GUILLEN DE BROCAR, ARNALD

See Imprints: Guillen de Brocar, Alcala, 1514-1517.

GUJARATI TYPE FOUNDRY

Cabinet Shelf No.

See Specimen Book, Types. India

GUILLERETE (Stephano)

Cabinet X Shelf 3 No. 14

Bibliographical note, with printer mark, Guillerete, Rome, 1506-24.

see KRISTELLER, Dr. Paul. Italienischen buchdrucker...p.56

GUILMAIN, RENÉ

Cabinet RR Shelf 6 No. 16

Fabrication du papier de ses origines au 19e siècle. (Papermaking from the earliest times to the 19th century. Issued in 5 parts, illus.). n.p., n.d.
Part I. Types d'appareils primitifs. (Primitive tools)
" 2. La fabrication en Asie. Illus.
"3 & 4 " " en Europe. "
" 5. Le matériel mécanique de papeterie...

Parts loose, in folder; 13-3/4 x 11¼ in.

GULDEMUND, HANS

Cabinet Y Shelf 3 No. 98

Nürnberger brief-maler, Hans Guldemund. von Walter Fries. (Bibliographical account of illustrated books, colored, or printed by Guldemund, 1521-1555)

Article in Zeitschrift für Buchkunde, vol. I, 1924, p.36.

GULDENSCHAFF, JOHANN

Cabinet B Shelf 2 No. 8

(Illustrated books printed by Guldenschaff, Cologne, 1479-90)

see SCHRAMM, ALBERT. (Der) Bilderschmuck der frühdrucke...Leipzig, 1924.

GULYAS, PAUL

Cabinet 26 Shelf 1 No. 20

(Der) Wiener buchdrucker Rafael Hoffhalter und sein sohn in Ungarn. (The Vienna printer Rafael Hoffhalter and his son in Hungary in 1563-

Article in the "Gutenberg-Gesellschaft Jahrbuch" 1930, pp.198-208.

GUMEIL, Diego de and Peter Michael

Cabinet X Shelf 3 No. 19

Bio-bibliographical sketch, with printer mark, de Diego (Sevilla), 1491-1494, 1494-1518.

see
HAEBLER, KONRAD. (Spanish and Portuguese printer marks...p.xi)

GURSCH, EMIL

Cabinet Shelf No.

See Specimen Books, Types. Germany.

GUTENBERG

See also Printers' Celebrations.

GUMIEL, GIEGO de

Cabinet 75 Shelf 2 No. 6

Printer, Valencia, 1515, his work.

See Transactions of the Bibliographical Society, "The Library," Vol. VI, 1925-1926, pp. 11-13.

GUSMAN, PIERRE

Cabinet J Shelf 5 No. 16

(La) Gravure Francaise au 18e siècle. Avec une suite de 44 estampes. Paris, n.d. circa 1916.

Portfolio; 18 x 13 in.

GUTENBERG, JOHANN.

Cabinet E Shelf 3 No. 5

See Adamo, Melchiore. Vitae Germanorum philosophorum. p.l.

GUMMED PAPER

Cabinet P Shelf 2 No. 47.01

Suggestions (110) new gummed paper. Mid-States Gummed Paper Company, Chicago, 1934.

Illus. Brochure.

GUSMAN, PIERRE

Cabinet K Shelf 6 No. 36

L'Illustration du livre Francais (1478-1934). Étude historique, tec.nique et critique. Par Pierre Gusman. Bulletin Officiel des Maitres Imprimeurs de France. Paris (Noel, 1934)

On the evolution of book illustration in France. Section devoted to processes and specimens of color printing.

Paper; $12\frac{1}{2}$ x $9\frac{1}{4}$ in.

GUTENBERG, JOHANN

Cabinet L Shelf 2 No. 9

Alphabet which served as a model for Gutenberg's type, concerning the. Brief account.

See IMPERIAL ROYAL PRINTING OFFICE. Austria.
Buchschriften des mittelalters...Wien, 1852, p.19

GUMUCHIAN et CIE

Cabinet PF Shelf 5 No. 40

Reliures du 15e au 19e siècle, en vente a la librairie Gumuchian et Cie. Paris, 1930. Catalogue XII.

Half morocco; 13 x 10 x 1-7/8 in.

GUSTAFSON, DAVID

Cabinet S Shelf 2 No. 9

American printing industry:,Bulletin No.3. Who's Who in printing in the United States and Canada [in 2 parts]. By David Gustafson. Published by the author. Pittsburgh, 1933.

Paper; 9 x 6 in.

GUTENBERG, JOHANN

Cabinet W Shelf 2 No. 1

Appel au monde civilisé pour celebré dignement la fête seculaire de l'art de l'imprimerie par l'erection d'un monument en l'honneur de son inventeur Jean Gensfleisch ... Mayence, 1832. Pamphlet.

Bound in vol. "Gutenberg, inventeur de l'imprimerie. Mélangés", item 21.

GUPPY, HENRY

Cabinet U Shelf 5 No. 36

Stepping stones to the art of typography. With fourteen facsimiles. Reprinted from "The Bulletin of the John Rylands Library," vol. 12, No. 1, January 1928. Manchester.

Half morocco; 10-1/8 x $6\frac{1}{2}$ x $\frac{1}{2}$ in.

GUTCH, JOHN MATHEW

Cabinet L Shelf 3 No. 11

Observations or notes upon the writings of the ancients, upon the materials which they used and upon the introduction of the art of printing. Being from papers read before The Philosophical and Literary Society, 1827. By J.M. Gutch. Bristol: Printed by J.M. Gutch, 1827.

Boards; 10 x $6\frac{1}{2}$ in.

GUTENBERG, JOHANN.

Cabinet 14 Shelf 2 No. 1

Bible of 42-lines. Mainz [1450-1455] One leaf.

Bound in with Bibliographical Essay by A. Edward Newton, New York, 1921.

GURMUKKI

Cabinet II Shelf 3 No. 63 Box

Language characters.

See AMERICAN BIBLE SOCIETY. Gummurukki ...

GUTENBERG.

Cabinet AA Shelf 3 No. 21

Linde, A. Van der: Gutenberg. (Brochure of 40 pages, dated Den Haag, 1870; in Dutch).
Autographed by the author: A.L.S. bound in.

Half morocco; 9 x $5\frac{3}{4}$ in.

GUTENBERG, JOHANN.

Cabinet 14 Shelf 2 No. 2

Bible of 42 lines [Mainz, 1450-1455] Facsimile, 2 vols. Leipzig: Insel-Verlag, 1913.

GUTENBERG, JOHANN

Cabinet Y Shelf 4 No. 4

(Bio-bibliographical notes relating to Gutenberg. With consideration of the types used by him in printing his great Bible)

see VOULLIÉME, ERNST . (Die) Deutschen drucker des fünfzehnten jahrhunderts...p.70

GUTENBERG, JOHANN

Stack A Shelf 1 & 2 Number 66

Bullen, Henry Lewis: A defense of Johann Gutenberg, inventor of typography. In The Inland Printor, Vol. LXVI, p. 190. Illus.

GUTENBERG, JOHANN

Cabinet W Shelf 2 No. 140

Delon, Ch.: Gutenberg et l'invention de l'imprimerie. Par Ch. Delon. Deuzième édition. Paris, 1884. Illus.

Half morocco; 5-7/8 x 3-3/4 in.

GUTENBERG, JOHANN

Cabinet V Shelf 3 No. 15

(Biographical account of the inventor of movable types; his genealogy, his legal controversies, books printed by him)

see WERDET, EDMOND. Histoire du livre en France...lre partie, pp.214-271

GUTENBERG, JOHANN

Cabinet W Shelf 2 No. 1

Cenni sulla invenzione delle stampa: Statua innalzata a Guttenberg in Magonza. Articolo estrato dal Teatro Universale ... Torino, Tomo V, 1838 - n.205. Dal Stamperia Casali, Forli, 1841.

Item 24 in volume "Gutenberg l'inventeur de l'imprimerie - Melanges."

GUTENBERG, JOHANN

Cabinet Y Shelf 1 No. 53

Deutscher druck von 1456 in der Gutenbergtype: Die turkenbullen Pabst Calixtus III. In nachbildung herausgegeben und untersucht von Paul Schwenke. Mit eine geschichtlich-sprachlichen abhandlung von Hermann Degering. Berlin, 1911. Seltene druck der Königlichen bibliothek zu Berlin. Facsimiles.

Half morocco; 10½ x 7-1/8 x 3/8 in.

GUTENBERG, JOHANN

Cabinet X Shelf 5 No. 3

[Biographical account of the man and his invention]. n.a.n. Illus. account. Extract from unidentified periodical [1876].

p. 33 in vol. with binder's title "Scrap-Book, 1705-1891, relating to printing."

GUTENBERG, JOHANN

Cabinet Y Shelf 1 No. 42

(Coat-of-arms; Gutenbergs ancestry; monuments to Gutenberg, medals, etc. With descriptive account.)

See index to MEISNER, HEINRICH and JOHANN LUTHER (Die) Erfindung der buchdruckerkunst...

GUTENBERG, JOHANN

Cabinet W Shelf 2 No. 1

Didot, Ambroise Firmin: Gutenberg (Jean ou Hans Gensfleisch). Extrait de la Nouvelle Biographie Génerale, publiée par MM. Firmin Didot, frères et fils. Paris, n.d.
Bio-bibliographical account.

Item 10 in volume "Gutenberg, l'inventeur de l'imprimere - Melanges."

GUTENBERG, JOHANN

Cabinet Y Shelf 1 No. 23

Biographical, bibliographical notes and comments. Gutenberg's invention,; legal controversies; his partnerships; false claims to his invention, etc. Illus.

See LINDE, ANTONIOUS van der. Geschichte der erfindung buchdruckkunst... Berlin, 1886. (see index vol.3)

GUTENBERG, JOHANN

Cabinet Y Shelf 3 No. 105

(Comparison of the art of Gutenberg-Bodoni-Morris. A lecture delivered at a meeting of printers in Switzerland, Sept. 13, 1924) Eine vergleichung ihre kunst. Vortrag an der versammlung des bildungsverbandes Schwarz buchdrucker. Karl J. Luthi. Berne 1925.

Stiff paper; 5-3/4 x 4-3/8 x ¼ in.

GUTENBERG, JOHANN.

Cabinet W Shelf 2 No. 15

Didot, Ambroise Firmin: Jean ou Hans Gensfleisch. Par Ambroise Firmin Didot. Extrait de la Nouvelle biographie generale.
Historical, biographical and bibliographical account.

Full morocco; 9¾ x 5¾ in.

GUTENBERG, JOHANN

Cabinet X Shelf 2 No. 25

(Biographical; with account of the Gensfleich family, the Gutenberg home in Mainz, Gutenberg's burial place, etc.)
Account in the "Gedenk-Buch der vierten jubelfeier der erfindung der buchdruck in Mainz". Mainz, 1840.

Boards; 9¾ x 6½ in.

GUTENBERG, JOHANN

Cabinet Y Shelf 1 No. 47

(Coster to Gutenberg: The earliest impressions in Holland and the invention of printing) von Coster zu Gutenberg: Der hollandische frühdruck und die erfindung des buchdruckes. Gottfried Zedler. Mit 28 doppeltafeln und 49 abbildungen, darunter 8 typentafeln. Leipzig, 1921.

Stamped cloth; 11-3/8 x 8-7/8 x 1¼ in.

GUTENBERG, JOHANN

Cabinet X Shelf 2 No. 22

Dinglestedt, Franz: Sechs jahrhundert aus Gutenberg's leben. Kleine gabe zum grossen feste. Cassel, 1840. Illus.
A poem in six cantos. The historical events of the century are sung under the dates of the centenaries of the invention of printing.

Half morocco; 14¼ x 10-3/8 x 3/8 in.

GUTENBERG, JOHANN.

Cabinet Shelf No.

See Biographies, Printers. (Neumeister, Johann) Les pérégrinations de J. Neumeister, compagnon de Gutenberg en Allemagne....

GUTENBERG, JOHANN

Cabinet V Shelf 2 No. 48

Debuts de l'imprimerie a Strasbourg, recherches sur les travaux mysterieux de Gutenberg dans cette ville, et sur le proces qui lui fut intente en 1439 a cette occasion. Paris. 1840.

Half morocco; 10-3/8 x 6-7/8 in.

GUTENBERG, JOHANN.

Cabinet W Shelf 2 No. 1

Discours prononcé a la barre de l'assemblée Nationale, au nom des imprimeurs, par Anacharsis Cloots, Paris, 1792. Pamphlet.

A plea to recognize Gutenberg as one of the greatest benefactors of man, and to allow him a niche of recognition in the French Pantheon.

Bound in volume "Gutenberg, inventeur de l'imprimerie, Melanges," item 20.

GUTENBERG, JOHANN

Cabinet W Shelf 2 No. 1

(Discovery of the Gutenberg Bible dated 1457. Note on the). Memoire sur la decouverte d'un exemplaire de la Bible connu sous le nom de Gutenberg. Par Dom. Maugerard. Socìetè Royale des Science [Paris]. Dec. 24, 1789. Manuscript in pamphlet form.

Item 3 in volume "Gutenberg inventeur de l'imprimerie - Melanges."

GUTENBERG, JOHANN

Cabinet X Shelf 2 No. 59

(Documental records relating to Gutenberg) Die urkundlichen nachrichten über Johann Gutenberg. von Karl Schorbach in Strassburg.

See HARTWIG, OTTO (Compiler) Festschrift...Mainz, 1900, pp.133-256

GUTENBERG, Johann

Cabinet 14 Shelf 2 No. 4

DONAT FRAGMENT in the Book Museum, Leipzig. In reproduction from the Art Shop of Max Breslauer, Leipzig, 1926.

Item in manila envelope.

GUTENBERG, JOHANNES

Cabinet X Shelf 2 No. 60

Drama in vier akten

See FICTION, PRINTING. Gutenberg...

GUTENBERG, JOHANN.

Cabinet W Shelf 2 No. 1

Die Druckerie zu Eltville in Rheingan und ihre erzeugnisse, von F.W. E.Roth, Augsburg,1886. (Trans. The press at Eltville and its products.)

Includes an account of Gutenberg's second impression and its relation to the Eltville press.

Bound in volume "Gutenberg inventeur de l'imprimerie. Melanges," item 13.

GUTENBERG, JOHANN

Cabinet S Shelf 4 No. 68.01

Earlier work of Gutenberg, the. By Joel Eno. A review of Otto Hupp's argument. March 1903. Excerpt from The Literary Collector, vol.5. With facsimiles.

In box marked "Pamphlets and excerpts relating to Gutenberg"

GUTENBERG, JOHANN

Cabinet T Shelf 6 No. 9

Earliest efforts of the printing press at Strasburg and Mayence from 1436 to 1467, Gutenberg

See HUMPHREYS, NOEL. History of the art of printing...London, 1867, p.68

GUTENBERG, JOHANN

Cabinet W Shelf 2 No. 36

Eloge historique de Jean Gensfleisch dit Guttenberg, premier inventeur de l'art typographique à Mayence. Par J. F. Nee de la Rochelle. Paris, 1811. Portrait.

Tree calf; 8-3/8 x 5¼ in.

GUTENBERG, JOHANN

Cabinet Y Shelf 1 No. 45

Erfinder der buchdruckerkunst. von Albrecht Thoma. Munchen, 1900. Mit 8 abbildungen in tondruck nach originalen von maler Fritz Bergen, 8 shriftproben, 1 siegelbild, 1 wappen und 1 portrait.

Cloth, lithograph on front cover; 9 x 6¼ x 1 in.

GUTENBERG, JOHANN.

Cabinet Y Shelf 2 No. 19

Erfinder der buchdruckerkunst. Ein vorbild für die deutsche jugend. von Philipp Körber. Nürnberg, n.d. [after 1833]. Frontispiece steel engraving.

Paper boards; 6¾ x 4-3/8 x 3/8 in.

GUTENBERG, JOHANN

Cabinet Y Shelf 1 No. 11

Erfinder der buchdruckerkunst. Eine historische skizze mit mehreren zeichnungen und facsimile autographisch ausgefuhrt von den zöglingen der Strassburger Industrie-Schule. Strassburg, 1840. In lithography.

Half morocco; 9-3/4 x 7-3/4 x ¼ in.

GUTENBERG, JOHANN

Cabinet X Shelf 2 No. 26

Erfindung der buchdruckerkunst... Thuringisch-Erfurter gedenkbuch der vierten saecularfeier. Erfurt am 26 und 27 Juli, 1840.

Half morocco; 8 x 7/8 x 6 in.

GUTENBERG, JOHANN

Cabinet Y Shelf 1 No. 29

Erfindung der buchdruckerkunst nach den neuesten forschungen. Dem deutschen volk. Dargestellt von Prof. Karl Faulmann. Wien, 1891. Facsimiles.
Biographical historical account; includes genealogy of the Gensfleisch family.

Cloth; 9¼ x 6-5/8 x ½ in.

GUTENBERG, JOHANN

Cabinet W Shelf 2 No. 1

Esquisse historique de Gutenberg. Par J.P. Gama. Paris, 1857. Pamphlet.
Bio-bibliographical account.

Item 8 in volume "Gutenberg, l'inventeur de l'imprimerie - Melanges."

GUTENBERG, JOHANN

Cabinet W Shelf 2 No. 1

Essai d'Annales de la vie de Jean Gutenberg, inventeur de la typographie. Par Jér. Jerome Oberlin. Strasbourg, 1801. Frontispiece portrait. Pamphlet.
Bio-bibliographical.

Item 4 in volume "Gutenberg, l'inventeur de l'imprimerie - Melanges."

GUTENBERG, JOHANN

Cabinet W Shelf 2 No. 25

Essai d'annales de la vie de Jean Gutenberg, inventeur de la typographie. Par Jér. Jacques Oberlin. Strasbourg, 1801.

Half morocco; 8¾ x 5¾ in.

GUTENBERG, JOHANN

Cabinet Y Shelf 1 No. 5

Essai sur les monumens typographiques de Jean Gutenberg, Mayencais, inventeur de l'imprimerie. Mayence l'an 10 [1802]. Portrait of Gutenberg, engraved title, engraved dedication plate, facsimiles.
Bibliographical historical account. p.90: Chronological list of the works from the press of Fust and Schoeffer, 1454-1478.

Boards; 9¾ x 7-7/8 x ½ in.

GUTENBERG, JOHANN

Cabinet Y Shelf 2 No. 13

Falkenstein, Dr. Karl. Geschichte der Buchdruckerkunst in ihrer Entstehung und Ausbildung. (A memorial of the fourth centenary celebration of the invention of printing.) Leipzig, 1840.

Boards; 11¾ x 9¼ in.

GUTENBERG, JOHANN

Cabinet T Shelf 3 No. 2

Family of Gutenberg; Gutenberg's first experiments on printing; law suit, etc.

Account in DIBDIN'S Bibliographical Decameron...London, 1817, vol.1, pp.305-330.

GUTENBERG, JOHANN

Cabinet X Shelf 2 No. 21.01

Festgedichte. Allen verehren Gutenberg's und seiner kunst. Zur feier des vierten jubel-festes. Dresden, 1840.
Poetry in honor of Gutenberg, in celebration of the fourth centenary of printing.

Paper boards; 12½ x 9½ in.

GUTENBERG, JOHANN

Cabinet X Shelf 2 No. 61

Festrede zur feier der 450 jahr erfindung der buchdruckerkunst. von Dr. Paul Johannes Rée. Nürnberg, 1890. Pamphlet.

Item in manila envelope.

GUTENBERG, JOHANN

Cabinet X Shelf 2 No. 59

Festschrift zum 500 jahrigen geburtstag von Johann Gutenberg...Herausgegeben von Otto Hartwig. Mainz am 24 Juni 1900. Illus. (Memorial volume celebrating the 500th anniversary of the invention of printing).

Cloth; 11¾ x 9 in.

GUTENBERG, JOHANN

Cabinet X Shelf 2 No. 60

Festschrift zur feier des 500 jahrigen geburtstages. Gutenberg-Feier in Mainz. K. G. Bockenheimer, Mainz, 1900.
Celebration number in honor of the 500th anniversary of the birth of Gutenberg. Includes seven separate essays by as many authors: Bio-bibliographical historical accounts.

Embossed cloth; 10 x 7 x 1 in.

GUTENBERG, JOHANN

Cabinet S Shelf 1 No. 135

(The) Fichet letter, the earliest document ascribing to Gutenberg the invention of printing. By Douglas C. McMurtrie. With reproduction of the letter in collotype and a translation of the text by W. A. Montgomery New York, 1927.

Boards; 11½ x 8-1/8 in.

GUTENBERG, JOHANN

Cabinet W Shelf 2 No. 1

(Fichet's letter (1st January 1472?) to Robert Gaguin, in which he mentions Gutenberg, declaring him to have been the original inventor of the art of printing). Latin text. Edited by Ludwig Sieber. Basel, 1887. Pamphlet.

Item 16 in volume "Gutenberg, l'inventeur de l'imprimerie - Melanges."

GUTENBERG, JOHANN

Cabinet CC Shelf 1 No. 45

Figuier, Mme. Louis. Gutenberg: Drame historique. En cinq actes et en prose. Paris, 1869.

GUTENBERG, JOHANN

Cabinet Y Shelf 1 No. 25

(First books printed by Gutenberg, the 36 and 42 line Bibles; a study in the method of production) Gutenbergs früheste druckpraxis. Dargestellt von Karl Dziatzko. Mit 8 lichtdrucktafeln. Berlin, 1890.

Boards; morocco back, 9¾ x 6½ in.

GUTENBERG, JOHANN

Cabinet U Shelf 4 No. 86

First master printer: His acts, and his most remarkable discourses, and his death. From the German, by C. O. W. (n. p. n. d.)

Half morocco; 8-3/8 x 5-7/8 x 5/8 in.

GUTENBERG, JOHANN

Cabinet U Shelf 2 No. 51

First printing press of Johann Gutenberg, seen and described by Francis Fry, typefounder.

Account in Theodor Fry's "Memoire of Francis Fry", 1887, p.65

GUTENBERG, JOHANN

Cabinet Y Shelf 1 No. 9

Franklin und Gutenberg. Eine festgabe zum vierten jubilaum der erfindung der buchdruckerkunst...von Karl Preusker, Leipzig, 1840. With a lithographed title, showing the portraits of Gutenberg and Franklin, and the statue of the former at Mainz.

Half morocco; 8-5/8 x 5¼ x ¼ in.

GUTENBERG, JOHANN

Cabinet S Shelf 4 No. 68.01

From Gutenberg to the Cuneo Press: An historical sketch of the printing press. By Otto Mauric ~~Faker~~ Fokert. Chicago, Illinois, The Cuneo Press, 1933. Illus.

Brochure in box labelled "Pamphlets and Excerpts relating to Gutenberg"

GUTENBERG, JOHANN

Cabinet Y Shelf 1 No. 25

Fruheste druckerpraxis. Auf grund einer mit hölfer der gerren Dr. Phil. W. Bahrdt, Dr. Phil. Karl Meyer und Cand. Phil. J. Schnorrenberg ausgefuhrten vergleichung der 42 zeiligen und 36 zeiligen Bibel.
Bibliographical account.

Half morocco; 9-3/4 x 6½ x 5/8 in.

GUTENBERG, JOHANN

Cabinet W Shelf 2 No. 1

Fust vs. Gutenberg (Law suit of Fust against Gutenberg). Der prozess Fust's gegen Gutenberg in jahre 1455. von Ludw. Wilhelm Mayr. Munchen 1858. Pamphlet.

Item 2 in volume "Gutenberg, inventeur de l'imprimerie - Melanges."

GUTENBERG, JOHANN

Cabinet E Shelf 3 No. 31

See Garzoni, Tomaso. Piazza Universale...pp. 647-8.

GUTENBERG, JOHANN

Cabinet X Shelf 2 No. 18

Gedenkbuch an die festlichen tage der inauguration des Gutenberg-Denkmals zu Mainz am 13, 14, 15, and 16 August 1837. ... Mainz, 1837.
Biographical.

Paper, 8½ x 5-3/8 x 5/8 in.

GUTENBERG, JOHANN.

Cabinet X Shelf 2 No. 25

Gedenkbuch der vierten jubelfeier der erfindung der buchdruckerkunst in Mainz. Mainz, 1840.
Includes an account of the edifices of Mayence and their connection with the early history of printing, by J. Wetter; an historical sketch of printing in Mayence, by Schaab.

Paper boards; 9½ x 6½ x ¾ in.

GUTENBERG, JOHANNES

Cabinet X Shelf 2 No. 20

Gedenk-Buch zur vierten jubelfeier der erfindung der buchdruckerkunst begangen zu Frankfurt am Main am 24ten und 25ten Junius 1840. Eine festgabe herausgegeben von den buchdruckern, schriftgiessern und buchhändlern.
Celebration of the fourth centenary of printing.
A collection of essays, poetry, historical notes, etc. by various writers.

GUTENBERG, JOHANN

Cabinet X Shelf 2 No. 59

(Genealogy of the Gaensfleisch family)
Genealogie des Mainzer Geschlechtes Gansfleisch. von Gustav F. Schenk.

see HARTWIG, OTTO (Compiler) Festschrift...Mainz, 1900, pp.65-131

GUTENBERG, JOHANN cont'd

Cabinet Shelf No.

Half morocco; 8-1/8 x 5 x 3/8 in.

GUTENBERG, JOHANN

Cabinet Y Shelf 1 No. 7

Geschichte der erfindung der buchdruckerkunst. Eine für jedermann verständliche kurze darstellung der durch die neuesten forschungen gewonnenen resultate. von. Ph. H. Külb, Mainz, 1837. Frontispiece: Lithographic view of the statue at Mayence. At the end, two drawings of the bassi-relievi.
Condensed account of the invention of printing.

cont'd

GUTENBERG, JOHANNES

Cabinet X Shelf 2 No. 60

(Glory of Gutenberg, to the : a literary study).
Vom Thume Joannes Gutenberg. Ein litterargeschichtliche studie. von Heinrich Heidenheimer, Mainz, 1900.

Essay in book with title "Gutenberg-Feier, Mainz, 1900"... By K.G. Bockenheimer

---

GUTENBERG, JOHANN

Cabinet X Shelf 2 No. 37

Gott zu lob, drey christliche danck predigten wegen ders im jahr 1440 durch Gottliche eingebung in Strassburg erfunden hochwerthen buchdrucker-kunst ... Johann Schmidt. Strassburg, 1641.
This is a sermon preached on the occasion of the celebration of the second centenary of the invention of printing.

Boards; 8 x 6½ x ½ in.

GUTENBERG, JOHANN.

Cabinet 14 Shelf 2 No. 10

See Gottschalk, Paul. Buchkunst (Die) Gutenbergs und Schöffers.

GUTENBERG, JOHANN

Cabinet W Shelf 3 No. 22

Gutenberg, 1400-1467. Par Gustave Ringel. (Illustrated historical biblio. account) Extract from "Le livre d'or des peuples. Plutarque Universel". n.p. n.d.

In folder marked "Gutenberg, Johann. Various items relating to" (French text)

GUTENBERG, JOHANN.

Cabinet W Shelf 2 No. 1

Gutenberg, Jean, 1450, par E.J. Delecluze, Paris, n.d. Pamphlet, pp. 43.

Bound in volume "Gutenberg inventeur de l'imprimerie. Melanges," item 7.

GUTENBERG, JOHANN

Cabinet S Shelf 5 No. 4

(The) Gutenberg Anniversary, 1400-1900. By Theodore Low DeVinne, in the Outlook, May 5, 1900. Illus.
Historical.

Item 15 and 16 in collection "Various printers and their plants; excerpts from Magazines I."

GUTENBERG, JOHANN

Cabinet 26 Shelf 1 No. 20

Gutenberg im roman und drama. Ein stoffgeschichtlicher versuch. von Paul Alfred Merbach.

Article in the "Gutenberg-Gesellschaft Jahrbuch" 1930, pp.77-103.

GUTENBERG, JOHANN

Cabinet 26 Shelf 1 No. 19

Gutenberg und die nacherfinder. von Otto Hupp. Illus.
Bibliographical historical account of Gutenberg's invention, and of his succeeding inventors.
Article in the "Gutenberg-Gesellschaft Jahrbuch 1929, pp.31-100.

GUTENBERG, JOHANN

Cabinet Y Shelf 1 No. 12

Gutenbergs-Album. Herausgegeben von Dr. Heinrich Meyer. Braunschweig, 1840. Has portraits of Gutenberg.
Miscellaneous collection; includes an appendix of Oriental compositions, executed in twenty-six different languages and types.

Cloth; 8-7/8 x 5-3/4 x 7/8 in. See also Y/1/13

GUTENBERG, JOHANN

Cabinet W Shelf 2 No. 1

Helbig, Henri: Une decouverte pour l'histoire de l'imprimerie. Les plus anciens caracters de Gutenberg, et ce qui en est advenu.- Albert Pfister imprimeur a Bamberg.- Le Bible de 36 ligne. Bruxelles, 1855.
A discovery for the history of printing. What became of Gutenberg's first types. etc.

Item 11 in volume "Gutenberg l'inventeur de l'imprimerie - Melanges."

GUTENBERG, JOHANN

Cabinet W Shelf 4 No. 35

Histoire de l'invention de l'imprimerie ... par J.F.Lichtenberg; avec une préface de M.J.G. Schweighäuser. Strassbourg et Paris, 1825. Portrait of Gutenberg, and facsimiles of his types.
The author rejects the Coster Haarlem legend.

Boards; 9 x 5½ x ½ in.

GUTENBERG, JOHANN

Cabinet W Shelf 2 No. 1

(History of printing, from its origin to the present time). Gutenberg, oder geschichte der buchdruckerkunst von ihren ursprung bis zur gegenwart. Von Otto August Schulz. Ein festgabe zur vierten secularfeir der typensdruck. Leipzig, 1840. Illus.

Item 5 in volume "Gutenberg, l'inventeur de l'imprimerie - Melanges."

GUTENBERG, JOHANN

Cabinet Y Shelf 1 No. 3

Hochverdiente und aus bewahrten Urkunden wohlbeglaubte Ehren-Rettung Johann Guttenberg's, eingebohrnen Burger's in Mayntz, aus dem alten Rheinlandischen Adelichen Geschlechte derer von Gorgenloch, genannt Gaensfleisch, wegen der ersten erfindung der nie gnug gepriesenen Buchdrucker-Kunst in der Stadt Mayntz, zu unvergaenglichen Ehren der Teutschen Nation...von Johann David Kohler. Leipzig, 1741.
Documentary evidence in favor of Gutenberg

cont'd

GUTENBERG, JOHANN cont'd

Cabinet Y Shelf 1 No. 3

as the inventor of printing. Includes quotations from various works in which the invention is mentioned, and commentaries on each citation, by the author. Also includes genealogy of the Sorgenloch-Gaensfleisch family.

Half morocco; 8-5/8 x 7 x ½ in.

GUTENBERG, JOHANN

Cabinet 26 Shelf 1 No. 20

Holländische frühdruck und die ersten versuche Gutenberg's in Strassburg. von Gottfried Zedler.

Article in the "Gutenberg-Gesellschaft Jahrbuch" 1930, pp.53-72.

GUTENBERG, JOHANN

Cabinet W Shelf 2 No. 1

L'Inventeur de l'imprimerie - Melanges [Miscellaneous pamphlets all relating to the invention of printing, its development and progress. Bound in one volume. Each item numbered (23 pamphlets.)

(No cards for item 12)
Boards; morocco back; 9¾ x 6-3/8 x 2¼ in.

GUTENBERG, JOHANN

Cabinet S Shelf 4 No. 68.01

Inventor of printing, Gutenberg the. By Rev. L.F. Van Cleve. Excerpt from the Ladies' Repository, May, 1862.

In box marked "Pamphlets and excerpts relating to Gutenberg"

GUTENBERG, JOHANN

Cabinet Y Shelf 1 No. 92.02

Huldigung an Gutenberg: Eine festdichtung zu seinem angedenken. Kleine druck der Gutenberg-Gesellschaft No.6 n.d.

Play, theatrical, about the invention of printing.

With other items in manila envelope.

GUTENBERG, JOHANN

Cabinet W Shelf 2 No. 1

L'Invention de l'imprimerie a Strasbourg, par J. Gutenberg. Courte notice publiée a l'occasion du quatriéme anniversaire séculaire de cette invention célébre a Strasbourg les 24, 25 et 26 Juin, 1840. [Le Roux, printer].

Item 22 in volume "Gutenberg, l'inventeur de l'imprimerie - Melanges."

GUTENBERG, JOHANN

Cabinet W Shelf 2 No. 1

Jean Gutenberg, 1450: L'Imprimerie. [The history, invention and development of the art of printing]. By E.J. Delécuze. Paris, n.d. Pamphlet.

Item 7 in volume "Gutenberg, l'inventeur de l'imprimerie - Melanges."

GUTENBERG, JOHANN

Cabinet Y Shelf 1 No. 92.02

Huldigung an Gutenberg: Eine festdichtung zu seinem angedenken. von Herbert Eulenberg. Gutenberg-Gesellschaft Nr. 6.n.d.

Play theatrical, in celebration of the invention of printing.

In box marked Gutenberg-Gesellschaft, Mainz, 1927--Various Pamphlets.

GUTENBERG, JOHANN

Cabinet Y Shelf 1 No. 92

(Invention dream of Gutenberg.) Gutenbergs schöpfertraum. Erzahlung von Hans Bleyer-Hörtl. Mainz, 1930. Verlag der Gutenberg-Gesellschaft. Pamphlet.

With other items in manila envelope.

GUTENBERG, JOHANN

Cabinet W Shelf 2 No. 147

(Jean ou Hans Gensfleisch). Par M. Ambroise Firmin Didot. Extrait de la Nouvelle Biographie Générale. Paris, 1858.

Bound in with Wallon's "Notice sur la vie et les travaux de ... Didot. Paris, 1886.

Half morocco; 11 x 9 in.

GUTENBERG, JOHANN

Cabinet Y Shelf 1 No. 35

Hupp, Otto. Ein Missale speciale, vorläufer des psalteriums von 1457. Beitrag sur geschichte der ältesten druckwerke. Munchen, 1898. [Bound in with]: Gutenberg's erste drucke. Ein weiterer beitrag...von Otto Hupp. Munchen, 1902.

Bibliographical study of Gutenberg's supposed first printed work.

Half morocco; 12¼ x 9-1/8 x 5/8 in.

GUTENBERG, JOHANN

Cabinet S Shelf 4 No. 68.01

Invention of printing, Johann Gutenberg and the. By Karl Dziatsko. Translated from the German by E.F. Kunz. July, 1903.

Excerpt from the Literary Collector.

Portrait of J.G. from a woodcut by an unknown master of the 16th cent.

In box marked "Pamphlets and excerpts relating to Gutenberg."

GUTENBERG, JOHANN

Cabinet S Shelf 1 No. 33

John Gutenberg. By Theodore Low DeVinne. An Article extracted from a magazine ... [n.n.] Pittsburgh, Pa. 1912. Illus.

Historical account.

Item I in volume "Writings of Theodore Low DeVinne."

Half morocco; 9¾ x 6-5/8 in.

GUTENBERG, JOHANN

Cabinet W Shelf 2 No. 1

Inauguration du monument de Gutenberg a Strasbourg. La fête durera trois jours, les 24, 25 et 26 juin 1840. Programme.

Item 23 in volume "Gutenberg, l'inventeur de l'imprimerie - Melanges.

GUTENBERG, Johann

Cabinet V Shelf 3 No. 2

See Invention of Printing: Lettre sur l'origine de l'imprimerie servant de réponse...Strasbourg, 1761.

GUTENBERG, JOHANN

Cabinet S Shelf 5 No. 24

John Gutenberg. By Theodore Low DeVinne. An excerpt from Scribner's Monthly, May, 1876. Illus.

Bio-bibliographical account.

pp. 1-13 in collection "Printing Excerpts."

GUTTENBERG, JOHANN

Cabinet R Shelf 2 No. 4

Inventeur de l'imprimerie, bienfait immense; grande impulsion donnee au genie de l'homme. Par Daunou. [1834].

In vol. Montyon et Franklin, Societe, 1833 1834." [pp. n.n.]

Tooled calf; 8¾ x 5-3/8 x 1-1/8 in.

GUTENBERG, JOHANN.

Cabinet Shelf No.

See Invention of Printing. Pérégrinations de J. Neumeister, compagnon de Gutenberg en Allemagne en Italie et en France (1463-1468)....Par A. Claudin. Paris, 1880.

GUTENBERG, JOHANN

Cabinet S Shelf 4 No. 60

John Gutenberg and the art of printing. By Emily C. Pearson, Boston, 1871. Illus.

A popular history of the invention and progress of printing.

Cloth; 7¾ x 5½ in.

GUTENBERG, JOHANN

Cabinet W Shelf 2 No. 1

(Jubilee celebrations 1540 to 1882, for the invention of printing. A bibliographical essay). Die jubelfeste der buchdruckerkunst und ihre literatur. Ein bibliographische versuche. Von Louis Mohr. Wien, 1882. Pamphlet.

Item 19 in volume "Gutenberg, l'inventeur de l'imprimerie - Melanges."

GUTENBERG, JOHANN

Cabinet S Shelf 5 No. 24

Jubilee of the Printing Press. By Charles Whibley. An excerpt from The North American Review, Dec. 1900.
On the occasion of the five hundredth anniversary of the birth of Gutenberg at Mainz.

Pp. 76-86 in collection "Printing Excerpts."

GUTENBERG, JOHANN

Cabinet Y Shelf 1 No. 3

Koehler, Johann David. Hochverdiente und aus bewahrten urkunden wohlbeglaubte ehrenrettung Johann Guttenbergs...Leipzig, 1741. Illus.
At the end are several poetical effusions, some in Latin, also quotations from various books relating to the invention of printing.

Half morocco; $8\frac{3}{4}$ x 7 x $\frac{1}{2}$ in.

GUTENBERG, JOHANN

Cabinet Y Shelf 1 No. 41

Leben und werk Gutenberg's. (Life and works of Johann Gutenberg)
pp.1-73 in "Gutenberg und seine berühmsten nachfolger"...von Alfred Borckel. Frankfurt a.M. 1900

Cloth; $8\frac{1}{2}$ x 5-5/8 in.

GUTENBERG, JOHANN

Cabinet X Shelf 2 No. 60

(Life in Mainz in the 15th century. The corporation quarrels and the part in them of the Gensfleisch family. Bio-historical accounts)

See BOCKENHEIMER, K.G. (Compiler). Gutenberg-feier in Mainz, 1900...

GUTENBERG, JOHANN

Cabinet T Shelf 2 No. 44

Life of Johann Gutenberg.

See MARSHALL, DAVID. Printing, and account of its invention...London and Paris, 1877, p.31

GUTENBERG, JOHANN

Cabinet Y Shelf 1 No. 33

(Life, work, and fame of Gutenberg). Sein leben, sein werk, sein rhum. Zur errinerung an die 500 jahrige geburt des erfinders der buchdruckerkunst. Mit 34 abbildungen. von Alfred Börckel. Giessen, 1897. Portraits and facsimiles.

Cloth; $11\frac{1}{4}$ x 8 x 3/8 in.

GUTENBERG, JOHANN

Cabinet W Shelf 2 No. 151

Louis Leriche. Les étapes de Gutenberg: Comédie en quatre actes avec chants, pour jeunes gens. Par L. Leriche, preface par Charles Bult. Illus. par Fernand Fau & A. Humbert. Musique composé par Augusta Holmes. Paris, 1889.

Boards; 11 x 9 in.

GUTENBERG, JOHANN

Cabinet V Shelf 5 No. 10

See Madden, J. P. A. Lettres d'un Bibliographe. Versailles, 1873, 1874. pp. 39-71.

GUTENBERG, JOHANN

Cabinet X Shelf 2 No. 59

Mainz, 1900. Festschrift zum 500 jahrigen geburtstag. Illus. and facsimiles.
This birthday celebration number contains bio-bibliographical historical essays by several authors. Artricles on printing in Italy, Germany, France, Spain and Portugal, etc.

Cloth; $11\frac{3}{4}$ x 9 x $1\frac{1}{2}$ in.

GUTENBERG, JOHANN

Cabinet Y Shelf 1 No. 92

Mainz als Gutenbergstadt. von A. Ruppel Kline-Druck Nr. 8 der Gutenberg-Gesellschaft. Pamphlet.

With other items in manila envelope.

GUTENBERG, JOHANN

Cabinet Y Shelf 1 No. 79

(The Mainz fragment from the Last Judgment: a section from German Sibylline literature). Das Mainzer fragment vom Weltgericht: ein ausschnitt aus dem deutschen Siblyllen-buch. von Dr. Edward Schröder. Mainz, 1908. Verlag der Gutenberg-Gesellschaft.
One of four bibliographical studies, by four authors, in one volume.

Boards; $11\frac{1}{2}$ x 8-3/4 x 3/4 in.

GUTENBERG, JOHANN

Cabinet Y Shelf 5 No. 65

Marlow, F. (Wolfram). Gutenberg. Drama in fünf aufzügen. Leipzig, 1840.

Half morocco; 8 x $5\frac{3}{4}$ x 7/8 in.

GUTENBERG, JEAN

Cabinet B Shelf 3 No. 2

Mémoire de Jean Gutenberg. Hommage de l'Imprimerie Nationale et de la Bibliotheque Nationale. Paris, 1900.
(With 17 plates)

Morocco; 17 x 13 in.

GUTENBERG, JOHANN.

Cabinet W Shelf 2 No. 1

Memoire sur le decouverte d'un exemplaire de la bible connu sous le nom de Guttenberg (manuscript), par Dom. Maugerard, Dec. 24, 1879: Societe Royale des Sciences de Metz.

Bound in volume "Gutenberg inventeur de l'imprimerie. Melanges," item 3.

GUTENBERG, JOHANN

Cabinet AA Shelf 1 No. 22

Micheletti, Gio. Battista: Presagi scientifici sull'arte della stampa. Aquila, 1814.
Strongly in favor of Gutenberg. The author also comments on the advantages gained by mankind since the discovery of printing.

Boards; $8\frac{1}{2}$ x $5\frac{1}{2}$ in.

GUTENBERG, JOHANN

Cabinet W Shelf 1 No. 147

Missel Special de Constance, oeuvre de Gutenberg avant 1450: Premier livre imprimé connu. Etude liturgique et critique. Par E. Misset. Paris, 1899.

Half morocco; $9\frac{3}{4}$ x $6\frac{1}{2}$ in.

GUTENBERG, JOHANN

Cabinet S Shelf 5 No. 9

(N'est) Pas l'inventeur de l'imprimerie. (Gutenberg is not the inventor of printing). By Arthur Hubens. Excerpt from La Revue de Holland, June, 1917.

Bound in collection "Various printers - excerpts and brochures", item 13.

GUTENBERG, JOHANN

Cabinet W — Shelf 2 — No. 1

(Ein) Neuer druck Gutenberg's in Deutscher sprache (Newly discovered Gutenberg imprint [The Kalender of 1460] in the German language.) By Albert Cohn. Excerpt from Neuer Anzeiger für Bibliographie. January, 1884.
Bibliographical invention controversy concerning a falsely dated calender.

Item 15 in volume "Gutenberg, l'inventeur de l'imprimerie - Melanges."

GUTENBERG, JOHANN

Cabinet 26 — Shelf 1 — No. 15

(New Gutenberg discovery: Documents relating to the suit of Claus Schott v. Gutenberg, 1436-7) Neue Strassburger Gutenbergfunde. Von Carl Schorbach, Baden-Baden, 1926
p. 14 Gutenberg-Gesellschaft Jahrbuch, 1926. Mainz.

GUTENBERG, JOHANN

Cabinet W — Shelf 2 — No. 1

Nouveau dètails sur la vie de Gutenberg. Tires des archives de l'ancien chapitre de Saint - Thomas a Strasbourg. Par C. Schmidt. Strasbourg, 1841.

Item 6 in volume "Gutenberg, l'inventeur de l'imprimerie - Melanges."

GUTENBERG, JOHANN

Cabinet W — Shelf 2 — No. 1

Un nouveau document sur Gutenberg, par A. Claudin, Paris, 1883.
An account of an early document in which the typographers, Gering, Krantz and Friburger proclaim Gutenberg the actual inventor of printing.

Item 14 in volume "Gutenberg inventeur de l'imprimerie. Melanges."

GUTENBERG, JOHANN

Cabinet W — Shelf 2 — No. 1

(Notes on the invention of printing, and the erection of statues to Gutenberg in Mainz and Strasbourg) Cenni sulla invenzione della stampa ... Forli, 1841.

Bound in vol. "Gutenberg l'inventeur de l'imprimerie. Melanges." item 24.

GUTENBERG, JOHANN.

Cabinet E — Shelf 3 — No. 43

See reference to in Pancirollus, Guido. Rerum memorabilium sive deperditarum....p.311 Frankfort a.M., 1631.

GUTENBERG, JOHANN

Cabinet V — Shelf 6 — No. 14

(Pictorial history of the invention of printing).

see
ICONOGRAPHIE de l'IMPRIMERIE
Bulletin Officiel...Paris, 1927, pp.62-82

GUTENBERG, JOHANN

Cabinet 26 — Shelf 1 — No. 20

Original brief Gutenbergs aus dem Jahre 1438, ein angeblicher. von A. Ruppel.

Article in the "Gutenberg-Gesellschaft Jahrbuch" 1930, pp.73-76.

GUTENBERG, Johann

Cabinet 69 — Shelf 1 — No. 40

Portrait and biographical note.

See Early Printing in France. Lyons, 1573. Antoine Gryphe. La Prosopographie...p.469.

GUTENBERG, JOHANN

Cabinet W — Shelf 2 — No. 93

Premier maître imprimeur: Ses faits et discours les plus dignes d'admiration, et sa mort. Ce récit fidèle, écrit par Fr. Dingelstedt est traduit de l'Allemand en Français par Gustave Revilliod. Geneva, 1858.
A novel with a supposed historical background.

Boards; 12 x 8 in.

GUTENBERG, JOHANN

Cabinet 81 — Shelf 2 — No. 39

Printer Guttenberg, the. [Translated for the Albany Argus, by W.G.B.] Newspaper excerpt, circa 1859.

See MUNSELL, JOEL. "Printers Scraps", Vol.X, pp.36-40.

GUTENBERG, JOHANN

Cabinet W — Shelf 2 — No. 36

See Printing, Historical. Née de la Rochelle, J. F. Eloge historique de Jean Gensfleisch ...Paris, 1811.

GUTENBERG, JOHANN

Cabinet X — Shelf 5 — No. 3

Printing in the 15th and in the 19th centuries. n.a.n. Excerpt from The Penny Magazine of the Society for the Diffusion of Useful knowledge. Nov. 30 to Dec. 31, 1837. Illus.
Biographical historical account, with description of the festival at Mayence on the erection of a Statue of Gutenberg.

p. 25 in vol. with binder's title "Scrap-Book, 1705-1891, relating to printing."

GUTENBERG, JOHANN

Cabinet W — Shelf 2 — No. 1

Procès de Guttemberg: Dissertations sur quelques points curieux. Par Paul L. Jacob. Paris,,1847. Pamphlet.
Extracts from original documents which claim to establish the facts concerning the exact date of the invention of moveable types by Gutenberg.

Item 1 in volume "Gutenberg, inventeur de l'imprimerie - Melanges."

GUTENBERG, JOHANN

Cabinet Y — Shelf 2 — No. 7 — 3 vols.

Schaab, Carl A. Geschichte der erfindung der buchdruckerkunst durch Johaan Gensfleisch genannt Gutenberg zu Mainz...mit... ungedruckten urkunden, welche die genealogie Gutenberg's, Fust's und Schoffer's in ein neuen licht stellen. Mainz, 1830-1831. 3 vols. Portraits, and folding plate. Chronological index, and general index in vol.3.

Half morocco, each vol. $8\frac{3}{4}$ x $5\frac{1}{2}$ in.

GUTENBERG, JOHANN

Cabinet 39 — Shelf 2 — No. 35

See Printing, Historical. [Origin and development of typography]. An account in Latin in which Gutenberg is mentioned. See page 370.

GUTENBERG, JOHANN

Cabinet X — Shelf 1 — No. 55

Schoepflin, Jo. Daniel: Vindiciae typographicae. Argentorati, 1760. Facsimiles.
The author here declares that Gutenberg made his first experiments at Strasburg. Information supposed to have been drawn from original documents.

Full morocco; 9-5/8 x $7\frac{1}{2}$ x $\frac{3}{4}$ in.

GUTENBERG, JOHANN

Cabinet Y — Shelf 1 — No. 92

Schopfertraum Gutenbergs. Erzählung von Hans Bleyer-Härtl. Mainz 1930, Verlag der Gutenberg-Gesellschaft.

In box marked Gutenberg-Gesellschaft, Mainz 1927--Various Pamphlets

GUTENBERG, JOHANN.

Cabinet 14 Shelf 2 No. 3

See Schwenke, Paul Dr. Gutenbergs, Johannes. Zweiundvierzig zeilige Bibel.

GUTENBERG, JOHANN

Cabinet R Shelf 6 No. 1

True story about Gutenberg's invention of printing. Complete in seven sheets. Drawn by B.A. Wikstrom, New York, 1882. Illus.

Humorous account in verse.

Half morocco; 16 x 12 in.

GUTENBERG, JOHANN

Cabinet 26 Shelf 1 No. 21

[Which was Gutenberg's first printed book? A study of the types used in printing the Psalter, the 42 and 36 line Bible] Ein zahlembeweis für Gutenberg. von Otto Hupp.

Essay in "Gutenberg-Gesellschaft Jahrbuch, 1931", pp.9-27.

GUTENBERG, JOHANN.

Cabinet 14 Shelf 2 No. 3

See Schwenke, Paul Dr. Gutenbergs, Johannes. Zweiundvierzig zeilige Bibel.

GUTENBERG, JOHANN

Cabinet Y Shelf 1 No. 15

Sur Gutenberg et le fragment de sa presse trouvé dans la maison où il a établi sa première imprimerie. Traduit d'un manuscrit. Ch. Klein. Mayence, 1856.

Discovery of the fragment of a press supposed to have belonged to Gutenberg.

Boards; 8¼ x 5¼ x ¼ in. See also Y/1/16

GUTENBERG, JOHANN

Cabinet Y Shelf 1 No. 64

(What did Gutenberg invent? Reflections on the early technique of typecasting). Was hat Gutenberg erfunden? Ein rückblick auf die frühtechnik des schriftgusses. Gustav Mori, Frankfort a.M., 1921. Facsimiles.

Paper; 9 x 6¼ x ¼ in.

GUTENBERG, JOHANN

Cabinet W Shelf 2 No. 1

(The) Signature of Gutenberg. Found in the Letters of Indulgence for 1454 and 1455. Described by P. De Villiers. London, 1878. Pamphlet.

Signed copy. Presentation to A. Claudin author of the Monuments Typographiques." etc.

Item 17 in volume "Gutenberg, l'inventeur de l'imprimerie - Melanges."

GUTENBERG, JOHANN

Cabinet X Shelf 2 No. 58

[Types used for the 42 and 36 line Bibles printed by Gutenberg, a study of the]

See SCHWENKE, PAUL Untersuchungen...Berlin, 1900

GUTENBERG, JOHANN

Cabinet W Shelf 2 No. 73

Winaricky, Charles: Jean Gutenberg ne en 1412 a Kuttenberg en Boheme... Par Charles Winaricky Traduit du Manuscrit Allemand par Jean de Carro. Bruxelles, 1847.

These pages go to prove the usual account of Gutenberg's parentage erroneous, and that he was born in a small town in Bohemia.

Half morocco; 7½ x 4-7/8 in.

GUTENBERG, JOHANN

Cabinet W Shelf 2 No. 67

Schmidt, Charles: Nouveau détails sur la vie de Gutenberg, tirés des archives de l'ancien chapitre de Saint Thomas à Strasbourg. Strasbourg, 1841.

GUTENBERG, JOHANN

Cabinet Y Shelf 2 No. 10

Wetter, Johann. Kritische geschichte der erfindung der buchdruckerkunst durch Johann Gutenberg in Mainz, begleidet mit einer genauen prüfung...und einer neuen untersuchung der ansprüche der stadt Harlem...Mainz, 1836. Facsimiles.

"A valuable work, in which many of the documents relating to the invention of printing are reproduced in the original text." B & W.

cont'd

GUTENBERG, JOHANN

Cabinet W Shelf 2 No. 1

Wittig, Jvo. von Hammelburg in Mainz. By Falk. Excerpt from Centralblatt für Bibliothekswesen. Leipzig, n.d.

Adverse to Hessel who in his new book "Haarlem the birth place of printing" claims Wittig to have been related to Gutenberg.

Item 18 in volume "Gutenberg l'inventeur de l'imprimerie - Melanges."

GUTENBERG, JOHANN.

Cabinet X Shelf 2 No. 39

(A) Strasbourg [1840] ou l'invention de l'imprimerie Divertissement en un acte, mêlé de chants et de danses, pour l'inauguration de la Statue de Gutenberg. [Par Vessiére et Gatry]. Impr. Silbermann. Strasbourg, 1840. With 1 lithogr., frontispiece, the monument of Gutenberg a Strasbourg.

Paper; 8-7/8 x 5-5/8 in. pp. 36.

GUTENBERG, JOHANN cont'd

Cabinet Shelf No.

Buchram; 9-1/8 x 5⅝ x 2¼ in.

GUTENBERG, JOHANN

Cabinet 26 Shelf 1 No. 7

Wohnort Gutenbergs in seinen letzten lebensjahren (Gutenbergs home in the latter part of his life). von A. Ruppel.

Article in the Gutenberg-Gesellschaft Jahrbuch 1928. pp.58-68.

GUTENBERG, JOHANN

Cabinet U Shelf 4 No. 87

Signature of Gutenberg. By P. DeVilliers, M.D. London, 1878. With folding sheet, facsimiles of the Letters of Indulgence of 1455.

The author analyzes the various strokes in the supposed signatures of Gutenberg.

Half morocco; 10¼ x 6½ x 3/8 in.

GUTENBERG, JOHANN

Cabinet Y Shelf 1 No. 61

(Typecasting, the invention of, and Gutenberg's earliest impressions). Gutenberg: die erfindung des typengusses und seine Frühdrucke. Georg Domel. Mit 19 beilagen. Koln, 1919. Facsimiles.

Author's signed copy.

Stamped cloth 9-3/4 x 6½ x 3/4 in.

GUTENBERG, JOHANN

Cabinet R Shelf 6 No. 1

Wikström, B. A. The true story about Gutenberg's invention of printing. Complete in seven sheets. Drawn by B. A. Wikström. New York 1882. I. H. Hamburger, publisher. Copper engravings.

Humorous account, in rhyme.

Half morocco; 16 x 12 in.

GUTENBERG, JOHANN.

Cabinet Y Shelf 1 No. 1

Zum gedachtnis an Johannes Gutenberg, 1468-1918. Dem toten zur ehr', den lebenden zur lehr'! von Johann Christ. Gottsched.
Illustrated bio-historical account. Excerpt from "Typographische Mitteilungen," Juni, 1918. Leipzig.

Item in box labelled "German pamphlets and excerpts relating to Gutenberg."

GUTENBERG, JOHANN

Cabinet Y Shelf 1 No. 46

Zedler, Gottfried. Gutenberg forschungen. Mit vier tafeln. Leipzig, 1901.
Gutenberg investigations: bio-bibliographical historical account.

Half morocco; 9¼ x 6-3/8 x 7/8 in.

GUTENBERG BIBLE (The)

Cabinet S Shelf 4 No. 68.02

(The) Melk copy of the Gutenberg Bible, to be sold by auction by order of the owner, Edward Goldstron, London, England, Feb.,15, 1926, at The Anderson Galleries, New York.
Description of the Bible by Seymour de Ricci.

Brochure catalogue, item in manila envelope

GUTENBERG, JOHANN

Cabinet X Shelf 2 No. 60

(Die) Zunftkampfe in Mainz und der anteil der familie Gensfleisch. von Dr. J.B. Seidenberger. Mainz, 1900.

See BOCKENHEIMER, K.G. (COMPILER). Gutenberg-Feier in Mainz, 1900... (see index)

Guttenberg Album

Cabinet Y Shelf 1 No. 13

Meyer, Heinrich, Braunschweig, 1840, herausgegeben von.
Includes portraits of Gutenberg, Fust, Schoeffer, Senefelder, etc. Ornamented with plates produced in all the various methods invented up to 1840. Has an appendix of 26 Oriental languages and types.

Embossed morocco; 12-3/8 x 9¾ in. See also Y/1/12

GUTENBERG BIBLE.

Cabinet e Shelf No.

See also
Bible Literature. Gutenberg Bible.

GUTENBERG, JOHANN (see also)

Cabinet Shelf No.

GENSFLEISCH

GUTENBERG ANNIVERSARY (The), 1400-1900.

Cabinet S Shelf 5 No. 4

Brief illus. account of the introduction of printing, by Theodore L. De Vinne, honorary vice-president of the Gutenberg Festival, in the Outlook, May 5, 1900.

Bound with other items in "Various printers and their plants", item 15 and 16, vol.1.

GUTENBERG BIBLE SALES

Cabinet 14 Shelf 2 No. 3

Gutenberg Bible sells for $106,000, Feb. 15, 1926. Dr. A. W. Rosenbach Pays High Price. Excerpt from N. Y. Times, Feb. 16, 1926. With a History of Previous Sales.

Secured in Dr. Paul Schwenke's Bibliography of the Gutenberg Bible and description of each of the surviving copies. Leipzig, 1925.

GUTENBERG, JOHANN & PETER (I) SCHOEFFER.

Cabinet 14 Shelf 2 No. 10

Buchkunst Gutenberg's und Schoeffers, mit einem einleitenden versuch über die entwicklung versuch ... von Paul Gottschalk, Berlin 1918. Facsimiles.

Buchram; 18 x 13 x ¾ in.

GUTENBERG BIBLE

Cabinet U Shelf 5 No. 38

Account of Dr. Schwenke's calculations on

see
PROCTOR, ROBERT. Bibliographical essays...London, 1905, pp.45-53

GUTENBERG-COSTER.

Cabinet U Shelf 1 No. 1c

Bibliographical tour, A, by J.H. Hessels.

An account of a tour undertaken for the examination and collation of certain copies which would establish the invention of printing for Haarlem.

In excerpts relating to printing from The Library, 1908, pp.282-307.

GUTENBERG (Le)

Cabinet 24 Shelf 2 No. 18

Lausanne, 1891.

see
PERIODICALS, PRINTING. Switzerland. Gutenberg (Le)

GUTENBERG BIBLE

Cabinet T Shelf 2 No. 7

(The) Lambeth Mazarine Testament. By the Rev. W. J. Loftie. Excerpt from Arch. Journ. Vol. 28, p. 341.
This item relates to the Lambert volume which contains the New Testament only.

In envelope.

GUTENBERG ALBUM

Cabinet Y Shelf 1 No. 19

Gutenberg-Album. Herausgegben von Friedrich W. Ruland Mayence, 1868. Thirty plates, facsimiles, with German and English text.
Book produced to perpetuate the relics relating to Gutenberg, found in his birthplace.

Embossed cloth; 13-5/8 x 10-7/8 x 7/8 in.

GUTENBERG ALBUM.

Cabinet 26 Shelf 2 No. 1

Announcements and prospectuses of "Gutenberg's-Album" published in Germany in 1840, in commemoration of the forthcoming celebration of the 400th anniversary of the invention of printing.

Journal fur Buchdruckerkunst, Nos.3,5,6,7, 12, bound in one vol. dated, 1838, 1839, 1840.

GUTENBERG BIBLE, The (Vollbehr Collection)

Cabinet S Shelf 4 No. 68.01

Library of Congress purchase. Brochure to commemorate an important event--the handing over of the Gutenberg Bible to Dr. Vollbehr at the Benedictine Monastery of St. Paul, Carinthia, Austria. Printed by the Stone Printing and Manufacturing Co., Roenoke, Virginia, 1930.

In box marked "Pamphlets relating to Gutenberg and the Gutenberg Bible"

GUTENBERG-COSTER CONTROVERSY

Cabinet AA Shelf 4 No. 6

Bausch, P.: Louwerijsz Janzn. Koster. Door P. Bausch. [Reprinted from the Publishers "Nieuwsblad"], 1922-1923. [Amsterdam], Facsimile.
A bibliographical study based on authorities in favor of Coster.

Half morocco; 10-3/8 x 6¾ x 3/8 in.

GUTENBERG-COSTER CONTROVERSY.

Cabinet AA Shelf 3 No. 43

Costerlegende ontward? Enkele opmerkingen. Naar aanleiding van Gottfried zedler's "Von Coster zu Gutenberg." Door K. Vos. Haarlem, 1922. Pamphlet.

Vos refutes Zedler's statements concerning Coster, and adds genealogy in proof of his discoveries in favor of Coster.

Bound in volume "De Coster Legende." 1856. 1904, 1922.

Half morocco; 11 x 7½ in.

GUTENBERG-COSTER CONTROVERSY

Cabinet U Shelf 4 No. 85

Hessels, J. H. The Gutenberg fiction: A critical examination of the documents relating to Gutenberg, showing that he was not the inventor of printing. London, 1912.

Cloth; 10 x 6¼ x 1 3/8 in.

GUTENBERG-COSTER CONTROVERSY.

Cabinet U Shelf 1 No. 1d

So-called Gutenberg documents, The, by J.H. Hessels.

In excerpts relating to printing from The Library, 1909, pp.53,106,165: 1911-12, pp.95, 152,180,207 of pencilled folios.

GUTENBERG-COSTER CONTROVERSY

Cabinet AA Shelf 3 No. 27

Bakker, W. L. Een woord in het geding "Haarlem-Mainz", Door W. A. P. F. L. Bakker, Haarlem, 1889.

Half morocco; 10 x 6-7/8 in.

GUTENBERG-COSTER CONTROVERSY

Cabinet AA Shelf 3 No. 7

Koning, Jacobus: Bijdragen tot de geschiedenis der Boekdrukkunst, door Jacobus Koning. Haarlem, 1818.

This is part I of a supplement to Koning's "Verhandelingen over den oorsprong ... der boekdrukkunst" ... Haarlem, 1816. Includes copies of the watermarks of the so-called Kosterian "Donatus." See also AA/3/6.

Half morocco; 9¼ x 5-3/8 in.

GUTENBERG-COSTER CONTROVERSY.

Cabinet AA Shelf 3 No. 45

Uit de strijdschriften over de Hollandesche uitvinding.

I: pp. 142-148 Hessels "Haarlem de geboortplaats der boekdrukkunst niet Mainz.

II: pp. 50-56 Ch. Enschede's "Technische onderzook naar de uitvinding van de boekdrukkunst"

For both items - In "Ontwikkeling der boekdrukkunst in Nederland" ... pp. 135-139.

GUTENBERG-COSTER CONTROVERSY

Cabinet AA Shelf 3 No. 21

Gutenberg, by Dr. A. van der Linde. (In Dutch.) The Hague, April 17, 1870.

Half morocco; 9 x 5¾ in.

GUTENBERG-COSTER CONTROVERSY

Cabinet AA Shelf 3 No. 20

Linde, M.A. Van der: De Haarlemsche Coster legende wetenschappelijk onderzocht. Door Dr. A. Van der Linde. Tweede uitgaff. 's Gravenhage, 1870.

The author restores Gutenberg to his proper place as the inventor of printing.

Boards; 9 x 5½ in.

GUTENBERG-COSTER CONTROVERSY

Cabinet Y Shelf 1 No. 22

Linde, A. van der. Gutenberg. Geschichte und erdichtung aus den quellen nachgewiesen. Stuttgart, 1878.

Documentary evidence relating to the history of Gutenberg family, and the invention of printing.

Half morocco; 10-3/8 x 7-3/4 x 2-1/8 in. See also Y/1/23

GUTENBERG-COSTER CONTROVERSY

Cabinet U Shelf 1 No. 1c

Hessels, J. H. A bibliographical tour.

In Excerpts relating to printing from "The Library," 1908. pp. 282-307.

GUTENBERG-COSTER CONTROVERSY

Cabinet W Shelf 4 No. 85

Linde, A. Van der: La legende Costérienne de Harlem: Nouvel examen critique par le Dr. A. Van der Linde, précédé d'une introduction historique par M. Ch. Ruelens. Bruxelles, 1871. Facsimiles

Half morocco; 9½ x 6-1/8 in.

GUTENBERG-COSTER CONTROVERSY

Cabinet AA Shelf 3 No. 7

See also Invention controversy

GUTENBERG-COSTER CONTROVERSY.

Stack A Shelf 1&2 Number 66

Defense of Johann Gutenberg, inventor of typography by Henry Lewis Bullen, in The Inland Printer, vol.LXVI, p.190. Illus.

GUTENBERG-COSTER CONTROVERSY

Cabinet AA Shelf 3 No. 22

Meurs, Dr. P. Van: De keulsche kronick en de Costerlegende van Dr. A. Van der Linde te zamen getoetst door Dr. P. Van Meurs. Haarlem, 1870.

An attack upon Van Linde and his conclusions derived from the Cologne Chronical of Ulrich Zell, 1499.

Half morocco; 9-3/8 x 5¾ in.

GUTENBERG-GESELLSCHAFT

Cabinet Y Shelf 1 No. 92.02

(Aims and purpose of the Gutenberg Society briefly related. In French, German, Italian, Spanish, English). Booklet.

With other items in manila envelope.

GUTENBERG-COSTER CONTROVERSY

Cabinet U Shelf 4 No. 83

Hessels, J. H. Gutenberg: Was he the inventor of printing? An historical investigation embodying a criticism of Dr. van der Linde's "Gutenberg". London, 1882.

Cloth; 9¼ x 5-3/4 x 1 in.

GUTENBERG-COSTER CONTROVERSY

Cabinet 18 Shelf 1 No. 15

Review of a controversial article which appeared in the "Boek" published in Holland.

In Zeitschrift für Bücherfreunde 1913-14, part 2, p.494 of Supplement ("Bieblatt.")

GUTENBERG-GESELLSCHAFT

Cabinet Y Shelf 1 No. 92.05

Bodonis, Giambattista typenkunst. Hermann Falk. Beilage zum 13 Jahresbericht der Gutenberg Gesellschaft. Mainz, 1915

Pamphlet in manila envelope

GUTENBERG GESELLSCHAFT

Cabinet 26 Shelf 1 No. 27

Buchillustrationen in dem ersten jahrzehnten des deutsches buchdruckes. Hans Koegler, June, 1911.

Lecture, printed in the Gutenberg-Gesellschaft yearly report, No.10.

Item in cloth covered box holding "Reports" 1902-1913.

GUTENBERG-GESELLSCHAFT

Cabinet Y Shelf 4 No. 58

Die deutsche schriftgiesserei. Eine historisch-ästhetische betrachtung. von Julius Rodenberg. Mainz 1927.

History of German type founding.

Half morocco; $9\frac{3}{4}$ x $6\frac{3}{4}$ x $\frac{1}{4}$ in.

GUTENBERG-GESELLSCHAFT

Cabinet Y Shelf 1 No. 92.05

(Gutenberg portraits, illustrated descriptive account of.) Uber Gutenberg bildnisse. von Adolph Tronnier. Beilage zum 12 Jahresbericht der Gutenberg-Gesellschaft. Mainz, 1913.

Pamphlet in manila envelope

GUTENBERG - GESELLSCHAFT

Cabinet Y Shelf 1 No. 92.05

Hymnus auf die druckkunst. von Victor Hugo. (In praise of printing). Druck, No. 1, Gutenberg-Gesellschaft. Mainz, 1926.

French and German text.

Pamphlet in manila envelope

GUTENBERG-GESELLSCHAFT

Cabinet Y Shelf 1 No. 92.05

(List of Gutenberg-Gesellschaft publications) Die Gutenberg-Gesellschaft und ihre publicationen. Mainz, 1928

Pamphlet in manila envelope

GUTENBERG GESELLSCHAFT

Cabinet C Shelf 2 No. 28

Liturgischen druckwerke Erhard Ratdolts

See SCHOTTENLOHER, KARL (Die) Liturgischen druckwerke Erhard Ratdolt...

GUTTENBERG GESELLSCHAFT

Cabinet 26 Shelf 1 No. 27

(Reports 1902-1913) Jahresberichte. Gutenberg-Gesellschaft, Mainze.

Pamphlets in cloth covered box stamped "Gutenberg-Gesellschaft. Jahresberichten, 1902-1913."

GUTENBERG-GESELLSCHAFT

Cabinet 26 Shelf 1 No. 28

Reports for the years 1914, 1915, 1916, 1917-18 1919-21, 1922.

Items in manila envelope.

GUTENBERG-GESELLSCHAFT

Cabinet Y Shelf 1 No. 92.04

Tatigkeits-Bericht der Gutenberg-Gesellschaft, 1910, 1912, 1925-26. Pamphlets.

Reports of the Gutenberg-Gesellschaft, with names of all members for years as above.

Items in manila envelope.

GUTENBERG-GESELLSCHAFT JAHRBUCH, 1926

Cabinet 26 Shelf 1 No. 15

[An international medium for investigations and information relating to the art of printing from Gutenberg's time to the present]. Illus. and facsimiles.

Seventeen articles by as many authors. German text.

Boards; 11-1/8 x 8-3/8 x 7-1/8 in.

GUTENBERG-GESELLSCHAFT JAHRBUCH, 1927.

Cabinet 26 Shelf 1 No. 16

Section A: The history of printing. Illus.
" B: Modern printing. Illus.
" C: Writing and types. Illus.
" D: Binding.

31 articles by as many authors.

Boards; 11-1/8 x 8-3/8 x 1 in.

GUTENBERG-GESELLSCHAFT JAHRBUCH. 1928

Cabinet 26 Shelf 1 No. 17

Cont: Chinese background of the European invention of printing. By T.F. Carter. Xylographische Donat...von Konrad Haebler Entwicklung des japanischen buchdrucks. von Morimoto. Etc. Etc.

Important and authoritative essays on the history of printing.

Boards; $11\frac{1}{2}$ x $8\frac{1}{2}$ x 1 in.

GUTENBERG-GESELLSCHAFT JAHRBUCH 1929

Cabinet 26 Shelf 1 No. 19

Collection of essays contributed by various writers. Among them are: Alten Chinischen buchdruckerkunst. von Dr. Ting Wen Yuan; Der erste lesebuch an den Lateinschulen. von Ernst Schultz; Gutenberg und die nacherfinder, von Otto Hupp, etc.

Boards; $11\frac{1}{4}$ x $8\frac{1}{2}$ x 1 in.

GUTENBERG-GESELLSCHAFT JAHRBUCH. 1930

Cabinet 26 Shelf 1 No. 20

Series of articles on the history of printing, early printers, early and modern typography, and types. By several writers among whom are C.H. Kleukens, Maurice Audin, Gottfried Zedler, A. Ruppel, John Clyde Oswald, etc.

Boards; 11 x $8\frac{3}{4}$ x 1-1/8 in.

GUTENBERG-GESELLSCHAFT JAHRBUCH, 1931.

Cabinet 26 Shelf 1 No. 21

(Printers, printing, type design, type founding, typography, bookbinding, bibliography, etc. Thirty essays by as many writers). Illus.

Boards, linen back; 11 x 8-3/8 x $1\frac{1}{4}$ in.

GUTENBERG-GESELLSCHAFT PUBLICATIONS

Cabinet Y Shelf 1 No. 99

Buchdruckpresse von Joannes Gutenberg bis Friedrich König. von Karl Dieterichs, Mainz 1930. Illus.

Brief history of printing presses from Gutenberg to Koenig.

Boards; $9\frac{1}{4}$ x 6 in.

GUTENBERG-GESELLSCHAFT PUBLICATIONS

Cabinet Y Shelf 1 No. 72

A-Canon Missae vom jahr 1458 in liturgischer beziehung. von Dr. Franz Falk.
B-Typographische und druckasthetische erlauterungen von Heinrich Wallau. Mainz, 1904. Verlag der Gutenberg-Gesellschaft. Facsimiles.

Boards; $11\frac{1}{2}$ x 8-3/4 x $\frac{1}{2}$ in.

GUTENBERG-GESELLSCHAFT PUBLICATIONS

Cabinet Y Shelf 1 No. 84

De Ricci, Seymour, Catalogue raisonné des premièrs impressions de Mayence (1445-1476). Par Seymour De Ricci. Mainz, 1911. Verlag der Gutenberg-Gesellschaft.

Boards; 11 1/2 x 8 3/4 x 5/8 in.

GUTENBERG-GESELLSCHAFT PUBLICATIONS

Cabinet Y
Shelf 1
No. 69

[Donat, 1451 and calender type of 1448: supplement and summary] Die Donat-und kalender-type: Nachtrage und ubersicht von Dr. Paul Schwenke. Mit einem abdruck des donattextes nach den altesten ausgaben, und mit 7 tafeln. Mainz 1903. Verlag der Gutenberg-Gesellschaft.

Boards; 11½ x 8-3/4 x ½ in.

GUTENBERG-GESELLSCHAFT PUBLICATIONS

Cabinet Y
Shelf 1
No. 92.05

Handpresse, die. Kleine Drucke No.lV, 1927

See KLEUKENS, CH. H. Handpresse...

GUTENBERG-GESELLSCHAFT PUBLICATIONS.

Cabinet Y
Shelf 1
No. 79

(Das) Mainzer fragment vom Weltgericht: ein ausschnitt aus dem deutschen Sibyllenbuche. von Edward Schroeder. (The Mainz fragment from the Last Judgement: A section from the German Sibylline book) [Probably a Gutenberg impression]. Mainz, 1908. Verlag der Gutenberg-Gesellschaft.

One of four bibliographical studies, by four authors, in one volume.

Boards; 11½ x 8-3/4 x 3/4 in.

GUTENBERG-GESELLSCHAFT PUBLICATIONS

Cabinet FF
Shelf 4
No. 26

(Die) Enstehung der frakturschrift. von Rudolf Kautzsch. Mainz, 1922. With facs.

Boards; 8$\frac{3}{4}$ x 5$\frac{1}{2}$ in.

GUTENBERG-GESELLSCHAFT PUBLICATIONS

Cabinet Y
Shelf 1
No. 91

(Incunabula, inquiry concerning: A lecture given on the 25th anniversary of the Gutenberg Museum, Mainz. 1925) Aufgabe der wiegendruckforschung: Festvortrag...von Erich V. Rath. Gutenberg-Museums, am 27 Juni 1925 in Mainz. Beilage zum 22 bis 24 jahresbericht der Gutenberg-Gesellschaft.

Paper; 3 x 6 in.

GUTENBERG-GESELLSCHAFT PUBLICATIONS

Cabinet Y
Shelf 1
No. 79

(Missal Printed by Peter Schoeffer and his son John) Die missaldrucke Peter Schoffers und sohnes Johann. von Dr. Adolph Tronnier. Mainz, 1908. Verlag der Gutenberg-Gesellschaft.

One of four bibliographical essays by four authors, in one vol.

Boards; 11$\frac{1}{2}$ x 8$\frac{3}{4}$ x $\frac{3}{4}$ in.

GUTENBERG-GESELLSCHAFT PUBLICATIONS

Cabinet Y
Shelf 1
No. 72

(First impression with Gutenberg's Donat-Kalender-type: The Mainz fragment of the last judgement). Das Mainzer fragment vom Weltgericht: der älteste druck mit der Donat-Kalender-type Gutenbergs. von Ed. Schröder, Gottfried Zedler, und Heinrich Wallau. Mainz, 1904. Verlag der Gutenberg-Gesellschaft.

Boards; 11½ x 8-3/4 x ½ in.

GUTENBERG-GESELLSCHAFT PUBLICATIONS

Cabinet Y
Shelf 1
No. 92

Johanniswunder: Ein festspiel zur Gutenbergfeier in Mainz. von Hans Ludwig Linkenbach. 1932.

Kleine druck der Gutenberg-Gesellschaft.

Paper; 8-3/8 x 5-7/8 in. Item in manila envelope.

GUTENBERG-GESELLSCHAFT PUBLICATIONS

Cabinet Y
Shelf 3
No. 58

(Modern typography in Germany) Die moderne buchkunst in Deutschland. von Dr. Johannes Schinnerer. Beilage zum 11 jagresbericht. Mainz, 1912. Facsimiles.

Half morocco; 9-3/8 x 7-1/8 x 3/8 in.

GUTENBERG-GESELLSCHAFT PUBLICATIONS

Cabinet Y
Shelf 1
No. 79

(Forty two line Bibletype in the Schoeffer Missale of 1493). Die 42 zeilige Bibeltype im Schöfferschen Missale Moguntium von 1493. vor Gottfried Zedler. Mainz, 1908. Verlag der Gutenberg-Gesellschaft. Facsimiles.

One of four bibliographical studies, by four authors, in one volume.

Boards; 11$\frac{1}{2}$ x 8$\frac{3}{4}$ x $\frac{3}{4}$ in.

GUTENBERG-GESELLSCHAFT PUBLICATIONS

Cabinet Z
Shelf 5
No. 57

Liturgischen druckewerke Erhard Ratdolts, aus Augsburg, 1485-1522...Einleitung von Dr. Karl Schottenloher. Mainz, 1922.

Cloth; 18$\frac{1}{2}$ x 12$\frac{1}{4}$ x $\frac{3}{4}$ in.

GUTENBERG-GESELLSCHAFT PUBLICATIONS

Cabinet Y
Shelf 1
No. 90

(Native home of the art of printing). Die heimatstadt der buchdruckkunst. von Dr. A. Ruppel. Verlag der Gutenberg-Gesellschaft, Mainz-Berlin, 1926.

Paper; 8-5/8 x 5-3/4 x ¼ in.

GUTENBERG-GESELLSCHAFT PUBLICATIONS

Cabinet Y
Shelf 1
No. 74

Gutenberg as (technician and artist: A lecture). Gutenberg, techniker und kunstler. Vortrag, gehalten in der mitglieder versammlung der Gutenberg-Gesellschaft. Mainz, juni 25, 1905. Pamphlet.

Included in the above: Fourth yearly report of the Gutenberg-Gesellschaft, with list of members.

Paper; 9-7/8 x 7-1/8 in.

GUTENBERG-GESELLSCHAFT PUBLICATIONS

Cabinet Y
Shelf 1
No. 92

Mainz als Gutenbergstadt. von A. Ruppel. Kleine druck Nr. 8 Pamphlet.

With other items in manila envelope.

GUTENBERG-GESELLSCHAFT Publications

Cabinet Y
Shelf 1
No. 85

(The Pfister, Bamberg impression, and the 36 line Bible) Die Bamberger Pfisterdruck und die 36 zeilige Bibel. von Dr. Gottfried Zedler. Mainz, 1911. Verlag der Gutenberg-Gesellschaft. Facsimiles.

Boards; 11½ x 8-3/4 x 5/8 in.

GUTENBERG GESELLSCHAFT PUBLICATIONS

Cabinet Y
Shelf 1
No. 90.01

Gutenberg's grab. von Dr. A. Ruppel. Mainz, 1930. Kleine druck Nr. 13.

Paper; 11$\frac{1}{2}$ x 8$\frac{1}{2}$ in.

GUTENBERG-GESELLSCHAFT PUBLICATIONS

Cabinet Y
Shelf 1
No. 73

(Das) Mainzer Catholicon: Die typographische einteiling des Catholicon, die shrift, der drucker. (The Mainz Catholicon: typographical classification, the type, the printer). von Dr. Gottfried Zedler. Mainz, 1905. Verlag der Gutenberg-Gesellschaft. With Facsimiles.

Boards; 11½ x 8-3/4 x ½ in.

GUTENBERG-GESELLSCHAFT PUBLICATIONS

Cabinet Y
Shelf 1
No. 57

(Portraits of Gutenberg, a lecture). Gutenberg-Bildnisse: Festvortrag von Dr. Adolph Tronnier ...in der mitglieder-versammling der Gutenberg-Gesellschaft in Mainz am 22 juni 1913. Illus.

Half morocco; 9-3/4 x 7-1/8 x ¼ in.

GUTENBERG-GESELLSCHAFT PUBLICATIONS

Cabinet Y Shelf 1 No. 92

(Report of proceedings for 1922-24: With a list of members) 22-24. Tätigkeitsbericht der Gutenberg Gesellschaft. Erstattet von dem 11. vorsitzenden Dr. Ruppel. Mainz, 1925.

Paper; 9¾ x 7 in. In manila envelope.

GUTENBERG-GESELLSCHAFT PUBLICATIONS

Cabinet Y Shelf 1 No. 65

Was hat Gutenberg erfunden? Ein ruckblick auf die frühtechnik des schriftgusses. von Gustav Mori. Mainz, 1921.

Half morocco; 9 x 6½ in.

GUTENBERG MUSEUM

Cabinet Y Shelf 4 No. 76

Account of the Gutenberg Museum, with mention of Theo. L. DeVinne's gifts to the Museum. Mainz, 1902-3. Brochure.

Item in manila envelope

GUTENBERG-GESELLSCHAFT PUBLICATONS

Cabinet Y Shelf 1 No. 79

(Schoeffer's, Peter, book advertising sheets). Zu den bücheranzeigen Peter Schoffers. von Dr. Wilhelm Velke. Mainz, 1908. Verlag der Gutenberg-Gesellschaft. Facsimiles

One of four bibliographical studies, by four authors, in one volume.

Boards; 11½ x 8-3/4 x 3/4 in.

GUTENBERG-GESELLSCHAFT PUBLICATIONS

Cabinet Y Shelf 1 No. 92.02

(World Museum of typography in the making) Das werdende weltmuseum der druckkunst. Kleine Druck Nr. 12. Pamphlet. Text in four languages.

With other items in manila envelope.

GUTENBERG- MUSEUM

Cabinet Y Shelf 1 No. 92.05

Kleiner Führer durch des Gutenberg Museum in Mainz. Abteilung 1.: Haus zum Römischen Kaiser. Zuzammengestellt von Dr. A. Ruppel u: und Dr. A. Tronnier, Mainz, 1934.

Illus. guide to the new house of the Gutenberg Museum, opened in 1933.

Brochure.

GUTENBERG-GESELLSCHAFT PUBLICATIONS No.22

Cabinet Y Shelf 1 No. 86.01

(Der) Strassburger frühdrucker Johann Mentelin (1458-1478). Studien zu seinem leben und werke. von Karl Schorbach. Mit 19 tafeln. Mainz, 1932.

paper; 11¾ x 8½ x 1¼ in.

GUTENBERG-GESELLSCHAFT PUBLICATIONS

Cabinet Y Shelf 1 No. 86

Zedler, Gottfried: Die Mainzer Ablassebriefe der jahre 1454 und 1455. (Letters of Indulgence). Verlag der Gutenberg-Gesellschaft, Mainz, 1913.

With 17 plates of facsimiles in separate cover. See Y/1/87

Paper; 11-3/4 x 8-3/4 x 3/8 in.

GUTENBERG-MUSEUM

Cabinet X Shelf 2 No. 57

Mainz, 1900: Gutenberg-Fest, zugleich errinerungs gabe an die eröffnung des Gutenberg-Museums am 23 Juni, 1901.

Account of the Gutenberg celebration held in Mainz in the year 1900, together with the names of the donors and list of donations for the new Gutenberg Museum.

Paper; 9¼ x 6¾ x ½ in.

GUTENBERG-GESELLSCHAFT PUBLICATIONS

Cabinet Y Shelf 1 No. 92.02

Türkenkalender für das jahr 1455. Eine druck-historische studie von Gustav Mori. Mainz 1928 Kleiner Druck Nr. 9b.

With other items in manila envelope.

GUTENBERG-GESELLSCHAFT PUBLICATIONS

Cabinet Y Shelf 1 No. 68

Zedler, Gottfried. (The earliest Gutenbergtypes). Die älteste Gutenbergtype. Mit 13 tafeln. Mainz, 1902. Verlag der Gutenberg-Gesells-chaft.

Bibliographical study of a newly discov-ered astronomical calender for 1448.

Boards; 11½ x 8-3/4 x ½ in.

GUTENBERG MUSEUM

Cabinet X Shelf 2 No. 57

[opening of the Gutenberg Museum: Programme of events] Gutenberg Fest zu Mainz im j[ahr] 1900: Zugleich erinnerungens-gabe an die eröffnung des Gutenberg-Museum, am 23 Juni, 1901. Mainz.

Paper; 9¼ x 6¾ in.

GUTENBERG-GESELLSCHAFT PUBLICATIONS

Cabinet Y Shelf 1 No. 92

Vier neue Gutneberg-vildnisse des Gutenberg-Museums Mainz. von Adolph Tronnier. (1930). Kleine Druck Nr. 11. Illus.

Description of four new portraits of Gutenberg.

Item in manila envelope.

GUTENBERG HALL, IN THE

Cabinet KK Shelf 2 No. 60.01

"Buchgewerbehaus"

see

PICTURES. Gutenberg Hall.

GUTENBERG MUSEUM

Cabinet Y Shelf 4 No. 76

(Prospectus of a forthcoming book in celebration of the 25th anniversary of the founding of the Gutenberg Museum. German text)

Gutenberg Festschrift zur feier des 25 jahrigen bestehens des Gutenberg Museums in Mainz. 1925.

Item in manila envelope

GUTENBERG-GESELLSCHAFT PUBLICATIONS

Cabinet Y Shelf 1 No. 92.02

Wandlungen in der schrift und in der kunst. von Adolf Kautzsch. 1928. Kline-Druck 10.

With other items in manila envelope.

(Le) GUTENBERG JOURNAL [Afterward] Le

Cabinet C Shelf 1 No. 15

Gutenberg et le Senefelder...Paris, 1859-1870

See PERIODICALS, PRINTING. France. Gutenberg (Le) Journal des imprimeurs...

GUTENBERG MUSEUM

Cabinet Y Shelf 1 No. 92.05

(Solicitation for funds towards maintenance of the Gutenberg Museum, Mainz. n.d. circa 1926

Has list of American patrons, illustration of the Museum, etc.

Double paged broadside, in envelope

GUTENBERG TO PLANTIN

Cabinet S Shelf 4 No. 43

(An) Outline of the early history of printing, 1450-1600. By George Parker Winship, Cambridge, Mass., 1926. Illus.

Cloth; 8½ x 5-5/8 in.

GUTHRIE, JAMES

Cabinet M Shelf 4 No. 5.05

Pear Tree Press

see IMPRINTS, England. Pear Tree Press...

GUYER, I. D.

Cabinet QQ Shelf 4 No. 39

Chicago, history of its commercial and manufacturing interests and industries... Chicago, 1862.

see p.66 and following for stereotyping; p.53-line engraving; p.90-bookbinding; p.99-lithographing; p.120-paper warehouses; p.130-publishing; p.139 wood engraving.

Morocco, 10½ x 8 x 5/8 in.

GUTENBERG ZEITSCHRIFT

Cabinet 24 Shelf 2 No. 10 & 11

Auer, M., Wien, 1855, 1856.

see PERIODICALS, PRINTING. Germany. Gutenberg.Zeitschrift...

GUTHRIE, STUART

Cabinet M Shelf 4 No. 5.05

Primer of Printing. By Stuart Guthrie. An extract from a forthcoming book. Article in The Book Craftsman. Spring Number, 1935.

With other items in manila envelope.

GUYOT, E.

Cabinet V Shelf 5 No. 23

Bruxelles, 1856-1880. History of the printing plant of E. Guyot.

See DeGEORGE, L. Historique de l'Imprimerie E. Guyot... Bruxelles, 1880.

GUTENBERG'S LAW SUIT IN 1439.

Cabinet V Shelf 2 No. 48

Debut de l'imprimerie à Strasbourg, ou Recherches sur les traveus mysterieux de Gutenberg dans cette ville, et sur le procès qui lui fut inventé en 1439 à cette occasion Par Léon de Laborde. Paris, 1840. Facsimiles of type and woodcuts.

Half morocco; 10½ x 6¾ x ½ in.

GUTIERREZ, Juan

Cabinet X Shelf 3 No. 19

Brief bio-bibliographical note, with printer mark, Gutierrez (Alcalá), 1558-1572.

see HAEBLER, KONRAD. (Spanish and Portugese printer marks...p.xxix

GUYOT, EUGÈNE ÉMILE

Cabinet W Shelf 5 No. 77

See Plants, Printing, Belgium.

GUTENBERG'S LAW SUIT In 1439.

Cabinet W Shelf 2 No. 1

See Gutenberg, Johann. Process de Gutenberg.

GUTNER (Jo. G.)

Cabinet X Shelf 1 No. 36

Typographiae Chemnitiensis primal plagulal

[In Wolf, "Monumenta Typographica", Vol. 2, p. 404]

GUZMAN, Francisco de

Cabinet X Shelf 3 No. 19

Brief bio-bibliographical note, with printer mark Guzman (Toledo), 1563-1578

See HAEBLER, KONRAD. (Spanish and Portugese printer marks...p.xxx

GUTENBERG'S TURKENKALENDER

Cabinet Y Shelf 1 No. 54

Facsimile with a bibliographical study of Gutenberg's 1455 Turkenkalender. By Gustav Mori.

Kleiner druck lXa and lXb. der Gutenberg Gesellschaft, Mainz, 1928.

Item in manila envelope

GUTTERWITZ, ANDREAS

Cabinet AA Shelf 5 No. 32

(Ett) Okänt Kopenhammstrych av ar 1582 (An unknown Kopenhagen imprint of 1582). Ragnar Dahlberg, Helsingfors, 1925.

Bibliographical essay in Collijn's "Bok-ock biblioteks historika studier ... Uppsala, 1925. pp. 295-301.

Boards; 11 x 8½ x 2 in.

GUZMAN, MELCHIOR DE

Cabinet AA Shelf 5 No. 1

See Cabrera Nunez de Guzman

GUTHRIE, JAMES

Cabinet M Shelf 4 No. 5.05

(The) Book Craftsman. James Guthrie editor. At the Pear Tree Press, Flansham, Bognor Regis, Sussex, England. Spring Number [1935] Specimen copy.

With other items in manila envelope.

GUYENNE

Cabinet Shelf No.

See Printing, Historical, France (Guyenne)

GWATKINS' TRAVELLER

Cabinet 43 Shelf 2 No. 17

Toronto, 1890

See PERIODICALS, PRINTING, Canada Gwatkins' Traveller...

GYLES, F. and E.

Cabinet See Specimen Books, Types. England

Shelf

No.

GYMNICH FAMILY OF PRINTERS

Cabinet X Bio-bibliographical notes, Gymnich family of printers, Cologne, 1517-1614.

Shelf 3 see HEITZ, PAUL.

No. 20 Kölner büchermarken...p.xxv

GYMNICUS, ARNOLD

Cabinet X Biographical note, with printer mark, Basel, circa 1562.

Shelf 3 see HEITZ, PAUL

No. 15 Basler büchermarken... pp.xxxvi, 103

H

HAARLEM, Enrico di (see)

Cabinet HENRICO (de Haarlem)

Shelf

No.

HAAS, GUILLAUME

Cabinet 83 See Specimen Books, Types. Switzerland.

Shelf 1

No. 2

HACKET, THOMAS

Cabinet T Books printed by Thomas Hacket, London, 1560-90. Bibliographical notes.

Shelf 2 in DIBDIN'S 'Typographical Antiquities" ...London, 1810-19, vol.IV, p.580

No. 6

[vol.4]

HAARLEM

Cabinet X (De) Typographicae artis inventione, et inventoribus, dissertatio. Marcus Zuerius Boxhorn. Lugduni, Batavorum, 1640.

Shelf 1 A dissertation on the invention and inventors of printing. Favors Haarlem. Reprinted in Wolf, "Monumenta Typographica", vol. I, pp. 813-865.

No. 9

Morocco; 7½ x 5½ x 3/8 in.

HAASE SÖHNE, GOTTLIEB

Cabinet See Specimen Books, Types. Bohemia.

Shelf

No.

HACKLEMAN, CHARLES W.

Cabinet MM Commercial engraving and printing. A manual of practical instruction and reference covering commercial illustrating, and printing by all processes...Published by Commercial Engraving Publishing Company, Indianapolis, Indiana (1921).

Shelf 7

No. 28 With more than 2000 illus.

Cloth; 9½ x 6½ x 2-1/8 in.

HAARLEM

Cabinet Y (Printing offices in Haarlem, 1483-1583. Historical notes and comments. also bio-biblio. study.)

Shelf 1

No. 23 See LINDE, ANTONIOUS van der. Geschichte der erfindung der buchdruckkunst ...Berlin, 1886, vol.1,p.183. See also index of above work, vol.3.

HACK, FRANS.

Cabinet 39 See Imprints, Holland. Elzevier, Ludwig and Frans Hack.

Shelf 2

No. 50

HACKSTAFF'S MONTHLY

Cabinet 21 Publication devoted to the graphic arts.

Shelf 2

No. 10 See PERIODICALS, PRINTING. United States Hackstaff's Monthly, etc.

HAARLEMSCHE COURANT.

Cabinet See Newspapers, Holland.

Shelf

No.

HACKERT, PHILIP

Cabinet RR (Don) Stefano Merola's paper mill. From the biographical sketch of Philip Hackert by Johann Wolfgang Goethe. New York: Japan Paper Company, 1931.

Shelf 5

No. 21

Boards; 8½ x 6¼ in.

HADEN, SEYMOUR

Cabinet K Mezzotint as a painter's art, on the revival of. By Seymour Haden. Illus. excerpt from Harper's New Monthly Magazine, Jan., 1885.

Shelf 5

No. 1 Item 5 in vol. with binder's title "Wood Engraving, Etc".

HADRIAN, JUNIUS

Cabinet I Shelf 1 No. 8

Portrait, with biography of the originator of the Coster legend.

See CLOQUIUS (or Cloucq), ANDREAS. Icones ...Lug. Batav. 1617, p.35.

HAEBLER, KONRAD.

Cabinet 75 Shelf 2 No. 5

Die deutschen buchdrucker des 15 jahrhunderts im auslande. Munich, 1924. Review of book with above title by V. S. (Victor Scholderer)

In Transactions of the Bibliographical Society, "The Library," Vol. V. 1924-1925, pp. 285-289.

HAEBLER, KONRAD

Cabinet Y Shelf 3 No. 69

(Incunabula and manuscripts. A collection of bio-bibliographical historical essays by I. Collijn; E. Crous; P. Schwenke; E. Voullieme, and others. Dedicated to K. Haebler on his 60th birthday. Wiegendruck und handschriften. Festgabe Konrad Haebler zum 60. geburtstage. Mit bildnes, tafeln, abbildingen im text. Leipzig, 1919.

Half vellum; 11½ x 8 x 1-3/8 in.

HAEBLER, KONRAD

Cabinet Y Shelf 3 No. 93

Beitrag sur geschichte des bucheinbandes im 16 jahrhundert: Die buchbinder von Zwickau. Illus.

Article in Hiersemann's "Werden und Wirken: Ein festgruss"...Leipzig, 1924, p.99

HAEBLER, KONRAD

Cabinet X Shelf 2 No. 59

Deutscher buchdrucker in Spanien und Portugal (German printers in Spain and Portugal)

see HARTWIG, OTTO (Compiler) Festschrift...Mainz, 1900, pp.393-405

HAEBLER, KONRAD.

Cabinet 18 Shelf 2 No. 1

(Introduction of Printing into Spain) Einfuhrung des Buchdrucks in Spanien.

In Zeitschrift für Bücherfreunde, 1915-16, part 2, p.177.

HAEBLER, KONRAD

Cabinet AA Shelf 5 No. 16

Bibliografía Ibérica del siglo XV. Enumeracion de todos los libros impresos en España y Portugal hasta el año de 1500. Con notas criticas. Por Conrado Haebler. Leipzig, 1903.

With alphabetic and chronological index of printers and printed books. See also AA/5/17.

Half morocco; 9½ x 6½ in.

HAEBLER, KONRAD

Cabinet Y Shelf 1 No. 92.02

Erfindung der druckkunst und ihre ausbreitung in den Ländern Europas. Vortrag in der Generalversammlung der Gutenberg-Gesellschaft am 22 Juni 1930. Pamphlet.

With other items in manila envelope.

HAEBLER, KONRAD

Cabinet K Shelf 1 No. 18

(Introduction to Lyell's "Early book illustration in Spain"... London, 1926.

Cloth; 11½ x 9 x 1¾ in.

HAEBLER, KONRAD.

Cabinet AA Shelf 5 No. 17

Bibliografía Ibérica del siglo XV. Segunda parte. Por Conrado Haebler. Leipzig, 1917.

Bibliographical account of printing in Spain in the 15th century. Second part is an addition to "Bibliografica Ibérica" published in 1903. See AA/5/16.

Half morocco; 9⅛ x 6½ in.

HAEBLER, KONRAD

Cabinet B Shelf 2 No. 23

Geschichte des spanischen frühdruckess. In stammbäumen. Mit 489 abbildungen. Leipzig, 1923. Facs., illus.

History of early Spanish printers and printing.

Cloth over boards; 16¾ x 13 x 1¾ in.

HAEBLER, KONRAD

Cabinet 9 Shelf 1 No. 1a & 1b

Italienische Wiegendruck in original-typenbeispielen. 120 Inkunabelproben. Beschrieben von Konrad Haebler, München, 1927. (2 Portfolios)

Cloth; 21½ x 17¼ in.

HAEBLER, KONRAD.

Cabinet 18 Shelf 1 No. 2

(Counterfeit money notices in the early period of printing) "Falsche Gulden" - Blätter aus der Frühzeit der Druckerkunst, von Konrad Haebler, Berlin. Illus.

In Zeitschrift für Bücherfreunde, 1907-8, part 1, p.219.

HAEBLER, KONRAD.

Cabinet 75 Shelf 2 No. 6

Geschichte des spanischen Fruhdruckes in Stammbaumen. Book with same title reviewed by V. Scholderer.

In Transactions of the Bibliographical Society, "The Library," Vol. VI, 1925-1926, pp. 99-104.

HAEBLER, KONRAD

Cabinet Y Shelf 4 No. 73

(Die) Italianischen fragmente vom Leiden Christi, das alteste druckwerk Italiens. (The Italian fragments of the "Leiden Christi", the earliest Italian printed work.) Ein untersuchung von Konrad Haebler. Verlag von Jacques Rosenthal. Munchen, 1927. Illus. pamphlet.

Beitrag zur Forschung (1)

Item in manila envelope.

HAEBLER, KONRAD

Cabinet Y Shelf 5 No. 60

Deutschen buchdrucker des 15 jahrhunderts im ausland. München, 1924. With facsimiles.

Bio-bibliographical historical account of German printers resident in foreign countries, and printing of the 15th century.

Paper; 14-1/8 x 10½ x 1¼ in.

HAEBLER, KONRAD.

Cabinet 20 Shelf 1 No. 18

(Greyff, Michel - printer of Calendars). Michel Greyff als Kalenderdrucker, von Dr. Konrad Haebler, Dresden, Dec., 1905, Many facsimiles

In Zeitschrift für Bücherfreunde, 1905-6, part 2, p.343.

HAEBLER, KONRAD.

Cabinet 75 Shelf 1 No. 3

Native printers in Spain in the fifteenth century. A paper read before the Bibliographical Society, June, 17, 1895.

In Trans. Biblio. Soc., Vol. III, 1895-1897. pp. 4-7.

HAEBLER, KONRAD

Cabinet 20 Shelf 2 No. 14

Neues vom Meister N.P. (Further information concerning N.P., 1549-1563).
An unidentified book binder who decorated his leather bindings by means of a roller stamp. (or printing between rollers?).

In Zeitschrift für Bücherfreunde, 1924, pp. 130-138.

HAEBLER, KONRAD

Cabinet AA Shelf 5 No. 12

Tipografia Iberica del siglo XV. Reproductions en facsimile de todos los caracteres tipograficos empleados en España y Portugal hasta el año de 1500. Con notas criticas y biograficas. Por Conrado Haebler ... La Haya - Leipzig, 1902.

Quarter russia; 15 x 12 in.

HAEBLER, KONRAD

Cabinet 26 Shelf 1 No. 17

Xylographische Donate. [Comparison of some Holland Donates to determine which one Gutenberg used as a model for his invention].
Article in the Gutenberg-Gesellschaft Jahrbuch 1920. pp.15-31.

HAEBLER, KONRAD.

Cabinet 18 Shelf 1 No. 5

(On the study of the types used in the XV century) Zur typenkunde des XV jahrkunderts.

In Zeitschrift fur Bucherfreunde, 1909, part 1, p.136.

HAEBLER, KONRAD

Cabinet S Shelf 5 No. 37

Type founding and commerce of type during the early years of printing.

Article in "Ars Typographica", vol.3, No No.1, July, 1926, p.5

HAEBLER, KONRAD

Cabinet AA Shelf 5 No. 32

Zwei Nurnberger tonformen (Two Nurnberg color forms). Bei Konrad Haebler. Uppsala, 1925. Facsimile.
Bibliographical essay in Collijns "Bokock biblioteks-historika studier ... pp.103-110.

Boards; 11 x 8½ x 2 in.

HAEBLER, KONRAD

Cabinet 00 Shelf 6 No. 28

(Presillanndt new Zeitung, 1515). Facsimile einer handschriftlichen "Neuen Zeitung" aus dem anfange des 16 jahrhunderts. 1515 New Zeitung aus Presillanndt. Mit einem geleitwort von Konrad Haebler. Leipzig, 1920.

Item in envelope.

HAEBLER, KONRAD.

Cabinet 18 Shelf 1 No. 6

(Unknown broadside of Bartholomaes Gothan). Ein unbekannte einblattdruck des Bartholomaeus Gothan. Facsimile.

In Zeitschrift für Bücherfreunde, 1908-9, part 2, p.357.

HAEGGSTROMSKA BOKTRYCHERIET

Cabinet AA Shelf 5 No. 27

See Plants, Printing. Sweden.

HAEBLER, KONRAD.

Cabinet 76 Shelf 2 No. 4

Printers of Spain and Portugal, early. Printed for the Bibliographical Society, March, 1897. Illus. Illus. Monograph IV.

Half morocco; 11 x 9 in.

HAEBLER, KONRAD

Cabinet Y Shelf 2 No. 2

Verlegomarked des Jean Petit. (Trade marks of the publisher.) Halle (Saale), 1914. Pamphlet.

In box labelled "German Pamphlets - History of Printing - Bibliography, etc."

HAENEL, EDUARD

Cabinet Shelf No.

see

I Specimen Books, Types. Germany
II " " Cuts. "
III Broadsides, Type Founders, "

HAEBLER, KONRAD.

Cabinet 75 Shelf 2 No. 1

Review of "The Haebler Festgabe," Wigendruck und Handschriften. A bibliographical tribute, by Victor Scholderer.

In Transactions of the Bibliographical Society, "The Library," Vol. I, 1920-1921, pp. 52-56.

HAEBLER, KONRAD

Cabinet 9 Shelf 1 No. 1

Westeuropäische wigendruck in original typenbeispielen. 60 Inkunabelproben, Niederländische, Französischer, Iberischer und Englisher Pressen. Beschrieben von Konrad Haebler, München, 1928.

60 Original pages of incunabula. With descriptive text.

Cloth portfolio; 21½ x 17¾ in.

HAGAR, WILLIAM JR. & COMPANY

Cabinet Shelf No.

See Specimen Books, Types. United States. Hagar, William Jr. & Co. New York.

HAEBLER, KONRAD

Cabinet X Shelf 3 No. 19

(Spanish and Portugese printer marks of the 15th and 16th centuries. Preceded by biographical notes) Spanische und Portugiesische bücherzeichen des XV und XVI. jahrhunderts. Strassburg, 1898. Illus.

Half cloth; 14¼ x 11¼ x ⅜ in.

HAEBLER, KONRAD

Cabinet Shelf No.

Wie ich inkunabelforscher wurde. Ein stückchen lebensgeschichte. Biog. with portrait. Printed by T. Tchudy & Co. St. Gall, Switzerland. With printer mark.

Article, supplement fo "Philobiblon", 5 Jahrgang, heft I, 1932.

HAGAR & CO., WILLIAM

Cabinet Shelf No.

See Specimen Books, Types. United States. Hagar & Co. William.

HAGENAU

Cabinet K, Shelf 1, No. 17

Anshelm, Thomas, 1516 - 1523

See Heitz, Paul, (Die) Zierinitialen in dem drucken der Thomas Anshelm...

HAGENAU (Alsace-Lorrain)

Cabinet X, Shelf 3, No. 13

(Printers and publishers devices, 15th to 18th centuries, Hagenau).

see HEITZ, PAUL. Elsässische büchermarken...

HAGENBACH, Peter

Cabinet X, Shelf 3, No. 19

Bio-bibliographical sketch, Hagenbach (Valencia), 1493-1509.

see HAEBLER, KONRAD. (Spanish and Portugese printer marks...p.xi

---

HAGER, HANS

Cabinet X, Shelf 3, No. 16

Brief bio-bibliographical note. Hager, printer, Zurich, 1524.

see HEITZ, PAUL. Zürcher büchermarken... p.6

HAGHEN, GOLFRIED VAN DER, Printer, Antwerp.

Cabinet S, Shelf 5, No. 6

An attempt to prove that "Haghen" was not the name of the man who printed the last corrected version of Tindale's Bible in The Bibliographer, Dec., 1881.

Bound with other items in "Various Printers and their Plants," item 23, vol.2.

HAHN, ULRIC

Cabinet S, Shelf 1, No. 29

See De Vinne, Theodore Low. Notable printers of Italy ... New York, 1910. p. 53.

HAIDA (Queen Charlotte Isl. Br. Columbia)

Cabinet II, Shelf 4, No. 2

[Language of a large body of American Indians settled around Alaska. Illustrative sketch of]. By John R. Swanton.

See BOAS, FRANZ. American Indian languages, handbook of...Bulletin 40, Washington, 1911, pp.209-277.

HAIGHT, A.V.

Cabinet EE, Shelf 1, No. 19

See SPECIMEN BOOKS TYPES. Printers'

HAILING, THOMAS

Cabinet EE, Shelf 2, No. 42

Specimens of general printing. Oxford works, Cheltenham, 1879.

Together with "Hailings Circular", a periodical for printers, with innumerable items of typographic interest. Illus. Following frontispiece, memorial broadside for George W. Child, president of New York Typographical Union No.6. With portrait.

Cloth, stamped; 12½ x 10 in.

HAILINGS CIRCULAR

Cabinet 38, Shelf 2, No. 17.01

Published by Thomas Hailing, Oxford Printing Works, Cheltenham.

See PERIODICALS, GREAT BRITAIN Hailings Circular...

HAINES, HENRY

Cabinet X, Shelf 4, No. 66

Treachery, baseness and cruelty displayed in the hardships and sufferings of Henry Haines, late printer of the Country Journal, or Craftsman...London: Printed for Henry Haines, 1740.

Half morocco; 7¾ x 4¾ in.

HAINES, JENNIE DAY

Cabinet 71, Shelf 1, No. 6

Weather Opinions: A Book of quotations with interleaves on weather subjects. Compiled by Jennie Day Haines. Typography designed by John Henry Nash. Published for Paul Elder & Company, and printed for them at the Tomaye Press in New York City, 1907.

Half morocco; 9½ x 7¼ in.

HAINS, LUDWIG

Cabinet AA, Shelf 5, No. 32

(Zur) Biographie Ludwig Hains. Bei Erich V. Rath, Bonn, 1925.

Essay in Collijns "Bok-ock biblioteks historika studier ... Uppsala, 1925. pp. 161-182.

Boards; 11 x 8½ x 2 in.

HAITI

Cabinet, Shelf, No.

See Early Printing in Spanish-America [Literature of] West Indies.

HAKLUYT SOCIETY (see)

Cabinet T, Shelf 5, No. 7

Hume, Rev. A. (Compiler). Learned societies and printing clubs...London, 1893, p.294

HAKLUYT SOCIETY (THE)

Stack 15, Shelf 4, Number 66

Publications of The Hakluyt Society. A catalogue of books, No. 515. Bernard Quaritch Ltd. London, 1936.

also catalogue of New & Standard books on Architecture and. The Allied Arts... Architectural Book Publishing Co., Inc., New York.

In envelope.

HALDEMAN-JULIUS, E.

Cabinet Q, Shelf 1, No. 3

(Biography) E. Haldeman-Julius: a psychography. By Isaac Goldberg. Excerpt from Stratford Monthly, Jan. 1925.

Item 12 in vol. with binder's title "Publishing Houses and Periodicals. Pamphlets."

HALDEMAN-JULIUS, E.

Cabinet NN, Shelf 2, No. 2.01

Sixty million books. Haldeman-Julius' first five years. By Herbert Flint and Viola Roseboro. Illus. excerpt from McClure's, Aug., 1924.

Item 19 in vol. with binder's title "Journalists and Journalism -- II. Pamphlets".

HALE, EDWARD E and EDWARD E. Jr.

Cabinet R Shelf 2 No. 32

Franklin in France. From original documents, most of which are now published for the first time. Boston, 1887. Illus. Portraits.

Orig. cloth bds., 9¾ x 7 ins., pp. (XVI), 3 leaves, 478.

HALFTONE PHOTOGRAPHY.

Cabinet Shelf No.

Making of a half-tone plate. A pictorial description.
Article in The British Printer, No. 257. Vol. XLIII, Jan. Feb. 1931. pp. 217-219.

HALIFAX GAZETTE, THE

Cabinet NN Shelf 2 No. 9

First newspaper in Canada

see

JOURNALISM, Canada Halifax Gazette...

HALE, SARAH JOSEPHA (Buel)

Cabinet R Shelf 3 No. 203

Brief biographical sketch of Mrs Hale, editor of Godey's Lady's Book.

see
MOORE, JOHN W. Historical, Biographical, and Miscellaneous Gatherings...p.493

HALFTONE PHOTOGRAPHY

Cabinet MM Shelf 6 No. 1

Preparation and consideration of halftone copy, by Harry W. Leggett, Ottawa. Published by Southam Press, Limited, Toronto. n.d. Pamphlet.

Bound with "Various items on printing," item 10.

HALIFAX GAZETTE
see also
First Occurrences, Canada: Halifax Gazette.

Cabinet Shelf No.

HALE, MRS. SARAH J.

Cabinet 80 Shelf 2 No. 40

Editor, Boston, 1833, Ladies Magazine.

See ~~Magazines~~ Periodicals, United States. Ladies Magazine and Literary Gazette. Edited by Mrs. Sarah J. Hale...

HALFTONE PLATES FOR 3-COLOR PROCESS

Cabinet I Shelf 2 No. 48.01

Plates for yellow, red and blue printing.

With other items in manila envelope

HALIFAX TYPOGRAPHICAL SOCIETY

Cabinet KK Shelf 6 No. 26

Scale of prices. Addressed to master printers of Halifax. Nov. 3, 1864.

Item in envelope.

HALE, MRS. SARAH J.

Cabinet 80 Shelf 2 No. 44

Editor, 1838, (Godey's) The Lady's Book, and Ladies American Magazine...

See ~~Magazine~~ Periodicals, United States. Lady's Book, and Ladies American Magazine...

HALF-TONE PROCESS

Cabinet Shelf No.

See PHOTO-ENGRAVING PROCESSES. [Half-tone].

HALL, CHARLES WINSLOW

Cabinet S Shelf 5 No. 6

(The) Printer and Publisher, 1470-1810. By C. W. Hall. Excerpt from National Magazine Jan., 1912. Illus.

Item 5 in collection "Various printers and their plants; excerpts from magazines," Vol. 2, 1918.

HALES, (J. W.)

Cabinet Q Shelf 1 No. 24

Publishers in Hampstead. Reprinted from Hampstead Annual, 1904-5). Illus.

Presentation copy from author to H. Buxton Forman. Autograph letter bound in.

Half morocco· 10½ x 7 x 3/8 in.

HALFTONES

Cabinet MM Shelf 6 No. 1

Preparation and consideration of halftone copy. A paper by Henry W. Leggett. Published by the Southam Press, Limited, Toronto and Montreal. n.d. circa 1912. Pamphlet.

Item 10 in book with binder's title "Various items on printing". Bound 1919.

HALL, CHARLES WINSLOW

Cabinet S Shelf 5 No. 4

(The) Printer and publisher: The discovery of printing, 1400-1440. Excerpt from the National Magazine, Dec. 1911.

Item 17 in collection "Various printers and their plants; excerpts from Magazines, I."

HALEVI, ISAAC BEN SAMUEL

Cabinet E Shelf 3 No. 34

Siah Yizhak. Prague, 1627. [Printer Unknown]

This is a Hebrew grammar based on phonetic laws.

Tooled Leather; 7-3/4 x 6 x 1 in.

HALIFAX

Cabinet X Shelf 5 No. 15

Imprint of P.K.Holden, Halifax, 1810.

See LIBERTY OF PRINTING. Apology for the liberty of the press...Halifax, 1810.

HALL, DAVID & Benjamin Franklin

Cabinet R Shelf 2 No. 100

Work-book of 1759-1766.

See Franklin, Benjamin & David Hall. Work-book...

HALL, DAVID and WILLIAM STRAHAN.

Cabinet R Shelf 5 No. 15

Correspondence between William Strahan [printer] and David Hall [the partner of Franklin], 1763-1777. From originals in the possession of the Historical Society of Pennsylvania.
In volume "Early printing and printers in America. Excerpts from Pennsylvania Magazines pp. 86-221.

Half morocco; 9-7/8 x 6-5/8 in.

HALL, FREDERICK JOHN

Cabinet Shelf No.

See Oxford University Press. Hall, Frederick, Controller of Oxford University Press.

HALL, FREDERICK JOHN

Cabinet U Shelf 2 No. 129

Printer to the University of Oxford, 1915-1925

See OXFORD UNIVERSITY PRESS. Hall, Frederick John...

HALL, ROBERT

Cabinet X Shelf 5 No. 25

(An) Apology for the freedom of the press and the general liberty. To which are prefixed remarks on Bishop Horsley's Sermon, preached on the 30th January, 1793. Huddersfield: Printed by William Moore, Westgate, 1819.
The fourth edition.

Half morocco; 8-5/8 x 5-3/8 in.

HALL, ROWLAND

Cabinet T Shelf 2 No. 6 [vol.4]

Books printed by Rowland Hall. London, 1559-1563. Bibliographical notes. With printer's device.

see

DIBDIN'S "Typographical Antiquities" ...London, 1810-19, vol.IV, p.410

HALL, MRS S. C.

Cabinet S Shelf 5 No. 24

(The) Printing Office of William Caxton. By Mrs. S. C. Hall. Pamphlet,"Houses and Haunts of the Wise and Good", Phila. 1854.

P. 40 in collection "Printing Excerpts."

HALL, SAMUEL, Printer

Cabinet Shelf No.

See Early printing in New England. Boston, 1791. Samuel Hall.

HALL, Samuel.

Cabinet A Shelf 3 No. 7

SEe Newspapers, Massachusetts; The Salem Gazette printed by him.

Bound in with other newspapers; leaf 33.

HALL, SAMUEL

Cabinet F Shelf 2 No. 88

Salem, 1774, S. Hall (Imprint)

See EARLY PRINTING IN NEW ENGLAND Salem, 1783...

HALL, SAMUEL
see also

Imprints.

HALL, THOMAS (Inventor) see

Cabinet FF Shelf 6 No. 19

TYPE WRITING MACHINES. Hall, Thomas

HALL, WILLIAM

Cabinet S Shelf 6 No. 8

Shepard Kollock, printer of the first New York directory. Excerpt from the Mag. of Am. History. Oct., 1886.

Item 13 in vol. with binder's title "Early printing and printers. Pamphlets".

HALL PRINTING COMPANY, W.F.,(Chicago, Ill.)

Cabinet Shelf No.

See Imprints, United States.

HALLE, GERMANY

See also Printers' Celebrations.

HALLEY, R.A.

Cabinet RR Shelf 4 No. 21

Paper making in Tennessee. By R.A. Halley.

Article in "The American Historical Magazine, and Tennessee Historical Quarterly", vol.IX, July, 1904, No.3, p.211.

Item in manila envelope.

HALLIDAY, JOHN

Cabinet X Shelf 5 No. 3

[Obituary]. At Edinburgh, aged 75, Mr. John Halliday, printer; during a period of sixty-one years was employed in the office of the Caledonian Mercury. He has left behind him some curious specimens of typography. Newspaper excerpt, n.n.n.d. [1826].

p. 43 in vol. with Binder's title "Scrap-Book, 1705-1891, relating to printing."

HALLOCK, GERARD

Cabinet NN Shelf 3 No. 9

Life of Gerard Hallock, Thirty-three years. Editor of the New York Journal of Commerce. New York. 1869.

Frontispiece. portrait.

Cloth: 7¾x5¼"

HALLOCK & CO., H.P.

Cabinet Shelf No.

See Specimen Books, Types. United States.

HALSEY, ROSALIE V.

Cabinet S Shelf 3 No. 106

Forgotten books of the American nursery. A history of the development of the American story-book. Boston, 1911. Printed by D.B. Updike, at the Merrymount Press, Boston, 1911 Illus.

Paper boards; 10-1/8 x $6\frac{3}{4}$ x 7/8 in.

HALSTEAD, MURAT

Cabinet NN Shelf 2 No. 9

Journalism, the varieties of. (Excerpted article from The Cosmopolitan, Dec., 1892)

Item 22 in vol. with binder's title "Newspapers, various excerpts".

HAMAN, (Johannes de Landois) see

HERTZOG, GIOVANNI

Cabinet Shelf No.

HAMBURG

Cabinet Y Shelf 2 No. 63

Printers of Hamburg, 1490-1522. Bio-bibliographical notes.

see

LAPPENBERG, J.M. Geschichte der buchdruckerkunst in Hamburg...

HAMBURG

Cabinet FF Shelf 3 No. 41

(Der) Schriftgiesserei Christian Elias Schurig in Hamburg 1773.

See BAUER, FRIEDRICH. (Der) Schriftgiesser Christian Elias Schurig...

HAMELIN, ERNEST

Cabinet X Shelf 4 No. 33.01

La liberté de l'imprimerie au point de vue des intérêts de l'industrie typographique. Paris et Montpellier. 1867. Booklet.

"Includes curious statistics of the number of printers in Paris and the books printed by them."

Item 26 in book with binder's title "French legislation relating to printing. Various items. vol. I, 1500-1872.

HAMER, DOUGLAS.

Cabinet 75 Shelf 2 No. 10

Bibliography of Sir David Lindsay, (1490-1555). Paper read before the Bibliographical Society 21 Jan. 1929. London, Facs.

A history of the printing of the successive editions of Lindsay's works; an addition the the history of Scottish printing before 1550.

In Trans. Biblio. Soc. "The Library", vol. 10, 1929-30. pp. 1-42.

HAMILTON, ADAM BOYD

Cabinet NN Shelf 2 No. 6

Memorial address for A.B. Hamilton. By William Henry Egle. Harrisburg, Pa., 1897.

Account of Hamilton's activities as printer, journalist, newspaper editor and publisher, writer. b.-1808--d.-1896.

Item 2 in bound collection "Biographies of Journalists".

HAMILTON, ALEXANDER

Cabinet OO Shelf 6 No. 65

Career of Alexander Hamilton, one of the founders of the Evening Post.

Article with portrait in New York Evening Post, New Building Supplement... April 13, 1907, p. 9.

HAMILTON, FREDERICK W.

Cabinet MM Shelf 6 No. 67

Abbreviations and signs: A primer of information about abbreviations and signs, with a list of those in most common use. "Typographic Technical Series for Apprentices", Part VI, No.37. United Typothetae of America. 1918.

Cloth; 8 x 5 in.

HAMILTON, FREDERICK W.

Cabinet MM Shelf 6 No. 76

Books before typography. A primer of information about the invention of the alphabet, and the history of book-making up to the invention of moveable types. "Typographic Technical Series for Apprentices". Part VIII, No.49. The United Typothetae of America, 1918. Illus.

Cloth; 8 x 5 in.

HAMILTON, FREDERICK W.

Cabinet MM Shelf 6 No. 78 & 79

Brief history of printing, a. Part I: The development of the industry. The great pioneers. A primer of information about the beginning of printing..."Typographic Technical Series for Apprentices", Part VIII, No.51. The United Typothetae of America, 1918.

Part II: The economic history of printing. MM/6/83. Part VIII, No.52 "Typographic Technical Series for Apprentices".

(cont'd)

HAMILTON, FREDERICK W. (cont'd)

Cabinet Shelf No.

Cloth; 8 x 5 in.

HAMILTON, FREDERICK W.

Cabinet MM Shelf 6 No. 81

Brief (A) history of printing in America; containing a brief sketch of the development of the newspaper and some notes on publishers who have contributed to printing. "Typographic Technical Series for Apprentices", Part VIII, No. 54. The United Typothetae of America, 1918.

Cloth; 8 x 5 in.

HAMILTON, FREDERICK W.

Cabinet MM Shelf 6 No. 64

Capitals. A primer of information about capitalization, with some practical hints as to the use of capitals. "Typographic Technical Series for Apprentices", Part VI, No.34. United Typothetae of America, 1918.

Cloth; 8 x 5 in.

HAMILTON, FREDERICK W.

Cabinet MM Shelf 6 No. 66

Compound words. A study of the principles of compounding, the components of compounds, and the use of the hyphen. "Typographic Technical Series for Apprentices" Part VI, No.36. United Typothetae of America, 1918.

Cloth; 8 x 5 in.

HAMILTON, FREDERICK W.

Cabinet MM Shelf 6 No. 65

Division of words. Rules...with remarks on spelling, syllabication and pronunciation. "Typographic Technical Series for Apprentices" Part VI, No.36. United Typothetae of America, 1918.

Cloth; 8 x 5 in.

HAMILTON, FREDERICK W.

Cabinet MM Shelf 6 No. 77

Invention of typography, The. A brief sketch of the invention of printing, and how it came about. "Typographic Technical Series for Apprentices", Part VIII, No.50. The United Typothetae of America, 1918. Illus.

Cloth; 8 x 5 in.

HAMILTON, FREDERICK W.

Cabinet MM Shelf 6 No. 68

Italic, the uses of. A primer of information regarding the origin and uses of italic letters. "Typographic Technical Series for Apprentices", Part VI, No.38. United Typothetae of America, 1918.

Cloth; 8 x 5 in.

HAMILTON, FREDERICK W.

Cabinet MM Shelf 6 No. 62

Word study, and English grammar. A primer of information about words their relations and their uses. "Typographic Technical Series for Apprentices", No.VI, No.32. United Typothetae of America, 1918.

Cloth; 8 x 5 in.

HAMILTON MANURACTURING CO.

Cabinet EE Shelf 4 No. 48

Printers' furniture and materials. Catalogue No.12. 1899-1900. The Hamilton Mfg. Co. Two Rivers, Wis. and Middletown, N.Y.

Has interior view of finishing department in main factory.

Boards; 11¼ x 8¼ in.

HAMILTON, FREDERICK W.

Cabinet MM Shelf 6 No. 70

Preparation of printers' copy. Suggestions for authors, editors and all who are engaged in preparing copy for the composing room. "Typograph Technical Series for Apprentices". Part VI, No.40. The United Typothetae of America. 1918.

Cloth; 8 x 5 in.

HAMILTON, G.

Cabinet F Shelf 4 No. 40

See Early Printing in Scotland. Edinburgh, 1757. G. Hamilton and John Balfour.

HAMILTON MANURACTURING COMPANY

Cabinet EE Shelf 4 No. 52

Printing plant equipment: Galley storage and lock-up section. Catalog No.17. [Issued 1931] Two Rivers, Wisconsin.

Embossed paper; 11 x 8½ in. With other items in manila envelope.

HAMILTON, FREDERICK W.

Cabinet MM Shelf 6 No. 71

(A) Printers' manual of style. Compiled by Frederick W. Hamilton. Typographic Technical Series for Apprentices. Part VI, No.41. The United Typothetae of America. 1918.

Cloth; 8 x 5 in.

HAMILTON, MILTON W.

Cabinet NN Shelf 6 No. 55

Spread of the newspaper press in New York before 1830, the. By M.W. Hamilton. Read before the N.Y. State Historical Association at Southhampton, Oct.7, 1932. Reprinted from New York History, vol.XlV, No.2, 1933.

Brochure, in manila envelope

HAMILTON MANUFACTURING COMPANY

Cabinet Shelf No.

see also Specimen Books, Wood Types. United States.

HAMILTON, FREDERICK W.

Cabinet MM Shelf 6 No. 80

Printing in England, a brief history of...From Caxton to the present time. "Typographic Technical Series for Apprentices", Part VIII, No.53. The United Typothetae of America, 1918.

Cloth; 8 x 5 in.

HAMILTON & BAKER

Cabinet EE Shelf 4 No. 46

Catalogue or printers' tools, cabinets, cases, stands, wood rule, etc., manufactured and for sale by Hamilton & Baker, Two Rivers, Wis. 1887-1888.

These are Hamilton's first and second catalogues.

In manila envelope.

HAMMANN, J.-M.-HERMAN

Cabinet I Shelf 2 No. 72

Arts graphiques destinés a multiplier par l'impression, considérés sous le double point de vue historique et pratique... Geneve - Paris, 1857.

Half morocco; 7 x 4-1/8 x 1 in.

HAMILTON, FREDERICK W.

Cabinet MM Shelf 6 No. 63

Punctuation: A primer of information about the marks of punctuation and their use both grammatically and typographically. "Typographic Technical Series for Apprentices", Part VI, No.33. United Typothetae of America, 1920.

Cloth; 8 x 5 in.

HAMILTON MANUFACTURING COMPANY

Cabinet EE Shelf 4 No. 53

Composing room economy. Plans of printing office equipment. Hamilton's modernized printing office furniture. Hamilton Mfg. Co. Two Rivers, Wis. 1908. Catalogue.

Boards; 11½ x 12-3/4 in.

HAMMERDEN, STEPHAN

Cabinet X Shelf 3 No. 20

Brief bio-bibliographical note, Hammerden, printer, Cologne, 1598-1613.

see

HEITZ, PAUL. Kölner büchermarken.... p.xxxiii

HAMILTON, FREDERICK W.

Cabinet MM Shelf 6 No. 82

Type and presses in America. A brief historical sketch of the development of type casting and press building in America. "Typographic Technical Series for Apprentices" Part VIII, No.55. The United Typothetae of America, 1918.

Cloth; 8 x 5 in.

HAMILTON MANUFACTURING COMPANY.

Cabinet EE Shelf 4 No. 50

History of this company, illustrated with interior and exterior views of the plant at Two Rivers, Wis. (1907).

In Catalogue No. 14, "Modern Cabinets, Furniture and Materials for Printers."

Imitation leather; 13 x 10 x ⅜ in.

HAMMOND, JAMES B (Inventor) see

Cabinet FF Shelf 6 No. 19

TYPEWRITING MACHINES. Hammond, James B...

HAMMOND MACHINERY BUILDERS

Cabinet FF, Shelf 1, No. 54.01

New Hammond Stereotyping Process, descriptive illustrated circular of. Kalamazoo, Michigan, 1935.

In envelope.

HAMPDEN GLAZED PAPER and CARD COMPANY

Cabinet RR, Shelf 6, No. 31

Sample book of "Sunburst Covers".

See PAPER, SAMPLES OF. Hampden Glazed Paper & Card Company...

HAMPSHIRE PAPER COMPANY

Cabinet, Shelf, No.

See Paper Mills, Massachusetts.

HAMPTON COMPANY, BEN B.

Cabinet LL, Shelf 4, No. 15

Advertising agency, an unusual. The Hampton Company, New York, 1906.

Illustrations showing interior views of executive offices and technical departments of Hampton Co. Has also specimens of advertising.

Boards; 11½ x 8-1/8 x ½ in.

HAMPTON INSTITUTE PRINTING SCHOOL (see)

Cabinet, Shelf, No.

SCHOOLS OF PRINTING, United States. Hampton Institute Printing Trade School...

HAMPTON INSTITUTE TRADE SCHOOL.

Cabinet S, Shelf 5, No. 1

See Schools of Printing, United States.

HAN, ULRICH

Stack D, Shelf 4, Number 62

Rome, 1470.

see INCUNABULA (loose leaves), Han, Ulrich...

HANCOCK, LA TOUCHE.

Cabinet I, Shelf 3, No. 1

American caricature and comic art. [Excerpt in 2 parts. The Bookman, Oct. and Nov. 1902]. Illus.

Item 17 in vol. with binder's title "Various Engravers and About Engravers."

HAND PRINTING PRESSES

Cabinet 79, Shelf 2, No. 27

First wood press introduced into Ecuador en 1750. Picture

see SANCHEZ, CARLOS ENRIQUE. (La) Imprenta en el Ecuador...Quito, 1935, p. 40.

HANDBOK I BOKTRYKERIKONSTEN főr Unga Săttare.

See Fahlgren, Carl I.

HANEMANN, CARL

Cabinet, Shelf, No.

See Specimen Books, Types. Germany

HANFORD, G.B.

Cabinet RR, Shelf 4, No. 39

Making newspaper from wood. Excerpt from the Engineering Magazine, Sept., 1892. Illus.

Item with other excerpts and pamphlets relating to paper. Folder; 10½ x 7½ x 1 in.

HANNETT, JOHN (pseud. John Andrews Arnett)

Cabinet, Shelf, No.

see ARNETT, JOHN ANDREWS

HANNOVER, EMIL

Cabinet Y, Shelf 3, No. 76

(von) Bozerian bis Trautz. (Mit 4 tafeln.) (Development of bookbinding; from Bozerian to Trautz)

pp. 99-205 in Loubier, Hans (Tribute to) Buch und bucheinband...Leipzig, 1923.

HANS von ERFURT (Hans Werlich)

Cabinet 26, Shelf 1, No. 16

(Printer of the Worms edicts, 1510 1532). Hans Werlich, genannt Hans von Erfurt, der drucker des Wormser edikts (1518-1532) von Karl Schottenloher, Munchen. Facsimiles.

pp. 53-57 Gutenberg-Gesellschaft Jahrbuch, 1927.

HANSARD, LUKE

Cabinet U, Shelf 2, No. 97

Biographical memoir of Luke Hansard, many years printer to the House of Commons. [London], 1829. Portrait, engraved by F. C. Lewis, after a painting by S. Lane.

Half morocco; 12½ x 10-1/8 x ½ in.

HANSARD, THOMAS C.

Cabinet T, Shelf 4, No. 13

History of the processes of manufacture and uses of printing, gas-light, pottery, glass and iron. With numerous illustrations. From The Encyclopedia Britannica. New York, 1864.

Cloth; 7-7/8 x 5-3/8 x 1-3/8 in.

HANSARD, THOMAS CURSON

Cabinet T, Shelf 5, No. 85

Treatises on printing and typefounding. By T.C. H. From the seventh edition of the Encyclopaedia Britannica. Edinburgh, 1841. Facsimiles.

Cloth; 8¾ x 5 x 1 in.

HANSARD, THOMAS CURSAN

Cabinet T Shelf 3 No. 12

Typographia: An historical sketch of the origin and progress of the art of printing; with practical directions for conducting every department in an office: with a description of stereotype and lithography. Illus. Biographical notices and portraits. London, 1825.

Half morocco; 9¼ x 6¼ x 2 in. See also T/3/13/

HANSIUS, KARL GOTTLOB

Cabinet Y Shelf 5 No. 3

Biographie Herrn Joh. Gottlob Immanuel Breitkopfs. Ein geschenk fur seine freunde. Leipzig, 1794. Portrait on title page.

Boards; 8¼ x 5-1/8 in.

HARDING, WARREN J.

Cabinet LL Shelf 6 No. 49 Box

Dedication of Harding Hall in the United States Government Printing Office. Washington, Friday, May 23, 1930. Illus. pamphlet.

In box labelled "Apprenticeship: Various items".

HANSARD, THOMAS CURSON

Cabinet T Shelf 3 No. 13

Typographia: an historical sketch of the origin and progress of the art of printing...London, 1867. [Monthly sections from the Printers Journal]

Special copy gathered and bound by Chas. H. Davy, Master-Printer. At the end of this bound collection are many miscellaneous items inserted relating to the history of printing.

Cloth; 10½ x 6-5/8 x 1½ in.

HARANG, F.

Cabinet 83 Shelf 1 No. 20

See Specimen Books, Types. France

HARDING, WARREN G., President, U.S.

Cabinet MN Shelf 2 No. 1

Governor Cox and Senator Harding give exclusive interviews to "The New Success." October, 1920.

Item 39 in book with binder's title "Journalists. Various Excerpts".

HANSARD, T. C.

See also Imprints.

HARBOR PRESS, THE see

Cabinet Shelf No.

IMPRINTS, United States.

HARDING HALL.

Cabinet Shelf No.

See Government Printing Offices, United States. Washington, D.C.

HANSARD AND SONS, LUKE

Cabinet QQ Shelf 3 No. 29

Imprint, London 1825.

see BUTLER, CHARLES. Erasmus, the life of...London, 1825.

HARDEL, AIMABLE-AUGUSTIN

Cabinet V Shelf 5 No. 2.01

Mémoire de A.A. Hardel, imprimeur libraire a Caen, 1834-1864. Pamphlet.

Item 12 in vol. with binder's title "French printers and printing. Pamphlets". Bound, 1932.

HARDINGH en Du MORTIER

Cabinet 83 Shelf 2 No. 12

See Specimen Books, Types, Holland.

HANSEN, HANS C. See

Cabinet Shelf No.

PATENTS, TYPE CASTING MACHINES

HARDIE, MARTIN

Cabinet I Shelf 2 No. 28

Etching, the British School of: Being a lecture delivered to the Print Collectors' Club by Martin Hardie, on July 8th 1921, with a foreword by Sir Frank Short...Printed in London by Sanders Phillips and Company, Ltd., at the Baynard Press, 1921. Illus.

Cloth; 9¾ x 7-3/8 in.

HARDMAN, THOS. H. (Compiler)

Cabinet OO Shelf 4 No. 14

Parliament of the press: The first Imperial Press Conference. Written and compiled by Thos. H. Hardman. With preface by the Rt. Hon. The Earl of Rosebery. Illustrated. London, 1909.

Cloth; 9¾ x 7½ x 1 in.

HANSEN, H.C. TYPE FOUNDRY

Cabinet Shelf No.

See Specimen Books, Types. United States. Hansen. (H.C.)

HARDING, COUPLAND, Editor

Cabinet 38 Shelf 2 No. 18½

Typo, Napier, N. Zealand

PERIODICALS, PRINTING, New Zealand Typo...

HARDOUYN, Pedro

Cabinet X Shelf 3 No. 19

Bio-bibliographical sketch, with printer mark, Hardouyn (Saragossa), 1528-1536.

see HAEBLER, KONRAD. (Spanish and Portugese printer marks...p.xviii

HARDY and SONS

Cabinet II
Shelf 4
No. 4

Imprint, Dublin, 1852.

See IMPRINTS, Ireland. Hardy and Sons...

HARLAND, JOHN

Cabinet MM
Shelf 4
No. 21

Printing Arts, the. An epitome of the theory practice, processes, and mutual relations, of engraving, lithography, & printing in black and in colours. With illustrations. Ward, Lock, Bowden and Co. 1892.

Cloth; 7½ x 5-1/8 x ¾ in.

HARLEIAN MISCELLANY

Cabinet U
Shelf 4
No. 4.01

Tracts, etc. a collection of

See TRACTS, ENGLISH. Harleian Miscellany ...

HARMSWORTH, ALFRED

Cabinet
Shelf
No.

See NORTHCLIFF (Lord)

HARO, ----

Cabinet RR
Shelf 3
No. 36

Rapport sur la papeterie, reliure, matériel des arts de la peinture et du dessin. Par M. Haro. Paris, Exposition Universelle Internationale de 1878. Illus.

Paper; 10¾ x 8-3/8 in.

HARO, Pedro Lopez de

Cabinet X
Shelf 3
No. 19

Brief bio-bibliographical note, with printer-publisher mark, Haro (Toledo-Madrid), 1580-1587.

see HAEBLER, KONRAD. (Spanish and Portugese printer marks...p.xxxvii

---

HARPEL, OSCAR H.

Cabinet EE
Shelf 1
No. 15

Harpel's typograph, or book of specimens containing useful information...and arranged for the assistance of master printers, amateurs, apprentices, and others By Oscar H. Harpel, typographic designer and printer. Cincinnati. Printed and published by the author. 1870.

Half morocco; 9½ x 6½ x 1 in.

HARPEL, OSCAR H. (Editor)

Cabinet [illegible]
Shelf 1
No. 46

Poets and poetry of printerdom: A collection of original, selected, and fugitive lyrics, written by persons connected with printing. Collected and edited by Oscar H. Harpel, printer and publisher, Cincinnati, 1875.

Cloth; 9¾ x 7 x 1-1/8 in.

HARPER, CHARLES G.

Cabinet K
Shelf 3
No. 15

Practical handbook of drawing for modern methods of reproduction. Illus. with drawings by several hands...(2nd. ed.) Revised. London, 1901.

Cloth; 8-7/8 x 5¾ in.

HARPER, FLETCHER

Cabinet Q
Shelf 1
Number 3

Biographical notes by L. C. Buttre. With portrait. Excerpt from American Portrait Gallery, Vol. I, N. Y., 1887.

Item 14 in vol. with binder's title "Publishing Houses and Periodicals. Pamphlets".

HARPER, FLETCHER

Cabinet 81
Shelf 2
No. 37

Publisher or the New York Daily Times. Case of The Daily Times for Contempt of Court. Newspaper report, Feb. 17, 1855. Excerpt.

Item in MUNSELL, JOEL. "Printers Scraps", Vol.VIII, p.41-47.

HARPER, J. HENRY

Cabinet Q
Shelf 2
No. 17

(The) House of Harper. A century of publishing in Franklin Square. By J. Henry Harper. With portraits. New York, 1912.

Cloth; 9 x 6 in.

HARPER, JAMES

Cabinet
Shelf
No.

See Publishing, United States; Down among the dead men.

HARPER, JAMES

Cabinet Q
Shelf 1
No. 1

"Down among the dead men". James Harper. Excerpt from "The Old Guard", March, 1870.

Item 4 in volume with binder's title "Publishing. Various Excerpts".

HARPER, JOHN

Cabinet S
Shelf 5
No. 19

American Publishing. [Brief historical an statistical account]. By John Harper, for "One hundred years of American Commerce" 1895.

In volume "Excerpts on American Printing, etc."

HARPER, LATHROP COLGATE

Cabinet S
Shelf 3
No. 104

(A) Maryland tract of 1646. By Lathrop Colgate Harper of New York. Bibliographical account of an important historical tract lacking name of author, publisher and printer. P. 143 in volume, Wilberforce Eames ... A tribute to. Cambridge, 1924.

HARPER AND BROTHERS

Cabinet Q
Shelf 2
No. 18

Centennial, 1817-1917, the Harper. A few of the greetings and congratulations. With fac-simile of title page of the first book with the Harper imprint.

Boards; 9-1/8 x 6¼ x 5/8 in.

HARPER AND BROTHERS

Cabinet Q
Shelf 2
No. 15

Harper establishment; or how the story books are made. New York, Harper & Brothers, publishers, 1855. Illus.

Cloth, stamped; 6⅞ x 5½ in.

HARPER & BROTHERS

Cabinet Q Shelf 2 No. 17

House of Harper. A century of publishing in Franklin Square. By J. Henry Harper. New York, 1912.

Cloth; 9 x 6 in.

HARPER & BROTHERS

Cabinet Q Shelf 1 No. 1

Visit to the publishing house of the Messrs. Harper & Brothers. By the Editor of the Ladies Repository
Excerpt from the Ladies Repository, Dec., 1853.

Item 10 in volume with binder's title "Publishing. Various Excerpts".

HARPER AND BROTHERS

Cabinet Q Shelf 2 No. 16

Visitor's guide to Harper and Brothers establishment New York, n. d. (1880)

Half morocco; $9\frac{1}{4}$ x 6 in.

HARPER & BROTHERS

Cabinet S Shelf 5 No. 12

see also
PUBLISHING HOUSES (Harper & Brothers' Centennial).
PUBLISHING, New York City.

HARPER BROTHERS, The

Cabinet Q Shelf 1 No. 1

Biographical sketch of brothers of a famous publishing house.
Excerpt from the National Repository, Sept., 1877.

Item 21 in volume with binder's title "Publishing. Various Excerpts".

HARPER BROTHERS

Cabinet Q Shelf 1 Number 3

(Brief compilation of chronicle and comment.) Harper Brothers. By Laura C. Holloway. Excerpt from "Famous American Fortunes," 1885.

Item 9 in vol. with binder's title "Publishing Houses and Periodicals. Pamphlets."

HARPER BROTHERS.

Cabinet G Shelf 5 No. 20

Imprint, 1846.
See Imprints, United States. Harper Bros.

HARPERS' MAGAZINE

Cabinet Shelf No.

See Periodicals, American (U.S.): Fifty years of Harpers' Magazine, by the editor.

HARPERS' MAGAZINE.

Cabinet Shelf No.

See Periodicals, American (U.S.), Harpers' magazine, by Henry Mills Alden.

HARPERS' MAGAZINE.

Cabinet Shelf No.

See Periodicals, American (U.S.); Harpers' Magazine: The making of a great magazine.

HARPERS' MAGAZINE.

Cabinet Shelf No.

See Periodicals, American (U.S.): Two generations, 1850-1917, by E.S. Martin.

HARPER'S NEW MONTHLY MAGAZINE (see)

Cabinet 31 Shelf 1 No. 9

PERIODICALS, ILLUSTRATED. Harper's New Monthly Magazine...

HARPERS' MONTHLY AND WEEKLY, New York, 1857.

Cabinet Shelf No.

See Periodicals, American: Harpers monthly and weekly.

HARPER'S WEEKLY

Cabinet OO Shelf 6 No. 44

(A) Journal of civilization. The first volume of Harper's Weekly. The year 1857. New York: Harper & Brothers, publishers.

Half morocco; $15\frac{3}{4}$ x $11\frac{1}{4}$ x 2 in.

HARRAP, CHARLES

Cabinet MM Shelf 2 No. 58

Metalography (Printing from metals) and off-set printing: Being a full consideration of the nature and properties of zinc and aluminum ...Second edition. Leicester, 1912.

Cloth; $7\frac{1}{2}$ x 5 in.

HARRILD R.

Cabinet DD Shelf 5 No. 69

Harrild's useful ornamental engravings for printers. London: R. Harrild, Printer, 20, Great Eastcheap. n.d. circa 1840. Pamphlet 14 lvs. with prices.

In box marked (Misc.) Wood types & Type Ornaments. Various printers and Type Founders.

HARRILD, R. (London, England)

Cabinet J Shelf 2 No. 44

see also
WOOD ENGRAVERS, ADVERTISEMENTS OF. (alphabetically arranged list)

HARPER'S WEEKLY

see also
Periodicals

HARRILD & SONS, Ltd.

Cabinet A — Shelf 3 — No. 89

See Roller Making, Great Britain.

HARRIS, G.F.

Cabinet II — Shelf 1 — No. 15

Specimen book of types, 1818.

See SPECIMEN BOOKS, TYPES. England. Harris...

HARRISON, H. W.

Cabinet K — Shelf 4 — No. 22

(The) Theory of pictorial art. A guide to the study of light, colour, line, and composition. By H. W. Harrison. With a foreword by W. L. Wyllie. London, 1931. Illus.

Boards, cloth back; 9¼ x 6-5/8 x ½ in.

HARRILD & SONS

Cabinet — Shelf — No.

see also Specimen Books, Cuts. England.

HARRIS, JOEL CHANDLER

Cabinet S — Shelf 2 — No. 101

Life and letters of Joel Chandler Harris. By Julia Collier Harris. With portraits and other illustrations. Boston: The Riverside Press, 1918.

Cloth; 9 x 6¼ in.

HARRISON, RICHARD

Cabinet T — Shelf 2 — No. 6

Books printed by R. Harrison, London, 1562. Bibliographical notes. With printer's device.

see DIBDIN'S "Typographical Antiquities"...London, 1810-19, vol.IV, p.559.

[vol.4]

HARRINGTON, H.F. and T. T. FRANKENBERG

Cabinet NN — Shelf 3 — No. 28

Essentials in journalism: A manual in newspaper making for college classes. By H. F. Harrington and T. T. Frankenberg. Boston. 1912. Frontispiece, 4 portraits of representative American editors.

Cloth: 8½x6"

HARRIS, JOEL CHANDLER

Cabinet NN — Shelf 2 — No. 2.01

New editor-in-chief (Clark Howell) of the "Constitution". Excerpt from the American Review of Reviews. May, 1897. With portraits.

Item 23 in vol. with binder's title "Journalists and Journalism -- II. Pamphlets".

HARRISON, THOS. G.

Cabinet NN — Shelf 5 — No. 7

Career and reminiscences of an amateur journalist and a history of amateur journalism. By Thos. G. Harrison, ex-president of the National and Western Amateur Press Associations. Indianapolis, Ind. 1883. With inscription (autograph) from author.

Cloth; 7 x 4½ in.

HARRIS, BENJAMIN

Cabinet X — Shelf 4 — No. 27

(A) Short but just account of the tryal of Benjamin Harris, upon an information brought against him for printing and vending a late seditious book...Printed in the Year 1679. [London]

Half morocco; 11½ x 7¾ in.

HARRIS, JULIA COLLIER

Cabinet S — Shelf 2 — No. 101

Life and letters of Joel Chandler Harris. With portraits and other illustrations. Boston, The Riverside Press, 1918.

Cloth; 9 x 6¼ in.

HARRISON and SONS

Cabinet U — Shelf 2 — No. 108

(The) House of Harrison and Sons, London, 1795--: Being an account of the family and firm of Harrison and Sons, printers to the king. London, 1914. Illus. portraits, facsimiles, etc.

Cloth; 10-3/8 x 7-7/8 x 7/8 in.

HARRIS, DAVID FRASER see

Cabinet C — Shelf 1 — No. 14

FLEMING & Co., Ltd. Caroline Park House...

HARRIS (Rendel) and JONES (Stephen)

Cabinet U — Shelf 4 — No. 48

Pilgrim Press. A bibliographical and historical memorial of the books printed at Leyden by the Pilgrim Fathers. Cambridge, 1922.

Cloth; 8¾ x 5¾ in.

HARRISON AND SONS

Cabinet X — Shelf 5 — No. 3

See Newspapers, Great Britain. The London Gazette [1661-1845].

HARRIS, EMERSON P. & FLORENCE HARRIS HOOKE

Cabinet NN — Shelf 3 — No. 40

(The) Community newspaper: Its promise and development. New York, 1923.

Cloth; 7½ x 5 x 1-3/8 in.

HARRIS AUTOMATIC PRESS CO.

Cabinet EE — Shelf 4 — No. 58

Catalogue of printing presses manufactures by Harris Automatic Press Co. General Office and Factory, Niles, Ohio. 1910.

Type written list.

Item in manila envelope.

HARRISON & SONS

see also Imprints.

HARRISEE, HENRY

Cabinet V — Shelf 1 — No. 19

(Les) Premiers incunables Bâlois et leurs dérivés Toulouse, Lyon, etc. 1471-1484: Essai de synthèse typographique. Par H. Harrisse, Paris, 1902. Seconde édition, revue et augmentée.
Historical bibliographical account.

Half morocco; 9-7/8 x 6-5/8 in.

HARRISSE, HENRY.

Cabinet S — Shelf 3 — No. 74

Printing in America [Mexico] a brief disquisition concerning the early history of. [By Henry Harrisse]. New York. Privately printed, 1866. Extracted from the Bibliotheca Americana Vetustissima, pp. 365-377.
Includes a list of works printed in America between the years 1540 and 1600.

Half morocco; 10½ x 7¼ in.

HARROGATE HERALD PRINTING OFFICE

Cabinet — Shelf — No.

See Plants, Printing. England.

HARSY, OLIVIER de

Cabinet V — Shelf 3 — No. 18

(Bio-bibliographical notes relating to Harsey, printer, Paris, 1556-1576).

see

WERDET, EDMOND. Histoire du livre en France...3me partie (2), p.107

HART, CHARLES HENRY

Cabinet R — Shelf 1 — No. 74

Who was the mother of Franklin's son: An inquiry demonstrating that she was Deborah Read, wife of Benjamin Franklin. Philadelphia, 1911.

Half morocco, 10 x 7 ins. pp. 7.

HART, CHARLES HENRY

Cabinet R — Shelf 1 — No. 1

Franklin in allegory. By C. H. Hart, in the Century Magazine, Dec., 1890.

Bound in volume "Franklin, excerpts from Magazines", item 6.

HART, FRANCIS

Cabinet — Shelf — No.

Imprint, 1871, New York City.

See Imprints, United States. Hart, Francis.

HART, FRANCIS

Cabinet EE — Shelf 4 — No. 63 Also 64 Dupl.

Imprint, 1860, New York.

See HOE, ROBERT, & Co. (Catalogue and price list, 1860).

HART, FRANCIS

Cabinet S — Shelf 1 — No. 50

Inventory of his printing plant.

See DeVinne, Theodore Low. Inventory of the printing plant.

HART, FRANCIS

Cabinet J — Shelf 1 — No. 6

Printer, stationer, 63 Cortlandt Street, New York.
His business card. circ 1860.

See SCRAP BOOK. Trade cards mostly issued by New York business houses.

HART, FRANCIS

Cabinet S — Shelf 1 — No. 51

Printing Office for sale: Catalogue of complete plant of Francis Hart, 4 Thames Street N.Y. City, circa 1849, offered for $7000. (4 pp.) foolscap.
The sale was not affected. Theodore L. De Vinne became a partner, and in 1883 he became sole owner.

p.19 of De Vinne Scrap Book No.2.

HART, FRANCIS

Cabinet LL — Shelf 5 — No. 26

Record of production of 22 printing presses operated in the press room of Francis Hart & Co., N. Y. City, (circa 1871) at a time when T.L. DeVinne was superintendent.
The book was opened by DeVinne, the writing in the heavier ink is his. H.L. Bullen, Nov. 19, 1928.

Boards; 8½ x 5-5/8 x 5/8 in.

HART, FRANCIS AND COMPANY

Cabinet 25 — Shelf 2 — No. 5

(The) Printers Miscellany, New York, 1859

See PERIODICALS, PRINTING. United States (The) Printers Miscellany ...

HART, FRANCIS and COMPANY (see)

Cabinet 61 — Shelf 1 — No. 2

PRINTING HOUSES, United States. DeVinne, Theodor L.& Co.-Late Francis Hart...

HART & CO., FRANCIS
see also

Imprints.

SPECIMEN BOOKS, TYPES. Printers'. (U.S.).

HART, HORACE

Cabinet U — Shelf 2 — No. 125

Notes on a century of typography at the University Press, Oxford, 1693-1794. With annotations and appendixes. Oxford, 1900. Illus.
Includes specimens, facsimiles of Fell ornaments, list of founts, documents referring to punches, matrices, etc.

Full morocco; 13¾ x 10¼ x 1-3/8 in.

HART, HORACE

Cabinet S — Shelf 6 — No. 9

Portrait of Horace Hart, printer, Oxford University Press, 1897.

See OXFORD UNIVERSITY PRESS. (The) Making of the Bible. By H.J.W. Dam...

HART, HORACE

Cabinet U — Shelf 1 — No. 1e

Red printing in the 1611 Bible, on the. By Horace Hart, with note by R. B. McKerrow.
Briefly outlines possible methods by which the red markings were obtained.

In Excerpts relating to printing from "The Library," 1911-12. p.81 of pencilled folios.

HART, HORACE

Cabinet 75 Shelf 2 No. 6

Rules for compositors and readers at the University Press, Oxford. By Horace Hart, M.A. London and Oxford. 1883: Comments and review of book with above title, by W.W. Greg.

In Transactions of the Bibliographical Society, vol. VI, 1925-1926. pp. 264-270. "The Library."

HART, HORACE

Cabinet U Shelf 2 No. 121

Stanhope, Charles (Earl), and the Oxford University Press. Oxford, 1897.
Account of Stanhope's secret process of stereotyping, his iron presses, ink rollers, the Stanhope cases, logotypes, etc.

Stamped cloth; 8-7/8 x 5-5/8 x 3/8 in.

HART, HORACE.
see also
Imprints, England. Oxford University Press. Horace Hart.

Cabinet Shelf No.

HART, JAMES P.

Cabinet II Shelf 4 No. 26

Orthography become phonography. A homographic introduction to the English language...By James P. Hart. New Haven, Ct. U.S.A. n.d.

Cloth; 7-3/4 x 4-5/8 in.

HART (T.) and STRAHAN (W.)

Cabinet Shelf No.

Specimen of the Printing-Letter of T. Hart and W. Strahan...

see SPECIMEN BOOKS, TYPES, PRINTERS Great Britain

HART PRINTING COMPANY.

Cabinet LL Shelf 5 No. 72

Practical printing price list. Always up-to-the-minute. For commerical and job printers. Hart Printing Co. Publishers. Danville, Va. n.d.

Limp cloth; 8½ x 4½ in.

HARTE, BRET.

Cabinet 73 Shelf 2 No. 8

Heathen Chinee. Plain language from truthful James, by Bret Harte. With an introduction by Ina Coolbrith. Also a note concerning the history of the manuscript. And a bibliography with notes by Robert Ernest Cowan. Librarian of the C.A. Clarke, Jr. Library.
Imprint: Printed by John Henry Nash for his friends, San Francisco, 1924.

Paper boards; 17 x 12½ ins. pp.22, not numbered.

HARTE, BRET

Cabinet 71 Shelf 1 No. 14

Tennessee's partner. By Bret Harte including an introduction by W. D. Armes. Photogravure frontispiece by Albertine R. Wheelan.
Imprint: The typography designed by John Henry Nash: The Tomoye Press, San Francisco, 1910 Published by Paul Elder and Co.

Boards; 6½ x 4-3/4 ins. pp. 38

HARTE, BRET.
See also
Periodicals, California: Overland Magazine.

Cabinet Shelf No.

HARTENBACH, RITSCHEL Von

Cabinet Shelf No.

See RITSCHEL Von HARTENBACH (J.)

HARTFORD COURANT (THE), Hartford, Conn., 1764-1909.

Cabinet A Shelf 2 No. 28

See Newspapers, anniversary issues. U.S.

HARTFORD COURANT (see)

Cabinet 61 Shelf 1 No. 1

NEWSPAPERS, United States. Literature of Hartford Courant...

HARTFORD TIMES, Hartford, Connecticut.

Cabinet A Shelf 2 No. 29

See Newspapers, special issues. U.S.

HARTL, HANS MEYER

Cabinet Y Shelf 1 No. 92

Gutenbergs Schöpfertraum. Erzählung. Mainz, Verlag der Gutenberg-Gesellschaft, 1930. Pamphlet.

HARTLEY, A.

Cabinet S Shelf 5 No. 14

Girls in country printing offices. By A. Hartley. An excerpt from The Bookkeeper, Feb. 1910. Illus.
An account of satisfactory and economical changes of benefit to the country printer proprietor.

Bound with other items in collection "Printing Processes", item 22.

HARTLEY, DOROTHY

Cabinet U Shelf 5 No. 94

(The) Old Book: A mediaeval anthology edited and illuminated by Dorothy Hartley. With an introduction by George Saintsbury. London, Alfred A. Knopf. 1930. Printed by Robert Maclehose & Co. The University Press, Glasgow.

Cloth; 10-3/8 x 7¼ x 1-1/8 in. In protective case.

HART'S LOCOMOTIVE, New York see NEWSPAPERS, ADVERTISING.

Cabinet NN Shelf 7 No. 41

HARTSHORNE, CHARLES HENRY

Cabinet T Shelf 4 No. 137

(The) Origin of printing. Being the substance of a lecture to the Northampton Mechanics Institute, December, 1851. Northampton (England): Thomas Phillips, Printer.

Brochure, in envelope.

HARTWIG, KONSTANTIN

Cabinet Y Shelf 1 No. 66

Schriftschneider und schriftgiesser in Nurnberg, 1690. Fraktur-Probe.
Specimens of his types, also portrait of K. Hartwig.
See Mori, Gustav. Schriftgiessergewerbe in Süddeutschland...Stuttgart, 1924. Plates XII and XIII

HARTWIG, OTTO (Compiler)

Cabinet X Shelf 2 No. 59

Festschrift zum 500 jahrigen geburtstage von Johann Gutenberg...Herausgegeben von Otto Hartwig. Mainz am 24 Juni, 1900. Illus.
Essays by several authorities on the subject of printing. Introduction, historical, by O. Hartwig.

Cloth; $11\frac{3}{4}$ x 9 in.

HARVARD LAMPOON

Cabinet NN Shelf 7 No. 1

Cambridge (Mass.) The Harvard Lampoon, Dec. 11, 1885.
One issue only.

Bound in vol. with binder's title "American Comic Papers", 1857 - 1891.

HARVARD LYCEUM (THE)

Cabinet 80 Shelf 2 No. 29

Cambridge, (Mass.), 1810.
See Periodicals, United States. Harvard Lyceum (The)...

HARVARD SCHOOL OF BUSINESS ADMINISTRATION

Cabinet 78 Shelf 2 No. 13

Printing ink. Two lectures delivered in the course on the technique of printing. By James A. Ullman. Cambridge, Mass. March 22 and 24. 1911. New York.

Cloth; 9 x 5-7/8 x ¼ in.

HARVARD UNIVERSITY

Cabinet C Shelf 2 No. 21

Advertising awards, 1925.
see ADVERTISING, TYPOGRAPHY. Harvard Advertising awards...

HARVARD UNIVERSITY

Cabinet LL Shelf 6 No. 75

Awards to be given for 1930...in advertising.
See ADVERTISING. Awards to be given and regulations...

HARVARD UNIVERSITY.
see also

Cabinet Shelf No.

Journalism, Four Harvard editors.

HARVARD UNIVERSITY PRESS

Cabinet G Shelf 2 No. 34.01

Books published at the Harvard University Press, Cambridge. 1927-28. Catalogues

Paper; 9 x 5/ in.

HARVARD UNIVERSITY PRESS.

Cabinet 67 Shelf 1 No. 0.1

See IMPRINTS, United States.

HARVARD UNIVERSITY PRESS

Cabinet LL Shelf 3 No. 1.01

Proof reader's marks and table for estimating copy. Cambridge: Harvard University Press, 1919.

Item 2 in vol. with binder's title "Proof-reading: Pamphlets". Bound, 1932.

HARVEY, CHARLES M.

Cabinet R Shelf 5 No. 148

(The) Dime Novel in Amerian life. By C. M. Harvey: An excerpt from The Atlantic, July 1907.

EXCERPT 8 in volume "Chap Books, Almanacs, Annuals, etc.

HARVEY, EDWARD HOOKER

Cabinet S Shelf 4 No. 51

Notes on the life of John Baskerville, an eighteenth century printer. By Edward Hooker Harvey, Cleveland: The Rowfant Club, 1901.
Bound in with The Plantin-Moretus Museum, by Frank Howard Neff.

Half morocco; $7\frac{1}{2}$ x 4-7/8 in.

HARVEY, GEORGE

Cabinet NN Shelf 7 No. 24

Journalism, politics and the university. Bromley Lectures, delivered by George Harvey at Yale University on March 12 and 16, 1908.

Cloth; $13\frac{1}{2}$ x $9\frac{1}{2}$ in.

HASE, OSCAR

Cabinet Y Shelf 2 No. 26

(Die) Koberger, seine darstellung des buchhändlerischen geschäftsbetriebes in der zeit des uberganges vom mittelalter zur neuzeit. von Oscar Hase. [second ed.] Leipzig, 1885. Facsimiles.

Boards; $9\frac{1}{4}$ x 6 x $1\frac{1}{4}$ in.

HASLUCK, PAUL N.

Cabinet PP Shelf 4 No. 30

Bookbinding. With numerous engravings and diagrams. Edited by P. N. Hasluck. London, 1907. Cassell and Company, Ltd...

Cloth; 7 x $4\frac{1}{4}$ in.

HASLUCK, PAUL N.

Cabinet K Shelf 3 No. 21

Decorative designs of all ages and for all purposes. With numerous engravings and diagrams. Edited by Paul N. Hasluck. London, 1903.

Cloth; 7 x 4-1/8 in.

HASPER, WILHELM

Cabinet LL Shelf 1 No. 20 Two copies

Handbuch der buchdruckerkunst. Nach eigener erfahrung und unter zuzichung der werke von Brun, Fournier, Hansard, Johnson, Savage, Bodoni und Taübel. Herausgegeben und mit zeichnungen begleitet von W. Hasper. Carlsruhe und Baden, 1835.

Original boards; $8\frac{3}{4}$ x 5-1/8 x 1 in. Second copy; cloth, $8\frac{1}{2}$ x 5 x $\frac{3}{4}$ in.

HASPER, WILHELM

Cabinet LL Shelf 1 No. 19

Kurzes practisches handbuch der buchdruckerkunst in Frankreich. Aus dem Französischen des M. Brun übersetzt, und mit nützen anmerkungen und zeichnungen begleitet. Carlsruhe und Baden, 1828.
A German translation of Brun's work "Manuel pratique"...

Boards; 7-3/8 x 4-5/8 x 3/4 in.

HASSE, F. C. A.

Cabinet X Shelf 2 No. 29

Kurtz geschichte der Leipziger Buchdruckerkunst im verlaufe ihres vierten jahrhunderts. Leipzig, 1840.
A brief history of the progress of printing in Leipzig. Fourth centenary celebration.

4 facs. block-books.
Half morocco; 8½ x 5-3/8 x 3/8 in.

HASWELL, ANTHONY

Cabinet R Shelf 5 No. 86

Printer-patriot-ballader: A biographical study with a selection of his ballads and an annotated bibliographical list of his imprints. By John Spargo. Rutland, Vt. 1925. Facsimiles.

Half morocco; 12½ x 9¾ in.

HASS, GUILLAUME.

Cabinet Shelf No.

See Specimen Books, Types, Switzerland.

HASSELBACH, NICHOLAS

Cabinet R Shelf 4 No. 143

First book printed in Baltimore-Town, Nicholas Hasselbach, printer. The book reprinted with a sketch of Hasselbach's life and work. By George W. McCreary ... Baltimore, 1903. Facsimile.

Boards; 8¾ x 6¼ in.

HATCH, HARRIS B.

Cabinet FF Shelf 1 No. 28

Electrotypes, how to know values in. n. p. (1915) Illus.
Published by the Royal Electrotype Company of Philadelphia, Pa.

Boards; 7-1/8 x 4½ in.

HASS, WILHELM (Son)

Cabinet F Shelf 3 No. 70

Basel, 1789. (Imprint)

See EARLY PRINTING IN SWITZERLAND. Basel, 1789. Wilhelm Hass dem Sohne...

HASSEL'S AUSTRALIAN MISCELLANY

Cabinet K Shelf 2 No. 22

Art & Letters: Hassel's Australian Miscellany, 1921-1922. The Hassel Press, Adelaide and Melbourne.
Illus., many in colors.

Boards; 11 x 8-7/8 in

HATCH, HARRIS B.

Cabinet MM Shelf 6 No. 54

Electrotyping and stereotyping: A primer of information about the processes of electrotyping and stereotyping. Part I, Electrotyping, by Harris B. Hatch; Part 2, Stereotyping, by A.A. Stewart. "Typographic Technical Series for Apprentices", Part 1, No.15. Published by the United Typothetae of America. 1918.

Cloth; 8 x 5 in.

HASS BANK NOTE ENGRAVING COMPANY

Cabinet I Shelf 2 No. 17

Machines versus engraving. An answer to an article by the editor of the Engravers Bulletin, issue of April 1914. A discourse on the degeneracy of the engraving business by present day methods. [By Paul E. Hass]. New York, 1914.

Item in manila envelope.

HASSLER, KONRAD DIETERICH

Cabinet Y Shelf 2 No. 90

(Die) Buchdrucker-Geschichte Ulm's: zur vierten säcularfeier der erfindung der buchdruckerkunst. von Dr. Konrad D. Hassler. Mit neuen beiträgen zur culturgeschichte, dem facsimile eines der ältesten drucke und artifischen beilagen, besonders zur geschichte der holzschneidekunst. Ulm, 1840.
History of printing; history of printing in Ulm; history of wood-engraving.

Half morocco; 12½ x 9-7/8 x 3/4 in.

HATCH, HARRIS B.

Cabinet FF Shelf 1 No. 27

Ten two-minute talks. Royal Electrotype Co. Philadelphia, Pa. 1910.

Boards; 8½ x 6 in.

HASSARD, JOHN, R. G.

Cabinet FF Shelf 5 No. 51

(The) Fast printing machine; An account of recent improvements in newspaper presses. Reprinted from the N. Y. Tribune. 1878. With folding plates.

Half morocco; 7½ x 5 x 3/8 in.

HASTINGS, HENRY M.

Cabinet LL Shelf 6 No. 26

Hastings graphic systems. Estimators hand-book... Estimators hand books No.333 and 340. Compiled and issued by Henry M. Hastings, 232 Federal Telegraph Building. Oakland, California, 1927.
Loose leaf.

Limp morocco; 7-7/8 x 5-3/4 in.

2 vols.

HATSUKADE, ITSUAKI.

Cabinet Y Shelf 2 No. 97

Reform der Japanischen nationalschrift. Geschichte der reformbestrebungen. With 11 figures.
Article in Gutenberg-Gesellschaft Jahrbuch, 1932, p. 27.

HASSE, A. R.

Cabinet S Shelf 6 No. 9

No. 15

New York in 1696: A note to accompany the proclamation of September 12, 1696. (Excerpt) The Literary Collection, Sept. 1903.
Has a reproduction of the proclamation broadside printed by William Bradford, 1696.

~~Item in box labelled "Excerpts and Brochures relating to printing and printers in America~~

HASTY, JOHN EUGENE.

Cabinet 73 Shelf 2 No. 1

If it were today. A playlet written for John Henry Nash on the occasion of his attempt to tell the Advertising Club of San Franciso why is the poor printer ...
Imprint: San Francisco: Printed by John Henry Nash in the month of May MDCCCCXXV.

Brochure No. 7 in John Henry Nash, Imprints, San Francisco, 1910-1927.

HATT, J. ARTHUR H.

Cabinet L Shelf 4 No. 43

Colorist the. Designed...to supply the much needed method of determining color harmony. Together with a system of color nomenclature and other practical information. By. J. Arthur H. Hatt. New York, 1908.
With color charts.

Cloth: 8-5/8 x 7 x ½ in.

HATTERSLEY, ROBERT.

Cabinet FF Shelf 2 No. 40

Inventor of type setting and distributing machine.

See Type Composing Machines, Hattersley.

Half morocco; 7-5/8 x 5 x 2 in.

HATTERSLEY, ROBERT (see)

Cabinet FF Shelf 6 No. 18

COMPOSING MACHINES.- Single Types. Hattersley...

HATTERSLEY COMPOSING AND DISTRIBUTING MACHINE

Cabinet FF Shelf 6 No. 76

See COMPOSING MACHINES (Single Types) Hattersley...

HATTON, JOSEPH

Cabinet MM Shelf 7 No. 8

Printing and bookbinding. [In British Manufacturing Industries, edited by Phillips Bevan, pp.33-74]. London, 1876.

Cloth; 6-5/8 x $4\frac{3}{4}$ x $\frac{3}{4}$ in.

HAUGHWOUT, E.V. and COMPANY

Cabinet C Shelf 1 No. 21

Printing machine manufacturers, New York, circa, 1872.

See PRINTING PRESSES. "Universal", specimens of printing...

HAUKINS, JOHN

Cabinet T Shelf 2 No. 6 [vol.3]

Books printed by John Haukins, London, 1530. Bibliographical notes.

see

DIBDIN'S "Typographical Antiquities" ...London, 1810-19, vol.iii, p.363

HAUSER, HANS

Cabinet B Shelf 2 No. 7

(Illustrated books printed by Hauser at Ulm, 1482-1499)

see

SCHRAMM, ALBERT. (Der) Bilderschmuck der frühdrucke...Leipzig, 1923.

HAUTH, DAVID

Cabinet X Shelf 3 No. 13

Brief bibliographical note, with printer mark, Hauth, Strassburg, 1635.

see

HEITZ, PAUL. Elsässische büchermarken...pp. xxviii, liii

HAÜY [Valentin]

Cabinet II Shelf 6 No. 1

Essai sur l'education des aveugles...A Paris; Imprimé par des enfans-aveugles...1786.

The essay is printed in raised types and the whole creditable book is announced on p.VIII to be the work of blind printers, some of whose names are given at end of book.

Calf; 10 x 8 in. pp.VIII, 126, 15, 36.

HAVANA

Cabinet Shelf No.

See Printing Historical, (Sp. America) Cuba. Havana.

HAVENS, MUNSON ALDRICH

Cabinet S Shelf 4 No. 57

Horace Walpole and the Strawberry Hill Press 1757-1789. With facsimiles. The Kirgate Press, Canton, Penn. 1901.

Boards, cloth back; 7-7/8 x $5\frac{3}{4}$ x 5/8 in. See also U/2/32.

HAVETTE, RENÉ

Cabinet L Shelf 3 No. 9.01

Conférence sur l'histoire documentaire de la sténographie. Faite par M. René Havette au 45em dîner de la Société Archéologique Le Vieux Papier, 25 Fevrier, 1908. Paris.

On pp.163-175 and account of the "Bulletin"...Artistique Le Vieux Papier.

Boards; $11\frac{1}{2}$ x $9\frac{1}{2}$ in.

HAVILAND, JOHN

Cabinet Shelf No.

See Early printing in England. London, 1632. John Haviland.

HAVRE, G. Van

Cabinet X Shelf 3 No. 8

Marques typographiques des imprimeurs et libraires Anversois. Recueillies par le Chev. G. Van Havre. Antwerp, 1883-1884. 2 Vols. Illus.

Biographical notes attached to each printer mark.

Maatschappij der Antwerpsche bibliophilen. uitgivenr. 13 & 14.

Half morocco; 9-3/4 x 6-1/8 in.

HAWAII

Cabinet 00 Shelf 6 No. 24

Newspapers, 1835-1871. A collection, bound as one volume.

Cloth; $17\frac{3}{4}$ x 12-1/8 in.

HAWAII MISSION PRESS.

Cabinet S Shelf 5 No. 25

History of the Hawaii Mission Press, with a bibliography of the early publication. By Howard M. Ballou and George R. Carter. Illus. Paper presented to the Hawaiian Historical Society, Aug. 27, 1908. Honolulu T.H. Papers of the Society, No. 14.

In box labelled "History of Printing, United States. Miscellaneous items."

HAWAIIAN ISLANDS

Cabinet R Shelf 5 No. 114

First printing house in Hawaii, completed Aug.30, 1823.

In the "Story of Three Old Buildings in Honolulu", by Mrs. R.W.Andrews. Honolulu, 1926, p.9

The first printing press arrived Aug.5, 1820. The first public printing was issued Dec. 24, 1821.

Illus. pamphlet. Item in manila envelope.

HAWAIIAN ISLANDS

Cabinet R Shelf 5 No. 114

Hawaiian Missions Centennial, 1820-1920. Honolulu, April 11-19, 1920. Official program for the events. Illus.

Has picture of the first printing house in Hawaii.

Pamphlet. Item in manila envelope

HAWAIIAN MISSION PRESS, The

Cabinet R Shelf 5 No. 113

History of the Hawaiian Mission Press, with a bibliography of the earlier publications. By Howard M. Ballou and George R. Carter. Honolulu, 1908. Facsimiles.
Papers of the Hawaiian Historical Society, No. 14.

Half morocco; 12¼ x 9⅛ in.

HAWKINS, RUSH C.

Cabinet S Shelf 1 No. 189

Catalogue of books mostly from the presses of the first printers showing the progress of printing with movable metal types through the second half of the 15th century. Collected by Rush C. Hawkins, catalogued by Alfred W. Pollard and deposited in the Annmary Brown Memorial at Providence, Rhode Island. University Press, Oxford, 1910. Printed at the cost of General Rush C. Hawkins.

Cloth; 11½ x 9 x 1¾ in.

HAWKS, NELSON C.

Cabinet FF Shelf 2 No. 31

Inventor of the American Point System of Type Bodies. Explanation of the Point System of Printing Types, with specimens in the office of the Island City Press, Alameda, Californi August, 1918.
The casting of types on point bodies originated in 1878 in the Pacific Type Foundry, San Francisco, of which N.C. Hawkes was manager.

Brochure, with frontispiece portrait of N.C. Hawks. Item in manila envelope.

HAWKERS LITERATURE. FRANCE

Cabinet S Shelf 6 No. 7

Histoire des livres populaires, ou de la litterature du colportage...depuis le 15em siècle. Par Charles Nisard, Paris, 1852.

Review of book with above title. Excerpt from Edinburgh Review. January, 1858.

Item (b) in book with binder's title: Early printed books: Various excerpts and pamphlets, 1854-1931.

HAWKINS, RUSH C.

Cabinet S Shelf 5 No. 18

(New) Light on the invention of printing By R. C. Hawkins. An excerpt from The Bookmart, Oct. 1886.
An account of a newly discovered document which tends to establish Gutenberg's claim to the invention of printing.

Bound in collection "Dawn of Printing", item 13.

HAWKS & SHATTUCKS

Cabinet 31 Shelf 2 No. 12

Occasional Typograph, 1890-93.

See PERIODICALS, PRINTING, United States Hawks & Shattucks Occasional Typograph...

HAWKING BOOKSELLERS

Cabinet V Shelf 4 No. 3

(France, 1670). Broadside : Royal decree prohibiti peddling of books to all but printers. Signed, De Ryantz.

Item inserted in l'Histoire de l'Imprimerie", par Jean de la Caille, Paris, 1689.

HAWKINS, RUSH C.

Cabinet S Shelf 5 No. 24

Some late statements about Early Printing. By Rush C. Hawkins. An excerpt from The Bibliographer, Feb. 1902.

pp. 15-22 in collection "Printing Excerpts".

HAWKS & SHATTUCK

see also Specimen Books, Types. United States. Hawks & Shattuck, San Francisco, 1889.
Specimen Books, Types. United States. Pacific States Type Foundry, Cal. circa 1899.

Cabinet Shelf No.

HAWKING, BOOKSELLING

Cabinet X Shelf 5 No. 15

Apology for the liberty of the press...

See CROWTHER, J. Apology for the liberty of the press...Halifax, 1810.

HAWKINS, [General] RUSH C.

Cabinet PP Shelf 2 No. 9

Titles of the first books from the earliest presses established in different Cities, Towns, and Monasteries in Europe, before the end of the 15th century, with brief notes upon their printers. Illustrated with reproductions of early types and first engravings of the printing press. New York and London, 1884.

Cloth; 12 x 9 x 7/8 in.

HAWTHORNE, NATHANIEL

Cabinet G Shelf 2 No. 29

(The) Golden Touch. By Nathaniel Hawthorne. The Grabhorn Press, San Francisco, 1927. Drawings by Valenti Angelo.

Boards; 9¼ x 5-3/4 x ¼ in. In protective case.

HAWKINS, ABDIEL

Cabinet I Shelf 2 No. 20

Glyphographic Office, London, n.d.

See GLYPHOGRAPHY. Instructions on glyphography...

HAWKINS, W. C.

Cabinet T Shelf 3 No. 40

(The) Church and Parish of Saint Bride, Fleet Street, Fourth edition, with a preface by Walter G. Bell. London: Printed by students of Saint Bride Foundation Printing School, Bride Lane. 1922.

Boards; 10¼ x 8 x ¼ in.

HAY, GEORGE.

Cabinet Shelf No.

See Hortensius (George Hay).

HAWKINS (General) RUSH C.

Cabinet 75 Shelf 2 No. 1

Biography of the founder of the "Annmary Brown" Library, Providence, R. I. By Alfred W. Pollard.

In Transactions of the Bibliographical Society, "The Library," Vol. I, 1920-1921, pp. 171-178.

HAWKS, NELSON C.

Cabinet Shelf No.

"Invention" of the American Point System by Nelson C. Hawks. By Henry Lewis Bullen.

Article with portrait, in The Inland Printer, vol. 83, August, 1929, p.65.

"HAYDOCK'S BIBLE"

Cabinet Shelf No.

See Bibles, "Haydock's Bible".

HAYEK, HENRY R.

Cabinet See Imprints, United States
Shelf
No.

HAZARD'S REGISTER OF PENNSYLVANIA

Cabinet 80 Philadelphia, 1833. Hazard's Register...vol. XI, No. 3, January 19, 1833, No. 264. Edited by Samuel Hazard.
Shelf 2 On p. 37 of this issue, report of the "Anniversary of the Philadelphia Typographical Society". Has a partial list of attendants at this meeting: Mathew Carey, William Duane, Richard Ronalds, Adam Ramage, etc.
No. 42
Item in manila envelope

HAZEWELL, CHARLES C.

Cabinet Conservative power of the Press...
Shelf 1
No. 42
See p.277, Breton's Voices of the Press ...New York, 1850.

HAYEZ, EDUARDUS

Cabinet FF Dissertatio inauguralis mathematica de literarum proportionibus...Bruxelles, 1829.
Shelf 5 Inserted at end: Schemes for assorting fonts for printing in Dutch language (manuscript based on researches of Spin, eminent Dutch printer)
No. 2.01 Also, "The Persian Alphabet", Rumanian, Hebrew, Greek, etc., each with proportions of characters in workable fonts.
Quarter calf; 10¼ x 8¼ in.

HAZELL, W. HOWARD

Cabinet LL Office organization for printers. By W. Howard Hazell. Issued by the Costing Committee of the Federation of Master Printers. London, 1919.
Shelf 5
No. 61
Cloth; 8-5/8 x 5½ x 3/8 in.

HEAL, AMBROSE.

Cabinet T Tradesmen's cards of the 18th century, London. An account of their origin and use. London: B.T. Batsford, Ltd. 1925. Illus.
Shelf 6
No. 49
Cloth, linen back; 10 x 7¼ x 1-3/8 in.

HAYEZ, EDUARDUS (cond,d)

Cabinet
Shelf Quarter calf; 10½ x 8¼
NO.

HAY, JOHN

Cabinet R Franklin in France. By John Hay in the Century Magazine, Jan., 1906. Portrait.
Shelf 1 Bound in volume "Franklin, excerpts from magazines", item 8.
No. 1

HEALTH OF PRINTERS

Cabinet X Wiechmann, Johann Theodor. Dissertatio inauguralis medica de morbis typographorum... Jena, 1792.
Shelf 1
No. 87
Cloth; 8 x 7 in.

HAYNES, MERRITT W.

Cabinet MM Methods of teaching related subjects in printing. Delivered at Conference on Printing Education, Washington D.C. June 28, 1932, By Merritt W. Haynes, Education Department. American Type Founders Company, Jersey City, N.J. Pamphlet.
Shelf 6
No. 100 (Env.)
Item in manila envelope.

HAZEL, WATSON & VINEY

Cabinet Aylesbury and London, England. Brief account of its origin in 1867.
Shelf Article in Caxton Magazine, vol.34, No.2, Feb. 1932, p.78.
No.

HEALTH OF PRINTERS

Cabinet JJ
Shelf 3 see also HYGIENE
No. 24 SANITATION

HAYNES, MERRITT WAY

Cabinet S (The) Students' History of Printing, giving the principal dates, personages, and events in the development of the typographic art from earliest times to the present, in Chronological order. First ed. New York, 1930. Illus.
Shelf 3
No. 94
Cloth; 8¾ x 5½ x ½ in.

HAZELL, WATSON & VINEY, LTD.

Cabinet T With the Colors: News about employees of Hazell, Watson & Viney, Ltd., who are serving king and country at home and abroad. Oct. 1914 to Dec. 1918.
Shelf 6
No. 40
Half morocco; 13 x 9½ x 1 in.

HEARST, GEORGE

Cabinet 73 Life of a California pioneer, George Hearst. By Mr. and Mrs. Froment Older. The frontispiece and headbands by William Wilke. Printed for William Randolph Hearst by John Henry Nash, San Francisco, 1933.
Shelf 2
No. 39
Vellum; 13¾ x 9 in.

HAZAÑAS Y LA RUA, DON JOAQUIN

Cabinet 26 Cuatro Alemanes compañeros impresores de Seville 1490-1503 (Four German journeymen printers at Seville).
Shelf 1 Bio-bibliographical essay.
No. 21
Article in "Gutenberg-Gesellschaft Jahrbuch, 1931", pp.201-211.

HAZELL WATSON AND VINEY.

Cabinet M see also Imprints, England. Hazel, Walson, and Viney. also Plants, Printing, England.
Shelf
No.

HEARST, PHOEBE APPERSON.

Cabinet 73 Life and personality. By Winifred Black Bonfils. The frontispiece and head bands by William Wilke. Printed for William Randolph Hearst by John Henry Nash. San Francisco, 1928.
Shelf 2
No. 38
Vellum; 13¾ x 9¼ x 1½ in.

HEARST, WILLIAM R.

Cabinet QQ Shelf 3 No. 1

American almanac...1903

see

ALMANACS. American almanac...

HAZELL, WALTER

Cabinet U Shelf 3 No. 27

Memoir of Walter Hazell, 1843-1919. By his son Ralph C. Hazell. Printed for private circulation by Hazell, Watson & Viney, Ltd. London, 1910. Portrait frontispiece.

Quarter Cloth; 8 x 5-3/8 x 3/8 in.

HEARTMAN, CHARLES F.

Cabinet R Shelf 5 No. 143

(The) New England Primer printed in America prior to 1830. A bibliographical checklist. Compiled by Charles Fred Heartman. Embellished with cuts. New York, 1915.

See also R/5/144.

Boards; 9¼ x 6½ in.

HEARST, WILLIAM RANDOLPH

Cabinet NN Shelf 2 No. 1

See BIOGRAPHIES, Editor-Journalists. Hearst...

HEARST, WILLIAM RANDOLPH

see also

Cabinet Shelf No.

Journalism, American (U.S.): Real Mr. Hearst, The.

HEARTMAN, CHARLES F.

Cabinet S Shelf 5 No. 12

(The) New England Primer printed in America prior to 1830. A bibliographical check list Compiled by Charles F. Heartman, New York, 1917. Heartman's Historical Series, No. 15.

Item 10 in collection "Pamphlets and excerpts relating to various typographical matters".

HEARST, WILLIAM R.

Cabinet NN Shelf 2 No. 1

Democratic candidate, the, Charles E. Hughes, the Republican candidate. Which? Excerpt from the Outlook, Oct. 20, 1906.

Item 25 in book with binder's title: "Journalists. Various Excerpts".

HEARTMAN, CHARLES F.

Cabinet R Shelf 4 No. 87

Check list of printers in the United States; from Stephen Daye to the close of the War of Independence, with a list of places in which printing was done. Compiled by Chas. F. Heartman, New York, 1915.

Boards; 9½ x 6½ in.

HEARTMAN, CHARLES F. (Publisher) see

Cabinet OO Shelf 3 No. 34

NEWSPAPERS, United States. Literature of. Notes toward a history...

HEARST, WILLIAM RANDOLPH

Cabinet 73 Shelf 1 No. 3

See Imprints, United States. Nash, John Henry: San Francisco, March 1929.

HEARTMAN, CHARLES F. (Compiler)

Cabinet 80 Shelf 1 No. 85

Almanacs printed in New Jersey prior to 1850, preliminary checklist of. Compiled by Charles F. Heartman. Metuchen, N.J., 1929.

Paper; 10¼ x 6-7/8 in. In manila envelope.

HEATH, T.T. (Inventor) see

Cabinet FF Shelf 6 No. 18

COMPOSING MACHINES - Matrix Method. Heath Matrix Typograph...

HEARST, WILLIAM RANDOLPH

Cabinet NN Shelf 2 No. 6

Myth, the Hearst. By Q. P.

Excerpt from World's Work, Oct., 1906.

Item 15 in bound collection "Biographies of Journalists".

HEARTMAN, CHARLES F.

Cabinet QQ Shelf 4 No. 22

Heartmans Historical Series, No. 35, Material towards a History of Andover, Vermont... Abby Maria Hemenway, Editor.[Copyright] Price 50 cents. Chicago, Ill., 1886. Reprinted for Heartmans Historical Series (No. 35), Perth Amboy, New Jersey, 1922.

Boards; 10-1/8 x 7 in.

HEATH, THOMAS T.

Cabinet S Shelf 2 No. 47

Johnston, William, in memoriam. Remarks made at a Bar meeting. Resolutions, reminiscences, letters, and newspaper notices. Cincinnati Ohio, The Heath Matrix Typograph Machine Print, 1891. Frontispiece.

Half morocco; 9½ x 6¼ in.

HEARST, WILLIAM RANDOLPH

Cabinet NN Shelf 2 No. 1

Tragedy of Hearst, By Robert L. Duffus. Excerpt from World's Work, Oct., 1922. Portraits.

Item 45 in book with binder's title: "Journalists. Various Excerpts".

HEARTMAN, CHARLES F.

Cabinet R Shelf 5 No. 144

(The) New England Primer issued prior to 1830. A bibliographical checklist...Embellished with a hundred cuts and now revised, greatly improved and arranged. With preface, introduction and index compiled by Charles F. Heartman ... 1922.

Boards; 11¼ x 7¾ in.

HEATON, Mrs. CHARLES

Cabinet J Shelf 2 No. 19

Dürer, Albrecht, of Nürnberg, the life of. With a translation of his letters and journal and an account of his works. Second edition, with portrait and 16 illustrations. London, 1881.

Cloth; 8½ x 6 x 1¼ in.

HEATON, JOHN L.

Cabinet 00 Shelf 3 No. 29

Story of a page: Thirty years of public service and public discussion in the editorial columns of The New York World. New York, 1913.
Has frontispiece portrait of Joseph Pulitzer, founder of the N. Y. World, 1883.

Boards, cloth back; 8-7/8 x 5-7/8 x 1½ in.

HEATON, Rev. W. J.

Cabinet U Shelf 1 No. 45

(The) Bible of the Reformation. Its translators and their work. With illustrations and facsimiles. London, 1910.

Cloth; 7¾ x 5¼ x 5/8 in.

HEATON, Rev. W. J.

Cabinet U Shelf 1 No. 46

Our own English Bible: Its translators and their work. The manuscript period. With fifty-six facsimiles and illustrations. London, 1913.

Cloth; 7¾ x 5¼ x 5/8 in.

HEATON, Rev. W. J.

Cabinet U Shelf 1 No. 47

Puritan Bible. The, and the contemporaneous Protestant versions. Being the third volume of "Our own English Bible; its translators and their work". By the Rev. W. J. Heaton. London, 1913. Illus.
Inserted: A.L.S. the author.

Cloth; 7½ x 5-1/8 x 1 in.

HEATWOLE, JOEL PRESCOTT

Cabinet S Shelf 5 No. 6

(A) Country print shop...The Northfield News: Its equipment and facilities for the doing of the high class in printing. Northfield, Minnesota, 1907. Illus. Booklet.

Item 7 in collection "Various printers and their plants; excerpts from magazines," Vol. 2, 1918.

HEAWOOD, EDWARD

Cabinet 75 Shelf 2 No. 9

Position on the sheet of early watermarks. [An historical bibliographical essay].
Brief mention of early printing, and sizes of paper.

In Trans. Bibl. Soc. "The Library," Vol. IX pp. 38-47. 1928-29.

HEAWOOD, E.

Cabinet 75 Shelf 2 No. 10

Sources of early English (15th and 16th centuries) paper supply. A paper for the Bibliographical Society, London, 1929.
Has list of paper marks, and facsimiles.

In Trans. Biblio. Soc. "The Library," vol. 10, 1929-30. pp. 282-307, 427-454.

HEBEL, J. WILLIAM.

Cabinet 75 Shelf 2 No. 5

Ling, Nicholas and Englands Helicon. A paper read before the Bibliographical Society.

In Trans. Biblio. Soc., "The Library," Vol. V, 1924-1925, pp. 153-160.

HEBREW

Cabinet L Shelf 2 No. 15

Origin and varieties of the Semitic alphabet. With specimens. By John C. C. Clarke. 2nd ed. Chicago, 1884.

Half morocco; 9-7/8 x 7 in.

HEBREW PRINTING

Cabinet X Shelf 1 No. 80

Annales Hebraeo-typographici ab an 1501-1540. Digessit notisque hist-criticis instruxit. Johannes Bernardus DeRossi. Parmae, 1799 : Ex Regio Typographeo.
Annales of Hebrew printing, printers, and types.

Half leather; 10¾ x 8 in.

HEBREW PRINTING

Cabinet X Shelf 1 No. 79

Annales Hebraeo-typographici, sec XV., descripsit fusoque commentario illustravit. Joh. Bern. DeRossi. Parma, 1795.
Annales of Hebrew printing, and a brief history of the origin of Hebrew types.

Boards; 12¼ x 9-1/8 in.

HEBREW PRINTING

Stack A Shelf 1 & 2 Number 82

Bullen, Henry Lewis: The liberty of Hebrew printing. (In Collectanea Typographica) The Inland Printer, Vol. 82, March, 1929, p. 90.

HEBREW PRINTING.

Cabinet 75 Shelf 2 No. 10

Catalogue of Hebrew printed books in the Bodleian Library. Reviewed by J. L. London, 1929.

In Transactions of Bibliographical Society, "The Library," vol. 10, 1929-30. pp. 108-10.

HEBREW PRINTING

Cabinet V Shelf 4 No. 2

Decouvre l'origine de l'impression Grecque et Hebraique...

See CHEVILLIER, ANDRE. Origine de l'imprimerie de Paris...[part IV]

HEBREW PRINTING

Cabinet X Shelf 1 No. 76

(De) Hebraicae typographiae ac primitiis; seu antiquis ac rarissimis Hebraicorum librorum editionibus seculi XV. Disquisitio historico-critica...Joh. Bernardi De Rossi. Recudi curavit G.F. Hufnagel, Erlangae, 1778.

Half morocco; 7-3/7 x 4-5/8 in.

HEBREW PRINTING

Cabinet Y Shelf 2 No. 68

Hebraischen druckereien und ihre druck. Mit benutzung der akten des Grossh. Badischen General-Landes-Archives. Karlsruhe i.B. 1898.

Historical, bio-bibliographical account of hebrew printing, mainly in Karlsruhe.

Cloth; 9 x 5¾ x ¼ in.

HEBREW PRINTING

Cabinet 18 Shelf 1 No. 13

Incunabula, a catalogue of Hebrew. Review of Catalogue 151, Rosenthal (bookseller), Munich. German text.

In Zeitschrift für Bücherfreunde, 1913, part 2, p.521 of "Beiblatt".

HEBREW PRINTING

Cabinet S Shelf 3 No. 84

Makers of Hebrew books in Italy. Being chapters in the history of the Hebrew printing press. By David Werner ~~Aram~~ Amram. Philadelphia, 1909. Illus.
Has printer marks, and bibliographies or lists of the printing from the more famous Hebrew presses.

Cloth; 9 x 5-7/8 in.

HEBREW PRINTING

Cabinet AA Shelf 2 No. 8

Manzoni, Giacomo: Annali tipografici del Soncino: Parte Prima nella quale si descrivono e illustrano le edizioni eseguite da Ciosue-Salomone, da Mosè ben Salomo e da Gherescom Soncino...nel secolo XV. a Soncino, a Casalmaggiore, a Napoli ... Tomo unico. Bologna, 1886.

Bibliographical, historical account.

Half morocco; 9¼ x 6 in.

HEBREW PRINTING

Cabinet X Shelf 1 No. 78

Typographia Hebraeo-Ferrariensi commentarius historicus, quo Ferrarienses judaeorum editiones Hebraicae, Hispanicae, Lusitanae recensentur...Joh. Bernardi De Rossi. Erlangae, 1781.

Origin and progress of Hebrew printing at Ferrara.

Half morocco; 6¾ x 4½ in.

HEBREW PRINTING IN ITALY. Literature

Cabinet Y Shelf 2 No. 2

Annalen der hebraischen typographie von Riva di Trento (1558-1562). Von E. Carmoly. Zweite auflage. Frankfurt am Main, 1868. Pamphlet.

Bio-bibliographical account. Has type specimens.

Item in box labelled "German Pamphlets - History of Printing - Bibliography, etc."

HEBREW PRINTING

Cabinet AA Shelf 3 No. 45

Ontwikkeling der boekdrukkunst in Nederland....

See PRINTING, HISTORICAL, Holland. Ontwikkeling der boekdrukkunst...Haarlem, 1923, p.177

HEBREW PRINTING IN BOHEMIA

Cabinet E Shelf 3 No. 34

Prague, 1627. [Printer unknown]. "Siah zizhak" By Samuel Halevi.

A Hebrew grammar based on phonetic laws.

Tooled morocco; 7¾ x 5-7/8 x ¾ in.

HEBREW TYPES

Cabinet V Shelf 4 No. 22

Le Bé, Guillaume. Paris and Venice, 1546-1574.

See Specimen Books, Types. France. Le Be, Guillaume.

HEBREW PRINTING.

Cabinet 50 Shelf 1 No. 10

Origine ac primitiis de hebraicae typographiae, seu antiquis ac rarissimus. Hebraicorum librorum, editionibus seculi XV. Disquitio historico-critica. Johannis Bernardi de-Rossi. Parmae. Ex regio typographeo. 1776.

Half morocco; 9¾ x 7½ in.

HEBREW PRINTING IN FRANCE.

Cabinet 40 Shelf 1 No. 22

Paris, 1548. Robert (I) Estienne.
Title: Thesaurus lingua sanctae. Ex R. David Kimcki ... contractior et emendatior.
Imprint: Ex officina Roberti Stephani typographi Regii. Ex privilegio Regio.

Tooled pigskin in buckram case; 9 x 6¼ x 3 in

HEBREW TYPES

Cabinet S Shelf 3 No. 104

Notes on the use of Hebrew type in non-Hebrew books, 1475-1520. By Alexander Marx.

Bibliographical account on p.381 of book "Wilberforce Eames...a tribute to. Cambridge, 1924.

HEBREW PRINTING

Cabinet Z Shelf 1 No. 50

Specimens of Hebrew printing types, circa 1820.

N.F. 8-15-74. See BELINFANTE (J.J. or A.C.?). Amsterdam, 1820. [Broadside specimen ...]

HEBREW PRINTING IN FRANCE

Cabinet E Shelf 2 No. 80

Paris, 1609, Guillaume (III) Le Be.
Title: Linguae hebraicae institutiones absolutissimae ... Johanne Quinquarboreo, authore ... Lutelia. 1609.

Limp vellum; 8¾ x 6½ x ¾ in.

HECKEL FAMILY OF PUBLISHERS

Cabinet 22 Shelf 1 No. 20

See Publishing, Germany. Dresden, 1526-1844.

Publishing house founded in 1681 and still continuing in 1844.

HEBREW PRINTING

Cabinet L Shelf 3 No. 32

Thesaurus typographiae hebraicae saeculi 15. Editor Prof. A. Freimann. Marx & Co. Verlag Berlin.

Consists of about 400 plates of facsimil of hebrew printing, with ornaments, etc. Published in 8 parts at intervals, 1924 to 1931.

Portfolios, p[...] wrappers.

HEBREW PRINTIN IN HOLLAND

Cabinet E Shelf 4 No. 44

Amsterdam, 1667. Joseph Athias.
Biblio Hebraica accuratissima notis...A Johanne Leusden. Amsterdami, 1657.

Vellum; 8¾ x 5 x 3¼ in.

HECKETHORN, CHARLES WILLIAM

Cabinet U Shelf 4 No. 35

(The) Printers of Basle in the 15th and 16th centuries: Their biographies, printed books and devices. London, 1897. Illus.

Cloth; 12 x 8-1/8 x 1½ in.

HEBREW PRINTING

Cabinet X Shelf 1 No. 77

(De) Typographia Hebraeo-Ferrariensi commentarius historicus, quo Ferrarienses Judacorum editiones hebraicae, hispanicae, lusitanae recensentur et illustrantur...Joh. Bernardi De Rossi. Parmae, 1780.

History of Hebrew printing in Ferrara.

Half morocco; 8-7/8 x 5-7/8 in.

HEBREW PRINTING IN ITALY

Cabinet 60 Shelf 1 No. 2

Venice, circa 1501, Aldus Manutius.

See FACSIMILES. Alphebutum Hebraicum ....

HÉDON, JULES

Cabinet L Shelf 1 No. 11

Lithographie a Rouen. Par Jules Hédon. Avec un portrait à l'eau-forte. Rouen, 1877.

No.64 Of 100 printed copies. Signed.

Paper; 9½ x 6½ in.

HEEMSKERCK, MARTIN van (engraver, 1498-1574)

Cabinet C Shelf 2 No. 4

Illustrations of van Heemskerck (of Holland), with biographical sketch.

See STIRLING-MAXWELL, Sir WILLIAM (The) Chief victories of Emperor Charles the Fifth...

HEINECKEN (Baron)

Cabinet I Shelf 1 No. 28

Idée générale d'une collection complette d'estampes. Avec une dissertation sur l'origine de la gravure et sur les premiers livres d'images. A Leipsic et Vienne. Chez Jean Paul Kraus. 1771.

Half calf; 7¾ x 5 in.

HEIR, MARTIN (Compiler)

Cabinet MM Shelf 7 No. 70

Twentieth Century Encyclopedia of Printing. Compiled by Martin Heir, editor The Graphic Arts Monthly. Chicago, 1930. Illus.

Introduction by Douglas C. McMurtrie.

Embossed leather; 9-3/8 x 6⅝ x 1¼ in.

HEARTMAN, CHARLES F. (Compiler)

Cabinet PP Shelf 2 No. 23 2 vols.

(The) Cradle of the United States, 1765-1789. A collection [1000 items] of contemporary broadsides, pamphlets...Alphabetically arranged. Bibliographically, historically, and sometimes sentimentally described by C.F. Heartman, Metuchen, N.J. 1922-23.

Boards; 11 x 7-5/8 in.

HEICHEN, PAUL

Cabinet Y Shelf 3 No. 33

(Printers and publishers from Gutenberg's time to the present day. A pocket manual) Taschen-Lexicon der buchdrucker u. buchhändler seit Gutenberg bis auf die gegenwart. Leipzig, 1884. Illus.

Half morocco; 5-3/4 x 3-3/4 x 3/4 in.

HEIR, MARTIN

Cabinet LL Shelf 6 No. 20

How to figure type composition by known factors. A new, easy, and labor-saving method of finding the number of items in any form of type matter. Also reference tables, weight of linotype composition, and other information of value to printers, publishers, and printing buyers. Evanston, Ill. 1914. Brochure.

Item 12 in book with binder's title "Various items on printing shop practice". Bound 1919.

HEIDENHEIMER, HEINRICH

Cabinet X Shelf 2 No. 60

(Vom) Rhume Joannes Gutenberg: eines litterargeschichteliche studie. (To the glory of Gutenberg: a literary study). Mainz, 1900. Buchdruckerei H. Prickarts.

Essay in book with title "Gutenberg-Feier, Mainz, 1900"...von K.G. Bockenheimer

HEINRICH, PH.

Cabinet Shelf No.

See Specimen Books, Types. United States. Heinrich, Ph. New York.

HEITZ, JOHANN (and successors)

Cabinet X Shelf 3 No. 13

Brief bibliographical note, Heitz, printer, Strassburg, 1719-1741.

see HEITZ, PAUL. Elsässiche büchermarken...p.xxx

HEILBRONN, FRANZ (RENNER) VON (see)

Cabinet Shelf No.

Renner (Franz) von Heilbronn

HEINTZMANN PRESS.

Cabinet Shelf No.

See Imprints, United States.

HEITZ, PAUL

Cabinet X Shelf 3 No. 15

Basler büchermarken bis zum anfang des 17 jahrhunderts. Herausgegeben von Paul Heitz. Mit vorbemerkungen und nachrichten über die Basler drucker von Dr. Chr. Bernoulli. Strassburg (Heitz u. Mundel), 1895.

Boards, cloth back; 14¼ x 11 in.

HEIM, JOSEPH

Cabinet J Shelf 5 No. 4

French typographical ornament from the 16th to the 18th centuries. [Reproductions of wood and copper by half tone process]. Josef Heim, Art Publisher. Vienna (Austria).

Portfolio, boards; 16½ x 12 in.

HEINEMANN, JULIUS & COMPANY.

Cabinet EE Shelf 4 No. 59

Illustrated price list.

See PRINTING EQUIPMENTS. Catalogue.

HEITZ, PAUL

Cabinet X Shelf 3 No. 13

Elsässische büchermarken bis anfang des 18 jahrhunderts. Herausgegeben von Paul Heitz. Mit vorbewerkungen und nachrichten über die drucker von Dr. Karl August Barack. Strassburg, 1892.

Boards, cloth back; 14¼ x 11 in.

HEIM, JOSEF

Cabinet LL Shelf 2 No. 8

Fromme's Graphischen Kalender, 1881, fur buch, stein-und kupferdrucker, schriftgiesser und verwandte kunstgenossen. Redigirt vom Josef Heim. Wien. Druck und Verlag von Carl Fromme, K.K. Hofbuchdruckerei. Illus.

Cloth; 5¼ x 3-3/8 x ½ in.

HEIR, MARTIN (Compiler)

Cabinet LL Shelf 5 No. 59

Printing estimator's red book. Published by Grand Rapids Printers Association. Grand Rapids, Mich. 1919.

Leather; 7 x 5-1/8 in.

HEITZ, PAUL

Cabinet RR Shelf 1 No. 8

Filigranes des papiers, contenus dans les archives de la ville de Strasbourg. Par Paul Heitz. Strasbourg, 1902.

39 plates, with about 1525 watermarks.

Half morocco; 13 x 9-3/4 x 3/8 in.

HEITZ, PAUL

Cabinet X, Shelf 3, No. 17

(Frankfort and Mainz printer and publisher marks, from the 15th to the 17th century) Frankfurter und Mainzer drucker-und verlegerzeichen bis in das 17 jahrhundert. Strassburg, 1896. Illus.

Half cloth; $14\frac{1}{4}$ x $11\frac{1}{4}$ x $\frac{3}{4}$ in.

HEITZ, PAUL

Cabinet X, Shelf 3, No. 21

Genfer buchdrucker-und verlegerzeichen im xv., xvi und xvii jahrhundert. [Alternating title] Marques d'imprimerus et de libraires de Geneve...von Paul Heitz. Strassburg, 1908.

Half cloth; 14-3/8 x $11\frac{1}{4}$ in.

HEITZ, PAUL

Cabinet X, Shelf 3, No. 20

Kölner büchermarken bis anfang des 17 jahrhunderts. Herausgegeben von Paul Heitz. Mit nachrichten über die drucker, von Otto Zaretzky. Strassburg, 1898.

Boards, linen back; $14\frac{1}{4}$ x $11\frac{1}{4}$ in.

HEITZ, PAUL

Cabinet K, Shelf 1, No. 17

(Die) Zierinitialen in den drucken der Thomas Anshelm (Hagenau 1516-1523).
Ein beitrag zur geschichte des holzschnittes. Mit 105 abbildungen. Strassburg, 1894.
20 plates.

Half morocco; $11\frac{1}{4}$ x $8\frac{1}{4}$ in.

HEITZ, PAUL

Cabinet X, Shelf 3, No. 16

(Zurich printer marks to the beginning of the 17th century. An illustrated bibliographical supplement to the works of C. Rudolphi's and S. Vogelin) Die Zürcher büchermarken bis zum anfang des 17. jahrhunderts. Ein bibliographischer und bildlicher nachtrag zu C. Rudolphi's and S. Vogelin's arbeiten uber zurcher druckerwerke. Zuzammengestellt. von P. Heitz. Zurich, 1895.

Half morocco; $14\frac{1}{4}$ x 11 in.

HELBIG, HENRI

Cabinet W, Shelf 2, No. 1

(Une) Decouverte pour l'histoire de l'imprimerie. Les plus anciens caracteres de Gutenberg et ce qui en est advenu. - Albert Pfister imprimeur a Bamberg.- Le Bible de 36 lignes. Par Henri Helbig. Bruxelles, 1855.

Item 11 in volume "Gutenberg l'inventeur de l'imprimerie - Melanges."

HELBIG, H.

Cabinet V, Shelf 4, No. 21

Notes et dissertations relatives à l'histoire de l'imprimerie: Extrait du tome XVIII de Bulletin du Bibliophile Belge. Bruxelles, n. d. [1863].

Cloth, 10 x $6\frac{1}{2}$ in.

HELBIG, H.

Cabinet V, Shelf 5, No. 23

Notes et dissertations relatives a l'histoire de l'imprimerie. Bruxelles [1863]. Pamphlet (Extrait du tome XVIII du Bulletin du Bibliophile Belge.

Item 15 in vol. with binder's title "Origin of Printing in France: Pamphlets".

HELBIG, H.

Cabinet W, Shelf 4, No. 42

Notice sur les descendants de Pierre Schoeffer qui exercèrent l'imprimerie à Bois-le-Duc de père en fils, depuis l'année 1541 jusqu'en 1796. Gand, 1846. With vignettes and a genealogical table.
Reprinted from the "Messager des Sciences Historiques et Archives des Arts de Belgique" 1846, pp. 433-445.

Half morocco; 8-7/8 x $5\frac{3}{4}$ in.

HELIOCHROMY

Cabinet I, Shelf 2, No. 3

Color photography.

See IVES, FREDERIC E. Heliochromy.

HELIOGRAPHY

Cabinet I, Shelf 2, No. 23

Gravure heliographique, galvanoplastie. Traite pratique. Par Guymet & Alker. Paris... Bruxelles, 1870.

Paper; $7\frac{1}{4}$ x $4\frac{1}{2}$ in.

HELIOGRAVURE

Cabinet I, Shelf 2, No. 42.01

Description of method, or heliogravure process. Excerpt from the Bulletin Officiel, 1925. Typescript translation.

Item in manila envelope

HELIOTYPE PROCESS

Cabinet I, Shelf 2, No. 25

Edwards, Ernest. The heliotype process. With twenty-eight illustrations. Boston, James R. Osgood and Company. 1876.

Boards; 12 x 10 x 5/8 in.

HELIOTYPE PROCESS

Cabinet I, Shelf 2, No. 24

What is heliotype? Description of the process. The Heliotype Company, Ltd., London, 1872. With 12 specimens.

Cloth; $9\frac{1}{4}$ x $6\frac{3}{4}$ x 3/8 in.

HELLER, ALFRED

Cabinet Y, Shelf 3, No. 44

Deutscher buchdruckerverein un sein werden in funfzig jahren (1869-1919)...Herausgegeben vom Deutschen Buchdrucker-Verein als Jubilaums-Festgabe, 1919.
With portraits and illus.

Boards; 13-1/8 x $9\frac{1}{2}$ in.

HELLER, ALFRED

Cabinet LL, Shelf 5, No. 55

Organisation der buchdruckerei, die. Leipzig, Carl Ernst Poeschel Verlag, 1916.

Half morocco; 9-1/8 x $6\frac{1}{4}$ x 7/8 in.

HELLER, JOHANN B.

Cabinet X, Shelf 2, No. 3.01

Wohlgemeynte gedancken uber fuhrung einer buchdruckerey, bey feyerung des 3 Jubel-Festes der buchdruckerkunst...Erffurt, 1740.
Frontispiece copper engraving, allegorical subject with portraits of Gutenberg, Fust and Schoeffer.

Half morocco; $7\frac{1}{4}$ x $4\frac{1}{4}$ x 3/8 in.

HELLER, JOSEPH

Cabinet K, Shelf 5, No. 8

Geshcichte der holzschneiderkunst von den altesten bis auf die neusten zeiten, nebst zwei beilagen enthaltend den ursprung der spielkarten und ein berzeichniss der sammtlichen xylographischen werke. Bamberg, 1823. Illus.
"One of the best German works on xylography, with a history of the origin of playing cards."

Boards; 8 x 4-3/4 x $1\frac{1}{4}$ in.

HELLEU, RENÉ

Cabinet W Shelf 1 No. 181

Table alphabétique des éditions d'art Edouard Pelletan suivi de catalogue des livres estampes originales et reproduction édités par René Helleu. Paris, 1919.

Half morocco; $8\frac{1}{2}$ x $6\frac{1}{2}$ in.

HELLWIG, WILHELM

Cabinet LL Shelf 2 No. 15.01

(Composition of chemical and mathematical formulas) Der satz chemischer und mathematischer formeln. von Wilhelm Hellwig. Leipzig, 1909. "Monographien des Buchgewerbes, III Band".

Half morocco; $6\frac{1}{4}$ x $4\frac{3}{8}$ x 3/8 in.

HELLWIG, WILHELM

Cabinet LL Shelf 3 No. 54

(Der) Satz und die behandlung fremder sprachen. Ein hilfsbuch für schriftsetzer und korrektoren. Vierte erweiterte auflage. Frankfurt a.M. 1920. Klimsche Graphische Bibliothek, Band VI.

Boards; 8-3/8 x 5-7/8 x 7/8 in.

HELYAE, HELYAS von Laufen

Cabinet Y Shelf 4 No. 4

Note on the Helyae press at Beromunster, 1470-1475)

see

VOULLIÉME, ERNST (Die) Deutschen drucker des fünfzehnten jahrhunderts...p.26

HEMENWAY, ABBY MARIA (Editor)

Cabinet QQ Shelf 4 No. 22

Material towards a history of Andover, Vermont... Abby Maria Hemenway, Editor. [Copyright] Price 50 cents. Chicago, 1886. Reprinted for Heartman's Historical Series (No. 35) Perth Amboy, New Jersey, 1922.

Boards; 10-1/8 x 7 in.

HEMERY, J. Fr.

Cabinet Shelf No.

See Specimen Books, Types, France,

Also Mozet.

HEMERY, J. FR.

Cabinet 83 Shelf 1 No. 21

See Specimen Books, Types. France.

HEMSWORTH, H. W.

Cabinet L Shelf 2 No. 8.01

Cuneorum Clavis. The primitive alphabet and language of the ancient ones of the earth... From the papers of the late Daniel Smith. Edited by H.W. Hemsworth, London, 1875.

Cloth; 9 x $5\frac{1}{2}$ in.

HENCHMAN, DANIEL (Publisher)

Cabinet F Shelf 1 No.

See Early Printing in New England. Boston, [v.d.] Printed for D. Henchman.

HENDERSON, JAMES D.

Cabinet S Shelf 2 No. 160

Miniature Books. By James D. Henderson, scrivener of the News - Letter of the LXIV mos. Leipzig, 1930. Limited to 260 copies.

Boards; 4-7/8 x 3 in.

HENDRIKSEN, F.

Cabinet S Shelf 5 No. 12

William Morris, born at Walthamstow, 1834, died October 3, 1896 in London. Excerpt from Tidsskriftet Bogvennen, Copenhagen, 1896. Biographical.

Item 25 in collection "Pamphlets and excerpts relating to various typographical matters."

HENRICO (de Haarlem)

Cabinet X Shelf 3 No. 14

Bibliographical note, with printer mark, Henrico de Haarlem, and Valbeck, Siena, 1488-9.

see

KRISTELLER, Dr. Paul. Italienischen buchdrucker...p.58

HENRICPETRI.

Cabinet Shelf No.

See Petri, Sebastian (Henricpetri).

HENRY, FRANK S.

Cabinet MM Shelf 6 No. 93

Essentials (The) of printing: A text book for beginners. New York, 1924. Illus.

Cloth; $7\frac{3}{4}$ x $5\frac{1}{2}$ x 5/8 in.

HENRY, FRANK S.

Cabinet MM Shelf 6 No. 59

Locking forms for the job press; containing useful information regarding the imposition of job forms; wooden and metal furniture, quoins, bearers, foundry guards, etc. "Typographic Technical Series for Apprentices", Part III, No.24, United Typothetae of America, 1918.

Cloth; 8 x 5 in.

HENRY, FRANK S.

Cabinet MM Shelf 6 No. 38

Printing: A textbook for printers' apprentices, continuation classes, and for general use in schools. First edition. New York, 1917. Illus.

Cloth; $7\frac{3}{4}$ x $5\frac{1}{4}$ x 1 in.

HENRY, GEORGE & CO.

Cabinet Shelf No.

See Imprints, England.

HENRY, NORRIS

Cabinet 80 Shelf 2 No. 36

New York, 1821, publisher.

See Periodicals, United States. Saturday Magazine...Published by E. Littell and Norris Henry...

HENSBERG, GERHARD

Cabinet X Shelf 3 No. 20

Cologne, 1550.

see HEITZ, PAUL. Kölner büchermarken...p.xxx

HERALD OF GOSPEL LIBERTY

Cabinet NN Shelf 7 No. 12

Our centennial year. Portsmouth, N. H. Herald of Gospel Liberty, 1808 - 1908.
Two numbers bound in one: No. I [Facsimile], 1808, No. 100, 1908, Dayton, Ohio.

Cloth; 12¾ x 8-7/8 in.

HERALDRY

Cabinet E Shelf 3 No. 28

See François, René. Essay des Merveilles de nature...[p.354-75]

HENTSCHEL, CARL

Cabinet I Shelf 2-b No. 2

Process engraver. The "What to be" books. Penny guides to trades and handicrafts for youths and girls. London, n.d. Booklet.

Paper; 5-3/8 x 3-3/8 in.

HERALD of LIBERTY.

Cabinet Shelf No.

See Newspapers, Maine.

HERALDRY

Cabinet 2 Shelf 2 No. 35

Marques d'honneur de la maison de Tassis. Alain Cartier, secretaire de Charles VII. Ray de France. Antwerp, Plantin-Moretus Press, 1645.

Paper boards; 15-1/8 x 9-3/4 x 1¼ in.

HENZE, ADOLPH

Cabinet FF Shelf 4 No. 8

Handbuch der schriftgiesserei und der verwandten nebenzweige: stereotypie, abklatschen, holzschneidekunst...proportion der buchstaben etc., fur schriftgiesser, buchdrucker, stempelschneider, xylographen, graveure und andere kunstgenossen. Mit 393 abbildungen auf 11 tafeln. Weinmar, 1844.
"Though now somewhat out of date, it is still one of the best books on type founding". B. & W.
Boards; 7-3/8 x 4-3/8 x 1 in.

HERALD of LIBERTY

Cabinet Shelf No.

See Newspapers, Pennsylvania

HERALDRY

Cabinet E Shelf 3 No. 22

Theater (The) of Honor and Knighthood.

See Favine, Andrew. The Theater etc.

HENZE, ADOLPH

Cabinet LL Shelf 1 No. 25

Handbuch der schriftgiesserei und der verwandten nebenzweige: Stereotypie, abklatschen, holzschneidekunst...proportion der buchstaben etc. für schriftgiesser, buchdrucker, stempelschneider, xylographen, graveure und andere. Weimar, 1844.
Lacks the 11 plates with 393 illus.
"Though now somewhat out of date, it is still one of the best books on typefounding". B. & W.

Boards; 6-7/8 x 4-3/8 x 3/4 in

HERALD of the TIMES

Cabinet Shelf No.

See Newspapers, New York State.

HERALDRY

Cabinet Shelf No.

SEE

COATS OF ARMS

HERALD, THE DAILY

Cabinet NN Shelf 7 No. 13

Bar Harbor, Maine, 1886.

see DAILY HERALD, THE.

HERALDRY

Cabinet 39 Shelf 2 No. 21

Alliances généalogiques des rois et princes de Gaule. Par Claude Paradin. [Printer Mark] À Lyon. Par Ian de Tornes. M.D.LXI.

Tooled morocco; 13½ x 8¼ x 2½ in. Brunet 4, 358.

HERBALS.

Cabinet 75 Shelf 2 No. 4

Bibliography.

See Bibliography. Herbals...

HERALD, THE NEW YORK see

Cabinet Shelf No.

JOURNALISM, United States

NEW YORK HERALD, The

HERALDRY

Cabinet 2 Shelf 2 No. 35

Chiflet, J. Les Marques d'honneur de la Maison de Tassis. A Anvers, en l'imprimerie Plantinienne de Balthasas Moretus. 1645.

Vellum over boards; 15-1/8 x 9¾ x 1¼ in.

HERBALS.

Cabinet 75 Shelf 2 No. 2

Bohemian herbal of 1562.

See Early Printing in Bohemia. Literature of. (Prague, 1562).

HERBALS, Early

Cabinet U Shelf 5 No. 52

Books on horticulture and botany, 1480 to 1750. By R. Weston.
See pp.229-237 in Bibliographical notes: The Gentleman's Magazine.

HERBERMANN, C.G.

Cabinet S Shelf 6 No. 8

New York's first directory, 1786, printed by Shepard Kollock. Bibliographical account. Excerpt from the "U.S. Cath. Hist. Soc. Historical Records & Studies, vol.V, No.1, Nov. 1907. Pamphlet.

Item 4 in vol. with binder's title "Early printing and printers. Pamphlets".

HERBERT, BENJAMIN BRIGGS

Cabinet NN Shelf 2 No. 31

National Editorial Association (N.E.A.). The first decennium...Discussions and Legislation as to newspaper work and interests. By B.B. Herbert, organizer and first president of the N.E.A. Chicago, 1896. Illus.

Cloth; 8-¾ x 6 in.

HERBERT, WILLIAM

Cabinet Shelf No.

See Ames, Joseph and Wm. Herbert. Typographical antiquities...

HERBERT, WILLIAM

Cabinet T Shelf 3 No. 2

Anecdotes relating to Wm. Herbert, author of the Typographical Antiquities.

In DIBDIN'S Bibliographical Decameron...London, 1817, vol.3, pp.321-6

HERBERT, WILLIAM

Cabinet T Shelf 2 No. 2 3 vols.

Typographical antiquities: Or an historical account of the origin and progress of printing in Great Britain and Ireland...from the year 1471 to 1600. Begun by the late Joseph Ames ...Considerably augmented by W. Herbert. London, 1785, 1786 and 1790. (3 vols.)

Quarter calf, each vol.; 10-5/8 x 8-3/8 in.

HERBORT, JOHANNES.

Cabinet D Shelf 1 No. 39

See Incunabula. Baysio, Guido de. Rosarium decretorum.

HERBST, HERMANN

Cabinet PP Shelf 4 No. 44

Bibliographie der buchbinderei-literature, 1924-1932. von Hermann Herbst. Leipzig, Verlag Karl W. Hiersemann, 1933.

Cloth; 10¼ x 8¼ in.

HERBST, JOHANN.

Cabinet Shelf No.

See Biographies, Printers. Oporinus,Johann [Johann Herbst]. Basle, 1507-1568.

HERDINGH & MORTIER

Cabinet Shelf No.

See Specimen Books, Types, Holland.

HERFKENS, F. JR. (Editor)

Cabinet 36 Shelf 2 No. 8

Advertentiebled

See PERIODICALS, PRINTING, Holland Advertentiebled...

HERFORDE, JOHN (and widow of)

Cabinet T Shelf 2 No. 6 [vol.3]

Books printed by John Herforde and his widow. London, 1544-1550. Bibliographical notes.

see

DIBDIN'S "Typographical Antiquities" ...London, 1810-19, vol.iii, p.554

HERGOTT, JOHANN

Cabinet Shelf No.

See Early Printing in Germany, Nurnberg, 1527; See also Bookselling, Herrgott, Johann.

HERHAN, LOUIS ETIENNE

Cabinet FF Shelf 1 No. 64

French stereotyping invention controversy.

See STEREOTYPING. French invention controversy...Grassal. Paris (1805).

HERHAN, LOUIS-ÉTIENNE

Cabinet FF Shelf 1 No. 105

Stereotyping experiments by Herhan, account of. With brief biographical note.

see

KUBLER, GEORGE A. Historical treatises...on stereotyping. New York, 1936 p. 105 and following.

HERING, A

Cabinet FF Shelf 1 No. 18

(Die) Galvanoplastik und ihre anwendung in der buch druckerkunst. Bearbeitet von A. Hering. Leipzig, 1870. Illus.

Half morocco; 7 x 5 in.

HÉRISSANT, Claude

Cabinet V Shelf 3 No. 18

(Bio-bibliographical notes relating to Herissant family of printers-booksellers, Paris, 1654-1763)

see

WERDET, EDMOND. Histoire du livre en France...3me partie (2), p.220

HERLUISON, H.

Cabinet L Shelf 1 No. 17

Débuts de la lithographie a Orléans [France]. Par H. Herluison. Conservateur du Musée Historique de l'Orleans et du Musée de Jeanne-d'Arc. Orléans, 1902. Illus.

With a list of Orleans artists and their lithographic productions.

Brochure, in manila envelope

HERING, K.F. and COMP.

Cabinet See SPECIMEN BOOKS, TYPES. Printers'. Germany.

Shelf

No.

HERRING, RICHARD

Cabinet RR Paper and paper making, ancient and modern. By Richard Herring. Third edition. With an introductory preface by the late Rev. George Croly. London, 1863.

Shelf 4

No. 13

Cloth; 9 x 6 in.

'S-HERTOGENBOSCH (Bois-le-Duc)

Cabinet AA Printers and publishers, 16th to 18th century

see VERREYT, CH. C.V. (De) Boekdrukkers en uitgevers te 's-Hertogenbosch...

Shelf 3

No. 14.02

HERNANDEZ, M. G. HIJOS de

Cabinet See Specimen Books, Types. Spain.

Shelf

No.

HERRING, RICHARD

Cabinet RR Paper and paper making, ancient and modern. By Richard Herring. With an introduction by the Rev. George Croly. LL.D. London, 1856. (2nd ed.) Frontis.

Shelf 3

No. 34

Cloth; 9 x 5½ x 3/4 in.

HERTZOG, GIOVANNI (J. Hamen de Landois)

Cabinet X Bibliographical note, with printer mark, Hertzog, Venice, 1487-1501.

see KRISTELLER, Dr. PAUL. Italienischen buchdrucker...p.86

Shelf 3

No. 14

HEROLT, GEORGE

Cabinet S See De Vinne, Theodore Low. Notable printers of Italy ... New York, 1910. p. 58.

Shelf 1

No. 29

HERRING, RICHARD

Cabinet RR Practical guide to the varieties and relative values of paper. Illustrated with samples of nearly every description, and especially adapted to the use of merchants...To which is added a history of the art of paper making. London, 1860. Illus.

Shelf 1

No. 1

Cloth; 13 x 10 x 1-5/8 in.

HERWAGEN, JOHANN (Sr. and Jr.)

Cabinet X Biographical sketch, with printer mark, Herwagen father and son, Basel, 1523-1559, 1553-1565.

see HEITZ, PAUL. Basler büchermarken... pp.xxix-xxx, 77-83

Shelf 3

No. 15

HERRICK, C. A.

Cabinet U Early New Englanders: What did they read? [Evidence gathered from wills and inventôries to show that the early settlers did not confine their reading to the Bible alone]. London, 1918.

Shelf 1

No. 1j

In Excerpts relating to printing from "The Library," 1918-19. pp. 1-17 of pencilled folios.

HERRINGMAN, HENRY

Cabinet E See Early Printing in England. London, 1661.

Shelf 4

No. 30

HESS, ANDREA

Cabinet D See Incunabula. Chronica Hungarorum. Buda, 1473.

Shelf 1

No. 21

HERRICK PRESS, The

Cabinet DD Cut book, the Herrick Press. Published by The Herrick Press, Chicago, Ill. n.d.

Shelf 5

No. 23

Brochure, in manila envelope.

HERRMANN, CARL

Cabinet FF (Composing machines, history and development of). Geschichte der setzmaschine und ihre entwickelung bis auf die heutiger zeit. Mit vielen illustrationen. von Carl Herrmann. Im selbstverlage des verfassers: Wien (1900)

Shelf 6

No. 44

Paper; 9 x 6 x 3/8 in. Item in manila envelope.

HESS, ELMER C. (Compiled)

Cabinet QQ Official congressional directory. For the use of the United States Congress. First edition, May, 1929. Compiled under the direction of the joint committee of printing. By Elmer C. Hess.

Shelf 5

No. 4

Cloth; 9¼ x 6 x 1 in.

HERRIN NEWS PRESS, THE

Cabinet See Imprints, United States. Herrin News Press, The. Hal W. Trovillion.

Shelf

No.

HERTFORT, JOHN

Cabinet T Memoire of John Hertford, St. Albans, 1534-1538

see AMES, JOSEPH and WM. HERBERT Typographical Antiquities...vol.3, pp.1435-1436.

Shelf 2

No. 2

HESSELS, J. A.

Cabinet U (A) Bibliographical tour. The author describes a tour through Belgium and Holland, which was undertaken for the examination and collation of the several editions of the "Speculum...presumably printed at Haarlem in the 15th century.

Shelf 1

No. 1c

In Excerpts relating to printing from "The Library," 1908, pp. 282-307.

HESSELS, J.H.

Cabinet AA Shelf 3 No. 45

See Gutenberg-Coster Controversy. Uit de strijdschriften over de Hollandsche uitvinding.

HESSELS, J.H.

Cabinet AA Shelf 3 No. 26

Haarlem de geboorteplaats de boek-drukkunst niet Mainz. Door J.H. Hessels. Haarlem, 1888 Bibliographical study, favors Coster.

Half morocco; 10 x 7 in.

HEUKELOM DZ. F.

Cabinet II Shelf 2 No. 52

(Auction sale catalogue of printing materials, machinery and types from the printing house of F. Heukelom. Amsterdam, 1864).

Item in manila envelope.

HESSELS, J. H.

Cabinet U Shelf 1 No. 1d

Gutenberg documents, So-called. Bibliographical account communicated to "The Library," 1909.

In Excerpts relating to printing from "The Library," pp. 53-106 of pencilled folios.

HESSELS, J. H.

Cabinet 75 Shelf 1 No. 9

Invention of printing, some notes on the: Summary of a paper read before the Bibliographical Society, February 18th,1907.

In Trans. Biblio. Soc., Vol. IX, 1906-1908, pp. 11-14.

HEWITT, JOHN

Cabinet S Shelf 5 No. 14

Who made possible the greatest advance in the art preservative by his foresight and hearty co-operation with the printers of the world. An excerpt from the National Magazine, Sept. 1911.
Biographical.

Bound with other itesm in collection "Printing Processes", item 14.

HESSELS, J. H.

Cabinet U Shelf 4 No. 85

(The) Gutenberg Fiction: A critical examination of the documents relating to Gutenberg, showing that he was not the inventor of printing. London, 1912.

Cloth; 10 x $6\frac{1}{2}$ x 1-3/8 in.

HESSELS, J.H.

Cabinet U Shelf 1 No. 1d

So-called Gutenberg documents, The, by J.H. Hessels.

In Excerpts relating to printing from The Library, 1909, pp.53, 106,165: 1911-12, pp.95,152,180,207 of pencilled folios.

HEYMER, FRIEDRICH

Cabinet Shelf No.

See SPECIMEN BOOKS, TYPES. Printers'. Germany.

HESSELS, J. H.

Cabinet U Shelf 4 No. 83

Gutenberg: Was he the inventor of printing? An historical investigation embodying a criticism on Dr. Vander Linde's "Gutenberg". London, 1882.

Cloth, leather back; 9 x 5-3/8 x $1\frac{1}{4}$ in.

HESTER, ANDREW

Cabinet T Shelf 2 No. 6 [vol.3]

Bio-bibliographical notes relating to Andrew Hester, printer-bookseller, London, 1550.

see
DIBDIN'S "Typographical Antiquities" ...London, 1810-19, vol.iii, p.535

HEYNY, CHRISTMAN

Cabinet Y Shelf 4 No. 4

(Note on the Heyny press at Augsburg, 1481)

see
VOULLIÉME, ERNST. (Die) Deutschen drucker des fünfzehnten jahrhunderts...p.7

HESSELS, J. H. translator

Cabinet U Shelf 4 No. 81

(The) Haarlem legend of the invention of printing by Lourens Janszoon Coster, critically examined by Dr. A. van der Linde. From the Dutch by J. H. Hessels. London, 1871.

Half morocco; 9-3/4 x 6-3/8 x 5/8 in.

HETHERINGTON, H.

Cabinet A Shelf 3 No. 1

Imprint, London, March 14, 1840.

See Periodicals, England. Odd Fellow (The)...1840.

HEYWOOD, JOHN

Cabinet Shelf No.

See Specimen Books, Types. England

HESSELS, J. H.

Cabinet U Shelf 4 No. 84

Haarlem the birth-place of printing. Not Mentz. London, 1887.

Cloth; 10-1/8 x $6\frac{1}{4}$ in.

HEUER, FREDERIC

Cabinet 78 Shelf 2 No. 99

Rouleaux (Les) d'imprimerie: Historique, technique fabrication. Paris, 1901

Half morocco, 9 5/8 x $6\frac{1}{2}$ x $\frac{1}{2}$ in

HIBBERT, JULIAN

Cabinet FF Shelf 4 No. 6

Book of Orphic Hymns...Printed in uncial letters as a typographical experiment, and published for the sum of 3/6 in the year 1827. Printed and published by Julian Hibbert, No. I, Fitzroy Place, Kentish Town.

Half calf; 8-3/8 x $5\frac{1}{4}$ x 3/8 in.

HIBBERT, JULIAN. Printer

Cabinet FF — Shelf 2 — No. 10

See Greek Printing. England. Hibbert, Julian. Kentish-Town, 1828.

HICKOK, W.O., and COMPANY

Cabinet EE — Shelf 4 — No. 60

Catalogue complete bindery outfits. Perfected rulers' equipment. The W.O. Hickok Mfg. Co., Harrisburg, Pa. 1896.

Two catalogues without date: Catalogue No.62 and 66, in same folder, also 1875 catalogue.

In manila envelope.

HICHBORN, WILLIAM

Cabinet QQ — Shelf 3 — No. 22

Trip of the ancients. A memoir of events...By William Hichborn, Malden, 1897.

Preceding contents a brief note "To my relative and friend, Samuel Tilden, Managing Editor of the Malden Evening Press".

Cloth; $7\frac{3}{4}$ x 5 in.

HICKOK (W.O.) MANUFACTURING COMPANY

Cabinet PP — Shelf 5 — No. 11

Catalogue, improved paper ruling machines and bookbinders' machinery. Harrisburg, Penna. 1890. With prices.

Portrait frontispiece; exterior view of factory.

Im. leather; $10\frac{3}{4}$ x 7 x $\frac{3}{4}$ in.

HIDALGO, DIONISIO

Cabinet AA — Shelf 5 — No. 4

Tipografía Española, ó historia de la introducción, propagación y progresos del arte de la imprenta en Españo ... autor Fray Francisco Mendez ... Segunda edición corregida y adicionada por Don Dionisio Hidalgo. Madrid, 1861.

Half morocco; 9-3/4 x $6\frac{1}{2}$ in.

HIERAT, ANTON

Cabinet X — Shelf 3 — No. 20

Brief bio-bibliographical note, Hierat, publisher, Cologne, 1597-1627.

see HEITZ, PAUL. Kölner büchermarken...p.xxvi

HIERATIC WRITING see HIEROGLYPHICS

Cabinet — Shelf — No.

HIEROGLYPHICS

Cabinet K — Shelf 1 — No. 25

Bilder schriften der renaissance

See Volkmann, Ludwig. Bilder schriften der renaissance...Leipzig, 1923.

HIEROGLYPHICS.

Cabinet V — Shelf 6 — No. 29

Catalogue des signes hieroglyphiques des l'Imprimerie Nationale. 2nd. edition. Paris, 1873.

Half morocco; 10 x 7 x 3/8 in.

HIEROGLYPHICS

Cabinet L — Shelf 2 — No. 45

Egypt in the neolithic and archaic periods. By E.A. Wallis Budge. Illustrated. Second edition. London, 1904. Illus.

With several specimens of hieratic writing.

Cloth; $7\frac{3}{4}$ x 4-7/8

HIEROGLYPHICS

Cabinet K — Shelf 1 — No. 26

Egyptian book of the dead...With an introduction and complete translation. With 99 plates reporduced in facsimile. By Charles H. S. Davis, New York, 1894.

Cloth; $17\frac{1}{2}$ x $12\frac{1}{2}$ in.

HIEROGLYPHICS

Cabinet GG — Shelf 1 — No. 48

Original cutting of hieroglpphic type faces) Hieroglyphen in originalschnitte. Berthold A-G. Berlin S.W. Bauer & Co., Stuttgart. n.d.

Paper; $11\frac{1}{2}$ x $7\frac{3}{4}$ in. Item in manila envelope.

HIEROGLYPHICS see also Writing

Cabinet — Shelf — No.

HIERONYMUS

Cabinet D — Shelf 2 — No. 42

Commentaria in Biblia. Venice 1498. Joannes et Gregorius de Gregoriis. (2 vols.)

Gesamt-Kat. ; Hain 8581.

Calf; 12[illegible] x $9\frac{1}{2}$ in.

HIERONYMUS, (St. Jerome)

Cabinet D — Shelf 2 — No. 38

Epistolae de San Hieronymo volgare. Ferrara, 1497. Per Lorenzo de Rossi.

Gesamt-Kat. Brunet [illegible]98.

Full morocco, gilt; 12[illegible] x 9-1/8 x 1[illegible] in.

HIERONYMUS.

Cabinet D — Shelf 1 — No. 47

Vitas Patrum. De laude et effectu virtutem... Venice, 1483. Ottaviano Scottus.

Gesamt-Kat. ; Hain 8599. Parchment, 8-3/4 x $6\frac{1}{4}$ x 2 ins.

HIERONYMUS (S. Eusebius)

Cabinet 14 — Shelf 2 — No. 21 — 2 Vols.

Epistolae, cum praefat. Joan. Andreae episc. Aleriensis. Romae per Conrad Swaynheym et Arnold Pannarts. 1468.

Full morocco; each vol. $16\frac{1}{4}$ x $11\frac{1}{4}$ x 3 ins. Hain 8551-8552.

HIERSEMANN, KARL WILHELM

Cabinet Q — Shelf 1 — No. 2

Biographical comments.

see BRESLAUER, MARTIN. Sum Gedenken. Karl Wilhelm Hiersemann.

HIERSEMANN, KARL W.

Cabinet 75 Shelf 2 No. 6

Gesamtkatalog der Wiegendrucke. Herausgegeben von der Kommission fur den Gesamtkatalog der Wiegendrucke. Band I. Abana-Alexius. Leipzig, 1925. Review of book with above title, by Alfred W. Pollard.

In Transactions of the Bibliographical Society, "The Library," Vol. VI, 1925-1926, pp. 285-88.

HIERSEMANN, KARL W.

Cabinet Y Shelf 3 No. 93

Werden und Wirken: Ein festgruss Karl W. Hiersemann. Zugesandt am 3 Sept. 1924, zum 70ten geburtstag und 40 jahrigen bestehen seiner firma. Leipzig, 1924.
No.25 of 50 copies printed.

A tribute to Hiersemann on his 70th birthday. Contains many articles related to the history of the arts of the book.

Boards; 11 x 7-7/8 in.

HIERSEMANN, KARL W.

Cabinet 75 Shelf 2 No. 5

Werden und Wirken. Ein Festgruss...zum siebzigsten Geburtstag. Book with above title reviewed by Victor Scholderer.

In Transactions of the Bibliographical Society, "The Library," Vol. V, 1924-1925, pp. 376-379.

HIGDEN (Ranulphus)

Cabinet 17 Shelf 2 No. 4

Polychronicon, 1482.

see

INCUNABULA. Polychronicon.

HIGHTON, ALBERT H.

Cabinet LL Shelf 3 No. 40

Practical proof reading. Chicago, United Typothetae of America, 1926. Illus.

HIGHTON, ALEXANDER G.

Cabinet Shelf No.

See Imprints, United States. Highton, Alexander G. Newark, N.J.

HIGHTON, ALEX. G., Inc

Cabinet P Shelf 2 No. 57

Newark, New Jersey, 1935.

see

ADVERTISING TYPOGRAPHY. Highton ....

HIGMAN, JEAN

Cabinet D Shelf 1 No. 63

Paris, 1497.

see

INCUNABULA (loose leaves) Higman...

HILDEBRAND, JOHANN CHRISTOPH

Cabinet LL Shelf 1 No. 21

Handbuch für buchdrucker-lehrlinge...Nebst einem alphabetischen bezeichnisse von 709 druckkereien in 317 Städten. Herausgegeben von Joh. Chr. Hildebrand. Eisenach, 1835.

Boards; 7-1/8 x 4¼ x ½ in.

HILDEBURN, CHARLES R.

Cabinet R Shelf 5 No. 19 2 Vols.

(A) Century of printing: The issues of the press in Pennsylvania 1685-1784. By Charles R. Hildeburn. Philadelphia, 1885 and 1886. 2 vols.
Has chronological list of printers in Pennsylvania before 1785.

HILDEBURN, CHARLES R.

Cabinet R Shelf 5 No. 15

(The) First book printed South of Massachusetts. Nt Leed's Temple of Wisdom, but William Penn's Excellent Privilege of Liberty and Property: A lost work by the Founder of Pennsylvania. By C. R. Hildeburn.
In volume "Early printing and printers in America. Excerpts from Pennsylvania Magazine p. 61.

Half morocco; 9-7/8 x 6-5/8 in.

HILDEBURN, CHARLES R.

Cabinet R Shelf 3 No. 178

Sketches of printers and printing in Colonial New York. By C.R. Hildeburn, New York, 1895. Illus., portraits, and facsimiles.
Includes a chronological list of New York printers, 1693 to 1789, on pp. XIII and XIV.

Half vellum and boards; 7-3/4 x 5¼ in.

HILDRETH, E.L. and COMPANY

Cabinet EE Shelf 1 No. 55

Specimens of type in the office of E.L. Hildredth & Co. (Incorporated), at Brattleboro, Vermont, 1932.

Boards; 9 x 6 x ⅝ in.

HILL, A. F.,

Cabinet NN Shelf 3 No. 12

Secrets of the Sanctum: An inside view of an editor's life.

By A. F. Hill. Philadelphia. 1875.

Cloth: 7½x5¼"

HILL, BENJAMIN THOMAS

Cabinet R Shelf 4 No. 25 2 Vols.

Thomas, Isaiah. The Diary of Isaiah Thomas, 1805-1828. Edited with an introduction and notes by Benjamin Thomas Hill. Worcester, Mass. Published by the American Antiquary Society. 1909. 2 vols.

Cloth; 10 x 6¼ in.

HILL, GEORGE BIRKBECK

Cabinet LL Shelf 3 No. 1.01

Boswell's proof-sheets. (Excerpt from the "Atlantic", Nov., 1894.)

Item 6 in vol. with binder's title "Proofreading: Pamphlets". Bound, 1932.

Hill, John

Cabinet F Shelf 2 No. 102

The power of water-dock against the scurvy; with marks to know that disease in all its states; instances of its being mistaken for other disorders; and rules of life for those afflicted with it, by the late Sir John Hill ... First American from the tenth London edition. Salem, Printed by Joshua Cushing, 1801.
24 p. 19½cm.

In envelope.

HILL, JOHN ALEXANDER

Cabinet Q Shelf 2 No. 27

Some of the writings of John A. Hill. Memorial volume. Privately printed for his friends. (New York, n.d. after 1905)
With portrait

Boards; 8-5/8 x 5-5/8 in.

HILL, JOHN C.

Cabinet LL Shelf 3 No. 3

Manual of style for composing room. By John C. Hill, Proof-Reading Department, The Stone Printing and Mfg. Co. Roanoke, Va. 1901. Pamphlet; 9¼ x 5¾ in.

Item in book with binder's title "Punctuation, Greek Composition, Office Style".

HILLIARD, WILLIAM

Cabinet 80 Shelf 2 No. 23

Cambridge (Mass.) 1804. Imprint of Wm. Hilliard.

See PERIODICALS, United States. Literary Miscellany (The)....Cambridge (Mass.) 1804.

HINGSTON, EDWARD P.

Cabinet NN Shelf 1 No. 5

(The) Genial showman: Reminiscences of the life of Artemus Ward, and pictures of a showman's career in the western world. With numerous illustrations. Third edition. London (1870). Col. frontispiece.

Chatto and Windus advertisements at end of book.

Half morocco; 7-5/8 x 5½ x 1-3/4 in.

HILL, JOSEPH

Cabinet U Shelf 5 No. 68

Book makers of old Birmingham; authors, printers and booksellers. Birmingham, 1907. illus. facs.

Stamped cloth; 10¾ x 8-5/8 in.

HIMES, GEORGE H.

Cabinet R Shelf 4 No. 163

History of the Press of Oregon, 1839-1850. By George H. Himes. Portland, 1902. Excerpt from The Quarterly of the Oregon Historical Society. Vol. III, No. 4, 1902.

Half morocco; 9½ x 6¼ in.

HINGSTON, EDWARD P.

Cabinet NN Shelf 1 No. 6

(The) Genial showman. Being reminiscences of the life of Artemus Ward, and pictures of a showman's career in the western world. By Edward P. Hingston. New York, Harper Brothers, 1870.

Cloth; 9¼ x 5-3/4 in.

HILL, LAWRANCE L.

Cabinet QQ Shelf 3 No. 16

Los Angeles in three centuries, 1631-1929.

see CALIFORNIA. Los Angeles in three centuries...

HIND, A.M.

Cabinet J Shelf 3 No. 19

Engraving & etching, a short history of. For the use of collectors and students. With a full bibliography, classified list and index of engravers. With frontispiece in photogravure, and 110 illustrations in the text. Boston, 1908.

Cloth; 9½ x 6½ x 1¾ in.

HIRSCH, CAROL CHRISTIAN

Cabinet X Shelf 1 No. 44

Librorum ab anno I. usque annum L. Seculi XVI. typis exscriptorum ex libraria quadam supellectile, Norimbergae privatis sumptibus in communem usum collecta et observata Millenarius I-IV. speciminis loco ad supplendos annalium typographicorum labores editi. Norimbergae, 1746-49. 4 parts. [Our copy lacks part I].

Historical bibliographical of printing from the year 1501 to 1550.

Bound in with Orlandi's "Artis Typograph-

cont'd

HILL, ROWLAND.

Cabinet FF Shelf 2 No. 40

[Inventor of first printing press to print on both sides of a continuous web(roll) of paper--the Web Perfectory Press.]

See Inventions, Patents for. Abridgments of specifications, Vol. I...London, 1859. pp. 192,193, No. 6762, 1835.

Half morocco; 7-5/8 x 5 x 2 in.

HIND, A.M.

Cabinet J Shelf 3 No. 19

Short history of engraving and etching. For the use of collectors and students. With full bibliography, classified list and index of engravers. By A.M. Hind. With frontispiece in photogravure and 110 illustrations in the text. Boston, 1908.

Cloth; 9-3/8 x 6-3/8 x 1¾ in.

HIRSCH, CAROL CHRISTIAN cont'd

Cabinet X Shelf 1 No. 44

icae progressibus 1457-1500".

Boards, vellum back; 8-5/8 x 7 x 1½ in.

HILL, WILLIAM

Cabinet T Shelf 2 No. 6 [vol.4]

Books printed by Wm. Hill, London, 1584. Bibliographical notes.

see DIBDIN'S "Typographical Antiquities" ...London, 1810-19, vol.IV, p.322

HINDLEY, CHARLES

Cabinet U Shelf 2 No. 93

Life and times of James Catnach (late of Seven Dials). London, 1878. Colored illustrations, with 230 woodcuts, 42 of them by Bewick.

Cloth; 7¾ x 5-1/8 x 1-3/8 in.

HIRSCHFELD, A.B.PRESS

Cabinet P Shelf 5 No. 31.01

Type specimen book, and examples of typography. Denver: Typographic Studio, The A.B. Hirschfeld Press.

Boards; 17 x 12 in.

HILL, WILLIAM H.

Cabinet R Shelf 3 No. 188

Brief history of the printing press in Washington, Saratoga and Warren Counties State of New York. Together with A Check List of their Publications prior to 1825...Privately Printed. Fort Edward, New York, 1930. Printed by the Tory Press, Rutland, Vermont.

No. 27 of an edition of 54 copies.

Cloth; 9½ x 6-3/8 x ⅝ in.

HINDU

Cabinet II Shelf 3 No. 61

Language characters.

See LANGUAGE CHARACTERS. Examples of Hindu...

HIRTH, GEORGE

Cabinet Y Shelf 3 No. 98

See Biographies, Publishers.

HIST, JOHANN and KONRAD

Cabinet Y, Shelf 4, No. 4

(Note on Hist and his printing at Speyer, 1512-1515)

see

VOULLIÉME, ERNST. (Die) Deutschen drucker des fünfzehnten jahrhunderts...p.102

HISTOIRE DU LIVRE EN FRANCE

Cabinet V, Shelf 3, No. 15 to 19

See Werdet, Edmond. Histoire du livre en France, depuis les plus reculés jusqu 'en 1789. Paris, 1861-64. 5 Vols.

HISTORICAL DOCUMENTS RELATING TO PRINTING

Cabinet X, Shelf 5, No. 2

Broadsides, early 17th and 18th century documents relating to regulation of printing in Great Britain, Holland, Germany, Italy and France.

Hal morocco; 14½ x 10-1/3 x 1¼ in.

HISTORICAL Society of McLean Co. Illinois.

Cabinet QQ, Shelf 3, No. 14

McLean County Historical Society. Bloomington, Ill.

see

McLEAN COUNTY HISTORICAL SOCIETY...

HISTORICAL SOCIETY OF PENNSYLVANIA

Cabinet R, Shelf 3, No. 71

Publications of the Historical Society of Pennsylvania, 1852 to 1869. Includes a collection of addresses, circulars, cards of admission, and history of the Society.

In this there are items relating to "Early Printing in New York", "Early Printing in Pennsylvania," William Bradford, and Andrew Bradford.

Half morocco; 9¼ x 6 in.

HISTORICAL SOCIETY OF WISCONSIN (see)

Cabinet, Shelf, No.

State Historical Society of Wisconsin...

HISTORISCH SPEL DER BOEKDRUKKUNST see

Cabinet AA, Shelf 4, No. 6.01

VAN ARUM, Gebroeders.

HISTORY OF PRINTING (see)

Cabinet, Shelf, No.

PRINTING, Historical

HISTORY OF PRINTING PRESSES

Cabinet, Shelf, No.

See PRINTING PRESSES. (History of)

HISTORY OF TYPEFOUNDING AND TYPES (see)

Cabinet, Shelf, No.

SPECIMEN BOOKS, Types

also see TYPES, Printing

TYPES, Printing. Literature of

HITCHCOCK, FREDERICK H. (Editor)

Cabinet S, Shelf 4, No. 99

(The) Building of a book: A series of practical articles ... With an introduction by Theodore L. DeVinne. Edited by Frederick H. Hitchcock. New York, 1906.

Cloth; 8½ x 5½ in.

HITCHCOCK, FREDERICK H.

Cabinet MM, Shelf 7, No. 36

How to build a good book from your manuscript, containing suggestions of value for authors and others whose works are ready for printing...Issued by The Special Book Department of Braunworth & Company. New York, 1925. Illus.

Presentation copy by the author.

Boards; 7¾ x 5¼ x 3/8 in.

HITTORP, GOTTFRIED

Cabinet X, Shelf 3, No. 20

Brief bio-bibliographical sketch, Hittorp, publisher, Cologne, 1490-1573.

see

HEITZ, PAUL. Kölner büchermarken.... p.xxvi

HITZ, JOHN

Cabinet II, Shelf 4, No. 32

Bell, Alexander Melville. By John Hitz, Superintendent of the Volta Bureau, Washington D.C. 1905. With portrait frontispiece.

Bound in with two other items on Bell's "Visible Speech".

Half morocco; 11½ x 8½ in.

HOAG AUTOMATIC PRESS COMPANY

Cabinet EE, Shelf 4, No. 61

Circulars and specimens showing the range of work done on the Hoag Automatic Press. San Francisco, Calif. Factory, Hartford, Conn. 1910.

Items in manila envelope.

HOARD, WILLIAM DEMPSTER

Cabinet Q, Shelf 2, No. 29

Life of William Dempster Hoard. By George William Rankin, Fort Atkinson, Wisconsin. Wm. D. Hoard & Sons Co., 1925. Illus.

Cloth; 9-1/8 x 5-5/8 in.

HOARE, H. W.

Cabinet U, Shelf 1, No. 43

Evolution of the English Bible. A historical sketch of the successive versions from 1382 to 1885. Second edition. With portraits and specimen-pages from old Bibles. London, 1902.

Cloth; 8-1/8 x 5-3/8 x 1½ in.

HOARE, H. W.

Cabinet S, Shelf 4, No. 120

Lineage of the English Bible. By H. W. Hoare. An excerpt from Harper's Monthly Magazine, March, 1902. Illus.

Item 7 in volume "About the Bible: Excerpt from Magazines."

Half morocco; 10¼ x 6-7/8 in.

HOBART, JAMES F.

Cabinet RR · Shelf 4 · No. 39

Paper-making industry, the. By James F. Hobart. Excerpt from Engineering Magazine, Jan., 1892.

Item with other excerpts and pamphlets relating to paper. Folder; 10½ x 7½ x 1 in.

HOBART & HOBBINS

Cabinet FF · Shelf 2 · No. 32

New England Type, Stereotype and Electrotype Foundry, Boston. Circular dated March 30, 1864, issued by Hobart & Robbins announcing a deep cut in prices necessitating them to with-draw from the Type Founders Association of the United States.

Item in manila envelope.

HOBART & ROBBINS

Cabinet DD · Shelf 3 · No. 23

See SPECIMEN BOOKS, TYPES, United States. New England Type Foundry...

HOBBIES

Cabinet · Shelf · No.

See Collectors' Hobbies.

HOBBY CLUB OF NEW YORK.

Cabinet 73 · Shelf 2 · No. 3

Curiosities of early economic literature. An address to his fellow members. By R. A. Seligman. Privately printed by John Henry Nash. San Francisco, 1920.

Boards; 15½ x 11 in.

HOBSON, CHARLES W.

Cabinet LL · Shelf 6 · No. 73

Manchester Guardian Advertising Review; a brief notice of some of the theories and principles of advertisement and of the contributary arts. Arranged and produceed by Charles W. Hobson, July 16, 1924.

Half morocco; 15¾ x 11¼ in.

HOBSON, G. D.

Cabinet 75 · Shelf 2 · No. 5

Bookbindings with painted plaquettes, on a group of. By G. D. Hobson. June, 1924.

In Transactions of the Bibliographical Society, "The Library," Vol. [illegible], 1924-1925 pp. 47-58.

HOCHFEDER, KASPER

Cabinet Y · Shelf 4 · No. 4

(Note on Hochfeder and his printing at Nuremberg, 1490, and Metz, 1498)

see

VOULLIÉME, ERNST (Die) Deutschen drucker des fünfzehnten jahrhunderts...p.93, also p.84, also p.57

HODGE, ALLEN and CAMPBELL

Cabinet 80 · Shelf 2 · No. 15

Congressional Record (The), New York, 1790. [Printers and proprietors]. Hodge, Allen and Campbell.

(1 issue only).

Item in manila envelope.

HODGKIN, JOHN ELIOT

Cabinet T · Shelf 1 · No. 73 · 3 vols.

Rariora: Being notes of some of the printed books, manuscripts, historical documents, medals, engravings, pottery, etc., etc. collected (1858-1900) By John Eliot Hodgkin. London. 3 vols.

Vols. 2 and 3 especially contain much valuable material relating to printing, including facsimile plates and illustrations.

Cloth; each volume, 11¼ x 8-3/4 in.

HODGSON, C.F. & SON

Cabinet EE · Shelf 2 · No. 45

See SPECIMEN BOOKS, TYPES. Printers'. Gr. Britain

HODGSON, THOMAS

Cabinet FF · Shelf 1 · No. 72

(An) Essay on the origin and progress of stereotype printing; including a description of the various processes. Newcastle; Printed by and for S. Hodgson. 1820.

Signed copy.

Half Russia; 9 x 5⅝ in.

HODNETT, EDWARD

Cabinet 72 · Shelf 2 · No. 43

English woodcuts, 1480-1535. Illustrated Monograph No. XXII. London: Printed for The Bibliographical Society at the Oxford University Press, 1935 (for 1934).

Boards, linen back; 11 x 8-7/8 in.

HODSON, JAMES SHIRLEY

Cabinet KK · Shelf 3 · No. 2

Printing trade charities, a history of the. By James Shirley Hodson...London, 1883. Frontispiece.

Cloth; 8½ x 5-5/8 x ½ in.

HOE, PETER J.

Cabinet FF · Shelf 1 · No. 19

Autograph on title page of Hoe's "Hints on electrotyping and stereotyping". New York, 1875.

Cloth; 8½ x 5¾ in.

HOE, RICHARD M.

Cabinet S · Shelf 1 · No. 84

Biographical obituary notice. Excerpt from New York Herald, June 9, 1886.

Item inserted in book with title "R. HOE & CO.'S PROGRESS, 1834-1888". Tucker.

HOE, RICHARD MARCH

Cabinet 81 · Shelf 2 · No. 35

Complimentary dinner to Col. Richard M. Hoe, Jan. 28, 1851. In connection with installation of first 8-feeder Type-Revolving (Lightning) Press in office of N.Y. Sun. Excerpts, newspaper clippings.

Items in MUNSELL, JOEL. "Printers Scraps", Vol.VI, pp.21-26.

HOE, RICHARD, M.

Cabinet 17 · Shelf 2 · No. 1

History of the House of R.M. Hoe, 1784-1877. Typescript.

Item on fol.1 of HENRY STEVEN'S "Typographical Miscellanies", vol.1-A

HOE, RICHARD M.

Cabinet FF Shelf 3 No. 64

(History of the Web Perfecting Presses and Folding devices.) Richard M. Hoe et el. complainants v. Boston Daily Advertiser Corporation et el, defendants...Boston, 1886. Illus., and diagrams.

Boards; 11 x 7½ in.

HOE, ROBERT

Cabinet PP Shelf 2 No. 10

Bookbinding as an art. An address. Printed in Transactions of the Grolier Club. Part I, 1885. p.42.

Paper; 9½ x 7-1/8 in.

HOE, ROBERT

Cabinet 81 Shelf 2 No. 39

Reminiscence of Robert Hoe. By Laurie Todd. Newspaper clipping, circa 1854.

Item in MUNSELL, JOEL. "Printers Scraps." Vol.X, p.16.

HOE, RICHARD MARCH.

Cabinet FF Shelf 2 No. 40

Patent issued to him in Great Britain, through his agent and in the name of his agent, William Newton, for his "Lightning Type-revolving cylinder press, No. 11, 688, May 4, 1847.

See Inventions, Patents for. Abridgments of specifications,Vol.I,...London, 1859.

This press was the fastest in the world until 1860, when it gave way to the web perfecting press of Bullock.

Half morocco; 7-5/8 x 5 x 2 in.

HOE, ROBERT

Cabinet FF Shelf 6 No. 2 (2 vols.)

(Bookbindings) 176 historic and artistic bookbindings dating from the 15th to the present time. Pictured by etchings, artotypes, and lithographs after the originals selected from the library of Robert Hoe. (2 vols.) Dodd, Mead & Company, New York, 1895. The DeVinne Press.

One of 200 copies only, all printed upon Imperial Japanese paper.

Half morocco; 14 x 11 in.

HOE, ROBERT

Cabinet S Shelf 1 No. 80

(A) Short history of the printing press, and of the improvements in printing machinery from the time of Gutenberg up to the present day. Printed and published for Robert Hoe, New York, 1902. Illus.

Half morocco; 10¾ x 8-1/8 in.

HOE, RICHARD M.

Cabinet 27 Shelf 1 No. 5

Printing press patent, the Hoe. [Communication to the editor of the Printers' Circular]

Item in the Printers' Circular, vol.5, No.1, March, 1870, p.15

HOE, ROBERT

Stack A Shelf 1 & 2 Number 66

Bullen, Henry Lewis. Episode in the life of Robert Hoe, founder of the firm of R. Hoe & Company. Account in The Inland Printer, Vol. LXVI, 621. Portrait.

HOE, R. & Company

Cabinet Q Shelf 5 No. 11

Established 1803. Present location, 504-520 Grand Street, New York. Brief historical account of the house of R. Hoe & Co.

see

BONNER, WILLIAM THOMPSON. New York, the World's Metropolis...p.555

HOE, RICHARD MARCH.

Stack Shelf Number

See Printing Presses. Hoe, Richard March, and the evolution of fast printing presses.

HOE, ROBERT.

Stack A Shelf 1&2 Number 66

Episode in the life of Robert Hoe, founder of the firm of R. Hoe & Co., by Henry Lewis Bullen, in The Inland Printer, vol. LXVI, p. 621. Portrait of Richard March Hoe.

HOE, R. and Company

Cabinet FF Shelf 1 No. 1

Hints to stereotypers and electrotypers. New York, 1871. Brochure.

Item 4 in vol. with binder's title "Electrotyping and Stereotyping Pamphlets".

HOE, RICHARD MARCH

Cabinet 17, 19, 20 Shelf No.

Typographical Miscellanies (37 vols.). Compiled for the R.M. Hoe Library, by Henry Stevens.

see

SCRAP BOOKS RELATING TO PRINTING. Typographical Miscellanies....

HOE, ROBERT

Cabinet MM Shelf 5 No. 35

Origin, progress and present condition of R. Hoe & Co.

See pp.214-215 MacKellar's American Printer...Philadelphia, 1866.

HOE, ROBERT, & COMPANY

Cabinet EE Shelf 4 No. 73

(Bulletins, various numbers.) Electrotyping and photo-engraving machinery, stereotyping machinery, machinery for postage and revenue stamps, bank notes, etc. n.d.

Several bulletins bound in one vol.

Half morocco loose leaf binder; 8½ x 12¼ in.

HOE, RICHARD M. and COMPANY

Cabinet S Shelf 1 No. 84

Rise and Progress of a great firm - New Grand Street Offices - New fire-proof factory on Sheriff St. - The old works - Hoe's saws and presses - The Perfecting Press.

Excerpt from the N.Y. Daily TRIBUNE, July 6, 1869.

Item in envelope inserted in book with title "R. HOE & Co.'S PROGRESS, 1834-1888". Tucker.

HOE, ROBERT

Cabinet QQ Shelf 3 No. 31

Reference to his distress on his arrival in New York from England and his eventual success.

In THORBURN, GRANT. Life and writings...New York, 1852, pp. 55-58.

HOE, ROBERT & COMPANY.

Cabinet EE Shelf 4 No. 74

(Catalogue, n.d.). Automatic curved stereotype plate finishing and cooling machine. Four in one. Patented. R. Hoe & Co.'s. New York.

Item in manila envelope.

HOE, ROBERT & COMPANY.

Cabinet EE Shelf 4 No. 74

(Catalogue, n.d.). The "Unique" Press, single-plate, single-roll, stereotype newspaper press ... (Patent applied for), R. Hoe & Co. New York.

Item in manila envelope.

HOE, ROBERT, & Co.

Cabinet EE Shelf 4 No. 63 Also 64 Dupl.

(Catalogue and price list, 1860) Single and double cylinder and type revolving printing machines, power presses, Adams patent, Washington and Smith hand presses, etc. New York...and on Foundry Street, Boston, Mass. Francis Hart & Co., Printers, N.Y.

Paper; 9¾ x 6-3/8 in. In manila envelope.

HOE, ROBERT, & CO.

Cabinet EE Shelf 4 No. 65 2 copies

(Catalogue and price list, 1867). Printing machines, power presses (Adam's Patent) Washington and Smith hand presses, self-inking machines, etc...New York...Boston...London. Francis Hart & Co., Printers. New York.

Cloth; 10¾ x 7½ x ½ in.

HOE, ROBERT, & Co.

Cabinet EE Shelf 4 No. 66

(Catalogue and price list, 1871). Manufacturers of type-revolving, perfecting, single and double cylinder and Adams' printing machines ...New York...London.

Cloth; 13-1/8 x 10¼ x 3/8 in.

HOE, ROBERT, & Co.

Cabinet EE Shelf 4 No. 67

(Catalogue and price list, 1873) Printing machines...Every article connected with the art of letter-press, copper-plate, and lithographic printing and bookbinding, stereotyping and electrotyping, always on hand. New York...London.

Preface dated Jan. 1873.

Cloth; 13¾ x 11 x 3/8 in.

HOE, ROBERT, & Co.

Cabinet EE Shelf 4 No. 70

(Catalogue, 1879) Printing presses, printing materials, bookbinders' machinery, and saws. Electrotypers' and stereotypers' machinery... Illus. pamphlet.

Item in manila envelope.

HOE, ROBERT, & Co.

Cabinet EE Shelf 4 No. 68

Catalogue, 1881, of printing presses and printers' materials. New York, 504 Grand Street. 1881.

Paper; 10[illegible] x 7[illegible] x 3/8 in.

HOE, ROBERT, & Co.

Cabinet EE Shelf 4 No. 69

Catalogue, 1881, of stereotyping and electrotyping machinery. R. Hoe & Co., New York, 1881.

Boards; 10¾ x 7¼ in.

HOE, ROBERT, & Co.

Cabinet EE Shelf 4 No. 70

Catalogue and price list, 1886-7. R. Hoe & Co's catalogue of printing presses.

On pp.45-50 "Hints on make-ready for cylinder presses".

Item in manila envelope.

HOE, ROBERT, & Co.

Cabinet EE Shelf 4 No. 72

(Catalogue, illus. n.d. circa 1897) R. Hoe & Co.'s patent type and stereotype fast newspaper pamphlet and book perfecting machines.

Item in manila envelope.

HOE, ROBERT, & Co.

Cabinet EE Shelf 4 No. 71

Catalogue, 1897, and price list of printing materials. Pamphlet.

Item in manila envelope.

HOE, ROBERT, & Co.

Cabinet EE Shelf 4 No. 71

Catalogue of machinery and materials for electrotyping, stereotyping and photo-engraving. New York, 1898.

Printed by The DeVinne Press.

On p. following index, views of the main offices and works in New York and London.

Pamphlet in manila envelope.

HOE, ROBERT, & Co.

Cabinet EE Shelf 4 No. 71

(Catalogue and price list, [illegible]) Improved printing presses. Illus. pamphlet.

On front page a view of main entrance to R. Hoe & Co.'s office on Grand Street, N.Y.

Item in manila envelope.

HOE, ROBERT, & Co.

Cabinet EE Shelf 4 No. 72

(Catalogue, 19[illegible]0) R. Hoe & Co.'s improved stop-cylinder, two-color, two-revolution and flat bed perfecting presses.

On cover of this pamphlet a reproduction of the first American [illegible] of Gutenberg. On last page, a view of the Hoe works in New York.

Item in manila envelope.

HOE, ROBERT, & Co.

Cabinet EE Shelf 4 No. 72

(Catalogue and price list. circa 1900) Improved rotary offset presses for printing from zinc or aluminum plates.

Item in manila envelope.

HOE, ROBERT & COMPANY

Cabinet EE Shelf 4 No. 74

Catalogue, 1901. Single large cylinder, news and job and flat-bed newspaper presses.

Item in manila envelope.

HOE, ROBERT, & Co.

Cabinet EE Shelf 4 No. 72

(Catalogue, 1902) Improved lithographic, metal-printing and rotary aluminum presses. Pamphlet.

Has pictures of models to R. Hoe & Co.

In manila envelope.

HOE, ROBERT, & Co.

Cabinet EE Shelf 4 No. 72

(Catalogue, 1903) Patented improved two-roll, three-roll and four-roll two plate wide also double supplement newspaper perfecting presses.

Pamphlet in manila envelope.

HOE, ROBERT, & Co.

Cabinet EE Shelf 4 No. 72

(Catalogue, 1903) A few of R. Hoe & Co.'s newspaper perfecting presses with fast speed rotary folders, and the latest patented improvements.

Item in manila envelope.

HOE, ROBERT & COMPANY.

Cabinet S Shelf 5 No. 14

(The) Master Printer's Return: What Gutenberg saw amid the roar of a modern printing wonderland. By Harrison Houghton. Published by R. Hoe & Co. New York, 1913. Illus.

Bound with other items in collection "Printing Processes." item 8.

HOE, ROBERT & COMPANY.

Cabinet S Shelf 1 No. 84

Stephen D. Tucker's narrative of his life long connection with Robert Hoe & Co., New York, 1913. Typewritten manuscript, not published

In latter years Mr. Tucker was a member of the firm.

Half morocco; oblong, 8½ x 13¼ in.

HOE, ROBERT, & Co.

Cabinet EE Shelf 4 No. 72

(Catalogue and price list, 1910) Some of the rotary electrotype presses...Patented and manufactured by R. Hoe & Co. New York - London. (2 pamphlets)

Item in manila envelope.

HOE, R. and Company

Cabinet EE Shelf 4 No. 74

Newspaper printing presses. Bulletin No.251. Two-Plate-Wide Machines. R. Hoe & Co. New York-London...n.d.

Half morocco, oblong; 8½ x 11-3/4 in.

HOE, ROBERT, & Co.

Cabinet EE Shelf 4 No. 72

What may be seen in the Government Printing Offices. Booklet which shows some of the improved machines supplied to the various printing departments of the United States Government. R. Hoe & Co. New York, London. Illus. booklet.

Has views of the Hoe & Co.'s works in London.

Item in manila envelope.

HOE, R. and Company

Cabinet FF Shelf 1 No. 19

Hints on electrotyping and stereotyping... New York. R. Hoe & Co., 1875. Illus.

Has autograph of Peter J. Hoe on title page.

Cloth; 8½ x 5¾ in.

HOE, R. & Company

Cabinet FF Shelf 6 No. 7

Patent newspaper stop and cylinder presses. (Engravings with descriptions). New York, 1881.

With prices.

Oblong, cloth; 12 x 17-7/8 in.

HOEPLI, ULRICO

Cabinet AA Shelf 2 No. 40

(Incunabula. Manuscripts. Books with woodcuts of the 16th century. Sale catalogue) Manuscritti, incunabuli e libri figurati del secólo XVI. 18 Giugno, 1930. Vendita all'Asta Milano, 1930.

pp.136 of descriptive bibliographical text; 114 plates, facsimiles and reproductions.

Paper; 12¼ x 9-3/8 x 1¼ in.

HOE, ROBERT. & Company

Cabinet FF Shelf 1 No. 87

Hints on electrotyping and stereotyping. R. Hoe & Co. New York. 1875 Illus.

Cloth; 9-1/8 x 6¼ x 3/8 in.

HOE, R. and COMPANY

Cabinet S Shelf 1 No. 84

Presses and printing machinery., R. Hoe and Co.'s. Excerpt from "THE DAILY PICAYUNE", Sunday Nov.14, 1875.

Item in envelope inserted in book with title "R. HOE & Co.'s PROGRESS" 1834-1888. Tucker.

HOEVEN, A. VAN DER, Typefoundry

See Specimen Books, Types, Holland

HOE, ROBERT & COMPANY

Cabinet S Shelf 1 No. 77

History of Robert Hoe & Company, New York. By Stephen D. Tucker; copied accurately from the original Ms. in the possession of Edwin D. Tucker. 1900. Portrait of R. Hoe bound in. Holograph letter signed Eugene Smith to S. D. Tucker.

Half morocco; 11-1/8 x 8¾ in.

HOE, ROBERT & COMPANY.

Cabinet EE Shelf 4 No. 63

Price list, 1871. Reduced price list for printers, electrotypers, stereotypers, lithographers, and binders. R. Hoe & Co., New York, 31 Gold Street, 1871.

Cloth; 7½ x 4-3/8 in. Item in Manila Envelope.

HOEYNCK, F. A.

Cabinet Y Shelf 2 No. 47

Geschichte der kirchlichen liturgie des bisthums Augsburg. Mit beilagen; Monumenta liturgiae Augustanae. Augsburg, 1889.

Historical account of the earliest liturgies from the bishopric of Augsburg, 1489-1584.

Boards; 9¼ x 6¼ x 7/8 in.

HOE, ROBERT, & CO.

Cabinet EE Shelf 4 No. 62 2 copies

List of prices of printing materials, etc. New York. 1854.

On front and back cover, pictures of the Hoe factories on Gold and Broome Streets.

Half morocco; 9¼ x 6 x 3/8 in. Second copy, original paper cover; in manila envelope.

HOE, ROBERT & COMPANY.

Cabinet Shelf No.

See PRINTING PRESSES. Degener & Weiler. George P. Gordon, R. Hoe & Co.

HÖFER, CONRAD

Cabinet Y Shelf 2 No. 55

Beitrag zu einer geschichte des Coburgs buchdrucks im 16 jahrhundert. Ein bibliographischer versuch. Coburg, 1906. With facsimiles.

Brief history of 16th century Coburg printing.

Half morocco; 9½ x 6½ x 3/8 in.

HOFFHALTER, RAFAEL

Cabinet
Shelf
No.

See Early Printing in Hungary. Literature. The Vienna printer Rafael Hoffhalter...

HOFFMANN, JOHN DANIEL

Cabinet X
Shelf 1
No. 38

Typographiis earumque initiis et incrementis in regno Poloniae et Magno Ducata Lithuaniae, cum variis observationibus rem literariam et typographicam utriusque gentis aliqua ex parte illustrantibus. Dantisci, 1740.
History of printing in Poland, literary and typographical observations.

Apud Georgium Marcum Knochium.
Boards, half calf: $8\frac{1}{2}$ x 7 x 3/8 in.

HOFFMEISTER, HEINRICH

Cabinet
Shelf
No.

see also
Specimen Books, Types. Germany.

HOFFMAN, EMIL R., AND ALFRED W. (Inventors)

Cabinet FF
Shelf 6
No. 19

see
TYPE WRITING MACHINES. Hoffman, Emil R...

HOFFMANN, JOSEPH FRANCIS IGNATIUS

Cabinet FF
Shelf 3
No. 9

Polytipe of Mm. Hoffmann, graveurs, 1783-1787. Documents communique et annotes par J. Guiffrey.

Excerpt in manila envelope.

HOFMAN, GREGORIUM

Cabinet B
Shelf 1
No. 19

See Early printing in Germany. Worms, 1551.

HOFFMAN, FRANCOIS-IGNACE-JOSEPH

Cabinet FF
Shelf 1
No. 105

Account of Hoffman's experiments with stereotyping methods in 1783.

see
KUBLER, GEORGE A. Historical treatises...on stereotyping. New York, 1936, pp. 28-38.

HOFFMANN, PAUL

Cabinet L
Shelf 1
No. 21

Wilhelm Reuter; ein beitrag zur geschichte der lithographie. von Paul Hoffmann. Gedruckt auf Veranlassung der H. Berthold Messinglinienfabrik und Schriftgiesserei. Berlin, 1924. Illus.

No.227 of 500 printed copies.

Boards; 11-1/8 x 8-3/8 in.

HOFMANN, HANS

Cabinet Y
Shelf 4
No. 4

(Note on Hofmann and his printing at Nuremberg, 1490)

see
VOULLIÉME, ERNST (Die) Deutschen drucker des fünfzehnten jahrhunderts...p.92

HOFFMAN, Francois-Ignace-Joseph

Cabinet V
Shelf 3
No. 18

(Bio-bibliographical notes referring to Hoffman, printer and inventor, Paris, 1783)

see
WERDET, EDMOND. Histoire du livre en France...3me partie (2), p.340

HOFFMANNSCHEN BUCHDRUCKEREI

Cabinet J
Shelf 4
No. 20

Krais, Felix. Stuttgart, 1902. Imprint.

See IMPRINTS. Germany. Hoffmannschen Buchdruckerei: Felix Krais...

HOGENFORST, A.

Cabinet EE
Shelf 5
No. 70 & 71

(Catalogue and price list of machines and materials for every branch of the printing industry) Maschinenfabrik. A. Hogenforst. Leipzig. n.d. circa 1900. Specialität maschinen und apparate fur die gesammte buchdruck-industrie; stereotypie, galvanoplastik... Gegründet 1869.
Has exterior view of factory.

Cloth; 11-?/8 x $8\frac{1}{4}$ x 3/8 in. EE/5/71 in manila envelope.

HOFFMAN, WALTER JAMES

Cabinet L
Shelf 2
No. 33

Beginnings of writing, the. By Walter James Hoffman. With an introduction by Prof. Frederick Starr. New York, 1895. Illus.

Cloth; $7\frac{1}{2}$ x 5 x 7/8 in.

HOFFMEISTER, HEINRICH

Cabinet FF
Shelf 4
No. 24

Enstehung (die) einer schrift. von Heinrich Hoffmeister. Frankfurt A. M. Monographien des Buchgewerbes, VIII Band, Leipzig, 1913.

How type is made, illustrated description

Half morocco; 6-5/8 x $4\frac{3}{8}$ in.

HOGER, KARL and KARL TROJAN

Cabinet LL
Shelf 2
No. 9

Almanach für buchdrucker. 1881. Wien. I Jahrgang.

Cloth; 6 x 4-1/8 x 3/8 in.

HOFFMAN, WALTER JAMES

Cabinet PP
Shelf 3
No. 43.01

Graphic art of the Eskimos. Based upon the collections in the National Museum, Washington D.C.

pp.739-937 of Smithsonian Institution Annual Report for year ending June 30th. 1895.

Cloth; 9 x $6\frac{1}{4}$ x 3 in.

HOFFMEISTER, HEINRICH

Cabinet Y
Shelf 3
No. 132

(Types, the making of) Die entstehung einer schrift. von H. Hoffmeister. Frankfurt a.M. n.d. Monographien des Buchgewerbes. Leipzig. Band VIII.

Paper; 6-3/8 x 4-5/8 in.

HÖGER, KARL

Cabinet LL
Shelf 2
No. 10

Almanach für buchdrucker. II Jahrgang, Wien, 1882. Frontispiece portrait of Fr. Koenig.
Historical and technical notes. Has names and addresses of contemporary printers, machine & printing material manufacturers, etc., in Austria, Hungary and other European towns and cities.

Cloth; 5-7/8 x $4\frac{1}{4}$ x $\frac{1}{2}$ in.

HOHENWANG, LUDWIG

Cabinet Y, Shelf 4, No. 4

(Note on the Hohenwang press at Augsburg, 1476-1487)

see
VOULLIÉME, ERNST. (Die) Deutschen drucker des fünfzehnten jahrhunderts...p.4

see also p.21

HOHLWEIN, LUDWIG

Cabinet L, Shelf 5, No. 9

(German commercial art and Ludwig Hohlwein. Compiled and edited by H.K. Frenzel. With an introduction by Dr. Walter F. Schubert. Translated by Herman George Scheffauer. Berlin, 1926. Illus.

228 plates of specimens of poster printing, labels, advertisements, prospectuses, book-covers, etc.

Cloth; 12 x 9 x 1 in.

HOLBEIN, HANS

Cabinet J, Shelf 2, No. 26

(The) Celebrated Hans Holbein's alphabet of death. Illustrated with old borders engraved on wood...selected by Anatole de Montaiglon. Paris: Printed for Edwin Tross, 1856.

Half morocco; 7¾ x 5-1/8 x ¼ in.

HOLBEIN, HANS THE YOUNGER

Cabinet J, Shelf 2, No. 27, 2 Vols.

Chamberlain, Arthur B. Hans Holbein, the Younger. With 252 illustrations, including 24 in colour. In two volumes. London, 1913.

Cloth; 11½ x 9½ in.

HOLBEIN, HANS

Cabinet K, Shelf 6, No. 33

Dance of Death, subject of the wood engravings of Hans Holbein. Excerpt from The Columbian, July, 1844.

Brief description of the different groups in these drawings.

Item I in vol. with binder's title "Wood engravers: Various excerpts."

HOLBEIN, HANS

Cabinet I, Shelf 1, No. 35

Dance of Death, the designs for. Exhibited in engravings on wood, with a dissertation on the several representations of that subject. By Francis Douce...London, 1833. With 49 plates.

Half morocco; 9 x 5⅞ in.

HOLBEIN, HANS

Cabinet S, Shelf 1, No. 105

Drawings for Erasmus: Praise of Folly.

See BULLEN, HENRY LEWIS. Erasmus... March, 1932.

HOLBEIN, HANS

Cabinet 5, Shelf, No. 26

Engraving (1 plate, facsimile reprint)

Fac. in Cabinet 5, portfolio 26.

HOLBEIN, HANS

Cabinet K, Shelf 6, No. 39.01

Essai bibliographique sur les différentes éditions des Icones Veteris Testamenti d' Holbein. Par G. Duplessis. Lu dans la séance du 25 juillet, 1883.
Pamphlet.

Item 2 in bound collection with binder's title ENGRAVERS AND WOOD ENGRAVERS

HOLBEIN, HANS

Cabinet T, Shelf 3, No. 2

First printed editions of the "Dance of Death" by Holbein; account of the editions of the Veteris Testamenti Icones, etc.

In DIBDIN'S Bibliographical Decameron...London, 1817, vol.1, pp.174-80

HOLBEIN, HANS.

Cabinet 20, Shelf 1, No. 19

(Five unknown wood engravings by Hans Holbein) Fünf unbekannte Holzschnitte Hans Holbeins, von W.L.Schreiber, Potsdam, Apr., 1906. Illus.

In Zeitschrift für Bücherfreunde, 1906-7, part 1, p.26.

HOLBEIN, HANS, Engraver.

Cabinet D, Shelf 3, No. 47

Frontispiece, signed.

See Early Printing in Switzerland. Basle, 1516. Johannes Froben.

HOLBEIN, HANS

Cabinet J, Shelf 4, No. 15

Hans Holbein, the younger. By Gerald S. Davis. London, 1903. Illus.

Bio-bibliographical.

Cloth; 15-1/8 x 10¼ x 2 in.

HOLBEIN, HANS.

Cabinet 69, Shelf 1, No. 12

See Illustrated Books, Early. Icones historiam...Lugduni, Apud Frellonium, 1547.

HOLBEIN, HANS (The younger)

Cabinet D, Shelf 3, No. 38

Marginal drawings of Hans Holbein the younger. Basle 1515.

See Facsimiles. Erasmi, Rotterdami: Encomium moriae...Basle, 1931.

HOLBEIN, HANS

Cabinet 13, Shelf, No. 3

Original drawings, imitations of. By Hans Holbein, in the collection of His Majesty, for the portraits of illustrious persons of the court of Henry VIII. With biographical tracts. Published by John Chamberlain... London: Printed by W. Bulmer and Co. Shakspeare Printing Office, 1792.

Morocco, gilt; 21½ x 17 in.

HOLBEIN, HANS.

Cabinet D, Shelf 3, No. 55

Title pages to the second edition of Thomas More's Utopia, printed by John Froben, Basel, 1518.

See Early Printing in Switzerland, Basle, 1518.

HOLBEIN, HANS

Cabinet K, Shelf 5, No. 3

(Wood engravings of Hans Holbein and John Bewick)

see
GARRISON, WENDELL P. Holbein and John Bewick...

HOLBEIN, HANS

Cabinet U Shelf 5 No. 52

Works ornamented by, or from the designs of, Hans Holbein.
See pp.270-2 in Bibliographical Notes: The Gentleman's Magazine.

HOLBEIN SOCIETY

Cabinet D Shelf 3 No. 61

Tewrdannchk: A reproduction of the edition printed at Augsburg in 1519. Edited by W. Harry Rylands. With an introduction by George Bullen. Printed for the Holbein Society. London, 1884.

Cloth $14\frac{1}{2}$ x $10\frac{1}{4}$ x $2\frac{3}{4}$ in.

HOLDEN, EDWARD S.

Cabinet L Shelf 3 No. 16

Studies in Central American picture-writing. By Edward S. Holden. Smithsonian Institution, Washington, D.C., 1880. Illus.

Quarter morocco; 11-1/8 x $7\frac{1}{2}$ in.

HOLDEN, RALPH and EARNEST ELMO CALKINS

Cabinet LL Shelf 4 No. 16

Modern Advertising. New York, 1907.
Illus. practical and technical text book.

Cloth; 7-3/4 x 5-3/8 x 1 in.

HOLDERMANN JEAN-BAPTISTE

Cabinet II Shelf 4 No. 49

Grammaire Turque, ou methode courte et facile pour apprend la langue Turque. A Constantinople, 1730.

This is the first European book printed i in Constantinople. Printer, Ibraham Mutafarrika.

Contemporary style native binding; half calf; 8-3/8 x 6 x 7/8 in.

HOLL, LEONHARD

Cabinet D Shelf 1 No. 63

Ulm, circa 1482.

see INCUNABULA (loose leaves) Holl, Leonhard...

HOLLAND, JOSIAH GILBERT

Cabinet Q Shelf 1 No. 1

Biographical sketch, with portrait of the editor-in-chief of the Century Magazine.
Excerpt from the "Century", Dec., 1881

Item 14 in volume with binder's title "Publishing. Various Excerpts".

HOLLAND, JOSIAH GILBERT.

Cabinet Shelf No.

See Publishing, New York City: Holland, J.C. (First publisher of The Century Magazine, New York.)

HOLLAND

Cabinet II Shelf 6 No. 2

Amsterdam, 1808. [Lesson book for blind children of Holland. Printed in embossed types].

Half morocco; $8\frac{1}{4}$ x 7 x 3/8 in.

HOLLAND

Cabinet Y Shelf 1 No. 23

(Diffusion of printing in the Low Countries (Holland and Belgium) Bio-bibliographical notes and comments.

See LINDE, ANTONIOUS van der. Geschichte der erfindung ... Berlin, 1886, vol.1, p.293 (see also index, vol.3)

HOLLAND

Cabinet AA Shelf 3 No. 14.02

s-Hertogenbosch (Bois-le-Duc)

see VERREYT, CH. C.V. (De) Boekdrukkers en uitgevers te 's-Hertogenbosch...

HOLLAND.

Cabinet I Shelf 4 No. 18

Histoire de la gravure dans les anciens Pays-Bas ... des origines jusqu'a 1500.

See DELEN, A.J.J. Histoire de la gravure ... Paris et Bruxelles, 1924.

HOLLAND

Cabinet OO Shelf 2 No. 30

Journalism in Zeeland

See ABRAHAMS, H.P. Pers in Zeeland 1758-1900...

HOLLAND

Cabinet I Shelf 5 No. 1 2 Portfol.

(Miniature work of the 14th to 16th centuries)

See BYVANCK, A.W. et HOOGEWERFF, C.J. Miniature Hollandaise...

HOLLAND

Cabinet KK Shelf 2 No. 61.01

(Printers' Co-operative society.)

see CO-OPERATIVE SOCIETIES. (Holland ...

HOLLAND

Cabinet Shelf No.

Schools of Printing in Holland

See SCHOOLS OF PRINTING, Holland

HOLLAND

Cabinet U Shelf 5 No. 28

Spread of printing in Holland (see) DUFF, E. GORDON. Early printed books...p.95

HOLLAND

Cabinet MM Shelf 2 No. 26

[Technique of make ready for different sizes. Dutch description, entirely in Mss., without date or place]. Letter-zetters luywagen... door Christian Sigismund Matthaeus, Studios Typograph.

Tooled leather; 8-5/8 x 6-1/8 x $\frac{1}{4}$ in.

HOLLAND

Cabinet K Shelf 1 No. 19

Trade marks, guild medals, etc., reproductions of.

See Dirks, J. Atlas van platen... Haarlem, 1879.

HOLLAND

Cabinet K Shelf 6 No. 23

Woodcuts of the 15th century, Dutch and Flemish.

see SCHRETLEN, M. J. Dutch and Flemish woodcuts...

HOLLAND

Cabinet AA Shelf 3 No. 54

Zutphen, St. Walburgskerk (and its chained Library)

see MEINSMA. K. O. Catalogus van de Librye....

HOLLAND

see also

Early Printing in Holland.
Liberty of Printing, Holland.

HOLLAND LAND COMPANY

Cabinet QQ Shelf 3 No. 33

Travels in the years 1791 and 1792 in Pennsylvania, New York and Vermont. Journals of John Lincklaen, agent of the Holland Land Company. With a biographical sketch, and notes. New York, 1897.

Cloth; 8½ x 6 in.

HOLLAR, WENZEL, Engraver.

Cabinet E Shelf 4 No. 49

~~See Engraving, Early. Faithhorn, William and W. Hollar. London, 1668.~~ Hollar, Wenzel. Gt. Brit.

HOLLE, LIENHART

Cabinet B Shelf 2 No. 7

(Illustrated books printed by Holler, Ulm, 1480-1492)

see SCHRAMM, ALBERT. (Der) Bilderschmuck der frühdrucke...Leipzig, 1923.

HOLLE, LIENHART

Cabinet Y Shelf 4 No. 4

(Note on Holle and his printing at Ulm, 1480)

see VOULLIÉME, ERNST. (Die) Deutschen drucker des fünfzehnten jahrhunderts...p.119

HOLLENBECK PRESS

See Imprints.

HOLLEY, O.L.

Cabinet R Shelf 3 No. 28

Benjamin Franklin, The life of. By O.L.Holley. Philadelphia [1885?]. Illus.
The wood engravings depicting scenes in the life of B.F. are from the originals by Alex. Anderson, son of a N.Y. master printer and a contemporary of B.F.

Cloth; 7½ x 4¾ in.

HOLLINS COLLEGE

Cabinet QQ Shelf 4 No. 13

Hollins, Virginia.

see COLLEGES, United States. Hollins College...

HOLLISTON MILLS, INC.

Cabinet PP Shelf 4 No. 40

Bookbinding as an art, historical sketch of. By Meiric K. Dutton. Norwood (Mass.) The Holliston Mills, Inc. 1926.

Cloth; 8¾ x 5-7/8 x ¾ in.

HOLLISTON MILLS

Cabinet PP Shelf 4 No. 1

Sample book of Span-o-tone.

see BOOK BINDING. Sample book...

HOLLOWAY, R. EMORY

Cabinet S Shelf 2 No. 96

Walt Whitman's history of Brooklyn just found. "Personal chrolicles and gossip", as Poet calls them, were written long before he achieved distinction in literary world. By R. Emory Holloway.
Illus. excerpt from The New York Times, Sept.17, 1916.

Item in manila envelope.

HOLMAN, LOUIS A.

Cabinet J Shelf 2 No. 22

Dürer, Albert: the man in his own eyes and in the eyes of his neighbors, with a complete list of his prints from wood, copper, and iron. (Goodspeeds Monographs No.5) Boston, 1922.

Portrait frontispiece.

Half morocco; 7-7/8 x 5 in.

HOLMAN, LOUIS A.

Cabinet B Shelf 3 No. 5

Graphic processes; intaglio, relief, planographic. A series of actual prints. Selected and arranged with notes, by Louis A. Holman. Boston, 1926.

Portfolio; 19 x 13¾ in.

HOLMAN, LOUIS A.

Cabinet QQ Shelf 3 No. 25

Old maps and their makers. Considered from the historical and decorative standpoints. A survey of a huge subject in a small space. By Louis A. Holman. Second revised edition. Boston, 1926. Illus.

Boards; 8 x 5¾ in.

HOLMAN, WORTHINGTON C.

Cabinet LL Shelf 4 No. 12

Ginger talks. The talks of a sales manager to his men. By W.C. Holman, editor of "Salesmanship" Chicago, 1905.

Cloth; 8½ x 5-1/8 x ¾ in.

HOLME, CHARLES (Editor)

Cabinet J "Studio" Ltd., London, 1917.

See "STUDIO" LTD. London, 1917. The Graphic Arts of Great Britain....

Shelf 3

No. 12

HOLT, HENRY

Cabinet NN (A) Young man's oracle. The editor of the "Unpopular Review" recalls his relations with the "Nation" in its early days and his friendship with E. L. Godkin.

Shelf 7

see NATION, THE. Semi - centennial number, 1863 - 1915, p. 45.

No. 16

HOLTZAPFEL & CO.

Cabinet FF Amateur printing, apparatus for.

Shelf 5

See Printing Presses. Cowpers Parlour Printing Press...London, 1846.

No. 42

HOLME, FRANK

Cabinet K Training of an illustrator. By Frank Holme of the Chicago Daily News. Compliments of the Daily News, Chicago, 1899. Illus. brochure

Shelf 3

No. 14

Item in manila envelope.

HOLT, JOHN

Cabinet X New York, 1770 (Imprint), John Holt

see LIBERTY OF PRINTING, United States Zenger, John Peter (1770)....

Shelf 4

No. 64

HOLTZAPFFEL AND COMPANY

Cabinet MM Printing apparatus for the use of amateurs. Containing full and practical instructions for the use of Cowper's parlour printing press. Also the description of larger presses on the same principle, and various other apparatus for the amateur typographer. The whole manufactured and sold by Holtzapffel & Co. London, Illus. 1846.

Shelf 3

No. 27

Has price list of printing apparatus.

Cloth; 9 x $5\frac{3}{4}$ in.

HOLMES, JOHN H. (Editor Boston "Herald")

Cabinet NN Journalism, the new and the old. Excerpt from Munsey's, April, 1897.

Shelf 2

No. 7

Item 27 in bound collection "Journalism. Excerpts, etc."

HOLT, JOHN

Cabinet R Printer and postmaster: Some facts and documents (1721-1784) relating to his career. By Victor Hugo Paltsits. New York Public Library. 1920. Brochure.

Shelf 4

Has inventory of printing materials, etc.

No. 87.01

Envelope

Item in manila envelope.

HOLTZAPFEL and COMPANY

see also

Cabinet Specimen Books, Types. England.

Shelf

No.

HOLMES, R. R.

Cabinet PP Specimens of Royal Fine and Historical Book - binding, selected from the Royal Library, Windsor Castle. 152 plates printed in facsimile by W. Griggs. With an introduction and notes by R. R. Holmes. London, 1893.

Shelf 6

No. 1

Cloth, stamped; 15 x $11\frac{1}{4}$ x $1\frac{1}{2}$ in.

HOLTROP, J. W.

Cabinet I Confessionale ou Beichtspiegel nach den zehn geboten ... [Reproduction and account of a unique 15th century Block Book of Ten Commandments. Introduction by J. W. Holtrop.] La Haye, 1861.

Shelf 3

No. 29

Boards; $10\frac{1}{2}$ x 7 in.

HÖLTZEL, HIERONYMUS

Cabinet Y (Note on Höltzel and his printing at Nuremberg, 1500-1520)

Shelf 4

see VOULLIÉME, ERNST (Die) Deutschen drucker des fünfzehnten jahrhunderts...p.94

No. 4

HOLMES, THOMAS J.

Cabinet S (The) Surreptitious printing of Cotton Mather's manuscripts. By J..Thomas Holmes, Librarian of William G. Mather's Library, Cleveland, Ohio.

Shelf 3

Bibliography.

P. 149 in volume, Wilberforce Eames ... A Tribute to. Cambridge, 1924.

No. 104

HOLTROP, JOHN WILLIAM

Cabinet W Monuments typographiques des Pays-Bas du Quinzième Siècle. Collection de facsimile d'apres les originaux conserves a la Bibliotheque royale de la Haye et ailleurs. La Haye 1868. Facsimile

Shelf 5

At the end a map of Holland in the 15th. cent., also a chronological tableof the towns where printing was exercised in the 15th cent., in Holland, with the name of the printers.

No. 57

Boards; $14\frac{1}{2}$ x 11 in.

HOLBORCH, CONRAD WINTERS DE

Cabinet V Catalogue of his impressions: Bible attributed to Ulrich Zell, printed by him.

Shelf 5

See Madden, J.P.A. Lettres d'un Bibliographe. Tome IV, 183 to 193: Tome VI, 20 to 24.

No. 11

HOLT, DANIEL

Cabinet X Printer of The Newark Herald, Newark [upon Trent] 1794.

Shelf 5

See Liberty of Printing. Great Britain. Holt, Daniel.

No. 4

HOLTROP, JOHN WILLIAM

Cabinet W Thierry Martens d'Alost. Étude bibliographique. Par J. W. Holtrop. La Haye, 1867.

Shelf 4

The book is an inquiry into the question whether Thierry Martens was really the first printer of Belgium.

No. 79

Half morocco; 9-1/8 x $5\frac{1}{2}$ in.

HOMER LEE BANK NOTE COMPANY

Cabinet S Engravers and printers of bonds and stock certificates. Excerpt from Paper and Press, Phil., Oct., 1888.

Shelf 5

No. 1

Bound in collection "Various printing plants Brochures", item 12.

HOMESPUN, HENRY jr. (Solomon Southwick)
1819

Cabinet NN | Shelf 7 | No. 19.01

Plough Boy, The. Vol.1, June 5th. to May 27, 1820. By Henry Homespun, jr. Albany N.Y.

Boards, morocco back: 11[illegible] x 9[illegible] in.

HONATE, BENIGNO and JOH. ANTONIO DE.

Cabinet D | Shelf 1 | No. 31

See Incunabula. Durandus. Speculum Judiciale, Milan, 1478.

HONDT, PIERRE DE

Cabinet F | Shelf 5 | No. 1

See Early Printing in Holland. Haye (La) 1729. Pierre de Hondt.

HONE, WILLIAM

Cabinet M | Shelf 2 | No. 39.04

Imprint of W. Hone, London, 1819

See IMPRINTS, England. Hone, William ...

HONE, WILLIAM

Cabinet X | Shelf 5 | No. 22

(The) Three trials of William Hone, for publishing three parodies; viz. The late John Wilke's Catechism...on three ex-officio informations at Guildhall, London, during three successive days, before three special juries, etc. London: Printed by & for William Hone, London, 1818.

Boards; 9 x 5-7/8 in.

HONIG, LOUIS

Cabinet 71 | Shelf 1 | No. 86

(The) Arrogant Youth; Being a family music play in two acts. The book & lyrics by Louis Honig, the music by Rudy Seiger...And now imprinted in the City of San Francisco...by John Henry Nash...November, 1928.

Boards; $12\frac{1}{2}$ x 9 in.

HONOLULU ADVERTISER.

Cabinet 66 | Shelf 1 | No. 4

Anniversary issue, 75th birthday, July 2, 1931. Illus.

With biography of first editor and founder.

Cloth; 23 x $17\frac{1}{4}$ in.

HONOLULU STAR-BULLETIN

Cabinet | Shelf | No.

See Newspapers, Hawaii.

HOOCHSTRATEN, JOHANNES.

Cabinet 75 | Shelf 2 | No. 9

Printer of English books at Antwerp, 1525--brief bio-bibliographical account.

See Kronenberg, M. W. English printing, early 16th century, in the low Countries... p. 155 and fol.

HOOLE MACHINE & ENGRAVING WORKS

Cabinet EE | Shelf 4 | No. 78

(Catalogue) Brass stamp and rolls, tools and machinery. New York City, n.d. (circa 1890) Pamphlet.

Item in manila envelope.

HOOREBEKE, L. MINARD-VAN

Cabinet QQ | Shelf 5 | No. 18

Description de méreau et autres objects anciens des gildes et corps de metiers, églises eti Par L. Minard-Van Hoorebeke. Gand. 1877-1878 (2 vols. illus.)
Flemish guilds and their emblems.

Boards, cloth back; $13\frac{1}{2}$ x $10\frac{1}{4}$ in.

HOORN, JAN.

Cabinet E | Shelf 4 | No. 81

See Early Printing in Holland. Amsterdam, 1685. Hieronymus Sweerts.

HOOVER, HERBERT

Cabinet QQ | Shelf 5 | No. 12

Hoover and his times. Looking back through the years. By Edwin Emerson. Illustrated by contemporary cartoons. New York, 1932.

Presentation copy.

Cloth; $8\frac{1}{2}$ x 5-5/8 x $1\frac{1}{4}$ in.

HOPE, FREDERICK WILLIAM, REV.

Cabinet OO | Shelf 4 | No. 2

Catalogue of a collection of early newspapers and essayists, formed by the late John Thomas Hope, and presented to the Bodleian Library by the late Rev. Frederick William Hope. Oxford, 1865.

Cloth; 9 x $5\frac{3}{4}$ x 5/8 in.

HOPKINS, CLAUDE C.

Cabinet LL | Shelf 5 | No. 13

Advertising, My life in. New York, 1927.

A business story of instructive interest.

Cloth; 8-3/4 x 5-5/8 x $1\frac{1}{4}$ in.

HOPKINS VS. WOOD.

Cabinet FF | Shelf 1 | No. 107

Inventors of stereotype plate making machines. And the all important question as to which is the real and true inventor of the Junior Autoplate. n. d. n. p. Ms.

Item in manila envelope

HOPKINSON & COPE (Albion Works)

Cabinet EE | Shelf 5 | No. 72

(Catalogue 1861) Printing presses and machines, steam engines, machinery for bookbinders etc. Manufactured by Hopkinson & Cope. Albion Works. New North Street, Finsbury, London.

Illus., and with prices.

Half morocco; $9\frac{3}{4}$ x $6\frac{1}{2}$ x $\frac{1}{4}$ in.

HORAE

Cabinet 75 | Shelf 1 | No. 7

Devotional books printed by the earliest English printers. Bibliography of some. A paper read by the Rev. F. A. Gasquet, Jan. 18, 1904.

In Trans. Biblio. Soc. Vol. VII, 1902-1904. pp. 163-189.

HORAE

Cabinet | Shelf | No.

see also

BOOKS OF HOURS.

HORATIUS, FLACCUS (Quintus)

Cabinet 68 | Shelf | No. 12

Printed by Pierre Didot the Elder, Paris, 1799. Decorations by Percier (Charles)

This book of Horace has been called by Dibdin "One of the noblest and magnificent editions"

Morocco; 19 x 14¼ in. In protective case

HORATIUS, FLACCUS.

Cabinet F | Shelf 4 | No. 95

Quintus Horatius Flaccus. Editio stereotypa. Paris, 1800.

Imprint: Ex Officina Stereotypa. Petri Didot natu maj. et Firmin Didot. Anno VIII (1800)

Vellum; 6¼ x 3-7/8 x 1¼ in. Brunet 3, 323.

HORGAN, S.H.

Cabinet NN | Shelf 2 | No. 2

Brief notice of S.H. Horgan's pictorial contribution to the American Press. With Portrait. Article by Valerian Gribayedoff.

Item 10 in vol. "Journalism and Journalists". Bound 1918.

HORGAN, S.H.

Stack A | Shelf 1&2 | Number 72

Bullen, Henry L., in Europe, by H. Horgan in the Inland Printer, vol. LXXII, p. 642.

A tribute to Mr. Bullen on his departure for Europe.

HORGAN, STEPHEN H.

Cabinet 79 | Shelf 2 | No. 17

(The) First book printed in North America. Excerpt from U. S. Cath. Hist. Society Hist. Researches & Studies, Vol. 5, Part 2, April, 1909.

In envelope.

HORGAN, STEPHEN H.

Cabinet I | Shelf 2 | No. 49

Glossary of words and terms used in the photo-engraving business. Submitted to the 31st Annual Convention of the American Photo-Engravers Association. Washington D.C., July 14, 15, 16, 1927. Pamphlet.

Includes signed letter, S.H. Horgan.

Item in manila envelope.

HORGAN, STEPHEN H.

Cabinet | Shelf | No.

Half-tone screen: An historical article in British & Colonial Printer, Vol. III, New Series 202, Sept. 8, 1932. p. 230.

HORGAN, STEPHEN H.

Cabinet I | Shelf 2 | No. 46

Horgan's half-tone and photomechanical processes. Published by The Inland Printer Company. Chicago, 1913. Illus.

Frontispiece portrait of the author.

Cloth; 8¾ x 5-7/8 x 1¼ in.

HORGAN, STEPHEN H.

Cabinet | Shelf | No.

Is this the oldest printed book in the world? (China, A.D. 868). Illus.

Article in Inland Printer, vol. 86, Nov. 1930. p. 57.

HORGAN, STEPHEN HENRY

Cabinet 79 | Shelf 2 | No. 16

(The) Oldest American book: A technical appreciation of the first American printers. New York: The United States Catholic Historical Society, 1928. Doctrina Breve of Bishop Zumarraga, Mexico, 1544.

Cloth; 9½ x 6-3/8 in.

HORGAN, STEPHEN H.

Cabinet I | Shelf 2 | No. 48

Photo-engraving primer. Concise instructions for apprentice engravers, or for those seeking simple yet practical knowledge of line and half tone engraving...American Photographic Publishing Co. Boston, Mass. 1920. Illus.

Cloth; 8 x 5¾ x 3/8 in.

HORGAN, STEPHEN H.

Cabinet A | Shelf 2 | No. 91

Progress of engraving and process work -- Boston the home of the first American engravers -- Pioneer of the first illustrated weekly paper...By Stephen H. Horgan.

Illus. article in the Graphic Arts Section of the Boston Evening Transcript, August 29, 1922, part four, p.5.

HORGAN, S.H.

Cabinet I | Shelf 2 | No. 53

Three-color processwork. A brief outline of the knowledge a photoengraver must possess to undertake three color block-making.

See Section VII, div. B. p.34_, AMSTUTZ, N.S. Anstutz' hand-book of photoengraving ...1907.

HORN BOOKS

Cabinet S | Shelf 6 | No. 7

See Blumenthal, Walter Hart. Curious books... 1921.

HORNBOOKS

Cabinet S | Shelf 5 | No. 26.01

Collection of hornbooks given by James C. McGuire to The New York Public Library. Bibliographical account with a foreword by James C. McGuire. New York, 1927. Illus. brochure.

Item in manila envelope.

HORN BOOKS

Cabinet S | Shelf 5 | No. 12

(Denmark). Horn books and primers in. Bildrag til ABC-litteraturens historie I Danmark Af Julius Clausen. Excerpt from Tidsskriftet. Copenhagen, 1896.

Bound in collection "Pamphlets and excerpts relating to typographical matters, item 25.

HORN BOOKS

Cabinet T | Shelf 4 | No. 9

History of horn books. By Andrew W. Tuer, London, 1896. (2 vols.) Illus.

Seven horn books are enclosed in built up recesses in these books.

Vellum; 10½ x 8 in.

HORN BOOKS

Cabinet S Shelf 5 No. 18

Horn Books, by George A. Plimpton, in The Independent, Aug., 1912. Illus.

Mr. Plimpton of the firm of Ginn & Company, has the largest collection of these early school books, and in the item above essays to trace the history of these "tools of teaching."

Bound in collection "Dawn of Printing," item 10.

HORNKEN, LUDWIG

Cabinet X Shelf 3 No. 15

Biographical sketch, with printer device, Hornken. Basel, 1513 --

see

HEITZ, PAUL

Basler büchermarken... pp.xxiv, 59

HORNE, THOMAS HARTWELL.

Cabinet PP Shelf 1 No. 29

Introduction to the study of bibliography. To which is prefixed a memoir on the public libraries of the antients. Illustrated with engravings (2 Vols.) London, 1814. Printed by G. Woodfall.

Half calf; 9 x 5¼ in.

HORN BOOKS

Cabinet P Shelf 2 No. 56

Reproduction of an early Horn Book, with brief history of same. A Christmas Greeting from Charles R. Capone, designer-typographer, Boston, Mass. n.d. circa 1919.

In envelope.

HORNKEN, LUDWIG

Cabinet X Shelf 3 No. 20

Brief bio-bibliographical note, Hornken, Cologne, 1512-1516.

see

HEITS, PAUL.

Kölner büchermarken...p.xxi

HORNING, HANS

Cabinet FF Shelf 4 No. 28

(Das) Schriftgiessereigewerbe der gegenwart. Inaugural dissertation zur erlangung der Doctorwurde de hohen philosophischen... von Hans Horning. Heidelberg, 1923. Brochure, with 3 plates.

Item in manila envelope

HORN BOOKS

Cabinet Shelf No.

See also

I. Chap Books
II. Children's Books.
III. School Books.

HORNE, HERBERT P.

Cabinet M Shelf 2 No. 34

See Imprints, England. Florence Press The. Chatto & Windus.

See also Types; Printing.

HORNSCHUCH, D. JEROME

Cabinet LL Shelf 3 No. 5.01

(Der) Bey buchdruckerey wohl unterwiesene corrector, oder: kurtzer unterricht fur diejenigen die werke so gedruckt werden corrigiren wollen....von D.H.H. Frankfurth und Leipzig, 1739.

Facing title page, a copper engraving.

Hornschuch, a learned proof reader of the 17th century, proposes here to instruct authors in the art of preparing copy for the press.

Half morocco; 7½ x 4¼ x ½ in.

HORNBY, CHARLES H.ST. JOHN

Cabinet M Shelf No.

See Imprints, England. Ashendene Press, The.

HORNE, HERBERT P.

Cabinet G Shelf 4 No. 14

See Imprints, United States. Updike, Daniel Berkeley. The Merrymount Press, 1907. Erasmus against war. Type and decorations designed by H.P. Horne.

HORNSCHUCH, D. JEROME

Cabinet Y Shelf 3 No. 29

(Die) Buchdruckerey wohl unterwiesene corrector, oder kurtzer unterricht für diejenigen, die werke, so gedruckt werden, corrigiren wollen ...Frankfurth und Leipzig, 1739.

Hornschuch who was a learned 17th century proofreader, here gives brief historical sketches of the inventors and the invention of printing, and instructions for authors on how to prepare copy for the press.

Boards, morocco back; 6-7/8 x 4¼ x ¼ in.

HORNBY, C. St. John

Cabinet U Shelf 5 No. 24

Private press of C. St.John Hornby

see

POLLARD, A. W. Fine Books ...London, 1912, pp.88, 306

HORNE, THOMAS HARTWELL

Cabinet U Shelf 4 No. 2

Introduction to the study of bibliography. To which is prefixed a memoir on the public library of the antients. Illustrated with engravings. (vol.1). London: Printed by G. Woodfall, 1814.

Half morocco; 9½ x 6 in.

HORNSCHUCH, D. (Jerome)

Cabinet LL Shelf 3 No. 52

Der bey buchdruckerey wohl interwiesene corrector ....Franckfurth und Leipzig, 1739.

Bound in with "Ehren gedichte auf die edle freye kunst-buchdruckerey...Franckfurth und Leipzig, 1739.

Paper; 7-3/8 x 4½ in.

HORNCKEN. LUDOVIC

Cabinet X Shelf 3 No. 14

Bibliographical note, with printer mark, Horncken Milan, 1513.

see

KRISTELLER, Dr. Paul.

Italienischen buchdrucker...p.22

HORNE, THOMAS HARTWELL

Cabinet U Shelf 4 No. 2

Introduction to the study of bibliography. To which is prefixed a memoir on the public libraries of the antients. Illustrated with engravings. vol. 1. London, 1814.

Half morocco; 9½ x 6 x 2-3/8 in.

HORNSCHUCH, D. JEROME

Cabinet LL Shelf 1 No. 6

Der bey Buchdruckerey wohl unterwiesene corrector...Frankfurth und Leipzig, 1739.

Bound in back of vol.II of Gessner's: Die so nothig als nutzlich Buchdruckerkunst... Leipzig, 1740-1745.

HORNUNG, CLARENCE PEARSON

Cabinet S Shelf 5 No. 46

Bookplates by Harold Nelson. Arranged and edited by C.P. Harnung. With a foreword by John Malcolm Bullock. New York. Caxton Press, Inc, 1929.

Boards; $11\frac{1}{4}$ x $8\frac{1}{2}$ x 3/8 in.

HORNUNG, CLARENCE P.

Cabinet S Shelf 5 No. 47

Trade-Marks designed by C.P. Hornung. New York. Caxton Press, 1930. Numbered and signed copy.

Cloth; $8\frac{1}{4}$ x 7-1/8 x 5/8 in. In board protective case.

HORST, PETER

Cabinet X Shelf 3 No. 20

Cologne, 1551-1591

see HEITZ, PAUL.
Kölner büchermarken...p.xxx

HORTENSIUS (GEORGE HAY).

Cabinet X Shelf 4 No. 104

Essay on the liberty of the press. Respectfully inscribed to the Republican printers throughout the United States. By Hortensius. Philadelphia. Printed at the Aurora Office. [Benjamin Franklin Bache], 1799.

Half morocco; $8\frac{1}{2}$ x $5\frac{1}{4}$ x $\frac{1}{4}$ in.

HOSPIANUS, RODOLPHUS.

Cabinet 39 Shelf 2 No. 35

(De) Templis et rebus ad ea spectantibus. Geneva, sumplibus Joannis Antonii & Samuelis de Tournes. 1672.

Calf; 14 x $8\frac{1}{2}$ x $1\frac{1}{4}$ in.

HOTOT, FABIAN

Cabinet X Shelf 4 No. 8

Orleans (France, 1594. (Imprint of F. Hotot)

see PRINTING, HISTORICAL. France. (Edict of the King of France, 1594)...

HOTTEN, JOHN CAMDEN

Cabinet LL Shelf 4 No. 6.01

See Larwood, Jacob and John Camden Hotten... London, 1866.

HOUDOY, JULES

Cabinet V Shelf 1 No. 88

Imprimeurs Lilloise: Bibliographie des impressions Lilloise 1595-1700. Par Jules Houdoy. Paris, 1879.

Half morocco; 11 x 7 x $1\frac{1}{4}$ in.

HOUGHTON, ASA

Cabinet 80 Shelf 1 No. 48

Almanacs, 1806, 1910. Keene, New Hampshire.

See ALMANACS. Houghton's Genuine Almanac, 1806 and 1810...

HOUGHTON, H.O

Cabinet Q Shelf 1 No. 1

Biographical sketch, with portrait.

Excerpt from the Book Buyer, March, 1897.

Item in volume with binder's title "Publishing. Various Excerpts"

HOUGHTON, HENRY OSCAR

Cabinet S Shelf 5 No. 9

Biographical narrative. By Julius H. Ward. Excerpt from the New England Magazine, Oct, 1895.

Bound in collection "Various printers- excerpts and brochures", item 12.

HOUGHTON, HENRY OSCAR

Cabinet S Shelf 2 No. 20

Biographical outline, A. By Horace E. Scudder. Cambridge. The Riverside Press, 1897. Portraits.

Half vellum; 9 x 6 in.

HOUGHTON, HENRY O.

Cabinet R Shelf 3 No. 161

Early Printing in America: An address delivered before the Vermont Historical Society. At Montpelier, October 23, 1894, by H.O.Houghton, Montpelier, 1894.
Historical and biographical account.

Half morocco; $8\frac{3}{4}$ x 5-7/8 in.

HOUGHTON, L.

Cabinet U Shelf 3 No. 103

Illustrator forgotten, [Bibliographical account] By L. Housman.

See vol. I, pp.275-92 in Bibliographica... London, 1895-1897.

HOUGHTON, THOMAS SHAW

Cabinet MM Shelf 3 No. 28

Printers' (The) practical every-day-book, calculated to assist the young printer to work with ease and expedition. Fourth Ed. London, 1849. Illus.
Copy in this library incomplete. Lacks ten (10) pages, 129-139.

Boards; $6\frac{3}{4}$ x $4\frac{1}{4}$ x 3/8 in.

HOUGHTON, THOS. SHAW

Cabinet MM Shelf 3 No. 28.01

(The) Printers' practical every day book. Lancashire: To be had only from the author near Preston. 1857.

Cloth; 6-3/8 x 4-1/8 x 3/8 in.

HOUGHTON, THOMAS SHAW, and GEO. MARSHALL

Cabinet MM Shelf 3 No. 29

Printers' (The) practical every day book, by T.S. Houghton; with emendations and additions by Geo. Marshall. Preston. n.d. (1875).
"This is a stereotype reprint of the major part of Houghton's Manual, with several serious omissions and a few unimportant... interpolations by Mr. Marshall" Bigmore & Wyman.

Cloth; $6\frac{1}{2}$ x $4\frac{1}{4}$ x $\frac{1}{2}$ in.

HOUGHTON, MIFFLIN COMPANY

Cabinet S Shelf 3 No. 5 & 6

Riverside Press, Cambridge, Mass., a brief description of. Pamphlet, n.d.

Has pictures of factory, exterior and working departments.

Half morocco; $5\frac{3}{4}$ x $5\frac{3}{4}$ in.

HOUGHTON, MIFFLIN AND COMPANY

Cabinet Q Shelf 1 No. 14

(A) Sketch of the firm of Houghton Mifflin & Company, Publishers. Together with a description of The Riverside Press at Cambridge, Massachusetts. Boston, 1889. Illus.

Buckram; 9 x 6-1/8 x 3/8 in.

HOUDLED, EMILE

Cabinet Z Shelf 2 No. 37

See Specimen Books, Types. France.

HOUBLOUP, ----.

Cabinet III Shelf 2 No. 47

Théorie lithographique, ou manière facile d'apprendre a imprimer soi-même, contenant six planches représentent onze sujets. Paris, 1825.

pp.15-20 are incorrectly bound in before p.9 (beginning of chap.I).

Quarter morocco, (incorrectly lettered "Houbloud") 7-7/8 x 5-1/8 in.

HOUSE, G.C.

Cabinet 80 Shelf 1 No. 14

Boston printer: Imprints of 1809, 1810, 1811, 1814, 1815.

See ALMANACS. Farmer's Almanac...E.C. House, Printer.

HOUSE ORGANS. Paper Manufacturers

Cabinet LL Shelf 4 No. 2

Acorn (The) trophy contest. Robert Smith Printing Company wins the award for effective direct advertising.

Account in "The Acorn" Chicago Paper Company. Special Convention and Direct Mail Issue, June 1917.

Item 6 in book with binder's title "Various items on advertising".

HOUSE ORGANS, TYPE FOUNDERS. Germany

Cabinet GG Shelf 5 No. 32 Box

Weisert, Otto, Stuttgart, n.d. circa 1904. Schrift und Schmuck. Blätter für die Buch Industrie. Erscheint in zwangloser folge als hausjournal. Erstes-Heft - Zweites Heft.

Two issues only in this Library.

Paper; $11\frac{1}{4}$ x 9 in. In box labelled "Otto Weisert Stuttgart. Type Specimens. Miscellany, v.d."

HOUSE ORGANS

Cabinet Shelf No.

See also

I - Advertising. House Organs.
II - Periodicals, Printers.
III - " Type Founders.
Etc., Etc.

HOUSEHOLD WORDS (Charles Dickens) see

Cabinet NN Shelf 2 No. 14

PERIODICALS, Great Britain.

HOUSEHOLD WORDS

Cabinet Shelf No.

Weekly journal, A, conducted by Charles Dickens.

See Periodicals, British: Unknown Public, The.

HOUSTON, EDWIN JAMES

Cabinet R Shelf 2 No. 79

Franklin as a man of science and an inventor. Benjamin Franklin Trust Funds to Boston and Philadelphia. By E. J. Houston. In Journal of Franklin Institute, April and May, 1906. Illus.

Half morocco; $9\frac{1}{4}$ x $6\frac{1}{4}$ in.

HOUSTON, WILLIAM (Inventor) see

Cabinet FF Shelf 6 No. 19

COMPOSING MACHINES. Houston, William...

HOUT, JAN VAN

Cabinet Shelf No.

See Jan Van Hout.

HOW AND PARSONS.

Cabinet 78 Shelf 1 No. 4

Specimens of How and Parsons' Printing inks. Manufactory, Orange Street. Southwark. London, 1840. Prices.

Examples of advertising and book work in black and colors.

Paper; $9\frac{3}{4}$ x $6\frac{1}{4}$ in.

HOWARD, FRANK

Cabinet L Shelf 4 No. 20

Colour as a means of art, being an adaptation of the experience of professors to the practice of amateurs. By Frank Howard, London, 1838.

With 17 colored plates, printed by Willoughby and Co., London.

Cloth; 8 x 5 x 5/8 in.

HOWARD, JOHN GALEN

Cabinet 71 Shelf 1 No. 27

Brunelleschi: A poem by J. S. Howard, Printed by Taylor, Nash and Taylor, under the supervision of John Henry Nash. San Francisco, 1913.

Boards; 10 x 6-7/8 in. pp. 93.

HOWE, EBER D.

Cabinet R Shelf 3 No. 220

Recollections of a pioneer printer. By Eber D. Howe. In Annals of Cuyahoba County, 1895. Vol. III. No. 4, pp. 505-516.

The above item is from a pamphlet published in 1878, entitled: Autobiography and recollections of a pioneer printer.

Cloth; $8\frac{3}{4}$ x 6 in.

HOWE, GEORGE

Cabinet QQ Shelf 1 No. 164

First printer in Australia, 1802-1821.

see AUSTRALIA (First printer in Australia)....

HOWE, J. & CO.

Cabinet 82 Shelf 1 No. 30

Specimen of printing types and ornaments from the letter-foundry of J. Howe & Co. Philadelphia, 1830.

Half morocco; $9\frac{1}{4}$ x $5\frac{3}{4}$ in. Original covers bound in.

HOWE & CO., J.
see also
Specimen Books -- Types --- U. S.

HOWELLS, WILLIAM DEAN

Cabinet NN Shelf 2 No. 11

(The) Country printer. Illustrated excerpt from "Scribners Magazine", May, 1893.

Autobiographical

Item 3 in bound collection with binder's title "About various newspapers".

HOYT, AZOR, b. 1799 - d. 1881

Cabinet NN Shelf 7 No. 9

Printer, New York City, 1826. Brief biography of, with portrait.

see CHRISTIAN ADVOCATE, THE. Centennial Number, 1826 - 1926, p. 28.

HOWE, S.G.

Cabinet II Shelf 6 No. 12

Letter to the editor of the North British Advertiser (Scotland) from S.G. Howe, superintendent of the Perkins Institution and Massachusetts Asylum for the Blind. Boston, 1841. Pamphlet.

On the subject of printing for the blind.

With other items in manila envelope.

HOWELLS, WILLIAM D.

Cabinet S Shelf 5 No. 24

(The) Country printer. By W. D. Howells [Autobiographical]. An excerpt.

pp. 112-131 in collection "Printing Excerpts

HRADISCH, JOHANN von (see)

Cabinet Y Shelf 2 No. 17

Enders, Johann Nepomuk

HOWELL, CLARK, Editor.

Cabinet See Journalism, American (U.S.): Seven superpen.

Shelf Editor of The Atlanta Constitution.

No.

HOWES, H. WILSON

Cabinet KK Shelf 3 No. 20

Hands across the sea. Some leaves from my diary. Being a descriptive account of the Fraternal Delegacy to the 27th Convention of the Printing Pressmen and Assistants' Union of North America, held at Pressmens' Home, Hale Springs, Rogersville, Tennessee, June 19, to 26, 1916...London, 1916.
Portraits, illus.

Cloth; 9-1/8 x 6-1/8 in.

HUBBARD, ELBERT

Cabinet QQ Shelf 3 No. 23

Bigotry bacillus: being a preachment by Elbert Hubbard.
Done in print by the Roycrofters at the Roycroft Shop, in East Aurora, Erie County, N. Y. Feb., 1899.

Paper; 9 x $5\frac{3}{4}$ in.

HOWELL, GEORGE R.

Cabinet S Shelf 2 No. 19

Biographical sketch of Joel Munsell. By George R. Howell. To which is appended a genealogy of the Munsell family, by Frank Munsell. Boston, 1880. Portrait.

Half morocco; 9-7/8 x $6\frac{1}{4}$ in.

HOWLAND, PAUL Jr.

Cabinet EE See SPECIMEN BOOKS, TYPES. Printers'

Shelf 1

No. 20

HUBBARD, ELBERT

Cabinet S Shelf 3 No. 154

(The) Book of the Roycrofters: Being a history and some comments by Elbert Hubbard and Elbert Hubbard II. Done into a booklet by the Roycrofters themselves at their shops ing East Aurora, State of New York, 1921. Illus.

Half morocco; $9\frac{3}{4}$ x $6\frac{1}{4}$ in.

HOWELLS, WILLIAM DEAN

Cabinet S Shelf 4 No. 10

(The) Country printer: An essay by William Dean Howells. Privately Printed, n.d. [1896].
With portrait.
Autobiographical account.

Boards; 8-1/8 x $5\frac{1}{4}$ in.

HOYER, E.

Cabinet RR Shelf 4 No. 7

Papier. Étude sur sa composition, analyses et essais. Par E. Hoyer. (Paper: a study of composition, analysis, and experiments. Translated from the German.) Paris, 1884. With 2 folding plates.

Cloth; $10\frac{1}{4}$ x $6\frac{1}{2}$ in. Orig. wrappers bound in.

HUBBARD, ELBERT

Cabinet QQ Shelf 2 No. 19

Imprint (The Roycrofters), East Aurora, 1911.

see IMPRINTS, United States. Hubbard, Elbert...

HOWELLS, WILLIAM D.

Cabinet S Shelf 3 No. 143

(The) Country Printer. By W. D. Howells. Illus Excerpt from Scribner's Magazine, May, 1873.
Autobiographical account.

Half morocco; $9\frac{3}{4}$ x $6\frac{1}{2}$ in.

HOYOIS, EMMANUEL

Cabinet EE Shelf 3 No. 32

Specimen des caractères de la typographie d'Em. Hoyois, à Mons, rue de Nimy, No.163. 1839.

Half morocco; $10\frac{1}{4}$ x $7\frac{3}{4}$ x $\frac{5}{8}$ in.

HUBBARD, ELBERT

Cabinet S Shelf 3 No. 155

Interesting personality, an: Elbert Hubbard. (By himself). Excerpt from Cosmopolitan Magazine, Jan., 1902.
Illus. and portraits.

Item in envelope

HUBBARD, ELBERT

Cabinet — Shelf — No.

see also

Printing Plants: Roycroft Press.

HUBBARD, HARLAN PAGE (See)

Cabinet 61 — Shelf 1 — No. 1

Advertising. Hubbard's Newspaper Agency...

HUBBARD, HESKETH.

Cabinet I — Shelf 3 — No. 6

How to distinguish prints: written and illustrated by members of The Print Society, and edited by Hesketh Hubbard. Publishing by The Print Society...Woodgreen Common, in the County of Wiltshire, England, 1926.

HÜBEL & DENCK see

Cabinet — Shelf — No.

BOOKBINDING FIRMS. Germany

HUBER, AMBROSIUS

Cabinet Y — Shelf 4 — No. 4

(Note on Huber and his printing at Nuremberg, 1498-1503)

see

VOULLIÉME, ERNST. (Die) Deutschen drucker des fünfzehnten jahrhunderts...p.93

HUBER, J.M., Inc.

Cabinet 78 — Shelf 2 — No. 41

Black printing inks: an instructive sample book. J.M. Huber Inc., Manufacturers of Fine Inks. Main Office: 460 West 34th Street, New York City.

Cloth; 11 x 8½ in.

HUBER, J. M., Inc .

Cabinet 78 — Shelf 1 — No. 71

Ink. The story of News Ink. J. M. Huber, Inc. Manufacturers of printing inks ... New York City, 1928. Views of Ink-Making Plant.

Black, green, and brown shown by illustrations and newspaper work.

Half morocco; 7-7/8 x 10-1/8 in.

HUBER, MICHAEL.

Cabinet 78 — Shelf 1 — No. 49

Farbenfabriken, München, 1780-1930. Denkschrift zum 150 jährigen bestehen Michael Huber. Illus. portraits.

Half morocco; 12¼ x 9¼ in.

HUBER, WOLFGANG

Cabinet 5 — Shelf — No. 26

Engravings (early 16th century, German). Facsimile reprints of woodcuts by W. Huber.

Facs. in Cabinet 5, portfolio 26

HUBER PRINTING PRESS COMPANY

Cabinet EE — Shelf 4 — No. 79

Catalogues of printing presses, 1902.

See PRINTING PRESSES. LITHOGRAPHIC. Catalogue. Huber-Hodgeman...

HUBERT, EMILE

Cabinet KK — Shelf 4 — No. 11

Historique (1842 - 92) de l'association libre des compositeurs et imprimeurs typographes de Bruxelles. Bruxelles. P. Weissenbruch, Imprimeur du Roi. 1892.

On the history of this printers society. Bound with other items.

Boards, cloth back; 9 x 6 in.

HUBLOU, FRANCOIS JOSEPH

Cabinet W — Shelf 5 — No. 47

Vincent, J. B. Notice sur un imprimeur Belge (Hublou). Par J. B. Vincent, Bruxelles, 1858. Extrait du tome XIII du. Bulletin Bibliophile Belge. 1857.

Half morocco; 9 x 5¾ in.

HÜBNER, JULIUS

Cabinet RR — Shelf 4 — No. 29

Cantor Lectures on paper manufacture. By Julius Hübner, F.C.S. (Director of the dyeing, printing, and paper-making department at the Municipal School of Technology, Manchester.) Delivered before the Society of Arts on February 2nd, 9th, 16th and 23rd, 1903. London, 1903. Illus.

Half morocco; 10-1/8 x 6-3/4 in.

HUCK & CO., J.M.

Cabinet — Shelf — No.

See Specimen Books, Types. Germany.

HUDSON (Mrs. Barzillai), Publisher.

Cabinet — Shelf — No.

"The first woman publisher," 1749-1807. See Newspapers, anniversary issues; The Hartford Courant, Hartford, Connecticut: 145th anniversary issue.

HUDSON, FREDERIC

Cabinet NN — Shelf 3 — No. 4

Journalism in the United States, from 1690 to 1872. By Frederic Hudson, New York, 1873.

Preceded by a brief history of European journalism, list of first newspapers, etc.

Has authors A.L.S. inserted.

Cloth; 8-5/8 x 5-5/8 in.

HUDSON, FREDERIC

Cabinet NN — Shelf 2 — No. 12

Journalism in the United States, from 1690 to 1872.

Review of book with above title. Excerpt from Harper's Magazine, March, 1873.

Item 25 in vol. with binder's title "Various Newspapers and Periodicals".

HUDSON, WILLIAM C.

Cabinet OO — Shelf 3 — No. 28

Random recollections of an old political reporter. With an introduction by St. Clair McKelway. New York, 1911. Portraits.

Hudson was staff-writer for 44 years on political subjects in the Brooklyn Daily Eagle.

Cloth; 7¾ x 5½ in.

HUE, FERNAND

Cabinet W
Shelf 3
No. 19

Lemercier, imprimeur-lithograph, officier de la Légion d'Honneur. Biographie avec un portrait... Auteur, Fernand Hue. Paris, 1884.

Half morocco; 11-1/8 x 7½ in.

HUEY, EDMUND BURKE

Cabinet FF
Shelf 3
No. 82

Psychology and pedagogy of reading: with a review of the history of reading and writing and of methods, texts, and hygiene in reading. New York, 1910. Illus.

Cloth; 7¾ x 5¼ in.

HUGHES, THOMAS

Cabinet Q
Shelf 3
No. 9

Memoir of Daniel Macmillan. By Thomas Hughes London, 1882. With portrait.

Cloth; 7¾ x 5¼ x 1 in.

HUGHES & KIMBER, Ltd.

Cabinet EE
Shelf 5
No. 73

Catalogue of machinery and materials for letter-press, lithographic & copperplate printers and bookbinders. Established 1820. West Harding Street, Fetter Lane. London, E.C. n.d. After 1873.

Illus. and prices. Frontispiece view of the London factory of Hughes & Kimber.

Cloth stamped; 9½ x 6-5/8 x ½ in.

HUGHES and KIMBER
see also

Cabinet
Shelf
No.

Specimen Books, Types. England.

HUGO, HERMANNUS

Cabinet 2
No. 1
No. 30

De prima scribendi origine et universa rei literariae antiquitate....scribebat Hermannus Hugo.

Imprint: Antverpiae, Ex Officina Plantiniana, apud Balthasarem & Ioannem Moretus M.DC.XVII (1617)

Chapter 34, p.210: The invention of Typography.

Tooled morocco; 7¼ x 4-3/4 x 1-1/8 in.

HUGO, HERMANNUS cont'd

Cabinet
Shelf
NO.

Tooled morocco; 7¼ x 4½ x 1-1/8 in.

HUGO (Rev.) THOMAS

Cabinet K
Shelf 5
No. 14

Bewick collector. A descriptive catalogue of the works of Thomas and John Bewick; including cuts in various states for books and pamphlets...The whole described from the originals, and illustrated with 112 cuts. By Thomas Hugo...The possessor of the collection. London, 1866.

Cloth; 9-1/8 x 6 x 1¼ in.

HUGO (Rev.) THOMAS

Cabinet K
Shelf 5
No. 15

Bewick collector. A supplement to a descriptive catalogue of the works of Thomas and John Bewick...Illustrated with 180 cuts. By Thomas Hugo, the possessor of the collection. London, 1868.

Cloth; 9-1/8 x 5¾ x 1-1/8 in.

HUGO, VICTOR

Cabinet Y
Shelf 1
No. 92.05

Ceci tuera cela. (Hymnus auf die drukkunst.

See PRAISE OF PRINTING. Hugo, Victor ...

HUGO, THOMAS

Cabinet J
Shelf 4
No. 1

Bewick's woodcuts: impressions of upwards of 2000 wood-blocks, engraved, for the most part by Thomas and John Bewick...with an introduction, a descriptive catalogue of the blocks, and a list of the books and pamphlets illustrated. By Thomas Hugo...the owner of the collection. London, 1870.

Half leather; 17¼ x 10-7/8 x 2-1/8 in.

HUGO, VICTOR

Cabinet 21
Shelf 2
No. 3

Liberty of the press. Victor Hugo's estimate of it.

In "The Printer", Vol. IV, p. 97.

HUGUETAN, JEAN

Cabinet W
Shelf 1
No. 01

See Imprints, France. Huguetan, Jean. Lyon, 1642

HUIDEKOPER, HARM JAN

Cabinet S
Shelf 2
No. 87

Tiffany, Nina Moore and Francis: Harm Jan Huidekoper. Cambridge: Riverside Press, 1904. Illus.

Biographical account gathered from early newspaper files and letters; in which there are references to early printers and printing in America.

Cloth; 8¾ x 6¼ in.

HUILLIER (l'), PIERRE.

Cabinet 69
Shelf 1
No. 51

See Early Printing in France. Paris, 1584.

HUISH, MARCUS B.

Cabinet M
Shelf 2
No. 3

American pilgrims way in England. By Marcus B Huish. Illus. by Elizabeth M. Chettie. The Fine Arts Society. Printed by R. & R. Clark, Limited, Edinburgh.

Cloth; 12½ x 9 x 2¼ in.

HÜLLE, HERMANN

Cabinet Y
Shelf 4
No. 53

Über den alten Chinischen typendruck und seine entwickelung in den landern des fernen Ostens. Gedruckt auf veranlassung der H. Berthold. [Berlin] 1923.

On Chinese types and their development in Far Eastern countries.

Paper; 9-3/8 x 6¾ in. Bound in Chinese manner in folding protective case.

HÜLLE, HERMANN

Cabinet II
Shelf 3
No. 46

Uber den alten Chinesischen typendruck und seine entwicklung in den ländern des fernen ostens. Gedruckt als Privatdruck der Berthold'schen Hansdruckerei. (Berlin) 1923. Pamphlet.

Relates to development of Chinese printing types in the far East.

Item in Chinese style board cover; 9½ x 6¼ in.

HULLMANDEL (Charles)

Cabinet L Shelf 1 No. 7

Art of drawing on stone, giving a full explanation of the various styles, of the different methods to be employed to ensure success, and of the modes of correcting, as well as the several causes of failure. London, 1824.
With 19 lithographic plates.

Boards; 11¼ x 7¾ in.

HULLMANDEL, CHARLES (Translator)

Cabinet L Shelf 1 No. 8

Manual of lithography...London, 1832.

See RAUCOURT, de CHARLEVILLE
Manual of lithography...London, 1832

HULSHOF, ABRAHAM

Cabinet Y Shelf 3 No. 76

(Bookbinding in the Carthusian monastery at Utrecht, 1466-1470) Uitgaven voor de boekerij van het Karthuizerklooster te Utrecht in de jaren 1466-1470.

pp.170-175 in Loubier, Hans (Tribute to) Buch und bucheinband...Leipzig, 1923.

HULST, FELIX, van

Cabinet W Shelf 4 No. 44

Christopher Plantin. Par Felix Van Hulst, 2m édition. Liège, 1846. Lithographed portraits of Plantin and Raphelengius.

Half morocco; 9-3/4 x 6½ in.

HUMANIST'S LIBRARY

Cabinet Shelf No.

SEE IMPRINTS: Updike, D. B.

[HUMBERT De.] Mr. le MAJOR H.

Cabinet I Shelf 1 No. 19

Abregè historique de l'origine et des progrez de la gravure et des estampes en bois, et en teille douce. Par Mr. le Major H. A Berlin, chez Haude & Spener, 1752.

Half morocco; 6½ x 3¾ in.

HUME, Rev. A. (Compiler)

Cabinet T Shelf 5 No. 7

Learned Societies and Printing Clubs of the United Kingdom: Being an account of their respective origin, history...Compiled from official documents by the Rev. A. Hume... With a supplement by A. I. Evans. London, 1853.

Cloth; 8 x 4-7/8 x 1-1/8 in.

HUMOR, PRINTERS'

Cabinet Shelf No.

See
I - PRINTERS' HUMOR.
II - POETRY OF PRINTING.

HUMPHREYS, HENRY NOEL

Cabinet T Shelf 6 No. 9

History of the art of printing, from its invention to its widespread development in the middle of the 16th. century; preceded by a short account of the origin of the alphabet, and the successive methods of recording events...With 100 illus. produced in photolithography by Day & Son, London, 1867.

Full morocco, gilt tooled, 13½ x 9¾ x 1¾ in.

HUMPHREYS, HENRY NOEL

Cabinet T Shelf 6 No. 10

History of the art of printing, from its invention to its wide-spread development in the middle of the 16th century...Illustrated by 100 facsimiles in photolithography, executed under the direction of the author. Second issue. London, 1868.

Stamped cloth; 14 x 9¾ x 2 in.

HUMPHREYS, HENRY NOEL

Cabinet T Shelf 6 No. 11

Masterpieces of the early printers and engravers. A series of facsimiles from rare and curious books remarkable for illustrative devices, beautiful borders, decorative initials, printers marks, elaborate title-pages, etc. London, 1870.

Stamped cloth; 14½ x 10¼ x 1¼ in.

HUMPHREYS, HENRY NOEL

Cabinet L Shelf 3 No. 14

Origin and progress of the art of writing: a connected narrative of the development of the art...By Henry Noel Humphreys. Illustrated by a number of specimens of the writing of all ages, and a series of facsimiles from autograph letters from the 15th to the 19th century. London, 1853.

Cloth; 10¼ x 7½ in.

HUNGARIAN PRINTERS' TRADE UNION

Cabinet KK Shelf 2 No. 57

(History of fifty years of Hungarian Printers' Trade Union) Egyesült Erövel...Novitzky N. Laszlo. Budapest, 1911. Illus.

Cloth; 10½ x 7-3/8 x 1-3/8 in.

HUNGARY

Cabinet Y Shelf 3 No. 101

(Bookmaking, modern in Hungary. Illus. article)

see DEUTSCHER VEREIN FUR BUCHWESEN U. SCHRIFTUM...Jahrbuch 1933-34, p.73

HUNGARY

Cabinet J Shelf 5 No. 24

[History of art and painting in Hungary from 1667 to 1900. With reproductions in black and white and colored] A Magyar képirás üttöröi. Irta Malonyay Dezso...Budapest. Franklin-Tarsulat. 1905.

Boards; 16 x 11¼ x 1½ in.

HUNGARY

Cabinet 26 Shelf 1 No. 16

Leutschau 1625-1715, the Brewer family of printers in.

See "Gutenberg-Gesellschaft Jahrbuch, 1927", pp.91-95.

HUNGARY

Cabinet 26 Shelf 1 No. 16

Pressburg, 1715-1848, the Royer family of printers.

See "Gutenberg-Gesellschaft Jahrbuch, 1927", pp.85-90.

HUNGARY

Cabinet 26 Shelf 1 No. 16

Pressburg, 1715, the Royer family of printers.

Article in GUTENBERG-GESELLSCHAFT JAHRBUCH, 1927, pp.91-95

HUNGARY

Cabinet 26 Shelf 1 No. 21

(Reprints of 17th century German devotional writings. A bibliographical essay)

See "EARLY PRINTING IN HUNGARY. Literature of. (Reprints...

HUNGARY

Cabinet NN Shelf 2 No. 13

What the people read in.

see NEWSPAPERS, Hungary. Literature of

HUNT, HAYWOOD H.

Cabinet Shelf No.

See Imprints, United States.

HUNGARY

Cabinet *T Shelf 5 No. 135

(A) Short history of printing in Hungary

See PEDDIE, R. A. Printing, a short history of the art...p.245

HUNGARY (see also)

Cabinet Shelf No.

EARLY PRINTING in Hungary
INCUNABULA. Chronicra Hungarorum, 1473.
IMPRINTS, Hungary
LANGUAGE CHARACTERS, Hungary
MODERN PRINTING, Hungary
NEWSPAPERS, Hungary
PRINTING, HISTORICAL, Hungary
SPECIMEN BOOKS, TYPES, Hungary
TYPOGRAPHY, Hungary

HUNT, S.

Cabinet Q Shelf 1 No. 18

Centennial of the Methodist Book Concern. New York, 1889.

Half morocco; 9 x $5\frac{3}{4}$ in.

HUNGARY

Cabinet C Shelf 1 No. 4

Specimens of printing from the printing office of "Vilagossag" Co., Ltd. Budapest, Hungary (1924)

Portfolio; $16\frac{1}{2}$ x $13\frac{3}{4}$ in.

HUNNEWELL, JAMES FROTHINGHAM

Cabinet S Shelf 4 No. 12

Triumphs of early printing: A paper read at the Annual Meeting of The Club of Odd Volumes, at the University Club, Dec. 26, 1901, by the President, James Frothingham Hunnewell. Boston, 1902.

Half boards; 3-7/8 x 7 in.

HUNT, WILLIAM

Cabinet OO Shelf 5 No. 7

Then and now; or, fifty years of newspaper work. With an appendix. Hull...London, 1887. With frontispiece portrait.

Cloth; $7\frac{1}{2}$ x 5 x 7/8 in.

HUNGARY

Cabinet LL Shelf 2 No. 43

(Text book of printing, for pressmen and compositor) Fuchs Zsigmond: A gepterem...Budapest, 1910. Illus.

Cloth; $10\frac{1}{2}$ x $7\frac{1}{2}$ x 1-3/8 in.

HUNSCOT, JOSEPH

Cabinet X Shelf 4 No. 15

Petition of Joseph Hunscot, stationer, to both the Houses of Parliament...in vindication of himself and the Company of Stationers; against divers scandalous libels against the Government...As it was presented to both Houses the 11 and 12 of June, 1646. [London]

Half morocco; $7\frac{1}{4}$ x $8\frac{1}{2}$ x 3/8 in.

HUNTER, DARD

Cabinet Shelf No.

Ancestry given in "Cornell Hunter, (12), joins Chillicothe Century Club.

Illus. article in American Press, vol. 50, No.3, Dec. 1931, p.20.

HUNGARY

Cabinet II Shelf 1 No. 74

[Type Foundry, the first in Hungary. Established 1890].
Specimen book of printing types. Has price list of 1907.

See also II/1/73.

Cloth, stamped; 12 x $9\frac{1}{4}$ x 7/8 in.

HUNT, F. KNIGHT

Cabinet OO Shelf 5 No. 1 (2 vols.)

(The) Fourth Estate: Contributions towards a history of newspapers, and of the liberty of the press. In two vols...London, 1850.

Cloth; 8 x 5-1/8 in.

HUNTER, DARD

Cabinet S Shelf 6 No. 6

Books of Dard Hunter. By Nelson Antrim Crawford. Excerpt from the American Mercury, August, 1924. Pasted in, an excerpt from the N.Y. Evening Post, May 26, 1931: "To Dard Hunter belongs the palm of bookcraft". By Lewis Sherwin.

Item (1) in book with binder's title "Printing and printing offices."

HUNGARY

Cabinet 26 Shelf 1 No. 17

Vergangenheit der buchdruckerkunst im Burgenland. von Andre Csatkai.
Article, German text, in the Gutenberg-Gesellschaft Jahrbuch 1928, pp.172-174.

HUNT, GAILLARD

Cabinet QQ Shelf 4 No. 40

History of the Seal of the United States. Washington, D. C., Department of State, 1919. With plates, some in colors.

Half morocco; $9\frac{3}{4}$ x $7\frac{1}{2}$ in.

HUNTER, DARD

Cabinet RR Shelf 6 No. 8

Literature of papermaking, 1390-1800. By Dard Hunter. (The Mountain House, Chillicothe, Ohio) 1925.

Limited edition. Illus., facs.

Portfolio with ties; 17 x $12\frac{1}{4}$ in.

HUNTER, DARD

RR 6 11

Old papermaking. By Dard Hunter. Chillicothe, Ohio, At the Mountain House Press, 1923. Illus.

No. 63, signed by the author, edition of 200 copies.

HUNTER, DARD

Cabinet RR Shelf 6 No. 38

Old papermaking in China and Japan. By Dard Hunter, Chillicothe, Ohio, at the Mountain House Press, 1932. Illus.

No. 14 of 200 copies printed.

Half linen; 17¼ x 11¾ in. In slip case.

HUNTER, DARD

Cabinet RR Shelf 6 No. 10

(A) Papermaking pilgrimage to Japan, Korea and China. Pynson Printers. New York, 1936. Illus.

No. 196, signed by the author, edition of 370 copies.

Partial contents: Papermaking materials, papermaking moulds, the pilgrimage, Japanese papers, bibliography, description of illustrations, descriptions of specimens of paper.

Boards, morocco back; 11-3/8 x 9¼. In slip case.

HUNTER, DARD

Cabinet RR Shelf 3 No. 30

Paper-making through eighteen centuries. By Dard Hunter. New York, 1930. Illus.

Printed by William Edwin Rudge.

Cloth; 9½ x 6½ x 1-3/8 in.

HUNTER, DARD

Cabinet Shelf No.

see also

Imprints, United States.

HUNTER, DARD

Cabinet RR Shelf 6 No. 9

Primitive papermaking. An account of a Mexican sojourn and of a voyage to the Pacific Islands in search of information, implememts, and specimens relating to the making and decorating of bark-paper. By Dard Hunter. Chillicothe, Ohio. At the Mountain House Press, 1927.

With original specimens of native papers, and facsimiles.

Signed and numbered copy.

Portfolio with ties; 17 x 12 in.

HUNTER, JOSEPH

Cabinet RR Shelf 1 No. 3

Specimens of marks used by the early manufacturers of paper, as exhibited in documents in the public archives in England. Communicated by Joseph Hunter. February 18, 1858.

Cloth; 12 x 9½ x 3/8 in.

HUNTINGTON, HENRY EDWARDS

Cabinet S Shelf 5 No. 48

Founder of the Henry E. Huntington Library, San Marino, California. [Biographical]. By Robert O. Schad. Reprinted from The Huntington Library Bulletin, No. 1, May, 1931. Illus., portrait.

In envelope.

HUNTINGTON, HENRY E.

Cabinet Shelf No.

See LIBRARIES, Private.

HUONDER, ANTON

Cabinet Y Shelf 3 No. 20

(Die) Verdienst der katholischen Heidenmission um die Buchdruckerkunst in überseeischen Ländern vom 16.-18 Jahrhundert. Xaverius Verlagsbuchhandlung A.-G. Aachen, 1923.

(On the history of Mission printing in all countries.

Cloth; 8 x 5-1/8. pp.114. Original covers bound in.

HUPA LANGUAGE

Cabinet II Shelf 4 No. 2

Athapascan (Hupa). By Pliny Earle Goddard.

See BOAS, FRANZ. American Indian languages, handbook of...Bulletin 40, Washington, 1911, pp.91-158.

HUPFUFF, MATTHIAS

Cabinet X Shelf 3 No. 13

Brief bibliographical note, with printer mark, Hupfuff, Strassburg, 1492-1520.

see

HEITZ, PAUL. Elsässische bücher-marken...p.xvii, plate vii.

HUPFUFF, MATHIS

Cabinet Y Shelf 4 No. 4

(Note on Hupfuff and his printing at Strasbourg, 1498-1516)

see

VOULLIÉME, ERNST. (Die) Deutschen drucker des fünfzehnten jahrhunderts...p.113

HUPP, OTTO

Cabinet 26 ~~Y~~ Shelf 1 No. 19 ~~95.01~~

Gutenberg und die nacherfinder. Illus.

Bibliographical account of Gutenberg's invention, and of his succeeding inventors.

Article in the "Gutenberg-Gesellschaft Jahrbuch 1929, pp.31-100.

HUPP, OTTO

Cabinet 26 ~~Y~~ Shelf 1 No. 21 ~~27~~

(Gutenberg's first printed book? A comparitive study of the types used for the Psalter, the 42 and 36 line Bibles.) Ein zahlenweis für Gutenberg.

Essay in "GUTENBERG-GESELLSCHAFT JAHRBUCH, 1931", pp.9-27.

HUPP, OTTO

Cabinet Y Shelf 1 No. 35

(Ein) Missale speciale, vorläufer des psalteriums von 1457. Beitrag sur geschichte der ältesten druckwerke. Munchen, 1898. [Bound in with]: Gutenberg's erste drucke. Ein weiterer beitrag...von Otto Hupp, Munchen, 1902.

Bibliographical study of Gutenberg's supposed first printed work.

Half morocco; 12¼ x 9-1/8 x 5/8 in.

HUPROYE (Estienne de la) le Jeune

Cabinet V Shelf 5 No. 23

Sur un imprimeur de Troyes au 16e siècle. Par M. Alexis Socard. [Excerpt, Troyes, 1862].

Item 3 in vol. with binder's title "Origin of Printing in France: Pamphlets".

HURLBUT, STEPHEN A.

Cabinet G Shelf 3 No. 53

Song of S. Peter Damiani, The. Edited from the Vatican Ms., with a New translation by Stephen A. Hurlbut.

Imprint: The St. Alban's Press, Mount Saint Alban. Washington, D.C. M.D.CCCCXXVIII.

Boards; 8¾ x 5-3/4 x ¼ in.

HURLBUT'S PAPERMAKER GENTLEMAN

Cabinet RR Shelf 4 No. 42

Published by Hurlbut Paper Co., South Lee, Mass.

See PERIODICALS, PAPERMAKERS. Hurlbut's Papermaker...

HURUS, Hans and Paul

Cabinet X Shelf 3 No. 19

Bio-bibliographical sketch, with printer mark, Hurus (Saragossa), 1485-1499.

see HAEBLER, KONRAD. (Spanish and Portugese printer marks...p.i

---

HURUS, PABLO and Juan.

Cabinet 75 Shelf 2 No. 6

Printers of illustrated books at Zaragoza, 1491.

See Lyell, James P. R. Notes on Early book-illustration in Spain.

HUSBAND, EDWARD

Cabinet X Shelf 4 No. 17

London, 1649 (Imprint)

see LIBERTY OF PRINTING. Great Britain, Act (1649)...

HUSNER, GEORG

Cabinet Y Shelf 4 No. 4

(Note on Husner and his printing at Strasbourg, 1473)

see VOULLIÉME, ERNST. (Die) Deutschen drucker des fünfzehnten jahrhunderts...p.107

HUSNER, GEORG.

Cabinet D Shelf 4 No. 62

Strassburg, circa 1476.

see also INCUNABULA (loose leaves) Husner...

HUSSEY, H.

Cabinet QQ Shelf 3 No. 8

Australian Colonies; together with notes of a voyage from Australia to Panama. Descriptions of Tahiti and other Islands in the Pacific, and a tour through some of the States of America in 1854. By H. Hussey. London.

Presentation copy signed by author.

Hussey was one of the earliest master printers in Adelaide, arriving there in 1839.

Paper; 6-3/8 x 4½ x ½ in.

HUSSEY, H.

Cabinet QQ Shelf 3 No. 7

More than half a century of Colonial life and Christian experience. With notes of travel, lectures, publications, etc. By H. Hussey. Adelaide (Australia) 1897. Illus.

Autobiographical account of a preacher-printer-publisher.

Cloth; 7½ x 5 x 1-1/8 in.

HUSUNG, MAX JOSEPH

Cabinet Y Shelf 3 No. 76

(Development of pictures representing months in calenders) Über die entwicklung der monatsbilder in kalendern.

pp. 13 to 39 in Loubier, Hans (Tribute to) Buch und bucheinband...Leipzig, 1923.

HUSZ, MATHIEU.

Cabinet I Shelf 4 No. 9

Lyons, 1483. Imprint.

See FACSIMILES. Jacques de Voragine, la legende doree en francais ...

HUTCHINGS PRINTING HOUSE

Cabinet C Shelf 1 No. 24

Imprint of 1871, Hutchings Printing House, Hartford Conn.

See MALLORY, WHEELER AND COMPANY. Catalogue of door knobs...

HUTCHINS, HENRY CLINTON

Cabinet S Shelf 3 No. 162

Robinson Crusoe and its printing, 1719-1731. A bibliographical study. By Henry C. Hutchins. With a foreword by A. Edward Newton. New York, 1925. Illus.

Cloth; 10 x 7¾ in.

HUTCHINS, SAMUEL

Cabinet S Shelf 4 No. 107

(An) Old printer's reminiscences: Samuel Hutchins being The Author. Old Cambridge, 1869. Illus.

A series of autobiographical essay excerpted from magazines, cut and pasted on leaved to form a book. Each subject with its extra illustrations fitted into their proper relation to the subject. Occasional explanatory notes in the authors own hand writing.

Half morocco; 8 x 5 in.

HÜTER, SIMON.

Cabinet E Shelf 1 No. 46

See Early Printing in Germany. Frankfort a.M. 1566. Sigmund Feyerbend, Simon Hüter and Georg Rabner.

HUTTON, RICHARD HOLT

Cabinet OO Shelf 5 No. 10

"Spectator, The", Richard Holt Hutton of. A monograph. Edinburgh, 1899.

Cloth; 7¾ x 5¼ x ½ in.

HUTTON, WILLIAM

Cabinet Q Shelf 3 No. 13

Life of William Hutton

see JEWITT, LLEWELLYNN. Hutton, William, life of...

HUTZ, Leonard

Cabinet X Shelf 3 No. 19

Bio-bibliographical sketch, with printer mark, Hutz (Valencia), 1493-1506.

see HAEBLER, KONRAD. (Spanish and Portugese printer marks...p.xii

---

[HUYOT, ADOLPHE JOSEPH?]

Cabinet I Shelf 3 No. 15

Engraver, Paris, 1839-83. Examples of his works.

See ENGRAVING, LITERATURE OF. [French Engravings and Engravers] ... Paris, 1888.

HUZARD (Mme.)

Cabinet X Shelf 5 No. 43

Imprint of Mme. Huzard, Paris, 1834

See LIBERTY OF PRINTING, France.
(Le) l'Etat reel de presse...Par M.C. Leber, Paris, 1834.

HYALL, NICHOLAS

Cabinet T Shelf 2 No. 6 [vol.4]

Books printed by N. Hyall, London, 1548-1552.
Bibliographical notes.

see

DIBDIN'S "Typographical Antiquities"... London, 1810-19, vol.IV, p.230

HYALOGRAPHY.

Cabinet 26 Shelf 2 No. 3

See Engraving, Glass. Art of printing, etc.

HYDRAULIC PRESSES

Cabinet Z Shelf 3 No. 43

Presse Hydraulique, advertised and illus. with prices, by Ch. Giroudot Fils, Paris. [circa, 1840].

p. 401 in "Miscellaneous Collection of French Type Specimens." ... 1829-1844.

HYGIENE

Cabinet AA Shelf 1 No. 26

Buniva, Michele Francesco. Igiene dé tipografi ... Saggio offerto a questa nella sua adunanza del 23 gennaio 1825. Torino, 1825.

Half morocco; 8¼ x 5¼ in.

HYGIENE

Cabinet JJ Shelf 3 No. 24

Health of printers: a study in industrial hygiene. By George A. Stevens, statistician. Excerpt from Report of Labor Statistics. New York, 1906.

Cloth; 9 x 6 in.

HYGIENE

Cabinet KK Shelf 2 No. 56

Über die gesundheitsverhältnisse der buchdrucker ...von Dr. med. Albrecht Eduard Burckhardt. n. p. Oktober, 1889.
(Supplement to "Eingabe des Vereins schweizerischer Buchdruckereibesitzer...fur Reduktion der taglichen Arbeitszeit im Buchdruckergewerbe. [Bern] 1889.

Boards; 11 x 8¾ in.

HYGINUS (CAIUS JULIUS).

Cabinet 29 Shelf 1 No. 15

Poeticon astronomicon [Sentinnus (Jacobus) and Santritter (J.L.)]. Venice, Erhard Ratdolt. 1482.
Title printed in red.

Gesamt-Kat; Zapf. 159; Essling 285.

Vellum; 8½ x 6 x ½ in.

HYGINUS (CAIUS JULIUS)

Cabinet 29 Shelf 1 No. 24

Poeticon astronomicon. Venice. Erhard Ratdolt. 1485.

Boards; 8¾ x 6-3/8 x ½ in.

HYMNOLOGY.

Cabinet Shelf No.

(A) Hymnological Library. Account of what is the most extensive collection, at Church House, Westminster, England. Dr. Julian collection.

Article in South African Printer & Stationer, Vol. 12, No. 7, July 1932, p. 263.

HYPNEROTOMACHIA

Cabinet QQ Shelf 4 No. 12

Strife of love in a dream...

see

LANG, ANDREW. Strife of love in a dream...

HYPNEROTOMACHIA
SEE ALSO

Cabinet Shelf No.

POLIPHILO. Hypnerotomachia...

I

IAGGARD, WILLIAM

See Jaggard, William

IBANAG, (Philippine Islands)

Cabinet II | Shelf 4 | No. 1

Saint Luke, the Gospel of. n.d. circa 1907. Booklet.

Item in manila envelope.

IBARRA, ANTONIO and PINEDA JOSÉ de

Cabinet 79 | Shelf 1 | No. 5

Guatemala, 1660-1679.

See Medina's La imprenta Guatemala... Santiago de Chile, 1910. [Introduction to]

IBARRA, JOACHIN.

Cabinet F | Shelf 5 | No. 44

See Early Printing in Spain. Madrid, 1772. Joachin Ibarra.

IBARRA, JOACHIN. La viuda de

Cabinet AA | Shelf 5 | No. 3

See Imprints, Spain. Ibarra, Joachin: La viuda de. Madrid, 1796.

ICAZBALCETA, JOAQUIN GARCIA

Cabinet 79 | Shelf 2 | No. 14

Bibliografia Mexicana del siglo XVI. Primera parte. Catalogo razonado de libros impresos en Mexico en 1539 á 1600, con biografias de, autores y otras ilustraciones. Precedido de una noticia acerca de la introduccion de la imprenta en Mexico. Mexico, 1886.

Half morocco; 12 x $8\frac{3}{4}$ in.

ICELAND

Cabinet T | Shelf 5 | No. 135

(A) Short history of printing in Iceland

See PEDDIE, R.A. Printing, a short history of the art...p.232

ICELAND

Cabinet AA | Shelf 5 | No. 41

See Printing, Historical, Iceland.
See also Early Printing in Iceland.

ICONES (PORTRAITS, or BOOKS OF EMBLEMS)

Cabinet | Shelf | No.

See cards with following sub-heads:

PORTRAITS
EMBLEMS

EMBLEMS. Literature of.

ICONOGRAPHIC ENCYCLOPEDIA.

Cabinet I | Shelf 3 | No. 2

Arts and sciences, the iconographic encyclopedia of. Translated from the German...Beautifully illustrated with nearly 600 steel, wood and lithographic prints, from the original plates ...Published by special arrangement with F.A. Brockhaus, Leipzig, Germany. Iconographic Publishing Company, Philadelphia, 1885.

Vol. III only, treats of "Sculpture and Painting."

Stamped Cloth; $10\frac{3}{4}$ x $7\frac{1}{4}$ x $1\frac{3}{4}$ in.

ICONOGRAPHIE DE l'IMPRIMERIE

Cabinet V | Shelf 6 | No. 14

Bulletin Officiel des Maitres Imprimeurs. Paris, 1927. l'Imprimerie glorifiée par les poétes et par les litterateurs. Illus.

(Printing glorified in literature and poetry)

Half morocco; $12\frac{1}{8}$ x 9-$\frac{3}{4}$ in.

IDE, SIMEON

Cabinet R | Shelf 3 | No. 203

Biography

see BIOGRAPHIES, Printers. Ide, Simeon...

IDE, SIMEON

Cabinet R Shelf 4 No. 131

Yeoman, freeman, pioneer printer. By Louis W. Flanders. With a genealogy of the Ide family ...Bibliography of the imprints [1814-1879] of Simeon Ide. Rutland, Vermont. 1931. Has frontispiece portrait.

Cloth; 9-3/8 x 6-1/8 x $1\frac{1}{4}$ in.

IDEOGRAPHS

Cabinet K Shelf 5 No. 7

CHINESE

See Design. Chinese book of design; ideagraphs...

IDEOGRAPHS

Cabinet K Shelf 4 No. 1 & 2

(Symbolic significance of ideographs)

See Bayley, Harold. Lost language of symbolism...London, 1912 (2 vols.)

IDEOGRAPHS, CHINESE

Cabinet Shelf No.

See LANGUAGE CHARACTERS. Examples of. Chinese ideographs...

IESI, (Italy).

Cabinet Y Shelf 2 No. 97

First printer in Iesi. Federico De'Conti.

See SCHOLDERER, VICTOR. Federico de'Conti...

IFAN, CHARLES

Cabinet M Shelf 1 No. 61

Le Prote (overseer), étude-causerie, publiée dans le Courrier du Livre d'Aout, 1901, à Novembre 1904. Bordeauz. Imprimerie G. Delmas, 1904. Presented by G. Delma Delmas, Esq.

Cloth; 10 x $6\frac{1}{2}$ x 1 in.

IFERN, PEDRO

Cabinet Shelf No.

See Specimen Books, Types. Spain.

IHM, BERNHARD A.

Cabinet L Shelf 4 No. 12

Bunten farben in der buchdruckerei und insbesonderer derem druck auf der schnellpresse. Ein handbuch zur practischen erlernung und forthilfe herausgegeben von Bernhard A.Ihm. Zweite auflage. Wien & Leipzig. 1874.

With 48 plates of color printing.

Half morocco; 11 x 8 in.

IHM, BERNHARD A.

Cabinet 78 Shelf 1 No. 45

(Die) Bunten farben in der buchdruckerei, und insbesondere deren druck auf der schnellpresse. Ein praktisches handbuch. Vienna, 1874. Second edition. With 48 plates of examples.

"A valuable work on color printing by the steam press."

Paper boards; 10-7/8 x $7\frac{1}{2}$ x $\frac{3}{4}$ in.

IIBEI, KUMIHIGASHI

Cabinet Y Shelf 3 No. 99

(Handbook for paper production. Facsimile of edition published in Japan in 1798). "Kamisuki Choho-ki." Kumihigashi Iibei, Naniwa (Osaka) 1798. (Japanese text. Illus. by Seichuan Takei).

Reproduced by the Deutsche Buchmuseum, Leipzig, 1925. With concluding remarks by Albert Schramm.

Paper; $8\frac{3}{4}$ x 6-1/8 in.

ILES, GEORGE

Cabinet QQ Shelf 2 No. 24

Leading American Inventors. With 15 portraits and many illustrations. [Series] Biographies of leading Americans. Edited by W.P. Trent, New York, 1912.

see other side of this card for names of inventors.

Cloth; 8 x $5\frac{1}{4}$.

ILES, GEORGE

Cabinet QQ Shelf 2 No. 24

Leading American Inventors. With 15 portraits and many illustrations. [Series] Biographies of leading Americans. Edited by W.P. Trent, New York, 1912.

Included in this book of inventors are the following:

John and Robert Stevens; Robert Fulton; Eli Whitney; Thomas Blanchard; Samuel Morse; Charles Goodyear; John Ericsson; Cyrus H. McCormick; C.L. Sholes; Benjamin C. Tilghman; Ottmar Mergenthaler.

Cloth; 8 x $5\frac{1}{4}$ in.

ILIVE, JACOB.

Cabinet F Shelf 4 No. 4

Oration spoke at Joyners Hall in Thames Street: On Monday, Sept. 24, 1733. Pursuant to the Will of Mrs. Jane Ilive...By her son and executor. London: Printed for T. Cooper in Ivy Lane. 1733. [Price 1 s.]

Mrs. Ilive was wife of the typefounder Jacob Ilive, who wrote the above oration. See Reed; pp. 346-9.

Half morocco; 8 x 5 in.

ILIVE, JACOB

Cabinet F Shelf 4 No. 4

Dialogue between a Doctor of the Church of England, and Mr. Jacob Ilive, upon the subject of the Oration...1733.

Bound in with the Oration spoke at Joyners-hall in Thames Street, on Monday, Sept. 24, 1733.

Half morocco; 8 x 5 in.

ILLINOIS

Cabinet Shelf No.

Early printing in Illinois.

See EARLY PRINTING IN AMERICA (U.S.) Literature (Illinois)

ILLINOIS

Cabinet Shelf No.

Early printing in Illinois.

See McMurtrie. Pioneer printing in Illinois.

ILLINOIS

Cabinet NN Shelf 6 No. 20

Newspapers, 1808-1897

see NEWSPAPERS, United States. Literature. Illinois and Missouri newspapers...

ILLINOIS

Cabinet NN Shelf 6 No. 6

Newspapers and periodicals of Illinois, 1814 - 1879. By Franklin William Scott. Bibliographical Series, Vol. I. Collections of the Illinois State Historical Library, Vol. VI, Springfield, Ill. 1910. Illus.

Cloth; 9 x 6 x 2-1/8 in.

ILLINOIS

Cabinet NN Shelf 7 No. 14

Early newspapers in Illinois.

see

BOSS, HENRY R. Illinois, early newspapers in...Chicago, 1870.

ILLINOIS.

Cabinet Shelf No.

See Newspapers, special issues: The Inter-Ocean, Chicago Day.

ILLINOIS PRESS ASSOCIATION

Cabinet KK Shelf 5 No. 89

Annual reports for 1895, 1909, 1922 - 25.

3 pieces in board holder; 9 x 6 in.

ILLINOIS PRESS ASSOCIATION see

Cabinet Shelf No.

ASSOCIATIONS, EDITORS'. Illinois...

ILLINOIS PUBLISHER

Cabinet KK Shelf 5 No. 90

Official publication of the Illinois Press Association. Springfield Ill., March, 1917, May 1918, August, 1918.

3 issues in envelope.

ILLINOIS STATE JOURNAL.

Cabinet 66 Shelf 1 No. 5

Centennial issue, 1831-1931.

See NEWSPAPERS, ANNIVERSARY ISSUES. Illinois State Journal.

ILLINOIS TYPE-FOUNDING CO.

Cabinet Shelf No.

See Specimen Books, Types. United States. Illinois Type-Founding Co.

ILLUMINATED BOOKS

Cabinet M Shelf 4 No. 23

Book of Common Prayer...Illuminated and illustrated with the engravings from Works of Great Painters. The vignettes, initials, borders, and ornaments, designed by Owen Jones, Architect. London: Vizetelly Bros. & Co., printers and engravers, 1845.

Morocco, tooled, gilt; 9⅜ x 6½ x 1¾ in.

ILLUMINATED BOOKS

Cabinet G Shelf 1 No. 52

Cranbrook Papers by the Cranbrook Society, Detroit, Mich. 1901. First Book. Printed and illuminated entirely by hand, on paper made by hand in U.S. Types, Jenson Old Style as designed by the late William Morris.

Half vellum; 11¼ x 8-3/4 ins. pp.(6), 1oo.

ILLUMINATED BOOKS

Cabinet 68 Shelf No. 7

Griechische buchmalerei. von Hans Gerstinger, Wien, 1926. In two parts

Part 1, Text
" 2, Plates

Boards; 20 x 15 in.

ILLUMINATED BOOKS.

Cabinet 70 Shelf 1 No. 19

Horae Beatae Virginis Mariae ad usum Romanum. Simon Vostre. Paris, 1520. Printed on vellum.

Calf; 7¼ x 4⅝ x 1¼ in.

ILLUMINATED BOOKS.

Cabinet 29 Shelf 2 No. 6

Hore dive vgis Maris scdum usum Romanum. Paris, 1511. Thielman Kerver. Printed on vellum, many woodcut borders.

Calf; 7 x 4½ x 1½ in.

ILLUMINATED BOOKS

Cabinet 68 Shelf No. 9

Italian 15th and 16th centuries choral books, Capital letters selected from. Engraved in outline...The Arundel Society, London, 1862.

Portfolio; 22½ x 17½ in.

ILLUMINATED BOOKS

Cabinet 68 Shelf No. 8

(Masterpieces of book illumination)

See LEIDINGER, Georg. Meisterwerke der buchmalerei...Munchen, 1920.

ILLUMINATED BOOKS

Cabinet 29 Shelf 1 No. 41

Paris, 1503: Thielman Kerver.
Title: Hore intemerate Virginis marie secundu usum Romanum [Printer Mark]
Colophon: Ces présentes heures...furet achévees le V iour de Janier l'an mil cinq ces et troys. Par Thielman Kerver imprimeur...de Paris. Pour Gillet Remacle, aussi libraire demourant sur le pont saint Michela a lenseigne dela Licorne. [1503]

Calf; 7-3/8 x 5 x 1¼ in.

ILLUMINATED BOOKS

Cabinet D Shelf 1 No. 31

Speculum Judiciale, Durandus, Milan, 1478.

Type work by Benignus and Johan Antonius de Honate.

Gesamt-Kat. ; Hain 6510; large-fol.

ILLUMINATED BOOKS
see also

Cabinet Shelf No.

Imprints, United States. Grabhorn Press, San Francisco, 1926.

ILLUMINATED BOOKS [Literature of]

Cabinet S Shelf 5 No. 18

Famous Breviary, A (Grimaldis), by Mrs.J.W.Davis, in Harpers' New Monthly Magazine, Feb.1880. Illus.

Brief desceriptive account of the book, its possible origin, the patron, Cardinal Grimini, and the contributing artists.

Bound in collection "Dawn of Printing," item 5.

ILLUMINATED BOOKS [Literature of]

Cabinet 20 Shelf 1 No. 19

(Style and composition of French miniatures in the time of Charles V.) Über stil und komposition der französischen miniaturen aus der Zeit Karls V. von Frankreich von Fritz Hoeber Berlin, Aug., 1906. Illus.

In Zeitschrift für Bücherfreunde, 1906-7, part 1, p.187.

ILLUMINATED MANUSCRIPTS.

Cabinet Shelf No.

See MANUSCRIPTS, ILLUMINATED.

ILLUMINATING.

Cabinet V Shelf 2 No. 50

Enlumineurs, les relieurs, les libraires, et les imprimeurs de Toulouse, 1480-1530. Documents et notes pour servir a leur Histoire. Par A. Claudin. Paris, 1893-1894. Two parts.

Morocco; $8\frac{3}{4}$ x $5\frac{3}{4}$ x $\frac{1}{2}$ in.

ILLUMINATING

Cabinet V Shelf 4 No. 18

Lacroix, Paul, Éduard Fournier, et Ferdinand Seré. Le livre d'or des metiers: Histoire de l'imprimerie et des arts et professions qui se rattachent a la typographie...Calligraphie, enluminure...Paris, 1852. Illus.

Half morocco; $11\frac{1}{4}$ x $7\frac{3}{4}$ in.

ILLUMINATING

Cabinet N Shelf 1 No. 24

MIDDLETON, J. HENRY: Illuminated Manuscripts in Classical and Mediaeval Times, their Art and their Technique.
Cambridge: at the University Press: 1892.

Original cloth; 10-3/4 x 7½ ins.; pp.xxiv 270. Illustrated.

ILLUMINATION

Cabinet K Shelf 2 No. 25

(Les) Arts au Moyen Age...Par Paul Lacroix. Paris, 1871.

see pp.457-487

Morocco, gilt; 11-3/8 x 8-3/8 in.

ILLUMINATION

Cabinet C Shelf 2 No. 3

Initial letters on vellum, collection of original illuminated. Scrap book collection.

Folder; $18\frac{1}{2}$ x 13-5/8 in.

ILLUMINATION

Cabinet 68 Shelf No. 15

Irish Biblical manuscripts, remarks on some illuminations in. Communicated by the Rev. James Henthorn Todd. n.p.n.d.
With 4 plates

Temporary wrapper, tied.

ILLUMINATION

Cabinet L Shelf 5 No. 27.01

"Pochoir" or stencil method of color application.

see
SAUDÉ, JEAN. Traité d'enluminure d'art au pochoir...

ILLUMINATORS

Cabinet V Shelf 4 No. 18

Ecrivans-enlumineurs...[illus. historical account of copyists and illuminators].

See BOOK MAKING. Le livre d'or des metiers...Paris, 1852.

ILLUSTRATED BIBLES [Literature of]

Cabinet 18 Shelf 1 No. 1

(Bible illustrations by Jost Amman, 1573) Jost Amman's Bibelbilder von 1573 von W.L. Schreiber, Potsdam.

Brief account of the man, his work, and some of his contemporary printers and publishers.

In Zeitschrift für Bücherfreunde, 1906-7, part 2, p.267.

ILLUSTRATED BOOKS. [15th cent. In Library]

Cabinet 29 Shelf 1 No. 25

Augsburg, 1488.
Title: Astrolabium. Johannes Angeli. Augsburg: Erhard Ratdolt, 1488.

Boards; 8-3/4 x 6½ x 1 in.

ILLUSTRATED BOOKS. [15th cent. In Library]

Cabinet D Shelf 2 No. 43

Basle, 1498. Stultifera Navis. Sebastien Brant. (Translated by Jacob Locher). Printed by Johann Bergmann de Olpe. Basle.

Gesamt-Kat. ; Hain 3751.

Full morocco, gilt; 8¼ x 6¼ x 1 in.

ILLUSTRATED BOOKS [15th century. In Library]

Cabinet J Shelf 5 No. 19

(Der) Edelstein von Ulrich Boner...Bamberg, 1461.

Facsimile of the first book printed in Germany with date and wood engravings. (In Berlin bei Bruno Cassirer. 1908.

Boards, linen back; 15-3/8 x 11 in.

ILLUSTRATED BOOKS. [15th cent. In Library]

Cabinet D Shelf 2 No. 35

Ferrara, 1497. Jacobus Philippus (Foresti)
Title: Claris mulieribus. Lorenzo Rossi.
More than 170 woodcuts, chiefly portraits of women, and printer's device.
This is the first illustrated book from the Ferrara Press.

Gesamt-Kat. ; Hain 2813; Proctor 5762.

Morocco; 12 x 8½ x 1 in.

ILLUSTRATED BOOKS. [15th cent. In Library]

Cabinet 10 Shelf 2 No. 14

Nuremberg Chronicle. Anthony Coburger, 1593.

There are more than 2000 wood cuts in this book, of which many were designed and engraved by Wohlgemut, the master of Albert Durer.

Original covers; 18½ x 13 x 3½ ins.

ILLUSTRATED BOOKS. [15th cent. In Library]

Cabinet D Shelf 2 No. 35

Venice, 1479.
Title: Bergomensis Jac. Phil. (Foresti). De claris selectisque mulieribus. Ferrara. 1479. Laurenti Rubeis.

Morocco; 12 x 8¼ x 1¼ in. Hain 2813.

ILLUSTRATED BOOKS. [15th cent. In Library]

Cabinet 29 Shelf 1 No. 23

Venice, 1485: Erhard Ratdolt.
Title: Fasciculus temporum. Venice: Erhard Ratdolt, 1485.

See Incunabula. [Rolewinck, Werner] Fasciculus temporum, etc.

ILLUSTRATED BOOKS. [15th cent. In Library]

Cabinet D — Venice, 1492:
Title: Bergomensis, Jac: Phil. (Foresti). Supplementum. Chronicarum. Venice, 1492.
Shelf 2 — Bernardino Rizzo da Novara.
No. 19

Gesamt-Kat. ; Hain 2809.

Modern binding; 12½ x 9 x 1½ in.

ILLUSTRATED BOOKS. [16th cent. In Library]

Cabinet E — Frankfurt aM. 1566.
Thurnier-Buch, von anfang, ursachen, Ursprung und herkommen der Thurnier...[George Ruxner]
Shelf 1 — Frankfurt a.M. 1566.
This book, the illustrations of which are attributed to Jost Amman, has the imprint of
No. 46 — George Rabner, Sigmund Feyerabent, and Simon Huter.

Vellum over boards; 12 x 8 x 1-3/4 in. Brunet vol.4. 1471.

ILLUSTRATED BOOKS. [16th cent. In Library]

Cabinet 69 — Lyons, 1550:
Title: Emblemata D. A. Alciati ... Lugd. apud Guliel Rovilium. 1550. Lugduni, Excudebat
Shelf 1 — Mathias Bonhomme.
Copper engravings.
No. 18

Vellum; 7 x 4-3/4 x 3/4 in.

ILLUSTRATED BOOKS. [16th cent. In Library]

Cabinet 2 — Antwerp 1595. Descriptio publicae gratulationis spectaculorum et ludorum in adventu Sereniss. Principis Ernisti....auctore Ioanne Bochio.
No. 2 — Antwerp: Ex officina Plantiniana apud viuduam et Ioannem Moretum. M.D.XCV. (1595). Full p. wood engravings.
No. 22 — The engravings were executed by Pierre van der Borcht, who it is said designed many of the Initial Majuscules for Christopher Plantin.

Leather; 15 x 9-3/4 x 7/8 in.

ILLUSTRATED BOOKS. [16th cent. In Library]

Cabinet I — Frankfort a.M. 1568. Sig Feyerabent.
Title: [Panoplia] Omnium illiberalium mechanicarum aut sedentariarum artium genera continens
Shelf 1 — ...per Hartman Schopperum. (Jost Amman, illustrator). Frankfort a.M, 1568: Sigmund Feyerabent.
No. 5

Full morocco; 5¾ x 3½ x ¾ in.

ILLUSTRATED BOOKS. [16th cent. In Library].

Lyons, 1554-1577. Jean de Tournes.
Cabinet 39 — Title: [His old and new testaments bound together, the first dated 1554, the latter 1577.] Illus.
Shelf 2
No. 9

Morocco; 6¼ x 4½ x 7/8 in.

ILLUSTRATED BOOKS (16th century)

Cabinet J — L'Art du dessin...de Jean Cousin. Paris, n.d. circa 1550.
Shelf 4 — Title page and 24 plates, copperplate engravings.
No. 5

Half morocco; 15¾ x 12 x ½ in.

ILLUSTRATED BOOKS. [16th cent. In Library]

Cabinet I — Frankfort A.M. 1574. De onmibus illiberalibus sive mechanicis articus ... Hartmanno Schoppero. [Jost Amman, illus.]. Impressum
Shelf 1 — ... Sigismundi Caroli Feyerabent, 1574.
No. 6

Tooled leather; with clasps, 6½ x 3-3/4 x 1-1/8 in.

ILLUSTRATED BOOKS. [16th cent. In Library]

Cabinet 39 — [Lyons, 1577?] Jean de Tournes.
Thesaurus amicorum....Apud Ioann Tornaesium np. nd. [Lyons, 1577?]
Shelf 2 — [Portrait medallions (184) each in wood cut borders. Accompanying mottoes in various
No. 13 — languages each with appropriate type]

Boards; 6-3/4 x 4¼ in.

ILLUSTRATED BOOKS. [16th cent. In Library]

Cabinet D — Augsburg, 1531: Heynrich Stayner.
Title: Cicero Officia Officia M.T.C. Gedruckt ... durch Heynrich Stayner (Steiner).
Shelf 4 — Wood-cuts by Burgkmair and borders by Weiditz.
No. 39

Boards; 12 x 8¼ x 5/8 in.

ILLUSTRATED BOOKS. [16th cent. In Library]

Cabinet E — Geneva, 1580: Jean Laon.
Title: Incones id est verae imagines virorum... Theodore de Beze...Geneva, Ioannem Laonium.
Shelf 2 — 1580.
No. 32 — See Early Printing in Switzerland. Geneva, 1580. Jean de Laon.

ILLUSTRATED BOOKS. [16th cent. In Library]

Cabinet 39 — Lyons, 1558: Bernard Salomon.
Title: Illustratione de gli epitaffi et medaglie antichi, di M. Gabriel Symoni.
Shelf 2 — In Lione, per Giovan di Tournes, M.D.LVIII Wood cuts and borders by Bernard Salomon.
No. 14

Limp vellum; 8½ x 6¼ x½

ILLUSTRATED BOOKS. [16th cent. In Library]

Cabinet E — Cremona, 1585: Ercoliano Bartoli.
Title: Cremona fedelissima citta et nobilissima Colonia de Romani rappresentata in disegna
Shelf 1 — ...da Antonio Campo. Cremona, 1585. In Cremona in casa dell'auttore. Per Hippolito Trombe et Hercoliano Bartoli.
No. 65

Morocco; 15-3/4 x 10¼ x 1/8 in. Brunet 1, 1526.

ILLUSTRATED BOOKS. [16th cent. In Library]

Cabinet E — Geneva, 1581: Théodore de Beze.
Title: Vrais pourtraits des hommes illustrés en piète et doctrine...plus quarante quatre
Shelf 2 — emblemes chrestiens. Traduicts du latin de Théodore de Beze. [Printer Mark]. Geneva Par Jean de Laon.
No. 33

Calf; 8 x 6 x 1 in. Brunet 1, 843.

ILLUSTRATED BOOKS. [16th cent. In Library]

Cabinet 39 — Lyons, 1559: Jean de Tournes.
Title: Vita et metamorfoso d'Ovidio, figurata & abbreviata...da Gabriello Symeoni.....
Shelf 2 — A Lione, per Giovanni de Tornes nella via Resina. 1559.
Illus. by Bernard Salomon.
No. 19

Tooled calf; 7 x 4-3/4 x 5/8 in. Brunet 4, 287 Updike 1, 203-4.

ILLUSTRATED BOOKS. [16th cent. In Library]

Cabinet D — Fano, 1507: Soncino (Gerson ben Moses)
Title: Vigerius. (Marcus Cardinal). Decachordum Christianum. Fano. Hieronymus Soncinus
Shelf 3 — (Gerson ben Moses), 1507. Fano, (Italy)
Handsome woodcuts, and borders signed FV
No. 15 & 16 — (Florio Vavassore?)

Morocco, blind tooled; 12½ x 8¼ x 2 in. 2 copies.

ILLUSTRATED BOOKS. [16th cent. In Library]

Cabinet 69 — Lyons, 1547: Hans Holbein.
Title: Incones historiarum veteris testamenti.... Lugduni, Apud Ioannem Frellonium. 1547.
Shelf 1 — [Woodcuts designed by Hans Holbein].
No. 12

Calf; 7-3/8 x 5¼ x 3/8 in.

ILLUSTRATED BOOKS. [16th Cent. In Library]

Cabinet 69 — Lyons, 1561. Guillaume Roville.
Title: Description de Limagne d'Auvergne en forme de dialogus...Traduit du livre Italien de
Shelf 1 — Gabriel Symeon en langue Francoyse par Antoine Chappuys...A Lyon, par Guillaume Roville. 1561. (Illus. of medals, emblems,
No. 35 — etc.)

Boards; 8½ x 6¼ x ½ in. Brunet, 5, 391.

ILLUSTRATED BOOKS. [16th cent. In Library]

Cabinet 69 Shelf 2 No. 13

Lyons, 1572: Hugues Sambin.
Title: Oeuvre de la diversité des termes dont on use en Architecture...Par Hugues Sambin. À Lyon, par Jean Durant. M.D.LXXII.

Boards; 13-3/8 x 8-3/4 x 3/8 in. Brunet 5, 104.

ILLUSTRATED BOOKS. [16th cent. In Library]

Cabinet 70 Shelf 1 No. 26

Paris, 1525: Pierre Rosset.
Title: Horae.
Superbly illustrated Book of Hours printed by Rosset.

Tooled leather; 8-3/4 x 6 x 1 in.

ILLUSTRATED BOOKS. [16th cent. In Library]

Cabinet D Shelf 3 No. 21

Venice, 1511: Lazzaro Soardo.
Title: Plauti (M) linguaelati nae Principis comodiae XX. Venice, 1511. Lazzaro de Soardi.

Calf; 12½ x 8¼ x 2 in.

ILLUSTRATED BOOKS. [16th cent. In Library]

Cabinet 69 Shelf 1 No. 48

Lyons, 1581: Gulielmum Rovillium.
Title: Promptuarii iconum insigniorum a seculo hominum...Ludguni. Apud Gulielmum Rovillium. 1581.

[Portraits on medals representing important personages of antiquity.]

Vellum; 9½ x 7 x 2¼ in. Brunet 4, 900.

ILLUSTRATED BOOKS. [16th cent. In Library]

Cabinet 70 Shelf 2 No. 11

Paris, 1532: Gerard Morrhy.
Title: Fine, Oronce: Protomathesis. Opus varium [In five parts: arithmetic, geometry, cosmography...] Parisiis, anno 1532. Excusam est impensis Gerhardi Morrhii & Ioannis Petri.....

[The wood-cut title-border, diagrams, ornaments, large ititials, were all designed by the author.]

Vellum; 14½ x 10½ x 2 in.

ILLUSTRATED BOOKS. [16th cent. In Library]

Cabinet E Shelf 1 No. 3

Venice, 1535.
Title: Supplementum supplementi delle croniche del Venerando Padre Frate Jacobo Philippo. Venice, 1535: Bernardino Bindoni.

See Early Printing in Italy. Venice, 1535. Bernardino Bindoni.

ILLUSTRATED BOOKS. [16th cent. In Library]

Cabinet D Shelf 3 No. 60

Nurnberg, 1519: Hans Schonsperger.
Title: Theuerdank, Die geuerlicheiten und einsteil der geschichten des. von Melchior Pfinzing. Nurnberg, 1519. Hans Schonsperger.
Woodcuts by Beck, Schaufelein, Burgkmair, Traut etc.

Panzer 958; Brunet 5, 767; Proc.10939.

Plush over boards; 14-3/8 x 9-3/8 x 2½ in.

ILLUSTRATED BOOKS. [16th cent. In Library]

Cabinet 69 Shelf 1 No. 1

Paris, 1539: Denys Janot.
Title: Le théâtre des bons engins, auquel sont contenuz cent emblems moraulx. Composé par Guillaume de la Perrière Tolosain...De l'imprimerie de Denys Ianot, imprimeur & Libraire. Paris, 1539.

Morocco; 6½ x 4¼ x ½ in.

ILLUSTRATED BOOKS. [16th Cent. In Library]

Cabinet E Shelf 1 No. 6

Venice, 1542, P. Virgilii maronis...Venetiis apud haeredes Luceantonii Iuntae Florentini. Anno a Partu Virginis 1562, mense Ianvario.

Leather covered boards; 12 x 8 3/4 x 3 in.

ILLUSTRATED BOOKS. [16th cent. In Library]

Cabinet 70 Shelf 2 No. 8

Opera Vergiliana ... exposita a Servio, Donato, Mancinello et Probo cum abnot. Beroaldi Aug. Dathi. Calderini, Jodoci Badii Ascensii ... Lugduni, in Typographaria officina Ioannis Crespini, Anno. M.D.XXXIX.

Tooled leather over wood covers; 13 x 8¾ x 3 in.

ILLUSTRATED BOOKS. [16th cent. In Library]

Cabinet 69 Shelf 2 No. 3

Paris, 1560. Richard Roux.
Title: Annales et croniques de France. Nicole Gilles...Corrigées et annotés par le Seigneur Denis Sauvage. À Paris, par Iean Ruelle... Imprimées à Paris, par Richard Roux...

Calf; 13¼ x 8½ x 1½ in. Brunet 2,1596.

ILLUSTRATED BOOKS. [16th cent. In Library]

Cabinet E Shelf 1 No. 11

Venice, 1544: Francesco Marcolini.
Title: Comedia di Dante Aligieri. Venice, 1544: Francesco Marcolini.

Calf; 9½ x 6¼ x 2½ in.

ILLUSTRATED BOOKS. [16th cent. In Library]

Cabinet 29 Shelf 2 No. 9

Paris, 1523. Thielman Kerver [Widow]
Title: Hore deipare virginis marie secudu usum Romanu. Paris. 1523. Thielman Kerver [Widow]. Finiuntur hore...Parisiis, opera & impensis vidue defuncti...Thielmani Kerver, in vico sancti Jacobi, ad signum Unicornis....Anno dni M.D.XXIII die XXX Martii....

Vellum; 6½ x 4-1/8 x 1 in.

ILLUSTRATED BOOKS. [16th cent. In Library]

Cabinet 29 Shelf 2 No. 14

Paris, 1561. Jacques Kerver.
Title: Poliphile. Hypnerotomachie...nouvellement traduict de langue Italien en Francois. À Paris, pour Iaques Kerver...M.X.LXI. Imprimé pour Iaques Kerver...par Iehan le Blanc, le XI iour de Iuillet, l'an M.D.LXI. [large printer mark]

Calf; 13¼ x 9 x 1-1/8 in. Brunet 4, 779.

ILLUSTRATED BOOKS. [16th cent. In Library]

Cabinet E Shelf 1 No. 10

Venice, 1544: Francesco Marcolini.
Title: Serlio, Sabastiano. Il terzo libro...nel quale si figurano, e descrivono di antiquita de Roma... Venice: Francesco Marcolini, 1544.

Boards; 14¼ x 9-3/4 x 1 in. See Essling, vol. III, 670.

ILLUSTRATED BOOKS. [16th Cent. In Library]

Cabinet 70 Shelf 1 No. 23

Paris, 1524; Philippe Le Noir.
Title: Illustrations de Gaule et singularitez de Troye. Fratris Petri...Philippe Le Noir.

Morocco over boards, clasps; 10 3/4 x 7 3/4 x 1 3/4.

ILLUSTRATED BOOKS. [16th cent. In Library]

Cabinet E Shelf 2 No. 47

Strassburg, 1590: Bernard Jobinus.
Title: Incones sive imagines virorum literis illustrium. Nicolai Reusneri.

See Early Printing In Germany. Strassburg, 1590. Bernard Jobinus.

ILLUSTRATED BOOKS (17th cent. In Library)

Cabinet I Shelf 1 No. 13 & 14

Amsterdam, 1694: Johannes en Gaspaares Luiken.
Title: Het menselyk bedrye...

100 copper engraved plates of trades and professions.

Vellum; 8 x 6½ in.

ILLUSTRATED BOOKS. [17th cent. In Library]

Cabinet 2 Shelf 1 No. 45

Antwerp, 1634. Plantin-Moretus Press.
Title: De symbolis heroicis. Libri IX. Auctore, Silvestro Petrasancta, Romano E. Soc, Jesu. Antverpiae, ex officina Plantiniana, Balthasaris Moreti.
Title page engraved by Gallo after a design by Rubens.

Morocco; $8\frac{1}{2}$ x 6-3/8 x 1-5/8 in.

ILLUSTRATED BOOKS. [17th cent. In Library]

Cabinet E Shelf 3 No. 76

Paris, 1644: Cl. Mellau.
Title: Les Sainctes Metamorphoses....A Paris De l'Imprimerie de P. Moreau.

Morocco; $15\frac{1}{4}$ x $10\frac{1}{2}$ x 2 in.

ILLUSTRATED BOOKS (18th cent. In Library)

Cabinet I Shelf 1 No. 15

Abraham à S. Clare. Wurtzburg, 1711.

Copper engravings describing 177 trades and professions. (2 vols.)

Half calf, each vol., 6-5/8 x 4-1/8 x 2-3/8 in.

ILLUSTRATED BOOKS. [17th cent. In Library]

Cabinet 2 Shelf 1 No. 46

Antwerp, 1634. Sacrum sanctuarium crucis et patientiae crucifixorum emblematicis imaginibus ornatum...Antverpiae, ex officina Plantiniana Baltharis Moreti. 1634.
Book of emblems.

Calf; $8\frac{3}{4}$ x $6\frac{1}{2}$ x $2\frac{1}{2}$ in. Brunet 1, 955

ILLUSTRATED BOOKS. [17th cent. In Library]

Cabinet I Shelf 5 No. 21

Paris, 1651. Traitte de la peinture de Léonard de Vinci. Traduit d'Italian en François par R.F.S.D.C. À Paris, de l'Imprimerie de Jacques Langlois.

Morocco; 15-3/4 x 11-3/4 x 1 in.

ILLUSTRATED BOOKS 18th century (In library

Cabinet 9 Shelf 2 No. 1 to 9

Ercolano (le) Antichita di...1757, 1792, Naples, regia stampa

See BAJARDI, OTTAVANIO-ANTONIO. Antichita (le) di Ercolano...

ILLUSTRATED BOOKS. [17th cent. In Library]

Cabinet 39 Shelf 1 No. 4

Leyden, 1626. Bonaventura and Abraham Elzevier.
Title: Schoonhovius. Emblemata...Lugduni Batavorum. Ex officina Elzeviriana. Anno 1626.

Vellum; $8\frac{1}{4}$ x $6\frac{1}{4}$ x 1-3/8 in.

ILLUSTRATED BOOKS. [17th cent. In Library]

Cabinet E Shelf 4 No. 12

2 vols.

Paris, 1653: Sebastien Cramoisy.
Title: Biblia Sacra...See Early Printing in France. Paris, 1653. Sebastien Cramoisy.

ILLUSTRATED BOOKS. [18th cent. In Library]

Cabinet 30 Shelf 1 No. 30

London, 1795. Bewick Brothers.
Title: Bewick brothers wood engravings in "Poems" by Goldsmith and Parnell. Printed by W. Bulmer London, 1795.

Calf, tooled; 12 x 9-3/8 x $1\frac{1}{2}$ in.

ILLUSTRATED BOOKS [17th cent. In Library]

Cabinet 13 Shelf No. 6

Academie de l'espee...Gérard Thibault, 1628. [n.p.] Leyden?

Plates engraved by Bolswert, Crisp, de Pas, etc.

Consult Pieters "Annales de l'imprimerie Elzevirienne", p.117, for verication of imprint of above volume.

Calf, gilt; $22\frac{1}{2}$ x $17\frac{1}{2}$ in.

ILLUSTRATED BOOKS. [17th cent. In Library]

Cabinet E Shelf 4 No. 53

Paris, 1671. Les figures et l'abbrege de la vie, de la mort et des miracles de Saint Francois de Paule. Par Ant. Donde. Paris chez Francois Muguet.
Portraits, head and tail pieces, and full page engravings.

Full morocco; $14\frac{1}{4}$ x 10 x 1 in. Brunet 2, 809.

ILLUSTRATED BOOKS. [18th cent. In Library]

Cabinet 30 Shelf 1 No. 32

London, 1796. Thomas Bewick. Their wood engravings in Somerville's "The Chase, A poem." London, 1796. Printed by W. Bulmer and Co.

Tree calf; 11-3/4 x 9-3/8 x $1\frac{1}{4}$ in.

ILLUSTRATED BOOKS. [17th cent. In Library]

Cabinet E Shelf 3 No. 88

London, 1676. Printed for Thom. Bassett and R. Chiswell.
Title: The theatre of Great Britain...Geography and atlas of the world. By John Speed.
Imprint: Printed for Thomas Bassett and Richard Chiswel. 1766.

Half morocco; $17\frac{1}{4}$ x $12\frac{1}{4}$ x $1\frac{1}{2}$ in.

ILLUSTRATED BOOKS. [17th cent. In Library]

Cabinet E Shelf 3 No. 26

Venice, 1625. Fr. Valesio.
Title: Illustrium Anachoretarum elogia sive religiosi viri musaeum. Auctore D. Iacobo Cavacio. [Full page engravings by Fr. Valesio]. Venetiis in typographia Pinelliana. Superiorum permissu. 1625.

Vellum; $10\frac{1}{2}$ x 8-1/8 x 1-1/8 in.

ILLUSTRATED BOOKS. [18th cent. In Library]

Cabinet F Shelf 4 No. 79

3 vols.

Paris, 1745. Charles, Nicolas Cochin I.
Title: Virgilii Opera, 3 vols. Engravings by Cochin. Lutetiae Parisiorum. Sumptibus Ant. Urb. Coustelier. 1745.

Morocco; gilt; 6 x $3\frac{1}{2}$ x 7/8 in. Brunet 5, 1291.

ILLUSTRATED BOOKS. [17th Cent. In Library]

Cabinet 69 Shelf 1 No. 60

Paris, 1600.
Title: Tableau des riches inventions, couvert du voile des feintes amoureuse qui sont representees dans le Songe de Poliphile. Par Beroalde (de Verville). Paris. Matthiew Guillmot. 1600.

Half morocco; $10\frac{1}{2}$ x $7\frac{1}{2}$ x 3/4 in. Brunet 4, 779.

ILLUSTRATED BOOKS. [17th Century].

Cabinet E Shelf 4 No. 57

Venice, 1672, Isabella Picini and Francesco Cassioni. [Wood Engravings].
Title: Historie cronologiche della vera origine de titti gl'ordine equestri. Bernardino Giustiano ... Venetia, 1672.

Vellum; $10\frac{1}{2}$ x $7\frac{1}{2}$ x $1\frac{1}{2}$ in.

ILLUSTRATED BOOKS. [19th cent. In Library]

Cabinet G Shelf 1 No. 17

Boston, 1896-1897. Will Bradley.
Title: Bradley his book, Springfield and Boston, 1896, 1897.

Vol. 1, Nos. 1,2,3,4,
" 2, " 1,2,3,4, all issued.

Half mor. $11\frac{1}{4}$ x $8\frac{1}{2}$ ins., $1\frac{1}{4}$ in. thick.

ILLUSTRATED BOOKS [19th cent. in Library

Cabinet 68 Shelf No. 1

Choix des plus celebres maisons de plaisance de Rome...dessinees par Charles Percier. A Paris, de l'Imprimerei de P.Didot l'aine, 1809.

Copper engravings

Half pigskin; 22 x 15¾ in.

ILLUSTRATED BOOKS. [19th cent. In Library]

Cabinet 30 Shelf 1 No. 42

London, 1813: W. Bulmer & Co.
Title: Hobbinol. Field Sports and the Bowling Green, by W. Summerville. Printed by Bulmer and Co. for R. Ackerman, London, in the Strand.

Half morocco; 12 x 9¼ in. pp.118.

ILLUSTRATED BOOKS (20th cent.)

Cabinet B Shelf 2 No. 25

Collezione di vetri antichi. Ordinati e descritti da Giorgio Sangiorgi...Milan-Roma, 1914.

Printed at Bergamo "Dall' Istituto Italiano d'Arte Grafichi".

Cloth; 15¾ x 12½ in.

ILLUSTRATED BOOKS (19th century. In Library)

Cabinet I Shelf 5 No. 26

Dante illustrations by Doré 1861. His drawings reproduced by the then leading wood engravers The binding designed probably by John Leighton ("Luke Limner") and executed by J. & J. Leighton then at 40 Brewer St., Golden Square, London, W.I. This volume was exhibited in the International Exhibition 1862. Printed in Paris, 1861, by Lahure & Co.
Parigi: Libreria di L. Hachette e Cie, 1861.

Morocco, gilt, tooled; 16-7/8 x 12 x 2

ILLUSTRATED BOOKS. [19th cent. In Library]

Cabinet M Shelf 1 No. 46

London, 1864: Chiswick Press.
Title: Testament of our Lord and Saviour, Jesus Christ. With engravings on wood from designs by Fra Angelico...and others. London, The Chiswick Press. Charles Whittingham. Printer, R. Clay. London, 1864.

Half morocco; 11-3/4 x 9 x 2-1/8 in.

ILLUSTRATED BOOKS (20th cent. In Library)

Cabinet K Shelf 5 No. 31

Destiny: a novel in pictures. By Otto Nückel. New York, 1930.

About 300 wood engravings.

Cloth; 8 x 6-3/4 x 1-1/8 in.

ILLUSTRATED BOOKS 19th century

Cabinet T Shelf 3 No. 3

Dibdin, Thomas Frognall. A bibliographical antiquarian and picturesque tour in France and Germany. London. Printed for the author by W. Bulmer and W. Nichols, Shakspeare Press, 1821 (3 vols. illus.)

Morocco, gilt; 10¼ x 6¾ in.

ILLUSTRATED BOOKS. [19th cent. In Library]

Cabinet 50 Shelf 1 No. 58

Parma, 1800. Giambattista Bodoni.
Title: Pitture di Antonio Allegri detto Il Corregio Parma nel Regal Palazzo. MDCCC. Co'tipi Bodoniani.

Boards; 10-3/4 x 7-3/4 x 3/4 in.

ILLUSTRATED BOOKS. [20th cent. In Library]

Cabinet M Shelf 1 No. 53

Gullivers Travels into Lilliput and Brobdingnag. Illusted by Jean de Bosschère. London. [1920]. William Heineman, publisher.
Plates in color and many black and white illustrations.

Cloth; 10¾ x 8¼ x 5/8 in.

ILLUSTRATED BOOKS (19th century) In Library

Cabinet T Shelf 6 No. 9

Humphreys, Noel: A history of the art of printing ...With 100 illus. produced in photo-lithography by Day & Son, Ltd., under the direction of the author. London, 1867.

Morocco, gilt; 13½ x 9¾ in.

ILLUSTRATED BOOKS [19th cent. In Library]

Cabinet 49 Shelf 1 No. 6

Parma, 1809. Giambattista Bodini.
Title: Le Piu insigni pitture Parmensi indicate agli amatori delle belle arti. Parma, dalla Tipografia Bodoniana, 1809.

Half morocco; 12¼ x 9 x 1¼ in. Brooks 1059.

ILLUSTRATED BOOKS. [20th cent. In Library]

Cabinet M Shelf 1 No. 20

London, 1918: The Beaumont Press.
Title: Six illustrations designed and hand-colored by Michel Sevier for The tale of Igor...The Beaumont Press, London, 1918.

Boards; 9-1/8 x 5-7/8 x 3/8 in.

ILLUSTRATED BOOKS. [19th cent. In Library]

Cabinet M Shelf 3 No. 12

Lee Priory, 1820. Engravings on wood at Lee Priory, printed on Chinese paper, with verses. Kent: Printed at the private press of Lee Priory; by John Warwick, 1820.

Paper boards; 10¼ x 8-1/8 x 3/8 in.

ILLUSTRATED BOOKS(19th century. In Library)

Cabinet C Shelf 2 No. 18

Holends knappen. Illustrirt von Heinrich Lesler und Joseph Urban. Gesellschaft für Verfielfältigende Kunst. Wien, 1898.

Cloth; 19 x 14½ in.

ILLUSTRATED BOOKS. [20th cent. In Library]

Cabinet G Shelf 1 No. 23

New York, 1906: Will Bradley.
Title: Peter Poodle. Toy maker to the King, by Will Bradley.
An illustrated book for children, which includes many pictures, chapter titles, and headings.

Board; 11¼ x 9 in.

ILLUSTRATED BOOKS. 19th cent. In Library

Cabinet 30 Shelf 1 No. 35

London, 1804: Bulmer & Co.
Title: Outlines from the figures and compositions upon Greeks, Roman, and Etruscan vases. Drawn and engraved by Mr. Kirk. Printed by W. Bulmer and Co., Cleveland-Row, St. James, MDCCCIV.

Morocco; tooled, gilt edges; 12 x 9¼ in.

ILLUSTRATED BOOKS (19th century)

Cabinet C Shelf 1 No. 6

(Der) Teppich die lebens...von George Stefan. Berlin, 1899.
[Decorations by Melchoir Lechter. Printed by Otto V. Holten in Berlin.]

Cloth over board; 15½ x 17 in.

ILLUSTRATED BOOKS (20th cent. In Library)

Cabinet L Shelf 4 No. 55

New York, 1924: Tony Sarg.
Title: Sarg's,Tony, book for children from six to sixty. Published by Greenberg Inc., N. Y. 1924.

Boards; 11¾ x 8 in.

ILLUSTRATED BOOKS [20th cent. in Lib

Cabinet 64 Shelf 1 No. 1

(Die) Nibelunge. Berlin, 1898-1904. Illus. by Joseph Sattler. Reichsdruckerei, Berlin.

Morocco; 22¾ x 15¾ in.

ILLUSTRATED BOOKS, [Literature of]

Cabinet Y Shelf 3 No. 120

(Augsburg 15th century book illustration, studies of) Schwäbische federzeichnungen. Studien zur buchillustration Augsburgs im XV jahrhundert. von Hellmut Lehmann-Haupt. Leipzig, 1928.

Stamped cloth; 9 x 5-3/4 x 1-1/8 in.

ILLUSTRATED BOOKS Literature

Cabinet U Shelf 3 No. 103

Chinese illustrated books. By Robert K. Douglas. [Illus. article].

See BOOKS ABOUT BOOKS. Bibliographica: papers on books...vol.2, p.452.

ILLUSTRATED BOOKS. 20th century. In Library

Cabinet G Shelf 1 No. 51

Revelation of St. John the Divine, in reprint of the English edition of 1525 (with illustrations of Albrecht Durer), printed at the Cranbrook Press, Detroit, Mich., 1901.

Half vellum; 11¼ x 8¾ in.

ILLUSTRATED BOOKS Literature

Cabinet 72 Shelf 2 No. 43

Bibliography of illustrated (English) 1480-1535.

see HODNETT, EDWARD. English woodcuts, 1480-1535...p. 73.

ILLUSTRATED BOOKS Literature of

Cabinet P Shelf 4 No. 26

Cleland illustrates his first book. Brief notice of. Excerpt from Publishers' Weekly, Sept. 1935.

In envelope.

ILLUSTRATED BOOKS (20th century)

Cabinet C Shelf 1 No. 1

Sports et divertissements. Music de Rik Satie. Dessins de Ch. Martin. Publications Lucien Vogel, Paris (1914)

Plates illuminated by Jean Saude, by his stencil (pochoir) process.

Boards; 15¾ x 17½ in.

ILLUSTRATED BOOKS. Literature

Cabinet U Shelf 3 No. 103

Brandt, Sebastian, the illustrated books of. By Gilbert R. Redgrave.

Bibliographical.

See vol. 2, p.47 Bibliographica...London, 1895-1897.

ILLUSTRATED BOOKS Literature of

Cabinet J Shelf 2 No. 14

Cousin, Jean, books illustrated by. Bio-bibliographical account...

See Didot, Ambroise Firmin. Etude sur Jean Cousin...Paris, 1872.

ILLUSTRATED BOOKS. Literature of

Cabinet K Shelf 6 No. 39.01

Abbotsford Edition of the Waverley Novels. Edinburgh and London, 1842-1844. Review of book with above title. An excerpt.

Item 7 in bound collection with binder's title ENGRAVERS AND WOOD ENGRAVERS.

ILLUSTRATED BOOKS Literature of

Cabinet K Shelf 6 No. 39.01

Buchillustration in religiösen Druckwerken. Illus. excerpt from "Die Religion in Geschichte und Gegenwart. Handwörterbuch. Tubingen. n.d.

Item 22 in bound collection with binder's title ENGRAVERS AND WOOD ENGRAVERS.

ILLUSTRATED BOOKS [Literature of]

Cabinet Y Shelf 3 No. 38

Baer, Dr. Leo. Die illustrierten historienbücher des 15 jahrhunderts. Ein beitrag zur geshcichte des fromschnittes (A contribution to the history of form cutting, and early illustrated histories). Strassburg im Elsass, 1903.

Half morocco; 12 x 8-1/8 x 1-3/4 in.

ILLUSTRATED BOOKS Literature of

Cabinet K Shelf 4 No. 6

(Alciati's book of emblems, bibliographical study of editions 1531 to 1781)

See Duplessis, Georges. Livres a gravures du 16th siecles...

ILLUSTRATED BOOKS. Literature of

Cabinet K Shelf 6 No. 39.01

Carteggio inedito d'Artisti dei Secoli 14, 15, 16. Publicato ed illustrato con documenti pure inediti dal D. Gio. Gaye. Firenze, 1839. (3 vols.)
Review of book with title as above.

Item 7 in bound collection with binder's title ENGRAVERS AND WOOD ENGRAVERS

ILLUSTRATED BOOKS Literature of

Cabinet K Shelf 6 No. 23

Dutch and Flemish, 15th century.

see SCHRETLEN, M. J. Dutch and Flemish woodcuts of the 25th century...

ILLUSTRATED BOOKS Literature of

Cabinet J Shelf 2 No. 1

Amman, Jost, 1564 to 1586, books illustrated by. Bibliography.

See BECKER, (CARL). Amman, Jobst, Zeichner... Leipzig, 1854.

ILLUSTRATED BOOKS Literature of

Cabinet K Shelf 6 No. 28

Childrens' books and their illustrators. By Gleeson White. "The Studio". Special Winter Number, 1897-8. London. Illus.

Paper; 11 3/4 x 8 1/2 in.

ILLUSTRATED BOOKS. Literature of

Cabinet AA Shelf 2 No. 14.03

Editions de Luxe du xvie au xixe siécle. Vente aux Enchères, 11-12 Juin, 1929. A Zurich, chez Ulrico Hoepli, Libraire. Illus. catalogue.

Half morocco; 9½ x 7. Original wrappers bound in.

ILLUSTRATED BOOKS Literature of

Cabinet K Shelf 6 No. 23

Dutch and Flemish, 15th century.

see

SCHRETLEN, M. J. Dutch and Flemish woodcuts of the 15th century...

ILLUSTRATED BOOKS Literature of

Cabinet U Shelf 5 No. 24

French illustrated books, early

see

POLLARD, A. W. Fine Books... London, 1912, p.143

ILLUSTRATED BOOKS. [Literature of]

Cabinet 18 Shelf 1 No. 5

(Germany). (Artists of modern book decoration). Hugo Steiner-Prag. Deutscher Buchkunstler der gegenwart, von Friedrich Stelle, Leipzig. Illus.

In Zeitschrift für Bücherfreunde, 1909, part 1, p. 81.

ILLUSTRATED BOOKS, [Literature of]

Cabinet 75 Shelf No.

(England). On the Herbarius and Hortus Sanitatis: A paper read before the Bibliographical Society, by Joseph Frank Payne, Jan. 21, 1901 Illus.

In Transactions of the Bibliographical Society, vol. VI, pp. 65-126, 155-157.

ILLUSTRATED BOOKS. Literature of

Cabinet PP Shelf 1 No. 42

(French illustrated books of the 18th century). Les livres illustrés francais du dix-huitième siècle. Par Max Sander. Bibliographies de poche ... III. Sous le patronage de la Société Suisse des Bibliophiles. Stuttgart [1926].

Cloth; 7-7/8 x 4-7/8 x 5/8 in.

ILLUSTRATED BOOKS. [Literature of]

Cabinet 18 Shelf 1 No. 10

(Germany). (Modern decorators of the book: George Belwe and his class at the Koniglichen Akademie für Graphische Kunst und Buchgewerbe Deutscher Buchkunstler der gegenwart, von Johannes Schinnerer, Leipzig. Illus.

In Zeitschrift fur Bucherfreunde, 1911, part 1, p.1.

ILLUSTRATED BOOKS. Literature

Cabinet U Shelf 3 No. 103

Florentine book illustrations of the 15th and early 16th centuries. By Paul Kristeller.

See vol. 2, pp.81, 227 Bibliographica... London, 1895-1897.

ILLUSTRATED BOOKS. Literature of.

Cabinet PP Shelf 1 No. 40

(French 19th century). Die illustrierten französischen bücher des 19 jahrhunderts von Max Sander. Mit 8 bildnissen. Unter dem patronat der Schweizer Bibliophilen gesellschaft. Stuttgart, [1924].
Has biographies of illustrators. French German text.

Cloth; 7-7/8 x 4-7/8 x 5/8 in.

ILLUSTRATED BOOKS Literature of

Cabinet 26 Shelf 1 No. 16

Gravelot's werk als buchillustrator. von Richard Oehler, Breslau.

Illus. article with list of Gravelot's works. In GUTENBERG-GESELLSCHAFT JAHRBUCH, 1927, p.105

ILLUSTRATED BOOKS Literature of

Cabinet K Shelf 6 No. 18

Florentine books with woodcuts, an annotated list of.

see

KRISTELLER, PAUL, Early Florentine woodcuts...London, 1897. pp. 1-179.

ILLUSTRATED BOOKS Literature of

Cabinet U Shelf 5 No. 24

German and Dutch illustrated books, early

see

POLLARD, A. W. Fine Books... London, 1912, p.100

ILLUSTRATED BOOKS, Literature.

Cabinet I Shelf 3 No. 3

Guide de l'Amateur de livres à vignettes du 18e siècle. Second édition. Par Henry Cohen. Paris, 1873.

Frontispiece etching by J. Chauvet.

Half morocco; 9¼ x 5-7/8 x 1-1/8 in.

ILLUSTRATED BOOKS. Literature

Cabinet J Shelf 5 No. 29

(France, 14th to 19th centuries, illustrated history of engraving in).

See COURBOIN, FRANCOIS. Histoire illustrée ... Paris, 1923.

ILLUSTRATED BOOKS Literature

Cabinet 26 Shelf 2 No. 15

(German illustrated books, modern) German text.

Illus. article in Jahrbuch IX, 1935, p. 69, Deutscher Verein für Buchwesen und Schrifttum.

ILLUSTRATED BOOKS Liter.

Cabinet K Shelf 5 No. 8

(History of wood engraving, 1300 to 1823.)

see

HELLER, JOSEPH. Geschichte der holzschneiderkunst...Bamberg, 1823.

ILLUSTRATED BOOKS. Literature

Cabinet U Shelf 3 No. 103

French Books of Hours, 1486-1500, the illustrations in. By Alfred W. Pollard. Bibliographical account, illus.

See vol. 3, p.430 Bibliographica... London, 1895-1897.

ILLUSTRATED BOOKS [Literature of]

Cabinet Y Shelf 3 No. 65

German printing, 1473-1800, art in. From the collection of Ida Schoeller. Exhibited in Leipzig, 1914) Die kunst im deutschen buchdruck. Aus der sammlung Ida Schoeller in Duren, ausgestellt in der Gruppe Bibliphilie der Weltaustellung für Buchgewerbe und Graphik. Leipzig, 1914. Mit einem geleitwort von Otto Zaretsky. Weimar, 1915. Illus.

Half vellum; 12-3/4 x 10 x 1 in.

ILLUSTRATED BOOKS Literature of

Cabinet K Shelf 6 No. 39.01

Illuminated ornaments, drawn from ancient manuscripts. By Henry Shaw; with descriptions by Sir Frederick Madden. London, 1833.
Review of book with title as above.

Item 7 in bound collection with binder's title ENGRAVERS AND WOOD ENGRAVERS

ILLUSTRATED BOOKS Literature of

Cabinet K (Italian 15th and 16th century illustrated editions of Savonarola's writings)

Shelf 6 see GRUYER, GUSTAVE. Illustrations des écrits de Jérome Savonarole....Paris, 1879.

No. 16

ILLUSTRATED BOOKS. [Literature of]

Cabinet 75 Lyons, 16th century, books printed at. See Early Printing in France (Literature of). Books printed at Lyons.

Shelf 2

No.

ILLUSTRATED BOOKS Literature of

Cabinet K Pictorial Bible, The; being the Old and New Testament...Illustrated with many hundred woodcuts. London, 1839. (4 vols.) Review of books with title as above.

Shelf 6

No. 39.01

Item 7 in bound collection with binder's title ENGRAVERS AND WOOD ENGRAVERS.

ILLUSTRATED BOOKS

Cabinet AA (Italian illustrated books, early) Catalogue... a Tommaro De Marinis.

Shelf 2 See DeMARINIS, TOMMARO. Catalogue d'une collection d'anciens livres a figures...

No. 42

ILLUSTRATED BOOKS. Literature of

Cabinet I Manuel de l'amateur de la gravure sur bois et sur metal au 15e siècle ... Par. W.L. Schreiber Leipzig et Berlin, 1891-1910. [9 vols. of text, 3 of facsimiles].

Shelf 5 Vols. I to V bibliographical text only. " VI to VIII Reproductions.

No. 7 to 15 Half morocco; vols. I to V measure 10 x 7 in. " " " VI to VIII " 17 x 13 in.

9 vols.

ILLUSTRATED BOOKS. Literature of.

Cabinet U Pollard, Alfred W. Early illustrated books. A history of the decorations and illustration of books in the 15th and 16th centuries. London, 1893.

Shelf 5

No. 21

Half morocco; $8\frac{1}{2}$ x $5\frac{1}{4}$ x $1\frac{1}{4}$ in.

ILLUSTRATED BOOKS Literature of

Cabinet U Italian illustrated books, early

Shelf 5 see POLLARD, A. W. Fine Books ... London, 1912, p.123

No. 24

ILLUSTRATED BOOKS. Literature of

Cabinet 1 [Manuscripts, illustrated or illuminated, from the 9th to about the 14th century].

Shelf 5 See MANUSCRIPTS, ILLUMINATED. Literature of.

No. 5

ILLUSTRATED BOOKS Literature of

Cabinet K Some illustrated books of the 15th and 16th centuries. By W. Roberts. Illus. excerpt from The Book-Lover, April, 1904.

Shelf 6

No. 39.01

Item 23 in bound collection with binder's title ENGRAVERS AND WOOD ENGRAVERS.

ILLUSTRATED BOOKS Literature of

Cabinet U Japanese illustrated books. By R.K. Douglas. [illus. article]

Shelf 3 See BOOKS ABOUT BOOKS. Bibliographica: Papers on books...vol.3, p.I.

No. 103

ILLUSTRATED BOOKS Literature of

Cabinet K Monumens des Arts du Dessin chez les peuples tant anciens que modernes. Recueilles par Vivant Denon. Paris, 1829. (4 vols.)

Shelf 6 Review of book with title as above.

No. 39.01

Item 7 in bound collection with binder's title ENGRAVERS AND WOOD ENGRAVERS

ILLUSTRATED BOOKS. Literature of

Cabinet 75 Some notes on illustrated books. A paper read before the Bibliographical Society by Alfred W. Pollard. Nov. 19, 1900. Illus.

Shelf 1

No. 6

In Trans. Biblio. Soc. Vol. VI, pp. 29-61. 1900-1902.

ILLUSTRATED BOOKS. Literature of.

Cabinet I Le livre Belge a gravures ... Imprime en Belgique avant le 18e siecle ... Par le Dr. M. Funck. Paris et Bruxelles. 1925. Illus.

Shelf 3

No. 28

Paper; 10 x $6\frac{3}{4}$ x $1\frac{1}{4}$ in.

ILLUSTRATED BOOKS. [Literature]

Cabinet Y Nurnberg, 1521-1555, Hans Guldemund. Account of books illustrated or printed by Hans Guldemund. By Walter Fries.

Shelf 3 Article in Zeitschrift fur Buchkunde, vol. I, 1924, p.36.

No. 98

ILLUSTRATED BOOKS. [Literature of]

Cabinet 75 (Spain). Book illustration in Spain,early. With an introduction by Dr. Konrad Haebler. Book with above title reviewed by Alfred W. Pollard.

Shelf 2

No. 7

In Trans. Biblio. Soc. "The Library," vol. VII, pp. 325-6. 1926-1927.

ILLUSTRATED BOOKS [Literature of]

Cabinet AA Le livre illustré au 15e siècle. Avec 344 figures sur 220 planches dont une en couleurs... Florence. Leo S. Olschki, editeur. 1926.

Shelf 2 Illustrated descriptive list of 15th century books; block books, etc.

No. 14

Cloth; 10 x 6-7/8 x 1 in.

ILLUSTRATED BOOKS. [Literature of].

Cabinet V Origines des livres Francais du quinsieme siecle, et marche de la gravure sur bois a leur illustration.

Shelf 3 Bio-bibliographical historical. Has list of illustrated books. p. 207 in Didot's Essai typographique ... sur l'histoire de la gravure sur bois. Paris 1863.

No. 12

Boards; leather back; $9\frac{1}{2}$ x 6 in.

ILLUSTRATED BOOKS Literature

Cabinet U Spanish illustrated books, early

Shelf 5 see POLLARD, A. W. Fine Books... London, 1912, p.143

No. 24

ILLUSTRATED BOOKS Literature of

Cabinet K Shelf 6 No. 39.01

Travels of Sir John Mandeville. Perhaps the first travel book to see print. A clever and artistic compilation.
Illus. excerpt from Travel Magazine, March, 1927.

Item 35 in bound collection with binder's title ENGRAVERS AND WOOD ENGRAVERS

ILLUSTRATED JOURNALISM

Cabinet K Shelf 6 No. 20

American newspapers and magazines, illustrated.
see
LINTON, W. J. History of wood engraving in America...London, 1882.

ILLUSTRATED NEW ENGLAND FAMILY MAGAZINE

Cabinet 80 Shelf 2 No. 58

Boston, 1846.
see
PERIODICALS, United States New England Family Magazine...

ILLUSTRATED BOOKS. [Literature of].

Cabinet U Shelf 1 No. 1c

(Venetian). Etudes sur l'art de la gravure sur bois a Venise ... de la fin du XVe siecle et du commencement du XVIe ... Par Prince d'Essling. Paris 19--. Book with title as above reviewed by A. W. Pollard.

In "Excerpts relating to printing from "The Library," 1908. pp. 104-110.

ILLUSTRATED JOURNALISM.

Cabinet 26 Shelf 2 No. 6

(European illustrated newspapers) Die europaischen bilderzeitungen.

In German.

Journal fur Buchdruckerkunst, 1853, No.10, cols. 109-111.

ILLUSTRATED NEWS, THE

Cabinet OO Shelf 6 No. 42

Barnum & Beach's Paper. The Illustrated News. Jan. - July, 1853. New York.

Engraved title page.

Half morocco; $15\frac{3}{4}$ x $11\frac{1}{4}$ x 1-1/8 in.

ILLUSTRATED BOOKS Literature of

Cabinet I Shelf 5 No. 16 to 20

(Venetian illustrated books of the 15th and beginning of the 16th centuries)

See ESSLING (Prince d') Études sur l'art de la gravure sur bois a Venise...

ILLUSTRATED JOURNALISM Ref.

Cabinet Shelf No.

Pennsylvania Gazette, 1754, published the drawing of a snake cut in eight parts. It symbolized the divided colonies, and under it he wrote "Join or Die". This woodcut illus. the earliest specimen of newspaper pictorial feature.

In REED, PERLEY ISAAC, Writing Journalistic Features. New York, 1935, p. 5.

Book not in Library.

ILLUSTRATED NEWS, THE

Cabinet J Shelf 5 No. 17

Gems of wood engravings from The Illustrated News.

See CHATTO, WILLIAM A. Gems of wood engraving...London, 1849.

ILLUSTRATED BOOKS Literature of

Cabinet K Shelf 5 No. 22

(Wood engravings of the 15th and 16th centuries, books with.) Livres à figures sur bois des 15e et 16e siècles. Paris: Théophile Belin. 1911.
Illus. catalogue.

Paper; $9\frac{1}{2}$ x $6\frac{1}{4}$ x $\frac{1}{2}$ in.

ILLUSTRATED JOURNALISM see also

Cabinet Shelf No.

JOURNALISM ILLUSTRATED.

ILLUSTRATED NEWS, The

Cabinet NN Shelf 2 No. 13

Parent of all weekly illustrated journals. Brief account of its career, and its founder, Herber Ingram. By J.M. Bullock.
Excerpt from The Lamp, April, 1903.

Item 21 in bound collection with binder's title "Various newspapers and periodicals"

ILLUSTRATED BOOKS Literature of

Cabinet K Shelf 5 No. 32

Woodcut books of the 16th century. Illustrations by the famous old masters...Catalogue 226, Gilhofer & Ranschburg. Vienna. Illus.

Paper; 10-1/8 x $7\frac{1}{4}$ x $\frac{1}{2}$ in.

ILLUSTRATED JOURNALISM, Humorous

Cabinet Shelf No.

See Journalism, illustrated, humorous: How your Sunday smile is made.

ILLUSTRATED NEWSPAPERS

Cabinet Shelf No.

see
JOURNALISM, ILLUSTRATED
NEWSPAPERS-ILLUSTRATED

ILLUSTRATED BROADSIDES see

Cabinet Shelf No.

BROADSIDES

ILLUSTRATED LONDON NEWS

Cabinet OO Shelf 6 No. 4 & 5

Coronation Number, 1911.
see
PERIODICALS, ILLUSTRATED (Great Britain). Illustrated London News.

ILLUSTRATED PERIODICALS see

Cabinet Shelf No.

PERIODICALS, Illustrated

ILLUSTRATION

Cabinet K Shelf 6 No. 1

Advertising Art. Sixth Annual of. From advertisements shown at the Exhibition of the Art Directors Club, Art Center, New York, May 4 to 31, 1927. Illus.

Cloth; 11½ x 8 x 7/8 in.

ILLUSTRATION

Cabinet K Shelf 1 No. 14 2 vols.

Berlins graphischen gelegenheitskunst. von Walter von Zur Westen. Berlin, 1912 (2 vols).

Decorative typography: ex-libris, invitations, programs etc.

Morocco; 12½ x 9 in.

ILLUSTRATION

Cabinet K Shelf 1 No. 4

Callot (?), circa 1630, some original copper-plates.

Fastened together to form a book; paper, leather back; 8½ x 11 in.

ILLUSTRATION

Cabinet 27 Shelf 2 No.

Aldine Typographic Art Journal.

See PERIODICALS, PRINTING. United States Aldine (The(...

ILLUSTRATION

Cabinet K Shelf 5 No. 1

Bible illustration, early history. By W. C. Prime. Illus. excerpt from "Harper's New Monthly Magazine," April, 1880.

Item 3 in vol. with binder's title "Wood Engraving, Etc."

ILLUSTRATION

Cabinet L Shelf 1 No. 50

(Les) Cartes a jouer du 14e au 20e siècle...Par Henry-René d'Allemagne. Paris, 1906.(2 vols.)

Contains 300 reproductions of cards of which 956 are in colors; 12 large colored plates, 25 phototype plates and upwards of 500 illustrations in the text.

Pictorial boards; 13 x 10-3/8 in.

ILLUSTRATION

Cabinet K Shelf 1 No. 13

ART YEAR BOOK, 1884. Prepared and published by the New England Institute, Boston, Mass.

This Art Year Book was made for the N. E. M. & M. I. By Arthur B. Turnure, of the Art Age Press, New York.

Boards; 12¼ x 9-5/8 x 5/8 in.

ILLUSTRATION

Cabinet K Shelf 3 No. 11

Bird's-eye views, examples of. By Edward W. Spofford, illustrator. New York, 1910.

Cloth, oblong; 7-1/8 x 9-7/8 in.

ILLUSTRATION

Cabinet K Shelf 2 No. 35

Cartoon history of Abraham Lincoln.

see SHAW, ALBERT. Abraham Lincoln: His path to the presidency...

ILLUSTRATION

Cabinet K Shelf 2 No. 22

Australia. Art and Letters: Hassel's Australia Miscellany, 1921-1922. Adelaide & Melbourne.

Illus., many in colors.

Boards; 11 x 8-7/8 in.

ILLUSTRATION

Cabinet A Shelf 3 No. 89

Book, Magazine and Art Illustration, p.20, special graphic art number of The Times Sept. 10, 1912.

ILLUSTRATION

Cabinet K Shelf 1 No. 10

(Color prints of Pellerin. Épinal, France, 17--) Les images d'Épinal. Par René Perrout. Préface de Maurice Barres. Edition de la Revue Lorraine Illustrée. Nancy, 1912.

Portfolio: 13-3/8 x 10¼ in.

ILLUSTRATION

Cabinet J Shelf 2 No. 7

Beardsley, Aubrey Vincent, 1872 - 1898

See Biographies, Illustrators, Beardsley, Aubrey...

ILLUSTRATIONS

Cabinet G Shelf 1 No. 20

Bradley, Will. The Wayside Press, Cambridge, Mass 1898. A print shop established by Will Bradley for the printing of choice books and the higher classes of commercial work is now a part of the University Press.

Brochure; 8 x 6 ins., pp.33.

ILLUSTRATION

Cabinet K Shelf 3 No. 18

Conférence sur le croquis-calque. Faite a Paris au Cercle de la Librarie, le 12 Decembre, 1903. Par F. Thibadeau. (Paris)

Discourse on the art and methods of decorative typography.

Cloth; 8 x 5-3/8 in.

ILLUSTRATION.

Cabinet I Shelf 4 No. 19 2 Vols.

(Beginning of illustration and printing. Earliest specimens illustrated).

See WEIGEL, T. O. and DR. AD. ZESTERMANN. Anfange der druckerkunst...Leipzig, 1866.

ILLUSTRATION

Cabinet J Shelf 2 No. 10

CALDECOTT, RANDOLPH, his early art career. By Henry Blackburn. With 172 illustrations. Fourth edition. London, 1887.

Cloth; 8¾x6½x1 in.

ILLUSTRATION

Cabinet 18 Shelf 1 No. 16

[Contemporary Graphic Arts at the International Exhibition in Leipzig, 1914] Die zeitgenossische graphic....von Dr. Hans Wolf. Illus.

In the Zeitschrift fur Bucherfreunde, 1914-15, part I, p.129.

ILLUSTRATION

Cabinet K Shelf 2 No. 24

Engravings after the designs of Adrien Van de Venne of Holland, 16th century, for Cats book of moral emblems, by John Leighton and Dalziel...London, 1860.

Moral emblems of all ages and nations From J. Cats and Robert Farlie...By John Leighton, London, 1860.

Cloth, embossed; 10-7/8 x 8 in.

ILLUSTRATION

Cabinet RR Shelf 1 No. 7

French book and newspaper illustration, 1871-1894. Brief account of.

See VACHON, MARIUS. Arts et les industries du papier...Paris, 1894.

ILLUSTRATION

Cabinet J Shelf 5 No. 24

[Hungary History of painting, 1667 to 1900. With reproductions in black and white and colored] A Magyar képirás úttörői. Irta Malonyay Dezső...Budapest. Franklin-Társulat, 1905.

Boards; 16 x 11¼ x 1½ in.

ILLUSTRATION

Cabinet JJ Shelf 2 No. 13

Evolution of illustrating. By H.M. Duncan.

Illus. article in United Typothetae Official Souvenir. Eighth Annual Convention, Philadelphia, Sept.,1894, p.80.

Stiff paper; 10½ x 7-3/8. In envelope.

ILLUSTRATION

Cabinet K Shelf 5 No. 2

Gavarni: A Parisian prince of the pencil. By A. Rhodes. Excerpt from Scribner's, May, 1873. Illus.

Item 5 in vol. with binder's title "Wood engravers and illustrators".

ILLUSTRATION

Cabinet K Shelf 2 No. 17

Illustrations to catalogue 727. Catholic Theology Joseph Baer & Co. Frankfort am Main. n.d.

Item in manila envelope

ILLUSTRATION

Cabinet J Shelf 5 No. 22

Figaro photographe. Edition unique. Supplement du Figaro. A l'occasion de la première Exposition Internationale de Photographie. Paris, 1887. Illus.

History of photography and photographic processes.

Cloth; 16¾ x 12¾ in.

ILLUSTRATION

Cabinet Y Shelf 2 No. 23

(German, the illustrative art in the 15th and early 16th century. Copperplate engraving, wood engraving, etc.)

See LORCK, CARL B. Handbuch der geschichte...Leipzig, 1882-1883 [see index of this work]

ILLUSTRATION

Cabinet J Shelf 4 No. 16

Illustrations, typographiques (Deuxieme volume). Recueil de vignettes, alphabets...Gravés et polytypes. Par H. Porret. Paris, n.d. 1800?

Boards, oblong; 10-5/8 x 13-3/8 in.

ILLUSTRATION

Cabinet J Shelf 5 No. 21 also 22

Figaro-Salon, 1887. Par Albert Wolff. Paris.

Illustrations from the Figaro. With descriptive text.

Cloth; 16-7/8 x 13 in.

ILLUSTRATION

Cabinet K Shelf 2 No. 30

Half-tone illustrations (245), some in color

see McCLELLAND, NANCY. Historic wall papers...Philadelphia, 1924.

ILLUSTRATION

Cabinet K Shelf 1 No. 9

L'Imagerie Orleanaise. Par Auguste Martin. Onvrage precede d'une etude sur les origines et les sources d'inspiration des imagiers. Par Pierre Louise Ducharte. Notices biographiques par le Dr. Maurice Gersonnin. Paris (1928)

Half morocco; 11½ x 8-7/8 x 1 in.

ILLUSTRATION

Cabinet K Shelf 2 No. 1

(France, origin and evolution of illustration in).

see DUCHARTE,LOUIS and SAULNIER, RENE L'Imagerie populaire...Paris, 1925

ILLUSTRATION.

Cabinet I Shelf 4 No. 20 2 vols.

History of German illustration, from its beginning to the present time) Geschichte der deutschen illustration vom ersten auftreten des formschnittes bis auf die gegenwart von Th. Kutschmann. Goslar und Berlin. (1899). 2 vols.

Cloth; 12½ x 9½ in.

ILLUSTRATION

Cabinet C Shelf 2 No. 20

(Die) Konigliche Akademie für Graphische Kunste und Buchgewerbe. Leipzig, 1913.

Plates, with examples of decorative printing.

Portfolio; 19 x 13¼ in.

ILLUSTRATION

Cabinet K Shelf 2 No. 3

French almanachs, 1600-1895

see GRAND-CARTERET, JOHN Almanachs Francais, bibliographie...Paris, 1896

ILLUSTRATION

Cabinet K Shelf 3 No. 5

(History of popular picture making) Histoire de l'imagerie populaire. Par Champfleury. Paris, 1869. Illus.

Paper; 7-3/8 x 4-5/8 in.

ILLUSTRATION

Cabinet K Shelf 2 No. 19

Kostbare privat-sammlung von kufferstichen und holzschnitten alter meister des xv bis xvii jahrhunderts. Gilhofer & Ranschburg, Lucerne, 1927.

Illus. catalogue of copperplate and wood engravings of the old masters.

Paper; 11¾ x 8-5/8 in.

ILLUSTRATION

Cabinet K Shelf 4 No. 18

Libermann's Max. Graphishche kunste. Herausgegeben vom Max J. Friedlander. Mit 98 abbildungen. Dresden, 1900.

Boards, cloth back; 9¾ x 7½ x ½ in.

ILLUSTRATION

Cabinet J Shelf 5 No. 25

(Original prints in black and white and in colors. 50 plates.)

See ENGRAVINGS. L'Estampe moderne... Premiere volume, 1897-1898. Préface par Léonce Bénédite. Paris.

ILLUSTRATION

Cabinet K Shelf 3 No. 35

Pictures as a commercial asset. Address by A.J. Powers, before the New York Employing Printers Association, Feb.15, 1926. Privately printed. Brochure, illus.

Boards; 6-3/8 x 4-5/8 in.

ILLUSTRATION

Cabinet RR Shelf 6 No. 32

Linweave Limited Editions. Specimens of a variety of techniques valuable to students of printing. Copyright 1931. The P.P. Kellogg & Co. Division, United States Envelope Company.

Boards; 12¼ x 9 in.

ILLUSTRATION

Cabinet L Shelf 5 No. 11

(Paris, 1927, special Christmas number of l'Illustration.)
l'Illustration. Noel. With numerous examples of color printing work.

Cloth; 16¼ x 12 in.

ILLUSTRATION

Cabinet J Shelf 3 No. 3

(Poster printing)

See PENNELL, JOSEPH. Liberty-Loan Poster: A text book....1918.

ILLUSTRATION

Cabinet 27 Shelf 2 No. 5

Major & Knapp Illustrated Monthly, vol.1, 1870. Published by Major & Knapp Engraving, Manufacturing and Lithographic Co., New York.

Half morocco; 15 x 11¾ in.

ILLUSTRATION

Cabinet J Shelf 3 No. 5

Pennell, Joseph, a memorial exhibit of his works. With an account by his wife, Elizabeth Robins Pennell, Washington, 1927. Library of Congress. Illus.

Half morocco; 9¼ x 6 x 3/4 in.

ILLUSTRATION

Cabinet K Shelf 3 No. 15

Practical handbook of Drawing for modern methods of reproduction. By Charles G. Harper. Illus. with drawings by several hands... (2nd. ed.) London, 1901.

Cloth; 8-7/8 x 5¾ in.

ILLUSTRATION

Cabinet L Shelf 5 No. 20

Modern illustrative methods, three: duograph, colortype, half-tone. Colortype Company, W. Kurtz, President. 32-32 Lafayette Place, New York, 1894.

Item in folder; 14½ x 10¼ in.

ILLUSTRATION

Cabinet J Shelf 3 No. 4

Pennell, Joseph. Adventures of an illustrator, mostly in following his authors in America and Europe. Published ... Boston, 1925. Illus. Has a list of Pennell's works.

Cloth; 12-1/8 x 8-3/4 x 1½ in.

ILLUSTRATION

Cabinet J Shelf 5 No. 20

Printers' trade cards. Collection. Specimens of color printing, engraving. lithography. Scrap book.

In linen case; 17¾ x 11½ in.

ILLUSTRATION.

Cabinet I Shelf 3 No. 1

Modern methods of illustration, some. By Jas. B. Carrington. Excerpt from the "Bookman," August 1905. Illus.

Item 21 in vol. with binder's title:"Various Engravers and About Engravers."

ILLUSTRATION

Cabinet J Shelf 3 No. 2

Pennell, Joseph. Die moderne illustration. Aus dem Englischen von L. und K. Burger. Autorisierte ausgabe: Mit 170 illustrationen. Leipzig, 1901.

Paper; 8¾ x 6 x 1 in.

ILLUSTRATION

Cabinet J Shelf 5 No. 23

(Proofs of reproductive printing processes)
Proeven van reproductie in boekdruk. Haarlem, 1907. Joh. Enschede en Zonen

Pictorial paper cover; 17-7/8 x 11-3/8 in.

ILLUSTRATION

Cabinet C Shelf 1 No. 9

Modern movement in illustration. Brief illus. article.

See MANCHESTER GUARDIAN. Craft of printing, the...May 23, 1922, p.XII

ILLUSTRATION

Cabinet L Shelf 1 No. 34

(Photography and modern book illustrating)
L'Illustration du livre moderne et la photographie. Par Jules Pinsard. Avec preface de Victor Breton. Paris, 1897. Illus.

Half morocco; 11½ x 8-1/8 in.

ILLUSTRATION

Cabinet K Shelf 2 No. 28

Rackham's, Arthur book of pictures. With an introduction by Sir Arthur Quiller-Couch. London (1913)

44 plates

Cloth; 11¾ x 8-7/8 in.

ILLUSTRATION

Cabinet K Shelf 1 No. 11

Rococco engravings, 18th century.

See Jessen, Dr. Peter. Rococco engravings...London, 1922.

ILLUSTRATION

Cabinet K Shelf 4 No. 22

Theory of pictorial art. A guide to the study of light, colour, line, and composition. By H. W. Harrison. With a foreword by W. L. Wyllie. London, 1931. Illus.

Boards, cloth back: 9¼ x 6-5/8 x ½ in.

ILLUSTRATION, BOOK

Cabinet 18 Shelf 1 No. 13

[American picture books] Von amerikanischer Bilderbuch. von Ernst Eisele. New York, 1913. Illus.

In Zeitschrift fur Bucherfreunde, 1913, part 2, p. 253.

ILLUSTRATION

Cabinet K Shelf 2 No. 20

(Russian Graphic Arts)

see KUSMIN, M. and WSEWOLD WAYNOFF. Russische graphische kunst...

ILLUSTRATION

Cabinet K Shelf 3 No. 14

Training of an illustrator. By Frank Holme of the Chicago Daily News, Chicago, 1899. Illus. brochure.

Item in manila envelope

ILLUSTRATION, BOOK

Cabinet I Shelf 2 No. 16

Aquatint engraving: a chapter in the history of book illustration. By S.T. Prideaux. London, 1909. Illus.

Cloth; 9-5/8 x 6¼ x 2 in.

ILLUSTRATION

Cabinet K Shelf 4 No. 24 (8 parts)

"Savoy, The". Illustrated Quarterly. Edited by Arthur Symons, London. Nos. 1 to 8, first and last number. Jan.-Dec. 1896.

With drawings, wood-engravings, etchings, lithographs, by Beardsley, Pennell, Beerbohm, etc.

Bound in pictorial covers.

ILLUSTRATION.

Cabinet 18 Shelf 2 No. 1

(War Scenes) Kriegsgraphik, von Julius Zeitler, Leipzig. Illus.

Briefly describes the work and style of the artists who illustrated the "World War."

In Zeitschrift für Bücherfreunde, 1915-16, part 2, p.157.

ILLUSTRATION, Book.

Cabinet 18 Shelf 1 No. 16

(Art and industry of the book at the Leipzig Book Exhibition, 1914). Buchgewerbe und Buchkunst auf der Leipziger Bucherweltausstellung, 1914 von Julius Zeitler. Illus.

In Zeitschrift für Bücherfreunde, 1914. part 1, p. 138.

ILLUSTRATION

Cabinet K Shelf 6 No. 32

Some original illustrations prepared by The Youth's Companion for its advertisers. Boston, n. d. circa 1895.

Artists proofs.

Cloth, oblong; 8-1/8 x 12½ x ½ in.

ILLUSTRATION.

Cabinet R Shelf 5 No. 148

War-time envelopes. By Pleasant E. Todd. Excerpt from the Monthly Illustrator, 1895.

Excerpt 17 in volume "Chap books, Almanacs, Annuals, etc.

ILLUSTRATION, Book.

Cabinet 18 Shelf 1 No. 6

(Art of the book as shown in the collection of Wilhelm Metzler). Die Buchkunst der Sammlung Wilhelm Metzler sur Frankfurt A.M., von Fritz Hoeber, Strassburg. Facsimiles.

In Zeitschrift für Bücherfreunde, 1908-9, part 2, pp. 419-459.

ILLUSTRATION

Cabinet L Shelf 5 No. 11

(Special Christmas number of L'Illustration, Paris, 1927)

See Color Printing. L'Illustration. Noel, 1927...

ILLUSTRATION see also

Cabinet Shelf No.

BOOKMAKING

WOOD ENGRAVING

ILLUSTRATION, BOOK

Cabinet K Shelf 3 No. 32

Arts of the book. A guide to an exhibition of the. By W.M. Ivins Jr. The Metropolitan Museum of Art, New York, May-Sept., 1924. Illus.

Paper; 8½ x 5½ in.

ILLUSTRATION

Cabinet 00 Shelf 4 No. 53

Technique of illustration printing. By R. B. Fishenden.

Article in LONDON MERCURY, THE. Special printing number, Nov. 1931, Vol.25, No. 145, pp. 81-84.

ILLUSTRATION, BOOK

Cabinet K Shelf 5 No. 25

Altdeutsche buchillustration, die.

see WORRINGER, WILHELM. Buchillustration, die altdeutsche...Munchen, 1921.

ILLUSTRATION, BOOK

Cabinet U Shelf 4 No. 35

Basle book illustration of the 15th and 16th centuries.

See HECKETHORN, CHARLES WILLIAM. The printers of Basle in the 15th and 16th centuries...

ILLUSTRATION BOOK

Cabinet L
Shelf 4
No. 26

Baxter's book illustration

See Lewis, C. T. Courtney, George Baxter, the picture printer...London, n.d.(circa 1925) (See index).

ILLUSTRATION, BOOK

Cabinet J
Shelf 4
No. 1

Bewicks woodcuts, impressions of upwards of 2000 wood-blocks.

See HUGO, THOMAS. Bewick's woodcuts... London, 1870.

ILLUSTRATION, BOOK

Cabinet
Shelf
No.

Bible illustration, early history of. By W. C. Prime. Illus. excerpt from Harper's New Monthly Magazine, April, 1880.

Item 4 in vol. labeled "Excerpts relating to wood engraving and engravers".

ILLUSTRATION, BOOK

Cabinet B
Shelf 2
Nos. 1 to 18

Bibliographical, historical account of 15th century German book illustration.

See SCHRAMM, ALBERT. (Der) Bilderschmuck der frühdrucke...

ILLUSTRATION, BOOK.

Cabinet I
Shelf 3
No. 1

Book illustration, old and new, Cantor Lectures on. By J. Comyns Carr. Delivered before the Society of Arts, May, 1882. London. Pamphlet.

Item 10 in vol. with binder's title "Various Engravers and About Engravers."

ILLUSTRATION, BOOK

Cabinet U
Shelf 5
No. 54

(Book illustration through the centuries)

See Bouchot, Henri, (The) Book: its printers...London, 1890

ILLUSTRATION, Book.

Cabinet V
Shelf 6
No. 8

See Brunel, Georges. Le livre à travers les ages ...Paris, 1894. P. 29.

Essay by Paul Chaux and Léon Vidal.

ILLUSTRATION, BOOK

Cabinet K
Shelf 3
No. 30

(Die) Buchornamentik im 15 und 16 jahrhundert. von Hans Wolff. Monographien des Buchgewerbes. v Band. Leipzig, 1911. Illus.

Half morocco; 6½ x 4-3/4 in.

ILLUSTRATION, BOOK

Cabinet K
Shelf 4
No. 15

Cantor lectures on book illustration, old and new. By J. Comyns Carr. Delivered before the Society of Arts, May, 1882.

Half morocco; 10¼ x 6-3/4 x 3/8 in.

ILLUSTRATION, BOOK.

Cabinet I
Shelf 3
No. 1

Chapter on book illustrations, by B. B. Chamberlain. An excerpt from the Ladies'Repository, Oct. 1869. Illus.

Brief historical account which traces the progress of the art from its supposed origin down to the 18th century.

Item 14 in vol. with binder's title:"Various Engravers and About Engravers."

ILLUSTRATION, Book.

Cabinet 18
Shelf 1
No. 8

(Children's Picture Books.) Bibliophilie in der Kinderstube von Max Brahn, Leipzig, Many col. illus.

Former crude methods and products compared with the newer methods of machine processes.

In Zeitschrift für Bücherfreunde, 1910. part 2, p. 303.

ILLUSTRATION, BOOK

Cabinet K
Shelf 4
No. 7

(Collection of articles on book making, illustration, types, bookbinding, etc.) Kunstgewerbe. Ein bericht uber entwicklung und tatigkeit der handwerker - u. kunstgewerbeschulen in Preussen. Herausgegeben vom Bund der Kunstgewerbeschulmänner. Verlag Ernst Wasmuth. Berlin (1922) With 208 plates.

Boards: 10 x 7½ x 5/8 in.

ILLUSTRATION, Book.

Cabinet 18
Shelf 1
No. 16

(Contemporary graphic art at the International Exhibition of the book industry and graphic arts in Leipzig, 1914.) Die Zeitgenossische Graphik auf der Internationalen Ausstellung fur Buchgewerbe und Graphik in Leipzig von Hans Wolff. Illus.

In Zeitschrift fur Bucherfreunde, part 1, page 129.

ILLUSTRATION, BOOK

Cabinet J
Shelf 3
No. 32 (env.)

D'Alencon, Godard, Paris, 1830.

See DIMIER, LOUIS. (Le) Bois d'illustration au 19e siecle...

ILLUSTRATION, BOOK

Cabinet K
Shelf 5
No. 2

Darley, Felix O. C. American illustrator circa 1840. With portrait.

see BIOGRAPHIES, ILLUSTRATORS. Darley...

ILLUSTRATION, BOOK

Cabinet K
Shelf 3
No. 31

(Les) Decorateurs du livre. Par Charles Saunier. Paris, 1922. Avec 24 planches hors text

Modern French book illustration

Paper; 9 x 5 x ½ in.

ILLUSTRATION BOOK

Cabinet K
Shelf 4
No. 19

(La) Decorazione del libro. 90 disegni del pittore Dardo Battaglini. Prefazione del Cav. Cesare Ratta di Bologna, Edizione della Casa d'Arte "Ariel" Alessandria. n.d. circa 1924.

Paper; 9½ x 7¾ in.

ILLUSTRATION, BOOK

Cabinet K
Shelf 1
No. 15

Deutsche bucherillustrationen der gothik und fruhrenaissance (1560-1530). von Richard Muther. (2 vols. in one) München, 1884.

Boards, morocco back; 14½ x 10½ x 1-5/8 in.

ILLUSTRATION, BOOK

Cabinet K Shelf 2 No. 12

Deutschland, die entwicklung die modernen buchkunst in.

see GRANTOFF, OTTO. Entwicklung der modernen buchdruckunst...Leip zig, 1901

ILLUSTRATION, BOOK.

Cabinet K Shelf 1 No. 20

France, the new book illustration in. By Leon Pichon. Translated from the French by Herbert B. Grimsditch. Special Winter number of "The Studio", London, 1924.

Paper; $11\frac{1}{2}$ x 8-1/8 x $\frac{1}{4}$ in.

ILLUSTRATION, BOOK

Cabinet J Shelf 4 No. 23

(German book illustration of the first half of the 16th century).

See GEISBERG, MAX. Deutsche buchillustration in der ersten halfte des 16e jahrhunderts ...

ILLUSTRATION, BOOK

Cabinet G Shelf 3 No. 52

Dwiggins, W.A. Form letters: Illustrator to author...an assortment of opinions about the proper function of illustration, and the relation between pictures and text. New York, William Edwin Rudge, 1930.

Half cloth; 9-5/8 x $6\frac{1}{2}$ x $\frac{1}{4}$ in.

ILLUSTRATION, BOOK

Cabinet U Shelf 3 No. 103

French Books of Hours, 1486-1500, the illustrations in. By A.W. Pollard. [Illus. biblio. account].

In BOOKS ABOUT BOOKS. Bibliographica: Papers about books...vol.3, p.430.

ILLUSTRATION, BOOK.

Cabinet I Shelf 3 No. 1

German peoples artist, 1803-1884, Ludwig Richter ...

See RICHTER, LUDWIG. German peoples' artist ...

ILLUSTRATION, BOOK

Cabinet C Shelf 2 No. 4

Emperor Charles the Fifth, the victories of. Designed by Martin Heemskerck, 1555. Now illustrated with portraits, prints and notes By Sir William Stirling Maxwell. London and Edinburgh, 1870.

Cloth over boards; 18-3/8 x $13\frac{1}{2}$ in.

ILLUSTRATION, BOOK

Cabinet J Shelf 4 No. 8

(French 16th century.) La gravure dans le livre et l'ornament. La gravure en France au 16e siècle. Par J. Lieure. Paris et Bruxelles. 1927. G. Vanoest, Editeur.

72 plates of illustration.

Paper; 13 x 9-7/8 x $1\frac{1}{4}$ in.

ILLUSTRATION, BOOK.

Cabinet 1 & 5 Shelf Portfolios Nos. 1 to 41

German single-plate woodcuts of the first half of the 16th century, facsimile reprints of.

See GEISBERG, MAX (Editor) (German single-plate woodcuts ... Hugo Schmidt Verlag, Munchen, 1923-1930.

ILLUSTRATION, BOOK

Cabinet J Shelf 3 No. 13

English illustrated books, before 1860, 1857-1864.

See WHITE, GLEESON. English illustration 'The Sixties'...pp.95-112.

ILLUSTRATION, BOOK

Cabinet J Shelf 4 No. 22

French (1925). Livre d'or du bibliophile. Première année.

Specimens of decorative printing. Collective efforts of several artists, printers, publishers, etc.

Paper; 13 x $10\frac{1}{4}$ x 1 in.

ILLUSTRATION, Book.

Cabinet 26 Shelf 2 No. 5

Gotta, Johann Friedrich, 1846, printer and publisher, Munich. Illus. prospectus.

Supplement to Journal fur Buchdruckerkunst, 1846-53, No.45.

ILLUSTRATION, Book

Cabinet U Shelf 5 No. 24

English woodcut illustrations, early

see POLLARD, A. W. Fine Books.. ..London, 1912, p.250

ILLUSTRATION, BOOK.

Cabinet K Shelf 5 No. 24

(German book illustration, early) Die altdeutsche buchillustration. von Wilhelm Worringer. Mit 105 abbildungen nach holzschnitten. Zweite auflage. Munchen, 1919.

Pictorial boards; 10 x 8 in.

ILLUSTRATION, BOOK

Cabinet 26 Shelf 1 No. 16

Gravelot's werk als bücherillustrator. von Richard Oehler. [With list of books illustrated by Gravelot].

Illustrated essay in "Gutenberg-Gesellschaft Jahrbuch, 1927", pp.105-115.

ILLUSTRATION, Book

Cabinet K Shelf 6 No. 36

Francais, illustration du livre (1478-1934). Étude historique, technique et critique. Par Pierre Gusman. Bulletin Officiel des Maitres Imprimeurs de France. Paris, 1934. (Noel)

Evolution of book illustration in France with one section devoted to processes and specimens of color printing.

Paper; $12\frac{1}{4}$ x $9\frac{1}{2}$ in.

ILLUSTRATION, BOOK

Cabinet 26 Shelf 1 No. 27

(German book illustration in the first century of printing) Buchillustrationen in den ersten jahrzehnten des deutschen buchdruckes.

Lecture by Hans Koegler, at Gutenberg-Gesellschaft meeting at Mainze, June 25, 1911 and printed in the Society's yearly report, No. 10

Item in cloth covered box holding Reports 1902-1913

ILLUSTRATION, BOOK

Cabinet FP Shelf 3 No. 33

(History and art of the book, many articles relating to the).

See LIBRARIES. Congrès Internationale des bibliothecaires...Paris, 1925.

ILLUSTRATION, BOOK

Cabinet J Shelf 4 No. 15

Holbein, books illustrated by.

See DAVIES, GERALD S. Hans Holbein... London, 1903.

ILLUSTRATION, Book.

Cabinet S Shelf 5 No. 12

(The) Illustration of books. By George Wharton Edwards, in the Outlook, Dec. 4, 1897.

Bound in collection "Pamphlets and excerpts relating to typographical matters," item 12.

ILLUSTRATION BOOK

Cabinet K Shelf 6 No. 34

Italian illustration, the rebirth of. By Gardner Teall. Excerpt from the Bookman, Jan. 1914. Illus.

Item 8 in vol. with binder's title "Wood Engraving. Various excerpts".

ILLUSTRATION, BOOK

Cabinet J Shelf 2 No. 27

Holbeins designs for book illustrations for the Basel publishers.... Initial letters and alphabets, trade-marks and devices for printers....

See Chamberlain, Arthur B. Hans Holbein the Younger... London, 1913, Vol.I, p.187.

ILLUSTRATION, Book

Cabinet S Shelf 1 No. 33

Illustration of books, The. By George Wharton Edwards. An excerpt from "The Outlook,"n.d. Item 10 in volume "Writings of Theodore Low DeVinne."

Half morocco; 9¾ x 6-5/8 in.

ILLUSTRATION, Book.

Cabinet U Shelf 5 No. 22

Italy 15th century: Italiam book illustrations. By Alfred W. Pollard. London, 1894.

Morocco; 10½ x 7-1/8 x ½ in.

ILLUSTRATION, BOOK

Cabinet S Shelf 1 No. 105

Holbeins drawings for Erasmus Praise of Folly.

See BULLEN, HENRY LEWIS. Erasmus...Excerpt American Book Collector, March, 1932.

ILLUSTRATION, BOOK.

Cabinet K Shelf 4 No. 21

(Das) Illustrierte buch des 19 jahrhunderts in England, Frankreich und Deutschland, 1790-1860. von Arthur Rumann. Mit 235 abbildungen. Leipzig, 1930.

Cloth; 10½ x 7½ x 1¼ in.

ILLUSTRATION, BOOK

Cabinet J Shelf 4 No. 3.01

Japanese. List of choice-colour-printed books and albums...

See BINYON, LAURENCE and SEXTON, J.J. O'BRIEN. Japanese colour prints...pp.211-225.

ILLUSTRATION, BOOK

Cabinet AA Shelf 3 No. 53

Holland, 1923.

see PANNEKOEK, G. H. JR. De Verluchting van het boek...

ILLUSTRATION, BOOK

Cabinet J Shelf 4 No. 21

Italian book illustration (circa 1925-6) Two incomplete unidentified publications, with specimens of book illustration, trade and social printing, color printing etc. Librum IV and V.

In folder; 14½ x 11¼ in.

ILLUSTRATION, Book.

Cabinet 18 Shelf 2 No. 1

(Jean Paul and the contemporary art of the book) Jean Paul und die Buchkunst der gegenwart, von Georg Witkowski. Illus.

In Zeitschrift für Bücherfreunde, 1915-16, p. 279.

ILLUSTRATION, BOOK

Cabinet U Shelf 3 No. 103

Houghton, L. a forgotten book-illustrator. By L. Housman.

Bibliographical account.

See vol. I, pp.275-92 in Bibliographica... London, 1895-1897.

ILLUSTRATION, BOOK

Cabinet K Shelf 4 No. 17

Italian book illustrations, chiefly of the 15th century. By Alfred W. Pollard. London, 1894. Illus.

Imitation leather; 10½ x 7-1/8 x ½ in.

ILLUSTRATION, Book

Cabinet M Shelf 2 No. 46

Kerver, Thielman, Paris, 1522.

see LINOTYPE MACHINERY LTD. London. Calendar for the year 1923...

ILLUSTRATION, BOOK

Cabinet K Shelf 6 No. 34

Illustrated Books, by W. M. Ivins, Jr. Excerpt from the Bulletin of the Metropolitan Museum of Art, June, 1918. Illus.

Bound in volume "Wood Engraving: Various excerpts," item 7.

ILLUSTRATION, BOOK

Cabinet AA Shelf 2 No. 19.01

(Italian book of the 19th century).

See BERTIERI, RAFFAELLO. (Il) Libro Italiano nel novecento...

ILLUSTRATION, BOOK

Cabinet K Shelf 4 No. 20

Le livre illustre au XVe siecle. Avec 344 figures sur 220 planches dont une en couleurs et 3 en bistre, plus 15 figures dans le texte dont 2 en couleurs. Leo S. Olschki. Florence, 1926.

Has tables of artists, printers, block-books, places of printing, etc.

Paper: 9-5/8 x 6¾ x 1 in.

ILLUSTRATION, BOOK

Cabinet 26 Shelf 2 No. 15

(Modern German book illustration.) Über Bilderbücher. von Emmy Zweybrück-Prochaska.

Illus. article in Jahrbuch IX, 1935, p. 69, Deutscher Verein für Buchwesen und Schrifttum.

ILLUSTRATION, Book.

Cabinet I Shelf 3 No. 1

Picture and the text, The. by Professor Robert MacDougall, in The Popular Science Monthly, September 1914.

Item 8 in vol. with binder's title; "Various Engravers and About Engravers."

ILLUSTRATION, BOOK

Cabinet B Shelf 2 No. 17

Reproductions of illustrations used by Anton Koberger, 1482-1500

see SCHRAMM, ALBERT (Die) Bilderschmuck der fruhdruck. Band XVll... Leipzig, 1934.

ILLUSTRATION, BOOK

Cabinet K Shelf 3 No. 28

Modern methods of illustrating books.

see WHEATLY, HENRY B. (Editor). Modern methods...London, 1887

ILLUSTRATION, Book.

Cabinet I Shelf 3 No. 1

Picture books of olden days, by Mary E. Allen: An excerpt from the Cosmopolitan, January, 1899. Illus.

Item 25 in vol. with binder's title: "Various Engravers, and About Engravers."

ILLUSTRATION, Book.

Cabinet U Shelf 1 No. 1h

Some early illustrated sermon books, by G. J. Gray. Illus.

In excerpts relating to printing from The Library, 1915-17, pp.64-77 of pencilled folios.

ILLUSTRATION BOOK

Cabinet K Shelf 5 No. 30

(Modern wood engraving in France and other European countries, also North and South Americas).

see

AVERMAETE, ROGER. (La) Gravure sur bois moderne...Paris, 1928.

ILLUSTRATION, BOOK.

Cabinet Y Shelf 3 No. 40

(Poliphilo, the anonymous master of, and Italian book illustration of the 14th century) Der anonyme meister des Poliphilo: Eine studie zur italianischen buchillustration und zur antike in der kunst des quattrocento. von Jos. Poppelreuter. Strassburg, 1904.

Half morocco; 11½ x 8 in.

ILLUSTRATION, BOOK.

Cabinet K Shelf 1 No. 18

Spain, early book illustration in. By James P. R. Lyell. With an introduction by Dr. Konrad Haebler. Illustrated with numerous reporductions. London, 1926.

Cloth; 11½ x 9 x 1¾ in.

ILLUSTRATION, BOOK.

Cabinet I Shelf 3 No. 1

Natural history, the first illustrated. By Leonard Larkin. [Excerpt from Strand Magazine, Feb. 1916].

Item 13 in vol. with Binder's title:"Various Engravers and About Engravers."

ILLUSTRATION, BOOK

Cabinet L Shelf 4 No. 18

Practical hints on decorative printing.

See Savage, William. Practical hints on decorative printing...London, 1822.

ILLUSTRATION, BOOK

Cabinet J Shelf 4 No. 13

Steinlen, Paris, 1913. L'Oeuvre gravé et lithographie de Steinlin. Catalogue descriptive...

See STEINLEN. L'Oeuvre gravé et lithographie de...

ILLUSTRATION, BOOK

Cabinet K Shelf 3 No. 29

Notes on book illustration. By Charles Gerring. Opusculum x: Nottingham Sette of Odde Volumes. Privately printed. Nottingham, January 1898. Illus.

Half morocco; 5[illegible] x 4-5/8 in.

ILLUSTRATION, Book.

Cabinet 18 Shelf 1 No. 9

(Prestorius, Emil. Modern German book illustrators). Deutsche Buchkunstler der gegenwart Emil Prectorius, von Kurt Wolff, Leipzig, Illus.

In Zeitschrift fur Bucherfreunde, 1910-11, part 1, p. 373.

ILLUSTRATION, BOOK

Cabinet J Shelf 3 No. 27

(Wood engravings of Antoine Verard)

See RENOUVIER, J. Gravures sur bois dans les livres d'Anthoine Verard...

ILLUSTRATION, BOOK

Cabinet J Shelf 3 No. 1

Pennell, Joseph. Ilustration of books. A manual for the use of students, notes for a course of lectures at the Slade School, University College. New York - London (1895)

Cloth; 7½ x 4-7/8 x 5/8 in.

ILLUSTRATION, BOOK

Cabinet K Shelf 3 No. 33

Prints and books. Informal papers. By William M. Ivins Jr. Cambridge (Mass.), 1926. Illus.

Boards, linen back; 8-1/8 x 5-3/8 in.

ILLUSTRATION, BOOK (see also)

Cabinet Shelf No.

COLOR PRINTING

ILLUSTRATION, BOOK. Literature of

Cabinet V Shelf 3 No. 15

(Ancient methods of manuscript and book illustration.)

see

WERDET, EDMOND. Histoire du livre en France...lre partie, pp.129-142

ILLUSTRATION, COMIC

Cabinet K Shelf 5 No. 1

Early political caricature in America. By Jos. B. Bishop. Illus. excerpt from "The Century Magazine", June, 1893.

Item 15 in vol. with binder's title "Wood Engraving, Etc".

ILLUSTRATION, Comic.

Cabinet 18 Shelf 2 No. 2

(World War as seen in comic illustrations: The animal in satire and caricature during the World War.) Der Weltkrieg im Scherzbilde: Das tier in der satire und karikatur des Weltkrieges, von Ernst Schultz-Besser, Leipzig, Illus.

In Zeitschrift fur Bucherfreunde, 1916-17, part 2, p. 231.

ILLUSTRATION, Caricature.

Cabinet 18 Shelf 2 No. 1

(World War in comic pictures) Der weltkrieg im Scherzbilde, von Ernst Schulz-Besser, Leipzig. Illus.

In Zeitschrift für Bücherfreunde, 1915-16, p.205.

ILLUSTRATION, Comic.

Cabinet 18 Shelf 2 No. 3

(German war contractor in caricature.) Der Kriegslieferant in der karikature, von Fritz Hansen, Berlin. Illus.

In Zeitschrift für Bücherfreunde, 1917-18, part 1, p. 63.

ILLUSTRATION, COMIC.

Cabinet Shelf No.

see also

I - CARICATURE.
II - CARTOONISTS.
III- BIOGRAPHIES, CARTOONISTS.

ILLUSTRATION, COMIC.

Cabinet I Shelf 3 No. 1

American caricature and comic art, by La Touche Hancock: Two excerpts from The Bookman, Oct. 1902.

Item 17 in vol. with binder's title:"Various Engravers, and About Engravers."

ILLUSTRATION, COMIC

Cabinet K Shelf 5 No. 1

Japanese caricature...

see

CARICATURE. Japanese caricature...

ILLUSTRATION, Early, [Literature of]

Cabinet 18 Shelf 1 No. 14

[Devotional pictures of the Catholic Church] Beitrage zur Geschichte des katholischen Andachtsbildes von C. Benziger in Bern. Illus.

In Zeitschrift für Bücherfreunde, 1913-14, part I, p.65.

ILLUSTRATION, Comic.

Cabinet I Shelf 3 No. 1

Cartoons and their makers, by R. K. Munkittrick. An excerpt from Munsey's Magazine, Aug., 1904. Illus.

The editor of Judge writes of the leading American cartoonists and their achievements.

Item 20 in vol. with binder's title:"Various Engravers and About Engravers."

ILLUSTRATION, Comic.

Cabinet I Shelf 3 No. 1

Nast, Thomas and his cartoons, by Arthur Bartlett Maurice, in The Bookman, March, 1902. Illus.

Item 12 in vol. with binder's title:"Various Engravers and About Engravers."

ILLUSTRATION, Early. [Literature of].

Cabinet U Shelf 1 No. 1f

"Fasciculus Temporum," The edition printed by Arnold Ther Hoernen in 1474: An account by A.G.W. Murray.

This is probably the first or second illustrated book printed in Cologne.

In Excerpts relating to printing from "The Library," 1912-13, p. 93 of pencilled folios.

ILLUSTRATION, COMIC

Cabinet K Shelf 5 No. 2

"Cham" Comte, de Noe, 1830-1879, by R. Whiteing, in "Scribner's Magazine", March, 1880.

Bound in volume "Wood engravers and illustrators: Excerpts from magazines," item 10.

ILLUSTRATION, COMIC

Cabinet K Shelf 5 No. 2

Oberlender, Adolf, humorist. [Illus. biographical sketch. With portrait.] By Charles Stuart Pratt. Excerpt from The Cosmopolitan Magazine, Sept., 1890.

Item 7 in vol. with binder's title "Wood engravers and illustrators".

ILLUSTRATION, Early. [Literature of]

Cabinet 18 Shelf 1 No. 12

(Four broadsides concerning the comets of 1680). Vier einblattdruck uber der Kometen von jahr 1680, von Paul Gulyas, Budapest.

These broadsides are in the library in Budapest in which place the author declares there are others of early date which were printed in Hungary.

In Zeitschrift für Bücherfreunde, 1912, part 2, p.328.

ILLUSTRATION, COMIC

Cabinet K Shelf 5 No. 1

Curiosities of ancient caricatures. By J. Holt Schooling. Illus. excerpt from the "Strand Magazine", Sept., 1898.

Item 11 in vol. with binder's title "Wood Engraving, Etc".

ILLUSTRATION, COMIC

Cabinet K Shelf 5 No. 1

Present campaign in cartoon. By Marmaduke Humphrey. Illus. excerpt from "Godey's Magazine", Oct. 1896.

Item 12 in vol. with binder's title "Wood Engraving, Etc".

ILLUSTRATION, Early. [Literature of]

Cabinet 75 Shelf 1 No. 6

"Herbarius" and "Hortus Sanitatis," on the. A paper read before the Bibliographical Society, Jan. 21, 1901. By J. F. Payne. Illus.

Description of the earliest literature devoted to the illustration of Natural History.

In Trans. Biblio. Soc. Vol. 6, 1900-1902, pp. 63-126.

ILLUSTRATION, Early. [Literature of]

Cabinet 20 Shelf 1 No. 18

Illustrationen in Stephan Arndes Bible 1494 und andere Lubecker Holzschnitte, von Axel L. Romdahl, Stockhom, Jan., 1906. Illus.

In Zeitschrift für Bücherfreunde, 1905-6, part 1, p. 391.

ILLUSTRATION, Early [Literature of]

Cabinet 75 Shelf 1 No. 3

Oppenheim Press, (1494) some early book illustration of the. By Gilbert R. Redgrave. Read before the Bibliographical Society, May 20, 1895. Illus.

In Trans. Biblio. Soc. vol. 3, 1895-1896. p. 71-80.

ILLUSTRATION Literature of

Cabinet U Shelf 5 No. 21

Early illustrated books: a history of the decoration and illustration of books in the 15th and 16th centuries. By Alfred W. Pollard. London, 1893. Illus.

Half morocco; $8\frac{1}{2}$ x $5\frac{1}{4}$ in.

ILLUSTRATION, Early. [Literature of]

Cabinet 18 Shelf 1 No. 9

(Illustrators and some publishers of the works of Hans Sachs). Uber einege verleger und illustratoren des Hans Sachs, von Reinhard Buchwald, Leipzig, Illus.

In Zeitschrift für Bücherfreund, 1910-11, part 1, p. 233.

ILLUSTRATION, Early. [Literature of]

Cabinet 18 Shelf 1 No. 9

(Representation of the sky and natural sciences in the printed broadsides of the 15th to the 18th century) Himmels-und naturerscheinungen in Einblattdrucken des XV bis XVIII Jahrhunderts von Wilhelm Hess, Bamberg. Illus.

In Zeitschrift für Bücherfreunde, 1910-11, part 1, pp.301, 388.

ILLUSTRATION, Periodicals

Cabinet 26 Shelf 2 No. 5

Prospectus and proof sheets of the "Illustrirte Naturgeschichte des Thierreichs," Leipzig, 1846, pp.4.

Supplement to Journal fur Buchdruckerkunst, 1846-53, No.14.

ILLUSTRATION, Early. [Literature of]

Cabinet 20 Shelf 1 No. 16

Italy. (Venetian book illustration, wood engraving, prior to 1500). Venetianische Buchillustration in Holzschnitt vor 1500, von Dr. Emil Gigas, Kopenhagen.

Richly illustrated with facsimiles from the more famous works of the early printers, Ratdolt and others.

In Zeitschrift fur Bucherfreunde, 1904-5, pp. 377-417.

ILLUSTRATION, Early. [Literature of]

Cabinet 18 Shelf 1 No. 7 & 9

(Sky and the Natural phenomena as depicted in the Broadsides of the XV to the XVIII century). Himmels und Naturerscheinungen in Einblattdrucken des XV bis XVIII. Jahrhunderts von Wilhelm Hess, Bamberg. Illus.

In Zeitschrift für Bücherfreunde, 1910, part 1, pp. 1, 75: 1910-11, part 1, pp.301, 342, 388.

ILLUSTRATION, Posters.

Cabinet I Shelf 3 No. 1

Some recent London posters. By Alfred Yockney: An excerpt from the International Studio, February, 1915. Illus.

Item 37 in vol. with binder's title:"Various Engravers and About Engravers."

ILLUSTRATION, EARLY [Literature of]

Cabinet W Shelf 3 No. 60

2 Vols.

Les Le Rouge de Chablis, calligraphes et miniaturists, graveurs et imprimeurs. Etude sur les débuts de l'illustration du livre au XVe siècle. Par Henri Monceaux. Paris, 1896. 2 Vols. With 200 Facsimiles.

Half morocco; 11-1/8 x $7\frac{1}{2}$ in.

ILLUSTRATION, Early. [Literature of]

Cabinet 75 Shelf 2 No. 6

(Spain). Notes on early book-illustration in Spain. A paper read before the Bibliographical Society. By James P. R. Lyell, London, Feb. 16, 1925. Facsimile, and biographies of printers, also chronological descriptive account of the introduction of printing in the provinces of Spain.

In Trans. Biblio. Soc., "The Library," 1925-1926, vol. VI, pp. 1-41.

L'ILLUSTRATION (Paris) see

Cabinet 00 Shelf 6 No. 31

PERIODICALS, ILLUSTRATED. France

ILLUSTRATION, Early. [Literature of]

Cabinet 20 Shelf 2 No. 6

(Luther portrait. An unknown?). Ein unbekanntes Lutherbild? von August Schnizlein in Rothenburg. Illus.

In Zeitschrift fur Bucherfreunde, 1917-18, part 2, p. 175.

ILLUSTRATION, Early. [Literature of]

Cabinet 18 Shelf 1 No. 2

(Transformation of some Luther portraits in the illustrated books of the 16th century). Die Wandlungen eines Lutherbildnisses in der buchillustration des XVI, jahrhunderts von Alfred Hagelstange, Magdeburg. Illus.

In Zeitschrift für Bücherfreunde, 1907-8, part 1, p. 97.

ILLUSTRATIONS

Cabinet NN Shelf 4 No. 9

Nash, Thomas. 1872.

See GREELEY, HORACE. What I know about farming...1872.

ILLUSTRATION, Early. [Literature of]

Cabinet W Shelf 1 No. 187

Maitres Suises (dessinateurs et graveurs) de l'illustration et de l'ornementation du livre de 1475 a 1914 ...

See Lonchamp, F. A. Manuel de Bibliophile Suisse ... pp. 127 - 171.

ILLUSTRATION, Early. [Literature of]

Cabinet 20 Shelf 2 No. 19

Weltchronik des Rudolf von Ems: Ein Lieblingsbilderbuch des Mittelatlers. Von Dr. Karl Löffler of Stuttgart. (A favorite picture book of the Middle Ages). Illus.

In Zeitschrift für Bücherfreunde, 1927, pp. 1-11.

ILLUSTRATORS

Cabinet K Shelf 6 No. 39.01

Darley, Felix Octavius Carr, 1822-1888.

see WEITENKAMPF, FRANK. "Illustrated by Darley"...

ILLUSTRATORS

Cabinet 26 Shelf 1 No. 17

Doré, Gustave, als buch illustrator. von Albert Kolb.
Article in Gutenberg-Gesellschaft Jahrbuch 1928. pp.118-141.

ILLUSTRATORS

Cabinet U Shelf 3 No. 103

Houghton, Arthur Boyd., a forgotten book illustrator. By Laurence Housman. Article, illus.

See BOOKS ABOUT BOOKS. Bibliographica: Papers on books...vol.I, p.275.

ILLUSTRATORS

Cabinet J Shelf 3 No. 6.01

Notable American illustrators, a book of. Written and arrangrd by Nathan G. Horwitt. New York, 1926. Illus.
Presented with the compliments of the Walker Engraving Company.

Boards; $12\frac{1}{2}$ x $9\frac{1}{2}$ in.

ILLUSTRATORS

Cabinet 26 Shelf 1 No. 17

Oronce Fine as an illustrator of books. By A.F. Johnson.
Article in the Gutenberg-Gesellschaft Jahrbuch 1928. pp.107-9.

ILLUSTRATORS

Cabinet 26 Shelf 2 No. 15

Schrödter, Adolph als Illustrator. von Werner Kruse.
Illus. article in Jahrbuch IX, 1935, p. 93, Deutscher Verein für Buchwesen und Schrifttum.

ILLUSTRATORS.
see also
Biographies, Illustrators.

Cabinet Shelf No.

"ILLUSTRIRTE ZEITUNG"

Cabinet 00 Shelf 6 No. 27

Leipzig, 75th anniversary, 1834-1909. History of the firm, with portraits of founders and successors of the "Illustrirte Zeitung".

Cloth; $16\frac{1}{4}$ x 12 in.

ILLYRIAN

Cabinet Shelf No.

See Alphabets. Servian

ILOKANO (PHILIPPINE ISLANDS)

Cabinet II Shelf 4 No. 1

Gospel of Saint Luke. Manila, 1911. American Bible Society. Pamphlet.

Item in manila envelope.

IMBERT, JEAN

Cabinet F Shelf 4 No. 65

Jugement de Paris. Poeme en IV chants. Par Mr. Imbert. Title and frontispiece engraved by Moreau, many other engravings by various artists.
Imprint: Amsterdam, 1772. n. pr. n.
Includes: Idylles de Saint-Cyr (attributed to Dorat), 1771 also, Phrosine Melidore, 1772. Each with separate title page.

Morocco, gilt; 8-5/8 x $5\frac{3}{4}$ x 1-1/8 in.

IMITATION A JESUS-CHRIST see KEMPIS, THOMAS a.

Cabinet N Shelf 1 No. 15

IMMIG, CORNS & ZOON

Cabinet AA Shelf 4 No. 8

Gedenkboek der Corns. Immig & Zoon van 1873-1908, Printer and engravers, Rotterdam and Amsterdam. Illus.
Brief history of printing, and outline of the firms progress.

Cloth; 13 x $9\frac{1}{2}$ in.

"IMPARTIAL CITIZEN"

Cabinet X Shelf 5 No. 6

Dissertation upon the constitutional freedom of the press in the United States. By an Impartial Citizen...Boston: Printed by David Carlisle, for Joseph Nancrede, No.49, Marlborough Street. 1801.

Half morocco; 8-7/8 x $5\frac{1}{2}$ in.

IMPARTIAL GAZETTE, THE see GREENFIELD (MASS.) GAZETTE. ("The Impartial Intelligencer")

Cabinet Shelf No.

IMPARTIAL INTELLIGENCER

Cabinet A Shelf 3 No. 5

Greenfield, Massachusetts. 1792.

See "NEWSPAPERS, Massachusetts". Impartial Intelligencer...

IMPERIAL ACADEMY OF SCIENCES. Russia

Cabinet II Shelf 2 No. 7

Printing establishment and type foundry.

See SPECIMEN BOOKS, TYPES. Russia. Imperial Academy...

IMPERIAL CHINESE GAZETTE

Cabinet NN Shelf 6 No. 2

Newspaper in which edicts from the palace are published. The Imperial Chinese Gazette is probably the oldest publication in the world. Copy in this Library of date Sept.12, 1903.

Item in manila envelope

IMPERIAL GOVERNMENT PRINTING BUREAU

Cabinet 62 Shelf 2 No. 14

Japan, 1923.

See GOVERNMENT PRINTING OFFICES. Japan

IMPERIAL PRESS, THE, Cleveland (Ohio)

Cabinet See Imprints, United States. Imperial Press.

Shelf

No.

IMPERIAL ROYAL PRINTING OFFICE

Cabinet Y (Vienna, 1804-1904. Historical account. Issued on the occasion of the centennial celebration). Die Hof-und Staats-Druckerei von der gründung bis zur gegenwart. 1804-1904. Illus.

Shelf 5

No. 34

Half morocco; 16¼ x 12 1/8 x 1 in.

IMPERIAL ROYAL TYPE FOUNDRY

Cabinet GG (Vienna, Austria) Alfabete des gesammte erdkreises. Wien. 1855.

Shelf 3

No. 15

Collection of printing types of all languages precisely graded and calculated according to points by a tipometric system.

Boards; 14 x 10½ in.

IMPERIAL PRESS, THE

Cabinet S (A) Critique: The Imperial Press. Cleveland, Ohio. By George French. Cleveland, Ohio. 1902. Illus.

Shelf 3

No. 32

Cloth; 7¼ x 4¾ in.

IMPERIAL ROYAL PRINTING OFFICE

Cabinet I (Vienna, Austria) Polygraphische apparat...von Alois Auer. Wien, 1853.

Shelf 2

No. 10

Description of the different processes in use at the K.K. hof und Staatsdruckerei at Vienna.

Paper; 9½ x 6-1/8 x ½ in.

IMPOSITION

Cabinet T Arrangement of the pages of a sheet in their proper order, some examples

Shelf 3

No. 21

See DICTIONARIES OF PRINTING Savage, William...London, 1841, pp.327-410

IMPERIAL PRINTING OFFICE, Germany

Cabinet BERLIN

Shelf

No.

See GOVERNMENT PRINTING OFFICES, Germany (Berlin)...

IMPERIAL ROYAL PRINTING OFFICE

Cabinet 83 Vienna (Austria). Specimen characterum latinorum existentium in Caesarea ac Regio-Aulica Typorum Fusura apud Joannem Thomam Trattner, Caesareo-Regio Aulicum Typographum et Bibliopolam. Vindobone, 1759. [Four parts, each with separate title page; 3 with date of 1760.]

Shelf 1

No. 50

Boards; 8-7/8 x 7 x ½ in.

IMPOSITION

Cabinet MM Beknopte en volledige handleiding tot het overslaan van drukvormen, ten gebruike van letterzetters. In vrije verzameld en bewerkt maar het fransch, door H. Le Blansch. S'Gravenhage, bij Leopold Loebenberg. 1844.

Shelf 2

No. 28

Half morocco, oblong, 5 x 7-1/8 x ½ in.

IMPERIAL ROYAL PRINTING OFFICE

Cabinet B Vienna (Austria) Album...Die Vereinignung der graphischen kunst. Aus der Graphischen und Staats-Druckerei in Wien, 1851.

Shelf 1

Nos. 1-2-3-4-

4 massive volumes showing all the types and ornaments in use in this printing establishment. Beautifully printed.

Morocco; gilt; 22 x 15¾ in.

IMPERIAL ROYAL PRINTING OFFICE, Austria

Cabinet L Buchschriften des mittelalters mit besonders berucksichtigung der deutschen, und zwar vom sechsten jahrhundert bis zu erfindung der buchdruckerkunst...von einem mitgliede der K.K. Hof-und Staatsdruckerei zu Wien, 1852.

Shelf 2

No. 9

With 23 plates of alphabets.

Cloth; 9½ x 6¼ in.

IMPOSITION

Cabinet MM Bidwell, Geo. H. The printers' new hand-book. A treatise of the imposition of forms, with tables of signatures, etc. New York, 1875.

Shelf 5

No. 29

Cloth; 6 x 3¾ x 3/8 in.

IMPERIAL ROYAL PRINTING OFFICE

Cabinet GG Vienna (Austria) Alfabete des gesammten erdreises aus der K.K. Hof-und Staatsdruckerei in Wien. Zweite auflage. Wien, 1876.

Shelf 3

No. 16

A collection of printing types of every known language, precisely graded and calculated according to points, by a tipometric system.

Paper; 14 x 10¼ in. In folder labelled: K.K. Hof-und Staatsdruckerei in Wien, 1876. Specimens of Types.

IMPERIAL ROYAL PRINTING OFFICE Austria

Cabinet L Specimens of all the types in use at the K.K. Hof-und Staatsdruckerei, Wien, 1879.

Shelf 2

No. 13

See FAULMANN, CARL. Buch der Schrift ...Wien, 1878

IMPOSITION

Cabinet MM Book impositions, useful information concerning. Including all the modern layouts and practical advice to the printer and publisher. Compiled and published by J.F. Tapley Co. New York, 1914. Pamphlet.

Shelf 6

No. 2

Item in book with binder's title "Text books of Stump, Tapley, and Sergeant". Bound 1919.

IMPERIAL ROYAL PRINTING OFFICE

Cabinet Y Vienna (Austria) (Historical account of the K.K. Hof-und Schriftsdruckerei in Vienna. In French, German, Italian, and English). Geschichte der K.K. Hof-und Schriftsdruckerei in Wien. Von einem typographen dieser anstalt ...Wien, 1851.

Shelf 5

No. 26

Half morocco; 9-3/8 x 6 x 2¼ in.

IMPERIAL ROYAL PRINTING OFFICE

Cabinet 83 Vienna (Austria).

Shelf 1

No. 50

See SPECIMEN BOOKS, TYPES. Austria. Trattner...Vienna, 1759.

IMPOSITION

Cabinet MM Diagrams of imposition.

Shelf 3

No. 37.01

See GOULD, JOSEPH. Compositors guide and pocket book...London, 1878.

IMPOSITION

Cabinet LL, Shelf 1, No. 1

Formatbuchlein darinnen angesetzte figuren wieman die columen auszschiessen soll in allen gemeinen formaten mit sambt deren abtheillungen...Mit besten fleiss auffgesetze von J.L. V. (Hans Ludwig Vietor). Anno Christi MDCLIII (1753). Nach erfindung der kunst Buchdruckerey das CCXIII.

Vel., oblong, 7¼ x 4-7/8 in.

IMPOSITION

Cabinet MM, Shelf 6, No. 101

Imposition simplified: the most useful schemes pictorially represented; with diagrams for the measurement of margin, table of bookwork furnitures. By George Ruse. London, n.d.

Cloth; 4 x 2-5/8 x ¼ in. In manila envelope.

IMPOSITION

Cabinet MM, Shelf 6, No. 26

Inductive method of learning stonework. A simplified system for acquiring the art of preparing forms...By John W. Barr. Cincinnati. Published by the author, 1909.

Pamphlet 8 x 5½ in., with 47 folded diagrams in case, each having instructions written on it.

Cloth case; 9 x 7 x 2¾ in.

IMPOSITION

Cabinet MM, Shelf 6, No. 8

Lee, Charles W. The Stoneman: The science and art of imposition. Chicago, Ill. 1904.

Boards; 6 x 4 in.

IMPOSITION

Cabinet MM, Shelf 1, No. 31

Lefèvre, Théotiste: Recueil d'impositions exécutées en caractères mobiles, suivi d'une nouvelle classification de la casse Francaise. Deuxieme édition, avec appendice. Paris, 1848.

Oblong boards, morocco back; 4¾ x 6 x 7/8 in.

IMPOSITION

Cabinet MM, Shelf 6, No. 59

Locking forms for the job press: containing useful information regarding the imposition of job forms...By Frank S. Henry. "Technical Series for Apprentices". Part III, No.24. United Typothetae of America, 1918.

Cloth; 8 x 5 in.

IMPOSITION

Cabinet MM, Shelf 6, No. 2

Manual (A) on imposition of forms, and printers' ready reckoner...J.H. Sergeant, Publisher, New York, N.Y. Price 50 cents. Pamphlet.

Item in book with binder's title "Text books of Stump, Tepley, and Sergeant". Bound 1919.

IMPOSITION

Cabinet MM, Shelf 1, No. 9

Manuel des impositions typographiques, ou l'on trouve...la manier de composer l'Anglaise, et celle de corriger les épreuves d'imprimerie. Extrait du grand ouvrage de M. Momoro. Troisième édition, corrigée et augmentée. A Bruxelles, 1819. De l'Imprimerie de F. Visscher.

Boards; 8-1/8 x 4-7/8 x 3/8 in.

IMPOSITION

Cabinet MM, Shelf 3, No. 12

Mason, William. The printer's assistant: containing a sketch of the history of printing... select schemes for difficult imposition... Fourth edition. London, 1823.

Half morocco; 8 x 4-7/8 in.

IMPOSITION

Cabinet LL, Shelf 1, No. 2

Neu vorgestelltes auf der löblichen kunst buchdruckerey gebrauchliches format-buch worinnen allerhand nachrichtungs figuren die Columnen recht auszuschiessen...Durch Daniel Michael Schmatzen. Sulzbach, 1684, Druckts Johann Holst.

Bound in with Schmatz "Depositio Cornuti", 1684.

Leather; 6-7/8 x 4¼ x ½ in.

IMPOSITION

Cabinet EE, Shelf 4, No. 12

Newspaper and pamphlet folding.

See BROWN FOLDING MACHINE COMPANY. Catalogue.

IMPOSITION

Cabinet 75, Shelf, No.

Notes on concel leaves. By R. W. Chapman. Illus.

In Transactions of the Bibliographical Society. "The Library." vol. V. pp. 249-58.

IMPOSITION

Cabinet MM, Shelf 2, No. 2

Nouveau manuel des impositions. La manière d'imposer et les modeles d'impositions...Par Arnold Muller. Paris, n.d. circa 1901.

Paper; 7-5/8 x 5-1/8 in.

IMPOSITION

Cabinet LL, Shelf 1, No. 3

(Nuremberg, 1721). Neu-eingerichtetes und auf der loblichen buchdruckerey-kunst fehr nutzliches Format-Buchlein [etc].

In Ernesti, "Die wol-eingerichtete buchdruckerey"...Nuremberg, 1721.

These pages are reprinted in the 1733 edition of Ernesti (LL/1/4), with the same pagination.

IMPOSITION

Cabinet MM, Shelf 1, No. 75, Box

Prospetto dei segni correzione tipografica e dei modi di disporre per la stampa i formati piu in uso. Milano, 1870. Tip. Giacomo Agnelli. Folded plate.

In box labelled "Text Books of Printing. French and Italian. Brochures, Pamphlets, etc.

IMPOSITION

Cabinet MM, Shelf 2, No. 27

[Techinque of make-ready for different sizes from folio to 64 mo.] Mss. no title, date or place.

Morocco; 6¼ x 4-1/8 x 5/8 in.

IMPOSITION

Cabinet MM, Shelf 6, No. 102

Theory and practice of book imposition, using the systems of groups-of-four as originally introduced by the author, Charles J. Schott. Seattle, Wash., 1910.

Limp morocco; 6 x 3 in.

IMPOSITION

Cabinet MM, Shelf 1, No. 39

Traité pratique de l'imposition, ou moyen mécanique d'imposer en imprimerie. Par Auguste Bourles. Sisteron, 1864.

Cloth; 9 x 6-3/8 x 1 in.

IMPOSITION

Cabinet MM Shelf 5 No. 28

Treatise on the imposition of forms: embracing a system of rules and principles for laying the pages, applicable to all forms; with instructions for making margin and register... also tables of signatures, etc. By Geo. H. Bidwell. New York: Raymond & Caulon, 1865.

Cloth; 6 x 3-7/8 in.

IMPOSITION

Cabinet MM Shelf 6 No. 22

Treise, F.J. Imposition: a handbook for printers. Chicago, The Inland Printer, Publishers. 1907. Illus.

Limp morocco; 6 x 3¾ in.

IMPOSITION

Cabinet MM Shelf 4 No. 5

Typographers handy bookwork test cards. Thirty two (32) cards with detailed schemes for the construction of book forms in various sizes. By Charles Blackshaw. London, n.d. circa 1860.

In protective case, cloth; 4¾ x 3-3/8 x 7/8 in.

IMPOSITION

Cabinet MM Shelf 5 No. 57

Williams, T.B. Hints on imposition, an illustrated guide for printer and pressman in the construction of book forms. Also other matter pertaining to letter-press printing. Buffalo, 1895.

Flexible levant; 6 x ¾ in.

IMPOSITION OF TYPE FORMS

Cabinet LL Shelf 1 No. 8

Engraved schemes of Impositions, on wood.

On pp.2-192, in Gessner's "Der in der Buchdruckerei wohl unterrichtete Lehr-Lunge ...Leipzig, 1743.

Vellum; 6-7/8 x 4¼ x 1-5/8 in.

IMPOSITION OF TYPE FORMS

Cabinet LL Shelf 1 No. 6

Leipzig, 1740, pp.2-32, Gessner's text book of printing, vol.I.

IMPRENSA NACIONAL (Nova Goa. India)

Cabinet EE Shelf 3 No. 77

See SPECIMEN BOOKS, TYPES. Printers'. India.

IMPRENSA NACIONAL (Rio de Janeiro)

Cabinet EE Shelf 3 No. 74

See GOVERNMENT PRINTING OFFICES. South America.

IMPRENTA REAL

Cabinet AA Shelf 5 No. 5

See Government Printing Offices, Spain; see also Imprints, Spain.

IMPRENTA REAL (Madrid)

Cabinet Shelf No.

See Specimen Books, Types. Spain.

IMPRENTA REAL (Mexico)

Cabinet F Shelf 1 No. 101

See Early Printing in Mexico: Mexico City, 1735.

(1)'IMPRIMERIE DE LA RÉPUBLIQUE

Cabinet V Shelf 6 No. 17

Opinion de J.G. Lacuée relative à l'Imprimerie de la Republique. Séance du 19 Prairial, au V. (1795-1804).

In opposition to the maintanance of a government printing office.

Item 1 in book with binder's title "French legislation relating to l'Imprimerie Nationale". vol. I, Paris 1795-1905.

(1)'IMPRIMERIE DE LA REPUBLIQUE.

Cabinet V Shelf 6 No. 19

Rapport fait par Brival ... sur une rèsolution du 11 pluviose, relative a l'imprimerie de la Republique. Séance du 16 Floreal, an V. Paris. [1795?].

Half morocco ; 8½ x 5¾ in.

IMPRIMERIE DE MONSIEUR

Cabinet F Shelf 4 No. 92

Paris, 1785. Precis historique de la vie de M. de Bonnard. Par M. Garat. A. Paris, de l'Imprimerie de Monsieur.

Quarter morocco; 5-3/4 x 3-3/8 x 3/8 in.

(1)'IMPRIMERIE IMPERIAL

Cabinet V Shelf 6 No. 17

Décret qui rétablit provisoirement l'Imprimerie impériale dans l'état réglé par les Décrets des 24 Mars 1809 et 28 janvier 1811.

Item 2 in book with binder's title "French legislation relating to l'Imprimerie Nationale" vol. I, Paris, 1795-1905.

IMPRIMERIE IMPERIALE

Cabinet X Shelf 5 No. 17

Decret Imperiale. Sur l'administration et la police de l'Imprimerie Imperiale. Au Palais des Tuileries [Paris], le 28 Janvier, 1811.

Boards; 8-3/8 x 5¼ in.

(1)'IMPRIMERIE IMPERIALE

Cabinet X Shelf 4 No. 33

Décret Imperiale, 1813, portant institution d'éléves compositeurs pour les langues orientales. Du 22 Mars, 1813. Signé Napoleon.

Concerning teaching oriental languages to apprentices at the government printinf office at Paris.

Item 2 in vol. French legislation affecting printing, 1799-1832. Various items.

IMPRIMERIE IMPÉRIALE

Cabinet V Shelf 4 No. 15

See Dupont, Paul. Histoire de l'Imprimerie. Paris, 1854. vol. 2, p. 461

IMPRIMERIE IMPERIALE.

Cabinet V Shelf 6 No. 26

Exposition Universelle de 1855. Quelques details sur les produits de l'Imprimerie Imperiale de France. Par M. D'Escodeca de Boisse. Paris, 1855.

Boards; 9¼ x 9-7/8 in.

IMPRIMERIE NATIONALE

Cabinet C Shelf 2 No. 4.01

l'Academie des inscriptions...de l'Institute de France. Paris, 1900 [Imprint of the] l'Imprimerie Nationale..

Printed in the Garamond types of 1550. Cochin decorations, 1753.

Paper; 19½ x 13 in.

L'IMPRIMERIE NATIONALE.

Cabinet V Shelf 4 No. 28

Débuts de l'Imprimerie Nationale: L'Imprimerie Royale.

See pp. 73-131 in Christian's "Débuts de l'imprimerie en France." Paris, 1905.

Has many specimens of types engraved for, and used at the Imprimerie Nationale.

Half morocco; 11¼ x 8 x 1¼ in.

IMPRIMERIE IMPÉRIALE

Cabinet V Shelf 6 No. 27

(Les) Grandes usines de France. L'Imprimerie Imperiale. (3e partie.-Composition, tirage, etc.) Par Turgan. Paris, 1860. Dessiné par E. Bourdelin. Gravé par H. Linton.

Interior views of various departments: specimens of types: tools: marks used by the Imprimerie Impériale.

Cloth; 11 x 8 in.

IMPRIMERIE NATIONALE

Cabinet V Shelf 6 No. 24

Bernard, Auguste. Notice historique sur l'Imprimerie Nationale. Par Aug. Bernard. Paris, 1848.

The contents include: Origine and invention of printing: notices of the appointed government printers: type designers: list of types engraved for l'Imprimerie nationale 1809-1847.

Boards; 5¼ x 3½

IMPRIMERIE NATIONALE.

Cabinet V Shelf 4 No. 14

See Dupont, Paul. Notice historique sur l'imprimerie. Paris, 1849. p. 105.

IMPRIMERIE IMPERIALE

Cabinet V Shelf 3 No. 14

History of: See Dupont, Paul. Histoire de l'Imprimerie. Paris, 1854. Vol. 2, Chap. XVI, p. 46.

IMPRIMERIE NATIONALE

Cabinet V Shelf 6 No. 25

(Le) Budget de 1874 et L'Imprimerie Nationale. Observations présentees...Par la Chambre Syndicale des Imprimeurs de Paris. Pamphlet.

Item in folder marked "L'Imprimerie Nationale. Various Pamphlets. Paris, 1874--

---

IMPRIMERIE NATIONALE

Cabinet V Shelf 6 No. 23

Duprat, F.A. Précis historique sur l'Imprimerie Nationale et ses types. Par F.A. Duprat. Paris, 1848.

The author was the "Chef-du-Service" of the foundry department, and controller of the letter press-work of the Nationale Printing Office at Paris.

Half morocco; 9-1/8 x 6 in.

IMPRIMERIE IMPERIALE

Cabinet V Shelf 6 No. 20

Marcel, Jean Jacques. Oratio Dominaca C L. linguae characteribus expressa. Edente J.J. Marcel, typographeii imperialis administro generali. Parisiis, typis imperialibus. Anno Repar. Sal. 1805.

Specimens of the different types used in the Imprimerie Imperial.

Half leather; 11¾ x 9-1/8 in.

IMPRIMERIE NATIONALE

Cabinet V Shelf 6 No. 33

Catalogue des signes chinois. Corps 10. Paris, Imprimerie Nationale. 188[illegible].

pp. 117 with two broadsides showing all the Chinese caracteres produced or used at the Imprimerie Nationale.

Half morocco; 9¾ x 6¼ in.

(l)'IMPRIMERIE NATIONALE

Cabinet V Shelf 6 No. 5

[Historical, statistical, and biographical account, 1640 to 1823].

See Chap. XII, pp.39-54 of Dupont's Essais pratiques d'imprimerie...Paris, 1849.

IMPRIMERIE IMPERIALE

Cabinet V Shelf 3 No. 14

Premiers directeurs ... L'Imprimerie Impérial après la revolution de Juillet ... Plaintes des imprimeurs contre son monopole ... Benefices ...

See Chap. XVI, tome 2, Dupont's "Histoire de l'Imprimerie." (2 vols.) Paris, 1854.

Half morocco; 7-- x 5-1/8 in.

IMPRIMERIE NATIONALE.

Cabinet V Shelf 6 No. 29

Catalogue des signes hieroglyphiques. 2nd edition. Paris, 1873.

Half morocco; 10 x 7 x 3/8 in.

IMPRIMERIE, NATIONALE

Cabinet V Shelf 6 No. 25

L'Imprimerie Nationale. Par Arthur Legrand. Extrait de la Revue Brittannique, numéro d'aout 1885. Paris.

In folder marked "L'Imprimerie Nationale. Various Pamphlets." Paris, 1874--

---

IMPRIMERIE IMPERIAL

Cabinet Shelf No.

see also

I. Laws relating to Printing. France.
II. Printing shop management. France.

---

l'IMPRIMERIE NATIONALE

Cabinet C Shelf 2 No. 13

(Copper engravings provided for the former Imprimerie Royale. Frontispieces, portraits, fleurons, head and tail pieces, etc.) l'Imprimerie Nationale, Paris, 1889.

Half calf; 20 x 13-7/8 in.

IMPRIMERIE NATIONALE

Cabinet V Shelf 6 No. 31

Imprimerie Nationale dans ses rapports avec l'état et avec l'industrie privée. Paris, 1883. n.n.

Report on conditions of labor in State and private industries.

Half morocco; 10-3/4 x 6¼ in.

IMPRIMERIE NATIONALE

Cabinet V, Shelf 6, No. 25

L'Imprimerie Nationale en 1874. (Historical account signed J.G.) Extract from "Mélanges, Mai 1874."

In folder marked "Imprimerie Nationale. Various Pamphlets." Paris 1874-1900.

IMPRIMERIE NATIONALE

Cabinet V, Shelf 6, No. 34

Réponse de l'Imprimerie Nationale aux attaques de ses adversaires. 1792-1896. Paris, 1896. Imprimé aux frais du personnel de l'Imprimerie Nationale avec l'autorisation de M.J. Darlan, Garde des Sceaux.
Pamphlet bound in :"Note soumis à messieurs les représentants par les délégues de la typographie et de la lithographie." Paris, 1851.

Cloth; 10 x 6½ x 7/8 in.

---

(1)'IMPRIMERIE NATIONALE EGYPTIENNE

Cabinet 26, Shelf 1, No. 21

Aperçu historique...(Brief historical account.)

Essay in "Gutenberg-Gesellschaft Jahrbuch, 1931", pp.275-77.

L'IMPRIMERIE NATIONALE

Cabinet QQ, Shelf 2, No. 1 (5 vols.)

Imprint, Paris, 1793, L'Imprimerie Nationale.

see IMPRINTS, France. L'Imprimerie Nationale...

IMPRIMERIE NATIONALE

Cabinet V, Shelf 6, No. 30

Specimens des types divers de l'Imprimerie Nationale: Types Étrangers. Paris, 1878.
"These types comprise an assortment that is probably unrivalled." B & W.

Vellum manuscript over boards; 11-5/8 x 9 x 1-1/8 in.

Imprimerie Nouvelle (Association Ouvriere)

Cabinet KK, Shelf 4, No. 40

(Les) Delegues de la typographie Parisienne au Congres du Havre...Paris, 1881.
Fourth National Congress. Report of delegates.

Paper; 7¼ x 4½ x ¼ in. With other items in envelope.

---

(1)'IMPRIMERIE NATIONALE

Cabinet V, Shelf 6, No. 17

Note administrative. Reponse au discours prononcé par M. Chaumié...22 Fevrier, 1906. in fine Arthur Christian.
Considers administration irregularities, questions of profit, deficit, etc.

Item 16 in book with binder's title "French legislation relating to l'Imprimerie Nationale". vol. I, Paris 1795-1905.

IMPRIMERIE NATIONALE

Cabinet V, Shelf 6, No. 35

Visite à l'Imprimerie Nationale. Par Jules Claretie. Paris, 1904. Engraved head and tail pieces. Text within borders.
Presentation copy signed by the author.

Half morocco; 10½ x 7-3/4 in.

IMPRIMERIE ROYALE

Cabinet V, Shelf 6, No. 21

Album typographique de l'Imprimerie royale Paris, 1830.
I: Écritures les plus remarquables des peuples anciens et modernes, imprimées en caractères mobiles.
II: Les cartes géographiques
III: Color Printing.

Tooled calf; 13½ x 9-3/4 x ½ in.

IMPRIMERIE NATIONALE

Cabinet V, Shelf 6, No. 32

Ouvrages publies de 1823 a 1886. Avec l'indication de leur date, et des sommes despensees pour leur impression. Paris, Janvier 1887. Comite des impressions gratuites.
Contains an extract from the regulations of 1877, in regard to gratuitous printing.

Cloth; 12½ x 9½ x 3/8 in.

IMPRIMERIE NATIONALE

Cabinet V, Shelf 6, No. 25

Vitrines de l'Imprimerie Nationale (a) l'Exposition Universelle et Internationale de 1900. Paris.
Catalogue of items exhibited. Includes a brief history of l'Imprimerie Nationale, also a chronological table of 1640 to 1895 of the managers of l'Imprimerie Nationale.

In folder marked "L'Imprimerie Nationale. Various Pamphlets." Paris. 1874--

---

L'IMPRIMERIE ROYALE

Cabinet FF, Shelf 5, No. 35

Anisson le fils. Description d'une nouvelle press executee pour le service du Roy. A Paris, de l'Imprimerie Royale, 1783. With colored plates.

Autographed letter inserted signed Anisson le fils, le inventeur. See also FF/5/36.

Full morocco gilt; 10½ x 8 in.

L'IMPRIMERIE NATIONALE

Cabinet KK, Shelf 4, No. 16

Proposition de loi...1902.

see SOCIETIES, PRINTERS'. France. Proposition de loi...

IMPRIMERIE NATIONALE.

Cabinet V, Shelf 5, No. 1

Vitrines de l'Imprimerie Nationale. Exposition Universelle et International de Saint-Louis en 1904. Pamphlets catalogue.
Includes:- Tableau des directors de l'Imprimerie Nationale depuis sa fondation jusqu'à ce jour.

Bound in volume "French Typographical Pamphlets", item 13: Item 14 is an English Translation.

IMPRIMERIE ROYALE.

Cabinet X, Shelf 4, No. 32

Arrest, 1775 ... qui ordonne la suppression de l'imprimerie établie a l'Hotel a la Guerre a Versailles, et sa réunion à l'Imprimerie Royale. Du 22 Mai, 1775. Signé de M,[al] Du Muy.

Item 22 in volume with binder's title: French Legislation Affecting Printing, 1573-1810.

L'IMPRIMERIE NATIONALE

Cabinet KK, Shelf 4, No. 40

Question du personnel ouvrier de l'Imprimerie Nationale dévant le parlement, la presse, et l'opinion publique. Paris, 1887. Pamphlet.

With other items in envelope.

L'IMPRIMERIE NATIONALE (see also)

Cabinet, Shelf, No.

IMPRINTS, France

L'IMPRIMERIE ROYALE

Cabinet X, Shelf 4, No. 32

Arrest (du 22 Mai, 1775) qui ordonne la suppression de l'imprimerie établie a l'Hôtel de la Guerre a Versailles, et sa réunion à l'Imprimerie Royale. Signé, M. Du Muy.

Item 22 in volume with binder's title: French Legislation Affecting Printing, 1573-1810.

(1)'IMPRIMERIE ROYALE

Cabinet X Shelf 4 No. 33

Arrêté, du 9 Janvier, 1824, relatif au reglement des comptes de M. Anisson. Signé De Peyronnet.
Concerning the accounts of Anisson, director of the Imprimerie Royale.

Item 5 in vol. with title "French legislation affecting printing, 1799-1832. Various items.

(1)'IMPRIMERIE ROYALE

Cabinet X Shelf 4 No. 33

Décision du 15 Avril 1828, relative...en ce qui concerne le cumul des pensions des ouvriers et ouvrieres...Signé Cte. Portalis.

Item 10 in vol. with title "French legislation affecting printing, 1799-1833. Various items".

IMPRIMERIE ROYALE

Cabinet 83 Shelf 1 No. 25

Luce, Louis, 1771: Essai d'un nouvelle typographie, ornée de vignettes...inventés, dessinés et exécutés par L. Louce, graveur du Roy, pour son Imprimerie Royale. Paris, 1771.

Calf; 10-1/8 x 8 x 1-1/8 in.

(1)'IMPRIMERIE ROYALE

Cabinet X Shelf 4 No. 33

Arrêté du 25 Novembre 1825, portant reglement sur le surveillance des ouvrages imprimés à l'Imprimerie Royale. Signé L. de Villebois.

Item 8 in vol. with title "French legislation affecting printing, 1799-1833. Various items"

IMPRIMERIE ROYALE

Cabinet V Shelf 6 No. 18

Essai historique. Sur l'origine des caractères Orienteux de l'imprimerie royale, sur les ovrages qui ont été imprimés à Paris, en Arabe, en Syriaque...et sur les caractères Grecs de Francois 1er appelés communément Grecs du Roi. Par M. de Guignes. n. d. [circa 1780]

Half morocco; 10-7/8 x 8½ in.

IMPRIMERIE ROYALE.

Cabinet V Shelf 6 No. 22

Notice sur les types étrangers. Du spécimen de l'Imprimerie Royale. Paris, 1847.
Brief historical sketches of the various types represented. Includes a chart of the Roman caracters used by the government printing office, from 1640 to 1846; with notices concerning the engravers.

Boards; 12¼ x 9 in.

IMPRIMERIE ROYALE

Cabinet V Shelf 6 No. 28

Arrêté qui porte á 6 francs la journee des correcteurs, et qui les met à la disposition de l'administration jusqu'a neuf heures du soir...Paris, le 19 Oct. 1829. Signé de Villebois.
Regulating the hours of work of proof readers.
Pamphlet attached to inside cover of Bernard's "Histoire de l'Imprimerie Royale" ...Paris, 1867.

Half morocco; 9-3/8 x 6¼ x 1-1/8 in.

cont'd

(1)'IMPRIMERIE ROYALE

Cabinet V Shelf 6 No. 17

Extrait du rapport fait à la Chambre des Députés, en 1822, par M. de Bourienne.

Concerning the method of re-establishment and administration.

Item 4 in book with binder's title "French legislation relating to l'Imprimerie Nationale". vol. I, Paris, 1795-1905.

(1)'IMPRIMERIE ROYALE

Cabinet X Shelf 4 No. 33

Ordonnance du roi, 1814, portant qu'a partir du 1 Janvier 1815, l'Imprimerie Royale cessera d'étre regie aux frais de l'État. Du 28 Decembre. Signé Louis.
Concerning maintanance charges of the L'Imprimerie Royale.

Item 3 in vol. French legislation affecting printing, 1799-1832. Various items.

(1)'IMPRIMERIE ROYALE

Cabinet X Shelf 4 No. 33

Arrêté du 18 fevrier 1832. Distribution aux pièces, a raison du sixième du prix reglé pour la composition - Mode à suive pour l'exécution de cette mesure. Signé Lebrun.
Concerning new regulations for payment of compositors.

Item 11 in vol. with title "French legislation affecting printing, 1799-1833. Various items".

IMPRIMERIE ROYALE.

Cabinet T Shelf 4 No. 50

Historical essay on the origin of Oriental characters in the Royal Printing-House, on the works which have been printed at Paris, in Arabic, Syriac, Armenian, etc., and on the Greek characters of Francis I. commonly called the King's Greek. Translated from the French of Joseph de Guignes. London, 1789. 2 Vols. in 1.
Extracts of manuscripts in the library of the King of France.

Half calf; 8-3/8 x 5¼ x 2-3/8 in.

(1)'IMPRIMERIE ROYALE

Cabinet X Shelf 4 No. 33

Ordonnance du Roi, 1816, relative à la formation d'une seule caisse commune de pensions de retraite et de secours en faveur des employés et ouvriers de l'Imprimerie Royale ...A Paris, le 3 Juillet, 1816. Signe Louis. A Paris, de l'Imprimerie Royale.

Item 4 in vol. with title "French legislation affecting printing, 1799-1832. Various items.

IMPRIMERIE ROYALE

Cabinet V Shelf 6 No. 25

Caractères orientaux de l'Imprimerie Royale en 1787. Par Deguignas. Paris, 13 Juin 1787.
A letter addressed to the Bulletin de la Société de l'Histoire de Paris et de l'Ile-de-France. [1889]. Extract.

In folder marked "L'Imprimerie Nationale. Various Pamphlets". Paris, 1874--

L'IMPRIMERIE ROYALE

Cabinet KK Shelf 4 No. 29

Instruction sur la ténue du régistre des attachements des travaux par l'Inspecteur des batiments de l'Imprimerie royale. Du 14 Janvier, 1826. (Excerpt)

With other items in envelope.

(1)'IMPRIMERIE ROYALE

Cabinet V Shelf 6 No. 17

Ordonnance (No. 8119) du roi concernant l'Imprimerie royale. Au chateau des Tuileries, le 12 Janvier 1820.

Item 3 in book with binder's title "French legislation relating to l'Imprimerie Nationale". vol. I, Paris 1795-1905.

IMPRIMERIE ROYALE

Cabinet Z Shelf 5 No. 16

Catalogue des caractères Chinois de l'Imprimerie Royale, gravés en Chine en 1838. Paris, Imprimerie Royale, 1841.

Paper boards, calf back; 16½ x 10½ x 1-3/4 in.

IMPRIMERIE ROYALE

Cabinet V Shelf 4 No. 12

Lettre-Patentes de Francois Ier en date du 17 janvier 1538, qui instituent le premier Imprimeur Royal pour le Grec.
See Crapelet, G. A. Progrès de l'Imprimerie en France au XVI siecle...Paris, 1836.

IMPRIMERIE ROYALE. (Imprint).

Cabinet E Shelf 3 No. 64

Paris, 1640. De Imitatione Christi, libri IV. Parisiis. Anno MDCXL. E. Typographia Regia

Morocco; 15¼ x 10½ x 2 in. Bigmore and Wyman 1, p. 357.

IMPRIMERIE ROYALE

Cabinet V Shelf 4 No. 28

See Printing, Historical, France. Christian, Arthur. Débuts de l'imprimerie en France: L'Imprimerie Nationale...Paris, 1905.

IMPRINTS, Australia

Cabinet QQ Shelf 3 No. 4

Specialty Press Pty. Ltd. Melbourne, 1921.
Title: A young man and a nail can, MacRobertson.
Imprint on back cover: The Specialty Press Pty. Ltd. Melbourne...The Photographs in this booklet by Allan Studios, Smith Street, Collingwood.

Quarter morocco; $8\frac{3}{4}$ x $11\frac{1}{4}$ x $\frac{3}{4}$ in.

IMPRINTS, Belgium

Cabinet V Shelf 5 No. 5

Gaborrie, Armond. Brussels, 1795.
Title: Mémoire sur l'origine et la premier usage des signatures et des chiffres...Par le citoyen C. de la Serna.
Imprint: Bruxelles. Des presses d'Armand Gaborrie An IV. (1795).

Boards, half leather; $8\frac{1}{2}$ x $5\frac{1}{2}$ in.

(1)'IMPRIMERIE ROYALE

Cabinet X Shelf 4 No. 33

Rapport au roi du 20 Août 1824. Application des exercices des élèves et compositeurs en langues orientales a la formation d'un collection d'ouvrages orientaux...Signé De Peyronnet. Approuvé. Signé Louis.
Plea for the king's approbation to utilize the oriental types in l'Imprimerie Royale to print oriental classics.

Item 6 in vol. with title "French legislation affecting printing, 1799-1833. Various items.

IMPRINTS, Austria.

Cabinet D Shelf 3 No. 8

Baumgarten, Conrad. Ölmutz, 1502.

See Early Printing in Austria. "Olmutz, 1502. Conrad Baumgarten.

IMPRINTS, Belgium.

Cabinet 2 Shelf 1 No. 39

Moretus, Balthasar (I), widow, John (III) Moretus, and John Meurs: Plantin-Moretus Press. Antwerp, 1627-30.

See Early Printing in Belgium. Antwerp, 1627 and 1630. Plantin-Moretus Press.

IMPRIMERIE ROYALE

Cabinet 83 Shelf 1 No. 27

Spécimen des caractères, vignettes...et fleurons. Paris, 1819.
Includes such types, vignettes etc., engraving of which was begun before the year 1812.

Boards; 12 x $9\frac{1}{4}$ x 1-3/4 in.

IMPRINTS, Austria

Cabinet C Shelf 2 No. 18

Kais.-Konigl. Hof-und Staatsdruckerei. Wien, 1898.
Title: Rolands Knappen. Illustriet von Heinrich Lesler un Joseph Urban.
Imprint: Aus der Kaiserlich-Koniglichen Hof-und Staatsdruckerei.

Cloth; 19 x $14\frac{1}{2}$ in.

IMPRINTS, Belgium.

Cabinet 2 Shelf 1 No. 22

Moretus, John (I): Plantin-Moretus Press, Antwerp, 1599.

See Early Printing in Belgium. Antwerp, 1599. Plantin-Moretus Press: John Moretus.

IMPRIMERIE ROYALE

Cabinet 83 Shelf 1 No. 28

Spécimen de caractères nouvelles frappés, et de caractères de gravure étrangère. n.d. [1820]
"Septembre 1823" written by hand on the fly leaf.

Boards; 11 x $8\frac{1}{4}$ x 3/8 in.

IMPRINTS, Austria

Cabinet X Shelf 1 No. 62

Schulz, George Ludwig, Vienna, 1764.
Title: Commentatio de primis Vindobonae typographis.
Imprint: Vindobonae, typis Georgii Ludovici Schulzii, typogr. Academici.

Has printer mark of J. Winterburger, first printer in Vienna.

Half morocco; $8\frac{1}{4}$ x 6-7/8 in.

IMPRINTS, BELGIUM.

Cabinet 2 Shelf 1 No. 25

Moretus, John (I): Plantin-Moretus Press, Antwerp, 1602.

See Early Printing in Belgium: Antwerp, 1602. Plantin-Moretus Press.

(1)'IMPRIMERIE ROYALE
see also

Cabinet Shelf No.

I - (1)'IMPRIMERIE IMPERIALE
II - " NATIONALE
III - EARLY PRINTING IN FRANCE. Paris, 1642.
IV - SPECIMEN BOOKS, TYPES. France.

IMPRINTS, Austria

Cabinet E Shelf 5 No.

Trattner, Joh. T. Vienna, 1766-1790.
Title: Lambecius, Petrus: Commentarorum de augustissima bibliotheca caesarea vindobonensi...(9 vols. illus.)
Imprints: Typis et sumptibus Joan. Thomae nob. de Trattnern, augustae aulae typographi, et bibliopolae vindobonensis.

Calf; 15 x $9\frac{1}{2}$ in. each vol.

IMPRINTS, Belgium.

Cabinet 2 Shelf 1 No. 16

Moretus, John (III) and widow of Balthasar (I) Moretus: Plantin-Moretus Press, Antwerp, 1590.

See Early PRinting in Belgium. Antwerp, 1590. Plantin-Moretus Press.

IMPRIMERIE ROYALE du LOUVRE

Cabinet V Shelf 6 No. 28

Histoire de l'Imprimerie Royale du Louvre. Par Auguste Bernard. Paris, 1867.

Half morocco; 9-3/8 x $6\frac{1}{4}$ x 1-1/8 in.

IMPRINTS, Belgium

Cabinet 17 Shelf 2 No. 2

Belleri, Petri, Antwerp, 1591, 1623, 1660, 1666.
(Imprints on fragments of folio pages. With printer's device)

Items on fols. 87-90 of HENRY STEVEN'S "Typographical Miscellanies", vol.2 B-1

IMPRINTS, Belgium.

Cabinet Shelf No.

Plantin, Christopher and his successors, 1555-1876. See Plantin Collections in cabinets 2 and 6.

IMPRINTS, Belgium.

Cabinet 2 Shelf 1 No. 47

Plantin, Christopher, Antwerp, 1564.
Title: Prophetae ... [Printer Mark].
Imprint: Antverpiae, ex officina Christophori Plantini.

Leather, gilt, gauffered (chased) edges; 4¾ x 2-3/8 x 1-5/8 in.

IMPRINTS, BELGIUM

Cabinet L Shelf 5 No. 1

Plantin, Christopher, Antwerp, 1569.

See Perret, Clement. Exercitatio alphabetica nova et utilissima...

IMPRINTS, Belgium

Cabinet 2 Shelf 1 No. 11

Plantin, Christopher, Antwerp, 1585.
Title: Lipsi. Saturnalium sermonum libri duo, qui di gladiatoribus. Noviter correcti, aucti, & formis aeneis illustrati.
Imprint: Antverpiae, apud Christophorum Plantinum 1585.

Tree claf; 8¼ x 5¾ x ½ in.

IMPRINTS, Belgium

Cabinet 2 Shelf 2 No. 13

Plantin-Moretus Press. Antwerp, 1582.
Title: Hugonis Donelli, Iurisconsulti Commentarii Ad titulos digestorum qui infra scripta sunt ...
Imprint: Ex officina Christophori Plantini, M.D.LXXXIII.

Vellum; 13½ x 9 x 1½ in.

IMPRINTS, Belgium

Cabinet 2 Shelf 1 No. 50

Plantin Moretus Press. Widow & heirs of Balth. Moretus. Antwerp, 1677.
Title: Officum B. Mariae Virg. Illus.
Imprint: Antwerpiat. Ex Officina Plantiniana. Apud Viduam & Heredes Balth. Moreti.
Signatures a to y, untrimmed and unbound.

In morocco case; 4¾ x 3½ x 2 in.

IMPRINTS, Belgium.

Cabinet 6 Shelf 2 No. 18

Plantin-Moretus Press: Albert-Francis Moretus, Antwerp, 1835.
Title: Officium Beatae Mariae Virginis.
Imprint: Antverpia, ex Typographia Plantiniana, apud Albertum Moretus. M.D.CCC.XXXV.
A complete set folded sigs., not trimmed nor sewn; copper illus., black and red; size of pp.4 x 2 in.
In box containing other incompleted items after printing.

IMPRINTS, Belgium.

Cabinet 6 Shelf 2 No. 18

Plantin-Moretus Press: Edward-Joseph Moretus Antwerp, 1866.

Title: Horae Diurne.....S. Francisci
Imprint: Antverpiae, ex Archytypographia Plantiniana, M.D.CCC.LXVI.
Complete set folded sigs. not trimmed nor sewn; in black and red; size of pp. 7¼ x 4 in.
In box containing other items incompleted after printing.

IMPRINTS, Belgium.

Cabinet 2 Shelf 1 No.

Plantin-Moretus Press.

See Early Printing in Belgium. Antwerp v.d. Also see Early Printing in Holland, Leyden, v.d.

IMPRINTS, Belgium

Cabinet X Shelf 4 No. 3 also X/4/4

Sassenus, Serv. Louvain, 1546 - 1550

see PRINTING, HISTORICAL, Belgium. (Ordinance of Charles V, 1550)

IMPRINTS, Canada.

Cabinet F Shelf 1 No. 121

Mesplet (Fleury) and Charles Berger. Montreal, 1776.
Title: Réglement de la confrerie de l'adoration perpétuelle du S. Sacrement...
Imprint: A Montreal: Chez F. Mesplet & C. Berger. Imprimeurs & Libraires; près le Marché 1776.
First book printed in Canada.

Limp morocco; 4½ x 3¼ x 1/8 in. Thomas 2, p.181.

IMPRINTS, Canada. Miscellaneous

Cabinet G Shelf 2 No. 88

Description of and guide to Jasper Park. Ottawa. Department of the Interior. Illus.

Flexible linen; 9¾ x 6¾ in.

IMPRINTS, China

Cabinet II Shelf 3 No. 45

Commercial Press Ltd., Shanghai, ca. 1913.

See CHINA. Commercial Press Ltd. Shanghai, ca. 1913. Catalogue...

IMPRINTS, China.

Cabinet R Shelf 3 No. 231

Commercial Press, Limited. Shanghai, 1919.
Title: The history of Chinese Printing [Chinese text]. Edited by Y.S.Sen.
Imprint: Commercial Press, Limited.

Half morocco; 7¾ x 5¼ in.

IMPRINTS, China

Cabinet II Shelf 3 No. 43

Presbyterian Mission Press, Hankow and Shanghai. n.d.

See PRESBYTERIAN MISSION PRESS. National Phonetic edition of "Pilgrims Progress".

IMPRINTS, China

Cabinet EE Shelf 3 No. 83

Presbyterian Mission Press, Shanghai. circa 1900

See SPECIMEN BOOKS, TYPES. Printers'. China.

IMPRINTS, England

Cabinet E Shelf 3 No. 52

Alsop, Bernard and Thomas Fawcet. London, 1633.
See Early Printing in England. London, 1633. Bernard Alsop and Thomas Fawcet.

IMPRINTS, ENGLAND

Cabinet J Shelf 1 No. 23

Angus, George, Newcastle on Tyne (1825)

See Angus, George (Printer) Impressions of a numerous collection of ancient wood cuts...

IMPRINTS, England

Cabinet M Shelf 2 No. 53

Aquila Press [George W. Jones] London, 1930.
Title: The grand inquisition. By F.M. Dostoevsky.
Imprint: The Aquila Press. 1930.
Colophon....Printed in Linotype Estienne type... by George W. Jones at the Sign of the Dolphin London.

Boards, vellum back; 9¾ x 6½ x 3/8 in.

IMPRINTS, England

Cabinet M
Shelf 2
No. 52

Aquila Press, London, 1930.
Title: The odes and sonnets of Garcilaso de la Vega...
Imprint: The Aquila Press, 1930.
Colophon: ... Linotype Estienne Old Face, and has been printed for the Aquila Press by the designer, George W. Jones at The Sign of the Dolphin...London.

Boards, vellum back; 11-5/8 x 8 x 5/8 in.

IMPRINTS, England

Cabinet M
Shelf 1
No. 4

Ashendene Press, The. St. John Hornby, Hertford, 1896.
Title: The poems of John Milton.
Imprint on page following: This book....was imprinted by me, St. John Hornby...with types cast from matrices given to the University of Oxford by Bishop Fell, 1670 (?).....
Printed for my friends.

Linen over boards; 8¾ x 6½ x 3/8 in.

IMPRINT, England

Cabinet M
Shelf 1
No 5

Ashendene Press, The. St. John and Cicely Hornby, Chelsea, 1904.
A book of songs and poems from the Old Testament and the Apocrypha. Printed in red and black with hand-painted initials.
Colophon: Printed by St. John & Cicely Hornby with the help of Meysey Turton & E. Faulkner at the Ashendene Press, Shelley House, Chelsea, in the spring of the year, 1904.
Printer Mark.

Vellum; 7½ x 5¼ x ½ in.

IMPRINTS, England

Cabinet M
Shelf 5
No. 3

Ashendene Press, St. John Hornby, London, 1920.
Title: Decameron di Messer Giovanni Boccaccio, Cittadino Fiorentino.
Imprint: Nella stamperia Ashendiniana: Shelley House, Chelsea, 1920.
The colophon states that the printing of this book was commenced in October 1913, but owing to The Great War, it was only finished in December, 1920.

Paper boards, linen back; 16 x 11¼ x 1-3/4 in

IMPRINTS, England

Cabinet M
Shelf 5
No. 4

Ashendene Press, St. John Hornby, London, 1923.
Title: The Faerie Queene. By Edmund Spenser.
Colophon: Printed at the Ashendene Press, at Shelley House, Chelsea, by C.H. St. J. Hornby. The printing was begun in the month of January of the year 1922 and finished in the month of November of the following year ....Printer Mark......

Vellum boards, leather back; 17 x 12 x 2½ in.

IMPRINTS, England

Cabinet M
Shelf 1
No. 1

Ashendene Press (St. John and Cicely Hornby)
Title: Hand-list of the books printed at the Ashendene Press, Chelsea, London, Shelley House, 1895-1925.

Brochure, with other items in manila envelope

IMPRINTS, England

Cabinet M
Shelf 5
No. 5
2 vols.

Ashendene Press, The: St. John Hornby, 1927-28.
Title: Historie of Don Quixote of the Mencha: Translated out of the Spanish by Thomas Shelton. 2 vols.
Colophon:...First printed for E. Blount in 1620. Now newly reprinted by Charles H. St. John Hornby assisted by G. Faulkner...at his private press called The Ashendene Press, Shelley House in the county of London. The printing was begun in May...1927 and ended

cont'd

IMPRINTS, England cont'd

Cabinet M
Shelf 5
No. 5

...in July 1928. The borders and initials were designed by Louis Powell...Laus deo. Printer mark.

Full morocco; 17 x 12 in.

IMPRINTS, England

Cabinet M
Shelf 1
No. 3

Austin, Stephen. Hertford, 1855.
Title: Sakoontala; or the lost ring. Translated into English prose by Monier Williams, M.A. Illus. and polychrome borders taken from illuminated MSS. Designer, T. Sulman, Jr., engraver, George Measom.
Imprint: Printed and published by Stephen Austin bookseller to the East-India College, M.DCCC.LV.

Boards, decorated paper gilt edges; 9 x 7 x 1½ in.

IMPRINTS, England

Cabinet M
Shelf 1
No. 6

Astolat Press, The. A.C. Curtis. Guildford, 1902.
Title: The Prioresses Tale. From The Canterbury Tales by Geoffrey Chaucer. Printer Mark.
Printed upon Japanese vellum.

Parchment over boards; 8¾ x 6-3/8 x ½ in.

IMPRINTS, England

Cabinet QQ
Shelf 3
No. 30

Baker, William, London, 1811.

see BAKER, WILLIAM. Peregrinations of the mind...London, 1811.

IMPRINTS, England

Cabinet W
Shelf 1
No. 144

Ballantyne Press, The. Charles Ricketts: London, 1898.
Title: De la typographie et de William Morris. Par Lucien Pissarro et Charles Ricketts.
Colophon: "Ce livre fut commence par Lucien Pissarro en Avril 1897 et acheve au Ballantyne Press sous le direction de Charles Ricketts le 2 janvier 1898."

Boards; 7-7/8 x 5¼ in.

IMPRINTS, England

Cabinet Q
Shelf 1
No. 26

Ballantyne Press (Ballantyne & Company Ltd.) London, 1910.
Title: The romance of bookselling. By Frank A. Mumby. London, 1910.
Imprint: Printed by Ballantyne & Company Ltd. at The Ballantyne Press, London.

Cloth; 9 x 6 x 2¼ in.

IMPRINTS, England

Cabinet M
Shelf 1
No. 7

Astolat Press, The. A.C. Curtis, Guildford, 1903.
Title: The story of Elayne. The fair maid of Astolat. By Sir Thomas Malory. Printer Mark A.C. Curtis, Guildford, MDCCCCIII. Printed in black and red. Ornamental Initials.

Boards; 7¼ x 4½ x ¼ in.

IMPRINTS, ENGLAND

Cabinet L
Shelf 4
No. 17

Barnard, J. G. London, 1807
Title: Essay on transparent prints...By Edward Orme.
Imprint. London:..1807. J. G. Barnard. Printer. 57, Snow Hill.

Quarter morocco: 14½ x 10½ x ¾ in.

IMPRINTS, England

Cabinet 30
Shelf 1
No. 1

Baskerville, John, London, 1758. Paradise Lost, The author John Milton. Printed by John Baskerville for J. and R. Tonson in London.

Half calf; 9¼ x 6 in. pp.(27) LXIX, 416

IMPRINTS, England

Cabinet 30
Shelf 1
No. 1

Baskerville, John, London, 1758. Paradise Regained, a poem in 4 books....Printed by John Baskerville for J. and R. Tonson in London.

Half calf, 9¼ x 6 in. pp.390

IMPRINTS, England

Cabinet 30
Shelf 1
No. 3

Baskerville, John. Birmingham, 1761. D. Junii Juvenalis et auli Persii Flacci satyrae. Birminghamiae: types Johannis Baskerville, MDCCLXI. Printed red line borders.

Morocco; 12 ¼ x 9¾ in. pp.240

IMPRINTS, England.

Cabinet 30 Shelf 2 No. 2

Baskerville, John. Cambridge, 1763. The Holy Bible, containing the Old Testament and the New ... Cambridge, Printed by John Baskerville Printer to the University, 1763.

IMPRINTS, England

Cabinet 30 Shelf 1 No. 4

Baskerville, John. Birmingham, 1766. The works of Virgil. Englished by Robert Andrews. Birmingham. Printed by John Baskerville for the author. MDCCLXVI.

Half morocco; 10 x 6¼ in. pp.(5),16,536.

IMPRINTS, England

Cabinet 30 Shelf 1 No. 5

Baskerville, John, Birmingham, 1772. Catulli, Tibuli, et propertii opera. Birminghamiae, Typis Johannis Baskerville, MDCCLXXII.

Orign. Calf; 7 x 4½ in. pp.276

IMPRINTS, England.

Cabinet F Shelf 4 No. 16

Bassam, Robert. London, 1794.

See Early Printing in England. London, 1794. Robert Bassam.

IMPRINTS, England

Cabinet RR Shelf 2 No. 3

Baxter, J., Lewes, 1809.

See PAPER. Sister arts...Lewes, 1809.

IMPRINTS, England

Cabinet M Shelf 1 No. 19.01

Baynard Press, The. Sanders Phillips & Co., Ltd., London, n.d.

Title: The Baynard book of badges.

Brochure; 10¼ x 6-3/8 in.

IMPRINTS, England

Cabinet M Shelf 1 No. 18

Baynard Press, The. Sanders Phillips & Company, London, n.d.

Title: The Flying Wheel. By Robert Finch [An account, with interior and exterior views, of a large manufactory of silk hosiery].

Colophon: Printed in London at The Baynard Press by Sanders Phillips & Co., Ltd.

Boards; 11 x 8½ x ½ in.

IMPRINTS, England

Cabinet K Shelf 2 No. 27

Baynard Press, The. Sanders Phillips & Co., London, 1900.

Title: A collection of fine old engravings after Sir Henry Raeburn...

Colophon: Printed at the Baynard Press, Sanders Phillips & Co., Ltd., Chryssell Road, London, S.W.9

Cloth; 10¾ x 8¼ in.

IMPRINTS, England

Cabinet I Shelf 2 No. 28

Baynard Press, The. Sanders Phillips & Co. London, 1921.

Title: The British School of Etching...a lecture delivered by Martin Hardie, R.E., on July 8th, 1921, published by the Print Collectors Club. Illus.

Colophon: Printed in London by Sanders Phillips and Company Ltd. At the Baynard Press. November, 1921.

Linen over boards; 10 x 7½ x 3/8 in.

IMPRINTS, England

Cabinet J Shelf 2 No. 21

Baynard Press, The. Sanders Phillips & Co. London, 1922.

Title: Albert Dürer his life and work...With notes on watermarks, a chronological list of his woodcuts and engravings and illustrations of his work. A lecture by T.D. Barlow.

Colophon: Printed in London by Sanders Phillips and Company, Ltd. At the Baynard Press.

Boards; 9¼ x 6½ x 3/8 in.

IMPRINTS, England

Cabinet M Shelf 1 No. 17

Baynard Press, The. Sanders Phillips & Co. Ltd., London, 1922.

Title: International Theater Exhibition. Catalogue and Bibliography. Illus.

Colophon: Printed in London at The Baynard Press by Sanders Phillips & Co., Ltd.

Boards; 9¼ x 6¼ x ½ in.

IMPRINTS, England

Cabinet M Shelf 1 No. 19

Baynard Press, The. London, 1922.

Title: The Savoy Orpheans. Published privately at the Savoy, London 1924. Color decorations.

Colophon: This book has been printed at The Baynard Press...The type has been distributed.

Boards; 10 x 7¼ x ¼ in.

IMPRINTS, England

Cabinet I Shelf 2 No. 29

Baynard Press, The: Sanders Phillips & Co., London, 1924.

Title: British Mezzotints: Being a lecture delivered....Nov. 7th, 1924. By Sir Frank Short. Publication No.4. Published by The Print Collectors' Club. Illus.

Colophon: Printed in London by Sanders Phillips & Co., Ltd., at The Baynard Press, Chryssell Rd., S.W. 9.

Boards; 10 x 7½ x 3/8 in.

IMPRINTS, England

Cabinet M Shelf 1 No. 20

Beaumont Press, The. London, 1918.

Title: The tale of Igor. Adapted from the Russian by Helen de Vere Beauclerk. With six illustrations designed and hand-colored by Michel Sevier.

Imprint: 1918. London. C.W. Beaumont, 75 Charing Cross Road, W.C.

Colored boards, linen back; 9 x 6 x 3/8 in.

IMPRINTS, England

Cabinet M Shelf 1 No. 21

Beaumont Press, The. Cyril W. Beaumont, London, 1919.

Title: Eclogues: A Book of Poems by Herbert Read.

Colophon:...The cover and the decorations designed by Ethelbert White. The Typography and binding arranged by Cyril W. Beaumont. Printed by hand on his Press in the City of Westminster. Completed December the twentieth MDCCCCXIX. Printer Mark.

Decorated paper boards, linen back; 7-7/8 x 5¼ x ¼ in.

IMPRINTS, England

Cabinet M Shelf 1 No. 22

Beaumont Press, The. C.W. Beaumont, London, 1922.

Title: The good-humored ladies. By Carlo Goldoni ...Translated by Richard Aldington...Embellished with cuts by Ethelbert White

Imprint: London: Published by C.W. Beaumont at 75 Charing Cross Road, MDCCCCXXII. Printer Mark and Colophon on last page.

Decorated boards, linen back; 9 x 7 x ½ in.

IMPRINTS, England

Cabinet M Shelf 1 No. 23

Beaumont Press, The. C.W. Beaumont. London, 1922.

Title: Thamar Karsavina. By Valerien Svetlov. Translated by H. De Vere Beauclerk & Nadia Evrenov. Edited by Cyril W. Beaumont. Colored decorations.

Imprint: 1922 London. C.W. Beaumont. 75 Charing Cross Road W.C. 2.

Colored boards, vellum back; 12-3/8 x 8½ x 1-3/8 in.

IMPRINTS, England

Cabinet M Shelf 1 No. 24

Beaumont Press, The. London, 1923.

Title: To nature: New Poems by Edmund Blunden

Colophon:...The cover decorations and initial letters designed by Randolph Schwabe. The typography and binding arranged by Cyril William Beaumont, printer, in the City of Westminster. Completed on the thirtieth day of June, MDCCCCXXIII. Printer Mark.

Boards; 9 x 5¾ x 3/8 in. Tomkinson, Modern Presses, p.14.

IMPRINTS, England

Cabinet M, Shelf 1, No. 25

Beldornie Press: G.E. Palmer, London, 1842.
Title: Chrestoleros. Seven Books of Epigrams written by T.B. Imprinted at London by Richard Bradocke.......1598.
Colophon: Reprinted at the Beldornie Press, by G.E. Palmer, for Edwd. V. Utterson, in the year MDCCCXLII.

Paper boards; 5-7/8 x 4½ x ¾ in.

IMPRINTS, England

Cabinet M, Shelf 1, No. 26

Bensley, Thomas. Bolt-Court, Fleet Street, London, 1794.
Title: Q. Horatii Flacci, quae supersunt recensuit et notulis. Instruxit Gilbertus Wakefield, A.B...Londini: Impensis Kearsley, M.DCC.XCIV. 2 vols.
Colophon: Typis T. Bensley.

Calf; 8-1/8 x 5¼ x 1-1/8 in. See Timperley, p.940.

IMPRINTS, England

Cabinet M, Shelf 1, No. 27

Bensley, T. London, 1809.
Title: Gertrude of Wyoming; a Pennsylvanian tale and other poems. By Thomas Campbell...
Imprint: London: Printed by T. Bensley, Bolt Court. Published by the author by Longman, Hurst, Rees and Orme, Paternoster Row, 1809.

Calf and marbled boards; 11¾ x 9½ x ½ in.

IMPRINTS, England

Cabinet M, Shelf 5, No. 7

Bensley, Thomas. London, 1809.
Title: Poems on the abolition of the slave trade. Written by James Montgomery, James Grahame, and E. Benger. Embellished with engravings from pictures painted by R. Smirke, Esq. R.A.
Imprint: London: Printed for R. Bowyer, the proprietor, No.80, Pall Mall, by T. Bensley, Bolt Court, Fleet Street, 1809.

Paper boards; 14¾ x 11¾ x 1¼ in.

IMPRINTS, England

Cabinet L, Shelf 1, No. 46

Bensley and Son, London, 1816

See SINGER, SAMUEL WELLER. Researches into the history of playing cards...London, 1816.

IMPRINTS, England

Cabinet M, Shelf 1, No. 28

Bensley and Son. London, 1817.
Title: The institutions of physiology. By J. Fred. Blumenbach...translated from the Latin of the third and last edition...by John Elliotson, M.D...Second Edition.
Imprint: London: printed by Bensley and Son, Bolt Court, Fleet Street for S. Cox and Son...1817. This is the first book printed on a cylinder press.

Half calf; 9 x 5¾ x 1-1/8 in.

IMPRINTS, England

Cabinet M, Shelf 5, No. 8

Bentley, Samuel. London, 1838.
Title: The ceremonies to be observed at the Royal Coronation of Her Most Sacred Majesty, Queen Victoria, in the Abbey Church of Westminster. June 28, 1838.
Colophon: Printed by Samuel Bentley, Dorset Street, Fleet Street, London.

Half morocco; 13½ x 8½ in.

IMPRINTS, England

Cabinet M, Shelf 1, No. 29

Bentley, Wilson and Fley. London, 1848.
Title: L'Allegro and Il Penseroso. By John Milton. With thirty illustrations designed expressly for The Art-Union of London, 1848. The full page wood engravings are by 16 of the leading contemporary engravers.

Calf tooled; 11¼ x 8¾ x ½ in.

IMPRINTS, England

Cabinet M, Shelf 1, No. 30

Birmingham Guild of Handicraft Press. Birmingham, 1895.
Title: The Sonnets of William Shakespeare.
Colophon...With decorations by Ernest G. Treglown, engraved on wood by Charles Carr, of the Birmingham Guild of Handicraft Press; printed on the press at the same Guils; and published...in the city of London, MDCCCXCV

Cloth; 9 x 7 x 5/8 in. Tomkinson, Bibliography of modern press, p.186.

IMPRINTS, England

Cabinet F, Shelf 4, No. 3

Bowyer, William, Sr. London, 1709.

Title: An English-Saxon homily on the birth-day of St. Gregory....By Elizabeth Elstob. Engraved frontispiece by S. Gribelin.
Imprint: London: Printed by W. Bowyer M.DCC.IX.

Leather; 8¾ x 5½ x ¾ in.

IMPRINTS, England

Cabinet X, Shelf 1, No. 24

Bowyer, William, London, 1717
Title: Historia Typographorum Parisiensium... (Michel Maittaire)
Imprint: Londini: Apud Christophorum Bateman, ipsius impensis: Typis Gulielmi Bowyer.

Morocco; 7¾ x 4¾ in.

IMPRINTS, England

Cabinet F, Shelf 4, No. 5

Bowyer, William and John Nichols. London, 1772.
Title: The poems of Mark Akenside, M.D.
Imprint: London, printed by W. Bowyer and J. Nichols; and sold by J. Dodsley, in Pall Mall, 1772.

Leather; 8¾ x 5-3/8 x 1½ in.

IMPRINTS, England.

Cabinet K, Shelf 4, No. 44

Bradbury & Evans, London, circa 1856.

See ENGRAVING, BANK NOTE. Specimens of bank note printing...

IMPRINT, England

Cabinet 13, Shelf, No. 3

Bulmer, W. and Co. Shakspeare Printing Office. London, 1792
Title: Imitations of original drawings by Hans Holbein...
Imprint: Printed by W. Bulmer and Co. Shakspeare Printing Office, 1792.

Morocco, gilt; 21½ x 17 in.

IMPRINTS, England

Cabinet 30, Shelf 1, No. 30

Bulmer, William and Co., Shakspeare Printing Office, London, 1795. Poems by Goldsmith and Parnell. Printed by W. Bulmer and Co. Types executed by William Martin. Illus. with many wood engravings, by Thomas and John Bewick.

This book is "meant to combine the various beauties of Printing, Typefounding, Engraving, and Paper-making."

cont'd

IMPRINTS, England cont'd

Cabinet 30, Shelf 1, No. 30

Tooled calf; 12 x 9¼ in. pp.(XX) 76 (XV) (VII) 126.

IMPRINTS, England

Cabinet 30, Shelf 1, No. 31

Bulmer, William & Co. Shakespeare Printing Office London, 1795. Poems by Goldsmith and Parnell Printed by W. Bulmer & Co. The types were executed by William Martin.

A book the purpose of which is "meant to combine the various beauties of Printing, Typefounding, Engraving, and Paper-making."

Tooled calf; 12 x 9¼ in. pp.(XX) 76 (XV) (VII), 126.

IMPRINTS, England

Cabinet 30, Shelf 2, No.

Bulmer, W. and Co., London, 1795. The poetical works of John Milton. Printed by W. Bulmer and Co. Shakspeare Printing-Office from the Types of W. Martin, vols. 2 and 3 only. Steel engravings of R. Westall.

Full morocco; 17 x 13 in.

IMPRINTS, England

Cabinet 30 Shelf 1 No. 32

Bulmer, W. and Co., Shakspeare Printing Office, London, 1796. The Chase: A poem by William Somerville, Illus. by Thomas and John Bewick.

Includes a foreword by W. Bulmer "To the patrons of fine printing."

Calf; $11\frac{3}{4}$ x $9\frac{1}{4}$ in. pp. (XV) (V) 76.

IMPRINTS, England

Cabinet 30 Shelf 1 No. 33

Bulmer, William and Co., London, 1800. The fathers revenge: A tragedy. By Frederick, Earl of Carlisle. Printed by W. Bulmer & Co., Shakspeare Printing Office. Steel engravings (6) by R. Westall.

Calf; $11\frac{1}{2}$ x $9\frac{1}{4}$ in. pp.163.

IMPRINTS, England

Cabinet 30 Shelf 1 No. 34

Bulmer, W. and Co., London, 1802. Anacreontis Odaria ad textus Barnesiani fidem emendata. Londini, sumptibus editoris execudebant Gul. Bulmer et soc. MDCCCII. Printed in Greek. Illus. Steel engravings.

Calf; $8\frac{1}{4}$ x $5\frac{3}{8}$ in. pp.130.

IMPRINTS, ENGLAND

Cabinet I Shelf 1 No. 32

Bulmer, W. and Co., London, 1803.

See BOYDELL, JOHN and JOSIAH. Alphabetical catalogue of plates...Printed by W. Bulmer & Co.

IMPRINTS, England

Cabinet 30 Shelf 1 No. 35

Bulmer, W. and Co., London, 1804. Outlines from the figures and compositions upon Greek, Roman and Etruscan vases. Borders and outlines drawn and engraved by Mr. Kirk. Printed by W. Bulmer and Co., Cleveland-Row St. James's MDCCCIV.

Full morocco, tooled, gilt edges; 12 x $9\frac{1}{2}$ in. pp.XVII, 47, 120 plates.

IMPRINTS, England

Cabinet 30 Shelf 1 No. 35. 01

Bulmer, W. and Co. London, 1804.
Title: Rasselas, by Dr. Johnson. Printed with patent types in a manner never before attempted. Rucher's Edition. Banbury...1804.
Last page: London. Printed by W. Bulmer and Co. Cleveland-Row, St James's.

Half morocco; $8\frac{1}{2}$ x $5\frac{1}{4}$ x 5/8 in.

IMPRINTS, England

Cabinet 30 Shelf 1 No. 39

Bulmer, W. and Co., London, 1807. Richardi Bentleii et doctorum virorum epistolae, partim mutuae. Accedit Richard Dawesii ad Joannem Taylorum. Londoni, typis Bulmerianis, MDCCCVII. Portraits (2) and facsimile (1)

Half morocco; $12\frac{1}{4}$ x 10 in. pp.330.

IMPRINTS, England.

Cabinet 30 Shelf 1 No. 40 2 vols.

Bulmer, William. London, 1808.
Title...Utopia. By Sir Thomas More...A new edition with copious notes...and a biographical and literary introduction by T.F. Dibdin.
Imprint: London, 1808. Printed by William Bulmer at the Shakspeare Press, Cleveland Row, for William Miller.

Boards; 8 x $5\frac{1}{4}$ x 7/8 in. each vol.

IMPRINTS, England

Cabinet 30 Shelf 1 No. 42

Bulmer, W. and Co., Shakspeare Printing-Office, London, 1813. Hobbinol. Field Sports and the Bowling Green, by W. Sommerville, London: Printed by William Bulmer and Co. for R. Ackerman, in the Strand. Decorations by Nesbit and Thurston.

Half morocco; 12 x $9\frac{1}{4}$ in. pp.118.

IMPRINTS, England

Cabinet T Shelf 3 No. 2

Bulmer, W. & Co., London, 1817
Title: Bibliographical Decameron...By Thomas F. Dibdin.
Imprint: London. Printed for the author, by W. Bulmer & Co. 1817. (3 vols. illus.)

Morocco, tooled, gilt, $11\frac{7}{4}$ x $7\frac{3}{4}$ in.

IMPRINTS , England

Cabinet T Shelf 3 No. 3

Bulmer, W. and N. Nichols, Shakspeare Press, London, 1821
Title: Bibliographical tour...by Thomas F. Dibdin
Imprint: Printed for the author by W. Bulmer and N. Nichols, Shakspeare Press, London, 1821. (3 vols.) Illus.

Morocco, gilt, $10\frac{1}{4}$ x $6\frac{3}{4}$ in.

IMPRINTS, ENGLAND

Cabinet RR Shelf 1 No. 13

Burton, T. London, 1800.

See KOOPS, MATTHIAS. Historical account of the substances...

IMPRINTS, England

Cabinet D Shelf 1 No. 22

Cambridge University Press, 1905
Title: The story of Queen Anelida and the false Arcite. By Geoffrey Chaucer. Printed at Westminster by William Caxton about the year 1477.
Imprint: Cambridge, at the University Press, MDCCCCV 1905.

Facsimile.

Boards: $10\frac{1}{2}$ x 7 in.

IMPRINTS, England

Cabinet U Shelf 2 No. 142

Cambridge University Press, 1906, John Clay.
Title: John Sieberch. Bibliographical notes, 1886-1905. By Robert Bowes and G.J. Gray. With fecs.
Imprint: Printed by John Clay, printer to the University of Cambridge...1906.

Boards; 8-1/8 x 6 in.

IMPRINTS, England

Cabinet M Shelf 1 No. 31

Cambridge University Press, The. 1919. J.B. Peace, director.
Title: A journey to America in 1834. By Robert Heywood of The Pike, Bolton. Privately printed, 1919.

Boards, linen back; $8\frac{3}{4}$ x 5-5/8 x 3/8 in.

IMPRINTS, England

Cabinet M Shelf 1 No. 32

Cambridge University Press, The. 1919. J.B. Peace, director.
Title: The litany of the elves. By J.C. Lawson, M.A. Cambridge University Press. 1919.
Colophon: Cambridge: Printed by J.B. Peace, M.A. of The University Press.

Boards; $10\frac{1}{2}$ x $7\frac{3}{4}$ x $\frac{1}{4}$ in.

IMPRINTS, England

Cabinet M Shelf 1 No. 33

Cambridge University Press, The. 1922. J.B. Peace, director.
Title: The beggar's opera. Its predecessors and successors. By Frank Kidson. University Seal.
Imprint: Cambridge. At The University Press, 1922.

Cloth over boards; 7 x $4\frac{3}{4}$ x 3/8 in.

IMPRINTS, England

Cabinet M Shelf 1 No. 34

Cambridge University Press, The. 1923. W. Lewis, printer.
Title: Devotions upon emergent occasions. By John Donne.
Imprint: Cambridge, at The University Press. MDCCCCXXIII.

Boards, cloth back; $8\frac{3}{4}$ x 7 x 1 in.

IMPRINTS, England

Cabinet M, Shelf 1, No. 35

Cambridge University Press, 1924. W. Lewis, printer.
Title: A bibliography of Sir Thomas Browne, Kt. M.D. By Geoffrey Keynes...Many facsimile title pages.
Colophon under the University seal: Printed by W. Lewis at The University Press, MCMXXIV.
All the plates and blocks for the illustrations were prepared by Messrs. Emery Walker, Ltd.

Cloth; 10¼ x 8-3/4 x 1 in.

IMPRINTS, England

Cabinet B, Shelf 3, No. 10

Cambridge University Press (Walter Lewis), 1924.
Title: Four centuries of fine printing...1500-1914. With an introductory text and indexes by Stanley Morison. London, 1924
[Imprint on last page] Printed by Walter Lewis at the University Press, Cambridge.

Morocco; 18¾ x 15½ x 1-7/8 in.

IMPRINTS, England

Cabinet M, Shelf 3, No. 29

Cambridge University Press, 1925: W. Lewis.
Title: Nonesuch Books for Christmas 1925, for Spring 1926: With a handlist of books hithertó published by the Press....16 Great James Street, W.C.
Colophon: Cambridge. Printed by W. Lewis at the University Press.

Boards; 7½ x 5-3/8 in.

IMPRINTS, England

Cabinet M, Shelf 1, No. 38

Caradoc Press, The. George and Hesba D. Webb. Bedford Park. Chiswick, 1902,
Title: In Praise of Wisdom.
Colophon:...Designed, engraved, printed and bound & published by H.G. Webb & his wife H.D. Webb at The Caradoc Press....finished December in the year of the crowning of our sovereign Lord, King Edward the Seventh MDCCCCII. Device.

Vellum; 6 x 3 in. Tomkinson, Bibliography of Modern presses p.23

IMPRINTS, England

Cabinet M, Shelf 1, No. 37

Caradoc Press, The. George Webb, Bedford Park, Chiswick, 1905.
Title: The Compleate Angler....
Colophon: The end of the Complete Angler by Isaak Walton reprinted...The ornaments, initials and etchings designed and engraved by H.G. Webb and the whole printed and bound at the Caradoc Press. Bedford Park, Chiswick, London, MDCCCCV. Printed in red and black.

Mottled and glazed calf; 9 x 6 in.

IMPRINTS, ENGLAND

Cabinet L, Shelf 4, No. 23

Cassell & Company, Limited, La Belle Sauvage, London, E. C. (n.d. circa 1880).

See Color Printing. Illustrated book pigeons...By Robert Fulton.

IMPRINTS, England

Cabinet 17, Shelf 2, No. 6

Cawod (John), John Waly and R. Tottell, London, 1557.
Large 8vo. title page. Wood engraving with monogram and imprint.

Item in HENRY STEVNE'S "Typographical Miscellanies", vol.6-C, p.40

IMPRINTS, England

Cabinet M, Shelf 1, No. 40

Chiswick Press, The. C. Whittingham, College House, Chiswick, London, 1823.
Title: The dramatic works of William Shakspeare With a glossary. Illus.
Imprint: Chiswick: Printed by C. Whittingham, College House; for.....1823.

Morocco, gilt; 7 x 4¼ x 1½ in.

IMPRINTS, England

Cabinet I, Shelf 1, No. 35

Chiswick Press (C. Wittingham), London, 1833.

See DOUCE, FRANCIS. Dance of Death: Exhibited in elegant engravings...London, 1833.

IMPRINTS, England

Cabinet M, Shelf 1, No. 41

Chiswick Press, The. C. Whittingham, Chiswick, 1842.
Title: The deformed, Jessy Bell, and other poems. By Mary St. Aubyn. Printer Mark: the Aldus dolphin and anchor. London: William Pickering. 1842. Printed by C. Whittingham, Chiswick.
Colophon: C. Whittingham, Chiswick.

Cloth; 7 x 4¾ x 1 in.

IMPRINTS, England

Cabinet M, Shelf 5, No. 10

Chiswick Press. Charles Whittingham. Chiswick, 1844.
Title: The book of Common Prayer...according to the use of the Church of England...London: William Pickering, 1844.
Colophon: Printed by C. Whittingham. Printer Mark.

Vellum boards; 13½ x 9¼ x 2⅝ in.

IMPRINTS, England

Cabinet M, Shelf 1, No. 42

Chiswick Press, Charles Whittingham (nephew) London, 1844.
Title: The diary of Lady Willoughby...Imprinted for Longman, Brown, Green, Paternoster Row, ...in the City of London, 1844.
Colophon: Printed by Charles Whittingham at the Chiswick Press. Printer Mark.

Paper over boards; ~~8-5/8~~ x 7 x 1¼ in.

IMPRINTS, England

Cabinet J, Shelf 2, No. 18

Chiswick Press, Charles Whittingham, London, 1844.
Title: The Passion of our Lord Jesus Christ, pourtrayed by Albert Durer...
Colophon: Printed by Charles Whittingham at the Chiswick Press, 15 July 1844.

Has printer mark.

Leather; 8 x 5⅛ in.

IMPRINTS, England

Cabinet M, Shelf 1, No. 44

Chiswick Press, The. C. Whittingham (nephew), London, 1845.
Title: Decii Junii Juvenalis Aquinatis satirae Decem et sex. Auli Persii Flacci, satirae sex. Londini, MDCCCXLV. Printed in black and red. Text enclosed within borders.
Colophon: Excudebat Carolus Whittingham, 1845. Printer Mark.

Calf, gilt; 11-1/8 x 8-3/8 x 1 in.

IMPRINTS, England

Cabinet M, Shelf 1, No. 43

Chiswick Press, The. C. Whittingham (Nephew) London, 1846.
Title: Diary of Lady Willoughby...The fourth edition. Imprinted for Longman, Brown, Green & Longmans, Paternoster Row, London, 1846.
Colophon: Printed by C. Whittingham, Chiswick.

Decorated paper over boards; 7 x 4⅝ x ¾ in.

IMPRINTS, England

Cabinet M, Shelf 1, No. 45

Chiswick Press, The. C. Whittingham (nephew) London, 1848.
Title: Order for the administration of the Holy Communion...of the Church of England. Device, London: William Pickering. 1848.
Colophon: Printed by C. Whittingham, Chiswick.

Paper over boards, 8½ x 6¼ x 5/8 in.

IMPRINTS, England

Cabinet S, Shelf 4, No. 88

Chiswick Press (C. Wittingham), London, 1853.
Title: Catalogue of my English library. Collected and described by Henry Stevens.
Imprint: London, Printed by C. Wittingham, Nov. 1853.

Cloth; 6¾ x 4¼ x 3/8 in.

IMPRINTS, England

Cabinet M, Shelf 1, No. 46

Chiswick Press, The. Charles Whittingham. London, 1864.
Title: The New Testament of our Lord and Saviour Jesus Christ. With engravings on wood from designs of Fra Angelico...and others. London: Longman, Green, Longman, Roberts and Green, 1864. Printer, R. Clay. Includes wood engraved marginal ornaments, Initial Letters, Medallions, etc.

Half morocco; 11¾ x 9 x 2-1/8 in.

IMPRINTS, England

Cabinet M Shelf 1 No. 48

Chiswick Press. Whittingham and Wilkins, London, 1868.
Title: Bishop Ken's Christian Year...Printer Mark. London. Basil Montague Pickering, 196, Piccadilly, 1868.
Colophon: Printed by Whittingham and Wilkins, Tooks Court, Chancery Lane.
Text within borders, most of them designed by the daughter of C. Whittingham.

Boards; 9 x 6¾ x 1-3/8 in.

IMPRINTS, England

Cabinet M Shelf 1 No. 50

Chiswick Press. London, 1899.
Title: Some hints on pattern designing. By William Morris.
Colophon: Printed at the Chiswick Press with the Golden type designed by William Morris for the Kelmscott Press, and finished on the fourth day of October, 1899....

Boards; 8¾ x 5¾ x ¼ in.

IMPRINTS, England

Cabinet 17 Shelf 2 No. 6

Clark, Charles. London, circa 1842. (Loose leaflets, with imprints of)

Items in HENRY STEVENS "Typographical Miscellanies", vol.6-C, pp.137-139

IMPRINTS, England

Cabinet M Shelf 5 No. 24

Chiswick Press (Wittingham and Wilkins), London, 1868.
Title: The Order for the Administration of the Holy Communion...
London: Sold by Thomas Bosworth, 215 Regent Street. 1868.
Imprint: Chiswich Press:- Printed by Whittingham and Wilkins, Tooks Court, Chancery Lane.

Full morocco: 14¾ x 9½ in.

IMPRINTS, England

Cabinet M Shelf 1 No. 57

Chiswick Press. London, 1900.
Title: The sonnets of John Keats.
Colophon: This edition...with decorated borders and initials by Christopher Dean, was published by George Bell and Sons....London, and printed at the Chiswick Press, MDCCCXCVIII and reprinted MDCCCC. Device.

Boards; 6½ x 5-1/8 x 3/8 in.

IMPRINTS, ENGLAND

Cabinet L Shelf 4 No. 21

Clay. R. Printer, Bread Street Hill, London, 1858.

See Kingsley, Charles. Glaucus... Cambridge (England) 1858.

IMPRINTS, England

Cabinet U Shelf 2 No. 66

Chiswick Press: Whittingham & Wilkins. London, 1872-75.
Title: Chiswick Press. Literary Almanack.
Imprint: London: Printed by Whittingham & Wilkins. Tooks Court, Chancery Lane, E.C.

Half morocco; 9¾ x 7½ x 5/8 in.

IMPRINTS, England

Cabinet U Shelf 3 No. 45

Chiswick Press, London, 1901.
Title: Art and its producers, and The arts and crafts of today: two a ddresses delivered before the National Association for the Advancement of Art. By William Morris.
Imprint: The Chiswick Press, London, 1901.

Boards; 8½ x 5¾ in.

IMPRINTS, England.

Cabinet M Shelf 1 No. 53

Clay & Sons, Limited, Richard. London and Suffolk, 1920.
Title: Gulliver's Travels into Lilliput and Brobdingnag. Illustrated by Jean de Bosschère. London, 1920.
Colophon: Printed in Great Britain by Richard Clay & Sons, Limited, Brunswick St. Stamford St., and Bungay Suffolk.

Cloth; 10¾ x 8½ x 5/8 in.

IMPRINTS, England

Cabinet T Shelf 5 No. 23

Chiswick Press: Charles Whittingham, London, 1878.

See BIBLIOGRAPHY. Photo-bibliography... By Henry Stevens of Vermont. London, 1878.

IMPRINTS, ENGLAND

Cabinet U Shelf 3 No. 63

Chiswick Press, Charles Whittingham & Co. London, 1902.
Title: Ecce mundus: Industrial ideals and the book beautiful. By T.J. Cobden-Sanderson.
Colophon: Printed at the Chiswick Press: Charles Whittingham & Co. London.

Boards; 8½ x 6 in.

IMPRINTS, England

Cabinet M Shelf 1 No. 54

Clay & Sons, Richard. Bungay, Suffolk. 1929.
Title: Compendium maleficarum. Collected in 3 books...by Brother Francesco Maria Guzzo... Translated by E. A. Ashwin. London, 1929. Illus.
Imprint follows title page: Printed in Great Britain by Richard Clay & Sons, Limited, Bungay Suffolk.

Cloth; 10¾ x 7¾ x 1 in.

IMPRINTS, England

Cabinet 76 Shelf 2 No. 1

Chiswick Press, London, 1894.
Title: Erhard Ratdolt and his work at Venice. By Gilbert R. Redgrave.

Half morocco; 11 x 9 in.

IMPRINTS, England

Cabinet M Shelf 1 No. 52

Chiswick Press. Charles T. Jacobi, London, 1909.
Title: An address delivered by Past Master Selwyn Image before the Art Worker's Guild.
Colophon: London; Printed, with the permission of the Trustees, in the Golden Type designed by by Past Master William Morris, by Charles T. Jacobi at the Chiswick Press....March 25, 1909.

Paper; 9 x 6-1/8 in.

IMPRINTS, England

Cabinet M Shelf 2 No. 4

Cloister Press, The. Heaton Mersey, Manchester, 1921.
Title: Catherine. A Romantic Poem by R.C.K. Ensor. London. Sidgwick & Jackson Ltd.
Colophon: At the Cloister Press. Heaton Mersey near Manchester.
Printed in A.T.F. Co. Garamond types; their first use in England.

Paper; 7 x 4½ x ¼ in.

IMPRINTS, England

Cabinet M Shelf 1 No. 49

Chiswick Press. C. Whittingham and Co., London, 1899.
Title: Of The Imitation of Christ. In four books by Thomas A Kempis...London, Kagan Paul...
Illustrations and title-page designed wood by Miss Clemence Housman.
Colophon: Chiswick Press: Charles Whittingham and Co. Took's Court, Chancery Lane, London Printer mark.

Vellum; 9 x 6 x 1½ in.

IMPRINTS, England

Cabinet Q Shelf 1 No. 25

Chiswick Press, Charles Wittingham and Griggs Ltd. London, 1924.
Title: William Pickering, publisher. A memoir ...By Geoffrey Keynes. London, 1924. Illus.

Cloth boards; 10¼ x 7¾ x 5/8 in.

IMPRINTS, England

Cabinet M Shelf 2 No. 5

Cloister Press, The. Heaton Mersey, Manchester, 1921.
Title: Thoughts in Hospital. By Lawrence Pilkington. Longmans, Green & Co....London, 1921.
Colophon: At the Cloister Press, Heaton Mersey, near Manchester.

Paper boards; 7½ x 5-1/8 in.

IMPRINTS, England

Cabinet M | Shelf 2 | No. 6

Cloister Press, The. Manchester, 1922.
Title: Sixe Idillia. That is sixe small or pretty poems, or aeglogves, chosen out of.... Theocritus and translated into English verse. Illus.
Colophon: Printed in England at The Cloister Press, Heaton Mersey, Manchester.

Boards; 12 x $8\frac{3}{4}$ x $\frac{1}{4}$ in.

IMPRINTS, England

Cabinet M | Shelf 2 | No. 7

Clowes, William and Sons, London, 1883.
Title: Living English Poets, MDCCCLXXXII. Second edition. Device. London: Kegan Paul, Trench & Co., 1, Paternoster Square, Illus.
Colophon: London. Printed by William Clowes and Sons, Limited, Stamford Street and Charing Cross.

Calf, tooled, gilt; $8\frac{3}{4}$ x 5 x $1\frac{1}{2}$ in.

IMPRINTS, England

Cabinet M | Shelf 2 | No. 8

Cooke, J.P. London [1800?]
Title: Poetry of nature...of the Caledonian Bards. The typographical execution in a style entirely new, and decorated with the superb ornaments of the celebrated Caslon. n.d.
Colophon: Londini: Typis, J.P. Cooke.
The text of this book is entirely in script.

Boards; 8 x $6\frac{1}{2}$ x $\frac{3}{4}$ in.

IMPRINTS, England

Cabinet | Shelf | No.

Cooper and Wilson, London, 1799.

see
FRY, EDMUND. Pantographia...London, 1799

IMPRINT, England

Cabinet U | Shelf 2 | No. 10

CURLL, E., at Pope's-Head, Rose Street, Covent Garden, London, 1741.

See BIOGRAPHIES, Printers.
Barber, John, impartial histor y...London, 1741.

IMPRINTS, England

Cabinet M | Shelf 2 | No. 9

Curwen Press, The. London, n.d.
Title: Apropos the Unicorn: A few candid notes. By Joseph Thorp. Published by The Curwen Press. Plaistow, London, E. 13. Col. Illus.
Following last page: The Device of the Curwen Press.
Has specimen of "Some letters from the Curwen Press Poster Types."

Paper covers; $5\frac{3}{4}$ x $3\frac{1}{2}$ in.

IMPRINTS, England

Cabinet M | Shelf 2 | No. 11

Curwen Press, The. London, 1923.
Title: A garland of Elizabethan Sonnets. Text within decorative borders.
Colophon: Printed at The Curwen Press, Plaistow.

Decorated paper over boards; $7\frac{3}{4}$ x 6 x $\frac{1}{4}$ in.

IMPRINTS, England

Cabinet M | Shelf 2 | No. 10

Curwen Press, The. London, 1923.
Title: A new pilgrimage. Published privately at the Savoy Hotel, London, 1923.
Brief account of the Shrine of London: The Abraham Lincoln Room, at The Hotel Savoy. Has illus. of bust of Abraham Lincoln.
Colophon: Printed at the Curwen Press.

Boards; 9-1/8 x 6 in.

IMPRINTS, England

Cabinet M | Shelf 2 | No. 14

Curwen Press, The. London, 1924.
Title: A bibliography of the first editions of books by William Butler Yeats. Compiled by A.J.A. Symons. The First Edition Club.... London, W.C. 1, 1924.
Imprint: Made and printed in England at the Curwen Press, Plaistow, London, E. 13.

IMPRINTS, England

Cabinet M | Shelf 2 | No. 15

Curwen Press, The. London, 1924.
Title: Catalogue Raisonne of books printed at The Curwen Press, 1920-1923. With an introduction by Holbrook Jackson. The Medici Society Limited.
Has specimen pages, title pages, and illus.
Colophon: Printed at The Curwen Press. Plaistow. E.13. With device.

Boards; 8-7/8 x 6 x $\frac{1}{4}$ in.

IMPRINTS, England

Cabinet M | Shelf 2 | No. 13

Curwen Press, The. London, 1924.
Title: The discovery: A comedy in five acts, written by Mrs. Frances Sheridan...London. Chatto & Windus. 1924.
Imprint: Printed in England at the Curwen Press. Plaistow, E. 13.

Paper over boards; 8 x 5-1/8 x $\frac{1}{2}$ in.

IMPRINTS, England

Cabinet K | Shelf 6 | No. 13

Dalziel Brothers: Camden Press. London, 1865.

see
WOOD ENGRAVINGS. Dalziels' Illustrated Goldsmith...London, 1865.

IMPRINTS, England

Cabinet E | Shelf 3 | No. 78

Daniel, Roger. Cambridge, 1644.
Title: Apxaionomia, sive de precis Anglorum legibus libro...in lucern vocati, Gulielmo Lambardo, interprete. [Bibliography of the laws of the British kings, years 712 to 1135]
Imprint: Cantabrigiae: Ex officina Rogeri Daniel, celeberrimae Academiae Typographie, 1644.

Calf; 14 x $9\frac{1}{4}$ in.

IMPRINTS, England

Cabinet M | Shelf 2 | No. 16

Daniel Press, The. H. Daniel, Oxford, 1885.
Title: Love's Graduate. A comedy by John Webster.
Imprint: Printed at The Private Press of H. Daniel. Fellow of Worcester College. Oxford, 1885.

Boards; $8\frac{3}{4}$ x 7 in.

IMPRINTS, England

Cabinet M | Shelf 2 | No. 17

Daniel Press, The. Oxford, 1901.
Title: Through human eyes. Poems by A Buckton.
Imprint: Daniel: Oxford: 1901.

Paper; $9\frac{1}{2}$ x $7\frac{1}{4}$ in.

IMPRINTS, England

Cabinet M | Shelf 2 | No. 18

Daniel Press, The. H. Daniel, Oxford, 1919.
Title: The recreations of his age. By Sir Nicholas Bacon.
Imprint: Daniel: Oxford: MCMIII (Issued 1919)
This book was issued by Leslie Chaundy, bookseller, Oxford, who purchased upon the death of Dr. Daniel all the remaining works of the Daniel Press.

Paper; 10 x 7-3/8 in.

IMPRINTS, England

Cabinet X | Shelf 4 | No. 45

Darby, J. London, 1698.

see
LIBERTY OF PRINTING. Great Britain. Letter to a member of parliament....

IMPRINTS, England

Cabinet T | Shelf 5 | No. 1

Davidson, G.H. London, 1837.
Title: Inquiry into the nature and form of books of the ancients...By John Andrews (J. Hannett).
Imprint: London: G.H. Davidson, Printer, Tudor Street, Blackfriars Bridge.

Levant, stamped; $6\frac{1}{2}$ x $4\frac{3}{4}$ x $\frac{5}{8}$ in.

IMPRINTS, England

Cabinet 68 Shelf No. 10

Day and Son, London, 1856
Title: The grammar of ornament...By Owen Jones.
Imprint: Printed in colours by Day and Son. London, 1856.

Morocco; gilt, 22¾ x 15 x 2 in.

IMPRINTS, England

Cabinet L Shelf 3 No. 4

Dicey, William, London, 1737
Title: Fables and other short poems...
Imprint: Printed and sold by William and Cluer Dicey...

With 100 copperplate engravings.

Calf, stamped; 8½ x 5¾ in.

IMPRINTS, England.

Cabinet PP Shelf 1 No. 6

Edwards, R. London, 1806
Title: The bibliographical miscellany...By Adam Clark
Imprint: London: Printed for W. Baynes, Paternoster Row (by R. Edwards, Printer)...

Half calf; 7½ x 4½ x 1-5/8 in.

IMPRINTS, England

Cabinet E Shelf 2 No. 12

Daye, John. London 1573.
Title: Johannis Parkhursti ludicra sive epigrammata Juvenilia.
Imprint: Londini apud Johannem Dayeum, Typographum. An.1573.

IMPRINTS, England

Cabinet M Shelf 2 No. 20

Doves Press, The. T.J. Cobden-Sanderson and Emery Walker, n.d.

Prospectuses.

In buckram case; 10½ x 7½ x 1½ in.

IMPRINTS, England.

Cabinet M Shelf 2 No. 21

Eragny Press. Lucien and Esther Pissarro. London, 1901.
Title: Emile Verhaeren. Les Petits vieux.
Colophon: Le frontispiece en conleur et les lettres ornees ont ete dessines par Lucien Pissarro et graves sur bois par Lucien et Esther Pissarro. Printer Mark.

Paper over boards; 4-7/8 x 6-3/8 x 3/8 in.

IMPRINTS, England

Cabinet M Shelf 3 No. 18

De La More Press, The. Alexander Moring. London, n.d.
Title: The Cloud, Skylark, and Ode to the West Wind, By P.B. Shelley.
Imprint: London: At the De La More Press, 32 George Street, Hanover Square, W.

Booklet, limp cloth; 5¾ x 3-5/8 in.

IMPRINTS, England

Cabinet M Shelf 5 No. 12

Doves Press, The. T.J. Cobden-Sanderson and Emery Walkers. London, 1903-1904.
Title: The English Bible containing the Old and New Testament....now reprinted...For The Syndics of The University Press, Cambridge. 5 vols.
Colophon: Printed by T.J. Cobden-Sanderson and Emery Walker at The Doves Press. No. 1 The Terrace, Hammersmith...vol. 1 dated Dec. 1902. vol. II, Oct. 15, 1903. vol. III, May 13, 1904. vol. IV, Sept. 1, 1904. vol. V, Oct. 19, 1904.
Vellum boards; 13 x 9¼ in.

IMPRINTS, England

Cabinet M Shelf 2 No. 22

Eragny Press, The. Lucien and Esther Pissarro. London, 1902.
Title: Choix de sonnets de P. De Ronsard.
Colophon: Le frontispiece a ete dessine et grave sur bois par Lucien Pissarro. La bordure et les lettres ornees ont ete dessinees par L. Pissarro et gravess sur bois par Esther Pissarro...acheve d'imprimer en Juillet 1902 sur leurs presses, The Brook, Hammersmith, London, W. Printer Mark.

Boards; 8¼ x 5-7/8 x ½ in.

IMPRINTS, England

Cabinet M Shelf 3 No. 17

De La More Press. Alexander Moring, London, 1895.
Title: The nut-brown maid. From the original version in the famous Percy Ballad.
Colophon: Printed by The De La More Press, Ltd. 32 George Street, Hanover Square, London, W. n.d.

Booklet, limp cloth; 5¾ x 3-5/8 in.

IMPRINTS, England

Cabinet M Shelf 2 No. 19

Doves Press, The. Cobden-Sanderson and Emery Walker. London, 1907.
Title: Areopagitica; A speech of Mr. John Milton for the liberty of unlicenc'd printing.....
Colophon: Printed at the Doves Press by T.J. Cobden-Sanderson and Emery Walker...Compositors: J.H. Mason and W. Jenkins. Pressmen: Richard Cobden-Sanderson and A.H. Lewis Published June MDCCCCVII.

Parchment; 9¼ x 6½ x ½ in.

IMPRINTS, England

Cabinet M Shelf 2 No. 23

Eragny Press, The. Lucien and Esther Pissarro, London, 1903.
Title: C'est D'Auccassin et de Nicolete.
Colophon: The frontispiece has been designed and engraved by Lucien Pissaro. This is the last book printed in the Vale Type by Esther and Lucien Pissarro at the Eragny Press, The Brook, Hammersmith, May, 1903. Printer Mark.

Printed paper over boards; 8¾ x 6 in.

IMPRINTS, England

Cabinet M Shelf 3 No. 19

De La More Press. Alexander Moring, London, 1902.
Title: Hand and Soul. By Dante Gabriel Rosetti.
Imprint: London: At the De La More Press, 298 Regent Street, W. 1902.

Booklet, paper; 5¾ x 3-5/8 in.

IMPRINTS, England

Cabinet R Shelf 1 No. 33

Dryden Press (J. Davy & Sons), London, 1881.
Benjamin Franklin's life and writings: A bibliographical essay on the Steven's collection of books and manuscripts relating to Doctor Franklin, by Henry Stevens, London 1881. Illus.

Cloth; 11¼ x 7¾ in. pp. (VIII), 40.

IMPRINTS, England

Cabinet M Shelf 2 No. 24

Eragny Press, The. Lucien and Esther Pissarro. London, 1911.
Title: Poems tires du livre de jade. By Judith Gautier. Col. illus. by L. Pissarro.
Colophon: In this, the 14th book printed in the Brook Type, the colored illustrations and ornaments have been designed by Lucien Pissarro & engraved on the wood by Lucien & Esther Pissarro. The book has been printed by E. and L. Pissarro at their Eragny Press. September 1911...Printer Mark.

cont'd

IMPRINTS, England

Cabinet M Shelf 3 No. 20

De La More Press. Alexander Moring, London, 1904.
Title: Goethe on Shakespeare. Being selections from Carlyles translation of Wilhelm Meister.
Imprint: London: At The De La More Press, 32 George Street, Hanover Square, W. 1904.

Booklet, limp boards; 5¾ x 3-5/8 in.

IMPRINTS, England

Cabinet E Shelf 4 No. 7

Du-Gardianis, London, 1651.
Title: Joannis Miltoni, Angli, pro populo Anglicano defensio...
Imprint: Londini, typis Du-Gardianis. Anno Domini 1651.

Calf; 13 x 9 x 1 in. Brunet 3, 1731.

IMPRINTS, England cont'd

Cabinet M Shelf 2 No. 24

Printed on Roman vellum in red, grey and gold.

Limp lambskin, Japanese fashion; 7-5/8 x 5-1/8 in.

IMPRINTS, England

Cabinet M Shelf 2 No. 32

Essex House Press, The. C.R. Ashbee, Campden, Gloucestershire, v.d.
Prospectuses from The Essex House Press.

In Buckram case; 10 x 7½ x 1½ in.

IMPRINTS, England cont'd

Cabinet M Shelf 2 No. 28

Drawings by E.H. New and other designs reproduced from the 1750 edition. Caslon Type.

Linen boards; 12 x 9 x 1¼ in.

IMPRINTS, England

Cabinet E Shelf 3 No. 7

Field, Richard. London, 1616.

See Early Printing in England. London, 1616, Richard Field.

IMPRINTS, England

Cabinet M Shelf 2 No. 25

Essex House Press, The. C.R. Ashbee, London, 1901.
Title: American sheaves and English seed corn being a series of addresses delivered in the United States 1900-1901, by C.R. Ashbee.
Colophon: Here endeth...printed under my care at the Essex House Press, in the same year, and now issued...
"Endeavour" type in black and red.

Vellum: 8½ x 6-1/8 in.

IMPRINTS, England

Cabinet M Shelf 2 No. 29

Essex House Press, The. C.R. Ashbee, Gloucestershire, 1904.
Title: The Imitation of Christ by Thomas a Kempis.
Colophon:...This book has been printed at the Essex House Press, Campden, Glos., under the care of C.R. Ashbee, by whom also is the block which was cut on the plank by Alec. Miller. A.D.MDCCCCIIII.
Printed in Prayer Book type.

Brown calf with tabs; 11¾ x 8⅝ x 1 in.

IMPRINTS, England

Cabinet QQ Shelf 4 No. 16

Field & Tuer, London, n.d. circa 1870.
Title: Curiosities of ale and beer...By John Bickerdyke.
Imprint: London, Field & Tuer, the Leadenhall Press. E.C., n. d. circa 1870.

Parchment; 10¼ x 6-5/8 x 1½ in.

IMPRINTS, England

Cabinet M Shelf 2 No. 26

Essex House Press, The. C.R. Ashbee, London, 1901.
Title: An endeavour towards the teaching of John Ruskin and William Morris. Wood engravings & cuts.
Colophon:...Being an account of the work and aims of the Guild of Handicraft by C.R. Ashbee, is the first book printed at the Essex House Press in the new type designed by him...An. Dom. MDCCCCI.

Vellum; 8¼ x 6 in.

IMPRINTS, England

Cabinet M Shelf 2 No. 30

Essex House Press, The. C.R. Ashbee, Gloucestershire, 1905.
Title: Browning's Flight of the Duchess.
Colophon: Here ends R. Browning's Flight of the Duchess....Printed among the great poems of the Language under the care of C.R. Ashbee at the Essex House Press, Campden, Gloucestershire, 1905.

Vellum; 7½ x 5 in.

IMPRINTS, England

Cabinet NN Shelf 5 No. 9

Field & Tuer, Ye Leadenhalle Presse. London, circa 1881.

see
WILLIAMS...Journalistic jumbles, or trippings in type...

IMPRINTS, England.

Cabinet M Shelf 2 No. 27

Essex House Press, The. C.R. Ashbee, London, 1901.
Title: Milton's Comus.
Colophon: Printed under the care of C.R. Ashbee, at the Essex House Press, with a wood block frontispiece by Reginald Savage, A.D.MDCCCCI ......
Caslon type in black and red. Printed on vellum.

Vellum; 7½ x 5 in.

IMPRINTS, England

Cabinet M Shelf 2 No. 31

Essex House Press, The. C.R. Ashbee. Campden, Gloucestershire, 1909.
Title: The Private Press: A study in idealism. To which is added a bibliography of the Essex House Press.
Colophon:....has been printed by the courtesy and at the expense of the Club of Odd Volumes Boston, Mass. The Essay is in substance an address....delivered before the Club by C.R. Ashbee in February of the present year and now printed by him at the Norman Chapel ...Nov., 1909

Boards; 10¼ x 8 in. cont'd

IMPRINTS, England

Cabinet T Shelf 4 No. 92

Field & Tuer, Ye Leadenhalle Press, London, 1884.
Title: Quads for authors, editors and devils. Edited by And. W. Tuer. Enlarged edition.
Imprint: London: Field and Tuer. (Ye Leadenhalle Press) Simpkin: Hamilton. 1884.
Inserted in back cover is a facsimile miniature edition, the size of which is 1-5/8 x 1-1/8 in.

Vellum; 6 x 4-3/4 in.

IMPRINTS, England

Cabinet M Shelf 5 No. 15

Essex House Press. C.R. Ashbee, London, 1901.
Title: The Prayer Book of Edward VII. [American ed.]
Colophon: Here ends the authorized American edition...The designs and the types are those of the English edition...and are the work of C.R. Ashbee...The printing was done at the Plimpton Press, Norwood, Massachusetts under the supervision of Angus F. Mackay....

Morocco; 14¾ x 11 in.

IMPRINTS, England cont'd

Cabinet M Shelf 2 No. 31

Reproductions of initials, cuts, and devices. Printed in black and red in "Endeavour" type.

Boards; 10½ x 8 in.

IMPRINTS, England

Cabinet D Shelf 1 No. 23

Figgins, Vincent and James. London, 1855.
Title: Game and Playe of Chesse. Facsimile of the third book printed by or for Caxton probably in 1474. [Reproduction of the first work printed in England]. Printed and published by James and Vincent Figgins. London, 1855.

Calf; 11¼ x 8-3/8 x 7/8 in.

IMPRINTS, England

Cabinet M Shelf 2 No. 28

Essex House Press, The. C.R. Ashbee, Gloucestershire, 1903.
Title: The life and works of Sir Christopher Wren. From the Parentalia or Memoirs by his son Christopher.
Colophon...first published in 1750 and now reprinted at the Essex House Press, Campden, Gloucestershire, 1903....edited from the original by Ernest J. Enthoven and carried out under the supervision of C.R. Ashbee.

cont'd

IMPRINTS, ENGLAND

Cabinet L Shelf 4 No. 22

Evans, Edmund. London, 1869.

See Color Printing. Gems from painters and poets...London (1869).

IMPRINTS, England

Cabinet M Shelf 4 No. 2.0b

First Edition Club, London W.C. Relating to the history of the. Wirh rules and list of exhibtors and books published. n.d. circa 1928.

Small brochures, in manila envelope.

IMPRINTS, ENGLAND

Cabinet T Shelf 1 No. 65

Fisher, S. London, 1797
Title: Typographical Antiquities...Extracted from the best authorities by Henry Lemoine.
Imprint: Printed and sold by S. Fisher, No. 10, St. John's Lane, Clerkenwell, London.

Half morocco, $7\frac{1}{2}$ x 4-5/8 in.

IMPRINTS, England

Cabinet L Shelf 3 No. 11

GUTCH, JOHN MATHEW, Bristol, 1827.

See GUTCH, JOHN MATHEW. Observations on notes upon the writings of the ancients ...

IMPRINTS, England

Cabinet E Shelf 4 No. 30

Herringman, Henry. London, 1661.

See Early Printing in England. London. 1661.

IMPRINTS, England

Cabinet E Shelf 2 No. 58

Fisher, Thomas. London, 1600.
Title: A midsommer nights dream...William Shakespeare [Facsimile].
Imprint: Imprinted London, for Thomas Fisher.

Boards; $8\frac{3}{4}$ x 6-1/8 x $\frac{1}{2}$ in.

IMPRINTS, England.

Cabinet K Shelf 4 No. 41

Hansard, T. C. London, 1819.

See BANK NOTE PRINTING. Report ... on the mode of preventing the forgery of bank notes ...

IMPRINTS, England

Cabinet A Shelf 3 No. 1

Hetherington, H. London, 1840.

See Periodicals, England. Odd Fellow (The)...1840.

IMPRINTS, England

Cabinet M Shelf 2 No. 33

Fleuron Limited. London, 1927.
Title: Fleuron Books: A list of Fleuron Books to be published in the Autumn 1927.

Paper; 7-1/8 x $4\frac{3}{4}$ in.

IMPRINTS, England

Cabinet QQ Shelf 3 No. 29

Hansard and Sons, Luke. London, 1825.

see BUTLER, CHARLES. Erasmus, the life of ...

IMPRINTS, England

Cabinet FF Shelf 2 No. 10

Hibbert, Julian. Kentish-Town, 1828

See Greek Printing, England. Hibbert ...

IMPRINTS, England

Cabinet F Shelf 4 No. 23

Gent, Thomas. York, 1735.
Title: Annales Regioduni Hullini: or, the History of Kingston-upon-Hull...Faithfully collected by Thomas Gent.
Imprint: Sold at the Printing-Office, near the Star in Stone-Gate. York.

Leather; $7\frac{3}{4}$ x 5 x 1 in.

IMPRINTS, England

Cabinet E Shelf 3 No. 47

Haviland, John. London, 1632.
Title: The essays or counsels, civill and morall, of Francis Lo. Verulam, Viscount St. Alban. (Francis Bacon)
Imprint: Printed by John Haviland, in the little old Bayley, 1632.

Calf; $7\frac{1}{2}$ x $5\frac{1}{2}$ x 1-1/8 in.

IMPRINTS, ENGLAND

Cabinet FF Shelf 1 No. 58

Hodgson, S. Newcastle, 1819.
Title: Biographical memoirs of William Ged:
Imprint Newcastle; Printed by S. Hodgson. Union Street. 1819

Half morocco; $7\frac{3}{4}$ x $5\frac{1}{4}$ in.

IMPRINTS, England

Cabinet M Shelf 2 No. 35

Golden Cockerel Press, The. Waltham Saint Lawrence, Berkshire, 1923.
Title: The XI Books of the Golden Asse of Lucius Apuleius...Translated out of Latine in English, by W. Adlington.
Colophon: Printed at the Golden Cockerel Press... and finished on the 13th day of August, 1923. Seen through the Press by G.S. Taylor.

Boards; $10\frac{1}{4}$ x 7-7/8 x $1\frac{1}{4}$ in.

IMPRINTS, England

Cabinet M Shelf 2 No. 38

Hazel, Watson and Viney, Ld., London and Aylesbury, 1922.
Title: The Liar. A comedy in three acts. By Carlo Goldoni. Translated...By Grace Lovat Fraser. Decorations by C. Lovat Fraser. Introduction by E. Gordon Craig.
Imprint: Printed in Greek Britain by Hazell, Watson & Viney Ld., London and Aylesbury.

Cloth; $9\frac{1}{4}$ x 7 x $\frac{1}{2}$ in.

IMPRINTS, England

Cabinet M Shelf 2 No. 39.04

Hone, William, London, 1819
Title: The political house that Jack built. With 13 cuts. Fourth edition.
Imprint: London. Printed by and for William Hone, Ludgate Hill, 1819.

Brochure, in manila envelope

IMPRINTS, England

Cabinet M Shelf 2 No. 36

Golden Cockerel Press, The. Robert Gibbings Waltham Saint Lawrence, Berkshire, 1927.
Title: Men & Manners by William Shenstone....
Colophon: This book was printed by Robert Gibbings at the Golden Cockerel Press....& completed on the 27th day of April, 1927.... Printer Mark.

Decorated paper over boards; $7\frac{3}{4}$ x $5\frac{1}{4}$ x 5/8 in.

IMPRINTS, England

Cabinet M Shelf 2 No. 39

Henry, George and Co., London, 1850.
Title: The Holy Bible, translated from the Latin Vulgate...with useful notes, critical, historical controversial and explanatory...By the late Rev. Geo. Leo Haydock...Two vols. in one. Illus.
Imprint: London: George Henry and Co., 64 Bartholomew Close. [1850]

Tooled calf; $12\frac{1}{2}$ x $9\frac{3}{4}$ x 4 in.

IMPRINTS, England

Cabinet E Shelf 2 No. 66

Islip, Adam. London, 1602.

See Early Printing in England. London, 1602. Adam Islip.

IMPRINTS, England

Cabinet E Shelf 3 No. 22

Jaggard, William. London, 1623.

See Early Printing in England. London, 1623.

Jaggard printed the Shakespeare First Folio. Preface to this book is an interesting defense of his ability as a printer.

IMPRINTS, England

Cabinet M Shelf 2 No. 43

Jones, Geo. W. The Dolphin Press. London, 1922.
Title: The Hour of Magic and other poems by W.H. Davis. Decorated by William Nicholson. Publishers Mark, Jonathan Cape, London.
Colophon:...Now printed for the first time in Garamond Type at The Sign of The Dolphin & published at Eleven Gower Street by Jonathan Cape, September, MDCCCCXXII.

Boards; 7⅞ x 5¼ in.

IMPRINTS, England

Cabinet M Shelf 2 No. 49

Jones, Geo. W. The Dolphin Press, London, 1924.
Title: A short history of the Castle Lodge of Harmony No.26...Constituted 22nd January 1724.
Imprint: Privately printed by Brother George W. Jones at The Sign of The Dolphin in Gough Square, Fleet Street, London, E. C.4, England, 1924.

Cloth; 10¼ x 6½ x ⅜ in.

IMPRINTS, England

Cabinet M Shelf 2 No. 61

Jones, George W., at the Sign of the Dolphin 1921, 1924, 1925, 1929.

Collection of menus, catalogues, etc.

Items in manila envelope

IMPRINTS, England

Cabinet M Shelf 2 No. 44

Jones, Geo. W. The Dolphin Press. London, 1922.
Title: Richard Vincent Sutton: A record of his life together with extracts from his private papers.
Colophon: Printed by George W. Jones at The Sign of The Dolphin in Gough Square, Fleet Street, London, and finished this Eleventh Day of November, One Thousand Nine Hundred and Twenty-Two.

Boards, cloth back; 11¼ x 8¾ x 1¼ in.

IMPRINTS, England

Cabinet M Shelf 5 No. 17

Jones, Georg W. London, 1927.
Broadside: First page of the Mainz Psalter of 1457 printed by Fust and Schoeffer. Reproduced by wood cutting from the original copy on vellum in the King's Library of the British Museum...A remembrance of the International Typographic Council, Sept. 14, 1927.

In folder marked "Broadsides, Printers (Various) England. 1927--

IMPRINTS, England

Cabinet M Shelf 2 No. 40

Jones, Geo. W. The Dolphin Press, London, 1918.
Title: Pearl: An English Poem of the fourteenth Century.
Colophon: Here ends Pearl: re-set in Modern English by Israel Gollancz, and dedicated by him to the British Red Cross Society... imprinted in the Humanistic Types (by exclusive arrangement...) by Geo. W. Jones at The Sign Dolphin, in Gough Square, Fleet Street, London, in the year one thousand 1918 Device

Boards; 9¾ x 7¼ x ½ in.

IMPRINTS, England.

Cabinet M Shelf 2 No. 46

Jones, George W, The Sign of The Dolphin, London. 1923.
Title: A Calendar for the year 1923 containing twelve plates representing the twelve ages of man, which appeared in a Book of Hours printed by Thielman Kerver in Paris in 1523.
Imprint: Published by Linotype & Machinery Ltd. Kingsway, London.

(Cont'd.)

IMPRINTS, England

Cabinet M Shelf 2 No. 50

Jones, George W: The Sign of the Dolphin. London, 1928.
Title: Catalogue of the Library of Constance Astley at Brinsop Court, Herefordshire.
Colophon...printed by George W. Jones at the Sign of the Dolphin, London. The type for the text in Linotype Granjon Old Face... The printing of the Catalogue was completed on the sixteenth day of November, one thousand and nine hundred and twenty-eight. [One of fifty copies. Presented to the Library by Mrs. Astley]

Vellum; 13¼ x 9½ in. cont'd

IMPRINTS, England

Cabinet M Shelf 2 No. 41

Jones, Geo. W. The Dolphin Press, London, 1919.
Title: The Grammar School of King Edward the 6th .....in Stratford-Upon-Avon. Illus.
Colophon: This Brochure...has been printed in his Venezia type, a facsimile of that used by Nicolas Jenson in Venice in 1470, by Geo. W. Jones at The Sign of the Dolphin in Gough Square, Fleet Street, London, E.C., One Thousand Nine Hundred and Nineteen.

Paper; 11¼ x 8 in.

Cabinet M Shelf 2 No. 46

Colophon: Composed on the Linotype Composing Machine in the Benedictine Series of Type ... Printed on a Miehle by George W. Jones. ...

Boards; 11 x 7 x ¼ in.

IMPRINTS, England cont'd

Cabinet M Shelf 2 No. 50

Library by Mrs. Astley].

Vellum; 13¼ x 9½ in.

IMPRINTS, England

Cabinet M Shelf 2 No. 42

Jones, Geo. W. The Dolphin Press, London, 1921.
Title: The Deserted Village. By Oliver Goldsmith.
Colophon: The production of the woodcuts in this edition, which are facsimiles of those engraved by the Bewicks for Bulmer's 1795 edition, has been superintended by Geo. W. Jones, who has linotyped the work and printed it on a Miehle Press at his office at The Sign of the Dolphin.....London.

Paper 12¼ x 9 in

IMPRINTS, England

Cabinet M Shelf 2 No. 47

Jones, Geo. W. The Dolphin Press. London, 1924.
Title: Gilgamesh: A dream of the eternal quest. By Zabelle C. Boyajian. Illus. by the author ...
Imprint: Printed and published by George W. Jones at The Sign of The Dolphin in Gough Square, Fleet Street, London, MCMXXIV.

Cloth; 12½ x 10¼ x 1 in.

IMPRINTS, England

Cabinet M Shelf 2 No. 51

Jones, George W. "The Sign of the Dolphin," London, 1929.
Title: A distinguished family of French printers of the 16th century. Henri & Robert Estienne Mergenthaler Linotype Company. Brooklyn, New York, 1929.
Colophon: Printed in London by George W. Jones at "The Sign of the Dolphin." in Gough Square.

Boards; vellum back; 13-3/8 x 8-5/8 in. In protective case.

IMPRINTS, England

Cabinet M Shelf 2 No. 45

Jones, Geo. W. The Dolphin Press, London 1922.
Title: Brasiliae Britannia. An illustrated Record of British participation...to commemorate the Centenary of Brazilian Independence, 1822-1922. With photographs.
Colophon: Printed by Geo. W. Jones at The Sign of The Dolphin, Gough Square, Fleet Street, London, E.C.

Paper board; 11½ x 8½ in.

IMPRINTS, England

Cabinet M Shelf 2 No. 48

Jones, Geo. W. The Dolphin Press, London. 1924.
Title: The pavilion of his majesty's Government, The British Empire Exhibition, 1924. With photographs.
Colophon: Printed by Geo. W. Jones, at The Sign of The Dolphin...London, E.C. and published by H.M. Stationery Office.

Paper board; 11½ x 8½ in.

IMPRINTS, England

Cabinet T Shelf 6 No. 59

Jones, George W. At the sign of the Dolphin London, 1929.
Title: Henri and Robert Estienne. A distinguished family of printers of the 16th century n.a.n.
Imprint: London, Linotype Machinery Ltd. 1929. Printed by George W. Jones.

Boards; 13-3/8 x 8½ in.

IMPRINTS, England

Cabinet M Shelf 2 No. 53

Jones, George W. The Sign of the Dolphin. London, 1930.
Title: The Grand Inquisitor. By F.M. Dostoevsky. Translated by S.S. Koteliansky. The Aquila Press.
Colophon...Printed in Linotype Estienne type... by George W. Jones at the Sign of the Dolphin. London.

Boards; vellum back; 9¾ x 6½ x 3/8 in.

IMPRINTS, England

Cabinet M Shelf 2 No. 52

Jones, George W. The Dolphin Press, London, 1930.
Title: The odes and sonnets of Garcilaso de la Vega. An English verse rendered by James Cleugh. The Aquila Press, 1930.
Colophon:...the first book to appear in this country in Linotype Estienne Old Face type, and has been printed for the Aquila Press by the designer, George W. Jones.

Boards, vellum back; 11-5/8 x 8 x 5/8 in.

IMPRINTS, England

Cabinet M Shelf 2 No. 54

Jones, George W: The Sign of the Dolphin. London, 1930.
Title: A true description of all trades. Published in Frankfort in the year 1568. With six of the illustrations by Jobst Amman.
Imprint: Mergenthaler Linotype Co. New York, 1930.
Colophon: Printed in linotype Granjon.
"George W. Jones of London, is the author and printer of this exquisite and interesting little book. He is also the owner of the woodcuts." H.L.B. Oct. 1930.

Boards; 7-3/4 x 5-1/8 x ½ in.

IMPRINTS, ENGLAND.

Cabinet M Shelf 2 No. 57

Jones, Geo. W. At The Sign of The Dolphin. London, 1931.
Title: The Georgics of Vergil. Translated by R. D. Blackmore.
Imprint: London. Published by George W. Jones.

Printed in Linotype Estienne, designed by Geo. W. Jones.

Quarter vellum; 11-3/8 x 7¾ x ¾ in.

IMPRINTS, England

Cabinet M Shelf 2 No. 58

Jones, George W. The Sign of the Dolphin. London, n.d., (1931).
Title: The message of one of England's greatest poets to a printer and printers...Portrait frontispiece.
Colophon:..Printed in Linotype Estienne roman and italic by its designer, George W. Jones ...

Boards; 11 x 7-5/8 x ½ in.

IMPRINTS, England

Cabinet M Shelf 2 No. 56

Jones, Geo. W. The Sign of the Dolphin. London, 1931.
Title: Robert Granjon, 16th century typecutter and printer. Mergenthaler Linotype Co. Brooklyn, New York.
Colophon: Press of George W. Jones, at the Sign of the Dolphin in Gough Square, London, England.
Has device of Robert Granjon.

Boards, vellum back; 13½ x 8½ in. In slip case.

IMPRINTS, England.

Cabinet M Shelf 2 No. 55

Jones, Geo. W. At the Sign of the Dolphin Press, 1931.
Set of plates from the work "The Leonard Gow Collection of Chinese Porcelain"

In Folder; 13 x 10¼ in.

IMPRINTS, England

Cabinet M Shelf 5 No. 18

Jones, Geo. W. The Sign of the Dolphin. London, 1932.
Title: Dr. Johnson Calendar for 1932. From Geo. W. Jones.

Color illustrations.

Item in manila envelope.

IMPRINTS, ENGLAND

Cabinet M Shelf 2 No. 59

Jones, George W. at The Sign of the Dolphin. London, 1932.
Title: Souvenir menu of presentation dinner to Alderman Sir George Wyatt Truscott, Bt.
In celebration of fifty years service to The Corporation of London.
Imprint: Press of George W. Jones at The Sign of the Dolphin in Gough Square.

Booklet, paper; 11¼ x 7¾ in. Item in envelope.

IMPRINTS, England

Cabinet M Shelf 2 No. 60

Jones, Geo. W., at The Sign of The Dolphin London, 1932.
Title: Souvenir menu of presentation dinner to Alderman Sir George Wyat Truscott, Pt.

Item in envelope.

IMPRINTS, England

Cabinet M Shelf 2 No. 62

Jones, George W., at the Sign of the Dolphin London, 1933.
Title: Royal College of Arts Students' Magazine. June, 1923, New Series, No.VI.
Imprint, with printer mark, on back cover.

Brochure; 10 x 6 in.

IMPRINTS, England

Cabinet E Shelf 2 No. 83

Kellam, Lawrence. Doway, 1609-1610.
Title: The Holy Bible. Faithfully translated into English...By the English College of Doway. 2 vols.
Imprint: Printed at Doway by Lawrence Kellam at the signe of the holie Lamb.

Vellum; 8-7/8 x 7 in. each vol.

IMPRINTS, England

Cabinet M Shelf 5 No. 23

Kelmscott Press. William Morris, Kelmscott, v.d.

Prospectuses and Proof Sheets.

Boards; 15½ x 12¼ in.

IMPRINTS, England

Cabinet M Shelf 3 No. 8

Kelmscott Press. William Morris. Kelmscott, v.d.
Prospectuses of the Kelmscott Press, Upper Mall, Hammersmith: Items with specimens of Golden Troy and Chaucer types.

Buckram case; 9-1/8 x 7¼ x ¾ in.

IMPRINTS, England

Cabinet M Shelf 3 No. 3

Kelmscott Press. William Morris. Kelmscott, 1892.
Title: The defense of Guenevere, and other poems by William Morris.
Colophon: Here ends...by William Morris; and printed by him at the Kelmscott Press, 14, Upper Mall. Hammersmith; & finished on the 2nd day of April, of the year 1892. Printer Mark.
Printed with Morris' Golden Types in black and red.

Half morocco; 8½ x 5-7/8 x 3/4 in.

IMPRINTS, England

Cabinet M Shelf 3 No. 2 3 vols.

Kelmscott Press, William Morris, Kelmscott, 1892.
Title: The Golden Legend of William Caxton. 3 vols.
Colophon: Here ends this new edition...printed by me William Morris at the Kelmscott Press, Upper Mall, Hammersmith, in the County of Middlesex, and finished on the 12th day of September of the year 1892.
Golden type with wood cut title and two woodcuts designed by Sir E. Burne-Jones.

Boards; 11-3/4 x 8½ in.

IMPRINTS, England

Cabinet M Shelf 3 No. 5

Kelmscott Press. William Morris, Kelmscott, 1893.
Title: Maud, a monodrama. By Alfred Lord Tennyson.
Colophon: Printed by William Morris at the Kelmscott Press, Upper Mall, Hammersmith, in the Country of Middlesex, and finished on the 11th day of August, 1893.
Golden type in black and red.

Limp vellum; 8¼ x 5¾ in.

IMPRINTS, England

Cabinet M Shelf 3 No. 4

Kelmscott Press. William Morris. Kelmscott, 1893.
Title: The poems of William Shakespeare printed after the original copies...
Colophon: Here ends...and printed by me William Morris at the Kelmscott Press, Upper Mall. Hammersmith, in the County of Middlesex, and finished on the 17th day of January, 1893. Printer Mark.

Limp vellum; 8¼ x 5¾ x 1 in.

IMPRINTS, England

Cabinet M Shelf 3 No. 6

Kelmscott Press. William Morris, Kelmscott, 1896.
Title: Laudes Beatae Mariae Virginis. [Latin poems].
Colophon: These poems are taken from a Psalter written by an English scribe...early in the 13th century. Printed by William Morris at the Kelmscott Press, Upper Mall, Hammersmith in the County of Middlesex......7th day of July, 1896. Printer Mark. Sold by William Morris at the Kelmscott Press.

cont'd

IMPRINTS, England cont'd

Cabinet M Shelf 3 No. 6

One of two books printed in which three colors were used by Morris.

Paper boards; 11½ x 8½ in.

IMPRINTS, England

Cabinet M Shelf 5 No. 20

Kelmscott Press. William Morris, 1896.
Title: The works of Geoffroy Chaucer.
Colophon: Here ends the books of...ornamented with pictures designed by Sir Edward Burne Jones, and engraved on wood by W.H. Hooper, Printed by me, William Morris, at the Kelmscott Press, Kelmscott, in the County of Middlesex. Finished on the 8th day of May, 1896.

Boards; 17 x 11¼ x 2½ in. In Cloth protective case.

IMPRINTS, England

Cabinet M Shelf 5 No. 22

Kelmscott Press. William Morris, Kelmscott, 1897.
Title: Facsimile Trial Pages. Kelmscott Edition of Froissart's Chronicles. Printed for Frederic & Bertha Goudy in June 1920, at the shop of William Rudge, New York City, by Thomas Hughes and Hugh Grannum.

Paper Boards; 17 x 12 in.

IMPRINTS, England

Cabinet M Shelf 3 No. 7

Kelmscott Press, William Morris. Kelmscott, 1897.
Title: The Waters of the Wondrous Isles. By William Morris.
Colophon:....It was printed at the Kelmscott Press.....and finished on the first day of April, 1897. The borders and ornaments were designed entirely by William Morris.... Kelmscott Mark. Sold by the Trustees of the late William Morris.
Chaucer Type in double columns; printed in black and red.

Limp vellum; 11¼ x 8¼ in.

IMPRINTS, England

Cabinet M Shelf 3 No. 9

Lanston Monotype Corporation, Ltd., London, 1928.
Title: Ben Jonson's English Grammar first published in 1640. Now reprinted 1928. With a prefatory note by Strickland Gibson, M.A. Facsimile title page.
Imprint: Printed and published by the Lanston Monotype Corporation Ltd., M.CM.XXVIII.
Includes specimen sheets of Poliphilus and Blado Italic types which were used in this reprint.

Paper boards; 6-3/4 x 4¼ in.

IMPRINTS, England

Cabinet M Shelf 3 No. 10

Lee Priory Press, Sir Egerton Brydges, proprietor; Johnson and Warwick, printers, Kent, 1813.
Title: The poems of Sir Walter Raleigh: Now first collected with introduction by Sir Egerton Brydges, K.J. Printed at the Private Press of Lee Priory by Johnson and Warwick, 1813.
Colophon: Printed by John Warwick, at the Private Press of Lee Priory.

Boards leather back & corners; 12 x 9-1/8 x 1-1/8 in.

IMPRINTS, England

Cabinet M Shelf 3 No. 11

Lee Priory Press. Sir Egerton Brydges, proprietor; John Warwick, printer, Kent, 1817.
Title: List of pictures at The Seat of T.B. Brudges Barrett, Esq., at Lee Priory in the Country of Kent.
Imprint: Printed at the Private Press at Lee Priory, by John Warwick. 1817.

Half morocco; 9 x 6 in.

IMPRINTS, England

Cabinet M Shelf 3 No. 12

Lee Priory Press. Sir Egerton Brydges, proprietor; John Warwick, printer, Kent, 1820.
Title: The Engravings on wood at Lee Priory printed on Chinese paper, with verses.
Imprint: Kent. Printed at the Private Press of Lee Priory. By John Warwick. 1820.

Boards; 10¼ x 8 in.

IMPRINTS, England

Cabinet M Shelf 3 No. 13

Lee Priory Press, Sir Egerton Brydges, proprietor; John Warwick, Printer, Kent, 1821.
Title: Letters from the Continent. By Sir Egerton Brydges, Bart, K.J. 2 vols.
Imprint: Kent. Printed at the private press of Lee Priory; by John Warwick. 1821.

Boards; 9¼ x 5-7/8 in.

IMPRINTS, ENGLAND.

Cabinet K Shelf 4 No. 44

Leighton, John, London, 1856.
Specimens of bank note printing.

Items in manila envelope.

IMPRINTS, England

Cabinet U Shelf 5 No. 70

London School of printing. 1923.
Title: Romance of the printing craft. A lecture delivered by R.A. Austen-Leigh. Oct. 12, 1923, at Stationers Hall.
Imprint: Printed by students of the London School of Printing, 61 Stamford Street, London, S.E. I.

Half morocco; 11-7/8 x 8-7/8 x ½ in.

IMPRINTS, England

Cabinet M Shelf 3 No. 14

London School of Printing. 1926-27.
Title: The romance of printing. Address by R.A. Austen-Leigh at Stationers' Hall, London E.C.4.
Imprint Colophon: Monotype set and printed by students of the London School of Printing and Kindred Trades, 61 Stamford Street, London, S.E. Session 1926-27.

Paper; 10¼ x 7 in.

IMPRINTS, England

Cabinet M Shelf 3 No. 15

Macbeth, Donald: The Artist's Press, Balham, London, 1921.
Title: The old Snuff House of Fribourg & Treyer. At the sign of The Rasp & Crown. London, S.W. 1720-1920. By George Evans. Illus.
Imprint preceding title page.....produced and printed by Donald Macbeth at the Artist's Press, Balham, London, S.W. January, 1921.

Boards; 9-7/8 x 6¾ in.

IMPRINTS, England.

Cabinet QQ Shelf 1 No. 12

McCreery, John Liverpool, 1803.
Title: The press, a poem published as a specimen of typography. By John McCreery.
Imprint: Liverpool: Printed by J. McCreery, Houghton-Street, and sold by Cadell and Davis, Strand, London. 1803.

Half morocco; 12 x 9½ x ½ in.

IMPRINTS, England

Cabinet M Shelf 3 No. 16

McCreery, J. Liverpool, 1805.
Title: The life and pontificate of Leo the Tenth. In four volumes. By William Roscoe. Portraits.
Imprint: Liverpool; printed by J. McCreery; for J. Cadell and W. Davis, Strand, London, 1805.
Has references concerning the introduction of printing in certain parts of Italy, establishment of the Greek Press in Rome, and the origin of engraving on copper.

Calf; 10¾ x 8½ in.

IMPRINTS, England

Cabinet I Shelf 1 No. 34

M'Creery, John, London, 1816, Imprint with printer mark.

See OTTLEY, WILLIAM YOUNG. Inquiry into the origin and early history of engraving... 2 vols. London, 1816.

IMPRINTS, England

Cabinet QQ Shelf 1 No. 13

McCreery, John. London, 1828.
Title: The press, a poem, in two parts, with other pieces. By John McCreery. Second edition. London. William Pickering.
Imprint: J. M'Creery, Tooks Court, Chancery Lane, London.

Half calf; 8 x 5-1/8 in.

IMPRINTS, ENGLAND.

Cabinet PP Shelf 1 No. 30

Manning and Smithson. London, 1834.
Title: A bibliographical catalogue of books privately printed ... By John Martin.
Imprint: London: J. and A. Arch; Payne and Foss; J. Rodwell, 1834.
Page 563: London: Printed by Manning and Smithson, London House Yard.

Calf; $8\frac{1}{2}$ x $5\frac{1}{2}$ x $1\frac{1}{4}$ in.

IMPRINTS, England

Cabinet PP Shelf 2 No. 3

Nicol, William, Shakspeare Press. London, 1823.
Title: A descriptive catalogue of the books printed in the 15th century...By T.F. Dibdin.
Imprint: London: Printed for the author by William Nicol, Shakspeare Press, 1823.

Boards, leather back; 10-7/8 x 7-1/8 x 1-1/8 in.

IMPRINTS, England

Cabinet M Shelf 3 No. 25

Nonesuch Press. Francis Meynell. London, 1924.
Title: The complete programme of the Nonesuch Press for MCXXIV. Printer Mark. 30 Gerrard Street, Soho, London.

$\frac{3}{4}$ Morocco; $12\frac{1}{2}$ x $8\frac{1}{4}$ in.

IMPRINTS, England

Cabinet 78 Shelf 1 No. 1

Martin, John. London, 1660.
Title: De atramentis cujuscunque generis... Auctore Pedro Mario Caneparìo.
Imprint: Londini, excudebat J.M. Impensis Jo. Martin, Ja. Alestry...ad insigne Campana, in Coemeterio Paulino, 1660.

Calf; 7-7/8 x 5-7/8 x 1-3/8 in. [Arber, T.C. 1., p.398].

IMPRINTS, England

Cabinet L Shelf 3 No. 7

Nichols, John, London, 1784

See EARLY PRINTING IN ENGLAND. London, 1784, John Nichols...

IMPRINTS, England

Cabinet M Shelf 3 No. 24

Nonesuch Press, The. Francis Meynell, London, 1924.
Title: The complete works of William Wycherley. Edited by Montague Summer. 4 vols.
Imprint: Soho. The Nonesuch Press. 30 Gerrard Street, W. MCMXXIV.

4 vols. Boards, linen backs; $10\frac{1}{4}$ x $7\frac{3}{4}$ in.

IMPRINTS, England

Cabinet F Shelf 4 No. 25

Martin, Robert [Successor to Baskerville], Birmingham, 1767.
Title: The chase: A poem by William Somerville.
Imprint: Birmingham: Printed by Robert Martin, and sold by A. Donaldson at his shop... London, 1767.

Paper boards; 9 x $6\frac{1}{4}$ x $\frac{3}{4}$ in.

IMPRINTS, England

Cabinet T Shelf 1 No. 27

Nichols, J. Son and Bentley. London, 1818.
Title: Life and errors of John Dunton.
Imprint: Printed by and for J. Nichols, Son and Bentley. London, 1818. (2 vols.)

Binding by Hayday: Calf, paneled, gilt edges; $8\frac{3}{4}$ x $5\frac{1}{2}$ in.

IMPRINTS, England

Cabinet M Shelf 3 No. 26

Nonesuch Press. Francis Meynell, London, 1924. (Curwen Press)
Title: Genesis. Twelve woodcuts by Paul Nash with the first chapter of Genesis. The Nonesuch Press. Soho (London), MCMXXIV.
Following title page:...The cuts are printed from the wood and the text is in Rudolf Koch's Neuland type...The Curwen Press for the Nonesuch Press.

Paper boards; $10\frac{1}{2}$ x $7\frac{1}{2}$ in.

IMPRINT, England

Cabinet M Shelf 3 No. 31

Meynell, Francis. London, 1930
Title: A.M. A keepsake for the A.I.G.A. from Francis Meynell. February 1930
Colophon: Printed and made in England in the types of Janson (Jenson) under the care of Francis Meynell.

Paper; 5-3/4 x 3-3/4 in.

IMPRINTS, England

Cabinet F Shelf 4 No. 10

Nicholson, John (Bookseller), London, 1715. [Printer unknown].
Title: The history of many memorable things lost ...(vol.2)
Imprint: London, printed for John Nicholson in Little-Britain, and sold by John Morphew.

Leather; $6\frac{1}{2}$ x 3-7/8 x $\frac{3}{4}$ in.

IMPRINTS, England

Cabinet M Shelf 3 No. 22

Nonesuch Press, The. Francis Meynell, London, 1924, Kynoch Press.
Title: Henry Vaughan. Silurist. Poems from Poems, Olor Iscanus....An Essay from The Mount of Olives. Two letters from MSS in the Bodleian Library.
Imprint: This edition printed in England with Baskerville type....by the Kynoch Press.

Paper boards; $10\frac{1}{2}$ x 7 x $\frac{3}{4}$ in.

IMPRINTS, England

Cabinet PP Shelf 4 No. 9

Minshall, N., Oswestry, 1811.

see BOOKBINDING. (The) Whole art of book-binding...Oswestry, 1811.

IMPRINTS, England

Cabinet M Shelf 3 No. 23

Nonesuch Press, The: Francis Meynell, London n.d. (Pelican Press)
Title: Plato's Symposium or Supper. Newby translated by Francis Birrell & Shane Leslie.
Imprint: Printed by The Pelican Press.

Paper boards; $6\frac{1}{2}$ x $4\frac{1}{2}$ x $\frac{3}{4}$ in.

IMPRINTS, England

Cabinet M Shelf 3 No. 27

Nonesuch Press. Francis Meynell, London, 1924. (Kynoch Press)
Title: The Receipt Book of Elizabeth Raper... Written in 1756-1770 and never before printed Soho: The Nonesuch Press, 1924. Nonesuch device.
Colophon: Printed at The Kynoch Press. Birmingham for The Nonesuch Press, Soho. F.M. finx.

Cloth boards; $9\frac{1}{2}$ x 6 in.

IMPRINTS, England

Cabinet X Shelf 1 No. 23

Motte, Benj. London, 1709.

See EARLY PRINTING IN ENGLAND. London, 1709.

IMPRINTS, England

Cabinet M Shelf 3 No. 21

Nonesuch Press, The. Francis Meynell, London 1923. (Pelican Press)
Title: The Book of Ruth. Translated out of the original tongues....by His Majesty's special command. London: The Nonesuch Press, MCMXXIII. [Printed by the Pelican Press]
Colophon:....The type is a new modification of William Caslon's roman and italic. The borders are enlarged from copies of those designed in the mid-sixteenth century by Bernard Salomon for Jean de Tournes. Numbered copy.
Batik paper in slip case; 8-3/4 x $5\frac{1}{2}$ in.

IMPRINTS, England

Cabinet M Shelf 4 No. 2

Nonesuch Press. Francis Meynell. London, 1925-1926. (Westminster Press).
Title: The Anatomie of Melancholy. By Robert Burton. 2 vols.
Imprint: The illustrations were made by E. McKnight Kauffer; the typography was arranged by Francis Meynell; and the printing executed by the Westminster Press.....

Paper over boards: 12 x $7\frac{3}{4}$ in.

IMPRINTS, England

Cabinet M Shelf 3 No. 29

Nonesuch Press, The. Francis Meynell, London, 1925-26.
Title: Nonesuch Books for Christmas 1925, for Spring, 1926...
Colophon: Cambridge, Printed by W. Lewis at the University Press.

Boards; 7½ x 5-3/8 in.

IMPRINTS, England

Cabinet X Shelf 4 No. 46

Oxford, 1699.

see LIBERTY OF PRINTING, Great Britain. Letter to a member of Parliament...

IMPRINTS, ENGLAND

Cabinet P Shelf 5 No. 33

Oxford University Press, Oxford, England. John Johnson, Printer, 1925.
Title: Specimens of Oxford books printed in Fell type, 1674-1925.
Imprint...Printed at the University Press, Oxford England. By John Johnson, Printer to the University.

Cloth; 18 x 11½ in.

IMPRINTS, England

Cabinet M Shelf 3 No. 28

Nonesuch Press, The. Francis Meynell, London, 1925. (Curwen Press).
Title: Songs of the Gardens. Edited by Peter Warlock. [Printed by the Curwen Press in Caslon type]
Imprint: The Nonesuch Press [London] 1925.

Parchment boards; 10¼ x 7¼ in. See Tomkinson, Bibliography of Modern Presses, p.136.

IMPRINTS, England

Cabinet F Shelf 4 No. 21

Oxford; Clarendon Press, 1771.
Title: Tracts relating to the antiquities and laws of England. By W. Blackstone. 3rd edd. Oxford, printed at the Clarendon Press. 1771.

Leather; 11 x 8½ x 1½ in.

IMPRINTS, ENGLAND

Cabinet L Shelf 2 No. 47

Oxford University Press, Oxford, England. John Johnson, Printer, 1928.
Title: Innermost Asia ... by Sir Aurel Stein.
Colophon: Printed in England at the University press Oxford by John Johnson Printer to the University.

IMPRINTS, England

Cabinet M Shelf 3 No. 30

Nonesuch Press, The. Francis Meynell, 1927.
Title: Prospectus and Retrospectus of the Nonesuch Press editions, 16 Great James Street, London. The Nonesuch device.
Imprint: Made and printed in Scotland by R. & R. Clark Limited Edinburgh.

Boards; 11-1/8 x 8¾ in.

IMPRINTS, England

Cabinet LL Shelf 3 No. 5

Oxford University Press: Horace Hart. n.d. (circa 1880)
Title: Office manual for the use of workmen in the printing house of Theo L. DeVinne & Co. New York.
Imprint on last page: Oxford: Horace Hart, Printer to the University.

Cloth; 5½ x 3 x ½ in.

IMPRINTS, England

Cabinet U Shelf 2 No. 133

Oxford University Press (John Johnson, printer), 1929.
Title: Oxford nearly visited. A fantasy by David McCord.
Imprint: Privately printed for the Cygnet Press of Cambridge, Mass., by the University Press, Oxford. 1929.
Illus. brochure.

Paper; 9 x 7 in.

IMPRINTS, England

Cabinet M Shelf 3 No. 30

Nonesuch Press (London). The 1928 Prospectus of Nonesuch Books. Issued in New York by Random House.

With 1927 Prospectus in temporary boards.

IMPRINTS, England

Cabinet J Shelf 4 No. 17

Oxford University Press, Oxford: Horace Hart, 1900-1909.

See TYPE FACSIMILE SOCIETY. Publications of the Society...1900-1909.

IMPRINTS, England

Cabinet 67 Shelf 2 No. 86

Oxford University Press: John Johnson & Bruce Rogers. 1930
Title: The rime of the ancient mariner. By Coleridge.
Imprint Colophon: Printed at the Oxford University Press by John Johnson. Designed by Bruce Rogers.

Boards; 9¼ x 6 x 3/8 in.

IMPRINTS, England

Cabinet E Shelf 2 No. 73

Norton, John. London, 1607.
Title: A world of wonders of a preparation treatise to the Apologie for Herodotus... written in Latin by Henry Stephen... translated out of the best corrected French copie. [Printer mark].
Imprint: London, imprinted for John Norton, 1607.

Calf; tooled; 11⅝ x 7-7/8 in.

IMPRINTS, England

Cabinet M Shelf 4 No. 3

Oxford University Press. Horace Hart, 1907.
Title: The Historical Pageant, June 27 - July 3, 1907. With illustrations. Printed for the Pageant Committee.
Imprint following title page: Oxford: Printed at The University Press with the ancient types (Circ. 1677) of Bishop Fell, by Horace Hart, printer to The University.

Half morocco; 10-1/8 x 1¼ x 7¾ in.

IMPRINTS, England

Cabinet F Shelf 4 No. 13

Palmer, Samuel, London, 1725.
Title: Wollaston Religion of Nature
Imprint: London, Printed by Samuel Palmer, 1725

This is the book upon which B. Franklin is supposed to have worked as a compositor when in London.

Calf; 9½ x 7-7/8 in.

IMPRINTS, England

Cabinet X Shelf 4 No. 13

Oulton, R. and G. Dexter, London, 1641

See PYM, JOHN. Speech delivered Jan., 25th.....London, 1641

IMPRINTS, England

Cabinet M Shelf 4 No. 4

Oxford, Clarendon Press. Horace Hart, 1913.
Title: Trecentale Bodleianum. A memorial volume for the three hundredth anniversary of the funeral of Sir Thomas Bodley, March 29, 1613....
Imprint: Oxford. At the Clarendon Press, MDCCCCXIII.

Boards; 7-5/8 x 5¼ in.

IMPRINTS, England

Cabinet F Shelf 4 No. 14

Palmer, Samuel, London, 1726.
Title: Wollaston Religion of Nature
Imprint: London, Printed by Samuel Palmer, in Bartholomew Close, 1726.

On this book Franklin worked as a compositor at Palmer's in 1725.

Morocco, gilt; 11½ x 9 in.

IMPRINTS, England

Cabinet M | Shelf 4 | No. 5.05

Pear Tree Press, Flansham, Bognor Regis, Sussex, England, 1935.
The Book Craftsmen. Edited by James Guthrie.

With other items in manila envelope.

IMPRINTS, England

Cabinet M | Shelf 4 | No. 5.05

Pear Tree Press (James Guthrie), 1935
Title: A circular of works and projects from the Pear Tree Press, Flansham, Bognor Regis, Sussex England.

A prospectus. In manila envelope with other items.

IMPRINTS, England

Cabinet M | Shelf 4 | No. 5

Peckham Press. Cooper & Budd Ltd. London, S.E. n.d.
Title: Letterpress Printing. Some examples of modern work. Printer mark.

Paper boards; 12½ x 10-1/8 x ¾ in.

IMPRINTS, England

Cabinet M | Shelf 3 | No. 23.01

Pelican Press, London, 1924
Title: The pervigilium Veneris
Imprint: London, Grant Richards Ltd.
Colophon with printer mark: The Pelican Press
Copy No.270

Paper; 10½ x 6½ in.

IMPRINTS, England

Cabinet M | Shelf 3 | No. 23

Pelican Press. Francis Meynell, London, 1924.
Title: The Symposium or Supper of Plato. Translated by Francis Birrell and Shane Leslie. The Nonesuch Press. Mark.
Imprint following title: Printed by the Pelican Press on Arnold unbleached hand-made paper. Numbered copy.
Printed in Garamond type.

Boards; 6½ x 4¼ in.

IMPRINTS, England

Cabinet F | Shelf 4 | No. 27

Raikes, Robert. Glocester, 1775.
Title: An humble address...By Josiah Tucker.
Imprint: Glocester: Printed by R. Raikes. 1775.

Half morocco; 8 x 4-7/8 in.

IMPRINTS, England

Cabinet F | Shelf 4 | No. 2

Rhodes, Henry. London, 1700-1702.

See Early Printing in England. (Example) London, 1700-1702, Henry Rhodes.

IMPRINTS, England

Cabinet M | Shelf 4 | No. 6

Riccardi Press. Chas. T. Jacobi, London, 1909.
Title: The thoughts of the Emperor Marcus Aurelius Antoninus. Translated by George Long. Illustrated by Russell Flint.
Colophon....Imprinted....by kind permission of Messrs. George Bell & Sons in the Riccardi Press Fount by Chas. T. Jacobi...The book is published for The Medici Society Ltd: London, MCMIX.

Paper boards; 11 x 8¼ x 7/8 in.

IMPRINTS, England

Cabinet M | Shelf 4 | No. 7

Riccardi Press. Chas. J. Jacobi, London, 1911.
Title: Everyman: A morality play. Illustrated after drawings by John H. Amschewitz. London Philip Lee Warner, publisher to the Medici Society Ltd.
Colophon: Here ends the treatise....imprinted.... in The Riccardi Press Fount, by Charles T. Jacobi....Grafton Street, Bond Street, W. MDCCCCXI.

Paper boards; 10-3/4 x 8-1/8 x ½ in.

IMPRINTS, ENGLAND

Cabinet FF | Shelf 5 | No. 19

Riccardi Press, 1923.
Title: On type Faces. Examples of the use of type for the printing of books...With an introduction by Stanley Morison... Published jointly by the Medici Society and the fleuron. London. 1923.

No. 24 of 750 copies

Boards, cloth back; 11½ x 9¾ in.

IMPRINTS, England

Cabinet M | Shelf 1 | No. 11

Ricketts, Charles. The Ballantyne Press. London, 1898.
Title: The Sonnets of Sir Philip Sidney.
Colophon: Here ends...The ornaments designed & cut on the wood by Charles S. Ricketts under whose supervision the book has been printed at the Ballantyne Press.

Boards; 9¼ x 6 x ½ in.

IMPRINTS, England

Cabinet M | Shelf 1 | No. 10

Ricketts, Charles. Ballantyne Press. London, 1898.
Title: The World at Auction.
Colophon: Here ends the World at Auction by Michael Field. The decorations are designed and cut on the wood by Charles Ricketts, under whose supervision the book has been printed at the Ballantyne Press....

Boards; 9½ x 6 x 5/8 in.

IMPRINTS, England

Cabinet M | Shelf 1 | No. 13

Ricketts, Charles. The Ballantyne Press, London n.d. [1903?]
Ecclesiastes: Or, The preacher.
Colophon:...composed in the fount known as the King's Fount, designed by Charles Ricketts, and printed under his supervision for Messrs. Hacon & Ricketts by the Ballantyne Press.

Boards; 11¾ x 8 x ½ in.

IMPRINTS, England

Cabinet M | Shelf 1 | No. 12

Ricketts, Charles. The Ballantyne Press, London, 1903.
The Kingis Quair, By King James of Scotland.
Colophon: Here ends...composed in the fount called the King's Fount, designed by Charles Ricketts, and printed under his supervision at the Ballantyne Press, London, MCMIII.

Boards; 9¼ x 5¾ x ½ in.

IMPRINTS, England

Cabinet M | Shelf 4 | No. 8

Rivingtons, London, 1923.
Title: A Calendar of Verse. With an introduction by George Saintsbury. New edition. London: Rivingtons.

Calf, gilt edges; 5¼ x 4-1/8 x 1¾ in.

IMPRINTS, England

Cabinet QQ | Shelf 3 | No. 39

Roffe, Edwin, Rochester Press. Somers' Town, 1862.

see
ROFFE, EDWIN. Times tunefull tabor ...Somers' Town, 1862.

IMPRINTS, England

Cabinet 67 | Shelf 2 | No. 30

Rogers, Bruce. The Mall Press. (Emery Walker, et al), Hammersmith, 1917.
Title: Of the Just Shaping of Letters. By Albrecht Durer, Translated by R.T. Nichol from the latin text of the edition of 1535.
Imprint: New York: The Grolier Club, MCMXVII.

Paper boards; 12½ x 8½ in. Warde, 126.

IMPRINTS, England.

Cabinet 67 | Shelf 1 | No. 30

Rogers, Bruce. Cambridge. [1918].
Title: Address at the unveiling of the Roll of Honour of the Cambridge Tipperary Club. 1916. By M. R. James. Cambridge [1918]. Pamphlet. Warde 132.

In box labelled "Bruce Rogers. Imprints. Miscellany."

IMPRINTS, England

Cabinet 67 | Shelf 2 | No. 32

Rogers, Bruce, University Press, Cambridge, 1918. A collection of books about cats. With notes by Percy L Babington.

Georgian old style types. Title page in red, and black, with border (Warde 134)

Boards; 9 x 5¾ in. pp.20.

IMPRINTS, England

Cabinet K | Shelf 5 | No. 26

St. Dominic's Press; H.D.C. Pepler, Ditchling. Sussex, 1920.

see

BEEDHAM, R. JOHN. Wood engraving ...1920.

IMPRINTS, England

Cabinet M | Shelf 4 | No. 14

Shakespeare Head Press. B. H. Newdigate. Stratford-upon-Avon, 1923.
Title: Shakespeare's The Tragedie of Cymbeline. Printed from the Folio of 1623. London, 1923.
Publishers' Advertisement follows....printed at the Shakespeare Head Press, Stratford-upon-Avon under the direction of Mr. B.H. Newdigate....The line blocks are by Messrs. Emery Walker, Ltd.

Tooled morocco; 13 x 9¾ x 1¼ in.

IMPRINTS, England

Cabinet 67 | Shelf 2 | No. 31

Rogers, Bruce. University Press, Cambridge, 1918. On Friendship: 16th century verses. Privately printed for A.T. Bartholomew and B.R. Autographed by B.R.

Caslon Italic type. Brochure (Warde 129)

IMPRINTS, England

Cabinet M | Shelf 4 | No. 10

St. Dominic's Press. H.D.C. Pepler. Ditchling, Sussex, 1924.
Title: Horae Beatae Virginis Mariae. Juxta ritum sacri ordinis praedicatorum. Jussu Editae.
Imprint: Typographia S. Dominici, Ditchling in Anglia. Anno Domini MCMXXIII.

Linen; 11⅜ x 8-7/8 x ½ in.

IMPRINTS, England

Cabinet M | Shelf 4 | No. 12

Shakespeare Head Press. Bernard H. Newdigate, 1923.
Title: Stratford-upon-Avon: Report on future development....The University Press of Liverpool Ltd. Hodder & Stoughton Ltd. London, 1923. Illus.
Imprint: Printed and made at the Shakespeare Head Press. Stratford-upon-Avon.

Paper boards; 12½ x 10¼ in.

IMPRINTS, England

Cabinet 67 | Shelf 2 | No. 35

Rogers, Bruce, University Press, Cambridge, England, 1919. Spare your good. (T. Marshe? ab.1555) Reprinted from the only known copy with an introduction by E. Gordon Duff.

Centaur types. Two facsimiles of woodcuts. (Warde 140)

Orig. stiff paper bound in full morocco binding; 9¼ x 6¼ in. pp.22.

IMPRINTS, England

Cabinet M | Shelf 4 | No. 9

St. Dominic's Press. H.D.C. Pepler, Ditchling, Sussex. 1924.
Title: Libellus Lapidum...The first part of a collection of verses and wood-engraving made by H.P. and D.J.
Imprint: Printed & published at S. Dominic's Press,Ditchling, Sussex and at 350 Oxford Street, London, W.1. A. MCMXXIV. D

Paper; 7 x 4-7/8 in.

IMPRINTS, England

Cabinet M | Shelf 4 | No. 13

Shakespeare Head Press. B.H. Newdigate. Stradford-upon-Avon, 1923.
Title: Tragedie of Macbeth: The Players' Shakespeare.
Publishers' Advertisement: The volumes have been printed at the Shakespeare Head Press.... under the direction of Mr. B.H. Newdigate and the colored illustrations have been carried out by Messrs. Whittingham & Griggs. The line blocks are by Emery Walker....

Vellum over boards; 13 x 9¼ in.

IMPRINTS, England

Cabinet 67 | Shelf 2 | No. 62

Rogers, Bruce. University Press, Cambridge, 1924. The Common Weal. Six lectures...by W. Cunningham.

Old Style types. On title page B.R. has written with pencil "I think this is the first book I turned out at Camb. B.R."

Boards, linen back; 8 x 5¼ in. pp.117.

IMPRINTS, England

Cabinet T | Shelf 2 | No. 6

Savage, William, London, 1810

see

DIBDIN'S "Typographical Antiquities" ...London, 1810-19, vol.i

---

IMPRINTS, England

Cabinet M | Shelf 4 | No. 15

Shakespeare Head Press, B.H. Newdigate. Stratford-upon-Avon, 1924.
Title: Ernest Gimson; His life & work. Stratford-upon-Avon, at the Shakespeare Head Press. London: Ernest Benn Ltd......Oxford: Basil Blackwell.
Imprint:....Printed in England at the Shakespeare Head Press Stratford-upon-Avon. The Collotype plates have been printed at the Sussex House, Kelmscott, England, by Emery Walker Ltd.

Paper boards; 12 x 8-3/4 x 1-1/8 in.

IMPRINTS, England

Cabinet E | Shelf 4 | No. 49

Roycroft, Thomas. London, 1668.

See Early Printing in England. London, 1668.

IMPRINTS, England

Cabinet M | Shelf 4 | No. 10.03

(The) Scholartis Press, London, 1929.
Title: The Scholartis Press, list for. May-July, 1929. With a full description of all previous publications, including those which are out of print.

Brochure, in manila envelope

IMPRINTS, England

Cabinet M | Shelf 4 | No. 16

Shakespeare Head Press (B.H. Newdigate), Stratford-upon-Avon.
Title: Shakespeare's loves labor's lost. Newly printed from the folio of 1623.
Imprint: The Publishers Advertisement, Ernest Benn. Limited, London, 1924.

Prospectus, in manila envelope.

IMPRINTS, England

Cabinet PP | Shelf 1 | No. 5

Ruff, H. Glocester, 1802
Title: An introduction to the knowledge of rare and valuable editions of the Greek and Roman classics...By T.F.Dibdin.
Imprint: Glocester, printed by H. Ruff...1802

Half morocco (by Zaehnsdorf) 7-7/8 x 5 in.

IMPRINTS, England

Cabinet M | Shelf 4 | No. 11

Shakespeare Head Press. Arthur Henry Bullen. Stratford-upon-Avon, 1921.
Title: Shakespeare's Sonnets. Stratford-upon-Avon: at the Shakespeare Head. Oxford: Basil Blackwell.
Following title page: The text of this edition was printed by the late A.H. Bullen at the Shakespeare Head Press....The foreword and note were printed in 1921.

Paper boards; 7-1/8 x 5¼ x 1 in.

IMPRINTS, England

Cabinet E | Shelf 2 | No. 26

Singleton, Hugh. London, 1579.

See Early Printing in England. London, 1579.

IMPRINTS, England

Cabinet E Shelf 4 No. 74

Bowle, Andrew. London, 1681.

See Early Printing in England. London, 1681.

IMPRINTS, England

Cabinet M Shelf 4 No. 16

Stanton Press. Richard Stanton Lambert. Wembley Hill, Middlesex, 1922.
Title: Orchestra, or a Poeme of Dauncing, by Sir John Davis.
Colophon: This book has been decorated with woodcuts by Elinor Lambert, and printed by Richard Stanton Lambert and Elinor Lambert at their Stanton Press...where copies are sold by the owners of the Press.

Paper boards; 10 x 8 x ½ in.

IMPRINTS, England

Cabinet M Shelf 5 No. 60

Strawberry Hill Press, 1753.

see FIRST OCCURRENCES. Strawberry Hill Press...

IMPRINTS, England

Cabinet M Shelf 4 No. 17

Strawberry Hill Press. Horace Walpole. 1758.
Title: A Parallel; In the manner of Plutarch.... By the Reverend Mr. Spence.
Imprint: Printed at Strawberry-Hill by William Robinson; and sold by Messieurs Dodsley, at Tully's Head, Pall Mall. For the Benefit of Mr. Hill. MDCCLVIII.

¼ Morocco; 7¼ x 4½ x 3/8 in.

IMPRINTS, England

Cabinet M Shelf 4 No. 18

Strawberry-Hill Press. Horace Walpole, 1760.
Title: M. Annaei Lucani. Pharsalia cum notis Hugonis Grotii, et Richardi Bentleii.....
Imprint: Strawberry-Hill, MDCCLX.

Calf; 11¾ x 9-1/8 x 1¾ in. Brunet 3, 1200.

IMPRINTS, England

Cabinet M Shelf 4 No. 19

Strawberry-Hill Press. Horace Walpole, 1781.
Title: The Muse Recalled, an ode...By William Jones, Esq;
Imprint: Strawberry-Hill: Printed by Thomas Kirgate, MDCCLXXXI.

Half morocco; 9¾ x 8 in.

IMPRINTS, England

Cabinet M Shelf 4 No. 20

Sun Engraving Company, London, 1924.
Title: Everybody's Book of The Queen's Doll House. Edited by A.C. Benson, C.V.D. and Sir Lawrence Weaver. The Daily Telegraph and Methuen & Co. Ltd., London.
London: Printed in Photogravure and Color by The Sun Engraving Company, Ltd. London and Watford.
This is a description of the Queen's Doll House exhibited in the British and Colonial Exposition at Wembley in 1925--the most

Cloth; 10 x 7½ x 1 in. cont'd

IMPRINTS, England cont'd

Cabinet M Shelf 4 No. 20

notable of all the exhibits.

Cloth; 10 x 7½ x 1 in.

IMPRINTS, England

Cabinet F Shelf 4 No. 8

Tonson, Jacob and John Watts. London, 1713.
Title: Vita Sallustii. By Michael Maittaire.
Imprint: Londini: Ex Officina Jacobi Tonson & Johannis Watts. 1713. Cum privilegio.
"The Maittaire's Classicks would alone have immortalized his memory (John Watt's) both for correctness and neatness." Plomer's booksellers & printers, 1668-1725.

Leather; 6-1/8 x 3¾ x ⅝ in.

IMPRINTS, England

Cabinet E Shelf 4 No. 75

Tooke, Benjamin? London, 1681-85.
Title: Leabhuir...The books of the Old Testament translated into Irish...By Doctor William Bedel, 1685 [With the New Testament in the Irish character, translated by William O'Donnell. London, 1681]
Imprint: Printed at London, Anno Dom. MDCLXXXV

Calf; 9½ x 7½ x 3¼ in.

IMPRINTS, England

Cabinet Shelf No.

University Press, Cambridge

see IMPRINTS, England. Cambridge University Press

IMPRINTS, England

Cabinet M Shelf 4 No. 21

Vale Press: Charles Ricketts, London, v.d.
Propectuses: Lists of Vale editions.

Paper board case; 9-5/8 x 7 in.

IMPRINTS, England

Cabinet M Shelf 4 No. 22

Vizetelly Brothers & Co., London, 1842.
Title: Ancient Spanish Ballades...Translated with notes by J.G. Lockhart, Esq. With numerous illustrations from drawings...The borders and ornamental vignettes by Owen Jones, architect. London: John Murrey. Edinburgh: W. Blackword & Sons.
Colophon: London. Vizetelly Bros. & Co. printers and engravers 135 Fleet Street.

Morocco, embossed; 9¾ x 7-7/8 x 1-1/8 in.

IMPRINTS, England

Cabinet M Shelf 4 No. 23

Vizetelly Brothers & Co., London, 1845.
Title: The Book of Common Prayer.....According to the use of the United Church of England and Ireland. With notes. Illuminated and illustrated with engravings from the works of the great painters. The vignettes, initials, borders, and ornaments are designed by Owen Jones, architect. London: John Murray, MDCCCXLV.
Imprint: London, Vizetelly Brothers & Co. Printers and Engravers.

Morocco, tool ed, gilt; 9½ x 6½ x 1-3/4 in.

IMPRINTS, England

Cabinet II Shelf 3 No. 64

Walter, John. London, 1786.

John Walter was the founder of the London Times.

See ELPHINSTON, JAMES. Propriety ascertained...London, 1786.

IMPRINTS, England

Cabinet M Shelf 4 No. 24

Westminster Press. Gerard Meynell, London, 1916.
Title: A Carol and other Rhymes. By Edward Johnston. London. Douglas Pepler. Hampshire House Workshops. Hampshire Hog Lane, Hammersmith, 1916.
Colophon: Printed at the Westminster Press, 411a Harrow Road. London, W.

Cloth; 5¼ x 4¼ in.

IMPRINTS, England

Cabinet M Shelf 4 No. 25

Westminster Press. Gerard Meynell, 1921.
Title: Weeping-Cross and other Rimes by A.H. Bullen. London. Sidgwick & Jackson, Ltd. 1921.
Colophon: The Westminster Press. Harrow Road, London.

Paper boards; 6¾ x 4-1/4 in.

IMPRINTS, England

Cabinet M Shelf 4 No. 26

Westminster Press, The. Gerard Meynell, London, 1924.
Title: Elizabethans. By A.H. Bullen. London: Chapman and Hall Ltd., 1924.
Imprint: Printed in Great Britain at The Westminster Press, 411 Harrow Road. London, W.9. 1924.

Cloth boards, gold stamped; 9-1/8 x 6 x 1-1/8 in.

IMPRINT, ENGLAND

Cabinet FF Shelf 1 No. 63

Wilson, A. London, 1804
Title: An abstract of the whole Christian Religion. By J. Anastasius Freylinghausen... The first book stereotyped by the new (Stanhope) process.
Imprint: London, stereotyped and printed by A. Wilson ...1804

Boards; $10\frac{3}{4}$x$7\frac{1}{4}$ in.

IMPRINTS, France.

Cabinet 70 Shelf 2 No. 3

Bade, Josee (Badius Ascensius). Paris, 1524.
Title: De Asse et partibus eius libri quinquorum Gulielmi Budei. Paris, 1524.

Vellum; 12 x $8\frac{1}{2}$ x $1\frac{1}{2}$ in.

IMPRINTS, France.

Cabinet 40 Shelf 2 No. 1

Blaublom Ludovico. Paris, 1530.
See Early Printing in France. Paris, 1530. Simon de Colines. Ludovico Blaublom.

IMPRINTS, England

Cabinet Q Shelf 1 No. 25

Wittingham, Charles and Griggs, Ltd. The Chiswick Press, 1924.

see
IMPRINTS, England. Chiswick Press, Charles Wittingham...

IMPRINTS, France.

Cabinet 69 Shelf 1 No. 15

Badius, Conrad. Paris, 1548.
Title: Theodori Bezae Vezelli poemata [Ascensian Press device].
Imprint: Lutetiae. Ex officina Conradi Badii sub prelo Ascensiano, e regione gymnasii D. Barbarae. 1548.

Mottled calf; $6\frac{3}{4}$ x 4-1/8 x 3/8 in. Brunet I 841.

IMPRINTS, France.

Cabinet 69 Shelf 1 No. 18

Bonhomme, Mathias. Lyons, 1550.
Title: Alciati, D. A. Emblemata ...
Imprint: Lugd. Apud Guliel. Rovilium.
Colophon: Excudebat Mathias Bonhomme.

Vellum; 7 x $4\frac{3}{4}$ x $\frac{3}{4}$ in. Brunet I, 148.

IMPRINTS, England

Cabinet F Shelf 4 No. 1

Woodfall, Henry. London, 1704.
Title: Monsieur de Pourceaugnac...done into English from a Comedy of Moliere's...for the diversion of the French King in 1679.
Imprint: Printed for William Davis, at the Black Bull against the Royal Exchange and Bernard Lintott...in Fleet Street, 1704.

Cloth covered boards; $8\frac{1}{2}$ x $6\frac{1}{2}$ in.

IMPRINTS, France.

Cabinet 70 Shelf 1 No. 2

Badius, Josse (Ascensius). Paris, 1507.
Title: Prima pars operu Baptiste Mantuani ...
Imprint: Venudatur in vico Sancti Jacobi in aedibus Ascensianis, et sub Pelicano.
Colophon: Finis Exedibus Ascensianis. nonis Septembriis 1507.
Title page with first Badius mark, the second earliest known picture of a printing office.

Vellum; $6\frac{1}{4}$ x $4\frac{1}{4}$ x $1\frac{1}{2}$ in.

IMPRINTS, France.

Cabinet 69 Shelf 2 No. 1

Bonhomme, Matthieu. Lyons, 1552.
Title: Aemylii Fereti Praelectiones. [Printer Mark].
Imprint: Lugduni, apud Mathiam Bonhomme. 1552.
Bound in with another item printed by G. Roville, Lyons, 1550.

Vellum; 13 x $8\frac{1}{2}$ x 2 in. In protective case.

IMPRINTS, England.

Cabinet PP Shelf 1 No. 29

Woodfall, G. London, 1814.
Title: An introduction to the study of bibliography ... By Thomas Hartwell Horne. (2 vols)
Imprint: London. Printed by F. Woodfall, for T. Cadell and W. Davis, Strand, 1814.

Half calf; 9 x $5\frac{1}{4}$ in.

IMPRINTS, France.

Cabinet 70 Shelf 1 No. 30

Badius, Josse (Ascensius). Paris, 1526.
Title: Contemptu rerum fortuitarum libri tres
" II: Latinae linguae floseuli ad operis D. Gulielmi Budei ... [Printer mark].
Imprint: Venundantur in officina Ascensiana, cum gratia et privilegio in triennium.

Boards; $7\frac{1}{2}$ x 5-5/8 x $\frac{3}{4}$ in.

IMPRINTS, France

Cabinet 69 Shelf 1 No. 30

Breton, Richard and Philippe Danfrie. Paris, 1558.
Title: Le discourse de la Court [Printed in a peculiar "Civilite Type", probably the first use of these types].
Imprint: À Paris. De l'Imprimerie de Philippe Danfrie et Richard Breton...

Calf; $6\frac{1}{2}$ x 3/8 in.

IMPRINTS, England

Cabinet M Shelf 4 No. 27

Wynkyn de Worde, London, 1852-1853.
Title: The maner of the tryumphe of Caleys and Bulleyn...Printed by Wynkyn de Worde, 1532-33.
[Facsimile] Bibliotheca Curiosa. Edited by Edmund Goldsmid. Privately printed, Edinburgh, 1884.

Cloth; 7 x $4\frac{1}{2}$ in.

IMPRINTS, France

Cabinet 17 Shelf 2 No. 2

Belleri (Balthazeris), Douay, 1616.
Title page (folio), with a fine etching of St. Paul.
Imprint: Dvaci, Ex Officina Typographia Balthazaris Belleri.

Item on fol.86 of HENRY STEVEN'S "Typographical Miscellanies", vol.2, B-1

IMPRINTS, France.

Cabinet E Shelf 2 No. 85

Cardon, Horatio. Lyon, 1612-13.

See Early Printing in France. Lyon, 1612-13. Horatio Cardon.

IMPRINTS, France

Cabinet K Shelf 1 No. 28

Attaignant, Pierre, Paris, 1528.

See FACSIMILES
Music printing and manuscripts, 12th to 16th century...(Plate XXVI)

IMPRINTS, France

Cabinet 17 Shelf 2 No. 2

Berthelin, Jean, Touen, 1660.
Fragment of title folio, with imprint and printer's device.

Item on fols. 120-121 of HENRY STEVEN'S 'Typographical Miscellanies", vol.2, B-1

IMPRINTS, France.

Cabinet 70 Shelf 1 No. 41

Chevallon, Claude, Paris, 1532. Psalmo/ rum omnium ivxta Hebraica veritate....autore Ioanne Cãpensi (etc) [Printers mark]: C. Chevallon Parisiis, ex officina Claudñ Chevallõn, Anno 1532.

Calf, $4\frac{3}{4}$ x 3-1/8 ins., 1 in. thick.

IMPRINTS, France.

Cabinet 69 | Shelf 1 | No. 8

Chevallon, Claude (Veuve) [Charlotte Guillard]. Paris, 1540.
Title: Les apothegmes ., translatez de la Latin en Francois par lesleu Macault.
Imprint: On les vend a Paris au Soleil dor, en la rue Saint Jacques.
Printer's name appears in the privilege which follows title page.

Morocco; 4-7/8 x 3 x 1½ in.

IMPRINTS, France

Cabinet N | Shelf 1 | No. 15

Claye, J. et L. Perrin, Paris, 1858.

see KEMPIS, THOMAS a. Imitation a Jesus-Christ...

IMPRINTS, France

Cabinet X | Shelf 4 | No. 32

Coignard, Jean Baptiste, Paris, 1707

See LIBERTY OF PRINTING, France Arrest du Conseil d'Estat (1706)...

IMPRINTS, France.

Cabinet 40 | Shelf 2 | No. 19

Colines, Simon de. Paris, 1526.
Title: Sarzosi Cellani Aragonei, in acquatorem Planetarum.
Imprint: Parisiis. Apud Simonem Colinaeum. 1526.
[Two books in one. The first book in the volume, printed by Andreas Wechel. Paris, 1564].

Calf; 13 x 9 x 2¾ in.

IMPRINTS, France.

Cabinet 40 | Shelf 1 | No. 9

Colines, Simon de. Paris, 1530.
Title: Aediloquium ceu Disticha, partibus Aedium urbanarum & rusticarum suis....Gotofredo Torino.
Imprint: Parisiis, apud Simonem Colineum. 1530.

Morocco, hand tooled (by Lortic); 6¼ x 4 x ¼ in. Brunet 5, 888-9.

IMPRINTS, France.

Cabinet 40 | Shelf 1 | No. 78

Colines, Simon de. Paris, 1530-1.
Title 1: L. Fenestellae de magistratibus Romanarum libellus ...
" 2: Historia de vita et moribus imperatorum Romanorum ...
Imprint: Parisiis apud Simonem Colinseum, 1530-1531.
Woodcut title page in "maniere criblé," by Geofroy Tory.

Boards; 7 x 4½ x 1 in.

IMPRINTS, France.

Cabinet 40 | Shelf 2 | No. 1

Colines, Simon de. Paris, 1530.
Title: Veterinariae medicinae libri II. Johanne Ruellio.
Imprint: Parisiis apud Simonem Colinseum.
Colophon: Parisiis, ex chalcographia Ludovici Blaublomii Gandivi, impensis Simonis Colinaei. 1530.

Boards; 13-1/8 x 8-7/8 in.

IMPRINTS, France.

Cabinet 40 | Shelf 1 | No. 77

Colines, Simon de. Paris, 1531.
Title: Silii Italici Clarissimi poetae de bello punici ...
Imprint: Parisiis. Apud Simonem Colinaeum, 1531.

Vellum; 6¾ x 4-3/8 x 1½ in. Brunet 5, 383.

IMPRINTS, France.

Cabinet 40 | Shelf 2 | No. 8

Colines, Simon de. Paris, 1536.
Title: De natura stirpium libri tres Ioanne Ruellio authore. [Title within a border in the manner of Geofroy Tory].
Imprint: Cum privilegio. Parisiis, ex officina Simonis Colinaei. 1536.

Morocco; 15 x 10 x 2½ in. Brunet 4,1451.

IMPRINTS, France

Cabinet 40 | Shelf 2 | No. 21

Colines, Simon. Paris, 1544.
Title: Orontii Finaei Delphinatis, regii mathematicarum Lutetiae professoris. Quadrature Circuli, tandem inventa et clarissime demonstrata ...
Imprint: Lutetiae Parisiorum, apud Simon Colinaeum. 1544.

Vellum manuscript, with straps, 12-7/8 x 8-5/8 x ½ in.

IMPRINTS, France.

Cabinet 40 | Shelf 2 | No. 22

Colines, Simon. Paris, 1544.
Title: Orontii Finaei Delphinatis. Regii mathematicarum Lutetiae professoris, in sex priores libros geometricorum elementorum Euclidia ... interpretatione latina Bartholamaei Zamberti Veneti. Omnia ad fidem ... per eunde Orontium recognita.
Imprint: Lutetiae parisiorum, apud Simonem Colinaeum 1544. Cum privilegio regis. Virescit vulnere virtus.
Boards; 11¾ x 8-3/8 x 5.8 in.

IMPRINTS, France.

Cabinet 40 | Shelf 1 | No. 81

Colines, Simon de. Paris, 1554.
Title: Martialis epigrammaton, libri 14 ...
Imprint: Parisiis. Apud Simonem Colinaeum. 1544. With printer mark.

Calf; 4½ x 2¾ x 7/8 in.

IMPRINTS, France.

Cabinet E | Shelf 4 | No. 48

Coste, (Veuve) Nic de la. Paris, 1668.

See Early Printing in France. Paris, 1668.

IMPRINTS, France

Cabinet F | Shelf 4 | No. 79 | 3 vols.

Coustelier, Ant. Urban (II). Paris, 1745.
Title: Vergilii Opera... (3 vols.)
Imprint: Lutetiae. Parisiorum. Sumptibus Ant. Urb. Coustelier.
Includes printer mark. Copper-plate engravings by Cochin.

Morocco, gilt; 6 x 3½ x 7/8 in. Brunet 5, 1291.

IMPRINTS, France.

Cabinet E | Shelf 3 | No. 82

Cramoisy, Sebastien (II). Paris, 1648.

See Early Printing in France, Paris, 1648.

IMPRINTS, France.

Cabinet E | Shelf 4 | No. 12 | 2 vols.

Cramoisy, Sebastien. Paris, 1653.

See Early Printing in France. Paris, 1653. Sebastien Cramoisy.

IMPRINTS, France

Cabinet 68 | Shelf | No. 2

Crapelet, (Charles), Paris, 1802
Title: Oiseaux dores ou reflets metalliques. (2 vol.)
Imprint: A Paris, de l'Imprimerie de Crapelet. An X1 (1802)
Plates printed in natural coloring with metallic reflections.

Calf, gilt; 20 x 13½ in.

IMPRINTS, France.

Cabinet 70 | Shelf 2 | No. 8

Crespin, Jean. Lyons, 1529.
Title: Opera Virgiliana cum decem commentis ...
Colophon: Lugduni, in typographaria officina Ioannis Crespini, anno Virginei partus. 1529.

Tooled leather over board; 13 x 8¾ x 3 in.

IMPRINTS, France

Cabinet J Shelf 2 No. 25

Curmer, L. Paris, 1866-7.

See FOUCQUET, JEHAN. Vie et les oeuvres de...

IMPRINTS, FRANCE

Cabinet I Shelf 1 No. 10

Des-Hayes, Pierre, Paris, 1645, for A. Bosse.

See BOSSE, ABRAHAM. Traicte de manieres de graver...A Paris, 1645 (De l'Imprimerie de Pierre Des-Hayes).

IMPRINTS, France.

Cabinet F Shelf 5 No. 34

Didot, Pierre, l'aine. Paris, 1795.

Title: M. Annaei Lucani Pharsalia ex optimo exemplaribus emendata.
Imprint: Parisiis: Studio et impensis Ant. Aug. Renouard. Typis P. Didot natu majoris. An. Reipubl. III.

Tooled leather; 14¾ x 10 x 1¾ in. Brunet 3, 1200.

IMPRINTS, France

Cabinet B Shelf 3 No. 6

Danel, L. Lille, 1899.
Title: Collection Dutuit. Livres et manuscrits.
Imprint: Imprimé par L. Danel de Lille, 1899.
With printer's device

Boards; 18-3/8 x 12½ x 1-7/8 in.

IMPRINTS, France

Cabinet FF Shelf 1 No. 73

Didot, J. l'aine. Paris, 1822.

See STEREOTYPING. Nouveau procédé...Par P. Arnaud Leroux. Paris, 1822.

IMPRINTS, France.

Cabinet F Shelf 5 No. 36

Didot, Pierre l'ainé. Paris, 1796.

Title: Jérusalem delivrée (par Tasso) en vers Francois. Par L.P.M.F. Baour-Lormian. 2 vols Full page engravings by C.N. Cochin.
Imprint: A Paris, de l'Imprimerie de P. Didot l'ainé. L'an IV de la République. 1796.

Half cloth; 13 x 10 x 1½ in. Brunet 5, 667.

IMPRINTS, France.

Cabinet 69 Shelf 1 No. 30

Danfrie, Philippe and Richard Breton. Paris, 1558.
Title: Le discourse de la Court. [Printed in a peculiar "Civilite Type"].
Imprint: A Paris. De l'Imprimerie de Philippe Danfrie et Richard Breton ...

Calf; 6½ x 4 x 3/8 in.

IMPRINTS, France

Cabinet 13 Shelf No.s. 7-7a-7b 7c.

Didot, Firmin fréres, Paris, 1839-41

Title: Paléographie universelle...Par M. Silvestre (4 parts)
Imprint: Paris: Typographie de Firmin Didot fréres.

Half morocco; 24½ x 17 in.

IMPRINTS, FRANCE

Cabinet 68 Shelf No. 12

Didot, Pierre the Elder, Paris, 1799

See HORATIUS, FLACCUS (Quintus). Printed by Pierre Didot the elder...

IMPRINTS, France.

Cabinet 69 Shelf 1 No. 57

Danfrie, Philippe. Paris, 1597.
Title: Declaration de l'usage du graphometre ...
Imprint: A Paris, chez ledict Danfrie ...
Curious work in cursive characters created by Robert Granjon, and now known as "Civilitee,"

Morocco; 7¾ x 5 x ½ in. Brunet 2, 485.

IMPRINTS, France

Cabinet QQ Shelf 1 No. 9

Didot, Francois Ambroise. Paris, 1784.
Title: Épitre sur les progrès de l'imprimerie. Par Didot, fils ainé.
Imprint: À Paris, imprimé chez Didot l'ainé, avec les italiques de Firmin, son second fils. 1784.

Half morocco; 8-3/4 x 5-3/8 in.

IMPRINTS, France

Cabinet F Shelf 4 No. 95

Didot, Pierre [Son of Ambroise-Firmin II]. Paris, 1800.
Title: Quintus Horatius Flaccus Edita stereotypa. Parisiis, ex Officina Stereotypa Petri Didot natu maj., et Firmin Didot. Anno VIII (1800).

Vellum; 6¼ x 3-7/8 x 1¼ in. Brunet 3, 323.

IMPRINTS, FRANCE

Cabinet FF Shelf 3 No. 23

DeBerny et Cie., Paris, 1822.
Title: DeBerny. Appreciation de son oeuvre.
Imprint: Paris. Rue Visconti, 17, pres le palais des Beaux-Arts, 1882.

Has frontispiece portrait of Alex. DeBerny.

Morocco, gilt; 10½ x 8 in.

IMPRINTS, France

Cabinet F Shelf 4 No. 91

Didot, Françoise-Ambroise II. Paris, 1785.
Title: Idées d'un militaire...Par M. Fossé. [Several colored engravings by Bonnet who claimed to have been the inventor of this crayon stipple method].
Imprint: De l'Imprimerie de Franc. Amb. Didot l'ainé. À Paris. 1785.

Cloth; 11-3/4 x 9 x 1 in.

IMPRINTS, France

Cabinet 68 Shelf No. 1

Didot, Pierre l'ainé, Paris, 1809
Title: Choix des plus célèbres maisons de plaisance de Rome...
Imprint: A Paris, de l'Imprimerie de P. Didot l'ainé.

With copper engravings, designs of Percier.

Half pigskin, 22 x 15¾ in.

IMPRINTS, FRANCE

Cabinet J Shelf 2 No. 13.01

Demasso, Francoise, Lyon, 1672.

Title: La vraye science de la pourtraicture. Par Jean Cousin.
Imprint: A Lyon, chez Francoise Demasso, rue Merciere, a l'Ensigne de la Juste Paix.

Boards, oblong; 7 x 9½ in.

IMPRINTS, France.

Cabinet F Shelf 5 No. 24

Didot, Francois-Ambroise l'aine. Paris, 1788.
Title: Fables de la Fontaine...De l'Imprimerie de Didot l'aine.
Colophon: Cette edition a été imprimée...avec les nouveaux caracteres de la fonderie de Didot l'aine, gravés par Firmin son 2d fils. ...

Morocco gilt; 12½ x 9¼ x 2-1/8 in. Brunet 3, 751.

IMPRINTS, France

Cabinet MM Shelf 1 No. 22

Didot Pere et Fils, Firmin. Paris, 1825.
Title: Manuel pratique de la typographie Francaise. Par W. Brun.
Imprint: A Paris, chez Firmin Didot Pere et Fils.

Tooled morocco; gilt; 6-1/8 x 4 x ⅝ in.

IMPRINTS, FRANCE

Cabinet D Shelf 4 No. 54

Dolet, Estienne, Lyon, 1540.
Title: La chirugie de Paulus Aegineta...
Imprint: Ches Estienne Dolet. A Lyon, 1540

With printer mark on title page

Vellum; 6½ x 4¼ in.

IMPRINTS, France.

Cabinet 40 Shelf 1 No. 10

Estienne, Francois (I). Paris, 1539.
Title: Vita beatissimi patris D. Petri Caelestini Quinti, pontificis Maximi ...
Imprint: Parisiis. Apud Franciscum, 1539.

Vellum; 9¼ x 6½ x ¾ in.

IMPRINTS, France.

Cabinet 40 Shelf 1 No. 6

Estienne, Robert (Stephanus) Paris, 1526.
Title: Prisciani libellus de accentibus.
Imprint: Parisiis. Ex officina Roberti Stephani e regione scholae decretorum. 1526.

Tooled morocco; 6¼ x 4¼ x 3/8 in.

IMPRINTS, France.

Cabinet 69 Shelf 1 No. 7

Dolet, Etienne. Lyons, 1540.
Title: Les gestes de Francoys de Valois Roy de France ...
Imprint: A Lyon, ches Estienne Dolet, 1540.

Half morocco; 7½ x 6 x 3/8 in.

IMPRINTS, France

Cabinet K Shelf 1 No. 28

Estienne, Francois, Paris, 1567.

See FACSIMILES.
Music printing and manuscript, 12th to 16th century...Plate XXV11

IMPRINTS, France.

Cabinet 40 Shelf 1 No. 8

Estienne, Robert I. Paris, 1536. [Various botanical-medical works, bound together, of which his brother Charles (Carolus) was author.]
First title: De re horteli libellus, vulgaria herbarum, florum...Parisiis: Ex officina Roberti Stephani, M.D.XXXVI. pp.96 xv.
Second title: Seminariu sive plantarium arborum.. [no imprint: colophon dated July 21, 1536] pp. 107, xvii.
Third title: De vasculis libellus.... Parisiis: Ex officina Rob. Stephani M.D.XXXVI, pp.56 vii.

cont'd

IMPRINTS, FRANCE

Cabinet V Shelf 6 No. 5

Dupont, Paul. Paris, 1849.
Title: Essais pratiques d'imprimerie...
Imprint: Imprimerie Paul Dupont.

Boards; 14 x 10½ in.

IMPRINTS, France.

Cabinet 40 Shelf 1 No. 1

Estienne, Henri I (Stephanus). Paris, 1507.
Title: Joannes Damascenus: Theologica...de orthodoxae fidei.
Colophon: Sancti patris Ioannis Damasceni....cosummatus est et absolutus: efformatusqe Parisiis per Henricum Stephanum...Anno domini virtutum et fidei autoris, millesimo quingentesimo septimo, decima quinta (April 15, 1507)

Calf; 8¼ x 3-3/4 x 1 in.

IMPRINTS, France cont'd

Cabinet Shelf No.

Third Title: De vasculis libellus....Parisiis: Ex officina Rob. Stephani M.D.XXXVI, pp.56 vii.
Fourth title: De re vestiaria libellus...secunda editio. [Same imprint as on third title] pp.68, viii. [Colophon dated May 3, 1536.]

Stamped leather; 7 x 4⅝ in.

IMPRINTS, France.

Cabinet 69 Shelf 2 No. 19

Du Puys, Jacques. Paris, 1580.
Title: Recueil des roys de France ... Par Jean de Tillet. [Printer Mark].
Imprint: A Paris, chez Jacques du Puys, Libraire jure en l'Universite de Paris. 1580.

Mottled calf; 12½ x 8½ x 1⅜ in.

IMPRINTS, France.

Cabinet 40 Shelf 1 No. 36

Estienne, Henri. Paris, 1554.
Title: Anacreon ab Henrico Stephano luce et Latinitate nunc primum donatae.
Imprint: Lutetiae. Apud Henricum Stephanum. 1554.

Morocco; 8 x 5¾ x 5/8 in.

IMPRINTS, France

Cabinet 40 Shelf 2 No. 10

Estienne, Robert (I) Paris, 1538.
Title: M. Tulli Ciceronis epistolae.
Imprint: Ex officina Roberti Stephani M.D.XXXVIII

Old leather; 14¼ x 10-1/8 x 3-1/4 ins.

IMPRINTS, France.

Cabinet 69 Shelf 2 No. 13

Durant, Jean. Lyons, 1572.
Title: De la diversite des termes dont on use en architecture. Par Hughes Sambin.
Imprint: A Lyon. Par Jean Durant, 1572.

Boards; 13-3/8 x 8¾ x 3/8 in. Brunet 5, 104. Baudrier 1, p.139.

IMPRINTS, France.

Cabinet 40 Shelf 1 No. 72

Estienne, Jacques. Paris, 1768.
Title: Le spectacle de la nature ... seconde partie.
Imprint: A Paris, chez les Freres Estienne, rue S. Jacques, a la Vertu. 1768.

Leather; 6¾ x 4 x 1-1/8 in.

IMPRINTS, France.

Cabinet 40 Shelf 2 No. 13

Estienne, Robert (I). Paris, 1539.
Title: M.T. Ciceronis. Opera.
Imprint: Ex officina Roberti Stephani.
Colophon: Excudebat Robertus Stephanus. Parisiis. Ann. 1539. Idib. Augusti.

Leather; 14¾ x 10-1/8 x 2½ in.

IMPRINTS, France.

Cabinet 40 Shelf 1 No. 30

Estienne, Charles, Paris. 1551-1552.
Title (1). Apologia ...
" (2). Altera apologia pro rege christianissimo contra Caesarianos ...
Colophon, 1 and 2: Lutetia, apud Carolum Stephanum Typographum Regium ... 1551-1552.
Both items bound together.

Vellum; 8¾ x 6-3/8 x 3/8 in.

IMPRINTS, France.

Cabinet 40 Shelf 2 No. 5

Estienne, Robert I. Paris, 1532.
Title: P. Virgilii Maronis Opera.
Imprint: Parisiis. Ex Officina Roberti Stephanii 1532.

Morocco, gilt; 12¾ x 8¼ x 2-1/8 in.

IMPRINTS, France.

Cabinet 40 Shelf 1 No. 12

Estienne, Robert. Paris, 1543.
Title: C. Suetonii tranquilli XII Caesares ...
Imprint: Parisiis. Ex officina Roberti Stephani typographi Regii, 1543.

Calf; 6¾ x 4¼ x 7/8 in.

IMPRINTS, France.

Cabinet 40 Shelf 1 No. 11

Estienne, Robert. Paris, 1543.
Title: Libri de rustica M. Catonis ...
Imprint: Parisiis. Ex officina Roberti Stephani typographi Regii. 1543.

tooled and gilt morocco; 6¾ x 4-3/8 x 1 in.

IMPRINTS, France

Cabinet 40 Shelf 2 No. 20

Estienne, Robert (I). Paris, 1544.
Title: Ecclesiasticae Historiae. [Greek text].
Imprint: Lutetiae. Parisiorum. Ex officina Roberti Stephani typographi Regii, Regiis typis. 1544.

Calf; 13-3/4 x 10 x 2-3/4 in.

IMPRINTS, France.

Cabinet 40 Shelf 1 No. 51

Estienne, Robert II, Paris, 1568.
Title: Edict du roy ...
Imprint: A Paris, par Rob. Estienne Imprimeur du Roy. 1568.

Half morocco; 6¾ x 4-3/8 x 3/8 in.

IMPRINTS, France.

Cabinet 40 Shelf 1 No. 15

Estienne, Robert (I). Paris, 1544.
Title: Dion Cassius Nicaeus Aelius Spartianus ... Johannis Baptiste Egnati ... annotationes.
Imprint: Parisiis. Ex officina Roberti Stephani typographie Regii.

Leather; 6½ x 4¼ x 7/8 in.

IMPRINTS, France.

Cabinet 40 Shelf 1 No. 22

Estienne, Robert I. Paris, 1548.
Title: Thesaurus linguae sanctae. Ex R. Kimchi
Imprint: Ex officina Roberti Stephani typographi Regii.

Tooled pigskin in buckram case; 9 x 6¼ x 3 in

IMPRINTS, France.

Cabinet 40 Shelf 1 No. 54

Estienne, Robert II. Paris, 1569.
Title: Novum Testamentum ex bibliotheca regia [Greek text].
Imprint: Lutetiae: Ex officina Roberti Stephani Typographi regii. 1568.
Colophon: Excudebat Rob. Stephanus ... 1569.

Morocco; 5 x 3½ x 1-5/8 in.

IMPRINTS, France cont'd

Cabinet 40 Shelf 1 No. 8

Fourth title: De re vestiaria libellus...secunda editio. [Same imprint as on third title] pp.68, viii. [Colophon dated May 3, 1536.]

Stamped leather; 7 x 4-3/4 in.

IMPRINTS, France.

Cabinet 40 Shelf 1 No. 27

Estienne, Robert (I). Paris, 1549.
Title: Jovius Paulus. Vitae duodecim vicecomitum Mediolani principum ...
Imprint: Lutetia. Rob. Stephanus. 1549.
In this book are the engravings; initials and printers device, signed by Geoffroy Tory.

Vellum; 10 x 6-7/8 x 7/8 in.

IMPRINTS, France.

Cabinet 40 Shelf 1 No. 25

Estienne, Robert. Paris, 1548-1550.
Title I: Seminarium et plantarium ... Carolus Stephanus ...
Imprint: Parisiis, ex officina Rob. Stephani, 1548.
Title II: Caroli Stephani, de nutrimentis.
Imprint: Parisiis, ex officna Rob. Steph. 1550.
Bound in with other item printed by Melchior and Gaspar Trechsel, Lyons, 1535.

Tooled leather; 6-3/4 x 4½ x 1-3/4 in.

IMPRINTS, France.

Cabinet 40 Shelf 1 No. 16

Estienne, Robert. Paris, 1544-45.
Title: Valerii Maximi dictorum factorum que memorabilium exemple ... (Printer Mark).
Imprint: Lutetiae, ex officina Roberti Stephani Typographie Regii. 1544.

Calf; 6¾ x 4¼ x 7/8 in.

IMPRINTS, France.

Cabinet 40 Shelf 2 No. 16

Estienne, Robert (I), Paris, 1550.
Title: Novum Testamentum ... [Greek text].
Imprint: Lutetiae, ex officina Roberti Stephani typographi Regii, Regiis typis.

Calf; 13¼ x 9 x 1¾ in.

IMPRINTS, France.

Cabinet 70 Shelf 1 No. 8

Eustace, Guillaume. Paris, 1511.

See Early Printing in France. Paris, 1511. Guillaume Eustace.

IMPRINTS, France.

Cabinet 40 Shelf 1 No. 19

Estienne, Robert. Paris, 1546.
Title: La coltivatione di Luigi Alamanni ...
Imprint: Stampato a Parigi da Ruberto Stephano. Regio stampatore. 1546.

Morocco; gilt tooling; 8-4/8 x 53/4 x 7/8 in.

IMPRINTS, France.

Cabinet 40 Shelf 1 No. 29

Estienne, Robert (I), Paris, 1551.
Title: Dionis Nicae rerum Romanarum ... [Greek and Latin text].
Imprint: Lutetiae, ex officina Roberti Stephani, typographi Regii, Regiis typis.

Vellum; 9¾ x 6¾ x 2 in.

IMPRINTS, France

Cabinet X Shelf 4 No. 34

Fournier, L. A Auxerre, 1791.
Title: Loi, le Juin 28, 1791, relative a brochure arguée de faux...
Imprint: A Auxerre, de l'Imprimerie de L. Fournier, Imprimeur du Département de l'Yonne.

Items 107, 109, 114 in book with binder's title "French legislation relating to printing. Various items. vol. II, 1640-1793".

IMPRINTS, France.

Cabinet 40 Shelf 2 No. 28

Estienne, Robert (I). Paris, 1548.
Title: Dionis a Romanarum historiarum ...
Imprint: Lutetiae : ex officina Rob. Stephani, typographi regii, typis regiis. 1548.

Calf; 13¼ x 9 x 1½ in.

IMPRINTS, France.

Cabinet 40 Shelf 1 No. 32

Estienne, Robert. Paris, 1552.
Title: Ad censures theologorum ...
Imprint: Oliva Roberti Stephani 1552.

Morocco; 7-1/8 x 4-5/8 x 3/4 in.

IMPRINTS, France

Cabinet X Shelf 4 No. 32

Fournier, L., Auxerre, 1793.

See LIBERTY OF PRINTING, France Decret (du 28 Fevrier, 1793)...

IMPRINTS, France.

Cabinet 69 Shelf 1 No. 12

Frellon, Jean. Lyons, 1547.
Title: Icones historiarum veteris testamenti ...
Imprint: Lugduni, apud Ioannem Frellonium. 1547.

Calf; 7-3/8 x $5\frac{1}{4}$ x 3/8 in.

IMPRINTS, France.

Cabinet 69 Shelf 1 No. 33

Frellon, Jean (II). Lyons, 1560-62.
Title: Scholia Pauli Manutii.
Imprint: Lugduni, apud Joannem Frellonium. [Printer Mark].
Bound in with two additional commentaries each with own title page, printer mark, and imprints dated 1562. Colophon of last two sections: "Lugduni, excudebat Symphorianus Barbierus."

Calf; 6-7/8 x $4\frac{1}{4}$ x $2\frac{1}{2}$ in. Baudrier V, 252.

IMPRINTS, France.

Cabinet 69 Shelf 1 No. 23

Gaultherot, Vivant, Paris, 1553.
Title: Apiani. Cosmographia ...
Imprint: Parisiis. Veneunt apud Viventium Gaultherot, via Jacobea: Sub insignia D. Martini.

Half vellum; 9x $6\frac{1}{4}$ x $\frac{3}{4}$ in.

IMPRINTS, France.

Cabinet 70 Shelf 1 No. 5

Gering, Ulrich and Berthold Rembolt. Paris 1508.
Title: Beatissimi Gregorii ... In septe psalmos penitentiales ... [Rembolt device on title page.
Colophon: In Sole aureo Parisiis vicos Sorbonico opera Udalrici Gering et Berchtoldi Rebolt socio [ri]. 1508. Marcii.

Mottled paper over boards; 8-3/8 x $5\frac{3}{4}$ x 3/8"

IMPRINTS, France.

Cabinet 70 Shelf 1 No. 45

Giunta, Jacques and Franciscus. Lyons, 1533-4
Title I: Eusebius historia.
Colophon: Impressa lugduni per Benedictum Bonnyn calcographum. Sumptibus Jacobi. ç. Francisci de Giuncta, sociorum, Florentini, 1533.
Title II: Historia Tripertita. Cassiodorun.
Imprint: Veneun Lugduni apud Jacubu Giuncti in vico Mercuriali. 1534. Printer marks.

Calf; $7\frac{1}{4}$ x $4\frac{3}{4}$ x $1\frac{1}{2}$ in. Blaudelaire 6, 150.

IMPRINTS, France.

Cabinet F Shelf 4 No. 85

Grangé. Paris, 1773.
Title: Chefs-D'Oeuvre dramatiques....Par M. Marmontel.
Imprint: A Paris, de l'Imprimerie de Grangé, rue de la Parcheminerie, 1773. Avec approbation et privilege du roi.

Paper Boards; $11\frac{3}{4}$ x $9\frac{1}{4}$ x 1 in.

IMPRINTS, France.

Cabinet 69 Shelf 1 No. 13

Groulleau, Estienne (I). Paris, 1547.
Title: La cyropedie de Xenophon. [Printer Mark].
Imprint: A Paris, de l'Imprimerie d'Estienne Groulleau, demourant ... a l'enseigne Saint Jan Baptiste, contre Sainte Genevieve des Ardants. 1547.

Morocco; $9\frac{1}{4}$ x $6\frac{1}{2}$ x 7/8 in.

IMPRINTS, France.

Cabinet 69 Shelf 1 No. 40

Gryphe, Antoine. Lyons, 1573.
Title: La prosopographie ou description des personnes insignes ... Par Antoine du Verdier.
Imprint: A Lyon, par Antoine Gryphius, 1573. [Printer Mark].
This book is an attempt at an illustrated dictionary of universal biography.

Calf; $9\frac{1}{4}$ x 6-7/8 x 2 in.

IMPRINTS, France.

Cabinet 70 Shelf 2 No. 6

Gryphe, Sebastien. Paris, 1528.
Title: Adiorum opus des Erasmi Roterodami ...
Imprint: Sebastianus Gryphius Germanus, excudebat Lugduni, anno. 1528.

Calf; $12\frac{3}{4}$ x 9 x $1\frac{1}{2}$ in.

IMPRINTS, France.

Cabinet 70 Shelf 1 No. 49

Gryphe, Sebastien. Lyons, 1535.
Title: Stephani Doleti dialogus de imitatione Ciceroniana ... Printer Mark.
Imprint: Lugduni apud Seb. Gryphium.M.D.XXXV.

Calf; $8\frac{3}{4}$ x 6 x $\frac{1}{2}$ in. Gresswell's I, 296.

IMPRINTS, France.

Cabinet 70 Shelf 2 No. 15 (2 vols.)

Gryphe, Sebastian. Lyons, 1536-38.
Title: Commentariorum linguae latinae ... Stephano Doleto ... (2 vols.)
Imprint: Lugduni, apud Seb. Gryphium. 1563.

Calf; $13\frac{1}{2}$ x 9-3/8 x $2\frac{1}{2}$ in.

IMPRINTS, France

Cabinet 70 Shelf 1 No. 55

Gryphius, Sebastien. Lyons, 1552.
Title: Aonii Palearii verulani di animorum imortalitate. Libri III.
Imprint: Apud Seb. Gryphium. Lugduni, 1552.

Paper cover; 6-5/8 c $4\frac{1}{4}$ in.

IMPRINTS, France.

Cabinet 69 Shelf 1 No. 26

Gryphe. Sebastien. Lyons, 1555.
Title: Nicolai Leonici Thomaei. De varia historia. Libri tres.
Imprint: Apud Seb. Gryphium. Lugduni, 1555.
Bound in with Libanius [Greek text], printed at Lyons by Jean Gullieron, 1614.

Boards; leather back; $4\frac{3}{4}$ x 3-7/8 x 1 in.

IMPRINTS, France.

Cabinet 70 Shelf 2 No. 23

Guillard, Charlotte. Paris, 1544.
Title: D. Hilarii ... Lucubrationes olim per Des. Erasmum ... nunc denuo virgilantissima cura emendatae. [With printer device].
Imprint: Parisiis. Ex officina Carolae Guillard, sub Sole aureo, via ad divum Jacobum, 1544.

Boards; $13\frac{1}{2}$ x 9-1/8 x $1\frac{1}{2}$ in.

IMPRINTS, France

Cabinet 69 Shelf 1 No. 60

Guillemot, Matthieu (I) Paris, 1600.
Title: Le tableau des riches inventions...qui sont representées dans le Songe de Poliphile ...exposées par Beroald [de Verville].
Imprint: À Paris chez Mattieu Guillemot. 1600.

Half morocco; $10\frac{1}{2}$ x $7\frac{1}{2}$ x 3/4 in. Brunet 4, 779.

IMPRINTS, France

Cabinet W Shelf 1 No. 01

Huguetan, Jean. Lyon, 1642.
Title: Essay des merveilles de nature...Par René François.
Imprint: À Lyon, chez Jean Huguetan, rue Mercière, au plat d'é ain. MDCXLII.
p. 300: L'Imprimerie
p. 377: Paper

Vellum; $6\frac{1}{2}$ x 4 x $1\frac{1}{4}$ in.

IMPRINTS, France.

Cabinet 69 Shelf 1 No. 51

Huillier (l'), Pierre. Paris, 1584.
Title: De la vicissitude on variete des choses en l'univers ... Par Loys le Roy dict Regius. [Printer Mark].
Imprint: A Paris, A l'Olivier de Pierre l'Huillier M.D.LXXXIIII. Avec privilege du Roy.

Vellum; 6-5/8 x $4\frac{1}{4}$ x $1\frac{1}{2}$ in. Brunet 3,1000-1.

IMPRINTS, France

Cabinet F Shelf 4 No. 92

Imprimerie de Monsieur, Paris, 1785.
Title: Precis historique de la vie de M. de Bonnard. Par M. Garat.
Imprint: A Paris, de l'imprimerie de Monsieur. 1785.

Quarter morocco; $5\frac{3}{4}$ x 3-3/8 x 3/8 in.

IMPRINTS, France

Cabinet QQ Shelf 2 No. 1 (5 vols.)

L'Imprimerie Nationale, Paris, 1793.
Title: Troisième recueil. Pieces imprimées d'après le décret de la Convention Nationale...(5 vols.)
Imprint: A Paris, de l'Imprimerie Nationale. 1793.

Boards, tree-calf back; 8 x 5 in.

IMPRINTS, France

Cabinet B Shelf 3 No. 2

Imprimerie Nationale, Paris, 1900
Title: A la memoire de Jean Gutenberg... (With 17 plates)
Imprint: Paris. Imprimerie Nationale. Juin, 1900.

Morocco; 17 x 13 in.

IMPRINTS, France

Cabinet C Shelf 2 No. 4.01

l'Imprimerie Nationale, Paris, 1900
Title: l'Académie des Inscriptions...de l'Institute de France à l'Académie Royale des Sciences de Prusse.

Printed in the Garamond types of 1550. Cochin decorations of 1753.

Paper; $19\frac{1}{2}$ x 13 in.

IMPRINTS, France

Cabinet E Shelf 3 No. 64

Imprimerie Royale.Paris, 1640.

See Early Printing in France. Paris, 1640.

IMPRINTS, France.

Cabinet E Shelf 3 No. 72

(L)'Imprimerie Royale. Paris, 1642.

See Early Printing in France. Paris, 1642.

IMPRINTS, France

Cabinet X Shelf 4 No. 32

L'Imprimerie Royale, Paris, 1725

See LIBERTY OF PRINTING, France Arrest (Avril 10, 1725)...

IMPRINTS, France.

Cabinet F Shelf 4 No. 82

Imprimerie Royale: Paris, 1750.
Title: Oeuvres de M. de Crebillon,de l'Academie Francaise. 2 vols. with engravings designed by F. Boucher, Peintre du Roy.
Imprint: A Paris, de l'Imprimerie Royale. 1750.

Leather; $10\frac{1}{4}$ x $8\frac{3}{4}$ x $1\frac{1}{4}$ in. Brunet 2, 412.

IMPRINTS, France

Cabinet EE Shelf 3 No. 51

Jannon, Jean. Sedan, 1633.

See Early Printing in France. Sedan, 1633.

IMPRINTS, France.

Cabinet 69 Shelf 1 No. 1

Janot, Denys. Paris, 1539.
Title: Le theatre des bons engins, auquel sont contenuz cent emblems moraulx. Compose par Guillaume de la Perriere ...
Colophon: Imprime a Paris par Denys Janot ... [Printer Mark].

Morocco; $6\frac{1}{2}$ x $4\frac{1}{4}$ x $\frac{1}{2}$ in.

IMPRINTS, France

Cabinet F Shelf 5 No. 18

Jombert, Charles-Antoine. Paris, 1755.
Title: Fables choisies mises en vers par J. de la Fontaine. (2 vols. with full page etchings)
Imprint: A Paris, 1755. De l'Imprimerie de Charles-Antoine Jombert.

Leather; $16\frac{1}{2}$ x $11\frac{1}{4}$ x $2\frac{1}{2}$ in.

IMPRINTS, FRANCE

Cabinet I Shelf 1 No. 18

Jorry, Sebastien, Paris, 1750.

See CHRIST, J. FRED. Dictionnaire des monogrammes...

IMPRINTS, France.

Cabinet 69 Shelf 1 No. 26

Jullieron, Jean. Lyons, 1614.
Title: Libanii sophistae characteres ... [Greek and Latin text].
Imprint: Lugduni typis Joannis Jullieron. Bound in with a 1555 item printed by Sebastien Gryphe.

Boards, leather back; $4\frac{3}{4}$ x 3-7/8 x 1 in.

IMPRINTS, France

Cabinet 29 Shelf 2 No. 14

Kerver, Jacques. Paris, 1561.
Title: Hypernotomachie, ou, discours du songe de Poliphile ... traduit de langage Italian en France.
Imprint: A Paris. Pour Jacques Kerver a la Licorne, rue S. Jacques, 1561.

Tree calf; $13\frac{1}{2}$ x 9 x $1\frac{1}{2}$ in.

IMPRINTS, France.

Cabinet 29 Shelf 2 No. 13

Kerver, Jacques, Paris, 1561.
Title: Polygraphie, et Universelle escriture cabalistique de M. I. Tritheme Abbé ...
Imprint: Pour Iagues Kerver demeurant en la ruë sainct Iaques, à l'enseigne de la Licorne, 1561.

Calf; 10 x 8 x 2-1/8 in.

IMPRINTS, France

Cabinet 29 Shelf 1 No. 41

Kerver, Thielman. Paris, 1503.
Title: Hore intemerate virginis marie secundum usum Romanum...[Printer's device].
Colophon...furet achevées par Thielman Kerver imprimeur et libraire...de Paris. Illuminated, printed on vellum.

Calf; 7-3/8 x 5 x $1\frac{1}{4}$ in.

IMPRINTS, France.

Cabinet 29 Shelf 2 No. 3

Kerver, Thielman. Paris, 1507.
Title: Decretales dni pape Gregorii noni ...
Colophon: ... Impresse Parisiis solerti cura Thielmani Kerver Impressoris ac librorii ... Parisienso. Anno dni 1507. nonis Januarii.

Calf; $9\frac{1}{4}$ x $6\frac{3}{4}$ x $2\frac{1}{4}$ in.

IMPRINTS, France.

Cabinet 29 Shelf 2 No. 6

Kerver, Thielman, Paris, 1511.
Title: Hore dive vgis Marie scdm̄ verūsum Romanū. [Title page composed of the Kerver wood cut printers device. Printed on vellum. Illuminated initial letters].
Colophon: Finit offici bte marievirgis scdm̄ usum Romanū...Imp̄ssum parissi Thielmanu Kerver. Anno dn̄i M.CCCCCXI Die xxiiii Iulii.

Full morocco; 7 x 4-3/8 in. In protective case.

IMPRINTS, France.

Cabinet 29 Shelf 2 No. 9

Kerver, Thielman [Widow]. Paris, 1523.
Title: Hore deipare virginis marie secundum usum Romanum.
Colophon: Finiuntur hore ... Parisiis, opera ac impensis vidue defuncti ... Thielmani Kerver ... Anno dni 1523 die 30 Martii ...

Vellum; $6\frac{1}{2}$ x 4-1/8 x 1 in.

IMPRINTS, France

Cabinet 29 Shelf 1 No. 44

Kerver, Thielman. Paris, 1506.
Title: Decretum aurem domini Gratiani...
Colophon:...expensis et opera Johannis parui et Thielmani Kerver bibliopolarum parisiensium in vico diva Jacobi...1506. Octobris 21.

Boards; 9-7/8 x 7¼ x 3/4 in.

IMPRINTS, France.

Cabinet E Shelf 2 No. 80

Le Be (Guillaume III). Paris, 1609.

See Early Printing in France. Paris, 1609.

IMPRINTS, France.

Cabinet 70 Shelf 1 No. 16

Lenoire, Michel. Paris, 1518.
Title: Le rebours de Matheolus [Facsimile lithographed on veneered wood].
Colophon: ... Nouvellement imprime a Paris par Michel Le Noir...

Morocco; 7½ x 4¾ x 6/8 in.

IMPRINTS, France.

Cabinet 70 Shelf 1 No. 15

La Barre, Nicolas de. Paris, 1518.
Title: La mer des croniques et mirouer historical iadis composé en latin par Robert Gaguin...Nouvellement translaté...Printer Mark
Imprint: on les vent en la rue des carmes a lenseigne sainct iehan Baptiste. Illus.

Calf; 10½ x 7½ x 1¼ in.

IMPRINTS, FRANCE

Cabinet J Shelf 2 No. 13

Le Be, Guillaume, Paris, 1647.

See Cousin, Jean. Science de la pourtraicture... Paris, 1647.

IMPRINTS, France

Cabinet 70 Shelf 1 No. 23

Le Noir, Philippe. Paris, 1524.
Title: Les illustrations de Gaule et Singularitez de Troye. Fratris Petri....Illus.
Imprint: Cy les vend à Paris par Philippe Lenoir marchāt libraire et relieur...rue Sainct Jaques à lenseigne de la Rose blanche couronnée. [There are four parts to this volume; each with Lenoir imprint, colophon, and printer mark].

Morocco over boards, clasps; 10-3/4 x 7-3/4 x 1-3/4 in.

IMPRINTS, France

Cabinet I Shelf 1 No. 9

Langlois, Francois, Paris, 1642.

See TAVERNIER, MELCHIOR. Methodes universelles pour faire des perspectives...

IMPRINTS, France

Cabinet 29 Shelf 2 No. 14

Leblanc, Jean. Paris, 1561.
Title: Poliphile. Hypnerotomachie...nouvellement traduict de langue Italien en François...
Imprint: Imprimé pour Jaques Kerver...par Jehan Le Blanc, le XI jour de Juillet, l'an 1561.

Calf; 13¼ x 9 x 1-1/8 in. Brunet 4, 779.

IMPRINTS, France.

Cabinet E Shelf 4 No. 27

Léonard, Frederic. Paris, 1660.

See Early Printing in France. Paris, 1660.

IMPRINTS, France.

Cabinet I Shelf 5 No. 21

Langlois, Jacques, Paris, 1511.
Title: Traite de la peinture de Leonardo Da Vinci.
Imprint: A Paris, De l'Imprimerie de Jacques Langlois, Imprimeur ordinaire du Roy, au mont Sainct Generiefue, vis a vis la Fonteine, a la Reyne de Paix.
With many copper engravings.

Half morocco; 18½ x 11 x ¾ in.

IMPRINTS, France.

Cabinet F Shelf 5 No. 16

Le Breton. Paris, 1751.

See Early Printing in France. Paris, 1751. Le Breton.

IMPRINTS, France (Alsace-Lorraine)

Cabinet X Shelf 2 No. 38

Levrault (the widow of), Strassburg, 1840.

See CELEBRATIONS, Printers. 1840, Strassburg...

IMPRINTS, France

Cabinet I Shelf 5 No. 21

Langlois, Jacques, Paris, 1651.

See Early Printing in France. Paris, 1651.

IMPRINTS, France.

Cabinet 70 Shelf 1 No. 43

Lecoq. Jean II. Troyes [1533 or 1544?].
Title: la vie de Saincte Marguerite Vièrge et martyre. [Facsimile].
Imprint: Imprimé à Troyes chez Jean Lecoq, n.d. Printer Mark.
The design of the printer mark is said to indicate that this booklet must have been printed by the widow Lecoq. Thibaut Trumen, or Jean II. Lecoq.

Marbled paper; 7¼ x 4-7/8 in.

IMPRINTS, France

Cabinet QQ Shelf 1 No. 10

Lottin, Jean-Roch, Paris, 1785.
Title: Plainte de la typographie...Par Henri Estienne, IIe du nom.
Imprint: A Paris, chez Jean-Roch Lottin de S.-Germain, imprimeur-libraire ordinaire de la ville.

Morocco; 9½ x 7½ in.

IMPRINTS, France

Cabinet V Shelf 4 No. 4

Laulne, Jean de. Paris, 1694.
Title: L'Origine de l'imprimerie de Paris...Par André Chevillier.
Imprint: Paris, chez Jean de Laulne, rue de la Harpe, proche le College d'Harcourt...M.D.C.XCIV. Bound in with another item printed by Jean de la Caille, Paris, 1689.

Calf; 10-1/8 x 7¼ x 1¼ in.

IMPRINTS, FRANCE

Cabinet X Shelf 4 No. 35

Lemercier, Paris, 1731

See LIBERTY OF PRINTING. France. Edit du roy...Lemercier, Paris, 1731

IMPRINTS, France

Cabinet F Shelf 5 No. 31

Maisonneuve, Defer de. Paris, 1793.
Title: Galatee, roman pastoral; imite de Cervantes, par M. de Florian...Edition ornee de figures en couleur, d'apres les dessins de Monsiau.
Imprint: A Paris, chez Defer de Maisonneuve, rue du Foin S. Jacques.

Leather, gilt; 13¾ x 10¼ x 1 in. Brunet 2, 1307.

IMPRINTS, France.

Cabinet E Shelf 4 No. 21

Moreau, Adrien. Paris, 1658.

IMPRINTS, France

Cabinet X Shelf 4 No. 36

Muguet, Francois, Paris, 1702

See LIBERTY OF PRINTING, France Lettres patentes (2 Octobre 1701)...

IMPRINTS, FRANCE

Cabinet J Shelf 4 No. 14

Pichon, Léon, Paris, 1925.

See WOOD ENGRAVINGS. Hermann, Paul. Conseils obscurs...Paris, 1925.

IMPRINTS, France

Cabinet E Shelf 3 No. 76

Moreau, Pierre. Paris, 1644.

See Early Printing in France. Paris, 1644.

IMPRINTS, France

Cabinet X Shelf 4 No. 32

Muguet, Hubert, Paris, 1716.

See LIBERTY OF PRINTING. France Arrest (1716)...

IMPRINTS, France.

Cabinet D Shelf 2 No. 53

Pigouchet, Philippe, Paris, 1500. Guillermus Altissiodorensis. Summa in IV libros sententiarum, per Vaultier et Dur. Gerlier.
Colophon: Summa aurea.....Impressa est Parisiis maxima Philippi Pigoucheti cura, impensis vero Nicolai vaul/tier et Durandi gerlier alme universitatis Parisiensis librariorum inratorum (etc) [Has two Pigouchet printer marks]
Wood, covered with decorated calf; folio 11½ x 8½ ins. 2½ ins. thick. Hain 8324.

IMPRINTS, France.

Cabinet 69 Shelf 1 No. 43

Morel, Frederic. Paris, 1575.
Title: Octo cantica sacra e sacris bibliis latino carmoni expressa. Io. Matthaeo Toscano.
Imprint: Parisiis, Ex officina Federici Morelli. Typographi Regii, 1575.

Calf; 6-7/8 x 4-3/8 x ½ in.

IMPRINTS, France.

Cabinet 69 Shelf 1 No. 5

Neobar, Conrad. Paris, 1539.
Title: Aristoteles: Rhetoric. [Greek text, and printer mark].
Imprint: Parisiis. Per Conradum Neobarium. Regium Typographum.
Bound in with another Greek item with the imprint of Adrien Turnebe, and the colophon of Guillaume Morel. Paris, 1555.

Calf; gilt edges; 10½ x 8 x 1½ in.

IMPRINTS, France

Cabinet QQ Shelf 1 No. 31

Pinard, J. Paris, 1827.
Title: Eloge en vers de l'imprimerie. Par un Typographe. Paris, Ambroise Dupont et Ce, Libraires.
Imprint: Imprimerie et fonderie de J. Pinard, rue d'Anjou-Dauphine.

Half cloth; 9 x 5-7/8 x ¼ in.

IMPRINTS, France.

Cabinet E Shelf 3 No. 60

Morel, Gilles. Paris, 1638.
Title: Interpretatione div. Scripturae epistolarum ... Isiodorus Pelusiota. [Greek and Latin text].
Imprint: Paris, Aegid Morellius.

Calf; 13¼ x 9½ x 2¼ in. Brunet 3, 464.

IMPRINTS, France.

Cabinet E Shelf 3 No. 28

Osmont, Jean. Rouen, 1626.

See Early Printing in France. Rouen, 1626. Jean Osmont.

IMPRINTS, France.

Cabinet 2 Shelf 1 No. 20

Plantin-Moretus Press: Hadrian Perier. Paris, 1598.

See Early Printing in France. Paris, 1598. Plantin-Moretus Press: Hadrian Perier.

IMPRINTS, France.

Cabinet 70 Shelf 2 No. 11

Morrhy, Gerard and Jean Pierre. Paris, 1532.
Title: Orontii Finei. Protomathesis: Opus varium.
Colophon: Excusum est autem ipsum opus Parisiis in vico Sorbonico, impensis Gerardi Morrhi et Ioannis Petri ...

Vellum; 14½ x 10½ x 2 in.

IMPRINTS, France

Cabinet C Shelf 3 No. 2

Panckoucke, C.L.F., Paris, 1827
Title: La science du bonhomme Richard. Par Benj. Franklin.
Imprint: Paris, Imprimé par C.L.F. Panckoucke, 1827.

Half morocco; 20 x 15½ in.

IMPRINTS, France.

Cabinet 70 Shelf 2 No. 2

Rembolt, Berthold. Paris, 1514.
Title: Cornucopie. D. Nicolai Perotti ... [Printer mark].
Imprint: Venundat ubi nuper impressum est Parrhisiis in via regia ad divum Jacobum sub Sole aurea ...
Colophon: Impressum ... per magistrum Bartholdum Rembolt, Germano.

Tooled leather; 4¾ x 10 x 2½ in.

IMPRINTS, France.

Cabinet E Shelf 4 No. 53

Muguet, Francois. Paris, 1671.

See Early Printing in France. Paris, 1671.

IMPRINTS, France.

Cabinet 40 Shelf 1 No. 64

Patisson, Mamert and Robert Estienne. Paris, 1587.
Title: Premieres ouvres de Philippes des Portes
Imprint: A Paris, par Mamert Patisson, Imprimeur du Roy, chez Robert Estienne.

Vellum; 5¾ x 3-3/8 x 1¼ in.

IMPRINTS, France.

Cabinet 70 Shelf 1 No. 26

Rosset, Pierre. Paris [1525].
Title: Horae [Engraved title pages with border and printer mark].
Imprint: ... faictes a Paris pour Pierre Rosset, libraire demourant en la rue me.sue a lesei. du faulcheur. n.d.

Tooled leather; 8¾ x 6 x 1 in.

IMPRINTS, France.

Cabinet 69 Shelf 2 No. 3

Roux, Richard. [For Jean (I) Ruelle]. Paris, 1560.
Title: Les annales et croniques de France ... Corrigees par le Seigneur Denis Sauvage.
Colophon; ... Imprimees a Paris, par Richard Roux Imprimeur, demourant en la rue Sainct Victor a l'Enseigne Sancte Catherine. 1560.

Calf; 13¼ x 8½ x 1½ in. Brunet 2, 1596.

IMPRINTS, France

Cabinet H Shelf 5 No. 36

Schmied, F.-L, Paris (1929)
Title: Suetone. Les douze Cesars. Traduction inedite de Joseph Esteve. Preface de Louis Barthou de l'Academie Francaise.
Imprint: Chez F.-L. Schmied, peint-Graveur et imprimeur, rue Halle 74 Bis, Paris.

Presentation copy to Henry Lewis Bullen

Boards, cloth back; 11¼ x 7¾ in.

IMPRINTS, France

Cabinet X Shelf 4 No. 36

Thierry, Denis, Paris, 1687.

See LIBERTY OF PRINTING, France
Edit du roy (21 Aoust, 1686)...

IMPRINTS, France.

Cabinet 69 Shelf 1 No. 28

Roville, Guillaume and Mathieu Bonhomme, Lyons, 1556.
Title I: Orlando furioso de M. Ludovico Ariosto. [Printer Mark]. A Lyon en casa de Gulielmo Roville.
Title: II:Exposicion de todos los lugares difficultosos ... [Printer Mark]. En Leon, en casa de Gulielmo Rovillio.

(Cont'd)

IMPRINTS, France

Cabinet C Shelf 3 No. 4

Simon, E. fils, Strasbourg, 1840
Title: Fètes de Gutenberg. Lithographie de cortége...
Imprint: Strasbourg: E.Simon fils, Imp. Lith.

Half calf; 13 x 20½ in.

IMPRINTS, France.

Cabinet 70 Shelf 1 No. 27

Tory, Geofroy. Paris, 1525.
Title: Heures a la louange de la Vierge Marie ... [Printer mark. Paris, 1525]. Geofroy Tory.
Imprint: a vendre par maistre Geofroy Tory de Bourges, libraire demorant a Paris sus Petit Pont ioignant lhostel Dieu, a lenseigne du Pot Casse.

Old calf; gold tooled; 8¾ x 5½ x 1 in.

Cabinet Shelf No.

Colophon following second title: Fue impresso el present libro en la inclita cuidad de Leon en casa de Mathias Bonhomme.

Morocco; 9¼ x 6½ x 1-5/8 in.

IMPRINTS, France

Cabinet X Shelf 4 No. 32

Simon, Pierre, Paris, 1735 (Imprint)

See LIBERTY OF PRINTING, France
Arrest du Roy (2 Avril, 1735)...

IMPRINTS, France.

Cabinet 70 Shelf 1 No. 37

Tory, Geofroy. Paris, 1529.
Title: Champ Fleury...
Imprint: a Paris sus Petit Pont a lenseigne du Pot Casse par maistre Geofroy Tory de Bourges, libraire et autheur du dict livre ... [With printer mark].

Tooled leather; 10 x 7 x 1 in.

IMPRINTS, France.

Cabinet 69 Shelf 2 No. 1

Roville, Guillaume. Lyons, 1550.
Title: Ioannis Corasii Tolosatis, iurisconsulti clarissimi ... Pandectarum ...
Imprint: Lugduni, apud Gulielmum Rovillium ... 1550.
Bound in with another item printed by Matthieu Bonhomme, Lyons, 1552.

Vellum; 13 x 8½ x 2 in. In protective case.

IMPRINTS, France.

Cabinet F Shelf 5 No. 20 n.o.s.

Simon, Pierre-Guillaume. Paris, 1766.
Title: Bibliothèque des artistes et des amateurs ...Par l'Abbé Petity. 3 Vols. Illus.
Imprint: Paris, chez P. G. Simon, Imprimeur du Parlement. Rue de la Harpe, à Hercule.
Head pieces, allegories, vignettes, in copper, wood and types, are of unusual merit.
The contents are virtually the same as that in the "Encyclopédie Élementaire", 1767, by the same author, which is in V/5/4.
Tree calf; each 10¼ x 8½ in. Brunet 4,533.

IMPRINTS, France.

Cabinet 39 Shelf 2 No. 3

Tournes, Jean de (I), Lyons, 1547.
Title: Il Dante ... novamente revisto & stampato.
Imprint: In Lione, per Giovan di Tournes.

Morocco; 5¼ x 5¼ x 1¼ in. Vingtrinier 209.

IMPRINTS, France.

Cabinet 69 Shelf 1 No. 35

Roville, Guillaume. Lyons, 1561.
Title: Description de la l'image d'Auvergne en forme de dialogue ...
Imprint: A Lyon, par Guillaume Roville, 1561.

Boards; 8½ x 6½ x ½ in. Brunet 5,391.

IMPRINTS, France

Cabinet F Shelf 5 No. 28

Société Litteraire-Typographique. Paris, 1789.
Title: La Henriad, poeme de Voltaire,
Imprint: De l'Imprimerie de la Société Litteraire-Typographique. 1789.

Leather; 12½ x 10 x 2¼ in. Brunet 5, 1360.

IMPRINTS, France.

Cabinet 39 Shelf 2 No. 5

Tournes, Jean (I) de. Lyons, 1550.
Title: Physionomie naturelle. Extraite de plusieurs philosophes anciens ...
Imprint: A Lyon, par Jean de Tournes.

(Bound by Lortic) Full morocco; 6½ x 4¼ in.

IMPRINTS, France.

Cabinet 69 Shelf 2 No. 8

Roville, Guillaume. Lyons, 1566.
Title: Biblia Sacra ... cum Hebraicorum, Caldeorum et Graecorum nominum interpretatione ...
Imprint: Lugduni, apud Guliel. Rovillium, 1566.

Vellum; 16¼ x 10½ x 3¾ in.

IMPRINTS, France

Cabinet I Shelf 1 No. 9

Tavernier, Melchior, Paris, 1642.

See TAVERNIER, MELCHIOR. Methodes universelles pour faire des perspectives...

IMPRINTS, France.

Cabinet 39 Shelf 2 No. 7

Tournes, Jean (I) de. Lyons, 1552.
Title: M. Vitruvii Pollionis de Architectura ... [Printer Mark].
Imprint: Lugduni, apud Joan. Tornaesium. 1552.

Boards; 9¾ x 6-5/8 x 1 in. Brunet 5, 1327.

IMPRINTS, France.

Cabinet 39
Shelf 2
No. 9

Tournes, Jean (I) de. Lyons, 1554.
Title: Figure des vecchio testamento, con versi Toscani. Per Damian Maraffi. [Printer's device].
Imprint: In Lione, per Giovanni di Tournes. 1554.
Bound in with "Figure de Nuovo Testamento" Lyons, 1577. V Jean de Tournes.

Morocco; 6¼ x 4½ x 7/8 in.

IMPRINTS, France.

Cabinet 39
Shelf 2
No. 11

Tournes, Jean (I) de. Lyons, 1555.
Title: La Cyropedie de Xenophon de la vie & institution de Cyrus Roy des Perses. Traduite de Grec par Iaques des Comtes de Vintemille Rhodien....A Lion, par Ian de Tournes. M.D.LV.

Vellum; 9¼ x 6 x 1 in.

IMPRINTS, France.

Cabinet 39
Shelf 2
No. 13

Tournes, Jean (I) de. [Lyons, 1557?].
Title: Thesaurus amicorum. Variis iconibus ...
Imprint: Apud Joannn. Torneasium ...
Portraits medallions (184) with mottoes in various languages each with appropriate type. Wood cut borders.

Boards; 6-3/4 x 4¼ x 1¼ in.

IMPRINTS, France

Cabinet 39
Shelf 2
No. 15

Tournes, Jean (I) de. Lyons, 1558.
Title: D. Magni Ausonii. Burdigalensis Poëtae. Augustorum praeceptoris virique Consularis opera....
Imprint: Lugduni, apud Ioan Tornaesium, M.D.LVIII.

Morocco, gilt: 6½ x 4 x 3/4 in.

IMPRINTS, France.

Cabinet 39
Shelf 2
No. 14

Tournes, Jean (I) de. Lyons, 1558.
Title: Illustratione degli epitaffi et medaglie antichi, di Gabriel Symeoni.
Imprint: In Lione, per Giovan di Tournes M.D.LVIII.

Wood cuts and borders by Bernard Salomon.

Limp vellum; 8½ x 6¼ x ½ in.

IMPRINTS, France

Cabinet 39
Shelf 2
No. 19

Tournes, Jean (I) de. Lyons, 1559.
Title: La vita et metamorfoso d'Ovidio..... abbraviato da Gabriello Symeoni.
Imprint: Giovanni di Tornes, Lyons, 1559.

Tooled calf; 7 x 4-3/4 x 5/8 in. Updike I, 203-4.

IMPRINTS, France.

Cabinet 39
Shelf 2
No. 21

Tournes, Jean (I) de. Lyons, 1561.
Title: Alliances genealogiques des rois et princes de Gaule ... Par Claude Paradin. [Printer's Device].
Imprint: A Lion par Jan de Tournes, 1561.
Illustrated with wood cut heraldic devices.

Tooled morocco; 13½ x 8¼ x 2½ in. Brunet 4, 358.

IMPRINTS, France.

Cabinet 39
Shelf 2
No. 9

Tournes, Jean (I) de. Lyons, 1577.
Title: Figure de Nuovo Testamento. Illustrate de versi vulgari Italiani. [Wood engravings]
Imprint: In Lione, per Gio. Di Tournes, MCLXXVII.

Bound in with "Vecchio Testamento", 1554. Lyons, Jean de Tournes.
Morocco; 6¼ x 4½ x 7/8 in.

IMPRINTS, France.

Cabinet 40
Shelf 1
No. 25

Trechsel, Melchior and Gaspar. Lyons, 1535.
Title: Lexicon di partibus aedium Francisci Marii Grapaldi. [With printer mark of Simon Vincent].
Imprint: Lugduni, apud haeredes Simonis Vicentii
Colophon: Excudebant Lugduni Melchior et Gaspar Trechsel fratres, 1535.
Bound in with two items of Robert Estienne, Paris 1548 and 1550.

Tooled leather; 6¾ x 4½ x 1¾ in.

IMPRINTS, France.

Cabinet 69
Shelf 1
No. 21

Turnèbe, Adrien. Paris, 1552.
Title: Aeschyli Tragodiae sex [Greek Text]. Printer Mark.
Imprint: Parisiis. Ex officina Adriani Turnèbi, Typographia Regii. 1552. Typis Regis.

Contemporary pigskin; 6¾ x 4 x ½ in. Brunet I, 77.

IMPRINTS, France.

Cabinet 69
Shelf 1
No. 5

Turnebe, Adrien and Guillaume Morel. Paris, 1555.
Title: Aristoteles. [Greek and Latin text].
Imprint: Parisiis. 1555. Apud Adrianum Turnebum
Colophon: Excudebat ... Guil. Morelius.
Bound in with another Aristotle item printed in Greek and printed by Conrad Neobar Paris, 1539.

Calf, tooled gilt edges; 10½ x 8 x 1½ in.

IMPRINTS, France.

Cabinet E
Shelf 3
No. 77

Typographia Regia. Paris, 1644.

See Early Printing in France. Paris, 1644.

IMPRINTS, France

Cabinet QQ
Shelf 2
No. 6

Valade, fils ainé, de l'Imprimerie de. Paris, 1792.

see

SACHTLEBEN, JEAN HENRI. L'Art d'économiser le bois...

IMPRINTS, France.

Cabinet 70
Shelf 2
No. 18

Vascosan, Michael. Paris, 1538.
Title: Appianus Alexandrinus. De civilibus Romanorum bellis historiarum libri quinque ... [Two title pages, each with picture of Ascensian Press.]
Imprint: Parisiis, ex officina Michaelis Vascosani.

Calf; 13 x 8½ x 1¼ in.

IMPRINTS, France.

Cabinet 60
Shelf 2
No. 18

Vascosan, Michel. Paris, 1540.
Title: Jacobi Lodoici Strebaei in dialogos M.T. Ciceronis ... Commentaria.
Imprint: Parisiis. Ex officina Michaelis Vascosani, sub fonte, in via quae est ad divum Jacobum, 1540.
Bound in with a 1554 Paul Manutius item.

Vellum; 13 x 9 x 1-3/8 in.

IMPRINTS, France.

Cabinet 70
Shelf 2
No. 20

Vascosan, Michael. Paris, 1542.
Title: M. Fabii Quintiliani. Institutionum oratoriarum libri XII. [two parts; Second title with the Ascensian mark].
Imprint: Ex officina Michaelis Vascosani, in via quae est ad D. Jacobum sub fontis insigni 1542.

Calf; 13½ x 9 x 1¾ in.

IMPRINTS, France.

Cabinet 69
Shelf 2
No. 14

Vascosan, Michel de. Paris, 1572.
Title: Plutarch: Les oeuvres morales et melées. Translatées du Grec en Francois (2 vols.)
Imprint: A Paris, de l'Imprimerie de Michel Vascosan. 1572.

Vellum; 15½ x 10 x 2in. Brunet 4, 737.

IMPRINTS, France.

Cabinet 70
Shelf 1
No. 34

Vidoue, Pierre. Paris, 1528.
Title: Les XXI epistres Davide translatée de latin in Fracoys par monseignr Dangoulesme [Publishers device]. Ils se vende en la bontique de Galliot, Patis, MDXVIII.
Colophon:...imprimées à Paris, par Pierre Vidoue, pour Galliot du pre...de Paris, ayāt sa bouticque au premier pillier de la grande salle du pallais.

Morocco; 5-3/8 x 3¼ x ½ in.

IMPRINTS, France.

Cabinet E Shelf 4 No. 34

Vitre, Antoine. Paris, 1662.

See Early Printing in France. Paris,1662.

IMPRINTS, France

Cabinet 70 Shelf 1 No. 19

Vostre, Simon. Paris, 1520.
Title: Horae Beatae Virginis ad usum Romanum.
[Printed on vellum, illuminated. Printer mark].
Imprint: Les presentes heures a l'usaige de Rome ...ont est faictes a Paris pour Symo Vostre, Libraire demourat a leseigne s. ioh levagel.

Calf; 7¼ x 4¾ in.

IMPRINTS, France.

Cabinet 69 Shelf 1 No. 10

Wechel, Christian. Paris, 1542.
Title: Clarissimi viri D. Andreae Alciati emblematum libellus ... [Printer Mark].
Imprint: Parisiis. Apud Christianum Wechelum, sub scuto Basiliensi, in vico Jacobeo; et sub Pegaso, in vico Bellovacensi. 1542.

Half morocco; 6-1/8 x 4 x ½ in. Brunet 1,147

IMPRINTS, France.

Cabinet 40 Shelf 2 No. 19

Wechel, Andreas, Paris, 1564.
Title: Gorraeus (J). Definitionum medicarum ... Wechelum, sub Pegaso, in voco Bellovaco. 1564.
[Two books bound in one. Second book in the volume printed by Simon de Colines. Paris, 1526.]

Calf; 13 x 9 x 2-3/4 in.

IMPRINTS, France.

Cabinet 40 Shelf 2 No. 19

Wechel, Andreas. Paris, 1564.

See Early Printing in France. Paris, 1564. Andreas Wechel.

IMPRINTS, France

Cabinet I Shelf 1 No. 4

Wechel, Christian, Paris, 1535.
Title: Albertus Durer, Nurembergensis pictor... adeo exacte quatuor his suarum Institutionum Geometricarum libris...
Imprint: Paris: Christian Wechel, 1535.

With printer mark.

Boards, leather back; 12¾ x 8½ x 5/8 in.

IMPRINTS, Germany

Cabinet D Shelf 3 No. 11

Anshelm, Thomas. Pförzheim, 1503.

Title: De laudibus Sancte Crucis. Rabanus.
Imprint: Pforcheim in aedibus Thome Anshelmi Martio mense. MD.III.

Parchment over boards; 12¼ x 8¼ x 3¼ ins.
Brunet IV, 1035.

IMPRINTS, Germany

Cabinet 10 Shelf 2 No. 10

Augsburg Monastery of SS. Ulrich and Afra. circa 1478. Salomon, episcopus Constantiensis Glossae ex illustrissimis collectae auctoribus incipiunt soeliciter.
"The work is a glossary of Hebrew, Greek and Latin; its author, Salomon von Romschwag was abbot of St. Gall in 890."

Stamped pigskin; 16 x 11 x3½ in.

IMPRINTS, Germany

Cabinet F Shelf 4 No. 52

Bauch, Christian. Breslau, 1711.
Title: Vitae illustrum virorum...
Imprint: Vratislaviae, sumptibus Christiani Bauchii, 1711.

Vellum; 5-3/4 x 4-1/8 x 1½ in.

IMPRINTS, Germany

Cabinet 17 Shelf 2 No. 2

Beerwaldinis -- Leipzig. n.d.
(Wood engraving from a title page. With printer's device and imprint: "Gedruckt zu Leipzig. Typis Beerwaldinis".

Item on fol.82 of HENRY STEVEN'S "Typographical Miscellanies", vol.2, B-1

IMPRINTS, Germany

Cabinet 17 Shelf 2 No. 2

Bencard, Caspari, Augsburg, 1712.
Fragment of title, rubricated. With imprint.

Item on fol.96 of HENRY STEVEN'S "Typographical Miscellanies", vol.2 B-1

IMPRINTS, Germany

Cabinet FF Shelf 3 No. 46

Berthold, H. Ges. M.B.H. Wien, 1924.

See FRITZ, GEORGE. Geschichte der Wiener schriftgiesserien, 1482-1923...

IMPRINTS, Germany

Cabinet L Shelf 1 No. 21

Berthold Schriftgiesserei, Berlin, 1924

See HOFFMANN, PAUL. Wilhelm Reuter...

IMPRINTS, Germany

Cabinet FF Shelf 3 No. 41

Berthold, H. Schriftgiesserei. Berlin, 1928.

See BAUER, FRIEDRICH. Der Schriftgiesser Christian Elias Schurig in Hamburg 1773...

IMPRINTS, Germany

Cabinet Y Shelf 2 No. 1

Bielcken, Johann Felix. Frankfurt und Leipzig, 1721 (Imprint)

See WERTHER, JOHANN DAVID Wahrhaffitige nachrichten...

IMPRINTS, Germany

Cabinet 17 Shelf 2 No. 2

Bielckii, Jo. Felicio, Jena, 1711.
Fragments of title pages, rubricated. With printer's imprint and monogram "FB", and printer device.

Items on fols. 135-138 of HENRY STEVEN'S "Typographical Miscellanies", vol.2, B-1

IMPRINTS, GERMANY

Cabinet FF Shelf 5 No. 2

Breitkopf, J. G. I. Leipzig, 1756 - 1757.

See Music Printing. Breitkopf...

IMPRINTS, Germany.

Cabinet 10 Shelf 2 No. 6

Coburger, Anthony. Nuremburg, 1473. Boethius (Anicius Manlius Severinus) De Consolatione Philosophie Nuremberg:
Colophon: Hic liber Boccij de csolatione philosophie in textu latina alemanicaqz lingua... finit feliciter. Anno domini M.CCC.LXXIII. XXIIII mensis July. Condidit hoc ciuis alunis Nurembergensis öpus arte sua Antonius Coburger.

Original boards; 16-3/4 x 12 x 3 ins.

IMPRINTS, Germany.

Cabinet 10 Shelf 2 No. 8

Coburger, Anthony. Nuremberg, 1480. Biblia latina.
Colophon: Anno incarnationis dn̄ice Millesimoqua/dringetesimo octuagesimo. Mai vero Kl/ octavodecimo...In oppido Nurnbergū per Antonius Coburger pfati/oppido incolam industria cuius q̈ dilegetis-/sime fabresactum. finit feliciter.

Original boards; 16-3/4 x 11½ x 4-3/4 ins.

IMPRINTS, Germany.

Cabinet E Shelf 1 No. 40

Egenolff, Christian. Frankfort a M., 1564.

See Early Printing in Germany. Frankfort, 1564.

IMPRINTS, Germany

Cabinet I Shelf 1 No. 6

Feyerabend, Karl. Frankfort a M., 1574.

See Early Printing in Germany. Frankfort a M., 1574.

IMPRINTS, Germany

Cabinet 10 Shelf 2 No. 14

Coburger, Anthony. Nuremberg, 1493.

See Incunabula, Schedel, Hartman, Nuremberg Chronicle.

IMPRINTS, GERMANY.

Cabinet E Shelf 1 No. 39

Egenolff, Christian (Successors), Frankfurt a.M. 1564.

See EARLY PRINTING IN GERMANY. Frankfort A.M. Christian Egenolff (Successors).

IMPRINTS, Germany

Cabinet X Shelf 1 No. 87

Fiedleriana, ex Offician. Jena, 1792.

See WIECHMANN, JOHANN THEODOR Dissertqtio...

IMPRINTS, Germany.

Cabinet I Shelf 5 No. 23

Durer, Albrecht, Nurnberg, 1511.

See DURER, ALBRECHT. Apocalipsis cum figuris ... 1511.

IMPRINTS, Germany.

Cabinet F Shelf 4 No. 55

Endter, Johann Andreas. Nurnberg, 1762.
Title: Herrn Johann Arndts... Sech Bucher vom Wahren Christenthum...Nebst dasselben Paradiessgartlein...
Imprint: Nurnberg, zu finden in der Johann Andrea Endterischen Buchhandlung, 1762.

Leather; 9 x 7¼ x 3½ in.

IMPRINTS, Germany.

Cabinet E Shelf 2 No. 67

Forster, [Georg?] Amberg [Bavaria] 1602.

See Early Printing in Germany. Amberg, 1602.

IMPRINTS, GERMANY

Cabinet I Shelf 1 No. 2

Durer, Albrecht, Nuremberg, 1525.
Title: Underweisung der messung, mit der zirckel und richtscheyt...
Imprint: Durch Albrecht Durer zu zamen getzogē, und zu nutz alle...figuren in truck gebracht im jar 1525.
See also colophon.

Half morocco; 12¼ x 8-5/8 x ⅝ in.

IMPRINTS, Germany.

Cabinet E Shelf 1 No. 46

Feyerabend, Sigmund and Simon Hüter, Frankfort a M., 1566.

See Early Printing in Germany. Frankfort a M., 1566.

IMPRINTS, Germany

Cabinet Y Shelf 1 No. 3

Fritschen, Gaspar, Leipzig, 1741.

See Koehler's Hochverdiente...chrenrettung Johann Gutenbergs...Leipzig 1741.

IMPRINTS, GERMANY

Cabinet I Shelf 1 No. 3

Durer, Albrecht (Widow), Nuremberg, 1532.
Title: Alberti Dureri clarissimi pictoris et geometrae de symetria...
Colophon: Norimbergaer excudebatur opus...M.D. XXXII. In aedib. viduae Durerianae.

Half morocco; 11-5/8 x 7¾ x 5/8 in.

IMPRINTS, Germany

Cabinet I Shelf 1 No. 5

Feyerabend, Sigmund. Frankfurt a.M. 1568.

See EARLY PRINTING IN GERMANY. Frankfurt, a.M. 1568, Sigmund...

IMPRINTS, Germany

Cabinet K Shelf 1 No. 28

Fyner, Conrad. Esslingen, 1473. (see)

FACSIMILES. Music printing and manuscript, 12th to 16th century... (plate Vlll)

IMPRINTS, Germany

Cabinet E Shelf 1 No. 38

Egenolph, Christian, Strassburg, 1530.

See EARLY PRINTING IN GERMANY. Strassburg, 1530, Christian Egenilph...

IMPRINTS, Germany.

Cabinet I Shelf 1 No. 5

Feyerabend, Sigmund. Frankfort a M, 1568.

See Illustrated Books, [16th Century. In library] [Panoplia] omnium illberalium mechanicarum....

IMPRINTS, Germany

Cabinet X Shelf 1 No. 19

Gleditsch & Söhne, Jo. Frider. Leipzig, 1710.

This imprint on Pater's De Germania miraculo...Leipsiae, 1710.

IMPRINTS, Germany

Cabinet K Shelf 1 No. 28

Grevenbruch, Gerardus, Cologne, 1603 (see)

FACSIMILES. Music printing and manuscript, 12th to 16th century... (plate V1)

IMPRINTS, Germany.

Cabinet E Shelf 2 No. 47

Jobinus, Bernard. Strassburg, 1590.

See Early Printing in Germany. Strassburg, 1590.

IMPRINTS, Germany.

Cabinet 10 Shelf 2 No. 4

Mentelin, Johann. Strassburg, 1472.

See Incunabula. Astesanus de Ast. Summa de casibus conscientia.

IMPRINTS, GERMANY

Cabinet I Shelf 1 No. 15

Hertzen, Hiob. Wurtzburg, 1711.

See ABRAHAM a S. CLARA. "Etwas für alle" ... Wurtzburg, 1711.

IMPRINTS, GERMANY

Cabinet I Shelf 1 No. 7

Kauffmann, Paul, Nurenberg, 1596.

See LENCKER, HANS. Perspectiva literaria ...Gedruckt zu Nurmberg, durch Paulum Kauffmann, 1596.

IMPRINTS, Germany

Cabinet K Shelf 1 No. 28

Oglin, Erhard, Augsburg, 1507

See
FACSIMILES
Music printing and manuscript, 12th to 16th century...(Plate XXV)

IMPRINTS, Germany

Cabinet J Shelf 4 No. 20

Hoffmannschen Buchdruckerei: Felix Krais. Stuttgart, 1902.
Title: Die graphishen kunst der gegenwart. von Theodor Goebel. Illus.
Imprint: Stuttgart. Verlag von Felix Krais. 1902
" Papier fur text...Druck der Hoffmauschen Buckdruckerei Felix Krais.

Cloth; 14¼ x 10½ x 2⅝ in.

IMPRINTS, Germany.

Cabinet 10 Shelf 2 No. 6

Koberger, Anton. Nuremberg, 1473.

See Incunabula. Boethius (Annius Manlius Severinus).

IMPRINTS, Germany

Cabinet K Shelf 1 No. 28

Petreio, Johan. Nurnberg, 1536 (see)

FACSIMILES. Music printing and manuscript, 12th to 16th century... (plate V11)

IMPRINTS, Germany

Cabinet C Shelf 1 No. 6

Holten, Otto V., Berlin, 1899
Title: Stefan, George. Der teppich die lebens...
Colophon...(Translated) The decorative initials, borders, and full page illustrations by Melchior Lechter. Printed by Otto V. Holten, Berlin. 300 copies printed. this is No.32. Plates destroyed after publication.

Cloth over boards; 15½ x 17 in.

IMPRINTS, Germany.

Cabinet D Shelf 2 No. 47

Koelhoff, Johann [the younger]. Cologne, 1499.

See Incunabula. Chronica van der hilliger Stat van Coellen.

IMPRINTS, Germany

Cabinet K Shelf 1 No. 28

Peyser, Georium, Wurtzburg, 1481 (see)

FACSIMILES. Music printing and manuscripts, 12th to 16th century... (plates XV11, XV111)

IMPRINTS, Germany.

Cabinet 14 Shelf 2 No. 2 2 vols.

Insel-Verlag, Leipzig, 1913. Facsimile of Bible of 42 lines [Johann Gutenberg, Mainz, 1450-1455]

IMPRINTS, Germany.

Cabinet E Shelf 3 No. 5

Lacellori, Johann. Heidelberg, 1615.

See Early Printing in Germany. Heidelberg, 1615. Johann Lacellori.

IMPRINTS, Germany.

Cabinet D Shelf 2 No. 16

Quentell, Heinrich, Cologne: [1491]

See Incunabula. Gouda, Gulielmus de. Tractatus.

IMPRINTS, Germany.

Cabinet E Shelf 3 No. 31

Jennis, Lucas. Frankfort a.M., 1626.

See Early Printing in Germany. Frankfort, 1626.

IMPRINTS, Germany

Cabinet K Shelf 1 No. 28

Le Signerre, Guillaume, Milan, 1496. (see)

FACSIMILES. Music printing and manuscript, 12th to 16th century...(plate 1X)

IMPRINTS, Germany.

Cabinet D Shelf 2 No. 17

Quentell, Heinrich. Cologne, Germany, 1499.

See Incunabula. Sabunde, Raimundus de. Viola anima.

IMPRINT, GERMANY.

Cabinet D Shelf 2 No. 18

Quentell, Peter. Venice, 1538.
Title: Des Ertzstiffts Coeln Reformation.
Colophon: Gedruckt durch den Ersamen Peter Quentell, Burger der Stat Coeln. 1538.
Title within wood engraved border.

Paper boards; 12-1/8 x $8\frac{1}{4}$ x $\frac{3}{4}$ in.

IMPRINTS, Germany

Cabinet 29 Shelf 1 No. 25

Ratdolt, Erhard. Augsburg, 1488.
Title: Angeli. Astrolabium...
(Imprint) Colophon:..Ergardi Ratdolt Augustesis viri solertis: eximia industria mira imprimendi arte qua nuper veneciis nunc Auguste vindelicorum excellit...Novembris 1488.

Boards; 8-3/4 x $6\frac{1}{2}$ x 1 in.

IMPRINTS, Germany

Cabinet 29 Shelf 1 No. 28

Ratdolt, Erhard. Augsburg, 1490.
Title: Aliaco: Concordantia astronomie...
Colophon: Opus...qua nuper venetiis nunc Auguste Vindelicorum...Erhardi Ratdolt foelicia conspice signa testata artificem qua valet ipse manum. 1490.

Mottled paper over boards; 8-1/8 x $6\frac{1}{4}$ x $\frac{1}{2}$ in.

IMPRINTS, Germany.

Cabinet 29 Shelf 1 No. 31

Ratdolt, Erhard. Augsburg, 1494.
Title: Psalterium.
[Imprint] Colophon: Hie endet der psalter ... gedrucker czu Augsburg von maister Erharte Ratdolt ... 1494.

Tooled leather over boards, with part of original clasps; $8\frac{3}{4}$ x $6\frac{1}{4}$ x $1\frac{1}{2}$ in.

IMPRINTS, Germany

Cabinet 29 Shelf 1 No. 34

Ratdolt, Erhard. Augsburg, 1503.
Title: Missale Pataviense.
[Colophon with printer mark facing p. 305]
Erhardi Ratdolt felicia conspice signa testata artifecem qua velet ipse manum.
Printed in red and black throughout.

Tooled pigskin with clasps; 9-3/4 x $7\frac{1}{4}$ x 2-3/4 in.

IMPRINTS, Germany

Cabinet 29 Shlef 1 No. 35 and 36

Ratdolt, George Augsburg, 1515.
Title: Breviarium Ratisbonense.
Colophon...Auguste vindelicorum impressus ast. Sed expensis et sumptubus Georg Ratdolt. Anno 1515.
Printed throughout in red and black.
See also 29/1/35, second copy on same shelf.

Pigskin, tooled; $7\frac{1}{2}$ x 5 x $2\frac{1}{4}$ in.

IMPRINTS, Germany

Cabinet B Shelf 3 No. 8

Reichsdruckerei, Berlin, 1884-7
Title: Druckschriften des 15 bis 18 jahrhunderts. (Facsimiles of printing types, 15th to 18th centuries. 100 plates)
Imprint: Berlin. Reichsdruckerei, 1884-1887.

Half morocco; $18\frac{3}{4}$ x $12\frac{1}{2}$ X 1-3/8 in.

IMPRINTS, Germany

Cabinet 64 Shelf 1 No. 1

Reichsdruckerei, Berlin, 1898-1904.
Title: Die Nibelunge.
Colophon (translation): Letter, full-page illus., decorations by Joseph Sattler. Cut and casting of types, plates for full-page illus, paper with water mark, from the studios of the Reichsdruckerei...Published by J.A. Stargardt, Berlin, 1898-1904.

Morocco; $22\frac{1}{4}$ x $15\frac{3}{4}$ in.

IMPRINTS, Germany

Cabinet K Shelf 1 No. 23

Rhaw, Georg. Wittenberg, 1523. (see)

FACSIMILES. Music printing and manuscript, 12th to 16th century...(plate X)

IMPRINTS, Germany.

Cabinet D Shelf 4 No. 38

Rodler, Hieronymo. Siemeren [Hundsrück], 1531.

See Early Printing in Germany, Siemeren.

IMPRINTS, Germany.

Cabinet E Shelf 3 No. 43

Rotell, Caspar. Frankfort a.M., 1631.

See Early Printing in Germany. Frankfort a.M., 1631. Caspar Rotell.

IMPRINTS, GERMANY

Cabinet J Shelf 2 No. 11

Schelter & Giesecke. Leipzig, 1923.

See APEL, THEODOR. Drei briefe...1923.

IMPRINTS, Germany.

Cabinet 14 Shelf 1 No. 15

Schoeffer, Ives, Mainz, 1541.

See Early Printing in Germany. Mainz, 1541. Ives Schoeffer [Grandson of Peter Schoeffer]

IMPRINTS, Germany.

Cabinet 14 Shelf 1 No. 15

Schoeffer, Ives, Mainz, 1541.

See Early Printing in Germany. Mainz, 1541. Ives Schoeffer [Grandson of Peter Schoeffer I]

IMPRINTS, Germany.

Cabinet 14 Shelf 1 No. 5

Schoeffer, Johann I. Mainz, 1515.

See Early Printing in Germany. Mainz, 1515. Johann Schoeffer I.

IMPRINTS, Germany.

Cabinet 14 Shelf 1 No. 7

Schoeffer, Johann (I).Mainz, 1518.

See Early Printing in Germany. Mainz, 1518. Johann Schoeffer I.

IMPRINTS, Germany.

Cabinet 14 Shelf 1 No. 9

Schoeffer, Johann(I) Mainz, 1530.

See Early Printing in Germany, Mainz, 1530.

IMPRINTS, Germany.

Cabinet 14 Shelf 1 No. 11

Schoeffer, Johann I. Mainz, 1531.

See Early Printing in Germany. Mainz, 1531. Johann Schoeffer I.

IMPRINTS, Germany.

Cabinet 14 Shelf 2 No. 4

Schoeffer, Peter. Mainz, 1458 and 1484.

See Incunabula, Canon Missal and Missale Cracoviense.

IMPRINTS, Germany.

Cabinet 14 Shelf 2 No. 15

Schoeffer, Peter I. Mainz, 1472. Gratianus. Decretum [With a commentary]
Colophon: Anno incarnationis dñice M.CCCCLXXII. Idibo augustiis...ingeniosa imprimēdi! cūctipotēte adspirāti deo Petrus Schoiffer de gernssheym suis consignando scutis! feliciter consummairt. Printer mark!

Gesamt-Kat. ; Full Morocco, 19 x 14¼ x 3 ins.

IMPRINTS, Germany.

Cabinet 14 Shelf 2 No. 16

Schoeffer, Peter I. Mainz, 1472. Gratianus. Decretum [Second copy; unrubricated and unilluminated, on unusually thick paper: compare with adjoining copy.]

Full leather; 19 x 13¾ x 4¼ ins.

IMPRINTS, Germany

Cabinet D Shelf 4 No. 37

Schoeffer, Peter II. Strassburg 1531, son of Peter Schoeffer, asst. to Gutenberg and successor to Gutenberg's Mainz printing office.
Title: Eyn new kunstlichs wolgegründts disierbuch ...von Ulrich Kern.
Has woodcut designs, tables for calculations (Some in black and red)
Colophon with printer mark: Inn...Strassburg truckts Peter Schaffer bei Hansen Schwyntzern am 1st Aprilis, 1531.

cont'd

IMPRINTS, Germany (cont'd)

Cabinet D Shelf 4 No. 37

Morocco; 12 x 7¾ in.

IMPRINTS, Germany.

Cabinet 14 Shelf 1 No. 14

Schoeffer, Peter II. Worms, 1527.

See Early Printing in Germany. Worms, 1527. Peter Schoeffer II.

IMPRINTS, Germany

Cabinet K Shelf 1 No. 28

Schoeffer, Peter, Mainz, 1512. (see)

FACSIMILES. Music printing and manuscript, 12th to 16th century... (plate 111)

IMPRINTS, Germany

Cabinet D Shelf 3 No. 61

Schonsperger, Hans. Augsburg, 1519.
Title: Tewrdanckh [Facsimile] Holbein Society. London, 1884.
Colophon: Gebruckt in der Kayserlichen Stat Augspurg durch den eltern Hansen Schonsperger ... 1519.

Morocco; 14½ x 10¼ x 2¾ in.

IMPRINTS, Germany

Cabinet D Shelf 3 No. 60

Schönsperger, Johannes. Nürnberg, 1519.

See Early Printing in Germany. Nürnberg, 1517, Schönsperger, Johannes.

IMPRINTS, Germany.

Cabinet D Shelf 1 No. 29

Sorg, Anton. Augsburg, 1476.

See Incunabula. Bonaventura [St.]. Speculum beatae Mariae virginis.

IMPRINTS, GERMANY

Cabinet K Shelf 4 No. 21

Spamererschen Buchdurckerei in Leipzig, 1930.

See RÜMANN, ARTHUR (Das) Illustrierte buch des 19 jahrhunderts...Leipzig, 1930.

IMPRINTS, Germany.

Cabinet D Shelf 4 No. 39

Steiner, Heinrich. Augsburg, 1531.

See Early Printing in Germany. Augsburg, 1531. Heinrich Steiner.

IMPRINTS, Germany.

Cabinet D Shelf 4 No. 40

Steiner (or Stayner) Heinrich, Augsburg, 1533.

See Early Printing in Germany. Augsburg, 1533. Heinrich Steiner.

IMPRINTS, Germany.

Cabinet D Shelf 1 No. 51

Strassburg, 1487. [Printer unknown]. Sermones Dormi secu/re uel Dormi fino cura.
Colophon: Ad laudem et hono/rem omipotentis dei vginisqz matris....Impressi Argentine an-/no dni M.CCCCLXXXVII [1487] Finiti circa festum/ Sancti Iohannis baptiste.

11½ x 8½ ins., ¾ ins. thick.

IMPRINTS, Germany

Cabinet K Shelf 1 No. 28

Stüchs, Jeorius, Nurnberg, 1492. (see)

FACSIMILES
Music printing and manuscript, 12th to 16th century...(plate XX1)

IMPRINTS, Germany.

Cabinet E Shelf 2 No. 35

Wechel, Andrea. Frankfort, 1584.

See Early Printing in Germany. Frankfort, 1584.

IMPRINTS, Germany

Cabinet Y Shelf 3 No. 125

Westermann, George, Braunschweig, 1855.

see MINIATURE BOOKS. Fouqué... Berlin, 1852

IMPRINTS, Germany.

Cabinet D Shelf 1 No. 18

Zainer, Günther, Augsburg, 1472.

See Incunabula, Isiodorus [S. Hispalensis Episcopi] Etymologiarum lib. XX. n.p.

IMPRINTS, Germany.

Cabinet X Shelf 2 No. 37

Zetner, Eberhard. Strassburg, 1641.

See Early Printing in Germany. Strassburg.

IMPRINTS, Holland

Cabinet N Shelf 2 No. 18.01

Boosten & Stols te Maastricht, 1925

see PRIVATE PRESSES, Holland. Catalogus der Tentoonstelling...

IMPRINTS, Holland.

Cabinet 39 Shelf 1 No. 23

Elzevier, Abraham. Leyden, 1683-1712.
A collection of pages including title pages, taken from books printed by him.

9¼ x 7 in.

In folder.

IMPRINTS, Holland

Cabinet II Shelf 3 No. 8

Armenische Drukkerey. Amsterdam, 1696.
Title: Thomas A. Kempis. [In Armenian].
Imprint: Amsterdam, 1696.

Morocco; gilt goffered; 4-7/8 x 3 x 1-1/8 in.

IMPRINTS, Holland.

Cabinet D Shelf 3 No. 37

Borne, Theodorici (Dirk) de Borne, Daventry, 1515.

See Early Printing in Holland. Daventry, 1515.

IMPRINTS, Holland.

Cabinet 39 Shelf 1 No. 4

Elzevier, Bonaventura and Abraham. Leyden, 1626.
Title: Schoonhovius. Emblemata.
Imprint: Lugduni Batavorum, ex officina Elzeviriana. 1622.

Vellum; 8¼ x 6¼ x 1-3/8 in. Pieters 74, 13.

IMPRINTS, Holland.

Cabinet E Shelf 4 No. 44

Athias, Joseph. Amsterdam, 1667.

See Early Printing in Holland. Amsterdam, 1667.

IMPRINTS, Holland.

Cabinet E Shelf 3 No. 12

Casteleyn, Vincent. Haarlem, 1620.

See Early Printing in Holland. Haarlem, 1620.

IMPRINTS, Holland.

Cabinet 39 Shelf 1 No. 12

Elzevier, Daniel. Amsterdam, 1665.
Title: Arnold Vinnii. In quatro libros Institutionum Imperialium. Commentarius. [Printer's device].
Imprint: Amstelodami, apud Danielem Elzevirium. 1665

Half morocco; 9½ x 7¾ x 2-3/8 in. Pieters 229, 8.

IMPRINTS, Holland

Cabinet E Shelf 4 No. 18

Blaeu, Johan. Amsterdam, 1657.

See Early Printing in Holland. Amsterdam, 1657.

IMPRINTS, HOLLAND

Cabinet I Shelf 1 No. 8

Cloquius, Andreas. Leyden, 1617.

See CLOQUIUS (or Cloucq), ANDREAS. Icones ...Lug. Batav. 1617.

IMPRINTS, Holland.

Cabinet 39 Shelf 1 No. 15

Elzevier, Daniel. Amsterdam, 1671.
Title: Polydori Vergilii de rerum inventoribus. libri VIII ...
Imprint: Amstelodami, apud Danielem Elzevirium, 1671.

Calf; 5-3/8 x 3 x ½ in. Pieters, 255, 18.

IMPRINTS, Holland.

Cabinet 39 Shelf 1 No. 24

Blaeu, Johann, Ludwig and Daniel Elzevier, Amsterdam, 1663.
Title: Corpus Juris Civilis ... Gothofredi [2 vols in one].
Imprint: Amstelodoma, Apud Joannem Blaeu, Ludovicum & Danielem Elzevirios ... 1663.

Calf; 16 x 10 x 4¼ in. Pieters 221; Brunet 3, 608.

IMPRINTS, Holland.

Cabinet AA Shelf 3 No. 4

Conradi, Petrus and Volkert vander Plaats junior, Amsterdam and Harlingen, 1762.
Title: De vryheid der drukpers ... [Anon]
Imprint: Te Amsterdam, by Petrus Conradi. Te Harlingen, by V. van der Plaats. 1782.

Half morocco; 8-7/8 x 5⅛ in.

IMPRINTS, Holland.

Cabinet 39 Shelf 1 No. 16

Elzevier, Daniel. Amsterdam, 1671.
Title: Reflexions, sentences, ou maxims royales et politiques. Traduites par le Rev. Pere D'Obeilh.
Imprint: A Amsterdam, chez Daniel Elzevier. 1671.

Vellum; 5¼ x 3-1/8 x 1 in.

IMPRINTS, Holland

Cabinet RR Shelf 3 No. 4

Blusse, A. en Zoonen, Dortrecht
Title: Volledige beschrijving alle konsten... Door P.J. Kastelijn.
Imprint: A. Blusse en Zoonen, Dortrecht.

Half morocco; 8½ x 5½ in.

IMPRINTS, HOLLAND

Cabinet I Shelf 1 No. 11

Danckersz, Danckert, Amsterdam, 1664.

See BOSSE, ABRAHAM. Perspective op regellose...Anno 1664.

IMPRINTS, Holland.

Cabinet 39 Shelf 1 No. 20

Elzevier, Daniel. Amsterdam, 1674.
Title: Catalogus librorum qui in bibliopolio Danielis Elsevirii venales extant. [Printer device].
Imprint: Amstelodami, ex Officina Elzeviriana. 1674.

Vellum; 5½ x 3¼ x 1½ in. Pieters, p. LV.

IMPRINTS, Holland.

Cabinet 39 Shelf 2 No. 48

Elzevier, Daniel: Amsterdam, 1678.

Title: Lettres choisies du Sr. de Balsac.
Imprint: À Amsterdam. Chez les Elzeviers, 1678.

Vellum; 5-3/8 x 3 x $1\frac{1}{4}$ in.

IMPRINTS, Holland.

Cabinet 39 Shelf 1 No. 3

Elzevier, Isaac. Leyden, 1622.
Title: Tabacologia ... Per Johannem Neanorum. [Printer's device].
Imprint: Lugduni Batavorum, ex officina Isaaci Elzeviri. Jurati Academiae Typographi, 1622.

Calf; $8\frac{3}{4}$ x $6\frac{1}{4}$ x $1\frac{1}{4}$ in. Pieters 56, 9.

IMPRINTS, Holland.

Cabinet 39 Shelf 1 No. 25

Elzevier, Johann [Widow of]. Leyden, 1663.
Title: Biblia ...
Imprint: Tot Leyden. By de Weduwe van Joannes Elzevier, 1663.

Calf, tooled with iron corners and clasps, 19 x 12 x 6 in. Pieters, 153.

IMPRINTS, Holland.

Cabinet 39 Shelf 2 No. 50

Elzevier, Ludwig and Frans Hack. Leyden and Amsterdam, 1648.
Title: Historia naturalis Brasiliae ...
Imprint: Lugdun. Batavorum, apud Franciscum Hackium et Amstelodami, apud Lud. Elzevirium 1648.

Paper, vellum back, 15-3/4 x 10 in.

IMPRINTS, Holland.

Cabinet 39 Shelf 1 No. 7

Elzevier, Ludwig and Daniel. Amsterdam, 1659.
Title: Corvino: Posthumus Pacianus, seu definitiones. [Printers' device].
Imprint: Amstelaedami, apud Ludovicum & Danielem Elzevirirot.

Vellum; $5\frac{1}{2}$ x 3 x $1\frac{1}{2}$ in. Pieters 216, 3.

IMPRINTS, Holland.

Cabinet 39 Shelf 1 No. 24

Elzevier, Ludwig and Daniel. Johaen Blaeu. Amsterdam, 1663.
Title: Corpus Juris Civilis, pandectis ... Gothofredi ... (2 vols. in one).
Imprint: Amstelodama, Apud Joannem Blaeu, Ludovicum & Danielem Elzevirios. Lugd. Batavorum apud Franciscum Hackium, 1663.
Colophon, end of first part, p. 796: Amsterdami, Typis Ludovici & Danielis Elzeviriorum.
Calf; 16 x 10 x $4\frac{1}{4}$ in. Pieters 221; Brunet 3, 608.

IMPRINTS, Holland.

Cabinet 39 Shelf 2 No. 47

Elzevier, Peter. Utrecht, 1670.
Title: Prima Scaligerana, nusquam antehac edita, cum praefatione T. Fabri.
Imprint: Ultrajecti, apud Petrum Elzevirium, M.DC.LXX.
Peter Elzevier, grandson of Josse, was not a printer, he was a publisher of books. This is probably a false Elzevier.
See Willems re "False Elzeviers."

Calf; $6\frac{1}{4}$ x 4 x 5/8 in.

IMPRINTS, Holland

Cabinet 13 Shelf No. 6

Elzevier Printing Office, Leyden, 1628
Title: Academie de l'espee...Girard Thibault [n.p.]

Consult Pieters "Annales de l'imprimerie Elsevirienne", p. 117 for authenticity of above imprint.

IMPRINTS, Holland.

Cabinet 39 Shelf 1 No. 10

Elzevier, ex officina. Amsterdam, 1664. [Ludwig and Daniel].
Title: Varenio. Geographia generalis ...
Imprint: Amstelodami. Ex officina Elzeviriana, 1664.

Half morocco; $5\frac{1}{2}$ x 3 x $1\frac{1}{4}$ in. Ledeboer 31.

IMPRINTS, Holland

Cabinet X Shelf 1 No. 41

Enschede, Isaac & Joannes. Haarlem 1742.
Title: Annus tertius saecularis inventae artis typographicae...Auctore Joanne Christiano Seiz.
Imprint: Urbe nobilissimae artis typographicae inventrice. Apud Isaacum et Joannem Enschede, urbis ejusdem typographos publicos.

Calf; 8 x 5 x 1 in.

IMPRINTS, HOLLAND

Cabinet FF Shelf 3 No. 1

Enschede, Isaak en Johannes, Haerlem, 1761.
Title: Haerlemse Zangen...overgebragt doo J. J. D.

Imprint: Te Haerlem, Gedrukt ter Musicq-Drukkery van Isaak en Johannes Enschede. 1761.

Half mor. oblong; $9\frac{1}{2}$ x $11\frac{1}{2}$ in.

IMPRINTS, Holland

Cabinet F Shelf 4 No. 66

Enschedé, Johannes en Zoonen. Haarlem, 1778.
Title: Extract uit de Resolutien van de Edele Mogenden Heeren Raaden van Staate der Vereenigde Nederlanden. Donderdag den 28 Augusti, 1777.
Colophon: Te Haarlem. Gedrukt ter Boekdrukkery van Johannes Enschedé en Zoonen.
(Printed with the same types which were used in 1578 by Aelbert Hendricxz.)

Calf, gilt; 12-7/8 x $8\frac{3}{4}$ in.

IMPRINTS, Holland

Cabinet QQ Shelf 5 No. 14.01

Enschede, Joh. en Zonen, Haarlem, 1933
Title: The nativity of our Lord...

Brochure in manila envelope

IMPRINTS, Holland

Cabinet E Shelf 3 No. 16

Erpenius, Thomas. Leyden, 1622.

See Early Printing in Holland. Leyden, 1622.

IMPRINTS, Holland.

Cabinet D Shelf 4 No. 27

Eynhoven, Christopher. Antwerp, 1525.
Provinciale Constitutiones. William Lyndwood.

See Early Printing in Holland. Antwerp, 1525.

IMRPINTS, Holland.

Cabinet E Shelf 4 No. 68

Gaesbeeck, Daniel. Leyden, 1678.

IMPRINTS, Holland

Cabinet F Shelf 4 No. 60

Gazinet, Gysbregt. S'Gravenhagen, 1717.
Title: De schoonste of het ontzet van Schevening; Bly-spel.
Imprint: In s'Gravenhage. By Gysbregt Gazinet. Boekverkooper in t'Kort-Agterom, 1717.

Half morocco; $6\frac{1}{4}$ x 4 in.

IMPRINTS, Holland

Cabinet F Shelf 5 No. 1

Hondt, Pierre de. La Hague, 1729.
Title: Oeuvres de Nicolas Boileau.
Imprint: A La Haye, chez Pierre de Hondt. 1729.

Leather; $14\frac{3}{4}$ x $9\frac{1}{2}$ x 2 in.

IMPRINTS, Holland.

Cabinet E Shelf 2 No. 65

Leyden, 1602. [Frans van Mieris.]

See Early Printing in Holland. Leyden,1602 [Frans van Mieris]

IMPRINTS, Holland.

Cabinet 14 Shelf 1 No. 20

Schoeffer, Johann III. Bois-le-Duc, 1585. Die Gulden Letanien. Woodcut.

Boards; $5\frac{1}{2}$ x 3-3/4 x 1/8 in.

IMPRINTS, Holland.

Cabinet E Shelf 1 No. 35

Zuren, Jan van. Haarlem, 1561.

See Early Printing in Holland. Haarlem, 1561. Jan van Zuren.

IMPRINTS, HOLLAND

Cabinet I Shelf 1 No. 13 & 14

Luiken, Johannes and Gaspaares. Amsterdam, 1694.

See LUIKEN, JOHANNES and GASPAARES. "Het menselyk bedrye...t'Amsterdam, 1694.

IMPRINTS, Holland.

Cabinet E Shelf 4 No. 52

Smetius, Reynier. Nijmegen. Batavia, 1671.

See Early Printing in Holland. Nimwegen, 1671. Reynier Smetius.

IMPRINTS, Hungary.

Cabinet D Shelf 1 No. 21

Hess, Andrea. Budae, 1473.

See Incunabula. Chronica Hungarorum.

IMPRINTS, Holland

Cabinet II Shelf 3 No. 4

Lutchmans, S. en J. Te Leyden, 1840.

See WEIJERS, H.E. Nieuwe proeve om al de arabische letters...

IMPRINTS, Holland.

Cabinet E Shelf 4 No. 81

Sweerts, Hieronymus. Amsterdam, 1685.

See Early Printing in Holland. Amsterdam, 1685.

IMPRINTS, Hungary

Cabinet D Shelf 1 No. 21

Hess, Andrea, Buda. 1473.

See Incunabula. Chronica Hungarorum.

IMPRINTS, Holland.

Cabinet 2 Shelf 1 No. 15

Raphelengen, Francis: Plantin-Moretus Press, Leyden, 1590.

See Early Printing in Holland. Leyden, 1590. Plantin-Moretus Press: Francis Raphelengen.

IMPRINTS, Holland.

Cabinet D Shelf 1 No. 34

Veldener Joh. Utrecht, 1479.

See Incunabula. Gregorious. Magnus. Papa. Homelien.

IMPRINTS, Ireland.

Cabinet M Shelf 1 No. 36

Candle Press, The. Colm O'Lochlain. Dublin, 1920.

Title: The Book of Saint Ultain: A collection of of picutres and poems by Irish artists and writers. This book has been compiled and arranged by Katherine MacCormack: designed by and printed under the direction of Colm O'Locklain, M.A.

Imprint: Published by The Candle Press...Dublin. Paper; 11-7/8 x $8\frac{1}{2}$ in.

IMPRINTS, Holland

Cabinet AA Shelf 3 No. 1

Rooman (or Roman) Adriaen. Haarlem, 1611-1641

Title: Beschryvinge ende lof der Stad Haerlem in rijm bearbeyd ... door Samuel Ampzing ... Mitsgaders P. Scriverii Laurenkranz voor L. Koster, eerste vinder van der Boekdruckerye. Haerlem, 1628.

Imprint: Adrien Rooman, Ordinaris Stads-Boekdruck er. Te Haerlem, 1628. Printer Mark.

IMPRINTS, HOLLAND

Cabinet X Shelf 1 No. 32

Wetstenios, R.J.and G. Smith. Amsterdam, 1730

Title: Prolegomena ad Novi Testamenti Graeci...

Imprint: Amsteladami, apud R.&J. Wetstenios & G. Smith, 1730.

Vellum; $10\frac{1}{4}$x8x$\frac{3}{4}$ in.

IMPRINTS, Ireland

Cabinet L Shelf 2 No. 5

Greisberg and Campbell, Dublin, 1815

See CARMICHAEL, ANDREW. Essay on the invention of alphabet writing...

Cabinet Shelf No.

Plates by Vander Velde, one giving a view of the market place with the house of Coster.

Vellum; $7\frac{1}{2}$ x $5\frac{3}{4}$ x $2\frac{1}{4}$ in.

IMPRINTS, Holland

Cabinet N Shelf 2 No. 18.02

Zilverdistel Press (The Silver Thistle), Dr. J.E. Van Royen, The Hague, 1918.

Title: Een boecxken gemaket van suster bertken die lvij. jaren...tot Utrecht.

Entirely hand set with types designed by Pissarro. No.19 Of 70 printed copies.

Boards; $6\frac{3}{4}$ x $4\frac{3}{4}$ in.

IMPRINTS, IRELAND

Cabinet II Shelf 4 No. 4

Hardy and Sons. Dublin, 1852.

Title: Irish Testament, translated into the Irish language by William O'Donnell.

Colophon: Dublin: Hardy and Sons, Typ. 23, Upper Sackville-Street.

Cloth; $5\frac{3}{4}$ x $3\frac{1}{2}$ x 5/8 in.

IMPRINTS, Ireland

Cabinet C Shelf 2 No. 8

Vize, T.M., Cork, 1788

See LARKIN, GEORGE. Essay on the origin...of printing. Cork, 1778.

IMPRINTS, Ireland

Cabinet Q Shelf 2 No. 13

[West, William]. Cork, 1835.
Title: Three hundred and fifty years retrospection...
Imprint: Cork: Printed by and for the author, 67 South Mall, 1835.

Cloth; 8½ x 5½ in.

IMPRINTS, Italy.

Cabinet E Shelf 2 No. 38

Accolti, Vincento. Rome, 1585.

See Early Printing in Italy. Rome, 1585.

IMPRINTS, Ireland.

Cabinet M Shelf 1 No. 37

Candle Press, The. Colm O'Lochlain, Dublin, 1922.
Title: Clann Lir. A story of Ancient Ireland. Decorated by Austin Molloy: printed in the Petrie type.

Colophon, and Printer Mark on last page.

Paper; 9-3/4 x 7¼ in. Tomkinson, Bibliography. Modern Presses p.21.

IMPRINTS, Italy

Cabinet F Shelf 4 No. 72

Albrizzi, Giambatista. Venice, 1753.
Title: Dissertationi Vossiane.
Imprint: In Venezia, per Giambatista Albrizzi Q. Gir.

Boards; 10-5/8 x 8 x 1¼ in.

IMPRINTS, Italy.

Cabinet F Shelf 5 No. 14

Albrizzi Press. Venice, 1764.

Title: Componimenti poetici per l'ingresso solenne....il Signor Lodovico Manin. Engraved frontispiece, borders, head and tail pieces, n.a.n.
Colophon: Nella Stamperia Albrizzi. Con privilegio del Ecc^mo Senato per tutti li rami che adornano le di lui stampe.

Paper; 14½ x 10¼ x ½ in.

IMPRINTS, Italy

Cabinet 60 Shelf 1 & 2 No.

Aldine Imprints (Aldus, Paulus and Aldus II Manutius and Andreae Asulani (or Asola). Venice and Rome. Includes imprints of the Academie Veneta, which were printed by Paulus Manutius in the printing house in Venice founded by his father. 1507 to 1588.

IMPRINTS, Italy.

Cabinet 60 Shelf 2 No. 1

Aldine Press. Aldus Manutius. Venice, 1500.
Title: Epistola devotissime de Sancta Catharina da Siena. Illum. and wood engravings.
Imprint: Stampata in la inclita cita de Venetia in casa de Aldo Manutio Romano adi XV Septembrio 1500.

Mottled paper over boards; calf back; 12¾ x 9 x 3 in. Renouard I, p. 55.

IMPRINTS, Italy

Cabinet 60 Shelf 1 No. 2

Aldine Press, Aldus Manutius, Venice, 1501.

See FACSIMILES. Alphabetum Hebraicum ...

IMPRINTS, Italy.

Cabinet 60 Shelf 1 No. 5

Aldine Press, Venice, 1509. Aldus Manutius and Andrea Asola.
Title: C. Crispi Sallusti de Conivratione Catilinae ...
Colophon: Venetiis in aedibus Aldi et Andrea Asulani soceri. Mense Aprili, 1509. With printer mark.

Tooled calf; 6½ x 4 x 7/8 in. Renouard I, p. 133.

IMPRINTS, Italy.

Cabinet 60 Shelf 2 No. 5

Aldine Press. [Manutius] Aldi et Andreae [d'Asola] Soceri. Venice, 1514.
Title: Suida [Greek].
Colophon: Venetiis in aedibus Aldi et Andreae Soceri. Mense Feb. M.V.XIIII.

Vellum, stamped; 13½ x 8½ x 2-3/8 in. Brunet 5, 587; Renouard. Annales ... des Aldes I, p.153

IMPRINTS, Italy.

Cabinet 60 Shelf 1 No. 9

Aldine Press, Venice, 1515. Aldus Manutius and Andrea Asola.
Title: M. Annei Lucani civilis bellis ...
Colophon: Venetiis aedibus Aldi et Andreae soceri, Mense Iulio 1515. Printer mark.

Vellum; 6¼ x 3½ x 1-1/8 in. Brunet 3, 1199; Renouard I, p. 171

IMPRINTS, Italy.

Cabinet 60 Shelf 2 No. 8

Aldine Press [Manutius]. Aldi et Andreae [d'Asola] Soceri. Venice, 1516.
Title: Rhodiginus, Ludovicus Coelius. Lectionum antiquarum libri XVI.
Colophon: Venetiis in aedibus Aldi, et Andreae Soceri. Mense Februario M.D.XVI. [Printer Mark].

Vellum; gilt edges; 12½ x 8¾ x 2¾ in. From the Library of William Morris, with his label

---

IMPRINTS, Italy.

Cabinet 60 Shelf 1 No. 12

Aldine Press: Aldo Manutius et Andrea [di Asola] Soceri. Venice, 1518.
Title: Sacrae scripturae veteris novaéque omnia [Greek Bible: Old and New Testament].
Colophon: Venetiis in aedib. Aldi et Andrea Soceri. M.D.XVIII. Mense Februario. [Printer Mark.]

Blind Stamped Vellum over Boards; 12 x 8¼ x 2-3/4 in.

IMPRINTS, Italy.

Cabinet 60 Shelf 1 No. 15

Aldine Press. Aldus Manutius and A. Asola, Venice, 1520.
Title: Polybii historiarum ... Nicolas Perotto interprete.
Colophon: Venetiis in Aedebus Aldi et Andreae soceri, mense Decembri, 1520. Printer mark.

Calf; 12 x 8¼ x ¾ in.

IMPRINTS, Italy.

Cabinet 60 Shelf 2 No. 12

Aldine Press. Aldus Manutius & Andreae d'Asolani. Venice, 1528.
Title: Paulas Aegineta. Opera medica [Greek Text]
Colophon: Venetiis in aedibus Aldi et Andreae Asolani soceri. Mense Augusto 1528.
Bound in with Aetius Amidenus "Librorum medicinalum." Venice, 1534.

Vellum over boards; 12½ x 8½ x 2¼ in. Brunet 1,59; Renouard I, p. 251.

IMPRINTS, Italy.

Cabinet 60 Shelf 2 No. 12

Aldine Press. Aldus Manutius & Andreae Asulani. Venice, 1534.
Title: Aetius Amidenus. Librorum medicinalum [Greek Text].
Colophon: Venetiis in aedibus haeredum Aldi Manutii & Andreae Asulani. Mense Sept, 1500.
Bound in with another Aldine item printed in 1528.

Vellum over boards; 12½ x 8½ x 2¼ in. Brunet 1, 103; Renouard 1, 267.

IMPRINTS, Italy.

Cabinet 60 Shelf 1 No. 19

Aldi Filio, (Paul Manutius), Venice, 1546.
Title: De oratore Ciceronis.
Imprint: Corrigente Paulo Manutio, Aldi Filio. Venetiis.
Three vols. in one, LARGE PAPER, 8-1/8 x 5½ in. ruled in red, unimpaired margins.

Calf; 8-3/8 x 5¾ x 1-7/8 in.

IMPRINTS, Italy.

Cabinet 60 Shelf 1 No. 22

Aldine Press. Aldi Filii [The sons of Aldo] Venice. 1548.
Title: Le Epistole famigliari di Cicerone, tradotte ... della lingua volgare. Ristampete di nuovo. [Printer Mark] Con privilegio ... M.D.XLVIII.
Colophon: In Vinegio, nell'anno M.D.XLVIII. In casa de'figliuoli di Aldo.

Half morocco, modern; 6¾ x 4-1/8 x 1¼ in. Brunet 2,46. Renouard, Annales ... des Adles I - p. 339.

IMPRINTS, Italy.

Cabinet 60 Shelf 1 No. 35

Aldine Press; Academia Veneta, Paul Manutius. Venice, 1559.
Title: Summa librorum quos in omnibus scientiis ac nobilioribus artibus variis linguis conscriptos.
Imprint: Academia Veneta. 1559.

Morocco; 8 x 5½ x ¼ in. Brunet 5, 592] Goldsmid Vol. II, p. 57.

IMPRINTS, Italy.

Cabinet 60 Shelf 1 No. 47

Aldine Press. Aldus Manutius. Venice, 1585.
Title: Vicissitudine o mutabile varieta della cose ... Luigi Regio, Francese: Tradotta dal Sig ... Cato.
Imprint: In Vinetia, 1585. Presso Aldo.
Engraved title page, also printer mark.

Boards; 8 x 6 x 1 in.

IMPRINTS, Italy.

Cabinet 60 Shelf 2 No. 15

Aldine Press. Paulus Manutius. Venice, 1551.
Title: Petri Bembi Cardinalis. Historiae Venetiis.
Colophon: Venetiis, apud Aldi filios. 1551.

Vellum over boards; 12¼ x 8⅛ x 1-5/8 in. Brunet I,767; Renouard I, 364.

IMPRINTS, Italy.

Cabinet 60 Shelf 2 No. 21

Aldine Press: Paul Manutius, Rome, 1562-3.
Title: Theodoretus. In visiones Danielis prophetae commentarius. J.B. Gabio interp.
Imprint: Romae, M.D.LXII. Apud Paulum Manutium, Aldi. F.
Bound in with two other Paul Manutius imprints: "In canticum cantorum" and "In Ezechielem Prophetem."

Morocco; 13½ x 9¼ x 1¾ in. Renouard II, 18 & 28.

IMPRINTS, Italy.

Cabinet D Shelf 1 No. 49

Battibovis, Nicolaus. Venice, 1486.

See Incunabula. Lucanus, Marcus Annaes. Pharsalia.

IMPRINTS, Italy.

Cabinet 60 Shelf 2 No. 18

Aldine Press: Paulus Manutius. Venice, 1554.
Title: Iovatae Rapicii Brixiani di numero oratorio libri quinque ... [Printer Mark].
Colophon: Venetiis, in aedibus Pauli Manutii, Aldi filii, M.D.LIIII.
Bound with a 1540 Vascosan item.

Vellum; 13 x 9 x 1-3/8 in.

IMPRINTS, Italy.

Cabinet 60 Shelf 2 No. 23

Aldine Press: Paul Manutius. Rome, 1563.
Title: Caecilii Cypriani ... Opera.
Imprint: Romae, M.D.LXIII, apud Paulum Manutium, Aldi F. Cum privilegio Pii IV, Pont Max.

Calf; 12½ x 8¾ x 1¾ in. Renouard II, 29; Brunet 2, 459.

IMPRINTS, ITALY

Cabinet FF Shelf 5 No. 1

Bertelli, Francesco, Padua, 1656.

See Early Printing in Italy. (Example) Padua, 1656. Francesco Bertelli.

IMPRINTS, Italy.

Cabinet 60 Shelf 1 No. 28

Aldine Press. Paul Manutius. Venice, 1556.
Title: Athenagora ... Tradotto in lingua Italiana da Girolamo Faleti.
Imprint: Aldus in Venetia 1556.

Parchment 8 x 5¾ x ½ in. Goldsmid, The Aldine Press, no. 455.

IMPRINTS, Italy.

Cabinet 60 Shelf 1 No. 39

Aldine Press, Paul Manutius. Rome, 1563.
Title: Francisci Vargas ... Rerum status a consiliis, ... Reponsum.
Imprint: Romae, 1563. Apud Paulum Manutium, Aldi F. In aedibus populi Romani.

Limp vellum, calf back; 7-5/8 x 5-5/8 x ⅜ in

IMPRINTS, Italy

Cabinet AA Shelf 2 No. 36

Bertieri, Raffaello: Milano, 1928.
Title: L'Arte tipografica in Italia nella terza Fiera Internazionale...Catalogue.
Colophon: Scritto da Augusto Calabi. Stampata de Raffaello Bertieri col nuovo carattere "Paganini"...April, 1928.

Half morocco; 9-1/8 x 6½ in.

IMPRINTS, Italy.

Cabinet 60 Shelf 1 No. 30

Aldine Press, Paul Manutius. Venice, 1558.
Title: Archimedis ... nuper in latinum conversa, et commentariis.
Imprint: Cum privilegio in annos X. Venetiis, apud Paulum Manutium, Aldi F. 1558.

Three quarter morocco; 11¾ x 7-7/8 x 1 in. Brunet 1, 384; Renouard II, p. 417?

IMPRINTS, Italy.

Cabinet 60 Shelf 2 No. 26

Aldine Press: Paul Manutius. Venice, 1566.
Title: T. Livii, Patavini, historiarum ab urbe condita ... Secunda editio.
Imprint: Venetiis, Apud Paulum Manutium, Aldi, F. 1566.

Calf; 12½ x 8½ x 2¾ in. Renouard II, 62.

IMPRINTS, Italy

Cabinet L Shelf 5 No. 17

Bertieri e Vanzetti, Milan, 1922-3

see COLOR PRINTING. Bertieri e Vanzetti...

IMPRINTS, Italy.

Cabinet 60 Shelf 1 No. 31

Aldine Press: Academia Venetia [Paul Manutius Venice, 1558.
Title: De dei locutione Marci Antonii Mattae. Astensis oratio.
Imprint: In Academia Veneta. 1558.

Vellum; 8¼ x 6 x ½ in. Renouard II, p. 221.

IMPRINTS, Italy.

Cabinet 60 Shelf 1 No. 42

Aldine Press: Aldus Manutius Jr. Venice, 1571.
Title: Epistolarum Pauli Manutii. Libri X.
Imprint: Venetiis, 1571. In aedib. Manutianis. Aldus Junior.

Vellum; 6¼ x 4¼ x 1¾ in. Goldsmid "Aldine Press," No. 674.

IMPRINTS, Italy

Cabinet AA Shelf 2 No. 42

Bertieri e Vanzetti, Milan, 1925.
Title: Catalogue d'une collection d'anciens livres à figures Italiens appartenant a Tammaro de Marinis. Préface de Seymour de Ricci.
Imprint: Milano. Bertieri e Vanzetti, Imprimeurs - Editeurs.

Paper; 13 x 9½ x 1½ in.

IMPRINTS, Italy.

Cabinet E Shelf 1 No. 3

Bindoni, Bernardino. Venice, 1535.

See Early Printing in Italy.

IMPRINTS, Italy.

Cabinet 50 Shelf 1 No. 14

Bindoni, Francesco and Mapheo Pasini. Venice 1547.
Title: Regula del S. Benedetto tradutta ... [With wood cut on title-page and printers' device on the last leaf.]
Colophon: Stampata in Venegia per Francesco di Alessandro Bindoni, & Mapheo Pasini, compagni. 1547.

Morocco; 5-7/8 x 3¾ x ½ in.

IMPRINTS, Italy.

Cabinet D Shelf 4 No. 53

Blado, Antonio. Rome, 1534.

See Early Printing in Italy. Rome, 1534. Antonio Blado.

IMPRINTS, Italy

Cabinet 17 Shelf 2 No. 3

Blado, Antonio, Rome, 1586.
(Folio page: Register and index. With printer device and imprint)

Item on fol.7 of Henry Steven's "TYPOGRAPHICAL MISCELLANIES", vol. 3-B-2

IMPRINTS, Italy.

Cabinet 50 Shelf 1 No. 1

Bodoni, Giambattista. Parma, 1769.
Title: Le festa d'Apollo celebrate sul teatro di Corte nell'Agosto del MDCCLXIX per le auguste sequite nozze tra il Reale Infante Don Ferdinando e la R. Arciduchessa Infanta Maria Amalia.
Imprint: Parma nella Stamperia Reale.

Leather; 9½ x 7¼ x 7/8 in. Brooks No. 8.

IMPRINTS, Italy.

Cabinet 50 Shelf 1 No. 2

Bodoni, Giambattista. Parma, 1771.
Title: Fregi e majuscule incise e fuse da Giambattista Bodoni.
Imprint: A Parma nella stamperia stessa.

Original paper cover, 7-7/8 x 4¾ x 3/8 in. In cloth protective case.

IMPRINTS, Italy.

Cabinet 50 Shelf 1 No. 4

Bodoni, Giambattista. Parma, 1773.

Title: Giornata Villereccia. Poemetto in tre canti in tenui labor. Virg. Georg. IV.

Imprint: Parma. Dalla Stamperia Reale. 1773. [Engraved frontispiece]

Paper; 8-3/4 x 5-3/4 x 3/8 in. Brooks No. 38

IMPRINTS, Italy.

Cabinet 50 Shelf 1 No. 3

Bodoni, Giambattista. Parma, 1773.
Title: La marcia. Commedia del signor abate Francesco Marucchi di Milano.
Imprint: Parma. Dalla Stamperia Reale.

Half morocco; 11¼ x 8 x ¾ in.

IMPRINTS, Italy.

Cabinet 50 Shelf 1 No. 5

Bodoni, Giambattista. Parma, 1773.

Title: Saggio di poesie Italiane dell'Abate Vincenzio Cammillo Alberti.
Imprint: Parma dalla Stamperia Real. MDCCLXXIII. [Vignette on title page and 13 decorative tail pieces. Last page numbered 86 by mistake.]

Original boards; 10 x 8¼ x 3/8 in. Brooks No.34.

IMPRINTS, Italy.

Cabinet 50 Shelf 1 No. 7

Bodoni, Giambattista. Parma, 1774.
Title: Pel solenne battesimo di S.A.R. Ludovico, Principe di Parma....
Colophon: Impresso nella R. Stamperia di Parma. L'Anno di nostra salute riparata MDCCLXXIV Il giorno 18 di Aprile. [Preface by Bodoni, followed by twenty inscriptions in as many exotic types and languages with their Latin equivalents.]

Half morocco; 11¼ x 8½ x 3/8 ins. Brooks No.50

IMPRINTS, Italy

Cabinet 50 Shelf 2 No. 3

Bodoni, Giambattista. Parma, 1775.

Title: Epithalamia exoticis linguis reditta.
Imprint: Parmae ex Regio Typographeo. [Many beautiful copperplate engravings, head and tail pieces.]

Full morocco; gilt; 17½ x 13 x 1½ ins. [Brooks No.70.

IMPRINTS, Italy.

Cabinet 50 Shelf 1 No. 10

Bodoni, Giambattista. Parma, 1776.
Title: Joh. Bernardi De-Rossi in Parm. Acad. Publ. Ling. Orient. Profess ...
Imprint: Parmae ex Regio Typographeo MDCCLXXVI.

Half morocco; 8-7/8 x 5-7/8 in. Brooks, Bodoniane, F157.

IMPRINTS, Italy.

Cabinet 50 Shelf 1 No. 13

Bodoni, Giambattista. Parma, 1778.

Title: Elogio Funebre. Recitato dal signor conte Antonio Cerati...nelle solenni esequie.... monsignore Corrado Tarasconi Smeraldi...
Colophon: Parma. Dalla Reale Stamperia (1778) Con approvazione.

Original calf; 11 x 8 x ½ in.

IMPRINTS, Italy.

Cabinet 50 Shelf 1 No. 15

Bodoni, Giambattista. Parma, 1779.

Title: Atti della solenne coronazione fatta in campidoglio della insigne poetessa Dna. Maria Maddalena Morelli Fernandez...[Many vignettes, borders, head & tail pieces.]
Colophon: Impresso nella Stamperia Reale di Parma il di XXX Giugno dell'anno di nostra riparata salute M.DCC.LXXIX.

Flowered Japanese paper; 8½ x 5-7/8 x 7/8 in. Brooks No.135

IMPRINTS, Italy

Cabinet X Shelf 1 No. 77

Bodoni, Giam. Battista: Ex Regio Typographeo, Parma, 1780.
Title: Joh. Bernardi De Rossi. De Typographia Hebraeo-Ferrariensi...
Imprint: Parma. Ex Regio Typographeo.

Half morocco; 8-7/8 x 5-7/8 in.

IMPRINTS, Italy.

Cabinet 50 Shelf 1 No. 17

Bodoni, Giambattista. Parma, 1783.

Title: Gestorum ab Episcopis Salutiensibus.... Iosephus Ioachimus Lovera. Patricius Saviliamensis. [Ornaments, borders, etc.]

Colophon: Parmae. Ex regio typographeo MDCCLXXXIII.

Calf; 9½ x 6¾ x 1 in. Brooks No.228.

IMPRINTS, Italy.

Cabinet 50 Shelf 1 No. 19

Bodoni, Giambattista. Parma, 1784.

Title: Il calendario di corte per l'anno bissestile MDCCLXXXIV.

Imprint: Parma. Nella Stamperia Reale. [Has a map of the City of Parma]

Morocco; 4¾ x 2¾ x 5/8 in. Brooks No.1386.

IMPRINTS, Italy.

Cabinet 50 Shelf 1 No. 21

Bodoni, Giambattista. Parma, 1785.
Title: ...Anacreontis Teii Odaria praefixo commentario quo poetae genus traditur ...
Imprint: Parmae. Ex Regio typographeio. [Printed in Majuscule types.]

Half morocco; 12- x 9-1/8 x 1 in. Brooks, No. 287.

IMPRINTS, Italy.

Cabinet 50 Shelf 1 No. 22

Bodoni, Giambattista. Parma, 1785.

Title: Lettre de J.B.Bodoni, Typographe du Roi d'Espagne et Directeur de l'Imprimerie de S.A.R. l'Infant Duc de Parme à Monsieur le Marquis de Cubieres. [Printed in French with an Italian version of the same letter.]

Half morocco; $11\frac{3}{4}$ x 8 x $\frac{1}{4}$ in. Brooks No.292.

IMPRINTS, Italy.

Cabinet 50 Shelf 1 No. 24

Bodoni, Giambattista, Parma, 1786. Gli Amori pastorali di Dafni e Cloe....Crisopoli, Impresso co'carrateri Bodoniana.

It is curious to find the words "co'tipi Bodoniana" (With Bodoni types) which appears once again in 1789 and never in books printed after 1790." Brooks, No.309.

Full morocco, tooled, Gilt edges, 12 x $8\frac{1}{4}$ x 1-1/8 in. pp. XVIII.245.

IMPRINTS, Italy.

Cabinet 50 Shelf 1 No. 25

Bodoni, Giambattista. Parma, 1786.

Title: Characterum ethicorum Theophrasti Eresii capita duo hactenus anecdota quae ex cod. MS. Vaticano saeculi XI graece edidit latine vertit praefatione...Christophorus Amadutius.

Imprint: Parmae. Ex Regio Typographeo. [Fleuron on title page.]

Orig. boards; 11 x 8 x 3/8 x in. Brooks No. 315.

IMPRINTS, Italy.

Cabinet 50 Shelf 1 No. 28

Bodoni, Giambattista. Parma, 1788.

Title: Osservazioni di Ennio Quirino Visconti su due Musaici antichi istoriati.

Imprint: In Parma. Dalla Reale Tipografia, MDCCLXXXVIII. [Engraving on title page by Bossi and two folded engravings by Cecchini]

Mottled calf; $8\frac{1}{2}$ x $5\frac{3}{4}$ x $\frac{1}{2}$ in. Brooks No.359.

IMPRINTS, Italy.

Cabinet 50 Shelf 1 No. 29

Bodoni, Giambatista. Parma, 1788.

Title: Serie de Caratteri Greci di Giambatista, Bodoni, 1788.

Boards; $9\frac{1}{4}$ x 6 x 3/8 in. Brooks, No.355.

IMPRINTS, Italy.

Cabinet 50 Shelf 2 No. 5

Bodoni, Giambattista. Parma, 1788.

Title: Serie di Majuscole e caratteri cancelleres-schi.[Without name or place. Contains a series of Russian, Greek, and other types. "I have had the great pleasure of receiving. ..It is one of the most beautiful that Art has hitherto produced. B. Franklin"]

Half morocco; 20 x $13\frac{1}{2}$ x 1 ins. Brooks No. 357; Updike II, p.166.

(Dup. with covers) -ed. For Bodoni...

IMPRINTS, Italy.

Cabinet 50 Shelf 1 No. 34

Bodoni, Giambattista, Parma, 1789. Aminta: Favola boschereccia di Torquato Tasso. Crispoli Impresso co'caratteri Bodoniani. Portrait on the frontispiece.

This is the second book with the words "co' tipi Bodoniani", The types were specially designed and cast. Brooks No.379.

Half morocco; $11\frac{1}{2}$ x $9\frac{1}{4}$ ins., pp.142.

IMPRINTS, Italy.

Cabinet 50 Shelf 1 No. 36

Bodoni, Giambattista. Parma, 1791.

Title: Anakreontoz...praefixo commentario quo Poetae genus traditur et bibliotheca Anacreonteia. Additis var. lect. [Oval medal].

Imprint: Parmae in Aedibus Palatinis, 1791.

Morocco, gilt edges; 6 x 4-3/8 x 1 in. Brooks No.422. Brunet I, 252.

IMPRINTS, Italy.

Cabinet 50 Shelf 1 No. 37

Bodoni, Giambattista, Parma, 1791.

Title: Saggio di memorie du la Tipografia Parmense del secolo XV del Padre Ireneo Affo... [Ornament].

Imprint: Parma dalla Stamperia Reale. M.DCC.XCI [2 copies; one original binding].

Half morocco; 10 x $8\frac{1}{4}$ x $\frac{1}{2}$ ins. Brooks No.435

IMPRINTS, Italy

Cabinet 50 Shelf 2 No. 8

Bodoni, Giambattista. Parmae, 1792.

Title: Britannia, Lathmon, Villa Bromhamensis, [By John Trenor].

Imprint: Parmae. In Aedibus Palatinis. Typis Bodonianis. 1792.

Full morocco; 18 x 12 in. Brooks. 470.

IMPRINTS, Italy.

Cabinet 50 Shelf 1 No. 40

Bodoni, Giambattista. Parma, 1792.

Title: Le Stanze di Messer Angelo Poliziano di nuovo pubblicate.

Imprint: Parma nel Regal Palazzo MDCCXCII Co'tipi Bodoniani.

Orig. mottled calf; 11-3/4 x $8\frac{1}{2}$ x 3/4 in. Brooks, No.451.

IMPRINTS, Italy.

Cabinet 50 Shelf 1 No. 42

Bodoni, Giambattista, Parma, 1793.

Title: La tavola di Cebete Tebano. [This is the second title; the first part of the book being a Greek Version of the same subject].

Imprint: Parma nel Regal Palazzo MDCCXCIII. co' tipi Bodoniani.

Calf; $7\frac{1}{2}$ x 5 x $\frac{1}{2}$ in. Brooks No. 510.

IMPRINTS, Italy.

Cabinet 49 Shelf 1 No. 4

Bodoni, Giambattista. Parma, 1794.

Title: La Gerusalemme liberate di Torquato Tasso.

Imprint: Parma, nel regal Palazzo, MDCCXCIV. Co'tipi Bodoniani.

Copy presented to H.L. Bullen, by A. Lobetti Bodoni, grandson of Bodoni's sister.

Paper covers; 15 x 10 x 1 in. Brooks No.563.

IMPRINTS, Italy.

Cabinet 50 Shelf 1 No. 44

Bodoni, Giambattista. Parma, 1794.

Title: Pel Virgilio. Stampato in Parma in due volumi. Ottavo, 1794.

Sonnets in praise of printing in which the names of Aldo, Gryph and Giolito are mentioned, also "Alcippo" being the Arcadian name for G. Bodoni.

Brochure, paper covers. Brooks 543.

IMPRINTS, Italy.

Cabinet 50 Shelf 1 No. 45

Bodoni, Giambattista. Parma, 1794.

Title: The Seasons. By James Thomson.

Imprint: Parma. Printed by Bodoni. MDCCXCIV.

Paper boards; leather back; $11\frac{1}{2}$ x 9 x 1 in. Brooks No.531.

IMPRINTS, Italy

Cabinet X Shelf 1 No. 79

Bodoni, Giam, Battista: Ex Regio Typographeo, 1795.

See De ROSSI, Johannes Bernardus Annales Hebraeo-typographici...

IMPRINTS, Italy.

Cabinet 50 Shelf 1 No. 48

Bodoni, Giambattista, Parma, 1795.

Title: Scherzi poetici e pittorici. (At the end) Parma, co' tipi Bodoniani.

Title and illustrations by Rosaspina are colored. Book dedicated to D. Allessandro de Sousa e Holstein.

Brooks, 599.

Half morocco; 12-3/8 x $9\frac{1}{2}$ x 1-1/8 in.

IMPRINTS, Italy.

Cabinet 50 Shelf 1 No. 52

Bodoni, Giambattista. Parma, 1796.

Title: Poesie di Maria Luisa Cicci. Tra gli Arcadi Erminia Tindaride.

Imprint: Parma. Co'tipi Bodoniani. 1796. [This is one of only two copies printed on vellum].

Boards; 6-3/4 x $4\frac{1}{2}$ x 3/4 in. In case. Brooks No.627.

IMPRINTS, Italy.

Cabinet 50 | Shelf 1 | No. 55

Bodoni, Giambattista. Parma, 1799.

Title: Odi dell' Abate Giuseppe Parini gia divolgate

Imprint: Parma. Co'tipi Bodoniani, 1799.

Boards; 6½ x 4½ x 5/8 in. Brooks No.760.

IMPRINTS, Italy.

Cabinet 50 | Shelf 2 | No. 9

Bodoni, Giambattista. Parmae, 1800.

Title: Aesopi Phrygii Fabulae Graecae latine conversae.

Imprint: Ex Regio Typographeo. M.D.CCC.

Printed in two columns, Greek and Latin version.

Calf; 16 x 11½ in. Brunet I, 87; Brooks Edizioni Bodoniane, 796.

IMPRINTS, Italy.

Cabinet 50 | Shelf 1 | No. 59

Bodoni, Giambattista. Parma, 1800.

Title: Per le nozze del nobil uomo Signor Conte Alessandro Bonacossi....

Imprint: Parma. Co'tipi Bodoniani, MDCCC.

Boards; 6-3/4 x 4½ x ½ in. Brooks No.764.

IMPRINTS, Italy.

Cabinet 50 | Shelf 1 | No. 58

Bodoni, Giambattista, Parma, 1800.

Title: Pitture di Antonio Allegri detto Il Correggio.

Imprint: Parma nel Regal Palazzo. MDCCC. Co'tipi Bodoniani.

Boards; 10-3/4 x 7-3/4 x 3/4 in. Brooks 777

IMPRINTS, Italy

Cabinet 50 | Shelf 2 | No. 14

Bodoni, Giambattista, Parma, 1803.

See BODONI, MARGHERITA. Letters di...

IMPRINTS, Italy

Cabinet 50 | Shelf 2 | No. 13

Bodoni, Giambattista. Parma, 1806-1807.

Title: Bodoniana 2. Bodoni in honor of Napoleon.

Imprints. [Various].

Scrap book collection of broadsides.

Bodoniana 2: Half morocco; 18½ x 13 in.

IMPRINTS, Italy.

Cabinet 50 | Shelf 2 | No. 11

Bodoni, Giambattista. Parma, 1806.

Title: Oratio Dominica in CLV linguas versa et exoticis characteribus plerumque expressa.

Imprint: Parmae typis Bodonianis. MDCCCVI. [Oratio Dominica in 155 languages with appropriate type for each.]

Full morocco; 17 x 11 x 2 ins. Brooks No.1003; Updike II p.168-169.

IMPRINTS, Italy.

Cabinet 49 | Shelf 1 | No. 6

Bodoni, Giambattista, Parma, 1809.

Title: Le piu insigni pitture Parmensi indicate agli amatori delle Belle Arti.

Imprint: Parma dalla Tipografia Bodoniana. MDCCCIX.

Half morocco; 12¾ x 9 x 1½ in. Brooks, No.1059.

IMPRINTS, Italy

Cabinet AA | Shelf 1 | No. 21

Bodoni (Vedova). Parma, 1814.

Title: In morte del Cavaliere Giambattista Bodoni, Sommo tipografo. Avvenuta il 30 Novembre, 1813.

Imprint: Parma. Presso la vedova Bodoni. 1814.

Half morocco; 9¼ x 6½ in.

IMPRINTS, Italy

Cabinet L | Shelf 3 | No. 4.02

Cartolari, Baldassarre di Francesco, Roma, 1540.

Title: Libro nuovo d'imparare a scrivere... Composto per Giovambattista Palatino

Colophon: Stampata in Roma, appresso Campo di Fiore, nella casa de M. Benedetto Gionta, per Baldassarre di Francesco Cartolari, Perugino. 1540.

Printed from wood blocks and type

Boards, russia back; 8 x 5½ in.

IMPRINTS, Italy.

Cabinet 49 | Shelf 1 | No. 10

Bodoni, Giambattista. Parma, 1818.

Title: Di Q. Orazio Flacco satira V. Traduzione italiana con rami allusivi.

Imprint; Parma. Co'tipi Bodoniani. MDCCCXVIII.

Half morocco; 12 x 9 x ¼ in. Brooks No.1212

IMPRINTS, Italy.

Cabinet 49 | Shelf 1 | No. 9

Bodoni, Giambattista. Parma, 1818.

Title: Manuale tipografico del cavaliere G. Bodoni.

Imprint: Parma, presso la Vedova MDCCCXVIII. [2 vol.]

Includes specimens of more than 250 different type designs.

Boards; 13 x 9¼ x 2 in. Brooks, 1216, Brunet I, 1027-8.

IMPRINTS, Italy.

Cabinet 50 | Shelf 1 | No. 66

Bodoni, Giambattista. Parma, 1827.

Title: Sullo stato attuale della Tragedia in Italy. Discorso di Antonio Beduschi.

Imprints: Parma. Co'tipi Bodoniani. MDCCCXXVII.

Printed on yellow toned paper. There were two editions printed simultaneously - one on white paper, and this one. H. L. Bullen.

Boards; 9-3/8 x 6¼ in. Brooks, 1294.

IMPRINTS, Italy

Cabinet QQ | Shelf 1 | No. 8

Braglia, Giuseppe, Casalmaggiore, 1777.

Title: La stampa. Poemetto in ottava rima...

Imprint: Casalmaggiore. Per Giuseppe Braglia Stamp. della Città all'Inseg. di Virgilio. 1777.

Half vellum; 8¼ 5 x ½ in.

IMPRINTS, Italy.

Cabinet D | Shelf 4 | No. 19

Calliergi [or Kaliergi], Zaccaria.

See Early Printing in Italy. Rome, 1522.[Calliergi....]

IMPRINTS, Italy

Cabinet F | Shelf 5 | No. 49

Cambiagi, Gaetano. Florence, 1791.

Title: La typografia per...Luisa Maria, Principessa de Napoli.

Imprint: Firenze, 1791. Per Gaetano Cambiagi, Stampatore Granducale.

With copper engravings, head and tail pieces.

Calf; 16 3/4 x 10 1/4 in.

IMPRINTS, Italy

Cabinet PP | Shelf 3 | No. 3

Cannetti, Gio. Batista. Rome, 1803.

See LAWS RELATING TO PUBLISHING. Rome, 1803...

IMPRINTS, Italy.

Cabinet D | Shelf 1 | No. 33

Cinquinis, Francisci di. Rome, 1479.

See Incunabula. (Ulmeus) de Bergamo Apologia religionis.....

IMPRINTS, Italy

Cabinet F Shelf 5 No. 51

Civelli, Giuseppi. Milan, 1868.
Title: Ghirlanda di Margarite...agli eccelsi sposa Umberto e Margarita di Savoia. Da Giuseppi Civelli.
Imprint colophon: Impressa nelle stabilimento Civelle in Milano.

Every page with border around text. Specimen of decorative color printing.

Cloth; 18 x 12½ in.

IMPRINTS, Italy.

Cabinet E Shelf 1 No. 17

Giolito, Gabriel. Venice, 1549.

See Early Printing in Italy. Venice, 1549.

IMPRINTS, Italy.

Cabinet E Shelf 1 No. 6

Giunta (Heirs of Luc Antonio), Venice, 1542.

See Early Printing in Italy.

IMPRINTS, Italy

Cabinet 10 Shelf 1 No. 1

Emericus de Spira, Johannes. Venice, 1499-1500.

See Incunabula Graduate Romanum.

IMPRINTS, Italy.

Cabinet E Shelf 2 No. 31

Giolito, Gabriel. Venice, 1558.

See Early Printing in Italy. Venice, 1558.

IMPRINTS, Italy.

Cabinet E Shelf 1 No. 56

Giunta. Florence, 1568.

See Early Printing in Italy. Florence, 1568.

IMPRINTS, Italy

Cabinet X Shelf 1 No. 88

Fulgon, Anton, Rome, 1793.
Title: De prima typographiae Hispanicae aetate specimen. Auctore Raymundo Diosdado Cabellero.
Imprint: Romae: apud Antonium Folgonium.

Half morocco; 9-5/8 x 5-3/8 in.

IMPRINTS, Italy.

Cabinet 10 Shelf 1 No. 1

Giunta, Lucantonio, Venice, 1499-1500.
Graduale Romanum [Edited by Franciscus de Brugis]
Colophon: Explicit graduale dñicale impressum Venetiis/ cura atqz impēsz nobil Viri luce ãtonii de giunta florentini...anno incarnationis dñice/ M.CCCCLXXXXIX.IIIj Kl octobris

Original boards, covered with red vellum, brass bosses, 23 x 15¾ x 5 ins.

IMPRINTS, Italy.

Cabinet E Shelf 2 No. 70

Giunta (Philip) and brothers. Flornece, 1604.

See Early Printing in Italy. Florence, 1604. [Giunta].

IMPRINTS, Italy.

Cabinet E Shelf 3 No. 37

Gherardus. Vincentius [Propaganda Fide]. Rome, 1628.

See Early Printing in Italy. Rome, 1628.

IMPRINTS, Italy

Cabinet D Shelf 3 No. 30

Giunta, Luca Antonio, Venice, 1514.

See Early Printing in Italy.

IMPRINTS, Italy.

Cabinet D Shelf 2 No. 42

Gregoriis, Joannes and Gregorius de. Venice, 1498.

See Incunabula. Hieronymus. Commentaria in Biblia.

IMPRINTS, Italy.

Cabinet E Shelf 1 No. 4

Giolito, Gabriel de Ferrari (Comin da Trino). Venice, 1540.
Title: I sei primi libri del Eneide di Vergilio, tradotti...Tolomei de Borghesi...[Title with in border].
Colophon:..Stampato in Vinetia per Comin de Trino ...nel anno MDXL. Adi XII del mese de Otto bre...

Half morocco; 6 x 4 in.

IMPRINTS, Italy.

Cabinet D Shelf 4 No. 16

Giunta, Luca Antonio. Venice, 1520.

See Early Printing in Italy. Venice, 1520. Luca Antonio Giunta.

IMPRINTS, Italy

Cabinet E Shelf 2 No. 16

Guerra, Domenico and Giambattista. Venice, 1574.

See Early Printing in Italy. Venice, 1574.

IMPRINTS, Italy.

Cabinet E Shelf 1 No. 15

Giolito, Gabriel. Venice, 1547.

See Early Printing in Italy. Venice, 1547.

IMPRINTS, Italy.

Cabinet D Shelf 4 No. 22

Giunta, Luca Antonio. Venice, 1523.

See Early Printing in Italy. Venice, 1523. Luca Antonio Giunta. Missale.

IMPRINTS, Italy.

Cabinet D Shelf 1 No. 39

Herbert, Johannes. Venice, 1481.

See Incunabula. Baysio, Guido de. Rosarium decretorum.

IMPRINTS, ITALY

Cabinet R Shelf 2 No. 25

Istituto Italiano d'Arte Bergamo, 1914

See ILLUSTRATED BOOKS. Collezione di vetri antichi...Milan-Rome, 1914

IMPRINTS, Italy

Cabinet L Shelf 2 No. 17

Landi Press, Florence, 1897.

See SPITTA, WILHELM. Egyptian alphabet...

IMPRINTS, Italy.

Cabinet E Shelf 2 No. 30

Marcolini, Francesco. Venice, 1551.

See Early Printing in Italy. Venice, 1551.

IMPRINTS, Italy.

Cabinet D Shelf 4 No. 30

Janiculo, Tolomeo, Vicenza, Venice, 1529. Dante/ de la volgare/ eloquenzia. (Printers mark. T.IA).
Last page: Stampata in Vicenza per Tolomeo Janiculo da Bressa/ nel anno MDXXIX./ del mese di Genaro./ Con la grazia, e prohibizione come ne l'altre.

11 x 6¾ x ¼ in.

IMPRINTS, Italy.

Cabinet D Shelf 3 No. 36

Liechtenstein, Pietro. Venice, 1515.

See Early Printing in Italy. Venice, 1515. Pietro Liechtenstein.

IMPRINTS, Italy

Cabinet AA Shelf 2 No. 28

Marescotti, Georgio. Florence, 1587 or 1588
Title: Oratio de Francisci Medices Etruriae ducis laudibus habita ab Aldo Manutius ... [Aldus Manutius, author] XII. Kal. Dec. 1587
Imprint: Florentiae. Ex typographia Georgii Marescotti. With printer marks.

Full morocco; gilt; 7-5/8 x 5½ x ¼ in.

IMPRINTS, Italy

Cabinet D Shelf 4 No. 31

Janiculo, Tolomeo. Vicenza, 1529

See EARLY PRINTING IN ITALY. Vicenza, 1529, Tolomeo Janiculo...

IMPRINTS, Italy

Cabinet K Shelf 1 No. 28

Locatello, Boneto, Venice, 1501. (see)

FACSIMILES. Music printing and manuscript, 12th to 16th century...(plate XV)

IMPRINTS, Italy

Cabinet K Shelf 1 No. 28

Mattia Moravo, Neapoli, 1477 (see)

FACSIMILES. Music printing and manuscript, 12th to 16th century... (plate Xll)

IMPRINTS, ITALY.

Cabinet 6 Shelf 1 No. 4

Jenson, Nicolas. Venice, 1472.
Title: Plinius Secundus (Caius), Historia naturalis ...
With 35 large initials illuminated in gold, and 100 smaller capitals in red and blue.

Morocco; 15¾ x 11 x 4 in.

IMPRINTS, Italy

Cabinet 68 Shelf No. 11

Manfre, Giovanni (Typographia Seminarii), Pavia, 1732.
Title: Numismata virorum illustrium ex Barbadica gente.
Imprint: Patavia, ex Typographia Seminarii, apud Joannem Manfre.

Boards; 23¼ x 16 in.

IMPRINTS, ITALY

Cabinet F Shelf 4 No. 76

Molini, Giuseppi e Co. Florence, 1827.
Title: Il decameron di Messer Giovanni Boccaccio.
Imprint: Firenze, 1827. Impresso Giuseppe Molini e Co.

Engraving on title page and frontispiece.

Vellum; 5¼ x 3 x 1-5/8 in.

IMPRINTS, Italy.

Cabinet 6 Shelf 1 No. 8

Jenson, Nicolas. Venice, Italy. 1479.

See Incunabula. Bonifacius VIII (Benedetto Gaetana) Liber sextus decretalium.

IMPRINTS, Italy.

Cabinet E Shelf 1 No. 10

Marcolini, Francesco. Venice, 1544.

See Early Printing in Italy.

IMPRINTS, Italy

Cabinet II Shelf 3 No.

Monastery of Saint Lazarius, Venice, 1837 and 1872.

See SAINT LAZARE (Venice) CONVENT OF.

IMPRINTS, Italy

Cabinet D Shelf 2 No. 48

Kallierges, Zakarias, Venice, 1499.
See Incunabula. Etymologikum magnum graece.

IMPRINTS, Italy.

Cabinet E Shelf 1 No. 11

Marcolini, Francesco. Venice, 1544.

See Early Printing in Italy.

IMPRINTS, Italy.

Cabinet E Shelf 1 No. 54

Niccolini, Vincenzo (Also known as Vicenzo da Sabbio)

See Early Printing in Italy. Brescia, 1568. Vicenzo da Sabbio.

IMPRINTS, Italy

Cabinet S Shelf 5 No. 43

Officina Bodoni, The. Verona, 1929.
Title: The operations of a hand press during the first six years of its work.
Imprint Colophon: Printed by The Officina Bodoni at Verona...in the original types of Giambattista Bodoni...Sept. 1929.

Cloth; 12 x 8½ x ½ in.

IMPRINTS, Italy

Cabinet F Shelf 4 No. 75

Palese, Carlo. Venice, 1784.
Title: Orazione per ingresso di sua eccellenza il Signor...e Signore di Ascalona. Engraved frontispiece signed, Daniotto.
Imprint: In Venezia nella stamperia di Carlo Palese. 1784.

Paper; 11¾ x 8¾ in.

IMPRINTS, Italy.

Cabinet D Shelf 3 No. 45

Porrus, Petrus-Paulus, Genoa, 1516.

See Early Printing in Italy. Genoa, 1516. Petrus-Paulus Porrus.

IMPRINTS, Italy.

Cabinet D Shelf 2 No. 20

Paganinis, Hieronymus (Jerome) de. Venice, 1492.

See Incunabula. Biblia Latina [Edited by Petrus Angelus, de Monte Ulmi]

IMPRINTS, Italy

Cabinet K Shelf 1 No. 28

Petrucci, Ottaviano de' (Venice), 1502. (see)

FACSIMILES. Music printing and manuscript, 12th to 16th century.... (Plate XXIV)

IMPRINTS, Italy.

Cabinet 29 Shelf 1 No. 1

Ratdolt, Erhard; Bernard Pictor, Peter Loslein. Venice, 1476.
Title: Monteregio. Kalendarium.
Imprint: ... I nomi di impressori son qui da basso ... Bernardus Pictor, Petrus Loslein, Erhard Ratdolt. Venice, 1476.

Vellum; 10¼ x 7½ x ½ in.

IMPRINT, Italy

Cabinet I Shelf 1 No. 1

Paganinus de Paganinus. Venice, 1509.
Title: Divia Proportione...Lucas Paciolo.
Colophon: Venetiis impressum per probum virum Paginnum de paganinis de Briscia...Anno Redemptionis nostre M.D.IX. klen. Iunii.

Two colophons, identical, except for a slight variation of the date designation.

Vellum; 12 x 8-1/8 x 1-1/8 in.

IMPRINTS, Italy.

Cabinet D Shelf 3 No. 27

Petrucci, Ottaviano. Fossombrone, 1513.

See Early Printing in Italy. Fossombrone.

IMPRINTS, Italy

Cabinet 29 Shelf 1 No. 4

Ratdolt, Maler (Pictor) and Loslein. Venice, 1477.
Title: Appianus. Historia Romano. (2 parts). Red border.
Colophon: Impressum est hoc opus Venetiis per Bernardu pictorem & Erhardum Ratdolt de Augusta una cum Petro Löslein de Langencen correctore ac socio. Laus Deo. M.CCCC.LXXVII

Morocco; 11½ x 8½ x 3 in.

IMPRINTS, Italy.

Cabinet D Shelf 3 No. 18

Paganinis (de) Paganinus, Venice, 1509. Euclidis. megarensis philo/sophi.... A. Paganius Paganinus characteribus elegantissimis accuratissime imprimebat.

Boards; 12 x 8 x 1 ins.

IMPRINTS, Italy.

Cabinet D Shelf 3 No. 27 & 28

Petrucci, Ottaviano. Fossombrone, 1513.

See Early Printing in Italy. Fossombrone, 1513. Ottaviano Petrucci. Paulina de recta Paschae celebratione.

IMPRINTS, Italy.

Cabinet 29 Shelf 1 No. 5

Ratdolt, Erhard. Maler (Pictor) and Loslein. Venice, 1477.
Title: Appianus. Historia Romana. [2 parts]. Black Border.
Colophon: Impressum est hoc opus Venetiis per Bernardum Pictorem, Erhardum Ratdolt, cum Petro Loslein ...

Morocco; 11½ x 8½ x 3 in.

IMPRINTS, Italy.

Cabinet D Shelf 4 No. 20

Paganini, Alexander, Venice, 1522.

See Early Printing in Italy. Venice, 1522: Alex. Paganinus.

IMPRINTS, Italy.

Cabinet E Shelf 3 No. 26

Pinelli [Antonio?] Venice, 1625.

See Early Printing in Italy. Venice, 1625.

IMPRINTS, Italy.

Cabinet 29 Shelf 1 No. 3

Ratdolt, Erhard, Bernhard Pictor, Peter Loslein. Venice, 1477.
Title: Dionysius [Periegetes]. De situ orbis.
Colophon: Impressum est hoc opusculum Venetiis per Bernardum Pictore & Erhardum Ratdolt ... cum Petro Loslein.

Vellum; 8½ x 6¼ x ¼ in.

IMPRINTS, Italy.

Cabinet F Shelf 5 No. 12

Pagliarini, Niccolo and Marco. Rome, 1758.
Title: Componimenti poetici per le felicissime nozze di sua eccellenza il Signor Giovanni Correr.... Many engraved initials, vignettes head pieces, etc.
Imprint: In Roma MDCCLVIII. Dalla Stamperia di Pallade. Appresso Niccolo e Marco Pagliarini Con licenza.

Paper boards; 14½ x 10 x ½ in.

IMPRINTS, Italy.

Cabinet D Shelf 3 No. 44

Porrus, Petrua-Paulus, Genoa, 1516.

See Early Printing in Italy. Genoa, 1516. Petrus-Paulus. Porrus.

IMPRINTS, Italy.

Cabinet 29 Shelf 1 No. 7

Ratdolt, Erhard. Pictor (Maler) and Loslein Venice, 1478.
Title: Mela, Pomponius. Cosmographia.
(Imprint) Colophon: Impressum ... Venetiis per Bernardum Pictorem & Erhardum Ratdolt ... cum Petro Loslein correctore ac socio. 1478.

Morocco; 8 x 6 x 5/8 in.

IMPRINTS, Italy.

Cabinet 29 Shelf 1 No. 8

Ratdolt, Erhard. Venice, 1478.
Title: Francisci Mataratis ... De compendis versibus.
(Imprint) Colophon: Erhardus Ratdolt ... confecit ... Anno christi 1468. Venetiis [Colophon misdated].

Morocco; $8\frac{1}{2}$ x 6 x $\frac{1}{4}$ in.

IMPRINTS, Italy.

Cabinet 29 Shelf 1 No. 12

Ratdolt, Erhard. Venice, 1482.
Title: Euclide. Elementa geometriae ...
(Imprint) Colophon: Erhardus Ratdolt Augustensis impressor solertissimus. Venetiis, 1482.

Vellum over boards with clasps, 12 x 8 x $1\frac{1}{2}$"

IMPRINTS, Italy

Cabinet 29 Shelf 1 No. 16

Ratdolt, Erhard. Venice, 1482.
Title: Sacrobusto, Joannes de. Sphaera Mundi.
(Imprint) Colophon: Impressum hoc est opusculum ... diligentia Erhardi Ratdolt Augustensis. Anno Salutis 1482.

Boards covered with leaf from a 15th cent. book; $8\frac{1}{4}$ x $5\frac{3}{4}$ x $\frac{1}{2}$ in.

IMPRINTS, Italy.

Cabinet 29 Shelf 1 No. 15

Ratdolt, Erhard. Venice, 1482.

See Incunabula. Hyginus (Caius Julius) Poeticon astronomicon.

IMPRINTS, Italy.

Cabinet 29 Shelf 1 No. 20

Ratdolt, Erhard. Venice, 1483.
Title: Eusebius. Chronicon ...
(Imprint) Colophon: Erhardus Ratdolt Augenstensis solerti vir ingenio maxima ... hoc volumine impressit Venetiis. 1483. Idibus Septembris.

Morocco; $9\frac{1}{4}$ x $6\frac{1}{2}$ x $1\frac{1}{2}$ in.

IMPRINTS, Italy.

Cabinet 29 Shelf 1 No. 24

Ratdolt, Erhard. Venice, 1485.
Title: Hyginus. Poeticon Astronomicon.
Colophon: ... Impressum est presens opusculii per Erhardum Ratdolt de Augusta: Venetiis. 1485.

Boards; $8\frac{3}{4}$ x $6\frac{1}{2}$ x $\frac{1}{2}$ in.

IMPRINTS, Italy.

Cabinet 29 Shelf 1 No. 23

Ratdolt, Erhard. Venice, 1485.
Title: [Rolewinck, Werner]. Fasciculus temporum
Colophon: Erhardus Ratdolt Augustensi impressioni paravit, 1485. Venetiis.

Gesamt-Kat. Zapf. 168; Hain 6937.

Boards; 10 x 8 x $\frac{1}{2}$ in.

IMPRINTS, ITALY

Cabinet 9 Shelf 2 No. 1 to 9

Regia Stampa, Napoli, 1752-92.

See BAJARDI, Ottaviano-Antonio. Antichita (le) di Ercolano...

IMPRINTS, Italy

Cabinet F Shelf 4 No. 78

Regiis Typis. Milan, 1816.
Title: Dionysii Helicarnassi Romanarum Antiquitatem. codicum Ambrosianorum ab Angelo Maio...
Imprint: Mediolani. Regiis Typis. 1816.

With portrait frontispiece.

Calf gilt; 12 x 9 x 7/8 in.

IMPRINTS, ITALY.

Cabinet D Shelf 2 No. 19

Rizzo (Rizus), Bernardino da Novara, Venice, 1492.

See Incunabula, Bergomensis. [Jac.Phil.] Supplementum Chronicarum.

IMPRINTS, Italy.

Cabinet F Shelf 4 No. 70

Remondini, Giovanni Battista. Bassano, 1744.

Title: Verita eterna esposte in lezioni...Raccolte dal P. Carlo Gregorio Rosignoli.
Imprint: In Bassano: Nella Stamperia Remondini, con Licenza de' Superiori.
The printing house of Remondini continued in the family until 1860.

Vellum; 6-1/8 x $3\frac{1}{4}$ x 1 in. See Arneudo, Dizionario Grafiche, p.1812.

IMPRINTS, Italy.

Cabinet PP Shelf 1 No. 28

Remondini e Figli, Giuseppe. Bassano, 1800.
Title: Catalogo dei libri impressi nella tipografia della dita Giuseppe Remondini e Figli di Venezia.
Imprint: Bassano, 1800.

Remondini a Venetian family of printers who also operated in Bassano, where the business existed until 1860.

Half morocco; 7-7/8 x 5-3/8 x 7/8 in.

IMPRINTS, Italy.

Cabinet D Shelf 1 No. 44

Renner, Franciscus de Heilbronn, Venice, 1482.

See Incunabula, [illegible]. Nicolaus de, Liber qui dicitur supplementum.

IMPRINTS, Italy.

Cabinet D Shelf 2 No. 38

Rossi, Lorenzo (da Valenza). Ferrara, Italy, 1497.

See Incunabula. Hieronymus, S. Epistolae.

IMPRINTS, Italy.

Cabinet D Shelf 1 No. 28

Rubeis, Jacobus. Also known as Rosso or Rossi. Venice, 1476.

See Incunabula. Geminiano...

IMPRINTS, Italy.

Cabinet D Shelf 2 No. 35

Rubeis, Laurentii (da Valenza). Also known as Lorenzo Rossi, or Rosso de valencia. Ferrara, 1497.

See Incunabula. Jacobus Philippus (Foresti). Bergomensis. De claris selectisque mulieribus.

IMPRINTS, Italy.

Cabinet E Shelf 2 No. 30

Salicato, Atobello. Venice, 1580.

See Early Printing in Italy. Venice, 1580. Atobello Silicato.

IMPRINTS, Italy

Cabinet K Shelf 3 No. 1

Salvioni, Giovanni M. Rome, circa 1730

see ENGRAVINGS, COPPERPLATE. Vignettes (125)...

IMPRINTS, Italy.

Cabinet E Shelf 2 No. 9

Salviani, Horatio. Naples, 1573.

See Early Printing in Italy. Naples, 1573.

IMPRINTS, Italy

Cabinet K Shelf 1 No. 28

Scoto, Octavuano, Venice, 1482 (see)

FACSIMILES. Music printing and manuscript, 12th to 16th century...(plate XlV)

IMPRINTS, Italy.

Cabinet 14 Shelf 2 No. 21 2 vols.

Sweynheym & Pannartz. Rome, 1468.

See Incunabula. Hieronymus (Eusebius) Epistolae.

IMPRINTS, Italy.

Cabinet F Shelf 5 No. 6

Salvioni, Maria Giovanni: Stampator Vaticano. Rome, 1736.

See Early Printing in Italy. Rome, 1736. Giovanni Maria Salvioni.

IMPRINTS, Italy.

Cabinet D Shelf 1 No. 47

Scotus, Ottaviano: Venice, 1483.

See Incunabula. Hieronymus. Vitas Patrum. De laude de effectu virtutem.

IMPRINTS, Italy

Cabinet F Shelf 5 No. 50

Tipografia Societa Letteraria. Pisa, 1811.
Title: La secchia rapita di Alessandro Tassoni.
Imprint: Pisa, dalla Tipografia Della Societa Letteraria.

Half calf; $15\frac{1}{4}$ x $9\frac{3}{4}$ x $1\frac{1}{4}$ in.

IMPRINTS, Italy.

Cabinet E Shelf 3 No. 37

S. Cong. de Propaganda Fide, Rome, 1628.

Title: Odegia [in Greek]
Imprint: In Roma, nella stampa della S. Cong. de propag. Fide. MDCXXVIII.

IMPRINTS, Italy.

Cabinet E Shelf 2 No. 22

Sessa, Giambattista and Marchio. Venice, 1578.

See Early Printing in Italy. Venice, 1578.

IMPRINTS, Italy.

Cabinet E Shelf 1 No. 21 2 vols.

Torrentino, Lorenzo. Florence, 1553.

See Early Printing in Italy. Florence, 1553.

IMPRINTS, Italy.

Cabinet D Shelf 1 No. 26

Schall, Johannes, Mantua, 1475.

See Incunabula. Paulus de S. Maria. Incipit dialogus qui vocatur, etc.

IMPRINTS, Italy.

Cabinet D Shelf 3 No. 21

Soardi, Lazzaro de. Venice, 1511.

See Early Printing in Italy. Venice, 1511.

IMPRINTS, Italy.

Cabinet E Shelf 1 No. 21 2 vols.

Torrentinus, Laurentius. Florence, 1553.

See Early Printing in Italy.

IMPRINTS, Italy

Cabinet 14 Shelf 1 No. 17

Schoeffer, Peter II. Venice, 1542.

See Early Printing in Italy. Venice, 1542. Peter Schoeffer II. Opera Toscane.

IMPRINTS, Italy.

Cabinet D Shelf 3 No. 15 and 16

Soncino, Hieronymo. Fano, 1507.

See Early Printing in Italy. Fano, 1507. Hieronymus Soncinus.

IMPRINTS, Italy

Cabinet F Shelf 4 No. 77

Stamperia Reale. Torino, 1842.
Title: Per le Auguste nozze di S.A.R. Vittorio Emanuele, Duca di Savoia...
Imprint: Torino, Stamperia Reale, 1842.

A famous printing office founded in 1740 in Torino under the patronage of Carlo Emanuele III.

Boards; 12 x $9\frac{1}{4}$ x $\frac{1}{2}$ in.

IMPRINTS, Italy.

Cabinet D Shelf 1 No. 41

Scotto (Scotus) Ottaviano, Venice, 1481.

See Incunabula. Iivius Titus. Quarte Deca di Titolivio.

IMPRINTS, Italy.

Cabinet D Shelf 3 No. 56

Soncino, Hieronymus. Ortona, 1515.

See Early Printing in Italy. Ortona, 1515. Girolamo Soncino.

IMPRINTS, Italy.

Cabinet 6 Shelf 1 No. 8

Torresanus. Andreas, de Asula. Venice, 1483.

See Incunabula. Clement V. Constitutiones.

IMPRINTS, Italy

Cabinet 10 Shelf 2 No. 12

Tortis, Baptista de. Venice, 1504.

See Early Printing in Italy, Venice. 1504, Baptista de Tortis.

IMPRINTS, Italy.

Cabinet E Shelf 1 No. 65

Tromba, Ippolito and Ercoliano Bartoli. Cremona, 1585.

See Early Printing in Italy. Cremona.

IMPRINTS, Italy.

Cabinet D Shelf 1 No. 55

Turre, Peter de, Rome, 1490.

See Incunabula. Ptolemaei Cosmographia.

IMPRINTS, Italy

Cabinet F Shelf 5 No. 6

Vatican Press: Giovanni Maria Salvioni. Rome, 1736.
Title: Parentalia Mariae Clementinae...
Colophon: In Roma. Appresso Giovanni Maria Salviani, stampatore Vaticano.

Paper boards, leather back; $16\frac{3}{4}$ x $11\frac{3}{4}$ in.

IMPRINTS, Italy.

Cabinet D Shelf 4 No. 35

Vavassore, Andrea. Venice, 1530?

See Early Printing in Italy. Venice, 1530? Andrea Vavassore.

IMPRINTS, Italy

Cabinet K Shelf 1 No. 28

Verovio, Simone, Rome, 1586 (see)

FACSIMILES. Music printing and manuscript, 12th to 16th century... (plate V)

IMPRINTS, ITALY

Cabinet C Shelf 1 No. 17

Vincenzi, Gem. e Compagno, Modena, 1814
Title: Saggio tipografico...
Imprint; Modena. Presso Gem Vincenzi e Compagno, 1814.

Boards; $17\frac{1}{2}$ x $12\frac{1}{2}$ in.

IMPRINTS, Italy.

Cabinet D Shelf 2 No. 31

Zanis, Bartholomaeus de. Venice, 1496.

See Incunabula. Plutarchus. Vitae illustrium virorum.

IMPRINTS, Italy.

Cabinet F Shelf 5 No. 9

Zempel, Joannes. Rome, 1763-65.
Title: P. Virgilii Maronis...ab Antonio Ambrogi Florentino S.J. Italico versus reddita... Aere incisis et cl. virorum illustrata. 3 vols.
Imprint: Excudebat Joannes Zempel prope montem Jordanum Venantii Monaldini Bibliopolae sumptibus.

Paper boards; 17 x 12 in. Brunet 5, 1306.

IMPRINTS, JAPAN

Cabinet L Shelf 5 No. 14

Tokyo Tsukiji Type Foundry, Tokyo, 1906.
Title: Masterpieces of great painters of Japan, thirty. Published by the Kokka Company, Tokyo.
Imprint: Press work of The Tokyo Tsukiji Type Foundry, Tokyo.

Silk; $16\frac{3}{4}$ x $11\frac{3}{4}$ in . See also 2/5/16

IMPRINTS, Mexico.

Cabinet E Shelf 2 No. 77

Balli, Jeronimo. Mexico, 1609.
Title: Ortografia castellane ... Por Mateo Aleman.
Imprint: Con previlejio por diez anos. En Mexico. En la emprenta de Jeronimo Balli. Ano, 1609.
Medina, La imprenta en Mexico II, 244.

Calf; 8 x $5\frac{1}{8}$ in.

IMPRINTS, Mexico.

Cabinet E Shelf 3 No. 61

Calderon, Bernardo, Mexico, 1638.
Title: Tratado del estado de las Philipinas. Por el Don Geronimo de Banuelos y Carrillo.
Imprint: En Mexico, con licencia de su Excelencia, en la imprenda Bernardo Calderon, impressor, y mercardor de libros.
Medina, La imprenta en Mexico II, 498.

Old Leather with ribbon ties, $7\frac{1}{4}$ x $5\frac{3}{4}$ in. In protective case.

IMPRINTS, Mexico

Cabinet F Shelf 1 No. 101

Imprenta Real: Mexico City. 1735.
Title: Vida del venerable padre Don Pedro...
Imprint: Con Licencia: En Mexico: En la Imprenta Real del Superior Gobierno...

Hand tooled calf; $8\frac{1}{2}$ x $6\frac{1}{4}$ in. Medina IV, 3364, p.400.

IMPRINTS, Mexico

Cabinet F Shelf 1 No. 105

Jauregui, Joseph. Mexico, 1770.
Title: Description del barreno ingles...
Imprint: Impresso en Mexico en la Imprenta del Lic. D. Joseph de Jaurequi. Los caracteres de esta impression han sido fabricado en esta ciudad por D. Francisco Favier de Ocampo.

Half morocco; 7-7/8 x 5-7/8 in. Medina VI, 5322, p.47.

IMPRINTS, New Zealand

Cabinet M Shelf 1 No. 8

Avery, Thomas and Sons. New Plymouth, N.Z. 1928.
Title: Maori artistry. By W. Page Rowe, member of Board of Maori arts. Printed under the authority of The Board of Maori Ethnological Research. Illus.
Imprint: New Plymouth, N.Z. Printed by Thomas Avery & Sons Limited, Devon Street.

Printed linen over boards; 10 x $6\frac{1}{4}$ x 3/8 in.

IMPRINTS, New Zealand

Cabinet M Shelf 4 No. 30

Avery, Thomas and Sons. New Plymouth, 1936.
Title: The discovery of Dinoris...By T. Lindsay Buick. Illus.
Imprint: New Plymouth, N. Z. Thomas Avery and Sons Limited. 1936.

Cloth; $8\frac{1}{4}$ x 5-1/8

IMPRINTS, PACIFIC ISLANDS.

Cabinet II Shelf 3 No. 55

Honolulu, 1841. Na Na Misionari Mea Pai.

See PACIFIC ISLANDS. Honolulu Imprint, 1841 ...

IMPRINTS, PACIFIC ISLANDS.

Cabinet II Shelf 3 No. 56

Honolulu, Oahu, 1845. Mea Pai Palapala a na Misionari ...

See PACIFIC ISLANDS. Honolulu Imprint, 1845 ...

IMPRINTS, Peru.

Cabinet F
[Imprenta Real?]; Lima, 1784.

Shelf 1
No. 106 (107?)

See Early Printing in Spanish America Peru, Lima, 1789, 1784.

IMPRINTS, Scotland

Cabinet C
Clark, R., Edinburgh, 1870
Title: The chief victories of Charles the Fifth. Designed by Martin Heemskerck in 1555...
Imprint: Printed by R. Clark, Edinburgh, 1870
Shelf 2
No. 4

Illustrated with portraits, prints, and notes by Sir William Stirling Maxwell.

Cloth over boards; 18-3/8 x 13½ in.

IMPRINTS, Scotland

Cabinet Q
Donaldson, Alexander, Edinburgh, 1767.
Title: Considerations on the nature and origin of literary property...
Imprint: Edinburgh; Printed by Alexander Donaldson, 1767.
Shelf 2
No. 2

Half morocco; 7-7/8 x 5 in.

IMPRINTS, Philippine Islands

Cabinet II
American Bible Society. Manila, 1904.

Shelf 3
See AMERICAN BIBLE SOCIETY. Gospel of Saint Luke in Cebuan...

No. 25

IMPRINTS, Scotland

Cabinet M
Clark, R. & R. Limited, Edinburgh, 1907.
Title: The American Pilgrim's Way in England.... By Marcus B. Huish. L.L.B. Illustrated by Elizabeth M. Chetti. London. The Fine Arts Society...1907.
Colophon: Printed by R. & R. Clark, limited. Edinburgh.
Shelf 2
No. 3

Cloth over boards; 12¾ x 9½ x 2¾ in.

IMPRINTS, Scotland

Cabinet F
Foulis, Robert and Andrew. Glasgow. 1751.
Title: Boetius. Consolationis philosophiae.
Imprint: Glasguae: In aedibus Academicis. Excudebant Robertus et Andreas Foulis. Academiae Typographi, 1751.
Shelf 4
No. 43

Leather; 7¾ x 6 x ½ in. Brunet 1, 1035.

IMPRINTS, POLAND

Cabinet X
Knoch, G. M., Dantisci, 1740
Title: De Typographiis in regno Poloniae et magno ducatu Lithuaniae...
Shelf 1
Imprint: Dantisci, 1740. apud Georgium Marcum Knochium

No. 38
With printer mark

Boards, morocco back; 8½ x 7 in.

IMPRINTS, Scotland

Cabinet M
Clark, R. & R. Edinburgh, 1927.

Shelf 3
See Imprints, England. Nonesuch Press, The. Francis Meynell, 1927.

No.

IMPRINT, Scotland

Cabinet F
Foulis, Robert and Andrew. Glasgow, 1756.
Title: Euclidis elementorum libri priories sex ex versione Latina Federici Commandini, curante a Roberto Simson, M.D.
Shelf 4
Imprint: Glasguae, in aedibus Academicis excudebant Robertus et Andreas Foulis. Academiae Typographi 1756.
No. 45

Leather; 11¾ x 9¼ x 1¾ in. Brunet 2, 1082.

IMPRINTS, Portugal

Cabinet L
De Carvalho, Bernardo da Costa. Lisboa Occidental, 1718 or 1822?
Title: Nova excola para aprender a ler...Por Manuel de Andrade de Figueiredo.
Shelf 3
Imprint: Lisboa Occidental. Na Officina de Bernardo da Costa de Carvalho, Impressor lo Serenissimo Senher Infante.
No. 3

Tree calf; 12 x 8¼ in.

IMPRINTS, Scotland

Cabinet M
Clark, Limited, R. and R. Edinburgh, 1927.
Title: Prospectus and retrospectus of the Nonesuch Press editions.
Shelf 3
Imprint: Made and printed in Scotland by R. & R. Clark, Ltd. Edinburgh.
No. 30

Boards; 11-1/8 x 8¼ in.

IMPRINTS, Scotland

Cabinet F
Foulis, Robert and Andrew. Glasgow, 1758.
Title: Publii Vergilii Maronis. Bucolica, Georgica, et Aeneis. Ex editione Petri Burmanni.
Shelf 4
Imprint: Glasguae: In aedibus Academicis. Excudebant Robertus et Andreas Foulis. Academiae Typographi. 1758.
No. 47

Half morocco, gilt; 6-3/8 x 4 x 1¼ in. Brunet 5, 1293.

IMPRINTS, Scotland

Cabinet M
Ballantyne, James. Kelso, 1802.
Title: The economy of human life. In two parts. By R. Dodsley.
Shelf 1
Imprint: Kelso: Printed by James Ballantyne for W. Creech, Bell and Bradfute, Manners and Miller, and A. Constable, Edinburgh, 1802.
No. 9

Calf; 6¾ x 5¼ x ⅜ in.

IMPRINTS, Scotland

Cabinet M
Constable, T. and A. Edinburgh, 1894.
Title: The life of Sir Thomas Bodley written by himself. Publishers device. Privately reprinted for John Lane and his friends. Christmas, 1894.
Shelf 1
Colophon: Reprinted by T. and A. Constable, printers to Her Majesty. Edinburgh.
No. 55

Paper boards; 6¾ x 4½ in.

IMPRINTS, Scotland

Cabinet F
Foulis, Robert and Andrew. Glasgow, 1763.
Title: Dionysii Longini de sublimitate commentarius.
Shelf 4
Imprint: Glasguae: In aedibus Academicis excudebant Robertus et Andreas Foulis.
No. 49

Morocco, gilt; 8½ x 6-3/8 x 1-1/8 in. Brunet 3, 1152.

IMPRINTS, Scotland.

Cabinet M
Ballantyne Press, Edinburgh, 1911.
Title: The Holy Bible, containing the Old and New Testament and the Apocrypha. Translated out of the original tongues in the year of Our Lord 1911. [3 vols.]
Shelf 1
Imprint: The Ballantyne Press, London and Edinburgh.
No. 14

Tooled calf, each vol. 9½ x 6 in.

IMPRINTS, Scotland

Cabinet PP
Constable, T. and A. Edinburgh, 1896.
Title: Foreign bookbindings in the British Museum...descriptions by Wm. Younger Fletcher. London, Kegan Paul...& Company Ltd. 1896.
Shelf 6
Imprint facing preface: Edinburgh: T. and A. Constable, Printers to Her Majesty.
No. 3

Cloth; 13 x 11¼ x 1-3/4 in.

IMPRINTS, Scotland

Cabinet U
Glasgow University Press. 1931.
Title: The Glasgow University Press, 1638-1931. With some notes on Scottish printing in the last three hundred years. By James Maclehose.
Shelf 1
Imprint: Glasgow: At the University Press. 1931.
No. 83

Boards, linen back; 9 x 5¾ x 1¼ in.

IMPRINTS, Scotland

Cabinet F Shelf 4 No. 40

Hamilton, G., and John Balfour. Edinburgh.
Title: Phaedri...Ex recension Alexandri Cuningamii, Scoti.
Imprint: Edinburgi, apud G. Hamilton & John Balfour, Academiae Typographos. 1757.

Morocco; $7\frac{1}{2}$ x $4\frac{3}{4}$ x $\frac{1}{2}$ in. Brunet 4, 589.

IMPRINTS, Scotland

Cabinet U Shelf 5 No. 94

Maclehose, Robert and Co., Ltd. The University Press, Glasgow 1930.
Title: The old book. A mediaeval anthology. Edited and illuminated by Dorothy Hartley.
Imprint: London. Alfred A. Knopf, 1930.

Cloth; 10-3/8 x $7\frac{1}{4}$ x 1-1/8 in. In protective case.

IMPRINTS, Scotland

Cabinet E Shelf 3 No. 55

Raban, Edward, Aberdeen, 1635.

See Early Printing in Scotland. Aberdeen, Edward Raban.

IMPRINTS, Scotland

Cabinet M Shelf 5 No. 27

Turnbull and Spears: Edinburgh, 1901.
Title: Florentine Villas. By Janet Ross. With reproductions in photogravure from Zocchis etchings, and many line drawings by Nelly Erichsen. London. J.M. Dent & Co., New York. Dutton & Co. MDCCCCI.
Colophon: Turnbull and Spears, printers, Edinburgh.

$\frac{3}{4}$ Morocco and Vellum; $17\frac{1}{4}$ x $12\frac{1}{2}$ x 2 in.

IMPRINTS, Scotland

Cabinet F Shelf 4 No. 36

Watson, James. Edinburgh, 1706-1711.
Title: A choice collection of comic and serious Scots poems.
Imprint: Printed by James Watson, and sold at his shop next door to the Red-Lyon, opposite to the Lucken-Booths.
There are three title pages, of which the first one is a substitution of more than a century later date.

Russia; $7\frac{1}{4}$ x $4\frac{1}{2}$ x 1 in.

IMPRINTS, Spain

Cabinet AA Shelf 5 No. 1

Bedmar, Lucas Antonio de. Madrid, 1675.
Title: Discurso legal, historico, y politico en prueba del origen ... del arte de la imprenta ... Don Melchor de Cabrera Nunez de Guzman.
Imprint: En Madrid, en la Oficina Lucas Antonio de Bedmar, 1675.

Boards; $11\frac{1}{2}$ x 7-3/4 in.

IMPRINTS, Spain

Cabinet D Shelf 4 No. 5

Brocar, Arnald Guillen de. Alcalá, 1514-17.
Title: Complutensian Polyglot Bible. 6 vols.
Colophon: [Vol. 6]:...noviter impssa in hac pclarissima coplutensi universtate. De mādatc ...F.Francisci Ximenez de Cineros...Industrie & soletie honorabilis viri Arnaldi Guilielmi de Brocario artis impressoria magistri. Anno dñi. M.D.XV...

Calf, each vol., 15 x $10\frac{1}{2}$ x 2 in.

IMPRINTS, Spain

Cabinet E Shelf 4 No. 97

Cabrera, Vincente. Valencia, 1695.

See Early Printing in Spain. Valencia, 1695.

IMPRINTS, Spain

Cabinet AA Shelf 5 No. 2

Espinosa de los Monteros, Antonio. Segovia, 1778.
Title: Provision Reale ... Para que se establezcan una imprenta: ... Baxo la dirección de Don Antonio Espinosa de los Monteros, gravador de la Casa de la Moneda. Segovia.
Imprint: Impresa en Segovia en la misma Imprenta Año, 1778.

Calf; 8 x 5-7/8 in.

IMPRINTS, Spain

Cabinet F Shelf 5 No. 44

Ibarra, Joachin: Madrid, 1772.

Title: La conjuración de Catilina y la guerra de Jugurta. Por Cayo Sallustio Crispo.
Colophon: En Madrid: Por Joachin Ibarra. Impresor de Camara del Rei Nuestro Senor.

Leather, gilt: 14 x $10\frac{1}{2}$ x 1-3/4 in. Brunet 5, 91. Updike 2, 55.

Duplicate in cabinet 7.

IMPRINTS, Spain

Cabinet AA Shelf 5 No. 3

Ibarra, Joachin: La Viuda de. Madrid, 1796.
Title: Typographia Española, ó historia de la introducción ... su autor Fray Francisco Mendez. Tome I. [The second vol. was never published]
Imprint: Madrid 1796. En la imprneta de la viuda de D. Joachin Ibarra.

Tree calf; 8 x $6\frac{1}{4}$ in.

IMPRINTS, SPAIN

Cabinet AA Shelf 5 No. 5

Imprenta Real, Madrid, 1799.
Title: Reglamento para la dirección y gobierno de la Imprenta Real.
Imprint: Madrid. En la misma Imprenta Real, año de 1799.

Marbled boards; 8 x $5\frac{1}{2}$ in.

IMPRINTS, Spain

Cabinet K Shelf 1 No. 28

Sanchez, Francisco, Madrid, 1578 (see)

FACSIMILES. Music printing and manuscript, 12th to 16th century... (plate IV)

IMPRINTS, Spain

Cabinet KK Shelf 3 No. 42

Siguenza y Vera, Juan Josef. Madrid, 1813.

see
SOCIETIES, PRINTERS'. Spain. Compañia de impresores y libreros...Siguenza y Vera, 1813.

IMPRINTS, Switzerland

Cabinet 17 Shelf 2 No. 2

Bebelium (Joan) of Basle, 1526.
(A final index page to a Bible (?). Device on obverse.

Item on fol.78 of HENRY STEVEN'S "Typographical Miscellanies", vol.2, B-1

IMPRINTS, Switzerland.

Cabinet D Shelf 2 No. 43

Bergmann, Johann (de Olpe) Basel, 1498.

See Incunabula. Brant. Sebastien. Stultifera Navis....

IMPRINTS, Switzerland

Cabinet 17 Shelf 2 No. 2

Berjon (Matthae), Geneva, 1630.
Folio title, with device and imprint.

Item on fols. 109-11 of HENRY STEVEN'S "Typographical Miscellanies", vol.2, B-1

IMPRINTS, Switzerland

Cabinet 17 Shelf 2 No. 2

Bertschii, Jacobi (& Joh. Rodolphi Genatheil) Basel, 1677-1683.
Title pages, folios, with printer mark and imprint.

Items on fols. 123-124 of HENRY STEVENS "Typographical Miscellanies", vol.2, B-1

IMPRINTS, Switzerland.

Cabinet E Shelf 1 No. 42

Crespin, Jean. Geneva, 1564.

See Early Printing in Switzerland. Geneva, 1564.

IMPRINTS, Switzerland.

Cabinet 40 Shelf 1 No. 55

Estienne, Henri. Geneva, 1569.
Title: Epistola Henrici Stephani ... Index librorum qui ex officina eiusdem Henrici Stephani hactenus profierunt.
Imprint: Anno M.D.LXIX. Excudebat Henricus Stephanus.

Morocco; 7 x 4¼ x ¼ in.

IMPRINTS, Switzerland.

Cabinet 40 Shelf 2 No. 42

Estienne, Henri (II) [Geneva, 1572?].
Title: Thesaurus graecae linguae. ab Henrico Stephano constructus ... [Printer Mark]
Imprint: Henr. Stephani Oliva. Cum privilegio Caes. maiestatis, et Christianiss Gallisrum regis.

Morocco; 15¼ x 9¾ x 2¾ in.

IMPRINTS, Switzerland.

Cabinet D Shelf 4 No. 23

Curio [or Schaffner] Velentinus. Basel, 1523.

See Early Printing in Switzerland. Basel, 1523.

IMPRINTS, Switzerland.

Cabinet 40 Shelf 1 No. 55

Estienne, Henri. Geneva, 1569.

See Early Printing in Switzerland. [Geneva] 1569.

IMPRINTS, Switzerland.

Cabinet 40 Shelf 1 No. 58

Estienne, Henri (II). Geneva, 1574.

See Early Printing in Switzerland. Geneva, 1574.

IMPRINTS, Switzerland.

Cabinet E Shelf 1 No. 30

Episcopius, Eusebius. Basel, 1569.

See. Early Printing in Switzerland. Basel, 1569.

IMPRINTS, Switzerland.

Cabinet 40 Shelf 1 No. 44

Estienne, Henri (II). [Geneva]. 1566.
Title: L'Introduction au traite de la conformite des merveilles anciennes avec les modernes. [Estienne printer mark, without the printer's name].
Imprint: L'an M.D.LXVI, au mois de Novembre.

Morocco; 5 x 3¾ x 1-7/8 in.

IMPRINTS, Switzerland.

Cabinet 40 Shelf 1 No. 60

Estienne, Henri (II). Geneva, 1576.

See Early Printing in Switzerland. [Geneva], 1576.

IMPRINTS, Switzerland.

Cabinet E Shelf 1 No. 28

Episcopius, Nicolaus, the younger. Basel, 1555.

See Early Printing in Switzerland: Basel, 1555.

IMPRINTS, Switzerland.

Cabinet 40 Shelf 1 No. 44

Estienne, Henri (II). Geneva, 1566.

See Early Printing in Switzerland. [Geneva] 1566.

IMPRINTS, Switzerland.

Cabinet 40 Shelf 1 No. 48

Estienne, Henri (II) and Ulrich Fugger. Geneva, 1567.
Title: Polemonis, Himerii et aliorum declamationes nunc primum editae ...
Imprint: Excudebat Henr. Stephanus, illustris viri Huldrichi Fuggeri typographus, 1567.

Old vellum; 9½ x 6-3/8 x ½ in.

Imprints, Switzerland

Cabinet 40 Shelf 1 No. 56

Estienne, Henri: Geneva, 1569.
Title: Artis typographicae...Epitaphia Graeca & Latino doctorum quorundum typographorum, ab eodem scripta...Autore Henrico Stephano. Printer Mark.
Imprint: Anno M D LXIX. Excudebat Henricus Stephanus.

Half morocco; 8½ x 6 in.

IMPRINTS, Switzerland.

Cabinet 40 Shelf 1 No. 48

Estienne, Henri (II). Geneva. 1567.

See Early Printing in Switzerland. Geneva 1567.

IMPRINTS, Switzerland.

Cabinet 40 Shelf 1 No. 68

Estienne, Paul. Geneva, 1599.

See Early Printing in Switzerland. Geneva, 1599.

IMPRINTS, Switzerland.

Cabinet 40 Shelf 1 No. 56

Estienne, Henri. [Geneva], 1569.
Title: Artis typographicae Querimonia ... autore Henrico Stephano. Epitaphia Graeca et Latin doctorum quorundam typographorum, ab eodem scripta.
Imprint: Anno M.D.LXIX. Excudebat Henricus Stephanus.

Morocco; 8½ x 6 in.

IMPRINTS, Switzerland.

Cabinet 40 Shelf 2 No. 38

Estienne, Henri (II) [Geneva], 1570.
Title: Conciones, sive orationes, ex Graecis Latinisque historicis excerptae ...
Imprint: Anno M.D.LXX. Excudebat Henricus Stephanus.

Vellum; 12½ x 8 x 1¾ in.

IMPRINTS, Switzerland.

Cabinet 40 Shelf 1 No. 32

Estienne, Robert (I) (Stephanus). Geneva, 1552.

See Early Printing in Switzerland [Geneva] 1552.

IMPRINTS, Switzerland

Cabinet J Shelf 5 No. 5

Fick, Jules Guillaume, Geneva, 1863.

See FICK, JULES GUILLAUME. Anciens bois ...

IMPRINTS, Switzerland.

Cabinet 40 Shelf 1 No. 33

Fick, Jules-Guillaume, Geneva 1866.
Title: Les censures des theologiens de Paris ... avec la response d'iceluy Robert Estienne. Traduictes de Latin en Francais. L'Olivier de Robert Estienne 1552.
Colophon: Réimprimé par Jules-Guillaume Fick. Geneva, 1866.

Vellum: 9½ x 6¼ x 1½ in.

IMPRINTS, Switzerland.

Cabinet E Shelf 1 No. 2

Froben, Jerome and Nicolaus Episcopius.

See Early Printing in Switzerland. Basel, 1535. Jerome Froben and Nicolaus Episcopius.

IMPRINTS, Switzerland.

Cabinet D Shelf 2 No. 25

Forben, Johann, Basle, 1494.

See Incunabula. Gregorious IX. Decretales.

IMPRINTS, Switzerland.

Cabinet D Shelf 3 No. 47

Froben, Johannes, Basel, 1516.

See Early Printing in Switzerland, Basle, 1516.

IMPRINTS, Switzerland.

Cabinet D Shelf 3 No. 55

Froben, John, Basel, Switzerland, 1518.

See Early Printing in Switzerland. Basle, 1518.

IMPRINTS, Switzerland.

Cabinet E Shelf 2 No. 42

Froschauer, Christopher. 1586.

See Early Printing in Switzerland. Zurich, 1586.

IMPRINTS. Switzerland

Cabinet D Shelf 4 No. 55

Isingrin, Michele, Basle, 1540 (Imprint)

See VIRGIL , POLYDORUS. (De) Rerum inventoribus...1540

IMPRINTS, Switzerland.

Cabinet E Shelf 2 No. 32

Laon, Jean de. Geneva, 1580.

See Early Printing in Switzerland. Geneva, 1580.

IMPRINTS, Switzerland.

Cabinet E Shelf 2 No. 33

Laon, Jean de. Geneva, 1581.

See Early Printing in Switzerland. [Geneva] 1581.

IMPRINTS, Switzerland

Cabinet E Shelf 1 No. 22

Parcum Jacob, Basle, 1554.

See Early Printing in Switzerland. Basle, 1554, Jacob Parcum.

IMPRINTS, Switzerland.

Cabinet E Shelf 2 No. 5

Petri, Sebastien Henri. Basel, 1572.

See Early Printing in Switzerland. Basel, 1572.

IMPRINTS, Switzerland

Cabinet K Shelf 1 No. 28

Pfortzheim, Jacob, Basle, 1510. (see)

FACSIMILES
Music printing and manuscript, 12th to 16th century...(plate XXII)

IMPRINTS, Switzerland.

Cabinet E Shelf 2 No. 48

Preux, Jean le. Geneva, 1590.

See Early Printing in Switzerland. Geneva, 1590.

IMPRINTS, Switzerland.

Cabinet D Shelf 1 No. 43

Richel, Bernhard. Basel, 1482.

See Incunabula. Rolewinck, Werner. Fasciculus temporum.

IMPRINTS, Switzerland

Cabinet 10 Shelf 2 No. 1

Ruppel V. Hanau, Berthold. Basle, 1468-70.

See Incunabula. Durandus, Gulielmus. Rationale divinorum officiorum.

IMPRINTS, Switzerland.

Cabinet 39 Shelf 2 No. 26

Tournes, Jean [Antoine] de. Geneve, 1612.
Title: Xenophontis ...
Imprint: Apud Ioann. Tornaesium, 1612, Geneuae.

Vellum; 4-7/8 x 3-1/8 x 1½ in.

IMPRINTS, Switzerland.

Cabinet 39 Shelf 2 No. 35

Tournes, Jean Antoine and Samuel de. Geneva 1672.
Title: Rodolphi Hospiniani de Templis ...
Imprint: Genevae, sumptibus Joannis Antonii and Samuelis de Tournes.

Calf; 14 x 8½ x 1¼ in.

IMPRINTS, Switzerland.

Cabinet 39 Shelf 2 No. 40

Tournes, Samuel de, Geneva, 1684.

Title: Lucii Annaei Flori rerum Romanarum. Libri quatuor. Cum notis Davidis Constantii [Printer Mark]

Imprint: Geneva, apud Samuelem de Tournes M.DC.LXXXIV.

Old leather; 5-3/4 x 3½ x 1½ in.

IMPRINTS, United States.

Cabinet G Shelf 1 No. 6

American Type Founders Company, Jersey City, April 28, 1923: Second Annual Show Shackamaxon Country Club, Westfield, New Jersey. Pamphlet.

9½ x 6¼ ins. pp.24.

IMPRINTS, United States

Cabinet R Shelf 2 No. 1

Bache, Benjamin Franklin. Philadelphia, 1792.

Title: Eulogium on Benjamin Franklin, L.L.D. ... delivered March 1, 1791, in the German Lutheran Church of Philadelphia, 1791 ... [Many Portraits].

Imprint: Printed by Benjamin Franklin Bache, Philadelphia, 1792.

Half morocco; 9 x 6 in.

IMPRINTS, SWITZERLAND

Cabinet E Shelf 2 No. 47

Valdkirch, Conrad. Basel, 1589.

See Early Printing in Switzerland. Basel, 1589.

Bound in with an Icones by Bernard Jobinus. Strassburg, 1590.

IMPRINTS, United States.

Cabinet G Shelf 1 No. 5

American Type Founders Company, Jersey City, 1924: Club Book. Shackamaxon Country Club, Westfield, New Jersey. Constitution-By-Laws. House and Golf Rules, 1924.

Board, 7 x 5 ins., pp.80.

IMPRINTS, United States.

Cabinet X Shelf 4 No. 104

Bache, Benjamin Franklin. The Aurora Office, Philadelphia, 1799.

Title: Essay on the liberty of the press ... by Hortensius [George Hay].

Imprint: Philadelphia. Printed at the Aurora Office. 1799.

Half morocco; 8½ x 5¼ x ¼ in.

IMPRINTS, Switzerland.

Cabinet E Shelf 4 No. 61

Widerholt, Johann Hermann. Geneva, 1674.

See Early Printing in Switzerland. Geneva, 1674.

IMPRINTS, United States.

Cabinet G Shelf 1 No. 7

American Type Founders Co. Jersey City, 1931

Title: Ernest Frederick Eilert,Printer. 1881-1931 Testimonial dinner sponsored by Printers' Supply Salesmen's Guild, New York, Wednesday Evening, February 25,1931. Hotel Astor.

Imprint-Colophon: Printed for Printers' Supply Salesmen's Guild of New York with the compliments of the American Type Founders Company.

(Cont'd)

IMPRINTS, United States

Cabinet JJ Shelf 3 No. 8

Baker, Godwin & Co., New York, 1855.

see LIBRARIES, TYPOGRAPHIC. New York Typographical Library...

IMPRINTS, United States.

Cabinet G Shelf 1 No. 3

Advertisers Paper Mills: W. A. Dwiggins, New York, 1913.

Title: Caslon flowers: An appreciation. Paper read before the printers of Boston.

Imprint, frontispiece: ... The displays of Caslon flowers are arranged by Mr. Dwiggins ... The text is composed in the original Caslon Old Style, cast from imported matrices.

Boards; 10¼ x 7 in.

Cabinet Shelf No.

[Printed under the supervision of Wadsworth A. Parker, Manager of the Typographic Department in Jersey City.]

Boards; 7-3/8 x 5-1/8 in.

IMPRINTS, United States

Cabinet JJ Shelf 3 No. 10

Baker & Godwin, New York, 1861.

see BAKER, PETER C. European recollections...New York, 1861.

IMPRINTS, United States.

Cabinet G Shelf 1 No. 4

Alumni Press, University of Michigan, The. Ann Arbor, 1928.

Title: The papers of Lord George Germain. By Randolph G. Adams.

Imprint: Printed at The Alumni Press University of Michigan, Ann Arbor.

Boards; 12½ x 9¾ x 3/8 in.

IMPRINTS, United States

Cabinet G Shelf 1 No. 50.04

Aries Press (Spencer Kellogg, jr.), Village of Eden, New York.

Prospectuses, 1925, 1926, 1927

In envelope.

IMPRINTS, United States

Cabinet JJ Shelf 3 No. 4

Barlow, B.R., New York City, 1847

see SOCIETIES, PRINTERS'. United States. New York Typographical Society...

IMPRINTS, United States

Cabinet JJ Shelf 4 No. 15

American Type Founders Company, Jersey City, 1915.

Time: Fifty years of the Typothetae, April 13, 1915.

Colophon: This book was arranged in Cloister Types by the Typographic Department of the American Type Founders Company after plans by Edmund G. Gress....

Half morocco; 9½ x 6½ in.

IMPRINTS, United States

Cabinet G Shelf 1 No. 7.05

Athenaeum Press, The. (Ginn & Co.) Boston, 1929

Title: Friends. A Primer. By Mary E. Pennell and Alice M.Cusack. Illustrated by Marguerite Davis.

Imprint: The Athenaeum Press. Ginn and Company proprietors. Boston.

Cloth; 7½ x 5½ in.

IMPRINTS, United States.

Cabinet G Shelf 1 No. 11

Bartlett-Orr Press, New York, n.d. Impressions: A printed messenger.

Boards, 6½ x 4¾ ins., ¼ in. thick (2) pp.4 (2)

IMPRINTS, United States.

Cabinet G Shelf 1 No. 8

Bartlett-Orr Press, New York, 1905.
Title: Evolution of the Machine Shop. By James Hartness. Copyright 1905, by the Jones & Lamson Machine Company. Springfield, Vermont, U.S.A.
Colophon: Bartlett & Company. The Orr Press, New York.

Limp leather; 6-1/8 x 4 in.

IMPRINTS, United States.

Cabinet G Shelf 1 No. 13

Bartlett-Orr Press, New York, 1926. Edward Dean Adams, by Edward E. Bartlett. Privately printed, New York, 1926.

Two hundred and fifty copies printed: This is No.36.

Half mor. in case, 9¼ x 6½ ins., pp.38.

IMPRINTS, United States.

Cabinet G Shelf 1 No. 25

Beran, C. Raymond. San Francisco.
Title: The Heathen Chinee. By Bret Harte.
Colophon: Printed in San Francisco, California. 1930. Composition and design by C. Raymond Beran. Wood cuts by Edgar Vaughan Simpson.

Paper; 9-7/8 x 7 in.

IMPRINTS, United States.

Cabinet G Shelf 1 No. 9

Bartlett-Orr Press, New York, 1907. The Hartness Flat Turret Lathe, made in two sizes for both Bar and Chuck work. Jones & Lamson Machine Co., Springfield, Vt. Catalogue. Illus.

Flexible mor. gilt, 9¼ x 6½ ins. pp.151.

IMPRINTS, UNITED STATES

Cabinet L Shelf 5 No. 27

Bartlett Orr Press, New York, 1927.

See Color Printing. Bartlett Orr Press, New York, 1927.

IMPRINTS, United States.

Cabinet G Shelf 5 No. 4

Berrien-Durstine, Inc., New York, 1917. Slants: The fifth of a series of publications from this agency...together with a collection of advertisements prepared by this agency illustrating the importance we attach to copy. Illus.

Paper covers; 16½ x 12 ins., pp.12.

IMPRINTS, United States.

Cabinet G Shelf 1 No. 10

Bartlett-Orr Press, New York, 1910. The car of 1911: Being the latest edition of the Locomobile Book. Catalogue. Illus.

Paper covers, 8 x 6 ins., pp.254.

IMPRINTS, United States.

Cabinet G Shelf 1 No. 14

Bartlett-Orr Press, New York, 1928.
Title: "Ever Thine"...From the travel letters of J.W. Muller.
Imprint: Made into book form...for the diversion of friends of the Bartlett Orr Press. New York, 1928.

Boards; 8¼ x 5¼ in.

IMPRINT, United States.

Cabinet F Shelf 2 No. 12

Billmeyer, Michael. Germantown, 1798.
Title: Kirchen-formularien der evangelische-reformirten gemeinen.
Imprint: Germantown: Gedruckt bey Michael Billmeyer, 1798.

Paper covers; 7¼ x 4¼ in.

IMPRINTS, United States

Cabinet R Shelf 6 No. 11

Bartlett-Orr Press, New York, 1915.
See Printing Crafts Building. Prospectus of...

IMPRINTS, United States

Cabinet G Shelf 5 No. 3

Bartlett Orr Press, New York, 1929.
Title: Fleetwood coach work. [Fleetwood Body Corporation advertising brochure.]
Imprint: Printed in U. S. A. By Bartlett Orr Press, from designs by Lucian Bernhard.

Boards; 12½ x 12¼ in.

IMPRINTS, United States.

Cabinet F Shelf 2 No. 46

Billmeyer, Michael: Germantown, 1809.
Title: Der psalter des königs und propheten David ... D. Martin Luther. Die siebente auflage.
Imprint: Germantown: Gedruckt bey Michael Billmeyer.

Calf; 5½ x 3-1/8 x 1-1/8 in.

IMPRINTS, United States

Cabinet G Shelf 1 No. 11.01

Bartlett Orr Press, New York City, 1921.
Title: Dinner tendered to Wallace B. Donham...
Imprint-Colophon: Designed and printed by Bartlett Orr Press, New York City.

This is a menu and includes notes by W.B. Donham on "The present status of education for the graphic arts...

Boards; 7 x 4½ in.

IMPRINTS, United States

Cabinet F Shelf 2 No. 48

Bell, Robert. Philadelphia, 1770.
Title: History of the reign of Charles the Fifth, Emperor of Germany. By William Robertson... Volume the third.
Imprint: America. Printed for the subscribers. The history is preceded by an address concerning copyright.

Leather; 8¼ x 5¼ x 1⅞ in. Evans 4, 11837; p.250

IMPRINTS, United States

Cabinet C Shelf 1 No. 26

Blakeley Printing Company, Chicago, Ill., 1893.

See BANCROFT, HUBERT HOWE. (The) Book of the Fair...Chicago, Ill., 1893

IMPRINTS, United States.

Cabinet G Shelf 1 No. 12

Bartlett-Orr Press, New York, 1924. The significance of Art in America, by Michael Friedsam, with a foreword, An appreciation of a dominating principle, by Eduard E. Bartlett.

A new years greeting.

Boards 7 x 4⅜ ins. pp.8

IMPRINTS, United States

Cabinet G Shelf 1 No. 14.01

Bentley Press (Wilder Bentley), Pittsburg, 1931.
Title: The Frankeleyns Tale. By Geoffrey Chaucer.
Imprint: The Bentley Press: Pittsburg, 1931

Boards; 8-5/8 x 4½ x ¼ in.

IMPRINTS, United States

Cabinet G Shelf 3 No. 84

Bookman Press, The. Pratt Institute, Brooklyn, N.Y., 1934.

See PRATT INSTITUTE FREE LIBRARY. Bookman Press, The...

IMPRINTS, United States.

Cabinet R Shelf 5 No. 11

Bowen, Daniel. Philadelphia, 1839.
Title: A History of Philadelphia.
Imprint: Philadelphia: Printed and published by Daniel Bowen, 1839.

Cloth; 9 x 5-7/8 in.

IMPRINTS, United States

Cabinet F Shelf 2 No. 5

Bradford, William. Philadelphia, 1754.
Title: The life and death of riches and poverty.
Imprint: Philadelphia. Printed and sold by W. Bradford, at the Sign of the Bible, in Second Street. 1754.

Half morocco; 6¼ x 3-3/4 in.

IMPRINTS, United States.

Cabinet G Shelf 1 No. 17

Bradley (Will) His book. Springfield and Boston, 1896, 1897.

Vol. 1, Nos. 1,2,3,4,
Vol. 2, " 1,2,3,4, all issued.

Half mor. 11¼ x 8½ ins., 1¼ ins. thick.

IMPRINTS, United States.

Cabinet F Shelf 2 No. 77

Boyle, John: Boston, 1774.

Title: Seven Sermons.....By Robert Russell. At Wardhurst in Sussex. Fifty-first edition.
Imprint: London, printed. Boston, reprinted and sold by J. Boyle in Marlborough Street, 1774,

Half board and leather: 5-7/8 x 3½ in.
Evans 5, 13593, p.69.

IMPRINTS, United States

Cabinet QQ Shelf 1 No. 7

Bradford, William. Philadelphia, 1758.
Title: The American Magazine.
Imprint: Printed and sold by William Bradford, at the Corner-House in Front and Market-Streets.

Half morocco; 8½ x 5¼ in.

IMPRINTS, United States.

Cabinet G Shelf 1 No. 16

Bradley, Will. The Wayside Press, Springfield, Mass. n.d. Commercial Designs re-printed from Bradley: His book. Broadsides (16).

Cardboard covers, 12 x 9½ ins.

IMPRINTS, United States.

Cabinet F Shelf 2 No. 10

Bradford, Thomas: Philadelphia, 1796.

Title: A New Year's Gift to Democrats....by Peter Porcupine [William Cobbett].
Imprint: Philadelphia: Published by Thomas Bradford, printer, bookseller and stationer, No.8, South Front Street. 1796.

Boards; cloth back; 8¾ x 5½ in.

IMPRINTS, United States.

Cabinet F Shelf 2 No. 7

Bradford, William. [Grandson of the First Printer in Philadelphia and New York], Philadelphia, 1758.
Title: The grants, concessions, and original constitutions of the province of New Jersey between 1664, and 1682...By Aaron Leaming and Jacob Spicer.
Imprint: Philadelphia. Printed by W. Bradford, printer to the King's Most Excellent Majesty for the Province of New Jersey.

cont'd

IMPRINTS, United States

Cabinet G Shelf 1 No. 24

Bradley, Will. The Wayside Press, Springfield, Mass. 1897.
Collection of brochures, commercial designs, etc.

Boards; 11½ x 9¼ in.

IMPRINTS, United States

Cabinet R Shelf 2 No. 5

Bradford, William, Philadelphia, 1685-1692. New York, 1694-1714.
Bibliographical excerpt from the New York Times Book Review, Sunday, Dec. 22, 1935.

Pasted on back cover of book R/2/5.

IMPRINTS, United States cont'd

Cabinet Shelf No.

Original calf; 11¾ x 7½ in. Evans 3,8205, p.204

IMPRINTS, United States.

Cabinet G Shelf 1 No. 18

Bradley, Will. The Wayside Press, Springfield, Mass., 1897. A portfolio of printing: Being a collection of proofs of some of the commercial work done at the Wayside Press.

11 x 8 ins., pp.12.

IMPRINTS, United States

Cabinet R Shelf 5 No. 2.01

Bradford, William, New York and Philadelphia.
Facsimile of imprints, 1693 to 1726.

With misc. collection of items in envelope.

IMPRINTS, United States.

Cabinet G Shelf 1 No. 15

Bradley, Will. University Press. Cambridge, Mass. 1895. Fringilla, or tales in verse by D. Blackmore. With sundry decorative pictures by Will Bradley.

Boards, 9 x 6 ins., ½ in. thick, pp.125.

IMPRINTS, United States.

Cabinet G Shelf 1 No. 19

Bradley, Will. The University Press, Cambridge, Mass. 1898.
Title: Little, Brown & Company's list of autumn Publications. 1898.
Colophon: Arranged and Printed by Will Bradley at The University Press. Cambridge, U.S.A.

Paper covers; 10-3/4 x 5-3/4 in.

IMPRINTS, United States.

Cabinet F Shelf 2 No. 3

Bradford, William (II): Philadelphia, 1747.
Title: An exhortation of the inhabitants of the province of South Carolina...By S.H. (Sophia Hume)
Imprint: Philadelphia: Printed by William Bradford [1747].

Leather; 7½ x 4¾ in. Evans 2, 5974; p.335.

IMPRINTS, United States

Cabinet G Shelf 1 No. 17.01

Bradley, William: The Wayside Press, Springfield, Mass.
Bradley His Book for July, 1896

This number is missing from bound volume, G/1/17

IMPRINTS, United States.

Cabinet G Shelf 1 No. 20

Bradley, Will. The Wayside Press, Cambridge, Mass., 1898. A print shop established by Will Bradley for the printing of choice books and the higher classes of commercial work is now a part of the University Press. John Wilson & Son, Inc.

Brochure, 8 x 6 ins., pp.33.

IMPRINTS, United States.

Cabinet G Bradley, Will. The American Chap Book. Issued monthly by the American Type Founders Co., Jersey City, 1904-1905.

Shelf 1 Vols. 1 and 2, Sept. 1904 to Aug. 1905. With supplements.

No. 21-2 Each vol. in separate board case, 7 x 4½ ins. 1½ ins. thick.

IMPRINTS, United States.

Cabinet G Bradley, Will, New York, 1906. Peter Poodle: Toy maker to the King, by Will Bradley

Shelf 1 Board; 11¼ x 9 ins., 1 in. thick, pp.166.

No. 23

IMPRINTS, United States

Cabinet F Braud, Denis, New Orleans ? 1764.
Title: Lettre d'un officier de la Louisiane a M...
Shelf 4 Imprint: A la Nouvelle Orleans, M.Dcc.LXlV
No. 80 The authenticity of this imprint is disputed. (see McMurtrie: Early printing in New Orleans. Also see letters in envelope containing the disputed imprint.

Quarter morocco; 6-3/8 x 3¾ in.

IMPRINTS, United States.

Cabinet G Bray & Beran: San Francisco, 1929.
Shelf 5 Title: The Declaration of Independence.
No. 5 Colophon: This brochure was designed and produced in San Francisco by C. Reymond Beran at the press of Bray & Beran during the month of June 1929.

Boards; 13¾ x 10½ in.

IMPRINTS, United States.

Cabinet F Brown, Samuel: New York City, 1766.

Shelf 3 Title: Theological Theses... By Isaac Sigfrid and Daniel Wyttenbach....
No. 16 Imprint: New York. Printed and sold by Samuel Brown at the foot of Pat-Baker's-Hill, between the New-Dutch Church and Fly-Market, 1766.

Half russia; 6½ x 4¼ in. Evans 10493, p.78.

IMPRINTS, United States.

Cabinet G Bruce, David and George, New York, 1809. The Reign of Grace, from its rise to its consummation. By Abraham Booth. The second American Ed. Printed for John Tiebont.

Shelf 1 No. 26 Original calf binding, 7 x 4 ins. 1¼ ins. thick, pp.306.

IMPRINTS, UNITED STATES

Cabinet FF Bruce, David & George. New York, 1815.
Title: The Holy Bible...
Shelf 1 Imprint: New York: Stereotyped and printed by D. & G. Bruce. No. 27 William Street.

No. 69 The first American stereotype Bible.

Morocco; 6¾ x 4 x 1-5/8 in.

IMPRINTS, United States.

Cabinet G Bruce, David and George, New York, 1909. John De Lancaster, A novel. Printed for M & W. Ward. vol. 1 only.

Shelf 1 No. 27 Original binding, 7 x 4¼ ins., ¾ in. thick, pp.292

IMPRINTS, United States

Cabinet S Buddy, Lewis: The Kirgate Press, Canton, Penn. 1901.
Shelf 4 Title: Horace Walpole and the Strawberry Hill Press, 1757-1789.
No. 57 Imprint: Lewis Buddy 3rd. The Kirgate Press.

Boards, cloth back; 7-7/8 x 5¾ x 5/8 in. See also U/2/32.

By Munson Aldrich Havens.

IMPRINTS, United States.

Cabinet G Butts, Isaac R., Boston, Mass., 1839. Memoir of Nathaniel Bowditch. From the press of Isaac R. Butts.

Shelf 1 No. 28 Boards, 11½ x 9 ins., ¾ in. thick, pp.168.

IMPRINTS, United States

Cabinet F Carey, Mathew. Philadelphia, 1792.
Title: Epicteti Enchiridion.
Shelf 1 Imprint: Philadelphiae: Impensis Mathaei Carey.
No. 88 This is the first book printed with Greek types in America.

Calf; 5¾ x 3½ in. Not in Evans.

IMPRINTS, United States

Cabinet K Carey and Hart, Philadelphia, 1846

Shelf 2 No. 29 see KEEPSAKES, or, GIFT BOOKS. Diadem, the, for 1846...

IMPRINTS, United States

Cabinet 80 Carlisle, David. Boston 1806, 1807.

Shelf 1 See ALMANACS. Farmer's Almanac (Robert B. Thomas), 1806 and 1807.

No. 12

IMPRINTS, United States.

Cabinet G Carlisle Indian School Press, Carlisle, Pa., 1910. A collection of printing.

Shelf 1 Brochures, Invitations, Magazines, etc.

No. 30 Buchram, 11½ x 9 ins., 1½ ins. thick.

IMPRINTS, United States

Cabinet G Carnegie Institute of Technology, Pittsburgh, 1917. Founders Day Exhibition. A catalogue. Illus.

Shelf 1 No. 29 Boards 8½ x 5¾ ins. pp.18.

IMPRINTS, United States.

Cabinet G Carr Horace. At the Printing Press. Cleveland, 1915. Bernard Shaw on Typography.

Shelf 1 No. 31 Half morocco, 8¼ x 5¼ ins., 11 lvs., Original paper bound in.

IMPRINTS, United States.

Cabinet G Carr, Horace, at Cleveland, Ohio, March, 1927. The Mather Literature, by Thomas Holmes. Privately printed for William Gwinn Mather.

Shelf 1

No. 32 Half morocco; 7½ x 4½, pp.63.

IMPRINTS, United States.

Cabinet G Carr, Horace. Cleveland, Ohio, 1930.
Title: Increase Mather, his works: Being a short title catalogue of the published writings that can be ascribed to him. Compiled by Thomas J. Holmes.
Shelf 1 Imprint: Cleveland. For private distribution.
No. 33 Colophon: Printed by Horace Carr, at Cleveland, Ohio, in May, 1930.

Quarter Morocco, in paper board case; 10¼ x 6-7/8 in.

IMPRINTS, United States.

Cabinet F Shelf 3 No. 2

Carter, John: Providence, 1774.
Title: English liberties, or the free-born subject's inheritance...Compiled first by Henry Care, and continued....by William Nelson.
Imprint: Providence, Rhode Island: Printed and sold by John Carter, at Shakespear's Head, in Meeting-Street, near the Court House, 1774.
Leather; $6\frac{3}{4}$ x $4\frac{3}{4}$ x $1\frac{1}{2}$ in. Evans 5, 13185, p.14.

IMPRINTS, United States.

Cabinet G Shelf 1 No. 34

Carteret Press, Newark, New Jersey, 1915.
Rubaiyat of Omar Khayyam. Wood engravings in color by Rudolf Ruzicka.

Orig. Bds., Linen Back, $8\frac{1}{2}$ x $5\frac{1}{2}$ ins. pp. (2) 26 (2)

IMPRINTS, United States.

Cabinet G Shelf 1 No. 34.01

Caxton Company, The. Cleveland, Ohio, 1915.
Title: A buyer of printing. Some confessions. by David Gibson.
Imprint: The Caxton Company, Cleveland.

Boards; 8-1/8 x $5\frac{1}{4}$ in.

IMPRINTS, United States

Cabinet S Shelf 1 No. 151

Caxton Company, Cleveland, Ohio, 1920.
Title: Christmas in Caxton's Time, as prevailed through the festive season during the lifetime of this illustrious printer.
Imprint: Made up and presented with the seasons greetings of the Caxton Company at Cleveland Ohio, Xmas, 1920.

Half morocco; 11-1/8 x $7\frac{3}{4}$ in.

IMPRINTS, United States

Cabinet S Shelf 5 No. 46

Caxton Press. New York, 1929.
Title: Bookplates by Harold Nelson. Arranged by Clarence Hornung, with a foreword by John Malcolm Bulloch.
Imprint: New York. Caxton Press, Inc. 1929.

Boards; $11\frac{1}{4}$ x $8\frac{1}{2}$ x 3/8 in.

IMPRINTS, United States

Cabinet S Shelf 5 No. 47

Caxton Press, New York, 1930.
Title: Trade Marks designed by Clarence P. Hornung.
Imprint: New York. Caxton Press.
Numbered and signed copy.

Cloth; $8\frac{1}{4}$ x 7-1/8 x 5/8 in. In board protective case.

IMPRINTS, United States.

Cabinet G Shelf 1 No. 35

Cedar Tree Press, The. Boston, Mass., 1925
Poems for young people, by Martha B. Thomas.

Boards, 9 x $6\frac{1}{4}$ ins., 5/8 in. thick, pp.47.

IMPRINTS, United States

Cabinet QQ Shelf 2 No. 16

Cheltenham Press, New York, 1918.
Title: Brooks Brothers Centenary, 1818-1918.
Imprint: Printed for Brooks Brothers at the Cheltenham Press, New York, 1918.

Boards; 6-7/8 x 4-7/8

IMPRINTS, United States.

Cabinet G Shelf 1 No. 36

Cheltenham Press, The, New York, 1926.
A history of fifty feet in New York, from 1644 to 1926. Copyright by The Bank of America. Illus.

Boards, $7\frac{1}{2}$ x $4\frac{3}{4}$ ins., $\frac{1}{4}$ in. thick, pp.90.

IMPRINTS, United States

Cabinet F Shelf 3 No. 24

Childs, Francis, and John Swaine. New York City, 1789-91.
Title: Acts of the First Congress of the United States...
Imprint: New York. Printed by Francis Childs and John Swaine, printers to the United States.

Paper boards; $12\frac{3}{4}$ x $8\frac{1}{2}$ in. Evans 8, 23902.

IMPRINTS, United States

Cabinet LL Shelf 4 No. 14.02

Chimes Press (William Colvard), Los Angeles, California, 1924.
Title: Selling creative advertising. By George O. Mc.Carthy.
Imprint: Chimes Press. Los Angeles, California, 1924.

Boards; $12\frac{1}{4}$ x $9\frac{1}{4}$ in.

IMPRINTS, United States

Cabinet JJ Shelf 3 No. 9

Clayton and Pagan, New York City, 1875

see
SOCIETIES, PRINTERS'. United States.
New York Typographical Society. Constitution and by-laws...1875

IMPRINTS, United States.

Cabinet G Shelf 1 No. 37

Cleland, Thomas Maitland, Boston, 1900. The Lady of Shalott, printed in Priory text type in black and red. Wood engravings.

Boards, $6\frac{1}{2}$ x $4\frac{3}{4}$ ins., $\frac{1}{4}$ in. thick.

IMPRINTS, United States.

Cabinet G Shelf 1 No. 39

Cleland, Thomas Maitland, at The Cornhill Press, Boston, 1901. The Shrine of Death and the Shrine of Love, by Lady Dilke. Illus. Types: Old Style Antique.

Boards, $7\frac{3}{4}$ x 6 ins., $\frac{1}{2}$ in. thick, n.p.

IMPRINTS, United States.

Cabinet G Shelf 1 No. 38

Cleland, Thomas Maitland, The Cornhill Press, Boston, 1901. Blind Love, by Lawrence Housman.

Boards, $6\frac{1}{4}$ x $5\frac{1}{4}$ ins., $\frac{1}{4}$ in. thick. Printed with Caslon Old Style types with original initial and end pieces.

IMPRINTS, United States.

Cabinet G Shelf 1 No. 40

Cleland, Thomas Maitland, New York, 1915. The Locomobile Book: Designed and executed by T.M. Cleland, Illus.

Boards, 12 x $9\frac{1}{4}$ ins., $\frac{1}{2}$ in. thick, pp.31.

IMPRINTS United States

Cabinet G Shelf 1 No. 44

Cleland, Thomas Maitland. Boston 1916.
Biographical sketch of Giambattista Bodoni of Parma delivered by T.M. Cleland at a meeting of The Society of Printers in Boston. April 22, 1913.

Boards; $9\frac{1}{4}$ x $6\frac{1}{4}$ x 3/8 in.

IMPRINTS, United States.

Cabinet G Shelf 1 No. 41

Cleland, Thomas Maitland, New York,1916.
The Book of the Locomobile. Designed and exectuted by T.M. Cleland. Illus.

Boards, $12\frac{1}{2}$ x $9\frac{1}{2}$ ins., $\frac{1}{4}$ in. thick, pp.36.

IMPRINTS, United States.

Cabinet G Shelf 1 No. 42

Cleland, Thomas Maitland, New York, 1917. The book of the Locomobile, Designed and executed by T.M. Cleland. Illus.

Boards, $12\frac{1}{2}$ x $9\frac{1}{2}$ ins. thick, pp.36.

IMPRINTS, United States.

Cabinet G Shelf 5 No. 6

Cleland, Thomas Maitland, Detroit, 1927: The new Cadillac. This book was designed and illustrated by T.M. Cleland, prepared and printed by Evans-Winter-Hebb Inc., Detroit.

Thin boards, 14 x 10 ins., pp.31.

IMPRINTS, United States

Cabinet G Shelf 1 No. 50.03

Colophon, New York, 1935. Pynson Printers Prospectus for the year of 1935, giving list of contibuting editors, etc.

Item in manila envelope.

IMPRINTS, United States

Cabinet P Shelf 4 No. 26

Cleland, Thomas M., New York, 1917.
Title: What is amateurism ?...by Max H. Behr.
Imprint: One of twenty-five copies printed from type on hand made paper by T. M. Cleland.

Brochure, in envelope.

IMPRINTS, United States.

Cabinet G Shelf 1 No. 47

Cleland, Thomas Maitland, Philadelphia, n.d. Algerian covers, made by A.M. Collins Mfg. Co. Specimens of covers designed and decorated by T.M. Cleland. Brochure.

Paper, $10\frac{1}{2}$ x 8 ins., $\frac{1}{4}$ in. thick.

IMPRINTS, United States.

Cabinet G Shelf 1 No. 50

Commonwealth Press, The. Worcester, Mass. 1927.
Title: Norton Hall ... Norton Company. Worcester, Massachusetts, 1927.
Colophon: ... Reproductions for this book are wood engravings by Howard McCormick. Typography and printing by The Commonwealth Press of Worcester, Massachusetts.

Paper boards; 11-1/8 x 8-3/4 in.

IMPRINTS, United States.

Cabinet G Shelf 1 No. 43

Cleland, Thomas Maitland, New York, 1918. The book of the Locomobile, Designed and executee by T.M. Cleland.

Boards, 1o x $7\frac{1}{2}$ in. $\frac{1}{4}$ in. thick, pp.47.

IMPRINTS, United States.

Cabinet G Shelf 1 No. 49

Clerk's Press, The, Rev. Charles C. Bubb, Cleveland, Ohio, 1911-12.

Collection of booklets printed on small hand press with types which includes music, devised and made by C. Bubb.

Boards 7 x $5\frac{1}{2}$ ins., $\frac{1}{2}$ in. thick.

IMPRINTS, United States

Cabinet P Shelf 4 No. 17

Condé Nast Press (Lester Douglas, typographer), Greenwich, Conn., 1932.

see DOUGLAS, LESTER. (The) Battle of the Fifty Books...

IMPRINTS, United States.

Cabinet G Shelf 1 No. 45

Cleland, Thomas Maitland, New York, 1922. The Ampico: A descriptive catalogue. Designed and decorated by T.M. Cleland.

Paper covers, 13 x 10 ins., $\frac{1}{4}$ in. thick, pp.18.

IMPRINTS, United States.

Cabinet X Shelf 4 No. 101

Cobbett, William (Peter Porcupine). Philadelphia, 1798.
Title: The democratic judge, or equal liberty of the press ...
Imprint: Philadelphia: Published by William Cobbett, oposite Christ-Church, March, 1798.

Paper boards, leather back; 8-3/8 x $5\frac{1}{4}$ in.

IMPRINTS. United States

Cabinet NN Shelf 3 No. 25

Cooke, Robert Grier, Press of. New York. 1905.

See Cooke, Robert Grier (Compiler). Casual essays of The Sun...

IMPRINTS United States

Cabinet G Shelf 1 No. 48

Cleland, Thomas Maitland, New York, 1924. The compromise of the king of the Golden Isles by Lord Dunsany, New York. Designed and printed by T.M. Cleland, for The Grolier Club, 1924.

Boards, cloth back; $11\frac{1}{4}$ x $8\frac{3}{4}$ x $\frac{1}{8}$ in. pp.25.

IMPRINTS, United States.

Cabinet F Shelf 3 No. 46

Collins, Isaac: Trenton, New Jersey, 1791.
Title: The Holy Bible, containing the Old and New Testament....
Imprint: Trenton: Printed and sold by Isaac Collins, 1791.
The first Bible printed in New Jersey.

Leather; 11 x 9 x in. Evans 8, 23184, p.124.

IMPRINTS, United States.

Cabinet G Shelf 1 No. 54

Cranbrook Press, Detroit, Mich., 1901. The dictes and sayings of the philosophers. First printed in England by William Caxton in 1477, and now emprinted at the Cranbrook Press, Jan. 19, 1901. Illus, with initials and original borders.

Half vellum. $11\frac{1}{4}$ x $8\frac{3}{4}$ ins., pp.125.

IMPRINTS, United States.

Cabinet G Shelf 1 No. 46

Cleland, Thomas Maitland. New York, 1924. Ornaments in Jade, by Arthur Machen. Printed by the Pynson Printers under the direction of T.M. Cleland.

Authors autograph.

Black Linen Boards in care 10 x $9\frac{1}{2}$ ins., $\frac{1}{2}$ in. thick (5) pp.46 (3)

IMPRINTS, United States

Cabinet QQ Shelf 1 No. 39

Collins, T.M. & P.G. Philadelphia, 1847.
Title: Tems fortnight ramble...By Thomas MacKellar. Published by Carey and Hart. Phila.
Imprint: T.M. & P.G. Collins, printers. No.I, Lodge Alley.

Half morocco; 7 x $4\frac{1}{4}$ x 7/8 in.

IMPRINTS, United States.

Cabinet G Shelf 1 No. 52

Cranbrook Press, Detroit, Mich. 1901. Cranbrook Papers.Printed and illuminated entirely by hand, on paper made by hand in U.S. Types Jenson Old Style, as designed by the late William Morris.

Half vellum, $11\frac{1}{4}$ x $8\frac{3}{4}$ ins. pp.(6), 100.

IMPRINTS, United States.

Cabinet G Shelf 1 No. 51

Cranbrook Press, George C. Booth, Detroit, Mich. 1901. The Revelation of St. John the Divine, from the earliest English version by William Tyndale, first printed in 1525, with Albrecht Durer's illustrations now newly imprinted.

Half vellum, $11\frac{1}{4}$ x $8\frac{3}{4}$ ins. pp.46, with 16 full page plates.

IMPRINTS, United States.

Cabinet G Shelf 1 No. 54.04

Cummings, E.E. New York, 1928.
Title: Christmas Tree.
Imprint: Copyright, 1928 by E. E. Cummings, New York.

A good piece of stunt printing.

Boards; $7\frac{3}{4}$ x $5\frac{1}{4}$ x $\frac{1}{4}$ in.

IMPRINTS, United States.

Cabinet G Shelf 1 No. 57

Daniels, Abraham G. Boston, 1918. Memories of Ohabei Shalom. Privately issued in commemoration of Temple Ohabei Shalom, in Boston, Feb. 26, 1918. Brochure.

Boards, $6\frac{3}{4}$ x $5\frac{1}{4}$, lvs. 14.

IMPRINTS, United States.

Cabinet G Shelf 1 No. 51

Cranbrook Press, Detroit, Mich., 1901.
Title: Revelation of St. John the Divine, in reprint of the English edition of 1525. (with illustrations of Albrecht Durer).

Half vellum; $11\frac{1}{4}$ x 8-3/8 in.

IMPRINTS, United States.

Cabinet G Shelf 1 No. 55

Currier & Harford, New York, 1926. Nowel: Being certain presumably Elizabethen verses with pictures by Walter Dorwin Teague, now printed for the friends of the artist and of Currier & Harford.

Stiff paper, 13 x 10 ins. pp.6.

IMPRINTS, United States.

Cabinet G Shelf 1 No. 58

Detterer, Ernst, F. Chicago, Ill., Dec., 1925. When all the world is kin, by H.W. Mabie. Designed and printed by Ernst F. Detterer, the Department of Printing Arts of the Art Institute of Chicago. Brochure.

Block pattern cover paper, 8 x 6 ins., pp. 6.

IMPRINTS, United States.

Cabinet G Shelf 1 No. 53

Cranbrook Press, Detroit, Mich., 1901. Three Wise Men: Extracts from the works of Marcus Aurelius. Francis Bacon, and Benjamin Franklin.

Half vellum; $11\frac{1}{4}$ x 8-3/4 ins. pp. 132.

IMPRINTS, United States

Cabinet G Shelf 1 No. 56.01

Cushing, Frank Myrle. Los Angeles, 1932.
Title: Bicentennial Edition. Valedictory Address of George Washington. With an introduction by John J. Cushing. Published in commemoration of the Two Hundredth Anniversary of George Washington, 1732-1931.
Imprint: Los Angeles. Printed by Frank Myrle Cushing, 1932.
No.II of XV copies. Has signature of printer.

(cont'd)

IMPRINTS, United States

Cabinet G Shelf 1 No. 58.05

DeVinne, Theo. Low. New York, 1884.
Title: An antidote against melancholy...
Imprint: At New-York. Printed by T.L.D.V. for Pratt Manufacturing Company...Christmas, MDCCCLXXXIV.

Half morocco; 8-7/8 x 7-1/8 x 5/8 in.

IMPRINTS, United States

Cabinet G Shelf 5 No. 24

Crocker Company Inc., H.S., San Francisco, California, 1920.

see IMPRINTS, United States. Garnett, Porter, etc.

IMPRINTS, United States.

Cabinet G Shelf 1 No. 56

Cushing, John D. and Thomas C. Jr., Salem, Mass. 1822. The ruins of Paestum and other compositions in verse.

Half morocco, $9\frac{1}{2}$ x 7 ins., $\frac{1}{2}$ in. thick, pp. 128.

IMPRINTS, United States.

Cabinet G Shelf 1 No. 59

DeVinne Press, The. New York, 1891.
Title: The women of the French Salons. By Amelia Gere Mason.
Imprint: T. Fisher Unwin, London: The Century Co. New York, 1891. The DeVinne Press.

Stamped morocco; $10\frac{3}{8}$ x $7\frac{1}{4}$ x $1\frac{1}{4}$ in.

IMPRINTS, United States

Cabinet F Shelf 3 No. 54

Crouch, Charles. Charles-Town, 1770.
Title: A discourse on the death of Rev. George Whitefield. By Josiah Smith.
Imprint: Charles-Town: Printed by Charles Crouch. 1770.

Half morocco; 7-3/4 x 4-3/4 in. Evans 4, 11862. p.254.

IMPRINTS, United States

Cabinet G Shelf 1 No. 56.03

Cygnet Press, Cambridge, Massachusetts, 192[illegible]

Prospectus with Cygnet Press device, designed by Dwiggins.

Small brochure in manila envelope.

IMPRINTS, United States

Cabinet PP Shelf 3 No. 6

DeVinne Press, The. New York, 1892.
Title: Four private libraries of New York. By Henri Pene DuBois. Preface by Octave Uzanne. New York, 1892.
Imprint colophon: The DeVinne Press. February, 1892.

Cloth; $9\frac{1}{4}$ x $6\frac{1}{4}$ in.

IMPRINTS, United States

Cabinet F Shelf 1 No. 7

Crump, T. Boston, 1717.
Title: The nature and manner of man's blessing God...A sermon preached by John Barnard.
Imprint: Printed by T. Crump for Samuel Gerrish. Boston, 1717.

In morocco case; $6\frac{1}{2}$ x 4 in. Evans 1, 1865, p.253.

IMPRINTS, United States

Cabinet K Shelf 6 No. 11

Damrell & Morre. Boston, Mass., 1853.
Title: Views of America...The Holy Land, Etc. New York: Published by J. Milton Emerson & Co. 1853.
Imprint: Damrell & Moore, Printers and Binders, Boston.
[Copperplate printing].

Morocco, gilt; 10-7/8 x 8-3/8 x 1-3/4 in.

IMPRINTS, United States

Cabinet PP Shelf 4 No. 22

De Vinne Press. New York, 1892.
Title: Roger Payne and his art: A short account of his life and work as a binder. By Wm. Loring Andrews.
Imprints: New York. Printed at the De Vinne Press. 1892.

Cloth; $8\frac{1}{4}$ x 5-1/8 x 3/8 in.
In protective case.

IMPRINTS, United States

Cabinet R Shelf 3 No. 38

DeVinne Press, New York, 1894.
Title: Facsimile of Poor-Richard's Almanack for 1773. With an introduction by John Bigelow, and notes on the portraits.
Imprint: The Duodecimos. At end of volume: The DeVinne Press. Printer marks.

Full morocco, gilt; $7\frac{1}{4}$ x $5\frac{1}{4}$ in.

IMPRINTS, United States

Cabinet G Shelf 1 No. 60

DeVinne Press, The. New York, 1902.
Title: The nonnes preestes tale of the Cok and Hen. By Geoffrey Chaucer. New York. The Grafton Press. 1902.
Colophon: ... printed by Theodore L. DeVinne & Co. ...

Boards; 9 x $6\frac{3}{4}$ x 3/8 in.

IMPRINTS, United States.

Cabinet F Shelf 1 No. 58

Draper, Richard: Boston, 1760:
Title: A discourse occasioned by the death of the honorable Stephen Sewall, Esq....By Jonathan Mayhew.
Imprint: Boston. Printed by Richard Draper, in Newbury Street, Edes & Gill in Queen-Street, and T. & J. Fleet, in Cornhill, M.DCC.LX.

Half morocco; $7\frac{1}{2}$ x $4\frac{3}{4}$ in. Evans 3, 8666; p.262.

IMPRINTS, United States

Cabinet S Shelf 1 No. 21

DeVinne Press, The. New York, 1895.
Title: Description of early printed books owned by the Grolier Club.
Imprint: Printed for The Grolier Club, New York, May, 1895. [Following title page] The DeVinne Press.

Quarter calf; 12 x 8 x $\frac{1}{2}$ in.

IMPRINTS, United States.

Cabinet G Shelf 1 No. 61

Dickinson, Samuel Nelson, Boston, Mass. 1841, Sketches from a student's window, by S.G. Goodrich.

Cloth, 8 x 5 ins., pp.311.

IMPRINTS, United States

Cabinet JJ Shelf 3 No. 13

Dutton & Wentworth, Boston, 1826.

see SOCIETIES, PRINTERS' United States. Franklin Typographical Society...Boston, 1826.

IMPRINTS, United States

Cabinet PP Shelf 2 No. 34

DeVinne, Theodore Low, New York, 1895.
Title: Description of the early printed books owned by The Grolier Club...Illus.
Imprint: Printed for The Grolier Club, New York, May, 1895.
Facing introduction: The DeVinne Press.

Cloth, pigskin back; 12 x 8 in.

IMPRINTS, United States.

Cabinet F Shelf 1 No. 48

Draper, John: Boston, 1739.
Title: A sermon preached....By John Barnard.... Prefaced by Samuel Phillips.
Imprint: Boston. Printed by John Draper, for D. Henchman in Cornhill, 1739.

Half morocco; 6-1/8 x 4 in. Not in Evans.

IMPRINTS United States

Cabinet G Shelf 1 No. 3

Dwiggins, W.A., New York, 1913.
Title: Caslon Flowers: An appreciation by W.A. Dwiggins. A paper read before The Society of Printers, Boston.
Imprint: The Advertisers Paper Mills, New York, 1913. Illus.

Boards; $10\frac{1}{4}$ x 7 in.

IMPRINTS, New York. United States

Cabinet PP Shelf 6 No. 2 (2 vols.)

DeVinne Press, The. New York, 1895.
Title: 176 historic and artistic bookbindings ...selected from the library of Robert Hoe ...(2 vols.) Dodd, Mead & Co. New York, 1895.
Imprint facing preface: The DeVinne Press. New York.
Printed on Imperial Japanese paper. One of two hundred copies only.

Half morocco; 14 x 11 in.

IMPRINTS, United States

Cabinet F Shelf 1 No. 50

Draper, John. Boston, 1740.
Title: The doctrine of predestination...By William Cooper.
Imprint: Boston. Printed by J. Draper for J. Edwards and H. Foster, in Cornhill. 1740.

Leather; $6\frac{1}{2}$ x 4 in. Evans 2, 4497. p.155.

IMPRINTS, United States

Cabinet QQ Shelf 4 No. 8

Eastburn, John H., Boston, 1835.

see MASSACHUSETTS HISTORICAL SOCIETY. Collections...1835.

IMPRINTS, United States

Cabinet R Shelf 3 No. 178

De Vinne Press, The. New York, 1895.
Title: Sketches of printers and printing in Colonial New York. By Charles R. Hildeburn. New York: Dodd, Mead & Company, 1895.
Imprint facing preface: The DeVinne Press.

With portraits and reproductions of titles.

Boards; $7\frac{3}{4}$ x 5 x 7/8 in.

IMPRINTS, United States.

Cabinet F Shelf 1 No. 53

Draper, John: Boston, 1750.
Title: A sermon preached at Boston....By Samuel Phillips.
Imprint: Boston, New England: Printed by John Draper, printer to his honor the Lieutenant Governor and Council, 1750.

Half morocco; 8-5/8 x $5\frac{1}{2}$ in. Not in Evans.

IMPRINTS, United States.

Cabinet G Shelf 1 No. 62

Eaton, James Kent, Inc., printers, Boston, 1927. The Puggsley Papers, by Thomas Hood, with reproduction of wood-engraving by Thomas Bewick, Printed for friends by J.K. Eaton.

Boards, 9 x 6 ins., pp.10.

IMPRINT, United States

Cabinet EE Shelf 4 No. 71

DeVinne Press, New York, 1898.
Title: R. Hoe & Co.'s catalogue of machinery and materials for electrotyping...
Imprint under copyright: The DeVinne Press, New York.

Pamphlet in manila envelope.

IMPRINTS, United States

Cabinet F Shelf 1 No. 55

Draper, John. Boston, 1755.
Title: A day of darkness. A sermon preached by Samuel Checkley.
Imprint: Boston, N.E. Printed by John Draper, printer to his Excellency the Governor and the Honorable His Majesty's Council. 1755.

Half morocco; $7\frac{1}{4}$ x $4\frac{3}{4}$ in. Evans 3, 7383, p.100.

IMPRINTS, United States.

Cabinet F Shelf 2 No. 79

Edes, Benjamin and John Gill, Boston, 1774.
Title: The misery and duty of an oppress'd and enslav'd people.....By Samuel Webster.
Imprint: Boston: Printed by Edes and Gill, in Queen Street. 1774.

Half leather; 8 x 5 in. Evans 5, 13758, p.94.

IMPRINTS, United States.

Cabinet F Shelf 2 No. 81

Edes, Benjamin: Watertown, 1775.

Title: A sermon presented before the Honorable House of Representatives [July 19, 1775]. By William Gordon.
Imprint: Watertown. Printed and sold by Benjamin Edes. 1775.

Half morocco; 7¾ x 5 in. Evans 5, 14073, p. 136.

IMPRINTS, United States.

Cabinet G Shelf 1 No. 64

Elm Tree Press, Woodstock, Vermont, 1909 Copa: The hostess of the inn. Edited by Charles L. Dana and John Cotton Dana.

Boards, 9¼ x 6 ins., pp.44.

IMPRINTS, United States.

Cabinet G Shelf 1 No. 70

Elm Tree Press, Woodstock, Vt., 1914. Essay on bibliography and on the attainments of a librarian by Elder, Translated by Mrs. Schuyler van Rensselaer. The librarian's series, Number four.

Boards, Linen back, 8½ x 5½ ins., pp. (4) 48.

IMPRINTS, United States.

Cabinet F Shelf 2 No. 83

Edes, Benjamin and Son: Boston, 1786.

Title: The shortness and afflictions of human life. By John Steele.
Imprint: Edinburgh printed: Boston re-printed and sold by B. Edes & Son, No.42 Cornhill, 1786.

Half morocco; 8¼ x 5¼ in. Evans, 7, 20008, p.71.

IMPRINTS, United States.

Cabinet G Shelf 1 No. 66

Elm Tree Press, The, Woodstock, Vt. 1909. The old librarian's almanack: A very rare pamphlet published in New Haven, Conn, 1773, and now reprinted for the first time. The librarians series. Edited by J.C.Dana and Henry W. Kent, No.1. Includes facsimile.

Boards, 9 x 5½ ins., ¼ in. thick, pp.20.

IMPRINTS United States

Cabinet G Shelf 1 No. 73

Elston Press, The. Clarke Conwell. New Rochelle. New York, 1902-3.
A collection of prospectuses from this Press.

Blue Buckram Case; 10 x 7½ x 1¾ in.

IMPRINTS, United States

Cabinet R Shelf 4 No. 4

Eliot, John Jr. Boston, 1811.
Title: An address to the Grand Lodge of Massachusetts, by Isaiah Thomas.
Imprinted: Printed by John Eliot, Jr. Boston, 1811.

Half morocco; 9¼ x 5-7/8 in.

IMPRINTS, United States.

Cabinet G Shelf 1 No. 67

Elm Tree Press, Woodstock, Vt., 1910. The library and the librarian: A selection of articles from the Boston Evening Transcript and other sources by E.L. Pearson. Librarian's series, No.2.

Boards, 8½ x 5½ ins., pp.87.

IMPRINTS, United States.

Cabinet G Shelf 1 No. 72

Emmett, Mary and Burton, Valley Cottage, New York, 1925. The gift of the magi; A Christmas story by O. Henry. Brochure.

Paper covers, 6 x 4¾ ins., pp.16.

IMPRINTS, United States

Cabinet GG Shelf 4 No. 33

Elliot, S. Alfred, Washington, D. C., 1828.

see
PATENTS, UNITED STATES. List of patents granted...

IMPRINTS, United States.

Cabinet G Shelf 1 No. 71

Elm Tree Press, Woodstock, Vt., 1910. The training of a librarian, by F. A. Ebert: Translated from the second, 1820, German Ed. Librarians series, No. 5.

Boards; 8¾ x 5½ in.

IMPRINTS, United States

Cabinet F Shelf 5 No. 48

Ephrata Press, The. Ephrata, Pennsylvania, 1748.
Title: Der blutige schau-platz oder Martyrer.... von T.J.V. Braght.
Imprint: Ephrata in Pensylvanien. Drucke und verlags der Bruderschaft. 1748.

Leather, metal corners; 15 x 9-3/4 x 4-3/4 in. Evans 2, 6256. p.371

IMPRINTS, United States.

Cabinet G Shelf 1 No. 65

Elm Tree Press, Woodstock, Vt., Dec. 25, 1905. Mosaics. Being certain sayings of various wise men. Leaflet.

8½ x 5 ins., 8 lvs.

IMPRINTS, United States.

Cabinet G Shelf 1 No. 68

Elm Tree Press, The, Woodstock, Vt., 1911. Pervigilium veneris a poeta latino incognito in metro eodem anglice reddidit, Elizabeth Hickman du Bois. Delineamenta a Dela F. Mussy. Woodstock verdemontani, typis et sumptibus preli Ulmei, XCMXI. Illum.

Publishers proof.

Boards, 11½ x 8 ins., pp.28.

IMPRINTS, United States.

Cabinet F Shelf 2 No. 15

Ephrata Press, The. [Peter Miller]: Ephrata 1770.
Title: Christliches Gemuths-Gesprach von dem Geistlichen und seligmachenden Glauben...
Imprint: Ephrata: Typis Societatis. Anno MDCCLXX.

Leather clasp; 6½ x 4 in. Thomas History of Printing, 2; p.87.

IMPRINTS, United States.

Cabinet G Shelf 1 No. 63

Elm Tree Press, Woodstock, Vt., 1906. Agamemnon, with an introduction by the editors, Charles L. Dana and John Cotton Dana.

Boards, 9¼ x 6 ins., pp.XII, (1), 71, (2)

IMPRINTS, United States.

Cabinet G Shelf 1 No. 69

Elm Tree Press, Woodstock, Vt., 1912. Origines Golfianal: The birth and early childhood of golf as revealed in a manuscript from a Scottish monastry. Edited by Arthur V. Taylor. With illus. and facsimiles.

Boards, linen back, 8½ x 5½ ins., pp.59.

IMPRINTS, United States.

Cabinet F Shelf 2 No. 17

Ephrata Press, The: Ephrata, Penn. 1786.
Title: Chronicum Ephratense...Zusamen getragen von Br. Lamech u Agrippa.
Imprint: Ephrata: Gedruckt Anno MDCCLXXXVI.

Half morocco; 9½ x 8 x 1 in. Sachse German Sectarian.

IMPRINTS, United States.

Cabinet G Shelf 1 No. 74

Eskew, William, Portsmouth, Ohio, 1921. The book of Ruth. Done as a labor of love by William Eskew at his little printshop. Brochure.

Boards, 9 x 6 ins., pp.6.

IMPRINTS, United States.

Cabinet G Shelf 1 No. 75

Evans-Winter-Hebb Inc., Detroit, Mich. An exacting clientele. Brochure.

Boards, 6½ x 5 ins., pp (1) 4 (1)

In envelope

IMPRINTS, United States.

Cabinet G Shelf 5 No. 6

Evans-Winter-Hebb Inc. Detroit, 1927. The new Cadillac. This book was designed and illustrated by T. M. Cleland, prepared and printed by Evans-Winter-Hebb Inc., Detroit.

Thin boards; 14 x 10 in.

IMPRINTS, United States.

Cabinet G Shelf 1 No. 76

Evans-Winter-Hebb, Detroit, Mich., 1927. Color creations from nature's studios. Brochure.

13 x 9½ ins., pp.30. (2 copies)

IMPRINTS, United States.

Cabinet G Shelf 1 No. 77

Evans-Winter-Hebb, Detroit, Mich., Feb., 1928. The Crest. Published and copyrighted by the Cadillac Motor Car Co., Detroit, Mich. Brochure, Illus.

10 x 7¼ ins., pp.20.

IMPRINTS, United States

Cabinet G Shelf 2 No. 6

Fine Arts Press, University of Oregon, John Henry Nash. 1927.
Title: Education & the State. Prince L. Campbell's philosophy of public education.
Imprint: Eugene. The University of Oregon. Fine Arts Press, 1927.
The book was composed by the senior students of the class of typography. John Henry Nash Fine Arts Press.

Boards; 12-5/8 x 9-1/8 in.

IMPRINTS, United States.

Cabinet F Shelf 2 No. 73

Fleet, Thomas: Boston, 1754.
Title: Some distinguishing characters of the extraordinary and ordinary Ministers of the Church of Christ.....By Edward Wigglesworth, D.D.
Imprint: Boston: Printed and sold by Thomas Fleet, at the Heart and Crown in Cornhill, 1754.

Half morocco; 7 x 4¼ in. Evans, 3, 7338, p.94.

IMPRINTS, United States.

Cabinet F Shelf 2 No. 75

Fleet, Thomas and John: Boston, 1776.
Title: Observations on the nature of civil liberty.....By Richard Price.
Imprint: London printed 1776. Boston re-printed and sold by T. and J. Fleet.

Half morocco; 7-3/8 x 4-5/8 in. Evans, 5, 15032, p.272.

IMPRINTS, United States.

Cabinet G Shelf 2 No. 4

Flebron Press, The, private press of L.A.Braverman, Cincinnati, Ohio. 1924. Aucassin & Nicolette, Illustrations by Glen Tracy.

Boards, 7 x 4¼ ins., ½ in. thick, pp.74.

IMPRINTS, United States

Cabinet G Shelf 1 No. 78

Foster, Roe and Crone, Chicago, Ill., circa 1880.
Title: "Art Fakes" (Specimens of typography)
Imprint: Foster, Roe and Crone, Art Printers, Chicago, Ill.

Brochure, in envelope.

IMPRINTS, United States.

Cabinet F Shelf 2 No. 63

Fowle, Daniel and Zechariah. Boston, 1755.
Title: The duty of God's People when engaged in War: A sermon.....By Samuel Checkley.
Imprint: Printed and sold by D. Fowle in Ann Street, and Z. Fowle in Middle Street, below the Mill Bridge, 1755.

Half calf; 7½ x 5-7/8 in. Evans, 3, 7384, p.100.

IMPRINTS, United States.

Cabinet F Shelf 2 No. 65

Fowle, Daniel. Portsmouth, New Hampshire, 1756.
Title: Good news from a Far Country....By Jonathan Parsons.
Imprint: Portsmouth, in New Hampshire: Printed and sold by Daniel Fowle, 1756.
This is the first book printed in New Hampshire.

Leather; 7 x 4½ in. Evans 3, 7746; p.146.

IMPRINT, United States.

Cabinet F Shelf 2 No. 67

Fowle, Daniel. Portsmouth, 1760:
Title: Preaching Christ the great business of the Gospel-Ministry.....By Samuel Haven.
Imprint: Portsmouth: Printed and sold by Daniel Fowle, 1760.

Half leather; 7¾ x 4-7/8 in. Evans 3, 8616; p.256.

IMPRINTS, United States.

Cabinet F Shelf 2 No. 70

Fowle, Daniel and Robert. Portsmouth, New Hampshire, 1765.
Title: An impartial examination of Mr. Robert Sandeman's letters on Theron and Aspasio.... By Samuel Langdon.
Imprint: Portsmouth,,in New Hampshire, N.E.: Printed by Daniel & Robert Fowle, MDCCLXV.

Cloth, 9 x 5½ in. Evans 4, 10035; p.19.

IMPRINTS, United States.

Cabinet F Shelf 1 No. 72

Franklin, B., and Hugh Merideth, Philadelphia, 1728.
Title: The History of the Rise, increase and progress of the Christian people called Quakers....by William Sewel.
Imprint: Philadelphia: Printed and sold by Samuel Keimer in Second Street, 1728.
This book was completed by Franklin and Meredith; their work commencing from page 533.

cont'd

IMPRINTS, United States. cont'd

Cabinet Shelf No.

Leather; 12 x 7⅜ in. Evans I, 3104; p.397.

IMPRINTS, United States

Cabinet F Shelf 1 No. 75

Franklin, Benjamin, Philadelphia, 1730
Title: Mystische und sehr geheyne spruche...
Imprint: Zu Philadelphia: Gedruckt bey B. Franklin in jahr 1730.

This is a reprint of the first printed book in the German language in America, and the earliest book with the imprint "B. Franklin"

Half morocco; 7½ x 5¼ in.

IMPRINTS, United States

Cabinet F Shelf 1 No. 79

Franklin, Benjamin. Philadelphia, 1742.
Title: The charters of the Province of Pensilvania and City of Philadelphia.
Imprint: Philadelphia. Printed and sold by B. Franklin.

Calf; 11½ x 7¼ x 1-7/8 in. Evans 2, 5033, p.217.

IMPRINTS, United States.

Cabinet R, Shelf 1, No. 94

Franklin, Benjamin. Passports printed by Benjamin Franklin on his Passy Press. Printed by Bruce Rogers for the William L. Clements Library, Ann Harbor, Nov., 1925. Three broadsides in facsimile.

Boards; $12\frac{1}{2}$ x $9\frac{1}{4}$ in.

IMPRINTS, United States.

Cabinet 86, Shelf 1, No. 3.01

Franklin, James, Newport, 1728.

Title: The Rhode Island Almanack for the year, 1728...Being the first ever published for that Meridian. By Poor Robin (J.F.)

Imprint: Newport, Printed and sold by James Franklin at his printing-house, etc. Facsimile, John Carter Brown Library, Providence, 1911).

Half morocco; $6\frac{1}{4}$ x 5 in.

IMPRINTS, United States.

Cabinet F, Shelf 3, No. 20

Gaine, Hugh: New York City. 1768.

Title: Every man his own lawyer...[By Jacob Giles.]

Imprint: New York: Printed by Hugh Gaine, printer, bookseller and stationer, at the Bible and the Crown, in Hanover Square. 1768.

Leather; $7\frac{1}{2}$ x 5 in. Evans, 4, 10935, p.136.

IMPRINTS, United States

Cabinet R, Shelf 1, No. 3

Franklin, Benjamin. Philadelphia, 1743.

Title: A proposal (of American Philosophical Society) for promoting useful knowledge among the British Plantations in America. Broadside (facsimile). Franklin was the writer and printer of this item.

Imprint: Benjamin Franklin, the writer of this proposal, offers himself to serve...Philadelphia, May 14, 1743.

In Volume "Frankliniana", p. 49.

IMPRINTS, United States

Cabinet F, Shelf 1, No. 69

Franklin, James. Newport, 1752.

Title: Catechism and confession of faith...

Imprint: Newport. Printed by James Franklin, at the Town-School-House.

Original leather; 6-1/8 x $4\frac{1}{4}$ x $\frac{1}{2}$ in. Not in Evans.

IMPRINTS, United States.

Cabinet F, Shelf 3, No. 22

Gaine, Hugh: New York City, 1785.

Title: Poems upon several occasions. By the Rev. Mr. John Pomfret...

Imprint: London printed: New York reprinted by Hugh Gaine, at the Bible, in Hanover Square. 1785.

Paper boards; $6\frac{1}{2}$ x 4 in. Evans 6, 19195, p.375.

IMPRINTS, United States

Cabinet F, Shelf 1, No. 81

Franklin, Benjamin. Philadelphia, 1744.

Title: M.T. Cicero's Cato Major, or his discourse of old age [Translated]. With explanatory notes [by James Logan].

Imprint: Philadelphia. Printed and sold by B. Franklin. 1744.

Gilt morocco; 8-1/8 x $5\frac{1}{2}$ x 3/8 in. Evans 2, 5361, p.258.

IMPRINTS, United States

Cabinet A, Shelf 3, No. 7

Franklin, James. Newport, R. I. 1760.

The Newport Mercury, March 11, 1760. No. 91

Imprint: Printed by J. Franklin.

Bound in with other newspapers; leaf 5.

IMPRINTS, United States

Cabinet II, Shelf 3, No. 35.01

Gales and Seaton. Washington, 1832.

See CHEROKEE NATION. Opinion of the Supreme Court of the United States...

IMPRINTS, United States

Cabinet 80, Shelf 1, No. 5

Franklin, Benjamin, Philadelphia, 1749

Title: Poor Richard Almanack...By Richard Saunders (Philom)

Imprint: Philadelphia: Printed and sold by B. Franklin, and D. Hall.

Facsimile reprint of this almanac.

With other items in manila envelope

IMPRINTS, United States

Cabinet R, Shelf 3, No. 155

Franklin, James .. Newport, 1828.

Title: Rhode-Island Almanack ... By Poor Robin [A facsimile].

Imprint: Printed and sold by J. Franklin, at his Printing-House ... near the Union-Flag Tavern, 1728.

Half morocco; $8\frac{1}{4}$ x 5 in.

IMPRINTS, United States

Cabinet G, Shelf 5, No. 24

Garnett, Porter (Press of H.S. Crocker Co., San Francisco, Calif., 1920.

Title: (2) Memorials

Imprint: Press of H.S. Crocker Co. Inc. San Francisco. Decorations and typography by Porter Garnett.

Brochures, in envelope.

IMPRINTS, United States

Cabinet F, Shelf 1, No. 65

Franklin, James. Boston, 1718.

Title: A sermon delivered by Thomas Prince M.A. at his ordination...Together with the charge of Increase Mather.

Imprint: Boston. Printed by J. Franklin for S. Gerrish, and sold at his shop near the Old Meeting House, 1718.

Paper boards, leather back; 7-3/8 x 5-1/8 in. Evans 1, 1996, p.269.

IMPRINTS, United States

Cabinet R, Shelf 2, No. 92

Franklin Printing Company. Philadelphia, 1914.

Title: The Youthful Franklin ... By James M. Beck, LL.D.

Imprint: Printed at the shop of Franklin Printing Company: Founded by Benjamin Franklin in 1727. Philadelphia, U.S.A.

Half morocco; $8\frac{3}{4}$ x $5\frac{1}{2}$ in.

IMPRINTS, United States.

Cabinet G, Shelf 2, No. 7

Geer, Elihu. Hartford, Conn. 1845.

Title: Transactions of the Hartford County Agricultural Society for 1843 and 1844.

Imprint: Hartford: Press of Elihu Geer, 26 State St. 1845.

Paper; 9 x 5-5/8 in.

IMPRINTS, United States

Cabinet F, Shelf 1, No. 68

Franklin, James. Boston, 1721.

Title: English liberties, or the free-born's subject's inheritence...Compiled by Henry Care.

Imprint: Boston. Printed by J. Franklin for N. Buttolph and D. Henchman, and sold at their shops. 1721.

Calf; $6\frac{1}{2}$ x 4-1/8 in. Evans 1, 2208, p.292.

IMPRINTS, United States.

Cabinet G, Shelf 2, No. 5

Fry & Kammerer, Philadelphia, 1807. The Columbiad. A poem. Illus. Steel Engravings.

The earliest American book which may be classed as "fine." The types were specially designed for it on a new body which was named Columbian = 16 point, H.L.B.

Full mor. $11\frac{1}{4}$ x $9\frac{1}{2}$ ins., $1\frac{1}{2}$ in. thick, pp. (XVI) 454

IMPRINTS, United States.

Cabinet G, Shelf 2, No. 8

Georgian Press, The. New York, 1927. B.R. America's typographic playboy, by Carl Purington Rollins, M.A., Printed by Richard W. Ellis. Illus.

Boards, 8 x $5\frac{1}{4}$ ins., pp. 13 (2)

IMPRINTS, United States

Cabinet G Shelf 2 No. 8

Georgian Press (Richard W. Ellis), Westport, Connecticut, 1928.
Title: A note on the Georgian Press, June, 1928.

On last page of this small folder, A.L.S.

Item in manila envelope.

IMPRINTS, Unites States

Cabinet S Shelf 2 No. 37

Gilliss Press, New York, 1899.
Title: Sextodecimos et Infra. By W. A. Loring. New York, 1899.
Colophon: The Gilliss Press device.

Paper, gilt; $7\frac{3}{8}$ x 4-5/8 in.

IMPRINTS, United States

Cabinet S Shelf 2 No. 38

Gilliss Press, The. New York, 1902

See Gilliss, Walter. Story of a motto...

IMPRINTS, United States.

Cabinet G Shelf 2 No. 9

Gillis Press, The, Walter Gillis, New York, 1923. The culprit fay and other poems by J. Rodman Drake, New York, The Grolier Club, MCMXXIII. Illus.

Paper bds., 9 x 6 ins., $\frac{1}{4}$ in. thick, pp. XV (1) 49.

IMPRINTS, United States.

Cabinet G Shelf 2 No. 10

Ginn & Company, Boston, The New England Primer. Twentieth Century reprint, n.d. Illus.

Boards, 5 x $3\frac{1}{2}$ ins., pp.72, not numbered.

IMPRINTS, United States

Cabinet G Shelf 4 No. 54

Golden Eagle Press (The) S. A. Jacobs. Fleetwood, Mount Vernon, New York, 1935.
Title: The Count. By Joseph Kling.
Imprint: Fleetwood, Mt. Vernon, N. Y. 1935.

One hundred copies printed.

Boards; $6\frac{1}{2}$ x $4\frac{1}{2}$ in.

IMPRINTS, United States.

Cabinet G Shelf 2 No. 11

Goudy, Fred W. and Bertha. The Village Press. Park Ridge, Ill. Dec., 1903. The Blessed Damosel, by Dante G. Rossetti. Reprinted from the Germ for February M.DCCC.L. Printed and bound by F. and B. Goudy.

Parchment covered bds. $6\frac{1}{4}$ x 4 ins., pp.16, (2) plates. 2 copies. Another copy for 1905 with hand colored initials, head and tail pieces.

IMPRINTS, United States.

Cabinet G Shelf 2 No. 12

Goudy, Fred W. and Will H. Ransom. The Village Press. Park Ridge, Illinois, 1903. Printing: An essay by William Morris and Emery Walker.

Boards, $9\frac{1}{4}$ x 7 ins., pp.17.

IMPRINTS, United States.

Cabinet G Shelf 2 No. 14

Goudy, Fred W. and Bertha. Village Press. Hingham, Mass., Nov., 1904. Good king Wenceslas: A carol by Dr. Neal. Pictures by Arthur Gaskin. Reprinted from the edition issued by Cornish Brothers. Double border and title from drawings by Will Dwiggins.

Boards $6\frac{1}{4}$ x 5 ins., pp.20.

IMPRINTS, United States.

Cabinet G Shelf 2 No. 13

Goudy, Fred W. and Bertha. The Village Press. Hingham, Mass., 1904. Rabbi Ben Ezra, by Robert Browning. Printed by hand. Frontispiece and decorations designed and cut on wood by Will Dwiggins.

Boards, 8 x 5-1/8 ins., pp (2) 24.

IMPRINTS, United States.

Cabinet G Shelf 2 No. 16

Goudy, Fred W. and Bertha. The Village Press, Hingham, Mass., 1904. The ninety-first psalm Reprinted from the text of the authorized version of the English Bible. Rubricated.

Boards, 4 x $3\frac{1}{4}$ ins., lvs. 10.

IMPRINTS, United States.

Cabinet G Shelf 2 No. 18

Goudy, Fred W. and Bertha, Village Press, Hingham, Mass., 1905. Lyf of Seynt Kenelme from Caxton's Golden Legend. With drawings taken from "The Quest."

Boards, $6\frac{1}{2}$ x 5 ins., pp.16.

IMPRINTS, United States.

Cabinet G Shelf 2 No. 17

Goudy, Fred W. and Bertha. The Village Press, Hingham, Mass., 1905. Massachusetts an old and prosperous democracy; An address by Charles W. Eliot.

Boards 6 x $4\frac{3}{4}$ ins., pp.16.

IMPRINTS, United States.

Cabinet G1 Shelf 5 No. 7

Goudy, Frederick W. and Bertha S. The Village Press, New York, 1911. The door in the wall, and other stories by H.G. Wells. This book has been set by B. Goudy, with types and decorations designed by F. Goudy, under whose supervision it has been printed by Norman T.A. Munder & Co., Baltimore, Photogravures from photographs.

Boards; 15 x $11\frac{1}{4}$ ins., pp.153.

IMPRINTS, United States.

Cabinet G Shelf 5 No. 8

Goudy, Frederick W. and Bertha M., New York City, 1919. Art and the great war. By A.E. Gallatin. This book has been set by Bertha M. Goudy from types and decorations designed by F. W. Goudy and printed in the shop of William E. Rudge. Engravings by the Beck Engraving Co. 100 illus.

Full morocco; $15\frac{1}{2}$ x 12 ins., pp.288.

IMPRINTS, United States.

Cabinet G Shelf 2 No. 15

Goudy, Fred W. and Bertha. The Village Press, Park Ridge, Ill., 1924. A dissertation upon Roast Pig. by Charles Lamb. Printed in the Village Type - the third book issued from the Press.

Boards $6\frac{1}{4}$ x $4\frac{1}{2}$, pp.52.

IMPRINTS, United States.

Cabinet G Shelf 2 No. 19

Goudy, Fred and Bertha, Village Press, Marlborough-on-Hudson, New York, 1924. Three Essays, by Augustine Birrell. Composed by Mrs. Goudy with types designed by Mr.Goudy.

Boards, $11\frac{3}{4}$ x $8\frac{1}{2}$ ins., pp.XVI.

IMPRINTS, United States

Cabinet S Shelf 6 No. 15

Government Printing Office, (George Henry Carter, Public Printer), Washington, D. C. 1932.

see ASHLEY, FREDERICK W. (The) Vollbehr Incunabula and the Book of Books...

IMPRINTS, United States

Cabinet S Shelf 4 No. 26

Grabhorn, Florence and Edwin, Indianapolis, The Studio Press. 1918.
Title: Typography of Shakspere's Midsommer Nightes Dreame. By Mark Harvey Liddell.
Colophon: Printed in the City of Indianapolis, U.S.A. by Florence and Edwin Grabhorn at Their shop, The Studio this 10th Oct. 1918.

Half morocco; 7-7/8 x $5\frac{3}{4}$ x $\frac{1}{4}$ in.

IMPRINTS, United States.

Cabinet G Shelf 2 No. 23

Grabhorn, Edwin and Robert, San Francisco, 1921. To a girl dancing, by George Sterling.

Boards, $10\frac{1}{4}$ x 7 ins., pp.8, not numbered.

IMPRINTS, United States.

Cabinet G Shelf 2 No. 30

Grabhorn Press. San Francisco, 1929.
Title: A letter written by Thomas Jefferson to his daughter Martha dated Nov. 28, 1783.
Colophon: Printed at the Grabhorn Press for Alfred Sutro ... for members of the Roxburgh Club of San Francisco.

Paper wrapper, $13\frac{1}{4}$ x 10-3/8 in.

IMPRINTS, United States.

Cabinet G Shelf 2 No. 20

Grabhorn, Edwin & Robert. Studio Press in Indianapolis, Dec., 1919. A defense of the dilettante, by G.C. Calvert. Rubricated initials.

This is the last work done at the Studio Press in Indianapolis - H.L.B.

Boards; $12\frac{1}{4}$ x 9 ins., pp.18.

IMPRINTS, United States.

Cabinet G Shelf 2 No. 26

Grabhorn, Edwin, The Grabhorn Press, San Francisco, 1924. Old French Title Pages, by Andrew Lang. Printed in San Francisco, Feb., 1924, for members of the American Institute of Graphic Arts, Wood-cuts and rubricated initials.

Boards $5\frac{3}{4}$ x 4 ins., pp.12.

IMPRINTS United States

Cabinet G Shelf 2 No. 31

Grabhorn, Edwin & Robert. San Francisco, 1930.
Title: Eden Anto. By Antonio Fogazzaro. Translated by Theo. Wesley Koch. The Roxburghe Club of San Francisco.
Colophon:...Printed in the month of June, 1930. by Edwin and Robert Grabhorn, members of the Club. The illustrations are by René Cockinga.

Paper boards with ribbon ties; $11\frac{1}{4}$ x $7\frac{3}{4}$ x $\frac{1}{4}$ in.

IMPRINTS, United States.

Cabinet G Shelf 2 No. 21

Grabhorn, Edwin and Robert, San Francisco, San Francisco, 1920. The Rill from the Town Pump, by Nathaniel Hawthorne, Vignette and head piece printed in blue.

Paper, $8\frac{1}{2}$ x $5\frac{1}{2}$ ins., 2 lvs., pp.16 (1).

IMPRINTS, United States.

Cabinet G Shelf 5 No. 9

Grabhorn, Edwin and Robert, San Francisco, 1926. The book of Job. Printed by E. and R. Grabhorn. Frontispiece by Valenti Angelo.

Boards, $17\frac{1}{4}$ x $11\frac{3}{4}$ ins., pp.XXIX.

IMPRINTS, United States.

Cabinet G Shelf 2 No. 31.01

Grabhorn, E. & R. San Francisco, 1931.
Title: The Santa Fe Trail to California, 1849-1852. The Journal and drawings of H.M.T. Powell. Edited by Douglas S. Watson.
Imprint: Three hundred copies printed for The Book Club of California by E. & R. Grabhorn. San Francisco, 1931.
With folded maps and plates.

Cloth, pigskin back; 16 x 9-3/8 x $1\frac{1}{2}$ in.

IMPRINTS, United States.

Cabinet G Shelf 2 No. 24

Grabhorn, Edwin & Robert, San Francisco, 1921. Early printing in America, a reprint from American Encyclopedia of Printing published in Phila. in 1871.

Boards, $8\frac{1}{2}$ x $5\frac{1}{2}$, pp.14.

IMPRINTS, United States.

Cabinet G Shelf 2 No. 27

Grabhorn Press, San Francisco, 1926. The Book of Ruth. Printed at the Grabhorn Press. Illuminated by Valenti Angelo.

Boards, $7\frac{1}{2}$ x $5\frac{3}{4}$ ins., pp.8, not numbered.

IMPRINTS, United States.

Cabinet G Shelf 2 No. 32

Grassby, Percy, Boston, 1915. Centenary 1825-1925. New Bedford Institution for Savings. Printed for private distribution. Typography and wood engravings, by Grassby.

Boards, $9\frac{1}{2}$ x $6\frac{1}{4}$ ins., pp.28 numbered, pp. 16, not numbered.

IMPRINTS, United States.

Cabinet G Shelf 2 No. 25

Grabhorn, Edwin & Robert, San Francisco, 1921. A gracious visitation by E.F. Dawson, with an appreciation by Ambrose Bierce. Printed for the Book Club of California.

Marbled Cloth, 9 x 6 ins., pp (6) 69.

IMPRINTS, United States.

Cabinet G Shelf 2 No. 28

Grabhorn, Edwin and Robert, San Francisco, 1927.
Title: A Journey to Lower Oregon & Upper California 1848-49. By Rev. Samuel C. Damon.
Colophon: Copies of this book printed for John J. Newbegin, San Francisco, in November M.CMXXVII, by Edwin, and Robert Grabhorn. Frontispiece and initials by Valenti Angelo.

Half calf; 10 x 7 x $\frac{3}{4}$ in.

IMPRINTS, United States

Cabinet F Shelf 1 No. 13

Green, Bartholomew: Boston, 1706.
Title: Considerations to prevent murmurings and promote patience in Christians...A lecture by Benj. Wadsworth.
Imprint: Boston. N. E. Printed by B. Green. Sold by Nicolas Boone at his shop. 1706.

Cloth case; 6 x $4\frac{1}{4}$ in. Evans I, 1282, p.186.

IMPRINTS, United States.

Cabinet G Shelf 2 No. 22

Grabhorn, Edwin and Robert. San Francisco, 1921. "Prayer" by C.K. Field. Printed for The Book Club of California.

Boards, 8 x $5\frac{1}{4}$ ins., pp.8, not numbered.

IMPRINTS, United States.

Cabinet G Shelf 2 No. 29

Grabhorn, Edwin and Robert: The Grabhorn Press. San Francisco, 1927.
Title: The Golden Touch. By Nathaniel Hawthorne. Printed by Edwin and Robert Grabhorn. April, 27. San Francisco. Drawings by Valenti Angelo.

Boards; $9\frac{1}{4}$ x 5-3/4 x $\frac{1}{4}$ in. In protective case.

IMPRINTS, United States

Cabinet F Shelf 1 No. 14

Green, Bartholomew. Boston, 1708.
Title: Sacremental meditations upon divers select places of Scriptures...John Flavel.
Imprint: Boston in N. E. 1708. Printed by B. Green, for Benj. Eliot, sold at his shop.

Leather; $5\frac{1}{2}$ x $3\frac{1}{2}$ in. Evans 1, 1351, p.195.

IMPRINTS, United States

Cabinet F · Shelf 1 · No. 15

Green, Bartholomew Jr. Boston, 1725.
Title: The reasonableness of reformation. By John Flavell.
Imprint: Boston, N. E. Reprinted by B. Green. Jun for D. Henchman at the shop at Cornhill, 1725.

Leather; $5\frac{1}{2}$ x $3\frac{1}{4}$ in. Evans I, 2634, p.342.

IMPRINTS, United States

Cabinet F · Shelf 1 · No. 17

Green, Bartholomew and Samuel Kneeland. Boston, 1726.
Title: A compleat body of Divinity...By Samuel Willard.
Imprint: Boston in New-England: Printed by B. Green and S. Kneeland for B. Eliot and D. Henchman, and sold at their shops. 1726.

Leather; $13\frac{1}{2}$ x $8\frac{1}{2}$ x 3 in. Evans 1, 2828. p.365.

IMPRINTS, United States

Cabinet F · Shelf 1 · No. 18

Green, Bartholomew. Boston, 1727.
Title: The duty of a people to pray to, and bless God for their Rulers...A sermon preached... in New England, May 31st, 1727.
Imprint: Boston in N.E. Printed by B. Green. Sold by Samuel Gerrish, at the lower end of Corn-hill, 1727.

Half morocco; 7 x $4\frac{1}{4}$ in. Evans 1, 2841, p.366.

IMPRINTS, United States

Cabinet F · Shelf 1 · No. 23

Green, Bushell and Allen. Boston, 1743.
Title: Marrow of modern divinity. By E. Fisher. Tenth edition.
Imprint: Boston. Printed by Green, Bushell, and Allen, for D. Henchman in Cornhill.

Leather; 5-3/4 x $3\frac{1}{2}$ in. Evans 2, 5182, p.236.

IMPRINTS, United States

Cabinet F · Shelf 1 · No. 22

Green (John). Bushell and [Bezoune] Allen. Boston, 1743.
Title: Some brief Sacramental meditations.
Imprint: Boston. Printed by Green, Bushell, and Allen, for D. Henchman, in Cornhill. 1743.

Leather; 5-7/8 x 4-7/8 x 7/8 in. Evans 2, 5315, p.253.

IMPRINTS, United States

Cabinet F · Shelf 1 · No. 31

Green, John and Joseph Russell. Boston, 1758.
Title: A rejoinder to the Reverend Mr. Robert Abercrombie...By B. J. Parsons and D. McGregore.
Imprint: Boston. Printed and sold by Green and Russell at their printing-office in Queen Street. 1758.

Half morocco; $7\frac{1}{2}$ x 5 in. Evans 3, 8224, p.207.

IMPRINTS, United States

Cabinet F · Shelf 1 · No. 37

Green, John, and Joseph Russell. Boston, 1761.
Title: Pietas et gratulatio Collegii Cantabrigiensis apud Novamglos.
Imprint: Bostoni-Massachusettensium. Typis J. Green et J. Russell. 1761.
This is the first printing with Greek types executed in the North American Colonies.

Full morocco; 10-1/8 x 8 in. Evans 3, 8877, p.286.

IMPRINTS, United States

Cabinet F · Shelf 1 · No. 9

Green, Samuel and Marmaduke Johnson. Cambridge, 1663.
Title: The first American Bible. A leaf [Original] from a copy translated into the Indian language by John Eliot. With an account of the two printers by George Parker Winship.
Imprint: Boston, Printed by D. B. Updike, 1929.

Stamped cloth; 7-7/8 x 6 x $\frac{1}{4}$ in.

IMPRINTS, United States

Cabinet F · Shelf 1 · No. 10

Green, Samuel. Cambridge, 1682.
Title: A seasonable discourse...by Urian Oakes, late pastor of the Church and president of Harvard College.
Imprint: Cambridge. Printed by Samuel Green, 1682.

Half morocco; $7\frac{1}{4}$ x $5\frac{5}{8}$ x 3/8 in. Evans 325, vol.1, p.54

IMPRINTS, United States.

Cabinet F · Shelf 2 · No. 92

Hall, Samuel: Boston, 1791.
Title: New version of the Psalms of David.... By N. Brady and N. Tate.
Imprint: Boston: Printed and sold by Samuel Hall, No.53 Cornhill. 1791.

Paper boards; $6\frac{1}{2}$ x $3\frac{1}{2}$ in. Not in Evans.

IMPRINTS, United States

Cabinet QQ · Shelf 4 · No. 8

Hall, Samuel, Boston, 1798.

see MASSACHUSETTS HISTORICAL SOCIETY. Collections...1835.

IMPRINTS, United States.

Cabinet G · Shelf 5 · No. 10

Hall (W.F.) Printing Company, Chicago, n.d. Research: A series of brochures on Chicago, its acticities and development. W.F. Hall Printing Company, Chicago. The world's greatest printing plant of catalogs and magazines Col. illus.

Paper, 16 x $12\frac{1}{4}$ ins., pp.8, not numbered.

IMPRINTS, United States

Cabinet PP · Shelf 4 · No. 23

Harbor Press, The, 142 East 32nd Street, New York.
Title: Extracts from the diary of Roger Payne.
Imprint: New York. The Harbor Press, 1928.

Printed for the members of the American Institute of Graphic Arts.

Boards; $7\frac{3}{4}$ x $4\frac{3}{4}$ x $\frac{1}{4}$ in.

IMPRINTS, United States.

Cabinet G · Shelf 5 · No. 20

Harper & Bros., New York, 1846. Illuminated Bible containing the old and new testaments. Embellished with sixteen hundred historical engravings by J. A. Adams, more than fourteen hundred of which are from original designs by J. G. Chapman.

Embossed morocco; $13\frac{1}{2}$ x 10 x 3 in.

IMPRINTS, United States

Cabinet EE · Shelf 4 · No. 63 Also 64 Dupl.

Hart, Francis. New York, 1860.

See HOE, ROBERT. (Catalogue and price list, 1860).

IMPRINTS, United States

Cabinet L · Shelf 5 · No. 25

Hart, Francis and Company, New York City, 1871.
Title: The printers' price list...By Theo. L. DeVinne.
Imprint: New York: Francis Hart and Company, 63 Cortland St.

Leather; $7\frac{1}{2}$ x 5-1/8 x 1 in.

IMPRINTS, United States.

Cabinet G · Shelf 2 · No. 34

Harvard University Press, Cambridge,1923. Doctor Johnson: A study in eighteenth century humanism. By Percy Hazen Houston. Portrait.

Cloth and boards, $9\frac{3}{4}$ x $6\frac{1}{2}$ ins., pp.28.

IMPRINTS, United States.

Cabinet 67 · Shelf 1 · No. 0.1

Harvard University Press, Cambridge, Mass., 1925.
Bruce Rogers, Designer of books. With a list of books printed under Mr. Rogers' supervision. By Frederic Warde.

Includes facsimile pages, borders, decorations, initials, etc.

Linen covered boards, 9 x 6 ins., pp.74, and 17? plates.

IMPRINTS, United States

Cabinet G Shelf 2 No. 34.01

Harvard University Press. Cambridge, 1927-28

See BIBLIOGRAPHY OF PRINTING. Harvard University Press...

IMPRINTS, United States.

Cabinet G Shelf 2 No. 38

Herrin News Shop: Violet & Hal Trovillion. Herrin, Illinois, 1930.
Title: Another Tussie-Mussie, collection of flower and garden sentiments in prose and verse.
Colophon: Set and printed in the City of Herrin Illinois at the shop of the Herrin News ...

Paper boards; 7 x 4-3/8 in.

IMPRINTS, United States.

Cabinet G Shelf 2 No. 42

Hunter, Dard. Marlborough-on-Hudson, 1916. The etching of contemporary life, by F. Weitenkampf. With an original etching by Ernest D. Roth. The paper was made by Dard Hunter who himself, designed the type face, cut the punches in steel, struck the matrices, and cast the types in a hand mould.

Boards, 12 x 8½ ins., pp.6, not numbered.

IMPRINTS, United States

Cabinet G Shelf 2 No. 35

Hayek, Henry R. Portland, Oregon, 1928.
Title: Between the golden Sun. By Henry R. Hayek.
Imprint facing title: Press of Henry R. Hayek. 311 Pine Street, Portland, Oregon. His mark.

With a special tribute to Henry Lewis Bullen from the author "In appreciation...of the great service he has rendered the printers of America"...
Paper over boards; 12-3/4 x 9-3/4 x ½ in.

IMPRINTS, United States.

Cabinet G Shelf 2 No. 39

Highton, Alexander G., Newark, New Jersey. Refined printing for advertising purposes. with specimens of work, n.d.

Boards, 8¾ x 5½ ins., pp.8. In envelope

IMPRINTS, United States

Cabinet C Shelf 1 No. 24

Hutchings Printing House, Hartford, Conn, 1871.

See MALLORY, WHEELER AND COMPANY. Catalogue of door knobs...

IMPRINTS, United States.

Cabinet G Shelf 2 No. 36

Heintzemann Press, Boston, Mass.,1917. Our family-fireside commencement: An American message of Christmas good cheer. By Brad Stephens. Gift book, published by Print, Brad Stephens & Company, and the Heintzemann Press.

Boards, 6 x 4½ ins., pp.12.

IMPRINTS, United States.

Cabinet G Shelf 2 No. 40

Hollenbeck Press, The. Indianapolis, founded M.DCCC.LXVII (1867). The unseen specification. Second printing.

Boards, paper back, 5¾ x 4¼ ins., pp.15.

IMPRINTS, United States.

Cabinet S Shelf 4 No. 94

Imperial Press, [George French], Cleveland, 1903.
Title: Printing in relation to graphic art. By George French.
Imprint: Cleveland: The Imperial Press.

Boards; 8¼ x 5¼ x 5/8 in.

IMPRINTS, United States

Cabinet F Shelf 1 No. 25

Henchman, Daniel Boston, 1737.
Title: A faithful servant of Christ described and rewarded...Tuesday lecture in Harvard College. By Edward Wigglesworth.
Imprint: Boston. Printed for D. Henchman, 1737.

Half morocco; 7-3/4 x 4½ in. Evans 2, 4209, p.121

IMPRINTS, United States

Cabinet 80 Shelf 1 No. 14

House, E.G. Boston, 1809-1815.

See ALMANACS. United States. Farmer's Almanac...E.G. House, Printer.

IMPRINTS, United States

Cabinet II Shelf 3 No. 31

Indian Territory: Park Hill: Mission Press, 1850.

See BIBLES. Cherokee...Fifth edition. 1850.

IMPRINTS, United States

Cabinet F Shelf 1 No. 25.01

Henchman, D. Boston, 1746.
Title:...A sermon at the South Church in Boston Nov. 27, 1746. By Thomas Prince.
Imprint: Boston. Printed for D. Henchman in Cornhill, 1746.

Half morocco; 8 x 6 in.

IMPRINTS, United States

Cabinet QQ Shelf 2 No. 19

Hubbard, Elbert (The Roycrofters), East Aurora, 1911.
Title: One thousand and one epigrams selected from the writings of Elbert Hubbard.
Colophon:..Evolved in idle moments by Fra Albertus, and gathered together and done into a printed volume by the Roycrofters at their shop, at East Aurora, 1911.

Tooled morocco; 6 x 4½ x ½ in.

IMPRINTS, United States

Cabinet S Shelf 2 No. 3

Inslee, Samuel and Anthony Car. New York City, 1772.
Title: The American Village. A poem by Philip Freneau. [Facsimile].
Imprint: New York: Printed by S. Inslee and A. Car, on Moor's Wharf, 1772.

Half vellum; 9 x 6-3/4 in.

IMPRINTS, United States

Cabinet G Shelf 2 No. 37

Herrin News Press, The. Hal W. Trovillion. Herrin, Ill. 1928. Favorite Fragments: Being a collection of inspiring passages and sentiments. Printer Mark.
Colophon:...Set and printed in the city of Herrin, Illinois, at the shop of The Herrin News. Dec. MCMXXVIII for Violet and Hal W. Trovillion and type distributed. signed copy.

Paper over boards; 6-7/8 x 4½ x 3/8 in.

IMPRINTS, United States.

Cabinet G Shelf 2 No. 41

Hunt, Haywood H., Printer, San Francisco, 1921. "Castles," Being a Christmas thought by Charles Dickens. Decorations by W.F.Rauschnabel. Designed and privately printed from handset Cloister Old Style Type. Brochure.

9¼ x 6 ins., pp.12, not numbered.

IMPRINTS, United States.

Cabinet G Shelf 2 No. 43

Japan Paper Co., New York, 1921. Privately printed books and their personal value as Christmas gifts.

Boards, 8 x 6 ins., pp (1) 7 (1)

IMPRINTS, United States.

Cabinet G Shelf 2 No. 44

Japan Paper Company, New York, 1927. Outlanders, whence come ye last? by William Morris. Privately printed, Christmas, 1927.

Boards, 7¾ x 5 ins., pp.8 not numbered.

IMPRINTS, United States.

Cabinet G Shelf 2 No. 45

Jaquish, O. W., designer of calendars, books, etc. New York, n.d. The origin of registering days: Calendars, Brochure, Illus.

Paper brochure; 5½ x 4-1/8 in.

IMPRINTS, United States.

Cabinet G Shelf 2 No. 46

Johnson, Henry Lewis. The Graphic Arts Company, Boston, Mass., 1917. President Wilson's were message to the senate. April 2, 1917.

Boards; 9 x 6 in.

IMPRINTS, United States

Cabinet F Shelf 1 No. 71

Keimer, Samuel. Philadelphia, 1720-1721.
Title: The Independent Whig [No.1, Jan. 20, 1720; No.53, Jan. 4, 1721].
Reprinted from the London edition [Thomas Gordon], in weekly numbers.

Marbled boards; 8 x 6 x 7/8 in. Evans 1, 2536, p.331.

IMPRINTS, United States.

Cabinet F Shelf 1 No. 72

Keimer, Samuel, Philadelphia, 1728.

See Early Printing in Pennsylvania. Philadelphia, 1728: Samuel Keimer.

IMPRINTS, United States

Cabinet Q Shelf 1 No. 8

Kellogg, Andrew H., New York, 1903.
Title: Three centuries of English booktrade bibliography. By A. Growoll. New York: Published for The Dibdin Club.

Half morocco; 9¾ x 6¼ x 1 in.

IMPRINTS, United States.

Cabinet G Shelf 2 No. 47

King, Geo. W. & Son. Worcester, Mass. 1930.
Title: He Is Nothing But A Boy. By Unknown Author.
Colophon:... printed at "The Home of Distinctive Printing." Geo. W. King & Son, whose press is located in Worcester, Massachusetts.

Paper boards; 5¾ x 3-1/8 in.

IMPRINTS, United States.

Cabinet G Shelf 2 No. 56

Kettredge, W.A. Oswald Press, New York, 1917. The Allyn Family. A Genealogical and historical sketch. Privatley printed, Illus.

Embossed coat of arms on board cover, 10½ x 7-3/4 ins., pp.20 with 5 plates.

IMPRINTS, United States

Cabinet F Shelf 1 No. 34

Kneeland, Daniel and John. Boston, 1760.
Title: A sermon after the death of Mr. John Noyes. By Jedidiah Jewett.
Imprint: Boston. Printed by D. and J. Kneeland in Queen Street.

Half leather; 7 x 4-5/8 in. Not in Evans.

IMPRINTS, United States.

Cabinet F Shelf 1 No. 35

Kneeland, Daniel and John. Boston, 1763.

Title: A new version of the Psalms of David....
Imprint: Boston: Printed by D. and J. Kneeland, for J. Edwards, in Corn-Hill. MDCCLXIII.

Leather; 6 x 3-5/8 x 1-1/8 in. Evans, 3, 9344; p.345.

IMPRINTS, United States.

Cabinet F Shelf 1 No. 43

Kneeland, John and Seth Adams. Boston,1769.

Title: A discourse occasioned by the death of the Reverend Dr. Joseph Sewall....By Charles Chauncy, Pastor of the First Church in Boston.
Imprint: Boston, N.E. Printed and sold by Kneeland and Adams, in Milk Street, MDCCLXIX.

Half leather; 7¼ x 4½ in. Evans 3, 11206; p.170.

IMPRINTS, United States.

Cabinet F Shelf 1 No. 28

Kneeland, Samuel. Boston, 1752.

Title: A defence of the Divine Right of infant baptism....By Peter Clark, A.M. Pastor of a Church in Salem.
Imprint: Boston, New England: Printed and sold by S. Kneeland, in Queen Street. 1752.

Leather; 7¾ x 4-7/8 x 1-3/8 in. Evans?

IMPRINTS, United States.

Cabinet F Shelf 1 No. 39

Kneeland, Samuel. Boston, 1763.

Title: Animadversions on the Reverend Mr. Croswell's late letter....By A. Cumming, A.M.
Imprint: Boston: Printed and sold by S. Kneeland in Queen Street, M.DCC,LXIII.

Half leather; 7¼ x 5 in. Evans?

IMPRINTS, United States

Cabinet F Shelf 1 No. 20

Kneeland, Samuel and Timothy (2) Green. Boston, 1741.
Title: An answer to the Rev. Mr. Garden's three letters to Mr. Whitefield.
Imprint: Boston. Printed and sold by S. Kneeland and T. Green, over against the prison in Queenstreet. 1741.

Half morocco; 7¼ x 4½ in. Evans 2, 4705. p.179.

IMPRINTS, United States

Cabinet F Shelf 1 No. 25.01

Kneeland, S. and T. Green. Boston, 1746.

See PRINCE, THOMAS.. Sermon delivered in Boston, August 14, 1746.

IMPRINTS, UNITED STATES

Cabinet K Shelf 1 No. 26

Knickerbocker Press, The: G. B. Putnam's Sons. New York, 1894.
Title: The Egyptian Book of the Dead... By Charles H. S. Davis.
Imprint: Electrotyped, printed and bound by The Knickerbocker Press, New York, G. B. Putnam's Sons.

Cloth; 17½ x 12½ in.

IMPRINTS, United States.

Cabinet G Shelf 5 No. 11

Laboratory Press, The. Pittsburgh, Pa. v.d.
Collection of brochures and broadsides.

Boards; 17½ x 13-3/8 in.

IMPRINTS, United States.

Cabinet G Shelf 2 No. 50

Laboratory Press, The. Pittsburgh, Pa. 1929
Title: The outlook for typography. By Daniel Berkeley Updike.
Imprint: Pittsburgh. The Laboratory Press.

Boards; 8¼ x 5¾ in.

IMPRINTS, United States.

Cabinet G Shelf 2 No. 49

Laboratory Press, The: Carnegie Institute of Technology. Pittsburgh, Pa. 1929.
Title: A Prayer for Fools ... By Giovanni Papini..
Imprint: Pittsburgh. The Laboratory Press 1929.

Boards; $9\frac{1}{4}$ x $6\frac{1}{4}$ in.

IMPRINTS, United States.

Cabinet G Shelf 2 No. 51

Laboratory Press, The. Pittsburgh, Pa. 1929.
Title: Tsang-Lang discourse on poetry. Yen Yu
Imprint: Pittsburgh. The Laboratory Press, 1929.

Boards; 9-5/8 x $6\frac{1}{2}$ in.

IMPRINTS, United States.

Cabinet G Shelf 2 No. 52

Laboratory Press, The. Pittsburgh, Pa. 1929.
Title: Two passages from the journal of Henry Marston ...
Imprint: Pittsburgh. The Laboratory Press, 1929.

Boards; 9-7/8 x 7 in.

IMPRINTS, United States.

Cabinet G Shelf 2 No. 48

Laboratory Press, The: Carnegie Institute of Technology. Pittsburgh, Pa. 1929.
Title: What the "L" books of 1923 looked like to Carl Purrington Rollins.
Imprint: The Laboratory Press: Pittsburgh.

Boards; 7 x $5\frac{1}{2}$ x $\frac{1}{4}$ in.

IMPRINTS, United States

Cabinet G Shelf 2 No. 53

Laboratory Press, The. (Porter Garnett) Pittsburgh, 1930.
Title: Selections from Poe's Marginalia.
Imprint: Pittsburg, the Laboratory Press.
Colophon: Printed on hand press by students. Type: Caslon Old Face, and a version of French Taille-Douce by the American Type Founders Co.
Presentation copy.

Boards; $8\frac{1}{2}$ x 6 in.

IMPRINTS, United States.

Cabinet G Shelf 2 No. 55

Laboratory Press (The), Porter Garnett, Carnegie Institute of Technology. Pittsburg, Pa.
Title: What is it? An aesthetical investigation to which is added some "Donts" for beginners and others. By Porter Garnett.
Imprint: Pittsburg. The Laboratory Press, 1931.

Boards; 7-3/4 x 5-5/8 in.

IMPRINTS, United States

Cabinet G Shelf 2 No. 55.01

Laboratory Press, Carnegie Institute of Technology, Pittsburgh, Pa. 1934
Title: The fine book, a symposium...Edited with an introduction bu Porter Garnett.
Imprint: Pittsburg: The Laboratory Press. M.CM. XXlV.

Morocco; $8\frac{1}{4}$ x $5\frac{1}{4}$ in.

IMPRINTS, United States

Cabinet G Shelf 4 No. 53

Laboratory Press (Carnegie Institute of Technology), Porter Garnett, Pittsburgh, Pa. 1935
Title: A conspectus of type design from 1454 to the present day.
Pamphlet.

In envelope.

IMPRINTS, United States

Cabinet G Shelf 4 No. 53.01

Laboratory Press (Porter Garnett), Pittsburgh, Pa., 1935.
Title: A Laboratory Press Anthology [Unfinished] Compiled by Porter Garnett.
Imprint: Pittsburgh: The Laboratory Press, 1935.

Boards: $9\frac{1}{2}$ x $6\frac{1}{2}$ in.

IMPRINTS, United States.

Cabinet G Shelf 2 No. 64

Lakeside Press, The, R.R. Donnelley & Sons Co. Chicago. Humanist Sermons, edited by Curtis W. Reese.

Boards, cloth back; 8-3/4 x $5\frac{1}{2}$ ins., 1-1/8 in. thick. pp.261.

IMPRINTS

Cabinet U Shelf 2 No. 4

Lakeside Press. Donnelley, R.R. & Sons Company. Chicago, Ill. 1901.
Title: Thomas Berthelet, royal printer and bookbinder to Henry VIII...By Cyril Davenport.
Imprint: Printed for the Caxton Club by R.R. Donnelley & Sons Company at the Lakeside Press, Chicago.

Boards; $12\frac{1}{2}$ x $9\frac{3}{4}$ in.

IMPRINTS, United States.

Cabinet G Shelf 2 No. 57

Lakeside Press (The), Chicago, 1912. The Squire's recipes. A reprint of an old volume issued for the Brothers of the Book.

Boards, mor. back, 6 x $4\frac{1}{2}$ ins., pp.25, not numbered. 5 blank.

IMPRINTS, United States.

Cabinet G Shelf 2 No. 59

Lakeside Press, The, R.R. Donnelley & Sons Company, Chicago, 1925. Great University Memorials: With a reference to plans for the development of the University of Chicago, Illus.

Boards, $11\frac{1}{2}$ x $10\frac{1}{2}$ in., pp.29 with 14 plates not numbered.

IMPRINTS, United States.

Cabinet G Shelf 2 No. 61

Lakeside Press, The. R.R. Donnelley & Sons Co., Chicago, 1925. Palmer House, Old and new, an historical sketch, by Wallace Rice, Illus.

Boards; 11 x $8\frac{1}{4}$ ins., pp.60.

IMPRINTS, United States.

Cabinet G Shelf 2 No. 60

Lakeside Press, The. R.R. Donnelley & Sons Co., Chicago, 1925. Sketches of speeches by David R. Fargan. Privately printed.

Cloth, $8\frac{1}{4}$ x $5\frac{3}{4}$ ins., pp.221.

IMPRINTS, United States.

Cabinet G Shelf 2 No. 58

Lakeside Press (The), 1925. R.R. Donnelley & Sons Company, Chicago. Tamarit, Some notes concerning this historical Catalonian Town, privately printed. Illus.

Buckram, 14 x 10 ins., pp.89.

IMPRINTS, United States.

Cabinet G Shelf 2 No. 63

Lakeside Press, The, R.R. Donnelley & Sons Co., Chicago, 1926. The Florentine Book Fair, The book section of the Exposition of decorative arts. Notes gathered by T.W. Koch, Colored reproductions, wood blocks, etchings etc.

Cover, paper $6\frac{1}{2}$ x 5 ins., pp.121.,

IMPRINTS, United States.

Cabinet G Shelf 2 No. 62

Lakeside Press, The. R.R. Donnelley & Sons Co. Chicago, 1926. Reading,a vice or a virtue? 15 reproductions from etchings, paintings, wood blocks, pencil drawings, and pen-and-ink sketches. Brochure.

$6\frac{1}{2}$ x $4\frac{1}{4}$ ins., pp.54.

IMPRINTS, United States.

Cabinet G Shelf 2 No. 66

Lakeside Press, The, R.R. Donnelley & Sons Co. Chicago, 1927. Foot Prints, by H.R.Hamilton. Privately printed.

Cloth, 8 x $5\frac{1}{4}$ ins., pp.220.

IMPRINTS, United States

Cabinet G Shelf 2 No. 69.01

Lakeside Press, R.R. Donnelley & Sons Company, Chicago, Ill., 1935

Title: Catalogue of a loan exhibition of drawings and paintings by Grant Wood.

Brochure, $7\frac{1}{4}$ x 6-3/8 in.

IMPRINTS, United States

Cabinet PP Shelf 4 No. 29

Literary Collector Press, The. Greenwich, Conn., 1905.

Title: Bookbinding for bibliophiles...By Fletcher Battershall.

Imprint: Greenwich, Conn: The Literary Collector Press, 1905.

Boards; 9 x 6 in.

IMPRINTS, United States.

Cabinet G Shelf 2 No. 65

Lakeside Press, The. R.R. Donnelley & Sons Company, Chicago, 1927. The point of view; An anthology of religion, from the works of Paul Carus.

Boards, $7\frac{1}{4}$ x 5 ins., $\frac{3}{4}$ in. thick, pp.211.

IMPRINTS, United States

Cabinet QQ Shelf 4 No. 37

Landis, David Bachman, Lancaster, Pa., 1914.

see LANDIS, DAVID BACHMAN. Lancaster Lyrics...

IMPRINTS, United States.

Cabinet G Shelf 5 No. 12

Little, J. J. New York, 1898.

Title: Catalogue de Luxe of the modern masterpieces gathered by the late connoisseur, William H. Stewart ... The American Art Association, 1898.

Imprint: J. J. Little & Co., Astor Place, New York.

Cloth; $14\frac{1}{2}$ x $11\frac{1}{4}$ x 1 in.

IMPRINTS, United States.

Cabinet G Shelf 2 No. 67

Lakeside Press, The. R.R. Donnelley & Sons Co., Chicago, 1928. A tour through time colony. The story of the New Ford Car. Announcing the New Ford Car. Who pays for economical planning? Booklets.

IMPRINTS, United States

Cabinet G Shelf 4 Number 54

Lauck, Harold. Lexington, Va.
Two items, pamphlets, 1932 and 1934.

I: In praise of print. By Frederick W. Ashley.

II: "A look back". The story of the Vollbehr Collection of Incunabula.

In envelope.

IMPRINTS, United States.

Cabinet G Shelf 2 No. 70

Lord Baltimore Press, The. Baltimore, Md., 19[illegible]. Human interest stories as told by an employing printer, Nathan Billstein. Brochure.

Boards, $7\frac{1}{4}$ x $4\frac{3}{4}$ ins., pp.25.

IMPRINTS, United States

Cabinet G Shelf 2 No. 68

Lakeside Press, R.R. Donnelley & Sons, Chicago, 1929.

Title: Charles Nodier. Francesco Colonna. A fanciful tale of the writing of the Hypnerotomachia translated by Theodore Wesley Koch.

Imprint: Chicago, privately printed 1929.

Colophon: Printed by R.R. Donnelley & Sons Company at the Lakeside Press.

Cloth; $9\frac{1}{2}$ x $6\frac{1}{2}$ in. In protective case.

IMPRINTS, United States.

Cabinet F Shelf 2 No. 86

Leverett, Thomas: Boston, 1775.

Title: A discourse preached December 15, 1774... By William Gordon.

Imprint: Boston: Printed for and sold by Thomas Leverett, in Corn-Hill. 1775.

Half morocco; 7 x $4\frac{3}{4}$ in. Evans 5, 14073, p.136.

IMPRINTS, United States

Cabinet R Shelf 1 No. 68

Los Angeles Club of Printing House Craftsmen, 1935.

see CLARY, WILLIAM W. Franklin, B...

IMPRINTS, United States.

Cabinet G Shelf 2 No. 68.01

Lakeside Press, R. R. Donnelley & Sons Co. Chicago, Ill. (William A. Kittredge, typographer). 1929.

Title: Log of the Auxiliary Schooner Yacht "Northern Light." ...Alaska-Arctic Expeditior 1927.

Imprint: Privately printed. Chicago: 1929. (This book is a printer's sample. Not for publication. Presentation Copy.)

Cloth; $11\frac{1}{2}$ x $8\frac{1}{2}$ x $1\frac{1}{4}$ in.

IMPRINTS, United States

Cabinet G Shelf 4 No. 30.01

Limited Edition Club, New York, 1929. The Monthly Letter of.

Folder, in manila envelope.

IMPRINTS, United States

Cabinet S Shelf 1 No. 112

Ludlow Typograph Company. Chicago, Ill. 1928

Title: The last will and testament of the late Nicolas Jenson ... Venice, Sept., A.D. 1480.

Colophon: ... This book is Ludlow-set in a new type designed by Ernst Detterer ... and printed by the Ludlow Typograph Company of Chicago, Nov., 1928.

Boards; $11\frac{1}{2}$ x 8 in.

IMPRINTS, United States

Cabinet G Shelf 2 No. 69

Lakeside Press, The R.R. Donnelley & Sons. Co. Chicago, Ill. 1930.

Title: Pattie's personal narrative.

Imprint: Chicago. The Lakeside Press, R.R. Donnelley & Sons Co. Christmas, 1930.

Cloth; 6-7/8 x $4\frac{1}{4}$ x $1\frac{1}{2}$ in.

IMPRINTS, United States

Cabinet M Shelf 5 No. 60

Limited Editions Club, New York and London. 1935-36.

Samples: A book containing many fine pages from the books to be published by the L. E. C. in its Seventh Series, with a note on Book Collecting by Sinclair Lewis.

Spiral binding, paper; 13-5/8 x $9\frac{1}{2}$ in.

IMPRINTS, United States

Cabinet G Shelf 2 No. 76.04

McCaffrey, Frank (Acme Press, Seattle, 1926.

Title: What he left to the world: being the last will and testament of Charles Lounsbury.

Imprint: Printed as a wrok of inspiration by Frank McCaffrey and Jay F. Horst of the Acme Press, Seattle.

Brochure, in manila envelope.

IMPRINTS, United States.

Cabinet G Shelf 2 No. 75

McCaffrey, Frank. Seattle, Washington, 1928.
Crashing Through Japan's Back Door.
An adventure of Herbert A. Schoenfeld.
First book printed by Frank McCaffrey.

Japanese cloth covers in case; 9 x $6\frac{1}{2}$ x $\frac{1}{2}$ in.

IMPRINTS, UNITED STATES.

Cabinet G Shelf 2 No. 76.03

McCaffrey, Frank, (Dogwood Press), Seattle, 1932.
Title: On being a printer craftsman. By Frank McCaffrey.
Imprint: Printed in Seattle at his Dogwood Press, 1932.

Boards; $8\frac{3}{4}$ x $6\frac{1}{2}$ in.

IMPRINTS, United States.

Cabinet G Shelf 2 No. 78

McCallister, Donald (Young & McCallister) Los Angeles, California, 1927.
Title: A city home set in a country garden. By Edward F. O'Day...Illus.
Colophon: A City Home set in A Country Garden was printed for Western States Properties Inc., by Young & McCallister of Los Angeles in the month of August, 1927.

Boards; 13 x $9\frac{1}{2}$ x $\frac{1}{4}$ in.

IMPRINTS, United States

Cabinet R Shelf 6 No. 109

McCaffrey, Frank, Seattle, Washington, 1931.
Title: Early printing in Wisconsin. By Douglas C. McMurtrie.
Imprint: Published and printed by Frank McCaffrey...

Cloth; 12 x $8\frac{1}{2}$ in.

IMPRINTS, United States.

Cabinet G Shelf 5 No. 13

McCallister, Bruce. Los Angeles, 1928.
Title: The will of Charles Lounsberry. [Broadside].
Imprint: For certain of his friends who expressed a desire to have a copy of this altogether worthy document the Will of Charles Lounsberry was set in type and printed by Bruce McCallister in the month of January, 1928.

Boards; 19 x $12\frac{3}{4}$ in.

IMPRINTS, United States

Cabinet G Shelf 2 No. 80.02

McCallister, Donald. (Son of Bruce) Hollywood, California, 1932.
Title: Three youthful trappers.
Imprint: Narrated and done into a book by Donald McCallister.

Boards; 8-1/8 x $5\frac{3}{4}$ x $\frac{1}{4}$ in.

IMPRINTS, United States.

Cabinet G Shelf 2 No. 76.02

McCaffrey, Frank (Dogwood Press), Seattle, 1931.
Title: Oscar Wilde's Happy Prince.
Imprint: Printed by Frank McCaffrey at his Dogwood Press in Seattle, 1931.

Boards, $10\frac{1}{4}$ x 7 x $\frac{1}{4}$ in.

IMPRINTS, United States

Cabinet G Shelf 2 No. 79

McCallister, Bruce. Los Angeles, 1929.
Title: The Zamorano Club.
Imprint: Printed for the Zamorano Club by Bruce McCallister, in the month of September, 1929.

Boards; 8-7/8 x 6 x $\frac{1}{4}$ in.

IMPRINTS, United States.

Cabinet G Shelf 2 No. 81

McDonald, Thomas W. and Edward S. Smith. Los Angeles, California, 1928-1929.
Title: Reflections. An expression of appreciation for the Frank Wiggins Trade School.
Colophon: Reflections was conceived, planned, written, set into type in the homes of two former students of the Printing Department of Frank Wiggins Trade Schools. ...

Boards; $8\frac{1}{2}$ x $6\frac{1}{2}$ in.

IMPRINTS, United States

Cabinet G Shelf 2 No. 76.01

McCaffrey, Frank (Dogwood Press), Seattle, 1931.
Title: The psychology of printing types. By Henry Lewis Bullen.
Imprint: Printed by Frank McCaffrey at his Dogwood Press [which is in Seattle] for the pleasure of doing, and as a keepsake for the friends of Henry Lewis Bullen. n.d.

Boards; 12 x 9-1/8 x $\frac{1}{4}$ in.

IMPRINTS, United States

Cabinet G Shelf 2 No. 8.01

McCallister, Bruce. Los Angeles, 1931.
Title: California Hills, and other wood engravings by Paul Landacre. From the original blocks. Foreword by Arthur Millier. 1931: Bruce McCallister. Los Angeles.
No.185 of an edition of 500 copies.
Signed by the artist.

Boards; $12\frac{3}{4}$ x $9\frac{3}{4}$ in.

IMPRINTS, United States

Cabinet K Shelf 3 No. 22

Manas Press, The. Rochester, N.Y., 1915

see BRAGDON, CLAUDE. Projective ornament...

IMPRINTS. United States

Cabinet G Shelf 2 No. 76

McCaffrey, Frank; Dogwood Press, Seattle, 1931.
Title: Two warriors, By Edward Lincoln Smith.
Imprint: Seattle, 1931. Printed by Frank McCaffrey at his Dogwood Press.

Boards, leather back; 7-3/8 x $4\frac{3}{4}$ in.

IMPRINTS, United States.

Cabinet G Shelf 2 No. 80

McCallister, Bruce, Virginia and Donald. Hollywood, California, 1931.
Title: The Yarn of Nancy Bell. By W.S. Gilbert.
Imprint-Colophon:...done by Bruce, Virginia and Donald McCallister. Virginia did the covers and decorations, Bruce and Donald set the type. Press work by Harold Young.

Boards; 9-5/8 x 6-3/8 x $\frac{1}{4}$ in.

IMPRINTS, United States.

Cabinet F Shelf 2 No. 94

Manning & Loring: Boston, 1793.
Title: New version of the Psalms of David. By N. Brady and N. Tate.
Imprint: Printed at Boston by Manning & Loring for J. Thomas and E.T.Andrews, Faust's statue, No.45, Newbury Street, 1793.

Leather; 7-1/8 x $4\frac{1}{4}$ x $1\frac{1}{4}$ in. Not in Evans.

IMPRINTS. United States

Cabinet G Shelf 2 No. 76.05

McCaffrey, Frank: The Dogwood Press at Seattle, Washington, 1931.
Title: Washington from Life. By Edmond S. Meany.
Imprint: Seattle, 1931. Printed by Frank McCaffrey at his Dogwood Press. Illus.

Cloth, morocco back; $12\frac{1}{2}$ x 9-3/4 in.

IMPRINTS, United States.

Cabinet G Shelf 2 No. 77

McCallister, Donald (Young & McCallister). Los Angeles, California, 1927.
Title: Bel-Air. A picturesque domain of homes. Administration Building. Stone Canyon & Chalon Roads Bel-Air. Los Angeles, California. Illus.

Brochure; $8\frac{1}{2}$ x $6\frac{1}{4}$ in.

IMPRINTS, United States.

Cabinet G Shelf 2 No. 72

Marchbanks Press, New York, 1914. Jingle's from the postman's pack to a blue-eyed boy. Illustrated by Jay Chambers. Privately printed for Clem Irwin Orr. Booklet.

Boards $7\frac{1}{2}$ x $5\frac{3}{4}$, pp.18, not numbered.

IMPRINTS, United States.

Cabinet G Shelf 2 No. 71

Marchbanks Press, New York, 1914. Round about the Christmas Tree, by W.M. Thackeray. Privately printed for Thomas Nast Fairbanks. Booklet.

Boards, 7½ x 5 ins., pp.23.

IMPRINTS, United States.

Cabinet G Shelf 2 No. 73

Marchbanks Press, The, New York, 1926. The great adventure, by Kendall Banning. Cut on title page. Authors authograph.

Boards, linen back, 8¾ x 6¼ ins., pp.44, Dup. copy, not signed.

IMPRINTS, United States.

Cabinet G Shelf 2 No. 74

Marchbanks Press, The, New York, 1927. Even better steam generation, by Gerald B. Gould and Douglas Henderson.

Boards, linen back, 8¾ x 5¾ ins., pp.44

IMPRINTS, United States.

Cabinet G Shelf 2 No. 82

Martin, Lambert & Co., New York, 1838. A newly opened treasury of heavenly incense.

This is on our shelves as an extreme and ugly example of printing with heavy modern Roman types, which effected a reaction in favor of Old Style Roman to the fore in 1844 the only surviving old style series that had been saved in the type founders Caslon Old-style.

Original bds. 8¾ x 5½ ins., pp.612.

IMPRINTS, United States

Cabinet Q Shelf 5 No. 51

Mathewson, Frank & Emily, Springfield, Mass., 1904.

Title: The story of the two friars...By Eugene Field.

Imprint: Privately printed and made into a booke for Miles C. Holden at the shop of Frank & Emily Mathewson, which is in Springfield, Mass.

Paper; 8¾ x 6¼ in., pp. 10.

In envelope.

IMPRINTS, United States.

Cabinet G Shelf 2 No. 83

Matthew-Northrup Works, Buffalo, for acquaintance sake: A pictorial journey through the Manufacturers and Traders National Bank of Buffalo, n.d.

Boards, 10 x 7 ins., pp.15.

IMPRINTS, United States.

Cabinet G Shelf 2 No. 84

Matthew-Northrup Works, Buffalo, New York. May-June 1926.

Clement Comments: Consolidation number. Published by J.W. Clement Co. combined with The Matthew-Northrup Works, New York, Buffalo. Cleveland. Photographs.

Half morocco; 8½ x 5½ in.

IMPRINTS, United States

Cabinet F Shelf 1 No. 60

Mecom, Benjamin [Nephew of B. Franklin]. Boston, 1760.

Title: The interest of Great Britain considered ...[By Benjamin Franklin].

Imprint: London printed 1760. Boston reprinted by B. Mecom, and sold at the New Printing Office near the Town-House. 1760.

Half morocco; 7¼ x 4½ x ½ in. Evans 3, 8601, p.254.

IMPRINTS, United States.

Cabinet G Shelf 2 No. 85

Mergenthaler Linotype Co. Brooklyn, N. Y, 1930.

Title: A true description of all trades. Published in Frankfurt in the year 1568. With six of the illustrations by Jost Amman.

Imprint: Mergenthaler Linotype Co. Brooklyn, N.Y. 1930.

Boards; 7¾ x 5¼ x ¼ in.

IMPRINTS, United States.

Cabinet G Shelf 2 No. 85.01

Mergenthaler Linotype Company. Brooklyn, N.Y. 1931.

Title: Contemporary Title Pages ...

Imprint: Brooklyn, New York. Mergenthaler Linotype Company, 1932.

Paper; 6¼ x 4 x ½ in.

IMPRINTS, United States

Cabinet G Shelf 4 No. 28.01

Mergenthaler Linotype Company, Brooklyn, N.Y. 1935

Title: A bakers' dozen of Emblems. Drawings by W. A. Dwiggins, and Verses by Wm. Rose Benét ... and Electra. A new Linotype face from the hand of the said W.A.D.

Imprint: Mergenthaler Linotype Company, etc.

Pamphlet. In envelope.

IMPRINTS, United States.

Cabinet G Shelf 2 No. 86

Merrell & Hastings, Utica, 1825. Questions on the historical parts of the New Testament Second revised edition.

Original bds., 5-3/4 x 3-3/4 ins., pp.144.

IMPRINTS, UNITED STATES

Cabinet L Shelf 4 No. 35

Metcalf and Company, Cambridge (Mass.) 1857.

See Color Printing. Pearls and other tales...Boston, 1857.

IMPRINTS, United States

Cabinet G Shelf 2 No. 87

Metropolitan Press, Truman Bailey. Fairfax Cone, and Hartley Jackson. San Francisco, December, 1927. The fountain of gold by Lafcadio Hearn, done in hand-set type, with hand-colored illustrations.

Boards; 13 x 10 in.

IMPRINTS, United States

Cabinet G Shelf 2 No. 89

Cincinnati, Ohio. Mullane. The Book of Candies. The John Mullane Co., n.d. Colored illus.

Boards; 7 x 5 in. pp.37.

IMPRINT, United States

Cabinet FF Shelf 2 No. 24

Munder, Norman T.A. and Company, Baltimore, 1912.

Title: Type spacing, by E.R. Currier.

Impirnt: J.M. Bowles [Publisher], New York.

Has Currier Press printer mark on title page.

Boards; 8-3/4 x 6 in.

IMPRINTS, United States.

Cabinet G Shelf 3 No. 3

Munder, Norman T.A. and Company, Baltimore, 1914. Dinner to Hon. William Howard Taft and Dr. William Henry Welch, Baltimore, Md., Saturday, Feb., 28th.

Lithographic borders, portraits, menu and guest list.

Boards; 8½ x 5-3/4 ins., lvs. 8.

IMPRINTS, United States.

Cabinet G Shelf 3 No. 4

Munder, Norman T.A. & Co., Printers, Baltimore Descriptive Catalogue of a printing exhibit at The Panama-Pacific International Exhibition, San Francisco, 1915.

Boards, 9¼ x 6 ins., pp.28. Dup. copy in paper covers.

IMPRINTS, United States

Cabinet L Shelf 2 No. 28

Munder, Norman T.A. and Co., Baltimore, Md. 1921.
Title: The story of the alphabet. By Otto F. Egge
Imprint: Compliments of Norman T. Munder & Co., Baltimore, Md.

Boards; 9¾ x 3-7/8 in.

IMPRINTS, United States.

Cabinet G Shelf 3 No. 5

Munder, Norman T.A. and Company, Baltimore, 1922. Benjamin Franklin, Printer. Printed especially for the American Institute of Graphic Arts. Portrait from the painting by Joseph Siffrein Duplessis (1725-1802) Decorations by Edward Edwards. Brochure.

Half morocco, 9¾ x 7¼ ins., pp.3.

IMPRINTS, United States.

Cabinet R Shelf 4 No. 146

Munder, Norman T.A., Baltimore, Md., 1922.
Title: A history of printing in Colonial Maryland 1686-1776. By L. C. Wroth.
Imprint, last page:...The book was printed for the Typothetae of Baltimore by Norman T. A. Munder & Company, in their shop at 109 Market Place, Baltimore, Maryland...Each copy of this limited edition has been signed by the author this 3rd day of June 1922.

Full morocco; 10-1/8 x 7½ in. In protective case.

IMPRINTS, United States

Cabinet G Shelf 5 No. 23

Munder, Norman T., Baltimore, Md., 1935.
Title: The Constitution of the United States of America -- The Declaration of Independence. (Facsimiles)
Imprint: The first reduced facsimile in legible form. Made and published by Norman T. A. Munder, Baltimore, 1935.

Brochure, in envelope.

IMPRINTS, United States.

Cabinet G Shelf 2 No. 92

Munder-Thomsen Company, Baltimore, 1905. The burning of Peggy Stewart: Religious toleration in Maryland. Issued by the Municipal Art Society, Illus. Brochure.

8 x 5¾ ins., pp.119.

IMPRINTS, United States.

Cabinet G Shelf 2 No. 93

Munder-Thomsen Company, Baltimore, 1909. A sermon preached in Emmanuel Church. Printed in Church text types in black and red.

Paper, 11 x 8½ ins., pp.48.

IMPRINTS, United States.

Cabinet G Shelf 2 No. 94

Munder-Thomsen, Company, Baltimore, 1913. The Woolworth Building by Montgomery Schuyler. Privately printed. Illus.

Boards, 13 x 7¾ ins., pp.14, not numbered, 11 full plates.

IMPRINTS, United States

Cabinet JJ Shelf 3 No. 12

Munroe & Francis, Boston, 1802.

see

SOCIETIES, PRINTERS'. United States Boston Franklin Association...1802.

IMPRINTS, United States

Cabinet QQ Shelf 1 No. 43

Munsell, Joel, Albany, 1868.
Title: A collection of songs of the American Press...Compiled by Charles Munsell.
Imprint: Albany, N.Y. 1868.

Morocco, gilt; 6¾ x 4¾ x 7/8 in.

IMPRINTS, United States

Cabinet QQ Shelf 3 No. 42

Munsell's Steam Press, Frank Munsell. Albany, N. Y., 1871.
Title: Chips for the chimney corner. Gathered by Frank Munsell.
Imprint: Albany, N.Y., Munsell's Steam Press, 1871

Note: This volume of miscellany has been set in type by a lad twelve years of age.

Cloth; 7 x 4¾ x ½ in.

IMPRINTS, United States

Cabinet QQ Shelf 1 No. 54

Murdock Press, The. San Francisco, 1902.
Title: Songs of the press. By Bailey Millard...
Imprint: Printed at San Francisco. The Murdock Press.

One of 100 copies for private circulation.

Boards; 8 x 5½ in.

IMPRINTS, United States

Cabinet G Shelf 3 No. 6

Museum Press, (H.W. Kent) Metropolitan Museum of Art, printing department, New York, 1916. Amycus et Celestin, by Anatole France. Printed with Bruce Rogers' Centaur Types. Wood-cuts by Timothy Cole.

Half morocco; 8¼ x 5½ in. pp.14.

IMPRINTS, United States

Cabinet G Shelf 3 No. 7

Museum Press (H.W. Kent), Metropolitan Museum of Art, printing department, New York, 1919. The great procession from the Church of Our Lady at Antwerp, as seen by Albrecht Durer, about 1620. Decorations in tint.

Half morocco; 8¼ x 5½ in. pp.6, (last blank)

IMPRINTS, United States.

Cabinet 71 Shelf 1 No. 1

Nash, John Henry, San Francisco. Printing done by John Henry Nash: Miscellaneous.

A scrap book.

Half morocco; 12½ x 9¼ ins.

Cards for items 1-5.

IMPRINTS, United States.

Cabinet 73 Shelf 1 No. 3

Nash, John Henry. San Francisco, n. d.
Title: The Ideal Book. By T. J. Cobden-Sanderson

Broadside; 8-3/4 x 7 in.

Item 5 in John Henry Nash: His Work. San Francisco, v. d.

IMPRINTS, United States.

Cabinet 73 Shelf 2 No. 1

[Nash, John Henry. San Francisco, n. d.]

Title: Napa Wine. By Robert Louis Stevenson.

Brochure 3: In John Henry Nash, Imprints. San Francisco, 1910-1927.

IMPRINTS, United States.

Cabinet 73 Shelf 1 No. 3

Nash, John Henry, San Francisco, v.d. Purgatorio XXXIV. The Comedy of Dante Alighieri.

A trial sheet.

Item 3 in John Henry Nash: His Work, San Francisco, v.d.

IMPRINTS, United States.

Cabinet 73 Shelf 1 No. 3

Nash, John Henry. San Francisco, n. d.
Title: We are closing this printing shop of ours ...(Signed) John Henry Nash.

Printed within red border.

Item 1, in John Henry Nash: His Work. San Francisco, v. d.

IMPRINTS, United States.

Cabinet 73 · Shelf 1 · No. 1

Nash, John Henry, San Francisco, 1901-1925. An anthology of effort. By J.H. Nash, Pamphlet.

Mr. Nash's expression of gratitude to those who assisted him in the preparation of "El Toison de oro" which received first award in the Graphic Arts Competition of 1926.

Item 4 in John Henry Nash: His Work, 1901-1925.

IMPRINTS, United States.

Cabinet 73 · Shelf 1 · No. 1

Nash, John Henry, San Francisco, 1901-1925. The rime of the ancient mariner. By Samuel Taylor Coleridge. Illustration on title page of "The Phantom Ship", reproduced by Charles D. Robinson. Brochure, 16 x 11 ins.

Item 6 in John Henry Nash: His Work, 1901-1925.

IMPRINTS, United States

Cabinet 71 · Shelf 1 · No. 10

Nash, John Henry. San Francisco, 1909.
Title: Rubaiyat of Omar Khayyam.
Imprint: ... Paul Elder and Company, in the fair city of San Francisco in the year 1909. And this book was imprinted under the skillful direction of John H. Nash.

Stamped boards; 8 x $5\frac{1}{2}$ in

IMPRINTS, United States.

Cabinet 73 · Shelf 1 · No. 1

Nash, John Herny, San Francisco, 1901-1925. Bene dictum Benedict: Printed by J.H. Nash of "The Vatican" for the joy of doing.... It is dedicated to a child of The Family & friend of "The Vatican", Louis Welch.

The "Vatican" is a coterie of booklovers centering around J.H. Nash.

Item 7 in John Henry Nash: His Work, 1901-1925.

IMPRINTS, United States.

Cabinet 71 · Shelf 1 · No. 2

Nash, John Henry: The Tomoye Press. New York, 1901.
Title: The love sonnets of a hoodlum. By Wallace Irwin. With an introduction by Gelet Burgess.
Imprint: Paul Elder and Company. San Francisco and New York. The Tomoye Press.

Linen, 7 x $5\frac{1}{4}$ in.

IMPRINTS, United States.

Cabinet 71 · Shelf 1 · No. 8

Nash, John Henry. The Tomoye Press, San Francisco, 1909. Sonnets, by Fanny P. Palmer. Printed for Paul Elder & Co., by the Tomoye Press under the direction of J.H. Nash.

Boards, 8 x 6 ins., pp.38.

IMPRINTS, United States.

Cabinet 73 · Shelf 1 · No. 1

Nash, Johm Henry, San Francisco, 1901-1925, A Bodoni keepsake. Handset in an American rendition of Bodoni type, the recutting done by Morris Fuller Benton. Brochure, with portrait of Bodoni.

Item 8 in John Henry Nash: His Work, 1901-1925.

IMPRINTS, United States

Cabinet 71 · Shelf 1 · No. 89

Nash, John Henry, 1904-1930, list of books etc., printed by J.H.N., and exhibited at the Paterson Free Public Library, fom May 27 1930.

The collection of Nash items in this exhibition the property of Mrs. H. Hand of Paterson.

Lists in manila envelope.

IMPRINTS, United States.

Cabinet 71 · Shelf 1 · No. 9

Nash, John Henry, The Tomoye Press, San Francisco, 1909. The Tocsin, a drama of the Renaissance. By Esther B. Tiffany. Printed for Paul Elder & Co. by the Tomoye Press, under the direction of J.H. Nash.

Boards; 8-7/8 x 6 ins., pp.72.

IMPRINTS, United States.

Cabinet 73 · Shelf 1 · No. 1

Nash, John Herny, San Francisco, 1901-1925. George Sterling: An appreciation, by Henry Louis Mencken. Decorative border by William Wilke. Broadside.

Item 9 in John Henry Nash: His work, 1901-25.

IMPRINTS, United States.

Cabinet 71 · Shelf 1 · No. 3

Nash, John Henry. The Tomoye Press, New York, 1906.
Title: Ye Gardeyne boke ... Gathered and arranged by Jennie Day Haines.
Imprint: ... Decorations by Spencer Wright. Published by Paul Elder and Company and printed for them by the Tomoye Press, New York, under the direction of Harry Nash, in the year 1906

Stamped cloth; $9\frac{1}{2}$ x $6\frac{1}{2}$ x 5/8 in.

IMPRINTS, United States.

Cabinet 71 · Shelf 1 · No. 2.05

Nash, John Henry: The Tomoye Press. San Francisco, 1910.
Title: By the Way. By Agness Greene Foster.
(Imprint) Colophon: Published by Paul Elder & Co. and printed for them by the Tomoye Press, in the City of San Francisco, under the direction of J. H. Nash. April, 1910.

Cloth; 7 x $4\frac{1}{4}$ x $\frac{3}{4}$ in.

IMPRINTS, United States.

Cabinet 73 · Shelf 1 · No. 1

Nash, John Henry, San Francisco, 1901-1925. Gutenberg. A reproduction of a portrait in oil after the original (artist unknown). Sent out by the Zellerbach Paper Company to the friends and patrons of their house.

Includes facsimile page from the Gutenberg 42 line Bible.

Item 5 in John Henry Nash: His Work, 1901-1925.

IMPRINTS, United States.

Cabinet 71 · Shelf 1 · No. 5

Nash, John Henry. San Franicsco, 1907.
Title: The case of Summerfield. By W. H. Rhodes. With an introudction by Geraldine Bonner. Photogravure frontispiece from an oil painting by Galen J. Perrett.
Colophon.....Typography designed by J.H. Nash.... Published by Paul Elder and Company, and done into a book for them at the Tomoye Press in the City of New York MCMVII.

Paper boards; 6-3/4 x $4\frac{1}{2}$ in.

IMPRINTS, United States.

Cabinet 73 · Shelf 2 · No. 1

Nash, John Henry. The Tomoye Press, San Francisco, 1910.
Title: Light through the Valley. By James Henry MacLafferty. Paul Elder and Company, Publishers.
Colophon: Printed for them by the Tomoye Press, under the direction of J. H. Nash, in the City of San Francisco, 1910.

Brochure 1, in John Henry Nash, Imprints, San Francisco, 1910-1927.

IMPRINTS, United States.

Cabinet 73 · Shelf 1 · No. 1

Nash, John Henry, San Francisco, 1901-1925. John Henry Nash, His Work.

A Scrap Book containing brochures, broadsides, facsimile page from the Gutenberg's 42 line Bible, etc.

Half morocco; 19-3/4 x 13 ins.

IMPRINTS, United States.

Cabinet 71 · Shelf 1 · No. 6

Nash. John Henry. San Francisco, 1907.
Title: Weather Opinions: A book of quotations with interleaves on weather subjects. Compiled and arranged by Jennie Day Haines.
Colophon:..The frontispiece in color by Gordon Ross. The typography designed by J. H. Nash. Published by Paul Elder & Company, and printed for them by the Tomoye Press in New York City, 1907.

Half morocco; $9\frac{1}{8}$ x $7\frac{1}{4}$ in.

IMPRINTS, United States.

Cabinet 71 · Shelf 1 · No. 13

Nash, John Henry. The Tomoye Press. San Francisco, 1910.
Title: My Soul's Cathedral and other poems. By James Henry MacLafferty.
Colophon:..Designed and executed by J. H. Nash at the Tomoye Press...in the year nineteen hundred and ten...

Boards; 8 x $5\frac{1}{2}$ in. pp. 22

IMPRINTS, United States.

Cabinet 71 Shelf 1 No. 15

Nash, John Henry. The Tomoye Press, San Francisco, 1910. Obil, keeper of camels. By Lucia C. Bell. Printed for Paul Elder and Company by the Tomoye Press, under the direction of J.H. Nash.

Boards, $7\frac{1}{4}$ x $5\frac{1}{2}$ ins., pp.26.

IMPRINTS, United States.

Cabinet 71 Shelf 1 No. 18

Nash, John Henry. Tomoye Press, San Francisco, 1911.
Title: Recipe for a Happy Life. Written by Margaret of Navarre in the 1500.
Colophon: ... Published by Paul Elder and Company ... and printed for them by their Tomoye Press under the care of John Henry Nash. San Francisco, 1911.

Stamped paper boards; $8\frac{1}{4}$ x 7 x 3/8 in.

IMPRINTS, United States

Cabinet 71 Shelf 1 No. 25

Nash, John Henry, San Francisco, 1913.
Title: The Fall of Ug: A Masque of Fear. By Rufus Steele. Music by Herman Perlet...Being the Eleventh Grove Play of the Bohemian Club of San Francisco...Autographed copy.
Imprint: Taylor, Nash & Taylor, San Francisco.

Paper Boards; $6\frac{3}{4}$ x $5\frac{1}{4}$ in.

IMPRINTS, United States.

Cabinet 71 Shelf 1 No. 16

Nash, John Henry, San Francisco, 1910. Sonnets from the Portugese by E.B. Browning. Put to press under the watchful eye of J.H. Nash, typographer. Decorations by Harold Sichel.

Boards, $7\frac{1}{2}$ x $5\frac{3}{4}$ ins.,pp.76

IMPRINTS, United States.

Cabinet 71 Shelf 1 No. 22

Nash, John Henry. San Francisco, 1912.
Title: The atonement of Pan. A Music drama. Book by Joseph H. Redding, music by Henry Hadley. Produced by members of the Bohemian Club....August the tenth, nineteen,hundred and twelve.
Imprint: Printed by Taylor, Nash & Taylor, San Francisco.

Half morocco $9\frac{1}{4}$ x $6\frac{1}{4}$ in.

IMPRINTS, United States

Cabinet QQ Shelf 1 No. 59

Nash, John Henry (Taylor, Nash & Taylor) San Francisco, 1913.
Title: A tragedy in printer's ink. By Wallace Irwin.
Imprint: San Francisco. Taylor, Nash & Taylor. 1913.

Boards; $9\frac{3}{4}$ x $7\frac{3}{4}$ in.

IMPRINTS, United States.

Cabinet 71 Shelf 1 No. 14

Nash, John Henry. The Tomoye Press, San Francisco, 1910. Tennessee's partner. By Bret Harte including an introduction by W.D. Armes. Photogravure frontispiece by Albertine R. Wheelan. The typography designed by J.H. Nash. Published by Paul Elder and Co.

Boards, $6\frac{1}{2}$ x $4\frac{3}{4}$ ins., pp.38.

IMPRINTS, United States.

Cabinet 73 Shelf 1 No. 1

Nash, John Henry. San Francisco, 1912.
Title: Lines to the devil. By Wallace Irwin. Written for Taylor, Nash & Taylor, San Francisco, and sent out by them as an example of their typography and letter press. Illus.

Item 1 in John Henry Nash, His work, 1901-1925.

IMPRINTS, United States.

Cabinet 71 Shelf 1 No. 30

Nash, John Henry. Taylor, Nash and Taylor, San Francisco, 1914. A bibliography of the history of California and the Pacific West, 1510-1906. By Robert Ernest Cowan. Printed for The Book Club of California by Taylor Nash and Taylor.

Boards, linen back, $10\frac{1}{2}$ x 8 ins., pp.318.

IMPRINTS, United States

Cabinet 71 Shelf 1 No. 17

Nash, John Henry: The Tomoyé Press, San Francisco, 1910.
Title: To friendship. By Agness Greene Foster. Paul Elder & Co. San Francisco.
Colophon: Printed by The Tomoye Press, in the City of San Francisco, under the direction of J. H. Nash ... March, 1910.

Paper; $8\frac{1}{4}$ x 4-7/8 in.

IMPRINTS, United States.

Cabinet 71 Shelf 1 No. 21

Nash, John Henry. Taylor, Nash and Taylor, San Francisco, 1912. What Christmas is as we grow older. By Charles Dickens, Presentation copy from the publishers, Taylor, Nash and Taylor. Illus.

Boards, 5-7/8 x $4\frac{1}{2}$ ins., pp.11.

IMPRINTS, United States

Cabinet 71 Shelf 1 No. 32

Nash, John Henry: San Francisco, 1914.
Title: An Interpretation of Maeterlinck's Blue Bird. By Lida Morse Staples. With a memorial note by Anna B. Newbegin.
Colophon.....were printed by Taylor, Nash and Taylor, San Francisco, during the month of February, 1914.

Paper boards; 9-1/8 x 6-1/8 in.

IMPRINTS, United States

Cabinet 71 Shelf 1 No. 19

Nash, John Henry: The Tomoye Press, San Francisco, 1911.
Title: Abelard and Heloise: The love letters: A poetical rendering by Ella Costillo Bennett
Colophon: ... Published by Paul Elder and Company and done into a book for them at their Tomoye Press, under the direction of John Henry Nash San Francisco, 1911.

Stamped paper boards; 8 x 5 x 3/8 in.

IMPRINTS, United States.

Cabinet 71 Shelf 1 No. 26

Nash, John Henry, San Francisco, 1913. A Hal Christmas. Printed for R.L. by Gilbert Mabbott, London, 1647, and reprinted by Taylor, Nash & Taylor for private distribution.

Boards, 10 x 8 ins., pp.10.

IMPRINTS, United States.

Cabinet 71 Shelf 1 No. 31

Nash, John Henry, Taylor, Nash and Taylor, San Francisco, 1914. The very pleasant and delectable tale of Cupid and Psyche. Translated from the Latin by Walter Pater. Frontispiece by Ray F. Coyle.

Boards, linen back, $7\frac{3}{4}$ x 5 ins., pp.34.

IMPRINTS, United States.

Cabinet 71 Shelf 1 No. 20

Nash, John Henry: Tomoye Press. San Francisco, 1911.
Title: Comfort found in good old books. By George Hamlin Fitch.
Colophon: ... Published by Paul Elder and Company and printed for them by their Tomoye Press in San Francisco under the direction of John Henry Nash. June, 1911.

Stamped cloth; 7 x $4\frac{1}{4}$ x 5/8 in.

IMPRINTS, United States.

Cabinet 71 Shelf 1 No. 27

Nash, John Henry; Taylor, Nash and Taylor, San Francisco, 1913. Brunelleschi: A poem by John Galen Howard. Printed by Taylor, Nash and Taylor, under the supervision of J. H. Nash.

Boards 10 x 6-7/8 ins., pp. 93.

IMPRINTS, United States.

Cabinet 71 Shelf 1 No. 36

Nash, John Henry, San Francisco, 1915.
Title: Discoveries and inventions: A lecture by Abraham Lincoln delivered in 1860.
Colophon:...The fronispiece is by Ray F. Coyle. Printed by the Blair-Murdock Co., San Francisco, under the direction of John Henry Nash, 1915.

Paper boards; $8\frac{1}{2}$ x 6 in.

IMPRINTS, United States.

Cabinet 71 Shelf 1 No. 35

Nash, John Henry, Taylor, Nash & Taylor, San Francisco, 1915. The Lady Isis in Bohemia. Printed by Taylor, Nash and Taylor of San Francisco for Jeremiah Lynch, and by him presented to the members of the Bohemian Club Illus. by Bohemian Dan Sweeney.

Limp boards, $11\frac{1}{2}$ x $8\frac{1}{4}$ ins., pp.23. Illus. pp.4.

IMPRINTS, United States.

Cabinet 71 Shelf 1 No. 40

Nash, John Henry, San Francisco, 1916. The man with the hoe. By Edwin Markham. Printed for The Book Club of California by John Henry Nash. Decorations by Ray F. Coyle.

Boards, linen back, 11 x $7\frac{3}{4}$ ins. pp.12.

IMPRINTS, United States.

Cabinet 71 Shelf 1 No. 1

Nash, John Henry, San Francisco,1919. The ideal book, or book beautiful, By T.J. Cobden-Sanderson. Printed by J.H. Nash for the Zellerbach Paper Company, and sent forth by them as a gift offering to the friends and patrons of their house.

Brochure $12\frac{1}{4}$ x $9\frac{1}{4}$ ins., pp.9.

Item I in "Printing done by John Henry Nash"

IMPRINTS, United States.

Cabinet 71 Shelf 1 No. 1

Nash, John Henry, -- Blair-Murdock Company -- San Francisco, 1915. The lights go out -- The last day and night of the Panama-Pacific International Exposition", accompanied by a facsimile of the Toast of Woodrow Wilson, President of the U.S.A., in his handwriting. Pamphlet.

Item 2, in "Printing done by John Henry Nash."

IMPRINTS, United States.

Cabinet 71 Shelf 1 No. 41

Nash, John Henry. San Francisco, 1916.
Title: What the Birds Did at Hazel's Orchard. by Eduard Eichenberg.
Imprint: San Francisco: Printed for John F. Newbegin by John Henry Nash, 1916.

Paper Boards; $7\frac{3}{4}$ x $5\frac{3}{4}$ in.

IMPRINTS, United States.

Cabinet 71 Shelf 2 No. [illegible]5 4 vols.

Nash, John Henry. San Francisco, 1920-1928.
Title: Library of William Andrews Clark, Jr. [Bibliography]: Modern English Literature. Collated and compiled by Robert Ernest Cowan and William Andrews Clark, Jr. Los Angles.
Imprint: San Francisco, Printed by John Henry Nash, 1920-,1921, 1927, 1928.

Boards, each volume, $10\frac{1}{4}$ x $7\frac{1}{4}$ in.

IMPRINTS, United States.

Cabinet 71 Shelf 1 No. 34

Nash, John Henry, San Francisco, 1915. The legacy of the exposition: An interpretation of the intellectual and moral heritage etc... San Francisco, 1915. Printed for the Exposition by John Henry Nash.

Boards, linen back, $9\frac{1}{2}$ x $7\frac{1}{4}$ ins., pp.187.

IMPRINTS, United States.

Cabinet 71 Shelf 1 No. 44

Nash, John Henry, San Francisco, 1917. Barney Mc Gee, By Richard Hovey. Frontispiece by Ray F. Coyle. Printed by J. H. Nash for his friends.

Boards, 12 x $9\frac{1}{2}$ ins. pp. 10.

IMPRINTS, United States.

Cabinet 71 Shelf 2 No. 19 4 Vols.

Nash, John Henry. San Francisco, 1920-1925.
Title: Early English Literature, 1519-1700. Collated and compiled by Robert Ernest Cowan and William Andrews Clark, Jr., Los Angeles.
Imprint: Printed by John Henry Nash for the Library of William Andrews Clark, Jr. [4 vols.]

Boards; each volume, $10\frac{1}{4}$ x $7\frac{1}{2}$ in.

IMPRINTS, United States.

Cabinet 71 Shelf 1 No. 33

Nash, John Henry: The Blair-Murdock Co. San Francisco, 1915.
Title: Little literary lights. Personal Preferences in art, literature, flowers: By Augustin S. MacDonald. San Francisco, 1915.

Paper boards; 7-6/8 x $5\frac{1}{4}$ in.

IMPRINTS, United States.

Cabinet 71 Shelf 1 No. 43

Nash, John Henry, San Francisco,1917. Descriptive catalogue of the Goewey collection of Browning pictures, 1908-1918. Together with an introductory paper.

Boards, $11\frac{3}{4}$ x $8\frac{1}{2}$, pp.40.

IMPRINTS, United States.

Cabinet 71 Shelf 2 No. 27

Nash, John Henry. San Francisco, 1920-1923.
Title: Cruikshank and Dickens, with supplemental volume "The posthumous papers of the Pickwick Club." Collated and compiled by Robert Ernest Cowan and William Andrews Clark, Jr. 3 vols.
Imprint: San Francisco. Printed by John Henry Nash.

Boards, each volume, $10\frac{1}{4}$ x $7\frac{1}{4}$ in.

IMPRINTS, United States.

Cabinet 71 Shelf 2 No. 1 (5 vols.)

Nash, John Henry. San Francisco, 1916-22.
Title: Library of Charles W. Clark: Catalogue of Library. Vol. 2, 1916, Vol. 3, 1917, Vol. 4 1918, Vol. 5, 1919. Vol. 7, 1922.
Imprint: Printed for Charles W. Clark by John Henry Nash. San Francisco.

Boards, each volume; $11\frac{1}{2}$ x $8\frac{1}{2}$ in.

IMPRINTS, United States.

Cabinet 71 Shelf 1 No. 1

Nash, John Henry, San Francisco,1917. A loan exhibition of Incunabula, held by The Book Club of California. This collection loaned by Mr. Charles W. Clark, San Mateo.

Catalogue.

Item 3 in "Printing done by John Henry Nash"

IMPRINTS, United States.

Cabinet 73 Shelf 2 No. 3

Nash, John Henry. San Francisco, 1920.
Title: Curiosities of early economic literature. An address to his fellow members of the Hobby Club of New York. By Edwin R. A. Seligman.
Imprints: San Francisco. Privately printed by John Henry Nash, MDCCCCXX.

Boards, $15\frac{1}{2}$ x 11 in.

IMPRINTS, United States.

Cabinet 71 Shelf 1 No. 39

Nash, John Henry, San Francisco, 1916. The ideal book or book beautiful, by Cobden-Sanderson. Privately printed by J.H. Nash. Decorations by Ray F. Coyle.

Boards, 10 x $7\frac{3}{4}$ ins., pp.13.

IMPRINTS, United States.

Cabinet 73 Shelf 1 No. 1

Nash, John Henry, San Francisco, 1918. A canticle of praise. By Witter Bynner. Brochure.

Printed in red and black within green lined margins. Illus. on title page by Lawrence B. Haste.

Item 2 in John Henry Nash: His Work, 1901-25.

IMPRINTS, United States.

Cabinet 71 Shelf 1 No. 47

Nash, John Henry, San Francisco, 1920. Ecclesiastes, or the preacher. Printed by J.H.Nash "for the joy of doing."

Boards, 12 x 7 ins., pp. 17.

IMPRINTS, United States.

Cabinet 71 Shelf 1 No. 48

Nash, John Henry, San Francisco, 1920. Ruth St. Denis: Pioneer and Prophet. Being a history of her cycle of oriental dances. By Ted Shawn. Printed by J.H. Nash. Decorations by W.F. Rauschnabel. Signed by Ruth St. Denis, 2 vols.

Boards, linen backs, 13 x 10 ins., $\frac{3}{4}$ in. thick.

IMPRINTS, United States.

Cabinet 71 Shelf 2 No. 15

Nash, John Henry. San Francisco, 1922.
Title: The Library of William Andrews Clark, Jr. Compiled and arranged by Robert Ernest Cowan and William Andrews Clark, Jr.
Imprint: San Francisco: Printed by John Henry Nash, 1922.

Boards, $10\frac{1}{2}$ x $7\frac{1}{2}$ in. pp. 179 Numbered copy 23.

IMPRINTS, United States.

Cabinet 71 Shelf 1 No. 68

Nash, John Henry, San Francisco, 1924.
Title: Memorial motions in Court upon the death of Charles Stetson Wheeler. Portraits.
Imprints: San Francisco; John Henry Nash, 1924.

Marbled paper boards; $9\frac{1}{2}$ x 6-3/8 in.

IMPRINTS, United States.

Cabinet 71 Shelf 2 No. 57

Nash, John Henry. San Francisco, 1921.
Title: The Kelmscott and Doves Presses. [Bibliography]. Compiled by Robert Ernest Cowan... With an Introduction by Alfred W. Pollard.
Imprint: San Francisco: Printed by John Henry Nash. 1921.

Boards, $10\frac{1}{2}$ x $7\frac{1}{2}$ in.

IMPRINTS, United States.

Cabinet 71 Shelf 1 No. 57

Nash, John Henry, San Francisco,1922. Life of Dante. Translated from the Italian by Philip Henry Wickstead. Printed by J.H. Nash for his friends. Dedication to Charles W.Clark and William Andrew Clark "whose recognition and patronage have ever encouraged the quest for higher attainment in the art of typography."

Marbled boards, $12\frac{1}{2}$ x 9 ins., pp.53.

IMPRINTS, United States.

Cabinet 71 Shelf 1 No. 67

Nash, John Henry. San Francisco, 1924.
Title: Some letters from Oscar Wilde to Alfred Douglas. With illustrative notes by Arthur C. Dennison, Jr., and Harrison Post, and an essay by A.S. Rosenbach. Facsimile.
Imprint: Printed by J.H. Nash, for William Andrews Clark, Jr.

IMPRINTS, United States.

Cabinet 71 Shelf 1 No. 54

Nash, John Henry, San Francisco, 1921. Quattrocentisteria: How Sandro Botticelli saw Simonetta in the Spring. By Maurice Hewlett. Printed by J.H. Nash for The Grolier Club. New York, 1921.

Boards, linen back, 12 x $8\frac{1}{2}$ ins., pp.19.

IMPRINTS, United States.

Cabinet 73 Shelf 2 No. 1

Nash, John Henry. San Francisco, 1923.
Title: Eight o'clock: Being a four-color engraving of the painting by Clarkson Dye, together with a word picture of Old San Francisco by Walter H. Gardner. Picture is in broadside collection.
Imprint: San Francisco: Printed for Howard J. Griffith of the American Engraving Color Plate Company by John Henry Nash. MDCCCCXXIII Brochure No. 5, in John Henry Nash. Imprints, San Francisco, 1910-1927.

IMPRINTS, United States.

Cabinet 73 Shelf 1 No. 3

Nash, John Henry. San Francisco, 1924. Verse. Written by Anacreon. Censored to meet the Volstead Act. Corrected by J. H. Nash

Item 5, in John Henry Nash, His Work, San Francisco, V.D.

IMPRINTS, United States.

Cabinet 71 Shelf 1 No. 53

Nash, John Henry, San Francisco,1921. The Sonneteering of Petrarchino. Copyright by Walter M. Hill, Chicago. Printed by J.H. Nash, San Francisco.

Boards, $9\frac{1}{4}$ x $5\frac{3}{4}$ ins., pp.20.

IMPRINTS, United States.

Cabinet 71 Shelf 1 No. 63

Nash, John Henry, San Francisco, 1923. The Silverado Squatters. By R.L. Stevenson Printed by J.H. Nash, from hand-set types which have been distributed. Title-page portrait and illustrative head-bands by H.W. Willard.

Boards, 12-3/4 x 9 ins., pp.99.

IMPRINTS, United States.

Cabinet 73 Shelf 1 No. 3

Nash, John Henry, San Francisco, 1925, Christmas A greeting. Printed for Mr. and Mrs. Roy T. Porte.

Item 4 in John Henry Nash: His Work, San Francisco, V.D.

IMPRINTS, United States.

Cabinet 71 Shelf 2 No. 33

Nash, John Henry. San Francisco, 1922 to 1931.
Title: Wilde and Wildeiana. A bibliography ... William A. Clark Jr. Los Angeles (5 vols.)
Imprint: Printed by John Henry Nash, San Francisco.

Supplement. 1v. 1923.

Boards, linen backs; $10\frac{1}{4}$ x $7\frac{1}{2}$ in.

IMPRINTS, United States.

Cabinet 73 Shelf 2 No. 7

Nash, John Henry. San Francisco, 1924.
Title: Green symbols. By Mark Daniels.
Imprint: San Francisco. Printed by John Henry Nash, 1924.

Boards; $12\frac{1}{2}$ x 9 in.

IMPRINTS, United States.

Cabinet 73 Shelf 1 No. 3

Nash, John Henry. San Francisco, 1925.
I: Christmas Greeting. Yuba Manufacturing Company.
II: Publishers prospectus: John Howell announces the publication of "Brunelleschi", and order form for same.

Item 6 in John Henry Nash: His Work, San Francisco. v.d.

IMPRINTS, United States.

Cabinet 71 Shelf 2 No. 33

Nash, John Henry. San Francisco, 1922-31.
Title: Wilde and Wildeiana [A bibliography]. Collated and compiled by Robert Ernest Cowan and William Andrews Clark, Jr. Los Angeles. 5 volumes with supplemental volume.
Imprints: Printed by John Henry Nash, San Francisco.

Boards, each volume $10\frac{1}{2}$ x $7\frac{1}{4}$ in.

IMPRINTS, United States

Cabinet 73 Shelf 2 No. 8

Nash, John Henry. San Francisco, 1924.
Title: The heathen Chinee. By Bret Harte. With an introduction, and historical note concerning the history of the manuscript. Bibliography and notes by R. E. Cowan, Librarian of the W. A. Clark, Jr. Library in Los Angeles.
Imprint: Printed by John Henry Nash for his friends.

Boards, 17 x $1\frac{1}{2}$ in.

IMPRINTS, UNITED STATES

Cabinet 73 Shelf 1 No. 3

Nash, John Henry. San Francisco, 1925.
Title: Franklin keepsake. Text by John Eugene Hasty.
Imprint: Given by the Zellerbach paper Company... Printed by John Henry Nash, September, 1925. [Broadside].

Item on p.30 of scrap book, "JOHN HENRY NASH: HIS WORK."

IMPRINTS, United States.

Cabinet 73 Shelf 2 No. 13

Nash, John Henry. San Francisco, 1925.
Title: Gray's Elegy in a country church yard. [Facsimile 1751 ed., and reprint]. With a foreword by William Andrews Clark, Jr., and frontispiece by William Wilke.
Imprint: Printed for William Andrews Clark, Jr., by John Henry Nash in San Francisco, 1925.

Paper boards, facsimile, $9\frac{3}{4}$ x $7\frac{3}{4}$ in, reprint 12 x $9\frac{1}{4}$ in. Both in one slip case.

IMPRINTS, United States.

Cabinet 73 Shelf 2 No. 1

Nash, John Henry. San Francisco, 1926.
Title: An Address before the American Association of Advertising Agencies at Washington, October the 27th, 1926, at Eight p.m., by President Coolidge.
Imprint: Printed by John Henry Nash of San Francisco.

Brochure 6: In John Henry Nash, Imprints, San Francisco, 1910-1927.

IMPRINTS, United States.

Cabinet 73 Shelf 1 No. 1

Nash, John Henry, San Francisco, 1926. Claude Garamond and his place in the renaissance. By Edward F. O'Day.

Mr. Nash comments upon the revival of Garamond types through the influence of Henry Lewis Bullen with the co-operation of Morris Fuller Benton.

Item 11 in John Henry Nash; His work, 1901-25

IMPRINTS, United States.

Cabinet 73 Shelf 2 No. 1

Nash, John Henry. San Francisco, 1925.
Title: If it were today. A playlet written by John Eugene Hasty for John Henry Nash....
Imprint: San Francisco: Printed by John Henry Nash in the month of May MDCCCCXXV.

Brochure No. 7. in John Henry Nash, Imprints San Francisco, 1910-1927.

IMPRINTS, United States.

Cabinet 73 Shelf 2 No. 1

Nash, John Henry. San Francisco, 1926.
Title: An Address before The American Association of Advertising Agencies at Washington...by President Coolidge. Printed by John Henry Nash of San Francisco.
Printed in a new italic designed by Morris Fuller Benton.

Brochure No.6. In John Henry Nash Imprints, San Francisco, 1910-1927.

IMPRINTS, United States.

Cabinet 71 Shelf 1 No. 79

Nash, John Henry, San Francisco, 1926. An introduction: Oliver Goldsmith and the deserted Village. By William Andrews Clark, Jr. Printed for William Andrews Clark, Jr.,

Introduction and bibliography, 1 vol., $12\frac{1}{4}$ x 9 ins., pp. 24. Facsimile of first edition 1770. 1 vol. 9 x $7\frac{1}{2}$ ins., pp. 23. Both in one case.

IMPRINTS, United States.

Cabinet 71 Shelf 1 No. 73

Nash, John Henry. San Francisco, 1925.
Title: Sonnets from the Portugese. By E. B. Browning. Biographical note by Edward F. O'Day. Portrait in dry point by John J. E. Stoll.
Imprint: Printed by John Henry Nash. San Francisco, 1925.

Boards, $12\frac{1}{2}$ x 9 in.

IMPRINTS, United States.

Cabinet 71 Shelf 1 No. 78

Nash, John Henry, San Francisco, 1926. An address before The American Association of Advertising Agencies at Washington....by President Coolidge.

The Lightface Cloister Italic used in this copy is a new cutting of Morris Fuller Benton, finished in Dec., 1926.

Boards; 14 x 9 ins., (2 copies?)

IMPRINTS, United States.

Cabinet 71 Shelf 1 No. 79

Nash, John Henry, San Francisco, 1926. An introduction: Oliver Goldsmith and the deserted Village. By William Andrews Clark, Jr. Printed for William Andrews Clark, Jr., John Henry Nash.

Introduction and bibliography, 1 vol., $12\frac{1}{4}$ x 9 ins., pp. 24. Facsimile of first edition 1770. 1 vol. 9 x $7\frac{1}{2}$ ins., pp. 23. Both in one case.

IMPRINTS, United States.

Cabinet 73 Shelf 2 No. 1

Nash, John Henry. San Francisco, 1925.
Title: Sonnets preceding the Inferno, Purgatorio, and Paradiso of the Comedy of Dante Alighieri of Florence. By Henry Wadsworth Longfellow.
Imprint: San Francisco: Printed for Aurelia Henry Reinhardt by John Henry Nash, MDCCCCXXV.

Brochure No.4, in John Henry Nash, Imprints, San Francisco, 1910-1927.

IMPRINTS, United States.

Cabinet 73 Shelf 2 No. 1

Nash, John Henry. San Francisco, 1926.
Title: Among quiet friends. By Alexander Inglis in the Pasadena Star-News, MDCCCCXXVI.
Colophon: Two hundred & fifty copies of this booklet were printed for Mrs. George M. Millard by John Henry Nash of San Francisco.

Brochure No.2, in John Henry Nash, Imprints, San Francisco, 1910-1927.

IMPRINTS, United States.

Cabinet 73 Shelf 1 No. 3

Nash, John Henry, San Francisco, 1926. Merry Christmas. Yuba Manufacturing Company. Printed by J.H. Nash.

Item 6 in John Henry Nash: His Work, San Francisco, v.d.

IMPRINTS, United States.

Cabinet 73 Shelf 1 No. 3

Nash, John Henry, San Francisco, 1925.
Title: El Toison de Oro: The Golden Fleece.
Imprint: This Broadside was written by Edward F. O'Day for Howard Griffith of the American Engraving & Color Plate Company as letter-press for a four-color reproduction... Printed by John Henry Nash of San Francisco MDCCCCXXV.

Item 7 in John Henry Nash: His Work. San Francisco v.d.

IMPRINTS, United States.

Cabinet 73 Shelf 1 No. 3

Nash, John Henry, San Francisco, 1926. "And on Earth peace to men of Good Will." By George Sterling. Reproduction of painting by Dan Sweeney. Borders by Edision Bills. Printing by John Henry Nash.
Broadside, folded, $12\frac{1}{2}$ x $9\frac{1}{2}$ in.

Item 2 in John Henry Nash: His Work, San Francisco, V.D.

IMPRINTS, United States.

Cabinet 73 Shelf 2 No. 17

Nash, John Henry. San Francisco, 1926. Nicolas Jenson, printer of Venice...By Henry Lewis Bullen, Librarian of The Typographic Library and Museum at Jersey City. The type is a recutting of Jenson's Roman Letter by Morris Fuller Benton.
Imprint: San Francisco. Printed by John Henry Nash. MDCCCCXXVI.

Boards; $16\frac{1}{2}$ x $10\frac{1}{2}$ in.

IMPRINTS, United States.

Cabinet 73 Shelf 1 No. 1

Nash, John Henry, San Francisco, 1925. Treasure: A broadside printed by J.H. Nash as a tribute to the president and the trustees of Mills College.

Item 3 in John Henry Nash: His Work, 1901-1925.

IMPRINTS, United States.

Cabinet 71 Shelf 1 No. 77

Nash, John Henry, San Francisco, 1926. An appreciation of James Wood Coffroth. Written for his son, by Edward F. O'Day, and printed by John Henry Nash. Portrait by William H. Wilke.

Marbled boards, $12\frac{1}{2}$ x 9 ins., pp.65.

IMPRINTS, United States.

Cabinet 73 Shelf 1 No. 1

Nash, John Henry, San Francisco, 1926. Retrospect: In Los Angeles. By Ina Coolbrith. Printed for Ernest Dawson by J.H. Nash of San Francisco in the month of December MDCCCCXXV.

Broadside.

Item 12 in John Henry Nash: His work, 1901-1925.

IMPRINTS, United States.

Cabinet 73 Shelf 2 No. 18

Nash, John Henry. San Francisco, 1926.
Title: To remember Ray Frederick Coyle. Six reproductions of his work, with a sonnet by George Sterling, and a foreword by John Henry Nash.
Imprint: Printed by John Henry Nash for his friends, MCMXXVI.

Boards, $15\frac{1}{2}$ x $12\frac{1}{2}$ in.

IMPRINTS, United States.

Cabinet 73 Shelf 2 No. 1

Nash, John Henry. San Francisco, 1927.
Title: The friendship of R. L. Stevenson and Jules Simoneau. Written by Edward F. O'Day. With portraits.
Imprint: Printed for Howard F. Griffith, president of the American Engraving...Company by John Henry Nash of San Francisco. December 1927.

Brochure No. 8. In John Henry Nash, Imprints San Francisco, 1910-1927.

IMPRINTS, UNITED STATES

Cabinet 73 Shelf 1 No. 3

Nash, John Henry. San Francisco, 1927.
Title: Caremond keepsake...Presented by the Zellerboch Paper Company to the members of the American Institute of Graphic Arts.
Imprint: The story is by Edward F. O'Day. Printed by John Henry Nash in San Francisco. February 1927.

Item 31 in scrapbook, "JOHN HENRY NASH: HIS WORK".

IMPRINTS, United States.

Cabinet 71 Shelf 1 No. 80

Nash, John Henry, San Francisco, 1927. Sonnets from the Portuguese, by E.B. Browning. With some observations and a bibliographical note by William Andrews, Clark, Jr., Frontispiece by William Wilke. Printed for W.A. Clark, Jr.

Biographical note, 1 vol. facsimile (1847), 1 vol. Both in one case.

Paper; 6 x 4 in.

IMPRINTS, United States.

Cabinet 73 Shelf 2 No. 27

Nash, John Henry: San Francisco, 1927.
Title: The Testimony of the Suns. By George Sterling. Including comments, suggestions and annotations by Ambrose Bierce.....
Imprint: San Francisco: Printed for The Book Club of California by John Henry Nash, 1927.

Marbled paper boards; $14\frac{1}{2}$ x 9-6/8 in

IMPRINTS, United States.

Cabinet 73 Shelf 2 No. 23

Nash, John Henry, San Francisco, Christmas, 1927. A Toast to the Ladies, by Edward H. Hamilton.

"To be permitted to print it in my shop and make it better known is an honor I profoundly appreciate," J.H.N.

Broadside, in cover; $17\frac{1}{2}$ s $10\frac{3}{4}$ ins.

IMPRINTS, United States

Cabinet 73 Shelf 2 No. 28

Nash, John Henry Fine Arts Press at the University of Oregon, 1927.
Title: Education & the State. Prince L. Campbells philosophy of public education
Imprint: Eugene. The University of Oregon Fine Arts Press, 1927.
The book was composed by the senior students of the class of typography. John Henry Nash Fine Arts Press.

Boards; 12-5/8 x 9-1/8 in.

IMPRINTS, United States

Cabinet 71 Shelf 1 No. 86

Nash, John Henry; San Francisco, 1928.
Title: The Arrogant Youth: Being a family music play in two acts.
Imprint:...Done at the family farm, in the Portola Valley...and now imprinted in the City of San Francisco...by John Herry Nash. November, 1928.

Boards; $12\frac{1}{2}$ x 9 in.

IMPRINTS, United States.

Cabinet 73 Shelf 1 No. 3

Nash, John Henry. San Francisco, 1928. A Christmas Greeting.
Imprint: Written by Edward F. O'Day and printed by John Henry Nash of San Francisco for the Yuba Manufacturing Company of San Francisco .....In the month of December nineteen hundred & twenty-eight.

Item 10 in John Henry Nash: His Work. San Francisco, v.d.

IMPRINTS, United States.

Cabinet 73 Shelf 2 No. 32

Nash, John Henry. San Francisco, 1928.
Title: A Christmas Sermon. By Robert Louis Stevenson.
Imprint: Printed for William Andrews Clark, Jr. By John Henry Nash, San Francisco, November, MCMXXVIII.
Reprinted by permission of Charles Scribn er's Sons, New York.

Boards, $16\frac{1}{2}$ x $10\frac{1}{2}$ in.

IMPRINTS, United States.

Cabinet 71 Shelf 1 No. 85

Nash, John Henry: San Francisco, 1928.

Title: An Invocation. By Ambrose Bierce: With a critical introduction by George Sterling.
Imprint: Printed for The Book Club of San Francisco by John Herny Nash of San Francisco, 1928.

Linen covered boards; 11 x 7-5/8 in.

IMPRINTS, United States

Cabinet 73 Shelf 2 No. 38

Nash, John Henry, San Francisco, 1928.
Title: Life and personality of Phoebe Apperson Hearst. By Winifred Black Bonfils.
Imprint: Printed for William Randolph Hearst by John Henry Nash.

Vellum; $13\frac{3}{4}$ x $9\frac{1}{4}$ x $1\frac{1}{2}$ in.

IMPRINTS, United States.

Cabinet 73 Shelf 2 No. 37

Nash, John Henry. San Francisco, 1928.
Title: A pleasaunt morn at La Estancia. By Templeton Crocker.
Imprint: Printed by John Henry Nash of San Francisco. 1928.

Paper Boards, 10 x $7\frac{1}{2}$ in.

IMPRINTS, United States.

Cabinet 73 Shelf 2 No. 33

Nash, John Henry. San Francisco, 1928.
Title: Pope's Essay on criticism. [Facsimile, 1711 ed., and reprint, 1928].
Colophon: Printed in facsimile for William Andrews Clark, Jr., by John Henry Nash in the City of San Francisco, 1928.

Paper boards; facsimile, 9 x $6\frac{1}{4}$ in., reprint $12\frac{1}{2}$ x $9\frac{1}{4}$ in. Both in one slip case.

IMPRINTS, United States

Cabinet 73 Shelf 2 No. 47

Nash, John Henry. San Francisco, 1929.
Title: All for love: or the world well lost. By John Dryden.
Imprint: San Francisco: Printed for William Andrews Clark, Jr. by John Henry Nash, 1929.
This also includes a facsimile of the original 1678 edition.

Boards; 12-5/8 x $9\frac{1}{4}$ x $\frac{3}{4}$ in. In protective case; $13\frac{1}{4}$ x 9-3/8 x 1-7/8 in.

IMPRINTS, United States

Cabinet 73 Shelf 1 No. 3

Nash, John Henry. San Francisco, 1929.
Title: Announcement: Cornelius Cole, California pioneer and United States Senator ... By Catherin Coffin Phillips. San Francisco. (A prospectus).
Imprint: Printed by John Henry Nash. 1929.

Item 14 in Scrap Book: John Henry Nash, His Work. San Francisco, V.D.

IMPRINTS, United States.

Cabinet 73 Shelf 1 No. 3

Nash, John Henry: San Francisco, March, 1929.
Title: Announcing a public showing of the life and personality of Phoebe Apperson Hearst. By Winifred Black Bonfils.
Printed for William Randolph Hearst by John Henry Nash.

Item 11 in John Henry Nash; His Work. San Francisco, v.d.

IMPRINTS, United States.

Cabinet 73 Shelf 1 No. 3

Nash, John Henry. San Francisco, 1929.
Title: Archbishop Hanna on the Vatican Library. By John Henry Nash.
Colophon: In honor of fine printing of the past, for the joy of present doing...this broadside has been created through the cooperation of a group of members of the San Francisco Club of Printing House Craftsmen. April, 1929.

Item 13 in John Henry Nash: His work. San Francisco.V.D.

IMPRINTS, United States.

Cabinet 73 — Shelf 1 — No. 3

Nash, John Henry. San Francisco, 1929.
Title: Besides the Straits of Carquinez. By Edward F. O'Day. Broadside.
Colophon: Text by Edward F. O'Day. The design by Dan Sweeney. Woodcutting by William Wilke. Printing by John Henry Nash. San Francisco, 1929.

Item 9 in John Henry Nash: His Work, San Francisco, v.d.

IMPRINTS, United States.

Cabinet 71 — Shelf 1 — No. 18

Nash, John Henry. Tomoye Press, San Francisco, 1911.
Title: Recipe for a Happy Life. Written by Margaret of Navarre in the 1500.
Colophon: ... Published by Paul Elder and Company ... and printed for them by their Tomoyé Press under the care of John Henry Nash. San Francisco, 1911.

Stamped paper boards; $8\frac{1}{4}$ x 7 x 3/8 in.

IMPRINTS, United States.

Cabinet 71 — Shelf 1 — No. 1

Nash, John Henry. San Francisco, [1929].
Title: Summer Time.
Imprint: John Henry Nash, Printer. 447 Sansome Street, San Francisco.

Item 5 in "Printing done by John Henry Nash San Francisco".

IMPRINTS, United States

Cabinet 71 — Shelf 1 — No. 88

Nash, John Henry. San Francisco, 1929.
Title: Cobden-Sanderson and the Doves Press. ... By Alfred W. Pollard, and Edward Johnston. [Printers' prospectus].
Imprint: San Francisco. Printed by John Henry Nash. 1929.

Paper cover brochure; $12\frac{3}{4}$ x $8\frac{1}{4}$ in.

IMPRINTS, United States.

Cabinet 73 — Shelf 2 — No. 43

Nash, John Henry. San Francisco, 1929.
Title: Immortal little Willie. By Eugene Field. Illus. by Dan Sweeney.
Colophon: Printed by John Henry Nash of San Francisco for understanding mothers and fathers...February, of the year Nineteen Hundred and Twenty-Nine.

Marbled paper boards; $17\frac{1}{4}$ x $12\frac{1}{4}$ in.

IMPRINTS, United States.

Cabinet 71 — Shelf 2 — No. 41

Nash, John Henry. San Francisco, 1929.
Title: This book announces the publication in folio volumes of the Comedy of Dante Alighieri...A translation in the rime form of the original by Melville Best Anderson.
Imprint: San Francisco. Printed by John Henry Nash, MCMXXIX.

Boards, $13\frac{3}{4}$ x $9\frac{1}{4}$ in.

IMPRINTS, United States

Cabinet 71 — Shelf 1 — No. 89

Nash, John Henry. San Francisco, 1929.
Title: Cobden-Sanderson and the Doves Press: The history of the Press and the story of its types told by Alfred W. Pollard ...
Imprint: San Francisco. Printed by John Henry Nash, 1929.

Vellum; $12\frac{1}{2}$ x 8-3/8 x $\frac{3}{4}$ in. In paper board protective case.

IMPRINTS, United States.

Cabinet 73 — Shelf 1 — No. 3

Nash, John Henry: San Francisco, January, 1929.
An inspiring message of typographic interest: Written for Zellerbach Paper Company by Edward F. O'Day and imprinted by John Henry Nash of San Francisco from a recutting of type of William Bulmer done by Morris Fuller Benton.

Item 12 in John Henry Nash: His Work: San Francisco, v.d.

IMPRINTS, United States.

Cabinet 71 — Shelf 2 — No. 38

Nash, John Henry. San Francisco, California, 1930.
Title: Father Damien: An open letter to the Reverend Dr. Hyde of Honolulu. By Robert Louis Stevenson. Sydney, 1890.
Colophon: Printed in facsimile for William Andrews Clark, Jr. by John Henry Nash in San Francisco, California, 1930.
Reprint, large copy in same edition, and in same protective case.

Boards; 8-3/8 x $5\frac{1}{2}$ x $\frac{1}{4}$ in. In case: 13 x $9\frac{1}{4}$ by $1\frac{1}{2}$ in.

This is no. 92 of an edition of 250 copies

IMPRINTS, United States

Cabinet 73 — Shelf 2 — No. 45

Nash, John Henry. San Francisco, 1929.
Title: Cornelius Cole. California pioneer and United States Senator ... By C. C. Phillips.
Imprint: San Francisco: Printed by John Henry Nash. 1929.

Cloth; $10\frac{3}{4}$ x 7-7/8 x $1\frac{1}{4}$ in. In Cloth covered protective case.

IMPRINTS, United States

Cabinet 73 — Shelf 2 — No. 44

Nash, John Henry. San Francisco, 1929.
Title: Memorial address on the life and character of Abraham Lincoln /.. By George Bancroft on the 12th February, 1866. With an introduction by John Drinkwater.
Imprint: Printed for The Book Club of California by John Henry Nash, San Francisco, 1929.

Boards; $11\frac{3}{4}$ x $8\frac{1}{4}$ x $\frac{1}{2}$ in.

IMPRINTS, United States.

Cabinet 73 — Shelf 1 — No. 3

Nash, John Henry. San Francisco, 1930.
Title: For all our friends ... Merry Christmas and a Happy New Year. The officers and directors of The Hibernia Bank. San Francisco [Engraving by William Wilke].
Imprint: San Francisco: Printed by John Henry Nash.

Leaf No. 22 in "John Henry Nash: His Work. San Francisco."

IMPRINTS, United States.

Cabinet 73 — Shelf 2 — No. 1

Nash, John Henry. San Francisco, 1929.
Title: A dinner to honor William Sproule and Paul Shoup. Announcement: Folded broadside in envelope.
Imprint: San Francisco. John Henry Nash, Printer

Item 9; In John Henry Nash, Imprints, San Francisco, 1910-1927.

IMPRINTS, United States

Cabinet 73 — Shelf 2 — No. 46

Nash, John Henry. San Francisco, 1929.
Title: The Psalms of the singer David.
Imprint colophon: Here ends ... A book done for the joy of doing by John Henry Nash, Printer of San Francisco ... Christmastide of 1929. The Frontispiece and the ornamental borders were designed and executed by William Wilke.

Cloth; 15-7/8 x 9-5/8 x $\frac{1}{2}$ in.

IMPRINTS, United States.

Cabinet 73 — Shelf 1 — No. 3

Nash, John Henry. San Francisco, 1930.
Title: The ghost that walked amid the cases has hied him to more ghostly places. [Vacation broadside].
Imprint: John Henry Nash (et al.), printer, San Francisco.

Leaf 18 in "John Henry Nash: His Work."

IMPRINTS, United States.

Cabinet 73 — Shelf 1 — No. 2

Nash, John Henry. San Francisco, 1929.
Title: Granddaughter of a California Pioneer. By Edward F. O'Day. With a reproduction from a drawing.
Colophon: Designed and printed by John Henry Nash for Howard J. Griffith....San Francisco, January, Nineteen Hundred and Twenty-Nine.

Boards; 18-3/4 x $12\frac{1}{2}$ in.

IMPRINTS, United States.

Cabinet 73 — Shelf 2 — No. 42

Nash, John Henry. San Francisco, 1929.
Title: Speech delivered by Leland W. Cutter at a dinner given in San Francisco to William Sproule and Paul Shoup...On January the tenth, nineteen hundred and twenty-nine.
Colophon: Imprinted by John Henry Nash of San Francisco, for S P. Eastman.

Boards; 13 x $9\frac{1}{2}$ in.

IMPRINTS, United States.

Cabinet 73 — Shelf 1 — No. 3

Nash, John Henry. San Francisco, 1930.
Title: In mellow mood. (Broadside).
Imprint: San Francisco, Printed by John Henry Nash for his friends, 1930.

On folio 33 of book "John Henry Nash: His Work."

IMPRINTS, United States.

Cabinet 73 Shelf 2 No. 51

Nash, John Henry. San Francisco, 1930.
Title: Laudes Virgilianae. Auctore Henricò Woods e Soc. Jesu.
Imprint: A Joanne Henrico Nash A.M. Littl. D. E. prelo suo amicorum gratia. Editae Sancti Francisci in California.

Paper boards; 12 x $7\frac{3}{4}$ in.

IMPRINTS, United States.

Cabinet 73 Shelf 1 No. 3

Nash, John Henry. San Francisco, 1930.
Title: The trial of the wine-brewers: An essay by Joseph Addison. With an introduction by Edward F. O'Day. [Prospectus].
Imprint: San Francisco: Printed by John Henry Nash, 1930.

Leaf 21 in "John Henry Nash: His Work. San Francisco, v.d "

IMPRINTS, United States

Cabinet 73 Shelf 1 No. 3

Nash, John Henry. San Francisco. 1931.
Title: Christmas Greetings from William Andrews Clark, Jr. Los Angeles. 1931.

Brochure, $12\frac{1}{2}$ x 9 in. Item on p.27 of scrap book labelled "John Henry Nash: His work".

IMPRINTS, United States.

Cabinet 71 Shelf 2 No. 16

Nash, John Henry. San Francisco, 1930.
Title: Library of William Andrews Clark Jr. Index to authors and titles. Compiled and arranged by Robert Ernest Cowan and William Andrews Clark, Jr.
Imprint: San Francisco: Printed by John Henry Nash, 1930.

Paper boards; 10-3/8 x $7\frac{3}{4}$ x $1\frac{3}{4}$ in.

IMPRINTS, United States.

Cabinet 73 Shelf 1 No. 3

Nash, John Henry. San Francisco, 1930.
Vacation broadside [beginning with]: "Castles of Spain!" ...
Imprint: John Henry Nash and his co-workers in Sansome Street, in the almost free city of San Francisco.

In volume "John Henry Nash: His Work." Leaf 17.

IMPRINTS, United States

Cabinet 73 Shelf 1 No. 3

Nash, John Henry, San Francisco, 1931.
Title: Emendatio mechanica plagularium: An announcement of importance to advertisers, printers, authors & poets from John Henry Nash.
An announcement of vacation time of the printing office of J.H.N.

Folded broadside, item 26, in "John Henry Nash: His work, San Francisco, v.d."

IMPRINTS, United States.

Cabinet 73 Shelf 2 No. 52

Nash, John Henry. San Francisco, 1930.
Title: Mr. Strahan's dinner party. A comedy in one act. With prologue and epilogue by A. Edward Newton, and a note by Edward F. O'Day With portraits of B. Franklin and Dr. Johnson.
Imprint: San Francisco: Printed for the Book Club of California by John Henry Nash, 1930.

Boards; 14 x $9\frac{1}{4}$ x $\frac{3}{4}$ in.

IMPRINTS, United States.

Cabinet 73 Shelf 2 No. 50

Nash, John Henry. San Francisco, 1930.
Title: The Visitor ... By Hugh A. Studdert Kennedy.
Imprint: San Francisco. Printed by John Henry Nash, 1930.
Has printer mark on title page.

Marbled paper boards; $11\frac{3}{4}$ x 8-3/8 x $\frac{1}{2}$ in.

IMPRINT, United States.

Cabinet 73 Shelf 1 No. 3

Nash, John Henry. San Francisco, 1931.
Title: How Old Am I? By Henrietta Heron.
Sent out at Christmas by The Nash Family.

Item on p. 28 of scrap-book labelled, John Henry Nash: His Work, San Francisco.

IMPRINTS, United States.

Cabinet 73 Shelf 1 No. 3

Nash, John Henry. San Francisco, 1930.
Title: The Nineteenth Psalm of Israel's great poet David.
Imprint: I have made this rendition in a folded broadside as an offering to the cause of the Jewish Community Center ... John Henry Nash [Imprinted 1930].

Leaf 19 in "John Henry Nash: His Work. San Francisco."

IMPRINTS, United States.

Cabinet 73 Shelf 1 No. 3

Nash, John Henry. San Francisco, 1930.
Title: The Visitor ... By Hugh A. Studdert Kennedy. (Prospectus) With J.H.N. Printer Mark.
Imprint: San Francisco. Printed by John Henry Nash. 1930.

p. 16 in "John Henry Nash - His work."

IMPRINTS, United States.

Cabinet 73 Shelf 2 No. 54

Nash, John Henry. San Francisco, 1931.
Title: Life of Saint Francis of Assisi. Translated by Miss E. B. Salter.
Imprint: And now imprinted by John Henry Nash on the 25th anniversary of the disaster of 1906 ... San Francisco, 1931.
Drawings by William Wilke. No. 216 of an edition of 385 copies.

Boards; 16 x 9-7/8 x 3/8 in.

IMPRINTS, UNITED STATES

Cabinet 73 Shelf 1 No. 8

Nash, John Henry, San Francisco, 1930.
Title: The Nuremberg Chronicle...A monograph by Henry Lewis Bullen.
Imprint: Printed for the Book Club of California by John Henry Nash, San Francisco, 1930.

Boards; 18-3/4 x 12-3/4 in.

IMPRINT, United States.

Cabinet 73 Shelf 1 No. 3

Nash, John Henry. San Francisco, 1931.
Title: Bene Dictum, Benedicte! (Broadside).
Imprint:...Printed for John Henry Nash of The Vatican for the joy of doing ...

On folio 34 of book "John Henry Nash: His Work."

IMPRINTS, United States.

Cabinet 73 Shelf 1 No. 5

Nash, John Henry. San Francisco, 1931.
Title: The Sermon on the Mount ...
Imprint: Printed for Edward L. and Estelle Doheny by John Henry Nash of San Francisco.

Boards; 19 x 10-5/8 in.

IMPRINTS, United States

Cabinet 73 Shelf 2 No. 53

Nash, John Henry. San Francisco, 1930.
Title: The trial of the wine-brewers. An essay by Joseph Addison. From the Tatler, Thursday Feb. 9, 1709. Introduction by Ed. F. O'Day. Decorations are by William Wilke.
Imprint: San Francisco: Printed by John Henry Nash, 1930.

Boards; $11\frac{3}{4}$ x 8-1/8 in.

IMPRINTS, United States.

Cabinet 73 Shelf 2 No. 56

Nash, John Henry. San Francisco, 1931.
Title: Bibliography of the history of California. By Robert Ernst Cowan and Robert Grannis Cowan [Prospectus of].

Item in manila envelope.

IMPRINTS, United States

Cabinet 73 Shelf 1 No. 6

Nash, John Hrnry. San Francisco, 1931.
Title: The songs of Solomon.
Imprint: This broadside was done from types, ornaments and rules by John Henry Nash in the City of Saint Francis by the Golden Gate at Christmas 1931, in the sincere hope that it will give pleasure to his friends.

Boards; 19 x $11\frac{1}{4}$ in.

IMPRINTS, United States

Cabinet 73 Shelf 1 No. 3

Nash, John Henry. San Francisco, 1931.
Title: Vergil...By Melville Best Anderson.
Imprint: San Francisco. Printed by John Henry Nash. (Prospectus).

Type -- a recutting of the letters of G. Bodoni by the Bauer Type Foundry. Frankfort a.M. Germany.

Item on folio 35 of scrap book "John Henry Nash, his book. San Francisco, v.d."

IMPRINTS, United States

Cabinet 73 Shelf 2 No. 57

Nash, John Henry. San Francisco, 1932.
Title: Portsmouth Plaza. The cradle of San Francisco. By Catherine Coffin Phillips.
Imprint: San Francisco: Printed by John Henry Nash, 1932.

Type: Elzevir, specially cut and refitted by Morris Fuller Benton of the American Type Founders Company, Jersey City, N.J.

Illustrations in wood-block style, by William Wilkie.

Boards, vellum back; 10-3/4 x 7½ x 2 in.

IMPRINTS, United States

Cabinet 73 Shelf 2 No. 59

Nash, John Henry, San Francisco, 1934
Title: A certain young man of Assisi. By May Southworth. With illustrations by Will Wilke.
Imprint: San Francisco. Imprinted bv John Heary Nash. (With Nash device)

Boards; $10\frac{3}{4}$ x $8\frac{3}{4}$ in.

IMPRINTS, United States

Cabinet 73 Shelf 1 No. 3

Nash, John Henry. San Francisco, 1932.
Title: About these United States. Longfellow.
Imprint: San Francisco: Printed by John Henry Nash. Border by William Wilke. 1932.

Broadside on fol. 37 or scrap book labelled "John Henry Nash: His work, v.d."

IMPRINTS, UNITED STATES

Cabinet 73 Shelf 1 No. 3

Nash, John Henry. San Francisco, Calif. 1932.
Title: Portsmouth Plaza: The cradle of San Francisco. [Broadside, prospectus].
Imprint: This is a preliminary announcement... John Henry Nash, 447 Sansome Street, San Francisco.

Item on p.29 of scrap book "John Henry Nash: His work".

IMPRINTS, United States

Cabinet 73 Shelf 1 No. 3

Nash, John Henry, San Francisco, 1934
Title: William Caxton an English printer. (Proof sheets, printed in black, and in colors). By Henry Lewis Bullen.
Imprint: The Zellerback Paper Company is presenting this Keepsake to friends and patrons... Printed by John Henry Nash in the City of San Francisco, January, 1934.

On folio 41 of vol. labelled: John Henry Nash: His work. San Francisco, v.d.

IMPRINTS, UNITED STATES.

Cabinet 73 Shelf 1 No. 3

Nash, John Henry. San Francisco, 1932.
Title: A bad case of jitters: A printer dreams a terrible dance of death. By John Henry Nash, Printer.
Imprint: August 15, 1932. John Henry Nash.

Broadside, $15\frac{3}{4}$ x $10\frac{1}{2}$ in. Item on fol. 32 of scrap book "John Henry Nash: His Work."

IMPRINTS, United States

Cabinet 73 Shelf 2 No. 58

Nash, John Henry, San Francisco, 1933
Title: Bibliography of the history of California, 1510-1930. By Robert E. and Robert G. Cowan.
Imprint: San Francisco: Printed by John Henry Nash. 1933.

2 vols with index in protective case.

IMPRINTS, United States

Cabinet 73 Shelf 1 No. 9

Nash, John Henry, San Francisco, Calif. 1935
Title: The Last Will anf Testament. Written by Williston Fish for Harpers Weekly, 1898.
Imprint: San Francisco: Printed by John Henry Nash, 1935.

Boards; $22\frac{1}{2}$ x $11\frac{3}{4}$ in.

IMPRINTS, United States.

Cabinet 73 Shelf 1 No. 7

Nash, John Henry. San Francisco, 1932.
Title: Biblia Sacra. Vulgate editionis ... Sancti Francisci, 1932.
(The Vulgate of St. Jerome: A prospectus)

Presentation copy.

Boards; $18\frac{1}{4}$ x $12\frac{1}{4}$ in. In protective case.

IMPRINTS, United States

Cabinet 73 Shelf 2 No. 39

Nash, John Henry, San Francisco, 1933
Title: George Hearst, life of a California pioneer. By Mr. and Mrs. Froment Older.
Imprint: The frontispiece and headbands by William Wilke. Printed for William Randolph Hearst by John Henry Nash, San Francisco, 1933.

Vellum; $13\frac{3}{4}$ x 9 in.

IMPRINTS, United States

Cabinet 73 Shelf 2 No. 60

Nash, John Henry, San Francisco, 1935.
Title: The Templeton Crocker Collection of seventy books from the famous Aldine Press, 1494 - 1595. With a foreword by John Eugene Hasty. Exhibited in The John Henry Nash Library, June 17 - 28, 1935.
Imprint: Printed by John Henry Nash.

Brochure, oblong; 10 x $4\frac{3}{4}$ in.

IMPRINTS, United States

Cabinet 73 Shelf 1 No. 3

Nash, John Henry. San Francisco, 1932.
Title: Christmas greetings from William Andrews Clark, Jr. The Lords Prayer from the Sermon on the Mount. The Last Supper is by Dagnan Bouvere.
Imprint: Reproduced...for William Andrew Clark Jr. by John Henry Nash of San Francisco.

Broadside on fol. 36 of scrap book labelled: "John Henry Nash: His work, v.d."

IMPRINTS, United States

Cabinet 71 Shelf 2 No. 39

Nash, John Henry, San Francisco, 1933
Title:Ode on the Pleasure arising from Vicissitud Left unfinished by Mr. Grey...With an introduction by Leonard Whibley.
Imprint: San Francisco: Printed for William Andrews Clark, Jr. by John Henry Nash, 1933

With facsimile . In protective case

IMPRINTS, United States.

Cabinet G Shelf 2 No. 90

New York, 1910. Walter Pater's conclusions to his book The Renaissance. Privately printed. Booklet.

Paper; $6\frac{1}{2}$ x 5 in.

IMPRINTS, United States

Cabinet 73 Shelf 2 No. 55

Nash, John Henry. San Francisco, 1932.
J.H.N. announces a bibliography of the history of California. By Robert Ernest Cowan and Robert Granniss Cowan.
A prospectus.

Item in manila envelope.

IMPRINTS, United States.

Cabinet G Shelf 4 No. 6.03

Nash, John Henry Fine Arts Press. University of Oregon, 1933.

See IMPRINTS, United States. University of Oregon: John Henry Nash Fine Arts Press ...

IMPRINTS, United States.

Cabinet G Shelf 2 No. 91

Newark, New Jersey, 1915. Poems of encouragement. Privately printed. With a foreword by Thomas L. Raymond.

Boards; 8 x 5 in. (3), pp.14.

IMPRINTS, United States

Cabinet G, Shelf 3, No. 7.03

Oriole Press (Joseph Ishill), Berkeley Heights, N.J., 1927.
Title: Elisee and Elie Reclus...Compiled, edited and printed by Joseph Ishill. Illus.
Imprint: Privately printed at the Oriole Press...

"These samples were printed on a rusty, worn-out "Favorite" press which was abandoned in a shed in the vicinity of Berkeley Heights, N.J. The Garamond type is cast by The American Type Founders".

Brochure, in manila envelope

IMPRINTS, United States

Cabinet F, Shelf 3, No. 35

Patten, Nathaniel. Hartford, 1789.
Title: A view of the internal evidence of the christian religion.
Imprint: Hartford: Printed by Nathaniel Patten. 1789.

Leather; 6½ x 4 x 1 in. Evans 7, 21904, p. 327.

IMPRINTS, United States.

Cabinet G, Shelf 3, No. 12

Polytype Press (S.A. Jacobs) New York, 1925. Natives of Rock: XX poems, by Glenway Wescott. Printed in types newly adopted for this edition. Decorations by Pamela Bianco.

Boards, 9-3/4 x 6 ins., pp. 24, not numbered lvs. 7.

IMPRINTS, United States.

Cabinet G, Shelf 3, No. 8

Oswald, John Clyde, New York, 1924. Merrie Tales of the mad men of Gotham, emprynted with wadparker types by mee, at the Signe of the Lion of St. Marks in New York Town. Booklet.

Boards; 6-3/4 x 5 ins., pp.8.

IMPRINTS, United States.

Cabinet G, Shelf 3, No. 9

Perry-Estabrook Press (The), Inc., Cambridge, Mass., 1924. Skilled labor, the Puritan heritage by Roy Griffith, with etching by the author.

Boards, 11 x 8 ins., pp.14.

IMPRINTS, United States

Cabinet G, Shelf 3, No. 13

Polytype Press (S.A. Jacobs), New York 1926. Is 5 by E.E. Cummings. Printed by Samuel Aiwaz Jacobs.

Boards; 8½ x 5½ in. pp.115.

IMPRINTS, United States

Cabinet F, Shelf 3, No. 33

Parker, James and Company. New Haven, 1757.
Title: Some remarks on Mr. President Clop's history.
Imprint: New Haven. Printed by J. Parker and Company, 1757.

Half morocco; 8 x 5½ in. Evans 3, 7881, p.163

IMPRINTS, United States.

Cabinet G, Shelf 3, No. 10

Peter Pauper Press, Larchmont, 1928.
Title: Faithless Sally Brown and Faithless Nelly Gray: Two ballads by Thomas Hood, with engravings by Herb Roth.
Imprint: Larchmont - Peter Pauper Press, 1928.

Boards; 9½ x 6-3/8 in.

IMPRINTS, United States.

Cabinet F, Shelf 2, No. 89

Powars and Willis: Boston, 1784.

Title: The benevolence of the Diety....By Charles Chauncy, D.D. Senior Pastor of the First Church of Christ in Boston.
Imprint: America: Massachusetts. Boston: Printed by Powars & Willis, MDCCLXXXIV.

Half russia; 8 x 5 in. Evans 6, 18397: p.276.

IMPRINTS, United States

Cabinet G, Shelf 3, No. 8.01

Parker, Wadsworth A. Specimen Printing Dept. American Type Founders Co., Jersey City, N.J., 1931.
Title: Testimonial dinner to E.F. Eilert, Feb., 25, 1931. Hotel Astor. With portrait frontispiece.
Imprint: Printed for Printers' Supply Salesmen's Guild of New York, with compliments of the A.T.F. Co.

Boards, gilt; 7½ x 5-1/8 x ¼ in.

IMPRINTS, United States.

Cabinet F, Shelf 1, No. 4

Pierce, Richard: Boston, 1685.

See Early Printing in New England. Boston. 1685: Richard Pierce.

IMPRINTS, United States.

Cabinet G, Shelf 3, No. 14

Prairie Press, The., Ralph Fletcher, Chicago, 1904. The book of Ruth. Taken from an edition of the Bible printed at Oxford in 1680. Printed for the designer and illustrator Ralph Fletcher Seymour.

Embossed linen covers, 9½ x 6-3/4 ins., pp.28.

IMPRINTS, United States

Cabinet S, Shelf 1, No. 130

Parks, William. Williamsburg, Va., 1730.
Title: Typographia, an ode to Printing...
Imprint: Williamsburg: Printed by William Parks 1730. Photographic reprint.
This is the first book printed in the American Colonies relating to the Art of Printing.

Boards; 10½ x 7-1/8 in. In protective case.

IMPRINTS, United States

Cabinet S, Shelf 5, No. 41

Plandome Press (Douglas C. McMurtrie). New York, 1927.
Title: A history of California newspapers.
Imprint: Plandome Press. Imprinted at New York, N.Y. 1927.

Boards; 7½ x 5 x 1 in.

IMPRINTS, United States.

Cabinet G, Shelf 4, No. 43

Press in the Forest, J.W. Wright, Carmel-by-the-sea, California, 1925. The Whim horse, by J.W. Wright. Typography and binding by the author. Full page drawing by Ralph Fullerton Mocine.

Boards, 7¼ x 5¼ ins., pp.29.

IMPRINTS, United States

Cabinet G, Shelf 3, No. 8.02

Parnassus Press, Lew Ney, Brooklyn, N.Y. 1933.
Title: With the makers...Compiled by Benjamin Musser.
Imprint: Designed and printed by Lew Ney in his Type Shop, Brooklyn, N.Y.

Paper; 6¼ x 4½ in. Item with other Parnassus items in manila envelope

---

IMPRINTS, United States.

Cabinet G, Shelf 3, No. 11

Polytype Press (S.A. Jacobs) New York, 1923. Tulips and Chimneys, by E.E. Cummings.

First book printed in 14-point Linotype Caslon Oldstyle.

Boards, cloth back, 8½ x 6½ ins., pp.125.

IMPRINTS, United States

Cabinet G, Shelf 3, No. 82.01

Press of Egyptian Publications at Herrin, Ill 1934.
Title: In casa mia...
Colophon: One hundred and thirty nine copies were privately printed for Violet and Hal W. Trovillion, at the Press of the Egyptian Publications at Herrin, Ill. Christmas, 1933.

Boards; 7¾ x 5¼ in.

IMPRINTS, United States.

Cabinet G Shelf 3 No. 16

Princeton University Press, Princeton, N.J. 1922. The apple tree table and other sketches by Herman Melville. Book designed by Frederique Warde.
A.L.S. inserted.

Boards; 8-7/8 x 5¾ in.

IMPRINTS, United States.

Cabinet G Shelf 3 No. 15

Princeton University Press, Princeton, N.J., 1922, John Marr and other poems by Herman Melville. Book designed by Frederique Warde.

Boards, 8-7/8 x 5¾ ins., pp.329.

IMPRINTS, United States.

Cabinet G Shelf 3 No. 18

Princeton University Press, Princeton, N.J., 1923. A catalogue of books published by the Princeton University Press. Brochure.

Paper, 8 x 5 ins., pp.95.

IMPRINTS, United States.

Cabinet G Shelf 3 No. 17

Princeton University Press, Princeton, N.J., 1923. Dedication of McCormick Hall, Princeton, June 16. Brochure. Illus.

A.L.S. Frederique Warde, director of the press at the time.

Paper, 10 x 7¼ ins., pp.24.

IMPRINTS, United States

Cabinet G Shelf 3 No. 19

Princeton University Press, Princeton, N.J., 1924. Survivals in the fine art of printing. An exhibition arranged and catalogued by Frederique Warde. Brochure.

Half morocco; 8 x 5¼ in. pp.15.

IMPRINTS, United States

Cabinet G Shelf 3 No. 20

Princeton University Press, Princeton, N.J.: Harvey Hopkins Dunn. 1927.
Title: Twenty-fifth anniversary class of 1902. University of Pennsylvania. Philadelphia, Portraits.
Colophon. ... Designed by Harvey Hopkins Dunn, and printed at the Princeton University Press

Boards; 6-3/8 x 4-3/8 x ½ in.

IMPRINTS, United States.

Cabinet G Shelf 3 No. 21

Pynson Printers, New York, 1923. April Twilights, by Willa Cather.

Edition, signed by the author.

Boards, 9 x 6 ins., pp.66. In Case.

IMPRINTS, United States.

Cabinet K Shelf 1 No. 30

Pynson Printers, New York, 1924. A book of American trade-marks and devices, compiled and designed by Joseph Sinel.

Boards, 12½ x 9½ ins., pp.64.

IMPRINTS, United States.

Cabinet G Shelf 3 No. 22

Pynson Printers, New York, 1924. The Squire's Home-made Wines, as described and set forth in the Journal of Thomas Hoggson, Gent, 1765. Set and printed in the city of New York at the shop of the Pynson Printers.

Boards, 6¼ x 4-3/4 ins., pp.37.

IMPRINTS, United States.

Cabinet G Shelf 5 No. 14

Pynson Printers, New York, 1925. Plans and designs for the Roosevelt Memorial in the City of Washington. Illus.

Boards, 14 x 11½ ins., pp.19, with 5 full plates.

IMPRINTS, United States.

Cabinet G Shelf 3 No. 24

Pynson Printers, New York, 1925. Twin peas in a pod. Privately printed for Ernst Elmo Calkins and Angie Cushman Calkins.

Boards 8¼ x 6½ ins., pp.23.

IMPRINTS, United States

Cabinet G Shelf 3 No. 22.01

**Pynson Printers, New York, 1929.
Title: Check List of Pynson Printer Imprints. New York, 1929.**

Item in manila envelope.

IMPRINTS, United States

Cabinet J Shelf 4 No. 24

**Pynson Printers, The. New York, 1929.
Title: Decorative work of T.M. Cleland...
Imprint: New York. The Pynson Printers. MCMXXIX.**

Cloth; 12½ x 9½ x ⅝ in.

IMPRINTS, United States

Cabinet RR Shelf 6 No. 10

Pynson Printers, New York, 1936.

see HUNTER, DARD. (A) Papermaking pilgrimage to Japan, Korea, etc.

IMPRINTS, United States

Cabinet G Shelf 3 No. 24.03

Random House, New York, 1928-1929, announcements for.

A note informs us that the Random House (publishers) was incorporated in 1927. The announcements deal with the imprints of the Random House , Crosby Gaige, Nonesuch Press, Golden Cockerel Press, Peter Davies, Haslewood, Fleuron, Sign of the Black Manikin, all publishing limited editions.

Item in mani[illegible] envelope.

IMPRINTS, United States.

Cabinet G Shelf 3 No. 26

Ransom, Will, Private Press, Chicago, 1923. Ye Beatyfycatyon of ye novyce, by C.B.Reed. Designed, set, printed on a hand presse and bound by ye personal labour of Will Ranson wyth ye help of Morris Jaral. Illustrations by A.E. Philbrick.

7 x 4½ ins., pp.24, not numbered.

IMPRINTS, United States.

Cabinet G Shelf 3 No. 25

Ransom, Will, Chicago, 1923. XXXI Hymns to the Star Goddess, who is not. By XIII, which is Achad. The sixth book from the private press of Will Ransom, "Maker of Books," assisted by Morris Jaral.

Autographed copy.

Boards, 8 x 6 ins., pp.38.

IMPRINTS, United States

Cabinet G Shelf 5 No. 21

Read Printing Co., New York. n.d. circa 1900.
Title: T.R. Emerson Shoe Company: Authentic Styles.

Container with plates.

Boards; 17-3/4 x 11-3/8 in.

IMPRINTS, United States.

Cabinet G, Shelf 3, No. 27

Read Printing Company, The. New York, 1914. The conquest of fire ... Together with the first historical collections of famous masterpieces and rare prints of the World's great conflagrations, New York Underwriters Agency.

Board; 11 x 8¼. in.

IMPRINTS, United States

Cabinet G, Shelf 3, No. 28

Redfield-Kendrick-Odell Co. New York, 1923.

Title: A printed exhibit of Bodoni type. Redfield-Kendrick-Odell Co., 311 West 43rd St. [Has portrait of Bodoni, and acknowledgment to Mr. Henry Lewis Bullen for the use of his article "G. Bodoni, Printer and Typefounder."]

Boards; 10¼ x 7-3/8 x 3/8 in.

IMPRINTS, United States

Cabinet G, Shelf 3, No. 29

Ridgeville Press, The, Evanston, Ill., 1905. The mocking bards: A collection of parodies made by Ralph A. Lyon. Published. designed, executed by direction of Earle Nelson Low. The Ridgeville Press.

Boards; 7¼ x 4¾ in. pp.69.

IMPRINTS, United States.

Cabinet 67, Shelf 1, No. 1

Rogers, Bruce. Indianapolis, 1895. Notes: Critical and Biographical. By R.B. Gruelle. Collection of W.T. Walters.

Old Style Antique types. Initials, headbands and title-page designed by B.R. Rubricated. (Warde 3)

Half morocco, 9¼ x 6¼ ins., pp.216 (6)

IMPRINTS, United States.

Cabinet 67, Shelf 1, No. 4

Rogers, Bruce, Riverside Press, Boston, 1900. Rubaiyat of Omar Khayyam. By Edward Fitzgerald.

Printed in Brimmer types. Red and black (Warde 13.)

Boards buckram back, 9 x 6 ins., pp.159

IMPRINTS, United States.

Cabinet 67, Shelf 1, No. 25, 26, 27

Rogers, Bruce. Riverside Press, Boston, 1902, 03, 04. The Essays of Montaigne (translated) by John Florio. With Bibliography and Notes by George B. Ives.

Montaigne types. Woodcut portraits, borders and initials. 3 vols. (Warde 33)

Boards, cloth back, in cases 15 x 10 ins.

IMPRINTS, United States.

Cabinet G, Shelf 5, No. 15

Rogers, Bruce. Riverside Press, Cambridge, 1902. Pan Sive Natura. Prospectus sent out by Houghton Mifflin & Co.

Title page printed in black within a red border with figures.

Marbled board, linen back, 17 x 11-3/4 ins.

IMPRINTS, United States.

Cabinet 67, Shelf 1, No. 8

Rogers, Bruce. Riverside Press, Boston, 1902. Prothalamion: Epithalamion. By Edmund Spenser.

Brimmer Italic types. Decorations in old red on India paper from drawings by Edwin H. Blashfield. (Warde 32)

Morocco, decorated, 11¾ x 7½ ins., pp.28.

IMPRINTS, United States.

Cabinet 67, Shelf 1, No. 7

Rogers, Bruce. Riverside Press, Boston, 1902. A report of the last sea fight of the Revenge By Sir Walter Raleigh.

Montaigne types, trial fount. With a woodcut after Howard Pyle, woodcut border and initial Printed by hand. (Warde 27)

Boards, 12 x 7¾ ins., pp.19 (4)

IMPRINTS, United States.

Cabinet 67, Shelf 1, No. 14

Rogers, Bruce, Riverside Press, Boston, 1903. Fifteen sonnets of Petrarch. Selected and translated by T.W. Higginson.

Caslon Italic types. Woodcut title in red and black; text within red rules.

Boards, 7½ x 4¼ ins., pp.XV.

IMPRINTS, United States.

Cabinet 67, Shelf 1, No. 11

Rogers, Bruce, Riverside Press, Boston, 1903. The History of Oliver and Arthur. Done into English by William Leighton and Eliza Barrett.

Priory Text type. Facsimile woodcuts on title and in the text. Printed in red and black. (Warde 30)

Boards, cloth back 10½ x 7½ ins., pp.108.

IMPRINTS, United States.

Cabinet 67, Shelf 1, No. 13

Rogers, Bruce. Boston, 1903. Instructions concerning erecting of a library. By Gabriel Naudens. Interpreted by Jo. Evelyn. Introduction by John Cotton Dana

Brimmer types. Printed in red and black (Warde 36)

Boards, leather back 7 x 5 ins., pp.160.

IMPRINTS, United States.

Cabinet 67, Shelf 1, No. 10

Rogers, Bruce. Riverside Press, Boston, 1903. My Cookery Books. By Elizabeth R. Pennell.

Modern types. Reproductions and facsimiles. (Warde 38)

Marbled boards, buckram back, 10 x 7¾ ins., pp.171.

IMPRINTS, United States.

Cabinet 67, Shelf 1, No. 12

Rogers, Bruce. Riverside Press, Boston, 1903. Songs and Sonnets of Pierre de Ronsard. Translated into English by Curtis H. Page. With and Introductory Essay & notes.

Caslon Italic types. Title border and decorations in red (Warde 37)

Boards, 7½ x 4½ ins., pp.137.

IMPRINTS, United States.

Cabinet 67, Shelf 1, No. 20

Rogers, Bruce. Riverside Press, Boston, 1904. Documents relating to the purchase and exploration of Louisiana. By Thomas Jefferson and William Dunbar.

Caslon types. Portrait and folding map. (Warde 48)

Cloth, paper label. 9½ x 6½ ins., pp.189,76

Imprints, United States.

Cabinet 67, Shelf 1, No. 28

Rogers, Bruce. Riverside Press. Cambridge, 1904. Life of Dante. By Giovanni Boccacio. Translated by P.H. Wickstead.

Montaigne types. Woodcut portrait. Printed by hand in red and black.

Boards, 12¾ x 8¾ ins., pp.73.

IMPRINTS, United States.

Cabinet 67, Shelf 1, No. 17

Rogers, Bruce. Riverside Press, Boston, 1904. The Parlement of foules. By Geoffrey Chaucer.

French Gothic type. Printed in red, blue, and black. Initials gilded. (Warde 44)

Boards 9¼ x 6 ins., pp.XXVII.

IMPRINTS, United States.

Cabinet 67, Shelf 1, No. 24

Rogers, Bruce. Riverside Press, Boston, 1905. A consolatorie letter or discourse. By Plutarch. Translated by Philemon Holland.

Brimmer types (Warde 54)

Boards, linen back, 9¾ x 5¾ ins., pp.31.

IMPRINTS, United States.

Cabinet 67 · Shelf 2 · No. 1

Rogers, Bruce, Riverside Press. Boston, 1905. A sentimental journey through France and Italy, by Mr. Yorich (Laurence Sterne)

Brimmer types. Woodcut vignettes on title. (Warde 57)

Boards, Buckram back, 9¼ x 6 ins., pp.231.

IMPRINTS, United States.

Cabinet 67 · Shelf 2 · No. 29

Rogers, Bruce, Riverside Press, Boston, 1906. Theocritus. Translated by C.S. Calverley.

Brimmer italic types. Woodcut decorations. (Warde 69)

Decorated boards 10 x 6 ins., pp.172.

IMPRINTS, United States.

Cabinet 67 · Shelf 2 · No. 14

Rogers, Bruce, Riverside Press, Boston, 1909. The Complete Angler. By Izaak Walton. A prospectus.

Riverside Caslon types. Vignette on title with decorative border.

IMPRINTS, United States.

Cabinet 67 · Shelf 1 · No. 23

Rogers, Bruce. Riverside Press, Boston, 1905. Sions Sonets. Periphrased by Francis Quarles

Brimmer types. Printed in red and black (Warde 55)

Boards, 6-5/8 x 4¼ ins., pp.125.

IMPRINTS, United States.

Cabinet 67 · Shelf 2 · No. 6

Rogers, Bruce. Riverside Press, Boston, 1907. Earl Percy's dinner table. By Harold Murdock.

Caslon types. Frontispiece portrait by Sidney L. Smith on India paper (Warde 79)

Boards, 10¼ x 7-1/8 ins., pp.77.

IMPRINTS, United States.

Cabinet 67 · Shelf 2 · No. 17

Rogers, Bruce. Riverside Press, Boston, 1909. Geofroy Tory. By Auguste Bernard. Translated by George B. Ives.

Riverside Caslon types. With reproductions (Warde 94)

Boards, 11¼ x 7¾ ins., pp.332 (4)

IMPRINTS, United States.

Cabinet R · Shelf 1 · No. 64

Rogers, Bruce. Riverside Press, Cambridge, 1906. The autobiography of Benjamin Franklin with illustrations. Boston and New York, published by Houghton Mifflin & Company, MDCCCCVI. Portrait and 27 plates.

Boards, cloth back, reproduction of medallion on front and back covers, (11¼ x 7¾ ins.)

IMPRINTS, United States.

Cabinet 67 · Shelf 2 · No. 7

Rogers, Bruce, Riverside Press, Boston, 1907. Hydriotaphia: Urne-Buriall, by Sir Thomas Browne.

Brimmer types. Woodcut border on title (Warde 72)

Crimson sheepskin, stamped in gold. 9¾ x 7¼ ins., pp.54.

IMPRINTS, United States

Cabinet 67 · Shelf 2 · No. 33

Rogers, Bruce [Cambridge] 1910.
Title: LXXV Sonnets. William Wordsworth
Imprint: The Riverside Press

Warde No. 103

Boards, cloth back; 8½ x 6-3/8 in.

IMPRINT, United States.

Cabinet · Shelf · No. Frame on Wall

Rogers, Bruce, Riverside Press, Cambridge, 1906. In Congress July 4th, 1776. The unanimous declaration of thirteen United States of America.

Broadside printed in Montaigne capitals.

IMPRINTS, United States.

Cabinet 67 · Shelf 2 · No. 8

Rogers, Bruce. Riverside Press, Boston, 1907. Some unpublished correspondence of David Garrick. Edited by George Pierce Baker.

Oxford types. Portraits. (Warde 74)

Buckram 9½ x 6½ ins., pp.140.

IMPRINTS, United States.

Cabinet 67 · Shelf 2 · No. 20

Rogers, Bruce, Riverside Press, Boston, 1911. The Constitution of the United States of America.

Montaigne types (Warde 111)

Boards, 11¼ x 7¾ ins.

IMPRINTS, United States.

Cabinet 67 · Shelf 2 · No. 3

Rogers, Bruce, Riverside Press, Cambridge, 1906. Paul et Virginie. Par Bernardin de Saint-Pierre.

French Didot type. Woodcuts by M. Lamont Brown after copperplates in first edition. Warde No.68.

Boards, 11¼ x 7½ ins., pp.154.

IMPRINTS, United States.

Cabinet 67 · Shelf 2 · No. 5

Rogers, Bruce, Riverside Press, Boston, 1907. The Sonnets of Henry Wadsworth Longfellow, with an introduction by Ferris Greenslet.

Caslon types (Warde 76)

Boards paper label, 7¾ x 5¼ ins., pp.82.

IMPRINTS, United States

Cabinet R · Shelf 1 · No. 22

Rogers, Bruce: The Riverside Press, 1914.
Title: Franklin and his Press at Passy: An account of the books, pamphlets and leaflets printed there ... By Luther S. Livingston.
Imprint: The Grolier Club, New York, 1914.

Boards; 9¾ x 6½ in.

IMPRINTS, United States.

Cabinet G · Shelf 5 · No. 16

Rogers, Bruce. Riverside Press. Cambridge, 1906. The song of Roland. Translated by Isabel Butler.

French Gothic and Civilité types. Printed by hand in red, blue, brown and black. Illustrations hand colored (Ward 71)

Half morocco, 17 x 11½ ins., pp.XXXIV.

IMPRINTS, United States.

Cabinet 67 · Shelf 2 · No. 12

Rogers, Bruce, Riverside Press, Boston, 1908. The banquet of Plato. Translated by Percy Bysshe Shelley.

Montaigne types (Warde 67)

Boards, 7¾ x 5¼ ins., pp.149.

IMPRINTS, United States.

Cabinet 67 · Shelf 2 · No. 24

Rogers, Bruce. At the Montague Press, Montague Mass., 1915. An account of descriptive catalogues of Strawberry Hill Sale Catalogues. Together with a bibliography. By Percival Merrit.

Walpole and Riverside Caslon types. With plates and facsimiles (Warde 123)

Marbled boards, linen back, 8-3/4 x 5-7/8 ins., pp.72.

IMPRINTS, United States

Cabinet 67 Shelf 2 No. 35

Rogers, Bruce. Cambridge University Press. England, 1919.
Title: Spare your good (London, T. Marshe.? ab. 1555).. Reprinted from the only known copy with an introduction by E. Gordon Duff.
Imprint: Cambridge. Printed at the University Press. 1919.
Warde, 140.

Morocco; 9-1/8 x 6-3/8 x 3/8 in. In protective case.

IMPRINTS, United States.

Cabinet 68 Shelf 2 No. 42

Rogers, Bruce. At the printing house of W.E. Rudge, 1921. The red path and the wounded bird. By John Freeman.

Monotype Caslon types. (50 on handmade paper) for Dunster House Bookshop. Cambridge (Warde 148)

Boards, linen back, 10 x 6½ ins., pp.30.

IMPRINTS, United States.

Cabinet 67 Shelf 2 No. 46

Rogers, Bruce. At the Printing House of W.E. Rudge, New York, 1922. Priapus and the Pool. By Conrad Aiken.

Linotype Original Old Style type

Boards, 8-3/4 x 6½ ins.

IMPRINTS, United States.

Cabinet 67 Shelf 2 No. 39

Rogers, Bruce. At the Printing House of W.E. Rudge, 1920. The Journal of Madam Knight. With an introduction by G.P. Winship.

Garamond types. Title-page in red and black. Map. First book printed in A.T.F. Co.'s Garamond types, as restored to use of printers after being in disuse for 125 years.

Board, 8¼ x 5 ins., pp.72.

IMPRINTS, United States

Cabinet 67 Shelf 2 No. 41-01

Rogers, Bruce. At the Printing House of William E. Rudge, Mount Vernon, N.Y. 1921.
Title: A selection of books from the library of the late John William White. Cambridge, 1921. Pamphlet. Warde (150)
Printed in red and black. 1000 copies for Dunster House Bookshop.

Half morocco; 9 x 5½ x 3/8 in.

IMPRINTS, United States.

Cabinet 67 Shelf 2 No. 45

Rogers, Bruce. At the printing house of W.E. Rudge, New York, 1922. A project of Universal and perpetual peace. B. Pierre-Andre Gargoz. Reprinted with an English Version by G. Simpson Eddy.

Monotype Caslon types. Rubricated title, decorations and facsimiles (Warde, 159)

Boards, buckram back, 7¼ x 4¼ ins., pp.24, 1-46, 1-4

IMPRINTS, United States.

Cabinet 67 Shelf 2 No. 43.01

Rogers, Bruce. New York, 1920. A visit from Saint Nicholas. By Clement C. Moore. Printed as a holiday remembrance by Bruce Rogers and W. E. Rudge, Mount Vernon, N.Y.
Original Old Style Italic Types. Illustrations by Florence W. Ivins, hand colored (Warde 146).

Decorated boards; 8½ x 6 in., pp. 9.

IMPRINTS, United States.

Cabinet 67 Shelf 2 No. 41

Rogers, Bruce. At the printing house of W.E. Rudge, New York, 1921. Several reasons. By Increase Mather. With an introduction by G. Lyman Kittredge. Privately printed for W. Gwinn Mather.

Garamond types. Rubricated title. (Warde 147)

IMPRINTS, United States.

Cabinet 67 Shelf 2 No. 52

Rogers, Bruce. At the Press of W.E. Rudge, New York, 1923. The Ballad of William Sycamore. By Stephen Vincent Benet.

Original Old Style Italic types within typographic borders (Warde 174)

Boards, 8 x 5½ ins., pp.9.

IMPRINTS, United States.

Cabinet 67 Shelf 2 No. 43

Rogers, Bruce. At the press of W.E. Rudge, 1921. Night and Moonlight. By Henry D. Thoreau.

Garamond types. With a woodcut in colors by Florence W. Ivins. (Warde 151)

Boards, 6-3/4 x 4¼ ins., pp.23.

IMPRINTS, United States.

Cabinet 67 Shelf 2 No. 43.02

Rogers, Bruce. William E. Rudge, Mount Vernon, N. Y. 1921.
Title: A visit from St. Nicholas. By C.C. Moore.
Imprint: Boston: The Atlantic Monthly Press, 1921
Colophon: Designed by Bruce Rogers and printed by William E. Rudge ... The text is that of the original (1837) edition. The woodcuts are by Florence W. Ivins.

Boards; 8-5/8 x 5-7/8 in.

IMPRINTS, United States.

Cabinet 67 Shelf 2 No. 53

Rogers, Bruce. At the Press of W.E. Rudge, New York, 1923. Jocelin of Brakelond. From Past and Present. By Thomas Carlyle.

Monotype Caslon types. Rubricated title-page (Warde 168)

Boards, 7¼ x 4½ ins., pp.156.

IMPRINTS, United States

Cabinet S Shelf 3 No. 148

Rogers, Bruce, New York, 1921.
Title: Modern fine printing in America. An essay by A. E. Gallatin. New York, 1921.
Imprint lacking.

Boards; 9-5/8 x 6-7/8 in. Warde 152

IMPRINTS, United States.

Cabinet 67 Shelf 2 No. 47

Rogers, Bruce. At the Printing House of W.E. Rudge, New York, 1922. American Water-Colorists. By A.E. Gallatin. Illus.

Bodoni types (Warde 158)

Boards, buckram back, 11 x 8-1/8 ins., pp. 24, plates, 30.

IMPRINTS, United States.

Cabinet 67 Shelf 2 No. 55

Rogers, Bruce. At the Printing House of W.E. Rudge, 1923. Monotype, Vol.9, No.6, Private Presses in England, etc. Printed for the Monotype Company.

Garamond types, with typographic decorations. Text and rubricated title within ruled margins (Warde 173)

Boards, 10¼ x 7½ ins., pp.23.

IMPRINTS, United States.

Cabinet 67 Shelf 2 No. 40

Rogers, Bruce. New York, 1921.
Title: Printing and the Renaissance ... By John Rothwell Slater. Rochester, N. Y.
Imprint: New York. William Edwin Rudge, 1921. (Printer Mark).
Colophon: Designed by Bruce Rogers and printed from Monotype Caslon Type by William Edwin Rudge, Mount Vernon, New York, Dec. 1921.

Boards; 9¾ x 6½ in. Warde 149.

IMPRINTS, United States.

Cabinet 67 Shelf 2 No. 44

Rogers, Bruce. At the Press of William Edwin Rudge, New York, 1922. The Bride of Huitzil: An Aztec legend. By Hervey Allen. Typography by Bruce Rogers. Decorations by Bernhardt Wall.

Monotype Caslon types (Warde 162)

Boards, cloth back, 9¾ x 5-7/8 ins., pp.35 (1)

IMPRINTS, United States.

Cabinet 67 Shelf 2 No. 51

Rogers, Bruce. At the Press of W.E. Rudge, New York, 1923. The Pierrot of the Minute. By Ernest Dowson. Printed for the Grolier

Deberny type and vignettes (Warde 170)

Boards, 7¼ x 4½ ins., pp.48.

IMPRINTS, United States.

Cabinet 67 Shelf 2 No. 54

Rogers, Bruce. At the Press of W.E. Rudge, New York, 1923. Ralph Herne. By W.H. Hudson.

Monotype Caslon types and ornaments (Warde 172)

Boards, cloth back, $9\frac{1}{2}$ x 6 ins., pp.160.

IMPRINTS, United States.

Cabinet 67 Shelf 2 No. 61

Rogers, Bruce. At the Printing House of W.E. Rudge, New York, 1924. The Construction of Roman Letters, By Albrecht Durer.

Centaur type. Reproductions within red rules (Warde 178). Library copy has inscription "To Henry Lewis Bullen, with the affectionate regard of Bruce Rogers."

Boards, 7-7/8 x $4\frac{3}{4}$ ins., pp.39 (2 copies)

IMPRINTS, United States.

Cabinet 67 Shelf 2 No. 63

Rogers, Bruce. At the Printing House of W.E. Rudge, New York, 1924. Edmund Burke. By John Morley.

Caslon types (Warde 181)

Boards, cloth covered $9\frac{3}{4}$ x $6\frac{1}{4}$ ins., pp.254

IMPRINTS, United States.

Cabinet 67 Shelf 2 No. 65

Rogers, Bruce. At the Printing House of W.E. Rudge, New York, 1924. Men of letters of the British Isles. Portrait medallions by T. Spicer-Simon, with Critical Essays by Stuart P. Sherman.

Garamond types. (Warde 188)

Boards, holland back, $11\frac{3}{4}$ x $8\frac{1}{4}$ ins., pp.133.

IMPRINTS, United States.

Cabinet 67 Shelf 2 No. 64

Rogers, Bruce. Harvard University Press, Cambridge, Mass., 1924. The portraits of Increase Mather. With some notes on Thomas Johnson, and English Mezzotinter, by K.B. Murdock. Privately printed for William Gwinn Mather.

John Baskerville types. Colored fontispiece and other portraits (Warde 199)

Boards, morocco back, gilt top, 10 x $7\frac{1}{2}$ ins., pp.70.

IMPRINTS, United States.

Cabinet 67 Shelf 2 No. 60

Rogers, Bruce. At the Printing House of W.E. Rudge, New York, 1924. The Symbol and the Saint. By Eugene Field. Printed privately for B.R.

Deberny types, with typographic decorations. (Warde 183)

Boards, $7\frac{1}{4}$ x $4\frac{1}{2}$ ins., pp.18.

IMPRINTS, United States.

Cabinet 67 Shelf 2 No. 74

Rogers, Bruce. At the Printing House of W.E. Rudge, New York, 1925. Christmas Epithalamium By Hervey Allen.

Text and title printed within red decorative borders.

Boards, paper label, 8 x 5-3/4 ins., lvs.17.

IMPRINTS, United States.

Cabinet 67 Shelf 2 No. 70

Rogers, Bruce. At the Printing House of W.E. Rudge, New York, 1925. Joseph Conrad: The Man. By Elbridge L. Adams.

Monotype Scotchtype (Warde, 189)

Boards, 8-3/4 x 5-3/4 ins., pp.72.

IMPRINTS, United States

Cabinet R Shelf 1 No. 94

Rogers, Bruce: Harvard University Press, Cambridge, Mass., 1925.
Title: The Passports printed by Benjamin Franklin at his Passy Press.
Colophon: Printed by Bruce Rogers...for the William L. Clements Library (Ann Harbor), 1925.

Boards; $12\frac{1}{2}$ x $9\frac{1}{4}$ in.

IMPRINTS, United States.

Cabinet 67 Shelf 2 No. 75

Rogers, Bruce. At the Printing House of W.E. Rudge, New York, 1925. Roderigo of Bivar. By T. Sturge Moore.

Boards, $9\frac{1}{4}$ x 6 ins., pp.51.

IMPRINTS, United States.

Cabinet 67 Shelf 2 No. 72

Rogers, Bruce. At the Printing House of W.E. Rudge, 1925. Skallagrim. An operetta, by Richard W. Saunders. Privately printed.

Boards, 8-3/4 x 5-6/8 ins., pp.53.

IMPRINTS, United States.

Cabinet 67 Shelf 2 No. 73

Rogers, Bruce. At the Printing House of W.E. Rudge, 1925. Studies on modern painters. By Arthur Symons.

Title page printed in red and black with typographic ornament.

Boards, linen back, $9\frac{3}{4}$ x $6\frac{1}{2}$ ins., pp.88.

IMPRINTS, United States

Cabinet 67 Shelf 2 No. 71

Rogers, Bruce. At the Printing House of W.E. Rudge, New York, 1925. XXVIII Sonnets, By Mrs. W.L. Putnam.

Boards, linen back, $8\frac{3}{4}$ x 6-1/8 ins., lvs.28

IMPRINTS, United States.

Cabinet 67 Shelf 2 No. 81

Rogers, Bruce. At the Printing House of W.E. Rudge, New York, 1926. Amy Lowell: A mosaic. By George H. Sargent.

Boards, linen back, 8-7/8 x $5\frac{1}{2}$ ins., pp.28.

IMPRINTS, United States.

Cabinet 67 Shelf 2 No. 80

Rogers, Bruce. At the Printing House of W.E. Rudge, New York, 1926. Peronnik the fool. By George Moore.

Printed in red and black.

Boards, 9 x 6 ins., pp.68.

IMPRINTS, United States.

Cabinet 67 Shelf 1 No. 29

Rogers, Bruce. At the Printing House of W.E. Rudge, New York, 1927. Champ fleury By Geofroy Tory. Translated into English and annotated by George B. Ives. The Grolier Club.

Boarus, $12\frac{1}{2}$ x $8\frac{3}{4}$ ins., pp.208.

IMPRINTS, United States.

Cabinet 67 Shelf 2 No. 82

Rogers, Bruce. At the Printing House of W.E. Rudge, New York, 1927. Persephone, By John Drinkwater.

Black and gold plaque on first page. Gold head initials.

Boards $10\frac{1}{4}$ x 7 ins., pp.14.

IMPRINTS, United States

Cabinet F Shelf 2 No. 53

Rogers, Gemaliel and Daniel Fowle. Boston, 1743.
Title: The fulfilling of the Scripture...
Imprint: Boston, New England: Printed by Rogers and Fowle for Walter McAlpine near the Mill Bridge. 1743.

Leather; $6\frac{3}{4}$ x 4 x 2 in. Evans 2, 5185, p.237

IMPRINTS, United States

Cabinet F Shelf 2 No. 55

Rogers, Gamaliel and Daniel Fowle. Boston, 1744.
Title: Nicodemus: or, a treatise against the fear of man...
Imprint: Boston. Printed by Rogers and Fowle, for N. Procter at the Bible and Dove in Ann-Street. 1744.

Leather; 5½ x 3 x ½ in. Evans 2, 5394, p.262.

IMPRINTS, United States.

Cabinet G Shelf 3 No. 33

Rollins, Carl Purington, Yale University Press, New Haven, 1924. Anchors of tradition, A presentment of some little known facts, by C. Hazard.

This is the A.I.G.A. Medal Book of 1925.

Linen, 9 x 6 ins., pp.242.
Z232
R65
1924
H33

IMPRINTS, United States.

Cabinet G Shelf 3 No. 36

Rudge, William Edwin, New York, 1918. And a little child shall lead them, by Leigh M. Hodges. Printed in the shop of W.E. Rudge, for his friends.

Boards, 10 x 7 ins., pp.4

IMPRINTS, United States

Cabinet F Shelf 2 No. 57

Rogers, Gamaliel and Daniel Fowle. Boston, 1747.
Title: The imperfection of the creature: By John Bernard.
Imprint: Boston. New England: Printed and sold by Rogers and Fowle in Queen Street, and sold by D. Gookin in Marlborough Street.

Leather; 8 x 5 x 1-1/8 in. Evans 2, 5905, p.325.

IMPRINTS, United States.

Cabinet G Shelf 3 No. 34

Rollins, Carl Purington. Yale University Press, New Haven. May, 1928.
Title: The Trust Company Corner. A history from earliest times, 1638-1928. By Dean B. Lyman Jr. The Union and New Haven Trust Company.

Boards; 9½ x 6¼ x 3/8 in.

IMPRINTS. United States

Cabinet J Shelf 2 No. 30

Rudge, William Edwin. New York, 1921.
Title: Considerations on engraving. By Timothy Cole.

Imprint: New York. William Edwin Rudge, 1921.

Boards; 9-1/8 x 5-7/8 in.

IMPRINTS, United States

Cabinet F Shelf 2 No. 59

Rogers, Gamaliel and Daniel Fowle. Boston, 1748.
Title: A sermon on the death of John Stoddard ...By Jonathan Edwards.
Imprint: Boston. Printed by Rogers and Fowle for J. Edwards in Cornhill.

Half calf; 7¼ x 4-3/8 in. Evans 2, 6130, p.355.

IMPRINTS, United States

Cabinet EE Shelf 5 No. 2

Rounds & James. Chicago (1869).
Title: Press Catalogue. A.B. Taylor's Son & Co.
Imprint: Rounds & James, Printers. Chicago.
Electrotyped and bound by Rounds & James, and by them printed on the "Chicago" Taylor Drum Cylinder Press.

Cloth, stamped; 9-3/8 x 6¼ x 3/8 in.

IMPRINTS, United States.

Cabinet G Shelf 3 No. 37

Rudge, William Edwin, New York City. 1920. Outdoors: A booklet, illus.

Paper, 12½ x 9¼ ins., pp.16, not numbered.

IMPRINTS, United States.

Cabinet G Shelf 3 No. 30

Rogers & Company Press, New York, 1922. Schenley Apartments. A description with text and plates. Rubricated large initial.

Board, 12½ x 10 ins., pp.16, In case.

IMPRINTS, United States

Cabinet QQ Shelf 3 No. 23

Roycroft Shop (Elbert Hubbard), East Aurora, N. Y., 1899.

see HUBBARD, ELBERT. Bigotry bacillus...

IMPRINTS, United States

Cabinet QQ Shelf 3 No. 12

Rudge, William Edwin, New York City, 1920.
Title: Political summary of the United States, 1789-1920.
Imprint: Published by the shop of William Edwin Rudge, New York City.

Boards; 8 x 5¼ x ¼ in.

IMPRINTS, United States.

Cabinet G Shelf 3 No. 31

Rollins, Carl Purington, at the Dyke Mill, Montague, Mass., 1917. Benjamin Franklin's dialogue with the gout. With an account of the first editions by Luther S. Livingston. Cambridge, Mass.

Full morocco, tooled, 8 x 5¼ ins., pp.16, (6), numbered.
2232
R65
1917
F85

IMPRINTS, United States.

Cabinet G Shelf 3 No. 46

Rudge, William Edwin, New York, n.d. A series of quaint astronomical Nativity Folders. Designed by Edna Leslie Freeman. To be published monthly by the printing house of William Edwin Rudge. New York. Illus. in colors.

Half morocco; 7¾ x 5¼ x ½ in.

IMPRINTS, United States.

Cabinet G Shelf 3 No. 38

Rudge, William, Edwin, New York City, 1921. In Flanders Fields by John McCrae. Booklet illuminated by Ernst Clegg.

Boards, 9¼ x 6½ ins., pp.6, with 4 plates.

IMPRINTS, United States.

Cabinet G Shelf 3 No. 32

Rollins, Carl Purington, New Haven, 1923. A lodging for the night: A story of mediaeval paris, by R.L. Stevenson.

Printed at the invitation of The Grolier Club.

Boards, 8¼ x 5-3/8 ins., PP.50.
Z1008
G89
1923
St48

IMPRINTS, United States.

Cabinet G Shelf 3 No. 35

Rudge, William Edwin, New York, 1916. Cabinets of the Presidents and the speakers of the House of Representatives, by E.F. Clymer.

Boards 8½ x 5 ins., pp.38 (2)

IMPRINTS, United States

Cabinet K Shelf 4 No. 13.01

Rudge, William Edwin. New York, 1922.
Title: Art in industry. By Charles R. Richards.
Imprint following p.499: Printing House of William Edwin Rudge, New York.

Cloth; 9½ x 6-1/8 x 1½ in. See also K/4/13.02 (1929 ed.)

IMPRINTS, United States.

Cabinet G Shelf 3 No. 40

Rudge, William Edwin, New York,1922. Kidd: A moral opuscule. Verse by Richard J. Walsh. Illustrations by George Illian.

Boards, 9½ x 7 ins., pp.22, not numbered.

IMPRINTS, United States

Cabinet 00 Shelf 6 No. 36

Rudge, William Edwin. New York, 1925.
Title: A portrait gallery of American editors... By Doris Ulmann.
Imprint: New York: William Edwin Rudge, 1925.

Boards, linen back; 16¼ x 11¼ x 1 in.

IMPRINTS, United States

Cabinet G Shelf 3 No. 48

Rudge, William Edwin, New York, 1929.
Title: The Christmas Dinner. From the Sketch Book by Washington Irving. Illustrations by Gordon Ross.
Colophon: For the friends of the printing house of William E. Rudge. Typography and binding designed by Frederic Warde.

Boards; 8¾ x 6-7/8 x 3/8 in. In protective case.

IMPRINTS, United States.

Cabinet G Shelf 3 No. 39

Rudge, William Edwin, New York City, 1922. The Three Kings, by Henry W. Longfellow. Booklet.

Boards, 8¾ x 5¾ ins., pp.7 with (1) col. plate.

IMPRINTS, United States.

Cabinet 67 Shelf 2 No.

Rudge, William Edwin. New York, 1925.
See Imprints, Rogers, Bruce. At the Printing House of W. E. Rudge, 1925.

IMPRINTS, United States

Cabinet A Shelf 1 No. 22

Rudge, William Edwin. New York, 1929.
Title: The Morning Post and Daily Advertiser. Saturday, August 17, 1776. [London]. A facsimile.
This issue contains the Declaration of Independence, the first report to reach the British Nation.

Buckram; 19 x 14 x 1-3/4 in.

IMPRINTS, United States.

Cabinet G Shelf 3 No. 42

Rudge, William Edwin, New York, 1923. Goudy: An address by Temple Scott at a meeting of the American Institute of Graphic Arts, May 22nd. Printed from Monotype (Goudy) Garamond. Booklet.

Boards 7¾ x 4 ins., pp.13.

IMPRINTS, United States

Cabinet R Shelf 1 No. 97

Rudge, William Edwin: New York, 1926.
Title: Benjamin Franklin in oil and bronze. By John Clyde Oswald.
Imprint: New York: William Edwin Rudge, 1926.

Printed cloth; 12½ x 9½ in.

IMPRINTS, United States

Cabinet G Shelf 3 No. 51

Rudge, William Edwin. (Frederic Warde, typographer) Mount Vernon, N.Y. 1930.
Title: A Christmas Carol. By Charles Dickens. 2 vols.
Imprint: For the friends of William Edwin Rudge.
Colophon: Original Baskerville was used in this book for the first time. Typography by Frederic Warde.

Morocco; gilt tooling; 6-3/4 x 4½ in. Two vols. in bound protective case.

IMPRINTS, United States.

Cabinet G Shelf 3 No. 41

Rudge, William Edwin, New York, 1923. O little town of Bethlehem. Set unto the tune composed by L.H. Redner. Printed for his friends by W.E. Rudge, Mount Vernon, N.Y. Christmas, 1923. Booklet, rubricated.

Boards, 8¼ x 6 ins., pp. 12, not numbered.

IMPRINTS, United States.

Cabinet G Shelf 3 No. 45

Rudge, William Edwin, New York, 1926. Insects and Greek poetry, by Lafcadio Hearn. Booklet.

Boards, 7 x 4¼ ins., pp.20.

IMPRINTS, United States.

Cabinet G Shelf 3 No. 49

Rudge, William E. New York, 1930.
Title: Catalogue of an exhibition of the private papers of James Boswell from Malahide Castle Held at the Grolier Club, New York, Dec. 18, 1930 to Feb. 7th, 1931.
Colophon: Printing House of William Edwin Rudge, Inc. New York.

Paper; 9-3/8 x 6¼ x 5/8 in.

IMPRINTS, United States.

Cabinet G Shelf 3 No. 43

Rudge, William Edwin, New York,1924. A Carol Printed by William Edwin Rudge for his friends. Christmas. Booklet pp.

Boards 8 x 5 ins., pp.4

IMPRINTS, United States

Cabinet G Shelf 3 No. 52

Rudge, William Edwin, New York, 1927.
Title: New poems by Ford Madox Ford. (Autographed by author)
Imprint: William Edwin Rudge. New York, 1927.

Boards; 9¼ x 6-1/8 x ¼ in.

IMPRINTS, United States

Cabinet G Shelf 3 No. 52

Rudge, William Edwin. New York, 1930.
Title: Form letters: Illustrator to author. W.A. Dwiggins.
Colophon: Two hundred and fifty copies printed by William Edwin Rudge, Mount Vernon, New York. Numbered and signed.

Half cloth; 9-5/8 x 6½ x ¾ in.

IMPRINTS, United States.

Cabinet G Shelf 3 No. 44

Rudge, William Edwin, New York, 1925. Eight Songs of William Blake. Printed by W.E. Rudge for his friends. Christmas booklet.

Boards, 7½ x 4¼ ins., lvs. 13.

IMPRINTS, United States.

Cabinet G Shelf 3 No. 47

Rudge, William Edwin, Mount Vernon, 1928.
Title: The Christmas Trail. By Frederick L. Collins. Illustrated by Howard McCormick
Imprint: Printed by William Edwin Rudge, Inc., at Mount Vernon, New York, for their friends Christmas, 1928.

Decorated paper over boards; 10 x 7-1/8 x 3/8 in.

IMPRINTS, United States.

Cabinet G Shelf 3 No. 52.02

Rudge, W. E. (Frederic Warde) New York, 1931.
Title: Christmas Day. From the sketch book of Geoffrey Crayon, Gent. By Washington Irving. New York: Privately printed, 1931.
Colophon: Two hundred and forty-five copies were privately printed for George A. Nelson, 1931, by Frederic Warde.

Boards; 7½ x 4¾ in. In Slip case.

IMPRINTS, United States

Cabinet G Shelf 3 No. 52.01

Rudge, William, E. New York, 1931.
Title: Verses. By Barry Vail [John Barry Ryan]
Imprint on page following title page: Designed and printed for Charles Scribner's Sons by the printing house of William Edwin Rudge, Inc. New York.
"Printed by W.E. Rudge, Inc. under direction of Mr. Patterson of that firm". H.L.B.

Boards; 8-1/8 x 5¼ x ½ in.

IMPRINTS, United States

Cabinet G Shelf 3 No. 50

Rudge, William Edwin (III). New York, 1930.
Title: Christmas at Little America.
Imprint: Privately printed. Mount Vernon: New York, 1930.

Paper boards; 8¾ x 5-7/8 x ¼ in.

IMPRINTS, United States

Cabinet G Shelf 3 No. 53.03

Rudge, William Edwin III. Mount Vernon, N.Y. 1931.
Title: Christmas. By Washington Irving. From The Sketch Book. Privately Printed, 1931. Illus.
Colophon: Printed by William Edwin Rudge III and Frederick G. Rudge to carry on a tradition to all of father's and our friends.

Boards; 7-3/8 x 4-5/8 in. In slip case.

IMPRINTS, United States

Cabinet G Shelf 3 No. 53

St. Albans Press. Mount St. Alban, Washington, D.C. 1928.
Title: The song of St. Peter Damiani. On the joys of Paradise ... A new translation by Stephen A. Hurlbut.
Imprint: The St. Albans Press. Mount St. Alban. Washington, D.C.

Boards; 8¼ x 5-5/8 in.

IMPRINTS, United States

Cabinet G Shelf 3 No. 54

St. Albans Press. Mount St. Alban, Washington, D.C. 1930.
Title: Kalendarium anno, 1930. Bimillenialí vergiliano.
Imprint: The St. Albans Press. Washington, D.C.

Temporary board binder

IMPRINTS, United States

Cabinet G Shelf 3 No. 55

Salt House Press: Baltimore, Maryland. 1929, 1930.
Various pamphlets and inserts.

Boards; 7 x 9¾ in.

IMPRINTS, United States

Cabinet F Shelf 2 No. 21

Sauer, Christopher (I) Germantown, 1739.
Title: Zionitischer Weyrauchs-Hugel oder Myrrhen Berg Woeinnen allerley liebeiches und wohl seichendes apotheker kunst...zu finden.
Imprint: Germantown. Gedruckt bey Christoph Sauer. 1739.
This is said to be the first book printed with German types in the United States.

Original leather binding; 6½ x 4¼ x 2-7/8 in. Evans 2, 4466, p.151.

IMPRINTS, United States

Cabinet F Shelf 2 No. 24

Sauer, Christopher (II). Germantown, 1751-2.
Title: Ausbund, das ist, etliche schone Christliche lieder...
Imprint: Germantown: Gedruckt bey Christoph Sauer, 1751.
A second title page at end of the book, with imprint "Gedruckt im jahr 1752".

Leather, with clasps; 6½ x 4 x 2-3/8 in. Evans 3, 6632, p.2.

IMPRINTS, United States

Cabinet F Shelf 2 No. 27

Sauer, Christopher (II). Germantown, 1757.
Title: Some gospel treasures...By John Everard.
Imprint: London printed in 1653, and now reprinted in Germantown by Christopher Sower, 1757.

Original leather; 8¼ x 6¾ x 2¼ in. Evans 3, 7889, p.164.

IMPRINTS, United States

Cabinet F Shelf 2 No. 30

Sauer, Christopher (II). Germantown, 1759.
Title: A discourse on mistakes concerning religion...By Thomas Bromley.
Imprint: London printed: Germantown reprinted by Christopher Sower. 1752.

Quarter morocco; 7-1/8 x 4¾ x ¾ in. Not in Evans.

IMPRINTS, United States

Cabinet F Shelf 2 No. 29

Sauer, Christopher (II). Germantown, 1759.
Title: The way to the Sabbath of rest...
Imprint: Germantown. Reprinted and sold by Christopher Sower; also sold by Solomon Fussell and Jonathan Zane in Philadelphia, 1759.

Leather; 7¾ x 1½ in. Evans 3, 8309, p.219.

IMPRINTS, United States

Cabinet F Shelf 2 No. 33

Sauer, Christopher (II). Germantown, 1762.
Title: Gesang-Buch...
Imprint: Germantown, gedruckt bey Christoph Sauer, auf kosten vereinigter Freunden. 1762.

Leather, with clasps; 7½ x 5¼ x 2 in.

IMPRINTS, United States

Cabinet F Shelf 2 No. 36

Sauer, Christopher (II) Germantown. 1770.
Title: Ein Geistliches Magazine...Zweite theile
Imprint: Germantown. Gedruckt bey Christoph Saur. 1777.
No. 12, p.136 of this publication has note in German as follows: Printed with the first types that were cast in America.

Half morocco; 8⅝ x 5⅝ in.

IMPRINTS, United States

Cabinet F Shelf 2 No. 38

Sauer, Christopher (II). Germantown, 1774.
Title: The ready reckoner, or trader's useful assistant. Seventh edition...By D. Fenning.
Imprint: London printed, Germantown reprinted by Christopher Sower, 1774.

Leather; 6½ x 4 x 1-1/8 in.

IMPRINTS, United States.

Cabinet F Shelf 2 No. 40

Sauer, Christopher (II). Germantown, 1776.

Title: Biblia, das ist die ganze Heilige Schrift alten und neuen Testaments.....
Imprint: Germantown: Gedruckt und zu finden bey Christoph Sauer, 1776.

Original leather over boards; 10½ x 8 x 3-7/8 in.

IMPRINTS, United States

Cabinet F Shelf 2 No. 44

Sauer, Samuel. Philadelphia, 1791.
Title: Der neue hoch Deutsche Americanische Calender auf das jahr Christi, 1792.
Imprint: Chestnut Hill, Gedruckt und zu finden bey Samuel Sauer.
Preceding title page a full page wood engraving showing a printing office with furniture.

Half morocco; 7-7/8 x 6½ x ¼ in. Seidensticker, p.128.

IMPRINTS, United States

Cabinet NN Shelf 7 No. 17

Scott, Geo. P. and Company. New York City, 1834 - 1835.

see
NEW YORK MIRROR...Vol. XII, 1834 - 1835, Geo. P. Scott & Co., Printers.

IMPRINTS, United States.

Cabinet G Shelf 3 No. 56

Seaver-Howland Press, Boston, Mass., 1915. A miscellaneous collection of "Waverley Chap Books," and others.

In cardboard box.

IMPRINTS, United States.

Cabinet G Shelf 3 No. 57

Shaw, William Walter. Los Angeles, 1926.
Title: Reveries of a drummer. A book of verse. By William Walter Shaw. With drawings by Addison Johnson.
Imprint: Los Angeles: Sixth Avenue Publishing Co. (The type composition and make up was done by the author, a retired printer. Set in Announcement Roman).

Imit. Leather; 7-7/8 x 5¼ in.

IMPRINTS, United States.

Cabinet G Shelf 3 No. 58

Shumaker, F.W., New York, 1925. Pinellas Country Club, Belleair, Florida. This book is printed from original wood cuts designed and executed by S. Garnett Goesle and Herbert F. Roese. The cover is by Reginal Farr.

Tooled Morocco, 10 x 13 ins., lvs. 18.

IMPRINTS, United States

Cabinet G Shelf 3 No. 59

Smith & Porter Press, Boston: 1925. Seven versions of the Gettysburg Address. Privately Printed. Booklet.

Boards; 7½ x 5¼ in.

IMPRINTS, United States

Cabinet JJ Shelf 3 No. 1

Southwick and Crooker, New York City, 1802

see EARLY PRINTING IN NEW YORK CITY

IMPRINTS, United States.

Cabinet G Shelf 3 No. 60

Southworth Press, Portland, Maine, 1924. Lucifer or the heavenly truce by George Santayana. The head-pieces, initial letters, and end-papers have been designed and the typography has been arranged by Pierre de Chaignon la Rose, and the printing under his direction.

Cloth covers, 4 to. pp.128.

IMPRINTS, United States.

Cabinet G Shelf 3 No. 61

Sparrell Print, The, Boston, 1901. Heartsease Hymns, by W.P. McKenzie. Typography by the Sparrell Print.

Boards, 8¼ x 6½ ins., pp.53.

IMPRINTS, United States.

Cabinet G Shelf 3 No. 62

Sparrell Print, Boston, Mass., 1903. The sower and other poems, by W.P. McKenzie. The title-page and initial letters in this book were designed and drawn by Miss E.H. McLeuthlin. The type is Cheltenham Old Style, designed by Bertram G. Goodhue.

Boards, 7 x 5 ins., lvs. 28.

IMPRINTS, United States.

Cabinet G Shelf 3 No. 63

Stephens, Brad & Co., Boston, Mass., n.d. It was a famous victory by Robert Southey. Printed by the Heintzemann Press and Brad Stephens & Co., as a Christmas remembrance for their friends. Booklet.

Boards, 6¼ x 4¼ ins., pp.8.

IMPRINTS, United States.

Cabinet G Shelf 3 No. 64

Stephens, Brad., Boston, Mass., 1921. The Whistle, by B. Franklin. Extract from a letter written by Franklin to Mme. Brillon, Nov., 1779. Published by Brad Stephens & Company. Booklet. Colored. Illus.

Boards, 6 x 4 ins., pp.8, not numbered.

IMPRINTS, United States.

Cabinet S Shelf 5 No. 66

Stone, Edward L. Roanoke, Virginia, 1931.
Title: A book-lover's bouquet.
Colophon: ...printed in Centaur type designed by Bruce Rogers, with the Foreword in Arrighi Italic designed by Frederic Warde, Edward L. Stone "seeing it through the press" of the Stone Printing and Manufacturing Co., Roanoke, Va.

Cloth; 6¾ x 4-3/8 x ¼ in.

IMPRINTS, United States

Cabinet S Shelf 1 No. 130

Stone Printing and Mfg. Co. Roanoke, Virginia, 1926.
Title: Typographia, an ode on printing ... Printed by William Park, Williamsburg, 1730.
Imprint: Photographic reprint by the Stone Printing Co. Roanoke, Virginia. For the American Institute of Graphic Arts, New York, 1926,

Boards; 10½ x 7-1/8 in. In protective case.

IMPRINTS, UNITED STATES

Cabinet J Shelf 3 No. 6

Rudge, William Edwin, Inc. New York City, 1931.

See PENNELL, JOSEPH. Catalogue of the lithographs of...

IMPRINTS, United States

Cabinet S Shelf 4 No. 68.01

Stone Printing and Manufacturing Co. Roanoke, Virginia, 1930.
Title: The great Gutenberg Bible. The St. Paul copy of. Brochure.
Imprint colophon: Printed by the Stone Printing and Manufacturing Company, Roanoke, Virginia, under the direction of Edward L. Stone.

In box marked "Pamphlets Relating to Gutenberg and the Gutenberg Bible"

IMPRINTS, United States

Cabinet G Shelf 3 No. 65

Stone, Edward L. Roanoke, Virginia (Stone Printing and Mfg. Co.). 1931.
Title: The President's camp on the Rapidan.
Colophon: Designed and printed by The Stone Printing and Mfg. Co. Under the direction of Edward L. Stone...The type used for the text is Centaur, designed by Bruce Rogers.

Paper; 11 x 8½ in. In folder.

IMPRINTS, United States

Stack G Shelf 3 Number 65.02

Stone, Edward L. Stone Printing and Manufacturing Co., Roanoke, Virginia. 1933
Title: Caverns of Virginia. By William M. McGill.
Imprint: University, Virginia, 1933
Colophon: Designed printed and bound by the Stone Printing and Manufacturing Company, under the direction of Edward L. Stone.

Boards, linen back; 10¾ x 7½ in. In slip case

IMPRINTS, United States

Cabinet G Shelf 3 No. 65.01

Stone Printing Co. (Edward L. Stone) Roanoke, Virginia, 1933
Title: Historic shrines of Virginia. By William E. Carson...
Colophon:..The designing, printing and binding have been done by the Stone Printing and Manufacturing Company, Roanoke, Virginia, U.S.A., under the immediate supervision of Edward L. Stone.

Boards; 11¾ x 7-7/8 in.

IMPRINTS, United States

Cabinet G Shelf 3 No. 66

(The) Stratford Press, S. A. Jacobs. New York 1929.
Title: The Twisted Tree. By M. & H. Bedford-Jones.
Imprint: Designed and printed by S. A. Jacobs. The Stratford Press: American Book Bindery Inc. New York.
[The book is printed throughout on birch-veneer].

Boards; 8-5/8 x 5¼ in.

IMPRINTS, United States.

Cabinet G Shelf 3 No. 67

Stratford Press-American Book Bindery. S.A. Jacobs. New York City, 1930.
Title: The Ideal Book: A tract on calligraphy printing and illustration and on the book beautiful as a whole. [T.J.Cobden-Sanderson].
Colophon: This tract ... is issued on the occasion of the thirtieth anniversary of its first appearance. The book is designed by S.A.Jacobs printed and bound at the Stratford Press-American Book bindery, 75 Varick Street.
Cloth; 8-3/8 x 6 x ¼ in.

IMPRINTS, United States

Cabinet G Shelf 2 No. 31.02

Studio Press (Edwin Grabhorn), Indianapolis, Indiana. Notice of removal. n. d.

In envelope.

IMPRINTS, United States.

Cabinet G Shelf 3 No. 71

Taylor & Taylor, San Francisco, 1915. In the court of the ages. By Edward Robeson Taylor. Poems in commemoration of the Panama-Pacific Exposition. Illus.

Boards, 8¼ x 4¼ ins., pp.35.

IMPRINTS, United States.

Cabinet G Shelf 3 No. 72

Taylor & Taylor, San Francisco, 1916. Yosemite: An Ode. By George Sterling. A cover in color after the painting by H.J. Breuer, and illustrations from photographs.

8-5/8 x 5¾ ins., pp.16.

IMPRINTS, United States.

Cabinet J Shelf 1 No. 17

Sutton, James & Co., New York, 1874.

See ALMANACS. Aldine almanac, the, 1874. A brochure of American art...

IMPRINTS, United States.

Cabinet G Shelf 3 No. 70

Taylor & Taylor, San Francisco, 1915. In the Keith Room at the Exposition. By Edward Robeson Taylor. Portrait.

A eulogistic poem of the man and his work as an artist.

Item 3, in Taylor & Taylor, San Francisco, 1915.

IMPRINTS, United States.

Cabinet G Shelf 3 No. 75

Taylor & Taylor, San Francisco, 1917-18. T & T Imprints, printed and published by Taylor & Taylor. The cover design made up entirely of type founders material, monogram, and forum type designed by F. Goudy. Main text in Kennerley Old Style also designs by Goudy as also title page and headings in main article.

Half morocco, 12½ x 9½ ins.

IMPRINTS, United States

Cabinet F Shelf 3 No. 28

Swords, T. and J. Pearl Street, 1798.
Title: The Botanic Garden. A poem in two parts. [by Erasmus Darwin].
Imprint: New York. Printed by T. and J. Swords, printers to the Faculty of Physic of Columbia College.

Calf; 8½ x 5½ x 1¼ in.

IMPRINTS, United States.

Cabinet G Shelf 3 No. 70

Taylor & Taylor, San Francisco, 1915. The Sylvan Cabin. A Lincoln Ode. By Edward Smyth Jones. Published by the author. Printed by Taylor & Taylor. Brochure. Illus.

Item I in Taylor & Taylor, San Francisco, 1915.

IMPRINTS, United States

Cabinet G Shelf 3 No. 75.01

Taylor & Taylor. San Francisco, 1922.
Title: Catalogue of the retrospective loan exhibition of European tapestries held in the San Francisco Museum of Art. By Phyllis Ackerman. With a preface by J. Nilsen Laurvik.
Printers Note: In the making of the type design for the cover, the printer has introduced an illuminated 15th century woodcut by an unknown master etc.
Paper; 10¾ x 7 in.

IMPRINTS, United States.

Cabinet G Shelf 3 No. 70

Taylor & Taylor, San Francisco, n.d. The Rieber Laboratories. A statement of affairs. Printed by Taylor & Taylor. Pamphlet, pp.24.

Item 4, in Taylor & Taylor, San Francisco, 1915.

IMPRINTS, United States.

Cabinet G Shelf 3 No. 73

Taylor & Taylor, San Francisco, 1916. Gold: A forest play, by Frederick S. Myrtle, and presented by the members of the San Francisco Bohemian Club. Color reproductions by L. Maynard Dixon, The decorations in black and white by Dan Sweeney.

Boards, colored, 8 x 5½ ins., pp.58.

IMPRINTS, United States

Cabinet G Shelf 3 No. 67.08

Taylor-Nash-Taylor, San Francisco, 1913
Title: Brunelleschi: A poem. By John Galen Howard. San Francisco, John Howell, 1913.
Colophon: Four hundred and eight copies of this book were printed by Taylor, Nash and Taylor, San Francisco, in November, 1913.

This is copy No.86

Boards: 10 x 6¼ in.

IMPRINTS, United States

Cabinet QQ Shelf 1 No. 59

Taylor, Nash & Taylor. San Francisco, 1913.
Title: A tragedy in printer's ink. By Wallace Irwin.
Imprint: San Francisco, Taylor, Nash & Taylor. 1913.

Boards; 9¾ x 7¾ in.

IMPRINTS, United States.

Cabinet G Shelf 3 No. 70

Taylor & Taylor, San Francisco, 1916. Netsuke: A catalogue of the Ney Wolfskill Loan Collection: Japanese section. Golden Gate Park.

Item 2, in Taylor & Taylor, San Francisco, 1915.

IMPRINTS, United States.

Cabinet G Shelf 3 No. 68

Taylor, Nash & Taylor, San Francisco, 1914-16. T.N.T. Imprints, printed and published by Taylor, Nash & Taylor, San Francisco, Calif.

This is a collection of monthly publications issued for the purpose of promoting the use of Direct Advertising.

Half morocco, 10 x 6¾ ins.

IMPRINTS, United States.

Cabinet G Shelf 3 No. 69

Taylor & Taylor, San Francisco, 1915. Apollo: A music drama. Book and lyrics by Frank Pixley. Music by E.F. Schneider. A Grove Play of the Bohemian Club of San Francisco. Printed by T & T.

Boards, embossed figure, 8 x 5½ ins., pp.49.

IMPRINTS, United States.

Cabinet G Shelf 3 No. 74

Taylor & Taylor, San Francisco, 1916. T. & T. Imprint for the Winter MCMXVI and XVII. The policy of this house. A statement by Taylor & Taylor.

Boards 6¾ x 4 ins., pp.44.

IMPRINTS, United States.

Cabinet G Shelf 3 No. 76

Thatcher, Ralph Henry. San Francisco, 1921. Old Christmas, by George Wither. Privately printed and presented by R.H. Thatcher Rubricated.

Boards, 8¾ x 5¾ ins., pp.6.

IMPRINTS, United States

Cabinet R Shelf 4 No. 1

[Thomas, Isaiah]. Worcester, Mass., 1781.
Title: An oration in Free Masons-Hall, Lancaster, Massachusetts ... June 24, 1779 ... By Brother Isaiah Thomas.
Imprint: Printed at Worcester, MDCCLXXXI (1781).

Limp morocco ; $8\frac{1}{4}$ x $5\frac{3}{4}$ in.

IMPRINTS, United States.

Cabinet F Shelf 3 No. 11

Thomas, Isaiah. Worcester, 1795.

Title: Elegiac sonnetts. By Charlotte Smith.
Imprint. Printed at Worcester by Isaiah Thomas, sold by him in Worcester, and by said Thomas and Andrews in Boston. 1795.
Colophon: From the Old Press of Isaiah Thomas at Worcester.
Printed on paper the first manufactured by the editor, I.T.
Leather; 5-7/8 x $4\frac{3}{4}$ x 5/8 in. Evans 10, 29523, p.200.

IMPRINTS, United States.

Cabinet F Shelf 3 No. 51

Timothy, Lewis. Charlestown, (S. Carolina), 1737.
Title: Collection of Psalms and Hymns.
Imprint Charles-Town, printed by Lewis Timothy.
Facsimile reprint.

Cloth; 7 x $4\frac{3}{4}$ x 3/8 in.

IMPRINTS, United States

Cabinet NN Shelf 5 No. 40

Thomas, Isaiah, Worcester (Mass.) 1783 - 1784.

see
NEWSPAPERS, Massachusetts. (Thomas's) Massachusetts Spy, or Worcester Gazette...

IMPRINTS, United States

Cabinet R Shelf 4 No. 3 2 Vols.

Thomas, Isaiah Jun. Worcester, Mass., 1810.
Title: History of printing in America ... By Isaiah Thomas, printer, Worcester. 2 Vols.
Imprint: From the Press of Isaiah Thomas, Jun. Isaac Sturtevant, printer. Worcester, 1810.

Leather; 9 x $5\frac{1}{2}$ in.

IMPRINT. United States

Cabinet NN Shelf 3 No. 23

Tomoye' Press, The.
San Francisco. 1904.
Title: Extra!! Fairy tales up to now.

Imprint: Paul Elder, San Francisco.
Publishers: The Tomoye' Press.

Boards: 8x4-5/8". In slip case.

IMPRINTS, United States

Cabinet F Shelf 3 No. 5

Thomas, Isaiah. Worcester Mass., 1787.
Title: The history of Goody Twoshoes...The first Worcester Edition. Illus.
Imprint: Printed at Worcester, Massachusetts. By Isaiah Thomas, and sold wholesale and retail at his book store.

Half morocco; $4\frac{1}{2}$ x 3 x $\frac{1}{2}$ in.

IMPRINTS, United States.

Cabinet G Shelf 5 No. 17 2 vols.

Thompson, John, and Abraham Small. [Hot-Press of John Thompson]. Philadelphia, 1798.
Title: The Holy Bible, containing the Old and New Testaments: Together with the Apocryphe. 2 vols.
Imprints: Philadelphia, Printed for John Thompson & Abraham Small, [from the Hot-Press of John Thompson].

Calf; each vol; $16\frac{3}{4}$ x $10\frac{1}{4}$ in.

IMPRINTS, United States

Cabinet G Shelf 3 No. 83

Tomoye Press, New York City, 1907
Title:Weather opinions... Compiled and arranged by Jennie Day Haines.
Imprint: Paul Elder and Company, San Francisco and New York.

See colophon for Tomoye Press imprint.

Boards; $9\frac{3}{4}$ x $7\frac{1}{4}$ in.

IMPRINTS, United States.

Cabinet F Shelf 3 No. 6

Thomas, Isaiah. Worcester, 1789.

Title: Elements of general history. Translated from the French of Abbe Millot. First American edition. Vol.5.
Imprint: Printed at Worcester, Massachusetts by Isaiah Thomas, Sold at his Bookstore in Worcester and by him and Company in Boston, 1789.

Leather; $8\frac{1}{4}$ x $5\frac{1}{2}$ x $1\frac{3}{4}$ in. Evans 7, 21965-6, p.336.

IMPRINTS, United States

Cabinet G Shelf 3 No. 77.01

Times-Mirror Printing and Binding House, Los Angeles, 1927.
Title: Twelve good men and true. (Biographical) sketches, with portraits)
Imprint:Printed by Times-Mirror Printing and Binding House, Los Angeles, for its friends.

No 23 of 75 copies printed.

Morocco, gilt; $11\frac{1}{2}$ x 9 in.

IMPRINTS, United States

Cabinet G Shelf 3 No. 78

Trezise, F.J., Chicago, 1910. Elegy written in a country churchyard, by Thomas Gray. Lettered and done into a book by F.J. Trezise.

Boards, $7\frac{3}{4}$ x $5\frac{1}{4}$ ins., lvs., 22.

IMPRINTS, United States.

Cabinet F Shelf 3 No. 8

Thomas, Isaiah and Ebenezer T. Andrews: Boston, 1791.

Title: An eulogy on the honorable James Bowdoin, Esq. Late President of the American Academy of Arts and Sciences...By John Lowell.
Imprint: Printed at Boston, by Isaiah Thomas and Ebenezer T. Andrews at Faust's Statue, No.45 Newbury Street, 1791.

Half morocco; $11\frac{1}{2}$ x 9 in. Evans 8, 23513, p.172.

IMPRINTS, United States.

Cabinet G Shelf 3 No. 77

Times-Mirror Printing & Binding House, Los Angeles, 1928.
Title: Twelve Pioneers of Los Angeles. By William H. Cline.
Colophon: This completes of history....printed by Sim W. Crabill, at The Times-Mirror Printing and Binding House, Los Angeles. The typography and design are by W. Irvin Brennan; drawings by Arthur Treichler.

Full morocco; $11\frac{3}{4}$ x 8-7/8 in.

IMPRINTS, United States

Cabinet G Shelf 3 No. 80

Tri-Arts Press, (F.W. Shaefer.) New York? 1932?
Title: B. Franklin's morals of chess. [Reprinted from an 1802 edition].
Imprint: Designed by F.W. Shaefer at the Tri-Arts Press. n.p. n.d.

Boards; 5-1/8 x 5-3/8 x $\frac{1}{4}$ in. In case.

IMPRINTS, United States.

Cabinet F Shelf 3 No. 9

Thomas, Isaiah: Worcester, 1791.
Title: The Holy Bible...with engraved frontispiece.
Imprint: Printed at the Press at Worcester, Massachusetts by Isaiah Thomas. Sold by him in Worcester, and by him and Company at Faust's Statue, No.45 Newbury Street, Boston.

Leather; $11\frac{3}{4}$ x $9\frac{1}{4}$ x $3\frac{1}{2}$ in. Evans 8,23185, p.125.

IMPRINTS, United States

Cabinet 80 Shelf 1 No. 5

Times-Mirror Printing And Binding Company, Los Angeles, 1933
Facsimile reproduction of Poor Richard's Almanac for 1733.

Reprint the complete number of "Three Minutes", January, 1933, the house organ of the Times&Mirror Co.

With other items in manila envelope

IMPRINTS, United States

Cabinet G Shelf 3 No. 81

Trovillion, Violet and Hal. Herin, Illinois, 1925.
Title: Vagaries from Munthe.
Imprint: Printed and published by Violet and Hal Trovillion. Herrin, Illinois, 1925.

Boards; 7 x $3\frac{1}{2}$ in.

IMPRINTS, United States

Cabinet G Shelf 3 No. 82

Trovillion, Violet & Hal. Herrin, Ill., 1932.
Title: The selfish giant. A tale from Oscar Wilde.
Imprint: Printed and published by Violet & Hal Trovillion. Herrin, Illinois. Christmas, 1932.

Boards; $7\frac{3}{4}$ x $5\frac{1}{2}$ in.

IMPRINTS, United States

Cabinet G Shelf 4 No. 2

University Press (Welch, Biglow & Co.) Cambridge, Mass., 1865.
Bibliographical Tracts. No. I. Spurious reprints of early books. Boston, 1865. From the Boston Daily Advertiser, March 24, 1865.
(130 copies printed)

Brochure, in envelope.

IMPRINTS, United States

Cabinet R Shelf 3 No. 129

University Press, The: Cambridge, Mass. 1921.
Title: Stephen Daye and his successors ... (Printer Mark) 1639-1921. Illus.
Imprint: Cambridge, Massachusetts, 1921.

Boards; 8 x $5\frac{1}{4}$ in.

IMPRINTS, United States

Cabinet JJ Shelf 3 No. 7

Trow, John F., New York, 1850.

see
CELEBRATIONS, PRINTERS'. 1850, New York City...

IMPRINTS, United States.

Cabinet G Shelf 4 No. 3

University Press, The. John Wilson and Son, Cambridge, Mass., 1897. Shakespear's Sonnets. Ornamental designs by Bertram Grosvenor Goodhue.

Board, 8 x 6 ins., pp.164.

IMPRINTS, United States.

Cabinet G Shelf 4 No. 5

University Press, The. Cambridge, Mass., 1924. Choate School, Brookline, Mass. An illustrated and descriptive prospectus. Brochure.

Paper $8\frac{1}{4}$ x 6 ins., pp.30.

IMPRINTS, United States

Cabinet G Shelf 3 No. 79

Typographic Laboratory (Henry Lewis Johnson) Boston, Massachusetts, 1931.
Title: The luck of roaring camp. By Bret Harte. Privately printed: Boston, Massachusetts, 1931.
Imprint: A project designed and executed at The Typographic Laboratory, Boston, Mass. By Charles W. Johnson [a pupil].

Boards; $7\frac{3}{4}$ x 5-3/8 in.

IMPRINTS, United States

Cabinet Q Shelf 1 No. 6

University Press: John Wilson and Son, Cambridge, Mass., 1900.
Title: Early Boston bookseller, 1642-1711. By George Emery Littlefield. Boston: The Club of Odd Volumes, 1900.
Imprint: University Press. John Wilson and Son, Cambridge, Mass., U.S.A.

Boards, leather back; $9\frac{3}{4}$ x $6\frac{1}{2}$ in.

IMPRINTS, United States.

Cabinet G Shelf 4 No. 6

University Press of Sewanee, Tennessee, 1905. Milton's ode on the Morning of Christ's Nativity.

Boards, 7 x $4\frac{1}{4}$ ins., pp.32.

IMPRINTS, United States

Cabinet QQ Shelf 5 No. 12.01

U.S. Government Printing Office, Washington, D.C.
Title: The Declaration of Indipendence, and the Constitution of the U.S. of America.
Imprint: United States Government Printing Office, Washington, D. C., 1934.
Inserted in the above item, A/L.S., George H. Carter, Public Printer, 1934.

Brochure.

IMPRINTS, United States.

Cabinet G Shelf 4 No. 4

University Press, The. John Wilson and Son. Cambridge, Mass., 1902. The history of over sea, done into english by W. Morris. Decorations by Louis Rhead.

Decorated covers, $10\frac{1}{2}$ x 8 ins., pp.14.

IMPRINTS, United States.

Cabinet G Shelf 4 No. 7

Updike, D.B., The Merrymount Press, Boston,1899. The king's lyrics, by Fitzroy Carrington. Printed for R.H. Russell. Portraits.

Boards, $6\frac{1}{2}$ x 4 ins., pp.127.

IMPRINTS, United States

Cabinet PP Shelf 3 No. 14

University of Chicago Press. Chicago. Ill., 1915.
Title: Public libraries...in ancient Rome. By Clarence Eugene Boyd.
Imprint: The University of Chicago Press, Chicago, Ill., 1915.

Cloth; 9 x 5-3/4 in.

IMPRINTS, United States

Cabinet S Shelf 4 No. 16

University Press, The. Cambridge, Mass., 1909.
Title: Ideals for printers: A collection of sentiments about printing and kindred subjects ...
Imprint: Christmas, 1909: The Cambridge University Press, Cambridge, Mass.

Half morocco; $7\frac{1}{4}$ x $4\frac{1}{2}$ in.

IMPRINTS, United States.

Cabinet G Shelf 5 No. 18

Updike, D. B., The Merrymount Press, Boston, 1900 Description of the Pastoral Staff belonging to the diocese of Albany, N. Y. The decorations of this volume were designed by Bertram G. Goodhue, of Boston.

Boards, morocco back; $15\frac{1}{2}$ x $12\frac{1}{4}$ in. (With 6 full plates.)

IMPRINTS, United States

Cabinet G Shelf 4 No. 6.03

University of Oregon. John Henry Nash Fine Arts Press. 1933.
Title: The ideal book or book beautiful. By Thomas James Cobden-Sanderson.
Imprint: University of Oregon : John Henry Nash Fine Arts Press.

Boards; $10\frac{3}{4}$ x $7\frac{1}{2}$ in.

IMPRINTS, United States.

Cabinet G Shelf 1 No. 44

University Press. Cambridge, Mass. 1916.
Title: Giambattista Bodoni of Parma: a biographical sketch of the Italian printer, and delivered by Thomas M. Cleland before the Society of Printers in Boston, April 22, 1913. Printed by the University Press. Boston, 1916. [Portrait of Bodoni].

Boards; $9\frac{1}{4}$ x $6\frac{1}{4}$ x 3/8 in.

IMPRINTS, United States.

Cabinet G Shelf 4 No. 8

Updike, D.B. The Merrymount Press, Boston, 1902. Four addresses, by Henry Lee Higginson.

Boards, 7-7/8 x $4\frac{3}{4}$ ins., pp.106.

IMPRINTS, United States.

Cabinet G Shelf 4 No. 9

Updike, D.B., The Merrymount Press, Boston,1902. Thoreau, the poet-naturalist. Limited edition, with etchings and engravings by Sydney L. Smith.

Boards, linen back, $8\frac{1}{2}$ x $5\frac{3}{4}$ ins.,pp.396.

IMPRINTS, United States.

Cabinet G Shelf 4 No. 14

Updike, Daniel Berkeley. The Merrymount Press. Boston, 1907. Erasmus against War. With an introduction by John W. Mackail. Types and decorations by Herbert P. Horne.

Boards, $9\frac{3}{4}$ x $5\frac{3}{4}$ ins., pp.64.

IMPRINTS, United States

Cabinet R Shelf 4 No. 17

Updike, D. B., The Merrymount Press, Boston, 1912.
Title: Isaiah Thomas, printer, writer and collector ... By Charles Lemuel Nichols.
Imprint: Printed for The Club of Odd Volumes. Boston, 1912. At end of Book: The Merrymount Press, Boston.

Boards; $9\frac{3}{4}$ x $6\frac{1}{2}$ in.

IMPRINTS, United States.

Cabinet G Shelf 4 No. 10

Updike, D.B., The Merrymount Press,Boston, 1904. A notable libel case: The criminal persecution of Theodore Lyman Jr., by Daniel Webster in the Supreme Judicial Court of Massachusetts, Nov., 1828. Josiah H. Benton,Jr. Illus.

Boards, linen back, $9\frac{1}{2}$ x 6 ins., pp.117.

IMPRINTS, United States.

Cabinet G Shelf 4 No. 15

Updike, Daniel Berkeley. The Merrymount Press 1907. The history of libraries in the seventeenth and eighteenth centuries. Edited by John Cotton Dana and Henry W. Kent.

Boards, $6\frac{3}{4}$ x 4 ins., pp.121.

IMPRINTS, United States.

Cabinet G Shelf 4 No. 20

Updike, D.B., The Merrymount Press, Boston,1913. Records of Journeys to Venice by Albrecht Durer. Edited by Roger Fry. This volume with title page by W.A. Dwiggins, was printed by D.B. Updike.

Boards, $9\frac{3}{4}$ x $6\frac{1}{4}$ ins., pp.117.

IMPRINTS, United States.

Cabinet G Shelf 4 No. 11

Updike, Daniel Berkeley, The Merrymount Press, Boston, 1905. The melody of God's Love: A new unfolding of the twenty-third psalm, by Oliver Huckel. Rubricated head-initials.

Board 7-5/8 x $5\frac{1}{4}$ ins., pp.50.

IMPRINTS, United States.

Cabinet G Shelf 4 No. 18

Updike, D.B., The Merrymount Press, Boston, 1908. Catalogue of a memorial exhibition of the works of Augustus Saint-Gandens, The Metropolitan Museum of Art, New York.

Half morocco, 8 x 5 ins., pp.82.

IMPRINTS, United States.

Cabinet G Shelf 4 No. 21

Updike, D.B., The Merrymount Press, Boston,1913. The story of George Crowninshield's yacht, Cleopatra's Barge. Compiled from Journals, letters, and log-book by Francis B. Crowninshield. Privately printed. Illus.

Linen covered boards, $11\frac{1}{4}$ x $8\frac{1}{2}$ ins., pp.259.

IMPRINTS, United States.

Cabinet G Shelf 4 No. 12 2 vols.

Updike, Daniel Berkeley. The Merrymount Press, Boston, 1906. The life of Benvenuto Cellini, written by himself. Translated by John Addington Symonds. With forty original portraits and views. Brentano's New York.

Decorated boards, $9\frac{1}{2}$ x 6 ins., vol.1, pp.386, vol.2, pp.359.

IMPRINTS, United States.

Cabinet G Shelf 4 No. 17

Updike, D.B., The Merrymount Press, Boston, 1908. The maid's forgiveness. A ply by John Jay Chapman.

Boards $7\frac{1}{4}$ x 5-1/8 ins., pp.93.

IMPRINTS, United States.

Cabinet G Shelf 4 No. 22

Updike, D.B., The Merrymount Press, Boston, 1914. A platonick discourse upon love. By Pica Della Mirandola. This volume with title page by T.M. Cleland was printed by D.B. Updike.

Boards, linen backs, $9\frac{1}{2}$ x $6\frac{1}{4}$ ins., pp. XXVII, 83,(2).

IMPRINTS, United States.

Cabinet G Shelf 4 No. 13

Updike, Daniel Berkeley. The Merrymount Press, Boston, 1906. Madame De Treymes, by Edith Wharton. Illus. Charles Scribner's Sons.

Decorated boards, 8 x 5 ins., pp.146.

IMPRINTS, United States.

Cabinet G Shelf 4 No. 19

Updike, D.B., The Merrymount Press, Boston, 1909. Christus. A story of love, by Grace Hoffman White. Privately printed.

Boards, 8 x 5 ins., pp.64.

IMPRINTS, United States.

Cabinet G Shelf 4 No. 23

Updike, D.B., The Merrymount Press, Boston,1915. The Johnny-Cake papers of "Shepherd Tom," by Thomas Robinson Hazard. Illustrations by Rudolf Ruzicka.

Boards, 9 x 6 ins., pp.429.

IMPRINTS, United States.

Cabinet G Shelf 4 No. 16

Updike, D.B., The Merrymount Press, Boston, 1907. A Christmas anthology. Carols and poems old and new. Composition and electrotype plates by D.B. Updike.

Boards $7\frac{3}{4}$ x $5\frac{1}{4}$ ins., pp.84.

IMPRINTS, United States

Cabinet QQ Shelf 1 No. 58

Updike, D.B. The Merrymount Press, Boston, Mass., 1911.
Title: Depositio cornuti typographici...Reprinted as acted at the Grolier Club, Jan. 28, 1909.
Imprint at end of book: Two hundred and fifty copies were printed by D.B. Updike at The Merrymount Press, Boston, in the Month of February, 1911.

Boards, cloth back; $9\frac{1}{2}$ x 6-1/8 in. In protective case.

IMPRINTS, United States

Cabinet Q Shelf 1 No. 5

Updike, D. B. The Merrymount Press, Boston, 1917.
Title: The Boston book market. By Worthington Chauncey Ford. Boston. The Club of Odd Volumes.
Imprint: D. B. Updike. The Merrymount Press, Boston.

Boards; $9\frac{3}{4}$ x 6-5/8 in.

IMPRINTS, United States.

Cabinet G Shelf 4 No. 24

Updike, D.B., The Merrymount Press, Boston,1917. Parochial libraries of the eighteenth century in Christ Church, Boston. Privately printed at the Merrymount Press in the year of our Lord MDCCCCXVII.

Marbled paper bds., $8\frac{1}{2}$ x $5\frac{3}{4}$ ins., pp.81.

IMPRINTS, United States

Cabinet G Shelf 4 No. 26

Updike, Daniel B., The Merrymount Press, Boston, 1923.
Title: Pro vita monastica...By Henry Dwight Sedgwick.
Imprint: The Atlantic Monthly Press. Printed by D.B. Updike.

Cloth; 8-3/8 x $5\frac{3}{4}$ in.

IMPRINTS, United States

Cabinet F Shelf 1 No. 9

Updike, Daniel Berkeley. The Merrymount Press. Boston, 1929.
Title: The first American Bible. A leaf [Original] with an account of the two printers, Samuel Green and Marmaduke Johnson. [1663]. By George Parker Winship.

Stamped cloth; 7-7/8 x 6 x $\frac{1}{4}$ in.

IMPRINTS, United States

Cabinet K Shelf 5 No. 23

Updike, D.B., The Merrymount Press, Boston, 1917.
Title: The wood engravings of Rudolph Ruzicka. By W. M. Ivins, Jr.

Pictorial boards; 7 x $4\frac{1}{2}$ in. Item in envelope.

IMPRINTS, United States

Cabinet L Shelf 1 No. 20

Updike, D. B. The Merrymount Press, Boston, Mass., 1923.

See BROWN, BOLTON. Lithography...

IMPRINTS, United States

Cabinet G Shelf 4 No. 30

Updike, D. B. The Merrymount Press, Boston, 1929.
Title: The Limited Editions Club ... Illustrated by the foremost artists and made into volumes of beauty ... [Prospectus].
Imprint: Printed by D. B. Updike. The Merrymount Press, Boston.

Boards; 8-3/4 x 5-3/4 in.

IMPRINTS, United States.

Cabinet G Shelf 4 No. 25

Updike, D.B., The Merrymount Press, 1918. Portraits of Whistler. A critical study and an iconography by A.E. Gallatin. With 40 illus.

Boards, linen back, 11 x 8 ins., pp.81.

IMPRINTS, United States

Cabinet S Shelf 3 No. 82

Updike, Daniel Berkeley: The Merrymount Press, Boston, 1924.
Title: A Dissertation upon English typographical founders and foundries. By Edward Rowe Mores...[A reprint of original 1779 edition]
Imprint: Edited [and printed] by D. B. Updike. New York, The Grolier Club, 1924.

Linen boards; $9\frac{3}{4}$ x 6 in.

IMPRINTS, United States

Cabinet QQ Shelf 1 No. 38

Van Benthuysen, C. & Co. Albany, 1845.
Title: Poems by Frederick Wing Cole.
Imprint: Albany: C. Van Benthuysen & Co.

Cloth; 7 x $5\frac{1}{4}$ x $\frac{1}{2}$ in.

IMPRINTS, United States

Cabinet S Shelf 1 No. 139

Updike, Daniel Berkeley: The Merrymount Press, Its aims, work and equipment. Boston, 1919.
Descriptive pamphlet, with partial bibliography of Merrymound Press Imprints.

Half morocco; 11-1/8 x $8\frac{1}{4}$ in.

IMPRINTS, United States

Cabinet S Shelf 4 No. 83

Updike, Daniel Berkeley: The Merrymount Press Boston, 1924.
Title: In the day's work. By Daniel Berkeley Updike. Limited edition. Cambridge, Harvard University Press.
Imprint: Printed by D.B. Updike. The Merrymount Press, Boston, U.S.A.

Marbled linen boards; 8-7/8 x $5\frac{3}{4}$ in.

IMPRINTS, United States

Cabinet JJ Shelf 3 No. 3

Van Winkle, C.S., New York City, 1811.

see
SOCIETIES, PRINTERS'. United States.
New York Typographical Society...1811

IMPRINTS, United States

Cabinet S Shelf 3 No. 81

Updike, D. Berkeley: The Merrymount Press, Boston, 1922.
Title: Printing types, their history, forms and use ... By Daniel B. Updike. 2 Vols.
Imprint: D. B. Updike; The Merrymount Press, Boston, Mass.
Cambridge University Press, 1922.

Cloth; $9\frac{1}{2}$ x $6\frac{1}{4}$ in.

IMPRINTS, United States.

Cabinet G Shelf 4 No. 29

Updike, Daniel B. The Merrymount Press, Boston, 1928.
A chronological list of books printed at the Kelmscott Press. With illustrative material from a collection made by William Morris and Henry C. Marillier, now in the library of Marsden J. Perry of Providence, Rhode Island.
Colophon: Printed at the Merrymount Press, Boston in the month of May, MDCCCCXXVIII.
Half morocco $8\frac{1}{2}$ x 5-7/8 in.

IMPRINTS, United States.

Cabinet G Shelf 4 No. 31

Walpole Printing Office. Edmund B. Thompson and Peter Beilenson. New Rochelle, N. Y. 1930.
Title: Horace Walpole and his printing office at Strawberry Hill. (Pamphlet.
Colophon: Printed at the Walpole Printing Office, Edmund B. Thomson and Peter Beilenson.

Paper cover; 6 x $3\frac{1}{2}$ in.

IMPRINTS, United States.

Cabinet G Shelf 4 No. 27

Updike, D.B. The Merrymount Press, Boston,1923. Dr. Johnson: A play by A.E. Newton, Esq. Boston. The Atlantic Monthly Press, MDCCCCXXIII. Photo eng. 17.

Autographed edition.

Boards, linen back, 9 x 6-7/8 ins., pp.120.

IMPRINTS, United States.

Cabinet G Shelf 4 No. 28

Updike, Daniel B. The Merrymount Press, Boston, 1928.
Title: The Complete Angler....by Izaak Walton. Decorations by W.A. Dwiggins. Boston. C.E. Goodspeed & Co., 1928.
Colophon:.....printed by D.B. Updike, The Merrymount Press, Boston,in the month of April, 1928.

Decorated boards; 7 x $4\frac{3}{4}$ x $1\frac{1}{4}$ in.

IMPRINTS, United States

Cabinet G Shelf 4 No. 31

Walpole Printing Office, New Rochelle, N.Y. (Peter Beilenson & Edmund Thompson.

Two small advertising brochures, 1930 and 1934.

In envelope.

IMPRINTS, United States

Cabinet G · Shelf 4 · No. 31.01

Walpole Printing Office (P.C. Duschnes) New Rochelle, N.Y. 1932
Title: The notorious jumping frog of Calaveras County...By Mark Twain.
Imprint: Philip C. Duschnes, New York, 1932.
Colophon: This edition consists of 200 copies... and printed for private distribution by Philip C. Duschnes. Walpole Printing Office.

Boards; $7\frac{1}{4}$ x 4-3/8 in.

IMPRINTS. United States

Cabinet NN · Shelf 3 · No. 10

Walsh, John P., Cincinnati, 1869.
His stereotyped editions.
Stereotyping at the Franklin Type Foundry, Cincinnati, Ohio.

See Fitzgerald, Joseph. Caseine: Being rural meditations...

IMPRINTS, United States.

Cabinet G · Shelf 4 · No. 32

Walton, Perry. Boston, Mass. 1929.
Title: Paul Revere's own story: An account of his Ride as told in a letter to a friend, together with a brief sketch of his career. Compiled by Harriet E. O'Brien. Facsimile. Portrait.
Imprint: Privately printed by Perry Walton [Boston, Mass.]. 1929.

Boards; $11\frac{1}{4}$ x $8\frac{1}{2}$ in.

IMPRINTS, United States.

Cabinet F · Shelf 1 · No. 111

Wands, William W. Lansingburgh, Rensselaer County, 1797.
Title: The American Accomptant; being a plain practical and systematic compendium of Federal Arithmetic....By Chauncy Lee.
Imprint: Lansingburgh: Printed by William W. Wands, 1797.

Leather; 6-7/8 x 4-1/4 x 1-1/4 in.

IMPRINTS, United States

Cabinet G · Shelf 4 · No. 33.01

Warde, Frederic, New York, 1929.
Title: New Year's Eve. By Charles Lamb.
Imprint: New York. Privately printed.
Colophon: Two hundred and forty-five copies privately printed for George A. Nelson, Christmas, 1929. Typography by Frederic Warde.

Boards: $6\frac{3}{4}$ x $4\frac{1}{2}$ in.

IMPRINTS, United States

Cabinet G · Shelf 3 · No. 51

Warde, Frederic. New York 1930.
Title: A Christmas Carol. By Charles Dickens.
Imprint: Printed for the friends of William Edwin Rudge, Mount Vernon N. Y.
Colophon...Typography and binding by Frederic Warde.

Morocco, gilt tooling; 6-3/4 x $4\frac{1}{4}$ in. Two vols. in board protective case.

IMPRINTS, United States.

Cabinet G · Shelf 4 · No. 33

Warde, Frederic. New York, 1930.
Title: Christmas Eve. From the Sketch Book of Geoffrey Crayon, Gent. By Washington Irving. New York. Privately printed. 1930.
Colophon: Printed for George A. Nelson. Christmas 1930. Typography by Frederic Warde.

Boards; 7-5/8 x 5 in.

IMPRINTS, United States.

Cabinet G · Shelf 3 · No. 52.02

Warde, Frederic, New York, 1931.

See Imprints, United States. Rudge, W. E. (Frederic Warde).

IMPRINTS, United States

Cabinet G · Shelf 4 · No. 34

Watts, John. Philadelphia, 1806.
Title: Xenophontis de Cyri institutis
Imprint: Execudebat Johannis Watts, impensis Wm. Payntell et Soc.
This is the first Greek book printed from the first Greek type cast in the United States of America.

Calf; 9 x $5\frac{1}{2}$ in.

IMPRINTS, UNITED STATES

Cabinet FF · Shelf 1 · No. 68

Watts & Co., J. New York, 1813.
Title: The Larger Catechism...Revised by Alex. McLeod.
Imprint: New York: Stereotyped and printed by J. Watts & Co., June 1813.

The first book ever stereotyped in America.
Half morocco; $6\frac{3}{4}$ x 4 x 5/8 in.

IMPRINTS, United States

Cabinet G · Shelf 4 · No. 35

Watts, John & Co. New York, 1813.
Title: The Larger Catechism...with proofs from the scripture revised by Alexander M'Leod, D.D. The first book ever stereotyped in America.
Imprint: New York. Stereotyped and printed by J. Watts & Co. for Whiting & Watson, Theological and classical Booksellers. June 1813.

Calf; 7-1/8 x $4\frac{1}{4}$ in.

Ex Cab. 40

IMPRINTS, United States

Cabinet G · Shelf 4 · No. 36

Webster, Charles R. and George. Albany, 1802.
Title: A farewell sermon delivered September 26th 1802 in the North Dutch Church, Albany. By John B. Johnson...
Imprint: Albany: Printed by Charles R. and George Webster. 1802.

Half morocco; 9-5.8 x $5\frac{3}{4}$ in.

IMPRINTS, United States

Cabinet C · Shelf 4 · No. 50

Wheatstalk Press. Carl I. Wheat. Palo Alto, Alta California, 1928.
Title: Poker as it was played in Deadwood in the fifties. Author unknown.
Colophon: Of this Episode...one hundred impressions have been struck by Carl I. Wheat at his wheatstalk press...this year of our Lord the one thousand nine hundred twenty and eight...
Paper; $9\frac{1}{4}$ x $6\frac{1}{4}$ in.

IMPRINTS, United States.

Cabinet G · Shelf 4 · No. 37

Windsor Press, The. Johnson Brothers, San Francisco, 1927. A catalog of books printed in editions de luxe by the Brothers Johnson at the Windsor Press. A Prospectus. Brochure.

$10\frac{1}{4}$ x $6\frac{1}{2}$ ins., pp.8, not numbered.

IMPRINTS, United States.

Cabinet G · Shelf 4 · No. 38

Windsor Press, The. Johnson Brothers, San Francisco, 1927. A child of Adam, by James Sydney Johnson, San Francisco, The Windsor Press.

Boards, $7\frac{1}{4}$ x $4\frac{3}{4}$ ins., pp.47.

IMPRINTS, United States.

Cabinet G · Shelf 4 · No. 39

Windsor Press, The. Johnson Brothers, San Francisco, 1927. The press of the renaissance in Italy: An essay written by James Sydney Johnson. Printed by the Brothers Johnson with illustrations adapted from the "Hypnerotomachi Poliphili," of Aldus Manutius.

Boards, 11 x $7\frac{1}{2}$ ins., pp.30.

IMPRINTS, United States

Cabinet G · Shelf 4 · No. 40

Windsor Press, The. Johnson Brothers, San Francisco, 1929.
Title: Nocturn in St. Gaudens. By James Sydney Johnson.
Imprint: Herein printed for the American Institute of Graphic Arts by The Windsor Press. San Francisco, A. D. Mcmxxix.

Boards; 8-5/8 x 6-1/8 x $\frac{1}{4}$ in.

IMPRINTS, United States.

Cabinet G · Shelf 4 · No. 41

Windsor Press: Cecil and James Johnson. San Francisco, 1930.
Title: The Book of Ruth.
Imprint: Privately printed: The Windsor Press.

Vellum; 5-1/8 x $3\frac{3}{4}$ in.

IMPRINTS, United States.

Cabinet G Shelf 5 No. 19

Woodward & Tiernan Printing Co., St. Louis. The Grand Canyon in Arizona. Advertising brochure Illus. n.d.

Paper, 15 x 12 ins., lvs. 8.

IMPRINTS, United States.

Cabinet G Shelf 4 No. 45

Wright, J.W. The Press in the Forest. California, 1926.

Title: Thanks Giving. By J.W. Wright.
Colophon: The types hand-set by the author, and the pages printed and made into this book by him in his shop which is in Carmel-by-the-Sea. California. The month of the Quail. Autographed copy.

Paper boards, leather back; 6 x 4-3/8 in.

IMPRINTS, United States

Cabinet G Shelf 4 No. 52

Yale University Press, New Haven, Conn., 1927.
Title: The parable against persecution...By Benjamin Franklin.[Reprint from the edition of 1775?]. Boston: Brad Stephens.
Imprint: ... Composition by Carl Purrington Rollins. At the Yale University Press, 1927.

Brochure.

IMPRINTS, United States

Cabinet S Shelf 3 No. 43

Woolly Whale Press, The (Geo. W. VanVechten Jr. and CharlesH. Richards) New York, 1933
Title: The story of the Village Type. By Frederic W. Goudy.
Imprint: New York. The Press of the Woolly Whale, 1933

Boards, cloth back; 9¼ x 6¼ in.

IMPRINTS, United States

Cabinet F Shelf 3 No. 40

Wyckoff, Cornelius P. Schenectady, 1797.
Title: Letters on Missions. By Melville Horne.
Imprint: Schenectady. Printed by C. P. Wyckoff, in State-Street. 1797.

Leather; 6¾ x 4½ x ½ in.

IMPRINTS, Anonymous

Cabinet S Shelf 5 No. 67

Privately printed: California, 1930
Title: Sub-rosa, or the rape of the printerie.

Paper; 9¼ x 6¾ in.

IMPRINTS, United States.

Cabinet G Shelf 4 No. 42

Wright, J.W.: The Press in the Forest. California, 1916.

Title: The long ago.
Imprint: The Press in the Forest. Carmel-by-the Sea. California.

Checked muslin over paper boards; 7¼ x 5¼ in

IMPRINTS, United States.

Cabinet G Shelf 4 No. 49

Wynkoop-Hallenbeck-Crawford Co., New York,1921. The American Triumvirate. Printed by Wynkoop-H-C., Co. for presentation to its personal and business friends.

Boards, 12 x 9¼ ins., pp.45.

IMPRINTS, Anonymous

Cabinet X Shelf 4 No. 40

London, 1693
Title: Reasons humbly offered for the liberty of unlicens'd printing...
Imprint: London: Printed in the year 1693...

Half morocco; 8¼ x 6¼ in.

IMPRINTS, United States.

Cabinet G Shelf 4 No. 47

Wright, J.W. The Press in the Forest, California, 1926.

Title: The Gipsy Wagon. By J.W. Wright.
Imprint: The Press in the Forest, publishers. Carmel-by-the-sea, California.

Paper; 8 x 5-3/4 ins.

IMPRINTS, United States.

Cabinet G Shelf 4 No. 48

Wynkoop Hallenbeck Crawford Co., New York, 1921. Some notes on catalog making, by Samuel Graydon. With a foreword by Ernest Elmo Calkins.

Boards, 8 x 5¼ ins., pp.29.

IMPRINTS, Anonymous. (Holland).

Cabinet F Shelf 4 No. 63

Amsterdam, 1769.
Title: Les saisons, poeme... [Par James Thomson]. Frontispiece, head, and tail pieces engraved by Chaufford etc.

Leather; 7-1/8 x 5 x 1-7/8 in.

IMPRINTS, United States.

Cabinet G Shelf 4 No. 44

Wright, J. W: The Press in the Forest. California, 1926.

Title: No gifts and other stories. By J. W. Wright.
Imprint:....The types handset by the author. Likewise printed and done into a book by him in his shop which is called The Press in The Forest in Carmel-by-the Sea. California. In the month of fairy lanterns.

Paper boards; 8 x 5½ in.

IMPRINTS, United States

Cabinet QQ Shelf 4 No. 38

Wynkoop, Hallenbeck, Crawford Co., New York, 1924.
Title: Fifth Avenue old and new, 1824 - 1924. By Henry Collins Brown. Illus. In commemoration of the 100th anniversary of the founding of Fifth Avenue.
Imprint: Produced by the Wynkoop, Hallenbeck, Crawford Co., New York City.

Pictorial boards; 12¼ x 9-1/8 in.

IMPRINTS, Anonymous. Holland

Cabinet F Shelf 4 No. 65

Amsterdam, 1771, 1772.
Title: Jugement de Paris. Poème in IV chants. Par Jean Imbert..
Imprint: Amsterdam, 1772.
Includes three other items, each with separate title page.

Morocco, gilt; 8-5/8 x 5-3/4 x 1-1/8 in.

IMPRINTS, United States.

Cabinet G Shelf 4 No. 46

Wright, J.W. The Press in the Forest, California, 1926.
Title: Smith's Pharmacy. By J.W. Wright.
Colophon: The writer set the types by hand and printed these pages from them. Bound into a book by him in his shop which is called The Press in the Forest. In Carmel-by-the-Sea. California. In the month of the Blue Lupin. MCMXXVI.

Paper boards; 7-7/8 x 5-3/8 in.

IMPRINTS, United States.

Cabinet G Shelf 4 No. 51

Yale University Press. New Haven, 1926. James Durand, an able seaman of 1812. Published with the co-operation of the Navel Order of the United States. Illus.

Linen bds., 8 x 5¼ ins., pp.139.

IMPRINTS, Anonymous. (United States).

Cabinet G Shelf 2 No. 3

Fairbanks Company, Thomas N. New York, 1930
Title: An introduction to a conclusion.
Imprint: New York. Privately printed, 1930.
Colophon: Privately printed for distribution to the friends of the Thomas N. Fairbanks Company. Import Division, U.S. Envelope Company.

Paper boards; 10 x 6 in. Protective case.

IMPRINTS, CURIOUSITIES OF see
CURIOSITIES OF IMPRINTS

Cabinet
Shelf
No.

IMPRINTS, FICTITIOUS
see also
FALSE IMPRINTS.

Cabinet
Shelf
No.

IMPRINTS, Fictitious.

Cabinet W
Shelf 1
No. 51

Imprimeurs imaginaires et libraires supposes. Par Gustave Brunet. Paris, 1866.

Cloth; 8½ x 5½ x 1¼ in.

INCUNABULA

Cabinet 29
Shelf 1
No. 28

Aliaco, (Petrus de). Concordantia astronomie cum theologia. Augsburg, Erhard Ratdolt, 1490.
Title: Cōcordātia astronomie cū theologia/cōcordātia astronomie cū hystorica/narratione. Et elucidariū....Petri de Aliaco car/dinalis Cameracensis.
Colophon: Opus...Ioannis Angeli...diligēti correctione. Erhardique Ratdolt mira imprimendi arte: qua nuper Venetiis nūc Auguste Vindel-

cont'd

INCUNABUALA cont'd

Cabinet 29
Shelf 1
No. 28

icorum excellit nominatissimus 4 nonas Januarii. 1490. [Red printer mark follows]: Erhardi Ratdolt foelicia conspice signa/ Testata artificem qua valet ipse manum.

Mottled paper over boards; 8-1/8 x 6¼ x ½ in. Zapf p.95; Hain I, 834.

INCUNABULA

Cabinet 29
Shelf 1
No. 25

Angeli, Johannes: Astrolabium. Augsburg: Erhard Ratdolt, 1488.
Title: Astrolabium planu in tabulis Ascendens/...
Dedication: Erhardus ratdolt Augustēn. impressor Albert rheni/ palatino:...Bavarie duci potentissimo....
Colophon: Opus Astrolabii plani in tabulis: a Johā/ne Angeli artium liberaliū magistro a no/uo elaboratū:...Erhardi rat/dolt Augustēsis viri solertis: eximia industria: mira

cont'd

INCUNABULA cont'd

Cabinet 29
Shelf 1
No. 25

imprimendi arte: qua nup ve/neciis nunc Auguste vindelicorū excellit nominatissimus. Vigesimoseptimo kalen/dus Novembris M.CCCC.LXXXVIII/

Gesamt-Kat; 1900. Hain 1100. Brunet 1,290.

Boards; 8-3/4 x 6½ x 1 in.

INCUNABULA

Cabinet D
Shelf 1
No. 37

Antoninus. Summa confessionum. De restitutionibus. Venice, [1480].Johann de Colonia.
Incipit sūmula confessionis utilissi/ma; in qua agitur qūo se haberer debe-/at confessor erga penitentem in cofessi/onibus audiendis; (etc)

Gesamt-Kat. 2112.

Original binding with chain, original enclosing case; 9½ x 6½ x 1-3/4 in.

In Glass Case.

INCUNABULA

Cabinet 29
Shelf 1
No. 4

Appianus. Historia Romana. Part I and II. Venice: Ratdolt, Maler (Pictor) and Löslein. 1477. Borders in red.
Title: of Part I: P. Candidi in libros Appiani sophiste Alexandrini ad Nico-/laum quintū summu pontificem. Prefatio incipit felicissime.
Colophon: Impressum est hoc opus Venetiis per Bernardu picto-/rem & Erhardum ratdolt de Augusta una cum Petro/Löslein de Langencen correctore ac socio. Laus Deo/M.CCCCLXXVII.

cont'd

INCUNABULA cont'd

Cabinet 29
Shelf 1
No. 4

Title of Part II: Additum Alfonsum Aragonum & utrius qz Sicilie/regem in libros civilu belborū....
Colophon of Part II: Identical with that of Part I.

Gesamt-Kat. 2290. Hain 1307. Redgrave 4. Morocco; 11½ x 8½ x 3 in.

INCUNABULA

Cabinet 29
Shelf 1
No. 5

Appianus. Historia Romana. Parts I and II. Venice. Ratdolt, Maler (Pictor) and Löslein. 1477. Borders in black [2nd copy]

For particulars see card 29/1/4.

Ex cab. 52

INCUNABULA

Cabinet 10
Shelf 2
No. 4

Astesanus de Ast. Summa de casibus conscientia. [Strassburg: Johann Mentelin, 1472]
Text: [V] enerando in xp̄o p̄ri et/ dñi. Johanni Gaye/ Tano de urbe divina pui-/dentia dignissimo sacro-/ sancte romane eccl'ie sc̄i/ theodori dyacono. cardia/li.
No colophon; 364 leaves, 2 cols. 62 lines
Index preceding text: [C] V piens ego fr̄ astaxanq cō/pilator huis sume ad hono-/rem dei (etc.)

cont'd

INCUNABULA cont'd

Cabinet 10
Shelf 2
No. 4

Stamped pigskin, with brass bosses; 17 x 12 x 4¾ in.

INCUNABULA

Cabinet 6
Shelf 1
No. 6

Augustinus, Aurelius: De civitate dei Venice: Nicolas Jenson, 1475.
First line, following index (pp.28) and blank leaf: Aurelij Augustiniēpi de civitate dei.
Colophon: Aurelij Augustini opus de civita/te dei feliciter explicit: consectuz uene/tijs ab egregio & diligēti magistro Ni/colao ienson; Petro Mozenicho prin/cipe: Anno a nativitate domini mile/simo quadringētesimo septuagesimo/quinto: sexto nonas octobres.

cont'd

INCUNABULA cont'd

Cabinet 6
Shelf 1
No. 6

First book printed by Jenson in Gothic types.
Perfect copy.

Original stamped vellum on boards with clasps; 11¾ x 9 x 3 in. Hain 1,2051.

INCUNABULA

Cabinet D
Shelf 1
No. 44

Ausimo, Nicolaus de. Liber qui dicitur supplementum. Venice, 1482. Ranner, Franciscus de Heilbronn.
Colophon: Impressum est hoc opusculum/ Venetiis per Franciscū renner de/Hailbrunn M.CCCC.LXXXII/ Laus deo.

Gesamt-Kat. ; Hain 2164; Orig. parch., 7 x 5 ins., 3-1/8 ins. thick.

INCUNABULA

Cabinet D
Shelf 1
No. 39

Baysio, Guido de. Rosarium decretorum. Venice. Johann Herbort [for Johann of Cologne & Co.] 1481.
Colophon: Exactum insigne hoc opus ductū auspitiis/optimoz, Iohannis de Colonia Nicolai ienson sociorūue/....prodesse uolunt...delectare/poete. Huiusce aut operis artifex extitit sūmus in hac arte/mgr̄ Ioanes de Selgenstat alemānz. qui sua solertia ac ui/gi liis diuoqz impremēdi caractere facile

cont'd

INCUNABULA cont'd

Cabinet D
Shelf 1
No. 39

supeminet oīs./Olympiadibus dñicis Anno vero millesimo, CCCCLXXXI/tertiás nonas apriles. [With printer mark]. Illum.

Gesamt-Kat.3-3747 ; Hain 2717; Large-fol.

Orginial binding, tooled vellum; 18 x 11½ in

In ex cab. 13

INCUNABULA

Cabinet D · Shelf 2 · No. 35

Bergomensis. (Foresti) Jacobus Philippus. De claris selectisque mulieribus. Ferrara; Laurentii Rubeis, 1497.
Colophon: Opus de claris selectisqz plurimis mulieribus a fratre Ja. Philippo Bergomense editum....Ferrari Ĩpressus/ Opera ẽ impensa magistri Laurentii de Rubeis de Valentia. tertio kal' maias./ anno salutis nr̃e M.CCCCLXXXXVII. Religioso Inuictiss, qz principe: Diuo hereu/ le: Duce secundo:
cont'd

INCUNABULA

Cabinet D · Shelf 2 · No. 20

Biblia Latina. [Edited by Petrus Angelus de Monte Ulmi] Venice, 1492. Hieronymus de Paganinis.
Colophon:....Impressa vero in felici/Venetorum civitate sumptibus arte Hieronymi de Pa-/ganinis Brixiensis. Anno gratie millesimo quadringente/ simo nonagesimo secundo: Septimo Idus septembris.

Gesamt-Kat. ; Hain 3112, 3114. Full calf; Proctor 8856; 6-7/8 x 4-3/4 x 2½ in.

INCUNABULA

Cabinet D · Shelf 2 · No. 43

Brant, Sebastien. Stultifera navis....per Iacobum Locher...in latinum traducta eloquium. Basel, J. Bergmann de Olpe,1498.
Colophon: Finis stultifere navis/Finis narragonice navis per...et nova quadā exactaqz emendatione elimate. Atqz sup additis q/busdam novis admirandisqz fatuor generibus sup/generibus sup/plete: In lauditissima Germanie urbe Basiliensi:/ nup op & pmotione Iohãnis Bergman de Olpe/ Anno o salutis nr̃e.
cont'd

INCUNABULA

Cabinet D · Shelf 2 · No. 19

Bergomensis [Jac. Phil.] Supplementum chronicarum. Venice, 1492. Bernadino Rizzo.
Text: Opus preclarum Supplementum chro/nicharum vulgo appellatum....
Colophon: Ac sic demū deo auxiliante...Hac q̃ppe in exordio huis op̄is me facere....auctū per me opus fuit idi/bus octobris anno a natali xp̄iano 1486 in civitate nostra Bergomi.... Impressum autem Venetiis per magistrum Bernardinus ricium de novaria anno a nativita/
cont'd

INCUNABULA

Cabinet 10 · Shelf 2 · No. 6

Boethius (Annius Manlius Severinus). Nuremberg, 1573. Anthony Koberger.
Text: Incipit Tabula sup libris Boety de con/solatione philosophie secundum ordinem/ alphabeti.
Colophon: Hic liber Boecii de c̃solatione philosophie in textu/latina aleman icaqz lingua refertus ac translatu...finit feliciter. Anno domini/M.CCCC LXXIII mensis July/ Conditit hoc Civis alūnis Nurembergensis/
cont'd

INCUNABULA cont'd

Cabinet D · Shelf 2 · No. 43

M.CCCCXCVIII, Kl: Martii. Printer mark.

Gesamt-Kat. ; Hain 3751; Crimson morocco gilt; 8¼ x 6¼ x 1 in.

INCUNABULA cont'd

Cabinet D · Shelf 2 · No. 19

te dñi M.CCCC.LXXXXII die decimo quinto Februarii....

Gesamt-Kat. ; Hain 2809; modern binding; 12½ x 9 x 1½ in.

In ex cab. 5

INCUNABULA cont'd

Cabinet 10 · Shelf 2 · No. 6

Opus arte sua Antonius Coburger.

Gesamt-Kat. ; Hain 3398. Original boards; 16½ x 11¼ x 2¾ ins.

INCUNABULA

Cabinet 14 · Shelf 2 · No. 4

Canon Missae (1458), Fust and Schoeffer, Mainz. Printed on vellum, and in two colors, with handsome initials. Lacking some folios Another incomplete copy of this missale is in the Bodleian Library. In our copy 18 pp. of the Canon Missal of 1458 are inserted in the Missale Cracoviense, 1484, Peter Schoeffer, Mainz.

Original boards, stamped calf with bronze bosses; 16¼ x 11¼ x 3½ in.

INCUNABULA

Cabinet 10 · Shelf 2 · No. 8

Biblia latina. Nuremberg: Antonius Coburger, 1480. Illuminated.
Text: Incipit epl̃a sancti hieronimi ad Paulinu presbiterum de omnibus divine historie libris.
Colophon: Anno incarnationis dñice. Millesimoqua/dringentesimooctuagesimo. Mai vero Kl/octavodecimo...In oppido Nurnbergn per Antonius Coburger pfati/oppidi incolam industria cuius q̃ dilig ẽtis-/sime fabresactum. finit feliciter.
cont'd

INCUNABULA

Cabinet D · Shelf 1 · No. 29

Bonaventura [St.]. Speculum beatae Mariae virginis. Augsburg, 1476: Anton Sorg.
Colophon: Devotissimi...fratris Bonavẽture/tractatus super gaudiosa ambasiata...explicit feliciter. Non quidem cyro/graphatus sed p fide dignum virū Anthonium sorg conduem/ Augustensem qz̄ diligenter impressus. Anno... M.CCCC.LXXVI. pridi Kalendis marciis.

Gesamt-Kat. . Hain 3566; boards; 12 x 8¼ x ½ in.

INCUNABULA

Cabinet 60 · Shelf 2 · No. 1

Catarina da Siena. Epistole ed orazioni. [Edited by Bartholomeo da Alzano]. Venice: Aldus Manutius, 1500.
Title: Epistole devotissime de/ sancta Cathari-/na da Siena/ Sappia ciascuno...queste Epistole....per il venerabile servo di Dio frate Bartholomeo da Alzano...essendo stampate... Venetia...[Illuminated].
Colophon: Stampato in la Inclita Cita de Venetia in Casa De Aldo Manutio/ Romano a di XV.
cont'd

Ex cab. 9

INCUNABULA cont'd

Cabinet 10 · Shelf 2 · No. 8

Gesamt-Kat;

Original boards, stamped leather 16¾ x 11¼ x 4¾ ins.

INCUNABULA

Cabinet 6 · Shelf 1 · No. 8

Bonifacius VIII. Sextus Decretalium. Venice: Andreas Torresanus and Bartholomaeus de Blavis, 1483.
First lines (Sig. a): [c]irca lecturā arboris diversis oli/diversuz modū tenentibus: Jo./de deo hispanus....
On Sig. a 2 has table of consanguinity.
Title lines (Sig. a 4): Incipit sextus liber decretalium/ Bonifacius Episcopus servus./
With the incorrect Colophon: Sexti libri decretalium opus perutile enecleatius emenda/tum atqz castigatum im-
cont'd

INCUNABULA cont'd

Cabinet 60 · Shelf 2 · No. 1

Septembrio. M.CCCCC.

Half morocco; 12½ x 8½ x 3 in. Hain 4688. Essling II, 1230.

INCUNABULA cont'd

Cabinet D · Shelf 2 · No. 35

ferrariesibus legiptime Imperante. [Printers mark follows].

Gesamt-Kat. Hain 2813; Proctor 5762.

Morocco; 12 x 8¼ x 1 in.

INCUNABULA cont'd

Cabinet 6 · Shelf 1 · No. 8

pensa idustriaqz singulari Nicolai/Jenson Gallici Venetijs impressuz feliciter explicit Olym/piadibz domini nostri iesu christi M.CCCC.LXXIX. nono ca/lendarum decembris.

Bound in with another volume in same format and types printed by Jenson's successors in 1483. Jenson died in 1480.

Gilt russia; 17 x 11½ x 1-3/4 in. Hain 1

INCUNABULA

Cabinet D · Shelf 2 · No. 47

Chronica van der hilliger Stat van Coellen, Die. Cologne, 1499. Johann Koelhoff, [the younger].
Colophon: Dye slossrede dis boichs/....Ind hait gedruckt/mit groissem ernst ind vliss Iohan Koelhoff Burger in Coellen. ind vollendet opsent/ Bartholomeus auent des heiligen Apostles Anno vursz/ Got have lof tzo aller tzijt und. ewichlich.

Gesamt-Kat. ; Hain 4989. Original covers; folio

12½ x 8-3/4 in.

INCUNABULA

Cabinet 6 Shelf 1 No. 8

Clement V. Constitutiones una cum apparatu Joannis Andreae. Venice: Bartholomei de Alexandria and Andreeqz de Asula, 1483.
Title line (Sig. A-2): Incipiunt constitutiones clementis/pape quinto vna cum apparatu do/mini ioannis andree/
Colophon, preceding epilogue, pp.15 (Sigs. H, H2, H3, H4, and 9 pp. without Sig. signs), headed "Incipiunt decretales extrauagantes que emanarum/post sextum/De electione & electi

cont'd

INCUNABULA cont'd

Cabinet 10 Shelf 2 No. 1

This printer worked with Gutenberg in Mainz on the great Bible and was a witness in the lawsuit Fust vs Gutenberg.

Gesamt-Kat. Hain 6463.

INCUNABULA

Cabinet 29 Shelf 1 No. 20

Eusebius. Chronicon. [With the continuations of Prosper and Matthaeus Palmerius. Edited by J.L. Santritter.] Venice: Erhard Ratdolt, 1483.
Title: Eusebii caesariensis episcopi chronicon id/ est temporum breviarium incipit.../quem Hieronymus praesbiter divino/ eius ingenio latinum facere...
Colophon: Erhardus Ratdolt Augenstensis solerti vir ingenio maxima/...hoc volumine de

cont'd

Ex Cab. 54

INCUNABULA cont'd

Cabinet 6 Shelf 1 No. 8

pot estate/Bonfacius octavus./: Clemantarium opus perutile enucleatius castigatum elima/ tuqz: Impensa atqz diligentia singulari Bartholomei de ale-/xandria Andreeqz de asola socioq Venetiis impressum felici/ter exp explicit: Anno salutis christiane. M.CCCC.LXXXIII. tertio ca-/lendas Novembris.

Bound in with another volume in same format and types, printed by Jenson in 1480. Gilt russia; 17 x 11½ x 1-3/4 in. Hain 2, 5431

INCUNABULA

Cabinet D Shelf 1 No. 31

Durandus. Speculum Judiciale. Milan. 1478. Benignus et Johan Ant. de Honate.
Begins as follows: Incipit prima pars Speculi suilhelmi dura/ti cu Iohannis Andree additioibus fuis....positis...post q̄nta d̄ eo variis Ī locis ip̄ssione fac/taz nūc p Beninū et Iohanne antonius et hona/te fratres sexte impressione Mli diligentissime/. [With miniature painting.]
Gesamt-Kat. ; Hain 6510. Original covers with metal corners; 17 x 11½ x 4¼ ins.

In Ex. Cab. 13

INCUNABULA Cont'd

Cabinet 29 Shelf 1 No. 20

temporib'/ additiones: nō paruo studio impensisqz emendatissime im-/pressit Venetiis ...1483. Idibus Septembris.

Gesamt-Kat. ; Zapf p.164. Hain 6717. Redgrave 36. Morocco; 9¼ x 6½ x 1½ in.

INCUNABULA.

Cabinet D Shelf 1 No. 5

Damasceni, Petrus. Liber de laudibus ac festis Gloriosae virginis. [Cologne Götz, ca. 1475].
Begins: "Incipit liber de laudibus ac festis Gloriose virginis matris marie alias Marionale Dictus per Doctores eximeos editus et compilatus," at end, "Explicit Petrus Damasceni de laudibus gloriose virginis Marie
Mentioned in Hain, 5918. Parchment; 10½ x 7¾ x ½ in.

INCUNABULA

Cabinet D Shelf 2 No. 48 In ex. cab. 9.

Etymologikum magnum graece. Venice, 1499. Zakarias Kallierges.
Colophon in Greek [trans] Etymologikum magnum typis expressum explicit jam cum Deo Venetiis sumtibus...Domini Nicolai Blasti Cretensis...Iabore et dexteritate Zachariae Calliergi Cretensis, in gratiam...Anno nativitatis Christi 1499. Metagitionis (Julii) stantis die octava [Printers Mark]

Gesamt-Kat. Hain 6691. Vellum 15¼ x 10 x 2 in.

INCUNABULA

Cabinet 29 Shelf 1 No. 21

Eusebius. Chronicon. Venice: Erhard Ratdolt, 1483 [2nd copy]

For particulars see card 29/1/20.

INCUNABULA

Cabinet 29 Shelf 1 No. 3

Dionysius [Periegetes]. De situ orbis. Venice: Ratdolt, Maler (Pictor), Löslein, 1477.
Title: Eloquentissimi viri domini Antonii Becharie veronensis proemium in/Dyonisii traductionem....
Colophon: Impressum est hoc opusculum Venetiis/ per Bernardū pictorē & Erhardū ratdolt/de Augusta una cū Petro loslein de Langencen eor correctore ac socio. Laus deo/

cont'd

Ex. Cab. 52

INCUNABULA

Cabinet 29 Shelf 1 No. 12

Euclide. Elementa geometriae. Venice: Erhard Ratdolt. 1482.
p.1, verso: Erhardus ratdolt Augustensis impressor serenissimo/ alme urbis venete Principe Joanni. Mocenico.S.
Title: Preclarissimus liber elementorum Euclidis perspi/ cacissimi: in artem Geometrie incipit...
Colophon:....Erhardus ratdolt Augustensis impressor/solertissimus venetiis impressit Anno

cont'd

Ex Cab. 54

INCUNABULA

Cabinet 6 Shelf 1 No. 2

Eusebius, Pamphilius: De euangelica praeparatione. Venice: Nicolaus Jenson, 1470.
First lines: [E]usebium Pamphili de euvangelica praeparatione/latinum ex graeco..../
Colophon: Hoc Ienson ueneta Nicolaus in urbe uolumen/Prompsit: cui foelix gallica terra parens./Scire placet tempus. Mauro christophorus vrbi/ Dux erat. aequa animo musa retecta suo est./Quid magis artifecem peteret Dux: christus: et auctor:/Tres facit

cont'd

INCUNABULA cont'd

Cabinet 29 Shelf 1 No. 3

M.CCCC.LXXVII.
Has autograph, and ex-libris of Gilbert R. Redgrave.

Gesamt-Kat. . Hain 6226. Essling 255. Redgrave 6. Vellum; 8½ x 6¼ x ¼ in.

INCUNABULA cont'd

Cabinet 29 Shelf 1 No. 12

salutis. M.CCCC.LXXXII. Octavis Calen/ Iuñ.

Gesamt-Kat; . Hain 6693. Zapf. p.160. Essling 282. Redgrave 26. Original vellum covered boards with clasps; 12 x 8 x 1½ ins.

INCUNABULA cont'd

Cabinet 6 Shelf 1 No. 2

aeternos ingeniosa manus./M.CCC.LXX.

This the first book printed by Jenson.

Stitched only; in morocco slip case; 14 x 10¼ x 2 in. Hian 2, 6699.

INCUNABULA

Cabinet 10 Shelf 2 No. 1

Durandus, Gulielmus. Rationale divinorum officiōrum. n.p.d. [Basel: Berthold Ruppel V. Hanau, circa 1477].
Text: Incipit raeionale divinorum officiorum.
Colophon ends: misericordissimū indicē p peccatis meis devotas oraciones essundant. Deo gracias.
60 lines, 207 leaves of Gothic types.
Original pigskin, 2 clasps; 16¼ x 11-3/4 x 3 in.

cont'd

INCUNABULA.

Cabinet 29 Shelf 1 No. 13

Euclide. Elementa geometria. Venice: Erhard Ratdolt. 1482. [2nd copy].

For particulars see card 29/1/12.

Ex Cab. 54

INCUNABULA

Cabinet D Shelf 1 No. 28

Geminiano (Dominicus de Sancto). Prima pars lecturae super VI decretalium... Impressa Venetiis per magistrum Jacobum de Rubeis: Anno 1476, 4 id. Sept.

Hain-7539, Gesamt-Kat.

Original boards; 17 x 14¼ x 3½ in.

INCUNABULA

Cabinet D
Shelf 2
No. 16

Gouda, Gulielmus de. Tractatus de expositione missae. Cologne: [1491. Heinrich Quentell].
Colophon: Tractatulus fratris Guilhelmi de Gouda. ordinis mino/rum de observantia de expõne misse et de modo celebrãdi finit feliciter. Impressus Colonie circa summum cuilibet facer/doti summa necessarius.

Gesamt-Kat. ; Hain 7828.

Paper board; 8-1/8 x 5-3/8 in.

INCUNABULA

Cabinet 13
Shelf
No. 4

Graduale Romanum [Edited by Franciscum de Brugis]. Venice Luc Ant. Giunta, 1499-1500.
Colophon: Explicit graduale canonicle? Impressum Venetiis cura atqz impesa nobil' viri Luce ãtonij de giunta florentini: arte aut Joanis emerici de Spira: Anno incarnationis canonice 1499, 4 kal. Octobris. (2 tomes)

Gesamt-kat. Br. M. (V) p. 541

cont'd.

INCUNABULA cont'd

Cabinet 13
Shelf
No. 4

Vol. I, 23 x 15½. Morocco with brass bosses.
Vol. II, 23 x 15¾, paper over boards, with brass bosses.

INCUNABULA

Cabinet 14
Shelf 2
No. 15

Gratianus. Decretum [With a commentary] 13 August, 1472 [Rubricated and illuminated]
Text: Incipit discordantium canonũ con/cordia, etc.
Colophon: Anno incarnationis dñice MCCCCLXXII. Idibo augustiis...hoc presens Gratiani decretum...arte quada ingeniosa imprimẽdi! cũctipotẽte adspirãti deo Petrus schoiffer de gernsheym suis consignando scutis! feliciter consummairt. Printer mark.

INCUNABULA cont'd

Cabinet 14
Shelf 2
No. 15

Gesamt-Kat. Full morocco,
19 x 14¼ x 3 ins.

Hain 7885.

INCUNABULA

Cabinet 14
Shelf 2
No. 16

Gratianus, Decretum. [With commentary]. Mainz: Peter Schoeffer, 1472 [second copy; entirely without rubrication and illumination]
Text: Incipit discordantium canonũ con/cordia [etc]
Colophon: Same as 14/2/15.
The variation in thickness from same work adjoining (14/2/15) is due to extra thickness of paper.
Full leather; 19 x 13¾ x 4¼ in.

INCUNABULA

Cabinet D
Shelf 1
No. 34

Gregorious. Magnus. Papa. Homelien. Without indication of typographer or place [Utrecht, Joh. Veldener], 1479/
F. 1: Dit is die prologues of die voersprake in sin/ to Gregorious omelie in duutschen/. F. 212 recto; Hier eynden ende gaen wt allen/ sinte gregorious omelien van den son/nendaghen ende sommighe ander ty-/ den. Ende hier volghen nae allen/ sijn omelien vernolghende vanden/heijlighen./

cont'd

INCUNABULA cont'd

Cabinet D
Shelf 1
No. 34

F. 310 recto (number 308): Dit boec is gheprint int iaer doe men screef M.CCCC.LXXIX op den tweentwintichste dach/ in april. deo gracias.

Campbell 854 p. 236. Proctor 8856.

Boards, leather back; 9 x 6 x 1½ in.

INCUNABULA

Cabinet D
Shelf 2
No. 25

Gregorious IX. Decretales. Basle, (with commentaries by Sebastien Brant) 1494. Johann Froben.
Title: Decretalium dñi pape Gre-/gorii noni cõpilatio accurata/ diligentia emendata sũmoqz/studio elaborata et cũ scriptu/ris sacris aptissime xordata.
Colophon: Param erat o ingeniosa inventus:...Hac sibi cõpediosam pĩnciã Johãnes Froben de Hammel-/burg litterarie officine sollers indagator...Anno salutisere incarnatiõrs

cont'd

INCUNABULA cont'd

Cabinet D
Shelf 2
No. 25

nõagesimoquarto: supra millesimũquadringentismũqz auspicato susceptam: Idibus maiis felici/fine cõsummavit (etc)

Gesamt-Kat. ; Haeckerthorn p. 92

Original covers with part of clasps; 9 x 6¼ x 3-1/8 ins.

INCUNABULA

Cabinet D
Shelf 2
No. 53

Guillermus Altissiodorensis. Summa in IV libros sententiarum, Paris, 1500. Philippe Pigouchet.
Title page with two differing printers marks;
Imprint: Summa aurea in quattor libros... ..Impressa est Parissiis maxima Philippi Pigoucheti cura. Impensis vero Nicolai vaultier et Durandi gerlier alme universitatis Parisiensis librarorium.

Hain 8324. Tooled leather over boards; 11-3/8 x 8½ x 2½ in.

INCUNABULA cont'd

Cabinet D
Shelf 2
No. 52

HAIN 8324

Tooled leather over boards; 11-3/8 x 8½ x 2½ in.

INCUNABULA

Cabinet D
Shelf 2
No. 42

Hieronymus. Commentaria in Biblia. Venice, 1498. Joannes and Gregorius de Gregoriis. 2 vols.
Colophon: Finiut...hac...oper: ea quip̃pe diligentia emedata...Habes itaq̃z studiossime lector Ioanis & Graegorii de Gregoriis/fretus officio ea nouiter ĩpressa cõmentaria:....Venetiis p praefatos fratres Joannẽ & Gregoriũ de Gregoriis. Anno dni, 1498, die, 25 Augusti, Cum privilegio...Imprimere valeat nec

cont'd

INCUNABULA cont'd

Cabinet D
Shelf 2
No. 42

alibi impressa in terras excellentissimo venetorum dominio subditas venalia asserre sub poenis in ipso contentis [Has printer mark]

Gesamt-Kat. ; Hain 8581, Calf, fol. 2 vols.

Calf; 12¾ x 9½ in.

INCUNABULA

Cabinet 14
Shelf 2
No. 21
2 vols.

Hieronymus (Eusebius). Epistolae [Edited by Joannes Andrea, Bishop of Aleria] 2 vols. Rome: Sweynheym and Pannartz, 1468 (vol.2) 1470 (vol.1) [Two editions were issued . Here we have a vol. of each edition in which however,the work is complete.]
Vol.1: Io Andree Ep̃i Alerieñ ad Paulũ II. Venetum Pontificẽ Maximũ in epistolae [S] Acrosanctam Romanam ecclesiam: cuius omnipotens deus: ad temporum/ nostrorũ felicitatem: [etc]

INCUNABULA cont'd

Cabinet 14
Shelf 2
No. 21
2 vols.

Colophon, vol.1: Impressum Rome opus in domo Petr Petri & Francisci de Maximis, iuxta campum flore/presidentibus magistris Conrado Sweynheym & Arnoldo/Panartz. Anno dominici/ natatis. M.CCCC.LXX...Urbe & Ecclesia florent.
Vol.2: [A]nte omnia muneru oim largitori deo ac sanctis eius:
Colophon vol.2: Eusebii/Hieronymi doctoris eximu secũdum epistolarum explicit volumen/anno

cont'd

INCUNABULA cont'd

Cabinet 14
Shelf 2
No. 21

Christi M.CCCC.LXVIII. Indictione prima die vero XIII mensis /decembris (etc)

Full morocco: each vol.16¼ x 11-3/4 x 3 ins. Hain 8551 8552.

Vol. 1 contains a dedication to the reigning Pope in which the art of printing and the printers (S and P) are eulogized.

Gesamt-Kat. , Hain 8552. See Br. Mus. Rome, pp. 5, 10.

INCUNABULA

Cabinet D
Shelf 2
No. 38
In ex. cab. #5

Hieronymus, S. Epistolae. L pistole de San Hieronymo volgare. Ferrara, per Lorenzo di Rossi da Valenza, 1497.
Colophon: Impressa e la presente opera...ne la inclita & florentis/sima cita de Ferrara: per maestro Lorenzo/ di Rossi da Valenza: ne gli anni...M.CCCCXCVII. A. di: XII/de Octobre.....

cont'd

INCUNABULA cont'd

Cabinet D
Shelf 2
No. 38

Gesamt-Kat. Hain 8566 .Brunet 998;

Full morocco, gilt; 12¾ x 9-1/8 x 1⅜ in.

INCUNABULA

Cabinet D
Shelf 1
No. 47

Hieronymus. Vitas Patrum. De laude et ef-fectū virtutem. Venice, 1483: Ottaviano Scotus.
Colophon: Impressum venetijis per Octavianum/ scotu modoetiensem sextodecimo ka/lēdas Martii. M.CCCCLXXXIII. Joanne/ mocenico in-clyto Venetian Duce.

Gesamt-Kat. . Hain 8599. Parchment covers, 8¾ x 6¼ ins., 2 ins. thick.

INCUNABULA

Cabinet 29
Shelf 1
No. 15

Hyginus (Caius Julius). Poeticon Astronomi-con. [Sentinnus (Jacobus) and Santritter (J.L.)]. Venice; Erhard Ratdolt. 1482.
Title: Printed in red: Clarissimi Uiri Iginij Poeticon Astronomicon/opus utilissimu. Foe-liciter Incipit...
Colophon: Hoc Augustensis ratdolt germanus Erhar-dus/ Dispositis signis undiqz pressit opus/.. .Anno salutis. 1482. Priedie Idus. Octobris. Venetiis.

cont'd

INCUNABULA cont'd

Cabinet 29
Shelf 1
No. 15

Gesamt-Kat; . Zapf. p.159. Essling 285. Hain 9062. Redgrave 30. Vellum; 8½ x 6 x ½ in.

INCUNABULA

Cabinet 29
Shelf 1
No. 24

Hyginus (Caius Julius). Poeticon Astronomi-con. Venice, 1485.
Title: Clarissimi Uiri Hyginii Poeticon Astro/ nomicon. Opus utilissimum Foelicter in/cipit. De mundi & sphere...Hyginius M. Fabio Pluri-mā salutē.
Colophon: Anno salutisere incarnationis Millesimo quadringentesimo/ octogesimo quinto mensis Ianuarii die vigesima secunda. Im/pressum est presens opusculu per Erhardū Radtolt de

cont'd

INCUNABULA cont'd

Cabinet 29
Shelf 1
No. 24

Augusta/. Venetiis.

Gesamt-Kat; . Zaph.p.167. Essling 286. Hain 9063. Redgrave 48. Boards; 8¾ x 6½ x ½ in.

INCUNABULA

Cabinet D
Shelf 1
No. 18

Isiodori (S. Hispalensis Episcopi). Etymolo-giarum libri XX. [Augustae-Vindel]. Gunther Zainer, 1472. [Rubricated capitals, etc., wood cut].
Colophon: Isidori iunioris hispalensis episcopi, Ethimologiarum libri numero viginti-finiunt soeliciter. Per Gintherum zainer ex Reutlin-gen progenitum. literis impressi ahenis. Anno ab incarnatione domini Millesimo Qua-dringentesimo Septuagesimo secundo Decima-

cont'd

INCUNABULA cont'd

Cabinet
Shelf
No.

nona die Mensis novēbris.
Old morocco; 12 x 8¼ x 2⅜ ins.
Gesamt-Kat. Hain 9273; Brunet 3,463.

INCUNABULA

Cabinet 6
Shelf 1
No. 10

Joannes Carthusiensis [Giov. de Dio]: Nosce te [etc]. [Venice]: Nicolas Jenson, 1480.

First lines: Ego Philippus rota iuris utriusqz doctor: licet/omnium minimus.....
Colophon: Actum hoc opus ex inclyta: atqz famo-sa officina/ Nicolai Ienson Gallici: olym-piadibus dnicis/Anno uidelicet. M.CCCCLXXX. qrtas Kledas Iulias.

Recent boards; 8¼ x 5-3/4 x 7/8 ins.
Hain 3,9388

INCUNABULA

Cabinet D
Shelf 1
No. 41

Livius, Titus. Venice. Ottaviano Scotto. 1481.
Title: Quarta Deca di Titolivio.
Colophon: Finita la quarta Deca de Titolivio pa-dova/no hystorico dignissimo ipressa per maestro/Octaviano scoto in la dictione de Sixto quarto/potifice maximo ac Ioanne mo-zenico principe/celeberrimo nel. M.CCCCLXXXI adi XXVIII de giu/gno in Venetia.

Gesamt-Kat. ; Hain 10146. 12 x 8½ x 2in

INCUNABULA

Cabinet D
Shelf 1
No. 49

Lucanus, Marcus Annaes. Pharsalia [With the commentary ascribed to Omnibonus Leonicenus.] Venice, 1486. Nicolaus Battibovis.
Colophon: Finit opus Lucano cum cōmētariis Omni-boni vicētini impressū venetiis Nicolae battibove alexādrino anno domini MCCCCLXXXVI. tertio idus maii regnante inclyto principe marco barbadico. Examen voluminis. Quaterni sunt signati....Y Z &.

cont'd

INCUNABULA cont'd.

Cabinet D
Shelf 1
No. 49

Gesamt-Kat. ; Hain 10238; vellum over boards, 11¼ x 8-5/8 x 1½ ins.

INCUNABULA

Cabinet D
Shelf 1
No. 26

Maria (Paulus de S.) Incipit dialogus qui vocatur Scrutiniuz scripturar [etc.] Mantua, Johannes Schall, 1475.
Colophon: Nota cp iste libellus videtur fuisse ...et cum diligenti emeda per me Johannem/ Schallus artiū doctorē Mantue impressus sub annis pre/fati domī nostri Jhesu xpi M.CCCC.LXXV. regnante ibidem etc.

Gesamt-Kat. Brunet 4, 451,- Hain 10765

Half morocco; 12 x 8¼ x 2½ in.

INCUNABULA

Cabinet 29
Shelf 1
NO. 8

Martaratius, Franciscus. De compendis ver-sibus...Jac. Sentini de...lyricis carmini-bus tractalulus. Venice: Erhard Ratdolt. i.e., 1482.
Title: Francisci Mataratii Perusini...ad/Petrum Paulum Cornelium...componendis...opusculum.
Colophon: Erhardus ratdolt Augustensis probatis-simus librarie artis exa/ctor summa confecit ...Anno christi M.CCCCLXVIII. VII ca/len. Decembris. Venetiis [colophon misdated]

cont'd

INCUNABULA cont'd

Cabinet 29
Shelf 1
No. 8

Gesamt-Kat; . Hain 10889. Zapf, p.156. Redgrave 15. Morocco; 8½ x 6 x ¼ in.

INCUNABULA

Cabinet 29
Shelf 1
No. 7

Mela, Pomponius. Cosmographia. Venice. Ratdolt, Maler (Pictor) and Löslein, 1478.
Title (in red): Pomponij Melle, Cosmographi de/ situ orbis liber primus. Prooemium.
Colophon: Impressum est hoc opusculum Venetiis per/Bernardū pictorem & Erhardum ratdolt de/ Augusta una cū Petro Löslein de Langen-sen/ correctore ac socio. Laus Deo M.CCCC.LXXVIII.

cont'd

INCUNABULA cont'd

Cabinet 29
Shelf 1
No. 7

Gesamt-Kat. Zapf, p.156. Hain 11016. Redgrave 11.
Morocco; 8 x 6 x 5/8 in.

INCUNABULA

Cabinet 14
Shelf 2
No. 4

Missale Cracoviense, Mainz: Peter Schoeffer, 1484, Nov. 10.
Colophon: Missale presens factore petro/Schoffer de gernszheym Im/pressorie artis magistro In/ inclita civitate mogūtina eius/dem artis in-ventrice elimatri-/reqz prima...millesimoqua-dringentesi/om octouagesimoquarto. deci-/ma die novembris se ititer est/cōsummatum.
Printer mark of Fust and Schoeffer in red.
The Canon proper to this book is missing

cont'd

INCUNABULA cont'd

Cabinet 14 | but in its place is Schoeffers' famous, rarer and finer Canon Missal of 1458.

Shelf 2 | Original boards, stamped calf, with bronze bosses; 16¼ x 11¼ x 3½ ins.

No. 4 | Gesamt-Kat. ; De Ricci, Impressions de Mayence, p.66.

INCUNABULA

Cabinet 29 | Shelf 1 | No. 31

Psalterium. Augsburg: Erhard Ratdolt, 1494.
Title: Psalterium cum appa/ratu vulgari famili-ari-/ter appresso/ Lateinisch psalter mit deteutschen nutzliche/dabei gedruckt.
Colophon: Hie endet der psalter...gedrucker czu/ Augspurg von maister Erharte ratdolt... M.CCCC.XCIIII.
Page facing colophon: Erhardi Ratdolt felicia conspicc signa/ Testata artificem qua valet ipse manum.[Followed by Printer mark in red]

cont'd

INCUNABULA

Cabinet D | Shelf 1 | No. 43

Rolewinck, Werner. Fasciculus temporum. Basel, 1482. Bernhard Richel.
Colophon: Chronica q̄ dicit...edita in alma universitate colonie agrippine sup rhenum./... Sepius quidem iā imp̄ssa sed neglig̃tia correctoř/ in diversis locis a vero originali minus iuste em̄data... per Bernardū Richel civem Basilieñ. Sub anno dñi M.CCCC.LXXXII. X. Kl. m̄s marcii...

Gesamt-Kat. . Hain 6932; boards; 11¾ x 8 x 1 in.

INCUNABULA

Cabinet 29 | Shelf 1 | No. 1

Monteregio, Joannes de. Kalendarium.Venice: Bernhard Pictor, Petrus Löslein & Erhard Ratdolt, 1476.
Title: Questa opra da ogni parte e un libro doro/ Non fu piu preciosa gemma mai Dil Kalendario ...Ioanne de monte regio questo fexe..... I nomi di impressori/ son qui da basso di rossi colori./ Venetiis 1476./ Bernardus pictor de Augusta/ Petrus loslein de Langencen/ Erhardus ratdolt de Augusta.

cont'd

INCUNABULA cont'd

Cabinet 29 | Shelf 1 | No. 31

Gesamt-Kat. Hain 13510.
Boards, tooled leather, with part of original clasps; 8-3/4 x 6¼ x 1½ in.

INCUNABULA

Cabinet 29 | Shelf 1 | No. 23

[Rolewinck, Werner]. Fasciculus temporum. Venice: Erhard Ratdolt. 1485.
Dedication: Nicolao mocenico magnifici.D.Francisci/ Patricio Veneto: Erhardus ratdolt salutē.
Text: Fasciculus temporū omnes antiquoz chroni/cas strictim complectens felici numine incipit./ Prologus:
Colophon: Erhardus Ratdolt Augustensi impressioni paravit:/ Anno salutis M.CCCC.LXXXV.VI. idus. Septembris/ Venetiis inclyto principe

cont'd

INCUNABULA cont'd

Cabinet 29 | Shelf 1 | No. 1

Gesamt-Kat. Hain 13789; Essling 248. Redgrave 2. Vellum; 10½ x 7½ x ½ in.

INCUNABULA

Cabinet D | Shelf 1 | No. 55

Ptolemaei (Claudius) Cosmographia: Registrum alphabeticum/super octo libros Ptolo-/mei incepit feliciter. Rome, 1490; Peter de Turre.
Colophon: Hoc opus....impressum fuit et completum Rome anno....M.CCCC.LXXXX...arte ac impensis Petri de Turre; folio.

Gesamt-Kat. Brunet 4, 954. Hain, 13541. Calf; 16-3/8 x 11 x 1½ in.

In vestibule

INCUNABULA cont'd

Cabinet 29 | Shelf 1 | No. 23

mocenico.

Gesamt-Kat. . Zapf, p.168. Essling 280. Hain 6935. Redgrave 52. Boards; 10 x 8 x ¼ in.

INCUNABULA

Cabinet D | Shelf 1 | No. 33

Paulus (Ulmeus) de Bergamo: Apologia religionis fratrum heremitarum ordinis S. Augustini contra falso impugnantes. Rome 1479. Francisci de Cinquinis.
Colophon: Impressum Rome in domo nobilis Francisci de Cinquinis apud Sanctam Mariam de p̄plo anno dñi 1479 die 18, mensis Julii.

Gesamt-Kat. ; Hain, 10328; B. M. IV, p. 76. Boards; 9 x 6¼ x ½ in.

INCUNABULA

Cabinet 29 | Shelf 1 | No. 14

Regiomontanus (Joh. Muller) Kalendarium. Venice: Erhard Ratdolt, 1482.
Title: In laudem operis huius praeclari a Johanne/ de monte regio editi germanor decoris et nostrae aetatis astronomorū principe Jacobi Sentini/ Ricinensis Carmina.
Metrical colophon: C. Iohannes Lucilis santritter helbrōnēsis/ Lectori. S./ Cui dedit ingeniū divina potentia: et artes qui bene daedalis

cont'd

INCUNABULA

Cabinet 6 | Shelf 1 | No. 16

Sabellicus, Marcus Antonius. Rerum Venetarum decades. Venice: Andreae de Torresanis de Asula, 1487.
Title lines (Sig. a iii, preceded by summary of contents (pp.11) and preface (pp.2): M. Antonii Sabellici rervm Venetarvm ab vrbe condita ad Marcvm Barbadicvm Sereniss./Venetarvm Principem et Senatvm/liber primus primae decades/foeliciter incipit.
Colophon, preceding pp.4 of errata set in Jen-

cont'd

INCUNABULA

Cabinet 6 | Shelf 1 | No. 4

Pliny (the second) Caius: Naturalis Historiae Venice: Nicolas Jenson, 1472.
Title: following preface (3 pp.): Caii Plynii secundi Natvralis Historiae.
Colophon preceding epilogue of the editor (3 pp.) Caii Plynii secvndi Natvralis Historiae libri tri-/cesimiseptimi et vltimi finis impressi Venetiis/per Nicolaum Ienson Gallicum M.CCCC.LXXII/Nicolao Trono inclyto Venetiarvm Duce.
In eighteenth century mor: 16 x 11 x 4 in. Hain: 4, 13089.

INCUNABULA cont'd

Cabinet 29 | Shelf 1 | No. 14

solus in orbe tenet/hoc augustensis ratdolt germañ erhardus/ Dispositis signis undiqz pressit opus./...Anno S. 1482. Idus 5. Augusti. Venitiis.

Gesamt-Kat. Hain 13777. Redgrave 29.

Morocco; 8½ x 6½ x ¼ in.

INCUNABULA cont'd

Cabinet 6 | Shelf 1 | No. 16

son's Gothic Types: Hoc opus Impressum Venetiis Arte & industria optimi/uiri Andreae de Torresanis de Asula Anno/M.CCCLXXXVII. Die. XXI/Madii Augustino Bar/badico Inclyto/ principe.

Printed in Jenson's Roman and Gothic Types.
Morocco; 16-3/4 x 11½ x 2¼ in. "Brunet 5, 6." Hain 4, 14053.

INCUNABULA

Cabinet D | Shelf 2 | No. 31

Plutarchus. Vitae illustrium virorum. Venice, 1496: Bartholomaeus de Zanis.
Colophon: Viroř illustrium vitae ex Plutarcho Graeco in latinū versae: solertiqz cura emendatae soeliciter expliciunt:/ Venetiis imp̄ssae Bartolameū de Zanis de Portefio Anno nři saluatoris, 1496, die octo Mēsis Iunius. [2 parts in 1 vol.]

Gesamt-Kat. . Hain 13130; Vellum covered boards; 12¼ x 8-1/8 x 2¼ ins.

INCUNABULA

Cabinet 29 | Shelf 1 | No. 14.01

Regiomantanus (Joh. Muller). Kalendarium. Venice: Erhard Ratdolt, 5 id Aug. 1482.
Printed throughout in red and black.
First page with Ratdolt's knotwork border.
Last page has metal pointer. This pointer not referred to by Redgrave.
Hain 13777. Proctor 4386. Redgrave Ratdolt 29.
Copy with Redgrave's ex-libris, also his signature.

Vellum; 8-1/8 x 6-1/8 in.

INCUNABULA

Cabinet D | Shelf 2 | No. 17

Ierlandus Sabunde, Raymundus de. Viola anima p̄ modum dyalogi. Cologne, 1499: Heinrich Quentell.
Colophon: Finit dyalogus de misteriis sacre passionis christi.../ in septe/ distinctus dyalogus Colonie Imp̄sis honesti viri Henrici/ Quentell faustissime iam p̄mo impressus. Anno natalicii sal/uatoris nostri. M.CCCC.XCIX. Die. XXIX. Mesis Maii.......

Gesamt-Kat; . Hain 14070; mottled calf, 8 x 5½ x ¾ in.

INCUNABULA

Cabinet 29 Shelf 1 No. 16

Sacrobusto [Joann s de]. Sphaera Mundi. Venice: Erhard Ratdolt, 1482.
Title: Nouiciis adolescētib: ad astronomica remp: capessendā aditū/ impetrātib': p brevi recto qz tramite a vulgari vestigio semoto:/ Joannis de sacro busto sphericū opusculu...
Colophon: Impressum hoc est opusculu mira arte e diligentia Erhardi/Ratdolt Augustensis. r. Nōn. Iulij Anno Salutis 1482.

cont'd

INCUNABULA
Donatus

Cabinet D Shelf 1 No. 12

Terence, Publius Terentius (Afer) Carthigine natus servivit Rome...vindelino Spirensi 1472.
Colophon: Raphael Zouensonius Tergestinus poeta/ vindelino Spirensi suo sal/ Qui cupit obstrusam frugem gustasse Terenti/ Donatum querat noscere gramaticu Quem Vindelinus signis impressit ahensis/ Vir bonus: & claro preditus ingenio.

Gesamt-Kat ; Hain 6383; Brunet 5,701.

INCUNABULA

Cabinet 17 Shelf 2 No. 4

Polycronicon, Higdins. (Caxton, 1482.) 2 lvs. Rubricated initials and marginal marks.

Item on fols. 30, 31 of HENRY STEVEN'S "Typographical Miscellanies", Vol. 4.

Hain 8659

INCUNABULA cont'd

Cabinet 29 Shelf 1 No. 16

Gesamt-Kat; Hain 14110. Essling 258. Redgrave 27. Boards covered with leaf from a 15th century book; 8¼ x 5-3/4 x ½ in.

INCUNABULA

Cabinet D Shelf 1 No. 51

[VERDENA, Johannes de]. Sermones Dormi secu/ re uel Dormi fino cura. Strassburg, 1487. unknown. [Johann (Reinhard) Gruninger].
Colophon: Ad laudem et hono/rem omnipotentis dei Text: Tabula siue directoriu sermonu/ Dormi Vginisqz matris eius/ gloriose necnō vtilitate totiū ecelesie finiunt...Impressi Argentine. An-/no dñi M.CCCCLXXXVII. Finita circa festum/ sancte Iohannis baptiste.
Gesamt-Kat. Hain 15959. Boards; 11½ x 8½ x ¾ in.

INCUNABULA (loose leaves)

Cabinet D Shelf 1 No. 63

Eggestein, Heinrich. Strassburg, circa 1472.

(5 large fols. from a Gratianus, with a commentary, rubricated initials and paragraph marks.)

In portfolio labeled "Specimens of Early Printing. 1468-1498".

INCUNABULA

Cabinet 10 Shelf 2 No. 10

Salomon. Epistola prelibaticia in sequentis/operis commendationem brevi/ bus absoluta incipit soeliciter/: Salemonis ecclesie Constantiensis/ epī glosse ex illustrissimis collecte/ auctoribus incipiunt soeliciter. [Augsburg: Monastery of SS. Ulrich and Afra, circa, 1474].
Text: Latine quidam loq/ & propie/ al's apte nō/ solu oratoribus [etc].

cont'd

INCUNABULA (loose leaves)

Cabinet D Shelf 4 No. 62

Amerbach, Johann. Basel, circa 1486.

(1 fol. from a Missal, Goth. type).

In portfolio labeled "Incunabula, Original Leaves".

INCUNABULA (loose leaves)

Cabinet D Shelf 4 No. 62

Greyff, Michael. Reutlingen, circa 1486.

(3 fols., Gothic type, many marginal notes).

In portfolio labeled "Incunabula. Original Leaves".

INCUNABULA cont'd

Cabinet 10 Shelf 2 No. 10

No colophon.

Gesamt-Kat. ; Hain 14134. Stamped pigskin; 16 x 11 x 3¼ in.

INCUNABULA (loose leaves)

Cabinet D Shelf 4 No. 62

Pämler, Johann. Augsburg, circa 1484.

(Some fols. from a Canon of the Mass. Gothic type).

In portfolio labeled "Incunabula. Original Leaves".

INCUNABULA

Cabinet 14 Shelf 2 No. 1

Bible of 42 lines. Mainz: Johann Gutenberg [1450-1455]

One leaf.

Bound in with Bibliographical Essay by A. Edward Newton, New York, 1921.
Full morocco; 16½ x 11¾ x 3/8 ins.

Gesamt-Kat.

INCUNABULA

Cabinet 10 Shelf 2 No. 14

Schedel, Hartman. Nuremberg Chronicle. Anthony Coburger, Nuremberg, 1493.
Title: Registrum hujus operis libri cronicarum cum figuris et imagibus ab inici mundi.
Colophon: ....Hunc librum dominus Antho/nius koberger Nuremberge impressit Adhibitis tame vi/ris mathematicis pingendiqz arte peritissimis Michaele/ wolgemut et wilhelmo Pleydenwurff. quaru solerti acu/ratissimaque animadversione tum civitatum illustrium/ virorum figure in-

cont'd

INCUNABULA (loose leaves)

Cabinet D Shelf 4 No. 62

Cato (Dionysius), Moralizatus. Speculum regiminis. n. p. n. d.

(9 leaves, without mark of identification as to printer, date, place of printing. Gothic type, probably before 1500.

In portfolio labeled "Incunabula. Original Leaves".

INCUNABULA (loose leaves)

Cabinet D Shelf 4 No. 62

Han, Ulric, Rome, 1470.

(14 fols., roman type).

In portfolio labeled "Incunabula, Original Leaves".

INCUNABULA cont'd

Cabinet 10 Shelf 2 No. 14

serte sunt. Consummatu autem duodeci/ma mensis Julii. Anno salutis nre 1493.

Original covers; 18½ x 13 x 3½ ins.
Gesamt-Kat. ; Hain 14508.

INCUNABULA

Cabinet 17 Shelf 2 No. 4

(The) Arte and Crafte to know well to dye. Translated from the French. Printed by Wm. Caxton, 1490.
Ten loose pages, having six woodcuts.

Items on fols. 35, 36 of HENRY STEVEN'S "Typographical Miscellanies", vol.4

INCUNABULA (loose leaves)

Cabinet D Shelf 1 No. 63

Higman, Jean, Paris, circa 1497.

(5 fols. of a Missale, gothic types, rubricated).

In portfolio labeled "Specimens of Early Printing, 1468-1498".

INCUNABULA (loose leaves)

Cabinet D Shelf 1 No. 63

Holl, Leonhard. Ulma, circa 1482.

(3 fols. from the Cosmographia of Ptolomeus, with roman type.)

In portfolio labeled "Specimens of Early Printing, 1468-1498".

INCUNABULA (loose leaves)

Cabinet D Shelf 1 No. 63

Mentelin, Johann, Strassburg, 1468.

(Some large fols., gothic type, with the peculiar letter R, initial spaces blank.

In portfolio labeled "Specimens of Early Printing, 1468-1498".

INCUNABULA (loose leaves)

Cabinet D Shelf 1 No. 63

Rubeus, Jacobus, Venice, 1477.

(2 fols. from Justianus. With a commentary; red and blue paragraph marks, types gothic. Hain 9564; B. M. (V, p. 216).

In portfolio labeled "Specimens of Early Printing, 1468-1498".

INCUNABULA (loose leaves)

Cabinet D Shelf 4 No. 62

Husner, Georg. Strassburg, circa 1476.

(2 fols. from Nider: In expositione decalogi. 2 cols. Goth. type).

In portfolio labeled "Incunabula, Original Leaves".

INCUNABULA (loose leaves)

Cabinet D Shelf 4 No. 62

Miscomini, Antonio (Bartolommeo da Bologna) Florence, 1489.

(15 folios, printing in Roman and Greek types).

In portfolio labeled "Incunabula, Original Leaves".

INCUNABULA.

Cabinet D Shelf 1 No. 35

Biblia latina cum glossa ordinaria Walafridi Stabouis et interlineari Anselmi Laudunensis. (Strassburg, Adolph Rusch of Ingweiler for Ant. Koberger of Nurnberg. circa 1479).

Three leaves from the third volume. With holiday greetings The Ampersand Press, Los Angeles, 1930.

In folder; 20 x 13¼ in.

INCUNABULA (loose leaves)

Cabinet D Shelf 1 No. 64

Jenson, Nicolaus, Venice, 1470-1478.

(Many original folios from theological and judicial works. Printed by Jenson between the years 1470-1478, printed in gothic type, rubricated.)

In portfolio labeled "Jenson Printing, 1470-1478".

INCUNABULA (loose leaves)

Cabinet D Shelf 4 No. 62

Pachel, Leonard & Ulrich Scinzenzeler, Milan, 1479.

(14 folios from Decretalium of Florentinus Paule. Gothic Type.

In portfolio labeled "Incunabula, Original Leaves".

INCUNABULA (loose leaves)

Cabinet D Shelf 1 No. 63

Stanchi, Antonio de Valentia, Venice, 1486.

(3 large fols., printed in two colors. gothic type.)

In portfolio labeled "Specimens of Early Printing, 1468-1498".

INCUNABULA (loose leaves)

Cabinet D Shelf 1 No. 63

Koberger, Anton. Nuremberg, circa 1477.

(5 large fols. from Summa Theologia, Antoninus, gothic type, rubricated.

In portfolio labeled "Specimens of Early Printing. 1468-1498".

INCUNABULA (loose leaves)

Cabinet D Shelf 1 No. 63

Paganinus de Paganinis, Hieronymus. Venice, circa 1498.

(1 fol. of original edition of a theological work. Gothic type).

In portfolio labeled "Specimens of Early Printing, 1468-1498".

INCUNABULA (loose leaves)

Cabinet D Shelf 4 No. 62

Ulrich and Afra, SS. Augsburg, 1474.

(11 folios from Utino, Sermones... Roman type. Hain No. 16130).

In portfolio labeled "Incunabula, Loose Leaves".

INCUNABULA (loose leaves)

Cabinet D Shelf 4 No. 60

Kreusner, Frederic. Nuremberg, 1493.

(8 pp. from the Roseum Memoria. Hain 13991.

No. 16 in Portfolio "Specimens of Early Printing".

INCUNABULA (loose leaves)

Cabinet D Shelf 4 No. 62

Paltaschis, Andreas de and Boninus de Boninis, Venice, 1478.

(4 fols. from a Lactantius (Hain 9813), Roman and Greek types).

In portfolio labeled "Incunabula, Original Leaves".

INCUNABULA (loose leaves)

Cabinet D Shelf 1 No. 63

Wencker, Claus (Nicolaus), Strassburg, 1473.

(Several large fols. from Concordia Evangelistarum, Chrysopolita).

In portfolio labeled "Specimens of Early Printing, 1468-1498".

INCUNABULA (loose leaves)

Cabinet D Shelf 4 No. 62

Kunne, Albert aus Duderstadt. (Imprint. Memmingen, 1486).

(15 folios from a liturgical work. Gothic type). - possibly Paulus (Attavanti) Florentinus. Breuiarium totius juris canonici

In portfolio labeled "Incunabula. Original leaves".

INCUNABULA (loose leaves)

Cabinet D Shelf 4 No. 62

Prüss, Johann, Strassburg [1484].

(2 fols. printed Gothic type, rubricated).

In portfolio "Incunabula. Original Leaves".

INCUNABULA

Cabinet D Shelf 1 No. 57

Wynkyn de Worde, London, 1493-1527. Two leaves (four pages) from the original edition of Wynkyn de Worde's "Golden Legend"

Two other leaves of same book are in frame over exhibition cabinet #13.

INCUNABULA (loose leaves)

Cabinet D Shelf 4 No. 63

Wynken de Worde. London.

(1 fol. with woodcut, from The lyf of the Evangelists.)

In portfolio labeled "Specimens of Early Printing, 1460-1498".

INCUNABULA (loose leaves)

Cabinet D Shelf 1 No. 63

Zainer, Johann. Ulm, 1474.

(4 original fols., Old Testament, Gothic type, initials in outline. Many marginal notes).

In portfolio labeled "Specimens of Early Printing, 1468-1498".

INCUNABULA (loose leaves)

Cabinet D Shelf 1 No. 63

Zainer, Gunther, Augsburg, circa 1476.

(6 large fols., gothic type, rubricated).

In portfolio labeled "Specimens of Early Printing, 1468-1498".

INCUNABULA (loose leaves)

Cabinet D Shelf 4 No. 62

Zell, Ulrich, Cologne circa 1475.

(5 fols. from Caesarius Cistercien... Hain No. 4230. Gothic types, rubricated).

In portfolio labeled "Incunabula, Original Leaves".

INCUNABULA

Cabinet 9 Shelf 1 No. 1

England. Original pages of incunabula

See HAEBLER, KONRAD. Westeuropäische wiegendruck...München, 1928

INCUNABULA

Cabinet 9 Shelf 1 No. 1

France. Original pages of French presses

See HAEBLER, KONRAD. Westeuropäische wiegendruck...München, 1928

INCUNABULA

Cabinet 9 Shelf 1 No. 1a & 1b

(Italien incunabula, original specimen pages. 120 examples, with descriptive text by Konrad Haebler. 2 Portfolios)

Italianische Wiegendruck...Beschrieben von Konrad Haebler, München, 1927.

Cloth; $21\frac{1}{2}$ x $17\frac{1}{4}$ in.

INCUNABULA

Cabinet 9 Shelf 1 No. 1

Netherlands

See HAEBLER, KONRAD. Westeuropäische wiegendruck...München, 1928

INCUNABULA

Cabinet 9 Shelf 1 No. 1

Spain. Original pages of incunabula

See HAEBLER, KONRAD. Westeuropäische wiegendruck...München, 1928

INCUNABULA, Calendars. [Literature of]

Cabinet 20 Shelf 1 No. 18

(Greyff, Michel as a printer of calendars) Michel Greyff als Kalendardrucker, von Dr. Konrad Haebler, Dresden, Dec., 1905. Many facsimiles.

In Zeitschrift für Bücherfreunde, 1905-6, part 2, p.343.

INCUNABULA, Facsimiles

Cabinet 14 Shelf 2 No. 2 2 vols.

Bible of 42 lines Johann Gutenberg, Mainz, 1450-1455 . Facsimile. 2 vols. Leipzig: Insel-Verlag, 1913, with bibliographical history of this Bible by Dr. Paul Schwenke (See 14/2/3), editor of this facsimile, but not published until 1923, owing to intervention of Great War.

See letter from publishers of July 4, 1913, re printer and method of reproduction, inserted in vol.1, in front.

cont'd

INCUNABULA cont'd

Cabinet 14 Shelf 2 No. 2 2 vols.

Stamped Morocco; each vol. 17 x 13 x $3\frac{3}{4}$ ins.

INCUNABULA, Facsimiles

Cabinet D Shelf 1 No. 21

Chronica Hungarorum. Impressa Budae. Andrea Hess, 1473. Facsimile [with history] of the first book printed in Hungary. Folio. Colophon: Finita Bude Anno dñi M.CCCC.LXXIII/ in vigilia penthecostes: per Andrea Hess.

Hain; 4994
Gesamt-Kat. Half morocco, $12\frac{1}{4}$ x 9 x 5/8 ins.

"With an explanatory essay by Wilhelm Fraknoi" -ed. Early Printing in Hungary.

INCUNABULA, FACSIMILES

Cabinet T Shelf 6 No. 5

Collection of fac-similes from one hundred works.

See Sotheby, Samuel. Typography of the 15th century...

INCUNABULA, Facsimiles

Cabinet T Shelf 6 No. 5

Collection of fac-similes from one hundred works.

see SOTHEBY, SAMUEL. Typography of the 15th century...

INCUNABULA, Facsimiles

Cabinet D Shelf 1 No. 23

Game and playe of the chesse. William Caxton, 1474. Cologne? or Bruges? Facsimile, by Vincent and James Figgins. London 1885.

The types were especially cut and cast for this "Tribute in memory of Wm. Caxton," in facsimile of Caxton's first types.

Stamped calf; 11-3/8 x $8\frac{1}{4}$ x 3/4 in.

INCUNABULA, Facsimiles

Cabinet T Shelf 2 No. 94.01

"Pylgremage of the Sowle". Printed by Caxton at Westminster, June 6, 1483. A hitherto unknown copy. Now in the possession of Wm. H. Robinson, London (1932).

Bibliographical description with facsimile pages.

Brochure; 12 x 10; pp. 11

INCUNABULA (Facsimile)

Cabinet D Shelf 1 No. 22

(The) Story of Queen Anelida and the false Arcite. By Geoffrey Chaucer. Printed at Westminster by William Caxton about the year 1477.

Facsimile reprint: Cambridge, at the University Press, 1905.

Boards; $10\frac{1}{2}$ x 7 in.

INCUNABULA, Facsimiles

Cabinet B Shelf 3 No. 14

(Facsimile, German and Italian.) Monumenta Germaniae et Italiae typographica...In getreuen nachbildungen. Herausgegeben von der Direction der Reichsdruckerei. Auswahl und text von K. Burger, Berlin, 1892-1913.
[10 parts, 300 plates]

Portfolio; 17¼ x 13½ in.

INCUNABULA Literature of

Cabinet 79 Shelf 1 No. 39

American Incunabla. Printing In Mexico in the 16th century.

see VALTON, EMILIO. Impresos Mexicanos del siglo XVI...

INCUNABULA Literature of

Cabinet PP Shelf 6 No. 4

Bohatta, Hanns. Katalog der inkunabeln der fürstlich Liechtenstein'schen Fideikommiss-Bibliothek und der Hauslabsammlung...Wien: Gilhofer & Ranschburg, 1910.
Bibliographical description of 351 incunabula.

Paper; 13 x 9¼ x 1½ in.

INCUNABULA, Facsimiles

Cabinet J Shelf 5 No. 18

Facsimiles of early printed books in the British Museum. Selected pages from representative specimens of the early printed books of Germany, Italy, France, Holland, and England, exhibited in the King's Library. London, 1897.

32 plates with descriptive text.

Portfolio; 15½ x 11¼ in.

INCUNABULA Literature of

Cabinet Y Shelf 3 No. 76

(Die) Anfänge des antiquadrucks in Deutschland und seinen nachbänden. von Ernst Crous. (A comparative study of incunabula printing types)

Illus. essay in Loubier's "Buch und bucheinband"...Leipzig, 1923, p.33

Boards; 12¼ x 9¾ in.

INCUNABULA. Literature of.

Cabinet Y Shelf 3 No. 39

(Books about incunabula: Bibliography). "Inkunabeln."

See MUHLBRECHT, OTTO. Bücherliebhaberei ... Berlin, 1896, pp. 166-9.

INCUNABULA (Facsimile)

Cabinet D Shelf 1 No. 58

Utraquist Passional of 1495, Prague, Jan Kamp ?

See D/1/59 for bibliographical information relating to the "Passional"

Tooled leather; 12¼ x 8¼ x 2¼ in.

INCUNABULA Literature of

Cabinet Y Shelf 2 No. 45

Augsburg incunabula, bibliographical notes.

See METZGER, G.C. Augsburgs älteste druckdenkmale...Augsburg, 1840.

INCUNABULA (Literature of)

Cabinet S Shelf 3 No. 91

Books in the cradle. (See Chap. IV) The Kingdom of the Book. By William Dana Orcutt, Boston, 1927. Illus., facsimiles, printer marks.
Bibliographical, historical account.

Cloth; 9 x 6 in.

INCUNABULA (Facsimiles)

Cabinet C Shelf 1 No. 2

Earliest printed books, facsimiles of. (13 plates

Half morocco; 12¼ x 14¾ in.

INCUNABULA. [Literature of]

Cabinet 75 Shelf 2 No. 1

Austrian Monastic Library, Incunabula of an. A review by Stephen Gaselee.

In Transactions of the Bibliographical Society, "The Library," Vol. I, 1920-1921, pp. 56-58.

INCUNABULA, LITERATURE OF.

Cabinet I Shelf 4 No. 4

Books printed in Holland. Low Countries and Germany during the 15th century. Bibliographical account.

See p. 126 - Sotheby's "Specimen of Mr. S. Leigh Sotheby's Principia Typographica ... London, 1858.

INCUNABULA, Literature of

Cabinet 75 Shelf 1 No. 1

Aldrich, Stephen, J; reads a paper on "Incunabula" before the Bibliographical Society, Feb. 20 1893.
Mr. Aldrich points out the necessity of expanding the works of Maittaire, Hains, Panzer, especially in the field of 15th century Spanish books.

In Transactions of the Bibliographical Society, vol. 1, pp. 107-121. 1892-1893.

INCUNABULA, Literature of

Cabinet V Shelf 1 No. 19

(Basle). Les premiers incunables Bâlois et leurs dérivés: Toulouse, Lyon, Vienne-en-Dauphine, Spire, Eltvil, etc. 1471-1484: Essai de synthèse typographique. Par Henry Harrisse... Seconde édition, revue et augmentée. Paris, 1902.

Half morocco; 9-7/8 x 6-5/8 in.

INCUNABULA [Literature of]

Cabinet U Shelf 1 No. 1f

See Bookselling. Bibliographical notes from the privy purse expenses of King Henry VII.

INCUNABULA, Literature of

Cabinet Y Shelf 2 No. 15

Alphabetical list of places where printing was practiced before and up to the year 1500. With titles of first issues, names of printers.

See REICHART, GOTTFRIED Druckorte des xv jahrhunderts...p.3

INCUNABULA. LITERATURE OF

Cabinet T Shelf 6 No. 17

Bible and its transmission. Being an historical and bibliographical view of the Hebrew and Greek texts, and the Greek, Latin and other versions of the Bible (both Ms and printed) prior to the Reformation. By Walter Arthur Copinger. With 28 facsimiles. London, 1897.

Boards, vellum back; 15-3/8 x 12½ x 2 in.

INCUNABULA. [Literature of]

Cabinet 75 Shelf 1 No. 4

(Brescia). An incunabulum of Brescia, hitherto ascribed to Florence. Communicated by R. C. Christie to the Bibliographical Society.

In Trans. Biblio. Soc., Vol. IV, 1896-1898. pp. 233-237.

INCUNABULA [Literature of]

Cabinet 20 Shelf 1 No. 17

Breviaruim Grimani, Das, 1489: Brief account (in German) of this early printed book of 1580 pages each one of which is decorated with all the animate and inanimate things of the earth, all in colors ture to nature.

In Zeitschrift für Bücherfreunde, 1905-6, part 1, p.254.

INCUNABULA. [Literature of]

Cabinet 75 Shelf 2 No. 5

Catalogue of the British Museum.

See Crous, Ernst. On the incunabula catalogue.

INCUNABULA [Literature of]

Cabinet 26 Shelf 1 No. 16

(Contribution to the technical knowledge of Incunabula) Technische beitrage zur inkunabelkunde. von Adolf Schmidt, Darmstadt. Illus.

pp. 9-23 Gutenberg-Gesellschaft Jahrbuch, 1927.

INCUNABULA. [Literature of]

Cabinet 75 Shelf 2 No. 5

British Museum collection of incunabula, building up of. Paper read before the Bibliographical Society, by Alfred W. Pollard. Oct, 20. 1924.

In Trans. Biblio. Soc., Vol. V, 1924-1925, "The Library," pp. 193-214.

INCUNABULA Literature of

Cabinet U Shelf 4 No. 27

Cataloguing fifteenth century books. By John P. Edmond.

Article in The Edinburgh Bibliographical Society proceedings. Sessions 1906-1907 1907-1908, pp.9-12.

Half morocco; 9-5/8 x 8 in.

INCUNABULA Literature of

Cabinet Y Shelf 2 No. 97

[Corrected sheet of 1473, Peter Schoeffer's]. Frühes korrekturblatt aus des Schofferschen offizin. Mit 2 facs. von Carl Wehmer.

Article in Gutenberg-Gesellschaft Jahrbuch, 1932, p.118.

INCUNABULA, LITERATURE OF

Cabinet PP Shelf 2 No. 20

Carvalho, David N. collection. A catalogue of the incunabula consisting of a sequence of dated books, 1470-1499. Together with a number of 16th century books compiled and annotated by Henrietta C. Bartlett. New York, 1911.

Cloth; 9¼ x 6¼ x ¾ in.

INCUNABULA Literature of

Cabinet PP Shelf 3 No. 23

Check list of books printed during the 15th century. Compiled by Pierce Butler. The Newberry Library. Chicago, Ill., 1924.

Paper; 10¼ x 7 x ¾ in.

INCUNABULA [Literature of]

Cabinet AA Shelf 2 No. 26

Cosentini, Francesco: Gli Incunaboli ed i tipografi Piedmontesi del secolo XV. Indici bibliografici. Museo Nazionale del Libro. Torino, 1914.

Half morocco; 8-3/4 x 6¼ in.

INCUNABULA, Literature of

Cabinet PP Shelf 2 No. 14

Catalogue des incunables de la Bibliotheque Mazarine. Par Paul Marais, et A. Dufresne de Saint-Léon. Paris, 1893.

Also "Supplement". PP/2/15.

Half morocco; 10 x 6½ x 2¼ in.

INCUNABULA. Literature of

Cabinet Y Shelf 4 No. 61

(Chronological list of books printed before 1500)

In Bohatta's "Einführung die buchkunde ...Vienna, 1928.

INCUNABULA - Literature of.

Cabinet V Shelf 6 No. 2

Description des lettres d'indulgence du Pape Nicolas V, pro regno Cypri, imprimées en 1451. Par Léon de Laborde. Paris, 1840. Facsimiles, and wood engravings.

The wood blocks, which were engraved by the author, were destroyed after publication.

Boards; 14 x 11-3/4 in.

INCUNABULA. Literature of

Cabinet PP Shelf 2 No. 12

Catalogue des incunables de la Bibliotheque Publique de Dijon. Par M. Pellechet. Dijon, 1886.

Has list of printers mentioned in the catalogue. Classification by Countries, Towns, Cities.

Paper; 9-7/8 x 6½ x 3/8 in.

INCUNABULA. [Literature of]

Cabinet Y Shelf 2 No. 57

(Cologne imprints, 1464 to 1500) Der buchdrucks Kölns bis zum ende des 15th jahrhunderts. Ein beitrag zur inkunabelbibliographe. von Ernst Voullième. Bonn, 1903.

Boards; 9 x 6-1/8 x 1¼ in.

INCUNABULA, Literature of

Cabinet PP Shelf 2 No. 34

Description of the early printed books owned by The Grolier Club...

See GROLIER CLUB, THE. Description of the early printed books...

INCUNABULA. Literature of

Cabinet I Shelf 5 No. 11 & 12 (7-15)

(Catalogue of illustrated books printed in the 15th century at Germany, Switzerland, Austria-Hungary and Scandinavia. With bibliographical and critical notes).

See SCHREIBER, W. L. Manuel de l'amateur de la gravure ... Vol. V.

INCUNABULA Literature of

Cabinet U Shelf 5 No. 24

Color printing in incunabula

see POLLARD, A. W. Fine Books... London, 1912, pp.129, 253

INCUNABULA. Literature of

Cabinet PP Shelf 2 No. 3

Descriptive catalogue of the books printed in the 15th century, lately forming part of the library of the Duke di Cassano Serra...By the Reverend Thomas Frognall Dibdin. London, printed by William Nicol, Shakespeare Press. 1823.

Has auction prices.

Boards, leather back; 10-7/8 x 7-1/8 x 1-1/8 in.

INCUNABULA [Literature of]

Cabinet 18 Shelf 1 No. 6

(Earliest possessions in the University Library in Lemgo) Die altesten Bestande der Lemgoer Gymnasialbibliothek von Ernst Weissbrodt, Lemgo. Illus.

In Zeitschrift für Bücherfreunde, 1908-9, part 2, p.489.

INCUNABULA Literature

Cabinet 26 Shelf 2 No. 12

Farbenschmuck der Wiegendrucke, Der. von Karl Schottenloher.

Illus. essay in Jahrbuch IV, 1930, p. 81 Des Deutschen Vereins für Buchwesen und Schrifttum.

INCUNABULA Literature

Cabinet B Shelf 2 Nos. 1 to 18

(German book illustration. Illustrated historical bibliographical studies)

See SCHRAMM, ALBERT. (Der) Bilderschmuck der frühdrucke...

INCUNABULA Literature of

Cabinet U Shelf 5 No. 28

Early printed books. By E. Gordon Duff. London, 1893. Illus.

Cloth; 8-3/8 x 5-1/8 in.

INCUNABULA, Literature of

Cabinet U Shelf 1 No. 1f

"Fasciculus Temporum." The edition printed by Arnold Ther Hoernen in 1474: An account by A.G.W. Murray.
This is probably the first or second illustrated book printed in Cologne.

In Excerpts relating to printing from "The Library," 1912-13, p. 93 of pencilled folios

---

INCUNABULA Literature of

Cabinet B Shelf 3 No. 11

German incunabula in the British Museum. 152 facsimile plates.

see MORISON, STANLEY. German incunabula...

INCUNABULA [Literature of]

Cabinet 20 Shelf 1 No. 19

See Early Printing in Germany (Literature of) Cologne, 1479. Die Kolner bilderbibel

---

INCUNABULA [Literature of]

Cabinet T Shelf 5 No. 34

Fifteenth-century books: a guide to their identification. With a list of Latin names of towns and an extensive bibliography of the subject. By Robert Alex. Peddie. London, 1913.

Cloth; $7\frac{1}{2}$ x 5 x 3/8 in.

INCUNABULA Literature of

Cabinet Y Shelf 4 No. 4

(German printers of the 15th century; identification of types used by them) Die deutschen drucker des fünfzehnten jahrhunderts. Kurzgefasste einführung in die monumenta germaniae et Italiae typographica. von Dr. Ernst Voulliéme. Berlin, 1916.

Half morocco; $10\frac{3}{4}$ x $7\frac{1}{2}$ in.

INCUNABULA [Literature of]

Cabinet 20 Shelf 1 No. 17

See Early Printing in Holland (Literature of) Leeu, Geraert, Antwerp, 1491.

INCUNABULA Literature of

Cabinet U Shelf 5 No. 40

Founts of type and woodcut devices used by printers in Holland in the 15th century, a list of the. By Henry Bradshaw.

In Bradshaw's "Collected Papers"... Cambridge, 1889, p.258

INCUNABULA. Literature.

Cabinet 75 Shelf 2 No. 6

Gesamtkatalog der Wiegendrucke...

See Hiersemann, Karl W. Gesamtkatalog ... Leipzig, 1925.

INCUNABULA. Literature of

Cabinet I Shelf 5 No. 16 to 20 5 vols.

Etudes sur l'art de la gravure sur bois a Venise. Les livres a figures Ventiens de la fin du 15 siecle et du commencement du 16e. Par Prince d'Essling. Florence-Paris. 1907, 1908, 1909, 1914.

Half morocco; $17\frac{1}{2}$ x 12 in.

INCUNABULA [Literature of]

Cabinet 75 Shelf 1 No. 12

General catalogue of incunabula. A paper read by Ernst Crous, before the Bibliographical Society, Dec. 16, 1912.

In Trans. Biblio. Soc., Vol. XII, 1911-1913, pp. 87-99.

INCUNABULA, Literature of

Cabinet Y Shelf 1 No. 23

Geschichte der erfindung der buchdruckkunst. von Antonious van der Linde, Berlin, 1886. (3 vols. illus.)

Half morocco; 13 x 10-1/8 in.

INCUNABULA Literature of

Cabinet B Shelf 3 No. 8

(Facsimiles of printing types used from the 15th to the 18th century)

see FACSIMILES. Printing types...

INCUNABULA Literature of

Cabinet Y Shelf 2 No. 95

Geographical and chronological histpry of incunabula.

See TEICHL, Dr. Robert. (Der) Wiegendruck im kartenbild...

INCUNABULA Literature of

Cabinet T Shelf 2 No. 6

Great Britain (England, Ireland, Scotland), History of printing in. With a register of books printed. Bibliographical notes.

see DIBDIN'S "Typographical Antiquities" ...London, 1810-19, vols. 1-1V

INCUNABULA, [Literature of]

Cabinet AA Shelf 2 No. 23

Guida del Museo del Libro con indice bibliografico dei facsimili degli incunabuli. Torino, 1913.

Half morocco; 7¼ x 5 in.

INCUNABULA. Literature of

Cabinet 75 Shelf 2 No. 2

Incunabula of Klosterneuburg, The: A review of book with same name, by S. Gaselee.

In Transactions of the Bibliographical Society, "The Library, "Vol. II, 1921-22, pp. 63-66.

INCUNABULA [Literature of]

Cabinet Shelf No.

See Libraries, Holland. Meermanno-Westreenianum in La Haye.

INCUNABULA, [Literature of]

Cabinet 14 Shelf 2 No. 10

Gutenberg, Johann. Die buchkunst Gutenbergs und Schöffers, mit einem einleitenden versuch über die entwickling der buchkunst von ihren frühesten anfangen....von Paul Gottschalk, Berlin, 1918. With facsimiles.

Buchram; 18 x 13 x ½ in.

INCUNABULA. Literature of

Cabinet W Shelf 3 No. 115

(Les) Incunables de la Bibliothèque de l'Arsenal. Par Daniel Bernard [Bibliographical excerpt. Paris, 1880].

Item I in vol. with binder's title "Pamphlets Relating to Books - II. Bound 1932".

INCUNABULA, LITERATURE OF

Cabinet PP Shelf 2 No. 19

List of books printed in the 15th century in the John Carter Brown Library and the General Library of Brown University, Providence, R.I. (G.P. Winship, bibliographer), Oxford: printed at the University Press, 1910.

Boards; 11½ x 9 in.

INCUNABULA Literature of

Cabinet L Shelf 3 No. 32

(Hebrew incunabula, typography of. Facsimiles)

See FRIEMANN, A.(Editor) Thesaurus typographiae hebraicae...

INCUNABULA Literature

Cabinet Y Shelf 2 No. 39

Inkunabelsammlungen und ihr wissenschaftlicher wert. Bemerkungen zur sammlung Vollbehr. von Dr. Ernst Schulz. München 1927.

Boards; 9 x 6½ in.

INCUNABULA. Literature of

Cabinet PP Shelf 1 No. 38

List of George Dunn collection.

See Jenkinson, Francis. List of incunabula collecyed by George Dunn...

INCUNABULA, LITERATURE OF.

Cabinet I Shelf 4 No. 18

Histoire de la gravure dans les anciens Pays-Bas etdans les Provinces Belges. Des origines jusqu'a la fin du 18e siecle. Par A.J.J. Delen. Paris et Bruxelles, 1924. [Part I]. With 66 plates of reproductions.

Paper; 13 x 10 x 1½ in.

INCUNABULA [Literature of]

Cabinet Y Shelf 1 No. 91

(Inquiry concerning incunabula. A lecture given on the 25th anniversary of the Gutenberg-Museum, Mainz, 1925) Aufgabe der wiegendruckforschung. Festvortrag. von Erich V. Rath. Gutenberg-Museums, am 27 Juni 1925 in Mainz. Beilage zum 22 bis 24 jahresbericht der Gutenberg-Gesellschaft.

Paper; 9 x 6 in.

INCUNABULA. Literature.

Cabinet 75 Shelf 2 No. 5.01

List of incunabula collected by George Dunn. Arranged to illustrate the history of printing, by Francis Jenkinson. Supplement to the Bibliographical Society's Transactions. No.3. In Volume of Supplements 1-5, 1921-1926.

Boards, linen back; 8-7/8 x 7 x 1-3/4 in.

INCUNABULA. Literature of.

Cabinet Y Shelf 2 No. 38

[History of the incunabula period of printing].

See BOGENG, G.A.E. Geschichte der buchdruckerkunst ... p. 209.

INCUNABULA [Literature of]

Cabinet V Shelf 3 No. 20

See Invention of Printing. (Paeile, Ch.): Essai historique et critique sur l'invention de l'imprimerie. Paris, 1859.

INCUNABULA. Literature of

Cabinet D Shelf 2 No.

List of incunabula in the Typographic Library and Museum Jersey City. Compiled by Henry Lewis Bullen, Jan., 1933.

2 copies, typescript.

Items in manila envelope.

INCUNABULA Literature

Cabinet B Shelf 2 No^{s} 1 to 18

(Illustrations in the early printed books. Bio-bibliographical lists and comments. Illus.)

see SCHRAMM, ALBERT. (Die) Bilderschmuck der frühdrucke...

INCUNABULA. [Literature of]

Cabinet 75 Shelf 1 No. 12

Inventory of incunabula in Great Britain and Ireland, by Ernst Crous.

In Trans. Biblio. Soc., Vol. XII, pp. 177-209, 1911-1913.

INCUNABULA Literature of

Cabinet K Shelf 6 No. 23

List of incunabula in which the works of the Dutch and Flemish woodcutters are to be found.

see SCHRETLEN'S Dutch and Flemish woodcuts of the 15th century...p. 61 - 65.

INCUNABULA [Literature of]

Cabinet 18 Shelf 1 No. 17

(List of the impressions of the "Historia Septem Sapientum Rome") Verzeichnis der drucke der "Historia septem sapientum Rome," von Friedrich Moldenhauer.

In Zeitschrift für Bücherfreunde, 1914-15, part 2, p.226.

INCUNABULA [Literature]

Cabinet 75 Shelf 1 No. 13

Medical books to 1480, printed: Summary of a paper read by Sir William Osler, before the Bibliographical Society, January 19, 1914.

In Trans. Biblio. Soc., Vol. XIII, 1913-1915, pp. 5-8.

INCUNABULA Literature of

Cabinet T Shelf 1 No. 73

Notice of some of the characteristics of the works of the earliest printers.

See HODGKIN, JOHN ELIOT. "Rariora"... London, 1858-1900, vol.2,

INCUNABULA Literature of

Cabinet Y Shelf 3 No. 19

(Mainz Ecclesiastical Acts of 1480, printed by Johan Numeister).
Der pergamentdruck der Agenda Ecclesiae Moguntinensis von 1480. Bibliographische beschreibung von Dr. Ernst Kelchner. Frankfurt an Main, 1885. Druck von Gebrüder Knauer. facs.

Half morocco; 10-5/8 x 7 x 3/8 in.

INCUNABULA, Literature of

Cabinet W Shelf 1 No. 147

Missel spécial de Constance, oeuvre de Gutenberg avant 1450: Le premier livre imprimé connu. Étude liturgique et critique. Par E. Misset Paris, 1899.

Half morocco; 9-3/4 x 6½ in.

INCUNABULA [Literature of]

Cabinet V Shelf 1 No. 19

Premiers incunables Bâlois et leurs dérivés: Toulouse, Lyon, Vienne-en-Dauphine, Spire, Eltvil, etc. 1471-1484. Essai de synthèse typographique. Par Harry Harrise. Second edition. Paris, 1902. Type facsimiles.

Half morocco; 9-1/8 x 6-5/8 x ½ in.

INCUNABULA Literature

Cabinet U Shelf 3 No. 103

Mainz Psalter of 1457. By Russell Martineau.

Illus. bibliographical account.

See vol. I, pp.309-323 in Bibliographica... London, 1895-1897.

INCUNABULA Literature of

Cabinet S Shelf 6 No. 7

Monuments of printing, 1455-1500: A catalogue... The Rosenbach Company. New York City, January, 1931.

Item (1) in book with binder's title "Early printed books, various excerpts and pamphlets". 1854-1931.

INCUNABULA [Literature of]

Cabinet Shelf No.

See Printing, early: Incunabula of an Austrian monastic library, The.

INCUNABULA Literature

Cabinet AA Shelf 2 No. 40

Manuscritti, Incunabuli e libri figurati del secolo XVI. Vendita all'Asta, 18 Giugno 1930. Milano. Ulrico Hoepli. With 114 plates, facsimiles and reproductions.
Catalogue. Sale of rare manuscripts, incunabula, books with woodcuts of the 16th century. Editiones Principes. Includes estimated prices.

Paper; 12¼ x 9-3/8 x 1¼ in.

INCUNABULA [Literature of]

Cabinet Y Shelf 2 No. 77

Munchens wiegendruck, 1482-1500. Ein bibliographische verzeichnis mit neun typentafeln. Zusammengestellt von Ernst Weil. Munchen, 1923.

Boards; 9½ x 6¼ x 3/8 in.

INCUNABULA Literature of

Cabinet U Shelf 5 No. 38

Proctor, Robert. Bibliographical essays. Printed at the Chiswick Press, 1905.

With portrait frontispiece, and 6 plates.

Half morocco; 10¼ x 7 in.

INCUNABLE, Literature of

Cabinet W Shelf 1 No. 129

Marais, Paul. Catalogue des incunable de la Bibliothèque Mazarine. Par Paul Marais et A. Dufresne de Saint-Léon. Paris, 1893.

Half morocco; 10 x 6½ in.

INCUNABULA, Literature of

Cabinet AA Shelf 3 No. 3

Naamlyst van boeken in de Neederlanden gedrukt, beginnende met 1472 en eindigende met't jaar 1500. (A list of books printed in the Netherlands from 1472 to the first part of 1500).
See following p. 118 in Meerman's "Uitvinding der boekdrukkunst" ... Amsteldam, 1767.

INCUNABULA Literature of

Cabinet X Shelf 1 No. 70

Romae XV saeculi, specimen historicum typographiae. Opera et studio P. Francisci Zver. Laire. Romae, 1778.

With specimen of Swyenheyn and Pannartz printing.

Half morocco; 8-3/8 x 5-7/8 in.

INCUNABULA. [Literature of]

Cabinet 76 Shelf 2 No. 19

Medical books 1467-1480: A study of the earliest printed. By Sir William Osler. Printed for the Bibliographical Society, at the Oxford University Press, 1923.
Illus. monograph XIX.

Boards; 11 x 9 in.

INCUNABULA [Literature]

Cabinet 75 Shelf 2 No. 7

Notes on three incunabula acquired by the British Museum. By Victor Scholderer.

In Transactions of the Bibliographical Society, "The Library," Vol. VII, 1926-1927, pp. 221-224.

INCUNABULA [Literature of]

Cabinet Shelf No.

See Scholderer, Victor: Notes on three incunabula etc.

INCUNABULA, [Literature of]

Cabinet Y Shelf 3 No. 100

Schramm, Albert. Die inkunabeln. Deutsches Buchmuseum, Leipzig, 1925. Facsimiles.
A catalogue, with bibliographical and historical notes.

Paper; 12 x 9-1/8 x ¼ in.

INCUNABLE Literature

Cabinet 26 Shelf 1 No. 19

Technique de certain illustrated incunables. Tirage separe des gravures et du text figures en Lamelles metalliques. Par Auguste Vincent.

Article in the "GUTENBERG-GESELLSCHAFT JAHRBUCH" 1929, pp.101-.08.

INCUNABULA [Literature of]

Cabinet 18 Shelf 1 No. 6

(Unknown broadside of Bartholomaeus Gothan). Ein unbekannte einblattdruck des Bartholomaeus Gothan, by Konrad Haebler, Berlin, Facsimile.

In Zeitschrift für Bücherfreunde, 1908-9, part 2, p.357.

INCUNABULA Literature

Cabinet 26 Shelf 1 No. 19

Small private collections of incunabula and their future. By Stephen Gaselee.

Article in the "Gutenberg-Gesellschaft Jahrbuch" 1929, pp.303-311.

INCUNABULA, Literature of

Cabinet 26 Shelf 1 No. 16

Technische beiträge zur inkunabelkunde. von Adolf Schmidt, Darmstadt. [Essay].

See Gutenberg-Gesellschaft Jahrbuch, 1927, pp.9-23.

INCUNABULA [Literature of]

Cabinet 18 Shelf 1 No. 5

(Unknown German "Horae B.M.V. of the 15th century.) Ein unbekannte deutsche Ausgabe des Horae B.M.V. aus dem XV Jahrhundert von Otto Zaretzki, Cologne. Facsimile.

An account of the only known German Horae printed by Marcus Reinhard in Kirchheim, 1491.

In Zeitschrift für Bücherfreunde, 1909, part 1, p.22.

INCUNABULA [Literature of]

Cabinet S Shelf 1 No. 116

Some noteworthy firsts in Europe during the 15th century. By Miriam E. Lone. With illustrations. New York, Lathrop C. Harper, 1930.

Cloth; 8-5/8 x 5¾ in. In protective case.

INCUNABULA, Literature of.

Cabinet W Shelf 3 No. 116 & 117 2 Vols.

Trésors des bibliothèques de France .. Publiés sous, la direction de M.R. Cantinelli et M. Emile Dacier. Paris, 1925-7. G. Van Oest Editeur. Illus.

Half morocco; 12 x 9 in.

INCUNABLA Literature of

Cabinet D Shelf 1 No. 59

Utraquist Passional of 1495. (Bibliographical account) By Zdenek V. Tobolka. Prague, 1926.

Paper; 12¼ x 8 in. Item in case.

INCUNABULA. Literature of

Cabinet 75 Shelf 2 No. 3

Spanish incunable, an unrecorded. By Stephen Gaselee.

In Transactions of the Bibliographical Society, "The Library," Vol. III, 1922-23, pp. 304-6.

INCUNABULA, [Literature of]

Cabinet 20 Shelf 2 No. 16

Tschechische Inkunabeln. Von Paul Krasnopolski of Prag. Facsimile, printer mark and wood engraving.

In Zeitschrift für Bücherfreunde, 1925, pp. 95-102

INCUNABULA (Literature of)

Cabinet 75 Shelf 1 No. 2

Virgiliana: A list of editions of Virgil printed during the 15th century. Compiled by W. A. Copinger. The Bibliographical Society.

In Trans. Biblio. Soc. vol. 2. 1893-1894. pp. 125-226.

INCUNABULA, Literature of

Cabinet 75 Shelf 2 No. 2

Speculum Historiale: Notes on the edition printed in the monastery of S.S. Ulrich and Afra, by S. Gaselee.

In Transactions of the Bibliographical Society, "The Library," vol. II, pp. 115-16. 1921-22.

INCUNABULA Literature of

Cabinet B Shelf 3 No. 7

(Two hundred incunabula in the Department of Prints, Bibliothèque Nationale, Paris)

see BOUCHOT, HENRI. Bibliothèque Nationale.- Les deux cents incunables...

INCUNABULA Literature of

Cabinet S Shelf 6 No. 15

Vollbehr Collection.

see ASHLEY, FREDERICK W. (The) Vollbehr Incunabula...

INCUNABULA Literature of

Cabinet U Shelf 5 No. 24

Study of incunabula; the word "incunabula" misleading; points of incunabula

see POLLARD, A. W. Fine Books ...London, 1912, pp.12, 77, 78

INCUNABULA, Literature of.

Cabinet Y Shelf 2 No. 97

Typen und der Gesamtkatalog der Wiegendrucke. Eine kritik. von Ernst Consentius.

Article in Gutenberg-Gesellschaft Jahrbuch, 1932. p. 55.

INCUNABULA Literature of

Cabinet S Shelf 4 No. 68.02

Vollbehr incunabula at the National Arts Club of New York, from August 23 to Sept., 1926. By George Parker Winship.

Brochure, with other items in manila envelope

INCUNABULA Literature of

Cabinet Y Shelf 3 No. 69

Wiegendruck und handschriften. Festgabe Konrad Haebler zum 60 geburtstage. Mit bildness, tafeln, und abbildungen in text. Leipzig, 1919.

Collection of bibliographical essays by several authorities in their varied fields of research.

Half vellum; 11½ x 8 x 1-3/8 in.

INCUNABULA, PRICES OF [Literature of]

Cabinet AA Shelf 2 No. 41

Sander, Max: Prices of Incunabula. With an introduction, list of booksellers, table of rate of exchange, and numbers given by Hain, Copinger and Reichling. Milan, 1930.

Boards; 9-7/8 x 7¼ x ¾ in.

INDEPENDENT CHRONICLE.

Cabinet Shelf No.

See Newspapers, Massachusetts.

INDEPENDENT CHRONICLE (The) and UNIVERSAL ASVERTISER.

Cabinet Shelf No.

See Newspapers, Massachusetts.

INDEPENDENT CHRONICLE OF 1778

Cabinet NN Shelf 2 No. 13

Boston newspaper of the Revolution

see

NEWSPAPERS, United States. Lit. Boston newspaper of 1778

INDEPENDENT POSTAL LEAGUE, THE

Cabinet NN Shelf 3 No. 30

Postal riders and raiders.

See Gantz, W.H. Postal riders.

"INDEPENDENT REFLECTOR"

Cabinet QQ Shelf 3 No. 13

New York, 1753, a brief consideration of.

see

LIVINGSTON, WILLIAM. Brief consideration of New York...

INDEPENDENT WHIG

Cabinet F Shelf 1 No. 71

Philadelphia, 1720-1721. Independent Whig. [No.1. Jan. 20, 1720. No.53. Jan. 4, 1721]. Printed and sold by S. Keimer in Philadelphia.

Reprinted from the London edition [Thomas Gordon], in weekly numbers.

Marbled boards; 8 x 6 x 7/8 in. Evans 1, 2536, p.331.

INDEX APPROBATIONUM

Cabinet II Shelf 4 No. 59

Löwenstein, Dr. Leopold. Index Approbationum. Bearbeitet von...Bezirksrabbiner in Mosbach. J. Kauffmann Verlag, Frankfurt, am Main. 1923.

Paper; 9-3/8 x 6½ x 5/8 in.

INDEX BIBLIOGRAPHICAL SOCIETY TRANSACTIONS

Cabinet 75 Shelf 2 No. 10.01

Volumes I - X (4th series) 1932 "The Library".

Boards, linen back; 8-3/4 x 6-3/4 x ½ in.

INDEX LIBRORUM PROHIBITORUM

Cabinet X Shelf 4 No. 78

Benedict XIV. jussus editus: Romae 1770. Ex Typographia Reverendae Cameriae Apostolicae. Pamphlet inserted with list of additional prohibitions issued on the 14th May, 1779.

Vellum; 11¼ x 8 x 1-7/8 in.

INDEX LIBRORUM PROHIBITORUM

Cabinet X Shelf 4 No. 78-01

Clementis X. Pontificis Maximi. Index...Rome, ex Typographia Rev-Cam-Apost. 1670.

Vellum; 6¾ x 3-7/8 x 7/8 in.

INDEX LIBRORUM PROHIBITORUM

Cabinet Shelf No.

see also
Forbidden Books
Liberty of Printing

INDEX TO BIBLIOGRAPHICAL PAPERS

Cabinet 76 Shelf 1 No. 18.01

Published by The Bibliographical Society and The Library Association, London, 1877 - 1932. By George Watson Cole. Published for The Bibliographical Society of America at The University of Chicago Press, Chicago Illinois.

Paper; 8-5/8 x 6-7/8 x 1 in.

INDIA

Cabinet Q Shelf 7 No. 16

Asian Printers' and Stationers' Annual

see

DIRECTORIES, PRINTERS' (The) Asian Printers' and Stationers' Annual...

INDIA

Cabinet MM Shelf 7 No. 4

Dictionary of terms used in printing. By H. Morgan, Government Printing Establishment. Madras, 1863.

Cloth; 8¾ x 5¼ in. Second copy MM/7/60.

INDIA

Cabinet NN Shelf 2 No. 13

Newspapers of India, 1780-1908. By S. M. Mitra. Excerpt article from The Nineteenth Century, Aug., 1908.

Item 9 in bound collection with binder's title "Various newspapers and periodicals"

INDIA

Cabinet NN Shelf 2 No. 2

Press in India, 1780-1908, the. By S.M. Mitra. Excerpt from The 19th Century, Aug., 1918.

Item 17 in vol. "Journalists and Journalism". Bound, 1918.

INDIA

Cabinet 00 Shelf 6 No. 33

press law in India. Memorandum of the Press Association of India. August, 1919.

Paper; 13 x 8-1/8 in. In envelope.

INDIA

Cabinet Y Shelf 2 No. 97

Printing in India today. (1932.) Its national aspect. By Nitindranath Ganguly.

Brief article in Gutenberg-Gesellschaft Jahrbuch, 1932, 269.

INDIA

Cabinet Shelf No.

see also

I - EARLY PRINTING IN INDIA.
II - PRINTING, HISTORICAL, India.
III - SPECIMEN BOOKS, TYPES. "
IV - JOURNALISM, India.

INDIA (British) see

Cabinet 62 Shelf 2 No.

GOVERNMENT PRINTING OFFICES. India, British

INDIA (BRITISH)

Cabinet MM Shelf 7 No. 5

Letterpress printing. Composing and proof-reading A practical manual for Indian artisans. By T. Fisher. Madras, 1906. Illus.

Text book of printing.

Cloth; 9-7/8 x 6-7/8 x $1\frac{1}{4}$ in.

INDIA (British)

Cabinet 00 Shelf 5 No. 31

Sketch of the history and influence of the press in British India...

see

STANHOPE, LEICESTER. (The) Press in British India...London, 1823.

INDIA (Nova Goa, a Portuguese possession)

Cabinet EE Shelf 3 No. 77

Imprensa Nacional. Nova Goa, 1887. Specimen de typos.

Boards, leather back; 11-5/8 x 7-3/4 x 3/4 in. See also EE/3/78.

INDIAN (American)

Cabinet Shelf No.

Cherokee.

See CHEROKEE (Indian Territory)

INDIAN (American)

Cabinet QQ Shelf 4 No. 26

Eliot's, John, first Indian teacher and interpreter. Cockenoe - De - Long Island, and the story of his career from the early records. By William Wallace Tooker, New York, 1896. Illus.

No. 17 of 215 copies printed.

Cloth; 9-3/8 x $6\frac{1}{2}$ in.

INDIAN (American)

Cabinet RR Shelf 4 No. 3

Nipmucks, the tribe to which James Printer belonged, who assisted John Eliot in the preparation of the Indian Bible.

See CRANE, JOHN C. Nipmucks and their country...

INDIAN (American)

Cabinet QQ Shelf 4 No. 27

Umatillas. Weyekin stories (Titwatit Weyekishnim) By J. M. Cornelison, Missionary to the Umatillas: San Francisco, Cal., n. d. circa 1910. Booklet.

Item in manila envelope.

INDIAN LANGUAGE (American)

Cabinet II Shelf 3 No. 63 Box

Chinook.

See LANGUAGE CHARACTERS. Examples of. Chinook jargon language...1889.

INDIAN LANGUAGE

Cabinet Shelf No.

Choctaw.

See LANGUAGE CHARACTERS. Example of. Choctaw language.

INDIAN LANGUAGE

Cabinet Shelf No.

Cree.

See LANGUAGE CHARACTERS. Examples of. Cree.

INDIAN LANGUAGE (American)

Cabinet II Shelf 3 No. 63

Creek or Muskokee.

See FLEMING, REV. JOHN. Short Sermon... Boston, 1835.

INDIAN LANGUAGE

Cabinet Shelf No.

Dakota.

See LANGUAGE CHARACTERS. Examples of. Dakota.

INDIAN LANGUAGE (American)

Cabinet II Shelf 3 No. 63

Muskokee or Creek.

See FLEMING, REV. JOHN. Short Sermon... Boston, 1835.

INDIAN LANGUAGE (American)

Cabinet II Shelf 4 No. 53

Winnebago language.

See BIBLES. Winnebago (Indian) Script. The Four Gospels...1907.

INDIAN LANGUAGES (American)

Cabinet II, Shelf 4, No. 2

Handbook of American Indian languages. By Frank Boas. Part I. With illustrative sketches. By [several writers]. Smithsonian Institution, Bureau of American Ethnology, Bulletin 40. Washington, 1911.

Cloth; 9¼ x 6 x 2¼ in.

INDIAN LANGUAGES

Cabinet II, Shelf 4, No. 1.01

Specimen of the Mountaineer, or Sheshatapoosh-shoish, Skoffie, and Micmac languages.

pp.16-23 in Collections of the Massachusetts Historical Society for the year 1799. Vol.VI. of the first Series. Boston, Reprinted, 1846.

Boards; 9-5/8 x 6 x ⅜ in.

INDIAN (American) LANGUAGES
see also

Cabinet, Shelf, No.

LANGUAGE CHARACTERS. Examples of...

INDIAN SHORTHAND WRITERS OF BRITISH COLUMBIA.

Cabinet S, Shelf 5, No. 6

In the Pacific Magazine, Dec. 1906, by Lillian E. Zeh.

Bound with other items in "Various printers and their plants", item 16, vol.2.

INDIAN TERRITORY, CHEROKEE

Cabinet, Shelf, No.

See CHEROKEE.

INDIANAPOLIS NEWS

Cabinet OO, Shelf 3, No. 24

Panama libel case. Newspaper slander case of President Roosevelt. [vs.] Delavan Smith and Charles R. Williams, publishers of The Indianapolis News. Indianapolis, Ind., 1909.

Half morocco; 9¾ x 7 x ⅜ in.

INDIANAPOLIS NEWS
see also
Newspapers.

INDIANS, (American)

Cabinet S, Shelf 3, No. 140

How Indians write. By Frederick E. MacGregor. Illus. Excerpt from Century Magazine, Jan. 1893.

P. 25 in volume with binders title "Books about Books." ... Collected by the Typographic Library, Jersey City, 1912.

INDIANS (American)

Cabinet II, Shelf 2, No. 35.02

Old settlers or Western Cherokee Indians. Senate Document N.77, 54th Congress, 1st. Session, 1896.

Pamphlet in "Senate Documents", vol.3. See index.

Calf; 9 x 6

INDIANS, PRINTING FOR

Cabinet S, Shelf 3, No. 104

(The) Eliot Indian Tracts. By George Parker Winship, Librarian of the Harry Elkins Widener Collection, Harvard College Library.
P. 179 in volume. Wilberforce Eames ... A tribute to. Cambridge, 1924.

INDULGENCES

Cabinet 75, Shelf 2, No. 9

Caxton Indulgence, The New. [Printed before Dec. 13, 1476]. By Alfred W. Pollard. London June, 1928. "The Library." With facsimile.

In Trans. Bibl. Soc. "The Library," Vol. IX pp. 86-89. 1928-29

INDULGENCES, Letters of

Cabinet Y, Shelf 1, No. 87

(Facsimiles) Die Mainzer Ablassebriefe der jahre 1454 und 1455. von Dr. Gottfried Zedler. Verlag der Gutenberg-Gesellschaft, Mainz, 1913. Plates only (17).
For accompanying text. See Y/1/86.

Boards; 14½ x 10-3/4 in.

INDULGENCES, Letters of

Cabinet, Shelf, No.

See Incunabula. Description des lettres d'indulgence du Pape Nicolas V...imprimées en 1451.

INDULGENCES. Letters of

Cabinet Y, Shelf 3, No. 9

(Printed Letters of Indulgences, 1454-1455).
Ueber die gedruckten Literae Indulgentiarum Nicolai V. Pont. M. Pro Regno Cypri. Mit einer lithographischen tafel. Aus dem Serapeum, 1843, besonders abgedruckt. von Johann D. F. Scotzmann. Leipzig, 1844.

Cloth; 9-3/8 x 5-1/8 x ¼ in.

INDUSTRIAL AMERICA

Cabinet QQ, Shelf 4, No. 4

Manufacturers and inventors of the United States ...A biographical and descriptive exposition of National progress. Illustrated with portraits and views on steel. New York: Atlantic Publishing and Engraving Company, 1876.
p.367-Playing Cards, A. Dougherty
" 381-Printing Ink Manufacture, J. C. Lightbody & Co.
" 387-Printing Presses, Geo. P. Gordon.
" 392-Printing type, James Conner's Sons.
Morocco; 11¾ x 9¼ x 2-1/8 in.

INDUSTRIAL ART

Cabinet S, Shelf 6, No. 12

Claims of Industrial Art, considered with reference to certain tendencies in Education. An address by Leslie W. Miller, Principal of the School of Art of the Pennsylvania Museum, before the Philobiblon Club of Philadelphia, Feb.27, 1908.
Printed and Published by the Boston School of Printing, Boston, Mass.

Brochure, in manila envelope.

INDUSTRIAL ART

Cabinet QQ, Shelf 4, No. 11

Report of Commission appointed by the Secretary of Commerce to visit and report upon the International Exposition of Modern Decorative and Industrial Art in Paris, 1925.

Report on the"Art and industries of the book" by W. E. Rudge, p. 82.

Paper; 9¼ x 5¾ x 3/8 in.

INDUSTRIAL ART (see also)

Cabinet, Shelf, No.

DESIGN

INDUSTRIAL EDUCATION, PRINTING see

Cabinet Schools of Printing

Shelf

No.

INGERSOLL, L. D.

Cabinet NN Shelf 4 No. 11

Life of Horace Greeley; Founder of the New York Tribune, with extended notices of many of his contemporary statesmen and journalists. Chicago, Ill. 1873. Illus.

Leather: 9¼x6½"

INITIAL LETTERS

Cabinet J Shelf 5 No. 13

Collection of Initial letters and borders, originals on wood and copper. Scrap Book.

Cloth; 18 x 13¼ in.

~~INDUSTRIAL EDUCATION SURVEY~~

Cabinet LL Shelf 6 No. 2

Printing Trade. Report of the Committee. Authorized by the Board of Estimate and Apportionment. New York City, 1918. Illus.

Cloth; 9-1/8 x 5-7/8 in.

INGRAM, HERBERT

Cabinet NN Shelf 2 No. 13

Founder of modern illustrated journalism, Herbert Ingram. Brief account, with portrait. Excerpt from The Lamp, April, 1903.

Item 21 in boumd collection with binder's title "Various newspapers and periodicals".

INITIAL LETTERS

Cabinet K Shelf 1 No. 6

Collection of initial letters, head and tail pieces, medallions with decorative borders etc. Photographic reproductions. Armand Guerint, Editor, Paris.

In portfolio: 12¾ x 9½ in.

INDUSTRIAL GRAPHIC ARTS LIBRARY AND MUSEUM

Cabinet (see)

TYPOGRAPHIC LIBRARY AND MUSEUM

Shelf

No.

INITIAL LETTERS

Cabinet J Shelf 4 No. 24

Cleland's, T.M., chapter initials for book and catalogue. Illustration of.

See CLELAND, THOMAS MAITLAND. Decorative work of...New York, 1929.

INITIAL LETTERS

Cabinet J Shelf 5 No. 14

Collection of initial letters, originals, on wood and copper. Scrap Book.

Portfolio, boards; 17-7/8 x 12¾ in.

~~INDUSTRIAL HYGIENE~~ see

Cabinet

HYGIENE

Shelf

SANITATION

No.

INITIAL LETTERS

Cabinet J Shelf 5 No. 14.01

Collection of early initial letters, n.d., somewhat classified. Woodcuts, steel engravings, etc.

Mounted on temporary plates. In folder.

INITIAL LETTERS

Cabinet K Shelf 2 No. 5

Collection of ornamental initial letters. Engravings, wood and copperplate. Scrap book collection.

Calf; 10 x 7¾ in.

INDUSTRIAL INFORMATION CO., of New Jersey

Cabinet Q Shelf 4 No. 14

Reference-Directory, 1895.

see DIRECTORIES, PRINTERS'. Industrial Information Co....

INITIAL LETTERS

Cabinet K Shelf 1 No. 5

Collection of early initials, head and tail pieces, vignettes, etc. In album with binder's title "Collection of early initial ornaments".

Half morocco; oblong, 9¼ x 12¼ x ¾ in.

INITIAL LETTERS

Cabinet K Shelf 4 No. 3

Copperplate engravings, probably 17th and 18th century. Scrap book collection of typographic decorative material.

Half morocco; 9¼ x 7-1/8 x ¾ in.

INDUSTRY see

Cabinet

BUSINESS

Shelf

BUSINESS HOUSES

No.

INITIAL LETTERS.

Cabinet I Shelf 4 No. 13

Collection of facsimiles of the types, woodcuts and capital letters used by early printers. London, 1840.

42 plates.

Boards; 14-3/8 x 9-7/8 in.

INITIAL LETTERS

Cabinet K Shelf 1 No. 16

(Decorative initial letters of the 15th to 19th century. A collection of plates, illustrated).

See Gerlach, Martin (Editor). Das Alte buch...Wien- Leipzig (1912 ?)

INITIAL LETTERS

Cabinet T Shelf 2 No. 6 [vol.i]

Earliest known instances of small initials; capital letters, their origin and progress; those used by Caxton; account of grotesque initial letters.

see

DIBDIN'S "Typographical Antiquities" ...London, 1810-19, vol.i, pp.xxvii-xlii

INITIAL LETTERS

Cabinet X Shelf 2 No. 59

(Fust and Schoeffers Psalter initials printed in two colors)
Die zweifarbigen initialen der Psalterdruck von Johann Fust und Peter Schoeffer. von Heinrich Wallau.

see HARTWIG, OTTO (Compiler) Festschrift...Mainz, 1900, pp.261-304

INITIAL LETTERS

Cabinet K Shelf 3 No. 25

Lettere iniziale. Racolta di lettere che servirono nella stampa varie opera. Tipogr. Volpe Padova, n.d. circa 1766.

Collection of copperplate ornamental initials.

Boards, oblong; $3\frac{3}{4}$ x 9-1/8 in.

INITIAL LETTERS

Cabinet Shelf No.

See Early Printing in Germany. Dresden, The earliest printing in.

INITIAL LETTERS

Cabinet K Shelf 4 No. 5

(History of ornamental initial letters, 15th to 18th century) Iniziali istoriate e iniziale fiorite o arabescate. Origine e evoluzione Studiata da Giuseppe Boffito. (Barnibita) Firenze, 1925.

Paper; 10 x 7 x $\frac{1}{4}$ in.

INITIAL LETTERS

Cabinet L Shelf 2 No. 9

(Mediaeval alphabets, illustrated and described.)

See IMPERIAL ROYAL PRINTING OFFICE. Austria
Buchschriften des mittelalters...Wien, 1852.

INITIAL LETTERS.

Cabinet 75 Shelf 2 No. 3

Eliot's Court Press. Decorative blocks and initials. By Henry R. Plomer. Facsimile.

In Transactions of the Bibliographical Society, "The Library," 1922-23, Vol. III, pp. 194-209.

INITIAL LETTERS

Cabinet J Shelf 4 No. 15

Holbein's initial letters "The Alphabet of Death".

See DAVIES, GERALD S. Hans Holbein... London, 1903. Plate facing p.194.

INITIAL LETTERS

Cabinet K Shelf 1 No. 22

Miscellaneous collection of initials, borders, ornaments, and other decorative typographical material.
Specimens mounted, 50 plates.

In box

INITIAL LETTERS

Cabinet 75 Shelf 1 No. 7

English printed books, initial letters in early. A paper read by Charles Sayle before the Bibliographical Society, Nov. 17, 1902.

In Trans. Biblio. Soc. Vol. VII, pp. 15-47 1902-1904.

INITIAL LETTERS

Cabinet C Shelf 2 No. 3

Illuminated initial letters on vellum, original. Scrap book collection.

Folder; $18\frac{1}{2}$ x 13-5/8 in.

INITIAL LETTERS

Cabinet L Shelf 3 No. 3

Nova escola para aprender a ler, escriver...Par Manoel de Andrade de Figueiredo. Lisboa Occidental. Na Officina de Bernardo da Costa de Carvalho, Impressor...(1718 or 1722).

Several plates of plain and ornamental letters.

Tree calf; 12 x $8\frac{1}{4}$ in.

INITIAL LETTERS

Cabinet U Shelf 2 No. 142

Facsimiles of some of the initial letters used by John Siebərch, the first Cambridge (England)printer.

In "Bibliographical notes, 1886-1905. By Robert Bowes and C.J. Grey...London, 1906.

Boards; 8-1/8 x 6 in.

INITIAL LETTERS.

Cabinet 6 Shelf 1 No. 4

Jenson, Nicolas. Venice, 1472. [Illuminated initial letters 35].

See PLINIUS SECUNDUS (Caius). Historia naturalis ... Venice, 1472

INITIAL LETTERS.

Cabinet I Shelf 5 No. 5

[Ornamental letters from the beginning of the 9th to the 11th century. Shown in reproduction].

See MERTON, ADOLF. Buchmalerei in St. Gallen ... Leipzig, 1923.

INITIAL LETTERS

Cabinet K Shelf 6 No. 19

Français du 15e siècle, gravures sur bois tirées des livres. À Labitte. Paris, 1868.

see
plates 58, 59, 60.

Boards; $11\frac{1}{2}$ x $9\frac{1}{4}$ in.

INITIAL LETTERS

Cabinet K Shelf 3 No. 24

Kurzgefasste handbuch...

see
ENGELHARDT, RUDOLF. (Der) Initial: Kurzgefasste handbuch...

INITIAL LETTERS

Cabinet U Shelf 3 No. 103

Pictorial and heraldic initials, some. By Alfred W. Pollard. [Illus. biblio. account].

See BOOKS ABOUT BOOKS. Bibliographica: Papers about books...vol.3, p.232.

INITIAL LETTERS

Cabinet C Shelf 2 No. 2

Plantin's decorative initial letters, head and tail pieces, etc.

See ROOSES, MAX. Plantin, Christophe, imprimeur Anverois...Anvers, 1883.

INITIAL LETTERS

Cabinet I Shelf 1 No. 1

Woodcut initials used in Paciolo's "Divina proportione...Venice, 1509. Printed by Paganinus de Paganinus.

Vellum; 12 x 8-1/8 x 1-1/8 in.

INITIALS

Cabinet U Shelf 3 No. 103

Italian printers, initial blocks of some. By A.J. Butler.

Illus. bibliographical account.

See vol. I, p.418 Bibliographica... London, 1895-1897.

INITIAL LETTERS

Cabinet K Shelf 4 No. 8

Printed initial letters. Illustrated historical account, brief.

See Glazier, Richard. Manual of historic ornament...pp. 151, 5, 7, 9, 21, 81, 93, 107, 131.

INITIAL LETTERS

Cabinet K Shelf 1 No. 17

(Die) Zierinitialen in den drucken des Thomas Anshelm (Hagenau 1516-1523).
Ein beitrag zur geschichte des holzschnitts.
Mit 105 abbildungen. von Paul Heitz.
Strassburg, 1894.
20 plates.

Half morocco; 11¼ x 8¾ in.

INITIALS

Cabinet 18 Shelf 1 No. 16

Meseck, Felix. The etched initials of.

In Zeitschrift fur Bucherfreunde, 1914-15, part I, p.132.

INITIAL LETTERS

Cabinet T Shelf 3 No. 2

Progress of art displayed in initial letters from illuminated Mss., engravings of from early books.

In DIBDIN'S Bibliographical Decameron...London, 1817, vol.1, p.cxiii; vol.2, pp.316-20

INITIALS

Cabinet M Shelf 2 No. 31

See Ashbee, C.R. Private Press, The: A study in idealism.

INITIALS

Cabinet 10 Shelf 2 No. 10

Notable set of large woodcut initials in Salomon. Epistola prelibaticia in sequentis operis commendationem brevibus absoluta incipit soeliciter. [Augsburg: Monoastery of S.S. Ulrich and Afra, circa 1478]

Stamped pigskin, 16 x 11 x 3¼ ins.

INITIAL LETTERS

Cabinet J Shelf 5 No. 1

(Reproductions. Collection of initial letters, printers ornaments, title pages, etc.)

See L'ART POUR TOUS. Encyclopedie de l'art industriel...Paris, 1861 to 1903.

INITIALS.

Cabinet 75 Shelf 2 No. 6

Designed by G. E. Milner for use in "The Library"

See pp.91-4 in Transactions of the Bibliographical Society, "The Library," Vol. VI, 1925-26.

INITIALS

Cabinet M Shelf 1 No. 39

Ornaments and initials designed and engraved by George Webb at The Caradoc Press, Bedford Park, Chiswick, London. 1905.

See Imprints, England. Caradoc Press, The.

INITIAL LETTERS

Cabinet L Shelf 3 No. 14

Series of capital letters from the 7th to the 17th century.

See HUMPHREYS, HENRY NOEL. Origin and progress of the art of writing ...London, 1853. (plates 23, 24)

INITIALS

Cabinet 14 Shelf 1 No. 7

See Early Printing in Germany. Mainz, 1518. Johann Schoeffer (1)

INITIALS

Cabinet M Shelf 2 No. 22

Pissarro, Lucien. His borders and ornamental initials, engraved on wood for The Sonnets of P. De Ronsard, Printed at the Eragny Press, Hammersmith, London. July, 1902.

Boards; 8½ x 5-7/8 x ½ in.

INITIAL LETTERS.

Cabinet I Shelf 5 No. 16 to 20

(Venice, 15th century). Initiales ornees tirees de livres illustres Venetiens du XVe siecle et du commencement du XVIe.

See ESSLING (Prince d'). Etudes sur l'art de la gravure sur bois a Venise ... Vol. IV, pp. 187-194.

INITIALS

Cabinet 70 Shelf 2 No. 11

See Illustrated Books, 16th cent....
Fine, Oronce: Protomathesis. Opus varium.

INITIALS

Cabinet W Shelf 4 No. 148

Plantin, Christophe; Initials engraved for, and used by him.
I Alphabet employées dans le Psalterium.
II " engraved by Arnold Nicolai in 1563.
III " engraved on wood from the designs of Pierre van der Borcht. etc.
See Celebrations, Printers (Antwerp 1520-1920) Sept. études.

INITIALS

Cabinet W Shelf 4 No. 113

Plantin, Chriostpher: The initials and decorative pieces used by him.
In Max Rooses. Christopher Plantin, imprimeur Anversois. Anvers, 1890.

INITIALS

Cabinet 6 Shelf 2 No. 9

Plantin-Moretus: A collection of woodcut initials printed from the original blocks in Plantin-Moretus Museum.
In Index Characterum Architypographiae Planinianae, with a preface by Max Rooses, Antwerp, 1905.

Half morocco; 14-3/4 x 11½ in.

INITIALS

Cabinet U Shelf 3 No. 103

Pollard, Alfred W. Some pictorial and heraldic initials (Illus. biblio. account).

See vol. 3, p.232 "Bibliographica"... London, 1895-1897.

INITIALS

Cabinet 20 Shelf 2 No. 6

[Thanner, Jacob, the printer of Luther's 1517 resignation thesis] Die Drucker von Luthers Ablassthesen von Otto Günther in Leipzig. Illus.

In Zeitschrift fur Bucherfreunde, 1917-18, part 2, p.259.

INITIALS AND TITLE PAGES.

Cabinet S Shelf 5 No. 17

(The) Record of the first modern Art competition. By J. M. Bowles. Illus. excerpt from Modern Art. Indianapolis. Jan, 1895.

Item 23 in collection "Miscellaneous items relating to printing; excerpts from magazines 1918.

INJUNCTIONS AGAINST LABOR UNIONS see

LABOR QUESTIONS

Cabinet Shelf No.

INK

Cabinet W Shelf 1 No. 64

Encre de Chine, son origine possible.
See Geraud, H. Essai sur les livres dans l'antiquité ... Paris, 1840. pp. 43-50.

INK

Cabinet 26 Shelf 2 No. 5

(Manufacture of printing ink, The) Die fabrikation der buchdruckerschwartz. In Wochentlicher anziger, 1846, vol.1, No.2.

Supplement to Journal fur Buchdruckerkunst, 1846-53, No.84.

INK INDUSTRY, BRIBERY IN

Cabinet 78 Shelf 1 No. 79

(An) Inquiry before the Federal Trade Commission in Washington, November 24, 1917. Verbatim Report: not published.
Typewritten leaves.
Carbon copy [also in Library] 78/1/80.

Half morocco; 11 x 8½ in.

INK INDUSTRY, BRIBERY IN.

Cabinet 78 Shelf 1 No. 80

(An) Inquiry before the Federal Trade Commission in Washington, November 24, 1917. Verbatim Report: not published.
Carbon copy: Original typewritten Mms, 78/1/79.

Half morocco; 11 x 8½ in.

INKING ROLLERS see

ROLLERS, INKING

Cabinet Shelf No.

INK MANUFACTURERS

Cabinet Shelf No.

Johnson Co., Charles Eneu; A brief history of. A romantic tale of ink developments.
Article in the United States Publisher and Printer, vol.9, Jan. 1931, p.18.

INK MANUFACTURERS, France.

Cabinet Z Shelf 3 No. 43

Amyot, Marius. rue St-Julien-le-Pauvre, 5, 1834.
Ancienne fabrique d'encre d'imprimerie, fondée par M. Cavaignac en 1790. Encre de toutes couleurs.
With prices.

pp. 315, 316, 321, 322, 329, 330 in Miscellaneous collection of French type specimens...1829- - 1844.

INK MANUFACTURERS, France.

Cabinet Z Shelf 3 No. 43

Beaulès ---- Fabricant d'encres pour la typographie et la lithographie, rue Saint-Julien, No. 4. [Paris, 1835].
Specimens of black and colors. With prices.

pp. 317-320, 374-375 in Miscellaneous collection of French type specimens ... 1829-1844.

INK MANUFACTURERS, France.

Cabinet Z Shelf 3 No. 43

Briquet et Cie. Gabriel, rue du Jardinet, 8, à Paris. [circa 1839]. Fabrique d'encre d'imprimerie. Prix des encres. Circular.

pp. 333-334 in Miscellaneous collection of French type specimens ... 1829-1844.

INK MANUFACTURERS, France.

Cabinet Z Shelf 3 No. 43

Cornault et Amyot, rue St-Julien-le-Pauvre, 5, a Paris, 1834.
Ancienne fabrique d'encre d'imprimerie. créée par M. Cavaignac en 1790.
With prices.

p. 321 in Miscellaneous collection of French type specimens ... 1829-1844.

INK MANUFACTURERS, France.

Cabinet Z Shelf 3 No. 43

Doré et Comp., 27 rue, Coquillière, à Paris. Fabrique d'encres d'imprimerie. [1828]. Prix courant. Circulars.

pp. 324-326, 376. In Miscellaneous collection of French type specimens ... 1829-1844.

INK MANUFACTURERS, France.

Cabinet Z Shelf 3 No. 43

Francois et Arnal. Barrière Fontainsbleu, 20. [Paris, 1839].
Fabrique d'encres typographique de toutes couleurs. Circular, with prices.

p. 325 in Miscellaneous collection of French type specimens ... 1829-1844.

INK MANUFACTURERS, France.

Cabinet Z Shelf 3 No. 43

Frény et Cie, rue du Jardinet, 8, Paris, 1839.
Encres d'imprimerie perfectionnées et brevétées contre le jaunissement. Prix courant. Circular.

p. 323 in Miscellaneous collection of French type specimens ... 1829-1844.

INK MANUFACTURERS, France.

Cabinet Z Shelf 3 No. 43

Lorilleux (Maison), rue du Cimitière-Saint-André-des-Arcs, 14. à Paris. [circa 1839]. Fabrication en grand de toutes les qualités d'encres, de rouleaux et ustensiles d'imprimerie. Circular with illus. of interior view of ink mill.
Prices.

pp. 327-328 in Miscellaneous collection of French type specimens ... 1829-1844.

INKS

Cabinet 78 Shelf 1 No. 92

Outline history of inks. Prepared by C.E. Waters.
Circular of the Bureau of Standards, No. 400. Issued Dec., 30, 1932. Washington D.C.

Pamphlet in box labelled "Pamphlets and excerpts relating to inks and ink making.

INK MANUFACTURERS, France.

Cabinet Z Shelf 3 No. 43

Jennings, H. C. à Champerret, commune de Neuilly, pres Paris. Dépôt Central à Paris, Chez E. Meyer, 49 rue de Seine. [circa, 1839].
Encres typographiques par les nouveaux procedes. Prix courant. Circular.

pp. 331-332 in Miscellaneous collection of French type specimens ... 1829-1844.

INK MANUFACTURERS, Germany.

Cabinet 78 Shelf 1 No. 49

Huber, Michael: Denkschrift zum 150 jährigen bestehen der farbenfabriken. München. 1780-1930. Illus., portraits.

Half morocco; 12¼ x 9¼ in.

INKS

Cabinet 78 Shelf 1 No. 76

Traite des vernis, ou l'on donne la maniere d'encomposer un qui ressemble parfaitment a celui de la Chine...A Paris, 1723. (Par P. Bonnani)

Boards, leather back; 7 x 4 x ½ in.

INK MANUFACTURERS, France.

Cabinet 78 Shelf 1 No. 37

Lorilleux et Co. Ch: The oldest and largest manufacturers of printing ink in the world. Head office 16, rue Suger, Paris, VIe. Saint Louis Exhibition, 1904. Printed in Paris, 1908.
A short chronicle of the firm with pictures of buildings and portraits of the officers.

Paper; 6 x 9½ in.

INK MANUFACTURERS, Germany.

Cabinet 78 Shelf 1 No. 47

Janecke, Gebr. & Fr. Schneemann. Hannover, 1886.
See Goebel, Theodor. "Unser farbe" ... St. Gallen, 1886.

INKS, PHOTOGRAVURE.

Cabinet Shelf No.

Casting and stock-keeping of photo-gravure inks. By R. B. Fishenden.

Article in BRITISH and COLONIAL PRINTER and STATIONER, Vol. 11, No. 196, July 28, 1932, pp. 84, 86, 88.

INK MANUFACTURERS, France.

Cabinet 78 Shelf 1 No. 36

Lorilleux et Cie. Paris, [1908?]. Printing Inks. Nine factories, forty branches. London, n.d.
Pictures of buildings, interior and exterior and portraits of officers. Includes a short chronicle of the first specialized printing ink factory in France, 1818.

Boards; 9½ x 6 in.

INK MANUFACTURERS, United States.

Cabinet 73 Shelf 1 No. 69

Ault & Wiborg Co.'s Printing Ink Plant in Cincinnati, Ohio, 1918.
Brief account of this house founded in 1878. With portraits of the founders, executive and sales force; also interior and exterior views of factories.
Black and colors shown by book work, and book illustrations.

Half morocco; 14¼ x 11¾ in.

INKS, PRINTING

Cabinet 78 Shelf 2 No. 42

Amtyco Printing Inks for sale by the American Type Founders Co. Circular, Practical Suggestions. Issued in 1935.
These inks were not made by the American Type Founders Co.

Item in manila envelope

INK MANUFACTURERS, France.

Cabinet 0 Shelf 1 No. 84

Lorilleux & Cie. Ch. (Pictures, interior and exterior views of the manufacturing palnt at Puteaux, Chantilly)

See EXHIBITIONS PRINTING. France. (Paris, 1911) 2em. Exposition...

INK MANUFACTURERS. United States

Cabinet QQ Shelf 4 No. 4

Lightbody, John Grant, New York, 1876. Biographical sketch, with survey of the ink industry. Portrait.

see INDUSTRIAL AMERICA. Manufacturers ...New York, 1876, p. 381.

INKS, PRINTING

Cabinet Shelf No.

Aniline printing, ink consumption in. Translated from the German by Reginald Steed.

Illustrated article in Buch und Werbekunst, heft 11, 9 jahrgang, 1932, pp.349-351.

INK MANUFACTURERS, France.

Cabinet 78 Shelf 1 No. 38

Lorilleux et Co. Firm founded in 1818. Nine factories, forty branches. London, n.d. [Printed in Paris, 1908?]. Specimen brochure
Includes a brief chronicle of the firm, its founder and successors. With portraits, and views of factories.
Signed copy "Pierre Ch- Lorilleux."

Paper; 9-3/8 x 6 in. Second copy, cloth; 78/1/39; also. 78/1/40.

INK MANUFACTURERS, United States.

Cabinet 78 Shelf 2 No. 10

Ullman Company, Sigmund. A modern printing ink factory. By A.L. Ralston in The American Printer. n.d. [After 1898].
Includes exterior view of the ink factory at 146th Str. and Park Ave. New York.

Cloth; 6-1/8 x 4½ in.

INKS, PRINTING

Cabinet Shelf No.

Arsenic in printing inks: some necessary knowledge, by James Scott.

Illus. article in Caxton Magazine, June, 1931, No.6. vol. 33, pp.321-323.

INKS, Printing

Cabinet A, Shelf 3, No. 89

Article on, p.32 special graphic arts number of The Times, Sept. 10, 1912.

INKS, PRINTING

Cabinet U, Shelf 5, No. 36

Chinese ink, method of making.

see GUPPY, HENRY. Stepping stones to typography...Manchester, 1928, p.26

INKS, Printing

Cabinet S, Shelf 5, No. 19

DeVinne, Theodore Low: American Printing. Written for "One hundred years of American Commerce", 1895. pp. 314-19.
Historical technical account of printing and printing inks.

In volume with binders title: "Excerpts on American printing", etc.

INKS, Printing

Cabinet 78, Shelf 1, No. 68

Ault & Wiborg Co. "Inkology" A Journal for printers and lithographers. Cincinnati, Ohio, 1904-5. [Vol. I only].

Cloth; 12-1/8 x 9¼ x 3/4 in.

INKS, PRINTING

Cabinet MM, Shelf 2, No. 40

Colour and colour printing as applied to lithography. Containing an introduction to the study of colour, an account of the general and special qualities of pugments employed, their manufacture into printing inks...By W.D. Richmond. Fourth edition. London, n.d. circa 1880.

Cloth; 7½ x 5 x ½ in.

INKS, PRINTING

Cabinet, Shelf, No.

Driers, the use of. Information issued by Lorilleux & Bolton, Ltd. London.

Article in The Printers' Register, vol. 71, No.828, June 6, 1932, p.IV.

INKS, PRINTING

Cabinet 78, Shelf 2, No. 41

Black printing inks: an instructive sample book. J.M. Huber Inc., New York, 1935.

Cloth; 11 x 8½ in.

INKS, Printing

Cabinet MM, Shelf 2, No. 16

Composizione degl'inchiostri odierni, inchiostri mat, bronze, doppia tinta, etc.
(Historical, technical account. Has portraits of the ink manufacturers, Francisco Orsenigo & Pierre Lorilleux, also interior views of an ink factory.)
pp.461-470 in Dalmazzo's Tipografia. Storia, tecnica, moderna...Torina, 1914.

INKS, Printing.

Cabinet 78, Shelf 1, No. 92

L'Encre et le papier. Par Gillot Saint-Evre. Conferences scientifiques et litteraires des facultes de Poitiers. Niort, 1867. Pamphlet.

Item in box labelled "Pamphlets and excerpts relating to inks and ink making."

INKS, PRINTING

Cabinet 78, Shelf 1, No. 92

British Standard Trichromatic Inks. Approved by the Federation of Master Printers, Federation of Master Process Engravers, Society og British Printing Ink Makers. August 1st. 1929

Specimen folder

Item in box labelled; "Pamphlets relating to inks and ink making".

INKS, Printing

Cabinet L, Shelf 4, No. 18

Coster, the various sorts of ink used by; colored inks; receipe for making a fine black, etc.

see SAVAGE, WILLIAM. Practical hints on decorative printing....London, 1822, pp.2, 6, 41, 42, 100

INKS, PRINTING

Cabinet 78, Shelf 1, No. 85

Encyclopedia of printing inks.

see KRIEGEL, HARRY G. Encyclopedia of printing inks...New York City, 1932.

INKS, Printing

Cabinet 78, Shelf 1, No. 1

Canepario, Petro Mario: De Atramentis cujuscunque generis. Opus sane novum, hactenus a nemine promulgatum. In sex descriptiones digestum. Lodnini, 1660.
The first book to describe inks of all kinds.

Calf; 7-7/8 x 5-7/8 x 1-3/8 in.

INKS, Printing

Cabinet 78, Shelf 1, No. 87

Davids & Co. Thaddeus. The history of ink, including its etymology, chemistry, and bibliography. New York, n.d. Printed by Francis Hart & Co. 63 Cortlandt Street.

Stamped cloth; 7-3/4 x 5¼ in.

INKS, PRINTING

Cabinet, Shelf, No.

Fading of colors. Discussed by Mr. G.F. Jones of Lorilleux and Bolton Ltd.

Brief article in Typographical Circular, No.956, May, 1932, p.101.

INKS, Printing

Cabinet 78, Shelf 1, No. 73

Carvalho, David N. Forty centuries of ink, or a chronological narrative concerning ink and its backgrounds. New York, 1904. New York.

Cloth; 9½ x 6¼ x 1-3/8 in.

INKS, PRINTING

Cabinet T, Shelf 3, No. 2

Definition and antiquity of ink; Cuneperius, his work upon ink, etc.

In DIBDIN'S Bibliographical Decameron...London, 1817, vol.1, pp.5-7

INKS, Printing

Cabinet 78, Shelf 1, No. 47

Goebel, Theodor. Unsere farbe: Historisch und technisch betrachtet. St. Gallen, 1886.
Historical technical account. With three folding plates, illustrations showing interior and exterior views of the ink manufacturing house of Janecke & Schneemann in Hannover.

Stamped cloth; 6-1/8 x 4-3/8 x ¼ in.

INKS, Printing

Cabinet W Shelf 1 No. 189

Histoire de l'encre. See Book Making."Etapes d'un livre"... par Léon Thevenin et G. Lemierre. Paris, 1922. pp.33-39.

INKS, Printing

Cabinet 78 Shelf 1 No. 92 Box

Lithographic ink pigments, light fastness of. By William D. Appel...Robert F. Reed. Research paper No.100. Reprint from Bureau of Standards Journal of Research, vol. 3, Sept, 1929.

U. S. Department of Commerce. Bureau of Standards.

With other items in box labelled "Pamphlets & excerpts relating to inks and ink making".

INKS, PRINTING

Cabinet 78 Shelf 1 No. 92

Practical facts for printers. Compiled from practical experience and observations of printers...Copyrighted by Lee A. Riley, 1899. Paper booklet.

Item in box labelled "Pamphlets & excerpts relating to ink and ink making".

INKS, Printing

Cabinet 78 Shelf 1 No. 45

Ihm Bernard A. Die bunten farben in der buchdruckerei, und insbesonderer deren druck auf der schnell-presse. Ein praktisches handbuch Vienna, 1874. Second edition.

"A valuable work on color printing by the steam press."

Paper boards; 10-7/8 x 7½ x 3/4 in.

INKS, Printing

Cabinet Shelf No.

Metallic inks, practical and reliable suggestions for the use of. Excerpt from the "American Ink Maker".

Article in The Inland Printer, vol. 88, March, 1932, p.66.

INKS, Printing.

Cabinet 78 Shelf 1 No. 92

Pressman's ink manual, containing basic facts on colors and color mixtures. By Julius Frank. New York, 1928. Pamphlet.

In box labelled "Pamphlets and excerpts relating to inks and ink making."

INKS, Printing

Cabinet S Shelf 5 No. 23

Ingredients and composition - Old inks - The process of manufacture etc.

Historical and technical summary in Brochure "Great American Industries of the United States." Hartford, Conn. 1872.

Item 2 in volume with binders title "Various items relating to printing." Bound, 1919.

INKS, Printing

Cabinet S Shelf 5 No. 23

Method of mixing inks for printings; p.459 of "Great American Industries of the U.S.", Hartford, 1875.

Item 2, in bound volume of "Various items relating to printing."

INKS, PRINTING

Cabinet 78 Shelf 1 No. 92

Principles of color mixing for embossing and plate printing. Compiled by Standard Ink & Color Co. 129 Atkins Ave. Brooklyn, N.Y. 1926.

Pamphlet in box labelled "Pamphlets and excerpts relating to inks and ink making".

INKS, Printing.

Cabinet 78 Shelf 1 No. 92

Ink secrets for pressmen. Philip Ruxton, Ink makers. ... New York, 1928. Pamphlet.

Item in box labelled "Pamphlets and excerpts relating to inks and ink making."

INKS, Printing

Cabinet 78 Shelf 1 No. 2

Mitchell (C. Ainsworth and Hepworth, T.C.) Inks their composition and manufacture, including methods of examination and a full list of English patents. With illustrations and plates. London, 1904.

Cloth; 8 x 5-3/4 in.

INKS, Printing.

Cabinet 78 Shelf 1 No. 92

Roosen, Herman D. How one man turned the trick. The story of H. D. Roosen and what he did with one thousand dollars. By Shelton Chauncey. Excerpt from "Business America," June, 1914.

Item in box labelled "Pamphlets and excerpts relating to Inks and Ink Making."

INKS, Printing.

Cabinet FF Shelf 2 No. 40

Lamp Black, process of making. See Inventions, Patents for. Abridgments of specifications, Vol. I...London, 1859.p.157, No. 4601 (1821).

Half morocco; 7-5/8 x 5 x 2 in.

INKS, Printing

Cabinet 26 Shelf 2 No. 4

Mixing of printing inks: A brief outline of proper ingredients and quantities and methods by G. Rogmann.

In German language.

Journal fur Buchdruckerkunst, 1845, No.14, cols. 177-181; No.15, cols. 185-195.

INKS, Printing

Cabinet 78 Shelf 1 No. 88

Roret-Manuels, Nouveau manuel complet de la fabrication des encres. Telles que encres a ecrire, de chine, de couleur, d'impression typographique et lithographique etc. Par MM. de Champour et F. Malepeyre. Paris, 1856.

Half morocco; 6-1/8 x 4 x 7/8 in.

INKS, PRINTING

Cabinet 78 Shelf 1 No. 32

Lefranc, A. Paris, 1878. Specimen des encres d'imprimerie de A. Lefranc, 4 rue de l'Abbaye. G. Fouquet, Directeur. Usine a Vapeur a Issy -sur-Seine.

Boards, morocco back; 12-1/8 x 10¼ x 1 in.

INKS, Printing

Cabinet 26 Shelf 2 No. 1

(Necessity of cleaning the lamp black in order to produce a good printing black.) Reinigung des kienrusses, als notwendigstes erfordniss zur darstellung einer guten buchdruckerschwartze. R. Fr. Hergt, Coblenz.

Journal fur Buchdruckerkunst, Nov., 1838, No.11, cols.167-9.

INKS, PRINTING

Cabinet 78 Shelf 1 No. 89

Ruxton, Philip. New York, 1907. Ruxton's Three Color Process Chart.

Item in manila envelope.

INKS, Printing

Cabinet MM Shelf 6 No. 52

Ruxton, Philip: Printing inks: their composition, properties and manufacture..."Typographic Technical Series for Apprentices", Part 1, No.12. Published by the United Typothetae of America, 1918.

Cloth; 8 x 5 in.

INKS, Printing

Cabinet 78 Shelf 1 No. 77

Underwood, Norman & Thomas Sullivan. Chemistry and technology of printing inks. New York, 1915. Illus.

Cloth; 8-5/8 x 5-7/8 x 3/4 in.

INKS, Printing. [Specimen Books, England].

Cabinet 78 Shelf 1 No. 22

Mander Brothers. Wolverhampton, England, 1903. Price list of printing inks manufactured by Mander Brothers. [Together with] Illustrations of printing inks made by Mander Brothers.

Stiff paper; 8½ x 6-3/8 x 5/8 in.

INKS, Printing.

Cabinet 78 Shelf 1 No. 3

Seymour, Alfred: Modern printing inks. A practical handbook for printing ink manufacturers and printers. With six engravings. London, 1910.

Morocco; 8-5/8 x 5½ x ½ in.

INKS, Printing.

Cabinet 78 Shelf 1 No. 83

Wiborg, Frank B. Printing ink, a history. With a treatise on modern methods of manufacture and use. New York and London, 1926. Illus.

Cloth; 9 x 5-7/8 x 1-1/8 in.

INK, Printing. [Specimen Books, England].

Cabinet 78 Shelf 1 No. 15

Morrell, H. London [1851?]. Morrell's specimens of printing inks. Colored inks made to pattern. Roller maker to the trade. 149 Fleet Street. London. With prices.

Cloth; 9-5/8 x 6¼ x 3/8 in. Typothetae Copy.

INKS, PRINTING.

Cabinet Shelf No.

Some faults of printing inks. Microscopical investigations. By James Scott. Illus.

Article in The Caxton Magazine, Vol. 34, No. 8, August, 1932, pp. 385-387.

INKS, Printing. (Metallic)

Cabinet Shelf No.

Metallic inks, recent thought on; as used in the modern plant. By A.W. Barrett.
Has portrait of.

Article in The Inland Printer, vol. 88, March, 1932, p.55.

INKS, Printing. [Specimen Books. England]

Cabinet 78 Shelf 1 No. 6

Parsons, Fletcher and Co. London, 22 Broad St. [1843?]. Specimens of printing inks manufactured by Parsons, Fletcher & Co.
Various examples of book work in black and colors.

Paper; 12½ x 10 x 3/16 in. See also 78/1/7.

INKS, Printing

Cabinet 78 Shelf 2 No. 13

Ullman, James A. Printing ink. Two lectures delivered in the course on the technique of printing. Graduate School of Business Administration, Harvard University, Cambridge, Mass. March 22 and 24, New York, 1911.

Cloth; 9 x 5-7/8 x ½ in.

INKS, PRINTING. (Metallic).

Cabinet Shelf No.

On using metallic inks. By W. H. Barrett.

Article (copied from Inland Printer) in South African Printer & Stationer, Vol. 12, No. 7, July, 1932, pp. 245, 247, 249.

INKS, Printing. [Specimen Books, England].

Cabinet 78 Shelf 1 No. 7

Parsons, Fletcher and Co. London. [1843?]. Specimens of printing inks manufactured by Parsons, Fletcher and Co. London.
Engraving on cover "Gutenberg and Faust's first proof from moveable types."

Stiff paper; 10-5/8 x 7-3/8 in.

INKS, PRINTING

Cabinet L Shelf 4 No. 18

Various sorts used by Coster,-accounts of colored inks,-recipe for making a fine black.

See Savage, William. Practical hints on decorative printing...London, 1822, pp.2,6, 41, 42, 100. (See index

INKS, Printing. [Specimen Books, England].

Cabinet 78 Shelf 1 No. 17

Foster, & Winstone. London, 1851. Specimens of printing inks, machine, letter-press, and lithographic, manufactured by Foster & Winstone, 100 Shoe Lane, Fleet Street. London, 1851. With prices.

Half morocco; 8½ x 5½ x 3/8 in.

INKS, PRINTING. (Specimen Books, England)

Cabinet 78 Shelf 1 No. 8

Parsons, Fletcher & Co. London, n.d. circa, 1845. Specimen of printing inks manufactured by.
On front cover "Proben von druckfarben.. On last page cover, picture of Columbian Press, Clymer & Dixon, London.

Paper; 12¼ x 10 in.

INKS, Printing

Cabinet 78 Shelf 2 No. 9

Ullman, Sigmund Company. Our doubletone inks in theory and practice. Second ed. New York. Copyright, 1903. Brochure.

Paper; 6-3/8 x 5-1/8 in.

INKS, Printing. [Specimen Books, England].

Cabinet 78 Shelf 1 No. 4

How & Parsons. London, 1840. Specimens of How & Parsons printing inks. Manufactory, Orange Street, Southwark, London. With prices.
Examples of advertising and book work in black and colors.

Paper; 9¾ x 6¼ in.

INKS, Printing. [Specimen Books, England].

Cabinet 78 Shelf 1 No. 10

Shackell and Edwards. London, 1849. Specimen of printing inks in every variety of color. Manufactured by Shackell and Edwards. No. 35 Coppice Row, Clerkenwell.

Paper; 8-3/8 x 5-3/8 in.

INKS, Printing. [Specimen Books, England]

Cabinet 78 Shelf 1 No. 12

Shackell and Edwards. London, 1853. Specimen of printing inks manufactured by Shackell & Edwards, Coppice Row, Clerkenwell, London.
Examples of book and advertising work.

Cloth; 10-1/8 x 6¼ x 3/8 in.

INKS, Printing. [Specimen Books, England].

Cabinet 78 Shelf 1 No. 9

Shackell and Lyons. No. 35 Coppice Row, Clerkenwell, London. [1849?]. Specimen of printing inks in a variety of colors. Includes prices.

Morocco; 9 x 5¾ x 3/8 in.

INKS, Printing. [Specimen Books, France]

Cabinet 78 Shelf 1 No. 31

Lefranc et Cie. Paris, 1853: Encres typographiques de Lefranc et Cie, fabricants. 4 Rue de l'Abbaye-Saint-Germain. A Paris. Extrait du Specimen. [With prices].
Examples in black and colors.

Cloth; 12 x 9-3/8 x 5/8 in.

INKS, Printing. [Specimen Books, France]

Cabinet 78 Shelf 1 No. 40

Lorilleux et Cie. Encres d'Imprimerie. Paris, 1818-1908. [still active].
Examples of inks with brief chronicle of firm, the first specialized ink factory in France. With portraits of the founder, Rene Pierre Lorilleux, and successors.

Paper; 9-7/8 x 7-1/8 in. See also 78/1/38 - 78/1/39.

INKS, Printing. [Specimen Books, France]

Cabinet 78 Shelf 1 No. 36

Lorilleux & Co. Paris, n.d. [1908?]. Printing Inks. London n.d. Pictures of buildings and portraits of officers.
This is a short chronicle of the first specialized printing ink factory in France, 1818.

Boards; 9½ x 6 in.

INKS, Printing. [Specimen Books, Germany]

Cabinet 78 Shelf 1 No. 55

Berger & Wirth. Farbenbabriken. Leipzig, n.d. [1898]. Filialen : Berlin, Barmen, Florenz, London, New York. St. Petersburg.
Book of samples.

Cloth folder, stamped; 7¼ x 4-7/8 x 1 in.

INKS, Printing. [Specimen Books, Germany].

Cabinet 78 Shelf 1 No. 48

Jänecke, Gbr. & Fr. Schneemann. Hannover & New York, 1896. Graphischer abreiss - kalender von Gebr. Jänecke & Fr. Schneemann, buch-und steindruckfarben-fabriken. Hannover & New York. Zusammengestellt von Theofor Goebel.
With prices.

Stamped cloth; 7¼ x 5 x ¾ in.

INKS, PRINTING [Specimen Books, Scotland]

Cabinet C Shelf 1 No. 14

Fleming & Co., Ltd. Caroline Park House and Roystoun Castle, a descriptive and historical account. By David F. Harris. [Together with] - Specimens of fine illustration inks. Printed at the manufactory, Caroline Park, Edinburgh, 1896.
Caroline Park House became and is the head office of A.B. Fleming & Co., Ltd., inkmakers, in whose interest this volume is issued.

Cloth; 17 x 11¾ in.

INKS, Printing. [Specimen Books, U.S.]

Cabinet 78 Shelf 1 No. 60 2 copies

American Type Founders Company: Albert Nathan & Co.'s, printing inks, varnishes and bronze powders. Selling agent, A.T.F. Co. [1895].
Black and colors: Printed in the Specimen Printing Dept. of A.T.F. Co., Philadelphia.

Cloth; 5-5/8 x 9½ x 1 in.

INKS, Printing. [Specimen Books, U.S.]

Cabinet 78 Shelf 1 No. 64

Ault & Wiborg Co. Specimens of black and colored printing inks manufactured by. Cincinnati, n.d.

Paper; 4 x 6 x ½ in.

INKS, Printing. [Specimen Books, U.S.]

Cabinet 78 Shelf 1 No. 62

Ault & Wiborg Co. Some letter press proofs of regular goods. Cincinnati, January 1, 1901.

Limp cloth; 5½ x 8½ x 5/8 in.

INKS, Printing. [Specimen Books, U.S.]

Cabinet 78 Shelf 1 No. 63

Ault & Wiborg Co. Poster Album. Cincinnati, May, 1902.
With prices.

Cloth; 12 x 9¼ x ½ in.

INKS, Printing. [Specimen Books, U.S.]

Cabinet 78 Shelf 1 No. 67

Ault & Wiborg Co. A few of our regular (stock) shades of inks for half-tone work, including some of our justly celebrated duplex colors. Cincinnati. [1903].

Paper; 9½ x 12 x ¼ in.

INKS, PRINTING, United States

Cabinet 78 Shelf 1 No. 58

Berger & Wirth, New York. Specimen book of fine printing inks. n.d.

Paper; 10 x 7-3/4 in.

INKS, Printing [Specimen Books, U.S.]

Cabinet 78 Shelf 1 No. 57

Berger & Wirth. Fine color and printing ink makers. New York, Broome Street 403-405. Color chart of "Ink suitable for every branch of the Graphic Arts."

Cloth, printed; 9 x 6 in.

INKS, Printing. [Specimen Books, U.S.]

Cabinet 78 Shelf 1 No. 56

Berger & Wirth. New York, n.d. [1900?]. Specimen of "Fine Printing Inks."
Black and colors shown by book illustrations.

Paper; 10¼ x 7¾ in.

INKS, Printing. [Specimen Books, U. S.]

Cabinet 78 Shelf 2 No. 17

Buffalo Printing Ink Works. New Specimen Book. Various shades and colors. n.d. With prices.

Cloth, printed; 5 x 6¼ x 7/8 in.

INKS, PRINTING, SPECIMEN BOOKS, United States

Cabinet 78 Shelf 2 No. 36

Chicago Printing Ink Co., Foster, Roe & Crone, Chicago. Ill. circa 1880. Sample of ink manufactured by Foster, Roe & Crone.

Paper; 8¼ x 6-7/8 in. In board folder.

INKS, Printing. [Specimen Books, U.S.]

Cabinet 78 Shelf 2 No. 20

Daniels, Ralph. Practical color matching system. Blue section. Printed with cover blue V. Factory 1820-22-24 Blake St., Denver, Colorado, n.d.

Paper pamphlet; 9½ x 6 in. See also 78/2/21.

INKS, Printing. [Specimen Books, U.S.]

Cabinet 78 Shelf 2 No. 21

Daniels, Ralph. Practical color matching system. Second section including browns, greens, reds, and miscellaneous shades. Factory 1820-22-24 Blake St. Denver, Colorado, n.d.

Stiff paper; 9½ x 6 x 3/8 in. See also 78/2/20.

INKS, Printing. [Specimen Books, U.S.]

Cabinet 78 Shelf 1 No. 71

Huber, J. M. Inc. The story of news ink. New York City, 1928. Views of ink-making plant interior and exterior.

Black, green and brown shown by illustrations and newspaper work .

Half morocco; 7-7/8 x 10-1/8 in.

INKS, Printing. [Specimen Books. U.S.]

Cabinet 78 Shelf 1 No. 54

Jaenecke Printing Ink Co. Newark N.J.-New York-Chicago. n.d. [1900]. Specimens of Jaenecke's [inks] for typo and lithographic printing. Newark N.J. Price list of black, and colored printing and lithographic ink.

Cloth; 4½ x 7-3/4 x 5/8 in.

INKS, Printing. [Specimen Books, U.S.]

Cabinet 78 Shelf 2 No. 40

Levey, Fred'k H. Company. Printing ink specimens. New York, n.d. [1910].

With prices.

Limp cloth; 6-1/8 x 9-1/8 x ½ in.

INKS, Printing. [Specimen Books, U.S.]

Cabinet 78 Shelf 2 No. 33

Morrill, Geo. H. and Co. Printing and lithographic inks. Boston, New York, Chicago, n.d. [1903].

Cloth; 8-7/8 x 10-7/8 x 5/8 in. See also 78/2/34.

INKS, Printing. [Specimen Books, U. S.]

Cabinet 78 Shelf 2 No. 34

Morrill, Geo. H. Co. Printing and lithographic inks. Head Office, Norwood, Mass. n.d. [circa, 1904].

Includes the history of the plant, with views, interior and exterior, and portraits of founder and successors.

Cloth; 5½ x 9¼ x 1¼ in. See also 78/2/33.

INKS, Printing. [Specimen Books, U.S.]

Cabinet 78 Shelf 2 No. 31

Okie, F. E. Company. "Art Colors." n.d. Philadelphia, Pa.

Cloth; 8-7/8 x 7½ x 3/8 in. See also 78/2/30.

INKS, Printing. [Specimen Books, U.S.]

Cabinet 78 Shelf 2 No. 30

Okie, F. E. Company. Fine printing inks manufactured by. Kenton Place. Philadelphia, Pa. n.d. [With prices].

Cloth; 6 x 9¼ x ½ in. See also 78/2/31.

INKS, Printing. [Specimen Books, U.S.]

Cabinet 78 Shelf 2 No. 15

Peckett, J. W. Specimen book of printing inks. New York 75 Fulton Street, n. d. [1890].

With prices.

Stamped cloth; 7¾ x 5¼ x ½ in.

INKS, Printing. [Specimen Books, U. S.]

Cabinet 78 Shelf 2 No. 38

Ruxton, Philip, Incorporated. Printing inks. A hand book for the printer. New York, 1907.

Contains history of the firm.

Boards; 12¼ x 9¼ x 5/8 in.

INKS, Printing. [Specimen Books, U.S.]

Cabinet 78 Shelf 2 No. 3

Ullman, Sigmund. Specimens (250) of German printing inks and Bronze powders manufactured and imported by S. Ullman. New York, 1890.

With prices.

Morocco, stamped; 9 x 6¼ x 1¼ in.

INKS, Printing. [Specimen Books, U.S.]

Cabinet 78 Shelf 2 No. 6

Ullman, Sigmund. German printing inks and bronze powders. New York, n.d. [Before 1897]

Black and colors. Specimen leaves all with name of the firm of Gebr. Jänecke & Fr. Schneemann. Hannover.

Stamped cloth; 8 x 6 x 7/8 in.

INKS, Printing. [Specimen Books, U.S.]

Cabinet 78 Shelf 2 No. 7

Ullman Co., Sigmund. Specimens of some of our superior printing inks. Sigmund Ullman Co. 146th Street and Park Av. New York, N. Y. 1898.

Paper; 2-7/8 x 6 x ½ in.

INKS, Printing. [Specimen Books, U.S.]

Cabinet 78 Shelf 2 No. 8

Ullman, Sigmund. Specimens of 292 printing inks and bronze powders. With a complete catalog and price list. New York, 146th Street and Park Av. n.d. [After 1898].

Paper; 5¼ x 7-1/8 x ½ in.

INKS, Printing. [Specimen Books, U.S.]

Cabinet 78 Shelf 2 No. 9.01

Ullman Co. Sigmund. Specimens of doubletone inks manufactured by Sigmund Ullman Co. Inventors and sole manufacturers of doublestone inks. New York. 146th St. and Park Ave. 1903. DeVinne Press Series.

Paper; 6-7/8 x 10-3/4 in.

INKS, PRINTING (Specimen Books. U.S.)

Cabinet 78 Shelf 2 No. 11

Ullman Company, Sigmund. Specimens of high grade colored inks. New York, n.d. circa 1905

Imitation leather, gilt; 9½ x 7¼ in.

INKS, Printing. [Specimen Books, U.S.]

Cabinet 78 Shelf 2 No. 25

Wade, H. D. Specimens of printing inks. Black and colored. New York, 50 Ann Street. n.d. With prices.

Specimens are pasted into book, Typothetae copy.

Quarter morocco; 10½ x 8¾ in.

INKS, Printing. [Specimen Books, U. S.]

Cabinet 78 Shelf 2 No. 24

Wade, H. D. & Co. New York, 1887. Printing inks. [Black and colors].

Cloth; 9-7/8 x 8½ x 3/8 in.

INKS, Printing. [Specimen Books, U.S.]

Cabinet 78 Shelf 2 No. 26

Wade's Standard Printing Inks. Manufactured in every variety of black and colors. H. D. Wade & Co. Nos. 111 Fulton St. and 50 Ann Street, New York. n.d. :[1880?].

Morocco; 5½ x 8¼ x ¾ in.

INKS, Printing. [Specimen Books, U.S.]

Cabinet 78 Shelf 2 No. 27

Wade's standard printing inks manufactured by H.D.Wade &Co. New York. n.d. [1881?].

Cloth; 5½ x 8¾ x ¾ in.

INKS (for) PRINTING PROCESSES

Cabinet Shelf No.

Problems of printers and inkmakers; a lecture by R.F. Bowles: relates among other matters to fading, spraying on fast rotary presses, mottling and spotting, scumming, printing on celluloid, etc.

Articles in British and Colonial Printer, (vol. 167, Dec. 18, 1930, p. 212, Dec. 25, 1930, p.1250) also, vol. 108, Jan. 8, 1931, p.42.

INKS, Writing.

Cabinet FF Shelf 2 No. 40

See Inventions, Patents for, Inks, Writing.

INLAND DAILY PRESS ASSOCIATION

Cabinet Shelf No.

Fifty years of Inland history, 1885-1934. By George M. Purcell, publisher of Bloomington (Indiana) World. Illus.

Article in Editor and Publisher, Feb. 23, 1935, vol.67, No.41, pp.8,9,61,62. Also report of Fiftieth Birthday Anniversary, Feb.20, in same issue, pp.1-7, 45. By George A. Brandenburg. Illus.

INLAND PRINTER, THE

Cabinet MM Shelf 6 No. 102

Vest pocket manual of printing. A convenient reference book...Chicago, 1905.

Morocco; 5-3/4 x 2-3/4 x ¼ in. With other items in manila envelope.

INLAND TYPE FOUNDRY

Cabinet C Shelf 2 No. 22

Portfolios (2) of individual showings of type faces made by The Inland Type Foundry, St. Louis, Mo. n.d.

Portfolio; 19½ x 14¾ in.

INLAND TYPE FOUNDRY

Cabinet 41 Shelf 1 No. 1 to 11

Practical Printer, 1901-1911

See PERIODICALS, PRINTING, United States Practical Printer...

INLAND TYPE FOUNDRY

Cabinet QQ Shelf 1 NO. 53

Printers' wit and humor: a string of jokes and anecdotes...used as matter for point-set type specimens. With a preface explaining the point-set system...Third edition. St. Louis, 1902.

Cloth; 7½ x 5½ in.

INLAND TYPE FOUNDRY

Cabinet Shelf No.

see also Specimen Books, Types. United States. First Occurrences. Standard Line Type Book.

INNES, J.

Cabinet X Shelf 4 No. 102

Liberty of the Press. Article reprinted from the supplement of the Encyclopaedia Britannica. London: Printed by J. Innes, 1790.

Half morocco; 8¼ x 5¼ in.

"INSATSUTAIKWAN"

Cabinet L Shelf 5 No. 13

Japanese color printing, specimens by various Japanese printers. Book published with title of "Insatsutaikwan". Preface by Swada Iozo, President of the Japan Society of Printers. Nov., 1915.

Laced silk over board 15¼ x 10½ x 7/8 in.

INSEL-VERLAG

Cabinet 14 Shelf 2 No. 2 2 vols.

See Imprints, Germany. Insel-Verlag, Leipzig, 1913.

INSEL-VERLAG

Cabinet Y Shelf 5 No. 22

[List of all the publications of the Insel-Verlag, Leipzig, 1899-1924) Verzeichnis aller veröffentlichungen des Insel-Verlags. With facsimiles.

Boards; 8½ x 5-5/8 x ¾ in.

INSETSU-KIOKU

Cabinet Shelf No.

See Specimen Books, Types. Japan

INSLEE, SAMUEL

Cabinet 3 Shelf 2 No. 3

See Imprints, United States. Inslee, Samuel.

INSOMUCH, JOHN, Great Britain

Cabinet Shelf No.

St. Albans monastery. First printer, John Insomuch, 1480.

See p.196, vol. I. Horne's Introduction to the study of bibliography...London, 1814.

INSTITUTE OF PRINTERS AND KINDRED TRADES

Cabinet KK Shelf 2 No. 26

British Empire, Institute of Printers and Kindred Trades. Constituted 1898. Terms of membership. Pamphlet.

Includes list of trades eligible to enter this society, officers 1898 - 99, and provisional by - laws.

Item in envelope.

INSTITUTE OF PRINTERS AND KINDRED TRADES OF THE BRITISH EMPIRE.

Cabinet Shelf No.

see also

SOCIETIES, PRINTERS. Great Britain.

INSTITUTE OF PRINTERS...OF THE BRITISH EMPIRE

Cabinet KK Shelf 1 No. 19

see

SOCIETIES, PRINTERS'. Great Britain.

INSTITUTIONS FOR THE BLIND

Cabinet W Shelf 1 No. 37

(France). L'Institution Royale des jeunes aveugles de Paris. [An introductory chapter relating the history of Blind Institutions]. Se Guillé (Doctor). Essai sur l'instruction des aveugles...Paris, 1817. pp. 11-30.

INSTITUTO ARGENTINO DE ARTES GRAFICAS

Cabinet KK Shelf 3 No. 41

Estatutos, 1927

See SOCIETIES . PRINTERS. South America. Instituto Argento...

INSULANI (MENAPII, GUILL.)

Cabinet X Shelf 1 No. 36

Statera chalcographiae, qua bona ipsius & mala simul appenduntur et numerantur, Basil, 1547-8

[Printed in Work, "Monumenta Typographica", vol. I, p. 1046]

INSURANCE.

Cabinet Shelf No.

(Insuring printing plants in Great Britain). Questions and answers on insurance policies, by Frank Colebrook.

Opening of a department relating to insurance in Caxton Magazine, Vol. 33, No. 9, Sept., 1931, p. 508.

INTAGLIO PRINTING

Cabinet A Shelf 3 No. 89

Rembrandt Intaglio Printing Company, Lancaster, England; a full page advertisement on p.35 special graphic arts number of The Times,, Sept. 10, 1912.

This firm first to introduce rotary photogravure printing on direction of Karl Klick of Vienna.

INTAGLIO PROCESS ENGRAVING

Cabinet A Shelf 3 No. 89

Photo mechanical Intaglio Engraving, p. 21, special graphic arts number of The Times, Sept. 10, 1912.

INTAGLIOTYPE AND GRAPHOTYPE ENGRAVING CO.

Cabinet I Shelf 2 No. 26

Prospectus of the...Engraving Company. New York, 1864. Pamphlet, illus.

Bound in with 3 pamphlets issued by the Moss Engraving Co., of New York, 1880-1884.

Cloth; $12\frac{3}{4}$ x 9-7/8 x 3/8 in.

INTELLINGENCER and WEEKLY ADVERTISER, LANCASTER.

Cabinet Shelf No.

See Newspapers, Pennsylvania.

INTERNATIONAL BENJAMIN FRANKLIN SOCIETY.

Cabinet R Shelf 1 No. 3

First prospectus of constitution, by-laws, and form of application for membership, New York 1893.

In Frankliniana, p.46.

INTERCHANGEABLE SYSTEM

Cabinet Shelf No.

See SYSTEMS OF TYPE BODIES.

INTERNATIONAL ASSOCIATION OF PRINTING HOUSE CRAFTSMEN

Cabinet Shelf No.

Constitutions, By-laws, Reports, etc..

See SOCIETIES, PRINTERS. United States. International Association of Printing House Craftsmen...

INTERNATIONAL ASSOCIATION OF TYPOGRAPHICAL ENGRAVERS & FOUNDERS. PARIS, 1859.

Cabinet FF Shelf 3 No. 21

See Type Designs Protection. International Association, etc.

INTERNATIONAL BROTHERHOOD OF BOOKBINDERS OF NORTH AMERICA.

Cabinet Shelf No.

See SOCIETIES, BOOKBINDERS.

INTERNATIONAL CONGRESS OF PRINTERS'.

Cabinet KK Shelf 1 No. 1

(France) First International meeting of printers. Organized by a committee of editors and held at the Grand Hotel, Paris, on Tuesday, 20th August 1878. Reprinted for private circulation, from the "Printing Times & Lithographer".

The speeches, report, the banquet, etc.

Half morocco; $9\frac{1}{2}$ x $7\frac{3}{4}$ in.

INTERNATIONAL CONGRESS OF PRINTERS

Cabinet KK Shelf 1 No. 6

(Germany) Zweite Internationaler Buchdrucker - kongress. Köln, 4 - 8 September, 1928.

Speeches, and reports from the several attending countries.

see also

KK/1/5

Half morocco; 11-7/8 x 9 in.

INTERNATIONAL CONGRESS OF PRINTERS

Cabinet KK Shelf 1 No. 4

(Sweden) Proceedings at the International Congress of Master Printers in Gothenberg. June 4 to 6, 1923. Illus.

Paper; 9½ x 6½ in.

INTERNATIONAL CORRESPENDENCE SCHOOL

Cabinet LL Shelf 5 No. 4

Advertisers handbook, the. A book of reference dealing with plans, copy, typography, illustrations,...and other details of advertising management. 1st ed., 9th impression. Scranton, Pa. International Textbook Company. 1910. Illus.

Cloth; 5-3/8 x 3½ x 3/4 in.

INTERNATIONAL COST CONGRESS

Cabinet JJ Shelf 2 No. 39

Official program of the 3rd International Cost Congress, Sept. 4 to 6, 1911, Denver, Colo.

Paper; 11 x 8 in.

INTERNATIONAL COST CONGRESS

Cabinet LL Shelf 6 No. 16

Standard uniform cost finding system. Devised by American Printers' Cost Commission, 1910. (First) Cost Congress held at Chicago, Ill. Oct. 18, 20, 1909.

Together with sample sheets, cost finding forms, etc.

Buckram; 11¼ x 8-3/4 x 3/4 in.

INTERNATIONAL COST CONGRESS OF EMPLOYING PRINTERS

Cabinet Shelf No.

See PRINTING ACCOUNTANCY. Proceedings of International Cost Congress...

INTERNATIONAL CRAFTSMEN CLUBS

Cabinet JJ Shelf 4 No. 40

Proceedings and annual reports for years, 1921, 1922, 1923, 1926, 1930, 1932.

Also constitution and by-laws, 1921. In all 7 pieces.

Boards; 10½ x 6-3/4 in.

INTERNATIONAL PHOTO-ENGRAVERS UNION

Cabinet Shelf No.

See SOCIETIES, PRINTERS. International etc.

INTERNATIONAL PRESSMANS' UNION

Cabinet JJ Shelf 1 No. 24

Hearings on industrial relations...Washington, D. C. April 8 and 9, 1914.

see

LABOR QUESTIONS. Hearing on industrial relations...

(The) INTERNATIONAL PRINTER

Cabinet 35 Shelf 2 No. 1 to 8

Successor to Paper and Press. Founded by Wm. M. Patton, Philadelphia.

See PERIODICALS, PRINTING, United States (The) International Printer..

INTERNATIONAL PRINTING PRESSMEN & ASSISTANTS UNION.

Cabinet JJ Shelf 2 No. 34

Conference between the...United Typothetae of America, and officers of the I. P. P. A. U. Niagara Falls, Canada, Tuesday, Sept. 10, 1907. Pamphlet.

Included in proceedings of U.T.A., 1907. (see JJ-2-33).

Item in manila envelope.

INTERNATIONAL PRINTING PRESSMAN AND ASSISTANTS

Cabinet Shelf No.

Union of North America.

See SOCIETIES, PRINTERS. International Printing Pressmen's etc.

INTERNATIONAL PRINTING PRESSMEN UNION OF N.A.

Cabinet P Shelf 2 No. 53

(The) Book of Art Printing, 1932

see

TYPOGRAPHY. (The) Book of Art Printing...

North America
INTERNATIONAL STEREOTYPERS' AND ELECTROTYPERS UNION

Cabinet JJ Shelf 6 No. 73

Constitution and By-laws, 1911, and Annual Convention Souvenirs for years, 1906, 1908.

Also National Electrotypers Association of America:

I - Constitution and By-laws.
II - Annual Meeting, Milwaukee, 1898.

Items in manila envelope.

INTERNATIONAL STEREOTYPERS & ELECTROTYPERS UNION

Cabinet Shelf No.

see also

SOCIETIES, STEREOTYPERS.

INTERNATIONAL TRADE COMPOSITION ASSOCIATION

Cabinet Shelf No.

Boston, Massachusetts. Official Bulletin of the I.T.C.A.

see

Periodical Record

INTERNATIONAL TYPOGRAPHICAL UNION

Cabinet JJ Shelf 1 No. 51

Childs - Drexel Home for Union Printers. Memorial souvenir, dedication. Colorado Springs, Colorado, May 12, 1892. Printed in Boston. Illus., portraits.

Cloth, gilt tops; 12½ x 9½ in.

INTERNATIONAL TYPOGRAPHICAL UNION

Cabinet JJ Shelf 1 No. 50

Childs - Drexel Home for Union Printers and allied crafts, Colorado Springs, Colorado, erected and maintained by the I. T. U. Published by the I. T. U., Indianapolis, 1898. Illus.

Historical sketch.

Half morocco; 6½ x 4¾ in.

INTERNATIONAL TYPOGRAPHICAL UNION

Cabinet JJ Shelf 1 No. 5

Constitution and By - Laws as issued in 1878, 1890, 1891, 1893, 1900, 1904, 1905, 1909, 1911, 1913.

10 Issues

In portfolio; 6½ x 4½ in.

INTERNATIONAL TYPOGRAPHICAL UNION

Cabinet JJ Shelf 1 No. 46

Course of instruction in printing. Conducted by The Inland Printer Technical School... By authority of the I. T. U. (1908).

Outline of course, with enrollment blank, first prospectus, etc.

Cloth; 9 x 6-1/8 x $\frac{1}{4}$ in.

INTERNATIONAL TYPOGRAPHICAL UNION

Cabinet JJ Shelf 1 No. 24

Hearings...at Washington, D. C., April 8 and 9, 1914.

see
LABOR QUESTIONS. Hearings of the United Typothetae of America...

INTERNATIONAL TYPOGRAPHICAL UNION

Cabinet JJ Shelf 1 No. 51

History of the I. T. U.

see
CHILDS - DREXEL HOME FOR UNION PRINTERS. Memorial souvenir...1892, pp. 35 - 47.

INTERNATIONAL TYPOGRAPHICAL UNION

Cabinet JJ Shelf 1 No. 4

History of the Typographical Union. Compiled by authority...by George A. Tracy (Indianapolis). Published by the International Typographical Union, 1913. With portraits.

Morocco flexible; $9\frac{1}{4}$ x 6-1/8 in.

INTERNATIONAL TYPOGRAPHICAL UNION

Cabinet NN Shelf 2 No. 9

See Journalism California: Long winning fight against the close shop, A.

INTERNATIONAL TYPOGRAPHICAL UNION

Cabinet JJ Shelf 1 No. 52

Labor's post of combat must not be abandoned before the enemy. Messages commending the members of the I. T. U. for their patriotic services in the war for the triumph of justice and liberty. Vol. I, 1918. I. T. U. Indianapolis, Indiana.

Boards, leather back; 5-5/8 x 8 x $\frac{3}{4}$ in.

INTERNATIONAL TYPOGRAPHICAL UNION

Cabinet JJ Shelf 1 No. 6

Proceedings of annual convention. 26th annual session, held in Detroit, Mich., June, 1878.

Half morocco; 9-1/8 x 5-7/8 in.

INTERNATIONAL TYPOGRAPHICAL UNION

Cabinet JJ Shelf 1 No. 7

Report of proceedings of 30th annual session held in St. Louis, Mo., June, 1882.

Half morocco; $9\frac{1}{4}$ x 5-7/8 x $\frac{3}{4}$in.

INTERNATIONAL TYPOGRAPHICAL UNION

Cabinet JJ Shelf 1 No. 8

Report of proceedings of the 32nd annual session held in New Orleans, La., June, 1884.

Half morocco; $9\frac{1}{4}$ x 5-7/8 x $\frac{3}{4}$ in.

INTERNATIONAL TYPOGRAPHICAL UNION

Cabinet JJ Shelf 1 No. 9

Proceedings. Sessions 34 - 35, 1886 - 1887.

Cloth; 9-1/8 x 6 x $1\frac{1}{2}$ in.

INTERNATIONAL TYPOGRAPHICAL UNION

Cabinet JJ Shelf 1 No. 10

Report of proceedings of the 36th to 39th sessions, 1888 - 1891.

Cloth; $9\frac{1}{4}$ x $6\frac{1}{4}$ x 2-1/8 in.

INTERNATIONAL TYPOGRAPHICAL UNION

Cabinet JJ Shelf 1 No. 12

Report of proceedings. 40th annual session, held in Philadelphia, Pa., June, 1892.

Paper; 9 x 6 in.

INTERNATIONAL TYPOGRAPHICAL UNION

Cabinet JJ Shelf 1 No. 13

Report of proceedings, 41st annual session. Chicago, Ill., June, 1893.

Paper; 9 x 6 in.

INTERNATIONAL TYPOGRAPHICAL UNION

Cabinet JJ Shelf 1 No. 16

Reports of Proceedings of Annual Conventions. Sessions 44 - 48, 1898 - 1902.

44th Session, Syracuse, 1898.
45th " Detroit, 1899.
46th " Milwaukee, 1900.
47th " Birmingham, Ala.1901.
48th " Cincinnati,Ohio.1902.

Buckram; $9\frac{1}{2}$ x $6\frac{1}{2}$ x $1\frac{1}{4}$ in.

INTERNATIONAL TYPOGRAPHICAL UNION

Cabinet JJ Shelf 1 No. 17

Reports of proceedings of Annual Conventions. Sessions 49 - 51, 1903 - 1905.

49th Session, Washington, D. C., 1903.
50th " St. Louis, Mo., 1904.
51st " Toronto, Canada. 1905.

Buckram; $9\frac{3}{4}$ x $6\frac{3}{4}$ x $1\frac{1}{4}$ in.

INTERNATIONAL TYPOGRAPHICAL UNION

Cabinet JJ Shelf 1 No. 18

Reports of proceedings of Annual Conventions.

52nd Session, Colorado Springs, 1906.
53rd " Hot Springs, 1907.
54th " Boston, 1908.

Buckram; $9\frac{3}{4}$ x $6\frac{3}{4}$ in.

INTERNATIONAL TYPOGRAPHICAL UNION

Cabinet JJ Shelf 1 No. 20

Report, 56th Annual Session, Aug. 8 - 13, 1910. Minneapolis, Minn.

Paper; $12\frac{1}{4}$ x $9\frac{1}{4}$ in.

INTERNATIONAL TYPOGRAPHICAL UNION

Cabinet JJ Shelf 1 No. 28

Report of proceedings of Annual Convention. 64th Session, August 12 to 17, 1918, at Scranton, Pennsylvania. Official Souvenir, Illus.

Pictorial paper; 9-3/8 x 12 x $\frac{1}{2}$ in.

INTERNATIONAL TYPOGRAPHICAL UNION

Cabinet JJ Shelf 1 No. 29

Report of proceedings, 65th Session, Albany, N. Y., August 9th to 14th, 1920. Golden Jubilee. 70th Anniversary Souvenir. Illus.

Pictorial paper; 9½ x 12½ x ½ in.

INTERNATIONAL TYPOGRAPHICAL UNION

Cabinet JJ Shelf 1 No. 26

Report of proceeding of Annual Session, Quebec, Canada, August 8 - 13, 1921.

Supplement to Typographical Journal, August, 1921.

Paper; 9½ x 6-5/8 x 7/8 in.

INTERNATIONAL TYPOGRAPHICAL UNION

Cabinet JJ Shelf 1 No. 34

Reports of officers to 74th Annual Convention held at Seattle, Washington, Sept. 9 - 14, 1929. Supplement to Typographical Journal.

Paper; 9½ x 6½ in.

INTERNATIONAL TYPOGRAPHICAL UNION

Cabinet JJ Shelf 1 No. 11

Souvenir of the 40th annual session. Philadelphia, Pa., June 13th to 18th, 1892. Published by the Philadelphia Typographical Union, No. 2, 1892. Illus. portraits.

Pictorial cover; 11¼ x 9 in.

INTERNATIONAL TYPOGRAPHICAL UNION

Cabinet JJ Shelf 1 No. 14

Official souvenir of the 41st session of the International Typographical Union, at Chicago, June 12 - 17, 1893. Illus.

Cloth, oblong; 9-3/8 x 12½ in.

INTERNATIONAL TYPOGRAPHICAL UNION

Cabinet JJ Shelf 1 No. 15

Official souvenir of the 44th annual session, at Syracuse, N. Y. October 10 - 15, 1898. Portraits, illus.

Business meeting, historical biographical sketches, etc.

Half morocco; oblong; 9½ x 12½ x ½ in.

INTERNATIONAL TYPOGRAPHICAL UNION

Cabinet JJ Shelf 1 No. 19

Official convention souvenirs, 1906 - 1909.

52-Session, Aug. 13-18, 1906. Colorado Springs
53 " " 10-17, 1907. Arkansas, Ark.
54- " " 10-15, 1908. Boston, Mass.
55- " " 9-14, 1909. St. Joseph, Mo.

All bound in one volume.

Buckram; 12 x 9¼ x 1-7/8 in.

INTERNATIONAL TYPOGRAPHICAL UNION

Cabinet JJ Shelf 1 No. 21

Official Souvenir. 57th Convention. August 14 - 19, 1911, San Francisco.

Paper; 12 x 9 in.

INTERNATIONAL TYPOGRAPHICAL UNION

Cabinet JJ Shelf 1 No. 22

Convention souvenir. 58th Convention, Cleveland, Ohio, August 12 - 17, 1912.

Articles on business matters, labor questions, etc.

Paper; 12½ x 9¼ in.

INTERNATIONAL TYPOGRAPHICAL UNION

Cabinet JJ Shelf 1 No. 23

Convention souvenir. International Typographical Union, 60th session, Providence, R. I., Aug. 10 - 15, 1914. Illus. Souvenir.

Pictorial paper; 12¼ x 9¼ in.

INTERNATIONAL TYPOGRAPHICAL UNION

Cabinet JJ Shelf 1 No. 25

Official Convention Souvenirs, 1915 - 1917.

61-convention(1915) Aug. 9-14, Los Angeles.
62- " (1916) " 14-19, Baltimore, Md.
63- " (1917) " 13-18, Colorado Springs, Col.

Cloth; 9¼ x 12 x 1½ in.

INTERNATIONAL TYPOGRAPHICAL UNION

Cabinet JJ Shelf 1 No. 30

Souvenir Blue - Book. The 66th Annual Convention at Quebec, Canada. (1920). Illus.

Pictorial paper; 9¼ x 12 in.

INTERNATIONAL TYPOGRAPHICAL UNION

Cabinet JJ Shelf 1 No. 31

Souvenir of 69th Annual Convention. Toronto, Canada, August 11 to 16, 1924. Illus.

Pictorial paper; 8¼ x 11 in.

INTERNATIONAL TYPOGRAPHICAL UNION

Cabinet JJ Shelf 1 No. 32

Souvenir of 70th Annual Convention. Kalamazoo, Mich., August 10 - 15, 1925. Illus.

Pictorial paper; 9-3/8 x 12½ in.

INTERNATIONAL TYPOGRAPHICAL UNION

Cabinet JJ Shelf 1 No. 33

Souvenir of 74th Annual Convention. Seattle, Washington, 1929. Illus.

Cloth; 9¼ x 12 in.

INTERNATIONAL TYPOGRAPHICAL UNION

Cabinet JJ Shelf 1 No. 35

Souvenir of 75th Annual Convention held at Houston, Texas, Sept. 8 - 13, 1930. Illus.

Paper; 9½ x 12¼ in.

INTERNATIONAL TYPOGRAPHICAL UNION

Cabinet JJ Shelf 1 No. 47

Suggested plan of instruction for teaching printing in the public schools. Also I. T. U., Unit 1 - Lesson 1
" 1 - " 2
" 1 - " 3

6 pieces in one envelope.

INTERNATIONAL TYPOGRAPHICAL UNION

Cabinet JJ Shelf 1 No. 45

Union Printers Home, Colorado Springs, Colorado. Eight views, postcards.

In envelope

INTERNATIONAL TYPOGRAPHICAL UNION

Cabinet JJ Shelf 1 No. 27

Union Printers' Home, Silver Anniversary, 1892 - 1917. Souvenir of The 63rd International Typographical Union Convention. Held at Colorado Springs, Colorado, August 13 - 18, 1917.

Fully illustrated with portraits of leading printers.

Paper; 9½ x 12¼ x ½ in.

INTERTYPE CORPORATION

Cabinet Shelf No.

Specimen Books, Types. United States. Intertype (etc.)

Composing Machines. Catalogue. Intertype.

INTRODUCTION OF PRINTING

Cabinet R Shelf 4 No. 172

Canada, introduction of printing into. A brief history by Aegidius Fauteux. Published by the Rolland Paper Company, Montreal, 1930. Illus. facs.

Cloth; 9½ x 6¼ x 7/8 in. In protective case.

INTERNATIONAL TYPOGRAPHICAL UNION

see also

Cabinet Shelf No.

SOCIETIES, PRINTERS', United States

INTRODUCTION OF PRINTING

Cabinet Y Shelf 2 No. 15

Alphabetical list of places where printing was practiced before and up to the year 1500. With titles of first issues, names of printers.

See REICHART, GOTTFRIED Druckorte des xv jahrhunderts...p.3

INTRODUCTION OF PRINTING.

Cabinet V Shelf 4 No. 27

(Canada, Quebec). Débuts de l'imprimerie. Par Raoul Renault. Québec: Imprimé pour l'auteur, 1905 Illus. Wood engravings, and facsimile title page of the Catéchisme de Sens, 1765, the first book printed in Canada.

Half morocco; 10¼ x 7-3/4 in.

~~INTERNATIONALER GRAPHISCHER MUSTER-AUSTAUSCH~~

Cabinet 19 Shelf No.

(Periodical of the) Deutscher Buchdrucker-Vereins, Leipzig, 1889-1897.

See PERIODICALS, PRINTING. Germany. Internationaler Graphischer, etc.

INTER-OCEAN (The)

Cabinet Shelf No.

See Newspapers, special issues.

INTRODUCTION TO PRINTING

Cabinet T Shelf 1 No. 48

Chronological table of the introduction of printing in European countries.

See LUCKOMBE, PHILIP. Concise history of the origin of printing...p.37

INTERNATIONAL TYPOGRAPHICAL UNION

Cabinet Shelf No.

(United States and Canada). Unions divided on 5 day week plan.

(Incident of the business depression of 1930-1931).

Article in Editor & Publihser, vol. 64, pp. 11. May 23, 1931

INTRODUCTION OF PRINTING

Cabinet Y Shelf 3 No. 25

America, (U.S.) Notizen uber die einfuhrung und erste ausbreitung der buchdruckerkunst in America. von J. F. Fabricius. Hamburg, 1841.

Half morocco; 6-7/8 x 4-3/8 x ¼ in.

INTRODUCTION OF PRINTING

Cabinet V Shelf 5 No. 10

(Cologne). Printing introduced in by Nicolas Jenson (?)

See Madden. J.P.A. Lettres d'un Bibliographe. Tome 2, 1873. pp. 121-132.

INTER - OCEAN, CHICAGO see

Cabinet Q Shelf 7 No. 53

CARRIERS' ADDRESSES.

INTRODUCTION OF PRINTING

Cabinet T Shelf 5 No. 29

Bolton, the introduction of printing into...

See SCHOLES, JAS. C. Bolton bibliography ... Manchester, 1886, p.50

INTRODUCTION OF PRINTING

Cabinet S Shelf 5 No. 25

(Connecticut) First book printed in Connecticut by Timothy Green. 1709. Brief note.

Excerpt from Historical Magazine, June, 1858.

In box labeled History of Printing, United States. Miscellaneous items.

INTERTYPE CORPORATION

Cabinet FF Shelf 6 No. 63

Annual Report of Fiscal year ended December 31, 1929.

Item in manila envelope.

INTRODUCTION OF PRINTING

Cabinet V Shelf 5 No. 23

Bordeaux, 1486.

See GAULLIEUR, ERNEST. L'Imprimerie a Bordeaux en 1486...

INTRODUCTION OF PRINTING

Cabinet 00 Shelf 5 No. 3 (2 vols.)

Dates of introduction of printing into various countries...

see Chap. I, pp. I-86, in MADDEN'S History of Irish periodical literature... London, 1867. [2 vols.].

INTRODUCTION OF PRINTING

Cabinet V Shelf 3 No. 21

(European Cities). Imprimerie en Europe aux XV e et XVIe siècles: Les premières productions typographiques et les premiers imprimeurs. Par Leon De George. Paris, 1892.

Chronological account of the first productions of the first printers in all parts of Europe.

Half morocco; 6-1/8 x 4 x ½ in.

INTRODUCTION OF PRINTING

Cabinet V Shelf 6 No. 13

(France, Paris). Brief notices chronoligically arranged, 1470 to 1790. With facsimile of the first book printed in Paris.

In the Bulletin Officiel de l'Union Syndicate des Maitres Imprimeurs. December, 1925.

Paper; 12½ x 9¼ x 1 in.

INTRODUCTION OF PRINTING

Cabinet T Shelf 1 No. 65

(Great Britain) Caxton, to the present time; including, among a variety of curious matter. Its progress in the provinces; with chronological lists of eminent printers in England, Scotland, and Ireland.

Account in "Typographical Antiquities"... By Henry Lemoine. London, 1797.

Half morocco; 7½ x 5-5/8 x 3/8 in. See also T/1/66

INTRODUCTION OF PRINTING

Cabinet V Shelf 3 No. 11

(European Cities) Imprimeries qui existent ou ont existe en Europe. [Additional Supplements 2]: Notice sur les imprimeries ... hors de l'Europe. Par H. Ternaus - Compans. Paris, 1843.

Boards; 8½ x 5¼ in.

INTRODUCTION OF PRINTING

Cabinet W Shelf 3 No. 37

(France. Paris). Épitre adressée a Robert Gaguin le Ie janvier 1472 par Guillaume Fichet, sur l'introduction de l'imprimerie a Paris. Reproduction heliographique de l'exemplaire unique possedé par l'Universite de Bâle. Paris, 1889.

With historical and explanatory preface signed L.D.

Boards; 10 x 6¾ in.

INTRODUCTION OF PRINTING.

Cabinet V Shelf 4 No. 23

(Great Britain). Origines (Les) de l'imprimerie et son introduction en Angleterre. D'après de recentes publicationes Anglaises. Par A. Quantin. Paris, 1877. With author's ex-libris, and printer mark.

Half morocco; 11-3/4 x 8¼ in.

INTRODUCTION OF PRINTING

Cabinet V Shelf 3 No. 15

(European Cities): Tableau chronologique de l'introduction de l'imprimerie dans les principales villes de l'Europe pendant le XVe siècle; les noms des imprimeurs et l'indication de leurs premiers ouvrages.

See Werdet, Edmond. Histoire du Livre en France: Origines du livre-manuscrit, 1275-1470. partie I, p. 352. Paris, 1861

INTRODUCTION OF PRINTING

Cabinet V Shelf 4 No. 20

(France, Paris). Histoire de la typographie: Extrait de l'Encyclopedie modern. Par Ambroise Firmin Didot. Paris, 1882. pp.735-914.

Cloth; 9 x 5-3/4 in. See also V/4/19.

INTRODUCTION OF PRINTING

Cabinet T Shelf 2 No. 45

(Great Britain). Willima Caxton at Westminster. Fac-similes illustrating the labours of William Caxton, and an introduction of printing into England. With a memoir of our first printer, and bibliographical particulars of the illustrations. By Francis Compton Price. London, privately printed. 1877. [The four-hundredth anniversary].

Half morocco; 11-3/8 x 8-7/8 x ½ in.

INTRODUCTION OF PRINTING

Cabinet Y Shelf 2 No. 13

Falkenstein, Dr. Karl. Geschichte der buchdruckerkunst in ihre entstehung und ausbildung... Mit nachbildungen von typen alter beruhmter officinen. Leipzig, 1840.

Numerous fac-simile plates, and at end specimens of Oriental types, also chronological table of places where printing was introduced.

Boards; 11¾ x 9¼ in.

INTRODUCTION OF PRINTING.

Cabinet Shelf No.

(France). See Mellottée, Paul. Histoire economique de l'imprimerie. Tome I. Paris, 1905.

INTRODUCTION OF PRINTING.

Cabinet V Shelf 3 No. 14

L'Imprimerie dans les divers contrées de la terre (The progress of printing in all parts of the world.)

See Chap. VIII tome, I, Dupont's "Histoire de l'Imprimerie." (2 vols.) Paris, 1854.

Half morocco; 7½ x 5-1/8 in.

INTRODUCTION OF PRINTING

Cabinet V Shelf 4 No. 28

France: Chronology of first impressions, and the printers who introduced printing in the towns and provinces.

See pp. 44-68: Débuts de l'Imprimerie en France. Par Arthur Christian, Paris, 1905.

Half morocco; 11¼ x 8 x 1¼ in.

INTRODUCTION OF PRINTING

Cabinet V Shelf 3 No. 19

French Provinces, 1470 to 1700: Chronological index, and alphabetic table of towns.

See Werdet, Edmond, Histoire du Livre en France. Propagation...de l'imprimerie dans les provinces. Partie 4, Paris, 1862.

INTRODUCTION OF PRINTING

Cabinet V Shelf 3 No. 21

L'Imprimerie en Europe aux 15 e et XVIe siecles: Les premières productions typographiques et les premiers imprimeurs. Par Léon DeGeorge. Paris, 1892.

Half morocco; 6-1/8 x 4 x ½ in.

INTRODUCTION OF PRINTING

Cabinet V Shelf 5 No. 2.01

France: Guillaume Fichet et sa famille...[Brief account].

See COUDERC, C. Documents inedits sur Guillaume Fichet...

INTRODUCTION OF PRINTING

Cabinet S Shelf 5 No. 25

(Georgia) Printing introduced in Savannah, 1785, by James Johnston. Brief note.

Excerpt from Historical Magazine, June, 1858.

In box labeled History of Printing, United States. Miscellaneous items.

INTRODUCTION OF PRINTING

Cabinet AA Shelf 1 No. 8

(Italy, Venice). Venezia la prima città fuori della Germania dove si esercitò l'arte della stampa Dissertazione a S. E. il signore Gio: Girolamo Zuccato...di D. Jacopo M.ª Paitoni. Edizione seconda, riveduta, e corretta In Venezia 1772. Apresso Tommaso Betinelli. (The first city after Germany in which the art of printing was practised.)

Half morocco; 8 x 5¾ in.

INTRODUCTION OF PRINTING

Cabinet MM Shelf 3 No. 15

List of places where, and the persons by whom, the art of printing was received prior to the year 1500.

See Johnson, J. Typographia...London, 1824, vol.I, pp.58-64.

INTRODUCTION OF PRINTING

Cabinet S Shelf 5 No. 25.01

New York, 1693, William Bradford.

see

CELEBRATIONS, PRINTERS. United States 1893, New York...

INTRODUCTION OF PRINTING

Cabinet AA Shelf 5 No. 14

(Spain). Introducción y establecimiento de la imprenta en las coronas de Aragon, y Castilla, y de los impresores de los incunables Catalanes. Por S. Sanpere y Miguel. Barcelona, 1909.

Half morocco; 7 x 5 in.

INTRODUCTION OF PRINTING.

Cabinet 75 Shelf 2 No. 8

(Mexico, introduction of printing into: with a list of printers). McMurtrie, Douglas C. The first typefounding in Mexico. A paper for the Bibliographical Society, June, 1927.

In Trans. Biblio. Soc., "The Library," Vol. VIII, 1927-1928, pp. 307-9.

INTRODUCTION OF PRINTING

Cabinet 81 Shelf 2 No. 36

North America, introduction of printing into. - Pioneers of the profession. (Excerpt, newspaper clipping, Albany, Jan., 18, 1846.

Item in MUNSELL, JOEL. "Printers Scraps", vol.VII., p.2.

INTRODUCTION OF PRINTING

Cabinet 26 Shelf 1 No. 16

(Spanish America) Die einführung in den Spanishen Kolonien Südamerikas. von Carla von Müller. [Bio-bibliographical essay].

Item in "Gutenberg-Gesellschaft Jahrbuch, 1927", pp.116-125.

INTRODUCTION OF PRINTING

Cabinet 79 Shelf 2 No. 11

Mexico (Spanish-America) Introduction de la imprenta en America. Carta que al Sr. D. José Gestoso y Perez divige J.T. Medina. Santiago de Chile, 1910.

Cloth; $10\frac{1}{4}$ x 7 in. Chiappa 190

INTRODUCTION OF PRINTING

Cabinet V Shelf 5 No. 23

Notice sur les imprimeries qui existent ou ont existe hors de l'Europe. Par H. Ternaux-Compans. Paris, n.d. [1842].

Alphabetic arrangement of notes relative to the introduction of printing in the United States, Canada, South America, India, Africa, Asia, etc.

Item I in vol. with binder's title "Origin of Printing in France: Pamphlets".

INTRODUCTION OF PRINTING

Cabinet NN Shelf 2 No. 35

United States. Brief notes on the introduction of printing into every State of the Union. With brief biographical sketches.

see

NELSON, WILLIAM. Notes toward the history of American newspapers, vol.1.

INTRODUCTION OF PRINTING.

Cabinet Y Shelf 2 No. 38

[Names of printers and places, alphabetical list of].

See BOGENG, G. A. E. Geschichte der buch druckerkunst ... pp. 647-666.

INTRODUCTION OF PRINTING

Cabinet S Shelf 5 No. 25

(Ohio), Cincinnati, 1795, printing introduced by S. Freeman. Brief note.
Excerpt from Historical Magazine, June, 1858.

In box labeled History of Printing, United States. Miscellaneous items.

INTRODUCTION OF PRINTING

Cabinet AA Shelf 5 No. 3

(Spain). Tipografia Española, ó historia de la introducción, propagación y progresos del arte de la imprenta en España. Su autor Fray Francisco Mendrez. Tomo I. Madrid, 1796.
The second volume of this history was never published, because of the loss of the manuscript.

Tree calf; 8 x $6\frac{1}{4}$ in.

INTRODUCTION OF PRINTING

Cabinet R Shelf 5 No. 150 & 151

New Hampshire, Portsmouth, 1756.

See NEW HAMPSHIRE. Portsmouth, 1756-1856, centennial anniversary...

INTRODUCTION OF PRINTING

Cabinet V Shelf 5 No. 2.01

Paris, Ulrich Gering, and account of the introduction of printing into.

See ALKAN Ainé. Memoire sur le projet d'elever une statue...a Ulrich Gering...Paris, 1879.

INVENTION CONTROVERSY

Cabinet V Shelf 5 No. 1

(Avignon). Documents inédits sur les origines de la typographie, Communication de M. l'abbé Requin: An excerpt from "Bulletin historique et philologique", Paris, 1890.

Documentary evidence to prove that printing was attempted in Avignon in 1444.

Bound in volume "French Typographical Pamphlets", item 11.

INTRODUCTION OF PRINTING

Cabinet 79 Shelf 2 No. 19

(New Mexico. Santa Fe) 1835, Antonio Jost Martinez, memorias. Por Pedro Sanchez. Santa Fe, N.M. 1903.

Stamped cloth; $7\frac{1}{2}$ x $5\frac{1}{4}$ in.

INTRODUCTION OF PRINTING

Cabinet S Shelf 5 No. 25

(Peru) First Peruvian book, printed at Lima, 1621. Brief note.
Excerpt from Historical Magazine, June, 1858.

In box labeled History of Printing, United States. Miscellaneous items.

INVENTION CONTROVERSEY

Cabinet 75 Shelf 1 No. 3

Bibliography of Books relating to Gutenberg-Coster Controversey.

In Trans. Biblio. Soc., Vol. III, 1895-1896, pp. 85-152.

INVENTION CONTROVERSY

Cabinet X Shelf 1 No. 9

Boxhorn, Marcus Zuerius: De typographicae artis inventione, & inventoribus, dissertatio. Lugduni Batavarum, 1640.
A dissertation on the invention and the first inventors of printing. Favors Haarlem. Reprinted in Wolf, "Monumenta Typographica", vol. 1, pp. 813-865.

Full morocco; 7½ x 5½ x 3/8 in.

INVENTION CONTROVERSY

Cabinet X Shelf 1 No. 5

Mallinkrot, Bernard. Ortu ac progressu artis typographicae: Dissertatio historica in quae praeter alia pleraque ad calcographices negocium spectantia de auctoribus et loco inventionis praecipuè inquiritur, proque Moguntinis contra Harlemenses...Coloniae Agrippinae...1640. Portraits of the author, Gutenberg, and Fust.
A collection of testimonies relative to the discovery of printing.

Vellum; 8 x 6¼ in.

INVENTION CONTROVERSY

Cabinet X Shelf 1 No. 33

Munch-Schaubert-Negelein: Primaria quaedam documenta de origine typographiae. Quorum partem primam sub praesidio Christiani Gottlibii Schwarzii...Disquisitione Academicae subiicit Benedictus Guil. Munch. Altdorfi [1740]. II Partem alteram...Jo. Guil. Schaubert. Altdorfi 1740 . III Partem tertiam...Gustavus P. Negelein. Altdorfi [1740]. Three parts each with own title. 1 vol
Three viewpoints based on documentary evidence.

Half morocco; 8-5/8 x 7-1/8 x 3/4 in.

INVENTION CONTROVERSEY

Cabinet T Shelf 1 No. 73

Brief sketch of the contentions of the advocates of Gutenberg. Taken from documents. Numerous facsimiles.

See HODGKIN, JOHN ELIOT. "Rariora",,, London, 1858-1900, vol. 2, p.3 and fol.

INVENTION CONTROVERSIES

Cabinet X Shelf 1 No. 66

Meerman, Gerardo: Origines typographicae. Hague Comitum, Parisiis, Londini, 1765. With plates. 2 vols. in one. Latin text.
The author consulted German, Spanish, French, Italian. Swiss, English and Dutch authors who treated of typography, in order to substantiate his claim in favor of Coster.

Stamped vellum; 10-5/8 x 8-3/4 x 2¼ in.

INVENTION CONTROVERIES cont'd

Cabinet Shelf NO.

Three viewpoints based on documentary evidence.

Half morocco; 8-5/8 x 7-1/8 x 3/4 in.

INVENTION CONTROVERSY.

Cabinet V Shelf 3 No. 2

Dissertation ... Pour éclaircir quelques traits de l'histoire de l'imprimerie, et prouver que Guttemberg n'en est pas l'inventeur; par Fournier le jeune. Paris, 1758.
Bound in with three other tracts, with separate titles, related to the same subject.

Calf; 7¼ x 4¾ x 1¾ in.

INVENTION CONTROVERSY

Cabinet Shelf NO.

Vellum; 8 x 6¼ in.

INVENTION CONTROVERSY

Cabinet S Shelf 5 No. 18

New light on the invention of printing [Rush C. Hawkins]. Excerpt from The Bookmart, Oct. 1886.

Bound in collection "Dawn of Printing", item 13-14.

INVENTION CONTROVERSIES

Cabinet T Shelf 1 No. 24

Ducarel vs. Meerman re invention of printing and its introduction into England.

See DUCAREL, ANDRÉ COLLÉE Letters to Meerman...London, 1781.

INVENTION CONTROVERSY

Cabinet AA Shelf 3 No. 3

Meerman, Gerard: Uitvinding der boekdrukkunst getrokken uit het latynsch werk, met ene vorrede en aanteekenigen van H. Gockinga; hierachter is gevoegt ene lijst der boeken in de Nederlanden gedrukt voor't jaar MD. Amsteldam, 1767, Portrait of Coster.

Boards; 11 x 9 in.

INVENTION CONTROVERSY

Cabinet X Shelf 1 No. 103

Reber, Francis. De primordiis artis imprimendi ac praecipue de inventione typographiae Harlemensi...Berolini, 1856.
"A University thesis, in opposition to the claims of Haarlem.

Boards; 8½ x 5½ in.

INVENTION CONTROVERSY

Cabinet AA Shelf 3 No. 6

Koning, Jacobus: Verhandeling over den oorsprong, de uitvinding, verbetering en volmaking der boekdrukkunst. Door Jacobus Koning. Harlem, 1816. Facsimile.
A prize essay; favors Coster. See also AA/3/7.

Half morocco; 8-3/4 x 5¼ in.

INVENTION CONTROVERSY

Cabinet X Shelf 1 No. 6

(Mentelin,John) Iacobi Menteli, patricii Castro-Theodoricensis de vera typographiae origine paraensis, ad...D. Bernardum A. Malinkrot. Parisiis, 1650. Latin Text.
Concerning the true history of typography, and John Mentelin, the inventor. Reprinted in Wolf "Monumenta Typgraphica", vol. II, pp. 237-365.

Calf; 8-7/8 x 6-3/8 x 5/8 in.

INVENTION CONTROVERSY

Cabinet AA Shelf 3 No. 9

Scheltema, Jacobus en Jacobus Konig: Vier brieven gewisseld tusschen Mr. J. Scheltema en J. Konig over de laatste tegenspraak van het regt van Haarlem op de uitvinding de drukkunst. Te Haarlem, 1823.

Half leather; 8-3/4 x 5 in.

INVENTION CONTROVERSY

Cabinet W Shelf 4 No. 35

Lichtenberg, Johann F: Histoire de l'invention de l'imprimerie, pour servir de défense à la ville de Strassbourg, contre les prétentions de Harlem; avec une préface de M.J.G. Schweighäuser. Strassbourg et Paris: 1825. Portrait of Gutenberg, and facsimiles of his types.
The author rejects the Coster Haarlem legend.

Boards; 9 x 5½ x ⅛ in.

INVENTION CONTROVERSY

Cabinet AA Shelf 3 No. 22

Meurs, Dr. P. Van. De Keulsche Kronick en de Coster Legende van Dr. A. van de Linde, te zamen getoetst. Haarlem, 1870.
Meurs for Coster, van der Linde favors Gutenberg.

Half morocco; 9½ x 5¾ in.

INVENTION CONTROVERSY

Cabinet 14 Shelf 1 No. 7

Schoeffer, Johann I, Mainz, 1518. Livius Historia (etc)

Contains the preface by Carbachius, in which the Invention of Printing is attributed to the father of the printer, Peter Schoffer I.

INVENTION CONTROVERSY

Cabinet AA Shelf 3 No. 1

Scriverius, Petrus: Laure-crans voor Laurens Coster van Haerlem, erste vinder vande boekdruckery. Tot Haerlem, by Adriaen Rooman, ordinaris Stads-Boekdrucker, 1628.
Bound in with Ampzing "Beschryving ende lof der Stad Haerlem." Haerlem, 1628.

Vellum; 7½ x 5-3/4 x 2¼ in.

INVENTION CONTROVERSY

Cabinet AA Shelf 3 No. 13.01

Tweetal bijdragen, betrekklijk de boekdrukkunst. s'Gravenhage, 1844.)Privately printed) A.D.Schinkel.

Favors Coster

Half morocco, 9½ x 6 in.

INVENTION CONTROVERSY

Cabinet LL Shelf 1 NO. 22

Typographia oder die buchdruckerkunst eine erfindung der Deutschen; bei gelegenheit der vierten Harlemer secularfeier zur ehre dieser Kunst in erinnerung gebracht. Essen, 1823.
Combats the Dutch pretensions.
Item at end of Ritschl von Hartenbach's "Neues system geographische charten"... Leipzig, 1840.

Boards; 7 x 4½ x 3/8 in.

INVENTION CONTROVERSY

Cabinet AA Shelf 3 No. 5

Westreenen, van Tiellandt, W. H. J.: Verhandeling over de uitvinding der boekdrukkunst; in Holland oorspronkelijk uitgedacht, te Straatsburg verbeterd in te Menz voltood. Door W. H. J. van Wetreenen. 's Hage, 1809.

Half morocco; 8-7/8 x 5-1/8 in.

INVENTION OF PRINTING

Cabinet QQ Shelf 2 No. 23

(Account, Dutch text, of the invention and progress of printing. With 1 plate)

See FOKKE, AREND. Museum der voornaamste uitvindingen...Amsteldam, n.d. circa 1795, pp.54-65.

INVENTION OF PRINTING

Cabinet T Shelf 2 No. 28

Account of the invention of printing and of the modes and materials used for transmitting knowledge before that took place [together with the] life of William Caxton. Published under the superintendence of The Society for the diffusion of useful knwoledge. London, 1828.

Half morocco; 9-1/8 x 6 x 3/8 in.

INVENTION OF PRINTING

Cabinet E Shelf 1 No. 3

Account under date 1458 in "Supplementum supplementi delle croniche" By Bergomensis. Venice, 1535.

Vellum leaves, over boards; 11¾ x 8½ x 2⅛ in.

INVENTION OF PRINTING.

Cabinet E Shelf 1 No. 43

Allusions to the art of printing, having first passed through Portugal into India and from thence to Europe.
See p. 381 for allusion, and back of book for translation. "Istorie di Mons. Giovio" Venice, 1564. Cavalli.

Parchment; 8¼ x 6 x 1⅝ in.

INVENTION OF PRINTING

Cabinet X Shelf 5 No. 3

Anecdotes of early printers and printing. A letter to the editor of "The Gentleman's Magazine, Oct. 1829. By Shirley Woolmer An excerpt.

p. 37 in vol. with binder's title "Scrap Book, 1705-1891, relating to printing."

INVENTION OF PRINTING

Cabinet X Shelf 1 No. 41

Annus tertius saccularis inventae artis typographicae, sive brevis historica ennarratio de inventione nobilissima artis typographicae...Harlemi, apud Isa cum et Joannem Enschedé. [1741].
An account of the third centenary celebration at Haarlem of the invention of printing, with plates representing the statue of Coster, his house and medals commemorative of him. Includes also a list of works relating to the invention of printing.

cont'd

INVENTION OF PRINTING cont'd

Cabinet Shelf No.

Calf; 7-7/8 x 5 x 1 in.

INVENTION OF PRINTING.

Cabinet V Shelf 4 No. 7

Art de l'Imprimerie; son histoire ... Excerpt from "Arts et Metiers." [Paris, 1773].

Boards; 10¾ x 8½ x 1 in.

INVENTION OF PRINTING

Cabinet V Shelf 1 No. 14

(Avignon) Histoire du livre et de l'imprimerie a Avignon du XIVe au XVIme siècle. Par Pierre Pansier. Avignon, 1922.
Chap. VIII. p.161 for Procope Waldfoghel.

Half morocco; 10-1/8 x 6½ x 2 in. 3 vols. in one.

INVENTION OF PRINTING

Cabinet X Shelf 4 No. 48

Benefit and invention of printing, by John Fox... anno 1684: where he shews, when and by whom printing was invented...London, printed and sold by T. Sowle, 1704.

Boards; 8-3/8 x 6¼ in.

INVENTION OF PRINTING

Cabinet X Shelf 1 No. 1

Bergellanus, Joannes Arnuldus: De Chalcographie inventione, poema encomiasticum. Moguntiae, 1541. Latin text. Title page with the earliest picture of a compositor at his case, in the act of setting type.
The author assigns the year 1450, and Strasburg as the locality of the first printer, Gutenberg.

Half morocco; 7-3/4 x 6-1/8 x ¼ in.

INVENTION OF PRINTING

Cabinet W Shelf 2 No. 1

Bernard, August. Archéologie typographique: Voyage typographico en Allemagne et en Belgique. (Extrait du tome 1er, 2e serie, du Bulletin Bibliophile Belge). Bruxelles, 1853.

Item 9 in volume "Gutenberg, l'inventeur de l'imprimerie - Melanges."

INVENTION OF PRINTING

Cabinet X Shelf 1 No. 3

Besoldu, Christophorus. De bombardis: ac item de typographia, dissertatio historica. (Invention of artillery and also of printing). n.p. 1620.
The author is of the opinion that we are not indebted to the Chinese for the discovery of typography. He does not decide upon the respective claims of Strasburg, Mainz, and Haarlem.

Half morocco; 7-7/8 x 6-1/8 x ¼ in.

INVENTION OF PRINTING

Cabinet U Shelf 5 No. 11

Blades, William: On the present aspect of the question.-Who was the inventor of printing? Being a paper read at a meeting of the Library Association at Birmingham, Sept. 20-23, 1887. London [Privately Printed].
Includes a list of books published upon the subject since 1868.

Half morocco; 11-1/8 x 7¼ x 3/8 in.

INVENTION OF PRINTING.

Cabinet Y
Shelf 3
No. 39

(Books for and against Gutenberg as the inventor of printing). Schriften für und gegen Gutenberg als erfinder.

See MUHLBRECHT, OTTO. Bücherliebhaberei ... Berlin, 1896, pp. 156-66.

INVENTION OF PRINTING

Cabinet X
Shelf 1
No. 100

Bossch, Hermann. Memoria Hieronymi de Bosch rite celebrata a David Jacobi van Lennep, et Carmen de inventae typographiae laude Kostero Harlemensi potenter tandem asserta. Amstelodami, 1817.

Songs in praise of printing, and of Coster the inventor.

Half morocco; 10-3/4 x 9¼ x 3/8 in.

INVENTION OF PRINTING (Gee)

Cabinet U
Shelf 5
No. 54

Bouchot, Henri. (The) Book: its printers.... London, 1890, pp. 1-41

INVENTION OF PRINTING

Cabinet T
Shelf 1
No. 54

Bowyer, William: The origin of printing, in two essays: I. The substance of Dr. Middleton's Dissertation on the origin of printing in England. II. Mr. Meerman's account of the First invention of the Art. An appendix is annexed...London, printed for W. Bowyer and J. Nichols. 1774.

Half calf; 8-3/4 x 5½ x 5/8 in. See also T/1/55.

INVENTION OF PRINTING

Cabinet 79
Shelf 2
No. 27

Brief notes on the invention and development of printing.

see

SANCHEZ, CARLOS ENRIQUE. (La) Imprenta en el Ecuador...Quito, 1935, p. 13 and fol.

INVENTION OF PRINTING.

Cabinet V
Shelf 1
No. 40

Bruges, sur l'invention de l'imprimerie a. Par H. Rommel. St. Augustin, 1892.

Bound in with another item "L'oeuvre de Jean Brito" by Louis Gilliodts-van Severen.

Half morocco; 9 x 5¾ x ½ in.

INVENTION OF PRINTING

Cabinet V
Shelf 4
No. 3

See Caille, Jean de la (Printer, Author). Histoire de l'imprimerie et de la librairie... Paris, 1689.

See also V/4/2.

INVENTION OF PRINTING

Cabinet W
Shelf 2
No. 1

Caselli, Scipione: Cenni sulle invenzione della stampa e inaugurazione della statue di Guttemberg in Magonza e Strasburgo. Con note aggiunta. Forli, 1841. Pamphlet.

Item 24 in volume "Gutenberg, l'inventeur de l'imprimerie - Melanges."

INVENTION OF PRINTING

Cabinet X
Shelf 2
No. 8

(Celebration of the third centenary of the invention of printing. Has brief biographical notices in the speeches on this occasion. Nuremberg, 1740)

Acta des zum feyerlich andenken der buchdruckerkunst. Nurnberg, 1740. [Edited by J.B. Röder]

Half morocco; 14 x 8½ in.

INVENTION OF PRINTING

Cabinet AA
Shelf 1
No. 42

Cennini, Di Bernardi e dell'arte della stampa in Firenze nei primi cento anni dall'invenzione di essa...Giuseppe Ottino, Firenze, 1871.

Half morocco; 8-3/4 x 6 in.

INVENTION OF PRINTING

Cabinet V
Shelf 4
No. 2

Chevillier, André. Origine de l'imprimerie... Dissertation historique et critique. Divisée en quatre parties... Paris, 1694.

Bound in with Histoire de l'imprimerie et de librairie... Par Jean Caille. Paris 1689.

Calf; 10-1/8 x 7¼ x 1¼ in. See also V/4/23.

INVENTION OF PRINTING

Cabinet S
Shelf 3
No. 175

(China) Invention of printing in China and its spread Westward. By Thomas Francis Carter. Columbia University Press, New York, 1925.

Cloth; 9½ x 7¼ x 1¼ in.

INVENTION OF PRINTING

Cabinet 26
Shelf 1
No. 17

Chinese background of the European invention of printing. By Thomas F. Carter.

Article in the Gutenberg-Gesellschaft Jahrbuch, 1928. pp.9-14.

INVENTION OF PRINTING

Cabinet U
Shelf 5
No. 24

Cologne Chronicle, its story of the invention of printing.

see

POLLARD, A. W. Fine Books... London, 1912, p.34

INVENTION OF PRINTING

Cabinet 26
Shelf 1
No. 21

(Concerning the history of the invention of printing) Anmerkungen zur erfindungsgeschichte der buchdruckerkunst. Von G.A.E. Bogeng.

Essay in "Gutenberg-Gesellschaft Jahrbuch, 1931", pp.38-72.

INVENTION OF PRINTING

Cabinet AA
Shelf 3
No. 11

Coster, Lourens Janszoon. Aanmerkingen op de gedenkschriften wegens het vierde Eeuwgetijde van de uitvinding der boekdrukkunst, door Lourens Janszoon Koster... 'sGravenhage, 1824.

Celebration, fourth century of printing, the invention of Coster.

Half morocco; 9 x 5½ in.

INVENTION OF PRINTING

Cabinet JJ
Shelf 3
No. 2

Coster, Laurens Janzoon, favored as the inventor of printing in an address presented to the Faustus Association, Boston, Mass., by John Russell, Oct. 4, 1808.

Half morocco; 9½ x 6 x ¾ in.

INVENTION OF PRINTING.

Cabinet X
Shelf 2
No. 12

Coster, Laurens Janszoon. Het derde Jubeljaar der uitgevondene boekdrukkunst der Laurens Jansz. Koster...Door Johann Christian Seiz. Gedrukt by Isaack en Johannes Enschede, 1740.

An account of the third centenary celebration at Haarlem of the invention of printing. With plates representing the statue of Coster, his house, and medals commemorative of him. Includes also, a list of works relating to the invention of printing.

(Cont'd)

Cabinet
Shelf
No.

A Latin translation of the above will be found in Cabinet X/1/41.

Half morocco; 8½ x 5½ x 1 in.

INVENTION OF PRINTING

Cabinet RR
Shelf 2
No. 11

Découverte de l'imprimerie.

See PIZZETTA, J. Histoire d'ume feuille de papier...Paris, 1868. p.71-96.

INVENTION OF PRINTING

Cabinet U
Shelf 4
No. 1

Discovery of the art of printing: Literary history of the Middle Ages...and the state of learning from the close of the reign of Augustus, to its revival in the 15th century. By Rev. Joseph Berington. London, 1814.

Calf; 11¼ x 8-7/8 x 1-3/4 in.

INVENTION OF PRINTING.

Cabinet X
Shelf 2
No. 10

Coster, Laurens Janszoon. Lof der drukkunst te Haerlem uitgevonden door, omtrent het jaer 1440. Jakob Kortebrant, Te Delf, Pieter vander Kloot, 1740. Interesting printing mark

Eulogium of Coster in verse, written in Dutch. Includes a list of towns and the date when, it is stated, printing was introduced.

Half morocco; 9½ x 7½ x ½ in.

INVENTION OF PRINTING

Cabinet AA
Shelf 3
No. 2

Het derde jubeljaar der uitgevondene boekdrukkonst...Door Johann Christiaan Seiz. Haarlem. Gedrukt by Isaak en Johannes Enschede. 1740.

This is a Dutch version of "Annus Tertius" by the same author. See X/1/41.

Morocco; 8¼ x 5 x 1 in.

INVENTION OF PRINTING

Cabinet W
Shelf 2
No. 1

(A) Discovery relating to the history of printing: Gutenberg's first types, and what became of them - Albert Pfister, printer at Bamberg.- The 36 line Bible. [French text] By Henri Helbig. Bruxelles, 1855.

Item 11 in volume "Gutenberg, l'inventeur de l'imprimerie - Melanges."

INVENTION OF PRINTING

Cabinet U
Shelf 5
No. 42

Coster, Laurence Janszoon the claims of considered--Claims based on tradition--evidence of the types, etc.

In Skeen's "Early typography". Ceylon, 1872, p. 201

INVENTION OF PRINTING

Cabinet V
Shelf 4
No. 8

Des Roches, J. Nouvelles recherches sur l'origine de l'imprimerie dans lesquelles on fait voir que le premier idée en est due aux Brabancons. Lués à la Séance de 8 Janvier. Bruxelles. l'Academie de Bruxelles, 1777.

Half morocco; 10 x 8 in.

INVENTION OF PRINTING.

Cabinet V
Shelf 5
No. 8

Documents sur l'Art d'Imprimer a l'aide de planches en bois, de planches en pierre et de types mobiles, invente en Chine, bien longtemps avant que l'Europe en fit usage; extraits des livres Chinois. Par Julien Stanislas. Paris, 1847.

Bound in volume "Five French Typographical Items, 1809-1862".

INVENTION OF PRINTING.

Cabinet V
Shelf 3
No. 6

(Daunou, Pierre Francois). Analyse des opinions diverses sur l'origine de l'imprimerie. Par Daunou ... Paris, Frimaire, An XI (1802).

Boards, leather back; 8-1/8 x 5-1/8 x 3/8 in.

INVENTION OF PRINTING

Cabinet S
Shelf 1
No. 9

DeVinne, Theo. L. The invention of printing. A Collection of facts ... descriptive of early prints and playing cards, the block-books of the fifteenth century, the legends of Lourens Janszoon Coster, of Harlem, and the work of John Gutenberg and his associates. By Thos. L. Devinne. New York, 1876. Illus. See also S/1/10.

Half morocco; 9½ x 6¾ in.

INVENTION OF PRINTING

Cabinet D
Shelf 2
No. 47

Earliest known book that refers to the invention of printing by Gutenberg. It was printed in 1499.

See Incunabula. Chronica van der hilliger Stat van Coellen. p.312.

INVENTION OF PRINTING

Cabinet T
Shelf 1
No. 73

Dawn of typography documents. Numerous facs.

See HODGKIN, JOHN ELIOT. "Rariora"... London, 1858-1900, vol.2.

INVENTION OF PRINTING

Cabinet Y
Shelf 3
No. 79

DeVinne, Theodore Low. Der schlussel zur erfindung der typographie. Ein abschnitt aus dem werke "The invention of printing". New York, 1876. Aus dem Englischen ubersetzt von Dr. Oscar Jolles. (Key to the discovery of printing: An extract from The invention of Printing by T. L. DeVinne. Translated from the English by Dr. Oscar Jolles, Berlin, 1921.

Boards; 11½ x 8¼ x ¼ in.

INVENTION OF PRINTING

Cabinet Y
Shelf 1
No. 23

Earliest witnesses (1460-1517) and commentators on the invention ov printing. Citations from original documents.

See LINDE, ANTONIOUS van der. Geschichte der erfindung...Berlin, 1886. See vol.3, p.723 and following.

INVENTION OF PRINTING.

Cabinet V
Shelf 6
No. 2

Débuts de l'imprimerie à Mayence et à Bamberg, ou description des lettres d'indulgence ... imprimées en 1454. Par Léon de Laborde. Paris, 1840. Facsimiles.

Boards; 14 x 11¾ in.

INVENTION OF PRINTING

Cabinet S
Shelf 5
No. 4

Discovery of printing, 1400-1440, the...By Charles Winslow Hall. Illus. excerpt from the National Magazine, "Nobility of the Trades Series", Dec., 1911, Jan., 1912.

Item 17 in vol. with binder's title "Various printers and their plants", vol. I; also Vol. 2, S/5/6, item 5.

INVENTION OF PRINTING

Cabinet U
Shelf 5
No. 28

Early printed books. By E. Gordon Duff. London, 1893. Illus.

Invention of printing, pp.1-38

Cloth; 8-3/8 x 5-1/8 in.

INVENTION OF PRINTING

Cabinet D Shelf 4 No. 55

Early references (1540) to the invention of printing. In Polydori Vergilii...De rerum inventoribus. Libri VIII. Basileae. 1540.

See pp. 105-6

Boards; 6½ x 4-1/8 x 1¼ in.

INVENTION OF PRINTING

Cabinet T Shelf 1 No. 42

Enquiry into the origin of printing in Europe... By a Lover of Art. London, 1752.

The book is mainly concerned with wood and chiaroscuro printing. The work is by John Baptist Johnson.

Half morocco; 7¾ x 5 in.

INVENTION OF PRINTING

Cabinet AA Shelf 3 No. 14

Enschedé, Joh. en Zonen: Uitvinding der boekdrukkunst. Haarlem. Joh. Enschedé en Zonen 1854. Portrait of Coster. Illus.

Coster is here credited with the invention of printing, Gutenberg with its improvement, Schoeffer with its perfecting.

Leather; 7-1/8 x 5-3/8 in.

INVENTION OF PRINTING

Cabinet X Shelf 2 No. 38

(Die) Erfindung der buchdruckerkunst, ihre ersten anfänge und ihre ent-wickeling. Nebst einem berichte uber die vierte säkularfeier dieser erfindung in Strassburg. Ein gedenk-und lesebüchlein für volk und schule. C. Kuntz. Strassburg, 1840.

Morocco; 5½ x 3½ x 3/8 in.

INVENTION OF PRINTING

Cabinet X Shelf 2 No. 31

Erfindung der buchdruckerkunst und ihre folgen ... von C.L.Schwabe, Leipzig, 1840.

Boards; 6-3/8 x 4-1/8 in.

INVENTION OF PRINTING

Cabinet Y Shelf 2 No. 28

Erfindung der buchdruckerkunst. Zum funfhundertsten geburtsday Johann Gutenbergs. Mit 15 kunstbeilagen und 100 abbildungen. Beilefeld und Leipzig. 1900.

Limp cloth; 10-1/8 x 7 x 3/8 in.

INVENTION OF PRINTING

Cabinet Y Shelf 1 No. 92.02

Erfindung der druckkunst und ihre erste ausbreitung in den Landern Europas. Vortrag von Dr. Konrad Haebler in der Generalversammlung der Gutenberg Gesellschaft am 22 Juni 1930. Pamphlet.

With other items in manila envelope.

INVENTION OF PRINTING

Cabinet 26 Shelf 1 No. 17

Erfindung Gutenbergs und der Chinische und frühhollandische bucherdruck. von Gottfried Zedler.

Article in the Gutenberg-Gesellschaft Jahrbuch 1928. pp. 50-57.

INVENTION OF PRINTING.

Cabinet X Shelf 5 No. 3

Essay on the invention of printing. By W. Williams n.d.n.p. Newspaper clipping [1794]

p. 41 in vol. with binder's title "Scrap-Book, 1705-1891, relating to printing."

INVENTION OF PRINTING

Cabinet S Shelf 5 No. 37

Essence of Gutenberg's invention. By Gustav Mori.

Illus. article in ARS TYPOGRAPHICA, vol.2, No.2, Oct.,1925, p.101

INVENTION OF PRINTING

Cabinet V Shelf 6 No. 8

Étapes (Les) de l'imprimerie. Par L. de Belfort de la Roque. [Illus. of an early printing office, after the design of Jean Stradamus, at Bruges.]

See Brunel, Georges. Le livre à travers les ages. Paris, 1894. pp.18-22.

INVENTION OF PRINTING.

Cabinet V Shelf 5 No. 10

Étude sur Gutenberg et sur Schoiffer. Par J.P.A. Madden. Versailles, 1874. In "Lettres d'un Bibliographe." Tomes II - III. 1873-4.

Half morocco; 9-5/8 x 6-3/8 x 1-1/8 in.

INVENTION OF PRINTING

Cabinet L Shelf 1 No. 46

Evidence of Junius, Coornhert, and Guicciardini, in favor of Coster.

See SINGER, SAMUEL WELLER Researches into the history of playing cards ...London, 1816 [index]

INVENTION OF PRINTING

Cabinet Y Shelf 2 No. 13

Falkenstein, Dr. Karl. Geschichte der buchdruckerkunst...Ein denkmal zur vierten säcular-feier der erfindung der typographie. Leipzig, 1840. Numerous facsimiles, and specimens of Oriental types.

"This history is the most important of the works published in Germany, although not always correct in its historical data." B. & W.

Boards; 11¾ x 9¼ x 1¾ in.

INVENTION OF PRINTING.

Cabinet E Shelf 4 No. 27

Faxarda, Didaco Saavedra. Idea ... Symbolis CI Paris, 1660.

Following dedication: Picture of a printing press, and an account of the invention of printing addressed to the reader.

Vellum; 5¼ x 8 x 1 in.

INVENTION OF PRINTING

Cabinet U Shelf 5 No. 24

Fichet, Guillaume, letter on invention of printing.

See POLLARD, A.W. Fine Books... London, 1912, pp.33, 44, 70

INVENTION OF PRINTING

Cabinet S Shelf 1 No. 135

(The) Fichet letter, the earliest document ascribing to Gutenberg the invention of printing. By Douglas C. McMurtrie. With reproduction of the letter in collotype and a translation of the text by W.A. Montgomery. New York, 1927.

Boards; 11½ x 8-1/8 in.

INVENTION OF PRINTING

Cabinet W Shelf 2 NO. 1

(Fichet's letter (1 January 1472?) to Gaguin, in which he mentions Gutenberg, declaring him to have been the original inventor of the art of printing). Guillermi Fichet ... quam ad Robertum Gaguinum de Gutenberg et de artis impressoriae in Gallia primordiis nec non de orthographiae utilitate conscripsit. Epistola ... Edidit Ludovicus Sieber. Basileae, 1887.

Item 16 in volume "Gutenberg, l'inventeur de l'imprimerie - Melanges."

INVENTION OF PRINTING

Cabinet V Shelf 1 No. 13

(France) Origines de l'imprimerie en France: Premiers essais à Avignon en 1444. Par A. Claudin, Paris, 1898.

Half morocco; 9-1/8 x 5-3/4 x 3/8 in.

INVENTION OF PRINTING

Cabinet AA Shelf 3 No. 21

Gutenberg. Door Dr. A. van der Linde. (Dutch text) The Hague, April 17, 1870.

Half morocco; 9 x 5¾ in.

INVENTION OF PRINTING

Cabinet X Shelf 2 No. 60

Gutenberg in Mainz; seine erfindung und seine werke

See BOCKENHEIMER, K.G. Gutenberg-Feier in Mainz, 1900, p.73.

INVENTION OF PRINTING

Cabinet V Shelf 4 No. 17

Frère, Ed.: Considérations sur les origines typographiques. Par Ed. Frère. Rouen, 1850.

Half morocco; 9½ x 6¼ in.

INVENTION OF PRINTING

Cabinet AA Shelf 5 No. 139

Gutenberg, Johann.

See Scheibler, H. Bogtrykkerkunstens og avidernes historie ... Kristiania, 1910.

INVENTION OF PRINTING

Cabinet V Shelf 5 No. 1

Gutenberg inventeur de l'Imprimerie: 1400-1469. Par A. De Lamartine. Paris, 1853. Pamphlet. pp. 49.

Bound in volume "French Typographical Pamphlets", item I

INVENTION OF PRINTING

Cabinet T Shelf 2 No. 70

From cylindrical records of Babylon and Persepolis to the first printed Bible.

Chapter 1, in "Caxton and the art of printing". London: The Religious Tract Society (1850)

Half morocco; 6-1/8 x 3¾ in.

INVENTION OF PRINTING

Cabinet S Shelf 4 No. 60

Gutenberg and the art of printing. By Emily C. Pearson. Boston, 1871. Illus.

A popular history of the invention and progress of printing.

Cloth; 7¾ x 5¼ in.

INVENTION OF PRINTING

Cabinet W Shelf 2 No. 1

Gutenberg (Jean ou Hans Gensfleisch), par M. Ambroise Firmin-Didot. Extrait de la nouvelle Biographie Génerale, publiée par MM. Firmin Didot, frères et fils. Paris, n.d.

Bio-bibliographical account.

Item 10 in volume "Gutenberg, l'invention de l'imprimerie - Melanges."

INVENTION OF PRINTING

Cabinet X Shelf 2 No. 25

Gedenk-buch der vierten jubelfeier der erfindung der buchdruckerkunst. Mainz, 1840.

Includes biographies of Gutenberg, Fust and Peter Schoeffer.

Boards; 9¾ x 6½ in.

INVENTION OF PRINTING

Cabinet W Shelf 2 No. 1

(Gutenberg and the invention of printing at Mainz: with an inquiry concerning the claims of Haarlem, Strassburg, Bamberg)

See SCHULZ, OTTO AUGUST. Gutenberg oder geschichte der buchdruckerkunst...pp.2-15

INVENTION OF PRINTING

Cabinet S Shelf 4 No. 68.01

Gutenberg, Johann, and the invention of printing. By Karl Dziatsko. Translated by E.F. Kunz. July, 1903. Excerpt from the Literary Collector.

With portrait from a woodcut by an unknown master of the 16th cent.

In box marked "Pamphlets and excerpts relating to Gutenberg".

INVENTION OF PRINTING

Cabinet X Shelf 1 No. 19

(De) Germaniae miraculo optimo, maximo typis, literarum, earumque differentiis, Dissertatio ...Paulus Pater. Prostat Lipsiae, anno 1710.

Favors Gutenberg.

Half morocco; 9 x 7¼ x 3/8 in.

INVENTION OF PRINTING

Cabinet Y Shelf 1 No. 16

Gutenberg den erfinder der buchdruckerkunst und das in ersten durckhause aufgefundene fragment der erste druckerpresse. von Karl Klein. Mainz, 1857.

Discovery of a fragment of a press supposed to have belonged to Gutenberg.

Boards; 7-1/8 x 5 x 3/8 in. See also Y/1/15

INVENTION OF PRINTING

Cabinet W Shelf 2 NO. 1

Gutenberg, Johann, et l'invention de l'imprimerie a Strasbourg. Courte notice publiee a l'occasion de quatrieme anniversaire seculaire de cette invention celebre a Strasbourg les 24, 25 et 26 juin, 1840. Le Roux, printer. Pamphlet.

Item 22 in volume "Gutenberg, l'inventeur de l'imprimere - Melanges."

INVENTION OF PRINTING

Cabinet Y Shelf 2 No. 7 3 vols.

Geschichte der erfindung der buchdruckerkunst durch Johann Gensfleisch, genannt Gutenberg zu Mainz...von Carl A. Schaab. Mainz, 1830-1831. (3 vols.). vol. 1, portrait of Gutenberg; vol. II, 3 folding plates and portrait of Fust; vol. III, portrait of Schöffer. Chronological index, and general index in vol. 3.

Half morocco, each vol. 8¾ x 5½ in.

INVENTION OF PRINTING

Cabinet W Shelf 2 No. 140

Gutenberg et l'invention de l'imprimerie. Par Ch. Delon. Deuzième édition. Paris, 1884. Illus.

Half morocco; 5-7/8 x 3-3/4 in.

INVENTION OF PRINTING

Cabinet U Shelf 5 No. 42

Gutenberg, Johann, first attempts at typography, etc.

See Skeen, William. Early typography ...Ceylon, 1872, pp. 36-68.

INVENTION OF PRINTING

Cabinet Y Shelf 2 No. 23

(Gutenberg, Johann; his ancestore; in Strasburg; in Mainz; his death; monuments erected to him, etc.)

See LORCK, CARL B. Handbuch der geschichte...Leipzig, 1882-1883, pp. 23-36

INVENTION OF PRINTING

Cabinet W Shelf 2 No. 1

Guttemberg. Procès de: Dissertations sur quelques points curieux. Par Paul L. Jacob. Paris, 1847. Pamphlet.
Claims to establish the exact date of the invention of moveable types by Gutenberg.

Item 1 in volume "Gutenberg, inventeur de l'imprimerie - Mélanges."

INVENTION OF PRINTING

Cabinet MM Shelf 6 No. 77

Hamilton, Frederick W. The invention of typography. A brief sketch of the invention of printing, and how it came about. "Typographic Technical Series for Apprentices", Part VIII, No.50. The United Typothetae of America. Illus.

Cloth; 8 x 5 in.

INVENTION OF PRINTING.

Cabinet Y Shelf 1 No. 1

Gutenberg, Johann, zum gedachtnis an, 1468-1918. Dem toten zur ehr', den lebenden zur lehr'! von Johann Christ. Gottsched.
Illustrated bio-historical account. Excerpt from "Typographische Mitteilungen," Juni, 1918. Leipzig.

Item in box labelled "German pamphlets and Excerpts relating to Gutenberg."

INVENTION OF PRINTING

Cabinet X Shelf 1 No. 59

Guttenbergio, Joanne, de typographia Moguntiae inventa...

See QUIRINI, ANGELO MARIA (Card.) Liber singularis...Lindaugiae, 1761, pp. 2-43

INVENTION OF PRINTING

Cabinet T Shelf 4 No. 137

Hartshorne, Charles Henry. The origin of printing. Being the substance of a lecture delivered to the Northampton Mechanics Institute, December, 1851. Northampton (England): Thomas Phillips, Printer.

Brochure, in envelope

INVENTION OF PRINTING.

Cabinet X Shelf 5 No. 3

Gutenberg, John [Biographical account of the man and his invention]. n.a.n. Illus. account. Extract from unidentified periodical [1876].

Item 33 in vol. with binder's title "Scrap-Book, 1705-1891, relating to printing."

INVENTION OF PRINTING

Cabinet Y Shelf 4 No. 61

(Gutenberg-Coster) Buchgeschichte die grundlagen der erfindung Gutenbergs).

pp.1-70 of Bohatta's "Einfuhrung in die buchkunde"...Vienna, 1928.

INVENTION OF PRINTING

Cabinet V Shelf 4 No. 21

Helbig, H. Notes et dissertations relatives a l'histoire de l'imprimerie: Extrait du tome XVIII du Bulletin du Bibliophile Belge. Bruxelles, n. d. [1863].

Cloth; 10 x 6½ in.

INVENTION OF PRINTING

Cabinet L Shelf 4 No. 18

Gutenberg, John, not the inventor of printing.

See Savage, William. Practical hints on decorative printing...London, 1822, p.1.

INVENTION OF PRINTING

Cabinet V Shelf 3 No. 15

Gutenberg, Fust, Schoeffer. [Biographical sketch of each, with a critical examination relating to the discovery and the discoverer of printing].
See Werdet, Edmond. Histoire du Livre en France. depuis les plus reculés jusqu'en 1789...Origines du livre-manuscrit, 1275-1470. Part I, Paris 1861. pp. 214 to 293.

INVENTION OF PRINTING

Cabinet U Shelf 1 No. 1c

Hessels, J. A. Bibliographical tour. [1907].
The author in order to strengthen his theory concerning Coster as the inventor of printing, undertakes the tour for the purpose of examining and collecting various editions of the "Speculum."

In Excerpts relating to printing from "The Library,", 1908, pp. 282-307.

INVENTION OF PRINTING.

Cabinet T Shelf 1 No. 45

[Gutenberg proofs ... Invention of printing claimed by Lawrence Coster, n.p.n.d. Anonymous. Prior to 1839].
Favors Gutenberg in this brief account of the invention of typography.

Half morocco; 10 x 6-7/8 x ¼ in.

INVENTION OF PRINTING

Cabinet X Shelf 2 No. 35

Gutenbergs-Jubiläum des neunzehnten jahrhunderts. Offenbach, 1837. Programm, von Georg Stuchrad.
An account of the Offenbach celebration in 1837, and the invention of printing in Germany.

Half morocco; 7-7/8 x 4-7/8 x 5/8 in.

INVENTION OF PRINTING.

Cabinet V Shelf 6 No. 3

Histoire de l'invention de l'imprimerie par les monuments. Album typographique exécuté à l'occasion de Jubilé Européan de l'invention de l'imprimerie [Par E. Duverger]. Paris, 1840. Facsimile, representations of early type founding apparatus, portraits of Gutenberg, engraving of a type-mould made by Garamond.

Boards; 13½ x 10½ in..

INVENTION OF PRINTING

Cabinet 26 Shelf 1 No. 19

Gutenberg und die nacherfinder. von Otto Hupp. Illus.
Bibliographical historical account of Gutenberg's invention, and of his succeeding inventors.
Article in the "Gutenberg-Gesellschaft Jahrbuch" 1929, pp.31-100.

INVENTION OF PRINTING

Cabinet V Shelf 2 No. 48

See Gutenberg's Law Suit in 1439. Debut de l'imprimerie a Strasbourg.....Par Leon de Laborde.

INVENTION OF PRINTING

Cabinet V Shelf 4 No. 20

Histoire de la typographie: Extrait de l'Encyclopédie modern. Par Ambroise-Firmin Didot. Paris, 1882.

Cloth, 9 x 5¾ in. See also V/4/19..

INVENTION OF PRINTING

Cabinet T Shelf 5 No. 77

Historical essay on the origin of printing. Translated from the French of Serna-Santander, M. de la, by T. Hodgson. Newcastle, 1819.
Favors Gutenberg.

Calf; 7½ x 5 x ½ in.

INVENTION OF PRINTING.

Cabinet E Shelf 4 No. 30

Humane industry; or a manual of most useful arts. (Several authors). London, 1661.
For allusions to printing see p. 62 of above book.

Half morocco; 6-1/2 x 4-1/2 x 5/8 in.

INVENTION OF PRINTING

Cabinet L Shelf 1 No. 46

Junius's account of Coster's discovery of printing at Haarlem.

See SINGER, SAMUEL WELLER. Researches into the history of playing cards...London, 1816, p.110

INVENTION OF PRINTING

Cabinet T Shelf 1 No. 31

History of printing from its first invention in the City of Mentz to its first progress and propagation...By S. Palmer, printer. London, 1732.

Calf; 10 x 8 x 1½ in.

INVENTION OF PRINTING

Cabinet AA Shelf 3 No. 43

Iets over de uitvinding der boekdrukkunst. Door J. Smits. Dordrecht, 1856 (Notes concerning the invention of printing). Pamphlet.
Bound in volume "De Coster Legende." 1856, 1904, 1922.

Half morocco; 11 x 7½ in.

INVENTION OF PRINTING

Cabinet Y Shelf 1 No. 3

Koehler, Johann David. Hochverdiente und aus bewahrten urkunden wohlbeglaubte ehrenrettung Johann Guttenbergs...Leipzig, 1741.

Beginning at p.43, quotations from several source books which relate to the invention of printing. Also at end several poetical effusions, some in Latin.

Half morocco; 8¾ x 7 x ½ in.

INVENTION OF PRINTING

Cabinet T Shelf 1 No. 65

History, origin, and progress of the art of printing, from its invention in Germany to the end of the 17th century.
Account in "Typographical Antiquities"... By Henry Lemoine...London, 1797.

Half morocco; 7½ x 5-5/8 x 3/8 in. See also T/1/66

INVENTION OF PRINTING

Cabinet W Shelf 1 No. 115

Imprimerie: See p. 141 in "Le livre et les arts qui s'y rattachent ... Par M. P. Louisy." Paris, 1886. Illus. Printer marks, facsimile etc.

INVENTION OF PRINTING

Cabinet W Shelf 4 No. 07

Konig, Jacques. Dissertation sur l'origine l'invention et le perfectionnement de l'imprimerie. Par Jacques Konig. Traduit du Hollandais Amsterdam, 1819. Specimens of early types and portraits of Koster and his son.

Half morocco; 9¼ x 5½ in.

INVENTION OF PRINTING

Cabinet U Shelf 5 No. 24

Holland, and the invention of printing.

see
POLLARD, A. W. Fine Books... London, 1912, p.32

INVENTION OF PRINTING

Cabinet PP Shelf 3 No. 1

L'Invention de l'imprimerie. (Brief account)

See LE GALLOIS (le sieur) Traité de plus belles bibliotheques...Paris, 1680, pp.153, 156-164.

INVENTION OF PRINTING

Cabinet AA Shelf 3 No. 7

Koning, Jacobus. Bijdragen tot de geschiedenis der boekdrukkunst...Haarlem, 1818.
With portrait of Coster on p.52.

Half morocco; 9¼ x 5-3/8 in.

INVENTION OF PRINTING

Cabinet 26 Shelf 1 No. 20

Holländische frühdruck und die ersten versuche Gutenberg's in Strassburg. von Gottfried Zedler.
Biblio-historical account of the first Holland printing, and Gutenberg's first experiments.

Article in the "Gutenberg-Gesellschaft Jahrbuch" 1930. pp.53-72.

INVENTION OF PRINTING

Cabinet AA Shelf 2 No. 21

Invenzione della stampe e Giovanni Guttemberg. Scoperta delle matrici.--Pamfilo Castaldi e i caratteri mobili.
See Lambiasi, Enrico: Aldo Pio Manuzio, tiopgrafo ... Studio storico--critico. Rome, 1911. P. 11

INVENTION OF PRINTING

Cabinet AA Shelf 3 No. 6

Koning, Jacobus. Verhandeling, over den oorsprong, de uitvinding, verbetering en volmaking der boekdrukkunst. Haarlem, 1816.

Half morocco; 8¾ x 5¼ in.

INVENTION OF PRINTING

Cabinet 2 Shelf 1 No. 30

Hugo, Hermannus. De prima scribendi origine... Antverpiae, ex officina Plantiniana, apud Balthasarem et Ioannem Moretos. 1617.
Chap. 34 of the above work "De inventione Typographiae".

Tooled morocco; 7¼ x 4¾ x 1-1/8 in.

INVENTION OF PRINTING.

Cabinet E Shelf 4 No. 52

Joannes Cuthenbergus natione Theutonicus ... hane imprimendarum literarum artem excogitavit, ...
The above account of the invention of printing by a citizen of Mainz, will be found on p. 141 of Polydorus "De rerum inventoribus" Noviomagi, 1671.

Vellum; 5 x 3 x 1½ in.

INVENTION OF PRINTING

Cabinet AA Shelf 4 No. 6

Koster, Louwerijsz Janzn. Door P. Bausch. [Reprinted from the Publisher's "Nieuwsblad"] 1922-1923. [Amsterdam]. Facsimile.
A bibliographical study based on authorities in favor of Coster.

Half morocco; 10-3/8 x 6¾ x 3/8 in.

INVENTION OF PRINTING

Cabinet V Shelf 3 No. 5

See Lambinet Pierre. Origine de l'impirmerie d'apres les titres authentiques...Paris, 1810.

INVENTION OF PRINTING

Cabinet U Shelf 5 No. 24

Mainz and the invention of printing.

see POLLARD, A. W. Fine Books... London, 1912, p.44

INVENTION OF PRINTING

Cabinet V Shelf 5 No. 23

(Mentel, John, native of Schlestadt)

See DURLAN, A. Quelques mots sur l'origine de l'imprimerie...Schlestadt, 1840.

INVENTION OF PRINTING

Cabinet 60 Shelf 1 No. 47

Leroy, Louis (Luigi Regio): Vicissitudine o mutabile varieta delle cose ... Tradotta dal Sig. Cavalier Hercole Cato. In Vineta, 1585 Presso Aldo.

pp. 54 and 274. Here the invention is accredited to the Portugese. An account follows of writing and writing materials, and a full description of the process of printing, types, etc.

Boards; 8 x 6 x 1 in.

INVENTION OF PRINTING

Cabinet V Shelf 4 No. 5

Marchand, Prosper. Histoire de l'origine et des premiers progres de l'imprimerie. [Second part]: Histoire de l'imprimerie; second partie, contenant diverses pieces importantes pour la confirmation de la premier. La Haye, 1740. Frontispiece is an allegorical copper plate engraving by Schley, 1739.

Includes Maittaires "Dissertatio de origine Typographiae" concerning the introduction of printing in England

Calf; 10-1/8 x 8-1/8 x 1 in.

INVENTION OF PRINTING

Cabinet X Shelf 1 No. 6

Mentelin, Jacques. De vera typographiae origine Paraenesis, ad sapientissimum virum D. Bernardum a Malinkrot, Monasteriensem Decanum. Paris, 1650. Robert Ballard, Printer.

Calf; 8-3/4 x 6½ x ½ in.

INVENTION OF PRINTING

Cabinet V Shelf 3 No. 2

Lettre sur l'origine de l'imprimerie servant de réponse aux Observations publiées par M. Fournier, sur l'ouvrage de M. Schoepflin, intitulé: Vindiciae Typographicae. Strasbourg, 1761.

Bound in with Observations...Paris, 1760, and Dissertation sur l'origine de graver en bois. Paris, 1758.

Leather; 7½ x 4¾ x 1¾ in. See also V/3/3 .

INVENTION OF PRINTING

Cabinet X Shelf 1 No. 65

Meerman, Gerard: Conspectus originum typographicarum a Meerman proxime in lucem edendarum. In usum amicorum typis descriptus [Amsterdam] 1761.

Privately printed, as the porspectus of the "Origines typographiques" of 1765.

Half morocco; 6-3/4 x 4¼ x 3/8 in.

INVENTION OF PRINTING

Cabinet 26 Shelf 1 No. 20

Métallographie et le problème du livre. Par Maurice Audin. I. Le point de vue technique; les origines de l'imprimerie et la xylogravure...

Article in the "Gutenberg-Gesellschaft Jahrbuch" 1930, pp.11-52.

INVENTION OF PRINTING

Cabinet X Shelf 1 No. 94

Lichtenberger, Johann Friedrick: Initia typographica. Argentorati, 1811.

Favors Gutenberg.

Tree calf; 9-1/8 x 7½ in.

INVENTION OF PRINTING

Cabinet V Shelf 3 No. 8

Meerman, Baron Gerard. De L'Invention de l'imprimerie ... suivi d'une notice chronologique et raisonée des livres avec et sans date imprimé avant l'année 1501, dans les dix-sept Provinces des Pays-Bas, par M. Jacques Visser. Paris, 1809.

Half morocco; 9½ x 5¾ in.

INVENTION OF PRINTING

Cabinet AA Shelf 1 No. 41

Monumenti a Vittorino de Rambaldoni e Panfilo Castaldadi in Feltre. Tipografia Sociale Panfilo Castaldi, 1869.

Biographical historical account, addresses made at the unveiling of the monument, eulogies in praise of printing, etc.

Half morocco; 11-7/8 x 8 in.

INVENTION OF PRINTING

Cabinet Y Shelf 1 No. 23

Linde, Antonious van der. Geschichte der erfindung der buckdruckkunst. Berlin, 1886. (3 vols. illus.)

See vol.1, p.53 and fol. of this work for information concerning the various legal controversies in relation to the invention.

Half morocco; 13 x 10-1/8 in.

INVENTION OF PRINTING

Cabinet V Shelf 3 No. 7

Meerman, Baron Gerard: Plan du traite des origines typographiques. Traduit de Latin en Francois. A Amsterdam, et se trouve a Paris, chez Aug. Mart. Lottin ... 1762.

Plan for the treatise on the origin of printing. Favors Coster.

Boards; 9¼ x 5¼ in. See also V/3/8 .

INVENTION OF PRINTING

Cabinet E Shelf 4 No. 30

Mysterie of Printing: Also of Printing-Presses. P. 62 in: Human industry, or a history of most Manual Arts...n.a.n. London, Printed for Henry Herringman...1661.

Half morocco; 6½ x 4¼ x 5/8 in.

INVENTION OF PRINTING

Cabinet AA Shelf 3 No. 21

Linde, A. Van der: Gutenberg. (Brochure of 40 pages, dated Den Haag, 1870, in Dutch).

Autographed by the author: A.L.S. bound in.

Half morocco; 9 x 5¾ in.

INVENTION OF PRINTING

Cabinet T Shelf 5 No. 80

Memoir on the origin of printing. In a letter addressed to John Topham. By Ralph Willett. Newcastle, 1817.

This memoir "satisfactorily" establishes the claim of Mainz to the honor of the invention.

Calf; 7½ x 407/8 x ½ in.

INVENTION OF PRINTING

Cabinet V Shelf 5 No. 23

Notes et dissertations relatives à l'histoire de l'imprimerie. P.H. Helbig. Bruxelles [1863] (Extrait du tome XVIII du Bulletin du Bibliophile Belge).

Item 15 in vol. with binder's title "Origin of Printing in France: Pamphlets".

INVENTION OF PRINTING

Cabinet T Shelf 5 No. 112

Notes on the history and progress of printing. Invention of movable type and the printing press--Johann Gutenberg...A royal craft. By F. H. S. Ellis, London, n. d. Illus.

See pp.7-16

Cloth; $6\frac{3}{4}$ x $4\frac{1}{4}$ in.

INVENTION OF PRINTING

Cabinet T Shelf 5 No. 85

Origin and history of the art of printing

See HANSARD, THOMAS CURSON Treatises on printing...pp.3-56

INVENTION OF PRINTING

Cabinet AA Shelf 1 No. 39

Panfilo Castaldi da Feltre e l'invenzione dei caratteri mobili per la stampa. Dissertazione dei signori ... Bernardi ... Zanghellini ... Valsecchi. Milano, 1866. Illus.

Half morocco; 12 x 8½ in.

INVENTION OF PRINTING

Cabinet W Shelf 2 No. 1

Nouveau document sur Gutenberg. Temoinage d'Ulric Gering, le premier imprimeur parisien, et de ses compagnons en faveur de l'invention de l'imprimerie. Par A. Claudin Extrait du Livre. 4e Année. pp. 369-72. Paris, 1883.

New Gutenberg document: Testimony of Ulric Gering and his contemporary printers.

Item 14 in volume "Gutenberg, l'inventeur de l'imprimerie - Melanges."

INVENTION OF PRINTING

Cabinet AA Shelf 1 No. 40

Origine e del primato della stampa tipografica. De Giovanni Praloran. Milano, 1868. Frontispiece, statue of Panfilo Castaldi.

Italy here claims the invention of printing through Castaldi.

Half morocco; 9-3/4 x 6½ in.

INVENTION OF PRINTING

Cabinet E Shelf 1 No. 38

Passage on the invention of printing, by Konrad Peutinger, Strassburg, 1530, In "De mirandis Germaniae antiquitatibus...

See folio 10, recto of book with above title. English translation of Latin passage inserted in envelope on front cover.

Boards; 8 x 5-3/8 in.

INVENTION OF PRINTING

Cabinet W Shelf 2 No. 25

See Oberlin, Jerome Jacques. Essai d'annales de la vie Jean Gutenberg....Strasbourg, 1801.

INVENTION OF PRINTING

Cabinet W Shelf 3 No. 27

(Les) Origines légendaires de l'imprimerie. Par Fernand Mitton. Extrait de L'Intermédiaire du Bibliophile, Paris. 24 Jan. 1925.

Item F in vol. with binder's title "Eight French typographic items."

INVENTION OF PRINTING.

Cabinet V Shelf 1 No. 3

Pérégrinations de J. Neumeister, compagnon de Gutenberg en Allemagne, en Italie et en France (1463-1468). Son établissement définitif a Lyon (1485-1507) Par A. Claudin. Paris, 1880.

[Chap.III in Claudin's Origines de l'imprimerie en Languedoc 1480-1481]

Half morocco; 10 x $6\frac{3}{4}$ x 1 in.

INVENTION OF PRINTING

Cabinet U Shelf 4 No. 15

(The) Oldest type-printed book in existence: A disquisition on the relative antiquity of the Pfister and Mazarin (Gutenberg) Bibles and the 63-line A Catholicon: Prefaced by a brief history of the invention of printing. By George Washington Moon. London 1901. Facsimiles.

Half morocco; 11 x 9 in.

INVENTION OF PRINTING

Cabinet U Shelf 4 No. 5

Ottley, William Young: Inquiry concerning the invention of printing...Including also notices of the early use of wood engraving in Europe, the Block Books, etc. With an Introduction by J. Ph. Berjeau. London, 1863. Numerous wood-engravings.

Quarter morocco and cloth; 11-3/4 x 9¼ x 1½ "

INVENTION OF PRINTING

Cabinet V Shelf 6 No. 3

[Pictorial history of the invention of printing] Histoire de l'invention de l'imprimerie par les monuments. Album typographique execute a l'occasion du Jubile Europeen...[D. B. Duverger.] Paris, 1840.

Half morocco; $13\frac{3}{4}$ x $10\frac{1}{2}$ in.

INVENTION OF PRINTING

Cabinet WQ Shelf 1 No. 7

On the invention of letters and the art of printing. Addrest to Mr. Richardson in London, the author and printer...(In the American Magazine, Phila., March, 1758, pp.281-287. Printed and sold by William Bradford.)

Half morocco; $8\frac{1}{2}$ x $5\frac{1}{4}$ in.

INVENTION OF PRINTING

Cabinet V Shelf 3 No. 20

(Paeile, Ch.): Essai historique et critique sur l'invention de l'imprimerie. Paris. [Lille printed], 1859.

The author favors the claims of Haarlem as the birthplace of Printing.

Boards, leather back; 9 x $5\frac{1}{2}$ x 1 in.

INVENTION OF PRINTING

Cabinet T Shelf 6 No. 9

Practical origin of printing with moveable types, and the claims of Koster of Haarlem.

See HUMPHREYS, NOEL. History of the art of printing...London, 1867, p.45

INVENTION OF PRINTING

Cabinet T Shelf 3 No. 13

On the present aspect of the question, who was the inventor of printing ? By William Blades. [Excerpted article]

Excerpt attached to back cover of Hansards Typographia...London, 1867

INVENTION OF PRINTING

Cabinet F Shelf 4 No. 10

Pancirollus, Guido. History of memorable things lost. Written originally in Latin, and now done into English...2 vols.

To this English edition is added, first, a supplement to the chapter of printing, showing the time of its beginning...London, 1717.

Leather; 6½ x 3-7/8 x 3/4 in.

INVENTION OF PRINTING

Cabinet AA Shelf 1 No. 40

Praloran, Giovanni: Delle origine e del primato della stampa tipografica. Milano, 1868. Woodcut frontispiece of statue of Castaldi.

It is in this book that the claims of Italy to the invention of printing through Castaldi are developed.

Half morocco; 9-3/4 x 6½ in.

INVENTION OF PRINTING

Cabinet AA Shelf 1 No. 22

Presagi scientifici sull'arte della stampa, de Gio battista Micheletti. Aquila, 1814.
Strongly in favor of Gutenberg, with explanatory text enumerating the benefits acquired by mankind since the discovery of printing.

Boards; ½ vellum; 8½ x 5½ in.

INVENTION OF PRINTING

Cabinet V Shelf 3 No. 14

See Printing, Historical. Dupont, Paul: Histoire de l'Imprimerie. Paris, 1854. Chap. II, Vol. 1, p. 23.

INVENTION OF PRINTING

Cabinet AA Shelf 3 No. 20

Roest, M. De "Wetenschappelijke moraliteit" van Dr. A. van der Linde, een poosje maar te luchten gehangen, ten gerieve der lezers van diens Spectator-opstellen en boek over "de Haarlemsche Costerlegende". Amsterdam, 1870
Bound in at end of Linde's de Haarlemsche Costerlegende.

Boards; 9 x 5½ in.

INVENTION OF PRINTING.

Cabinet I Shelf 4 No. 5

Principia Typographica: The block books, issued in Holland, Flanders and Germany, during the 15th century, exemplified and considered in connexion with the origin of printing, to which is added an attempt to elucidate the character of the paper marks of the period ...3 vols. By Samuel Leigh Sotheby. London, 1858.

Half morocco; 14½ x 10 x ¾ in.

INVENTION OF PRINTING

Cabinet V Shelf 3 No. 4

See Printing, Historical. Lambinet, Pierre. Recherches historical...sur l'origine de l'imprimerie...Bruxelles [1799]

INVENTION OF PRINTING

Cabinet QQ Shelf 2 No. 17

Romance of commerce, the. By H. Gordon Selfridge. With illustrations. London, 1923.
Refers to printing, invention of printing on pp. 18, 20, 34, 83, 117, 374, 375.

Cloth; 8-7/8 x 5-7/8 x 2-1/8 in.

INVENTION OF PRINTING

Cabinet T Shelf 2 No. 44

Printing: An account of its invention and of William Caxton, the first English printer. By David Marshall, Esq. London and Paris, 1877.

Half morocco; 11-7/8 x 8¼ x 3/4 in.

INVENTION OF PRINTING

Cabinet T Shelf 5 No. 91

Printing: Its antecedents, origin, and results. By Adam Stark, London, 1855.

Cloth; 7¼ x 5 x ½ in.

INVENTION OF PRINTING

Cabinet E Shelf 4 No. 52

Sardi, Alexandri...1671.

See SARDI, ALEXANDRI Rerum inventoribus...

INVENTION OF PRINTING

Cabinet QQ Shelf 2 No. 26

Printing and the invention of the gun.

see
FISKE, BRADLEY A. Invention: the master-key...New York, 1921, p.101

INVENTION OF PRINTING

Cabinet U Shelf 5 No. 11

Printing, who was the inventor of? On the present aspect of the question. Being a paper read at a meeting of the Library Association at Birmingham. By William Blades. London, 1887.
Includes a list of books published upon the subject since 1868.

Half morocco; 11-1/8 x 7¼ x 3/8 in.

INVENTION OF PRINTING

Cabinet AA Shelf 3 NO. 13

Scheltema, Jacobus: De Geloofwaardigheid van Adrianus Junius gehandhaafd, ten opzigte van zijne berigten aangaande de uitvinding en beoefening der boekdrukkunst te Haarlem; door Jacobus Schneltema. [Utrecht]. 1834.
Junius was the first (1588) to name Coster as the inventor of printing. See also DeVinne "The invention of printing." pp.330-346.

Half morocco; 8-5/8 x 5¼ in.

INVENTION OF PRINTING

Cabinet V Shelf 3 No. 9

See Printing, Historical, Delandine, Antoine Francois. Histoire abrégée de l'imprimerie ou précis sur son origine...

INVENTION OF PRINTING

Cabinet W Shelf 2 No. 1

Proces de Guttemberg: Dissertations sur quelques points curieux. Par Paul L. Jacob. Paris, 1847. Pamphlet.
Extracts from original documents which claim to establish the facts concerning the exact date of Gutenberg's Invention.

Item 1 in volume "Gutenberg l'inventeur de l'imprimerie - Melanges."

INVENTION OF PRINTING

Cabinet AA Shelf 3 No. 12

Scheltema, Jacobus: Levens-schets van Laurens Janszoon Koster, door Mr. Jacobus Scheltema ... [Amsterdam], 1834.

Half morocco; 8¾ x 5½ in.

INVENTION OF PRINTING

Cabinet V Shelf 3 No. 12

See Printing, Historical. Didot, Ambroise Firmin: Essai sur la typographia... Paris, 1851.

INVENTION OF PRINTING

Cabinet X Shelf 2 No. 3

(Remarkable discourse between the first inventors of printing from the realm of the tomb, to vindicate the claims of Mainz. In the 3rd jubilee celebration of the discovery. Erfurt, 1740). Merkwürdiges gesprach im reich der todten zwischen den ersten erfindern...Der stadt Mayntz der ruhm von der erfindung vindiciret wird...In dem 3 buchdrucker jubilaeo...Erfurt, 1740. Portraits.

Half morocco; 7-5/8 x 4-7/8 x 3/8 in.

INVENTION OF PRINTING

Cabinet U Shelf 4 No. 88

Schoeffer, Peter, at work. By Alfred W. Pollard. (Illus. exerpt)

Item in manila envelope

INVENTION OF PRINTING

Cabinet X, Shelf 1, No. 36

Schrag, J. Adam. Historia typographiae Argentorati inventae.
Latin text. Printed in Wolf's "Monumenta typographica"...vol. 2, pp.1-67.

Schrag's theory is that Mentel invented printing in Strassbourg.

INVENTION OF PRINTING

Cabinet MM, Shelf 3, No. 17

Typographia; or the printer's instructor, including an account of the origin of printing... By John Johnson. London, 1824. (v.1 only)

T/3/7, MM/3/15, MM/3/16. Other copies 9 x 5-7/8 in., each with v.1-2.

Half morocco; 5 x 3-1/8 in.

INVENTION OF PRINTING

Cabinet W, Shelf 4, No. 32

Vries, A. de: Eclaircissemens sur l'histoire de l'invention de l'imprimerie...Par A. de Vries Traduit de Hollandais par J.J.F. Noordziek. La Haye, 1843.
Bound in with "Arguments des Allemands en faveur de leur prétention"...Par A. de Vries, La Haye, 1845.

Boards; ¼ Calf; 9¼ x 6 in. See also W/4/33.

INVENTION OF PRINTING.

Cabinet 75, Shelf 1, No. 9

Some notes on the invention of printing. Summary of a paper read before the Bibliographical Society by Dr. J. H. Hessels, February 18, 1907.

In Trans. Biblio. Soc., Vol. IX, 1906-1908, pp.11-14.

INVENTION OF PRINTING

Cabinet Y, Shelf 3, No. 4

Typographischen seltenheiten nebst beyträgen zur erfindungsgeschichte der buchdruckerkunst (Typographical rarities, together with information on the history and invention of printing) von. Gotthelf Fischer. Nurnberg und Mainz, 1801-1804. In 6 parts with numerous plates.

Half morocco; 8-7/8 x 5-7/8 x 3 in.

INVENTION OF PRINTING

Cabinet Y, Shelf 2, No. 1

Wahrhafftige nachrichten der so alt als beruhmten buchdruckerkunst, in welchem vom ursprung und fortgang der buchdruckereyen 1440 an bis jetzo 1720...von Johann David Werther. Leipzig 1721.
Curious information concerning the invention

Half vellum; 8-5/8 x 6-5/8 x 1¼ in.

INVENTION OF PRINTING

Cabinet W, Shelf 2, No. 1

Strasbourg. L'invention de l'imprimerie a Strasbourg par J. Gutenberg. Courte notice publiée a l'occasion du quatriéme anniversaire séculaire de cette invention célébré a Strasbourg les 24, 25 et 26 Juin 1840 [Le Roux, printer].

Item 22 in volume "Gutenberg, l'inventeur de l'imprimeire - Melanges."

INVENTION OF PRINTING

Cabinet 26, Shelf 1, No. 21

[Typography and stereotyping, or the evolution of printing] Typographie et stereotypie. Par Maurice Audin.

Essay in the "Gutenberg-Gesellschaft Jahrbuch, 1931", pp.28-37.

INVENTION OF PRINTING

Cabinet AA, Shelf 3, No. 5

Westreenen, W.H.J. van. Verhandeling over de uitvinding der boekdrukkunst in Holland, oorspronkelijk uitgedacht; te Straatsburg verbeterd; en te Mentz voltooid. 's Hage, 1809.

Half morocco; 8-7/8 x 5-1/8 in.

INVENTION OF PRINTING.

Cabinet F, Shelf 4, No. 10

Time of its beginning, and the first book printed in each city before the year 1500.

See Pancirollus, Guido. History of memorable things lost. vol.2, p.338.

INVENTION OF PRINTING

Cabinet K, Shelf 5, No. 11

(Various opinions concerning the invention of printing)

see
JACKSON, JOHN. Treatise on wood engraving...London, 1839, pp.145 - 200 (also index)

INVENTION OF PRINTING

Cabinet Y, Shelf 5, No. 125

Wetter, Johann: (Facsimiles of original documents intended to accompany Wetter's History of the invention of printing. 13 plates). XIII tafeln facsimiles zu Wetter's geschichte der erfindung der buchdruckerkunst. Mainz, 1838.

Half morocco; 12-3/4 x 14½ in.

INVENTION OF PRINTING

Cabinet MM, Shelf 1, No. 13

Traité de l'imprimerie: Origine, invention et progrès de cet art. Chez Bertrand-Quinquet. Paris (1799), an VII. Illus.

Tree calf; 10½ x 8-1/8 x 1 in.

INVENTION OF PRINTING

Cabinet Y, Shelf 2, No. 5

(Various opinions on the invnetions and inventors of printing) Geschichte der erfindung der buchdruckerkunst...von Johann Gottlob. Immen. Breitkopf, Leipzig, 1779.

Half calf; 8½ x 7 in.

INVENTION OF PRINTING

Cabinet K, Shelf 2, No. 26

Who was the inventor of printing ?...Improvement of typographical processes up to the 16th century.

See
LACROIX, PAUL. Arts of the Middle Ages...London, 1875, p.485

INVENTION OF PRINTING

Cabinet R, Shelf 6, No. 1

True story about Gutenberg's invention of printing. Complete in seven sheets. Drawn by B. A. Wilström. New York, 1882. Copper engravings.
Humorous account in rhyme.

Half morocco; 16 x 12 in.

INVENTION OF PRINTING

Cabinet E, Shelf 4, No. 52

Vergil (Pol.) De rerum inventoribus. Libri VIII. Noviomagi Batavorum (Nimwegen, Holland). Reinerei Smetii, 1671.

Bound in with "De rerum inventoribus...By Alexandri Sardi.

Invention notes on p.141 of Vergil, and p.2 of Sardi's.

Vellum; 5 x 3 x 1½ in.

INVENTION OF PRINTING

Cabinet T, Shelf 1, No. 61

Willett, Ralph: A memoir of the origin of printing. London, 1793.

Half morocco; 12 x 9 x 3/8 in.

INVENTION OF PRINTING.

Cabinet 75 Shelf 1 No. 13

Wimpheling (Jacob), his references to the beginnings of printing.

See Scholderer, Victor. Wimpheling, Jacob, an early Strassburg humanist, pp. 93-5

INVENTION OF PRINTING

Cabinet D Shelf 3 No. 13

Wimpheling's "Epithoma rerum Germanicarum." See Chap. LXV.

In this account mention is made of Gutenberg, Mentelin and Adolph Rusch.

INVENTION OF PRINTING

Cabinet W Shelf 4 No. 48

Winaricky, Charles: Jean Gutenberg, ne en 1412 a Kuttenberg en Boheme ... Essai historique et critique, par le Révérend Charles Winaricky, traduit du manuscrit Allemand par Jean de Carro. Bruxelles, 1847.

Morocco; 7 x 4½ in.

INVENTION OF PRINTING

Cabinet X Shelf 1 No. 36

Wolf, John Christian: Monumenta Typographica... Hamburg, 1740. (2 vols.)

Collection of dissertations, poems and memoirs relating to the discovery, development, and dispersion of the printing art.

Boards, morocco back; 7-3/8 x 4½ x 2 in.

INVENTION OF PRINTING

Cabinet S Shelf 3 No. 172 2 Vols.

Work of the first printers in Holland and Germany, 1440-1528. Books and their makers during the Middle Ages ... By George Haven Putnam, New York, 1897-1898. 2 Vols. See Vol. I, p. 348.

Cloth; 9¼ x 6½ in.

INVENTION OF PRINTING.

Cabinet I Shelf 4 No. 5

Zell, Ulric, Printer at Cologne. His communication to the author of the Cologne Chronicle respecting the invention of printing.

See SOTHEBY, SAMUEL LEIGH. Principia Typographica ... London, 1858, Vol. I, pp. 129-133, also index Vol. III.

INVENTIONS

Cabinet QQ Shelf 2 No. 36

Dirigible Aérostat, now known as the Zeppelin, named after the German inventor. Actually the Dirigeable was invented in 1789, or earlier by Capt. le Baron Scott of the French army. In the absence of engines Scott's invention was directed with sails. In 1789, Scott published a book (pp.354), dedicated to Montgolfier Bros., inventors of the ordinary gas balloon.

In envelope to which this item refers

cont'd

INVENTIONS cont'd

Cabinet QQ Shelf 2 No. 26

will be found an advertisement of Capt. Scott's book, also an electro of the illustration of the various types of Scott's Dirigibles.

In envelope.

INVENTIONS

Cabinet QQ Shelf 2 No. 30

Great Facts: A popular history and description of the most remarkable inventions during the present century. By Frederick C. Bakewell. Illustrated with numerous engravings. London 1859.

On p.67-photography; p 219-paper making; p228-printing machines; p.246-lithography.

Cloth, embossed: 7-3/8 x 5 in.

INVENTIONS

Cabinet Shelf No.

Green, Buford, inventor of the "Semagraph" or Electric Eye.

See Composing Machines [Semagraph]

INVENTIONS

Cabinet QQ Shelf 2 No. 27

Electric motor

see

DAVENPORT, THOMAS. Biography of....

INVENTIONS

Cabinet QQ Shelf 2 No. 23

(History of inventions related to the arts and crafts; playing-cards, bookbinding, printing, engraving, etc.)

See FOKKE, AREND. Museum der voornaamste uitvindingen...

INVENTIONS

Cabinet QQ Shelf 2 No. 25

History of wonderful inventions. Illustrated with numerous engravings on wood. [in 2 parts] New York: Harper & Brothers, 1849.

pp.49 to 76 on the history of the invention of printing.

Cloth; 7¼ x 5¼

INVENTIONS

Cabinet QQ Shelf 2 No. 26

Invention the master-key to progress. By Rear-Admiral Bradley A. Fiske. New York, 1921. Illus.

On p.101, brief outline of the invention of printing.

Cloth; 8¼ x 5-5/8.

INVENTIONS

Cabinet QQ Shelf 2 No. 29

Wonderful inventions: from the mariner's compass to the electric telegraph cable. By John Timbs. With numerous engravings. London, n.d. circa 1868.

pp.54-75, printing

Cloth; 7-3/8 x 5

INVENTIONS, AMATEUR PRINTING (see)

Cabinet Shelf No.

AMATEUR PRINTING INVENTIONS

INVENTIONS, PATENTS FOR.

Cabinet FF Shelf 2 No. 40

Abridgments of specifications relating to Printing [issued by Great Britain]. Vol. I. London: at the Great Seal Patent Office, 1859.

Complete copies of most of the specifications are obtainable from the Patent Office, London.

Half morocco; 7-5/8 x 5 x 2 in.

INVENTIONS, PATENTS FOR.

Cabinet FF Shelf 2 No. 40

Anastatic Printing. See Inventions, Patents for, Abridgments of specifications, Vol. I ... London, 1859, pp. 29, 248, No. 10,219 (1844) "Obtaining reversed facsimiles on metallic surfaces from designs."

Half morocco; 7-5/8 x 5 x 2 in.

INVENTIONS, PATENTS FOR.

Cabinet FF Shelf 2 No. 40

Bagmaking Machines, with printing attachments. See Inventions, Patents for. Abridgments of specifications, Vol. I...London, 1859. p.348 No. 541 (1853) and 435, No. 1194, (1854). The latter bya Frenchman, A.E.L. Bellford.

Half morocco; 7-5/8 x 5 x 2 in.

INVENTIONS, PATENTS FOR

Cabinet Paper, pasteboard, etc.

Shelf

See PATENTS FOR INVENTIONS RELATING TO PAPER.

No.

Cabinet Shelf No.

ing cylinder, which he failed to do. Hoe, using ordinary types, wedged them around the cylinder by making the column rules wedge-shaped and holding each page in a curved chase, with a bottom, called a "turtle."

Half morocco; 7-5/8 x 5 x 2 in.

INVETNIONS, PATENTS FOR

Cabinet FF Shelf 3 No. 36

British patents, 1617 to 1913. List of specifications of British patents relating to the preparation of typographical printing surfaces.

See Legros...and Grant. Typographical printing surfaces...London, 1916, pp. 581-667.

INVENTIONS, PATENTS FOR

Cabinet 80 Shelf 2 NO. 21

Printers' types, for making. A description of various machines and engines invented by Mr. Apollos Kinsley, now in the City of New York.

Article in The American Review and Literary Journal...Vol.I, No.I, Jan.-March, 1801, pp.127-8.

In manila envelope.

INVENTIONS, PATENTS FOR.

Cabinet FF Shelf 2 No. 40.

Types, Wedge-Shaped. See Inventions, Patents for. Abridgments of specifications, Vol. I ...London, 1859. p. 126, No. 3610 (1812). (Patent granted to Wm. Caslon for casting type 3-16 in. high, to be fitted into adjustable "stands" to bring them to type height--thus to secure "economy of weight and space.")

Half morocco; 7-5/8 x 5 x 2 in.

INVENTIONS, PATENTS FOR.

Cabinet FF Shelf 2 No. 40

Inks, Writing. See Inventions, Patents for. Abridgments of Specifications, Vol. I; pp. 82, 83, No. 258 (1688). "A new invencion of makeing a certaine powder, which being put into faire water, beer, ale or wine, doth immediately turne the same into very good block writing ink...can be afforded very cheape."

Half morocco; 7-5/8 x 5 x 2 in.

INVENTIONS, PATENTS FOR.

Cabinet FF Shelf 2 No. 40

Type Casting Apparatus. See Inventions, Patents for. Abridgments of specifications, Vol. I ...London, 1859. p. 109, No. 2931, (1806); p. 114, No. 2979 (1806); p. 115, No. 3033 (1807); p. 117, No. 3194 (1809); p. 165, No. 4326 (1823); p. 166, No. 4850, (1823); p. 177 No. 5658 (1828); p. 185, No. 6076 (1831); p. 203, No. 7585 (1838).

In 1838 the Bruce machine was perfected and patented in America, but not patented abroad. The foregoing citations relate to

(Cont'd.)

INVENTIONS, PATENTS FOR.

Cabinet FF Shelf 2 No. 40

Wall Paper, methods of printing. See Inventions Patents for. Abridgments of specifications, Vol. I...London, 1859. p. 28 (when and by whom invented, 1620); p. 89, No. 1007, (1772) p. 99, No.1748-III (1790); p.101, No.1953 (1793); p. 129, No.3777 (1814); pp.163-201. Nos.4783,7411 (1823-1837); pp. 191-192, Nos. 6728,6762, (1834,1835); p.217, No.8458 (1840); pp.274,276. No.11,526 (1847); pp.280 282,No.11,883 (1847); pp.286-288, No.12,248 (1848); pp. 306-308, No. 12,898, (1850);

INVENTIONS, PATENTS FOR

Cabinet L Shelf 1 No. 13

Lithography: list of patents, 1802 to 1889

See LORILLEUX, CH. Traité de la lithographie...Paris, 1889, pp.352-372.

Cabinet Shelf No.

attempts prior to that of David Bruce, jr., of New York. For subsequent efforts see the Index, p. 614.

Half morocco; 7-5/8 x 5 x 2 in.

Cabinet Shelf No.

pp. 339,340, No.1061 (1852); pp. 356-357, No. 857 (1853).

For other related patents see the Index, p. 623.

Half morocco; 7-5/8 x 5 x 2 in.

INVENTIONS, PATENTS FOR.

Cabinet FF Shelf 2 No. 40

Numbering or Paging Machines. See Inventions, Patents for. Abridgments of specifications, Vol. I ... London, 1859, pp. 183, 184, No. 6065 (1831); pp. 218,219, No. 8538 (1840); pp. 253,254, No. 10,543 (1845); pp. 279,280, No. 11,812 (1847); pp. 296,297, No. 12,653 (1849); pp. 305,306, No. 12,994, (1850); p. 347, No. 514 (1853); pp. 586-588, No. 1400 (1857). This latter appears to be the earliest mention of an apparatus to work with and in type forms.

(Cont'd)

INVENTIONS, PATENTS FOR.

Cabinet FF Shelf 2 No. 40

Types, incorrosive. See Inventions, Patents for. Abridgments of specifications, Vol. I...London, 1859, p. 567, No. 2980 (1856). "Aluminum is rendered capable of being used without being alloyed with other metals in and for [among other articles] printers' types.

Half morocco; 7-5/8 x 5 x 2 in.

INVENTIONS, PATENTS FOR.

Cabinet FF Shelf 2 No. 40

[Web Perfecting Press.] "Certain improvements in methods of letterpress printing by machinery." Issued to Rowland Hill, 1835.

See Inventions, Patent for. Abridgments of specifications, Vol. I...London, 1859. pp. 192,193, No. 6762, 1835.

Half morocco; 7-5/8 x 5 x 2 in.

Cabinet Shelf No.

Half morocco; 7-5/8 x 5 x 2 in.

INVENTIONS, PATENTS FOR.

Cabinet FF Shelf 2 No. 40 Vol I

Types, Wedge-shaped. See Inventions, Patents for Abridgments of specifications, Vol. I... London, 1859. p. 97, No. 1748, 2d par. (1790)

Types intended to be arranged around cylinders, as we now use curved stereotypes. This patent of an all rotary printing press to use types wedged around the form cylinder anticipated the Hoe type-revolving "Lightning" press of Richard M. Hoe of New York, 1847. Nicholson's invention depended upon a means of holding the types around the print-

(Cont'd.)

INVENTIONS RELATING TO PRINTING

Cabinet See Patents for Inventions Relating to Printing.

Shelf

No.

INVENTORIES, PRINTING HOUSES

Cabinet W Shelf 3 No. 114

Angouleme (France) 1660. Inventaire d'un imprimeur libraire. [Excerpt].

Item 5 in vol. with binder's title "Pamphlets Relating to Books - I. Bound, 1932".

INVENTORIES. Printing Houses.

Cabinet 22 Shelf 1 No. 14

See Bookselling, Early. Leipzig, 1581. Lorenz Finckelthaus.

INVENTORIES, PRINTING HOUSES. United States

Cabinet R Shelf 4 No. 87.01

Holt, John, printer and postmaster.

See Paltsits, Victor Hugo. John Holt, printer and postmaster...New York, 1920.

INVENTORIES, PRINTING PLANTS. France

Cabinet V Shelf 6 No. 28

Imprimerie Royale. Extrait de l'inventaire de l'Imprimerie Royale fait en 1691-1791.
See Bernard, Auguste. Histoire de l'Imprimerie Royale du Louvre. Paris, 1867. pp. 278-287.

INVENTORIES, PRINTING PLANTS, United States

Cabinet S Shelf 1 NO. 50

Hart, Francis, New York [1847]. Printing Office for sale in the City of New York. Leaflet, 4 pp.
Theodore Low DeVinne worked as a journeyman printer at the Hart plant, and eventually became sole owner.
In DeVinne's Scrap Book, p. 11.

INVENTORS

Cabinet QQ Shelf 2 No. 24

Leading American inventors, By George Iles. With 15 portraits and many illustrations. Edited by W.P. Trent. New York, 1912.

Considers the inventions of John and Robert Stevens, Robert Fulton, Eli Whitney, Thomas Blanchard, Samuel Morse, Goodyear, Ericsson, Cyrus Hall McCormick, C.L. Sholes, E. Howe, B.C. Tilghman, O. Mergenthaler

Cloth; 8 x 5½.

INVENTORS

Cabinet Shelf No.

Rogers, John Raphael, inventor of the Typograph Composing Machine. Biographical sketch, with portrait.

Article by Henry Lewis Bullen, in The Inland Printer, vol.73, No.1, April, 1924, p.65

INVENTORS

Cabinet Shelf No.

Scudder, Wilber Stevens, inventor of the monoline composing machine. Biographical sketch, with portrait.

Article by Henry Lewis Bullen, in The Inland Printer, vol.73, April,1924,p.65

INVENTORS see also

Cabinet Shelf No.

BIOGRAPHIES, INVENTORS

IONA CLUB (see)

Cabinet T Shelf 5 No. 7

HUME, REV.A. (Compiler). Learned Societies and printing clubs...London, 1853, p.249

IOVIUS, PAULUS

See Jovius, Paulus

IOWA

Cabinet S Shelf 2 No. 104

See Early Printing in Iowa.

IOWA

Cabinet NN Shelf 6 No. 8

Journalism in Iowa, early.

see ALDRICH, CHARLES. Early journalism in Iowa...

IOWA

Cabinet NN Shelf 3 No. 8

Valley and the shadow: comprising the experiences of a blind ex-editor, a chapter on Iowa journalism. . .

By J. M. Dixon. New York. 1868.

Cloth: 7½x5"

IPENBUUR & VAN SELDAM

Cabinet FF Shelf 4 No. 17

Boek-Plaat-Steen drukkerij. Amsterdam, 1902. Specimens of types used by them.
Together with "De boekletter in Nederland. Door J. W. Enschede.

Cloth: 8¾ x 5-7/8 in.

IPSWICH

Cabinet U Shelf 1 No. 1d

See Early Printing in England.

IRELAND, ALEXANDER.

Cabinet PP Shelf 1 No. 9

Book-Lover's Enchiridion: Thoughts on the solace and companionship of books ... gathered from the best writers of every age, and arranged in chronological order ... London, 1884.

Cloth; 6¾ x 4¼ in.

IRELAND, ALLEYNE

Cabinet NN Shelf 3 No. 31

Joseph Pulitzer.
Reminiscences of a secretary.
By Alleyne Ireland.
New York, 1914.
With portraits.

Cloth: 8¼x5¾x1-1/8"

IRELAND

Cabinet T Shelf 2 No. 2

Ancient printers of Ireland, memoirs of, together with lists of the books printed by them.

see
AMES, JOSEPH and WM. HERBERT
Typographical Antiquities...

IRELAND

Cabinet OO Shelf 5 No. 3 (2 vols.)

History of Irish periodical literature, from the end of the 17th to the middle of the 19th century...By Richard Robert Madden, London, 1867. [2 vols.]

Cloth; $8\frac{3}{4}$ x $5\frac{3}{4}$ in.

IRELAND

Cabinet OO Shelf 5 No. 3 (2 vols.)

Printing of early Irish newspapers, etc., ...

see
MADDEN'S History of Irish periodical literature...London, 1867. [2 vols. index].

IRELAND

Cabinet PP Shelf 3 No. 12

Books in early Irish monasteries, the use of.

See SAVAGE, ERNEST A. English libraries old...London, 1911. p.1-

IRELAND

Cabinet M Shelf 1 No.

See Imprints, Ireland. Candle Press, The.

IRELAND

Cabinet S Shelf 2 No. 151

Sixteenth century: Early printing in Ireland. By P. P. Lennox.
Excerpt from the Catholic University Bulletin, March, 1909.

In envelope.

IRELAND.

Cabinet 75 Shelf 1 No. 15

Brian Boru and the Irish manuscript tradition. A paper read before the Bibliographical Society By M. G. R. Redgrave. Oct.21, 1918.

In Trans. Biblio. Soc. Vol. XV, pp. 133-135. 1917-1919.

IRELAND

Cabinet 18 Shelf 2 No. 1

[Ireland's contribution to the art of the book] Die verdienste Ireland um Schrift und buckwesen, von Ernst Schultze, Hamburg, 1915.

In Zeitschrift fur Bucherfreunde, 1915-16, Part I, p.82.

IRISH

Cabinet L Shelf 2 No. 4

Alphabet Irlandaise...1803

See MARCEL, J.J. Alphabet Irlandais ...(1803)

IRELAND.

Cabinet U Shelf 1 No. 1d

Care of books in early Irish monasteries. (Historical, bibliographical account). By Ernest A. Savage. London, 1909.

In Excerpts relating to printing from "The Library," 1909. p. 156 of pencilled folios.

IRELAND.

Cabinet 75 Shelf 2 No. 4

Irish characters in print, 1571-1923. By E. W. Lynam. A paper for the Bibliographical Society, London, March, 1924. Facsimiles.

In Trans. Biblio. Soc. Vol. IV, 1923-1924. pp. 286-325. "The Library."

IRISH

Cabinet II Shelf 4 No. 5

[Book of short stories] By Padraic Conaine. Mantan terten, Tta...

Printed in Irish characters. Probably of date 1930.

Boards; $7\frac{1}{4}$ x 5 x $\frac{1}{2}$ in.

IRELAND.

Cabinet 76 Shelf 1 No. 17

Dictionary of printers and booksellers, 1726-1775.

See BIBLIOGRAPHICAL SOCIETY, England. Dictionary of the printers ... from 1726 to 1775. Printed for the Bibliographical Society, 1932 (for 1930).

IRELAND

Cabinet U Shelf 5 No. 24

Printing in Ireland

see
POLLARD, A. W.
Fine Books...London, 1912, p.242 sq.

IRISH

Cabinet II Shelf 4 No. 3

Language, Irish characters of.

See BRITISH AND FOREIGN BIBLE SOCIETY. Irish Testament...London, 1820.

IRELAND

Cabinet S Shelf 2 No. 151

Folk books of the last century, Irish. (Bibliographical account).
Excerpt from the Catholic World, Aug., 1866. From Dublin University Magazine.

In evnelope.

IRELAND

Cabinet T Shelf 5 No. 50

Printing in Irish characters

See
BRADSHAW, HENRY. Letters written by......

IRISH

Cabinet E Shelf 4 No. 75

Leabhuir....The books of the Old and New Testament translated into Irish by....Dr. William Bedel. London, 1685 [With the New Testament in the Irish Character, translated by William O'Donnell. London, 1681.

Calf; $9\frac{1}{2}$ x $7\frac{1}{4}$ x $3\frac{1}{4}$ ins.

IRISH

Cabinet II Shelf 4 No. 4

Testament translated into Irish by William O'Donnell. Printed at Dublin; Hardy and Sons, Typ. 1852.

Cloth; 5¾ x 3½ x 5/8 in.

IRWIN, WALLACE

Cabinet 73 Shelf 1 No. 1

Lines to the devil. By Wallace Irwin. Illus. by Igoe. Written fro Taylor, Nash & Taylor. San Francisco, and sent out by them as an example of their typography and letter press.

Item 1 in John Henry Nash, His Work. 1901-1925.

ISEGHEM, A. F. van

Cabinet W Shelf 4 No. 55

Biographie de Thierry Martens d'Alost, premier imprimeur de la Belgique, suivie de la bibliographie de ses éditions. Par A.F. van Iseghem. Malines et Alost, 1852. Apendix dated 1854.

Boards; 8¼ x 5½ in.

IRISH ARCHAEOLOGICAL SOCIETY (see)

Cabinet T Shelf 5 No. 7

Hume, Rev. A. (Compiler). Learned societies and printing clubs...London, 1853, p.263

IRWIN, WALLACE.

Cabinet 71 Shelf 1 No. 2

Love sonnets of a hoodlum. With an introduction by Gelett Burgess. The Tomoye Press. [John Henry Nash]. New York, 1901.

Linen, 7 x 5¼ in.

ISEGHEM, A.F. van

Cabinet W Shelf 4 No. 55

Thierry Martens d'Alost, premier imprimeur de la Belgique, biographie de, suivi de la bibliographie de ses éditions.

Paper boards; 8¼ x 5-1/8 x 1 in.

IRMISCH, LINUS

Cabinet MM Shelf 7 No. 65

Wörterbuch der buchdrucker und schriftgiesser. Etwa 1700 fachgewerbliche und fachgesellschaftliche wörter und redensarten. Sprachlich und sachlich kurz erläutert. Braunschweig, 1901.

Buckram; 8 x 5¼ x ½ in.

IRWIN, WALLACE

Cabinet 4Q Shelf 1 No. 59

Tragedy in printer's ink. To which are added a few quotations taken from letters and magazines commenting on good printing. San Francisco, Taylor-Nash & Taylor. 1913.

A poem.

Boards; 9¾ x 7¾ in.

ISENGRIN, MICHAEL

Cabinet X Shelf 3 No. 15

Biographical sketch, with printer mark, Isingrin, Basel, 1500-1578.

see

HEITZ, PAUL. Basler büchermarken... pp.xxxi, 85,87

IRON TYPE

Cabinet Shelf No.

See SPECIMEN BOOKS, IRON TYPE.

ISAAC, FRANK

Cabinet 76 Shelf 2 No. 30

Types, English and Scottish printing, 1501-35, 1508-41, 1535-58, 1552-58. Collected and annotated. Printed for the Bibliographical Society at the Oxford University Press. 1930, 1932 (2 vols.)

Facsimiles & Illustrations No. II.
" " " " III.

Boards; 11¼ x 9 in.

ISERMANN, A.

Cabinet FF Shelf 1 No. 84

Anleitung zur stereotypen - giesserei in Gyps- und papiermatrizen. Leipzig. 1869 Illus.

Guide to stereotyping by means of plaster of Paris and the paper processes.

Half morocco; 6¾ x 4¾ in.

IRVING, WASHINGTON

Cabinet G Shelf 3 No. 48

(The) Christmas dinner. From the Sketch Book. Illustrations by Gordon Ross. Typography and binding by Frederic Warde. For the friends of the printing house of William Edwin Rudge, New York, 1929.

Boards; 8¾ x 6-7/8 x 3/8 in. In protective case.

ISAAC, FRANK

Cabinet 75 Shelf 2 No. 9

Wynkyn de Worde, and the types used by him, 1501-34. The Bibliographical Society, London, 1928. With facsimiles.

An attempt to date more closely the undated books from English presses.

In Trans. Bibl. Soc. "The Library" vol. IX pp. 395-409. 1928-1929.

ISERMANN, A.

Cabinet I Shelf 2 No. 7

Chemitypie, anleitung zur. Nach eigenen erfahrungen bearbeited von A. Isermann... Leipzig, 1869.

Introduction to method of electrotyping.

Half morocco; 6½ x 4¾ in.

IRWIN, R.B.

Cabinet II Shelf 6 No. 17

Reading tests for partially blind. Cleveland, Ohio, 1919-1920.

A series of tests conducted by R.B. Irwin, Supervisor of the Department for the Blind.

Half morocco; 11¼ x 5¾ x ½ in.

ISACSON, OSCAR L.

Cabinet AA Shelf 5 No. 30

(Flowers from my garden of memories.) Blomster fran minnenas örtagård. Oscar L. Isacson. boktryckare. Göteborg, 1923.

Auto-biographical reminiscenses of a master printer.

ISHILL, JOSEPH

Cabinet G Shelf 3 No. 7.03

Elisee and Elie Reclus...fragments and letters, with woodcuts by Louis Moreau. Compiled, edited and printed by Joseph Ishill, Berkeley Heights, N.J., 1927.

"These samples were printed on a rusty worn-out "Favorite" press which was abandoned in a shed in the vicinity of Berkeley Heights,N.J. The Garamond type is cast by the American Type Founders".

Brochure, in manila envelope.

ISIDORUS (S, Hispalensis Episcopi)

Cabinet D Shelf 1 No. 18

Etymologiarum libri XX., Epistolae III. Augsburg, Günther Zainer, 1472.

The earliest edition with a date.

Gesamt-Kat. ; Hain 9273, Brunet 10846; folio.

ISIDORUS, PELUSIOTA (ST.)

Cabinet E Shelf 3 No. 60

Interpretatione div. Scripturae epistolarum libri V. (gr. and lat.). Paris, Aegid Morellius. 1638.

Calf; $13\frac{1}{4}$ x $9\frac{1}{2}$ x $2\frac{1}{4}$ in. Brunet 3, 464.

ISINGRIN, MICHELE

Cabinet D Shelf 4 No. 55

Imprint of 1540, Michele Isingrin, Basle.

See VIRGIL , POLYDORUS. (De) Rerum inventoribus...Basle, 1540

ISLAMIC BOOK, THE see

Cabinet U Shelf 5 No. 87

ARNOLD, THOMAS W. and Prof. A. GROHMANN. Islamic Book, the...

ISLIP, ADAM

Cabinet E Shelf 2 No. 66

See Early Printing in England. London, 1602. Adam Islip.

ISLIP, ADAM

See Imprints.

ISOTYPE

Cabinet I Shelf 2 No. 44

Half tone process, Isotype a new.

See TURATI, COUNT VITTORIO. Isotypie... circa 1909.

ISRAEL, JOHN (Editor-Printer)

Cabinet A Shelf 3 No. 9

His newspaper The Herald of Liberty, vol.II, No. 78, Aug. 5th 1799. (one copy)

Item on folio 4 in vol. labelled "Early printing in Pennsylvania".

ISSAVERDENZ, P. JACQUES

Cabinet T Shelf 5 No. 14

Island of San Lazzaro, or the Armenian Monastery near Venice. (An account of the founding and the founder of this institution). Venice: Armenian typography of San Lazzaro, 1879. Illus.

Cloth; 7-3/8 x $4\frac{3}{4}$ in.

ISSHIKI JOB PRINTERS

Cabinet EE Shelf 3 No. 80

See SPECIMEN BOOKS, TYPES. Printers. Japan.

ITALIAN COMMERCIAL PRINTING, 1924

Cabinet N Shelf 5 No. 27

Specimens of Italian commercial printing of 1924

Items in bundle, brown paper

ITALIAN CORPORATE STATE, THE

Cabinet KK Shelf 3 No. 46

Pitigliani, Fausto. New York, 1934.

On occupational associations, their historical evolution and relation to the State. Includes chapters on the paper and printing industries.

Cloth; 9 x 6 in.

ITALIC. Specimen

Cabinet 60 Shelf 1 No. 22

Aldine Italic (various).

See books in cabinet 60/1/22.

ITALIC. Specimen

Cabinet D Shelf 4 No. 53

Blado, Antonio. Rome 1534.

See Early Printing in Italy. Rome, 1534. Antonio Blado.

ITALIC. Specimen

Cabinet 67 Shelf 1 No. 12

Caslon Italic used by Bruce Rogers in Fifteen Sonnets of Petrach. Houghton Mifflin. New York, 1903.

Also 67/1/14.

Boards; $7\frac{1}{2}$ x $4\frac{1}{4}$ x 3/8 in.

ITALIC

Cabinet QQ Shelf 1 No. 9

Didot, Firmin, Paris, 1784. Early Modern Roman Italic made by him. Used in: Épitre sur les progrès de l'imprimerie. Par Didot, fils ainé. A Paris, Imprimé chez Didot l'aine, avec les italiques de Firmin, son second fils. 1784.

Half morocco; 8-3/4 x 5-3/8 in.

ITALIC

Cabinet Shelf No.

Garamond Italics. American Type Founders Company.

See Specimen Book of 1923.

ITALIC. Specimen

Cabinet CC Shelf 5 No. 22

Goudy Modern Italic; Goudy Open; Italian Old Style, etc. Specimens.

Box

In box labelled Box "A" Goudy, The Valley Letter Foundry, 1926-1931."

ITALIC — Specimen
Cabinet 67 · Shelf 2 · No. 52

Old Style Italic. Bruce Rogers.

See Imprints. United States. Rogers, Bruce...1923. Ballad of William Sycamore.

ITALIC — Specimen
Cabinet BB · Shelf 3 · No. 36

Original Old Style Italic in 18-pt. American Type Founders Company.

Specimen sheets.

With other items in manila envelope.

ITALIC see also
Cabinet · Shelf · No.

TYPES, Printing. Literature
Italic Types...

ITALICS
Cabinet D · Shelf 4 · No. 31

Arrighi di Vicenza, Ludovico. Type-specimen broadside of the Arrighi italics. With printer mark of Tolomeo Janiculo, Vicenza, 1529.
Inserted in back of Trissino's "Epistola", etc.

ITALICS
Cabinet FF · Shelf 3 · No. 48

Garamond type. A printed exhibit. Redfield-Kendrick-Odell Co. New York, 1927.

Boards; 10¼ x 7¼ x 3/8 in.

ITALICS
Cabinet V · Shelf 4 · No. 4

Invented by Aldus Manutius. Brief account of the printing character.

See CHEVILLIER, ANDRÉ. l'Origine de l'Imprimerie de Paris...Paris, 1694, pp. 115, 116.

ITALIC TYPES — Literature
Cabinet 26 · Shelf 1 · No. 21

Essay on 18th century Italic type. By A.F. Johnson. Illus.

Article in "Gutenberg-Gesellschaft Jahrbuch, 1931", pp.262-268.

ITALIC TYPES — Literature
Cabinet MM · Shelf 6 · No. 68

Uses of italic. A primer of information regarding the origin and uses of italic letters. By Frederick W. Hamilton. "Typographic Technical Series for Apprentices". Part VI, No.38. United Typothetae of America, 1918.

Cloth; 8 x 5 in.

ITALY
Cabinet AA · Shelf 2 · No. 36

L'Arte tipografico in Italia: Nella terza Fiera Internazionale del libro a Firenze nel 1928. Augusto Calabi. Stampato da Raffaello Bertieri.

Half morocco; 9-1/8 x 6½ in.

ITALY
Cabinet X · Shelf 2 · No. 59

(German printers in Italy in the 15th century)
I tipographi tedeschi in Italia durante il secolo XV. Demetrio Marzi.

see HARTWIG, OTTO (Compiler) Festschrift...Mainz, 1900, pp.407-453

ITALY
Cabinet K · Shelf 4 · No. 20

(Illustrated book of the 15th century)

See Olschki, Leo S. Le livre illustre au XV siecle...Florence, 1926.

ITALY
Cabinet 9 · Shelf 1 · No. 1a & 1b

Incunable, original specimen pages of

See HAEBLER, HAEBLER. Italianische Wiegendruck...

ITALY
Cabinet X · Shelf 1 · No. 59

(Rome, first books printed in)

See QUIRINI, ANGELO MARIA (Card.) Liber singularis...Lindaugiae, 1761

ITALY
Cabinet PP · Shelf 3 · No. 14

Rome, public libraries in ancient.

See BOYD, CLARENCE EUGENE. Public libraries...in Rome.

ITALY.
Cabinet 75 · Shelf 2 · No. 1

Spanish books printed in Italy.

See Transactions of the Bibliographical Society, "The Library," Vol. I, 1920-1921, p. 85.

ITALY
Cabinet U · Shelf 5 · No. 28

Spread of printing in Italy (see)

DUFF, E. GORDON. Early printed books...p.59

ITALY
Cabinet J · Shelf 4 · No. 21

Typographic designs (circa 1924-5)

See TYPOGRAPHY, DECORATIVE. Italian (circa 1925-6) Two incomplete...

ITALY
Cabinet K · Shelf 6 · No. 31

Xilografia... [A monthly devoted to the art of wood engraving. Each number with 10 original woodcuts. Edited by Francesco Nonni. Faenza. 1924-5].
7 issues, not consecutive.

ITALY

Cabinet | Shelf | No.

see also

I - Journalism, Italy
II - Newspapers, Italy
III - Periodicals, Italy
IV - Early Printing in Italy
V - " " " " [Lit. of]
VI - Imprints, Italy
VII - Incunabula, Italy
VIII - Printing, Historical, Italy
IX - Specimen Books, Types. Italy.
X - Societies, Printers'. Italy.

ITINERANT PRINTERS

Cabinet 26 | Shelf 1 | No. 21

(Four German journeymen printers at Seville, 1490-1503) Cuatro Alemanes compañeros impresores de Sevilla, 1490-1503, de Don Joaquin Hazañas y la Rua.

Bio-bibliographical essay.

Article in the "Gutenberg-Gesellschaft Jahrbuch, 1931", pp.201-211.

ITINERANT PRINTERS

Cabinet 26 | Shelf 1 | No. 21

(Hungerian printers of the 15th century in Europe) Ungarische buchdrucker des XV jahrhunderts im Auslande. von Joseph Fitz.

Essay in the "Gutenberg-Gesellschaft Jahrbuch, 1931", pp.109-121.

ITINERANT PRINTERS

Cabinet AA | Shelf 3 | No. 25

Antwerpsche drukkers in den vreemde: Bio-bibliographische schetsen. Door Alfons de Decker Antwerpen, 1931. Facsimile, printers marks.

Half morocco; 9 x 6½ in.

ITINERANT PRINTERS

Cabinet Y | Shelf 1 | No. 23

France, German printers in (15th century)

See LINDE, ANTONIOUS van der. Geschichte der erfindung ...Berlin, 1886, vol.3, p.717

ITINERANT PRINTERS

Cabinet W | Shelf 4 | No. 124

(Les) Imprimeurs Belges à l'étranger. Liste géographique des imprimeurs et libraires Belges établis a l'étranger depuis les origines de l'imprimerie jusqu' a la fin du XVIIIe siècle. Nouvelle édition ... facsimiles. Gand, 1922.
Biographical.

Half morocco; 9½ x 6¾ in.

ITINERANT PRINTERS

Cabinet V | Shelf 5 | No. 23

Charney, Jean de, 1507-1513. Les perigrinations d'un imprimeur.

See CLAUDIN, A. Origines de l'imprimerie a Sisteron...

ITINERANT PRINTERS.

Cabinet 75 | Shelf 2 | No.

Gerardus de Lisa, a Fleming in Venetia [1461]. Gerardus de Lisa, printer, bookseller, schoolmaster, and musician. By Victor Scholderer. A paper read before the Bibliographical Society, London, Nov. 18, 1929.
Bio-bibliographical.

In Trans. Biblio. Soc. "The Library," vol. 10, 1929-30. pp. 253-272.

ITINERANT PRINTERS.

Cabinet V | Shelf 1 | No. 109

Imprimeurs et libraires étrangers a Lyon.

See BAUDRIER, JULIEN. Bibliographie. Lyonnaise ... VIe serie. 1904. p. 491.

ITINERANT PRINTERS

Cabinet AA | Shelf 5 | No. 33

Denmark printers 1482-1552. Dansk-Bibliografi: Med saerligt hensyn til Dansk bogtrykkerkunst historie. Af Lauritz Nielsen, København og Kristiania, 1919. Facsimiles, reproductions letters, types, borders, vignettes, etc.
Bio-bibliographical historical account. pp. 155-160.

Half morocco; 11¾ x 9¼ in.

ITINERANT PRINTERS.

Cabinet Y | Shelf 5 | No. 60

(German 15th century printers in foreign countries). Deutschen buchdrucker des 15 jahrhunderts im Auslande. von Konrad Haebler. München, 1924. Facsimiles.

ITINERANT PRINTERS

Cabinet Y | Shelf 1 | No. 23

Italy, German printers in (15th century)

See LINDE, ANTONIOUS, van der. Geschichte der erfindung ... Berlin, 1886, vol.3, p.715

ITINERANT PRINTERS

Cabinet Y | Shelf 5 | No. 60

Deutschen buchdrucker des 15 jahrhunderts im auslande. von Conrad Haebler. Munchen, 1924. Facs.
Bio-bibliographical account of German printers resident in foreign countries, and printing of the 15th century.

Paper; 14-1/8 x 10½ x 1¼ in.

ITINERANT PRINTERS

Cabinet 26 | Shelf 1 | No. 21

(German printing office in Seville, 1491-1500. Menard Ungut and Stanislao Polono). Un taller Aleman de imprenta en Sevilla en el siglo XV. Por Francisco Collantes de Teran.

Bio-bibliographical essay.

Item in "Gutenberg-Gesellschaft Jahrbuch, 1931", pp.146-65.

ITINERANT PRINTERS

Cabinet 26 | Shelf 1 | No. 20

[Moravus, Matthias of Olmütz, the first printer in Genoa, 1474, in Naples 1475-1491] Nota per Mattia Moravo. Di Tamaro di Marinis. Illus.
Bio-biblio. account.

Article in the "Gutenberg-Gesellschaft Jahrbuch" 1930, pp.104-114.

ITINERANT PRINTERS

Cabinet 26 | Shelf 1 | No. 19

Enrico di Colonia ed altri tipografi Tedeschi a Bologna nel sec XV. Di Albano Sorbelli.
Article in the "Gutenberg-Gesellschaft Jahrbuch" 1929, pp.109-128.

ITINERANT PRINTERS

Cabinet | Shelf | No.

History of the famous itinerant printers, known as "Missouri Press Printers".

Article in the Publishers Auxiliary, 67th year, No.27, July, 1932, pp.1 and 7

ITINERANT PRINTERS

Cabinet AA | Shelf 5 | No. 32

(Pedersen, Christiern; Danish printer in Paris, 1507) To Danske palaeotyper trykte in Paris. Sofus Larsen, Kopenhamn, 1925. Facsimiles.
Bio-bibliographical essay in Collijn's "Bok-ock biblioteks historika studier ... Upsala, 1925. pp. 183-197.

Boards; 11 x 8½ x 2 in.

ITINERANT PRINTERS

Cabinet W Shelf 4 No. 63

Recherches sur la vie et les travaux de quelques imprimeurs Belges et Néerlandais établis à l'étrangère pendant le XVe siècle...Par P.C. van der Meersch. Tome premier. Gand, 1856. Facsimiles.

Half morocco; 10 x 6½ in.

ITINERANT PRINTERS

Cabinet Y Shelf 1 No. 23

Spain, German printers in (15th century)

See LINDE, ANTONIOUS van der. Geschichte der erfindung...Berlin, 1886. vol.3, p.719

ITINERANT PRINTERS

Cabinet S Shelf 3 No. 167

"Tramp Printer," A memorial to the ... A collection of old time literature of great interest to anyone in the printing trade. Compiled and printed by John Gordon at The Gordon Press, South Brewer, Maine, 1927. Illus.

Boards; 7 x 4¾ in.

ITINERANT PRINTERS.

Cabinet I Shelf 4 No. 5

Veldener, Johann: View of his labours as a printer at the several places at which he practised his art ...

See SOTHEBY, SAMUEL LEIGH. Principia Typographica ... London, 1858, Vol. I, p. 190-1, also index Vol. III.

ITINERANT PRINTERS, Belgium

Cabinet W Shelf 4 No. 65

Recherches sur la vie et les travaux de quelques imprimeurs Belges, établis a l'etranger pendant les XV et XVIe siècles. Par P.C. Van der Meerch. Gand, 1844 to 1846.

Bio-bibliographical, historical account of the printers, Antonius Mathias, Arnoldus, Pierre de Keysere and others.

Half morocco; 9 x 6-1/8 in.

ITINERANT PRINTERS, Germany

Cabinet 20 Shelf 2 No. 18

Deutscher Buchdrucker des 15. Jahrhunderts im Auslands. Von Dr. Otto Glauning in Leipzig.

In Zeitschrift für Bücherfreunde, 1925, pp. 42-44.

ITINERANT PRINTERS, Italy

Cabinet V Shelf 2 No. 40

Les Imprimeurs rouennais en Italy au XVe siècle: Discours prononcé à la Séance générale de la Société de l'Histoire de Normandie. Par Emile Picot. Rouen, 1911.

3/4 morocco; 9-3/4 x 6½ x ½ in.

ITINERANT PRINTERS, Italy.

Cabinet 20 Shelf 2 No. 10

(Laurentii, Nikolaus, 1477-1486).

See Printing, Historical, Italy (Florence) Nikolaus Laurentii...

ITINERARIES (see)

Cabinet Shelf No.

MAPS

IVES, FREDERIC E.

Cabinet J Shelf 2 No. 28

Autobiography of an amateur inventor. Frederic E. Ives. Privately printed. (Philadelphia) 1928. Illus. portraits.

Cloth; 9-3/4 x 6 in.

IVES, FREDERIC E.

Cabinet S Shelf 2 No. 49

Autobiography of an amateur inventor. By Frederic E. Ives. Privately printed. Philadelphia, 1928. Frontispiece portrait, illus., and diagrams.

Cloth; 8-7/8 x 6 in.

IVES, FREDERICK EUGENE

Cabinet S Shelf 5 No. 9

See Color Printing. Ives, Frederick Eugene: A tribute ...

IVES, FREDERIC E.

Cabinet I Shelf 2 No. 53

Half-tone and trichromatic process theories. 1902.

See Section VII, div. A. p.331, AMSTUTZ, N.S. Amstutz' hand-book of photo-engraving ...1907.

IVES, FREDERIC E.

Cabinet I Shelf 2 No. 39

Heliochromy, a new principle in. By Frederic E. Ives. Philadelphia: Printed by the author. 1889. Frontispiece portrait.

Cloth; 9-1/8 x 7 x ¼ in.

IVES, FREDERIC

Cabinet L Shelf 1 No. 35

Krömskop color photography. With chapters on the nature of light and theory of color. By some of the first authorities. London, 1898 Illus.

Cloth; 6¾ x 4¾ in.

IVES, FREDERIC E.

Cabinet 61 Shelf 1 No. 5

Photo-engraving. A wonderful stage of advancement and achievement in art printing. The Ives process of photo-electrotyping.

Illus article in "The Paper World", vol.18, No.5, May 1889, p.1.

IVES, GEORGE B. (Translator)

Cabinet 67 Shelf 1 No. 29

Champ Fleury. By Geofroy Tory. Translated into English and annotated by George B. Ives. The Grolier Club, New York, 1927.

Printed at Mount Vernon. Wm. Edw. Rudge printing house, under the direction of Bruce Rogers.

Boards; 12½ x 8¾ x 1¼ in.

IVES, GEORGE B.

Cabinet LL Shelf 3 No. 37.01

Text, type and style: A compendium of Atlantic usage. By George B. Ives. The Atlantic Monthly Press. Boston, 1921.

Cloth; 7½ x 5¾ in.

IVES, GEORGE B. (Translator)

Cabinet S Shelf 1 No. 187

Tory, Geofroy, painter and engraver...An account of his life and works, by Auguste Bernard, translated by George B. Ives. The Riverside Press (Bruce Rogers), 1909. Illus.

Boards; $11\frac{1}{4}$ x $7\frac{3}{4}$ x $1\frac{1}{2}$ in. In slip case

IVES, GEORGE B. (Translator)

Cabinet 67 Shelf 2 No. 17

Tory, Geoffroy: Painter, engraver, first Royal Printer...By Auguste Bernarde. The Riverside Press, 1909 [Bruce Rogers, printer].

No.285 of 370 copies printed. Warde 94.

Boards; 11-3/8 x 7-5/8 x $1\frac{3}{4}$ in. In slip case.

IVINS, WILLIAM M. Jr.

Cabinet K Shelf 3 No. 32

Arts of the book. A guide to an exhibition of the. By W. M. Ivins Jr. The Metropolitan Museum of Art. New York, 1924. Illus.

On p.95 "The Book: A list of important dates"

Paper; $8\frac{1}{2}$ x $5\frac{1}{2}$ x $\frac{1}{2}$ in.

IVINS, WM. M. JR.

Cabinet K Shelf 6 No. 34

Illustrated books. "Article by) Wm. M. Ivins Jr. Illus. excerpt from The Bulletin of the Metropolitan Museum of Art. June, 1918.

Item 7 in vol. with binder's title "Wood Engraving. Various Excerpts".

IVINS, WILLIAM M. Jr.

Cabinet K Shelf 3 No. 33

Prints and books. Informal papers. By William M. Ivins Jr. Cambridge (Mass.), 1926. Illus.

Boards, linen back; 8-1/8 x 5-3/8 in.

IVINS, WILLIAM M., jr.

Cabinet 75 Shelf 2 No. 7

Prints and books: informal papers. Cambridge [Mass.]: Howard University Press, 1926. Brief review of book with above title.

In Transactions of the Bibliographical Society, "The Library," Vol. VII, 1926-27, p. 432.

IVINS, W. M. Jr.

Cabinet K Shelf 5 No. 23

Ruzicka, Rudolph, the wood engravings of. Newark, New Jersey. 1917. Frontispiece. D.B. Updike, The Merrymount Press, Boston.

Pictorial boards; 7 x $4\frac{1}{2}$ in. Item in envelope.

IVORY, JAMES

Cabinet X Shelf 5 No. 57

Authorized Master Printer for Scotland, 1859

See LIBERTY OF PRINTING, Great Britain (Scotland 1859)....

IVY PAPER MILL

Cabinet RR Shelf 4 No. 42

Story of Ivy Paper Mill, Delaware County, Pa. Illus. account in "Hurlbut's Papermaker Gentleman", vol.1, No.3, July, 1933.

Item in box labelled "Hurlbut's Papermaker Gentleman"

J

JAAGER, J. FLUIT de

Cabinet AA — Shelf 3 — No. 8

Morgenwandeling van Laurens Janszoon Koster in der hout bij Haarlem anno 1423. [Verse]. Dordrecht, 1823.
Celebration at Dordrecht of the fourth century of printing, invented by Coster at Haarlem.

Morocco; 9 x $5\frac{1}{2}$ in.

JACKETS, BOOK see

Cabinet — Shelf — No.

BOOK JACKETS

JACKSON, ALFRED.

Cabinet 75 — Shelf 2 — No. 10

Rowe's edition. [1709]. of Shakespeare. A paper for the Bibliographical Society. London, 1929. Illus.

In Trans. Biblio. Soc. "The Library," Vol. 10, 1929-30. pp. 455-473.

JACKSON, FRANCIS and JOHN Jr.

Cabinet U — Shelf 5 — No. 49

Biographical bibliographical notes relating to these early 18th century York printers, John Jr. and son Francis Jackson.

see DAVIES, ROBERT
(A) Memoir of The York Press...1868, pp. 312-320

JACKSON, FRANK G.

Cabinet K — Shelf 3 — No. 20

Decorative design: an elementary text book of principles and practice. By Frank G. Jackson. (7th thousand). London, 1905. Illus.

Cloth; 8-$\frac{3}{4}$ x 5-5/8 in.

JACKSON, FRANK G.

Cabinet K — Shelf 3 — No. 19

Theory and practice of design. An advanced text book on decorative art. With 700 illustrations. 4th ed. London, 1903.

Cloth; 9 x 6 in.

JACKSON, HOLBROOK.

Cabinet U — Shelf 5 — No. 92

Bibliomania, the anatomy of. In Two volumes. London, The Soncino Press, 1930.
This is Vol. I; Vol. 2 will follow some time later.

Cloth; $9\frac{1}{2}$ x 6 x $1\frac{1}{2}$ in.

JACKSON, HOLBROOK

Cabinet U — Shelf 3 — No. 91

Catalogue raisonne of books printed at the Curwen Press, 1920-1923. With an introduction by Holbrook Jackson, London, 1924. Facsimiles.

Boards; 8-3/4 x 6 x $\frac{3}{4}$ in.

JACKSON, HOLBROOK

Cabinet S — Shelf 5 — No. 37.01

(The) Revival of printing: an illuminating chapter from "The Eighteen Nineties".

Illus. article in ARS TYPOGRAPHICA, vol.1, No.1, 1918.

JACKSON, HOLBROOK and STANLEY MORISON

Cabinet U — Shelf 5 — No. 33

(A) Brief survey of printing history and practice. London: At the Office of the Fleuron, 1923.

Signed copy.

Boards; $8\frac{3}{4}$ x $5\frac{3}{4}$ in.

JACKSON, JOHN

Cabinet K — Shelf 5 — No. 11

Treatise on wood engraving, historical and practical [By W. A. Chatto]. With upwards of 300 illustrations, engraved on wood, by John Jackson. London, 1839.

Half morocco; 10-1/8 x 7 x 2-3/8 in.

JACKSON, JOHN

Cabinet K — Shelf 5 — No. 12

Treatise on wood engraving, historical and practical. With upwards of 300 illustrations envraved on wood by John Jackson. The historical portion by W. A. Chatto. 2nd edition. London, 1861.

Morocco, gilt; $10\frac{1}{2}$ x $7\frac{1}{4}$ x 1-3/4 in.

JACKSON, JOHN BAPTIST

Cabinet T Shelf 1 No. 42

Origin of printing in Europe, an inquiry into the ...By a "Lover of Art". London, 1752.
The book is mainly concerned with wood and chiaroscuro printing.

Half morocoo; 7-3/4 x 5 in.

JACKSON, WILLIAM H.

Cabinet FF Shelf No. 3 21.04

"Units-to-Pica" method of copy-fitting. Devised by William H. Jackson. New York, 1932.

Brochure, in manila envelope, with other items

JACOBI, CHARLES T.

Cabinet T Shelf 4 No. 80

Books and printing, some notes on: A guide for authors, and others. New and englarged edition. London, Charles Whittingham & Co. 1902.

Includes type specimens; samples of paper; a glossary of bibliographical and typographical terms, etc.

Cloth; 9¼ x 6 x 1-1/8 in.

JACKSON, MARGARET TALBOT

Cabinet PP Shelf 3 No. 38

Museum, the. A manual of the housing and care of art collections. By Margaret Talbot Jackson. New York...1917. Illus.

Cloth; 7-5/8 x 5 x 1-1/8 in.

JACKSONVILLE REPUBLICAN

Cabinet A Shelf 3 No. 5

See Newspapers, Alabama.

JACOBI, CHAS. T.

Cabinet EE Shelf 2 No. 37

Chiswick Press, London. Style and Custom of the Chiswick Press, emended June, 1913. Marked "Private". Signed Chas. T. Jacobi.

Folded broadside. Inserted in book "A selection of types in use at the Chiswick Press".

JACKSON, MASON

Cabinet OO Shelf 4 No. 6

Pictorial Press, The. Its origin and progress. By Mason Jackson. With 150 illustrations. London, 1885.

Cloth; 9 x 5-5/8 x 1¼ in.

JACOB, PAUL L.

Cabinet W Shelf 2 No. 1

Procès de Guttemberg: Dissertations sur quelques points curieux ... Par Paul L. Jacob. Paris, 1847. Pamphlet.
Extracts from original documents which claim to establish the facts concerning the date of the invention of moveable types by Gutenberg.

Item 1 in volume "Gutenberg, inventeur de l'imprimeur - Melanges."

JACOBI, CHAS. T.

Cabinet T Shelf 5 No. 109

Gesta typographica, or a medley for printers and others. Collected by Chas. T. Jacobi. London, 1897.
Brief biographical historical notes on printers and printing.

Boards; linen back; 7 x 4½ x ½ in.

JACKSON, ROBERT

Cabinet X Shelf 5 No. 3

[Obituary]. Robert Jackson, 1743-1810, printer of the Dumfries Journal. A newspaper excerpt. n.n.

p. 41 in vol. with binder's title "Scrap-Book, 1705-1891, relating to printing."

JACOB, P. L. (BIBLIOPHILE).

Cabinet W Shelf 2 No. 79

Recherches bibliographiques sur les livres rares et curieux. Paris, 1880.
Bibliographical account of French books printed at Strassburg in the 16th century, French books lost, and of rare and curious books of the 15th, 16th and 17th centuries.

Half morocco; 8½ x 5½ x 7/8 in.

JACOBI, CHARLES T.

Cabinet M Shelf 1 No.

See Imprints, England. Chiswick Press, Charles T. Jacobi.
" also Imprints, England, Riccardi Press.

JACKSON, W.W.

Cabinet Shelf No.

Type designer and punch cutter.

See Typefounding, Werner, Nicholas Joseph ...

JACOBI, CHARLES T.

Cabinet T Shelf 4 No. 67

Books and printing. Some notes on: A guide for authors and others. By Charles T. Jacobi. Chiswick Press, London, 1892. First edition.
Includes type specimens; samples of paper; a glossary of bibliographical and typographical terms, etc.

Cloth; 9-1/8 x 5-7/8 x 5/8 in.

JACOBI, CHARLES T.

Cabinet T Shelf 4 No. 85

Modern book-printing. Cantor lectures on. By Charles T. Jacobi (of the Chiswick Press). Delivered before the Society of Arts on Feb. 22 and 29, 1904. London, 1904. Illus.

Half morocco; 10-1/8 x 6-5/8 x ½ in.

JACKSON, WILLIAM H.

Cabinet MM Shelf 6 No. 103

"Units-to-Pica" method of copy-fitting, the Jackson. New York, 1932.

Boards; 7 x 4½ in.

JACOBI, CHARLES T.

Cabinet T Shelf 4 No. 80

Books and printing. Some notes on: A guide for authors, publishers, and others. New and enlarged edition. London: Charles Whittingham & Co. 1902.
Includes type specimens; samples of paper; a glossary of bibliographical and typographical terms, etc.

Cloth; 9¼ x 6 x 1-1/8 in.

JACOBI, CHARLES THOMAS (Compiler)

Cabinet MM Shelf 3 No. 49

Printers' (The) handbook of trade recipes, hints, & suggestions relating to letterpress and lithographic printing, bookbinding, statioery, engraving, etc. With many useful tables, and an index. London, The Chiswick Press, 1887.

Cloth; 7½ x 5-1/8 x ¾ in.

JACOBI, CHARLES THOMAS (Compiler)

Cabinet MM Shelf 3 No. 51

Printers' (The) handbook of trade recipes, hints, and suggestions relating to letterpress and lithographic printing, bookbinding, stationery, process work, etc. Third edition, revised and enlarged. London, 1905.

Cloth; 7-3/8 x 5¼ x 1-1/8 in.

JACOBI, CHARLES THOMAS

Cabinet MM Shelf 7 No. 64

Printers' vocabulary: a collection of some 2500 technical terms, phrases, abbreviations and other expressions mostly relating to letterpress printing, many of which have been in use since the time of Caxton. London: The Chiswick Press, 1888.

Cloth; 7¾ x 5¼ x ½ in.

JACOBI, CHARLES THOMAS

Cabinet MM Shelf 3 No. 50

Printing: A practical treatise on the art of typography as applied more particularly to the printing of books. With upwards of 150 illustrations, and many useful tables, together with glossarial index of technical terms and phrases. London: Geo. Bell & Sons. 1890.

Cloth; 7-1/8 x 4¾ x 1 in.

JACOBI, CHARLES THOMAS

Cabinet MM Shelf 3 No. 52

Printing. A practical treatise on the art of typography, as applied more particularly to the printing of books. Sixth edition. (Revised and enlarged). London: 1919. Illus.

Cloth; 7¼ x 5¼ x 1¼ in.

JACOBI, CHAS. T.

Cabinet R Shelf 1 No. 90

Printing and printers of Franklin's time. By Chas. T. Jacobi, in The American Printer Franklin Number, Jan. 20, 1923. p. 60 Illus.

Half morocco; 12 x 8-7/8 in.

JACOBI, CHAS. T.

Cabinet R Shelf 1 No. 90

Printing and printers of Franklin's time, by Chas. T. Jacobi, in The American Printer: Franklin number, Jan.20, 1923, p.60. Portraits.

Half morocco; 12 x 8-7/8 in.

JACOBI, CHARLES T.

Cabinet 75 Shelf 1 No. 1

Printing of modern books: A paper read before the Bibliographical Society by Charles T. Jacobi, June, 19, 1893.

In Trans. Biblio. Soc., Vol. I pp. 187-204, 1892-1893.

JACOBI, CHARLES T. see also

Cabinet Shelf No.

AUTOGRAPHS

JACOBI, MATTHIAS

Cabinet X Shelf 3 No. 20

Cologne, 1566

see HEITZ, PAUL. Kölner büchermarken...p.xxxi

JACOBS, MICHEL

Cabinet L Shelf 4 No. 54

Art of colour, the. By Michel Jacob. Garden City, New York. 1924. Illus.

Cloth: 11 x 7-7/8 x 5/8 in.

JACOBS, S. A.

Cabinet G Shelf 4 No. 54

Golden Eagle Press, The.

see IMPRINTS. United States. Golden Eagle Press (The) S. A. Jacobs...

JACOBS, S.A.

Cabinet Shelf No.

See also Imprints, United States. The Stratford Press, S.A. Jacobs.

JACOBUS PHILIPPUS (Foresti) BERGOMENSIS

Cabinet Shelf No.

See Bergomensis (Foresti) Jacobus Philippus.

JACQUEMIN

Cabinet V Shelf 6 No. 22

Roman types engraved by Jacquemin, 1818. Specimens.

See Imprimerie Royale. Notice sur les types étrangers...Paris, 1847.

JACQUES, CH.

Cabinet J Shelf 3 No. 32

Gravure et imprimerie en taille-douce. [Illus. excerpt from "Magazine Pittoresque"] n.d. circa 1860.

Gives an exact idea of the operations necessary for engraving and printing from copper plates. Illus. show interior of engravers studio, printing office with men working at the press, engraving tools, etc.

Item in manila envelope.

JAGGARD, WILLIAM

Cabinet U Shelf 4 No. 56

Birth and growth of printing. With illuminated facsimile of the Gutenberg Bible, and a portrait of Caxton. Liverpool, 1908.

Cloth; 9½ x 6½ in.

JAGGARD, WILLIAM

Stack A Shelf 1 & 2 Number 71

Defence of William Jaggard, Printer. by Henry Lewis Bullen in The Inland Printer Collectanea Typographica April, 1923, p. 65. Vol.71 Illus.

JAGGARD, WILLIAM

Cabinet E Shelf 3 No. 22

See Early Printing in England. London, 1623. William Jaggard.

Jaggard printed the Shakespeare First Folio.

Preface to this book has a defence of his ability as a printer which had been questioned by an author with whom he had quarreled.

JAGGARD, WILLIAM

Cabinet U Shelf 1 No. 1d

False dates in Shakespearian quartos. Bibliographical communication by W. Jaggard, for "The Library," 1909.

In Excerpts relating to printing from "The Library," p. 71 of pencilled folios.

JAGGARD, WILLIAM

Cabinet 75 Shelf 2 No. 9

Interrupted printing of Shakespeares First Folio. [Also] A note on the typography of the running titles of the First Folios. Papers by Edwin Eliott Willoughby. London, the Bibliographical Society, 1928.

In Trans. Bibl. Soc. "The Library" vol. IX pp. 262-66, 385-87. 1928-1929.

JAGGARD, WILLIAM

Cabinet U Shelf 1 No. 1c

(On) Certain false dates in Shakespearian quartos Bibliographical account by W. W. Greg. "The Library," London, 1908. With facsimiles.

In Excerpts relating to printing from "The Library," 1908. pp. 113-131.

JAGGARD, WILLIAM

Cabinet T Shelf 1 No. 12

Preface to Vincent's "A discovery of errours. 1622"; in which he (Jaggard) justifies his printing house. [Typewritten manscript].

Paper board binder; 10-3/4 x 8-5/8 in.

JAHN, HUGO (Compiler)

Cabinet MM Shelf 7 No. 69

Dictionary of graphic arts terms. A book of technical words and phrases used in the printing and allied industries. Published by the United Typothetae of America, 1928.

Cloth; 8 x 5-1/8 x ½ in.

JAILLOT, ALEXIUS HUBERTUS.

Cabinet 75 Shelf 2 No. 3

Engraver of maps 1632-1712.

See Early Printing in France. Literature. Listes generales des postes de France, etc.

JAMAICA

Cabinet R Shelf 4 No. 176

See Printing, Historical, West Indies.

JAMES, ELIANOR

Cabinet X Shelf 5 No. 2

To the Honourable House of Commons. May it please your Honours ... Therefore I humbly beseech you to take off this tax from paper ... [London, n.d.]. Broadside.

Item 22 in volume "Historical documents relating to printing."

JAMES, J.A.

Cabinet 21 Shelf 2 No. 2.01

Western Advertiser, Cincinnati, Ohio, 1839.

see PERIODICALS, TYPE FOUNDERS. Western Advertiser...

JAMES, JOHN

Cabinet X Shelf 5 No. 3

Letter Founder, London, 1773: To be sold at auction, the genuine stock and utensils of Mr. John James, Letter Founder, lately deceased. Newspaper clipping.

p. 37 in vol. with binder's title "Scrap Book, 1705-1891, relating to printing."

JAMES, MONTAGUE RHODES.

Cabinet 75 Shelf 2 No. 7

Greek manscripts in England before the Renaissance. Paper read before the Bibliographical Society, November 15, 1926.

In Trans. Biblio. Soc., "The Library", Vol. VII, 1926-1927, pp. 337-353.

JAMES, M. R.

Cabinet 75 Shelf 2 No. 2

Royal manuscripts at the British Museum, The.

In Transactions of the Bibliographical Society, "The Library, " Vol. II, 1921-1922 pp.193-200.

JAMES, PRINTER see

Cabinet 21 Shelf 2 No. 1

PRINTER, JAMES.

JAENECKE PRINTING INK CO.

Cabinet 78 Shelf 1 No. 54

Specimens of Jaenecke's [inks] for typo and lithographic printing. Newark, N.J. n.d. [1900]. Price list of black, and colored, printing, and lithographic ink.

Cloth; 4½ x 7-3/4 x 5/8 in.

JANECKE, GEBR. & FR. SCHNEEMANN.

Cabinet 78 Shelf 1 No. 47

Ink manufacturers in Hannover: Illustrations (3 folded plates) showing interior and exterior views of their factory in Goebel's "Unserer farbe. Historisch und technisch betrachtet," St. Gallen, 1886.

Stamped cloth; 6-1/8 x 4-3/8 x ¼ in.

JÄNECKE, GBR. et FR. SCHNEEMANN.

Cabinet 78 Shelf No.

See Inks, Printing. [Specimen Books, Germany].

JANICULO, TOLOMEO

Cabinet D Shelf 4 No. 31

Imprint, colophon, and printer mark of Tolomeo Janiculo, Vicenza, 1529.

See EARLY PRINTING IN ITALY. Vicenza, 1529, Tolomeo Janiculo...

JANIN-CLEMENT.

Cabinet V Shelf 1 No. 67

Recherches sur les imprimeurs Dijonnais et sur les imprimeries de département de la Coté-D'Or. Par Clément-Janin. Dijon, 1873.

See clément-Janin.

Paper; 8¾ x 6 in.

JANISCH, J.N.

Cabinet X Shelf 2 No. 1.01

Abhandlung von der buchdrucker-kunst...Bey gelegenheit des dritten jubel-jahrs... Bremen, 1740.

A treatise on typography and the early products of the printing press. Celebrating the third century of the invention of printing.

JANNET, P.

Cabinet W Shelf 5 No. 43

Spécimen des nouveaux caractères destinés a l'impression de la Biblitheque Elzevirienne, suivi du plan de la collection. Paris, chez P. Jannet, 1856.

Half morocco; 7½ x 4½ in.

JANNET, P.

Cabinet W Shelf 1 No. 81

Specimen des nouveaux caracterès destinès a l'impression de la Bibliotheque Elzevirienne, suivi du Plan de la Collection. Chez P. Jannet, Paris, 1856.

The type "Elzevirienne" was especially designed for P. Jannet, for use in his own publications.

Half morocco; 6-3/8 x 4 in.

JANNON, JEAN

Cabinet E Shelf 3 No. 51

See Early Printing in France. Sedan, 1633. Jean Jannon.

JANNON, JEAN

Cabinet S Shelf 3 No. 128

(The) Type Specimen (1621) of Jean Jannon, Paris & Sedan. Designer and engraver of the Caractères de l'Université now owned by the Imprimerie Nationale, Paris. Edited in facsimile, with an introduction by Paul Beaujon (Beatrice Warde), Paris, 1927.

Paper boards; 9¾ x 6-5/8 in.

JANOT, DENYS

Cabinet 69 Shelf 1 No. 1

See Early Printing in France. Paris, 1539.

JANSEN, HENDRIK

Cabinet I Shelf 1 No. 33

Essai sur l'origine de la gravure en bois et en taille-douce, et sur la connoissance des estampes des 15 et 16 siecles; ou il est parle aussi de l'origine des cartes a jouer et des cartes geographiques. Suivi de recherches sur l'origine du papier...ansi que sur l'origine et le premier usage des signatures et des chiffres dans l'art de la typographie. Tome premier, avec 20 planches. Paris, 1808.

Half morocco; 8-7/8 x 5 x 1-3/4 in.

(cont'd)

JANSON, HENDRIK (cont'd)

Cabinet I Shelf 1 No. 33

Half morocco; 8-7/8 x 5 x 1¾ in.

JANSEN, HENDRIK

Cabinet I Shelf 1 No. 33.01

Essai sur l'origine de la gravure en bois et en taille-douce, et sur la connaissance des estampes des XvIe et XVIe siecles...Suivi de recherches sur l'origine du papier de coton et de lin; sur la calligraphie depuis les plus anciens manuscrits...2 vols.

vol.1, Paris 1808. 5 leaves, pp.lV, 404, 2 leaves of table and errata

vol.2, Paris 1808, pp.373.

Tree calf; 8½ x 5 in.

JANSEN, REINIER

Cabinet R Shelf 5 No. 27

See Smith, Joseph. Short biographical notices of William Bradford, Reinier Jansen ... London, 1891.

JANSEN, McCLURG and COMPANY (see)

Cabinet 61 Shelf 1 No. 1

PUBLISHING, United States. Chicago publishing...

JAN VAN DOESBORGH.

Cabinet Shelf No.

See Doesborgh, Jan van

JAPAN

Cabinet E Shelf 2 No. 9

See Acosta, Emmanuel (Compiler) Historia rerum a Societate in Oriente ... 1573.

JAPAN

Cabinet J Shelf 5 No. 15

L'Art Japonais. Par Louis Gonse. Paris, 1883.

Illustrated descriptive prospectus of forthcoming book with title as above.

Paper; 14-3/8 x 10¾ in. In folder.

JAPAN

Cabinet S Shelf 5 No. 17

Arts of wood cutting and wood cut printing in Japan. By S. R. Kochler. Excerpt from "Paper and Press," n.d. Illus.

Thorough explanation of the process by a member of the Smithsonian National Museum, in collaboration with T. Tokuno, chief of the Bureau of Engraving and Printing of the Ministry of Finance, Tokio.

Item 2 in collection "Miscellaneous items relating to printing; excerpts from magazines, 1918.

JAPAN

Cabinet 00 Shelf 6 No. 21

"Asahi" The Osaka and Tokyo, 1930.

see

NEWSPAPERS, SPECIAL ISSUES. Japan. The "Asahi"...1930.

JAPAN

Cabinet FF Shelf 5 No. 9

Benton Matrix Machine, the first sent to Japan.

See Benton, Lynn Boyd. Instructions for setting up...

JAPAN

Cabinet K Shelf 5 No. 1

Caricature, Japanese...

see

CARICATURE. Japanese caricature...

JAPAN

Cabinet J Shelf 5 No. 26

(Catalogue of the treasures in the Emperor's Royal Art Gallery, Tokyo. "The Kokka Yoho". Published by the Imperial Government Printing Bureau in the early part of the Meiji Era (1880). Now out of print, and presented by S. Sugi on behalf of Dr. Yano, head of the Bureau, to the Typographic Library and Museum, Jersey City, 1935.

Covered in figured silk; 13 x 9¾ in. In protective folder.

JAPAN

Cabinet K Shelf 5 No. 5

Designs suggested or in use for purposes similar to our book marks. Text and designs lithographed in imitation of block book printing.

Limp cloth, oblong; 7-3/8 x 10¼ x 1¼ in.

JAPAN

Cabinet Q Shelf 7 No. 16

Imperial Printing Office, brief account of the. In the Asian Printers' and Stationers' Annual and Directory, 1923. Bombay (India) p.13

Boards; 9 x 6-1/8 in.

JAPAN

Cabinet J Shelf 4 No. 3.01

Color prints, Japanese.

See BINYON, LAURENCE and SEXTON, J.J. O'BRIEN. Japanese colour prints...

JAPAN

Cabinet L Shelf 5 No. 16.01

Fashion Magazine, equivalent to our "Vogue". Printed in Japan. Nice example of modern color printing in year 1935.

Paper cover

JAPAN

Cabinet EE Shelf 4 No. 137

Japanese catalogue of printing machinery and materials. Tokyo, 1920. Illus.

Paper; 10 x 7¼ x ½ in.

JAPAN

Cabinet K Shelf 5 No. 1

Color prints, Japanese...

see COLOR PRINTING. Japanese color printing...

JAPAN

Cabinet E Shelf 2 No. 9

First Japanese characters printed in Europe, 1573.

See Early Printing in Italy. Naples, 1573. Horatio Salviani.

JAPAN

Cabinet OO Shelf 2 No. 38

Journal of Sinological Studies.

See PERIODICALS, JAPAN

JAPAN

Cabinet J Shelf 3 No. 31

Color prints, Japanese...

See KEANE, WILLIAM LAWRENCE. Japanese color prints...

JAPAN

Cabinet BB Shelf 4 No. 12

First Japanese embassy from the Japanese government to the U.S. Government. 1860.
Their signatures, and newspaper notices of their visit to the typefoundry of MacKellar, Smiths and Jordan, Philadelphia.
See Specimen Books, Types. United States. MacKellar, Smiths, & Jordan. Philadelphia, 1871.

JAPAN

Cabinet Shelf No.

Journalism of Japan.

see JOURNALISM, JAPAN

JAPAN

Cabinet K Shelf 6 No. 39.01

Color print revival, Japans. By E.A.U. Valentine. Illus. excerpt from International Studio, May, 1923.

Item 28 in bound collection with binder's title ENGRAVERS AND WOOD ENGRAVERS

JAPAN

Cabinet 62 Shelf 2 No. 14

Imperial Government Printing Bureau.

See GOVERNMENT PRINTING OFFICES, Japan...

JAPAN

Cabinet L Shelf 5 No. 16

(The) Kokka: An illustrated monthly journal

see PERIODICALS, ILLUSTRATED (Japan The Kokka...

JAPAN

Cabinet L Shelf 5 No. 13

Color printing, specimens by vari us Japanese printers. Book published under the title of "Insatsutaikwan". With a preface by Sawada Yazo, "Le Directeur de la Societe d'Imprimerie du Japon". Nov.,1915.

Laced silk over board; 15¾ x 10½ x 7/8 in.

JAPAN

Cabinet Q Shelf 1 No. 4

Imperial Library at Tokio, Japan.

see GRIFFIS, WILLIAM ELLIOT. (The) New World of books in Japan...

JAPAN.

Cabinet I Shelf 3 No. 1

Kuniyoshi, the art of.

See Kuniyoshi (Engraver) Art of Kuniyoshi.

JAPAN

Cabinet RR Shelf 4 No. 39

Manufacture of paper in Japan, the. Excerpt from The Athenaeum and "Living Age", Dec., 9, 1871.

Item with other excerpts and pamphlets relating to paper. Folder; 10½ x 7½ x 1 in.

JAPAN

Cabinet NN Shelf 6 No. 2.01

Newspaper, the first said to have been printed in Japan with moveable wooden types. "Shimbun Zassiji, January 30th 1870.

In envelope.

JAPAN

Cabinet K Shelf 6 No. 39.01

Print-artists, the Japanese Bohemia of. By W.G. Blaikie Murdoch. Illus. excerpt from "Asia", Sept.,1923.

Item 32 in bound collection with binder's title ENGRAVERS AND WOOD ENGRAVERS

JAPAN

Cabinet L Shelf 5 No. 14

Masterpieces of great painters of Japan, thirty. Published by The Kokka Company. Toky, 1906. Press work by the Tokyo Tsukiji Type Foundry Tokyo.

Specimens of color printing.

Silk; 16¾ x 11¾ in.

JAPAN

Cabinet 44 Shelf 1 & 2 No.

Nippon Printing World, 1913-

See PERIODICALS, PRINTING, Japan Nippon Printing World...

JAPAN

Cabinet NN Shelf 2 No. 13

PRinter's copy, a page of corrected.

See PROOF READING, Japan. Page of...

JAPAN

Cabinet E Shelf 2 No. 38

See Mendoça, Joanne Gonzales de.. Historia de las cosas mas notables...

JAPAN

Cabinet RR Shelf 6 No. 38

Old papermaking in China and Japan. By Dard Hunter. Chillicothe, Ohio, 1932. Illus. No. 14 of 200 copies printed.

Half linen; 17¼ x 11-3/4 in. In slip case.

JAPAN

Cabinet R Shelf 3 No. 232

See Printing, Historical, Japan. Early History of printing in Japan ... 1881.

JAPAN

Cabinet R Shelf 3 No. 233

Motogi, Nagahisa, Japan's pioneer printer and inventor of types for Japanese characters. By Shigeri Magata, director of the Tokyo Tsukiji Type Foundry. Feb., 1893. With portrait.

Half morocco; 7-7/8 x 5 in.

JAPAN

Cabinet OO Shelf 6 No. 21

Paper industry. Illus. statistical article.

see NEWSPAPERS, SPECIAL ISSUES. Japan. (The) "Asahi"...1930, p. 169.

JAPAN

Cabinet 44 Shelf 2 No. 15

Printing Art Year Book.

see PERIODICALS, PRINTING. Japan Printing Art Year Book...

JAPAN

Cabinet K Shelf 6 No. 39.01

New Year Cards of the 18th century

see TABLADA, JOSE JUAN Japanese New Year Cards...

JAPAN

Cabinet C Shelf 2 No. 15.

Pictorial art, one hundred masterpieces of Japanese. Selected by the members of the faculty of The Tokyo Fine Art School. Tokyo, 1919. 2 vols.

Silk over boards; 19½ x 13½ in. Protective portfolio, Japanese style.

JAPAN.

Cabinet Y Shelf 2 No. 97

Reform de Japanischen nationalschrift. Geschichte der reformbestrebungen. Von Itsuaki Hatsukade. With 11 figures.

Article in Gutenberg-Gesellschaft Jahrbuch, 1932. p. 27.

JAPAN

Cabinet NN Shelf 4 No. 50

Newspaper evangelism in Japan

see PIETERS, ALBERTUS. Seven years of newspaper evangelism in Japan...

JAPAN

Cabinet AA Shelf 4 No. 30

(Popular history of printing: Japan, China, Korea. Japanese text, by Hisashito Makayama 2 vol. Illus. circa 1926)

Mss. outline translation of above book AA/4/31

Cloth; 9 x 5¾ in.

JAPAN

Cabinet 44 Shelf 2 No. 18

(A) Statistical survey on the Japanese type characters. Report No. 2. By Nobuo Nakamura. Research Bulletin of the Government Printing Bureau, Tokyo. June 1935.

Brochure, in envelope.

JAPAN

Cabinet Y Shelf 2 No. 23

Statistics of printing in Japan, brief.

See LORCK, CARL B. Handbuch der geschichte...Leipzig, 1882-1883 (part 2, pp. 110)

JAPAN.

Cabinet I Shelf 3 No. 1

[Wood Engraving in Japan]. Estampes Japonaises. Hiroshighe--Toyokuni--Kounyoshi--Kounisasa--Keisai Yeisen. [Article by Gaston Migeon.] Excerpt from Art et Décoration, February, 1914. Illus.

Item 31 in vol. with binder's title:"Various Engravers and About Engravers."

JAPAN ADVERTISER

Cabinet 00 Shelf 6 No. 20

Enthronement Edition. The Japan Advertiser. Benjamin W. Fleisher, Publisher and Editor. Tokyo, November 1928. Illus.

Cloth; 17 x $12\frac{1}{4}$ x $\frac{3}{4}$ in. In protective case.

JAPAN

Cabinet FF Shelf 5 No. 9.01

"Tanshiko", or Simplex printing machine based on the typewriter principle. By Sukekazu Wada, Managing Director of the Tanshiki Printing Co., Ltd. Tokyo, Japan, 1935.

Illus. pamphlet (2)

In envelope.

JAPAN

Cabinet J Shelf 3 No. 30

Wood engravings, Japanese, their history, technique and characteristics. By William Anderson. New edition. London, 1908. Illus.

Cloth; 6 x $4\frac{1}{2}$ x 5/8 in.

JAPAN PAPER COMPANY

Cabinet R Shelf 4 No. 14

Achievement; a treatise on one of the factors of the advancement of the art of printing, with examples. New York, 1920. Frontis.

List of contemporary printing, books etc., printed on Japan Paper Company's paper, and exhibited by the A.I.G.A.

Boards; 9 x 6-1/8 in. In slip case.

JAPAN.

Cabinet BB Shelf 4 No. 12.01

Visit of the Japanese Embassy to MacKellar, Smiths & Jordan's Type Foundry, Philadelphia, March 23, 1872. [Clippings from the press].

Also first rough proof of types cast from matrices made for the Imperial Government of Japan.

Items in manila envelope.

JAPAN

Cabinet J Shelf 3 No. 29

Wood engravings, Japanese; their history, technique and characteristics. By William Anderson, London, 1895. Illus.

Cloth; $10\frac{1}{2}$ x $7\frac{1}{4}$ in.

JAPAN PAPER COMPANY

Cabinet RR Shelf 6 No. 23

Hand-made papers from Italy, France, England, Spain, and Sweden, price list and samples of Japan Paper Company, New York, 1923.

Paper boards; $13\frac{1}{2}$ x 10-3/8 in.

JAPAN

Cabinet K Shelf 6 No. 39.01

War as seen by Japanese artists, the. Illus. excerpt from the Outlook, July 2, 1904.

Item 5 in bound collection with binder's title ENGRAVERS AND WOOD ENGRAVERS

JAPAN

Cabinet K Shelf 5 No. 4

Woodcuts of Japanese warriors, etc. Ei o Sanjuro Kassen. Sadahida, Koka, 1848. This is a block book printed and found prior to the introduction of typography in Japan.

Paper; 7-1/8 x $4\frac{3}{4}$ x $\frac{1}{2}$ in.

JAPAN PAPER COMPANY

Cabinet RR Shelf 6 No. 24

Hand made papers, Japanese, Italian, etc. Portfolio of samples. Japan Paper Company, Book No.44.

Paper board portfolio; 14-7/8 x 11 in.

JAPAN

Cabinet K Shelf 5 No. 6

Wood-cutting and wood-cut printing. By T. Tokuno. Washington, D. C. 1894. Smithsonian Institute.

From Report of the U. S. National Museum for 1892, pp. 221 - 144, with plates IV - XIII.

Half morocco; 9-3/4 x $6\frac{1}{4}$ in.

JAPAN.

See also

Cabinet Shelf No.

I EARLY PRINTING IN JAPAN. (Literature of)
II JOURNALISM, Japan.
III TYPE FOUNDING, Japan
IV PRINTING, HISTORICAL, Japan.
V SPECIMEN BOOKS, TYPES, Japan.
VI TYPES, PRINTING (Literature of)
VII PAPER MAKING, Japan.
VIII PLANTS, PRINTING, Japan.

JAPAN PAPER COMPANY

Cabinet RR Shelf 4 No. 2

Italian hand made paper making [Brief historical account] Japan Paper Company, New York, n.d. circa 1910. Pamphlet.

Item I in bound collection of pamphlets and excerpts on paper and paper making. "About Papers".

JAPAN

Cabinet K Shelf 5 No. 28

(Wood engravers of Yédo, and Japanese wood engravers)

see

BUSSET, MAURICE. (La) technique moderne du bois gravé...Paris (1925), p. 51.

JAPAN see also

Cabinet Shelf No.

PUBLISHING, Japan

JAPAN PAPER COMPANY

Cabinet RR Shelf 4 No. 2

Normandy vellum (from France.) Carried in stock by Japan Paper Company, Importers...New York.

Item 3 in bound collection of pamphlets and excerpts on paper and paper making. "About Papers".

JAPAN PAPER COMPANY

Cabinet RR Shelf 6 No. 18

Portfolio of hand made papers, samples.

Boards; 14-3/4 x 11 x 1 in.

JAPAN PAPER COMPANY

Cabinet RR Shelf 1 No. 42

Prices and samples of various papers; hand made, tissue papers, Japanese paper tapes, etc. Price lists of May 1, 1916 and Sept. 1, 1926. Japan Paper Company, New York.

Items in manila envelope.

JAPAN PAPER COMPANY

Cabinet RR Shelf 4 No. 47

Samples of hand-made Japanese vellum from the Shidzuoka Mill. Japan Paper Company, New York & Philadelphia.

Japanese vellum; 8-3/4 x 6 in.

JAPAN PAPER COMPANY

Cabinet RR Shelf 4 No. 47

Samples of imported paper sold by the Japan Paper Company.

17 items, with 1 dup. and 3 price lists, tied together.

In box with other items.

JAPAN PAPER COMPANY

Cabinet S Shelf 5 No. 3

Small brochure announcing this company's removal into new offices at 109 East 31st, New York City. Illus.

Bound in collection "Printers and their Plants," item 1.

JAPAN PAPER COMPANY.

Cabinet Shelf No.

See also Imprints, United States.

JAPANESE

Cabinet II Shelf 4 No. 8

Book (3 parts) in a contemporary Japanese binding, cloth with ivory tab fasteners. (circa 1890).

Cloth; 10 x 7 x $1\frac{1}{2}$ in.

JAPANESE

Cabinet II Shelf 4 No. 10

Book, novel? history? On cover "New York, Oct. 3, 1885, M. Kurumschi. My Dear Friend".

Gauze over paper; 9 x $5\frac{7}{8}$ x $\frac{3}{4}$ in.

JAPANESE

Cabinet E Shelf 2 No. 9

First European explanation of Japanese Characters Illus. On p. 246 of book entitled "Rerum a Socièiate Jesu in Oriente ... Naples, 1573.

Vellum over boards; $8\frac{1}{2}$ x $6\frac{1}{4}$ x $1\frac{1}{4}$ in.

JAPANESE

Cabinet II Shelf 4 No. 11

Language characters: Various Japanese. Subject? Place? Date?

Paper; 5-7/8 x 7 x 1-1/8 in.

JAPANESE

Cabinet II Shelf 4 No. 7

"Homa-ji" for writing and printing the Japanese language. Various early efforts toward a reformed alphabetical system.

Articles include: Letter from H. Koyama of the Imperial Printing Bureau, Tokyo.
II. A booklet of Romaji A.B.C.
III. Romanized Japanese Periodical
IV. Booklet of reformed Kanas.
V. Japanese paper recording the reformed Kanas.

(cont'd)

JAPANESE (cont'd)

Cabinet II Shelf 4 No. 7

VI. Present style Japanese book.

Items in manila envelope.

JAPANESE

Cabinet II Shelf 4 No. 9

Said to be first Japanese book printed from individual engraved characters, circa 18th century. An experiment which proved less satisfactory than printing from pages wholly engraved.

Paper; 10-7/8 x 8 x 3/8 in.

JAPANESE BOOKS.

Cabinet PP Shelf 1 No. 37

(Bibliography). Descriptive account of the Chinese, Tibetan, Mongol, and Japanese books in the Newberry Library. Chicago, Ill. 1913.

Cloth; $8\frac{3}{4}$ x $5\frac{3}{4}$ x 3/8 in.

JAPANESE PRINTER (The)

Cabinet 44 Shelf 2 No.

See PERIODICALS, PRINTING. Japan

JAPANESE PRINTS

Cabinet L Shelf 5 No. 12

Printed in colors from wood blocks by rubbing (no impression) 50 plates.

Paper; 14 x $9\frac{1}{2}$ x $\frac{1}{2}$ in.

JAPANESE PRINTS

Cabinet L Shelf 5 No. 15

Reproductions. Examples of color printing. With K. Ohashi's best wishes. (Tokyo, 1906?)

5 plates.

Paper; 2-3/8 x 10 in.

JAPANESE VISIT TO PHILADELPHIA

Cabinet Shelf No.

Diary of the Japanese visit to Philadelphia in 1872, containing descriptions of the manufacturing establishments inspected by them...Philadelphia, 1872.

p. 37, account of a visit to the type foundry of MacKellar, Smiths & Jordan.

Cloth; $9\frac{3}{4}$ x $6\frac{3}{4}$ x 3/8 in.

JAPANESE WOOD ENGRAVINGS

Cabinet 20 Shelf 1 No. 17

See Wood Engraving colored. (Critical essay on Japanese colored wood engraving and perspective problems.)

JAQUISH, O.

Cabinet FF Shelf 5 No. 2

Short talk on covers: Covers and bookmaking. n. p. n. d.

Boards; 10 x 6¾ x 3/8 in.

JARROLD FAMILY OF PRINTERS

Cabinet U Shelf 3 No. 73

(The) House of Jarrolds, 1823-1923 [Established 1770]. A brief history of one hundred years. Printed at their works, The Empire Press, Norwich, 1924. Portraits and Illus.

Half morocco; 9-5/8 x 6¼ x 5/8 in.

JASPER, FRIEDRICH

Cabinet Y Shelf 5 No. 68

(Viennese printer of the early 20th century. Friedrich Jasper, on his 80th birthday. A contribution to the history of printing in Vienna). Ein Wiener buchdrucker um die wende des zwanzigsten jahrhunderts. Ein beitrag zu Wiens buchdruckergeschichte. von Carl Junker, Wien, 1927. Portrait.

Paper; 11½ x 8-5/8 x 3/8 in.

JAUGEON

Cabinet V Shelf 4 No. 28

Theories on letter designing: Brief descriptive sketch, based on Jaugeon's book entitled: Description et perfection des arts et metiers: Des arts de construire les caractères, de graver les poincons de lettres, d' imprimer les lettres etc. Illus.

See pp. 273-276: Débuts de l'Imprimerie en France. Par Arthur Christian. Paris, 1905

Half morocco; 11¼ x 8 x1¼ in.

JAUREGUI, JOSEPH.

Cabinet Shelf No.

See Early Printing in Mexico. Mexico, 1770, Joseph Jauregui.

JAVA

Cabinet 26 Shelf 2 No. 2

See Specimens, Types, Holland. Enschede, Joh. and Zohnen.

JAVAJI, TUKARAM

Cabinet Shelf No.

See Specimen Books, Types. India

JAVAL, M.

Cabinet V Shelf 5 No. 15

Evolution de la typographie considerée dans ses rapports avec l'hygiene de la vue. Par M. Javal. En la Revue Scientifique, June 25, 1881. p. 802.

A study of type forms, with a brief history of type development.

Cloth; 11¾ x 8½ in.

JBANEZ, Sebastian

Cabinet X Shelf 3 No. 19

Brief bio-bibliographical note, with printer mark, Jbanez (Madrid), 1570-1595.

see

HAEBLER, KONRAD. (Spanish and Portuguese printer marks...p.xxxiv

---

JEBB, R. C.

Cabinet 00 Shelf 4 No. 29

Ancient organs of public opinions. An address delivered before the members of the Phi B.K. Society at Harvard College, June, 26, 1884, by R.C. Jebb. Cambridge (England): Printed at The University Press.

Brochure; in envelope with other items.

JEFFERSON, THOMAS

Cabinet G Shelf 2 No. 30

Letter written by T. Jefferson to his daughter Martha dated Nov. 28, 1783. Printed at the Grabhorn Press for Alfred Sutro ... for members of the Roxburgh Club of San Francisco, 1929.

Paper wrapper; 13½ x 10-3/8 in.

JEFFRIES, B. JOY

Cabinet FF Shelf 3 No. 79

Our eyes and our industries. By B. Joy Jeffries, A.M., M.D. (Harvard). Boston, 1887. Illus. pamphlet.

Item in manila envelope.

JEHNE, PAUL

Cabinet Y Shelf 5 No. 92

(Printers' Medals) Über buchdruck-medaillen. Nach einem älterem werke beschrieben vervollständigt und neu geordnet. von Paul Jehne. Dippoldiswalde, 1907.

Cloth; 8¾ x 5-5/8 x 5/8 in.

JENKINS, CHARLES F.

Cabinet R Shelf 3 No. 83

Guide book to historic Germantown. Prepared for the Site and Relic Society. By C. F. Jenkins, Germantown, 1904. Illus.

Contains information concerning early Pennsylvania printers, Sauer (Sower) and others. pp. 44, 109: "Type first made in America." p. 45: "Paper making, first in America." p. 130.

Boards; 6½ x 4¾ in.

JENKINSON, FRANCIS.

Cabinet 75 Shelf 2 No. 5.01

List of the incunabula collected by George Dunn. Arranged to illustrate the history of printing. Supplement to the Bibliographical Society's Transactions. No. 3. In Volume of Supplements 1-5, 1921-1926.

Boards, linen back; 8-7/8 x 7 x 1¾ in.

JENKINSON, FRANCIS.

Cabinet PP Shelf 1 No. 38

List of the incunabula collected by George Dunn arranged to illustrate the history of printing. Printed at the Oxford University Press for the Bibliographical Society. London, 1923.

Supplement to the Biblio. Soc. Trans. No. 3.

Half morocco; 8¾ x 7-1/8 x ½ in.

JENKINSON, FRANCIS.

Cabinet 75 Shelf 2 No. 7

Memoire, A. by H. F. Stewart, reviewed by Stephen Gaselee.

In Transactions of the Bibliographical Society, "The Library," Vol. VII, 1926-1927, pp. 98-103.

JENKINSON, FRANCIS.

Cabinet 75 Shelf 2 No. 7

Ulrich Zell's early quartos. A paper read at Cambridge as a Sanders Lexture. Dec. 4, 1908.

In Transactions of the Bibliographical Society, "The Library," Vol. VII, 1926-27, pp. 46-66.

JENKINSON, HILARY.

Cabinet 75 Shelf 2 No. 3

Elizabethan handwritings. A paper read before the Bibliographical Society January 16th, 1922 Facsimiles.

In Trans. Biblio. Soc., "The Library," Vol. 3 1922-23, pp. 1-34.

JENKINSON, HILARY.

Cabinet 75 Shelf 1 No. 13

English current writing and early printing. A paper read before the Bibliographical Society, February 15th, 1915. Illus.

In Trans. Biblio. Soc., Vol. XIII, 1913-15, pp. 273-275.

JENKINSON, RICHARD C.

Cabinet PP Shelf 1 No. 44

Collection of books chosen to show the work of the best printers. Book II. The Public Library. Newark, New Jersey, 1929. (Catalogue).

Boards; 8 x 5 x ¾ in.

JENNINGS, H. C.

Cabinet Shelf No.

See Ink Manufacturers, France.

JENNIS, LUCAS.

Cabinet E Shelf 3 No. 31

See Early Printing in Germany. Frankfort a.M., 1626. Lucas Jennis.

JENNIS, LUCAS
SEE ALSO

Imprints.

JENSEN, PHIL. HANS

Cabinet L Shelf 3 No. 27

Geschichte der schrift. von Dr. Phil. Hans Jensen. Mit 303 abbildungen. Hannover, 1925.

Cloth; 12-3/8 x 9¼ in.

JENSON, NICOLAS

Cabinet S Shelf 5 No. 25.02

Artist - printer, Venice, 1465-1481. [Biographical account]. by Louis K. Comstock, Montclair, Dec., 25, 1928.

Pamphlet in box labelled "Pamphlets and excerpts relating to printers, their plants, and other typographical matters". Box No.2.

JENSON, NICOLAS

Cabinet Q Shelf 2 No. 30

Artist-printer-publisher. Biographical sketch of Jenson.

See PUBLISHING. Aldus, Froben, Jenson ... Montclair, 1928.

JENSON, NICOLAS

Cabinet X Shelf 3 No. 14

Bibliographical notes, with printer marks, Jenson Venice, 1470.

see

KRISTELLER, Dr. PAUL. Italienischen buchdrucker...p.90

JENSON, NICOLAS

Cabinet 26 Shelf 1 No. 16

Brief biographical notes, with a historical account of Jenson Roman type faces. Illus.

See Essay by Audin in Gutenberg-Gesellschaft Jahrbuch, 1927, pp.26-42.

JENSON, NICOLAS

Cabinet 73 Shelf 2 No. 17

Bullen, Henry Lewis. Nicolas Jenson, printer of Venice: His famous type designs and some comments upon the printing types of the early printers. By Henry L. Bullen, Librarian of the American Typographic Library and Museum at Jersey City. Printed by John Henry Nash, San Francisco, 1926.

Boards; 16⅛ x 10½ in.

JENSON, NICOLAS

Cabinet S Shelf 1 No. 29

See De Vinne, Theodore Low. Notable printers of Italy ... New York, 1910. p. 72.

JENSON, NICOLAS

Cabinet AA Shelf 1 No. 17

Esame sui principe della Francese ed Italiana Tipografia, ovvero storia critica di Nicolas Jenson ... da Giacomo Sardini. Lucca. Vol. I, 1796, Vol. II, 1797, Vol. III, 1798: Bound in one Vol.

Plates, facsimiles of the types used by Jenson, etc.

Boards, vellum back; 15 x 10½ in.

JENSON, NICOLAS

Cabinet 27 Shelf 2 No. 26

(History of the Celebrated Cloister Type Family from its earliest use by Nicolas Jenson in Venice in 1470 to its revival by the American Type Founders Co. in 1895, at the suggestion of Henry L. Bullen). Mr. Morris Benton recut Jenson's Roman and designed the Italic and other additions to Jenson's design. Narrative of Cloister Oldstyle, Cloister Oldstyle Italic and Cloister Title. By Henry Lewis Bullen.

see THE AMERICAN BULLETIN, April, 1914, page 4.

JENSON, NICOLAS

Cabinet V Shelf 5 No. 10

In what school did Nicolas Jenson learn printing?

See Madden, J. P. A. Lettres d'un Bibliographe Deuxième Série. 1873. [Letter 15].

JENSON, NICOLAS.

Cabinet 6 Shelf 1 No. 8

See Incunabula. Bonifacius VIII (Benedetto Gaetana)

JENSON, NICOLAS

Cabinet 6 Shelf 1 No. 2 Vault

See Incunabula. Eusebius Pamphilius. De evangelica praeparatione. Venice, Nicolaus Jenson, 1470.

JENSON, NICOLAS

Cabinet AA Shelf 1 No. 17

Types used by Jenson: The Roman majusculi, the minusculi, the abbreviations and punctuation marks, Greek fonts, and blackletter fonts.
See Sardini, Giacomo. Esame sui principi della Francese ed Italiana tipografia ...

JERROLD, WALTER

Cabinet T Shelf 5 No. 110

Triumphs of the printing press. London, n.d. Illus.
Historical account of printing from its origin to 1884.

Cloth; 7½ x 5 x ¾ in.

JENSON, NICOLAS

Cabinet 6 Shelf 1 No. 10

See Incunabula. Joannes Carthusiensis. [Giov. di Dio]......

JENSON, NICOLAUS

Cabinet D Shelf 1 No. 64

Venice, 1470-1478. (Some original folios, Jenson printing. Gothic type, rubricated.)

In portfolio labeled "Jenson Printing, 1470-1478".

JERSEY JOURNAL (THE)

Cabinet LL Shelf 5 No. 8.02

Contest of printing lay-out for an advertisement. Specimens.

In envelope.

JENSON, NICOLAS

Cabinet 6 Shelf 1 No. 4

See Incunabula. Pliny (the second), Caius: Naturalis Historiae. Venice, nicolas Jenson, 1472.

JENSON, NICOLAS

See also Imprints.

JERSEY JOURNAL (The)

Cabinet A Shelf 2 No. 64

See Newspapers, anniversary issues.

JENSON, NICOLAS

Cabinet S Shelf 1 No. 112

(The) Last will and testament of the late Nicolas Jenson, printer, who departed this life at the City of Venice in the month of September A.D., 1480.
This book is Ludlow-Set in a new type designed by Ernst Detterer ... and printed by the Ludlow Typograph Company of Chicago, Nov. 1928.

Boards; 11½ x 8 in.

JERMAIN, FRANCES D.

Cabinet L Shelf 2 No. 18

Alphabet, in the path of the. An historical account of the ancient beginnings and evolution of the modern alphabet. By Frances D. Jermain, Fort Wayne, Indiana, 1906. Illus.

Stamped cloth; 8 x 6 in.

JESSEN, PETER

Cabinet Y Shelf 5 No. 99

Führer für die sonderausstellung die kunst im neuren buchdruck. Kunstgewerbe Museum, Berlin, Dezember 1904-Januar 1905. (Text by Peter Jessen)
Guide to an exhibition of modern printing.

Half morocco; 7-1/8 x 5¼ in.

JENSON, NICOLAS

Cabinet I Shelf 1 No. 33

(Paper marks in the different papers used by Jenson, explanation of the). Explication des marques des différentes especes de papier dont s'est servi le célèbre imprimeur Nicolas Jenson.
See p.340 of JANSEN'S Essai sur l'origine de la gravure... Tome I, Paris, 1808.

JERROLD, DOUGLAS

Cabinet 00 Shelf 4 No. 15

"Punch" (The London) and Douglas Jerrold. By Walter Jerrold. London, 1910. With portraits and illus.

Cloth; 9-1/8 x 6 x 1½ in.

JESSEN, PETER

Cabinet L Shelf 3 No. 35

Meister der schreibkunst aus drei jahrhunderten. Ausgewahlt, von Peter Jessen, Stuttgart, 1923.
Masters of the art of writing, 16th to 18th century. With 200 plates of specimens.

Boards; 13 x 10 in.

JENSON, NICOLAS

Cabinet Shelf No.

See Printing, Historical, France. (Tours) Les origines de l'imprimerie à Tours, 1467-1550. .....

JERROLD, WALTER

Cabinet 00 Shelf 4 No. 15

"Punch" (London) and Douglas Jerrold. London, 1910. With portraits and illus.

Cloth; 9-1/8 x 6 x 1½ in.

JESSEN, PETER

Cabinet K Shelf 1 No. 12

Meister des ornamentstichs: Gothik und Renaissance. 200 bildtafeln. Ausgewahlt von Peter Jessen. (BandI) Berlin, n. d. circa 1926.
200 plates of design.

Boards, cloth back; 13½ x 9-7/8 x 1 in.

JESSEN, PETER

Cabinet K Shelf 4 No. 9

Ornamentstich. Geschichte der vorlagen des kunsthandwerks seit dem mittelalter. von Peter Jessen. Berlin, 1920. Illus.

History of decorative design and ornament.

Boards, linen back; 9½ x 6-3/8 x 7/8 in.

JESSEN, PETER

Cabinet Y Shelf 5 No. 107

(The) Public Art Library; formerly the Library of Art and Crafts Museum in Berlin. A farewell message). Die Staatliche kunstbibliothek in Berlin. Ein abschiedswort von Peter Jessen. Berlin, 1924. Brochure.

Paper; 9-5/8 x 6-5/8 in.

JESSEN, DR. PETER

Cabinet K Shelf 1 No. 11

Rococco engravings, two hundred plates of the 18th century selected by Dr. Peter Jessen, and reproduced in collotype. London,1922.

One of an edition of 250 copies.

Cloth: 13½ x 10¼ x 7/8 in.

JESUIT PRESS (1580) see

Cabinet U Shelf 5 No. 24

POLLARD, A. W. Fine Books...London, 1912, p.228

JETTINGER, CARL A.

Cabinet NN Shelf 3 No. 39

How and what to write as news. A book for correspondents and editors.

By Carl A. Jettinger. Salt Lake City, Utah. 1921. Porte Publishing Company.

Leatherette: 7½x5¼"

JEUNESSE, AUG.

Cabinet V Shelf 5 No. 14

L'Imprimerie et les livres. Historique. La Librairie à l'Expostion de 1867. La matérial: machines à composer. La fonderie en caractères. Clichage etc. Paris, 1874. Chaps. I to IV by Aug. Jeunesse in Gobin's L'Art de Peindre la Parole.

Paper; 10 x 6½ in.

JEUNESSE, AUG.

Cabinet V Shelf 5 No. 14

Stereotypie...

See ENGRAVING PROCESSES, METHODS OF. [Stereotypie.] Par Aug. Jeunesse. Paris, 1874.

JEWETT, CHARLES C.

Cabinet FF Shelf 1 No. 82

Construction of catalogues of libraries and their publication by means of separate stereotyped titles, with rules and examples. Second edition: published by the Smithsonian Institute, 1853.

Cloth; 9¼ x 6½ in.

JEWETT, JOHN L.

Cabinet JJ Shelf 3 No. 6

Franklin - his genius, life, and character: An oration delivered before the New York Typographical Society, on the occasion of the birthday of Franklin at the Printer's Festival, held January 17, 1849. Published by order of the Society. New York.

Cloth; 9-1/8 x 5⅝ x ¾ in.

JEWETT, JOHN L.

Cabinet CC Shelf 1 No. 42

Franklin: his genius, life, and character. An oration delivered before the New York Typographical Society, on the occasion of the birthday of Franklin, at the Printers' Festival, held Jan. 17, 1849.

See p.185, Brenton's Voices of the Press ...New York, 1850.

JEWITT, LLEWELLYN

Cabinet Q Shelf 3 No. 13

Hutton, William, the life of, and the history of the Hutton family. Edited from the original manuscripts, with addition of numerous notes ...With original portraits. London, 1872.

Cloth; 7-1/8 x 4-7/8 in.

JOANNES DAMASCENUS

Cabinet 40 Shelf 1 No. 1

Theologia Damasceni: Joannis Damasceni de orthodoxa fide liber, interprete Jacobo Fabro Stapulensi. Parisiis, per Henrieum Stephanum, 1507.

Calf; 8¼ x 3½ x 1 in.

JOBARD, J.B.A.M.

Cabinet O Shelf 1 No. 93

L'Exposition de 1839, rapport de. Industrie Française, typographie, lithographie et reliure. Bruxelles, 1842.

Half morocco; 8-3/4 x ½ in.

JOBIN, BERNHARD

Cabinet X Shelf 3 No. 13

Brief bio-bibliographical note, with printer mark Jobin, Strassburg, 1572-1595.

see

HEITZ, PAUL. Elsässische büchermarken...p.xxv, plate xxxvii-xl

JOBINUS, BERNARD

Cabinet E Shelf 2 No. 47

See Early Printing in Germany. Strassburg, 1590. Bernard Jobinus.

JOCELYN, SIMEON S. (Whitney & Jocelyn)

Cabinet J Shelf 2 No. 44

see

WOOD ENGRAVERS, ADVERTISEMENTS OF (Alphabetically arranged list)

JOFFRE, Juan

Cabinet X Shelf 3 No. 19

Bio-bibliographical sketch, with printer mark, Joffre (Valencia), 1502-1528.

see

HAEBLER, KONRAD. (Spanish and Portuguese printer marks...p.xv)

JOHANN de SPIRA

Cabinet Shelf No.

See Giovanni da Spira.

JOHANNES [Carthusiensis Giov. de Dio].

Cabinet 6 Shelf 1 No. 10

Nosce te ipsum. [First line begins]: Ego Phillipus rota iuris utruisqum doctor... Venice, Nicolai Jenson, 1480.
Lacks title page.

Boards; $8\frac{1}{4}$ x $5\frac{3}{4}$ x 7/8 in.

JOHANNES DE COLONIA

Cabinet D Shelf 1 No. 37

See Incunabula. Antoninus...Venice [1474]

JOHANNISBERT MASCHINENFABRIK

Cabinet Shelf No.

See MASCHINENFABRIK JOHANNISBERG.

JOHN OF WESTPHALIA.

Cabinet 75 Shelf 2 No. 9

Books from his press...Alost, 1473.

See Kronenberg, M. E. English printing (early 16th century) in the Low Countris ... pp. 153-, 154 and fol.

JOHN, J. SÖHNE

Cabinet Shelf No.

See Specimen Books, Types. Germany.

JOHN CARTER BROWN LIBRARY, THE.

Cabinet S Shelf 3 No. 79

[List] of books printed in Lima, 1585-1800. Books printed in Lima and elsewhere in South America after 1800. The Merrymount Press, Boston, 1908.

Boards; $10\frac{1}{4}$ x 7 in.

JOHN CARTER BROWN LIBRARY

Cabinet S Shelf 3 No. 80

Stillwell, Margaret B. The influence of William Morris. As shown by an exhibition of books from the later English Presses at the John Carter Brown Library in Dec., 1911. Providence, R. I. Reprinted 1912.

Half morocco; $6\frac{1}{2}$ x 4-7/8 in.

JOHN CARTER BROWN LIBRARY, The.
See also
Libraries, Private.

Cabinet Shelf No.

JOHN RYLANDS LIBRARY (see)

Cabinet Shelf No.

Rylands, John

JOHNE-WERK, A.-G.

Cabinet EE Shelf 4 No. 80.01

(Catalogue, 1929. paper cutting machine, the "Perfecta") The "Perfecta, the most powerful accurate and rapid guillotine ... Johne-Werk A.-G., Bautzen (Germany). Represented in the U.S.A. by Messrs. H. H. Heinrich, Inc., 15 Park Row, New York.

Pamphlet in manila envelope.

JOHNS, JAMES

Cabinet G Shelf 4 No. 30.06

Brief sketch or outline of the history of the town of Huntington; Chittendon County, Vermont. Compiled by James Johns, 1859. (Mss. photostat).

Original document in the Vermont Historical Society.

Boards; 9 x 6-3/8 in.

JOHNS, JAMES.

Cabinet NN Shelf 5 No. 4

Vermont Autograph and Remarker. Huntington, Vt May 31, 1861. Edited and pen-made by Johns. pp. 4, each page 4-1/8 x 6-1/8 in.

Paper boards; $6\frac{3}{4}$ x $4\frac{1}{4}$ in.

JOHNSON, A. F.

Cabinet 75 Shelf 2 No. 8

Basle ornaments on Paris books, 1519-36. By A. F. Johnson. London, Dec., 1927. Illus.

In Transactions of the Bibliographical Society, vol. VIII, 1927-1928. pp. 355-360.

JOHNSON, A. F.

Cabinet U Shelf 4 No. 33

Basle, The first century of printing at. With fifty illustrations. In series of handbooks "Periods of Typography", edited by Stanley Morison. London, 1926.

Linen over boards; 9-7/8 x $7\frac{1}{2}$ x 3/8 in.

JOHNSON, ALFRED FORBES.

Cabinet 75 Shelf 2 No. 3

Books printed at Lyons in the 16th century. A paper read before the Bibliographical Society, October 16th, 1922.

In Trans. Biblio. Soc., "The Library," Vol. III, 1922-23, pp. 145-174.

JOHNSON, ALFRED FORBES

Cabinet 76 Shelf 2 No. 42

Catalogue of engraved and etched title-pages, down to the death of William Faithorn, 1691. Compiled by A.F. Johnson. Bibliographical Society (England), 1934 (for 1933).
Facsimiles and Illustrations No.1V

Boards, linen back; 11 x 9 x $1\frac{1}{4}$ in.

JOHNSON, A. F. (compiler) see

Cabinet 84 Shelf 1 No. 1a

CATALOGUE OF SPECIMENS OF PRINTING TYPES...

JOHNSON, A.F.

Cabinet 75 Shelf 2 No. 9

Classification of Gothic types. [With facsimile specimens, 15th century]. A paper read before the Bibliographical Society, 17 Dec. 1928.

In Trans. Bibl. Soc. "The Library," vol. IX pp. 357-80. 1928-1929.

JOHNSON, ALFRED FORBES.

Cabinet 76 Shelf 2 No. 29

German Renaissance title-borders. Selected by A. F. Johnson. Printed for the Bibliographical Society at the Oxford University Press, 19091
Facsimiles and Illustrations No. I

Board; 11¼ x 9.in.

JOHNSON, A. F.

Cabinet 75 Shelf 2 No. 7

Periods of typography. Italian 16th century. London, 1926. Book with above title reviewed by A. W. Pollard.

In Transactions of the Bibliographical Society "The Library," Vol. VII, 1926-1927, p. 111.

JOHNSON, G. J.

Cabinet S Shelf 4 No. 90

(The) Printing Press as a power for good. Illustrated by many facts, incidents, and experiences, gathered casually from various sources. By G. J. Johnson, Philadelphia: American Baptist Publication Society, 1885.

Half morocco; 6-7/8 x 4½ in.

JOHNSON, A. F.

Cabinet U Shelf 4 No. 31

Italian [Printing] 16th century, The. With fifty illustrations. In series of handbooks "Periods of Typography", edited by Stanley Morison, London, 1926.

Boards; 9-7/8 x 7½ x 3/8 in.

JOHNSON, A. F.

Cabinet K Shelf 6 No. 30

Woodcut writing books, (Illus. article)

see

WOODCUT ANNUAL (British) 1930. pp. 17-29.

JOHNSON, H.T.

Cabinet FF Shelf 6 No. 81

Brief biographical notices. Excerpts from the Inland Printer, vol.35,p.564, July,1905. With portrait.

Mr. Johnson died in May, 1932. Much of the material relating to Type Composing Machines was gathered by him.

Items in envelope.

JOHNSON, A.F.

Cabinet 26 Shelf 1 No. 21

Italic type in the 18th century. Illus. essay.

Article in the "Gutenberg-Gesellschaft Jahrbuch, 1931", pp.262-268.

JOHNSON, A.P. (Compiler)

Cabinet LL Shelf 4 No. 21 (6 vols.)

Advertising, Library of. Fundamental principles, Advertising mediums; Methods of Appeal; Mediums and Publications; Type; Department Store and Retail Advertising; Selling Advertising; Show Window Display and Specialty Advertising...Compiled and edited by A.P. Johnson. Chicago, 1913. (6 vols. Illus.)

Cloth; 10¼ x 7 in.

JOHNSON, H.T.

Cabinet FF Shelf 6 No. 61

Fifty years of mechanical composition. By H.T. Johnson. Reprinted from Jubilee Number of "Printers Register", July, 1913.

Presentation copy signed and dated "April 1919" by the author.

Cloth; 7-3/8 x 4⅝ x 3/8 in.

JOHNSON, A.F.

Cabinet 26 Shelf 1 No. 17

Oronce Fine as an illustrator of books.
Bibliographical account.
Article in the Gutenberg-Gesellschaft Jahrbuch 1928. pp.107-9.

JOHNSON, BENJAMIN

Cabinet QQ Shelf 3 No. 37

Publisher, Philadelphia, 1804. Brief biographical notes concerning Johnson in letter and inscription in Bible.

see

BIBLES. Philadelphia, 1804...

JOHNSON, H.T.

Cabinet FF Shelf 6 No. 18

Fifty years of mechanical composition. Article in the Printer's Register, July 7, 1913.
Excerpt on folio 176 of scrap book compiled by Hohn S. Thompson.

Scrap Book.

JOHNSON, A. F.

Cabinet 75 Shelf 2 No. 7

Periods of typography. The first century of printing at Basle. London, 1926. Book with above title reviewed by A. W. Pollard.

In Transactions of the Bibliographical Society, "The Library," Vol. VII, 1926-27, p. 111.

JOHNSON, EDMUND C.

Cabinet T Shelf 4 No. 58

Tangible typography; or, how the blind read. London, 1853.
The book includes an account of various systems, and a list of the books which have been printed in them.

Full morocco, gilt; 8-5/8 x 5½ x ½ in.

JOHNSON, HENRY

Cabinet FF Shelf 2 No. 3

Introduction to logography: or the art of arranging and composing for printing with words intire, their radices and terminations,instead of single letters. By his Majesty's Royal Letters Patent. Printed logographically, and sold by J. Walter,bookseller,Charing-Cross. London,n.d. before 1783 ?

Probably an advance copy, as inscription on fly-leaf reads:"To be dedicated if the author can obtain permission, to the King's most excellent Majesty."

Half calf; 8 x 5 in.

JOHNSON, A.F.

Cabinet U Shelf 4 No. 34

Periods of Typography: French 16th century printing. With fifty illustrations. London: Ernest Benn, Ltd., 1928.

Boards; 9¾ x 7-3/8 in.

JOHNSON, EDMUND C.

Cabinet II Shelf 6 No. 8

Tangible typography: or, how the blind read. By Edmund C. Johnson. London: 1853.

Has ten specimen pages of shorthand alphabet for the blind, on the phonetic principle, various systems.

Cloth; 9 x 5-3/4 in.

JOHNSON, HENRY

Cabinet FF Shelf 2 No. 4

Introduction to logography, or the art of arranging and composing for printing with words intire, their radices and terminations, instead of single letters. By Henry Johnson, London: printed logographically, and sold by J. Walter. 1783

Half calf; 8¼ x 5½ in.

JOHNSON, HENRY LEWIS (Editor)

Cabinet 43 Shelf 1 No.

(The) Engraver and Printer, Boston, Mass., 1893-

See PERIODICALS, PRINTING, United States (The) Engraver and Printer...

JOHNSON, HENRY LEWIS

Cabinet LL Shelf 3 No. 1 Box

Master art of democracy, the.
An article on the art of printing. Set up in dummy form. Includes another article "The benefits of printing" by Henry Lewis Bullen.

Four "dummy" sheets in box labelled "Proof Reading: Various items".

JOHNSON, JAMES SYDNEY.

Cabinet G Shelf 2 No. 38

Child of Adam, A. Printed in San Francisco by the Johnson Brothers, The Windsor Press, 1927

Boards, 7¾ x 4-3/4 ins.,pp.47.

JOHNSON, HENRY LEWIS (Editor)

Cabinet 43 Shelf 1 No.

(The) Graphic Arts, Boston, Mass.

See PERIODICALS, PRINTING, United State (The) Graphic Arts...

JOHNSON, HENRY LEWIS

Cabinet 27 Shelf 2 No. 27

The master art of democracy (printing). Article by Henry Lewis Johnson.

see THE AMERICAN BULLETIN, December, 1915, p. 2.

JOHNSON, JAMES SYDNEY.

Cabinet G Shelf 4 No. 39

Press of the Renaissance in Italy: An essay. Printed by the Brothers Johnson, San Francisco, 1927. Illustrations adapted from the "Hypnerotomachia Poliphili", of Aldus Manutius.

Boards, 11 x 7½ ins., pp.30

JOHNSON, HENRY LEWIS

Cabinet NN Shelf 7 No. 25

Graphic Arts, The. Prospectus of a new monthly magazine for the printers of America. Edited by Henry Lewis Johnson. Published by National Arts Publishing Company, 200 Summer Street, Boston, 1910. With portraits.

Half morocco; 12¾ x 9½ in.

JOHNSON, HENRY LEWIS

Cabinet RR Shelf 2 No. 28

Parsons handbook of letter-headings. An authoritative manual of text matter, principles of arrangement and standards in style. By Paper Company, Holyoke, Mass. n.d.

Boards, oblong; 5-3/4 x 8-3/4 x 3/8 in.

JOHNSON, JOHN

Cabinet U Shelf 2 No. 130

(The) Printer, his customers and his men. By John Johnson, Printer to the University of Oxford. With a foreword by Hugh R. Dent. Issued as a Supplement to the December 1933 issue of the Members Circular of the British Federation of Master Printers, London.

Brochure, in manila envelope.

JOHNSON, HENRY LEWIS.

Stack A Shelf 1&2 Number 72

His latest work for printers, by Henry Lewis Bullen, in The Inland Printer, vol. LXXII, p. 317. Portrait.

Brief biographical account of the former editor of "Printing Art."

JOHNSON, HENRY LEWIS (Editor)

Cabinet 45 Shelf 1 and 2 No.

Printing Art (The). Issued by the University Press Cambridge, U.S.A. Henry Lewis Johnson, editor.

See PERIODICALS, PRINTING, United States Printing Art (The)...

JOHNSON, JOHN.

Cabinet T Shelf 6 No. 61

Printers' preceptor, a: One hundred years ago. Thoughts on "Typographia." H.W. Westbrook. n.p.n.d.
Illus. brief bio-bibliographical account.

Brochure in box labelled "English printing and printers. Shakespeariana. Misc. v.d."

JOHNSON, HENRY LEWIS.

Cabinet P Shelf 2 No. 36.01

Historic design in printing. Reproductions of book covers, borders, initials, decorations, printers' marks and devices comprising reference material for the designer, printer, advertiser and publisher. With introduction and notations by Henry Lewis Johnson. Boston: The Graphic Arts Company, 1923.

This is a duplicate of P/2/36 in another form.

Cloth; 12¼ x 9 1/8 x ¾ in.

JOHNSON, HENRY LEWIS

Cabinet P Shelf 2 No. 37.01

Resources for motifs in book and catalogue covers. Second part. Illus.
From The New England Printer, August, 1924.

In envelope.

JOHNSON, JOHN

Cabinet T Shelf 3 No. 7 2 vols.

Typographia, or the Printers' Instructor: Including an account of the origin of printing, with biographical notices of the printers of England, from Caxton to the close of the 16th century: A series of ancient and modern alphabets, and the Domesday characters; together with an elucidation of every subject connected with the art. By J. Johnson, printer. London, 1824. 2 vols.

Half morocco; each vol. 9 x 5-7/8 x 1½ in.

JOHNSON, HENRY LEWIS (Typographic Laboratory)

Cabinet G Shelf 3 No. 79

Imprint, 1931.

See Imprints, United States. Typographic Laboratory.

JOHNSON, HENRY LEWIS

Cabinet 43 Shelf 1 No. 7

Services of Henry Lewis Johnson to the Printing Industry. By Henry Lewis Bullen, Oct.16, 1911.
With a confidential relation of the condition of the National Arts Publishing Company, a Massachusetts (Boston) Corporation.

Small brochure on first blank page of vol.1, The Graphic Arts, 1911.

JOHNSON, JOHN

Cabinet MM Shelf 3 No. 15 2 vols.

Typographia, or the printers' instructor: including an account of the origin of printing, with biographical notes of the printers of England, from Caxton to the close of the 16th century, a series of ancient and modern alphabets and Domesday characters, together with an elucidation of every subject connected with the art. London, 1824. 2 vols.
Has portrait of Caxton and devices of printers.

(cont'd)

JOHNSON, J. (cont'd)

Cabinet MM Shelf 3 No. 15

Large paper, printed within ornamental borders.

Half morocco gilt; 9 x 5-7/8 in.

JOHNSON, LAWRENCE & Co. see also

BIOGRAPHIES, TYPE FOUNDERS

see also: SPECIMEN BOOKS, TYPES. United States.
" " " WOOD TYPES

Cabinet Shelf No.

JOHNSON, Dr. (Samuel)

Cabinet FF Shelf 2 No. 8

Rasselas, Prince of Abissinia. Printed with patent types, in a manner never before attempted. Rusher's edition, Banbury: 1804.

Philip Rusher patented this "new mode" in 1802, and put it to practical test in 1804, by the publication of this book.

Boards; 9 x 5½ in. See also FF/2/9 (second copy)

JOHNSON, JOHN

Cabinet MM Shelf 5 No. 5

Typographia. An abridgment of Johnson's Typographia, or the printers' instructor: With an appendix. Boston: C.L. Adams, print. 1828. Illus.

Title within engraved borders.

Half morocco; 7-3/8 x 4¾ x 1 in.

JOHNSON, LOUIS K. (Inventor) see

Cabinet FF Shelf 6 No. 19

COMPOSING MACHINES. Johnson, Louis K...

JOHNSON, DR. (Samuel)

Cabinet 30 Shelf 1 No. 35.01

Rasselas, prince of Abissinia. By Dr. Johnson. Printed with patent types, in a manner never before attempted. Rusher's Edition. Banbury, 1804. Printed by W. Bulmer and Co. London.

Half morocco; 8½ x 5¼ x 5/8 in.

JOHNSON, LAWRENCE

Cabinet 21 Shelf 2 No. 1

Obituary notice.

In "The Printer", vol. 2, May, 1860, p. 279.

JOHNSON, MARMADUKE

Cabinet F Shelf 1 No. 9

See Early Printing in Massachusetts. Cambridge 1663. Samuel Green and Marmaduke Johnson.

JOHNSON, Dr. SAMUEL see also

Cabinet Shelf No.

NEWTON, A. EDWARD.
Strahan's (Mr.) dinner party...

JOHNSON, LAWRENCE

Cabinet 21 Shelf 2 No. 2

Obituary notice additional to that of May 1860. With portrait.

In "The Printer", Vol. 3, No. 5, Oct., 15, 1860.

JOHNSON, PHILIP

Cabinet S Shelf 5 No. 25.02

Japanese Gutenberg, The. [Motogi Nagahisa, the first Japanese typefounder and printer] Excerpt from the Book-Lover, Nov.-Dec- 1901.

Pamphlet in box labelled "Pamphlets and excerpts relating to printers, their plants, and other typographical matters". Box No.2.

JOHNSON BROTHERS.

Cabinet Shelf No.

See Imprints, United States. Windsor Press, The.

JOHNSON, LAWRENCE

Cabinet FF Shelf 1 No. 55

Stereotyping, Philadelphia, 1827-68. Lawrence Johnson, manuscript journal of agreements made with publishers for type composition, etc.

Boards; 10 x 7¾ in.

JOHNSON, ROBERT

Cabinet I Shelf 2 No. 32

Retouching photographic negatives, the art of... Twelfth edition revised and rewritten by T.S. Bruce and Alfred Braithwaite. Revised and enlarged, by Arthur Hammond. Boston, Mass., 1930.

Cloth; 9-1/8 x 6 x ¾ in.

JOHNSON TYPE FOUNDRY

Cabinet Shelf No.

See Specimen Books, Types. United States. MacKellar, Smiths & Jordan. Philadelphia.

JOHNSON, LAWRENCE

Cabinet 25 Shelf 2 No. 4

Typographical Advertiser. Published by L. Johnson, MacKellar, Smiths, & Jordan, Philadelphia, 1855-

See PERIODICALS, TYPE FOUNDING. United States. Typographic Advertiser...

JOHNSON, ROBERT UNDERWOOD

Cabinet S Shelf 1 No. 50

(A)Great Printer [Theodore Low DeVinne]. By R.U. Johnson. Excerpt from The Literary Review. Jan. 20, 1923.
Biographical eulogy.
p. 25 in DeVinne Scrap Book. Souvenirs of the Typothetae of New York.

Half morocco; 13½ x 10¾ in.

JOHNSTON, DANIEL S. B.

Cabinet NN Shelf 6 No. 19

Minnesota journalism in the territorial period. Read in a series of five papers at monthly meetings of the Executive Council, Feb.10 and Nov.10, 1902; Feb.9 and Oct.12, 1903; Feb.8, 1904. By Daniel S.B. Johnston. Minnesota Historical Society. Illus.

Together with Minnesota journalism from 1858 to 1865. Read, April 10, 1905, Nov.12, 1906, and March 11, 1907.

Half morocco; 9 x 6 in.

JOHNSTON, JAMES.

Cabinet 75 Shelf 2 No.

First printer in the royal colony of Georgia. A paper by Douglas C. McMurtrie, for the Bibliographical Society, London, Jan. 1929. Historical.

In Trans. Biblio. Soc. "The Library," vol. 10, 1929-30.

JOHNSTON, JAMES.

Cabinet 75 Shelf 2 No. 10

Printer, the first in Georgia, 1762.

See Early Printing in America. Literature of. (Georgia, 1762). James Johnston.

JOHNSTON, JAMES

Cabinet R Shelf 4 No. 169

See Printing, Historical, Georgia.

JOHNSTON, PAUL.

Cabinet S Shelf 3 No. 67

Biblio-Typographica: A survey of contemporary fine printing style. Published by Covici Friede. New York, 1930.

Cloth; 10½ x 7-1/8 x 1-1/8 in.

JOHNSTON, PAUL

Cabinet 26 Shelf 2 No. 15

(Die) Entwicklung des schönen Druckes in den U.S.A.

Illus. article in Jahrbuch IX, 1935, p. 13, Deutscher Verein für Buchwesen und Schrifttum.

JOHNSON & SMITH.

See Specimen Books -- Types -- U. S.

JOHNSTON, WILLIAM

Cabinet S Shelf 2 No. 47

Printer, lawyer, judge, 1804-1891, Cincinnati, O. In Memoriam.

Half morocco; 9½ x 6¼ in.

JOHNSTON, WILLIAM DAWSON

Cabinet PP Shelf 3 No. 15

History of the Library of Congress. Vol.I, 1800-1864. Illustrated. Washington: Government Printing Office, 1904.

Cloth; 10½ x 7½ x 2¼ in.

JOHNSTON, WILLIAM G.

Cabinet S Shelf 2 No. 46

Life and reminiscences from birth to manhood. By W. G. Johnston. Pittsburgh, 1901. Portraits.

Cloth; 9½ x 6½ in.

JOKES, PRINTERS'

Cabinet Shelf No.

See PRINTERS' HUMOR.

JOLIET DAILY NEWS (The)

Cabinet A Shelf 1 No. 67

See Newspapers, anniversary issues.

JOLLES, Dr. OSCAR

Cabinet Y Shelf 4 No. 62

Die deutsche schriftgiesserei: Eine gewerbliche bibliographie. Unter mitwirkung von Friedrich Bauer, Gustav Mori... Gedruckt auf veranlassung der Schriftgiesserei H. Berthold A-G in Berlin, 1923.

Bibliography of type founding in Germany.

Boards; 9½ x 6-3/4 in.

JOLLES, Dr. OSCAR.

Cabinet Y Shelf 4 No. 63

Drei reden zu seinem gedenken. Geboren den 10 Nov. 1860 in Berlin, abgeschieden den 11 Marz 1929. (Memorial addresses in honor of Dr. Jolles, printed by Berthold Type Foundry. Berlin, 1929).

Paper boards; 11¾ x 8-7/8 x ½ in.

JOLLES, DR. OSCAR (Translator)

Cabinet Y Shelf 3 No. 79

(Invention of printing. Key to the discovery of. An abstract from "The invention of printing" by Theodore Dow DeVinne, and translated by Dr. Oscar Jolles) Der schlüssel zur erfindung der typographie. Ein abschnitt aus dem werke "The invention of printing", by T. L. DeVinne. New York, 1876. Übersetzt von Dr. O. Jolles. Berlin, 1921.

Boards; 11½ x 8¼ x ¼ in.

JOLLES, Dr. OSCAR

Cabinet FF Shelf 3 No. 40

Portrait of Dr. Jolles, who in 1899 became head of the Berthold Type Foundry in Berlin.

See p.41 in Berthold Schriftgiesserei. (History... 1858-19210.

JOLLES, Dr. OSCAR

Cabinet Y Shelf 5 No. 57

(Unger, Johann Friedrich, 1750-1804, Berlin. Brief biography of the type designer and type founder. Special issue of the Berthold Type Foundry, printed by them in Unger-Fraktur from the original matrices). Beiträge zur lebensgeschichte Johann Friedrich Ungers. Berlin, 1924. Portrait.

Boards; 14¼ x 10-5/8 in.

JOMBERT, CHARLES ANTOINE

Cabinet V Shelf 3 No. 18

(Bio-bibliographical notes relating to Jombert family of printers-publishers, Paris, 1700-1772)

see

WERDET, EDMOND. Histoire du livre en France...3me partie(2), p.306

JOMBERT, CHARLES-ANTOINE

Cabinet Shelf No.

See Early printing in France. Paris, 1755.

JONES, GARTH A.

Cabinet S Shelf 5 No. 17

Master of line, A: Note on decorative title pages and the work of an English designer. Facsimile reproductions, in Arts and Decoration, Nov., 1911.

Bound in collection "Miscellaneous items relating to printing," item 7.

JONES, IFANO

Cabinet U Shelf 5 No. 89

History of printing and printers in Wales to 1810, and of successive and related printers to 1923. Also a history of printing and printers in Monmouthshire to 1923. By Ifano Jones, Cardiff, 1925.

Cloth; 10 x 6-3/8 in.

JONES, OWEN.

Cabinet M Shelf 4 No.

See Imprints, England. Vizetelly Bros., & Co., London,

JONES, GEORGE W.

Stack A Shelf 1 & 2 No. 82

See Bullen, Henry Lewis. Jones, George W. Master Printer of London.

JONES, JOHN ELBRIDGE

Cabinet R Shelf 4 No. 170

Utah, the story of printing and publishing in. Reprint from the "Utah resources and Activities". Published 1933.

Metaloid cover. Brochure in envelope

JONES, PHILIP L.

Cabinet LL Shelf 3 No. 33

Script and Print. A practical primer for use in the preparation of manuscript and print. Philadelphia, 1910.

Cloth; 6-7/8 x 4 in.

JONES, GEORGE W. (Author)

Cabinet M Shelf 2 No. 54

True description of all trades. Published in Frankfort in the year 1568. With six of the illustrations of Jobst Ammon . Mergenthaler Linotype Co. Brooklyn, New York, 1930.

"Jones, author of the Introductory Essay, and printer of this exquisite and interesting little book," H. L. B. Oct. 1930.

Boards; $7\frac{3}{4}$ x 5-1/8 x $\frac{1}{4}$ in.

JONES, JOHN M., Co.

Cabinet EE Shelf 4 No. 81

Modern printers machinery manufactured by the John M. Jones Co., Palmyra, New York, n.d.

Catalogue, illus., of Job Presses, Paper Cutters; the Lightning Jobber etc.

Pamphlet in manila envelope.

JONES, WILLIAM

Cabinet M Shelf 4 No. 19

Muse Recalled: An ode occasioned by The nuptials of Lord Viscount Althorp and Miss Lavinia Bingham, eldest daughter of Charles Lord Lucan, March VI, M.DCC.LXXXI. Strawberry-Hill: Printed by Thomas Kirgate.

Half morocco; $9\frac{3}{4}$ x 8 in.

JONES, GEO. W.

Cabinet Shelf No.

See also Imprints, England. Jones, Geo. W. The Dolphin Press, v.d.

JONES, LEUKIN

Cabinet A Shelf 3 No. 1

Imprint, London, 1839-40.

See Periodicals, England. Paul Pry: A Swindler's Register...1839-1840.

JONES, SAMUEL

Cabinet Shelf No.

See Paper Mills.

JONES, HORATIO GATES

Cabinet R Shelf 3 No. 71

Andrew Bradford, founder of the Newspaper Press in the Middle States of America: An address delivered at the Annual Meeting of the Historical Society of Pennsylvania. Feb., 9, 1869.

Bound in with publications of the Historical Society of Pennsylvania. No. 11.

Half morocco; $9\frac{1}{2}$ x 6 in.

JONES, OWEN

Cabinet 68 Shelf No. 10

(The) Grammar of ornament. Illustrated by examples from various styles of ornament. One hundred folio plates drawn on stone by E. Bedford, and printed in colours by Day and Son, London, 1856.

Morocco, gilt; $22\frac{3}{4}$ x 15 x 2 in.

JONSON, BEN.

Cabinet M Shelf 3 No. 9

English Grammar, first published in 1640. Now reprinted by the Lanston Monotype Corporation, Ltd., London, 1928.

Has facsimile title page, and specimens of Poliphilus and Blado Italic types used in this reprint.

Paper boards; $6\frac{3}{4}$ x $4\frac{1}{4}$ in.

JONES, HORATIO GATES

Cabinet R Shelf 5 No. 2.02

Bradford (The) Prayer Book of 1710. Some account of. "The Book of Common Prayer", printed by William Bradford. The first edition of that book ever printed on the American Continent. Privately printed for Horatio Gates Jones, 1870.

Brochure, in envelope.

JONES, OWEN

Cabinet J Shelf 5 No. 6

Grammar of ornament. By Owen Jones. Illustrated by examples from various styles of ornament. One hundred and twelve plates. London, 1856.

Cloth, gilt; 13-3/8 x 9-3/8 x $1\frac{3}{4}$ in.

JORDAN, C.W.

Cabinet I Shelf 2 No. 2

Treatise on anastatic printing, or the art of reprinting from prints on paper, detailing a simple process invented by the author. With various applications and modifications. Transfers to zinc and stone, invention of litho-cylindrical printing, etching in relief, etc. London, 1853.

Cloth; 8-1/8 x 5-3/4 in.

JOSEPHSON, AKSEL G.S.

Cabinet IP Shelf 3 No. 41

Bibliographies of bibliographies chronologically arranged. With occasional notes and an index. By Aksel G.S. Josephson. Chicago, Ill. 1901. Pamphlet.

Item in manila envelope.

JOSSE FAMILY OF PRINTERS, BOOKSELLERS

Cabinet V Shelf 3 No. 18

(Bio-bibliographical notes relating to this family of Paris, 1627-1737)

see WERDET, EDMOND. Histoire du livre en France...3me partie (2), p.175

JOST de NECKER

Cabinet 5 Shelf No. 28

Engravings, 1510-1539 (4 plates), facsimile reprints of woodcut.

Facs. in Cabinet 5, portfolio 28

JOUAUST, D.

Cabinet Q Shelf 1 No. 2

Publishing House, Paris.

see PUBLISHING, France. Jouaust, D...

JOUAUST, D.

Cabinet W Shelf 3 No. 27

See Typography (Fine), France. Jouaust, D.

JOURNAL DE TREVOUX

Cabinet W Shelf 3 No. 115

Paris, 1775.

See PROSPECTUSES, BOOKSELLERS. France, 1775. Memoires...

JOURNAL DES DEBATS

Cabinet 00 Shelf 1 No. 14.01

(History of this newspaper, 1814-1914)

See PEREIRE, ALFRED. (Le) Journal des Débats...

JOURNAL FÜR BUCHDRUCKERKUNST, SCHRIFTGIESSEREI und Die vervandten Fächer.

Cabinet 28 Shelf No.

See PERIODICALS, PRINTING. Germany. Journal für Buchdruckerkunst...

JOURNALISM

Cabinet NN Shelf 2 No. 7

Address delivered by Frank A. Munsey at Yale University, Jan.12, 1903.

Item 12 in bound collection "Journalism. Excerpts, etc."

JOURNALISM

Cabinet NN Shelf 2 No. 2.02

Address delivered by Mr. Munsey before the Merchants' Club of Boston on Dec., 16, in which he sketches a splendid journalism for the future...[Excerpt from Munsey's, Feb. 1903].

Item 8 in vol. with binder's title "Journalists and Journalism -- III. Pamphlets".

JOURNALISM

Cabinet NN Shelf 2 No. 4

Adventures of a special correspondent. By Gibson Willets. Excerpt from The National Magazine, March, 1906. Illus.

Item 16 in vol. "Journalists and their work".

JOURNALISM

Cabinet 61 Shelf 1 No. 4

Agricultural publications. The Phelps Publishing Co., Springfield, Mass. Conspicuous success and how it happened. A lesson in journalism.

Illus. article in "The Paper World", vol.13, No.3, Sept.,1886.

JOURNALISM

Cabinet NN Shelf 2 No. 16

American journalism today. By Chester T. Crowell. Excerpt from the American Mercury, June, 1924.

Item 15 in vol. with binder's title; "Journalism: Pamphlets. Bound, 1932".

JOURNALISM

Cabinet NN Shelf 3 No. 29

American Newspaper The. By James Edward Rogers. The University of Chicago Press. Chicago, Illinois. 1912.

Boards; cloth back: 7-3/8x4-7/8x7/8"

JOURNALISM

Cabinet NN Shelf 2 No. 9

American newspapers on themselves, in Chambers' Journal, Nov. 8, 1884: Comments on the American newspapers' characteristic, bombastic method of advertising their political views, etc.

Bound with other items in "Newspapers, various excerpts", item 19.

JOURNALISM.

Cabinet U Shelf 1 No. 18

Amphlett and Samuel Taylor Coleridge, by William E.A. Axon.

Brief review of a book "The Newspaper Press in part of last century...by J.Amphlett, sometime styled the Father of the Press.

In excerpts relating to printing from The Library, 1911-12, pp.34-39 of pencilled folios

---

JOURNALISM

Cabinet 00 Shelf 4 No. 29

Ancient organs of ~~tXXX~~ public opinions. An address delivered before the members of the Phi B.K. Society of Harvard College, June, 26, 1884. By R.C. Jebb, Cambridge (England): Printed by The University Press.

Brochure, in envelope with other items.

JOURNALISM

Cabinet 00 Shelf 4 No. 26.01

Anonymous journalism. References to.

see "TIMES", The London. History of the Times...1935, pp.150, 205, etc.

JOURNALISM

Cabinet 81 Shelf 2 No. 40

Anonymous writing. English, French, and American press contrasted. Excerpt, newspaper clipping.

Item in MUNSELL, JOEL. "Printers Scraps", Vol.XI, pp.7-8.

JOURNALISM

Cabinet 00 Shelf 4 No. 27

Australian newspapers; The Evening News, 1867-1926. A record of progress of a great Australian newspaper. Sydney, N.S.W., Australia.

Has spedimens of advertisements, views of printing plant, executive offices etc.

Boards; 11 x $8\frac{3}{4}$ x 5-7/8 in.

JOURNALISM

Cabinet Shelf No.

[Bache, Benjamin Franklin, editor, The Aurora, grandson of B. Franklin. Philadelphia 1798].

See Liberty of Printing. United States. [Bache, Benjamin Franklin]---

---

JOURNALISM

Cabinet NN Shelf 7 No. 16

Beginnings of modern journalism. Early records of the "London Gazette". (By David Harrison Stevens).

see NATION, THE. Semi - centennial, 1863-1915, p. 68.

JOURNALISM

Cabinet NN Shelf 3 No. 42.01

Bennett, James Gordon. Memoirs and times of.

By a Journalist. New York. 1855.

Frontispiece.

Cloth: $7\frac{1}{2}$x$5\frac{1}{4}$x1-3/8"

JOURNALISM

Cabinet NN Shelf 2 No. 2.01

Bennett, James Gordon and the Herald. By James Parton. [Excerpt from the North Am. Review, Boston, 1867.

Item 3 in vol. with binder's title "Journalists and Journalism -- II. Pamphlets".

JOURNALISM

Cabinet NN Shelf 3 No. 37

Bing, Phil C.: The country weekly. A manual for the rural journalists and for the students of the country field.

New York. D. Appleton & Co. 1917

Cloth: $7\frac{1}{4}$x$5\frac{1}{4}$"

JOURNALISM

Cabinet NN Shelf 2 No. 6

Biography gone mad (Bennett and Greeley) [Critical of the gossiping habits of the American Press as compared with the habits of British journals.]

Excerpt from Blackwoods, March, 1856.

Item 1 in bound collection "Biographies of Journalists".

JOURNALISM

Cabinet NN Shelf 3 No. 36

Bleyer, Willard Grosvenor. The profession of journalism. A collection of articles on newspaper editing and publishing, taken from the Atlantic Monthly. Boston. 1916.

Cloth: $7\frac{1}{4}$x$5\frac{1}{4}$"

JOURNALISM

Cabinet NN Shelf 3 No. 35

Bleyer, Willard Grosvenor. Types of news writing. Boston. 1916. Houghton-Mifflin Company.

Cloth: $8\frac{1}{4}$x$5\frac{1}{2}$x1"

JOURNALISM

Cabinet 00 Shelf 3 No. 37

Bok, Edward W., editor-author. The greatest word in English.

[Brief talk to editors]. Excerpt from The Mentor, June 1, 1921, Vol. 9, No. 5, p. 31.

Cloth; $10\frac{1}{4}$ x 7 in.

JOURNALISM

Cabinet NN Shelf 2 No. 2.02

Boston Courier, biography of the. [Excerpt from the Historical Magazine, Feb., 1866].

Item 15 in vol. with binder's title "Journalists and Journalism -- III. Pamphlets".

JOURNALISM

Cabinet 61 Shelf 1 No. 1

(The) Boston Herald : A story of journalistic enterprise. With portrait of R.M. Pulsifer, senior publisher and proprietor.

Article in The Paper World, vol.3, No.3, Sept., 1881, p.1

JOURNALISM.

Cabinet 66 Shelf 1 No. 1

Boston-Herald-Traveler. New building and anniversary number. 85th anniversary of the Herald, 106th birthday of the Traveler. Story of these two newspapers. Sunday, Sept. 13, 1931. Illus.

Cloth; $22\frac{1}{2}$ x $17\frac{1}{2}$ in.

JOURNALISM

Cabinet NN Shelf 3 No. 24

Boynton, H. W.: Journalism and literature, and other essays. Boston and New York. 1904.

Cloth: $7\frac{1}{2}$x5"

JOURNALISM

Cabinet 61 Shelf 1 No. 6

(The) Brattleboro (Vt.) Household: a notable success in journalism. Geo. E. Crowell, pioneer in journalism devoted to the interests of the American housewife.

Article, with portrait in "The Paper World, vol.20, No.2, Feb., 1890.

JOURNALISM

Cabinet NN Shelf 5 No. 24

(The) Bread Line: a story of a paper. By Albert Bigelow Paine, New York, 1900.

Cloth; 7 x $4\frac{1}{2}$ in.

JOURNALISM

Cabinet NN Shelf 7 No. 30

Brooklyn Daily Eagle, 1841-1893, a history of the ...

see NEWSPAPERS, Anniversary ISSUES. United States Brooklyn Daily Eagle...

JOURNALISM

Cabinet 61 Shelf 1 No. 1

Burdette, Robert Jones. The "Burlington Hawkeye Man". Modern specialities in journalism.

Illus. article in "The Paper World", vol.1, No.10, Oct., 1880, p.7

JOURNALISM

Cabinet NN Shelf 3 No. 19

Byxbee, O.F.: Establishing a newspaper: a handbook for the prospective publisher, including suggestions for the financial advancement of existing daily and weekly journals.
Chicago. 1901.

Cloth: $7\frac{1}{4}$x$5\frac{1}{2}$"

JOURNALISM

Cabinet QQ Shelf 3 No. 9

California, 1846. Account of first newspaper in English issued by Rev. Walter Colton, at Monterey.
Three years in California. By Rev. Walter Colton. With illustrations, New York, 1850.
See p. 38 and after.

Cloth; $7\frac{3}{4}$ x $5\frac{1}{4}$ in.

JOURNALISM

Cabinet NN Shelf 1 No. 19

Career of a journalist. By William Salisbury. Drawings by O. Theodore Jackman. New York, 1908.

Cloth; $8\frac{1}{4}$ x $5\frac{1}{2}$ in.

JOURNALISM

Cabinet Q Shelf 7 No. 53

Carriers Addresses.
It was the general custom of publishers of newspapers to give to their carriers at New Year's printed addresses, which in turn the carriers presented to their customers, expecting and generally receiving a gift of money in return --A New Years Gift.

See Collection of these addresses in envelope xx in Cabinet Q/7/53 etc.

JOURNALISM

Cabinet NN Shelf 2 No. 5

Case for the newspapers, The. By W.P. Hamilton. Excerpt from The Atlantic Monthly, May, 1910. The layman's ignorance of the ethical code governing the publication or suppression of news.

Item 18 in vol. "Various aspects of Journalism".

JOURNALISM

Cabinet NN Shelf 2 No. 5

Case of the reporter, The, by Hugo Munsterberg, in McClure's, Feb., 1911. The reporters case presented under the following headings: Misrepresenting speeches, faked interviews.

Bound with other items in "Various aspects of Journalism", item 27.

JOURNALISM

Cabinet NN Shelf 2 No. 2.02

Catholic Press, The. By William C. Murphy, Jr. [Excerpt from the American Mercury, Dec., 1926].

Item 19 in vol. with binder's title "Journalists and Journalism -- III. Pamphlets".

JOURNALISM

Cabinet OO Shelf 3 No. 25

Century Club of American newspapers. St. Louis. The St. Louis Republic. 1909. Illus.
Has also chronology of the origin of newspapers. Bound in, leaf of Republic, July 10, 1910, 102nd anniversary, with further histories.

Cloth; $8\frac{3}{4}$ x 12 x 3/8 in.

JOURNALISM

Cabinet 61 Shelf 1 No. 1

Childs, George William of the Philadelphia Public Ledger.

Illus article in "The Paper World", vol.1, No.6, June, 1880, p.1

JOURNALISM,

Cabinet 66 Shelf 1 No. 2

Chillicothe News-Advertiser, 100th anniversary. Monday, Nov. 16, 1931. Chillicothe, Ohio.
Has history of newspapers, with portraits and biographical notes of founder, editors, etc.

Cloth; $22\frac{3}{4}$ x $16\frac{1}{2}$ in.

JOURNALISM

Cabinet NN Shelf 4 No. 48

Clark, Joseph I.C.
My life and memories.

With illustrations.
New York. 1925.

Cloth: 9x6x$1\frac{1}{2}$"

JOURNALISM

Cabinet NN Shelf 4 No. 43.01

Collection from the newspaper writings of Nathaniel Peabody Rogers. Concord, 1847. With frontis. portrait.

Cloth; $7\frac{3}{4}$ x 5 in.

JOURNALISM

Cabinet NN Shelf 2 No. 2

College of Journalism, The, by Joseph Pulitzer, in The North American Review, May, 1904: This is Mr. Pulitzer's reply to an article criticising the College of Journalism (Columbia University) of which he was the founder.

Bound with other items in "Journalists and Journalism", item 8.

JOURNALISM

Cabinet NN Shelf 2 No. 5

Confessions of a reporter. By Howard Ardsley. Excerpt from The Pacific Monthly, July, 1911.

Item 29 in vol. "Various aspects of Journalism".

JOURNALISM

Cabinet NN Shelf 3 No. 13

Congdon, Charles T.
Reminiscences of a journalist.

Boston. 1880.

Cloth: $7\frac{3}{4}$x$5\frac{1}{4}$"

JOURNALISM

Cabinet QQ Shelf 1 No. 42

Conservative power of the press. By Charles C. Haxewell.

See p.277 Brenton's Voices of the Press ...New York, 1850.

JOURNALISM

Cabinet NN Shelf 2 No. 2.01

"Constitution", new editor-in-chief of the. By Joel Chandler Harris. Excerpt from the American Review of Reviews. May, 1897. With portraits.

Item 23 in vol. with binder's title "Journalists and Journalism -- II. Pamphlets".

JOURNALISM

Cabinet NN Shelf 3 No. 25

Cooke, Robert Grier (Compiler). Casual essays of The Sun: editorial articles on many subjects, clothed with the new philosophy of the bright side of things. From the Press of Robert Grier Cooke. New York. 1905.

Cloth: 8-5/8x5¼x1¼"

JOURNALISM

Cabinet OO Shelf 3 No. 37

Dana - master of facts...Intimate picture of, by Chester S. Lord. With portrait.

Excerpt from The Mentor, June 1, 1921, Vol. 9, No. 5, p. 29.

Cloth; 10¼ x 7 in.

JOURNALISM.

Cabinet 66 Shelf 1 No. 3

Edisoniana: Papers announcing death of Thomas Alva Edison, with biographical and appreciative articles. Issued Oct, 19-22, 1932. Illus.
Times and Herald Tribune. (New York).
San Francisco Chronicle.
Globe-Democrat and Post-Dispatch (St. Louis)
Tribune, Daily News (Chicago),
Etc.

Cloth; 21 x 17 ¾ in.

JOURNALISM

Cabinet NN Shelf 2 No. 9

Country newspapers. Article by E.W. Howe. Excerpt from "Century Magazine", Sept., 1891.

Item 15 in volume with binder's title "Newspapers, various excerpts".

JOURNALISM

Cabinet NN Shelf 2 No. 7

Dana (Charles A.), on journalism. By H.T.P. Excerpt from the Bookman, Nov., 1895.

Item 26 in bound collection "Journalism, Excerpts, etc."

JOURNALISM

Cabinet NN Shelf 4 No. 12.03

Editorial chair of the Tribune. [Excerpt from Putnam's Magazine, May, 1868] With portrait of Horace Greeley drawn by Th. Nast.

With other Tribune items in manila envelope

JOURNALISM

Cabinet NN Shelf 2 No. 16

Country press, the changing. By C. M. Harger. Excerpt from Scribner's, April, 1924.

Item 11 in vol. with binder's title; "Journalism: Pamphlets. Bound, 1932".

JOURNALISM

Cabinet NN Shelf 2 No. 29

Defence of Cyrus Barton, against the attacks of Hon. Isaac Hill upon the establishment of the New-Hampshire Patriot and State Gazette. [New-Hampshire Patriot, Extra, Sept.,7, 1840]

With other items in manila envelope

JOURNALISM

Cabinet 81 Shelf 2 No. 37

Editorial difficulties, about. Scrap book of newspaper excerpts collected by Joel Munsell, Albany. N.Y., prior to 1860.

Half morocco; 8-7/8 x 7½ in.

JOURNALISM

Cabinet NN Shelf 2 No. 2.01

Cox (James M.) Events in the career of. By George MacAdam. Excerpt from World's Work, Nov. 1920.

Item 24 in vol. with binder's title "Journalists and Journalism -- II. Pamphlets".

JOURNALISM

Cabinet NN Shelf 2 No. 9

Development of newspaper making, The, by Edward Arden, in The Chatauguan, June, 1899.

Bound with other items in "Newspapers, various excerpts", item 28.

JOURNALISM

Cabinet NN Shelf 7 No. 42

Editors of 1422 B. C. keen as newsmen. Egyptian scarabs, tabloids of their era, went in for big front-page events. Shown at Museum here. Amen-hotpe III got out extra when he buitl mile-long lake for queen in 15 days. Unsigned article, excerpt from the N. Y. Times of May, 1936.

In envelope.

JOURNALISM

Cabinet NN Shelf 3 No. 43

Crockett, Albert Stevens.

When James Gordon Bennett was Caliph of Bagdad. New York. 1926.

With portraits.

Cloth: 7½x5-1/8x1-3/8"

JOURNALISM

Cabinet Shelf No.

Directory (Eighth Annual) of Feature and Picture Syndicate of U.S. and Canada.

In Editor and Publisher, vol. 64, No.15, August 29, 1931, pp.42-66.

JOURNALISM

Cabinet NN Shelf 2 No. 5

Effect of the daily press (The) on the development of Christian character. By Rev. D.E. Marvin, D.D. Excerpt from The Editorial Review, Aug. 1909.

Item 6 in vol. "Various aspects of Journalism".

JOURNALISM

Cabinet NN Shelf 3 No. 17

Dana, Charles A.: The art of newspaper making. Three lectures. New York. 1895.

Cloth: 7¼x4¾"

JOURNALISM

Cabinet A Shelf 2 No. 11

Early journalism West of the Mississippi. By James Melvin Lee.

See NEWSPAPERS, ANNIVERSARY ISSUES (U.S.) Arkansas Gazette, 100 years, 1819-1919... p.45

JOURNALISM

Cabinet NN Shelf 2 No. 2.01

English and American journalism. By Henry Watterson. (The veteran editor of the Louisville Courier-Journal pronounces an expert opinion upon the newspapers and newspaper-making of Britain and the United States.

Item 14 in vol. with binder's title "Journalists and Journalism -- II. Pamphlets".

JOURNALISM

Cabinet NN Shelf 2 No. 4

Episodes of journalism. By Francis E. Leupp. Excerpt from The Century Magazine. June, 1902.

Item 23 in "Journalists and their work".

JOURNALISM

Cabinet 61 Shelf 1 No. 5

Evening journalism seen in the history of The Springfield Daily Union.

Illus. article in "The Paper World", vol.16, No.1, Jan., 1888

JOURNALISM

Cabinet NN Shelf 2 No. 2.01

First newspaper printed in america.

See NEWSPAPERS, UNITED STATES. Literature of. First newspaper...

JOURNALISM

Cabinet NN Shelf 2 No. 7

([Ethics and correct reports, France, 1832] Du journalism. Art.1. Revue Encyclopedique. Publiee par MM. H. Carnot et P. Leroux.- Paris, Sept., 1832.

Review of the above article excerpted from Westminister Review, Jan., 1833.

Item 9 in bound collection "Journalism. Excerpts, etc."

JOURNALISM

Cabinet A Shelf 3 No. 1

Evening papers (the). Its place in journalism. By Neil Munro.

Article in The Evening News, Glasgow, Sept. 17, 1923. The Jubilee Supplement.

Item on folio 24 of vol. labelled "Early printing in Great Britain and Europe".

JOURNALISM

Cabinet NN Shelf 3 No. 10

Fitzgerald, Joseph. About newspapers (pp. 182-240 of book with title) "Caseine: being rural meditations."

By J. Fitzgerald, Cincinnati.

Published for the author by John P. Walsh, 190 Sycamore St. 1869.

Cloth: 7-3/8x4¾x7/8"

JOURNALISM

Cabinet NN Shelf 2 No. 7

Ethics of modern journalism. By Charles B. Connolly.

Excerpt from the Catholic World, July, 1902.

Item 10 in bound collection "Journalism. Excerpts, etc."

JOURNALISM

Cabinet NN Shelf 2 No. 16

Experiment of a Christian daily [Topeka "Daily Capital"] By Charles M. Sheldon.

Excerpt from the Atlantic, Nov., 1924.

Item 6 in vol. with binder's title; "Journalism: Pamphlets. Bound, 1932".

JOURNALISM

Cabinet NN Shelf 2 No. 2.02

(42) Pictures of Davy Crockett help run the Dallas "News"...By George W. Gray.

A story of success, with portrait of George B. Dealy, President of the Dallas News.

Item 22 in vol. with binder's title "Journalists and Journalism -- III. Pamphlets".

JOURNALISM

Cabinet NN Shelf 2 No. 2

Europe, leading journals and journalism in. By Wm. T. Coggeshall. Excerpt from The Ladies Repository, Jan., 1857.

Item 12 in vol. "Journalists and Journalism". Bound, 1918.

JOURNALISM

Cabinet NN Shelf 3 No. 23

Extra !! Fairy tales up to now. Paul Elder, the San Francisco Publisher, brings to light the details of the tragedy. San Francisco. 1904.

Boards: 8x4-5/8". In slip case.

JOURNALISM

Cabinet NN Shelf 2 No. 10

Four and twenty hours in a newspaper office. Article by Harold King. Excerpt from "Once a Week"., Sept.26, 1863; Feb. 6, 1864.

Item 10 in bound collection with binder's title "Description of various newspapers".

JOURNALISM,

Cabinet NN Shelf 2 No. 7

Europe, newspaper press of. By H. R. Chamberlain.

Excerpt from The Chautaugan, Oct., 1894.

Item 29 in bound collection "Journalism. Excerpts, etc."

JOURNALISM

Cabinet NN Shelf 2 No. 5

Falsehood in the Daily Press. By James Parton. Excerpt from Harper's New Monthly Magazine, July, 1874.

Item 13 in vol. "Various aspects of Journalism".

JOURNALISM

Cabinet 00 Shelf 5 No. 1 (2 vols.)

(The) Fourth Estate: Contributions towards a history of newspapers, and of the liberty of the press. By F. Knight Hunt. In two vols...London, 1850.

Cloth; 8 x 5-1/8 in.

JOURNALISM

Cabinet Shelf No.

European Editors Paris Tribune (an historical article relating to)

In article "Grads" mourn Paris Tribune passing. By Bernhard Ragner, managing editor, 1926-1929. In Editor and Publisher, Nov. 24, 1934, pp.10 and 39

JOURNALISM

Cabinet NN Shelf 2 No. 2

First editor, The: A rainy-day retrospect, by A. Gilman, in Putnam's Magazine, March, 1869.

Bound with other items in "Journalists and Journalism", item 5.

JOURNALISM

Cabinet NN Shelf 2 No. 9

Fourth Estate, The: Contributions towards a history of newspapers, and the liberty of the press, by F. Knight Hunt, London, 1850: A review of the book with same title in the Eclectic, Aug., 1850. From the North British Review.

Bound with other items in "Newspapers, various excerpts", item 6.

JOURNALISM

FRANCE: See also Hatin, Eugene

JOURNALISM

Cabinet NN Shelf 3 No. 27

Given, John L.
Making a newspaper.
New York. 1907.

Cloth: 7½x5¼"

JOURNALISM

Cabinet NN Shelf 4 No. 15

Greeley, Horace, the comic life of

See GREELEY, HORACE. Comic life of Horace Greeley...

JOURNALISM

Cabinet X Shelf 4 No. 82

Freedom of the press, and privileges of the Commons, considered: in a letter to a country friend. London: Printed for J. Bell, 1771.

On the qualities of reporters, their ignorance, etc.

Half morocco; 7¼ x 4⅝ in.

JOURNALISM

Cabinet NN Shelf 2 No. 9

Gleanings from an old Southern newspaper. Article by W.P. Trent. Excerpt from "The Atlantic", Sept., 10, 1910.

Item 8 in volume with binder's title "Newspapers, various excerpts".

JOURNALISM

Cabinet 61 Shelf 1 No. 2

Green, Charles Gordon, and the Boston Post. Article, with portrait.

Item in "The Paper World", vol.5, No.2, Aug., 1882.

JOURNALISM

Cabinet NN Shelf 2 No. 5

Freedom of The Press, vindicated, The. By B.J. Lossing, in Harper's New Monthly Magazine, July 1878.

Item 31 in vol. "Various aspects of Journalism".

JOURNALISM

Cabinet NN Shelf 2 No. 4

Going through the newspaper mill. By Roy S. Durstine. Excerpt from The Outlook, July 5, 1913. Experiences of the average journalist, during his apprenticeship period.

Item 19 in vol. "Journalists and their work".

JOURNALISM

Cabinet NN Shelf 2 No. 34.01

Half a Century of New York Newspaper Life. Personal reminiscences of famous editors of the Sixties. How Tweed's Fire Engine Company turned a compositor into a reporter, etc. By (Major) George F. Williams.
Excerpt from the N.Y. Sun, November 23, 1913.

With other items in manila envelope

JOURNALISM

Cabinet NN Shelf 2 No. 2.02

French provincial news. [Brief unsigned article]. Excerpt from Household Words, July 24, 1855.

Item 5 in vol. with binder's title "Journalists and Journalism -- III. Pamphlets".

JOURNALISM

Cabinet 61 Shelf 1 No. 1

Goodwin, George, publisher of the Connecticut Courant. Account of the man and newspaper founded in 1775.

Illus article in "The Paper World", vol.2, No.4, April, 1881.

JOURNALISM

Cabinet NN Shelf 3 No. 28

Harrington, H. F. and T. T. Frankenberg. Essentials in journalism. A manual in newspaper making for college classes. Boston. 1912. Ginn & Company.
Frontispiece, 4 portraits of representative American editors.

Cloth: 8½x6"

JOURNALISM

Cabinet NN Shelf 2 No. 2.02

From Confucius to "The Daily News". By Carrol K. Kichener. Excerpt from the Catholic World, April, 1926.

Item 7 in vol. with binder's title "Journalists and Journalism -- III. Pamphlets".

JOURNALISM

Cabinet NN Shelf 2 No. 4

Great business operations. The collection of News, by T.B. Connery. Excerpt from The Cosmopolitan, May, 1897. Illus.

Item 14 in vol. "Journalists and their work".

JOURNALISM

Cabinet NN Shelf 3 No. 40

Harris, Emerson P. and Florence Harris Hooke.

The community newspaper: Its promise and development.

New York. 1923.

Cloth: 7½x5x1-3/8"

JOURNALISM

Cabinet NN Shelf 2 No. 9

Gentlemen of the press. Article by S.R.Fiske. Excerpt from "Harpers' New Monthly Magazine' Feb., 1863.

Item 3 in volume with binder's title "Newspapers, various excerpts".

JOURNALISM

Cabinet NN Shelf 2 No. 2.01

(A) Great newspaper [Chicago Tribune] and its owner [James Keeley]. Excerpt from "Business America", June 1914. With portrait.

Item 18 in vol. with binder's title "Journalists and Journalism -- II. Pamphlets".

JOURNALISM

Cabinet NN Shelf 7 No. 24

Harvey, George. Journalism, politics and the university. Bromley Lectures, delivered at Yale University on March 12 and 16, 1908.

Cloth; 13½ x 9½ in.

JOURNALISM

Cabinet NN Shelf 2 No. 7

Headlines and how we make them. By Victor S. Yarros.
Excerpt from the "Oth Century Magazine, March, 1912.

Item 18 in bound collection "Journalism. Excerpts, etc."

JOURNALISM.

Cabinet 18 Shelf 1 No. 14

(History and development of trade and socialistic publications.) Zur entwicklung und geschnichte des sozialistischen Buchhundels und arbeitspresse, von Ernst Drahn: A brief review of book with same title.

In Zeitschrift für Bücherfreunde, 1913-14, part 1, p.166, of Supplement ("Beiblatt")

JOURNALISM

Cabinet NN Shelf 2 No. 4

How the newspapers handle National Conventions. By Trumbull White. Excerpt from Appleton's, June, 1908.

Item 21 in vol. "Journalists and their work"

JOURNALISM

Cabinet 81 Shelf 2 No. 39

Herald, the, and the Tribune: Journalism, its progress. Excerpt from the N.Y. Herald, July 31st, 1849.

Item in MUNSELL, JOEL. "Printers Scraps", Vol.X, pp.94-95.

JOURNALISM

Cabinet 00 Shelf 4 No. 52

History of journalism. By Wm. Talbot Allison...Being a lecture delivered Aug. 9, 1921 to the Conference of Western Journalists at the Manitoba Agricultural College, Winnipeg.

Half morocco; 9½ x 5½ x 3/8 in.

JOURNALISM

Cabinet NN Shelf 2 No. 7

How to conduct a local newspaper. By John A. Cockerill.
Excerpt from Lippincott's, Sept., 1906.

Item 16 in bound collection "Journalism. Excerpts, etc."

JOURNALISM

Cabinet NN Shelf 2 No. 33

High Schools, newspaper writing in. Containing an outline for the use of teachers. By L.B. Flint. Department of Journalism in the University of Kansas, 1914.

Pamphlet bound in with "Lectures of Journalism". University of Kansas, Lawrence, 1917.

Half morocco; 10 x 7 in.

JOURNALISM

Cabinet NN Shelf 2 No. 2.02

History of newspapers published in New Hampshire, 1756 to 1840.

See NEWSPAPERS. UNITED STATES. Literature of. New Hampshire, 1756 to 1840...

JOURNALISM

Cabinet NN Shelf 2 No. 4

How we got our news, by W.F.G. Shanks, in Harper's New Monthly Magazine, March, 1867.

Item 1 in vol. "Journalists and their work."

JOURNALISM

Cabinet NN Shelf 2 No. 33

High Schools, newspaper writing in. Containing an outline for the use of teachers. By L.N. Flint. Department of Journalism in the University of Kansas. 1917.
Pamphlet bound in with "Lectures of Journalism", University of Kansas, Lawrence, 1914.

Half morocco; 10 x 7 in.

JOURNALISM

Cabinet NN Shelf 2 No. 7

Honest newspaper possible, is an ? By a New York Editor.
Excerpt from The Atlantic, Oct.,1908.

Item 15 in bound collection "Journalism. "Excerpts, etc."

JOURNALISM

Cabinet S Shelf 3 No. 143

Howells, William D. The Country Printer. Illus Excerpt from Scribner's Magazine, May, 1873.
Autobiographical account.

Half morocco; 9¾ x 6½ in.

JOURNALISM

Cabinet Shelf No.

High spots on the horizon: Concerning over production of graduates in journalism.

Article in the Publishers Auxiliary, 67th year, No.2, Jan. 9, 1932, p.5.

JOURNALISM.

Cabinet 66 Shelf 1 No. 4

Honolulu Advertiser, The. 75th Birthday issue, July 2, 1931. Illus.
Has history of this newspaper, biography of its founder, etc.

Cloth; 23 x 17¼ in.

JOURNALISM, United States

Cabinet 00 Shelf 3 No. 31

Hubbard, Elbert & Alice, In Memoriam. Done into a book and printed at The Roycrofters at Their Shop which is in East Aurora, Erie County, New York. 1915. Illus.

Half morocco; 7-3/8 x 5¼ x 1 in.

JOURNALISM

Cabinet R Shelf 3 No. 203

Historical, biographical, and miscellaneous gatherings in the form of disconnected notes relative to printers, printing, publishing, and editing ... from the discovery of the art, or from 1420 to 1886. By John W. Moore. Concord, N.H., 1886.

Cloth; 9¼ x 6¼ in.

JOURNALISM

Cabinet NN Shelf 2 No. 4

How a newspaper syndicate works. By an ex-syndicator. Excerpt from The Booklovers Magazine, June, 1904.

Item 20 in vol. "Journalists and their work".

JOURNALISM.

Cabinet 66 Shelf 1 No. 5

Illinois State Journal. Centennial, 1831-1931. Springfield, Illinois.
Has illustrated history of this newspaper, with biographies of its founders and successors.

Cloth; 23 x 17¾ in.

JOURNALISM

Cabinet NN Shelf 2 No. 5

Independent Press, The. Its opportunities and duties. By Samuel Bowles, editor of The Springfield Republican. Excerpt from The North American Review, July, 1906.

Item 21 in vol. "Various aspects of Journalism".

JOURNALISM

Cabinet NN Shelf 2 No. 4

Journalism as a profession. By Walter Avenel. Excerpt from The Forum, May, 1898. Data presented to prove that the profession of journalism is underpaid and undesirable for serious young men.

Item 12 in vol. "Journalists and their work".

JOURNALISM.

Cabinet 66 Shelf 1 No. 12

Last issue of New York World, sold to Scripps-Howard Chain of Newspapers, Feb. 27, 1931. with first issues of the (Evening) New York World-Telegram, Feb. 27, 1932.

Cloth; $22\frac{3}{4}$x $17\frac{1}{2}$ in.

JOURNALISM

Cabinet NN Shelf 3 No. 28.01

Industrial publishing. The foundation, principles functions, methods, and general practice. Based upon lessons of an educational course. Edited and revised by Horace M. Swetland. New York City (1923)

Cloth; $8\frac{1}{2}$ x 5-1/8 in.

JOURNALISM

Cabinet NN Shelf 2 No. 2

Journalism as exemplified by Mr. Bagehot, by John Arbuckle, in Scribner's, Oct., 1879: Comments upon Mr. Bagehot's particular journalistic style.

Bound with other items in "Journalists and Journalism", item 9.

JOURNALISM

Cabinet 00 Shelf 3 No. 31

Law and the newspaper. By Frederick W. Lehmann. The University of Missouri Bulletin, Vol. 18, No. 32. Journalism Series 15. Columbia, Miss., Dec. 1917.

Cloth; $9\frac{1}{4}$ x 6-1/8 in.

JOURNALISM

Cabinet 00 Shelf 3 No. 27

Influence of newspaper presentation upon the growth of crime and other anti-social activity. A dissertation...for the decree of Doctor of Philosophy. By Frances Fenton. The University of Chicago, 1911.

Half morocco: $9\frac{1}{2}$ x $6\frac{3}{4}$ x $\frac{1}{2}$ in.

JOURNALISM

Cabinet NN Shelf 2 No. 5

Journalism: Its rewards and opportunities. By Truman A. De Weese. Excerpt from The Forum, Dec., 1898.

Item 8 in "Various aspects of Journalism".

JOURNALISM

Cabinet NN Shelf 2 No. 33

Lectures delivered at Kansas Newspaper Week, under the auspices of the Department of Journalism, University of Kansas, May 10 to 14, 1914.

Bound in with two pamphlets by L.N. Flint (of the Department of Journalism, dated 1917, 1918.

Half morocco; 10 x 7 in.

JOURNALISM

Cabinet NN Shelf 2 No. 7

Interviewing, the art of. By A.E. Watrous. Excerpt from Lippincott's, Sept.,1890.

Item 13 in bound collection "Journalism. Excerpts, etc."

JOURNALISM

Cabinet NN Shelf 5 No. 9

Journalistic jumbles, or trippings in type. Being notes on some newspaper blunders, their origin and nature; with numerous examples. London, Field & Tuer, Ye Leadenhalle Presse, E. C. [n. d. circa 1881].

Boards; 4-5/8 x 5-5/8 in.

JOURNALISM

Cabinet NN Shelf 2 No. 2.02

"Ledger", Philadelphia, and George W. Childs.

See CHILDS, GEORGE W. [Biographical sketch, with portrait]...

JOURNALISM

Cabinet NN Shelf 3 No. 39

Jettinger, Carl A.: How and what to write as news. A book for correspondents and editors. Salt Lake City. 1921. Porte Publishing Company.

Leatherette: $7\frac{1}{2}$x$5\frac{1}{4}$"

JOURNALISM

Cabinet NN Shelf 1 No. 2.01

Kendall, George Wilkins, war correspondent in Mexico, 1846-47. (An article with portrait, in N.Y.Sun, July 26, 1914): Americna newspaper men real pioneers in reporting war news

Excerpted article in manila envelope.

JOURNALISM

Cabinet NN Shelf 2 No. 4

Letter to a young journalist whose education has been neglected, A, by W.P.A., in Scribner's Magazine, Oct., 1872.

Item 9 in vol. "Journalists and their work".

JOURNALISM

Cabinet NN Shelf 2 No. 5

Journalism as a career. By C.M. Harger. Excerpt from The Atlantic Monthly, Feb., 1911.

Item 9 in vol. "Various aspects of Journalism".

JOURNALISM

Cabinet 00 Shelf 5 No. 4

Knight, Charles [1791-1873], passages from the life of. Boston: Estes & Lauriat, 1874.

American edition, published with introduction by James Thorne, after the death of Mr. Knight.

Cloth; $7\frac{1}{2}$ x $5\frac{3}{4}$ x 1-3/8 in.

JOURNALISM

Cabinet Shelf No.

Liberty or licence? - An open letter to the newspaper editors and publishers of America. By Frank Parker Stockbridge, Editor.

See American Press, vol. 50, No.5, Feb. 1932, p.11.

JOURNALISM

Cabinet JJ Shelf 5 No. 13

Louisville (Ky.) Brief history of the press in. Louisville Printing Pressmen's Union. No. 28. November 14, 1904.

See page 36 and fol.

Printed stiff paper; 12¾ x 9¾ x ¼ in.

JOURNALISM

Cabinet NN Shelf 2 No. 4

Managing editor, The, by Julius Chambers, in Lippincott's, Feb., 1892: A brief analysis of the editor's responsibilities.

Item 2 in vol. "Journalists and Their Work". Bound 1918.

JOURNALISM.

Cabinet NN Shelf 2 No. 1

Mr. Munsey on Journalism: An address at Yale University, in Munsey's magazine, March, 1903.

Bound with other items in "Journalists, various excerpts," item 18.

JOURNALISM

Cabinet NN Shelf 3 No. 26

Luce, Robert. Writing for the press: A manual. 5th Edition. Boston. 1907.

Cloth: 7½x5-1/8x1"

JOURNALISM

Cabinet NN Shelf 6 No. 55

Men who make daily newspapers and opinion in the Metropolis. Excerpt from the New York Herald, Sunday, May 14, 1893.
Broadside (2pp.) covered with silk Portraits and personal sketches or workers on the World, Sun, Tribune, Times, and Advertiser.

Item in manila envelope

JOURNALISM

Cabinet NN Shelf 2 No. 2.02

Mr. Munsey, the rise and fall of. By Rowland Thomas. Excerpt from The Nation, April 2, 1924.

Item 28 in vol. with binder's title "Journalists and Journalism -- III. Pamphlets".

JOURNALISM.

Cabinet Shelf No.

McFadden, Bernarr: How (in 1931) he proposed to give his millions for charity. With portrait.

Article in Editor & Publisher, Vol. 64, No. 20, Oct. 3, 1931.

JOURNALISM

Cabinet NN Shelf 2 No. 16

Menace to journalism. By Roscoe E. Brown. Excerpt from the North American Review, November, 1921.

Item 13 in vol. with binder's title; "Journalism: Pamphlets. Bound, 1932".

JOURNALISM

Cabinet NN Shelf 2 No. 2.01

Mitchell, John Ames, a reminiscent story of the man who made "Life". By Thomas L. Masson. Excerpt from the Bookman, Feb., 1919.

Item 13 in vol. with binder's title "Journalists and Journalism -- II. Pamphlets".

JOURNALISM

Cabinet NN Shelf 2 No. 1

Magazine literature. By the Editor (John Inman) Excerpt from The Columbian Magazine, Jan. and July, 1844.

Item 13 in book with binder's title "Journalists, Various excerpts".

JOURNALISM

Cabinet NN Shelf 2 No. 4

Metropolitan newspaper reporter. By A.F. Matthews. Excerpt from the Chautauquan, Nov., 1893.

Item 22 in vol. "Journalists and their works".

JOURNALISM

Cabinet 61 Shelf 1 No. 2

Modern American journalism, as illustrates by Charles A. Dana in the conduct of the New York Sun. With portrait.

Article in "The Paper World", vol.4, No.1, Jan., 1882.

JOURNALISM

Cabinet NN Shelf 2 No. 5

Making a choice of a profession: The profession of Journalism. By Albert Shaw. Excerpt from The Cosmopolitan, June, 1903.

Item 7 in vol. "Various aspects of Journalism".

JOURNALISM

Cabinet NN Shelf 2 No. 16

Mexican journalism. By Charles E. Hodson. Excerpt from the Catholic World, July, 1888.

Item 3 in vol. with binder's title; "Journalism: Pamphlets. Bound, 1932".

JOURNALISM

Cabinet NN Shelf 2 No. 16

Modern journalism. [Unsigned article] Excerpt from Living Age, Auf.7, 1852.

Item 12 in vol. with binder's title; "Journalism: Pamphlets. Bound, 1932".

JOURNALISM

Cabinet Shelf No.

Making of a newspaper man. By Selah M. Clarke and Harold M. Anderson.

First chapter of a to be continued story in The American Press, 50th year, No.4, pp.1, 2.

JOURNALISM

Cabinet KK Shelf 5 No. 100-101-102

Michigan Bulletin: Official Paper of the Michigan Press Association.

See PERIODICALS, JOURNALISM Michigan Bulletin...

JOURNALISM

Cabinet NN Shelf 2 No. 2

Modern newspaper, The, by John Addison Porter, editor of The Hartford Post: A lecture delivered in Charter Oak Hall, Hartford, Jan. 22, 1894. Pamphlet.

Item I in vol. "Journalists and Journalism". Bound 1918.

JOURNALISM

Cabinet NN Shelf 2 No. 10

(The) Modern newspaper. A review of three books dealing with the history of journalism. Excerpt from "The British Quarterly Review", April, 1872.

Item 8 in bound collection with binder's title "Description of various newspapers".

JOURNALISM

Cabinet NN Shelf 2 No. 2

New Journalism, The, by T.P. O'Connor, in the New Review, Oct., 1889.

Bound with other items in "Journalists and Journalism", item 6.

JOURNALISM

Cabinet OO Shelf 3 No. 44

New York Times. Manual for advertisers. Rules with instructions to agents. Second edition, 1926. Brochure.

Paper; 10 x 7 in. In envelope.

JOURNALISM

Cabinet NN Shelf 2 No. 5

Modern newspaper as it might be. By A. Maurice Low. Excerpt from Yale Review, Jan., 1913. Considers the influence of the newspaper in shaping the mental and active life of a people.

Item 23 in Vol. "Various aspects of Journalism".

JOURNALISM

Cabinet NN Shelf 2 No. 7

New journalism and the old. By John H. Holmes (Editor of the Boston "Herald") Excerpt from Munsey's, April, 1897.

Item 27 in bound collection "Journalism. Excerpts, etc."

JOURNALISM

Cabinet NN Shelf 4 No. 12.03

New York Tribune, The. Where and how it is made. Facts for advertisers. Philadelphia Offices. n.d. [May 31, 1876]. With frontispiece.

Brochure in manila envelope with other Tribune items.

JOURNALISM

Cabinet NN Shelf 3 No. 18

Munson, A.J. Making a country newspaper. Being a detailed statement of the essentials to success in newspaper making. Chicago. 1899.

Cloth: 7¾x5½"

JOURNALISM

Cabinet NN Shelf 2 No. 2.02

New York Dailies, The. By Hugh Kent. [Excerpt from the American Mercury, Nov., 1926].

Item 16 in vol. with binder's title "Journalists and Journalism -- III. Pamphlets".

JOURNALISM

Cabinet NN Shelf 4 No. 12.03

New York Tribune. 50th anniversary of the founding of, 1841-1891, April, 10. Programme of exercises.

In manila envelope, with other items.

JOURNALISM

Cabinet NN Shelf 2 No. 4

National Press Club of Washington. By Earl Hamilton Smith. Excerpt from The National Magazine, Aug., 1915. Illus.

Item 17 in vol. "Journalists and their work".

JOURNALISM

Cabinet NN Shelf 2 No. 16

New York Newspapers. Excerpt (unsigned article) from **Living Age, Sept., 1866.**

Item 4 in vol. with binder's title; "Journalism: Pamphlets. Bound, 1932".

JOURNALISM

Cabinet NN Shelf 4 No. 18

(The) New York "Tribune" in the draft riots. The story of a member of the staff who assisted in the arming of the "Tribune" Office. By James R. Gilmore ("Edmund Kirke"). Periodical excerpt, n.n.n.d.

With other items in manila envelope

JOURNALISM

Cabinet NN Shelf 2 No. 5

Nationale newspaper, a great. By Harry Thurston Peck. Excerpt from the Cosmopolitan, Dec., 1897.

A severe criticism of the press.

Item 10 in vol. "Various Aspects of Journalism".

JOURNALISM

Cabinet KK Shelf 6 No. 11

New York Press Association, authorized history of 50 years, 1853 - 1903. By A. O. Bunnell, Secretary. Dansville, N. Y. n. d. (1910) Illus.

see also ASSOCIATIONS, NEWSPAPER. New York Press Association...

Cloth; 10¼ x 7 in.

JOURNALISM

Cabinet NN Shelf 5 No. 3.01

New York World, the end of. A post - mortem by its intangible assets. James W. Barrett, of the City Desk Editor. New York, 1931. Illus. facs. portraits.

Cloth; 8-1/8 x 5¼ x 1¼ in.

JOURNALISM

Cabinet KK Shelf 6 No. 26

(The) Nebraska Editor, Beaver City, Nebraska

See PERIODICALS, JOURNALISM. (The) Nebraska Editor...

JOURNALISM

Cabinet OO Shelf 3 No. 44

New York Times, educational value of. Compendium of excerpts from letters of prominent American educators. New York, 1926. Brochure.

With other items in envelope.

JOURNALISM

Cabinet NN Shelf 3 No. 42

News writing for high schools. By Leo A. Borah, in the School of Journalism of the University of Washington. Boston. 1925. Allyn & Bacon.

Cloth: 7½x5¼"

JOURNALISM

Cabinet NN Shelf 3 No. 14

Newspaper libel:
A handbook for the press.

By Samuel Merrill...Boston. 1888

Cloth: 7¼x5¼"

JOURNALISM

Cabinet NN Shelf 5 No. 20

Newspaper reporting in olden time and today. By John Pendleton. London, 1890.

Cloth; 7 x 4¾ in.

JOURNALISM

Cabinet NN Shelf 2 No. 5

Newspapers and trouble makers. By Lindsay Denison. Excerpt from Hampton's Broadway Magazine, Oct., 1908. On editing "tainted, manufactured or doctored news".

Item 25 in "Various aspects of Journalism".

JOURNALISM

Cabinet 33 Shelf 1 No. 23

(The) Newspaper Man, 1892-3

See PERIODICALS, PRINTING, United States (The) Newspaper Man...

JOURNALISM

Cabinet A Shelf 1 No. 22

NEWSPAPER Tax Stamps (British) on several newspapers in this volume.

JOURNALISM

Cabinet NN Shelf 2 No. 5

Newspapers' contempt for the public, The. By a City Editor. Excerpt from The World Today, Nov., 1907. One City Editor interviews another.

Item 14 in vol. "Various aspects of Journalism".

JOURNALISM

Cabinet NN Shelf 2 No. 9

Newspaper methods yesterday and today. Article by Geo. F. Spinney. Excerpt from "Pearson's Magazine", May, 1910.

Item 10 in volume with binder's title "Newspapers, various excerpts".

JOURNALISM

Cabinet NN Shelf 2 No. 16

(The) Newspaper, the magazine and the public. Interview with Richard Watson Gilder, by Clifton Johnson.
Excerpt from The Outlook, Feb.4, 1899. With portrait.

Item 7 in vol. with binder's title; "Journalism: Pamphlets. Bound, 1932".

JOURNALISM

Cabinet NN Shelf 2 No. 16

Newspapers gone to seed. By James Parton. Excerpt from the Forum, March, 1866.

Item 5 in vol. with binder's title; "Journalism: Pamphlets. Bound, 1932".

JOURNALISM

Cabinet NN Shelf 2 No. 5

Newspaper morals. By H.L. Mencken. Excerpt from Atlantic Monthly, March, 1914.

Mencken's opinions concerning the means of educating the ignorant reader public.

Item 15 in vol. "Various aspects of journalism".

JOURNALISM

Cabinet NN Shelf 2 No. 9

(The) Newspaper-the World's diary Article by Jas. Melvin Lee. Excerpt from "Munsey's Magazine", Dec., 1916.

Item 9 in volume with binder's title "Newspapers, various excerpts".

JOURNALISM

Cabinet NN Shelf 2 No. 7

Newspapers here and abroad. By E.L. Godkin. Excerpt from North American Review, Feb., 1890.

Item 11 in bound collection "Journalism. Excerpts, etc."

JOURNALISM

Cabinet NN Shelf 2 No. 5

Newspaper of the future, the. By Noah Brooks. Excerpt from the Forum, July, 1890.

Item 3 in vol. "Various aspects of Journalism".

JOURNALISM

Cabinet 37 Shelf 1 & 2 No.

Newspaperdom: a trade journal for makers of newspapers, 1892 to 1925.

See PERIODICALS, PRINTING, United States Newspaperdom...

JOURNALISM

Cabinet R Shelf 5 No. 35

Newspapers of Lancaster County (Pennsylvania). Paper read before the Lancaster County Historical Society, May 2, 1902, by F.R. Diffenderffer and printed in Proceedings, vol. VI, No.8.
Pasted in at back; three newspaper articles, "Our early German printers".

Cloth; 9¾ x 6 in.

JOURNALISM

Cabinet NN Shelf 2 No. 2.02

Newspaper press in Ohio. [Article signed W.T.C. Excerpt from the Historical Magazine, April, 1859].

Item 12 in vol. with binder's title "Journalists and Journalism -- III. Pamphlets".

JOURNALISM

Cabinet NN Shelf 2 No. 9

Newspapers and the public, by Chas. Dudley Warner, in The Forum, April, 1890: In this account the responsibility for the vulgarity of a portion of the American press is shifted from the editors shoulder to that of the public.

Bound with other items in "Newspapers, various excerpts", item 23.

JOURNALISM

Cabinet NN Shelf 2 No. 9

Newspapers, their use and abuse; in which it is questioned whether the free press is not an evil that should be abated. Excerpt from "The Republic", June, 1873.

Item 1 in bound collection with binder's title "Newspapers, various excerpts".

JOURNALISM

Cabinet NN Shelf 2 No. 2.01

O'Connor, Joseph, editor, author, poet, who deceased at Rochester, N.Y., October 9th, 1908. Sketch of his life. [Excerpt from the Jour. Am. Irish Hist. Soc., vol. 8, 1909].

Item 5 in vol. with binder's title "Journalists and Journalism -- II. Pamphlets."

JOURNALISM

Cabinet 81 Shelf 2 No. 34

Partisan press and newspaper statistics. Celebrated printing offices, reporters and reporting. Vol.V, of "Printers Scraps" collected by Joel Munsell, of Albany, N.Y., prior to 1860.

Half morocco; 8-3/4 x 7-1/8 in.

JOURNALISM

Cabinet 25 Shelf 1 No. 4

"Pointers". A magazine of newspaper comment, vols. XVI-XVIII, 1910-1912. Published monthly by Barnhart Brothers & Spindler, Kansas City, Mo.

Cloth; 10½ x 7½ in.

JOURNALISM

Cabinet KK Shelf 6 No. 18

Ohio Associated Dailies

see ASSOCIATIONS, NEWSPAPERS. Ohio Associated Dailies...

JOURNALISM

Cabinet NN Shelf 3 No. 20

Pendleton, John. How to succeed as a journalist. London: Grant Richards The "How to" Series. 1902.

Cloth: 7½x5"

JOURNALISM

Cabinet NN Shelf 2 No. 9

Plan for an endowed Journal, A, by Hamilton Holt, in The Independent, Aug. 8, 1912: An address delivered by Mr. Holt at the First National Newspaper Conference.

Bound with other items in "Newspapers, various excerpts", item 26.

JOURNALISM

Cabinet NN Shelf 2 No. 9

(The) Omaha Bee, and contemporary journalism. Excerpt from the "Editorial Review", Aug., 1911.

Item 16 in volume with binder's title "Newspapers, various excerpts".

JOURNALISM

Cabinet NN Shelf 2 No. 4

Personal intelligence fifty years ago: by Ellen Mackay Hutchinson, in Harper's New Monthly Magazine, Feb., 1891: Items culled from various early periodicals.

Item 4 in vol. "Journalists and their work". Bound 1918.

JOURNALISM

Cabinet NN Shelf 2 No. 1

Political portraits with pen and pencil: William Cullen Bryant. Excerpt from the Democratic Review, March, 1842. Portrait.

Item 5 in vol. with binder's title "Journalists, Various items".

JOURNALISM

Cabinet NN Shelf 2 No. 16

Our changing journalism. By Bruce Bliven. Excerpt from the Atlantic, Dec., 1923.

Item 9 in vol. with binder's title: "Journalism: Pamphlets. Bound, 1932".

JOURNALISM

Cabinet NN Shelf 2 No. 5

Pest of the period, the. A chapter of the morals and manners of journalism. By Richard Grant White. Excerpt from The Galaxy, Jan., 1870.

Item 2 in vol. "Various aspects of journalism".

JOURNALISM

Cabinet NN Shelf 3 No. 41

Porte, Ray T.: The new publisher: A tale of twelve cities. Salt Lake City, Utah. 1924.

Leatherette: 7-3/8x5-1/8x¾"

JOURNALISM

Cabinet NN Shelf 5 No. 14

Our Joshua as a reporter. By Brother Jonathan... Fredericton, N. B. 1884.

Cloth; 7½ x 5 in.

JOURNALISM

Cabinet NN Shelf 2 No. 2.02

Philadelphia's Johnny Inkslingers. By Isaac R. Pennypacker. [Excerpt from the American Mercury, Nov., 1925].

Item 14 in vol. with binder's title "Journalists and Journalism -- III. Pamphlets".

JOURNALISM

Cabinet NN Shelf 3 No. 30

Postal riders and raiders.

By The man on the ladder (W.H. Gantz). Issued by The Independent Postal League. Chicago. 1912.

Frontispiece.

Cloth: 8-1/8x5-5/8x1-1/8"

JOURNALISM

Cabinet NN Shelf 2 No. 2.01

Parisian journalism of to-day. Excerpt from the Eclectic, Feb., 1874.

Item 11 in vol. with binder's title "Journalists and Journalism -- II. Pamphlets".

JOURNALISM

Cabinet QQ Shelf 1 No. 51

"PI". A compilation of odds and ends relating to workers in sanctum and newsroom. Culled from the scrap-book of a compositor. Hamilton, Ont....1890.

Half morocco; 6½ x 5¼ in.

JOURNALISM

Cabinet NN Shelf 2 No. 2.02

Power and character of the press [Unsigned article: Excerpt from Emerson's Magazine, Jan., 1858.

Item 6 in vol. with binder's title "Journalists and Journalism -- III. Pamphlets".

JOURNALISM

Cabinet NN Shelf 2 No. 16

(The) Press

Unsigned article; excerpt from the Democratic Review, April 1, 1852.

Item 2 in vol. with binder's title; "Journalism: Pamphlets. Bound, 1832".

JOURNALISM

Cabinet NN Shelf 2 No. 4

Press as a news gatherer, The. By the manager of the Associated Press, William Henry Smith, Excerpt from The Century Magazine, Aug., 1891. Includes an account of the origin of The Associated Press, and the good it has accomplished.

Item 18 in vol. "Journalists and their work".

JOURNALISM

Cabinet NN Shelf 2 No. 5

Public opinion, making of. By Rollo Ogden. Excerpt from The Century Magazine, March, 1904.

Lunch table talk of a senator, a college president, a doctor of divinity, and an editor.

Item 12 in vol. "Various aspects of journalism".

JOURNALISM

Cabinet 00 Shelf 5 No. 16

Press, The, and its story. An account of the birth and development of journalism up to the present day, with the history of all the leading newspapers...also the story of their production from wood-pulp to the printed sheet. By J. D. Symon. With 26 illus. London, 1914. Seeley, Service & Co. Ltd.

Cloth; 7-7/8 x 5-1/8 x $1\frac{3}{4}$ in.

JOURNALISM

Cabinet 00 Shelf 3 No. 37

(The) Press the greatest power in the world. By George Creel. [Illus. excerpt from The Mentor, June 1, 1921, Vol. 9, No. 5. Has portraits of Pres. Harding, Geo. W. Childs, founder of the Philadelphia Public Ledger, James G. Bennett, etc.

Cloth; $10\frac{1}{4}$ x 7 in.

JOURNALISM

Cabinet 25 Shelf 1 No. 5 and following

(The) Publishers' Guide: a monthly journal for all all departments...

See PERIODICALS, PUBLISHERS. (The) Publishers Guide...

JOURNALISM

Cabinet NN Shelf 2 No. 16

Press and periodical literature of the United States. By "S"

Excerpt from the Quarterly Register, March, 1849.

Item 1 in vol. with binder's title; "Journalism: Pamphlets. Bound, 1892".

JOURNALISM

Cabinet NN Shelf 3 No. 45

Printing for the journalists. A handbook for reporters, editors, and students of journalism.

By Eric W. Allen. New York. 1928. Illus.

Borzoi Handbooks of Journalism

Cloth: $7\frac{1}{2}$x5x$\frac{3}{4}$"

JOURNALISM

Cabinet NN Shelf 2 No. 5

Quack Journalism. By Mrs. L.H. Harris. Excerpt from Putnam's Monthly, May, 1907.

Item 26 in vol. "Various aspects of Journalism".

JOURNALISM

Cabinet NN Shelf 2 No. 5

Press and public men, The. By H.V. Boynton. Excerpt from The Century Magazine, Oct., 1891.

Item 22 in vol. "Various aspects of Journalism".

JOURNALISM

Cabinet NN Shelf 2 No. 5

Problem of the Associated Press, The. By An Observer. Excerpt from The Atlantic Monthly, July, 1914.

Item 17 in vol. "Various aspects of Journalism".

JOURNALISM

Cabinet NN Shelf 3 No. 21

Ralph, Julian. The making of a journalist. New York. 1903.

Cloth: 8x$5\frac{1}{2}$"

JOURNALISM

Cabinet S Shelf 5 No. 17

(The) Press and Southern progress. An excerpt from The Forensic Quarterly, Sept. 1910.

Improved journalistic conditions attributed to modern inventions.

Bound in collection Miscellaneous items relating to printing; excerpts from magazines," 1918.

JOURNALISM

Cabinet NN Shelf 2 No. 2.01

(The) Provincial editor's outlook. By Arthur Reed Kimball.

Item 16 in vol. with binder's title "Journalists and Journalims -- II. Pamphlets".

JOURNALISM

Cabinet 00 Shelf 3 No. 28

Random recollections of an old political reporter. By William C. Hudson...For 44 years staff writer on the Brooklyn Daily Eagle. With an introduction by St. Clair McKelway. New York, 1911. With portraits.

Cloth; $7\frac{3}{4}$ x $5\frac{1}{2}$ in.

JOURNALISM

Cabinet NN Shelf 2 No. 5

Press and the professors, the. By G. Stanley Hall. Excerpt from Appleton's Magazine, March, 1909.

Criticism of the "news fakirs of the daily press".

Item 24 in Vol. "Various aspects of Journalism".

JOURNALISM

Cabinet QQ Shelf 4 No. 36

Public-Ledger, 1836-1866, historical account, illustrated.

see

VANSANT, I.L. Royal road to wealth.... circa 1866, p.115

JOURNALISM

Cabinet NN Shelf 2 No. 2.01

Raymond, Henry J. and the "Times". By Augustus Maverick. Excerpt from the Galaxy, Aug., 1869.

Item 8 in vol. with binder's title "Journalists and Journalism -- II. Pamphlets".

JOURNALISM

Cabinet NN Shelf 2 No. 7

(The) Reader, the reporter and the news. By Shepard A. Margen.
Excerpt from The Outlook, June 3, 1911.

Item 17 in bound volume "Journalism. Excerpts, etc."

JOURNALISM

Cabinet KK Shelf 6 No. 16

Republican Editorial Association of New York. Annual reports for years 1895, 1897, 1898, 1900, 1901, 1902, 1903 - 06, 1907.

(8 pieces - 8 titles) business meetings, historical biographical sketches and notes.

Paper board holder; 10¾ x 6½ in.

JOURNALISM

Cabinet NN Shelf 3 No. 12

Secrets of the sanctum, an inside view of an editor's life.

By A. F. Hill, Philadelphia. 1875.

Cloth: 7½x5½"

JOURNALISM

Cabinet NN Shelf 2 No. 7

Recent phases of journalism. By Frank C. Bray.
Excerpt from the Chautaugan, March, 1902.

Item 2 in bound collection "Journalism. Excerpts, etc."

JOURNALISM

Cabinet NN Shelf 7 No. 16

Reviewing, the hazards of. The founder of the "American Journal of Philology" relates the inner history of reviewing for the "Nation". By Basil L. Gildersleeve.
see
NATION, THE. Semi - centennial, 1863 - 1915, p. 49.

JOURNALISM

Cabinet NN Shelf 2 No. 2.02

See the papers! The malady of American journalism. By a Newspaper Man. Excerpt from Harper's Magazine, June, 1925.

Item 9 in vol. with binder's title "Journalists and Journalism -- III. Pamphlets".

JOURNALISM

Cabinet NN Shelf 2 No. 4

Reminiscences of an editor. Excerpt from the Forum, Jan., 1896.

Item 13 in vol. "Journalists and their work".

JOURNALISM

Cabinet NN Shelf 5 No. 30

Robbins, Sir Alfred. The Press. Benn's Sixpenny Library. London, n. d. circa 1928. Paper booklet.

Paper; 6½ x 4-1/8 in. In board folder.

JOURNALISM

Cabinet NN Shelf 2 No. 16

Seeing a manuscript through the press. By Robert Cortes Halliday.
Excerpt from the Bookman, July, 1922.

Item 14 in vol. with binder's title; "Journalism: Pamphlets. Bound, 1932".

JOURNALISM

Cabinet NN Shelf 2 No. 4

Reporter, some experiences of a. By A.E. Watrous. Excerpt from Lippincott's, May, 1897.

Item 3 in vol. "Journalists and their work".

JOURNALISM.

Cabinet 66 Shelf 1 No. 11

Sac Sun, The. (Sac City, Iowa.) 1871-1931. 60th Anniversary Edition, Thursday, June, 25, 1931. Illus. facsimile, portraits.

Cloth; 22¾ x 17½ in.

JOURNALISM

Cabinet NN Shelf 3 No. 33

Seitz, Don. C.: Training for the newspaper trade.
By D.C. Seitz, business manager of the "New York World".
Philadelphia... 1916.
J.B. Lippincott Co. Illus.

Cloth: 7¾x5"

JOURNALISM

Cabinet NN Shelf 2 No. 4

Reporters, by George J. Mansey. Excerpt from The Cosmopolitan, June, 1890.

Item 8 in vol. "Journalists and their work".

JOURNALISM

Cabinet Q Shelf 1 No. 1

Sergent, John Osborne. Some interesting reminiscences of the past fifty years.
Excerpt from the Harvard Register, June, 1881. With portrait.

Item 18 in volume with binder's title "Publishing, Various Excerpts".

JOURNALISM

Cabinet NN Shelf 3 No. 22

Shuman, Edwin L. Practical journalism: A complete manual of the best newspaper methods. New York. 1903.

Frontispiece.

Cloth; 7¾ x 5¼ in.

JOURNALISM

Cabinet NN Shelf 2 No. 4

Reporters of the sea. By W.F.G. Shanks. Excerpt from Harper's New Monthly Magazine, July, 1868.

Item 11 in vol. "Journalists and their work".

JOURNALISM

Cabinet NN Shelf 2 No. 9

Scientific analysis of "The Press". Article by Alvan A. Tenney. Excerpt from "The Independent", Oct., 17, 1912.

Item 18 in volume with binder's title "Newspapers, various excerpts".

JOURNALISM

Cabinet NN Shelf 7 No. 39

(The) Silver Standard of 1847.

see

NEWSPAPERS, United States. Connecticut.

(The) Silver Standard...

JOURNALISM

Cabinet NN Shelf 2 No. 10

Simultaneous newspapers of the 20th century. By Alfred Harmsworth, editor of the London Daily Mail.
(Excerpt from the North American Review, Jan., 1911.)

Item 5 in bound collection with binder's title "Description of various newspapers".

JOURNALISM

Cabinet NN Shelf 7 No. 29

Spirit of the Fair. Printed and published by John F. Trow, 1864, New York City. Editorial staff; Macdonough, Mrs. C.E. Butler, Mrs. Edward Cooper, C.A. Bristed, Messrs Dewey, Gerard jr., Sedgwick, etc.
A literary daily paper, first issued April 5, last issue April 23, 1864. One vol.

Half morocco; $9\frac{1}{2}$ x 12.

JOURNALISM

Cabinet NN Shelf 3 No. 11

Studies in literature: George D. Prentice, poet-journalist. By George W. Griffin. Philadelphia, 1871. 2d ed.

Paper; $7\frac{1}{2}$ x $4\frac{3}{4}$ in.

JOURNALISM

Cabinet 00 Shelf 4 No. 29

(A) Sketch of the political history of the past three years in connexion with "The Press Newspaper", and the part it has taken on the leading questions of the time. London, Press Office, 1856.

Brochure, in envelope

JOURNALISM

Cabinet 61 Shelf 1 No. 5

Springfield Republican (The), its founders and conductors. A new newspaper home

Illus. article in "The Paper World", vol.18, No.1, Jan., 1889

JOURNALISM

Cabinet NN Shelf 2 No. 9

Study in independent Journalism, A, by Geo. S. Merriam, in The Century, Oct., 1885.

Bound with other items in "Newspapers, various excerpts", item 25.

JOURNALISM.

Cabinet NN Shelf 7 No. 7.01

Smith, Major Orlando Jay, founder and president of the American Press Association.

See AMERICAN PRESS ASSOCIATION.
Announces the death of .... Major Orlando J. Smith ... Dec. 26, 1908.

JOURNALISM

Cabinet 61 Shelf 1 No. 2

"Starting a newspaper". A romantic chapter of daily journalism. The very late Baltimore Times.

Article in "The Paper World", vol.4, No.2, Feb., 1882.

JOURNALISM

Cabinet NN Shelf 2 No. 9

Sunday newspapers. Article by Rev, Prof. Herric Johnson: An address at the Washington Sabbath Conference,Dec.,13, 1888.
Excerpt from "Our Day, Feb., 1889.

Item 5 in volume with binder's title "Newspapers, various excerpts".

JOURNALISM

Cabinet NN Shelf 2 No. 5

Some humors of Yellow Journalism. By Hugh Logan. Excerpt from The Van Norden Magazine, Feb., 1907.

Item 11 in vol. "Various aspects of Journalism".

JOURNALISM

Cabinet NN Shelf 2 No. 5

Status of journalism, the. By Arthur Lynch. Excerpt from The Outlook, Aug. 12, 1901.
A critical comparison of French, British, and American newspapers.

Item 16 "Various aspects of journalism".

JOURNALISM

Cabinet NN Shelf 2 No. 5

Suppression of important news, The. By Edward Alsworth Ross. Excerpt from The Atlantic Monthly, March, 1910.

Item 19 in vol. "Various aspects of Journalism".

JOURNALISM

Cabinet NN Shelf 2 No. 5

Some phases of contemporary Journalism. By John A. Cockerill. Excerpt from The Cosmopolitan, Oct., 1892.

Item 20 in vol. "Various aspects of Journalism".

JOURNALISM

Cabinet 00 Shelf 3 No. 29

Story of a page: Thirty years...in the editorial columns of The New York World. By John L. Heaton. New York, 1913.

Has frontispiece portrait of Joseph Pulitzer, founder of the N. Y. World, 1883.

Boards, cloth back; 8-7/8 x 5-7/8 x $1\frac{1}{2}$ in.

JOURNALISM

Cabinet NN Shelf 2 No. 2.02

Tabloid a day, a. By Abel Kandel. [Excerpt from the Forum, March, 1927.]

Item 10 in vol. with binder's title "Journalists and Journalism -- III. Pamphlets".

JOURNALISM

Cabinet NN Shelf 2 No. 5

Some weaknesses of Modern Journalism. By Oswald Garrison Villard. An address delivered at Kansas Newspaper Week, under the auspices of the Department of Journalism, University of Kansas, May 10 to 14, 1914. In the University of Kansas News - Bulletin, Nov., 2, 1914.

Item 32 in vol. "Various aspects of Journalism".

JOURNALISM

Cabinet 00 Shelf 5 No. 17

Street of ink, the. An intimate history of journalism. By H. Simonis. With eighty portraits and other illustrations. London, 1917. Cassell and Company, Ltd.

Cloth; $8\frac{3}{4}$ x $5\frac{3}{4}$ x $1\frac{1}{2}$ in.

JOURNALISM

Cabinet NN Shelf 2 No. 2.02

Tabloids, the. By Richard G. de Rochemont [Excerpt from the American Mercury, Oct., 1926].

Item 18 in vol. with binder's title "Journalists and Journalism -- III. Pamphlets".

JOURNALISM

Cabinet NN Shelf 2 No. 2.02

Tabloids, some facts about the. By Hubert Malkus. [Illus. excerpt from Success Magazine, Dec., 1926].

Item 24 in vol. with binder's title "Journalists and Journalism -- III. Pamphlets".

JOURNALISM

Cabinet NN Shelf 3 No. 44

Training of a journalist. An address. By Frederick Peaker. A paper read before the International Association of Journalists, at a Conference held in London, June, 1927. Pamphlet.

Item in manila envelope.

JOURNALISM

Cabinet NN Shelf 6 No. 55

United Amateur Press Association of America. Year Book 1933-1934. Published for the Association by Vincent B. Haggerty, 21 Stegman Court, Jersey City, N.J.

Brovhure, in manila envelope

JOURNALISM

Cabinet NN Shelf 2 No. 2.01

Taylor, General Charles H. What he is, and what he has done -- His place in journalism, and his influence as creator, and manager of a great daily newspaper. By Frank A. Munsey. [Excerpt from Munsey's.] With portrait.

Item 17 in vol. with binder's title "Journalists and Journalism -- II. Pamphlets".

JOURNALISM

Cabinet V Shelf 3 No. 23

2 vols.

(Les) Travailleurs du livre et du journal. Par G. Renard. Paris, 1925.

History of the development of printing in France. The influence of labor and other conditions which accelerated or retarded newspaper and book production, etc.

Half morocco; $7\frac{1}{4}$ x 4-5/8 in.

JOURNALISM

Cabinet NN Shelf 2 No. 16

Unprintable.- when, if ever, and why. By Stuart P. Sherman.
Excerpt from the Atlantic, July, 1923.

Item 10 in vol. with binder's title; "Journalism: Pamphlets. Bound, 1932".

JOURNALISM

Cabinet NN Shelf 2 No. 5

Telling the good (which) men do. By Wilder D. Quint. Excerpt from The New England Magazine, Sept., 1909.

An account of the origin and successful career of The Christian Science Monitor. Illus.

Item 30 in vol. "Various aspects of Journalism".

JOURNALISM

Cabinet NN Shelf 4 No. 12.02

Tribune Association, The. Organization and by-laws. New York, 1872.
With 2 portraits, Horace Creeley

Brochure, in manila envelope

JOURNALISM

Cabinet NN Shelf 2 No. 2.02

[Van Anden, Isaac, and the Brooklyn "Eagle".] Biographical excerpt from "Sketches of men of progress", New York, 1870-71.

Item 25 in vol. with binder's title "Journalists and Journalism -- III. Pamphlets".

JOURNALISM

Cabinet QQ Shelf 2 No. 12

Thayer, John Adams. Out of the rut. The Smart Set Edition. With an added chapter. New York, 1912.

Life story of a pioneer in periodical journalism, with brief notes of other journalistic personalities-Cyrus Curtis, Frank Munsey, Thomas Lawson, etc.

Half morocco; $9\frac{3}{4}$ x $6\frac{3}{4}$ in.

JOURNALISM

Cabinet NN Shelf 4 No. 12.03

Tribune Association presented with a portrait of Whitelaw Reid, Dec.12, 1899. Program of exercises. Brochure, with frontispiece.

With other items in manila envelope.

JOURNALISM

Cabinet NN Shelf 2 No. 9

Varieties of Journalism, The, by Murat Halstead, in Cosmopolitan, Dec., 1892.

Bound with other items in "Newspapers, various excerpts", item 22.

JOURNALISM

Cabinet NN Shelf 3 No. 32

Thorpe, Merle. The coming newspaper. New York. 1915.

A collection of essays by representative American editors, and edited by Merle Thorpe, Professor of Journalism.

Cloth: 7x5x1-1/8"

JOURNALISM

Cabinet NN Shelf 4 No. 12.03

Tribune Club, proceedings of the. Presentation--Anniversary Dinner. New York, 1855.
Honor guest, Franklin J. Ottarson, chief editor of the N.Y. Tribune, city department.

With other Tribune items, in manila envelope

JOURNALISM

Cabinet NN Shelf 2 No. 2.02

"Variety" [Sime Silverman's theatrical newspaper] By Hugh Kent. Excerpt from the American Mercury, Dec., 1926.

Item 17 in vol. with binder's title "Journalists and Journalism -- III. Pamphlets".

JOURNALISM.

Cabinet 66 Shelf 1 No. 10

Times, the story of the New York, 1851-1931, 80th anniversary, Sept. 18, 1851. All rag edition.
Has portraits, also facsimile of issue of Sept. 18, 1851.

Cloth; $22\frac{1}{2}$ x 18 in.

JOURNALISM

Cabinet NN Shelf 2 No. 9

Twenty-four hours in a newspaper office. Article by Arnot Reid. Excerpt from "The Nineteenth Century", March, 1887.

Bound with other items in collection with binder's title "Newspapers, various excerpts" item,7

JOURNALISM

Cabinet OO Shelf 6 No. 65

Villard, Henry, and journalism. A civil war correspondent - ownership of The Evening Post acquired by him in 1881.

Article with portrait in New York Evening Post New Building Supplement... April 13, 1907, p. 13.

JOURNALISM

Cabinet NN Shelf 2 No. 40

[Walter, John: one of the proprietors of the "London Times"] First impressions of America. London: Printed for Private Circulation, 1867. Preface dated, Bearwood, Nov., 1867.

Cloth; 7¼ x 4¾ in.

JOURNALISM

Cabinet NN Shelf 2 No. 9

Western Journalism, by Z.L. White, in Harpers' New Monthly Magazine, Oct., 1888: Includes biographical sketches of editors and founders of the various newspapers of the West. Portraits.

Bound with other items in "Newspapers, various excerpts", item 21.

JOURNALISM

Cabinet NN Shelf 2 No. 2

Your daughter's career, if she wants to be a newspaper woman, by Rose Young, in Good Housekeeping, Sept., 1915.

Bound with other items in "Journalists and Journalism", item 16.

JOURNALISM

Cabinet Shelf No.

War correspondents. G.W. Kendall who went to Mexico with U.S. Army in 1846, was first war correspondent.

Article in the Publisher's Auxiliary, 66th year, No. 45, Nov. 7, 1931, pp. 1 and 6.

JOURNALISM

Cabinet NN Shelf 2 No. 5

What a daily nespaper might be made. By Wm. M. Payne. Excerpt from The Forum, Nov., 1893.

Item 5 in vol. "Various aspects of Journalism".

JOURNALISM (see also)

Cabinet Shelf No.

AMATEUR PRINTING
JOURNALISM (various countries)
LIBEL
LIBERTY OF THE PRESS
NEWSPAPERS
PERIODICALS
ASSOCIATIONS, NEWSPAPER

JOURNALISM

Cabinet 00 Shelf 3 No. 39

Warren, Low. Journalism. With an introduction by Alan Pitt Robbins, news editor of "The Times." London, 1922. Illus.

History and text book. Frontispiece "The earliest known picture of an editor at work."

Cloth; 9 x 5¾ x 1-1/8 in.

JOURNALISM

Cabinet NN Shelf 2 No. 5

What a newspaper should be. By J.C. Croly. Excerpt from Putnam's, March, 1868.

Item 4 in vol. "Various aspects of Journalism".

JOURNALISM, Australia

Cabinet 00 Shelf 6 No. 12

"The Bulletin" in Australia. By John Dalley. Sydney, January 29, 1930.

On p. 32 of Jubilee Number of "The Bulletin", 1880-1930.

Cloth; 16 x 10¾ in.

JOURNALISM

Cabinet NN Shelf 2 No. 2.01

Watterson, Henry. An outline of the most striking and interesting personality in the American journalism of today. By Elisha Jay Edwards. Excerpt from Munsey's. Jan. 1906. With portrait.

Item 14 in vol. with binder's title "Journalists and Journalism -- II. Pamphlets".

JOURNALISM

Cabinet NN Shelf 2 No. 2.02

What a youngster [Herschel Jones] learned from his grandfather's newspaper. By James H. McCullough. Excerpt from the American Magazine, Jan., 1924.

With portrait of Herschel Jones, owner of the Minneapolis "Journal"

Item 21 in vol. with binder's title "Journalists and Journalism -- III. Pamphlets".

JOURNALISM, Australia.

Cabinet A Shelf 3 No. 39

Sydney Morning Herald: Centenary Supplement, 1831-1931. A century of Journalism.

History of this newspaper, illustrated with exterior views of buildings, working departments, etc.

Buckram; 25½ x 20½ in.

JOURNALISM

Cabinet 61 Shelf 1 No. 2

Weed, Thurlow, an old time journalist. Article with portrait.

Item in "The Paper World", vol.4, No.3, March, 1882.

JOURNALISM

Cabinet NN Shelf 2 No. 38.01

Wisconsin Agriculturist, Racine, Wis., 1926. Set of 15 photographs of the organization, and premises.

Items in manila envelope

JOURNALISM, Australia

Cabinet 00 Shelf 4 No. 47

Sydney Morning Herald and The Sydney Mail. A record of the years from 1831. John Fairfax & Sons Limited. Sydney (1926). Illus. brochure.

In envelope.

JOURNALISM

Cabinet NN Shelf 1 No. 13

Weed, Thurlow and Edwin Croswell. (Biographical sketch) Excerpts, newspaper clipping. n.d. circa 1874.

In envelope vol.I "The life of Thurlow Weed. Autobiography". Edited by his daughter, Harriet A. Weed. Boston, 1883.

JOURNALISM

Cabinet Shelf No.

Women journalists.

See Women Journalists.

JOURNALISM, Austria. Literature of

Cabinet NN Shelf 2 No. 13

Great newspapers of Continental Europe, Austria. By Eugene Limedorfer.

Excerpt from The Bookman, April, 1900.

Item 32 in bound collection with binder's title "Various newspapers and periodicals".

JOURNALISM, Belgium.

Cabinet 18 Shelf 2 No. 1

(Newspapers in Belgium. The history of) Aus der Geschichte das Zeitungwesens in Belgien. von Toni Kellen, Essen, 1915.

In Zeitschrift fur Bucherfreunde, 1915-16, part I, p.144.

JOURNALISM, Canada

Cabinet 00 Shelf 4 No. 48

Halifax, 1751. Early journalism in Nova Scotia. A paper read by J. J. Stewart, Dec. 8, 1887.

On p. 91 of the Collections of the Nova Scotia Historical Society for the year 1887-88, Vol. VI, Halifax, N. S.

Boards; $8\frac{3}{4}$ x 5-7/8 in.

JOURNALISM, Canada.

Cabinet A Shelf 1 No. 31

Picton Gazette. Picton, Ontario, 1830-1930. One hundred years of service. Centenary issue, which includes a history of this newspaper.

Buckram; $22\frac{1}{2}$ x $17\frac{1}{4}$ in.

JOURNALISM, Belgium

Cabinet 00 Shelf 3 No. 35

Secret press in Belgium, the. By Jean Massart. Translated by Bernard Miall. New York (1918). Illus.

Cloth; 7-5/8 x 5 x $\frac{3}{4}$ in.

JOURNALISM, Canada

Cabinet NN Shelf 2 No. 9

Halifax Gazette: the first newspaper established in Canada. (Excerpted article from The Canadian Antiquarian, July, 1885)

Item 24 in vol. with binder's title "Newspapers, various excerpts".

JOURNALISM, Canada

Cabinet Shelf No.

Southam, William, Canadian printer and publisher. Noted Canadian publisher dies in 88th year: a brief biography.

Article in Editor & Publisher, vol. 64, No.42, March, 1932, p.44.

JOURNALISM, Bulgaria

Cabinet NN Shelf 2 No. 16

What the people read in Bulgaria. By O. Leonard. Illus. excerpt from the American Review of Reviews, March, 1905.

Item 22 in vol. with binder's title; "Journalism: Pamphlets. Bound 1932".

JOURNALISM, Canada

Cabinet 00 Shelf 4 No. 50

(A) History of Canadian journalism in the several portions of the Dominion, with a sketch of the Canadian Press Association, 1859-1908. Edited by a Committee of the Association. Toronto, 1908. Portraits.

Cloth; $9\frac{3}{4}$ x 6-3/8 x 1 in.

JOURNALISM, Canada

Cabinet NN Shelf 2 No. 16

What the people read in Canada. By P.T. McGrath. Excerpt from the American Review of Reviews, June, 1906.

Item 19 in vol. with binder's title: "Journalism: Pamphlets. Bound, 1932".

JOURNALISM, Canada

Cabinet NN Shelf 2 No. 2

Canadian Journalists and Journalism, by W.B. Harte, in The New England Magazine, Dec., 1891. Portraits.

Bound with other items in "Journalists and Journalism", item 18.

JOURNALISM, Canada.

Cabinet A Shelf 2 No. 21a

History of the newspaper press. In the special Centenary Issue of the Quebec Gazette. June 21, 1864. vol.102.

Buckram, 23 x $8\frac{1}{2}$ x $\frac{1}{2}$ in.

JOURNALISM

CHINA. A Collection of Chinese Newspapers and Magazines issued in 1920, and supposed to be complete, as per envelope attached to card in classification CHINA.

This collection is in a stout box with a view to its preservation without opening for at least half a century, when it is hoped that it will have great value and interest in connection with the history of Journalism in China.

JOURNALISM, Canada

Cabinet 00 Shelf 4 No. 49

Canadian newspaper directory, containing accurate lists of all the newspapers and periodicals published in the Dominion of Canada and Province of Newfoundland. Montreal: T. F. Wood & Co., Publishers, 1876.

Preceded by "Observations on Canadian journalism, with a sketch of its rise and growth." By James V. Wright.

Half morocco; 8-5/8 x 5-7/8 x $\frac{1}{2}$ in.

JOURNALISM, Canada

Cabinet 00 Shelf 4 No. 51

Imperial Press Conference in Canada, The. By Robert Donald. Foreword by Viscount Burnham...London-New York-Toronto, n. d. (circa 1920). Illus. and portraits.

Cloth; $9\frac{1}{2}$ x $6\frac{1}{4}$ x $1\frac{1}{2}$ in.

JOURNALISM, China

Cabinet 00 Shelf 6 No. 17

Shanghai, 1850-1910.

see NEWSPAPERS, ANNIVERSARY ISSUES. China. Shanghai. Special supplement...

JOURNALISM, Canada.

Cabinet NN Shelf 2 No. 8

Four early Canadian journalists, by Wilfred Campbell, author of "The Canadian Lake Region": A brief sketch of the careers and affairs of Huge Scobie, J. Sheridan Hogan, John Lowe, and Brown Chamberlain.

Bound with other items in "Various Editors", item 17.

JOURNALISM, Canada

Cabinet Shelf No.

(Ontario). Extinct early Ontario newspapers (1793-1830).

A list in Printing Review of Canada, vol. 7, No.3, Aug. 1931, p.26.

JOURNALISM, Denmark

Cabinet NN Shelf 2 No. 13

Great newspapers of Continental Europe: Scandinavian newspapers. By Daniel Kilham Dodge.

Item 35 in bound collection with binder's title "Various newspapers and periodicals"

JOURNALISM, England

Cabinet KK Shelf 1 No. 25

"Leeds Mercury, The". Two centuries of journalistic work.

see "LEEDS MERCURY, THE". Two centuries of journalistic work...

JOURNALISM, France

Cabinet NN Shelf 2 No. 13

French journals and journalists, the history of. Excerpt from "American Eclectic", April 1851.

Item 8 in volume with binder's title "Various newspapers and periodicals"-1

JOURNALISM, France

Cabinet NN Shelf 2 No. 2

Paris Press, the thunderer of the. Excerpt from Harper's New Monthly Magazine, May, 1884.

Item 13 in vol. "Journalists and Journalism". Bound, 1918.

JOURNALISM, Finland

Cabinet NN Shelf 2 No. 13

What the people read in Poland and Finland. Excerpt article from "The American Reviews of Reviews", July, 1904. Illus.

Item 37 in volume with binder's title "Various newspapers and periodicals".

JOURNALISM, France Literature of

Cabinet NN Shelf 2 No. 13

Great newspapers of Continental Europe; France. By Adolph Cohn.
Excerpt from The Bookman, Feb., 1900.

Item 31 in bound collection with binder's title "Various newspapers and periodicals".

JOURNALISM, France

Cabinet NN Shelf 2 No. 1

Parisian journalists, by Junius Henri Browne, in Harper's Magazine, Oct., 1875: Brief character sketches of five of the most important journalists of the period. Portraits.

Bound with other items in "Journalists, various excerpts", item 38.

JOURNALISM, France.

Cabinet V Shelf 1 No. 28

(Bordeaux) La Presse Bordelaise pendant la Révolution. Bibliographie historique. Vingt-cinq fac-similes de titres de Journaux, portraits...Par Ernest Labadie. Bordeaux, 1910.

Paper; 10 x 6½ x 1 in.

JOURNALISM, France

Cabinet OO Shelf 1 No. 14.01

Journal des Débats, politiques et littéraires, 1814-1914...Avec vingt reproductions. Paris, 1914. (Actually published in 1924)

Includes list of collaborators .

Half morocco; 11½ x 9¼ in.

JOURNALISM, France.

Cabinet NN Shelf 2 No. 12

Parisian newspapers, notes on. By Brander Matthew.
Excerpted illus. article. n.d. circa 1861.

Item 20 in vol. with binder's title "Various Newspapers and Periodicals".

JOURNALISM, France

Cabinet NN Shelf 2 No. 16

Catholic press in France, the. By Denis Gwynn.
Excerpt from the Catholic World, Oct., 1923.

Item 18 in vol. with binder's title; "Journalism: Pamphlets. Bound, 1932".

JOURNALISM, France

Cabinet Q Shelf 1 Number 2

Jounal des Savants and the Journal de Trevoux. Brief historical account. Excerpt from Living Age, May 19, 1866.

Item 4 in volume with binder's title, "Publishers and Publishing. Pamphlets."

JOURNALISM, France

Cabinet OO Shelf 1 No. 21

Travailleurs du livre et du journal. Par G. Renard.

See pp.217-236

Paper; 7-7/8 x 4-5/8 x ⅝ in.

JOURNALISM, France Literature

Cabinet OO Shelf 4 No. 5

Douay, 1563. An early news-sheet. The Russian invasion of Poland in 1563. An exact facsimile of a contemporary account in Latin, published at Douay. Together with an introduction and historical notes, and a full translation into English. London: Chatto and Windus, Publishers. 1874.
Only 250 copies printed.

Boards; 8¼ x 5½ in.

JOURNALISM, France

Cabinet NN Shelf 2 No. 2

Notes on Parisian newspapers, by Brander Matthews. in The Century Magazine, Dec., 1887. Illus.

Bound with other items in "Journalists and Journalism", item 15.

JOURNALISM, France

Cabinet NN Shelf 2 No. 8

Veuillot, Louis, a pugilist of the press. By Albert Rhodes.
Excerpt from the Galaxy, March, 1876.

Item 12 in volume with binder's title: "Various Editors".

JOURNALISM, France

Cabinet NN Shelf 2 No. 2

French Journalists and Journalism, by Arthur Hornblow, in The Cosmopolitan, Dec., 1892. Portraits.

Bound with other items in "Journalists and Journalism", item 19.

JOURNALISM, France

Cabinet NN Shelf 2 No. 2

Paris journalism and journalists. Article signed J.C. Excerpt from Am. Whig Review. March-April, 1852.

Items 2 & 3 in vol. "Journalists and Journalism". Bound 1918.

JOURNALISM, France

Cabinet NN Shelf 2 No. 16

What the people read in France.
Excerpt from the American Review of Reviews, March, 1904.

Item 21 in vol. with binder's title; "Journalism: Pamphlets. Bound, 1932".

JOURNALISM, Germany

Cabinet NN
Shelf 2
No. 12

Allgemeine Zeitung, Augsburg.: A correspondents account of his visit to the office of the. Excerpt from "Harper's New Monthly Magazine", Jan., 1868.

Item 15 in bound collection with binder's title "Various newspapers and periodicals"

JOURNALISM, Germany

Cabinet 22
Shelf 1
No. 3

(Beginning of the German Newspaper Press, 1609-1650.) Anfange der deutschen zeitungspress, von Julius Otto Opel. Facsimiles of title and text pages.

In Archiv für Deutschen Buchhandels, vol.3, pp.268.

JOURNALISM, Germany

Cabinet 18
Shelf 1
No. 5

(Concerning a Museum of Newspapers). Uber Zeitungmuseen, von Stephan Kekule.

Museum is here recommended as an aid for research in studying the history of any people or nation.

In Zeitschrift für Bücherfreunde, 1909, part 1, p.1.

JOURNALISM, Germany.

Cabinet NN
Shelf 2
No. 12

German newspapers. Article by Stephen Powers. Excerpt from "Harper's New Monthly Magazine" Jan.,1868.

Account of a visit to the offices and with the editors of the "Allegemeine Zeitung" and other leading newspapers of Germany.

Item 3 inbound collection with binder's title "Description of various newspapers".

JOURNALISM, Germany   Literature of

Cabinet NN
Shelf 2
No. 13

Great newspapers of Continental Europe. By Henry W. Fischer.
Excerpt from The Bookman, Jan., 1900

Item 30 in bound collection with binder's title "Various Newspapers and Periodicals"

JOURNALISM, Germany.

Cabinet 18
Shelf 1
No. 15

[History of Hamburg newspapers]. Zur Geschichte des hamburgischen Zeitungswesens. von G. Kowalewski, Hamburg, 1913. With facsimile.

Bibliographical comments with some references to the printers of these early newspapers.

In Zeitschrift fur Bucherfreunde, 1913-14, part 2, p.355.

JOURNALISM, Germany.

Cabinet 22
Shelf 1
No. 8 & 9

(Leipzig, History of the character of the earliest Leipzig newspapers.) Zur altesten geschichte des altesten zeitungswesens in Leipzig, von Albrecht Kirchhoff.

In Archiv für Deutschen Buchhandels, vol. VIII, 49; vol.IX, 250.

JOURNALISM, Germany.

Cabinet 22
Shelf 1
No. 8

(Leipzig, 1609. The earliest account of the beginning of the newspaper press in Leipzig.) Zur altesten geschichte des Leipziger Zeitungswesens, von Albrecht Kirchhoff.

In Archiv fur Deutschen Buchhandles, 1883, vol.VII, pp.49, 118, vol.IX, p.250, vol.IX, p.250.

JOURNALISM, Germany.

Cabinet 22
Shelf 1
No. 19

(Rostock, 1625-1795. The Rostock Newspapers of the 17th century.) Die Rostocker zeitungen des 17th jahrhundert, von Wilhelm Stieda.

Includes an account of postal assistance and of the various types of periodicals including trade papers.

In Archiv für Deutschen Buchhandels, vol. XIX, p.67-178.

JOURNALISM, Germany

Cabinet NN
Shelf 2
No. 13

What the people read in Germany: An excerpt from The American Review of Reviews, Aug., 1904. Illus.

Bound with other items in "Various newspapers and periodicals", vol.1, item 36.

JOURNALISM, Great Britain

Cabinet NN
Shelf 5
No. 8

(The) Agony Column of the "Times", 1800 - 1870. With an introduction, Edited by Alice Clay. London, 1881.

Cloth; 6-5/8 x $4\frac{3}{4}$ x 1 in.

JOURNALISM, Great Britain

Cabinet 00
Shelf 6
No. 1

Amalgamated press, the romance of. By George Dilnot. London, 1925.

Has portraits, illustrations of printing works, publishing houses, paper making operations, printing presses, etc.

Half morocco; 13-1/8 x $10\frac{1}{4}$ x $1\frac{1}{4}$ in.

JOURNALISM, Great Britain

Cabinet NN
Shelf 4
No. 41

Bussey, H. Findlater.

Sixty years of Journalism. Anecdotes and reminiscences.

Bristol. London. 1906.

Cloth: $7\frac{1}{2}$x5"

JOURNALISM, Great Britain

Cabinet 00
Shelf 4
No. 2

Catalogue of a collection of early newspapers and essayists formed by the late John Thomas Hope, and presented to the Bodleian Library by the late Rev. Frederick William Hope. Oxford, 1865.

Cloth; 9 x $5\frac{3}{4}$ x 5/8 in.

JOURNALISM, Great Britain

Cabinet 00
Shelf 3
No. 38

Central News, London, 1871-1921. A record of the celebrations, August, 1921.

Limp leather; 9-7/8 x 5-5/8 in.

JOURNALISM, Great Britain

Cabinet NN
Shelf 2
No. 8

Chambers, William and Robert (Edinburgh, Scotland From the Dublin University Magazine.
Excerpt from the Eclectic, March, 1851.

Item 13 in volume with binder's title: "Various Editors".

JOURNALISM, Great Britain

Cabinet S
Shelf 5
No. 9

Commonweal, The: William Morris' Commonweal, by Leonard D. Abbott, in The New England Magazing, June, 1899. Facsimile Headings, reduced sizes.

Mr. Morris edited this paper for a period of five years, and resigned after its socialistic policies became too intolerant.

Bound in collection "Various Printers - Excerpts and Brochures," item 8.

JOURNALISM, Great Britain

Cabinet 00
Shelf 4
No. 9

Cooper, Charles A. An editor's retrospect: fifty years of newspaper work. London, 1896.

Cloth; p x $5\frac{3}{4}$ x $1\frac{1}{4}$ in.

JOURNALISM, Great Britain

Cabinet 00 Shelf 5 No. 9

"Daily News" (The) Jubilee: A political and social retrospect of fifty years of the Queen's reign. By Mr. Justin McCarthy and Sir John R. Robinson. Illustrated. London 1896.

Cloth, printed; $7\frac{1}{2}$ x 4-7/8 x 7/8 in.

JOURNALISM, Great Britain

Cabinet 00 Shelf 6 No. 2

First newspapers of England printed in Holland, 1620-1621. A faithful reproduction made from the originals...The Hague, 1914.

In cloth folder; $16\frac{1}{4}$ x 11-3/8 in.

JOURNALISM, Great Britain ([illegible])

Cabinet 00 Shelf 4 No. 38

Glasgow press, the early. A paper read to the members of The Old Glasgow Club, by Michael Graham, on March 19, 1906. Glasgow.

Half morocco: $8\frac{5}{8}$ x $6\frac{3}{4}$ x $\frac{1}{2}$ in.

JOURNALISM, Great Britain (Scotland)

Cabinet 00 Shelf 4 No. 41

Dundee Courier. The progress and development of W. & D. C. Thomson's Publications. Dundee, 1899. Illus. brochure. [Also] The pageant of the press, being a tour through the new offices of the Dundee Courier. Dundee, 1907. Illus. [Also] The new home of the Dundee Courier. Dundee, 1905. Illus. brochure.

Four brochures bound in one vol.

Cloth; $8\frac{3}{4}$ x 10 x $\frac{1}{2}$ in.

JOURNALISM, Great Britain

Cabinet NN Shelf 2 No. 7

[First power of the State! Sovereign, Lords, Commons, and -- the Press!] Journalism. By a resident at Paris.

Excerpt from the American Review, Sept. 1846.

Item 3 in bound collection "Journalism. Excerpts, etc."

JOURNALISM, Great Britain

Cabinet A Shelf 3 No. 93

Gloucester Journal, The history of. 1722-1922. By Roland Austin, Librarian of the Gloucester Library.

In the Gloucester Journal-Bi-centenary Historical Supplement. April 8th, 1922.

Buckram; 22 x 19 x $\frac{1}{2}$ in.

JOURNALISM, Great Britain

Cabinet NN Shelf 2 No. 1

Editor of The Times, The, George E. Buckle, by Isis, in The Young Man, Jan., 1897: A character sketch. Portrait.

Bound with other items in "Journalists, various excerpts", item 37.

JOURNALISM, Great Britain

Cabinet 00 Shelf 5 No. 8

Fleet Street, 1846-1890. By Walter Wellsman. Read before the City of London Tradesmen's Club, London, on Thursday, October 9, 1890.

Presentation copy "With the compliments of the author".

Half morocco; $5\frac{3}{4}$ x $4\frac{3}{4}$ x $\frac{1}{4}$ in.

JOURNALISM, Great Britain

Cabinet NN Shelf 2 No. 11

Greatest newspaper in the world, the:-The London Times. Illustrated historical account. By "ALondon Editor". Excerpt from the "Outlook" 28 Nov., 1908.

Item 5 in volume with binder's title "About various newspapers".

JOURNALISM, Great Britain

Cabinet 00 Shelf 4 No. 7 (2 vols.)

English newspapers: chapters in the history of journalism. By H. R. Fox Bourne. (2 vols.) London, 1887.

Cloth; 9 x 5-3/4 x $1\frac{1}{2}$ in.

JOURNALISM, Great Britain

Cabinet 00 Shelf 5 No. 6

Frost, Thomas. Reminiscences of a country journalist. New edition. London, 1888.

Cloth; $8\frac{1}{4}$ x $5\frac{3}{4}$ x 1-1/8 in.

JOURNALISM, Great Britain

Cabinet NN Shelf 2 No. 13

Historical sketches of British periodicals...

see

PERIODICALS, Great Britain. Historical sketches...

JOURNALISM, Great Britain

Cabinet NN Shelf 5 No. 2

Examiner (the) for the year 1711. To which is prefixed a letter to the Examiner. London. Printed for John Morphew. 1712.

Reprint of political and literary tracts issued weekly during the years 1710 - 11.

Leather; $5\frac{1}{4}$ x $3\frac{3}{4}$ in.

JOURNALISM, Great Britain

Cabinet 00 Shelf 4 No. 37

"Glasgow Herald", 1845-1895. Fifty years of newspaper life: being chiefly reminiscences of that time. By Alexander Sinclair. Printed for private circulation. (Glasgow, 1895)

Morocco; $8\frac{3}{4}$ x 7 x $1\frac{1}{4}$ in.

JOURNALISM, Great Britain

Cabinet 00 Shelf 5 No. 2 (2 vols.)

History of British Journalism, from the foundation of the newspaper press in England to the repeal of the stamp act in 1855, with sketches of press celebrities. By Alexander Andrews. In two vols., with index. London, 1859.

Cloth; 8 x 5 x 1 in.

JOURNALISM, Great Britain

Cabinet 00 Shelf 5 No. 12

Fifty years of Fleet Street, being the life and recollections of Sir John R. Robinson. Compiled and edited by Frederick Moy Thomas. London, 1904. McMillan and Co.

Portrait frontispiece.

Cloth; 9-1/8 x 5-7/8 x $1\frac{1}{2}$ in.

JOURNALISM, Great Britain

Cabinet 00 Shelf 4 No. 35

"Glasgow Herald". Centenary of. Banquet in St. Andrew's Hall, Glasgow, Friday, Jan. 27, 1882.

Stamped cloth; 8-3/8 x 6-3/8 x 3/8 in.

JOURNALISM, Great Britain

Cabinet 00 Shelf 4 No. 13

History of English journalism to the foundation of the Gazette. By J. B. Williams. With illustrations. London, 1908.

Cloth; 9 x 6-1/8 x $1\frac{1}{2}$ in.

JOURNALISM, Great Britain

Cabinet A Shelf 3 No. 89

History of The Times, London: pp. 23 and 25 of special graphic arts number of The Times, Sept. 10, 1912.

JOURNALISM, Great Britain

Cabinet 00 Shelf 4 No. 19

(The) King's journalist, 1659-1689. Studies in the reign of Charles II. By J. G. Muddiman. With 14 illus. London,(1923).

Life of Henry Muddiman, the first editor of the "London Gazette".

Cloth; $8\frac{3}{4}$ x 6 x $1\frac{1}{2}$ in.

JOURNALISM, Great Britain

Cabinet NN Shelf 2 No. 1

Lord Northcliffe, "The World's greatest expert in human nature, by Isaac F. Marcosson, in The American Magazine, Jan., 1922.

Bound with other items in "Journalists, various excerpts", item 51.

JOURNALISM, Great Britain

Cabinet 00 Shelf 5 No. 7

Hunt, William. Then and now; or, fifty years years of newspaper work. With an appendix. Hull...London, 1887. With frontispiece portrait.

Cloth; $7\frac{3}{8}$ x 5 x 7/8 in.

JOURNALISM, Great Britain

Cabinet 00 Shelf 5 No. 15

Labouchere, Henry, the life of. By Algar Labouchere Thorold...New York and London. G. P. Putnam's Sons. 1913.

With portrait. Newspaper clippings at end of book.

Cloth; $9\frac{1}{4}$ x $5\frac{3}{4}$ x 2 in.

JOURNALISM, Great Britain

Cabinet NN Shelf 2 No. 7

Lurking literature of London.

Excerpt from Chamber's Journal, Jan.26 1856.

Item 24 in bound collection "Journalism. Excerpts, etc."

JOURNALISM, Great Britain

Cabinet 00 Shelf 5 No. 10

Hutton, Richard Holt of "The Spectator". A monograph. Edinburgh, 1899.

Cloth; $7\frac{3}{4}$ x $5\frac{1}{4}$ x $\frac{1}{2}$ in.

JOURNALISM, Scotland

Cabinet 00 Shelf 4 No. 43

Lennox, John, and the "Greenock Newsclout"; a fight against the taxes on knowledge. By William Stewart. Glasgow, 1918.

Reprinted with additions from the "Scottish Historical Review".

Paper; $8\frac{1}{2}$ x 7 x $\frac{1}{4}$ in.

JOURNALISM, Great Britain

Cabinet 00 Shelf 5 No. 18

Manchester Guardian, the. A century of history. By William Haslam Mills. London, 1921. Illus. Chatto and Windus.

Portrait frontispiece of Ch. Prestwich Scott, editor of The Manchester Guardian since 1872.

Boards, cloth back; 9 x $5\frac{3}{4}$ x 1 in.

JOURNALISM, GREAT BRITAIN

Cabinet 00 Shelf 4 No. 10

Irish journalism, fifty years of. By Andrew Dunlop. Dublin, 1911

Cloth; 7-7/8 x 5 x 1-3/8 in.

JOURNALISM, Great Britain

Cabinet 00 Shelf 4 No. 8

London Daily Press, The. By H. W. Massingham. With illustrations and portraits. New York ...Chicago, 1892.

The Leisure Hour Library.-New Series

Cloth; $7\frac{1}{4}$ x 4-3/4 x 5/8 in.

JOURNALISM, Great Britain

Cabinet 00 Shelf 5 No. 11

Memoirs of M. de Blowitz [Paris correspondent for the London "Times"] New York, 1903. Illus.

Cloth; $9\frac{1}{4}$ x $6\frac{1}{4}$ x $1\frac{1}{4}$ in.

JOURNALISM, Great Britain

Cabinet NN Shelf 2 No. 16

Journalism in England, 1773-1850.

Excerpts from the Ladies' Repository, May-June, 1858.

Item 27 in vol.with binder's title "Journalism: Pamphlets", Bound, 1932.

JOURNALISM, Great Britain

Cabinet 00 Shelf 5 No. 19.01

Lord Northcliffe: a memoire. By Max Pemberton. London, n.d. (1926).

Frontispiece portrait.

Cloth; $8\frac{1}{2}$ x $5\frac{1}{2}$ x $1\frac{1}{2}$ in.

JOURNALISM, Great Britain

Cabinet 00 Shelf 4 No. 1

Mercurius Politicus, comprising the sum of foreine intelligence, with the affairs now on foot in the three nations of England, Scotland, and Ireland. For information of the people. London: Printed by Thomas Newcomb, 1656-1657.

Comprises Nos. 331, 335, 338-340 for 1656.
" " 367-369, 391, 329, 394, 398, 399-400, 402, 403, 405 for 1657.

Half leather; $9\frac{1}{4}$ x $7\frac{1}{2}$ x $\frac{5}{8}$ in.

JOURNALISM, Great Britain

Cabinet NN Shelf 2 No. 2

Journalistic London, by Jos. Hatton, in Harper's New Monthly Magazine, Oct.-Dec., 1881 and Jan., 1882: A brief account of the great English literary and journalistic centres, with sketches of some of the important editors and journalists. Illus. with many portraits.

Bound with other items in "Journalists and Journalism", item 14.

JOURNALISM, Great Britain

Cabinet 00 Shelf 5 No. 19

Lord Northcliff, the real. Some personal recollections of a private secretary, 1902-1922. London, 1922. Cassell & Co. Ltd. 1922.

With portrait frontispiece. Clippings pasted on back cover.

Cloth; $7\frac{1}{2}$ x $5\frac{1}{4}$ x 7/16 in.

JOURNALISM, Great Britain

Cabinet 00 Shelf 5 No. 14

My life's pilgrimage. By Thos. Catling, formerly editor of "Lloyd's Weekly Newspaper". Introduction by The Right Honourable Lord Burnham. With illustrations. London, 1911.

Cloth; 8-7/8 x $5\frac{1}{2}$ x $1\frac{3}{4}$ in.

JOURNALISM, Great Britian

Cabinet 00 Shelf 4 No. 4

Newspaper Press, The. Its origin, progress and present position. By James Grant. In 3 vols. London, 1871-2.

Cloth; 9 x 5-5/8 in.

JOURNALISM, Great Britain

Cabinet 00 Shelf 5 No. 20

Pearson, Sir Arthur, the life of. Newspaper proprietor and founder of St. Dunstan's Hostel...By Sidney Dark. London, n. d. (1922). With portraits.

Cloth; $8\frac{3}{4}$ x 6 x $1\frac{3}{4}$ in.

JOURNALISM, Great Britain

Cabinet 00 Shelf 4 No. 40

Story of the "Scotsman": a chapter in the annals of British journalism. Edinburgh: Printed for private circulation. 1886. Brochure.

Together with "The Scotsman. New buildings, Edinburgh, 1905". Illus.

Cloth; $8\frac{3}{4}$ x $10\frac{1}{4}$ x $\frac{1}{2}$ in.

JOURNALISM, Great Britain

Cabinet NN Shelf 2 No. 1

Northcliffe, Lord, by J. St. Loe Strachy, in The Outlook, Sept., 13th, 1922.

Bound with other items in "Journalists, various excerpts", item 50.

JOURNALISM, Great Britain

Cabinet NN Shelf 2 No. 9

Philosophy of Journalism, The: A review of a book, The Fourth Estate: Contribution towards a history of newspapers, in Chamber's Edinburgh Journal, June 29, 1850.

Bound with other items in "Newspapers, various excerpts", item 17.

JOURNALISM, Great Britain

Cabinet 00 Shelf 4 No. 26.01

"The Thunderer" [London Times] in the making. The history of the Times, 1785-1841. London. Written, Printed anf Published at The Office of The Times, Printing House Square, 1935. Illus.

Cloth; 10 x 6 in.

JOURNALISM, Great Britain

Cabinet NN Shelf 2 No. 1

Northcliffe, by Eric Fisher Wood, in The Century, Oct., 1917: An attempt to describe the peculiar characteristics of this English editor.

Bound with other items in "Journalists, various excerpts", item 49.

JOURNALISM, Great Britain

Cabinet 00 Shelf 4 No. 15

"Punch" (London) and Douglas Jerrold. By Walter Jerrold. London, 1910. With illus. and portraits.

Cloth; 9-1/8 x 6 x $1\frac{1}{2}$ in.

JOURNALISM, Great Britain.

Cabinet NN Shelf 4 No. 26

"The Times". The Story of:

By William Dodgson Bowman. London, 1931. Illus.

Cloth: $8\frac{3}{4}$x$5\frac{1}{2}$x1-3/8"

JOURNALISM, Great Britain

Cabinet NN Shelf 2 No. 1

Northcliffe: Living, dying, dead, by Mark Sullivan, from World's Work, Oct., 1922.

Bound with other items in "Journalists, various excerpts", item 48

JOURNALISM, Great Britain

Cabinet 00 Shelf 5 No. 5

Reminiscences of a country journalist. By Thomas Frost. London, 1886.

Cloth; 9 x5-7/8 x $1\frac{1}{4}$ in.

JOURNALISM, Great Britain

Cabinet NN Shelf 2 No. 13

(A) Visit to The London Times. Excerpt from the "National Magazine", Dec., 1852.

Item 3 in volume with binder's title"Various newspapers and periodicals"-1.

JOURNALISM, Great Britain

Cabinet A Shelf 3 No. 89

Origin and growth of the British Newspaper 1622-1714; pp. 13-15 special graphic arts number of The Times, Sept. 10, 1912.

JOURNALISM, Great Britain

Cabinet 00 Shelf 4 No. 39

Russel, Alexander, editor of "Scotsman," Edinburgh, for 31 years. Memorial volume of extracts from newspapers. Printed for private circulation, 1876.

Cloth; 9 x 6 x $\frac{1}{2}$ in.

JOURNALISM, Great Britain

Cabinet 00 Shelf 4 No. 18

War-time, the press in. With some account of the Official Press Bureau. An essay. By Sir Edward Cook. London, 1920.

Cloth; $7\frac{3}{4}$ x 5-1/8 x $\frac{3}{4}$ in.

JOURNALISM, Great Britain

Cabinet 00 Shelf 4 No. 14

Parliament (A) of the Press. The first Imperial Press Conference. Written and compiled by Thos. H. Hardman. With preface by The Earl of Rosebery. Illus. London, 1909.

Cloth; $9\frac{3}{4}$ x $7\frac{1}{2}$ x 1 in.

JOURNALISM, Great Britain

Cabinet 00 Shelf 5 No. 13

Sixty years in the wilderness; some passages by the way. By Henry W. Lucy. With a portrait [frontispiece] by J. S. Sargent. Second impression. London, 1909.

Cloth; $8\frac{1}{2}$ x 6 x 1-3/8 in.

JOURNALISM, Great Britain

Cabinet NN Shelf 2 No. 1

What interests people, by Viscount Northcliffe, in The American Magazine, Jan., 1922.

Bound with other items in "Journalists, various excerpts", item 51.

JOURNALISM, Great Britain

Cabinet NN Shelf 2 No. 16

What the people read in Great Britain. By Harry Jones.
Illus. excerpt from the American Review of Reviews, Sept., 1905.

Item 23 in vol. with binder's title "Journalism: Pamphlets. Bound, 1932".

JOURNALISM, Great Britain (Ireland)

Cabinet 00 Shelf 5 No. 3 (2 vols.)

History of Irish periodical literature, from the end of the 17th century to the middle of the 19th century, its origin, progress, and results...By Richard Robert Madden. [2 vols.] London, 1867.

Cloth; 8⅝ x 5⅝ in.

JOURNALISM, Great Britain

Cabinet A Shelf 3 No. 29

Scotsman, the. Centenary supplement. Jan. 25, 1917.

See Newspapers, Scotland Anniversary Issues: The Scotsman.

JOURNALISM, Holland

Cabinet 00 Shelf 2 No. 29

Belasting op de nieuwspapieren (1674-1896... Amsterdam, 1895.
Two items bound in one. the work of W. P. Sautijn Kluit.

Cloth; 9¼ x 6¼., pp.181, 284. Original cove covers bound in.

JOURNALISM, Holland

Cabinet 00 Shelf 2 No. 28

Kluit, W.P. Sautijn. (Collection of pamphlets bound in one volume. Each part devoted to a bibliographical historical account of early Holland newspapers and periodicals.) Amsterdam, 1872-1882. Edited by W.P. Sautijn Kluit.

Half morocco; 9½ x 6½.

JOURNALISM, Holland

Cabinet W Shelf 5 No. 130

(La) Librairie, l'imprimerie et la presse en Holland à travers quatre siècles. Documents pour servir à l'histoire de leurs relations internationales. Recueillis et annotés par W. P. Van Stockum Jr. La Haye, 1910.

Tooled calf; 14¼ x 11 in.

JOURNALISM, Holland

Cabinet 00 Shelf 2 No. 30

Pers in Zeeland, 1758-1900, de. Door H.P. Abrahams. s'Gravenhage, 1912. with portrait and facsimile.

Half morocco; 10 x 6½ in pp.405.

JOURNALISM, Hungary

Cabinet NN Shelf 2 No. 13

Telephoni Ujseg (Telephone News)

See Newspapers, Hungary. Literature of. Telephone News...

JOURANLISM, Hungary

Cabinet NN Shelf 2 No. 13

What the people read in Hungary

see
NEWSPAPERS, Hungary. Literature of

JOURNALISM, India

Cabinet NN Shelf 2 No. 13

India, the Press in, 1780-1908. Article by S.M.Mitra. Excerpt from "The Nineteenth Century", Aug., 1908.

Item 9 in volume with binder's title "Various newspapers and periodicals"-1

JOURNALISM, India

Cabinet NN Shelf 2 No. 2

Press in India, The. 1780-1908, by S.M. Mitra, in The Nineteenth Century, Aug., 1908: A brief historical account.

Bound with other items in "Journalists and Journalism", item 17.

JOURNALISM, India

Cabinet 00 Shelf 6 No. 33

Press law in India. Memorandum of the Press Association of India. August, 1919.

Paper; 13 x 8-1/8 in. In envelope.

JOURNALISM, India (British)

Cabinet 00 Shelf 5 No. 31

Sketch of the history and influence of the press in British India. Containing remarks on the effects of a free press... By Leicester Stanhope. London, 1823.

Half leather; 8-7/8 x 5¼ x ⅝ in.

JOURNALISM, Italy

Cabinet NN Shelf 2 No. 13

Great newspapers of Continental Europe: Italian newspapers. By Frederic Faber Cooper.
Excerpt from The Bookman, June, 1900.

Item 34 in bound collection with binder's title "Various newspapers and Periodicals".

JOURNALISM, Italy

Cabinet X Shelf 5 No. 123.01

Missione del giornalismo nel Regime. S.E. Benito Mussolini. (The mission of journalism under the regime. A discourse to newspaper proprietors, Oct., 10, 1928.)

See Benedetti, Giulio. Codice della... Milano, 1930, p.5.

JOURNALISM, Italy.

Cabinet NN Shelf 2 No. 13

What the people read in Italy: An excerpt from The American Review of Reviews, Sept. 1904. Illus.

Bound with other items in "Various newspapers and periodicals", vol.1, item 38.

JOURNALISM, Japan

Cabinet 00 Shelf 6 No. 21

(The) Magazine king of the Orient. Mr. Seiji Noma. Nine large magazines under his control. [Illus. article].

see
NEWSPAPERS, SPECIAL ISSUES. Japan. (The) "Asahi"...1930, p. 17.

JOURNALISM, JAPAN

Cabinet NN Shelf 2 No. 7

Martin, Frank L. Journalism of Japan. University of Missouri Bulletin, vol.19, No.10, April, 1918. Illus.

Item 8 in bound collection "Journalism. Excerpts, etc."

JOURNALISM, Japan.

Cabinet NN Shelf 2 No. 13

What the Japanese are reading: The literature of a serious minded nation. Article by Harold Bolce. Excerpt from "The Booklovers Magazine Nov., 1904. Illus.

Item 11 in volume with binder's title "Various newspapers and periodicals"-1

JOURNALISM, Portugal

Cabinet NN Shelf 2 No. 16

What the people read in Portugal. Illustrated. Excerpt from the American Review of Reviews, May, 1905.

Item 16 in vol. with binder's title; "Journalism: Pamphlets. Bound, 1932".

JOURNALISM, South Africa

Cabinet NN Shelf 7 No. 32

Mathers, Edward P. A press paper describes the founder, conductor and proprietor of the newspaper "South Africa".

see NEWSPAPERS, South Africa. "South Africa". A weekly for all interested... London (1903) p. 96.

JOURNALISM, Mexico

Cabinet 00 Shelf 5 No. 34

History of Mexican journalism, the. By Henry Lepidus. University of Missouri Bulletin, Volume 29, No. 4. Jan. 21, 1928. Illus.

Half morocco; 9 x 6 x ½ in.

JOURNALISM, Russia

Cabinet NN Shelf 2 No. 16

Conducting a Russian newspaper. By Wolf von Schierbrand. Excerpt from World's Work, January, 1903.

Item 26 in vol. with binder's title "Journalism: Pamphlets. Bound, 1932".

JOURNALISM, South America

Cabinet NN Shelf 7 No. 35

"Aurora de Chile, 1812 - 1813. Reimpresion paleografica... con una introducción por Julio Vicuña Cifuentes. Santiago de Chile, 1903.

Cloth; 13-5/8 x 10¼ x 1 in.

JOURNALISM, Mexico

Cabinet 79 Shelf 2 No. 21

(La) Imprenta y la prensa en Mexico. See pp.593 to 603 in Obregon's Mejico viejo...Mexico 1900.

Printed Cloth; 9-5/8 x 6-3/8 x 1-7/8 in.

JOURNALISM, Russia

Cabinet NN Shelf 2 No. 13

Great newspapers of Continental Europe: Russian newspapers. By V.S.Y. Excerpt from The Bookman, May, 1900

Item 33 in bound collection with binder's title "Various newspapers and Periodicals".

JOURNALISM, South America

Cabinet NN Shelf 2 No. 16

What the people read in South America. Illus. excerpt from the American Review of Reviews, Jan., and March, 1906.

Item 20 in vol. with binder's title; "Journalism: Pamphlets. Bound, 1932".

JOURNALISM, New Zealand

Cabinet 00 Shelf 6 No. 16

New Zealand Free Lance, 25th Anniversary, 1900-1925. Wellington, 1925.

Cloth; 16¾ x 10-7/8in.

JOURNALISM, Russia

Cabinet NN Shelf 2 No. 11

Religious press of Russia, the. By Andrew J. Shipman. (Excerpt from The Messenger, Oct.,1906

Item 6 in bound collection with binder's title "About various newspapers".

JOURNALISM, South America, Argentine

Cabinet NN Shelf 2 No. 13

Newspaper with many functions, The (La Prensa), by Bernard Michlejohn, in The World's Work, Feb., 1902: An historical account of the paper, with description of building, equipment, editors, and civic activities. Illus.

Bound with other items in "Various newspapers and periodicals", vol. 1, item 41.

JOURNALISM, New Zealand

Cabinet NN Shelf 7 No. 33

Otago Punch, The. Printed and published by Chas. Francis. From Sept. 1, 1866 to Jan. 19, 1867, Dunedin, New Zealand.

Read printed notice on p. 1 following cover.

Half calf; 11 x 8½ x 5/8 in.

JOURNALISM, RUSSIA.

Cabinet Shelf No.

Russian Press gives false view of United States. By Frank Parker Stockbridge.

Article in The American Press, 49th year, No. 11. August 1931, pp. 1, 42, 44.

JOURNALISM, South America, Argentine

Cabinet 79 Shelf 2 No. 23

(La) Prensa y el progreso. Por B. Borghese. Buenos Aires, 1884. Includes a brief account of the history of printing, and biographies of celebrated early printers; Johann Gutenberg, Estienne Dolet, Panfilo Castaldo, Giambattista Bodoni, etc.

Cloth; 7-7/8 x 5-3/8 x ¾ in.

JOURNALISM, Poland.

Cabinet NN Shelf 2 No. 13

What the people read in Poland and Finland. Excerpt article from "The American Review of Reviews", July, 1904. Illus.

Item 37 in volume with binder's title "Various newspapers and periodicals".

JOURNALISM, Russia

Cabinet NN Shelf 2 No. 16

What the people read in Russia. With illustrations of some representative Russian newspapers. Excerpt from Review of Reviews, May, 1905.

Item 16 in vol. with binder's title; "Journalism: Pamphlets. Bound, 1932".

JOURNALISM, South America, Venezuela

Cabinet 79 Shelf 2 No. 24

Tachira, 1845-1883: La imprenta en el Tachira. Por Luis F. Briceño, Caracas, 1883. Brief account of printing and journalism.

Cloth 12½ x 8½ in.

JOURNALISM. Spain

Cabinet NN Shelf 2 No. 16

What the people read in Spain. With illustrations of some representative Spanish publications.
Excerpt from the American Review of Reviews, May 1905.

Item 16 in vol. with binder's title; "Journalism: Pamphlets. Bound, 1932".

JOURNALISM, Turkey

Cabinet 00 Shelf 5 No. 32

Development of modern Turkey as measured by its press, the. By Ahmed Emin. New York, 1914.
Columbia University "Studies in History, Economics and Public Law", Vol. 59, No. I, Whole No. 142.

Half morocco; $9\frac{3}{4}$ x $6\frac{1}{2}$ x $\frac{1}{2}$ in.

JOURNALISM, United States

Cabinet NN Shelf 6 No. 22

Albany Minerva, 1828, Nos.1 to 8.
The only volume issued. No.8, April 8, 1828, announces the expiration of this publication which "was got up merely for a Winter's pastime".
Pasted in front; a letter dated 1879, signed by J. Munsell.

Half morocco; $9\frac{1}{2}$ x 6-1/8 in.

JOURNALISM, United States

Cabinet NN Shelf 5 No. 10

(The) American newspaper: An essay read before the Social Science Association, at Saratoga Springs, Sept. 6, 1881, By Charles Dudley Warner. Boston, 1881.

Cloth; $4\frac{3}{4}$ x $3\frac{1}{4}$ x $\frac{1}{4}$ in.

JOURNALISM, United States

Cabinet NN Shelf 2 No. 7

American Press, The. By Henry King.
Excerpt from The Chautaugan, Feb.,1896

Item 31 in bound collection "Journalism. Excerpts, etc."

JOURNALISM United States

Cabinet NN Shelf 6 No. 1

American Press Association. Hand book. Description of service, list of features, with some useful suggestions about plates. New York, June 1, 1889. Pamphlet.

With other item in envelope.

JOURNALISM, United States.

Cabinet Shelf No.

Anaconda Standard. Battle of mining giants. [Daly and Clark] ends in Montana merger. With portraits of Marcus Daly and W. A. Clark.

Article in The American Press, 49th year, No. 11, August 1931, p. 3.

JOURNALISM, United States

Cabinet NN Shelf 2 No. 12

Analysis (Brief) of the American Newspaper's distinguishing marks: From Chamber's Journal in the Living Age, March, 29, 1845.

Bound in with other items "Various Newspapers and Periodicals", item 13.

JOURNALISM, United States

Cabinet 00 Shelf 6 No. 55

Arkansas (Little Rock), 1819-1919.

see NEWSPAPERS, ANNIVERSARY ISSUES. Arkansas Gazette, 1819-1919.

JOURNALISM, United States

Cabinet NN Shelf 6 No. 3

Arkansas Press for a hundred years, history of the. By Fred W. Allsopp. Little Rock, Arkansas, 1922. Illus.

Cloth; $8\frac{1}{2}$ x $5\frac{3}{4}$ x 1-3/8 in.

JOURANLISM, United States

Cabinet NN Shelf 1 No. 8

Artemus Ward (Charles Farrar Browne) A biography and bibliography. By Don. C. Seitz. Harper & Brothers, New York, 1919. Illus.

Cloth; 9 x 6 x $1\frac{1}{2}$ in.

JOURNALISM, United States

Cabinet KK Shelf 5 No. 4

Associated Press reports, 4th to 15th, 1897 to 1915. (incomplete)

Cloth; $9\frac{1}{4}$ x 6 in. each vol.

JOURNALISM. United States.

Cabinet NN Shelf 4 No. 47

Atkinson, Wilmer. An autobiography of the founder of the Farm Journal Philadelphia.
Wilmer Atkinson Company, 1920. Illus.

Has frontispiece portrait.

Cloth: 8x$5\frac{1}{4}$x$1\frac{1}{2}$"

JOURNALISM, United States,

Cabinet NN Shelf 2 No. 8

Bailey, Gamaliel, a pioneer editor, by J.E. Snodgrass, in the Atlantic Monthly, June, 1866: An account of his association with the pioneer advocate of freedom, James G. Birney, the editor of The Cincinnati Philanthropist, 1883.

Bound with other items in "Various Editors", item 3.

JOURNALISM, United States

Cabinet NN Shelf 7 No. 6

Baltimore American, The. A brief review of its history. Its long record of usefulness and enterprise, 1773 - 1894. Souvenir edition, 121st. anniversary. Illus.

Morocco; 13-5/8 x 10-7/8 x $\frac{3}{4}$ in.

JOURNALISM, United States

Cabinet S Shelf 5 No. 21

Beginning of Journalism in America: A group of pre-revolutionary editors, by G.G. W. Benjamin, in Magazine of American History, Jan., 1887. Has portraits, also reduced facsimile reproductions of some of the earliest newspapers in America.

Bound in "Excerpts relating to printing in America," pp. 1 - 28.

JOURNALISM, United States

Cabinet NN Shelf 2 No. 2

Beginnings of Journalism in America, by S.G.W. Benjamin, in Magazine of American History, n.d. Portraits, also facsimile, reduced sizes, of first pages of the earliest American newspapers.

Bound with other items in "Journalists and Journalism", item 23.

JOURNALISM, United States

Cabinet NN Shelf 2 No. 1

Bennett, James Gordon. By James Creelman, in The Cosmopolitan, May, 1902.

Bound with other items in "Journalists, various excerpts", item 19.

JOURNALISM, United States.

Cabinet NN Shelf 2 No. 1

Bennett, James Gordon, by Henry Fish, in Munsey's Magazine, 1895.

Bound with other items in "Journalists, various excerpts," item 30.

JOURNALISM, United States.

Cabinet NN Shelf 2 No. 1

Bennett, James Gordon, in Every Saturday, May 6, 1871: A biographical sketch of the founder of The New York Herald, Portrait.

Bound with other items in "Journalists, various excerpts", item 47.

JOURNALISM, United States

Cabinet NN Shelf 2 No. 1

Bennett, James Gordon, The late. In The Phrenological Journal, July, 1872.

Bound with other items in "Journalists, various excerpts", item 11.

JOURNALISM, United States.

Cabinet NN Shelf 2 No. 1

Bennett, James Gordon, the Monte Cristo of modern journalism, by George Jean Nathan, in Outing, March, 1909.

Bound with other items in "Journalists, various excerpts," item 31.

JOURNALISM, United States

Cabinet NN Shelf 2 No. 1

Bennett of The Herald, by Leo L. Redding, in Everybody's, June, 1914: An account dealing with Mr. Bennet's so-called Idiosyncrasies.

Bound with other items in "Journalists, various excerpts," item 34.

JOURNALISM, United States.

Cabinet NN Shelf 2 No. 1

Bennett's, James Gordon, scintillations, by Paul Peebles, in The Galaxy, Aug., 1878.

Bound with other items in "Journalists, various excerpts", item 7.

JOURNALISM, United States

Cabinet NN Shelf 1 No. 23

Bierce, Ambrose. a biography of. By Carey McWilliams. New York, 1929. (Albert & Charles Boni, Publishers)

Cloth; $9\frac{1}{4}$ x 6 x $1\frac{1}{2}$ in.

JOURNALISM, United States

Cabinet NN Shelf 6 No. 48

"Bill Arp" (Charles H. Smith). From the Uncivil War to Date, 1861 - 1903. Memorial edition. Atlanta, Ga., 1903. Portrait frontispiece.

Cloth; $9\frac{1}{2}$ x $6\frac{1}{4}$ x $1\frac{1}{4}$ in.

JOURNALISM, United States

Cabinet NN Shelf 4 No. 8

(The) Biter bit, or the Robert Macaire of journalism.
Being a narrative of some of the blackmailing operations of Charles A. Dana's "Sun". By James B. Mix, Washington. 1870.
Also: The Comic life of Horace Greeley. New York. 1872. Illus.
Also: The House that Tweed built. Cambridge. 1871. Illus.
Three campaign items bound as one.
Cloth: 9-7/8x7"

JOURNALISM, United States.

Cabinet NN Shelf 2 No. 3

Blackmailing operations of Charles A. Dana's "Sun." History of a moral Journalist. Printed in Washington, D.C., 1870.

Bound with other items in "Journalists and Journalism", item 2.

JOURNALISM, United States

Cabinet NN Shelf 2 No. 37

Bleyer, Willard Grosvenor. Main currents in the History of American journalism. Boston, 1927. Illus.

Cloth; $8\frac{1}{4}$ x 5-5/8 in.

JOURNALISM, United States

Cabinet NN Shelf 4 No. 30

"Boston Herald, The", and its history:
How, when, and where it was founded.

A glimpse into its different departments. Thirty-two years of journalism in Boston. 1878. Illus.

Cloth: 8-1/8x6"

JOURNALISM, United States.

Cabinet S Shelf 5 No. 21

Boston newspaper of the Revolution, 1778, A. By Horatio King, in Magazine of American History An account of The Independent Chronicle and the Universale Advertiser, printed by Powars and Willis.

Bound with other items in "Excerpts relating to printing in America," pp. 103-107.

JOURNALISM, United States,

Cabinet NN Shelf 2 No. 13

Boston newspaper of the Revolution, A. 1778, by Horatio King, in The Magazine of American History, Oct., 1888: An account of The Independent Chronicle and the Universal Advertiser.

Bound with other items in "Various newspapers and periodicals", vol. 1, item 42.

JOURNALISM, United States

Cabinet NN Shelf 2 No. 28

Boston newspapers, 1704-1780, chech-list of. By Mary Farwell Ayer. With bibliographical notes by Albert Matthews. Publications of the Colonial Society of Massachusetts, vol. IX. Boston, 1907.

Cloth; 9-5/8 x $6\frac{3}{4}$ in.

JOURNALISM, United States

Cabinet NN Shelf 6 No. 16

Boston Transcript (The), and William Durant. Sixty years of service. Complimentary dinner to Wm. Durant, by his fellow-employees of the Boston Transcript Company. Feb., 19, 1894, at the Copley-Square Hotel, Boston. Privately printed. Portrait frontispiece.

Cloth; 9 x $6\frac{3}{4}$ in. See also NN/6/16

JOURNALISM, United States

Cabinet NN Shelf 6 No. 43

Bowles, Samuel, the life and times of. By George S. Merriam. In 2 vols. New York, 1885. Portrait.

S. Bowles II, founder and editor of the Springfield (Mass.) "Republican".

Cloth; $8\frac{1}{4}$ x $5\frac{3}{4}$ in.

JOURNALISM, United States.

Cabinet S Shelf 5 No. 21

Bradford, John and the Kentucky Gazette founded in 1787: The first newspaper West of the Alleghanies. By W. H. Perrin, in Magazine of American History. Illus.

Bound with other items in volume "Excerpts relating to printing in America", pp. 89-95.

JOURNALISM, United States.

Cabinet NN Shelf 2 No. 1

Brisbane, Arthur, gives an exclusive interview to The New Success, by Ada Patterson, in The New Success, Oct., 1920: This is said to be the first interview ever given by Mr. Brisbane

Bound with other items in "Journalists, various excerpts", item 29.

JOURNALISM, United States

Cabinet NN Shelf 7 No. 7

Brooklyn Daily Eagle 60th anniversary, 1841-1901, Oct. 26, 1901. [And its founder], Isaac Van Anden. Illus., portraits, facsimiles.

Half morocco; 11-5/8 x 8-7/8 in.

JOURNALISM, United States

Cabinet NN Shelf 2 No. 13

Brooklyn Daily Eagle, The. Established in 1841. A sketch of its career.
Excerpt from The Editorial Review, Nov. 11, 1911.

Item 13 bound collection with binder's title "Various newspapers and periodicals".

JOURNALISM, United States.

Cabinet NN Shelf 2 No. 1

Bryant, William Cullen, by Gen. Jas. Grant Wilson, in The National Repository, Sept., 1877. Portrait.

Bound with other items in "Journalists, various excerpts", item 24.

JOURNALISM, United States.

Cabinet NN Shelf 2 No. 1

Bryant, William Cullen: An account of his life and activities as journalist and poet, in Harper's Magazine, Feb., 1862.

Bound with other items in "Journalists, various excerpts," item 17.

JOURNALISM, United States

Cabinet NN Shelf 2 No. 8

(Bryant, William Cullen.) Among the makers of American literature: William Cullen Bryant, poet and journalist, by Elizabeth Anna Semple, in The Craftsman, July, 1911.

Bound with other items in "Various Editors", item 31.

JOURNALISM, United States.

Cabinet NN Shelf 2 No. 1

Bryant, William Cullen: Brief biographical sketch in The International Magazine, Dec. 1851. Portrait, etching.

Bound with other items in Journalists, various excerpts", item 20.

JOURNALISM, United States.

Cabinet NN Shelf 2 No. 1

Bryant's centennial, by Wm. R. Thayer, in American Review of Reviews, Oct., 1894: an account which considers Bryant's merit as the first American Poet, as well as his influence on the journalistic literature of his time. Portraits.

Bound with other items in "Journalists, various excerpts," item 44.

JOURNALISM, United States,

Cabinet R Shelf 3 No. 102 2 Vols.

Buckingham, Joseph T. Personal memoirs and recollections of editorial life. By J. T. Buckingham. 2 Vols. Portrait.
Vol. I: The New England Galaxy
Vol. II: The Boston Courier.

Cloths; 7-3/8 x 4-5/8 in.

JOURNALISM, UNITED STATES

Cabinet NN Shelf 3 No. 5

Buckingham's reminiscences. Anecdotes, person memoirs, and biographies of literary men, connected with newspaper literature, from 1690 to 1800. By Joseph T.Buckingham. With steel portraits of Isaiah Thomas and Benjamin Russell. Boston. 1852. (2 vols. illus.)

Paper: 7½x4-5/8"

JOURNALISM, United States

Cabinet NN Shelf 4 No. 39

Buel, Jesse. Eulogy on the life and character of the late Judge Jesse Buel, pronounced before the New York State Agricultural Society, at their annual meeting, on the 5th February, 1840.

By Amos Dean. Albany. 1840.

Half Morocco: 8½x5½"

JOURNALISM, United States

Cabinet NN Shelf 6 No. 44

(Buffalo, N. Y.) Journalism. A paper read before the Buffalo Historical Society, at a Club Meeting, held...Jan. 24, 1876, by George J. Bryan, Editor and Proprietor of the Buffalo Evening Post.
Bound in with other items.

Cloth; 9 x 6 x ¾ in.

JOURNALISM, United States

Cabinet NN Shelf 6 No. 23

Buffalo, periodical press of, 1811-1915.

see BUFFALO HISTORICAL SOCIETY. Periodical Press of Buffalo...

JOURNALISM, United States.

Cabinet NN Shelf 2 No. 1

Bundy, Major J.M., editor of the New York Evening Mail, in the Phrenological Journal, Dec., 1873. Portrait.

Bound with other items in "Journalists, various excerpts", item 16.

JOURNALISM, United States

Cabinet NN Shelf 2 No. 4

Business of a great newspaper, the. By Lincoln Steffens. Excerpt from Scribner's Magazine, Oct., 1897. Illustrated by W.R. Leigh.

Item 6 in vol. "Journalists and their work".

JOURNALISM, United States

Cabinet NN Shelf 4 No. 17

By-laws and organization of The Tribune Association. New York. 1872.

Cloth, Gile: 8x5-3/8"

JOURNALISM, United States

Cabinet NN Shelf 2 No. 6

Cahan, Abraham: Socialist-Journalist-Friend of the Ghetto. By Ernest Poole.
Excerpt from The Outlook, Oct.,28, 1911. With portrait.

Item 12 in bound collection "Biographies of Journalists".

JOURNALISM. United States

Cabinet NN Shelf 2 No. 3

California. A full and authentic account of the murder of James King, editor of the San Francisco Evening Bulletin...Compiled from the columns of the Alta California of May 15 (1856). Pamphlet.

Item I in vol. "Journalists and Journalism". Pamphlets.

JOURNALISM, United States

Cabinet NN Shelf 2 No. 8

California journalism, its origin and progress. By M.H. de Young. With portrait of H.de Young.
Excerpt from Lippincott's, Sept., 1892

Item 9 in volume with binder's title: "Various Editors".

JOURNALISM, United States

Cabinet NN Shelf 6 No. 5

California, journalism in. By John P. Young. Pacific Coast and Exposition Biographies. Chronicle Publishing Company, San Francisco, California (1915). Illus.

Cloth; 9¼ x 6 x 1¼ in.

JOURNALISM, United States,

Cabinet A Shelf 3 No. 52

California newspapers, a history of. By E.C. Kemble. In the Sacramento Daily Union, D3c. 25, 1858.
This best of all early histories of newspapers in California occupies 33 columns of the Daily Union in Nonpareil (6 pt) types.
At this writing (May 1931) only two copies of the above issue of the Daily Union are known to have survived - this one and one in the State Library in Sacramento.

JOURNALISM, United States

Cabinet NN Shelf 2 No. 9

California's long winning fight against the closed shop. Article by Harrison Gray Otis. Excerpt from "World's Work, Dec., 1907.

Account of a seventeen years' conflict between the Los Angeles Times and the Typographical Unions.

Item 30 in bound collection with binder's title "Newspapers, various excerpts".

JOURNALISM, United States

Cabinet NN Shelf 2 No. 23

Catalogue of the...periodicals published in the United States (in 1850).
arranged by States, alphabetically.

Cloth; 9 x 5¾ in.

JOURNALISM, United States,

Cabinet NN Shelf 2 No. 8

Chamberlain, Edwin Martin: Memorial addresses on the life and character of E.M. Chamberlain, delivered at Boston, Thursday Evg., April 7, 1892. Chamberlain was an active worker in labor movement and editor of the labor paper, "The Echo".

Bound with other items in "Various Editors" item 6.

JOURNALISM, United States

Cabinet S Shelf 5 No. 21

Cherokee Indians, Journalism among. By George E. Foster. Excerpt from the Magazine of American History.

Bound with other items in volume "Excerpts relating to printing in America," pp. 97-102.

JOURNALISM, United States. Literature

Cabinet NN Shelf 2 No. 15

Cherokee Indians, journalism among. By Geo. E. Foster.
Excerpt

Item 4 in vol. with binder's title "Early American Newspapers--Excerpts--Bound, 1919".

JOURNALISM, United States

Cabinet NN Shelf 2 No. 2

Cherokee. Journalism among the Cherokee Indians, by G.E. Foster, in The Magazine of American History, July, 1887. An account of the invention of the Cherokee alphabet, the inventor, first printed newspaper, the editors and printers.

Bound with other items in "Journalists and Journalism, item 22.

JOURNALISM, UNITED STATES

Cabinet II Shelf 3 No. 36

Cherokee Nation, biography of Hon. William P. Ross of the. By Mrs. Wm. P. Ross. Fort Smith, Ark., 1893. With portrait.

Cloth; 8-3/8 x 6 in.

JOURNALISM, United States.

Cabinet A Shelf 1 No. 65

(Chicago). History of growth of journalism in Chicago. An interesting sketch of the City's leading newspapers.
See Newspapers, Anniversary Issues; Chicago Journal.

Buckram; 22 x 18 x ½ in.

JOURNALISM, United States.

Cabinet NN Shelf 2 No. 9

Chicago newspapers and their makers, by Willis J. Abbot, in American Review of Reviews, June, 1895: Illustrated biographical sketches.

Bound with other items in "Newspapers, various excerpts", item 32.

JOURNALISM, United States,

Cabinet NN Shelf 2 No. 9

Chicago Record-Herald, The: The history of the growth and success of this newspaper. An account in the department of Contemporary Journalism of the Editorial Review, July, 1912.

Bound with other items in "Newspapers, various excerpts", item 27.

JOURNALISM, United States,

Cabinet A Shelf 3 No. 54

Chicago, reporting world events for: How that feat is performed by the men of the Daily News foreign service. By Paul Scott Mowrer.
p.16, second section, of Chicago Daily News, Special Issue, June and July, 1929.

Buckram; 21-5/8 x 17¾ x ¾ in.

JOURNALISM, United States

Cabinet NN Shelf 2 No. 7

Chicago, the daily newspapers of. By F. Leroy Armstrong.
Excerpt from The Chautaugan, Oct.,1894

Item 30 in bound collection "Journalism. Excerpts, etc."

JOURNALISM, United States.

Cabinet NN Shelf 2 No. 6

Chiefs of the American Press, by James Creelman, in Cosmopolitan, Nov., 1894. Portraits.

Bound with other items in "Biographies of Journalists," item 4.

JOURNALISM, United States,

Cabinet NN Shelf 2 No. 1

Childs, George W. by James Parton, in Every Saturday, Aug. 27, 1870: An account concerning G.W. Child's purchase of The Public Ledger, Philadelphia, 1864.

Bound with other items in "Journalists, various excerpts", item 46.

JOURNALISM United States

Cabinet NN Shelf 4 No. 29

Childs, George W. "Recollections". Philadelphia. 1890.

With portrait.

Cloth: 7¼x5"

JOURNALISM, United States

Cabinet NN Shelf 2 No. 1

Childs, George W., and the Philadelphia "Public Ledger". By James Parton. Excerpt from "Every Saturday", August 27, 1870. With portrait.

Item 46 in book with binder's title: "Journalists. Various Excerpts".

JOURNALISM, United States.

Cabinet NN Shelf 2 No. 1

Church, William C. (Col.), editor-in-chief of the United States Army and Navy Journal, by Col. L.L.Langdon, in United Service, March, 1891, A brief biographical sketch.

Bound with other items in "Journalists, various excerpts," item 27.

JOURNALISM, United States

Cabinet A Shelf 1 No. 101

Cincinnati Daily Gazette. 1879.

See NEWSPAPERS. Anniversary Issues. U.S.

JOURNALISM, United States

Cabinet 00 Shelf 5 No. 2 (2 vols.)

Colonial Press-North America; Benjamin Franklin and his brother James...Slow progress of the American Press.

see Chap. XXI, p. 298, Vol. I. ANDREWS History of British Journalism...London, 1859.

JOURNALISM, United States

Cabinet NN Shelf 5 No. 16

Concerning printed poison. By Josiah W. Leeds. Philadelphia, 1885.

Concerning demoralizing journalism.

Cloth; $6\frac{3}{4}$ x $5\frac{1}{4}$ in.

JOURNALISM, United States

Cabinet NN Shelf 2 No. 11

Country newspaper, the olden time. By Helen Everton Smith. Article in "The American Historical Register", Nov., 1894.

Item 4 in bound collection with binder's title "About various newspapers".

JOURNALISM, United States

Cabinet NN Shelf 2 No. 1

Daily Press, The, by Sumner L. Fairfield, in North American Review, June 1833: an attack against the abusive defamatory and unprincipled character of American newspapers.

Bound with other items in "Journalists, various excerpts", item 6.

JOURNALISM, United States

Cabinet NN Shelf 4 No. 22

Dana, Charles A., The Life of:

By James Harrison Wilson. New York. 1907.

Frontispiece portrait.

Cloth: $8\frac{1}{2}$x$5\frac{1}{2}$"

JOURNALISM, United States.

Cabinet Shelf No.

Dana, Charles Anderson, when he ruled the New York Sun.

Has picture of the bronze plaque by Saint-Gaudens.

Article in Editor & Publisher, vol. 64, p.13 May 23, 1931.

JOURNALISM, United States

Cabinet NN Shelf 2 No. 8

De Costa, William Hickling, b. 1825, d. 1878. In memoriam. Privately printed, Charlestown (Mass.) 1878. With portrait.

De Costa edited and established the "Charlestown Advertiser".

Item 2 in Vol. "Various Editors: Excerpts and Pamphlets".

JOURNALISM, United States

Cabinet NN Shelf 2 No. 1

Dennie, Joseph (Oliver Oldschool). Life of Joseph Dennie, Esq., in the Port Folio, May, 1816: Brief eulogistic biographical sketch of the editor, founder of the Port Folio, Boston, 1801.

Bound with other items in "Journalists, various excerpts", item 1.

JOURNALISM, United States

Cabinet NN Shelf 6 No. 18

Detroit News, 1873-1917. A record of progress. By Lee A. White. Pastel illustrations by James Scripps Booth. Detroit, Michigan. Copyrighted 1918. Illus. with interior and exterior views of the Detroit News Building.

Boards, linen back; $10\frac{1}{4}$ x $8\frac{1}{4}$ in.

JOURNALISM, United States.

Cabinet NN Shelf 2 No. 11

Development of the American newspaper. Article by Walter L. Hawley of the New York Sun. Excerpt from "The Popular Science Monthly". Illus.

Item 1 in bound collection with binder's title "About various newspapers".

JOURNALISM, United States

Cabinet NN Shelf 6 No. 11

Dingley, Nelson, Jr. An autobiography of. Lewiston (Maine): Published at the Journal Office, 1874.

Half morocco; 8-3/8 x 6 in.

JOURNALISM, United States.

Cabinet NN Shelf 3 No. 8

Dixon, J. M., The valley and the shadow, comprising the experience of a blind ex-editor, a literary biography, a chaper on Iowa journalism, etc. New York. 1868.

Cloth: $7\frac{1}{2}$x5"

JOURNALISM, United States

Cabinet NN Shelf 2 No. 19

Duane, William. By Allen C. Clarke. Read before the Columbia Historical Society, Washington, D.C., February 13, 1905.

Has frontispiece portrait

Cloth; $9\frac{3}{4}$ x $6\frac{1}{2}$ in.

JOURNALISM, United States

Cabinet Q Shelf 1 No. 2

Early American magazines. Historical account. Excerpt from New Princeton Review, July, 1887.

Item 5 in volume with binder's title, "Publishers and Publishing. Pamphlets."

JOURNALISM, United States.

Cabinet R Shelf 4 No. 136

Early Press of Iowa. By John Springer, Iowa City Iowa, 1880.

Historical, biographical account of Iowa printers, printing, and newspapers.

Half morocco; $9\frac{3}{4}$ x $6\frac{1}{4}$ in.

JOURNALISM, United States.

Cabinet NN Shelf 2 No. 2

Editorial chair of The Tribune, in Putnam's magazine, May, 1868: A biographical account of Horace Greeley, his career as an editor, his political relations, etc.

Bound with other items in "Journalists and Journalism", item 4.

JOURNALISM, United States

Cabinet 00 Shelf 6 No. 65

Famous editors of The Evening Post: Coleman, Bryant, Legett, Godwin, Bigelow, Schurz, Godkin, White.

Article with portraits in The New York Evening Post: Special supplement, Saturday April 13, 1907. On p. 10 and following.

Cloth; 16 x 10-7/8 in.

JOURNALISM, UNITED STATES

Cabinet NN Shelf 3 No. 1

Goddard, William. The partnership; or the history of the rise and progress of the Pennsylvania Chronicle, etc. Philadelphia: Printed and sold by William Goddard, in Arch Street, between Front and Second Streets. 1770

Half morrocco: $7\frac{1}{2}$x$4\frac{3}{4}$"

JOURNALISM, United States.

Cabinet NN Shelf 2 No. 1

Editors of the younger generation, by Zona Gale, in The Critic, April, 1904. Portraits.

Bound with other items in "Journalists, various excerpts," item 33.

JOURNALISM, United States

Cabinet NN Shelf 6 No. 45

Fifty years in journalism, embracing recollections and personal experiences with an autobiography. By Beman Brockway, Watertown N. Y., 1891. With portrait.

Cloth; 9 x $6\frac{1}{4}$ x $1\frac{1}{4}$ in.

JOURNALISM, United States.

Cabinet NN Shelf 2 No. 1

Godkin, Edwin Lawrence, by Wendall P. Garrison, in The Book Buyer, Feb., 1896: Brief biographical sketch of the editor of The New York Evening Post. Engraved portrait.

Bound with other items in "Journalists, various excerpts", item 28.

JOURNALISM, United States

Cabinet NN Shelf 2 No. 8

Editors Table.-- Our corps editorial (The Ladies Repository, Jan., 1871.

Excerpted article with portraits and brief biographical sketches of notable contemporary editors.

Item 18 in volume with binder's title: "Various Editors".

JOURNALISM, United States.

Cabinet NN Shelf 2 No. 13

First newspapers in America, by Lyman Horace Weeks, and Edwin M. Bacon, in The Connecticut Magazine, No. 3, 1908: An illustrated historical account of the first products of the Printing Press in America.

Bound with other items in "Various newspapers and periodicals," vol. I, item 26.

JOURNALISM, United States

Cabinet NN Shelf 2 No. 8

(Godkin, Edwin Lawrence). Mr. Godkin and his book, by H.T.Peck, in The Bookman, Feb., 1896: An account of the man, also a review of the book "Reflections and Comments," by E.L. Godkin. Halftone portrait.

Bound with other items in "Various Editors", item 15.

JOURNALISM, United States.

Cabinet NN Shelf 2 No. 1

Editors that I have known, by Alex. Wilder in Belford's, Aug., 1890: Brief personal sketches of Horace Greeley, and James Gordon Bennett, with an outline of the policies of their respective newspapers.

Bound with other items in "Journalists, various excerpts", item 2.

JOURNALISM, United States

Cabinet NN Shelf 2 No. 3

Fitchburg, Mass., sketch of journalism in. By James F.D. Garfield, Reprinted from "Fitchburg, Past and Present". Press of Blanchard & Brown, Fitchburg, 1888. Pamphlet. Illus.

Item 4 in vol. "Journalists and Journalism". Pamphlets".

JOURNALISM, United States

Cabinet 00 Shelf 3 No. 42

"Good old days, the." Being some newspaper reminiscences, with a little salt of Kentucky journalism in the last century. Address delivered by Urey Woodson at the 62nd Annual Meeting of the Kentucky Press Association. June 25-27, 1931. Paducah, Ky. Illus. portraits.

Brochure, in envelope.

JOURNALISM, United States.

Cabinet NN Shelf 2 No. 12

Evening Post (The): A sketch of the history and growth of a newspaper of prominence: in Editorial Review, Aug., 1909.

Bound with other items in "Various newspapers and periodicals", item 6.

JOURNALISM. United States

Cabinet NN Shelf 1 No. 20

Flint, Timothy, pioneer, missionary, author, editor, 1780-1840. The story of his life. By John Ervin Kirkpatrick. Cleveland, Ohio, 1911.

Cloth; $9\frac{1}{2}$ x 6 3/8 x $1\frac{1}{2}$ in.

JOURNALISM, United States.

Cabinet NN Shelf 2 No. 1

Governor Cox and Senator Harding give exclusive interview to The New Success, by Albert Sydney Gregg, in The New Success, Oct., 1920.

Bound with other items in "Journalists, various excerpts", item 39.

JOURNALISM, United States

Cabinet NN Shelf 2 No. 8

Famous Editors, by William S. Bridgman. The early days of the newspaper and the review, in Munsey's, Mar., 1904. Has an account of the editors who have left their mark in the world of journalism from 1661-1878. Halftone portraits.

Bound with other items in "Various Editors", item 22.

JOURNALISM, United States,

Cabinet NN Shelf 2 No. 3

Full and authentic account of the murder of James King, of Wm., editor of The San Francisco Evening Bulletin, by James P. Casey. Compiled from the columns of the Alta California and originally written for that paper, by Frank F. Fargo, 1850. Pamphlet.

Bound with other items in "Journalists and Journalism", item 1.

JOURNALISM, United States

Cabinet NN Shelf 4 No. 16

Greeley, Horace.
Fiftieth anniversary of the founding of "The Tribune," celebrated April 10, 1891, at the Metropolitan Opera House. New York.

Cloth: 10 x 6-3/4 in.

JOURNALISM, United States

Cabinet NN Shelf 4 No. 7

Greeley, Horace.
Recollections of a busy life. - to which are added Miscellanies.

With portrait and other illustrations.
New York. 1869.

Cloth: 9x6¼"

JOURNALISM, United States

Cabinet NN Shelf 2 No. 6

Hamilton, Adam Boyd, Memorial address by William Henry Egle. Harrisburg, Pa., 1897.

Account of Hamilton's activities as printer, journalist, publisher, writer. b.1808-d.1896

Item 2 in bound collection "Biographies of Journalists".

JOURNALISM, United States

Cabinet NN Shelf 2 No. 12

An historical and statistical account by Franklin Matthews in the Chatauquan, Nov., 1894.

Bound with other items in "Various newspapers and periodicals", item 21.

JOURNALISM, United States

Cabinet NN Shelf 4 No. 12

Greeley, Horace and journalism.
(From The Tribune, Dec. 3)

See Greeley, Horace, Memorial of - New York. 1873. 232

JOURNALISM, United States

Cabinet NN Shelf 2 No. 1

Hearst, William Randolph. By Arthur Brisbane. [Excerpt from series] "Captains of Industry", The Cosmopolitan, May, 1902.

Item 19 in book with binder's title "Journalists. Various Excerpts".

JOURNALISM, United States

Cabinet NN Shelf 2 No. 27

Historical digest of the provincial press, 1704-1707...

see
WEEKS, HORACE L., and EDWIN M. BACON. Historical digest...

JOURNALISM, United States

Cabinet NN Shelf 7 No. 27

Greeley, Horace as a journalist. An address by Wm. H. McElroy: on the one hundreth anniversary of the birth of Horace Greeley, first President Typographical Union No. 6. New York, 1911. With portrait.
See p. 17.

With other items in box labeled "Horace Greeley. Various items"

JOURNALISM, United States

Cabinet NN Shelf 2 No. 6

Hearst myth, the. By "Q.P".
Excerpt from World's Work, Oct., 1906.

Item 15 in bound collection "Biographies of Journalists".

JOURNALISM, United States.

Cabinet NN Shelf 2 No. 11

History of American journalism. Excerpt from unidentified periodical, n.d.

Item 2 in bound collection with binder's title "About various newspapers".

JOURNALISM, United States

Cabinet NN Shelf 4 No. 11

Greeley, Horace, founder of the New York Tribune, with extended notices of many of his contemporary statesmen and journalists. By L.D. Ingersoll. Chicago, Ill., 1873. Illus.

Leather; 9¼ x 6 ½ in.

JOURNALISM, United States.

Cabinet NN Shelf 2 No. 1

Hearst, the man of mystery, by Lincoln Steffen, in The American Magazine, Nov., 1906.

Bound with other items in Journalists, various excerpts," item 42.

JOURNALISM, United States,

Cabinet S Shelf 5 No. 21

History of a Newspaper: The Pennsylvania Gazette, Paul L. Ford, in Magazine of American History, April, 1887.

Bound with other items in "Excerpts relating to printing in America", pp.84-88.

JOURNALISM, United States

Cabinet NN Shelf 2 No. 7

Greeley campaign, the humor and tragedy of. By Henry Watterson.
Excerpt from The Cnetury, Nov., 1912. With portraits.

Item 28 in bound collection "Journalism. Excerpts, etc."

JOURNALISM, United States.

Cabinet NN Shelf 2 No. 1

Hearst, Mr. the real. By James Creelman, in Pearson's Magazine, Sept., 1906: Character sketch with brief account of his family life. Illus.

Bound with other items in "Journalists, various excerpts," item 41.

JOURNALISM, United States,

Cabinet A Shelf 3 No. 52

History of California Newspapers: Included as a Christmas offering to the readers of the Sacramento Daily Union. Double Sheet. Sacramento: vol. XVI, No. 2417, Dec. 25, 1858

Buckram; 24½ x 18¼ x ½ in.

JOURNALISM, United States

Cabinet NN Shelf 2 No. 6

Group of pre-revolutionary editors, A: Beginnings of journalism in America, by G.G. W. Benjamin, in Magazine of American History, Jan., 1887.

Bound with other items in "Biographies of Journalists", item 10.

JOURNALISM, United States

Cabinet NN Shelf 2 No. 12

Herald, The---Onward!
Excerpt from the Democratic Review, Nov., and Dec., 1852. With portrait of James Gordon Bennett.

Item 2 in vol. with binder's title "Various Newspapers and Periodicals".

JOURNALISM, United States

Cabinet NN Shelf 2 No. 2

History of Rutland newspapers, by Chauncy K. Williams.

An excerpt from unidentified publication, n.d.

Item 2 in vol. "Journalists and Journalism". Bound, 1918.

JOURNALISM, United States

Cabinet NN Shelf 4 No. 25

History of The New York Times, 1851-1921.

By Elmer Davis. New York. 1921. Illus.
Has signature of

Cloth: $8\frac{3}{4}$x$5\frac{1}{2}$x$1\frac{1}{2}$

JOURNALISM, United States

Cabinet NN Shelf 6 No. 7

(Illinois) Chicago Tribune 75th birthday, 1922. The W - G - N - A hand book of newspaper administration, editorial, advertising... depicting in word and picture "how its done" by the World's greatest newspaper. Published by The Chicago Tribune in commemoration of its 75th birthday. June 10, 1922.

Cloth; 9-5/8 x $6\frac{1}{4}$ x 1-1/8 in.

JOURNALISM, United States

Cabinet NN Shelf 6 No. 9

Kansas newspapers 1854 to 1916, a history of... William E. Connelley, Secretary Kansas State Historical Society and Department of Archives. Topeka, 1916. Illus.

Cloth; 9 x 6 x 1 in.

JOURNALISM, United States

Cabinet OO Shelf 6 No. 59

History of the "Open Shop" in Los Angeles. October 1, 1929. Booklet reprinted from the Los Angeles Times, which published it in a series of daily articles beginning October 1, 1920, the 19th anniversary of the destruction of the Times Building by dynamite. Illus.

Cloth; $10\frac{1}{2}$ x $11\frac{1}{4}$ in.

JOURNALISM, United States

Cabinet S Shelf 5 No. 21

Influence of early American Press: Notable editors between 1776 and 1800, by S. C. W. Benjamin, in Magazine of American History, Feb. 1887. Portraits and reduced facsimile reproductions of some early newspapers.

Bound with other items in "Excerpts relating to printing in America", pp. 29-59.

JOURNALISM, United States

Cabinet NN Shelf 2 No. 1

Kendall, George Wilkins (of New Orleans Picayune) In the International Magazine, May, 1851: Brief personal record. Portrait.

Bound with other items in "Journalists, various excerpts", item 23.

JOURNALISM, United States

Cabinet NN Shelf 2 No. 11

Howells, William Dean: The country printer. Excerpt from "Scribners M agazine, May, 1893.

Autobiographical

Item 3 in collection with binder's title "About various newspapers".

JOURNALISM, United States

Cabinet NN Shelf 6 No. 8

Iowa, early journalism in : The founding of the Hamilton Freeman at Webster City, in 1857. By Charles Aldrich.
Article in The Iowa Historical Record of the State Historical Society, at Iowa City, Jan. 1893, Vol. 1X, No. 1, p. 394.

Cloth; $9\frac{3}{4}$ x $6\frac{1}{4}$ in.

JOURNALISM, United States.

Cabinet NN Shelf 4 No. 44

Klopsch, Louis, life work of.

Romance of a modern knight of mercy.

By Charles M. Pepper. With numerous illustrations. The Christian Herald. New York (1910)

Cloth: $9\frac{1}{4}$x$6\frac{1}{4}$"

JOURNALISM, United States

Cabinet NN Shelf 3 No. 4

Hudson, Frederic. Journalism in the United States, 1690-1872. New York, 1873.

Has A.L.S. the author inserted.

Cloth; 8-5/8 x 5-5/8 in.

JOURNALISM, United States.

Cabinet NN Shelf 2 No. 8

Journalists and journalism of New York, The, by Frank A. Munsey, in Munsey's Magazine, Jan. 1892: Mr. Munsey's comments on the changing conditions of editorial and business methods over those of earlier days. Portraits of thirteen editors.

Bound with other items in "Various Editors". item 16.

JOURNALISM, UNITED STATES

Cabinet NN Shelf 2 No. 1

Kohlsaat, Hermann H., of Chicago, and his part in the political history-making of 1896, by Walter Wellman, in American Review of Reviews, Jan., 1897: A brief life story of the editor of the Chicago Times-Herald.

Bound with other items in "Journalists, various excerpts", item 32.

JOURNALISM, United States

Cabinet NN Shelf 6 No. 6

Illinois, 1814 - 1879, newspapers and periodicals of. By Franklin William Scott. Bibliographical Series, Vol. I, Collections of the Illinois State Historical Library, Vol. VI, Springfield, Ill., 1910. Illus.

Cloth; 9 x 6 x 2-1/8 in.

JOURNALISM, United States

Cabinet NN Shelf 2 No. 8

(The) Kansas City Star, the best newspaper in America. By Charles H. Crasty.
Excerpt from The World's Work, June, 1919. With portrait of W.R.Nelson, founder of the Kansas City Star.

Item 29 in volume with binder's title: "Various Editors".

JOURNALISM, United States

Cabinet NN Shelf 4 No. 46

Leach, Frank A.
Recollections of a newspaper man. A record of life and events in California. San Francisco. 1917.

Frontispiece, portrait and other illus.

Cloth: 9x6-1/8x1-3/8"

JOURNALISM, United States Literature

Cabinet QQ Shelf 3 No. 14

Illinois (Bloomington.) Transactions of the McLean County Historical Society...Meeting of May 29, 1900. Edited by Ezra M. Prince. Vol. III. Bloomington, Illinois. 1900. Illus.

Cloth; 8-7/8 x 6 x $\frac{1}{2}$ in.

JOURNALISM, United States

Stack Shelf Number

Kansas journalism, the story of.

Radio talks by Prof. E.C. Rogers, Kansas State College, reported in The Publishers Auxiliary, 68th year, No.38, Sept.23, 1933, pp.1 and 6

JOURNALISM, United States.

Cabinet NN Shelf 2 No. 1

Leland, William Wallace (with portrait), in Hunt's Merchants' Magazine, May, 1857. W.W. Leland in 1849 became part owner of the Pacific News, California, and by himself undertook the publication of the Marysville Herald, California.

Bound with other itmes in "Journalists, various excerpts", item 3.

JOURNALISM, United States.

Cabinet S Shelf 2 No. 7 4 vols.

Liberator, The. Boston, 1831. Edited by William Lloyd Garrison and Isaac Knapp. Printer, Stephen Foster.
For account of the above weekly see Garrison, William Lloyd. Story of his Life... London 1885-1889. pp.219-276.

JOURNALISM, United States.

Cabinet NN Shelf 8 No. 6

Lyon, Matthew (Col.). A picturesque politician of Jefferson's time, by J. Fairfax McLaughlin, in The Century, April 1903: Incidents in the life of Col. Matthew Lyon, who was the founder and editor of The Farmers Library, and a newspaper, The scourge of Aristocracy, for which he cast his own type and made his own paper.

Bound with other items in "Biographies of Journalists." item 7.

JOURNALISM, United States

Cabinet NN Shelf 7 No. 2-3-4

(Maine, Wiscasset) The Seaside Oracle. Wiscasset, Maine, Publisher and Proprietor, Joseph Wood.
In this library: Seaside Oracle,
Vol. I-III, 1869 - 71.
" IV 1872
" VI-VII-VIII, 1874 - 6.
Pasted in vol. I, are 2 letters April 5, and 13, 1909 containing bibliographical information concerning "The Seaside Oracle", and signed by Joseph Wood.
Vols. 1869 - 71 and vols. 1874 - 76, Buckram bindings, Vol. 1872 half morocco. Sizes of volumes vary.

JOURNALISM, United States

Cabinet NN Shelf 4 No. 43

Little adventures in newspaperdom.

By Fred W. Allsop, Little Rock, Ark. 1922. Illustrated.

Signature of the author.

Leatherette: 7¾x5½"

JOURNALISM, United States.

Cabinet NN Shelf 2 No. 8

McClure, A.K. the editor in chief, by A.K. McClure, in Lippincott's, Jan., 1892.

Brief autobiographical sketch by the editor himself.

Bound with other items in "Various Editors", item 14.

JOURNALISM, United States

Cabinet NN Shelf 7 No. 15

Marin Journal, The. New Era Edition. San Rafael Marin County. California, March 25, 1909.

Cloth; 13¾ x 10 in.

JOURNALISM, United States.

Cabinet NN Shelf 2 No. 1

Lorimer, George Horace, original easy boss, by Irvin S. Cobb, in The Bookman, Dec., 1918: A plain statement of the facts concerning the one-time editor of The Saturday Evening Post.

Bound with other items in "Journalism, various excerpts", item 26.

JOURNALISM, United States

Cabinet Shelf No.

McLean, William L. proprietor Philadelphia Bulletin; a biography with portrait. Also editorial on McLean and expressions of tribute to his memory.
In Editor & Publisher, pp.5, 28, 43, and 44, Aug. 1, vol.64, No.11.

JOURNALISM, United States

Cabinet NN Shelf 2 No. 26

Massachusetts periodicals, 1689-1783. Chronologically arranged list of the.

see

WEEKS, HORACE L., and EDWIN M. BACON. Historical digest of the provincial press... Boston, 1908

JOURNALISM, United States.

Cabinet NN Shelf 2 No. 12

Louisville Courier Journal, (The): A brief sketch of the history and growth of this newspaper, in the Editorial Review, Nov., 1910

Bound with other items in "Various newspapers and periodicals", item 7.

JOURNALISM, United States,

Cabinet Shelf No.

McLean, William L. 36 years owner of the Philadelphia Evening Bulletin: A brief biography; with portrait.

Article in The American Press, 49th year, No. 11, August 1931, p. 34.

JOURNALISM. United States

Cabinet NN Shelf 1 No. 23

Memoirs of an editor: fifty years of American Journalism. By Edward P. Mitchel. New York, 1924. Illus. Charles Scribner's Sons.

Cloth 9 x 6¼ x 1¾ in.

JOURNALISM, United States

Cabinet NN Shelf 2 No. 13

Lowell Offering. Article by Harriet H Robinson. Excerpt from the "New England Magazine", Dec., 1889.

Historical account of a periodical published and edited entirely by women in 1845.

Item 25 in volume with binder's title "Various newspapers and periodicals"

JOURNALISM, United States

Cabinet NN Shelf 6 No. 10

Maine, 1785 - 1872. History of the press of Maine. Edited by Joseph Griffin. Second issue of the Press of Maine, 1872, with a supplement, 1874. Brunswick: From the press established A. D. 1819. Illus.

Cloth; 9-3/8 x 6 x 1-1/8 in.

JOURNALISM, United States.

Cabinet NN Shelf 2 No. 2

Memorial address upon the services of Morton McMichael, as editor, public officer, and citizen, by John W. Forney, in accordance with the invitation of the journalists of Philadelphia. Pamphlet.

Bound with other items in "Journalists and Journalism, Item 7.

JOURNALISM, United States.

Cabinet NN Shelf 2 No. 8

Lyon, Matthew, The life and services of: An address pronounced Oct., 29, 1858, before the Vermont Historical Society, by Pliny H. White.
Matthew Lyon edited and published "The Farmer's Library and The Farmer's Gazette, both in Vermont.

Bound with other items in "Various Editors, item 1.

JOURNALISM, United States

Cabinet NN Shelf 6 No. 12

Maine,(Paris). The semi - centennial of The Oxford Democrat. January 8, 1884. Printed at the Oxford Democrat Office. 1884.
By Wm. B. Lapham.

Half morocco; 8¾ x 6 x 3/8 in.

JOURNALISM, United States.

Cabinet NN Shelf 2 No. 6

Men who make the New York "Sun", The, by E.J. Edwards, in Munsey's Oct., 1893. Illus. with halftone portraits.

Bound with other items in "Biographies of Journalists", item 14.

JOURNALISM. United States.

Cabinet NN Shelf 3 No. 16

Miller, Charles Grant: Don Piatt, his work and his ways. Cincinnati. 1893.

With frontispiece portrait.

Cloth: 8x5½"

JOURNALISM, United States.

Cabinet NN Shelf 2 No. 1

Murphy, Thomas D., who made a nation wide success in a small town in Iowa, by Edward Mott Woolley, in World's Work, Feb., 1914: brief sketch of the editor of the Independent, Red Oak, Iowa.

Bound with other items in "Journalists, various excerpts", item 35.

JOURNALISM, United States

Cabinet 00 Shelf 6 No. 54

New Bedford Mercury, 1807-1907. One hundredth anniversary supplement. New Bedford, Mass. Aug. 7, 1907. Illus. and portraits of founder, his successors, journalists, etc.

Cloth; 15½ x 11¼ in.

JOURNALISM, United States

Cabinet NN Shelf 6 No. 19

Minnesota journalism, 1858-1865.

see JOHNSTON, DANIEL S.B. Minnesota journalism...

JOURNALISM, United States

Cabinet NN Shelf 7 No. 16

Nation, The, 1865 - 1915, semi - centennial number, New York, Thursday, July 8, 1915. Portraits.

Includes articles as follows: Two editors, E. L. Godkin and W. P. Garrison (By Viscount Bryce).- The founding of the Nation. (Henry James).- The Nation and its ownership. (O. G. Villard).- Fifty years of books.(G. H. Putnam.- Former editors of the Nation.(E. L. Godkin).- etc.

Cloth; 12¼ x 9-1/8 x 3/8 in.

JOURNALISM, United States

Cabinet NN Shelf 6 No. 13

New Bedford (Mass.) newspapers, 1792 - 1860. Brief history.

Item in City Document No. 9. Tenth annual report of the trustees of the Free Public Library. New Bedford, 1862.

Half morocco; 9¾ x 5⅝ x ¼ in.

JOURNALISM, United States

Cabinet NN Shelf 6 No. 21

Missouri County Press, history of the. By Minnie Organ.

Three articles excerpted from The Missouri Historical Review, vol.IV, Nos.1-3, 1910.

Cloth; 9½ x 6¾ in.

JOURNALISM, United States

Cabinet NN Shelf 2 No. x28x 31

National Editorial Association (N.E.A.)

see HERBERT, BENJAMIN BRIGGS. National Editorial Association...Chicago, 1896

JOURNALISM, United States

Cabinet NN Shelf 2 No. 8

(New England) Joseph Dennie and Royall Tyler. Damon and Pythias among our early journalists. By S. Arthur Bent. Excerpt from the New England Magazine, Aug., 1896.

Item 27 in Vol. "Various Editors. Excerpts and Pamphlets".

JOURNALISM, United States

Cabinet NN Shelf 5 No. 22

Missouri Press Association. The Missouri Editor, printed on steamer Belle Memphis, Mississippi River, June 6-11, 1896, during excursion of Missouri Press Association from St. Louis to Memphis. Illus. Vol. 1, Nos. 1-5, all issued

After p. 12, No. 5 issue, picture of an improvised printing office.

Morocco; 6½ x 3¾ x ½ in.

JOURNALISM,United States

Cabinet KK Shelf 5 No. 44

National Editorial Association. Report of conventions, 1902 to 1930. Illus.

Each volume with articles on journalism, technicalities of production, brief biographies of editors, etc.

Original covers bound in. Cloth; 8¼ x 5½ in.

JOURNALISM, United States.

Cabinet NN Shelf 4 No. 31

New England, 1787 - 1815. Newspapers and newspaper writers in. Read before the New England Historic, Genealogical Society, Feb. 4, 1880.

By Delano A. Goddard. Boston. 1880.

Cloth: 8-1/8x6"

JOURANLISM, United States.

Cabinet NN Shelf 2 No. 6

Modern superman, A: A character sutdy of the late Joseph Pulitzer, by Alleyne Ireland, in American Magazine, April 1912.

Bound with other items in "Biographies of Journalists", item 13.

JOURNALISM, United States

Cabinet NN Shelf 2 No. 13

(The) National Intelligencer and its editors, Joseph Gales and Henry Seaton. Excerpt from the Atlantic, Oct.,1860.

Item 7 in bound collection with binder's title "Various newspapers and periodicals"

JOURNALISM, United States

Cabinet NN Shelf 2 No. 8

New England editors in the South. By George Frederick Mellen.

Excerpt from the New England Magazine, Feb., 1903.

Item 25 in volume with binder's title: "Various Editors".

JOURNALISM, United States

Cabinet NN Shelf 6 No. 47

Monody on certain members of the "Press Club" (Believed to bear date about A. D. 1900). By Charles J. Peterson, Philadelphia. Privately printed for F. J. Dreer. Illus.

Pasted in newspaper clippings of biographical obituaries for C. J. Peterson, proprietor of Peterson's "Ladies National Magazine".

Half morocco; 9-1/8 x 7-3/8 x 3/8 in.

JOURNALISM, United States.

Cabinet NN Shelf 4 No. 45

Nelson, William Rockhill. The story of a man a newspaper and a city. By members of the staff of the Kansas City Star. Cambridge. Printed at The Riverside Press. 1915. Portraits and illus.

Cloth: 9x6"

JOURNALISM, United States

Cabinet NN Shelf 4 No. 1 3 vols

New Jersey Archives. First series, Vol. 11, 1894; Vol. 12, 1895; Vol. 19, 1897. Newspaper extracts

Some account of American newspapers, 1704-1739, Vol. I 1740-1750, Vol. II 1751-1755, Vol. III

Cloth: 9x6-1/8"

JOURNALISM, United States.

Cabinet NN Shelf 2 No. 13

(The) New Orleans Item. Brief historical sketch of this newspaper founded in 1878. Excerpt from the "Editorial Review", Feb.,1878.

Item 14 in volume with binder's title "Various newspapers and periodicals"-1

JOURNALISM, United States

Cabinet QQ Shelf 3 No. 13

New York, brief consideration of...1753.

see LIVINGSTON, WILLIAM. Brief consideration of New York...

JOURNALISM, United States

Cabinet NN Shelf 6 No. 26

New York City, 1869, the daily press and the weekly press.

see BROWNE, JUNIUS HENRI (The) Great Metropolis; a mirror of New York...1870. (pp.295, 311, 491, 399, 214, 150)

JOURNALISM, United States

Cabinet NN Shelf 2 No. 7

New York Daily, a study of a. By Byron C. Mathews.
Excerpt from The Independent, Jan.13, 1910.

Item 23 in bound collection "Journalism. Excerpts, etc."

JOURNALISM, United States,

Cabinet R Shelf 4 No. 63

New York during the last half century: A discourse in commemoration of the Fifty-third Anniversary of the New York Historical Society. ... By John W..Francis, M.D. New York, 1857.
See pp. 206-221 for data on newspapers, journalism, publishing and authorship.

Half morocco; 9¼ x 6-1/8 in.

JOURNALISM, United States.

Cabinet A Shelf 1 No. 89

New York Evening Post, The. 1801-1901.

See Newspapers. Anniversary Issues.

JOURNALISM, United States

Cabinet NN Shelf 2 No. 9

New York Herald: a sketch of the daily routine of the.
(Excerpt from the Illustrated Magazine of Art, Feb., 1853)

Item 31 in vol. with binder's title "Newspapers, various excerpts".

JOURNALISM, United States.

Cabinet NN Shelf 2 No. 12

New York Herald, 1863: The newspaper press of American (The), by R. B. in Temple Bar, Jan., 1863: a brief account which includes an attack against the abuses of James Gordon Bennett.

Bound with other items in "Various newspapers and periodicals", item I.

JOURNALISM, United States.

Cabinet NN Shelf 2 No. 1

New York Journalists: E.L. Godkin, by Eugene Benson, in The Galaxy, June, 1869.

Bound with other items in "Journalists, various excerpts", item 8.

JOURNALISM, United States.

Cabinet NN Shelf 2 No. 1

New York Journalists: Parke Godwin, by Eugene Benson, in The Galaxy, Feb., 1869.

Bound with other items in "Journalists, various excerpts," item 9.

JOURNALISM, United States.

Cabinet NN Shelf 2 No. 1

New York Journalists: W.H. Hurlbut, by Eugene Benson, in The Galaxy, Jan., 1869. He was editor of New York World.

Bound with other items in "Journalists, various excerpts," item 10.

JOURNALISM, United States

Cabinet NN Shelf 4 No. 33

New York press and its makers in the 18th Century.
By Charlotte M. and Benjamin Ellis Martin.
Half Moon Series.
Copyright 1898 by G.P. Putnam's Sons. New York.

Cloth: 8-3/8x5-5/8"

JOURNALISM, United States

Cabinet NN Shelf 6 No. 27

New York Press Association. Authorized history for fifty years, 1853-1903. By A.O. Bunnell, Secretary.

Cloth; 10-1/8 x 6¾ in.

JOURNALISM, United States

Cabinet NN Shelf 5 No. 21

New York Press Club. Constitution, by - laws and list of members. Instituted December 4, 1874. New York: Printed by P. F. McBreen, 1891.

Cloth; 6-5/8 x 4-3/8 in.

JOURNALISM, United States

Cabinet NN Shelf 6 No. 46

(New York State. Chautauqua Co.) Editorial miscellanies. The pioneer press of Chautauqua County. [Read before the Fredonia Historical Society, March 14, 1879, by W. McKinstry. Frontspiece.
Also Letters published in the Fredonia Censor at various times between 1842 and 1894.

Cloth; 9-1/8 x 6-1/8 x 1 in.

JOURNALISM, United States (N. Y. C.)

Cabinet 00 Shelf 6 No. 66

New York Times, The. Jubilee Number, 1851-1901. Illus.
Has history of this newspaper, articles on early New York journalism and journalists, portraits with brief biographies of some famous editors, etc.

Cloth; 16 x 11¼ in.

JOURNALISM, United States

Cabinet 00 Shelf 3 No. 52

New York Tribune. The organization and by-laws of The Tribune Association. New York, 1872. With portraits.

Cloth, stamped; 11½ x 9¼ in.

JOURNALISM, United States.

Cabinet NN Shelf 2 No. 9

New York Tribune in the draft riots, The, by James R. Gilmore ("Edmund Kirke"), in McClure's, Oct., 1895: The story of a member of the staff who assisted in arming the Tribune office.

Bound with other items in "Newspapers, various excerpts", item 20.

JOURNALISM, United States

Cabinet NN Shelf 2 No. 9

New York World, The: a journal of duality. By Oswald G. Villard.
(Excerpt from The Nation, Oct.25, 1922)

Item 33 in vol. with binder's title "Newspapers, various excerpts".

JOURNALISM United States

Cabinet S Shelf 2 No. 87

Newspapers, periodicals, and editors in the 18th century. Historical data concerning journalism in America.

See Tiffany, Nina Moore and Francis. Harm Jan Huidekoper. Cambridge, 1904.

JOURNALISM, United States,

Cabinet NN Shelf 2 No. 10

Ohio State Journal, The: An account of the history and growth of this newspaper. In the department of Contemporary Journalism of the Editorial Review, Sept. 1912.

Bound in collection "Description of various newspapers", item 6.

JOURNALISM, United States

Cabinet NN Shelf 6 No. 28

(New York) "World". Who's who on the "World". Character is given to a paper by the men and women who write it. (New York, 1922)
Brief biographical sketches of The World staff. With portraits.

Half morocco; 10 x $7\frac{3}{4}$ x $\frac{3}{4}$ in.

JOURNALISM, United States

Cabinet NN Shelf 2 No. 16

North Carolina, the first newspaper in.
Excerpt from Magazine of American History, Nov., 1889.

Item 25 in vol. with binder's title "Journalism: Pamphlets. Bound, 1932".

JOURNALISM, United States

Cabinet NN Shelf 6 No. 33

(Ohio) Toledo Commercial, The. Editor James M. Comly.

see COMLY, JAMES M. In Memoriam...1887.

JOURNALISM, United States

Cabinet NN Shelf 2 No. 7

Newspaper in 1761, the New York Gazette, printed by W. Weyman in Broad Street. [Bibliographical account], by Henry A. Auchincloss.
Excerpt from Knickerbocker, April, 1855

Item 7 in bound collection "Journalism. Excerpts, etc."

JOURNALISM, United States.

Cabinet R Shelf 4 No. 155

North Carolina, the pre-Revolutionary printers of...By Stephen B. Weeks. (Lacks title page, n.d. (1915).

See also R/4/154.

Half morocco; 9-1/8 x 6 x 3/8 in.

JOURNALISM, United States.

Cabinet R Shelf 4 No. 157

(The) Ohio Valley Press before the war of 1812-15 By R. G. Thwaites. Worcester, Mass. 1909.

Half morocco; $9\frac{1}{2}$ x $6\frac{1}{2}$ in.

JOURNALISM, United States

Cabinet NN Shelf 2 No. 12

Newspapers and editors (Journalism in the United States from 1690 to 1872. By Frederic Hudson).
Review of book with above title. Excerpt from Harpers New Monthly Magazine, March, 1873.

Item 25 in vol. with binder's title "Various Newspapers and Periodicals".

JOURNALISM, United States

Cabinet NN Shelf 2 No. 15

Notable editors between 1776 and 1800. Influence of the early American Press. By S.G.W. Benjamin.
Excerpt from the Magazine of American History, Feb., 1887. Has portraits and facs.

Item 6 in vol. with binder's title "Early American Newspapers-Excerpts-Bound, 1919".

JOURNALISM, United States

Cabinet NN Shelf 6 No. 32

Ohio Valley Press before the war of 1812 - 15. By Reuben Gold Thwaites. Reprinted from the Proceedings of the American Antiquarian Society, for April, 1909. Worcester, Mass. The Davis Press. Facs.

Half morocco; 10 x $6\frac{3}{4}$ in.

JOURNALISM, United States,

Cabinet A Shelf 1 No. 56

Newspapers of Connecticut and the men who made them. Biographical historical account, in the "Hartford Courant" 140th anniversary issue, (1764-1904). Oct. 29, 1904.

Buckram; 23 x $17\frac{3}{4}$ x $\frac{1}{4}$ in.

JOURNALISM, United States

Cabinet NN Shelf 5 No. 26

Notes on Journalism: History of the Morning Herald and other Titusville papers. By Edwin C. Bell. Titusville, 1910.

Half morocco; 6-1/8 x $4\frac{1}{4}$ in.

JOURNALISM, United States

Cabinet NN Shelf 7 No. 19

Oklahoma Press and the Oklahoma Press Association, history of the. Dedicated at the Silver Jubilee Convention of the Oklahoma Press Association at Woodward, Oklahoma, June 6 and 7, 1930. History by J. B. Thoburn. Compiled and supervised by John Windsor Sharp. Illus.

Embossed leatherette; $10\frac{3}{4}$ x $7\frac{3}{4}$ x 7/8 in.

JOURNALISM, United States

Cabinet NN Shelf 2 No. 9

Newspapers of the United States. Article in "The Republic", June, 1873.

Includes a list of first issues of newspapers in every State

Item 2 in volume with binder's title "Newspapers, various excerpts".

JOURNALISM United States

Cabinet KK Shelf 6 No. 21

Ohio Associated Dailies. Annual reports.

see ASSOCIATIONS, NEWSPAPER. Ohio Associated Dailies...

JOURNALISM, United States

Cabinet NN Shelf 5 No. 18

Olden Time Series, No. 4. Quaint and curious advertisements. Gleanings chiefly from old newspapers of Boston and Salem, Massachusetts Selected and arranged with brief comments. By Henry M. Brooks. Boston, 1886. Illus.

Cloth; 7 x 4-7/8 in.

JOURNALISM, United States,

Cabinet NN Shelf 2 No. 8

O'Meara, James, California Journalist, by Francis L. O'Meara, for the Journal of the American-Irish Historical Society, July, 1917: Brief sketch of his life and work.

Bound with other items in "Various editors" item 4.

JOURNALISM, UNITED STATES

Cabinet NN Shelf 3 No. 46

"One Day". This volume is designed to show how one copy of the Evening Bulletin appears when published in book form.

The Evening Bulletin. Philadelphia. 1929.

Cloth: 7-3/4 x 5½ x 1-1/8"

JOURNALISM, United States.

Cabinet R Shelf 3 No. 175

(Onondago County). Fitch, Charles E: The press of Onondaga. A lecture delivered before the Onondago Historical Association, by Charles E. Fitch Syracuse, 1868:

Has list of newspapers, with dates of publication of all the newspapers in Onondago County. pp. 11-12.

Half morocco; 9 x 6 in.

JOURNALISM, United States

Cabinet NN Shelf 2 No. 7

Our leading journals, with some account of their beginning. By Wm. T. Coggeshall.

Excerpt from the Ladies Repository, Aug., 1856.

Item 22 in bound collection "Journalism. Excerpts, etc."

JOURNALISM, United States

Cabinet NN Shelf 2 No. 3

(The) Paper Trust. The advance in prices of paper - its causes and the remedy. Missouri Editorial Association, St. Louis. Feb. 8th, 1900. Address by W.D. Thomas, the Fulton, Mo., Sun. Pamphlet.

Item 5 in vol. "Journalists and Journalism". Pamphlets.

JOURNALISM, United States

Cabinet NN Shelf 2 No. 36

Payne, George Henry. History of journalism in the United States. New York, 1920.

Cloth; 8 x 5-3/8 in.

JOURNALISM, United States

Cabinet NN Shelf 6 No. 35

(Pennsylvania, Beaver County, 1805 - 1893) History of the newspapers of...

see

READER, FRANCIS S. History of newspapers of Beaver County, Pennsylvania ...New Brighton, Pa., 1905.

JOURNALISM, United States

Cabinet 00 Shelf 3 No. 57

Philadelphia Press, The.

see

SPECIMEN BOOKS, TYPES (Newspapers)

JOURNALISM, United States.

Cabinet NN Shelf 2 No. 18

Philadelphia Public Ledger, (The): A history of the 75 years career of this newspaper; Editorial Review, Feb. 1911.

Bound with other items in "Various newspapers and periodicals", item 18.

JOURNALISM, United States

Cabinet NN Shelf 2 No. 25

Philadelphische Zeitung, the first German newspaper printed and published in America, by Benjamin Franklin.

Account by Julius F. Sachse, Philadelphia, 1900.

Half morocco; 9-3/8 x 6¼ in.

JOURNALISM, United States.

Cabinet R Shelf 3 No. 220

Pioneer press of Cleveland: An address by John C. Covert to theEarly Settlers Association of Cuyahoga County. In Annals of Cuyahoga County. 1897 Vol. III. No. 6, pp. 861-871.

Cloth; 8¾ x 6 in.

JOURNALISM, United States,

Cabinet R Shelf 5 No. 93

Pioneer Press of Kentucky, from the printing of the first paper West of the Alleghanies, Aug. 11, 1787, to the establishment of the daily press in 1830. Written for the Filson Club, Louisville, Ky., 1888.

Cloth; 11¼ x 9 in.

JOURNALISM, United States

Cabinet NN Shelf 2 No. 13

(The) Pittsburgh Gazette-Times. Brief historical sketch of this newspaper founded in 1786. Excerpt from the "Editorial Review", Sept., 1911.

Item 15 in volume with binder's title "Various newspapers and periodicals"-1

JOURNALISM, United States

Cabinet NN Shelf 7 No. 19.01

Plough Boy, The. Vol.1, 1819-20. Albany N.Y. Edited by Henry Homespun jr. (Solomon Southwick).

Boards, morocco back; 11¾ x 9¼ in.

JOURNALISM, United States

Cabinet NN Shelf 2 No. 1

Political portraits with pen and pencil: William Cullen Bryant, in Democratic Review, March, 1842, with steel engraving.

Bound with other items in "Journalists, various excerpts", item 5.

JOURNALISM, United States.

Cabinet NN Shelf 3 No. 7

Pomeroy, Mark M., life of "Brick" Pomeroy, editor of Lacrosse (Wis.) Democrat and of the Democrat, New York City. A representative young man of America...

By Mrs. Mary E. Tucker. With portrait. New York. 1868.
Has autograph of Pomeroy.
Cloth: 7½x5"

JOURNALISM, United States

Cabinet NN Shelf 3 No. 15

Pomeroy, Mark M.
Early life of "Brick" Pomeroy. (Second title): Wholesale mining in Colorado. (Third title): Better than Gold.(Fourth title): Ourselves and neighbors. New York. 1881 to 1891.

Four items in one volume.
Cloth: 8x5¾"

JOURNALISM, United States

Cabinet NN Shelf 1 No. 14

Poore, Ben. Perley. Perleys reminiscences of sixty years in the National Metropolis. Illustrated. Vols. I and II. Hubbard Brothers, Publishers. Philadelphia, 1886.

Has frontispiece portrait.

Cloth; 9¼ x 6½ x 2 in.

JOURNALISM. United States

Cabinet NN Shelf 1 No. 2

Porter, William T., the life of. By Francis Brinley. New York, 1860. Portrait frontispiece.

Copy has Porter's signature.

Cloth; 8 x 5 in.

JOURNALISM, United States

Cabinet S Shelf 5 No. 17

Press and Southern progress, The, by George F. Milton, in The Forensic Quarterly, Sept., 1910.

Brief account of improved journalistic conditions due to the modern inventions within fifty years.

Bound in collection "Miscellaneous items relating to printing," item 11.

JOURNALISM, United States

Cabinet NN Shelf 2 No. 1

Pulitzer, Joseph, of the New York.World. By Arthur Brisbane. Biographical account. With portrait. Excerpt from the "Cosmopolitan, May, 1902.

Item 19 in book with binder's title "Journalists. Various Excerpts".

JOURNALISM, United States

Cabinet NN Shelf 4 No. 27

"Post, The Evening". A century of journalism.

By Allan Nevins. New York. 1922. Illus.

Cloth: 9x6-1/8x1¼"

JOURNALISM, United States.

Cabinet NN Shelf 2 No. 12.

Press in the United States (The), by F.P. Stanton, in the Continental, Nov.1862.

Bound with other items in "Various newspapers and periodicals", item 4.

JOURNALISM, United States

Cabinet NN Shelf 2 No. 7

Raymond, Henry J., and journalism. [Biographical account of the founder of the New York Times] By L.J. Jennings.

Excerpt from the Galaxy, April, 1870.

Item 6 in bound collection "Journalism. Excerpts, etc."

JOURNALISM, United States

Cabinet NN Shelf 2 No. 6

Prentice, George D. [Brief account of this editor His political career and character] By Junius Henry Browne.

Excerpt from Harper's New Monthly Magazine, Jan., 1875.

Item 6 in bound collection "Biographies of Journalists".

JOURNALISM, United States

Cabinet NN Shelf 2 No. 9

Providence Journal (The), and Senator Anthony. Article by Rev. S.L. Caldwell, D.D. Excerpt from "The New England Magazine", April-May, 1887. With portraits

Item 13 in bound collection with binder's title "Newspapers, various excerpts".

JOURNALISM, United States

Cabinet NN Shelf 1 No. 9

Raymond, Henry J.,and The New York Press for thirty years. Progress of American journalism from 1840 to 1870. With portraits, illustrations, and appendix. By Augustus Maverick. Hartford, Conn. 1870.

Cloth; 9 7/8 x 6 x 1 5/8 in.

JOURNALISM, United States.

Cabinet NN Shelf 2 No. 3

Prentice, George Dennison: A memorial address delivered before the legislature of Kentucky, on Wednesday, Feb., 2, 1870. By Henry Watterson.

G.D. Prentice established and edited the Louisville Journal.

Bound with other items in "Journalists and Journalism", item 3.

JOURNALISM, United States

Cabinet NN Shelf 4 No. 28

"Public Ledger, The". Account of the proceedings connected with the opening June 2, 1867, of the Public Ledger Building, Philadelphia. Philadelphia: George W. Childs, 1868. Illus., portrait.

Cloth: 8¼x5-5/8x7/8"

JOURNALISM, United States.

Cabinet NN Shelf 2 No. 1

Raymond, Henry J., editor of the New York Daily Times, in The United States Magazine, Jan., 1857. Engraved portrait.

Bound with other items in "Journalists, various excerpts", item 15.

JOURNALISM, United States.

Cabinet NN Shelf 2 No. 8

Prentice, George D: A record of his life and work, by Junius Henri Browne, in Bedford's Magazine, Jan., 1891.

Bound with other items in "Various Editors", item 8.

JOURNALISM, United States.

Cabinet NN Shelf 2 No. 1

Pulitzer, Joseph - Master Journalist, by James Creelman, in Pearson's Magazine, March, 1909. Illus. from photographs.

Bound with other items in "Journalists, various excerpts", item 22.

JOURNALISM, United States.

Cabinet NN Shelf 2 No. 1

Raymond, Henry J., founder and editor of the Times: An account of his character and career, in the Living Age, July 17, 1869.

Bound with other items in "Journalists, various excerpts", item 4.

JOURNALISM, United States,

Cabinet NN Shelf 2 No. 6

Prentice, George D. and Kentucky thirty-five years ago, by James Freeman Clarke, in Old and New, June, 1870.

Bound with other items in "Biographies of Journalists", item 5.

JOURNALISM. United States

Cabinet NN Shelf 3 No. 31

Pulitzer, Joseph. Reminiscences of a secretary. By Alleyne Ireland. New York. 1914. With portraits.

Cloth: 8¼x5¼x1-1/8"

JOURNALISM, United States

Cabinet NN Shelf 2 No. 9

Recent tendencies in American Journalism. Article by E.V.Smalley. Excerpt from The Manhattan", April 1, 1884.

Item 14 in bound collection with binder's title "Newspapers, various excerpts".

JOURNALISM, United States,

Cabinet NN Shelf 2 No. 6

Reid, Whitelaw. An account of the career of the editor of The Tribune, in Scribner's Magazine, Aug., 1874.

Bound with other items in "Biographies of Journalists", item 3.

JOURNALISM, United States

Cabinet NN Shelf 6 No. 37

(Rhode Island) Providence Journal, half a century with. Being a record of the events and associates connected with the past fifty years of the life of Henry R. Davis, secretary of the company. Compiled and issued by The Journal Company, 1904. For private distribution. Illus.

Cloth; 9¾ x 6¾ x 1-1/8 in.

JOURNALISM, United States,

Cabinet NN Shelf 2 No. 10

Rochester Advertiser: The first daily newspaper in the West, and the first telegraph line between the Atlantic and the Mississipi Valley. An excerpt from the Historical Magazine, Jan., 1907.

Bound in collection "Description of various Newspapers", item 11.

JOURNALISM. United States

Cabinet NN Shelf 1 No. 22

Reid, Whitelaw, the life of. By Royal Cortissoz. New York, 1921. (2 Vols.) Illus.

Cloth; 9 1/8 x 6¼ in.

2 Vols.

JOURNALISM, United States

Cabinet NN Shelf 6 No. 36

(Rhode Island) Providence Journal, 1820 - 1870, semi - centennial of. January 3, 1870. Providence. By William E. Richmond.
Together with "Providence fifty years ago". (By Edwin E. Stone)

Half morocco; 10 x 6-1/8 x ¼ in.

JOURNALISM, United States

Cabinet NN Shelf 2 No. 8

Rosenwaters and the (Nebraska) "Bee": an account of the founder of the Omaha Bee.
Excerpt from the American Review of Reviews, June, 1896.

Item 30 in volume with binder's title "Various Editors".

JOURNALISM, United States

Cabinet NN Shelf 2 No. 12

Religious journalism in England and America. Article by Herbert W. Horwell. Excerpt from the "Forum", July, 1901.

Item 5 in bound collection with binder's title "Various newspapers and periodicals".

JOURNALISM, United States.

Cabinet NN Shelf 2 No. 1

Rice, Allen Thorndike, editor of North American Review: In memoriam, by William H. Ridenig, In North American Review, June, 1889.

Bound with other items in "Journalism various excerpts," item 14.

JOURNALISM, United States

Cabinet OO Shelf 6 No. 58

Sacramento Bee. James McClatchy Edition, 1857-1903.
Has portrait of McClatchy, the founder of the "Bee", pictures of the buildings and offices, brief biographies of editors, list of Sacramento newspapers, with dates of foundings, etc.

Cloth; 17-3/8 x 12½ in.

JOURNALISM, United States.

Cabinet R Shelf 4 No. 57

Reminiscences of printers, authors and booksellers in New York. By John W. Francis.
Excerpt from The International Magazine, March, 1852; pp. 253-266.

Bound half morocco; 9½ x 6¼ in.

JOURNALISM, United States

Cabinet NN Shelf 2 No. 8

Ridder, Herman: Necrology, in the Journal of the American-Irish Historical Society, July, 1916. This item includes an account of the editor's connection with the Katholisches Volksblatt, The Catholic News and the New Yorker Staats-Zeitung. Halftone portrait.

Bound with other items in "Various editors", item 5.

JOURNALISM, United States

Cabinet NN Shelf 2 No. 9

San Antonio Express, and contemporary journalism. Excerpt from The Editorial Review, April, 1912.

Item 12 in boumd collection with binder's title "Newspapers, various excerpts".

JOURNALISM, United States

Cabinet NN Shelf 1 No. 1

Reminiscences of the last sixty-five years. By E.S. Thomas, formerly editor of the Charleston (S.C.) City Gazette, and lately of the Cincinnati Daily Evening Post. In two volumes, Hartford. Printed by Case, Tiffany and Burnham, 1840.

Cloth; 8¼ x 5-1/8 in.

2 Vols.

JOURNALISM, United States

Cabinet NN Shelf 5 No. 11

Ripley, George. By Octavius Brooks Frothingham. Fourth edition. American men of letters [Series], edited by Charles Dudley Warner. Boston, 1884. Frontispiece.

Cloth; 7-1/8 x 4-5/8 x 1-1/8 in.

JOURNALISM, United States

Cabinet NN Shelf 6 No. 24

Scrap Book containing clippings from newspapers (1866-1869). Contemporary opinions concerning editors and their papers, with accounts of the beginning of newspapers, history of printing, type making, etc.

Items pasted over New York Board of Health Report for 1866.

Leatherette; 9¾ x 6¼ in.

JOURNALISM, United States

Cabinet NN Shelf 2 No. 9

Reminiscences of the New York Evening Post. By William C. Bryant, 1851.

Bound with other items in vol. with binder's title "Newspapers, various excerpts", item 11

JOURNALISM, United States

Cabinet NN Shelf 2 No. 13

Rise of Metropolitan Journalism, The. 1800-1840 by Charles H. Levermore: An excerpt from The American Historical Review, April, 1901: Briefly outlines the modern journalistic spirit, and its influence on all political parties.

Bound with other items in "Various newspapers and periodicals," vol. 1, item 40.

JOURNALISM, United States

Cabinet NN Shelf 6 No. 25

Scrap Book of clippings from newspapers, 1867-68., relating to journalism, journalists, newspapers. Many references to Horace Greeley

Clippings pasted over a school report.

Boards; 9 x 6 in.

JOURNALISM, United States

Cabinet NN Shelf 7 No. 23

Scripps - Howard buys the "World". Feb. 27, 1931. Consolidation of Morning, Evening and Sunday New York World and New York World as "New York World - Telegram", six day, evening newspaper. Price $5,000,000.
Articles in Editor and Publisher, The Fourth Estate. New York, Feb. 28, and March 7, 1931.

In board folder; 14 x 11 in.

JOURNALISM, United States.

Cabinet NN Shelf 2 No. 1

Seven super-pens, in Everybody's, March, 1916: Brief biographical sketches of the editors of The Emporia (Kansas) Gazette, The Atlanta Constitution, New York World, New York Evening Journal, San Francisco Bulletin, and The Birmingham News, Portraits.

Bound with other items in "Journalists, various excerpts," item 40.

JOURNALISM, United States

Cabinet KK Shelf 6 No. 22

South Carolina Press.

see
ASSOCIATIONS, NEWSPAPERS. South Carolina State Press Association...

JOURNALISM, United States

Cabinet OO Shelf 3 No. 51

Scripps-Howard interests buy New York World. Pulitzer Morning, Evening and Sunday newspapers absorbed by New York Telegram. March, 1931.
Excerpts from newspapers giving all the details of the transaction. With portraits.

Item in envelope.

JOURNALISM, United States

Cabinet NN Shelf 2 No. 16

Significance of the newspaper in the U.S. By Wm. Morton Fullerton.
Excerpt from the New Review, June, 1915.

Item 24 in vol. with binder's title; "Journalism: Pamphlets. Bound, 1932".

JOURNALISM, United States see

Cabinet OO Shelf 3 No. 56

SPECIMEN BOOKS, TYPES (Newspapers).

JOURNALISM, United States

Cabinet OO Shelf 3 No. 51

Scripps-Howard News (Sept.,1929). Special edition. The story of Scripps-Howard. A study in personality and achievement.

Booklet, with other items in manila envelope.

JOURNALISM, United States.

Cabinet NN Shelf 2 No. 1

Smith, Roswell, by Washington Gladden and others, in The Century Magazine, June, 1892: Brief account of the life and part played by R. Smith in establishing The Century and St. Nicholas' Magazine.

Bound with other items in "Journalists, various excerpts," item 36.

JOURNALISM, United States.

Cabinet R Shelf 3 No. 101 2 vols.

Specimens of newspaper literature. With personal memoirs, anecdotes, and reminiscences. By J. T. Buckingham. Boston, 1852. 2 Vols.
Vol. I: Biography of Isaiah Thomas, with portrait.
Vol.II: Biography of Benj. Russell, with portrait.
Very reliable history of printers, printing and newspapers in Massachusetts.

Cloth; 7-3/4 x 5 in.

JOURNALISM, United States

Cabinet OO Shelf 6 No. 46

Seaside Oracle, The. Vols. V-VI, 1873-1874. Published every Saturday. Joseph Wood, Editor, Wiscasset, Me.

Cloth; 17-7/8 x 13 x 1-1/8 in.

JOURNALISM, United States.

Cabinet NN Shelf 2 No. 13

Some aspects of pioneer California journalism. By J.M. Scanland. Excerpt from The Bookman May 1906. Illus.

Bound with other items in "Various newspapers and periodicals. Excerpts from magazines". item 24.

JOURNALISM, United States.

Cabinet S Shelf 4 No. 3 2 Vols.

Specimens of newspaper literature: With personal memoirs, anecdotes and reminiscences. By Joseph T. Buckingham. Boston, 1850. Second Edition 1852 (2 Vols.) Illus., portrait of I. Thomas, specimens, etc.
Historical, literary, and biographical of the earliest American printers.

Cloth; 8-1/8 x 5 in. See also S/4/4.

JOURNALISM, United States

Cabinet NN Shelf 1 No. 10

Seaton, William Winston of the "National Intelligencer". A biographical sketch with passing notices of his associates and friends. Boston, 1871.

Cloth; 7-3/4 x 5¼ x 1-1/8 in.

JOURNALISM, United States

Cabinet 00 Shelf 6 No. 53

South Carolina, 1731-1903.

see
NEWSPAPERS, ANNIVERSARY ISSUES. News and Courier (The), Charlestown, S.C.

JOURNALISM, United States

Cabinet NN Shelf 2 No. 8

Steedman, Maj. Gen. James B. Oration at the unveiling of the monument to. By Gen. John C. Smith. At Toledo, Ohio, May 26, 1887. Pamphlet.
Steedman worked as printer on several newspapers.

Item 7 in Vol. "Various Editors. Excerpts and Pamphlets".

JOURNALISM, United States

Cabinet NN Shelf 2 No. 18

Senate documents, Feb., 26, 1880...in the case od Willaim Duane.

see
DUANE, WILLIAM. Senate documents...

JOURNALISM, United States

Cabinet NN Shelf 6 No. 38

(South Carolina) Newspaper press of Charleston, S. C. A chronological and biographical history embracing a period of 140 years. By William L. King. Charleston, S. C. 1882.

Cloth; 7-5/8 x 4¾ x 5/8 in.

JOURNALISM, United States

Cabinet NN Shelf 1 No. 16

Stillman, William James. Autobiography of a journalist. In two volumes. Boston and New York. Houghton, Mifflin & Company, 1901.

Portrait frontispiece, each volume.

Cloth; 8-3/4 x 6-1/8 in.

JOURNALISM, United States

Cabinet NN Shelf 1 No. 21

Stone, Melville E. M.E.S. His Book ... New York, 1918.

See STONE, MELVILLE E. M.E.S. His Book ...

JOURNALISM, United States

Cabinet KK Shelf 6 No. 23

Tennessee Press Association. Annual reports for years, 1890, 1891, 1895.

3 pieces) Business meetings, historical
3 titles) biographical sketches. With portraits.

Items in envelope.

JOURNALISM, United States,

Cabinet NN Shelf 2 No. 8

Those Kansas Editors, by Charles Moreau Harger, in The Independent, Feb. 24, 1910: A brief summary of the editorial interests of five Kansas editors. Halftone portraits.

Bound with other items in "Various Editors", item 20.

JOURNALISM, United States

Cabinet NN Shelf 2 No. 24

Streeter, Gilbert L. An account of the newspapers and periodicals published in Salem, from 1768 to 1856. Salem, 1856.

Half morocco; 9 x 5½ in.

JOURNALISM, United States,

Cabinet NN Shelf 2 No. 13

Tennessean and American, The, (Nashville), in the Editorial Review, Dec., 1910: A brief historical sketch of the successful career of this newspaper, founded 1812.

Bound with other items in "Various newspapers and periodicals," vol.1, item 17.

JOURNALISM, United States.

Cabinet NN Shelf 2 No. 12

Times (The) Sketch of the history and growth of a newspaper of prominence ... Excerpt from the Editorial Review, Oct., 1909.

Item 9 in volume "Various newspapers and periodicals."

JOURNALISM, United States

Cabinet OO Shelf 3 No. 30

Sun, The [New York] Eleventh annual outing and games of the Sun Employees' Pleasure Association. Sunday, Aug. 13, 1913. Edited by Dudley Pollard.

Program of the event. Includes poetry of printing, and other journalistic items.

Boards, 12 x 8 in.

JOURNALISM, United States

Cabinet KK Shelf 6 No. 24

Texas Press Association. Annual reports for years, 1894, 1895.

2 pieces) Business meetings, historical
2 titles) biographical notes, etc.

Items in envelope.

JOURNALISM, United States.

Cabinet NN Shelf 2 No. 1

Tragedy of Hearst, The. by Robert L. Duffus, in Worlds' Work, Oct., 1922. Illus.

Bound with other items in "Journalists, various excerpts," item 45.

JOURNALISM, United States

Cabinet NN Shelf 4 No. 23

"Sun" New York. Farewell dinner to the old "Sun" building. July 11, 1915. Second edition. Illus., portraits, etc.

Essays and poetry by several "Sun" associates.

Half morocco: 10½x6¾"

JOURNALISM, United States

Cabinet NN Shelf 6 No. 39

Texas Press Association, history of the. By F. B. Baillio.

To which is added A history of the early newspaper press of Texas. By the late Judge A. B. Norton...Dallas, Texas, 1916.

Cloth; 8¾ x 5-7/8 x 1 in.

JOURNALISM, United States.

Cabinet S Shelf 5 No. 21

Transition period of the American Press: Leading editors early in this century, by Benjamin Ellis Martin, in Magazine of American History 1887. Illus.

Bound with other items in "Excerpts relating to printing in America." pp. 61-83.

JOURNALISM, United States

Cabinet NN Shelf 4 No. 24

"Sun", story of the. New York, 1833-1918. By Frank M. O'Brien, with an introduction by Edward Page Mitchell, editor of "The Sun" New York. Illus. and facs.

Cloth: 8¾x5¾x1-7/8

JOURNALISM, United States

Cabinet Shelf No.

Texas Press, History of.

See BULLEN, HENRY LEWIS. History of the Texas Press.

JOURNALISM, United States

Cabinet NN Shelf 2 No. 6

Transition period of the American Press. Leading editors early in this century. By Benjamin Ellis Martin.

Excerpt from Magazine of American History, April, 1887. Illus.

Item 9 in bound collection "Biographies of Journalists".

JOURNALISM, United States

Cabinet NN Shelf 5 No. 13

Taylor, Bayard. By Albert H. Smyth. American men of letters. Edited by Charles Dudley Warner. Boston and New York, 1896. Frontispiece.

Cloth; 7 x 4-5/8 x 1 in.

JOURNALISM, United States,

Cabinet S Shelf 5 No. 6

Thomas, Isaiah, The Patriot Printer, by Frank R. Bechelder; in the New England Magazine, Nov., 1901. Illus.

Bound with other items in "Various Printers and their Plants", item 12, vol. 2.

JOURNALISM, United States

Cabinet NN Shelf 2 No. 15

Transition period of the American Press: Leading editors early in this century. By Benjamin Ellis Martin.

Excerpt from the Magazine of American History, vol.xvii, April, 1887, No.4. With portraits and facsimiles.

Item 1 in vol. with binder's title: "Early American Newspapers--Excerpts. Bound 1919".

JOURNALISM, United States, .

Cabinet NN Shelf 2 No. 13

Troy Times, The, in the Editorial Review Oct., 1910: A brief historical sketch of the successful career of this newspaper, founded 1851.

Bound with other items in "Various newspapers and periodicals", Vol. 1, item 16.

JOURNALISM, United States

Cabinet NN Shelf 2 No. 6

Vigorous politician of the olden time, A. Colonel Matthew Lyon, by John Gilmer Speed, in Harpers', Apr., 1894.

Bound with other items in "Biographies of Journalists", item 8.

JOURNALISM, United States

Cabinet NN Shelf 2 No. 6

Watterson, Henry, the last of the personal journalists. By Jas. M. Rogers. Excerpt from Booklovers Magazine, March, 1905. With portraits.

Item 11 in bound collection "Biographies of Journalists".

JOURNALISM, United States

Cabinet NN Shelf 4 No. 42

Twenty years in a newspaper office.

By Fred W. Allsop. Consisting principally of random sketches of things seen, heard and experienced on the "Arkansas Gazette".

Illustrated. Little Rock, Ark. 1907

Cloth: 8x5¼"

JOURNALISM, United States.

Cabinet NN Shelf 2 No. 8

Virginia Editor, The, by a Virginian, in Harper's. Dec. 1856: A description of an average Virginian editor's appearance and character.

Bound with other items in "Various Editors", item 10.

JOURNALISM, United States

Cabinet NN Shelf 2 No. 20

Webb, James Watson, editor, 1829, the New York Courier and Enquirer. Brief biographical sketch. Published by the N.Y. and Hartford Publishing Co., 41 Park Row (Times Bldg.) New York, n.d. circa 1870.

Has brief notices of contemporary journalistic activities.

Half morocco; 10½ x 8-3/8 in.

JOURNALISM, United States,

Cabinet S Shelf 5 No. 6

(A) Typographic Galaxy [Connecticut newspaper publishers, 1709-1893]. By Marcus A. Casey. Excerpt from The Connecticut Quarterly, No. I, 1896.

Bound in collection "Various printers and their plants; excerpts from magazines", vol. 2, 1918. Item 19.

JOURNALISM, United States

Cabinet NN Shelf 2 No. 8

Wall, Caleb Arnold, (of the Worcester Spy) with the Worcester County Press. 1837 - 1887. Proceedings at the semi - centennial anniversary. Worcester, Mass., 1887. Pamphlet.

Item 11 in Vol. "Various Editors. Excerpts and Pamphlets"

JOURNALISM, United States

Cabinet NN Shelf 5 No. 12

Webster, Noah. By Horace E. Scudder. Boston, 1885. With portrait. Biography

Cloth; 7-1/8 x 4¾ x 1 in.

JOURNALISM, United States

Cabinet NN Shelf 6 No. 50

Ups and downs of a country editor. Mostly downs. By S. A. Fackler. n. p. n. d. Illus.

Paper; 9 x 5¾ x 3/8 in.

JOURNALISM, United States

Cabinet NN Shelf 1 No. 12

"Warrington" pen-portraits. A collection of personal and political reminiscences from 1848 to 1876, from the writings of William S. Robinson. Boston. Edited and published by Mrs. W.S.Robinson. 1877.

Portrait frontispiece.

Cloth; 8¼ x 6 x 1 3/8 in.

JOURNALISM. United States

Cabinet NN Shelf 1 No. 13

Weed, Thurlow, the life of.

Vol. I: Autobiography of Thurlow Weed. Edited by his daughter, Harriet A. Weed, Boston, 1883.
Vol.II: Memoir of Thurlow Weed. By his grandson, Thurlow Weed Barnes, Boston, 1884.

With portraits, steel engravings.
Cloth; 9½ x 6¼ in.

JOURNALISM, United States

Cabinet NN Shelf 5 No. 4

Vermont Autograph and Remarker. Huntington, Vermont, May 31, 1861. Edited and pen made by James Johns. pp. 4, each page 4-1/8 x 6-1/8 in.

Paper boards; 6¾ x 4¼ in.

JOURNALISM, UNITED STATES

Cabinet NN Shelf 2 No. 4

Washington News. By Ben Perley Poore. Excerpt from Harper's New Monthly Magazine, Jan., 1874. A brief account of some of the early Washington newspaper correspondents; with notes on the newspapers with which they were connected. Illus.

Item 5 in vol. "Journalists and their work".

JOURNALISM, United States

Cabinet NN Shelf 2 No. 1

Weed, Thurlow, 1797. Printer-journalist and a self-made man. By T. P. Thorpe. Excerpt from Appleton's Journal, New York, Aug. 8, 1874. Portrait.

Item 43 in vol. "Journalists. Various excerpts

JOURNALISM, United States

Cabinet NN Shelf 2 No. 8

(Vermont) Rev. Samuel Williams. A famous editor of a hundred years ago. By Mason A. Green. Excerpt from the New England Magazine, June, 1895. Portrait.

Item 21 in vol. Various Editors. Excerpts and Pamphlets".

JOURNALISM, United States

Cabinet NN Shelf 2 No. 7

Washington Post, The. Contemporary journalism. (History of this newspaper established in 1877)

Excerpt from the Editorial Review, Aug., 1910.

Item 21 in bound collection "Journalism. Excerpts, etc."

JOURNALISM, United States,

Cabinet R Shelf 3 No. 170

(Western New York). History of the press of Western New York, together with proceedings of the printers' festival, held on the 141st anniversary of the birthday of Franklin, by Frederick Follett. Rochester, 1847.

Cloth; 9½ x 6 in.

JOURNALISM, United States.

Cabinet NN Shelf 2 No. 1

Which? William R. Hearst, Democratic candidate, Charles E. Hughes, Republican candidate: character studies, in the Outlook, Oct. 20, 1906.

Bound with other items in "Journalists, various excerpts", item 25.

JOURNALISM. United States

Cabinet NN Shelf 1 No. 17

Wise, Isaac M. Reminiscences. Translated from the German and edited with an introduction by David Philipson. Cincinnati, 1901. Portraits.

Cloth, stamped; 8 3/8 x 5 7/8 x 1 3/8 in.

JOURNALISM, College

Cabinet NN Shelf 2 No. 7

College literature and journalism. By Cleveland F. Bacon.
Excerpt from the Critic, July, 1900. Illus.

Item 19 in bound collection "Journalism. Excerpts, etc."

JOURNALISM. United States

Cabinet NN Shelf 1 No. 15

Wilkie, Franc B. ("Polinto") Personal reminiscences of thirty-five years of journalism. Chicago (1891)

Cloth; 8 x 5½ x 1-1/8 in.

JOURNALISM, United States

Cabinet NN Shelf 5 No. 3

"World, The", its history and its new home. The Pulitzer Building, New York City, 1860 - 1890. Illus., portrait.

Half morocco; 5-7/8 x 8¾ in.

JOURNALISM, College

Cabinet NN Shelf 2 No. 8

Harvard editors (4): Edward S. Martin, Ellery Sedgwick, F.H. Simonds and Mark Sullivan.
Excerpt from the Harvard Graduate Magazine, Dec., 1916.

Item 23 in volume with binder's title: "Various Editors".

JOURNALISM, United States

Cabinet NN Shelf 6 No. 49

Williams, David Rogerson [Editor Charlston, S.C. 1801], the life and legacy of. By Harvey Toliver Cook, New York, 1916. Portrait frontspiece.

Cloth; 9½ x 6¼ x 1¼ in.

JOURNALISM, United States

Cabinet NN Shelf 4 No. 49

Worcester County Press, proceedings at the semi-centennial anniversary of the connection of Caleb Arnold Wall (of the Worcester Spy), May 18, 1887. Worcester, 1887.

Brochure in manila envelope

JOURNALISM, COLLEGE — Example of

Cabinet NN Shelf 7 No. 1

Harvard Lampoon. Cambridge (Mass.) December 11, 1885.
One issue only.

Bound in vol. with binder's title "American Comic Papers", 1857 - 1891.

JOURNALISM, United States

Cabinet NN Shelf 1 No. 11

Winans, William H. Reminiscences and experiences in the life of an editor. Newark, N.J. 1875.

JOURNALISM, United States

Cabinet Shelf No.

See also

I - NEWSPAPERS
II - " Anniversary Issues.
III - PERIODICALS.

JOURNALISM, COLLEGE

Cabinet NN Shelf 2 No. 12

(History and growth of) College journalism. By C.F. Thwing.
Excerpt from Scribners, Oct., 1878.

Item 12 in vol. with binder's title "Various Newspapers and Periodicals".

JOURNALISM, United States

Cabinet KK Shelf 6 No. 25

Wisconsin Editorial Association, annual reports for years, 1885, 1872, 1894.

3 pieces) Business, historical, biographical
3 titles) sketches, etc.

Items in manila envelope.

JOURNALISM, Agricultural (see)

Cabinet Shelf No.

AGRICULTURAL JOURNALISM

JOURNALISM, College.

Cabinet NN Shelf 2 No. 12

Student periodicals at Columbia, 1813-1911, by Isadore Gilbert Mudge, Sept.1911.

Bound with other items in "Various newspapers and periodicals", item 22.

JOURNALISM. United States

Cabinet NN Shelf 1 No. 18

Wise, Isaac Mayer. The founder of American Judaism. A biography. By Max B. May. Illustrated. New York, 1916.

Cloth; 6 3/8 x 6 in.

JOURNALISM, Amateur (see)

Cabinet Shelf No.

AMATEUR JOURNALISM
also AMATEUR NEWSPAPERS
AMATEUR PRINTING

JOURNALISM, COMIC — Example of

Cabinet NN Shelf 7 No. 1

Chatter: Weekly newspaper conducted by Julian Ralph. Price 5 cents.

One issue only; Vol. I, No. 18, May 14, 1890.

Bound in vol. with binder's title "American Comic Papers", 1857 - 1891.

JOURNALISM, COMIC Example of

Cabinet NN Shelf 7 No. 1

"Dubuque Grit". To the interest of the farmers and workingmen. Vol. I, No. I, Jan. 3, 1891. Dubuque, Iowa. Illus.

One issue only, bound in vol. with binder's title "American Comic Papers", 1857 - 1891.

JOURNALISM, COMIC Examples of

Cabinet NN Shelf 7 No. 1

Merryman's Monthly. J. C. Haney & Co., Publishers, New York.
Two issues; Sept. n. d.-Nov. 1864.

Bound in vol. with binder's title "American Comic Papers", 1857 - 1891.

JOURNALISM, COMIC Examples of

Cabinet NN Shelf 7 No. 1

Nick - Nax. Levinson and Haney, Publishers, N. Y. Miscellaneous numbers, Aug. 1858 to Feb. 1869.

Bound in vol. with binder's title "American Comic Papers", 1857 - 1891.

JOURNALISM, COMIC Example of

Cabinet NN Shelf 7 No. 1

"Racket". Published by The Racket Publishing Company. New York City. Andrew Miller, Manager. - James S. Metcalf, Editor.
One issue only; No. 11, May 17, 1890.

Bound in vol. with binder's title "American Comic Papers", 1857 - 1891.

JOURNALISM, COMIC Example of

Cabinet NN Shelf 7 No. 1

Yankee Notions. Miscellaneous numbers. Vols. 5 to 17. n. d. Probably, 1860 - 89. New York.
First published by T. W. Strong, 98 Nassau Str., later; The American News Company, 121 Nassau Str.

Bound in vol. with binder's title: "American Comic Papers, 1857 - 1891.

JOURNALISM, COMIC. Example of

Cabinet NN Shelf 7 No. 1

"Yours Truly". Our illustrated quarterly. Five cents a copy. n. p., n. d.

Item bound in vol. with binder's title "American Comic Papers", 1857 - 1891.

JOURNALISM, Comic (see)

Cabinet Shelf No.

JOURNALISM, Humorous

JOURNALISM, Curious

Cabinet S Shelf 5 No. 21

Newspaper Curiosities. An excerpt in Harper's New Monthly Magazine, Sept. 1867.
Descriptive historical account.

Bound with other items in Excerpts relating to printing in America". pp. 116-124.

JOURNALISM, GERMAN - AMERICAN

Cabinet NN Shelf 6 No. 29

New - Yorker Staats - Zeitung: An epitome of sixty - five years (1834 - 1899) of progress. A success unprecedented in the history of American publications printed in foreign languages. New York, 1922. Illus.

Half morocco; $9\frac{1}{4}$ x 6 in.

JOURNALISM, Humorous

Cabinet NN Shelf 2 No. 7

America, the comic paper in. By William H. Shelton
Excerpt from The Critic, Sept., 1901. Illus.

Item 25 in bound collection "Journalism. Excerpts, etc."

JOURNALISM, Humorous

Cabinet NN Shelf 2 No. 16

American comic journalism. By Brander Matthews.
Excerpt from the Bookman, Nov., 1918.

Item 8 in vol. with binder's title: "Journalism: Pamphlets. Bound, 1932".

JOURNALISM, Humorous

Cabinet NN Shelf 2 No. 7

As we see ourselves: journalism and humor. By Benj. A. Heydrick.
Excerpt from the Chautaugan, March, 1912.
With portraits, Lyman Abbot, Joseph Pulitzer, Henry Watterson, S. S. McClure, Norman Hapgood, etc.

Item 1 in bound collection "Journalism. Excerpts, etc."

JOURNALISM, Humorous

Cabinet NN Shelf 2 No. 12

Brief account of Comic Journalism, by C.D. Shanly, Atlantic, Feb., 1867.

Bound with other items in "Various newspapers periodicals", item 3.

JOURNALISM, Humorous

Cabinet NN Shelf 2 No. 2

Browne, Charles Farrar (Artemus Ward), at Cleveland, by C.C. Ruthrauff, Scribner's magazine, Oct., 1878: Brief account of the editor's career, with some specimens of his journalistic repartee.

Bound with other items in "Journalists and Journalism", item 11.

JOURNALISM, Humorous

Cabinet NN Shelf 2 No. 14

Cockney's Calender, The. By Douglas Story.
"Punch"- The famous men who have been its editors and cartoonists.
(Excerpt from Munsey's, dec., 1902. Illus.

Item 10 in bound collection with binder's title "Periodicals, various excerpts".

JOURNALISM, HUMOROUS

Cabinet NN Shelf 2 No. 2.02

Funny paper, the real mission of the. By Ernest Brennecke. [Excerpt from the Century, March, 1924].

Item 11 in vol. with binder's title "Journalists and Journalism -- III. Pamphlets".

JOURNALISM, Humorous

Cabinet NN Shelf 2 No. 13

German comic paper, the "Fliegende Blatter". Article by William D. Ellwanger and Charles M. Robinson. Excerpt from"TheCentury Magazine July, 1894.

Item 10 in volume with binder's title "Various newspapers and periodicals"-1

JOURNALISM, Humorous

Cabinet NN Shelf 2 No. 10

How your Sunday smile is made. By Wm. Haynes.
(Excerpt from Van Norden, Feb., 1909)

Item 9 in bound collection with binder's title "Description of various newspapers".

JOURNALISM, Humorous

Cabinet NN Shelf 2 No. 7

Humor of the colored supplement. By Ralph Bergengren.
Excerpt from The Atlantic, Aug.,1906.

Item 14 in bound collection "Journalism. Excerpts, etc."

JOURNALISM, Humorous

Cabinet Shelf No.

Ward, Artemus (Charles F. Browne).

See BROWNE, CHARLES FARRAR. (pseud. Artemus Ward).

JOURNALISM, ILLUSTRATED

Cabinet J Shelf 5 No. 21 also 22

Figaro-Salon. 1887. Paris.

See WOLFF, ALBERT. Figaro-Salon, 1887...

JOURNALISM, Humorous

Cabinet NN Shelf 2 No. 1

Mitchell, John Ames, By Edward S. Martin, in The Book Buyer, April 1, 1896: A brief account of the founder and editor of "Life." Portrait, half tone.

Bound with other items in "Journalists, various excerpts", item 12.

JOURNALISM, Illustrated

Cabinet NN Shelf 7 No. 1

American comic papers, 1857 - 1891.

The following: Yankee Notions. - Nick - Nax. - Merryman's. - The Harvard Lampoon. - Racket. - Chatter. - Dubuque Grit. - Yours Truly.

Bound in vol. with binder's title "American Comic Papers", 1857 - 1891.

JOURNALISM, ILLUSTRATED

Cabinet 00 Shelf 6 No. 57

Frank Leslie's Illustrated Newspaper, No. I, Vol. I, Dec. 15, 1855, New York.

Cloth; 16 x 11 in.

JOURNALISM, Humorous

Cabinet NN Shelf 2 No. 14

Paper of all sorts. Excerpt from "Harper's", March, 1858.
Brief biographical sketches of the men who indirectly or indirectly were influential in the development of comic literature and comic illustration.

Item 22a in bound collection with binder's title "Periodicals, various excerpts".

JOURNALISM, Illustrated

Cabinet NN Shelf 1 No. 3

Artemus Ward, his book. With many comic illustrations. New York, 1862.

Cloth; 7½ x 5 x 1 in.

JOURNALISM, Illustrated

Cabinet 00 Shelf 3 No. 39

Genesis of the illustrated press...

see
Chap. XX, p. 217, WARREN'S "JOURNALISM"...London, 1922.

JOURNALISM, Humorus

Cabinet NN Shelf 2 No. 12

"Punch, Mr". Some precursors and competitors. By Sir F. C. Burnard.
Excerpt from The Pall Mall Magazine, Jan-Feb., 1903. Illus.

Item 16 in vol. with binder's title "Various Newspapers and Periodicals".

JOURNALISM, ILLUSTRATED

Cabinet K Shelf 2 No. 35

Cartoon history of Abraham Lincoln. By Albert Shaw. New York, 1929. (2 vols.)

Cloth; 11 x 8¾ in.

JOURANLISM, ILLUSTRATED

Cabinet 00 Shelf 6 No. 3

Graphic illustrated newspaper, the. Vol. I, Dec. 1869 to June 1870. London.

Cloth; 16½ x 12¼ x 2 in.

JOURNALISM, Humorous

Cabinet NN Shelf 2 No. 14

"Punch". The origin of the London Punch. By "Fusbos".
(Excerpt from The Great Republic, July, 1859)

Item 24 in bound collection with binder's title "Periodicals, various excerpts".

JOURNALISM, ILLUSTRATED

Cabinet C Shelf 3 No. 13 to 26

(The) Daily Graphic: An illustrated evening newspaper, New York, March 4, 1873, vol.1, 1-21, to 1879.
First daily illustrated newspaper. Pictures made by photo-lithographic process, were printed a day or more in advance on one side of each signature. The other side of the signatures were completed on day of issue.

Half morocco; 20¾ x 14¼ in.

JOURNALISM, Illustrated

Cabinet NN Shelf 2 No. 10

How your Sunday smile is made. Article by Wadsworth Haynes. Excerpt from "Van Norden-The World Mirror", Feb.,1909.

Item 9 in bound collection with binder's title "Description of various newspapers".

JOURNALISM, Humorous

Cabinet NN Shelf 2 No. 13

"Punch London". By T. B. Fox.
Excerpt article from the Atlantic Monthly, Dec., 1858.

Item 1 in vol. with binder's thtle "Various Newspapers and Periodicals".

JOURNALISM, ILLUSTRATED

Cabinet J Shelf 3 No. 13

English newspapers and periodicals of the 'Sixties'. Historical account.

See WHITE, GLEESON. English illustration 'The Sixties'... pp.9-88.

JOURNALISM, ILLUSTRATED

Cabinet OC Shelf 6 No. 4 & 5

Illustrated London News. Coronation Number, 1911. Published at 172 Strand, W.C.
This copy has advertisements at front and back. No. 00/6/4 is a specially bound copy, without advertisements.

Boards; 16½ x 11-3/8 x ½ in.

JOURNALISM, ILLUSTRATED

Cabinet J Shelf 5 No. 17

Illustrated London News, The., gems of wood engravings from...

See CHATTO, WILLIAM A. Gems of wood engraving, from The Illustrated News...London, 1849.

JOURNALISM, ILLUSTRATED.

Cabinet I Shelf 3 No. 1

Newspaper art and artists. By Katherine Louise Smith. [Illus. excerpt from The Bookman, August, 1901].

Item 19 in vol. with binder's title:"Various Engravers and About Engravers."

JOURNALISM, Illustrated.

Cabinet I Shelf 3 No. 1

Newspaper illustrator's story, The. by Max de Lipman: An excerpt from Lippincott's Magazine, 1892. Illus.

Brief autobiographical account.

Item 3 in vol. with binder's title: "Various Engravers and About Engravers."

JOURNALISM, Illustrated

Cabinet NN Shelf 2 No. 9

Newspapers, illustrated: a new mania in journalism. From the Gentleman's Magazine. Excerpt from Living Age, Apr. 30, 1870.

Item 4 in vol. with binder's title "Newspapers, various excerpts"

JOURNALISM, Illustrated

Cabinet NN Shelf 2 No. 2

Pictorial Journalism, by V. Gribayedoff. In The Cosmopolitan Magazine, Aug., 1891: An attempt to trace the origin of daily newspaper illustration.

Bound with other items in "Journalism and Journalists", item 10.

JOURNALISM, ILLUSTRATED

Cabinet 00 Shelf 4 No. 6

Pictorial Press, The. Its origin and progress. By Mason Jackson. With 150 illustrations. London, 1885.

Cloth; 9 x 5-5/8 x 1¼ in.

JOURNALISM, Illustrated.

Cabinet NN Shelf 2 No. 10

Romance of press photography. Article by Walter T. Roberts. Excerpt from "The Strand Magazine", Nov., 1910.

Item 7 in bound collection with binder's title "Description of various newspapers".

JOURNALISM, Illustrated

Cabinet NN Shelf 2 No. 13

Weekly newspapers, illustrated. Article by J.M. Bulloch. Excerpt from "The Lamp", April, 1903.

Item 21 in volume with binder's title "Various newspapers and periodicals".

JOURNALISM, ILLUSTRATED (Great Britain)

Cabinet 00 Shelf 6 No. 7

Daily Mail, London. "News of the future", Jan. 1, 2000" issue. London, 1928.

Extra illustrated, printed on colored paper.

Buckram; 16½ x 12½ in.

JOURNALISM, ILLUSTRATED United States

Cabinet 00 Shelf 6 No. 43

Ballou's Pictorial Drawing-Room Companion, Boston, Jan. - June, 1857, Vol. 12.

Issue of Feb. 21, View of building with business signs of P. Low, bookbinder, John Andrews, wood engraver. April, 1857, p. 237, article "The Press". April, 1857, p. 263, Ballou's Publishing House. May 16, p. 317, article "Book Making".

Half morocco; 15-3/8 x 11¼ x 1¼ in.

JOURNALISM, ILLUSTRATED United States

Cabinet 00 Shelf 6 No. 41

Carpet-Bag, The. A literary journal; published weekly, for the amusement of its readers. Vol. I, 1851. Published by Wilder, Pickard & Co. Boston.

On p. 7 an announcement: "The new type...was cast at the foundry of Messrs. Hobart & Robbins in this city"...

Half morocco; 15¾ x 11¼ x 1½ in.

JOURNALISM, ILLUSTRATED United States

Cabinet 00 Shelf 6 No. 44

Harper's Weekly, a Journal of Civilization ~~of~~. The first volume, the year 1857. New York: Harper & Brothers, publishers.

Half morocco; 15¾ x 11½ x 2 in.

JOURNALISM, ILLUSTRATED United States

Cabinet 00 Shelf 6 No. 42

Illustrated News (Barnum & Beach's Paper). New York, Vol. 1, Jan. - July, 1853.

With engraved title page.

Half morocco; 15¾ x 11¼ x 1-1/8 in.

JOURNALISM, Negro.

Cabinet Shelf No.

Negro editors run weeklies upon distinctly high plane.

Article in The American Press, p. 34, July, 1931, vol. 49, No. 10.

JOURNALISM, Religious

Cabinet NN Shelf 2 No. 32

(The) Centennial of religious journalism. 2nd ed. By J. Pressley Barrett. Christian Publishing [illegible] Association, Dayton, Ohio, 1908. Illus.

Cloth; 8 x 5½ in.

JOURNALISM, Religious

Cabinet NN Shelf 7 No. 9

Christian Advocate, The, 1826 - 1926.

see CHRISTIAN ADVOCATE, THE. Centennial Number, 1826 - 1926.

JOURNALISM, Religious

Cabinet NN Shelf 5 No. 41

Christian Register, The. Boston, Mass., April 1821 to Aug. 9, 1822, Vol. I, Nos. I to 52. Printed by John Cotton, Jr. & Co.

Half calf; 19 x 12 in. Vol. lying flat on shelf.

JOURNALISM, Religions

Cabinet NN Shelf 7 No. 12

Herald of Gospel Liberty, 1808 - 1908. Portsmouth and Dayton, Ohio. Our Centennial.

No. I, 1808 is in facsimile.

Cloth; 12¾ x 8-7/8 in.

JOURNALISM, Religious

Cabinet NN Shelf 2 No. 8

Men who furnish the "Quarterlies", "Advocates", etc. Portraits with brief biographical notes.
Excerpt from the Ladies Repository, Jan., 1871.

Item 18 in volume with binder's title: "Various Editors".

JOURNALISM, Religious

Cabinet NN Shelf 2 No. 12

New York's first Catholic newspaper. By Thomas F. Meehan.
Excerpt from U.S. Catholic Historical Scoeity, Historical Records...vol.3, part 1, Jan., 1903.

Item 19 in vol. with binder's title "Various Newspapers and Periodicals".

JOURNALISM, RELIGIOUS

Cabinet NN Shelf 4 No. 50

Pieters, Albertus. Seven years of newspaper evangelism in Japan. Published under the auspices of the Association for the Promotion of Newspaper Evangelization. Kyobunkwan (Japan), 1919.

Pamphlet

In envelope.

JOURNALISM, Religious

Cabinet NN Shelf 2 No. 7

Pioneer efforts in Catholic journalism in the United States (1809-1840). By Paul J. Foik. Notre Dame.
Excerpt from the Catholic Historical Review, Oct., 1915.

Item 20 in bound collection "Journalism. Excerpts, etc."

JOURNALISM, Religious

Cabinet NN Shelf 2 No. 12

Pioneer efforts in Catholic journalism in the United States (1809-1840). By Poil J. Foik.
Excerpt from the Catholic Historical Review, Oct., 1915.

Item 8 in vol. with binder's title "Various Newspapers and Periodicals".

JOURNALISM, Religious

Cabinet NN Shelf 2 No. 12

Religious journalism in England and America. Article by Herbert W. Horwill. Excerpt from "The Forum", July, 1901.

Item 5 in bound collection with binder's title "Various papers and periodicals".

JOURNALISM, SCHOOLS OF.

Cabinet Shelf No.

High spots on the horizon: Concerning over production of graduates in journalism.

Article in the Publishers' Auxiliary, 67th year, No.2, Jan. 9, 1932, p.5.

JOURNALISM, SCHOOLS OF.

Cabinet Shelf No.

Missouri School of Journalism, University of, acquires three country weekly newspapers as fields of practise for its students.
Article in United States Publisher and Printer, vol. 9, Jan. 1931, p.18.

JOURNALISM, SCHOOLS OF

Cabinet NN Shelf 2 No. 4

Reid, Whitelaw. Schools of journalism, and the schemes of special instruction for it. Excerpt from Scribner's Magazine, June, 1872.

Item 7 in vol. "Journalists and their work".

JOURNALISM, Society

Cabinet NN Shelf 2 No. 12

Evolution of the Society Journal, by Mrs.Rogers, A.Pryor, Cosmopolitan, Sept., 1891.

Bound with other items in "Various newspapers and periodicals", item 11.

JOURNALISM, SOCIETY

Cabinet NN Shelf 7 No. 17

New York Mirror. A weekly journal...Vol. XII, 1834 - 1835.

A weekly founded in 1823 by Samuel Woodworth; it afterwards became the property of Geo. P. Morris and N. P. Willis.

Half Calf; $14\frac{1}{4}$ x $10\frac{1}{2}$ x $1\frac{1}{2}$ in.

JOURNALISM, Sunday (GUIDE CARD)

Cabinet Shelf No.

See Sunday Journalism.

JOURNALISM, Trade.

Cabinet NN Shelf 2 No. 14

Railroad trade journalism. Article by Frank Chapin Bray. Excerpt from the "Chatauqua", June, 1904.

Item 12 in bound collection with binder's title "Periodicals, various excerpts".

JOURNALISM, WOMEN'S

Cabinet NN Shelf 2 No. 13

Lowell Offering. By Harriet H. Robinson.
Excerpt from the New England Magazine, Dec., 1889.
(Historical account of a periodical of 1845, edited by women, with contributing articles by factory girls.

Item 25 in bound collection with binder's title "Various newspapers and periodicals", (1)

JOURNALISTS

Cabinet NN Shelf 3 No. 34

(Bibliography) Masters of American Journalism. By Julia Carson Stockett, White Plains, N.Y. and New York City. 1916.
"Bibliographies prepared by graduates of the Library School at the University of Wisconsin".

Bound with other items.

Half morocco; $7\frac{3}{4}$ x $5\frac{1}{4}$ in.

JOURNALISTS

Cabinet NN Shelf 3 No. 34

(Bibliography) Some great American newspaper editors. By Margaret Ely. White Plains, N.Y. and New York City. 1916.

Bibliographies prepared as graduation requirements at the Library School of the University of Wisconsin.

Bound with other items.

Half morocco; $7\frac{3}{4}$ x $5\frac{1}{4}$ in.

JOURNALISTS

Cabinet NN Shelf 3 No. 38

Fenton, Sagie Velle, co-editor on "The Logansport Times", Logansport, Indianapolis.

See FENTON, SAGIE VELLE. Some Verses, travel letters...Indianapolis. 1917.

JOURNALISTS

Cabinet NN Shelf 2 No. 15

Notable editors between 1776 and 1800. Influence of the early American press. By S. G. W. Benjamin.
Excerpt from American Magazine of History, Feb., 1887.

Item 6 in vol. with binder's title "Early American News[illegible]rs-Excerpts-Bound, 1919".

JOURNALISTS

Cabinet NN — [Washington newspaper correspondents, brief account of. With portraits].

Shelf 2 — Portraits as follows: Poore; Cobright; Simonton.

No. 4 — See JOURNALISM, United States. Washington News. By Ben Perley Poore.

JOURNALISTS

Cabinet — Women journalists.

Shelf — see WOMEN JOURNALISTS

No.

JOVIUS, PAULUS (Paolo Giovo)

Cabinet E — (Dell') Istorie di mons Paolo Giovo da Coma vescovo de nocera. Traddote per M. Lodovico Domenichi...[Printer mark]. In Venetia appresso Giorgio de Cavalli. 1564.

Shelf 1 — Part 2: La Selva de varia istoria de Carlo Passi ... e seconda parte delle istoria de Monsig Giovo. Venetia, appresso Giogio de' Cavalli 1562.

No. 43

Allusions to the history of printing on p. 381 of part I: p. 42 of part 2.

Parchment; 8¼ x 6 x 2 in.

JOVIUS, PAULUS

Cabinet E — Allusions to the history of printing on p. 381 of part I: p. 42 of part 2.

Shelf 1

No. 43 — Parchment; 8¼ x 6 x 2 in.

JOVIUS, PAULUS.

Cabinet 40 — Vitae duodecim vicecomitum Mediolani principum. Lutetia, Rob. Stephanus, 1549.

Shelf 1 — Has ten large wood-cuts signed by Geoffroy Tory; some initials and printers device also by Tory.

No. 27

Vellum; 10 x 6-7/8 x 7/8 in.

JOY, CHARLES A.

Cabinet RR — Paper, the manufacture of. By Professor Charles A. Joy.

Shelf 1 — Illustrated excerpt from Frank Leslie's Popular Monthly, Aug., 1877.

No. 25

Item 9 in vol. with binder's title "Various item on paper".

JOYE, GEORGE (otherwise Clerke, or Clarke)

Cabinet T — Bio-bibliographical note.

Shelf 2 — see DIBDIN'S "Typographical Antiquities" ...London, 1810-19, vol.iii, p.553

No. 6 [vol.3]

JOYNER, GEORGE

Cabinet T — Fine printing: Its inception, development, and practice. With twelve artistic supplements illustrating the tendency of fine work. London, 1895.

Shelf 4

No. 71

Morocco; gilt; 9-7/8 x 7½ x 1 in.

JOYNER, GEORGE (Compiler)

Cabinet MM — Practical printing; a handbook of the art of typography. The original work by John Southward...In 2 vols. London, The "Printers Register", 1911.

Shelf 3

No. 46 2 vols.

Cloth; 8¼ x 5¼ x 1½ in.

JOYNSON'S PAPER MILL

Cabinet X — See Paper Mills, Great Britain

Shelf 5

No. 3

JUCHOFF, RUDOLF

Cabinet X — (Printer and bookseller marks of the 15th century. The Netherlands, England, Spain, Bohemia, Moravia and Poland). Drucher und verlegerzeichen des XV jahrhunderts in den Nederlanden, England, Spanien...Munchen, 1927. Illus.

Shelf 3 — Bio-bibliographical description.

No. 52 — Stamped boards; 10¼ x 8-3/8 x ½ in.

JUCUNDUS (see)

Cabinet — FROELICH, JACOB

Shelf

No.

JUDD & GLASS

Cabinet MM — Counsels to authors, and hints to advertisers. London: Judd & Glass, Grays Inn Road, 1856.

Shelf 7 — With three engravings showing interior views of the composing room, press room, and bookbindery of the firm of Judd & Glass, printers.

No. 6

Cloth; 7-3/8 x 4-7/8 x ¼ in.

JUDEX (Matthaeus), pseud. (see)

Cabinet — RICHTER, MATTHIAS

Shelf

No.

JUDGE, ARTHUR W.

Cabinet L — Stereoscopic photography. Its application to science, industry and education.

Prospectus of book with title as above.

Shelf 1

No. 42

With other items in manila envelope

JUGG, RICHARD.

Cabinet 75 — London printer, 1547-1577. Bio-bibliographical brief account.

Shelf 2 — See Early Printing in England. Literature of. Printers and publishers of "The Birth of Mankind." p. 34.

No. 8

JUGGE, JOAN (widow of Richard)

Cabinet T — Books printed by Joan Jugge, London, 1579-80. Bibliographical notes.

Shelf 2 — see DIBDIN'S "Typographical Antiquities" ...London, 1810-19, vol.lV, p.268

No. 6 [vol.4]

JUGG, RICHARD

Cabinet T — Memoire of R. Jugg, with a list of books printed by him, 1547-1577

Shelf 2 — see AMES, JOSEPH and WM. HERBERT Typographical Antiquities...vol.2, pp. 713-729

No. 2

JUGGE, RICHARD and JOHN

Cabinet T Shelf 2 No. 6 [vol.4]

Books printed by the Jugge family. London, 1547-1577. Bibliographical notes.

see

DIBDIN'S "Typographical Antiquities" ...London, 1810-19, vol.lV, p.241

JUGOSLAVIA

Cabinet T Shelf 5 No. 135

(A) Short history of printing in Jugoslavia

See PEDDIE, R. A. Printing, a short history of the art...p.275

JUILLIOT, FRANCOIS

Cabinet V Shelf 3 No. 18

(Bio-bibliographical notes relating to Juilliot, printer and bookseller, Paris, 1606-1620.

see

WERDET, EDMOND. Histoire du livre en France...3me partie (2), p.150

JULIEN, STANISLAS

Cabinet V Shelf 5 No. 2

Documents sur l'Art d'Imprimer à l'aide de planches de bois, de planches en pierre, et de types mobiles, inventé en Chine, bien longtemps avant que l'Europe en fit usage; extrait des livres Chinois. Paris, 1847. Pamphlet, pp.16.

Bound in volume "Five French Typographical Items, 1809-1862."

JULLIEN, Inventor

Cabinet Shelf No.

See Exhibitions, Printing. Antwerp, 1884. Pictures and description of the two printing presses invented by M. Jullien.

JULLIERON, JEAN.

Cabinet 69 Shelf 1 No. 26

See Early Printing in France. Lyons, 1614. Jean Juillieron.

JUNGBLUT & COMPANY

Cabinet Shelf No.

See Specimen Books, Cuts. United States

JUNIUS, HADRIAN.

Cabinet 2 Shelf 1 No. 13

(History of Holland) Hadriani Iunii. Hornani, medici. Batavia: In qua praeter gentis & insulae antiquitatem originem, docora, mores...Printer Mark.

Imprint: Ex officina Plantiniana apud Franciscum Raphelengium, 1588.

In this book (pp.253-255) the claim was first advanced that the honor of the invention of printing belonged to Holland and not to Germany.

3/4 morocco; 8½ x 6-1/8 x 1¼ in.

JUNIUS, HADRIAN.

Cabinet Shelf No.

3/4 morocco; 8½ x 6-1/8 x 1¼ in.

JUNIUS, HADRIAN

Cabinet L Shelf 1 No. 46

Invention of printing, Junius's account of. Leyden, 1588.

See SINGER, SAMUEL WELLER. Researches into the history of playing cards...London, 1816, p.110.

JUNIUS, HADRIANUS

Cabinet Y Shelf 1 No. 23

(Notes and comments on the Junius contributions to the Coster legends.)

See LINDE, ANTONIOUS van der. Geschichte der erfindung der buchdruckkunst ...Berlin, 1886, vol.1, p.217. (see also vol.3 index of the above work)

JUNIUS, ADRIEN

Cabinet T Shelf 3 No. 2

Notice of Junius book of emblems; his documents respecting the art of printin.

in DIBDIN'S Bibliographical Decameron...London, 1817, vol.1, pp.271-2, 347, 362

JUNIUS, HADRIAN

Cabinet AA Shelf 3 No. 13

Scheltema, Jacobus De Geloofwaardigheid van Adrianus Junius gehandhaafd, ten opzigte van van zijne berigten aangaande de uitvinding en beoefening der boekdrukkunst te Haarlem; door Jacobus Scheltema. [Utrecht]. 1834.

Junius was the first writer (1588) to name Coster as the inventor of printing. See also DeVinne "The invention of printing". pp. 330-346.

Half morocco; 8-5/8 x 5¼ in.

JUNIUS, HADRIANUS

Cabinet T Shelf 1 No. 73

Testimony of Junius on the origin of printing.

See HODGKIN, JOHN ELIOT. "Rariora"... (1858-1900) London, vol.2, p.6.

JUNKER, CARL

Cabinet Y Shelf 5 No. 68

Jasper, Friedrich, a Vienna printer of the early 20th century. On his 80th birthday, Jan. 22, 1927. A contribution to the history of printing in Vienna) Ein Wiener buchdrucker um die wende des zwanzigsten jahrhunderts. Ein beitrag zu Wiens buchdruckergeschichte. Wien, 1927. Portrait frontispiece.

Paper; 11½ x 8-5/8 x 3/8 in.

JUNTA, Juan de

Cabinet X Shelf 3 No. 19

Bio-bibliographical sketch, with printer mark, Junta (Salamanca), 1526-1558.

see

HAEBLER, KONRAD. (Spanish and Portuguese printer marks...p.xiv

---

JUSSERAND, JEAN J.

Cabinet R Shelf 1 No. 3

Franklin, Benjamin: An oration by His Excellency, J. J. Jusserand. LL.D., the French Ambassador of the 158th commencement of the University of Pennsylvania, June 17, 1914.

Excerpt from "Old Penn Weekly Review" in volume "Frankliniana", p. 35.

JUSTIANUS

Cabinet 39 Shelf 1 No. 24

Corpus Juris Civilis...Addito textu Graeco... cum notis Dionsjii Gothofredi...Amstelodami, apud Joannem Blaeu, Ludovicum & Danielem Elzevirios, 1663. 2 vols. in one.

Calf; 16¼ x 10 x 4¼ ins. See Pieters, Annales Elzevirienne, p.221; Brunet 3, 608.

JUSTINIANUS

Cabinet E Shelf 1 No. 21

Digestorum seu Pandectarum libri quinquaginta ... Florentiae In officina Laurentii Torrentini Ducalis Typographi 1553 ...
See also E/1/25.

2 vols. Morocco; $16\frac{1}{2}$ x $10\frac{1}{2}$ x 3 in. Brunet 3, 615.

JUSTINIANUS

Cabinet E Shelf 4 No. 68

Sacratissimi principis institutionum libri quatuor ... Lugd. Batab. Apud Danillem Gaesbeeck. 1678.

Morocco; $5\frac{3}{4}$ x $3\frac{1}{4}$ x $\frac{3}{4}$ in.

JUTKINS, A. J.

Cabinet QQ Shelf 3 No. 34

Hand-book of prohibition. Chicago, 1884.

On p. 147, notice of R. W. Nelson's work as Secretary of the National Prohibition Home Protection Party, 1882-4. Portrait of Nelson on p. 136.

Cloth; 8 x $5\frac{1}{2}$ in.

JUVENALIS, DECIUS-JUNIUS

Cabinet E Shelf 3 No. 77

Satyrae. Parisiis, e typ. Regia, 1644.

Morocco; $14\frac{1}{2}$ x $10\frac{1}{2}$ x $1\frac{1}{4}$ in.

JUVENILE LITERATURE.

Cabinet Shelf No.

See CHILDRENS' BOOKS.

K

KABLE BROTHERS COMPANY

Cabinet NN — Mount Morris, Illinois, Kable Brothers Company, Publication Printers.

Shelf 2 — see PLANTS, PRINTING. United States. Kable Bros...

NO. 34.01

KACHELOFEN, KONRAD and JOHANNES

Cabinet 26 — See Early Printing in Germany, Literature of. Leipzig.

Shelf 1

No. 19

KACHELOFER, KONRAD

Cabinet Y — (Notes relating to the Kachelofer press and printing, Freiberg in Saxony, 1496)

Shelf 4 — see VOULLIÉME, ERNST. (Die) Deutschen drucker des fünfzehnten jahrhunderst...p.47

No. 4

KADE, EMIL.

Cabinet X — Vierte säcularfeier der buchdruckerkunst zu Leipzig am 24, 25, 26 Juni 1840. Eine Denkschrift im auftrage des Comité zur feier der erfindung der buchdruckerkunst. Leipzig, 1841.

Shelf 2

No. 32

Half morocco; 11 x 8-7/8 x ½ in.

Breitkopf and Härtel.

KAEMPFFERT, WALDEMAR

Cabinet RR — Discovering new facts about paper. The story of the greatest paper research laboratory. The first of a series issued by the American Writing Paper Company. Holyoke, Mass., 1920.

Shelf 1

No. 10

Paper boards; 14 x 10-3/4 in.

KAEMPFFERT, WALDEMAR

Cabinet PP — (The) Museum of Science and Industry founded by Julius Rosenwald. An institute to reveal the techinal ascent of man. By Waldemar Kaempfert, director. Reprinted from the Scientific Monthly of June, 1929. Illus.

Shelf 3

No. 48

Item in manila envelope

KAEPPELIN, D.

Cabinet V — Lithographie, chromo-lithographie, autographe, gravure sur pierre...Paris, 1874.

Shelf 5 — Descriptive illustrated essay in L'Art de peindre la parole...Par MM. Gobin, Jeunesse, Kaeppelin...Paris, 1874, pp.77-101.

No. 14

Paper; 9-7/8 x 6¼ in.

KAESTLIN, HERMANN

Cabinet Y — (Note on the Kaestlin press at Augsburg, 1479-1485)

Shelf 4 — see VOULLIÉME, ERNST. (Die) Deutschen drucker des fünfzehnten jahrhunderts...p.6

No. 4

KAESTNER, OTTO

Cabinet — Gravir-Anstalt. Otto Kaestner

Shelf

No. — See SPECIMEN BOOKS, BRASS TYPES. Germany. Kaestner, Otto...

See also SPECIMEN BOOKS, CUTS. Germany

KAHN, ALEXANDER NICHOLS

Cabinet C — (The) Printers' vade mecum. An indispensable desk book for printers...Copyright, 1906, by Alex. N. Kahn, New York, 1908.

Shelf 1

No. 22

Cloth; 14¾ x 18¼ in.

KAIS. u. KON. HOF-SCHRIFTGIESSEREI

Cabinet — See cards with following sub-heads:

Shelf

No.

I - SPECIMEN BOOKS, TYPES. Austria. K.K. Hof-und Staatsdruckerei.
II - SPECIMEN BOOKS, TYPES. Austria. Poppelbaum. K.K. Hof-und Staatsdruckerei.
III - IMPERIAL ROYAL PRINTING OFFICE. Vienna (Austria)
IV - IMPERIAL ROYAL TYPE FOUNDRY. (Vienna)

KAIS. u. KON. HOF-STAATSDRUCKEREI

Cabinet — (Vienna. Austria)

Shelf — See cards with following sub-heads:

No.

I - IMPERIAL ROYAL PRINTING OFFICE.
II - GOVERNMENT PRINTING OFFICES. Austria.

KAISER'S SÖHNE, L.

Cabinet EE Shelf 5 No. 74

Schuellpressen-Fabrik Mödling. vorm L. Kaiser's Söhne. Möbling bei Wien. n.d.

Illus. catalogues of printing presses. Includes views of the main factory at Mobling.

Items in manila envelope.

KALÁP, METHOD

Cabinet 26 Shelf 1 No. 17

(Die) Industrie-druckerei in Prag 1923-1927. (With specimens of type, book composition and book illustration).

Article, German text, in the Gutenberg-Gesellschaft Jahrbuch 1928. pp. 180-1, plates 43 to 50.

KALKHOFF COMPANY, Printers

Cabinet Shelf No.

See Plants, Printing. United States (New York City).

KALLIERGOS (Zacharias)

Cabinet X Shelf 3 No. 14

Bibliographical note, with printer mark, Kalliergos, Venice, 1499.

see KRISTELLER, Dr. Paul. Italienischen buchdrucker...p.78

KALLIERGES, ZACHARIAS.

Cabinet D Shelf 2 No. 48

Imprint, Venice, 1499.

See INCUNABULA. Etymologicum magnum graece ...

KAMLOOPS WAWA (The), Alphabet.

Cabinet S Shelf 5 No. 6

See Indian Shorthand writers of British Columbia, in the Pacific Magazine, Dec., 1906, by Lillian E. Zeh, illustrated.

Bound with other items in "Various printers and their plants," item 16, vol.2.

KAMLOOPS (B.C.) WAWA

Cabinet II Shelf 3 No. 47

Polyglot paper, printed in English, French and Chinook. Published by D. & J. Sadlier & Co., Montreal, Canada. 1895.

Includes a system of shorthand as the written language of the Chinooks.

Cloth; 7 x 4¾ x ½ in.

KAMPMANN, C.

Cabinet K Shelf 3 No. 10

(Die) Graphischen künste. von C. Kampmann. Mit zahlreichen abbildungen und beilagen. Dritte, vermehrte und verbesserte auflage. Leipzig, 1909. Illus.

Text book of reproduction methods; wood engraving, chemical processes, photo-mechanical process, etc.

Cloth; 6-1/8 x 4-1/8 in.

KANDLER, P.

Cabinet AA Shelf 1 No. 49

Antonio Turini, primo stampatore in Trieste nel 1625 ... Lettera di P. Kandler all consigliere municipale ... con documenti. Trieste, 1860. Pamphlet.

Documentary history of the first printer in Trieste.

Item 3 in volume "Four Italian Typographic Items."

Half morocco; 9¾ x 6½ in.

KANE, HOPE FRANCES

Cabinet R Shelf No. 2 3

Franklin, James Sr.(b.1696-d.1735), of Boston and Newport. With facs., and illus. of Franklin press.

Article in "The American Collector", Oct., 1926, vol.3, No.1, p.17

KANSAS

Cabinet NN Shelf 2 No. 16

Journalism and the Topeka Daily Capital.

see JOURNALISM. Experiment of a Christian Daily...

KANSAS

Cabinet R Shelf 4 No. 144

Mystery of the Meeker Press. By Kirke Mechem.

Article in Kansas Historical Quarterly, Vol. IV, No. 1, Feb., 1935, pp. 61 - 73, (This article clarifies the history of the first printing press used in Kansas, which was undoubtedly the press set up by the Baptist Shawnee Mission Press, set up by Jonathan Meeker in Feb., 1834. The Mission was in the suburbs of what is now Kansas City.)

Item in manila envelope.

KANSAS

Cabinet NN Shelf 6 No. 9

Newspapers, 1854 to 1916, history of.

see CONNELLEY, WILLIAM E. Kansas newspapers, history of...Topeka, 1916.

KANSAS

Cabinet NN Shelf 2 No. 34.01

Newspapers in Kansas: their politics, circulation, editors, etc.

Excerpt article from the N.Y. Herald, April 25, 1858.

With other items in manila envelope.

KANSAS.

Cabinet Shelf No.

Oklahoma editor has first Newspaper Press ever used in Kansas; taken there in 1833.

An article in The Publisher's Auxiliary 65th year, No. 45, Nov. 8. 1930.

KANSAS

Cabinet Shelf No.

University of Kansas

see UNIVERSITY OF KANSAS

KANSAS

See also under Newspapers.

EARLY PRINTING IN AMERICA (U.S.) Literature of. Kansas...

KANSAS CITY "STAR"

Cabinet NN Shelf 2 No. 8

Best newspaper in America.

see JOURNALISM. United States. (Missouri) The best newspaper...

KANSAS CITY STAR

Cabinet NN Shelf 4 No. 45

Nelson, William Rockhill.
The story of a man, a newspaper, and a city.
By members of the staff of the Kansas City Star.
Printed at the Riverside Press. Cambridge. 1915. Illus.

Cloth: 9x6"

KANSAS CITY STAR (The),
See also
Cabinet Newspapers, special issues.
Shelf
No.

KANSAS CITY TYPE FOUNDRY

Cabinet See Specimen Books, Types. United States
Shelf
No.

KANSAS CITY TYPE FOUNDRY, ELECTROTYPE & STEREOTYPE

Cabinet Shelf No.

See
Specimen Books, Types. United States
" also " " Cuts. " "

KANSAS EDITORIAL ASSOCIATION

Cabinet KK Shelf 5 No. 91

Annual reports for years 1893, 1899, 1902, 1904, 1905, 1906, 1907.

7 titles, 7 items.

In board holder; 9 x 6¼ in.

KANSAS EDITORIAL ASSOCIATION

Cabinet KK Shelf 5 No. 92

Annual reports for years 1908, 1909, 1919, 1920, 1921, 1922, 1923.

Also copy of the association house organ for February 1924.

In board holder; 9-1/8 x 6¼ in.

KANT, IMMANUEL

Cabinet Y Shelf 3 No. 22

(Bookmaking and public taste, Kant's opinion on). Ueber die buchmacherey. Zwey briefe an Herrn Friedrich Nicolai von Immanuel Kant, Königsburg, 1798.

Cloth; 7¼ x 4 x ¼ in.

KAPP, FRIEDRICH.

Cabinet 22 Shelf 1 No. 1

(German-Americen printing and publishing 1683-1872) Der Deutschamerikanische buchdruck und buchhandel im vorigen jahrhundert.

In "Archive für geschichte Deutschen buchhandels," vol. 1, 1878, pp. 56-77.

KARABACEK, JOSEPH von (see)

Cabinet Ritter von Karabacek
Shelf
No.

KARPINSKI, LOUIS C.

Cabinet S Shelf 3 No. 104

Colonial American arithmetics. By Louis C. Karpinski of the University of Michigan.
Bibliographical essay with list of arithmetics and arithmetical works published in America up to 1775.
P. 243 in volume, Wilberforce Eames ... A tribute to. Cambridge, 1924.

KARWEYSSE, JAKOB

Cabinet Y Shelf 4 No. 4

(Notes on the Karweysse 15th century press at Marienburg)

see
VOULLIÉME, ERNST (Die)
Deutschen drucker des fünfzehnten jahrhunderts...p.81

KASTELEIJN, P.J.

Cabinet RR Shelf 3 No. 3

Volledige beschreiving van alle konsten... Nagende stuk. De Papier-Maaker. Met plaaten. Te Dortrecht, 1792. Blussé.

This is the Dutch edition taken from the French of De La Lande.

Half morocco; 8½ x 5½ in.

KASTENBEIN, CHARLES (Inventor) see

Cabinet FF Shelf 6 No. 19

COMPOSING MACHINES. Kastenbein, Charles...

KAUP, W. J.

Cabinet FF Shelf 5 No. 8

Modern automatic type making methods: Refinement of machine design, unique method for determination of accuracy of matrix. The microscope a factor of machine installation. (Lynn Boyd Benton's Invention).
Excerpt from American Machinist, Dec. 16, 1909. Illus.

Cloth; 12 x 9 in.

KAUTZSCH, RUDOLF

Cabinet FF Shelf 4 No. 26

(Die) Enstehung der frakturschrift. von Rudulf Kautzsch. Mainz, 1922. Beilage... der Gutenberg-Gesellschaft. facs.

Boards; 8¾ x 5½ in.

KAUTZSCH, RUDOLF

Cabinet Y Shelf 5 No. 97

(Modern printing: Essays on printing in England, Denmark, Holland, America, and Germany) Die neue buchkunst: Studien im inland und ausland. Herausgegeben von Rudolf Kautzsch. Weimar, 1902.

Boards; 9-3/8 x 6½ x 7/8 in.

KAUTZSCH, RUDOLF

Cabinet Y Shelf 1 No. 92.02

Wandlungen in der schrift und in der kunst. Rede bei der jubelfeier Deutscher Schriftgiessereien in Frankfurt A.M, Dezember 1, Gesellschaft. Illus.
Kleinedruck 10.

With other items in manila envelope.

KAVMOR PLATEN PRESS

Cabinet EE Shelf 4 No. 3

(Prospectus. Illus.)

See AUTOMATIC PLATEN PRESS Co. (Prospectus)

KAY, JOHN

Cabinet RR — Paper, its history. By John Kay. London: Smith, Kay & Co., 1893.
Shelf 2
No. 37

Cloth; 7¼ x 5 x 3/8 in.

KEANE, WILLIAM LAWRENCE

Cabinet J — Japanese color prints. The famous artists of the popular school. By W.L. Keane. With reproductions of prints in the writer's possession [Excerpt from "The Century Magazine", Oct., 1912.]
Shelf 3
No. 31

Item in manila envelope.

KEARNEY, WILLIAM

Cabinet U — Bio-bibliographical note relating to Kearney, printer, Dublin, 1571.
Shelf 1
No. 111

see
McDIX, E.R. Dublin printing...p.23

KEELEY, JAMES (Editor)

Cabinet NN — Chicago Tribune.
Shelf 2
No. 2.01

See JOURNALISM. (A) Great newspaper [Chicago Tribune] and its owner...

KEIMER, S.

Cabinet X — London, 1715. Case of libel against S. Keimer, copy from the records.
Shelf 4
No. 73

see
LIBERTY OF PRINTING. Great Britain. Copies taken from the records....London, 1763, p.19

KEIMER, SAMUEL

Cabinet S — [Biographical sketch]. By Henry Simpson. From "Lives of eminent Philadelphians", Phila. 1859.
Shelf 5
No. 25.01

Pamphlet in box labelled "Colonial printing and printers. Miscellaneous items".

KEIMER, SAMUEL

Cabinet F — Independent Whig, Philadelphia, 1720.
Shelf 1
No. 71

One of the earliest Philadelphia publications, printed by Keimer, Franklin' old rival. It is a sort of a regular reprint of an English Serial publication.

Half calf; 8 x 6 in.

KEIMER, SAMUEL

Cabinet X — [Persecutions of S. Keimer, by whom B. Franklin was employed prior to 1728]. A brand plucked from the burning: Exemplified in the unparallel'd case of Samuel Keimer...London, 1718.
Autobiographical in content.
Shelf 4
No. 50

Half morocco; 6¼ x 4 x 3/8 in.

KEIMER, SAMUEL

Cabinet R — See Smith, Joseph. Short biographical notices of William Bradford ... and Samuel Keimer. London, 1891.
Shelf 5
No. 27

KEIMER, SAMUEL.
See also
Early Printing in Pennsylvania. Philadelphia, [v.d.]. Samuel Keimer.
also Imprints, United States.
" Biographies, Printers.

Cabinet
Shelf
No.

KELCHNER, ERNEST

Cabinet W — Catalogue de l'Officine des Elzevier (1628). Reproduction heliographique d'apres d'exemplaire de la bibliotheque de Frank-fort-sur-le-Mein. Avec une introduction par Ernesr Kelchner, Paris, 1880.
Shelf 5
No. 104

Parchment; 7½ x 5 in. Item in manila envelope

KELCHNER, Dr. ERNST

Cabinet Y — (Mainz Ecclesiastical Acts of 1480, printed on parchment) Der pergamentdruck der Agenda Ecclesiae Moguntinensis von 1480. Bibliographisch beschrieben. Frankfurt am Main, 1885. Facsimiles.
Shelf 3
No. 19

Half morocco; 10-5/8 x 7 x 3/8 in.

KELCHNER, Dr. ERNST

Cabinet Y — (The) Marienthal impressions, 1463-, now in the Municipal Library in Frankfurt a.M. A bibliographical study, with facsimiles). Die Marienthaler drucke der Stadt-Bibliothek ...Bibliographisch beschreiben. Mit funf facsimile-tafeln. Frankfurt a.M, 1883.
Shelf 5
No. 134

Half morocco; 14-7/8 x 11 x ½ in.

KELE, RICHARD

Cabinet T — Books printed by R. Kele, London, 1552. Bibliographical notes.
Shelf 2
No. 6 [vol.4]

see
DIBDIN'S "Typographical Antiquities" ...London, 1810 - 1819, vol.lV, p.302

KELLAM, LAWRENCE

Cabinet — See Early Printing in England. Doway, 1609-1610. Lawrence Kellam.
Shelf
No.

KELLER, HELEN

Cabinet II — Keller (Miss) celebrates a sight-giver, Louis Braille. Article by Miss Keller. Portrait of Helen Keller and Louis Braille
Shelf 6
No. 27

Excerpt from The New York Times Magazine, Nov. 17, 1929.

In envelope.

KELLER, JOHANN

Cabinet Y — (Note on the Keller press at Augsburg, 1478-1486)
Shelf 4
No. 4

see
VOULLIÉME, ERNST. (Die) Deutschen drucker des fünfzehnten jahrhunderts...p.5

KELLOG, Leonard.

Cabinet A — See Newspapers, New York State: Herald of the Times, printed by him.
Shelf 3
No. 11

Bound in with other newspapers; leaf 28.

KELLOGG, A.N.

Cabinet LL Shelf 4 No. 7

Kellogg's Auxiliary Hand-Book: containing a history of auxiliary printing; with opinions of publishers. And Day-Book and Journal combined: being a model system of keeping advertising accounts; together with various useful articles, tables, and calendars. Chicago: A.N. Kellogg, 1878.

Cloth; $9\frac{1}{4}$ x $6\frac{1}{4}$ in.

KELLOGG, A. N. NEWSPAPER COMPANY

Cabinet NN Shelf 6 No. 53

List 1919, family weekly newspapers of the better class. Kellogg's Lists. Established 1865. Chicago, New York.

Paper; $9\frac{1}{2}$ x 7-3/8 in.

KELLOG, ANDREW H.

See Imprints.

KELLOGG, CHARLES W.

Stack A Shelf 1&2 Number 72

Kellogg succeeds Henry Lewis Bullen: Brief biography in The Inland Printer, vol. Vol.LXXII, p. 488.

KELLOGG, R.S.

Cabinet RR Shelf 1 No. 24

Paper age, a. Illustrated excerpt from "American Forests", Dec., 1924.

Item in manila envelope.

KELLOGG and WESTERN LISTS (The) see

Cabinet Q Shelf 7 No. 2 and 4

DIRECTORIES, Newspapers. Western Newspaper Lists.

Also Western Newspaper Union...

KELLOGG'S AUXILIARY HAND-BOOK.

Cabinet LL Shelf 4 No. 7

...Containing a history of auxiliary printing; with opinions of publishers: And day-book and journal combined. Being a system of keeping advertising accounts. Chicago, 1878.

At end of book contemporary advertisements, type founders, ink makers, paper makers, advertising agency, etc.

Cloth; 9-3/8 x $6\frac{1}{4}$ x 5/8 in.

KELLOGG'S LISTS

See Advertising.

KELLS, BOOK OF

Cabinet PP Shelf 3 No. 12

Book of Kells, 7th century, description of.

See SAVAGE, ERNEST A. English libraries, old...London...Chicago, 1911. pp.14, 15, 16, 20.

KELLS, BOOK OF

Cabinet S Shelf 6 No. 9

Most beautiful book in the world. [Illus. description]. By Mary Denver Hoffman. Excerpt from "Scribner's", Oct., 1910.

Item 17 in vol. with binder's title "Early printing and printed books. Pamphlets. Bound, 1932.

KELLY, JAMES

Cabinet T Shelf 4 No. 52

Printers' Carnival and other poems. Airdrie, 1875. Glasgow.

This item is supposed to consist of the poetical effusions of a company of printers assembled at what is in the trade familiarly known as a "G.I." (or General Indulgence) to welcome the entry of an apprentice into manhood. B. & W.

Cloth; 6-3/4 x 4-3/8 x 7/8 in.

KELLY, WILLIAM J. (Editor, 1891 to end)

Cabinet 25 Shelf 2 No. 19 to 22

(The) American Art Printer, bi-monthly to April, 1890; monthly thereafter. C.E. Bartholomew, publisher, New York.

Vols. 1 to lV, 1887, to July, 1891.

Cloth, 14 X 11 in.

KELLY, WILLIAM J. (Editor)

Cabinet 25 Shelf 2 No. 18

American Model Printer, monthly. New York. Vol.1 (Oct. 1879) to (Nov., 1884)

Cloth, morocco back; 14 x 11 in.

KELLY, WM. J.

Cabinet MM Shelf 5 No. 56

Presswork. A practical handbook for the use of pressmen and their apprentices. Chicago, Ill. The Inland Printer Company. 1894.

Frontispiece portrait of the author.

Cloth; $7\frac{3}{4}$ x 5-3/8 x 3/8 in.

KELLY PRESS

Cabinet BB Shelf 3 No. 32

Circulars, pamphlets, and specimens. Salesman's portfolio. n.d.

Boards; $13\frac{1}{4}$ x 11 x 3/4 in.

KELLY'S DIRECTORIES, LTD.

Cabinet Shelf No.

Historical and descriptive article in British Printer, Vol. 45, No. 266, July-August, 1932. pp. 67, 68, 69-71. Illus.

KELLY'S DIRECTORY (see)

Cabinet Q Shelf 7 No. 29

DIRECTORIES, PRINTERS'. Kelly's Directory...

KELMAN, J.L.

Cabinet MM Shelf 6 No. 24

Simplex type computer, by inches or pica measures. Indispensable to the printer, compositor, and publisher. Published by J.L. Kelman, Chicago. 1908.

Cloth; $9\frac{1}{2}$ x 7-3/8 in.

KELMSCOTT PRESS, THE.

Cabinet See Bibliography. Chronological list of books printed at the Kelmscott Press...

Shelf

No.

KELMSCOTT PRESS

Cabinet 71 See Bibliography. Kelmscott and Doves Presses. Compiled by Robert Ernest Cowan...1921.

Shelf 2

No. 37

KELMSCOTT PRESS

Cabinet S Bibliography of the Kelmscott Press: Addendum to the publications published in "The Book Buyer" for Nov. 1895. By Ernest Dressel North.

Shelf 1 Item 9 in volume "Writings of Theodore Low DeVinne."

No. 33

Half morocco; 9¾ x 6-5/8 in.

KELMSCOTT PRESS

Cabinet T Facsimiles of initial letters, border, and types: the "Golden" type, the "Chaucer", and "Troy" types.

Shelf 4 See STEELE, ROBERT T. (The) Revival of printing...London, 1912. pp.13, 16, 19, 22.

No. 111

KELMSCOTT PRESS, THE

Cabinet M Kelmscott Press, The. William Morris, Kelmscott, 1896.

Shelf 5 Title: The Works of Geoffroy Chaucer.

No. 21 This is a specimen copy in special binding by Leighton.

Pigskin, tooled. In Cloth protective case. 17 x 11¼ x 2½ in.

KELMSCOTT PRESS, THE

Cabinet S Kelmscott Press work and other recent printing. By Charles F. Richardson. Excerpt from the "Bookman", Nov., 1896.

Shelf 6

No. 8

Item 12 in vol. with binder's title "Early printing and printers". Pamphlets".

KELMSCOTT PRESS, THE

Cabinet S (The) Kelmscott Press Work and other recent printing. By Charles F. Richardson. Excerpt from The Bookman, n. d.

Shelf 5

No. 4

Item 19 in collection "Various printers and their plants; excerpts from Magazines,I."

KELMSCOTT PRESS, THE

Cabinet S (The) Kelmscott Style. By Theodore Low DeVinne. Excerpt from The Bibliographier, Jan. 1902. Illus.

Shelf 5

No. 12

Item 23 in collection "Pamphlets and excerpts relating to various typographical matters."

KELMSCOTT PRESS

Cabinet U List (annotated) of all the books printed at the Kelmscott Press.

Shelf 3

No. 61

See SPARLING, H. HALLIDAY (The) Kelmscott Press and William Morris ...London, 1924, p.148

KELMSCOTT PRESS, THE

Cabinet S (The) New printing. By Albert Louis Cotton. Excerpt from The Contemporary Review, 1898.

Shelf 5

No. 9

Bound in collection "Various printers - excerpts and brochures", item 4.

KELMSCOTT, PRESS

Cabinet U (A) Note by William Morris on his aims in founding the Kelmscott Press, together with a short description of the Press by S. C. Cockerell, and an annotated list of the books printed thereat. London, March 4, 1898. Illus.

Shelf 3

No. 41 This was the last book printed at the Kelmscott Press.

Boards; 8-1/8 x 5-3/4 x 3/8 in.

KELMSCOTT PRESS, THE

Cabinet S Rinder, Frank. The Kelmscott Press. Excerpt from Book-Lover, Jan-Feb. 1902. With portrait of William Morris.

Shelf 6

No. 6

Item (n) in book with binder's title "Printing and printing offices".

KELMSCOTT PRESS

Cabinet U Summary list of the books issued from the Kelmscott Press.

Shelf 3 See FORMAN, H. BUXTON. Books of William Morris...Chicago, 1897. pp.155, 219-224.

No. 38

KELMSCOTT PRESS

See also

Cabinet Biographies, Printers: Morris, William. also Imprints, England.

Shelf

No.

KELOTYPE MACHINE (Mw. M. Kelly) see

Cabinet FF COMPOSING MACHINES (Single Types). Kelotype Machine...

Shelf 6

No. 69

"KELSO MAIL"

Cabinet U Facsimile, reduced, of first page, first issue. No.I, April 13, 1797.

Shelf 2 See "BALLANTYNE PRESS, THE". (The) Ballantyne Press and its founders, 1796-1908 ...p.4.

No. 63

KEMBLE, E.C.

Cabinet S See California, a history of California newspapers and the note "Explanatory" inserted opposite title page, in which the author's name is given.

Shelf 5

No. 41

KEMBLE, E. C.

Cabinet A History of California Newspapers. In Sacramento Daily Union, Dec. 25, 1858.

Shelf 3 This best of all early histories of newspapers in California occupies 33 columns of the Daily Union in nonpareil (6 pt.) types.

No. 52 At this writing (May 1931) only two copies of the above issue of the Daily Union are known to have survived - this one and one in the State Library in Sacramento.

KEMPEN, GOTTRFRIED & JOHANN von

Cabinet X Shelf 3 No. 20

Brief bio bibliographical notes, von Cologne, 1525-1660.

See HEITZ, PAUL. Kölner büchermarken...p. xxviii

KEMPEWERK NURNBERG

Cabinet EE Shelf 5 No. 75

(Catalogue printing presses and materials). Maschinenfabrik. Stereotypie, Chemigraphic, Galvanoplastik, Buchdruck...n.d. After 1883.

With prices.

Item in manila envelope.

KEMPIS (Thomas a)

Cabinet II Shelf 3 No. 8

Armenian printing of the works of Thomas A Kempis Printed at Amsterdam, 1696. (Armenische Drukkerey).

Morocco, gilt goffered; 4-7/8 x 3 x 1-1/8 in.

KEMPIS, THOMAS A.

Cabinet N Shelf 1 No. 15

Imitation de Jesus-Christ. Appendice a. Notice de Jules Janin...Histoire de l'orementation des manuscrits par Ferdinand Denis. L. Curmer, editeur; Lemercier, imprimeur-lithographe; J. Claye et L. Perrin, imprimeur-typographes. Paris, 1858. (2 Vols.)

Morocco, tooled, gilt, 11 x 7-1/8 in.

KEMPIS, THOMAS OF

Cabinet 2 Shelf 1 No. 31

Imitatione Christi de. Libri quatuor..... Antverpiae: Ex officina Plantiniana, apud Balthasarum & Ioannem Moretus. 1617.

Vellum; 5-7/8 x 3¼ x 1-3/4 in.

KEMPIS, THOMAS a

Cabinet AA Shelf 5 No. 32

Nelson, Axel: Richard de Bury och Thomas a Kempis By Axel Nelson. Uppsala, 1925.

Bio-bibliographical essay in Collijn's "Bok-och-biblioteks-historika studier ... pp. 59-70. [Swedish text].

Boards; 11 x 8½ x 2 in.

KENDELL, GEORGE WILKINS

Cabinet NN Shelf 1 No. 2.01

Journalist, war correspondent in Mexico, 1846-47.

see JOURNALISM. Kendell, George Wilkins....

KENNARD, JOSEPH SPENCER

Cabinet S Shelf 4 No. 13

(Some) Early printers and their colophons. By Joseph Spencer Kennard, Philadelphia, 1902.

Illuminated vellum; 9 x 5¾ in.

KENNARD, T.

Cabinet 80 Shelf 2 No. 28

Boston, 1810, imprint

See Periodicals, United States. Omnium Gatherum for April, 1810.

KENNEDY, HUGH A STUDDERT.

Cabinet 73 Shelf 1 No. 3

(The) Visitor: Of his coming and of his sojourning and concerning the manner of his going away. (A prospectus). Printed by John Henry Nash. San Francisco, 1930.

p. 16 in "John Henry Nash - His Work."

KENNEDY, HUGH A STUDDERT.

Cabinet 73 Shelf 2 No. 50

(The) Visitor: Of his coming and of his sojourning and concerning the manner of his going away. San Francisco. Printed by John Henry Nash, 1930.

Has printer mark on title page.

Marbled paper boards; 11¾ x 8-3/8 x ½ in.

KENNEDY, JAMES B.

Cabinet JJ Shelf 3 No. 23

Beneficial features of American Trade Unions. By James B. Kennedy. John Hopkins University Studies, series XXVI, Nos. 11-12. Baltimore, November - December, 1908.

Cloth; 9½ x 6 in.

KENNY, DANIEL J. (Comp.)

Cabinet NN Shelf 3 No. 6

American Newspaper Directory and Record of the Press - In the United States and British Provinces of North America. Also a concise general view of the origin, rise and progress of newspapers. New York. 1861.

Cloth: 7-5/8x5"

KENNY, JAMES

Cabinet Shelf No.

See Specimen Books, Cuts. United States.

KENT, H.W.

Cabinet Shelf No.

See Imprints, United States. Museum Press.

KENT, HENRY W.

Cabinet S Shelf 3 No. 104

Chez Moreau de St.-Méry, Philadelphie. Publications of Moreau de St.-Méry. By Henry W. Kent, Grolier Club, New York. With a list of Imprints enlarged by George Parker Winship.

Bio-bibliographical account.

P. 57 in volume, Wilberforce Eames ... A tribute. Cambridge, 1924.

KENT, HENRY W.

Cabinet PP Shelf 5 No. 20

Spencer Collection, The. Collection of modern book bindings. The New York Public Library, New York, 1914.

Descriptive catalogue, preceded by Mr. Kent's historical preface.

Half morocco; 10½ x 7½ x 3/8 in.

KENTUCKY.

Cabinet R Shelf 5 No. 93

See Early Printing in America, (Kentucky). Pioneer Press of Kentucky ... by W. H. Perrin.

KENTUCKY

Cabinet History of Kentucky journalism. By Victor B. Portmann.

Shelf

Article in The Publishers' Auxiliary, Oct. 27, 1934, p.7

No.

KENTUCKY GAZETTE, The

Cabinet S Bradford, John and the Kentucky Gazette, 1787.

Shelf 5

See Journalism, United States. Kentucky. Bradford, John...

No. 21

KENTUCKY GAZETTE

Cabinet NN Historical account of this newspaper established by John Bradford, 1787.

Shelf 2

No. 15

Item 5 in vol. with binder's "Early American Newspapers-Excerpts-Bound, 1919"

KENTUCKY PRESS ASSOCIATION see

Cabinet

ASSOCIATIONS, JOURNALISTS'

Shelf

No.

KENYON, F. G.

Cabinet S Bible came down to us, How the: By F. R. S Kenyon. An excerpt from Harpers Magazine, Nov., 1910. Illus.

Shelf 4

Item 6 in volume "About the Bible: Excerpts from Magazines."

No. 120

Half morocco; 10¼ x 6-7/8 in.

KENYON, SIR, FREDERIC.

Cabinet 75 Papyrus Book, The. Paper read before the Bibliographical Society, 15 March 1926.

Shelf 2

No. 7

In Trans. Biblio. Soc., "The Library," Vol. VII, 1926-1927. pp. 121-135.

KEPPEL, FREDERICK

Cabinet J Gentle art of resenting injuries. Being some unpublished correspondence addressed to the author of "The Gentle Art of Making Enemies". Privately printed and copyrighted. By Frederick Keppel, New York, 1904. Booklet.

Shelf 3

No. 21

Has authors signature.

Paper; 7-3/8 x 4½ in. Item in manila envelope

KEPPEL, FREDERICK

Cabinet J Golden age of engraving, the. A specialists story about fine prints. With 262 illustrations showing the progress of the art from the year 1465 to the year 1910. Third edition. New York, 1910.

Bibliography at end.

Shelf 3

No. 20

Cloth; 9½ x 6¾ in.

KEPPEL, FREDERICK

Cabinet J Golden age of engraving: An introductory essay on the old engravers. Reprinted by permission from Harpers Magazine. New York, 1878. Pamphlet.

Shelf 3

No. 21

Paper; 11 x 7¾ in. In manila envelope.

KEPPEL, FREDERICK

Cabinet K Golden age of engraving. By F. Keppel. Illus. excerpt from Harper's New Monthly Magazine. Aug., 1878.

Shelf 5

No. 1

Item 4 in vol. with binder's title "Wood Engraving, Etc."

KEPPEL, FREDERICK

Cabinet J Whistler, one day with. By Fred. Keppel. Reprinted from "The Reader" of January, 1904. Frederick Keppel & Co. New York, 1908. Booklet.

Shelf 3

No. 21

Paper; 5¾ x 3½ in. Item in manila envelope.

KERR, R. W.

Cabinet 62 History of the Government Printing Office, at Washington, D.C., with a brief record of the public printing for a century, 1789-1881. By R.W. Kerr, of the Government Printing Office. Illus. Lancaster, Pa., 1881.

Shelf 2

No. 24

Cloth; 9½ x 6 in.

KERR, ROBERT

Cabinet U Smellie, William: Memoirs of the life writings, and correspondence of W. Smellie, late printer in Edinburgh. Edinburgh, 1811. 2 vols.

Smellie was the original projector, editor and publisher of the Encyclopedia Britannica.

Shelf 2

No. 81

2 vols.

Calf, each vol., 8-5/8 x 5½ x 1-3/8 in.

KERROUX, L.G.F.

Cabinet I Translator of Blaerts..."Nieuwe manier om plaettekningen...Leiden, 1772.

Shelf 1

French translation from the Dutch. This edition has Dutch text with alternating French.

No. 29

Half morocco; 8¼ x 5 in.

KERSTEN, PAUL

Cabinet PP [Book binder, Berlin, circa 1870. Life and works of Paul Kersten]. Paul Kersten von Ernst Collin. Berlin, 1925.

Shelf 5

With portrait, and illus.

No. 21

Boards; 10 x 6½ x ½ in.

KERVER, JACQUES.

Cabinet 29 See Early Printing in France. Paris, 1561. Jacques Kerver.

Shelf 2

No. 13

KERVER, JACQUES

Cabinet X (Exclusive extension of ten year privileges granted to Kerver, to print Bibles and Missales, opposed by other Paris printers, 1573)

Shelf 4

No. 32

See LIBERTY OF PRINTING, Franc Arrests.(1573)...

KERVER, THIELMAN

Cabinet T Books printed by Kerver, with his device; Kerver first to introduce italic type in France; account of Missals printed by Kerver, etc.

Shelf 3

No. 2

In DIBDIN'S Bibliographical Decameron... London, 1817, vol.1, pp.92-3; vol.2, pp. 50-3

KERVER, THIELMAN

Cabinet 29 · Shelf · No.

See Early Printing in France. Paris, [v.d.] Thielman Kerver.

KESCHEDT, PETER

Cabinet X · Shelf 3 · No. 20

Brief bio-bibliographical note, Keschedt, printer, Cologne, 1593.

see

HEITZ, Paul. Kölner büchermarken.... p.xxxiii

KESSLER, NIKLAUS

Cabinet X · Shelf 3 · No. 15

Bio-bibliographical sketch, with printer mark, Kessler, Basel, 1488 --

see

HEITZ, PAUL. Basler büchermarken... pp.xvi, 6

KESSLER, NICOLAUS

Cabinet Y · Shelf 4 · No. 4

(Note on the Kessler press at Basel, 1485-1509)

see

VOULLIÉME, ERNST (Die) Deutschen drucker des fünfzehnten jahrhunderts...p.21

KESTLIN, HERMANN

Cabinet Y · Shelf 2 · No. 45

(Augsburg, 1481, book printed by Kestlin. Bibliographical note)

See METZGER, G. C. Augsburgs älteste druckdenkmale...Augsburg, 1840, p.58

KETTEL, T.P.

Cabinet RR · Shelf 4 · No. 39

Paper: its manufacture; materials, progress, inventions. Excerpt from "Eighty years progress of the United States". Hartford, 1869.

Item with other excerpts and pamphlets relating to paper. Folder; 10½ x 7½ x 1 in.

KEUFER, A.

Cabinet W · Shelf 1 · No. 109

Rapport du délégué de l'imprimerie a l'Exposition de Boston. [A. Keufer]. Paris, Imprimerie Nouvelle (Association Ouvrière). 1884.

Cloth; 9-7/8 x 6½ in. Bound in volume "Rapport sur l'imprimerie, Boston et Bruxelles, 1884-1885.

KEYBOARD FINGERING

Cabinet · Shelf · No.

See Linotype. Keyboard fingering.

KEYNES, GEOFFREY

Cabinet 75 · Shelf 2 · No. 3

Bibliography of William Blake, New York, 1921. A review of book with above title.

In Transactions of the Bibliographical Society, "The Library," Vol. III, 1922-23, pp. 58-61.

KEYNES, GEOFFREY

Cabinet U · Shelf 2 · No. 75

Pickering, William, publisher born 1796, died 1854. A memoir and hand-list of his editions. London, The Fleuron, 1924. Facsimiles.

See also U/2/73.

Cloth; 10¼ x 7-5/8 x 3/4 in.

KEYNES, GEOFFREY

Cabinet Q · Shelf 1 · No. 25

Pickering, William, publisher. A memoir and a hand-list of his editions. London: at the office of The Fleuron, 1924. Illus.

Cloth boards; 10¼ x 7¾ x 5/8 in/

KEYSER, MARTINUS DE

Cabinet 75 · Shelf 2 · No. 9

English books printed by him at Antwerp. 1528-35. Account of the.

See pp. 159-160, Transactions of the Bibliographical Society, "The Library," Vol. IX, 1928-29,

---

KEYSER, PIERRE DE ET ARNAUD

Cabinet W · Shelf 5 · No. 23

See Printing, Historical, Belgium. (Gand). Documents pour servir a l'histoire......par Aug. Voisin...Gand, 1840.

KEYSERE, ROBERT DE

Cabinet W · Shelf 4 · No. 127

L'Humaniste-imprimeur, Robert de Keysere, et sa soeur Clara, la miniaturiste, XV-XVI siècles, Par Victor Vander Haeghen. Gand, 1908. With one facsimile.

Half morocco; 9¼ x 6 in.

KEYSERER, PIERRE de

Cabinet W · Shelf 4 · No. 65

Imprimeur à Paris, de 1473-1479.

See Meersch, P.C. Van der : Recherches sur la vie et les travaux de quelques imprimeurs Belges ... Gand, 1844 - 46. pp. 121-169.

KEYSERER, PIERRE de

Cabinet W · Shelf 4 · No. 43

Recherches sur la vie et les travaux de Pierre de Keyserer, imprimeur a Paris, de 1473-1479. Par P. C. Van der Meersch. Gand, 1846.

Biographical and bibliographical account.

Half morocco; 9-7/8 x 6¼ in.

KEYSTONE PRINTING COMPANY OF PITTSBURG

Cabinet LL · Shelf 6 · No. 20

(A) Suggestion offered by the Keystone Printing Co. of Pittsburg. A plan for collective advertising in the general interest of the printing industry. Pittsburg 1916.

Item 17 in book with binder's title "Various items on printing shop practice". Bound 1919.

KEYSTONE TYPE FOUNDRY.

Cabinet EE · Shelf 4 · No. 82

Catalogue of printing material. Miscellaneous tools, machinery, bookbinders' supplies... n.d. Philadelphia, New York...

Paper; 12 x 9 x 3/8 in.

KEYSTONE TYPE FOUNDRY

Cabinet DD Shelf 2 No. 17

C.I.F. Price List, No. 5. Containing private code, instructions for ordering type, tools, material and machinery for printers. Philadelphia n.d. Pamphlet.

In folder marked Price Lists, Export. Keystone Type Foundry.

KEYSTONE TYPE FOUNDRY

Cabinet FF Shelf 3 No. 65

Circuit Court of the United States. Maine. Keystone Type Foundry vs. Portland Publishing Company. Pleadings and proofs. Portland, Maine, 1910.

Important type design suit.

Half morocco; 10¾ x 8-1/8 in.

KEYSTONE TYPE FOUNDRY (Agent)

Cabinet EE Shelf 4 No. 23

Cottrell Single Revolution Press. New Series Two Rollers. Manufactured by C.B. Cottrell & Sons Co. Westerly, R.I.

Pamphlets in manila envelope.

KEYSTONE TYPE FOUNDRY

Cabinet MM Shelf 6 No. 102

Useful information for the printer...Printed by and with the compliments of the Keystone Type Foundry. Philadelphia, etc., n.d. Booklet.

With other items in manila envelope.

KEYSTONE TYPE FOUNDRY

Cabinet Shelf NO.

See also

Specimen Books, Types. United States.

KEYSTONE TYPE FOUNDRY OF CALIFORNIA

Cabinet Shelf No.

See Specimen Books, Types. United States. Hawks & Shattuck, San Francisco, 1889.

KIDDER PRESS MFG. Co.

Cabinet EE Shelf 4 No. 83

Designers and builders of printers', box makers' and other machinery. Office and works, 24 to 34 Norfold Avenue. Boston, Mass. Sept. 1888.

Catalogue, illus., and price list of Kedder Presses.

Item in manila envelope.

KIDSON (or Kytson) JOHN

Cabinet T Shelf 2 No. 6 [vol.4]

Books printed by Kidson, London, circa 1558. Bibliographical notes.

see

DIBDIN'S "Typographical Antiquities" ...London, 1810-19, vol.1V, p.541

KIEFFER, CARL

Cabinet X Shelf 3 No. 13

Brief bio-bibliographical note, Kieffer. printer, Strassburg, 1587-1590.

see

HEITZ, PAUL. Elsässiche büchermarken...p.xxvi

KIKABHOY HURIVALUBHDAS & Son, SHAH

Cabinet Shelf NO.

See Specimen Books, Types. India.

KIMBERLY-CLARK CO.

Cabinet R Shelf 6 No. 14

See Paper Making, United States ... 1872-1922.

KIMBERLY-CLARK COMPANY

Cabinet MM Shelf 7 No. 41

Rotogravure, how and when to use it. Kimberly-Clerk Company. Neenah, Wisconsin, n.d. circa 1925.

Cloth; 11-5/8 x 8¾ x 3/8 in.

KINCHIUS, JOHANN

Cabinet Shelf No.

See Early Printing in Germany, Cologne, 1639.

KING, FRANCIS S.

Cabinet Shelf No.

See Biographies, engravers. King, Francis S.

KING, GEO. W. and SON.

Cabinet Shelf No.

See Imprints, United States. King, Geo. W. and Son. Worcester, Mass.

KING, HENRY

Cabinet NN Shelf 2 No. 7

American Press, The. By Henry King. (Historical account of the progress of newspapers in the U.S.)

Excerpt from The Chautaugan, Feb., 1896

Item 31 in bound collection "Journalism. Excerpts, etc."

KING, HORATIO

Cabinet S Shelf 5 No. 21

Boston newspaper of the Revolution, 1778. An account of the Independent Chronicle and the Universale Advertiser, printed by Powars and Willis. By Horatio King in Magazine of American History, 1887.

Bound with other items in "Excerpts relating to printing in America, pp. 103-107.

KING, JAMES

Cabinet NN Shelf 2 No. 3

Editor of the San Francisco Bulletin.

See JOURNALISM, United States. California. A full and authentic account of the murder of James King...

KING, MARIE WEST

Cabinet 71 Shelf 1 No. 18

Recipe for a happy life. Written by Margaret of Navarre in the year 15 hundred. Amplified by a compilation from the works of many writers ... Published by Paul Elder and Company ... and printed for them by their Tomoyé Press under the care of John Henry Nash. San Francisco, 1911.

Stamped paper boards; $8\frac{1}{4}$ x 7 x 3/8 in.

KING, MOSES

Cabinet G Shelf 5 No. 22

Views of New York, King's. 400 illustrations. Copyright 1905. By Moses King.

Printed cloth; $15\frac{3}{4}$ x 10 x 5/8 in.

KING, PRATHER

Cabinet S Shelf 5 No. 23

Mailing a newspaper. By Prather King. An excerpt from the Technical World, Mar. 1907. Illus.

Item 7a, in volume with binders title "Various items relating to printing." Bound, 1919.

KING, WILLIAM L.

Cabinet NN Shelf 6 No. 38

(The) Newspaper press of Charleston S. C. A chronological and biographical history embracing a period of 140 years. By William L. King. Charleston, S. C. 1882.

Cloth; 7-5/8 x $4\frac{3}{4}$ x 5/8 in.

KING, SELL & RAILTON

Cabinet EE Shelf 2 No. 48

See SPECIMEN BOOKS, TYPES. Printers'. Gr. Britain.

KING'S PRINTERS

Cabinet U Shelf 5 No. 49

Bio-bibliographical notes relating to the King's printers at York, early 17th century.

see DAVIES, ROBERT (A) Memoir of The York Press...1868, pp.38-55

KINGS' PRINTERS

Cabinet V Shelf 6 No. 38

France, 1558-1790.

see AUDIN, MARIUS. Causeries Typographiques No.11...

KINGS' PRINTERS (see also)

Cabinet Shelf No.

GOVERNMENT PRINTERS

GOVERNMENT PRINTING OFFICES

KING'S PRINTERS' PATENTS

Cabinet X Shelf 5 No. 53

Report from Select Committee of King's Printers' Patents: with the minutes of evidence, and evidence, and appendix. Ordered by The House of Commons to be printed. 8 August, 1832-1837

Half morocco; 14 x $8\frac{1}{2}$ in.

KING'S PRINTERS' PATENTS (see also)

Cabinet Shelf No.

GOVERNMENT PRINTING OFFICES

KINGSLEY, CHARLES

Cabinet L Shelf 4 No. 21

Glaucus; or wonders of the shore. Fourth edition corrected and enlarged; with coloured illustrations. Cambridge (England) 1858.

Printed by R. Clay. Bread Street Hill, London.

Cloth, gilt; 6-5/8 x $4\frac{3}{4}$ x $\frac{3}{4}$ in.

KINGSLEY, ELBRIDGE

Cabinet K Shelf 6 No. 39.01

American wood engraver, Elbridge Kingsley. With a portrait and two original wood engravings. Excerpt from Scribner's Magazine, July, 1895.

Items 17 and 19 in bound collection with binder's title ENGRAVERS AND WOOD ENGRAVERS

KINGSLEY, ELBRIDGE

Cabinet K Shelf 5 No. 3

Originality in wood engraving. With engravings by the author. Illus. excerpt from "The Century Magazine", Aug., 1889.

Item 6 in vol. labeled "Excerpts relating to engraving and engravers".

KINGSTON, JOHN

Cabinet T Shelf 2 No. 6 [vol.4]

Books printed by Kingston, London, 1553-1582. Bibliographical notes.

see DIBDIN'S "Typographical Antiquities" ...London, 1810-19, vol.IV, pp.463-484

KINGSTON CHRONICLE.

Cabinet Shelf No.

See Newspapers, New York State.

KINSLEY, A.W. & Co.

Cabinet Shelf No.

See Specimen Books, Types, United States, Franklin Letter-Foundry (A.W. Kinsley & Co.)

KINSLEY, APOLLOS

Cabinet 80 Shelf 2 No. 21

Printers' types, for making. A description of various machines and engines invented by Mr. Apollos Kinsley, now resident in the City of New York.

Article in The American Review and Literary Journal...Vol.I, No.I, Jan.-March, 1801, pp.127-8.

In manila envelope.

KINSLEY, APOLLOS

Cabinet Shelf No.

See also material from Newton C. Brainard in vertical file of biographical material.

KIRCHER, E. WILHELM GOTTL.

Cabinet LL Shelf 1 No. 16

Anweisung in der buchdruckerkunst so viel davon das drucken betrifft. Zum unterricht für drucker und ihre lehrlinge. Herausgegeben von E. Wihl. Gottl. Kircher, buchdrucker in Braunschweig und Goslar. Mit Kupfern und holzschnitten. Braunschweig, 1793.

Boards; 7¼ x 4-1/8 in.

KIRCHHEIM IM ELSASS

Cabinet Y Shelf 4 No. 4

(Notes relating to the 15th century Kirchheim press at Neu-Klein-Troyga, in Elsass.)

see

VOULLIÉME, ERNST. (Die) Deutschen drucker des fünfzehnten jahrhunderts...p.56

KIRGATE, THOMAS

Cabinet M Shelf 4 No.

See Imprints, England. Strawberry-Hill Press. Horace Walpole, 1781.

KIRGATE PRESS, THE

Cabinet S Shelf 4 No. 57

See Imprints, United States. Buddy, Lewis. The Kirgate Press.

KIRK, MR. (Engraver).

Cabinet 30 Shelf 1 No. 35

See Illustrated Books. [19th cent. In Library]. Bulmer, W. and Co., London, 1804.

"KIRKE, EDMUND" (see)

Cabinet Shelf No.

Gilmore, James R. ("Edmund Kirke")...

KIRKPATRICK, JOHN ERVIN

Cabinet NN Shelf 1 No. 20

Flint, Timothy. pioneer, missionary, author, editor, 1780-1840. The story of his life. Cleveland, Ohio, 1911. Illus.

Cloth; 9½ x 6-3/8 x 1½ in.

KIRSCHMANN, AUGUST

Cabinet FF Shelf 4 No. 18

Antiqua oder fraktur ? (Lateinishche oder schrift). Eine kritische studie. Monographien des Buchgewerbes. Band I. Leipzig, 1907.

Paper; 6½ x 4½ in.

KIRSCHMANN, AUGUST

Cabinet FF Shelf 4 No. 19

Antiqua oder Fraktur (Lateinische oder deutsche schrift). Eine kritische studie. Zweite umgearbeitete und erganzte auflage. "Monographien des Buchwerbes. I Band. Leipzig, 1912.

Half morocco; 6-5/8 x 4¾ in.

KISHORE PUBLISHING HOUSE, Lucknow, India.

Cabinet S Shelf 5 No. 6

See Native Publishing House in India (A). An account in Harpers Magazine, August 1887, by the Rev., John F. Hurst, D.D.

Bound with other items in "Various Printers and their Plants," item 13, vol.2.

KISLING, J. G.

Cabinet Y Shelf 5 No. 40

(History of the firm of Kisling in Osnabrück, 1709-1909) Geschichte der firma J. G. Kisling zu Osnabrück. Festschrift zur feier des 200 jahrigen bestehens der buchdruckerei. Illus. Onsabrück, 1909.

Limp cloth; 12¼ x 9½ in.

KISSEL, CLEMENS.

Cabinet K Shelf 4 No. 32

Symbolic bookplates. Twenty-five ex-libris. Designed and drawn by Clemens Kissel. Mayence. London, 1894. Printed in Germany.

Half morocco; 9½ x 7¼ x ½ in.

KISTLER, BARTHOLOMAEUS

Cabinet Y Shelf 4 No. 4

(Note on Kistler and his printing at Strasbourg, 1497)

see

VOULLIÉME, ERNST (Die) Deutschen drucker des fünfzehnten jahrhunderts...p.113

KITCHEN, GEORGE

Cabinet X Shelf 5 No. 115

L'Estrange, Sir Roger: a contribution to the history of the press in the 17th century. With 11 full-page plates. London: Kegan Paul, Etc., 1913.

Cloth; 8-3/4 x 5-3/4 in.

KITTREDGE, GEORGE LYMAN

Cabinet S Shelf 3 No. 104

(The) Ballad of Lovewell's fight. By George Lyman Kittredge of Harward University. Bibliographical account concerning the author [Joshua Coffin, 1792-1864] of the above song.

P. 93 in volume Wilberforce Eames ... A tribute to. Cambridge, 1924.

KITTREDGE, WILLIAM A.

Cabinet R Shelf 6 No. 13

(The) Lakeside Press announces that William A. Kittredge is now in charge of its Design and Typography. R. R. Donnelley and Sons Co. Chicago, 1922.

Half morocco; 16-1/8 x 10½ in.

KITTREDGE, W. A.

Cabinet Shelf No.

See also Imprints, United States. Kittredge, Oswald Press, New York. also Lakeside Press, The. R. R. Donnelley & Sons, Chicago, Ill.

KJAER, S.

Cabinet JJ Shelf 3 No. 41

Productivity of labor in newspaper printing. (Bulletin prepared by S. Kjaer for the United States Bureau of Labor Statistics, Bulletin No. 475, March, 1929. Washington, D. C. Illus.

Paper; 9-1/8 x 5-7/8 x ⅛ in.

KLEECK, MARY VAN

Cabinet PP, Shelf 4, No. 36

Women in the bookbinding trade. Introduction by Henry R. Seager. New York, Survey Associates, Inc. 1913. Illus.

Cloth; 8 x 5½ x 1 in.

KLEERKOOPER, M. M.

Cabinet AA, Shelf 4, No. 5, 2 vols.

(De) Boekhandel te Amsterdam voornamelijk in de 17e eeuw... s' Gravenhage, 1914-16. 2 vols.

Book publishing in Amsterdam in the 17th century, history of.

Half morocco; 9¼ x 6½ in.

KLEIDOGRAPH

Cabinet II, Shelf 6, No. 12

Illustrated description.

See PRINTING FOR THE BLIND. (The) Kleidograph...

KLEIN, HENRY OSCAR (Translator)

Cabinet L, Shelf 1, No. 36

Three colour photography...By Arthur Freiherrn von Hübl. Translated by Henry Oscar Klein. London, 1904.

Cloth; 8¾ x 5½ in.

KLEIN, KARL

Cabinet Y, Shelf 1, No. 16

Gutenberg den erfinder der buchdruckerkunst und kas im ersten druckhause aufgefundene fragment der erste druckerpresse. von Karl Klein. Mainz, 1857.

Discovery of the fragment of a press supposed to have belonged to Gutenberg.

Boards; 7-1/8 x 5 x 3/8 in. See also Y/1/15

KLEIN, FORST & BOHN

Cabinet EE, Shelf 5, No. 96

Maschinenfabrik Johannisberg. Geisenheim a. Rh. 1897.

See GOEBEL, THEODOR (Die) Maschinenfabrik Johannisberg....

KLEINWECHTER (V)

Cabinet X, Shelf 1, No. 36

Actus saecularis II in laudem typographiae.

[Printed in Wolf, "Monumenta Typographica" vol. I, pp. 1005-1014].

KLEMPERER, VICTOR Von

Cabinet 26, Shelf 1, No. 16

Bämler, Johann, der Augsburger drucker als rubrikator. [Essay, with facsimiles].

See the Gutenberg-Gesellschaft Jahrbuch, 1927, pp.50-52.

KLEMPERER, VICTOR von

Cabinet 26, Shelf 1, No. 19

Kachelofen, Konrad und Johannes. Illus. facsimiles and printer marks.

Bio-bibliographical account of two celebrated 15th century Leipzig printers.

Article in the "Gutenberg-Gesellschaft Jahrbuch" 1929, pp.134-151.

KLENZ, HEINRICH

Cabinet LL, Shelf 3, No. 53

Die deutsche druckersprache. Strassburg, 1900. (German printing terms).

At end of book, pp.115-128, poetry of printing.

Half morocco; 8¾ x 5½ in.

KLEPPNER, OTTO

Cabinet LL, Shelf 4, No. 36

Advertising procedure. By Otto Kleppner, Advertising Manager, Prentice-Hall, Inc. New York, 1925. Illus.

Cloth, 9¼ x 6¼ x 1½ in.

KLETTENBERG, JOH. ERAM. GEO. von

Cabinet X, Shelf 2, No. 14

See, Munden, D. Christian...Danck-Predigt, welche am dritten Jubel-Fest.

KLETZKER TYPELINE MACHINE (see)

Cabinet FF, Shelf 6, No. 75

COMPOSING MACHINES (Slug Lines) Kletzker...

KLEUKENS, CH. H.

Cabinet 26, Shelf 1, No. 20

Buchdrucker und buchfreund, ein heikles thema vorgetragen einer vereinigung von bücherfreunden im September 1929 zu Mainz.

A lecture: Printer and the friend of the book, a delicate subject.

Article in the "Gutenberg-Gesellschaft Jahrbuch" 1930, pp.347-351.

KLEUKENS, CH.H.

Cabinet Y, Shelf 1, No. 92.05

Handpresse (die). Drucke der Ernst Ludwig Presse zu Darmstadt., hergestellt Juni, 1927 durch Ch.H. Kleukens. [Illus. hand presses 15th to 19th centuries]

No.IV der kleinen Drucke der Gutenberg-Gesellschaft, Mainz.

Brochure, in manila envelope with other items.

KLEUKENS, F.W. (Type Designer)

Cabinet, Shelf, No.

See Specimens, Types. Germany. Kleukens, T.W.

KLEUKENS, FRIEDR. WILH.

Cabinet Y, Shelf 5, No. 104

(Ernst Ludwig Press, and the Kleukens Brothers.)

See WIHLISCH, ALBERT. (Die) Drucke der Ernst Ludwig Presse...

(KLIEN, WILLIAM L.)

Cabinet LL, Shelf 3, No. 21

Why we punctuate, or, reason versus rule in the use of marks. By a Journalist. St. Paul and Minneapolis, 1897.

Cloth; 7¾ x 5½ x ¾ in.

KLIETSCH, KARL

Cabinet J Shelf 2 No. 29

Erfinderder heliogravure und des rakeltiefdrukes. von Prof. Karl Albert. Mit 25 tafeln in dem von Klietsch erfundenen techniken herstellt. Wien, 1927.

Boards; 9-7/8 x 8 x ½ in.

KLIMSCH, KARL

Cabinet Q Shelf 7 No. 45

Adressbuch der buch und steindruckereien und der damit verwandten geschaftszweige in Deutschland, Oesterreich u. der Schweiz. 1876. Frankfurt a.M. Verlag von Klimsch & Co.

Bound in with "Das urheberrecht des Deutschen Reich. von A.W. Volkmann. (Concerning German copyright)

Half morocco; 9¾ x 6-3/8 in.

KLIMSCH and COMPANY

Cabinet EE Shelf 5 No. 76

[Catalogue and price list of ruling machines, "Universal" engraving machine, etc. machines invented by Karl and Charles Klimsch. Frankfort a.M.].

Item in manila envelope.

KLIMSCHE GRAPHISCHE BIBLIOTHEK

Cabinet FF Shelf 5 No. 66

Handbuch fur buchdrucker. von Friedrich Bauer. Klimsche Graphische Bibliothek. Bank IX. Frankfurt a. M. 1921. Illus.

Boards; 9½ x 6½ x 1-3/8 in.

KLINGER, JULIUS and ANKER, HANNS

Cabinet K Shelf 3 No. 23

(Die) Groteskilinie und ihre spiegelvariation im modernen ornament und in der decorationsmalerei. Herausgegeben von Julius Klinger und Hanns Anker. Berlin-Koln. n.d.

Consists of 64 plates of decorative motives, mostly printed in colors.

In portfolio, cloth; 6¾ x 8¾ in.

KLINGSPOR, GEBR. (SCHRIFTGIESSEREI)

Cabinet FF Shelf 5 No. 17

(Die) Schriftgiesserei in Schattenbild. Wie bei Gebr. Klingspor in Offenbach a. M. eine druckschrift insteht. Offenbach am Main, 1918.

A series of silhouettes cut by Rudolf Koch, showing how the Klingspors made type.

Oblong boards; 9-5/8 x 12½ in.

KLINGSPOR, GEBR.

Cabinet Shelf No.

See also Specimen Books, Types. Germany.

KLINKHARDT, JULIUS

Cabinet Shelf No.

See Specimen Books, Types. Germany

KLOBERG (CARL)

Cabinet Shelf No.

See Specimen Books, Types. Germany.

KLOPSCH, CHARLES M.

Cabinet NN Shelf 4 No. 44

Life work of Louis Klopsch. Romance of a modern knight of mercy. By Charles M. Pepper. With numerous illustrations. The Christian Herlad. New York. (1910).

Cloth: 9¼ x 6½"

KLUIT, W. P. SAUTIJN

Cabinet 00 Shelf 2 No. 29

Belasting op de nieuwspapieren (1674-1869). Nagelaten geschriften. (Overgenomen uit de Bijdragen tot de Geschiedenis van den Nederlandschen Boekhandel. dl.V) Amsterdam, 1895.

Together with: Nagelaten geschriften van W.P. Sautijn Kluit. Uitgeven door W.N. Du Rieu. Amsterdam, 1896.

Cloth; 9¼ x 6¼, pp.181, 284. Original covers bound in.

KLUIT, W.P. SAUTIJN (Editor)

Cabinet 00 Shelf 2 No. 28

(Early Holland newspapers. Collection of pamphlets bound in one volume. Each item devoted to historical bibliographical information relating to newspapers and periodicals in Holland. Amsterdam, 1872-1882.)

Half morocco; 9½ x 6½ in.

KLUIT, W. P. SAUTIJN, Editor

Cabinet Q Shelf 2 No. 31

Nieusbladen voor den boekhandel. Door W.P. Sautijn Kluit.

Bijdragen tot de geschiedenes van den nederlandschen boekhandel. 2e deel, Amsterdam: P.N. Van Kampen & Zoon, 1885.

Periodicals of bookselling.

Paper; 9 x 5-7/8 in.

KNAUFFT, ERNEST

Cabinet K Shelf 3 No. 13

Drawing for printers. A practical treatise on the art of design, and illustrating in connection with typography. Containing complete instruction...for the beginner as well as the most advanced student. By Ernest Knaufft. Chicago, 1899. Illus.

Cloth; 7½ x 5⅛ in.

KNEELAND, DANIEL and JOHN.

Cabinet F Shelf 1 No.

See Early Printing in New England. Boston, [v.d.] Daniel and John Kneeland.

KNEELAND, JOHN.

Cabinet F Shelf 1 No.

See Early Printing in New England. Boston, 1763: Daniel and John Kneeland.

See also Early Printing....1769, John Kneeland.

KNEELAND, SAMUEL

Cabinet Shelf No.

See Early Printing in New England. Boston, [v.d.]

KNEELAND, SAMUEL.

Cabinet F Shelf 1 No. 17

See Early Printing in New England. Boston, 1726: Bartholomew Green and Samuel Kneeland.

KNEELAND, SAMUEL

See also

Imprints, Green and Kneeland.

KNEELAND AND ADAMS

Cabinet 80 Shelf 1 No. 45

Printers, Boston, 1772 (Imprint)

See ALMANACS. Nathanael Low's Almanack, 1772...

KNER, EMERICH

Cabinet 26 Shelf 1 No. 19

(Hand composition and machine composition in book work) Handgemachtes buch und maschinenbuch.

Article in the "Gutenberg-Gesellschaft Jahrbuch" 1929, pp.221-237.

KNER, EMERICH

Cabinet 26 Shelf 1 No. 20

Kozma, Ludwig, als buchkunstler. Illus.

An appreciative account of the man and his work, Ludwig Kozma, Hungarian artist typographer.

Article in the "Gutenberg-Gesellschaft Jahrbuch" 1920, pp.298-327.

KNICKERBOCKER, OR, NEW YORK MONTHLY MAGAZINE

Cabinet 80 Shelf 2 No. 41

New York, 1833, Peabody & Co.

See Periodicals, United States, Knickerbacker, or...

KNICKERBOCKER PRESS, THE (G. B. Putnam's Sons)

Cabinet K Shelf 1 No. 26

Imprint of 1894

See Imprints, United States, Knickerbocker Press, The

KNICKERBOCKER PRESS, THE

Cabinet S Shelf 3 No. 46

Putnam, George P. & Sons. New Rochelle, New York. Illustrated and descriptive account of the Knickerbocker Press Printing and Bindery, New Rochelle, 1918.

Half morocco; 8-3/8 x 5½ in.

THE KNICKERBOCKER PRESS

See also

Printing Plants

KNICKERBOCKER TYPE FOUNDRY

Cabinet Shelf No.

See Specimen Books, Types. United States

KNIGHT, CHARLES

Cabinet Q Shelf 1 No. 1

Biographical sketch of Charles Knight, publisher. By Alexander Strahan.

Excerpt, with portrait from "Good Words", Sept.,1, 1867.

Item 16 in volume with binder's title "Publishing. Various Excerpts".

KNIGHT, CHARLES

Cabinet 17 Shelf 2 No. 4

Caxton, William, biography of the first English printer. London, 1844.

(The whole book as above, 240 pages, on fols. 48-67 of Henry Steven's TYPOGRAPHICAL MISCELLANIES, vol.4

KNIGHT, CHARLES

Cabinet J Shelf 3 No. 14

Color printer, Charles Knight as a. Points of resemblance between him and Baxter...

See LEWIS, COURTNEY. Story of picture printing in England during the 19th century ...pp.31-36.

KNIGHT, CHARLES.

Cabinet DC Shelf 2 No. 1

See Color Printing. Knight, Charles, London, 1791-1873.

KNIGHT, CHARLES

Cabinet T Shelf 5 No. 88

(The) Old printer and the modern press. London, 1854. Illus.

First part is a compact narrative of the state of knowledge before the invention of printing, and a personal biography of Caxton: The second part, the progress of the newspaper press up to 1854.

Stamped cloth; 7 x 4½ x 1 in.

KNIGHT, CHARLES (Printer-Publisher)

Cabinet 00 Shelf 5 No. 4

Passages from the life of Charles Knight. Boston: Estes & Lauriat, 1874. [Autobiography].

American edition, published with introduction by James Thorne after the death of Mr. Knight.

Cloth; 7½ x 5¾ x 1-3/8 in.

KNIGHT, CHARLES

Cabinet Q Shelf 1 No. 1

Passages of a working life during half a century. By Charles Knight, London, 1864.

Review of book with title as above. Exerpt from the "Eclectic", Dec., 1864.

Item 20 in volume with binder's title "Publishing. Various Excerpts".

KNIGHT, CHARLES

Cabinet S Shelf 5 No. 6

(The) Printer. Review of Chas. Knight's article with same title. In The London Magazine, n. d. circa, 1854.

Item 1 in collection "Various printers and their plants; excerpts from magazines," Vol. 2, 1918.

KNIGHT, CHARLES

Cabinet S Shelf 5 No. 18

(The) Printer's Devil. By Chas. Knight. In Magazine of Foreign Literature, reprinted from the Quarterly Review. March, 1840. Excerpt.

Bound with other items in "Dawn of Printing" item 4.

KNIGHT, CHARLES

Cabinet NN Shelf 7 No. 34

(The) "Printing Machine"; or companion to the library, and register of progressive knowledge. Vol. I, London 1834. Charles Knight [Publisher].

"Printing Machine", a literary publication, afterwards merged with the periodical "The Library of Useful Knowlege".

Cloth; $11\frac{3}{4}$ x $7\frac{1}{2}$ x $\frac{3}{4}$ in.

KNIGHT, CHARLES

Cabinet Q Shelf 3 No. 12

Shadows of the old booksellers. London, 1865.

Cloth; 8 x $5\frac{1}{4}$ in.

KNIGHT, CHARLES

Cabinet X Shelf 5 No. 42

(The) Struggles of a book against excessive taxation. London (1850).

Concerns cost of material and production.

Brochure.

KNIGHT, CHARLES

Cabinet T Shelf 2 No. 42

William Caxton, the first English printer. A biography. By Charles Knight. New edition. London, 1877. Frontispeice portrait. Illus.

Half morocco; 7-1/8 x 4-7/8 x 1 in.

KNIGHT,CHARLES.

Cabinet Shelf Nó.

See also
Publishing, Great Britain: Knight, Charles.
Author-Booksellers: Knight, Charles

KNIGHT, EDWARD H.

Cabinet S Shelf 5 No. 23

(The) First Century of the Republic [Fifth Paper] Mechanical progress: printing. By Edward H. Knight. Washington, D.C. 1875. Illus. excerpt from Harper's.

Includes a brief summing up of the invention of type founding, the first type foundries, processes of printing, and printing machinery.

Item 4, in bound volume "Various items relating to printing."

KNIGHT, EDWARD, H.

Cabinet S Shelf 5 No. 23

Printing: Mechanical progress. The first century of the Republic (U. S.) An Excerpt from Harper's Magazine, March, 1875.

Item 4 in volume with binders title "Various items relating to printing." Bound, 1919.

KNIGHT & LEONARD COMPANY

Cabinet L Shelf 4 No. 42

"Artistic printers". Chicago, 1887.

See Color Printing. Baltimore & Ohio Annual for 1887.

KNIGHT ERRANT (Sir John Carr) see

Cabinet Shelf No.

CARR (Sir John)

KNIGHT'S PICTORIAL GALLERY OF ARTS

Cabinet T Shelf 6 No. 52

(The) Arts contributory to writing [and printing] books and music. London, 1860.

Illus. excerpt from Knight's Pictorial Gallery. Has pictures of writing materials, type founding tools, printing offices, printing presses, printers' marks, etc.

In folder; 14 x $10\frac{3}{4}$ in.

KNOBLOCHTZER, HEINRICH

Cabinet AA Shelf 5 No. 32

Bibliographie Heinrich Knoblochtzers in Heidelberg. Ernst Voulliéme, Berlin, 1925. Facsimile, repro. types.

Bibliographical essay in Collijns "Bokock biblioteks-historika studier ... Uppsala, 1925. pp. 137-151.

Boards; 11 x $8\frac{1}{2}$ x 2 in.

KNOBLOCHTER, HEINRICH

Cabinet Y Shelf 4 No. 4

(Note on Knoblochter and his printing at Strasbourg, 1479)

see
VOULLIÈME, ERNST. (Die) Deutschen drucker des fünfzehnten jahrhunderts...p.107

KNOBLOUCH, JOHANN

Cabinet Y Shelf 4 No. 4

(Note on Knoblouch and his printing at Strasbourg, 1497)

see
VOULLIÉME, ., ERNST. (Die) Deutschen drucker des fünfzehnter jahrhunderts...p.115

KNOBLOUCH, JOHANN (father and son)

Cabinet X Shelf 3 NO. 13

Brief bio-bibliographical note, with printer marks, Knoblouch, Strassburg, 1497-1528, 1529-1558.

see
HEITZ, PAUL. Elsässische büchermarken...p.viii, plate ix-xi

KNORR AND HIRTH

Cabinet Y Shelf 5 No. 43

(History of the firm of Knorr & Hirth, 1875-1900. Munich). Rückblicke und erinnerungen anlässlich ihres 25 jährigen jubiläums. Herausgegeben von der buch-und kunstdruckerei Knorr & Hirth, verlag der Münchner neuesten nachrichten. München, 1900. Illus.

Half morocco; 12 x 8-7/8 x $\frac{3}{4}$ in.

KNORR & HIRTH, München

See also
Printing Offices

KNUDSEN, C.W.

Cabinet II Shelf 3 No. 63 Box

English demotic alphabet, a plea for the. Printed in pronouncing orthography. South Norwalk, Conn. 1881. Paper booklet.

Item in box labelled "MIXCELLANEOUS LANGUAGE CHARACTERS: EXAMPLES".

KNUTTEL, W.P.C.

Cabinet AA Shelf 3 No. 39

Verboden boeken in de Republiek der Vereenigde Nederlanden. Beredeneerde catalogus. Door Dr. W.P.C. Knuttel. 'S-Gravenhage, 1914.

Bibliographical account of prohibited books in Holland, 16th and 17th centuries. Nijhoff.

Half morocco; $9\frac{1}{2}$ x 6 in.

KAY, JOHN

Cabinet RR Paper, its history. By John Kay. London: Smith, Kay & Co., 1893.

Shelf 2

No. 37

Cloth; 7¼ x 5 x 3/8 in.

KEIMER, SAMUEL

Cabinet F Independent Whig, Philadelphia, 1720.

One of the earliest Philadelphia publications, printed by Keimer, Franklin's old rival. It is a sort of a regular reprint of an English Serial publication.

Shelf 1

No. 71

Half calf; 8 x 6 in.

KELCHNER, Dr. ERNST

Cabinet Y (The) Marienthal impressions, 1463-, now in the Municipal Library in Frankfurt a.M. A bibliographical study, with facsimiles). Die Marienthaler drucke der Stadt-Bibliothek ...Bibliographisch beschreiben. Mit funf facsimile-tafeln. Frankfurt a.M, 1883.

Shelf 5

No. 134

Half morocco; 14-7/8 x 11 x ½ in.

KEANE, WILLIAM LAWRENCE

Cabinet J Japanese color prints. The famous artists of the popular school. By W.L. Keane. With reproductions of prints in the writer's possession [Excerpt from "The Century Magazine", Oct., 1912.]

Shelf 3

No. 31

Item in manila envelope.

KEIMER, SAMUEL

Cabinet X [Persecutions of S. Keimer, by whom B. Franklin was employed prior to 1728]. A brand plucked from the burning: Exemplified in the unparallel'd case of Samuel Keimer...London, 1718.

Autobiographical in content.

Shelf 4

No. 50

Half morocco; 6¼ x 4 x 3/8 in.

KELE, RICHARD

Cabinet T Books printed by R. Kele, London, 1552. Bibliographical notes.

Shelf 2

see

No. 6 [vol.4]

DIBDIN'S "Typographical Antiquities" ...London, 1810 - 1819, vol.IV, p.302

KEARNEY, WILLIAM

Cabinet U Bio-bibliographical note relating to Kearney, printer, Dublin, 1571.

Shelf 1

see

McDIX, E.R. Dublin printing...p.23

No. 111

KEIMER, SAMUEL

Cabinet R See Smith, Joseph. Short biographical notices of William Bradford ... and Samuel Keimer. London, 1891.

Shelf 5

No. 27

KELLAM, LAWRENCE

Cabinet See Early Printing in England. Doway, 1609-1610. Lawrence Kellam.

Shelf

No.

KEELEY, JAMES (Editor)

Cabinet NN Chicago Tribune.

Shelf 2

See JOURNALISM. (A) Great newspaper [Chicago Tribune] and its owner...

No. 2.01

KEIMER, SAMUEL.

See also

Cabinet Early Printing in Pennsylvania. Philadelphia, [v.d.]. Samuel Keimer.

also Imprints, United States.

Shelf " Biographies, Printers.

No.

KELLER, HELEN

Cabinet II Keller (Miss) celebrates a sight-giver, Louis Braille. Article by Miss Keller. Portrait of Helen Keller and Louis Braille

Shelf 6

Excerpt from The New York Times Magazine, Nov. 17, 1929.

No. 27

In envelope.

KEIMER, S.

Cabinet X London, 1715. Case of libel against S. Keimer, copy from the records.

Shelf 4

see

LIBERTY OF PRINTING. Great Britain. Copies taken from the records....London, 1763, p.19

No. 73

KELCHNER, ERNEST

Cabinet W Catalogue de l'Officine des Elzevier (1628). Reproduction heliographique d'apres d'exemplaire de la bibliotheque de Frankfort-sur-le-Mein. Avec une introduction par Ernesr Kelchner, Paris, 1880.

Shelf 5

No. 104

Parchment; 7½ x 5 in. Item in manila envelope

KELLER, JOHANN

Cabinet Y (Note on the Keller press at Augsburg, 1478-1486)

Shelf 4

see

VOULLIÉME, ERNST. (Die) Deutschen drucker des fünfzehnten jahrhunderts...p.5

No. 4

KEIMER, SAMUEL

Cabinet S [Biographical sketch]. By Henry Simpson. From "Lives of eminent Philadelphians", Phila. 1859.

Shelf 5

No. 25.01

Pamphlet in box labelled "Colonial printing and printers. Miscellaneous items".

KELCHNER, Dr. ERNST

Cabinet Y (Mainz Ecclesiastical Acts of 1480, printed on parchment) Der pergamentdruck der Agenda Ecclesiae Moguntinensis von 1480. Bibliographisch beschrieben. Frankfurt am Main, 1885. Facsimiles.

Shelf 3

No. 19

Half morocco; 10-5/8 x 7 x 3/8 in.

KELLOG, Leonard.

Cabinet A See Newspapers, New York State: Herald of the Times, printed by him.

Shelf 3

Bound in with other newspapers; leaf 28.

No. 11

KANSAS CITY STAR

Cabinet NN Shelf 4 No. 45

Nelson, William Rockhill.
The story of a man, a newspaper, and a city.
By members of the staff of the Kansas City Star.
Printed at the Riverside Press.
Cambridge. 1915.
Illus.

Cloth: 9x6"

KANT, IMMANUEL

Cabinet Y Shelf 3 No. 22

(Bookmaking and public taste, Kant's opinion on).
Ueber die buchmacherey. Zwey briefe an Herrn Friedrich Nicolai von Immanuel Kant.
Königsburg, 1798.

Cloth; $7\frac{1}{4}$ x 4 x $\frac{1}{4}$ in.

KASTENBEIN, CHARLES (Inventor) see

Cabinet FF Shelf 6 No. 19

COMPOSING MACHINES. Kastenbein, Charles...

KANSAS CITY STAR (The),
See also

Cabinet Shelf No.

Newspapers, special issues.

KAPP, FRIEDRICH.

Cabinet 22 Shelf 1 No. 1

(German-American printing and publishing 1683-1872) Der Deutschamerikanische buchdruck und buchhandel im vorigen jahrhundert.

In "Archive für geschichte Deutschen buchhandels," vol. 1, 1878, pp. 56-77.

KAUP, W. J.

Cabinet FF Shelf 5 No. 8

Modern automatic type making methods: Refinement of machine design, unique method for determination of accuracy of matrix. The microscope a factor of machine installation. (Lynn Boyd Benton's Invention).
Excerpt from American Machinist, Dec. 16, 1909. Illus.

Cloth; 12 x 9 in.

KANSAS CITY TYPE FOUNDRY

Cabinet Shelf No.

See Specimen Books, Types. United States

KARABACEK, JOSEPH von (see)

Cabinet Shelf No.

Ritter von Karabacek

KAUTZSCH, RUDOLF

Cabinet FF Shelf 4 No. 26

(Die) Enstehung der frakturschrift. von Rudulf Kautzsch. Mainz, 1922. Beilage... der Gutenberg-Gesellschaft. facs.

Boards; $8\frac{3}{4}$ x $5\frac{1}{2}$ in.

KANSAS CITY TYPE, ELECTROTYPE & STEREOTYPE FOUNDRY

Cabinet Shelf No.

See
Specimen Books, Types. United States
" also " " Cuts. " "

KARPINSKI, LOUIS C.

Cabinet S Shelf 3 No. 104

Colonial American arithmetics. By Louis C. Karpinski of the University of Michigan.
Bibliographical essay with list of arithmetics and arithmetical works published in America up to 1775.
P. 243 in volume, Wilberforce Eames ... A tribute to. Cambridge, 1924.

KAUTZSCH, RUDOLF

Cabinet Y Shelf 5 No. 97

(Modern printing: Essays on printing in England, Denmark, Holland, America, and Germany) Die neue buchkunst: Studien im inland und ausland. Herausgegeben von Rudolf Kautzsch. Weimar, 1902.

Boards; 9-3/8 x $6\frac{1}{2}$ x 7/8 in.

KANSAS EDITORIAL ASSOCIATION

Cabinet KK Shelf 5 No. 91

Annual reports for years 1893, 1899, 1902, 1904, 1905, 1906, 1907.

7 titles, 7 items.

In board holder; 9 x $6\frac{1}{4}$ in.

KARWEYSSE, JAKOB

Cabinet Y Shelf 4 No. 4

(Notes on the Karweysse 15th century press at Marienburg)

see
VOULLIÉME, ERNST (Die)
Deutschen drucker des fünfzehnten jahrhunderts...p.81

KAUTZSCH, RUDOLF

Cabinet Y Shelf 1 No. 92.02

Wandlungen in der schrift und in der kunst. Rede bei der jubelfeier Deutscher Schriftgiessereien in Frankfurt A.M, Dezember 1, Gesellschaft. Illus.
Kleinedruck 10.

With other items in manila envelope.

KANSAS EDITORIAL ASSOCIATION

Cabinet KK Shelf 5 No. 92

Annual reports for years 1908, 1909, 1919, 1920, 1921, 1922, 1923.

Also copy of the association house organ for February 1924.

In board holder; 9-1/8 x $6\frac{1}{4}$ in.

KASTELEIJN, P.J.

Cabinet RR Shelf 3 No. 3

Volledige beschreiving van alle konsten... Negende stuk. De Papier-Masker. Met plaaten. Te Dortrecht, 1792. Blussé.

This is the Dutch edition taken from the French of De La Lande.

Half morocco; $8\frac{1}{2}$ x $5\frac{1}{8}$ in.

KAVMOR PLATEN PRESS

Cabinet EE Shelf 4 No. 3

(Prospectus. Illus.)

See AUTOMATIC PLATEN PRESS Co. (Prospectus)

KINSLEY and COMPANY, A.W.

Cabinet See Specimen Books, Types. United States. Franklin Letter-Foundry.

Shelf

No.

KOBERGER, ANTON

Cabinet Y (Nuremberg, Anton Koberger in. Biographical account, with portrait.

Shelf 1

No. 41

See BÖRCKEL, ALFRED. "Gutenberg und seine berühmsten nachfolger"...pp.102-115

KOBIAN, VALENTIN

Cabinet X Brief bibliographical note, with printer mark, Kobian, Hagenau (Alsace-Lorraine), 1502-1542.

Shelf 3

No. 13

see HEITZ, PAUL. Elsässische büchermarken...p.xxii, plate lxviii

KÖBEL, JACOB.

Cabinet 75 Oppenheim Press, The, 1494?

Shelf 1

No. 3

See Redgrave, Gilbert R. Oppenheim Press, [Jacob Köbel].

KOBERGER, ANTON

Cabinet U Nuremberg printer, largest; the illustrated books of Koberger

Shelf 5

No. 24

see POLLARD, A.W. Fine Books ...London, 1912, pp.63, 108, 183

KOCH, JOHANN (Meister)

Cabinet Y (Brief note on the Koch press at Basel, 1479-)

Shelf 4

No. 4

see VOULLIÉME, ERNST (Die) Deutschen drucker des fünfzehnten jahrhunderts...p.20

KOBELL, FRANZ von

Cabinet FF (Die) Galvanographie, eine methode, gemalde tuschbilder durch galvanisbhe kupferplatten in drucke zu vervielfaltigen. Mit abbildungen des galvanischen apparates und abdrucken von acht galvanographischen platten auf 7 tafeln. Munchen, 1842.

Shelf 1

No. 4

Half levant, 12 x 9 in.

KOBERGER, ANTON

Cabinet D Die Teutsche Bibel, Nuremberg, 1483. 23 leaves.

Shelf 1

No. 63

In portfolio.

KOCH, RUDOLF

Cabinet U Book of signs which contains all manner of symbols used from the earliest times to the middle ages by primitive peoples and Early Christians. Collected, drawn and explained by R. Koch. Translated from the German by Vyvyan Holland. London, The First Edition Club, 1930.

Shelf 3

No. 113

Cloth; $9\frac{1}{4}$ x 7 x 3/8 in.

KOBERGER, ANTON

Cabinet Y [Brief biographical account, illus. German text] von Albert Schramm.

Shelf 4

No. 51

In "Die Zeugkiste", Leipzig, 1923, p.13.

Stamped cloth; 7-7/8 x 5-5/8 x 3/4 in.

KOBERGER, ANTON

Cabinet 10 See Incunabula. Biblia latina. Nuremberg; Antonius Coburger.

Shelf 2

No. 8

KOCH, THEODORE WESLEY (Translator)

Cabinet G Nodier, Charles. Francesco Collona: A fanciful tale of the writing of the Hypnerotomachia. Translated by T.W. Koch, Chicago, 1929. Printed by R.R. Donnelley & Sons Company, at the Lakeside Press.

Shelf 2

No. 68

Cloth; $9\frac{1}{2}$ x $6\frac{1}{2}$ in. In protective case.

KOBERGER, ANTHONY

Cabinet Y (Die) Koberger, Seine darstellung des buchhändlerischen geschäftsletriebes in der zeit des uberganges vom mittelatler zur neuzeit, von Oscar Hase. [second ed.] Leipzig, 1885. Facsimiles.

Shelf 2

No. 26

Boards; $9\frac{1}{4}$ x 6 x $1\frac{1}{4}$ in.

KOBERGER, ANTON.

Cabinet 10 See Incunabula. Boethius (Annius Manlius Severinus) Nuremberg, 1473.

Shelf 2

No. 6

KOHLER, JOHANN DAVID

Cabinet Y Hochverdiente und aus bewährten urkunden wohlbeglaubte ehren-rettung Johann Guttenbergs...Leipzig, 1741. Illus.

Shelf 1

No. 3

At the end several poetical effusions, some in Latin.

Half morocco; $8\frac{3}{4}$ x 7 x $\frac{1}{2}$ in.

KOBERGER, ANTON

Cabinet Y (Note on Koberger and his printing at Nuremberg, 1470-)

Shelf 4

No. 4

see VOULLIÉME, ERNST (Die) Deutschen drucker des fünfzehnten jahrhunderts...p.87

KOBERGER, ANTON (see also)

Cabinet

Shelf

No.

EARLY PRINTING IN GERMANY. Example Koberger...

EARLY PRINTING IN GERMANY. Literat

INCUNABULA

KOEHLER, S.R.

Cabinet K White - line engraving for relief - printing in the 15th and 16th centuries. By S. R. Koehler, Curator, Section of Graphic Arts (Smithsonian Institute). Washington, D. C. 1892.

Shelf 6

No. 17

From Report of the National Museum for 1890.

Bound in with Lewis' "Schrotblätter"; or prints in the "Manière Criblée". Phila. 1904 Half morocco; 9-3/4 x $6\frac{1}{4}$ x $\frac{1}{4}$ in.

KOELHOFF, JOHANN

Cabinet X Shelf 3 No. 20

Bibliographical notes, with printer mark, Koelhoff, Cologne, 1490-1493.

see HEITZ, PAUL. Kölner büchermarken...p.xv

KÖNIG, FRIEDRICK

Cabinet FF Shelf 5 No. 49

Friedrick König und die erfindung der schnellpresse. Ein gedenkblatt zum 17 April, 1875, vom Theod. Goebel. Braunschweig, 1875. (Reprinted from the Journal fur Buchdruckerkunst).

Quarter morocco; 8 x 5-1/8 x ½ in.

KOENIG, FREDERICK

Cabinet FF Shelf 5 No. 48

Inventor of the steam-printing machine. By Samuel Smiles. (Excerpt from MacMillan's Magazine. Eclectic. March, 1870.) Brochure.

Biographical

Item in manila envelope

KOELHOFF, JOHANNES

Cabinet B Shelf 2 No. 8

(Illustrated books printed by Koelhoff, Cologne, 1487-92)

see SCHRAMM, ALBERT (Der) Bilderschmuck der frühdrucke...Leipzig, 1924.

KOENIG, FRIEDRICH

Cabinet FF Shelf 5 No. 64

Goebel, Theodor. Friedrich Koenig und die erfindung der schnellpresse. Ein biographisches denkmal. Zweite auflage. Stuttgart, 1906. Illus.

Cloth; 8½ x 6 in.

KOENIG, FRIEDRICH

Cabinet Y Shelf 5 No. 85

(Memoir of the inventor of the cylinder printing machine, compiled from original sources) Friedrich Koenig und die erfindung der schnellpresse. Ein biographisches denkmal. von Theodor Goebel. Stuttgart, 1883. Illus.

Stamped cloth; 13 x 9¾ x 7/8 in.

KOELHOFF, JOHANN

Cabinet Y Shelf 4 No. 4

(Note on the Koelhoff press at Cologne, 1472)

see VOULLIÉME, ERNST. (Die) Deutschen drucker des fünfzehnten jahrhunderts...p.31

also p.37

KOENIG, FREDERICK

Cabinet EE Shelf 5 No. 77

[History of the printing press, from 1441 to the first cylinder press invented by Fredr. Koeing in 1811].

Illus. catalogue and history. Koenig & Bauer maschinenfabrik, Kloster Oberzell in Wurzburg, 1902.

Pamphlet in manila envelope.

KOENIG, FREDERIC

Cabinet V Shelf 5 No. 13

(La) Presse méchanique et son inventeur, Fredr. Koenig.

See MADDEN, J.P.A. Lettres d'un bibliographie...Paris, 1886, pp.109-127

KOELHOFF, JOHANN [The Younger]

Cabinet D Shelf 2 No. 47

See Incunabula. Chronica van der hilligen Stat van Coellen.

KOENIG, FRIEDRICH

Cabinet X Shelf 5 No. 3

Invention of printing by steam: The Times, London, Nov. 29, 1814, the first newspaper printed by steam. Excerpt from unidentified publication, n.d.

Koenig was inventor of first power printing press.

p. 27 in vol. with binder's title "Scrap Book, 1705-1891, relating to pr inting."

KOENIG, FREDERIC ?

Cabinet L Shelf 4 No. 18

Printing machine of Mr. Koenig, account of.

See Savage, William, Practical hints on decorative printing...London, 1822, pp.17, 75.

KOENIG, FRIEDRICH

Stack A Shelf 1 & 2 Number 82

See Bullen Henry Lewis. Inventor's (The) account of the invention of the Cylinder Press.

KOENIG, FREDERICK.

Cabinet FF Shelf 2 No. 40

Inventor of first flat-bed cylinder press.

See Inventions, Patents for. Abridgments of specifications, Vol. I...London, 1859. Patents issued to him, pp. 121 (1810), 123, 126, 131 (1814)

Half morocco; 7-5/8 x 5 x 2 in.

KOENIG, FRIEDRICH.

Cabinet 26 Shelf 2 No. 1

See Printing Presses, Koenig, Friedrich.

KOENIG, FREDERICK

Cabinet FF Shelf 5 No. 50

First printing with a power printing press invented and used by Frederick Koenig. See: Sig. H. part 2, commencing p. 113 of the "Annual Register" Principal occurrences in the year 1810, London, 1811.

Has portrait and clippings pasted in.

Tree calf; 8¾ x 5¼ x 1½ in.

KOENIG, FREDERICK

Cabinet S Shelf 5 No. 23

Inventor of the steam printing machine [Biographical sketch]. By Samuel Smiles. Excerpt from Macmillan's, Dec. 1869.

Item 3 in volume with binders title "Various items relating to printing." Bound, 1919.

KOENIG & BAUER

Cabinet EE Shelf 5 No. 78

(Catalogue of printing presses) Zweitourenschnellpresse "Sturmvogel"...fur feinsten illustrations- u. Autotypiedruck. Katalog ausgabe No.165. Koenig & Bauer, G.M.B.H. Wurzburg.

With prices, Frontispiece view of the entire Koenig & Bauer works.

Item in manila envelope.

KOENIG & BAUER

Cabinet EE Shelf 5 No. 77

Maschinenfabrik Kloster Oberzell in Wurzburg, alteste schnellpressenfabrik, gegrundet 1817 durch Friedrich Koenig, Erfinder der Schnellpresse. 1902.
Illus. account of the development of the printing press, from the hand press of 1441 to the first cylinder press invented by Fredr. Koenig in 1811 and following to the three revolution press and latest 1930 development.

Item in manila envelope.

KOENIG & BAUER (CONT" D

Cabinet EE Shelf 5 NO. 77

Item in manila envelope

KOENIG & BAUER

Cabinet Y Shelf 5 No. 109

(Printing machinery manufactory. Souvenir Book. History of the house, and the inventions of Friedrich Koenig.) Gedenkbuch der druckmachinen-fabrik von Koenig & Bauer zur Kloster Oberzell bei Würzburg. Oberzell, 1898. Illus. and portrait.

Stamped cloth; 12¼ x 15¼ x 5/8 in.

KOHLER, ANDREAS

Cabinet Y Shelf 1 No. 66

Fraktur-Probe des schriftschneiders und schriftgiessers Andreas Köhler. Nürnberg 1710. Specimens of types. Broadside.
See Mori, Gustav. Schriftgiesser-gewerbe in Süddeutschland...Stuttgart, 1924. Plate XV.

KOHLER, JOHANN

Cabinet Shelf No.

See Specimen Books, Types. Germany. Various type-founders of Nuremberg, 1721-1733.

KOHLER, JOHANN DAVID

Cabinet Y Shelf 1 No. 3

Hochverdiente und aus bewahrten Urkunden wohlbeglaubte Ehren-Rettung Johann Guttenberg's, eingebohrnen Burger's in Mayntz, aus dem alten Rheinlandischen Adlichen Geschlechte derer von Gorgenloch, genannt, Gaensfleisch, wegen der ersten erfindung der nie gnug gepriesenen Buchdrucker-Kunst in der Stadt Mayntz, zu unvergaenglichen Ehren der Teutschen Nation...von Johann David Kohler. Leipzig, 1741.
Documentary evidence in favor of Guten- (cont'd)

KOHLER, JOHANN DAVID cont'd

Cabinet Y Shelf 1 No. 3

berg as the inventor of printing. Includes quotations from various works in which the invention is mentioned, and the commentaries of each citation by the present author. Also includes genealogy of the Sorgenloch-Gaensfleisch family.

Half morocco; 8-5/8 x 7 x ½ in.

KOHLSAAT, HERMANN H.

Cabinet NN Shelf 2 No. 1

See BIOGRAPHIES, Editors. Kohlsaat...

KOKKA, THE

Cabinet L Shelf 5 No. 16

Illustrated mont ly journal, Japan

See Periodicals, Illustrated (Japan) The Kokka...

"KOKKA YOHO, THE"

Cabinet J Shelf 5 No. 26

Catalogue of Japanese Art Treasures

see JAPAN. Catalogue of treasures...

KOLB, ALBERT

Cabinet 26 Shelf 1 No. 20

(Die) Anfänge der drukkunst in Nancy. The beginning of printing in Nancy, Alsace Lorraine, 1572-1600). Illus.
Bio-bibliographical account.

Article in the"Gutenberg-Gesellschaft Jahrbuch" 1930, pp.209-225.

KOLB, ALBERT

Cabinet 26 Shelf 1 No. 17

Doré, Gustave, als buchillustrator.
Article in the Gutenberg-Gesellschaft Jahrbuch 1928. pp.118-141.

KOLKHOFF COMPANY

Cabinet R Shelf 6 No. 11

See Printing Plants, New York City.

KOLLARII, ADAMI FRANC.

Cabinet EE Shelf 5 No.

(Ad) Petri Lambecuii commentariourm de augusta bibliotheca caes. vindobonensi Libros VIII Supplementorum. Liber primus. Posthumus. Vindobonae. Typis et sumpt. Joan. Thomae nob. de Trattnern, anno 1790. Illus.
This book is the posthumus supplement to the previous eight books by Lambecus, all edited by Killari.

Calf; 15 x 9½ in. each vol.

KOLLICKER, PETER

Cabinet Y Shelf 4 No. 4

(Note on the Kollicker press at Basel, 1470-1486)

see VOULLIÉME, ERNST. (Die) Deutschen drucker des fünfzehnten jahrhunderts...p.20

KOLLOCK, SHEPHARD, Printer

Cabinet R Shelf 4 No. 133

Genealogy of the Kollock Family of Sussex County, Delaware, 1657-1897. By Edwin Jaquett Sellers. Philadelphia, 1897.
Kollock was a celebrated printer of the Revolutionary period, and founder of "The New Jersey Journal," 1779, and "The New York Gazeteer and Country Journal," New York City, 1783.
For detailed account of Kollocks' activities, see Nelson's "New Jersey printers and printing." ... April, 1911. pp. 18-21.

KOLLOCK, SHEPARD

Cabinet R Shelf 4 No. 121

See Nelson, William: New Jersey printers in the 18th century ... April, 1911, p. 18.

KOLLOCK, SHEPARD

Cabinet S Shelf 6 No. 8

Printer of first New York directory, 1786.

See EARLY PRINTING IN AMERICA (U.S.) Literature. (New York City, 1786) Shepard Kollock...

KÖLNISCHE ZEITUNG, Geschichte der..

See Newspapers.

"KOLNISCHEN ZEITUNG" see

Cabinet CO Shelf 6 No. 29

NEWSPAPERS, Germany (Literature of) "Kolnischen Zeitung".

KOMARECK, J. M.

Cabinet Y Shelf 1 No. 2

Faust von Mainz. Ein gemahlde aus der mitte der funfzehnten jahrhunderts. In vier aufzuegen Leipzig, 1794.
A drama in four acts.

Half morocco; 6¾ x 4¼ x 3/8 in.

KONIG, FRIEDRICH.

Stack A Shelf 1 & 2 Number 69

See Biographies, press builders, Konig Friedrich.

KONIG, JACOBUS en JACOBUS SCHELTEMA

Cabinet AA Shelf 3 No. 9

Vier brieven gewisseld tusschen Mr. Jacobus Scheltema en Jacobus Konig over de laatste tegenspraak van het regt van Haarlem op de utivinding der drukkunst. Te Haarlem, 1823.
Invention controversy.

Half leather; 8-3/4 x 5 in.

KONIG, JACQUES.

Cabinet W Shelf 4 No. 07

Dissertation dur l'origine, l'invention et le perfectionnement de l'imprimerie. Par Jacques Konig. Traduit du Hollandais. Amsterdam, 1819. Specimens of early types and portraits of Koster and his son.

Half morocco; 9¼ x 5½ in.

KÖNIG, SAMUEL

Cabinet X Shelf 3 No. 15

Brief biographical note, with printer mark, Konig, Basel, 1568-1580.

SEE HEITZ, PAUL. Basler büchermarken...pp.xxxviii, 107

KÖNIGLICHE MUSEEN -- Berlin

Cabinet Y Shelf 5 No. 99

Kunstgewerbe Museum. Führer für die sonderausstellung die kunst im neuren buchdruck. Dezember 1904-Januar 1905. (Text by Peter Jessen)
Guide to an exhibition of modern printing.

Half morocco; 7-1/8 x 5¼ in.

KONING, JACOBUS

Cabinet AA Shelf 3 No. 7

Bijdragen tot de geschiedenis der Boekdrukkunst, door Jacobus Koning. Haarlem 1818.
This is part I of a supplement to Koning's "Verhandelingen over den oorsprong ... der boekdrukkunst" ... Haarlem 1816. Includes copies of the watermarks of the so-called Kosterian "Donatus." See also AA/3/6.

Half morocco; 9¼ x 5-3/8 in.

KONING, JACOBUS

Cabinet AA Shelf 3 No. 6

Verhandeling over den oorsprong, de uitvinding, verbetering en volmaking der boekdrukkunst. Door Jacobus Koning. Haarlem, 1816. Facsimile.
A prize essay of the history of printing. For the Holland Society of Sciences. This essay favors Coster. See also AA/3/7.

Half morocco; 8-3/4 x 5¼ in.

KONNINKLIJKE NEDERLANDSCHE STOOMDRUKKERII

Cabinet EE Shelf 3 No. 55

See SPECIMEN BOOKS, TYPES. Printers'. Holland.

KONKLE, BURTON ALVA

Cabinet S Shelf 5 No. 52

Life of Chief Justice Ellis Lewis, 1798-1871: Of the first Elective Supreme Court of Pennsylvania. Philadelphia, 1907. Illus.
Biography. Maj. Lewis, founded the first newspaper in Harrisburg, Ellis Lewis served as apprentice on this paper afterwards became co-editor of "The Gazette" at Williamsport, Penna.

Cloth; 9-3/4 x 6 x 1¼ in.

KÖNNECKE, GUSTAV

Cabinet Y Shelf 2 No. 85

Hessisches buchdruckerbuch: Enthaltend nachweis aller bisher bekannt gewordenen buchdruckereinen des jetsigen regierungsbezirks Cassel und des kreises Biedenkopf. Marburg in Hessen, 1894. With printer marks.
Bio-historical account of printers and printing in the Northern and Southern part of Germany, Cassel, Hanau, Marburg etc.

Stamped cloth; 8¼ x 5¾ x 1½ in.

KOOPMAN, HARRY LYMAN

Cabinet QQ Shelf 4 No. 25

Booklover and his books, the. By Harry Lyman Koopman. Boston, 1917. Frontspiece.

Cloth; 9¾ x 6¾ in.

KOOPMAN, HARRY LYMAN

Cabinet S Shelf 3 No. 104

(The) Clerk of Breukleyn. By Harry Lyman Koopman, Library of the Brown University Library. May, 1924.
An ode to a book lover.
See p. V in volume Eames, Wilberforce: Bibliographical Essays...Cambridge, 1924.

KOOPMAN, HARRY LYMAN

Cabinet S Shelf 3 No. 106 No. 5

(The) Mastery of books: Hints on reading and the use of libraries. By Harry Lyman Koopman, A. M. Librarian of Brown University. American Book Company, New York, 1896.

Cloth; 7½ x 5¼ x ½ in.

KOOPMAN, H.L.

Cabinet S Shelf 6 No. 8

Modern American printing. [Excerpt from the American Mercury, May, 1924].

Item 10 in vol. with binder's title "Early printing and printers. Pamphlets".

KOOPMAN, HENRY LYMAN

Cabinet U Shelf 1 No. 1d

Simplified spelling from the printer's standpoint: Reprinted from the book with title Orthographic Reform in "The Printing Art." (University Press, Cambridge, Mass.)

In Excerpts relating to printing from "The Library," pp. 1-8 of pencilled folios.

KOOPS, MATTHIAS

Cabinet RR Shelf 6 No. 39

Engraving on paper made from straw by Mr. Koops, 1800.

Portfolio, 17½ 14 in.

KOOPS, MATTHIAS

Cabinet RR Shelf 3 No. 3.01

Historical account of the substances which have been used to describe events, and to convey ideas, from the earliest date, to the invention of paper. Printed on the first useful paper manufactured soley from straw. Printed by T. Burton, London, 1800. [1st edition].

Half morocco; 10 x 6-3/8 x ½ in.

KOOPS, MATTHIAS

Cabinet RR Shelf 1 No. 13

Historical account of the substances which have been used to describe events, and to convey ideas, from the earliest date, to the invention of paper. Printed on the first useful paper manufactured soley from straw. London, 1800.
Printed by T. Burton.

Half morocco; 11½ x 6-3/4 x ½ in.

KOOPS, MATTHIAS

Cabinet RR Shelf 3 No. 4

Historical account of substances which have been used to describe events, and to convey ideas, from the earliest date to the invention of paper. Second edition. Printed on paper manufactured solely from straw. By Matthias Koops. London: Printed by Jacques and Co., 1801. Frontispiece.

Half calf; 8¼ x 5¼ x 7/8 in.

KOOPS, MATTHIAS

Cabinet Shelf No. With Dups. 491.02

Historical account of the substances which have been used to describe events, and to convey ideas, from the earliest date to the invention of paper. Second edition. Printed on paper re-made from old printed and written paper. By Matthias Koops. London, 1801. Frontispiece. Printed by Jacques and Co.
Appendix, p. 259, printed on paper made from wood.
Half calf; 8¼ x 5¼ x 7/8 in.

KÖPFEL, WOLFGANG

Cabinet X Shelf 3 No. 13

Brief bio-bibliographical note, with printer mark, Köpfel, Strassburg, 1522-1554

see
HEITZ, PAUL. Elsässische büchermarken...p.xix, plate xvi-xx

KÖRBER, PHILIPP.

Cabinet Y Shelf 2 No. 19

Gutenberg der erfinder der buchdruckerkunst. Ein vorbild für die deutsche jugend. Nürnberg, n.d. [After 1833]. Frontispiece steel engraving.

Paper boards; 6¾ x 4-3/8 x 3/8 in.

KOREA

Cabinet II Shelf 4 No. 12

American Bible Society. The Gospel of St. Luke in Korean. 1910.

Paper; 7-3/8 x 5 in.

KOREA

Cabinet FF Shelf 3 No. 9

Evolution of modern printing and the discovery of movable metal type by the Chinese and Koreans in the 14th century. By Judson Daland. Reprinted from The Franklin Institute. vol. 212, No. 2, Aug. 1931. Illus. brochure.

Item in manila envelope

KOREA

Cabinet Shelf No.

History of printing in Korea

See PRINTING, HISTORICAL. Korea...

KORTEBRANT, JAKOB.

Cabinet X Shelf 2 No. 10

Lof der drukkunste, te Haerlem uitgevonden door Laurens Janszoon Koster ... Te Delf, Pieter vander Kloot, 1740. With interesting printer mark.
Eulogium of Koster in verse, written in Dutch. Includes some historical matter followed by a list of towns and the date when, it is stated, printing was introduced.

Half morocco; 9½ x 7½ x ½ in.

KOSTER

See under Coster, Laurens Janszoon.

KOZMA, LUDWIG

Cabinet 26 Shelf 1 No. 20

Buchkunstler, Ludwig Kozma als. von Emerich Kner. Illus. article.
An appreciative account of the man and his work, Ludwig Kozma, Hungarian artist typographer.

Article in the "Gutenberg-Gesellschaft Jahrbuch" 1930, pp.298-327.

KRAIS, FELIX

Cabinet J Shelf 4 No. 20

Imprint, Stuttgart, 1902.

See IMPRINTS, Germany. Hoffmannschen Buchdruckerei: Felix Krais...

KRAMER & FUCHS.

Cabinet Shelf No.

See Specimen Books, Types, Germany. Bauer'sche Giesserei (Kramer & Fuchs).

KRANTZ, CAMILLE

Cabinet W Shelf 1 No. 132

Exposition Internationale de Chicago en 1893: Imprimerie et Librairie: Rapports publies sous la direction de M. Camille Krantz ... Paris, Imprimerie Nationale, 1894.
Complete reports on the exhibits of printing and printing processes from Europe, and the United States.

Half morocco; 11-5/8 x 7-7/8 in.

KRASNOPOLSKI, PAUL

Cabinet 26 Shelf 1 No. 16

Prager druck bis 1620. (Printing in Prague to the year 1620).

article in GUTENBERG-GESELLSCHAFT JAHRBUCH, 1927, pp.72-84

KRAUS (J.C.)

Cabinet X Shelf 1 No. 36

Epistola de laudibus typographiae e lingua germanica latine reddita A.J.G.Suchsdorfio.

[In Wolf, "Monumenta Typographicae", vol. ii, p. 700]

KRAUSE, KARL (Maschinen Farbik)

Cabinet EE Shelf 5 No. 83

(Catalogue, n.d. English text for export trade. Stamped on cover "Sole agents" John Dickinson & Co., Ltd. Bombay) Karl Krause. Leipzig. Specialty: Labor-saving machinery for printiers, bookbinders. n.d. about 1912.

Boards; 6¼ x 9¼ in.

KRAUSE, KARL (Maschinen-Fabrik)

Cabinet EE Shelf 5 No. 81

(Catalogue, 1900, Machinery for printers, bookbinders and allied trades) Maschinen für die gesammte papier-industrie. Leipzig, 15 December, 1900.

Boards; 6¼ x 9¼ x 5/8 in.

KRAUSE, KARL

Cabinet EE Shelf 5 No. 82

(Catalogue, 1902. Complete catalogue of machinery and tools used in the paper making, industry, and allied trades.) Maschinen für die gesammte papierindustrie. Karl Krause, Leipzig.

Stamped on cover: Kampe & Co., London.

Embossed cloth; 12-3/4 x 9-3/4 x 1 in.

KRAUSE, KARL (Maschinenfabrik)

Cabinet EE Shelf 5 No. 84.01

Jubiläumschrift (1855-1905). Karl Krause und sein werk. Zür feier des Jubilaums des fünfzigjährigen bestehens der fabrik. Geschildert von Theodor Goebel. Leipzig: Verlag der Maschinenfabrik Karl Krause. 1905. Portraits, illus.

Printed silk over board; oblong, 12¾ x 15⅝

KRAUSE, KARL

Cabinet Y Shelf 5 No. 111

Karl Krause und sein werk. Die machinenfabrik in Leipzig. Zur feier des jubiläums des fünfzigjährigen bestehens der fabrik. Geschildert von Theodor Goebel. Leipzig, 1905. Fully illustrated.

Issued on the 50th anniversary of the establishment.

Stamped cloth; 12½ x 15⅝ in.

KRAUSE, KARL see also

Cabinet Shelf No.

PRINTING EQUIPMENTS. Catalogue.

KRAUSE, L.W.

Cabinet X Shelf 2 No. 21

Beschreibung der feier des vierten säcular-feste der erfindung der buchdruckerkunst. (Description of the celebrations on the 400th anniversary of printing). Berlin, 1840.

Morocco; 6-1/8 x 4-3/8 x ¼ in.

KRAWANY, FRANZ

Cabinet RR Shelf 3 No. 18

Internationale papier-statistik. von K. K. Kommerzialrat, Franz Krawany...Berlin-Wien (1910)

Statistics of paper, paper-makers, paper merchants and of firms manufacturing or dealing in paper making tools and implements, for all countries.

Cloth; 10-3/8 x 7-5/8 x 1-1/8 in.

KREBS, BENJAMIN

Cabinet Shelf No.

See Specimen Books, Types. Germany.

KREUSNER, FREDERIC

Cabinet D Shelf 4 No. 60

Nuremberg, 1493.

see INCUNABULA (loose leaves) Kreusner, Frederic...

KRIEGEL, HARRY G.

Cabinet 78 Shelf 1 No. 85

Encyclopedia of printing: Lithographic inks and accessories. Secrets, formulae and helpful hints for craftsmen in the graphic arts. Published by Harry G. Kriegel, president of t the Superior Printing Ink Company, New York City, 1932.

Cloth; 8¼ x 5¾ in.

KRISTELLER, PAUL

Cabinet U Shelf 3 No. 103

Books with wood cuts printed at Pavia.

Illus. bibliographical account.

See vol. I, p.347 in Bibliographica... London, 1895-1897.

KRAUSE, KARL (Fabrica de Maguinas)

Cabinet EE Shelf 5 No. 84

(Catalogue, n.d. about 1913. Spanish text for export trade. Machines for printers, bookbinders...and allied trades).

Paper; 6-3/8 x 9-3/8 in. In manila envelope.

KRISTELLER, PAUL

Cabinet K Shelf 6 No. 18

Early Florentine woodcuts. With an annotated list of Florentine illustrated books. By Paul Kristeller. London, 1897.

On pages following page 184, are 193 reproductions of important woodcuts. "This is an exhaustive compilation, preceded by a comprehensive introduction". No. 175 of 300 copies printed.

Quarter morocco; 11½ x 9-1/8 x 1¼ in.

KRISTELLER, PAUL

Cabinet U Shelf 3 No. 103

Florentine book-illustrations of the 15th and early 16th centuries.

Bibliographical.

See vol. 2, pp.81, 227 Bibliographica... London, 1895-1897.

KRISTELLER, Dr. PAUL

Cabinet X Shelf 3 No. 14

(Die) Italienischen buchdrucker und verlegerzeichen bis 1525. Strassburg, 1893. Illus.

Italian printer and publisher marks to the year 1525.

Half cloth; 14¾ x 11¼ in.

KRISTELLER, PAUL

Cabinet U Shelf 3 No. 103

Woodcuts as bindings (Bibliographical account)

See vol. I, p.249 in Bibliographica... London, 1895-1897.

KROBER, ERNST

Cabinet Y Shelf 3 No. 98

Buchbinderhandwerks in Leipzig, die anfänge des. (The beginning of hand book binding in Leipzig, 1494-1543).

Illus. article in Zeitschrift für Buchkunde, vol. I, 1924, p.83.

KRŌMSKŌP COLOR PHOTOGRAPHY (see)

Cabinet L Shelf 1 No. 35

IVES, FREDERIC. Krōmskōp...

KRONENBERG, M.E.

Cabinet 75 Shelf 2 No. 9

English printing, early 16th cent., in the Low Countries. A paper read before the Bibliographical Society, 19 March 1928.
Bibliographical account of the productions of the presses of Jan van Doesborch, C. van Ruremund, etc.

In Trans. Bibl. Soc. "The Library" vol. IX pp. 139-163.

KRONENBERG, M.E.

Cabinet AA Shelf 3 No. 47

Nederlandsche bibliographie van 1500 tot 1540, door Wouter Nijhoff en M.E. Kronenberg, 'S-Gravenhage, 1923-40.
Bibliography with alphabetic lists of places and printers with their addresses. v.1-2.

Half morocco; 10-1/8 x 6½ x 3½ in.

KRONENBERG, M. E.

Cabinet B Shelf 2 No. 21

Nederlandsche bibliographie, van 1500 tot 1540. Door Wouter Nijhoff en M.E. Kronenberg... s-Gravenhage, 1925. Afl. 1-4.

With other items in box.
Supplement to AA/3/47 v.1

KRONHEIM, JOSEPH MARTIN

Cabinet J Shelf 3 No. 14

Account of the man and his work as a color printer.

See LEWIS, COURTNEY. Story of picture printing in England during the 19th century ...pp.174-

---

KRONHEIM AND CO.'s

Cabinet FF Shelf 1 No. 81

Patent process of stereotyping; printed from plates produced without either picking or turning. Specimens of Kronheim & Co's. London: Foundry, No. 3, Earl Street, Blackfriars. 1844.

Cloth; 10¾ x 8½ x 3/8 in.

KRUELL, GUSTAV

Cabinet J Shelf 2 No. 33

American portrait engraver on wood, Gustav Kruell. By Ralph Clifton Smith. Champlain, N. Y. 1929. Illus. portraits.

Includes a chronological list of the works of Gustav Kruell.

Cloth, linen back; 10-5/8 x 7-5/8 x ½ in.

KRUELL, GUSTAV

Cabinet K Shelf 6 No. 33

American wood-engravers, Gustav Kruell.
Illustrated biographical article. Excerpt from Scribner's Magazine, Feb., 1895.

Item 4 in vol. with binder's title "Wood engravers: Various excerpts."

KRUELL, GUSTAV, Engraver.

Cabinet Shelf No.

See Biographies, engravers, Kruell, Gustav.

KRUG, LUDWIG

Cabinet 5 Shelf No. 27

Engravings (early 16th century, German), facsimile reprints of woodcut.

Facs. in Cabinet 5, portfolio 27

KRÜGER, OTTO

Cabinet MM Shelf 2 No. 62

Lithographischen verfahren und der offsetdruck. Mit 146 abbildungen im text und 21 mehrfarbigen tafeln. Leipzig, 1926.

Cloth; 9¼ x 6¼ x 1 in.

KRUGER, THOMAS.

Cabinet Shelf No.

See Bookbinding, Early. Kruger, Thomas. Der Wittenberger Bookbinder.

KRUITWAGEN, B.

Cabinet AA Shelf 3 No. 46

Erasmus en zijn drukkers-uitgevers. Een fragment uit hun breifwisseling. Bewerkt door B. Kruitwagen. Amsterdam, 1923.
A showing of the "Amsterdam" Lettergieterei new type designed by S.-H. de Roos, "Erasmus Mediaevel".

Half morocco; 9½ x 6-3/8 in.

KUBLER, GEORGE A.

Cabinet FF Shelf 1 No. 105

Historical treatises, abstracts and papers on stereotyping. New York, 1936. Illus.

Boards; 9¼ x 6; pp. VII, 169.

KUBLER, GEO. A.

Cabinet FF Shelf 1 No. 104

(A) Short history of stereotyping. New York City 1927. Illus.
Chapters include I - Origin of the art of printing.
II - Block printing
III - Discovery of the art of printing.

Boards; 9 x 6 x ½ in.

KUHL, ERNEST

Cabinet 75 Shelf 2 No. 9

Stationers' Company and censorship. (1599-1601). The Bibliographical Society, London 1928.

In Trans. Bibl. Soc. "The Library," vol. IX pp. 388-94. 1928-1929.

KÜHL, GUSTAVE

Cabinet L Shelf 3 No. 21

Psychology of writing, marginal notes on the. By Dr. Gustave Kuhl. Translated by John Burnhoff. Published and printed by Rudharsche Giesserei, Offenbach a. M. 1905
Brochure. With some specimens of gothic letters.

Item in manila envelope.

KULB, P. H.

Cabinet Y Shelf 1 No. 7

Geschichte der erfindung der buchdruckerkunst. Eine für jedermann verständliche kurze darstellung der durch die neuesten forschungen gewonnenen resultate. Mainz, 1837. Frontispiece: Lithographic view of the statue at Mayence. At the end two drawings of the bassi-relievi.
Condensed account of the invention of printing.

Half morocco; 8-1/8 x 5 x 3/8 in.

KUNERA-PERS (The Kuners Press)

Cabinet N Shelf 2 No. 18.01

List of books printed at this press in Holland, 1922-1935

see

PRIVATE PRESSES, Holland. Catalogus...

KUNIYOSHI (Engraver).

Cabinet I Shelf 3 No. 1

Art of Kuniyoshi. By Hamilton Easter Field. Excerpt from Art and Decoration, March, 1917 With portrait and illus.

Item 34 in vol. with binder's title:"Various Engravers and About Engravers."

KUNNE, ALBERT (de Duderstadt)

Cabinet D Shelf 4 No. 62

Memmingen, 1486.

see

INCUNABULA. (Loose leaves) Kunne, Albert...

KUNNE von Duderstadt, ALBRECHT

Cabinet Y Shelf 4 No. 4

(Notes on the Kunne 15th century press at Memmingen)

see

VOULLIÉME, ERNST (Die) Deutschen drucker des fünfzehnten jahrhunderts...p.82

KUNSTGEWERBE MUSEEN, Berlin (see)

Cabinet Y Shelf 5 No. 99

Königliche Museen, Berlin. Kunstgewerbe Museen...

KUNTZ, C.

Cabinet X Shelf 2 No. 38

Gutenberg. Die erfindung der buchdruckerkunst, ihre ersten anfänge und ihre entwickelung. Nebst einem berichte über die vierto säkularfeier dieser erfindung in Strassburg, 1840. Ein gedenk-und lesebüchlein für volk und schule. Strassburg, 1840.

The history of the invention of printing in Strassburg, and its development, together with a report of the celebrations on the occasion of the 4th centenary of printing.

Wittwe Levrault

Morocco; 5½ x 3½ x 3/8 in.

cont'd

KUNTZ, C. cont'd

Cabinet X Shelf 2 No. 38

Morocco; 5½ x 3½ x 3/8 in.

KÜNZEL (Hermann), pseud. Alex. Waldow (see

Cabinet Shelf No.

WALDOW, ALEXANDER

KURREIN, MAX

Cabinet FF Shelf 5 No. 68

(Tools and working methods for making presses). Die werkzeuge und arbeitsverfahren der pressen. Mit benutzung des buches. "Punches, dies, tools for manufacturing in presses". von Joseph V. Woodworth. Zweite auflage. Mit 1025 abbildungen im text...Berlin, verlag von Julius Springer, 1926.

Cloth; 9¼ x 6¼ x 1½ in.

KUSMIN, M. and WSEWOLOD WOYNOFF

Cabinet K Shelf 2 No. 20

Russische graphische kunst., D. I. Mitrochin. Staats-Verlag, Moskau, 1922. Illus.

Paper; 11¾ x 9-1/8 in.

KÜSTERMANN & CO. (Press Builders, Germany)

Cabinet EE Shelf 5 No. 85

(Catalogue of printing presses and printing materials. Includes of brief history of this house. Has portrait of Ferd. H. Kustermann, b. 1835, d. 1908). Machinen und Werkzeuge, zur herstellung von schrift, einfassungen, füllmaterial, linien. Kustermann & Comp. Berlin N. 20. (1915).

Paper; 9-3/8 x 7-3/4 in. Item in manila envelope.

KUSTERMANN & COMPANY (see)

Cabinet FF Shelf 3 No. 9.01

TYPE FOUNDING MACHINERY. Kustermann...

KUTSCHMANN, TH.

Cabinet I Shelf 4 No. 20 2 vols.

Geschichte der deutschen illustration vom ersten auftreten des formschnittes bis auf die gegenwart von Th. Kutschmann. Goslar und Berlin. (1899). 2 vols.

History of German illustration, from its origin to the present time.

Cloth; 12½ x 9½ in.

KUTTENBERG

Cabinet Shelf No.

See Printing, Historical, Bohemia.

KWAGUL

Cabinet II Shelf 4 No. 2

American Indians. Illustrative sketch of their language, "Kwakwala". By Franz Boas.

See BOAS FRANZ. American Indian languages, handbook of...Bulletin 40, Washington, 1911, pp.427-557.

KYNGE, JOHN

Cabinet T Shelf 2 No. 6 [vol.4]

Books printed by John Kynge. London, 1550-1560. Bibliographical notes.

see

DIBDIN'S "Typographical Antiquities" ...London, 1810-1819, vol.IV, p.236

KYNOCH PRESS

Cabinet Shelf No.

See Imprints, England. Nonesuch Press. Francis Meynell.

" also Imprints, England. Kynoch Press, Birmingham.